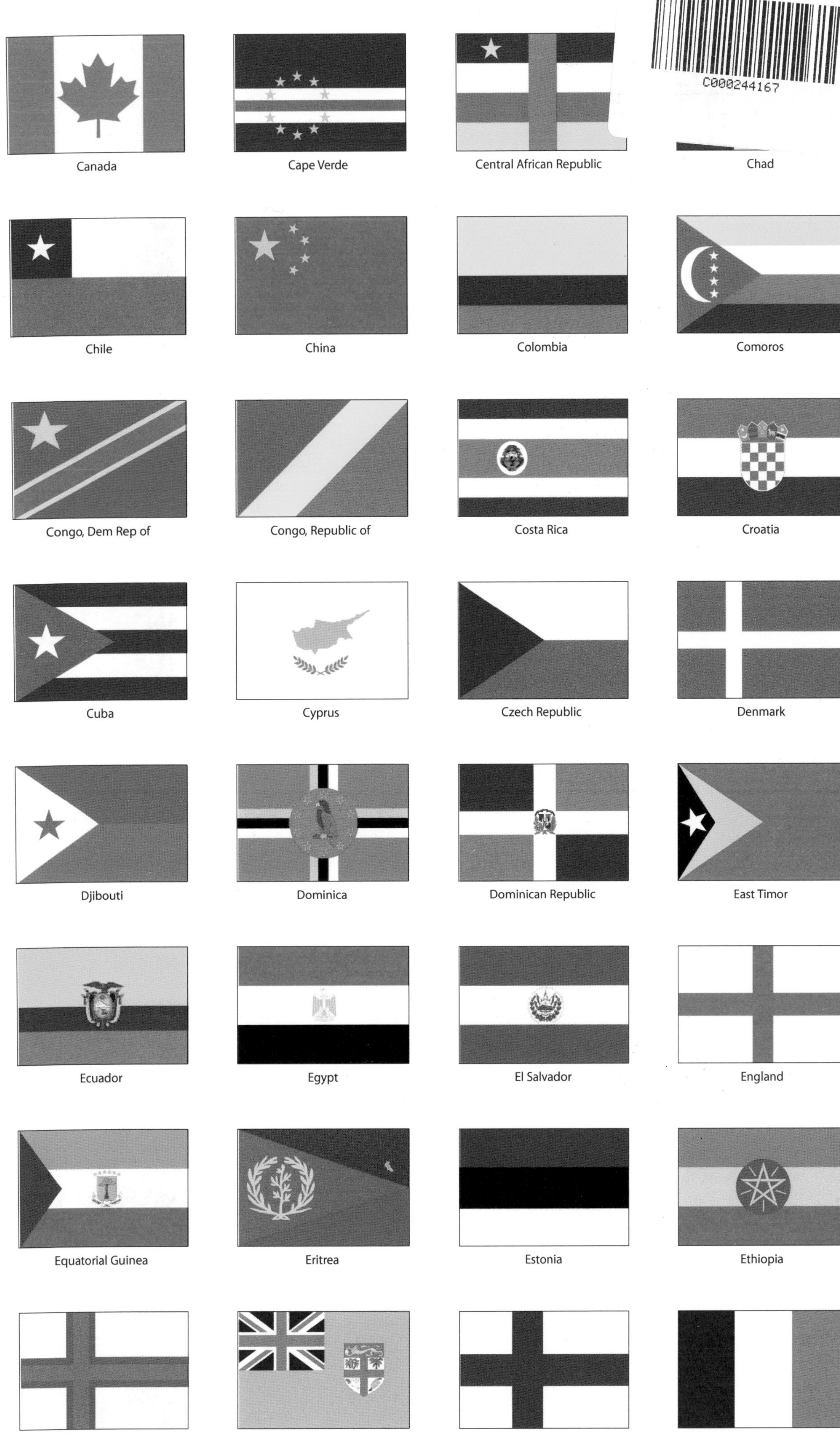
Canada
Cape Verde
Central African Republic
Chad
Chile
China
Colombia
Comoros
Congo, Dem Rep of
Congo, Republic of
Costa Rica
Croatia
Cuba
Cyprus
Czech Republic
Denmark
Djibouti
Dominica
Dominican Republic
East Timor
Ecuador
Egypt
El Salvador
England
Equatorial Guinea
Eritrea
Estonia
Ethiopia
Faroe Islands
Fiji
Finland
France

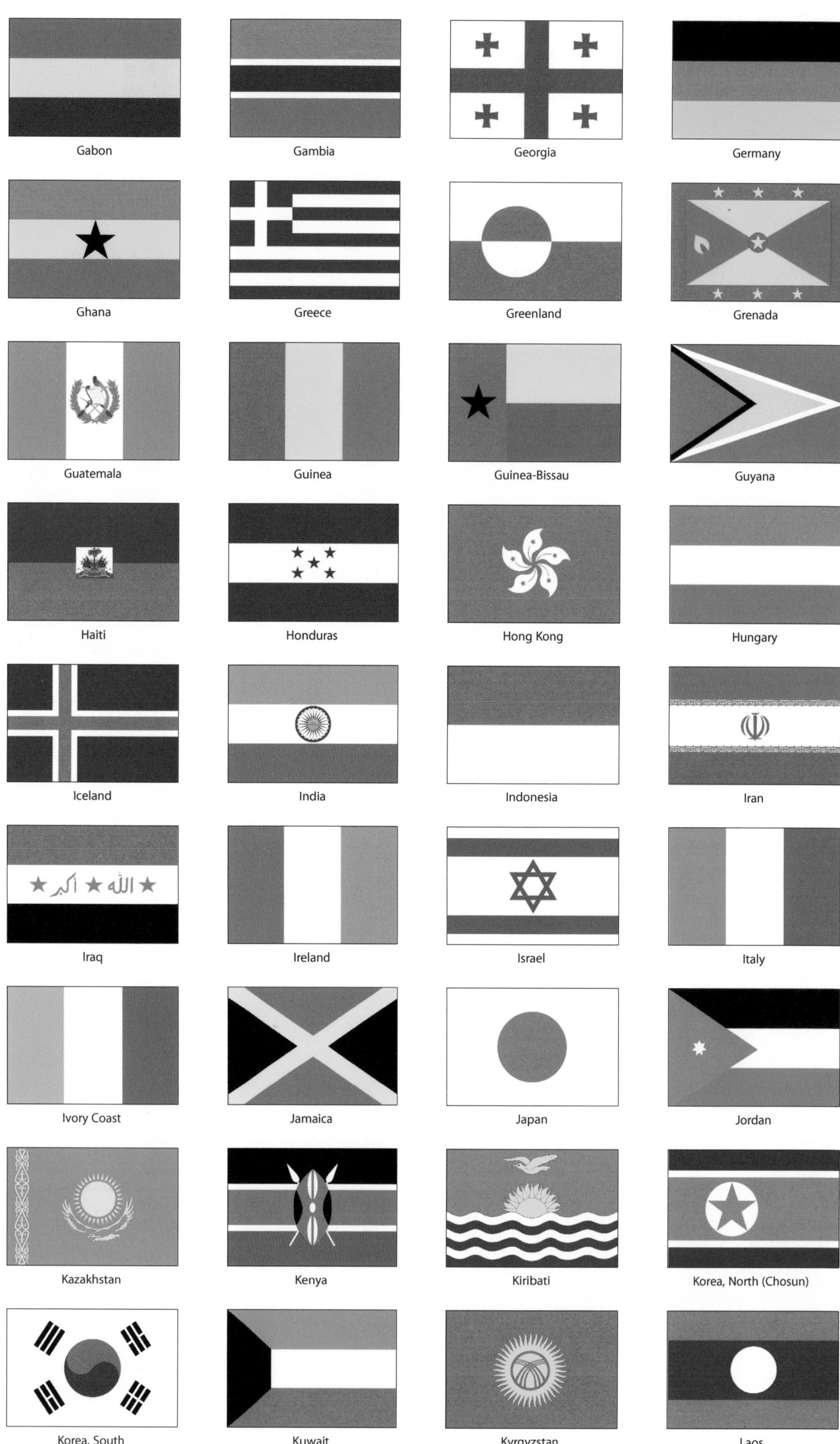
Gabon
Gambia
Georgia
Germany
Ghana
Greece
Greenland
Grenada
Guatemala
Guinea
Guinea-Bissau
Guyana
Haiti
Honduras
Hong Kong
Hungary
Iceland
India
Indonesia
Iran
الله أكبر
Iraq
Ireland
Israel
Italy
Ivory Coast
Jamaica
Japan
Jordan
Kazakhstan
Kenya
Kiribati
Korea, North (Chosun)
Korea, South
Kuwait
Kyrgyzstan
Laos

AUTHOR'S NOTE

This sixth edition of the *A to Z of almost Everything* has been exhaustively and painstakingly updated and rationalised to accommodate new, and for the expansion of existing, material. No sections have been omitted although I have taken heed of the feedback from the general public and trimmed areas that might not necessarily be as helpful as I originally imagined. To that end I have removed my duplicate sorts of data throughout the book and more specifically the very obscure capitals from my gazetteer. This has enabled me to introduce a plethora of new facts across every section.

For this edition every section through Abbreviations, Art, Astronomy, Britain, Cinema, Famous People, Literature, Music, Nature, Politics, Science, Sport, and Transport has been revised and added to as new terms become en vogue, young artists flourish, planetary moons continue to be discovered, films win awards and chemical elements previously unnamed are now given nomenclature - albeit temporary in some cases

The Current Affairs section again covers three years, rather than the usual two, and the sporting record inevitably highlights the magnificent London Games of 2012 as does the sports section itself.

The Geography section is always a major undertaking and two countries, Libya and Burma (Myanmar) have new flags and of course I have introduced the flag of South Sudan.

My cut-off point for new information is usually the December of the previous year of publication but I have endeavoured to maintain records right up to going to press in October 2013 so you will notice many of the lists are updated to 2013 unless the event takes place after this date.

The general revision of the book is the most extensive yet and although no information has been lost I have tweaked the sections and adjusted the format to cram in as much useful information as possible and consequently the book has a rather different, perhaps fresher look.

I hope you will be edified and entertained when dipping in to the book.

As always I have done my utmost to achieve 100 per cent accuracy, but if I have fallen short or you would like to suggest new topics or discuss existing ones, then please write to me via my website.

Back cover questions answers:

Michael Crawford (see page 53)
Alistair Carmichael (see page 703)
Charon, Hydra, Kerberos, Nix, Styx (see page 33)

SIXTH EDITION

Also by Trevor Montague

A to Z of Sport

A to Z of Britain and Ireland

A to Z of British (and Irish) Popular Culture

MONTAGUE PUBLISHING

First published in Great Britain in 2001 by Little, Brown
Second edition published in 2003
Third edition published in 2005
Fourth edition published in 2007
Fifth edition published in 2010
Sixth edition published in 2013

A CIP catalogue record for this book
is available from the British Library.

ISBN 978-0-7481-9998-3

Printed and bound by CPI Group (UK) Ltd, Croydon, CR0 4YY

Papers used by Clowes are natural, renewable and recyclable products sourced from well-managed forests and certified in accordance with the rules of the Forest Stewardship Council.

Introduction to the First Edition by Magnus Magnusson KBE

Trevor Montague is a Masterminder. That is to say, in 1995 he became one of the 1,231 bravehearts who appeared on the television *Mastermind* during its twenty-five-year run. But Trevor Montague is much more than that: he is that not-quite-so-rare-now animal, a quiz addict.

Trevor is also a begetter of quiz-teams. There is an unofficial *Mastermind* mafia which meets every month in the Grape Street wine bar in London, and from its regulars Trevor puts together formidable scratch teams of veteran Masterminders to take part in all and any quiz challenges. Trevor is also the question-setter of the fledgling British Quiz Championship which is a part of the annual Mind Sports Olympiad at London's Olympia.

That in itself is a sign of the immense and growing popularity of quizzes of all kinds on television, on radio, in pubs, in the Civil Service, and now even on the Internet. And it has given rise to Trevor's most ambitious project yet – *An A–Z of Almost Everything*: a massive factfile of information calculated to be of value to anyone and everyone interested in quizzes.

But how does one define 'General Knowledge' as opposed to 'Specialised Knowledge'? Indeed, when does 'Specialised Knowledge' become 'General Knowledge'? With the staggering growth of pub quiz-teams and television game-shows over recent years, the reservoir of what used to be considered 'General Knowledge' has expanded out of all recognition. Over the twenty-five years of *Mastermind*, for instance, questions which would once have come into the specialised category became demoted to the General Knowledge sets. I tried to make that very point, as subtly as possible, in the last round of the last Final of the last *Mastermind* series (in Kirkwall Cathedral, Orkney, in 1997): the last question echoed the very first question I had asked, in the University of Liverpool back in 1972:

Q: During the Spanish Civil War, which town in the Basque country was destroyed by German bombers, an event which was commemorated in a painting by Picasso?

A: Guernica

When that question was first asked in 1972, it was in a set of specialised questions on 'The Visual Arts'; in 1997 it was in a General Knowledge set.

So, what exactly makes up an A–Z of Everything? For Trevor, everything is grist to his insatiable mill. He has produced a monster factfile on an astonishing array of subjects from abbreviations to zodiac, embracing Americanisms, animal adjectives, assassination attempts, *Carry On* films, dubbed singing voices, famous dogs, gestation periods, London postal areas, middle names, nursery rhymes, obituaries, pub names, quantum theory, Schrödinger's cat, sculptors, trains, Visigoth rulers and zip codes.

I can think of few subjects which have been omitted, except perhaps for some of the classic *Mastermind* offerings which never made it to the screen: 'orthopaedic bone cement in total hip-replacement'; 'self-service petrol stations from 1963–68'; 'perfect squares from 992–9801'; and 'motorway routes to anywhere in mainland Britain from Letchworth'.

To put together this weighty tome, Trevor called upon his network of friends and colleagues in the Mastermind Club – that remarkable association of survivors of the Black Chair. The Club membership represents an astonishing reservoir of knowledge which its owners are always ready to impart to others. Many is the time I found myself marooned in a hotel without reference books and phoned friends in the Club to check on some vital detail which I needed for an occasion in the next morning.

The quiz cognoscenti who will avidly devour this book may well start off feeling superior ('I know that, of course!'), but I am pretty sure that even they will find much to intrigue them in this shrine of serendipity.

CONTENTS

ABBREVIATIONS

A & E Accident and Emergency
A & P Advertising and Promotion
A & R Artists and Repertoire / Recording
AA Automobile Association; Alcoholics Anonymous
AAA Amateur Athletic Association; Anti-Aircraft Artillery
AAM Air-to-Air Missile
ABC Atomic, Biological and Chemical; American Broadcasting Company; Australian Broadcasting Commission
ABH Actual Bodily Harm
ABM Anti-Ballistic Missile
ABRACADABRA ABbreviations and Related ACronyms Associated with Defense, Astronautics, Business and RAdio-electronics
ABS Anti-lock Braking System
ABTA Association of British Travel Agents
AC Alternating Current; Audit Commission
A/C Account
ACAS Advisory Conciliation and Arbitration Service
ACCA Association of Certified and Corporate Accountants
ACLU American Civil Liberties Union
ACM Air Chief Marshal
ACPO Association of Chief Police Officers
ACPOS Association of Chief Police Officers in Scotland
ACT Advance Corporation Tax
ACTT Association of Cinematograph, Television and Allied Technicians
ACV Air-Cushion Vehicle
AD Anno Domini
ADC Aide-De-Camp
ADCM Archbishop of Canterbury's Diploma in Church Music
ADHD Attention Deficit Hyperactivity Disorder
ADSL Asymmetric Digital Subscriber Line
AEEU Amalgamated Engineering and Electrical Union
AEGIS Aid for the Elderly in Government InstitutionS
AEU Amalgamated Engineering Union
AFP Agence France Press
AFR Automatic Fingerprint Recognition
AFV Armoured Fighting Vehicle
AG Attorney General; Adjutant General
AGM Air-to-Ground Missile; Annual General Meeting
AGR Advanced Gas-cooled Reactor
AH Anno Hegirae (from 622 AD, the start of the Muslim calendar)
AI Artificial Intelligence; Amnesty International; Artificial Insemination
AID Artificial Insemination by Donor
AIDS Acquired Immune Deficiency Syndrome
AIM Alternative Investment Market
AKA Also Known As
ALGOL ALGOrithmic Language
ALICE Autistic and Language-Impaired Children's Education
ALWR Advanced Light Water Reactor
AM Ante Meridiem; Amplitude Modulation
AMCST Associate, Manchester College of Science and Technology
AMICE Associate Member of the Institute of Civil Engineers
ANC African National Congress
ANPR Automatic Number Plate Recognition
ANZAC Australian and New Zealand Army Corps
AOL America On Line
AONB Area of Outstanding Natural Beauty
AP Associated Press; Artist's Proof
APEX Advance Purchase EXcursion; Association of Professional, EXecutive, Clerical and Computer Staff
APR Annual / Annualised Percentage Rate
APT Advanced Passenger Train
APWR Advanced Pressurised Water Reactor
ARCO Associate of the Royal College of Organists
ARCS Associate of the Royal College of Science
ARP Association of Retired Persons; Air-Raid Precautions
AS Advanced Subsidiary (Education)
ASA Advertising Standards Authority; Amateur Swimming Association
ASAP As Soon As Possible
ASB Alternative Service Book
ASBM Air-to-Surface Ballistic Missile
ASBO Anti-Social Behaviour Order
ASCII American Standard Code for Information Interchange
ASDA ASsociated DAiries
ASDE Airport Surface Detection Equipment
ASDIC Anti-Submarine Detection Investigation Committee
ASEAN Association of South East Asian Nations
ASH Action on Smoking and Health
ASLEF Associated Society of Locomotive Engineers and Firemen
ASSC Accounting Standards Steering Committee
ASSR Autonomous Soviet Socialist Republic
ASTMS Association of Scientific, Technical and Managerial Staff
AT & T American Telephone and Telegraph Company
ATC Air Traffic Control; Air Training Corps
ATM Automated Teller Machine; Asynchronous Transfer Mode
ATOL Air Travel Organisers Licence
ATS Auxiliary Territorial Service; Automated Traffic Signal
ATV Associated TeleVision
AUC Anno Urbis Conditae (in the year of the founding of the city); Ab Urbe Condita (years since the foundation of Rome)
AUEW Amalgamated Union of Engineering Workers (now AEU)
AUT Association of University Teachers
AVR Army Volunteer Reserve
AWACS Airborne Warning And Control System
AWOL Absent WithOut Leave / Absent Without Official Leave
AWP Amusement With Prizes
AWRE Atomic Weapons Research Establishment
BA Bachelor of Arts; British Airways
BAA British Airports Authority
BAC British Aircraft Corporation
BACS Bankers' Automated Clearing Service
BACUP British Association of Cancer-United Patients
BAF British Athletics Federation
BAFTA British Academy of Film and Television Arts
BALPA British AirLine Pilots' Association
BANANA Build Absolutely Nothing Anywhere Near Anyone
BAOR British Army Of the Rhine
BARB British Audience Research Bureau; Broadcasters' Audience Research Board
BART Baronet
BART Bay Area Rapid Transit
BASIC Beginners All-Purpose Symbolic Instruction Code
BAT British American Tobacco Company
BBBC British Boxing Board of Control
BBC British Broadcasting Corporation
BBFC British Board of Film Censors / Classification (new title)
BC Before Christ; British Colombia
BCC British Chamber of Commerce
BCE Before Common / Christian Era
BCh(D) / BDS Bachelor of Dental Surgery
BEBO Blog Early Blog Often
BEC Building Employers' Confederation
BECTU Broadcasting, Entertainment and Cinematograph Technicians Union
BEF British Expeditionary Force
BEM British Empire Medal
BES Business Expansion Scheme
BEST British Expertise in Science and Technology
BFI British Film Institute
BFPO British Forces Post Office
BHF British Heart Foundation
BHI British Horological Institute
BIFU Banking, Insurance and Finance Union
BIM British Institute of Management
BIT BInary DigiT
BLitt Bachelor of Letters
BLOG weB LOG
BMA British Medical Association
BMJ British Medical Journal
BMR Basal Metabolic Rate
BMX Bicycle Motocross
BOAC British Overseas Airways Corporation
BOGOFF Buy One, Get One For Free

BOOTP BOOTstrap Protocol
BPD Barrels Per Day
BPS Bits Per Second; Bytes Per Second
BRCS British Red Cross Society
BSA Birmingham Small Arms
BSAD British Sports Association for the Disabled
BSB British Satellite Broadcasting
BSc Bachelor of Science
BSE Bovine Spongiform Encephalopathy
BSI British Standards Institution
BSL British Sign Language
BST British Summer Time
BSW British Standard Whitworth
Bt Baronet
BTEC Business and Technology Education Council
BTP British Transport Police
BUNA BUtadiene and NAtrium (synthetic rubber)
BUPA British United Provident Association
BUS Broadcast and Unknown Server
BVM Blessed Virgin Mary
BWIA British West Indian Airways
BWR Boiling Water Reactor
BYO Bring Your Own
CAA Civil Aviation Authority
CAB Citizens Advice Bureau
CAD Computer Aided Design
CADD Computer Aided Design and Drafting
CAFOD CAtholic Fund for Overseas Development
CAL Computer Aided Learning
CAMRA CAMpaign for Real Ale
CAN Christian Advertising Network
Cantab Cantabrigiensis (of Cambridge)
CAP Computer Aided Publishing; Common Agricultural Policy
CARE Co-operative for American Relief Everywhere
CAT Computerised Axial Tomography
CB Companion of the order of the Bath
CBC Canadian Broadcasting Corporation
CBD Central Business District
CBE Commander of the Order of the British Empire
CBI Confederation of British Industry
CBS Columbia Broadcasting System
CCRC Criminal Cases Review Commission
CCTV Closed Circuit TeleVision
CDI Compact Disc Interactive
CDS Chief of the Defence Staff
CE Christian Era; Common Era
CEO Chief Executive Officer
CERN Conseil Européen pour la Recherche Nucléaire
CET Central European Time; Common External Tariff
cf *confer* (compare)
CFC ChloroFluoroCarbon
CFS Chronic Fatigue Syndrome (see ME)
CGM Conspicuous Gallantry Medal
CGS Centimetre-Gramme-Second; Chief of General Staff
CH Companion of Honour
CHP Combined Heat and Power
CIA Central Intelligence Agency
CICB Criminal Injuries Compensation Board
CID Criminal Investigations Department
CIPFA Chartered Institute of Public Finance and Accountancy
CIS Commonwealth of Independent States (former Soviet republics)
CITES Convention on International Trade in Endangered Species
CIWF Compassion In World Farming
CJD Creutzfeldt-Jakob Disease
CLA Country Landowners' Association
CM Chirurgiae Magister (Master of Surgery)
CMEA Council for Mutual Economic Assistance
CND Campaign for Nuclear Disarmament
CNN Cable News Network
COBOL COmmon Business-Oriented Language
COBRA Cabinet Office Briefing Room A
COD Cash On Delivery
COHSE Confederation Of Health Service Employees (Now UNISON)
COI Central Office of Information
COMECON COuncil for Mutual ECONomic aid / assistance
COMINTERN COMmunist INTERNational
CPRE Council for the Protection of Rural England
CPS Crown Prosecution Service; Characters Per Second
CPSA Civil and Public Services Association
CPU Central Processing Unit
CRC Carbon Reduction Commitment
CRE Commission for Racial Equality
CRT Cathode Ray Tube
CS (gas) Carson and Staughton
CSA Child Support Agency
CSE Certificate of Secondary Education
CSO Central Statistical Office
CT Computerised Tomography
CTO Cancelled To Order (Philately)
CTS Counter Terrorist Search
CTT Capital Transfer Tax
CURE Care, Understanding, REsearch
CV Curriculum Vitae; Cardio Vascular
CVD Compact Video Disc
CVO Commander of the Royal Victorian Order
CVP Climate, Vegetation and Productivity
CWU Communication Workers' Union
CYP Children and Young Persons
DA District Attorney
DAB Digital Audio Broadcasting
DAGMAR Defining Advertising Goals for Measured Advertising Results
D & C Dilatation and Curettage
DAR Daughters of the American Revolution
DAT Digital Audio Tape
DBE Dame Commander of the Order of the British Empire
DBS Direct Broadcasting by Satellite
DC Direct Current; District of Columbia
DCL Doctor of Civil Law
DCM Distinguished Conduct Medal
DCMG Dame Commander of the Order of St Michael and St George
DCMS Department for Culture, Media and Sport
DD Doctor of Divinity
DDS Doctor of Dental Surgery
DDT DichloroDiphenylTrichloro-ethane
DECC Department of Energy and Climate Change
DEFRA Department for Environment, Food and Rural Affairs
DERV Diesel-Engined-Road Vehicle
DFC Distinguished Flying Cross
DFM Distinguished Flying Medal
DHTML Dynamic HyperText Mark-up Language
DIF Data Interchange Format
DINKY Double Income No Kids Yet
DipSW Diploma in Social Work
DLitt Doctor of Letters
DLR Docklands Light Railway
DNA DeoxyriboNucleic Acid
DOA Dead On Arrival
DORA Defence Of the Realm Act (1914)
DOS Disc Operating System
DPA Data Protection Act
DPP Director of Public Prosecutions
DQL Data Query Language
DSA Driving Standards Agency
DSC Distinguished Service Cross
DSL Digital Subscriber Line
DSM Distinguished Service Medal
DSO Distinguished Service Order
DSS Department of Social Security
DTI Department of Trade and Industry
DTLR Department of Transport, Local Government and the Regions
DTP Desk-Top Publishing
DVD Digital Versatile / Video Disc
DVLA Driver Vehicle Licensing Authority
DVM Doctor of Veterinary Medicine
DWI Drinking Water Inspectorate
DWP Department for Work and Pensions
DWT Denarius WeighT (pennyweight); Dead Weight Tonnage
EAROM Electrically Alterable Read Only Memory

EBRD European Bank for Reconstruction and Development
EBV Epstein-Barr Virus
EC European Commission/Community
ECG ElectroCardioGram / Graph
ECGD Export Credit Guarantee Department
ECHR European Court of Human Rights; European Convention on Human Rights
ECJ European Court of Justice
ECO English Chamber Orchestra
ECSC European Coal and Steel Community
ECT Electro-Convulsive Therapy
ECU European Currency Unit
EDI Electronic Data Interchange
EDM Early Day Motion
EDP Electronic Data Processing
EEC European Economic Community
EEG ElectroEncephaloGram / Graph
EFA European Fighter Aircraft; Extended File Attribute
EFTA European Free Trade Association
EFTS Electronic Funds Transfer System
e.g. exempli gratia (for example)
EHF Extremely High Frequency
EIB European Investment Bank
EIS Educational Institute of Scotland
E-Mail Electronic Mail
EMF Electro-Motive Force; European Monetary Fund
EMI Electro-Magnetic Interference
EMS European Monetary System
EMU ElectroMagnetic Unit; European Monetary Union
ENEA European Nuclear Energy Agency
ENG Electronic News Gathering
ENIAC Electronic Numerical Integrator Analyser and Computer
ENO English National Opera
ENSA Entertainments National Service Association
ENT Ear, Nose and Throat
EOC Equal Opportunities Commission
EPCOT Experimental Prototype Community Of Tomorrow
ER Elizabeth Regina
ERA Engine Room Artificer (navy)
ERM Exchange Rate Mechanism
ERNIE Electronic Random Number Indicator Equipment
EROM Erasable Read Only Memory
ESA European Space Agency
ESF European Social Fund
ESP ExtraSensory Perception
ESSO Standard Oil
et seq. et sequentia (and the following)
ETA Estimated Time of Arrival; Euzkadi Ta Askatasuna (Basque separatist organisation)
ETD Estimated Time of Departure
EU European Union
EVA ExtraVehicular Activity
EWCB England and Wales Cricket Board
E-ZINE Electronic magaZINE
FANY First Aid Nursing Yeomanry
FAO Food and Agriculture Organisation; For Attention Of
FAP File Access Protocol
FAQ Frequently Asked Questions
Fax Facsimile transmission
FBI Federal Bureau of Investigation
FBOU Fellow of the British Ornithologists' Union
FCO Foreign and Commonwealth Office
FGS Fellow of the Geographical Society
FHS Fellow of the Heraldry Society
FIA Fellow of the Institute of Actuaries
FICE Fellow of the Institution of Civil Engineers
FIFA Fédération Internationale de Football Association
FIFO First In, First Out
FILO First In, Last Out
FIRST Fixed Interest Rate Savings Tax free
FMCG Fast Moving Consumer Goods
FOIA Freedom Of Information Act
FOREST Freedom Organisation for the Right to Enjoy Smoking Tobacco
FORTRAN Formula Translation
FPN Fixed Penalty Notice
FRAM Fellow of the Royal Academy of Music
FRAS Fellow of the Royal Astronomical Society
FRBS Fellow of the Royal Botanical Society
FRCGP Fellow of the Royal College of General Practitioners
FRCM Fellow of the Royal College of Music
FRCOG Fellow of the Royal College of Obstetricians and Gynaecologists
FRCP Fellow of the Royal College of Physicians
FRHS Fellow of the Royal Horticultural Society
FTP File Transfer Protocol
FTSE Financial Times Stock Exchange
FTW For The Win
FWTK FireWall Tool Kit
FYI For Your Information
GAA Gaelic Athletic Association
GATT General Agreement on Tariffs and Trade
GBE Knight or Dame Grand Cross of the Order of the British Empire
GBH Grievous Bodily Harm
GC George Cross
GCB Knight or Dame Grand Cross of the Order of the Bath
GCHQ Government Communications Headquarters
GCS Glasgow Coma Scale
GCSE General Certificate of Secondary Education
GCVO Knight or Dame Grand Cross of the Royal Victorian Order
GDBA Guide Dogs for the Blind Association
GDP Gross Domestic Product
Gestapo GEheime STAatsPOlizei
GIF Graphics Interchange Format
GIFT Gamete IntraFallopian Transfer
GMB Grand Master Bowman
GMT Greenwich Mean Time
GNP Gross National Product
GNVQ General National Vocational Qualification
GPMU Graphical, Paper and Media Union
GPS Global Positioning System
GRAS Generally Regarded As Safe
GRU Glavnoye Razvedyvatelnoye Upravleniye (military counterpart of KGB in former Soviet Union)
GSOH Good Sense Of Humour
HB Hard Black (pencil)
HBM Her / His Britannic Majesty
HCF Highest Common Factor
HDRA Henry Doubleday Research Association (Gardening)
HDTV High-Definition TeleVision
HF High Frequency
HGV Heavy Goods Vehicle
HIV Human Immunodeficiency Virus
HJ Hic Jacet (here lies, seen on gravestones)
HMCE Her/His Majesty's Customs and Excise
HMSO Her / His Majesty's Stationery Office
HNC Higher National Certificate
HND Higher National Diploma
HOLMES Home Office Large Major Enquiry System (police computer system)
HOTOL HOrizontal Take-Off and Landing
HRH Her/His Royal Highness
HSH Her / His Serene Highness
HSV Herpes Simplex Virus
HTHL Horizontal Take-Off Horizontal Landing
HTML HyperText Mark-up Language
HTTP HyperText Transfer Protocol
HTVL Horizontal Take-Off Vertical Landing
HWM High Water Mark
IATA International Air Transport Association
ib. ibidem (in the same place)
IBA International Broadcasting Authority
ibid. Ibidem (in the same place)
ICAEW Institute of Chartered Accountants of England and Wales
ICAO International Civil Aviation Organisation
ICBM InterContinental Balistic Missile
ICU Intensive Care Unit
IDDS Insulin Dependent Diabetic Syndrome
i.e. id est (that is)
IFAW International Fund for Animal Welfare
IFOR Implementation FORce

IFS Institute for Fiscal Studies
IGC Inter-Governmental Conference
IGY International Geophysical Year
ILO International Labour Organisation
IM Instant Message
IMAP Internet Message Access Protocol
IMO International Maritime Organisation
INRI Iesus Nazarenus Rex Iudaeorum (Jesus of Nazareth King of the Jews)
INSET INSErvice Training
INST INSTant (current month)
INTEGRAL INTErnational Gamma-Ray Astrophysics Laboratory
INTERPOL INTERnational Criminal POLice Organisation
IOM Isle Of Man
IOTA Infrared-Optical Telescope Array; International Occultation Timing Association
IOW Isle Of Wight
IPA International Phonetic Alphabet
IQ Intelligence Quotient
IRC International Red Cross
IRS Internal Revenue Service
IRSF Inland Revenue Staff Federation
ISA Individual Savings Account
ISBN International Standard Book Number
ISH Information Super Highway
ISO In Search Of; International Organisation for Standardisation
ISP Internet Service Provider
ISY International Space Year
IT Information Technology
ITA Initial Teaching Alphabet
ITC Independent Television Commission
ITU International Telecommunications Union; Intensive Therapy Unit
ITV Independent TeleVision
IV Intra Vires (within power); IntraVenous
IVF In Vitro Fertilisation
IWC International Whaling Commission
J & B Justerini and Brooks
JCR Junior Common Room
JCS Joint Chiefs of Staff
JP Justice of the Peace
JPEG Joint Photographic Experts Group
JPL Jet Propulsion Laboratory
JRDF Joint Rapid Deployment Force
KBE Knight Commander of the Order of the British Empire
KCVO Knight Commander of the Royal Victorian Order
KG Knight of the Order of the Garter
KGB Komitet Gosudarstvennoi Bezopasnosti (State Security Committee in former Soviet Union)
KT Knight of the Order of the Thistle
LACS League Against Cruel Sports
LAN Local Area Net (computer Internet)
LASER Light Amplification by Stimulated Emission of Radiation
LAUTRO Life Assurance and Unit Trust Regulatory Organisation
LBO Leveraged BuyOut
LCD Liquid Crystal Display
LCE London Commodities Exchange
LCJ Lord Chief Justice
LCM Lowest Common Multiple
LDOS Lord's Day Observance Society
LDV Local Defence Volunteers (Home Guard)
LED Light Emitting Diode
LEM Lunar Excursion Module
LGV Light Goods Vehicle
LH Liquid Hydrogen
LIDAR LIght Detection And Ranging
LIFFE London International Financial Futures and options Exchange
LIFO Last In, First Out
LIFT London International Festival Theatre
LILO Last In, Last Out
LLD Doctor of Laws
LMS / LMSR London, Midland and Scottish Railway
LNER London and North Eastern Railway
LORAN Long RAnge Navigation
LOX Liquid OXygen
LSD Librae Solidi Denarii; LySergic Acid Diethylamide
LSE London School of Economics
LSO London Symphony Orchestra
LULU Locally Unacceptable Land Use
LWM Low Water Mark
M & B May and Baker (forerunner of antibiotics)
MAD Mutually Assured Destruction
MADD Mothers Against Drunk Driving
MAFF Ministry of Agriculture Fisheries and Food
MANWEB Merseyside And North Wales Electricity Board
MASER Microwave Amplification by Stimulated Emission of Radiation
Mb Mega Bit
MB Mega Byte
MBA Master of Business Administration
MBE Member of the Order of the British Empire
MBO Management BuyOut
MBR Master Boot Record
MCC Marylebone Cricket Club
MCS Marine Conservation Society
ME Myalgic Encephalomyelitis (see CFS)
MEP Member of the European Parliament
MFH Master of Fox Hounds
MFN Most Favoured Nation
M. ft. mistura fiat (let a mixture be made)
MIDAS Missile Defence Alarm System
MIG Mortgage Indemnity Guarantee
MIPS Millions of Instructions Per Second
MIRAS Mortgage Income Relief At Source
MIRV Multiple Independently targeted Re-entry Vehicle
MIT Massachusetts Institute of Technology
MKS Metre Kilogram Second
MLR Minimum Lending Rate
MM Messieurs; Military Medal
MMR Measles, Mumps, Rubella
MNR Marine Nature Reserve
MO Modus Operandi
MOBO MOther BOard; Music Of Black Origin
MOMA Museum Of Modern Art
MOD Ministry Of Defence
MOMI Museum Of Moving Image
MORI Market and Opinion Research Institute
MoT Ministry of Transport
MP Member of Parliament; Military Police
MPEG Moving Picture Experts Group
MPLA Movimento Popular de Libertação de Angola (Popular Movement for the Liberation of Angola)
MPV Multi-Purpose Vehicle
MRI Magnetic Resonance Imaging
MRSA Methicillin Resistant Staphylococcus Aureus
MRT Magnetic Resonance Tomography
MSF Manufacturing, Science and Finance (Union)
MSP Member of Scottish Parliament
MST Mountain Standard Time
MWA Member of the Welsh Assembly
MWGM Most Worthy Grand Master (Masons)
NAACP National Association for the Advancement of Colored People
NAAFI Navy, Army, and Air Force Institutes
NABISCO NAtional BIScuit COmpany
NACODS National Association of Colliery Overmen, Deputies and Shotfirers
NACRO National Association for the Care and Resettlement of Offenders
NALGO National Association of Local Government Officers (now UNISON)
NAO National Audit Office
NARAS National Academy of Recording Arts and Sciences
NASA National Aeronautics and Space Administration
NASDAQ National Association of Securities Dealers Automatic Quotation
NAS / UWT National Association of Schoolmasters / Union of Women Teachers
NATO North Atlantic Treaty Organisation
NB Nota Bene (note well)
NBC National Broadcasting Company
NBL National Book League
NCCL National Council for Civil Liberties

NCDL National Canine Defence League
NCIS National Criminal Intelligence Service
NCVO National Council for Voluntary Organisations
NCVQ National Council for Vocational Qualifications
NEDC National Economic Development Council (Neddy)
NEET Not in Employment, Education or Training
NFT National Film Theatre
NFU National Farmers' Union
NGA National Graphical Association (now merged with SOGAT to form GPMU)
NHI National Health Insurance
NICE National Institute for health and Clinical Excellence
NIDDS Non-Insulin-Dependent Diabetic Syndrome
NIMBY Not In My Back Yard
NIREX Nuclear Industry Radioactive waste Executive
NMRI Nuclear Magnetic Resonance Imaging
NORWICH (K)Nickers Off Ready When I Come Home
NP Notary Public
NPT Non-Proliferation Treaty
NRA National Rifle Association; National Rivers Authority
NSPCC National Society for the Prevention of Cruelty to Children
NUCPS National Union of Civil and Public Servants (now the PCS)
NUJ National Union of Journalists
NUMAST National Union of Marine, Aviation and Shipping Transport Officers
NUPE National Union of Public Employees (now UNISON)
NUS National Union of Students
NUT National Union of Teachers
NVQ National Vocational Qualification
NW Neighbourhood Watch
NYO National Youth Orchestra
NYT National Youth Theatre
O & M Organisation and Method
OAPEC Organisation of Arab Petroleum-Exporting Countries
OAS Organisation of American States
OAU Organisation of African Unity
OBE Officer of the Order of the British Empire; Out-of-Body Experience
OBO Ore Bulk Oil (carrier)
OCR Optical Character Recognition
OECD Organisation for Economic Co-operation and Development
OED Oxford English Dictionary
OFFER OFFice of Electricity Regulation
OFGAS OFfice of GAS Supply
OFGEM OFfice of Gas and Electricity Markets
OFSTED OFfice for STandards in EDucation
OFTEL OFfice of TELecommunications
OFWAT Office of Water Services
OHMS On Her / His Majesty's Service
OM Order of Merit
OMOV One Member One Vote
ONO Or Near Offer
OP Opposite Prompt side (theatre); Out of Print (publishing)
op. cit. *opere citato* (in the work cited)
OPCS Office of Population Censuses and Surveys
OPEC Organisation of Petroleum-Exporting Countries
OS Old Style; Ordnance Survey
OSP Obiit Sine Prole (died without issue)
OST Office of Science and Technology
OT Old Testament
OUDS Oxford University Dramatic Society
OXFAM OXford Committee for FAMine Relief
Oxon Oxoniensis (of Oxford)
P & O Peninsular and Oriental Steamship Company
PABX Private Automatic Branch eXchange
PACE Police And Criminal Evidence act
parSec parallax second (3.26 light-years)
PAL Phase Alternating Line
PAN Personal Area Network
PAS Power-Assisted Steering
PAYE Pay As You Earn
PBX Private Branch eXchange
PC Personal Computer; Privy Council; Police Constable; Prince Consort; Politically Correct
PCA Police Complaints Authority
PCB Printed Circuit Board
PCS Public and Commercial Services Union
PCT Primary Care Trust
PDA Personal Digital Assistant. Public Display of Affection
PDF Portable Document File; Package Definition File
PDSA People's Dispensary for Sick Animals
PEP Personal Equity Plan
pH potential of Hydrogen ions
PIA Personal Investment Authority (replaced LAUTRO)
PIN Personal Identification Number
PIPO Parallel In, Parallel Out
Pixel Picture Element
PLA Port of London Authority
PLC Public Limited Company
PLO Palestine Liberation Organisation
PLR Public Lending Rights
PM Post Mortem
PMT Pre-Menstrual Tension
PNMPB Police National Missing Persons Bureau
POP Post Office Protocol
POS Point Of Sale
POW Prisoner Of War
PP Per Procurationem (by proxy); Parallel Port
PPI Pixels Per Inch
PPS Parliamentary Private Secretary
PPV Pay Per View
pro tem. pro tempore (for the time being)
PROM Programmable Read Only Memory
PRP Profit-Related Pay
PRS Performing Rights Society
PS Post Scriptum
PSBR Public Sector Borrowing Requirement
PSDR Public Sector Debt Repayment
PSV Public Service Vehicle
PTI Physical Training Instructor
PTO Please Turn Over
PTSD Post-Traumatic Stress Disorder
PVC PolyVinylChloride
QA Quantitative Analysis; Quality Assurance
QANTAS Queensland And Northern Territory Aerial Service
QARANC Queen Alexandra's Royal Army Nursing Corps
QARNNS Queen Alexandra's Royal Naval Nursing Service
QBD Queen's Bench Division
QC Queen's Counsel; Quality Control
QED Quod Erat Demonstrandum (which was to be demonstrated)
QGM Queen's Gallantry Medal
QMG QuarterMaster General
QMV Qualified Majority Voting
QPM Queen's Police Medal; Quality and Performance Management
QSO Quasi-Stellar Object (quasar)
QUANGO QUasi-Autonomous Non-Governmental Organisation
qv quod vide (which see)
RAC Royal Automobile Club
RADA Royal Academy of Dramatic Art
RADAR RAdio Detection And Ranging
RAEC Royal Army Educational Corps
RAFVR Royal Air Force Voluntary Reserve
RAM Random-Access Memory
RAMC Royal Army Medical Corps
RAOC Royal Army Ordnance Corps
RAVC Royal Army Veterinary Corps
RBA Royal Society of British Artists
RC Roman Catholic; Red Cross
RCA Radio Corporation of America
RCM Royal College of Music
RCMP Royal Canadian Mounted Police
RCN Royal College of Nursing
REM Rapid Eye Movement
REME Royal Electrical and Mechanical Engineers
RFA Royal Fleet Auxiliary
RFDS Royal Flying Doctor Service
RH Relative Humidity
RHA Regional Health Authority
RHS Royal Historical / Horticultural / Humane Society

RIBA Royal Institute of British Architects
RKO Radio-Keith-Orpheum
RMT (National Union of) Rail, Maritime and Transport Workers
RNA RiboNucleic Acid
RNAS Royal Naval Air Service
RNIB Royal National Institute for the Blind
RNID Royal National Institute for the Deaf
RNLI Royal National Lifeboat Institution
RNR Royal Naval Reserve
ROC Royal Observer Corps
ROI Return On Investment
ROM Read-Only Memory
ROSPA ROyal Society for the Prevention of Accidents
RP Received Pronunciation
RPI Retail Price Index
RRP Recommended Retail Price
RSC Royal Shakespeare Company
RSI Repetitive Stress/Strain Injury
RSM Regimental Sergeant Major
RSPB Royal Society for the Protection of Birds
RSPCA Royal Society for the Prevention of Cruelty to Animals
RSV Revised Standard Version (Bible)
RSVP Répondez S'il Vous Plaît
RTA Road Traffic Accident
RTE Radio Telefis Eireann
RTS Royal Television Society
RTZ Rio Tinto Zinc Corporation Ltd
RUC Royal Ulster Constabulary
RYS Royal Yacht Squadron
SA Sociedad Anónima (Spanish: limited company); Société Anonyme (French: limited company)
SAD Seasonal Affective Disorder
SAE Stamped Addressed Envelope
SAFE Saving Animals From Extinction
SALT Strategic Arms Limitation Talks
SANE Schizophrenia – A National Emergency
SARS Severe Acute Respiratory Syndrome
SAS Special Air Service
SATB Soprano, Alto, Tenor, Bass
SATS Standard Assessment TestS
SBS Special Boat Squadron; Sick Building Syndrome
SCM State Certified Midwife
SCO Scottish Chamber Orchestra
SCR Senior Common Room
SCREAM Society for the Control and Registration of Estate Agents and Mortgage brokers
SCUBA Self-Contained Underwater Breathing Apparatus
SDA Severe Disability Allowance
SDI Strategic Defence Initiative
SDLP Social Democratic and Labour Party
SDP Social Democratic Party
SEA Single European Act
SEC Securities Exchange Commission
SEN Special Educational Needs; State Enrolled Nurse
SERPS State Earnings-Related Pension Scheme
SETI Search for Extra-Terrestrial Intelligence
SFO Serious Fraud Office
SHAPE Supreme Headquarters Allied Powers in Europe
SHF Super High Frequency
SI Système International (of units); Statutory Instrument
SIB Securities and Investments Board
SIG Special Interest Group
SIM Subscriber Identity Module
SIPP Self-Invested Personal Pension
SJ Society of Jesus (Jesuits)
SLBM Submarine-Launched Ballistic Missile
SLDP Social and Liberal Democratic Party
SLR Single Lens Reflex
SMMT Society of Motor Manufacturers and Traders
SMP Statutory Maternity Pay
SMS Short Message Service
SMTP Simple Mail Transfer Protocol
SNAFU Situation Normal All Fouled / Fucked Up
SNCF Société Nationale des Chemins de Fer français
SNP Scottish National Party
SOCO Scene Of Crime Officer
SOGAT Society Of Graphical and Allied Trades (now merged with NGA to form GPMU)
SOM Start Of Message
SONAR SOund Navigation And Ranging
SOS Save Our Souls
SOWETO SOuth WEstern TOwnships (South Africa)
SP Sine Prole (without issue)
SPCK Society for Promoting Christian Knowledge
SPF Sun Protection Factor
SPG Special Patrol Group
SPQR Senatus PopulusQue Romanus (the Senate and People of Rome)
SRA Squash Rackets Association
SRN State Registered Nurse
SS SchutzStaffel
SSP Statutory Sick Pay
SSSI Site of Special Scientific Interest
SST SuperSonic Travel
START STrategic Arms Reduction Talks
STD Subscriber Trunk Dialling; Sexually Transmitted Disease
STOL Short TakeOff and Landing
STRIVE Society for The Preservation of Rural Industrial and Village Enterprises
STROBE Satellite TRacking Of Balloons and Emergencies
STV Single Transferable Vote
SVQ Scottish Vocational Qualification
SWALK Sealed With A Loving Kiss
SWAPO South West African People's Organisation
SWAT Special Weapons And Tactics
TA Territorial Army
TAMBA Twins And Multiple Births Association
TASS Technical, Administrative and Supervisory Section (of AUEW); Telegrafnoye Agentsvo Sovetshkovo Soyuza (news agency)
TAURUS Transfer and AUtomated Registration of Uncertified Stock
TAVR Territorial and Army Volunteer Reserve
TAVRA Territorial Auxiliary and Volunteer Reserve Association
TBA To Be Advised / Agreed / Announced / Arranged
TCCB Test and County Cricket Board
TEC Training and Enterprise Corporation
TEFL Teaching English as a Foreign Language
TELEX TELeprinter EXchange
TES Times Educational Supplement
TGWU Transport and General Workers Union
3GL Third Generation Language
TIFF Tag Image File Format (computing)
TIROS Television and InfraRed Observation Satellite
TLD Top Level Domain
TLR Twin Lens Reflex
TLS Times Literary Supplement
TM Transcendental Meditation; Trade Mark
TNT TriNitroToluene
Toc H Talbot House (Christian aid organisation)
TSB Trustee Savings Bank
TT Tuberculin Tested; Tourist Trophy
TUC Trades Union Congress
TVP Textured Vegetable Protein
TWAIN Technology Without Any Interesting Name
24/7 Twenty-Four Hours a Day, Seven Days a Week
TWOC Take WithOut Consent
UA Unitary Authority
UAE United Arab Emirates
UCAS Universities and Colleges Admissions Service (replaced UCCA in 1993)
UCATT Union of Construction, Allied Trades and Technicians
UCCA Universities Central Council on Admissions (replaced by UCAS in 1993)
UCLA University of California Los Angeles
UDA Ulster Defence Association
UDC Urban Development Corporation (e.g. Docklands) Urban District Council
UDI Unilateral Declaration of Independence
UDM Union of Democratic Mineworkers
UDP United Democratic Party; Ulster Democratic Party
UDR Ulster Defence Regiment
UEFA Union of European Football Associations

UFC Universities' Funding Council
UFO Unidentified Flying Object
UGC University Grants Committee
UHF Ultra High Frequency
UHT Ultra High Temperature; Ultra Heat Treatment
UKAEA United Kingdom Atomic Energy Authority
ULCC Ultra Large Crude Carrier
ULTRA Unrelated Live Transplant Regulatory Authority
UMIST University of Manchester Institute of Science and Technology
UNCTAD United Nations Conference on Trade And Development
UNESCO United Nations Educational, Scientific and Cultural Organisation
UNHCR United Nations High Commission for Refugees
UNICEF United Nations Children's Fund (formerly United Nations International Children's Emergency Fund)
UNITA União Nacional para a Independencia Total de Angola (National Union for the Total Independence of Angola)
UNITAR United Nations Institute for Training And Research
UNPROFOR United Nations Protection Force
UNRRA United Nations Relief and Rehabilitation Administration
UPC Universal Product Code
UPU Universal Postal Union
URL Uniform Resource Locator
USB Universal Serial Bus
USDAW Union of Shop, Distributive and Allied Workers
USM Unlisted Securities Market
USSR Union of Soviet Socialist Republics
UUP Ulster Unionist Party
UV Ultra Violet
UVF Ulster Volunteer Force
VASCAR Visual Average Speed Computer And Recorder
VAT Value Added Tax
VC Victoria Cross
VDU Video / Visual Display Unit
VHF Very High Frequency
VHS Video Home System
vix. vixit (she / he lived)
viz. videlicet (namely)
VLF Very Low Frequency
VLT Very Large Telescope
VOD Video On Demand
VOIP Voice Over Internet Protocol
VOOs Violent Offender Orders
VR Virtual Reality
VRY ViceRoY
VSO Voluntary Service Overseas
VSOP Very Special Old Pale
VTOL Vertical TakeOff and Landing
WAGS Wives And GirlfriendS
WAN Wide Area Net (computer Internet)
WAP Wireless Application Protocol
WASP White Anglo-Saxon Protestant
WCC World Council of Churches
WDCS Whales and Dolphins Conservation Society
WEA Workers' Educational Association
WEU Western European Union
WFP World Food Programme
WFTU World Federation of Trade Unions
WHAM Winning Hearts And Minds (Vietnam propaganda slogan)
WHO World Health Organisation
WIBF Women's International Boxing Federation
WIMP Windows Icons Menus Pointing (computing); Weakly Interacting Massive Particle
WMD Weapons of Mass Destruction
WMO World Meteorological Organisation
WOMAN World Organisation for Mothers of All Nations
WORM Write Once Read Many (times)
WPAN Wireless Personal Area Network
WPBSA World Professional Billiards and Snooker Association
WRAC Women's Royal Army Corps
WRAF Women's Royal Air Force
WRNS Women's Royal Naval Service
WRP Worker's Revolutionary Party
WRVS Women's Royal Voluntary Service
WSPA World Society for the Protection of Animals
WTO World Trade Organisation
WVS Women's Voluntary Service
WWF World Wide Fund for Nature (formerly World Wildlife Fund)
WWW World Weather Watch; World Wide Web
WYSBYGI What You See Before You Get It
WYSIWYG What You See Is What You Get
YAHOO Yet Another Hierarchical Officious Oracle
YCNAC Young Conservative National Advisory Committee
YHA Youth Hostels Association
YMCA Young Men's Christian Association
YOC Young Ornithologists' Club
Y2K Year 2000
YTD Year To Date
YUPPIE Young Upwardly mobile / Urban Professional
YWCA Young Women's Christian Association
ZANU Zimbabwe African National Union
ZAPU Zimbabwe African People's Union
ZEBRA Zero-Energy Breeder-Reactor Assembly
ZEG Zero Economic Growth
ZENITH Zero-Energy NITrogen-Heated thermal reactor
ZIP Zone Improvement Plan; Zigzag In-line Package
ZPG Zero Population Growth

NB: The TGWU merged with Amicus (itself a merger of MSF and AEEU) on 1 May 2007 to form Unite, the largest trade union in the UK.

ARCHITECTURE

Famous Architects

Aalto, Alvar (1898–1976) Finnish architect and designer whose work included the Hall of Residence, Massachusetts Institute of Technology, the Finlandia Concert Hall, Helsinki and Nordic Centre in Reykjavik. He also invented bent plywood furniture in 1932.

Abercrombie, (Sir) Patrick (1879–1957) English architect and pioneer of town planning in Britain, brother of the poet Lascelles Abercrombie. His major work was the replanning of London (County of London Plan, 1943, and Greater London Plan, 1944).

Adam, Robert (1728–92) Scottish architect and interior designer, leader of the British Neo-Classical revival. Famous works include the interiors of Harewood House, Luton Hoo, Syon House and Osterley Park. He worked with his brother James Adam, on the Adelphi near Charing Cross, largely rebuilt in 1936.

Alsop, Will (1947–) Northampton-born architect with practices in London, Beijing, Singapore, Toronto and Shanghai. Alsop's book *SuperCity* was particularly controversial, suggesting a futuristic conurbation stretching along the M62 corridor from Liverpool to Hull. Alsop's design of Peckham Library won the Stirling Prize in 2000 and the Sharp Centre for Design in Toronto won him the RIBA Worldwide Award in 2004. More recent designs include an arts gallery The Public, West Bromwich and Stratford Docklands Light Railway Station.

Archer, Thomas (1668–1743) Along with Vanbrugh and Hawksmoor, the third member of the great triumvirate of English Baroque architects. The north elevation at Chatsworth with its pilastered bow front is his best-known remaining work. Born in Tamworth, Archer's work was chiefly in ecclesiastical architecture. He designed the church of St Paul's, Deptford (1712–30), the church of St John's, Westminster (1714–28) and Birmingham Cathedral (1709–15).

Baker, (Sir) Benjamin (1840–1907) Civil engineer and designer knighted for his work on designing the Forth Rail Bridge (1883–90). Baker worked in partnership with Sir John Fowler and their collaboration is probably most famous for the London Underground system, completed in 1890.

Barry, (Sir) Charles (1795–1860) British architect of the Neo-Gothic Houses of Parliament (1840–60), which were completed after his death by his son Edward Middleton Barry. Other works included the church of St Peter, Brighton; Travellers' Club, Pall Mall; the Reform Club, London; King Edward's School, Birmingham, and the Manchester Athenaeum. His fifth son Sir John Wolfe-Barry (1836–1918) was engineer of Tower Bridge and Barry Docks.

Bramante, Donato (1444–1514) Italian High Renaissance architect, born near Urbano. Designed the new Basilica of St Peter's as well as the Belvedere courtyard, the Tempietto di S Pietro in Montorio and the Palazzo Caprini.

Brown, Lancelot (1716–83) English landscape-gardener and architect, nicknamed 'Capability' due to his stock reply to clients that their gardens had 'excellent capabilities'. Works include the gardens at Blenheim, Kew, Stowe, and Warwick Castle.

Brunel, Isambard Kingdom (1806–59) English engineer and inventor, born in Portsmouth, son of Sir Marc Isambard Brunel. His numerous works include the original Thames Tunnel, Clifton and Hungerford Suspension Bridges, and the Saltash Bridge over the Tamar. His ship designs include the *Great Western* (1838), the *Great Britain* (1845) and the *Great Eastern*, in collaboration with John Scott Russell.

Chambers, (Sir) William (1723–96) Swedish-born, Scottish architect. He popularised Chinese influence (Kew Garden pagoda) and designed Somerset House, London (1776).

Cockerell, Charles Robert (1788–1863) English architect, son of Samuel Pepys Cockerell. He designed the Taylorian Institute at Oxford, Fitzwilliam Museum at Cambridge, and Ashmolean Museum, Oxford.

Foster, Norman (Lord Foster of Thames Bank)
(1935–) British architect of the high-tech school. His best-known buildings include the Willis Faber office, Ipswich (1975), the Sainsbury Centre for the visual arts, Norwich (1978), the Hong Kong and Shanghai Bank, Hong Kong (1986), the Stansted Airport Terminal Building (1991), the American Air Museum, Duxford, Cambridgeshire (1998), the Millennium Footbridge, London (1999), 30 St Mary Axe (Swiss Reinsurers building aka The Gherkin), London (2004), the Millau Viaduct, France (2004 – the tallest bridge in the world), the Palace of Peace and Reconciliation, Astana, Kazakhstan (2006), the new Wembley Stadium, Terminal 3 of the Beijing Capital International Airport, and the Willis Building (all completed in 2007). Lord Foster, who was knighted in 1990 and appointed to the Order of Merit in 1997, also designed the National Police Memorial in The Mall, London (2005).

Fowler, (Sir) John (1817–98) Civil engineer and designer who worked in partnership with Benjamin Baker on the Forth Rail Bridge (1883–90) and the London Underground system (1890). He was made a baronet in 1890.

Fuller, Richard Buckminster (1895–1983) American architect who invented the Geodesic Dome. Examples of his works are at the Union Tank Car Repair Shop, Louisiana (1958), and the US Pavilion, Montreal Exhibition (1967).

Gaudí, Antonio (1852–1926) Spanish architect, noted for his flamboyant style. His work on the Church of the Holy Family in Barcelona begun in 1883 was unfinished at his death.

Gehry, Frank (1929–) Born Frank Owen Goldberg, in Toronto, Canada. Architect who moved to California when he was 17 and became a naturalised American citizen. Known for his curvaceous free-form sculptural style, often encompassing titanium sheathing for his buildings. His best-known buildings include the Frederick Weisman Museum of Art, University of Minnesota (1990), the Dancing House, Prague (aka Fred and Ginger) the Nationale-Nederlanden building (in conjunction with Croatian-Czech architect Vlado Milunić), the Guggenheim Museum, Bilbao, Spain (1997), the Walt Disney Concert Hall, Los Angeles (2003) and the Jay Pritzker Pavilion in Millennium Park, Chicago (2004). Known for his recurrent fish theme in his buildings and also his jewellery and furniture designs. Gehry was portrayed in an episode of *The Simpsons*.

Gibbs, James (1682–1754) Scottish Neo-Classical architect whose works include St Martin-in-the-Fields, London (1722), and the Radcliffe Camera, Oxford (1737).

Grimshaw, Sir Nicholas (1939–) Baron Grimshaw of Peterloo is noted for several modernist buildings including the railway terminal at London's Waterloo station (1993), the Eden Project, Cornwall (2001), the National Space Centre, Leicester (2001), the Thermae Bath Spa, Bath (2006) and the London School of Economics New Academic Building (2008). In 2004, he was elected President of the Royal Academy.

Hadid, Zaha (1950–) British architect born in Baghdad, Iraq. Became the first woman to win the $100,000 Pritzker Architecture Prize, in 2004. Her projects to date include the Vitra Fire Station (1994) and the LFone pavilion (1999), in Weil am Rhein, Germany, the Mind Zone at the Millennium Dome, London (1999), a ski jump in Innsbruck, Austria (2002), the Contemporary Arts Centre, Cincinnati (2003), the Maggie's Centre at the Victoria Hospital, Kirkcaldy, Scotland (2006), the London Aquatics Centre (2011) and the Riverside Museum, Glasgow (2011). She won the Stirling Prize in 2010, for the Maxxi in Rome, and in 2011 for the Evelyn Grace Academy, a Z-shapes school in Brixton. Appointed DBE in 2012.

Hawksmoor, Nicholas (1661–1736) English Baroque architect born in Nottingham. He designed many London churches including St George's, Bloomsbury, and Christ Church, Spitalfields. Assisted Vanbrugh at Blenheim Palace and Castle Howard and was clerk to Wren.

Jones, Inigo (1573–1652) English architect, born in London. The founder of Classical English architecture whose innovations include the introduction of the proscenium arch and movable scenery to the English stage. In 1616 he designed the Queen's House at Greenwich. Other commissions included the rebuilding of the Banqueting Hall at Whitehall, the nave and transepts and a large Corinthian portico of old St Paul's, Marlborough Chapel, the Double-Cube room at Wilton, and possibly the York Water Gate. Jones also laid out Covent Garden and Lincoln's Inn Fields.

Kent, William (1684–1748) Born in Yorkshire. After studying painting in Rome became a leading light in the introduction of the Palladian style of architecture into Britain. He designed many public buildings in London, including the Royal Mews in Trafalgar Square, the Treasury buildings and the Horse Guards block in Whitehall (1745). An example of his gardens is at Stowe House in Buckinghamshire and his artistry is visible in the Gothic screens at Westminster Hall and Gloucester Cathedral. He also designed the interiors of Burlington House and Chiswick House in London.

Lasdun, (Sir) Denys Louis (1914–2001) English architect whose works include the Royal College of Physicians, London; University of East Anglia, Norwich; National Theatre, London; and the European Investment Bank in Luxembourg.

Le Corbusier (1887–1965) Pseudonym of Charles Édouard Jeanneret, Swiss-born French architect, famous for his proclamation that the house is a habitable machine to be designed to functional criteria. His works include the Palace of the Nations, Geneva; and Cité Radieuse, Marseilles; as well as the town plan for Chandigarh, India.

Lutyens, (Sir) Edwin Landseer (1869–1944) English architect whose designs ranged from the picturesque of his early country houses, including Marsh Court, Stockbridge, and the restoration of Lindisfarne Castle, which owed much to the Arts and Crafts movement, to those in the Renaissance style such as Heathcote, Ilkley and Salutation, Sandwich. He finally evolved a classical style exhibited in the Cenotaph, Whitehall, which reached its height in his design – never built – for Liverpool Roman Catholic Cathedral. Other works include the Viceroy's House, New Delhi, and the British Embassy in Washington.

Mackintosh, Charles Rennie (1868–1928) Scottish architect, designer, and water colourist. Outstanding exponent of the Art Nouveau style in Scotland. Born in Glasgow, the son of a police superintendent, he married Margaret Mackintosh in 1900. His output included the Glasgow School of Art, Cranston tearooms, and houses such as Hill House in Helensburgh. By the end of World War I he had given up architecture for a career in water colours, mainly in France.

Mies Van Der Rohe, Ludwig (1886–1969) German-born American architect, born in Aachen. A pioneer of glass skyscrapers and high-rise flats, he also designed tubular-steel furniture, particularly the 'Barcelona Chair'. Became professor of architecture at the Illinois Institute of Technology in Chicago and designed two glass apartment towers on Lake Shore Drive, and the Seagram Building in New York. He also designed the Washington DC Public Library and two art galleries in Berlin.

Nash, John (1752–1835) British architect who designed Regent's Park and its terraces, Regent Street and Marble Arch. He also recreated Buckingham Palace from old Buckingham House and rebuilt Brighton Pavilion in oriental style. Trafalgar Square and St James's Park were also laid out by Nash.

Paxton, (Sir) Joseph (1801–65) British architect and garden superintendent to the Duke of Devonshire. By far his most famous work was the design of the Great Exhibition Building of 1851, the Crystal Palace, the first example of a prefabricated industrialised building on a large scale.

Pei, Ieoh Ming (1917–) Known as I. M. Pei. Chinese-born American architect whose works include the John Hancock Tower, Boston; the Mile High Center, Denver, the glass pyramid at the Louvre, the Museum of Islamic Art, Doha, Qatar and the Macao Science Center .

Piano, Renzo (1937–) Born in Genoa, Italy, and graduated from the University of Milan in 1964. The Italian designer and lecturer is best-known for his partnership with Richard Rogers (1970–78) during which time they designed the Pompidou Centre in Paris. He received the Pritzker Prize in 1998 and has designed buildings in Italy, France, the United States, Germany, Japan, and notably Dakar, Senegal. His most recent high-profile project is the Shard (aka the London Bridge Tower). Standing 309.6 metres (1,016 ft) high, the Shard is the tallest completed building in the European Union, and the second-tallest free-standing structure in the UK, after the 330-metre (1,083 ft) concrete tower at the Emley Moor transmitting station.

Pugin, Augustus Welby Northmore (1812–52) British architect and leader of the Gothic revival movement, a fine example of his style being the church of St Giles in Cheadle, Staffordshire. Pugin was employed by Sir Charles Barry to work on the Houses of Parliament and although controversy surrounds his precise input he certainly designed its Gothic interiors and the clocktower in which Big Ben hangs.

Rogers, Richard (Lord Rogers of Riverside) (1933–) Florence-born British architect whose works include the Pompidou Centre in Paris (1977), the Lloyd's building, London (1986) the Channel 4 Headquarters, London (1994), the European Court of Human Rights, Strasbourg (1995), the Millennium Dome (1999), Terminal 4 at Barajas Airport, Madrid (2005) and the National Assembly for Wales (2006). He was created a life peer in 1996. Founder member with Norman Foster and their wives of 'Team 4'. He has been chosen as the architect of Tower 3 of the new World Trade Center in New York. Pioneer of 'Bowellism' whereby internal features such as lifts and pipes were made visible on the outside of the structures in order to maximize space to appreciate his exhibitions. Married to Ruth Rogers, chef and co-owner of The River Café restaurant in west London.

Saarinen, Eero (1910–61) Finnish-born American architect whose works include the American Embassy in London and Dulles Airport near Washington DC.

Scott, (Sir) George Gilbert (1811–78) English architect, born in Gawcott, Bucks. His works include the Albert Memorial, St Pancras station, and the Episcopal Cathedral in Edinburgh.

Scott, (Sir) Giles Gilbert (1880–1960) English architect, grandson of Sir George Gilbert Scott. Won a competition in 1903 for the design of the Anglican Cathedral in Liverpool (consecrated 1924). Other works include the new Bodleian Library at Oxford and the new Cambridge University Library. He also planned the new Waterloo Bridge and was responsible for the rebuilding of the House of Commons after World War II.

Shaw, Norman (1831–1912) English architect born in Edinburgh. Worked with his partner William Eden Nesfield (1835–88) in many styles ranging from Gothic Revival to Neo-Baroque, but became an acknowledged leader in the trend away from the Victorian style back to traditional Georgian design, leading to the English Domestic Revival. His major buildings include the Old Swan House, Chelsea (1876), New Scotland Yard (1888), the Gaiety Theatre, Aldwych (1902, now demolished), and Piccadilly Hotel (1905). He also designed the garden suburb at Bedford Park, London.

Smirke, (Sir) Robert (1781–1867) English architect, son of Robert Smirke (1752–1845) the painter and book illustrator. His works in London include Covent Garden Theatre (destroyed), British Museum, King's College and the Royal College of Physicians (now Canada House).

Soane, (Sir) John (1753–1837) English architect, born near Reading, the son of a mason. His works included the Bank of England, the Dulwich Picture Gallery and his own house in Lincoln's Inn Fields, London which he bequeathed to the nation.

Spence, (Sir) Basil Urwin (1907–76) Scottish architect, born in India. His works include the conversions at Queen's College, Cambridge; the pavilions for the Festival of Britain and the British Embassy in Rome. His best-known work is his prize design for the new Coventry Cathedral (1951).

Sullivan, Louis (1856–1924) Architect born in Boston, Massachusetts but studied in Paris. Won the New Exposition building contract (1886) with Dankmar Adler (1844–1900). Sullivan was an early pioneer of the skyscraper: e.g. the Wainwright building in St Louis (1891). His experimental, functional skeleton constructions of skyscrapers and office blocks, particularly the Stock Exchange, Chicago, earned him the title 'Father of Modernism'.

Tange, Kenzo (1913–2005) Japanese architect who designed the National Gymnasium for the Tokyo Olympics and the city plan for the new Nigerian capital of Abuja (completed 1986).

Telford, Thomas (1757–1834) Began life as a stonemason but appointed as surveyor of public works for Shropshire in 1786. Telford is famous for his road-building and bridge-building, particularly those over the River Severn, but he also built the Caledonian Canal (1803–22).

Utzon, Jørn (1918–2008) Danish architect born in Copenhagen. Came to prominence after winning a competition to design Sydney Opera House in 1956. The building, completed between 1957 and 1973, is one of the most famous landmarks of the 20th century. Other works include the Municipal Theatre in Zurich (1964) and the Kuwait Parliamentary Building (1983). His awards include the gold medal of the Royal Institute of British Architects (1978), the Alvar Aalto medal (1982), the Fritz Schumacher prize (1988) and the Pritzker Prize (2003).

Vanbrugh, (Sir) John (1664–1726) English playwright and Baroque architect, born in London, the son of a tradesman. Educated in France and commissioned into Lord Huntingdon's regiment, he suffered imprisonment in the Bastille as a suspected spy. His major architectural work was Blenheim Palace at Woodstock, Oxfordshire, which was so disliked by the Duchess of Marlborough that she refused to pay him for some time.

Wilkins, William (1778–1839) Son of an architect, he was educated at Cambridge and established a reputation as an enthusiastic Greek revivalist with the publication of his *Antiquities of Magna Graecia.* In London he built St George's Hospital at Hyde Park Corner (1827–8) and the National Gallery in Trafalgar Square (1832).

Wren, Christopher (1632–1723) Wren was educated at Westminster School and Wadham College, Oxford, and became a fellow of All Souls, Oxford. He became professor of astronomy at Gresham College, London, 1657, before returning to Oxford to take up a similar position. The chapel at Pembroke College, Cambridge, 1663, was the first design of Wren's to be built and later that year he began designs for Sheldonian Theatre at Oxford. Following the Great Fire he designed over 50 London churches including St Paul's (1675–1710). Other works included the Ashmolean Museum at Oxford, Chelsea Hospital, Greenwich Observatory, parts of Hampton Court Palace, Royal Exchange, and parts of the Royal Naval College, Greenwich. Wren was a founder of the Royal Society, was knighted in 1673, and became MP for Plympton in 1685, Windsor in 1689, and finally, Weymouth in 1701.

Wright, Frank Lloyd (1867–1959) American architect, born in Richland Center, Wisconsin. Studied civil engineering at Wisconsin University, but the collapse of a newly-built wing of the Wisconsin State Capitol caused him to apply engineering principles to architecture. After setting up in practice in Chicago he became known for low-built prairie-style bungalows like Robie House. His best-known public buildings include the Imperial Hotel in Tokyo (1916–20), the 'Falling Water' weekend retreat at Mill Run in Pennsylvania (1936), the Johnson Wax office block in Racine, Wisconsin (1936), Florida Southern College (1940) and the Guggenheim Museum of Art in New York (1959), in which the exhibits line the walls of a continuous spiral ramp.

Wyatt, James (1746–1813) Born in Staffordshire, he closely followed the style of Robert Adam in his early days, so much so that Adam accused him of plagiarism. Wyatt won a competition to redesign the Pantheon in Oxford Street (1772) and his reputation was made. Fonthill Abbey in Wiltshire displays the extravagant Gothic Revival country house he built for William Thomas Beckford.

Zumthor, Peter (1943–) Swiss architect, winner of the 2009 Pritzker Prize, best known for the design of the Vals Spa hotel complex in Graubünden, Switzerland (1996) and the Kunsthaus Bregenz (art museum) in Austria (1997).

Architectural Terms

Abacus The top member of a capital, usually a square or rounded slab of stone or marble

Acanthus Conventionalised acanthus leaf used to decorate Corinthian and Composite capitals

Adobe Sun-dried brick mainly of clay; also the name of buildings constructed of such bricks

Architrave Lowest part of an entablature, resting immediately upon the abacus (flat slab) on the capital of a column. The term also describes the moulding around the exterior of an arch or the various parts surrounding a door or window

Art Deco Popular design style of the 1920s and at its height in the 1930s, characterised by geometrical shapes, bold outlines and zigzag forms

Ashlar Hewn and squared stones prepared for building

Astragal Small convex moulding usually with a semi-circular cross-section

Atrium Inner courtyard of a home or other building that is open to the sky or covered by a skylight

Baluster Short post or pillar in a series that supports a rail, thus forming a balustrade

Bauhaus German school of architecture and design founded by Walter Gropius in 1919 and closed in 1933

Bay, bow and oriel windows These windows project out from the front or side of a house. Oriel windows generally project from an upper storey, supported by a bracket. Bay windows are angled projections that rise up from the ground on the first floor. Bow windows are rounded projections, often formed of the window glass itself

Brickwork: Types English Bond: Bricklaying with alternate courses of headers and stretchers. Flemish Bond: Bricklaying with courses of alternate headers and stretcher. Monk Bond: Bricklaying with courses alternating with pairs of stretchers

Buttress Structure of wood, stone or brick built against a wall to strengthen or support it

Campanile A free-standing bell-tower

Cantilever Horizontal projection from a building, such as a step, beam, balcony or canopy, that is without external bracing and appears self-supporting

Capital Head of a column, usually featuring mouldings or carvings

Cartouche Scroll-shaped ornament or corbel. Term also describes a tablet representing a scroll with rolled-up ends or edges, with or without an inscription

Caryatid Female figure used as a pillar to support an entablature

Clerestory Row of windows in the upper part of the wall of a church that divides the nave from the aisle, set above the aisle roof

Column Tall, often slightly tapering, cylinder usually surmounted by an entablature and forming part of an arcade or colonnade, or standing alone as a monument
Console Ornamental flat-sided bracket or corbel, usually incorporating a volute at each end
Corbel Projection of stone or timber jutting out from a wall to support weight
Corinthian Column One of the five classical orders of architecture, characterised by a bell-shaped capital having carved ornamental decorations of acanthus leaves
Cornice Horizontal, usually moulded projection crowning the outside of a building or structure, especially the uppermost part of an entablature, above the frieze. Term also applies to an ornamental moulding running round the wall of a room near the ceiling
Cupola Rounded vault or dome forming part of a roof of a building. Term also describes the ceiling of a dome
Curtain Wall External non-loadbearing wall composed of repeated modular elements generally of glass in metal framing. These are prefabricated then erected on site.
Cyma Moulding in a section of two contrasting curves, either cyma recta or cyma reversa
Dado The plain portion of a pedestal between the base and the cornice. Term also describes the lower part of an interior wall when faced or coloured differently from the upper part
Dome: Geodesic Invented by Richard Buckminster Fuller, the geodesic dome, built with lightweight rods arranged as linked hexagons, is the only practical kind of building that has no limiting dimensions, i.e. beyond which the structural strength must be insufficient
Dome: Onion A dome larger in diameter than the drum it is set upon, its height also usually exceeding its width. These bulbous structures taper smoothly to a point. A good example of onion domes are those atop St Basil's Cathedral in Moscow
Doric Column Greek-style column with only a simple decoration around the top, usually a smooth or slightly rounded band of wood, stone or plaster
Dormer Window Window placed vertically in a sloping roof that has a tiny roof of its own. Most often seen in second-floor bedrooms
Ell Single-storey extension to a building, usually at right angles
Engaged Column Column that is attached to the wall so that only a half to three-quarters of its circumference stands visible
Entablature The part of a classical temple above the columns, having an architrave, a frieze, and a cornice
Fanlight Fan-shaped window over a door or other window
Flute Vertical channelling in the shaft of a column
Flying Buttress Buttress, usually on an arch, which slants upwards to a wall from a pier or other support
Frieze Central member of the classical entablature
Gable Triangular upper portion of a wall at the end of a pitched roof
Gargoyle Grotesque carving, usually in the form of a human or real or fantastic animal mouth, head, or body projecting from the gutter of a building, especially in Gothic architecture, and used as a spout to drain off rainwater
Gazebo Building or structure that commands a view, i.e. a summer-house or balcony
Gothic Style of architecture prevalent in western Europe from the 12th to the 16th century, of which familiar features include the pointed arch and the flying buttress
Greek Orders The three original classical orders of architecture, i.e. Doric, Ionic and Corinthian
Groin The edge formed by the intersection of two vaults. Term also describes an arch supporting a vault
Hammerbeam Horizontal beam in timber roof situated as a tie beam but in two sections with main opening in the centre
Hypocaust Hollow space under the floor where hot air was sent from a furnace to provide heating in Roman houses
Keystone The wedge-shaped block or central voussoir at the summit of an arch built of stone
Kouros Sculptured representation of a youth on Ionic architecture
Lancet High, narrow window with a lancet arch
Lancet Arch An arch with a head resembling the blade of a lancet (surgical knife)
Lintel Horizontal stone slab or timber beam spanning an opening and supported on columns or walls
Loggia Covered area on the side of a building that opens on one or more sides
Lunette Semicircular panel, often ornamented in the form of stone, wood or glass
Mansard Roof in which each face has two slopes, the lower one steeper than the upper
Mezzanine Low storey between two others in a building, usually between the ground floor and the floor above. Term also describes the floor beneath the stage in a theatre, from which the traps are worked
Mullion Vertical bar dividing the lights in a window, especially in Gothic architecture
Niche Artificially constructed wall recess often holding a statue or urn
Ogee Moulding consisting of a continuous double curve, especially with the upper part concave and the lower part convex
Ogee Arch Arch formed by two contrasted ogees which meet at its apex, often called a pointed or Gothic arch
Ogive The diagonal groin or rib of a vault, two of which cross each other at the vault's centre; or any pointed arch
Oriel Porch or balcony at the head of an outdoor staircase
Oriel Window Large polygonal recess with a window, projecting from upper storey of a building, and supported from the ground or on corbels
Palladian Window A window with three openings, the central one arched and wider than the others
Pediment Triangular part crowning the front of a building in the classical style, usually situated over a portico and consisting of a flat recessed field, framed by a cornice and often ornamented with sculptures
Pergola Covered walk in a garden, usually formed by a double row of posts or pillars with joists above and covered by climbing plants
Pier Solid support designed to sustain vertical pressure, e.g. a doorpost or gatepost; also a massive supporting column, holding up a nave or a bridge
Porte-cochere Large covered entrance for vehicles leading into a courtyard
Portico Formal entrance to a classical temple, church, or other building, consisting of columns at regular intervals supporting a roof often in the form of a pediment, a covered walkway
Porticus Addition on north or south side of a church of the Anglo-Saxon period, resembling an aisle or transept and containing a chapel
Prefabrication The manufacture of whole buildings or components cast in a factory or on site before being placed in position
Purlin Horizontal beam along the length of a roof, resting on principals (pairs of angled supporting beams that meet at the top) and supporting the common rafters
Quoin Dressed stones at the corners of a building
Rib A curved member supporting a vault or defining its form. The term also describes the curved pieces of stone, timber or metal strips forming the framework of a dome or the arched or flat beam or girder supporting a bridge
Roman Orders The two classical orders of architecture, i.e. Tuscan and Composite, which were added to the earlier Greek orders
Rotunda Building with a circular interior and plan, especially one with a dome, e.g. the Pantheon in Rome

Rustication Style of masonry in which the surface of the blocks is roughened. Rustication also refers to masonry cut in massive blocks separated from each other by deep joints

Soffit Underside of any architectural element such as an arch, beam or stair

Spandrel Originally, a space between timbers supporting a building, but now refers to the almost triangular space between one side of the outer curve of an arch and the rectangle formed by the mouldings enclosing it. The term also applies to the area of support between a set of steps and the ground

Stucco Fine plaster usually made from gypsum and pulverised marble, for covering walls and ceilings

Stupa Domed structure erected as a Buddhist burial mound

Styles Regency, Baroque, Palladian, Rococo, International

Telamon Male figure used as a pillar to support an entablature or other structure

Terrazzo Floor or wall finish made by setting marble or other stone chips into a layer of mortar and polishing the surface

Tracery Ornamentation in the upper part of a Gothic window, consisting of a perforated design or of an intersecting pattern, formed by the elaboration of the mullions. Tracery also refers to the interlaced work of a vault or panel

Transom Horizontal supporting or strengthening crossbar in any structure but usually refers to a window frame

Tuscan Order Simplest of the five classical orders of architecture, resembling the Doric, but devoid of all ornaments

Tympanum Triangular space between the sloping and horizontal cornices of a classical pediment

Vault Continuous arch, or a series of arches radiating from a central point or line, used to form a roof over a space inside a building

Venetian Window Composite window with three separate openings, the central one being arched and taller than the others

Volute Spiral scroll characteristic of Ionic capitals and also used in Corinthian and Composite capitals

Voussoir Each of the wedge-shaped or tapered stones forming an arch or vaulting

Wainscoting Decorative panelling applied to the lower half of an interior wall; usually wood in a plain design but may be painted

Wattle-and-Daub Walling made from vertical timber stakes woven horizontally with branches and reeds. The whole is then surfaced with mud

Wonders of the World: Ancient Colossus of Rhodes: bronze statue of Apollo erected c 280 BC; Hanging Gardens of Babylon: adjoining Nebuchadnezzar's palace 60 miles south of Baghdad; Pharos of Alexandria: lighthouse erected c 270 BC; Pyramids of Gizeh (Giza) near Cairo: Zoser, at Saqqara built c 2650 BC; Cheops built c 2580 BC (both still standing); Statue of Zeus: marble statue, built by Phidias c 430 BC, in the plains of Elis, Olympia; Temple of Artemis at Ephesus: Ionic temple built c 350 BC and burned by the Goths in AD 262; Tomb of Mausolus at Halicarnassus: built by the widowed Queen Artemisia c 350 BC

Pritzker Architecture Prize

The most prestigious award in the world of architecture is the Pritzker Architecture Prize, often referred to as 'architecture's Nobel'. Inaugurated in 1979 by the wealthy Pritzker family of Chicago through their Hyatt Foundation, and awarded each year to a living architect for lifetime achievement. The presentation ceremonies move around the world each year, paying homage to the architecture of other eras and also to works of previous winners. The bronze medallion awarded to each Laureate is based on the designs of Chicago architect Louis H Sullivan, widely acknowledged as the father of the skyscraper. On one side is the name of the prize and the winner's name and on the other the words 'firmness, commodity and delight'. These are the three conditions for good architecture referred to by Henry Wotton, England's first ambassador to Venice, in his 1624 treatise, *The Elements of Architecture*, which was a translation of Marcus Vitruvius' work, *Ten Books of Architecture*, dedicated to the Roman Emperor Augustus. The panel of judges (usually between six and ten) consists of internationally respected architects and design experts.

The complete list of Pritzker Architecture Prize winners is as follows:

1979 Philip Johnson (USA) presented at Dumbarton Oaks, Washington, DC
1980 Luis Barragán (Mexico) presented at Dumbarton Oaks, Washington, DC
1981 James Stirling (Great Britain) presented at the National Building Museum, Washington, DC
1982 Kevin Roche (USA) presented at the Art Institute, Chicago, Illinois
1983 Ieoh Ming Pei (USA) presented at the Metropolitan Museum of Art, New York
1984 Richard Meier (USA) presented at the National Gallery of Art, Washington, DC
1985 Hans Hollein (Austria) presented at the Huntington Library, Art Collections and Botanical Gardens, San Marino, California
1986 Gottfried Boehm (Germany) presented at Goldsmiths' Hall, London, England
1987 Kenzo Tange (Japan) presented at the Kimbell Art Museum, Fort Worth, Texas
1988 Gordon Bunshaft (USA) and Oscar Niemeyer (Brazil) presented at the Art Institute, Chicago, Illinois
1989 Frank Gehry (USA) presented at Todaiji Buddhist Temple, Nara, Japan
1990 Aldo Rossi (Italy) presented at Palazzo Grassi, Venice, Italy
1991 Robert Venturi (USA) presented at Palacio de Iturbide, Mexico City, Mexico
1992 Alvaro Siza (Portugal) presented at the Harold Washington Library Center, Chicago, Illinois
1993 Fumihiko Maki (Japan) presented at Prague Castle, Czech Republic
1994 Christian de Portzamparc (France) presented at The Commons, Columbus, Indiana
1995 Tadao Ando (Japan) presented at the Grand Trianon and Chateau of Versailles, France
1996 Rafael Moneo (Spain) presented at the construction site of the Getty Center, Los Angeles, California
1997 Sverre Fehn (Norway) presented at the construction site of the Guggenheim Museum, Bilbao, Spain
1998 Renzo Piano (Italy) presented at the White House, Washington, DC
1999 Lord Foster of Thames Bank (Great Britain) presented at the Altes Museum, Berlin, Germany
2000 Rem Koolhaas (Netherlands) presented at the Jerusalem Archaeological Park, Israel
2001 Jacques Herzog and Pierre de Meuron (Switzerland) presented at Thomas Jefferson's Monticello, Virginia
2002 Glenn Murcutt (Australia) presented at Michelangelo's Campidoglio, Rome, Italy
2003 Jørn Utzon (Denmark) presented at the Royal Academy of Fine Arts of San Fernando, Madrid, Spain
2004 Zaha Hadid (Great Britain) presented at the State Hermitage Museum of St Petersburg, Russia
2005 Thom Mayne (USA) presented at the Jay Pritzker Pavilion, Millennium Park, Chicago, Illinois
2006 Paulo Mendes da Rocha (Brazil) presented at the Dolmabahce Palace, Istanbul, Turkey
2007 Lord Rogers of Riverside (Great Britain) presented at the Banqueting House, London, England
2008 Jean Nouvel (France) presented at the Library of Congress, Washington, DC
2009 Peter Zumthor (Switzerland) presented at the Legislative Palace of the City Council, Buenos Aires
2010 Kazuyo Sejima and Ryue Nishizawa (Japan) presented at Ellis Island
2011 Eduardo Souto de Moura (Portugal) presented at the Andrew W. Mellon Auditorium, Washington, D.C.
2012 Wang Shu (China) presented at the Great Hall of the People, Beijing
2013 Toyo Ito (Japan) presented at the John F. Kennedy Presidential Library and Museum, Boston

Art

There are a number of points to be considered with reference to the following section. The history of art is a complex subject and although it is traditional to fix a label on artists and their works, in fact not only is it often impossible to identify a painter with any one group, it is also just as precarious to attach one term to the whole oeuvre of an artist. Even the historical styles overlap in many instances. The problem is that painters do not like to be pigeonholed, as styles and moods change and very often one style or school may become defunct or develop into something else. In researching this section I have also found that the nationalities of artists, especially those of the Low Countries, are open to interpretation, dependent not only on place of birth or naturalisation but also on style. I have endeavoured to qualify any contentious entries so as to give a more complete picture of the nature of the artist and his or her work. A problem when listing artworks is that not only are particular subjects covered as 'stock' pieces by numerous artists (such as The Adoration of the Magi) but also many individual artists often paint more than one version of a particular work – for example, Cézanne painted several versions of The Card Players and Millet painted several versions of The Sower. The final observation I have to offer in this web of intrigue is that when I came to list paintings in alphabetical order it occurred to me that many have alternative titles. For instance Vermeer's The Kitchen-Maid is listed in reputable sources with the alternative titles of The Milkmaid, The Maid with a Milk Jug, The Cook, The Maid-Servant Pouring Milk and The Servant Pouring Milk.

Famous Artists and Sculptors (selected work at end of each entry)

Abbate, Niccolo dell' (c1512–71) Italian Mannerist landscapist. *Rape of Proserpine.*

Albers, Josef (1888–1976) German-born founder of American Bauhaus in 1933. *Homage to the Square* series.

Alma-Tadema, (Sir) Lawrence (1836–1912) Dutch-born British painter of Classical genre. *The Visit, Parthenon Frieze.*

Altdorfer, Albrecht (c1480–1538) German painter and engraver, a pioneer of copperplate etching. *Landscape with a Bridge.*

Amigoni, Jacopo (c1682–1752) Venetian history and portrait painter. The altarpiece of Emmanuel College, Cambridge, is his.

André, Carl (1935–) American Minimalist sculptor famous for his 120 bricks (*Equivalent VIII*) in the Tate.

Andrea del Sarto (1486–1530) Florentine High Renaissance painter. His original name was Andrea D'Agnolo, but his father's family (from Lanfranchi) were tailors, hence del Sarto. *Madonna of the Harpies*; *St John the Baptist*; *A Young Man.*

Angelico, Fra (c1387–1455) Florentine religious painter and Dominican (monastic name Giovanni da Fiesole). *Annunciation*; *St Lawrence Receiving the Treasure of the Church*; *The Coronation of the Virgin.*

Antonello da Messina (c1430–79) Sicilian Renaissance landscapist. *St Sebastian*; *Salvator Mundi*; *A Man.*

Appel, Karel (1921–2006) Dutch Abstract Expressionist who founded the CoBrA group. *The Horseman.*

Arp, Jean (1886–1966) French artist, co-founder of Dadaism. Aka Hans Arp. Arp's first wife was the artist Sophie Taeuber-Arp (1889-1943)

Avercamp, Hendrick (1585–1634) Deaf and dumb Dutch landscapist. *Winter Landscape with Ice Skaters.*

Bacon, Francis (1909–92) Dublin-born figurative painter, influenced by Surrealism and violent imagery; studied under Graham Sutherland. *Three Studies for a Crucifixion; Triptych inspired by the Oresteia trilogy of Aeschylus.*

Baily, Edward Hodges (1788–1867) English sculptor whose most famous work is his Nelson for the column in Trafalgar Square.

Baldung (aka Grien), Hans (1484–1545) German religious painter of the macabre. Selected works: *A Man*; *Allegorical Figure.*

Balla, Giacomo (1871–1958) Italian Futurist who signed the Futurist Manifesto (1910) but by 1930 adopted a more conventional style of painting. *Dynamism of a Dog on a Leash.*

Bambi Graffiti Unknown female street artist said to be a famous London-based pop star. Best known for her stencilled images of Amy Winehouse and David Beckham, in 2011 she commemorated the wedding of Prince William and Kate Middleton with the satirical slogan 'A Bit Like Marmite' across their chests.

Banksy Bristol-born artist who has managed to keep his identity relatively unknown. Thought to have been born Robert (or Robin) Banks or Robin Gunningham in 1974/5, he first achieved fame by sticking fake objects to walls of museums and art galleries. In April 2006 he protested at the way BT has been replacing the classic telephone kiosk by placing one in Soho, London with a pickaxe embedded in it. His best known work was painted on the side of a sexual health clinic in Bristol later in 2006. *Well Hung Man* depicts a naked man dangling from a window as a suspicious husband peers out. Banksy's works are currently selling for huge prices and almost always depict an ironic view of life, occasionally making a political or social statement. In 2010 he made his debut as a film director in the acclaimed documentary *Exit Through the Gift Shop*, telling the story of Thierry Guetta, a French immigrant in Los Angeles who is obsessed with filming his every life experience and who eventually becomes a noteworthy street artist.

Barocci, Federico (1530–1612) Born Federico Fiori, and nicknamed Il Baroccio. *The Circumcision*; *Madonna of the Rosary; Ecce Homo.*

Bassano, Jacopo (c1510/17–92) Italian Mannerist and specialist in religious scenes. *The Holy Family*; *The Adoration of the Magi*; *Adoration of the Shepherds; The Good Samaritan*; *Calvary; Flight into Egypt; Susannah and the Elders.*

Beardsley, Aubrey Vincent (1872–98) Brighton-born art nouveau artist. Became famous for his fantastic posters and illustrations for *Morte d'Arthur*, Wilde's *Salome*, *Pope's Rape of the Lock*, as well as for the *Yellow Book* magazine (1894–6) and his own *Book of Fifty Drawings.* With Wilde he is regarded as leader of the 'Decadents' of the 1890s. Died of TB at Menton, France, having embraced Catholicism.

Beckmann, Max (1884–1950) German figurative painter and draughtsman who emigrated to the USA in 1947. *Night.*

Beechey, Sir William (1753–1839) English portraitist who was knighted for George III and the Prince of Wales Reviewing Troops.

Beerbohm, Max (1872–1956) English writer and caricaturist famous for his watercolours of Oscar Wilde and Edward VII.

Bell, Vanessa (1879–1961) English painter and decorative designer, a member of the Bloomsbury group, and the sister of Virginia Woolf.

Bellini Family Jacopo (c1400–70) founder of Venetian Renaissance art. His sons were Gentile (1429–1507), a portrait and panorama painter, and Giovanni (c1430–1516), the first Renaissance master of Venetian art, who taught both Giorgione and Titian. Selected works (Giovanni): *Descent into Limbo*; *Doge Leonardo Loredan*; *Pietà.*

Bellotto, Bernardo (1720–80) Venetian topographical artist, nephew of Canaletto. Painted a masterly interior of King's College Chapel, Cambridge. *View of Dresden.*

Bernini, Gian Lorenzo (1598–1680) Italian sculptor, architect and painter, born in Naples. Patronised by Cardinal Scipione Borghese. He designed the monumental baldacchino (choir canopy) for Saint Peter's in the Vatican. Although frequently used by Pope Urban VIII he was less popular with Innocent X, who preferred Alessandro Algardi. His most famous works include the Cornaro Chapel in the church of Santa Maria della Vittoria, the tomb of Alexander VII in Saint Peter's and the small Jesuit church of San Andrea al Quirinale, all in Rome. He was buried in Rome in the church of Santa Maria Maggiore.

Bevan, Robert Polhill (1865-1925) Hove-born artist famous for his paintings of horses. Founding member of the Camden Town Group, the London Group, and the Cumberland Market Group. Friend of, and influenced by, Gauguin. Married Polish painter Stanisława de Karłowska in 1897. Best-known paintings include: *Breton Churchyard* (1893), *Breton Mother and Child* (1894), *Horse Sale at the Barbican* (1912), *The Feathered Hat* (1915), *Mare and Foal* (1917), *A Devon Cottage* (1920) and *Mount Stephen* (1924). In 1913 *The Cabyard, Night* (1910) was bought by the Contemporary Art Society to become the only painting acquired for a public collection during his lifetime.

Bewick, Thomas (1753–1828) English wood engraver, born a farmer's son in Ovingham, Northumberland. His *History of British Birds* (1797–1804) was his masterpiece and the Bewick's Swan was named in his honour shortly after his death.

Blake, Peter (1932–) British Pop artist of the 1960s (now more conventional) famous for the cover of The Beatles' album *Sergeant Pepper's Lonely Hearts Club Band* (1967). Knighted in 2002; in 2006, he designed the cover for *Stop the Clocks* - Oasis' greatest hits album. *Toy Shop*; *Montgomery Clift was a Twin; The Owl and the Pussycat; Portrait of David Hockney in a Hollywood Spanish Interior; Self Portrait with Badges.*

Blake, Quentin (1932-) English cartoonist, illustrator and children's author best known for his illustration of books written by Roald Dahl.

Blake, William (1757–1827) English painter and poet. *Heads of the Poets*; *The Circle of the Lustful*; 20 illustrations to Dante's *Divine Comedy.*

Bonington, Richard Parkes (1802–28) English topographical watercolourist. *View of Normandy.*

Bonnard, Pierre (1867–1947) French landscape painter who also specialised in domestic scenes. Bonnard joined the Nabis, who included Denis and Vuillard, with whom he formed the Intimiste group. *Women with a Dog.*

Bosch, Hieronymus (c1450–1516) Netherlandish painter of the macabre, best known for his triptych *The Garden of Earthly Delights* (Prado, Madrid). *The Adoration of the Magi; The Ship of Fools; Christ Mocked; The Crowning with Thorns.*

Botticelli, Sandro (1445–1510) Florentine allegorical painter with distinctive linear style. *Mars and Venus; La Primavera; The Birth of Venus.*

Boucher, François (1703–70) French Rococo court painter and decorator to Louis XV; also director of the famous French tapestry workshop the Gobelins. *Diana after her Bath; Reclining Girl; Madame de Pompadour.*

Boudin, Eugène Louis (1824–98) French 'plein-airiste' - collections of his work are in the Musée de Doctor Faure, Aix-les-Bains, and the Musée des Beaux-Arts Jules Chéret, Nice. *Deauville; Harbour of Trouville; Corvette Russe; Beach Scene.*

Bourgeois, Louise (1911–2010) Born in Paris and studied under Léger before moving to New York in 1938. Regarded in later life as one of the most important artists working, she explored her ideas in painting, sculpture, printmaking, installation and performance, using various media from wood and stone to latex and rubber. In 2000 she was commissioned to exhibit the first of the annual Unilever Series at the Turbine Hall of Tate Modern. The installation consists of three steel towers, entitled *I Do, I Undo* and *I Redo.* Each tower is 9m high; *I Do* and *I Redo* are encircled by spiral staircases while *I Undo* has an additional staircase in its core. Bourgeois was famous for her drawings and sculpture of spiders.

Brancusi, Constantin (1876–1957) Romanian sculptor, born in Pestisani, near Turgujiu. In his youth he was a shepherd boy in the Carpathians. Brancusi worked in Rodin's atelier and produced his *The Kiss* (1908) 22 years after Rodin's. His *Sleeping Muse* (1910) also shows Rodin's influence, but is the first of his characteristic highly polished egg-shaped carvings. The *Prodigal Son* (1925) shows the influence of African sculpture. Brancusi was a pioneer of modern abstract sculpture. *Adam and Eve; Flying Turtle.*

Brangwyn, Sir Frank (1867–1956) Welsh painter, initially apprenticed to the Socialist designer William Morris. He presented a collection of his work to the city of Bruges in 1936 which is now housed in the Brangwyn Museum, and there is a substantial collection in the McManus Gallery, Dundee, and Brangwyn Hall, Swansea. *British Empire Panels* (Swansea Guildhall).

Braque, Georges (1882–1963) French pioneer of Cubism, with Picasso, who designed scenes for two Diaghilev ballets, *Les Fâcheux* and *Zéphyr et Flore.* Braque was the first man to have his work exhibited in the Louvre during his lifetime. *Still Life with Playing Cards; The Woman Musician; The Candlestick; L'Estaque, l'embarcadère; Piano and Lute; Violin and Jug.*

Bronzino, Agnolo (1503–72) Florentine Mannerist and portraitist. *Noli Me Tangere; Venus, Cupid, Folly and Time; Portrait of Don Garzia de Medici ; Eleanora da Toledo with Her Son; Christ in Limbo.*

Brouwer, Adriaen (c1605–38) Flemish-born low-life painter who studied at Haarlem under Frans Hals and is regarded as 'culturally' Dutch, although eventually settling in Antwerp, where he died of the plague. *A Boor Asleep; Interior of an Alehouse; Man with a Pointed Hat.*

Brown, Ford Madox (1821–93) French-born British painter associated with Pre-Raphaelites and William Morris in particular. He completed twelve frescoes for Manchester Town Hall, just before his death. His most famous picture, *Work,* was first exhibited at a retrospective exhibition held in London but is now hung in Manchester. Brown was the early tutor of Dante Gabriel Rossetti. *The Last of England.*

Brueghel, Jan (1568–1625) Flemish painter (nicknamed 'Velvet'); son of 'Peasant' Brueghel. *Still Life with Garland of Flowers.*

Brueghel the Elder, Pieter (c1520–69) Flemish allegorical and religious painter of the Antwerp School, nicknamed 'Peasant' Brueghel. *Adoration of the Magi; Death of the Virgin; Peasant Dance; The Massacre of the Innocents; The Tower of Babel; The Way to Calvary.*

Brueghel the Younger, Pieter (c1564–1636) Flemish painter nicknamed 'Hell' because of fantastic treatments of fire and grotesque imagery. The son of Pieter 'Peasant' Brueghel and famous for numerous copies after his father such as the *Tower of Babel* and *Way to Calvary.*

Burne-Jones, Sir Edward Coley (1833–98) British painter associated with Pre-Raphaelites and the Arts and Crafts Movement. *Adoration of the Magi (tapestry); Perseus* series; *Legend of the Briar Rose* series; *King Cophetua and the Beggar Maid.*

Calder, Alexander (1898–1976) American kinetic sculptor, abstract painter and illustrator of children's books. Calder invented the mobile.

Canaletto, Antonio (1697–1768) Venetian topographical artist who was the uncle of Bellotto. Canaletto was associated with his views of London and Venice, where the entrepreneur Joseph Smith was responsible for popularising his work. *View of the Grand Canal,* Venice; *View of the City of London from Richmond House; Stonemason's Yard; Piazza San Marco Looking East from South of the Central Line.*

Canova, Antonio (1757–1822) Venetian Neoclassicist sculptor whose work includes *The Three Graces* and *Daedalus and Icarus.*

Caravaggio, Michelangelo Merisi da (c1573–1610) Italian Baroque painter who fled Rome in 1606 after killing a man and spent the rest of his life as a refugee, moving between Naples, Sicily and Malta. *Adoration of the Shepherds; The Young Bacchus; Beheading of St John; Supper at Emmaus;* La Zingara (The Fortune-Teller); *Boy Bitten by a Lizard; The Calling of St Matthew; Crucifixion of St Peter.*

Caro, (Sir) Anthony (1924–) English sculptor. Assistant to Henry Moore between 1951 and 1953 specialising in clay figures. From 1953 he was influenced by the American sculptor David Smith and began to use steel as his medium. He was knighted in 1987. In the 1990s he turned his attention to installation pieces, notably *Sea Music* (1991), located on Poole Quayside in Dorset, and *Chapel of Light* in the St Jean-Baptiste Church of Bourbourg in France. Married since 1949 to artist Sheila Girling. *The Tower of Discovery; Dream City; Black Cover Flat.*

Carpaccio, Vittore (c1450–1525) Venetian religious painter. His most characteristic work is seen in the nine subjects from the life of St Ursula, and in his masterpiece, *the Presentation in the Temple,* both now in the Accademia, Venice. *The Preaching of St Stephen; Courtesans.*

Carrà, Carlo (1881–1966) Italian Futurist who founded the Metaphysical School with de Chirico in 1917.

Carracci, Annibale (1560–1609) Most important of the family of Bolognese Mannerists. *The Butcher's Shop; Bacchus and Silenus; Coronation of the Virgin.*

Castagno, Andrea del (c1420–57) Florentine Early Renaissance fresco painter. *Dante; The Youthful David.*

Cézanne, Paul (1839–1906) French Post-Impressionist who married Hortense Fiquet (subject of many of his paintings) in 1886, the year his friendship with Émile Zola ended, due to the publication of Zola's *L'Oeuvre,* in which the central figure is unflatteringly Cézanne. *The Bather; The Lake at Annecy; Card Players; The Blue Vase; Uncle Dominic as a Monk; Boy in a Red Waist-Coat.*

Chagall, Marc (1887–1985) Russian-born figurative painter, active in France and the USA. The Musée Marc Chagall in Nice is entirely devoted to his work. *The Dead Man; I and the Village; Self Portrait with Seven Fingers; The Juggler.*

Champaigne, Philippe de (1602–74) Brussels-born French Baroque court painter to Louis XIII patronised by Cardinal Richelieu. After 1647 he was associated with the Jansenists, a strict Roman Catholic sect. *Ex Voto of 1662 (The Louvre, Paris); Cardinal Richelieu.*

Chapman Brothers Jake (1966–) and Dinos Chapman (1962–) are former assistants of Gilbert and George and are identified with the YBA movement. Their sculpture *Hell* (2000) consists of miniature figures of Nazis arranged in nine glass cases laid out in the shape of a Swastika.

Chardin, Jean-Baptiste Siméon (1699–1779) French still-life genre painter. *Grace before Meat; Housewife; The Young Schoolmistress.*

Chirico, Giorgio de (1888–1978) Italian Surrealist and co-founder of Metaphysical School with Carlo Carrà. *The Pink Tower.*

Christo (1935–) Bulgarian-born, American sculptor famous for his 'wrappings', e.g. of the Reichstag building. His full name is Javacheff Christo. Christo often worked in collaboration with his wife Jeanne-Claude (1935–2009).

Cimabue, Giovanni (c1240–1302) Florentine fresco painter who is accepted as the teacher of Giotto. *Madonna and Child.*

Claude (le) Lorrain (1600–82) French Classical landscapist (born Claude Gellée). *Village Fête; Aeneas at Delos; Ascanius Shooting the Stag of Sylvia; The Marriage of Isaac and Rebecca* (aka *The Mill*).

Close, Chuck (1940–) American painter and photographer who pioneered photorealism, the technique of producing a painting from a photograph. Close continues to paint despite being partially paralysed since 1988 following a spinal artery collapse.

Clouet the Younger, Jean (c1485–1541) French court painter to François I. *Guillaume Budé.*

Clouet, François (c1510–72) French court painter to Francis I, Henri II, Francis II, and Charles IX. *Elizabeth of Austria; Mary Queen of Scots; Portrait of Henri II.*

Constable, John (1776–1837) English landscapist, born in East Bergholt, Suffolk, the county where many of his most famous works are set. *Dedham Vale; The Haywain; Harnham Ridge from Archdeacon Fisher's House, Salisbury; Dedham Lock and Mill; The Leaping Horse;* Various depictions of *Salisbury Cathedral.*

Cook, Beryl (1926–2008) Beryl took up painting in her thirties and immediately chose a humorous niche. In 1975 the Plymouth Arts Centre exhibited her work and in 1979 her life was featured on LWT's *The South Bank Show*, bringing her popular acclaim. *Football on Looe Beach.*

Cooper, Samuel (c1608–72) English miniaturist whose Oliver Cromwell (Buccleuch College) was his most famous work.

Copley, John Singleton (1738–1815) American portraitist and history painter working in England from 1775. *Hugh Montgomery, 12th Earl of Eglinton*; *The Siege of Gibraltar*; *The Copley Family*; *Brook Watson and the Shark.*

Corot, Jean-Baptiste Camille (1796–1875) French landscapist. *Louis Robert as a Child*; *Avignon.*

Correggio, Antonio Allegri da (c1490–1534) Italian High Renaissance painter, active mainly in Parma. *The Adoration of the Kings; Ecce Homo*; *The Agony in the Garden*; *St Mary Magdalen*; *Danae*; *Ascension of Christ; Assumption of the Virgin; Four Saints; The Nativity (aka The Holy Night or Adoration of the Shepherds); Venus with Mercury and Cupid* (aka *The School of Love).*

Cortona, Pietro Berrettini da (1596–1669) Italian painter and architect, creator of Roman High Baroque. *The Rape of the Sabines*; *Allegory of Divine Providence and Barbarian Power* (a ceiling frescoe in the Galleria Nazionale, Rome).

Cotman, John Sell (1782–1842) English landscapist, co-founder of the Norwich School. *The Devil's Elbow*; *Greta Bridge*; *Seashore with Boats.*

Courbet, Gustave (1819–77) French Realist who joined the Paris Commune, was imprisoned for his part in the destruction of the Vendôme Column and died in exile in Switzerland. *Battle between Two Stags; Studio of the Painter: an Allegory of Realism*; *Les Demoiselles de Village*; *Bonjour, Monsieur Courbet* ; *Stream in a Ravine*; *Young Women on the Banks of the Seine.*

Craig-Martin, Michael (1941–) Dublin-born conceptual artist who influenced many of the so-called 'Young British Artists' while teaching at Goldsmiths College, London (1974–88). His best known work, *An Oak Tree*, consists of a glass of water placed on a small glass shelf of the type normally found in a bathroom. In 1989 a major retrospective of his work was held at the Whitechapel Art Gallery, London. He has done installations for the Projects exhibition series at the Museum of Modern Art, New York (1991) and at the Centre Pompidou in Paris (1994). He was a Trustee of the Tate Gallery, London, from 1989 to 1999. In 2006, the Irish Museum of Modern Art displayed 40 years of his work.

Cranach the Elder, Lucas (1472–1553) German court painter to the Elector of Saxony. He had three sons, one of them Lucas the Younger (1515–86) specialised in recreating his father's work. *A Young Girl*; *Adam and Eve*; Stag Hunt of the Elector Frederick the Wise; *A Crucifixion*; *Martin Luther; The Judgement of Paris; Hercules and Antaeus; Paradise; Venus and Cupid.*

Crome, John (1768–1821) English topographical artist and founding member of the Norwich Society (1803), now known as the Norwich School. *Yarmouth Jetty*; *The Beaters*; *Marlingford Grove.*

Cuyp, Aelbert (1620–91) Dutch landscapist who was greatly influenced by Jan van Goyen. He also painted animals, seascapes and still lifes. *River Scene with a View of Dordrecht* ; *Sunset after Rain*; *Resting Horsemen in a Landscape.*

Daddi, Bernardo (c1290–1348) Florentine Early Renaissance contemporary of Giotto. *Virgin and Child.*

Dali, Salvador (1904–89) Spanish Surrealist. Born in Figueras but lived in Paris and, from 1940, in the USA. Dali collaborated with Luis Buñuel on such Surrealist films as *Le Chien Andalou* (1928) and *L'Age d'Or* (1930). *Young Virgin Auto-Sodomized by the Horns of Her Own Chastity; Accommodations of Desire; Christ of St John of the Cross*; *Inventions of the Monsters*; *Galacidalacideoxyribonucleicacid*; *Inventions of the Monsters; Tuna Fishing (Homage to Meissonier); The Persistence of Memory* (aka *The Limp Watches).*

Daubigny, Charles-François (1817–78) French landscapist of the Barbizon School who was a pupil of Paul Delaroche. *Evening Landscape.*

Daumier, Honoré (1808–79) French caricaturist and political satirist. Most famous work: *The Washerwoman* (*The Laundress*)

David, Gerard (c1460–1523) Netherlandish painter who became dean of the Painters' Guild of Bruges in 1501. *The Transfiguration*; *The Marriage at Cana*; *The Tree of Jesse* .

David, Jacques-Louis (1748–1825) French Neo-classicist who voted in the National Convention for the death of Louis XVI and after Robespierre's death was twice imprisoned. He produced his masterpiece *The Rape of the Sabines* in 1799 and in 1804 became court painter to Napoleon, but was eventually banished as a regicide after the Bourbon restoration. *The Death of Marat; Death of Socrates*; *Madame Récamier*; *Napoleon Crowning Josephine; Three Women of Ghent; Oath of the Tennis Court.*

Degas, Edgar (1834–1917) French Impressionist painter and sculptor who specialised in dancers. *The Ballet Scene; Miss La La at the Cirque Fernando*; *The Dancing Class*; *L'Absinthe*; *The Dancer; Semiramis Founding Babylon; At the Races.*

Delacroix, Eugène (1798–1863) French Romantic painter. Delacroix's Paris studio-apartment is now a museum for his work. *The Abduction of Rebecca; The Death of Sardanapalus*; *Battle of Taillebourg*; Baron Schwiter; *The Execution of Faliero*; *Liberty Leading the People.*

Delaroche, Paul (1797–1859) French history painter whose *Children of King Edward* is housed in the Louvre.

Delaunay, Robert (1885–1941) French Cubist and exponent of Orphism, husband of the pioneer abstract painter Sonia Delaunay Terk (1885–1979). *L'Equipe de Cardiff*, various depictions of *The Eiffel Tower.*

Delvaux, Paul (1897–1994) Belgian Neo-Impressionist, Expressionist and Surrealist. *Sleeping Venus.*

Denis, Maurice (1870–1943) French painter, founder of the 'Nabis' group. *Hommage à Cézanne.*

Derain, André (1880–1954) French Fauvist painter and sculptor. *Mountains at Collioure*; *Blackfriars.*

Dix, Otto (1891–1969) German Expressionist painter, a leader of the Neue Sachlichkeit group. *Sylvia von Harden*; *Nude Girl in a Fur* .

Dobson, William (c1610–46) English portrait painter who succeeded Van Dyck as painter to the exiled Charles I (1641). *Endymion Porter* .

Doesburg, Theo van (1883–1931) Dutch artist and architect. Leader of De Stijl movement with Mondrian and devotee of a severe form of geometrical abstraction known as Neo-Plasticism. He was originally called Christian Emil Marie Kupper.

Domenichino (1581–1641) Bolognese artist. *Portrait of Monsignor Agucchi* ; *Sibyl* ; *Last Communion of St Jerome*; *Tobias.*

Domenico Veneziano (c1400–61) Florentine Early Renaissance painter. *St Lucy Altarpiece.*

Donatello (c1386–1466) Florentine sculptor whose work included his *David and St George Killing the Dragon* (properly, Donato di Niccolò.)

Dongen, Kees van (1877–1968) Dutch painter active in Paris. Fauvist and member of Die Brücke (The Bridge). *Women on the Balcony.*

Dossi, Dosso (c1479–1542) Ferrarese fresco painter. *The Christ Child Learning to Walk*; *The Sorceress Circe.*

Dou, Gerrit (or Gerard) (1613–75) Dutch painter and former collaborator with Rembrandt. Started the 'Fijnschilder' (fine painter) School in Leiden. *A Woman at a Window*; *The Young Mother; A Poulterer's Shop*; *The Astronomer; The Hermit*; *Night-School; Rembrandt's Mother.*

Duccio di Buoninsegna (c1260–c1318) Sienese painter. *Maestà*; *Rucellai Madonna*; *Christ Healing the Blind Man*; *The Annunciation.*

Duchamp, Marcel (1887–1968) French-born American painter and sculptor, brother of Jacques Villon. Inventor of the 'Ready-Made' and leader of the New York Dadaists. *The Bride Stripped Bare by her Bachelors, Even*, also known as *The Large Glass*; *Mona Lisa with Moustache and Goatee; Sad Young Man in a Train.*

Dufy, Raoul (1877–1953) French artist and designer, born in Le Havre. Dufy played a big part in popularising Fauvism. In 1911 he illustrated Guillaume Apollinaire's *Bestiary*. *Château and Horses.*

Dürer, Albrecht (1471–1528) German artist, born in Nuremberg, the son of a Hungarian goldsmith. Dürer is often considered the inventor of etching and was a supreme master of the woodcut. *Self Portrait in a Fur-collared Robe*; *A Young Man*; *Adoration of the Magi*; *Anna Selbdritt; Job and His Wife; Madonna with Musical Angels; The Feast of the Rose Garlands; Hercules Killing the Stymphalian Birds; Lucretia.*

Dyce, William (1806–64) Scottish painter and pioneer of state art education in Great Britain.

Dyck, (Sir) Anthony van (1599–1641) Anglo-Flemish court painter to Charles I of England and pupil of Rubens. Member of the Antwerp School. *Triple Portrait of Charles I*; *Portrait of the Earl of Strafford*; *The Lornellini Family; Carrying of the Cross; Samson and Delilah; Emmanuel Philibert; The Entry into Jerusalem; King Charles on Horseback; Lamentation for Christ; Cupid and Psyche.*

Eakins, Thomas (1844–1916) American painter and photographer, born in Philadelphia. His composite plates inspired Duchamp's *Nude Descending a Staircase*. *Max Schmitt in a Single Scull*; *Chess Players.*

Eliasson, Olafur (1967–) Born in Copenhagen, Denmark and attended the Royal Academy of Arts in Copenhagen from 1989 to 1995. He specialises in large installation works and *The Weather Project* is the fourth in the annual Unilever Series of commissions for the Turbine Hall at Tate Modern. Currently based in Berlin. In May 2009 Eliasson completed *The Parliament of Reality*, a permanent sculpture based on the Icelandic Althing. Situated at Bard College, New York, the man-made island project is surrounded by a 30ft circular lake and 24 trees. In 2011 he designed the facade of Harpa, Reykjavík's new concert hall and conference centre notable for its glass panels of different colours.

Elsheimer, Adam (1578–1610) German painter on copper. *St Paul on Malta*; *Judith and Holofernes*; *Tobias and the Angel*.

Emin, Tracey (1963–) Croydon-born modern artist who was brought up in Margate. Her best-selling autobiography is entitled *Exploration of the Soul.* In 1993, she opened 'The Shop' with fellow artist Sarah Lucas. In May 2004, a fire in a Momart storage warehouse in East London destroyed several of her works, including *The Hut* and *Everyone I Have Ever Slept With 1963–95*, consisting of a tent with a montage of names of old lovers embroidered on its walls. A recent public work is a neon artwork sign reading "More Passion"; installed outside the Terracotta Room at Number 10 Downing Street in August 2011. *Every Part of Me's Bleeding*; *People Like You Need to Fuck People Like Me; My Bed.*

Ensor, James (1860–1949) Belgian painter of the macabre and precursor of Surrealism. *Entry of Christ into Brussels.*

Epstein, (Sir) Jacob (1880–1959) American-born British sculptor, born a Russian-Polish Jew in New York. His early commissions included 18 nude figures for the façade of the British Medical Association building in the Strand (1907–8) and *Night and Day* (1929) for the London Transport Building in Westminster. These and later symbolic sculptures, such as the marble *Genesis* (1930), the *Ecce Homo* (1934) and the alabaster *Adam* (1939), resulted in accusations of indecency and blasphemy. His last two large commissioned works were *Christ in Majesty* (Llandaff Cathedral) and *St Michael and the Devil* (Coventry Cathedral).

Ernst, Max (1891–1976) German painter and sculptor who was a founder of the Surrealist movement. He invented the technique of frottage (pencil rubbings on canvas). *The Elephant Celebes*; *Le Grand Amoureux.*

Estes, Richard (1932–) US founder of the photorealism movement of the 1960s; *Telephone Booths* (1968) being one of the first examples.

Etty, William (1787–1849) English artist who specialised in nudes. *Monk Bar, York*; *The Combat*; *Somnolency*; *The Fairy of the Fountain.*

Eyck, Hubert van (c1366–1426) Flemish painter; the brother of Jan van Eyck.

Eyck, Jan van (c1389–1441) Netherlands painter, successively in the service of John of Bavaria, the Count of Holland and Philip the Good of Burgundy. *The Arnolfini Wedding*; *Adoration of the Lamb*; *The Madonna with Chancellor Rolin*; *Man in a Red Turban.*

Fabritius, Carel (1622–54) Dutch painter of still lifes and street-scenes. Worked under Rembrandt around 1641 and lived mainly at Delft, where he was killed in the explosion of the municipal ammunition depot. *View of Delft*; *An Old Man*); *The Goldfinch.*

Fairhurst, Angus (1966–2008) English installation and video artist known for his collaborations with Damien Hirst and Sarah Lucas. As a sculptor he was most famous for his gorillas. On the final day of his exhibition at Sadie Coles HQ in London in March 2008 he was found hanging from a tree near Bridge of Orchy in the Scottish Highlands, having taken his own life.

Fantin-Latour, Henri (1836–1904) French genre, still-life and Symbolist painter, born in Grenoble. *Flowers and Fruit*; *Homage to Delacroix.*

Feininger, Lyonel (1871–1956) American artist and cartoonist, born in New York of German immigrant parents. Taught at the Bauhaus at Weimar and Dessau, but when the Nazis came to power he returned to the USA and, with Gropius and Mies van der Rohe, founded the Chicago Bauhaus. *Sailing Boats*; *Gelmeroda III.*

Fini, Leonor (1908–96) Argentinian graphic artist often associated with the surrealist movement. Prolific painter of beautiful women but possibly best known for her flamboyant Parisian lifestyle. She was photographed nude in a swimming pool by Cartier-Bresson, a photo that sold for $305,000 in 2007.

Flanagan, Barry (1941–2009) Welsh sculptor, best known for his bronze statues of hares.

Fouquet, Jean (c1420–81) French court painter to Louis I. Pope Eugenius IV commissioned a portrait from him, now lost. *Etienne Chevalier with St Stephen*; *Madonna and Child*; *Charles VII.*

Fragonard, Jean-Honoré (1732–1806) French Rococo painter. *The Swing*; *Bathers.*

Frankenthaler, Helen (1928–2011) American Abstract Expressionist painter, who devised a technique for staining unprimed canvases with washes of colour. *Blue Territory.*

Freud, Lucian (1922–2011) German-born, English figurative painter. In his early years he was one of the Neo-Romantic group along with Minton, Craxton, Sutherland and Piper; but from the 1950s he developed a realist style. One of the most respected artists since World War II. Freud's work does not lend itself to be pigeon-holed in any particular style and includes portraits ranging from *Francis Bacon* in the Tate (stolen in 1988 whilst on exhibition in Germany) to the painting of a man in a raincoat with a yucca – *Interior in Paddington* (Walker Art Gallery, Liverpool). Sigmund Freud was the artist's grandfather. In 1948 he married Kitty Garman, the daughter of Jacob Epstein, and after the marriage was annulled in 1952 he married Lady Caroline Maureen Blackwood (marriage dissolved in 1957; she died in 1996). Freud is known to have sired numerous offspring by various mistresses. In May 2008, his 1995 portrait *Benefits Supervisor Sleeping* was sold at Christie's in New York for $33.6m, a world record by a living artist at the time.

Friedrich, Caspar David (1774–1840) German Romantic painter of nature, and particularly forest scenes. His works are included in the German Romantic collection in the Schinkel Pavilion at Schloss Charlottenburg and in the Neue National Galerie, both in Berlin. *Man and Woman Gazing at the Moon*; *Wreck of the Hope.*

(Dame) Elizabeth Frink (1930–93) English sculptress. The horror of war ran through her entire oeuvre. *Gogglehead*; *Arrival at Canterbury.*

Frith, William Powell (1819–1909) English genre painter who became the wealthiest painter of his time by selling both paintings and their copyright. *The Derby Day*; *The Railway Station.*

Fuseli, Henry (1741–1825) Swiss Romantic fantasy painter who took British citizenship and became professor of painting at the Royal Academy, and Keeper in 1804. *Lady Macbeth Sleepwalking*; *Titania and Bottom*; *The Three Witches from Macbeth*; *The Nightmare.*

Gabo, Naum (1890–1977) Russian-born, US artist; the brother of Antoine Pevsner, with whom he founded Constructivism.

Gaddi, Taddeo (c1300–66) Florentine painter and mosaicist who was Giotto's best pupil and also his godson. *Life of the Virgin.*

Gainsborough, Thomas (1727–88) English portrait and landscape painter, born in Sudbury, Suffolk. Married Margaret Burr, the illegitimate daughter of the 4th Duke of Beaufort. Most famous work: *The Blue Boy* (depiction of his friend Master Jonathan Buttall). *Harvest Wagon*; *Portrait of Mary, Countess Howe*; *The Watering Place*; *Mrs Graham*; *George III & Queen Charlotte*; *The Market Cart; The Morning Walk; Mrs Robinson (aka Perdita); The Painter's Daughters Chasing a Butterfly; Peasants Returning from Market; Woodcutter Courting a Milkmaid.*

Gaudier-Brzeska, Henri (1891–1915) French Cubist sculptor born in St Jean de Braye. Came to England in 1911 with his partner Sophie Brzeska (a Polish writer of almost twice his age he had met the previous year in a Paris library), and founded the London Group of Sculpture. In 1914 he signed the Vorticist Manifesto. Joined the French army at the outbreak of WWI and was killed in action. *Armour.*

Gauguin, Paul (1848–1903) French Post-Impressionist who gave up a stockbroking career to devote himself to painting. He evolved a style known as 'Synthetism' in a reaction against Impressionism. Lived in Tahiti 1891–1901 and then the Marquesas Islands. Fell out with his friend Van Gogh at Arles in 1888. *The Vision after the Sermon*; *Tahitian Women*; *La Seine au Pont d'Iéna; The King's Wife* (aka *Women with Mangoes*); *The Swineherd; When Shall We Be Married.*

Gentile da Fabriano (c1370–1427) Italian International Gothic painter (properly, Niccolo di Giovanni di Massio). *Adoration of the Magi*.

Gentileschi, Artemisia (c1597–c1651) Daughter of the Bolognese painter Orazio Gentileschi. *Self-portrait as Pittura*; *Susannah and the Elders.*

Gérard, François (1770–1837) French artist, born in Rome. *Cupid and Psyche; Battle of Austerlitz; Josephine Bonaparte.*

Géricault, Théodore (1791–1824) French Romantic history painter. He died following a fall from his horse. His tomb in Père Lachaise cemetery, Paris, has a brass relief of *The Raft of the Medusa. The Wounded Cuirassier*, *Mad Woman with a Mania of Envy*; *The Charging Chasseur.*

Gheeraerts, Marcus, the Younger (c1561–1636) Flemish portraitist. Court painter to Elizabeth I and James I of England (VI of Scotland). Portrait of Arabella Stuart in the Scottish National Portrait Gallery is possibly by Gheeraerts. *Sir Thomas Lee*; *William Camden.*

Ghirlandaio, Domenico (1449–94) Florentine Renaissance fresco painter (properly, Domenico di Tommaso Bigordi). *Life of the Virgin; Visitation of the Virgin*; *Old Man and His Grandson.*

Giacometti, Alberto (1901–66) Swiss sculptor and painter best known for his attenuated sculptures of solitary figures.

Gibson, John (1790–1866) Welsh Neo-classical sculptor whose *Tinted Venus* is in the Walker Art Gallery, Liverpool.

Gilbert & George (1943– / 1942–) English avant-garde artists, noted for painting their faces gold and wearing identical outfits. Their full names are Gilbert Proesch and George Passmore.

Gilbert, (Sir) Alfred (1854–1934) English sculptor and goldsmith, leader of the New Sculpture movement. *The Clarence Memorial* in Windsor is considered the climax of his work although *Eros* (Piccadilly Circus, London) his most famous. Other works include *Joule* (Manchester Town Hall); the *Alexandra Memorial* in Marlborough Road, London, and the *Queen Victoria* statue in Winchester.

Gill, Eric (1882–1940) English sculptor, engraver, writer and typographer, born in Brighton, the son of a clergyman. In 1909 he carved his first stone figure *The Madonna and Child.* Through the influence of Augustus John he exhibited at the Chenil Galleries, Chelsea (1911). He maintained a steady output for the rest of his life, during which he designed the classic typeface Gill. Joined the Fabian movement and eventually became Catholic. *Mankind*; *Stations of the Cross*; *Prospero and Ariel* (BBC Broadcasting House, London).

Gillray, James (1756–1815) English political and social caricaturist and printmaker, born in Chelsea, the son of a Lanark trooper. Gillray had a life-long partnership with the publisher Mrs Humphrey. From 1810 until his death he was hopelessly insane.

Giordano, Luca (1634–1705) Neapolitan decorative painter, precursor of Rococo and court painter to Charles II of Spain. Renowned for his speed of working, hence his nickname 'Luca Fa Presto' (Luke Go Quickly). *Apotheosis of the Medici.*

Giorgione (c1478–1510) Venetian Renaissance painter (properly, Giorgio Barbarelli). *The Adulteress before Christ*; *The Adoration of the Magi*; *The Tempest*; *Judgement of Solomon; Trial of Moses.*

Giotto di Bondone (c1266–1337) Florentine painter who introduced sculptural solidity into painting and heralded the Renaissance. He was a pupil of Cimabue, but because of confusion as to his early life it is not known for sure if the St Francis of Assisi frescoes were attributable to him. Often called the 'Father of Modern Painting'. Both he and Cimabue are mentioned by Dante. Legend says he drew a perfect circle freehand for the Pope. *The Arena Chapel murals* at S. Maria Annunziata dell'Arena, Padua; *Ognissanti Madonna; Lamentation.*

Giulio Romano (1492–1546) Roman Mannerist painter and architect. An indication of his fame is a mention in Shakespeare's *Winter's Tale. Isabella d'Este*; *Allegory of Immortality*; fresco decorations at the Palazzo del Te, Mantua.

Goes, Hugo van der (c1440–82) Flemish painter of religious subjects. *Adoration of the Shepherds*; *Death of the Virgin*; *Adoration of the Magi.*

Gogh, Vincent van (1853–90) Dutch Post-Impressionist. The Rijksmuseum Vincent van Gogh in Amsterdam houses over 700 of his paintings and drawings. *Cornfield and Cypress Trees*; *Irises*; *Church at Auvers; Pipe and Bandaged Ear (Self-portrait); The Chair and the Pipe (aka Van Gogh's Chair); In the Field; Skull of a Skeleton with Burning Cigarette.*

Gore, Spencer Frederick (1878–1914) English painter, born in Epsom, Surrey. Gore was a founder member and first president of the Camden Town Group (1911). *From a Window in Cambrian Road, Richmond.*

Gorky, Arshile (1904–48) Armenian-born US painter influenced by Cubism, Surrealism and Abstract Expressionism. Original name: Vosdanig Manoog Adoian. *The Liver Is the Cock's Comb.*

Gormley, Antony (1950–) At the forefront of a generation of British artists who emerged during the 1980s. *Another Place*, first exhibited on the beach at Cuxhaven, Germany in 1997, but now permanently erected on Crosby Beach, near Liverpool, consists of 100 nude cast iron figures in the artist's image which emerge from the sea at low tide. Public work in Britain can be seen in locations as diverse as the crypt at Winchester Cathedral and Birmingham city centre. In 1994 he won the Turner Prize and in 1997 was awarded the OBE for services to sculpture. His best-known work is *The Angel of the North* (see entry below). In May 2003 *Domain Field*, a room full of life-size depictions of the human form made out of stainless steel rods, was unveiled at the Baltic Arts Centre in Gateshead. The 2006 Sydney Biennale featured Gormley's *Asian Field*, an installation of 180,000 small clay figurines crafted by 350 Chinese villagers in five days from 100 tons of red clay. In July 2009 Gormley presented *One and Other*, a Fourth Plinth Commission, whereby members of the public chosen by lot were able to spend one hour on the vacant plinth in Trafalgar Square, London.

Goya y Lucientes, Francisco (1746–1828) Court painter to Charles IV of Spain. His series of etchings, *The Disasters of War*, describe the horrors of the Peninsular war in Spain. *Family of Charles IV*; *The Naked Maja*; *The Duke of Wellington*; *The Annunciation; The Madhouse.*

Goyen, Jan van (1596–1656) Dutch landscapist. *Cottages & Fishermen by a River*; *Leiden from North-East; Dordrecht from Papendrecht*.

Gozzoli, Benozzo (c1421–97) Florentine fresco painter, a pupil of Fra Angelico. *Journey of the Magi.*

Greco, El (1541–1614) Cretan-born Spanish Mannerist (properly, Domenico Theotocopoulos). *The Saviour*; *The Tears of St Peter*; *The Disrobing of Christ*; *Assumption of the Virgin; Trinity.*

Greuze, Jean-Baptiste (1725–1805) French genre and portrait painter. *The Broken Pitcher*; *Girl with Doves.*

Grimshaw, (John) Atkinson (1836–93) Leeds-born artist who specialised in nocturnal townscapes with gas lights and wet streets.

Gris, Juan (1887–1927) Spanish Cubist (properly, José Victoriano González). *Still Life with Dice*; *The Glass.*

Grosz, George (1893–1959) German-born American Expressionist and Dadaist whose depictions of the depravity of war were so graphic that the Nazis called him 'Cultural Bolshevist Number One'. Although starting as a Dadaist, he was a co-founder of the Neue Sachlichkeit movement. *Kristallnacht*; *To Oskar Panizza.*

Grünewald, Matthias (c1470/80–1528) German visionary artist (properly, Mathis Gothardt – although he occasionally added his wife's surname Neithardt to his own). Grünewald is the 'Mathis der Maler' of Hindemith's opera of that name. *The Isenheim Altarpiece*; *The Mocking of Christ*; *The Miracle of the Snow.*

Guardi, Francesco (1712–93) Italian topographical artist, born in Pinzolo. Pupil of Canaletto, and like his master famous for his views of Venice. *Ascent in a Balloon*; *The Doge Embarking on the Bucintoro*; *The Doge's Palace.*

Guardi, Giovanni (1699–1760) Venetian painter, born in Vienna, brother of Francesco Guardi.

Guercino (1591–1666) Bolognese early Baroque painter (properly, Gian-Francesco Barbieri). *The Incredulity of St Thomas*; *Susanna Bathing.*

Gursky, Andreas (1955–) German visual artist known for his digitally enhanced images often mounted to plexiglass. *Chicago Board of Trade II.*

Hals, Frans (c1580–1666) Dutch genre and portrait painter, born in Antwerp. *The Laughing Cavalier*; *Married Couple in a Garden*; *Aletta Hannemans*; *The Merry Toper*; *Merry Company; Hamlet (aka Young Man Holding a Skull); Nurse and Child.*

Hamilton, Gavin (1723–98) Scottish painter in Rome, who pioneered the depiction of Homeric subjects in a severe manner.

Hamilton, Richard (1922–2011) English artist who became a pioneer of Pop Art after attending the *This is Tomorrow* exhibition in Whitechapel Art Gallery, London, in 1956. He reconstructed Duchamp's *Bride Stripped Bare by her Bachelors, Even*, by consulting the original notes and studies by the artist. *Adonis in Y-Fronts; Just What Is It That Makes Today's Homes So Different, So Appealing.*

Heartfield, John (1891–1968) German painter, originally Helmut Herzfelde, a leading member of Berlin Dada and a lifelong pacifist.

Hepworth, (Dame) Jocelyn Barbara (1903–75) Born in Wakefield, West Yorkshire, her first marriage was to fellow sculptor John Skeaping and her second to painter Ben Nicholson. Noted for the strength and formal discipline of her carving, e.g. *Contrapuntal Forms*, exhibited at the Festival of Britain, 1951. Such pieces as *Wave* (1944) and *Mr & Mrs Ashley* (Havinden Collection, England) became increasingly open, hollowed out and variously perforated, so that the interior space became as important as the mass surrounding it. *Pelagos*; *Pendour*.

Hilliard, Nicholas (1537–1619) English miniature-painter at the courts of Elizabeth I and James I of England. *Young Man among Roses*; *Elizabeth I Playing a Lute*; *Self-portrait Aged 31.*

Hirst, Damien (1965–) Avant-garde artist, born in Bristol. Following a disappointing 'D' in his A-Level art exam went on to train at Goldsmiths College, London. Became known for his works which made use of parts or all of dead animals preserved in formaldehyde, such as *I Want You Because I Can't Have You* (1992), a series of fish behind a perspex casing enclosed within a steel, melamine and wood exterior, and *Mother and Child Divided* (1993) – four tanks containing the severed halves of a cow and calf. His 1994 exhibition contained a dead lamb *Away from the Flock*, suspended within a tank. In 1995 he was awarded the Turner Prize and in 1996 his New York exhibition 'No Sense of Absolute Corruption' (Gagosian Gallery), contained several large paintings, as well as earlier works including an 8.3ins porcelain ashtray full of cigarette butts entitled *Home Sweet Home.* In December 2004, *The Physical Impossibility of Death in the Mind of Someone Living* was sold for $12m, the most expensive work by a living artist ever sold, with the exception of some early work by Jasper Johns. He then beat this record in June 2007 when *Lullaby Spring*, a 3m wide cabinet with 6,136 pills, sold for $19.2m (but see Lucian Freud). Later in 2007 he created *For the Love of God*, a platinum human skull adorned with 8,601 diamonds weighing a total of 1,106.18 carats. Approximately £15m worth of diamonds were used and a price tag of £50m asked for. His representation of the British Union Flag formed the arena centrepiece for the 2012 Summer Olympics closing ceremony in London.

Hobbema, Meindert (1638–1709) Dutch landscapist and pupil of Jacob von Ruysdael. *The Avenue at Middleharnis*; *A Watermill*; *A Peasant Cottage on a Water* Course; *The Ruins of Brederode Castle.*

Hockney, David (1937–) Versatile Bradford-born artist. Californian swimming pools were prolifically painted in his early career, notably *A Bigger Splash* (1967). In the Seventies his style became more traditional with a series of portraits of couples such as *Mr and Mrs Clark and Percy* (1970 - depicting the fashion designer Ossie Clark and the textile designer Celia Birtwell shortly after their wedding at which Hockney was Clark's best man

– Percy is a white cat) and *My Parents* (1977), both displayed in Tate Britain, London. Hockney is also a celebrated graphic artist, photographer and stage designer of operatic productions. *Le Plongeur* (The Diver); *Rocky Mountains and Tired Indians.*

Hogarth, William (1697–1764) English painter and satirist, born in Smithfield, the son of a teacher. Studied under Sir James Thornhill and married Thornhill's daughter in 1729. *Lord George Graham in His Cabin*; *The Rake's Progress* series; *Self-portrait with His Pug; A Fishing Party; Garrick in the Character of Richard III.*

Hokusai, Katsushika (1760–1849) Japanese engraver and watercolourist whose work became extremely popular in England after the Anglo-Japanese trade agreements of the 1880s. His work influenced Whistler. Famous for the *Thirty-six Views of Mount Fuji* series displayed at the Art Institute of Chicago.

Holbein the Younger, Hans (c1497–1543) German portraitist who was court painter to Henry VIII. His father, Hans Holbein the Elder (c1460–1524), was also a painter of note. *The Ambassadors*; *Sir Thomas Moore*; *Jane Seymour* ; *Anne of Cleves; Erasmus in the Roundel; Henry VIII.*

Homer, Winslow (1836–1910) American painter, born in Boston. Began as an illustrator for magazines such as *Harper's Weekly* and *Ballou's Pictorial.* Worked for many years at his Prouts Neck studio in Maine, where the local sea area became a favourite subject for depiction. *Fog Warning*; *Pitching Quoits.*

Honthorst, Gerrit van (1590–1656) Dutch genre and night-scene painter who was the court painter to the Stadholder of Holland and Charles I of England. *Winter Queen* (Elizabeth of Bohemia); *Willem II, Prince of Orange*; *The Death of Seneca.*

Hooch (or Hoogh), Pieter de (1629–84) Dutch genre painter. *Backgammon Players; A Musical Party*; *A Courtyard in Delft*; *At the Linen Closet.*

Hoppner, John (1758–1810) English portraitist whose masterpiece was *The Countess of Oxford.*

Hopper, Edward (1882–1967) New York-born painter, mostly of urban scenes. *Early Sunday Morning*; *Model Reading; Room in Brooklyn.*

Hughes, Arthur (1830–1915) English painter associated with the Pre-Raphaelite Brotherhood, although never formally.

Hume, Gary (1962–) YBA member who came to prominence via his 'door paintings' (life-size representations of hospital doors). Known for his simplistic use of colour as in his 1996 work *Snowman* consisting of a head, body and background in three shades of red.

Hunt, William Holman (1827–1910) English painter and founder member of the Pre-Raphaelite Brotherhood. *The Scapegoat* ; *Claudio and Isabella*; *The Light of the World* (Keble College, Oxford).

Hunt, William Morris (1824–79) American Romantic painter who created a fashion in the USA for the luminous, atmospheric painting of the Barbizon School. *Girl at a Fountain* (Metropolitan Museum of Art, New York).

Huysum, Jan van (1682–1749) Dutch still-life painter. *Fruit, Flowers and Insects* (Alte Pinakothek, Munich).

Ibbetson, Julius Caesar (1759–1817) English landscapist who specialised in the scenery of the Lakes and his native Yorkshire.

Ingres, Jean Auguste Dominique (1780–1867) French Classical painter of portraits and history pictures. Ingres bequeathed much of his work to his home town of Montauban, and the collection is now housed in the town's Musée Ingres. His motto was 'A thing well drawn is well enough painted'. Ingres became a senator in 1862. *Madame Moitessier* ; *The Turkish Bath*; *Oedipus and the Sphinx.*

Inness, George (1825–94) American landscapist, later influenced by the Barbizon School. *The Delaware Valley*; *Rainbow after a Storm.*

Jackson, Alison (1970-) Hampshire-born artist best known for her lookalike photographs of celebrities. She won a BAFTA for directing the BBC2 comedy series *Doubletake.*

Jawlensky, Alexej von (1864–1941) Russian Expressionist working in Munich from 1896 and France from 1905. In 1924 he co-founded Der Blaue Vier (Blue Four group) with Kandinsky, Klee and Feininger. *Head of a Woman.*

John, Augustus Edwin (1878–1961) Welsh painter, born in Tenby. Graduated from the Slade School of Art, London, with his elder sister, Gwen John. His favourite themes were gypsies, fishing folk and wild, lovely, yet regal women. *Smiling Woman*; *Richard Hughes.*

John, Gwen (1876–1939) Welsh painter who worked as an artist's model and became Rodin's mistress. *A Corner of the Artist's Room.*

Johns, Jasper (1930–) American Neo-Dadaist painter and sculptor, a strong influence on Pop Art, whose sculptures are of everyday items. Throughout his career he has specialised in numerous drawings and prints of flags in various media. His 1987 etching with aquatint, *The Seasons (Summer)* is highly acclaimed, although his best-known work is probably *Flag* (1955). Although Lucian Freud had the world record auction sale by a living artist, Johns' *False Start* (1959) was bought privately for $80m in 2006. In "Mom and Pop Art", a 1999 episode of *The Simpsons*, Johns guest starred as himself. *Zero Through Nine.*

Jordaens, Jacob (1593–1678) Flemish low-life and religious painter. Pupil of Rubens. *Commerce and Industry Protecting the Fine Arts*; *Presentation in the Temple*; *The Fruit Seller.*

Jorn, Asger Oluf (1914–73) Danish Expressionist (properly, Asger Jorgensen). Founded the CoBrA group, which was named after COpenhagen, BRussels, Amsterdam. *The Lost World.*

Judd, Donald (1928–1994) American Minimalist artist and sculptor who has geometric boxes built especially to use in his work.

Kahlo, Frida (1907–54) Mexican painter noted for her communist sympathies, unconventional lifestyle and flamboyant dress sense. She also sported a small moustache and unibrow, which she exaggerated in self-portraits. Frida suffered polio when she was six and this, coupled with a serious road accident in 1925, left her suffering pain for much of her life. Frida married Mexican muralist and cubist painter Diego Rivera and they were known as 'the elephant and the dove' due to their difference in size. In 2002 Miramax released *Frida*, a film of her life starring Salma Hayek in the title role. *The Bus*; *Thinking of Death.*

Kandinsky, Wassily (1866–1944) Russian pioneer of abstract art who was influenced by the Fauves, Bauhaus, and Surrealists. He founded Der Blaue Reiter group with Franz Marc. *First Abstract Watercolour* ; *Blue Mountain*; *Composition II; Tempered Elan; White Line.*

Kapoor, Anish (1954–) Born in Bombay but lives and works in London. Renowned for his enigmatic sculptural forms that permeate physical and psychological space. His versatility and inventiveness have resulted in works ranging from powdered pigment sculptures and site-specific interventions on wall or floor, to gigantic installations both in and outdoors. Throughout, he has explored what he sees as deep-rooted metaphysical polarities: presence and absence, being and non-being, place and non-place and the solid and the intangible. His *Sky Mirror* sculptures, reflecting the sky and surroundings, have been shown in Nottingham (2004) and New York (2006). Kapoor is currently working on the Tees Valley Giants, with structural designer Cecil Balmond. The first of the five sculptures, *Temenos*, has been completed. If the project is completed it will become the world's biggest public art project. His best-known works to date are *Marsyas*, the third in the Unilever series of commissions for the Turbine Hall at the Tate Modern and the *ArcelorMittal Orbit* (see entry in current affairs section 28 October 2011). He was awarded the CBE in 2003.

Kauffmann, Angelica (1741–1807) Swiss Neo-classical painter in England who co-founded the Royal Academy (1768). She married the Venetian painter Antonio Zucchi. *Rinaldo and Armida*; *Euphrosyne Complains to Venus of the Wounds of Cupid.*

Kiefer, Anselm (1945–) German avant-garde artist whose work tends to concentrate on German history.

Kirchner, Ernst Ludwig (1880–1938) German Expressionist, influenced by Neo-Impressionism, Fauvism and Primitive art. *Die Brücke painters* – portraits of Otto Muller, Erich Heckel, Schmidt-Rotluff and Kirchner; *Japanisches Theater.*

Kitaj, Ron B. (1932–2007) US Pop artist, introducing cultural and political elements. Active in the UK. Committed suicide in 2007. *If Not . . . Not.*

Klee, Paul (1879–1940) Swiss painter and etcher. Blaue Reiter member and teacher at the Bauhaus. Described his work as 'taking a line for a walk'. *Death and Fire*; *Around the Fish; Ad Marginem.*

Klein, Yves (1928–62) French revolutionary Minimalist, painting only in blue. Klein was a celebrated exponent of judo and lived in Japan in 1952–3. *ANT 143 The Handsome Teuton.*

Klimt, Gustav (1862–1918) Austrian Art Nouveau painter, founder member of the Vienna Secession, 1898, artists who resigned as a group from conventional academic bodies. *Salome*; *The Kiss*; *Frau Adele Bloch-Bauer; Frau Fritza Riedler.*

Kline, Franz Joseph (1910–62) American artist who became an Abstract Expressionist around 1950, using black shapes on white canvas.

Kneller, (Sir) Godfrey (1646–1723) German portrait painter in England, court painter to William III and George I. Famous for painting 42 portraits of the members of the literary association called the Kit-Kat Club, now in the National Portrait Gallery, London. These pictures were painted between 1700 and 1720 and are of a size (36" x 28") now known as 'Kit-Kat' size. *Isaac Newton*; *James, Duke of Monmouth.*

Knight, (Dame) Laura (1877–1970) British artist best known for her beautifully tranquil beach and seaside paintings, paintings of the circus and of ballet. Elected a Royal Academician in 1936. Dame Laura was an official war artist who was sent to make portraits at the Nuremberg Trials.

Kokoschka, Oskar (1886–1980) Austrian Expressionist working in England and Switzerland. Signed many of his paintings 'OK'. *Still Life with Tortoise and Hyacinth*; *The Tempest* (aka *Bride of the Wind*); *Sir Stanley Unwin.*

Koninck, Philips de (1619–88) Dutch panoramic landscapist. *Landscape* (Hunterian Art Gallery, Glasgow).

Kooning, Willem de (1904–97) Dutch-born American Abstract Expressionist. *Woman I* (Museum of Modern Art, New York).

La Tour, Georges de (1593–1652) French artist of candle-lit scenes, active in Lorraine. *St Joseph the Carpenter*; *The Dice Players*; *St Jerome.*

La Tour, Maurice Quentin de (1704–88) French pastellist and portrait painter whose works are celebrated in the Musée Antoine Lecuyer in Saint-Quentin, France. *Mr and Mrs Angerstein*; *Madame de Pompadour*; *Lamentation over St Sebastian.*

Lancret, Nicholas (1690–1743) French Rococo genre and *fêtes galantes* painter in the style of Watteau. *Mademoiselle Camargo Dancing.*

Landseer, (Sir) Edwin Henry (1802–73) English animal painter and engraver – a favourite of Queen Victoria. Landseer is famous for his *Monarch of the Glen* and for sculpting the lions at the foot of Nelson's Column. Buried in St Paul's Cathedral, London. *Dignity and Impudence*; *The Rout (Defeat) of Comus.*

Lawrence, (Sir) Thomas (1769–1830) Bristol-born artist, the son of an innkeeper. In 1792 he became painter to George III. *Queen Charlotte.*

Le Brun, Charles (1619–90) French artist; first director of the Gobelins tapestry works. *Banker Jabach and His Family; The Chancellor Séguier.*

Le Nain Brothers Antoine (c1588–1648), Louis (c1593–1648) and Mathieu (c1607–77). French painters, born in Laon. All painted scenes of peasant life but did not sign work with their initials, thus making attributions almost impossible. *Peasant Children*; *A Blacksmith in His Forge.*

Lear, Edward (1812–88) English landscape painter, youngest of 21 children, famous for his nonsense verse.

Léger, Fernand (1881–1955) French Cubist who has a museum dedicated to him on the Côte d'Azur. *Homage to David*; *Woman and Still Life.*

Leighton, (Lord) Frederick (1830–96) English painter of classical subjects, who became the 1st Baron Leighton of Stretton, the first British artist to be awarded a peerage; Leighton is buried in St Paul's Cathedral, London. *The Garden of the Hesperides.*

Lely, (Sir) Peter (1618–80) Dutch portrait painter working in England. Court painter to Charles II. *Ladies of the Lake Family*; *The Windsor Beauties*; *Duchess of Cleveland.*

Leonardo da Vinci (1452–1519) Italian painter, sculptor, scientist and creator of the High Renaissance style. Worked in the pay of Cesare Borgia, son of Pope Alexander VI, as senior military architect and general engineer, and then for François I of France. *Mona Lisa* (aka *La Gioconda*); *The Virgin of the Rocks* (two versions, one in The Louvre and one in the National Gallery, London); *The Last Supper*; *The Annunciation; Salvator Mundi (Saviour of the World* – attributed to*).*

Leyster, Judith (1609–60) Dutch portrait painter, pupil of Hals. She married the painter Jan Molenaer (c1609–68). *The Lute-Playing Fool*.

Lichtenstein, Roy (1923–97) American Pop artist, whose works were inspired by comic strips. *Whaam!*; *In the Car.*

Liebermann, Max (1847–1935) German painter and etcher, leader of the German Impressionist school.

Limbourg Brothers (early 15th-century) Flemish family of miniature painters in the International Gothic style. The three brothers were Pol, Jehanequin and Hermann de Limbourg. *Les Très Riches Heures* (Musée Condé, Chantilly).

Lippi, Filippino (c1457–1504) Florentine painter of the transition from Early to High Renaissance. Son of Fra Filippo Lippi. *Vision of St Bernard.*

Lippi, Fra Filippo (c1406–69) Florentine fresco painter. Aka 'Fra Lippo Lippi'. *Annunciation*; *The Adoration of the Magi.*

Lissitzky, Eleazar M (1890–1941) Russian Constructivist painter, influenced by Malevich. *Victory over the Sun.*

Lorenzetti, Ambrogio (c1290/1300–c1348) Sienese landscapist and realist famous for his frescoes in the Palazzo Pubblico, Siena.

Lorenzo, Monaco (the Monk) (c1370–1425) Sienese painter in the International Gothic style who took holy orders in 1391.

Lotto, Lorenzo (c1480–1556) Italian Renaissance painter. *Portrait of Andreas Odoni*; *Madonna and Child with Saints*; *A Gentleman in His Study.*

Louis, Morris (1912–62) American Cubist until 1952 and then influenced by Jackson Pollock. He pioneered Colorfield painting, using bands of colour. Louis was further influenced by Helen Frankenthaler's *Mountains and Sea*, which prompted him to throw acrylic paint onto unprimed canvases to create brilliant patches of abstract colour. *Alpha-Phi.*

Low, (Sir) David (1891–1963) New Zealand-born British political cartoonist. Joined the *Evening Standard* in 1927. His most famous creation was 'Colonel Blimp', an embodiment of the die-hard British bigot.

Lowry, Laurence Stephen (1887–1976) Salford painter famous for his matchstick-like men and women. Lowry was only ever a part-time painter and worked most of his life as a clerk. *The Pond* (Tate Britain, London).

Lucas, Sarah (1962–) British modern artist who works with a variety of materials and media, including photographs, sculpture and installations. Her work often features images of herself in a confrontational stance, eg *Self Portrait: Eating a Banana* (1990) and *Divine* (1991). In 1993 she opened 'The Shop' with Tracy Emin in Bethnal Green and shares a similar level of notoriety in her work. Lucas is said to have declined nomination for the Turner Prize on several occasions. In 1996 she was the subject of a BBC documentary, *Two Melons and a Stinking Fish.*

Mabuse, Jan (c1478–1532) Flemish Mannerist allegorical painter (properly, Jan Gossaert). *The Adoration of the Kings*; *Little Girl.*

Macke, August (1887–1914) German painter and leader of Der Blaue Reiter group killed in action in WWI.

Maes, Nicolaes (1634–93) Dutch portrait and genre painter, pupil of Rembrandt.*The Idle Servant.*

Magritte, René (1898–1967) Belgian Surrealist, influenced by de Chirico. *Black Flag*; *Golconda; Threatening Weather.*

Malevich, Kasimir (1878–1935) Russian Suprematist, producing the first strictly geometrical art of the 20th century. *Woman with Water Pails.*

Manet, Edouard (1832–83) French precursor of Impressionism. *A Bar at the Folies Bergère; The Absinthe Drinker*, *Blonde with Bare Breasts; Music in the Tuileries Garden*; *Olympia*; *Le Déjeuner sur l'herbe*; *Skating; The Street Singer.*

Mantegna, Andrea (1431–1506) Italian Renaissance painter working in Padua and Mantua. Mantegna married a daughter of Jacopo Bellini. *The Triumph of Caesar*; *Crucifixion*; frescoes in the Camera degli Sposi, Palazzo Ducale, Mantua.

Marc, Franz (1880–1916) German Expressionist and member of Der Blaue Reiter. Marc was killed at Verdun. *Large Blue Horses*; *Red Woman.*

Marclay, Christian (1955–) American visual artist and composer often identified as the inventor of turntablism (term coined by DJ Babu in 1995 to describe a DJ that manipulates the stylus and mixer).

Martini, Simone (c1280–1344) Artist of the Sienese School. *Madonna with Angels and Saints, Maesta*; *Christ Returns to his Parents.*

Masaccio (1401–28) Florentine painter (properly Tommaso di Ser Giovanni di Simone dei Guidi), whose nickname literally means 'Hulking Tom'. *Madonna and Child*; *Crucifixion*; frescoes in the Brancacci Chapel, S. Maria del Carmine, Florence.

Masson, André (1896–1987) French Surrealist painter and graphic artist who was famous for working whilst in a state of trance.

Massys, Quentin (c1465–1530) Netherlandish portrait painter, influenced by Italian art. *Jesus and the Infant St John Embracing*; *Virgin and Child with Angels*; *The Entombment of the Lord; Money Changer and His Wife; The Old Man and the Courtesan; The Virgin in Prayer.*

Matisse, Henri (1869–1954) French painter who was leader of the Fauves, 1905–6, before changing his style. The Chapelle de Rosaire in Vence, France, was entirely designed and decorated by him. The Musée Matisse in Nice houses a collection donated by the artist's family. *The Painting Lesson*; *Interior with Aubergines; The Dinner Table; Open Window; Woman with the Hat; The Snail.*

Memling, Hans (c1430–94) Flemish biblical and portrait painter. *Bathsheba*; *St John*; *The Adoration of the Magi*.

Mengs, Anton-Raphael (1728–79) German painter, born in Bohemia, the son of a Danish artist. *Maria Luisa of Parma*; *Richard Wilson.*

Metsu, Gabriel (1629–67) Dutch genre painter, particularly of domestic scenes, a pupil of Dou. *The Sick Child*; *The Music Lesson*; *Woman at the Spinet*; *Artist and His Wife; The Duet ('Le corset bleu').*

Michelangelo Buonarotti (1475–1564) High Renaissance and later Mannerist painter, sculptor and architect, born near Florence, where he grew up. Patronised by Pope Julius II, for whom he decorated the ceiling of Sistine Chapel (1508–12). The marble statue of a nude David located at the Accademia Gallery in Florence is another iconic masterpiece.

Millais, (Sir) John Everett (1829–96) Southampton-born co-founder of the Pre-Raphaelite Brotherhood. In 1840 he became the youngest ever student at the Royal Academy, and in 1896 its President. *The Blind Girl*; *Christ in the House of His Parents*; *The Return of the Dove to the Ark*; *Ophelia*; *Autumn Leaves.*

Millet, Jean François (1814–75) French artist at Barbizon 1849. *The Angelus; The Gleaners*; *La Famille du Paysan*; *The Milkmaid; The Sower.*

Miró, Joan (1893–1983) Spanish Abstract painter, sculptor and ceramicist, influenced by Cubism and Surrealism. *Samurai*; *The Egg.*

Modigliani, Amedeo (1884–1920) Italian painter and sculptor, working in Paris from 1906. *Seated Nude.*

Moholy-Nagy, László (1895–1946) Hungarian-born, American experimental artist and photographer, influenced by Lissitzky and Constructivism. He developed kinetic art and taught at the Bauhaus and in Chicago. *Z IV* (Marlborough Gallery, London).

Mondrian, Piet (1872–1944) Dutch member of De Stijl and developer of Neo-Plasticism, who influenced the Bauhaus School. *Broadway Boogie Woogie*; *Victory Boogie Woogie; Composition in Black and White*; *Composition in Diamond Shape*; *The Grey Tree*; *The Red Cloud; The Red Tree; Woods near Oele; Still Life with Gingerpot.*

Monet, Claude (1840–1926) Father of Impressionism, whose *Impression: Sunrise* gave its name to the movement. Monet's *Déjeuner sur l'herbe* (Luncheon on the Grass) should not be confused with Manet's. *Field with Poppies*; *The Beach at Trouville*; *Rouen Cathedral: Sunset*; *Antibes; Haystacks at Giverny; Hyde Park, London; The River.*

Moore, Henry Spencer (1898–1986) English sculptor, born in Castleford, Yorkshire, the son of a coal-miner. Moore is best known for his reclining female figures, carved in wood and stone or cast in bronze. He was an official war artist 1940–42, during which time he produced a famous series of drawings of air-raid shelter scenes. His principal commissions included the *Madonna and Child* in St Matthew's Church, Northampton; the decorative frieze on the Time-Life building, London; and the massive reclining figures for the UNESCO building in Paris and the Lincoln Center in New York. Moore was awarded the Order of Merit in 1963.

Moreau, Gustave (1826–98) French Symbolist painter whose Paris home and studio is now the Musée Gustave Moreau. *The Apparition.*

Morisot, Berthe (1841–95) French Impressionist, granddaughter of Fragonard, who married Eugène, the brother of Manet. *Cradle.*

Moro, Antonio (c1519–76) Dutch court painter to the Habsburgs and Mary I of England, who knighted him as Sir Anthony More. *Queen Anna of Spain*); *Sir Henry Lee.*

Morse, Samuel (1791–1872) American painter and first President of the National Academy (1826), but better known for his invention of the electric telegraph. *House of Representatives*); *Lafayette.*

Moses, Anna Mary ('Grandma') (1860–1961) American Primitive artist who did not start to paint until she was 75 years old.

Motherwell, Robert Burns (1915–91) US artist who wed fellow Expressionist Helen Frankenthaler, 1955. *Elegy to the Spanish Republic XXXIV.*

Mucha, Alphonse (1860–1939) Czech painter, graphic artist and designer, chiefly known for his Art Nouveau illustration style, especially the posters for the actress Sarah Bernhardt. *Job and Lorenzaccio* (Victoria and Albert Museum, London).

Munch, Edvard (1863–1944) Norwegian Expressionist. Important collections of his work are at the Rasmus Meyers Samlinger, Bergen, and the Munch Museum and the National Gallery, Oslo. *The Scream* ; *Vampire*; *Ashes* ; *The Evening Hour; The Sick Child.*

Muñoz, Juan (1953–2001) Born in Madrid, Spain, and studied at the Central School of Art, London and the Pratt Centre, New York. A leading exponent of installation sculpture, he was commissioned to submit the second of the Unilever Series at the Turbine Hall at Tate Modern. The work, entitled *Double Bind* consisted of a series of optical illusions and spectacular follies. He died of a stomach haemorrhage in August 2001.

Murillo, Bartolomé Esteban (c1618–82) Spanish Baroque painter of religious and genre subjects. Born in Seville, Murillo fell from a scaffold when painting an altarpiece at Cadiz, and died shortly afterwards in Seville. *Virgin of the Rosary*; *The Two Trinities*, aka *The Holy Family*; *Boys with Fruit*; *Ecstasy of St Diego of Alcalá.*

Nash, Paul (1889–1946) English painter and co-founder of the Modern Movement. Nash was an official war artist in both world wars. *Landscape of the Vernal Equinox*; *Pillar and Moon*; *Totes Meer* (Dead Sea).

Nauman, Bruce (1941–) Born in Indiana, USA. After studying mathematics at university he has established himself as a leading installation artist. His large-scale video installation *Mapping the Studio II* (2001) has been acquired by the Tate and *Raw Materials*, consisting of 22 spoken texts from existing works to create an aural collage, is the fifth in the Unilever Series of commissions for the Turbine Hall at Tate Modern. He currently lives and works in New Mexico.

Newman, Barnett (1905–70) American painter who founded the 'subject of the Artist' school with William Baziotes, Rothko and Motherwell.

Nicholson, Ben (1894–1982) English Abstract painter who used a restricted palette of greys and muted tones. Married three times; his second wife was the sculptor Barbara Hepworth. *Still Life* (Glasgow Art Gallery & Museum); *White Relief* (Tate Britain, London).

Nolan, (Sir) Sidney (1917–92) Australian artist noted for his series of Ned Kelly paintings, begun in 1946.

Nolde, Emil (1867–1956) German Expressionist and printmaker (properly, Emil Hansen). His Art Nouveau house in Seebull, Germany, is now a museum. *Doubting Thomas*; *Death of Mary*; *The Flower Garden.*

Ofili, Chris (1968–) Born in Manchester but heavily influenced by his African roots. His controversial collage *The Holy Virgin Mary*, which featured a black Virgin Mary with elephant dung on one breast and cut-outs from pornographic magazines glued in the background, created a stir when exhibited in New York. He is currently based in Trinidad. *The Adoration of Captain Shit and the Legend of the Black Stars* Part 2.

O'Keeffe, Georgia (1887–1986) US Surrealist and Abstract painter who married photographer Alfred Stieglitz. In May 2001 her 1928 painting *Calla Lilies with Red Anemone* was sold at Christie's, New York, for $6,166,000, the top auction price for a work by a woman artist. *Black Iris.*

Oldenburg, Claes Thure (1929–) Swedish-born, US sculptor specialising in representing giant foodstuffs, such as hamburgers.

Oliver, Isaac (c1560–1617) French-born English miniaturist who married the half-sister of Marcus Gheeraerts the Younger. Oliver's work included a famous miniature of Elizabeth I of England that displeased her immensely. *Self Portrait* (National Portrait Gallery, London).

Opie, John (1761–1807) Cornish portrait and history painter, son of a carpenter. Nicknamed the 'Cornish Wonder'. Patronised by John Wolcot (the political satirist Peter Pindar). His first exhibited historical work was *The Assassination of James I of Scotland* (1786), followed by *The Murder of Rizzio* (1787), both destroyed by bombing in 1941. *Mary Wollstonecraft* (Tate Britain, London).

Oudry, Jean-Baptiste (1686–1755) French artist. *The Dog* (Burrell Collection, Glasgow); *The Calling of the Hounds* (Pitti Palace, Florence).

Palma Vecchio (c1480–1528) Venetian painter of *sacra conversazione* altarpieces (b. Jacopo Palma). *Venus and Cupid*; *The Assumption.*

Palmer, Samuel (1805–81) English landscapist and etcher, influenced by William Blake. *Coming from Evening Church.*

Parmigianino, Il (1503–40) Italian early Mannerist (properly, Girolamo Francesco Maria Mazzola). *The Marriage of St Catherine*; *Madonna with the Long Neck*; frescoes in S. Maria della Steccata, Parma.

Pasmore, Victor (1908–98) English portrait, still-life and landscape painter. Co-founder of the Euston Road School. In the late 1940s he turned towards abstract art. *Inland Sea*; *Wine Red.*

Pechstein, Max Hermann (1881–1955) Co-founder of German Expressionism and member of Die Brücke from 1906 before helping to found the rival Neue Sezession (New Secession). *Indian and Woman.*

Perugino, Pietro (c1445–1523) Umbrian painter (properly, Pietro di Cristoforo Vannucci). Perugino was the master of Raphael. *Virgin and Child.*

Pevsner, Antoine (1886–1962) Russian-born French Constructivist painter, brother of Naum Gabo.

Piazzetta, Giovanni Battista (1682–1754) Venetian painter, illustrator and designer. *Fortune Teller*; fresco *The Crucifixion* (Church of S. Maddalena de' Pazzi, Florence).

Picabia, Francis (1879–1953) French Cubist, Dadaist and Surrealist who also dabbled in Futurism. Married Gabrielle Buffet in 1909. *Udnie.*

Picasso, Pablo (1881–1973) Malaga-born painter and sculptor who embraced Surrealism and Expressionism. Picasso, along with Braque, pioneered Cubism. Picasso's blue period was from 1901 to 1904, followed by his pink period (1904–6) and a short brown period (1905–6). He was director of the Prado during the Spanish Civil War and joined the Communist Party in 1944. Picasso died in Mougins, France. The Musée Picasso in Antibes was decorated by him in 1946, and many works are in the Musée Picasso, Paris. His mural *War and Peace* is housed in the Musée National Picasso in Vallauris, and *Man with a Lamb* is in the public square. The Museo Pablo Picasso in Barcelona holds early works donated by the painter in 1970. *Three Dancers*; *Les Demoiselles d'Avignon*; *Guernica*; *Woman in an Armchair; The Soup; Woman with Pears.*

Piero della Francesca (c1419–92) Umbrian painter, scientist and mathematician. *The Nativity*; *Constantine's Dream*; *Federigo da Montefeltro.*

Piper, John (1903–92) English artist, born in Epsom, Surrey. Originally an abstract painter, he turned to Romantic realism under the influence of Palmer and the earlier English topographical painters. As an official war artist (1940–42), he painted many successful war pictures, but his design of the stained glass windows for Coventry Cathedral and Eton are his best-known works.

Pisanello, Antonio (c1390–1455) Italian painter and follower of the International Gothic style of Gentile da Fabriano. *The Vision of St Eustace*; *Lionello d'Este*; *St George and the Princess.*

Pisano, Andrea (c1290–c1349) Italian sculptor born in Pontadera and trained in Pisa. Considered the founder of the Florentine School of sculpture. Best known for his relief panels on the bronze south door of the Florence Baptistry. *Weaver* (Campanile, Florence cathedral); *Noah* (Museo dell'Opere del Duomo, Florence).

Pissarro, Camille (1830–1903) French Impressionist and Pointillist, born in St Thomas, West Indies. *Boulevard Montmartre by Night*; *Lower Norwood, London, Snow* (both National Gallery, London).

Pollaiuolo, Antonio (c1431–c1498) Florentine painter, sculptor, goldsmith and engraver, properly Antonio di Jacopo d'Antonio Benci, but took his name from his father's profession as a poulterer. Collaborated with his brother Piero (c1443–c1496) on the bronze tomb of Sixtus IV and the monument to Pope Innocent VIII, both in Saint Peter's, Rome. Other notable works include the bronze statuette *Hercules and Antaeus* in the Bargello, Florence, and the signed engraving *Battle of the Ten Nude Gods*. It is not always clear which brother should be credited with some of their oeuvre, but Piero, principally a painter, is thought to be responsible for at least three of the *Seven Virtues* in the Uffizi, Florence; three others were probably collaborations with Antonio, and the seventh by Botticelli.

Pollock, Jackson (1912–56) American Abstract Expressionist and early exponent of tachisme (action painting). *Full Fathom Five* was probably the first work of this controversial 'poured painting' style. Alcoholism and his death in a car crash added to Pollock's notoriety. His painting *No. 5, 1948* is reputed to be the most expensive ever sold at approximately $140m although Paul Cézanne's *The Card Players* is rumoured to have been bought by the Royal Family of Qatar for an estimated $250m in April 2011. *Enchanted Wood*; *Summertime: Number 9a*.

Pontormo, Jacopo Carrucci (1494–1557) Florentine early Mannerist. *Four Scenes from the Life of Joseph*; *Cosimo I de Medici*.

Poussin, Nicolas (1594–1665) French Classical landscapist who was court painter to Louis XIII. His oeuvre included mythological works and biblical subjects; he was an early exponent of history painting. *The Nurture of Jupiter*, *Tancred and Erminia*; *Inspiration of the Poet*; *The Adoration of the Golden Calf; Holy Family on the Steps*.

Primaticcio, Francesco (1504–70) Italian Mannerist painter, sculptor and architect. *The Rape of Helen*.

Puvis de Chavannes, Pierre (1824–98) French decorative, symbolic painter, noted for his murals. A number of huge canvases are set in to the walls of the grand staircase of the Musée de Picardie, Amiens. *Poor Fisherman* (Louvre, Paris).

Quelling, Arnold (1653–1686) English sculptor who collaborated with Grinling Gibbons on many works.

Quinn, Marc (1964–) Although not represented in the 1988 Damien Hirst-curated Freeze exhibition which brought the Young British Artists (YBAs) to public attention, Quinn is readily identified with the movement. He is best known for *Alison Lapper Pregnant*, a statue of an armless artist which adorned the fourth plinth at Trafalgar Square, London, until 2007. Quinn's signature piece is *Self* (1991), a frozen sculpture of the artist's head made from 10 pints of his own blood. He is also known for his Kate Moss sculptures. Quinn is married to author Georgia Byng.

Rackham, Arthur (1867–1939) English artist best known for his illustrations of Peter Pan and of Hans Christian Andersen's fairy tales.

Raeburn, (Sir) Henry (1756–1823) Scottish portraitist, elected to the Royal Academy in 1815. Best known work *The Reverend Robert Walker Skating on Duddingston Loch* aka *The Skating Minister* (National Gallery of Scotland, Edinburgh). *Lady Dalrymple*; *The MacNab*.

Ramsay, Allan (1713–84) Scottish portrait painter to George III of England.

Raphael (1483–1520) Italian High Renaissance painter who worked on a number of Papal commissions. Raphael (properly, Raffaello Santi or Sanzio) was born in Urbino. Leo X selected him to succeed Donato Bramante (a relative) as architect of St Peter's in 1514. His last work, the *Transfiguration* was left unfinished when he died. *Pope Julius II*; *The Madonna of the Goldfinch*; frescoes in the Vatican Palace, Rome.

Rauschenberg, Robert (1925–) US avant-garde artist specialising in works constructed from everyday rubbish. Also a noted Pop silk-screenist.

Ray, Man (1890–1976) American painter, photographer and film-maker; he co-founded the New York Dadaist movement.

Redon, Odilon (1840–1916) French Symbolist painter and graphic artist; a precursor of Surrealism. *Violette Heyman*.

Rembrandt Harmenszoon van Rijn (1606–69) Dutch painter, etcher and graphic artist whose home is now a museum in Amsterdam. Born in Leiden, the son of a prosperous miller, his first wife was Saskia van Ulenburgh (d. 1642). He failed to achieve financial security and, despite being the most famous painter of his time, died a pauper. *Balaam's Ass and the Angel; Portrait of Titus*; *The Night Watch (aka The Militia Company of Captain Frans Banning Cocq)*; *Christ before Pilate; Capture of Samson (aka The Blinding of Samson)*.

Reni, Guido (1575–1642) Bolognese Classical painter of Baroque religious works. *St John the Baptist* (Dulwich Gallery , London).

Renoir, Pierre Auguste (1841–1919) French Impressionist, born in Limoges. He visited Italy in 1880 and during the next few years painted a series of *Bathers* in a colder, more classical style, influenced by Ingres and Raphael. He then returned to hot reds, orange and gold to portray nudes in sunlight. Renoir's hands were crippled by arthritis in later years. His son Jean (1894–1979) became a great film director. *Bather; Umbrellas (Les Parapluies)*; *Dancer; Moulin de la Galette*; *Madame Charpentier and Her Children; La Loge* (aka *The Theatre Box*).

Reynolds, (Sir) Joshua (1723–92) English portraitist and art theorist. Co-founder and first President of the Royal Academy, 1768. Principal painter to George III of England, 1784. *Mrs Siddons as the Tragic Muse; Three Ladies Adorning a Term of Hymen: The Montgomerie Sisters*; *Admiral Lord Anson; The Pembroke Family*.

Ribera, Jusepe de (c1591–1652) Spanish Baroque painter, known as Lo Spagnoletto (The Little Spaniard). *Martyrdom of St Bartholomew*.

Richter, Hans (1888–1976) American painter, sculptor and film-maker, born in Berlin. Member of the Zurich Dadaists, 1917.

Rigaud, Hyacinthe (1659–1743) French Rococo painter. Portraitist to Louis XIV and Louis XV of France. A small collection of his works is housed in the Musée Rigaud, Perpignan. *Cardinal de Bouillon*; *Louis XIV*; *Louis XV* (both Musée de l'Histoire de la France, Versailles).

Riley, Bridget (1931–) English Op artist since the early 1960s. *Crest*; *Punjab; Winter Palace* - composed of vertical stripes of the same length and width covering the entire picture area.

Rodin, Auguste (1840–1917) French sculptor, born in Paris, the son of a clerk. Produced his first great work in 1864, *L'Homme au nez cassé*. In 1877 he made a tour of the French cathedrals and published *Les Cathédrales de la France* in 1914. From 1886 to 1895 he worked on *Les Bourgeois de Calais*. His statues include a nude Victor Hugo and Balzac in a dressing gown. His works are represented in the Musée Rodin, Paris; the Rodin Museum, Philadelphia; and the Victoria and Albert Museum, London, where there is a collection of his bronzes that he presented to the British nation in 1914. *Le Penseur* (The Thinker) (Musée Rodin, Paris); *Le Baiser* (The Kiss) (Tate Britain, London).

Romney, George (1734–1802) English portraitist and history painter, born in Lancashire. At the height of his fame he rivalled both Reynolds and Gainsborough and his later history paintings and portraits of Emma Hart (later Lady Hamilton) enhanced his reputation, but he eventually died insane. *Self-portrait* (National Gallery, London).

Rosa, Salvator (1615–73) Neapolitan Baroque and macabre painter. *Landscape* (National Gallery, London).

Rossetti, Dante Gabriel (1828–1882) Anglo-Italian painter and poet, brother of the poet Christina Rossetti. DG Rossetti was born in London and his mother was Frances Mary Lavinia Polidori, daughter of Gaetano Polidori and sister of Lord Byron's physician, Dr John Polidori. Rossetti was a co-founder of the Pre-Raphaelite Brotherhood. *St George and the Princess Sabra*; *Ecce Ancilla Domini*; *The Blessed Damozel*.

Rothko, Mark (1903–70) American Abstract Expressionist and co-founder of Colorfield painting. Latvian-born (properly, Marcus Rothkovitch). *Two Openings in Black over Wine*.

Rouault, Georges (1871–1958) French Expressionist painter often on religious themes. Many of his works were acquired by the art dealer Ambroise Vollard. *Head of Christ*; *Two Nudes*.

Rousseau, Henri (1844–1910) French Primitive painter, known as 'Le Douanier' due to his early occupation as a tax collector in the Paris customs office. *Banks of the Seine; The Child among Rocks*; *The Sleeping Gypsy*; *Cascade*.

Rousseau, Théodore (1812–67) French landscape painter whose best known work was *The Forest of Compiègne*.

Rubens, (Sir) Peter Paul (1577–1640) Flemish Baroque painter and diplomat of the Antwerp School. Rubens's Antwerp home is now a museum. He married his first wife, Isabella Brandt, in 1609 (d. 1626) and his second, Helen Fourment, in 1630. *The Judgement of Paris*; *Descent from the Cross*; *Peace and War*; *Portrait of Isabella Brandt*; *Apotheosis of James I*; *Helen Fourment with Two of Her Children*; *Miracle of St Bavo*.

Ruysdael, Jacob van (1628–82) Dutch landscapist whose work was only appreciated after his death. *Bentheim Castle; Jewish Cemetery*; *View on the Amstel Looking toward Amsterdam*; *Windmill at Wijk bij Duurstede*.

Ruysdael, Salomon van (c1600–70) Dutch realist landscapist, properly, Salomon de Goyer. Uncle of Jacob van Ruysdael. *River Scene*; *River Scene near Utrecht*; *Landscape with a Carriage and Horsemen at a Pool*.

Saenredam, Pieter Janszoon (1597–1665) Dutch architectural painter. *Interior of the Grote Kerk at Haarlem*; *Interior of the Nieuwe Kerk*.

Sargent, John Singer (1856–1925) American portraitist of fashionable London society from 1884. Born in Florence, Sargent was an official war artist during World War I. *Carnation, Lily, Lily, Rose*; *Madame Gautreau*; *The Three Vickers Sisters*; *Gassed.*

Sassetta, Stefano di Giovanni (c1392–1450) Sienese painter of altarpieces. *St Francis Renounces His Earthly Father*, *Journey of the Magi.*

Schiele, Egon (1890–1918) Austrian Expressionist painter who died in the influenza epidemic of 1918.

Sebastiano del Piombo (c1485–1547) Venetian painter. *Raising of Lazarus*; *The Madonna and Child with SS. Catherine and John the Baptist.*

Seurat, Georges Pierre (1859–91) French Pointillist. *Sunday Afternoon on the Island of the Grande Jatte*; *Circus*; *Bathers at Asnières.*

Sickert, Walter Richard (1860–1942) German-born, English painter, influenced by Degas and Whistler. Co-founder of the Camden Town Group. *The Lion of St Mark*; *View at Ramsgate.*

Signac, Paul (1863–1935) French painter akin to Seurat, but using mosaic-like patches of colour as opposed to dots.

Sisley, Alfred (1839–99) French landscape Impressionist of British parentage, noted for his subtle treatment of skies. *Flood at Port Marly*; *The Boat during the Flood.*

Smetham, James (1821–89) Yorkshire-born Pre-Raphaelite painter of landscapes who died insane.

Smith, David Roland (1906–65) American sculptor who specialised in welded metal pieces.

Snyders, Frans (1579–1657) Born in Antwerp. Pupil of Pieter Brueghel the Younger. He specialised in still life and animals, often assisting Rubens in hunting scenes. In 1611he married Margaretha de Vos, sister of Flemish painters Cornelis and Paul de Vos. *Stag Hunt.*

Soutine, Chaim (1893–1943) Lithuanian painter, in Paris from 1913, influenced by Die Brücke group. *Les Gorges du Loup sur Vence.*

Spencer, (Sir) Stanley (1891–1959) English painter of portraits, landscapes and religious works. Born in Cookham, Berkshire. Spencer was an official war artist in World War II. *The Garden at Cookham Rise.*

Steen, Jan (c1626–79) Dutch painter. *The Effects of Intemperance*; *Romping Couple*; *Anthony and Cleopatra; The World Upside-down*

Steer, Philip Wilson (1860–1942) Member of the New English Art Club. *Mrs Cyprian Williams and Her Daughters*; *The Last Chapter*.

Stella, Frank (1936–) American Abstract Expressionist and Minimalist. *Hyena Stomp.*

Streeter, Robert (1624–79) Pepys's famous history painter who became Charles II's serjeant-painter in 1660. The ceiling of Oxford's Sheldonian Theatre is one of his few remaining decorative works.

Stubbs, George (1724–1806) English animal painter and engraver, born in Liverpool. Stubbs specialised in painting horses. *Mares and Foals in a River Landscape* ; *Self-portrait* (National Portrait Gallery, London); *Molly Long Legs with a Jockey* (Walker Art Gallery, Liverpool).

Sutherland, Graham Vivian (1903–80) English portraitist and official war artist, WW2. His official portrait of Sir Winston Churchill was destroyed by Lady Churchill, as she detested it. The Graham Sutherland Gallery in Haverfordwest was devoted almost entirely to his work until 1996, when it was closed, and the nearly 800 works have been displayed at Tenby Art Gallery (1996), Bodelwyddan Castle (1997) and the Turner House Gallery, Penarth (1998 and 2000-1). *Somerset Maugham*; *Christ in Majesty* (tapestry in Coventry Cathedral).

Tanguy, Yves (1900–55) French Surrealist in the USA from 1939, influenced by de Chirico. *The Furniture of Time.*

Tàpies, Antoni (1923–2012) Spanish painter; a founder member of the Dau al Set (Die with the Seven) and El Paso groups.

Tatlin, Vladimir (1885–1953) Russian painter and designer, the founder of Constructivism.

Taylor-Wood, Sam (1967–) London-born conceptual artist, photographer and film-maker. In 2002 she was commissioned by the National Portrait Gallery to make a video portrait of David Beckham sleeping. Her debut as a film director was *Nowhere Boy*, the biopic of John Lennon (2009). Taylor-Wood married art dealer Jay Jopling in 1997 but they divorced in 2008. In June 2012 she married Aaron Johnson (b. 1990), the actor who played Lennon in *Nowhere Boy*. They took the name Taylor-Johnson.

Teniers, the Elder, David (1582–1649) Flemish genre painter whose best-known work is *Temptation of St Anthony.*

Teniers the Younger, David (1610–90) Flemish painter. Curator of Archduke Leopold Wilhelm's picture gallery in Brussels, and copyist of many of its masterpieces. *Archduke Leopold Wilhelm in His Gallery*; *The Dentist* ; *Interior with a Peasant*; *Peasants Playing Music; The Village Fête.*

Tenniel, (Sir) John (1820–1914) English illustrator and political satirist (especially in *Punch*), best known for his illustrations of Lewis Carroll's *Alice in Wonderland* and *Through the Looking Glass.*

Terborch, Gerard (1617–81) Dutch genre painter of domestic scenes. *A Man*; *A Woman Playing a Theorbo to Two Men*; *Woman at a Mirror.*

Terbrugghen, Hendrick (c1588–1629) Dutch religious and genre painter, influenced by Caravaggio. *Jacob, Laban and Leah.*

Thompson, Elizabeth (1846–1933) Swiss-born British painter. Specialised in painting battle scenes, notably of the Crimean War and Battle of Waterloo. Her sister was the essayist and poet Alice Meynell. In 1877 she married Sir William Francis Butler (1838–1910). *Scotland Forever!.*

Thornhill, (Sir) James (1675–1734) English Baroque painter, born in Melcombe Regis, Dorset. His paintings for the dome of St Paul's (1707), the hall at Blenheim Palace, Hampton Court and the Painted Hall at Greenwich Hospital – on a scale unrivalled in Britain in the 15th century – made his reputation. He was the father-in-law of William Hogarth. Knighted by George I (1720) and appointed serjeant-painter; from 1722 became MP for Melcombe Regis.

Thornycroft, (Sir) William Hamo (1850–1925) London-born sculptor. Works include public statues of General Gordon in Trafalgar Square; John Bright in Rochdale; and Cromwell outside the Houses of Parliament.

Tiepolo, Giambattista (1696–1770) Venetian Rococo painter whose frescoes are prominent in palaces and churches throughout Europe. *Allegory of Fortitude and Wisdom; Finding of Moses*; *Banquet of Anthony and Cleopatra.*

Tinguely, Jean (1925–91) Swiss sculptor who pioneered kinetic and auto-destructive art.

Tintoretto (1518–94) Venetian Mannerist (properly, Jacopo Robusti). The son of a silk dyer (*tintore*), hence his nickname of Tintoretto (Little Dyer). In March 2007 Miguel Falomir, a biographer of Tintoretto, suggested his real name was Jacopo Comin. *St George Killing the Dragon* (National Gallery, London); *Miracle of S. Marco* (Galleria dell'Accademia, Venice); *The Washing of the Feet* (Wilton House, Wiltshire).

Titian (c1487–1576) Venetian painter (properly, Tiziano Vecellio); renowned for his use of colour. The Prado in Madrid has a superb collection of his work, particularly the paintings done under the patronage of the Holy Roman Emperor, Charles V. Titian was buried in the Church of S. Maria dei Frari, Venice. *The Three Ages of Man*; *Venus, Cupid and a Lute Player*, *Ecce Homo*; *The Assumption of the Virgin.*

Toulouse-Lautrec, Henri de (1864–1901) French painter, graphic artist and lithographer who forsook his noble origins for the cafés of Montmartre. He was influenced by Degas and by Japanese prints. Much of his work is housed in the Musée Toulouse-Lautrec et Galerie d'Art Moderne, Albi, France. Best known for his posters of the Moulin Rouge and his extremely short legs. *Jane Avril at the Moulin Rouge*; *La Toilette*; *The Artist's Mother* ; *In the Circus Fernando: The Ringmaster* ; *At the Moulin de la Galette*; *At the Bar; At the Nouveau Cirque: The Dancer and Five Stuffed Shirts; Tête-à-Tête Supper.*

Turner, Joseph Mallord William (1775–1851) English Romantic landscapist and precursor of Impressionism. A superb collection of Turner's work is in the Clore Gallery, attached to the Tate Britain, London. Turner entered the Royal Academy at the age of 14 and was patronised by Lord Egremont of Petworth. He died in temporary lodgings in Chelsea under the assumed name of Booth. *Battle of Trafalgar* ; *Norham Castle, Sunrise*; *The Fall of the Clyde; The Field of Waterloo; Linlithgow Palace; St Mawes at the Pilchard Season; Venus and Adonis.*

Twygge, Richard (1476–1510) English painter on glass whose work can be seen in many Malvern buildings.

Uccello, Paolo (1397–1475) Florentine artist noted for his sophisticated use of perspective. *The Hunt* ; *The Rout of San Romano*; *The Deluge.*

Utrillo, Maurice (1883–1955) French painter, born in Montmartre, Paris, the illegitimate son of painter Suzanne Valadon. Adopted by the Spanish writer Miguel Utrillo, he began to paint at Montmagny in 1902. Utrillo specialised in Paris street scenes. Despite acute alcoholism and drug addiction, his output was astonishing. His 'White Period' paintings of about 1908–14 are much sought after. He signed his works 'Maurice Utrillo V', incorporating the initial of his mother's family name.

Van Loo, Charles André (Carle) (1705–65) Prolific French artist and Rococo decorator; principle painter to Louis XV from 1762; the most talented of the artistic Van Loo family.

Van Loo, Jean-Baptiste (1684–1745) French portrait painter in England also notable for historical subjects. Brother of Charles André.

Vasarely, Victor (1908–97) Hungarian-born, French precursor of Op art. The 16th-century Château de Gordes in Vaucluse, France, is now the Musée Didactique Vasarely. *Sirius II*; *Ondho*; *Supernovae.*

Vasari, Giorgio (1511–74) Italian Mannerist fresco painter, architect and biographer. His *Lives of the Artists* was first published in Florence in 1550. The Casa Vasari in Arezzo was decorated by him. *Allegory of the Immaculate Conception*; *Lorenzo the Magnificent* .

Velazquez, Diego Rodriguez de Silva y (1599–1660) Spanish Baroque genre and royal portrait painter to Philip IV of Spain. Born in Seville and pupil of Francisco Pacheco, whose daughter he married in 1618. *Las Meninas* (aka *Maids of Honour*); *An Old Woman Cooking Eggs*; *The Toilet of Venus*, known as *The Rokeby Venus*.

Velde, Esaias van de (c1591–1630) Dutch realistic landscapist who was the master of Jan van Goyen. *Ice Scene* (Alte Pinakothek, Munich).

Vermeer, Jan (1632–75) Dutch genre painter of domestic scenes. Born in Delft, the son of an art dealer, he married Caterina Bolnes, who was to bear him eleven children. Fewer than 40 of his paintings are known. During World War II, forged Vermeers were produced by Jan Van Meegeren, who for some time deceived the experts. *A Girl Reading a Letter at an Open Window*; *Head of Girl with a Pearl Earring; Woman with a Pearl Necklace; Girl Drinking Wine with a Gentleman; Woman Weighing Gold (aka Woman with a Balance).*

Veronese (c1528–88) Venetian biblical and allegorical painter (properly, Paolo Caliari). *The Adoration of the Kings; Hermes, Herse and Aglauros*; *Mars and Venus*; frescoes in the Palazzo Ducale, Venice; *Christ among the Doctors.*

Vigée-Lebrun, Elisabeth Louise (1755–1842) French painter famous for her female subjects such as Marie Antoinette. She did paint male subjects, notably the Prince of Wales and Lord Byron.

Villon, Jacques (1875–1963) French painter (real name Gaston Duchamp) who specialised in Cubist works.

Vlaminck, Maurice de (1876–1958) French Fauve who was also a noted violinist, author and racing cyclist. *Woody River Scene.*

Vouet, Simon (1590–1649) French Baroque history and portrait painter. Court painter to Louis XIII. *La Richesse.*

Vuillard, Edouard (1868–1940) French painter. Member of the Nabis in the 1890s. *The Mantelpiece*; *The Open Window.*

Wallinger, Mark (1959–) London-born member of the YBA movement. Best known for his sculpture for the fourth plinth in Trafalgar Square, London, *Ecce Homo* (1999), *State Britain* (2007), and for winning the competition to design the *Angel of the South.*

Wallis, Alfred (1855-1942) Devon-born artist who spent his working life as a fisherman, taking up painting when he was 67. Much of his work depicts Cornish seascapes in a naïve style and can be seen at Tate St Ives.

Warhol, Andy (1928–87) American Pop Art painter, graphic artist and film-maker, famous for the Campbell soup-can labels and magazine illustrations directly reproduced by silk-screen. His controversial films included *Sleep* (1963) and *Chelsea Girls* (1966). In 1968 he was shot and wounded by Valerie Solanis, an actress in one of his films. *Green Coca-Cola Bottles* (Whitney Museum of American Art, New York).

Waterhouse, John William (1849-1917) Italian-born English Pre-Raphaelite famous for depicting women from ancient mythology.

Watteau, Jean-Antoine (1684–1721) French Rococo painter of *fêtes galantes*. *The Music Party*; *Gilles*; *Mezzetin*; *L'Enseigne de Gerseint* (Gerseint's Signboard); *L'île de Cythère.*

Watts, George Frederick (1817–1904) English artist who first drew attention with his cartoon of Caractacus in the competition for murals for the new Houses of Parliament. In 1864 he married actress Ellen Terry but parted from her within a year. *Found Drowned*; *Hope.*

West, Benjamin (1738–1820) American Neo-classical painter, in England from 1763. Founding member of the Royal Academy and its President in 1792. Court painter to George III of England. *The Death of General Wolfe*; *The Apotheosis of Lord Nelson*; *Mrs Worrall as Hebe.*

Westmacott, (Sir) Richard (1775–1856) Leading Neo-classical sculptor of public monuments and statues. After studying in Italy he returned to London and became a favourite sculptor of the Committee of Taste. His most accomplished monument was a public subscription commission commemorating Charles James Fox, in Westminster Abbey. His bronze monuments include the *Achilles* at Hyde Park Corner, Park Lane.

Weyden, Rogier van der (c1399–1464) Netherlandish painter of portraits and altarpieces, noted for his technical brilliance and emotional intensity. *Lamentation (Pietà) over the dead Christ*; *Antoine de Bourgogne*; *Deposition*; *Bladelin Altarpiece; St Luke Painting the Virgin.*

Whistler, James Abbott McNeill (1834–1903) American painter who lived in London and Paris. The critic John Ruskin's vitriolic criticism of his contributions to the Grosvenor Gallery exhibition of 1877, accusing him of 'flinging a pot of paint in the public's face', provoked the famous lawsuit in which Whistler was awarded a farthing's damages. Famous for his evening scenes, called nocturnes, such as the well-known impression of Battersea Bridge in the Tate Gallery, London. Whistler often dressed as the typical stereotype of an artist. *Arrangement in Grey and Black, No. I: The Artist's Mother*; *Arrangement in Grey and Black, No. 2: Thomas Carlyle; Nocturne in Black and Gold: The Falling Rocket; Nocturne in Blue and Gold: Old Battersea Bridge; Miss Cicely Alexander: Harmony in Grey and Green; Symphony in Grey and Green: The Ocean; Symphony in White No. 1: The White Girl.*

Whiteread, Rachel (1963–) London-born sculptor and the first woman to win the Turner Prize. She is probably best known for *House* (1993), a large concrete cast of the inside of a Victorian house. In the autumn of 2005 her work *Embankment* was installed at the Tate Modern's Turbine Hall as part of the annual Unilever Series. It consists of 14,000 translucent, white polyethylene boxes stacked in a variety of ways.

Wilkie, (Sir) David (1785–1841) Scottish painter famous for his genre pictures in the Dutch style, eg, *Card Players*, and *Penny Wedding.*

Wilson, Richard (1714–82) Welsh Classical landscapist. The National Museum of Wales, Cardiff, holds an important collection of his British and Italian landscapes. In 1776 he became librarian to the Royal Academy. *Caernarvon Castle*; *Flora Macdonald*; *Hadrian's Villa.*

Wright, Joseph (1734–97) English genre and portrait painter who specialised in fireside portraits and industrial scenes. He is known as Wright of Derby. *A Philosopher Giving a Lecture on the Orrery*; *An Experiment on a Bird in the Air Pump*; *Sir Brooke Boothby.*

Wyeth, Andrew Newell (1917–97) American figurative painter of scenes in Pennsylvania. His *Christina's World* in the Museum of Modern Art, New York, is probably the most famous American picture of the mid 20th century. *Young America.*

Yeats, Jack Butler (1870–1957) Irish painter, born in London, brother of the poet William Butler Yeats. *Grief*; *The Two Travellers.*

Zincke, Christian Frederick (c1683–1767) German enamel portraitist in London from 1714.

Zoffany, Johann (1733–1810) German portraitist working in England from 1758, Italy from 1772 and India from 1783. Patronised by George III of England and a founder member of the Royal Academy. *Garrick, Ackman and Bransby in Lethe*; *The Bradshaw Family*; *Charles Towneley among His Marbles.*

Zurbarán, Francisco de (1598–1664) Spanish Baroque religious painter whose earliest known painting, *Immaculate Conception* dated 1616, suggests he was schooled in the same naturalistic style as Velazquez. *The Vision of St Peter Nolasco*; *Death of St Bonaventure.*

Painting Movements and Terms

Abstract Art Non-representational forms, relying on line, form and colour, rather than realistic depiction. Originally formulated by Kandinsky c1912, the art form was embraced by all media, including sculpture. The early years of English Abstract art are represented in the Jim Ede collection at Kettle's Yard, Cambridge, which includes a large collection by Henri Gaudier-Brzeska and works by Nicholson and Brancusi.

Abstract Expressionism American painting movement developed in the 1940s from Surrealism, in which the idea is to make painting a spontaneous act, devoid of premeditation. Jackson Pollock and Willem de Kooning are the foremost exponents of Action Painting (or Tachisme, as it is called in France), using riotous swirls and splatters of colour. Rothko, Motherwell and Gorky were also Abstract Expressionists.

Academic Painting Traditional and figurative painting, often representing the work of a school or academy.

Action Painting see Abstract Expressionism.

Alla Prima Describes the technique, general since the 19th century but considered freakish and slapdash before then, of completing the picture surface in one session in full colour and with such opacity that neither any previous drawing nor underpainting (if in existence) modifies the final effect. The French term is 'Au Premier Coup'.

Altarpiece Decorated screen or panel placed behind an altar. The number of panels is indicated by the words diptych (2), triptych (3) or polyptych (many).

Armory Show, 1913 This exhibition introduced New York to modern European painting and sculpture, including the work of Marcel Duchamp.

Arts and Crafts English aesthetic movement that grew out of disenchantment at the mass-produced and trite decorative arts that followed the Industrial Revolution. By 1861, the social reformer, poet and designer William Morris had co-founded a firm of interior decorators dedicated to recapturing the essence and quality of medieval craftmanship. Together with artists Edward Burne-Jones and Ford Madox Brown, and architect Philip Webb, Morris set out to produce hand-crafted jewellery, wallpaper, textiles, furniture and books. Many of Morris's wallpaper and furniture designs continue to be popular today.

Art Brut (Raw Art) Term coined by Jean Dubuffet, referring to spontaneous and untrained artworks, often by criminals or the mentally ill.

Art Nouveau (New Art) Art and design style developed at the end of the 19th century, incorporating angular or sinuous vegetable forms into furniture and architecture. The style had its roots in the Arts and Crafts Movement and was popular all over Europe and North America. Samuel Bing coined the term when he opened his Paris gallery under the name L'Art Nouveau in 1895, although in Germany it was known as 'Jugendstil', in Italy as 'Stile Floreale' or 'Stile Liberty', in Spain as 'Modernismo' and in Austria as 'Sezession'. Leading exponents included René Lalique (glassware), Louis Comfort Tiffany (lamps and jewellery), Alphonse Mucha (graphic design), Alfred Gilbert (sculpture), Charles Rennie Mackintosh (interiors, buildings, furniture), Victor Horta and Hector Guimard (architecture), and Klimt, Beardsley, Jan Toorop and Ferdinand Hodler (art).

Ashcan School Painting group preoccupied with depicting the low-life of New York in the early 20th century. George Wesley Bellows and his master, Robert Henri, were leading exponents.

Attribution An artwork is 'attributed' to an artist when its provenance has not been proven.

Au Premier Coup see Alla Prima.

Automatism The method of producing a painting spontaneously and without conscious control. Used by Surrealists such as Miró and Abstract Expressionists such as Pollock.

Avant-garde Literally 'Vanguard'. In the forefront of artistic development, often with a conscious rejection of traditional methods or prior art forms.

Barbizon School Mid-19th-century French school of landscape painting based in the village of Barbizon, near Fontainebleau. Members included Théodore Rousseau, Narcisse Diaz, Daubigny and Millet. As the precursors of Impressionism they painted *en plein air* observing light.

Baroque European style of art and architecture following the High Renaissance and Mannerism, c1600–1740. It was a particularly Catholic style, popular in Italy, France and Spain in churches and public buildings, and encouraged as an integral part of the Counter-Reformation to appeal to the emotions and the senses of a still largely illiterate population. It was also eminently suitable for dramatising the idea of the divine right of kingship, and was fostered by many monarchs, such as Louis XIV of France. Exponents included the sculptor Bernini and the painters Rubens and da Cortona.

Bauhaus School of modern art and design originally based in Weimar, founded and headed by the architect Walter Gropius in 1919. Its policy was to explore the avant-garde and to reforge the link between art and design and industry, which the Arts and Crafts Movement had largely surrendered. The Bauhaus moved to Dessau in 1925, and then to Berlin, where it was closed by the Nazis in 1933. The new Bauhaus was set up by László Moholy-Nagy in Chicago in 1937.

Blaue Reiter, Der (Blue Rider) German Expressionist group that exhibited in Munich in 1911 and 1912. Among its members was the Russian émigré Kandinsky, who developed one of the earliest forms of abstract painting, and Franz Marc. It was an early titlework of Kandinsky's which provided the name. Other key members were Georges Braque, Robert Delaunay, André Derain, Paul Klee, August Macke, Henri Rousseau and Maurice de Vlaminck. Representative works are at the Kunsthalle, Bielefeld, Germany.

Bloomsbury Group British group of the 1920s and 1930s, influenced by French Post-Impressionism and later developments. Members included Vanessa Bell, Roger Fry and Duncan Grant. Roger Fry staged the first Post-Impressionist exhibition in London in 1910.

Brücke, Die (The Bridge) Among the earliest of the German Expressionist groups, Die Brücke was founded in Dresden in 1905. Founding members were Fritz Bleyl, Erich Heckel, Ernst Ludwig Kirchner and Karl Schmidt-Rottluff. Later members were Emil Nolde, Max Pechstein and Otto Mueller. The group disbanded in 1913.

Cabinet Picture Small easel picture, usually not more than about 3 or 4 feet across, and often much less. The minor Dutch masters were the principal painters of this type of furniture picture at its best.

Camera Obscura Mechanical means of securing accuracy in drawing, particularly of topographical detail. Invented in the 16th century and consisting of an arrangement of lenses and mirrors in a darkened tent or box. The view seen through the lens is reflected through the mirrors on to a sheet of paper, so that all the observer has to do is to trace round the edges. Canaletto is known to have used the device in making studies for his 'Vedute' (views). Camera Lucida is a more sophisticated optical instrument incorporating a prism.

Camden Town Group British group formed in 1911 and influenced by the Post-Impressionists. Members included Sickert, Gore, Augustus John, Harold Gilman, Charles Ginner, Lucien Pissaro and Robert Bevan.

Capriccio A picture in which real scenes, forms and figures are rearranged to suit a particular composition.

Caravaggisti Those artists heavily influenced by the style of Caravaggio, particularly in his use of chiaroscuro – contrasting light and dark. A strong Dutch Caravaggist school in the 17th century included van Honthorst, Terborch and Dirk van Baburen.

Cartoon Originally a full-size preparatory drawing of an intended artwork (painting, fresco or tapestry).

Chiaroscuro (Italian, light and dark) Defined contrast of light and dark most particularly in candle-lit scenes. Term used to describe works by Rembrandt and Caravaggio.

Classicism The imitation of Classical art, i.e. the style of Ancient Greece or Rome. An ordered style based on the harmony of perspective and composition, devised in the early Renaissance period by Filippo Brunelleschi. Classicism influenced thinking in the Renaissance period, leading to the philosophies of Platonism and Humanism, and the stories of Homer and other ancients provided a host of popular subjects which were applied to portraits, history subjects (Titian, Jacques-Louis David) and landscape (Poussin, Claude) into the 18th century. The Stoicism of ancient Rome provided the inspiration for the Neo-classical reaction to the Rococo style in the 1780s. In the 19th century the more mundane details of life in ancient Greece or Rome became the vehicle for finely executed decorative works by Leighton, Alma-Tadema and Albert Moore.

CoBrA Painting group that drew members from Copenhagen, Brussels and Amsterdam, including Appel and Jorn; founded in 1948. Their style incorporated violent figurative forms with Action Painting. Collections are in the Stedelijk Museum, Amsterdam, the Stedelijk Van Abbe-Museum, Eindhoven, and the Museum voor Schone Kunsten, Ghent.

Collage Picture built up wholly or partly from pieces of paper, cloth or other material stuck on to the canvas or other ground. The word comes from the French *coller* (to stick). The device was much used by the early Cubists and by the Dadaists, such as Kurt Schwitters. In his last years Matisse used pieces of coloured paper as a complete substitute for painting.

Colorfield Painting American offshoot of Abstract Expressionism and Minimalism, exploring monochromes or restricted contrasts in paint. The original of this idea was Malevich's *Black Square* of 1913. Rothko and Klein were typical exponents.

Constructivism Russian abstract sculptural and architectural movement from 1917 to 1921, founded by Vladimir Tatlin and developed by Naum Gabo and Antoine Pevsner, whose interest centred on movement in space and a reflection of the modern age.

Counterproof Mirror-image reproduction made by damping an original drawing or engraving, laying a damp sheet of clean paper on it, and then running both through a press. It is sometimes done by an artist in order to bring a fresh eye to his/her work by seeing it in reverse, but it is also the commonest method of faking 'original' drawings. Such fakes are obviously easily detectable because of the reversal. An offset is the same as a counterproof but has a wider meaning, for example in printing.

Cubism In 1907 Picasso and Braque began what was perhaps the first major development in painting away from figurative art. They were influenced by African tribal masks and by Cézanne, who looked at the world in terms of subtle coloured planes. This was the basis of Facet Cubism (1907–9). Analytical Cubism (1910–12) further fragmented basic shapes from all angles, and Synthetic Cubism (1913–14) totally recreated new objects. Delaunay (see Orphism), Léger and Gris were prominent Cubists. Although, as a particular style of art, Cubism developed into other things, it changed forever the way objects, and even the human form, were looked at.

Dada Formulated as an anarchic form of Expressionism during World War I in Zurich, 1916, possibly by the poet Tristan Tzara. The main centres of Dada in Germany were in Berlin, Hanover and Cologne. Its purpose was to discomfit and enrage the viewer. One of its major exponents was Kurt Schwitters, whose *Elterwater Merz* is in the Hatton Gallery at the University of Newcastle upon Tyne. Other exponents included Man Ray, Jean Arp, Duchamp, Ernst, Hannah Hoch and Picabia. Dada eventually developed into Surrealism.

Euston Road School Originally known as the Fitzroy Street School, this was a London-based school of painting and drawing, 1937–9, established by Victor Pasmore, Claude Rogers and William Coldstream. It aimed to counteract the tendencies of Surrealism and abstract art by returning to more figurative and natural forms of expression. Exponents included Vanessa Bell, Eric Gill, Duncan Grant, Augustus John, Kenneth Martin, John Nash and Fred Uhlman.

Expressionism Early 20th-century painting movement that expressed highly charged emotions and thoughts through colour, violence, distortion and exaggeration. The German Expressionist groups were among the first so to characterise their work, which itself developed further into Dada and Abstract Expressionism.

Fauves (Wild Beasts) An initially derogatory label applied by the critics of artists such as Derain, Matisse, Rouault and Vlaminck when their work was exhibited in one room at the Paris Salon d'Automne of 1905. The distortion and flat patterns, along with the intensity of the colour, created a furore, and the Fauves were born. Matisse came to be regarded as their leader, although the movement itself had fallen apart by 1908 as a number of its members defected to Cubism.

Fête champêtre Typical Rococo scene of lovers in an ideal setting, as epitomised by Lancret and Fragonard.

Fête galante Pastoral masquerade in dreamlike setting, as painted by Lancret and Watteau.

Figurative Art Artworks that contain recognisable objects.

Found Object (objet trouvé) A Dadaist and Surrealist technique of taking any given object and displaying it as an art form, as in *Bicycle Wheel.*

Fresco Wall-painting using water-based paints on damp plaster, particularly in European churches and ancient Greek and Egyptian temples. Giotto was one of the masters of fresco painting.

Futurism Italian art movement developed in Venice c1909–15, embracing the machine and new technology. Balla, Carrà, Umberto Boccioni and Gino Severini were its leading exponents. The term was born in Paris, in an article in *Le Figaro* by the poet Filippo Marinetti (1876–1944). Although Futurism is sometimes used to mean any art more recent than 1900, as a discrete aesthetic movement it died early in World War I.

Genre Type of subject painting or, more particularly, paintings of everyday life in a naturalistic style, reported without idealisation. Extremely popular in 17th-century Holland.

German Expressionism Much of German Expressionism grew out of a painterly reaction to modernity, but most particularly to the horrors of World War I. Die Brücke was one of the first Expressionist groups, and the movement also embraced Der Blaue Reiter and Dada. Representative artists include Ernst Barlach, Beckmann, Grosz, Kirchner and Nolde.

German Romantic Painting Early 19th-century forerunner of the English Pre-Raphaelite school. Artists were inspired by the collection of 14th and 15th century painting at the home of Bernhard August von Lindenau, now the Staatliches Lindenau-Museum, Altenburg. Friedrich, Philip Otto Runge and the Nazarenes are typical exponents.

Gothic A generic term first used in the Renaissance period to describe the style of the 11th to 15th centuries. It was initially a critical term implying barbarism because the style made no reference to Classical precedents. In the 19th century medieval architecture and painting 'pre-Raphael' became the inspiration for a Victorian resurgence, led by the critic John Ruskin and the architect-designer A.W. Pugin, which produced 'Gothic' fantasies far removed from the original inspiration. William Morris, whilst also taking the medieval Gothic period for inspiration, went back to basics and developed the culture of craftsmanship and simple forms.

Grisaille A painting done in tones of grey to define shadows or modelling. Often used in *trompe l'oeil.*

Happening An art form developed from the 1960s in which an artist participates in an action that encompasses the whole purpose of the piece, and once over is gone. Similar to Performance Art. Largely developed by Joseph Beuys.

High Victorian Art The British art of the 1870s until the turn of the century, epitomised by the languid classical beauties of Albert Moore, Leighton and Alma-Tadema – fabulously painted, very beautiful and often low on meaning. Fine collections are in the Lady Lever Art Gallery, Port Sunlight; Birmingham Museum and Art Gallery; and the Tate Gallery, London, as well as at Leighton's House in Holland Park Road, London.

History Painting After portraiture, the painting of uplifting scenes from history, the Bible or allegory was the highest form of art according to Reynolds. It was also used very effectively for propaganda purposes by the Neo-Classical painters such as Jacques-Louis David. (See his *Death of Marat.*)

Hudson River School 19th-century American landscape painting school, highly Romantic in feeling and glorifying the wonders of nature. The name is properly applied to the period after 1825 when leading exponent Thomas Cole, painter of *The Voyage of Life*, settled in New York. Other members include Albert Bierstadt, Asher B. Osmond and Frederick Church.

Impasto Word used to describe the thickness of the paint applied to a canvas or panel. When the paint is so heavily applied that it stands up in lumps, with the tracks of the brush clearly evident, it is said to be 'heavily' impasted.

Impressionism Essentially the painting of light and its effects on nature and objects. Developed in France in the late 19th century and influential all over Europe. Monet's *Impression: Sunrise* (Musée Marmottan, Paris) of 1872 was the work that suggested the name of the movement. Other leading protagonists included Cézanne, Degas, Morisot, Pissarro, Renoir and Sisley. The Impressionist exhibitions were held between 1874 and 1886. Seurat and Paul Signac took Impressionism a stage further with Pointillism.

International Gothic Late 14th-century form of Gothic which spread throughout Europe. Leading exponents were Gentile da Fabriano and Pisanello.

Kinetic Art Art that relies on real or apparent movement.

Kitchen Sink School Term coined by art critic David Sylvester in 1954 , referring to a group of British social realist painters popular in mid-1950s who focused their work on the unglamorous. Members: John Bratby, Derrick Greaves, Edward Middleditch, Leslie Duxbury and Jack Smith.

Land Art, Earth Art Arrangements of earth mounds or natural elements in situ, often in rural areas. Developed in the USA from the 1960s as a reaction to materialistic Pop Art. Richard Long is a leading exponent. Grizedale Forest in Cumbria is one of the foremost sculpture parks here, specialising in sculpture within natural settings.

Maestà (Majesty) A term used to describe a painting of the Virgin and Child enthroned, with saints or angels.

Mannerism The style that succeeded the High Renaissance, c1520–1600, exemplified by exaggerated figure drawing. Bronzino, El Greco, Michelangelo, Parmigianino and Pontormo were all Mannerists.

Metaphysical School Surrealist art group formed in Ferrara in 1917 by Giorgio de Chirico and Carlo Carrà, which survived until 1920.

Minimalism American art movement in painting and sculpture, essentially paring ideas down to bare essentials. Exponents include Carl André and Richard Serra.

Mobile A form of sculpture invented in 1932 by Alexander Calder, and named by Marcel Duchamp. Usually a mobile consists of a number of shapes cut from wood, cardboard, plastic or metal, connected by wires or rods and suspended so that a gentle touch will cause the whole to revolve and produce transforming 3D patterns of planes, solids and colours, and sometimes sounds.

Modern Art Accepted as the course of art in the 20th century from Impressionism up to the present day, embracing all major artistic developments including Cubism, Expressionism, Surrealism, Abstract Art, Pop Art, Minimalism and Performance Art. Excellent British public collections are in the Tate Galleries in London, Liverpool and St Ives; and the Scottish National Gallery of Modern Art in Edinburgh.

Nabis (Prophets) French anti-Impressionist art group inspired by Paul Gauguin's use of outline and flat colour which exhibited from 1892 to 1899. Members included Pierre Bonnard, Maurice Denis, Paul Sérusier and Edouard Vuillard.

Nazarenes Group of early 19th-century German and Austrian Romantic religious painters, founded by Friedrich Overbeck and Franz Pforr.

Neo-classicism Often described as the art of the French Revolution, it was a late 18th-century reaction to the fussiness of the Rococo, embracing noble simplicity and stoic grandeur. Jacques-Louis David was its leading exponent in painting, and Antonio Canova in sculpture.

Neo-Expressionism Refers to an International art movement of the late 1970s and 1980s involving revival of expressionist concerns

Neo-Impressionism A pre-Cubist movement which examined Impressionism from a scientific standpoint rather than an aesthetic one. An offshoot of Neo-Impressionism was Pointillism.

Neo-Plasticism Name used by Mondrian & van Doesburg for their style of pure abstract art, first used in *De Stijl* magazine in 1917.

Neo-Romanticism British art movement existing before WW2, reviving the interest in the Romantic landscapes of Blake and Samuel Palmer

Neue Sachlichkeit An inter-war German brutal realism art style represented by Dix, Grosz and Christian Schad. The literal meaning is 'New Objectivity'. Name coined by G.F. Artlaub.

Newlyn School Group of British painters based in the fishing village near Penzance, Cornwall, and dedicated to Plein air, following the lead in France. The school was founded by Stanhope Forbes (1857-1947) and his wife Elizabeth (1857–1912). Other members included Walter Langley (1852–1922) and Laura Knight (née Johnson) and her husband Harold.

New English Art Club British art group founded in 1886, which included George Clausen, Stanhope Forbes, Sargent, Steer and Edward Stott's work. The Club is well represented in the collection at Cartwright Hall, Bradford.

Norwich School A group of early 19th-century landscape painters led by John Cotman and John Crome.

Novecento Italiano Italian art movement of the 1920s which encouraged a return to the renaissance art.

Novembergruppe Formed in Berlin 1918 and advocating art for the masses. Led by Max Pechstein and César Klein.

Omega Workshops Co-operative workshop-cum-showroom at 33 Fitzroy Square, London, founded by critic Roger Fry in 1913, for the production of painted furniture, textiles, artefacts and decorative commissions. Vanessa Bell and Duncan Grant produced designs for Omega.

Op Art (short for Optical Art) is a style of painting which manipulates overall patterns, using repeated shapes or undulating lines which give an optical illusion of movement and often dazzles the beholder. Victor Vasarely (1908–97) is often considered a precursor of the op art movement with his black and white geometrical paintings but the movement became established in the early 1960s by Bridget Riley when she began to use colour in her optical paintings. The term became popularised following the 1965 New York City exhibition 'The Responsive Eye' at the Museum of Modern Art.

Perspective Quasi-mathematical system for the representation of three-dimensional objects in spatial recession on a two-dimensional surface, i.e. for the creation of an independent pictorial space as a microcosm of nature. The basic assumption of all perspective systems is that parallel lines never meet, but they appear to do so; and that, further, all parallel lines going in any one direction meet at a single point on the horizon, known as a vanishing point.

Pietà (Pity) Painting or sculpture showing the dead Christ cradled in the lap of the Virgin Mary.

Plein air 19th- and 20th-century landscape painting carried out in the open air, depicting nature and light as realistically as possible, as opposed to the deliberate Classicism of Old Masters such as Claude Lorrain and Poussin. Plein airists included the Barbizon School, the Impressionists, the Pre-Raphaelites, Millais, Ford Madox Brown and William Holman Hunt.

Pointillism Also known as 'Divisionism'. Seurat developed the Neo-Impressionist technique of using tiny dots of colour to build up form and subject; most notably used in his *Sunday Afternoon on the Island of the Grand Jatte*.

Pop Art American-formulated art form embracing painting, graphic design and sculpture, and preoccupied with modern technology, materialism and advertising. Exponents included Warhol, Blake, Johns, Robert Rauschenberg, Hamilton, Hockney, Lichtenstein and Claes Oldenburg.

Post-Impressionism Roger Fry of the Bloomsbury Group coined the term when he staged the 'Manet and the Post-Impressionists' Exhibition in London in 1910. They were artists whose chief feature in common was that they had rejected naturalism in various ways, through form, colour and subject, and included Cézanne, Denis, Gauguin, van Gogh, Picasso, Rouault, Seurat, Paul Sérusier, and Vlaminck.

Pre-Raphaelite Brotherhood The dream of a new generation to return art to its original purity of form and colour by preferring truth to nature to the stylised ideals of the Royal Academy and the ground rules laid down by its first president, Reynolds. The group was formed in London in 1848 by the painters Dante Gabriel Rossetti, William Holman Hunt, Millais and James Collinson, the art critics William Michael Rossetti and Frederick Stephens, and the sculptor Thomas Woolner. The group itself was shortlived, as its members were following separate artistic paths by 1853, but its impact on contemporary Victorian art was far more long-lasting. Pre-Raphaelitism strongly influenced Ford Madox Brown, Burne-Jones, Augustus Egg, Frith, Hubert Herkomer, Watts, among others, and formed the basis of High Victorian Art. It was also a foundation stone of the Arts and Crafts Movement, led by William Morris, and the English Art Nouveau of Charles Rennie Mackintosh and the Glasgow School, Scottish painters of the late 19th century. The style also opened the way for a new class of art collectors in the form of major industrialists based in the north, important contemporary art galleries such as the Grosvenor Gallery, and satire in the form of Gilbert and Sullivan's *Patience* and the cartoons in *Punch*. Subject matter varies from the willowy and lush allegorical beauties of Rossetti and Burne-Jones to the real-life and religious subjects of Holman Hunt and Ford Madox Brown. Major collections of Pre-Raphaelite art are in the Tate Gallery, London; Walker Art Gallery, Liverpool; Lady Lever Art Gallery, Port Sunlight; Birmingham Museum and Art Gallery, and Manchester City Art Gallery.

Primitive Term applied to pre-Renaissance art and provincial or naive art by untrained artists often ignoring perspective (see Alfred Wallis).

Provenance The documented history – and hence authenticity – of an artwork: who created it, who owned it, etc.

Rayonism Combination of Cubism, Futurism and Orphism developed by Russian artists Mikhail Larionov and Natalia Goncharova in 1911.

Ready-Made Term coined by Duchamp for his found objects, such as the urinal he exhibited at the 1913 Armory Show, signed 'R. Mutt'.

Realism Term applied to the realistic painting of artists such as Courbet, using a precision of detail and natural colour without idealisation.

Renaissance The 'rebirth' of art and ideas in Italy after the Dark Ages and Gothic art, starting in the 14th century. It had repercussions around the European world on artistic expression, intellectual discussion, religious thought and scientific experiment. It was inspired by the rediscovery of the Classicism of the ancient civilisations of Rome and Greece in Italy and the rise of humanism. The Early Renaissance period, up to c1500, includes the artists Giotto, Duccio and Uccello, and the first experiments in art with perspective and painterly modelling. The High Renaissance saw the development of architecture, sculpture and painting by men such as Michelangelo, Leonardo, Raphael and Titian, leading to Mannerism and the late Renaissance of Correggio, Veronese and the sculptor Benvenuto Cellini. Dürer was responsible for introducing new ideas into Germany, and Holbein the Younger into England. France embraced Renaissance ideals following the rise of Italian influence after the marriage of Catherine de' Medici to the future Henri II in 1533.

Rococo 18th-century French decorative style, epitomised by the paintings of Rigaud, Boucher, Fragonard and Watteau. It illustrated the dream world in which the nobility wished to live, of sunlit *fêtes galantes*, garden swings, cherry-picking and whimsical shepherdesses. The French Revolution forced them to face an unpleasant reality. Rococo also influenced painters, architects and sculptors in Austria , Germany and Italy.

Romanticism The early 19th-century reaction to the cold formality of Neo-classicism, the style introduced a new depth of colour, expression and passion into painting not seen since Titian, particularly in the works of Delacroix and Géricault. Stylistically different Romanticists were William Blake, Constable, Friedrich, Fuseli, Turner, the Nazarenes and the Pre-Raphaelites.

Sacra conversazione A painting of the Virgin and Child, often with saints or family in an informal setting, first depicted by Fra Angelico in the 15th-century. The term literally means 'Holy Conversation'.

Slade School of Art London art school, founded 1871, that in the 1890s and under the professorship in 1918–30 of Henry Tonks produced some of the most important painters of British 20th-century art. Slade teachers and graduates included David Bomberg, Mark Gertler, Harold Gilman, Spencer Gore, Duncan Grant, Augustus John, Gwen John, Wyndham Lewis, Ambrose McEvoy, Paul Nash, C.R.W. Nevinson, Ben Nicholson, William Orpen, William Rothenstein, Matthew Smith, Stanley Spencer and Edward Wadsworth.

Socialist Realism A realistic if stylised art form officially sponsored and sanctioned for propaganda purposes in the Soviet Union, where it was first defined in 1932, and later in China and Cuba.

Stijl, De ('The style') Dutch 20th-century art movement which embraced painting, sculpture, graphic design, interior design and architecture. Exponents include Mondrian, van Doesburg, Bart van der Leck and the architects Rietveld and Jacobus Oud. De Stijl architecture includes the Zonnestraal Sanatorium by Johannes Duiker, and Rietveld's Schröder house at Utrecht.

Suprematism Malevich produced his first non-representational Suprematist painting in 1913, *Black Square*, exploring elementary forms and restricted contrasts of colour which in turn influenced Expressionism, Abstract Art and Colorfield Painting.

Surrealism Term coined in 1922 by the poet André Breton to describe the real and unreal world of waking and dreaming as depicted by the artist. Breton chose term from earlier description of a Chagall work by Guillaume Apollinaire. Developed from Dada and influenced by Sigmund Freud's ideas. Exponents included de Chirico, Dali, Duchamp, Ernst, Klee, Magritte, Miró, Man Ray and Tanguy.

Symbolism Late figurative style of painting, associated with the Art Nouveau period. Jan Toorop, Johan Thorn Prikker, Munch, Arnold Böcklin, Redon, Puvis de Chavannes, Rouault and Moreau were all exponents.

Tachisme Term often used synonymously with Abstract Expressionism, but it strictly refers to a French movement of the 1950s which consisted of paintings composed of large blobs of colour.

Tempera Although this term actually means any kind of binder which will serve to 'temper' powder colour and make it workable, in practice it is confined to egg tempera (using the yolk of the egg), which was until the late 15th century the commonest technique of painting easel pictures.

Tenebrism Sombrely atmospheric painting particularly as seen in the works of those early 17th-century painters, mostly Neapolitan and Spanish, who were much influenced by Caravaggio. The term literally means 'Dark colouring'.

Trompe l'oeil Illusionistic painting effect, such as painting a ceiling to look as if it is open to the sky. The term literally means 'Deceive the eye'.

Veduta (View) Detailed topographical painting of an existing place. Leading 'Vedutisti' were Guardi and Canaletto.

Vernissage The practice – once common, now discontinued – by which painters would enter an exhibition after the pictures had been hung but before it was open to the public, so that they could varnish and also retouch their pictures. Turner would often submit his pictures incomplete and take advantage of Vernissage (Varnishing Day). Nowadays the custom is merely to invite favoured patrons to see the pictures before the public are allowed in.

Vorticism Brief English movement from 1914 with similar influences to Futurism, led by Percy Wyndham Lewis.

Watercolour The English landscapists were particularly strong in their use of watercolour, especially the artists of the Norwich School, William Blake, Girtin, Bonington and Turner. Dante Gabriel Rossetti brought a new jewel-like richness to watercolour painting in the 1850s, which raised the medium from insipidity.

Young British Artists Movement having its foundation in the exhibition 'Freeze', organised while he was a student at Goldsmiths College, London, in 1988 by Damien Hirst, who became the most celebrated of the YBAs. Goldsmiths, which numbered Michael Craig-Martin among its teachers, encouraged new forms of creativity. Leading artists have preserved dead animals (Hirst), presented her own bed (Tracey Emin) and made sculpture from women's tights (Sarah Lucas). Artists include: Fiona Banner, Christine Borland, Mark Wallinger, Rachel Whiteread.

Famous Works of Art (permanently housed)

Painting	***Artist***	***Location***
Adam and Eve	Lucas Cranach	Courtauld Gallery, London
Adam and Eve	Dürer	Prado, Madrid
Adoration of the Lamb, The	Jan van Eyck	St Bavo Cathedral, Ghent
Adoration of the Magi, The	Jacopo Bassano	Kunsthistorisches Museum, Vienna
Adoration of the Magi, The	Botticelli	Uffizi, Florence (1475)
Adoration of the Magi, The	Dürer	Uffizi, Florence (1504)
Adoration of the Magi, The	Da Vinci	Uffizi, Florence (1481)
Adoration of the Magi, The	Lippi	Uffizi, Florence (1496)
Adoration of the Magi, The	Velazquez	Prado, Madrid (1619)
After Cézanne	Lucian Freud	National Gallery of Australia
Allegory of Spring (aka *La Prima vera*)	Botticelli	Uffizi, Florence
Ambassadors, The	Holbein the Younger	National Gallery, London
Anatomy Lesson of Dr Jan Deyman	Rembrandt	Rijksmuseum, Amsterdam
Anatomy Lesson of Dr Nicolaes Tulp	Rembrandt	Mauritshuis, The Hague
Andromeda	Rembrandt	Mauritshuis, The Hague
Annunciation, The	Jan van Eyck	National Gallery, Washington DC
Aristotle Contemplating a Bust of Homer	Rembrandt	Metropolitan Museum of Art, NY
Arnolfini Portrait, The	Jan van Eyck	National Gallery, London
Around the Fish	Klee	Museum of Modern Art, New York
At the Moulin Rouge	Toulouse-Lautrec	Art Institute of Chicago
Avenue at Middelharnis, The	Hobbema	National Gallery, London
Bar at the Folies-Bergère, A	Manet	Courtauld Gallery, London
Baron Schwiter	Delacroix	National Gallery, London
Bathsheba	Rembrandt	Louvre, Paris
Beggar's Opera, The	Hogarth	Tate Britain, London
Belle Jardinière, La	Raphael	Louvre, Paris
Belshazzar's Feast	Rembrandt	National Gallery, London
Bicycle Wheel	Duchamp	Museum of Modern Art, New York
Birth of Venus, The	Botticelli	Uffizi, Florence
Blue Rider, The	Kandinsky	Ernst Bührle Collection, Zürich
Boatbuilding near Flatford Mill	Constable	Victoria and Albert Museum, London
Boyhood of Raleigh, The	Millais	Tate Britain, London
Broadway Boogie Woogie	Mondrian	Museum of Modern Art, New York
Bubbles	Millais	Lady Lever Art Gallery, Port Sunlight
Burial of the Count de Orgaz	El Greco	Church of Santo Tomé, Toledo, Spain
Capt Woodes Rogers and Family	Hogarth	National Maritime Museum, Greenwich
Cartoons	Raphael	V&A, London
Charge of the Mamelukes, The	Goya	Prado, Madrid
Chess Players, The	Duchamp	Philadelphia Museum of Art
Christ Crowned With Thorns	Titian	Louvre, Paris
Christ Healing the Blind Man	Duccio	National Gallery, London
Christ in the House of His Parents	Millais	Tate Britain, London
Christ Nailed to the Cross	Gerard David	National Gallery, London
Christ on the Cross	Goya	Prado, Madrid
Christ on the Cross	Velazquez	Prado, Madrid
Christ Taking Leave of His Mother	Correggio	National Gallery, London
Christina of Denmark, Duchess of Milan	Holbein the Younger	National Gallery, London
Church at Blainville	Duchamp	Philadelphia Museum of Art
Clothed Maja, The	Goya	Prado, Madrid
Colossus, The	Goya	Prado, Madrid
Conversion of St Paul, The	Michelangelo	Pauline Chapel, Vatican
Conversion of St Paul, The	Caravaggio	Sta Maria del Popolo, Rome
Conversion of St Paul, The	Pieter Brueghel (Elder)	Kunsthistorisches Museum, Vienna
Cornfield, The	Constable	National Gallery, London
Coronation of the Virgin, The	Raphael	Vatican Museum, Rome
Country Festival near Antwerp	Teniers the Younger	National Gallery, London
Cripples, The	Pieter Brueghel (Elder)	Louvre, Paris
Crucifixion of St Peter	Michelangelo	Pauline Chapel, Vatican
Crucifixion Triptych	Francis Bacon	Tate Britain, London
Cupid and Psyche	François Gérard	Louvre, Paris
Danae	Correggio	Borghese Gallery, Rome

Danae	Rembrandt	Hermitage, St Petersburg
Dance of Four Breton Women	Gauguin	Neue Pinakothek, Munich
Death of the Virgin	Caravaggio	Louvre, Paris
Demoiselles d'Avignon, Les	Picasso	Museum of Modern Art, New York
Descent from the Cross	Rembrandt	Alte Pinakothek, Munich
Descent from the Cross	Rubens	Antwerp Cathedral
Ditchley Portrait of Elizabeth I	Marcus Gheeraerts (Younger)	National Portrait Gallery
Duke of Wellington, The	Goya	National Gallery, London
Early Sunday Morning	Hopper	Whitney Museum of American Art, NY
Ecce Homo	Bosch	Stadelsches Kunstinstitut, Frankfurt
Ecce Homo	Caravaggio	Galleria di Palazzo Rosso, Genoa
Ecce Homo	Correggio	National Gallery, London
Education of Cupid	Correggio	National Gallery, London
Execution of Faliero	Delacroix	Wallace Collection, London
Fable of Arachne (aka *The Spinners*)	Velazquez	Prado, Madrid
Fairy Feller's Master-Stroke	Richard Dadd	Tate Britain, London
Fight between Carnival and Lent	Pieter Brueghel (Elder)	Kunsthistorisches Museum, Vienna
Fighting Temeraire, The	Turner	National Gallery, London
Flatford Mill on the River Stour	Constable	Tate Britain, London
Football Players	Henri Rousseau	Guggenheim Museum, New York
Fortune-Teller (aka *La Zingara*)	Caravaggio	Louvre, Paris
From the Week of Hell '94	Emin	Tate Britain, London
Gardener, The	Cézanne	Tate Britain, London
Gilles and His Family	Watteau	Wallace Collection, London
Girl Asleep, A	Vermeer	Metropolitan Museum of Art, NY
Girl at a Window	Rembrandt	Dulwich Picture Gallery
Girl Balancing on a Ball	Picasso	Pushkin Museum, Moscow
Girl With a White Dog	Freud	Tate Britain, London
Girl with Bare Feet	Picasso	Picasso Museum, Paris
Goldfish and Sculpture	Matisse	Museum of Modern Art, New York
Good Samaritan, The	Hogarth	St Bartholomew's Hospital, London
Graham Children, The	Hogarth	National Gallery, London
Great Wave, The	Hokusai	British Museum, London
Greenwich Hospital from the North	Canaletto	National Maritime Museum, Greenwich
Grey Tree, The	Mondrian	Haags Gemeentemuseum, The Hague
Guernica	Picasso	Museo Reina Sofia, Madrid
Gypsy Girl	Hals	Louvre, Paris
Half-Past Three (The Poet)	Chagall	Philadelphia Museum of Art
Haywain, The (triptych)	Bosch	Prado, Madrid
Haywain, The	Constable	National Gallery, London
Holy Family (Doni Tondo)	Michelangelo	Uffizi, Florence
Holy Family	Turner	Tate Britain, London
Holy Family (aka *The Two Trinities*)	Murillo	National Gallery, London
Horatius Cocles Defending the Bridge	Le Brun	Dulwich Gallery, London
House by the Railroad	Hopper	Museum of Modern Art, New York
Hunters in the Snow	Pieter Brueghel (Elder)	Kunsthistorisches Museum, Vienna
I and the Village	Chagall	Museum of Modern Art, New York
Impression: Sunrise	Monet	Musée Marmottan, Paris
Jewish Bride, The	Rembrandt	Rijksmuseum, Amsterdam
Jewish Cemetery	Jacob van Ruysdael	Gemäldegalerie, Dresden
Jupiter and Io	Correggio	Kunsthistorisches Museum, Vienna
Kiss, The	Klimt	Österreichische Galerie, Vienna
Kitchen-Maid (aka The Milk Maid)	Vermeer	Rijksmuseum, Amsterdam
Lady of Shalott	John William Waterhouse	Tate Britain, London
Landscape with a Footbridge	Altdorfer	National Gallery, London
Last Judgement, The	Michelangelo	Sistine Chapel, Vatican
Last Supper, The	Dali	National Gallery, Washington DC
Last Supper, The	Holbein the Younger	Kunstmuseum, Basel, Switzerland
Last Supper, The (mural)	Leonardo da Vinci	S. Maria delle Grazie, Milan
Laughing Cavalier, The	Hals	Wallace Collection, London
Leda	Correggio	Berlin Museum
Liberty Leading the People	Delacroix	Louvre, Paris
Light of the World, The	Holman Hunt	Keble College, Oxford
Little Street, The	Vermeer	Rijksmuseum, Amsterdam
Luncheon in the Studio	Manet	Neue Staatsgalerie, Munich
Luncheon of the Boating Party, The	Renoir	Phillips Collection, Washington DC
Lute Player, The	Caravaggio	Hermitage, St Petersburg
Madame Charpentier and Her Children	Renoir	Metropolitan Museum of Art, NY
Mademoiselle Gachet at the Piano	Van Gogh	Kunstmuseum, Basel
Madonna in Glory, The	Giotto	Uffizi, Florence
Madonna of St Jerome, The	Correggio	National Gallery, Parma
Madonna of the Basket, The	Correggio	National Gallery, London
Madonna of the Goldfinch, The	Raphael	Uffizi, Florence
Madonna of the Rosary	Van Dyck	Oratorio del Rosario, Palermo
Madonna of the Star	Fra Angelico	Museo di San Marco, Florence
Madonna with Angels and Saints	Gerard David	Musée des Beaux-Arts, Rouen
Madonna with Chancellor Rolin, The	Jan van Eyck	Louvre, Paris
Madonna with the Carnation	Leonardo da Vinci	Alte Pinakothek, Munich
Maestà	Duccio di Buoninsegna	Cathedral Museum, Siena
Maids of Honour (aka *Las Meninas*)	Velazquez	Prado, Madrid
Man with a Straw Hat, The	Cézanne	Metropolitan Museum of Art, NY
Marriage at Cana	Veronese	Louvre, Paris
Mars and Venus	Botticelli	National Gallery, London
Massacre at Chios, The	Delacroix	Louvre, Paris
Merry Drinker, The	Hals	Rijksmuseum, Amsterdam
Milkmaid of Bordeaux, The	Goya	Prado, Madrid
Miss Harriet Cholmondeley	Hoppner	Tate Britain, London

Mocker Mocked, The	Klee	Museum of Modern Art, New York
Mona Lisa (aka *La Gioconda*)	Leonardo da Vinci	Louvre, Paris
Mr and Mrs Andrews	Gainsborough	National Gallery, London
Mrs Siddons	Gainsborough	National Gallery, London
My Parents	Hockney	Tate Britain, London
Naked Maja, The	Goya	Prado, Madrid
Nevermore	Gauguin	Courtauld Gallery, London
Night Watch, The	Rembrandt	Rijksmuseum, Amsterdam
Nighthawks	Hopper	Art Institute of Chicago
Nude Descending a Staircase, No 2	Duchamp	Philadelphia Museum of Art
Odalisque	Renoir	National Gallery of Art, Washington DC
Officer and Laughing Girl	Vermeer	Frick Collection, New York
Old Walton Bridge	Canaletto	Dulwich Gallery, London
Old Woman Cooking Eggs, An	Velázquez	National Gallery of Scotland, Edinburgh
Old Woman Praying	Rembrandt	Residenz Gallery, Salzburg
Old Women of Arles	Gauguin	Art Institute of Chicago
On the Balcony	Peter Blake	Tate Modern, London
Order of Release, The	Millais	Tate Britain, London
Painting (1946)	Francis Bacon	Museum of Modern Art, New York
Pantry, The	Hooch	Rijksmuseum, Amsterdam
Paris through the Window	Chagall	Guggenheim Museum, New York
Parting of Hero and Leander, The	Turner	National Gallery, London
Peasant Wedding	Pieter Brueghel (Elder)	Kunsthistorisches Museum, Vienna
Peter Denying Christ	Rembrandt	Rijksmuseum, Amsterdam
Piazza San Marco and the Colonnade	Canaletto	National Gallery, London
Potato Eaters, The	Van Gogh	Van Gogh Museum, Amsterdam
Primavera, La (aka *Allegory of Spring*)	Botticelli	Uffizi, Florence
Rabbi of Vitebsk (aka *The Praying Jew*)	Chagall	Art Institute of Chicago
Raft of the Medusa, The	Géricault	Louvre, Paris
Rain, Steam and Speed	Turner	National Gallery, London
Raising of Lazarus	Rembrandt	Los Angeles County Museum of Art
Raising the Cross	Rubens	Antwerp Cathedral
Rake's Progress, The	Hogarth	Sir John Soane's Museum, London
Rape of the Sabine Women, The	Poussin	Louvre, Paris
Repudiation of Hagar	Tiepolo	Rasini Collection, Milan
Return of the Dove to the Ark, The	Millais	Ashmolean Museum, Oxford
Return of the Prodigal Son	Rembrandt	Hermitage, St Petersburg
Rokeby Venus (aka *Toilet of Venus*)	Velázquez	National Gallery, London
Sabines, Les	Jacques-Louis David	Louvre, Paris
Sad Shower in New York	Emin	Tate Britain, London
St Jerome Curing the Lion	Dürer	Kunstmuseum, Basel
St Joseph the Carpenter	La Tour	Louvre, Paris
St Michael Vanquishing Satan	Raphael	Louvre, Paris
Scream, The	Munch	National Gallery, Oslo
Seven Deadly Sins, The	Bosch	Prado, Madrid
Shoeing	Landseer	Tate Britain, London
Shrimp Girl, The	Hogarth	National Gallery, London
Skittle Players outside an Inn	Steen	National Gallery, London
Sleeping Gypsy, The	Henri Rousseau	Museum of Modern Art, New York
Snail, The	Henri Matisse	Tate Modern, London
Spanish Singer	Manet	Metropolitan Museum of Art, NY
Standing by the Rags	Freud	Tate Modern, London
Starry Night, The	van Gogh	Museum of Modern Art, New York
Stoning of St Stephen	Rembrandt	Museum of Fine Arts, Lyons
Sunflowers	Van Gogh	National Gallery, London
Three Dancers	Picasso	Tate Modern, London
Three Flags	Johns	Whitney Museum of Art, New York
Three Graces	Raphael	Musée Condé, Chantilly
Three Lawyers in Conversation	Daumier	Phillips Collection, Washington DC
Triumph of Bacchus (aka *The Topers*)	Velázquez	Prado, Madrid
Triumph of the Innocents, The	Holman Hunt	Tate Britain, London
Tropical Forest with Monkeys	Rousseau, Henri	John Hay Whitney Collection, NY
Turkish Bath, The	Ingres	Louvre, Paris
Twittering Machine	Klee	Museum of Modern Art, New York
Two Haystacks	Monet	Art Institute of Chicago
Ugolino	Reynolds	Knole House, Sevenoaks, Kent
Vampire	Munch	Munch-Museet, Oslo
Van Gogh's Chair	Van Gogh	National Gallery, London
Venus and Adonis	Titian	Prado, Madrid
Venus of Urbino	Titian	Uffizi, Florence
View of Delft	Vermeer	Mauritshuis, The Hague
Wedding Dance, The	Pieter Brueghel (Elder)	Detroit Institute of Arts
Whaam!	Lichtenstein	Tate Modern, London
Wheatfields	van Ruysdael, Jacob	Metropolitan Museum of Art, NY
Whistler's Mother	Whistler	Musée d'Orsay, Paris
White Crucifixion	Chagall	Art Institute of Chicago
Windsor Beauties, The	Lely	Hampton Court Palace, London
Women of Algiers in Their Apartment	Delacroix	Louvre, Paris
Wounded Cuirassier, The	Géricault	Louvre, Paris
Wounded Heron, The	Watts	Watts Gallery, Compton, Surrey
Wreck of a Transport Ship	Turner	Gulbenkian Foundation, Lisbon
Yellow Christ, The	Gauguin	Albright-Knox Art Gallery, Buffalo, NY
Young Bacchus, The	Caravaggio	Uffizi, Florence
Young Woman Holding a Powder-Puff	Seurat	Courtauld Gallery, London
Young Woman Standing at a Virginal	Vermeer	National Gallery, London
Young Woman with a Water Jug	Vermeer	Metropolitan Museum of Art, New York
Zoological Garden	Klee	Klee Foundation, Bern

Art: General Information

Action Painting: aka	Abstract Expressionism
Adoration of the Magi (Botticelli)	The Medici family are depicted as the Magi
Ambassadors, The	Jean de Dinteville, French ambassador to the court of Henry VIII and Georges de Selve, bishop of Lavaur are believed to be the two ambassadors depicted amid the scientific instruments and skull.
Angel of the North: details	Sculpted by Antony Gormley and situated on the site of an old coal mine next to the A1 at Eighton Banks, Gateshead, Tyne and Wear. The 20m (65ft) high figure in steel with a copper mixture has a wingspan of 54m (175ft), a weight of 200 tonnes (100 tonnes for the body and 50 tonnes per wing), and cost £800,000 to construct, largely funded by National Lottery donations. As the surface oxidises to form a patina the sculpture has become a rich brown colour
Arnolfini Portrait	Aka *The Arnolfini Wedding.* Portrait of a black-robed Giovanni di Nicolao Arnolfini and his green-frocked wife (not pregnant just over-elaborate material) with their dog.
Art Deco	Refers to a decorative style of the 1920s and 1930s
Art Gallery: largest	The Hermitage in St Petersburg
Beggarstaff Brothers	Sir William Nicholson (1872–1949) and James Pryde (1866–1941), still-life and poster painters
Brueg(h)el: spelling	Pieter the Elder spelt the name with an 'H' until 1559 and his children resorted back to original spelling
Bubbles: subject	Millais' grandson, the future Admiral William James
Churchill Portrait (Sutherland)	Destroyed by Churchill's wife
Cire Perdue	Modern bronzes are made either in sand moulds or by the 'cire perdue' (lost wax) method, which consists of a model smaller than the mould, the space between being filled with wax and vent pipes inserted. The molten bronze is poured in the top and takes the place of the wax which has been melted out
Claude Lorrain Glass	Black convex glass used by artists to reflect the landscape in miniature and, in doing so, to merge details and reduce the strength of colour so that the artist is presented with a broad picture of the scene
Collage	Objects such as newspaper, string or cloth which are pasted onto paper or canvas. Picasso's *Still Life with Chair Caning* may have been the first example of collage
Correggio	Named from the town in Modena where he was born
Courtauld Gallery, London	Art museum in Somerset House, on the Strand - houses the art collection of the Courtauld Institute of Art, a self-governing college of the University of London.
Cranach the Elder, Lucas: epitaph	Pictor Celerrimus (swiftest of painters) is how Cranach is described on his tombstone
Cubism: first picture	*Les Demoiselles d'Avignon* by Picasso
Customs Officer: former	Henri Rousseau (hence his byname 'Le Douanier')
Dada: formed where	In a nightclub in Zurich (Cabaret Voltaire) 1916
Duke of Wellington (Goya)	Stolen in 1961 but later found
Fakers: famous	Tom Keating faked Samuel Palmer paintings; Hans van Meegeren faked Vermeers
Frottage	Technique employed by Surrealists such as Max Ernst, which involves placing a piece of paper over an object and rubbing the paper with chalk or charcoal
Green Lady, The	Popular name of Vladimir Tretchikoff's 'Chinese Girl' one of the best-selling art prints ever. The original painting was sold to British jeweller Laurence Graff for £982,050 in March 2013.
Hay-Wain, The: farm	Willy Lott's farm
I Want You: Recruiting Poster	James Montgomery Flagg
Intaglio	Term used to describe types of printing such as etching and engraving whereby the design is incised as opposed to relief printing, such as wood cutting, where the raised portion creates the design
Killed a man in argument	Caravaggio in 1606 forced to flee Rome after killing a man in fit of temper
Kiss, The	Sculpture by Rodin depicting Francesca da Rimini (aka Francesca da Polenta - 1255-85) immortalised in Dante's Inferno, and Paolo Malatesta locked in an amorous embrace after reading the story of Lancelot and Guinevere.
Knighted by Britain & Spain	Sir Peter Paul Rubens
Libel Action Against John Ruskin	James Whistler, for Ruskin's attack on his *Falling Rocket* (won the case but received only one farthing)
Madonna Rucellai	Now attributed to Duccio Di Buoninsegna: formerly thought to be a work of Cimabue (Vasari's attribution)
Magic Realism	Refers to a type of painting which combines a realistic technique with fanciful designs, as in the paintings of René Magritte and other surrealists. In its strict sense it refers to German realist art of the 1920s
Marsyas: details	The title refers to a satyr in Greek mythology who was flayed alive by the god Apollo. The PVC membrane has a fleshy quality and the dark red colour suggests something 'of the physical, of the earthly, of the bodily'. *Marsyas* confounds spatial perception, immersing the viewer in a monochromatic field of colour. It is impossible to view the entire sculpture from any one position. The sculpture comprises three steel rings joined together by a single span. The flute-shaped structure is 500ft long and 10 storeys high, filling the entire space of the Tate Modern's Turbine Hall
Montage	Form of collage but refers specifically to the use of components which are complete in themselves
Murdered His Father	Richard Dadd (1817–86) English literary painter later confined in an asylum
Myra (Hindley): painter	Marcus Harvey painted this controversial painting on display at the 'Sensations' exhibition of 1997
Obscene: exhibition closed as	Modigliani
Oil Painting: largest	Tintoretto's *Paradiso* in the Doge's Palace, Venice (30ft by 74ft)
Oil Painting: largest painted in the open air	David Hockney's *Bigger Trees Near Warter* is made up of 50 canvases totalling 40ft by 15ft
Old Master: definition	A European painter of skill who worked before the 19th century
Old Masters: highest price at auction	Rubens *(Massacre of the Innocents)* £49.5m ($76.6m) in 2002 at Sotheby's, London.

Orphism	Term coined by poet Apollinaire in 1912 to distinguish the fragmented use of colour from the Cubist approach
Painting: highest price at auction	Edvard Munch's *The Scream* (1895) sold at Sotheby's in New York City on 2 May 2012. The masterpiece is one of four versions created by Munch and the only one that is privately owned. The painting sold for $119,922,500.
Patina	Term used to describe the beautiful greenish surface alteration on a bust or statue caused by age
Pears Soap Advertisement	*Bubbles* by Sir John Everett Millais
Pentimento	Phenomenon of earlier painting showing through a layer or layers of paint on a canvas
Pink Boy	*Master Nichols* by Thomas Gainsborough, a portrait currently part of the Rothschild Collection at Waddesdon Manor, Aylesbury, Buckinghamshire
Pop Art: term coined by	The critic Lawrence Alloway
Post-Painterly Abstraction	Term coined by the critic Clement Greenberg in 1964 to refer to non-objective artists who were not members of the Abstract Expressionist movement
Primary Colours	The colours from which all other colours are made up i.e. Blue, Yellow and Red
Purism	Term coined in 1918 by Amédée Ozenfant in 'Après le Cubisme' which rejected decorative qualities of Cubism
Putto	A plump naked boy used as a decorative addition to painting and sculpture, especially in the Baroque
Quattrocento	The 15th century, especially with reference to Renaissance Italian Art (literally four hundred, i.e. short for 14 hundred)
Renoir's Nude Sitter	Renoir's maid, Gabrielle, would often sit as nude model for his paintings
Rheumatism Sufferer	In later life Renoir was forced to paint with the brush tied to his fingers
Rokeby Venus (Velázquez)	Slashed by suffragette in the National Gallery
Saturday Evening Post	Norman Rockwell was famous for the covers
Sculpture: highest price at auction	A life-sized bronze by Alberto Giacometti, *L'Homme qui marche* (Walking Man I) sold for $104,327,006 (£65,001,250) at Sotheby's in London (Feb 2010).
Scumbling	Term used to describe the effect when an opaque colour is applied over another colour but allows the original colour to show through
Secondary Colours	Aka Complementary Colours; produced when two primary colours are mixed together, i.e. Green, Orange & Violet
Sensation	Charles Saatchi's controversial 1997 exhibition at the Royal Academy which includes such items as Damien Hirst's *Tiger Shark, Bisected Pig* & *Thousand Years*; Marcus Harvey's *Myra*, and Tracey Emin's *Everyone I have ever slept with*
Stole Mona Lisa 1914	Vincenzo Perugia (sentenced to one year, 15 days imprisonment)
Stolen from National Gallery	*The Scream* (stolen in 1994 but returned 2 months later)
Tempest, The (Kokoschka)	Depicts the artist and Alma Mahler resting in a huge cockleshell in the midst of a raging sea
Thousand Years	Damien Hirst's rotting cow head in a smear of blood, beset by flies
Turner Prize winners	Sponsored by Channel 4 and awarded to a British artist under 50. Inaugurated in 1984, the prize is worth £20,000 to the winner and is awarded at a ceremony at Tate Britain where an exhibition of the short-listed artists is on display for several months before the prize is announced. The full list of winners is Malcolm Morley (1984), Howard Hodgkin (1985), Gilbert and George (1986), Richard Deacon (1987), Tony Cragg (1988), Richard Long (1989), Prize suspended (1990), Anish Kapoor (1991), Grenville Davey (1992), Rachel Whiteread (1993), Antony Gormley (1994), Damien Hirst (1995), Douglas Gordon (1996), Gillian Wearing (1997), Chris Ofili (1998), Steve McQueen (1999), Wolfgang Tillmans (2000), Martin Creed (2001), Keith Tyson (2002), Grayson Perry (2003), Jeremy Deller (2004), Simon Starling (2005), Tomma Abts (2006), Mark Wallinger (2007), Mark Leckey (2008), Richard Wright (2009), Susan Philipsz (2010), Martin Boyce (2011), Elizabeth Price (2012).
Van Gogh: only painting sold	*Red Vineyard* was the only painting he sold in his lifetime

Astronomy

Constellations

Latin name	English name
Andromeda	Andromeda
Antlia	Air Pump
Apus	Bird of Paradise
Aquarius	Water Bearer
Aquila	Eagle
Ara	Altar
Aries	Ram
Auriga	Charioteer
Boötes	Herdsman
Caelum	Chisel
Camelopardalis	Giraffe
Cancer	Crab
Canes Venatici	Hunting Dogs
Canis Major	Great Dog
Canis Minor	Little Dog
Capricornus	Sea Goat
Carina	Keel
Cassiopeia	Cassiopeia
Centaurus	Centaur
Cepheus	Cepheus
Cetus	Whale
Chamaeleon	Chameleon
Circinus	Compasses
Columba	Dove
Coma Berenices	Berenice's Hair
Corona Australis	Southern Crown
Corona Borealis	Northern Crown
Corvus	Crow
Crater	Cup
Crux	Southern Cross
Cygnus	Swan
Delphinus	Dolphin
Dorado	Swordfish or Goldfish
Draco	Dragon
Equuleus	Foal
Eridanus	River Eridanus
Fornax	Furnace
Gemini	Twins
Grus	Crane
Hercules	Hercules
Horologium	Clock
Hydra	Sea Serpent
Hydrus	Water Snake
Indus	Indian
Lacerta	Lizard
Leo	Lion
Leo Minor	Little Lion
Lepus	Hare
Libra	Scales
Lupus	Wolf
Lynx	Lynx
Lyra	Lyre
Mensa	Table
Microscopium	Microscope
Monoceros	Unicorn
Musca	Fly
Norma	Level
Octans	Octant
Ophiuchus	Serpent Bearer
Orion	Orion
Pavo	Peacock
Pegasus	Winged Horse
Perseus	Perseus
Phoenix	Phoenix
Pictor	Painter
Pisces	Fishes
Piscis Austrinus	Southern Fish
Puppis	Poop or Stern
Pyxis	Mariner's Compass
Reticulum	Net
Sagitta	Arrow
Sagittarius	Archer
Scorpius	Scorpion
Sculptor	Sculptor
Scutum	Shield
Serpens	Serpent
Sextans	Sextant
Taurus	Bull
Telescopium	Telescope
Triangulum	Triangle
Triangulum Australe	Southern Triangle
Tucana	Toucan
Ursa Major	Great Bear
Ursa Minor	Little Bear
Vela	Sails
Virgo	Virgin
Volans	Flying Fish
Vulpecula	Fox

The Traditional Planets

Planetary data	*Diameter km*	*miles*	*Maximum distance from Sun (millions) km*	*miles*	*Minimum distance from Sun (millions) km*	*miles*	*Sidereal period*	*Axial rotation period*
Mercury	4878	3031	69.4	43	46.8	29	88 days	58d 16h
Venus	12104	7521	109	67.6	107.6	66.7	224.7 days	243 days
Earth	12756	7927	152.6	94.6	147.4	91.4	365.26 days	23h 56m
Mars	6794	4222	249.2	154.5	207.3	128.5	687 days	24h 37m 23s
Jupiter	142800	88700	817.4	506.8	741.6	459.8	11.86 years	9h 50m 30s
Saturn	120000	74600	1512	937.6	1346	834.6	29.46 years	10h 14m
Uranus	52000	32300	3011	1867	2740	1699.0	84.01 years	16-28 hours
Neptune	48400	30000	4543	2817	4466	2769.0	164.79 years	18-20 hours
Pluto	2300	1430	7364	4566	4461	2766.0	248.5 years	6d 9h

NB: In 2006 the International Astronomical Union voted on a new definition for a planet. Pluto was subsequently relegated to the status of dwarf planet and is now considered as a prototype for a new category of trans-Neptunian objects. There are now only eight planets recognised by the IAU, while solar system objects classified as dwarf planets are: Ceres, Pluto Haumea, Eris and Makemake. Planets, according to the IAU definition, must be in orbit around the sun, be almost spherical, and must have cleared the neighbourhood around their orbits. Small Solar System Body (SSSB) is the new term used to describe objects in the solar system that are neither planets nor dwarf planets. The term encompasses all the classical asteroids, with the exception of Ceres; all trans-Neptunian objects (TNOs), with the exception of the aforementioned dwarf planets; all comets; and the remaining minor planets (i.e. the centaurs and Trojans).

Astronomers Royal

John Flamsteed	1675–1719
Edmund Halley	1720–1742
James Bradley	1742–1762
Nathaniel Bliss	1762–1764
Nevil Maskelyne	1765–1811
John Pond	1811–1835
Sir George Airy	1835–1881
Sir William Christie	1881–191
Sir Frank Dyson	1910–1933
Sir Harold Jones	1933–1955
Sir Richard Woolley	1956–1971
Sir Martin Ryle	1972–1982
Sir Francis Graham-Smith	1982–1990
Sir Arnold Wolfendale	1991–1995
Sir Martin Rees	1995–

Until 1972 the title of Astronomer Royal was given to the director of Greenwich Observatory. It is now an honorary title for an outstanding astronomer, who receives a stipend of approx £100 per year.

Planetary Satellites (named)

		Discovered	*Diameter km*	*miles*
Earth	Moon		3476	2160
Mars	Phobos	1877	27	17
	Deimos	1877	15	9
Jupiter	Ganymede	1610	5260	3270
	Callisto	1610	4800	3000
	Io	1610	3650	2268
	Europa	1610	3138	1950
	Amalthea	1892	270	168
	Himalia	1904	180	110
	Elara	1905	80	50
	Pasiphae	1908	50	30
	Sinope	1914	40	25
	Carme	1938	40	25
	Lysithea	1938	40	25
	Ananke	1951	30	19
	Leda	1974	20	12
	Thebe	1979	100	62
	Metis	1979	40	25
	Adrastea	1979	24	15
	Callirrhoe	1999	10	6
	Praxidike	2000	36	22.5
	Themisto	2000	8	5
	Megaclite	2000	5.4	3.5
	Iocaste	2000	5.2	3.4
	Kalyke	2000	5.2	3.4
	Taygete	2000	5	3.1
	Harpalyke	2000	4.3	2.6
	Chaldene	2000	3.8	2.2
	Isonoe	2000	3.8	2.2
	Erinome	2000	3.2	2
	Aitne	2001	4	2.5
	Autonoe	2001	4	2.5
	Hermippe	2001	4	2.5
	Thyone	2001	4	2.5
	Euanthe	2001	3	1.9
	Eurydome	2001	3	1.9
	Euporie	2001	2	1.25
	Kale	2001	2	1.25
	Orthosie	2001	2	1.25
	Pasithee	2001	2	1.25
	Sponde	2001	2	1.25
	Carpo	2003	4	2.5
	Cyllene	2003	4	2.5
	Eukelade	2003	4	2.5
	Helike	2003	4	2.5
	Aoede	2003	3	1.9
	Arche	2003	3	1.9
	Hegemone	2003	3	1.9
	Kallichore	2003	3	1.9
	Mneme	2003	3	1.9
	Thelxinoe	2003	3	1.9
	Herse	2003	2	1.25
	Kore	2003	2	1.25
Saturn	Titan	1655	5150	3200
	Iapetus	1671	1440	900
	Rhea	1672	1530	950
	Dione	1684	1120	700
	Tethys	1684	1050	650
	Enceladus	1789	500	310
	Mimas	1789	390	240
	Hyperion	1848	349	217
	Phoebe	1898	220	135
	Janus	1966	200	120
	Epimetheus	1980	140	90
	Prometheus	1980	140	90
	Pandora	1980	100	60
	Atlas	1980	40	25
	Helene	1980	35	22
	Calypso	1980	30	19
	Telesto	1980	24	15
	Pan	1990	20	12
	Siarnaq	2000	45	28
	Albiorix	2000	30	19
	Paaliaq	2000	25	15
	Ymir	2000	20	12
	Kiviuq	2000	17	10.6
	Tarvos	2000	16	10
	Ijiraq	2000	14	8.8
	Erriapo	2000	10	6
	Skathi	2000	8	5
	Mundilfari	2000	7	4.3
	Suttungr	2000	7	4.3
	Thrymr	2000	7	4.3
	Narvi	2003	6.6	4.1
	Pallene	2004	4	2.5
	Polydeuces	2004	3.5	2.2
	Methone	2004	3	1.9
	Bestla	2004	7	4.3
	Aegir	2004	6	3.8
	Bebhionn	2004	6	3.8
	Bergelmir	2004	6	3.8
	Fornjot	2004	6	3.8
	Hati	2004	6	3.8
	Farbouti	2004	5	3.1
	Fenrir	2004	4	2.5
	Daphnis	2005	7	4.3
	Hyrrokkin	2006	8	5
	Kari	2006	7	4.3
	Greip	2006	6	3.8
	Jamsaxa	2006	6	3.8
	Loge	2006	6	3.8
	Skoll	2006	6	3.8
	Surtur	2006	6	3.8
	Tarqeq	2007	7	4.3
	Anthe	2007	2	1.25
	Aegaeon	2008	0.5	0.31
Uranus	Oberon	1787	1600	1000
	Titania	1787	1600	1000
	Ariel	1851	1300	800
	Umbriel	1851	1100	700
	Miranda	1948	400	250
	Puck	1986	170	105
	Portia	1986	90	55
	Cressida	1986	70	40
	Juliet	1986	70	40
	Belinda	1986	50	30
	Bianca	1986	50	30
	Desdemona	1986	50	30
	Rosalind	1986	50	30
	Ophelia	1986	20	12
	Cordelia	1986	15	9
	Sycorax	1997	160	100
	Caliban	1997	80	50
	Prospero	1999	30	19
	Setebos	1999	30	19
	Perdita	1999	26.6	16.1
	Stephano	1999	20	12
	Trinculo	2001	20	12
	Ferdinand	2001	12	7.5
	Francisco	2001	12	7.5
	Mab	2003	24.8	14.9
	Cupid	2003	17.5	11
	Margaret	2003	11	6.8
Neptune	Triton	1846	2700	1678
	Proteus	1989	415	260
	Nereid	1949	300	190
	Larissa	1989	190	118
	Galatea	1989	160	100
	Despina	1989	150	95
	Naiad	1989	50	30
	Thalassa	1989	50	30
	Halimede	2002	62	38
	Neso	2002	60	36
	Sao	2002	44	27
	Laomedeia	2002	42	26
	Psamathe	2003	38	24
Pluto	Charon	1978	1207	750
	Hydra	2005	61	37
	Nix	2005	46	28
	Kerberos	2011	34	21
	Styx	2012	25	16

Astronomy and Space: Selected Data

Albedo Reflecting power of a planet or other non-luminous body

American in Space: 1st Alan Shepard in Freedom 7 (5 May 1961); duration of flight 15 minutes 28 seconds

American to Orbit the Earth: 1st John Glenn in Friendship 7 (20 Feb 1962); for 3 orbits, duration of flight 4 hrs 55 mins 23 secs

Animals in Space Laika (meaning 'barker' in Russian) the dog was the first animal in space aboard *Sputnik 2* (3 November 1957). The first monkey in space was Gordo aboard the US Army rocket *Jupiter AM-13* (13 December 1958). Both animals died during re-entry.

Aphelion Furthest distance of a planet from the Sun

Apogee Furthest point of the Moon from the Earth

Apollo 13: Crew James Lovell, Jack Swigert and Fred Haise. The service module exploded 55 hrs into the mission to the Moon, but the lunar module was used to reach home safely on 17 Apr 1970

Appleton Layer Highest region of the Ionosphere, extending from a height of about 150 to about 1,000 kilometres. It contains the highest proportion of free electrons and is the most useful region for long-range radio transmission. The layer is also called the F-region

Artificial Satellite: 1st *Sputnik 1*, launched by Soviet Union on 4 October 1957. *Sputnik* was an 83.6 kg metal sphere, transmitting signals for three weeks before failing batteries caused it to fall to Earth on 4 January 1958

Asteroid Another name for a minor planet. Eros, discovered in 1898, comes closer to the Earth (every 37 years) than anything except the Moon. The first asteroid to be discovered, Ceres, is also the largest and is now classified as a dwarf planet. All others are classified as Small Solar System Bodies, a term introduced by the IAU in 2006. The majority of asteroids have elliptical orbits in the Asteroid Belt; some have moons or are found in pairs known as binary systems.

Asteroid: brightest Vesta

Asteroid: largest 1. Ceres 2. Pallas 3. Vesta 4. Hygeia

Asteroid Belt The 4,000-plus minor planets (asteroids) that orbit the Sun between Mars and Jupiter

Astrolabe Ancient device for measuring heights of celestial bodies

Astronomical Unit Mean distance between the Earth and the Sun: 149,598,500 km

Baikonur Launch site for manned Soviet space flights in Kazakhstan

Baily's Beads Brilliant points seen around the Moon just before and after a total solar eclipse

Big Bang Theory First advanced by Georges Lemaître: idea that the universe began, 15-17 billion years ago, as a point of superdense matter that exploded and has been expanding ever since

Black Hole Region of immense gravitational pull around a massive collapsed star from which not even light can escape

Bolide A brilliant exploding meteor

Brightest Stars in the celestial sphere 1. Sirius 2. Canopus 3. Alpha Centauri 4. Arcturus 5. Vega. It is traditional to omit our own sun from this list although it is easily the brightest object in the sky.

***Cassini-Huygens* Probe** Launched from Cape Canaveral, Florida, October 1997, to seek out the moons of Saturn. The probe flew by the moon Phoebe on 11 June 2004. Several new moons were discovered, giving a total of 37

Cassini's Division Dark gap between rings A and B of Saturn discovered by Gian Domenico Cassini, among others

Celestial Sphere Imaginary sphere surrounding the Earth on which all heavenly bodies appear to move, and whose centre is the same as that of the Earth's globe

Challenger US space shuttle exploded 72 seconds after lift-off on 28 Jan 1986, killing all 7 crew members, including schoolteacher Christa McAuliffe

Chinaman in Space: 1st Lt Col Yang Liwei (October 2003)

Chromosphere Part of the Sun's atmosphere lying above the Photosphere

Coldest Planet Pluto

Comet: Shortest known orbital period Encke's Comet, 3.3 years

Comet: meaning From the Latin 'Coma', which means hair

Constellations 31 in Northern and 52 in Southern hemisphere, with 5 'floaters' overlapping. **Largest**: Hydra. **Smallest**: Crux Australis

Corona Outermost part of the Sun's atmosphere visible with the naked eye only during a total solar eclipse

Cosmogony Study of the origin and evolution of the universe

Cosmology Study of the universe considered as a whole

Declination Angular distance of celestial body north or south of celestial equator, corresponding to latitude on the Earth

Doppler Effect Apparent change in wavelength of the light from a luminous body in motion relative to the observer

D-region Lowest layer of the Ionosphere. Extends from a height of about 60 to about 90 kilometres, contains a low concentration of free electrons, and reflects low-frequency radio waves

Earth: mean distance from Sun 150 million kms (93 million miles)

Ecliptic Apparent yearly path of the Sun among the stars

Ephemeris Table showing the predicted positions of a celestial body such as a planet, comet or asteroid

Equinox Equinoxes are two points at which the ecliptic cuts the celestial equator; vernal equinox 21 Mar, autumnal 22 Sep

Eris Largest known dwarf planet and the ninth-largest body known to orbit the Sun. It is approximately 2,500 km (1,554 miles) in diameter and has 27 per cent greater mass than Pluto. It was identified in 2005 by Mike Brown and Chad Trujillo at the Palomar Observatory in San Diego, California. Dysnomia, also discovered in 2005 by Mike Brown, is the only known moon of Eris.

European Space Agency Created 1975 by merger of European Space Research Organisation and European Launcher Development Organisation. Members are Austria, Belgium, Denmark, Finland, France, Germany, Ireland, Italy, Netherlands, Norway, Spain, Sweden, Switzerland and the UK. Canada being non-European is deemed a co-operating state. Head Office is at 8–10 Rue Mario Nikis, 75738 Paris, France

Exosphere Outermost part of a planet's atmosphere

Expanding Universe Observation made by Edwin Hubble in 1929 that the universe appears to be expanding; this confirms the Big Bang Theory

Flocculi Patches on the Sun's surface: bright (calcium) and dark (hydrogen)

Galaxies Systems made up of stars, nebulae and interstellar matter, forming star families held together by their own gravitational pull and separate from other such galaxies

Gibbous Phase Phase of the Moon or planet when between half and full

Golf Shot on the Moon Alan Shepard made the first-ever golf shot on the moon on 6 February 1971, using a six-iron head attached to the handle of a rock sample collector

Great Red Spot Enormous red feature in the atmosphere of Jupiter, visible since the 17th century

Haumea Located beyond Neptune's orbit, Haumea is a dwarf planet discovered by Mike Brown in 2004. It has two moons, Hi'iaka and Namaka.

Heaviside Layer Region of the Ionosphere, extending from a height of 90 to about 150 kilometres. It reflects radio waves of medium wavelength. This layer is also called the E-region or Kennelly-Heaviside layer

Hertzsprung-Russell Diagram Diagram in which stars are plotted according to their spectral types and their absolute magnitudes

Hottest Planet Venus

Hubble Space Telescope Placed in the Earth's orbit by the space shuttle *Discovery* (24 April 1990)

Inferior Planets Mercury and Venus: closer to the Sun than the Earth is

Inner Planets The 4 planets that orbit the Sun within the Asteroid Belt; i.e. Mercury, Venus, Earth, Mars

Ionosphere Region of the Earth's atmosphere lying above the Stratosphere

Jupiter Galileo discovered satellites Callisto, Europa, Ganymede and Io. Atmosphere: hydrogen, ammonia and methane. Temperature can be as low as -200° C. Probes: *Pioneer 10* and *11* (1973/4); *Voyager 1* and *2* (1979); *Galileo* (1995); *Ulysses* (1992 and 2004); *Cassini* (2000); *New Horizons* (2007). *Galileo* (1995) remains the only spacecraft to orbit Jupiter, the other probes merely conducting flyby missions. Although there are 50 named moons there are at least 17 additional minor moons awaiting nomenclature

Kuiper Belt Region of the solar system beyond the orbit of Neptune and named after astronomer Gerard Kuiper (1905–73). The Kuiper Belt is home to the dwarf planets – Pluto, Makemake and Haumea

Largest Planet Jupiter

Light Year Distance travelled by light in a year: 9.4607 million million km. Light travels at 186,000 mps (7½ times round the Earth)

Local Group Group of more than two dozen galaxies, including our own galaxy. Largest member is the Andromeda Galaxy, M.31

Lunar Eclipse Passage of the Moon through the shadow cast by the Earth

Magnitude Measurement unit for the brightness of a star or planet

Mariner 9 US space probe to Mars in 1971

Mars Atmosphere nearest to our own, but there is no water on Mars. Also known as the 'Red Planet', it is the site of Olympus Mons, the highest known mountain in the solar system, and of Valles Marineris, the largest canyon. Probes: *Mariner 4, 6, 7, 8, 9* (1965–71); and *1* and *2* landed 1976; *Pathfinder* landed 1997

Mercury Atmosphere: non-existent – burnt off by closeness to Sun. Probe: *Mariner 10* (1974 & 1975)

Mesosphere Region of the Earth's atmosphere between the Stratosphere and the Thermosphere, sometimes called the D-region and characterised by a rapid decrease in temperature with height

Messier, Charles (1730–1817) French astronomer nicknamed the 'comet ferret' who compiled the first catalogue of galaxies, nebulae, and star clusters. The 103 items on his list were assigned 'Messier' numbers. Although these were replaced by New General Catalogue (NGC) numbers from 1888.

Meteor Particle or small rock moving around Sun and destroyed when entering atmosphere

Meteorite Larger object that reaches the ground without being destroyed

Metonic Cycle 19-year cycle (6940 days), observed by the fifth century BC Greek astronomer Meton of Athens, used as the basis for various civilisation's calendar systems. Aka Enneadecaeteris

Milky Way The galaxy of which our Sun is a member. It contains approx 100,000m stars, of which 5,776 are visible to the naked eye

Mir Advanced space station launched by the Soviet Union in 1986

Moon Mean distance from Earth: 384,000 km (239,900 miles). Diameter: 3,476 km (2,160 miles). Revolves around the Earth from west to east. First soft landing by Soviet *Luna 9*, launched on 31 Jan 1966, landed 3 Feb. First manned flight around the Moon: *Apollo 8* in Dec 1968. First manned landing and walk: *Apollo 11* on 20 Jul 1969. Last man on the Moon was Eugene Cernan in *Apollo 17* on 11 Dec 1972

Moon Walks 12 men, all American, have walked on the surface of the Moon, Neil Armstrong and Buzz Aldrin *(Apollo 11)*, Charles Conrad Jr and Alan Bean *(Apollo 12)*, Alan Shepard and Edgar Mitchell *(Apollo 14)*, David Scott and James Irwin *(Apollo 15)*, John Young and Charles Duke *(Apollo 16)*, Eugene Cernan and Harrison Schmitt *(Apollo 17)*

Moon's Rotation Rotates about its own axis in 29½ days, which is about the same time it takes to orbit the Earth. Hence the same face of the Moon is always presented to the Earth

Nadir Point on the celestial sphere directly below the observer, diametrically opposite the zenith

Nearest Galaxy Andromeda (2.3 million light years)

Nearest Planet to Earth Venus

Nearest Star to Earth Sun

Nearest Stars to Sun 1. Proxima Centauri (4.26 light years) 2. Alpha Centauri (4.34) 3. Barnard's Star (5.88)

Nebula Cloud of gas and dust in space

Neptune Discovered by JG Galle in 1846. Atmosphere: hydrogen, helium, methane, ammonia. First suggested name was 'Janus'. Probe: *Voyager 2* (1989). To date 13 moons have been discovered

Neutron Star Remnant of a star that once exploded as a supernova

Nova Star that suddenly flares up to many times its normal brilliancy and then fades back to obscurity

Occultation The obscuring of one celestial body by another

Oldest person in space John Glenn, aged 77, on 29 Oct 1998 (aboard space shuttle Challenger - returned on 6 November)

Oort Cloud Hypothesised spherical cloud of comets thought to lie beyond the Kuiper Belt, its outer extent defining the gravitational boundary of our solar system

Ophiuchus Often called the 13th constellation of the Zodiac

Orbit of the Earth: 1st Yuri Gagarin (12 April 1961). 1st American, John Glenn in *Mercury Friendship 7* (20 February 1962).

Orrery Model showing the Sun and the orbiting planets, capable of being moved mechanically to scale

Outer Planets The 4 planets that orbit the Sun beyond the Asteroid belt; i.e. Jupiter, Saturn, Uranus, Neptune

Ozone Layer Located in the Stratosphere approx 19-30 km above the surface of the Earth. Ozone is created when energetic solar radiation strikes molecules of oxygen and causes the oxygen atoms to split apart. These atoms can then reform with O^2 molecules to form ozone (O^3) – a process known as photolysis. Ozone absorbs most of the incoming solar UV radiation which can be harmful to life on Earth

Parsec Unit used to measure astronomic distances: 3.26 light years

Perigee Position of the Moon in its orbit when closest to the Earth

Perihelion Position in orbit of a planet when closest to the Sun

Photosphere The bright surface of the Sun

Planet Large body orbiting a star - name means 'Wanderer' in Greek

Pluto Atmosphere: tenuous. Discovered by Clyde Tombaugh 1930; named by Venetia Burney, it is currently thought to have 5 moons

Polaris Also called the Pole Star, it is 680 light years from the Earth

Quadrant Ancient astronomical instrument used for measuring the apparent positions of celestial bodies

Rings of Saturn Discs composed of ice and rock orbiting Saturn. Major subdivisions of the rings include the Roche Division and the Maxwell, Colombo, Bond and Dawes Gaps.

Rotating Backwards Venus (east to west)

Saturn Mean distance from the Sun: 1,427 million km (891 million miles). Atmosophere: mostly hydrogen and helium, some methane and ammonia. Christiaan Huygens discovered the rings in 1655. Cassini discovered 4 of the satellites. The satellite Phoebe revolves in the opposite direction to the others. Probes: *Voyager 1* and *2*, 1980–81; *Cassini-Huygens*, 1997–present. Saturn is now thought to have 62 moons, 53 named and 9 awaiting nomenclature

Second Space Flight Virgil 'Gus' Grissom, the second American in space aboard *Liberty Bell 7* (21 July 1961), became the first person to make two space flights aboard *Gemini 3* (23 March 1965)

Sirius Also called the 'Dog Star', it is 8.7 light years from the Earth

Solar Cycle Discovered by H. Schwabe in 1826. He found that there is an 11-year solar cycle of sunspot activity

Solar Eclipse Blotting out of the Sun by the Moon, so that the Moon is directly between the Earth and the Sun

Solar Flares Brilliant eruptions of hydrogen in Sun's atmosphere

Solar Wind Flow of ionised hydrogen and helium from the Sun

Solstices When Sun is at its maximum declination of 23 1/2 degrees

Space Flight: 1st Yuri Gagarin in *Vostok 1* (12 Apr 1961); duration of flight 1 hr 48 mins. 2nd, Alan Shepard in *Freedom 7* (5 May 1961), the first American in space

Space Flight: 1st Briton Helen Sharman (18 May 1991)

Space Station: 1st *Salyut 1*, launched on 19 April 1971 from Baikonur (orbited for 179.93 days). First US – Skylab in May 1973

Space Walk: 1st American Ed White (June 1965 from *Gemini IV*)

Space Walk: 1st US Woman Dr Kathryn Sullivan (1984 *Challenger*)

Space Walk: 1st Briton Michael Foale

Space Walk: 1st Untethered Bruce McCandless (USA) (3 Feb 1984)

Space Walk: 1st Woman Svetlana Savitskaya (USSR) (17 Jul 1984)

Stratosphere Region of the Earth's atmosphere lying above the Troposphere and below the Ionosphere

Sun Distance from the Earth: 149,597,900 km on average. Diameter: 1,392,000 km. Light takes 8 minutes 14.2 seconds to reach the Earth. Most common elements in the sun 1. Hydrogen 2. Helium 3. Oxygen

Sunspot Region of lower temperature and therefore less brilliance, on the surface of the Sun

Superior Planets Those whose orbits lie outside the Earth's

Supernova Cataclysmic explosion of a massive star, which ends its career as a patch of expanding gas with a neutron star at its centre

Syzygy Position of the Moon in its orbit when new or full

Telescope: Largest Gran Telescopio Canarias, La Palma 10.4m lens

Troposphere Lowest part of Earth's atmosphere, reaching to 11km

Umbra Cone of shadow cast by Earth. Also darkest part of a sunspot

United Kingdom Space Agency Replaced the British National Space Centre in April 2010. HQ Polaris House, North Star Avenue, Swindon, Wiltshire, SN2 1SZ

Unmanned Moon Landing: 1st *Lunik 2* (USSR) 1959. First US landing, *Ranger 4* in 1962, although this was a crash-landing

Uranus Atmosphere: hydrogen and helium. Discovered by William Herschel 1781. Probe: *Voyager 2* (1986). Currently there are 27 named moons, all named after characters from the works of William Shakespeare and Alexander Pope

Van Allen Radiation Belts Zones of charged particles around the Earth, held captive by the Earth's magnetic field

***Venera* Space Probes** Russian series commencing with *Venera 4* in 1967 to explore Venus, the first planetary probe

Venus Atmosphere is largely carbon dioxide. Probes: Russian *Venera* series (1962–71); US *Mariners 2, 5,* and 10; *Magellan* (1990). Aka Hesperus (evening star), Phosphorus (morning star)

Voyager Pair of US interplanetary probes launched to observe and transmit to Earth data about the outer planetary system. *Voyager* runs out of power around 2020. *Voyager 1* was Launched on 5 Sep 1977, flew by Jupiter in March 1979, reached Saturn in Nov 1980, then flew out of the solar system. *Voyager 2* was launched on 20 Aug 1977. It flew by Jupiter (Jul 1979), Saturn (Aug 1981), Uranus (Jan 1986) and Neptune (Aug 1989), then on into interstellar space

Walk in Space: 1st Alexei Leonov (18 Mar 1965)

Woman in Space: 1st Valentina Tereshkova (1963) 1st American woman, Sally Ride aboard the space shuttle *Challenger* (1983)

Youngest Man in Space Gherman Titov, aged 25yrs 10 months 25 days (6 August 1961)

Zenith Point on the celestial sphere directly above the observer

Zodiac Belt stretching around the sky 8 degrees to either side of ecliptic. The constellations Aries, Taurus, Gemini, Cancer, Leo, Virgo, Libra, Scorpius, Sagittarius, Capricornus, Aquarius and Pisces lies within this belt, and so do the apparent paths of the Sun and all the planets except Pluto, which sometimes moves outside

Britain

United Kingdom: Administration Centres

A restructure of the old County boundaries has been ongoing throughout the UK. Formerly there were 46 English County Councils, but this has been reduced to 27, all of which have the same Administrative Headquarters as before.

The other 19 Counties, along with parts of still existing Counties, have been restructured and are now known officially as Unitary Authorities. There are 92 such authorities at present, plus the 32 London Boroughs and the City of London Corporation.

A similar position exists in Scotland, Wales and Northern Ireland.

Northern Ireland's six Counties have been rationalised across 26 districts (the same number as there are Counties of the Irish Republic), although at present only the traditional six Counties plus Belfast City and Londonderry City have Lord-Lieutenants.

English County Councils (as at 31 Aug 2013)

County	*Admin Headquarters*	*County*	*Admin Headquarters*
Buckinghamshire	Aylesbury	Lincolnshire	Lincoln
Cambridgeshire	Cambridge	Norfolk	Norwich
Cumbria	Carlisle	Northamptonshire	Northampton
Derbyshire	Matlock	North Yorkshire	Northallerton
Devon	Exeter	Nottinghamshire	Nottingham
Dorset	Dorchester	Oxfordshire	Oxford
East Sussex	Lewes	Somerset	Taunton
Essex	Chelmsford	Staffordshire	Stafford
Gloucestershire	Gloucester	Suffolk	Ipswich
Hampshire	Winchester	Surrey	Kingston-upon-Thames
Hertfordshire	Hertford	Warwickshire	Warwick
Kent	Maidstone	West Sussex	Chichester
Lancashire	Preston	Worcestershire	Worcester
Leicestershire	Leicester		

NB: The five inhabited islands of the Scillies, i.e. St Mary's (Admin HQ), Tresco, Bryher, St Agnes and St Martin's, although not constituting a separate County, do however have their own Council.

London Boroughs

(these are also Unitary Authorities)

Council	*Admin Headquarters*	*Council*	*Admin Headquarters*
Barking & Dagenham	Dagenham	Hounslow	Hounslow
Barnet	Hendon	* Islington	Islington
Bexley	Bexleyheath	* Kensington and Chelsea #	Kensington
Brent	Wembley	Kingston-upon-Thames #	Kingston-upon-Thames
Bromley	Bromley		
* Camden	Camden	* Lambeth	Brixton
City of London	Guildhall, London	* Lewisham	Catford
Croydon	Croydon	Merton	Morden
Ealing	Ealing	Newham	East Ham
Enfield	Enfield	Redbridge	Ilford
* Greenwich	Woolwich	Richmond-upon-Thames	Twickenham
* Hackney	Hackney	* Southwark	Southwark
* Hammersmith & Fulham	Hammersmith	Sutton	Sutton
Haringey	Wood Green	* Tower Hamlets	Tower Hamlets
Harrow	Harrow	Waltham Forest	Walthamstow
Havering	Romford	* Wandsworth	Wandsworth
Hillingdon	Uxbridge	*Westminster City	Westminster

* denotes Inner London Borough
# denotes Royal Borough

Unitary Authorities (as at 31 Aug 2013)

Authority	*Headquarters*
Barnsley*	Barnsley
Bath and North East Somerset	Bath
Bedford	Bedford
Birmingham*	Birmingham
Blackburn with Darwen	Blackburn
Blackpool	Blackpool
Bolton*	Bolton
Bournemouth	Bournemouth
Bracknell Forest	Bracknell
Bradford*	Bradford
Brighton and Hove	Brighton
Bristol	Bristol
Bury*	Bury
Calderdale*	Halifax
Central Bedfordshire	Chicksands
Cheshire East	Sandbach
Cheshire West and Chester	Chester
Cornwall	Truro
Coventry*	Coventry
Darlington	Darlington
Derby	Derby
Doncaster*	Doncaster
Dudley*	Dudley
Durham	Durham
East Riding of Yorkshire	Beverley
Gateshead*	Gateshead
Halton	Widnes
Hartlepool	Hartlepool
Herefordshire	Hereford
Isle of Wight	Newport
Isles of Scilly	Hugh Town
Kingston-upon-Hull	Kingston-upon-Hull
Kirklees*	Huddersfield
Knowsley*	Huyton
Leeds*	Leeds
Leicester	Leicester
Liverpool*	Liverpool
Luton	Luton
Manchester*	Manchester
Medway Towns	Rochester
Middlesbrough	Middlesbrough
Milton Keynes	Milton Keynes
Newcastle-upon-Tyne*	Newcastle-upon-Tyne
North East Lincolnshire	Grimsby
North Lincolnshire	Brigg
North Somerset	Weston-Super-Mare
North Tyneside*	North Shields
Northumberland	Morpeth
Nottingham	Nottingham
Oldham*	Oldham
Peterborough	Peterborough
Plymouth	Plymouth
Poole	Poole
Portsmouth	Portsmouth
Reading	Reading
Redcar and Cleveland	Redcar
Rochdale*	Rochdale
Rotherham*	Rotherham
Rutland	Oakham
St Helens*	St Helens
Salford*	Swinton
Sandwell*	West Bromwich
Sefton*	Southport
Sheffield*	Sheffield
Shropshire	Shrewsbury
Slough	Slough
Solihull*	Solihull
Southampton	Southampton
Southend-on-Sea	Southend
South Gloucestershire	Thornbury
South Tyneside*	South Shields
Stockport*	Stockport
Stockton-on-Tees	Stockton-on-Tees
Stoke-on-Trent	Stoke-on-Trent
Sunderland*	Sunderland
Swindon	Swindon
Tameside*	Ashton-under-Lyme
Telford and Wrekin	Telford
Thurrock	Grays
Torbay	Torquay
Trafford*	Stretford
Wakefield*	Wakefield
Walsall*	Walsall
Warrington	Warrington
West Berkshire	Newbury
Wiltshire	Trowbridge
Windsor and Maidenhead	Maidenhead
Wigan*	Wigan
Wirral*	Wallasey
Wokingham	Wokingham
Wolverhampton*	Wolverhampton
York	York

* denotes Metropolitan Authority

Scottish Districts (Unitary Authorities)

Council	*Admin Headquarters*
Aberdeen	Aberdeen
Aberdeenshire	Aberdeen
Angus	Forfar
Argyll and Bute	Lochgilphead
Clackmannanshire	Alloa
Comhairlenan Eilean Siar	Stornoway
Dumfries and Galloway	Dumfries
Dundee	Dundee
East Ayrshire	Kilmarnock
East Dunbartonshire	Kirkintilloch
East Lothian	Haddington
East Renfrewshire	Glasgow
Edinburgh	Edinburgh
Falkirk	Falkirk
Fife	Glenrothes
Glasgow City	Glasgow
Highland	Inverness
Inverclyde	Greenock
Midlothian	Dalkeith
Moray	Elgin
North Ayrshire	Irvine
North Lanarkshire	Motherwell
Orkney	Kirkwall
Perth and Kinrosshire	Perth
Renfrewshire	Paisley
Scottish Borders	Melrose
Shetland	Lerwick
South Ayrshire	Ayr
South Lanarkshire	Hamilton
Stirling	Stirling
West Dunbartonshire	Dumbarton
West Lothian	Livingston

Welsh Districts (Unitary Authorities)

District Council	*Admin Headquarters*
Anglesey	Llangefni
Blaenau Gwent	Ebbw Vale
Bridgend	Bridgend
Caerphilly	Ystad Mynach
Cardiff	Cardiff
Carmarthenshire	Carmarthen
Ceredigion	Aberystwyth
Conwy	Conwy
Denbighshire	Ruthin
Flintshire	Mold
Gwynedd	Caernarfon
Merthyr Tydfil	Merthyr Tydfil
Monmouth	Cwmbran
Neath Port Talbot	Port Talbot
Newport	Newport
Pembrokeshire	Haverfordwest
Powys	Llandrindod Wells
Rhondda, Cynon, Taff	Cardiff
Swansea, City and County	Swansea
Torfaen	Pontypool
Vale of Glamorgan	Barry
Wrexham	Wrexham

Northern Irish Districts (Unitary Authorities)

District Council	*Admin Headquarters*
Antrim	Antrim
Ards	Newtownards
Armagh	Armagh
Ballymena	Ballymena
Ballymoney	Ballymoney
Banbridge	Banbridge
Belfast	Belfast
Carrickfergus	Carrickfergus
Castlereagh	Castlereagh
Coleraine	Coleraine
Cookstown	Cookstown
Craigavon	Craigavon
Derry	Derry
Down	Downpatrick
Dungannon	Dungannon
Fermanagh	Enniskillen
Larne	Larne
Limavady	Limavady
Lisburn	Lisburn
Magherafelt	Magherafelt
Moyle	Ballycastle
Newry and Mourne	Newry
Newtownabbey	Newtownabbey
North Down	Bangor
Omagh	Omagh
Strabane	Strabane

Shopping Centres

by Towns and Cities

Aberdeen	Bredero; The Academy; Trinity Mall
Accrington	Arndale Centre
Aldershot	The Arcade
Andover	Chantry
Ashford, Kent	Park Mall; County Square
Aylesbury	Hale Leys; Friar Square
Banbury	Castle Quay
Barking	Vicarage Field
Barnet	Brent Cross (Hendon)
Barnsley	Mall Alhambra
Barnstaple, Devon	Green Lanes
Basildon	Eastgate Centre
Basingstoke	Festival Place
Bath	Green Park
Bayswater	Whiteleys Centre
Bedford	Harpur
Belfast	Castle Court; Victoria Square
Bexleyheath	Broadway
Bideford	Atlantic Village; Pyramids
Birmingham	Bull Ring; City Plaza; The Fort
Blackburn	The Mall
Blackpool	Hounds Hill
Bolton	Crompton Place; Market Place
Bournemouth	Castle Point
Bracknell	Princess Square
Bradford	Kirkgate Mall
Brighton	Churchill Square
Bristol	Galleries; Clifton Arcade; Cabot Circus; Broadmead; The Mall at Cribbs Causeway
Bromley	Glades
Burgess Hill	The Martletts
Burnley	Charter Walk
Bury	Millgate
Cambridge	Grafton Centre; Castle Mall
Cardiff	St Davids; Queens Arcade; Capitol
Carlisle	The Lanes
Carmarthen	Greyfriars
Caterham	Church Walk
Chatham	Pentagon; Dockside
Chelmsford	Meadows; High Chelmer
Cheltenham	Regent Arcade; Beechwood Arcade
Chester	Grosvenor; The Forum
Chippenham	Borough Parade
Colchester	Culver Square; St John's Walk; Lion Walk
Coventry	Cannon Park; West Orchard; Lower Precinct
Cowley	Templars Square
Crawley	County Mall
Crewe	Market Centre
Croydon	Whitgift Centre; Centrale
Darlington	Cornmill Centre
Dartford	Orchards; Copperfields
Derby	Eagle Centre; Westfield Derby
Doncaster	Frenchgate Centre
Dorking	St Martin's Walk
Dover	De Bradelei Wharf
Dudley	Trident; Westfield Merry Hill
Dundee	Wellgate Centre; Overgate
Durham	Milburngate; Arnison Centre; Prince Bishops Centre
Eastbourne	Arndale Centre
Eastleigh	Swan
Edgware	Broad Walk
Edinburgh	Cameron Toll; Gyle; Princess Mall; St James Centre; Ocean Terminal

Ellesmere Port	Cheshire Oaks
Epsom	Ashley Centre
Exeter	Guildhall; Harlequins
Falkirk	Howgate Mall
Fareham	Market Quay
Farnborough	Kingsmead; Princes Mead
Finchley	O2 Centre
Fleet	Hart Centre
Gateshead	MetroCentre (largest in the UK)
Gillingham	Hempstead Valley
Glasgow	St Enoch; Sauchiehall Centre; Braehead Centre; Forge Centre; Buchanan Galleries; Silverburn Centre
Gloucester	Kings Square
Gravesend	St Georges; Thamesgate
Greenhithe, Kent	Bluewater (4th largest)
Grimsby	Freshney Place; Abbeygate
Guildford	Friary, White Lion Walk
Halifax	Woolshops
Hanley	The Potteries
Harlow	Harvey Centre
Harrogate	Victoria Shopping Centre
Hartlepool	Middleton Grange
Hastings	Priory Meadow
Hatfield	Galleria Outlet Centre
Havant	Meridian Centre
Hemel Hempstead	The Marlowes
Hereford	Maylord; The Atrium
High Wycombe	Chilterns; Eden
Hinckley, Leics	Britannia
Horsham	Swan Walk; Piries Place
Hounslow	Treaty Centre
Huddersfield	Kingsgate
Hull	North Point; Princess Quay; Prospect
Ilford	Exchange
Inverness	Eastgate Centre
Ipswich	Tower Ramparts
Kendal	Elephant Yard; Westmorland Shopping Centre
Kettering	Newlands
Kingston Upon Thames	Bentalls
Lancaster	St Nicholas; Marketgate
Leatherhead	Swan Centre
Leeds	Bramley Centre; Crossgates; Merrion Centre; White Rose; The Light; Victoria Quarter; Trinity
Leicester	Highcross; Beaumont; Fosse
Lincoln	Waterside
Liverpool	Clayton Square; Liverpool One; St John's Precinct
Livingston	The Centre
Lowestoft	The Britten Centre
Luton	Arndale Centre (now renamed The Mall)
Maidenhead	The Nicholsons Centre
Maidstone	The Corn Exchange; Chequers
Manchester	Arndale Centre; Trafford Centre (2nd largest)
Mansfield	Four Seasons
Middlesbrough	Captain Cook Square; Cleveland Mall
Milton Keynes	thecentre:mk; Midsummer Place
Morecambe	Arndale
Newbury	Kennet Shopping
Newcastle	intu Eldon Square; Metro Centre
Newton Abbot	Trago Mills
Northampton	Grosvenor Centre; Weston Favell; Peacock Place
Norwich	Castle Mall; Chapelfield
Nottingham	Broadmarsh; Victoria; Exchange
Nuneaton	Abbey Gate
Oldham	Spindles
Oxford	Westgate; Clarendon; Templars Square
Penzance	Wharfside
Peterborough	Queensgate; Rivergate Centre; Serpentine Green
Petersfield	Rams Walk
Piccadilly, London	The London Pavilion
Plymouth	The Armada Centre
Poole	Dolphin Centre
Portsmouth	Bridge; Cascades; Gun Wharf Quays
Preston	Fishergate; St Georges
Reading	Oracle; Broad Street Mall
Redditch	Kingfisher Centre
Redhill	Belfry
Renfrew	intu Braehead
Ringwood	Furlong Centre
Rochdale	Wheatsheaf
Romford	Liberty 2
Ross-on-Wye	The Maltings
St Albans	Christopher Place; The Maltings
St Helens	St Mary's Arcade; Church Square
Sale	Square Shopping Centre
Scarborough	Brunswick; Balmoral
Scunthorpe	The Parishes; The Foundry
Sheffield	Forum; Meadowhall; Crystal Peaks; The Moor
Shepherd's Bush	Westfield London (5th largest)
Shrewsbury	Darwin; Pride Hill
Skegness	Hildreds Centre
Skipton, North Yorks	Craven Court
Slough	Queensmere; Observatory Centre
Solihull	Mell Square; Touchwood
Southampton	Marlands; WestQuay; Bargate Centre
Southend	Victoria Plaza, Royals
Southport	Marble Place
Staines	Elmsleigh Centre
Stevenage	Westgate
Stockport	Mersey Way
Stockton	Teeside Park; Castlegate
Stoke-on-Trent	Potteries
Stratford (London)	Westfield Stratford City (3rd largest)
Street, Somerset	Clarks Village
Sunderland	Bridges
Sutton Coldfield	Sainsbury Centre; Gracechurch Centre
Sutton (Surrey)	St Nicholas; Times Square
Swansea	St Davids
Swindon	Brunel Centre
Thurrock	Lakeside
Torquay	Fleet Walk; Union Square
Tunbridge Wells	Royal Victoria Place
Uxbridge	The Chimes
Wakefield	The Ridings
Wandsworth	Arndale; Southside
Warrington	Cockhedge; Golden Square
Washington	The Galleries
Watford	Harlequin Centre
Wellingborough	Swansgate
Welwyn Garden City	Howard Centre
Weston-super-Mare	Sovereign
Wigan	Galleries; Marketgate
Winchester	Brooks
Woking	Peacock Centre; Wolsey Place
Wolverhampton	Mander Centre
Wood Green	Shopping Centre
Worcester	Crowngate
York	Coppergate; Swinegate; Monks Cross; Clifton Moor

Pub Names

Bear & Ragged Staff	Heraldic sign of the Earl of Warwick.
Blind Beggar	Situated in Whitechapel Road, London and famous as the site of Ronald Kray's murder of George Cornell.
Clachan Inn	Situated in Drymen nr Glasgow and dating from 1734; the oldest pub in Scotland.
Five Alls	Sign depicts a king with the caption 'I rule for all', a parson with 'I pray for all', a lawyer with 'I plead for all' a soldier with 'I fight for all' and a labourer with 'I work for all'.
Greyhound	Situated in Tinsley Green, Crawley and famous for hosting the World Marbles Championships at Easter.

Marquis of Granby	Named after John Manners, Marquis of Granby (1721–70). C-in-C of the British army in 1766.
Most Popular Name	No longer unequivocal as the boundaries blur as to what constitutes the name 'Pub'. Traditionally the Red Lion has topped most lists although The Crown has also been mentioned in despatches closely followed by The Royal Oak.
Nutshell	Situated in Bury St Edmunds; the smallest pub in England.
Red Lion	The badge of John of Gaunt. James I (VI of Scotland) ordered Red Lions to be displayed outside all public places as it is part of the Royal Arms of Scotland.
Royal Oak	Named after the oak tree that Charles II hid in after the battle of Worcester in 1651.
Skirrid, The	Situated in Llanvihangel, Crucorney, near Abergavenny, South Wales; the oldest pub in Wales.
Tan Hill Inn	Situated in Arkengarthdale, near Reeth, N. Yorks; the highest pub in Britain.
White Hart	Named after Richard II's heraldic symbol.
White Lion	Named after Edward IV's heraldic symbol.
Ye Olde Trip to Jerusalem	Situated in Nottingham, dates to time immemorial ie 1189 AD, the oldest pub in Britain.

There is now well under 60,000 pubs in Britain. Since 1988 they can remain open any time between 11am and 11pm, although new legislation permits 24-hour opening on application.

National Parks

	sq. miles
Brecon Beacons (1957)	519
Broads (1989)	117
Cairngorms (2003)	1,461
Dartmoor (1951)	368
Exmoor (1954)	268
Lake District (1951)	885
Loch Lomond and the Trossachs (2002)	720
New Forest (2005)	224
Northumberland (1956)	405
North York Moors (1952)	554
Peak District (1951)	555
Pembrokeshire Coast (1952)	240
Snowdonia (1951)	835
South Downs (2010)	628
Yorkshire Dales (1954)	683

The Peak District was the first British National Park to be established. The South Downs became the latest on 31 March 2010. Scotland has two National Parks, the first established in July 2002.

Prisons

Name	*Location*
* Aberdeen	Aberdeen
Acklington	Morpeth, Northumberland
** Addiewell	West Lothian
Albany	Newport, Isle of Wight
Aldington	Ashford, Kent (closed 1999)
** Altcourse	Liverpool
Armley	Leeds
** Ashfield	Bristol
Ashwell	Oakham, Leics (closed 2011)
* Askham Grange	Askham Richard, York
Aylesbury	Aylesbury, Bucks
Barlinnie	Glasgow (holds the most prisoners in Scotland, approx 1,000)
Bedford	Bedford
Belmarsh	Thamesmead, London
** Blakenhurst	Redditch, Worcs
Blantyre House	Cranbrook, Kent
Blundeston	Lowestoft, Suffolk
Brinsford	Wolverhampton
Bristol	Bristol
Brixton	Brixton, London
* Brockhill	Redditch, Worcs
* Bronzefield	Ashford
Buckley Hall	Rochdale, Lancs
Bullingdon	Bicester, Oxon
* Bullwood Hall	Hockley, Essex
Camp Hill	Newport, Isle of Wight
Canterbury	see Longport
Cardiff	Cardiff, South Wales
Castington	Morpeth
Castle Huntly	Longforgan, nr Dundee
Channings Wood	Newton Abbott, Devon
* Chelmsford	Chelmsford, Essex
Coldingley	Woking, Surrey
* Cookham Wood	Rochester, Kent
* Cornton Vale	Stirling
Crumlin Road	Belfast
Dartmoor	Princetown, Yelverton, Devon
Deerbolt	Barnard Castle
** Doncaster	Marshgate, Doncaster
Dorchester	North Square, Dorchester
** Dovegate	Uttoxeter
Dover	Dover, Kent
Downview	Sutton, Surrey
* Drake Hall	Eccleshall, Staffs
* Dumfries	Dumfries
Dungavel	Strathaven, Lanark
* Durham	Old Elvet, Durham
* East Sutton Park	Maidstone, Kent
* Eastwood Park	Falfield
Edinburgh	Edinburgh
Edmunds Hill	Newmarket, Suffolk
Elmley	Sheerness, Kent
Erlestoke House	Devizes, Wilts
Everthorpe	Brough, Yorks
Exeter	Exeter
Featherstone	Featherstone, Wolverhampton
Ford	Arundel, West Sussex
** Forest Bank	Pendlebury, Manchester
* Foston Hall	Ashbourne, Derby
Frankland	Brasside, Durham
Friarton	Perth
Full Sutton	Full Sutton, Yorks
Garth	Preston, Lancs
Gartree	Market Harborough, Leics
Gateside	Greenock
Glenochil	Clackmannanshire
Glen Parva	Leicester
Gloucester	Barrack Square, Gloucester
Grendon	Aylesbury, Bucks
Guys Marsh	Shaftesbury, Dorset
Haslar	Gosport, Hants
Hatfield	Hatfield, Doncaster
Haverigg	Millom, Cumbria
Hewell Grange	Redditch, Worcs
High Down	Sutton, Surrey
* Highpoint	Newmarket, Suffolk
Hindley	Wigan, Lancs
Hollesley Bay	Woodbridge, Suffolk

Name	Location
* Holloway	Parkhurst Rd, London
Holme House	Stockton-on-Tees
Hull	Hull, Yorks
Hydebank Wood	Belfast
** Kilmarnock	Kilmarnock
Kingston	Portsmouth
Kirkham	Preston, Lancs
Kirklevington Grange	Yarm, Cleveland
Lancaster Castle	Lancaster (closed 2011)
Lancaster Farms	Lancaster
Latchmere House	Richmond, Surrey (closed 2011)
Leicester	Leicester
Lewes	Lewes, East Sussex
Leyhill	Wotton-under-Edge, Glos
Lincoln	Lincoln
Lindholme	Doncaster
Littlehey	Huntingdon
Liverpool	Liverpool
Long Lartin	Evesham, Worcs
Longport	Canterbury, Kent
Longriggend	Airdrie
** Lowdham Grange	Lowdham, Notts
Low Moss	Glasgow
* Low Newton	Brasside, Durham
Maghaberry	Lisburn, Co Antrim
Magilligan	Londonderry
Maidstone	Maidstone
Manchester	Manchester
Maze (formerly 'Long Kesh')	Lisburn, Co Antrim
Moorland	Doncaster
Morton Hall	Lincoln
Mount	Hemel Hempstead
Mountjoy	Dublin
Mousehold	Norwich
* New Hall	Wakefield, Yorks
Noranside	Angus (closed 2011)
Northallerton	Northallerton, N. Yorks
North Sea Camp	Boston, Lincs
Norwich	Norwich
Nottingham	Nottingham
** Oakwood	Featherstone, Staffs (highest operating capacity in UK approx. 1605 although currently 1346 at 31/8/2013)
Onley	Rugby, Warks
** Parc	Bridgend, S. Wales (although less Capacity than Oakwood currently more inmates 1439 at 31/8/2013
Parkhurst	Newport, Isle of Wight

Name	Location
Penninghame	Newton Stewart
Pentonville	London
Perth	Perth
** Peterborough	Cambs - mixed prison
Peterhead	Aberdeenshire
Polmont	Falkirk
* Porterfield	Inverness
Portland	Portland, Dorset
Prescoed	Pontypool
Preston	Preston, Lancs
Ranby	Retford, Notts
Reading	Reading
* Risley	Warrington
Rochester	Rochester, Kent
** Rye Hill	Rugby, Warks
Send	Woking, Surrey
Shepton Mallet	Somerset
Shotts	Shotts, Lanarkshire
Shrewsbury	The Dana, Shrewsbury (closed 2013)
Spring Hill	Buckinghamshire
Stafford	Gaol Rd, Stafford
Standford Hill	Sheerness, Kent
Stocken	Stretton, Leics
Stoke Heath	Market Drayton, Shrops
* Styal	Wilmslow, Cheshire
Sudbury	Sudbury, Derbyshire
Swaleside	Isle of Sheppey, Kent
Swansea	Swansea
Swinfen Hall	Lichfield, Staffs
Thorn Cross	Warrington
Usk	Usk, Gwent
Verne, The	Portland, Dorset
Wakefield	Wakefield, Yorks
Wandsworth	London
Wayland	Thetford, Norfolk
Wealston	Wetherby, W. Yorks
Weare	Portland Harbour (ship closed 2005)
Wellingborough	Northants (closed 2012)
Werrington	Stoke-on-Trent
Wetherby	Wetherby, Yorks
Whatton	Notts
Whitemoor	March, Cambs
* Winchester	Winchester, Hants
** Winson Green	Birmingham
** Wolds, The	Brough, Yorks
Woodhill	Milton Keynes
Wormwood Scrubs	DuCane Rd, London
Wymott	Preston, Lancs

* denotes women's prison (or women's wing attached)

** denotes private prison

British Castles

Name	Location	General Information
Abergavenny	Gwent	Norman Motte & Bailey castle founded by Hamelin of Ballon between 1087 & 1100, rebuilt in stone C12, captured by Welsh. c1172, recaptured by William de Braose c1175, ordered to be destroyed by Charles I in 1645.
Aberystwyth	Ceredigion	Edwardian concentric castle erected 1277–90 under aegis of Edmund Crouchback and Master Giles of St George (after destruction in 1282 by Welsh). Held by Glyndwr 1404–9, slighted by Parliament in 1649.
Abinger	Surrey	Norman Motte & Bailey erected c1100. Wooden Donjon on stilts, excavated 1947–9.
Aboyne	Grampian	Motte castle erected C13, stone additions by 1300.
Acton Burnell	Shropshire	Fortified manor founded by Bishop Burnell c1284–90.
Airlie	Tayside	Enclosure castle founded by Ogilvy family c1432.
Alfred's Castle	Oxfordshire	Small Iron Age hill fort behind Ashdown Park in the civil parish of Ashbury.
Allington	Kent	Founded by Stephen of Penchester 1281 beside site of Norman Motte & Bailey. Altered C15 by Sir Henry Wyatt, restored by Lord Conway 1905–30. Now a Carmelite nunnery.
Alnwick	Northumberland	Norman castle founded by Gilbert de Tesson, C12 shell keep, seat of Percy family since 1309, remodelled by Salvin C19.
Alton	Staffordshire	Founded by Bertram de Verdon and built on a rocky precipice overlooking the River Churnet in the 12th century (Alton Towers is close by). Now a residential youth centre.

Amberley	West Sussex	Built for the Bishops of Chichester, licence to crenellate 1377. Partially ruined, now a private residence.
Amroth	Pembrokeshire	Norman Motte & Bailey, later rebuilt as a small 12th century stone castle. Part of the 14th century gateway remains. Situated near Tenby.
Anstey	Herts	C12 Motte & Bailey, now lost.
Appleby	Cumbria	Norman castle erected C12 by Henry II, restored by Lady Anne Clifford 1651.
Ardrossan	Strathclyde	Courtyard castle founded late C13, gatehouse improved C15/16.
Arundel	West Sussex	Norman castle, founded 1069 by Roger of Montgomery. Seat of Dukes of Norfolk.
Ashby de la Zouch	Leicestershire	Norman hall founded C12 by Zouch family. Converted into a castle 1474 by Lord Hastings, slighted by Parliament 1648. Now owned by English Heritage.
Astley	Warwickshire	C16 manor house damaged by fire in 1978 but reopened as a holiday let in 2012.
Auchen	Dumfries & Galloway	Castle founded C13, slighted by Bruce, rebuilt C14 as quadrangular castle.
Auckland	County Durham	Situated in Bishop Auckland. It is the residence of the Bishop of Durham and has been owned by the diocese for 800 years.
Ayr	Strathclyde	Castle founded C12 by William the Lion, besieged by English 1298.
Balmoral	Grampian	Private royal residence on Deeside designed by William Smith of Aberdeen 1853–6.
Balvenie	Grampian	Enclosure castle founded late C13 by Douglases, remodelled C16 by 4th Earl of Atholl.
Bamburgh	Northumberland	Norman castle with C12 tower keep erected by Henry II, besieged in 1095, 1462 and 1464, 'restored' by Lord Armstrong 1894–1905.
Bampton	Oxfordshire	Quadrangular castle founded 1315 by Aymer de Valence, now lost.
Banbury	Oxfordshire	Norman castle built C12 by Bishops of Lincoln, extended 1400, now lost.
Barnard Castle	Durham	Norman castle erected by Guy de Balliol c1100, C13 round keep, dismantled 1630 by Sir Henry Vane, now owned by English Heritage.
Barnstaple	Devon	Norman Motte & Bailey castle erected C11 by Judhael, C12 shell keep now lost.
Barnwell	Northants	Norman castle founded 1132 by Reginald de Moine. Rebuilt c1265, now ruined.
Barry	Vale of Glamorgan	Originally two stone buildings erected C13 to replace an earlier earthwork. Hall and gatehouse added C14. The remains of which still stand.
Bass of Inverurie	Grampian	Motte & Bailey castle founded c1180 by David, Earl of Huntingdon.
Beaumaris	Gwynedd	Concentric Edwardian castle erected by Master James of St George 1295–1330.
Bedford	Bedfordshire	Norman Motte & Bailey castle founded late C11, modified and enlarged C12, besieged by Henry III 1224 and destroyed shortly after.
Beeston	Cheshire	Built by Ranulf of Chester c1220, slighted in Civil War, owned by English Heritage.
Belvoir	Lincolnshire	Gothic style C19 castle, seat of Dukes of Rutland on site of Norman Motte & Bailey castle founded by Robert de Todeni C11, destroyed by King John.
Benington	Hertfordshire	Motte & Bailey fortress founded by Peter de Valoignes in 1136 but destroyed in 1212. Situated in Stevenage, the foundations of the keep and some earthworks still remain.
Berkeley	Gloucestershire	Norman castle founded by William Fitz Osbern pre-1086, current building erected 1154 by Robert Fitzhardinge.
Berkhamsted	Hertfordshire	Norman Motte & Bailey castle founded by Robert of Mortain, rebuilt by Thomas Becket 1155–65 and King John, rare double moat, now owned by English Heritage.
Berry Pomeroy	Devon	Norman castle probably founded C12.
Berwick	Northumberland	Founded C12 by the Scottish King David I, only the western wall remains.
Bewcastle	Cumbria	Built C11 on the site of a Roman fort, only part of the gatehouse still remains.
Bickleigh	Devon	Norman Motte & Bailey castle dismantled mid-C12; Courtenay family built fortified mansion on site C14.
Bishop's Stortford	Hertfordshire	Norman Motte & Bailey castle, now lost.
Blackness	Lothian	Tower castle founded C15, extended C16 with plan resembling that of a ship.
Blair	Tayside	Tower founded c1270, last castle to be besieged (1746), C18 mansion, seat of Dukes of Atholl.
Bodiam	East Sussex	Quadrangular moated castle built by Edward Dalyngrigge 1386, restored by Lord Curzon. National Trust property.
Bolingbroke	Lincolnshire	Built by Ranulf, Earl of Chester, c1220, now ruined.
Bolsover	Derbyshire	Norman castle founded by William Peverel, rebuilt by Smythson in Jacobean Romantic style, owned by English Heritage.
Bolton	North Yorkshire	Quadrangular castle built by Lord Scrope c1381–99, slighted during Civil War.
Bothwell	Strathclyde	Castle founded in 1270s by Moravia family, captured by Scots 1297, English 1301 & 1331, dismantled by Sir Andrew de Moravia 1337, rebuilt by Black Douglas in 1360s.
Bowes	County Durham	Tower castle built by the Earl of Richmond 1170–87, now owned by English Heritage.
Bramber	West Sussex	Norman castle founded by William de Braose c1070, slighted during Civil War, now owned by National Trust.
Brampton Bryan	Herefordshire	Motte castle cC12, curtain walls, and the ruins of the towers and square gatehouse remain following damage incurred during the English Civil War.
Brancepeth	County Durham	Norman castle replaced in 1820 by John Matthew Russell; improved in 1841 by Anthony Salvin for William Russell, High Sheriff of Durham. Now owned by the Dobson family.
Brecon	Powys	Norman castle founded 1090 by Bernard de Neufmarche, extended and fortified in stone C12, unsuccessfully besieged by Welsh 1216, 1233 & 1404.
Bridgnorth	Shropshire	Norman castle founded by Robert de Belleme C11, C12 keep erected by Henry II, slighted during Civil War.
Bristol	Bristol	Norman Motte & Bailey castle founded after Conquest; Tower Keep erected C12 by Stephen, destroyed in 1650s.
Bronllys	Powys	Norman Motte & Bailey castle founded C12, cylindrical tower added c1176 after a fire.
Brough	Cumbria	Norman castle founded by William Rufus c1095 in ruins of a Roman fort, destroyed 1174 by William the Lion, rebuilt by Theobald de Valoires, restored C17 by Lady Anne Clifford. Now owned by English Heritage.
Brougham	Cumbria	Norman castle built C12 by Hugh d'Albini, pulled down c1700, now owned by English Heritage.
Buckingham	Buckinghamshire	Norman Motte & Bailey castle now covered by a church.
Builth	Powys	Norman Motte & Bailey castle founded by Philip de Braose c1100, destroyed by Llywelyn ap Gruffyd 1260, rebuilt 1277–82 by Edward I under direction of Master James of St George, severely damaged by Glyndwr.

Bungay	Suffolk	Norman castle founded by Roger Bigod c1105, demolished 1176, shell keep & bailey erected c1295 by Roger Bigod.
Caerlaverock	Dumfries	Built c1280 to a triangular plan, captured by Edward I 1300, slighted by Bruce, rebuilt C15, now owned by Historic Scotland.
Caerleon	Gwent	Norman Motte & Bailey castle erected c1086, great tower added 1158–73.
Caernarfon	Gwynedd	Norman Motte & Bailey castle erected 1093 by Earl Hugh of Chester, destroyed by Welsh 1115, Edwardian castle on site constructed by Master James of St George 1283–1330, designed to resemble walls of Constantinople.
Caerphilly	Mid Glamorgan	Built by Gilbert de Clare, Earl of Gloucester, 1271–80 after original castle of 1267–70 destroyed by Llywelyn, now owned by Welsh Historic Mons.
Cainhoe	Bedfordshire	Norman castle founded by Nigel d'Albini, motte and 3 baileys.
Caister	Norfolk	Built by Sir John Fastolf 1432–6, made of brick and surrounded by a moat.
Caldicot	Gwent	Norman Motte & Bailey castle founded by Walter Fitzroger early C12, developed by de Bohun Earls of Hereford late C12/early C13, gatehouse extended c1385, repaired C19.
Calshot	Hampshire	Circular blockhouse with three storey central keep erected in 1540, to protect Southampton Water , using stone from Beaulieu Abbey. Now owned by English Heritage.
Camber	East Sussex	C16 Henrician Castle, built to protect the Rye anchorage. Owned by English Heritage.
Cambridge	Cambs	Norman castle founded by William I 1068, rebuilt 1284–98, slighted in 1647.
Canterbury	Kent	Norman Motte & Bailey castle founded by William I 1066, Keep erected early C12.
Cardiff	South Glamorgan	Norman Motte built C1080 by Robert Fitzhamon on site of Roman fort, shell keep erected C12, further additions by Gilbert de Clare C13, castle remodelled by William Burges for 3rd Marquess of Bute C19.
Cardigan	Ceredigion	Norman castle founded c1093, captured by Welsh c1170 and converted to stone, sold to John 1199, destroyed by Llywelyn the Great 1231, new castle built near original site by English in 1240s.
Carew	Pembrokeshire	Norman Motte & Bailey castle founded by Gerald de Windsor 1105, extended by Nicholas de Carew in C13, damaged by Parliamentary forces in 1645.
Carisbrooke	Isle of Wight	Norman castle founded by William Fitz Osbern c1070, extended by Baldwin de Redvers in 1130s gatehouse erected c1335, now owned by English Heritage.
Carlisle	Cumbria	Norman castle built by William Rufus in 1192, improved by David I of Scotland, rebuilt 1541 for Henry VIII by Stefan von Hashenperg, now owned by English Heritage.
Carmarthen	Carmarthenshire	Norman Motte & Bailey castle founded early C12, captured by Llywelyn the Great 1215, rebuilt and extended by English during C13, held by Glyndwr 1403–9.
Carreg Cennen	Carmarthenshire	Courtyard castle built in C13 on site of Roman fort, demolished by Yorkists 1462.
Castell y Bere	Gwynedd	Enclosure castle founded c1221 by Llywelyn the Great, captured by Edward I 1283, restored 1286–90, abandoned by 1300.
Castle Acre, priory	Norfolk	Norman castle founded by William de Warenne C11, stone keep rebuilt C1140, now owned by English Heritage.
Castle Bytham	Lincolnshire	Norman castle founded c1169, besieged and demolished 1221, rebuilt by William de Colville 1220s.
Castle Drogo	Devon	Granite castle designed by Edwin Lutyens 1910–30.
Castle Hedingham	Essex	Tower keep built by Aubrey de Vere III 1141 on site of late C11 timber castle, now owned by English Heritage.
Castle of Mey	Highlands	C16 Z-plan castle built by George Sinclair. Situated on the coast between Thurso and John O'Groats, the estate was bought by Her Majesty the Queen Mother in 1952.
Castle Rising	Norfolk	Tower keep built by William II d'Albini c1140, now owned by English Heritage.
Castle Rushen	Castletown, I.O.M.	Probably the best-preserved medieval castle in the British Isles. Built c1200; partly destroyed in a siege by Robert the Bruce in 1313, but rebuilt by Sir William Montacute in c1344. The castle chapel houses a clock presented by Queen Elizabeth I in 1597.
Cause	Shropshire	Norman Motte & Bailey castle founded by Roger Fitz Corbet, fortified in stone C12, demolished 1645.
Cawdor	Inverness	Built 1454, seat of Earls of Cawdor.
Cawood	North Yorkshire	Built C12, formerly a residence of the Archbishop of York. Only the gatehouse and the banqueting hall now remain
Chepstow	Gwent	Norman castle with stone keep founded by William Fitz Osbern 1070, extended C13, disused from 1690, now owned by Welsh Historic Monuments.
Chester	Cheshire	Norman Motte & Bailey castle built on site of Roman fortress, improved C13, now lost.
Chilham	Kent	Norman castle founded by Fulbert of Dover, octagonal keep built for Henry II 1171–5.
Chillingham	Northumberland	Built as monastery C12 but later developed into sturdy fortress with four towers. Billed as the most haunted castle in Britain by its present owners.
Chirk	Clwyd	Motte & Bailey castle founded mid-C12, new castle founded nearby by Roger Mortimer 1274–1310.
Christchurch	Dorset	Norman Motte & Bailey castle founded by Richard de Redvers c1100, ruins now owned by English Heritage.
Cilgerran	Pembrokeshire	Norman enclosure castle founded by Gerald of Windsor c1110, rebuilt c1233.
Clare	Suffolk	Norman Motte & Bailey founded by Richard Fitzgilbert, improved by Gilbert de Clare.
Clavering	Essex	Norman castle founded by Robert Fitz Wimarc c1050.
Claypotts	Tayside	Built C16.
Clifford's Tower	York	Quatrefoil keep on motte founded by Henry III 1245 on site of Norman castle of 1069, burnt down 1190 whilst housing Jewish refugees, rebuilt and blown down 1228, now owned by English Heritage.
Clitheroe	Lancashire	Norman castle founded by Roger de Poitou.
Clun	Shropshire	Norman castle founded by Roger de Say, tower keep built in motte C12 by William Fitz Alan.
Cockermouth	Cumbria	Built C13 by William de Fortibus, rebuilt by Anthony de Lucy in 1360, slighted in Civil War.
Coity	Mid Glamorgan	Norman castle founded by Payn de Turberville, extended late C12, altered C14.
Colchester	Essex	Norman castle founded by William the Conqueror 1076–80; largest Norman tower keep, partly demolished 1683.
Conisborough	Yorkshire	Norman castle founded by William de Warenne, rebuilt with cylindrical tower keep by Hamelin, Earl of Surrey c1180, now owned by English Heritage.

Conwy	Gwynedd	Edwardian castle erected by Master James of St George 1283–7.
Cooling	Kent	Double quadrangular castle founded in 1380s, erected by Henry Yevele.
Corfe	Dorset	Norman castle founded by William I c1080, great tower erected by Henry I, gloriette erected by John, dismantled in Civil War (1646), now owned by National Trust.
Coulthalley	Strathclyde	Founded C12, rebuilt c1375, altered c1415 and c1520, rebuilt after siege 1557.
Coventry	West Midlands	Built C11 by Ranulf Meschines, Earl of Chester, the 12th century Caesar's Tower still exists and is now part of St Mary's Guildhall. In November 1569, Mary, Queen of Scots was detained in Caesar's Tower.
Craignethan	Strathclyde	Built in C16 by Sir James Hamilton, fortified courtyards with provision for artillery surrounding tower house, slighted 1579.
Criccieth	Gwynedd	Enclosure castle founded early C13, probably by Llywelyn the Great, Edwardian additions to site 1290, ruined by Glyndwr 1404.
Crichton	Lothian	Castle founded by John de Crichton late C14, extended C15.
Croft	Herefordshire	Medieval quadrangular castle of C14, named after family who built it, now owned by National Trust.
Cruggleton	Dumfries & Galloway	Motte & Bailey castle founded C12, reinforced in stone C13.
Dartmouth	Devon	Artillery fort built 1481 by Dartmouth corporation to protect town, now owned by English Heritage.
Deal	Kent	Henrician artillery fort built in 1539–40, besieged 1648, now owned by English Heritage.
Deganwy	Gwynedd	Double Motte & Bailey castle founded c1090, taken by Henry III 1241 and rebuilt/extended, destroyed by Llywelyn 1257.
Denbigh	Clywd	Edwardian castle built by Henry de Lacy, designed by Master James of St George, 1282–1311, destroyed in 1650s.
Devizes	Wiltshire	Norman castle founded late C11, used as prison by Henry II and Henry III, demolished in Civil War.
Dinefwr	Carmarthenshire	Castle founded C12, rebuilt with cylindrical donjon C13, damaged by fire C18, modern castle constructed 1856.
Dirleton	Lothian	Founded by de Vaux family C12, stone buildings built C13, extended C14/C15.
Dolbadarn	Gwynedd	Castle with cylindrical donjon erected by Llywelyn the Great early C13, partially dismantled by Edward I in 1284.
Dolwyddelan	Gwynedd	Castle founded by Iorwerth Trwyndwn c1170, captured by English 1282 and repaired.
Donnington	Berkshire	Enclosure castle founded late C14 by Richard de Adderbury, destroyed in 1646, now owned by English Heritage.
Doune	Perth & Kinrosshire	Enclosure castle founded by Duke of Albany late 14th Century.
Dover	Kent	Norman castle founded 1066 by William I, rebuilt with tower keep designed by Maurice the Engineer for Henry II in 1180–9, concentric fortifications built at same time, besieged 1216, extra fortifications added C19.
Dudley	West Midlands	Norman Motte & Bailey castle founded by William Fitzansculf, destroyed by Henry II 1175, rebuilt c1270 by John de Somery, extended early C14 by John de Somery, slighted 1647.
Duffus	Grampian	Motte & Bailey castle founded by Freskin de Moravia C12, rebuilt c1300 in stone, north-west corner of Donjon slid down motte late C14.
Dumbarton	Strathclyde	Built upon Dumbarton Rock.
Dundonald	Strathclyde	Founded by Walter Stewart c1250, expanded by Robert II, 1371–90.
Dunstaffnage	Strathclyde	Enclosure castle built by MacDougall in the 13th century.
Dunstanburgh	Northumberland	Enclosure castle founded by Thomas, 2nd Earl of Lancaster 1313–16, altered by John of Gaunt, now owned by English Heritage.
Dunster	Somerset	Norman castle founded by William de Mohun, fortified manor built on site C14, owned by Luttrells from 1376, remodelled by Salvin C19, now owned by National Trust.
Dunvegan	Skye	Home of the Chiefs of Clan Macleod since foundation in C13.
Durham	County Durham	Norman castle founded by William I c1072, rebuilt C12 in stone, keep C14, rebuilt 1840, now used by University of Durham.
Edinburgh	Lothian	Wooden fortress founded by Malcolm III C11, rebuilt C12/13, taken by Edward I 1296, taken by Earl of Moray and destroyed 1313, rebuilt C14.
Edlingham	Northumberland	Castle founded by Sir William Felton late C12, triangular enclosure with separate tower.
Egremont	Cumbria	Norman castle built by William de Meschines in 1130.
Eilean Donan	Western Ross	Built in C13, probably by Alexander II, rebuilt in C20.
Etal	Northumberland	Castle with donjon and gatehouse tower at opposing corners, founded 1342 by Manners family, captured 1513 by James IV.
Ewloe	Clwyd	Castle founded 1146 by Owain Gwynedd, rebuilt in stone c1200 by Llywelyn the Great.
Ewyas Harold	Herefordshire	Norman castle built c1050, refortified by William FitzOsbern.
Exeter	Devon	Norman castle founded by William I in 1067 in corner of Roman walls, largely demolished in 1744, stone gatehouse c1068 still extant.
Eynsford	Kent	Norman enclosure castle fortified in stone c1088, extended C12.
Farleigh Hungerford	Somerset	Castle erected c1370–83 by Sir Thomas Hungerford, enlarged C15 by Walter Hungerford, now owned by English Heritage.
Farnham	Surrey	Norman Motte & Bailey founded by Henry de Blois C12, slighted by Henry II 1155, rebuilt late C12 with stone encasing motte, slighted 1648, now owned by English Heritage.
Flint	Clwyd	Edwardian castle erected by Master James of St George 1277–80, donjon separate from rest of castle, slighted 1646.
Ford	Northumberland	Quadrangular castle founded 1338 by William Heron, attacked by Scots 1385, 1513, 1549, rebuilt 1861 by Marchioness of Waterford.
Fotheringhay	Northants	Norman Motte & Bailey castle, famous as the site of Mary Queen of Scots' beheading.
Framlingham	Suffolk	Norman castle founded c1100 by Roger Bigod, destroyed by Henry II 1175, rebuilt as enclosure castle by Roger II Bigod c1189–1200.
Gidleigh	Devon	Fortified manor house built by William de Prouz c1324. Only ruined keep tower with two storeys, an undercroft and a first floor hall remain.
Glamis	Tayside	Family seat of the Earls of Strathmure and Kinghorne. Built late C14. The 6th Earl entertained James Stuart (the Old Pretender) here in 1715. Childhood home of HM Queen Elizabeth the Queen Mother, the youngest daughter of the 14th Earl. Also the birthplace of HRH the Princess Margaret in 1930.

Gloucester	Gloucestershire	Norman Motte & Bailey castle founded by William I, Great Tower built by Henry I c1112.
Goodrich	Hereford	Keep built mid-C12, converted into quadrangular castle by de Valence family late C13. Barbican erected C14, slighted 1646, now owned by English Heritage.
Greystoke	Cumbria	Original castle built C11 and once owned by Thomas Howard, 4th Duke of Norfolk, before being ruined in the English Civil War. Rebuilt by Anthony Salvin C19.
Grosmont	Gwent	Castle founded late C11, rebuilt in stone c1210, extended by Hubert de Burgh 1220–40.
Guildford	Surrey	Norman Motte & Bailey castle, keep erected on side of motte mid-C12.
Hadleigh	Essex	Enclosure castle founded by Hubert de Burgh C13, extended by Edward III 1361–70, now owned by English Heritage.
Hailes	Lothian	Founded C13, owned from C14 by Hepburns, besieged by Percys c1400.
Hallaton	Leicestershire	Norman Motte & Bailey castle, motte almost as large as bailey.
Harbottle	Northumberland	Motte & Bailey castle with shell keep erected 1159–60 by Robert d'Umfraville.
Harlech	Gwynedd	Edwardian concentric castle erected 1283–9 by Master James of St George, besieged 1294, 1401–5, 1408–9, 1468, 1647, now owned by Welsh Historic Monuments.
Hastings	East Sussex	Norman Motte & Bailey castle founded by William I 1066, appears in Bayeux Tapestry, later converted to stone, only C13 ruins extant.
Haughley	Suffolk	Norman Motte & Bailey castle, one of largest in Britain, dismantled by Henry II c1173.
Haverfordwest	Pembrokeshire	Norman castle founded c1120 by Gilbert de Clare, strengthened by William de Valence C13, besieged by Glyndwr 1405.
Hawarden	Clwyd	Norman Motte & Bailey castle, fortified in stone early C13, destroyed by Llywelyn 1265, rebuilt 1277, slighted 1647/8.
Hay-on-Wye	Powys	Norman Motte & Bailey castle founded early C12 by William Revell, destroyed by King John, C13 replacement built on different site, destroyed by Glyndwr.
Hedingham	Essex	Norman Motte & Bailey castle rebuilt C12. Former seat of the de Vere family, Earls of Oxford. Five storey keep remains. Privately owned and used for functions.
Helmsley	North Yorkshire	Norman castle founded by Robert de Mortain, held by Walter l'Espec and de Roos family, who constructed current structure 1186–1227. Enclosure castle with keep, keep heightened early C14, slighted 1644/5.
Hereford	Hereford	Norman Motte & Bailey castle possibly founded c1050, held by William Fitz Osbern 1066–71, stoneworks C13 with tower on motte, now destroyed.
Hermitage	Borders	Founded early C14, captured by Scots 1338, owned by the Douglases, who extended it C14/15.
Herstmonceux	East Sussex	Brick quadrangular castle founded 1441 by Sir Roger Fiennes, restored C20.
Hertford	Herts	Norman Motte & Bailey castle founded c1067 by William I, major works on castle C15, demolished C17.
Hever	Kent	Manor house founded 1270s, fortified 1340 by William de Hever and in 1384 by Sir John Cobham, bought by Boleyn family 1462 & modified, restored by Viscount Astor 1903–7.
Holt	Clwyd	Edwardian enclosure castle founded by John de Warenne 1280s, demolished late C17.
Hopton	Shropshire	Norman Motte & Bailey castle founded C12, donjon built by Walter de Hopton c1300.
Hornby	Lancashire	Originally built for the Neville family in the 13th century, the polygonal tower dates from the 16th century. Reconstructed C19 and now privately owned.
Huntingdon	Cambridgeshire	Norman Motte & Bailey castle founded 1069 by William I, 2nd motte added C12, demolished 1174 by Henry II.
Huntly	Grampian	Motte & Bailey castle founded C12, rebuilt in stone and extended by 1st Earl of Huntly C15, blown up by James VI 1594, rebuilt by 1st Marquis of Huntly c1600–06.
Hurst	Southampton	Henrician device fort built in 1544 on a shingle spit at the western entrance to the Solent. Charles I was imprisoned there in 1648 before being taken to London to his trial and execution. The castle was retained by the War Office until 1933 and then handed over to the Ministry of Works. It is now owned by English Heritage.
Inverlochy	Highland	Enclosure castle founded c1270–80.
Inverness	Highland	Founded C12, later reclad in stone. Destroyed by Young Pretender 1746.
Jedburgh	Borders	Motte & Bailey castle founded C12 by David I, destroyed c1410 by Regent Albany.
Kendal	Cumbria	Built cC12 but only one of the towers and the keep are still standing.
Kenilworth	Warwickshire	Enclosure castle with motte & donjon founded c1120 by William de Clinton, donjon rebuilt later C12, water defences added C13, besieged for 6 months 1266, remodelled by John of Gaunt 1370s, slighted 1649, now owned by English Heritage.
Kidwelly	Carmarthenshire	Norman castle founded by Roger, Bishop of Salisbury c1106, burnt by Welsh 1215, enclosure castle built 1270s, concentric curtain added C14.
Kiessimut	Barra, Western Isles	Enclosure castle of late C12/early C13, restored by MacNeils.
Kildrummy	Grampian	Enclosure castle of C13 on site of C12 Motte & Bailey castle.
Kirby Muxloe	Leicestershire	Unfinished quadrangular castle built by Lord Hastings c1480–3, now owned by English Heritage.
Knaresborough	North Yorkshire	Norman castle built C12 by Eustace Fitzjohn, improved by Edward II and III 1307–50, slighted 1648.
Lancaster	Lancashire	Norman castle built early C12 by Roger de Poitou, extended by King John, improved by Henry IV, partially demolished 1649.
Laugharne	Carmarthenshire	Founded C12, rebuilt in C13 and 14 including cylindrical keep.
Launceston	Cornwall	Norman Motte & Bailey castle of Dunheved, built by Robert of Mortain, rebuilt with shell keep C13 by Richard of Cornwall. George Fox imprisoned in gatehouse 1656, owned by English Heritage.
Leeds	Kent	Norman castle founded by the de Crevecoeur family, rebuilt by Edward I after 1278, restored C19.
Leicester	Leicestershire	Norman Motte & Bailey castle founded c1068, fortified in stone by 2nd Earl of Leicester mid-C12, improved by Henry IV and V.
Lewes	East Sussex	Norman double Motte & Bailey castle built by William de Warenne c1069–70, shell keep added C13, barbican added C14.
Lincoln	Lincolnshire	Norman Double Motte & Bailey castle founded by William 1 1068, shell keep (Lucy Tower) added C12.
Lindisfarne	Northumberland	Fort built on Holy Island C16 and reconstructed by Lutyens in 1901 and turned into an Edwardian fantasy house, sometimes called a "Gothic" castle. Gertrude Jekyll designed the gardens. Now owned by the National Trust.

Llandovery	Carmarthenshire	Norman Motte & Bailey castle founded early C12 by Robert Fitzpons, captured by Welsh 1116, recovered c1158, stonework added late C12, slighted by Cromwell.
Llansteffan	Carmarthenshire	Enclosure castle founded C12, captured by Welsh 1146, retaken by Henry II, given to William de Camville, strengthened c1192, extended C13, captured by Glyndwr 1403.
Loch Doon	Strathclyde	C13 enclosure castle erected on an island; moved to western shore of loch 1934-5.
Loch Leven	Tayside	Built on an island towards the western end of Loch Leven, the C13 building was the prison of Mary Queen of Scots from 17 June 1567 to 2 May 1568.
Longtown	Hereford	Norman Motte & Bailey castle founded C11, cylindrical donjon added on motte C14.
Ludgershall	Wiltshire	Norman Motte & Bailey castle founded late C11, unfinished donjon added mid-C12, replacement tower added c1200, now owned by English Heritage.
Ludlow	Shropshire	Norman enclosure castle with flanking towers erected c1086 by Roger de Lacy.
Lydford	Devon	Norman castle founded C11, donjon added C12 and extended with motte built around base C13.
Lympne	Kent	Norman castle founded 1080s, reconstructed C14.
Maiden Castle	Dorset	Lying two miles south of Dorchester, covering an area of 47 acres, the largest hill fort in Britain.
Manorbier	Pembrokeshire	Norman enclosure castle founded by Otto de Barri late C11, strengthened C12, birthplace of Giraldus Cambrensis 1146.
Marisco	Lundy	Remains of a moat, walls and keep of castle built by Henry III c1242.
Marlborough	Wiltshire	Norman Motte & Bailey castle, extended by Henry II, shell keep added by King John and added to by Henry III.
Middleham	North Yorkshire	Norman Motte & Bailey castle founded c1086, tower keep built on nearby site by Robert Fitzranulph c1170, quadrangular curtain added C13, slighted in Civil War, now owned by English Heritage.
Millom	Cumbria	Small rectangular castle built after a licence to crenellate was granted by Edward III in 1335. Now ruined but the great tower and walls survive.
Monmouth	Gwent	Norman Motte & Bailey castle founded by William FitzOsbern c1070, keep added on motte c1120–30, birthplace of Henry V 1387, slighted during Civil War.
Montacute	Somerset	Norman Motte & Bailey castle founded by Robert of Mortain 1069/70, dismantled C12 by Cluniac monks of Montacute Priory.
Montfichet	London	Norman Motte & Bailey castle founded by William I 1066/7, dismantled C13.
Montgomery (I)	Powys	Norman Motte & Bailey castle built by Roger de Montgomery c1071, dismantled C12.
Montgomery (II)	Powys	Enclosure castle founded 1223 by Baldwin de Boller, slighted 1649.
Morpeth	Northumberland	Norman Motte & Bailey castle founded late C11, destroyed by King John 1215, castle rebuilt in bailey mid-C13.
Mountsorrell	Leicestershire	Norman Motte & Bailey castle, dismantled 1217.
Neath	Neath Port Talbot	C12 motte & bailey built on an earlier earthwork. Only the Gatehouse and adjoining walls remain standing.
Neroche	Somerset	Norman enclosure castle founded C11 by Robert of Mortain, motte added early C12, shell keep added mid-C12.
Nether Stowey	Somerset	Norman Motte & 2 Bailey castle, tower keep added on motte mid-C12.
Newark	Nottinghamshire	Norman enclosure castle built by Bishop of Lincoln 1130s, major reconstruction early C13, slighted 1646.
New Buckenham	Norfolk	Built by William II d'Albini c1140, cylindrical tower keep (first in Britain), demolished by Sir Philip Knyvey 1649.
Newcastle	Vale of Glamorgan	Located in Bridgend, ruined fortress built C12. Only gateway and a piece of wall remain.
Newcastle	Tyne & Wear	Norman Motte & Bailey castle founded c1080, rebuilt with keep designed by Maurice the Engineer 1068–77.
Newport	Gwent	Norman castle founded C12, rebuilt C13, sacked by Glyndwr and rebuilt C15.
Norham	Northumberland	Norman Motte & Bailey castle founded c1120 by Ranulf Flambard, destroyed by Scots 1140s, rebuilt by Bishop Hugh of Durham 1158–74, taken by Scots 1513, now owned by English Heritage.
Northampton	Northants	Norman Motte & Bailey founded c1080, enlarged by Henry I, tower keep added c1170.
Norwich	Norfolk	Norman Motte & Bailey castle founded by William FitzOsbern for William I 1067, tower keep added on motte 1125–35, stone curtain added 1268–70, keep restored by Salvin 1834–9, now serving as museum (since 1894).
Nottingham	Nottinghamshire	Norman Motte & Bailey castle founded 1068 by William I, modified by Henry II. Keep built 1213, demolished 1651 by Colonel Hutchinson, renovated 1878 and now a museum.
Nunney	Somerset	Rectangular moated Great Tower with cylindrical towers at corners built 1373 by Sir John de la Mare, slighted 1645, now owned by English Heritage.
Oakham	Rutland	Norman Motte & Bailey, stone added C12, Great Hall built by Wakelin de Ferrers c1180.
Odiham	Hampshire	Octagonal keep built by King John 1207–12.
Ogmore	Mid Glamorgan	Norman castle founded c1110, stone donjon built late C12, fortified in stone C13.
Okehampton	Devon	Norman Motte & Bailey castle founded by Baldwin Fitzgilbert c1070, extended and tower built on motte early C14.
Old Sarum	Wiltshire	Iron Age fort occupied by the Romans who built a Motte and Bailey castle and cathedral inside its ramparts.
Ongar	Essex	Norman Motte & Bailey founded C12 by de Lucy family, stone tower built 1150s.
Orford	Suffolk	Castle with polygonal keep founded by Henry II 1165, now owned by English Heritage.
Oswestry	Shropshire	Norman Motte & Bailey castle founded C11 by Rainald de Bailleul, shell keep built C12.
Oxford	Oxfordshire	Norman Motte & Bailey castle founded c1071 by Robert d'Oilly, St George's Tower built on motte late C11, shell keep built on motte C12. The Queen officially opened the restored castle on 5 May 2006.
Oystermouth	West Glamorgan	Norman castle built c1100, destroyed 1215, rebuilt C13 by William de Braose.
Peel Castle	Peel, I.O.M.	Situated on St Patrick's Isle near Peel harbour and built by William Le Scrope in 1392. The castle houses the ruins of St German's Cathedral, named from Germanus a disciple of Patrick who is thought to have brought Christianity to the island.
Peel of Lumphanan	Grampian	Motte & Bailey castle founded C12, shell keep erected early C13.
Pembridge	Hereford	Castle founded C13 by Ralph de Pembridge, includes moat and cylindrical donjon, ruined in Civil War.

Pembroke	Pembrokeshire	Norman enclosure castle founded c1090 by Arnulf de Montgomery, extended and cylindrical donjon built by William Marshal early C13, slighted by Cromwell 1648/9.
Pendennis	Cornwall	Henrician artillery fort built to protect Falmouth, now owned by English Heritage.
Pendragon	Cumbria	C12 fortified tower, located in Mallerstang dale; enlarged C14 but now ruined.
Penhow	Gwent	Enclosure castle founded early C13 by Sir William St Maur.
Penrice	West Glamorgan	Norman enclosure castle founded c1100, stone castle raised on nearby site mid-C13, cylindrical donjon.
Penrith	Cumbria	Tower built C14, quadrangular castle erected on site c1397–9 by William Strickland, Bishop of Carlisle.
Pevensey	East Sussex	Norman castle built within the site of old Roman fort, founded C11 by Robert of Mortain, donjon added c1100 by William of Mortain, strengthened early C13, now owned by English Heritage.
Peveril	Derbyshire	Norman castle founded by William Peverel, also known as Peak Castle, improved by Henry II, tower keep erected 1176, now owned by English Heritage.
Pickering	North Yorkshire	Norman Motte & Bailey founded c1100, shell keep built c1218–36, improved early C14.
Picton	Pembrokeshire	Norman Motte & Bailey castle founded c1090 by William de Picton, enclosure castle built on nearby site mid-C13.
Piel	Cumbria	Concentric fortification with keep and 3 towers built on Piel Island in 1327 at the entrance to Barrow harbour to protect Furness Abbey, near to the site of an earlier C12 castle. Ruined by C16, but there is a well preserved keep and 2 baileys. Also known as Fouldry (or Fouldrey) Castle. Now owned by English Heritage.
Pleshey	Essex	Norman Motte & Bailey castle founded early C12, destroyed 1157, refortified 1167–80, donjon on motte.
Pontefract	West Yorkshire	Norman Motte & Bailey castle founded 1069 by Ilbert de Lacy, improved by Thomas, Earl of Lancaster, and John of Gaunt C14, destroyed 1649.
Portchester	Hampshire	Norman castle founded by Henry I c1120 in corner of old Roman fort, keep raised by Henry II, palace constructed for Richard II 1396–9, now owned by English Heritage.
Portland	Dorset	Henrician device fort built in 1539 to guard the Portland anchorage. Although neighbouring Weymouth was a Parliamentary stronghold during the English Civil War, Portland was a Royal Manor and as such supported King Charles and the castle was set siege upon several times. Now owned by English Heritage.
Powis	Powys	Castle founded C13 by Gruffydd, Baron de la Pole, destroyed in 1270s by Llywelyn the Last and rebuilt, modified by the Herberts after purchase in 1587, now owned by the National Trust.
Prudhoe	Northumberland	Built C12 on the site of C11 motte on south bank of the River Tyne. Gatehouse and keep date from 1175 and barbican added C14. A 19th century house has been built within the ruins. Now owned by English Heritage.
Raglan	Gwent	Norman Motte & Bailey founded c1070 by the Bloet family, major reconstruction C15, hexagonal Yellow Tower of Gwent built by Sir William ap Thomas, other works 1450–69 by Sir William Herbert, slighted 1646, now owned by Welsh Historic Monuments.
Ravenscraig	Fife	Coastal artillery fortress founded 1460 by James II, erected 1460–3.
Restormel	Cornwall	Norman castle founded C11 by Baldwin FitzUrstin, C12 shell keep built by Robert of Cardinham, now owned by English Heritage.
Rhuddlan	Clwyd	Norman Motte & Bailey castle founded c1070, Edwardian concentric castle erected nearby by Master James of St George 1282, slighted 1648.
Richards Castle	Hereford	Norman Motte & Bailey castle founded by Richard Fitzscrub pre-Conquest, stone tower built on motte c1175.
Richborough	Kent	Roman fort situated near Sandwich and thought to be the landing point of the Roman invasion armies in AD 43.
Richmond	North Yorkshire	Norman enclosure castle founded by Count of Penhievre 1071, late C11 stone hall (Scolland's Hall) built by Alan the Red, great tower added by Conan, Duke of Brittany, c1150–70, now owned by English Heritage.
Ripley	Harrogate, North Yorks	C19 castle owned by Sir Thomas Ingilby, a baronet, who inherited the stately home on his 18th birthday.
Rochester	Kent	Norman Motte & Bailey built by Bishop Gundulf c1080, stone curtain added c1088 and stone keep c1126–40 by William de Corbeuil, besieged by John 1215, recaptured by Louis of France 1216, keep repaired c1225 with cylindrical corner added, besieged by de Montfort 1264, captured by Wat Tyler 1381, now owned by English Heritage.
Rockingham	Northants	Norman Motte & Bailey castle founded by William I, improved by Henry II, gatehouse built by Edward I c1280, damaged in Civil War, alterations by Salvin C19.
Rothesay	Isle of Bute, Strathclyde	Motte & Bailey castle founded C12, shell keep erected C13.
Roxburgh	Borders	Motte & Bailey founded C12, captured 1314 by Scots and demolished, rebuilt by Edward III 1335–7, extended by Richard II, taken by Scots 1460 with loss of James II and destroyed.
Rufus	Dorset	C15 ruined castle overlooking Church Ope Cove on Portland, built on site of C11 Norman castle. Aka Bow and Arrow Castle.
Ruthin	Clwyd	Edwardian castle founded 1277, held by Prince Dafydd to 1282 when taken by Reginald de Grey, slighted 1647, converted into a hotel C19.
Saffron Walden	Essex	Norman Motte & Bailey founded C11 by Geoffrey de Mandeville, flint tower added C12.
St Andrews	Fife	Castle founded late C12, slighted by Andrew Moray 1337, rebuilt late C14, extended early C16, besieged and damaged 1546–7, John Knox amongst besieged.
St Briavels	Gloucestershire	Norman enclosure castle founded C12 by Milo Fitzwalter, tower added mid-C12, gatehouse built by Edward I c1292–3, keep collapsed 1752.
St Catherine's	Cornwall	C16 Henrician device fort built to protect Fowey Harbour. Owned by English Heritage.
St Donats	South Glamorgan	Double enclosure castle founded by the Stradlings c1300.
St Mawes	Cornwall	Henrician artillery fort built 1540 to protect Falmouth, now owned by English Heritage.
Saffron Walden	Essex	C12 castle built during the Anarchy. Flint core of three storey keep is all that remains.
Saltwood	Kent	Norman enclosure castle founded by Henry of Essex c1150–60, improved by Archbishop Courtenay of Canterbury 1380s, designed by Henry Yevele, rendered uninhabitable by an earthquake 1580, formerly owned by Alan Clark MP.
Sandal	West Yorkshire	Norman Motte & Bailey castle founded c1157, converted to stone c1200–80, besieged 1645 and slighted 1646.

Sauvey	Leicestershire	Motte & Bailey castle founded by King John early C13, disused from 1260s.
Scarborough	North Yorkshire	Norman castle founded c1136 by William of Aumale, keep built by Henry II, barbican added c1240, Piers Gaveston besieged 1312, now owned by English Heritage.
Scotney	Kent	Moated castle founded late C14 by Roger Ashburnham, only cylindrical turret remaining, now owned by National Trust.
Sherborne	Dorset	Norman enclosure castle founded by Roger, Bishop of Salisbury, c1107–35, I-shaped donjon added mid-C12, besieged and ruined 1645, now owned by English Heritage.
Shrewsbury	Shropshire	Norman Motte & Bailey castle founded by Roger de Montgomery c1067–9, converted to stone by Henry II, tower on motte collapsed c1270, altered by Thomas Telford C18 for Sir William Pulteney.
Skenfrith	Gwent	Norman Motte & Bailey castle founded late C11, cylindrical donjon and stone curtain walls built c1220–40 by Hubert de Burgh.
Skipsea	East Yorkshire	Norman Motte & Bailey castle founded c1086, motte separated from bailey by a marsh, destroyed by Henry III.
Skipton	North Yorkshire	Norman D-shaped enclosure castle founded c1080, extended with six round towers added by Robert Clifford c1310–14, besieged and severely damaged 1645, renovated by Lady Anne Clifford C17.
Southampton	Hampshire	Norman Motte & Bailey castle founded early C12, refortified C14 by Richard II with tower built by Henry Yevele.
South Mimms	Hertfordshire	Norman Motte & Bailey castle founded c1140–2 by Geoffrey de Mandeville, motte built around base of tower.
Stafford	Staffordshire	Norman Motte & Bailey castle founded c1070, destroyed by 1086, restored late C11, tower built on motte 1348 by Ralph, 1st Earl of Stafford, decayed C16.
Stamford	Lincolnshire	Norman Motte & Bailey castle founded late C11, shell enclosure built on motte C12, extended late C12.
Stirling	Stirling	Timber castle founded C12, taken 1296, 1297, 1298, 1299, 1304, 1314 (whence dismantled), rebuilt under the Stewarts C15.
Stogursey	Somerset	Norman enclosure castle founded late C11, improved by de Courcys C12, demolished c1216.
Stokesay	Shropshire	Fortified manor house crenellated by Lawrence de Ludlow 1291.
Sulgrave	Northants	Norman triangular enclosure castle founded late C11, stone tower added early C12.
Sutton Valence	Kent	Castle founded mid-C12 with great tower, altered by William de Valence C13.
Swansea	West Glamorgan	Norman Motte & Bailey castle founded by Henry Beaumont, burned 1115/6, C12 enclosure castle constructed nearby, rebuilt early C14, damaged by Glyndwr.
Sween	Strathclyde	Castle founded by McSwine family early C12, earliest stone castle in Scotland. Remodelled by Earls of Menteith C13 and extended by Lords of the Isles C14.
Tamworth	Staffordshire	Norman castle with shell enclosure founded early C12 by the Marmions.
Tantallon	Lothian	Founded by the 1st Earl of Douglas c1360, besieged by Stewarts 1492 and 1526, damaged by General Monck 1651.
Tattershall	Lincolnshire	Castle with Great Tower built in brick by Ralph, Lord Cromwell 1433–43, rescued by Lord Curzon 1911, now owned by National Trust.
Taunton	Somerset	Norman enclosure castle founded c1110 by William Gifford, tower and other buildings raised by Henry de Blois mid-C12, improved 1207.
Tenby	Pembrokeshire	Norman castle founded after 1153, sacked by Welsh 1187 and 1260.
Thetford	Norfolk	Norman Motte & Bailey castle founded C11, destroyed by Henry II 1174.
Thornbury	Gloucestershire	Last military castle built in England c1511 by Edward Stafford, Duke of Buckingham, never completed.
Threave	Dumfries and Galloway	Founded by Archibald, 3rd Earl of Douglas, c1370, extended c1454, taken by James II 1455.
Tickhill	South Yorkshire	Norman Motte & Bailey castle founded late C11 by Robert de Belleme, 11-sided tower built on motte c1178–80 by Henry II.
Tintagel	Cornwall	Norman castle built c1145 by Reginald, Earl of Cornwall, modified by Richard, Earl of Cornwall, C13, now owned by English Heritage.
Tonbridge	Kent	Norman Motte & Bailey castle founded 1080s by Richard Fitzgilbert, shell enclosure added C12, gatehouse built by Gilbert de Clare C13.
Totnes	Devon	Norman Motte & Bailey castle founded C11 by the Nonants, shell keep added C13.
Tower of London	London	Norman enclosure castle founded by William I 1067, White Tower built by Gundulf of Rochester 1078–c1100, concentric fortifications added C13 by Henry III & Edward I.
Trematon	Cornwall	Norman Motte & Bailey castle founded C11, shell keep added C12.
Tretower	Powys	Norman Motte & Bailey castle founded by Sir Miles Picard c1100, shell keep added by Simon Picard mid-C12, cylindrical donjon added by Roger Picard c1220.
Turnberry	Strathclyde	Cylindrical Tower castle of C13, childhood home of Robert Bruce.
Tutbury	Staffordshire	Norman Motte & Bailey castle founded by Henry de Ferrers, improved by John of Gaunt from 1350, added to C15, slighted 1646.
Tynemouth	Tyne and Wear	Enclosure castle crenellated by Robert de Mowbray 1296, gatehouse added 1390s.
Urquhart	Highland	Motte & Bailey castle founded c1150, taken by Edward I, in 1313 passed to Randolph, Earl of Moray, extended C14.
Usk	Gwent	Norman earthwork castle founded by de Clares c1138, rebuilt C14, slighted in Civil War.
Wakefield	West Yorkshire	Motte & 2 Bailey castle erected c1140–50, possibly by William de Warenne.
Wallingford	Oxfordshire	Norman Motte & Bailey castle erected c1071, stonework added C12, demolished 1652.
Walmer	Kent	C16 Henrician artillery fortress converted into a stately home and used since 1708 as the residence of the Lord Warden of the Cinque Ports, a position held by the Duke of Wellington and Winston Churchill. Now owned and managed by English Heritage.
Wardour	Wiltshire	Old Wardour castle – hexagonal construction founded by John, 5th Lord Lovell, 1393, damaged after siege 1644. New Wardour 'Castle' built 1769–76.
Wareham	Dorset	Norman castle with keep founded by Henry I, destroyed in Civil War.
Wark	Northumberland	Norman Motte & Bailey castle dismantled by David I of Scotland 1138, rebuilt by Henry II 1158, decayed C14.
Warkworth	Northumberland	Norman Motte & Bailey castle founded by Henry, Earl of Northumberland, c1140, taken by William the Lion 1173, rebuilt by Clavering family C13, multiangular tower added by Henry Percy mid-C14, owned by Percys 1332–1922, now owned by English Heritage.

Warwick	Warwickshire	Norman Motte & Bailey castle founded by William I 1068, shell keep added C12, rebuilt C14 by Thomas Beauchamp, unfinished additions by Richard III C15, repaired by Fulke Greville C17.
West Malling	Kent	Stone tower built c1100 by Bishop Gundulf of Rochester, now ruined.
White Castle	Gwent	Norman castle founded by Pain Fitzjohn, stone fortifications built c1184–6 by William de Braose, refortified by Edward I 1260s.
Whittington	Shropshire	Norman Motte & Bailey castle, improved by Fulke de Warenne from 1219 with tower built on motte.
Wigmore	Hereford	Norman Motte & Bailey castle founded c1067 by William FitzOsbern, shell keep built C12, reconstructed C14.
Winchester	Hampshire	Norman Motte & Bailey castle founded 1067 by William I, Domesday Book originally housed in castle, site destroyed 1141, rebuilt shortly after, donjon added by Henry II, cylindrical tower on motte and Great Hall added by Henry III, only the Great Hall presently remains.
Windsor	Berkshire	Norman Motte & 2 Bailey castle founded 1067 by William I, shell keep added by Henry I, site rebuilt in stone and keep improved by Henry II, major rebuilding by Edward III c1350–77 with keep raised, alterations by Wyatville for George IV C19, damaged by fire 1992.
Wolvesey	Hampshire	Ecclesiastical castle-palace founded c1100, rebuilt in quadrangular form with great tower by Henry of Blois c1135–70.
Woodcroft	Cambridgeshire	Converted Edwardian castle in the parish of Etton, Peterborough, built at the end of the 13th century. Remains of the castle include a front, a circular tower and a gatehouse.
Worcester	Worcestershire	Norman Motte & Bailey castle founded c1069, burned down 1113, rebuilt C12, motte levelled 1830.
Wressle	East Yorkshire	Quadrangular enclosure castle founded c1380 by Sir Thomas Percy, damaged in Civil War.
Yester	Lothian	Motte & Bailey castle founded C12, C13 tower erected on motte, extended C15.
York	North Yorkshire	Norman Motte & Bailey castle on Baile Hill founded by William I 1068–9, destroyed 1069 and rebuilt, now lost.

Castles: General Information

Adulterine Castles	Unlicensed private castles built by barons primarily during the Anarchy (1135–54) of King Stephen's reign
Berkeley Castle	Edward II murdered in south tower
Bolingbroke Castle	Henry IV born Apr 1366
Caernarfon Castle	Edward II born 25 Apr 1284
Cardiff Castle	Built on the site of a Roman fort. Robert Curthose imprisoned for 28 years
Carisbrooke Castle	Prison of Charles I 1647–8
Carlisle Castle	Prison of Mary Queen of Scots when she first entered England
Castle: Terms	
allure	Wall-walk along the top of the battlements: the basic fighting platform for archers and crossbowmen
bailey	A courtyard in a castle
barbican	An outer fortification in front of the gate of a castle
bartizan	Turret projecting from a tower or wall
bastion	Tower projecting from a wall length or junction of two walls, designed to cover dead ground
battlement	Parapet or wall with indentures or embrasures, originally for shooting through
berm	Space between curtain wall and moat
buttery	One of the 2 service rooms (the other is the kitchen), used for dispensing drinks
caponier	A covered gallery running across a ditch, housing guns to fire along the ditch
casemate	Armoured compartment in which guns are mounted
concentric	Possessing more than one curtain wall
counterscarp	Outer side of the moat
crenel	Openings formed in top of a wall or parapet between the merlons, having slanting sides as in a battlement
curtain wall	Wall around the perimeter of a castle or one of its courtyards
drawbridge	Bridge that may be raised to prevent access
embrasure	The opening in a wall behind a window or an arrow loop
forebuilding	Structure protecting the entrance to a tower
garderobe	Latrine
gatehouse	Guarded building above or beside an entrance gate
great tower	Most important tower also called the donjon and, since the 16th century, the keep
hourd	(also hoarding) Timber gallery carried on beams outside the battlements. Stones could be dropped on attackers via holes in the floor
keep	see great tower
loop	Slit in wall for firing arrows
machicolation	Permanent stone version of a hourd
mangonel	Stone-throwing siege machine
merlon	Length of protective parapet between the openings of a battlement
mews	Building or yard where the hawks are kept
moat	Wide, often water-filled ditch surrounding a castle preventing land access
motte	Large, usually round flat-topped mound which supported a tower
murder hole	Opening over an entrance passage
oubliette	Dungeon or pit under the floor, usually below ground level, reached by a trap-door
palisade	Strong wooden fence
portcullis	Iron or wooden grating hanging vertically in gateway of castle, set in grooves and able to be raised and lowered
postern	Subsidiary gate in the outer wall
rampart	Surrounding embankment of a castle
revetment	Facing of stones or sandbags to protect a wall or embankment

scarp	Side of a moat surrounding a castle cut nearest to and immediately below a rampart
trebuchet	Stone-throwing siege engine powered by counterpoise weights; successor to the mangonel, and far more powerful
turret	Small tower that projects from the wall of a castle
ward	Courtyard in a castle
Dover Castle	Known as the 'Key of England'
First Castles	Imported by the Normans after 1066, although four possible sites c1050 built by Norman friends of Edward the Confessor
Flint Castle	Richard II formally surrendered his crown to Henry Bolingbroke
Fotheringhay Castle	Richard III born 2 Oct 1452; Mary Queen of Scots executed 8 Feb 1587
Framlingham Castle	Mary Tudor proclaimed Queen while staying there
Henry VIII's reign: built	Calshot, Camber, Deal, Hurst, Pendennis, St Mawes, Sandgate, Southsea, Walmer
Keep: largest	Colchester castle
Largest Castle : England	Windsor
Scotland	Doune
Wales	Caerphilly
Leaning Keep	Bridgnorth, Shropshire
Lewes Castle	Two mottes
Ludlow Castle	King Edward IV made Royal property when he ascended the throne
Marlborough Castle	John Lackland was married in the castle chapel and Henry III was married in the chapel
Newark Castle	King John died of dysentery 19 Oct 1216
Oldest inhabited, UK	Berkeley, Gloucestershire
Pembroke Castle	Birthplace of Henry VII
Pontefract Castle	Richard II died c14 Feb 1400
Powys Castle	Clive of India Museum
Roman forts: built in	Pevensey and Portchester Castles built within old Roman forts
Sherborne Castle	Once owned by Sir Walter Raleigh
Stone-built: first	Chepstow, Gwent
Stone keep: first	Tower of London (White Tower) 1078; Colchester built c1087
Thornbury Castle	Last built for military purposes
Tintagel Castle	Linked with Arthurian legend
Towers of similar design :	Colchester and White Tower, London
	Castle Rising, Norwich and Falaise (Normandy)
	Castle Hedingham and Rochester
	Dover and Newcastle
Walmer Castle	Lord Warden of the Cinque Ports resides there; it houses a Madame Tussaud's Waxworks
Windsor Castle	Queen Mary's dolls' house, St George's Chapel, Royal Mausoleum Frogmore. Oldest royal residence still in regular use. Edward III born 13 Nov 1312. George III, George IV, William IV all died there

British Cathedrals

Name	*Location*	*General Information*
Aberdeen	Grampian	Dedicated to St Andrew. Seat of Episcopal diocese of Aberdeen and Orkney.
Aberdeen	Grampian	Dedicated to St Machar. Presbyterian cathedral founded 1424.
Aberdeen	Grampian	Dedicated to St Mary. RC Gothic revival Victorian cathedral.
Arundel	West Sussex	Dedicated to Our Lady and St Philip Howard. RC since 1965 for see of Arundel and Brighton, designed by J.A. Hansom.
Ayr	Ayrshire	RC cathedral, seat of Bishop of Galloway.
Bangor	Gwynedd	Founded by and dedicated to St Deiniol and extensively restored in 1866.
Birmingham	West Midlands	Dedicated to St Philip. Built by Thomas Archer 1715, became a cathedral 1905.
Birmingham	West Midlands	Dedicated to St Chad. RC cathedral from 1850, designed by Augustus Pugin 1841.
Blackburn	Lancashire	Dedicated to St Mary, became Anglican cathedral 1927.
Bradford	West Yorkshire	Dedicated to St Peter, designed by Sir Edward Maufe, became Anglican cathedral 1914.
Brechin	Tayside	Founded as a monastery by David I c1150. Dedicated to the Triune God.
Brecon	Powys	Benedictine priory of St John the Evangelist became cathedral 1923 for the see of Swansea and Brecon.
Brentwood	Essex	Dedicated to St Mary and St Helen, RC cathedral from 1917.
Bristol	Bristol	Dedicated to the Holy Trinity, Anglican cathedral founded 1142 but rebuilt by G.E. Street.
Bristol	Bristol	Dedicated to SS. Peter and Paul, RC cathedral, seat of Bishop of Clifton since 1850.
Bury St Edmunds	Suffolk	Dedicated to St James, Anglican cathedral designed by John Wastell / Gilbert Scott 1914, seat of Bishop of St Edmonsbury and Ipswich.
Canterbury	Kent	Dedicated to Christ, rebuilt 1174 by William of Sens.
Cardiff	Glamorgan	Dedicated to St David, RC cathedral from 1920, replacing Belmont, designed by Edward Pugin.
Carlisle	Cumbria	Dedicated to the Holy Trinity, original site of Church of the Augustinian priory, founded 1093.
Chelmsford	Essex	Dedicated to SS. Mary, Peter and Cedd, refurbished by Charles Nicholson 1913, became cathedral 1914.
Chester	Cheshire	Dedicated to Christ and Blessed Virgin Mary, Henry VIII gave cathedral status in 1541.
Chichester	West Sussex	Dedicated to the Holy Trinity, founded by Bishop Ralph de Luffa 1108.
Coventry	West Midlands	Dedicated to St Michael, designed by Basil Spence, dedicated 1962.
Derby	Derbyshire	Dedicated to All Saints, became Anglican cathedral 1927, designed by James Gibbs.
Dornoch	Highland	Founded by Gilbert de Moravia, Bishop of Caithness in C13. Dedicated to the Conception of the Blessed Virgin Mary.
Dunblane	Central	Built on the site of a Celtic Christian foundation, the church was established in C12. Also known as the Cathedral Church of St Blane and St Laurence.

Dundee	Tayside	Dedicated to St Paul. Seat of Episcopal Bishop of Brechin.
Dundee	Tayside	RC cathedral, seat of Bishop of Dunkeld.
Dunkeld	Tayside	Dedicated to St Columba. Partly destroyed during the Battle of Dunkeld in 1689.
Durham	Durham	Dedicated to Christ and Blessed Mary the Virgin c1093.
Edinburgh	Lothian	Dedicated to St Giles. High Kirk & National Church of Scotland.
Edinburgh	Lothian	Dedicated to St Mary. Episcopal cathedral.
Edinburgh	Lothian	RC cathedral, seat of Bishop of St Andrews and Edinburgh.
Elgin	Grampian	Founded in 1224, rebuilt in form of Jerusalem cross, now ruined.
Ely	Cambridgeshire	Dedicated to the Holy Trinity, founded by Simeon, Abbot of Ely, became cathedral 1109.
Exeter	Devon	Dedicated to St Peter, consecrated 1133 and rebuilt c1275.
Glasgow	Strathclyde	Dedicated to St Mary. Seat of Episcopal Bishop of Glasgow and Galloway.
Glasgow	Strathclyde	Dedicated to St Mungo (St Kentigern). Built in C12.
Gloucester	Gloucestershire	Dedicated to St Peter and Holy Trinity, founded 681, became cathedral 1541.
Guildford	Surrey	Dedicated to the Holy Spirit, Anglican cathedral designed by Sir Edward Maufe, completed 1968.
Hereford	Herefordshire	Dedicated to the Blessed Virgin Mary and St Ethelbert, founded 676 by Bishop Putta, restored 1908.
Inverness	Highland	Dedicated to St Andrew. Seat of Episcopal Bishop of Moray, Ross and Caithness. Part of the worldwide Anglican Communion.
Kirkwall	Orkney	Dedicated to St Magnus. Founded in 1137 by St Rognvald, a Viking ruler, in honour of his martyred uncle.
Lancaster	Lancashire	Dedicated to St Peter, built 1859, became RC cathedral 1924.
Leeds	West Yorkshire	Dedicated to St Anne, RC cathedral from 1878.
Leicester	Leicestershire	Dedicated to St Martin, redesigned by Sir Charles Nicholson 1927.
Lichfield	Staffordshire	Dedicated to the Blessed Virgin Mary and St Chad. Built in C13/14.
Lincoln	Lincolnshire	Dedicated to the Blessed Virgin Mary. Norman cathedral built by Geoffrey de Noiers.
Lismore	Strathclyde	Ruins of a C13/14 cathedral which fell into disrepair following the Reformation.
Liverpool	Merseyside	Dedicated to Christ. Neo-Gothic Anglican cathedral founded 1904 but completed 1978. Largest in the UK by floor area.
Liverpool	Merseyside	Dedicated to Christ the King. Roman Catholic Metropolitan cathedral completed 1967. Nicknamed 'Paddy's Wigwam'. Original design by Lutyens rejected on grounds of cost.
Llandaff	Cardiff	Dedicated to St Peter and St Paul. Founded by St Teilo, rebuilt by Bishop Urban C12.
London	London	Dedicated to St Paul. Designed by Sir Christopher Wren, built 1675–1710.
Manchester	Greater Manchester	Dedicated to St Mary, St Denys and St George. Cathedral founded 1847.
Middlesbrough	North Yorkshire	Dedicated to St Mary. RC cathedral completed 1986.
Millport	Great Cumbrae Island, Ayrshire	Collegiate Church of the Holy Spirit. Anglican church known as the Cathedral of the Isles.
Motherwell	Strathclyde	Roman Catholic cathedral designed by Edward Pugin.
Newcastle	Tyne & Wear	Dedicated to St Nicholas. C14 cathedral rebuilt by R.J. Johnson.
Newcastle	Tyne & Wear	Dedicated to St Mary. RC cathedral from 1850, seat of Bishop of Hexham and Newcastle.
Newport	Newport	Dedicated to St Woolos. Seat of Bishop of Monmouth.
Northampton	Northamptonshire	Dedicated to Our Lady and St Thomas. RC cathedral completed in 1864.
Norwich	Norfolk	Dedicated to the Holy Trinity. Norman cathedral founded by William I in 1068.
Norwich	Norfolk	Dedicated to St John the Baptist. RC cathedral from 1976, seat of Bishop of East Anglia.
Nottingham	Nottinghamshire	Dedicated to St Barnabas. RC cathedral from 1850, designed by Augustus Pugin 1842.
Oban	Strathclyde	Dedicated to St John. Seat of Episcopal Bishop of Argyll and the Isles.
Oban	Strathclyde	Roman Catholic cathedral, seat of Bishop of Argyll and the Isles. Dedicated to St Columba.
Oxford	Oxfordshire	Dedicated to St Frideswide. Smallest cathedral in England, also known as Christ Church.
Paisley	Strathclyde	Roman Catholic cathedral built in the 1930s and dedicated as St Mirin's Cathedral.
Perth	Perthshire	Dedicated to St Ninian. Seat of Episcopal Bishop of St Andrews, Dunkeld & Dunblane. Built 1849–90.
Peterborough	Cambs	Dedicated to St Peter, St Paul and St Andrew. Consecrated 1238 and became cathedral 1541.
Plymouth	Devon	Dedicated to St Mary and St Boniface. RC cathedral completed 1858.
Portsmouth	Hampshire	Dedicated to St Thomas of Canterbury. Founded in C12, became a cathedral in 1927.
Portsmouth	Hampshire	Dedicated to St John the Evangelist. RC cathedral from 1882.
Ripon	North Yorkshire	Dedicated to St Peter and St Wilfred. Built in the C15.
Rochester	Kent	Dedicated to Christ and the Blessed Virgin Mary. Medieval church renovated by Bishop Gundulf 1125–30.
Salford	Greater Manchester	Dedicated to St John the Evangelist. RC cathedral from 1850, designed by Matthew Hadfield.
Salisbury	Wiltshire	Dedicated to the Blessed Virgin Mary. Founded 1220 by Richard Poore replacing prior foundation at Old Sarum.
Sheffield	South Yorkshire	Dedicated to St Peter and St Paul. Built by Charles Nicholson.
Sheffield	South Yorkshire	Dedicated to Saint Marie. RC cathedral from 1980, designed by Matthew Hadfield. Seat of the Bishop of Hallam.
Shrewsbury	Shropshire	Dedicated to Our Lady Help of Christians and St Peter of Alcontara. RC cathedral built by Edward Pugin, completed 1856.
Southwark	London	Dedicated to St Saviour and St Mary Overie. Sir Arthur Blomfield rebuilt 1890s.
Southwark	London	Dedicated to St George. RC cathedral from 1850, rebuilt 1858.
Southwell	Nottinghamshire	Dedicated to the Blessed Virgin Mary.
St Albans	Hertfordshire	Dedicated to St Alban. Built in 1077 and designated a cathedral in 1877.
St Andrews	Fife	Medieval cathedral completed in 1144, now ruined.
St Asaph	Clwyd	Dedicated to St Asaph. Restored C19 by Gilbert Scott.
St Davids	Dyfed	Dedicated to St David & St Andrew. Norman cathedral restored in C19.
Swansea	Swansea	Dedicated to St Joseph. RC cathedral 1875, seat of Bishop of Menevia.
Truro	Cornwall	Dedicated to St Mary. Designed by J.L. Pearson 1879–1910.
Wakefield	West Yorkshire	Dedicated to All Saints. Designed by J.L. Pearson.
Wells	Somerset	Dedicated to St Andrew. Built C12 by Reginald de Bohun.
Westminster	London	Dedicated to the Most Precious Blood. RC cathedral designed by James Bentley 1895.
Winchester	Hampshire	Dedicated to Holy Trinity, St Peter, St Paul and St Swithin. Restored by Bishop Walkelin c1090.

Worcester	Worcester	Dedicated to Christ and Blessed Virgin Mary. Wulfstan restored Worcester cathedral 1084, improved C19.
Wrexham	Clwyd	Dedicated to Our Lady of Sorrows. RC cathedral built by Edward Pugin.
York Minster	North Yorkshire	Dedicated to St Peter. Thomas of Bayeux built St Peter's church c1070; restored C13.

NB: Although St Giles is known as Edinburgh Cathedral it does not have a cathedra so is technically a church. However, it is included in the listing because it has the same standing in Scotland as Westminster Abbey in England.

British Cathedrals: General Information

Arundel Screen Part of Chichester cathedral.
Bell Harry Tower Tower of Canterbury cathedral erected 1490.
Bell-tower: detached Chichester.
Birmingham Cathedral Edward Burne-Jones designed four windows in 1880 and William Morris made them.
Bishop's eye window Lincoln cathedral.
Black stone fonts Lincoln and Winchester both have black stone fonts from Belgium.
Canterbury Cathedral Tombs for Henry IV and Edward the Black Prince and Trinity Chapel Shrine of Thomas Becket. William of Sens fell from scaffolding and work completed by William the Englishman. T.S. Eliot's play *Murder in the Cathedral* first performed in the Chapter House in 1935. Destroyed by fire in 1174, rebuilt by William of Sens with stone from Caen. Based on the Monastic Church of St Etienne in Caen where Lanfranc had been Abbot.
Carlisle Cathedral Sir Walter Scott was married there.
Cathedral: definition Church that contains a cathedra, or throne of the bishop of the diocese.
Cathedral: longest Winchester 556 ft (169 m).
Cathedral: widest in England Manchester at 114 ft (35 m).
Cathedrals: shape Cruciform, traditionally.
Chichester Cathedral Houses tomb for Bishop Robert Sherburne, who died in 1536. Houses monument for Walter Huskisson, Chichester MP (dressed as Roman).
Chichester: windows Designed by Marc Chagall.
Christ Church Gateway Canterbury cathedral.
Clock with no face Salisbury cathedral.
Coventry Cathedral Tapestry of the Risen Christ by Graham Sutherland 1952. Statue of Christ being doomed (behold the man) by Jacob Epstein. Windows by John Piper. Benjamin Britten's *War Requiem* first performed.
Coventry Cathedral: Old Destroyed by bombing 1940.
Durham Cathedral Completed by Ranulf Flambard and houses tomb of St Cuthbert.
Gloucester Cathedral Contains tomb of Edward II, murdered in Berkeley castle; also tomb of Robert Curthose, Duke of Normandy.
Great Paul 17-ton bell in St Paul's.
Hedda Stone: Sculpture Peterborough Cathedral.
Hereford Cathedral Map of the World (Mappa Mundi) by Richard of Haldingham and Lafford C13, based on C5 work of Orosius. Africa is labelled as Europe, and vice versa. Jerusalem is centre of the world. Largest chained library (1,450 books) includes *Anglo-Saxon Chronicle*. Restored by Lewis Cottingham and Sir George Gilbert Scott. Houses shrine of St Thomas Cantilupe. Highpoint of Hereford is a tower, not a spire.
Highest Spire Salisbury cathedral 404 ft (123 m); 2nd highest spire is Norwich at 315 ft (96 m).
Inverted Arches Wells cathedral.
Largest Gothic Church York Minster, in England.
Lichfield Cathedral Houses the *Sleeping Children* statue. Three spires named The Ladies of the Vale. Name means Field of the Dead (Emperor Diocletian martyred 1,000 Christians). Previous name – Bishopric called the diocese of 'Lichfield and Coventry' until 1836.
Lincoln Highest spire 524 ft (160 m) until it was blown down in 1584.
Liverpool Anglican Designed by Sir Giles Gilbert Scott after winning competition.
Llandaff Cathedral Houses *Christ in His Majesty* by Jacob Epstein.
Longest Nave St Albans has England's longest nave at 348 ft (106 m).
Magna Carta: copies Lincoln and Salisbury cathedrals; the other two are in the British Library.
Mostyn Christ Bangor cathedral.
Nelson's Column Hereford cathedral had a Nelson's Column long before the London monument.
New Cathedrals of 1927 Isle of Wight and South Hampshire became Anglican Diocese, creating many new cathedrals.
Norwich Cathedral Edith Cavell buried. It also has the largest cloisters in England.
Old St Paul's The Norman cathedral was 600 ft (183 m) long; its spire was 490 ft (149 m) high.
Oldest clock (1380) Salisbury cathedral (no dial).
Peterborough Cathedral Catherine of Aragon buried there 1536 and Mary Queen of Scots 1587 (moved to Westminster Abbey).
Priest and people: face East, traditionally.
Ribbed Vault 1st Durham cathedral.
Ripon Cathedral Crypt by St Wilfred and Reredos by Ninian Comper.
Scott, Sir George Gilbert Restored Westminster Abbey, Ely, Lichfield and Salisbury cathedrals.
Smallest Cathedral St Asaph's, Clwyd.
Smallest Cathedral City In England – Wells. In UK – St David's
Southwark Cathedral John Harvard, founder of Harvard University, baptised 1607. Bunyan and Chaucer windows.
St Albans: dedicatee St Alban, Britain's first Christian martyr (executed circa 209).
St Augustine's Chair Canterbury cathedral.
St David's Cathedral Based on the Spanish Santiago de Compostela.
St Giles Cathedral Jenny Geddes flung stool at preacher for reading an Anglican text. John Knox, the religious reformer, was buried there in 1572. White stork's nest was recorded on roof in 1416, the only British breeding occurrence.
St Lucy's Chapel Oxford cathedral.
St Paul's Cathedral Henry Moore's statue *Mother and Child*. Bombed in December 1940. Statue of Queen Anne outside. St Paul's destroyed by fire in 1666. All Souls Chapel is memorial to Kitchener and other casualties of World War I. Whispering Gallery is famous for its acoustics. Frescoes on the inside of the dome by Sir James Thornhill. Houses Wellington's monument by Alfred Stevens and Nelson's statue by John Flaxman.
Three Spires Lichfield, Truro and St Mary's Edinburgh.
Triforium 1st Canterbury cathedral.
Twenty-four-hour clock Wells cathedral.
Wastell's Tower Canterbury cathedral.
Westminster Abbey Not a cathedral as such, as it lacks a Bishop's Throne. Official name is the Collegiate Church of St Peter. George II was last Sovereign to be buried in the Abbey, as Windsor Castle was subsequently used. Tombs include Henry III, Edward I, Edward III, Henry V, Elizabeth I, Mary Queen of Scots and the Unknown Warrior.
Westminster Cathedral Houses Eric Gill's *14 Stations of the Cross*.
Whispering Gallery St Paul's cathedral.
Winchester Cathedral Canute and other Danish kings are buried here. So are Jane Austen and Izaak Walton. When St Swithin's remains were transferred in 971 it rained for 40 days. Nave was built C14 by William of Wykeham and William of Edington.
Worcester Cathedral Houses the tomb of King John.
Wren's tomb inscription Lector, si monumentum requiris, circumspice – 'Reader, if you seek his monument, look around you.'
York Minster Great East window by John Thornton 1405–8; St Cuthbert's (bishop in 685) window 1440.

Top 100 Greatest Britons of All Time, as Voted by Internet and BBC Viewers

1 Winston Churchill
2 Isambard Kingdom Brunel
3 Diana, Princess of Wales
4 Charles Darwin
5 William Shakespeare
6 Isaac Newton
7 Elizabeth I
8 John Lennon
9 Horatio Nelson
10 Oliver Cromwell
11 Ernest Shackleton
12 James Cook
13 Robert Baden Powell
14 Alfred the Great
15 1st Duke of Wellington
16 Margaret Thatcher
17 Michael Crawford
18 Queen Victoria
19 Paul McCartney
20 Alexander Fleming
21 Alan Turing
22 Michael Faraday
23 Owain Glyndwr
24 Elizabeth II
25 Stephen Hawking
26 William Tyndale
27 Emmeline Pankhurst
28 William Wilberforce
29 David Bowie
30 Guy Fawkes
31 Leonard Cheshire
32 Eric Morecambe
33 David Beckham
34 Thomas Paine
35 Boudicca
36 Steve Redgrave
37 Thomas More
38 William Blake
39 John Harrison
40 Henry VIII
41 Charles Dickens
42 Frank Whittle
43 John Peel
44 John Logie Baird
45 Aneurin Bevan
46 Boy George
47 Douglas Bader
48 William Wallace
49 Francis Drake
50 John Wesley
51 King Arthur (mythical king)
52 Florence Nightingale
53 TE Lawrence
54 Robert Falcon Scott
55 Enoch Powell
56 Cliff Richard
57 Alexander Graham Bell
58 Freddie Mercury
59 Julie Andrews
60 Edward Elgar
61 Queen Elizabeth, the Queen Mother
62 George Harrison
63 David Attenborough
64 James Connolly
65 George Stephenson
66 Charlie Chaplin
67 Tony Blair
68 William Caxton
69 Bobby Moore
70 Jane Austen
71 William Booth
72 Henry V
73 Aleister Crowley (occult leader)
74 Robert the Bruce
75 Bob Geldof
76 The Unknown Soldier
77 Robbie Williams
78 Edward Jenner
79 David Lloyd George
80 Charles Babbage
81 Geoffrey Chaucer
82 Richard III
83 JK Rowling
84 James Watt
85 Richard Branson
86 Bono
87 John Lydon
88 Montgomery of Alamein
89 Donald Campbell
90 Henry II
91 James Clerk Maxwell
92 JRR Tolkien
93 Walter Raleigh
94 Edward I
95 Barnes Wallis
96 Richard Burton (actor)
97 Tony Benn
98 David Livingstone
99 Tim Berners Lee (WWW inventor)
100 Marie Stopes

CALENDAR

Wedding Anniversaries

1	Cotton / Paper	8	Bronze / Pottery	15	Crystal	50	Golden
2	Paper / Cotton	9	Pottery / Willow	20	China	55	Emerald
3	Leather	10	Tin	25	Silver	60	Diamond
4	Fruit / Flowers	11	Steel	30	Pearl	65	Blue Sapphire
5	Wood	12	Silk / Linen	35	Coral	70	Platinum
6	Sugar	13	Lace	40	Ruby	75	Gold or Diamond
7	Wool / Copper	14	Ivory	45	Sapphire		

NB: Wedding anniversaries are an area of frustration for quiz players because there are slight variations to many of the gifts that are traditionally given on wedding anniversaries, and to complicate matters even more, some of the gifts have changed over the years: e.g. diamonds were traditionally given on a 75th wedding anniversary but after Queen Victoria celebrated her 'Diamond' Jubilee in 1897, this became the established gift for a 60th anniversary, and the 75th which was previously Diamond then became Gold, as opposed to 'Golden' for a 50th. A more common cause of frustration is the gift for a first anniversary. Cotton was traditionally given, as the 'binding' of two people who have tied the knot, but as in the case of so many infrequently used customs it has become traditional to think of a first anniversary as a paper one, after the certificate of marriage. Neither is right or wrong, as they have never been observed for any reason other than a convenient question to ask in a quiz. In fairness, it would be better for quiz-setters to avoid the more controversial anniversaries – e.g. 1st, 2nd, 75th – or if insisting on using them, it would be advisable to phrase the question in the form 'If paper is a first anniversary, what is a second?'

Months of the French Revolutionary Calendar

(each month was divided into three 10-day weeks)

Vendémiaire	(Grape harvest)	23 Sep –22 Oct	Germinal	(Buds)	22 Mar –20 Apr
Brumaire	(Mist)	23 Oct –21 Nov	Floréal	(Flowers)	21 Apr –20 May
Frimaire	(Frost)	22 Nov –21 Dec	Prairial	(Meadows)	21 May –19 Jun
Nivôse	(Snow)	22 Dec –20 Jan	Messidor	(Harvest)	20 Jun –19 Jul
Pluviôse	(Rain)	21 Jan –19 Feb	Thermidor	(Heat)	20 Jul –18 Aug
Ventôse	(Wind)	20 Feb –21 Mar	Fructidor	(Fruit)	19 Aug –22 Sep

Months of the Jewish Calendar

Tishri	30 days	Adar*	29 days	Tammuz	29 days
Marheshvan	29 / 30 days	Ve-Adar†	30 days	Av	30 days
Kislev	29 / 30 days	Nisan	30 days	Elul	29 days
Tevet	29 / 30 days	Iyyar	29 days		
Shevat	30 days	Sivan	30 days		

*30 days in a leap year
†13th month every 3rd, 6th, 8th, 11th, 14th, 17th, & 19th year of a 19-year cycle
NB: The Jewish calendar places the creation at 3761 BCE.

Months of the Muslim Calendar

1	Muharram	30 days	5	Jumâda I	30 days	9	Ramadan	30 days
2	Safar	29 days	6	Jumâda II	29 days	10	Shawwal	29 days
3	Rabia I	30 days	7	Rajab	30 days	11	Dhâl-Qa'da	30 days
4	Rabia II	29 days	8	Shaaban	29 days	12	Dhâl-Hijja	29 days*

*30 days in a leap year
NB: The first day of the first month of the Islamic calendar (1 Muharram 1 AH) was Friday, 16 July AD 622 marking the Prophet's move from Mecca to Medina.

Other Calendars

Indian	Vikrama Era	Dates from 23 Feb 57 BC	**Japanese Days** (months are numbered)	Nichiyobi	Sun-day
	Saka Era	Dates from 3 Mar AD 78		Getsuyobi	Moon-day
	Buddhist Era	Dates from 543 BC		Kayobi	Fire-day
	Jain Era	Dates from 527 BC (death of Vardhamana)		Suiyobi	Water-day
				Mokuyobi	Wood-day
	Parsee Era	Dates from 16 Jun AD 632		Kinyobi	Metal-day
				Doyobi	Earth-day
Coptic	Egypt and Ethiopia; dates from 29 Aug AD 284				

Commemorative Days

Advent Sunday	Sunday nearest to 30 Nov
All Saints' Day	1 Nov
All Souls' Day	2 Nov
Andrew's Day, St	30 Nov
Ascensiontide	Ascension day to Whitsun Eve (10 days)
Ash Wednesday	The 1st day of Lent
Assumption	15 Aug
Australia Day	26 Jan
Barnabas's Day, St	11 Jun
Bartholomew's Day, St	24 Aug
Bastille Day	14 Jul
Burns Night	25 Jan
Calends / Kalends	First day of each month in ancient Roman Calendar
Cecilia's Day, St	22 Nov
Commonwealth Day	2nd Monday in March
Corpus Christi	Thursday after Trinity Sunday
Crispin's Day, St	25 Oct
David's Day, St	1 Mar
Easter Sunday	The 1st Sunday after the full moon following the vernal equinox
Epiphany	6 Jan
First day of year pre-1752	25 Mar
Francis of Assisi's Day, St	4 Oct
George Washington Day	17 Feb (USA)
George's Day, St	23 Apr
Giles' Day, St	1 Sept
Good Friday	Day before Easter Saturday
Holy Saturday	Last day of Lent
Immaculate Conception Day	8 Dec
Independence Day (USA)	4 Jul
John the Baptist's Day, St	24 Jun
John the Evangelist's, St	27 Dec
Labor Day (USA)	Equivalent to our May Day, First Monday of September
Lady Day	25 Mar
Lent	The 40 days between Ash Wednesday and Easter Saturday excluding Sundays
Low Sunday	The 1st after Easter
Luke's Day, St	18 Oct
Maggie Thatcher Day	10 Jan on Falkland Islands
Mark's Day, St	25 Apr
Martin Luther King Day (USA)	15 Jan
Martin's Day, St	11 Nov
Matthew's Day, St	21 Sept
Maundy Thursday	Day before Good Friday
May Day	Became public holiday in 1978
Michael's Day, St	29 Sept
Mothering Sunday	4th in Lent and 3rd before Easter
New Year's Day	Became public holiday in 1974
Nicholas' Day, St	6 Dec
Nones (Roman Calendar)	The 9th day before the ides of each month i.e. 7th of March, May, July and October and 5th of other months
Orangeman's Day	Celebrated by Irish protestants on 12 July
Palm Sunday	Sunday before Easter Sunday
Passion Sunday	Sunday before Palm Sunday
Patrick's Day, St	17 Mar
Paul's Day, St	29 Jun
Pentecost (Whit Sunday)	7th Sunday after Easter Sunday
Peter's Day, St	29 Jun
Shrove Tuesday	Day before Ash Wednesday
Stephen's Day, St	26 Dec
Swithin's Day, St	15 Jul
Sylvester's Day, St	31 Dec
Thomas' Day, St	21 Dec
Trafalgar Day	21 Oct
Trinity Sunday	1st Sunday after Whitsun
Twelfth Night	5 Jan
United Nations Day	24 Oct
Valentine's Day, St	14 Feb

English Quarter Days

Lady Day	25 March
Midsummer Day	24 June
Michaelmas	29 September
Christmas Day	25 December

NB: A useful mnemonic for remembering English Quarter Days is that three of the days end with the same number as letters in the month e.g. March has five letters so Lady Day is the 25th, June has four letters so Midsummer Day is 24th, September has nine letters so Michaelmas is 29th. Christmas Day should never be forgotten.

Scottish Quarter Days

Candlemas	28 February
Whitsuntide	28 May
Lammas	28 August
Martinmas	28 November

NB: Although the names of the four Scottish Quarter Days have remained the same, the dates changed in 1991. Candlemas used to be on 2 Feb, Lammas was 1 Aug and Martinmas was on 11 Nov. The date of Whitsuntide varied.

Birthstones

January	Garnet
February	Amethyst
March	Bloodstone or Aquamarine
April	Diamond
May	Emerald
June	Pearl, Agate Moonstone, or Alexandrite
July	Ruby or Cornelian
August	Sardonyx or Peridot
September	Sapphire or Chrysolite
October	Opal or Tourmaline
November	Topaz
December	Turquoise or Zircon

NB: Birthstones are also controversial, as once again some months have more than one stone. Attempts to introduce birthstones for each sign of the Zodiac have fallen largely out of use.

Chinese Years

Snake (serpent)	2001
Horse	2002
Sheep (ram)	2003
Monkey	2004
Rooster (cock)	2005
Dog	2006
Pig	2007
Rat	2008
Ox	2009
Tiger	2010
Rabbit	2011
Dragon	2012

NB: The calendar goes in 12-year cycles, so it continues Snake, 2013; Horse, 2014; and so on.

Watches at Sea

First Watch	8pm–midnight
Middle Watch	midnight–4am
Morning Watch	4am–8am
Forenoon Watch	8am–midday
Afternoon Watch	midday–4pm
First Dog Watch	4pm–6pm
Last Dog Watch	6pm–8pm

NB: A bell is rung every half-hour during a watch, which therefore ends on eight bells or four for a dog watch. The New Year is brought in with 16 bells. Incidentally 'Dog' is thought to be a corruption of 'dodge', which was introduced to enable easier rostering.

Zodiac

Aries	21 Mar–19 Apr
Taurus	20 Apr–20 May
Gemini	21 May–21 Jun
Cancer	22 Jun–22 Jul
Leo	23 Jul–22 Aug
Virgo	23 Aug–22 Sep
Libra	23 Sep–23 Oct
Scorpio	24 Oct–21 Nov
Sagittarius	22 Nov–21 Dec
Capricorn	22 Dec–19 Jan
Aquarius	20 Jan–18 Feb
Pisces	19 Feb–20 Mar

CINEMA

A–Z of Films

A.I. Artificial Intelligence (2001) Haley Joel Osment (David), Jude Law (Gigolo Joe), William Hurt, Brendan Gleeson, Frances O'Connor. Child robot searches for the mother who abandoned him. *Dir.* Steven Spielberg.

À Nous la Liberté (1931) Raymond Cordy, Henri Marchand. Factory owner is blackmailed about his past and is helped by an old prison friend. US title: *Freedom for Us. Dir.* René Clair.

Abbott & Costello Go to Mars (1953) Bud Abbott, Lou Costello, Mari Blanchard, Martha Hyer, Robert Paige. Despite the title, they land first in Louisiana and then on Venus! *Dir.* Charles Lamont.

Abbott & Costello Meet Captain Kidd (1952) Bud Abbott, Lou Costello, Charles Laughton, Leif Erickson. *Dir.* Charles Lamont.

Abbott & Costello Meet Dr Jekyll & Mr Hyde (1953) Bud Abbott, Lou Costello, Boris Karloff, Craig Stevens. This film starring Boris Karloff was given an 'X' certificate in its day. *Dir.* Charles Lamont.

Abbott & Costello Meet Frankenstein (1948) Bud Abbott, Lou Costello, Bela Lugosi, Lon Chaney Jnr. Dracula and the Wolf Man also -feature. GB title: *Abbott & Costello Meet the Ghosts. Dir.* Charles Barton.

Abbott & Costello Meet the Killer, Boris Karloff (1948) Bud Abbott, Lou Costello, Boris Karloff, Gary Moore. Boris Karloff is not the killer and appears very little. *Dir.* Charles Barton.

Abe Lincoln in Illinois (1940) Raymond Massey (Abraham Lincoln), Ruth Gordon. GB title: *Spirit of the People. Dir.* John Cromwell.

Abominable Dr Phibes, The (1971) Vincent Price, Joseph Cotten, Terry-Thomas. Dr Phibes, a disfigured musical genius, avenges his wife's death at the hands of surgeons. Sequel: *Dr Phibes Rises Again* (1972), starred Price, Terry-Thomas, Beryl Reid, John Thaw. *Dir.* Robert Fuest.

Abominable Snowman, The (1957) Peter Cushing, Forrest Tucker, Richard Wattis. US title: *The Abominable Snowman of the Himalayas. Dir.* Val Guest.

About a Boy (2002) Hugh Grant (Will Freeman), Nicholas Hoult, Sharon Small, Madison Cook, Jordan Cook, Toni Collette, Rachel Weisz. Layabout philanderer exploits single mothers but has responsibility, in the form of a 12-year-old boy, thrust upon him. Based on a Nick Hornby novel. *Dir.* Chris and Paul Weitz.

About Schmidt (2002) Jack Nicholson (Warren Schmidt), Hope Davis (Jeannie), Dermot Mulroney (Randall Hertzel), Kathy Bates (Roberta Hertzel), Len Cariou (Ray), Howard Hesseman (Larry), June Squibb (Helen Schmidt). A retired actuary has to deal with life as an aged widower. *Dir.* Alexander Payne.

Above and Beyond (1952) Robert Taylor (Colonel Paul Tibbets, who dropped the first atomic bomb on Japan). *Dirs.* Melvin Frank and Norman Panama.

Absence of Malice (1981) Paul Newman, Sally Field. *Dir.* Sydney Pollack.

Absent-Minded Professor, The (1961) Fred MacMurray, Tommy Kirk, Keenan Wynn, Ed Wynn. Lighter than air substance called 'Flubber' allows the Professor's Model-T Ford to fly. Sequel *Son of Flubber. Dir.* Robert Stevenson.

Absolute Beginners (1986) Eddie O'Connell, Patsy Kensit, David Bowie (Vendice Partners), Ray Davies, James Fox, Steven Berkoff, Mandy Rice Davies, Robbie Coltrane, Irene Handl, Eric Sykes, Lionel Blair. Teen life in 1958 London. *Dir.* Julien Temple.

Absolute Power (1997) Clint Eastwood, Gene Hackman, Ed Harris, EG Marshall, Laura Linney, Judy Davis. *Dir.* Clint Eastwood.

Accident (1967) Dirk Bogarde, Stanley Baker, Vivien Merchant, Michael York. Screenplay by Harold Pinter. *Dir.* Joseph Losey.

Accidental Hero (1992) Dustin Hoffman (Bernie Laplante), Geena Davis (Gale Gayley), Andy Garcia (John Bubber). Screenplay by David Webb Peoples, the writer of *Unforgiven* and *Blade Runner. Dir.* Stephen Frears.

Accidental Tourist, The (1988) William Hurt, Kathleen Turner, Geena Davis. Geena Davis won Academy Award for Best Supporting Actress. *Dir.* Lawrence Kasdan.

Accused, The (1988) Kelly McGillis (Kathryn Murphy), Jodie Foster (Sarah Tobias), Bernie Coulson. Jodie Foster won Academy Award for Best Actress. *Dir.* Jonathan Kaplan.

Ace in the Hole (1951) Kirk Douglas (Chuck Tatum), Jan Sterling (Lorraine), Porter Hall (Boot), Ray Teal (Sheriff). In order to boost newspaper sales a journalist delays the rescue of a man trapped in a cave. Aka: *The Big Carnival. Dir.* Billy Wilder.

Ace Ventura, Pet Detective (1994) Jim Carrey, Courteney Cox, Sean Young, Tone Loc. Ace is hired to recover the Miami Dolphins' dolphin mascot. *Dir.* Tom Shadyac.

Ace Ventura, When Nature Calls (1995) Jim Carrey, Ian McNeice, Simon Callow, Adewalé. Ace goes to Africa to find a sacred white bat. *Dir.* Steve Oedekerk.

Across the Pacific (1942) Humphrey Bogart (Rick Leland), Mary Astor (Alberta Marlow), Sydney Greenstreet (Dr Lorenz). Huston was called up mid-film and it was eventually completed by Vincent Sherman. *Dir.* John Huston.

Actress, The (1928) Norma Shearer, Ralph Forbes. This film was the opening attraction at London's Empire Theatre, Leicester Square. GB title: *Trelawney of the Wells. Dir.* Sidney Franklin.

Adam's Rib (1949) Spencer Tracy, Katharine Hepburn, Judy Holliday. *Dir.* George Cukor.

Adaptation (2002) Nicolas Cage (Charlie Kaufman/Donald Kaufman), Meryl Streep (Susan Orlean), Chris Cooper (John Laroche), Tilda Swinton (Valerie), Cara Seymour (Amelia), Brian Cox (Robert McKee), Judy Greer (Alice the Waitress), Maggie Gyllenhaal (Caroline). Cage plays twin brothers, a neurotic screenwriter with writer's block struggling to adapt a book about a Florida orchid-breeder and a happier individual who writes a script about a serial killer. *Dir.* Spike Jonze.

Addams Family, The (1991) Anjelica Huston (Morticia), Raul Julia (Gomez), Christopher Lloyd (Uncle Fester). Impostor arrives at the Addams family home purporting to be a long-lost elder brother. *Dir.* Barry Sonnenfeld.

Addams Family Values (1993) Anjelica Huston (Morticia), Raul Julia (Gomez), Christopher Lloyd (Uncle Fester). Sequel in which the Addams children try, unsuccessfully, to kill the new baby. *Dir.* Barry Sonnenfeld.

Addicted To Love (1997) Meg Ryan (Maggie), Matthew Broderick (Sam), Kelly Preston (Linda), Tcheky Karyo (Anton) *Dir.* Griffin Dunne.

Addiction, The (1996) Christopher Walken, Lili Taylor. *Dir.* Abel Ferrara.

Admirable Crichton, The (1957) Kenneth More, Cecil Parker, Sally Ann Howes, Diane Cilento, Peter Graves, Gerald Harper. US title: *Paradise Lagoon. Dir.* Lewis Gilbert.

Adolf Hitler – My Part In His Downfall (1972) Jim Dale (Spike Milligan), Spike Milligan (Milligan's father), Arthur Lowe, Bill Maynard. Notable for appearance of Spike Milligan playing the part of his father. *Dir.* Norman Cohen.

Adventure of Sherlock Holmes' Smarter Brother, The (1975) Gene Wilder, Marty Feldman, Madeline Kahn, Thorley Walters. *Dir.* Gene Wilder.

Adventures of Arsène Lupin, The (1956) Robert Lamoureux, Liselotte Pulver, Otto Hasse. Based on the Jewel Thief character created by Maurice Leblanc. *Dir.* Jacques Becker.

Adventures of Baron Munchausen (1989) John Neville, Eric Idle, Sarah Polley, Oliver Reed, Uma Thurman. *Dir.* Terry Gilliam.

Adventures of Barry Mackenzie, The (1972) Barry Crocker, Barry Humphries (Edna Everage), Peter Cook, Spike Milligan, Dennis Price. *Private Eye* comic strip fantasy. (The 1974 sequel was called *Barry Mackenzie Holds His Own.*) *Dir.* Bruce Beresford.

Adventures of Captain Marvel (1941) Tom Tyler (Billy Batson alias Captain Marvel). Assistant radio operator on scientific trip to Siam is endowed with superpowers by the mysterious 'Shazam' and battles against the evil 'Scorpion'. *Dir.* John English & William Witney.

Adventures of Mark Twain (1944) Fredric March (Twain), Alexis Smith, Alan Hale. *Dir.* Irving Rapper.

Adventures of Milo and Otis (1986) Narrated by Dudley Moore, the tale of a puppy in search of his friend, a -kitten. This film was the second most popular film ever made in Japan. *Dir.* Masanori Hata.
Adventures of Pinocchio, The (1996) Martin Landau, Jonathan Taylor Thomas, Geneviève Bujold, Griff Rhys Jones, Dawn French. *Dir.* Steve Barron.
Adventures of Priscilla Queen of the Desert (1994) Terence Stamp, Hugo Weaving, Bill Hunter, Guy Pearce. Two transvestites and a transsexual drive a bus from Sydney to Alice Springs for a cabaret gig. *Dir.* Stephan Elliott.
Adventures of Robin Hood, The (1938) Errol Flynn (Robin), Basil Rathbone (Guy of Gisbourne), Claude Rains (Prince John), Olivia de Havilland (Marian), Alan Hale (Little John), Ian Hunter (King Richard), Melville Cooper (Sheriff of Nottingham). Won Academy Awards for Music and Editing. *Dir.* William Keighley and Michael Curtiz.
Adventures of Robinson Crusoe, The (1953) Dan O'Herlihy (Crusoe), Jaime Fernandez (Friday). *Dir.* Luis Buñuel.
Adventures of Sherlock Holmes, The (1939) Basil Rathbone, Nigel Bruce, George Zucco (Moriarty), Mary Gordon (Mrs Hudson). GB title: *Sherlock Holmes. Dir.* Alfred Werker.
Adventures of Tom Sawyer, The (1938) Tommy Kelly (Tom), Jackie Moran (Huck), Ann Gillis (Becky Thatcher). *Dir.* Norman Taurog.
Advise and Consent (1962) Charles Laughton, Henry Fonda, Walter Pidgeon, Don Murray. *Dir.* Otto Preminger.
African Queen, The (1951) Humphrey Bogart (Charlie Allnutt), Katharine Hepburn (Rose Sayer), Robert Morley. Based on the CS Forester novel. Humphrey Bogart awarded the Best Actor Oscar. *Dir.* John Huston.
Agatha (1979) Vanessa Redgrave (Agatha Christie), Dustin Hoffman, Timothy Dalton. Tells the story of Agatha Christie's disappearance in 1926. *Dir.* Michael Apted.
Age of Innocence, The (1993) Daniel Day-Lewis, Michelle Pfeiffer, Winona Ryder, Richard E Grant. Wealthy lawyer falls in love with his wife's cousin. *Dir.* Martin Scorsese.
Agony and the Ecstasy, The (1965) Charlton Heston (Michelangelo), Rex Harrison (Pope Julius II). Based on the Irving Stone novel. *Dir.* Carol Reed.
Aida (1953) Sophia Loren, Lois Maxwell. Based on Verdi's opera. *Dir.* Clemente Fracassi.
Airborne (1993) Shane McDermott, Seth Green, Brittney Powell. Surfer moves to Cincinnati and becomes a rollerblade champion. *Dir.* Rob Bowman.
Airforce One (1997) Harrison Ford (President James Marshall), Jurgen Prochnow (General Radek), Gary Oldman (Korshunov) *Dir.* Wolfgang Petersen.
Airplane! (1980) Robert Stack, Lloyd Bridges, Leslie Nielsen, Peter Graves, Kareem Abdul-Jabbar, Julie Hagerty. (The 1982 sequel, *Airplane II*, was directed by Ken Finkleman.) *Dir.* J. Abrahams, David and Jerry Zucker.
Airport (1970) Burt Lancaster, Dean Martin, Jean Seberg, Helen Hayes (Best Supporting Actress Oscar). Based on the Arthur Hailey novel. *Dir.* George Seaton.
Al Capone (1959) Rod Steiger (Capone), Fay Spain, Nehemiah Persoff, Martin Balsam. *Dir.* Richard Wilson.
Aladdin (1992) Voices of Robin Williams (Genie), Linda Larkin (Jasmine), Scott Weinger (Aladdin). 'Whole New World' won Best Song Oscar (music by Alan Menken, lyrics by Tim Rice) *Dir.* John Musker and Ron Clements.
Alamo, The (1960) John Wayne (Davy Crockett), Richard Widmark (Jim Bowie), Laurence Harvey (Travis), Frankie Avalon (Smitty), Richard Boone (Houston) *Dir.* John Wayne.
Alamo, The (2004) Dennis Quaid (Sam Houston), Billy Bob Thornton (Davy Crockett), Jason Patric (Jim Bowie), Patrick Wilson (William Travis), Emilio Echevarria (Antonio Lopez de Santa Ana). Based on the 1836 battle. *Dir.* John Lee Hancock.
Albert RN (1953) Jack Warner, Anthony Steel, Robert Beatty, Anton Diffring. POWs build a life-like dummy to cover the absence of escapers. US title: *Break to Freedom. Dir.* Lewis Gilbert.
Albino Alligator (1997) Faye Dunaway, Matt Dillon. Villains hold a group of New Yorkers hostage in a bar. *Dir.* Kevin Spacey.
Alexander (2004) Colin Farrell (Alexander the Great), Jared Leto (Hephaestion), Angelina Jolie (Queen Olympias), Val Kilmer (King Philip II), Raz Degan (Darius III of Persia), Christopher Plummer (Aristotle), Anthony Hopkins (Ptolemy I Soter). *Dir.* Oliver Stone.
Alexander the Great (1956) Richard Burton (Alexander), Fredric March, Claire Bloom. *Dir.* Robert Rossen.
Alexander's Ragtime Band (1938) Tyrone Power, Alice Faye, Don Ameche, Ethel Merman. *Dir.* Henry King.
Alf Garnett Saga, The (1972) Warren Mitchell, Dandy Nichols. The Una Stubbs and Tony Booth parts were played by Adrienne Posta and Mike Angelis. *Dir.* Bob Kellett.
Alfie (1966) Michael Caine (Alfie), Vivien Merchant, Shirley Anne Field, Jane Asher, Millicent Martin, Shelley Winters. Theme song sung by Cher. *Dir.* Lewis Gilbert.
Alfie (2004) Jude Law (Alfie), Marisa Tomei (Julie), Omar Epps (Marlon), Nia Long (Lonette), Jane Krakowski (Dorie), Sienna Miller (Nikki), Tara Summers (Carol), Susan Sarandon (Liz). A reinvention of of the 1960s film. *Dir.* Charles Shyer.
Alfie Darling (1975) Alan Price, Jill Townsend, Joan Collins, Annie Ross, Hannah Gordon, Rula Lenska. Alan Price takes over the Michael Caine role as well as contributing the music. *Dir.* Ken Hughes.
Algiers (1938) Charles Boyer, Hedy Lamarr, Alan Hale. The famous line 'Come with me to the Casbah' was never actually said in this film. *Dir.* John Cromwell.
Ali (2001) Will Smith (Ali), Jamie Foxx (Drew 'Bundini' Brown), Jon Voight (Howard Cosell), Mario Van Peebles (Malcolm X), Ron Silver (Angelo Dundee), Mykelti Williamson (Don King), LeVar Burton (Martin Luther King Jr), Albert Hall (Elijah Muhammad), Giancarlo Esposito (Ali's father), Michael Michele (Veronica), Nona Gaye (Belinda). *Dir.* Michael Mann.
Ali G Indahouse (2002) Sacha Baron Cohen, Michael Gambon, Charles Dance, Kellie Bright (Me Julie), Martin Freeman. Black rapper becomes a national hero after becoming an MP. *Dir.* Mark Mylod.
Alice (1990) Mia Farrow, Joe Mantegna, Alec Baldwin, William Hurt. *Dir.* Woody Allen.
Alice Doesn't Live Here Any More (1974) Ellen Burstyn, Kris Kristofferson, Jodie Foster, Diane Ladd, Alfred Lutter. Ellen Burstyn won Academy Award for Best Actress. *Dir.* Martin Scorsese.
Alice in Wonderland (1933) Charlotte Henry (Alice), WC Fields (Humpty Dumpty), Cary Grant (Mock Turtle), Gary Cooper (White Knight). Ida Lupino was brought from the UK for the title role but ultimately not used. *Dir.* Norman Z McLeod.
Alice in Wonderland (2010) Mia Wasikowska (Alice Kingsleigh), Johnny Depp (Tarrant Hightopp - The Hatter), Helena Bonham Carter (Iracebeth of Crims - The Red Queen), Anne Hathaway (Mirana of Marmoreal - The White Queen), Matt Lucas (Tweedledee and Tweedledum). Voice actors: Stephen Fry (Chessur – The Cheshire Cat), Alan Rickman (Absolem The Caterpillar), Christopher Lee (The Jabberwocky), Paul Whitehouse (Thackery Earwicket - The March Hare), Michael Sheen (Nivens McTwisp - The White Rabbit), Barbara Windsor (Mallymkun - The Dormouse). Computer-animated and live action reinvention of the classic story. *Dir.* Tim Burton.
Alice's Adventures in Wonderland (1972) Fiona Fullerton (Alice), Michael Crawford (White Rabbit), Robert Helpmann (Mad Hatter), Dudley Moore (Dormouse), Spike Milligan (Gryphon), Peter Sellers (March Hare), Michael Hordern (Mock Turtle), Ralph Richardson (Caterpillar) *Dir.* William Sterling.
Alice's Restaurant (1969) Arlo Guthrie, Pat Quinn, James Broderick. *Dir.* Arthur Penn.
Alien (1979) Tom Skerritt, Sigourney Weaver, John Hurt, Ian Holm, Harry Dean Stanton. *Dir.* Ridley Scott.
Alien Resurrection (1997) Sigourney Weaver, Winona Ryder, Dominique Pinou, Ron Perlman. *Dir.* Jean-Pierre Jeunet.
Aliens (1986) Sigourney Weaver, Carrie Henn, Michael Biehn, Bill Paxton. Sequel to *Alien* which won Academy Award for Special Visual Effects. *Dir.* James Cameron.
Alien 3 (1992) Sigourney Weaver, Charles S Dutton, Charles Dance, Paul McGann. *Dir.* David Fincher.

All about Eve (1950) Bette Davis (Margo Channing), George Sanders (Addison de Witt; Best Supporting Actor, Anne Baxter (Eve), Marilyn Monroe (Miss Caswell). Won Best Film Oscar. As well as Oscars above, Joseph L Mankiewicz won Academy Awards for Writing & Directing. *Dir.* Joseph L Mankiewicz.
All Creatures Great and Small (1974) Anthony Hopkins, Simon Ward, TP McKenna. Sponsored by *Reader's Digest. Dir.* Claude Whatham.
All of Me (1984) Steve Martin (Roger Cobb), Lily Tomlin (Edwina Cutwater), Victoria Tennant (Terry Hoskins) *Dir.* Carl Reiner.
All or Nothing (2002) Timothy Spall, Lesley Manville, Alison Garland, James Cordon, Ruth Sheen, Marion Bailey. *Dir.* Mike Leigh.
All Quiet on the Western Front (1930) Lew Ayres (Paul Baumer), Louis Wolheim (Katczinsky). Based on novel by Erich Maria Remarque. *Dir.* Lewis Milestone.
All That Jazz (1979) Roy Scheider, Jessica Lange, Ann Reinking, Leland Palmer, Ben Vereen. Semi-autobiographical musical of Fosse's life which won Oscars for Editing, Art Direction, Musical Adaptation & Costume Design. *Dir.* Bob Fosse.
All That Money Can Buy (1941) Walter Huston (Mr Scratch), Edward Arnold (Daniel Webster). Bernard Herrmann won Oscar for his music for this Faustian version of Stephen Vincent Benet's *The Devil and Daniel Webster. Dir.* William Dieterle.
All the Fine Young Cannibals (1960) Robert Wagner, Natalie Wood, Pearl Bailey. A fine young pop group took their name from the title of this film. *Dir.* Michael Anderson.
All the King's Men (1949) Broderick Crawford, Joanne Dru, John Ireland, Mercedes McCambridge (Best Film Oscar). Academy Awards for Broderick Crawford (Best Actor) and Mercedes McCambridge (Best Supporting Actress). *Dir.* Robert Rossen.
All the President's Men (1976) Robert Redford, Dustin Hoffman, Jason Robards Jnr. Reconstruction of the White House link with the Watergate affair by the *Washington Post. Dir.* Alan J Pakula.
Almost an Angel (1990) Paul Hogan (Terry Dean), Elias Koteas (Steve), Linda Kozlowski (Rose Garner) *Dir.* John Cornell.
Alphabet Murders, The (1965) Tony Randall, Robert Morley, Anita Ekberg, Margaret Rutherford (cameo role as Miss Marple). Based on *The ABC Murders* by Agatha Christie. Notable for the fact that Randall plays several characters as well as Poirot. *Dir.* Frank Tashlin.
Always (1989) Richard Dreyfuss, Holly Hunter, Audrey Hepburn. Remake of the 1944 film *A Guy Named Joe* about a dead pilot's ghostly return to matchmake his girlfriend. *Dir.* Steven Spielberg.
Amadeus (1984) F Murray Abraham (Salieri), Tom Hulce (Mozart), Elizabeth Berridge (Constance Mozart). Filmed mainly in Prague. The part of Constance was originally Meg Tilly's but she was injured in a soccer match the day before shooting began. *Dir.* Milos Forman.
Amélie (2001) Audrey Tautou (Amélie), Mathieu Kassovitz (Nino Quincampoix), Rufus (Raphael Poulain). A young woman full of joie de vivre has a rejuvenating effect on the people of a French town. French title: *Le Fabuleux Destin d'Amélie Poulain. Dir.* Jean-Pierre Jeunet.
American Beauty (1999) Kevin Spacey (Lester Burnham), Annette Bening, Thora Birch, Wes Bentley. *Dir.* Sam Mendes.
American Gigolo (1980) Richard Gere, Lauren Hutton. Music by Giorgio Moroder. Christopher Reeve allegedly refused $1 million to play the lead. *Dir.* Paul Schrader.
American Graffiti (1973) Richard Dreyfuss, Ron Howard, Candy Clark. Film was set in 1962 California. *Dir.* George Lucas.
American in Paris, An (1951) Gene Kelly, Oscar Levant, Leslie Caron. *Dir.* Vincente Minnelli.
America's Sweethearts (2001) Julia Roberts, Billy Crystal, Catherine Zeta-Jones, John Cusack, Christopher Walken. *Dir.* Joe Roth.
Amityville Horror, The (1979) James Brolin, Margot Kidder, Rod Steiger, Don Stroud. (The 1982 film *Amityville II: The Possession* was in fact a prequel.) *Dir.* Stuart Rosenberg.
Amour (2012) Jean-Louis Trintignant (Georges Laurent), Emmanuelle Riva (Anne Laurent), Isabelle Huppert (Eva Laurent). The story of a couple's struggle with age-related illness which won the Oscar for Best Foreign Language Film. *Dir.* Michael Haneke.
An Education (2009) Carey Mulligan (Jenny Miller), Peter Sarsgaard (David Goldman), Dominic Cooper (Danny), Rosamund Pike (Helen), Emma Thompson (Miss Walters), Alfred Molina (Jack Miller), Olivia Williams (Miss Stubbs), Cara Seymour (Marjorie Miller). Written by Nick Hornby and Lynn Barber and set in England in 1961. Schoolgirl Jenny is given a lift home by David, an older man, and the two strike up a relationship. *Dir.* Lone Scherfig.
Anaconda (1997) Jennifer Lopez, Ice Cube, Jon Voight, Eric Stoltz. *Dir.* Luis Llosa.
Anastasia (1956) Ingrid Bergman, Yul Brynner, Helen Hayes. Bergman's award-winning performance was all the more noteworthy as this was her comeback after being ostracised for 'immoral behaviour'. *Dir.* Anatole Litvak.
Anchors Aweigh (1945) Frank Sinatra, Gene Kelly, Katherine Grayson. Notable for the homophonic spelling of the title and a memorable dance scene between Gene Kelly and Jerry Mouse. *Dir.* George Sidney.
And God Created Woman (1988) Rebecca DeMornay (Robin Shay), Frank Langella (Jim Tiernan), Donovan Leitch (Pete Moran). Remake of the 1957 classic starring Brigitte Bardot. *Dir.* Roger Vadim.
And Soon The Darkness (1970) Michele Dotrice, Pamela Franklin, Sandor Eles, John Nettleton. Cult film about 2 young nurses on a cycling holiday in France. *Dir.* Robert Fuest.
And Then There Were None (1945) Walter Huston, Barry Fitzgerald, Richard Haydn, Queenie Leonard. GB title: *Ten Little Niggers* (after the novel it was based on by Agatha Christie) *Dir.* René Clair.
And Then There Were None (1974) Oliver Reed, Richard Attenborough, Elke Sommer, Charles Aznavour, Herbert Lom. US title: *Ten Little Indians.* The writer Peter Welbeck is in fact Harry Alan Towers, a curious -character who has made a living out of remaking this film. *Dir.* Peter Collinson.
Angela's Ashes (1999) Emily Watson (Angela), Robert Carlyle, Joe Breen (Young Frank), Ciaran Owen (Adolescent Frank), Michael Legge (Grown-up Frank). Based on Frank McCourt bestseller about the life of a Roman Catholic writer brought up in poverty-stricken Limerick. Ultimately fails to capture the spirit and sense of identity of the Irish people but a touching story of triumph over adversity. *Dir.* Alan Parker.
Angels With Dirty Faces (1938) James Cagney, Pat O'Brien, Dead End Kids, Ann Sheridan, Humphrey Bogart. Memorable final scenes when the gangster goes to the electric chair. *Dir.* Michael Curtiz.
Animal Crackers (1930) Groucho Marx (Captain Spaulding), Chico, Harpo, Zeppo, and Margaret Dumont. Thieves covet a valuable oil painting unveiled at a swank party. *Dir.* Victor Heerman.
Anna and the King of Siam (1946) Irene Dunne, Rex Harrison, Linda Darnell. In 1862 an English governess arrives in Bangkok to teach the 67 children of the King. *Dir.* John Cromwell.
Anna Christie (1930) Greta Garbo, Charles Bickford, Marie Dressler. Prostitute falls in love with a seaman. This was the film in which Garbo first talked. *Dir.* Clarence Brown.
Anna Karenina (1935) Greta Garbo (Anna), Fredric March (Count Vronsky). Based on the Tolstoy novel. *Dir.* Clarence Brown. A 1948 British version starring Vivien Leigh was less successful although the 2012 Tom Stoppard film adaptation of the novel directed by Joe Wright and starring Keira Knightley as Anna Arcadievna Karenina, Aaron Taylor-Johnson as Count Alexei Vronsky and Jude Law as Alexei Karenin won an Oscar for Costume Design.
Anne of Green Gables (1934) Anne Shirley (Anne), Tom Brown. Based on the LM Montgomery novel set on Prince Edward Island and notable for the fact that its star changed her name from Dawn O'Day to Anne Shirley to play the part. *Dir.* George Nicholls Jnr.
Anne of the Thousand Days (1969) Richard Burton (Henry VIII), Geneviève Bujold (Boleyn) John Colicos (Thomas Cromwell). Highly acclaimed film with many Oscar nominations but no awards. *Dir.* Charles Jarrott.
Annie Get Your Gun (1950) Betty Hutton (Annie Oakley), Howard Keel, Edward Arnold. Judy Garland was originally cast but was fired after her displays of temperament. *Dir.* George Sidney.
Annie Hall (1977) Woody Allen, Diane Keaton, Paul Simon, Shelley Duvall. Oscars for Best Picture, Script, Direction Actress. Classic line by Woody Allen: 'Hey, don't knock masturbation. It's sex with someone I love'. *Dir.* Woody Allen.

Another Woman (1988) Gena Rowlands, Mia Farrow, Ian Holm, Gene Hackman. *Dir.* Woody Allen.
Anthony Adverse (1936) Fredric March, Olivia de Havilland, Claude Rains, Akim Tamiroff. Based on the novel by Hervey Allen, this film won minor Academy Awards. *Dir.* Mervyn Le Roy.
Antonia's Line (1995) Willeke van Ammelrooy, Els Dottemans, Jan Decleir. *Dir.* Marleen Gorris.
Antony and Cleopatra (1972) Charlton Heston, Hildegarde Neil, Fernando Rey, John Castle (Octavius). Based on Shakespeare's play. Both Olivier and Orson Welles were sought for the lead. *Dir.* Charlton Heston.
Antz (1998) Voices of Woody Allen, Dan Aykroyd, Anne Bancroft, Sharon Stone, Sylvester Stallone. *Dir.* Eric Darnell and Tim Johnson.
Anything Goes (1936) Bing Crosby, Ethel Merman, Charles Ruggles, Ida Lupino. PG Wodehouse adapted much of the script from the successful Broadway show but only 3 of Cole Porter's songs were retained. *Dir.* Lewis Milestone.
Anything Goes (1956) Bing Crosby, Donald O'Connor, Zizi Jeanmaire, Mitzi Gaynor. Same story of the stars of a musical comedy each signing a different female lead. *Dir.* Robert Lewis.
Apartment, The (1960) Jack Lemmon (CC Baxter), Shirley Maclaine (Fran Kubelik), Fred MacMurray (Jeff D Sheldrake). Insurance co. name: Consolidated Life. Last line of film by Miss Kubelik: 'Shut up and deal'. *Dir.* Billy Wilder.
Apocalypse Now (1979) Martin Sheen, Robert Duvall, Marlon Brando, Harrison Ford. Vittorio Storaro won Oscar for Photography. Harvey Keitel originally played Willard but was replaced by Martin Sheen. *Dir.* Francis Coppola.
Apollo 13 (1995) Tom Hanks, Bill Paxton, Kevin Bacon, Ed Harris, Emile Ann Lloyd. Won Oscar for Sound Effects. *Dir.* Ron Howard.
Arbitrage (2012) Richard Gere (Robert Miller), Susan Sarandon (Ellen Miller), Tim Roth (Det Bryer), Brit Marling (Brooke Miller). A hedge fund manager's life takes a turn for the worse following his attempt to cover up a fraud. *Dir.* Nicholas Jarecki.
Argo (2012) Ben Affleck (Tony Mendez), Bryan Cranston (Jack O'Donnell), Alan Arkin (Lester Siegel), John Goodman (John Chambers). Adapted from the book *The Master of Disguise* by CIA operative Tony Mendez, and Joshuah Berman's 2007 article "The Great Escape" in *Wired* magazine about the "Canadian Caper", in which Mendez led the rescue of six US diplomats from Tehran, Iran, during the 1979 Iran hostage crisis. The film won three Academy Awards. *Dir.* Ben Affleck.
Aria (1987) Theresa Russell, Nicola Swain, Jack Kyle, Marion Peters, Beverley D'Angelo, Elizabeth Hurley, John Hurt, Bridget Fonda. Ten episodes each based on a different opera. *Ten Directors*: Nicolas Roeg, Jean-Luc Godard, Charles Sturridge, Julien Temple, Bruce Beresford, Robert Altman, Franc Roddam, Ken Russell, Derek Jarman, Bill Bryden.
Around the World in Eighty Days (1956) David Niven, Cantinflas, Robert Newton, Shirley Maclaine. Although, winning a Best Film Oscar, this film is more notable for the galaxy of stars that had cameos., e.g. Sinatra, George Raft, John Mills, Noël Coward, Buster Keaton, Marlene Dietrich. *Dir.* Mike Anderson and Kevin McClory.
Arsenic and Old Lace (1942) released 1944. Cary Grant (Mortimer Brewster), Josephine Hull (Abby), Jean Adair (Martha), Raymond Massey (Jonathan), John Alexander (Teddy), Peter Lorre (Dr Einstein), Grant Mitchell (Rev Harper). Two old ladies poison unsuspecting visitors with elderberry wine and have their mad brother, who believes they are yellow fever victims, bury them in the cellar. Raymond Massey was imitating Boris Karloff. *Dir.* Frank Capra.
Arthur (1981) Dudley Moore (Arthur Bach), John Gielgud (Hobson), Liza Minnelli (Linda Marolla). Gielgud won Oscar as Best Supporting Actor and 'Best That You Can Do' won Best Song Oscar. *Dir.* Steve Gordon. A 2011 remake, directed by Jason Winer, with Russell Brand taking over the title role performed poorly at the box office.
Arthur 2: On the Rocks (1988) Dudley Moore (Arthur Bach), John Gielgud (Hobson), Liza Minnelli (Linda Marolla Bach). Brogan Lane, the ex-Mrs Moore, appears briefly as 'Cindy'. *Dir.* Bud Yorkin.
Artist, The (2011) Jean Dujardin (George Valentin), Bérénice Bejo (Peppy Miller), Uggie (Jack - the dog), John Goodman (Al Zimmer), Penelope Ann Miller (Doris Valentin), Malcolm McDowell (The Butler). Story of a fading silent film actor and his relationship with a rising young actress of talking films. The film won five Academy Awards. *Dir.* Michel Hazanavicius.
As Good As It Gets (1997) Jack Nicholson (Best Actor Oscar), Helen Hunt (Best Actor Oscar), Greg Kinnear. *Dir.* James L Brooks.
Ashanti (1979) Michael Caine, Omar Sharif, Peter Ustinov, Rex Harrison, William Holden. Wife of a member of the World Health Organisation is seized by slave traders in West Africa. *Dir.* Richard Fleischer.
Ask a Policeman (1938) Will Hay, Graham Moffatt, Moore Marriott. Classic written by Val Guest and remade by him in 1983 as the somewhat less popular *The Boys in Blue* starring Cannon and Ball. *Dir.* Marcel Varnel.
Asphalt Jungle, The (1950) Sterling Hayden (Dix Handley), Louis Calhern (Alonzo D Emmerich), Marilyn Monroe (Angela Phinlay) *Dir.* John Huston.
Assassination Bureau, The (1968) Oliver Reed, Diana Rigg, Telly Savalas, Curt Jurgens. In 1906, a woman journalist breaks up an international gang of professional killers by falling in love with their leader. *Dir.* Basil Dearden.
Assassins (1995) Sylvester Stallone, Antonio Banderas, Julianne Moore. Hitman decides to quit but is menaced by a younger rival. *Dir.* Richard Donner.
Associate, The (1996) Whoopi Goldberg (Laurel Ayres and 'male' alter ego Robert S Cutty), Dianne Wiest (Sally), Tim Daly, Eli Wallach. *Dir.* Donald Petrie.
Asterix and the Big Fight (1989) Voices of Bill Oddie, Bernard Bresslaw, Ron Moody, Sheila Hancock, Brian Blessed, Peter Hawkins. Asterix attempts to restore the village soothsayer's memory in order to make a potion to defeat the invading Romans. *Dir.* Philippe Grimond.
Atlantis: The Lost Empire (2001) Voices of Michael J Fox (Milo Thatch), Claudia Christian (Helga Sinclair), James Garner (Commander Rourke), John Mahoney (Preston B Whitmore), Corey Burton (Mole), Cree Summer (Princess Kida). Animated film in which a polyglot leads an expedition to discover Atlantis in 1914. *Dir.* Gary Trousdale and Kirk Wise.
Atonement (2007) Keira Knightley (Cecilia Tallis), James McAvoy (Robbie Turner), Saoirse Ronan (Briony Tallis, age 13), Romola Garai (Briony Tallis, age 18), Vanessa Redgrave (Older Briony), Brenda Blethyn (Grace Turner), Harriet Walter (Emily Tallis), Patrick Kennedy (Leon Tallis), Juno Temple (Lola Quincey). A young fledgling writer, Briony Tallis, irrevocably changes the course of several lives when she accuses her older sister's lover of a crime he did not commit. The film comprises four parts, corresponding to the four parts of the novel. Some scenes are shown several times from different perspectives. Screenplay by Christopher Hampton based on the British romance novel by Ian McEwan. *Dir.* Joe Wright.
Attila the Hun (1954) Anthony Quinn, Sophia Loren. *Dir.* Pietro Francisci.
August (1995) Anthony Hopkins, Leslie Phillips, Kate Burton. *Dir.* Anthony Hopkins.
Austin Powers in Goldmember (2002) Mike Myers (Austin Powers/Goldmember/Fat Bastard/Dr Evil), Beyoncé Knowles (Foxxy Cleopatra), Michael Caine (Nigel Powers), Seth Green (Scott Evil), Verne Troyer (Mini-Me), Michael York (Basil Exposition), Robert Wagner (No. 2), Mindy Sterling (Frau Farbissina). *Dir.* Jay Roach.
Austin Powers: International Man of Mystery (1997) Mike Myers, Elizabeth Hurley, Michael York, Mimi Rogers, Robert Wagner, Seth Green. *Dir.* Jay Roach.
Austin Powers: The Spy Who Shagged Me (1999) Mike Myers (Austin Danger Powers/Dr Evil/Fat Bastard), Robert Wagner (No 2), Elizabeth Hurley (Vanessa Kensington Powers), Heather Graham (Felicity Shagwell), Michael York (Basil Exposition), Rob Lowe (Young No. 2), Seth Green (Scott Evil). *Dir.* Jay Roach.
Autumn Leaves (1956) Joan Crawford, Cliff Robertson, Lorne Greene, Vera Miles. Spinster marries a young man who turns out to be a pathological liar and tries to murder her. *Dir.* Robert Aldrich.
Avatar (2009) Sam Worthington (Jake Sully), Zoe Saldana (Neytiri), Sigourney Weaver (Dr Grace Augustine), Stephen Lang (Col Miles Quaritch), Michelle Rodriguez (Trudy Chacon), Giovanni Ribisi (Parker Selfridge), Joel Moore (Norm Spellman), CCH Pounder (Moat), Wes Studi (Eytukan), Laz Alonso (Tsu'tey), Dileep Rao (Dr Max Patel), Matt Gerald (Cpl Lyle Wainfleet), Sean Anthony Moran (Pte Fike). Jake Sully, a paraplegic marine on Earth, is morphed into becoming one of the indigenous population of Pandora, in order to

communicate an evacuation order, but falls in love with the chief's daughter, Neytiri, and becomes torn between following his orders and protecting the world he feels is his home. The film is notable for its stunning 3D effects. *Dir.* James Cameron.

Aviator, The (2004) Leonardo DiCaprio (Howard Hughes), Cate Blanchett (Katharine Hepburn), Kate Beckinsale (Ava Gardner), John C Reilly (Noah Dietrich), Alec Baldwin (Juan Trippe), Alan Alda (Senator Ralph Owen Brewster), Ian Holm (Professor Fitz), Kelli Garner (Faith Domergue), Brent Spiner (Robert Gross), Jude Law (Errol Flynn), Matt Ross (Glenn Odekirk), Adam Scott (Johnny Meyer), Gwen Stefani (Jean Harlow), Willem Dafoe (Roland Sweet), Danny Huston (Jack Frye). Biopic of a 20-year period in the life of Howard Hughes. *Dir.* Martin Scorsese.

Awakening, The (1980) Charlton Heston, Susannah York, Jill Townsend, Stephanie Zimbalist. Based on Bram Stoker novel *Jewel of the Seven Stars* about an archaeologist who believes the spirit of an Egyptian queen has entered the soul of his daughter. *Dir.* Mike Newell.

Awakenings (1990) Robert De Niro (Leonard Lowe) Robin Williams (Dr Sayer) Max Von Sydow (Dr Ingham). Based on factual development in treatment of mental illness. Robin Williams broke De Niro's nose accidentally. *Dir.* Penny Marshall.

Awfully Big Adventure, An (1994) Georgina Cates, Hugh Grant, Alan Rickman, Peter Firth, Prunella Scales, Nicola Pagett. Romance in a Liverpool repertory theatre in 1947. *Dir.* Mike Newell.

Babe (1995) James Cromwell, Magda Szubanski, Roscoe Lee Browne (Narrator). Orphaned piglet is adopted by a sheepdog. Based on a book by Dick King-Smith. *Dir.* Chris Noonan.

Babe, The (1992) John Goodman, Kelly McGillis, Bruce Boxleitner. *Dir.* Arthur Hiller.

Babel (2006) Brad Pitt (Richard Jones), Cate Blanchett (Susan Jones), Mohamed Akhzam (Anwar), Peter Wight (Tom), Harriet Walter (Lilly), Michael Maloney (James). Abdullah, a goatherd, buys a high-powered calibre .270 Winchester M70 rifle and a box of ammunition from his neighbour Hassan to shoot the jackals that have been preying on his goats. Abdullah gives the rifle to his two young sons, Yussef and Ahmed (played by local non-professional actors Boubker Ait El Caid and Said Tarchini), and sends them out to tend the herd, with tragic consequences for a married couple on vacation in the Moroccan desert. The drama completes Gonzalez Iñarritu's Death Trilogy, with *Amores Perros* (2000) and *21 Grams* (2003). *Dir.* Alejandro Gonzalez Iñarritu.

Babette's Feast (1987) Stéphane Audran, Jean-Philippe Lafont, Jarl Kulle, Birgitte Federspiel. Best Foreign Language Oscar for this Danish film about a Lottery winner laying on an enormous banquet. The original story on which the film was based was written by Karen Blixen. *Dir.* Gabriel Axel.

Baby Doll (1956) Karl Malden, Eli Wallach, Carroll Baker. *Dir.* Elia Kazan.

Back to the Future (1985) Michael J Fox (Marty McFly), Christopher Lloyd (Dr Emmett Brown), Crispin Glover (George McFly). Notable for cameo roles by Billy Zane as Match, and Huey Lewis, who sings 'Power of Love'. *Dir.* Robert Zemeckis.

Back to the Future II (1989) Michael J Fox (Marty McFly), Christopher Lloyd (Dr Emmett Brown), Lea Thompson (Lorraine Baines). Crispin Glover refused to take part for less than $1 million so lookalikes were used. *Dir.* Robert Zemeckis.

Back to the Future III (1990) Michael J Fox (Marty / Seamus McFly), Christopher Lloyd (Dr Emmett Brown), Lea Thompson (Lorraine Baines / Maggie McFly). Set in the Wild West of the 1880s. *Dir.* Robert Zemeckis.

Backdraft (1991) Kurt Russell (Stephen McCaffrey), William Baldwin (Brian McCaffrey), Rebecca DeMornay (Helen McCaffrey) Robert De Niro (Donald Rimgale) Donald Sutherland (Ronald Bartel). Two brothers track down an arsonist and expose corruption in the fire department. *Dir.* Ron Howard.

Bad and the Beautiful, The (1952) Kirk Douglas (Jonathan Shields), Lana Turner (Georgia Lorrison), Walter Pidgeon (Harry Pebbel), Dick Powell (James Lee Bartlow). A director, a star, a screenwriter and an executive recall their experiences at the hands of a go-getting Hollywood producer. *Dir.* Vincente Minnelli.

Bad Day at Black Rock (1955) Spencer Tracy, Robert Ryan, Lee Marvin, Walter Brennan. Action takes place within 24 hours and concerns a one-armed stranger greeted with hostility by a town with something to hide. *Dir.* John Sturges.

Bad Education (2004) Fele Martinez (Enrique Goded), Gael Garcia Bernal (School Friend/Zahara), Daniel Giménez Cacho (Father Manolo), Lluis Homar (Sir Berenguer), Javier Camara (Paca), Petra Martinez (Mother), Raul Garcia Forneiro (Young Enrique). A director, inspired by meeting an actor who claims to be his childhood lover, makes a film based on his schooldays; its story concerns a transsexual who, as a boy, was abused by a priest and later attempted to blackmail him. *Dir.* Pedro Almodóvar.

Bad Influence (1990) Rob Lowe (Alex), James Spader (Michael Ball). Notable scene where Lowe tries to blow up a car by connecting a broken tail-light with a petrol tank is apparently a terrorist trick from which one important step was omitted. *Dir.* Curtis Hanson.

Badlands (1973) Martin Sheen, Sissy Spacek, Warren Oates. Teenage girl and garbage collector wander across America leaving a trail of murder. *Dir.* Terrence Malick.

Ballad of the Sad Café, The (1991) Vanessa Redgrave (Miss Amelia Evans), Keith Carradine (Marvin Macy), Rod Steiger (Reverend Willin). Tale of a Southern town run by the despotic Redgrave, based on the novella by Carson McCullers. The film was shot at Willie Nelson's farm. *Dir.* Simon Callow.

Bananas (1971) Woody Allen, Louise Lasser, Carlos Montalban, Sylvester Stallone (walk-on as mugger). When asked why he called the film *Bananas*, Allen replied, 'Because there are no bananas in it.' *Dir.* Woody Allen.

Bandit Queen (1994) Seema Biswas, Nirmal Pandey, Manjoj Baipal. Story of Phoolan Devi, a real-life Indian bandit and rape victim. *Dir.* Sheka Kapur.

Bandits (2001) Bruce Willis, Billy Bob Thornton, Cate Blanchett, Troy Garity. *Dir.* Barry Levinson.

Bank Dick, The (1940) WC Fields, Franklin Pangborn, Shemp Howard, Jack Norton. Fields wrote the script using his nom de plume of Mahatma Kane Jeeves, which derived from characters in old English plays. They would say 'M'Hat, M'cane, Jeeves'. GB title: *The Bank Detective*. *Dir.* Eddie Cline.

Barabbas (1962) Anthony Quinn, Silvano Mangano, Ernest Borgnine, Jack Palance. The eclipse of the Sun at the beginning was a real one filmed in Nice. *Dir.* Richard Fleischer.

Barb Wire (1996) Pamela Anderson Lee, Temuera Morrison, Victoria Rowell. Set in civil-war-ravaged USA in 2017. *Dir.* David Hogan.

Barbarella (1967) Jane Fonda, John Phillip Law, Milo O'Shea, David Hemmings, Marcel Marceau. Beautiful 40th-century astronaut prevents positronic ray from getting into the wrong hands. *Dir.* Roger Vadim.

Barbarian Invasions, The (2003) Rémy Girard (Rémy), Stéphane Rousseau (Sebastien), Marie-Josée Croze (Nathalie), Marina Hands (Gaelle), Dorothée Berryman (Louise), Johanne Marie Tremblay (Sister Constance), Dominique Michel (Dominique), Louise Portal (Diane). French-Canadian film set in Montreal. A dying philandering academic is gradually reconciled with his son, a wealthy city trader. *Dir.* Denys Arcand.

Barbarosa (1981) Willie Nelson (Barbarosa), Gary Busey (Karl), Isela Vega (Josephina). Old-style Western that was well received by critics. *Dir.* Fred Schepisi.

Barbary Coast (1935) Edward G Robinson, Miriam Hopkins, Joel McCrea, Walter Brennan. Set during the San Francisco gold rush. *Dir.* Howard Hawks.

Barefoot Contessa, The (1954) Humphrey Bogart (Harry Dawes), Ava Gardner (Maria Vargas), Edmond O'Brien (Muldoon). O'Brien won Best Supporting Actor Oscar. *Dir.* Joseph L Mankiewicz.

Barefoot in the Park (1967) Robert Redford (Paul Bratter), Jane Fonda (Corie Bratter), Charles Boyer (Victor Velasco), Mildred Natwick (Ethel Banks). Based on Neil Simon's play. *Dir.* Gene Saks.

Barkleys of Broadway, The (1949) Fred Astaire, Ginger Rogers, Oscar Levant. Judy Garland was originally cast but withdrew through illness. *Dir.* Charles Walters.

Barretts of Wimpole Street, The (1934) Norma Shearer (Elizabeth Barrett), Fredric March (Robert Browning), Charles Laughton (Edward Moulton-Barrett), Maureen O'Sullivan (Henrietta). The 1956 remake starred Jennifer Jones and Bill Travers. *Dir.* Sidney Franklin.

Basic Instinct (1992) Michael Douglas (Nick Curran), Sharon Stone (Catherine Tramell), George Dzundza (Gus), Jeanne Tripplehorn (Dr Beth Garner), Leilani Sarelle (Roxy). Famous for a scene where the knickerless Stone crosses her legs. *Dir.* Paul Verhoeven. Sharon Stone reprised her role in *Basic Instinct 2: Risk Addiction,* opposite David Morrissey as Dr Michael Glass. *Dir.* Michael Caton-Jones.

Basket Case (1982) Kevin Van Hentenryck, Terri Susan Smith, Beverly Bonner. First of 3 (to date) cult films – followed by *Basket Case II* (1990) and *Basket Case 3: The Progeny* (1992) – depicting Siamese twins with attitude. *Dir.* Frank Henenlotter.

Batman (1989) Michael Keaton (Batman), Jack Nicholson (Joker), Kim Basinger (Vicki Vale), Jerry Hall (Alicia) Jack Palance (Grissom). *Batman Returns* (1992) starred Danny De Vito as Penguin (Oswald Cobblepot). *Dir.* Tim Burton.

Batman and Robin (1997) George Clooney (Batman), Chris O'Donnell (Robin), Alicia Silverstone (Batgirl), Arnold Schwarzenegger (Mr Freeze), Uma Thurman (Poison Ivy). Schwarzenegger line: 'Revenge is a dish best served cold' originally heard in *Star Trek: The Wrath of Khan. Dir.* Joel Schumacher.

Batman Begins (2005) Christian Bale (Bruce Wayne/Batman), Michael Caine (Alfred), Liam Neeson (Henri Ducard), Katie Holmes (Rachel Dawes), Gary Oldman (Jim Gordon), Cillian Murphy (Dr Jonathan Crane), Tom Wilkinson (Carmine Falcone), Rutger Hauer (Earle), Ken Watanabe (Ra's Al Ghul), Mark Boone Jnr (Flass), Linus Roache (Thomas Wayne). The story of how Bruce Wayne became what he was destined to be: Batman. *Dir.* Christopher Nolan.

Batman Forever (1995) Val Kilmer (Batman), Tommy Lee Jones (Harvey Two-Face), Jim Carrey (Riddler), Chris O'Donnell (Robin), Nicole Kidman, Drew Barrymore. *Dir.* Joel Schumacher.

Battle of Britain (1969) Laurence Olivier (Dowding), Robert Shaw, Michael Caine, Christopher Plummer, Kenneth More, Susannah York, Trevor Howard, Ralph Richardson, Michael Redgrave, Edward Fox. *Dir.* Guy Hamilton.

Battle of the Bulge (1965) Henry Fonda, Robert Shaw, Robert Ryan, Telly Savalas, Ty Hardin. Story of the German counter-attack in the Ardennes in December 1944. *Dir.* Ken Annakin.

Battle of the River Plate (1956) John Gregson, Anthony Quayle, Peter Finch. US title: *Pursuit of the Graf Spee. Dir.* Emeric Pressburger & Michael Powell.

Beach, The (2000) Leonardo DiCaprio (Richard), Tilda Swinton (Sal), Virginie Ledoyen (Françoise), Guillaume Canet (Etienne), Robert Carlyle (Duffy), Peter Youngblood Hills (Zeph). American traveller discovers a hippy community living by a perfect beach on a remote island in Thailand. *Dir.* Danny Boyle.

Beaches (1988) Bette Midler (CC Bloom), Barbara Hershey (Hillary Whitney Essex). Singer visits her dying friend, a lawyer, and recalls their long and volatile friendship. *Dir.* Garry Marshall.

Bean (1997) Rowan Atkinson, Peter MacNicol, Pamela Reed, Burt Reynolds, John Mills, Peter Egan, Harris Yulin, Richard Gant, Tricia Vessey, Peter Capaldi, Andrew Lawrence. *Dir.* Mel Smith.

Beau Brummell (1954) Stewart Granger, Elizabeth Taylor, Robert Morley (George III), Peter Ustinov (Prince of Wales). Remake of the 1924 film starring John Barrymore and Mary Astor. *Dir.* Curtis Bernhardt.

Beau Geste (1939) Gary Cooper, Ray Milland, Brian Donlevy, Susan Hayward. Remake of the 1926 film starring Ronald Colman and based on PC Wren's novel. *Dir.* William Wellman.

Beautiful Mind, A (2001) Russell Crowe (John Nash), Jennifer Connelly, Ed Harris, Christopher Plummer, Paul Bettany. Biopic of Nobel Prize-winning mathematician John Nash's struggle against mental illness. Multiple Oscar-winning film. *Dir.* Ron Howard.

Beauty and the Beast (1991) Voices of Robby Benson (Beast), Paige O'Hara (Belle), Angela Lansbury (Mrs Potts). Disney classic which became the best-selling video of all time in the USA. *Dir.* Gary Trousdale & Kirk Wise.

Beavis and Butthead Do America (1996) Created by animator Mike Judge. Voices include Robert Stack and Bruce Willis. *Dir.* Mike Judge.

Becket (1964) Richard Burton (Becket), Peter O'Toole (Henry II), John Gielgud, Sian Phillips. Based on Jean Anouilh's bitter stage play. *Dir.* Peter Glenville.

Bed Sitting Room, The (1969) Ralph Richardson, Rita Tushingham, Michael Hordern, Arthur Lowe, Spike Milligan, Harry Secombe, Peter Cook, Dudley Moore. After a nuclear war, survivors turn into bed sitting rooms, cupboards and parakeets. *Dir.* Richard Lester.

Bedazzled (1967) Peter Cook, Dudley Moore, Michael Bates, Raquel Welch, Eleanor Bron. *Dir.* Stanley Donen. Short-order cook is saved from suicide by Mr Spiggott, who offers him seven wishes in exchange for his soul.

Bedknobs and Broomsticks (1971) Angela Lansbury, David Tomlinson, Bruce Forsyth, Tessie O'Shea. *Dir.* Robert Stevenson.

Beetlejuice (1988) Alec Baldwin (Adam), Geena Davis (Barbara), Michael Keaton (Betelgeuse), Winona Ryder (Lydia Deetz). *Dir.* Tim Burton.

Before Sunset (2004) Ethan Hawke (Jesse), Julie Delpy (Celine). Nine years after Jesse and Celine first meet they encounter one another on the French leg of Jesse's book tour. *Dir.* Richard Linklater.

Beguiled, The (1971) Clint Eastwood, Geraldine Page, Elizabeth Hartman, Darleen Carr. Wounded Union soldier hides out in a Confederate girls' school. *Dir.* Don Siegel.

Behind Enemy Lines (2001) Owen Wilson, Gene Hackman, Gabriel Macht, Charles Malik Whitfield, David Keith, Joaquim de Almeida. US naval pilot is shot down over Bosnia and hunted by Serbian troops. *Dir.* John Moore.

Beijing Bastards (1993) Cui Jian, Li Wei, Wu Gang, Bian Tianshuo. Original title: *Beijing Zazhong.* Story of disillusionment by the young Chinese. *Dir.* Zhang Yuan.

Being Human (1994) Robin Williams, John Turturro, Anna Galiena, Theresa Russell (as narrator). Box office flop about a father who fails to provide for his family in five historic eras. *Dir.* Bill Forsyth.

Being John Malkovich (1999) John Cusack, Cameron Diaz, Catherine Keener, John Malkovich. *Dir.* Spike Jonze.

Being There (1979) Peter Sellers, Shirley MacLaine, Melvyn Douglas. Melvyn Douglas won Best Supporting Actor Oscar for this film about a simple gardener who becomes philosopher and sage to the American people. *Dir.* Hal Ashby.

Bell, Book and Candle (1958) James Stewart, Kim Novak, Jack Lemmon, Hermione Gingold. Publisher slowly realises that his girlfriend is a witch. *Dir.* Richard Quine.

Belles of St Trinian's, The (1954) Alastair Sim, George Cole (Flash Harry), Joyce Grenfell, Beryl Reid, Irene Handl. Based on Ronald Searle's cartoons. *Dir.* Frank Launder.

Bells of St Mary's, The (1945) Bing Crosby (Father O'Malley), Ingrid Bergman (Sister Benedict). Sequel to *Going My Way. Dir.* Leo McCarey.

Belstone Fox, The (1973) Eric Porter, Rachel Roberts, Dennis Waterman, Jeremy Kemp, Bill Travers. Based on the novel *The Ballad of the Belstone Fox* by David Rook. *Dir.* James Hill.

Ben Hur (1925) Ramon Novarro, Francis X Bushman, Carmel Myers. Based on the Lew Wallace novel. Originally, Charles Brabin was director and George Walsh the star; both were replaced when Louis Mayer saw the first rushes. *Dir.* Fred Niblo.

Ben Hur (1959) Charlton Heston, Haya Harareet, Jack Hawkins, Stephen Boyd, Hugh Griffith. Multi-award-winning film but critics generally regard the 1925 silent epic as definitive. *Dir.* William Wyler.

Bend it Like Beckham (2002) Parminder K Nagra, Keira Knightley, Jonathan Rhys-Meyers, Anupam Kher, Shaznay Lewis. Teenage London girl wants to become a professional footballer but is thwarted by her Punjabi Sikh parents, who want her to study law. *Dir.* Gurinder Chadha.

Beneath the Planet of the Apes (1970) James Franciscus, Charlton Heston, Linda Harrison, Kim Hunter. Sequel to *Planet of the Apes. Dir.* Ted Post.

Benji (1974) Peter Breck, Edgar Buchanan, Christopher Connelly. Popular film about a stray mongrel dog who saves two kidnapped children. *Dir.* Joe Camp.

Benny Goodman Story (1955) Steve Allen (Goodman), Donna Reed, Berta Gersten, Harry James, Gene Krupa, Sammy Davis Snr. Steve Allen went on to host one of America's leading variety shows on television. *Dir.* Valentine Davies.

Beowulf (2007) Ray Winstone (Beowulf/Golden Man/Dragon), Angelina Jolie (Grendel's Mother), Anthony Hopkins (King Hrothgar), Crispin Glover (Grendel), John Malkovich (Unferth), Robin Wright Penn (Wealthow). IMAX 3D experience based on the anonymous epic poem *Beowulf.* The warrior Beowulf fights and defeats the monster Grendel, and later has to deal with Grendel's monstrous mother, who begins killing townsfolk out of revenge. *Dir.* Robert Zemeckis.

Bequest to the Nation (1973) Peter Finch, Glenda Jackson, Michael Jayston, Margaret Leighton, Anthony Quayle. US title: *The Nelson Affair.* Story of Nelson's long affair with the tempestuous Lady Hamilton. *Dir.* James Cellan Jones.

Bespoke Overcoat, The (1956) Alfie Bass, David Kossoff. Won Academy Award for Best Short Film and launched its stars as successful TV actors. *Dir.* Jack Clayton.

Best Exotic Marigold Hotel, The (2012) Judi Dench (Evelyn Greenslade), Bill Nighy (Douglas Ainslie), Penelope Wilton (Jean Ainslie), Maggie Smith (Muriel Donnelly), Tom Wilkinson (Graham Dashwood), Ronald Pickup (Norman Cousins), Celia Imrie (Madge Hardcastle), Dev Patel (Sonny). A group of British pensioners move to a retirement hotel in India, run by the young and enthusiastic Sonny Kapoor. *Dir.* John Madden.

Best Years of Our Lives, The (1946) Fredric March, Myrna Loy, Teresa Wright, Dana Andrews, Virginia Mayo, Hoagy Carmichael. Multi-award-winning film notable for the performance of Harold Russell, a veteran who had lost his hands; he had no previous acting experience. *Dir.* William Wyler.

Beverly Hillbillies, The (1993) Diedrich Bader, Dabney Coleman, Erika Elaniak, Cloris Leachman, Buddy Ebsen, Zsa Zsa Gabor, Dolly Parton. *Dir.* Penelope Spheeris.

Beverly Hills Cop (1984) Eddie Murphy (Axel Foley), Judge Reinhold (Det Billy Rosewood), Steven Berkoff (Victor Maitland). Detroit cop races to Los Angeles to track down the killers of his best friend. *Dir.* Martin Brest.

Beverly Hills Cop 2 (1987) Eddie Murphy (Axel Foley), Judge Reinhold (Det Billy Rosewood), Brigitte Nielsen (Karla Fry). Ironically Sylvester Stallone was to play Axel Foley in the original film and his ex Brigitte Nielsen appears in this sequel. *Dir.* Tony Scott.

Beverly Hills Cop 3 (1994) Eddie Murphy (Axel Foley), Judge Reinhold (Det Billy Rosewood), John Saxon. Cop discovers that the head of security at a Los Angeles theme park is a murderer. *Dir.* Tony Scott.

Beyond Bedlam (1994) Craig Fairbrass, Elizabeth Hurley, Keith Allen, Anita Dobson, Georgina Hale. *Dir.* Vadim Jean.

Beyond the Poseidon Adventure (1979) Michael Caine, Telly Savalas, Karl Malden, Sally Field. Not so much a sequel, more an alternative ending to the original. *Dir.* Irwin Allen.

Bible, The (1966) Michael Parks (Adam), Ulla Bergryd (Eve), Richard Harris (Cain), John Huston (Noah), George C Scott (Abraham), Peter O'Toole (the 3 Angels). Remembered for Huston's whispered commentary and the eye-catching photography as well as Toshiro Mayuzumi's musical interpretation. *Dir.* John Huston.

Big (1988) Tom Hanks (Josh Baskin), Elizabeth Perkins (Susan), Robert Loggia (MacMillan). Story of 12-yr-old who wishes he were 'Big' and wakes up 20 yrs older. Steven Spielberg was originally going to direct and Harrison Ford to star. *Dir.* Penny Marshall.

Big Business (1929) Oliver Hardy, Stan Laurel, James Finlayson. Laurel & Hardy classic about their failure to sell a Christmas tree to a belligerent householder. Memorable for the scene of mutual destruction. *Dir.* James W Horne.

Big Business (1988) Bette Midler (Sadie Shelton / Ratcliff), Lily Tomlin (Rose Shelton / Ratcliff). Story of twins mixed up at birth. *Dir.* Jim Abrahams.

Big Chill, The (1983) Tom Berenger (Sam), Glenn Close (Sarah), William Hurt (Nick), Jeff Goldblum (Michael), Kevin Kline (Harold), Meg Tilly (Chloe). Story of a students' reunion after the suicide of one of them. Kevin Costner plays the corpse, Alex, although only his hands, torso and legs are seen in the final version. *Dir.* Lawrence Kasdan.

Big Country, The (1958) Gregory Peck, Jean Simmons, Charlton Heston, Burl Ives, Carol Baker, Charles Bickford, Chuck Connors. Story of the Terrills' and the Hannesseys' feud over water rights. Burl Ives won Best Supporting Actor Oscar. *Dir.* William Wyler.

Big Fat Liar (2002) Frankie Muniz, Paul Giamatti, Amanda Bynes, Amanda Detmer, Lee Majors. *Dir.* Shawn Levy.

Big Fish (2003) Ewan McGregor (Ed Bloom (young)), Albert Finney (Ed Bloom (senior)), Billy Crudup (Will Bloom), Jessica Lange (Sandra Bloom (senior)), Helena Bonham Carter (Jenny (young and senior) and The Witch), Alison Lohman (Sandra Bloom (young)), Robert Guillaume (Dr Bennett (senior)), Matthew McGrory (Karl the Giant), Loudon Wainwright (Beamen), Steve Buscemi (Norther Winslow), Danny DeVito (Amos Calloway). A salesman, prone to telling fantastic tales, reconciles with his son. *Dir.* Tim Burton.

Big Hand for the Little Lady, A (1966) Henry Fonda, Joanne Woodward, Jason Robards, Kevin McCarthy, Charles Bickford, Burgess Meredith. GB title: *Big Deal at Dodge City* (though the action, in fact, takes place in Laredo). *Dir.* Fielder Cook.

Big Man, The (1990) Liam Neeson, Joanne Whalley-Kilmer, Billy Connolly, Ian Bannen. Unemployed miner becomes a bare-knuckle fighter. *Dir.* David Leland.

Big Sleep, The (1946) Humphrey Bogart (Philip Marlowe), Lauren Bacall (Vivian Sherwood Rutledge), John Ridgely (Eddie Mars), Martha Vickers (Carmen Sternwood). Based on Raymond Chandler's Novel but adapted by William Faulkner, Leigh Brackett and Jules Furthman. (Alternative version with 18 minutes of different footage exists.) *Dir.* Howard Hawks.

Big Sleep, The (1978) Robert Mitchum (Philip Marlowe), Sarah Miles, Richard Boone, Candy Clark, James Stewart, Edward Fox, Oliver Reed, Richard Todd. Remake of the 1946 film but set in London. *Dir.* Michael Winner.

Big Trouble in Little China (1986) Kurt Russell (Jack Burton), Kim Cattrall (Gracie Law). *Dir.* John Carpenter.

Bill and Ted's Excellent Adventure (1989) Keanu Reeves (Ted 'Theodore' Logan), Alex Winter (Bill S Preston). Napoleon, Billy the Kid, Socrates, Freud, Genghis Khan, Joan of Arc and Abe Lincoln are some of the famous people met on their journey. *Dir.* Stephen Herek.

Billy Bathgate (1991) Dustin Hoffman, Nicole Kidman, Bruce Willis. Based on EL Doctorow's novel. Teenager becomes an assistant to top gangster Dutch Schultz. *Dir.* Robert Benton.

Billy Budd (1962) Peter Ustinov, Robert Ryan, Terence Stamp, Melvyn Douglas, David McCallum. Based on Herman Melville's novel about the young Billy Budd, who kills the sadistic master-at-arms of a British warship in 1797. *Dir.* Peter Ustinov.

Billy Elliot (2000) Julie Walters (Mrs Wilkinson), Jamie Bell (Billy Elliot), Gary Lewis (Billy's Dad), Jamie Draven (Tony). Young son of a working-class miner has aspirations to become a ballet dancer. *Dir.* Stephen Daldry.

Billy Liar (1963) Tom Courtenay, Julie Christie, Wilfred Pickles, Leonard Rossiter. Written by Keith Waterhouse and inspired by *The Secret Life of Walter Mitty. Dir.* John Schlesinger.

Birdcage, The (1996) Robin Williams, Nathan Lane, Gene Hackman, Dianne Wiest. Remake of French film, *La Cage aux Folles.* Son of a homosexual club-owner persuades his father to act the heterosexual with his future very conservative in-laws. *Dir.* Mike Nichols.

Birdman of Alcatraz (1962) Burt Lancaster (Stroud), Karl Malden, Thelma Ritter, Edmond O'Brien, Neville Brand, Telly Savalas. True story of Robert Stroud, who spent nearly 60 years in prison and made a name for himself as an ornithologist. *Dir.* John Frankenheimer.

Birds, The (1963) Rod Taylor, Tippi Hedren, Jessica Tandy, Suzanne Pleshette. Birds turn against humans. Action takes place at Bodega Bay, California. *Dir.* Alfred Hitchcock.

Birdy (1984) Matthew Modine (Birdy), Nicolas Cage (Al Columbato). *Dir.* Alan Parker.

Birth of a Nation (1915) Lillian Gish, Henry B Walthall, Mae Marsh, Donald Crisp. Originally *The Clansman,* this story of US Civil War strife was the first big screen epic. *Dir.* DW Griffith.

Black Beauty (1994) Alan Cummings (voice), Sean Bean, David Thewlis, Jim Carter, Peter Davison, Eleanor Bron, Peter Cook. Story is told by the horse itself. *Dir.* Caroline Thompson.

Black Hawk Down (2001) Josh Hartnett, Eric Bana, Tom Sizemore, Ewan McGregor, Sam Shepard, William Fichtner. Graphic war film set in 1993 troubled Mogadishu. Won Oscars for sound and editing. *Dir.* Ridley Scott.

Black Narcissus (1946) Deborah Kerr, Sabu, Jean Simmons, Flora Robson. Anglo-Catholic nuns in the Himalayas have trouble with climate and morale. *Dir.* Michael Powell & Emeric Pressburger.

Black Robe (1991) Lothaire Bluteau, Aden Young, Sandrine Holt. Jesuit priest travels through Quebec to convert the Indians in the 17th century. *Dir.* Bruce Beresford.

Black Swan (2010) Natalie Portman (Nina Sayers/The Swan Queen), Mila Kunis (Lily/The Black Swan), Vincent Cassel (Thomas Leroy/The Gentleman), Barbara Hershey (Erica Sayers/The Queen), Winona Ryder (Beth MacIntyre/The Dying Swan), Benjamin Millepied (David Moreau/The Prince). Plot revolves around the casting of a production of Tchaikovsky's *Swan Lake* ballet by a prestigious New York City company. *Dir.* Darren Aronofsky.

Blackboard Jungle, The (1955) Glenn Ford, Anne Francis, Louis Calhern, Sidney Poitier, Vic Morrow. Notable for the music of Bill Haley and the Comets. *Dir.* Richard Brooks.

Blackmail (1929) Anny Ondra, Sara Allgood, Charles Paton. Hitchcock's first talkie involves a Scotland Yard inspector who finds his girl is involved in a murder but conceals the fact and is blackmailed. *Dir.* Alfred Hitchcock.

Blade Runner (1982) Harrison Ford (Deckard), Rutger Hauer (Roy Batty), Sean Young (Rachel), Daryl Hannah (Pris). Set in LA in 2019. Ridley Scott released his 'Director's Cut' in 1992 which had a more satisfactory conclusion. Based on the novel *Do Androids Dream of Electric Sheep?* by Philip K Dick. *Dir.* Ridley Scott.

Blair Witch Project, The (1999) Heather Donahue, Michael C Williams, Joshua Leonard. *Dir.* Daniel Myrick and Eduardo Sanchez.

Blair Witch 2: Book of Shadows (2000) Tristen Skyler, Stephen B Turner, Jeffery Donovan. *Dir.* Joe Berlinger.

Blazing Saddles (1974) Cleavon Little, Gene Wilder, Slim Pickens, Mel Brooks, Madeline Kahn. Black railroad worker and an alcoholic ex-gunfighter foil a crooked attorney. Famous for its beans scene. *Dir.* Mel Brooks.

Blind Shaft (2003) Li Yixiang (Song Jinming), Wang Shuangbao (Tang Zhaoyang). Set in northern China. Two workmen blackmail mine owners into paying them compensation for the deaths of their fellow workers due to deficiencies in their working environment. *Dir.* Li Yang.

Blind Side, The (2009) Sandra Bullock (Leigh Anne Tuohy), Tim McGraw (Sean Tuohy), Kathy Bates (Miss Sue), Quinton Aaron (Michael 'Big Mike' Oher), Lily Collins (Collins Tuohy), Jae Head (Sean 'SJ' Tuohy Jr), Ray McKinnon (Coach Cotton), Kim Dickens (Mrs Boswell), Adriane Lenox (Denise Oher), Catherine Dyer (Mrs Smith). American football drama written by John Lee Hancock, and based on Michael Lewis's 2006 book *The Blind Side: Evolution of a Game.* The true-life action concerns the rise of Mike Oher from his humble beginnings, his adoption by Sean and Leigh Anne Tuohy, and his eventual success as an offensive lineman playing for the Baltimore Ravens of the NFL. *Dir.* John Lee Hancock.

Blob, The (1958) Steve McQueen, Aneta Corseaut, Earl Rowe. *Dir.* Irwin S Yeaworth.

Blockheads (1938) Oliver Hardy, Stan Laurel, Billy Gilbert. Twenty years after WW1, Stan is still guarding a trench because nobody told him to stop. *Dir.* John G Blystone.

Blondie (1938) Arthur Lake, Penny Singleton, Daisy the Dog, Jonathan Hale. Mr & Mrs Small Town America, Dagwood Bumstead and wife Blondie, spawned many sequels. *Dir.* Frank R Strayer.

Blow (2001) Johnny Depp (George Jung), Penelope Cruz, Franka Potente, Rachel Griffiths, Jordi Molla. True-life story of a Boston boy who grows up in the 1970s to become the biggest smuggler of cocaine into the United States from Colombia. *Dir.* Ted Demme.

Blow Up (1966) David Hemmings, Sarah Miles, Vanessa Redgrave. London fashion photographer thinks he sees a murder, but the evidence disappears. *Dir.* Michelangelo Antonioni.

Blue Angel, The (1930) Emil Jannings, Marlene Dietrich (Lola). Story of a professor's infatuation with a nightclub singer. *Dir.* Josef von Sternberg.

Blue Bird, The (1940) Shirley Temple, Johnny Russell, Gale Sondergaard (the cat), Eddie Collins (the dog). Two children of a poor woodcutter seek the bluebird of happiness. *Dir.* Walter Lang.

Blue Bird, The (1976) Elizabeth Taylor (Mother, Maternal Love, Light & The Witch), Ava Gardner, Jane Fonda, George Cole. Remake of the 1940 classic. *Dir.* George Cukor.

Blue Dahlia (1946) Alan Ladd, Veronica Lake, William Bendix, Howard de Silva. Raymond Chandler story of a returning war veteran who finds his faithless wife murdered and himself suspected. *Dir.* George Marshall.

Blue Lagoon (1949) Jean Simmons, Donald Houston, Cyril Cusack. Shipwrecked boy and girl grow up on a desert island. *Dir.* Frank Launder.

Blue Lagoon (1980) Brooke Shields, Christopher Atkins, Leo McKern. Remake of the 1949 film. *Dir.* Randal Kleiser.

Blue Lamp, The (1949) Jack Warner, Jimmy Hanley, Dirk Bogarde, Dora Bryan. Famous for its opening shooting scene and the subsequent reincarnation of George Dixon for *Dixon of Dock Green,* which ran for 20 years on Television. *Dir.* Basil Dearden.

Blue Max, The (1966) George Peppard, James Mason, Ursula Andress, Jeremy Kemp. *Dir.* John Guillermin.

Blues Brothers, The (1980) John Belushi (Jake), Dan Aykroyd (Elwood), Carrie Fisher, Cab Calloway. *Dir.* John Landis.

Bob and Carol and Ted and Alice (1969) Robert Culp, Natalie Wood, Elliott Gould, Dyan Cannon. *Dir.* Paul Mazursky.

Body Heat (1981) William Hurt, Kathleen Turner, Richard Crenna, Ted Danson. Florida lawyer becomes involved with a married woman and they plot to kill her husband. *Dir.* Lawrence Kasdan.

Bodyguard, The (1992) Kevin Costner (Frank Farmer), Whitney Houston (Rachel Marron), Gary Kemp (Sy Spector). *Dir.* Mick Jackson.

Bonfire of the Vanities (1990) Tom Hanks (Sherman McCoy), Bruce Willis (Peter Fallow), Melanie Griffith (Maria Ruskin). Based on Tom Wolfe's novel of the same name. *Dir.* Brian de Palma.

Bonnie and Clyde (1967) Warren Beatty (Clyde Barrow), Faye Dunaway (Bonnie Parker), Gene Hackman (Buck), Estelle Parsons, Michael J Pollard, Gene Wilder. Estelle Parsons won Academy Award for Best Supporting Actress. *Dir.* Arthur Penn.

Boom! (1968) Elizabeth Taylor, Richard Burton, Noël Coward. Based on Tennessee Williams's play *The Milk Train Doesn't Stop Here Anymore. Dir.* Joseph Losey.

Borat: Cultural Learnings of America For Make Benefit Glorious Nation Of Kazakhstan (2006) Sacha Baron Cohen (Borat Sagdiyev), Ken Davitian (Azamat Bagatov), Luenell (Luenell), Pamela Anderson (as herself). Controversial comedy built around a character from Baron Cohen's television spoof. Kazakhstani TV talking head Borat (Cohen) is dispatched to the United States to report on the greatest country in the world. With a documentary crew in tow, Borat becomes more interested in locating and marrying Pamela Anderson. *Dir.* Larry Charles.

Born on the Fourth of July (1989) Tom Cruise (Ron Kovic), Kyra Sedgwick (Donna), Willem Dafoe, Tom Berenger. *Dir.* Oliver Stone.

Bourne Identity, The (2002) Matt Damon, Franka Potente, Chris Cooper, Clive Owen, Brian Cox. Story of a secret agent trying to piece together the threads of his life whilst suffering total amnesia. *Dir.* Doug Liman.

Bourne Legacy, The (2012) Jeremy Renner (Aaron Cross/Kenneth Kitsom), Rachel Weisz (Dr Marta Shearing), Edward Norton (Eric Byer), Albert Finney (Dr Albert Hirsch), Stacy Keach (Mark Turso). Jason Bourne does not appear in the film as Matt Damon, who played Bourne in the first three films, chose not to return for a fourth film. However, there are several references to him throughout the film. Aaron Cross, a member of Operation Outcome, a US Defense Department black ops program whose agents are genetically enhanced, goes on the run once Bourne's actions lead to the public exposure of Operations Treadstone and Blackbriar. *Dir.* Tony Gilroy.

Bourne Supremacy, The (2004) Sequel to *The Bourne Identity* in which Jason Bourne (Matt Damon), a former CIA assassin attached to their Special Activities Division, continues to suffer from psychogenic amnesia but begins to get flashbacks. *Dir.* Paul Greengrass.

Bourne Ultimatum, The (2007) Third film of the series based on the Robert Ludlum novel of the same name. Jason Bourne travels through Europe in search of his identity. *Dir.* Paul Greengrass.

Bowling for Columbine (2002) Documentary examining America's attitude towards guns, beginning with the shooting rampage by students at Columbine High School. Cleverly edited film to ensure the point is made effectively. *Dir.* Michael Moore.

Box of Moonlight (1996) John Turturro (Al Fountain), Sam Rockwell (The Kid). *Dir.* Tom DiCillo.
Boxing Helena (1993) Julian Sands, Sherilyn Fenn, Bill Paxton, Art Garfunkel. Most memorable for Kim Basinger being sued for changing her mind over starring in it. Court ordered her to pay $8 million but studio settled for $3 million. *Dir.* Jennifer Chambers Lynch.
Boys Don't Cry (1999) Peter Sarsgaard (John), Brendan Sexton III (Tom), Alison Folland (Kate). *Dir.* Kimberly Peirce.
Boys from Brazil, The (1978) Gregory Peck (Josef Mengele), Laurence Olivier, James Mason, Lilli Palmer. Based on the Ira Levin novel. *Dir.* Franklin Schaffner.
Brassed Off (1996) Peter Postlethwaite (Danny), Tara Fitzgerald (Gloria), Ewan McGregor. *Dir.* Mark Herman.
Brave (2012) Voices of Kelly Macdonald (Merida), Billy Connolly (King Fergus of Dunbroch), Emma Thompson (Queen Elinor), Julie Walters (The Witch), Robbie Coltrane (Lord Dingwall), Kevin McKidd (Lord MacGuffin/Young MacGuffin), Craig Ferguson (Lord Macintosh), John Ratzenberger (Gordon, the guard). Computer-animated fantasy produced by Pixar Animation Studios and distributed by Disney. Set in the Scottish Highlands, Merida, a skilled archer defies an age-old custom, causing mayhem in the kingdom. *Dir.* Mark Andrews and Brenda Chapman
Braveheart (1995) Mel Gibson, Sophie Marceau, Patrick McGoohan, Ian Bannen. *Dir.* Mel Gibson.
Brazil (1985) Jonathan Pryce, Robert De Niro, Michael Palin, Peter Vaughan, Bob Hoskins. *Dir.* Terry Gilliam.
Breaking the Waves (1996) Emily Watson, Stellan Skarsgard, Katrin Cartlidge, Jean-Marc Barr. Award-winning film set in Scotland. A woman humiliates herself in the hope of saving the life of her husband, paralysed in an oil rig accident. *Dir.* Lars von Trier.
Bridge on the River Kwai (1957) Alec Guinness (Colonel Nicholson), Sessue Hayakawa (Colonel Saito), William Holden (Shears), Jack Hawkins (Major Warden). Based on the novel by Pierre Boulle. *Dir.* David Lean.
Bridges of Madison County (1995) Clint Eastwood, Meryl Streep, Annie Corley. Written by Richard LaGravenese. *Dir.* Clint Eastwood.
Bridget Jones's Diary (2001) Renée Zellweger, Hugh Grant, Colin Firth, Gemma Jones, Jim Broadbent. Cameo performances by Jeffrey Archer and Salman Rushdie. *Dir.* Sharon Maguire.
Brief Encounter (1945) Celia Johnson (Laura Jesson), Trevor Howard (Alec Harvey), Stanley Holloway, Joyce Carey. Based on a Noël Coward play, *Still Life.* The theme music was Rachmaninov's Piano Concerto No 2 and the railway station was Carnforth. *Dir.* David Lean.
Brigadoon (1954) Gene Kelly, Cyd Charisse, Van Johnson. Scottish village awakens once every hundred years. *Dir.* Vincente Minnelli.
Bringing Up Baby (1938) Katharine Hepburn (Susan), Cary Grant (David Huxley), May Robson. The baby of the title was, in fact, a leopard. *Dir.* Howard Hawks.
Brokeback Mountain (2006) Heath Ledger (Ennis Del Mar), Jake Gyllenhaal (Jack Twist), Randy Quaid (Joe Aguirre), Valerie Planche (Waitress), David Trimble (Basque), Michelle Williams (Alma). Based on the E Annie Proulx story about a forbidden and secretive relationship between two cowboys and their lives over the years. The film won three Academy Awards: Best Achievement in Directing (Ang Lee), Best Achievement in Music Written for Motion Pictures, Original Score (Gustavo Santaolalla), Best Writing, Screenplay Based on Material Previously Produced or Published (Larry McMurtry and Diana Ossana). *Dir.* Ang Lee.
Broken Arrow (1996) John Travolta, Christian Slater, Samantha Mathis. *Dir.* John Woo.
Broken Embraces (2009) Penelope Cruz (Lena), Lluís Homar (Mateo Blanco/Harry Caine), Blanca Portillo (Judit), Jose Luis Gomez (Ernesto Martel), Tamar Novas (Diego), Ruben Ochandiano (Ray X), Angela Molina (Lena's mother). Harry Caine is a blind writer who shares his life with his agent Judit and her adult son Diego. Slowly, events in the present begin to bring back memories of the past. *Dir.* Pedro Almodovar.
Browning Version, The (1951) Michael Redgrave, Jean Kent, Nigel Patrick, Wilfrid Hyde-White, Bill Travers. Based on Terence Rattigan's one-act play. *Dir.* Anthony Asquith.
Browning Version, The (1994) Albert Finney, Greta Scacchi, Matthew Modine, Julian Sands, Michael Gambon. Ronald Howard's adaptation of Terence Rattigan play. *Dir.* Mike Figgis.
Brubaker (1980) Robert Redford, Yaphet Kotto, Jane Alexander, Morgan Freeman, Murray Hamilton. Setting: Wakefield Prison Farm. *Dir.* Stuart Rosenberg.
Brüno (2009) Sacha Baron Cohen (Brüno), Gustaf Hammarsten (Lutz), Clifford Bañagale (Diesel, Brüno's lover), Josh Meyers (Kookus). Irreverent comedy, the third such effort based on characters from *Da Ali G Show,* following *Ali G Indahouse* and *Borat.* Gay Austrian fashionista Brüno attempts to make it big in America. *Dir.* Larry Charles.
Bugsy Malone (1976) Scott Baio, Jodie Foster, Florrie Dugger. Parts are played by children and the guns fire ice cream. *Dir.* Alan Parker.
Bullitt (1968) Steve McQueen, Jacqueline Bisset, Robert Vaughn, Robert Duvall. Based on the novel *Mute Witness* by Robert L Pike. *Dir.* Peter Yates.
Burbs, The (1989) Tom Hanks, Bruce Dern, Carrie Fisher, Corey Feldman. *Dir.* Joe Dante.
Buster (1988) Phil Collins, Julie Walters (June Edwards), Larry Lamb, Stephanie Lawrence, Martin Jarvis. *Dir.* David Green.
Butch Cassidy and the Sundance Kid (1969) Paul Newman, Robert Redford, Katharine Ross. 'Raindrops Keep Falling on My Head' won Oscar for Best Song. *Dir.* George Roy Hill.
Butterfield 8 (1960) Elizabeth Taylor, Laurence Harvey, Eddie Fisher. Taylor won Best Actress Oscar for her role as a society call girl. The title *Butterfield 8* was her telephone number. *Dir.* Daniel Mann.
Cabaret (1972) Liza Minnelli, Joel Grey, Michael York. Based on the novel *Goodbye to Berlin* by Christopher Isherwood and John Van Druten's play *I Am a Camera. Dir.* Bob Fosse.
Cabin in the Sky (1943) Eddie 'Rochester' Anderson (Little Joe), Lena Horne (Georgia Brown), Ethel Waters (Petunia), Louis Armstrong. All black cast. *Dir.* Vincente Minnelli.
Cable Guy, The (1996) Jim Carrey, Matthew Broderick, George Segal. *Dir.* Ben Stiller.
Caché – see **Hidden** (2006)
Cactus Jack (1979) Kirk Douglas, Arnold Schwarzenegger, Ann-Margret. US title: *The Villain. Dir.* Hal Needham.
Caesar and Cleopatra (1945) Claude Rains, Vivien Leigh, Stewart Granger, Flora Robson. Britain's most expensive film to this date was based on George Bernard Shaw's comedy. *Dir.* Gabriel Pascal.
Caine Mutiny, The (1954) Humphrey Bogart (Capt Queeg), José Ferrer (Lt Barney Greenwald), Van Johnson (Lt Steve Maryk), Fred MacMurray (Lt Tom Keefer), Lee Marvin (Meatball), Claude Akins (Horrible). Based on Herman Wouk's novel. *Dir.* Edward Dmytryk.
Calamity Jane (1953) Doris Day, Howard Keel. Memorable for its opening rendition of 'The Deadwood Stage' and the Oscar-winning song 'Secret Love'. *Dir.* David Butler.
California Suite (1978) Michael Caine, Maggie Smith, Walter Matthau, Alan Alda, Jane Fonda, Bill Cosby, Richard Pryor. Misadventures of 4 groups of guests at the Beverly Hills Hotel. *Dir.* Herbert Ross.
Caligula (1979) Malcolm McDowell, John Gielgud, Peter O'Toole, Helen Mirren. *Dir.* Tinto Brass.
Callan (1974) Edward Woodward, Eric Porter, Carl Mohner, Catherine Schell, Peter Egan, Russell Hunter. Aka: *The Neutralizer. Dir.* Don Sharp.
Camille (1936) Greta Garbo (Marguerite Gautier), Robert Taylor (Armand Duval), Lionel Barrymore, Henry Daniell. Based on Alexandre Dumas' novel. *Dir.* George Cukor.
Candyman (1992) Virginia Madsen, Tony Todd, Xander Berkeley, Vanessa Williams. Story of a mythical hook-handed serial killer which had an unsuccessful 1995 sequel *Candyman: Farewell to the Flesh. Dir.* Bernard Rose.
Cape Fear (1991) Robert De Niro (Max Cady), Nick Nolte (Sam Bowden), Jessica Lange (Leigh Bowden), Robert Mitchum (Lt Elgart), Gregory Peck (Lee Heller). Notable for cameo roles of Mitchum, Peck and Martin Balsam, who were all in original 1962 film. *Dir.* Martin Scorsese.

Capote (2005) Philip Seymour Hoffman (Truman Capote), Clifton Collins Jnr (Perry Smith), Craig Archibald (Christopher), Bronwen Coleman (Barbara), Kate Shindle (Rose), David Wilson Barnes (Grayson), Catherine Keener (Harper Lee). In 1959, Truman Capote, a popular writer for the *New Yorker*, learns about the horrific and senseless murder of a family of four in Holcomb, Kansas. Inspired by the story material, Capote and his partner, Harper Lee, travel to the town to research for an article. However, as Capote digs deeper into the story, he is inspired to expand the project into what will prove his greatest work, *In Cold Blood*. Hoffman won the Academy Award for Best Actor for his portrayal of Capote. *Dir.* Bennett Miller.

Captain America (1944) Dick Purcell, Lionel Atwill, Lorna Gray. District Attorney in guise of Capt America battles The Scarab (in guise of a museum curator). *Dir.* John English.

Captain America (1989) Matt Salinger, Ronny Cox, Ned Beatty, Bill Mumy. Captain America is freed from his deep-ice captivity to battle arch-enemy The Red Skull. *Dir.* Albert Pyun.

Captain Corelli's Mandolin (2001) Nicholas Cage (Corelli), Penelope Cruz, John Hurt, Christian Bale, David Morrissey. *Dir.* John Madden.

Captains Courageous (1937) Spencer Tracy, Lionel Barrymore, Freddie Bartholomew, Mickey Rooney. Spoiled rich boy falls off a cruise liner and lives for a while among fisherfolk. *Dir.* Victor Fleming.

Caravaggio (1986) Nigel Terry, Sean Bean, Tilda Swinton, Robbie Coltrane. *Dir.* Derek Jarman.

Caretaker, The (1964) Alan Bates, Robert Shaw, Donald Pleasence. Based on Pinter's play about 2 men who invite a tramp to share their attic. US title: *The Guest. Dir.* Clive Donner.

Carnal Knowledge (1971) Jack Nicholson, Art Garfunkel, Candice Bergen, Ann-Margret, Rita Moreno. *Dir.* Mike Nichols.

Carousel (1956) Gordon Macrae, Shirley Jones, Cameron Mitchell. *Dir.* Henry King.

Carpetbaggers, The (1964) George Peppard, Alan Ladd, Carroll Baker, Martin Balsam, Elizabeth Ashley, Lew Ayres, Archie Moore, Leif Erickson. *Dir.* Edward Dmytryk.

Carrie (1952) Laurence Olivier, Jennifer Jones, Eddie Albert. Based on Theodore Dreiser's novel *Sister Carrie. Dir.* William Wyler.

Carrie (1976) Sissy Spacek, Piper Laurie, Amy Irving, John Travolta. Based on the Stephen King novel. *Dir.* Brian De Palma.

Carrington (1995) Emma Thompson (Carrington), Jonathan Pryce (Strachey), Janet McTeer (Vanessa Bell). Based on Lytton Strachey's book. *Dir.* Christopher Hampton.

Carry On Columbus (1992) Jim Dale (Chris Columbus), Bernard Cribbins (Mort), Maureen Lipman (Countess Esmerelda), Alexei Sayle, Julian Clary, Rik Mayall. Last of the series of Carry Ons. *Dir.* Gerald Thomas.

Carry On Sergeant (1958) Bob Monkhouse, William Hartnell, Kenneth Williams, Charles Hawtrey, Shirley Eaton, Kenneth Connor. First of the series of 30 *Carry Ons. Dir.* Gerald Thomas.

Cars (2006) Voices of Owen Wilson (Lightning McQueen), Paul Newman (Doc Hudson), Bonnie Hunt (Sally Carrera), John Ratzenberger (Mack/Hamm Truck/Abominable Snow Plow/PT Flea Car), Michael Keaton (Chick Hicks), Katherine Helmond (Lizzie). A hot-shot race car named Lightning McQueen gets waylaid in Radiator Springs, where he finds the true meaning of friendship and family. *Dir.* John Lasseter and Joe Ranft.

Carve Her Name With Pride (1958) Virginia McKenna (Violette Szabo), Paul Scofield, Jack Warner, Sydney Tafler. Based on RJ Minney's book about young British WW2 spy shot by a German firing squad. *Dir.* Lewis Gilbert.

Casablanca (1942) Humphrey Bogart (Rick Blaine), Ingrid Bergman (Ilse Lund), Paul Henreid (Victor Laszlo), Claude Rains (Captain Louis Renault), Sydney Greenstreet (Ferrari), Peter Lorre (Ugarte), Conrad Veidt (Major Strasser), Dooley Wilson (Sam). Closing line, 'Louis, I think this is the beginning of a beautiful friendship.' Ronald Reagan and Ann Sheridan were originally cast as the leads. *Dir.* Michael Curtiz.

Casanova (1976) Donald Sutherland, Tina Aumont, Cicely Browne. Aka *Fellini's Casanova. Dir.* Federico Fellini.

Casino (1995) Sharon Stone, Robert De Niro, Joe Pesci, James Woods. *Dir.* Martin Scorsese.

Casino Royale (1967) David Niven, Deborah Kerr, Orson Welles, Peter Sellers, Ursula Andress, Woody Allen, William Holden, Charles Boyer, Jean-Paul Belmondo, Peter O'Toole, John Huston, George Raft. Sir James Bond is called out of retirement to tackle the power of 'SMERSH'. Joe McGrath was originally the sole director but was fired after Sellers walked out and Huston, Ken Hughes, Robert Parrish, Val Guest and Richard Talmadge finished the film.This was the first James Bond book but clearly not the first film. *Dir.* John Huston & others.

Casino Royale (2006) Daniel Craig (James Bond), Eva Green (Vesper Lynd), Mads Mikkelsen (Le Chiffre), Judi Dench (M), Jeffrey Wright (Felix Leiter), Giancarlo Giannini (Mathis), Caterina Murino (Solange), Simon Abkarian (Alex Dimitrios), Isaach De Bankolé (Steven Obanno), Jesper Christensen (Mr White), Ivana Milicevic (Valenka), Tobias Menzies (Villiers), Claudio Santamaria (Carlos), Sebastien Foucan (Mollaka), Malcolm Sinclair (Dryden). *Casino Royale* introduces James Bond before he holds his license to kill. After two professional assassinations, he is elevated to '00' status. Bond's first 007 mission takes him to Uganda where he is to spy on a terrorist, Mollaka. Following a lead to the Bahamas, he encounters Dimitrios and his girlfriend, Solange. He learns that Dimitrios is involved with Le Chiffre, banker to the world's terrorist organisations. Secret Service intelligence reveals that Le Chiffre is planning to raise money in a high-stakes poker game in Montenegro, at Le Casino Royale. MI6 assigns 007 to play against him, knowing that if Le Chiffre loses, it will destroy his organisation. M places Bond under the watchful eye of the beguiling Vesper Lynd. The title song 'You Know My Name' is performed by Chris Cornell. Producer Michael G Wilson appears as the corrupt Montenegrin police chief, continuing his long-standing tradition of Bond film cameos dating from *Goldfinger*. Two major exclusions from the film are the characters of Q and Miss Moneypenny, making this only the second Bond film without Q (*Live and Let Die* being the other) and the first without Moneypenny. *Dir.* Martin Campbell.

Cassandra Crossing, The (1976) Sophia Loren, Richard Harris, Ava Gardner, Burt Lancaster, Martin Sheen, OJ Simpson. *Dir.* George Pan Cosmatos.

Cast a Dark Shadow (1955) Dirk Bogarde, Margaret Lockwood. Wife-murderer marries an ex-barmaid and tries again. *Dir.* Lewis Gilbert.

Cast a Giant Shadow (1966) Kirk Douglas, Angie Dickinson, Chaim Topol, John Wayne, Frank Sinatra, Yul Brynner, Gordon Jackson, Jeremy Kemp, Michael Hordern. Biopic of Colonel David Marcus's fight against the Arabs in the Israel of 1947. *Dir.* Melville Shavelson.

Castaway (1987) Oliver Reed (Gerald Kingsland), Amanda Donohue, Georgina Hale, John Sessions. Based on Lucy Irvine's autobiographical book. *Dir.* Nicolas Roeg.

Casualties of War (1989) Michael J Fox (Eriksson), Sean Penn (Sgt Meserve). Story of the gang rape of a Vietnamese girl. *Dir.* Brian De Palma.

Cat and the Canary, The (1939) Bob Hope (Wally Campbell), Paulette Goddard (Joyce Norman), Gale Sondergaard (Miss Lu). *Dir.* Elliott Nugent.

Cat Ballou (1965) Jane Fonda, Lee Marvin, Nat King Cole, Stubby Kaye. Oscar-winning performances by Lee Marvin as twin brothers. *Dir.* Elliot Silverstein.

Cat on a Hot Tin Roof (1958) Paul Newman (Brick), Burl Ives (Big Daddy), Elizabeth Taylor (Maggie). Based on the play by Tennessee Williams. *Dir.* Richard Brooks.

Cat People (1942) Simone Simon, Tom Conway, Kent Smith. Yugoslavian girl believes she can turn into a panther and deaths follow, although the monster is never seen. *Dir.* Jacques Tourneur.

Cat People (1982) Nastassja Kinski, Malcolm McDowell. Kinky version of the 1942 classic. *Dir.* Paul Schrader.

Catch Me If You Can (2002) Leonardo DiCaprio (Frank Abagnale Jnr), Tom Hanks (Carl Hanratty), Christopher Walken (Frank Abagnale Snr), Martin Sheen (Roger Strong), James Brolin (Jack Barnes), Nathalie Baye (Paula Abagnale), Amy Adams (Brenda Strong). True-life story of a con-man and his attempts to remain one step ahead of an FBI agent. *Dir.* Steven Spielberg.

Catch My Soul (1973) Richie Havens, Lance LeGault, Season Hubley, Tony Joe White. Rock and country musical version of *Othello*. *Dir.* Patrick McGoohan.
Catch 22 (1970) Alan Arkin (Yossarian), Martin Balsam, Richard Benjamin, Art Garfunkel, Bob Newhart, Orson Welles, Martin Sheen, Jon Voight, Anthony Perkins. Based on Joseph Heller's novel. *Dir.* Mike Nichols.
Catholic Boys (1985) Donald Sutherland (Brother Thadeus), John Heard (Brother Timothy). Originally called *Heaven Help Us*. *Dir.* Michael Dinner.
Cats & Dogs (2001) Jeff Goldblum (Professor Brody), Elizabeth Perkins (Mrs Brody), Alexander Pollock (Scott Brody), Miriam Margolyes (Sophie). Story of a Persian cat's attempt to conquer the world, mixing actors and animation. Voices of Tobey Maguire (Lou), Alec Baldwin (Butch), Susan Sarandon (Ivy), Charlton Heston (The Mastiff), Sean Hayes (Mr Tinkles), Joe Pantoliano (Peek), Jon Lovitz (Calico). *Dir.* Lawrence Guterman.
Catwoman (2004) Halle Berry (Patience Phillips/Catwoman), Benjamin Bratt (Tom Lone), Sharon Stone (Laurel Hedare), Lambert Wilson (George Hedare), Frances Conroy (Ophelia). *Dir.* Pitof.
Celebrity (1998) Kenneth Branagh, Hank Azaria, Judy Davis, Leonardo DiCaprio, Melanie Griffith, Winona Ryder. *Dir.* Woody Allen.
Celia (1989) Rebecca Smart (Celia), Nicholas Eadie (Ray). *Dir.* Ann Turner.
Cemetery Man (1994) Rupert Everett, François Hadji-Lazaro, Anna Falci. *Dir.* Michele Soavi.
Central Station (1998) Fernanda Montenegro, Marilia Pera, Vinicius de Oliveira, Soia Lira, Othon Bastos. *Dir.* Walter Salles.
Chain Reaction (1996). Keanu Reeves, Morgan Freeman, Rachel Weisz. *Dir.* Andrew Davis.
Chamber, The (1996) Gene Hackman (Sam Cayhall), Chris O'Donnell (Adam Hall), Faye Dunaway. *Dir.* James Foley.
Champ, The (1931) Wallace Beery, Jackie Cooper. Frances Marion won Oscar for Best Original Story. *Dir.* King Vidor.
Champ, The (1979) Jon Voight, Faye Dunaway, Ricky Schroeder. Remake of the 1931 classic. *Dir.* Franco Zeffirelli.
Champions (1983) John Hurt (Bob Champion), Edward Woodward (Josh Gifford). Story of a jockey's fight against cancer and his subsequent Grand National success in 1981. *Dir.* John Irvin.
Chance of a Lifetime (1950) Bernard Miles, Kenneth More, Hattie Jacques. *Dir.* Bernard Miles.
Changeling (2008) Angelina Jolie (Christine Collins), Jeffrey Donovan (Capt JJ Jones), John Malkovich (Rev Gustav Briegleb), Jason Butler Harner (Gordon Northcott), Michael Kelly (Det Lester Ybarra), Amy Ryan (Carol Dexter), Geoff Pierson (Sammy Hahn). Based on real-life events in 1928 Los Angeles. Christine Collins is a woman who is reunited with her missing son but is sure he is an impostor. The city authorities vilify her as an unfit mother and brand her delusional. *Dir.* Clint Eastwood.
Changing Lanes (2002) Ben Affleck, Samuel L Jackson, Kim Staunton, Toni Collette, Sydney Pollack, William Hurt, Amanda Peet. *Dir.* Roger Michell.
Chaplin (1992) Robert Downey Jnr, Dan Aykroyd (Mack Sennett), Geraldine Chaplin (Hannah Chaplin), Kevin Dunn (J Edgar Hoover), Kevin Kline (Douglas Fairbanks), John Thaw (Fred Karno), Marisa Tomei (Mabel Normand). *Dir.* Richard Attenborough.
Chariots of Fire (1981) Ben Cross (Harold Abrahams), Ian Charleson (Eric Liddell), Nigel Havers. Oscars include: Best Film, Costume Design, Music and Script (Colin Welland). *Dir.* Hugh Hudson.
Charley Varrick (1973) Walter Matthau, Joe Don Baker. A bank robber discovers he has stolen mafia money. *Dir.* Don Siegel.
Charley's Aunt (1941) Jack Benny, Kay Francis, Anne Baxter, Laird Cregar. Based on play by Brandon Thomas. *Dir.* Archie Mayo.
Charlie and the Chocolate Factory (2005) Johnny Depp (Willy Wonka), Freddie Highmore (Charlie Bucket), David Kelly (Grandpa Joe), Helena Bonham Carter (Mrs Bucket), Noah Taylor (Mr Bucket), Missi Pyle (Mrs Beauregarde), James Fox (Mr Salt), Deep Roy (Oompa Loompa), Christopher Lee (Dr Wonka), Adam Godley (Mr Teavee), Franziska Troegner (Mrs Gloop), Anna Sophia Robb (Violet Beauregarde), Julia Winter (Veruca Salt), Jordan Fry (Mike Teavee). Based on Roald Dahl's book of the same name. Spectacular, but ultimately inferior remake of *Willy Wonka and the Chocolate Factory* (1971). *Dir.* Tim Burton.
Charlie Chan (Series) Warner Oland (1931–37), Sidney Toler (1938–47), Roland Winters (1947–49). Based on Earl Derr Biggers's character. *Dir.* Various.
Charlotte Gray (2001) Cate Blanchett (Charlotte), Billy Crudup, Michael Gambon, James Fleet, Jack Shepherd. Based on a Sebastian Faulks bestseller about a young Scotswoman who becomes a spy in France during the Second World War. *Dir.* Gillian Armstrong.
Che! (1969) Omar Sharif (Che Guevara), Jack Palance (Castro). *Dir.* Richard Fleischer.
Cheech and Chong's Next Movie (1980) Cheech Marin, Thomas Chong, Evelyn Guerrero. GB title: *High Encounters of the Ultimate Kind*. *Dir.* Thomas Chong.
Cheyenne Autumn (1964) Richard Widmark, Carroll Baker, Karl Malden, Dolores del Rio, Sal Mineo, Edward G Robinson, James Stewart (Wyatt Earp). *Dir.* John Ford.
Chicago (2002) Richard Gere (Billy Flynn), Renée Zellweger (Roxie Hart), Catherine Zeta-Jones (Velma Kelley), Queen Latifah, Taye Diggs. Adaptation of Bob Fosse's 1975 Broadway musical about two dreamers Velma Kelley and Roxie Hart. Velma is the Windy City's top nightclub star until the night she guns down her cheating husband, after which she becomes an even bigger celebrity, thanks to smooth lawyer Billy Flynn. Roxie also desperately wants fame, so decides to shoot her abusive lover dead. After Roxie replaces her, an outraged Velma plots Roxie's demise. *Dir.* Rob Marshall.
Chicago Joe and the Showgirl (1990) Kiefer Sutherland (Ricky Allen), Emily Lloyd (Georgina Grayson), Patsy Kensit (Joyce Cook). *Dir.* Bernard Rose.
Children of a Lesser God (1986) William Hurt (James), Marlee Matlin (Sarah), Piper Laurie (Mrs Norman). Deaf woman falls in love with her speech therapist. *Dir.* Randa Haines.
Children of Men (2006) Clive Owen (Theodore Faron), Julianne Moore (Julian Taylor), Michael Caine (Jasper Palmer), Chiwetel Ejiofor (Luke), Charlie Hunnam (Patric), Claire-Hope Ashitey (Kee), Pam Ferris (Miriam). In 2027, in a chaotic world in which humans can no longer procreate, a former activist agrees to help transport a miraculously pregnant woman to a sanctuary at sea, where her child's birth may help scientists secure the future of humankind. *Dir.* Alfonso Cuarón.
Child's Play (1988) Catherine Hicks (Karen Barclay), Chris Sarandon (Mike Norris). Dying killer Brad Dourif's soul passes into a Chucky Doll. *Dir.* Tom Holland.
China Syndrome, The (1979) Jane Fonda, Jack Lemmon, Michael Douglas. *Dir.* James Bridges.
Chinatown (1974) Jack Nicholson, Faye Dunaway, John Huston, Roman Polanski, Diane Ladd. *Dir.* Roman Polanski.
Chitty Chitty Bang Bang (1968) Dick Van Dyke, Sally Ann Howes (Truly Scrumptious), Lionel Jeffries, Benny Hill, Robert Helpmann, Gert Frobe, James Robertson Justice. Roald Dahl adapted the original Ian Fleming story. *Dir.* Ken Hughes.
Chocolat (2000) Juliette Binoche (Vianne Rocher), Alfred Molina (Comte de Reynaud), Carrie-Anne Moss (Caroline Clairmont), Johnny Depp (Roux), Judi Dench (Armande Voizin), Lena Olin (Josephine Muscat). Based on Joanne Harris bestseller. *Dir.* Lasse Hallstrom.
Chorus, The (2004) Gérard Jugnot (Clément Mathieu), François Berléand (Rachin), Kad Merad (Chabert), Jean-Paul Bonnaire (La Père Maxence), Marie Bunel (Violette Morhange), Jean-Baptiste Maunier (Pierre Morhange), Maxence Perrin (Pépinot). Set in 1949, Clément Mathieu is hired by a boarding school for troubled children to supervise the students. Nothing, it would seem, can bring the children into line. Nothing, that is, until Mathieu introduces them to singing. Undoubtedly one of the films of the year. French title: *Les Choristes*. *Dir.* Christophe Barratier.
Chorus Line, A (1985) Michael Douglas (Zach), Alyson Reed (Cassie), Terrence Mann (Larry). *Dir.* Richard Attenborough.
Chorus of Disapproval (1989) Anthony Hopkins (Dafydd Ap Llewellyn), Jeremy Irons (Guy Jones), Prunella Scales (Hannah), Jenny Seagrove (Fay Hubbard). *Dir.* Michael Winner.
Christmas Carol: The Movie (2001) Simon Callow (Charles Dickens), voices of Kate Winslet (Belle), Nicolas Cage (Jacob Marley), Jane Horrocks (Ghost of Christmas Past), Simon Callow (Scrooge), Michael Gambon (Ghost of Christmas Present), Rhys Ifans (Cratchit), Juliet Stevenson (Mrs Cratchit/Mother Gimlet). Animated version – other than Callow's Dickens. *Dir.* Jimmy T Murakami.

Christopher Columbus: The Discovery (1992) Marlon Brando (Torquemada), Tom Selleck (King Ferdinand), Georges Corraface (Columbus), Rachel Ward (Queen Isabella), Catherine Zeta Jones (Beatriz). *Dir.* John Glen.

Chronicles of Narnia, The: Lion, the Witch and the Wardrobe, The (2005) Georgie Henley (Lucy), Skandar Keynes (Edmund), William Moseley (Peter), Anna Popplewell (Susan), Tilda Swinton (Jadis the White Witch), James McAvoy (Mr Tumnus, a Faun), Jim Broadbent (Professor Digory Kirke), Kiran Shah (Ginarrbrik), James Cosmo (Father Christmas), Judy McIntosh (Mrs Pevensie), Liam Neeson (voice of Aslan). CS Lewis's timeless adventure follows the exploits of the four Pevensie siblings – Lucy, Edmund, Susan and Peter – in Second World War England who enter the world of Narnia through a magical wardrobe while playing a game of hide-and-seek in the rural country home of an elderly professor. Won an Academy Award for Best Makeup. *Dir.* Andrew Adamson. The second film in the series, *The Chronicles of Narnia: Prince Caspian* (2008) included Ben Barnes as Prince Caspian and Eddie Izzard as the voice of Reepicheep, a swashbuckling mouse. The third film in the series, *The Chronicles of Narnia: The Voyage of the Dawn Treader* (2010), unlike the first two films, which were distributed by The Walt Disney Company, was distributed by 20th Century Fox and released in Digital 3D. The two younger Pevensie children are joined by their cousin Eustace Scrubb (played by Will Poulter) to help save Narnia from a corrupting evil that resides on a dark island. Simon Pegg replaced Eddie Izzard as the voice of Reepicheep because director Michael Apted thought that his voice was more suited to the mature and serious side of the valiant mouse.

Cincinnati Kid, The (1965) Steve McQueen, Edward G Robinson, Karl Malden, Ann-Margret, Tuesday Weld. Based on Richard Jessup's novel concerning battle for supremacy among stud poker experts. *Dir.* Norman Jewison.

Cinderella Man (2005) Russell Crowe (Jim Braddock), Renée Zellweger (Mae Braddock), Craig Bierko (Max Baer). The true story of James Braddock, a supposedly washed up boxer who came back despite crippling hand injuries to pursue his dream of winning the world heavyweight boxing championship in the 1930s. *Dir.* Ron Howard.

Citadel, The (1938) Robert Donat, Rosalind Russell, Ralph Richardson, Rex Harrison. Based on AJ Cronin's novel, which also spawned the TV series *Dr Finlay's Casebook. Dir.* King Vidor.

Citizen Kane (1941) Orson Welles (Kane), Joseph Cotten (Jedediah Leland), Agnes Moorehead (Kane's mother). Based loosely on the newspaper magnate William Randolph Hearst. Welles also co-wrote the script with Herman J Mankiewicz. *Dir.* Orson Welles.

City Hall (1996) Al Pacino, John Cusack, Bridget Fonda, Danny Aiello. *Dir.* Harold Becker.

City Heat (1984) Clint Eastwood (Lt Speer), Burt Reynolds (Mike Murphy), Madeline Kahn (Caroline Howley). Reynolds broke his jaw when a prop chair turned out to be a real one!. *Dir.* Richard Benjamin.

City of God (2003) Matheus Nachtergaele (Sandro Cenoura), Seu Jorge (Mane Galinha), Buscape (Alexandre Rodrigues). Set in the slums of Rio; a poor wretch, eager to improve himself, watches his contemporaries turn to drugs and crime. *Dir.* Fernando Meirelles.

City of Industry (1997) Harvey Keitel, Stephen Dorff, Timothy Hutton. *Dir.* John Irvin.

City Slickers (1991) Billy Crystal (Mitch Robbins), Daniel Stern (Phil Berquist), Jack Palance (Curly). Oscar for Jack Palance as Best Supporting Actor. *Dir.* Ron Underwood.

Class Act (1992) Christopher Reid, Christopher Martin, Karyn Parsons. Two students swap identities. *Dir.* Randall Miller.

Class Action (1991) Gene Hackman, Mary Elizabeth Mastrantonio, Colin Friels. Father and daughter, both lawyers, find themselves on opposing sides in the courtroom. *Dir.* Michael Apted.

Cleopatra (1934) Claudette Colbert, Henry Wilcoxon (Antony), Warren William (Caesar). *Dir.* Cecil B de Mille.

Cleopatra (1963) Elizabeth Taylor, Richard Burton, Rex Harrison. *Dir.* Joseph L Mankiewicz.

Click (2006) Adam Sandler (Michael Newman), Kate Beckinsale (Donna Newman), Christopher Walken (Morty), David Hasselhoff (Mr Ammer), Henry Winkler (Ted Newman), Julie Kavner (Trudy Newman), Sean Astin (Bill Rando), Joseph Castanon (Ben Newman, age 7), Jonah Hill (Ben Newman, age 17), Jake Hoffman (Ben Newman, age 22–30), Tatum McCann (Samantha Newman, age 5), Lorraine Nicholson (Samantha Newman, age 15), Katie Cassidy (Samantha Newman, age 28). A workaholic architect finds a universal remote that allows him to fast-forward and rewind to different parts of his life. Complications arise when the remote starts to overrule his choices. *Dir.* Frank Coraci.

Clockers (1995) Harvey Keitel, John Turturro, Delroy Lindo, Mekhi Phifer, Pee Wee Love, Sticky Fingaz. A clocker is a small-time crack dealer working on the streets. *Dir.* Spike Lee.

Clockwise (1986) John Cleese (Timpson), Alison Steadman (Gwenda), Penelope Wilton (Pat Garden). *Dir.* Christopher Morahan.

Clockwork Orange, A (1971) Malcolm McDowell, Adrienne Corri, Patrick Magee, Michael Bates, Warren Clarke. Based on Anthony Burgess's novel. *Dir.* Stanley Kubrick.

Close Encounters of the Third Kind (1977) Richard Dreyfuss, François Truffaut, Teri Garr. *Dir.* Steven Spielberg.

Closer (2004) Natalie Portman (Alice), Jude Law (Dan), Julia Roberts (Anna), Clive Owen (Larry), Nick Hobbs, Colin Stinton. Set in London, the story of four strangers and their chance meetings, instant attractions and subsequent betrayals. Based on the play by Patrick Marber. *Dir.* Mike Nichols.

Cloud Atlas (2012) Tom Hanks, Halle Berry, Jim Broadbent, Hugo Weaving, Jim Sturgess, Doona Bae, Ben Whishaw, James D'Arcy, Zhou Xun, Keith David, David Gyasi, Susan Sarandon, Hugh Grant. German production based on the 2004 novel *Cloud Atlas* by David Mitchell. The plotlines cover six time periods with actors taking various roles. *Dirs.* Lana and Andy Wachowski and Tom Tykwer.

Coal Miner's Daughter (1980) Sissy Spacek (Loretta Lynn), Tommy Lee Jones. *Dir.* Michael Apted.

Cocktail (1988) Tom Cruise (Brian Flanagan), Bryan Brown (Doug Coughlin), Elizabeth Shue (Jordan Mooney). *Dir.* Roger Donaldson.

Cocoanuts, The (1929) Four Marx Brothers, Margaret Dumont. First of the Marx Brothers films. *Dir.* Robert Florey and Joseph Santley.

Cocoon (1985) Don Ameche (Art Selwyn), Steve Guttenberg (Jack Bonner), Jessica Tandy (Alma Finley), Tahnee Welch, (Kitty). There was a 1988 sequel *Cocoon: The Return. Dir.* Ron Howard.

Cold Comfort Farm (1995) Kate Beckinsale (Flora Poste), Joanna Lumley, Stephen Fry, Eileen Atkins, Ian McKellen. *Dir.* John Schlesinger.

Cold Mountain (2003) Jude Law (Inman), Nicole Kidman (Ada Monroe), Renée Zellweger (Ruby Thewes), Donald Sutherland (Reverend Monroe), Ray Winstone (Teague), Brendan Gleason (Stobrod), Philip Seymour Hoffman (Veasey), Natalie Portman (Sara), Kathy Baker (Sally Swanger), Giovanni Ribisi (Junior), Eileen Atkins (Maddy), Charlie Hunnam (Bosie). Set in 1864 during the American Civil War, a Confederate soldier deserts to make his way back to the woman he fleetingly loved. *Dir.* Anthony Minghella.

Color of Money, The (1986) Paul Newman (Eddie Felson), Tom Cruise (Vincent), Mary Elizabeth Mastrantonio (Carmen). Sequel to *The Hustler. Dir.* Martin Scorsese.

Color of Night (1994) Bruce Willis, Jane March, Ruben Blades, Lesley Ann Warren, Scott Bakula. Psychiatrist takes over a group that includes the person who murdered a colleague. *Dir.* Richard Rush.

Color Purple, The (1985) Whoopi Goldberg (Celie), Danny Glover (Albert Johnson) Oprah Winfrey (Sofia), Willard Pugh (Harpo). Based on the novel by Alice Walker. *Dir.* Steven Spielberg.

Comfort and Joy (1984) Bill Paterson (Alan), Eleanor David (Maddy), CP Grogan (Charlotte). Ice cream empires are called 'Mr McCool' and 'Mr Bunny' and the music is by Mark Knopfler. *Dir.* Bill Forsyth.

Coming Home (1978) Jane Fonda, Jon Voight, Bruce Dern. *Dir.* Hal Ashby.

Commitments, The (1991) Robert Arkins (Jimmy Rabbitte), Andrew Strong (Deco Cuffe), Michael Aherne (Steve Clifford). Story of a Dublin soul band. *Dir.* Alan Parker.

Con Air (1997) Nicolas Cage, John Cusack, John Malkovich. *Dir.* Simon West.

Conspiracy Theory (1997) Mel Gibson (Jerry Fletcher), Julia Roberts (Alice Sutton). *Dir.* Richard Donner.

Constant Gardener, The (2005) Ralph Fiennes (Justin Quayle), Rachel Weisz (Tessa Quayle), Hubert Koundé (Arnold Bluhm), Danny Huston (Sandy Woodrow), Daniele Harford (Miriam), Bill Nighy (Sir Bernard Pellegrin). A widower is determined to get to the bottom of a potentially explosive secret involving his wife's murder, big business, and corporate corruption. Based on a John le Carré novel adapted for the screen by Jeffrey Caine. Rachel Weisz won an Academy Award for Best Supporting Actress. *Dir.* Fernando Meirelles.

Contact (1997) Jodie Foster (Ellie). Based on Carl Sagan's book. *Dir.* Robert Zemeckis.

Control Room (2004) Documentary on perception of the United States' war with Iraq, with an emphasis on Al Jazeera's coverage. *Dir.* Jehane Noujaim.

Cook, the Thief, His Wife and Her Lover, The (1989) Richard Bohringer (Richard the Cook), Michael Gambon (Albert the Thief), Helen Mirren (Georgina, His Wife), Alan Howard (Michael, Her Lover). *Dir.* Peter Greenaway.

Cool Hand Luke (1967) Paul Newman (Lucas Jackson), George Kennedy, Jo Van Fleet. Luke was imprisoned for sawing off a parking meter. Famous scene where Luke swallows 50 eggs in an hour. *Dir.* Stuart Rosenberg.

Cotton Club, The (1984) Richard Gere (Dixie Dwyer), Gregory Hines (Sandman Williams), Bob Hoskins (Owney Madden), Nicolas Cage (Vincent Dwyer). *Dir.* Francis Ford Coppola.

Courage under Fire (1996) Denzel Washington (Colonel Serling), Meg Ryan (Captain Karen Walden). Gulf War story. *Dir.* Edward Zwick.

Courtneys of Curzon Street, The (1947) Anna Neagle, Michael Wilding, Michael Medwin. *Dir.* Herbert Wilcox.

Cousins (1989) Ted Danson (Larry Kozinski), Isabella Rossellini (Maria Hardy), Sean Young (Tish Kozinski), Lloyd Bridges (Uncle Vince). *Dir.* Joel Schumacher.

Cowboy Way, The (1994) Woody Harrelson, Kiefer Sutherland, Ernie Hudson. *Dir.* Gregg Champion.

Craft, The (1996) Robin Tunney, Fairuza Balk. *Dir.* Andrew Fleming.

Crash (1996) James Spader (James), Deborah Unger (Catherine), Holly Hunter (Helen). *Dir.* David Cronenberg.

Crash (2004) Sandra Bullock (Jean Cabot), Matt Dillon (Officer John Ryan), Don Cheadle (Det Graham Waters), Michael Peña (Daniel), Jennifer Esposito (Ria), Art Chudabala (Ken Ho), Tony Danza (Fred), Keith David (Lt Dixon), Loretta Devine (Shaniqua Johnson), Marina Sirtis (Shereen). For two days in Los Angeles, a racially and economically diverse group of people pursue lives that collide with one another in unexpected ways. Won Academy Awards for Best Film, Original Screenplay and Best Film Editing. *Dir.* Paul Haggis.

Crazy Heart (2009) Jeff Bridges (Bad Blake), Maggie Gyllenhaal (Jean Craddock), Colin Farrell (Tommy Sweet), Robert Duvall (Wayne Kramer), Beth Grant (JoAnne), Sarah Jane Morris (Marissa Reynolds), Annie Corley (Donna), Tom Bower (Bill Wilson). Musical drama written by Scott Cooper and based on the 1987 novel of the same name by Thomas Cobb. Bad Blake, an alcoholic country music singer/songwriter, tries to turn his life around after beginning a relationship with young journalist Jean Craddock. *Dir.* Scott Cooper.

Crimes and Misdemeanors (1989) Caroline Aaron (Barbara), Alan Alda (Lester), Woody Allen (Cliff Stern), Claire Bloom (Miriam Rosenthal), Mia Farrow (Halley Reed), Anjelica Huston (Dolores Paley). *Dir.* Woody Allen.

Crimes of the Heart (1986) Diane Keaton (Lenny Magrath), Jessica Lange (Meg), Sissy Spacek (Babe). Three kooky sisters argue about which one of them is going to go completely mad, first. *Dir.* Bruce Beresford.

Critters (1986) Dee Wallace Stone, M Emmet Walsh, Billy Green Bush. Hair-ball creatures arrive from an asteroid and devastate Kansas. *Dir.* Stephen Herek.

Crocodile Dundee (1986) Paul Hogan (Mick Dundee), Linda Kozlowski (Sue Charlton), John Meillon (Wally Reilly). As so often the case with sequels, *Crocodile Dundee II* was not as big a hit. *Dir.* Peter Faiman.

Crocodile Dundee in Los Angeles (2001) Paul Hogan, Linda Kozlowski, Jere Burns, Jonathan Banks, Mike Tyson (as himself). Second sequel made 13 years after the previous one but similar plot. *Dir.* Simon Wincer.

Cromwell (1970) Richard Harris, Alec Guinness, Frank Finlay, Robert Morley. *Dir.* Ken Hughes.

Crossing Guard, The (1995) Jack Nicholson, David Morse, Anjelica Huston, Piper Laurie. Alcoholic jeweller plans to kill the man who killed his daughter in a drink driving incident. *Dir.* Sean Penn.

Crossroads (2002) Britney Spears (Lucy), Zoe Saldana (Kit), Justin Long, Dan Aykroyd, Anson Mount, Kim Cattrall, Taryn Manning (Mimi). Three girls go to Los Angeles following their graduation. *Dir.* Tamara Davis.

Crouching Tiger, Hidden Dragon (1999) Michelle Yeoh, Chang Chen, Zhang Ziyi, Chow Yun-Fat. *Dir.* Ang Lee.

Crow, The (1994) Brandon Lee, Ernie Hudson, Michael Wincott. Brandon Lee died in a shooting accident during filming. *Dir.* Alex Proyas.

Cruel Sea, The (1953) Jack Hawkins, Donald Sinden, Stanley Baker. Eric Ambler adapted Nicholas Monsarrat's novel. *Dir.* Charles Frend.

Crumb (1994) Robert Crumb, Charles Crumb, Maxon Crumb, Dana Crumb, Beatrice Crumb, Aline Kominsky. Documentary about the creator of Fritz the Cat and Mr Natural. *Dir.* Terry Zwigoff.

Cry Freedom (1987) Kevin Kline (Donald Woods), Denzel Washington (Steve Biko). *Dir.* Richard Attenborough.

Cry in the Dark, A (1988) Meryl Streep (Lindy Chamberlain), Sam Neill (Michael). True story of a mother, convicted of killing her baby, who maintained a dingo had run off with it. *Dir.* Fred Schepisi.

Crying Freeman (1995) Mark Dacascos, Julie Condra (Emu O'Hara). *Dir.* Christophe Gans.

Crying Game, The (1992) Stephen Rea (Fergus), Miranda Richardson (Jude), Forest Whitaker (Jody). *Dir.* Neil Jordan.

Curious Case of Benjamin Button, The (2008) Brad Pitt (Benjamin Button), Cate Blanchett (Daisy Fuller), Spencer Daniels (Benjamin Button, looking like a minor), Shiloh Jolie-Pitt (Benjamin Button, looking like a baby), Elle Fanning (Daisy Fuller, age 6), Madisen Beaty (Daisy Fuller, age 11), Taraji P Henson (Queenie), Julia Ormond (Caroline Fuller), Jason Flemyng (Thomas Button), Mahershalalhashbaz Ali (Tizzy Weathers), Jared Harris (Capt Mike), Elias Koteas (Monsieur Gateau), Ed Metzger (Theodore Roosevelt), Phyllis Somerville (Grandma Fuller), Josh Stewart (Pleasant Curtis), Tilda Swinton (Elizabeth Abbott). Fantasy adventure. A boy is born in New Orleans on 11 November 1918, just after the end of the Great War. The baby's mother dies shortly after giving birth, and the father, Thomas Button, abandons the infant on the porch of a nursing home. Queenie and Mr 'Tizzy' Weathers find the baby and Queenie, who is unable to conceive, decides to take it in as her own, naming it Benjamin. The plot revolves around the love between Benjamin and Daisy, whose grandmother resides at the nursing home, and the extraordinary life of a man who is unique in that as he gets older he looks younger. Based on Scott Fitzgerald's short story of the same name (although Benjamin is born in 1860 in the book). *Dir.* David Fincher.

Curse of the Pink Panther, The (1983) David Niven (Sir Charles Litton), Robert Wagner (George Litton), Herbert Lom (Dreyfus), Joanna Lumley (Chandra), Capucine (Lady Litton). David Niven's voice was dubbed by Rich Little. *Dir.* Blake Edwards.

Cutthroat Island (1995) Geena Davis (Morgan), Matthew Modine (William Shaw), Frank Langella. *Dir.* Renny Harlin.

Cyrano de Bergerac (1990) Gérard Depardieu, Anne Brochet, Vincent Perez. *Dir.* Jean-Paul Rappeneau.

Da Vinci Code, The (2006) Tom Hanks (Dr Robert Langdon), Audrey Tautou (Agent Sophie Neveu), Ian McKellen (Sir Leigh Teabing), Jean Reno (Captain Bezu Fache), Paul Bettany (Silas), Alfred Molina (Bishop Manuel Aringarosa), Jürgen Prochnow (Andre Vernet), Jean-Yves Berteloot (Remy Jean), Etienne Chicot (Lt Collet). Based on Dan Brown's best-selling novel, adapted for the screen by Akiva Goldsman. *Dir.* Ron Howard.

Daddy Longlegs (1931) Janet Gaynor, Warner Baxter. Orphan girl grows up to fall in love with a mysterious benefactor. *Dir.* Alfred Santell.

Daddy Longlegs (1955) Fred Astaire, Leslie Caron, Fred Clark. Musical remake of the 1931 film. *Dir.* Jean Negulesco.

Daleks: Invasion Earth 2150 AD (1966) Peter Cushing, Bernard Cribbins. *Dir.* Gordon Flemyng.

Dam Busters, The (1954) Michael Redgrave (Barnes Wallis), Richard Todd (Guy Gibson). *Dir.* Michael Anderson.

Damien: Omen Two (1978) William Holden, Lee Grant, Jonathan Scott-Taylor, Sylvia Sidney. *Dir.* Don Taylor.

Dance with a Stranger (1985) Miranda Richardson (Ruth Ellis), Rupert Everett (David Blakely), Ian Holm, Stratford Johns. *Dir.* Mike Newell.

Dances with Wolves (1990) Kevin Costner (Lt John J Dunbar), Mary McDonnell (Stands With a Fist), Graham Greene (Kicking Bird). *Dir.* Kevin Costner.

Dangerous Ground (1997) Elizabeth Hurley, Ice Cube. *Dir.* Darrell James Roodt.

Dangerous Liaisons (1988) Glenn Close (Marquise de Merteuil), John Malkovich (Vicomte de Valmont), Michelle Pfeiffer (Madame de Tourvel), Keanu Reeves (Chevalier Danceny), Uma Thurman (Cecile de Volanges). *Dir.* Stephen Frears.
Danny the Champion of the World (1989) Jeremy Irons (William Smith), Samuel Irons (Danny), Robbie Coltrane (Victor Hazell). Based on a Roald Dahl book. *Dir.* Gavin Millar.
Dante's Peak (1997) Pierce Brosnan, Linda Hamilton. *Dir.* Roger Donaldson.
Dark Knight, The (2008) Christian Bale (Bruce Wayne/Batman), Heath Ledger (The Joker), Aaron Eckhart (Harvey Dent/Two-Face), Michael Caine (Alfred Pennyworth), Maggie Gyllenhaal (Rachel Dawes), Gary Oldman (James Gordon), Morgan Freeman (Lucius Fox), Monique Gabriela Curnen (Det Anna Ramirez), Ron Dean (Det Michael Wuertz), Cillian Murphy (Jonathan Crane/The Scarecrow). Sequel to the 2005 film *Batman Begins. Dir.* Christopher Nolan.
Dark Knight Rises, The (2012) Christian Bale, Michael Caine, Morgan Freeman and Gary Oldman reprise their roles. Final installment in Nolan's Batman film trilogy has Selina Kyle/Catwoman (Anne Hathaway) and Bane (Tom Hardy) as super villains. *Dir.* Christopher Nolan.
Darkman (1990) Liam Neeson (Peyton Westlake / Darkman). Scientist left for dead by thugs re-emerges as Darkman. *Dir.* Sam Raimi.
Darling (1965) Julie Christie, Dirk Bogarde, Laurence Harvey. *Dir.* John Schlesinger.
Dave (1993) Kevin Kline, Sigourney Weaver, Frank Langella, Ben Kingsley. US President suffers a stroke and a Baltimore businessman is hired to impersonate him. *Dir.* Ivan Reitman.
David Copperfield (1934) Freddie Bartholomew (young David), Frank Lawton (David as a man), WC Fields (Micawber). Charles Laughton was original choice for Micawber but resigned after 2 days. *Dir.* George Cukor.
Day at the Races, A (1937) First of the high-budget Marx Brothers films. *Dir.* Sam Wood.
Day of the Beast (1995) Alex Angulo, Armando de Razza, Santiago Segura. Priest attempts to track down the Anti-Christ who is to be born in Madrid. *Dir.* Alex de la Iglesia.
Day of the Jackal, The (1973) Edward Fox, Michael Lonsdale, Alan Badel, Eric Porter. *Dir.* Fred Zinnemann.
Day of the Triffids, The (1962) Howard Keel, Kieron Moore, Janette Scott, Nicole Maurey. *Dir.* Steve Sekely.
Daylight (1996) Sylvester Stallone, Amy Brenneman, Viggo Mortensen, Karen Young, Claire Bloom. Diverse group of people are trapped in Manhattan's Holland Tunnel. *Dir.* Rob Cohen.
Days of Thunder (1990) Tom Cruise (Cole Trickle), Robert Duvall (Harry Hogge), Nicole Kidman (Dr Claire Lewicki). *Dir.* Tony Scott.
Dead Again (1991) Kenneth Branagh (Roman Strauss / Mike), Andy Garcia (Gray Baker), Derek Jacobi (Franklyn Madson), Emma Thompson (Margaret Strauss / Grace). *Dir.* Kenneth Branagh.
Dead Calm (1989) Sam Neill (John Ingram), Nicole Kidman (Rae Ingram), Billy Zane (Hughie Warriner). *Dir.* Phillip Noyce.
Dead Man Walking (1995) Susan Sarandon (Sister Helen Prejean), Sean Penn (Matthew Poncelet). *Dir.* Tim Robbins.
Dead Men Don't Wear Plaid (1982) Steve Martin, Rachel Ward, Carl Reiner, Reni Santoni. Bogart, Ladd, Bacall, Stanwyck also appear in film-clip editing. *Dir.* Carl Reiner.
Dead Poets Society (1989) Robin Williams (John Keating), Robert Sean Leonard, Ethan Hawke, Josh Charles. Keating's motto: 'Carpe Diem (Seize the Day)'. *Dir.* Peter Weir.
Dead Pool, The (1988) Clint Eastwood (Harry Callahan), Patricia Clarkson, Liam Neeson, Evan C Kim. Famous scene of a car chase involving a toy car. Jim Carrey has small part as a murder victim. *Dir.* Buddy van Horn.
Dead Ringers (1988) Jeremy Irons (Beverly / Elliot Mantle), Geneviève Bujold (Claire Niveau). Concerns identical twins, gynaecologists. *Dir.* David Cronenberg.
Dealers (1989) Paul McGann (Daniel Pasco), Rebecca DeMornay (Anna Schuman), Derrick O'Connor (Robby Barrell). TV series *Capital City* was a spin-off. *Dir.* Colin Bucksey.
Dear Diary (1994) Jennifer Beals, Nanni Moretti, Alexandre Rockwell. *Dir.* Nanni Moretti.
Death in Venice (1971) Dirk Bogarde, Bjorn Andresen, Silvana Mangano Gustav Mahler's music is memorable. *Dir.* Luchino Visconti.
Death of a Salesman (1985) Dustin Hoffman (Willy Loman), Charles Durning (Charley), Kate Reid (Linda), Stephen Lang (Happy), John Malkovich. Screenplay: Arthur Miller. Film was made for cable TV. *Dir.* Volker Schlondorff.
Death on the Nile (1978) Peter Ustinov, Bette Davis, Mia Farrow, David Niven, Maggie Smith. Agatha Christie novel with Hercule Poirot. *Dir.* John Guillermin.
Death Race 2000 (1975) David Carradine, Simone Griffeth, Sylvester Stallone. *Dir.* Paul Bartel.
Death Wish (1974) Charles Bronson, Hope Lange, Vincent Gardenia. Four follow-on films – 1981, 1985, 1987, 1993 -– similar plots. *Dir.* Michael Winner.
Deathtrap (1982) Michael Caine, Christopher Reeve, Dyan Cannon. From the play by Ira Levin. *Dir.* Sidney Lumet.
Deepstar Six (1989) Taurean Blacque, Nancy Everhard, Greg Evigan. Underwater thriller. *Dir.* Sean Cunningham.
Deer Hunter, The (1978) Robert De Niro, John Savage, Christopher Walken, Meryl Streep. Vietnam thriller that won 3 Oscars. *Dir.* Michael Cimino.
Defence of the Realm (1985) Gabriel Byrne (Nick Mullen), Greta Scacchi (Nina Beckman), Denholm Elliott (Vernon Bayliss), Robbie Coltrane (Leo McAskey). *Dir.* David Drury.
Defiant Ones, The (1958) Tony Curtis, Sidney Poitier, Theodore Bikel, Lon Chaney Jnr. Prison escape drama, with black and white prisoners chained together, that won 3 Oscars. *Dir.* Stanley Kramer.
Delinquents, The (1989) Notable only for being Kylie Minogue's debut feature. *Dir.* Chris Thomson.
Deliverance (1972) Burt Reynolds, Jon Voight, Ned Beatty. From James Dickey's novel. *Dir.* John Boorman.
Demolition Man (1993) Sylvester Stallone (John Spartan), Wesley Snipes (Simon Phoenix), Lori Petty, Nigel Hawthorne, Melinda Dillon. Futuristic thriller with Stallone as former cop released from suspended animation. *Dir.* Marco Brambilla.
Dennis the Menace (1993) Walter Matthau, Mason Gamble, Joan Plowright, Christopher Lloyd, Lea Thompson. Story of the 6-yr-old menace. *Dir.* Nick Castle.
Departed, The (2006) Leonardo DiCaprio (Billy Costigan), Matt Damon (Colin Sullivan), Jack Nicholson (Frank Costello), Mark Wahlberg (Dignam), Martin Sheen (Oliver Queenan), Ray Winstone (Mr French), Alec Baldwin (Ellerby), Robert Wahlberg (FBI Agent Frank Lazio), Kristen Dalton (Gwen). Two men from opposite sides of the law are undercover within the Massachusetts State Police and the Irish mafia, but bloodshed boils when the infiltration is discovered, and the pair are sent to find their enemy's identities. *Dir.* Martin Scorsese.
Desert Fox, The (1951) James Mason, Jessica Tandy, Cedric Hardwicke. Biography of Erwin Rommel. *Dir.* Henry Hathaway.
Desert Rats, The (1953) James Mason (Rommel), Richard Burton, Robert Newton. *Dir.* Robert Wise.
Desperado (1995) Antonio Banderas, Salma Hayek, Joaquin de Almeida, Cheech Marin, Quentin Tarantino. Man with guitar case full of weapons walks into a Mexican town and starts shooting. *Dir.* Robert Rodriguez.
Desperate Hours (1990) Mickey Rourke (Michael Bosworth), Anthony Hopkins (Tim Cornell), Mimi Rogers (Nora). *Dir.* Michael Cimino.
Desperate Measures (1998) Michael Keaton, Andy Garcia. Detective Frank Connor is forced to choose between his badge and his son. *Dir.* Barbet Schroeder.
Desperately Seeking Susan (1985) Madonna, Aidan Quinn, Rosanna Arquette. Madonna's first starring role. *Dir.* Susan Seidelman.
Destiny Turns on the Radio (1995) James LeGros, Dylan McDermott, Quentin Tarantino, James Belushi, Nancy Travis. Bank robber gets out of jail and travels to Las Vegas to reclaim his loot. *Dir.* Jack Baran.
Devil Rides Out, The (1968) Christopher Lee, Charles Gray, Patrick Mower. From Dennis Wheatley's novel. *Dir.* Terence Fisher.
Devil Wears Prada, The (2006) Meryl Streep (Miranda Priestly), Anne Hathaway (Andy Sachs), Emily Blunt (Emily). A naive young woman comes to New York and manages to get a job as assistant to ruthless and cynical Miranda Priestly, one of the city's biggest magazine editors. *Dir.* David Frankel.

Devils, The (1970) Vanessa Redgrave, Oliver Reed, Dudley Sutton, Gemma Jones. *Dir.* Ken Russell.

Devil's Own, The (1997) Harrison Ford (Tom O'Meara), Brad Pitt (Frankie McGuire). *Dir.* Alan J Pakula.

Diabolique (1996) Sharon Stone, Isabelle Adjani, Kathy Bates. Wife and mistress of unpleasant schoolmaster conspire to murder him. *Dir.* Jeremiah Chechnik.

Dial M for Murder (1954) Ray Milland, Grace Kelly, Robert Cummings. Shot in 3D but never released in 3D form. *Dir.* Alfred Hitchcock.

Diamonds Are Forever (1971) Sean Connery, Charles Gray (Blofeld), Jill St John (Tiffany Case), Lana Wood (Plenty O'Toole). Theme song sung by Shirley Bassey. *Dir.* Guy Hamilton.

Dick Tracy (1990) Warren Beatty, Madonna (Breathless Mahoney), Dick Van Dyke, Al Pacino (Big Boy Caprice), Dustin Hoffman (Mumbles), Charlie Korsmo (Kid), Kathy Bates (Mrs Green), James Caan (Spaldini). Won 3 Oscars. *Dir.* Warren Beatty.

Dictator, The (2012) Sacha Baron Cohen (President Prime Minister Admiral General Haffaz Aladeen/Alison Burgers/Efawadh). The cruel and egotistical dictator of the fictional Republic of Wadiya is kidnapped and replaced by a double, Efawadh. *Dir.* Larry Charles.

Die Another Day (2002) Pierce Brosnan (James Bond), Halle Berry (Jinx), Rick Yune (Zao), Madonna (Verity), Judi Dench (M), John Cleese (Q), Rosamund Pike (Miranda Frost), Michael Madsen (Damian Falco), Toby Stephens (Gustav Graves), Samantha Bond (Moneypenny). Theme song sung by Madonna. *Dir.* Lee Tamahori.

Die Hard (1988) Bruce Willis (John McClane), Bonnie Bedelia (Holly Gennaro McClane), Alan Rickman (Hans Gruber). 3 sequels followed. *Dir.* John McTiernan.

Diner (1982) Steve Guttenberg (Eddie), Daniel Stern (Shrevie), Mickey Rourke (Boogie), Kevin Bacon (Fenwick), Ellen Barkin (Beth), Timothy Daly (Billy). Five men on verge of manhood hang out at Fells Point Diner. *Dir.* Barry Levinson.

Dirty Dancing (1987) Patrick Swayze (Johnny Castle), Jennifer Grey (Baby Houseman). Variant on *Saturday Night Fever. Dir.* Emile Ardolino.

Dirty Dingus Magee (1970) Frank Sinatra, George Kennedy. Western comedy. *Dir.* Burt Kennedy.

Dirty Dozen, The (1967) Lee Marvin, Robert Ryan, Charles Bronson, Telly Savalas, Ernest Borgnine, Jim Brown, John Cassavetes, George Kennedy, Richard Jaeckel, Trini Lopez, Ralph Meeker, Clint Walker, Donald Sutherland. *Dir.* Robert Aldrich.

Dirty Mary, Crazy Larry (1974) Peter Fonda, Susan George, Roddy McDowall (uncredited). *Dir.* John Hough.

Dirty Rotten Scoundrels (1988) Steve Martin (Freddie Benson), Michael Caine (Lawrence Jamieson). Remake of *Bedtime Story* (1964). *Dir.* Frank Oz.

Distinguished Gentleman, The (1992) Eddie Murphy (Thomas Jefferson Johnson), Lane Smith (Dick Dodge), James Garner. *Dir.* Jonathan Lynn.

Django Unchained (2012) Jamie Foxx (Django Freeman), Christoph Waltz (Dr King Schultz), Leonardo DiCaprio (Calvin J. Candie), Kerry Washington (Broomhilda Von Shaft), Samuel L. Jackson (Stephen), Don Johnson (Spencer 'Big Daddy' Bennett), Ato Essandoh (D'Artagnan), Franco Nero (Amerigo Vessepi). Western. Django, a freed slave who, accompanied by Schultz (a German dentist and bounty hunter), is on a mission to rescue his wife Broomhilda from Calvin Candie, a cruel plantation owner . *Dir.* Quentin Tarantino.

DOA (1950) Edmond O'Brien, Pamela Britton, Neville Brand, Luther Adler. Title stands for 'Dead on Arrival' and concerns a professor, who has been poisoned by a slow-acting drug, in a race against time to track down his murderer. *Dir.* Rudolph Maté.

DOA (1988) Dennis Quaid (Dexter Cornell), Meg Ryan (Sydney Fuller), Charlotte Rampling (Mrs Fitzwaring). Remake of the 1950 classic. *Dir.* Rocky Morton and Annabel Jankel.

Doc Hollywood (1991) Michael J Fox (Dr Benjamin Stone), Julie Warner (Lou), Bridget Fonda (Nancy Lee), George Hamilton (Dr Halberstrom). Famous scene of Warner urinating to throw hunters off their prey's scent. *Dir.* Michael Caton-Jones.

Doctor and the Devils (1986) Timothy Dalton (Dr Thomas Rock), Jonathan Pryce (Robert Fallon), Twiggy (Jenny Bailey), Beryl Reid, TP McKenna, Patrick Stewart. Screenplay by Dylan Thomas. *Dir.* Freddie Francis.

Dr Dolittle (1967) Rex Harrison, Anthony Newley, Samantha Eggar, Richard Attenborough. Oscars for Best Song ('Talk to the Animals') and Special Effects. LB Abbott. *Dir.* Richard Fleischer.

Dr Dolittle (1998) Eddie Murphy (Dr Dolittle), Ossie Davis, Oliver Platt, Peter Boyle. *Dir.* Betty Thomas.

Dr Dolittle 2 (2001) Sequel to the 1998 film with similar cast. *Dir.* Steve Carr.

Doctor in the House (1954) Dirk Bogarde, Kenneth More, Kay Kendall, Donald Sinden. First of many *Doctor* stories, followed by TV series. *Dir.* Ralph Thomas.

Doctor No (1962) Sean Connery, Ursula Andress (Honeychile Rider), Joseph Wiseman (Dr No), Jack Lord. First of the James Bond stories to be filmed (James Bond theme by Monty Norman). *Dir.* Terence Young.

Dr Strangelove (1963) Peter Sellers, George C Scott. Black comedy Peter Sellers plays 3 parts. *Dir.* Stanley Kubrick.

Dr Who and the Daleks (1965) Peter Cushing, Roy Castle, Roberta Tovey, Jennie Linden. First *Dr Who* film; sequel in 1966. *Dir.* Gordon Flemyng.

Doctor Zhivago (1965) Omar Sharif, Julie Christie, Rod Steiger, Alec Guinness, Rita Tushingham, Geraldine Chaplin, Tom Courtenay, Adrienne Corri. Oscars for Maurice Jarre (Music), Freddie Young (Photography), and Robert Bolt (Screenplay). *Dir.* David Lean.

Dog Day Afternoon (1975) Al Pacino, John Cazale, Charles Durning, Chris Sarandon, Sully Boyar. *Dir.* Sidney Lumet.

Dog Soldiers (2002) Sean Pertwee (Sgt Harry Wells), Kevin McKidd, Emma Cleasby. Story of an army patrol in the Highlands of Scotland besieged by werewolves. *Dir.* Neil Marshall.

Dogville (2003) Nicole Kidman (Grace), Harriet Anderson (Gloria), Lauren Bacall (Ma Ginger), Jean-Marc Barr (The Man with the Big Hat), Paul Bettany (Tom Edison), Blair Brown (Mrs Henson), James Caan (The Big Man), Patricia Clarkson (Vera), Jeremy Davies (Bill Henson), Ben Gazzara (Jack McKay), Philip Baker Hall (Tom Edison Snr), Udo Kier (The Man in the Coat), Chloe Sevigny (Liz Henson), Stellan Skarsgard (Chuck), John Hurt (Narrator). Set in the 1930s. A woman flees from gangsters and is protected by the residents of a small town until they realise the risks involved. Innovative film methods are used including lines of white paint to depict streets and buildings in order to distinguish public and private behaviour. *Dir.* Lars von Trier.

Dolores Claiborne (1995) Kathy Bates, Jennifer Jason Leigh, Judy Parfitt, Christopher Plummer. Housekeeper acquitted of murder is then arrested for killing her boss. *Dir.* Taylor Hackford.

Donnie Brasco (1997) Al Pacino (Ben 'Lefty' Ruggiero), Johnny Depp (Donnie Brasco / Joe Pistone), Michael Madsen (Sonny). *Dir.* Mike Newell.

Don't Look Now (1973) Donald Sutherland, Julie Christie. Daphne du Maurier story, set in Venice. *Dir.* Nicolas Roeg.

Doors, The (1991) Val Kilmer (Jim Morrison), Meg Ryan (Pamela Courson), Billy Idol (Cat). *Dir.* Oliver Stone.

Double Indemnity (1944) Fred MacMurray, Barbara Stanwyck, Edward G Robinson, Tom Powers, Porter Hall, Jean Heather, Byron Barr. An insurance agent connives with the wife of a client to kill her husband and claim on the policy. Screenplay by Billy Wilder and Raymond Chandler based on the novel by James M Cain. *Dir.* Billy Wilder.

Down and Out in Beverly Hills (1986) Nick Nolte (Jerry Baskin), Richard Dreyfuss (Davie Whiteman), Bette Midler (Barbara Whiteman), Little Richard (Orvis Goodnight). *Dir.* Paul Mazursky.

Downhill Racer (1969) Robert Redford, Gene Hackman, Camilla Sparv. Plotless film about a skier. *Dir.* Michael Ritchie.

Dracula (1931) Bela Lugosi, Helen Chandler, David Manners. Numerous follow-on films from this Bram Stoker novel. *Dir.* Tod Browning.

Dracula 2001 (2000) Christopher Plummer (Van Helsing), Jonny Lee Miller, Justine Waddell, Gerard Butler (Dracula). US title: *Dracula 2000. Dir.* Patrick Lussier.

Dragnet (1987) Dan Aykroyd (Joe Friday), Tom Hanks (Streebek), Christopher Plummer (Whirley), Harry Morgan (Bill Gannon). *Dir.* Tom Mankiewicz.

Dragon: The Bruce Lee Story (1993) Jason Scott Lee, Robert Wagner, Michael Learned, Lauren Holly, Nancy Kwan. *Dir.* Rob Cohen.

Dragonheart (1996) Dennis Quaid, David Thewlis, Pete Postlethwaite, voice of Sean Connery. *Dir.* Rob Cohen.

Dream Team, The (1989) Michael Keaton (Billy Caulfield), Christopher Lloyd (Henry Sikorsky), Peter Boyle (Jack McDermott), Stephen Furst (Albert Ianuzzi). Four mental patients have to fend for themselves in Manhattan. *Dir.* Howard Zieff.

Dreamscape (1984) Dennis Quaid (Alex), Max Von Sydow (Paul), Christopher Plummer (Bob), Kate Capshaw (Jane), George Wendt (Charlie). *Dir.* Joseph Ruben.

Dressed to Kill (1980) Michael Caine, Angie Dickinson, Nancy Allen. Michael Caine plays a transvestite killer. *Dir.* Brian De Palma.

Dresser, The (1983) Albert Finney (Sir), Tom Courtenay (Norman), Edward Fox (Oxenby). *Dir.* Peter Yates.

Driven (2001) Sylvester Stallone (Joe Tanto), Burt Reynolds (Carl Henry), Kip Pardue (Jimmy Bly), Gina Gershon (Cathy Moreno), Stacy Edwards (Lucretia Clans). *Dir.* Renny Harlin.

Driving Miss Daisy (1989) Jessica Tandy (Daisy Werthan), Morgan Freeman (Hoke Colburn), Dan Aykroyd (Boolie). Won 4 Oscars. *Dir.* Bruce Beresford.

Drugstore Cowboy (1989) Matt Dillon (Bob Hughes), Kelly Lynch (Dianne Hughes), Heather Graham (Nadine), William S Burroughs (Tom the Priest). *Dir.* Gus Van Sant.

Dry White Season, A (1989) Donald Sutherland (Ben Du Toit), Janet Suzman (Susan), Susan Sarandon (Melanie Bruwer), Marlon Brando (Ian McKenzie). Set in apartheid South Africa. *Dir.* Euzhan Palcy.

Duchess, The (2008) Keira Knightley (Georgiana Cavendish, Duchess of Devonshire), Ralph Fiennes (William Cavendish, 5th Duke of Devonshire), Hayley Atwell (Lady Elizabeth 'Bess' Foster), Charlotte Rampling (Countess Spencer), Dominic Cooper (Charles Grey, 2nd Earl Grey), Aidan McArdle (Richard Brinsley Sheridan), Simon McBurney (Charles James Fox). Drama based on Amanda Foreman's biography of the C18 English aristocrat Georgiana Cavendish, Duchess of Devonshire, the Lady Di of her day. *Dir.* Saul Dibb.

Duck Soup (1933) The Marx Brothers, Margaret Dumont. According to *Time Out* the best Marx Bros film. *Dir.* Leo McCarey.

Duet for One (1986) Julie Andrews (Stephanie Anderson), Alan Bates (David Cornwallis), Max Von Sydow (Dr Louis Feldman), Liam Neeson (Totter). Famous violinist develops multiple sclerosis. *Dir.* Andrei Konchalovsky.

Duke Wore Jeans, The (1958) Tommy Steele, June Laverick, Michael Medwin. *Dir.* Gerald Thomas.

Dune (1984) Kyle MacLachlan (Paul Atreides), Francesca Annis (Lady Jessica), Sting (Feyd Rautha), Kenneth McMillan (Baron Harkonnen). Based on Frank Herbert's epic SF novel. *Dir.* David Lynch.

Dunkirk (1958) John Mills, Richard Attenborough, Bernard Lee. Directed by Barry Norman's father. Factual story. *Dir.* Leslie Norman.

Eagle Has Landed, The (1976) Michael Caine, Donald Sutherland, Jenny Agutter, Robert Duvall, Donald Pleasence (Himmler). Involves a Nazi plot to kill Churchill. *Dir.* John Sturges.

Earth Girls Are Easy (1988) Geena Davis (Valerie Dale), Jeff Goldblum (Mac), Jim Carrey (Wiploc), Julie Brown (Candy Pink). *Dir.* Julien Temple.

Earthquake (1974) Charlton Heston, Ava Gardner, Lorne Greene, George Kennedy. First film to use 'Sensurround'. Big box-office hit. *Dir.* Mark Robson.

East of Sudan (1964) Anthony Quayle, Sylvia Syms, Jenny Agutter. *Dir.* Nathan Juran.

Easter Parade (1948) Fred Astaire, Judy Garland, Ann Miller. Music by Irving Berlin. *Dir.* Charles Walters.

Easy Street (1917) Charles Chaplin, Edna Purviance, Albert Austin. Tramp is reformed by missionary and becomes a policeman. *Dir.* Charles Chaplin.

Eddie (1996) Whoopi Goldberg (Eddie), Frank Langella (Wild Bill Burgess), Dennis Farina (John Bailey). *Dir.* Steve Rash.

Educating Rita (1983) Michael Caine (Dr Frank Bryant), Julie Walters (Rita), Maureen Lipman (Trish), Michael Williams (Brian). From the play by Willie Russell; shot in Ireland for tax reasons. *Dir.* Lewis Gilbert.

Edward Scissorhands (1990) Johnny Depp, Winona Ryder (Kim Boggs), Dianne Wiest (Peg), Alan Arkin (Bill), Vincent Price (Inventor). *Dir.* Tim Burton.

Eiger Sanction, The (1975) Clint Eastwood, George Kennedy, Vonetta McGee. Art teacher returns to CIA post as an exterminator. *Dir.* Clint Eastwood.

8 Mile (2002) Eminem, Kim Basinger, Brittany Murphy, Mekhi Phifer. *Dir.* Curtis Hanson.

Eight and a Half (1963) Marcello Mastroianni, Claudia Cardinale, Anouk Aimée. Fellini self portrait. Best Foreign Film Oscar. (The 8 1/2 refers to the number of films Fellini had then made.) *Dir.* Federico Fellini.

18 Again! (1988) George Burns (Jack Watson), Charlie Schlatter (David Watson), Tony Roberts (Arnold). *Dir.* Paul Flaherty.

84 Charing Cross Road (1987) Anne Bancroft (Helene), Anthony Hopkins (Frank Doel), Judi Dench (Nora Doel). Based on a true story of the late Helene Hanff. *Dir.* David Jones.

Elephant (2003) Alex Frost (Alex), Eric Deulen (Eric), John Robinson (John McFarland), Elias McConnell (Elias), Jordan Taylor (Jordan), Timothy Bottoms (John McFarland's father), Matt Molloy (Mr Luce). Drama depicting real high school students and adult actors. Based on the Columbine High School killings of 1999 where two Colorado students killed 12 other students and a teacher. The action is set in Portland, Oregon. Executive producer was Diane Keaton. *Dir.* Gus Van Sant.

Elephant Boy (1937) Sabu, Wilfrid Hyde-White. Based on a Kipling novel, made a star of Sabu. *Dir.* Robert Flaherty.

Elephant Man, The (1980) Anthony Hopkins, John Hurt (John Merrick), Anne Bancroft, John Gielgud. *Dir.* David Lynch.

Elizabeth (1998) Cate Blanchett (Elizabeth I of England), Geoffrey Rush (Francis Walsingham), Christopher Eccleston (Thomas Howard, 4th Duke of Norfolk), Joseph Fiennes (Robert Dudley, 1st Earl of Leicester), Kathy Burke (Mary I of England), Richard Attenborough (William Cecil, 1st Baron Burghley), George Yiasoumi (Philip II of Spain), Emily Mortimer (Kat Ashley), Edward Hardwicke (Henry FitzAlan, 19th Earl of Arundel), Daniel Craig (John Ballard), James Frain (Alvaro de la Quadra), Kelly Macdonald (Lettice Knollys), Angus Deayton (Waad, Chancellor of the Exchequer), Wayne Sleep (Dance Tutor), John Gielgud (the Pope), Fanny Ardant (Mary of Guise), Vincent Cassel (Duc d'Anjou), Eric Cantona (Monsieur de Foix). Drama written by Michael Hirst based on the early reign of Queen Elizabeth I of England. *Dir.* Shekhar Kapur. A 2007 sequel, *Elizabeth: The Golden Age,* also directed by Kapur, was written by Hirst and William Nicholson and starred Clive Owen (Walter Raleigh) and Samantha Morton (Mary, Queen of Scots). Both Cate Blanchett and Geoffrey Rush reprised their earlier roles.

Elmer Gantry (1960) Burt Lancaster, Jean Simmons, Arthur Kennedy, Shirley Jones. Oscars for Lancaster, Jones and Brooks (writer). *Dir.* Richard Brooks.

Emma (1996) Gwyneth Paltrow, Toni Collette, Ewan McGregor, Greta Scacchi, Sophie Thompson, Phyllida Law. Rachel Portman won Oscar for Music. *Dir.* Douglas McGrath.

Emmanuelle (1974) Sylvia Kristel, Marika Green, Daniel Sarky. Big soft-porn cinema hit, spawned 6 sequels. *Dir.* Just Jaeckin.

Empire of the Sun (1987) Christian Bale (Jim), John Malkovich (Basie), Miranda Richardson (Mrs Victor), Screenplay by Tom Stoppard, from JG Ballard's autobiographical novel. *Dir.* Steven Spielberg.

Empire Strikes Back, The (1980) Mark Hamill, Harrison Ford, Carrie Fisher. Second of the *Star Wars* films. *Dir.* Irvin Kershner.

Enchanted April (1991) Miranda Richardson (Rose Arbuthnot), Joan Plowright (Mrs Fisher), Alfred Molina (Mellersh Wilkins), Josie Lawrence (Lottie Wilkins). A quartet of Edwardian ladies go on holiday in an Italian villa. *Dir.* Mike Newell.

Endless Summer, The (1966) Study of surfing round the world. Documentary which has become a cult among surfers. *Dir.* Bruce Brown.

Enemy at the Gates (2001) Joseph Fiennes (Danilov), Jude Law (Vassili Zaitsev), Rachel Weisz, Bob Hoskins, Ed Harris. Setting of the Siege of Stalingrad. *Dir.* Jean-Jacques Annaud.

Enforcer, The (1976) Clint Eastwood, Tyne Daly, Bradford Dillman. Third of the *Dirty Harry* films. *Dir.* James Fargo.

English Patient (1996) Ralph Fiennes (Count Almasy), Kristin Scott-Thomas, Juliette Binoche, Willem Dafoe, Colin Firth. Dying Hungarian count recalls his doomed affair with the English wife of a colleague. Based on Michael Ondaatje's book. Won 9 Academy Awards. *Dir.* Anthony Minghella.

Entertainer, The (1960) Laurence Olivier, Joan Plowright, Alan Bates, Albert Finney. *Dir.* Tony Richardson.

Equinox (1992) Matthew Modine, Lara Flynn Boyle, Marisa Tomei, Fred Ward, Lori Singer. Timid garage mechanic discovers he has a killer brother. *Dir.* Alan Rudolph.

Eraser (1996) Arnold Schwarzenegger, James Caan, James Coburn, Vanessa Williams. Agent for the Federal Witness Protection Program discovers he can trust no one. *Dir.* Charles Russell.

Erik the Viking (1989) Tim Robbins (Erik), Mickey Rooney (Erik's grandfather), Eartha Kitt (Freya), Terry Jones (King Arnulf), John Cleese. *Dir.* Terry Jones.

Erin Brockovich (1999) Julia Roberts, Aaron Eckhart, Albert Finney, Marg Helgenberger, Cherry Jones, Peter Coyote, Veanne Cox. *Dir.* Steven Soderbergh. (The film was made in late 1999, too late for the 2000 Oscars.) True story of a twice-divorced single parent lawyer who took on the might of the Pacific Gas and Electric, accusing them of contaminating a town's water supply.

Escape from Alcatraz (1979) Clint Eastwood, Patrick McGoohan, Jack Thibeau. *Dir.* Don Siegel.

Escape from LA (1996) Kurt Russell (Snake Plissken), Steve Buscemi. Set in year 2013. *Dir.* John Carpenter.

ET – The Extra Terrestrial (1982) Dee Wallace (Mary), Henry Thomas (Elliott), Drew Barrymore (Gertie). ET was 3 million light years from home. *Dir.* Steven Spielberg.

Eternal Sunshine of the Spotless Mind (2004) Jim Carrey (Joel Barish), Kate Winslet (Clementine Kruczynski), Kirsten Dunst (Mary), Mark Ruffalo (Stan), Elijah Wood (Patrick), Tom Wilkinson (Dr Howard Mierzwiak), Jane Adams (Carrie), David Cross (Rob). A man discovers that his former lover has had all memory of their romance erased from her mind and decides to do the same. *Dir.* Michel Gondry.

Ethan Frome (1993) Liam Neeson, Patricia Arquette, Joan Allen. Massachusetts community is setting for story of minister and his crippled driver. *Dir.* John Madden.

Etre et Avoir (2002) Georges Lopez (the teacher), Alizé (female student), Axel (male student), Guillaume (male student). English title: *To Be and to Have.* Documentary portrait of a one-room school in rural France. *Dir.* Nicolas Philibert.

Eureka (1983) Gene Hackman, Theresa Russell, Rutger Hauer, Jane Lapotaire, Mickey Rourke, Joe Pesci. Gold prospector strikes it rich, but at a price. *Dir.* Nicolas Roeg.

Every Which Way But Loose (1978) Clint Eastwood, Sondra Locke, Ruth Gordon. The 1980 sequel *Any Which Way You Can* is the same story. *Dir.* James Fargo.

Everyone Says I Love You (1996) Woody Allen, Julia Roberts, Drew Barrymore, Alan Alda, Goldie Hawn. *Dir.* Woody Allen.

Evil That Men Do, The (1984) Charles Bronson (Holland), Theresa Saldana, José Ferrer. *Dir.* J Lee Thompson.

Evil under the Sun (1982) Peter Ustinov, James Mason, Diana Rigg, Maggie Smith, Roddy McDowall. Agatha Christie novel starring Hercule Poirot. *Dir.* Guy Hamilton.

Evita (1996) Madonna, Antonio Banderas, Jonathan Pryce, Jimmy Nail. Best Song Oscar: 'You Must Love Me' (Andrew Lloyd-Webber & Tim Rice). *Dir.* Alan Parker.

Evolution (2001) David Duchovny, Julianne Moore, Orlando Jones, Seann William Scott, Ted Levine. *Dir.* Ivan Reitman.

Executive Suite (1954) Fredric March, William Holden, June Allyson, Barbara Stanwyck, Walter Pidgeon, Shelley Winters. Boardroom battle. *Dir.* Robert Wise.

Exorcist, The (1973) Ellen Burstyn, Max Von Sydow, Linda Blair, Lee J Cobb. *Dir.* William Friedkin.

Expresso Bongo (1959) Cliff Richard, Laurence Harvey, Sylvia Syms, Gilbert Harding. *Dir.* Val Guest.

Eyes Wide Shut (1999) Tom Cruise (Dr Bill Hayard), Nicole Kidman, Madison Eginton, Marie Richardson. *Dir.* Stanley Kubrick.

Fabulous Baker Boys, The (1989) Jeff Bridges (Jack Baker), Beau Bridges (Frank), Michelle Pfeiffer (Susie Diamond). Pianist brothers ginger up their act by taking on a singer. *Dir.* Steve Kloves.

Face (1997) Robert Carlyle, Ray Winstone, Damon Albarn. Five criminals undertake a robbery, one of them is a traitor. *Dir.* Antonia Bird.

Face Off (1997) John Travolta, Nicolas Cage. *Dir.* John Woo.

Fahrenheit 9/11 (2004) Michael Moore's view on what happened to the United States after September 11; and how the Bush administration allegedly used the tragic event to push forward its agenda for unjust wars in Afghanistan and Iraq. *Dir.* Michael Moore.

Faithful (1996) Cher, Chazz Palminteri, Ryan O'Neal, Paul Mazursky, Amber Smith. Hitman chats to his victim whilst waiting for the signal to kill. *Dir.* Paul Mazursky.

Falling Down (1993) Michael Douglas (D-Fens), Robert Duvall (Prendergast), Barbara Hershey (Beth), Tuesday Weld (Mrs Prendergast). *Dir.* Joel Schumacher.

Fan, The (1996) Robert De Niro (Gil Renard), Wesley Snipes (Bobby Rayburn), Ellen Barkin. Baseball fan kidnaps the son of a star player. *Dir.* Tony Scott.

Fantasia (1940) Cartoon characters to music of Bach, Tchaikovsky, Dukas, Stravinsky, Beethoven, Ponchielli, Schubert and Mussorgsky. *Dir.* Ben Sharpsteen.

Fantastic Voyage (1966) Stephen Boyd, Raquel Welch, Edmond O'Brien, Donald Pleasence, Arthur O'Connell, Arthur Kennedy. *Dir.* Richard Fleizcher.

Far From Heaven (2002) Julianne Moore (Cathy Whitaker), Dennis Quaid (Frank Whitaker), Dennis Haysbert (Raymond Deagan), Patricia Clarkson (Eleonor Fine). In a wealthy suburb during 1957 a wife discovers her marriage is a sham and develops a love for her black gardener. *Dir.* Todd Haynes.

Far from the Madding Crowd (1967) Julie Christie, Peter Finch, Alan Bates, Terence Stamp (Sgt Troy). Set in Victorian Wessex. *Dir.* John Schlesinger.

Farewell My Lovely (1944) Dick Powell, Claire Trevor, Anne Shirley, Mike Mazurki, Otto Kruger. Aka: *Murder My Sweet. Dir.* Edward Dmytryk.

Farewell My Lovely (1975) Robert Mitchum, Charlotte Rampling, John Ireland, Sylvia Miles. Remake of the Raymond Chandler classic. *Dir.* Dick Richards.

Fargo (1996) Frances McDormand, William H Macy, Steve Buscemi, Harve Presnell, Peter Stormare. Car salesman with money troubles hires criminals to kidnap his wife for ransom. Nothing goes to plan. *Dir.* Joel Coen.

Fast and the Furious, The (2001) Paul Walker, Vin Diesel, Michelle Rodriguez, Rick Yune, Jordana Brewster. *Dir.* Rob Cohen.

Fatal Attraction (1987) Michael Douglas (Dan Gallagher), Glenn Close (Alex Forrest), Anne Archer (Beth Gallagher), Fred Gwynne (Arthur). *Dir.* Adrian Lyne.

Father of the Bride (1950) Spencer Tracy, Elizabeth Taylor, Leo G Carroll. *Dir.* Vincente Minnelli.

Father of the Bride (1991) Steve Martin (George Banks), Diane Keaton (Nina Banks), Kimberly Williams (Annie Banks). Remake of the Spencer Tracy classic. *Dir.* Charles Shyer.

Father's Day (1997) Robin Williams (Dale), Billy Crystal (Jack), Nastassja Kinski (Colette), Charlie Hofheimer (Scott), Mel Gibson. *Dir.* Ivan Reitman.

Fear (1996) Reese Witherspoon, Mark Wahlberg. *Dir.* James Foley.

Ferris Bueller's Day Off (1986) Matthew Broderick (Ferris Bueller), Alan Ruck (Cameron Frye), Mia Sara (Sloane Peterson). *Dir.* John Hughes.

Fever Pitch (1996) Colin Firth, Ruth Gemmell, Neil Pearson. Obsession with Arsenal FC creates romantic problems for teacher. *Dir.* David Evans.

Few Good Men, A (1992) Tom Cruise (Lt JG Kaffee), Jack Nicholson (Colonel Jessep), Demi Moore (Lt Cdr Galloway), Kevin Bacon (Capt Ross), Kiefer Sutherland (Lt Kendrick). *Dir.* Rob Reiner.

Fiddler on the Roof (1971) Topol, Norma Crane, Molly Picon. Topol recreates his classic stage role. *Dir.* Norman Jewison.

Field, The (1990) Richard Harris (Bull McCabe), Sean Bean (Tadgh McCabe), Frances Tomelty (Widow), Brenda Fricker (Maggie McCabe), John Hurt (Bird O'Donnell), Tom Berenger (The American). *Dir.* Jim Sheridan.

Field of Dreams (1989) Kevin Costner (Ray Kinsella), Amy Madigan (Annie), James Earl Jones (Terence Mann), Burt Lancaster (Dr Moonlight Graham), Ray Liotta (Shoeless Joe Jackson). Famous line: 'If you build it, he will come'. *Dir.* Phil Alden Robinson.

Fierce Creatures (1997) John Cleese, Jamie Lee Curtis, Kevin Kline, Michael Palin, Ronnie Corbett, Robert Lindsay. Follow-up to *A Fish Called Wanda.* Fred Schepisi replaced Young as director for three weeks whilst refilming the final scenes. *Dir.* Robert Young.

Fifth Element, The (1997) Gary Oldman (Zorg), Bruce Willis (Will Dallas), Milla Jovovich (Leeloo), Ian Holm (Cornelius). Costumes by Jean-Paul Gaultier. *Dir.* Luc Besson.

51st State, The (2001) Samuel L Jackson (Elmo McElroy), Meatloaf (The Lizard), Robert Carlyle (Felix DeSouza), Sean Pertwee (Detective Virgil Kane), Ricky Tomlinson (Leopold Durant), Emily Mortimer (Dakota Phillips), Steven Walters (Blowfish). American inventor of a new drug goes to Liverpool to sell the formula for $20 million to a local drug baron. *Dir.* Ronny Yu.

Fight Club (1999) Brad Pitt (Tyler Durden), Edward Norton, Helena Bonham Carter, Meatloaf. *Dir.* David Fincher.

Final Fantasy: The Spirits Within (2001) Voices of Ming-Na, Alec Baldwin, Ving Rhames, Steve Buscemi, Peri Gilpin, Donald Sutherland, James Woods, Jean Simmons. Animation film about a female scientist in 2065 and her battle to rid the world of powerful aliens known as phantoms. *Dir.* Hironobu Sakaguchi and Moto Sakakibara.

Finding Nemo (2003) Voices of Albert Brooks (Marlin), Ellen DeGeneres (Dory), Alexander Gould (Nemo), Willem Dafoe (Gill), Brad Garrett (Bloat), Allison Janney (Peach), Austin Pendleton (Gurgle), Geoffrey Rush (Nigel), Barry Humphries (Bruce), Eric Bana (Anchor), Bruce Spence (Chum), Bill Hunter (Dentist). A neurotic clownfish goes in search of his adventurous son, who has been captured and placed on display in an aquarium. *Dirs.* Andrew Stanton and Lee Unkrich.

Finding Neverland (2004) Johnny Depp (JM Barrie), Kate Winslet (Sylvia Llewelyn Davies), Julie Christie (Mrs Emma du Maurier), Radha Mitchell (Mary Ansell Barrie), Dustin Hoffman (Charles Frohman), Kelly Macdonald (Peter Pan). The story of JM Barrie's friendship with a family who inspired him to create Peter Pan. *Dir.* Marc Forster.

Finian's Rainbow (1968) Fred Astaire, Petula Clark, Tommy Steele. Tommy Steele plays a leprechaun. *Dir.* Francis Ford Coppola.

Firm, The (1993) Tom Cruise (Mitch Deere), Gene Hackman, Jeanne Tripplehorn. Cruise is the new boy at a Memphis law firm run, unknown to him, by the Mafia. Based on bestseller by John Grisham. *Dir.* Sydney Pollack.

First Blood (1982) Sylvester Stallone (John Rambo), Richard Crenna (Trautman), Brian Dennehy (Teasle). Q Moonblood on the writing credits is Stallone. *Dir.* Ted Kotcheff.

First Great Train Robbery, The (1978) Sean Connery, Donald Sutherland, Lesley-Anne Down. Wayne Sleep makes his first movie appearance. *Dir.* Michael Crichton.

First Knight (1995) Sean Connery, Richard Gere, Julia Ormond, Ben Cross, John Gielgud. King Arthur story that lost money at the box office. *Dir.* Jerry Zucker.

Fish Called Wanda, A (1988) John Cleese (Archie Leach), Jamie Lee Curtis (Wanda), Kevin Kline (Otto), Michael Palin (Ken). Big box office hit, Oscar for Kevin Kline. *Dir.* Charles Crichton.

Fish Tank (2009) Katie Jarvis (Mia Williams), Michael Fassbender (Connor), Kierston Wareing (Joanne Williams), Rebecca Griffiths (Tyler Williams). Volatile 15-year-old Mia lives on an Essex council estate with her single mother Joanne and younger sister Tyler. Mia's only escape from her misery takes the form of street dance. *Dir.* Andrea Arnold.

Fisher King, The (1991) Robin Williams (Parry), Jeff Bridges (Jack Lucas), Amanda Plummer (Lydia), Ted Ross (Limo Bum), Tom Waits. *Dir.* Terry Gilliam.

Five Easy Pieces (1970) Jack Nicholson, Karen Black, Fannie Flagg. Jack Nicholson plays a pianist. *Dir.* Bob Rafelson.

Flash Gordon (1980) Topol, Max Von Sydow, Brian Blessed, Timothy Dalton. Music by Queen. *Dir.* Michael Hodges.

Flashdance (1983) Jennifer Beals (Alex Owens), Michael Nouri (Nick Hurley), Lilia Skala (Hanna Long). *Dir.* Adrian Lyne.

Flatliners (1990) Kiefer Sutherland (Nelson Wright), Julia Roberts (Rachel Mannus), Kevin Bacon (David Labraccio), William Baldwin (Joe Hurley). *Dir.* Joel Schumacher.

Fletch (1985) Chevy Chase (Fletch), Joe Don Baker (Chief Karlin). Sequel: *Fletch Lives* (1989). *Dir.* Michael Ritchie.

Flintstones, The (1994) John Goodman, Elisabeth Perkins, Rick Moranis, Rosie O'Donnell, Elizabeth Taylor. *Dir.* Brian Levant.

Fly, The (1958) David Hedison, Patricia Owens, Vincent Price, Herbert Marshall. Classic horror film. *Dir.* Kurt Neumann.

Fly, The (1986) Jeff Goldblum (Seth Brundle), Geena Davis (Veronica Quaife). David Cronenberg makes a cameo performance as the gynaecologist. *Dir.* David Cronenberg.

Fools Rush In (1997) Matthew Perry, Salma Hayek, Jon Tenney, Jill Clayburgh. *Dir.* Andy Tennant.

Footloose (1984) Kevin Bacon (Ren), Lori Singer (Ariel), John Lithgow (Reverend Shaw Moore). *Dir.* Herbert Ross.

For Me and My Gal (1942) Judy Garland, Gene Kelly, George Murphy. *Dir.* Busby Berkeley.

For the Boys (1991) Bette Midler (Dixie Leonard), James Caan (Eddie Sparks), George Segal (Art Silver). *Dir.* Mark Rydell.

For Your Eyes Only (1981) Roger Moore, Topol, Carole Bouquet (Melina), Julian Glover (Kristatos). Ian Fleming does not get credit of any kind for this film. (Theme song: Sheena Easton.) *Dir.* John Glen.

Forbidden Planet (1956) Walter Pidgeon, Anne Francis, Leslie Nielsen, Warren Stevens, Jack Kelly. Set in AD 2200 and follows the plot of Shakespeare's *The Tempest. Dir.* Fred M Wilcox.

Forever Amber (1947) Linda Darnell, Cornel Wilde, George Sanders (Charles II), Richard Greene, Jessica Tandy. Costume drama set in the reign of Charles II. *Dir.* Otto Preminger.

Forever Young (1992) Mel Gibson (Daniel), Jamie Lee Curtis (Claire), Elijah Wood (Nat), George Wendt (Harry). *Dir.* Steve Miner.

Forrest Gump (1994) Tom Hanks, Robin Wright, Gary Sinise, Sally Field, Hanna R Hall. Won 6 Oscars. *Dir.* Robert Zemeckis.

Fort Apache (1948) Henry Fonda, John Wayne, Shirley Temple, Victor McLaglen, Ward Bond. *Dir.* John Ford.

Fort Apache, the Bronx (1980) Paul Newman, Ed Asner, Ken Wahl, Danny Aiello. *Dir.* Daniel Petrie.

Fortune Cookie, The (1966) Walter Matthau, Jack Lemmon. GB title: *Meet Whiplash Willie. Dir.* Billy Wilder.

40 Days and 40 Nights (2002) Josh Hartnett (Matt), Shannyn Sossamon (Erica Sutton), Paulo Costanzo (Ryan), Adam Trese (John), Emmanuelle Vaugier, Vinessa Shaw. Computer whizz-kid gives up sex for Lent. *Dir.* Michael Lehmann.

48 Hrs (1982) Nick Nolte (Jack Cates), Eddie Murphy (Reggie Hammond), Annette O'Toole (Elaine). Sequel: *Another 48 Hrs* (1990). *Dir.* Walter Hill.

49th Parallel (1941) Eric Portman, Laurence Olivier, Leslie Howard, Raymond Massey, Glynis Johns. US title: *The Invaders. Dir.* Michael Powell.

Foul Play (1978) Goldie Hawn, Chevy Chase, Burgess Meredith, Rachel Roberts, Dudley Moore. Two innocents in San Francisco get involved in plot to assassinate the Pope. *Dir.* Colin Higgins.

Four for Texas (1963) Dean Martin, Frank Sinatra, Anita Ekberg, Ursula Andress, Charles Bronson, Victor Buono, 3 Stooges. *Dir.* Robert Aldrich.

Four Horsemen of the Apocalypse, The (1921) Rudolph Valentino, Alice Terry, Alan Hale, Wallace Beery. Young Argentinian fights for his father's country, France, in WWI. 1961 remake starred Glenn Ford. *Dir.* Rex Ingram.

Four Musketeers, The (Revenge of Milady), (1974) Michael York, Oliver Reed, Frank Finlay, Richard Chamberlain, Raquel Welch, Faye Dunaway, Charlton Heston. *Dir.* Richard Lester.

Four Weddings and a Funeral (1994) Hugh Grant (Charles), Andie MacDowell, Kristin Scott Thomas, Simon Callow. *Dir.* Mike Newell.

1492: Conquest of Paradise (1992) Gérard Depardieu (Columbus), Armand Assante (Sanchez), Sigourney Weaver (Queen Isabel). *Dir.* Ridley Scott.

Fourth Protocol, The (1987) Michael Caine (John Preston), Pierce Brosnan (Petrofsky), Joanna Cassidy (Vassileva). Thriller by Frederick Forsyth. *Dir.* John Mackenzie.

Fox, The (1968) Anne Heywood, Sandy Dennis, Keir Dullea. Based on DH Lawrence's novella. *Dir.* Mark Rydell.

Francis (1949) Donald O'Connor, Patricia Medina, Chill Wills (as voice of Francis the Mule). Series of sequels followed. *Dir.* Arthur Lubin.

Frankenstein (1931) Boris Karloff, Colin Clive, Mae Clarke, Edward Van Sloan. Series of sequels followed. *Dir.* James Whale.

Frankie and Johnny (1966) Elvis Presley, Donna Douglas, Nancy Kovack. *Dir.* Frederick De Cordova.

Frankie and Johnny (1991) Al Pacino (Johnny), Michelle Pfeiffer (Frankie). *Dir.* Garry Marshall.

Frantic (1988) Harrison Ford (Richard Walker), Betty Buckley (Sondra Walker), Emmanuelle Seigner. American cardiologist searching for his kidnapped wife in Paris becomes embroiled with Arabs. *Dir.* Roman Polanski.

Freebie and the Bean (1974) Alan Arkin, James Caan, Loretta Swit. *Dir.* Richard Rush.

French Connection, The (1971) Gene Hackman (Popeye Doyle), Roy Scheider, Fernando Rey. Oscars for Best Picture, Best Director, Best Actor (Hackman) and Ernest Tidyman took Oscar for Best Adapted Screenplay. *Dir.* William Friedkin.

French Lieutenant's Woman (1981) Meryl Streep, Jeremy Irons, Leo McKern, Peter Vaughan. Harold Pinter adaption of John Fowles's novel. *Dir.* Karel Reisz.

Frenzy (1972) Barry Foster, Jon Finch, Alec McCowen, Vivien Merchant, Anna Massey, Billie Whitelaw. Anthony Shaffer adapted *Goodbye Piccadilly, Farewell Leicester Square* by Arthur La Bern. *Dir.* Alfred Hitchcock.

Freshman, The (1990) Marlon Brando (Carmine Sabatini), Matthew Broderick (Clark Kellogg), Maximilian Schell (Larry London). *Dir.* Andrew Bergman.

Freud (1962) Montgomery Clift, Larry Parks, Susannah York, David McCallum. *Dir.* John Huston.

Friday the 13th (1980) Betsy Palmer, Adrienne King, Jeannine Taylor, Robbi Morgan. Others in series include part 4 *The Final Chapter* and the last (part 8), *Jason Takes Manhattan. Dir.* Sean S. Cunningham.

Fried Green Tomatoes at the Whistle Stop Cafe (1992) Kathy Bates (Evelyn Couch), Jessica Tandy (Ninny Threadgoode). *Dir.* Jon Avnet.

Friendly Persuasion (1956) Gary Cooper, Dorothy McGuire, Anthony Perkins. No script credit (the writer, Michael Wilson, was blacklisted). *Dir.* William Wyler.

Fright Night (1985) Chris Sarandon (Jerry Dandridge), Roddy McDowall (Peter Vincent). William Ragsdale (Charley Brewster). Present-day vampires. McDowall's character named as tribute to Peter Cushing and Vincent Price. *Dir.* Tom Holland.

Fright Night Part 2 (1988) Roddy McDowall, William Ragsdale. *Dir.* Tommy Lee Wallace.

Frisco Kid, The (1979) Gene Wilder, Harrison Ford, Leo Fuchs. *Dir.* Robert Aldrich.

Fritz the Cat (1971) First 'X'-rated cartoon, about the adventures of an alleycat in New York. *Dir.* Ralph Bakshi.

From Hell (2001) Johnny Depp (Inspector Fred Abberline), Heather Graham (Mary Kelly), Ian Holm, Robbie Coltrane. Twist on the Jack the Ripper story. *Dir.* Albert Hughes and Allen Hughes.

From Here to Eternity (1953) Burt Lancaster, Deborah Kerr, Frank Sinatra, Montgomery Clift. *Dir.* Fred Zinnemann.

From Russia with Love (1963) Sean Connery, Robert Shaw (Red Grant), Daniela Bianchi (Tatiana Romanova), Lotte Lenya (Rosa Kleb), Bernard Lee, Lois Maxwell, Pedro Armendariz.Theme song sung by Matt Monro. *Dir.* Terence Young.

Front Page, The (1931) Adolph Merjon, Pat O'Brien, Mary Brian, Walter Catlett, Edward Everett Horton. *Dir.* Lewis Milestone.

Front Page, The (1974) Walter Matthau, Jack Lemmon, Susan Sarandon, David Wayne, Vincent Gardenia. *Dir.* Billy Wilder.

Fugitive, The (1993) Harrison Ford (Dr Richard Kimble), Tommy Lee Jones (Lt Gerard). *Dir.* Andrew Davis.

Full Metal Jacket (1987) Matthew Modine (Private Joker), Adam Baldwin (Animal Mother), Dorian Harewood (Eightball), Vincent D'Onofrio (Private Pyle). *Dir.* Stanley Kubrick.

Full Monty, The (1997) Robert Carlyle (Gaz), Mark Addy (Dave), Tom Wilkinson (Gerald), Hugo Speer (Guy), Paul Barber (Horse), Steve Huison (Lomper). Unemployed Sheffield welders decide to become male strippers. *Dir.* Peter Cattaneo.

Funeral, The (1996) Christopher Walken, Isabelle Adjani, Chris Penn, Annabella Sciorra. *Dir.* Abel Ferrara.

Funeral in Berlin (1967) Michael Caine (Harry Palmer), Oscar Homolka, Eva Renzi, Hugh Burden. *Dir.* Guy Hamilton.

Funny Girl (1968) Barbra Streisand (Fanny Brice), Omar Sharif, Walter Pidgeon, Kay Medford. *Dir.* William Wyler.

Funny Lady (1975) Barbra Streisand, James Caan, Ben Vereen, Omar Sharif, Roddy McDowall. *Dir.* Herbert Ross.

Funny Thing Happened on the Way to the Forum, A (1966) Zero Mostel, Phil Silvers, Michael Crawford, Michael Hordern, Buster Keaton. *Dir.* Richard Lester.

Futureworld (1976) Peter Fonda, Blythe Danner, Yul Brynner, Arthur Hill, Stuart Margolin. *Dir.* Richard T Heffron.

Game, The (1997) Michael Douglas (Nicholas Van Orton), Sean Penn (Conrad Van Orton). *Dir.* David Fincher.

Games, The (1970) Stanley Baker, Michael Crawford, Ryan O'Neal, Charles Aznavour. Four men take part in the Rome Olympics marathon. *Dir.* Michael Winner.

Gandhi (1982) Ben Kingsley (Gandhi), Candice Bergen (Margaret Bourke-White), Edward Fox (General Dyer), Daniel Day Lewis (Colin). *Dir.* Richard Attenborough.

Gangs of New York (2002) Leonardo DiCaprio (Amsterdam Vallon), Daniel Day-Lewis (William 'Bill the Butcher' Cutting), Cameron Diaz (Jenny Everdeane), Jim Broadbent (William 'Boss' Tweed), Henry Thomas (Johnny Sirocco), Liam Neeson (Priest Vallon, Amsterdam's father), Brendan Gleeson (Walter 'Monk' McGinn), John C Reilly ('Happy' Jack Mulraney), David Hemmings (Mr Schermerhorn). In 1863, Amsterdam Vallon returns to the Five Points area of New York City seeking revenge against Bill the Butcher, his father's killer. *Dir.* Martin Scorsese.

Garden State (2004) Zach Braff (Andrew Largeman), Kenneth Graymez (Busboy), George C Wolfe (Restaurant Manager), Austin Lysy (Waiter), Gary Gilbert (Young Hollywood Guy), Jill Flint (Obnoxious Girl), Ian Holm (Gideon Largeman). A young man returns home for his mother's funeral after being estranged from his family for a decade. *Dir.* Zach Braff.

Gardens of Stone (1987) James Caan (Clell Hazard), Anjelica Huston (Samantha Davis), James Earl Jones (Goody Nelson). Vietnam War from the perspective of soldiers guarding Arlington National Cemetery. *Dir.* Francis Ford Coppola.

Gaslight (1940) Anton Walbrook, Diana Wynyard, Frank Pettingell, Robert Newton, Jimmy Hanley. Victorian schizophrenic tries to drive his wife insane because of his guilty past. *Dir.* Thorold Dickinson.

Gaslight (1944) Charles Boyer, Ingrid Bergman, Joseph Cotten, Angela Lansbury. Remake of the 1940 film. *Dir.* George Cukor.

Genevieve (1953) Dinah Sheridan, John Gregson, Kay Kendall, Kenneth More, Joyce Grenfell. Genevieve was a classic car (Darracq). *Dir.* Henry Cornelius.

Genghis Khan (1964) Omar Sharif, Stephen Boyd, James Mason, Telly Savalas, Françoise Dorléac. *Dir.* Henry Levin.

Gentleman Jim (1942) Errol Flynn, Alan Hale, Ward Bond. Based on the life of world heavyweight boxing champion Jim Corbett. *Dir.* Raoul Walsh.

Gentlemen Marry Brunettes (1955) Jane Russell, Jeanne Crain, Alan Young, Rudy Vallee. Sequel to *Gentlemen Prefer Blondes. Dir.* Richard Sale.

Gentlemen Prefer Blondes (1953) Jane Russell, Marilyn Monroe, Charles Coburn. Based on Anita Loos's novel. *Dir.* Howard Hawks.

Geordie (1955) Bill Travers, Alastair Sim, Stanley Baxter. Sickly Scottish boy becomes Olympic hammer thrower. *Dir.* Frank Launder.

George Raft Story, The (1961) Ray Danton, Julie London, Jayne Mansfield, Frank Gorshin, Neville Brand (Al Capone). GB title: *Spin of a Coin. Dir.* Joseph M Newman.

Georgy Girl (1966) James Mason, Lynn Redgrave, Charlotte Rampling, Alan Bates, Rachel Kempson. *Dir.* Silvio Narizzano.

Gerald McBoing Boing (1951) Cartoon written by Dr Seuss (Theodore Geisel), which won an Oscar. *Dir.* Robert Cannon.

Gerry (2003) Matt Damon, Casey Affleck, Gus Van Sant. Drama of two friends (Damon and Affleck) each called 'Gerry', who go hiking in a remote area and lose their way in the forbiddingly beautiful terrain. *Dir.* Gus Van Sant.

Get Carter (1971) Michael Caine, John Osborne, Ian Hendry, Britt Ekland. Based on Ted Lewis's novel *Jack's Return Home. Dir.* Mike Hodges. Remake starring Sly Stallone as Carter was made in 2000, directed by Stephen Kay. Caine had a small cameo as Cliff Brumby.

Get Shorty (1995) John Travolta, Gene Hackman, Rene Russo, Danny De Vito. Miami debt collector for the Mob goes to Las Vegas and discovers a talent for film production. *Dir.* Barry Sonnenfeld.

Getaway, The (1972) Steve McQueen, Ali MacGraw, Ben Johnson, Sally Struthers, Slim Pickens. *Dir.* Sam Peckinpah.

Getaway, The (1994) Alec Baldwin, Kim Basinger, Michael Madsen, James Woods. *Dir.* Roger Donaldson.

Ghost (1990) Patrick Swayze (Sam Wheat), Demi Moore (Molly Jensen), Whoopi Goldberg (Oda Mae Brown). *Dir.* Jerry Zucker.

Ghost in the Machine (1993) Karen Allen, Chris Mulkey, Ted Marcoux, Nancy Fish. *Dir.* Rachel Talalay.

Ghost World (2001) Thora Birch (Enid), Scarlett Johansson (Rebecca), Steve Buscemi (Seymour), Teri Garr (Maxine). Two teenagers leave high school and feel inadequate in the adult world. *Dir.* Terry Zwigoff.

Ghostbusters (1984) Bill Murray (Dr Peter Venkman), Dan Aykroyd (Dr Raymond Stantz), Harold Ramis (Dr Egon Spengler), Sigourney Weaver (Dana Barrett), Rick Moranis (Louis Tully). *Ghostbusters II* (1989), was sequel. Ramis and Aykroyd also wrote the screenplay. *Dir.* Ivan Reitman.

Ghosts from the Past (1997) Alec Baldwin (DeLaughter), Whoopi Goldberg (Myrlie), James Woods (Byron De La Beckwith). Original title: *Ghosts of Mississippi. Dir.* Rob Reiner.

GI Jane (1997) Demi Moore (Lt Jordan O'Neill), Anne Bancroft (Senator Lillian DeHaven). *Dir.* Ridley Scott.

Giant (1956) Rock Hudson, Elizabeth Taylor, James Dean, Mercedes McCambridge, Carroll Baker, Chill Wills, Rod Taylor, Earl Holliman. *Dir.* George Stevens.

Gigi (1958) Leslie Caron, Louis Jourdan, Maurice Chevalier, Hermione Gingold, Eva Gabor. *Dir.* Vincente Minnelli.

Gilda (1946) Rita Hayworth, Glenn Ford, George Macready. *Dir.* Charles Vidor.

Girl 6 (1996) Theresa Randle, Isaiah Washington, Spike Lee. Unsuccessful actress is employed as a sex chat operator. *Dir.* Spike Lee.

Girl With the Dragon Tattoo, The (2011) Daniel Craig (Mikael Blomkvist), Rooney Mara (Lisbeth Salander), Yorick van Wageningen (Nils Bjurman), Christopher Plummer (Henrik Vanger), Joely Richardson (Anita Vanger / Harriet Vanger). Mystery thriller based on the Swedish novel of the same name by Stieg Larsson. Story of journalist Mikael Blomkvist's investigation to find out what happened to a woman from a wealthy family who disappeared 40 years earlier. *Dir.* David Fincher.

Girls Girls Girls (1962) Elvis Presley, Stella Stevens, Laurel Goodwin. *Dir.* Norman Taurog.

Give My Regards to Broad Street (1984) Paul McCartney, Bryan Brown, Ringo Starr, Barbara Bach, Tracey Ullman, Ralph Richardson. *Dir.* Peter Webb.

Gladiator (2000) Russel Crowe (Maximus), Joaquin Phoenix (Commodus), Connie Nielson, Derek Jacobi, Richard Harris (Emperor Marcus Aurelius), Oliver Reed (Proximo). *Dir.* Ridley Scott.

Glass Menagerie, The (1950) Gertrude Lawrence, Jane Wyman, Kirk Douglas, Arthur Kennedy. Shy, crippled girl seeks escape from her shabby life in St Louis. *Dir.* Irving Rapper.

Glass Menagerie, The (1987) Joanne Woodward, John Malkovich, Karen Allen. Remake of earlier version of Tennessee Williams' play. *Dir.* Paul Newman.

Glass Mountain, The (1949) Michael Denison, Dulcie Gray, Tito Gobbi. Nino Rota's music score is memorable and haunting. *Dir.* Henry Cass.

Gleaming the Cube (1988) Christian Slater, Steven Bauer, Richard Herd. Skateboarding film. *Dir.* Graeme Clifford.

Glenn Miller Story, The (1954) James Stewart, June Allyson, Charles Drake, Louis Armstrong, Gene Krupa. *Dir.* Anthony Mann.

Gloria (1980) Gena Rowlands, John Adames, Buck Henry. *Dir.* John Cassavetes.

Glory (1989) Matthew Broderick (Col Robert G Shaw), Denzel Washington (Private Trip), Cary Elwes (Maj Cabot Forbes), Morgan Freeman (Sgt Maj John Rawlins). *Dir.* Edward Zwick.

Go-Between, The (1970) Alan Bates, Julie Christie, Michael Redgrave, Dominic Guard, Michael Gough, Margaret Leighton, Edward Fox. Harold Pinter adaptation of LP Hartley's novel. *Dir.* Joseph Losey.

Godfather, The (1972). Marlon Brando, Al Pacino, James Caan, Robert Duvall, Diane Keaton, Richard Conte. *Dir.* Francis Ford Coppola.

Godfather Part II, The (1974) Al Pacino, Robert De Niro, Diane Keaton, Robert Duvall, Lee Strasberg, Troy Donahue. The first sequel to win a Best Picture Oscar (and 5 others). *Dir.* Francis Ford Coppola.

Godfather Part III, The (1990) Al Pacino, Diane Keaton, Talia Shire, Andy Garcia, Eli Wallach, Sofia Coppola. *Dir.* Francis Ford Coppola.

Godzilla (1955) Raymond Burr, Takashi Shimura, Momoko Kochi. *Dir.* Inoshiro Honda.

Godzilla (1998) Matthew Broderick, Jean Reno, Maria Pitillo, Hank Azaria, Kevin Dunn, Michael Lerner, Harry Shearer. As a result of French nuclear tests in the Pacific, a giant lizard invades Manhattan. Remake of the Japanese classic. *Dir.* Roland Emmerich.

Goin' South (1978) Jack Nicholson, Mary Steenburgen, Christopher Lloyd, John Belushi. *Dir.* Jack Nicholson.

Going My Way (1944) Bing Crosby (Father O'Malley), Barry Fitzgerald, Rise Stevens, Gene Lockhart. *Dir.* Leo McCarey.

Golden Compass, The (2007) Daniel Craig (Lord Asriel), Nicole Kidman (Marisa Coulter), Dakota Blue Richards (Lyra Belacqua), Sam Elliott (Lee Scoresby, a Texan aeronaut), Eva Green (Serafina Pekkala, a witch queen), Tom Courtenay (Farder Coram), Christopher Lee (Magisterium's First High Councillor), Derek Jacobi (the Magisterial Emissary), Ian McKellen (voice of Iorek Byrnison, an armoured bear), Ian McShane (voice of Ragnar Sturlusson, king of the panserbjørner), Kathy Bates (voice of Hester, Lee Scoresby's dæmon), Kristin Scott Thomas (voice of Stelmaria, Lord Asriel's dæmon). Fantasy based on *Northern Lights,* the first novel in Philip Pullman's trilogy *His Dark Materials.* Lyra, an orphan living in a parallel universe in which a person's soul resides outside the body in an animal-like form called a 'dæmon', fights against the evil Magisterium in an attempt to rescue her friend who has been kidnapped. *Dir.* Chris Weitz.

Goldeneye (1995) Pierce Brosnan, Sean Bean (Alec Trevelyan), Izabella Scorupco (Natalaya Simonova), Famke Janssen (Xenia Onatopp), Judi Dench (M), Desmond Llewelyn (Q), Samantha Bond (Miss Moneypenny), Joe Don Baker (Jack Wade), Robbie Coltrane (Valentin). Title song written by Bono and The Edge and performed by Tina Turner. *Dir.* Martin Campbell.

Goldfinger (1964) Sean Connery, Honor Blackman (Pussy Galore), Gert Fröbe (Auric Goldfinger), Harold Sakatá (Oddjob), Bernard Lee, Lois Maxwell, Desmond Llewellyn, Shirley Eaton. Theme song sung by Shirley Bassey. *Dir.* Guy Hamilton.

Gone with the Wind (1939) Clark Gable, Vivien Leigh, Olivia de Havilland, Leslie Howard, Thomas Mitchell, Hattie McDaniel, Butterfly McQueen. *Dir.* Victor Fleming (with George Cukor, Sam Wood, B Reeves Eason).

Good Earth, The (1937) Paul Muni, Luise Rainer, Keye Luke. Chinese peasant grows rich but loses his wife. *Dir.* Sidney Franklin.

Good Morning, Vietnam (1987) Robin Williams (Adrian Cronauer), Forest Whitaker (Edward Garlick). *Dir.* Barry Levinson.

Good Mother, The (1988) Diane Keaton (Anna), Liam Neeson (Leo). *Dir.* Leonard Nimoy.

Good Son, The (1993) Macaulay Culkin, Elijah Wood, Wendy Crewson, Quinn Culkin. Ten-year-old boy is a sadistic killer. *Dir.* Joseph Ruben.

Good, the Bad and the Ugly, The (1966) Clint Eastwood, Eli Wallach, Lee Van Cleef. *Dir.* Sergio Leone.

Good Will Hunting (1997) Robin Williams, Matt Damon (Will Hunting), Ben Affleck, Minnie Driver, Stellan Skarsgard. Janitor is spotted as a mathematical genius. *Dir.* Gus Van Sant.

Good Year, A (2006) Russell Crowe (Max Skinner), Albert Finney (Uncle Henry Skinner), Freddie Highmore (Young Max Skinner). A British investment broker inherits his uncle's chateau and vineyard in Provence, where he spent much of his childhood, and discovers a new laid-back lifestyle. *Dir.* Ridley Scott.

Goodbye, Columbus (1969) Richard Benjamin, Ali MacGraw, Jack Klugman. Jewish librarian has an affair with daughter of a nouveau riche family. *Dir.* Larry Peerce.

Goodbye Girl, The (1977) Richard Dreyfuss, Marsha Mason, Quinn Cummings. Neil Simon story. *Dir.* Herbert Ross.

Goodbye, Mr Chips (1939) Robert Donat, Greer Garson, Paul Henreid, John Mills. James Hilton's novel adapted by RC Sherriff, Claudine West & Eric Maschwitz. *Dir.* Sam Wood.

Goodbye, Mr Chips (1969) Peter O'Toole, Petula Clark, Michael Redgrave, Sian Phillips. Musical remake of the 1939 classic. *Dir.* Herbert Ross.

Goodfellas (1990) Robert De Niro (James Conway), Ray Liotta (Henry Hill), Joe Pesci (Tommy De Vito), Lorraine Bracco (Karen Hill), Catherine Scorsese (Tommy's mother). *Dir.* Martin Scorsese.

Goonies, The (1985) Sean Astin (Mickey), Josh Brolin (Brand), Jeff Cohen (Chunk), Corey Feldman (Mouth). Screenplay by Chris Columbus, based on a Steven Spielberg story. *Dir.* Richard Donner.

Gorillas in the Mist (1988) Sigourney Weaver (Diane Fossey), Bryan Brown (Bob Campbell). *Dir.* Michael Apted.

Gorky Park (1983) William Hurt (Arkady Renko), Lee Marvin (Jack Osborne). Filmed mainly in Helsinki. *Dir.* Michael Apted.

Gosford Park (2001) Maggie Smith (Constance, Countess of Trentham), Michael Gambon (Sir William McCordle), Kristin Scott Thomas (Lady Sylvia McCordle), Camilla Rutherford (Isobel McCordle), Eileen Atkins (Mrs Croft), Jeremy Northam (Ivor Novello), Clive Owen (Robert Parks), Alan Bates (Jennings), Helen Mirren (Mrs Wilson), Stephen Fry (Inspector Thompson), Sophie Thompson (Dorothy), Derek Jacobi (Probert), Richard E Grant (George). Set in a country house in the 1930s, the weekend guests fall under suspicion when the host is killed twice! Julian Fellowes won an Oscar for his script. *Dir.* Robert Altman.

Grace of My Heart (1996) Illeana Douglas, John Turturro, Eric Stoltz, Patsy Kensit, Bridget Fonda, Matt Dillon. Based loosely on Carole King, with Illeana Douglas's voice dubbed by Kristen Vigard. *Dir.* Allison Anders.

Graduate, The (1967) Dustin Hoffman (Benjamin Braddock), Anne Bancroft (Mrs Robinson), Katharine Ross. *Dir.* Mike Nichols.

Gran Torino (2008) Clint Eastwood (Walt Kowalski), Bee Vang (Thao Vang Lor), Ahney Her (Sue, Lor Thao's older sister), Christopher Carley (Father Janovich), Doua Moua (Fong 'Spider'), Sonny Vue (Smokie), Brian Haley (Mitch Kowalski), Brian Howe (Steve Kowalski), Geraldine Hughes (Karen Kowalski), Dreama Walker (Ashley Kowalski), Michael E Kurowski (Josh Kowalski). Recently widowed Korean War veteran Walt Kowalski is alienated from his family and angry at the politically correct world. Walt's young Hmong neighbour, Thao, tries to steal Walt's prized 1972 Ford Gran Torino on a dare by his cousin for initiation into a gang. Walt develops a relationship with the boy and his family. Eastwood's son Scott (as Scott Reeves) has a small role as Trey. *Dir.* Clint Eastwood.

Grand Canyon (1991) Danny Glover, Kevin Kline, Steve Martin. Black truck driver and white lawyer form an unlikely friendship. *Dir.* Lawrence Kasdan.

Grand Hotel (1932) Greta Garbo (Grusinskaya), John Barrymore, Lionel Barrymore, Joan Crawford. Famous Garbo line: 'I want to be alone'. *Dir.* Edmund Goulding.

Grand Prix (1966) James Garner, Eva Marie Saint, Yves Montand. *Dir.* John Frankenheimer.

Grande Illusion, La (1937) Pierre Fresnay, Erich Von Stroheim, Jean Gabin. Three captured French WWI pilots have uneasy relationship with their German commandant. *Dir.* Jean Renoir.

Grapes of Wrath, The (1940) Henry Fonda, Jane Darwell, John Carradine, Grant Mitchell. From the John Steinbeck novel. Oklahoma farmers trek to California after dust bowl disaster of the Thirties. *Dir.* John Ford.

Grease (1978) John Travolta, Olivia Newton-John, Stockard Channing, Frankie Avalon, Jeff Conaway, Sha Na Na, Eve Arden, Sid Caesar. School: Rydell High. *Dir.* Randal Kleiser.

Grease 2 (1982) Maxwell Caulfield, Michelle Pfeiffer, Lorna Luft, Eve Arden, Sid Caesar. *Dir.* Patricia Birch.

Great Balls of Fire (1989) Dennis Quaid (Jerry Lee Lewis), Winona Ryder (Myra Gale Lewis), John Doe (JW Brown). Peter Cook is 'First English Reporter'. *Dir.* Jim McBride.

Great Caruso, The (1951) Mario Lanza, Ann Blyth, Jarmila Novotna, Alan Napier. *Dir.* Richard Thorpe.

Great Escape, The (1963) James Garner, Steve McQueen, Richard Attenborough, Charles Bronson, Donald Pleasence, James Coburn, David McCallum, Gordon Jackson, John Leyton. *Dir.* John Sturges.

Great Expectations (1934) Phillip Holmes (Pip), Jane Wyatt (Estella), Henry Hull (Magwitch), Alan Hale (Joe Gargery), Francis L Sullivan (Jaggers), Florence Reed (Miss Havisham). *Dir.* Stuart Walker.

Great Expectations (1946) John Mills, Bernard Miles, Finlay Currie, Martita Hunt, Valerie Hobson, Jean Simmons, Alec Guinness, Francis L Sullivan. *Dir.* David Lean.

Great Gatsby, The (1949) Alan Ladd, Macdonald Carey, Barry Sullivan. Based on novel by F Scott Fitzgerald. *Dir.* Elliott Nugent.

Great Gatsby, The (1974) Robert Redford, Mia Farrow, Karen Black, Sam Waterston, Lois Chiles. Screenplay by Francis Ford Coppola. Nelson Riddle gained Oscar for music. *Dir.* Jack Clayton.

Great Muppet Caper, The (1981) Diana Rigg, Charles Grodin, John Cleese, Peter Ustinov, Robert Morley, Trevor Howard. Peter Falk has cameo as a tramp. *Dir.* Jim Henson.

Great St Trinian's Train Robbery, The (1966) Frankie Howerd, Dora Bryan, Reg Varney, George Cole. *Dir.* Frank Launder.

Great Santini, The (1979) Robert Duvall, Michael O'Keefe, Blythe Danner, Julie Anne Haddock. *Dir.* Lewis John Carlino.

Great Scout and Cathouse Thursday, The (1976) Lee Marvin, Oliver Reed, Kay Lenz, Robert Culp, Elizabeth Ashley, Sylvia Miles, Strother Martin. *Dir.* Don Taylor.

Great Waldo Pepper, The (1975) Robert Redford, Bo Svenson, Bo Brundin, Susan Sarandon. *Dir.* George Roy Hill.

Great Waltz, The (1938) Fernand Gravet, Luise Rainer, Miliza Korjus. Biopic of Johann Strauss the Younger. *Dir.* Julien Duvivier.

Great White Hope, The (1970) James Earl Jones, Jane Alexander, Lou Gilbert, Hal Holbrook. Jack Johnson story (he's called Jefferson in the film). *Dir.* Martin Ritt.

Great White Hype, The (1996) Samuel L Jackson, Jeff Goldblum, John Rhys-Davies. *Dir.* Reginald Hudlin.

Great Ziegfeld, The (1936) William Powell, Luise Rainer (Anna Held), Myrna Loy (Billie Burke), Frank Morgan, Ray Bolger, Fanny Brice. Biopic of impresario Florenz Ziegfeld. *Dir.* Robert Z Leonard.

Greatest, The (1977) Muhammad Ali, Ernest Borgnine, Robert Duvall, Ben Johnson, James Earl Jones. *Dir.* Tom Gries.

Greatest Show on Earth, The (1952) Betty Hutton, Cornel Wilde, Charlton Heston, James Stewart, Dorothy Lamour, John Ringling North. *Dir.* Cecil B de Mille.

Greatest Story Ever Told, The (1965) Max Von Sydow, Dorothy McGuire, Claude Rains, José Ferrer, David McCallum, Charlton Heston, Sidney Poitier, John Wayne, Pat Boone, Telly Savalas, Angela Lansbury. Famous John Wayne line: 'Truly this man was the Son of God'. *Dir.* George Stevens.

Greed (1925) Gibson Gowland, Zasu Pitts, Jean Hersholt. Ex-miner dentist kills his wife and later in Death Valley kills her lover but is bound to him by handcuffs. Re-edited by June Mathis and notable for its original length of nearly 9 hours. *Dir.* Erich Von Stroheim.

Green Berets, The (1968) John Wayne, David Janssen, Jim Hutton, Aldo Ray, Patrick Wayne. Vietnam War film. *Dir.* John Wayne.

Gremlins (1984) Zach Galligan (Billy), Hoyt Axton (Rand Peltzer), Phoebe Cates (Kate), Keye Luke (Grandfather), Judge Reinhold (Gerald). Don't get them wet and never feed them after midnight. Sequel: *Gremlins II (The New Batch). Dir.* Joe Dante.

Greystoke: The Legend of Tarzan, Lord of the Apes (1984) Christopher Lambert (John Clayton / Tarzan), Ralph Richardson (Lord Greystoke), Andie MacDowell (Jane Porter). *Dir.* Hugh Hudson.

Gridlock'd (1997) Tim Roth (Stretch), Tupac Shakur (Spoon), Thandie Newton (Cookie). *Dir.* Vondie Curtis-Hall.

Grifters, The (1990) Anjelica Huston (Lily Dillon), John Cusack (Roy Dillon), Annette Bening (Myra Langtry). *Dir.* Stephen Frears.

Groundhog Day (1993) Bill Murray (Phil), Andie MacDowell (Rita). Weatherman Murray is cursed to live the same day over and over. *Dir.* Harold Ramis.

Groundstar Conspiracy, The (1972) George Peppard, Michael Sarrazin, James Olson. *Dir.* Lamont Johnson.

Group, The (1966) Joanna Pettet, Candice Bergen, Jessica Walter, Joan Hackett, Elizabeth Hartman, Kathleen Widdoes, Larry Hagman, Hal Holbrook, Robert Emhardt. *Dir.* Sidney Lumet.

Guarding Tess (1994) Shirley MacLaine, Nicolas Cage, Austin Pendleton, Richard Griffiths. Secret Service agent engages in battle of wills with a former First Lady. *Dir.* Hugh Wilson.

Guess Who's Coming to Dinner (1967) Spencer Tracy, Katherine Hepburn, Sidney Poitier, Katharine Houghton. Katherine Houghton is the niece of Katharine Hepburn. *Dir.* Stanley Kramer.

Gunfight at the OK Corral (1957) Burt Lancaster, Kirk Douglas, Jo Van Fleet, Rhonda Fleming, John Ireland. *Dir.* John Sturges.

Gunfighter, The (1950) Gregory Peck, Helen Westcott, Karl Malden. *Dir.* Henry King.

Guns of Navarone (1961) Gregory Peck, David Niven, Stanley Baker, Anthony Quinn, Anthony Quayle, James Darren, James Robertson Justice, Richard Harris. *Dir.* J Lee Thompson.

Guys and Dolls (1955) Frank Sinatra, Marlon Brando, Jean Simmons, Vivian Blaine, Stubby Kaye. *Dir.* Joseph L Mankiewicz.

Gypsy (1962) Rosalind Russell, Natalie Wood, Karl Malden. *Dir.* Mervyn Le Roy.

Hairspray (1988) Sonny Bono (Franklin Von Tussle), Ruth Brown (Motormouth Maybell), Divine (Edna Turnblad / Arvin Hodgepile), Deborah Harry (Velma Von Tussle), Ricki Lake (Tracy Turnblad), Pia Zadora (Beatnik chick). *Dir.* John Waters.

Half Moon Street (1986) Sigourney Weaver (Lauren Slaughter), Michael Caine (Lord Bullbeck). *Dir.* Bob Swaim.

Halloween (1978) Jamie Lee Curtis, Donald Pleasence (Dr Loomis). *Dir.* John Carpenter. The franchise was rebooted by the Rob Zombie-directed remakes *Halloween* (2007) and *Halloween II* (2009).

Halloween 2 (1981) Jamie Lee Curtis, Donald Pleasence (Dr Loomis). *Dir.* Rick Rosenthal.

Halloween 3: Season of the Witch (1983) Tom Atkins, Stacey Nelkin, Dan O'Herlihy. *Dir.* Tommy Lee Wallace.

Halloween 4: The Return of Michael Myers (1988) Donald Pleasence, Ellie Cornell, Danielle Harris. *Dir.* Dwight H Little.

Halloween 5: The Revenge of Michael Myers (1989) Donald Pleasence, Danielle Harris, Wendy Kaplan, Ellie Cornell, Donald L Shanks, Jeffrey Landman, Beau Starr. *Dir.* Dominique Othenin-Girard.

Halloween H2O (1998) Jamie Lee Curtis, Adam Arkin, Josh Harnett, Michelle Williams, Adam Hann-Byrd. *Dir.* Steve Miner.

Halloween: Resurrection (2002) Jamie Lee Curtis, Brad Loree, Busta Rhymes, Tyra Banks, Luke Kirby. When a group of teenagers win a contest to spend a night in Michael Myers's childhood home to be broadcast live on the internet, they believe they are in for a little fun and some free publicity. But it all goes frightfully wrong and the game turns into a battle for survival. *Dir.* Rick Rosenthal.

Hamlet (1948) Laurence Olivier, Eileen Herlie, Jean Simmons, Peter Cushing, Patrick Troughton. *Dir.* Laurence Olivier.

Hamlet (1990) Mel Gibson, Glenn Close, Alan Bates, Paul Scofield, Helena Bonham Carter, Ian Holm. *Dir.* Franco Zeffirelli.

Hancock (2008) Will Smith (John Hancock), Jason Bateman (Ray Embrey), Charlize Theron (Mary Embrey), Eddie Marsan (Kenneth 'Red' Parker Jr). Comedy telling the story of a bumbling vigilante superhero, John Hancock, whose reckless actions routinely cost the city of Los Angeles millions of dollars. Eventually one person he saves, Ray Embrey, decides to change Hancock's public image. *Dir.* Peter Berg.

Hand that Rocks the Cradle, The (1992) Rebecca DeMornay (Peyton Flanders), Annabella Sciorra (Claire Bartel), Matt McCoy (Michael Bartel). *Dir.* Curtis Hanson.

Handful of Dust (1988) James Wilby (Tony Last), Kristin Scott Thomas (Brenda Last), Anjelica Huston (Mrs Rattery), Stephen Fry (Reggie), Alec Guinness (Mr Todd), Judi Dench (Mrs Beaver). *Dir.* Charles Sturridge.

Hang 'em High (1967) Clint Eastwood, Inger Stevens, Pat Hingle. *Dir.* Ted Post.

Hangover, The (2009) Bradley Cooper (Phil Wenneck), Ed Helms (Stu Price), Zach Galifianakis (Alan Garner), Heather Graham (Jade), Sasha Barrese (Tracy Garner), Rachael Harris (Melissa), Jeffrey Tambor (Sid Garner), Bryan Callen (Eddie Palermo), Mike Tyson (as himself). Comedy following the exploits of four friends who travel to Las Vegas for a bachelor party, only to wake up the next morning not remembering a thing and missing the groom, whose wedding is scheduled to occur the next day! *Dir.* Todd Phillips.

Hannah and Her Sisters (1986) Woody Allen (Micky), Michael Caine (Elliot), Mia Farrow (Hannah), Carrie Fisher (April), Barbara Hershey (Lee), Maureen O'Sullivan (Hannah's mother). *Dir.* Woody Allen.

Hannibal Brooks (1968) Oliver Reed, Michael J Pollard. *Dir.* Michael Winner.

Hanover Street (1979) Harrison Ford, Lesley-Anne Down, Christopher Plummer, Alec McCowen, Max Wall. *Dir.* Peter Hyams.

Hans Christian Andersen (1952) Danny Kaye, Zizi Jeanmaire, Farley Granger. *Dir.* Charles Vidor.

Happiest Days of Your Life, The (1950) Alastair Sim, Margaret Rutherford, Joyce Grenfell, Richard Wattis. *Dir.* Frank Launder.

Happy Feet (2006) Voices of Elijah Wood (Mumble), Brittany Murphy (Gloria), Hugh Jackman (Memphis), Nicole Kidman (Norma Jean), Hugo Weaving (Noah the Elder), Robin Williams (Ramón/Lovelace), Johnny A Sanchez (Lombardo), Carlos Alazraqui (Néstor), Jeff Garcia (Rinaldo), Miriam Margolyes (Mrs Astrakhan). Into the world of Emperor penguins, who find their soul mates through song, a penguin is born who cannot sing. But instead he is blessed with a talent for tap dancing. *Dir.* George Miller.

Happy Hooker, The (1975) Lynn Redgrave (Xaviera Hollander). *Dir.* Nicholas Sgarro.

Hard Candy (2005) Patrick Wilson (Jeff Kohlver), Ellen Page (Hayley Stark), Sandra Oh (Judy Tokuda), Odessa Rae as Jennifer Holmes (Janelle Rogers), Gilbert John (Nighthawks Clerk). A mature 14-year-old girl meets a charming 32-year-old photographer on the Internet. Suspecting that he is a paedophile, she goes to his home in an attempt to expose him. *Dir.* David Slade.

Hard Day's Night, A (1964) Beatles, Wilfrid Brambell, John Junkin, Norman Rossington, Victor Spinetti, Brian Epstein. *Dir.* Richard Lester.

Hard Way, The (1991) Michael J Fox (Nick Lang), James Woods (John Moss), Annabella Sciorra (Susan). *Dir.* John Badham.

Harder They Fall, The (1956) Humphrey Bogart, Rod Steiger, Max Baer, Jan Sterling. Bogart's last film. *Dir.* Mark Robson.

Hardy Family (1936–58) Mickey Rooney, Lewis Stone, Fay Holden, Cecilia Parker, Sara Haden, Spring Byington, Lionel Barrymore. Howard Koch directed the last of the series: *Andy Hardy Comes Home. Dir.* George B Seitz.

Harry and Tonto (1974) Art Carney, Ellen Burstyn, Chief Dan George, Larry Hagman. Tonto was a cat. *Dir.* Paul Mazursky.

Harry Potter and the Chamber of Secrets (2002) Largely the same cast and characters as in *Philosopher's Stone* although new characters include Kenneth Branagh (Gilderoy Lockhart). *Dir.* Chris Columbus.

Harry Potter and the Deathly Hallows-Part 1 (2010) Additions to the usual suspects include Rhys Ifans as Xenophilius Lovegood, the eccentric father of the trio's friend Luna; Bill Nighy as Rufus Scrimgeour, the new Minister for Magic; and Warwick Davis as Griphook, a goblin and former employee at Gringotts Bank. Davis, who had previously played Professor Filius Flitwick, replaced Verne Troyer, who portrayed the character physically in the first film, though Davis had dubbed Griphook's lines.The story follows Harry's quest to find and destroy Lord Voldemort's secret to immortality – the Horcruxes. *Dir.* David Yates.

Harry Potter and the Deathly Hallows-Part 2 (2011) Additions to the usual suspects include Ciarán Hinds who assumes the role of Aberforth Dumbledore, Albus Dumbledore's brother and bartender of the Hog's Head inn; and Kelly Macdonald as Helena Ravenclaw, the ghost of Ravenclaw at Hogwarts. The eighth and final instalment in the Harry Potter film series. *Dir.* David Yates.

Harry Potter and the Goblet of Fire (2005) Daniel Radcliffe (Harry Potter), Emma Watson (Hermione Granger), Rupert Grint (Ron Weasley), Robbie Coltrane (Rubeus Hagrid), Ralph Fiennes (Lord Voldemort), Maggie Smith (Minerva McGonagall), Alan Rickman (Severus Snape), Miranda Richardson (Rita Skeeter), Gary Oldman (Sirius Black), Shirley Henderson (Moaning Myrtle), Robert Hardy (Cornelius Fudge), David Tennant (Barty Crouch Jnr), Eric Sykes (Frank Bryce), Mark Williams (Arthur Weasley), James Phelps (Fred Weasley), Timothy Spall (Wormtail – Peter Pettigrew), Oliver Phelps (George Weasley), Bonnie Wright (Ginny Weasley), Jeff Rawle (Amos Diggory), Robert Pattinson (Cedric Diggory), Jason Isaacs (Lucius Malfoy), Tom Felton (Draco Malfoy), Stanislav Ianevski (Viktor Krum), Michael Gambon (Albus Dumbledore), David Bradley (Argus Filch), Devon Murray (Seamus Finnigan), Frances de la Tour (Madame Olympe Maxime), Roger Lloyd Pack (Barty Crouch), Warwick Davis (Filius Flitwick), Jarvis Cocker (Band Lead Singer). Harry finds himself selected as an underaged competitor in a dangerous multi-wizardry school competition. *Dir.* Mike Newell.

Harry Potter and the Half-Blood Prince (2009) The sixth film in the Harry Potter series sees Jim Broadbent join the cast as Horace Slughorn, the newly appointed Hogwarts Potions master, while the rest of the cast reprise their earlier roles. *Dir.* David Yates.

Harry Potter and the Order of the Phoenix (2007) The fifth film in the Harry Potter series follows Harry in his fifth year at Hogwarts. The Ministry of Magic refuses to believe the return of Lord Voldemort and plants bureaucrat Dolores Umbridge (Imelda Staunton) as the new Defence Against the Dark Arts teacher. The other new main character is Bellatrix Lestrange (Helena Bonham Carter), one of Lord Voldemort's right-hand Death Eaters who leads the battle at the Department of Mysteries. *Dir.* David Yates.

Harry Potter and the Philosopher's Stone (2001) Daniel Radcliffe (Harry Potter), Rupert Grint (Ron Weasley), Emma Watson (Hermione Granger), Robbie Coltrane (Hagrid), Richard Griffiths (Uncle Vernon Dursley), Richard Harris (Albus Dumbledore), Ian Hart (Professor Quirrell / Voldemort), John Hurt (Mr Ollivander), Alan Rickman (Professor Snape), Fiona Shaw (Aunt Petunia Dursley), Maggie Smith (Professor McGonagall), Julie Walters (Mrs Weasley), John Cleese (Nearly Headless Nick), Richard Bremner (He Who Must Not Be Named), Tom Felton (Draco Malfoy). US title: *Harry Potter and the Sorcerer's Stone. Dir.* Chris Columbus.

Harry Potter and the Prisoner of Azkaban (2004) Daniel Radcliffe (Harry Potter), Rupert Grint (Ron Weasley), Emma Watson (Hermione Granger), Gary Oldman (Sirius Black), David Thewlis (Professor Lupin), Michael Gambon (Albus Dumbledore), Alan Rickman (Professor Severus Snape), Maggie Smith (Professor Minerva McGonagall), Robbie Coltrane (Rubeus Hagrid), Tom Felton (Draco Malfoy), Emma Thompson (Professor Sybil Trelawney), Julie Walters (Mrs Weasley), Timothy Spall (Peter Pettigrew), Julie Christie (Madame Rosmerta). Sirius Black, the wizard imprisoned for killing Harry's father, escapes and heads for Hogwarts in search of Harry. *Dir.* Alfonso Cuarón.

Harvey (1950) James Stewart (Elwood P Dowd), Josephine Hull (Veta Louise), Victoria Horne. *Dir.* Henry Koster.

Hawk the Slayer (1980) Jack Palance, John Terry, Bernard Bresslaw. *Dir.* Terry Marcel.

Head (1968) Monkees, Victor Mature. Written by Jack Nicholson & Bob Rafelson. *Dir.* Bob Rafelson.

Heading South (2006) Charlotte Rampling (Ellen), Karen Young (Brenda), Menothy Cesar (Legba), Lys Ambroise (Albert), Louise Portal (Sue), Jackenson Pierre Olmo Diaz (Eddy). On the sun-drenched island of Haiti in the 1970s, Brenda, Ellen and Sue, three North American women, are looking for flirtation, relaxation and respite from their colourless jobs and marriages. They find what they are looking for in Legba, an enigmatic local Adonis. *Dir.* Laurent Cantet.

Hear My Song (1992) Ned Beatty (Josef Locke: voice of Vernon Midgley), Adrian Dunbar (Mickey O'Neill), Shirley Anne Field (Cathleen Doyle), David McCallum (Jim Abbott). *Dir.* Peter Chelsom.

Heart Is a Lonely Hunter, The (1968) Alan Arkin, Sondra Locke, Stacy Keach. Based on Carson McCullers's story of a deaf mute. *Dir.* Robert Ellis Miller.

Heartbreak Ridge (1986) Clint Eastwood (Highway), Marsha Mason (Aggie). *Dir.* Clint Eastwood.

Heartburn (1986) Meryl Streep (Rachel), Jack Nicholson (Mark), Jeff Daniels (Richard), Stockard Channing (Julie). *Dir.* Mike Nichols.

Heat (1995) Al Pacino, Robert De Niro, Val Kilmer, Jon Voight. Based on TV movie: *L.A. Takedown.* First film in which the 2 stars actually filmed scenes together. *Dir.* Michael Mann.

Heathers (1989) Winona Ryder (Veronica Sawyer), Christian Slater (JD), Shannen Doherty (Heather Duke), Lisanne Falk (Heather McNamara), Kim Walker (Heather Chandler). *Dir.* Michael Lehmann.

Heaven and Earth (1993) Tommy Lee Jones, Joan Chen, Haing S Ngor, Debbie Reynolds. Vietnamese woman endures hardships and torments from both sides during the war. *Dir.* Oliver Stone.

Heaven Can Wait (1943) Don Ameche, Gene Tierney, Laird Cregar, Charles Coburn. *Dir.* Ernst Lubitsch.

Heaven Can Wait (1978) Warren Beatty, Julie Christie, James Mason (Mr Jordan), Dyan Cannon, Vincent Gardenia. Remake of *Here Comes Mr Jordan* (1941). *Dir.* Warren Beatty.

Heaven Knows, Mr Allison (1957) Robert Mitchum, Deborah Kerr. Marine and nun marooned on Pacific island during WW2. *Dir.* John Huston.

Heavenly Creatures (1994) Melanie Lynskey, Kate Winslet, Diane Kent. *Dir.* Peter Jackson.

Heavens Above (1963) Peter Sellers, Isabel Jeans, Ian Carmichael, Irene Handl, Eric Sykes, Bernard Miles. *Dir.* John Boulting.

Heaven's Gate (1980) Kris Kristofferson, Christopher Walken, John Hurt, Jeff Bridges. Famous Western, remembered as a box office disaster. *Dir.* Michael Cimino.

Hedda (1975) Glenda Jackson, Peter Eyre, Jennie Linden, Patrick Stewart, Timothy West. *Dir.* Trevor Nunn.

Heidi (1937) Shirley Temple, Jean Hersholt, Arthur Treacher. Based on Johanna Spyri's novel. *Dir.* Allan Dwan.

Heiress, The (1949) Olivia de Havilland, Ralph Richardson, Montgomery Clift, Miriam Hopkins, Ray Collins. Based on Henry James's novel *Washington Square* and the play of the same name by Ruth and Augustus Goetz. *Dir.* William Wyler.

Helen Morgan Story, The (1957) Ann Blyth, Paul Newman, Walter Woolf King (Ziegfeld). GB title: *Both Ends of the Candle. Dir.* Michael Curtiz.

Hellfire Club, The (1960) Keith Michell, Peter Arne, Adrienne Corri, Peter Cushing, David Lodge. *Dir.* Robert S Baker and Monty Berman.

Hello Dolly (1969) Barbra Streisand, Walter Matthau, Michael Crawford, Marianne McAndrew, Tommy Tune. Based on Thornton Wilder's play *The Matchmaker. Dir.* Gene Kelly.

Hell's Angels (1930) Ben Lyon, James Hall, Jean Harlow. *Dir.* Howard Hughes.

Hellzapoppin (1942) Ole Olsen, Chic Johnson, Hugh Herbert, Martha Raye, Mischa Auer. Montage of Mirth and Madness. *Dir.* HC Potter.

Help! (1965) Beatles, Leo McKern, Eleanor Bron, Victor Spinetti. *Dir.* Dick Lester.

Help, The (2011) Emma Stone (Eugenia "Skeeter" Phelan), Viola Davis (Aibileen), Bryce Dallas Howard (Hilly Holbrook), Octavia Spencer (Minny). Highly acclaimed film, set in Jackson, Mississippi, about a young white woman, Skeeter Phelan, and her relationship with two black maids, Aibileen Clark and Minny Jackson during the early 1960s. Skeeter decides to write a book from the point of view of the maids (referred to as "the help"), exposing the racism they are faced with as they work for white families. *Dir.* Tate Taylor.

Henry and June (1990) Fred Ward (Henry Miller), Uma Thurman (June Miller), Maria De Medeiros (Anaïs Nin). Censors created a new 'NC-17' rating to cover rude but artistically worthwhile films. *Dir.* Philip Kaufman.

Henry V (1944) Laurence Olivier, Robert Newton, Leslie Banks, Esmond Knight, Renée Asherson. *Dir.* Laurence Olivier.

Henry V (1989) Kenneth Branagh, Derek Jacobi, Brian Blessed, Ian Holm, Alec McCowen, Robbie Coltrane (Falstaff), Emma Thompson (Katherine). *Dir.* Kenneth Branagh.

Henry VIII and His Six Wives (1972) Keith Michell, Frances Cuka (Aragon), Charlotte Rampling (Boleyn), Jane Asher (Seymour), Jenny Bos (Cleves), Lynne Frederick (Howard), Barbara Leigh-Hunt (Parr). *Dir.* Waris Hussein.

Hercules (1997) Voices of: Tate Donovan (Hercules), Rip Torn (Zeus), James Woods (Hades), Danny De Vito (Philoctetes), Susan Egan (Meg). Cartoons by Gerald Scarfe. *Dir.* John Musker & Ron Clements.

Here Come the Huggetts (1948) Jack Warner, Kathleen Harrison, Susan Shaw, Petula Clark, Jimmy Hanley, Diana Dors. Britain's answer to the Hardys. *Dir.* Ken Annakin.

Here Comes Mr Jordan (1941) Robert Montgomery, Evelyn Keyes, Claude Rains. Much-copied plot about a prizefighter cum saxophonist arriving in heaven too early. *Dir.* Alexander Hall.

Hero (2004) Jet Li, Tony Leung Chiu-Wai, Maggie Cheung Man-Yuk. The Kingdom of Qin is the most ruthless and ambitious of China's seven warring states. Its king is the target of numerous assassins, including Broken Sword, Flying Snow and Sky. When Nameless kills all three he is offered an audience with the king and explains how he used the personal relationships of the assassins to expose their weaknesses. The king tells a different version of the same story. *Dir.* Yimou Zhang.

Heroes of Telemark, The (1965) Kirk Douglas, Richard Harris, Ulla Jacobsson, Roy Dotrice, Michael Redgrave. *Dir.* Anthony Mann.

Hidden (Caché) (2006) Juliette Binoche (Anne Laurent), Daniel Auteuil (Georges Laurent), Annie Girardot, Maurice Benichou, Bernard Le Coq, Daniel Duval, Denis Podalydes, Walid Afkir, Lester Makedonsky, Aissa Maiga. Georges, who hosts a TV literary review, receives packages containing videos of himself with his family – shot secretly from the street – and alarming drawings whose meaning is obscure. He has no idea who may be sending them. Gradually, the footage on the tapes becomes more personal, suggesting that the sender has known Georges for some time. Georges feels a sense of menace hanging over him and his family but, as no direct threat has been made, the police refuse to help. Another French film that is certain to be regarded as one of the most critically acclaimed of 2006. *Dir.* Michael Haneke.

High Anxiety (1977) Mel Brooks, Madeline Kahn, Cloris Leachman. Psychologist suspects his predecessor was murdered. *Dir.* Mel Brooks.

High Noon (1952) Gary Cooper (Will Kane), Grace Kelly, Thomas Mitchell, Lloyd Bridges, Lon Chaney. Tex Ritter sang Dimitri Tiomkin's theme tune. Action takes place during the 85 minutes of running time. *Dir.* Fred Zinnemann.

High School High (1996) Jon Lovitz (Mr Clark), Tia Carrere (Victoria). School is Marion Berry High. *Dir.* Hart Bochner.

Highlander (1986) Christopher Lambert (Connor MacLeod), Roxanne Hart (Brenda Wyatt), Sean Connery (Ramirez). *Highlander II: The Quickening* was the 1990 sequel. *Dir.* Russell Mulcahy.

His Girl Friday (1940) Cary Grant, Rosalind Russell, Ralph Bellamy, Gene Lockhart. Remake of *The Front Page* (1931). *Dir.* Howard Hawks.

History of Mr Polly, The (1949) John Mills, Sally Ann Howes, Megs Jenkins, Finlay Currie. Based on HG Wells's novel. *Dir.* Anthony Pelissier.

Hit, The (1984) John Hurt, Terence Stamp, Tim Roth, Laura Del Sol, Fernando Rey. *Dir.* Stephen Frears.

Hitch (2005) Will Smith (Alex 'Hitch' Hitchens), Eva Mendes (Sara). While helping his latest client woo the fine lady of his dreams, a professional 'date doctor' (Smith) finds the game doesn't quite work on the gossip columnist (Mendes) with whom he's smitten. *Dir.* Andy Tennant.

Hitler – The Last Ten Days (1973) Alec Guinness, Simon Ward, Doris Kunstmann, Diane Cilento, Eric Porter, Joss Ackland. *Dir.* Ennio de Concini.

Hobson's Choice (1953) Charles Laughton, Brenda de Banzie, John Mills, Helen Haye, Prunella Scales. Based on Harold Brighouse's play. *Dir.* David Lean.

Hoffa (1992) Jack Nicholson, Danny De Vito, Armand Assante. *Dir.* Danny De Vito.

Holiday Inn (1942) Bing Crosby, Fred Astaire, Walter Abel, Marjorie Reynolds. Won Oscar for the song 'White Christmas'. *Dir.* Mark Sandrich.

Hollywood or Bust (1956) Dean Martin, Jerry Lewis, Pat Crowley, Anita Ekberg. Last of the Martin & Lewis films. *Dir.* Frank Tashlin.

Home Alone (1990) Macaulay Culkin (Kevin McCallister), Joe Pesci (Harry), Daniel Stern (Marv), John Candy (Gus). *Dir.* Chris Columbus.

Home Alone 2: Lost in New York (1992) Macaulay Culkin (Kevin McCallister), Joe Pesci (Harry), Daniel Stern (Marv), Brenda Fricker (Pigeon Lady). *Dir.* Chris Columbus.

Homeboy (1988) Mickey Rourke (Johnny Walker), Christopher Walken (Wesley), Kevin Conway (Grazziano). *Dir.* Michael Seresin.

Honey, I Blew up the Kid (1992) Rick Moranis (Wayne Szalinski), Lloyd Bridges (Clifford Sterling), Marcia Strassman (Diane). 'Blew up' in as much as the baby grows to 100 feet tall. *Dir.* Randal Kleiser.

Honey, I Shrunk the Kids (1989) Rick Moranis (Wayne Szalinski), Matt Frewer (Big Russ Thompson), Marcia Strassman (Diane), Kristine Sutherland (Mae Thompson). *Dir.* Joe Johnston.

Honkytonk Man (1982) Clint Eastwood (Red Stovall), Kyle Eastwood (Whit), John McIntire (Grandpa). *Dir.* Clint Eastwood.

Honorary Consul, The (1983) Michael Caine (Charley Fortnum), Richard Gere (Dr Plarr), Bob Hoskins (Col Perez). US title: *Beyond the Limit. Dir.* John MacKenzie.

Hook (1991) Dustin Hoffman (Capt Hook), Robin Williams (Peter Banning / Pan), Julia Roberts (Tinkerbell), Bob Hoskins (Smee). *Dir.* Steven Spielberg.

Hoop Dreams (1994) William Gates, Arthur Agee, Emma Gates. *Dir.* Steve James.

Hooper (1978) Burt Reynolds, Sally Field, Brian Keith, Jan Michael Vincent, Adam West. Ageing stuntman decides on one last sensational stunt. *Dir.* Hal Needham.

Hoosiers (1986) Gene Hackman, Barbara Hershey, Dennis Hopper, Sheb Wooley. Triumphs of an Indiana high school basketball team. *Dir.* David Anspaugh.

Horse Feathers (1932) Groucho (Wagstaff), Chico, Zeppo, Harpo Marx, Thelma Todd. College football team needs to win. *Dir.* Norman Z McLeod.

Hostel (2005) Jay Hernandez (Paxton), Derek Richardson (Josh), Eythor Gudjonsson (Oli), Barbara Nedeljakova (Natalya), Jan Vlasák (The Dutch Businessman), Jana Kaderabkova (Svetlana), Jennifer Lim (Kana), Keiko Seiko (Yuki), Lubomir Bukovy (Alex), Petr Janis (The German Surgeon). Three backpackers head to a Slovakian city that promises to meet their hedonistic expectations, with no idea of the horror that awaits them. *Dir.* Eli Roth. Sequels - *Hostel : Part II* (2007) and *Hostel: Part III* (2011), the latter directed by Scott Spiegel.

Hotel Rwanda (2004) Don Cheadle (Paul Rusesabagina), Sophie Okonedo (Tatiana Rusesabagina), Nick Nolte (Colonel Oliver), Joaquin Phoenix (Jack). True story of hotel manager Paul Rusesabagina, who sheltered over a thousand Tutsis refugees during their struggle against the Hutu militia in Rwanda. *Dir.* Terry George.

Hound of the Baskervilles (1939) Basil Rathbone, Nigel Bruce, Richard Greene, John Carradine. *Dir.* Sidney Lanfield.

Hound of the Baskervilles (1959) Peter Cushing, André Morell, Christopher Lee, John Le Mesurier. *Dir.* Terence Fisher.

Hound of the Baskervilles (1977) Peter Cook (Sherlock Holmes), Dudley Moore (Watson), Denholm Elliott (Stapleton), Terry-Thomas (Mortimer), Max Wall, Spike Milligan, Penelope Keith. *Dir.* Paul Morrissey.

Hours, The (2002) Meryl Streep (Clarissa Vaughan), Julianne Moore (Laura Brown), Nicole Kidman (Virginia Woolf), Ed Harris (Richard Brown), Toni Collette (Kitty Barlowe), Claire Danes (Julia Vaughan), Jeff Daniels (Louis Waters), Stephen Dillane (Leonard Woolf). Explores how Woolf's novel *Mrs Dalloway* affects three generations of women, all of whom have dealt with suicides in their lives. *Dir.* Stephen Daldry.

House of Flying Daggers (2004) Takeshi Kaneshiro (Jin), Andy Lau (Leo), Ziyi Zhang (Mei), Dandan Song (Yee). Beautifully filmed martial arts film of undercover espionage and romance. *Dir.* Yimou Zhang.

Houseboat (1958) Cary Grant, Sophia Loren, Martha Hyer, Harry Guardino. *Dir.* Melville Shavelson.

Housesitter (1992) Steve Martin (Davis), Goldie Hawn (Gwen). One-night stand turns into a comic fatal attraction. *Dir.* Frank Oz.

How Green Was My Valley (1941) Walter Pidgeon, Maureen O'Hara, Roddy McDowall. Based on Richard Llewellyn's novel. *Dir.* John Ford.

How I Won the War (1967) Michael Crawford, John Lennon, Roy Kinnear, Lee Montague, Michael Hordern. *Dir.* Richard Lester.

How the West Was Won (1962) Debbie Reynolds, Carroll Baker, Lee J Cobb, Henry Fonda, James Stewart, Gregory Peck. Spencer Tracy was the narrator. *Dir.* Henry Hathaway, John Ford, George Marshall.

How to Marry a Millionaire (1953) Lauren Bacall, Marilyn Monroe, Betty Grable, William Powell, Cameron Mitchell. *Dir.* Jean Negulesco.

Howard's End (1992) Anthony Hopkins (Henry Wilcox), Vanessa Redgrave (Ruth), Helena Bonham Carter (Helen), Emma Thompson (Margaret Schlegel). The Howard's End of the title is a house. *Dir.* James Ivory.

Howling, The (1980) Dee Wallace, Patrick Macnee, Kevin McCarthy. *Dir.* Joe Dante.

Howling II: Your Sister Is a Werewolf (1985) Christopher Lee, Annie McEnroe, Reb Brown. Filmed in Czechoslavakia and not a sequel to *The Howling. Dir.* Philippe Mora.

Hud (1963) Paul Newman, Patricia Neal, Melvyn Douglas, Brandon De Wilde. *Dir.* Martin Ritt.

Hue and Cry (1946) Alastair Sim, Jack Warner, Harry Fowler. First of the Ealing comedies concerns crooks passing information in a boys' paper. *Dir.* Charles Crichton.

Hugo (2011) Asa Butterfield (Hugo Cabret), Ben Kingsley (Georges Méliès / Papa Georges), Chloë Grace Moretz (Isabelle), Sacha Baron Cohen (Inspector Gustave), Ray Winstone (Claude Cabret), Jude Law (Hugo's father), Christopher Lee (Monsieur Labisse), Emil Lager (Django Reinhardt), Ben Addis (Salvador Dalí), Robert Gill (James Joyce), Richard Griffiths (Monsieur Frick). 3D historical adventure film based on Brian Selznick's novel *The Invention of Hugo Cabret* about a boy who lives alone in the Gare Montparnasse railway station in Paris. The film won five Oscars. *Dir.* Martin Scorsese.

Hunchback of Notre Dame, The (1939) Charles Laughton, Cedric Hardwicke, Maureen O'Hara, Edmond O'Brien, Thomas Mitchell. Remake of the Lon Chaney 1923 film. *Dir.* William Dieterle.

Hunchback of Notre Dame, The (1956) Anthony Quinn, Gina Lollobrigida. French / Italian production of the classic story. *Dir.* Jean Delannoy.

Hunger, The (1983) Catherine Deneuve (Miriam), David Bowie (John), Susan Sarandon (Sarah Roberts). *Dir.* Tony Scott.

Hunt for Red October, The (1990) Sean Connery (Capt Marko Ramius), Alec Baldwin (Jack Ryan), Sam Neill (Capt Borodin). *Dir.* John McTiernan.

Hunter, The (1980) Steve McQueen, Eli Wallach, Ben Johnson. McQueen's last film. *Dir.* Buzz Kulik.

Hurlyburly (1998) Sean Penn (Eddie), Kevin Spacey (Mickey), Robin Wright Penn, Garry Shandling, Meg Ryan, Chazz Pálminteri, Anna Paquin. *Dir.* Anthony Drazan.

Hurt Locker, The (2008) Jeremy Renner (Sgt William James), Anthony Mackie (Sgt J T Sanborn), Brian Geraghty (Specialist Owen Eldridge), Ralph Fiennes (PMC Team Leader), Evangeline Lilly (Connie James), Christian Camargo (Lt Col John Cambridge), Guy Pearce (Staff Sgt Matt Thompson). Story of an American bomb disposal squad serving in Iraq. Multi-award-winning film written by Mark Boal. *Dir.* Kathryn Bigelow.

Husbands and Wives (1992) Woody Allen (Gabe Roth), Judith Lewis (Rain), Blythe Danner (Rain's mother), Mia Farrow (Judy Roth), Judy Davis (Sally). *Dir.* Woody Allen.

Hustler, The (1961) Paul Newman, Jackie Gleason, George C Scott, Piper Laurie. *Dir.* Robert Rossen.

Hustler White (1996) Tony Ward, Bruce LaBruce, Kevin Kramer. *Dir.* Bruce LaBruce.

I Accuse (1958) José Ferrer (Dreyfus), Anton Walbrook (Esterhazy), Emlyn Williams (Zola). Written by Gore Vidal. *Dir.* José Ferrer.

I Am a Camera (1955) Julie Harris, Laurence Harvey, Shelley Winters, Anton Diffring. John Collier adaptation of Isherwood stories and the stage play by John Van Druten. *Dir.* Henry Cornelius.

I Am a Fugitive from a Chain Gang (1932) Paul Muni, Glenda Farrell, Helen Vinson, Preston Foster. *Dir.* Mervyn Le Roy.

I Confess (1953) Montgomery Clift, Anne Baxter, Brian Aherne, Karl Malden. Priest hears confession of a murderer and has a dilemma. *Dir.* Alfred Hitchcock.

I Married a Witch (1942) Fredric March, Veronica Lake, Cecil Kellaway, Susan Hayward, Elizabeth Patterson. *Dir.* René Clair.

I Wanna Hold Your Hand (1978) Nancy Allen, Bobby diCicco, Marc McClure. *Dir.* Robert Zemeckis.

I Want to Live (1958) Susan Hayward, Simon Oakland, Virginia Vincent, Theodore Bikel. Based on the Barbara Graham story of a prostitute executed despite doubts as to her guilt. *Dir.* Robert Wise.

I Was a Male War Bride (1949) Cary Grant, Ann Sheridan, Marion Marshall. *Dir.* Howard Hawks.

dI Was Monty's Double (1958) John Mills, Cecil Parker, ME Clifton-James. US title: *Hell, Heaven and Hoboken. Dir.* John Guillermin.

Ice Age (2002) Voices of Ray Romano (Manfred), John Leguizamo (Sid), Denis Leary (Diego), Goran Visnjic (Soto), Jack Black (Zeke), Tara Strong (Roshan). Animated sloth, mammoth and sabre-toothed tiger combine to return a lost child to his tribe during the ice age. *Dir.* Carlos Saldanha and Chris Wedge.

Ice Age: Continental Drift (2012) The fourth instalment of the Ice Age series sees Scrat (voiced by Chris Wedge), an acorn-obsessed sabre-toothed squirrel, inadvertently cause the break up of Pangaea. Jennifer Lopez voices Shira, a Smilodon, and Diego's love interest. *Dirs.* Steve Martino and Mike Thurmeier.

Ice Age: Dawn of the Dinosaurs (2009) The third instalment of the Ice Age series has Sid being taken by a female Tyrannosaurus rex after stealing her eggs, leading the rest of the protagonists to rescue him in a tropical lost world inhabited by dinosaurs beneath the ice. The voice actors from the second film reprise their roles. *Dir.* Carlos Saldanha and Michael Thurmeier.

Ice Age: The Meltdown (2006) Voices of Ray Romano (Manny), John Leguizamo (Sid), Denis Leary (Diego), Seann William Scott (Crash), Josh Peck (Eddie), Queen Latifah (Ellie), Will Arnett (Lone Gunslinger Vulture), Jay Leno (Fast Tony), Joseph Bologna (Mr Start). Diego, Manny and Sid return in this sequel to the hit animation film, *Ice Age.* This time around the ice age is over and the ice is starting to melt, threatening to destroy their valley. So they must unite and warn everyone about the situation. *Dir.* Carlos Saldanha.

Ice Cold in Alex (1958) John Mills, Sylvia Syms, Anthony Quayle, Harry Andrews. *Dir.* J Lee Thompson.

Ice Station Zebra (1968) Rock Hudson, Patrick McGoohan, Ernest Borgnine, Jim Brown. Based on the Alistair MacLean story. *Dir.* John Sturges.

Ideal Husband, An (1999) Cate Blanchett, Minnie Driver, Rupert Everett, Peter Vaughan, Julianne Moore. *Dir.* Oliver Parker.

If (1968) Malcolm McDowell, David Wood, Richard Warwick, Arthur Lowe. *Dir.* Lindsay Anderson.

If These Walls Could Talk (1996) Demi Moore, Cher. TV movie. *Dir.* Nancy Savoka and Cher.

I'm All Right Jack (1959) Ian Carmichael, Peter Sellers, Irene Handl, Richard Attenborough, Terry-Thomas, Dennis Price, Margaret Rutherford. *Dir.* John Boulting.

Importance of Being Earnest, The (1952) Michael Redgrave, Michael Denison, Edith Evans, Margaret Rutherford, Dorothy Tutin. *Dir.* Anthony Asquith.

Importance of Being Earnest, The (2002) Rupert Everett, Colin Firth, Frances O'Connor, Reese Witherspoon, Judi Dench. *Dir.* Oliver Parker.

In Good Company (2004) Dennis Quaid (Dan Foreman), Topher Grace (Carter Duryea), Scarlett Johansson (Alex Foreman). A middle-aged advertising executive is faced with a new boss nearly half his age who is sleeping with his daughter. *Dir.* Paul Weitz.

In Search of the Castaways (1961) Maurice Chevalier, Hayley Mills, George Sanders, Wilfrid Hyde-White, Wilfrid Brambell. *Dir.* Robert Stevenson.

In the Bleak Midwinter (1995) Michael Maloney, Richard Briers, Julia Sawalha, Joan Collins, Jennifer Saunders. Story of a production of *Hamlet* in a village church. *Dir.* Kenneth Branagh.

In the Heat of the Night (1967) Sidney Poitier, Rod Steiger, Warren Oates. *Dir.* Norman Jewison.

In Which We Serve (1942) Noël Coward, Bernard Miles, John Mills, Richard Attenborough, Celia Johnson, Michael Wilding. Viewed as one of the best propaganda wartime films. *Dir.* Noël Coward and David Lean.

Inchon (1981) Laurence Olivier (General MacArthur), Jacqueline Bisset, David Janssen, Ben Gazzara, Richard Roundtree. *Dir.* Terence Young.

Incredible Journey, The (1963) Disney cartoon about 2 dogs and a cat and their 250-mile journey home after being separated from their owners. *Dir.* Fletcher Markle.

Incredible Shrinking Man, The (1957) Grant Williams, Randy Stuart, April Kent. Radioactive mist is the cause of the shrinking. *Dir.* Jack Arnold.

Incredible Shrinking Woman, The (1981) Lily Tomlin, Charles Grodin, Ned Beatty, Henry Gibson. A new perfume causes the diminution in this case. *Dir.* Joel Schumacher.

Incredibles, The (2004) Voices of Craig T Nelson (Mr Incredible/Bob Parr), Holly Hunter (Elastigirl/Helen Parr), Samuel L Jackson (Frozone/Lucius Best), Jason Lee (Syndrome/Buddy Pine), Dominique Louis (Bomb Voyage), Teddy Newton (Newsreel Narrator), Jean Sincere (Mrs Hogenson), Eli Fucile and Maeve Andrews (Jack Jack Parr), Wallace Shawn (Gilbert Huph), Spencer Fox (Dashiell 'Dash' Parr), Lou Romano (Bernie Kropp), Sarah Vowell (Violet Parr), Michael Bird (Tony Rydinger). Animation in which insurance man Bob Parr and his family try to live a quiet suburban life but are forced to adopt their former superhero guises in order to save the world. *Dir.* Brad Bird.

Indecent Proposal (1993) Robert Redford (John Gage), Demi Moore (Diana Murphy), Woody Harrelson (David Murphy), Billy Connolly (Auction MC). *Dir.* Adrian Lyne.

Independence Day (1996) Will Smith (Capt Steve Hiller), Bill Pullman (President Whitmore), Jeff Goldblum, Judd Hirsch, Harry Connick Jnr, Brent Spiner. Pilot and computer expert battle an alien force. *Dir.* Roland Emmerich.

Indiana Jones and the Kingdom of the Crystal Skull (2008) Harrison Ford (Dr Henry 'Indiana' Jones, Jr), Cate Blanchett (Irina Spalko), Shia LaBeouf (Henry 'Mutt Williams' Jones III), Karen Allen (Marion Ravenwood/Williams), Ray Winstone (George 'Mac' McHale), John Hurt (Harold 'Ox' Oxley), Jim Broadbent (Dean Charles Stanforth). The fourth film in the Indiana Jones series is set in 1957 and sees Jones and his sidekick, Mac, kidnapped by a group of Soviet agents led by the psychic Colonel Dr Irina Spalko. *Dir.* Steven Spielberg.

Indiana Jones and the Last Crusade (1989) Harrison Ford, Sean Connery (Professor Henry Jones), Denholm Elliott (Marcus Brody), John Rhys-Davies (Sallah), Julian Glover (Walter Donovan). *Dir.* Steven Spielberg.

Indiana Jones and the Temple of Doom (1984) Harrison Ford, Kate Capshaw (Willie Scott), Ke Huy Quan (Short Round). Prequel to *Raiders of the Lost Ark* (action takes place in 1935). *Dir.* Steven Spielberg.

Indiscreet (1958) Cary Grant, Ingrid Bergman, Phyllis Calvert, Cecil Parker, David Kossoff, Megs Jenkins. Not very indiscreet as it happens, as the loving couple are both single. *Dir.* Stanley Donen.

Informer, The (1935) Victor McLaglen, Heather Angel, Margot Grahame, Una O'Connor. Story of IRA allegiances. *Dir.* John Ford.

Inglourious Basterds (2009) Brad Pitt (Lt Aldo 'the Apache' Raine), Christoph Waltz (SS Col Hans 'The Jew Hunter' Landa), Eli Roth (Staff Sgt Donny Donowitz), Mélanie Laurent (Shosanna 'Emmanuelle Mimieux' Dreyfus), Til Schweiger (Hugo Stiglitz), B J Novak (PFC Smithson 'The Little Man' Utivich), Mike Myers (Gen Ed Fenech), Gedeon Burkhard (Cpl Wilhelm Wicki), Omar Doom (PFC Omar

Ulmer), Samm Levine (PFC Gerold Hirschberg), Michael Fassbender (Lt Archie Hicox), Rod Taylor (Winston Churchill), Diane Krüger (Bridget von Hammersmark), Sylvester Groth (Joseph Goebbels), Martin Wuttke (Adolf Hitler), Samuel L Jackson (Narrator), Harvey Keitel (voice-only – OSS Commander), Quentin Tarantino (unnamed Nazi footman), Bo Svenson (American colonel). The film develops over five chapters: Once Upon a Time . . In Nazi-Occupied France; Inglourious Basterds; A German Night in Paris; Operation Kino; Revenge of the Giant Face. The setting is first German-occupied France in 1941 and then Italy in the spring of 1944, where the take-no-prisoners 'Basterds' operate. The title of the film was inspired by the English title of director Enzo Castellari's 1978 war film, *The Inglorious Bastards*. *Dir.* Quentin Tarantino.

Inherit the Wind (1960) Spencer Tracy, Fredric March, Dick York, Florence Eldridge, Gene Kelly. Fictionalised account of the Scopes Monkey Trial of 1925 when a teacher was accused of teaching Darwin's Theory of Evolution and, consequently, blasphemy. *Dir.* Stanley Kramer.

Inn of the Sixth Happiness, The (1958) Ingrid Bergman, Curt Jurgens, Robert Donat. Biopic of the missionary Gladys Aylward and her work in China. *Dir.* Mark Robson.

Inner Circle, The (1991) Tom Hulce (Ivan Sanshin), Lolita Davidovich (Anastasia), Bob Hoskins (Beria), Alexandre Zbruev (Stalin). Cinema projectionist goes to work for Stalin. *Dir.* Andrei Konchalovsky.

Innerspace (1987) Dennis Quaid (Lt Tuck Pendleton), Martin Short (Jack Putter), Meg Ryan (Lydia Maxwell), Kevin McCarthy (Victor Scrimshaw). Version of *The Fantastic Voyage. Dir.* Joe Dante.

Insider, The (1999) Al Pacino (Lowell Bergman), Russell Crowe (Jeffrey Wigand), Rip Torn (John Scanlon), Christopher Plummer (Mike Wallace), Diane Venora (Liare Wigand) Michael Gambon (Thomas Sandefor). *Dir.* Michael Mann.

Insignificance (1985) Gary Busey (The Ballplayer), Tony Curtis (The Senator), Michael Emil (The Professor), Theresa Russell (The Actress), Will Sampson (The Elevator Attendant). Four people resembling Monroe, Einstein, McCarthy & Di Maggio meet in New York hotel. *Dir.* Nicolas Roeg.

Insomnia (2002) Al Pacino, Martin Donovan, Hilary Swank, Paul Dooley. Not to be confused with the 1997 Norwegian film of the same name. *Dir.* Christopher Nolan.

Inspector Calls, An (1954) Alastair Sim, Jane Wenham, Bryan Forbes, Arthur Young. *Dir.* Guy Hamilton.

International Velvet (1978) Nanette Newman, Tatum O'Neal, Anthony Hopkins, Christopher Plummer. *Dir.* Bryan Forbes.

Intersection (1994) Sharon Stone, Richard Gere, Martin Landau. *Dir.* Mark Rydell.

Intermezzo (1939) Leslie Howard, Ingrid Bergman, John Halliday, Edna Best, Cecil Kellaway. A virtuoso violinist has an affair with his musical protégée. *Dir.* Gregory Ratoff (William Wyler is thought to have assisted).

Intolerance (1916) Mae Marsh, Lillian Gish, Constance Talmadge. Four stories depicting intolerance and persecution through the ages. *Dir.* DW Griffith.

Invasion of the Body Snatchers (1956) Kevin McCarthy, Dana Wynter, Larry Gates, King Donovan, Carolyn Jones, Sam Peckinpah. Small American town is taken over by aliens. *Dir.* Don Siegel.

Invasion of the Body Snatchers (1978) Donald Sutherland, Brooke Adams, Leonard Nimoy, Jeff Goldblum, Kevin McCarthy, Don Siegel. San Francisco becomes the venue for the remake of the 1956 classic. *Dir.* Philip Kaufman.

Invictus (2009) Morgan Freeman (Nelson Mandela), Matt Damon (François Pienaar), Adjoa Andoh (Brenda Mazikubo), Julian Lewis Jones (Etienne Feyder), Matt Stern (Hendrik Booyens), Scott Eastwood (Joel Stransky). Drama based on Nelson Mandela's life during the 1995 Rugby World Cup in South Africa. *Dir.* Clint Eastwood.

Invisible Man, The (1933) Claude Rains (Dr Griffin), Gloria Stuart, Una O'Connor. *Dir.* James Whale.

Ipcress File, The (1965) Michael Caine (Harry Palmer), Nigel Green, Sue Lloyd, Gordon Jackson. The Michael Caine character was never named in the novel by Len Deighton. *Dir.* Sidney J Furie.

IQ (1994) Tim Robbins, Meg Ryan, Walter Matthau (Einstein), Stephen Fry, Keene Curtis (Eisenhower). *Dir.* Fred Schepisi.

Iris (2001) Judi Dench (Iris Murdoch), Jim Broadbent (John Bayley), Kate Winslet (Young Iris), Hugh Bonneville (Young John), Penelope Wilton (Janet Stone), Juliet Aubrey (Young Janet), Eleanor Bron, Joan Bakewell. Jim Broadbent won Oscar as Best Supporting Actor. *Dir.* Richard Eyre.

Irma La Douce (1963) Shirley MacLaine, Jack Lemmon, Lou Jacobi. Paris policeman falls for a prostitute and becomes her pimp. *Dir.* Billy Wilder.

Iron Lady, The (2011) Meryl Streep (Margaret Thatcher), Jim Broadbent (Denis Thatcher), Alexandra Roach (young Margaret Thatcher), Harry Lloyd (young Denis Thatcher), Iain Glen (Alfred Roberts), Olivia Colman (Carol Thatcher), Anthony Head (Geoffrey Howe), Nicholas Farrell (Airey Neave), Richard E. Grant (Michael Heseltine), Paul Bentley (Douglas Hurd), Robin Kermode (John Major), John Sessions (Edward Heath), Michael Pennington (Michael Foot), Angus Wright (John Nott), Julian Wadham (Francis Pym), Nick Dunning (Jim Prior), Reginald Green (Ronald Reagan). Controversial film looking back at the career of Britain's first woman Prime Minister – mainly told in flashback by an ageing dementia-ridden Mrs Thatcher. *Dir.* Phyllida Lloyd.

Iron Man (2008) Robert Downey Jr (Tony Stark/Iron Man), Terrence Howard (Lt Col James 'Rhodey' Rhodes), Jeff Bridges (Obadiah Stane/Iron Monger), Gwyneth Paltrow (Virginia 'Pepper' Potts). Based on the Marvel Comics character of the same name. Engineering genius and playboy Tony Stark, head of Stark Industries, a major military contracting company which he inherited when his parents died in a traffic accident, builds a suit of armour for protection after being captured and severely injured by terrorists. He becomes the superhero Iron Man. Paul Bettany voices JARVIS, Stark's personal Artificial Intelligence computer program, which assists him in the construction and programming of the Iron Man suit. *Dir.* Jon Favreau.

Ishtar (1987) Warren Beatty (Lyle Rogers), Dustin Hoffman (Chuck Clarke), Isabelle Adjani (Shirra Assel). Second biggest flop of all time. *Dir.* Elaine May.

Island of Dr Moreau (1977) Burt Lancaster, Michael York, Nigel Davenport, Barbara Carrera. Story of shipwrecked sailors on a Pacific Island in 1911. *Dir.* Don Taylor.

It Happened One Night (1934) Clark Gable, Claudette Colbert, Walter Connolly, Alan Hale, Ward Bond. *Dir.* Frank Capra.

It Takes Two (1995) Kirstie Alley, Steve Guttenberg, Mary-Kate and Ashley Olsen. *Dir.* Andy Tennant.

Italian Job, The (1969) Michael Caine, Noël Coward, Benny Hill, Rossano Brazzi, Irene Handl, Fred Emney, John Le Mesurier, Simon Dee, Robert Powell. Crooks stage a traffic jam in Turin to pull off a robbery. *Dir.* Peter Collinson.

It's a Mad Mad Mad Mad World (1963) Spencer Tracy, Jimmy Durante, Mickey Rooney, Phil Silvers, Terry-Thomas, Peter Falk, Buster Keaton, The 3 Stooges. Buried loot is the instigator of mayhem. *Dir.* Stanley Kramer.

It's a Wonderful Life (1946) James Stewart, Henry Travers (Clarence), Donna Reed, Lionel Barrymore, Thomas Mitchell. James Stewart's favourite film and many believe Frank Capra's finest. *Dir.* Frank Capra.

It's a Wonderful World (1939) James Stewart, Claudette Colbert, Frances Drake, Guy Kibbee. *Dir.* WS Van Dyke II.

Jack (1996) Robin Williams, Diane Lane, Jennifer Lopez, Bill Cosby. *Dir.* Francis Ford Coppola.

Jack the Bear (1993) Danny De Vito, Robert J Steinmiller Jnr, Miko Hughes. *Dir.* Marshall Herskovitz.

Jackal, The (1997) Bruce Willis (The Jackal), Richard Gere (Declan Mulqueen), Sidney Poitier (Preston), Diane Venora (Valentina Koslova), Mathilda May (Isabella). *Dir.* Michael Caton-Jones.

Jackie Brown (1998) Pam Grier (Jackie Brown), Samuel L Jackson (Ordell Robbie), Robert Forster (Max Cherry), Michael Keaton, Michael Bowen, Robert De Niro (Louis Gara). Air stewardess smuggles cash into America for a gun-runner. *Dir.* Quentin Tarantino.
Jagged Edge (1985) Jeff Bridges (Jack Forrester), Glenn Close (Teddy Barnes), Robert Loggia (Sam Ransom). *Dir.* Richard Marquand.
Jailhouse Rock (1957) Elvis Presley (Vince Everett), Judy Tyler (Peggy Van Alden), Mickey Shaughnessy, Vaughn Taylor, Jennifer Holden. After serving a stretch for manslaughter, young tearaway Vince Everett becomes a rock star. *Dir.* Richard Thorpe.
James and the Giant Peach (1996) Paul Terry, Joanna Lumley, Pete Postlethwaite. *Dir.* Henry Selick.
Jason X (2002) Kane Hodder (Jason), Lexa Doig (Rowan), Chuck Campbell (Tsunaron), Lisa Ryder (KAY-EM 14), Peter Mensah (Sgt Brodski), David Cronenberg (Dr Wimmer). Science fiction story set in the 25th century concerning students aboard a spaceship who revive a frozen serial killer. *Dir.* Jim Isaac.
Jaws (1975) Robert Shaw, Roy Scheider, Richard Dreyfuss, Lorraine Gary. Long Island resort: Amity. *Dir.* Steven Spielberg.
Jaws 2 (1978) Roy Scheider, Lorraine Gary. *Dir.* Jeannot Szwarc.
Jaws 3-D (1983) Dennis Quaid (Mike), Bess Armstrong (Kathryn), Simon MacCorkindale (Philip), Louis Gossett Jr (Calvin). *Dir.* Joe Alves.
Jaws: the Revenge (1987) Lorraine Gary (Ellen Brody), Lance Guest (Michael), Mario Van Peebles (Jake), Karen Young (Carla), Michael Caine (Hoagie). *Dir.* Joseph Sargent.
Jazz Singer, The (1927) Al Jolson, May McAvoy, Warner Oland. Notable for being the first talkie. *Dir.* Alan Crosland.
Jean de Florette (1987) Yves Montand (Cesar Soubeyran), Gérard Depardieu (Jean de Florette), Daniel Auteuil (Ugolin), Elisabeth Depardieu (Aimée), Ernestine Mazurowna (Manon). Sequel: *Manon des Sources. Dir.* Claude Berri.
Jennifer 8 (1992) Andy Garcia (John Berlin), Uma Thurman (Helena Robertson). Serial killer preys on blind women. *Dir.* Bruce Robinson.
Jerry Maguire (1996) Tom Cruise, Cuba Gooding Jnr. *Dir.* Phillip Noyce.
Jesus Christ Superstar (1973) Ted Neeley, Carl Anderson, Yvonne Elliman. Melvyn Bragg wrote the screenplay with Jewison. *Dir.* Norman Jewison.
Jewel of the Nile (1985) Michael Douglas (Jack), Kathleen Turner (Joan), Danny De Vito (Ralph). Film is dedicated to Diane Thomas, the writer of *Romancing the Stone. Dir.* Lewis Teague.
Jezebel (1938) Bette Davis, Henry Fonda. US Civil War epic. *Dir.* William Wyler.
JFK (1991) Kevin Costner (Jim Garrison), Sissy Spacek (Liz Garrison), Tommy Lee Jones (Clay Shaw), Joe Pesci (David Ferrie), Gary Oldman (Lee Harvey Oswald), Brian Doyle-Murray (Jack Ruby). *Dir.* Oliver Stone.
Jim Thorpe, All-American (1951) Burt Lancaster (Thorpe), Charles Bickford, Phyllis Thaxter.Truish story of the Native American who became a star footballer. *Dir.* Michael Curtiz.
Jingle All the Way (1996) Arnold Schwarzenegger (Howard Langston), Rita Wilson (Liz Langston), Jake Lloyd (Jamie Langston), Sinbad, James Belushi. *Dir.* Brian Levant.
Joan of Arc (1948) Ingrid Bergman, José Ferrer, Francis L Sullivan. *Dir.* Victor Fleming.
John Paul Jones (1959) Robert Stack, Charles Coburn (Benjamin Franklin), Bette Davis (Catherine the Great). Notable for its unending list of star cameos. *Dir.* John Farrow.
Johnny Belinda (1948) Jane Wyman, Lew Ayres, Charles Bickford, Agnes Moorehead. Deaf mute is raped and the local doctor is suspected of being the father of the baby. *Dir.* Jean Negulesco.
Joker Is Wild, The (1957) Frank Sinatra, Mitzi Gaynor, Eddie Albert, Jeanne Crain. The song 'All the Way' won an Academy Award. *Dir.* Charles Vidor.
Jokers, The (1967) Michael Crawford, Oliver Reed, Harry Andrews, James Donald, Daniel Massey, Michael Hordern, Frank Finlay, Rachel Kempson. Two brothers decide to 'borrow' and replace the crown jewels. *Dir.* Michael Winner.
Jolson Story, The (1946) Larry Parks (voice of Jolson), Evelyn Keyes. *Dir.* Alfred E Green.
Journey into Fear (1942) Joseph Cotten, Dolores del Rio, Orson Welles. Munitions expert finds himself in danger from assassins in Istanbul. *Dir.* Norman Foster.
Journey to Shiloh (1967) James Caan, Michael Sarrazin, Brenda Scott, Paul Petersen, Don Stroud, Harrison Ford. Seven young Texans leave home to fight in the Civil War. *Dir.* William Hale.
Journey to the Center of the Earth (1959) James Mason, Arlene Dahl, Pat Boone, Diane Baker. Film ends with the team being catapulted out of Stromboli. *Dir.* Henry Levin.
Judge Dredd (1995) Sylvester Stallone, Armand Assante, Diane Lane, Ian Dury, Max Von Sydow. Set in Mega City One in AD 2139. *Dir.* Danny Cannon.
Judgment at Nuremberg (1961) Spencer Tracy, Marlene Dietrich, Burt Lancaster, Richard Widmark, Maximilian Schell, Judy Garland, Montgomery Clift, William Shatner. *Dir.* Stanley Kramer.
Judgment in Berlin (1988) Martin Sheen (Herbert J Stern), Sam Wanamaker (Bernard Hellring). Director is Sean Penn's father. *Dir.* Leo Penn.
Juggernaut (1974) Richard Harris, David Hemmings, Omar Sharif, Anthony Hopkins. Transatlantic liner is threatened by a mad bomber. *Dir.* Richard Lester.
Jules et Jim (1962) Jeanne Moreau (Catherine), Oskar Werner (Jules), Henri Serre (Jim). A love triangle that develops with tragic consequences. *Dir.* François Truffaut.
Julia (1977) Jane Fonda, Vanessa Redgrave, Jason Robards Jnr, Maximilian Schell, Hal Holbrook. Based on Lillian Hellman's book *Pentimento. Dir.* Fred Zinnemann.
Julie & Julia (2009) Meryl Streep (Julia Child), Amy Adams (Julie Powell), Stanley Tucci (Paul Child), Chris Messina (Eric Powell), Linda Emond (Simone 'Simca' Beck), Helen Carey (Louisette Bertholle), Jane Lynch (Dorothy McWilliams), Mary Lynn Rajskub (Sarah), Joan Juliet Buck (Madame Bassart). Comedy depicting true-life events of chef Julia Child in the early years of her culinary career, contrasting her life with Julie Powell, who aspires to cook all 524 recipes from Child's cookbook (*Mastering the Art of French Cooking*) during a single year. *Dir.* Nora Ephron.
Julius Caesar (1953) John Gielgud (Cassius), Marlon Brando (Marc Antony), Louis Calhern (Julius Caesar), Edmond O'Brien (Casca), James Mason (Brutus), Greer Garson (Calpurnia), Deborah Kerr (Portia). *Dir.* Joseph L Mankiewicz.
Jumanji (1995) Robin Williams, Bonnie Hunt, Kirsten Dunst. Two children play a mysterious board game that releases, after 25 years, a child and some ferocious animals. *Dir.* Joe Johnston.
Jumpin' Jack Flash (1986) Whoopi Goldberg (Terry Doolittle), Tracey Ullman, James Belushi, Jonathan Pryce. *Dir.* Penny Marshall.
Jungle Fever (1991) Wesley Snipes (Flipper Purify), Annabella Sciorra (Angela Tucci), Spike Lee (Cyrus), Anthony Quinn (Lou Carbone), Samuel L Jackson (Gator Purify). *Dir.* Spike Lee.
Jurassic Park (1993) Richard Attenborough, Jeff Goldblum, Sam Neill, Laura Dern, Samuel L Jackson, Bob Peck. *Dir.* Steven Spielberg.
Jurassic Park III (2001) Sam Neill (Dr Alan Grant), William H Macy, Tea Leoni, Laura Dern. *Dir.* Joe Johnston.
Just a Gigolo (1978) David Bowie, Sydne Rome, Kim Novak, Marlene Dietrich, David Hemmings, Curt Jurgens. *Dir.* David Hemmings.
K-9 (1989) James Belushi (Thomas Dooley), Mel Harris (Tracy), Kevin Tighe (Lyman). Not the same K-9 as in *Dr Who. Dir.* Rod Daniel.
K-19: The Widowmaker (2002) Harrison Ford (Captain Alexi Vostrikov), Sam Spruell, Liam Neeson (Mikhail Polenin), Peter Sarsgaard (Vadim Ratchenko), George Anton (Konstantin Poliansky), Steve Cumyn, Steve Nicholson, Chris Redman, Tygh Runyan. Based on a true-life story which follows the fate of Captain Alexi Vostrikov who, at the height of the Cold War, is ordered to take over command of nuclear missile submarine K-19, pride of the Soviet Navy. His assignment: prepare the K-19 for sea and take her out on patrol – no matter what the cost. But problems with the K-19 arise that may lead to a core meltdown and explosion that will certainly kill all aboard,

and possibly trigger nuclear war. In a daring act of heroism, Vostrikov must choose between his orders from the Kremlin and the lives of his men and his country. *Dir.* Kathryn Bigelow.

Kaleidoscope (1966) Warren Beatty, Susannah York, Clive Revill, Eric Porter. Playboy breaks into card factory to mark the cards and so enable him to clean up. *Dir.* Jack Smight.

Kansas City (1996) Jennifer Jason Leigh, Miranda Richardson, Harry Belafonte. Woman kidnaps a politician's drug addicted wife in a bid to get her husband released by the gangsters holding him. *Dir.* Robert Altman.

Karate Kid, The (1984) Ralph Macchio (Daniel), Pat Morita (Miyagi), Elisabeth Shue (Ali), Martin Kove (Kreese), William Zabka (Johnny). *Dir.* John G Avildsen.

Karate Kid Part II, The (1986) Ralph Macchio, Pat Morita, Nobu McCarthy (Yukie), Danny Kamekona (Sato). *Dir.* John G. Avildsen.

Karate Kid III, The (1989) Ralph Macchio, Pat Morita (Miyagi), Robyn Lively (Jessica Andrews). *Dir.* John G Avildsen. The fourth and final film in the original Karate Kid series *The Next Karate Kid* (1994) (aka *The Karate Kid Part IV*) stars Hilary Swank as Julie Pierce as replacement for Ralph Macchio in the lead role. The film was directed by Christopher Cain. A 2010 remake of the original Karate Kid film starred Jackie Chan as Mr Han and Jaden Smith as Dre Parker – the karate kid. This film was directed by Harald Zwart.

Kate and Leopold (2001) Meg Ryan (Kate McKay), Hugh Jackman (Leopold), Liev Schreiber, Natasha Lyonne, Breckin Meyer. An English duke is transported from 1876 to the present day and falls in love. *Dir.* James Mangold.

Kelly's Heroes (1970) Clint Eastwood, Telly Savalas, Don Rickles, Donald Sutherland. *Dir.* Brian G Hutton.

Kentuckian, The (1955) Burt Lancaster, Dianne Foster, Walter Matthau, John McIntire. *Dir.* Burt Lancaster.

Kes (1969) David Bradley, Lynne Perrie, Colin Welland, Brian Glover. *Dir.* Ken Loach.

Key Largo (1948) Humphrey Bogart, Lauren Bacall, Claire Trevor, Edward G Robinson, Lionel Barrymore. *Dir.* John Huston.

Kickboxer (1989) Jean Claude Van Damme, Dennis Alexio, Tong Po (Michel Qissi). *Dir.* Mark DiSalle and David Worth.

Kid, The (1921) Charles Chaplin, Jackie Coogan, Edna Purviance. *Dir.* Charles Chaplin.

Kid for Two Farthings, A (1955) Celia Johnson, Diana Dors, David Kossoff, Primo Carnera, Sydney Tafler. *Dir.* Carol Reed.

Kid from Brooklyn, The (1946) Danny Kaye, Virginia Mayo, Eve Arden, Walter Abel. Timid milkman becomes a prizefighter. *Dir.* Norman Z McLeod.

Kid Galahad (1937) Edward G Robinson, Bette Davis, Humphrey Bogart, Harry Carey. *Dir.* Michael Curtiz.

Kid Galahad (1962) Elvis Presley, Lola Albright, Gig Young, Charles Bronson. *Dir.* Phil Karlson.

Kidnapped (1971) Michael Caine, Lawrence Douglas, Trevor Howard, Jack Hawkins, Donald Pleasence, Gordon Jackson. Other versions starred Warner Baxter and Freddie Bartholomew (1938), and Peter Finch and James MacArthur (1959). *Dir.* Delbert Mann.

Kids (1995) Lee Fitzpatrick, Sarah Henderson, Justin Pearce. Day in the life of teenagers includes sex and skateboarding. *Dir.* Larry Clark.

Kill Bill Vol. 1 (2003) Uma Thurman (The Bride/Black Mamba), Lucy Liu (O-Ren Ishii/Cottonmouth), Vivica A Fox (Vernita Green/Copperhead), Daryl Hannah (Elle Driver/California Mountain Snake), Michael Madsen (Budd/Sidewinder), David Carradine (Bill), Michael Parks (Sheriff), Sonny Chiba (Hattori Hanzo), Chiaki Kuriyama (Go Go Yubari), Gordon Liu Chia-hui (Johnny Mo). An assassin, left for dead by her former colleagues, awakens from four years in a coma to exact her revenge. *Dir.* Quentin Tarantino.

Kill Bill Vol. 2 (2004) Uma Thurman (The Bride/Black Mamba), Daryl Hannah (Elle Driver/California Mountain Snake), Michael Madsen (Budd/Sidewinder), David Carradine (Bill), Gordon Liu (Pai-Mei), Michael Parks (Esteban Vihaio), Perla Haney-Jardine (BB), Samuel L Jackson (Rufus), Bo Svenson (Reverend Harmony). An assassin continues seeking her revenge for the murder of her friends. *Dir.* Quentin Tarantino.

Killer: A Journal of Murder (1996) James Woods (Carl Panzram), Robert Sean Leonard (Henry Lesser). True story set in Leavenworth Prison, Kansas. *Dir.* Tim Metcalfe.

Killers, The (1946) Burt Lancaster, Edmond O'Brien, Ava Gardner. *Dir.* Robert Siodmak.

Killers, The (1964) John Cassavetes, Lee Marvin, Clu Gulager, Angie Dickinson, Ronald Reagan. Ronald Reagan's last film and the first in which he played a bad guy. *Dir.* Don Siegel.

Killing Fields, The (1984) Sam Waterston (Sydney Schanberg), Haing S Ngor (Dith Pran), John Malkovich (Al Rockoff). *Dir.* Roland Joffé.

Killing of Sister George, The (1969) Beryl Reid, Susannah York, Coral Browne, Patricia Medina, Roland Fraser. *Dir.* Robert Aldrich.

Kind Hearts and Coronets (1949) Dennis Price, Alec Guinness, Valerie Hobson, Joan Greenwood, Arthur Lowe. Alec Guinness plays the 8 members of the D'Ascoyne family. *Dir.* Robert Hamer.

Kind of Loving, A (1962) Alan Bates, June Ritchie, Thora Hird, Bert Palmer. Keith Waterhouse & Willis Hall adapted Stan Barstow's story. *Dir.* John Schlesinger.

Kindergarten Cop (1990) Arnold Schwarzenegger (John Kimble), Penelope Ann Miller (Joyce Paulmarie), Pamela Reed (Phoebe O'Hara), Linda Hunt (Miss Schlowski). *Dir.* Ivan Reitman.

King and I, The (1956) Yul Brynner, Deborah Kerr, Rita Moreno. *Dir.* Walter Lang.

King and I, The (1999) Voices of Miranda Richardson, Ian Richardson, Martin Vidnovic, Darrell Hammond. *Dir.* Richard Rich.

King David (1985) Richard Gere (David), Edward Woodward (Saul), Alice Krige (Bathsheba), Dennis Quilley (Samuel). *Dir.* Bruce Beresford.

King Kong (1933) Fay Wray, Robert Armstrong (Carl Denham), Bruce Cabot. *Dir.* Merian C Cooper & Ernest B Schoedsnack.

King Kong (1976) Jeff Bridges, Charles Grodin, Jessica Lange. Dino de Laurentiis production - something of a spoof. *Dir.* John Guillermin.

King Kong (2005) Naomi Watts (Ann Darrow), Jack Black (Carl Denham), Adrien Brody (Jack Driscoll), Thomas Kretschmann (Captain Englehorn), Colin Hanks (Preston), Andy Serkis (Kong/Lumpy), Evan Parke (Hayes), Jamie Bell (Jimmy), Lobo Chan (Choy), John Sumner (Herb), Craig Hall (Mike), Kyle Chandler (Bruce Baxter), Bill Johnson as William Johnson (Manny), Mark Hadlow (Harry), Geraldine Brophy (Maude). In 1933 New York, an ambitious movie producer coerces his cast and hired ship crew to travel to mysterious Skull Island, where they encounter Kong, a giant ape who is immediately smitten with leading lady Darrow. Won Academy Awards for Sound Mixing and Visual Effects. *Dir.* Peter Jackson.

King of Comedy, The (1983) Robert De Niro (Rupert Pupkin), Jerry Lewis (Jerry Langford), Diahnne Abbott (Rita). *Dir.* Martin Scorsese.

King of Kings (1961) Jeffrey Hunter, Robert Ryan, Siobhan McKenna. *Dir.* Nicholas Ray.

King Ralph (1991) John Goodman (Ralph Jones), Peter O'Toole (Sir Cedric Willingham), John Hurt (Lord Graves), Joely Richardson (Princess Anna), Leslie Phillips (Gordon), Julian Glover (King Gustav), Judy Parfitt (Queen Katherine). The whole of the Royal Family are wiped out, leaving a lounge pianist as King. *Dir.* David S Ward.

King Rat (1965) George Segal, Tom Courtenay, John Mills, James Fox, Leonard Rossiter. Based on James Clavell novel about collaboration in Changi POW camp during WW2. *Dir.* Bryan Forbes.

King Solomon's Mines (1950) Stewart Granger, Deborah Kerr, Richard Carlson. *Dir.* Compton Bennett.

King Solomon's Mines (1985) Richard Chamberlain, Sharon Stone, Herbert Lom, John Rhys-Davies. *Dir.* J Lee Thompson.

King's Row (1941) Ann Sheridan, Robert Cummings, Ronald Reagan (Drake), Claude Rains. Reagan took the name of his autobiography from a line in this film. *Dir.* Sam Wood.

King's Speech, The (2010) Colin Firth (King George VI), Geoffrey Rush (Lionel Logue), Helena Bonham Carter (Queen Elizabeth), Guy Pearce (King Edward VIII), Timothy Spall (Winston Churchill), Derek Jacobi (Archbishop Cosmo Lang), Jennifer Ehle (Myrtle Logue), Anthony Andrews (Stanley Baldwin), Claire Bloom (Queen Mary), Eve Best (Wallis Simpson), Freya Wilson (Princess Elizabeth), Tim Downie (The Duke of Gloucester), Roger Hammond (Dr. Blandine Bentham), Ramona Marquez (Princess Margaret), Michael Gambon (King George V). The relationship between King George VI and his Australian speech therapist Lionel Logue. The film won four Academy Awards. *Dir.* Tom Hooper.

Kingdom of Heaven (2005) Orlando Bloom (Balian), Liam Neeson (Godfrey), Michael Sheen (Priest), Nathalie Cox (Balian's Wife), Eriq Ebouaney (Firuz), Jouko Ahola (Odo), David Thewlis (Hospitaller). Balian of Ibelin travels to Jerusalem during the crusades of the 12th century, and there finds himself the defender of the city and its people. *Dir.* Ridley Scott.
Kinsey (2004) Liam Neeson (Alfred Kinsey), Laura Linney (Clara McMillen), Chris O'Donnell (Wardell Pomeroy), Peter Sarsgaard (Clyde Martin), Timothy Hutton (Paul Gebhard), John Lithgow (Alfred Seguine Kinsey), Tim Curry (Thurman Rice). Biopic of Alfred Kinsey, a pioneer in the area of human sexuality research. *Dir.* Bill Condon.
Kipps (1941) Michael Redgrave, Phyllis Calvert, Diana Wynyard, Michael Wilding. Turned into musical *Half a Sixpence. Dir.* Carol Reed.
Kismet (1955) Howard Keel, Ann Blyth, Vic Damone, Sebastian Cabot. Musical based on Borodin. *Dir.* Vincente Minnelli.
Kiss Me Kate (1953) Howard Keel, Kathryn Grayson, Ann Miller, Keenan Wynn. Musical version of *The Taming of the Shrew. Dir.* George Sidney.
Kiss of the Spider Woman (1985) William Hurt (Molina), Raul Julia (Valentin), Sonia Braga (Leni Lamaison / Marta). Flamboyant gay shares South American prison cell with a radical activist. *Dir.* Hector Babenco.
Kissin' Cousins (1963) Elvis Presley, Arthur O'Connell, Glenda Farrell, Jack Albertson. Presley plays 2 parts. *Dir.* Gene Nelson.
Kitty Foyle (1940) Ginger Rogers, Dennis Morgan, James Craig, Eduardo Ciannelli. *Dir.* Sam Wood.
Klansman, The (1974) Lee Marvin, Richard Burton, Cameron Mitchell, OJ Simpson, Linda Evans. *Dir.* Terence Young.
Klute (1971) Jane Fonda, Donald Sutherland, Roy Scheider. *Dir.* Alan J Pakula.
Knack, The (1965) Michael Crawford, Ray Brooks, Rita Tushingham. *Dir.* Richard Lester.
Knight's Tale, A (2001) Heath Ledger, Rufus Sewell, Paul Bettany (Chaucer), Laura Fraser, Mark Addy. *Dir.* Brian Helgeland.
Kotch (1971) Walter Matthau, Deborah Winter. *Dir.* Jack Lemmon.
Krakatoa, East of Java (1968) Maximilian Schell, Diane Baker, Brian Keith, Rossano Brazzi, Sal Mineo. Krakatoa is actually west of Java. *Dir.* Bernard Kowalski.
Kramer versus Kramer (1979) Dustin Hoffman, Justin Henry, Meryl Streep, Jane Alexander, Howard Duff. Based on an Avery Corman novel. *Dir.* Robert Benton.
Krays, The (1990) Gary Kemp (Ronnie), Martin Kemp (Reggie), Billie Whitelaw (Violet), Susan Fleetwood (Rose), Jimmy Jewell (Cannonball Lee), Tom Bell (Jack 'The Hat' McVitie). *Dir.* Peter Medak.
Kung Fu Panda (2008) Voices of Jack Black (Po, a giant panda), Dustin Hoffman (Master Shifu, a red panda), Angelina Jolie (Master Tigress, a South China tiger), Ian McShane (Tai Lung, a snow leopard), Lucy Liu (Master Viper, a green tree viper), Seth Rogen (Master Mantis), Jackie Chan (Master Monkey, a golden langur), David Cross (Master Crane, a red-crowned crane), Randall Duk Kim (Master Oogway, a tortoise), James Hong (Mr Ping, a goose), Dan Fogler (Zeng, a goose), Michael Clarke Duncan (Commander Vachir, a Javan rhinoceros). DreamWorks animation. The Valley of Peace in China is protected by the Furious Five – Tigress, Monkey, Mantis, Viper and Crane – a quintet of warriors trained in kung fu by the wise tortoise Master Oogway and his protégé, the red panda Master Shifu. The ruthless snow leopard Tai Lung is soon to escape from prison and return to the valley and a kung fu tournament is held to find the all-powerful Dragon Warrior. Po, a young giant panda and kung fu fanatic, unwittingly gatecrashes the end of the competition just as the Dragon Warrior is to be announced. *Dir.* Mark Osborne and John Wayne Stevenson. *Kung Fu Panda 2* (2011) was directed by Jennifer Yuh Nelson, the new villain, Lord Shen, voiced by Gary Oldman.
L-Shaped Room, The (1962) Leslie Caron, Tom Bell, Brock Peters, Cicely Courtneidge, Bernard Lee, Avis Bunnage, Pat Phoenix, Emlyn Williams. *Dir.* Bryan Forbes.
La Bamba (1987) Lou Diamond Phillips (Ritchie Valens), Esai Morales (Bob Morales), Rosana De Soto (Connie Valenzuela). *Dir.* Luis Valdez.
LA Confidential (1997) Danny De Vito (Sid Hudgens), Kim Basinger (Lynn Bracken), Kevin Spacey (Jack Vincennes), Russell Crowe (Bud White), Guy Pearce (Ed Exley). Hooker with a facial similarity to Veronica Lake gets mixed up in murder case. *Dir.* Curtis Hanson.
LA Story (1991) Steve Martin (Harris K Telemacher), Victoria Tennant (Sara McDowel), Iman (Cynthia), Richard E Grant (Roland), Marilu Henner (Trudi), Patrick Stewart (Maître d' at L'Idiot). *Dir.* Mick Jackson.
La Vie en Rose (2007) Marion Cotillard (Edith Piaf), Sylvie Testud (Mômone), Jean-Pierre Martins (Marcel Cerdan), Gérard Depardieu (Louis Leplée), Emmanuelle Seigner (Titine), Pascal Greggory (Louis Barrier), Caroline Sihol (Marlene Dietrich), Manon Chevallier (Edith age 5), Pauline Burlet (Edith age 10), Laurent Olmedo (Jacques Pills), Dominique Bettenfeld (Albert). The life story of French singer Edith Piaf was released in France as *La Môme* (literally 'The Kid', but 'La Môme Piaf' is 'The Little Sparrow'). *Dir.* Olivier Dahan.
Labyrinth (1986) David Bowie (Jareth), Jennifer Connelly (Sarah), Toby Froud (Toby), Shelley Thompson (Stepmother). *Dir.* Jim Henson.
Lady Caroline Lamb (1972) Sarah Miles, Jon Finch, Richard Chamberlain (Byron), Margaret Leighton, John Mills (Canning), Ralph Richardson (George III), Laurence Olivier (Wellington). *Dir.* Robert Bolt.
Lady Sings the Blues (1972) Diana Ross (Billie Holliday), Billy Dee Williams, Richard Pryor. *Dir.* Sidney J Furie.
Lady Vanishes, The (1938) Margaret Lockwood, Michael Redgrave, Dame May Whitty, Googie Withers. A 1979 remake starring Cybill Shepherd and Elliott Gould flopped. *Dir.* Alfred Hitchcock.
Lady with the Lamp, The (1951) Anna Neagle, Michael Wilding. *Dir.* Herbert Wilcox.
Ladykillers, The (1955) Alec Guinness, Katie Johnson, Peter Sellers, Herbert Lom, Frankie Howerd. *Dir.* Alexander Mackendrick.
Lake House, The (2005) Keanu Reeves (Alex Wyler), Sandra Bullock (Kate Forster), Shohreh Aghdashloo (Anna Klyczynski), Christopher Plummer (Simon Wyler). Offbeat romantic fantasy in which Kate, a lonely doctor who once occupied an unusual lakeside home, begins exchanging love letters with a frustrated architect, Alex, its former resident. The mailbox they use seems to defy the normal rules of physics. *Dir.* Alejandro Agresti.
Lamerica (1994) Enrico Lo Verso, Michele Placido. *Dir.* Gianni Amelio.
Land and Freedom (1995) Ian Hart, Rosana Pastor, Iciar Bollain. *Dir.* Ken Loach.
Lantana (2001) Anthony LaPaglia, Geoffrey Rush, Barbara Hershey, Kerry Armstrong. *Dir.* Ray Lawrence.
Lara Croft: Tomb Raider (2001) Angelina Jolie (Lara), Iain Glen, Noah Taylor, Leslie Philips, Chris Barrie, Daniel Craig. *Dir.* Simon West. Angelina Jolie's father Jon Voight is cast as her on-screen father in this film. Jolie reprised her role in the 2003 film *Lara Croft Tomb Raider: The Cradle of Life*, directed by Jan de Bont.
Lassie Come Home (1943) Roddy McDowall, Elizabeth Taylor, Donald Crisp. Based on an Eric Knight story. *Dir.* Fred M Wilcox.
Last Action Hero, The (1993) Arnold Schwarzenegger, Mercedes Ruehl, F Murray Abraham, Art Carney, Anthony Quinn. *Dir.* John McTiernan.
Last Boy Scout, The (1992) Bruce Willis (Joe Hallenbeck), Damon Wayans (Jimmy Dix), Chelsea Field (Sarah Hallenbeck). *Dir.* Tony Scott.
Last Dance (1996) Sharon Stone (Cindy Liggett), Rob Morrow (Rick Hayes). *Dir.* Bruce Beresford.
Last Detail, The (1973) Jack Nicholson, Otis Young, Randy Quaid, Clifton James. *Dir.* Hal Ashby.
Last Emperor, The (1987) John Lone (Pu Yi), Peter O'Toole (RJ), Joan Chen (Wan Jung). *Dir.* Bernardo Bertolucci.
Last Exit to Brooklyn (1990) Stephen Lang (Harry Black), Jennifer Jason Leigh (Tralala), Burt Young (Big Joe), Ricki Lake (Donna), Peter Dobson (Vinnie). Mark Knopfler of Dire Straits provided the film score. *Dir.* Uli Edel.
Last Hard Men, The (1976) Charlton Heston, James Coburn, Barbara Hershey, Christopher Mitchum. *Dir.* Andrew V McLaglen.
Last King of Scotland, The (2006) Forest Whitaker (Idi Amin), James McAvoy (Dr Nicholas Garrigan), Kerry Washington (Kay Amin), Gillian Anderson (Sarah Merrit). Based on the events of the Ugandan dictator Idi Amin's brutal and bloody regime as seen by his personal physician during the 1970s. The title comes from a reporter in a press conference who wishes to verify whether Idi Amin declared himself king of Scotland, a country the despot had a lifelong fascination with. *Dir.* Kevin Macdonald.

Last Man Standing (1996) Bruce Willis, Christopher Walken, Bruce Dern, Alexandra Powers. Set in Texas during the Depression of the 1930s, it concerns a gunman on the run and rival bootleggers. *Dir.* Walter Hill.
Last of the Dogmen (1995) Tom Berenger, Barbara Hershey, Kuttwood Smith, Steve Reevis. Bounty hunter discovers a group of Cheyenne in Montana. *Dir.* Tab Murphy.
Last of the Mohicans, The (1992) Daniel Day-Lewis (Hawkeye), Madeleine Stowe (Cora), Russell Means (Chingachgook), Eric Schweig (Uncas). *Dir.* Michael Mann.
Last Orders (2001) Michael Caine (Jack), Bob Hoskins (Ray), Tom Courtenay (Vic), David Hemmings (Lenny), Ray Winstone (Vince), Helen Mirren (Amy). Three elderly Londoners reminisce on past lives and loves as they gather for a trip to the seaside to scatter the ashes of a mutual friend. Based on a novel by Graham Swift. *Dir.* Fred Schepisi.
Last Picture Show, The (1971) Timothy Bottoms, Jeff Bridges, Cybill Shepherd, Ben Johnson, Cloris Leachman, Ellen Burstyn. *Dir.* Peter Bogdanovich.
Last Seduction, The (1994) Linda Fiorentino, Peter Berg, Bill Nunn, Bill Pullman. Woman leaves her husband taking with her a million dollars he made from a drug deal. *Dir.* John Dahl.
Last Summer (1969) Barbara Hershey, Richard Thomas, Bruce Davison, Cathy Burns, Ralph Waite. *Dir.* Frank Perry.
Last Tango in Paris (1972) Marlon Brando, Maria Schneider. *Dir.* Bernardo Bertolucci.
Last Temptation of Christ, The (1988) Willem Dafoe (Jesus), Harvey Keitel (Judas), Barbara Hershey (Mary Magdalene), David Bowie (Pontius Pilate). *Dir.* Martin Scorsese.
Last Tycoon, The (1976) Robert De Niro, Robert Mitchum, Tony Curtis, Jeanne Moreau, Jack Nicholson, Donald Pleasence. *Dir.* Elia Kazan.
Lavender Hill Mob, The (1951) Alec Guinness, Stanley Holloway, Sid James, Alfie Bass, Audrey Hepburn. Bank clerk masterminds bullion robbery by moulding Eiffel Towers in gold to be smuggled to France. *Dir.* Charles Crichton.
Lawless (2012) Shia LaBeouf (Jack), Tom Hardy (Forrest), Jason Clarke (Howard), Guy Pearce (Charlie Rakes). Set in the early 1930s, the brothers Jack, Forrest and Howard Bondurant, sell moonshine in Franklin County, Virginia, during Prohibition. *Dir.* John Hillcoat.
Lawrence of Arabia (1962) Peter O'Toole, Omar Sharif, Arthur Kennedy, Jack Hawkins, Alec Guinness. Screenplay by Robert Bolt. The film is unusual in that it has no women in credited speaking roles. Dir. David Lean.
Le Fils (2002) Olivier Gourmet (Olivier), Morgan Marinne (Francis), Isabella Soupart (Magali). A carpentry teacher working with delinquent boys takes on a youth who killed his son. *Dir.* Jean-Pierre Dardenne.
League of Gentlemen, The (1960) Jack Hawkins, Richard Attenborough, Roger Livesey, Bryan Forbes, Nigel Patrick, Nanette Newman. *Dir.* Basil Dearden.
Leaving Las Vegas (1995) Nicolas Cage, Elisabeth Shue, Julian Sands, Richard Lewis. Alcoholic writer goes to Las Vegas to drink himself to death. *Dir.* Mike Figgis.
Left-Handed Gun, The (1958) Paul Newman (Billy the Kid), John Dehner (Pat Garrett). *Dir.* Arthur Penn.
Legally Blonde (2001) Reese Witherspoon, Luke Wilson, Selma Blair, Matthew Davis, Victor Garber. *Dir.* Robert Luketic.
Legend of the Lone Ranger, The (1981) Klinton Spilsbury, Michael Horse, Christopher Lloyd, Matt Clark. *Dir.* William A Fraker.
Lemon Drop Kid, The (1951) Bob Hope, Marilyn Maxwell, Lloyd Nolan. Based on a Damon Runyon story. *Dir.* Sidney Lanfield.
Lemony Snicket: A Series of Unfortunate Events (2004) Jim Carrey (Count Olaf), Meryl Streep (Aunt Josephine), Jude Law (Lemony Snicket (voice)), Emily Browning (Violet Baudelaire), Liam Aiken (Klaus Baudelaire), Timothy Spall (Mr Poe), Billy Connolly (Uncle Monty). Three wealthy children's parents are killed in a fire. When they are sent to a distant relative, they find out that he is plotting to kill them and seize their fortune. Based on the books of Daniel Handler. *Dir.* Brad Silberling.
Lenny (1974) Dustin Hoffman (Lennie Bruce), Valerie Perrine. *Dir.* Bob Fosse.
Les Misérables (1995) Jean-Paul Belmondo, Michel Boujenah, Rufus. *Dir.* Claude Lelouch.
Les Misérables (2012) Hugh Jackman (Jean Valjean), Russell Crowe (Javert), Anne Hathaway (Fantine), Amanda Seyfried (Cosette), Eddie Redmayne(Marius Pontmercy), Aaron Tveit (Enjolras), Samantha Barks(Éponine), Isabelle Allen (Young Cosette), Daniel Huttlestone (Gavroche), Colm Wilkinson (Bishop Myriel), Helena Bonham Carter (Madame Thénardier), Sacha Baron Cohen (Thénardier). Based on the musical of the same name by Alain Boublil and Claude-Michel Schönberg which is in turn based on Les Misérables, the 1862 French novel by Victor Hugo. Won three Oscars. *Dir.* Tom Hooper.
Lethal Weapon (1987) Mel Gibson (Martin Riggs), Danny Glover (Roger Murtaugh), Gary Busey (Joshua). Vietnam veteran turned cop is unhinged by his wife's death and has a death wish. *Dir.* Richard Donner.
Lethal Weapon 2 (1989) Mel Gibson, Danny Glover, Joe Pesci (Leo Getz), Patsy Kensit (Rika Van Den Haas), Joss Ackland. South African drug runners unfortunately meet Martin Riggs. *Dir.* Richard Donner.
Lethal Weapon 3 (1992) Mel Gibson, Danny Glover, Joe Pesci, Rene Russo (Lorna Cole). *Dir.* Richard Donner. *Lethal Weapon 4* (1998) had the same main cast and director as the previous films.
Let's Make Love (1960) Yves Montand, Marilyn Monroe, Tony Randall, Wilfrid Hyde-White, Frankie Vaughan, Bing Crosby, Gene Kelly. Multi-millionaire learns he is to be burlesqued, so joins the cast. *Dir.* George Cukor.
Letter to Brezhnev (1985) Alfred Molina (Sergei), Peter Firth (Peter), Margi Clarke (Teresa), Tracy Lea (Tracy). Liverpool lass falls in love with a Russian sailor. *Dir.* Chris Bernard.
Liar Liar (1997) Jim Carrey (Fletcher Reede), Amanda Donohoe, Justin Cooper, Jennifer Tilly. *Dir.* Tom Shadyac.
Licence to Kill (1989) Timothy Dalton, Carey Lowell (Pam Bouvier), Anthony Zerbe (Milton Krest), Robert Davi (Frank Sanchez), Caroline Bliss (Moneypenny), Robert Brown (M), Talisa Soto (Lupe Lamora). Book title: *Licence Revoked.* Title song by Gladys Knight. *Dir.* John Glen.
Licensed to Kill (1965) Tom Adams, Veronica Hurst, Karel Stepanek. US title: *The Second Best Secret Agent in the Whole Wide World. Dir.* Lindsay Shonteff.
Life Aquatic With Steve Zissou, The (2004) Bill Murray (Steve Zissou), Owen Wilson (Ned Plimpton), Cate Blanchett (Jane Winslett-Richardson), Anjelica Huston (Eleanor Zissou), Willem Dafoe (Klaus Daimler), Jeff Goldblum (Alistair Hennessey), Michael Gambon (Oseary Drakoulias). Seeking revenge on the mythical shark that killed his partner, oceanographer Zissou assembles a crew including his estranged wife (Huston), a journalist (Blanchett), and a man who may or may not be his son (Wilson). *Dir.* Wes Anderson.
Life at the Top (1965) Laurence Harvey (Joe Lampton), Jean Simmons, Honor Blackman, Michael Craig, Margaret Johnston. *Dir.* Ted Kotcheff.
Life Is Beautiful (1997) Roberto Benigni, Nicoletta Braschi, Giustino Durano, Horst Buchholz. *Dir.* Roberto Benigni.
Life of Pi (2012) Gautam Belur (Pi -age 6), Ayush Tandon (Pi - age 13), Suraj Sharma (Pi - age 16), Irrfan Khan (Pi - adult), Tabu (Gita Patel - Pi's mother), Adil Hussain (Santosh Patel - Pi's father), Gérard Depardieu (the Cook), Rafe Spall (the Writer - Yann Martel). 16-year old Indian boy Piscine Molitor "Pi" Patel survives a shipwreck in which his family dies, and is stranded in the Pacific Ocean on a lifeboat with a Bengal tiger named Richard Parker. 3D live-action/computer-animated adventure drama film based on Yann Martel's 2001 novel of the same name. *Dir.* Ang Lee.
Lilo & Stitch (2002) Voices of Daveigh Chase (Lilo), Chris Sanders (Stitch), Tia Carrere, Zoe Caldwell, Ving Rhames. Lilo is a young Hawaiian girl who adopts a 'dog' named Stitch who is actually an alien genetic experiment gone horribly awry. Stitch has crash-landed on Earth, where he immediately begins wreaking havoc. Through her generosity, Lilo teaches Stitch the one thing he wasn't designed to do: to care about others. *Dir.* Dean DeBlois and Chris Sanders.
Limelight (1952) Charlie Chaplin, Claire Bloom, Buster Keaton, Sydney Chaplin. *Dir.* Charlie Chaplin.

Lincoln (2012) Daniel Day-Lewis (President Abraham Lincoln), Sally Field (First Lady Mary Todd Lincoln), Tommy Lee Jones (Thaddeus Stevens), Jared Harris (Lt-Gen Ulysses S. Grant). Historical drama covering the final four months of Lincoln's life, focusing on his efforts in January 1865 to have the 13th Amendment to the United States Constitution (abolition of slavery) passed by the United States House of Representatives. The film won two Academy Awards. *Dir.* Steven Spielberg.

Lion in Winter, The (1968) Katharine Hepburn (Eleanor of Aquitaine), Peter O'Toole (Henry II), Anthony Hopkins. *Dir.* Anthony Harvey.

Lion King, The (1994) Voices of Matthew Broderick, Rowan Atkinson, Whoopi Goldberg, Jeremy Irons, Robert Guillaume, James Earl Jones. Songs include: 'Can You Feel the Love Tonight', 'Circle of Life' & 'Hakuna Matata'. (Music by Elton John, lyrics by Tim Rice.) *Dir.* Roger Allers.

Liquidator, The (1965) Rod Taylor, Trevor Howard, David Tomlinson, Wilfrid Hyde-White, Derek Nimmo. *Dir.* Jack Cardiff.

List of Adrian Messenger, The (1963) George C Scott, Kirk Douglas, Clive Brook, Dana Wynter, Robert Mitchum, Frank Sinatra, Tony Curtis, Burt Lancaster. The cameos by the last 4 listed stars are debatable as they are unrecognisable. *Dir.* John Huston.

Lisztomania (1975) Roger Daltrey, Sara Kestelman, Paul Nicholas, Fiona Lewis, Ringo Starr. *Dir.* Ken Russell.

Little Big Man (1970) Dustin Hoffman, Martin Balsam, Faye Dunaway, Chief Dan George. *Dir.* Arthur Penn.

Little Caesar (1931) Edward G Robinson, Douglas Fairbanks Jnr, Glenda Farrell. *Dir.* Mervyn Le Roy.

Little Children (2006) Kate Winslet (Sarah Pierce), Patrick Wilson (Brad Adamson), Jennifer Connelly (Kathy Adamson), Gregg Edelman (Richard Pierce), Sadie Goldstein (Lucy Pierce), Ty Simpkins (Aaron Adamson), Noah Emmerich (Larry Hedges), Jackie Earle Haley (Ronald James McGorvey), Phyllis Somerville (May McGorvey), Raymond J Barry (Bullhorn Bob). A group of young married couples' lives intersect on the playgrounds, town pools and streets of their small community in potentially dangerous ways. *Dir.* Todd Field.

Little Dorrit (1987) Derek Jacobi (Arthur Clennam), Alec Guinness (William Dorrit), Max Wall (Flintwinch). There are 211 people named on the cast list, which is a record for a British film. *Dir.* Christine Edzard.

Little Foxes, The (1941) Bette Davis, Herbert Marshall, Teresa Wright, Dan Duryea. Based on a Lillian Hellman story. *Dir.* William Wyler.

Little Giants (1994) Rick Moranis, Ed O'Neil, John Madden. Wimp creates a young football team full of misfits. *Dir.* Duwayne Dunham.

Little Shop of Horrors (1986) Rick Moranis (Seymour Krelborn), Ellen Greene (Audrey), Vincent Gardenia (Mushnik), Steve Martin (Orin Scrivello, DDS). Voice of the plant (Audrey II): Levi Stubbs of the Four Tops. *Dir.* Frank Oz.

Little Women (1933) Katharine Hepburn, Paul Lukas, Joan Bennett, Frances Dee, Spring Byington. *Dir.* George Cukor.

Little Women (1949) June Allyson, Elizabeth Taylor, Peter Lawford, Margaret O'Brien, Janet Leigh, Mary Astor. *Dir.* Mervyn Le Roy.

Little Women (1994) Winona Ryder, Gabriel Byrne, Trini Alvarado, Samantha Mathis, Susan Sarandon. *Dir.* Gillian Armstrong.

Live and Let Die (1973) Roger Moore, Yaphet Kotto (Dr Kananga), Jane Seymour (Solitaire). Paul McCartney wrote and performed theme song. *Dir.* Guy Hamilton.

Living Daylights (1987) Timothy Dalton, Maryam d'Abo (Kara Milovy), Jeroen Krabbe (Gen Georgi Koskov), Joe Don Baker (Brad Whitaker), John Rhys-Davies (Gen Leonid Pushkin), Robert Brown (M), Desmond Llewellyn (Q), Caroline Bliss (Moneypenny), John Terry (Felix Leiter). Theme Song by A-Ha. *Dir.* John Glen.

Local Hero (1983) Burt Lancaster (Happer), Peter Riegert (Mac), John Gordon Sinclair (Ricky). TV series *Northern Exposure* was strongly influenced by this film. *Dir.* Bill Forsyth.

Loch Ness (1995) Ted Danson, Joely Richardson, Ian Holm, John Savident. US scientist tries to debunk the monster myth. *Dir.* John Henderson.

Lock Up (1989) Sylvester Stallone (Frank Leone), Donald Sutherland (Warden Drumgoole). *Dir.* John Flynn.

Logan's Run (1976) Michael York, Richard Jordan, Jenny Agutter, Farrah Fawcett-Majors, Peter Ustinov. Based on SF novel by William F Nolan. *Dir.* Michael Anderson.

Lolita (1962) James Mason, Shelley Winters, Sue Lyon, Peter Sellers. Lolita is 14 years old. *Dir.* Stanley Kubrick.

London Kills Me (1991) Justin Chadwick, Steven Mackintosh, Emer McCourt, Roshan Seth, Fiona Shaw. Down on his luck drug pusher is told he can have a job as a waiter if he can acquire a decent pair of shoes. *Dir.* Hanif Kureishi.

Loneliness of the Long Distance Runner, The (1962) Tom Courtenay, Michael Redgrave, James Bolam, Avis Bunnage. *Dir.* Tony Richardson.

Lonely Are the Brave (1962) Kirk Douglas, Walter Matthau, Gena Rowlands, Carroll O'Connor. Modern technology is pitted against a last rebel cowboy. *Dir.* David Miller.

Long and the Short and the Tall, The (1960) Laurence Harvey, Richard Todd, David McCallum, Richard Harris. US title: *Jungle Fighters*. *Dir.* Leslie Norman.

Long Good Friday, The (1980) Bob Hoskins, Helen Mirren, Dave King, Bryan Marshall, Eddie Constantine. *Dir.* John Mackenzie.

Long Goodbye, The (1973) Elliott Gould, Nina Van Pallandt, Sterling Hayden, Mark Rydell, Henry Gibson. *Dir.* Robert Altman.

Long Kiss Goodnight, The (1996) Geena Davis, Samuel L Jackson, Patrick Malahide. *Dir.* Renny Harlin.

Long Riders, The (1980) Stacy Keach, James Keach, David Carradine, Keith Carradine, Robert Carradine, Dennis Quaid, Randy Quaid. Story of the Younger, Miller and James boys. *Dir.* Walter Hill.

Longest Day, The (1962) John Wayne, Robert Mitchum, Henry Fonda, Robert Ryan, Roddy McDowall, Robert Wagner, Paul Anka, Fabian, Jeffrey Hunter, Rod Steiger, Red Buttons, Richard Burton, Sean Connery. *Dir.* Andrew Marton.

Look Back in Anger (1959) Richard Burton, Mary Ure, Claire Bloom, Edith Evans, Donald Pleasence. *Dir.* Tony Richardson.

Look Who's Talking (1989) John Travolta (James), Kirstie Alley (Mollie), Olympia Dukakis (Rosie), George Segal (Albert). Bruce Willis was the voice of Mikey. *Dir.* Amy Heckerling.

Look Who's Talking Too (1990) John Travolta, Kirstie Alley, Olympia Dukakis, Roseanne Arnold (voice of Julie), Mel Brooks (voice of Mr Toilet Man), Bruce Willis (voice of Mikey). *Dir.* Amy Heckerling.

Loot (1970) Richard Attenborough, Lee Remick, Hywel Bennett, Milo O'Shea, Dick Emery. *Dir.* Silvio Narizzano.

Lord of the Flies (1963) James Aubrey, Tom Chapin, Hugh Edwards. Remake in 1990 was directed by Harry Hook. *Dir.* Peter Brook.

Lord of the Rings (1978) Cartoon version of Tolkien's book with voices of Christopher Guard and John Hurt. *Dir.* Ralph Bakshi.

Lord of the Rings: The Fellowship of the Ring, The (2001) Ian McKellen (Gandalf), Elijah Wood (Frodo Baggins), Viggo Mortensen (Aragorn), Sean Astin (Sam), Cate Blanchett (Galadriel), Sean Bean (Boromir), John Rhys-Davies (Gimli), Liv Tyler (Arwen), Billy Boyd (Pippin), Christopher Lee (Saruman), Ian Holm (Bilbo Baggins), Andy Serkis (Gollum), Dominic Monaghan (Merry), Orlando Bloom (Legolas). Multiple Oscar winner concerning a hobbit who inherits a magic ring that could enslave all the people of Middle Earth unless it is destroyed. *Dir.* Peter Jackson.

Lord of the Rings: The Return of the King, The (2003) The third chapter in Tolkien's trilogy is the longest and most spectacular of them all. The former Fellowship of the Ring prepare for the final battle for Middle Earth, while the hobbits Frodo and Sam approach Mount Doom to destroy the cursed ring. The usual cast is reprised without Sean Bean, Brad Dourif, Christopher Lee, Karl Urban and David Wenham. *Dir.* Peter Jackson.

Lord of the Rings: The Two Towers, The (2002) The second chapter in the JRR Tolkien saga. The hobbits Frodo and Sam brave terrible dangers in an attempt to have the evil ring destroyed, while Aragorn, Legolas and their allies strive to rescue the abducted hobbits Pippin and Merry from the clutches of evil. The great wizard Gandalf also makes his miraculous return to aid in the struggle against the united towers of Saruman and Sauron (Sala Baker). *The Two Towers* has the same cast as *The Fellowship of the Ring* but new characters include Bernard Hill's Théoden, David Wenham's Faramir, Karl Urban's Éomer, and Brad Dourif as Grima Wormtongue. *Dir.* Peter Jackson.

Lost Highway (1997) Bill Pullman, Patricia Arquette, Balthazar Getty. *Dir.* David Lynch.

Lost Horizon (1937) Ronald Colman, HB Warner, Thomas Mitchell, Sam Jaffe. Remade in 1972 with Peter Finch in Colman role. *Dir.* Frank Capra.
Lost in Translation (2003) Bill Murray (Bob Harris), Scarlett Johansson (Charlotte), Giovanni Ribisi (John), Anna Faris (Kelly), Fumihiro Hayashi (Charlie), Catherine Lambert (Jazz Singer). A tired actor, making a whisky advert in Tokyo, meets a young married woman and they imagine how their lives could have been different. *Dir.* Sofia Coppola.
Lost Weekend, The (1945) Ray Milland (Don Birnam), Jane Wyman, Howard da Silva. *Dir.* Billy Wilder.
Lost World, The: Jurassic Park (1997) Jeff Goldblum (Dr Ian Malcolm), Julianne Moore, Pete Postlethwaite, Richard Attenborough (John Hammond). *Dir.* Steven Spielberg.
Love Is a Many-Splendored Thing (1955) Jennifer Jones, William Holden, Torin Thatcher. Sammy Fain & Paul Francis Webster won an Academy Award for the title song. *Dir.* Henry King.
Love Me Tender (1956) Richard Egan, Debra Paget, Elvis Presley, Neville Brand, James Drury. *Dir.* Robert D Webb.
Love Me Tonight (1932) Maurice Chevalier, Jeanette MacDonald, Charles Butterworth, Myrna Loy. *Dir.* Rouben Mamoulian.
Love on the Dole (1941) Deborah Kerr, Clifford Evans, George Carney. Based on Walter Greenwood's novel. *Dir.* John Baxter.
Love Story (1970) Ali MacGraw, Ryan O'Neal (Oliver Barrett IV), Ray Milland. 1978 sequel: *Oliver's Story. Dir.* Arthur Hiller.
Lust for Life (1956) Kirk Douglas (Vincent Van Gogh), Anthony Quinn (Paul Gauguin). *Dir.* Vincente Minnelli.
Mad Dog and Glory (1992) Robert De Niro, Uma Thurman, Bill Murray. Timid cop is given a present of a beautiful girl for a week by a gangster. *Dir.* John McNaughton.
Mad Max (1979) Mel Gibson, Joanne Samuel. *Dir.* George Miller.
Mad Max 2 (1981) Mel Gibson, Bruce Spence, Vernon Wells. *Dir.* George Miller.
Mad Max beyond Thunderdome (1985) Mel Gibson, Tina Turner, Angelo Rossitto, Helen Buday. *Dir.* George Miller.
Madagascar (2005) Voices of Ben Stiller (Alex), Chris Rock (Marty), David Schwimmer (Melman), Jada Pinkett Smith (Gloria), Sacha Baron Cohen (Julien). Spoiled by their upbringing and with no idea what wildlife is really like, four animals from New York Central Zoo escape, unwittingly assisted by four absconding penguins, and find themselves in Madagascar, among a bunch of merry lemurs. *Dir.* Eric Darnell and Tom McGrath. The production team and cast reprised their roles in the 2008 sequel, *Madagascar: Escape 2 Africa.*
Madame Bovary (1949) Jennifer Jones, Van Heflin, James Mason, Louis Jourdan. A 1991 remake starring Isabelle Huppert kept to the original plot a little better. *Dir.* Vincente Minnelli.
Made in America (1993) Whoopi Goldberg, Ted Danson, Will Smith. Black teenager, born by artificial insemination, discovers her father is a white car salesman. *Dir.* Richard Benjamin.
Madness of King George, The (1994) Nigel Hawthorne, Helen Mirren, Ian Holm, Amanda Donohoe, Rupert Everett, Rupert Graves. *Dir.* Nicholas Hytner.
Magic Christian (1969) Peter Sellers, Ringo Starr, Richard Attenborough, Laurence Harvey, Spike Milligan, Raquel Welch, John Cleese. Yul Brynner cameo as a transvestite nightclub singer. *Dir.* Joseph McGrath.
Magnificent Seven, The (1960) Yul Brynner, Steve McQueen, Robert Vaughn, James Coburn, Charles Bronson, Brad Dexter, Horst Buchholz. *Dir.* John Sturges.
Malcolm X (1992) Denzil Washington, Angela Bassett, Albert Hall, Al Freeman Jnr, Spike Lee. Based on the book *Autobiography of Malcolm X as told to Alex Haley. Dir.* Spike Lee.
Mame (1974) Lucille Ball, Beatrice Arthur, Robert Preston, Bruce Davison. *Dir.* Gene Saks.
Mamma Mia! (2008) Meryl Streep (Donna Sheridan), Amanda Seyfried (Sophie Sheridan), Pierce Brosnan (Sam Charmichael), Colin Firth (Harry Bright), Stellan Skarsgård (Bill Anderson), Julie Walters (Rosie Mulligan), Christine Baranski (Tanya Wilkinson), Dominic Cooper (Sky). Musical film adaptation of the 1999 West End musical of the same name, based on the songs of the pop group ABBA, with additional music by ABBA member Benny Andersson, who also has a cameo performance in the film as the piano player during 'Dancing Queen'. On the fictional Greek island of Kalokairi, 20-year-old bride-to-be Sophie Sheridan posts three wedding invitations to three different men, any of whom might be her father. *Dir.* Phyllida Lloyd.
Man and a Woman, A (1966) Anouk Aimée, Jean-Louis Trintignant. Best Foreign Film Oscar. Concerns a racing driver and a script girl who fall in love. *Dir.* Claude Lelouch.
Man Called Horse, A (1970) Richard Harris, Judith Anderson, Jean Gascon, Manu Tupou. Sequels: *Return of a Man Called Horse* (1976), & *Triumphs of a Man Called Horse* (1984). *Dir.* Elliot Silverstein.
Man for All Seasons, A (1966) Paul Scofield, Wendy Hiller, Susannah York, Robert Shaw, Orson Welles, John Hurt, Corin Redgrave. Events leading to the execution of Sir Thomas More. *Dir.* Fred Zinnemann.
Man in the Iron Mask, The (1939) Louis Hayward, Warren William (D'Artagnan), Alan Hale, Bert Roach, Joseph Schildkraut. King Louis XIV keeps his twin brother prisoner. *Dir.* James Whale.
Man of the Year (1995) Dirk Shafer, Vivian Paxton, Deidra Shafer. Documentary about events surrounding the homosexual Dirk Shafer's awarding of the 1992 *Playgirl* magazine's Man of the Year. *Dir.* Dirk Shafer.
Man on Wire (2008) Documentary film covering Philippe Petit's 1974 high-wire walk between the Twin Towers of New York's World Trade Center. Based on Petit's book, *To Reach the Clouds*, later republished with the new title *Man on Wire. Dir.* James Marsh.
Man Who Came to Dinner, The (1941) Bette Davis, Monty Woolley, Ann Sheridan, Jimmy Durante (spoofing Harpo Marx). *Dir.* William Keighley.
Man Who Could Work Miracles, The (1936) Roland Young, Ralph Richardson, Ernest Thesiger, George Sanders. Based on the HG Wells story. *Dir.* Lothar Mendes.
Man Who Fell to Earth, The (1976) David Bowie, Rip Torn, Candy Clark. *Dir.* Nicolas Roeg.
Man Who Knew too Much, The (1934) Leslie Banks, Edna Best, Peter Lorre. *Dir.* Alfred Hitchcock.
Man Who Knew too Much, The (1956) James Stewart, Doris Day, Bernard Miles. Remake of the 1934 film. *Dir.* Alfred Hitchcock.
Man Who Shot Liberty Valance, The (1962) John Wayne, James Stewart, Lee Marvin, Vera Miles. John Wayne shot Liberty Valance. *Dir.* John Ford.
Man Who Wasn't There, The (2001) Billy Bob Thornton (Ed Crane), Frances McDormand (Doris Crane), Michael Badalucco, James Gandolfini. Set in the 1940s. *Dir.* Joel Coen.
Man Who Would Be King, The (1975) Sean Connery, Michael Caine, Christopher Plummer (Kipling), Shakira Caine, Saeed Jaffrey. Based on a Rudyard Kipling story. *Dir.* John Huston.
Man with the Golden Arm (1956) Frank Sinatra, Kim Novak, Eleanor Parker, Arnold Stang. Golden Arm refers to the card-dealing expertise of the lead character. *Dir.* Otto Preminger.
Man with the Golden Gun (1974) Roger Moore, Christopher Lee (Scaramanga), Britt Ekland (Mary Goodnight), Maud Adams (Andrea Anders), Hervé Villechaize, Clifton James, Richard Loo. Title song performed by Lulu. *Dir.* Guy Hamilton.
Man without a Face, The (1993) Mel Gibson, Margaret Whitton, Fay Masterson, Viva. Boy remembers how he was helped to enter a military academy by a disfigured former teacher. *Dir.* Mel Gibson.
Manchurian Candidate, The (1962) Frank Sinatra (Capt./Maj. Bennett Marco), Laurence Harvey (Sgt Raymond Shaw), Janet Leigh (Eugenie Rose Chaney), Angela Lansbury (Mrs Iselin), Henry Silva (Chunjin). A former Korean War veteran is brainwashed by Communists into becoming a political assassin. *Dir.* John Frankenheimer.
Manchurian Candidate, The (2004) Denzel Washington (Ben Marco), Meryl Streep (Eleanor Shaw), Liev Schreiber (Raymond Shaw), Jon Voight (Senator Thomas Jordan). In the midst of the Gulf War, soldiers are kidnapped and brainwashed for sinister purposes. *Dir.* Jonathan Demme.

Mandy (1952) Jack Hawkins, Terence Morgan, Phyllis Calvert, Mandy Miller. Little deaf girl is sent to a special school. *Dir.* Alexander Mackendrick.
Manhattan (1979) Woody Allen, Diane Keaton, Meryl Streep, Mariel Hemingway. *Dir.* Woody Allen.
Manhattan Murder Mystery (1993) Woody Allen, Alan Alda, Anjelica Huston, Diane Keaton. *Dir.* Woody Allen.
Marathon Man (1976) Dustin Hoffman, Laurence Olivier, Roy Scheider, William Devane. *Dir.* John Schlesinger.
March of the Penguins (2005) French title *La Marche de l'empereur.* A look at the annual journey of Emperor penguins as they march – single file – to their traditional breeding ground. Morgan Freeman is the narrator of the English version. Won an Academy Award for Best Documentary Feature. *Dir.* Luc Jacquet.
Maria Full of Grace (2004) Catalina Sandino Moreno (Maria Alvarez), Yenny Paola Vega (Blanca). A young Colombian girl accepts a risky offer in order to escape her country for the United States. *Dir.* Joshua Marston.
Marnie (1964) Tippi Hedren, Sean Connery, Martin Gabel, Diane Baker. Rich man marries a kleptomaniac who sees red when she sees red! *Dir.* Alfred Hitchcock.
Mars Attacks! (1996) Jack Nicholson, Glenn Close, Annette Bening, Michael J Fox, Pierce Brosnan, Rod Steiger, Danny De Vito, Tom Jones. *Dir.* Tim Burton.
Marty (1955) Ernest Borgnine, Betsy Blair, Jerry Paris. *Dir.* Delbert Mann.
Mary of Scotland (1936) Katharine Hepburn, Fredric March, Donald Crisp. *Dir.* John Ford.
Mary Poppins (1964) Julie Andrews, Dick Van Dyke, Glynis Johns, David Tomlinson, Elsa Lanchester, Arthur Treacher. Among many other awards, the song 'Chim Chim Cheree' won the Oscar for Best Song. *Dir.* Robert Stevenson.
Mary Queen of Scots (1971) Vanessa Redgrave, Glenda Jackson, Trevor Howard, Patrick McGoohan, Nigel Davenport. *Dir.* Charles Jarrott.
M*A*S*H (1970) Donald Sutherland, Elliott Gould, Sally Kellerman, Robert Duvall, Gary Burghoff. *Dir.* Robert Altman.
Mask, The (1994) Jim Carrey, Amy Yasbeck, Peter Riegert. *Dir.* Charles Russell.
Master and Commander: The Far Side of the World (2003) Russell Crowe (Captain Jack Aubrey), Paul Bettany (Dr Stephen Maturin), Billy Boyd (Barrett Bonden), James D'Arcy (First Lt Thomas Pullings), Lee Ingleby (Hollom), George Innes (Joe Plaice), Mark Lewis Jones (Mr Hogg), Chris Larkin (Captain Howard, Royal Marines), David Threlfall (Killick), Max Pirkis (Lord Blakeney). Based on the Patrick O'Brian novels. Although his ship is almost destroyed in an attack, a British sea captain chases a superior French warship across the oceans. *Dir.* Peter Weir.
Matilda (1997) Danny De Vito, Mara Wilson (Matilda), Rhea Perlman, Pam Ferris. Based on Roald Dahl's bestseller. *Dir.* Danny De Vito.
Matter of Life and Death, A (1946) David Niven, Roger Livesey, Kim Hunter, Marius Goring, Raymond Massey, Abraham Sofaer. US title: *Stairway to Heaven. Dir.* Michael Powell.
Maverick (1994) Mel Gibson, Jodie Foster, James Garner, Graham Greene, James Coburn, Alfred Molina. *Dir.* Richard Donner.
Mean Creek (2004) Rory Culkin (Sam), Ryan Kelley (Clyde), Scott Mechlowicz (Marty 'Martini' Blank), Trevor Morgan (Rocky). When a teenager is bullied, his brother and friends lure the bully into the woods to seek revenge. *Dir.* Jacob Aaron Estes.
Mean Streets (1973) Robert De Niro, Harvey Keitel, Amy Robinson. *Dir.* Martin Scorsese.
Meet Me in St Louis (1944) Judy Garland, Margaret O'Brien, Tom Drake, Mary Astor. *Dir.* Vincente Minnelli.
Memoirs of a Geisha (2005) Ziyi Zhang (Chiyo/Sayuri), Suzuka Ohgo (Young Chiyo), Ken Watanabe (The Chairman), Kôji Yakusho (Nobu), Youki Kudoh (Pumpkin), Zoe Weizenbaum (Young Pumpkin). Nitta Sayuri reveals how she transcended her fishing-village roots and became one of Japan's most celebrated geisha. The film won three Academy Awards: Art Direction, Cinematography and Costume Design. *Dir.* Rob Marshall.
Men, The (1950) Marlon Brando, Teresa Wright, Everett Sloane, Jack Webb. Reissue title: *Battle Stripe. Dir.* Fred Zinnemann.
Men in Black II (2002) Tommy Lee Jones, Will Smith, Rip Torn. Sequel to *MIB (Men In Black). Dir.* Barry Sonnenfeld.
Men of Respect (1990) John Turturro, Katherine Borowitz, Dennis Farina, Peter Boyle, Rod Steiger. Gangster setting for Shakespeare's *Macbeth. Dir.* William Reilly.
Mercury Rising (1998) Bruce Willis, Alec Baldwin, Miko Hughes, Chi McBride, Kim Dickens, Robert Stanton, Carrie Preston, Bodhi Pine Elfman, LL Ginter, John Carroll Lynch, Peter Stormare. *Dir.* Harold Becker.
Mermaids (1990) Cher, Bob Hoskins, Winona Ryder. Daughter, torn between becoming a nun and her feelings for a handsome boy, resolves her difficulties with her flirtatious mother. *Dir.* Richard Benjamin.
Merry Christmas, Mr Lawrence (1982) David Bowie, Tom Conti, Ryuichi Sakamoto, Takeshi. *Dir.* Nagisa Oshima.
Metro (1997) Eddie Murphy (Scott Roper), Michael Rapaport, Kim Miyori. *Dir.* Thomas Carter.
Mexican, The (2001) Brad Pitt (Jerry Welbach), Julia Roberts (Samantha), James Gandolfini (Leroy). Incompetent crook is sent to Mexico to bring back a priceless pistol for his boss whilst his girlfriend is held as ransom. Gene Hackman as Arnold Margolese is uncredited. *Dir.* Gore Verbinski.
Miami Rhapsody (1995) Sarah Jessica Parker, Gil Bellows, Antonio Banderas, Mia Farrow, Paul Mazursky, Naomi Campbell. Woman contemplating marriage observes the marital errors being committed by her siblings and friends. *Dir.* David Frankel.
Miami Vice (2006) Colin Farrell (Det. James 'Sonny' Crockett), Jamie Foxx (Det. Ricardo 'Rico' Tubbs). Based on the 1980s TV action/drama. *Dir.* Michael Mann.
MIB (Men in Black), (1997) Tommy Lee Jones (K), Will Smith (J), Linda Fiorentino (Dr Weaver), Tim Blaney (voice of Frank the Pug), Rip Torn (Zed). SF film in which Will Smith performs title track & Snoop Doggy Dogg the soundtrack album. *Dir.* Barry Sonnenfeld.
Michael Clayton (2007) George Clooney (Michael Clayton), Tom Wilkinson (Arthur Edens), Tilda Swinton (Karen Crowder), Sydney Pollack (Marty Bach), Michael O'Keefe (Barry Grissom). Law firm brings in its gambling-addicted 'fixer' after a lawyer has a breakdown while representing a chemical company that he knows is guilty in a multi-billion-dollar action suit. *Dir.* Tony Gilroy.
Michael Collins (1996) Liam Neeson (Michael Collins), Aidan Quinn (Harry Boland), Julia Roberts (Kitty Kiernan). *Dir.* Neil Jordan.
Microcosmos (1996) French documentary film revolving around stag beetles' attempts to gain control of a twig. *Dir.* Marie Perennau & Claude Nuridsany.
Midnight Cowboy (1969) Dustin Hoffman, Jon Voight, Brenda Vaccaro, Sylvia Miles. *Dir.* John Schlesinger.
Midnight Express (1978) John Hurt, Brad Davis, Randy Quaid, Bo Hopkins. *Dir.* Alan Parker.
Midnight's Children (2012) Satya Bhabha, Shriya Saran, Siddharth Narayan, Anupam Kher, Shabana Azmi, Seema Biswas, Shahana Goswami, Samrat Chakrabarti, Rahul Bose, Soha Ali Khan, Anita Majumdar and Darsheel Safary. Film adaptation of Salman Rushdie's 1981 novel of the same name dealing with India's transition from British colonialism to independence. *Dir.* Deepa Mehta.
Midsummer Night's Dream, A (1935) James Cagney, Dick Powell, Jean Muir, Mickey Rooney, Olivia de Havilland. *Dir.* Max Reinhardt.
Midsummer Night's Dream, A (1996) Lindsay Duncan, Alex Jennings, Alfred Burke. *Dir.* Adrian Noble.
Mighty, The (1998) Sharon Stone, Gena Rowlands Harry Dean Stanton, Gillian Anderson, Meatloaf. *Dir.* Peter Chelsom.
Mighty Aphrodite (1995) Woody Allen, Helena Bonham Carter, Mira Sorvino, F Murray Abraham, Olympia Dukakis, Peter Weller, Claire Bloom, Michael Rapaport. Sportswriter's attempt to rescue the mother of his adopted son from life as a prostitute. *Dir.* Woody Allen.
Mighty Ducks, The (1992) Emilio Estevez, Joss Ackland, Lane Smith, Heidi King. Lawyer on community service for drink-driving adopts a hockey team. GB title: *Champions. Dir.* Stephen Herek.
Mighty Quinn, The (1989) Denzel Washington, James Fox, Mimi Rogers, M Emmet Walsh, Norman Beaton. Caribbean police investigate the murder of an American. *Dir.* Carl Shenkel.
Mike Bassett: England Manager (2001) Ricky Tomlinson (Mike Bassett), Amanda Redman, Bradley Walsh, Philip Jackson, Phil Jupitus, Pele (as himself). *Dir.* Steve Barron.

Milk (2008) Sean Penn (Harvey Milk), Emile Hirsch (Cleve Jones), Josh Brolin (Dan White), Diego Luna (Jack Lira), James Franco (Scott Smith), Alison Pill (Anne Kronenberg), Victor Garber (Mayor George Moscone), Denis O'Hare (State Senator John Briggs), Joseph Cross (Dick Pabich), Stephen Spinella (Rick Stokes), Lucas Grabeel (Danny Nicoletta), Jeff Koons (Art Agnos). Biographical film about rights activist Harvey Milk, the first openly gay man to be elected to public office in California. The film begins at Milk's 40th birthday and covers the last eight years of his life, including his move from New York City to settle in the Castro district of San Francisco in 1972 and his ultimate murder, alongside that of Mayor George Moscone, by former city supervisor Dan White in November 1978. *Dir.* Gus Van Sant.

Million Dollar Baby (2004) Clint Eastwood (Frankie Dunn), Hilary Swank (Maggie Fitzgerald), Morgan Freeman (Eddie 'Scrap-Iron' Dupris). Moving story set around a boxing gym, and in particular the relationship between a wannabe female fighter in her early 30s and her reluctant trainer. *Dir.* Clint Eastwood.

Million Pound Note, The (1953) Gregory Peck, Jane Griffiths, Ronald Squire, Joyce Grenfell, Wilfrid Hyde-White. Based on a Mark Twain story. *Dir.* Ronald Neame.

Minority Report (2002) Tom Cruise, Colin Farrell, Samantha Morton, Max von Sydow, Lois Smith. *Dir.* Steven Spielberg.

Miracle (2004) Kurt Russell (Herb Brooks), Patricia Clarkson (Patty Brooks), Noah Emmerich (Craig Patrick). Story of player-turned-coach Herb Brooks, who led the 1980 US Olympic hockey team to victory over the previously invincible Russians. *Dir.* Gavin O'Connor.

Miracle on 34th Street (1994) Richard Attenborough (Kris Kringle), Elizabeth Perkins, Robert Prosky. Remake of the 1947 film starring Edmund Gwenn (Kris Kringle) and Maureen O'Hara. *Dir.* Les Mayfield.

Miracle Worker, The (1962) Anne Bancroft, Patty Duke, Victor Jory. *Dir.* Arthur Penn.

Miranda (1947) Glynis Johns, Griffith Jones, Googie Withers, Margaret Rutherford, David Tomlinson. Sequel to this mermaid movie was *Mad About Men,* starring Johns and Donald Sinden. *Dir.* Ken Annakin.

Misery (1990) James Caan, Kathy Bates, Richard Farnsworth, Lauren Bacall. Disturbed fan kidnaps an injured novelist and forces him to write a novel. *Dir.* Rob Reiner.

Misfits, The (1961) Clark Gable, Marilyn Monroe, Montgomery Clift, Eli Wallach, Kevin McCarthy. Film about cowboys in the Nevada desert roping mustangs but more famous for its co-stars' imminent deaths. *Dir.* John Huston.

Mission, The (1986) Robert De Niro, Jeremy Irons, Ray McAnally, Liam Neeson, Cherie Lunghi. Music by Ennio Morricone. *Dir.* Roland Joffe.

Mission: Impossible (1996) Tom Cruise, Jon Voight, Kristin Scott-Thomas, Vanessa Redgrave. *Dir.* Brian De Palma.

Mission: Impossible II (2000) Tom Cruise (Ethan Hunt), Dougray Scott (Sean Ambrose), Thandie Newton (Nyah Nordoff-Hall), Ving Rhames (Luther Stickell), William Mapother (Wallis). A secret agent is sent to Sydney, to find and destroy a genetically modified disease called 'Chimera'. Incidentally, William Mapother is a cousin of Tom Cruise and Lee Anne De Vette. *Dir.* John Woo.

Mission: Impossible III (2006) Tom Cruise (Ethan Hunt), Ving Rhames (Luther Stickell), Philip Seymour Hoffman (Owen Davian), Billy Crudup (Musgrave), Michelle Monaghan (Julia Meade), Jonathan Rhys Meyers (Declan Gormley), Keri Russell (Lindsey Farris), Maggie Q (Zhen Lei), Laurence Fishburne (Theodore Brassel). Ethan Hunt comes face to face with a dangerous and sadistic arms dealer while trying to keep his identity secret in order to protect his girlfriend. Although the plot line and action sequences are improbable, this second sequel is critically acclaimed as the best of the three films. *Dir.* JJ Abrams.

Mission Impossible: Ghost Protocol (2011) Tom Cruise (Ethan Hunt), Simon Pegg (Benji Dunn), Michael Nyqvist (Kurt Hendricks aka Cobalt), Jeremy Renner (William Brandt), Paula Patton (Jane Carter), Michelle Monaghan (Julia Mead – Ethan's wife), Ving Rhames (Luther Stickell). The fourth film in the Mission: Impossible series Ethan infiltrate secret Moscow Kremlin archives and locate files identifying a Swedish nuclear strategist, codenamed Cobalt. *Dir.* Brad Bird.

Missionary, The (1983) Michael Palin, Maggie Smith, Trevor Howard, Michael Hordern, Denholm Elliott. *Dir.* Richard Loncraine.

Mississippi Burning (1988) Gene Hackman, Willem Dafoe, Frances McDormand. *Dir.* Alan Parker.

Missouri Breaks (1976) Marlon Brando, Jack Nicholson, Randy Quaid, Kathleen Lloyd. *Dir.* Arthur Penn.

Moby Dick (1956) Gregory Peck, Richard Basehart, Orson Welles, James Robertson Justice. Based on Herman Melville's novel. *Dir.* John Huston.

Mommie Dearest (1981) Faye Dunaway, Diana Scarwid, Steve Forrest, Howard da Silva (Louis B Mayer). Joan Crawford life story. *Dir.* Frank Perry.

Mona Lisa (1986) Bob Hoskins, Cathy Tyson, Michael Caine, Robbie Coltrane. *Dir.* Neil Jordan.

Money Train (1995) Wesley Snipes, Woody Harrelson, Jennifer Lopez. *Dir.* Joseph Ruben.

Monster (2003) Charlize Theron (Aileen Wuornos), Christina Ricci (Selby Wall), Bruce Dern (Thomas), Scott Wilson (Horton), Pruitt Taylor Vince (Gene), Lee Tergesen (Vincent Corey), Annie Corley (Donna Tentler). True-life crime story of Aileen Wuornos, a prostitute who shot at least six men. *Dir.* Patty Jenkins.

Monster's Ball (2001) Billy Bob Thornton (Hank Grotowski), Halle Berry (Leticia Musgrove), Heath Ledger (Sonny Grotowski), Peter Boyle, Sean Combs, Mos Def, Amber Rules. After a family tragedy, a racist prison guard re-examines his attitudes while falling in love with the African-American wife of the last prisoner he executed. *Dir.* Marc Forster.

Monty Python and the Holy Grail (1975) John Cleese, Graham Chapman, Terry Gilliam, Eric Idle, Michael Palin, Terry Jones. *Dir.* Terry Gilliam and Terry Jones.

Monty Python's Life of Brian (1979) The Python team spoof the life of Jesus of Nazareth. *Dir.* Terry Jones.

Monty Python's The Meaning of Life (1983) The Python team return to their roots with some original sketches. *Dir.* Terry Jones.

Moolaadé (2004) Fatoumata Coulibaly (Collé Gallo Ardo Sy), Maimouna Hélène Diarra (Hadjatou). Set in Burkina Faso, an examination of the subject of female circumcision. *Dir.* Ousmane Sembene.

Moon is Blue, The (1953) Maggie McNamara, David Niven, William Holden, Tom Tully, Dawn Addams. *Dir.* Otto Preminger.

Moonlighting (1982) Jeremy Irons, Eugene Lipinski, Jiri Stanislaw. Four Polish building workers arrive in London to renovate a house and hear of social unrest at home. *Dir.* Jerzy Skolimowski.

Moonraker (1979) Roger Moore, Lois Chiles (Holly Goodhead), Michael Lonsdale (Hugo Drax). Title song performed by Shirley Bassey. *Dir.* Lewis Gilbert.

Moonstruck (1987) Cher, Nicolas Cage, Vincent Gardenia, Olympia Dukakis, Danny Aiello. Young widow falls for the estranged brother of her husband-to-be. *Dir.* Norman Jewison.

Moonwalker (1988) Michael Jackson, Joe Pesci, Sean Lennon. *Dir.* Colin Chilvers.

Motorcycle Diaries, The (2004) Gael Garcia Bernal (Che Guevara), Rodrigo de la Serna (Alberto Granado). True story of a 23-year-old medical student from Argentina, Che Guevara, who travelled across South America on a motorcycle with his friend Alberto Granado in 1951–2, in a personal odyssey which would ultimately inspire him to become a revolutionary. *Dir.* Walter Salles.

Moulin Rouge (2001) Nicole Kidman, Ewan McGregor, Jim Broadbent, John Leguizamo (Toulouse-Lautrec), Matthew Whittet (Satie), Kylie Minogue (Green Fairy), Garry McDonald (The Doctor). *Dir.* Baz Luhrmann.

Mouse on the Moon, The (1963) Margaret Rutherford, Ron Moody, Bernard Cribbins, David Kossoff, Terry-Thomas, Michael Crawford. Sequel to *The Mouse That Roared*; concerning home-made wine making excellent rocket-fuel. *Dir.* Richard Lester.

Mouse That Roared, The (1959) Peter Sellers (three roles), Jean Seberg, David Kossoff, William Hartnell, Leo McKern. Tiny Duchy of Grand Fenwick is bankrupt, so decides to declare war on USA, be defeated, and then accept aid. *Dir.* Jack Arnold.

Move over Darling (1963) Doris Day, James Garner, Polly Bergen, Chuck Connors. Wife returns home after shipwreck to find her husband remarried. *Dir.* Michael Gordon.

Mr and Mrs Bridge (1990) Paul Newman, Joanne Woodward, Robert Sean Leonard, Blythe Danner, Simon Callow. Inhibited lawyer gradually erodes his wife's personality. *Dir.* James Ivory.

Mr & Mrs Smith (2005) Brad Pitt (John Smith), Angelina Jolie (Jane Smith). A bored married couple are surprised to learn that they are both assassins hired by competing agencies to kill each other. *Dir.* Doug Liman.

Mr Deeds Goes to Town (1936) Gary Cooper, Jean Arthur, Raymond Walburn, Margaret Seddon. Small-town poet inherits fortune and sets New York on its heels with his honesty. *Dir.* Frank Capra.

Mr Jones (1993) Richard Gere, Lena Olin, Anne Bancroft. Manic depressive begins an affair with his psychiatrist. *Dir.* Mike Figgis.

Mr Smith Goes to Washington (1939) James Stewart, Claude Rains, Jean Arthur, Thomas Mitchell, Edward Arnold. Senator exposes corruption in high places. *Dir.* Frank Capra.

Mrs Brown (1997) Billy Connolly (John Brown), Dame Judi Dench (Queen Victoria). *Dir.* John Madden.

Mrs Dalloway (1998) Vanessa Redgrave, Rupert Graves, Natascha McElhone, Michael Kitchen. *Dir.* Marleen Gorris.

Mrs Doubtfire (1993) Robin Williams, Sally Field, Pierce Brosnan, Robert Prosky. *Dir.* Chris Columbus.

Mrs Miniver (1942) Greer Garson, Walter Pidgeon, Teresa Wright. Multi-award winning film. *Dir.* William Wyler.

Mrs Pollifax – Spy (1970) Rosalind Russell, Darren McGavin. Written by CA McKnight, who was, in fact, Rosalind Russell. *Dir.* Leslie Martinson.

Much Ado about Nothing (1993) Kenneth Branagh, Emma Thompson, Richard Briers, Michael Keaton, Denzel Washington. *Dir.* Kenneth Branagh.

Mudlark, The (1950) Alec Guinness, Irene Dunne, Andrew Ray, Anthony Steel, Finlay Currie. Scruffy boy from the docks breaks into Windsor Castle to visit Queen Victoria. *Dir.* Jean Negulesco.

Mulholland Falls (1996) Nick Nolte, Melanie Griffith, Treat Williams, John Malkovich, Bruce Dern. *Dir.* Lee Tamahori.

Multiplicity (1996) Michael Keaton, Andie MacDowell, Ann Cusack. *Dir.* Harold Ramis.

Mummy, The (1932) Boris Karloff, Zita Johann, David Manners, Arthur Byron, Edward Van Sloan. Boris Karloff was billed as 'Karloff the Uncanny'. *Dir.* Karl Freund.

Mummy, The (1959) Peter Cushing, Christopher Lee, Yvonne Furneaux, Eddie Byrne, Felix Aylmer, John Stuart. *Dir.* Terence Fisher.

Mummy, The (1999) Brendan Fraser, Rachel Weisz, John Hannah, Arnold Vosloo, Kevin O'Connor. *Dir.* Stephen Sommers.

Mummy Returns, The (2001) Brendan Fraser, Rachel Weisz, John Hannah, Arnold Vosloo (The Mummy), Kevin O'Conner. *Dir.* Stephen Sommers. Acting debut of wrestling superstar 'The Rock' as The Scorpion King.

Mummy: Tomb of the Dragon Emperor, The (2008) Brendan Fraser (Rick O'Connell), Jet Li (Emperor Han), Maria Bello (Evelyn Carnahan O'Connell), John Hannah (Jonathan Carnahan), Luke Ford (Alex O'Connell), Michelle Yeoh (Zi Yuan). *Dir.* Rob Cohen. Sequel to the two Stephen Sommers' films.

Munich (2005) Eric Bana (Avner), Daniel Craig (Steve), Ciarán Hinds (Carl), Mathieu Kassovitz (Robert), Hanns Zischler (Hans), Geoffrey Rush (Ephraim), Michael Lonsdale (Papa), Marie-Josée Croze (Jeanette The Dutch Assassin). The world was watching in 1972 as 11 Israeli athletes were murdered at the Munich Olympics. This is the story of what happened next. *Dir.* Steven Spielberg.

Muppet Christmas Carol, The (1992) Michael Caine (Ebenezer Scrooge). *Dir.* Brian Henson.

Muppet Movie, The (1979) Charles Durning, Edgar Bergen, Bob Hope, Milton Berle, Mel Brooks, James Coburn, Dom DeLuise, Elliott Gould, Cloris Leachman, Telly Savalas, Orson Welles. *Dir.* James Frawley.

Muppet Treasure Island (1996) Tim Curry (Long John Silver), Billy Connolly (Billy Bones), Kevin Bishop (Jim Hawkins), Jennifer Saunders (Mrs Bluberidge). *Dir.* Brian Henson.

Muppets, The (2011) Musical comedy film, the seventh in the franchise. *Dir.* James Bobin.

Muppets From Space (1999) The sixth feature film to star The Muppets (see also *The Great Muppet Caper*). *Dir.* Tim Hill.

Muppets Take Manhattan, The (1984) Dabney Coleman, Art Carney, James Coco, Joan Rivers, Gregory Hines. *Dir.* Frank Oz.

Murder by Decree (1978) Christopher Plummer, James Mason, Anthony Quayle, David Hemmings, Susan Clark, John Gielgud, Donald Sutherland, Frank Finlay, Geneviève Bujold. Sherlock Holmes investigates the murders of 'Jack the Ripper'. *Dir.* Bob Clark.

Murder Most Foul (1964) Margaret Rutherford, Ron Moody, Charles Tingwell, Andrew Cruickshank, Megs Jenkins, James Bolam, Francesca Annis, Dennis Price, Terry Scott. Based on the Agatha Christie novel *Mrs McGinty's Dead*. *Dir.* George Pollock.

Murder on the Orient Express (1974) Albert Finney (Poirot), Ingrid Bergman, Lauren Bacall, Wendy Hiller, Sean Connery, Vanessa Redgrave, Michael York, Martin Balsam, Richard Widmark, Jacqueline Bisset, Jean-Pierre Cassel, Rachel Roberts, George Coulouris, John Gielgud, Anthony Perkins, Colin Blakely, Jeremy Lloyd, Denis Quilley. Agatha Christie story. *Dir.* Sidney Lumet.

Murders in the Rue Morgue (1932) Bela Lugosi, Sidney Fox, Leon Ames, Bert Roach, Brandon Hurst. *Dir.* Robert Florey.

Murders in the Rue Morgue (1971) Jason Robards Jnr, Herbert Lom, Lilli Palmer, Adolfo Celi, Michael Dunn. *Dir.* Gordon Hessler.

Muriel's Wedding (1994) Toni Collette, Bill Hunter, Rachel Griffiths, Jeanie Drynan. *Dir.* PJ Hogan.

Murphy's Law (1986) Charles Bronson, Carrie Snodgress, Kathleen Wilhoite, Robert F Lyons, Richard Romanus. *Dir.* J Lee Thompson.

Murphy's War (1971) Peter O'Toole, Sian Phillips, Philippe Noiret, Horst Janson. *Dir.* Peter Yates.

Music Lovers, The (1970) Richard Chamberlain, Glenda Jackson, Christopher Gable, Max Adrian, Isabelle Telezynska, Maureen Pryor, Andrew Faulds. Screenplay written by Melvyn Bragg. *Dir.* Ken Russell.

Music Man, The (1962) Robert Preston, Shirley Jones, Buddy Hackett, Hermione Gingold, Pert Kelton, Paul Ford. *Dir.* Morton da Costa.

Mutiny on the Bounty (1935) Charles Laughton, Clark Gable, Franchot Tone, Movita, Dudley Digges. *Dir.* Frank Lloyd.

Mutiny on the Bounty (1962) Trevor Howard, Marlon Brando, Richard Harris, Hugh Griffith, Tarita, Gordon Jackson. *Dir.* Lewis Milestone.

My Beautiful Laundrette (1985) Saeed Jaffrey, Roshan Seth, Daniel Day-Lewis, Shirley Anne Field. Based on the Hanif Kureishi work. *Dir.* Stephen Frears.

My Big Fat Greek Wedding (2002) Nia Vardalos, John Corbett, Michael Constantine, Andrea Martin. Low-budget, unlikely smash hit of the year. Apparently the wedding dress featured in the film was bought by a viewer for a pittance and sold following the film's success for an amount approaching the budget of the film!! *Dir.* Joel Zwick.

My Favourite Martian (1999) Christopher Lloyd, Jeff Daniels, Elizabeth Hurley, Daryl Hannah, Ray Walston. *Dir.* Donald Petrie. Based on the TV series starring Ray Walston and Bill Bixby.

My Super Ex-Girlfriend (2006) Uma Thurman (Jenny Johnson/G-Girl), Luke Wilson (Matt Saunders), Anna Faris (Hannah Lewis), Rainn Wilson (Vaughn Haige), Eddie Izzard (Professor Bedlam/Barry). When a regular guy (Luke Wilson) dumps a superhero (Uma Thurman), it's payback time! *Dir.* Ivan Reitman.

Mysterious Dr Fu Manchu, The (1929) Warner Oland played the Sax Rohmer character in early films in the series. *Dir.* Various.

Mystic River (2003) Sean Penn (Jimmy Markum), Tim Robbins (Dave Boyle), Kevin Bacon (Sean Devine), Laurence Fishburne (Whitney Powers), Marcia Gay Harden (Celeste Boyle), Laura Linney (Annabeth Markum), Kevin Chapman (Val Savage), Thomas Guiry (Brendan Harris), Emmy Rossum (Katie Markum). Situated in Boston, concerns the murder of the daughter of an ex-con and the interaction of three old friends whose lives were devastated by a previous tragedy. *Dir.* Clint Eastwood.

Naked (1993) David Thewlis, Lesley Sharp, Katrin Cartlidge, Greg Cruttwell. *Dir.* Mike Leigh.

Naked Edge, The (1961) Gary Cooper, Deborah Kerr, Peter Cushing, Michael Wilding, Diane Cilento. *Dir.* Michael Anderson.

Naked Gun, The: From the Files of Police Squad (1988) Leslie Nielsen, Priscilla Presley, Ricardo Montalban, OJ Simpson, George Kennedy. *Dir.* David Zucker.

Naked Gun 2 1/2, The: The Smell of Fear (1991) Leslie Nielsen, Priscilla Presley, Robert Goulet, OJ Simpson, George Kennedy. *Dir.* David Zucker.

Naked Gun 33 1/3, The: The Final Insult (1994) Leslie Nielsen, Priscilla Presley, Fred Ward, OJ Simpson, George Kennedy, Anna Nicole Smith. *Dir.* Peter Segal.

Naked in New York (1993) Eric Stoltz, Mary-Louise Parker, Ralph Macchio, Jill Clayburgh, Tony Curtis, Kathleen Turner, Timothy Dalton, Whoopi Goldberg, Quentin Crisp. *Dir.* Dan Algrant.
Naked Lunch (1991) Peter Weller, Judy Davis, Ian Holm, Roy Scheider, Julian Sands. Drug-addicted writer emulates William Tell with fatal results. *Dir.* David Cronenberg.
Name of the Rose, The (1986) Sean Connery (William of Baskerville), F Murray Abraham (Bernardo Gui), Christian Slater (Adso of Melk), Feodor Chaliapin (Jorge de Burgos), William Hickey (Ubertino de Casale). Based on Umberto Eco novel. *Dir.* Jean-Jacques Annaud.
Narrow Margin (1952) Charles McGraw, Marie Windsor, Jacqueline White, Queenie Leonard. Police try to guard a witness on a train from Chicago to LA. The 1990 remake starred Gene Hackman and Anne Archer. *Dir.* Richard Fleischer.
National Lampoon's Animal House (1978) John Belushi, Tim Matheson, Donald Sutherland, John Vernon. First of the series which continued with *Movie Madness* (1981), *Class Reunion* (1982), *Vacation* (1983), *European Vacation* (1985), *Christmas Vacation* (1989), *Loaded Weapon* (1993), and *Senior Trip* (1995). The Chevy Chase character in 3 of the films was Clark Griswold. *Dir.* John Landis.
National Velvet (1945) Mickey Rooney, Elizabeth Taylor, Anne Revere, Donald Crisp, Angela Lansbury. *Dir.* Clarence Brown.
Natural, The (1984) Robert Redford (Roy Hobbs), Robert Duvall (Max Mercy), Glenn Close (Iris), Kim Basinger (Memo Paris), Barbara Hershey (Harriet Bird), Robert Prosky (Judge), Joe Don Baker (The Whammer). Ups and downs of a baseball star. *Dir.* Barry Levinson.
Natural Born Killers (1994) Woody Harrelson, Juliette Lewis, Robert Downey Jnr, Tommy Lee Jones. Young couple become mass murderers while winning the affection of the media. *Dir.* Oliver Stone.
Ned Kelly (1970) Mick Jagger, Allen Bickford, Geoff Gilmour, Mark McManus. Story of the 19th-century Australian outlaw. *Dir.* Tony Richardson.
Nell (1994) Jodie Foster, Liam Neeson, Natasha Richardson. Two doctors endeavour to talk to a young woman who speaks a solitary language. *Dir.* Michael Apted.
Net, The (1995) Sandra Bullock, Jeremy Northam, Dennis Miller, Diane Baker. *Dir.* Irwin Winkler.
Network (1976) Peter Finch (Howard Beale), William Holden (Max Schumacher), Faye Dunaway, Robert Duvall, Ned Beatty. Peter Finch was awarded a posthumous Academy Award. *Dir.* Sidney Lumet.
Nevada Smith (1966) Steve McQueen, Karl Malden, Brian Keith, Suzanne Pleshette. Scenes from the early life of the *Carpetbaggers* character. *Dir.* Henry Hathaway.
Never Been Kissed (1998) Drew Barrymore, David Arquette, Michael Vartan, Leelee Sobieski, Jeremy Jordan. *Dir.* Raja Gosnell.
Never on Sunday (1959) Melina Mercouri, Jules Dassin. Original title: *Pote tin Kyriaki. Dir.* Jules Dassin.
Never Say Never Again (1983) Sean Connery, Klaus Maria Brandauer (Largo), Max Von Sydow (Blofeld), Alec McCowen (Q), Kim Basinger (Domino), Edward Fox, Rowan Atkinson, Barbara Carrera (Fatima). Remake of *Thunderball*, so titled because Connery vowed he would never make another Bond movie after *Diamonds Are Forever. Dir.* Irvin Kershner.
New York, New York (1977) Liza Minnelli, Robert De Niro, Lionel Stander, Barry Primus. *Dir.* Martin Scorsese.
New York Stories (1989) *Life Lessons*: Nick Nolte, Patrick O'Neal, Rosanna Arquette, Steve Buscemi, Debbie Harry, Peter Gabriel. *Dir.* Martin Scorsese. *Life without Zoe*: Talia Shire, Giancarlo Giannini, Heather McComb, Carmine Coppola. *Dir.* Francis Ford Coppola. *Oedipus Wrecks*: Woody Allen, Mia Farrow, Julie Kavner, Mae Questel, Mayor Ed Koch. *Dir.* Woody Allen. Teacher sets the 3 top boys an essay – topic: 'My Story about New York' and the 3 separately directed stories follow.
Next of Kin (1989) Patrick Swayze (Truman Gates), Liam Neeson (Briar Gates), Adam Baldwin (Joey Rosselini). *Dir.* John Irvin.
Niagara (1952) Joseph Cotten, Jean Peters, Marilyn Monroe. *Dir.* Henry Hathaway.
Nicholas and Alexandra (1971) Michael Jayston, Janet Suzman, Laurence Olivier, Jack Hawkins, Tom Baker, Michael Redgrave. Life of Tsar Nicholas II from 1904 until the execution of his family in 1918. *Dir.* Franklin Schaffner.
Nickelodeon (1976) Ryan O'Neal, Burt Reynolds, Tatum O'Neal, Brian Keith, Stella Stevens. Events leading up to the premiere of *The Birth of a Nation. Dir.* Peter Bogdanovich.
Night and Day (1946) Cary Grant (Cole Porter), Alexis Smith, Monty Woolley, Mary Martin, Jane Wyman, Eve Arden. *Dir.* Michael Curtiz.
Night and the City (1992) Robert De Niro (Harry Fabian), Jessica Lange (Helen Nasseros), Alan King (Boom Boom Grossman). Remake of the 1950 classic starring Richard Widmark and Gene Tierney. *Dir.* Irwin Winkler.
Night at the Museum (2006) Ben Stiller (Larry Daley), Robin Williams (Theodore Roosevelt), Dick Van Dyke (Cecil Fredericks), Mickey Rooney (Gus), Jake Cherry (Nick), Ricky Gervais (Dr McPhee), Owen Wilson (Jedediah Smith), Steve Coogan (Octavius), Patrick Gallagher (Attila the Hun). Comedy based on the 1993 children's book by Milan Trenc. Larry Daley is a divorced father with a list of failed business ventures. Desperate to win the support of his son Nick, he is hired as a night guard at the American Museum of Natural History. Stiller's real-life mother, actress Anne Meara, has a cameo as Debbie. *Dir.* Shawn Levy. Most of the leading actors reprised their roles in a 2009 sequel, *Night at the Museum 2* (also known as *Night at the Museum: Battle of the Smithsonian*).
Night at the Opera, A (1935) Groucho Marx, Chico Marx, Harpo Marx, Margaret Dumont. *Dir.* Sam Wood.
Night Crossing (1982) John Hurt, Jane Alexander, Beau Bridges, Ian Bannen. East Germans escape to the West via air balloon. *Dir.* Delbert Mann.
Night Falls on Manhattan (1997) Andy Garcia (Sean Casey), Ian Holm. *Dir.* Sidney Lumet.
Night in Casablanca, A (1946) Groucho Marx (Kornblow), Chico Marx, Harpo Marx, Lisette Verea (Beatrice). *Dir.* Archie Mayo.
Night of the Hunter (1955) Robert Mitchum, Shelley Winters, Lillian Gish, Peter Graves. Psychopathic preacher on the trail of hidden loot. *Dir.* Charles Laughton.
Night of the Iguana (1964) Richard Burton, Deborah Kerr, Ava Gardner, Sue Lyon. Disbarred clergyman becomes a courier in Mexico and is chased by teenage nymphomaniac. *Dir.* John Huston.
Night on Earth (1992) Winona Ryder (Corky), Gena Rowlands (Victoria Snelling), Giancarlo Esposito (Yo Yo). Five people take simultaneous taxi rides in 5 cities, i.e. LA, New York, Paris, Rome & Helsinki. *Dir.* Jim Jarmusch.
Night Porter, The (1973) Dirk Bogarde, Charlotte Rampling. Conductor's wife recognises porter as former SS officer. *Dir.* Liliana Cavani.
Night Shift (1982) Henry Winkler, Michael Keaton, Shelley Long, Gina Hecht, Kevin Costner (Frat Boy). *Dir.* Ron Howard.
Night They Raided Minsky's, The (1968) Jason Robards, Britt Ekland, Norman Wisdom, Bert Lahr. *Dir.* William Friedkin.
Night to Remember, A (1958) Kenneth More, Honor Blackman, David McCallum. *Dir.* Roy Baker.
Nightmare Before Christmas, The (1993) Voices of Danny Elfman, Chris Sarandon, William Hickey, Catherine O'Hara. Based on a Tim Burton story. *Dir.* Henry Selick.
Nightmare on Elm Street, A (1984) John Saxon, Ronee Blakley, Robert Englund (Freddie). *Dir.* Wes Craven.
Nightmare on Elm Street, A, 2: Freddy's Revenge (1985) Mark Patton, Clu Gulager, Hope Lange, Robert Englund. *Dir.* Jack Sholder.
Nightmare on Elm Street, A, 3: Dream Warriors (1987) Heather Langenkamp, Patricia Arquette, Robert Englund. *Dir.* Chuck Russell.
Nightmare on Elm Street, A, 4: The Dream Master (1988) Rodney Eastman, Danny Hassel, Robert Englund. *Dir.* Renny Harlin.
Nightmare on Elm Street, A: The Dream Child (1989) Lisa Wilcox, Kelly Jo Minter, Danny Hassel, Robert Englund. Last of the series called *Freddy's Dead: The Final Nightmare* (1991). *Dir.* Stephen Hopkins.
Nil by Mouth (1997) Ray Winstone (Ray), Kathy Burke (Valerie). *Dir.* Gary Oldman.
Nine and a Half Weeks (1986) Mickey Rourke, Kim Basinger. *Dir.* Adrian Lyne.
976–EVIL (1988) Stephen Geoffreys (Hoax), Sandy Dennis (Aunt Lucy). The title refers to the Devil's freephone number. *Dir.* Robert Englund.
9/30/55 (1977) Richard Thomas, Susan Tyrrell, Dennis Quaid. Title refers to the death of James Dean and the effect on an Arkansas student. *Dir.* James Bridges.

Nine to Five (1980) Jane Fonda, Dolly Parton, Lily Tomlin, Dabney Coleman, Sterling Hayden. Three office women plot to get rid of their boss. *Dir.* Colin Higgins.

1984 (1984) John Hurt (Winston Smith), Richard Burton (O'Brien), Suzanna Hamilton (Julia), Cyril Cusack (Carrington). A 1955 version starred Michael Redgrave and Edmond O'Brien. *Dir.* Michael Radford.

1941 (1979) Dan Aykroyd, Ned Beatty, John Belushi, Christopher Lee, Robert Stack, Lorraine Gary. Farce concerning a stray Japanese submarine terrorising Hollywood after Pearl Harbor. *Dir.* Steven Spielberg.

Ninotchka (1939) Greta Garbo, Melvyn Douglas, Bela Lugosi. *Dir.* Ernst Lubitsch.

Nixon (1995) Anthony Hopkins (Nixon), Joan Allen (Pat Nixon), Powers Boothe (Alexander Haig), Ed Harris (E Howard Hunt), Paul Sorvino (Henry Kissinger). *Dir.* Oliver Stone.

No Country For Old Men (2007) Tommy Lee Jones (Sheriff Ed Tom Bell), Javier Bardem (Anton Chigurh), Josh Brolin (Llewelyn Moss), Woody Harrelson (Carson Wells), Kelly Macdonald (Carla Jean Moss), Garret Dillahunt (Deputy Wendell), Tess Harper (Loretta Bell), Barry Corbin (Ellis), Stephen Root (Man who hires Wells), Rodger Boyce (Sheriff Roscoe Giddens), Beth Grant (Carla Jean's Mother), Ana Reeder (Poolside Woman), Kit Gwin (Sheriff Bell's Secretary), Zach Hopkins (Strangled Deputy), Chip Love (Man in Ford). Based on the 2003 novel by Cormac McCarthy. Hunter Llewelyn Moss stumbles upon the aftermath of a drug deal gone wrong in the Texan desert. Moss makes off with a case containing $2m and sets in motion a chain of events that leaves a bloody trail of carnage across the state as he is pursued by the psychopathic and totally dedicated hit man Anton Chigurh, who sometimes decides whether or not to kill a person by the simple toss of a coin. The darkest of film noirs, the film ultimately leaves the viewer unsatisfied as to its outcome but appreciative of its honesty. *Dir.* Ethan Coen and Joel Coen.

Nobody's Fool (1994) Paul Newman, Jessica Tandy, Bruce Willis, Melanie Griffith. A 60-yr-old handyman has a chance to make up for a disappointing life. *Dir.* Robert Benton.

Noises Off (1992) Carol Burnett (Dotty Otley / Mrs Clackett), Michael Caine (Lloyd Fellowes), Denholm Elliott, Julie Hagerty, Marilu Henner, Christopher Reeve. Adaptation of Michael Frayn's farce about a second-rate touring company. *Dir.* Peter Bogdanovich.

No Place To Go (*Die Unberührbare*) (2001) Hannelore Elsner (Hanna), Vadim Glowna, Tonio Arango, Michael Gwisdek, Bernd Stempel. *Dir.* Oskar Röhler.

North by Northwest (1959) Cary Grant, Eva Marie Saint, James Mason. *Dir.* Alfred Hitchcock.

North Dallas Forty (1979) Nick Nolte, Mac Davis, Charles Durning, Bo Svenson. Gruelling life of an American football player. *Dir.* Ted Kotcheff.

Notorious (1946) Cary Grant, Ingrid Bergman, Claude Rains, Louis Calhern. Lady marries a Nazi in Rio to help the American government. *Dir.* Alfred Hitchcock.

Notorious Bettie Page, The (2005) Gretchen Mol (Bettie Page). The story of Bettie Page, a successful 1950s American pin-up model, the target of a Senate investigation (based on her bondage photos). *Dir.* Mary Harron.

Notre Musique (2004) Sarah Adler (Judith Lerner), Nade Dieu (Olga Brodsky), Rony Kramer (Ramos Garcia). Divided into three 'kingdoms' – Enfer (Hell), Purgatoire (Purgatory) and Paradis (Paradise) – An insight into war and memory. *Dir.* Jean-Luc Godard.

Notting Hill (1999) Julia Roberts, Hugh Grant, Hugh Bonneville, Emma Chambers, Alec Baldwin. *Dir.* Roger Michell.

Nuns on the Run (1990) Eric Idle, Robbie Coltrane, Janet Suzman, Doris Hare. *Dir.* Jonathan Lynn.

Nun's Story, The (1959) Audrey Hepburn, Peter Finch, Edith Evans, Peggy Ashcroft. Belgian girl joins a strict order of nuns. *Dir.* Fred Zinnemann.

Nurse Edith Cavell (1939) Anna Neagle, George Sanders. Based on Reginald Berkeley's novel *Dawn*. *Dir.* Herbert Wilcox.

Nutty Professor, The (1996) Eddie Murphy (plays 7 roles), James Coburn, Jada Pinkett. *Dir.* Tom Shadyac.

Object of Beauty, The (1991) John Malkovich, Andie MacDowell, Joss Ackland, Bill Paterson, Jack Shepherd. *Dir.* Michael Lindsay-Hogg.

Objective Burma! (1945) Errol Flynn, James Brown, William Prince. Exploits of a US platoon during the Burma campaign. The film caused a furore among the Burma Star Organisation and nearly created a diplomatic fallout by failing to mention the British contribution. *Dir.* Raoul Walsh.

Obsession (1976) Cliff Robertson, Geneviève Bujold, John Lithgow. Widower meets the double of his dead wife. *Dir.* Brian De Palma.

Ocean's Eleven (1960) Frank Sinatra, Peter Lawford, Sammy Davis Jnr, Dean Martin, Richard Conte, Ilka Chase, Cesar Romero, Joey Bishop, Patrick Wymore, Akim Tamiroff, Henry Silva, Angie Dickinson. *Dir.* Lewis Milestone.

Ocean's Eleven (2001) George Clooney (Danny Ocean), Julia Roberts (Tess Ocean), Brad Pitt (Rusty Ryan), Matt Damon (Linus), Andy Garcia (Terry Benedict), Casey Affleck (Virgil Malloy), Scott Caan (Turk Malloy), Don Cheadle (Basher Tarr), Elliott Gould (Reuben Tishkoff), Carl Reiner (Saul Bloom). Remake of the 1960 film of the same name. *Dir.* Steven Soderbergh. A 2004 sequel, *Ocean's Twelve*, was a critical flop. Catherine Zeta-Jones was added to the cast as Europol agent Isabel Lehiri, although the 12th member of Danny's gang is his wife Tess. The remaining cast and director were the same. In *Ocean's Thirteen* (2007) Julia Roberts and Catherine Zeta-Jones do not reprise their roles, the three newbies being Eddie Jemison (Livingston Dell), Eddie Izzard (Roman Nagel) and Shaobo Qin (Mr Weng/The Amazing Yen).

Octopussy (1983) Roger Moore, Maud Adams (Octopussy), Louis Jourdan (Prince Kamel Khan), Steven Berkoff (Orlov), Robert Brown (M), Desmond Llewelyn (Q). Tennis player Vijay Amritraj appeared in a cameo. Title song performed by Rita Coolidge. *Dir.* John Glen.

Odd Couple, The (1968) Jack Lemmon (Felix Unger), Walter Matthau (Oscar Goldman). Written by Neil Simon. *Dir.* Gene Saks.

Odessa File, The (1974) Jon Voigt, Maria Schell, Maximilian Schell, Derek Jacobi. *Dir.* Ronald Neame.

Of Mice and Men (1939) Burgess Meredith, Lon Chaney Jnr, Betty Field, Charles Bickford. Itinerant worker looks after his immensely strong but mentally retarded cousin. The 1992 remake starred John Malkovich and Gary Sinise. *Dir.* Lewis Milestone.

Officer and a Gentleman, An (1982) Richard Gere (Zack Mayo), Debra Winger, Lou Gossett Jnr, David Keith, Lisa Blount. Oscars for Lou Gossett Jnr (Best Supporting), and song ('Up Where We Belong'). *Dir.* Taylor Hackford.

Oh What a Lovely War (1969) Ralph Richardson, Meriel Forbes, John Gielgud, Kenneth More, John Clements, Joe Melia, Paul Daneman, Jack Hawkins, Maggie Smith, John Mills, Michael Redgrave, Laurence Olivier, Susannah York, Dirk Bogarde, Phyllis Calvert, Vanessa Redgrave. Musical fantasia of World War I. *Dir.* Richard Attenborough.

O.H.M.S. (1936) John Mills, Wallace Ford, Anna Lee. British forces in China are joined by an American gangster on the run, who dies a hero. US title: *You're in the Army Now*. *Dir.* Raoul Walsh.

Oklahoma (1955) Gordon Macrae, Shirley Jones, Rod Steiger, Eddie Albert. *Dir.* Fred Zinnemann.

Oklahoma Kid, The (1939) James Cagney, Humphrey Bogart, Rosemary Lane, Donald Crisp, Ward Bond. *Dir.* Lloyd Bacon.

Old Gringo (1989) Jane Fonda (Harriet Winslow), Gregory Peck (Ambrose Bierce), Jimmy Smits (Tomas Arroyo). *Dir.* Luis Puenzo.

Old Man and the Sea, The (1958) Spencer Tracy, Felipe Pazos, Harry Bellaver. *Dir.* John Sturges.

Old Mother Riley (1935–52) Arthur Lucan (Riley), Kitty McShane (his daughter). Series of films with Lucan and his real-life wife playing mother and daughter. *Stars on Parade* was the first of the series and *Mother Riley Meets the Vampire* the last. *Dir.* Maclean Rogers.

Oliver! (1968) Ron Moody, Oliver Reed, Harry Secombe, Mark Lester, Shani Wallis, Jack Wild. *Dir.* Carol Reed.

Oliver Twist (1948) Alec Guinness, Robert Newton, Francis L Sullivan, John Howard Davies, Anthony Newley, Diana Dors, Mary Clare, Kay Walsh. *Dir.* David Lean.

Oliver's Story (1978) Ryan O'Neal, Candice Bergen, Nicola Pagett, Ray Milland. *Dir.* John Korty.

Omega Man, The (1971) Charlton Heston, Rosalind Cash, Anthony Zerbe. Based on the novel *I am Legend* by Richard Matheson. Set in 1977 Los Angeles after a germ warfare plague has decimated the world's population. *Dir.* Boris Sagal.

Omen, The (1976) Gregory Peck, Lee Remick, David Warner, Billie Whitelaw, Leo McKern, Patrick Troughton. Three inferior sequels were made. *Dir.* Richard Donner.

Omen, The (2006) Liev Schreiber (Robert Thorn), Julia Stiles (Katherine Thorn), Seamus Davey-Fitzpatrick (Damien), Michael Gambon (Bugenhagen), Mia Farrow (Mrs Baylock), Pete Postlethwaite (Father Brennan), David Thewlis (Keith Jennings), Amy Huck (Nanny), Giovanni Lombardo Radice (Father Spiletto), Baby Zikova, Baby Morvas, Baby Muller and Baby Litera (Damien, newborn), Tomas Wooler (Damien, age 2), Carlo Sabatini (Cardinal Fabretti), Bohumil Svarc (Pope). Faithful remake of the 1976 classic. *Dir.* John Moore.
On Deadly Ground (1994) Steven Seagal, Michael Caine, Joan Chen, Chief Irvin Brink. *Dir.* Steven Seagal.
On Golden Pond (1981) Henry Fonda, Katharine Hepburn, Jane Fonda, Dabney Coleman, Doug McKeon. *Dir.* Mark Rydell.
On Her Majesty's Secret Service (1969) George Lazenby, Diana Rigg (Tracy Vicenzo née Draco), Telly Savalas (Blofeld). *Avengers* fans note: not only does Diana Rigg become Mrs Bond but Joanna Lumley is one of the lovelies in the Swiss Alps and Honor Blackman is visible in a clip from *Goldfinger* in the opening titles. *Dir.* Peter Hunt. Theme song: 'We have all the time in the world' performed by Louis Armstrong.
On the Beach (1959) Gregory Peck, Ava Gardner, Fred Astaire, Anthony Perkins, Donna Anderson. Crew of serving American submarine wait for the devastation of atomic war to catch up with them in Australia. *Dir.* Stanley Kramer.
On the Buses (1971) Reg Varney, Doris Hare, Anna Karen, Michael Robbins, Stephen Lewis. Sequels: *Mutiny on the Buses* (1972), and *Holiday on the Buses* (1973). *Dir.* Harry Booth.
On the Double (1961) Danny Kaye, Dana Wynter, Wilfrid Hyde-White, Diana Dors, Margaret Rutherford, Allan Cuthbertson, Jesse White. American private is asked to impersonate a British Intelligence officer. *Dir.* Melville Shavelson.
On the Fiddle (1961) Alfred Lynch, Sean Connery, Wilfrid Hyde-White, Kathleen Harrison, Cecil Parker, Alan King, Eleanor Summerfield, Eric Barker, John Le Mesurier. US title: *Operation Snafu.* Wide boy and slow-witted gypsy's adventures in the RAF. *Dir.* Cyril Frankel.
On the Town (1949) Frank Sinatra, Gene Kelly, Jules Munshin, Ann Miller, Vera-Ellen, Betty Garrett. Gene Kelly directed the dance scenes. *Dir.* Stanley Donen.
On the Waterfront (1954) Marlon Brando, Eva Marie Saint, Rod Steiger, Lee J Cobb, Karl Malden. *Dir.* Elia Kazan.
Once (2007) Glen Hansard (Guy), Markéta Irglová (Girl), Darren Healy (Heroin Addict), Hugh Walsh (Timmy Drummer), Gerard Hendrick (Lead Guitarist), Alaistair Foley (Bassist), Geoff Minogue (Eamon), Bill Hodnett (Guy's Dad), Danuse Ktrestova (Girl's Mother), Mal Whyte (Bill), Marcella Plunkett (Ex Girlfriend), Niall Cleary (Bob). A modern-day musical about a busker and an immigrant and their eventful week in Dublin, as they write, rehearse and record songs that tell their love story. The two lead characters are unnamed but listed as Guy and Girl in the film credits. *Dir.* John Carney.
Once a Jolly Swagman (1948) Dirk Bogarde, Renée Asherson, Bonar Colleano, Bill Owen. US title: *Maniacs on Wheels.* Factory worker becomes a speedway rider. *Dir.* Jack Lee.
Once Around (1991) Richard Dreyfuss, Holly Hunter, Danny Aiello, Gena Rowlands, Laura San Giacomo. *Dir.* Lasse Hallstrom.
Once Bitten (1985) Lauren Hutton, Jim Carrey, Karen Kopins, Cleavon Little. Teenage sex problems are complicated by a visiting vampiress. *Dir.* Howard Storm.
Once More with Feeling (1960) Yul Brynner, Kay Kendall, Geoffrey Toone, Maxwell Shaw, Mervyn Johns. Volatile private life of an orchestral conductor. *Dir.* Stanley Donen.
Once Upon a Crime (1992) John Candy, James Belushi, Cybill Shepherd, Sean Young, Joss Ackland. *Dir.* Eugene Levy.
Once Upon a Horse (1958) Dan Rowan, Dick Martin, Martha Hyer, Leif Erickson, Nita Talbot, James Gleason. Two cowboys steal a herd of cattle but can't afford to feed them. The two stars later went on to revolutionise TV comedy with their *Laugh-in* shows. *Dir.* Hal Kanter.
Once Upon a Time in America (1984) Robert De Niro (Noodles), James Woods (Max), Elizabeth McGovern (Deborah), Treat Williams (Jimmy O'Donnell), Tuesday Weld (Carol), Joe Pesci (Frankie), Danny Aiello (Police Chief Aiello), William Forsythe (Cockeye). Story of 4 Jewish gangsters known as the 'Kosher Nostra', from 1922 to 1968. 228-minute film which has a 147-minute version. *Dir.* Sergio Leone.
Once Upon a Time in the West (1969) Henry Fonda, Claudia Cardinale, Jason Robards, Charles Bronson. Notable for its opening credits which last for the first 12 minutes of film time. *Dir.* Sergio Leone.
Once Were Warriors (1994) Rena Owen, Temuera Morrison. This film is the top NZ film as regards box office takings. *Dir.* Lee Tamahori.
One-Eyed Jacks (1961) Marlon Brando, Karl Malden, Pina Pellicer, Katy Jurado, Slim Pickens, Ben Johnson. Based on the novel *The Authentic Death of Hendry Jones* by Charles Neider. *Dir.* Marlon Brando.
One False Move (1992) Bill Paxton (Dale 'Hurricane' Dixon), Cynda Williams (Fantasia / Lila), Michael Beach (Pluto), Billy Bob Thornton (Ray Malcolm), Jim Metzler (Dud Cole). Two killers on the run with their black girlfriend go to Alabama where the sheriff is waiting. Cynda Williams and Billy Bob Thornton fell in love on set and married soon after. *Dir.* Carl Franklin.
One Fine Day (1996) Michelle Pfeiffer, George Clooney, Charles Durning. Two busy single parents fall in love. *Dir.* Michael Hoffman.
One from the Heart (1982) Frederic Forrest (Hank), Teri Garr (Frannie), Raul Julia (Ray), Nastassja Kinski (Leila). Rebecca DeMornay's screen debut in the restaurant scene with the line: 'Excuse me, I think those are my waffles'. First film for Coppola's Zoetrope studios. *Dir.* Francis Ford Coppola.
187 (1997) Samuel L Jackson (Trevor Garfield), Tony Plana. Title refers to the Californian penal code for murder. School: John Quincy Adams High. *Dir.* Kevin Reynolds.
101 Dalmatians (1996) Glenn Close, Jeff Daniels, Joan Plowright, Joely Richardson, Hugh Laurie. Live-action remake of the 1961 animated film. *Dir.* Stephen Herek. The sequel *102 Dalmatians* was released in 2000.
One Hundred Men and a Girl (1937) Deanna Durbin was the girl and the men were an orchestra. *Dir.* Henry Koster.
One Million Years BC (1966) John Richardson, Raquel Welch, Robert Brown. *Dir.* Don Chaffey.
One Woman or Two (1985) Gérard Depardieu (Julien Chayssac), Sigourney Weaver (Jessica Fitzgerald), Dr Ruth Westheimer (Mrs Heffner). Advertising woman uses an archaeologist as basis for a new campaign and falls in love. *Dir.* Daniel Vigne.
Onibaba (1964) Nobuko Otowa, Jitsuko Yoshimura, Kei Sato. Mother and daughter live by preying on stray soldiers. Aka: *The Hole. Dir.* Kaneto Shindo.
Operation Crossbow (1965) George Peppard, Tom Courtenay, John Mills, Sophia Loren, Lilli Palmer, Trevor Howard. *Dir.* Michael Anderson.
Ordinary People (1980) Donald Sutherland, Mary Tyler Moore, Timothy Hutton, Judd Hirsch. Oscars for Hutton, Redford and Alvin Sargent (screenplay). *Dir.* Robert Redford.
Othello (1965) Laurence Olivier, Frank Finlay, Maggie Smith, Derek Jacobi. The 1995 Oliver Parker film starred Laurence Fishburne and Ken Branagh (Iago). *Dir.* Stuart Burge.
Others, The (2001) Nicole Kidman (Grace), Christopher Eccleston (Charles), Fionnula Flanagan (Mrs Mills), James Bentley (Nicholas), Eric Sykes (Mr Tuttle), Elaine Cassidy (Lydia). Set in the 1940s. *Dir.* Alejandro Amenabar.
Our Man Flint (1965) James Coburn, Lee J Cobb. *Dir.* Daniel Mann.
Our Man in Havana (1965) Alec Guinness, Noël Coward, Burl Ives, Maureen O'Hara, Ralph Richardson. *Dir.* Carol Reed.
Out of Africa (1985) Robert Redford (Denys), Meryl Streep (Karen Blixen), Klaus Maria Brandauer, Michael Gough. *Dir.* Sydney Pollack.
Outbreak (1995) Dustin Hoffman, Rene Russo, Morgan Freeman, Donald Sutherland, Kevin Spacey. *Dir.* Wolfgang Petersen.
Outland (1981) Sean Connery, Peter Boyle, Kika Markham. *Dir.* Peter Hyams.
Outlaw Josey Wales, The (1976) Clint Eastwood, Chief Dan George, Sondra Locke. *Dir.* Clint Eastwood.
Outrageous Fortune (1987) Bette Midler (Sandy), Shelley Long (Lauren), Robert Prosky, Peter Coyote. *Dir.* Arthur Hiller.
Outsiders, The (1983) Matt Dillon (Dallas Winston), Ralph Macchio (Johnny Cade), Patrick Swayze (Darrel Curtis), Robb Lowe (Sodapop Curtis), Emilio Estevez (Two-Bit Matthews), Tom Cruise (Steve Randle). *Dir.* Francis Ford Coppola.

Over The Hedge (2006) Voices of Bruce Willis (RJ), Garry Shandling (Verne), William Shatner (Ozzie), Nick Nolte (Vincent), Catherine O'Hara (Penny), Avril Lavigne (Heather). A scheming raccoon fools a mismatched family of forest creatures into helping him repay a debt of food, by invading the new suburban sprawl that popped up while they were hibernating. *Dir.* Tim Johnson and Karey Kirkpatrick.

Over the Top (1987) Sylvester Stallone (Lincoln Hawk), Robert Loggia (Jason Cutler), Susan Blakely (Chris Hawk). *Dir.* Menahem Golan.

Overboard (1987) Goldie Hawn (Joanna / Annie), Kurt Russell (Dean Proffitt), Roddy McDowall (Andrew). *Dir.* Garry Marshall.

Owl and the Pussycat, The (1970) Barbra Streisand, George Segal, Robert Klein, Allen Garfield. *Dir.* Herbert Ross.

Paint Your Wagon (1969) Lee Marvin, Clint Eastwood (Pardner), Jean Seberg, Harve Presnell, Ray Walston. *Dir.* Joshua Logan.

Pal Joey (1957) Frank Sinatra, Rita Hayworth, Kim Novak. *Dir.* George Sidney.

Pale Rider (1985) Clint Eastwood (Preacher), Michael Moriarty, Carrie Snodgrass, Chris Penn, Richard Kiel. *Dir.* Clint Eastwood.

Paleface, The (1948) Bob Hope, Jane Russell, Robert Armstrong. Song 'Buttons and Bows' (music by J Livingston, lyrics by Ray Evans) won Oscar. Sequel was *Son of Paleface* and 1968 remake was *The Shakiest Gun in the West. Dir.* Norman Z Mcleod.

Pallbearer (1996) David Schwimmer, Gwyneth Paltrow, Michael Rapaport, Barbara Hershey. *Dir.* Matt Reeves.

Palm Beach Story, The (1942) Claudette Colbert, Joel McCrea, Rudy Vallee (Hackensacker), Robert Dudley (Weenie King). Engineer's wife travels to Florida with her sights set on a millionaire. *Dir.* Preston Sturges.

Palookaville (1996) Adam Trese (Jerry), William Forsythe (Sid), Vincent Gallo (Russ), Frances McDormand. Story of 3 bungling would-be criminals. *Dir.* Alan Taylor.

Panic Room (2002) Jodie Foster, Kristen Stewart, Forest Whitaker, Jared Leto, Dwight Yoakam. *Dir.* David Fincher.

Panther (1995) Kadeem Hardison, Bokeem Woodbine, Joe Don Baker, Nefertiti. Black Vietnam vet recalls his role in the Black Panther movement. *Dir.* Mario Van Peebles.

Paper, The (1994) Michael Keaton, Glenn Close, Marisa Tomei, Robert Duvall, Randy Quaid. *Dir.* Ron Howard.

Paper Chase, The (1973) Timothy Bottoms, Lindsay Wagner, John Houseman, Graham Bickel. Based on John Jay Osborn Jnr novel. Houseman won Oscar and film spawned a successful TV series of the same name. *Dir.* James Bridges.

Paper Moon (1973) Ryan O'Neal, Tatum O'Neal, Madeline Kahn, John Hillerman. Tatum O'Neal won an Oscar. *Dir.* Peter Bogdanovich.

Paper Tiger (1975) David Niven, Toshiro Mifune, Hardy Kruger, Ando, Ronald Fraser, Ivan Desny. Englishman becomes tutor to the son of a Japanese ambassador. *Dir.* Ken Annakin.

Papillon (1973) Dustin Hoffman, Steve McQueen. *Dir.* Franklin Schaffner.

Paradise (1991) Melanie Griffith (Lily Reed), Don Johnson (Ben Reed), Elijah Wood, Louise Latham. The first film that Griffith and Johnson starred in together. Remake of *Le Grand Chemin* directed in 1987 by Jean-Loup Hubert. *Dir.* Mary Agnes Donoghue.

Parallax View, The (1974) Warren Beatty, Paula Prentiss, William Daniels. Witnesses to political assassination are systematically killed. *Dir.* Alan J Pakula.

Paranormal Activity (2009) Katie Featherston (Katie), Micah Sloat (Micah). Horror film. Katie, a student, and her boyfriend Micah, a day trader, live in a two-storey tract house in suburban San Diego, California. Katie claims that a ghostly presence has haunted her since her youth and believes that it has followed her to their new home. Micah sets up cameras to record any movement within the house. *Dir.* Oren Peli. Sequels have been released annually and *Paranormal Activity 5* will be released on October 25th 2013.

Parenthood (1989) Steve Martin (Gil), Mary Steenburgen (Karen), Dianne Wiest (Helen), Jason Robards (Frank), Rick Moranis (Nathan), Tom Hulce (Larry), Keanu Reeves (Tod), Leaf Phoenix (Gary). Four generations of a large family have different approaches to parenthood. *Dir.* Ron Howard.

Parole Officer, The (2001) Steve Coogan (Simon Garden), Lena Headey, Om Puri, Steven Waddington, Ben Miller, Stephen Dillane, Jenny Agutter, Omar Sharif (Victor Bondarenko). *Dir.* John Duigan.

Passage to India, A (1984) Judy Davis (Adela Quested), Victor Banerjee (Dr Aziz), Peggy Ashcroft (Mrs Moore), James Fox (Richard Fielding), Alec Guinness (Godbole), Nigel Havers, Art Malik Richard Wilson (Turton), Saeed Jaffrey, Clive Swift, Roshan Seth. David Lean's first film for 14 years. It was also his last. *Dir.* David Lean.

Passion of the Christ, The (2004) Jim Caviezel (Jesus), Monica Bellucci (Mary Magdalen), Hristo Naumov Shopov (Pontius Pilate), Maia Morgenstern (Mary), Francesco De Vito (Peter), Luca Lionello (Judas), Mattia Sbragia (Caiaphas), Rosalinda Celentano (Satan). This truly graphic and disturbing film based on the last hours of Jesus Christ serves as both a *memento mori* and *memento vivere* to all who watch it. Dialogue in Aramaic, Latin and Hebrew with English subtitles. *Dir.* Mel Gibson.

Passport to Pimlico (1949) Stanley Holloway, Margaret Rutherford, Basil Radford, Sydney Tafler, Hermione Baddeley. Part of postwar London is discovered to belong to Burgundy and the residents find themselves free of rationing restrictions. Based on a real-life story whereby the Canadian government presented to Holland the room where Princess Juliana was to bear a child. *Dir.* Henry Cornelius.

Pat and Mike (1952) Spencer Tracy, Katharine Hepburn, Aldo Ray. Sports promoter takes on a female intellectual. *Dir.* George Cukor.

Patriot Games (1992) Harrison Ford (Jack Ryan), Anne Archer, Patrick Bergin, Sean Bean, Samuel L Jackson James Fox, Richard Harris, James Earl Jones, Thora Birch. *Dir.* Philip Noyce.

Patton (1969) George C Scott, Karl Malden, Michael Bates. Famous for Scott's refusal to collect his Oscar. *Dir.* Franklin Schaffner.

Patty Hearst (1988) Natasha Richardson, William Forsythe, Ving Rhames, Frances Fisher. *Dir.* Paul Schrader.

Peacemaker, The (1997) Nicole Kidman (Dr Julia Kelly), George Clooney (Lt Col Thomas Devoe). First film from Steven Spielberg's Dreamworks Studio. *Dir.* Mimi Leder.

Pearl Harbor (2001) Ben Affleck, Josh Hartnett, Kate Beckinsale, Cuba Gooding, Jon Voight, Dan Aykroyd, Alec Baldwin, James King, Tom Sizemore, *Dir.* Michael Bay.

Pearl of Death, The (1944) Basil Rathbone (Holmes), Nigel Bruce (Watson), Dennis Hoey, Miles Mander, Rondo Hatton. Based on Conan Doyle's 'The Six Napoleons'. *Dir.* Roy William Neill.

Peggy Sue Got Married (1986) Kathleen Turner (Peggy Sue), Nicolas Cage (Charlie Bodell), Jim Carrey (Walter Getz), Barry Miller, Catherine Hicks, Joan Allen, Helen Hunt (Beth Bodell). *Dir.* Francis Ford Coppola.

Pelican Brief, The (1993) Julia Roberts, Denzel Washington, Sam Shepard, John Heard, Robert Culp. Law student is stalked by hitmen after she suspects their involvement in murder of 2 judges. *Dir.* Alan J Pakula.

People vs Larry Flint, The (1996) Woody Harrelson (Larry Flynt, the self-styled King of Sleaze), Courteney Love, Edward Norton. Biopic of the publisher of soft porn mag *Hustler. Dir.* Milos Forman.

Perez Family, The (1995) Marisa Tomei, Alfred Molina, Anjelica Huston. *Dir.* Mira Nair.

Perfect (1985) John Travolta (Adam), Jamie Lee Curtis (Jessie), Anne De Salvo (Frankie). Journalist falls in love with aerobics teacher he is investigating. *Dir.* James Bridges.

Perfect Storm, The (1999) George Clooney, Mark Wahlberg, Diane Lane, Mary Elizabeth Mastrantonio, Michael Ironside. Six Massachusetts fishermen encounter a raging storm in their boat 'Andrea Gail'. *Dir.* Wolfgang Peterson.

Perfect World, A (1993) Clint Eastwood, Kevin Costner, Laura Dern. *Dir.* Clint Eastwood.

Performance (1970) James Fox, Mick Jagger, Anita Pallenberg, Allan Cuthbertson. *Dir.* Nicolas Roeg & Donald Cammell.

Perfume: The Story of a Murderer (2006) Ben Whishaw (Jean-Baptiste Grenouille), Dustin Hoffman (Giuseppe Baldini), Rachel Hurd-Wood (Laura Richis), Alan Rickman (Antoine Richis), John Hurt (Narrator). Set in C18 France, the film tells the story of Jean-Baptiste Grenouille, a young man with a discerning sense of smell who goes on a homicidal quest for the perfect scent. Based on the 1985 novel *Das Parfum* by German writer Patrick Süskind. *Dir.* Tom Tykwer.

Perils of Pauline, The (1934) Betty Hutton, John Lund, Billy de Wolfe. The career of silent serial queen Pearl White. *Dir.* George Marshall.

Personal Services (1987) Julie Walters (Christine Painter), Alec McCowen (Wing Commander Morton), Shirley Stellfox. Read 'Cynthia Payne' for Christine Painter. *Dir.* Terry Jones.

Peter's Friends (1992) Kenneth Branagh (Andrew), Alphonsia Emmanuel (Sarah), Stephen Fry (Peter), Hugh Laurie (Roger), Phyllida Law (Vera), Rita Rudner (Carol), Emma Thompson (Maggie). *Dir.* Kenneth Branagh.

Phantom of the Opera (1925) Lon Chaney, Mary Philbin, Norman Kerry. Remakes include 1943 version with Claude Rains, 1962 film with Herbert Lom and 1989 version with Robert Englund. *Dir.* Rupert Julian.

Phantom of the Opera, The (2004) Gerard Butler (The Phantom), Emmy Rossum (Christine), Patrick Wilson (Raoul), Miranda Richardson (Madame Giry), Minnie Driver (Carlotta), Ciarán Hinds (Firmin), Simon Callow (Andre), Victor McGuire (Piangi), Jennifer Ellison (Meg Giry), Murray Melvin (Reyer), Kevin McNally as Kevin R McNally (Buquet), James Fleet (Lefevre). A disfigured musical genius, hidden away in the Paris Opera House, terrorises the opera company for the unwitting benefit of a young protégée whom he trains and loves. Based on Andrew Lloyd Webber's stage adaptation of the Gaston Leroux novel. *Dir.* Joel Schumacher.

Phenomenon (1996) John Travolta, Kyra Sedgwick, Robert Duvall, Forest Whitaker, Brent Spiner. Simpleton is struck by a strange light which raises his IQ and his sensitivity. *Dir.* James Cameron.

Philadelphia (1993) Tom Hanks, Denzel Washington, Jason Robards, Mary Steenburgen, Antonio Banderas, Joanne Woodward, Robert Ridgely. Homosexual lawyer with AIDS sues his firm for unfair dismissal. *Dir.* Jonathan Demme.

Philadelphia Story, The (1940) Katharine Hepburn, Cary Grant, James Stewart, Ruth Hussey. *Dir.* George Cukor.

Pianist, The (2002) Adrien Brody (Wladyslaw Szpilman), Thomas Kretschmann (Captain Wilm Hosenfeld), Frank Finlay (the father), Maureen Lipman (the mother), Emilia Fox (Dorota), Ed Stoppard (Henryk), Julia Rayner (Regina), Jessica Kate Meyer (Halina), Ruth Platt (Janina). Based on the autobiography of Wladyslaw Szpilman, a Polish Jew who survived the Nazi occupation of World War II. A composer and pianist, he plays the last live music heard over Polish radio before the invasion. Eluding deportation, he remains in the devastated Warsaw ghetto and struggles to stay alive. *Dir.* Roman Polanski.

Piano, The (1993) Holly Hunter, Harvey Keitel, Sam Neill, Genevieve Lemon. *Dir.* Jane Campion.

Picnic (1955) William Holden, Kim Novak, Rosalind Russell, Susan Strasberg. *Dir.* Joshua Logan.

Picnic at Hanging Rock (1975) Rachel Roberts, Dominic Guard, Helen Morse, Vivian Gray. *Dir.* Peter Weir.

Picture of Dorian Gray, The (1945) Hurd Hatfield (Gray), George Sanders (Sir Henry), Donna Reed, Angela Lansbury. *Dir.* Albert Lewin.

Pierrepoint (2005) Timothy Spall (Albert Pierrepoint), Juliet Stevenson (Annie Pierrepoint), Eddie Marsan (James 'Tish' Corbitt), Mary Stockley (Ruth Ellis), Ben McKay (Timothy Evans). The life and times of Albert Pierrepoint, Britain's most prolific hangman and one of a family of hangmen. The film was also known as *The Last Hangman. Dir.* Adrian Shergold.

Pillow Talk (1959) Doris Day, Rock Hudson, Tony Randall, Thelma Ritter. First of the partnership films of Day and Hudson, this one concerning a party line love affair. *Dir.* Michael Gordon.

Pink Panther, The (1963) David Niven, Peter Sellers, Capucine, Claudia Cardinale, Robert Wagner. The seven sequels were *A Shot in the Dark, Inspector Clouseau, Return of the Pink Panther, The Pink Panther Strikes Again, The Revenge of the Pink Panther, Trail of the Pink Panther* and *Son of the Pink Panther. Dir.* Blake Edwards.

Pink Panther, The (2006) Steve Martin (Insp. Jacques Clouseau), Kevin Kline (Chief Insp. Dreyfus), Jean Reno (Gendarme Gilbert Ponton), Beyoncé Knowles (Xania). Inferior remake of the 1964 Peter Sellers classic. *Dir.* Shawn Levy.

Pirates of the Caribbean: At World's End (2007) The third film in the series sees Rolling Stone Keith Richards join the regular crew of the *Black Pearl* as Captain Teague, father of Captain Jack Sparrow. *Dir.* Gore Verbinski.

Pirates of the Caribbean: Curse of the Black Pearl, The (2003) Johnny Depp (Jack Sparrow), Geoffrey Rush (Barbossa), Orlando Bloom (Will Turner), Keira Knightley (Elizabeth Swann), Jack Davenport (Norrington), Kevin R McNally (Joshamee Gibbs), Zoe Saldana (Anamaria), Jonathan Pryce (Governor Weatherby Swann). *Dir.* Gore Verbinski.

Pirates of the Caribbean: Dead Man's Chest (2006) Johnny Depp (Jack Sparrow), Orlando Bloom (Will Turner), Keira Knightley (Elizabeth Swann), Jack Davenport (Norrington), Bill Nighy (Davy Jones), Jonathan Pryce (Governor Weatherby Swann), Lee Arenberg (Pintel), Mackenzie Crook (Ragetti), Kevin McNally (Gibbs), Stellan Skarsgård (Bootstrap Bill), Naomie Harris (Tia Dalma). *Dir.* Gore Verbinski.

Pirates of the Caribbean: On Stranger Tides (2011) The fourth film in the series sees Captain Jack Sparrow joined by Angelica (Penélope Cruz) in his search for the Fountain of Youth, confronting the infamous pirate Blackbeard (Ian McShane). *Dir.* Rob Marshall.

Pit and the Pendulum, The (1961) Vincent Price, Barbara Steele, John Kerr. *Dir.* Roger Corman.

Place in the Sun, A (1951) Montgomery Clift, Elizabeth Taylor, Shelley Winters, Raymond Burr. Man is offered the chance of a rich wife, but allows himself to be convicted and executed for the accidental death of his former fiancée. *Dir.* George Stevens.

Planes, Trains and Automobiles (1987) Steve Martin (Neal Page), John Candy (Del Griffith), Laila Robbins, Kevin Bacon. Yuppie attempts to get home to his family for a snowy Thanksgiving. *Dir.* John Hughes.

Planet of the Apes (1968) Charlton Heston, Roddy McDowall, Kim Hunter, James Whitmore. John Chambers won Oscar for Make-up. Sequels included *Beneath the Planet of the Apes* (1969), *Escape from the Planet of the Apes* (1970), *Conquest of the Planet of the Apes* (1972), and *Battle for the Planet of the Apes* (1973). *Dir.* Franklin Schaffner.

Platoon (1986) Tom Berenger (Sgt Barnes), Willem Dafoe (Sgt Elias), Charlie Sheen (Chris), Johnny Depp (Lerner), Forest Whitaker (Big Harold). *Dir.* Oliver Stone.

Play Misty for Me (1971) Clint Eastwood, Jessica Walter, Donna Mills, John Larch. *Dir.* Clint Eastwood.

Player, The (1992) Tim Robbins (Griffin Mill), Greta Scacchi (June Gudmundsdottir), Fred Ward (Walter Stuckel), Whoopi Goldberg (Det. Avery), Richard E Grant (Tom Oakley), Sydney Pollack (Dick Mellen). This satire on Hollywood also starred 65 other stars who accepted nominal fees, including, Steve Allen, Cher, James Coburn, Peter Falk, Teri Garr, Jeff Goldblum, Elliott Gould, Joel Grey, Anjelica Huston, Sally Kellerman, Jack Lemmon, Marlee Matlin, Nick Nolte, Malcolm McDowell, Burt Reynolds, Julia Roberts, Mimi Rogers, Annie Ross, Jill St John, Susan Sarandon, Rod Steiger, Lily Tomlin, Robert Wagner, Bruce Willis. *Dir.* Robert Altman.

Ploughman's Lunch, The (1983) Jonathan Pryce (James Penfield), Tim Curry (Jeremy Hancock), Charlie Dore (Sue Barrington). British journalist furthers his career by rewriting history. *Dir.* Richard Eyre.

Pocahontas (1995) Voices: Mel Gibson, Irene Bedard, David Ogden Stiers, Judy Kuhn, Billy Connolly. *Dir.* Mike Gabriel & Eric Goldberg.

Point Blank (1967) Lee Marvin, Angie Dickinson, Keenan Wynn, Carroll O'Connor. Based on the novel *The Hunter* by Richard Stark. *Dir.* John Boorman.

Point Break (1991) Patrick Swayze (Bodhi), Keanu Reeves (Johnny Utah), Gary Busey, Lori Petty. FBI man Reeves infiltrates a gang of surfers to investigate bank robberies. *Dir.* Kathryn Bigelow.

Pokemon: The First Movie (1999) Animation based on the popular Japanese characters. To date two subsequent sequels have arisen – *Pokemon 2: The Power of One; Pokemon 3 the Movie: Spell of the Unknown. Dir.* Kunihiko Yuyama.

Polar Express, The (2004) Tom Hanks (Hero Boy/Father/Conductor/Hobo/Scrooge/Santa Claus), Leslie Harter Zemeckis (Sister Sarah/Mother (as Leslie Zemeckis), Eddie Deezen (Know-it-All). Santa Claus does not exist. Or does he? For one doubting boy (voice of Daryl Sabara and Tom Hanks), an astonishing event occurs. *Dir.* Robert Zemeckis.

Police Academy (1984) Steve Guttenberg (Carey), Kim Cattrall (Karen), Bubba Smith (Moses), GW Bailey (Lt. Harris), David Graf (Tackleberry), Donovan Scott (Leslie). Sequels include *2: Their First Assignment*; *3: Back in Training*; *4: Citizens on Patrol*; *5: Assignment Miami Beach*; *6: City under Siege. Dir.* Hugh Wilson.

Poltergeist (1982) JoBeth Williams, Craig T Nelson, Beatrice Straight, Oliver Robbins, Dominique Dunne. Two inferior sequels were made. *Dir.* Tobe Hooper.

Pope Joan (1972) Liv Ullmann, Trevor Howard, Olivia de Havilland, Franco Nero, Maximilian Schell. *Dir.* Michael Anderson.

Pope Must Die, The (1991) Robbie Coltrane, Beverly D'Angelo, Herbert Lom, Alex Rocco, Annette Crosbie. *Dir.* Peter Richardson.

Popeye (1980) Robin Williams, Shelley Duvall, Ray Walston. *Dir.* Robert Altman.
Postcards From the Edge (1990) Meryl Streep, Shirley MacLaine, Dennis Quaid, Gene Hackman, Richard Dreyfuss, Annette Bening. *Dir.* Mike Nichols.
Postman Always Rings Twice, The (1981) Jack Nicholson, Jessica Lange, Anjelica Huston. Remake of the 1946 film starring Lana Turner & John Garfield. *Dir.* Bob Rafelson.
Precious (2009) Mo'Nique (Mary Lee Johnston), Gabourey Sidibe (Precious Jones), Paula Patton (Ms Blu Rain), Mariah Carey (Ms Weiss), Lenny Kravitz (Nurse John McFadden), Sherri Shepherd (Cornrows), Grace Hightower (Social Worker), Kimberly Russell (Katherine), Bill Sage (Mr Wicher), Sapphire (Day Care Woman). Set in Harlem in 1987, adaptation of the award-winning 1996 novel *Push* by Sapphire. Obese, illiterate black 16-year-old Claireece 'Precious' Jones lives with her dysfunctional mother, Mary. She has been raped and impregnated twice by her father, Carl, and also suffers physical, mental and sexual abuse from her mother. *Dir.* Lee Daniels.
Predator (1987) Arnold Schwarzenegger (Dutch), Carl Weathers (Dillon), Kevin Peter Hall (The Predator). *Predator 2* starred Danny Glover and Gary Busey. *Dir.* John McTiernan.
Prestige, The (2006) Hugh Jackman (Robert Angier), Christian Bale (Alfred Borden), Michael Caine (Cutter), Piper Perabo (Julia Angier), Rebecca Hall (Sarah Borden), Scarlett Johansson (Olivia Wenscombe), Samantha Mahurin (Jess), David Bowie (Nikola Tesla). Robert and Alfred are rival magicians. After Alfred performs the ultimate magic trick, Robert tries desperately to find out its secret and their rivalry knows no bounds. *Dir.* Christopher Nolan.
Prêt-à-Porter (1994) Anouk Aimée, Lauren Bacall, Kim Basinger, Sophia Loren, Marcello Mastroianni, Julia Roberts, Teri Garr, Tracey Ullman, Richard E Grant. Aka *Ready to Wear. Dir.* Robert Altman.
Pretty Woman (1990) Richard Gere (Edward Lewis), Julia Roberts (Vivian Ward), Ralph Bellamy (James Morse). *Dir.* Garry Marshall.
Prick up Your Ears (1987) Gary Oldman (Joe Orton), Alfred Molina (Kenneth Halliwell), Vanessa Redgrave (Peggy), Julie Walters (Elsie Orton), Lindsay Duncan (Anthea Lahr). *Dir.* Stephen Frears.
Prime of Miss Jean Brodie, The (1969) Maggie Smith, Robert Stephens, Pamela Franklin, Celia Johnson, Gordon Jackson. *Dir.* Ronald Neame.
Prince and the Pauper (1937) Errol Flynn, Claude Rains, Billy and Bobby Mauch, Montagu Love (Henry VIII). Edward VI changes place with a street urchin. *Dir.* William Keighley. The 1977 remake starred Mark Lester, Oliver Reed and Raquel Welch (*Dir.* Richard Fleischer).
Prince and the Showgirl (1957) Laurence Olivier, Marilyn Monroe, Sybil Thorndike. *Dir.* Laurence Olivier.
Prince of Tides, The (1991) Nick Nolte (Tom Wingo), Barbra Streisand (Susan Lowenstein), Blythe Danner, Kate Nelligan. *Dir.* Barbra Streisand.
Prisoner of Zenda (1952) Stewart Granger, James Mason, Deborah Kerr, Louis Calhern. *Dir.* Richard Thorpe. Remake of the 1937 classic starring Ronald Colman and Douglas Fairbanks Jr (*Dir.* John Cromwell). A further remake of 1979 starred Peter Sellers and Lynne Frederick (*Dir.* Richard Thorpe).
Private Function, A (1984) Michael Palin, Maggie Smith, Denholm Elliott, Richard Griffiths, Betty the Pig. *Dir.* Malcolm Mowbray.
Private Life of Henry VIII, The (1933) Charles Laughton, Elsa Lanchester, Robert Donat, Merle Oberon. *Dir.* Alexander Korda.
Private Parts (1996) Howard Stern (as himself), Mary McCormack (Alison). Screen biography of top US disc jockey. *Dir.* Betty Thomas.
Prizzi's Honor (1985) Jack Nicholson, Kathleen Turner, Robert Loggia, Anjelica Huston. *Dir.* John Huston.
Producers, The (1968) Zero Mostel, Gene Wilder, Kenneth Mars. The play within the film is *Springtime for Hitler. Dir.* Mel Brooks.
Prospero's Books (1991) John Gielgud, Michael Clark, Tom Bell, Mark Rylance. *Dir.* Peter Greenaway.
Psycho (1960) Anthony Perkins, Vera Miles, Janet Leigh, John Gavin, Martin Balsam. Shower stabbing scene was directed by Saul Bass. Two sequels also starring Perkins in 1983 and 1986. *Dir.* Alfred Hitchcock.
Pulp Fiction (1994) John Travolta, Samuel L Jackson, Uma Thurman, Harvey Keitel, Tim Roth, Bruce Willis, Rosanna Arquette. *Dir.* Quentin Tarantino.
Punchline (1988) Sally Field (Lilah Krytsick), Tom Hanks (Steven Gold), John Goodman (John Krytsick), Mark Rydell (Romeo), Kim Greist (Madeline Urie). As the title suggests the film examines the world of a stand-up comedian. *Dir.* David Seltzer.
Quadrophenia (1979) Phil Daniels, Mark Wingett, Philip Davis, Sting, Leslie Ash, Toyah Willcox. *Dir.* Frank Roddam.
Quantum of Solace (2008) Daniel Craig (James Bond), Judi Dench (M), Olga Kurylenko (Camille Montes), Giancarlo Giannini (René Mathis), Mathieu Amalric (Dominic Greene), Gemma Arterton (MI6 Agent Strawberry Fields), Jeffrey Wright (Felix Leiter). Sequel to *Casino Royale* (2006). Bond battles wealthy businessman Dominic Greene, a member of the Quantum organisation posing as an environmentalist who intends to stage a coup d'état in Bolivia to take control of the nation's water supply. Bond seeks revenge for the death of his lover, Vesper Lynd, and is assisted by Camille Montes, who is also on her own revenge mission. Jack White of The White Stripes and Alicia Keys collaborated on the theme song *Another Way to Die*, the first Bond music duet. *Dir.* Marc Forster.
Queen, The (2006) Helen Mirren (HM Queen Elizabeth II), Michael Sheen (Tony Blair), James Cromwell (Prince Philip), Sylvia Syms (HM The Queen Mother), Alex Jennings (Prince Charles), Helen McCrory (Cherie Blair). Based on events after the untimely death of Lady Diana Spencer, when Queen Elizabeth's restrained reaction causes a public relations debacle that Prime Minister Tony Blair must defuse. *Dir.* Stephen Frears.
Queen Christina (1933) Greta Garbo, John Gilbert, Ian Keith, Lewis Stone, Reginald Owen. Queen of Sweden roams the country to escape a political marriage. *Dir.* Rouben Mamoulian.
Quick and the Dead, The (1995) Sharon Stone, Gene Hackman, Leonard DiCaprio. *Dir.* Sam Raimi.
Quiet American, The (2002) Michael Caine, Brendan Fraser, Do Thi Hai Yen, Rade Sherbedgia. Set in Vietnam in 1952 during the Vietnamese liberation war against French rule, this is the story of a love triangle between a young CIA agent (Fraser), a beautiful young Vietnamese woman (Do Hai Yen) and a British reporter (Caine). Based on the Graham Greene novel. *Dir.* Phillip Noyce.
Quiet Man, The (1952) John Wayne, Maureen O'Hara, Barry Fitzgerald, Victor McLaglen, Ward Bond. *Dir.* John Ford.
Quigley Down Under (1990) Tom Selleck, Laura San Giacomo, Alan Rickman, Chris Haywood. In 1860s Australia, an American hired gun is outlawed. *Dir.* Simon Wincer.
Quiller Memorandum, The (1966) George Segal, Max Von Sydow, Alec Guinness, Senta Berger, George Sanders. *Dir.* Michael Anderson.
Quiz Show (1994) John Turturro, Ralph Fiennes, Rob Morrow, Paul Scofield, Martin Scorsese. *Dir.* Robert Redford.
Quo Vadis (1951) Robert Taylor, Deborah Kerr, Peter Ustinov, Leo Genn. *Dir.* Mervyn Le Roy.
Rabbit-Proof Fence (2002) Everlyn Sampi (Molly Craig), Tianna Sansbury (Daisy Craig), Laura Monaghan (Gracie Fields), David Gulpilil (Moodoo), Kenneth Branagh (AO Neville), Deborah Mailman (Mavis), Jason Clarke (Constable Riggs), Ningali Lawford (Molly's Mother). True story based on the book *Follow the Rabbit-Proof Fence* by Molly's daughter Doris Pilkington Garimara, concerning three young aborigine girls who are taken away from their mother to be integrated into white society in 1930s Australia. *Dir.* Phillip Noyce.
Radio Days (1987) Woody Allen (Narrator), Mia Farrow (Sally White), Seth Green (Little Joe), Julie Kavner (Mother), Michael Tucker (Father), Diane Keaton (New Year's singer). *Dir.* Woody Allen.
Rage, The: Carrie 2 (1999) Emily Bergl, Jason London, Dylan Bruno, Amy Irving, John Doe, Zachery Ty Bryan. *Dir.* Katt Shea.
Rage in Harlem, A (1991) Forest Whitaker, Gregory Hines, Robin Givens, Danny Glover. *Dir.* Bill Duke.
Raging Bull (1980) Robert De Niro, Cathy Moriarty, Joe Pesci. *Dir.* Martin Scorsese.
Raiders of the Lost Ark (1981) Harrison Ford, Karen Allen, John Rhys-Davies, Denholm Elliott. *Dir.* Steven Spielberg.
Railway Children, The (1970) Dinah Sheridan, William Mervyn, Jenny Agutter, Sally Thomsett, Bernard Cribbins. *Dir.* Lionel Jeffries.
Rain Man (1988) Dustin Hoffman (Raymond Babbitt), Tom Cruise (Charles Babbitt), Valerie Golino (Susanna). *Dir.* Barry Levinson.
Raising Arizona (1987) Nicolas Cage (HI), Holly Hunter (Ed), Trey Wilson (Nathan Arizona Sr), John Goodman (Gale). *Dir.* Joel Coen.

Raising Victor Vargas (2002) Victor Rasuk (Victor Vargas), Judy Marte (Judy Ramirez), Melonie Diaz (Melonie), Altagracia Guzman (Grandma), Silvestre Rasuk (Nino Vargas), Krystal Rodriguez (Vicki Vargas), Kevin Rivera (Harold), Wilfree Vasquez (Carlos). A 16-year-old in New York's Lower East Side struggles to come to terms with growing up. *Dir.* Peter Sollett.
Rambo (2008) After reprising the role of Rocky, 16 years after the last film, Stallone left a 20-year gap between the third and the fourth instalment of the Rambo franchise. *Dir.* Sylvester Stallone.
Rambo: First Blood Part II (1985) Sylvester Stallone, Richard Crenna, Steven Berkoff. Written by Sylvester Stallone & James Cameron. *Dir.* George Pan Cosmatos.
Rambo III (1988) Sylvester Stallone, Richard Crenna, Marc de Jonge. Written by Sylvester Stallone and Sheldon Lettich. *Dir.* Peter MacDonald.
Ran (1985) Tatsuya Nakadai, Satoshi Terao. Japanese version of *King Lear*. *Dir.* Akira Kurosawa.
Rango (2011) Voices of Johnny Depp (Rango - a chameleon), Isla Fisher (Beans - a desert iguana), Ned Beatty (Tortoise John - Mayor of Dirt - a desert tortoise), Alfred Molina (Roadkill - a nine-banded armadillo), Bill Nighy (Rattlesnake Jake), Harry Dean Stanton (Balthazar - a mole), Ray Winstone (Bad Bill - a Gila monster). Computer-animated action comedy western film. *Dir.* Gore Verbinski.
Ratatouille (2007) Voices: Patton Oswalt (Remy), Peter Sohn (Emile, Remy's older brother), Brian Dennehy (Django, father of Remy and Emile), Lou Romano (Alfredo Linguini), Janeane Garofalo (Collette Tatou), Ian Holm (Skinner), Peter O'Toole (Anton Ego), Brad Garrett (Chef Auguste Gusteau – his motto was 'anyone can cook'), John Ratzenberger (Mustafa, Gusteau's head waiter), Brad Bird (Ambrister Minion, Ego's butler). Computer animation produced by Pixar and distributed by Walt Disney Pictures. A rat named Remy dreams of becoming a chef and tries to achieve his goal by forming an alliance with a Parisian restaurant's garbage boy. The film's title refers to the traditional French dish which is served late in the film, but is also a play on words on the species of the main character. *Dir.* Brad Bird.
Ray (2004) Jamie Foxx (Ray Charles), CJ Sanders (young Ray Robinson), Regina King (Margie Hendricks), Kerry Washington (Della Bea Robinson), Clifton Powell (Jeff Brown), Aunjanue Ellis (Mary Ann Fisher), Harry Lennix, Terrence Dashon Howard, Larenz Tate (Quincy Jones), Sharon Warren. The life story of legendary singer Ray Charles, who went blind, aged seven, after witnessing his younger brother's accidental death. *Dir.* Taylor Hackford.
Reach for the Sky (1956) Kenneth More (Douglas Bader), Muriel Pavlow. *Dir.* Lewis Gilbert.
Reader, The (2008) Kate Winslet (Hanna Schmitz), Ralph Fiennes (Adult Michael Berg), David Kross (Young Michael Berg), Bruno Ganz (Professor Rohl), Lena Olin (Rose Mather and older Ilana Mather), Alexandra Maria Lara (Younger Ilana Mather), Vijnessa Ferkic (Sophie), Hannah Herzsprung (Julia, Michael's daughter), Karoline Herfurth (Martha), Burghart Klaußner (Judge). Set in Berlin and Neustadt, the film crosses three time frames to tell the story of the young Michael Berg's affair with an older woman, Hanna Schmitz, and his re-encounter with his former lover as she defends herself in a war-crime trial. Michael then realises Hanna's secret (she is a functional illiterate) and the devastating effect this has had on her life. The film adaptation was written by David Hare and based on the 1995 German novel of the same name by Bernhard Schlink. The concentration camp scenes were filmed at the Majdanek concentration camp, Lublin, Poland. *Dir.* Stephen Daldry.
Rear Window (1954) James Stewart, Grace Kelly, Raymond Burr. *Dir.* Alfred Hitchcock.
Rebecca (1940) Laurence Olivier, Joan Fontaine, George Sanders. *Dir.* Alfred Hitchcock.
Rebel without a Cause (1955) James Dean, Natalie Wood, Jim Backus, Sal Mineo, Dennis Hopper. *Dir.* Nicholas Ray.
Red Heat (1988) Arnold Schwarzenegger (Ivan Danko), James Belushi (Art Ridzik), Peter Boyle (Lou Donnelly). *Dir.* Walter Hill.
Red Sonja (1985) Arnold Schwarzenegger (Kalifor), Brigitte Nielsen (Red Sonja). *Dir.* Richard Fleischer.
Reds (1981) Warren Beatty (John Reed), Diane Keaton, Edward Herrmann, Jerzy Kosinski, Jack Nicholson. *Dir.* Warren Beatty.
Relic, The (1997) Tom Sizemore (D'Agosta), Penelope Ann Miller (Dr Margo Green). *Dir.* Peter Hyams.
Remains of the Day, The (1993) Anthony Hopkins, Emma Thompson, James Fox, Christopher Reeve, Peter Vaughan, Hugh Grant. *Dir.* James Ivory.
Repulsion (1965) Catherine Deneuve, Ian Hendry, John Fraser, Patrick Wymark. *Dir.* Roman Polanski.
Reservoir Dogs (1991) Lawrence Tierney, Harvey Keitel (Mr White), Tim Roth (Mr Orange), Eddie Bunker (Mr Blue), Michael Madsen (Mr Blonde), Steve Buscemi (Mr Pink), Quentin Tarantino (Mr Brown). *Dir.* Quentin Tarantino.
Resident Evil (2002) Milla Jovovich (Alice), Michelle Rodriguez (Rain), Eric Mabius (Matt), Michaela Dicker (Red Queen). Virus turns workers into flesh-eating zombies. *Dir.* Paul WS Anderson.
Return of the Swamp Thing (1989) Louis Jourdan (Dr Anton Arcane), Heather Locklear (Abby Arcane), Dick Durock (Swamp Thing). *Dir.* Jim Wynorski.
Return of the Jedi (1983) Mark Hamill, Harrison Ford, Carrie Fisher, Billy Dee Williams. *Dir.* Richard Marquand.
Revenge (1990) Kevin Costner (Jay Cochran), Anthony Quinn (Tiburon), Madeleine Stowe (Miryea). *Dir.* Tony Scott.
Revenge of the Pink Panther (1978) Peter Sellers, Herbert Lom, Dyan Cannon. *Dir.* Blake Edwards.
Reversal of Fortune (1990) Jeremy Irons (Claus Von Bulow), Glenn Close (Sunny Von Bulow), Julie Hagerty (Alexandra). *Dir.* Barbet Schroeder.
Revolution (1985) Al Pacino (Tom Dobb), Donald Sutherland (Sgt Major Peasy), Nastassja Kinski (Daisy). Notable for being the biggest flop of all time. *Dir.* Hugh Hudson.
Revolutionary Road (2008) Leonardo DiCaprio (Frank Wheeler), Kate Winslet (April Wheeler), Kathy Bates (Helen Givings), Kathryn Hahn (Milly Campbell), David Harbour (Shep Campbell), Michael Shannon (John Givings), Richard Easton (Howard Givings), Zoe Kazan (Maureen Grube), Jay O Sanders (Bart Pollock). Husband and wife Frank and April Wheeler move from New York City to Revolutionary Road in a middle-class Connecticut suburb, but become disillusioned with their lives. *Dir.* Sam Mendes.
Rhapsody in Blue (1945) Robert Alda (George Gershwin), Joan Leslie, Alexis Smith. *Dir.* Irving Rapper.
Richard III (1995) Ian McKellen, Annette Bening, Jim Broadbent, Robert Downey Jnr, Kristin Scott-Thomas, Maggie Smith, Nigel Hawthorne. Ian McKellen wrote the screenplay. *Dir.* Richard Loncraine.
Rififi (1955) Jean Servais, Carl Mohner, Jules Dassin. Famous for its 25 minutes of silence whilst robbery is taking place. *Dir.* Jules Dassin.
Right Stuff, The (1983) Sam Shepard (Chuck Yeager), Barbara Hershey (Glennis), Scott Glenn (Alan Shepard), Ed Harris (John Glenn), Fred Ward (Gus Grissom), Dennis Quaid (Gordon Cooper). *Dir.* Philip Kaufman.
Rise of the Planet of the Apes (2011) James Franco (Dr William Rodman), Freida Pinto (Caroline Aranha), John Lithgow (Charles Rodman), Andy Serkis (Caesar). Origin story in which Will Rodman's research into a cure for his father's dementia leads him into rearing a super-intelligent chimpanzee, Caesar. *Dir.* Rupert Wyatt.
Rising Sun (1993) Sean Connery, Harvey Keitel, Wesley Snipes, Mako. *Dir.* Philip Kaufman.
Road House (1989) Patrick Swayze, Kelly Lynch, Sam Elliott, Ben Gazzara, Marshall Teague. *Dir.* Rowdy Herrington.
Road to Hong Kong (1962) Bob Hope, Bing Crosby, Dorothy Lamour, Joan Collins, Peter Sellers, Frank Sinatra, Dean Martin, David Niven. Last of the seven *Road* films. *Dir.* Norman Panama.
Road to Perdition (2002) Tom Hanks (Michael Sullivan), Paul Newman (John Rooney), Jude Law (Maguire), Jennifer Jason Leigh (Annie Sullivan), Tyler Hoechlin (Michael Sullivan Jr) *Dir.* Sam Mendes.
Road to Singapore (1940) Bob Hope, Bing Crosby, Dorothy Lamour, Anthony Quinn. First of the seven *Road* films, destination followed by Zanzibar, Moscow, Utopia, Rio, Bali and Hong Kong. *Dir.* Victor Schertzinger.
Rob Roy (1995) Liam Neeson, Jessica Lange, John Hurt, Tim Roth. *Dir.* Michael Caton-Jones.
Robe, The (1953) Richard Burton, Jean Simmons, Michael Rennie, Victor Mature, Richard Boone. *Dir.* Henry Koster.
Robin Hood (1991) Patrick Bergin, Uma Thurman, Edward Fox. *Dir.* John Irvin.

Robin Hood: Men in Tights (1993) Cary Elwes, Richard Lewis, Roger Rees, Tracey Ullman, Mel Brooks, Isaac Hayes, Patrick Stewart. *Dir.* Mel Brooks.

Robin Hood: Prince of Thieves (1991) Kevin Costner, Morgan Freeman, Christian Slater, Alan Rickman, Sean Connery (uncredited). Title song: 'Everything I Do I Do for You' by Bryan Adams. *Dir.* Kevin Reynolds.

Robocop (1987) Peter Weller, Nancy Allen, Ronny Cox. *Dir.* Paul Verhoeven.

Rock, The (1996) Sean Connery, Nicolas Cage, Ed Harris. *Dir.* Michael Bay.

Rocking Horse Winner, The (1949) John Mills, Valerie Hobson, John Howard Davies, Cyril Smith. Based on a DH Lawrence short story. *Dir.* Anthony Pelissier.

Rocky (1976) Sylvester Stallone, Burgess Meredith, Talia Shire, Carl Weathers. Written by Sylvester Stallone. *Dir.* John G Avildsen.

Rocky II (1979) Stallone, Meredith, Shire, Weathers. Written and directed by Stallone.

Rocky III (1982) Stallone, Meredith, Shire, Weathers, Mr T, Hulk Hogan. Written and directed by Stallone.

Rocky IV (1985) Stallone, Dolph Lundgren, T Shire, Weathers, Brigitte Nielsen. Written and directed by Stallone.

Rocky V (1990) Stallone, Meredith, Shire, Burt Young, Sage Stallone. Written by Stallone. *Dir.* John G Avildsen.

Rocky Balboa (2006) Sylvester Stallone reprises the role of Rocky for the sixth time. Antonio Tarver, former world light-heavyweight champion, plays Mason 'The Line' Dixon, Rocky's opponent and current heavyweight champion of the world. *Dir.* Sylvester Stallone.

Rocky Horror Picture Show, The (1975) Tim Curry, Susan Sarandon, Meat Loaf, Little Nell. *Dir.* Jim Sharman.

Roman Holiday (1953) Gregory Peck, Audrey Hepburn, Eddie Albert, Hartley Power. *Dir.* William Wyler.

Roman Scandals (1933) Eddie Cantor, Gloria Stuart, Ruth Etting, Edward Arnold. *Dir.* Frank Tuttle.

Romancing the Stone (1984) Michael Douglas, Kathleen Turner, Danny De Vito, Zack Norman. *Dir.* Robert Zemeckis.

Rookie, The (1990) Clint Eastwood (Nick Pulovski), Charlie Sheen (David Ackerman), Raul Julia (Strom). *Dir.* Clint Eastwood.

Rookie of the Year (1993) Gary Busey, Thomas Ian Nicholas, Albert Hall, John Candy (uncredited). Young boy becomes pitcher for the Chicago Cubs after his arm is injured in an accident. *Dir.* Daniel Stern.

Room at the Top (1959) Laurence Harvey, Simone Signoret, Heather Sears, Donald Wolfit. Based on John Braine's novel. *Dir.* Jack Clayton.

Room with a View, A (1986) Maggie Smith (Charlotte Bartlett), Helena Bonham Carter (Lucy Honeychurch). Opens in Italy in 1907. *Dir.* James Ivory.

Rope (1948) James Stewart, John Dall, Farley Granger, Joan Chandler. Two homosexuals murder a friend for the thrill of it and hide his body in a trunk from which they serve cocktails to a party. *Dir.* Alfred Hitchcock.

Rose, The (1979) Bette Midler, Alan Bates, Frederic Forrest, Harry Dean Stanton. *Dir.* Mark Rydell.

Rosencrantz and Guildenstern Are Dead (1990) Gary Oldman (Rosencrantz), Tim Roth (Guildenstern), Iain Glen (Prince Hamlet). *Dir.* Tom Stoppard.

Running Man, The (1987) Arnold Schwarzenegger (Ben Richards), Maria Conchita Alonso (Amber Mendez), Yaphet Kotto (Laughlin), Jim Brown (Fireball). *Dir.* Paul Michael Glaser.

Rush Hour (1998) Jackie Chan (Lee), Chris Tucker (Carter), Tom Wilkinson, Elizabeth Pena, Mark Rolston, Tzi Ma, Philip Baker Hall. Chinese detective joins a disgraced LA cop in bringing a master criminal to justice. *Dir.* Brett Ratner.

Rush Hour 2 (2001) Jackie Chan (Lee), Chris Tucker (Carter), John Lone (Ricky Tan), Zhang Ziyi (Hui Li). Sequel set in Hong Kong. *Dir.* Brett Ratner.

Russia House, The (1990) Sean Connery, Michelle Pfeiffer, Roy Scheider, James Fox. *Dir.* Fred Schepisi.

Ruthless People (1986) Bette Midler, Danny De Vito, Judge Reinhold, Helen Slater. *Dir.* Jim Abrahams.

Ryan's Daughter (1970) Robert Mitchum, Sarah Miles, John Mills, Trevor Howard. *Dir.* David Lean.

Saint, The (1997) Val Kilmer (Simon Templar), Elisabeth Shue (Emma Russell). Roger Moore's voice heard on car radio. *Dir.* Phillip Noyce.

St Trinian's (2007) Rupert Everett (Miss Camilla Fritton, St Trinian's headmistress/Carnaby Fritton, Camilla's brother), Colin Firth (Geoffrey Thwaites, the Education Minister), Russell Brand (Flash Harry), Talulah Riley (Annabelle Fritton, the new girl), Gemma Arterton (Head Girl Kelly Jones), Tamsin Egerton (Chelsea Parker, posh totty no. 1), Paloma Faith (Andrea, the emo), Juno Temple (Celia, the 'trustafarian'), Kathryn Drysdale (Taylor, the chav), Lily Cole (Polly, the geek), Fenella Woolgar (Miss Cleaver, the sports teacher), Celia Imrie (Matron), Stephen Fry (Himself, the School Challenge presenter), Mischa Barton (JJ French, the PR guru, and previous head girl). The band members of Girls Aloud make cameo appearances as members of St Trinian's school band while Zöe Salmon makes a cameo appearance as an emo girl. The plot revolves around a stolen painting and St Trinian's success in the School Challenge quiz. *Dir.* Oliver Parker and Barnaby Thompson.

St Trinian's 2: The Legend of Fritton's Gold (2009) Much the same cast as the 2007 film although Everett's dual role is now of headmistress and Pirate Fritton, as the plot concerning a stolen ring begins 400 years ago and unearths the remarkable revelation that Pirate Fritton was in fact Shakespeare and a woman to boot! Miss Fritton's daughter, Annabelle, is now head girl although Kelly Jones returns to offer field advice. David Tennant plays Pomfrey, the main antagonist, and Sarah Harding has a more prominent role as Roxy (an independent girl with no allegiance to any of the school factions). The seventh film based on Ronald Searle's cartoons, the others being *The Belles of St Trinian's* (1954 – see entry), *Blue Murder at St Trinian's* (1957), *The Pure Hell of St Trinian's* (1960), *The Great St Trinian's Train Robbery* (1966 – see entry for the final film of the quartet), *The Wildcats of St Trinian's* (1980 – also directed by Frank Launder but different cast) and *St Trinian's* (2007), *St Trinian's 2* is the first of the genre without the appearance of the iconic Flash Harry. *Dir.* Oliver Parker and Barnaby Thompson.

Santa Claus: The Movie (1985) Dudley Moore (Patch), John Lithgow (BZ), David Huddleston (Claus), Burgess Meredith (Elf). *Dir.* Jeannot Szwarc.

Saturday Night and Sunday Morning (1960) Albert Finney, Shirley Anne Field, Rachel Roberts. Nottingham factory worker is dissatisfied with his lot. *Dir.* Karel Reisz.

Saturday Night Fever (1977) John Travolta, Karen Lynn Gorney, Barry Miller. *Dir.* John Badham.

Save the Last Dance (2001) Julia Stiles (Sara), Sean Patrick Thomas (Derek), Kerry Washington (Chenille), Fredro Starr (Malakai). Young white ballerina moves to Chicago and falls in love with a black youth. *Dir.* Thomas Carter.

Saving Private Ryan (1998) Tom Hanks, Edward Burns, Tom Sizemore, Matt Damon, Ted Danson, Harve Presnell. *Dir.* Steven Spielberg. (Author's Note: I believe this is the first work to be published which highlights a subtle continuity error. After losing one of the eight original platoon members all eight can be seen marching across a field, but fortunately become seven again on arrival at a radar station!)

Scandal (1989) John Hurt (Stephen Ward), Joanne Whalley-Kilmer (Christine Keeler), Bridget Fonda (Mandy Rice-Davies), Ian McKellen (John Profumo), Leslie Phillips, Britt Ekland, Jean Alexander, Jeroen Krabb, Michael Ironside. *Dir.* Michael Caton-Jones.

Scanners (1981) Stephen Lock, Jennifer O'Neill, Patrick McGoohan, Michael Ironside. *Dir.* David Cronenberg.

Scanners II: The New Order (1991) David Hewlett, Yvan Ponton, Raoul Trujillo. *Dir.* Christian Duguay.

Scanners III: The Takeover (1992) Liliana Komorowska, Valerie Valcis, Steve Parrish, Harry Hill. *Dir.* Christian Duguay.

Scarface (1983) Al Pacino (Tony Montana), Steven Bauer (Manny Ray), Michelle Pfeiffer (Elvira), Mary Elizabeth Mastrantonio (Gina), Robert Loggia (Frank Lopez), F Murray Abraham (Omar). *Dir.* Brian De Palma.

Scarlet Letter, The (1995) Demi Moore, Gary Oldman, Robert Duvall, Robert Prosky, Joan Plowright. Set in C17 Massachusetts; a settler's wife gives birth to an illegitimate daughter. Based on the Nathaniel Hawthorne novel, the scarlet letter is 'A' for adultery. *Dir.* Roland Joffé.

Scary Movie (2000) Marlon Wayans (Shorty), Shawn Wayans (Ray), Anna Faris (Cindy), Shannon Elizabeth (Buffy), Cheri Oteri (Gail Hailstorm). A killer murders high-school children in this horror-movie spoof. *Dir.* Keenen Ivory Wayans.

Scary Movie 2 (2001) Marlon Wayans (Shorty), Shawn Wayans (Ray), Anna Faris (Cindy), Regina Hall (Brenda), Chris Masterson (Buddy), Tim Curry (The Professor), Kathleen Robertson (Theo), James Woods (Father McFeely). Sequel concerning psychology professor who invites students to spend a weekend in a haunted house. *Dir.* Keenen Ivory Wayans.

Scenes from a Mall (1991) Bette Midler, Woody Allen, Paul Mazursky. *Dir.* Paul Mazursky.

Scent of a Woman (1992) Al Pacino, Chris O'Donnell, Gabrielle Anwar. Blind ex-officer takes young man under his wing. *Dir.* Martin Brest.

Schindler's List (1993) Liam Neeson, Ben Kingsley, Ralph Fiennes. *Dir.* Steven Spielberg.

School of Rock, The (2003) Jack Black (Dewey Finn), Joan Cusack (Rosalie Mullins), Mike White (Ned Schneebly), Sarah Silverman (Patty Di Marco), Joey Gaydos Jnr (Zack), Robert Tsai (Lawrence), Maryam Hassan (Tomika), Kevin Clark (Freddy Jones). A wannabe rock musician impersonates a teacher at an upmarket school and turns a class of ten-year-olds into a rock band. *Dir.* Richard Linklater.

Scooby-Doo (2002) Freddie Prinze Jr (Fred), Sarah Michelle Gellar (Daphne), Matthew Lillard (Shaggy), Linda Cardellini (Velma). Real-life version of the Hanna-Barbera cartoon. *Dir.* Raja Gosnell.

Scorpion King, The (2002) Dwayne Johnson, Steven Brand, Michael Clarke Duncan, The Rock (Mathayus/The Scorpion King), Kelly Hu, Bernard Hill. Spin-off from *The Mummy Returns. Dir.* Chuck Russell. A 2008 direct-to-DVD prequel, *The Scorpion King 2: Rise of a Warrior* (aka *The Scorpion King: Rise of the Akkadian*) was directed by Russell Mulcahy and starred Michael Copon as Mathayus.

Scream (1996) David Arquette, Neve Campbell (Sidney), Courteney Cox (Gale Weathers), Drew Barrymore. *Dir.* Wes Craven.

Screamers (1996) Peter Weller, Roy Dupuis, Jennifer Rubin, Ron White. Set in 2078 on the planet Sirius 6B where killer robots run amok. *Dir.* Christian Duguay.

Sea of Love (1989) Al Pacino (Frank Keller), Ellen Barkin (Helen Cruger), John Goodman (Sherman Touhy). Cop investigating murders of lonely hearts advertisers places an ad himself. *Dir.* Harold Becker.

Seabiscuit (2003) Tobey Maguire (Red Pollard), Jeff Bridges (Charles Howard), Chris Cooper (Tom Smith), Elizabeth Banks (Marcela Howard), Gary Stevens (George Woolf), William H Macy (Tick-Tock McGlaughlin), Kingston DuCoeur (Sam), Eddie Jones (Samuel Riddle). Based on Laura Hillenbrand's book about the true story of champion racehorse Seabiscuit. *Dir.* Gary Ross.

Searchers, The (1956) John Wayne (Ethan Edwards), Jeffrey Hunter (Martin Pawley), Vera Miles (Laurie Jorgenson), Natalie Wood (Debbie Edwards), Ward Bond (Rev. Capt. Samuel Johnston Clayton), Henry Brandon (Chief Cicatrice, aka Scar), Lana Wood (Debbie Edwards (child)). A civil war veteran spends years searching for his young niece, captured by Indians. *Dir.* John Ford.

Sebastiane (1976) Leonardo Treviglio, Barney James, Neil Kennedy, Ken Hicks. Title character is banished by Emperor Diocletian and suffers further tragedy. Dialogue is in Latin with English subtitles. *Dir.* Derek Jarman and Paul Humfress.

Secret Garden, The (1949) Margaret O'Brien, Herbert Marshall, Gladys Cooper, Elsa Lanchester, Dean Stockwell, Brian Roper. Adaptation of the novel by Frances Hodgson Burnett which was shot in black and white but the scenes in the garden were filmed in Technicolor. A 1993 remake starred Maggie Smith. *Dir.* Fred M Wilcox.

Secrets and Lies (1995) Timothy Spall, Phyllis Logan, Brenda Blethyn, Claire Rushbrook, Marianne Jean-Baptiste. *Dir.* Mike Leigh.

See No Evil, Hear No Evil (1989) Gene Wilder (Dave Lyons), Richard Pryor (Wally Karew). Pryor is blind and Wilder is deaf. *Dir.* Arthur Hiller.

Seize the Day (1986) Robin Williams, Joseph Wiseman. Based on a Saul Bellow novel. *Dir.* Fielder Cook.

Sense and Sensibility (1995) Emma Thompson, Alan Rickman, Kate Winslet, Hugh Grant, Hugh Laurie, Gemma Jones. Emma Thompson wrote the screenplay. *Dir.* Ang Lee.

September (1987) Denholm Elliott (Howard), Dianne Wiest (Stephanie), Mia Farrow (Lane), Elaine Stritch. *Dir.* Woody Allen.

Serendipity (2001) John Cusack, Kate Beckinsale, Jeremy Piven, Molly Shannon. *Dir.* Peter Chelsom.

Sgt Bilko (1996) Steve Martin, Dan Aykroyd. *Dir.* Jonathan Lynn.

Sgt Pepper's Lonely Hearts Club Band (1978) Peter Frampton, Bee Gees, George Burns, Frankie Howerd, Donald Pleasence, Paul Nicholas, Alice Cooper, Steve Martin, Earth Wind & Fire, Sandy Farina. *Dir.* Michael Schultz.

Seven (1995) Brad Pitt, Morgan Freeman, Richard Roundtree, Kevin Spacey. *Dir.* David Fincher.

Seven Brides for Seven Brothers (1954) Howard Keel, Jane Powell, Jeff Richards, Russ Tamblyn. *Dir.* Stanley Donen.

Seven Year Itch, The (1955) Tom Ewell, Marilyn Monroe, Sonny Tufts, Evelyn Keyes. *Dir.* Billy Wilder.

Seven Years in Tibet (1997) Brad Pitt, David Thewlis, BD Wong. *Dir.* Jean-Jacques Annaud.

Sex and the City (2008) Sarah Jessica Parker (Carrie Bradshaw), Kim Cattrall (Samantha Jones), Kristin Davis (Charlotte York Goldenblatt), Cynthia Nixon (Miranda Hobbes), Chris Noth (John James 'Mr Big' Preston), Jennifer Hudson (Louise), David Eigenberg (Steve Brady), Jason Lewis (Smith Jerrod), Evan Handler (Harry Goldenblatt), Willie Garson (Stanford Blatch), Mario Cantone (Anthony Marantino), Lynn Cohen (Magda), Candice Bergen (Enid Frick). Film adaptation of the television comedy series of the same name (itself based on the novel of the same name by Candace Bushnell) about four female friends: Carrie, Samantha, Charlotte and Miranda, dealing with their lives as 40-something year olds in New York City. *Dir.* Michael Patrick King.

Shadow, The (1994) Alec Baldwin, Penelope Ann Miller, Tim Curry. In the 1930s a former criminal battles against a descendant of Genghis Khan. *Dir.* Russell Mulcahy.

Shakespeare in Love (1998) Gwyneth Paltrow, Joseph Fiennes, Geoffrey Rush, Colin Firth, Ben Affleck, Judi Dench, Rupert Everett, Simon Callow, Martin Clunes, Antony Sher, Imelda Staunton. *Dir.* John Madden. Judi Dench won Best Supporting Actor Oscar although only on screen for eight minutes. Daniel Day-Lewis and Julia Roberts turned down the lead roles.

Shadowlands (1993) Anthony Hopkins, Debra Winger, John Wood. Biopic of CS Lewis and his love for an American woman. *Dir.* Richard Attenborough.

Shallow Hal (2001) Gwyneth Paltrow, Jack Black (Hal), Jason Alexander, René Kirby. Man who judges women on superficial looks is hypnotised to see only their inner beauty and falls for a 300lb woman. *Dir.* Bobby Farrelly and Peter Farrelly.

Shaun of the Dead (2004) Simon Pegg (Shaun), Kate Ashfield (Liz), Lucy Davis (Di), Nick Frost (Ed), Dylan Moran (David), Bill Nighy (Philip), Penelope Wilton (Barbara), Jessica Stevenson (Yvonne). Spoof horror movie concerning flesh-eating zombies which arrive in North London but are thwarted by a shop assistant and his dishevelled friend. Written by Simon Pegg & Edgar Wright. *Dir.* Edgar Wright.

Shawshank Redemption, The (1994) Tim Robbins, Morgan Freeman, Bob Gunton, James Whitmore. *Dir.* Frank Darabont.

Sheena, Queen of the Jungle (1984) Tanya Roberts, Ted Wass, Donovan Scott. *Dir.* John Guillermin.

Sheik, The (1921) Rudolph Valentino, Agnes Ayres. English heiress falls for a desert chieftain. Notable for two reasons: it was the film that made a star of Valentino; and it was based on the novel by EM Hull, often considered the first novel of the Romantic Fiction genre. *Dir.* George Melford.

Sherlock Holmes (2009) Robert Downey Jr (Holmes), Jude Law (Dr John Watson), Rachel McAdams (Irene Adler), Mark Strong (Lord Avery Blackwood), Kelly Reilly (Mary Morstan), Eddie Marsan (Inspector Lestrade), Hans Matheson (Lord Coward, Home Secretary), Geraldine James (Mrs Hudson), James Fox (Sir Thomas Blackwood). Modernisation of the classic Sir Arthur Conan Doyle stories made famous on film by Basil Rathbone in *The Hound of the Baskervilles, The Adventures of Sherlock Holmes* (1939 – see entry), *Sherlock Holmes and the Voice of Terror* (1942), *Sherlock Holmes and the Secret Weapon, Sherlock Holmes in Washington, Sherlock Holmes Faces Death, Crazy House* (1943), *The Spider Woman, The Scarlet Claw, The Pearl of Death* (1944), *The House of Fear, The Woman in Green, Pursuit to Algiers* (1945), *Terror by Night* and *Dressed to Kill* (1946). *Dir.* Guy Ritchie.

Sherlock Holmes: A Game of Shadows (2011) Robert Downey Jr (Holmes), Jude Law (Dr John Watson), Rachel McAdams (Irene Adler), Stephen Fry (Mycroft Holmes), Jared Harris (Professor James Moriarty). *Dir.* Guy Ritchie.

Shine (1996) Armin Mueller-Stahl, Geoffrey Rush, Noah Taylor, Lynn Redgrave, Googie Withers, John Gielgud. Based on the life of pianist David Helfgott. *Dir.* Scott Hicks.
Ship of Fools (1965) Vivien Leigh, Simone Signoret, Oskar Werner, Lee Marvin. German line *Vera Cruz* leaves for Bremerhaven with a mixed bag of passengers. *Dir.* Stanley Kramer.
Shirley Valentine (1989) Pauline Collins, Tom Conti, Julia McKenzie, Alison Steadman, Joanna Lumley, Bernard Hill. *Dir.* Lewis Gilbert.
Shooting Dogs (2005) John Hurt (Christopher), Hugh Dancy (Joe Connor), Dominique Horwitz (Capitaine Charles Delon), Louis Mahoney (Sibomana), Nicola Walker (Rachel), Steve Toussaint (Roland), David Gyasi (François), Susan Nalwoga (Edda), Victor Power (Julius), Jack Pierce (Mark), Musa Kasonka Jnr (Boniface), Kizito Ssentamu Kayiira (Pierre), Claire-Hope Ashitey (Marie). Touching but deeply disturbing film, based on a true story. An exhausted Catholic priest (Hurt) and a young idealistic English teacher (Dancy) find themselves caught in the 1994 Rwandan genocide where 800,000 were killed in 100 days. They must choose whether to stay with the thousands of Tutsis about to be massacred or flee for safety. *Dir.* Michael Caton-Jones.
Shooting Fish (1997) Dan Futterman, Stuart Townsend, Kate Beckinsale, Annette Crosbie, Jane Lapotaire. *Dir.* Stefan Schwartz.
Shooting Party, The (1984) James Mason (Ralph Nettleby), Dorothy Tutin, Edward Fox, Cheryl Campbell, John Gielgud. *Dir.* Alan Bridges.
Shootist, The (1976) John Wayne, Lauren Bacall, James Stewart, Ron Howard, Hugh O'Brian. *Dir.* Don Siegel.
Short Cuts (1993) Andie MacDowell, Bruce Davison, Jack Lemmon, Robert Downey Jnr. Lives of 9 dysfunctional suburban couples intertwine. *Dir.* Robert Altman.
Shrek (2001) Voices of Mike Myers (Shrek), Eddie Murphy (Donkey), Cameron Diaz (Princess Fiona), John Lithgow (Lord Farquaad), Vincent Cassel (Monsieur Hood). Animation in which an ugly green ogre agrees to rescue a princess in return for having his swamp vacated but falls in love with her. *Dir.* Andrew Adamson and Vicky Jenson.
Shrek 2 (2004) Voices of Mike Myers (Shrek), Eddie Murphy (Donkey), Cameron Diaz (Princess Fiona), Julie Andrews (Queen), Antonio Banderas (Puss in Boots), John Cleese (King), Rupert Everett (Prince Charming), Jennifer Saunders (Fairy Godmother), Aron Warner (Wolf), Cody Cameron (Pinocchio/Three Pigs), Conrad Vernon (Gingerbread Man/Cedric/Announcer/Muffin Man/Mongo), Christopher Knights (Blind Mouse), David P Smith (Herald/Man with Box), Kelly Asbury (Page/Elf/Nobleman/Nobleman's Son), Mark Moseley (Mirror/Dresser). Princess Fiona's parents invite her and Shrek to dinner to celebrate her marriage, unaware the newlyweds are both ogres. *Dir.* Andrew Adamson, Kelly Asbury, Conrad Vernon.
Shrek 3 (2007) The third film in the series sees Shrek, Donkey and Puss in Boots set out to find Arthur Pendragon, the heir to the dying King Harold. Justin Timberlake joins the usual cast as the voice of Arthur. *Dir.* Chris Miller and Raman Hui.
Shrek Forever After (2010) The fourth and final film in the series sees the fiendish Rumpelstiltskin (voiced by Walt Dohrn) conning King Harold (John Cleese), Queen Lillian (Julie Andrews) and the usual suspects in his bid to be King of Far Far Away. *Dir.* Mike Mitchell.
Sideways (2004) Paul Giamatti, Thomas Haden Church, Patrick Gallagher, Alex Kalognomos, Virginia Madsen, Joe Marinelli, Sandra Oh, Alysia Reiner. Comedy concerning Miles Faymond, a failed writer teaching junior high school English, and his best friend, Jack, an actor whose popularity is diminishing, who take a week-long drive up to 'wine country' in California to explore the nature of their failures. *Dir.* Alexander Payne.
Signs (2002) Mel Gibson (Graham Hess), Joaquin Phoenix (Merrill Hess), Cherry Jones (Officer Caroline Paski), Rory Culkin (Morgan Hess). A lapsed priest regains his faith after a supernatural experience. *Dir.* M Night Shyamalan.
Silence of the Lambs (1991) Jodie Foster (Clarice Starling), Anthony Hopkins (Dr Hannibal Lecter), Scott Glen. *Dir.* Jonathan Demme.
Silkwood (1983) Meryl Streep, Cher, Kurt Russell. Female worker in nuclear processing plant mysteriously dies before she denounces safety aspects of the plant. *Dir.* Mike Nichols.
Silverado (1985) Scott Glen, Kevin Costner, John Cleese, Kevin Kline, Rosanna Arquette, Danny Glover. *Dir.* Lawrence Kasdan.
Silver Linings Playbook (2012) Bradley Cooper (Patrizio "Pat Jr." Solitano), Jennifer Lawrence (Tiffany Maxwell), Robert De Niro (Patrizio "Pat Sr." Solitano), Jacki Weaver (Dolores Solitano). Comedy drama adapted from the novel of the same name by Matthew Quick. Pat Solitano suffers from bipolar disorder and after his release from a psychiatric hospital moves back in with his parents and sets out to to win back his estranged wife. Pat meets recently-widowed sex addict Tiffany Maxwell who vows to help Pat if he enters a dance competition with her. *Dir.* David O. Russell.
Single Man, A (2009) Colin Firth (George Carlyle Falconer), Julianne Moore (Charlotte), Nicholas Hoult (Kenny Potter), Matthew Goode (Jim), Jon Kortajarena (Carlos). Set in Los Angeles on 30 November 1962, a month after the Cuban missile crisis. A gay middle-aged English college professor struggles to find meaning in his life since the death of his partner, Jim. *Dir.* Tom Ford.
Single White Female (1992) Bridget Fonda (Allison Jones), Jennifer Jason Leigh (Hedra Carlson), Steven Weber. *Dir.* Barbet Schroeder.
Sirens (1994) Hugh Grant, Tara FitzGerald, Sam Neill, Elle MacPherson. *Dir.* John Duigen.
Sister Act (1992) Whoopi Goldberg, Maggie Smith, Harvey Keitel. *Dir.* Emile Ardolino.
Sister Act 2: Back in the Habit (1993) Whoopi Goldberg, Maggie Smith, James Coburn. *Dir.* Bill Duke.
16 Blocks (2006) Bruce Willis (Jack Mosley), Mos Def (Eddie Bunker), David Morse (Frank Nugent), Jenna Stern (Diane Mosley), Casey Sander (Captain Gruber), Cylk Cozart (Det. Jimmy Mulvey). An ageing cop (Willis) is assigned the straightforward task of escorting a fast-talking witness (Def) from police custody to a courthouse. There are however forces at work trying to prevent them from making it. *Dir.* Richard Donner.
Sixth Sense, The (1999) Bruce Willis (Malcolm Crowe), Toni Collette, Haley Joel Osment (Cole). *Dir.* M. Night Shyamalan.
Skyfall (2012) Daniel Craig (James Bond), Judi Dench (M), Javier Bardem (Raoul Silva - born Tiago Rodriguez), Ben Whishaw (Q), Naomie Harris (Eve Moneypenny), Ralph Fiennes (Gareth Mallory - Chairman of the Intelligence and Security Committee). The 23rd James Bond film centres on Bond investigating an attack on MI6. The theme song, sung by Adele, won an Oscar.
Sleeper (1973) Woody Allen, Diane Keaton, John Beck. *Dir.* Woody Allen.
Sleeping with the Enemy (1990) Julia Roberts, Patrick Bergin. *Dir.* Joseph Ruben.
Sleepless in Seattle (1993) Tom Hanks, Meg Ryan, Ross Malinger. *Dir.* Nora Ephron.
Sleepy Hollow (1999) Johny Depp (Ichabod Crane), Christina Ricci (Katrina Van Tassel), Michael Gambon (Bactus Van Tassel), Christopher Lee (Burgomaster), Christopher Walken (Hessian Horseman). *Dir.* Tim Burton.
Sliding Doors (1998) Gwyneth Paltrow, John Hannah, John Lynch, Jeanne Tripplehorn, Virginia McKenna. *Dir.* Peter Howitt.
Sliver (1993) Sharon Stone, William Baldwin, Tom Berenger, Martin Landau. Based on an Ira Levin novel. *Dir.* Philip Noyce.
Slumdog Millionaire (2008) Dev Patel (Jamal K Malik), Anil Kapoor (Prem Kumar, WWTBAM host), Freida Pinto (Latika), Madhur Mittal (Salim Malik, Jamal's elder brother), Saurabh Shukla (Sgt Srinivas), Ayush Mahesh Khedekar (Youngest Jamal), Tanay Hemant Chheda (Early Teenage Jamal), Rubina Ali (Youngest Latika), Tanvi Ganesh Lonkar (Early Teenage Latika), Azharuddin Mohammed Ismail (Youngest Salim), Ashutosh Lobo Gajiwala (Early Teenage Salim). This adaptation of Vikas Swarup's 2005 novel *Q & A* was nominated for ten Academy Awards and won eight. The film tells the story of how a young man from the Mumbai slums (Dev Patel) happens to know the answer to all the questions on the Indian version of *Who Wants to Be a Millionaire*, and the suspicion he is treated with by the authorities. Many of the young children who appear in the slum scenes (including Rubina Ali and Azharuddin Mohammed Ismail) are actual residents of the Mumbai slums. *Dir.* Danny Boyle.
Smile Pinki (2008) The story of a poor girl in rural India whose life is transformed when she receives free surgery to correct her cleft lip. *Dir.* Megan Mylan.
Smilla's Feeling for Snow (1997) Julia Ormond (Smilla), Gabriel Byrne, Richard Harris (Tork), Vanessa Redgrave, Bob Peck, Jim Broadbent, Robert Loggia. *Dir.* Bille August.
Sneakers (1992) Robert Redford, Dan Aykroyd, Ben Kingsley, River Phoenix, Sidney Poitier. Experts hired to recover electronic device that can penetrate the government's most secure computer systems. *Dir.* Phil Alden Robinson.

Snow Dogs (2002) Cuba Gooding Jr (Ted Brooks), James Coburn (Thunder Jack), Sisqo, Graham Greene, Michael Bolton (as himself). Dentist goes to Alaska to search for his roots. *Dir.* Brian Levant.
Snow White: A Tale of Terror (1997) Monica Keena (Lilli), Sam Neill (Baron Hoffman), Sigourney Weaver (Claudia).
Social Network, The (2010) Jesse Eisenberg (Mark Zuckerberg), Andrew Garfield (Eduardo Saverin), Justin Timberlake (Sean Parker). Adaptation of Ben Mezrich's book *The Accidental Billionaires*, portraying the founding of Facebook. *Dir.* David Fincher.
Some Like It Hot (1939) Bob Hope, Shirley Ross, Una Merkel, Gene Krupa. Sideshow owner runs out of money. *Dir.* George Archainbaud.
Some Like It Hot (1959) Tony Curtis, Jack Lemmon, Marilyn Monroe, Joe E Brown, George Raft. *Dir.* Billy Wilder.
Somebody up There Likes Me (1956) Paul Newman (Rocky Graziano), Pier Angeli, Sal Mineo, Steve McQueen. *Dir.* Robert Wise.
Something's Gotta Give (2003) Jack Nicholson (Harry Sanborn), Diane Keaton (Erica Barry), Keanu Reeves (Julian Mercer), Frances McDormand (Zoe), Amanda Peet (Martin), Jon Favreau (Leo), Paul Michael Glaser (Dave), Rachel Ticotin (Dr Martinez). While convalescing, a middle-aged playboy begins to develop feelings for his girlfriend's mother. *Dir.* Nancy Meyers.
Sommersby (1993) Richard Gere, Jodie Foster. Remake of *The Return of Martin Guerre. Dir.* Jon Amiel.
Son of Lassie (1945) Peter Lawford, Donald Crisp, Nigel Bruce. The first sequel to *Lassie Come Home. Dir.* S Sylvan Simon.
Son of the Pink Panther (1993) Robert Benigni, Herbert Lom, Claudia Cardinale, Burt Kwouk. *Dir.* Blake Edwards.
Song of Bernadette, The (1943) Jennifer Jones, Charles Bickford, William Eythe. *Dir.* Henry King.
Song to Remember, A (1944) Cornel Wilde, Merle Oberon, Paul Muni. Life and death of Chopin. *Dir.* Charles Vidor.
Sophie's Choice (1982) Meryl Streep, Kevin Kline, Josh Mostel. *Dir.* Alan J Pakula.
Sound of Music, The (1965) Julie Andrews, Christopher Plummer, Richard Haydn, Marni Nixon. *Dir.* Robert Wise.
Soylent Green (1973) Charlton Heston, Edward G Robinson, Leigh Taylor-Young. Set in 2022, the Soylent Green of the title is synthetic food. *Dir.* Richard Fleischer.
Space Jam (1996) Michael Jordan, Bugs Bunny, voice of Danny De Vito. *Dir.* Joe Pytka.
Space Truckers (1997) Dennis Hopper, Stephen Dorff, Debi Mazar, Charles Dance. Set in 2196; BMW's Bio-Mechanical Warriors. *Dir.* Stuart Gordon.
Specialist, The (1994) Sharon Stone, Sylvester Stallone, Rod Steiger, James Woods. *Dir.* Luis Llosa.
Speed (1994) Sandra Bullock, Keanu Reeves, Dennis Hopper, Jeff Daniels. *Dir.* Jan de Bont.
Spellbound (2002) Documentary following eight children taking part in the final of the US National Spelling Bee. *Dir.* Jeffrey Blitz.
Spiceworld (1997) Spice Girls, Richard E Grant. Originally called: *Five. Dir.* Bob Spiers.
Spider-Man (2002) Tobey Maguire (Peter Parker / Spider-Man), Willem Dafoe (Norman Osborn / The Green Goblin), Kirsten Dunst (Mary Jane Watson), James Franco (Harry Osborn), Cliff Robertson (Ben Parker), Rosemary Harris (May Parker). *Dir.* Sam Raimi.
Spider-Man 2 (2004) Tobey Maguire (Peter Parker/Spider-Man), Willem Dafoe (Norman Osborn/The Green Goblin), Kirsten Dunst (Mary Jane Watson), James Franco (Harry Osborn), Alfred Molina (Doc Ock/Dr Otto Octavius), Rosemary Harris (May Parker), Cliff Robertson (Ben Parker), JK Simmons (J Jonah Jameson), Donna Murphy (Rosalie Octavius), Daniel Gillies (John Jameson), Ted Raimi (Hoffman). While Peter Parker is beset with personal problems, his alter-ego confronts the brilliant Dr Octavius who has been transformed into 'Doctor Octopus' (aka Doc Ock), a multi-tentacled super-villain. *Dir.* Sam Raimi.
Spider-Man 3 (2007) The third and final film in the series sees Spidey pitched against two new adversaries, Flint Marko, a small-time crook who becomes Sandman (played by Thomas Haden Church), and Eddie Brock Jr, Peter's rival at the *Daily Bugle* who becomes Venom (played by Topher Grace). Other actors reprise their earlier roles. *Dir.* Sam Raimi. *The Amazing Spider-Man* (2012) is a reboot of the franchise starring Andrew Garfield as Peter Parker/Spider-Man and Rhys Ifans as Dr. Curt Connors/Lizard; directed by Marc Webb.
Spitfire Grill, The (1996) Ellen Burstyn, Marcia Gay Harden, Alison Elliott. *Dir.* Lee David Zlotoff.
Splash! (1984) Tom Hanks (Allen Bauer), Daryl Hannah (Madison), John Candy, Eugene Levy. *Dir.* Ron Howard.
Splitting Heirs (1993) Rick Moranis (Henry), Eric Idle (Tommy Patel), Barbara Hershey, Catherine Zeta Jones, John Cleese (Raoul P Shadgrind), Stratford Johns, Eric Sykes. *Dir.* Robert Young.
Spy Hard (1996) Leslie Nielsen (Agent WD-40), Andy Griffith, Nicollette Sheridan. *Dir.* Rick Friedberg.
Spy Who Loved Me, The (1977) Roger Moore, Barbara Bach (Major Anya Amasova), Curt Jurgens (Stromberg). Theme song 'Nobody Does it Better' performed by Carly Simon. *Dir.* Lewis Gilbert.
Stagecoach (1939) John Wayne, Claire Trevor, Thomas Mitchell, Andy Devine. The 1966 remake starred Ann-Margret & Bing Crosby. *Dir.* John Ford.
Stalag 17 (1953) William Holden, Don Taylor, Otto Preminger, Peter Graves, Neville Brand. *Dir.* Billy Wilder.
Stanley and Iris (1990) Jane Fonda, Robert De Niro. *Dir.* Martin Ritt.
Stanza del Figlio, La (2001) Nanni Moretti (Giovanni), Laura Morante (Paola). Apparent family bliss falls apart when the young son dies in an accident. *Dir.* Nanni Moretti.
Star! (1968) Julie Andrews, Richard Crenna, Daniel Massey (Noël Coward), Bruce Forsyth, Beryl Reid. Biopic of Gertrude Lawrence. *Dir.* Robert Wise.
Star Is Born, A (1937) Janet Gaynor, Fredric March, Adolphe Menjou, Andy Devine. *Dir.* William A Wellman.
Star Is Born, A (1954) Judy Garland, James Mason, Charles Bickford. *Dir.* George Cukor.
Star Is Born, A (1976) Barbra Streisand, Kris Kristofferson, Gary Busey, Paul Mazursky. *Dir.* Frank Pierson.
Star Trek (2009) Chris Pine (James T Kirk), Zachary Quinto (Spock), Leonard Nimoy (Spock Prime), Eric Bana (Nero), Bruce Greenwood (Pike), Karl Urban (Bones), Zoe Saldana (Uhura), Simon Pegg (Scotty), John Cho (Hikaru Sulu), Anton Yelchin (Chekov), Ben Cross (Sarek), Winona Ryder (Amanda Grayson), Chris Hemsworth (George Kirk), Jennifer Morrison (Winona Kirk). The film follows Kirk and Spock before they unite aboard the USS *Enterprise* to combat Nero, a Romulan from their future who threatens the United Federation of Planets. *Dir.* JJ Abrams.
Star Trek: First Contact (1996) Patrick Stewart, Jonathan Frakes, Brent Spiner, Michael Dorn, LeVar Burton. *Dir.* Jonathan Frakes.
Star Trek: Generations (1994) Patrick Stewart, William Shatner, Malcolm McDowell, Jonathan Frakes, Brent Spiner, Whoopi Goldberg. *Dir.* David Carson.
Star Trek: The Motion Picture (1979) William Shatner, Leonard Nimoy, DeForest Kelley, Persis Khambatta. *Dir.* Robert Wise.
Star Trek II: The Wrath of Khan (1982) William Shatner, Leonard Nimoy, DeForest Kelley, Ricardo Montalban. Sequel to TV episode 'Space Seed'. *Dir.* Nicholas Meyer.
Star Trek III: The Search for Spock (1984) William Shatner, Leonard Nimoy, DeForest Kelley, Robert Hooks. *Dir.* Leonard Nimoy.
Star Trek IV: The Voyage Home (1986) William Shatner, Leonard Nimoy, DeForest Kelley, Catherine Hicks, Jane Wyatt. *Dir.* Leonard Nimoy.
Star Trek V: The Final Frontier (1989) William Shatner, Leonard Nimoy, DeForest Kelley, David Warner. *Dir.* William Shatner.
Star Trek VI: The Undiscovered Country (1991) William Shatner, Leonard Nimoy, DeForest Kelley, David Warner, Christian Slater, Christopher Plummer. *Dir.* Nicholas Meyer.
Star Wars (1977) Mark Hamill, Harrison Ford, Alec Guinness, Carrie Fisher, Anthony Daniels (C3PO), Kenny Baker (R2D2), Dave Prowse. *Dir.* George Lucas.
Star Wars: Episode I – The Phantom Menace (1999) Liam Neeson, Ewan McGregor, Natalie Portman, Jake Lloyd, Frank Oz, Ray Park, Ian McDiarmid, Samuel L Jackson, Brian Blessed, Sofia Coppola, Pernilla August. *Dir.* George Lucas.
Star Wars: Episode II – Attack of the Clones (2002) Ewan McGregor (Obi-Wan Kenobi), Natalie Portman (Padme), Christopher Lee (Count Dooku), Hayden Christensen (Anakin Skywalker), Samuel L. Jackson (Mace Windu), Yoda (voice of Frank Oz), Kenny Baker (R2-D2), Anthony Daniels (C-3PO). *Dir.* George Lucas.

Star Wars Episode III: Revenge of the Sith (2005) Ewan McGregor (Obi-Wan Kenobi), Natalie Portman (Padmé), Hayden Christensen (Anakin Skywalker), Ian McDiarmid (Supreme Chancellor Palpatine), Samuel L Jackson (Mace Windu), Jimmy Smits (Senator Bail Organa), Frank Oz (Voice of Yoda), Anthony Daniels (C-3PO), Christopher Lee (Count Dooku), Keisha Castle-Hughes (Queen of Naboo), Kenny Baker (R2-D2), Peter Mayhew (Chewbacca), George Lucas (Baron Papanoida – uncredited). After three years of fighting in the Clone Wars, Anakin Skywalker (pre-Darth Vader) concludes his journey towards the Dark Side of the Force, putting his friendship with Obi-Wan Kenobi and his marriage at risk. *Dir.* George Lucas.

Starman (1984) Jeff Bridges, Karen Allen. Alien arrives in Wisconsin. *Dir.* John Carpenter.

Starship Troopers (1997) Casper van Dien, Dina Meyer, Denise Richards, Jake Busey, Michael Ironside. *Dir.* Paul Verhoeven.

Starter for 10 (2006) James McAvoy (Brian Jackson), Dominic Cooper (Spencer), James Corden (Tone), Simon Woods (Josh), Catherine Tate (Julie Jackson), Elaine Tan (Lucy Chang), Alice Eve (Alice Harbinson), Rebecca Hall (Rebecca Epstein), Charles Dance (Michael Harbinson), Lindsay Duncan (Rose Harbinson), Benedict Cumberbatch (Patrick Watts), Mark Gatiss (Bamber Gascoigne). Brian Jackson, a student in his first year at Bristol University, has been a fan of *University Challenge* since childhood and seizes upon the opportunity to join Bristol's *University Challenge* team. The film's title is taken from the quiz show's famous catchphrase 'Your starter for 10'. David Nicholls wrote the screenplay from his own novel of the same name. Tom Hanks was the producer. *Dir.* Tom Vaughan.

Stay Hungry (1976) Jeff Bridges, Sally Field, Arnold Schwarzenegger, Robert Englund. *Dir.* Bob Rafelson.

Staying Alive (1983) John Travolta, Cynthia Rhodes, Finola Hughes, Steve Inwood. Sequel to *Saturday Night Fever*, Tony Manero becomes a Broadway dancer. *Dir.* Sylvester Stallone.

Steaming (1985) Vanessa Redgrave (Nancy), Sarah Miles (Sarah), Diana Dors (Violet), Patti Love, Brenda Bruce. *Dir.* Joseph Losey.

Steel Magnolias (1989) Sally Field, Dolly Parton, Shirley MacLaine, Daryl Hannah, Olympia Dukakis, Julia Roberts, Tom Skerritt. *Dir.* Herbert Ross.

Stepford Wives, The (1974) Katharine Ross, Paula Prentiss, Nanette Newman, Patrick O'Neal. *Dir.* Bryan Forbes.

Stepford Wives, The (2004) Nicole Kidman (Joanna), Glenn Close, Christopher Walken, John Cusack, Joan Cusack, Matthew Broderick, Bette Midler. Inferior remake of the 1974 film based on Ira Levin's novel. *Dir.* Frank Oz.

Sting, The (1973) Paul Newman, Robert Redford, Robert Shaw. *Dir.* George Roy Hill.

Stormy Monday (1988) Melanie Griffith (Kate), Tommy Lee Jones (Cosmo), Sting (Finney), Sean Bean (Brendan). *Dir.* Mike Figgis.

Strange Days (1995) Ralph Fiennes (Lenny Nero), Angela Bassett, Juliette Lewis, Tom Sizemore, Michael Wincott. *Dir.* Kathryn Bigelow.

Strangers on a Train (1951) Farley Granger, Robert Walker, Ruth Roman, Patricia Hitchcock. *Dir.* Alfred Hitchcock.

Straw Dogs (1971) Dustin Hoffman, Susan George, Peter Vaughan, David Warner, TP McKenna. Based on Gordon M Williams novel *The Siege of Trencher's Farm*. *Dir.* Sam Peckinpah. A 2011 remake was directed, produced, and written by Rod Lurie.

Striptease (1996) Demi Moore (Erin Grant), Burt Reynolds (David Dilbeck). Strip club name: The Eager Beaver. *Dir.* Andrew Bergman.

Stuart Little (1999) Geena Davis (Mrs Little), Hugh Laurie (Mr Little), Jonathan Lipnicki (George Little), Dabney Coleman (Dr Beechwood), voices of Michael J Fox (Stuart Little), Nathan Lane. *Dir.* Rob Minkoff.

Stuart Little 2 (2002) Geena Davis (Mrs Little), Hugh Laurie (Mr Little), voice of Michael J Fox (Stuart Little). *Dir.* Rob Minkoff

Substitute, The (1996) Tom Berenger, Ernie Hudson, Diane Venora. Commando-trained man takes over teaching position when his girlfriend is beaten up. *Dir.* Robert Mandel.

Sudden Impact (1983) Clint Eastwood (Callahan), Sondra Locke (Jennifer Spencer), Pat Hingle. *Dir.* Clint Eastwood.

Suddenly Last Summer (1959) Katharine Hepburn, Elizabeth Taylor, Mongomery Clift. *Dir.* Joseph L Mankiewicz.

Summer Holiday (1962) Cliff Richard, Lauri Peters, Melvyn Hayes, Una Stubbs. *Dir.* Peter Yates.

Summer of '42 (1971) Jennifer O'Neill, Gary Grimes, Jerry Houser. *Dir.* Robert Mulligan.

Sunday, Bloody Sunday (1971) Glenda Jackson, Peter Finch, Murray Head. *Dir.* John Schlesinger.

Sundowners, The (1960) Robert Mitchum, Deborah Kerr, Glynis Johns, Peter Ustinov. *Dir.* Fred Zinnemann.

Sunset (1988) Bruce Willis (Tom Mix), James Garner (Wyatt Earp), Malcolm McDowell. *Dir.* Blake Edwards.

Sunset Boulevard (1950) William Holden, Gloria Swanson, Erich Von Stroheim, Cecil B de Mille, Buster Keaton, Hedda Hopper. *Dir.* Billy Wilder.

Sunshine State (2002) Edie Falco (Marly Temple), Angela Bassett (Desiree Perry), Jane Alexander (Delia Temple), Ralph Waite (Furman Temple), James McDaniel (Reggie), Timothy Hutton (Jack Meadows), Mary Alice (Eunice Stokes), Bill Cobbs (Dr Lloyd), Mary Steenburgen (Francine Pickney), Miguel Ferrer (Lester). Attempts by property companies to redevelop a small Florida coastal town meet resistance by local residents. *Dir.* John Sayles.

Super Mario Brothers (1993) Bob Hoskins, Dennis Hopper, John Leguizamo. *Dir.* Rocky Morton and Annabel Jankel.

Supergirl (1984) Faye Dunaway (Selena), Helen Slater (Supergirl / Linda Lee), Peter O'Toole (Zeitar), Peter Cook, Simon Ward, Brenda Vaccaro, Mia Farrow. *Dir.* Jeannot Szwarc.

Superman (1978) Christopher Reeve, Marlon Brando, Susannah York, Margot Kidder, Glenn Ford, Gene Hackman, Trevor Howard. *Dir.* Richard Donner.

Superman 2 (1980) Christopher Reeve, Susannah York, Margot Kidder, Gene Hackman, Ned Beatty, Terence Stamp. *Dir.* Richard Lester.

Superman 3 (1983) Christopher Reeve, Richard Pryor, Jackie Cooper, Margot Kidder, Pamela Stephenson, Robert Vaughn. *Dir.* Richard Lester.

Superman 4: The Quest for Peace (1987) Christopher Reeve, Gene Hackman, Jackie Cooper, Margot Kidder. *Dir.* Sidney J Furie.

Superman Returns (2006) Brandon Routh (Clark Kent/Superman), Kate Bosworth (Lois Lane), Kevin Spacey (Lex Luthor), James Marsden (Richard White), Parker Posey (Kitty Kowalski), Frank Langella (Perry White), Sam Huntington (Jimmy Olsen), Eva Marie Saint (Martha Kent). Superman returns from a long and painful visit to Krypton in order to save Metropolis once more. *Dir.* Bryan Singer.

Surviving Picasso (1996) Anthony Hopkins (Picasso), Natascha McElhone (Françoise). *Dir.* James Ivory.

Swallows and Amazons (1974) Virginia McKenna, Ronald Fraser, Simon West, Sophie Neville. *Dir.* Claude Whatham.

Sweeney Todd: The Demon Barber of Fleet Street (2007) Johnny Depp (Benjamin Barker/Sweeney Todd), Helena Bonham Carter (Mrs Lovett), Alan Rickman (Judge Turpin), Jamie Campbell Bower (Anthony Hope), Timothy Spall (Beadle Bamford), Sacha Baron Cohen (Davie Collins/Signor Adolfo Pirelli), Ed Sanders (Tobias 'Toby' Ragg), Laura Michelle Kelly (Beggar Woman/Lucy Barker), Jayne Wisener (Johanna Barker). Adaptation of Stephen Sondheim and Hugh Wheeler's Tony Award-winning 1979 musical thriller. It retells the Victorian melodramatic tale of Sweeney Todd, an English barber who murders his customers with a straight razor and, with the help of his accomplice, Mrs Lovett, turns their remains into meat pies. All the songs are by Sondheim and include 'The Worst Pies in London' (sung by Bonham Carter), 'Green Finch and Linnett Bird' (sung by Wisener), 'Ladies in Their Sensitivities' (sung by Spall) and 'No Place Like London' (sung by Bower and Depp). *Dir.* Tim Burton.

Sweet Charity (1969) Shirley MacLaine, Ricardo Montalban, Chita Rivera, Stubby Kaye, Sammy Davis Jnr. *Dir.* Bob Fosse.

Sweet Liberty (1986) Alan Alda, Michael Caine, Michelle Pfeiffer, Lilian Gish, Bob Hoskins. College professor is alarmed as he watches the Hollywood filming of his historical novel. *Dir.* Alan Alda.

Swing Shift (1984) Goldie Hawn, Kurt Russell, Fred Ward, Christine Lahti. *Dir.* Jonathan Demme.

Swiss Family Robinson, The (1960) John Mills, Dorothy McGuire, James MacArthur, Janet Munro. *Dir.* Ken Annakin.

Sword of Sherwood Forest (1960) Richard Greene, Peter Cushing, Richard Pasco, Niall MacGinnis, Oliver Reed. *Dir.* Terence Fisher.

Swordfish (2001) John Travolta (Gabriel Shear), Hugh Jackman, Halle Berry (Ginger), Don Cheadle, Vinnie Jones (Marco). Computer hacker is hired by a secret agent and thief to steal government funds. *Dir.* Dominic Sena.

Syriana (2005) George Clooney (Bob Barnes), Matt Damon (Bryan Woodman), Christopher Plummer (Dean Whiting), Chris Cooper (Jimmy Pope), Robert Foxworth (Tommy Barton), Nicky Henson (Sydney Hewitt). Convoluted and contrived film about the politics of the oil industry, explored through the lives of those personally involved and affected by it. Clooney won an Academy Award for Best Actor in a Supporting Role and thoroughly deserved it for putting on 50lb for the role. *Dir.* Stephen Gaghan.

Taking of Pelham 123, The (1974) Walter Matthau, Robert Shaw, Martin Balsam, Hector Elizondo. Four gunmen hold a New York subway train to ransom. *Dir.* Joseph Sargent.

Tale of Two Cities, A (1958) Dirk Bogarde, Dorothy Tutin, Christopher Lee, Donald Pleasence, Alfie Bass. Remake of 1935 classic. *Dir.* Ralph Thomas.

Talented Mr Ripley, The (1999) Matt Damon (Tom Ripley), Jude Law (Dickie Greenleaf), Gwyneth Paltrow (Marge Sherwood), Cate Blanchett (Meredith Logue), Philip Seymour Hoffman (Freddie Miles). *Dir.* Anthony Minghella. Anthony Minghella wrote the screen play based on Patricia Highsmith's novel. The film was also a remake of the 1960 classic French film *Purple Noon* (French: *Plein Soleil*) starring Alain Delon in the title role and directed by René Clément.

Tales from the Darkside: The Movie (1991) Debbie Harry is a cannibal waiting to eat a young boy once he has told her 3 stories. *The Wraparound Story*: Debbie Harry (Betty), Matthew Lawrence (Timmy). *Lot 249*: Christian Slater, Steve Buscemi, Robert Sedgwick, Julianne Moore. *Cat from Hell*: David Johansen, William Hickey. *Lover's Vow*: James Remar, Rae Dawn Chong, Robert Klein. *Dir.* John Harrison.

Talk Radio (1988) Eric Bogosian (Barry Champlain), Ellen Greene, Leslie Hope, Alec Baldwin. *Dir.* Oliver Stone.

Tall Guy, The (1989) Jeff Goldblum (Dexter King), Emma Thompson (Kate Lemon), Rowan Atkinson (Ron Anderson). *Dir.* Mel Smith.

Tango and Cash (1989) Kurt Russell, Sylvester Stallone, Jack Palance, Teri Hatcher, Michael J Pollard. *Dir.* Andrei Konchalovsky.

Tank Girl (1994) Lon Petty, Ice T, Naomi Watts, Malcolm McDowell. *Dir.* Rachel Talalay.

Tank Malling (1988) Ray Winstone, Jason Connery, Amanda Donohoe, John Conteh, Terry Marsh, Nick Berry. *Dir.* James Marcus.

Tap (1989) Gregory Hines, Suzanne Douglas, Sammy Davis Jnr (Little Mo). *Dir.* Nick Castle.

Taps (1981) Timothy Hutton, George C Scott, Sean Penn, Tom Cruise. *Dir.* Harold Becker.

Taras Bulba (1962) Yul Brynner, Tony Curtis, Christine Kaufmann, Sam Wanamaker. *Dir.* J Lee Thompson.

Tarnation (2004) Having documented his life since the age of 11, Jonathan Caouette weaves a psychedelic whirlwind of snapshots, Super-8 movies, answering machine messages, video diaries, early short films, snippets of '80s pop culture and dramatic re-enactments to create an epic portrait of an American family torn apart by dysfunction and reunited through the power of love. *Dir.* Jonathan Caouette.

Tarzan the Apeman (1981) Bo Derek, Miles O'Keeffe (Tarzan), Richard Harris, John Phillip Law, Wilfrid Hyde-White. *Dir.* John Derek.

Taste of Honey, A (1961) Rita Tushingham, Dora Bryan, Murray Melvin. Based on Shelagh Delaney play. *Dir.* Tony Richardson.

Taxi Driver (1976) Robert De Niro (Travis Bickle), Jodie Foster, Cybill Shepherd, Harvey Keitel. *Dir.* Martin Scorsese.

Teenage Mutant Ninja Turtles (1990) Judith Hoag (April O'Neil), Elias Koteas (Casey Jones), Josh Pais (Raphael), Michelan Sisti (Michelangelo), Leif Tilden (Donatello), David Forman (Leonardo). Michael Pressman's 1991 sequel: *Teenage Mutant Ninja Turtles II: The Secret of the Ooze. Dir.* Steve Barron.

10 (2002) Mania Akbari (Driver), Amin Maher (Amin), Roya Arabshahi, Katayoun Taleidzadeh, Mandana Sharbaf, Amerie Moradi. Thought-provoking film about 10 conversations between a woman driver and the people to whom she gives lifts over a period of two days in Tehran. *Dir.* Abbas Kiarostami.

Ten Commandments, The (1956) Charlton Heston (Moses), Yul Brynner, Edward G Robinson, Anne Baxter, Yvonne De Carlo. *Dir.* Cecil B de Mille.

Ten Little Indians (1965) Wilfrid Hyde-White, Dennis Price, Stanley Holloway, Shirley Eaton, Hugh O'Brian, Daliah Lavi, Fabian, Mario Adorf. Based on Agatha Christie's novel. *Dir.* George Pollock.

Ten Rillington Place (1971) Richard Attenborough, John Hurt, Judy Geeson. Account of the Christie murders of the 1940s. *Dir.* Richard Fleischer.

10 Things I Hate About You (1999) Heath Ledger, Julia Stiles, Joseph-Gordon Levitt, Andrew Keegan, Susan May Pratt. *Dir.* Gil Junger. Teenage comedy loosely based on Shakespeare's *The Taming of the Shrew.*

10 to Midnight (1983) Charles Bronson (Leo Kessler), Lisa Eilbacher (Laurie), Andrew Stevens, Gene Davis. *Dir.* J Lee Thompson.

Tender Mercies (1982) Robert Duvall, Tess Harper, Betty Buckley. Robert Duvall sang the songs himself. *Dir.* Bruce Beresford.

Tequila Sunrise (1988) Mel Gibson (McKussic), Michele Pfeiffer, Kurt Russell, Raul Julia. *Dir.* Robert Towne.

Terminator, The (1984) Arnold Schwarzenegger, Linda Hamilton, Michael Biehn. *Dir.* James Cameron.

Terminator 2: Judgment Day (1991) Arnold Schwarzenegger, Linda Hamilton, Edward Furlong. *Dir.* James Cameron.

Terms of Endearment (1983) Shirley MacLaine, Jack Nicholson, Debra Winger, Danny De Vito. *Dir.* James L Brooks.

Texas Chainsaw Massacre, The (1974) Marilyn Burns, Allen Danziger, Paul A Partain. *Dir.* Tobe Hooper.

Thelma and Louise (1991) Susan Sarandon (Louise Sawyer), Geena Davis (Thelma Dickinson), Harvey Keitel, Brad Pitt. *Dir.* Ridley Scott.

There Will Be Blood (2007) Daniel Day-Lewis (Daniel Plainview), Paul Dano (Paul Sunday/Eli Sunday), Dillon Freasier (Young HW Plainview), Russell Harvard (Adult HW Plainview), Colleen Foy (Adult Mary Sunday), Hans Howes (William Bandy), Kevin J O'Connor (Henry), Barry Del Sherman (HB Ailman), Randall Carver (Mr Bankside), Coco Leigh (Mrs Bankside), David Warshofsky (HM Tilford), Tom Doyle (JJ Carter), Hope Elizabeth Reeves (Elizabeth), Ciarán Hinds (Fletcher), Sydney McCallister (Young Mary Sunday), David Willis (Abel Sunday), Kellie Hill (Ruth Sunday), Christine Olejniczak (Mother Sunday). Tough and passionate oil man Daniel Plainview adopts HW, the son of one of his workers killed in an accident. The complex plot sees HW lose his hearing in another accident but become his stepfather's partner of convenience. The subplot revolves around Plainview's relationship with the Bible-bashing Eli Sunday, who is ultimately killed by Plainview with a bowling ball. *Dir.* Paul Thomas Anderson.

There's No Business Like Show Business (1954) Ethel Merman, Dan Dailey, Marilyn Monroe, Donald O'Connor, Johnny Ray, Mitzi Gaynor, Hugh O'Brian. *Dir.* Walter Lang.

They Died with Their Boots On (1941) Errol Flynn, Olivia de Havilland, Arthur Kennedy, Anthony Quinn, Sidney Greenstreet. Biopic of General Custer. *Dir.* Raoul Walsh.

They Shoot Horses, Don't They? (1969) Gig Young, Jane Fonda, Susannah York, Red Buttons. Tragedy during a six-day marathon dance contest in the 1930s. *Dir.* Sydney Pollack.

Thief of Baghdad (1940) Conrad Veidt, John Justin (died in 2002), Sabu, June Duprez. The visual effects make this the best version of this oft-filmed story. The 1924 film starred Douglas Fairbanks, the 1960 film Steve Reeves, and the 1978 film Roddy McDowall, Frank Finlay, Terence Stamp and Peter Ustinov. The 1924 film won Oscars for photography and art direction. *Dir.* Michael Powell, Ludwig Berger and Tim Whelan.

Thin Man, The (1934) William Powell, Myrna Loy, Maureen O'Sullivan. *Dir.* WS Van Dyke.

Thing, The (1951) Robert Cornthwaite, Kenneth Tobey, James Arness (the Thing). GB title: *The Thing from Another World. Dir.* Christian Nyby.

Thing, The (1982) Kurt Russell, A Wilford Brimley, TK Carter. Remake of the 1951 film, although this 'Thing' is a metamorphic creature that can now enter and take over the protagonists. *Dir.* John Carpenter.

Things To Do in Denver When You're Dead (1995) Andy Garcia (Jimmy the Saint), Christopher Walken, Christopher Lloyd. *Dir.* Gary Fleder.

Thinner (1987) Robert John Burke (William Halleck). Stephen King wrote the novel under the pseudonym Richard Bachman. *Dir.* Tom Holland.

Third Man, The (1949) Orson Welles (Harry Lime), Joseph Cotten, Trevor Howard, Alida Valli, Bernard Lee, Wilfrid Hyde-White. *Dir.* Carol Reed.

Thirteen (2003) Holly Hunter (Melanie), Evan Rachel Wood (Tracy), Nikki Reed (Evie Zamora), Jeremy Sisto (Brady), Brady Corbett (Mason), Deborah Kara Unger (Brooke), Kip Pardue (Luke), Sarah Clarke (Birdie), DW Moffett (Travis). A young teenager becomes a drug-taking delinquent under the influence of her new best friend. *Dir.* Catherine Hardwicke.
Thirty-Nine Steps, The (1935) Robert Donat, Madeleine Carroll, Peggy Ashcroft. *Dir.* Alfred Hitchcock.
Thirty-Nine Steps, The (1959) Kenneth More, Taina Elg, Barry Jones. *Dir.* Ralph Thomas.
Thirty-Nine Steps, The (1978) Robert Powell, Karen Dotrice, John Mills. *Dir.* Don Sharp.
This Is Spinal Tap (1984) Michael McKean (David St Hubbins), Christopher Guest (Nigel Tufnel), Harry Shearer (Derek Smalls), RJ Parnell (Mick Shrimpton), Rob Reiner (Marti DiBerti). Cameos by Anjelica Huston, Patrick Macnee and Billy Crystal. *Dir.* Rob Reiner.
This Sporting Life (1963) Richard Harris, Rachel Roberts, Alan Badel, William Hartnell, Arthur Lowe. *Dir.* Lindsay Anderson.
Thomas Crown Affair, The (1968) Steve McQueen, Faye Dunaway, Yaphet Kotto. *Dir.* Norman Jewison. The 1999 remake starred Pierce Brosnan in the title role and was directed by John McTiernan.
Thoroughly Modern Millie (1967) Julie Andrews, Mary Tyler Moore, James Fox. *Dir.* George Roy Hill.
Three Amigos! (1986) Chevy Chase (Dusty Bottoms), Steve Martin (Lucky Day), Martin Short (Ned Nederlander). *Dir.* John Landis.
Three Colours: Blue (1993) Juliette Binoche, Benoît Régent, Florence Pernel. First part of trilogy based on the colours of the French tricolour. *Dir.* Krzysztof Kieslowski.
Three Colours: Red (1994) Juliette Binoche, Irene Jacob, Jean-Louis Trintignant, Julie Delpy. Third part of trilogy based on the colours of the French tricolour. *Dir.* Krzysztof Kieslowski.
Three Colours: White (1993) Zbigniew Zamachowski, Julie Delpy, Juliette Binoche, Florence Pernel. Second part of trilogy based on the colours of the French tricolour. *Dir.* Krzysztof Kieslowski.
Three Days of the Condor (1975) Robert Redford, Faye Dunaway, Cliff Robertson, Max Von Sydow. *Dir.* Sydney Pollack.
Three Faces of Eve, The (1957) Joanne Woodward, Lee J Cobb. Introduced by Alistair Cooke. *Dir.* Nunnally Johnson.
Three Fugitives (1989) Nick Nolte (Dan Lucas), Martin Short (Ned Perry), Sarah Rowland Doroff, James Earl Jones. *Dir.* Francis Veber.
300 (2007) Gerard Butler (King Leonidas of Sparta), Lena Headey (Queen Gorgo of Sparta), Giovani Cimmino (Pleistarchus, son of Leonidas and Gorgo), Dominic West (Theron, a corrupt Spartan politician), David Wenham (Dilios, narrator and Spartan soldier), Vincent Regan (Capt Artemis, Leonidas' captain), Tom Wisdom (Astinos, Capt Artemis' eldest son), Andrew Pleavin (Daxos, Arcadian soldier), Andrew Tiernan (Ephialtes, deformed Spartan outcast), Rodrigo Santoro (King Xerxes of Persia), Stephen McHattie (loyalist Spartan politician), Michael Fassbender (Stelios, highly skilled Spartan soldier), Peter Mensah (Persian messenger), Kelly Craig (Pythia), Tyler Neitzel (Young Leonidas), Robert Maillet (Über Immortal, giant), Patrick Sabongui (Persian General). Adaptation of the graphic novel of the same name by Frank Miller recounting the Battle of Thermopylae, albeit in a fantasy style. *Dir.* Zack Snyder.
Three Kings (1999) George Clooney (Major Archie Gates), Ice Cube (Chief Elgin), Mark Wahlberg (Sgt Barlow). *Dir.* David O. Russell.
Three Men and a Baby (1987) Tom Selleck (Peter), Steve Guttenberg (Michael), Ted Danson (Jack), Nancy Travis. *Dir.* Leonard Nimoy.
Three Men and a Little Lady (1990) Tom Selleck, Steve Guttenberg, Ted Danson, Nancy Travis, Sheila Hancock. *Dir.* Emilio Ardelino.
Three Men in a Boat (1956) David Tomlinson, Jimmy Edwards, Laurence Harvey, Shirley Eaton, Jill Ireland. *Dir.* Ken Annakin.
Three Musketeers, The (1993) Charlie Sheen, Kiefer Sutherland, Chris O'Donnell, Rebecca DeMornay. *Dir.* Stephen Herek.
Three Musketeers, The (The Queen's Diamonds), (1973) Michael York, Oliver Reed, Richard Chamberlain, Frank Finlay, Raquel Welch, Geraldine Chaplin, Spike Milligan, Faye Dunaway, Charlton Heston, Christopher Lee. *Dir.* Richard Lester.
Throw Momma from the Train (1987) Danny De Vito (Owen), Billy Crystal (Larry), Kim Greist (Beth), Anne Ramsey (Momma), Kate Mulgrew, Rob Reiner, Annie Ross, Oprah Winfrey (as herself). *Dir.* Danny De Vito.
Thunderball (1965) Sean Connery, Adolfo Celi (Emilio Largo), Claudine Auger (Domino). Title song performed by Tom Jones. *Dir.* Terence Young.
Thunderbolt and Lightfoot (1974) Clint Eastwood, Jeff Bridges, George Kennedy, Catherine Bach. *Dir.* Michael Cimino.
THX 1138 (1970) Robert Duvall, Donald Pleasence. *Dir.* George Lucas.
Tiger Bay (1959) Hayley Mills, John Mills, Horst Buchholz, Megs Jenkins. *Dir.* J Lee Thompson.
Tightrope (1984) Clint Eastwood (Wes Block), Geneviève Bujold (Beryl Thibodeax), Alison Eastwood (Amanda). *Dir.* Richard Tuggle.
Time after Time (1980) Malcolm McDowell, David Warner, Mary Steenburgen. Jack the Ripper in modern San Francisco via HG Wells's time machine. *Dir.* Nicholas Meyer.
Time Bandits (1981) John Cleese (Robin Hood), Sean Connery (Agamemnon), Ian Holm (Napoleon), Ralph Richardson (God), David Warner (Satan). *Dir.* Terry Gilliam.
Time Machine, The (1960) Rod Taylor, Yvette Mimieux, Alan Young, Sebastian Cabot. Victorian scientist builds a machine which transports him to the year 802701. *Dir.* George Pal.
Time of Your Life (1948) James Cagney, William Bendix, Jeanne Cagney, Wayne Morris, Broderick Crawford, Ward Bond. Group of eccentrics meet in a San Francisco bar. *Dir.* HC Potter.
Time to Kill, A (1996) Sandra Bullock, Matthew McConaughey, Samuel L Jackson, Donald & Kiefer Sutherland. Ku Klux Klan still has power in small Mississippi town. *Dir.* Joel Schumacher.
Tin Cup (1996) Kevin Costner, Rene Russo, Don Johnson. *Dir.* Ron Shelton.
Tin Men (1987) Richard Dreyfuss (Bill 'BB' Babowsky), Danny De Vito (Ernie Tilley), Barbara Hershey (Nora). *Dir.* Barry Levinson.
Titanic (1997) Kate Winslet, Leonardo DiCaprio. Famous song: 'My Heart Will Go On' sung by Céline Dion. *Dir.* James Cameron.
To Be or Not to Be (1983) Mel Brooks (Frederick Bronski), Anne Bancroft (Anna), Tim Matheson (Lt Andre Sobinski), Charles Durning (Col Erhardt), José Ferrer (Prof Siletski), Christopher Lloyd (Capt Schultz). *Dir.* Alan Johnson.
To Catch a Thief (1955) Cary Grant, Grace Kelly. *Dir.* Alfred Hitchcock.
To Die For (1995) Nicole Kidman, Matt Dillon, Joaquin Phoenix, David Cronenberg, George Segal (uncredited). Fame-obsessed weather woman on local TV station describes how she murdered her husband. *Dir.* Gus Van Sant.
To Have and Have Not (1945) Humphrey Bogart, Lauren Bacall, Walter Brennan, Hoagy Carmichael. US charter boat captain in Martinique gets involved with Nazis. *Dir.* Howard Hawks.
To Kill A Mockingbird (1962) Gregory Peck (Atticus Finch), Mary Badham (Jean Louise 'Scout' Finch), Philip Alford (Jem Finch), John Megna (Dill Harris), Frank Overton (Sheriff Heck Tate), Brock Peters (Tom Robinson), Rosemary Murphy (Miss Maudie Atkinson), Robert Duvall (Arthur 'Boo' Radley). Kim Stanley was the narrator as the older Scout Finch. Screenplay by Horton Foote and based on Harper Lee novel about a black man, Tom Robinson, being falsely accused of rape and the attempt to defend him by Atticus Finch, the whole struggle seen through the eyes of his young daughter, Scout. Music by Elmer Bernstein. Won Oscars for Best Screenplay and Best Actor. *Dir.* Robert Mulligan.
To Sir with Love (1967) Sidney Poitier, Judy Geeson, Suzy Kendall, Lulu. *Dir.* James Clavell.
Tokyo Godfathers (2003) Voices of Toru Emari (Gin), Yoshiaki Umegaki (Hana), Ava Okamoto (Miyuki), Shozo Iizuka (Oota), Seizo Kato (Mother), Hiroya Ishimaru (Yasuo). Animated story concerning three motley vagrants, an alcoholic, a teenage runaway and a former drag queen, who discover an abandoned baby and wander the streets of Tokyo in search of its mother. *Dir.* Satoshi Kon.
Tom Brown's Schooldays (1940) Freddie Bartholomew, Jimmy Lydon, Cedric Hardwicke, Billy Halop, Gale Storm. The 1951 remake starred Robert Newton and John Howard Davies (Tom). *Dir.* Robert Stevenson.
Tom Horn (1979) Steve McQueen, Linda Evans, Slim Pickens. *Dir.* William Wiard.
Tombstone (1993) Kurt Russell, Val Kilmer, Sam Elliott, Charlton Heston. Narrated by Robert Mitchum. *Dir.* George P Cosmatos.
Tomorrow Never Dies (1997) Pierce Brosnan (James Bond), Michelle Yeoh (Wai Lin), Teri Hatcher (Paris Carver), Jonathan Pryce (Elliot Carver). Theme song sung by Sheryl Crow. *Dir.* Roger Spottiswoode.

Too Hot to Handle (1991) Kim Basinger (Vicki Rosemary Anderson), Alec Baldwin (Charley Raymond Pearl), Robert Loggia, Elisabeth Shue, Armand Assante. *Dir.* Jerry Rees.
Tootsie (1982) Dustin Hoffman (Michael Dorsey / Dorothy), Teri Garr, Dabney Coleman, Jessica Lange, Charles Durning, Bill Murray, Sydney Pollack, Geena Davis. *Dir.* Sydney Pollack.
Top Gun (1986) Tom Cruise (Maverick), Kelly McGillis (Charlie), Val Kilmer (Ice), Tom Skerritt (Viper), Anthony Edwards (Goose), Michael Ironside (Jester), John Stockwell (Cougar), Meg Ryan (Carole), Tim Robbins (Merlin), Barry Tubb (Wolfman), Clarence Gilyard (Sundown). *Dir.* Tony Scott.
Top Hat (1935) Fred Astaire, Ginger Rogers. *Dir.* Mark Sandrich.
Tora! Tora! Tora! (1970) Martin Balsam, Joseph Cotten, Jason Robards. Events leading up to Pearl Harbor. *Dir.* Richard Fleischer.
Torn Curtain (1966) Paul Newman, Julie Andrews. *Dir.* Alfred Hitchcock.
Total Eclipse (1995) Leonardo DiCaprio (Arthur Rimbaud, the 19th-century poet), David Thewlis (Verlaine). *Dir.* Agnieszka Holand.
Total Recall (1990) Sharon Stone, Arnold Schwarzenegger (Doug Quaid), Rachel Ticotin, Michael Ironside. *Dir.* Paul Verhoeven.
Touching the Void (2003) Brendan Mackey (Joe Simpson), Nicholas Aaron (Simon Yates), Ollie Ryall (Richard Hawking), Joe Simpson (as himself), Simon Yates (as himself), Richard Hawking (as himself). Based on Joe Simpson's book. Two mountaineers recall an accident during a climb in Peru that left one of them for dead. *Dir.* Kevin Macdonald.
Tough Guys (1986) Burt Lancaster (Harry Doyle), Kirk Douglas (Archie Long), Charles Durning, Eli Wallach. *Dir.* Jeff Kanew.
Towering Inferno, The (1974) Paul Newman, Steve McQueen, William Holden, Faye Dunaway, Fred Astaire, OJ Simpson, Robert Wagner, Jennifer Jones, Robert Vaughn, Richard Chamberlain. *Dir.* John Guillermin.
A Town Like Alice (1956) Virginia McKenna, Peter Finch, Takagi, Marie Lohr, Maureen Swanson, Jean Anderson. Life among women prisoners of the Japanese in Malaya. Based on Nevil Shute's novel. *Dir.* Jack Lee.
Toxic Avenger, The (1985) Andree Maranda, Mitchell Cohen, Pat Ryan Jnr. Archetypal Troma trash-fest. Ron Fazio took over the role of the supercharged weakling in the sequels. *Dir.* Michael Herz.
Toy Story (1995) Voices of Tom Hanks, Don Rickles, Jim Varney, Tim Allen, John Ratzenberger. First full-length computer-animated feature film. Song: 'You've Got a Friend in Me' (music and lyrics by Randy Newman). *Dir.* John Lasseter.
Toy Story 2 (1999) Voice of Woody (Tom Hanks), Buzz Lightyear (Tim Allen), Hamm (John Ratzenberger), Mr Potato Head (Don Rickles), Slinky Dog (Jim Varney). *Dirs.* Ash Brannan, Lee Unkrich and John Lasseter.
Toy Story 3 (2010) New characters include Lots-O'-Huggin' Bear (Ned Beatty), Mr Pricklepants (Timothy Dalton), Stretch (Whoopi Goldberg) and Ken (Michael Keaton). The plot concerns the uncertain futures of the toys as their owner, Andy, prepares to leave for college. Blake Clark took over the role of Slinky Dog after Jim Varney's death. Currently the highest-grossing animated film of all time worldwide (surpassing Shrek 2). *Dir.* Lee Unkrich.
Toys (1992) Robin Williams, Michael Gambon, LL Cool J, Joan Cusack, Donald O'Connor. *Dir.* Barry Levinson.
Trading Places (1983) Dan Aykroyd, Eddie Murphy, Ralph Bellamy, Don Ameche, Jamie Lee Curtis, Denholm Elliott. *Dir.* John Landis.
Trail of the Pink Panther (1982) Peter Sellers, Joanna Lumley, Herbert Lom, David Niven. *Dir.* Blake Edwards.
Trainspotting (1996) Ewan McGregor, Ewen Bremner, Jonny Lee Miller, Robert Carlyle, Kelly MacDonald. *Dir.* Danny Boyle.
Transformers (2007) Shia LaBeouf (Sam Witwicky), Megan Fox (Mikaela Banes), John Turturro (Agent Simmons), Jon Voight (John Keller, US Secretary of Defense), Josh Duhamel (Capt William Lennox), Tyrese Gibson (Technical Sergeant Robert Epps), Anthony Anderson (Glen Whitmann). Teenager Sam Witwicky is involved in a war between the heroic Autobots and the evil Decepticons, two factions of alien robots who can disguise themselves by transforming into everyday machinery. Peter Cullen voices Optimus Prime, the Autobot leader who comes to Earth to destroy the All Spark in order to end the war. *Dir.* Michael Bay. The second film in the live-action Transformers series was released in 2009; *Transformers: Revenge of the Fallen,* produced by Steven Spielberg, opened to a disappointing critical response but huge box office success.
Trapeze (1956) Burt Lancaster, Tony Curtis, Gina Lollobrigida, Sid James. *Dir.* Carol Reed.
Treasure Island (1990) Charlton Heston, Oliver Reed, Christian Bale, Christopher Lee, Richard Johnson. *Dir.* Raúl Ruiz. Earlier versions 1934 (*Dir.* Victor Fleming); 1950 (*Dir.* Byron Haskin).
Treasure of the Sierra Madre, The (1948) Humphrey Bogart, Walter Huston, Tim Holt, John Huston. *Dir.* John Huston.
Tree of Life, The (2011) Brad Pitt (Mr O'Brien), Sean Penn (Jack). Film chronicling the origins and meaning of life by way of a middle-aged Texan's boyhood memories of the 1950s, against a narrative backdrop of the origins of the universe and the inception and end of life on Earth. Despite winning several awards the global response was divided with mass walkouts commonplace. *Dir.* Terrence Malick.
Trial, The (1962) Orson Welles, Jeanne Moreau, Anthony Perkins. Joseph K is tried and condemned for an unspecified crime. *Dir.* Orson Welles. 1992 remake (*Dir.* David Jones) starred Anthony Hopkins & Kyle MacLachlan.
Trilogy: On the Run, An Amazing Couple, After Life (2002) Francois Morel (Alain Costes), Dominique Blanc (Agnes Manise), Gilbert Melki (Pascal Manise), Lucas Belvaux (Bruno Le Roux), Catherine Frot (Jeanne), Valerie Mairesse (Claire), Raphaele Godin (Louise). The lives of a left-wing revolutionary, who is now a school teacher, a policeman and his drug-addicted wife, and a lawyer and his suspicious wife become intertwined. Three films that total 5 1/2 hours viewing but stand alone although featuring the same characters. *Dir.* Lucas Belvaux.
Triplettes de Belleville, Les (2002) Voices of Jean-Claude Donda, Michel Robin, Monica Viegas. A club-footed old lady, an overweight dog and a trio of aged singers help rescue a cyclist who is kidnapped during the Tour De France. GB title: *Belleville Rendezvous. Dir.* Sylvain Chomet.
Trouble with Girls, The (1969) Elvis Presley, Marlyn Mason, Vincent Price. Manager of an educational medicine show (a chautauqua) gets involved in a murder. *Dir.* Peter Tewksbury.
Troy (2004) Brad Pitt (Achilles), Brian Cox (Agamemnon), Brendan Gleeson (Menelaus), Diane Kruger (Helen), Eric Bana (Hector), Orlando Bloom (Paris), Julian Glover (Triopas), John Shrapnel (Nestor), Sean Bean (Odysseus), Julie Christie (Thetis, mother of Achilles), Peter O'Toole (King Priam of Troy). An adaptation of Homer's great epic, the film follows the assault on Troy by the united Greek forces and chronicles the fates of the men involved. *Dir.* Wolfgang Petersen.
True Grit (1969) John Wayne, Kim Darby, Glen Campbell, Robery Duvall, Dennis Hopper. *Dir.* Henry Hathaway. The 2010 remake starred Jeff Bridges as US Marshal Reuben J. "Rooster" Cogburn and was directed by Joel & Ethan Coen.
True Lies (1994) Arnold Schwarzenegger, Jamie Lee Curtis, Tom Arnold, Charlton Heston. US secret agent pretends to be a computer salesman to his wife. *Dir.* James Cameron.
True Romance (1993) Christian Slater, Patricia Arquette, Dennis Hopper, Val Kilmer, Brad Pitt, Gary Oldman, Christopher Walken. Quentin Tarantino story about a shop assistant and a callgirl who go on the run with a case full of cocaine. *Dir.* Tony Scott.
True Stories (1986) David Byrne (Narrator), John Goodman (Louis Fyne), Annie McEnroe (Kay Culver). Famous for the club scene where a multitude of characters mime to Byrne's voice. *Dir.* David Byrne.
Truly, Madly, Deeply (1990) Juliet Stevenson (Nina), Alan Rickman (Jamie), Bill Paterson, Michael Maloney. *Dir.* Anthony Minghella.
Truman Show, The (1998) Jim Carrey, Laura Linney, Noah Emmerich, Ed Harris, Natascha McElhone. *Dir.* Peter Weir.
Tunes of Glory (1960) Alec Guinness, John Mills, Susannah York, Dennis Price, Kay Walsh, Duncan Macrae. *Dir.* Ronald Neame.
Tupac: Resurrection (2003) Home movies, photographs and recited poetry illuminate the life of Tupac Shakur, the godfather of gangsta rap. *Dir.* Lauren Lazin.
Turbulence (1997) Lauren Holly (Teri Halloran), Ray Liotta (Ryan Weaver), Brenda Gleeson (Stubbs). *Dir.* Robert Butler.
Turner & Hooch (1989) Tom Hanks, Mare Winningham, John McIntire. Cop teams up with a dog to solve a murder. *Dir.* Roger Spottiswoode.
Turning Point, The (1977) Anne Bancroft, Shirley MacLaine, Mikhail Baryshnikov, Tom Skerritt. *Dir.* Herbert Ross.

Twelfth Night (1996) Helena Bonham Carter, Richard E Grant, Nigel Hawthorne, Mel Smith, Imogen Stubbs. *Dir.* Trevor Nunn.
Twelve Angry Men (1957) Henry Fonda, Lee J Cobb, EG Marshall, Jack Warden, Ed Begley, George Voskovec, Jack Klugman, John Fiedler, Martin Balsam, Robert Webber, Edward Binns, Joseph Sweeney. *Dir.* Sidney Lumet.
Twelve Monkeys (1995) Bruce Willis, Brad Pitt, Madeleine Stowe, Christopher Plummer. Set in 2035; a convict is sent back to 1996 to discover cause of pandemic disease. *Dir.* Terry Gilliam.
Twelve O'Clock High (1949) Gregory Peck, Hugh Marlowe, Gary Merrill, Dean Jagger. *Dir.* Henry King.
28 Days (2000) Sandra Bullock (Gwen Cummings), Viggo Mortensen (Eddie Boone), Dominic West (Jasper), Diane Ladd (Bobbie Jean), Elizabeth Perkins (Lily), Steve Buscemi (Cornell). An alcoholic woman is sent to a rehabilitation centre to dry out, hence the title. *Dir.* Betty Thomas.
28 Days Later ... (2002) Cillian Murphy, Naomie Harris, Megan Burns, Brendan Gleeson, Noah Huntley. Not a sequel to *28 Days* but a science fiction drama concerning a deadly virus unleashed on the British public following a raid on a primate research centre. The virus causes a deadly rage. *Dir.* Danny Boyle.
21 Grams (2003) Sean Penn (Paul), Benicio Del Toro (Jack), Naomi Watts (Cristina), Charlotte Gainsbourg (Mary), Melissa Leo (Marianne), Clea DuVall (Claudia), Danny Huston (Michael), Paul Calderon (Brown). After her family are killed in a traffic accident, a middle-class housewife's life becomes intertwined with those of an academic and an ex-convict in ways that involve drug-taking, adultery and murder. *Dir.* Alejandro Gonzalez Iñarritu.
Twenty Thousand Leagues under the Sea (1954) Kirk Douglas, James Mason, Paul Lukas, Peter Lorre. *Dir.* Richard Fleischer.
Twilight (2008) Robert Pattinson (Edward Cullen), Kristen Stewart (Bella Swan), Peter Facinelli (Carlisle Cullen), Elizabeth Reaser (Esme Cullen), Ashley Greene (Alice Cullen), Jackson Rathbone (Jasper Hale), Nikki Reed (Rosalie Hale), Kellan Lutz (Emmett Cullen), Billy Burke (Charlie Swan), Cam Gigandet (James), Rachelle Lefèvre (Victoria), Edi Gathegi (Laurent), Sarah Clarke (Renée Dwyer), Matt Bushell (Phil Dwyer), Taylor Lautner (Jacob Black), Gil Birmingham (Billy Black). Romantic fantasy with screenplay by Melissa Rosenberg, based on the novel of the same name by Stephenie Meyer, focusing on the development of the relationship between human teenager Bella Swan and vampire Edward Cullen. Although Edward only consumes animal blood Bella is threatened by three nomadic vampires, James, Victoria and Laurent. Meyer makes a cameo appearance as a customer in the diner where Bella and her father frequently eat. *Dir.* Catherine Hardwicke.
Twilight Saga, The: Breaking Dawn – Part 1 (2011) The fourth installment of The Twilight Saga series was directed by Bill Condon.
Twilight Saga, The: Breaking Dawn – Part 2 (2012) The fifth installment of The Twilight Saga series was directed by Bill Condon.
Twilight Saga, The: Eclipse (2010) The third installment of The Twilight Saga series was directed by David Slade.
Twilight Saga, The: New Moon (2009) The second film in the Twilight Saga series sees many of the original cast reprising their roles. Michael Sheen plays Aro, the leader of an ancient Italian vampire coven known as the Volturi. *Dir.* Catherine Hardwicke.
Twilight Zone: The Movie (1983) Dan Aykroyd, Vic Morrow, Scatman Crothers, Kevin McCarthy. Four supernatural stories. *Dir.* John Landis, Steven Spielberg, Joe Dante, George Miller.
Twin Town (1997) Rhys Ifans, Llyr Evans, Keith Allen. *Dir.* Kevin Allen.
Twinky (1969) Charles Bronson, Susan George, Trevor Howard. 16-yr-old schoolgirl marries a dissolute 40-yr-old American author. *Dir.* Richard Donner.
Twins (1988) Arnold Schwarzenegger (Julius Benedict), Danny De Vito (Vincent Benedict). *Dir.* Ivan Reitman.
Twister (1996) Helen Hunt, Bill Paxton, Lois Smith. *Dir.* Jan de Bont.
Two Days in the Valley (1996) Danny Aiello, James Spader, Jeff Daniels, Teri Hatcher, Louise Fletcher, Keith Carradine. *Dir.* John Herzfeld.
Two Much (1996) Antonio Banderas, Melanie Griffith, Danny Aiello, Daryl Hannah. Art dealer, engaged to wealthy woman, invents a twin brother so that he can marry her sister. *Dir.* Fernando Trueba.
Two Mules for Sister Sara (1969) Clint Eastwood, Shirley MacLaine. *Dir.* Don Siegel.
2001: A Space Odyssey (1968) Keir Dullea, Gary Lockwood, Leonard Rossiter, Robert Beatty, Douglas Rain (voice of Hal). Film based on Arthur C Clarke story 'The Sentinel'. Computer: Hal 9000 stands for Holistic Algorithmic. Journeyed to moon of Jupiter, although it was to the rings of Saturn in the book. *Dir.* Stanley Kubrick.
2010 (1984) Roy Scheider, Helen Mirren, John Lithgow, Keir Dullea. *Dir.* Peter Hyams.
Two-Way Stretch (1960) Peter Sellers, Wilfrid Hyde-White, Lionel Jeffries, Bernard Cribbins, David Lodge, Beryl Reid, Irene Handl. Three convicts break out of jail to do a robbery. *Dir.* Robert Day.
Ultimate Warrior, The (1975) Yul Brynner, Max Von Sydow, Joanna Miles. Set in New York AD 2012. *Dir.* Robert Clouse.
Unfinished Life, An (2005) Robert Redford (Einar Gilkyson), Jennifer Lopez (Jean Gilkyson), Morgan Freeman (Mitch Bradley). A woman, down on her luck and desperate to provide care for her daughter, moves in with her father-in-law from whom she is estranged. Through time, they learn to forgive each other and heal old wounds. *Dir.* Lasse Hallström.
Unforgiven (1992) Clint Eastwood, Gene Hackman, Morgan Freeman, Richard Harris. *Dir.* Clint Eastwood.
Unforgiven, The (1960) Burt Lancaster, Audrey Hepburn, Audie Murphy. *Dir.* John Huston.
Universal Soldier (1992) Jean-Claude Van Damme, Dolph Lundgren. *Dir.* Roland Emmerich.
Unsinkable Molly Brown, The (1964) Debbie Reynolds, Harve Presnell, Ed Begley. *Dir.* Charles Walters.
Untouchables, The (1987) Kevin Costner, Sean Connery (Jim Malone), Robert De Niro (Al Capone), Andy Garcia. *Dir.* Brian De Palma.
Up (2009) Voices of Ed Asner (Carl), Jordan Nagai (Russell), Christopher Plummer (Charles F Muntz). Computer-animated comedy-drama concerning elderly widower Carl Fredricksen and a young over-eager 'wilderness explorer' named Russell, who fly to South America in a floating house suspended from helium balloons. *Dir.* Pete Docter and Bob Peterson.
Up in the Air (2009) George Clooney (Ryan Bingham), Vera Farmiga (Alex Goran), Anna Kendrick (Natalie Keener), Jason Bateman (Craig Gregory), Amy Morton (Kara Bingham), Melanie Lynskey (Julie Bingham), JK Simmons (Bob), Sam Elliott (Maynard Finch), Danny R McBride (Jim Miller), Zach Galifianakis (Steve). Adaptation of Walter Kirn's 2001 novel *Up in the Air.* Ryan Bingham visits workplaces around the United States in order to conduct employee layoffs but his livelihood becomes threatened by the internet. *Dir.* Jason Reitman.
Uptown Saturday Night (1974) Sidney Poitier, Bill Cosby, Harry Belafonte, Flip Wilson, Richard Pryor. Friends pursue crooks who have stolen a winning lottery ticket. *Dir.* Sidney Poitier.
Urban Cowboy (1980) John Travolta, Debra Winger. *Dir.* James Bridges.
Used Cars (1980) Kurt Russell, Gerrit Graham, Jack Russell. *Dir.* Robert Zemeckis.
Usual Suspects, The (1995) Gabriel Byrne, Stephen Baldwin, Kevin Spacey, Pete Postlethwaite. *Dir.* Bryan Singer.
V for Vendetta (2005) Hugo Weaving (V), Natalie Portman (Evey Hammond), John Hurt (Chancellor Adam Sutler), Rupert Graves (Dominic), Sinéad Cusack (Delia Surridge), Stephen Rea (Chief Inspector Eric Finch), Clive Ashborn (Guy Fawkes), Tim Pigott-Smith (Creedy), Stephen Fry (Gordon Deitrich). A shadowy freedom fighter known only as 'V' uses terrorist tactics to fight against his totalitarian society. *Dir.* James McTeigue.
Valentino (1977) Rudolf Nureyev, Leslie Caron, Michelle Phillips. *Dir.* Ken Russell.
Valley of the Dolls (1967) Barbara Parkins, Patty Duke, Susan Hayward, Sharon Tate, Martin Milner. *Dir.* Mark Robson.
Vanilla Sky (2001) Tom Cruise (David Aames), Penelope Cruz, Cameron Diaz, Kurt Russell, Jason Lee, Noah Taylor, Timothy Spall, Tilda Swinton. Accused of murder, a publishing tycoon explains to a prison psychiatrist how his life fell apart. *Dir.* Cameron Crowe.
Vera Drake (2004) Imelda Staunton (Vera Drake), Richard Graham (George), Eddie Marsan (Reg), Anna Keaveney (Nellie), Sam Troughton (David), Alex Kelly (Ethel). Abortionist Vera Drake finds her beliefs and practices clash with the morals of 1950s Britain, a conflict that leads to tragedy for her family. Extraordinary film veiled in secrecy throughout its unscripted filming which gives a dramatic heightening of its content. *Dir.* Mike Leigh.

Verdict, The (1982) Paul Newman, James Mason, Charlotte Rampling. *Dir.* Sidney Lumet.
Vertigo (1958) James Stewart (Detective John 'Scottie' Ferguson), Kim Novak (Madeleine Elster / Judy Barton), Barbara Bel Geddes (Marjorie 'Midge' Wood), Tom Helmore (Gavin Elster), Henry Jones (Coroner). A detective with a fear of heights is hired by old schoolfriend Gavin Elster to follow his wife Madeleine. Ferguson falls in love with her but she apparently falls to her death. Then he meets her double. *Dir.* Alfred Hitchcock.
Very Important Person (1961) James Robertson Justice, Stanley Baxter, Leslie Phillips. *Dir.* Ken Annakin.
Vice Versa (1988) Judge Reinhold, Fred Savage, Corinne Bohrer. *Dir.* Brian Gilbert.
Vicky Cristina Barcelona (2008) Javier Bardem (Juan Antonio Gonzalo), Penelope Cruz (María Elena), Scarlett Johansson (Cristina), Rebecca Hall (Vicky), Chris Messina (Doug), Patricia Clarkson (Judy Nash), Kevin Dunn (Mark Nash). Two American women, Vicky and Cristina, spend a summer in Barcelona, where they meet an artist who is attracted to both of them while still enamoured of his mentally and emotionally unstable ex-wife María Elena. *Dir.* Woody Allen.
Victor / Victoria (1982) James Garner, Julie Andrews, Robert Preston, John Rhys-Davies. *Dir.* Blake Edwards.
View to a Kill, A (1985) Roger Moore, Christopher Walken (Max Zorin), Grace Jones (May Day), Tanya Roberts (Stacey Sutton), Patrick MacNee, Fiona Fullerton, David Yip. Title song performed by Duran Duran. *Dir.* John Glen.
Vikings, The (1958) Kirk Douglas, Tony Curtis, Janet Leigh, Ernest Borgnine. Orson Welles was the narrator. *Dir.* Richard Fleischer.
Village of the Damned (1960) George Sanders, Barbara Shelley, Laurence Naismith. Village women simultaneously give birth to fair-haired, genius level, telepathic children with eerie results. *Dir.* Wolf Rilla.
Village of the Damned (1995) Christopher Reeve, Kirstie Alley, Linda Kozlowski, Mark Hamill. *Dir.* John Carpenter.
Villain (1971) Richard Burton, Ian McShane, Nigel Davenport, TP McKenna. *Dir.* Michael Tuchner.
VIPs, The (1963) Richard Burton, Elizabeth Taylor, Rod Taylor, Maggie Smith, Orson Welles, Louis Jourdan, Lance Percival. *Dir.* Anthony Asquith.
Virginian, The (1929) Gary Cooper, Walter Huston. 1946 remake starred Joel McCrea & Brian Donlevy. *Dir.* Victor Fleming.
Viva Las Vegas (1964) Elvis Presley, Ann-Margret. Presley plays a sports car racer. *Dir.* George Sidney.
Viva Zapata (1952) Marlon Brando, Anthony Quinn, Jean Peters, Joseph Wiseman. *Dir.* Elia Kazan.
Volcano (1997) Tommy Lee Jones (Mike Roark), Gaby Hoffmann, Don Cheadle, Anne Heche (Dr Amy Barnes). *Dir.* Mick Jackson.
Von Ryan's Express (1965) Frank Sinatra, Trevor Howard, Sergio Fantoni. *Dir.* Mark Robson.
Voyage to the Bottom of the Sea (1961) Walter Pidgeon, Robert Sterling, Joan Fontaine, Peter Lorre, Barbara Eden. Spawned a long-running TV series. *Dir.* Irwin Allen.
Wag the Dog (1998) Dustin Hoffman, Robert De Niro. *Dir.* Barry Levinson.
Wages of Fear, The (1953) Yves Montand, Folco Lulli, Peter Van Eyck, Charles Vanel. Nitro-glycerine is the substance transported over dangerous roads to put out oil well fire. *Dir.* Henri-Georges Clouzot.
Wait until Dark (1967) Audrey Hepburn, Alan Arkin, Richard Crenna, Efrem Zimbalist Jnr. *Dir.* Terence Young.
Walk the Line (2005) Joaquin Phoenix (Johnny Cash), Reese Witherspoon (June Carter), Ginnifer Goodwin (Vivian Cash), Robert Patrick (Ray Cash), Dallas Roberts (Sam Phillips), Dan John Miller (Luther Perkins), Larry Bagby (Marshall Grant), Shelby Lynne (Carrie Cash), Tyler Hilton (Elvis Presley), Waylon Malloy Payne (Jerry Lee Lewis), Shooter Jennings (Waylon Jennings), Sandra Ellis Lafferty (Maybelle Carter), Dan Beene (Ezra Carter), Clay Steakley (WS 'Fluke' Holland), Johnathan Rice (Roy Orbison), Johnny Holiday (Carl Perkins). Chronicles the first half of country music legend Johnny Cash's life, from his childhood on an Arkansas cotton farm to his rise to fame after recording alongside Elvis Presley, Jerry Lee Lewis and Carl Perkins at Sun Records in Memphis. Reese Witherspoon won an Academy Award as Best Actress for her role as the country singer's wife June Carter. *Dir.* James Mangold.
Walkabout (1970) Jenny Agutter, Lucien John, David Gulpilil. *Dir.* Nicolas Roeg.
WALL·E (2008) Voices of Ben Burtt (WALL·E), Elissa Knight (EVE), Jeff Garlin (Capt B McCrea), Fred Willard (Shelby Forthright), John Ratzenberger (John), Kathy Najimy (Mary), Sigourney Weaver (Axiom's computer). Computer-animated science-fiction film produced by Pixar Animation Studios. The plot concerns the title character, a robot (Waste Allocation Load Lifter Earth Class), who is designed to clean up a waste-covered Earth of the future. He eventually falls in love with another robot, EVE (Extraterrestrial Vegetation Evaluator), and follows her into outer space on an adventure that changes the destiny of both his kind and humanity. *Dir.* Andrew Stanton.
Wallace & Gromit in The Curse of the Were-Rabbit (2005) Voices of Peter Sallis (Wallace/Hutch), Ralph Fiennes (Victor Quartermaine), Helena Bonham Carter (Lady Campanula Tottington), Liz Smith (Mrs Mulch), Geraldine McEwan (Miss Thripp), Peter Kay (PC Mackintosh), Mark Gatiss (Miss Blight), Nicholas Smith (Reverend Clement Hedges), John Thomson (Mr Windfall). Wallace and his loyal dog, Gromit, set out to discover the mystery behind the garden sabotage that plagues their village and threatens the annual giant vegetable growing contest. The film won an Academy Award for Best Animated Feature. *Dir.* Steve Box and Nick Park.
War, The (1994) Kevin Costner, Elijah Wood, LaToya Chisholm. *Dir.* Jon Avnet.
War Games (1983) Matthew Broderick, Dabney Coleman, John Wood. *Dir.* John Badham.
War of the Roses, The (1989) Michael Douglas, Kathleen Turner, Danny De Vito. *Dir.* Danny De Vito.
War of the Worlds, The (1953) Gene Barry (Dr Clayton Forrester), Ann Robinson (Sylvia Van Buren), Les Tremayne (Maj. Gen. Mann), Robert Cornthwaite (Dr Pryor), Sandro Giglio (Dr Bilderbeck), Lewis Martin (Pastor Dr Matthew Collins). The film adaptation of the HG Wells story told on radio of the invasion of Earth by Martians. *Dir.* Byron Haskin. The 2005 Steven Spielberg film *War of the Worlds* was an inferior remake starring Tom Cruise as Ray Ferrier, who tries to save his family from alien tripod machines ripping up the tarmac of American cities. The film featured cameos by the original stars, Gene Barry and Ann Robinson, as grandparents.
Waterworld (1995) Kevin Costner, Dennis Hopper, Jeanne Tripplehorn. *Dir.* Kevin Reynolds.
Way We Were, The (1973) Robert Redford, Barbra Streisand, Patrick O'Neal. *Dir.* Sydney Pollack.
Wedding Banquet, The (1993) Mitchell Lichtenstein, Winston Chao, May Chin. *Dir.* Ang Lee.
Welcome II The Terrordome (1994) Suzette Llewellyn, Saffron Burrows. *Dir.* Ngozi Onwurah.
Welcome to the Dollhouse (1995) Heather Matarazzo, Victoria Davis. *Dir.* Todd Solondz.
We're No Angels (1954) Humphrey Bogart, Peter Ustinov, Aldo Ray, Basil Rathbone. *Dir.* Michael Curtiz.
We're No Angels (1989) Robert De Niro, Sean Penn, Demi Moore. Remake of the 1954 film. *Dir.* Neil Jordan.
West Side Story (1961) Natalie Wood, Richard Beymer, Russ Tamblyn, George Chakiris, Rita Moreno. *Dir.* Robert Wise.
Westerner, The (1940) Gary Cooper, Walter Brennan, Charlton Heston. *Dir.* William Wyler.
Westworld (1973) Yul Brynner, Richard Benjamin, James Brolin. *Dir.* Michael Crichton.
Whatever Happened to Baby Jane? (1962) Bette Davis, Joan Crawford, Victor Buono. *Dir.* Robert Aldrich.
What's New Pussycat? (1965) Peter O'Toole, Peter Sellers, Woody Allen, Ursula Andress, Capucine. *Dir.* Woody Allen.
What's Up Doc? (1972) Barbra Streisand, Ryan O'Neal. *Dir.* Peter Bogdanovich.
When Saturday Comes (1996) Sean Bean (Jimmy Muir), Emile Lloyd (Annie Doherty), Pete Postlethwaite. *Dir.* Maria Giese.
When We Were Kings (1996) Documentary of Muhammad Ali's defeat of George Foreman in Zaïre. *Dir.* Leon Gast.
Where Eagles Dare (1969) Richard Burton, Clint Eastwood, Mary Ure. Seven Allied agents land in Bavarian Alps to rescue officer from impregnable castle during World War II. *Dir.* Brian G Hutton.
Whistle down the Wind (1961) Hayley Mills, Bernard Lee, Alan Bates, Norman Bird. Three children think a murderer on the run is Jesus. *Dir.* Bryan Forbes.
White Christmas (1954) Bing Crosby, Danny Kaye, Rosemary Clooney, Dean Jagger. *Dir.* Michael Curtiz.
White Countess, The (2005) Natasha Richardson (Countess Sofia Belinskya), Ralph Fiennes (Todd Jackson), Vanessa Redgrave (Princess Vera Belinskya), Lynn Redgrave (Olga Belinskya), Madeleine Potter (Grushenka), Madeleine Daly (Katya), John Wood (Prince

Peter Belinsky). Set in 1930s Shanghai, where a blind American diplomat develops a curious relationship with a young Russian refugee who works odd – and sometimes illicit – jobs to support members of her dead husband's aristocratic family. Notable for being the final Merchant Ivory production. *Dir.* James Ivory.

White Heat (1949) James Cagney, Edmond O'Brien, Margaret Wycherly, Virginia Mayo. *Dir.* Raoul Walsh.

White Hunter, Black Heart (1990) Clint Eastwood (John Wilson), Jeff Fahey (Pete Verrill), Marisa Berenson (Kay Gibson), Timothy Spall (Hodkins). Fictionalised account of John Huston during the shooting of *The African Queen. Dir.* Clint Eastwood.

White Men Can't Jump (1992) Wesley Snipes, Woody Harrelson, Rosie Perez. *Dir.* Ron Shelton.

White Mischief (1987) Charles Dance, Greta Scacchi, John Hurt, Sarah Miles, Trevor Howard. *Dir.* Michael Radford.

White Nights (1985) Mikhail Baryshnikov, Gregory Hines, Helen Mirren, Isabella Rossellini. Best Song Oscar for 'Say You, Say Me' by Lionel Richie. *Dir.* Taylor Hackford.

White Ribbon, The (2009) Christian Friedel (school teacher), Ernst Jacobi (narrator/school teacher as an old man), Leonie Benesch (Eva), Ulrich Tukur (baron), Ursina Lardi (Baroness Marie-Louise), Fion Mutert (Sigmund), Michael Kranz (private tutor), Burghart Klaußner (pastor), Rainer Bock (doctor), Steffi Kühnert (Anna), Maria-Victoria Dragus (Klara), Leonard Proxauf (Martin), Levin Henning (Adolf), Johanna Busse (Margarete), Thibault Sérié (Gustav). Drama set in the Protestant village of Eichwald, Germany between July 1913 and 10 August 1914. The pastor, the doctor and the baron rule the roost over women, children and peasant farmers. The film's name derives from the puritanical pastor's persuasion to make his errant children wear white ribbons of purity to remind them of the path of righteousness from which they have strayed. The film ends with the assassination of the heir to the throne of the Austro-Hungarian Empire, Archduke Franz Ferdinand, in Sarajevo, and the declaration of war on Serbia by Austria–Hungary. *Dir.* Michael Haneke.

White Squall (1996) Jeff Bridges (Christopher 'Skipper' Sheldon). Boat: *The Albatross. Dir.* Ridley Scott.

Who Framed Roger Rabbit? (1988) Bob Hoskins (Eddie Valiant). Animation synchronised with live action. Christopher Lloyd (Judge Doom). Jessica Rabbit's speaking voice was Kathleen Turner and singing voice was Amy Irving. *Dir.* Robert Zemeckis.

Whoops Apocalypse (1986) Loretta Swit (President Adams), Peter Cook (Sir Mortimer Chris). *Dir.* Tom Bussmann.

Who's Afraid of Virginia Woolf? (1966) Richard Burton, Elizabeth Taylor, George Segal, Sandy Dennis. Based on Edward Albee's play. *Dir.* Mike Nichols.

Wicked Lady, The (1945) Margaret Lockwood, James Mason, Michael Rennie. The 1983 remake starred Faye Dunaway in the Lockwood role. *Dir.* Leslie Arliss.

Wild Bunch, The (1969) William Holden, Ernest Borgnine, Robert Ryan, Warren Oates, Edmond O'Brien. *Dir.* Sam Peckinpah.

Wild One, The (1954) Marlon Brando, Lee Marvin, Mary Murphy. The Garutso lens created the sharpness of photography. *Dir.* Laslo Benedek.

Willard (1971) Bruce Davison, Elsa Lanchester, Ernest Borgnine, Sondra Locke. Shy, introverted man breeds and trains rats to kill his enemies. *Dir.* Daniel Mann.

William Shakespeare's Romeo and Juliet (1996) Leonardo DiCaprio, Claire Danes, Brian Dennehy, Pete Postlethwaite. *Dir.* Baz Luhrmann.

Willy Wonka and the Chocolate Factory (1971) Gene Wilder (Willy Wonka), Jack Albertson (Grandpa Joe), Peter Ostrum (Charlie Bucket), Roy Kinnear (Mr Henry Salt), Julie Dawn Cole (Veruca Salt), Leonard Stone (Mr Sam Beauregarde), Denise Nickerson (Violet Beauregarde), Nora Denney as Dodo Denney (Mrs Teevee), Paris Themmen (Mike Teevee). Screen adaptation of Roald Dahl's famous book *Charlie and the Chocolate Factory.* The world is astounded when Willy Wonka, for years a recluse in his factory, announces that five lucky people will be given a tour of the factory and shown all the secrets of his amazing candy, and one will win a lifetime supply of Wonka chocolate. Young Charlie is the proud owner of one of the five golden tickets and along with four somewhat odious other children, gets the chance of a lifetime. Along the way, mild disasters befall each of the other children, but can Charlie beat the odds and grab the brass ring? *Dir.* Mel Stuart. See also *Charlie and the Chocolate Factory* (2005).

Wind in the Willows, The (1996) Steve Coogan (Mole), Eric Idle (Rat), Terry Jones (Toad), Stephen Fry, Julia Sawalha. *Dir.* Terry Jones.

Wind that Shakes the Barley, The (2006) Cillian Murphy (Damien), Padraic Delaney (Teddy), Liam Cunningham (Dan), Gerard Kearney (Donnacha), William Ruane (Gogan). A sympathetic look at Republicans in early 20th century Ireland, and in particular two brothers torn apart by anti-British rebellion. *Dir.* Ken Loach.

Winslow Boy, The (1948) Robert Donat, Cedric Hardwicke, Margaret Leighton, Wilfrid Hyde-White, Kathleen Harrison. Father endeavours to prove the innocence of naval cadet son, expelled for stealing postal order. *Dir.* Anthony Asquith.

Wish You Were Here (1987) Emily Lloyd, Tom Bell, Clare Clifford. *Dir.* David Leland.

Witches of Eastwick, The (1987) Jack Nicholson, Cher, Susan Sarandon, Michelle Pfeiffer. *Dir.* George Miller.

Witness (1985) Harrison Ford, Kelly McGillis, Lukas Haas, Alexander Godunov. *Dir.* Peter Weir.

Witness for the Prosecution (1957) Charles Laughton, Tyrone Power, Marlene Dietrich, Elsa Lanchester. *Dir.* Billy Wilder.

Wiz, The (1978) Diana Ross, Michael Jackson, Lena Horne, Richard Pryor. *Dir.* Sidney Lumet.

Wizard of Oz, The (1939) Judy Garland, Frank Morgan, Bert Lahr (Lion), Jack Haley (Tin Man), Ray Bolger (Scarecrow). *Dir.* Victor Fleming.

Wolf (1994) Jack Nicholson, Michelle Pfeiffer, James Spader, Kate Nelligan, Christopher Plummer. *Dir.* Mike Nichols.

Woman in a Dressing Gown (1957) Yvonne Mitchell, Anthony Quayle, Sylvia Syms, Andrew Ray. *Dir.* J Lee Thompson.

Women in love (1969) Glenda Jackson, Jennie Linden, Alan Bates, Oliver Reed. Famous for its nude wrestling scene between Bates and Reed. *Dir.* Ken Russell.

Working Girl (1988) Harrison Ford, Sigourney Weaver, Melanie Griffith, Alec Baldwin, Olympia Dukakis. *Dir.* Mike Nichols.

Working Girls (1986) Louise Smith, Ellen McElduff, Amanda Goodwin. *Dir.* Lizzie Borden.

World Is Not Enough, The (1999) Pierce Brosnan, Robert Carlyle (Renard), Sophie Marceau (Elektra), Denise Richards (Christmas Jones), Judi Dench (M), Robbie Coltrane, John Cleese (R). Theme song performed by Shirley Manson of Garbage. *Dir.* Michael Apted.

World of Suzie Wong, The (1960) William Holden, Nancy Kwan, Sylvia Syms, Michael Wilding, Jackie Chan. *Dir.* Richard Quine.

World Trade Center (2006) Nicolas Cage (John McLoughlin), Michael Pena as Michael Peña (Will Jimeno), Maria Bello (Donna McLoughlin), Connor Paolo (Steven McLoughlin), Anthony Piccininni (JJ McLoughlin), Alexa Gerasimovich (Erin McLoughlin), Morgan Flynn (Caitlin McLoughlin), Maggie Gyllenhaal (Allison Jimeno). Two Port Authority police officers become trapped under the rubble of the World Trade Center. *Dir.* Oliver Stone.

Wrong Box, The (1966) Ralph Richardson, John Mills, Michael Caine, Peter Cook, Dudley Moore, Peter Sellers, Tony Hancock, Nanette Newman. Two Victorian brothers are last survivors of a tontine agreement and try to kill each other. *Dir.* Bryan Forbes.

Wrong Man, The (1957) Henry Fonda, Vera Miles, Anthony Quayle. *Dir.* Alfred Hitchcock.

Wuthering Heights (1939) Laurence Olivier, Merle Oberon, David Niven, Flora Robson. *Dir.* William Wyler.

Wuthering Heights (1970) Timothy Dalton, Anna Calder-Marshall, Ian Ogilvy. *Dir.* Robert Fuest.

Wyatt Earp (1994) Kevin Costner, Dennis Quaid, Gene Hackman, Mark Harmon, Isabella Rossellini. *Dir.* Lawrence Kasdan.

X-Men: The Last Stand (2006) Patrick Stewart (Professor Charles Xavier), Hugh Jackman (Logan/Wolverine), Halle Berry (Ororo Munroe/Storm), Ian McKellen (Eric Lensherr/Magneto), Famke Janssen (Jean Grey/Phoenix), Anna Paquin (Marie/Rogue), Kelsey Grammer (Dr Hank McCoy/Beast), James Marsden (Scott Summers/Cyclops), Rebecca Romijn (Raven Darkholme/Mystique), Shawn Ashmore (Bobby Drake/Iceman), Aaron Stanford (John Allerdyce/Pyro), Vinnie Jones (Cain Marko/Juggernaut), Ben Foster (Warren Worthington III/Angel), Ellen Page (Kitty Pryde), Michael Murphy (Warren Worthington II). When a cure is found to treat mutations, lines are drawn among the X-Men, led by Professor Charles Xavier, and the Brotherhood, a band of powerful mutants organised under Xavier's former ally, Magneto. *Dir.* Brett Ratner. The third in a series of X-Men films; the first two, *X-Men* (2000) and *X–2* (2003), were directed by Bryan Singer. The series continued with *X-Men Origins: Wolverine* (2009) directed by Gavin Hood and *X-Men: First Class* (2011) directed by Matthew Vaughn (a prequel set primarily in 1962 during the Cuban Missile Crisis).

Xanadu (1980) Olivia Newton-John, Gene Kelly, Michael Beck. *Dir.* Robert Greenwald.

xXx (2002) Samuel L Jackson (Agent Gibbons), Vin Diesel (Xander Cage / Triple X), Marton Csokas (Yorgi), Asia Argento (Yelena). Spy thriller in which agents infiltrate a cult group, Anarchy 99, who have made a biological weapon named Silent Night. *Dir.* Rob Cohen.

Y Tu Mama También (2001) Maribel Verdu (Luisa Cortes), Gael Garcia Bernal (Julio Zapata). Two Mexican youths learn about life and love from an older woman while travelling to find the perfect beach. *Dir.* Alfonso Cuaron.

Yankee Doodle Dandy (1942) James Cagney, Walter Huston, Eddie Foy Jnr. Life story of dancer George M Cohan. *Dir.* Michael Curtiz.

Yanks (1979) Vanessa Redgrave, Richard Gere, Rachel Roberts. *Dir.* John Schlesinger.

Year of the Dragon, The (1985) Mickey Rourke, John Lone, Ariane. *Dir.* Michael Cimino.

Yearling, The (1946) Gregory Peck, Jane Wyman. *Dir.* Clarence Brown.

Yellow Rolls Royce, The (1964) Rex Harrison, Jeanne Moreau, Omar Sharif, Ingrid Bergman, Shirley MacLaine. Aristocrat, gangster and millionairess in turn own an expensive car. *Dir.* Anthony Asquith.

Yellowbeard (1983) Graham Chapman, Peter Cook, Marty Feldman, Eric Idle, John Cleese, Spike Milligan, Beryl Reid, Susannah York. *Dir.* Mel Damski.

Yentl (1983) Barbra Streisand, Mandy Patinkin, Amy Irving, Nehemiah Persoff. Barbra Streisand also co-wrote with Jack Rosenthal. *Dir.* Barbra Streisand.

You Only Live Twice (1967) Sean Connery, Akiko Wakabayashi (Aki), Tetsuro Tamba, Charles Gray, Donald Pleasence (Blofeld), Bernard Lee, Mie Hama (Kissy Suzuki). Theme song sung by Nancy Sinatra. *Dir.* Lewis Gilbert.

Young Adam (2003) Ewan McGregor (Joe Taylor), Tilda Swinton (Ella Gault), Peter Mullan (Les Gault), Emily Mortimer (Cathie Dimly). Set in the 1950s, concerning a Scottish drifter who brings death and mayhem to those who cross his path. Based on a novel by Alexander Trocchi. *Dir.* David Mackenzie.

Young Bess (1953) Jean Simmons, Stewart Granger, Charles Laughton (Henry VIII), Kay Walsh, Deborah Kerr. *Dir.* George Sidney.

Young Frankenstein (1974) Gene Wilder, Marty Feldman, Madeline Kahn, Gene Hackman. *Dir.* Mel Brooks.

Young Guns (1988) Emilio Estevez, Kiefer Sutherland, Charlie Sheen, Terence Stamp, Jack Palance, Patrick Wayne. *Dir.* Christopher Cain.

Young Guns II (1990) Emilio Estevez, Kiefer Sutherland, Lou Diamond Phillips, Christian Slater, James Coburn. *Dir.* Geoff Murphy.

Zardoz (1974) Sean Connery, Charlotte Rampling, John Alderton. Set in the year 2293. *Dir.* John Boorman.

Ziegfeld Follies (1946) Fred Astaire, Lucille Ball, Jimmy Durante, Fanny Brice, Lena Horne, Esther Williams, Judy Garland, Red Skelton, Gene Kelly. *Dir.* Vincente Minnelli.

Zorba the Greek (1964) Anthony Quinn, Alan Bates, Lila Kedrova. *Dir.* Michael Cacoyannis.

Zorro the Gay Blade (1981) George Hamilton, Lauren Hutton, Brenda Vaccaro, Ron Leibman, James Booth. *Dir.* Peter Medak.

Zulu (1964) Stanley Baker, Jack Hawkins, Michael Caine, James Booth, Ivor Emmanuel. *Dir.* Cy Endfield.

Zulu Dawn (1979) Burt Lancaster, Denholm Elliott, Peter O'Toole, John Mills. *Dir.* Douglas Hickox. Famous for being the last listed film in *Halliwell's Film Guide.*

NB: It is hoped that this is a fairly representative catalogue of cinematic history, but it is inevitable that some films of quality will not be listed.

Films: General Information

Abba hits featured *Muriel's Wedding, Mamma Mia!*

Acromegaly: sufferer Rondo Hatton (d.1946), often billed as 'The Brute Man' or 'The Creeper', suffered from this enlargement of the bones.

Aramaic dialogue *Passion of the Christ* (2004).

Archers: nickname Film-makers Michael Powell and Emeric Pressburger (and name of their film company).

Bafta Presidents The Duke of Edinburgh (1959–65), Earl Mountbatten of Burma (1966–72), The Princess Royal (1972–2001), Lord (Richard) Attenborough (2002–10), Prince William (2010–)

Barons Richard Attenborough (Richmond on Thames), Laurence Olivier (Brighton).

Benchley shorts Popular one-reel shorts delivered by Robert Benchley, sitting behind a desk, pontificating on aspects of modern living.

Bond Cars All four-wheeled transport driven by the six Bonds. *Dr No* (Sunbeam Alpine), *From Russia with Love* (Bentley Mark IV), *Goldfinger* (Aston Martin DB5), *Thunderball* (Aston Martin DB5), *Casino Royale* (black Bentley), *On Her Majesty's Secret Service* (Aston Martin DBS), *Diamonds Are Forever* (moon buggy and Ford Mustang Mach 1), *Live and Let Die* (double-decker bus and white Coronado), *The Man with the Golden Gun* (red AMC Hornet), *The Spy Who Loved Me* (white Lotus Esprit), *Moonraker* (MP Roadster), *For Your Eyes Only* (Lotus Esprit Turbo and Citroen 2CV), *Octopussy* (Mercedes 250SE), *Never Say Never Again* (black Bentley), *A View to a Kill* (Renault 11), *The Living Daylights* (Aston Martin DBS V8 Vantage as a coupé and as a soft-top Volante version, also drove an Audi 200 Quattro), *Licence to Kill* (Kenworth W900B Truck), *Goldeneye* (BMW Z3 Roadster and Aston Martin DB5), *Tomorrow Never Dies* (BMW 750iL and Aston Martin DB5), *The World Is Not Enough* (silver BMW Z8), *Die Another Day* (Aston Martin V12 Vanquish), *Casino Royale* (Aston Martin DBS and DB5), *Quantum of Solace* (Aston Martin DB5 V12, also drove Ford Edge and Volvo 540 TS), Skyfall (Aston Martin DB5, also drove Mercedes S65).

Bowery Boys Leo Gorcey, Huntz Hall, Bob Jordan, Gabriel Dell, Bernard Gorcey, David Gorcey, Billy Benedict, Bennie Bartlett.

Carry On Cleo: US video title *Caligula's Funniest Home Videos.*

Carry On films *Carry On Sergeant* (1958), *Carry On Nurse* (1959), *Carry On Teacher,* (1959), *Carry On Constable* (1960), *Carry On Regardless* (1961), *Carry On Cruising* (1962), *Carry On Cabby* (1963), *Carry On Cleo* (1964), *Carry On Spying* (1964), *Carry On Jack* (US title: *Carry On Venus*) (1964), *Carry On Cowboy* (1965), *Carry On – Don't Lose Your Head* (1966), *Carry On – Follow that Camel* (1966), *Carry On Screaming* (1966), *Carry On Doctor* (1968), *Carry On Up the Khyber* (1968), *Carry On Again Doctor* (1969), *Carry On Camping* (1969), *Carry On Up the Jungle* (1970), *Carry On Loving* (1970), *Carry On Henry* (1971), *Carry On at Your Convenience* (1971), *Carry On Abroad* (1972), *Carry On Matron* (1972), *Carry On Girls* (1973), *Carry On Dick* (1974), *Carry On Behind* (1975), *Carry On England* (1976), *Carry On Emmanuelle* (1978), *Carry On Columbus* (1992).

Celluloid film: innovator William Friese-Greene (1888).

Cinéma vérité Film technique that utilises raw, natural sound, hand-held cameras and little rehearsal.

Cinemascope: first film *The Robe* (1953).

Cinematic projections: early examples Stroboscope, zoetrope, thaumatrope and praxinoscope.

Cinerama: invented New York 1952.

Documentary: term coined by John Grierson (8 February 1926) while reviewing Robert Flaherty's ethnographic film *Moana* for the *New York Sun*.

Dolby Stereo: invented 1980.

Film à clef Film that appears to be a fictional work, but is in fact based on a true story.

Film festival: first Venice, 1932.

Film: first British feature *Oliver Twist* (Aug 1912).

Film: first before paying audience *Young Griffo v Battling Charles Barnett* (New York, 20 May 1895).

Film: first over one hour long *The Story of the Kelly Gang* (Melbourne, 24 Dec 1906).

Hitchcock cameos *The Lodger* (1926) Seen seated at desk in a newsroom, and later he's one of the onlookers watching arrest of Ivor Novello. *Blackmail* (1929) Bothered by a young boy on the Underground as he is trying to read a book. *Murder!* (1930) He is a passer-by on the street. *The Thirty-Nine Steps* (1935) Again, he is a passer-by on the street. *Young and Innocent* (1937) Appears as a clumsy press photographer. *The Lady Vanishes* (1938) Appears in a London railway station. *Rebecca* (1940) Appears standing outside a telephone booth while George Sanders is making a call. *Foreign Correspondent* (1940) Reading newspaper on the street, before Joel McCrea meets Van Meer (Albert Basserman). *Mr & Mrs Smith* (1941) On the street, unaware of Robert Montgomery. *Saboteur* (1942) At the news-stand. *Shadow of a Doubt* (1943) Holding a full house whilst playing poker on a train. *Lifeboat* (1944) Pictured in a before-and-after weight reduction advertisement in paper read by William Bendix. *Spellbound* (1945) Getting out of a crowded hotel lift. *Notorious* (1946) Drinking champagne at a party. *The Paradine Case* (1948) Carrying a cello case. *Rope* (1948) Crossing the street during the opening credits. *Under Capricorn* (1949) Seen first at Governor's house and then on steps of Government House. *Stage Fright* (1950) Turning round in the street to look at Jane Wyman, who's talking to herself. *Strangers on a Train* (1951) Boarding a train carrying a bass violin. *I Confess* (1953) Crossing the screen at the top of a long staircase. *Dial M for Murder* (1954) In a class reunion photo. *Rear Window* (1954) Winding a clock in the musician's apartment. *To Catch a Thief* (1955) On a bus, next to Cary Grant. *The Trouble with Harry* (1955) At an outdoor exhibition. *The Man Who Knew Too Much* (1956) Watching Arab acrobats in Marrakesh marketplace. *Vertigo* (1958) Crossing the street. *North by Northwest* (1959) Running to catch a bus, with the door slamming in his face. *Psycho* (1960) Standing outside the real-estate office, wearing a ten gallon hat. *The Birds* (1963) Exiting a pet shop, with 2 Scottie dogs. *Marnie* (1964) Coming out of a hotel room. *Torn Curtain* (1966) In hotel lobby with baby on his lap (his theme tune playing softly). *Topaz* (1969) Wheelchair-bound being attended by a nurse (in an airport). *Frenzy* (1972) Spectator in a crowd scene. *Family Plot* (1976) In silhouette behind the door of the Office of Vital Statistics.

Hollywood studio: first Centaur Film Company (Horsley).

Latin dialogue *Sebastiane* (directed by Derek Jarman), *Passion of the Christ* (directed by Mel Gibson).

Marilyn Monroe: film shooting when died *Something's Gotta Give.*

Miss Ohio winner Halle Berry (also Miss Teen All-American, and in 1986 was first runner-up in the Miss USA pageant, becoming the first African-American to represent the USA in Miss World).

Monarch acted in film Edward VIII (whilst Prince of Wales), *The Power of Right* & *The Warrior Strain* (1919). Prince Charles was the first member of the Royal Family to speak in a fiction film: *Grime Goes Green* (1990).

Movie camera: first patent William Friese-Greene (1888).

Oscar: first British Charles Laughton for *Private Life of Henry VIII* in 1934.

Oscar nominations: most without winning *The Color Purple* and *The Turning Point* each had 11 Oscar nominations but failed to win a single award.

Oscar nominations: records Meryl Streep was nominated for a record 15th time in the acting category as at 2009.

Oscar statuettes Designed by Cedric Gibbons and sculpted by George Stanley.

Oscars: film with most awards *Ben Hur* (1959), *Titanic* (1997), *The Lord of the Rings: The Return of the King* (2003): 11.

Oscars: films with most nominations *All About Eve* (1950) and *Titanic* (1998), each nominated in 14 categories.

Oscars: most won Walt Disney (26)

Pamela Stephenson: film sued for £3.5m *Hello, She Lied* (renamed *Miami Hustle*); replaced by Kathy Ireland.

Pearl and Dean: music called Asteroid.

Picasso painting in lieu of cash Robin Williams received a $7 million Picasso in lieu of earnings for *Aladdin.*

Pixar films Founded in 1979 as the Graphics Group and based in Emeryville, California. Steve Jobs (co-founder of Apple Inc.) became its majority shareholder in 1986. The Walt Disney Company bought Pixar in 2006. As at 31 December 2012 Pixar have released 13 films – *Toy Story* (1995), *A Bug's Life* (1998), *Toy Story 2* (1999), *Monsters, Inc.* (2001), *Finding Nemo* (2003), *The Incredibles* (2004), *Cars* (2006), *Ratatouille* (2007), *WALL-E* (2008), *Up* (2009), *Toy Story 3* (2010), *Cars* (2011) and *Brave* (2012). John Ratzenberger has voiced characters in all 13 films to-date.

Road films: first in colour *Road to Bali* (1952).

Road films: order Singapore, Zanzibar, Morocco, Utopia, Rio, Bali, Hong Kong.

Ronald Reagan films: include *Accidents Will Happen* (1938), *Angels Wash their Faces* (1939), *Bedtime for Bonzo* (1951), *Hellcats of the Navy* (1957), *Cattle Queen of Montana* (1954), *The Killers* (1964).

Smell-O-Vision: first film *The Scent of Mystery* (1959).

Sound film: first *Jazz Singer* (1927).

Tarzan: actors played Johnny Weissmuller 1932–48, Lex Barker 1949–53, Gordon Scott 1955–60, Jock Mahoney 1962–3, Mike Henry 1966–8. Also Miles O'Keeffe, Buster Crabbe, Frank Merrill, Christopher Lambert.

Third Man: famous quote 'In Italy for 30 years under the Borgias they had warfare, terror, murder and bloodshed, but they produced Michelangelo, Leonardo da Vinci and the Renaissance. In Switzerland, they had brotherly love, they had 500 years of democracy and peace – and what did they produce? The cuckoo clock.'

Triangle Film Corporation Formed in 1915 by DW Griffith, Thomas Ince and Mack Sennett.

United Artists Formed in 1919 by Mary Pickford, Douglas Fairbanks, Charlie Chaplin and DW Griffith. In November 2006, producer/actor Tom Cruise and his production partner, Paula Wagner, signed an agreement with the holding company, MGM, to run United Artists.

Videodrome: presenters Alex Cox, Mark Cousins.

Western film: first in USA *The Great Train Robbery* (directed by Edwin Porter, 1903).

First Films

Actor	Film
Danny Aiello	*Bang the Drum Slowly* (1973)
Claude Akins	*A Place in the Sun* (1951)
Alan Alda	*Gone Are the Days* (1963)
Woody Allen	*What's New Pussycat* (1965)
Kirstie Alley	*One More Chance* (1981)
June Allyson	*All Girl Revue* (1937)
Mädchen Amick	*The Borrower* (1989)
Dana Andrews	*Lucky Cisco Kid* (1938)
Harry Andrews	*Red Beret, The* (1952)
Julie Andrews	*Mary Poppins* (1964)
	As extra: *The Reluctant Debutante* (1958)
	Voice only: *Rose of Baghdad* (1952)
Gabrielle Anwar	*Manifesto* (1988)
Anne Archer	*The All-American Boy* (1970; released 1973)
Eve Arden	*Song of Love* (1929)
Alan Arkin	*Calypso Heat Wave* (1957)
George Arliss	*Devil, The* (1921)
Edward Arnold	*The Heart of Virginia Keep* (1916)
	Short: *When the Man Speaks* (1916)
Rosanna Arquette	*More American Graffiti* (1979)
	TV film: *Having Babies II* (1977)
Jean Arthur	*Cameo Kirby* (1923)
	Short: *Somebody Lied* (1923)
Armand Assante	*The Lords of Flatbush* (1974)
Fred Astaire	*Dancing Lady* (1933)
	Short: *Municipal Bandwagon* (1932)
Mary Astor	*Hope* (1922)
	Short: *The Beggar Maid* (1921)
Rowan Atkinson	*The Secret Policeman's Ball* (1979)
Richard Attenborough	*In Which We Serve* (1942)
Gene Autry	*In Old Santa Fe* (1934)
Dan Aykroyd	*Love at First Sight* (1976)
	Short and voice only: *The Gift of Winter* (1974)
Lew Ayres	*The Sophomore* (1929)
Charles Aznavour	*Les Disparus de Saint-Agil* (1938)
	US title: *Boys' School*
Lauren Bacall	*To Have and Have Not* (1944)
Kevin Bacon	*National Lampoon's Animal House* (1978)
Carroll Baker	*Easy to Love* (1953)
Joe Don Baker	*Cool Hand Luke* (1967)
Stanley Baker	*Undercover* (1943)
Alec Baldwin	*Forever Lulu* (1987)
	TV film: *Sweet Revenge* (1984)
William Baldwin	*Born on the Fourth of July* (1989)
Christian Bale	*Empire of the Sun* (1987)
	TV film: *Anastasia: Mystery of Anna* (1986)
Martin Balsam	*On the Waterfront* (1954)
Anne Bancroft	*Don't Bother to Knock* (1952)
Theda Bara	*A Fool There Was* (1914)
Javier Bardem	*El Picaro* (1974)
Brigitte Bardot	*Le Trou Normand* (1952)
Ellen Barkin	*The Diner* (1982)
Drew Barrymore	*Altered States* (1980)
Ethel Barrymore	*The Nightingale* (1914)
John Barrymore	*An American Citizen* (1913)
Lionel Barrymore	*Men and Women* (1914)
	Short: *Friends* (1969)
Kim Basinger	*Hard Country* (1981)
Alan Bates	*It's Never Too Late* (1956)
Kathy Bates	*Taking Off* (1971)
Anne Baxter	*Twenty Mule Team* (1940)
Sean Bean	*Caravaggio* (1986)
	TV film: *Winter Flight* (1984)
Warren Beatty	*Splendor in the Grass* (1961)
Bonny Bedelia	*The Gypsy Moths* (1969)
Harry Belafonte	*Bright Road* (1953)
Ralph Bellamy	*The Secret Six* (1931)
William Bendix	*Woman of the Year* (1942)
Tom Berenger	*The Sentinel* (1976)
Candice Bergen	*The Group* (1966)
Ingrid Bergman	*Munkbrogreven* (1934)
Halle Berry	*Jungle Fever* (1991)

Actor	Film
Juliette Binoche	*Liberty Belle* (1981)
Jacqueline Bisset	*The Knack* (1964)
Honor Blackman	*Daughter of Darkness* (1947)
Cate Blanchett	*Paradise Road* (1997)
	Australia-only release: *Police Rescue* (1994)
Claire Bloom	*The Blind Goddess* (1948)
Orlando Bloom	*Wilde* (1997)
Dirk Bogarde	*Dancing With Crime* (1947)
	As extra: *Come on George* (1939)
Humphrey Bogart	*A Devil with Women* (1930).
	As extra: *The Dancing Team* (1928)
Ernest Borgnine	*China Corsair* (1951)
Clara Bow	*Beyond the Rainbow* (1921)
Stephen Boyd	*Lilacs in the Spring* (1954) US title: *Let's Make Up*
Charles Boyer	*L'Homme du Large* (1920)
Kenneth Branagh	*High Season* (1986)
Marlon Brando	*The Men* (1950)
Walter Brennan	*Watch Your Wife* (1926)
Beau Bridges	*No Minor Vices* (1948)
Jeff Bridges	*The Company She Keeps* (1950) (as baby)
Lloyd Bridges	*They Dare Not Love* (1941)
Adrien Brody	*New York Stories* (1989) ('Life Without Zoe' segment)
Charles Bronson	*You're in the Navy Now* (1951)
	Aka *USS Teakettle* (as Charles Buchinski)
Mel Brooks	*Putney Swope* (1969)
	As narrator: *The Critic* (1963)
Pierce Brosnan	*The Long Good Friday* (1980)
	Short: *Resting Rough* (1979)
Yul Brynner	*Port of New York* (1949)
Sandra Bullock	*A Fool and His Money* (1988)
George Burns	*Lamb Chops* (1929)
Raymond Burr	*San Quentin* (1946)
Richard Burton	*The Last Days of Dolwyn* (1948)
Max Bygraves	*Bless 'em All* (1949)
Gabriel Byrne	*The Outsider* (1979)
	BFI 'Art' film: *On a Paving Stone Mounted* (1978)
James Caan	*Irma La Douce* (1963)
Nicolas Cage	*Fast Times at Ridgemont High* (1982)
	TV film: *The Best of Times* (1981)
	Both films as Nicolas Coppola
James Cagney	*Sinner's Holiday* (1930)
Michael Caine	*A Hill in Korea* (1956)
Simon Callow	*Amadeus* (1984)
John Candy	*Class of '44* (1973)
Claudia Cardinale	*Goha* (1957)
	Short: *Chaines d'Or* (1956)
Ian Carmichael	*Bond Street* (1948)
Leslie Caron	*An American in Paris* (1951)
David Carradine	*Taggart* (1965)
Keith Carradine	*A Gunfight* (1970)
Jim Carrey	*Introducing Janet* (1982)
	TV film: *Rubberface* (1981)
Richard Chamberlain	*The Secret of the Purple Reef* (1960)
Lon Chaney	*Storm and Sunshine* (1910)
Charlie Chaplin	*Charlie as a Piano Mover* (1910)
Cyd Charisse	*Something to Shout About* (1942)
	Short: *Rhumba Serenade* (1941)
Cher	*Wild on the Beach* (1965)
Maurice Chevalier	*Le Mauvais Garçon* (1921)
	Short: *Trop Crédule* (1908)
Julie Christie	*Crooks Anonymous* (1962)
John Cleese	*Interlude* (1968)
Montgomery Clift	*The Search* (1948)
George Clooney	*Grizzly II – The Predator* (1982)
Glenn Close	*The World According to Garp* (1982)
	TV film: *Orphan Train* (1979)
James Coburn	*Ride Lonesome* (1959)
Claudette Colbert	*For the Love of Mike* (1927)
George Cole	*Cottage to Let* (1941)
Joan Collins	*Lady Godiva Rides Again* (1951)

Actor	Film
Ronald Colman	*The Toilers* (1919) Short: *The Live Wire* (1917)
Sean Connery	*Lilacs in the Spring* (1954)
Tom Conti	*Flame* (1974)
Jackie Coogan	*Skinner's Baby* (1916)
Gary Cooper	*Blind Justice* (1923)
Harry H Corbett	*Never Look Back* (1952)
Kevin Costner	*Night Shift* (1982) (*Sizzle Beach, USA* made in late 70s but not shown till 1986)
Joseph Cotten	*Citizen Kane* (1941) Unreleased: *Too Much Johnson* (1938)
Tom Courtenay	*Loneliness of the Long Distance Runner* (1962)
Noël Coward	*Hearts of the World* (1918)
Broderick Crawford	*Woman Chases Man* (1937)
Joan Crawford	*Lady of the Night* (1925) Short: *Miss MGM* (1925)
Michael Crawford	*Soap Box Derby* (1957)
Richard Crenna	*The Pride of St Louis* (1952)
Bing Crosby	*King of Jazz* (1930) Short: *Ripstitch the Tailor* (1930)
Russell Crowe	*Blood Oath* (1990)
Tom Cruise	*My Bodyguard* (1980)
Penélope Cruz	*Jamón, Jamón* (1992)
Billy Crystal	*Rabbit Test* (1978) TV film: *Death Flight* (1977)
Macaulay Culkin	*Rocket Gibraltar* (1988)
Rory Culkin	*You Can Count On Me* (2000)
Robert Culp	*PT 109* (1963)
Jamie Lee Curtis	*Halloween* (1978) TV film: *Operation Petticoat* (1977)
Tony Curtis	*Criss Cross* (1948)
John Curtis	*Class* (1983)
Peter Cushing	*The Man in the Iron Mask* (1939)
Willem Dafoe	*Heaven's Gate* (1980)
Jim Dale	*6.5 Special* (1958)
Timothy Dalton	*The Lion in Winter* (1968)
Matt Damon	*Mystic Pizza* (1988)
Charles Dance	*The Spy Who Loved Me* (1977)
Jeff Daniels	*Ragtime* (1981)
Ted Danson	*The Onion Field* (1979)
Kim Darby	*The Restless Ones* (1965) As extra: *Bye Bye Birdie* (1963)
Sammy Davis Jr	*The Benny Goodman Story* (1956) Short: *Rufus Jones for President* (1933)
Bette Davis	*Bad Sister* (1931)
Geena Davis	*Tootsie* (1982)
Nancy Davis	*Shadow on the Wall* (1950)
Daniel Day-Lewis	*Sunday, Bloody Sunday* (1971)
Doris Day	*Romance on the High Seas* (1948) GB title: *It's Magic* Short: *My Lost Horizon* (1941)
Yvonne De Carlo	*Harvard Here I Come* (1941) GB title: *Here I Come* Short: *I Look at You* (1941)
Olivia De Havilland	*A Midsummer Night's Dream* (1935)
Rebecca DeMornay	*One From the Heart* (1982)
Robert De Niro	*Trois Chambres à Manhattan* (1966)
Danny De Vito	*Dreams of Glass* (1969)
James Dean	*Sailor Beware* (1951)
Judi Dench	*The Third Secret* (1964)
Catherine Deneuve	*Les Collégiennes* (1956)
Gérard Depardieu	*Le Beatnik et le Minet* (1965)
Johnny Depp	*A Nightmare on Elm Street* (1984)
Bruce Dern	*Wild River* (1960)
Laura Dern	*Teachers* (1984) As child actress: White Lightning (1973)
Brad Dexter	*The Asphalt Jungle* (1950)
Cameron Diaz	*The Mask* (1994)
Leonardo DiCaprio	*Critters 3* (1991)
Marlene Dietrich	*So Sind die Männer* (1922) Aka *Der Kleine Napoleon*
Matt Dillon	*Over the Edge* (1979)
Robert Donat	*Men of Tomorrow (1932)*
Amanda Donohoe	*Foreign Body* (1986) *Castaway* (1986) released at same time
Diana Dors	*The Shop at Sly Corner* (1946)
Kirk Douglas	*The Strange Love of Martha Ivers* (1946)

Actor	Film
Michael Douglas	*Hail, Hero* (1969) TV film: *The Experiment* (1968)
Robert Downey Jr	*Pound* (1970)
Richard Dreyfuss	*The Graduate* (1967)
Faye Dunaway	*The Happening* (1967)
Deanna Durbin	*Three Smart Girls* (1936) Short: *Every Sunday* (1936)
Robert Duvall	*To Kill a Mockingbird* (1962) TV film: *John Brown's Raid* (1960)
Clint Eastwood	*Revenge of the Creature* (1955) Short: *A Day in a Hollywood Star Factory* (1955)
Michael Elphick	*Fraulein Doktor* (1968)
Eminem	*Da Hip Hop Witch* (2000)
Edith Evans	*A Honeymoon for Three* (1915)
Douglas Fairbanks	*The Lamb* (1915)
Douglas Fairbanks Jr	*Stephen Steps Out* (1923)
Peter Falk	*Wind across the Everglades* (1958)
Colin Farrell	*The War Zone* (1999)
Mia Farrow	*John Paul Jones* (1959)
Marty Feldman	*The Bed Sitting Room* (1969)
Sally Field	*Moon Pilot* (1962)
Gracie Fields	*Sally in Our Alley* (1931)
WC Fields	*Janice Meredith* (1924) GB title: *The Beautiful Rebel* Short: *Pool Sharks* (1915)
Joseph Fiennes	*Stealing Beauty* (1996)
Ralph Fiennes	*Emily Brontë's Wuthering Heights* (1992) *A Dangerous Man – Lawrence after Arabia* (1991) was a TV film never released in cinemas
Peter Finch	*Dad and Dave Come to Town* (1938) Unreleased: *Magic Shoes* (1935)
Albert Finney	*The Entertainer* (1960)
Errol Flynn	*Dr H. Erben's New Guinea Expedition* (1932)
Henry Fonda	*The Farmer Takes a Wife* (1935)
Jane Fonda	*Tall Story* (1960)
Joan Fontaine	*No More Ladies* (1935) (as Joan Burfield)
Glenn Ford	*Heaven With a Barbed Wire Fence* (1939) Short: *Night in Manhattan* (1937)
Harrison Ford	*Dead Heat on a Merry-Go- Round* (1966)
George Formby	*By the Shortest of Heads* (1915)
Jodie Foster	*Napoleon and Samantha* (1972)
Edward Fox	*The Mind Benders* (1962)
James Fox	*The Miniver Story* (1950) (as William Fox)
Michael J Fox	*Letters From Frank* (1979)
Jamie Foxx	*Toys* (1992)
Tony Franciosa	*A Face in the Crowd* (1957)
Morgan Freeman	*Who Says I Can't Ride a Rainbow* (1971)
Clark Gable	*Forbidden Paradise* (1924)
Greta Garbo	*Fortune Hunter* (1921) Short: *How Not to Dress* (1921)
Andy Garcia	*Blue Skies Again* (1983) TV film: *Hill Street Blues* (1980) Pilot for series
Ava Gardner	*HM Pulham Esq* (1941) Short: *Fancy Answers* (1941)
Judy Garland	*Pigskin Parade* (1936) GB title: *Harmony Parade.* Short: *The Meglin Kiddie Revue* (1929) (billed as a Gumm sister)
James Garner	*Toward the Unknown* (1956) GB title: *Brink of Hell*
Greer Garson	*Goodbye Mr Chips* (1939) As extra: *21 Days* (1937) US title: *21 Days Together*
Richard Gere	*Report to the Commissioner* (1974) GB title: *Operation Undercover*
Mel Gibson	*Summer City* (1977)
John Gielgud	*Who is the Man?* (1924)
Lillian Gish	*Judith of Bethulia* (1914) Short: *Oil and Water* (1912)
Whoopi Goldberg	*Citizen (1982)* (released 1983)
Jeff Goldblum	*Death Wish (1974)*
Elliott Gould	*The Confession (1964)* GB title: *Quick, Let's Get Married!*

Actor	*Film*
Betty Grable	*Happy Days* (1929)
Stewart Granger	*A Southern Maid* (1933)
	As stand-in: *I Spy* (1933)
Cary Grant	*This Is the Night* (1932)
Hugh Grant	*Privileged* (1982)
Richard E Grant	*Withnail and I* (1986)
	TV film: *Honest, Decent and True* (1985)
Richard Greene	*Four Men and a Prayer* (1938)
Sydney Greenstreet	*The Maltese Falcon* (1941)
John Gregson	*Saraband for Dead Lovers* (1948)
Melanie Griffith	*Smith!* (1969)
Charles Grodin	*Rosemary's Baby* (1968)
	TV film: *The Meanest Men in the West* (1962)
Alec Guinness	*Great Expectations* (1946)
	As extra: *Evensong* (1934)
Gene Hackman	*Mad Dog Coll* (1961)
Larry Hagman	*Ensign Pulver* (1964)
	TV film: *The Member of the Wedding* (1958)
Susan Hampshire	*The Woman in the Hall* (1947)
Tony Hancock	*Orders Are Orders* (1954)
Tom Hanks	*He Knows You're Alone* (1980)
Daryl Hannah	*The Fury* (1978)
Oliver Hardy	*Outwitting Dad* (1913)
Jean Harlow	*Moran of the Marines* (1928)
Woody Harrelson	*Harper Valley PTA* (1978)
Ed Harris	*Coma* (1977)
	TV film: *The Amazing Howard Hughes* (1977)
Richard Harris	*Alive and Kicking* (1958)
Rex Harrison	*The Great Game* (1930)
Laurence Harvey	*House of Darkness* (1948)
Rutger Hauer	*Repelstweltje* (1973)
Ethan Hawke	*Explorers* (1985)
Jack Hawkins	*Birds of Prey* (1930)
Goldie Hawn	*The One and Only Genuine Original Family Band* (1968)
Will Hay	*Those Were the Days* (1934)
	Short: *Know Your Apples* (1933)
Susan Hayward	*Hollywood Hotel* (1937)
Rita Hayworth	*Cruz Diablo* (1934)
	Short: *La Fiesta* (1926) (as Rita Cansino)
Van Heflin	*A Woman Rebels* (1936)
David Hemmings	*Night and the City* (1950)
Ian Hendry	*Simon and Laura* (1955)
Audrey Hepburn	*Nederlan in 7 Lessen* (1948)
Katharine Hepburn	*A Bill of Divorcement* (1932)
Barbara Hershey	*With Six You Get Egg Roll* (1968)
Charlton Heston	*Peer Gynt* (1941)
Wendy Hiller	*Lancashire Luck* (1937)
Dustin Hoffman	*The Tiger Makes Out* (1967)
Paul Hogan	*Fatty Finn* (1980)
William Holden	*Prison Farm* (1938)
Judy Holliday	*Greenwich Village* (1944)
	Unreleased: *Too Much Johnson* (1938)
Stanley Holloway	*The Rotters* (1921)
Ian Holm	*Girls at Sea* (1958)
Bob Hope	*The Big Broadcast of 1938* (1938)
	Short: *Paree, Paree* (1934)
Anthony Hopkins	*The Lion in Winter* (1968)
	Short: *Changes* (1963)
Dennis Hopper	*Johnny Guitar* (1954)
Bob Hoskins	*Up the Front* (1972)
Leslie Howard	*The Happy Warrior* (1917)
	Short: *The Heroine of Mons* (1914)
Trevor Howard	*Volga-Volga* (1944) (dubbed voice)
Frankie Howerd	*The Runaway Bus* (1954)
Rock Hudson	*Fighter Squadron* (1948)
Holly Hunter	*The Burning* (1981)
Jeffrey Hunter	*A Date with Judy* (1948)
Isabelle Huppert	*Faustine et le Bel Été* (1971)
	GB title: *Faustine*
John Hurt	*The Wild and the Willing* (1962)
William Hurt	*Altered States* (1980)
	TV film: *Verna the USO Girl* (1978)
Anjelica Huston	*Sinful Davey* (1969)

Actor	*Film*
John Huston	*The Shakedown* (1928)
Jeremy Irons	*Nijinsky* (1980)
Burl Ives	*Smoky* (1946)
Glenda Jackson	*The Extra Day* (1956)
Gordon Jackson	*The Foreman Went to France* (1942)
Derek Jacobi	*Othello* (1965)
Sid James	*Black Memory* (1947)
Martin Jarvis	*Secrets of a Windmill Girl* (1965)
Lionel Jeffries	*Stage Fright* (1950)
Scarlett Johansson	*North* (1994)
Celia Johnson	*Dirty Work* (1934)
Don Johnson	*Good Morning ... and Goodbye!* (1967)
	GB title: *The Lust Seekers* (Russ Meyer epic!)
Angelina Jolie	*Looking to Get Out* (1982)
Al Jolson	*The Jazz Singer* (1927)
	Short: *April Showers* (1926)
Tommy Lee Jones	*Love Story* (1970)
Vinnie Jones	*Lock, Stock and Two Smoking Barrels* (1998)
Louis Jourdan	*Le Corsaire* (1939)
Boris Karloff	*The Dumb Girl of Portici* (1916)
Danny Kaye	*Up in Arms* (1944)
	Short: *Dime a Dance* (1937)
Stacy Keach	*The Heart Is a Lonely Hunter* (1968)
Buster Keaton	*The Saphead* (1920)
	Short: *A Reckless Romeo* (1917)
Diane Keaton	*Lovers and Other Strangers* (1970)
Michael Keaton	*Night Shift* (1982)
Howard Keel	*The Small Voice* (1948) (as Harold Keel)
Harvey Keitel	*Who's That Knocking at My Door* (1968)
	Unreleased: *Bring on the Dancing Girls* (1965)
Gene Kelly	*For Me and My Gal* (1942)
	GB title: *For Me and My Girl*
Grace Kelly	*Fourteen Hours* (1951)
George Kennedy	*The Little Shepherd of Kingdom Come* (1961)
Patsy Kensit	*For the Love of Ada* (1972)
Deborah Kerr	*Major Barbara* (1941)
	Contraband (1940) first film but scene was cut
Nicole Kidman	*Bush Christmas* (1982)
Val Kilmer	*Top Secret!* (1984)
Ben Kingsley	*Fear Is the Key* (1972)
Nastassja Kinski	*Falsche Bewegung* (1975)
	GB title: *Wrong Movement*
Eartha Kitt	*Casbah* (1948)
Kevin Kline	*Sophie's Choice* (1982)
Keira Knightley	*Star Wars Episode 1: The Phantom Menace* (1999)
Kris Kristofferson	*The Last Movie* (1971)
Alan Ladd	*Once in a Lifetime* (1932)
Veronica Lake	*All Women Have Secrets* (1939) (as Constance Keane)
Hedy Lamarr	*Geld auf der Strasse* (1930) (as Hedy Kiesler)
Christopher Lambert	*Le Bar du Téléphone* (1981)
Dorothy Lamour	*The Jungle Princess* (1936)
	Short: *The Stars Can't Be Wrong* (1936)
Burt Lancaster	*The Killers* (1946)
Michael Landon	*I Was A Teenage Werewolf* (1957)
Jessica Lange	*King Kong* (1976)
	Short: *Home Is Where the Heart Is* (1970)
Angela Lansbury	*Gaslight* (1944). GB title: *The Murder in Thornton Square*
Mario Lanza	*Winged Victory* (1944)
Charles Laughton	*Piccadilly* (1929)
	Short: *Bluebottles* (1928)
Stan Laurel	*Lucky Dog* (1917)
Jude Law	*Shopping* (1994)
Peter Lawford	*Poor Old Bill* (1930)
Bruce Lee	*Golden Gate Girl* (1941, aged 3 months)
	The Birth of Mankind (1946, first professional role)
Christopher Lee	*Corridor of Mirrors* (1948)

Actor	*Film*
Gypsy Rose Lee	*You Can't Have Everything* (1937) (as Louise Hovick)
Janet Leigh	*The Romance of Rosy Ridge* (1947)
Jennifer Jason Leigh	*Eyes of a Stranger* (1981)
Vivien Leigh	*Things Are Looking Up* (1934)
Jack Lemmon	*It Should Happen to You* (1953)
Jerry Lewis	*My Friend Irma* (1949)
Juliette Lewis	*Any Which Way You Can* (1980)
Jet Li	*Shaolin Temple* (1982)
Emily Lloyd	*Wish You Were Here* (1987)
Harold Lloyd	*Samson and Delilah* (1913)
Margaret Lockwood	*Lorna Doone* (1934)
Gina Lollobrigida	*L'Aguila Nera* (1946)
Herbert Lom	*Zena Pod Krizem* (1937)
Carole Lombard	*A Perfect Crime* (1921) (as Jane Peters)
Sophia Loren	*Cuori Sul Mare* (1950) (as Sofia Scicolone)
Peter Lorre	*Bomben auf Monte Carlo* (1931)
Rob Lowe	*The Outsiders* (1983) TV film: *Thursday's Child* (1982)
Myrna Loy	*Pretty Ladies* (1925)
Bela Lugosi	*Alarscobal* (1917)
Dolph Lundgren	*For Your Eyes Only* (1981)
Ida Lupino	*The Love Race* (1932)
James McAvoy	*The Near Room* (1995)
David McCallum	*Ill Met By Moonlight* (1956)
Jeanette MacDonald	*The Love Parade* (1929)
Roddy McDowall	*Grime Doesn't Pay* (1935)
Andie MacDowell	*Greystoke: The Legend of Tarzan Lord of Apes* (1984)
Malcolm McDowell	*If* (1968). *Poor Cow* (1967) first film but scene was cut
Kelly McGillis	*Reuben, Reuben* (1983)
Patrick McGoohan	*The Dam Busters* (1954)
Ali MacGraw	*A Lovely Way to Die* (1968) GB title: *A Lovely Way to Go*
Ewan McGregor	*Being Human* (1993) TV film: *Lipstick On Your Collar* (1993)
Virginia McKenna	*Father's Doing Fine* (1952)
Leo McKern	*Murder in the Cathedral* (1952)
Kyle MacLachlan	*Dune* (1984)
Victor McLaglen	*The Call of the Road* (1920)
Shirley MacLaine	*The Trouble with Harry* (1955)
Fred MacMurray	*Girls Gone Wild* (1929)
Patrick MacNee	*Sailors Three* (1940)
Steve McQueen	*Somebody up There Likes Me* (1956)
Ian McShane	*The Wild and the Willing* (1962)
Madonna	*A Certain Sacrifice* (1978)
Anna Magnani	*Scampolo* (1927)
Tobey Maguire	*This Boy's Life* (1993)
Lee Majors	*Strait-Jacket* (1964) (as Lee Yeary)
Karl Malden	*They Knew What They Wanted* (1940)
John Malkovich	*Places in the Heat* (1984) TV film: *Word of Honor* (1981)
Jayne Mansfield	*Prehistoric Women* (1950)
Fredric March	*The Devil* (1920)
Dean Martin	*My Friend Irma* (1949)
Steve Martin	*Sgt Pepper's Lonely Heart's Club Band* (1978) Short: *The Absent-Minded Waiter* (1977)
Lee Marvin	*Teresa* (1950)
Marx Brothers	*The Cocoanuts* (1929) Limited release: *Humorist* (1926)
Harpo Marx	*Too Many Kisses* (1925)
James Mason	*Late Extra* (1935) (The name of his fan club's news letter)
Raymond Massey	*The Crooked Billet* (1929) Aka *International Spy*
Marcello Mastroianni	*I Miserabili* (1947) As extra: *Marionette* (1938)
Walter Matthau	*The Kentuckian* (1955)
Jessie Matthews	*The Beloved Vagabond* (1923)
Victor Mature	*The Housekeeper's Daughter* (1939)
Virginia Mayo	*Stand by for Action* (1942) GB title: *Cargo of Innocents*
Melina Mercouri	*Stella* (1954)
Ethel Merman	*Follow the Leader* (1930)

Actor	*Film*
Bette Midler	*Hawaii* (1966)
Toshiro Mifune	*Shin Baka Jidai* (1946)
Sarah Miles	*Term of Trial* (1962)
Ray Milland	*The Plaything* (1929) (as Spike Milland)
Max Miller	*The Good Companions* (1933)
Spike Milligan	*Penny Points to Paradise* (1951)
Hayley Mills	*Tiger Bay* (1959)
John Mills	*The Midshipmaid* (1932) Limited release: *Words and Music* (1932)
Juliet Mills	*In Which We Serve* (1942) (as baby)
Liza Minnelli	*Easter Parade* (1948) (as baby)
Kylie Minogue	*The Delinquents* (1989)
Carmen Miranda	*A Voz do Carnaval* (1933)
Helen Mirren	*Herostratus* (1967)
Robert Mitchum	*Hoppy Serves a Writ* (1943)
Tom Mix	*The Heart of Texas Ryan* (1917) Short: *On the Little Big Horn* (1909)
Marilyn Monroe	*The Shocking Miss Pilgrim* (1946)
Yves Montand	*Etoile sans Lumière* (1945)
Demi Moore	*Choices* (1981)
Dudley Moore	*The Wrong Box* (1966) As narrator: *The Hat* (1964)
Julianne Moore	*Tales From the Darkside* (1990) TV film: *Money, Power, Murder* (1989) Limited release: *Slaughterhouse II* (1988)
Roger Moore	*Caesar and Cleopatra* (1945)
Jeanne Moreau	*Dernier Amour* (1948)
Kenneth More	*Look up and Laugh* (1935)
Robert Morley	*Marie Antoinette* (1938)
Zero Mostel	*DuBarry Was a Lady* (1943)
Paul Muni	*The Valiant* (1929)
Eddie Murphy	*48 Hrs* (1982)
Audie Murphy	*Beyond Glory* (1948)
Bill Murray	*Meatballs* (1979) Short: T*he Hat Act* (1976) Voice only: *Jungle Burger* (1975)
Anna Neagle	*Those Who Love* (1929) (as Marjorie Robertson)
Liam Neeson	*Excalibur* (1981)
Sam Neill	*Ashes* (1975)
Anthony Newley	*The Little Ballerina* (1947) Short: *Dusty Bates* (1947)
Paul Newman	*The Silver Chalice* (1954)
Jack Nicholson	*The Cry Baby Killer* (1958)
Leslie Nielsen	*The Vagabond King* (1956)
Leonard Nimoy	*Rhubarb* (1951)
David Niven	*There Goes the Bride* (1932)
Nick Nolte	*The Feather Farm* (1965)
Chuck Norris	*The Wrecking Crew* (1968)
Kim Novak	*The Veils of Baghdad* (1953)
Ivor Novello	*Call of the Blood* (1919)
Warren Oates	*Up Periscope!* (1958)
Merle Oberon	*The Three Passions* (1929)
Edmond O'Brien	*Prison Break* (1938)
Pat O'Brien	*Compliments of the Season* (1930)
Donald O'Connor	*Melody for Two* (1937)
Maureen O'Hara	*Kicking the Moon Around* (1938) as Maureen Fitzsimmons
Gary Oldman	*Remembrance* (1982)
Laurence Olivier	*Too Many Crooks* (1930)
Ryan O'Neal	*The Big Bounce* (1969) TV film: *This Rugged Land* (1962)
Tatum O'Neal	*Paper Moon* (1973)
Maureen O'Sullivan	*Song o' My Heart* (1930)
Richard O'Sullivan	*Dance Little Lady* (1954)
Peter O'Toole	*The Savage Innocents* (1959)
Al Pacino	*Me Natalie* (1969)
Jack Palance	*Panic in the Streets* (1950) (as Walter Palance)
Lilli Palmer	*Crime Unlimited* (1935)
Gwyneth Paltrow	*Shout* (1991)
Vanessa Paradis	*Noce Blanche* (1990)
Dolly Parton	*The Nashville Sound* (1970)
Gregory Peck	*Days of Glory* (1944)
Sean Penn	*Taps* (1981) TV film: *The Killing of Randy Webster* (1980)
George Peppard	*The Strange One* (1957) GB title: *End as a Man*

Actor	*Film*
Anthony Perkins	*The Actress* (1953)
Joe Pesci	*Hey, Let's Twist* (1961) (as Joe Ritchie)
Michelle Pfeiffer	*Falling in Love Again* (1979)
Leslie Phillips	*A Lassie from Lancashire* (1935)
River Phoenix	*Explorers* (1985) TV film: *Surviving* (1985)
Mary Pickford	*Through the Breakers* (1909)
Walter Pidgeon	*Mannequin* (1925)
Brad Pitt	*Cutting Class* (1989) TV film: *A Stoning in Fulham County* (1988)
Donald Pleasence	*The Beachcomber* (1954)
Christopher Plummer	*Wind Across the Everglades* (1958)
Sidney Poitier	*From Whence Cometh My Help* (1949)
Eric Portman	*The Girl from Maxim's* (1933)
Dick Powell	*Street Scene* (1931)
Robert Powell	*Robbery* (1967)
William Powell	*When Knighthood Was In Flower* (1922)
Tyrone Power	*Tom Brown of Culver* (1932)
Stefanie Powers	*Tammy Tell Me True* (1961)
Elvis Presley	*Love Me Tender* (1956)
Robert Preston	*King of Alcatraz* (1938)
Dennis Price	*A Canterbury Tale* (1944) As extra: *No Parking* (1938)
Vincent Price	*Service de Luxe* (1938)
Richard Pryor	*The Busy Body* (1966)
Bill Pullman	*Ruthless People* (1986)
Dennis Quaid	*Crazy Mama* (1975)
Anthony Quayle	*Moscow Nights* (1935)
Aidan Quinn	*Reckless* (1984)
Anthony Quinn	*The Milky Way* (1936)
George Raft	*Queen of the Night Clubs* (1929)
Luise Rainer	*Ja, der Himmel über Wien* (1930)
Claude Rains	*Build Thy House* (1920)
Charlotte Rampling	*The Knack and How to Get it* (1965)
Basil Rathbone	*Innocent* (1921)
Ronald Reagan	*Love Is on the Air* (1937) GB title: *The Radio Murder Mystery*
Robert Redford	*War Hunt* (1962). TV film: *In the Presence of Mine Enemies* (1960). (Charles Laughton played a rabbi in this film!)
Lynn Redgrave	*Tom Jones* (1963)
Michael Redgrave	*Secret Agent* (1936)
Vanessa Redgrave	*Behind the Mask* (1958)
Oliver Reed	*Value for Money* (1955)
Christopher Reeve	*Gray Lady Down* (1977)
Keanu Reeves	*The Prodigal* (1984). Video only: *Act of Vengeance* (1984)
Lee Remick	*A Face in the Crowd* (1957)
Burt Reynolds	*Angel Baby* (1961)
Debbie Reynolds	*June Bride* (1948)
Cliff Richard	*Serious Charge* (1959)
Joely Richardson	*The Charge of the Light Brigade* (1968)
Miranda Richardson	*Dance with a Stranger* (1984)
Natasha Richardson	*The Charge of the Light Brigade* (1968)
Ralph Richardson	*The Ghoul* (1933)
Brian Rix	*Reluctant Heroes* (1951)
Jason Robards Jnr	*The Journey* (1958)
Tim Robbins	*No Small Affair* (1984)
Julia Roberts	*Blood Red* (1988 but released 1990) *Baja Oklahoma* (shown in selected cinemas) 1988
Rachel Roberts	*Valley of Song* (1953)
Cliff Robertson	*Corvette K-225* (1943) GB title: *The Nelson Touch*
Dale Robertson	*The Boy with Green Hair* (1948)
Paul Robeson	*Body and Soul* (1924)
Edward G Robinson	*Arms and the Woman* (1916)
Flora Robson	*Gentleman of Paris* (1931)
Ginger Rogers	*Queen High* (1930) Short: *Campus Sweethearts* (1929)
Roy Rogers	*Way Up Thar* (1935) (as Dick Weston) Short: *Slightly Static* (1935) (as Leonard Slye)
Will Rogers	*Laughing Bill Hyde* (1918)
Gilbert Roland	*The Lady Who Lied* (1925)
Cesar Romero	*The Shadow Laughs* (1933)

Actor	*Film*
Mickey Rooney	*Orchids and Ermine* (1927) Short: *Not to Be Trusted* (1926)
Katharine Ross	*Shenandoah* (1965)
Isabella Rossellini	*A Matter of Time* (1976)
Leonard Rossiter	*The Two-Headed Spy* (1958)
Tim Roth	*Meantime* (1983) TV film: *Made in Britain* (1983)
Richard Roundtree	*What Do You Say to a Naked Lady* (1969)
Mickey Rourke	*1941* (1979). TV film: *Panic on Page One* (1979) Aka *City in Fear*
Gena Rowlands	*The High Cost of Loving* (1958)
Geoffrey Rush	*Hoodwink* (1981)
Jane Russell	*The Outlaw* (1943)
Kurt Russell	*The Absent-Minded Professor* (1961)
Rosalind Russell	*Forsaking All Others* (1934)
Theresa Russell	*The Last Tycoon* (1976)
Rene Russo	*Major League* (1989)
Margaret Rutherford	*Talk of the Devil* (1936)
Meg Ryan	*Rich and Famous* (1981)
Robert Ryan	*The Ghost Breakers* (1940)
Winona Ryder	*Lucas* (1986)
George Sanders	*Love, Life and Laughter* (1934)
Susan Sarandon	*Joe* (1970)
Telly Savalas	*The Young Savages* (1961)
John Saxon	*It Should Happen to You* (1953)
Greta Scacchi	*Das Zweite Gesicht* (1982) Short: *Dead on Time* (1981)
Roy Scheider	*The Curse of the Living Corpse* (1963) as Roy R Scheider
Maximilian Schell	*Die Letzte Brücke* (1954)
Romy Schneider	*Wenn der Weisse Flieder Wieder Blüht* (1953)
Arnie Schwarzenegger	*Hercules Goes Bananas* (1969) (as Arnold Strong)
Paul Scofield	*That Lady* (1955)
Kristin Scott-Thomas	*Under the Cherry Moon* (1986)
Randolph Scott	*Sharp Shooters* (1928)
George C Scott	*The Hanging Tree* (1959)
Steven Seagal	*Above the Law* (1988) GB title: *Nico*
Jean Seberg	*Saint Joan* (1957)
Harry Secombe	*Hocus Pocus* (1948)
George Segal	*The Young Doctors* (1961)
Tom Selleck	*Myra Breckinridge* (1970) *Judd for the Defense: The Holy Ground* (1969) was a made-for-TV film series
Peter Sellers	*Penny Points to Paradise* (1951) As extra: *Oliver Twist* (1948) Voice only: *The Black Rose* (1950)
Jane Seymour	*Oh What a Lovely War* (1969)
Omar Sharif	*The Blazing Sun* (1954) (as Omar el Cherif)
William Shatner	*The Brothers Karamazov* (1958) TV film: *The Defenders* (1957)
Robert Shaw	*The Lavender Hill Mob* (1951)
Norma Shearer	*Way Down East* (1920)
Charlie Sheen	*Grizzly II: The Predator* (1982) TV film: *The Execution of Private Slovik* (1974)
Martin Sheen	*The Incident* (1967)
Sam Shepard	*Renaldo and Clara* (1977) Voice only: *Easy Rider* (1969)
Cybill Shepherd	*The Last Picture Show* (1971)
Ann Sheridan	*Search for Beauty* (1934) (as Clara Lou Sheridan)
Dinah Sheridan	*I Give My Heart* (1934)
Brooke Shields	*Communion / Alice Sweet Alice* (1977)
Dinah Shore	*Thank Your Lucky Stars* (1943)
Simone Signoret	*Le Prince Charmant* (1942)
Phil Silvers	*Hit Parade of 1941* (1940) Short: *Here's Your Hat* (1937)
Alicia Silverstone	*The Crush* (1993) TV film: *Scattered Dreams* (1992)
Alastair Sim	*Riverside Murder* (1935)
Jean Simmons	*Give Us the Moon* (1944)
Frank Sinatra	*Las Vegas Nights* (1941) GB title: *The Gray City* Short: *Major Bowes' Amateur Theatre of the Air* (1935)

Actor	*Film*
Donald Sinden	*Portrait from Life* (1948)
Christian Slater	*The Legend of Billie Jean* (1985) TV film. *Living Proof: The Hank Williams Jr Story* (1983)
Maggie Smith	*Child in the House* (1956)
Will Smith	*Where the Day Takes You* (1992)
Jimmy Smits	*Running Scared* (1986) TV film: *Rockabye* (1986)
Wesley Snipes	*Wildcats* (1986)
Elke Sommer	*Das Totenschiff* (1958)
Ann Sothern	*Broadway Nights* (1927)
Sissy Spacek	*Prime Cut* (1972) As extra: *Trash* (1970)
James Spader	*Team-Mates* (1978)
Robert Stack	*First Love* (1939)
Sylvester Stallone	*Party at Kitty and Studs* (1970) Re-released as: *The Italian Stallion*
Terence Stamp	*Billy Budd* (1962)
Barbara Stanwyck	*Broadway Nights* (1927)
Imelda Staunton	*Comrades* (1987)
Anthony Steel	*Quartet* (1948)
Tommy Steele	*Kill Me Tomorrow* (1957)
Mary Steenburgen	*Goin' South* (1978)
Rod Steiger	*Teresa* (1951)
Inger Stevens	*Man on Fire* (1957)
Stella Stevens	*Say One for Me* (1959)
James Stewart	*The Murder Man* (1935) Short: *Important News* (1935)
Sting	*Quadrophenia* (1979)
Eric Stoltz	*Fast Times at Ridgemont High* (1982) TV film: *The Grass Is Always Greener over the Septic Tank* (1978)
Sharon Stone	*Stardust Memories* (1980)
The 3 Stooges	*Hollywood on Parade* (1930)
Meryl Streep	*Julia* (1977) Voice only: *Everybody Rides a Carousel* (1976)
Barbra Streisand	*Funny Girl* (1968)
Donald Sutherland	*The World Ten Times Over* (1963)
Kiefer Sutherland	*Max Dugan Returns* (1983)
Hilary Swank	*Buffy the Vampire Slayer* (1992)
Gloria Swanson	*Her Decision* (1918) Short: *The Romance of an American Duchess* (1915)
Patrick Swayze	*Skatetown USA* (1979)
Tilda Swinton	*Caravaggio* (1986) Uncredited: *Monty Python's Meaning of Life* (1983)
Eric Sykes	*Orders Are Orders* (1954)
Sylvia Syms	*My Teenage Daughter* (1955)
Russ Tamblyn	*Boy with Green Hair* (1948) (as Rusty Tamblyn)
Jacques Tati	*Retour à la Terre* (1938) Short: *Oscar, Champion de Tennis* (1932)
Elizabeth Taylor	*One Born Every Minute* (1942) Short: *Man or Mouse* (1942)
Robert Taylor	*Handy Andy* (1934)
Rod Taylor	*The Sturt Expedition* (1951) (as Rodney Taylor)
Shirley Temple	*The Red-Haired Alibi* (1932) Short: *War Babies* (1932)
Charlize Theron	*2 Days in the Valley* (1996) As extra: *Children of the Corn III: Urban Harvest* (1995)
Terry Thomas	*It's Love Again* (1936)
Emma Thompson	*The Tall Guy* (1989)
Sybil Thorndike	*Moth and Rust* (1921)
Uma Thurman	*Kiss Daddy Good Night* (1987)
Gene Tierney	*The Return of Frank James* (1940)
Richard Todd	*For Them That Trespass* (1948)
Marisa Tomei	*The Flamingo Kid* (1984)
Lily Tomlin	*Nashville* (1975)
David Tomlinson	*Garrison Follies* (1940) Short: *Name, Rank and Number* (1940)
Spencer Tracy	*Up the River* (1930) Short: *Taxi Talks* (1930)

Actor	*Film*
Bill Travers	*Conspirator* (1950)
John Travolta	*The Devil's Rain* (1975)
Claire Trevor	*Life in the Raw* (1933)
Tommy Trinder	*Almost a Honeymoon* (1938)
Jean-Louis Trintignant	*Si Tous les Gars du Monde* (1955) GB title: *Race for Life* Short: *Pechinef* (1955)
Forrest Tucker	*The Westerner* (1940)
Kathleen Turner	*Body Heat* (1981)
Lana Turner	*A Star Is Born* (1937)
Rita Tushingham	*A Taste of Honey* (1961)
Twiggy	*The Boy Friend* (1971)
Liv Ullman	*Fjol til Fjells* (1957)
Robert Urich	*Magnum Force* (1973)
Peter Ustinov	*Hullo Fame!* (1940)
Rudolph Valentino	*My Official Wife* (1914)
Rudy Vallee	*Vagabond Lover* (1929) Short: *Radio Rhythm* (1929)
Lee Van Cleef	*The Showdown* (1950)
Jean-Claude Van Damme	*Rue Barbar* (1983) US title: *Street of the Damned*
Dick Van Dyke	*Bye Bye Birdie* (1963)
Frankie Vaughan	*Ramsbottom Rides Again* (1957) Singing commentary: *Escape in the Sun* (1956)
Robert Vaughn	*The Ten Commandments* (1956)
Conrad Veidt	*Der Spion* (1916)
Monica Vitti	*Ridere, Ridere, Ridere* (1955)
Jon Voight	*The Hour of the Gun* (1967)
Erich Von Stroheim	*Captain McLean* (1914)
Max Von Sydow	*Bara en Mor* (1949)
Robert Wagner	*The Happy Years* (1950)
Christopher Walken	*Me and My Brother* (1968)
Clint Walker	*Mighty Joe Young* (1949) (as Norman Walker)
Eli Wallach	*Baby Doll* (1956) TV film: *Danger* (1952)
Julie Walters	*Educating Rita* (1983) Short: *Occupy!* (1976)
Rachel Ward	*Night School* (1980) GB title: *Terror Eyes*
Simon Ward	*If* (1968)
David Warner	*Loneliness of the Long Distance Runner* (1962)
Jack Warner	*The Dummy Talks* (1943)
Denzel Washington	*Carbon Copy* (1981) TV film: *Wilma* (1977)
Dennis Waterman	*Night Train for Inverness* (1959)
John Wayne	*Brown of Harvard* (1926)
Dennis Weaver	*Riders of Vengeance* (1952)
Sigourney Weaver	*Annie Hall* (1977)
Clifton Webb	*Polly with a Past* (1920)
Johnny Weissmuller	*Glorifying the American Girl* (1929)
Raquel Welch	*Roustabout* (1964)
Tuesday Weld	*The Wrong Man* (1956)
Orson Welles	*Citizen Kane* (1941) Short: *The Hearts of Age* (1934) Unreleased: *Too Much Johnson* (1938) As narrator: *Swiss Family Robinson* (1940)
Mae West	*Night after Night* (1932)
Joanne Whalley-Kilmer	*The Wall* (1982)
Forest Whitaker	*Fast Times at Ridgemont High* (1982)
Billie Whitelaw	*The Fake* (1953)
Pearl White	*The Life of Buffalo Bill* (1910)
Richard Widmark	*Kiss of Death* (1947)
Gene Wilder	*Bonnie and Clyde* (1967)
Cornel Wilde	*The Lady With Red Hair* (1940)
Michael Wilding	*Heads We Go* (1933) As extra: *Bitter Sweet* (1933)
Nicol Williamson	*Inadmissible Evidence* (1968) Short: *The Six-Sided Triangle* (1963)
Emlyn Williams	*The Frightened Lady* (1932)
Esther Williams	*Andy Hardy's Double Life* (1942)
Kenneth Williams	*Trent's Last Case* (1952)
Robin Williams	*Can I Do It 'til I Need Glasses* (1977)
Bruce Willis	*The First Deadly Sin* (1980) TV film: *Ziegfeld – The Man & His Women* (1978)

Actor	Film
Barbara Windsor	*Belles of St Trinian's* (1954)
Oprah Winfrey	*The Color Purple* (1985)
Debra Winger	*Slumber Party '57* (1976)
Kate Winslet	*Heavenly Creatures* (1994)
Shelley Winters	*What a Woman!* (1943) GB title: *The Beautiful Cheat*
Norman Wisdom	*A Date with a Dream* (1948)
Googie Withers	*The Girl in the Crowd* (1934)
Sir Donald Wolfit	*Down River* (1931)
Natalie Wood	*Happy Land* (1943) (as Natasha Gurdin)
James Woods	*The Visitors* (1971)
Edward Woodward	*Where There's a Will* (1955)
Joanne Woodward	*Count Three and Pray* (1955)
Fay Wray	*What Price Goofy* (1925) Short: *Gasoline Love* (1923)

Actor	Film
Teresa Wright	*The Little Foxes* (1941)
Jane Wyman	*The Kid from Spain* (1932) (as Sarah Jane Fulks)
Michael York	*The Mind Benders* (1962)
Susannah York	*Tunes of Glory* (1960)
Gig Young	*Misbehaving Husbands* (1940) (as Byron Barr)
Loretta Young	*The Only Way* (1917) (as Gretchen Young)
Robert Young	*The Black Camel* (1931)
Sean Young	*Stripes* (1981). TV film: *Jane Austen in Manhattan* (1980)
Pia Zadora	*Santa Claus Conquers the Martians* (1964)
Catherine Zeta-Jones	*Les Mille et Une Nuits* (1001 Nights) (1989)
Mai Zetterling	*Lasse-Maja* (1941)

NB: This is an area where many fine sources of information will inevitably differ, depending on the definition given of 'first film'. To give an example of the inherent dangers in answering questions on screen debuts, we can look at the early career of Orson Welles.

The 1941 classic, *Citizen Kane*, is often considered to be Welles's first film performance; but whilst it was certainly his first feature film, he did in fact do various film work before this. His potential was first spotted in his home-made film of 1934, *The Hearts of Age*, a film short that never went on general release. The unreleased film *Too Much Johnson* (1938) was shown to private audiences, although it was eventually lost to the world in a fire at Welles's Spanish home.

If narration is considered a film role, then the 1940 film *Swiss Family Robinson*, starring Thomas Mitchell and Freddie Bartholomew, could also be regarded as his big screen debut.

The approach taken in listing these is to cite an actor's debut in a film on general release and to mention prior work underneath. Many jobbing screen actors start their careers making 'film shorts', often shown before a main feature, but these films are rarely listed in cinema catalogues and are only included here if they predate a debut in a full-length feature. 'Made for television' films are treated in a similar vein.

Last Films

Actor	Film
Dev Anand	*Chargesheet* (2011)
Fred Astaire	*Ghost Story* (1981)
Mary Astor	*Hush, Hush, Sweet Charlotte* (1964)
Gene Autry	*It's Showtime* (1976)
Lew Ayres	*Letters from Frank* (1979) TV film: *Cast the First Stone* (1989)
George Baker	*Back to the Secret Garden* (2001)
Ingrid Bergman	*Autumn Sonata* (1978) TV film: *A Woman Called Golda* (1982)
Humphrey Bogart	*The Harder They Fall* (1956)
Ernest Borgnine	*The Man Who Shook the Hand of Vicente Fernandez* (2012)
Stephen Boyd	*The Squeeze* (1977)
Charles Boyer	*A Matter of Time* (1976)
Marlon Brando	*The Score* (2001)
Charles Bronson	*Death Wish V: The Face of Death* (1994) TV film: *Family of Cops III* (1998)
Yul Brynner	*Futureworld* (1976)
Horst Buchholz	*The Enemy* (2000)
George Burns	*Radioland Murders* (1994)
Raymond Burr	*Delirious* (1991) TV film: *Perry Mason: The Case of the Killer Kiss* (1993)
Richard Burton	*1984* (1984) TV film: *Ellis Island* (1984)
James Cagney	*Ragtime* (1981) TV film: *Terrible Joe Moran* (1984)
John Candy	*Canadian Bacon* (1995)
David Carradine	*Stretch* (2010)
Lon Chaney	*The Unholy Three* (1930)
Charlie Chaplin	*A Countess from Hong Kong* (1966)
Maurice Chevalier	*Monkeys Go Home* (1967) Voice only: *The Aristocats* (1970)
Diane Cilento	*The Boy Who Had Everything* (1985)
Montgomery Clift	*The Defector* (1966)
James Coburn	*Snow Dogs* (2002)
Claudette Colbert	*Parrish* (1961) TV film: *The Two Mrs Grenvilles* (1987)
Ronald Colman	*The Story of Mankind* (1957)

Actor	Film
Jackie Coogan	*The Prey* (1983)
Gary Cooper	*The Naked Edge* (1961)
Harry H Corbett	*Silver Dream Racer* (1980)
Joseph Cotten	*Rambo Sfida la Citta* (1982)
Noël Coward	*The Italian Job* (1969)
Broderick Crawford	*Liar's Moon* (1981)
Joan Crawford	*Trog* (1970) TV film: *We're Going to Scare You to Death* (1975)
Richard Crenna	*Wrongfully Accused* (1998) TV film: *Out of the Ashes* (2003)
Bing Crosby	*That's Entertainment* (1974)
Peter Cushing	*Biggles* (1986)
Bette Davis	*Wicked Stepmother* (1989) Short: *Hairway to the Stars* (1989)
Sammy Davis Jnr	*Tap* (1988) TV film: *The Kid Who Loved Christmas* (1990)
James Dean	*Giant* (1956)
Brad Dexter	*Secret Ingredient* (1990)
Marlene Dietrich	*Marlene* (1984)
Robert Donat	*The Inn of the Sixth Happiness* (1958)
Diana Dors	*Steaming* (1985)
Michael Clarke Duncan	*The Challenger* (2013)
Michael Elphick	TV film: *Ken Russell's Treasure Island* (1995)
Edith Evans	*Nasty Habits* (1976)
Douglas Fairbanks	*The Private Life of Don Juan* (1934)
Peter Falk	*American Cowslip* (2009)
Farrah Fawcett	*The Cookout* (2004)
Marty Feldman	*Yellowbeard* (1983)
Gracie Fields	*Madame Pimpernel* (1945)
WC Fields	*Sensations of 1945* (1944)
Peter Finch	*Network* (1976) TV film: *Raid on Entebbe* (1977)
Errol Flynn	*Cuban Rebel Girls* (1959)
Henry Fonda	*On Golden Pond* (1981) TV film: *Summer Solstice* (1981)
Glenn Ford	*Raw Nerve* (1991)

Actor	*Film*
George Formby	*George in Civvy Street* (1946)
Harry Fowler	*Chicago Joe and the Showgirl* (1990)
Anthony Franciosa	TV film: *Manifest Mysteries: Coronation* (2006)
Clark Gable	*The Misfits* (1961)
Greta Garbo	*Two-Faced Woman* (1941)
Ava Gardner	*Roma Regina* (1982)
Judy Garland	*I Could Go on Singing* (1963)
Greer Garson	*Directed by William Wyler* (1986)
Ben Gazzara	*Ristabbànna* (2011)
Lillian Gish	*The Whales of August* (1987)
Betty Grable	*How to Be Very Very Popular* (1955)
Stewart Granger	*Oro Fina (Fine Gold)* (1988) TV film: *Chameleons* (1989)
Cary Grant	*Elvis – That's the Way It Is* (1970)
Peter Graves	*Addams Family Values* (1993) TV film: *Jack's Family Adventure* (2010)
Dulcie Gray	*Welcome, Mr Beddoes* (1966)
Sydney Greenstreet	*Malaya* (1949) GB title: *East of the Rising Sun*
John Gregson	*The Tiger Lily* (1975)
Richard Griffiths	*Private Peaceful* (2012)
Larry Hagman	*The Flight of the Swan* (2011)
Tony Hancock	*The Wrong Box* (1966)
Oliver Hardy	*Meet Bela Lugosi and Oliver Hardy* (1952)
Jean Harlow	*Saratoga* (1937)
Richard Harris	*Harry Potter and the Chamber of Secrets* (2002)
Rex Harrison	*A Time to Die* (1983). Aka *Seven Graves for Rogan*
Jack Hawkins	*The Last Lion* (1973) TV film: *QB VII* (1974)
Susan Hayward	*The Revengers* (1972) TV film: *Say Goodbye, Maggie Cole* (1972)
Rita Hayworth	*Circle* (1976)
Will Hay	*My Learned Friend* (1943)
Van Heflin	*The Big Bounce* (1969) TV film: *The Last Child* (1971)
David Hemmings	*The League of Extraordinary Gentlemen* (2003)
Audrey Hepburn	*Always* (1989)
Katharine Hepburn	*Love Affair* (1994)
Charlton Heston	*My Father, Rua Alguem 5555* (2003)
Thora Hird	*Julie and the Cadillacs* (1999)
William Holden	*S.O.B.* (1981) TV film: *Mysteries of the Sea* (1981) (as narrator)
Judy Holliday	*Bells Are Ringing* (1960)
Stanley Holloway	*Journey into Fear* (1976)
Leslie Howard	*The First of the Few* (1942)
Trevor Howard	*The Dawning* (1988) Died whilst filming *Stille Nacht*, about the author of the carol 'Silent Night'
Frankie Howerd	*Sgt Pepper's Lonely Hearts Club Band* (1978)
Rock Hudson	*The Ambassador* (1984) TV film: *The Vegas Strip Wars* (1985)
Jeffrey Hunter	*Mafia Mob* (1969)
John Huston	*John Huston and the Dubliners* (1987)
Burl Ives	*Two Moon Junction* (1988)
Gordon Jackson	*The Whistle Blower* (1986) TV film: *Lady and the Highwayman* (1989)
Sid James	*Carry On Dick* (1974)
Celia Johnson	*The Prime of Miss Jean Brodie* (1968) TV film: *The Hostage Tower* (1980)
Al Jolson	*Rhapsody in Blue* (1945) Voice only: *Jolson Sings Again* (1949)
Jennifer Jones	*The Towering Inferno* (1974)
Boris Karloff	*The Incredible Invasion* (1969). Limited release: *House of Evil* (1972) Unseen footage: *Transylvania Twist* (1989)
Danny Kaye	*The Madwoman of Chaillot* (1969) Short: *Pied Piper* (1972) TV film: *Once They Marched through a Thousand Towns* (1981) US title: *Skokie*

Actor	*Film*
Buster Keaton	*A Funny Thing Happened on the Way to the Forum* (1966) Short: *The Scribe* (1966)
Howard Keel	*My Father's House* (2002)
Gene Kelly	*That's Entertainment III* (1994)
Grace Kelly	*Invitation to Monte Carlo* (1959) As narrator: *The Children of Theatre Street* (1978)
Deborah Kerr	*The Assam Garden* (1985)
Jack Klugman	*Camera Obscura* (2010)
Alan Ladd	*The Carpetbaggers* (1964)
Veronica Lake	*Flesh Feast* (1970)
Dorothy Lamour	*Creepshow 2* (1987)
Burt Lancaster	*Field of Dreams* (1989) TV film: *Separate but Equal* (1991)
Dinsdale Landen	*The Steal* (1994)
Mario Lanza	*For the First Time* (1959)
Charles Laughton	*Advise and Consent* (1962)
Stan Laurel	*Atoll K* (1951). GB title: *Robinson Crusoeland*
Peter Lawford	*Where Is Parsifal?* (1984)
Heath Ledger	*The Imaginarium of Doctor Parnassus* (2009)
Bruce Lee	*Game of Death* (1978, posthumously)
Gypsy Rose Lee	*The Trouble with Angels* (1966) TV film: *The Over the Hill Gang* (1969)
Vivien Leigh	*Ship of Fools* (1965)
Harold Lloyd	*The Sins of Harold Diddlebock* (1947) GB title: *Mad Wednesday*
Margaret Lockwood	*The Slipper and the Rose* (1976)
Carole Lombard	*To Be or Not to Be* (1942)
Peter Lorre	*Muscle Beach Party* (1964)
Myrna Loy	*Just Tell Me What You Want* (1980). TV film: *Summer Solstice* (1981)
Bela Lugosi	*Plan 9 from Outer Space* (1957)
Ida Lupino	*Deadhead Miles* (1982)
Jeanette MacDonald	*The Sun Comes Up* (1948) TV film: *Charley's Aunt* (1957)
Leo McKern	*Molokai – The Story of Father Damien* (1999)
Victor McLaglen	*The Italians Are Crazy* (1958)
Fred MacMurray	*The Swarm* (1978)
Philip Madoc	*Y Mabinogi* (2003) Short: *Hawk* (2011)
Anna Magnani	*Fellini's Roma* (1972)
Karl Malden	*Nuts* (1987)
Jayne Mansfield	*Mondo Hollywood* (1967)
Fredric March	*The Iceman Cometh* (1973)
Dean Martin	*Cannonball Run II* (1983) TV film: *Half Nelson* (1985)
Lee Marvin	*The Delta Force* (1986)
Marx Brothers	*Love Happy* (1950) Guest appearances in separate episodes of *The Story of Mankind* (1957) TV film: *Incredible Jewel Robbery* (1960) Later films didn't include all 3 main brothers
James Mason	*The Assisi Underground* (1984)
Raymond Massey	*MacKenna's Gold* (1969) TV film: *The President's Plane Is Missing* (1973)
Marcello Mastroianni	*Journey to the Beginning of the World* (1996)
Jessie Matthews	*Never Never Land* (1980)
Victor Mature	*Firepower* (1979) TV film: *Samson and Delilah* (1984)
Simon MacCorkindale	*13Hrs* (2010)
Patrick McGoohan	*Treasure Planet* (2002)
TP McKenna	*The Libertine* (2004) Short: *Death's Door* (2009)
Steve McQueen	*The Hunter* (1980)
Melina Mercouri	*Keine Zufallige Geschichte* (1983) US title: *Not by Coincidence*
Ethel Merman	*Airplane!* (1980)
Ray Milland	*The Sea Serpent* (1985)
Max Miller	*Asking for Trouble* (1943)
John Mills	*Bright Young Things* (2003)
Carmen Miranda	*Scared Stiff* (1953)

Actor	*Film*
Robert Mitchum	*Waiting for Sunset* (1997)
Tom Mix	*Rustlers' Roundup* (1933) Short film Series: *The Miracle Rider* (1935)
Marilyn Monroe	*The Misfits* (1961) (uncompleted) *Something's Got to Give*
Ricardo Montalban	*The Ant Bully* (2006)
Yves Montand	*IP5: L'Ile aux Pachydermes* (1992)
Kenneth More	*The Spaceman and King Arthur* (1979) TV film: *A Tale of Two Cities* (1981)
Robert Morley	*Istanbul* (1989) TV film: *The Lady and the Highwayman* (1989)
Zero Mostel	*Best Boy* (1979)
Paul Muni	*The Last Angry Man* (1959)
Audie Murphy	*A Time for Dying* (1969)
Anna Neagle	*The Lady Is a Square* (1959)
Paul Newman	*Cars* (2006)
Leslie Nielsen	*The Waterman Movie* (2013)
David Niven	*Curse of the Pink Panther* (1983)
Ivor Novello	*Autumn Crocus* (1934)
Warren Oates	*Blue Thunder* (1983)
Merle Oberon	*Interval* (1973)
Edmond O'Brien	*Dream No Evil* (1976)
Pat O'Brien	*Ragtime* (1981)
Laurence Olivier	*War Requiem* (1988)
Milo O'Shea	*Mystics* (2003)
Jack Palance	TV film: *Back When We Were Grownups* (2004)
Lili Palmer	*The Holcroft Covenant* (1985) TV film: *Peter the Great* (1986)
Fess Parker	*Smoky* (1966) TV film: *Climb an Angry Mountain* (1972)
Gregory Peck	*Cape Fear* (1991) TV film: *Moby Dick* (1998)
George Peppard	*The Tigress* (1992)
Anthony Perkins	*The Mummy Lives* (1992) TV film: *In the Deep Woods* (1992)
River Phoenix	*The Thing Called Love* (1993) Uncompleted: *Dark Blood* (1994)
Mary Pickford	*Star Night at the Cocoanut Grove* (1935)
Walter Pidgeon	*Sextette* (1977)
Donald Pleasence	*Halloween 6: The Curse of Michael Myers* (1995) Uncompleted: *Fotogrammi Mortal* (1996) (aka *Fatal Frames*). After he died his role was played by an actor in his face mask (as was Rossano Brazzi's, who also died). David Warbeck (the 'Milk Tray' man) died soon after release of the film
Eric Portman	*Deadfall* (1968)
Peter Postlethwaite	*Killing Bono* (2011)
Dick Powell	*Susan Slept Here* (1954)
William Powell	*Mister Roberts* (1955)
Tyrone Power	*Witness for the Prosecution* (1957)
Elvis Presley	*That's the Way It Is* (1970) TV film: *Elvis on Tour* (1972)
Robert Preston	*The Last Starfighter* (1984) TV film: *Outrage* (1986)
Dennis Price	*Theatre of Blood* (1973) Unreleased: *Son of Dracula* (1974) Aka *Count Downe* (also starred Ringo Starr)
Vincent Price	*Edward Scissorhands* (1990) TV film: *The Heart of Justice* (1992) Voice only: *The Thief and the Cobbler* (1995) Aka *Arabian Knight*
Richard Pryor	*Lost Highway* (1997)
Anthony Quayle	*King of the Wind* (1989)
George Raft	*The Man with Bogart's Face* (1979)
Claude Rains	*The Greatest Story Ever Told* (1965)
Basil Rathbone	*Hillbillies in a Haunted House* (1968)
Ronald Reagan	*The Killers* (1964)
Lynn Redgrave	*My Dog Tulip* (2009)
Michael Redgrave	*Nicholas and Alexandra* (1971) As narrator: *Roosevelt: The Power behind the Smile* (1975)

Actor	*Film*
Angharad Rees	*The Wolves of Kromer* (1998)
Christopher Reeve	*Village of the Damned* (1995) TV film: *Rear Window* (1998)
Lee Remick	*The Vision* (1987)
Natasha Richardson	*Wild Child* (2008)
Ralph Richardson	*Directed by William Wyler* (1986) (posthumously)
Pernell Roberts	*The Magic of Lassie* (1978) TV film: *Donor* (1990)
Rachel Roberts	*Charlie Chan and the Curse of the Dragon Queen* (1980) TV film: *The Hostage Tower* (1980)
Cliff Robertson	*Spider-Man 3* (2007)
Dale Robertson	*Aru heishi no kake* (1970) TV film: *Wind in the Wire* (1993)
Paul Robeson	*Paul Robeson: Tales of Manhattan* (1979)
Edward G Robinson	*Soylent Green* (1973)
Flora Robson	*Clash of the Titans* (1981)
Ginger Rogers	*The Confession* (1964) GB title: *Let's Get Married* TV film: *Harlow* (1964)
Will Rogers	*In Old Kentucky* (1935)
Gilbert Roland	*Barbarosa* (1982)
Cesar Romero	*The Player* (1992)
Jane Russell	*The Godfather and the Lady* (1975)
Rosalind Russell	*Mrs Pollifax – Spy* (1970) TV film: *The Crooked Hearts* (1972)
Margaret Rutherford	*Arabella* (1969)
Robert Ryan	*The Outfit* (1973)
George Sanders	*Psychomania* (1972)
Michael Sarrazin	*On the Road* (2012)
Telly Savalas	*Backfire* (1994)
Romy Schneider	*La Passante du Sans-Souci* (1981)
Randolph Scott	*Ride the High Country* (1962). GB title: *Guns in the Afternoon*
Jean Seberg	*The Wild Duck* (1976)
Peter Sellers	*Trail of the Pink Panther* (1982) (posthumous)
Robert Shaw	*Avalanche Express* (1979) (posthumous)
Norma Shearer	*Her Cardboard Lover* (1942)
Ann Sheridan	*Triangle on Safari* (1957) TV film: *Without Incident* (1957)
Dinah Shore	*Health* (1979) TV film: *Death Car on the Freeway* (1979)
Simone Signoret	*L'Etoile du Nord* (1982): As narrator: *Des 'Terroristes' à la Retraite* (1983)
Phil Silvers	*Hollywood Blue* (1980) aka *The Happy Hooker Goes to Hollywood*
Alastair Sim	*Escape from the Dark* (1976)
Jean Simmons	*Shadows in the Sun* (2009)
Robert Stack	*Killer Bud* (2001)
Barbara Stanwyck	*The Night Walker* (1965) TV film: *The Thorn Birds* (1983)
Anthony Steel	*The Monster Club* (1981)
Rod Steiger	*Poolhall Junkies* (2002)
James Stewart	*A Tale of Africa* (1981) TV film: *North and South II* (1986) Voice only: *An American Tail 2: Fievel Goes West* (1991)
The 3 Stooges	*Dr Death – Seeker of Souls* (1973)
Gloria Swanson	*Airport 1975* (1974)
Patrick Swayze	*Powder Blue* (2009)
Eric Sykes	*Son of Rambow* (2007)
Jacques Tati	*Traffic* (1971) Limited release: *Parade* (1974)
Elizabeth Taylor	*The Flintstones* (1994) TV film: *These Old Broads* (2001)
Robert Taylor	*The Glass Sphinx* (1968)
Shirley Temple	*A Kiss for Corliss* (1949)
John Thaw	*Chaplin* (1992) TV film: *Buried Treasure* (2001)
Terry Thomas	*Happy Birthday Harry!* (1981)
Sybil Thorndike	*Uncle Vanya* (1963)
Gene Tierney	*The Pleasure Seekers* (1964) TV film: *Daughter of the Mind* (1969)

Actor	*Film*
Richard Todd	*House of the Long Shadows* (1983)
Spencer Tracy	*Guess Who's Coming to Dinner* (1967)
Bill Travers	*Christian the Lion* (1973) TV film: *Bloody Ivory* (1979)
Tommy Trinder	*Barry McKenzie Holds His Own* (1974)
Lana Turner	*Witches' Brew* (1978; released 1985)
Robert Urich	*Jock – A True Tale of Friendship* (2001)
Peter Ustinov	*Luther* (2003)
Rudolph Valentino	*Son of the Sheik* (1926)
Rudy Vallee	*The Perfect Woman* (1978)
Lee Van Cleef	*Speed Zone* (1989)
Conrad Veidt	*Above Suspicion* (1943)
Erich Von Stroheim	*L'Homme Aux Cent Visages* (1956). GB title: *Man of a Thousand Faces*
Simon Ward	*Wuthering Heights* (1992) TV film: *Atrapa-la* (2000)
Jack Warner	*Dominique* (1978)
John Wayne	*The Shootist* (1976)
Dennis Weaver	*Throttle* (2005)
Clifton Webb	*Satan Never Sleeps* (1962)
Johnny Weissmuller	*Devil Goddess* (1955) Guest appearance: *That's Entertainment II* (1976)
Orson Welles	*Someone to Love* (1987) (posthumous)
Mae West	*Sextette* (1977)
Pearl White	*Perils of Paris* (1925)
Cornel Wilde	*Vultures in Paradise / Flesh and Bullets* (1983)
Michael Wilding	*Lady Caroline Lamb* (1972) TV film: *Frankenstein: The True Story* (1973)
Emlyn Williams	*The Walking Stick* (1970) TV film: *Past Caring* (1985)
Kenneth Williams	*Carry On Emmanuelle* (1978)
Nicol Williamson	*Spawn* (1997)
William Windom	*Yesterday's Dreams* (2005) Short: *Just* (2006)
Norman Wisdom	*Five Children and It* (2004) Short: *Expresso* (2007) Video: *Labrats* (2010)
Googie Withers	*Shine* (1996)
Sir Donald Wolfit	*The Charge of the Light Brigade* (1968)
Natalie Wood	*Brainstorm* (1981; released posthumously, 1983)
Fay Wray	*Summer Love* (1957). TV film: *Gideon's Trumpet* (1980)
Dana Wynter	*Le Sauvage* (1975) TV film: *The Return of Ironside* (1993)
Susannah York	*The Calling* (2009)
Gig Young	*Game of Death* (1978)
Mai Zetterling	*Morfars Resa* (1993)

Oscars (Academy Awards)

*Year	Best Film	Best Actor	Best Actress	Best Director
1929	Wings (1927)	Emil Jannings (The Way of All Flesh)	Janet Gaynor (Seventh Heaven)	Frank Borzage (Seventh Heaven) Lewis Milestone (Two Arabian Knights)†
1930	The Broadway Melody	Warner Baxter (In Old Arizona)	Mary Pickford (Coquette)	Frank Lloyd (The Divine Lady)
1931	All Quiet on the Western Front	George Arliss (Disraeli)	Norma Shearer (The Divorcee)	Lewis Milestone (All Quiet on the Western Front)
1932	Cimarron (1930)	Lionel Barrymore (A Free Soul)	Marie Dressler (Min and Bill)	Norman Taurog (Skippy)
1933	Grand Hotel	Fredric March (Dr Jekyll and Mr Hyde) Wallace Beery (*The Champ*)	Helen Hayes (The Sin of Madelon Claudet)	Frank Borzage (Bad Girl)
1934	Cavalcade (1932)	Charles Laughton (Private Life of Henry VIII)	Katharine Hepburn (Morning Glory)	Frank Lloyd (Cavalcade)
1935	It Happened One Night	Clark Gable (It Happened One Night)	Claudette Colbert (It Happened One Night)	Frank Capra (It Happened One Night)
1936	Mutiny on the Bounty	Victor McLaglen (The Informer)	Bette Davis (Dangerous)	John Ford (The Informer)
1937	The Great Ziegfeld	Paul Muni (The Story of Louis Pasteur)	Luise Rainer (The Great Ziegfeld)	Frank Capra (Mr Deeds Goes to Town)
1938	The Life of Emile Zola	Spencer Tracy (Captains Courageous)	Luise Rainer (The Good Earth)	Leo McCarey (The Awful Truth)
1939	You Can't Take It with You	Spencer Tracy (Boys Town)	Bette Davis (Jezebel)	Frank Capra (You Can't Take It With You)
1940	Gone with the Wind	Robert Donat (Goodbye Mr Chips)	Vivien Leigh (Gone with the Wind)	Victor Fleming (Gone with the Wind)
1941	Rebecca	James Stewart (The Philadelphia Story)	Ginger Rogers (Kitty Foyle)	John Ford (The Grapes of Wrath)
1942	How Green Was My Valley	Gary Cooper (Sergeant York)	Joan Fontaine (Suspicion)	John Ford (How Green Was My Valley)
1943	Mrs Miniver	James Cagney (Yankee Doodle Dandy)	Greer Garson (Mrs Miniver)	William Wyler (Mrs Miniver)
1944	Casablanca (1942)	Paul Lukas (Watch on the Rhine)	Jennifer Jones (The Song of Bernadette)	Michael Curtiz (Casablanca)
1945	Going My Way	Bing Crosby (Going My Way)	Ingrid Bergman (Gaslight)	Leo McCarey (Going My Way)
1946	The Lost Weekend	Ray Milland *(The Lost Weekend)*	Joan Crawford *(Mildred Pierce)*	Billy Wilder (The Lost Weekend)
1947	The Best Years of Our Lives	Fredric March (The Best Years of Our Lives)	Olivia de Havilland (To Each His Own)	William Wyler (The Best Years of Our Lives)
1948	Gentleman's Agreement	Ronald Colman (A Double Life)	Loretta Young (The Farmer's Daughter)	Elia Kazan (Gentleman's Agreement)
1949	Hamlet	Laurence Olivier (Hamlet)	Jane Wyman (Johnny Belinda)	John Huston (The Treasure of the Sierra Madre)
1950	All the King's Men	Broderick Crawford (All the King's Men)	Olivia De Havilland (The Heiress)	Joseph L Mankiewicz (A Letter To Three Wives)
1951	All about Eve	José Ferrer (Cyrano de Bergerac)	Judy Holliday (Born Yesterday)	Joseph L Mankiewicz (All About Eve)
1952	An American In Paris	Humphrey Bogart (The African Queen)	Vivian Leigh (A Streetcar Named Desire)	George Stevens (A Place in the Sun)
1953	The Greatest Show on Earth	Gary Cooper (High Noon)	Shirley Booth (Come Back Little Sheba)	John Ford (*The Quiet Man*)
1954	From Here to Eternity	William Holden (Stalag 17)	Audrey Hepburn (Roman Holiday)	Fred Zinnemann (From Here to Eternity)
1955	On the Waterfront	Marlon Brando (On the Waterfront)	Grace Kelly (The Country Girl)	Elia Kazan (On the Waterfront)
1956	Marty	Ernest Borgnine (Marty)	Anna Magnani (The Rose Tattoo)	Delbert Mann (Marty)
1957	Around the World in Eighty Days	Yul Brynner (The King and I)	Ingrid Bergman (Anastasia)	George Stevens (Giant)
1958	The Bridge on the River Kwai	Alec Guinness (The Bridge on The River Kwai)	Joanne Woodward (The Three Faces of Eve)	David Lean (The Bridge on the River Kwai)
1959	Gigi	David Niven (Separate Tables)	Susan Hayward (I Want To Live)	Vincente Minnelli (Gigi)
1960	Ben Hur	Charlton Heston (Ben Hur)	Simone Signoret (Room at the Top)	William Wyler (Ben Hur)
1961	The Apartment	Burt Lancaster (Elmer Gantry)	Elizabeth Taylor (Butterfield 8)	Billy Wilder (The Apartment)
1962	West Side Story	Maximilian Schell (Judgment at Nuremberg)	Sophia Loren (Two Women)	Jerome Robbins & Robert Wise (West Side Story)
1963	Lawrence of Arabia	Gregory Peck (To Kill a Mockingbird)	Anne Bancroft (The Miracle Worker)	David Lean (Lawrence of Arabia)
1964	Tom Jones	Sidney Poitier (Lilies of the Field)	Patricia Neal (Hud)	Tony Richardson (Tom Jones)
1965	My Fair Lady	Rex Harrison (My Fair Lady)	Julie Andrews (Mary Poppins)	George Cukor (My Fair Lady)
1966	The Sound of Music	Lee Marvin (Cat Ballou)	Julie Christie (Darling)	Robert Wise (The Sound of Music)
1967	A Man for All Seasons	Paul Scofield (A Man for All Seasons)	Elizabeth Taylor (Who's Afraid of Virginia Woolf)	Fred Zinnemann (A Man for All Seasons)
1968	In the Heat of the Night	Rod Steiger (In the Heat of the Night)	Katharine Hepburn (Guess Who's Coming To Dinner)	Mike Nichols (The Graduate)
1969	Oliver!	Cliff Robertson (Charly)	Katharine Hepburn (The Lion in Winter) Barbra Streisand (Funny Girl)†	Carol Reed (Oliver!)

*Year	Best Film	Best Actor	Best Actress	Director
1970	Midnight Cowboy	John Wayne (True Grit)	Maggie Smith (The Prime of Miss Jean Brodie)	John Schlesinger (Midnight Cowboy)
1971	Patton	George C Scott (Patton)	Glenda Jackson (Women in Love)	Franklin Schaffner (Patton)
1972	The French Connection	Gene Hackman (The French Connection)	Jane Fonda (Klute)	William Friedkin (The French Connection)
1973	The Godfather	Marlon Brando (The Godfather)	Liza Minnelli (Cabaret)	Bob Fosse (Cabaret)
1974	The Sting	Jack Lemmon (Save the Tiger)	Glenda Jackson (A Touch of Class)	George Roy Hill (The Sting)
1975	The Godfather Part II	Art Carney (Harry and Tonto)	Ellen Burstyn (Alice Doesn't Live Here Any More)	Francis Ford Coppola (The Godfather Part II)
1976	One Flew over the Cuckoo's Nest	Jack Nicholson (One Flew over the Cuckoo's Nest)	Louise Fletcher (One Flew Over the Cuckoo's Nest)	Milos Forman (One Flew over the Cuckoo's Nest)
1977	Rocky	Peter Finch (Network)	Faye Dunaway (Network)	John G Avildsen (*Rocky*)
1978	Annie Hall	Richard Dreyfuss (The Goodbye Girl)	Diane Keaton (Annie Hall)	Woody Allen (*Annie Hall*)
1979	The Deer Hunter	Jon Voight (Coming Home)	Jane Fonda (Coming Home)	Michael Cimino (*The Deer Hunter*)
1980	Kramer versus Kramer	Dustin Hoffman (Kramer versus Kramer)	Sally Field (Norma Rae)	Robert Benton (Kramer versus Kramer)
1981	Ordinary People	Robert De Niro (Raging Bull)	Sissy Spacek (Coal Miner's Daughter)	Robert Redford (Ordinary People)
1982	Chariots of Fire	Henry Fonda (On Golden Pond)	Katharine Hepburn (On Golden Pond)	Warren Beatty (Reds)
1983	Gandhi	Ben Kingsley (Gandhi)	Meryl Streep (Sophie's Choice)	Richard Attenborough (Gandhi)
1984	Terms of Endearment	Robert Duvall (Tender Mercies)	Shirley MacLaine (Terms of Endearment)	James L Brooks (Terms of Endearment)
1985	Amadeus	F Murray Abraham (Amadeus)	Sally Field (Places in the Heart)	Milos Forman (Amadeus)
1986	Out of Africa	William Hurt (Kiss of the Spider Woman)	Geraldine Page (The Trip to Bountiful)	Sydney Pollack (Out of Africa)
1987	Platoon	Paul Newman (The Color of Money)	Marlee Matlin (Children of a Lesser God)	Oliver Stone (Platoon)
1988	The Last Emperor	Michael Douglas (Wall Street)	Cher (Moonstruck)	Bernardo Bertolucci (The Last Emperor)
1989	Rain Man	Dustin Hoffman (Rain Man)	Jodie Foster (The Accused)	Barry Levinson (Rain Man)
1990	Driving Miss Daisy	Daniel Day Lewis (My Left Foot)	Jessica Tandy (Driving Miss Daisy)	Oliver Stone (Born on the Fourth of July)
1991	Dances with Wolves	Jeremy Irons (Reversal of Fortune)	Kathy Bates (Misery)	Kevin Costner (Dances with Wolves)
1992	Silence of the Lambs	Anthony Hopkins (Silence of the Lambs)	Jodie Foster (Silence of the Lambs)	Jonathan Demme (Silence of the Lambs)
1993	Unforgiven	Al Pacino (Scent of a Woman)	Emma Thompson (Howard's End)	Clint Eastwood (Unforgiven)
1994	Schindler's List	Tom Hanks (Philadelphia)	Holly Hunter (The Piano)	Steven Spielberg (Schindler's List)
1995	Forrest Gump	Tom Hanks (Forrest Gump)	Jessica Lange (Blue Sky)	Robert Zemeckis (Forrest Gump)
1996	Braveheart	Nicolas Cage (Leaving Las Vegas)	Susan Sarandon (Dead Man Walking)	Mel Gibson (Braveheart)
1997	The English Patient	Geoffrey Rush (Shine)	Frances McDormand (Fargo)	Anthony Minghella (The English Patient)
1998	Titanic	Jack Nicholson (As Good As it Gets)	Helen Hunt (As Good As it Gets)	James Cameron (Titanic)
1999	*Shakespeare in Love*	Roberto Benigni *(Life is Beautiful)*	Gwyneth Paltrow *(Shakespeare in Love)*	Steven Spielberg *(Saving Private Ryan)*
2000	*American Beauty*	Kevin Spacey *(American Beauty)*	Hilary Swank *(Boys Don't Cry)*	Sam Mendes *(American Beauty)*
2001	*Gladiator*	Russell Crowe *(Gladiator)*	Julia Roberts *(Erin Brockovich)*	Steven Soderbergh *(Traffic)*
2002	*A Beautiful Mind*	Denzel Washington *(Training Day)*	Halle Berry *(Monster's Ball)*	Ron Howard *(A Beautiful Mind)*
2003	*Chicago*	Adrien Brody *(The Pianist)*	Nicole Kidman *(The Hours)*	Roman Polanski *(The Pianist)*
2004	*The Lord of the Rings: Return of the King*	Sean Penn *(Mystic River)*	Charlize Theron *(Monster)*	Peter Jackson *(The Lord of the Rings: Return of the King)*
2005	*Million Dollar Baby*	Jamie Foxx *(Ray)*	Hilary Swank *(Million Dollar Baby)*	Clint Eastwood *(Million Dollar Baby)*
2006	*Crash*	Philip Seymour Hoffman *(Capote)*	Reese Witherspoon *(Walk the Line)*	Ang Lee *(Brokeback Mountain)*
2007	*The Departed*	Forest Whitaker *(Last King of Scotland)*	Helen Mirren *(The Queen)*	Martin Scorsese *(The Departed)*
2008	*No Country For Old Men*	Daniel Day-Lewis *(There Will Be Blood)*	Marion Cotillard *(La Vie en Rose)*	Joel and Ethan Coen *(No Country For Old Men)*
2009	*Slumdog Millionaire*	Sean Penn *(Milk)*	Kate Winslet *(The Reader)*	Danny Boyle *(Slumdog Millionaire)*
2010	*The Hurt Locker* (2008)	Jeff Bridges *(Crazy Heart)*	Sandra Bullock *(The Blind Side)*	Kathryn Bigelow *(The Hurt Locker)*
2011	The King's Speech	Colin Firth (The King's Speech)	Natalie Portman (Black Swan)	Tom Hooper (The King's Speech)
2012	The Artist	Jean Dujardin (The Artist)	Meryl Streep (The Iron Lady)	Michel Hazanavicius (The Artist)
2013	Argo	Daniel Day-Lewis (Lincoln)	Jennifer Lawrence (Silver Linings Playbook)	Ang Lee (Life of Pi)

* The Oscars are awarded for films made the previous year – e.g. the 1997 Best Film Oscar was awarded to *The English Patient*, which was a 1996 film release.
All of the above films were premiered in the year prior to the award unless the date is specifically given, since as on rare occasions a film has been released too late for consideration for a nomination, as in the case of Casablanca.

† Separate award for Comedy Director.

Oscars (Academy Awards) Continued

	Best Supporting Actor		Best Supporting Actress	
Year	*Actor*	*Film*	*Actress*	*Film*
1937	Walter Brennan	*Come and Get it*	Gale Sondergaard	Anthony Adverse
1938	Joseph Schildkraut	*The Life of Emile Zola*	Alice Brady	*In Old Chicago*
1939	Walter Brennan	*Kentucky*	Fay Bainter	*Jezebel*
1940	Thomas Mitchell	*Stagecoach*	Hattie McDaniel	*Gone with the Wind*
1941	Walter Brennan	*The Westerner*	Jane Darwell	*The Grapes of Wrath*
1942	Donald Crisp	*How Green Was My Valley*	Mary Astor	*The Great Lie*
1943	Van Heflin	*Johnny Eager*	Teresa Wright	*Mrs Miniver*
1944	Charles Coburn	*The More the Merrier*	Katina Paxinou	*For Whom the Bell Tolls*
1945	Barry Fitzgerald	*Going My Way*	Ethel Barrymore	*None but the Lonely Heart*
1946	James Dunn	*A Tree Grows in Brooklyn*	Anne Revere	*National Velvet*
1947	Harold Russell	*The Best Years of Our Lives*	Anne Baxter	*The Razor's Edge*
1948	Edmund Gwenn	*Miracle on 34th Street*	Celeste Holm	*Gentleman's Agreement*
1949	Walter Huston	*The Treasure of the Sierra Madre*	Claire Trevor	*Key Largo*
1950	Dean Jagger	*Twelve O'Clock High*	Mercedes McCambridge	*All the King's Men*
1951	George Sanders	*All about Eve*	Josephine Hull	*Harvey*
1952	Karl Malden	*A Streetcar Named Desire*	Kim Hunter	*A Streetcar Named Desire*
1953	Anthony Quinn	*Viva Zapata!*	Gloria Grahame	*The Bad and the Beautiful*
1954	Frank Sinatra	*From Here to Eternity*	Donna Reed	*From Here to Eternity*
1955	Edmond O'Brien	*The Barefoot Contessa*	Eva Marie Saint	*On the Waterfront*
1956	Jack Lemmon	*Mister Roberts*	Jo Van Fleet	*East of Eden*
1957	Anthony Quinn	*Lust for Life*	Dorothy Malone	*Written on the Wind*
1958	Red Buttons	*Sayonara*	Miyoshi Umeki	*Sayonara*
1959	Burl Ives	*The Big Country*	Wendy Hiller	*Separate Tables*
1960	Hugh Griffith	*Ben-Hur*	Shelley Winters	*The Diary of Anne Frank*
1961	Peter Ustinov	*Spartacus*	Shirley Jones	*Elmer Gantry*
1962	George Chakiris	*West Side Story*	Rita Moreno	*West Side Story*
1963	Ed Begley	*Sweet Bird of Youth*	Patty Duke	*The Miracle Worker*
1964	Melvyn Douglas	*Hud*	Margaret Rutherford	*The V.I.P.s*
1965	Peter Ustinov	*Topkapi*	Lila Kedrova	*Zorba the Greek*
1966	Martin Balsam	*A Thousand Clowns*	Shelley Winters	*A Patch of Blue*
1967	Walter Matthau	*The Fortune Cookie*	Sandy Dennis	*Who's Afraid of Virginia Woolf?*
1968	George Kennedy	*Cool Hand Luke*	Estelle Parsons	*Bonnie and Clyde*
1969	Jack Albertson	*The Subject Was Roses*	Ruth Gordon	*Rosemary's Baby*
1970	Gig Young	*They Shoot Horses Don't They?*	Goldie Hawn	*Cactus Flower*
1971	John Mills	*Ryan's Daughter*	Helen Hayes	*Airport*
1972	Ben Johnson	*The Last Picture Show*	Cloris Leachman	*The Last Picture Show*
1973	Joel Grey	*Cabaret*	Eileen Heckart	*Butterflies Are Free*
1974	John Houseman	*The Paper Chase*	Tatum O'Neal	*Paper Moon*
1975	Robert De Niro	*The Godfather Part II*	Ingrid Bergman	*Murder on the Orient Express*
1976	George Burns	*The Sunshine Boys*	Lee Grant	*Shampoo*
1977	Jason Robards	*All the President's Men*	Beatrice Straight	*Network*
1978	Jason Robards	*Julia*	Vanessa Redgrave	*Julia*
1979	Christopher Walken	*The Deer Hunter*	Maggie Smith	*California Suite*
1980	Melvyn Douglas	*Being There*	Meryl Streep	*Kramer vs. Kramer*
1981	Timothy Hutton	*Ordinary People*	Mary Steenburgen	*Melvin and Howard*
1982	John Gielgud	*Arthur*	Maureen Stapleton	*Reds*
1983	Louis Gossett Jr	*An Officer and a Gentleman*	Jessica Lange	*Tootsie*
1984	Jack Nicholson	*Terms of Endearment*	Linda Hunt	*The Year of Living Dangerously*
1985	Haing S Ngor	*The Killing Fields*	Peggy Ashcroft	*A Passage to India*
1986	Don Ameche	*Cocoon*	Anjelica Huston	*Prizzi's Honor*
1987	Michael Caine	*Hannah and Her Sisters*	Dianne Wiest	*Hannah and Her Sisters*
1988	Sean Connery	*The Untouchables*	Olympia Dukakis	*Moonstruck*
1989	Kevin Kline	*A Fish Called Wanda*	Geena Davis	*The Accidental Tourist*
1990	Denzel Washington	*Glory*	Brenda Fricker	*My Left Foot*
1991	Joe Pesci	*Goodfellas*	Whoopi Goldberg	*Ghost*
1992	Jack Palance	*City Slickers*	Mercedes Ruehl	*The Fisher King*
1993	Gene Hackman	*Unforgiven*	Marisa Tomei	*My Cousin Vinny*
1994	Tommy Lee Jones	*The Fugitive*	Anna Paquin	*The Piano*
1995	Martin Landau	*Ed Wood*	Dianne Wiest	*Bullets over Broadway*
1996	Kevin Spacey	*The Usual Suspects*	Mira Sorvino	*Mighty Aphrodite*
1997	Cuba Gooding Jr	*Jerry Maguire*	Julliette Binoche	*The English Patient*
1998	Robin Williams	*Good Will Hunting*	Kim Basinger	*L.A. Confidential*
1999	James Coburn	*Affliction*	Judi Dench	*Shakespeare in Love*
2000	Michael Caine	*The Cider House Rules*	Angelina Jolie	*Girl Interrupted*
2001	Benicio Del Toro	*Traffic*	Marcia Gay Harden	*Pollock*
2002	Jim Broadbent	*Iris*	Jennifer Connelly	*A Beautiful Mind*
2003	Chris Cooper	*Adaptation*	Catherine Zeta-Jones	*Chicago*
2004	Tim Robbins	*Mystic River*	Renée Zellweger	*Cold Mountain*
2005	Morgan Freeman	*Million Dollar Baby*	Cate Blanchett	*The Aviator*
2006	George Clooney	*Syriana*	Rachel Weisz	*The Constant Gardener*
2007	Alan Arkin	*Little Miss Sunshine*	Jennifer Hudson	*Dreamgirls*
2008	Javier Bardem	*No Country For Old Men*	Tilda Swinton	*Michael Clayton*
2009	Heath Ledger	*The Dark Knight*	Penelope Cruz	*Vicky Cristina Barcelona*
2010	Christoph Waltz	*Inglourious Basterds*	Mo'Nique	*Precious*
2011	Christian Bale	*The Fighter*	Melissa Leo	*The Fighter*
2012	Christopher Plummer	*Beginners*	Octavia Spencer	*The Help*
2013	Christoph Waltz	*Django Unchained*	Anne Hathaway	*Les Miserables*

Best Original Song

Year	Film	Artist	Song
1935	*The Gay Divorcee*	Con Conrad (composer), Herb Magidson (lyricist)	The Continental
1936	*Gold Diggers*	Harry Warren (composer), Al Dunin (lyricist)	Lullaby of Broadway
1937	*Swing Time*	Jerome Kern (composer), Dorothy Fields (lyricist)	The Way You Look Tonight
1938	*Waikiki Wedding*	Harry Owens	Sweet Leilani
1939	*The Big Broadcast*	Ralph Rainger (composer), Leo Robin (lyricist)	Thanks for the Memory
1940	*The Wizard of Oz*	Harold Arlen (composer), EY Harburg (lyricist)	Over the Rainbow
1941	*Pinocchio*	Leigh Harline (composer), Ned Washington (lyricist)	When You Wish upon a Star
1942	*Lady Be Good*	Jerome Kern (composer), Oscar Hammerstein II (lyricist)	The Last Time I Saw Paris
1943	*Holiday Inn*	Irving Berlin	White Christmas
1944	*Hello, Frisco, Hello*	Harry Warren (composer), Mack Gordon (lyricist)	You'll Never Know
1945	*Going My Way*	James Van Heusen (composer), Johnny Burke (lyricist)	Swinging on a Star
1946	*State Fair*	Richard Rodgers (composer), Oscar Hammerstein II (lyricist)	It Might As Well Be Spring
1947	*The Harvey Girls*	Harry Warren (composer), Johnny Mercer (lyricist)	On the Atchison, Topeka and the Santa Fe
1948	*Song of the South*	Allie Wrubel (composer), Ray Gilbert (lyricist)	Zip-A-Dee-Doo-Dah
1949	*The Paleface*	Jay Livingston (composer), Ray Evans (lyricist)	Buttons and Bows
1950	*Neptune's Daughter*	Frank Loesser	Baby, It's Cold Outside
1951	*Captain Carey U.S.A.*	Jay Livingston (composer), Ray Evans (lyricist)	Mona Lisa
1952	*Here Comes the Groom*	Hoagy Carmichael (composer), Johnny Mercer (lyricist)	In the Cool, Cool, Cool of the Evening
1953	*High Noon*	Dimitri Tiomkin (composer), Ned Washington (lyricist)	High Noon (Do Not Forsake Me, Oh My Darlin')
1954	*Calamity Jane*	Sammy Fain (composer), Paul Francis Webster (lyricist)	Secret Love
1955	*Three Coins in the Fountain*	Jule Styne (composer), Sammy Cahn (lyricist)	Three Coins in the Fountain
1956	*Love is a Many-Splendored Thing*	Sammy Fain (composer), Paul Francis Webster (lyricist)	Love is a Many-Splendored Thing
1957	*The Man Who Knew Too Much*	Jay Livingston (composer), Ray Evans (lyricist)	Whatever Will Be, Will Be (Que Sera, Sera)
1958	*The Joker Is Wild*	James Van Heusen (composer), Sammy Cahn (lyricist)	All The Way
1959	*Gigi*	Frederick Loewe (composer), Allan Jay Lerner (lyricist)	Gigi
1960	*A Hole in the Head*	James Van Heusen (composer), Sammy Cahn (lyricist)	High Hopes
1961	*Never on Sunday*	Manos Hadjidakis	Never On Sunday
1962	*Breakfast at Tiffany's*	Henry Mancini (composer), Johnny Mercer (lyricist)	Moon River
1963	*Days of Wine and Roses*	Henry Mancini (composer), Johnny Mercer (lyricist)	Days of Wine and Roses
1964	*Papa's Delicate Condition*	James Van Heusen (composer), Sammy Cahn (lyricist)	Call Me Irresponsible
1965	*Mary Poppins*	Richard M Sherman (composer), Robert B Sherman (lyricist)	Chim Chim Cher-ee
1966	*The Sandpiper*	Johnny Mandel (composer), Paul Francis Webster (lyricist)	The Shadow of Your Smile
1967	*Born Free*	John Barry (composer), Don Black (lyricist)	Born Free
1968	*Doctor Dolittle*	Leslie Bricusse	Talk to the Animals
1969	*The Thomas Crown Affair*	Michel Legrand, Alan Bergman, Marilyn Bergman	The Windmills of Your Mind
1970	*Butch Cassidy and the Sundance Kid*	Burt Bacharach (composer), Hal David (lyricist)	Raindrops Keep Fallin' On My Head
1971	*Lovers and Other Strangers*	Fred Karlin, Robb Royer [aka Robb Wilson] James Griffin [aka Arthur James]	For All We Know
1972	*Shaft*	Isaac Hayes	Theme from Shaft
1973	*The Poseidon Adventure*	Al Kasha (composer), Joel Hirschhorn (lyricist)	The Morning After
1974	*The Way We Were*	Marvin Hamlisch, Alan Bergman, Marilyn Bergman	The Way We Were
1975	*The Towering Inferno*	Al Kasha (composer), Joel Hirschhorn (lyricist)	We May Never Love Like This Again
1976	*Nashville*	Keith Carradine	I'm Easy
1977	*A Star is Born*	Barbara Streisand (composer), Paul Williams (lyricist)	Evergreen (Love Theme from A Star is Born)
1978	*You Light Up My Life*	Joseph Brooks	You Light Up My Life

1979	*Thank God It's Friday*	Paul Jabara	Last Dance
1980	*Norma Rae*	David Shire (composer), Norman Gimbel (lyricist)	It Goes Like It Goes
1981	*Fame*	Michael Gore (composer), Dean Pitchford (lyricist)	Fame
1982	*Arthur*	Burt Bacharach, Carole Bayer Sager, Christopher Cross, Peter Allen	Arthur's Theme (Best That You Can Do)
1983	*An Officer and a Gentleman*	Jack Nitzsche, Buffy Saint-Marie, Will Jennings	Up Where We Belong
1984	*Flashdance*	Giorgio Moroder, Keith Forsey, Irene Cara	Flashdance . . . What a Feeling
1985	*The Woman in Red*	Stevie Wonder	I Just Called to Say I Love You
1986	*White Nights*	Lionel Richie	Say You, Say Me
1987	*Top Gun*	Giorgio Moroder (composer), Tom Whitlock (lyricist)	Take My Breath Away
1988	*Dirty Dancing*	Franke Previte, John DeNicola, Donald Markowitz	(I've Had) The Time of My Life
1989	*Working Girl*	Carly Simon	Let the River Run
1990	*The Little Mermaid*	Alan Menken (composer), Howard Ashman (lyricist)	Under the Sea
1991	*Dick Tracy*	Stephen Sondheim	Sooner Or Later (I Always Get My Man)
1992	*Beauty and the Beast*	Alan Menken (composer), Howard Ashman (lyricist)	Beauty and the Beast
1993	*Aladdin*	Alan Menken (composer), Tim Rice (lyricist)	A Whole New World
1994	*Philadelphia*	Bruce Springsteen	Streets of Philadelphia
1995	*The Lion King*	Elton John (composer), Tim Rice (lyricist)	Can You Feel the Love Tonight
1996	*Pocahontas*	Alan Menken (composer), Stephen Schwartz (lyricist)	Colors of the Wind
1997	*Evita*	Andrew Lloyd Webber (composer), Tim Rice (lyricist)	You Must Love Me
1998	*Titanic (1997)*	James Horner (composer), Will Jennings (lyricist)	My Heart Will Go On
1999	*The Prince of Egypt*	Stephen Schwartz	When You Believe
2000	*Tarzan*	Phil Collins	You'll Be In My Heart
2001	*Wonderboys*	Bob Dylan	Things Have Changed
2002	*Monsters Inc*	Randy Newman	If I Didn't Have You
2003	*8 Mile*	Eminem	Lose Yourself
2004	*The Lord of the Rings: Return of the King*	Frances Walsh, Howard Shore, Annie Lennox	Into the West
2005	*The Motorcycle Diaries*	Jorge Drexler	Al Otro Lado Del Rio (To the other side of the river)
2006	*Hustle & Flow*	Three 6 Mafia	It's Hard Out Here For A Pimp
2007	*An Inconvenient Truth*	Melissa Etheridge	I Need to Wake Up
2008	*Once*	Glen Hansard and Marketa Irglova	Falling Slowly
2009	*Slumdog Millionaire*	AR Rahman and Gulzar	Jai Ho
2010	*Crazy Heart*	Ryan Bingham and T Bone Burnett	The Weary Kind
2011	*Toy Story 3*	Randy Newman	We Belong Together
2012	*The Muppets*	Bret McKenzie	Man or Muppet
2013	*Skyfall*	Adele Adkins and Paul Epworth	Skyfall

Recent winners of the lesser known categories follow

2011 Academy Awards
Original Screenplay: David Seidler, The King's Speech; Adapted Screenplay: Aaron Sorkin, The Social Network; Foreign Language Film: In a Better World (Denmark); Animated Feature: Toy Story 3; Cinematography: Wally Pfister, Inception; Costume Design: Colleen Atwood, Alice in Wonderland; Makeup: Rick Baker and Dave Elsey, The Wolfman; Visual Effects: Paul Franklin, Chris Corbould, Andrew Lockley and Peter Bebb, Inception; Short Film – Animated: The Lost Thing; Short Film – Live Action: God of Love; Original Score: Trent Reznor and Atticus Ross, The Social Network; Art Direction: Robert Stromberg and Karen O'Hara, Alice in Wonderland; Documentary Feature: Inside Job; Documentary Short Subject: Strangers No More; Sound Mixing: Lora Hirschberg, Gary A Rizzo and Ed Novick, Inception; Sound Editing: Richard King, Inception; Film Editing: Angus Wall and Kirk Baxter, The Social Network.

2012 Academy Awards
Original Screenplay: Woody Allen, Midnight in Paris; Adapted Screenplay: Alexander Payne, Nat Faxon, and Jim Rash, The Descendants; Foreign Language Film: A Separation (Iran); Animated Feature: Rango; Cinematography: Robert Richardson, Hugo; Costume Design: Mark Bridges, The Artist; Makeup: Mark Coulier and J. Roy Helland, The Iron Lady; Visual Effects: Rob Legato, Joss Williams, Ben Grossmann, and Alex Henning, Hugo; Short Film – Animated: The Fantastic Flying Books of Mr. Morris Lessmore; Short Film – Live Action: The Shore; Original Score: Ludovic Bource, The Artist; Art Direction: Dante Ferretti and Francesca Lo Schiavo, Hugo; Documentary Feature: Undefeated; Documentary Short Subject: Saving Face; Sound Mixing: Tom Fleischman and John Midgley, Hugo; Sound Editing: Philip Stockton and Eugene Gearty, Hugo; Film Editing: Angus Wall and Kirk Baxter, The Girl with the Dragon Tattoo.

2013 Academy Awards
Original Screenplay: Quentin Tarantino, Django Unchained; Adapted Screenplay: Chris Terrio, Argo; Foreign Language Film: Amour (Austria); Animated Feature: Brave; Cinematography: Claudio Miranda, Life of Pi; Costume Design: Jacqueline Durran, Anna Karenina; Makeup: Lisa Westcott and Julie Dartnell, Les Misérables; Visual Effects: Bill Westenhofer, Guillaume Rocheron, Erik-Jan De Boer and Donald R. Elliott, Life of Pi; Short Film – Animated: Paperman; Short Film – Live Action: Curfew; Original Score: Mychael Danna, Life of Pi; Art Direction: Rick Carter and Jim Erickson: Lincoln; Documentary Feature: Searching for Sugar Man; Documentary Short Subject: Inocente; Sound Mixing: Andy Nelson, Mark Paterson and Simon Hayes, Les Misérables; Sound Editing: Per Hallberg and Karen Baker Landers, Skyfall; and Paul N.J. Ottosson, Zero Dark Thirty (tied); Film Editing: William Goldenberg, Argo.

Computers

Common Terms

Artificial Intelligence A word coined in the USA in 1956 as the ultimate aim for electronic processing ability. Although great strides have been made towards a device that would simulate human thought processes, as yet, no such device exists and the term is used to describe advanced programs such as PROLOG which allows empirical evidence to guide future decisions.

ASCII American Standard Code for Information Interchange (computer code for representing alphanumeric characters.

Bebo Social networking website founded in January 2005 by Michael and Xochi Birch.

bit (binary digit) Smallest unit of data manageable by a computer.

bootstrap Technique for loading the first few program instructions into a computer main store to enable the rest of the program to be introduced from an input device.

busbar Group of electrical conductors maintained at low voltage, used for carrying data in binary form between the various parts of a computer or its peripherals.

byte Equivalent of eight bits (generally makes up a character of information). It is possible to have a six-bit byte.

computer: definition A machine that carries out a programmed sequence of instructions by translation of coded data. Digital computers use binary code which is represented by eletrical current being turned off and on. Analogue computers use continuous variables as opposed to the discreet data of digital machines. A simple example of an analogue computer would be a set of scales.

computer generations The developement of computers is sometimes viewed as falling into several phases or generations. First generation began with the ENIAC (electronic numerical integrator and calculator) modern computers designed by J. Presper Eckert and John W Mauchly, both of the University of Pennsylvania. Completed in 1946, this was first all-purpose, all-electronic digital computer. A special-purpose, all-electronic computing machine called Colossus had earlier been developed at Bletchley Park, in England, and was in operation by December 1943. The Colossus was designed (by the computer genius Alan Turing) to decipher codes generated by the German electromechanical enciphering devices known as Enigma machines. The successor to ENIAC was EDVAC (Electronic Discrete Variable Automatic Computer).

The 'second generation' of modern computers began in 1959, when machines employing semiconductor devices known as transistors became commercially available.

The 'third generation' of modern computers began in the late 1960s, when integrated circuits were imprinted on silicon chips. This permitted the construction of large 'mainframe' computers with much higher operating speeds.

The 'fourth generation' of modern computers began in the 1980s. This and subsequent generations have continued to develop very large-scale integration (VLSI) and have promoted the advancement of virtual reality (VR) and computer aided design (CAD).

The 'fifth generation' of modern computers is an ongoing general development of recent technological advances. Using recent engineering advances for example, computers are able to accept spoken word instructions (voice recognition) and imitate human reasoning. The ability to translate a foreign language is now commonplace.

Computer Programming languages (high-level)

ABAP Advanced Business Application Programming.

ADA Designed for dealing with real-time processing problems and used for military and other systems. It was named after Augusta Ada Byron, Lady Lovelace (assistant to Charles Babbage), and developed in the late 1970s by the US Defense Department.

AED Algol Extended for Design.

ALGOL ALGorithmic Orientated Language, principally used for scientific and mathematical problems (types: ALGOL 60 and ALGOL 68).

APL A Programming Language.

APT Automatically Programmed Tools.

ATLAS Abbreviated Test Language for Avionics Systems.

BASIC Beginners All-purpose Symbolic Instruction Code.

BCPL Basic Computer Programming Language.

BLISS Developed in 1970 by Wulf, Russell and Habermann. It was perhaps the best-known systems programming language before C.

BOO An object-oriented statically typed programming language developed in 2003.

C Introduced at Bell Laboratories in 1974 and originally developed for use in the UNIX operating system.

C Sharp Designed by Microsoft in 2001.

CHEY Chain Hypertext Emotion for You. Developed by Aleta Manske in late 1990.

COBOL COmmon Business-Oriented Language (developed in 1959).

COGO CO-ordinate GeOmetry.

COMAL COMmon Algorithmic Language.

CORAL Computer On-line ReAL time.

FORTH Name derives from an intention to provide a language for fourth-generation computers. It uses a notation called reverse polish, in which an operator is always preceded by its arguments. FORTH is popularly used for writing video game programs.

FORTRAN FORmula TRANslation (Invented in 1956).

GPSS General Purpose Systems Simulation.

LISP LISt Processor (introduced in 1960). Its basic entity is an s-expression (symbolic expression) which is either an atomic symbol or a list structure.

LOGO A simple, interactive language which is compact enough to run on most microcomputers but also embodies powerful programming facilities. It is used extensively for teaching programming to children.

ML Meta Language.

PASCAL ALGOL-related language named after the scientist-philosopher Blaise Pascal (1623–62). Pascal is a teaching language developed in the late 1960s.

PERL Practical Extraction and Report Language.

PL/1 Programming Language 1, a multipurpose programming language designed for solving both business and scientific problems.

PL/M Programming Language for Micro Computers.

PROLOG PROgramming in LOGic. There the emphasis is on description rather than on action, eg to find the greater of two input numbers, one would describe what 'greater of' meant and then query it with the given numbers as data.

SAIL Stanford Artificial Intelligence Language.

SIMULA SIMUlation LAnguage.

SNOBOL StriNg-Oriented symBOlic Language, provides facilities for the manipulation of strings of characters by pattern-matching expressions. SNOBOL is particularly applicable for text editing, linguistics and the compiling and symbolic manipulation of algebraic expressions.

SQL Structured Query Language.

Visual Basic Designed by Microsoft in 1998.

computer: makes and models: Commodore: Amiga and PET; Apple: Macintosh; Sinclair: Spectrum and ZX80 / 1; Packard Bell: Legend; DEC: Vax; IBM: PS/2; Acorn: BBC Micro; Digital: Equipment Corporation-PDP Series.

computer: mechanical pioneers Charles Babbage (1791–1871) designed computing machines that he called the 'Difference Engine' and 'Analytical Engine' in the 1820s and 30s. They were never built but the first practical programmed computer built by Georg Scheutz of Stockholm and exhibited at the Paris Exposition of 1855 was based on Babbage's Difference Engine. The mechanical adding machine developed by Blaise Pascal in 1642 which used a 10:1 gearing ratio to represent decimal columns, can be regarded as the ancestor of the computer.

computer programmer: first Ada Byron, Countess Lovelace, assistant to Charles Babbage (see computer mechanical pioneers), is generally recognised as the first 'computer programmer'.The first proposal for a computer language, however, was by German philosopher Gottfried Leibniz (1646–1716), who devised a system allowing logic statements to be dealt with mathematically, using the digit 0 for false and 1 for true.)

computer: types Micro, mini, mainframe (computers can also be categorised as digital and analog).

CPU Central Processing Unit; the electronic decision making device within a computer.

DTP Desktop Publishing; the production of high-quality printed matter using a desktop computer and a laser printer. Some examples of packages are Pagemaker and QuarkXpress, Adobe Illustrator, Microsoft Publisher, Corel Draw, GST and Serif.

exabyte one billion billion characters of information.

Facebook Social networking website founded in February 2004 by Mark Zuckerberg.

Friends Reunited Portfolio of social networking websites founded in 1999 by Steve and Julie Pankhurst.

gigabyte one billion characters of information.

GIGO Garbage In, Garbage Out. Computer user's proverb meaning if you use unreliable data you will get unreliable results.

Hardware The electronic and mechanical components of a computer are called the hardware; this includes the processing unit.

high-level language Computer programming language that is closer to human language or mathematical notation than to machine language.

home computer: first Apple-1; created by Steve Wozniak and Steve Jobs in 1977.

k Kilobyte (1,024 bytes).

Internet An international computer network linking computers from educational institutions, government agencies, and industry.

Lara Croft Heroine of the video game 'Tomb Raider'.

Laptops: first Became prevalent in 1987, although the first laptop machine with a full colour screen was developed in 1990.

Laser printer developed in 1987 using the principle of the Xerox copier.

LCD Liquid Crystal Display.

low-level language Computer-programming. language that is closer to machine language than to human language.

m Megabyte (1,024 kilobytes).

microprocessor: first Intel 4004.

modem Acronym for MOdulator DEModulator, a device used to enable computers to communicate with one another via telephone lines.

Moshi Monsters Website with more than 80 million registered users worldwide. Children choose from one of six virtual pet monsters (Divalo, Luvli, Katsuma, Poppet, Zommer and Furi) that they can create, name and nurture for navigation around Monstro City and take daily puzzle challenges to earn 'Rox' (virtual currency).

motherboard Printed circuit board through which all hardware and software devise send electronic to talk to each other.

MS-DOS MicroSoft Disc Operating System.

network Group of computers connected in order to share and exchange information.

nibble Equivalent of four bits.

OS Operating System: a program that controls the overall operation of a computer system, typically by performing such tasks as memory allocation, job scheduling and input/output control.

pixel Picture element: one of the number of very small dots that make up the picture on a visual display unit.

port Socket used to connect a computer to other devices.

punched card: inventor The American Dr Herman Hollerith (1860–1929) invented the punched-card system in 1890; his company, the Tabulating Machine Co. became IBM in 1924. Hollerith's device enabled a census to be taken in six weeks rather than the six years required by manual analysis. Mechanical punched cards had been suggested earlier by Charles Babbage; and the 'Jacquard Loom' of 1801 is an even earlier example of punched card principles but Hollerith patented the system and was the first to use electrical contacts.

RAM Random Access Memory; temporary storage space that is lost when the computer is switched off.

ROM Read-Only Memory; permanent storage device that holds data that cannot be altered by the user.

software the programs and operating information used by a computer.

spreadsheets: first The first spreadsheet program Visicalc was developed on the Apple-2 in 1979.

terabyte Approximately a thousand billion characters of information.

Turing Test Test for successful artificial intelligence that depends on a human not being able to tell that he or she is communicating with a computer. No computer has ever passed the Turing Test.

Twitter Online social networking service created in March 2006 by Jack Dorsey - its microblogging function enables its users to send and read text-based messages of up to 140 characters, known as "tweets".

VGA Video Graphics Array (Super VGA is the advanced array).

video games: 1st Pong (established in Italy in the early 1970s).

Video games: famous Super Mario Brothers by Nintendo, Sonic the Hedgehog by Sega, Donkey Kong by Atari, Tomb Raider by Eios, Duke Nukem by 3D Realms, The Sims by Maxis, Doom by Idoh and Temple Run by Imangi Studios - the controllable characters being explorers Guy Dangerous, Montana Smith and Karma Lee, escape artist Scarlett Fox, cop Barry Bones, conquistador Francisco Montoya and football star Zack Wonder. In Temple Run II the three chasing monkeys are replaced by one giant monkey Cuchanck. This version became the fastest app to hit 50 million downloads beating the record of Angry Birds by Rovio Entertainment – a game in which players launch birds at pigs stationed on or within various structures.

Wikipedia Founded in 2001 by Jimmy Wales and Larry Sanger.

Windows User-friendly operating system created by Microsoft.

World Wide Web A system of interlinked hypertext documents usually referred to as the 'Web'. The Web was created around 1990 by Englishman Sir Tim Berners-Lee working at CERN in Geneva. The Internet and the Web are not synonymous; the Internet is a collection of interconnected computer networks, linked by copper wires, cables and wireless connections. The Web is accessible via the Internet but is a collection of interconnected documents linked by hyperlinks and Uniform Resource Locators.

YouTube Video sharing website created in February 2005 by Steve Chen, Chad Hurley and Jawed Karim.

NB: Many computer acronyms (eg AI, DOS, WYSIWYG, VDU, and MIPS) can be found listed in the Abbreviations section

Internet Chat Abbreviations

AAMOF as a matter of fact
AFAIK as far as I know
AFK away from keyboard
AIM AOL instant messenger
ASAP as soon as possible
ASL? age, sex, location?
ATK at the keyboard
B4 before
BBIAB be back in a bit
BB4N bye bye for now
BBFN bye bye for now
BBL be back later
BBS be back soon
BEG big evil grin
BF boyfriend
BFN bye for now

BION	believe it or not
BOT	back on topic
BRB	be right back
BRB NC	be right back, nature calls
BRS	big red switch
BTW	by the way
BWL	bursting with laughter
CID	crying in disgrace
CRBT	crying real big tears
CSG	chuckle, snigger, grin
C U L8ER	see you later
C U L8TER	see you later
C YA	see ya (you)
DC'D	disconnected
DIKU	do I know you
EG	evil grin
FAQ	frequently asked questions
FCOL	for crying out loud
FFS	for fuck sake
FOAF	friend of a friend
FTF	face to face
F2F	face to face
FUBAR	fucked up beyond all recognition
FUD	fear, uncertainty and doubt
FWIW	for what it's worth
FYI	for your information
GF	girlfriend
GG	good game
GMTA	great minds think alike
GR8	great
GL	good luck
GTG	got to go
H&K	hugs and kisses
HAGN	have a good night
HAND	have a nice day
HB	hurry back
HLOL	hysterically laughing out loud
HTH	hope that helps
IAAA	I am an accountant
IAAL	I am a lawyer
IANALB	I am not a lawyer ... but
IC	I see
IJWTS	I just want to say
ILU	I love you
ILY	I love you
IMHO	in my humble opinion
IMY	I miss you
INPO	in no particular order
IOW	in other words
IRL	in real life
ISRN	I'll stop rambling now
ITA	I totally agree
ITFA	in the final analysis
IWALU	I will always love you
IWALY	I will always love you
J/K	just kidding
JK	joke
JMO	just my opinion
K	okay
KISS	keep it simple, stupid
KOL	kiss on lips
L8R	later
L8R G8R	later 'gator
LJBF	let's just be friends
LMAO	laughing my arse off
LOL	laughing out loud
LOLOL	laughing out loud online
LTNS	long time no see
LTNT	long time no type
LUVYA	love ya (you)
LY4E	love you for ever
M/F	male or female?
MOTD	message of the day
MSG	message
MYOB	mind your own business
NBD	no big deal
N1	nice one
NM	never mind
NP	no problem
NQA	no questions asked
NRN	no reply necessary
OAUS	on an unrelated subject
OMG	oh my god
OIC	oh I see
OTOH	on the other hand
12345	talk about school
PDS	please don't shout
PM	private message
PMBI	pardon my butting in
PML	pissing myself laughing
POV	point of view
PTMM	please tell me more
RHIP	rank has its privileges
ROFL	rolling on floor laughing
ROTF	rolling on the floor
ROTFL	rolling on the floor laughing
ROTFLMAO	rolling on the floor laughing my arse off
RTBM	read the bloody manual
RTFM	read the fucking manual
RTM	read the manual
RTSM	read the stupid manual
RYS	read your screen
SICS	sitting in chair sniggering
SLM	see last mail
SO	significant other
SS	so sorry
SUAKM	shut up and kiss me
SWIM	see what I mean
SWL	screaming with laughter
SYT	sweet young thing
TANJ	there ain't no justice
TCOB	taking care of business
TOBAL	there oughta be a law
TPTB	the powers that be
TSR	totally stupid rules
TTFN	ta ta for now
TTYL	talk to you later
TY	thank you
TYCLO	turn your caps lock off
TYVM	thank you very much
VG	very good
VN	very nice
WAEF	when all else fails
WB	welcome back
WG	wicked grin
WTF	what the fuck
WTG	way to go
WTGP	want to go private?
WTH	what/who the hell
WUWH	wish you were here
YGLT	you're gonna love this
YMMV	your mileage may vary
YW	you're welcome
:-)	smiling
:-0	shock
:'-(	crying
X=	fingers crossed
:-w	a liar – speaks with forked tongue
:=)	little Hitler
:*	kissing
:-X	kissing
$-)	greedy
:-L~~	drooling
}:	devil
<:-)	idiot
:-S	confused
:-(	sad

CURRENT AFFAIRS

Daily Record 2010

January

4 The Burj Khalifa Bin Zayid, formerly known as Burj Dubai, officially opened in Dubai, United Arab Emirates, and became the tallest man-made structure ever built, at 829.8 m (2,722 ft). Construction began on 21 September 2004, with the exterior completed on 1 October 2009.

6 Former Cabinet ministers, Geoff Hoon and Patricia Hewitt, published a joint letter highlighting deep divisions within the Labour Party just weeks before the General Election.

12 A massive 7.0-magnitude earthquake struck the Caribbean nation of Haiti, the western part of the island of Hispaniola, which is shared with the Dominican Republic. The quake's epicentre, near the town of Léogâne, was approximately 25 km (16 miles) west of Port-au-Prince, Haiti's capital. Haiti's worst quake in two centuries wrecked the presidential palace, UN HQ and other buildings, killing an estimated 316,000.

19 Kraft Foods took over Cadbury for an estimated £11.9 billion.

20 Blue Peter presenter Helen Skelton set out from Natua in Peru in a quest to row the entire length of the Amazon. (See entry 28 February).

28 Adam Crozier, the head of the Royal Mail, became chief executive of ITV.

29 Former Prime Minister Tony Blair gave evidence to the Chilcot inquiry into the Iraq War

February

1 Stephen Marshall, 38, the so-called Jigsaw Killer, was sentenced to life and ordered to serve a minimum of 36 years after changing his plea three weeks into his trial at St Albans Crown Court, Hertfordshire. Marshall stabbed a former work colleague to death and cut his body into pieces and also admitted that he had hacked up four other bodies.

3 The share price of Toyota dropped eight per cent on the US Stock Exchange as hundreds of thousands of cars were recalled globally following incidents of faulty brakes.

4 A report on MP's expenses was published by Sir Thomas Legg.

5 The Director of Public Prosecutions Keir Starmer QC announced that Labour MPs Elliot Morley, David Chaytor and Jim Devine, plus Conservative peer Lord Hanningfield had been charged under the Theft Act for irregularities in their expense claims. The four are set to appear before City of Westminster Magistrates Court on 11 March.

8 Metropolitan Police Commander Ali Dizaei was sentenced to four years, at Southwark Crown Court, for assaulting and falsely arresting Waad Al-Baghdadi. The controversial policeman, 47, was ordered to spend two years in prison and two years on licence.

11 Figures of library lending in Britain showed that Dame Jacqueline Wilson was the most popular library book author of the past decade and her best-known work, *The Story of Tracy Beaker*, about a troublesome 10-year-old in a children's home, was the most borrowed individual title during this period.

17 Dozens of students, including three British teenagers, were left floating on life rafts in the Atlantic for nearly two days after their boat sank off the coast of Brazil. Sarah Calascione, 19, Nicole Turner, 18, and Gabriella Haines, 16, were among 41 students and 23 crew aboard the SV *Concordia*, a 57-metre long Canadian sailing ship which capsized in bad weather off the coast of Rio de Janeiro.

21 Allegations of bullying against the Prime Minister Gordon Brown were made in a book serialisation in a Sunday newspaper.

28 Blue Peter presenter Helen Skelton arrived at Almerim, Brazil, in her kayak, having clocked up 2,010 miles on her solo journey in aid of Sport Relief. She became the first woman to paddle the length of the river. (See entry 20 January 2010).

March

1 Tory Party deputy chairman, Lord Ashcroft, revealed he was a 'non-dom' for UK tax purposes.

10 Mexican tycoon Carlos Slim Helu was named as the world's richest person with a fortune estimated at £37.5billion.

12 Television presenter Christine Bleakley became the first woman to water ski across the English Channel. The treacherous 22-mile crossing from Dover to Calais, took 100 minutes and raised hundreds of thousands of pounds for Sport Relief.

14 A Hungarian Vizsla named Yogi was named Best in Show at Crufts dog show at Birmingham's National Exhibition Centre.

21 A pastoral letter from the Pope to Irish Catholics apologising for child sex abuse scandals was read out during Mass throughout Ireland.

April

5 Gordon Brown announced a General Election would take place on May 6th

7 Camilla, Duchess of Cornwall, broke her left leg while hill-walking near Balmoral.

8 Presidents Obama and Medvedev signed a US-Russian Strategic Arms Limitation Treaty in Prague.

10 Poland's president Lech Kaczynski was among 96 passengers who died when the presidential plane crashed as it attempted to land at a Russian airport near Smolensk.

15 All airports in the UK were closed by the National Air Traffic Control Service (Nats) following the eruption of Eyjafjallajökull, an Icelandic volcano, which caused a vast cloud of volcanic ash to drift 1,000 miles south and hang between 20,000ft and 55,000ft.
The first of three television debates between the leaders of the UK's three main political parties ahead of the country's May general election was broadcast live on ITV 1. Prime Minister and Labour Party leader Gordon Brown, Conservative Party leader David Cameron and Liberal Democrats leader Nick Clegg went head-to-head in the 90-minute live debate, the first time the UK has featured a US-style debate between the leaders of its main political parties.

20 Metro-Goldwyn-Mayer announced it is to sell off its film assets including the James Bond franchise and a stake in two Hobbit movies. The once thriving Hollywood studio was formed in 1916 by Samuel Goldwyn and has the official motto *Ars Gratia Artis* (Art for Art's Sake) although its unofficial motto of *More Stars Than There Are In Heaven* is perhaps better known.
UK airports were given the all-clear to fly following six days of travel chaos causing tens of thousands of Brits to be stranded overseas and many others having to undergo horrendously long journeys via ship and ferry.
An oil rig, *Deepwater Horizon*, exploded off the Louisiana coast killing eleven workers.

27 The Greek economy was hovering on disaster as its debt rating was decreased to BB+ (a 'junk' status) by financial research institution Standard & Poor, amidst fears of default by the Greek government.

28 Gordon Brown unwittingly made national news headlines while canvassing on the streets of Rochdale. Gillian Duffy, who had popped out for a loaf of bread, had a chance encounter with the Prime Minister and questioned him on the national debt, education and the party's immigration policy. Mr Brown replied politely but was caught on microphone labelling Mrs Duffy a "bigoted woman".

29 The massive oil spill pouring from a ruptured oil rig in the Gulf of Mexico reached the coast of Louisiana, threatening an environmental catastrophe in the region. An estimated 35 million gallons of crude oil has spewed from the *Deepwater Horizon* rig and it is expected to take months to control the leakage.

May

2 The IMF and EU agreed austerity measures with the Greek Government with a view to a bail-out package.

3 BP shares plummetted after it was announced they would be responsible for any damage caused by the oil slick in the Gulf of Mexico.
Goodluck Jonathan, 52, became Nigeria's first Christian president following the death of Umaru Yar'Adua, the Muslim president since 2007.

5 A Picasso painting, *Nude, Green Leaves and Bust*, fetched \$106.5million (£70.6million) at Christie's in New York, making it the most expensive piece of art to sell at auction.

6 Nigel Farage, the former UK Independence Party leader, escaped with broken ribs and superficial injuries after a plane he was flying in crashed at Hinton-in-the-Hedges airfield, near Brackley, Northants when a Ukip banner was caught in the tail fin of the plane.

Michael Edwards was convicted of fatally stabbing his "husband" John in what is thought to be the first murder in a British same-sex marriage.

7 Britain's electorate woke up to a hung parliament for the first time since 1974. The Conservative Party fell some 20 seats short of an overall majority with David Cameron announcing a meeting with Lib Dem leader Nick Clegg with a view to making a deal to govern while present incumbent Gordon Brown refused to resign until all possibilities were considered.

8 Mohamed Al-Fayed sold the world-famous Harrods store in Knightsbridge to Qatar Holdings for a sum of £1.5 billion.

11 Gordon Brown formally resigned his position as Prime Minister and David Cameron immediately took office after announcing Britain was to have a full coalition government with the Liberal Democrats. Nick Clegg immediately became deputy prime minister, the first Liberal in a Cabinet post since Sir Archibald Sinclair was Secretary of State for Air in Churchill's wartime government.

12 Two Britons and an Irish citizen were among the victims of a plane crash in Libya that killed 103 people. The plane operated by the Libyan carrier Afriqiyah Airlines had flown from Johannesburg and crashed short of the runway at Tripoli airport before disintegrating. Although 58 Dutch people perished aboard Airbus A330 flight 8U771, miraculously a 10-year-old Dutch boy was the sole survivor and is recovering from multiple leg fractures in a Tripoli hospital.

13 David Cameron's first Cabinet included four Lib-Dem MPs and Baroness Warsi, Britain's first female Muslim Cabinet minister.

17 On the day that Parliament reconvened after the General Election it was announced that outgoing Chief Secretary to the Treasury, Liam Byrne, left his successor, Lib-Dem MP David Laws, a note reading "I'm afraid there is no money. Kind regards and good luck!"
Bonita Norris, 22, who only took up climbing last year, became the youngest British woman to conquer Mt Everest.

29 The new coalition Government suffered its first crisis with the resignation of David Laws just 17 days after his appointment as Chief Secretary to the Treasury. The *Daily Telegraph* disclosed that Laws had claimed up to £950 a month in parliamentary expenses for eight years to rent rooms in two London properties owned by his partner, James Lundie, a political lobbyist. MPs were banned from leasing accommodation from partners in 2006. Another Lib-Dem MP, Danny Alexander, 38, the former Scotland Secretary, replaced Laws.
The Eurovision song Contest, in Oslo, was won by Germany, with Lena Meyer-Landrut scoring 246 points with her quirky song *Satellite*. The UK entrant *That Sounds Good To Me*, penned by Stock, Aitken and Waterman, and sung by Josh Dubovie, came last of the 25 finalists, scoring a paltry ten points.

June

2 Derrick Bird, a 52-year-old taxi driver who was under investigation for tax evasion, took his own life after embarking on a killing spree in the Whitehaven area of Cumbria which left 12 dead and several injured. Bird's brother David and the family solicitor Kevin Commons were among the victims.

4 Naoto Kan became Japanese Prime Minister.

10 A mammoth structure designed by the sculptor Anish Kapoor was officially unveiled on the windswept docks of Middlesbrough. Temenos, meaning sacred ground in Greek, at 164 feet, towers above Britain's most famous tall sculpture, the Angel of the North, Anthony Gormley's winged statue in Gateshead, about 40 miles down the road, which stands a mere 65 feet off the ground. Temenos consists of two steel rings pulling a delicate mesh of steel cables, which are suspended above the dockside, dominating the post-industrial landscape.

15 David Cameron issued an apology after the Saville Enquiry Report (set up in 1998), into the events of Bloody Sunday in Northern Ireland, was published.

22 Chancellor of the Exchequer George Osborne delivered an austerity budget in order to reduce the escalating UK budget deficit. The cuts, which will make every household in Britain worse off, includes increasing VAT to 20 per cent, Capital Gains Tax to 28 per cent for high earners, freezing Child Benefit for three years, reducing Housing Benefit and cutting Child Tax Credit for all earning more than £40,000.

23 President Barack Obama sacked General Stanley McChrystal, the US commander in Afghanistan, over anti-Government comments made in a *Rolling Stone* magazine interview. General David Petraeus immediately replaced McChrystal.

24 Julia Gillard became Australia's first female prime minister after Kevin Rudd stepped down rather than face a Labour party ballot he seemed sure to lose. Miss Gillard, 48, was born in Barry, South Wales, but emigrated to Australia with her family in 1966 as part of the post-war £10 assisted package scheme.

25 Henry Perkins, 19, became the first Briton to graduate from Russia's Bolshoi Ballet Academy.

July

3 A fugitive gunman, Raoul Moat, 37, who was set free from Durham Prison 48 hours earlier was on the loose after shooting his ex-girlfriend Samantha Stobbart, 22, and fatally wounding her new lover Chris Brown, 29. Moat also shot and blinded PC David Rathband, 42, and issued a warning that all members of the Northumberland constabulary were targets.

8 Peter Phillips, the Queen's eldest grandson, announced that his Canadian wife Autumn is pregnant with their first child, due in December.

10 Raoul Moat was pronounced dead at Newcastle General Hospital after shooting himself in the early hours of the morning in Rothbury, Northumberland.

12 Film director Roman Polanski who was arrested at Zurich Airport last September, on a 1978 US warrant for having sex with 13-year-old Samantha Geimer, walked free after the Swiss government announced he would not be extradited on child sex charges.
The General Synod of the Church of England approved legislation to consecrate women bishops.

15 BP announced it had stemmed the flow of oil from the stricken *Deepwater Horizon* (see entry for 20 April)

19 Doctors at Queen Mary's Hospital in Sidcup were baffled after a black Nigerian couple, Ben and Angela Ihegboro, conceived a blue-eyed blonde baby girl, Nmachi, the name meaning "Beauty of God" in their native language. Neither Ben, 44, nor 35-year-old Angela have any mixed race family history.

20 Actress Lindsay Lohan began a 90-day prison sentence at the Century Regional Detention Facility in Lynwood, California, for violating terms of her 2007 drink-driving probation.

24 At least 18 people were killed when music fans at Germany's annual Love Parade stampeded inside a crowded underpass on the outskirts of Duisburg.

27 Jackie Cobell, 56, recorded the slowest-ever time to swim the Channel from Dover to Calais. The Tonbridge housewife took 28 hours and 44 minutes for the journey after losing her bearings and swimming an extra 40 miles.

28 Catalonia became the first mainland region of Spain to ban bullfighting.

30 A bike hire scheme designed to encourage thousands more cycle journeys in central London began today. More than 300 docking stations were set up in the capital to enable users to buy a key access via credit cards. The bikes are designed for short journeys and may be returned to any available station.

31 Chelsea Clinton, the daughter of the former President of the United States, married Marc Mezvinsky in New York.
A British-led team of oarsmen smashed a 114-year world record for rowing across the north Atlantic from New York to the Scilly isles. The new record set by Leven Brown, Don Lennox, Ray Carroll and Livar Nysted, is 43 days, 21 hours, 26 minutes and 48 seconds.

August

1 A 53ft-tall life-size model of a dinosaur was assembled on a Portsmouth beach. The sculpture of an Ultrasaurus is 72ft long and took three months to build after its 10 pieces were shipped from Serbia to Southsea.

2 Ongoing floods in Pakistan were the worst for 80 years. The United Nations rated the disaster the greatest humanitarian crisis in recent history, the official death toll of 1,781 being only part of the story as millions struggled for food and shelter.

5 Thirty three miners were trapped more than 700 yards below the surface when their main access tunnel collapsed in the shaft at San Jose, Chile. (See entry 13 October 2010).

7 Thousands queued patiently at 10.00am this morning as doors opened at the new Apple Store in Covent Garden. The impressive store offers three floors of Macs, iPhones, iPad and iPods, along with an array of lifestyle accessories.

9 Ed Stafford, 34, a former army captain, became the first man known to have walked the length of the Amazon. Mr Stafford set off from the river's source in Peru on 2 April 2008.

23 Gareth Williams, an employee of GCHQ seconded to the Secret Intelligence Service (MI6), was found dead in suspicious circumstances at a Security Services safe house flat in Pimlico, London. Williams' decomposing remains were discovered locked in a sports bag after police gained entry into his top floor flat in Alderney Street, Pimlico.
31 President Obama announced the end of US combat operations in Iraq

September
1 The mystery stunt driver on the television show *Top Gear* was unmasked as former SAS soldier Ben Collins. The BBC lost a High Court action against the disclosure of the racing driver dubbed The Stig, after it was made known that Collins was to publish his autobiography, The Man In the White Suit, later this month.
2 Thousands of residents and holidaymakers were forced to leave the east coast of America as Hurricane Earl headed towards land, generating winds of up to 145mph.
3 Errors in the HM Revenue and Customs tax code system for the previous fiscal year were announced causing more than 10 million people to have been taxed too much or too little.
5 The Basque separist group ETA announced a ceasefire.
7 Barclays announced Bob Diamond as its next chief executive.
The xx won the £20,000 Mercury Prize for their debut album *xx*.
14 George Michael was given an eight-week sentence for crashing his car while under the influence of cannabis. He was also fined £1,250 at Highbury Corner Magistrates Court in London and given a five-year driving ban. The 47-year-old singer was arrested in July in Hampstead, north London after driving his Range Rover into a branch of photographic store Snappy Snaps.
16 Pope Benedict XV1 arrived at Edinburgh International Airport and was met by the Duke of Edinburgh before attending a reception at Holyroodhouse Palace. Pope Benedict's apostolic journey to the United Kingdom will culminate on 19 September with the beatification of Venerable Cardinal John Henry Newman (1801-90).
25 Ed Milliband, 40, was elected Leader of the Labour Party with the support of 50.65% of the electoral college. In the final vote he beat his older brother David Milliband, 45, who gained 49.35% of the vote.
29 David Milliband quit front-line politics but pledged to support his brother from the back benches.

October
2 Actor David Birrell, 35, was hit in the face by a discharge from a gun at the Saturday matinee performance of Stephen Sondheim's *Passion* at the Donmar Warehouse, London. Mr Birrell, who plays Colonel Ricci, was hurt during a scene in which his character challenges another to a duel. He was taken to hospital where he was treated for a serious eye injury.
8 A kidnapped British aid worker, Dr Linda Nordgrove, was accidentally killed during a US rescue attempt in Afghanistan.
11 Lady Justice Hallett opened the inquest into the victims of the 7 July 2005 London Bombings.
12 The Man Booker Prize was won by Howard Jacobson for his tragi-comic novel *The Finkler Question*.
13 The thirty three miners trapped underground in a mine shaft in San Jose, Chile since 5 August, were lifted to safety.
17 Thousands of Australians travelled to Rome to witness the Pope canonise Mary MacKillop. Melbourne-born Mary, who died in 1909 aged 67, has been credited with curing two terminally ill women. She becomes Australia's first saint.
20 The Supreme Court ruled that German heiress Katrin Radmacher's prenuptial agreement with her former husband was binding, effectively forming a legal precedent in the UK.
George Osborne announced that from 2013 the current system of grants and Civil List funding of the Royal Family will be replaced by an all-in-one payment called the Sovereign Support Grant, funded entirely from the Crown Estate.
22 The Royal Navy's newest and largest attack submarine HMS Astute ran aground in the Kyle of Lochalsh, off Skye.
23 Australian journalist Julian Assange, founder of whistleblowing website Wikileaks, defended the release of almost 400,000 classified US documents about the war in Iraq, stating the exercise was performed in an effort to reveal the truth about the conflict and how innocent Iraqi civilians were killed.
27 The French National Assembly increased the pension age from 60 to 62 despite weeks of strikes and demonstrations.
28 The Office of National Statistics announced that Oliver and Olivia were the most common names for baby boys and girls in 2009.

November
8 Tamara Mellon, the co-founder of Jimmy Choo shoes, was among 32 new 'business ambassadors' appointed by David Cameron.
9 A symphony lost for 200 years that "changed the course of musical history" when it was finally rediscovered was played for the first time in London today. The discovery of Étienne Méhul's 4th symphony by David Charlton, Emiritus Professor of Music at the University of London, in Paris in 1979 proved that he invented the 19th century romantic "cyclic" symphony two decades before his compatriot Hector Berlioz, who was previously considered to have pioneered the form in his celebrated *Symphony Fantastique*. The symphony was performed by the Orchestra of the Age of Enlightenment at the Queen Elizabeth Hall at the Southbank Centre.
10 Student demonstrators brought violence to London's streets on a scale not seen since the poll tax riots of 20 years ago. More than 50,000 people brought Westminster to a standstill with a peaceful march past Parliament to protest against the proposal to increase tuition fees to up to £9,000 a year. The demonstration turned nasty when a crowd smashed its way into the Conservative Party's headquarters in Millbank. Cheered on by hundreds more outside, furniture was thrown through windows, the interior was trashed, a ceiling was pulled down and a fire extinguisher was thrown off the roof at police in the crowded courtyard below.
13 Burma's pro-democracy leader Aung San Suu Kyi was released from house arrest in Yangon (Rangoon). Her release came six days after Myan Mar (Burma) held its first elections in 20 years - they were won by the military but widely condemned as a sham. Ms Suu Kyi's National League for Democracy (NLD) won the election in 1990 but was never allowed to take power. She has been under house arrest or in prison almost continually ever since. World leaders have ceaselessly fought the Burmese regime in an effort to free Aung San Suu Kyi, who was the recipient of the Rafto Prize and the Sakharov Prize for Freedom of Thought in 1990 and the Nobel Peace Prize in 1991. In 1992 she was awarded the Jawaharlal Nehru Award for International Understanding by the Government of India and the International Simón Bolívar Prize from the Government of Venezuela.
14 Paul and Rachel Chandler, the retired Kent couple kidnapped from their yacht by Somali pirates 388 days ago, were released unharmed after a ransom was purportedly paid.
16 Prince William and Kate Middleton announced their engagement with plans to marry next spring.
Ireland failed to agree the terms of an international bail-out as its deficit rose to almost a third of the size of its economy.
19 Lord Young of Graffham, David Cameron's enterprise advisor, resigned after he was criticised by the Prime Minister for claiming that most people had "never had it so good" during the recession.
21 Ireland was forced to accept the terms of an international bail-out from the European Union in a deal designed to save the euro. EU and IMF officials will prepare the details of the three-year assistance package.
Tony Johnson, a retired Isle of Wight solicitor, and his mum Gene were named as the couple who found an ancient Chinese vase during a house clearance which eventually sold at auction for £53 million. The elaborate 18th century masterpiece was found in a house clearance in Pinner, North West London, after the death of Mrs Johnson's sister, Patricia Newman, whose husband Bill had been the owner. It had sat on a bookshelf for years propping up books.
23 The European Court of Human Rights ordered David Cameron to give prisoners the vote within six months after a jailed rapist, Robert Greens, successfully claimed his human rights had been infringed. The Government was ordered to pay Greens costs of £4,230 and to give all convicts the vote by May 2011.

December

6 Susan Philipsz walked away with Britain's most prestigious art award, the £25,000 Turner Prize, at the Tate Britain ceremony. The winning work, *Lowland*, is the first sound installation to be awarded the major prize, and consists of the artist's own voice singing and chanting 16th century Scottish laments.

9 Questions were raised about police handling of tuition fee protesters after a car carrying the Prince of Wales and the Duchess of Cornwall was attacked on its way to the annual *Royal Variety Show* at the London Palladium. A window was smashed and paint thrown at the vehicle amid reports that the duchess was prodded with a stick.

10 Chinese dissident, Liu Xiabo, who is serving an eleven-year prison sentence for subversion, was awarded the Nobel Peace Prize in Oslo.

21 For the first time in 372 years, the winter equinox and a total lunar eclipse occurred on the same day. A lunar eclipse is when the moon passes behind the earth so that the earth blocks the sun's rays from striking the moon. This phenomenon, occurring only when the Sun, Earth, and Moon are aligned exactly, tends to give the moon a reddish hue as the Earth casts a shadow over it.

22 Zara Phillips announced her engagement to rugby player Mike Tindall.

27 Mikhail Khodorkovsky, the former oil oligarch currently nearing the end of an eight-year prison sentence, was found guilty of embezzlement and laundering of stolen funds in a Moscow court. Judge Victor Danilkin said the former chief executive of oil company Yukos, and Platon Lebedev, his business partner, were guilty of illegally obtaining $25 billion (£16.3 billion) in oil revenues from the now defunct company. Police arrested 30 people outside the courtroom where supporters of Mr Khodorkovsky chanted "freedom" and "down with Putin". Vladimir Putin, the Russian prime minister and former president, dismantled Yukos after Mr Khodorkovsky challenged powerful forces in Russia's establishment and many believe Putin is determined to keep Khodorkovsky locked up indeterminably.

28 The Qingdao Haiwan Bridge in East China was completed. The world's longest sea bridge, stretching 26.4 miles and linking the main urban area of Qingdao city with Huangdao district, straddles the Jiaozhou Bay sea areas. The road bridge, which took four years and cost £5.5billion to build is almost three miles longer than the previous record-holder, the Lake Pontchartrain Causeway in Louisiana.

Sporting Record 2010

January

3 Phil Taylor won his 15th darts world championship with a 7-3 victory over Aussie Simon Whitlock at Alexandra Palace, London.

5 Flavio Briatore's life-time ban from Formula One, for allegedly ordering Nelson Piquet Jnr to crash during the 2008 Singapore GP, was lifted by a Paris court due to irregularities in the original decision. Renault's former technical director, Pat Symonds, who had been given a five-year ban, also had his suspension lifted.

7 For the second time in the series, England tailender Graham Onions survived a tense final over to earn his team a draw in the third Test in Cape Town. England lead the series 1-0.
Britain's team of Jamie Baulch, Roger Black, Iwan Thomas and Mark Richardson were awarded the gold medal for the men's 4x400m relay 13 years after they finished 0.18sec behind the winning US team during the Athens World Athletics Championships in 1997; the American team including Antonio Pettigrew who later admitted to drug offences, being disqualified retrospectively.

8 The African Cup of Nations football tournament was put in doubt following an attack on the Togo national team coach in Luanda that killed two members of the party and one Angolan. Togo immediately pulled out of the tournament.

9 In her first tournament since her comeback, Justine Henin was narrowly beaten 6-3, 4-6, 7-6 in the final of the Brisbane International by her great Belgian rival Kim Clijsters.

10 Martin Adams beat Dave Chisnall 7-5 to win the BDO World Darts Championship at Lakeside Country Club, Frimley Green, Surrey.
The African Cup of Nations football tournament began despite the attack on the Togo national team coach in Luanda that killed three people. In the opening match Mali came from four goals down with 11 minutes remaining to secure a 4-4 draw.
Arizona Cardinals gained a 51-45 victory over the Green Bay Packers; the highest-scoring postseason game in NFL history.

17 South Africa levelled the series - and retained the Basil D'Oliveira Trophy - with a crushing innings-and-74-run victory over England in the fourth Test at the Wanderers, Johannesburg.
Mark Selby beat Ronnie O'Sullivan 10-9 in snooker's Masters' final at Wembley.

19 David Sullivan and David Gold took a controlling interest in West Ham United for an estimated £20 million.

24 Greg Harlow, the fifth seed from Ely in Cambridgeshire, defeated unseeded Stewart Anderson from Scotland in straght sets to win the World Indoor Bowls championships at Potters Leisure Centre, Hopton-on-Sea.

28 Vice President and Prime Minister of the UAE and Ruler of Dubai H. H. Sheikh Mohammed bin Rashid Al Maktoum attended the opening of the Meydan Racecourse. The biggest and most expensive track in history has taken 34 months and at least $1.25bn to build.

30 Jessica Ennis broke the British 60 metres hurdles record at the Aviva International Match in Glasgow. The world heptathlon gold medallist from Sheffield produced the fastest time in the world this year of 7.95 seconds - beating world indoor champion Lolo Jones in the process and securing the match victory for Great Britain.
Serena Williams beat Justine Henin 6-4, 3-6, 6-2, to retain her Australian Open title.

31 Roger Federer beat Andy Murray in three sets at the Australian Open to win his 16th Grand Slam title. The Swiss star, 28, won 6-3 6-4 7-6 (13-11) at Melbourne Park to extend his lead at the head of the all-time Grand Slam winners' list.

February

5 Chelsea defender John Terry was stripped of the England captaincy following revelations about an affair he had with England team-mate Wayne Bridge's ex-girlfriend, Vanessa Perroncel.

6 In the opening matches of the Rugby Union Six Nations, Ireland beat Italy 29-11 at Croke Park and England beat Wales 30-17 at Twickenham.

7 The New Orleans Saints beat the Indianapolis Colts 31-17 at Super Bowl XLIV, played at the Sun Life Stadium, Miami.
France beat Scotland 18-9, at Murrayfield, in the Rugby Union Six Nations.

12 The Winter Olympics in Vancouver opened amid controversy following the death of 21-year-old Nodar Kumaritashvili from Georgia who crashed on the super-fast luge run.

13 In the Rugby Union Six Nations, France beat Ireland 33-10, in Paris; England beat Italy 17-12, in Rome and Wales beat Scotland 31-24, in Cardiff. Hours after the game Welsh rugby union star Andy Powell was arrested after driving a golf buggy towards a motorway and subsequently failing a breathalyser.

17 American Alpine skier Lindsey Vonn won the women's downhill competition in Vancouver. Britain's Chemmy Alcott finished 13th, her second top 15 Olympic placing.

19 Despite a protest over the tiny ridges in her helmet Britain's Amy Williams won the gold in the skeleton in Vancouver. The 27-year-old from Bath had never previously won a top-flight competition but led by a huge margin from the first to the fourth of the four runs and eventually gained an accumulative advantage of 0.56sec over the silver medallist. Amy's gold was the first individual success by a British athlete since skater Robin Cousins in Lake Placid 30 years ago.

20 Jenny Meadows broke Dame Kelly Holmes British indoor 800m record at the Grand Prix meeting at the NIA, Birmingham. Her victorious time of 1min 59.21sec took a tenth of a second off the old record.

21 Ian Poulter beat fellow English golfer Paul Casey 4 & 2 in the final of the WGC Accenture Match Play Championship in Arizona.
American Bode Miller won his first Olympic skiing gold medal with victory in the men's super-combined.

23 South African-born Craig Kieswetter's first game as an England cricketer resulted in a stirring 143 run knock during an 112 run victory over a Bangladeshi one-day XI in Fatullah. The 22-year-old Somerset wicket keeper and batsman has an Afrikaan father and Scottish mother.

24 Indian batsman Sachin Tendulkar became the first man to score a double century in a one-day international when he made exactly 200 during India's 153-run victory over South Africa in Gwallor.

26 In the Rugby Union Six Nations, France beat Wales 26-20, in Cardiff.

27 In a tackle reminiscent of the one that sidelined Arsenal team-mate Eduardo da Silva for 18 months, young up-and-coming star, Aaron Ramsey, 19, suffered a broken leg after a tackle by Stoke centre-half Ryan Shawcross. Arsenal went on to win the game 3-1 to get within

three points of Chelsea at the top of the table. Earlier in the day Manchester City beat the table-toppers 4-2 at Stamford Bridge with Chelsea finishing the match with nine men. The game was the first meeting between John Terry and Wayne Bridge since the City star announced mid-week that he would no longer be available to play for England due to his falling out with the former England captain. (See entry 5 February 2010).
In the Rugby Union Six Nations, Ireland beat England 20-16 at Twickenham, and Italy beat Scotland 16-12 at the Stadio Flaminio, Rome.
28 Canada finished top of the medal board in Vancouver when their ice hockey team beat USA to give them their 14th gold. Great Britain ended with the solitary medal won by Amy Williams in the skeleton.
Manchester United beat Aston Villa 2-1 in the Carling Cup final at Wembley.

March
3 England beat Egypt 3-1 in a friendly international football match at Wembley.
7 British tennis players suffered a humiliating defeat 3-2 by Lithuania and must now beat Turkey, who lost to Ireland in a relegation play-off, to avoid dropping into Europe/Africa Zone Group III - the lowest tier of the Davis Cup competition.
12 Great Britain won two gold medals at the World Indoor Athletics Championships in Doha courtesy of Jessica Ennis in the pentathlon with a score of 4,937 points and Dwain Chambers in the 60m with a world best time in 2010 of 6.48sec.
13 In the Rugby Union Six Nations, England and Scotland drew 15-15, at Murrayfield; Ireland beat Wales 27-12, in Dublin; and France beat Italy 46-20, in Paris.
Manny Pacquiao, the Filipino boxer who has won world titles in seven weight divisions, retained his WBO welterweight title with a one-sided points victory over Joshua Clottey of Ghana, at the Dallas Cowboys Stadium.
14 The opening Formula One GP of the season, in Bahrain, was won by Fernando Alonso of Spain driving a Ferrari Marlboro. Alonso's team-mate Felipe Massa finished second and Lewis Hamilton, in a Vodafone McLaren placed third. Current world champion Jenson Button, Hamilton's team-mate, finished just behind Michael Schumacher in seventh spot. The German seven-times champion made a satisfactory return to F1 although his team-mate Nico Rosberg out-qualified him and finished ahead of him in the race proper. Among the innovations for this year's championships is a new scoring system whereby ten drivers score points (25, 18, 15, 12, 10, 8, 6, 4, 2 and 1) and no refuelling is allowed, although pit-stops will be made as both a soft and hard compound tyre must be used.
David Beckham was ruled out of the World Cup after snapping an achilles tendon during AC Milan's 1-0 victory over Chievo.
Great Britain won two more medals in Doha via Jenny Meadows in the 800m (silver) and men's 4 x 400m (bronze).
16 Binocular, ridden by Tony McCoy and trained by Nicky Henderson, won the Champion Hurdle at Cheltenham.
17 On the second day of the Cheltenham Festival the Queen Mother Chase was won by Big Zeb, ridden by Barry Geraghty and trained by Colm Murphy.
John Lloyd resigned as Britain's Davis Cup captain following five successive defeats.
18 Big Buck's, ridden by Ruby Walsh and trained by Paul Nicholls won the World Hurdle at Cheltenham for the second year running.
19 Imperial Commander, ridden by Paddy Brennan and trained by Nigel Twiston-Davies, won the Cheltenham Gold Cup. Favourite Kauto Star eventually fell after making an horrendous blunder on the first circuit and second favourite Denman placed second.
20 In the final matches of the Rugby Union Six Nations, Wales beat Italy 33-10 at the Millennium Stadium, Scotland beat Ireland 23-20 at Croke Park, and France beat England 12-10 in Paris to finish champions.
21 Northampton Saints beat Gloucester 30-24 in rugby union's LV= Cup final at Sixways to secure their first domestic cup win since claiming the EDF Energy Trophy back in 2008. The Anglo-Welsh tournament is jointly managed by the Rugby Football Union (RFU) and Welsh Rugby Union (WRU).
25 Sir Chris Hoy won Britain's first gold medal at the 2010 World Track Cycling Championships in Copenhagen, with victory in the men's keirin.
27 Victoria Pendleton won Britain's second gold medal and her fourth consecutive sprint world title in Copenhagen.
Jenson Button, driving a McLaren, won the Australian Formula One GP in Melbourne.
Penitent, ridden by Johnny Murtagh and trained by William Haggas, won the Lincoln Handicap at Doncaster.
The world's richest horse race was won by Gloria de Campeao, ridden by Tiago Pereira and trained by Pascal Bary. The Dubai World Cup, at Meydan, resulted in the closest finish possible in a horse race with South African jockey Kevin Shea, riding Lizard's Point, convinced he had won only to be denied by a nose.
28 Ed Clancy won Britains third gold medal at the cycling world championships with success in the Omnium.

April
3 Britain's David Haye retained his WBA heavyweight crown with a ninth round stoppage of American John Ruiz at Manchester's MEN Arena.
Cambridge neat Oxford in the Xchanging Boat Race on the Thames.
4 Red Bull's German driver Sebastian Vettel won the Malaysian F1 GP in Kuala Lumpur.
6 World Player of the Year, Lionel Messi, scored all four goals during Barcelona's 4-1 win over Arsenal in the Champions League quarter final second leg at the Nou Camp. The stunning performance by the 22-year-old Argentinian striker gave his side a 6-3 aggregate victory.
8 Tiger Woods made his best-ever start at the US Masters with a four-under-par 68. In his first tournament for five months the world number one golfer lay two shots off the first round lead held by veteran Fred Couples.
9 At the halfway stage of the US Masters Britons Lee Westwwod and Ian Poulter led the field by two shots from a group of players, including Tiger Woods.
10 Don't Push It, ridden by AP McCoy and trained by Jonjo O'Neill, won the Aintree Grand National. The 14-time champion jockey, riding his first Grand National winner, was stopped by the police on exiting the race meeting and fined £60 and three points for phoning his mother on his mobile whilst driving.
11 American Phil Mickelson won the US Masters. Tiger Woods, on his return to golf following lurid revelations of his personal life, finished 4th.
14 Andy Murray lost 6-2, 6-1 to Philipp Kohlschreiber of Germany in the 2nd round of the Monte Carlo Masters, his third defeat in a row.
18 Jenson Button won the Chinese Formula One GP in Shanghai. McLaren scored their first one-two of the season with Lewis Hamilton finishing in second place.
19 Venezuelan Edwin Valero, the unbeaten world lightweight boxing champion, hanged himself whilst in police custody on suspicion of murdering his wife. Valero's professional record was outstanding winning all 27 bouts by knockout, the first 18 in the first round!
23 Steve Davis rolled back the years by beating the defending world snooker champion John Higgins 13-11 in the 2nd round at The Crucible.
24 Danish boxer Mikkel Kessler scored a unanimous points victory over Nottingham-based Carl Froch to win the WBC cruiserweight title in Herning.
AP McCoy won his 15th consecutive National Hunt jockey's championship with a season total of 195 winners.
25 Tsegaye Kebede of Ethiopia and Lilya Shobukhova of Russia were crowned men's and women's Virgin London Marathon Champions. The Ethiopian finished 9 secs outside the course record with a time of 2:05:19, while Shobukhova set a personal best of 2:22:00. Mara Yamauchi was first British woman home, in tenth place, after an horrific week spent travelling around Europe due to the volcanic cloud that disrupted her flight plans. Andrew Lemoncello was the first British man home in eighth place in 2:13:40. Princess Beatrice became the first member of the Royal family to complete the London Marathon, as part of a human "caterpillar" of 34 runners.
Chennai Super Kings were crowned Indian Premier League 3 champions after beating Mumbai Indians by 22 runs in the final in Mumbai.

May
1 Makfi, ridden by Christophe Lemaire and trained by Mikel Delzangles, won the 2,000 Guineas at Newmarket.
Floyd Mayweather scored a one-sided points victory over fellow American Shane Mosley in a non-title welterweight fight in Las Vegas.
As the final of the world snooker championship got underway the News of the World announced that current world champion John Higgins had contracted with them to accept money to throw key frames in future matches.
2 Special Duty, ridden by Stephane Pasquier and trained by Criquette Head-Maarek, won the 1,000 Guineas to complete a French-trained double of both Newmarket Classics. The race was surrounded in controversy after the original winner Jacqueline Quest, ridden by Tom Queally and trained by Henry Cecil, was relegated to second for impeding Special Duty.

Britain's Beth Tweddle successfully defended her uneven bars and floor titles at the European Gymnastics Championships at Birmingham's Indoor Arena.
Former England football manager Steve McClaren guided FC Twenty Enschede to the Eredivisie (Dutch championship) following a 2-0 win at NAC Breda.
Ulsterman Rory McIlroy won the Quail Hollow Championship in Charlotte, North Carolina two days before his 21st birthday. His maiden US Tour victory was gained in scintillating fashion with a final round of 62.
3 Neil Robertson of Australia beat Scotland's Graeme Dott 18-13 in the final of the World Snooker Championship at the Crucible, Sheffield.
In a rain-effected encounter England were defeated by West Indies in their opening World Twenty20 cricket match in Georgetown, Guyana. England captain Paul Collingwood was openly critical of the Duckworth-Lewis system after West Indies were given a relatively soft target in six overs after England had scored a huge total in their 20 overs. The controversy exists because the system was introduced for 50-over one-day internationals and can throw up skewed results in the shorter version of the game.
Swindon-based Australian Paul Tapner, 34, won the Badminton horse trials riding Inonothing.
4 England qualified for the Super Eight stage of the World Twenty20 after their match with Ireland was rained off without the Irish team being able to respond to the meagre total of 120 posted by England. In another farcical rain-effected match Ireland were 14-1 after three overs but five overs are required to be completed before a result can be ratified.
5 A 1-0 victory over Manchester City ensured Spurs' fourth place in the Premiership and a Champions League place for next season.
6 England beat Pakistan by six wickets in Bridgetown, Barbados, to begin their Super Eight campaign with victory.
8 The British-based Team Sky's Bradley Wiggins won the prologue time trial in the Giro'D'Italia to become the first wearer of the maglia rosa (pink jersey).
England beat South Africa in their second Super Eight match of the World Twenty20. Kevin Pietersen, who scored 53 off only 33 deliveries, immediately flew back to England for the birth of his first child.
9 Chelsea won the Premiership in style with an 8-0 drubbing of Wigan Athletic in their final match to ensure a one-point final lead over Manchester United.
Australian Red Bull driver Mark Webber won the Spanish Formula One Grand Prix at the Circuit de Catalunya.
10 England beat New Zealand in their third Super Eight match to top their group for the semi-finals of the World Twenty20.
11 Atletico Madrid defeated Fulham 2-1 in the Europa League final with a late extra time goal after the match finished 1-1 after 90 minutes.
13 England beat Sri Lanka by seven wkts to secure their place in the final of the World Twenty20. Kevin Pietersen, who had dashed back to England for the birth of his baby boy after the victory over South Africa in the Super Eight stage, top-scored with 42.
15 A Didier Drogba goal from a free kick gave Chelsea a 1-0 victory over Portsmouth in the English FA Cup final at Wembley while Dundee United scored three second-half goals to beat Ross County 3-0 in the Scottish Cup final at Hampden Park.
Amir Khan stopped Brooklyn-based Paulie Malignaggi in the eleventh round to retain his WBA light-welterweight crown at Madison Square Garden, New York.
16 England beat Australia by seven wkts in a one-sided final of the World Twenty20 in Barbados. Kevin Pietersen was named as player-of-the-tournament. There was some compensation for the Aussies when they later defeated New Zealand in a low scoring women's final.
Mark Webber won successive Formula One Grand Prix' with victory in Monaco.
FA chairman Lord Triesman, 66, resigned after a British newspaper claimed that he suggested Spain could end its bid for the 2018 World Cup if rival bidder Russia helped bribe referees at the 2010 South Africa World Cup.
American sprint ace Tyson Gay beat Tommy Smith's 44-year-old straight line 200m record on the streets of Manchester. Gay's time of 19.41sec eclipsed Smith's time by 0.09sec. Andy Turner of Great Britain also secured a world best time in the 200m hurdles.
Laura Davies won her 74th career golf title with victory in the German Open in Munich.
22 Inter Milan beat Bayern Munich 2-0 in the Champions League final in Madrid.
Blackpool beat Cardiff City 3-2 to book their place in the Premiership for next season.
Toulouse defeated Biarritz 21-10 in the Heineken Cup final at Stade de France.
Canford Cliffs, ridden by Richard Hughes and trained by Richard Hannon, won the Irish 2,000 Guineas at The Curragh.
23 Bethrah, ridden by PJ Smullen and trained by Dermot Weld, won the Irish 1,000 Guineas.
24 England beat Mexico 3-1 in a friendly football match at Wembley.
Phil Taylor beat James Wade 10-8 in the final of dart's Premier League at Wembley Arena. The event which was postponed overnight after a power cut at Wembley made history with Taylor exceeding an average of 110 per three darts in the final and hitting two nine-dart 501 legs, the first time this has ever been done in the same match.
Inter Milan football coach Jose Mourinho became the boss of Real Madrid.
29 Leicester beat Saracens 33-27 in rugby union's Guinness Premiership final at Twickenham while Ospreys beat Leinster in the first Magners League grand final at the RDS Arena, Dublin.
Czech Republic tennis star Tomas Berdych beat Andy Murray in straight sets in the third round of the French Open at Roland Garros.
30 Lewis Hamilton won the Turkish Formula One Grand Prix after a coming together of the two leading Red Bulls of Sebastian Vettel and Mark Webber gifted him the race.
England beat Bangladesh by 8 wickets in the first Test at Lord's.
England beat Japan 2-1 in a friendly football match in Graz.

June

1 Roger Federer was denied his 24th consecutive Grand Slam semi-final when he was defeated in four sets by Sweden's Robin Soderling in the last eight at the French Open.
The non-inclusion of Theo Walcott was the major surprise in England's final 23 for the World Cup.
2 Barry Hearn won the vote of the top 64 snooker players to be the man to guide the sport into a new commercial era. Hearn beat former Olympian John Davison 35-29 in the vote in Sheffield and will take a 51 per cent stake in World Snooker.
3 Liverpool FC manager Rafael Benitez resigned following criticism of his lack of success.
4 England football captain Rio Ferdinand was ruled out of the World Cup with a knee injury. Steven Gerrard is expected to replace Ferdinand as captain and Michael Dawson was immediately added to the squad as replacement centre back.
Snow Fairy, ridden by Ryan Moore and trained by Ed Dunlop won the Oaks at Epsom.
5 Workforce, ridden by Ryan Moore and trained by Sir Michael Stoute, won the Epsom Derby by seven lengths in a course record time of 2mins 31.33secs.
Francesca Schiavone of Italy beat Australian Samantha Stosur 6-4, 7-6 in the final of the French Open in Paris.
6 British golfer Justin Rose won his first tournament on the PGA Tour with a three-shot triumph in the Memorial Tournament at Jack Nicklaus Muirfield Village course in Ohio.
England defeated Bangladesh by an innings and 80 runs at Old Trafford to win the series 2-0.
Rafael Nadal beat Robin Soderling 6-4, 6-2, 6-4 to win the French Open title for the fifth time.
11 30-year-old Yorkshireman Ian Hutchinson became the first rider to win five races in a week at the Isle of Man TT competition
15-time champion NH jockey Tony "AP" McCoy, was awarded the OBE in the Queen's Birthday Honours List.
12 England began their World Cup campaign in Rustenburg with a 1-1 draw against USA after a goalkeeping error by West Ham's Rob Green gifted the Americans an equaliser. Broadcasters complained about the constant droning noise of the vuvuzelas (South African stadium horn sometimes called a lepatata) throughout the match.
13 Lewis Hamilton won the Canadian Formula One Grand Prix to take the lead in the world drivers' championship from his team-mate Jenson Button.
18 England were held to a goalless draw by Algeria in their second World Cup group game in Cape Town. Theories abound as to the lifeless performances by England players; some critcs suggested the players were over-the-top after long domestic seasons whilst others blame the formation and yet others the composition of the Jabulani ball invented by scientists at Loughborough University.
19 Chelsea striker Nicolas Anelka was sent home from the World Cup following a heated dressing room confrontation with the French team's head coach Raymond Domenech.

20 Graeme McDowell of Northern Ireland won the US Open Golf Championship at Pebble Beach, California.

21 On the opening day of Wimbledon defending champion Roger Federer survived a scare as Alejandro Falla of Colombia served for the match in the fourth set before the Swiss ace eventually won 5-7, 4-6, 6-4, 7-6, 6-0. In a later match Britain's 16-year-old junior champion Laura Robson put up a brave performance against Jelena Jankovic the Serbian former world No 1 before losing 6-3, 7-6.

22 England defeated Australia in the first of the summer's One Day International cricket matches, at the Rosebowl, Southampton, with the Irish batsman Eoin Morgan scoring an unbeaten 103 off 85 balls.

23 England beat Slovenia 1-0 in Port Elizabeth to finish runners-up in Group C and face Germany in the last-16 of the World Cup.

24 The longest tennis match in history was finally completed when American John Isner defeated French rival Nicolas Mahut 6-4, 3-6, 6-7, 7-6, 70-68. The match began two days ago but only four sets were managed before fading light stopped play. Resumption of play began at lunchtime yesterday but again fading light prevented a conclusion as the match reached 59 games all in the fifth and final set. Isner finally won after a further 20 games were played today. The total match time was 11 hours 5 minutes, the final set itself was longer than any other full match in history. There were also 215 aces in total - 112 by Isner and 103 by Mahut. On a remarkable day at Wimbledon the Queen attended for the first time since 1977 and watched Andy Murray defeat Finn Jarrko Nieminen in straight sets.

England defeated Australia in the second One Day International cricket match, in Cardiff, with Eoin Morgan again top scoring with 52 runs.

25 After his record-breaking exploits at Wimbledon John Isner was defeated by Dutchman Thiemo de Bakker 6-0, 6-3, 6-2.

27 England were beaten 4-1 by Germany in a last 16 World Cup match in Bloemfontein. A mistake by the assistant referee Mauricio Espinosa and referee Jorge Larrionda prevented England from equalising at 2-2 in the first half when a Frank Lampard shot, which was clearly over the goal line, was adjudged a no goal. Despite this error the England defence always looked brittle and the final score line was England's worst ever World Cup defeat.

Sebastian Vettel of Germany won the European Formula One GP in Valencia with an all-the-way victory from the McLarens of Lewis Hamilton and Jenson Button. Team-mate Mark Webber survived an horrific crash when his Red Bull flipped over after running into the back of Heikki Kovalainen's Lotus.

England won the best-of-five One-Day International series against Australia with their third victory against the tourists at Old Trafford.

Guy Williams won the DFS Showjumping Derby at Hickstead on Softrack Skip Two Ramiro. Mitchell and Tina Fletcher on Promised Land jumped the only two clear rounds but softrack was by far the quicker in the jump-off.

Cape Blanco, ridden by Johnny Murtagh and trained by Aidan O'Brien, won the Irish Derby at The Curragh.

30 Defending champion Roger Federer was beaten 6-4, 3-6, 6-1, 6-4 by Tomas Berdych of the Czech Republic in the Wimbledon quarter-finals.

July

2 Andy Murray was beaten 6-4, 7-6, 6-4 by Rafael Nadal in the men's singles semi-final at Wimbledon.

3 Serena Williams won her fourth Wimbledon singles title with a 6-3, 6-2 victory over Vera Zvonareva of Russia to retain the Venus Rosewater Dish.

3 Rafael Nadal won his second Wimbledon singles title beating Tomas Berdych 6-3, 7-5, 6-4 in the men's final.

5 Caster Semenya, the 19-year-old South African winner of the 800 metres at the World Athletics Championships last year, was cleared to run against women after passing a gender eligibility test.

6 Holland reached the World Cup final with a 3-2 victory over Uruguay in Cape Town.

7 Spain will face Holland in the World Cup final after a hard-fought 1-0 victory over Germany in Durban.

8 Britain's Mark Cavendish won Stage 5 of the 2010 Tour de France.

9 Mark Cavendish won his second successive stage of the Tour de France.

10 Bangladesh beat England in a One-Day International cricket match at Bristol; the first time the Asian rookies had beaten the home side in any form of the game.

Germany beat Uruguay 3-2 in the World Cup 3rd/4th Place Play-Off.

Great Britain defeated Turkey 3-0 in the Davis Cup Europe/Africa Group II playoff at Devonshire Park, Eastbourne.

11 Australian Red Bull F1 driver Mark Webber won the British Grand Prix at Silverstone.

Spain beat Holland 1-0 in the World Cup final in Johannesburg after Andres Iniesta scored the winner with four minutes of extra time remaining. English referee Howard Webb showed a record 14 yellow cards plus a red card to Dutchman Johnny Heltinga as Holland used cynical tactics in an attempt to unsettle the better footballing skills of the Spaniards.

15 Mark Cavendish won his third stage of the 2010 Tour de France but his ace lead-out man, Australian Mark Renshaw, was disqualified from the remainder of the tour after butting Julian Dean of New Zealand three times for leaning on him in the last 400 metres of the sprint.

16 Northern Ireland golfer Rory McIlroy who shot a first round 63 in yesterday's opening round of The Open Championship, equalling the lowest-ever round in a Major and beating the best-ever opening round in a Major, crashed back to earth in the almost hurricane winds of St Andrews stuttering to a second round 80. Louis Oosthuizen of South Africa missed the inclement weather and ended the day five shots clear of the field.

18 Louis Oosthuizen, 27, of South Africa finished the Open championship on 16 under par, seven strokes clear of runner-up Lee Westwood.

19 Chelsea and England midfielder Joe Cole, 28, signed for Liverpool FC on a free transfer.

In a controversial Stage 15 of the Tour de France Alberto Contador took the yellow jersey from Andy Schleck following the Luxembourg rider's misfortune at losing his chain whilst instigating an attack on the final climb. Tradition calls for no attacks of the yellow jersey holder if mechanical problems occur but the Spaniard took advantage of the situation to turn a 31 second deficit into an 8 second lead.

21 Australia were bowled out for 88 by Pakistan in the second neutral Test match, at Headingley.

22 Muttiah Muralitharan's place in the pantheon of cricketing gods was assured when he took his 800th and final Test match wicket during Sri Lanka's 10 wicket victory over India in Galle. Pragyan Ojha was Muri's 800th victim.

23 Mark Cavendish won his fourth stage of the 2010 Tour de France, his 14th in three Tours.

24 Pakistan beat Australia by three wickets at Headingley, the Asian team's first Test victory over the Aussies since 1995.

Alex 'Hurricane' Higgins, one of the finest snooker players of all time, died at his home after complications as a result from throat cancer.

Harbinger, ridden by Olivier Peslier and trained by Sir Michael Stoute, won the King George VI and Queen Elizabeth Stakes by a record 11 lengths at Ascot after Epsom Derby winner and stablemate, Workforce, flopped.

25 Fernando Alonso won the German Formula One Grand Prix, at Hockenheim. The Spanish driver's Ferrari team-mate Felipe Massa of Brasil led the race for most of the way but was controversially overtaken by Alonso in the final few laps.

Alberto Contador won the Tour de France by the 39 seconds he gained on Andy Schleck during Stage 15. The final stage into Paris was won by Britain's Mark Cavendish, his fifth stage victory of the 2010 Le Tour.

27 Britain's Mo Farah won gold in the 10,000mts on the opening night of the European Athletics Championships in Barcelona. Team-mate Chris Thompson secured the silver.

Andrew Murray parted company from Miles Maglagan, his tennis coach of the past three years.

28 Christophe Lemaitre of France, the first white man to break 10 seconds for the 100 metres, won the short sprint crown at the European Championships, beating Britain's Mark Lewis-Francis into second. Dwain Chambers, the pre-race favourite, was beaten into 5th although he gained the same time as his team-mate Lewis-Francis.

29 Phillips Idowu won Britain's second gold medal in Barcelona with victory in the triple jump.

Eoin Morgan, the Irish-born batting star, scored his maiden Test century for England on the first day of the first Test against Pakistan at Trent Bridge.

30 Andy Turner (110m hurdles), Dai Greene (400m hurdles) and Jessica Ennis (heptathlon) gained three more gold medals for the GB athletics team in Barcelona.

31 Mo Farah took double gold in Barcelona with victory in the 5,000mts. Great Britain's final medal tally was 19 (6 gold, 7 silver, 6 bronze).

August

1 James Anderson took a 10 wicket haul in the Trent Bridge Test Match to give England a resounding 354 run victory over Pakistan.

England's Ross Fisher won the Irish Open at Killarney by two strokes from Padraig Harrington. The women's British Open at Royal Birkdale was won by 21-year-old Taiwanese golfer Yani Tseng who became the youngest woman to win three Majors.
Australian Red Bull driver Mark Webber won the Hungarian Formula One Grand Prix at the Hungaroring, Budapest, to take the lead in the driver's championship.
6 Jamaican sprint sensation Usain Bolt suffered a rare defeat at the Diamond League meeting in Stockholm. American Tyson Gay won the 100mts in 9.84sec with Bolt second in 9.97sec.
8 Manchester United beat Chelsea 3-1 at Wembley in the traditional English football season opener, the FA Community Shield.
9 England beat Pakistan by nine wickets at Edgbaston to take a 2-0 lead in the four-match Test series.
Martin O'Neill resigned as Aston Villa boss following a dispute over transfer funds.
11 England beat Hungary 2-1 at Wembley in their first match since the World Cup debacle.
14 Hampshire scraped home in their first Twenty20 final at their home ground, the Rose Bowl, beating Somerset by losing fewer wickets in a tied match, both teams scoring 173 runs.
15 After a disappointing 7th in the 800m freestyle three days earlier Rebecca Adlington won gold in the 400m freestyle on the final day of the European Championships in Budapest. Since Hannah Miley's opening-day gold in the 400m medley the Great Britain team won five further gold medals including a one-two by Lizzie Simmonds and Gemma Spofforth in the 200m backstroke and another in the 100m backstroke where Gemma reversed the positions with Lizzie; success for Fran Halsall in the 100m freestyle and victory for Gemma Spofforth, Kate Haywood, Fran Halsall and Amy Smith in the women's 4x100m medley relay final. The British men had no victories.
Andy Murray beat Roger Federer 7-5, 7-5, in the final of the Toronto Masters.
Martin Kaymer of Germany won the US PGA after a three-hole play-off against American Bubba Watson. Watson's countryman Dustin Johnson would have also been in the play-off but was penalised two shots for grounding his club in a bunker on the 17th hole.
19 Mo Farah broke the British 5,000m record with a time of 12min 57.94sec at the Weltklasse meeting in Zurich.
21 Pakistan beat England by 4 wickets at the Brit Oval to reduce the deficit to 2-1 with a final match to play in the four-match series.
22 Kenyan David Rudisha broke the world 800m record at Berlin's ISATF meeting with a time of 1min 41.09sec.
Arjun Atwal became the first golfer born in India to win on the US PGA Tour by capturing the Wyndham Championship in Greensboro.
28 Warrington beat Leeds 30-6 in rugby league's Carnegie Challenge Cup final at Wembley.
Jonathan Trott and Stuart Broad shared a world record 332 runs for England's eighth wicket in the final Test at Lord's.
Kenya's David Rudisha broke the world 800m record for the second time in a week when he ran 1min 41.01sec at the Rieti GP in Italy.
29 On the day England beat Pakistan by an innings and 225 runs at Lord's, The News of the World exposed a multi-million pound cricket match-fixing ring which allegedly rigged the current Test match. Salman Butt, the captain of the Pakistan cricket team plus bowlers Mohammad Amir and Mohammad Asif, who are accused of delivering three blatant no-balls to order, have had their mobile phones seized by investigating police officers. Footage appears to show the players' fixer Mazhar Majeed taking £150,000 cash, and telling the newspaper reporters exactly when the no-balls would come.
Lewis Hamilton won the Belgian Formula One GP at Spa Francorchamps to maintain a three point lead over Mark Webber in the drivers' championship.
European Ryder Cup captain Colin Montgomerie named Edoardo Molinari, Padraig Harrington and Luke Donald as his three wild card picks controversially omitting Paul Casey and Justin Rose from his team.

September
1 The No10 seed, Victoria Azarenka, was taken to hospital after collapsing on court during her second-round US Open match against Gisela Dulko of Argentina. The Belarusian, 21, slumped to the ground while 1-5 and 15-30 down on the Grandstand court and, after receiving medical treatment, was taken off in a wheelchair with suspected concussion after injuring herself prior to the match.
The three Pakistan cricketers at the centre of the match-fixing scandal have been banished from their national team's 16-man squad for the forthcoming matches against England.
3 England beat Bulgaria 4-0 at Wembley in the first of their Euro 2012 qualifiers. In other matches Ireland beat Armenia 1-0, Northern Ireland beat Slovenia 1-0, Scotland drew 0-0 with Lithuania and Wales lost 1-0 against Montenegro.
5 The Pakistan cricket team were under scrutiny during the first Twenty20 international match against England in Cardiff. England won a low-scoring game by 5 wickets.
New Zealand beat England 13-10 to claim a fourth successive women's Rugby World Cup title at Twickenham.
Caroline Powell became the fourth New Zealander to win the Land Rover Burghley Horse Trials after a foot-perfect showjumping round on the veteran Lenamore.
Andy Murray was beaten in four sets by Swiss No 2 Stanislas Wawrinka in the 3rd round of the US Open in New York.
7 England beat Switzerland 3-1 in Basle in the second of their Euro 2012 qualifiers. In other matches Ireland beat Andorra 3-1 and Scotland beat Liechtenstein 2-1 with an injury time winner at Hampden Park.
England beat Pakistan by 6 wickets in the second Twenty20 international match at the Swalec Stadium, Cardiff.
US Ryder Cup captain Corey Pavin announced his four wild cards for his team to play against Europe as Zach Johnson, Stewart Cink, Rickie Fowler and Tiger Woods.
8 Scottish snooker player John Higgins was banned from the sport for six months and fined £75,000 after admitting bringing the game into disrepute although the match-fixing charges were withdrawn by World Snooker.
11 Arctic Cosmos, ridden by William Buick and trained by John Gosden, won the Doncaster St Leger.
Belgian tennis star Kim Clijsters retained her US Open title, defeating Vera Zvonareva, the Russian who beat her in the Wimbledon quarter final earlier in the year, 6-2, 6-1 at Flushing Meadows.
12 Fernando Alonso won the Italian Formula One Grand Prix at Monza.
13 Rafael Nadal won the rain-delayed men's US Open title, defeating Novak Djokovic 6-4, 5-7, 6-4, 6-2 in the final at Flushing Meadows.
16 On the day that Andrew 'Freddie' Flintoff announced his retirement from cricket, Nottinghamshire won the County Championship by winning more games during the season than Somerset, who also finished on 214 points but won only six games to the champion's seven.
18 Ian Bell scored a century for Warwickshire during his side's three wicket victory over Somerset in the CB40 final at Lord's.
19 Italian cyclist Vincenzo Nibali won the Tour of Spain, 43 seconds ahead of Ezequiel Mosquera. Britain's Mark Cavendish won the green jersey for being the highest points scorer of the tour, emulating the feat of Malcolm Elliott in 1989, the only other British winner of a points jersey in a major tour although when Elliott won the jersey in Spain it was a blue one.
20 Snooker genius Ronnie O'Sullivan completed a controversial 147 maximum during the World Open in Glasgow. Leading 2-0 in the best-of-five opening round match O'Sullivan potted a red and a black before enquirying of the referee Jan Verhaas if there was a bonus for a maximum break. On being told there was no bonus Ronnie duly potted the remaining reds with blacks and after potting the colours to the pink then shook the hand of his opponent Mark King and was about to leave the auditorium with the break on 140 but the frame and match won. Verhaas then pleaded with Ronnie to pot the black for the satisfaction of the audience and a reluctant O'Sullivan promptly smashed the black into the pocket to loud cheers and an assured share of the high break prize of £4,000.
22 England beat Pakistan by 121 runs in the fifth and deciding one day international of the NatWest series at the Rose Bowl. Man-of-the-match was Eoin Morgan with an unbeaten 107 runs.
24 Cornish cyclist Vin Cox, 34, officially became the fastest person to ride around the world. Vin completed the 18,225-mile 163-day tour of the globe on August 1st - cycling 112 miles per day.
25 Tomas Gollob of Poland became World Speedway Champion following his win in the Italian GP in Terenzano.
26 Fernando Alonso won the Singapore Formula One Grand Prix.
World snooker champion Neil Robertson beat Ronnie O'Sullivan 5-1 in the final of the World Open in Glasgow.
American golfer Jim Furyk won the PGA Tour Championship and the £7.2m jackpot for also gaining victory in the FedEx Cup.
Halifax beat Featherstone Rovers 23-22 with a dropped goal in "golden point" extra time in Rugby League's Championship Grand Finals day at the Halliwell Jones Stadium in Warrington.
29 Cyclist Emma Pooley of Great Britain won the world individual time-trial title in Geelong, Australia.

30 The UCI, cycling's world governing body, announced that Tour de France winner Alberto Contador tested positive for clenbuterol during this year's Tour.

October

1 Much of the first day of the Ryder Cup was washed out at Celtic Manor, Newport, and no points were scored by either the Americans or Europeans although all the fourballs were started.

2 USA led 6-4 at the end of the second day's play of the Ryder Cup although Europe were ahead in all six uncompleted matches.
Wigan beat St Helens 22-10 in rugby league's Super League Grand Final at Old Trafford.
Credit Swap, ridden by Jim Crowley and trained by Michael Wigham, won the Cambridgeshire at Newmarket.

3 Workforce, ridden by Ryan Moore and trained by Sir Michael Stoute, won the Prix de l'arc de Triomphe at Longchamp.
The Commonwealth Games opened in New Delhi, India.

4 Trailing 9½-6½ going into the delayed finale of the Ryder Cup, the Americans fought back superbly to take the match to the wire. Graeme McDowell of Northern Ireland held his nerve in the final singles match as Europe clung on to their overnight lead to beat United States 14½-13½ to regain the trophy.

5 Fran Hallsall won the home nation's first gold medal of the Commonwealth Games with victory in the 50m butterfly representing England.

10 Sebastian Vettel came home triumphant ahead of his Red Bull teammate Mark Webber in the Japanese Grand Prix in Suzuka.

12 In European Championship qualifying matches England drew with Montenegro 0-0, Republic of Ireland drew with Slovakia 1-1, Northern Ireland drew with Faeroe Islands 1-1, Wales lost to Switzerland 1-4 and Scotland lost to Spain 2-3.

14 England were beaten for second place in the Commonwealth Games medals table by India at the very last opportunity as the 2010 Games in Delhi closed. Saina Nehwal's badminton victory handed India their 38th gold medal, one more than England's tally of 37, as English badminton players lost three finals. Australia topped the medals table, winning 74 gold medals. Scotland's nine golds placed them 10th, Northern Ireland's three boxing titles earned them 13th, and Wales finished 15th.

15 John W Henry, owner of the Boston Red Sox baseball team, and his New England Sports Ventures Group took over Liverpool FC with a £300million deal.

17 Andy Murray beat Roger Federer 6-3 6-2 to win the Shanghai Masters and claim his second title of the year.

18 LaShawn Merritt, the Olympic and world 400metres champion, was banned for 21 months after testing positive for testosterone three times between October 2009 and January 2010.

22 After a week of uncertainty Manchester United forward Wayne Rooney signed a new five-year contract.

23 British gymnasts gained three medals at the world championships in Rotterdam. Beth Tweddle won gold in the uneven bars, Louis Smith silver on the pommel horse and Dan Purvis bronze on the floor.

24 Fernando Alonso won the inaugural Korean Formula One GP in Yeongam.
Italian golfer Matteo Manassero became the youngest winner on the European Tour with victory in the Castello Masters in Spain. Last year's British amateur champion – he was the youngest to lift that title too – at 17 years and 188 days, broke the previous record set by New Zealand's Danny Lee, who was 18 years and 113 days old when he won the 2008 Johnnie Walker Classic.

31 England's Lee Westwood became world number one for the first time, ending American Tiger Woods's 281-week reign at the top of the golf rankings.

November

6 Paul Hanagan became the first northern jockey since Steve Donaghue in 1923 to win the flat jockey's championship. In a gripping season finale Hanagan (191 winners) held off the late challenge of Richard Hughes (189) by riding two more winners.
In a sensational Breeder's Cup meeting at Churchill Downs, Kentucky, Goldikova won her third consecutive Breeder's Cup Mile while wonder horse Zenyatta failed by a head to make it a perfect 20 wins from 20 starts in the Breeder's Cup Classic after her jockey Mike Smith trailed the field by 50 yards after only two furlongs of the race.

7 German Formula One ace Sebastian Vettel came home triumphant ahead of his teammate Mark Webber of Australia in the Brazilian Grand Prix at Interlagos, Sao Paulo. The result ensured the constructor's championship for the English-based Red Bull team although the driver's championship, led by Fernando Alonso, will not be decided until next week's final race.
The Murray brothers, Andy and Jamie, won their first doubles title together with a 7-6, 5-7, 10-7 victory over Max Mirnyi of Belarus and India's Mahesh Bhupathi at the Valencia Open.

11 Ray Wilkins was sacked as Chelsea's assistant coach during half-time of a reserve match.

13 David Haye stopped Audley Harrison in the third round of their WBA title fight at the MEN Arena, Manchester.
England beat Australia 35-18 in a Rugby Union International at Twickenham.
Manny Pacquiao of the Philippines gained a one-sided points victory over Antonio Margarito of Mexico for the vacant WBC light-middleweight boxing title in Texas.

14 John Higgins made a triumphant return to professional snooker following his six-month ban for not reporting an illegal match-fixing approach, beating Shaun Murphy 4-2 in the final of the Euro Player's Tour Championship in Hamm.
Sebastian Vettel beat Fernando Alonso by four points to become Formula One world champion in an exciting final race at the Yas Marina Circuit on Yas Island, on the outskirts of Abu Dhabi. Although Alonso topped the points table going into the race he could finish only seventh behind his German rival, who converted his pole position into a race win.

17 England were beaten 2-1 by France in a friendly international football match at Wembley.

27 Ronnie O'Sullivan was in unstoppable from has he thrashed Shaun Murphy 7-1 in the final of snooker's Premier League at Potters Leisure Resort in Hopton on Sea, Norfolk.

28 England enjoyed a record-breaking drawn first Test at the Gabba. Alastair Cook's second innings of 235 was the highest score at the Brisbane ground, beating Don Bradman's 226 for Australia v South Africa in 1931. Alastair Cook and Jonathan Trott's unbeaten stand of 329 was the highest in Australia by an England pair for any wicket, eclipsing the 98-year old record of 323 set by Jack Hobbs and Wilfred Rhodes at the MCG in 1912.
Roger Federer beat Rafael Nadal 6-3, 3-6, 6-1 in the ATP World Finals at the O2 Arena.
British golfer Ian Poulter lost £350,000 on the flip of a coin in a farcical finish to the £11million Dubai World Championship. His hopes of winning the European Tour's richest event disappeared when he dropped a ball on his marker and suffered a one-shot penalty. The ball flipped his "lucky" platinum coin over on the second hole of a sudden-death play-off with Robert Karlsson, who was left with two putts from four feet to clinch the £776,000 winner's cheque.

December

2 Russia won the bid to host the 2018 World Cup after England crashed out in the first round of voting despite an impressive presentation by the prime minister David Cameron, David Beckham and Prince William.

6 Serbia won the Davis Cup for the first time in their history, beating France, the nine time champions, 3-2 in the final.

7 England beat Australia by an innings & 71 runs in Brisbane to take a 1-0 lead in the Ashes series.

11 Amir Khan made a third successful defence of his WBA light-welterweight boxing title with a hard-fought points win over Marcos Maldana of Argentina, in Las Vegas.

12 John Higgins beat Mark Williams 10-9 in a pulsating final of the UK Snooker Championship at Telford. Williams led 9-5 but Higgins won the last five frames, requiring snookers in one of them, to gain an improbable victory.
Europe defeated USA 11-8 in the annual Mosconi Cup pool competition at the York Hall, Bethnal Green.

13 Sam Allardyce was sacked as manager of Blackburn Rovers after refusing to have new signings imposed on him during the January transfer window.

19 Champion jump jockey AP McCoy, 36, was named as BBC Sports Personality of the Year.
Australia beat England by 267 runs in the third Ashes Test at the WACA, Perth, to level the series at 1-1 with two matches left to play.

27 Australian cricket captain Ricky Ponting was fined 40 per cent of his match fee (around £3,500), for arguing with umpire Aleem Dar over a not out decision for a caught behind appeal against Kevin Pietersen. Despite the controversy England ended the second day on 444-5 after bowling the Aussies out for 98.
29 England beat Australia by an innings & 157 runs at the Melbourne Cricket Ground to take a 2-1 lead in the series and thereby retain the Ashes.

Obituaries 2010

January
1 Jean Carroll, US comedienne, born Celine Zeigman, January 6th 1911
Max Salpeter, violinist, born April 16th 1908
5 Willie Mitchell, US record producer, born March 23rd 1928
Kenneth Noland, US abstract artist, born April 10th 1924
11 Eric Rohmer, French film director, born Jean-Marie Schérer, April 4th 1920
13 Teddy Pendergrass, US soul singer, born March 26th 1950
Ed Thigpen, US drummer, born September 28th 1930
16 Felice Quinto, Italian 'father of the paparazzo', born April 11th 1929
17 Erich Wolf Segal, US author, born June 16th 1937
19 William Pollock 'Bill' McLaren, rugby union commentator, born October 16th 1923
22 Jean Merilyn Simmons, actress, born January 31st 1929
Betty Wilson, Australian cricketer, born November 21st 1921
23 Earl Wild, US piano virtuoso, born November 26th 1915
24 Pernell Elvin Roberts, US actor, born May 18th 1928
26 Louis Auchincloss, US author, born September 27th 1917
27 Jerome David "JD" Salinger, US author, born January 1st 1919
28 Margaret Dale, US dancer, born Margaret Bolam, December 30th 1922
29 Ralph McInerny, author of the Father Dowling novels, born February 24th 1929
31 Paddie O'Neil, actress, born Adalena Nail, May 1st 1926

February
1 David Brown, US film producer, born July 28th 1916
3 John McCallum, Australian creator of Skippy the Bush Kangaroo, born March 14th 1918
Gil Merrick, goalkeeper, born January 26th 1922
5 Peter Calvocoressi, Karachi-born British author and head of air intelligence at Bletchley Park, born November 17th 1912.
Ian Carmichael, actor, born June 18th 1920
6 Johnny Dankworth, jazz musician, born September 20th 1927
7 Philip Klass, US science fiction writer (as William Tenn), born May 6th 1920
9 (Walter) Frederick Morrison, US inventor of the Frisbee, born January 23rd 1920
11 (Lee) Alexander McQueen, fashion designer, born March 16th 1969
13 Cy Grant, Guyanese actor, born November 8th 1919
Gareth Wigan, film executive, born December 2nd 1921
14 Dick Francis, author and jockey, born October 31st 1920
17 Kathryn Grayson, US singer and actress, born Zelda Hedrick, February 9th 1922
19 Lionel Jeffries, actor, born June 10th 1926
20 Alexander Haig, US Army general and politician, born December 2nd 1924
23 Mervyn Jones, author and journalist, born February 27th 1922
Wyn Morris, conductor, born February 14th 1929
26 Gai Eaton, Swiss author and diplomat, born January 1st 1921
27 Wendy Toye, ballerina, born May 1st 1917
28 Phillip Law, Australian Antarctic explorer, born April 21st 1912
Martin Benson, actor, born August 10th 1918

March
1 Kristian Digby, television presenter, born June 24th 1977
2 Winston Churchill, politician and journalist, born October 10th 1940
3 Michael Foot, politician, born July 23rd 1913
5 Philip Langridge, tenor, born December 10th 1939
6 Ole Schmidt, Danish composer, born July 14th 1928
Carol Marsh, actress, born Norma Lilian Simpson, May 10th 1926
8 Tony Imi, cinematographer, born March 27th 1937
10 George Webb, jazz pianist, born October 8th 1917
Corey Haim, Canadian actor, born December 23rd 1971
Merlin Olsen, US actor and American football player, born September 15th 1940
Simeon 'Tim' Holland, US backgammon champion, born March 3rd 1931
Evelyn Dall, US singer and actress, born Evelyn Fuss, January 8th 1918
14 Peter Graves, US actor, born Peter Aurness, March 18th 1926
17 Charlie Gillett, DJ and rock historian, born February 20th 1942
18 Fess Parker, US actor, born August 16th 1924
Joseph Ettedgui, Moroccan fashion designer, born February 22nd 1936
19 Lady Mary Clive, author, born Lady Mary Katherine Pakenham, August 23rd 1907
John Hicklenton, illustrator of the Judge Dredd comic series, born May 8th 1967
Gerald Drucker, double bass player, born August 5th 1925
20 Harry Carpenter, sports commentator, born October 17th 1925
22 Sir James Black, Nobel Prize-winning pharmacologist, born June 14th 1924
Diz Disley, Canadian jazz guitarist and cartoonist, born May 27th 1931
23 Blanche Thebom, US mezzo soprano, born September 19th 1915
24 Ron Hamence, Australian cricketer, born November 25th 1915
Jim Marshall, US photographer, born February 3rd 1936
27 Stephen Hearst, BBC Radio executive, born October 6th 1919
Vasily Smyslov, Russian chess champion, born March 24th 1921
28 Herb Ellis, US jazz guitarist, born August 4th 1921

April
1 John Forsythe, US actor, born John Freund, January 29th 1918

Penelope Hughes-Hallett, biographer, born Penelope Fairbairn, June 13th 1927
4 Alec Bedser, cricketer, born July 4th 1918
6 Corin Redgrave, actor, born July 16th 1939
David Quayle, co-founder of B&Q with Richard Block, born August 19th 1936
7 Christopher Cazenove, actor, born December 17th 1943
8 Bishop Abel Tendekayi Muzorewa, Zimbabwean politician, born April 14th 1925
Malcolm McLaren, former manager of the Sex Pistols, born January 22nd 1946
9 Kenneth McKellar, tenor, born June 23rd 1927
Meinhardt Raabe, US actor, born September 2nd 1915
10 Lech Kaczynski, president of Poland, born June 18th 1945
14 Greville Starkey, flat jockey, born December 21st 1939
18 Tom Fleming, actor, born June 29th 1927
19 Edwin Valero, Venezuelan boxing champion, born December 3rd 1981
20 Robert Natkin, US abstract painter, born November 7th 1930
21 Juan Antonio Samaranch, Spanish 7th President of the IOC, born July 17th 1920
23 Peter Porter, Australian poet, born February 16th 1929
25 Alan Sillitoe, novelist, poet and playwright, born March 4th 1928
26 Roy Baird, film producer, born September 3rd 1933
27 Peter Cheeseman, theatre director, born January 27th 1932
29 Avigdor Arikha, Romanian-born Israeli artist, born April 28th 1929
30 Gerry Ryan, Irish radio broadcaster, born June 4th 1956

May
2 Lynn Redgrave, actress, born March 8th 1943
3 Peter O'Donnell, creator of literary heroine Modesty Blaise, born April 11th 1920
5 Giulietta Simionato, Italian mezzo-soprano, born May 12th 1910
Umaru Yar'Adua, Nigerian president, born August 16th 1951
7 Pamela Green, first woman to appear naked in a British film, born March 28th 1929
9 Lena Horne, US singer, born June 30 th 1917
15 John Shepherd-Barron, inventor of the Automated Telling Machine, born June 23rd 1925
16 Hank Jones, US jazz pianist, born August 31st 1918
Ronnie James Dio, US rock singer with Black Sabbath, born Ronald Padavona, July 10th 1942
17 Yvonne Loriod, French pianist, born January 20th 1924
18 Shusaku Arakawa, Japanese artist and architect, born July 6th 1936
John Gooders, writer of bird books, born January 10th 1937
20 Lord (Leonard Gordon) Wolfson, philanthropist, born November 11th 1927
22 Martin Gardner, US writer, born October 21st 1914
24 Ray Alan, ventriloquist, born September 18th 1930
27 Reg White, Olympic sailor, born October 28th 1935
28 Gary Coleman, US actor, born February 8th 1968
29 Dennis Lee Hopper, US actor, born May 17th 1936
30 Joan Rhodes, music hall act 'The Mighty Mannequin', born April 13th 1921
31 Louise Bourgeois, French sculptress, born December 25th 1911
Chris Haney, Canadian co-creator of Trivial Pursuit, born August 9th 1950
Brian Duffy, photographer, born June 15th 1933

June
2 Giuseppe Taddei, Italian baritone, born June 26th 1916
3 Rue McClanahan, US actress, born February 21st 1934
Vladimir Arnold, Russian mathematician, born June 12th 1937
7 Stuart Cable, drummer with the Stereophonics, born May 19th 1970
8 Crispian St Peters, pop singer, born Robin Peter Smith, April 5th 1939
9 Marina Semyonova, Russian ballerina, born June 12th 1908
10 Sigmar Polke, German artist, born February 13th 1941
12 Egon Ronay, Hungarian-born food critic, born July 24th 1915
15 Bekim Fehmiu, Bosnian actor, born June 1st 1936
16 Maureen Forrester, Canadian contralto, born July 25th 1930
17 Andy Ripley, rugby union player and all-round sportsman, born December 1st 1947
Rosemary Lomax, first woman to train a winner at Royal Ascot (Precipice Wood), born November 7th 1928
18 Jose Saramago, Portuguese Nobel Prize-winning novelist, born November 16th 1922
19 Ursula Thiess, German actress, born Ursula Schmidt, May 15th 1924
21 Chris Sievey, creator of the papier mâché headed Frank Sidebottom, born in 1956
Russell Ash, author of The Top Ten of Everything, born June 18th 1946
24 Norman Hutchinson, Indian-born artist, born October 11th 1932
25 Alan Plater, dramatist, born April 15th 1935
Wu Guanzhong, Chinese artist, born July 5th 1919
26 Algirdas Brazauskas, Lithuanian politician, born September 22nd 1932
Spen King, designer of the Range Rover, born March 26th 1925

July
1 Alan Robb, radio presenter, born February 27th 1961
Geoffrey Hutchings, actor, born June 8th 1939
2 Dame Beryl Bainbridge, writer, born November 21st 1934
5 Cesare Siepi, Italian operatic bass, born February 10th 1923
9 Mark Bytheway, former Quizzing World Champion, born July 22nd 1963
10 Sugar Minott, Jamaican singer, born May 25th 1956
12 Harvey Pekar, US author, born October 8th 1939
Olga Guillot, Cuban singer "the queen of bolero", born October 9th 1922
Tuli Kupferberg, US founder of rock group The Fugs, born September 28th 1923
13 Wyn Knowles, former editor of Woman's Hour, born July 30th 1923
Gilly Coman, actress, born September 13th 1955
15 Hank Cochran, US Country and Western singer, born August 2nd 1935
21 Anthony Rolfe Johnson, tenor, born November 5th 1940
24 Alexander Gordon Higgins, snooker player, born March 18th 1949
28 David William, actor, born Bryan Williams, June 24th 1926
29 Martin Drew, jazz drummer, born February 11th 1944
31 Tom Mankiewicz, US scriptwriter, born June 1st 1942

Suso Cecchi D'Amico, Italian scriptwriter, born July 24th 1914
Tony Fox, Olympic oarsman, born July 27th 1928

August
1 Eric Tindill, New Zealand cricketer and rugby player, born December 18th 1910
2 Susan Benjamin, creator of Halcyon Days enamel boxes, born May 10th 1921
6 Phelps 'Catfish' Collins, US guitarist, born in 1944
8 Patricia Neal, US actress, born Patsy Lou Neal, January 20th 1926
Jack Parnell, bandleader and drummer, born August 6th 1923
10 Antonio Pettigrew, US Olympic sprint champion, born November 3rd 1967
14 Herman Leonard, US photographer, born March 6th 1923
Abbey Lincoln, US jazz singer, born Anna Marie Wooldridge, August 6th 1930
16 Bobby Thomson, baseball player, born October 25th 1923
17 Francesco Cossiga, Italian politician, born July 26th 1928
Edwin Morgan, poet, born April 27th 1920
22 Hope Bourne, author, born August 26th 1918
23 Tito Burns, showbusiness agent, born Nathan Bernstein, February 7th 1921
27 Corinne Day, photographer, born February 19th 1962
30 Nicholas Walter Lyell, politician, born December 6th 1938
31 Laurent Fignon, French cyclist, born August 12th 1960

September
3 Cyril Smith, politician, born June 28th 1928
5 Elizabeth Jenkins, novelist and biographer, born October 31st 1905
David Dortort, US writer, born David Katz, October 23rd 1916
6 Clive Donner, film director, born January 21st 1926
9 Bent Larsen, Danish chess champion, born March 4th 1935
11 Lord (Thomas Henry) Bingham of Cornhill, judge, born October 13th 1933
12 Claude Chabrol, French film maker, born June 24th 1930
14 Dodge Morgan, US sailor, born January 15th 1932
16 Helen Escobedo, Mexican sculptor, born Elena Fulda, July 28th 1934
17 Louis Marks, scriptwriter, born March 23rd 1928
18 Bobby Smith, footballer, born February 22nd 1933
19 László Polgár, Hungarian operatic bass, born January 1st 1947
21 Geoffrey Burgon, composer, born July 15th 1941
Grace Bradley, US actress, born September 21st 1913
Don Partridge, busker and pop star, born October 27th 1941
22 Eddie Fisher, US singer, born August 10th 1928
Alan Rudkin, boxer, born November 18th 1941
23 Catherine Walker, French-born British couturier, born June 27th 1945
24 Dick Griffey, US founder of the record label Solar, born November 16th 1938
26 Terry Newton, rugby league player, born November 7th 1978
Gloria Stuart, US actress, born Gloria Stewart, July 4th 1910
27 Kurt Albert, German pioneer of freestyle climbing, born January 18th 1954
28 Arthur Penn, US film director, born September 22nd 1922
29 Tony Curtis, US actor, born Bernie Schwartz, June 3rd 1925
David Marques, rugby player, born December 9th 1932
30 Robert Mark, police commissioner, born March 13th 1917
Stephen J Cannell, US television writer and producer, born February 5th 1941

October
4 Norman Wisdom, comedian and musician, born February 4th 1915
5 Roy Ward Baker, film director, born December 19th 1916
Moss Keane, Irish rugby union player, born July 27th 1948
7 Selma al-Radi, Iraqi archaeologist, born July 23rd 1939
8 Neil Richardson, composer of 'Approaching Menace' (Mastermind theme), born February 5th 1930
10 Joan Sutherland, Australian soprano, born November 7th 1926
Alison Stephens, mandolin player, born March 1st 1970
Eric Joisel, French sculptor, born November 15th 1956
11 Claire Rayner, broadcaster and agony aunt, born January 22nd 1931
13 Mary Malcolm, television announcer, born March 15th 1918
Marzieh, Iranian singer, born Ashraf os-Saadaat Morteza'I, in 1924
Eddie Baily, footballer, born August 6th 1925
14 Simon MacCorkindale, actor, born February 12th 1952
Malcolm Allison, football manager, born September 5th 1927
Benoit Mandelbrot, Polish mathematician, born November 20th 1924
15 Vera Rózsa, Hungarian mezzo-soprano, born May 16th 1917
17 Graham Crowden, actor, born November 30th 1922
19 Tom Bosley, US actor, born October 1st 1927
20 Ari Up, German punk rock singer, born Ariane Foster, January 17th 1962
Eva Ibbotson, Austrian children's author, born Maria Wiesner, January 21st 1925
Bob Guccione, US founder of Penthouse magazine, born December 7th 1930
Robert Katz, US writer, born June 27th 1933
21 Lady Spender, concert pianist, born Natasha Litvin, April 18th 1919
23 Leo Cullum, US cartoonist, born January 11th 1942
24 Andy Holmes, rower, October 15th 1959
Joseph Stein, US scriptwriter, born May 30th 1912
25 Gregory Isaacs, Jamaican singer, songwriter and producer, born July 15th 1951
27 Nestor Kirchner, Argentinian politician, born February 25th 1950
28 James MacArthur, US actor, born December 8th 1937
Paddy Mullins, Irish racehorse trainer, born January 28th 1919
29 Ronnie Clayton, footballer, born August 5th 1934
30 Harry Mulisch, Dutch novelist, born July 29th 1927
Douglas Argent, television producer and director, born May 21st 1921
31 Ted Sorensen, US President Kennedy's speech writer, born May 8th 1928

November
2 Rudolf Barshai, Russian viola player, born September 28th 1924
3 Viktor Chernomyrdin, Russian politician, born April 9th 1938
Jerry Bock, US songwriter, born November 23rd 1928
5 Shirley Verrett, US mezzo-soprano, born May 31st 1931
Jill Clayburgh, US actress, born April 30th 1944
8 Jack Levine, US painter, born January 3rd 1915
11 "Baby" Marie Osborne, US child actress, born Helen Alice Myres, November 5th 1911
Agostino 'Dino' De Laurentiis, Italian film producer, born August 8th 1919
12 Henryk Gorecki, Polish composer, born December 6th 1933
13 Luis Garcia Berlanga, Spanish film director, born June 12th 1921
17 Simona Pakenham, actress, born September 25th 1916
23 Ingrid Pitt, Polish actress, born Ingoushka Petrov, November 21st 1937
Joyce Howard, actress, born February 28th 1922
25 Bernard Matthews, founder of Bernard Matthews Farms Limited, born January 24th 1930
28 Leslie Nielsen, Canadian actor, born February 11th 1926
29 Mario Monicelli, Italian film director, born May 15th 1915
30 Peter Hofmann, German tenor, born August 22nd 1944
Patrick Pollen, artist in stained glass, born January 12th 1928
Monty Sunshine, jazz drummer, born April 8th 1928

December
1 Helen Boatwright, US soprano, born Helen Strassburger, November 17th 1916
3 Hugues Cuénod, Swiss tenor, born June 16th 1902
6 Tom Crowe, Irish radio broadcaster, born July 5th 1922
8 Walter Haeussermann, German rocket scientist, born March 2nd 1914
10 Michael Hagopian, Armenian film maker, born October 20th 1913
Professor John Fenn, US Nobel prize-winning chemist, born June 15th 1917
12 Tom Walkinshaw, Formula 1 team manager, born August 14th 1946
13 Enrique Morente, Spanish flamenco singer, born December 15th 1942
Bella Akhmadulina, Russian poet, born April 10th 1937
14 John Beharrell, amateur golfer, born May 2nd 1938
16 Blake Edwards, US film director, born July 26th 1922
Richard Adeney, flautist, born January 25th 1920
17 Captain Beefheart, US rock musician, born Donald Glen Vliet, January 15th 1941
Ralph Coates, footballer, born April 26th 1946
18 His Honour James Pickles, QC, born March 18th 1925
19 Anthony Howard, former editor of the New Statesman, born February 12th 1934
20 Brian Hanrahan, BBC news correspondent, born March 22nd 1949
John Alldis, conductor, born August 10th 1929
21 Enzo Bearzot, Italian football coach, born September 26th 1927
24 Elisabeth Beresford, creator of the Wombles, born (in Paris) August 6th 1926
25 Carlos Andrés Peréz, former Venezuelan president, born October 27th 1922
26 Teena Marie, US singer, born Marie Brockert, March 5th 1956
27 Keith Andrew, cricketer, born December 15th 1929
28 Avi Cohen, Israeli footballer, born (in Cairo) November 14th 1956
Hideko Takamine, Japanese actress, born March 27th 1924
30 Bobby Farrell, Aruban member of Boney M, born October 6th 1949

Daily Record 2011

January
1 Around 40 prisoners wearing balaclavas went on the rampage at Ford Prison, near Arundel, West Sussex, after being asked to provide breath tests. Inmates then set fire to accommodation and facility blocks, forcing prison warders to evacuate. Six accommodation blocks, a gymnasium, a mail room, a snooker room and a pool room including 10 newly-installed pool tables were all damaged, causing millions of pounds of damage. The disturbance started at midnight as the New Year beckoned and prisoners were finally brought under control by specially trained staff at 10pm.
4 VAT was increased by 2.5 per cent to its highest-ever level of 20 per cent.
7 David Chayter, the former Labour MP for Bury North, was jailed for 18 months for making false expenses claims to the House of Commons.
9 A US congresswoman was shot in the head and six other people were killed by a gunman in Arizona. Democratic Representative Gabrielle Giffords, 40, was shot during a public meeting in Tucson. Jared Lee Loughner, 23, was arrested for the assassination attempt.
10 Ninety-nine per cent of the population of Southern Sudan voted in favour of Independence.
11 Miriam O'Reilly, 53, former presenter of *Countryfile*, won her case of unfair dismissal against the BBC on the grounds of ageism.
A-level student Edward Woollard, 18, who hurled a fire extinguisher off the top of the Tory Party HQ during a tuition fees riot was jailed for two years and eight months.
14 Flash floods in the Australian state of Queensland claimed eight lives, with at least another 72 people missing.
President Zine El Abidine Ben Ali was forced to flee Tunisia after a general strike led to violent clashes.
17 Segways, the two-wheeled motorised vehicles once hailed as the future of transport, were banned from use on footpaths and pavements following the conviction of Phillip Coates for riding one on the pavement in his home town of Cudworth, Barnsley. Mr Coates was fined £75 plus costs. Segways can now only be used on private land as they do not comply with road traffic law.
18 Barclays Bank was fined £7.7m by the Financial Services Authority and ordered to pay £60m compensation to its customers for selling "low-risk" investments negligently.
A Christian couple, Peter and Hazelmary Bull, lost a court battle over their refusal to allow a homosexual couple to share a room at their Chymorvah Private Hotel in Marazion, near Penzance. Judge Andrew Rutherford ordered the couple to pay £3,600 in damages to civil partners Steven Preddy and Martyn Hall.
19 Andy Coulson resigned as David Cameron's director of communications in the wake of the phone hacking scandal prevalent during his time as editor of the News of the World.
20 Shadow Chancellor Alan Johnson resigned amid claims his wife had an affair with a bodyguard.
22 Australian soldier Corporal Benjamin Roberts-Smith, 32, was awarded the Victoria Cross, for single-handedly overpowering Taliban machine-gunners attacking his platoon last June in Afghanistan. Cpl Roberts-Smith is the second person to have received the Victoria Cross for Australia, which was created in 1991 and is a separate award from the British VC.
24 Thirty five people killed by a suspected suicide bomber in the arrival's hall at Moscow's Domodedovo airport, included two Britons and Ukrainian dramatist and poet, Anna Yablonskaya, who was on her way to get a prize for her play *The Pagans.*
25 Hizbollah-backed billionaire Najib Mikati became Lebanon's prime minister two weeks after the pro-American Saad Hariri's government fell. Under Lebanon's constitution the president has to be Christian, the prime minister, Sunni and the speaker Shia.
26 Tommy Sheridan, former leader of the Scottish Socialist party, was jailed for 3 years after hearing he had brought "the walls of the temple crashing down" by repeatedly lying on oath about his adultery in order to win a £200,000 defamation case against the *News of the World.*

February

7 Britain's coalition Government scrapped anti-social behaviour orders, first implemented by Tony Blair in 1998. Asbos will be replaced by measures that will give the police power to ban troublemakers from town centres and street corners; offenders under penalty of having their assets seized if found in breach.

8 Seventy-one-year-old grandmother Ann Timson foiled an armed gem's raid in Northampton town centre by walloping thieves with her handbag causing one to be detained and the other five to abort their crime.

10 Former Labour MP for Barnsley Central, Eric Illsley, was jailed for a year at Southwark Crown Court for fiddling his parliamentary expenses. Illsley admitted falsely claiming more than £14,000 between 2005 and 2008. In the same court former Labour MP for Livingstone, Jim Devine, was found guilty of netting more than £8,000 in bogus expenses. Devine, 57, accused his ex-office manager Marion Kinley, 48, of stealing £5,000 of it but this was found to be untrue. He will be sentenced next month.

11 After 18 days of anti-government protests President Hosni Mubarak finally agreed to step down from office, handing power over to the Egyptian army. The announcement was made by Vice-President Omar Suleiman amid rejoicing in Tahrir Square in Cairo, the centre of more than two weeks of "people power" demonstrations. South African-born journalist Lara Logan, the CBS network's chief foreign affairs correspondent, was describing the jubilation in the aftermath of the resignation when a wild bunch of Egyptian youths attacked her as she was preparing to file a live report for CNN from the square.

15 Simon Cremer, a 46-year-old floor-fitting company boss, who paraded employee Mark Gilbert through the streets of Witham in Essex wearing a cardboard sign saying "THIEF. I Stole £845. Am on my way to the police station" in October 2008, was forced to pay Mr Gilbert £5,000 in compensation and £8,000 legal costs. Mr Gilbert's original theft was dealt with by the police with a caution.

17 The world's hottest chilli was produced in the Lincolnshire town of Grantham. Tests by Warwick University rate the new variety at 1,067,286 on the Scoville Scale which is used to measure the heat of peppers. The former record-holder, the Indian Bhut Jolokia, is rated 1,041,427. The Lincs variety, bred by Nick Woods and Matt Simpson, is named Infinity for its "never-ending" burn, which cannot be quelled by even the best antidote, milk.

21 The wave of people power against corrupt dictatorships in north Africa reached the streets of Libya as thousands demonstrated in Tripoli, amid claims that Muammar Gaddafi, the ruler for the past 41 years, ordered his airforce to bomb unarmed civilians.

22 Colonel Muammar Gaddafi made a defiant speech from a building destroyed by an American air raid in 1986 that killed his adopted daughter. In his 75 minute diatribe the Libyan leader threatened death sentences against all those who challenged his authority.
An earthquake measuring 6.3 on the Richter scale devastated the city of Christchurch, New Zealand, causing 185 confirmed deaths.

24 Kate Middleton carried out her first official engagement, launching a new RNLI lifeboat, in Anglesey, North Wales.

26 After leading Fine Gael to victory in Ireland's 2011 General Election, Enda Kenny is all but assured of being elected Taoiseach when the 31st Dáil convenes on 9 March. The centre-right party trounced Fianna Fail, which has been the ruling party for the last fourteen years.

28 High Court judges Lord Justice Munby and Mr Justice Beatson remarked that there is no place in British law for Christian beliefs, when ruling on the case of a Christian couple, Eunice and Owen Johns, who were told that they could not be foster carers because of their view that homosexuality is wrong.

March

9 Enda Kenny is officially sworn in as Irish Taoiseach (prime minister).

10 The Dalai Lama announced his political retirement, from his exile capital of Dharamsala in northern India. Tenzin Gyatso, born in 1935, has held the position since 1950 and was recognised as the 14th incarnation in 1937.

11 An earthquake measured at 9.03 magnitude by the US Geological Survey, struck Japan at 2.46pm local time. The superquake triggered a tsunami that devastated Japan's Pacific coast with Sendai, 150 miles north of Tokyo, the worst affected area. Prime Minister Naoto Kan, immediately declared a state of emergency after an explosion at a nuclear plant in Fukushima, 100 miles north of Tokyo, created further problems with radiation levels increasing amid fears of a possible core meltdown unless cooling systems are repaired quickly. The official death toll was 15,883 although several thousand more were severely injured or missing.

14 Solicitor Hilary Thorpe, on behalf of her firm, Gaby Hardwicke of Eastbourne, made legal history by serving a summons via Facebook for the first time in Britain.

17 A United Nations Resolution, No 1973, was passed by the Security Council by 10 votes to nil, with 5 abstentions. The resolution established a no fly zone and authorisation of "any military or preventative measures" to protect Libyan civilians and civilian areas "while excluding a foreign occupation force of any form on any part of Libyan territory". The Security Council resolution was proposed by France, Lebanon, and the United Kingdom. Ten Security Council members voted in the affirmative (Bosnia and Herzegovina, Colombia, Gabon, Lebanon, Nigeria, Portugal, South Africa, and permanent members France, the United Kingdom, and the United States). Five (Brazil, Germany, and India, and permanent members China and Russia) abstained, with none opposed.

19 Forces from Britain, France, Canada and the United States launched Operation Ellamy, a series of bombing raids on Libyan airfields, tanks and air defence systems designed to stop Colonel Gaddafi deploying military equipment against his own people in a defiant act to remain in power. Military intervention began as French fighter jets flew reconnaissance flights over Libya and fired at a Libyan tank. The U.S. military designated its military operations as Operation Odyssey Dawn, and began by firing Tomahawk cruise missiles from U.S. Navy submarines at Libyan air defences.

20 A pair of the RAF's new F2 Typhoon Eurofighter fighter jets took off from southern Italy on their first patrols to enforce the UN-imposed no-fly zone over Libya.

23 Portugal's economy was in crisis after its parliament rejected an austerity package.

24 Sian O'Callaghan, 22, who had been missing for five days, was found murdered in a shallow grave near the White Horse of Uffington. Sian disappeared after partying with girl friends at the Suju club in Swindon High Street. A 47-year-old taxi driver Christopher Halliwell confessed to the murder and also to another in 2002. (see entry for 5 April 2011).
Syria's president Bashar Al-Assad was the latest Middle Eastern autocrat to face the wrath of his people when more than 20,000 protesters marched through the city of Daraa. At least 37 anti-government protesters were killed by the president's security forces.
Britain's worst sex attacker, Delroy Grant, was convicted of 29 offences of rape and burglary. The man known to police as the Night Stalker was finally caught in 2009, at least 17 years after he started terrorising south London residents, mostly pensioners.

25 The heart sign entered the Oxford English Dictionary as the first graphical symbol to signify a word in the reference work's 127-year history. Readers looking up the word "heart" will find the symbol listed as an entirely new usage, as a verb meaning "to love". Perhaps the most famous example, which is included in the latest edition of the dictionary, is the New York tourism advertising slogan: I [heart] NY. Its earliest recorded use is on a car bumper sticker printed in the US in 1984, which read: "I [heart] my dog's head."

26 Hundreds of thousands of protesters marched through London demonstrating against government spending cuts. Whilst Ed Miliband, the Labour Party leader, addressed a TUC rally of at least 250,000 peaceful protesters in Hyde Park an apparently co-ordinated attack began on shops and police in Oxford Street as a mob tried to storm into shops, including Topshop, BHS, and John Lewis. Department store Fortnum and Mason was occupied by 200 '"anti-cuts" protesters who smashed windows and knocked over displays. The Ritz hotel in Piccadilly was attacked with dustbins and a "Trojan horse" was set on fire in Oxford Circus.

30 Moussa Muhammad Koussa, who headed the Libyan intelligence agency from 1994 until being promoted to Minister of Foreign Affairs in the Libyan government in March 2009, resigned his position from the Gaddafi regime and flew to England to be questioned by, amongst others, Scottish prosecutors seeking answers about the Lockerbie bombing, which killed 270 people in 1988. At the time, Koussa was a leading member of the Libyan Bureau for External Security (the Mathaba) which was suspected to be responsible.

April

1 The cost of prescriptions in England rose by 20p to £7.40 per item. The other three UK countries all have free prescriptions.

4 United Nations and French helicopters fired missiles at the palace of Laurent Gbagbo, the former president of the Ivory Coast who has refused to relinquish power since being deposed last November. Soldiers loyal to Alassane Ouattara, the recognised president, gathered outside Abidjan ready to storm the city.

5 Human remains found at a second site by detectives investigating the murder of Sian O'Callaghan were identified by Wiltshire Police as those of Becky Godden, who would have been 29 yesterday, a Swindon girl who disappeared some eight or nine years ago. The remains were found during painstaking excavation work at a site at Baxter's Farm, Eastleach, around 17 miles from where Miss O'Callaghan's body was discovered. Becky had become "disconnected" from her family after developing a drug problem. (see entry for 24 March 2011).

6 Portugal became the third European Union country, after Greece and Ireland, to request an emergency bailout. Outgoing Portuguese Prime Minister Jose Socrates announced the request had become inevitable after lawmakers rejected a new package of austerity measures.

8 The *News of the World* admitted hacking into the phones of eight high profile people between 2004 and 2006. Tessa Jowell, the former Olympics minister, actress Sienna Miller, designer Kelly Hoppen, Miss Jowell's estranged husband David Mills, football pundit Andy Gray, former aide to Lord Prescott Joan Hammell, publicist Nicola Phillips and sports agent Sky Andrew, all stand to receive an apology and compensation from Rupert Murdoch's News International.

11 Laurent Gbagbo, the former president of the Ivory Coast, was captured by forces loyal to president-elect Allasane Ouattara after weeks of fighting.

13 Dee Caffari became the only woman to have sailed around the world non-stop three times when she finished the Barcelona World Race. The 38-year-old former PE teacher, from Titchfield, Hampshire, crossed the line off Barcelona, Spain, in sixth place, after spending nearly 103 days at sea in the two-handed 25,000-mile race along with her Spanish co-skipper Anna Corbella, 34, on board their 60ft boat *GAES Centros Auditivos*. Caffari has already successfully circumnavigated the globe twice solo, and now once double-handed.

16 University friends James Cooper, 25, and James Kouzaris, 24, were murdered in Newtown, a deprived part of the city of Sarasota, Florida. A 16-year-old boy, named by police as Shawn Tyson, was arrested and charged with two counts of murder.

19 Huddersfield-born Captain Lisa Head, 29, from 321 Explosive Ordnance Disposal, died in the Queen Elizabeth Hospital, in Birmingham, of wounds received in Helmand province. Captain Head was the first female officer to be killed in Afghanistan.

29 Prince William (b. 21 June 1982) and his long-term girlfriend Catherine Elizabeth 'Kate' Middleton (b. 9 January 1982) married at a service in Westminster Abbey watched by an estimated audience of two billion people around the world. The couple were formally declared married by the Archbishop of Canterbury Rowan Williams, the spiritual leader of the Church of England. William's full title now becomes: His Royal Highness Prince William Arthur Philip Louis, Duke of Cambridge, Earl of Strathearn, Baron Carrickfergus, Royal Knight Companion of the Most Noble Order of the Garter, Master of Arts. Kate becomes Catherine, Duchess of Cambridge and also Countess of Strathearn and Baroness Carrickfergus. The Duchess of Cambridge's wedding dress was designed by Sarah Burton, who took over as creative director of the Alexander McQueen label in May 2010, following its founder's suicide in February of that year.

May

2 Osama bin Laden, leader of al-Qaeda and mastermind of the September 11th terrorist attacks, was killed during an American ground operation in Abbotabad, Pakistan.

5 More than two thirds of people voted to keep the first-past-the-post system in what was the first UK-wide referendum for 36 years. In the first major test of opinion since the general election voters also went to the polls in council elections, and in assembly and parliament elections in Wales and Scotland. On what has been dubbed "Super Thursday" the Liberal Democrats were severely punished losing almost half their councillors in town halls across the country, while the Conservatives exceeded expectations. Alex Salmond's Scottish National Party won enough seats to form a historic majority in the Scottish Parliament for the next five years, thereby creating a case for Scottish home rule.

Engineer Vincent Tabak, the Dutch neighbour of Joanna Yeates, who was found strangled in a snowy lane on Christmas Day, pleaded guilty to manslaughter at the Old Bailey via video link from Long Lartin prison.

10 The Duke and Duchess of Cambridge began their honeymoon in the Seychelles.

12 Her Majesty the Queen's reign became the second-longest in British history, overtaking that of King George III. The Queen's 59 years and 110 days as monarch ranks behind Queen Victoria, who died in 1901 after 63 years and seven months on the throne.

13 Jennifer Mills-Westley, a 60-year-old grandmother of five from Norwich who had retired to the Spanish island of Tenerife in 2006 after working as a road safety officer at Norfolk County Council, was decapitated by 28-year-old unemployed Bulgarian Deyan Valentinov Deyanov in a supermarket in Los Cristianos. Deyanov, who has a history of mental illness, ran out into the street carrying the severed head shouting: "This is my treasure."

The Azerbaijan duo Eldar Gasimov and Nigar Jamal (known as Ell and Nikki) won the Eurovision Song Contest with their entry, *Running Scared*. Jedward did best of the home countries placing eighth with 119 points for their energetic bouncy song, *Lipstick*. The UK entry, *I Can*, performed by Blue, placed 11th with 100 points.

17 Her Majesty the Queen began a state visit to Ireland by laying a wreath at the Garden of Remembrance in Dublin's Parnell Square.

20 Former Cabinet minister Elliot Morley was jailed for 16 months for committing fraud, swindling £31,000 for mortgage payments from the public purse.

22 A tornado hit Joplin, Missouri killing 116 people and devastating 30 per cent of its buildings.

24 Fresh from a Guinness-drinking embrace of his ancestral roots in Ireland, US president Barack Obama continued his European tour with a state visit to Britain.

25 After last year's eruption of Eyjafjallajökull, a second Icelandic volcano, Grímsvötn, began spewing volcanic ash although the clouds are not expected to create the same amount of havoc to air travel.

28 Take That kicked off their sell-out tour in front of 55,000 fans at Sunderland's Stadium Of Light, the first of 29 dates which will see them perform to 1.75 million fans in the UK and Ireland. It was the group's first concert with Robbie Williams restored to the line-up.

31 Lord Taylor of Warwick was sentenced to 12 months imprisonment for claiming £11,277 expenses for a home in Oxford he never lived in. The former tory peer, the son of Jamaican immigrants, rose to become a barrister and the first black Conservative member of the Upper House. Lord Taylor is the first member of the House of Lords to be jailed over the expenses scandal.

June

4 Foreign Secretary William Hague held talks in Libya with rebel leaders as the UK escalated its military operations with air strikes by combat helicopters.

5 Following a rocket attack on his palace, the Yemen's battle-wounded president Ali Abdullah Saleh, was taken to Saudi Arabia for medical treatment. His temporary removal set off wild street celebrations in the capital Sanaa. The beleaguered president, who has maintained his power for 33 years has proven difficult to shunt from power and his deputy Abed Rabbo Mansour Hadi defiantly announced Saleh would return when fit.

6 The Duke and Duchess of Cambridge will move into a home at Kensington Palace in the coming weeks, St James's Palace announced.

7 *The Gruffalo* author Julia Donaldson was unveiled as the new Children's Laureate.

Tea Obreht picked up this year's Orange Prize for Fiction, becoming the youngest ever winner in the process. The 25-year-old, who was born in the former Yugoslavia but now lives in the United States, published her debut novel earlier this year. *The Tiger's Wife* is the story of a young doctor on a journey through the war-torn countries of the Balkans inspired by stories her grandfather told her as a child.

8 The Archbishop of Canterbury, Dr Rowan Williams, warned that the Government is committing Britain to fundamental reforms in health and education "for which no one voted".

Southern Cross Healthcare revealed plans to cut 3,000 jobs.

9 Former *Countdown* presenter Carol Vorderman was named winner of the Rear of the Year award.

10 Veteran entertainer Bruce Forsyth was awarded a knighthood in the Queen's Birthday Honours List.

German experts say, locally-grown bean sprouts are the cause of the European E.coli outbreak that has killed 29 people.

11 Ralph Vaughan Williams's *The Lark Ascending* came out top when more than 25,000 people submitted their top Desert Island Disc tracks to the Radio 4's show website. The Beatles were inevitably the most popular chosen artist among the thousands of votes but they failed to feature in the top eight tracks as listeners split their choices among the group's many classic songs.

17 India announced it is to build the world's tallest statue at a cost of more than £200 million. The statue of Sardar Patel, India's first home secretary and deputy prime minister, who is regarded as the unsung hero of the independence movement, will be 597ft high. The "Statue of Unity" will dwarf the world's current tallest statue, China's 420ft Spring Temple Buddha, and tower above New York's 151ft Statue of Liberty.

23 Former nightclub doorman Levi Bellfield was convicted of murdering schoolgirl Milly Dowler. Thirteen-year-old Milly vanished in Walton-on-Thames, Surrey, as she walked home from school on 21 March 2002. Her remains were found in Hampshire six months later. An Old Bailey jury found Bellfield, 43, guilty of abducting and murdering her after she walked past his home. In 2008 he was convicted of murdering two young women in west London and attempting to murder a third.

July

2 Allegations were made that the *News of the World* hacked into the voicemails of murder victim Milly Dowler, as well as victims of the 7/7 attacks and relatives of deceased British soldiers.

6 David Cameron announced to parliament that a public government inquiry would convene to further investigate the News of the World phone-hacking affair.

7 James Murdoch, the chairman of News International, announced the closure of the *News of the World* on Sunday, 10 July 2011, after 168 years of publication

8 The space shuttle *Atlantis* lifted off from Cape Canaveral, Florida on the final flight of the 30-year shuttle program. The 135th flight consists of a 13-day mission to the International Space Station. The STS-135 astronauts were: Commander Chris Ferguson, Pilot Doug Hurley, and Mission Specialists Sandy Magnus and Rex Walheim.

10 The *News of the World* published its 8,674th and final edition with the headline reading 'Thank You & Goodbye'. Rebekah Brooks, the chief executive of News International, revealed the company had no choice but to close the newspaper because worse revelations about the paper's activities were yet to emerge.

15 Britain's biggest Lotto winners were unveiled as Colin and Chris Weir from the Scottish seaside town of Largs. The couple scooped £161,653,000 in the EuroMillions draw.

Charlie Gilmour, the stepson of *Pink Floyd* guitarist David Gilmour, was jailed for 16 months for a series of offences, including hanging from a Union flag on the Cenotaph and leaping on the bonnet of a Jaguar car that was carrying Prince Charles and the Duchess of Cornwall.

17 Sir Paul Stephenson, the Metropolitan Police Commissioner, resigned admitting his links to former *News of the World* deputy editor Neil Wallis could hamper Operation Weeting, Scotland Yard's investigation into phone-hacking. Stephenson has also been criticised over his acceptance of a £12,000 luxury spa stay for free.

18 Former *News of the World* Journalist and phone hacking whistleblower Sean Hoare, 47, was found dead in his home in Watford. Mr Hoare was the first journalist to publicly claim that Andy Coulson, former editor of the *News of the World*, encouraged staff to hack phones. Metropolitan Police Assistant Commissioner John Yates resigned after growing pressure amid the phone-hacking scandal.

19 Whilst giving evidence to the House of Commons' culture, media and sport committee in the Wilson Room of Portcullis House, Rupert Murdoch, 80, the chairman of News Corp, was attacked by Left-wing campaigner Jonathan May-Bowles. The 26-year-old part-time stand-up comedian, who works under the name Jonnie Marbles, pushed a paper plate of shaving foam in the face of Mr Murdoch before himself being attacked by Wendi Deng, 42, the third wife of the newspaper magnate. May-Bowles was subsequently given a six week jail sentence.

21 The space shuttle *Atlantis* returned safely to the Kennedy Space Center, Florida. The Nasa programme using the world's first reusable spacecraft was ended by President Obama to save money. The iconic craft spearheaded America's longest-running space programme, launching the Hubble space telescope and building the International Space Station. The retired shuttles - *Atlantis, Enterprise, Discovery* and *Endeavour* - will now go to museums.

22 After detonating a massive bomb at the Government Building in the centre of Oslo which killed eight people, Anders Behring Breivik, a 32-year-old Norwegian political extremist caught a ferry to the nearby island of Utoya and commenced a shooting spree, killing a further 69 people, mainly student campers.

27 Anglers were in mourning after Britain's biggest freshwater fish died at St Ives Lakes in Cambridgeshire. The massive carp, dubbed The Fat Lady, was more than 30-years-old and weighed 61lb 6oz. The biggest fish is now Parrotface, a 57lb 12oz carp in Berkshire.

30 Zara Phillips, the Queen's grand-daughter, and Mike Tindall, 32, the England rugby captain, married at the Canongate Kirk on Edinburgh's Royal Mile. Zara's ivory silk faille and duchess satin gown was made by Stewart Parvin, the Royal couturier who dresses not only the Queen – who wore a peachy pink coat and matching dress – but also Princess Anne from his atelier in Belgravia. The 30 year-old Royal, once known as the "royal rebel", sprang a surprise when it emerged that she would not take Mr Tindall's name following their marriage.

August

2 Matthew Green became the first man in Britain to receive a complete plastic heart and walk out of hospital. The 40-year-old father from north London would almost certainly not have survived without the artificial organ that surgeons at Papworth Hospital in Cambridge transplanted into his chest cavity after removing most of his heart.

3 The trial against ousted Egyptian President Hosni Mubarak began in Cairo but was immediately adjourned until 15 August. Mr Mubarak was seen laying on a stretcher before being wheeled into the black defendant's cage.

4 The first three reels of a six-reel Alfred Hitchcock film were discovered at the New Zealand Film Archive. The White Shadow, first released in 1924, was thought lost to posterity.

5 The Royal Navy announced that Lt Cdr Sarah West, 39, will be promoted to commander from next January, becoming the first woman to be placed in command of a frontline warship, the Type 23 frigate HMS *Portland.*

6 Large areas of the north London borough of Tottenham was left in flames as rioters looted shops and burned cars and buildings; the shooting of 29-year-old Mark Duggan (a known offender from London's notorious Broadwater Farm Estate) by police whilst on a covert mission two days previously possibly sparking the action.

7 The London riots spread from Tottenham as shops were looted and cars damaged across Enfield, Walthamstow, Waltham Forest, Islington and Brixton.

8 On the third day of rioting and looting large areas of Croydon were destroyed including the iconic Reeves Corner shopping area. Other areas attacked included Hackney, Lewisham, and Clapham. Outside London riots began in Birmingham. A 32-year-old Polish woman, Monika Konczyk, was forced to jump from her blazing first floor flat window in Croydon after rioters torched the surrounding area.

9 Sixteen thousand police patrolled London to ensure that mob rule did not create the chaos of the previous three nights. Copycat rioters rampaged through Manchester and to lesser extents in Liverpool and the West Midlands. More than a thousand arrests were made with sentences expected to be the maximum allowable under the law.

15 British honeymooner Ian Redmond, 30, was killed by a shark off Anse Lazio beach on Praslin, the second largest island in the Indian Ocean archipelago of the Seychelles.

16 A neon artwork sign by artist Tracey Emin reading "More Passion" was installed outside the Terracotta Room at Number 10 Downing Street.

20 Flight Lieutenant Jon Egging, 33, was killed when his Hawk T1 jet plummeted to the ground as it and eight other Red Arrows left Bournemouth Air Festival to stage an afternoon fly-past over Christchurch in Dorset.

21 Rebel fighters streamed into Tripoli as Muammar Gaddafi's forces collapsed and crowds took to the streets to celebrate, tearing down posters of the Libyan leader. Although the dictator still remained defiant in broadcasts to the nation, intelligence sources are optimistic his regime is drawing ever closer to an end.

22 Actress Kate Winslet was among 20 guests forced to flee billionaire Richard Branson's luxury retreat of Necker Island in the Caribbean, as lightning during hurricane Irene set it ablaze.

25 Hurricane Irene was causing havoc on America's north east coast, with parts of New York having to be evacuated.

26 The killer of WPC Yvonne Fletcher was named as lowly diplomat Abdulmagid Salah Ameri, a junior officer at the Libyan People's Bureau when Yvonne, 25, died from a single bullet shot in London's St James' Square in April 1984. WPC Fletcher's death led to an 11-day armed siege and the expulsion of 30 Libyans – including Ameri.

A bomb hoax in the Canterbury branch of Marks & Spencer caused the town centre to be closed.

27 Darren Whitehead, 40, and Tony Dwight, 39, broke the record for travelling the 1,100 miles between John O'Groats and Land's End - by lawn mower. The five day journey broke the previous record by a day.

28 Andrew Holmes, from Halifax, West Yorkshire, broke the world record at the annual world bog snorkelling championships in Llanwrtyd Wells, Powys, covering two lengths of a 180ft (55m) trench in 1min 30.66sec.

September

1 Reports from Somalia estimate that more than half a million of the population will die of starvation in the last four months of the year unless United Nations aid reaches the famine-stricken African country.

7 Warrant Officer Class 1 Esther Freeborn, 35, became the first female bandmaster of the Life Guards, the senior regiment of the Army. Her first event as bandmaster will be the Lord Mayor's Parade in November.

12 Bernard Hogan-Howe, 53, was appointed as Metropolitan Police Commissioner.
David Walliams completed his eight-day 140-mile charity swim down the Thames, from Lechlade in Gloucestershire to Westminster Bridge in London. The 40-year-old comedy actor raised over £1m for sport Relief.

16 Colin Birch, 44, died in an "execution role play" after paying two women to kick away his ladder leaving him to hang from a tree in woods near Dartford in Kent.

18 Television presenter Jonathan Dimbleby admitted snorting cocaine and smoking cannabis in his early 20s; a revelation he made in defence of follies of youth, and in particular the accusation by an ex-prostitute that she once saw George Osborne take coke - a claim the Chancellor denies.

19 Kate Winslet won the Emmy for best actress in a mini-series for her role in *Mildred Pierce*.

20 The latest Darren Baker portrait shows the Queen looking relaxed in a royal blue dress, pearl necklace and black court shoes. She also wears a brooch with a spray of five poppies.

21 Rogue trader Kweku Adoboli, 31, attended City of London Magistrates' Court, standing accused of gambling away a record £1.5 billion from Swiss banking giant UBS.

22 Scientists at the CERN research centre, near Geneva, Switzerland, claimed they have recorded sub-atomic particles called neutrinos travelling faster than the speed of light.

29 Somerset angler Jonathan Avery caught a 245lb (111kg) catfish while on holiday in Spain. The 8ft 3in (2.5m) fish is the largest caught by a Brit although the world record for a catfish is 646lb (293kg), caught in Thailand in 2005. On the same day, 62-year-old retired policeman Reinhard Wuhrmann battled for three hours to catch an Atlantic halibut of the same length as the catfish but tipping the scales at just over 540lb - smashing the previous world record by an impressive 58lb.

October

1 The minimum wage was increased from £5.93 to £6.08 per hour for workers over 21. For 18-20 year olds the minimum wage was raised from £4.92 to £4.98 and for 16-17 year olds the rate was raised from £3.64 to £3.68.

2 Europe's newest princess, the South African former Olympic swimmer Charlene Lynette Wittstock (now Princess Charlene of Monaco), who married Prince Albert II in July, gave her first media interview since getting married.
The surviving members of *The Beatles* attended the film premiere of Martin Scorsese's documentary *George Harrison: Living in the Material World.*

3 Amanda Knox flew home to Seattle after being cleared of murdering British student Maredith Kercher in November 2007. Miss Knox served almost four years of her 26-year sentence. Her former boyfriend Raffaele Sollecito was also cleared of the murder in Perugia, Italy, in which now the only person convicted is Rudy Guede, an immigrant from the Ivory Coast, who is serving 16 years.

4 A heart disease and cancer-fighting "superbroccoli" developed by British scientists went on sale in the UK. The vegetable looks the same as normal broccoli but contains boosted levels of a health-giving nutrient, glucoraphanin, which is thought to protect the body against heart disease and some types of cancer. The new broccoli, called Beneforte, contains two to three times more glucoraphanin than standard broccoli. It will be sold at Marks & Spencer stores from today and will make an appearance on the shelves of other supermarkets next year.

9 Sir Paul McCartney wed his American fiancee Nancy Shevell at Marylebone register office in central London, the same venue where he married his first wife Linda 42 years ago. The date is particularly poignant because it would have been John Lennon's 71st birthday. Sir Paul's daughter Stella McCartney designed the bridal dress. Miss Shevell, 51, is independently wealthy, being heir to a haulage firm run by her father which is valued at £250 million. Sir Paul's younger brother Mike was best man at the ceremony and his daughter Beatrice, seven, from his marriage to Heather Mills acted as the sole bridesmaid.

10 Dave and Angela Dawes won £101m, Britain's third biggest lottery jackpot. The win makes the couple from Wisbech, Cambs, a million pounds better off than David Bowie, the 703rd richest person in the country.

14 Dr Liam Fox resigned as Defence Secretary as it emerged that he had asked a City financier to bankroll his unofficial adviser Adam Werritty. Philip Hammond was immediately promoted to the defence position as Justine Greening, a junior Treasury minister, took over his job as Transport Secretary.

20 Libyan dictator Colonel Muammar Gaddafi was killed after being captured by Libyan fighters and shot in the head after they overran his last bastion of resistance in Misrata, two miles west of his hometown of Sirte. "It's time to start a new Libya, a united Libya," Prime Minister Mahmoud Jibril declared. "One people, one future."

21 St Paul's Cathedral was closed after anti-capitalist protesters camped on its piazza.

23 Turkish Prime Minister Recep Tayyip Erdogan announced that hundreds had died after an earthquake registering a magnitude of 7.2 shattered buildings near the Turkish city of Van. Casualties are reported to be particularly high in the town of Ercis, close to the Iranian border, where dozens of buildings fell.

27 The Perth Mint in Australia cast the world's largest coin to mark the Commonwealth Heads of Government Meeting. The coin weighs more than a ton and is worth £35.1million.

28 The £22.7million, 376ft-tall ArcelorMittal Orbit, an Olympic tower built next to the main 2012 stadium in London, was completed and due to open next spring. The iconic steel spiral observation tower was designed by Cecil Balmond of engineering Group Arup and Anish Kapoor the Turner-Prize-winning sculptor.
St Paul's Cathedral reopened with a service held by the Dean, Graeme Knowles.

29 At the 2011 Commonwealth Heads of Government Meeting in Perth, Australia, the leaders of the Commonwealth realms agreed to introduce legislation to end male primogeniture of descendants of Charles, Prince of Wales, and to allow heirs to the throne to marry Roman Catholics. Friederike Thyra Marion Wilhelmine Dorothea von der Osten, 52, a German homoeopathic doctor from Halle, has been identified as the person who would be on the British throne if new rules on the royal succession had been adopted in the time of Queen Victoria.

30 According to a United Nations' estimate the world's population has exceeded 7 billion. All around the world nations were naming their candidates as the seven billionth baby - the British version was Peter Bashir Yansaneh, who made his entrance at St Thomas's, London at 6.58am, the time and date the UN predicted the landmark number would be reached.

31 The Dean of St Paul's, the Rt Rev Graeme Knowles, resigned amid controversy over protesters camped outside the cathedral.

November

4 Ruth Davidson, 32, was elected as the new leader of the Conservatives in Scotland.

5 Seven people died in a crash on the M5 motorway near Taunton in Somerset.

7 Michael Jackson's Texan physician, Dr Conrad Murray, who administered a powerful surgical anaesthetic to the singer hours before his death in June 2009, was convicted of involuntary manslaughter. The verdict came at the end of a six-week trial in which Murray was slammed for his 'unconscionable' professional behaviour and neglect of his celebrity patient. He will be sentenced on November 29th.

18 Adrian Prout, 49, who was jailed for life in January 2010, finally admitted killing his wife after failing a lie-detector test in Garth Prison, near Preston, Lancashire. Prout was escorted to Redhill Farm, in Redmarley, Gloucestershire to show police where he buried his wife's body.

20 Thousands of Xbox Live gamers were reportedly fooled by fraudsters into handing over their account details, in what appears to be a widespread phishing campaign. In the UK, gamers had lost an average of £100 and in some cases had been robbed of more than £200.
At the London Evening Standard Theatre Awards Benedict Cumberbatch and Jonny Lee Miller were both awarded best actor prizes for their sharing of the role of *Dr Frankenstein* at The National Theatre.

21 Essam Sharaf resigned as prime minister of Egypt.

25 Thomas Cook was saved from collapse after 17 banks poured in £200m. The beleaguered travel agent is however likely to make drastic staff cuts as part of its rationalisation programme.
29 The Britisn embassy in Tehran was stormed by a 200-strong mob who set the main building ablaze, looted the belongings of diplomats and tore down the Union flag.
Dr Conrad Murray was sentenced to the maximum penalty of four years of incarceration at the Los Angeles County Jail. (see entry for 7 November 2011).
30 Foreign Secretary William Hague announced the closure of the Iranian embassy in London in retaliation for the attack on its embassy in Tehran.

December
1 Speaking on World Aids Day, Barack Obama pledged the "beginning of the end of AIDS". The US President, speaking in Washington, promised to boost spending on treatment of the virus which has killed 30 million people.
4 Homosexual couples were given dispensation to seal civil partnerships in church from today.
5 Astronomers confirmed an extrasolar planet orbitting within the habitable zone of a Sun-like star. The possible super-Earth, is 600 light years away from Earth, in orbit around Kepler-22, a G-type star, and has been named Kepler 22-b.
6 Glasgow secured its third Turner Prize in a row as sculptor Martin Boyce won the £25,000 award. The city-based artist follows Glasgow-born Susan Philipsz last year and Richard Wright in 2009. Martin, 44, won the honour at the Baltic Centre for Contemporary Art in Gateshead for *Do Words Have Voice*, a quietly atmospheric, lyrically autumnal sculptural installation recalling a melancholy urban park with its square metallic trees and scattered paper leaves, surrounding the central piece based on a library desk.
7 The government of the Maldives temporarily banned the depositing of rubbish from its hotels onto an island used almost entirely as a garbage dump. Thilafishi, a man-made isle four miles from the capital Male became known as Rubbish Island after it become a dumping ground for leading tourist hotels in the 'tropical paradise.'
Kamal Ganzouri was sworn in officially for his second term as Egyptian prime minister after Essam Sharaf resigned last month.
8 Steph Warren, a chief examiner at Edexcel, one of Britain's biggest exam boards, was recorded boasting about the easiness of the company's GCSE geography tests. Another examiner, who works for Welsh exam board WJEC, was suspended after being secretly filmed revealing which history questions will be posed next year.
27 Harry was announced as Britain's favourite name for a boy in 2011 and Olivia the favourite girl's name.
28 North Korea's new leader, Kim Jong-un (the son of Kim Jong-il) went on sombre public display
30 Tuilaepa Sailele, the prime minister of Samoa, announced that the paradise island nation had skipped this day to move itself 24 hours into the future and put itself on the same weekday as Australia and New Zealand to help boost its economy by making trade with its neighbours easier. The date of December 30th 2011 was therefore wiped off calendars and Samoa's 180,000 citizens finished work on Thursday night and woke up on Saturday morning the 31st December. They also went from being the last people on Earth to ring in the New Year to being the first.

Sporting Record 2011

January
1 Phil Taylor, the 15-time world dart's champion, was beaten in the quarter finals of the 2011 tournament by Welshman Mark Webster. Although Taylor, who was runner-up in the BBC Sports Personality of the Year two weeks ago, averaged 102 per three darts he suffered a 5-2 defeat, his heaviest since first winning the championship.
3 Adrian Lewis landed the first-ever nine-dart finish en route to lifting the PDC World Darts Championship at Alexandra Palace. The 25-year-old Phil Taylor prodigy, now managed by 1983 world champion Keith Deller, beat Scotland's Gary Anderson 7-5 and hit 20 maximum 180s on the way to take his tally to 60, a tournament record.
6 Colombian golfer Camilo Villegas was disqualified from the Tournament of Champions in Kapalua, Hawai, for a rules violation that a television viewer called in after the opening round. Villegas was chipping up the slope to the 15th green when the ball twice rolled back toward him. The second time, Villegas walked over and casually swatted away some loose pieces of grass in front of the divot as the ball was still moving down the slope. This should have incurred a one-shot penalty but was not made clear at the time and the resultant signing of a wrong score brought automatic disqualification.
7 England beat Australia by an innings and 83 runs in Sydney to win the Ashes series 3-1.
8 *BBC Sports Personality of the Year* Tony McCoy won the Welsh National at Chepstow aboard Synchronised, trained by Jonjo O'Neill.
9 Martin Adams beat Dean Winstanley 7-5 to retain the BDO World Darts Championship at Lakeside Country Club, Frimley Green, Surrey.
10 Non-league Crawley Town FC reached the fourth round of the FA Cup for the first time in their history, beating Championship side Derby County 2-1 at Broadfield Stadium.
16 In an all Chinese snooker final, Ding Junhui defeated Marco Fu 10-4 to win the Masters at Wembley Arena.
17 Bowlers Alex Marshall and Paul Foster beat fellow Scots Andrew Barker and Michael Stepney, 3-8, 7-3, 2-0 in the final of the World Pairs Championship in Norfolk.
18 Spanish golfer José María Olazábal was appointed Ryder Cup captain and has the task of leading out the European team at Medinah in 2012 in defence of the trophy won by Colin Montgomerie at Celtic Manor.
19 For the second time in a fortnight golf was mired in a rules catastrophe, inviting ridicule and dismay. Irishman Padraig Harrington, appointed a Royal and Ancient ambassador just last week, was disqualified from the HSBC Championship in Abu Dhabi for inadvertently brushing his ball whilst retrieving his ball marker on the seventh green. Although the ball did not appear to move to the naked eye an eagle-eyed viewer spotted the slightest of rolls forward. There was no suggestion that Padraig was trying to gain any advantage from this position but ultimately he signed for the wrong score as a two-shot penalty was incurred retrospectively.
24 Co-hosts Andy Gray and Richard Keys were suspended from presenting their Sky football programme following sexist comments made about lineswoman Sian Massey which although made off-air were broadcast on Sky News. (note Gray was sacked the following day and Keys resigned the day after).
29 A 39th-minute goal by Matt Tubbs gave Crawley Town a 1-0 victory over Torquay United to become the first non-league club to reach the last 16 of the FA Cup since 1994.
Kim Clijsters beat Li Na in a pulsating final to win her first Australian Open and fourth Grand Slam title. Li had made history by becoming China's first Grand Slam singles finalist and made a strong start, but Clijsters powered back to win 3-6 6-3 6-3. It is the first time that three-time US Open champion Clijsters has won a major title outside of New York.
30 Nigel Bond won snooker's inaugural World Shoot-Out in Blackpool. The quickfire knockout event staged over three days consisted of players having 10 minutes to complete a frame, the first five minutes at a maximum of 20 seconds per shot and the second five minutes at 15 seconds per shot. Favourite Ronnie O'Sullivan was beaten in the semi-final by Robert Milkins. An investigation was undertaken as to unusual betting activity on the game between Jimmy Michie and his victor Marcus Campbell on the opening day.
Serbian tennis ace, Novak Djokovic (3) beat Britain's Andy Murray (5) 6-4, 6-2, 6-3 in the final of tha Australian Open Men's Singles Championship at the Rod Laver Arena, Melbourne. Murray, who also reached the final in 2010, has yet to win a set in any Grand Slam final, despite having now appeared in three.
Australia gained revenge for their Ashes defeat by trouncing England 4-1 in the seven-match One-Day International series, with two matches to play.
31 On the last day of football's January transfer window the British transfer record was broken when Fernando Torres joined Chelsea for £45 million up front plus £5 million potential add-ons to arrive at Liverpool's asking price of £50 million. The deal which was signed at 10.50pm (ten minutes before the deadline) also involved the transfer of Andy Carroll from Newcastle to Liverpool for an estimated £36 million, which would also have been a British transfer record.

February

4 In the opening rugby union Six Nations Championship match England defeated Wales 26-19 at the Millennium Stadium.
5 France beat Scotland 34-21 in Paris and Ireland defeated Italy 13-11 in Rome in the Six Nations.
6 The Green Bay Packers held off a spirited Pittsburgh Steelers fightback to win Super Bowl XLV, 31-25 in Dallas, Texas, for their first championship since 1997.
9 England beat Denmark 2-1 in an International friendly football match
Andy Murray lost 6-4, 6-1 to Cypriot Marcos Baghdatis in the first round of the World Tennis Tournament in Rotterdam. It was the Scotsman's first match since his straights set defeat in the final of the Australian Open last month.
10 Former England cricket all-rounder Trevor Bailey died in a fire in his retirement flat in Westcliff-on-Sea.
11 In the rugby union Six Nations Championship England defeated Italy 59-13 at Twickenham and Wales beat Scotland 24-6 at Murrayfield.
12 Racing was abandoned at Newbury after two horses collapsed and died in the paddock before the first race. Fenix Two, trained by Jonjo O'Neill, and Marching Song, trained by Andy Turnell, keeled over after stepping off the rubber parade mat and onto the grass. Although the first race took place it was decided that the whole area around the paddock was unsafe and the remainder of the meeting was cancelled. The accident is thought to have been caused by a severed underground electrical cable and a combination of metal horse-shoes and inability to earth electricity sufficiently because of the wide gait of horses.
In the rugby union Six Nations Championship France defeated Ireland 25-22 at the Aviva Stadium, Dublin.
Wayne Rooney scored the winning goal during Manchester United's 2-1 victory over local rivals Manchester City in a top-of-the-table Premiership clash at Old Trafford. The overhead volley is already being talked about as the goal-of-the-season.
15 Following AC Milan's 1-0 defeat by Tottenham at the San Siro, the Milan captain Gennaro Gattuso headbutted Spurs' assistant coach Joe Jordan.
19 Non-league Crawley Town were beaten 1-0 by Manchester United at Old Trafford in the fifth round of the FA Cup.
20 World No 1 Snooker player John Higgins successfully defended his Welsh Open title by beating Stephen Maguire 9-6 in the final - dedicating victory to his late father.
22 England narrowly scraped home in their opening World Cup cricket match against Holland. After the Dutch scored 292 for 6 in their 50 overs, England rattled off the runs with an over to spare.
26 In the rugby union Six Nations Championship England defeated France 17-9 at Twickenham while Wales beat Italy 24-16 at the Stadio Flaminio, Rome.
27 English golfer Luke Donald beat newly-minted world No 1 Martin Kaymer 3&2 to claim golf's Accenture World Matchplay Championship in Marana, Arizona.
In the rugby union Six Nations Championship Ireland defeated Scotland 21-18 at Murrayfield.
Surrey and England cricket Steven Davies 'came out' as homosexual, the first professional cricketer ever to do so.
England drew with India, both sides scoring 338 runs, in a World Cup group match in Bangalore, Andrew Strauss scoring a magnificent 158.
Birmingham beat Arsenal 2-1 in the Carling Cup final at Wembley, the Nigerian substitute Obafemi Martins celebrating his winning-goal with his traditional acrobatic display.

March

2 Ireland beat England by three wickets in a World Cup group match in Bangalore. A mixture of some sloppy fielding by England and great batting by Kerry O'Brien, who scored a century in 50 balls to create a new record in World Cup cricket, ensured victory for the Irish.
5 Mo Farah retained his 3,000 metres title at the European Indoor Athletics Championship in Paris, to give Great Britain their only men's gold medal.
6 Helen Clitheroe performed a similar feat to Mo Farah by winning the 3,000 metres title at the European Indoor Athletics Championship in Paris, her first international gold medal, achieved at the age of 37.
Croatia's Ivo Karlovic fired tennis' fastest serve ever during the Davis Cup tie against Germany. The 6ft 10in star clocked 156mph in Berlin, beating Andy Roddick's old record by 1mph.
12 Wales beat Ireland 19-13 in the Six Nations Championship match in Cardiff while Italy created a major shock by beating France 22-21 in Rome.
13 England kept their Six Nations Championship Grand Slam hopes alive with a hard-fought 22-16 victory over Scotland at Twickenham.
15 On the first day of the Cheltenham Festival, Hurricane Fly, ridden by Ruby Walsh and trained by Willie Mullins, won the Champion Hurdle.
16 Sizing Europe, ridden by Andrew Lynch and trained by Henry De Bromhead, won the Queen Mother Champion Chase at Cheltenham on a day that saw the Irish win six of the seven races.
17 Big Buck's, ridden by Ruby Walsh and trained by Paul Nicholls won the World Hurdle at Cheltenham for the third year running.
There were disgraceful scenes at the SECC in Glasgow as local hero Gary Anderson faced world darts champion Adrian Lewis in a Premier League match. Lewis was pelted with beer and coins throughout a match in which Anderson was visibly stunned by the treatment of Lewis. The match had been talked-up for months before by Anderson but although he was expecting partisan support he clearly felt this was unacceptable and almost gave the match to Lewis on a plate 8-3, after leading 2-0.
18 Long Run, ridden by amateur jockey Sam Waley-Cohen and trained by Nicky Henderson, won the Cheltenham Gold Cup from former winners, Denman and Kauto Star. Paul Nicholls saddled the second and third and also the fourth with What A Friend, part-owned by Sir Alex Ferguson.
19 Ireland destroyed England's rugby union Grand Slam hopes 24-8 in Dublin, but the visitors won the Six Nations after France beat Wales 28-9 in Paris in the tournament's final match. In the other match Scotland beat Italy 21-8 at Murrayfield.
20 Britain's top middle distance track star Mo Farah made his debut over the half marathon distance a winning one with victory in New York, in a time of 1hr 0min 23sec.
24 Britain's women's pursuit team of Wendy Houvenaghel, Laura Trott and Dani King, struck gold on the opening day of the World Track Championships in Apeldoorn, Holland.
25 Andy Murray's horrific run of form continued when he was again beaten in his opening match, this time 6-1, 7-5 by Alex Bogomolov Jr, at the Sony Ericsson Open in Miami. Since losing in the final of the Australian Open in January, the Scottish ace has failed to win a set in matches against Marco Baghdatis, Donald Young, the American world No 128, at the Indian Wells tournament a fortnight ago, and now another American, ranked No 118 in the world.
Sir Chris Hoy was beaten in the semi-final of the sprint by team-mate Jason Kenny at the world championships in Holland. Kenny went on to gain the silver medal, being beaten emphatically in the final by France's Gregory Bauge, whilst Hoy took the bronze.
26 In Euro 2012 qualifiers England beat Wales 2-0 at the Millennium Stadium, Cardiff, and Ireland beat FYR Macedonia 2-1 in Dublin.
England were ignominiously dumped out of cricket's World Cup at the quarter-finals stage following a 10 wicket loss to Sri Lanka in Colombo. After defeats by Ireland and Bangladesh in the group stages Sri Lanka were favourites to go through to the semis with home advantage but the manner of defeat was humiliating. England managed to score only 229 runs in their 50 overs despite only losing six wickets, Jonathan Trott, seemingly content to push singles throughout his top-scoring contribution of 86. In contrast the Sri Lankan openers Dilshan and Tharanga both scored centuries at a run a ball to thrash England inside 40 overs.
Oxford won the Xchanging Boat Race by four lengths in a time of 17min 32sec.
27 German FI world champion, Sebastian Vettel, won the Australian Grand Prix in Melbourne from his great rival Lewis Hamilton.
30 Catterick Bridge hosted the first flat race meeting of the season. Traditionally, the opening meeting of the season is at Doncaster on the Thursday before the Lincoln.

April

2 Sweet Lightning, ridden by Johnny Murtagh and trained by Michael Dods, won the first big handicap of the new flat season, the William Hill Lincoln, at Doncaster.
India won their second cricket World Cup final beating Sri Lanka by six wickets in Mumbai.
9 Ballabriggs, ridden by Jason Maguire and trained by Donald McCain, won the Grand National, 38 years after Donald's father Ginger trained Red Rum to his first Aintree victory.

10 Charl Schwartzel of South Africa won the US Masters at Augusta. Overnight leader Rory McIlroy, who began the round with a four shot lead, maintained his lead until a disastrous triple bogey on the 10th hole began a series of errors which ultimately led to a final round 80, ten strokes behind the winner.
German FI world champion, Sebastian Vettel, won the Malaysian Grand Prix in Kuala Lumpur.
13 Andy Murray not only won his first set of tennis since the Australian Open in January but also his first match; defeating Radek Stepanek 6-1, 6-4 in Monte Carlo.
Andy Murray beat Giles Simon of France 6-3, 6-3 in the third round of the Monte Carlo Masters.
15 Andy Murray beat Portugal's Frederico Gil in the quarter finals of the Monte Carlo Masters.
16 Amir Khan retained his WBA light-welterweight title after Paul McCloskey was controversially stopped in the sixth round after suffering a cut left eye causing the fight to go to the judges' scorecard.
Andy Murray was beaten 4-6, 6-2, 1-6 by Rafael Nadal in the semi finals of the Monte Carlo Masters.
Defending champion Neil Robertson was beaten in the first round of the snooker world championship by Judd Trump.
17 Lewis Hamilton won the Chinese Grand Prix in Shanghai from F1 Championship leader Sebastian Vettel, with Mark Webber pipping Jenson Button for third place after starting the race from 18th place on the grid.
Emmanuel Mutai captured the 2011 Virgin London Marathon with a new course record of 2:04:40. His Kenyan team-mate Mary Keitany clocked 2:19:19 to win the women's race.
18 Tottenham's Gareth Bale was named the Professional Footballers' Association Player of the Year. The 21-year-old became the fourth Welshman to be honoured, after Ian Rush, Mark Hughes and Ryan Giggs. Bale was also nominated for the PFA Young Player of the Year but that award went to 19-year-old Jack Wilshere of Arsenal.
21 Towcester National Hunt racecourse announced they will outlaw the use of the whip in all their meetings from October 5th.
22 West Ham midfielder Scott Parker, 30, was voted Player of the Year for 2011 by the Football Writers' Association.
24 Lee Westwood took over from Martin Kaymer as world No 1 golfer after winning the Indonesian Open. Fellow Englishman Luke Donald would have topped the rankings if he had won the Heritage tournament in Hilton Head, South Carolina, but he was beaten in a play-off and climbs to third in the table.
25 Mark Todd of New Zealand won his fourth Badminton three-day-event, at the age of 55, riding NZB Land Vision.
Organisedconfusion, ridden by Nina Carberry and trained by Arthur Moore, won the Irish Grand National at Fairyhouse.
27 Barney Gibson became England's youngest first-class cricketer, at the age of 15 years and 27 days, when making his senior debut as wicket-keeper batsman for Yorkshire v Durham.
30 Frankel, ridden by Tom Queally and trained by Henry Cecil, won the Qipco 2,000 Guineas at Newmarket in devastating fashion leading all the way and having the whole field in trouble by halfway, eventually winning by six lengths.

May
1 Blue Bunting, ridden by Frankie Dettori and trained by Mohammad Al Zarooni, won the Qipco 1,000 Guineas at Newmarket.
2 John Higgins beat Judd Trump 18-15 to claim his fourth World Snooker Championship at The Crucible, Sheffield.
5 Sara Stevenson, whose parents are both battling serious illness, won an emotional gold medal at the Taekwondo World Championships in Korea. The Doncaster fighter overcame home favourite Hwang Kyung-seon, the Olympic and world champion, in her semi-final before beating China's Yunfei Guo.
7 Manny Pacquiao, the best pound-for-pound fighter in the world, dominated from the first bell to the last to score a unanimous points decision over Shane Mosley and retain his WBO welterweight title.
8 German FI world champion, Sebastian Vettel, won the Turkish Grand Prix in Istanbul from his Red Bull team-mate Mark Webber.
Novak Djokovic beat Rafael Nadal 7-5, 6-4 in the final of the Madrid Masters to inflict a rare clay court defeat on the young Spaniard. Djockovic is yet to be beaten in 2011.
9 Belgian cyclist Wouter Weylandt was killed in a high-speed crash during Stage 3 of the Giro d'Italia.
10 Manchester City's 1-0 victory over Tottenham Hotspur ensured them a Champions League berth for next season.
Aussie Rules footballer Nathan Van Someren, who sports a towering gelled mowhawk, was sent off by referee Don Wheadon in the third quarter of the Simpson Tigers match against Otway Districts, because of his 'dangerous' hair-do, despite sporting the same spikey style for three years.
11 Celtic manager Neil Lennon was attacked by a fan on the touchline during Celtic's 3-0 win against Hearts at Tynecastle.
13 On a great day for Manchester football, fans celebrated Manchester City's 1-0 win over Stoke in the FA Cup final while earlier Manchester United sealed a record 19th league title with a 1-1 draw at Blackburn.
Andy Murray served for the match at 5-4 in the third set against Novak Djokovic but ultimately lost 6-1, 3-6, 7-6 in the semi-final of the Rome Masters.
14 Novak Djokovic beat Rafael Nadal 6-4, 6-4 in the final of the Rome Masters to maintain his unbeaten record in 2011. The Serbian ace is currently unbeaten in 37 matches, five matches short of John McEnroe's 42-0 record in 1984.
Following West Ham's 3-2 defeat by Wigan, condemning them to Championship football next season, their manager Avram Grant was sacked on the spot.
15 Samuel Wanjiru, Kenya's first Olympic marathon winner, striking gold at Beijing in 2008, died after falling from a balcony at his home. The man who was described by David Bedford as the greatest marathon runner of all time, had a personal best time of two hours, five minutes and 10 seconds, set when winning the 2009 London Marathon.
18 The Rugby Union disciplinary panel banned Leicester centre Manu Tuilagi for five weeks for his assault on Northampton wing, Chris Ashton, during last week's Premiership play-off semi-final.
19 Gary Anderson got his revenge on Adrian Lewis for recent defeats in the World Championship and the Premier League on St Patrick's Day. In a night of shocks Lewis beat Phil Taylor 8-3 in the first semi-final while Anderson beat Raymond van Barneveld 8-6 in the second. Gary won the Premier League title 10-4 at Wembley to earn his first televised title since joining the PDC two years ago.
21 Celtic beat Motherwell 3-0 in the Scottish Cup final.
Bernard Hopkins became the oldest world champion in boxing history when he defeated Canadian Jean Pascal on points for the WBC light-heavyweight crown in Montreal. As if to show his 18-year younger opponent exactly how fit he still was, Hopkins, 46, performed 10 press-ups during the fight.
Nathan Cleverly stopped late stand-in Aleksy Kuziemski in the fourth round after being confirmed as WBO champion when Juergen Braehmer pulled out of their fight at the 02 Arena. On the undercard, George Groves defeated James DeGale in a controversial points verdict to add DeGale's British super-middleweight title to his own Commonwealth championship.
22 On an exciting final day of football's Premiership, West Ham, Blackpool and Birmingham City were relegated.
Leinster beat Northampton 33-22 in the Heineken Cup final at the Millennium Stadium, Cardiff.
Ian Poulter beat his English countryman Luke Donald 2&1 in the final of the Volvo World Matchplay title in Casares, Spain.
AFC Wimbledon defeated Luton 4-3 on penalties after a goalless Blue Square Premier Play-off final.
German FI world champion, Sebastian Vettel, won the Spanish Grand Prix in Barcelona to extend his lead in the driver's championship.
23 Ryan Giggs was named by Liberal Democrat MP John Hemming as the married footballer at the centre of a gagging order. The Manchester United player is alleged to have conducted an affair with former Big Brother contestant Imogen Thomas.
26 On the fifth day of the French Open Andy Murray progressed to the third round at the expense of Italian Simone Bolelli, but the other two British tennis players, Heather Watson and Elena Baltacha, were beaten in the second round.
28 Barcelona beat Manchester United 3-1 in the Champions League final at Wembley.
Saracens were crowned English rugby's league champions for the first time when they overcame perennial finalists Leicester 22-18 in a gripping Premiership final at Twickenham.
29 Luke Donald beat Lee Westwood in a sudden-death play-off to win the BMW PGA Championship at Wentworth and thereby elevate himself above his English countryman to the coveted world No 1 ranking.
Spain's Alberto Contador claimed his second Giro d'Italia crown, holding off his closest rival by more than six minutes as the 21-stage cycle race concluded in Milan.

German Fl world champion, Sebastian Vettel, won the Monaco Grand Prix in Monte Carlo to extend his lead in the driver's championship to 58 points over nearest rival Lewis Hamilton.
Jonathan Trott scored 203 in England's first innings against Sri Lanka in Cardiff, the highest score by an England player against the tourists.
31 England won the first npower Test Match in Cardiff by an innings and 14 runs after Sri Lanka were bowled out in their second innings for 82 in just 24.4 overs.

June

3 Andy Murray was beaten in straight sets by Rafael Nadal in the French Open semi-finals. In the other semi-final Novak Djokovic was beaten for the first time in 2011, going down in four sets to Roger Federer.
Dancing Rain, ridden by Johnny Murtagh and trained by William Haggas, won the Investec Oaks at Epsom. In the same race Frankie Dettori was stood down for 10 days after failing to ride out a finish on favourite Blue Bunting who was denied third place on the line.
Mo Farah shattered the British and European 10,000m records with a winning time of 26min 46.57sec at the Prefontaine Classic meeting in Eugene, Oregon.
4 Pour Moi, ridden by Mickael Barzalona and trained by André Fabre, won the Investec Derby at Epsom. The Queen's horse, Carlton House, finished a gallant third after having a troubled run around Tattenham Corner.
Li Na became the first Chinese player to win a Grand Slam tennis title with a 6-4, 7-6 victory over defending champion Francesca Schiavone in the French Open final.
Carl Froch retained his WBC super-middleweight title with a comfortable points victory over former light-heavyweight world champion Glen Johnson. Froch will next face American Andre Ward in a world title unification bout later in the year which also doubles as the final of the World Super Sixes - a six-man tournament fought over the past two years.
England drew with Switzerland 2-2 in a European Championship qualifier after clawing there way back from a self-inflicted 2-0 deficit due to two freakish defensive errors.
5 Rafael Nadal beat Roger Federer in four sets to win his sixth French Open title to equal the feat of Bjorn Borg.
7 The second Test against Sri Lanka at Lord's ended in a draw.
10 Sixty-eight-year-old flat race trainer Henry Cecil was awarded a knighthood in the Queen's Birthday Honours List.
Andy Murray easily beat Andy Roddick in the semi-final of the ATP grass-court tournament at Queen's Club, London. In the other semi-final match Britain's James Ward lost to Jo-Wilfried Tsonga of France in two hard-fought sets.
11 Taylors Sky put an end to the red trap hoodoo to win a record sixth Greyhound Derby for master trainer Charlie Lister. The 7/4 favourite won, beating his own track record, in a time of of 28.17sec for the 480mts race. He also became the first Trap 1 winner in the history of the race since it moved to Wimbledon in 1981, after the closure of White City.
12 Bradley Wiggins became only the third British cyclist to win the Dauphine Libere. Only Brian Robinson (1961) and Robert Millar (1990) had previously won the Tour de France tune-up.
Jenson Button won the Canadian Formula One GP in Montreal, overtaking leader Sebastian Vettel on the final lap of an enthralling rain-effected race.
13 In a rain-delayed final Andy Murray beat Jo-Wilfried Tsonga of France 3-6, 7-6, 6-4 at Queen's Club, London.
16 Northern Ireland's Rory McIlroy led the US Open by three strokes with an opening round of 65 at the Congressional Country Club, Bethesda, Maryland.
Fame and Glory, ridden by Jamie Spencer and trained by Aidan O'Brien, won the Ascot Gold Cup.
17 Rory McIlroy continued his dominance of the US Open by posting a 66 on day two to move seven strokes clear of the field. McIlroy moved to -13 after the 17th hole, a US Open record, but unfortunately finished with a double bogey at the last to finish on 131, the lowest two-round score in US Open history.
19 Rory McIlroy duly won the US Open by eight shots with a record-breaking score of 16 under par. At 22 years of age, McIlroy became the youngest winner since Bobby Jones in 1923.
20 England drew the third Test against Sri Lanka, at the Rose Bowl, to take the three-match series 1-0.
25 Stuart Broad had an unhappy first match as England's new T20 captain, his side losing by nine wickets to Sri Lanka at Bristol.
26 German Fl world champion, Sebastian Vettel, won the European Grand Prix in Valencia to extend his lead in the driver's championship to 77 points.
Treasure Beach, ridden by Colm O'Donoghue and trained by Aidan O'Brien, won the Dubai Duty Free Irish Derby at The Curragh.
Tina Fletcher, 46, riding Promised Land, won the Carpetright Derby at Hickstead, jumping the only clear round - only the 53rd in the 51-year history of the competition.
A stunning 44-ball century from Kevin O'Brien helped Gloucestershire post the highest-ever total in domestic T20 cricket. Hamish Marshall also scored a ton in an opening stand of 192, another record for any wicket in domestic T20. Middlesex fell short of the required 255 to win, scoring 149 runs in their 20 overs.
29 Six-times Wimbledon champion Roger Federer was beaten 3-6, 6-7, 6-4, 6-4, 6-4 by Jo-Wilfried Tsonga of France in the quarter-finals, the first time he has been beaten in 178 Grand Slam matches when leading two sets to nil.

July

1 In the Wimbledon men's singles semi-finals, Rafael Nadal beat Andy Murray 5-7, 6-2, 6-2, 6-4, and Novak Djokovic beat Jo-Wilfried Tsonga 7-6, 6-2, 6-7, 6-3 to become the world number one for the first time.
2 Ukrainian boxer Wladimir Klitschko the WBO, IBF and IBO heavyweight champion, defeated WBA champion David Haye on points at the Imtech Arena, Hamburg.
In the ladies' singles final at Wimbledon, Petra Kvitova of the Czech Republic, defeated Maria Sharapova 6-3, 6-4. In the boy's singles final, Liam Broady of Great Britain was beaten 6-2, 4-6, 2-6 by Australian Luke Saville. The men's doubles final was won by American brothers Bob and Mike Bryan, beating Robert Lindstedt of Sweden and Horia Tecau of Romania 6-3, 6-4, 7-6
Philippe Gilbert of Belgium won the opening stage of the Tour de France.
Chorley athlete Helen Bleasdale, 19, leapt 4.70m in Mannheim, Germany to break the British pole-vault record and set a world record for her age group.
3 Novak Djokovic beat Rafael Nadal 6-4, 6-1, 1-6, 6-3 in the men's singles final at Wimbledon. Kveta Peschke of the Czech Republic and Katarina Srebotnik of Slovenia won the ladies' doubles final, defeating Sabine Lisicki of Germany and Sam Stosur of Australia 6-3, 6-1.
George Morgan of Great Britain and Mate Pavic of Croatia won the boy's doubles.
6 Isle of Man cyclist Mark Cavendish won his first stage of the 2011 Tour de France and his 16th in total.
8 On the day that Bradley Wiggins crashed out of Le Tour with a fractured collarbone, Stage 7 was won by sprinter Mark Cavendish.
Chris Tomlinson broke the British long jump record with a leap of 8.35m in Paris.
Rugby player-turned-discus thrower Lawrence Okoye threw 67.63m at the McCain UKA Challenge Jumpsfest and Throwsfest at Barnet Copthall stadium, Hendon, to break the British record.
Andy Murray triple-bageled Laurent Bram of Luxembourg 6-0, 6-0, 6-0 in Group Two of the Davis Cup's Euro-African Zone tie in Glasgow.
9 Luke Donald won the Scottish Open at Castle Stuart, Inverness.
Fernando Alonso won the British Formula One GP at Silverstone although Sebastian Vettel's second place meant he drew further clear in the driver's championship.
Hayley Turner's victory aboard Dream Ahead, trained by Michael Bell, in the Darley July Cup at Newmarket, gave her the distinction of being the first woman jockey to be an outright winner of a Group One race in Britain. Alex Greaves dead-heated for the Nunthorpe at York on Ya Malak in 1997.
England beat Sri Lanka by 16 runs at Old Trafford to win the NatWest Series 3-2 and in the process Graeme Swann became the first England bowler to be ranked the best in the world in one-day cricket.
10 Great Britain defeated Luxembourg 4-1 in the Davis Cup tie at the Braehead Shopping Centre, Glasgow.

13 Mark Cavendish won his third stage of Le Tour 2011; his 18th in total. The Isle of Man cyclist beat German rider Andre Greipel on Stage 11 and with it went to the top of the points table.
14 Tom Lewis, an amateur golfer from Welwyn Garden City, shared the first round lead in The Open championship with a five-under-par 65, the lowest-ever Open score by an amateur.
17 Darren Clarke became Northern Ireland's third major championship winner in the last 13 months with a four-round score of 275 (five under par) to win The Open, at Royal St George's, Sandwich, by three strokes. Clarke was the first player from Northern Ireland to lift the Claret Jug since Fred Daly won at Hoylake in 1947.
Mark Cavendish won his fourth stage of Le Tour 2011; his 19th in total.
19 Keri-Anne Payne won the open water 10k title at the World Aquatics Championship in Shanghai and thus sealed her qualification for the London Olympics.
22 European 5,000m champion Mo Farah set a new British record of 12 minutes, 53.11 seconds when winning the 5k at the Diamond League meeting in Monaco. Tiffany Ofili-Porter also raced to a British record of 12.60 seconds in the 100m hurdles as she finished third.
23 Kevin Pietersen scored 202 not out during England's first innings of 474-8 against India in the first Test at Lord's.
Mohamed bin Hamman, the former Fifa executive committee member, was banned for life from football after being found guilty of attempting to bribe Caribbean Football Union officials as he sought votes in his bid to challenge Sepp Blatter for the Fifa presidency.
Tragedy marred the victory of Nathaniel in King George VI and Queen Elizabeth Stakes at Ascot when Frankie Dettori's mount broke a cannon bone during the race and had to be put down.
Tyson Fury won a unanimous points decision over Dereck Chisora to take the British and Commonwealth heavyweight titles at Wembley Arena.
24 Australian cyclist Cadel Evans won the Tour de France for the first time. Isle of Man sprinter Mark Cavendish won the points race for accruing the highest-placed finishes, winning his fifth stage of the tour; the third year in a row he has taken the final stage on the Champs-Élysées, Paris.
Lewis Hamilton won the German Formula One Grand Prix at Hockenheim.
Amir Khan added the IBF light-welterweight title to his own WBA title when stopping American Zab Judah in the fifth round in Las Vegas.
Stuart Bingham won the first snooker ranking event of his career when winning the final four frames to beat World No 1 Mark Williams 9-8 in the Australian Goldfields Open at the Bendigo Stadium in Victoria, Australia.
England beat India by 196 runs in the first Test match at Lord's
27 Frankel, ridden by Tom Queally and trained by Sir Henry Cecil, won the Sussex Stakes at Goodwood in scintillating fashion to become officially the best horse in the world. Frankel beat Canford Cliffs, himself a champion miler, by an easy five lengths to earn the quote from Cecil that he is not only the best horse he has ever trained but also the best horse he has ever seen, including the likes of Brigadier Gerard, Mill Reef, Nijinsky and Shergar.
29 Rebecca Adlington added the world 800 metres freestyle title to her Olympic crown when she produced a blistering final length to overhaul the defending champion, Lotte Friis, at the World Aquatics Championship in Shanghai.
30 England were drawn against Montenegro, Ukraine, Poland, Moldova and San Marino in their bid to qualify for the 2014 World Cup in Brazil.
Stuart Broad took a hat-trick to fire England back into contention in the second Test against India at Trent Bridge.The tourists were in total control of the match, leading by 46 on 267-4, when Broad dismissed Yuvraj Singh for 62 to break his partnership of 128 with centurion Rahul Dravid. Then in his next over Broad had Mahendra Dhoni caught in the slips, Harbhajan Singh trapped leg before wicket and Praveen Kumar clean bowled in successive balls to send the crowd at his home ground into delirium. Broad was the 12th Englishman to take a hat-trick in Test cricket and the first since Ryan Sidebottom in Hamilton in 2008.
31 In his 200th Formula One race, Jenson Button won the Hungarian GP at the Hungaroring.
Ian Bell was run out off the final ball before tea during the second Test but was reinstated after the break at the request of Indian captain MS Dhoni. The controversial dismissal came about after Eoin Morgan clipped the ball from Ishant Sharma to the square leg boundary, where Praveen Kumar completed an awkward piece of fielding and hesitated before returning the ball to the middle. The spectators made noises to the effect that the ball had crossed the boundary ropes and the fielders were unsure. After grounding his bat for the third run Bell took off his gloves and began to walk off the field only to find he had been run out.
Liam Tancock won the third gold medal for Great Britain at the World Aquatics Championship, with victory in the 50m backstroke.
Perri Shakes-Drayton won the 400m hurdles title at the UK Trials and Championships to add to the flat 400m title she won the day before - a unique double.

August

1 England beat India by 319 runs at Trent Bridge to take a 2-0 lead in the four-match Test series.
4 HTC-Highroad team, the world's most successful cycling team, will cease to exist at the end of this year, having failed to line up a new sponsor amid rumours that their leading rider, Mark Cavendish would defect to Team Sky for 2012.
5 Michael Carberry hit an unbeaten triple century and shared in a mammoth 523-run stand with Neil McKenzie in Hampshire's County Championship Division One clash with Yorkshire. The stand was the third highest in the history of the Championship, the ninth highest in all first-class cricket and the highest ever third-wicket stand.
6 The annual Shergar Cup event at Ascot was won by Ireland for the third year in a row, although England's Paul Hanagan won the Silver Boot as top individual scorer in the handicaps.
7 Manchester Utd beat Manchester City 3-2 in the FA Community Shield, the season's curtain-raiser between the Premiership winners and the FA Cup holders.
10 England's friendly football match with Holland at Wembley was cancelled on safety grounds in the aftermath of the London riots.
12 Tiger Woods missed his first cut at the US PGA, and only his third at a major in 15 years as a professional.
13 England beat India by an innings and 242 runs at Edgbaston to lead the four-match Test series 3-0 and in the process become the newly-crowned No 1 Test side in the world.
14 Keegan Bradley, the nephew of six-times major winner Pat Bradley, won the 93rd US PGA golf championship in Atlanta after a play-off against fellow American Jason Dufner.
20 Trainer Barry Hills retired from horse racing after more than forty years; his final runner, One Lucky Lady, ridden by William Carson, winning at Bath.
21 Andy Murray became only the second player this year to beat Novak Djokovic. Murray won the Cincinnati Masters title after Djokovic, his opponent in the final, retired when trailing 3-0 in the second set, having lost the first set 6-4.
22 England beat India by an innings and 8 runs to win the Test series 4-0
25 Eoin Morgan made his debut as England cricket captain a winning one against his former Irish team. England won by 11 runs in a rain-affected match at Clontarf, Co Dublin, Morgan scoring a run-a-ball 59 to be named man-of-the-match.
27 Leicestershire won the FriendsLife T20 by 18 runs and qualified for the Champions League with beaten finalists Somerset. On a turning Edgbaston pitch, both rain-affected semi-finals were decided by super-over eliminators after ending in ties.
Wigan defeated Leeds 28-18 in the Rugby League Challenge Cup Final at Wembley.
28 On the second day of the World Athletics Championships in Daegu, South Korea, Usain Bolt, the overwhelming favourite for the 100m title, false-started and was disqualified, leaving his fellow Jamaican training partner Yohan Blake to run out an easy winner in 9.92sec. Earlier in the day South African amputee Oscar Pistorius came third in his heat to make the semi-finals of the 400m. There was disappointment for British fans as Mo Farah could only manage the silver in the men's 10,000m while several other athletes failed to progress as expected.
German FI world champion, Sebastian Vettel, won the Belgian Grand Prix at Spa Francorchamps to extend his lead in the driver's championship to 92 points.
29 Britain's Andy Turner won an unexpected bronze medal in the 110m hurdles in Daegu after the winner, Cuban Dayron Robles, was disqualified for impeding China's Liu Xiang, who was subsequently awarded the silver. The gold medal was awarded to American Jason Richardson.
30 In European Championship qualifying matches, England beat Bulgaria 3-0 in Sofia whilst Ireland drew 0-0 with Slovakia; Northern Ireland lost 1-0 to Serbia and Wales beat Montenegro 2-1, although still remain bottom of Group G.

September

1 Dai Greene won Great Britain's first gold medal in Daegu with victory in the 400m hurdles.
3 In European Championship qualifying Group 1, Scotland drew with the Czech Republic 2-2.
4 Mo Farah won Britain's second gold medal in Daegu with victory in the 5,000m.
At the world rowing championships in Bled, Slovenia, the British team finished with a record 14 medals, including seven golds.
Thomas Bjorn of Denmark won his second straight European Tour title with a final round 62 in the European Masters in Switzerland.
6 In European Championship qualifying matches, England beat Wales 1-0 at Wembley whilst Ireland drew 0-0 with Russia in Moscow to give themselves a fighting chance of qualifying from Group B. In other matches Northern Ireland lost 4-1 to Estonia and Scotland beat Lithuania 1-0.
9 Carolyn Still, 29, became chief executive of Blue Square Bet Premier club Mansfield Town FC.
10 Fly-half Jonny Wilkinson missed five penalties in a row as England gained a hard-fought 13-9 victory over Argentina, at the Otago Stadium, Dunedin, in their opening match of the Rugby Union World Cup in New Zeland. In other matches, South Africa beat Wales 17-16; Ireland beat USA 22-10 and Scotland beat Romania 34-24.
The year's final classic, the Doncaster St Leger, was won by Masked Marvel, ridden by William Buick and trained by John Gosden.
Alistair Brownlee of Great Britain was crowned ITU World Triathlon Champion, winning the grand final in Beijing. The Yorkshireman's brother, Jonathan, finished runner-up after placing third in the final race.
Juan Jose Cobo of Spain won the Spanish Vuelta (Tour of Spain) from Britain's Christopher Froome and Bradley Wiggins.
11 Samantha Stosur beat Serena Williams 6-2, 6-3 in the final of the Australian Open. Oliver Golding of Great Britain won the boy's singles.
German FI world champion, Sebastian Vettel, won the Italian Grand Prix at Monza to extend his lead in the driver's championship to 112 points.
12 Serbian Novak Djokovic won the rain-delayed men's US Open title, defeating Rafael Nadal 6-2, 6-4, 6-7, 6-1 in the final at Flushing Meadows.
13 Scotland beat Georgia 15-6 in a group match in the Rugby Union World Cup in New Zeland.
15 On the day that Middlesex secured promotion to the first division by winning Division Two, Lancashire ended a 77-year wait for cricket's county championship title by pipping Warwickshire for the title.
16 British heavyweight hope Tyson Fury kept his unbeaten record, stopping American Nicolai Firtha in the fifth round in Belfast.
17 Floyd Mayweather Jr. scored a controversial fourth-round knockout victory over Victor Ortiz in their WBC welterweight title fight in Las Vegas. Ortiz had just had a point deducted for a head-butt when Mayweather took this opportunity to land two knockout blows against the unguarded fighter. The unbeaten Mayweather, who had not fought for 16 months, now has a 42-0 record.
18 Ireland beat Australia 15-6 in a group match in the Rugby Union World Cup in New Zeland. In other matches Wales beat Samoa 17-10 and England beat Georgia 41-10.
Great Britain, under new captain Leon Smith, beat Hungary 5-0 in a Davis Cup Europe / Africa Zone Group Two tie in Glasgow.
Holland's Lars Boom won the Tour of Britain cycle race after sprinter Mark Cavendish was victorious on the final stage.
Great Britain & Ireland held off a strong Continental Europe fightback to claim victory on the final day of the Vivendi Seve Trophy at St-Nom-La-Bretèche, 15 miles west of Paris. Europe began the day 11½ points to 6½ down but pulled level at 11½ apiece before Great Britain & Ireland, captained by Paul McGinley, managed a 15½ to 12½ victory, their sixth in succession.
19 Lucy Garner of Great Britain won the women's junior cycling road race at the world championships in Copenhagen.
20 Emma Pooley of Great Britain lost her world time trial title in Copenhagen, placing third behind Judith Arndt of Germany.
21 Bradley Wiggins of Great Britain won the silver medal behind Tony Martin of Germany in the men's world time trial championship in Copenhagen; multi-champion Fabian Cancellara placing third.
22 Frank Warren launched his own boxing TV channel, Box Nation.
24 England ran in 10 tries during their 67-3 defeat of Romania in the Rugby Union World Cup.
Prince of Johanne, ridden by John Fahy and trained by Tom Tate, won the Cambridgeshire Handicap at Newmarket; the first leg of the Autumn Double.
25 Europe beat USA 15-13 in the Solheim Cup, the European women golfer's first victory in six years.
German FI world champion, Sebastian Vettel, won the Singapore Grand Prix.
Mark Cavendish won the men's road race world title in Copenhagen after a magnificent team effort by Great Britain, Bradley Wiggins leading the team out for most of the final lap.
Paula Radcliffe placed third in 2hr 23min 46sec behind Kenyan Florence Kiplagat in the Berlin Marathon. In the men's race Patrick Makau of Kenya broke the world record in a time of 2hr 3min 38sec.
26 Joe LaCava, who has been caddying for Dustin Johnson the past 12 months, joined Tiger Woods.
27 Argentinian striker Carlos Tevez was told he would never play for Manchester City ever again after refusing to play as a second half substitute during the 2-0 defeat by Bayern Munich in a Champions League match in Munich.
30 Manchester United goalkeeper David de Gea was tackled by security as he headed for the exit after CCTV filmed him scoffing a £1.19p doughnut at a Tesco Express in Altrincham, Greater Manchester.

October

1 England reached the quarter finals of the Rugby Union World Cup with a 16-12 victory over Scotland in Auckland. In other matches, Wales beat Fiji 66-0 in Hamilton and Ireland beat Italy 36-6 in Dunedin; both teams joining England in the knockout stage.
2 Andy Murray beat American Donald Young 6-2, 6-0 to win the Thailand Open in Bangkok.
Danedream, ridden by Andrasch Starke and trained by Peter Schiergen, became only the second German winner (Star Appeal being the first in 1975) of the Prix de l'arc de Triomphe at Longchamp.
5 American sprinter LaShawn Merritt's Olympic ban was overturned by the court of arbitration for sport, clearing the way for the reigning Olympic 400m champion to defend his title at next year's London Games. The move could also lead to renewed pressure on the British Olympic Association to drop a bylaw that bans drug cheats for life and provide the likes of cyclist David Millar and sprinter Dwain Chambers with a route to the 2012 Games.
6 Alexa Turness, from Holland Park, West London, landed a 215lb catfish, the biggest freshwater fish caught by a British woman anywhere in the world; beating the previous record by a pound. The 8ft 4in (2.52m) fish was caught on the River Segre in northern Spain, the same water as Jonathan Avery's British record a week earlier.
7 England reached the the finals of Euro 2012 with a 2-2 draw against Montenegro in Podgorica, despite the sending off of Wayne Rooney for kicking Miodrag Dzudovic.
8 In Rugby Union World Cup quarter final matches England were beaten 19-12 by France in Auckland while Wales defeated Ireland 22-10 in Wellington.
Leeds beat St Helens 32-16 in rugby league's Super League Grand Final at Old Trafford.
Frankie Dettori won his first Cesarewitch at Newmarket after 25 years of trying. The 25-1 shot Never Can Tell, trained by Jamie Osborne, made much of the running to win by a length and a half.
Brendan Dolan of Northern Ireland scored a nine-dart maximum during his 5-2 semi-final win over James Wade in the World Grand Prix in Dublin, the first time such a feat has been accomplished in the double in format.
9 Phil Taylor beat Brendan Dolan 6-3 in the final of the World Grand Prix.
Josef Vana won the 121st Velka-Pardubicka at Pardubice in the Czech Republic to take his astounding record in the race to eight wins as a jockey and nine as a trainer. For his mount, Tiumen, it was a hat-trick of wins in the race, eastern Europe's equivalent of the Grand National.
Andy Murray beat Rafael Nadal 3-6, 6-2, 6-0 in the final of the Japan Open in Tokyo
German FI world champion, Sebastian Vettel, retained his title after finishing third behind Jenson Button in the Japanese Grand Prix at Suzuka.
11 The Republic of Ireland beat Armenia 2-1 to qualify for the play-offs of Euro 2012
World road race champion Mark Cavendish signed for British-based cycling squad Team Sky.

13 Leading flat race jockey Richard Hughes gave up his riding licence in protest at the sport's new whip regulations which prevent a rider hitting the horse with the whip more than seven times during a race (eight times in a jumps race) and no more than five times in the final furlong.
Wayne Rooney was handed a three-match ban for his 'assault' on Miodrag Dzudovic during England's 2-2 draw with Montenegro last week. The ban rules Rooney out of the group stages of Euro 2012.
15 Wales were beaten 9-8 by France in the semi-finals of the Rugby Union World Cup in Auckland. The match was marred by the controversial sending off of Welsh captain Sam Warburton early in the first half. Ironically, the only other time Wales had reached the semi-final stage was the inaugural competition in 1987 when Huw Richards of Wales became the first man to be sent off in World Cup history.
James DeGale won the European super-middleweight title on a majority points decision over Piotr Wilczewski in Liverpool. In the main bout on the card Nathan Cleverly retained his WBO light-heavyweight title with a majority decision victory over local boy Tony Bellew.
Frankel, trained by Henry Cecil and ridden by Tom Queally, laid claim to being regarded as one of the best horses of all time with a four lengths victory in the Queen Elizabeth II Stakes at Ascot, his ninth win from nine starts.
16 Tom Lewis, 20, gained his first tour win in only his third professional tournament. The Welwyn Garden City golfer won the Portugal Masters with a closing 65 at Vilamoura.
20 Australia beat Wales 21-18 in the third place play-off of the Rugby Union World Cup.
22 New Zealand beat France 8-7 at Eden Park to win the 2011 Rugby Union World Cup.
23 Luke Donald topped the PGA Tour money list in America after winning the season-ending Disney Classic at Lake Buena Vista in Florida. The 33-year-old English golfer is bidding to become the first player to win the orders of merit on both sides of the Atlantic
Manchester City thrashed Manchester United 6-1 at Old Trafford to take a five-point lead in the Barclays Premier League.
25 England collapsed to a 95-run defeat by India in Calcutta to lose the One-Day International series 5-0.
Carlos Tevez was fined a record £792,000 by Manchester City for allegedly refusing to play against Bayern Munich last month.
30 Sebastian Vettel won the inaugural Indian Formula One GP in Delhi.
Rory McIlroy won the Shanghai Masters at Lake Malaren in a sudden-death play-off against Anthony Kim of the USA.
England bounced back from their One Day International beating by gaining victory in a Twenty20 match against India in Calcutta (Kolkotha).

November

1 Pakistan cricketers Salman Butt and Mohammad Asif were found guilty of their part in a "spot-fixing" scam after a trial at Southwark Crown Court. Former captain Butt, 27, and fast bowler Asif, 28, were both found guilty of conspiracy to cheat and conspiracy to accept corrupt payments. They plotted to deliberately bowl no-balls during a Lord's Test match against England last summer. Another bowler, Mohammad Amir, 19, admitted the charges prior to the trial.
3 Salman Butt, Pakistan's ex-Test captain, received a 30-month sentence at Southwark Crown Court, fast bowler Mohammad Asif 12 months and Mohammad Amir six months while Mazhar Majeed, the agent involved, was jailed for two years and eight months for his role in the scandal.
5 Ian Thorpe, the Australian multi-gold medal-winning swimmer made his return to the pool in the World Cup short-course meeting in Singapore, finishing seventh in the 100m individual medley final but failing to make the final of the 100m butterfly.
Paul Hanagan retained his Flat jockey's championship title ending the season with 165 winners, four in front of Brazilian rider Silvestre de Sousa. Martin Harley was crowned champion apprentice with 58 winners.
6 World No 1 squash player Nick Matthew of Great Britain retained his World Open title in Rotterdam, beating Frenchman Gregory Gaultier in the final 6-11, 11-9, 11-6, 11-4.
10 Newcastle United FC's home ground of St James' Park was temporarily renamed the Sports Direct Arena by owner Mike Ashley until the club can attract a sponsor.
11 The Republic of Ireland defeated Estonia 4-0 in the first leg of their Euro 2012 qualifier in Tallinn.
London will host the 2017 World Athletics Championships after defeating Doha's rival bid.
Andy Murray lost his 17-match winning run after a three-sets defeat to Tomas Berdych of the Czech Republic.
12 England beat world champions Spain 1-0 in a friendly football international at Wembley.
"Filipino boxing legend Manny Pacquiao retained his WBO welterweight title beating Mexican Juan Manual Márquez for the third time by way of a split points decision, at the MGM Grand in Las Vegas. In domestic fights, Tyson Fury picked himself up off the canvas in Round Two to stop Canadian-based heavyweight Neven Pajkic in three rounds to retain his Commonwealth title in Manchester and on the undercard middleweight Chris Eubank Jr - son of the former two-weight world champion - made his professional debut with a comfortable fourth-round stoppage win over Lithuania's Kirilas Psonko.
13 Lewis Hamilton won the Abu Dhabi Formula One Grand Prix.
14 Police announced that former Somerset and England cricketer Peter Roebuck committed suicide by jumping from the sixth floor of the Southern Sun Hotel in Newlands, Cape Town, South Africa.
15 The Republic of Ireland drew 1-1 with Estonia 4-0 in the second leg of their Euro 2012 qualifier at the Aviva Stadium, Dublin to win the tie 5-1 on aggregate.
England beat Sweden 1-0 in a friendly football international at Wembley; their first victory over the Swedes for 43 years.
16 Liverpool striker Luis Suarez was charged by the Football Association with racially abusing Manchester United defender Patrice Evra during the teams' 1-1 draw at Anfield on 15 October. Uruguayan Suarez, 24, denied Evra's claim that he used racist language to the French international.
20 The latest golf world rankings list three British men at the top; No 1 Luke Donald, No 2 Rory McIlroy and No 3 Lee Westwood.
26 Sebastian Vettel set a new seasonal record for Formula One pole positions, beating Nigel Mansell's 1992 mark, by posting the fastest time during qualifying for the Brazilian Grand Prix. The German lapped the Interlagos circuit in 1m 11.918s to take top spot for the 15th time in 19 races.
27 Mark Webber won the Brazilain GP after his team-mate Sebastian Vettel was forced to let him through early on in the race after developing gear box trouble. The final drivers' standings had Vettel top with 392pts, Button second with 270pts and Webber third with 258pts. Red Bull won the constructor's championship with 650pts from McLaren-Mercedes with 497pts.
Roger Federer won the end-of-season Barclays ATP World Tour Finals, beating Jo-Wilfried Tsonga 6-3, 6-7, 6-3 in the final.
Ronnie O'Sullivan beat China's Ding Junhui 7-1 to collect his 10th Premier League snooker title.
Harlequins beat Newcastle Falcons 39-8 at The Stoop to create an Aviva Premiership record by winning the first nine games of their season.
Gary Speed, the Wales international football team manager, was found dead at his home.

December

2 England were drawn against France, Sweden and Ukraine for Euro 2012, hosted by Poland and Ukraine, while the Republic of Ireland were grouped against Spain, Italy and Croatia.
4 Tiger Woods won his first tournament for two years with victory in the Chevron World Challenge at Thousand Oaks, California.
Spain beat Argentina 3-1 in the Davis Cup final at the Olympic Stadium, Seville, Spain.
6 Northern Ireland's Mark Allen found himself in front of a disciplinary board after criticising Barry Hearn's chairmanship of World Snooker.
7 In a bad night for Manchester, both City and United failed to qualify for the knockout stages of the Champions League. Basel beat United 2-1 to gain the runners-up spot behind Benfica in Group C while Manchester City beat top of Group A, Bayern Munich 2-0 but failed to qualify after Napoli beat Villareal to gain the second qualifying spot.
8 Virender Sehwag scored 219 runs during India's victory over West Indies, the highest score in one-day international history.
10 Amir Khan lost a majority points decision to American Lamont Peterson in Washington DC to lose his WBA and IBF world light-welterweight boxing titles.
11 Judd Trump beat Mark Allen 10-8 in the final of the UK Snooker Championship at The Barbican Centre, York.
American baseball was stunned by a positive drug test from Milwaukee's 'Mr Clean' Ryan Braun — the National League's MVP of the season. Braun is facing a 50-game suspension if his B-sample also tests positive for high levels of testosterone, which means he could not

play again until the end of May 2012. The 27-year-old star had helped the Milwaukee Brewers to their best season since 1982 as they reached the World Series semi-finals.
Luke Donald became the first golfer to top the money lists in Europe and America.
12 Jonny Wilkinson announced his retirement from international rugby.
14 Four jockeys were banned for their involvement in the largest race-fixing ring ever exposed in British racing history. Paul Doe and Greg Fairley were each banned for 12 years after being found guilty of conspiracy, giving inside information and stopping horses from obtaining their best possible placings. Jimmy Quinn was banned for six months for conspiracy and Kirsty Milczarek, the girlfriend of Kieren Fallon, was banned for two years by the British Horseracing Authority for committing 'corrupt or fraudulent' practices. Milczarek, known as Milkshake by fellow jockeys, was also found to have passed on information for reward.
17 Big Buck's, ridden by Ruby Walsh and trained by Paul Nicholls, won his 14th consecutive National Hunt hurdles race and in the process overtook Bula's record of 13 wins.
American Andre Ward proved he is the best super-middleweight in the world by uniting the WBC and WBA titles by beating Britain's Carl Froch on points in the final of Showtime's Super Six in Atlantic City, New Jersey.
20 Liverpool striker Luis Suarez was given an eight-match suspension and fined £40,000 after the Football Association found him guilty of misconduct after Manchester United defender Patrice Evra accused the Uruguay international of racially abusing him during the Premier League clash at Anfield on October 15.
22 Cyclist Mark Cavendish won the BBC Sports Personality of the Year title.
26 Kauto Star, ridden by Ruby Walsh and trained by Paul Nicholls, won the King George VI Chase at Kempton for the fifth time, eclipsing the feat of the mighty grey Desert Orchid, who won the race four times in five years.
28 A betting bungle saw odds of 28/1 offered on a horse seconds before it romped to victory. Voler La Vedette, ridden by Andrew Lynch, had been four lengths clear and approaching the winning post when the huge "in-running" odds were offered. He had gone off as 13-8 favourite on the course in Leopardstown, Ireland. There was fury when Betfair, which allows people to gamble against each other, later voided all bets — avoiding a £23million payout. No explanation was offered for the "obvious technical error".

Obituaries 2011

January

2 Peter Postlethwaite, actor, born February 16th 1946
Anne Francis, US actress, born Ann Marvak, September 16th 1930
Miriam Seegar, US actress, born September 1st 1907
3 (Valerie) Jill Haworth, actress, born August 15th 1945
4 Gerry Rafferty, singer / songwriter, born April 16th 1947
Gordon 'Dick' King-Smith, children's author and televsion presenter, born March 27th 1922
6 Gary Mason, boxer, born December 15th 1962
9 Peter Yates, film director, born July 24th 1929
10 Margaret Whiting, US country music singer, born July 22nd 1924
11 Terry Seabrooke, magician, born December 26th 1932
12 Joe Gores, US crime-writer, born December 25th 1931
13 Bea Seal, tennis player and referee, born January 13th 1914
15 Susannah York, actress, born Susannah Yolande Fletcher, January 9th 1939
Nat Lofthouse, footballer, born August 27th 1925
Michael Langham, theatre director, born August 22nd 1919
17 Brian Boobbyer, sportsman and Christian missionary, born February 25th 1928
20 Jean Le Patourel, archaeologist, born Hilda Bird, August 19th 1915
26 Charlie Louvin, US country singer, born Charles Elzer Loudermilk, July 7th 1927
28 Margaret Price, soprano, born April 13th 1941
29 Milton Babbitt, US composer, born May 10th 1916
30 John Barry, composer, born John Barry Prendergast, November 3rd 1933

February

2 Margaret John, actress, born December 14th 1926
3 Maria Schneider, French actress, born March 27th 1952
5 Brian Jacques, novelist, born June 15th 1939
6 Gary Moore, guitarist with Thin Lizzy, born April 4th 1952
10 Trevor Bailey, cricketer, born December 3rd 1923
Bill Justice, US cartoon animator, born February 9th 1914
11 Christian Lambertsen, US scientist who coined the term 'Scuba', born May 15th 1917
12 Kenneth Mars, US actor, born April 14th 1935
13 TP McKenna, Irish actor, born September 7th 1929
Reg Moores, developer of the radio microphone, born September 10th 1922
Paul Marcus, television director and producer, born May 30th 1954
14 George Shearing, jazz pianist, born August 13th 1919
David Friedman, US horror film maker, born December 24th 1923
16 Alfred Burke, actor, born February 28th 1918
John Ralph Merton, artist, born May 7th 1913
18 John Adewole, Sierra Leonean actor (the genie on the Sky Broadband advert), born in 1948
22 (William) Nicholas Courtney, actor, born in Cairo, December 16th 1929
Rosemary Gill, television producer, born December 7th 1930
23 Matthew Carr, artist, born February 5th 1953
26 Dean Richards, footballer, born June 9th 1974
Eugene Fodor, American violinist, born March 5th 1950
27 Betty Paul, actress, born Betty Percheron, May 21st 1921
Necmettin Erbakan, Turkish politician, born October 29th 1926
28 Jane Russell, US actress, born June 21st 1921
Annie Girardot, French actress, born October 25th 1931

March

4 Johnny Preston, US vocalist, born Johnny Preston courville, August 18th 1939
Simon van der Meer, Dutch Nobel Prize-winning physicist, born November 24th 1925
6 Louie Ramsay, South African-born British actress, born November 25th 1929
8 Richard Campbell, viola da gamba player and founder of 'Fretwork', born February 21st 1956
9 Erlund Hudson, artist, born Eleanor Hudson, February 18th 1912
10 Eddie Snyder, US songwriter, born February 22nd 1919
11 Hugh Martin, US composer, born August 11th 1914
Donny George, Iraqi archaeologist, born October 23rd 1950

Nancy Kominsky, US artist. Born Emanuella Agneta Circelli, September 24th 1915
Iris Kellett, Irish showjumper, born January 8th 1926
Celia Lipton, singer dubbed 'Britain's Judy Garland', born December 25th 1923
12 Joe Morello, US jazz drummer, born July 17th 1928
15 Peter Loader, cricketer, born October 25th 1929
Keith Fordyce, radio and television presenter, born Keith Fordyce Marriott, October 15th 1928
Smiley Culture, reggae singer, born David Victor Emmanuel, February 10th 1963
Yakov Kreizberg, Russian conductor, born October 24th 1959
17 Michael Gough, actor, born November 23rd 1916
18 Terence 'Jet' Harris, bass player with The Shadows, born July 6th 1939
Warren Christopher, US former Secretary of State, born October 27th 1925
Princess Antoinette of Monaco, born December 28th 1920
20 Johnny Pearson, musical director of Top of the Pops, born June 18th 1925
21 Jo Willy 'Pinetop' Perkins, US blues pianist, born July 7th 1913
22 George Walker, boxer and businessman, born April 14th 1929
23 Elizabeth Taylor, actress, born February 27th 1932
Fred Titmus, England and Middlesex cricketer, born November 24th 1932
Lanford Wilson, US playwright, born April 13th 1937
25 Lattimore Brown, US soul singer, born LV Brown, August 20th 1931
26 Geraldine Ferraro, US politician, born August 26th 1935
Diana Wynne Jones, children's author, born August 16th 1934
Harry Coover, US inventor of Cyanoacrylate (Super Glue), born March 6th 1917
27 Farley Granger, US actor, born July 1st 1925
Henry Reymond Fitzwalter 'HRF' Keating, crime novelist, born October 31st 1926
29 Robert Tear, tenor, born March 8th 1939
31 Edward Stobart, haulage boss, born November 21st 1954

April
3 Selwyn Goldsmith, architect, born December 11th 1932
Martin Horton, cricketer, born April 21st 1934
4 Juliano Mer-Khamis, Israeli actor, born May 29th 1958
Craig Thomas, novelist, born November 24th 1942
9 Sidney Lumet, US film director, born June 25th 1924
11 Angela Scoular, actress, born November 8th 1945
14 Trevor Bannister, actor, born August 14th 1936
15 Vincenzo La Scola, Italian tenor, born January 25th 1958
16 Gerry Alexander, Jamaican cricketer, born November 2nd 1928
Sol Saks, US writer - creator of TV series 'Bewitched', born December 13th 1910
17 Michael Sarrazin, Canadian actor, born May 22nd 1940
Eddie Leadbeater, Yorkshire and England cricketer, born August 15th 1927
Ken Taylor, screenwriter, born November 10th 1922
18 (George) Geoffrey Miller, US founder of Los Angeles Magazine, born August 1st 1936
19 Elisabeth Sladen, actress, born February 1st 1948
20 Jean MacLeod, romantic novelist, born January 20th 1908
Hubert Schlafly, US co-inventor of the teleprompter, born August 14th 1919
Tim Hetherington, photojournalist, born December 5th 1970
21 Gay Kindersley, National Hunt trainer, born June 2nd 1930
23 John Sullivan, scriptwriter, born December 23rd 1946
James Casey, radio producer and son of comedian Jimmy James, born August 16th 1922
Norio Ohga, Japanese businessman who commercialised the CD, born January 29th 1930
25 Poly Styrene, punk singer, born Marian Joan Elliot-Said, July 3rd 1957
26 Admiral of the Fleet Sir Henry Leach, First Sea Lord, born November 18th 1923
29 David Mason, trumpeter on The Beatles' Penny Lane, born in 1926
30 Professor Richard Holmes, military historian and broadcaster, born March 29th 1946
Alec Weeks, sports commentator and producer, born February 2nd 1927
Andy Dunkley, DJ known as The Living Jukebox, born July 13th 1942

May
1 Henry Cooper, boxing champion, born May 3rd 1934
Ted Lowe, snooker commentator, born November 1st 1920
2 Osama Bin Laden, Saudi Arabian terrorist, born March 10th 1957
3 Jackie Cooper, US actor, born John Cooperman, September 15th 1922
4 Mary Murphy, US actress, born January 26th 1931
5 Arthur Laurents, US director and playwright, born Arthur Levine, July 14th 1918
Dana Wynter, German-born British actress, born Dagmar Winter, June 8th 1931
6 Victoria Potts, painter, born Victoria Fitzwilliam-Lay, March 19th 1969
7 Severiano Ballesteros, Spanish golf champion, born April 9th 1957
Gunter Sachs, German playboy and third husband of Brigitte Bardot, born November 14th 1932
John Walker, US founder of the Walker Brothers, born John Maus, November 12th 1943
Big George (Webley), musician, bandleader, and broadcaster, born May 29th 1957
8 Jane White Cooke, US portrait painter, born January 10th 1913
13 Pam Gems, playwright, born Iris Pamela Price, August 1st 1925
15 Samuel Wanjiru, Kenyan marathon runner, born November 10th 1986
Bob Flanigan, US vocalist with The Four Freshmen, born August 22nd 1926
16 Edward Hardwicke, actor, born August 7th 1932
19 Garret FitzGerald, Irish politician, born February 9th 1926
Kathy Kirby, singer, born Kathleen O'Rourke, October 20th 1938
Alda Noni, Italian soprano, born April 30th 1916
21 Mala Sen, Indian writer of The True Story of Phoolan Devi, born June 3rd 1947
22 Breon O'Casey, artist son of playwright Sean O'Casey, born April 30th 1928
Suzanne Mizzi, Malta-born former Page 3 model, born December 1st 1967
24 Glyn Hughes, poet and novelist, born May 25th 1935
Edward John Carlos Plunkett (Lord Dunsany), Irish artist, born September 10th 1939
25 Leona Carrington, artist, born April 6th 1917
Terry Jenner, Australian cricketer, born September 8th 1944
26 Flick Colby, US choreographer of dance troupe Pan's People, born March 23rd 1946
27 Janet McLuckie Brown, impressionist, born December 14th 1923

Jeff Conaway, US actor, born October 5th 1950
Gil Scott-Heron, US poet and musician, born April 1st 1949
28 Dame Barbara Mills, former Director of Public Prosecutions, born August 10th 1940
30 Rosalyn Yalow, US Nobel Prize-winning scientist, born July 19th 1921
Giorgio Tozzi, US operatic bass, born George John Tozzi, January 8th 1923
31 Pauline Betz, US tennis player, born August 6th 1919
Hugh Stewart, producer, born December 14th 1910
Keith Irvine, interior designer, born October 14th 1928

June
2 Josephine Hart, Irish novelist, born March 1st 1942
3 Miriam Karlin, actress, born Miriam Samuels, June 23rd 1925
Andrew Gold, US vocalist, born August 2nd 1951
James Arness, actor, born James Aurness, May 26th 1923
Pat Jackson, film director, born March 26th 1916
4 Martin Rushent, record producer, born July 11th 1948
Donald Marland Hewlett, actor, born August 30th 1920
Lawrence Eagleburger, US politician, born August 1st 1940
8 Roy Skelton, voice of Zippy and George from the TV series Rainbow, born July 20th 1931
John Mackenzie, film director, born May 22nd 1928
9 Maqbool Fida 'MF' Husain, Indian billboard painter, born September 17th 1915
11 Jack Smith, 'Kitchen Sink' artist, born June 18th 1928
Gunnar Fischer, Swedish cinematographer, born November 18th 1910
12 Carl Gardner, US founder of singing group The Coasters, born April 29th 1928
Christopher Neame, film producer, born December 24th 1942
16 Larry 'Wild Man' Fischer, US busker, born November 6th 1944
18 Clarence Clemons, US saxophonist, born January 11th 1942
Frederick Chiluba, Zambian politician, born April 30th 1943
20 Ottilie Patterson, jazz singer, born January 31st 1932
Ryan Dunn, US stunt actor, born June 11th 1977
21 Arthur Budgett, Derby-winning racehorse trainer, born May 26th 1916
22 John Waite, South African cricketer, born January 19th 1930
Mike Waterson, folk singer, born January 16th 1941
23 Peter Falk, US actor, born September 16th 1927
24 Stanley Seeger, US art collector, born May 28th 1930
Colin Verity, maritime artist, born March 7th 1924
25 Margaret Tyzack, actress, born September 9th 1931
Michael Latimer, actor, born September 6th 1941
26 Ian Wheeler, jazz musician, born January 13th 1931
Marion Konyot, US vaudeville entertainer, born Marion Olive, May 25th 1925
Elaine Stewart, US actress and model , born Elsy Steinberg, May 31st 1930
27 Betty Callaway, ice dancing coach, born Betty Roberts, March 22nd 1928
28 Richard Fox, Irish jockey, born March 6th 1954
30 Jimmy Roselli, US vocalist, born December 26th 1925

July
2 Itamar Franco, Brazilian politician, born June 28th 1930
3 Anna Raymond Massey, actress, born August 11th 1937
George Blair, romantic fiction writer (Emma Blair), born August 12th 1942
Francis King, novelist, born March 4th 1923
4 Archduke Otto von Habsburg, Austrian politician, born November 12th 1912
5 Cy Twombly, US artist, born April 25th 1928
6 Josef Suk, Czech violinist, born August 8th 1929
8 Betty Ford, US former First Lady, born Elizabeth Ann Bloomer, April 8th 1918
9 Beverly Whitney Kean, Canadian actress, born Beverly Sutherland, September 10th 1921
10 Roland Petit, French choreographer, born January 13th 1924
11 Alex Hay, BBC golf commentator, born May 10th 1933
12 William Crozier, artist, born May 5th 1930
Sherwood Schwarz, US creator of Gilligan's Island, born November 14th 1916
14 Eric Delaney, drummer, born May 22nd 1924
15 Googie Withers, actress, born March 12th 1917
17 Juan Maria Bordaberry, Uruguayan politician, born June 17th 1928
Alex Steinwess, US inventor of the album sleeve, born March 24th 1917
19 Cec Thompson, rugby union player, born July 12th 1926
Sheila Burrell, actress, born May 9th 1922
20 Lucien Freud, artist, born December 8th 1922
21 Elliot Handler, US co-founder of Mattel, born April 9th 1918
22 Linda Christian, Mexican actress, born Blanca Welter Vorhauer, November 13th 1923
23 Amy Jade Winehouse, singer, born September 14th 1983
Robert Ettinger, US pioneer of Cryonics, born December 4th 1918
Fran Landesman, US poet, born Frances Deitsch, October 21st 1927
24 Dan Peek, US rock musician (with America), born November 1st 1950
25 Michael Cacoyannis, Greek film director, born June 11th 1922
26 Margaret Olley, Australian artist, born June 24th 1923
27 The Rev John Stott, Anglican clergyman, born April 27th 1921
Charles Gittens, America's first black Secret Service agent, born August 31st 1928
29 Richard Marsh, politician, born March 14th 1928
31 John Hoyland, abstract artist, born October 12th 1934

August
1 Stan Barstow, novelist, born June 28th 1928
2 Richard Pearson, actor, born August 1st 1918
3 Allan Watkins, cricketer, born April 21st 1922
Charles Aaron 'Bubba' Smith, US actor and American footballer, born February 28th 1945
Annette Charles, US actress, born Annette Cardona, March 5th 1948
4 Michael Bukht (aka Michael Barry), radio executive and TV chef, born September 10th 1941
6 John Wood, actor, born July 5th 1930
Roman Opalka, French conceptual artist, born August 27th 1931

7 Harri Holkeri, Finnish politician, born January 6th 1937
11 George Devol, US inventor of the robot arm, born February 20th 1912
12 Robert Robinson, broadcaster and writer, born December 17th 1927
13 Robert Breer, US artist, born September 30th 1926
14 Shammi Kapoor, Indian actor, born October 21st 1931
16 Huw Ceredig, actor, born June 22nd 1942
Shirley Eskapa, South African novelist, born July 30th 1934
19 Jimmy Sangster, scriptwriter, born December 2nd 1927
22 John Howard Davies, actor, born March 9th 1939
Nickolas Ashford, US pop star, born May 4th 1942
Jerry Leiber, US lyricist, born April 25th 1933
Murray Arbeid, fashion designer, born May 30th 1935
23 Sybil Jason, South African child actress, born November 23rd 1927
27 Norman Frederick 'NF' Simpson, dramatist, born January 29th 1919
28 Vic Carless, artist, born January 13th 1928
29 David 'Honeyboy' Edwards, US blues guitarist, born June 28th 1915
31 Ray Fisher, balladeer, born November 26th 1940

September
1 Cobina Wright, US actress, born August 14th 1921
5 Salvatore Licitra, Swiss operatic tenor, born August 10th 1968
Vann Nath, Cambodian artist, born in 1946
6 Wardell Quezergue, US bandleader and producer, born March 12th 1930
10 Cliff Robertson, US actor, born September 9th 1923
12 Wade Mainer, US banjo player, born April 21st 1907
13 Richard Hamilton, pioneer of pop art, born February 24th 1922
16 Norma Eberhardt, US fashion model, born in 1929
Ian Kemp, musicologist, born June 26th 1931
17 Kurt Sanderling, German conductor, born September 19th 1912
19 Donald 'Ginger' McCain, trainer of racehorse Red Rum, born September 21st 1930
20 Michael Jarvis, racehorse trainer, born August 14th 1938
Arch West, US inventor of Doritos, born September 8th 1914
22 Mohamed Mansur Ali Khan (The Nawab of Pataudi), cricketer, born January 5th 1941
Jonathan Cecil, actor, born February 22nd 1939
24 Emanuel Litvinoff, poet, born May 5th 1915
25 Wangari Maathai, Kenyan Nobel Peace Prize winner, born April 1st 1940
26 David Z Goodman, US screenwriter, born January 15th 1930
27 David Croft, television scriptwriter, born David John Sharland, September 7th 1922
Tatyana Lioznova, Russian film director, born July 20th 1924
29 Iain Sproat, politician, born November 8th 1938
30 Alexander Grant, New Zealand ballet dancer, born February 22nd 1925
Ralph Steinman, Canadian winner of the 2011 Nobel Prize for Medicine, born January 14th 1943

October
1 David Bedford, composer, born August 4th 1937
5 Graham Dilley, cricketer, born May 18th 1959
Bert Jansch, guitarist, born November 3rd 1943
Steve Jobs, US co-founder of Apple computers, born February 24th 1955
6 Diane Cilento, Australian-born actress, born October 5th 1933
Paul Dickson, film and television director, born January 18th 1920
7 George Baker, Bulgarian-born British actor, born April 1st 1931
9 Mark Kingston, actor, born April 18th 1934
Rob Buckman, doctor, comedian and television presenter, born August 22nd 1948
10 Ewald Osers, Czech-born British poet, born May 13th 1917
12 Dennis Ritchie, US co-creator of the Unix operating system, born September 9th 1941
13 Barbara Kent, Canadian actress, born December 16th 1907
14 John Clive 'JC' Hall, poet, born September 12th 1920
15 Betty Driver, actress, born May 20th 1920
16 Dan Wheldon, motor racing driver, born June 22nd 1978
17 Ramaz Chkhikvadze, Georgian actor, born February 28th 1928
19 Jon Weaving, Australian tenor, born February 23rd 1931
20 Colonel Muammar Gaddafi, Libyan dictator, born June 1942
Sue Lloyd, actress, born August 7th 1939
Barry Feinstein, US photographer, born February 4th 1931
Pamela Oldfield, author, born October 1st 1931
21 Edmundo Ros, Trinidadian bandleader, born December 7th 1910
22 Crown Prince Sultan Ibn Abdul-Aziz al Saud, heir to the Saudi throne, born 1926
Adrian Berg, landscape painter, born March 12th 1929
23 Herbert Hauptman, US Nobel Prize-winning chemist, born February 14th 1917
Marco Simoncelli, Italian motor cycle racer, born January 20th 1987
Begum Nusrat Bhutto, Iranian-born mother of Pakistani PM Benazir Bhutto, born March 23rd 1929
John Makin, pop singer who had Belgium No 1, Potverdekke! (Goddammit), born February 13th 1950
24 John McCarthy, US father of 'Artificial Intelligence', born September 4th 1927
Bruno Weber, Swiss architect, born April 19th 1931
28 Beryl Davis, big band singer, born March 16th 1924
29 Sir James Savile, disc jockey and television presenter, born October 31st 1926
31 Florian Albert, Hungarian footballer, born September 15th 1941

November
4 Norman Ramsey, US Nobel Prize-winning physicist, born August 27th 1915
6 Gordon Beck, jazz pianist, born September 16th 1935
7 Joe Frazier, US boxing champion, born January 12th 1944
Andrea True, US pop singer and porn star, born July 26th 1943
9 H Gobind Khorana, Pakistani Nobel Prize-winning scientist, born January 9th 1922
Richard Morant, actor, born October 30th 1945
11 Michael Garrick, jazz pianist, born May 30th 1933
12 Peter Roebuck, cricketer, born March 6th 1956

Evelyn Lauder, Austrian philanthropist, born August 12th 1936
15 Dulcie Gray, Malaysian-born British actress, born November 20th 1915
Jackie Leven, folk musician, born June 19th 1950
Karl Slover, Hungarian actor, born Karl Kosiczky, September 21st 1918
17 Peter Reading, poet, born July 27th 1946
18 David Langdon, cartoonist, born February 24th 1914
19 Michael Hastings, playwright, born September 2nd 1938
Basil Lewis D'Oliveira, South African-born England cricketer, born October 4th 1931
John Neville, actor-director, born May 2nd 1925
20 Shelagh Delaney, playwright, born November 25th 1939
22 Sena Jurinac, Bosnian soprano, born October 24th 1921
Paul Motian, US jazz drummer, born March 25th 1931
23 Gerald Laing, artist, born February 11th 1936
24 Ross MacManus, musician and father of Elvis Costello, born October 20th 1927
25 Vasily Alekseyev, Russian weightlifter, born January 7th 1942
27 Gary Speed, Welsh footballer and manager, born September 8th 1969
Ken Russell, film director, born July 3rd 1927
28 Ante Marković, last prime minister of Yugoslavia, born November 25th 1924
29 Helen Forrester, author, born June 6th 1919

December
1 Francois Lesage, French embroiderer, born March 31st 1929
Bill McKinney, US actor, born September 12th 1931
Christa Wolf, German author, born Christa Ihlenfeld, March 18th 1929
Ragnhild Hveger, Danish swimmer, born December 10th 1920
3 Dev Anand, Indian film actor, born September 26th 1923
4 Hubert Sumlin, US blues guitarist and singer, born November 16th 1931
Sócrates (de Oliveira), Brazilian footballer, born February 19th 1954
6 Dobie Gray, US soul singer, born July 26th 1940
7 Harry Morgan, US actor, born April 10th 1915
Jerry Robinson, US illustrator, born January 1st 1922
9 Roy Tattersall, cricketer, born August 17th 1922
12 Bert Schneider, US film producer, born May 5th 1933
John Gardner, composer, born March 2nd 1917
13 Russell Conwell Hoban, US writer, born February 4th 1925
14 Billie Jo Spears, US country singer, born January 14th 1937
15 Christopher Hitchens, journalist, born April 13th 1949
16 Nicol Williamson, actor, born September 14th 1936.
17 Kim Jong-il, North Korean dictator, born Yuri Irsenovich Kim, February 16th 1941
18 Václav Havel, Czech playwright and former President, born October 5th 1936
Ronnie Wolfe, scriptwriter, born August 8th 1922
23 Denise Darcel, French actress, born Denise Billecard, September 8th 1924
24 Johannes Heesters, Dutch actor, singer, and entertainer, born December 5th 1903
25 Sue Carroll, newspaper columnist, born December 6th 1953
George Robb, footballer, born June 1st 1926
30 Ronald Searle, cartoonist, born March 3rd 1920
Eva Striker Zeisel, Hungarian-born ceramicist, born Éva Amália Striker, November 13th 1906

Daily Record 2012

January
4 Two men found guilty of the 1993 racist murder of Stephen Lawrence in south-east London were jailed for life. Gary Dobson will serve a minimum of 15 years and two months, and David Norris 14 years and three months. Dobson, 36, and Norris, 35, were the first members of "The Firm" to be convicted over the fatal attack on Mr Lawrence by a group of white youths near a bus stop in Eltham on 22 April 1993.
7 A £33bn high-speed rail network was given the go-ahead by the government, despite strong opposition. Phase one of HS2, between London and Birmingham, should be running by 2026, later extending to northern England. The first phase of HS2 will include a connection to mainland Europe via the Channel Tunnel. On completion the network will include a direct link to Heathrow.
9 Celebrity chef Antony Worrall Thompson, of *Ready Steady Cook* fame, publicly apologised for shoplifting cheese and wine at a Tesco store in Henley-on-Thames over the Christmas period. The 60-year-old chef was issued with a formal caution by Thames Valley Police.
10 Pop singer Bryan Ferry, 66, married Amanda Sheppard, 29, on a beach in the Caribbean.
13 Thirteen people were confirmed dead after a cruise ship carrying 4,234 people ran aground off the coast of Italy. There were scenes of confusion as the *Costa Concordia* hit a sandbar near the island of Giglio creating panic among the passengers and crew. The ship had sailed earlier in the day from Civitavecchia port near Rome for a Mediterranean cruise and was due to dock in Marseille after calling at ports in Sicily, Sardinia and Spain. The ship's Italian owner, a subsidiary of Carnival Cruise lines, issued a statement saying there appeared to be "significant human error" on the part of the captain, Francesco Schettino, "which resulted in these grave consequences." Authorities were holding Schettino for suspected manslaughter following allegations he abandoned the stricken liner before all the 3,200 passengers had escaped. According to the Italian navigation code, a captain who abandons a ship in danger can face up to 12 years in prison.
18 The online encyclopaedia, Wikipedia, shutdown for 24 hours in protest at draft US laws to fight online piracy which they feel has the potential to censor and stifle social websites negatively.
Clothing chain, Peacocks, fell into administration with 249 staff at the company's head office at Capital Link in Cardiff being made redundant and many others soon to follow if a buyer is not found.
19 In a bleak post-Christmas for retailers, children's clothing retailer Pumpkin Patch went into administration.
21 Tudor Pack, 16, became Britain's youngest solo pilot after just 20 hours of training.
29 Royal Bank of Scotland boss Stephen Hester finally agreed to give back his bonus of nearly £1million following an announcement by the Labour Party that they would force a Commons vote to try to strip the RBS chief executive of the bonus. The RBS boss has presided over huge job cuts at the bailed-out bank - who are 82 per cent owned by the taxpayer - and had been under intense pressure since the bonus was announced on 26 January.
30 The 75th anniversary of the creation of Smarties was celebrated with the release of a limited-edition retro-style hexagon tube. The colourful chocolate treat first arrived in stores in 1937 under the name Smarties having been renamed from its previous incarnation of Chocolate Beans. They were made at the Nestle factory in York until production moved abroad in September 2006.
UBS rogue trader, Kweku Adoboli, 31, accused of losing £1.4 billion of the bank's funds, pleaded not guilty to the charges at Southwark Crown Court

February
1 Fred Goodwin joined the ranks of Robert Mugabe and Nicolae Ceausescu when his knighthood was removed by order of the Queen. The step was taken on the advice of a secretive Whitehall body responsible for the integrity of the honours system. The Forfeiture Committee

decided Mr Goodwin had brought the system into disrepute and his actions as Royal Bank of Scotland boss made it an exceptional case that merited him joining a shamed group of former dictators and criminals who have lost honours. The Cabinet Office said RBS's failure helped 'trigger the worst recession in the UK since the Second World War'. 'Fred Goodwin was the dominant decision maker at RBS at the time,' a statement added. 'The retention of a knighthood for services to banking could not be sustained.'

2 David Choe, a Korean-American graffiti artist who painted Facebook's offices, is set to become a multi-millionaire when the social network begins trading as a public company. Mr Choe, who first spray-painted the walls of Facebook HQ in 2005, accepted shares in payment for his work. Now the site is planning to float on the stock market, his share could be worth around $200m (£126m).

3 Energy Secretary Chris Huhne resigned following allegations by his ex-wife that she accepted speeding points on his behalf dating back to 2003. The Lib Dem MP and his ex-wife will face the charges of perverting the course of justice in court on March 2nd.
Cezanne's *The Card Players* became the world's most expensive artwork smashing the previous record of £88.7m for a Jackson Pollock. The 1890's painting was bought by the oil-rich Qatari royal family, who already own Harrods and the London Olympic Village, for £158m.

4 Six people were arrested during a protest at the Syrian embassy in London following reports of more than 200 people being killed by shelling in the Syrian city of Homs.

12 At the 54th Annual Grammy Awards, held at the Staples Center in Los Angeles, British vocalist, Adele, tied Beyoncé's record for most wins by a female artist in one night by walking away with six awards: Album of the Year and Best Pop Vocal Album for "21"; Record of the Year, Best Short Form Music Video and Song of the Year for "Rolling in Deep"; and Best Pop Solo Performance for "Someone Like You".

13 Extremist Muslim cleric Abu Qatada, once described as Osama bin Laden's right-hand man in Europe, was released from a British prison amid an outcry over security fears.

17 Jean-Claude Baumgartner, 50, who duped Peter Jones and Theo Paphitis into handing over £230,000 to develop a satnav for skiers, was jailed for two years and eight months. The Dragon's Den conman backed up his claim of a successful business on the reality show by falsifying emails and letters.

22 American journalist Marie Colvin who has worked for the British newspaper *The Sunday Times* since 1985 was killed while covering the siege of Homs in Syria. Colvin and award-winning French photographer Rémi Ochlik were killed by a rocket, while fleeing a temporary media building which was being shelled by the Syrian Army. The intrepid reporter was famous for her eye patch after losing the sight in her left eye due to a blast by a Sri Lankan Army rocket-propelled grenade on 16 April 2001 while crossing from a LTTE controlled area to a Government controlled area.

24 Chandra Bahadur Dangi, 72, at 21.5in (54.6cm) tall, entered the *Guinness World Records* as the shortest person in history. The Nepalese pensioner has a normal-sized head but an incredibly short body.

26 Following the demise of the *News of the World*, News International's best-selling newspaper, *The Sun*, went on sale on a Sunday for the first time.

27 The National Farmers' Union announced that 74 farms have been hit with the Schmallenberg virus this year. The virus, thought to have been spread from Germany by midges, attacks cattle but mainly lambs; the symptoms being deformities at birth and ultimately death.
Charlotte Church and her parents were awarded £600,000 damages and costs for having their phones hacked by the News of the World.

28 Barclays PLC revealed that it is the bank targeted by the British Treasury's action to shut down two methods of avoiding tax, a change in the law that could cost the bank up to 500 million pounds ($800 million). Insisting that its methods complied with existing law, Barclays said it had voluntarily informed tax officials that it had merely repurchased some of its debt "in a tax-efficient manner."

29 Davy Jones, the British member of the iconic manufactured 1960's pop group *The Monkees* (often cited as the first-ever boy band), died of a heart-attack in Florida.
PC David Rathband, who was shot and blinded by Raoul Moat in July 2010, was found dead at his home in an apparent suicide.
James Murdoch resigned as executive chairman of News International amid the phone hacking scandal that closed down the News of the World.

March

6 On the so-called Super Tuesday (the day on which the largest simultaneous number of state presidential primary elections are held in the United States) leading Republican candidate Mitt Romney, the former Governor of Massachusetts, won six of the 10 states that held primaries and caucuses i.e. Alaska, Idaho, Massachusetts, Ohio, Vermont and Virginia. His main rival, Rick Santorum, former senator of Pennsylvania, won three; North Dakota, Oklahoma and Tennessee while Newt Gingrich, the former Speaker of the U.S. House of Representatives, won Georgia. The fourth Republican candidate, Ron Paul, placed well in all ten states. The Democrats had races in seven states, six of which had Barack Obama as the sole candidate. Only Oklahoma had a competitive race although the outcome was an overwhelming victory for the incumbent President.

9 A headless and limbless torso dragged from Regent's Canal in London was identified as actress Gemma McCluskie, 29, who played Kerry Skinner in *Eastenders* in 2001. Her elder brother, Tony McCluskie, 35, was charged with the murder.

11 A Lhasa Apso called Elizabeth won Best in Show at Crufts at the Birmingham NEC.

14 Encyclopaedia Britannica announced it is to stop publishing print editions of its flagship encyclopaedia for the first time since the sets were originally published more than 200 years ago. The book-form of *Encyclopaedia Britannica* has been in print since it was first published in Edinburgh in 1768. It will stop being available when the current stock runs out, the company says. The Chicago-based company will continue to offer digital versions of the encyclopaedia.

15 A British boy, 11-year-old Sebastian Bowles, was among 22 children who died following a coach accident inside the Tunnel de Geronde near the town of Sierre in Switzerland.

16 Rowan Williams announced he is to step down as archbishop of Canterbury at the end of 2012 to take up a university position at Cambridge. Asked about his possible successor Mr Williams commented "It is a job of immense demands and I would hope that my successor has the constitution of an ox and the skin of a rhinoceros".
American actor George Clooney was arrested outside the Sudanese embassy in Washington DC whilst protesting against Sudan's president Omar al-Bashir's blockage of aid from the area near the border with South Sudan.

18 Apple, maker of the iPhone, iPad and iMac, overtook search-engine giant Google to become the world's most valuable brand. Microsoft placed third on the list closely followed by IBM. The top British company, Vodafone, placed 9th on the list.

20 The key points of the coalition government's 2012 Budget include a reduction in the 50p income tax rate for anyone earning more than £150,000 a year (this will be reduced to 45p from April 2013), a rise in personal allowance from £8,105 to £9,205 (also from April 2013) and an immediate 1% cut in corporation tax to 24% which will decrease to 22% by April 2014.

31 Burma's Nobel laureate Aung San Suu Kyi won a by-election for parliament, after a landmark vote gave her pro-democracy party its first foothold in government.

April

2 Leader of the national league for democracy Aung San Suu Kyi called for political unity as her party took 40 of the 44 seats it contested in the Burmese by-elections.

4 Jaguar announced that the long-awaited successor to the E-Type will go on sale next year. The 180mph F-Type will come in convertible and coupe versions with prices starting at £60,000. Powered by a three-litre turbo-charged V6 engine, it will shoot from 0-60mph in under five seconds.

6 A ban on tobacco displays in large shops and supermarkets came into force in England.

11 A looter who boasted 'I burned Reeves Corner' minutes after he set fire to a144-year-old furniture store in Croydon in August 2011, was sentenced to 11-and-a-half years in prison. Gordon Thompson, 34, used a cigarette lighter to set fire to a sofa in the window of the store which forced Monika Konczyk, who lived opposite, to jump from an upstairs window to escape the flames. The picture of her leap to safety set against the flames was beamed worldwide.

19 Politician Ann Widdecombe made her stage debut in Donizetti's comic opera *La Fille du Regiment* at the Royal Opera House. The 10-minute spoken role was most recently played by comedienne Dawn French. This opera is famous for the aria "Ah! mes amis, quel jour de fête!" (sometimes referred to as "Pour mon âme"), which has been called the "Mount Everest" for tenors. It features nine high Cs and comes comparatively early in the opera, giving the singer less time to warm up his voice. Luciano Pavarotti's stardom is reckoned from a

performance alongside Joan Sutherland at the Met, when he "leapt over the "Becher's Brook" of the string of high Cs with an aplomb that left everyone gasping."

27 BT announced the sale of sixty newly refurbished K6 telephone booths. The classic red cast iron boxes, designed by Sir Giles Gilbert Scott in 1936 for King George V's Silver Jubilee, will go on sale for £1,950 plus VAT and delivery.

30 Ironically, in the month the Government announced an official drought and instigated a hosepipe ban, April turned out to be the wettest on record.

May

3 Despite losing 405 council seats nationally, the Conservative Party could at least celebrate the victory of Boris Johnson over Ken Livingstone in the London mayorial election.

6 Socialist Francois Hollande won 52 percent of the vote to defeat the incumbent Nicolas Sarkozy in the presidential runoff, dominated by the eurozone crisis and unemployment.

8 Claire Lomas, 32, became the first person to complete a marathon with a bionic suit that enables the paralysed jewellery designer to walk. Claire finished the London Marathon after 16 days.

12 ITV's annual *Britain's Got Talent* series and £500,000 prize money was won by Ashleigh Butler, 17, and her performing dog, Pudsey.

15 Former News International boss Rebekah Brooks, 43, was charged with perverting the course of justice over the phone hacking enquiry and also stands accused of removing seven boxes of material from the News International archive. Her husband, racehorse trainer Charlie Brooks was also charged on two counts.

17 Sir Elton John marked the 40th anniversary of his hit *Rocket Man* by recording a special version for astronauts in space. The singer performed the ballad at his Million Dollar Piano Show in Las Vegas on 17 April - 40 years after it was released - and beamed the video to the International Space Station. He made the gesture after learning Dutch crew member Andre Kuipers is a big fan of the space-themed track, and regularly played it over the craft's airwaves.

18 Facebook was floated on the stock exchange with an opening valuation of $104bn (£66bn). Pop musician Bono's investment company stands to gain approximately £1 billion after purchasing a small interest in the social networking company in 2009.

19 Facebook founder and CEO Mark Zuckerberg updated his status to "married" after he and 27-year-old Priscilla Chan tied the knot at a small ceremony at his Palo Alto, California home.

20 The Surrey town of Staines officially changed its name to Staines-upon-Thames in an attempt to boost its riverside image. Councillors voted for the change last year after the town became synonymous with Sacha Baron Cohen's spoof rapper Ali G. The name officially changed at 14:00 BST and followed a day of celebrations, including a regatta, in the town.
Lockerbie bomber Abdelbaset Ali al-Megrahi, the only person convicted over the 1988 bombing of Pan Am flight 103 that killed a total of 270 people on board over the Scottish town where wreckage fell, died in Tripoli almost three years after he was freed from prison on compassionate grounds.

22 European judges defied Parliament by ordering Britain to give thousands of prisoners the vote. The unelected justices in Strasbourg backed a ruling declaring that the UK's blanket ban on lags voting breaches human rights. The decision — overwhelmingly opposed by MPs from all sides — could allow killers, rapists and thugs held in jails like London's Wormwood Scrubs to take part in elections.

26 Bookies' favourite Loreen triumphed for Sweden at the 57th Eurovision Song Contest, with her club track *Euphoria.* British entry Engelbert Humperdinck, 76, who opened the contest in Baku, with his ballad *Love Will Set You Free*, finished second from last. Ireland, who were represented by Jedward for the second year in a row, came 19th of the 26 finalists with their song *Waterline.*

29 Mitt Romney, the former Massachusetts governor, clinched the Republican nomination after scoring a big victory in Texas to secure the 1,144 delegates required to secure the GOP nomination for president.
Jacqueline Woodhouse, 42, was jailed for 21 weeks at Westminster Magistrates' Court for racially aggravated harassment. Woodhouse was also banned from using the Tube for five years following a drunken tirade targeted against black and Asian passengers that was witnessed by thousands when it went viral online.

30 The parents of six children killed in a house fire were remanded into custody at Crown Court today charged with their murder. Mick Philpott, 55, and his wife Mairead, 31, appeared at Nottingham Crown Court charged with murder following the blaze at the house on Victory Road in Allenton, Derby, on May 11. Their children Jade (10), and brothers John (9), Jack (7), Jessie (6), and Jayden (5) all died in the fire, and a sixth sibling Duwayne (13) died of his injuries in Birmingham Children's Hospital two days later.
Charles Taylor, the former Liberian president, was sentenced to 50 years in prison for aiding war crimes, in a judgment that sets a precedent for cases against heads of state who violate international law. After a five-year trial, the Special Court for Sierra Leone in The Hague convicted Mr Taylor on 11 charges of aiding and abetting rebel militias who committed vicious atrocities during the civil war in the west African country from 1998 to 2002. Mr Taylor supported the rebels, planned operations with them, and provided them with ammunition in exchange for blood diamonds from Sierra Leone's rich mines. Richard Lussick of Samoa, the presiding judge, noted when delivering the sentence that Mr Taylor's status as a head of state was an aggravating factor when considering the sentence.

June

2 Leanne Mitchell was crowned the winner of the BBC1 reality show, *The Voice.* Mentored by Sir Tom Jones, the 28-year-old singer from Lowestoft, Suffolk beat hot favourite Bo Bruce to land the £500,000 recording contract with Universal.

3 Recruitment manager and part time wrestler, Ricky Martin, won the BBC's *The Apprentice* with its £250,000 prize and partnership with Lord Sugar.

4 Canadian porn actor Luka Magnotta, 29, suspected of murdering and dismembering a Chinese student and mailing his body parts to Canada's top political parties, was reading about himself on the Internet when he was arrested at a cafe in Berlin.

5 The Jubilee celebrations, celebrating Her Majesty the Queen's 60 year reign, came to a frenzied climax as the Queen was met with a huge outpouring of adoration from a sea of people head-to-toe in red, white and blue who gathered below the balcony at Buckingham Palace. In what was the crowning event of a spectacular Bank Holiday weekend that saw one million people descend on a rainy London, a huge crowd sung themselves hoarse with a rousing rendition of *Land of Hope and Glory* and *God Save the Queen* as they marched to the gates of the Palace to watch the Royal Family acknowledge their affection. The Queen emerged to a deafening roar flanked by the Duke and Duchess of Cambridge, Prince Harry, Camilla and Prince Charles. The only senior member of the Firm missing was Prince Philip, who remains in hospital after being taken ill with a bladder infection hours before the previous evening's star-studded Jubilee concert, organised by Gary Barlow and set against the spectacular backdrop of Buckingham Palace.

9 Spain joined Greece, Ireland and Portugal in bowing to need for aid to survive the European debt crisis.
Prince Philip left hospital after recovering from a bladder infection.

12 An Australian coroner ruled that that a dingo - or dingoes - killed nine-week-old Azaria Chamberlain during a family camping trip to the Australian outback in 1982. The famous *Dingo Ate My Baby* headlines streamed around the world when the baby went missing prompted a Hollywood film (*A Cry in the Dark*) starring Meryl Streep and Azaria's mother Lindy served five years in jail for murdering her baby.

13 Texan banker Allen Stanford, who rose to prominence outside the US when he bankrolled international cricket competitions in the UK and Caribbean, was sentenced to 110 years in jail for operating a Ponzi scheme that defrauded investors of more than $7bn (£4.5bn).

14 *Usual Suspects* star Stephen Baldwin lost a highly publicised court battle to onetime business partner Kevin Costner, whom Baldwin accused of defrauding him and a friend over the sale of oil-cleanup technology to BP in the wake of the massive Gulf of Mexico oil spill in 2010.

15 Actor and director Kenneth Branagh and songwriter and television presenter Richard Stilgoe were knighted in the Queen's Birthday Honours list.

16 Prince William was presented with the Order of the Thistle, the highest honour in Scotland, in a bid to strengthen the Royal Family's ties north of the border. The move officially comes as part of his 30th birthday celebrations – but the timing ahead of a proposed referendum on Scottish independence in 2014 is thought to show the Queen's love and respect for her Scottish subjects.

Burmese pro-democracy leader Aung San Suu Kyi delivered her Nobel acceptance speech in Oslo more than two decades after it was awarded. Given the prize in 1991 – but by then under house arrest by Burma's military junta – it was left to her two sons, Alexander and Kim, to travel to Norway to receive the peace prize that year.

18 A curfew, between 9pm and 6am, came into force in Bangor, Gwynedd, affecting anyone under 16 not with an adult. The desperate remedy was instigated on a six-month trial after complaints from locals that they felt intimidated by gangs of youths.

24 Mohamed Morsi became Egypt's first democratically elected president although until a new constitution is written the Supreme Council of the Armed Forces (SCAF) will continue to maintain widespread control over the country just as it has since Hosni Mubarak's 30-year rule succumbed to a popular revolt last year.

27 Another milestone was reached in Northern Ireland's history as Queen Elizabeth II shook hands with former IRA commander turned Deputy First Minister Martin McGuinness at Belfast's Lyric Theatre.

July

3 On the day that Bob Diamond resigned as chief executive of Barclays after the bank admitted to rigging the London InterBank Offered Rate (LIBOR), Marcus Agius returned as chairman. Barclays agreed to pay US and British regulators $450 million dollars in penalties to settle the interest rate rigging scandal at the bank.

4 Scientists confirmed the discovery of a new subatomic particle that is consistent with the long-sought-after Higgs boson.

10 The body of Eva Rausing, 48, the wife of billionaire Hans Kristian Rausing whose family built the Tetra-Pak cartons empire, was found at Cadogan Place, Belgravia.

17 *Rogue Traders* TV star Dan Penteado was jailed for three months for fiddling nearly £25,000 in benefits, ironically while working for the BBC tracking down villains.

18 The world's most wanted Nazi, Ladislaus Csizsik-Csatary, was arrested in the Hungarian capital of Budapest. The 97-year-old war criminal is thought to have been responsible for the deportation of 15,700 Jews to Nazi death camps.

19 Defence Secretary Philip Hammond took delivery of the new F-35 Joint Strike Fighter at a ceremony in Fort Worth, Texas. The first of the UK's next generation stealth combat Short Take Off and Vertical Landing (STOVL) F-35 Joint Strike Fighters, manufactured by Lockheed Martin, will be known as Lightning II.

20 James Eagan, 24, was arrested on suspicion of killing 12 people and injuring 58 others in a shooting spree carried out in Theatre 9 at the Century 16's movie theatre during the midnight premier of Christopher Nolan's Batman movie *The Dark Knight Rises* in Aurora, a suburb of Denver, Colorado, USA. The PhD student in neuroscience at the University of Colorado-Denver dyed his hair red to resemble the Batman arch-villain The Joker and booby trapped his home in a carefully planned crime.

21 Eleven years after its launch, the British videogame *RuneScape* became the most popular in history with 200 million registered players. The free-to-play game, developed by Cambridge company Jagex, sees players travel through medieval kingdoms via magic spells or on ships in the fantasy world of Gielinor.

25 Ben Forster was crowned ITV's 'Superstar' after securing the role of Jesus in a new arena tour of the Andrew Lloyd Webber musical. Although Lord Webber and his panel of experts Mel C, Jason Donovan and Dawn French had input into the finalists it was the viewing public that ultimately chose the Sunderland-born singer as the winner. Former G4 singer Jonathan Ansell was controversially sent home early in the competition.

31 The world's biggest ever blackout brought half of India to a standstill, as a catastrophic power outage left 670 million people without electricity.

August

1 Hans Kristian Rausing, who failed to report the death of his wife, was sentenced to a 10-month suspended jail sentence that will require him to receive extensive treatment at a drug rehabilitation centre, plus a two-month suspended sentence for driving under the influence of drugs. For more than two months, the billionaire went about his business while the corpse of his wife Eva decomposed in their luxury home in central London. But the macabre pretense was dropped on July 9 when London police stopped Hans Kristian for driving erratically and, after finding drugs, searched his home. They found Eva's body in a fly-filled room under a pile of clothing and garbage bags that had been taped together. Her husband had used deodorizing power to try to minimize the smell.

6 In a triumphant technological tour de force by NASA, a plutonium-powered rover (aptly named *Curiosity*) the size of a small car was lowered at the end of 25-foot-long cables from a hovering rocket stage onto the surface of Mars on a quest for signs of whether the Earth's neighbour has evidence of past and present habitable environments. Only one other country, the Soviet Union, has successfully landed anything on Mars, and that spacecraft, *Mars 3* in 1971, fell silent shortly after landing.

10 A missing 12-year-old, Tia Sharp, was found dead in the loft of her gran's home in New Addington, near Croydon, south London.

17 Three members of Russian punk band Pussy Riot were jailed for two years after staging an anti-Vladimir Putin protest in a Moscow cathedral.

22 Tragic "locked in" victim Tony Nicklinson, 58, died after refusing food since he lost a legal battle to allow him to end his life.

23 Gang leader Ben Westwood, 33, was jailed for nine years for burglary offences and escaping the scene of a crime at a record 180 mph in a stolen Audi RS5.

24 Pictures of Prince Harry cavorting naked around a hotel room in Las Vegas emerged on a US celebrity website two days ago in clear breach of the prince's privacy. UK media sources refrained from printing the pictures initially but despite warnings from the Royal Family's lawyers the *Irish Herald* depicted the images yesterday and *The Sun* followed suit today.

South Korean firm Samsung was ordered to pay £632million in damages to Apple for copying products of the US technology giant. The decision of the Californian court sent shockwaves through the smartphone and tablet markets amid fears of an Apple monopoly of the market.

Norwegian right-wing fanatic Anders Breivik, 33, was declared sane and sentenced to 21 years in jail for his car bombing and shooting spree that left 77 dead in July 2011.

September

3 Prince Andrew Duke of York abseiled 785ft down the *London Shard*, at 1,016ft the tallest tower in Europe.

4 David Cameron reshuffled his cabinet, making thirteen changes in total - Grant Shapps replaced Baroness Warsi as Conservative party chairman, Andrew Mitchell replaced Patrick McLoughlin as Chief Whip, Maria Miller replaced Jeremy Hunt as Culture Secretary, Owen Paterson replaced Caroline Spelman as Environment Secretary, Chris Grayling replaced Kenneth Clarke as Justice Secretary, Jeremy Hunt replaced Andrew Lansley as Health Secretary, Justine Greening replaced Andrew Mitchell as International Development Secretary, Andrew Lansley replaced George Young as Leader of the Commons, David Jones replaced Cheryl Gillan as Welsh Secretary, Patrick McLoughlin replaced Justine Greening as Transport Secretary, Theresa Villiers replaced Owen Paterson as Northern Ireland Secretary, Kenneth Clarke was given the new position of Minister without Portfolio and Sayeeda Warsi similarly was given the new position of Senior Minister of State at the Foreign Office and Minister for Faith and Communities.

10 Three people were killed when a coach hit a tree on the A3 near Hindhead Tunnel in surrey en-route to Merseyside from the Bestival music festival on the Isle of Wight.

12 The 314ft high clock tower housing the 13.7 ton bell universally known as *Big Ben*, was renamed *Elizabeth Tower* to mark the Queen's 60 years on the throne. The historic name change, which came about after politicians backed a campaign by Conservative MP Tobias Ellwood, was officially made in Parliament by the House of Commons Speaker John Bercow.

14 French magazine, *Closer*, published exclusive pictures of the Duchess of Cambridge topless on the terrace of a private chateau owned by the Queen's nephew Lord Linley.

17 Education Secretary Michael Gove announced the replacement of GCSEs by a tougher "English Baccalaureate Certificate" which will be implemented in 2015.

18 Two unarmed female police officers were killed in a gun and grenade attack in Greater Manchester. PC Nicola Hughes, 23, and PC Fiona Bone, 32, were called to Abbey Gardens in Mottram to investigate what turned out to be a false report of a burglary. Dale Cregan, 29, later walked into Hyde police station and was detained in connection with the officers' deaths and two previous murders.

20 Chief Whip Andrew Mitchell stood accused of calling Downing Street security police "plebs" during a bad-tempered exchange.
23 The Deputy Prime Minister Nick Clegg entered the charts at number 143 with the spoof apology song (over university tuition fees) - *Nick Clegg Says I'm Sorry* - after the Liberal Democrat leader gave permission to the track's creator, satirical website www.thepoke.co.uk, to release it as a single. All profits from the song's success will be given to Sheffield Children's NHS Foundation Trust, of which his wife Miriam is a patron.
24 Nick Grimshaw replaced Chris Moyles as presenter of Radio 1's Breakfast Show.
28 A 15-year-old schoolgirl Megan Stammers, who ran off to France with her 30-year-old maths teacher Jeremy Foster, was found walking hand-in-hand with Foster in Bordeaux.

October
1 April Jones, a five-year-old who suffers from cerebral palsy, was believed to have been lured into a vehicle near her home in Machynlleth, Mid Wales. Police immediately began a search for her body and arrested a suspect.
3 Tesco announced its first trading loss in almost 20 years.
5 Islamic cleric Abu Hamza al- Masri was finally extradited from Britain after an eight-year battle.
6 Abu Hamza, whose fiery sermons allegedly inspired one of the September 11th 2001 plotters, was flown into the United States from RAF Mildenhall, Suffolk. Hamza later appeared in court in New York minus the hook that he has used since his hands were blown off by a bomb.
7 British scientist Sir John Gurdon, 79, was awarded the Nobel Prize for Physiology or Medicine for his work, carried out in 1962 when he was a student, concerning cells and their ability to be reprogrammed into a more immature state resulting in cloning.
9 Comedian Justin Lee Collins was found guilty of harassing ex-girlfriend Anna Larke and sentenced to 140 hours' community service and ordered to pay £3,500 in court fees.
12 Blind grandfather Colin Farmer, 61, was shot with a 50,000 volt Taser and then handcuffed behind his back despite yelling at a police officer "I'm blind, I'm blind". The shocking mistake was made after police were alerted that a man was on the loose with a sword. The attack on the retired architect took place in Chorley after the policeman apparently mistook Mr Farmer's white stick for a Samurai sword.
14 Austrian Felix Baumgartner, 43, skydived from a balloon 24 miles above sea level and in the process broke the sound barrier hitting 833.9mph on his descent.
16 Gary McKinnon, the 46-year-old autism sufferer who hacked into top secret computer systems at the Pentagon and Nasa from a North London house ten years ago, was saved from extradition by Home Secretary Theresa May as there was a "high risk" McKinnon would kill himself if he faced trial in America.
Seven paintings worth around £100million, including works by Picasso and Monet, were stolen from the Kunsthal Museum in the Dutch city of Rotterdam after thieves broke in at 3am.
Hilary Mantel became the first British author, and the first woman, to win the Man Booker Prize twice. Her best-selling novel, *Bring Up the Bodies*, beat five other titles and followed her success with *Wolf Hall* in 2009.
17 *Verity*, a controversial 66ft statue of a pregnant woman by artist Damien Hirst was unveiled in the seaside town of Ilfracombe, Devon, where it received a mixed reception from residents. The figure's stance is taken from Edgar Degas's late 19th century *Little Dancer of Fourteen Years* and is referenced by Hirst in his earlier bronze, *Virgin Mother*, from 2005. Verity holds the traditional symbols denoting justice - a sword and scales. The scales are hidden and off balance behind her back while the sword is held confidently in her upstretched arm.
19 On the day that Chancellor of the Exchequer George Osborne stood accused of travelling in a train's first class compartment when only having a standard ticket, Andrew Mitchell quit as chief whip, abandoning a month-long fight to save his career and fend off claims that he had referred to a police officer as a "pleb".
24 Hurricane Sandy, the largest Atlantic hurricane in diameter on record, began to devastate the Caribbean and the east coast of North America.
29 Hurricane Sandy, now officially designated a superstorm, entered the USA via New Jersey and wreaked havoc in surrounding areas, New York City almost grinding to a standstill.

November
1 Comet, the High Street electrical chain, collapsed into administration.
2 Senior Labour MP Denis MacShane quit as a Commons committee found him guilty of bogus expense claims.
3 The death toll from Sandy rose to almost 200 across North America and the Caribbean.
7 President Barack Obama was re-elected for a second term, defeating Republican challenger Mitt Romney. The Democrats retained their majority in the Senate, which they have held since 2007, and the Republicans kept control of the House of Representatives, which analysts fear could result in more of the gridlock that characterised Mr Obama's first term of office.
9 Old Etonian and Cambridge graduate Justin Welby, a former oil executive who was made a bishop just over a year ago, was confirmed as the next Archbishop of Canterbury. The 56-year-old Bishop of Durham will succeed Rowan Williams officially in a ceremony at Canterbury Cathedral on March 21st 2013.
11 The BBC's director general, George Entwistle, resigned after a BBC Newsnight film alleged child abuse by an unnamed Conservative politician - which was proved to be unfounded.
13 Terror suspect Abu Qatada was freed by a British judge who ruled that he could not be deported to Jordan - where he faces trial.
20 City trader Kweku Adoboli was jailed for seven years for perpetuating fraud resulting in the largest trading loss in British banking history - a total of £1.4billion.
21 The chief executive of the Royal Opera House and the BBC's former director of news, Tony Hall, was appointed the corporation's new director general.
27 Cyril Smith, former MP for Rochdale, Greater Manchester, who died two years ago aged 82, was accused of abusing children in care homes, although investigated three times by police but never charged with any offence.
29 SAS sniper Danny Nightingale, 37, who had been sentenced to 18 months military detention after pleading guilty to unlawfully possessing a Glock 9mm pistol and a large amount of ammunition, was freed by the Court of Appeal and his sentence reduced to 12-months suspended.

December
5 The former *It's A Knockout* presenter and football pundit Stuart Hall was the latest celebrity arrested in the police investigation into sexual abuse of young girls. Other celebrities investigated include Gary Glitter, Freddie Starr and Dave Lee Travis.
6 John McAfee, the founder of anti-virus software maker McAfee, was arrested for entering Guatemala illegally and is now expected to be deported to Belize, where police want to question him over the death of his neighbour.
PR guru Max Clifford was arrested in connection with sex offences dating back to 1977.
Starbucks, vowed to fork out £20m in tax over the next two years irrespective of profitability. The US coffee giant has recently been criticised along with Amazon.com and Google for legally dodging corporation tax in recent years.
7 Jacintha Saldanha, 46, committed suicide after transferring a prank call from Michael Christian and Mel Greig (two DJs from Sydney's 2Day FM radio station who made the call posing as Queen Elizabeth II and Prince Charles) to a colleague who described in detail the condition of the Duchess of Cambridge during her hospital stay for severe pregnancy sickness. Later, Jacintha was found hanging in her nurses' quarters at King Edward VII's Hospital by a colleague and a security guard.
9 James Arthur from Saltburn by the Sea in north Yorkshire won the *X Factor* final, beating favourite Jahmene Douglas to win the opportunity to compete for the Christmas No 1 spot.
12 Pope Benedict XVI sent his first tweet at the Twitter address @pontifex. It read: 'Dear friends, I am pleased to get in touch with you through Twitter. Thank you for your generous response. I bless all of you from my heart.'
14 Adam Lanza, 20, shot his mother in the head several times before heading to Sandy Hook Elementary School, Newtown, Fairfield County, Connecticut, where he killed 20 children and six adults, before taking his own life.
19 The top boys' name for 2012 was Harry and the top girls' name, Amelia

23 The Justice Collective's Hillsborough tribute single, *He Ain't Heavy, He's My Brother*, landed the top spot on the Official Christmas Singles Chart with sales of over 269,000.
29 Cyclist Bradley Wiggins and sailor Ben Ainslie received knighthoods in the New Year Honours while Paralympic cyclist Sarah Storey was awarded with a DBE. The illustrator Quentin Blake, famous for the Roald Dahl books, was also knighted.
30 James Arthur returned to the top of the charts with Impossible after being knocked off the top spot by the all-star Justice Collective over Christmas.
31 Lostprophets singer, Ian Watkins, 35, was remanded in custody until March 11th, accused of conspiracy to rape a one-year-old girl among other charges.

Sporting Record 2012

January

1 In two rivetting semi-finals in the PDC World Darts Championship at Alexandra Palace, Andy Hamilton beat Simon Whitlock 6-5 and current world champion Adrian Lewis came from 5 sets to one down against James Wade to also win 6-5, after Wade had a dart to take the match 6-3.
2 Adrian Lewis retained his World Darts Championship with a 7-3 victory over Andy Hamilton.
9 Thierry Henry capped his fairytale return to Arsenal by scoring the winning goal in the 1-0 victory over Leeds in the FA Cup 3rd round tie at the Emirates.
13 Amir Khan was granted a rematch with Lamont Peterson after the controversial decision in Washington DC last month.
15 Christian Kist completed a remarkable Lakeside debut by beating Tony O'Shea to take the BDO world darts title. Qualifier Kist, a road worker from the Netherlands, entered the tournament as a rank outsider. But the 25-year-old defeated O'Shea 7-5 in a thrilling final to win the £100,000 prize, reported to be 50 times his career earnings to date. Kist becomes the first non-English-speaking winner of a world darts title.
17 Andy Murray won his first round match at the Australian Open in Melbourne in four sets with new coach Ivan Lendl looking on and seemingly preventing Murray from adopting his usual prickly attitude and rantings at the player's box.
Pakistan spinner Saeed Ajmal took seven wickets to send England crashing to 192 all out on the first day of the first Test in Dubai.
19 Pakistan trounced England by 10 wickets in the first of three Test matches in Dubai to take a 1-0 lead in the series.
27 Andy Murray was beaten 6-3, 3-6, 6-7, 6-1, 7-5 by Novak Djokovic in the semi-finals of the Australian Open in Melbourne.
28 England were again humiliated by Pakistan in the second Test in Abu Dhabi. Requiring only 145 runs for victory in their second innings they were bowled out for a paltry 72.
Belarussian Victoria Azarenka beat Maria Sharapova 6-3, 6-0 to win the Australian Open.
In the only major shock of the FA Cup 4th round, Crawley Town beat Championship title contenders Hull 1-0 to emulate last year's feat of reaching the fifth round.
29 In a titanic match, Novak Djokovic beat Rafael Nadal 5-7 6-4 6-2 6-7 7-5 to defend his Australian Open title.
England's Robert Rock won the Abu Dhabi HSBC Championship after being paired with Tiger Woods for the final round.
Barry Hawkins won the second annual snooker shoot-out event in Blackpool.
30 Chris Robshaw, the 25-year-old Harlequins flanker, was announced as the new England rugby union captain.

February

1 Egyptian security forces were accused of standing by and doing nothing during a pitch invasion at a football match which left at least 74 people dead. Fans rushed onto the field in the seaside city of Port Said after the home team, Al Masry, beat Egypt's top club, the Cairo-based Al Ahly, 3-1, setting off clashes and a stampede. The melee after the league match was the worst case of football violence in the country and the deadliest worldwide since 1996. Interior Minister Mohammed Ibrahim told state TV that 13,000 Al Masry fans had stormed the field to attack around 1,200 Al-Ahly fans. A government spokesman said the massacre was carried out as a reprisal for the ousting of President Mubarak. A further 12 people were reported dead following the match as protesters clashed with police in Suez and in the capital's Tahrir Square.
3 John Terry was stripped of the England captaincy by the FA over his criminal charge for racially abusing Anton Ferdinand.
4 In the first matches of the 2012 Six Nations, France gave new boss Philippe Saint-Andre the perfect start as they avenged last year's humbling Six Nations defeat by Italy with a comfortable 30-12 victory in Paris. Stuart Lancaster's England team beat Scotland 13-6 in the Calcutta Cut match at Twickenham.
5 Wales chalked up a third consecutive win over Ireland thanks to a penalty by the stand-in kicker Leigh Halfpenny 13 seconds from time which gave them a 23-21 victory in Dublin.
6 Pakistan condemned England to their first Test series whitewash since the 2006/07 Ashes with a 71-run victory at the Dubai International Cricket Stadium sealing a 3-0 win overall.
The New York Giants beat New England Patriots 21-17 in a thrilling Super Bowl in Indianapolis. Giants quarterback Eli Manning was named MVP
England, represented by World champion Adrian Lewis and world No 1 Phil Taylor, won the World Cup of Darts after defeating Australia in the deciding leg of the final in Hamburg.
7 The Court of Arbitration for Sport (Cas) banned Alberto Contador for two years for doping. He was stripped of his 2010 Tour de France victory and, with his suspension running until 5 August, will miss this year's Tour and the Olympics. The Spaniard, 29, tested positive for clenbuterol during the 2010 Tour but has maintained that the failed test was a result of eating contaminated meat. Andy Schleck of Luxembourg, who finished second to Contador in the 2010 Tour de France, is set to be elevated to champion.
8 On the day that Spurs manager Harry Redknapp was cleared of tax evasion charges following a two-week trial in London, England manager Fabio Capello resigned in protest at John Terry being stripped of the England captaincy. Stuart Pearce, 49, was named as caretaker manager until a permanent appointment can be made with Redknapp the favourite for the job.
11 Luis Suarez, Liverpool's Uruguayan striker who was banned for eight games after racially abusing Patrice Evra four months ago, refused to shake hands with the Manchester United player before a Premiership clash at Old Trafford in which United won 2-1.
13 England beat Pakistan by 130 runs, captain Alastair Cook top scoring with a magnificent 137.
14 Rangers Football Club entered administration and as a result were automatically docked 10 points, effectively ending its Scottish Premier League challenge.
16 England beat Pakistan by 20 runs in the second One Day International in Abu Dhabi with Alastair Cook making history by scoring successive limited over centuries; the first England captain to perform such a feat.
18 Ding Junhui beat Mark Selby 9-6 in the final of the Welsh Open snooker event in Newport.
Kevin Pietersen scored his first international one-day century in more than three years as England beat Pakistan by nine wickets in Dubai to lead the four-match series 3-0.
19 Dereck Chisora failed to win the WBC heavyweight crown following a points loss to Vitali Klitschko in Munich. Chisora spat water towards Klitschko's brother, Wladimir, moments before the fight and was also involved in a post-fight scuffle with fellow heavyweight David Haye.
21 Kevin Pietersen scored his second successive international one-day century as England beat Pakistan by four wickets in the fourth and final match in Dubai.
26 Liverpool beat Cardiff City 3-2 on penalties in the Carling Cup final at Wembley after normal time finished at 1-1 and extra time at 2-2. Ironically Steven Gerrard missed the first Liverpool penalty but his cousin Anthony Gerrard missed the final penalty that led to Cardiff's defeat.
28 England beat Pakistan in the third Twenty20 international match in Abu Dhabi to take the series 2-1.
Dereck Chisora was hit with an indefinite ban by the WBC following his post-fight brawl with David Haye in Munich nine days ago.

29 England, captained by Spurs midfielder Scott Parker, were beaten 3-2 by Holland in an international friendly football match at Wembley. In other home country friendlies Northern Ireland lost 3-0 to Norway in Belfast, the Republic of Ireland drew 1-1 with the Czech Republic in Dublin, Scotland drew 1-1 with Slovenia in Koper, and Wales lost 1-0 to Costa Rica in Cardiff.

March

3 The Ukrainian heavyweight world champion Wladimir Klitschko, who holds the IBF, IBO, WBO and WBA championships, knocked out Jean-Marc Mormeck in the fourth round to retain his titles in Dusseldorf and claim his 50th knock out in 60 fights.

4 Chelsea sacked their manager Andre Villas-Boas after seven months in the job. The Portuguese ex-Porto boss was replaced temporarily by his assistant Roberto DiMatteo.
Rory McIlroy became World No 1 golfer after winning the Honda Classic at PGA National Resort & Spa in Palm Beach Gardens, Florida. A resurgent Tiger Woods posted a final round eight under par 62 to finish runner-up.
On a good day for Northern Ireland sportsmen Mark Allen won his first ranking title with a 10-1 victory over Stephen Lee in the final of the Haikou World Open in China.
In the Six Nations Championship France drew 17-17 with Ireland in Paris after being 17-6 down at half time.

10 In the Six Nations Championship Ireland beat Scotland 32-14 in Dublin while Wales beat Italy 24-3 in Cardiff.

11 Bradley Wiggins won the final time trial stage of the Paris-Nice to become the first Brit since Tommy Simpson in 1967 to win the overall title.
Team GB finished second in the table to USA at the World Indoor Athletics Championship with a total of nine medals including golds from Yamile Aldama in the triple jump and the women's 4 x 400 team.

13 On the first day of the Cheltenham Festival, Rock On Ruby, ridden by Noel Fehily and trained by Paul Nicholls, won the Champion Hurdle.

14 Finian's Rainbow, ridden by Barry Geraghty and trained by Nicky Henderson, won the Queen Mother Champion Chase at Cheltenham in a controversial finish with last year's winner, Sizing Europe having to swerve around the last fence at the last second after a flag was waved but the fence appeared jumpable.

15 Big Buck's, ridden by Ruby Walsh and trained by Paul Nicholls, won the World Hurdle at Cheltenham for the fourth year running.

16 Synchronised, ridden by AP McCoy and trained by Jonjo O'Neill, won the Cheltenham Gold Cup. Former winners, Kauto Star and Long Run were pulled up and placed third respectively.
India's Sachin Tendulkar became the first player to score 100 international centuries by compiling a ton during a one-day defeat against Bangladesh in Dhaka.

17 Master Overseer, ridden by Tom Scudamore and trained by David Pipe, won the Midlands Grand National at Uttoxeter.
Welsh fans were celebrating a third Six Nations Grand Slam in eight years after Wales beat France 16-9 at the Millennium Stadium. In other matches England beat Ireland 30-9 and Italy beat Scotland 13-6, to condemn them to the wooden spoon.
Fabrice Muamba, the Zaire-born former England youth player, suffered a cardiac arrest during the FA Cup quarter-final at White Hart Lane. The 23-year-old Bolton midfielder was immediately taken into intensive care and the match was abandoned.

18 Jenson Button won the opening F1 race of the season in Melbourne. His McLaren team-mate Lewis Hamilton was pipped for second by world champion Sebastian Vettel in a Red Bull.
England's Luke Donald regained the world No 1 spot he had lost to Rory McIlroy by winning the Transitions Championships in Florida. Donald won the tournament after emerging victorious from a four-way play-off against Jim Furyk, Robert Garrigus and Sang-Moon Bae after the quartet had all finished on 13 under par.

20 Carlos Tevez made his first appearance for Manchester City since last September in the 2-1 Premiership defeat of Chelsea which leaves the Manchester team only a point behind their fierce rivals Manchester United.

25 Fernando Alonso won a rain-affected Malaysian Formula One Grand Prix in Sepang.

29 England's status as the No 1 five-day team came under threat when they lost the first Test against Sri Lanka in Galle, their fourth-successive defeat.

31 Brae Hill, trained by Richard Fahey and ridden by Tony Hamilton, won the Lincoln Handicap at Doncaster. Dr Marwan Kookash, a big supporter of the all-weather racing at Southwell and Wolverhampton, owns the winner of the first big race of the flat season.

April

2 Welsh rugby union player Gavin Henson was sacked by his club Cardiff Blues after a drunken incident resulting in a six months ban from Airline Flybe.

7 England retained their position as the number one team in Test cricket after beating Sri Lanka by eight wickets in Colombo and thus drawing the two-match series. Despite a ten-wicket haul for Graeme Swann the man-of-the-match was Kevin Pietersen with a magnificent first innings 151 scored at almost a run a ball in difficult conditions.
After victory for the men's and women's pursuit teams Britain won its third gold medal at the World Track Championships in Melbourne when Victoria Pendleton picked herself up after crashing in the semi-final to eventually win sprint gold. In a controversial competition Vicky beat hot favourite Anna Meares of Australia in the semi-final and Lithuania's Simona Krupeckaite in the final after both her opponents were penalised for rule infringements.
Cambridge beat Oxford in a bizarre and chaotic University Boat Race which featured an intruder in the River Thames, a broken oar and an ailing oarsman. With Oxford in front at the half-way mark, 35-year-old Trenton Oldfield, a protester against the elitism of the race, was almost hit by the Oxford oars and the race had to be restarted. With Oxford again in front at the start of the re-run a clash of oars between the eights resulted in an Oxford rower snapping an oar which effectively ended the race as a spectacle when umpire John Garrett allowed the race to continue, blaming Oxford for the accident. The drama continued after the line when Oxford rower, Dr Alexander Woods collapsed in distress causing the victory ceremony to be cancelled.

8 American Bubba Watson won the US Masters in a sudden-death play-off with South African Louis Oosthuizen.
Great Britain won three more gold medals at the World Track Championships through Ben Swift in the scratch race, Laura Trott in the women's omnium and Sir Chris Hoy in the keirin.

12 On the opening day of the Aintree Grand National meeting, Big Buck's, ridden by Ruby Walsh and trained by Paul Nicholls, won his 17th-consecutive hurdles race.

14 Neptune Collonges, ridden by Daryl Jacob and trained by Paul Nicholls, won the Grand National but the race was marred by the death of the Gold Cup winner Synchronised who unseated Tony McCoy at Becher's but had to be put down after breaking his leg five fences later. Katie Walsh, the 27-year-old sister of top male jockey Ruby Walsh and daughter of trainer Ted Walsh, placed third on joint favourite Seabass, the highest-ever finish by a woman.
Italian youth footballer Piermario Morosini, 25, died of a heart-attack during a Serie B game at Pescara in which his side, Livorno were leading 2-0.

15 Nico Rosberg took his maiden Formula 1 victory with a dominant drive in the Chinese Grand Prix in Shanghai. The son of Finnish 1982 Formula One World Champion Keke Rosberg, who races for Germany, his mother's country of birth, led all the way in his Mercedes finishing over 20 seconds ahead of second-placed Jenson Button who fell back after a pit-stop error.

21 Kenyans Wilson Kipsang (2:04.44) and Mary Keitany (2:18.37) triumphed in the men's and women's races as 35,970 runners took part in the 2012 London Marathon. Lee Merrien (2:13.41) was the first British man to cross the line and Claire Hallissey (2:27.44) the first British woman. Shelly Woods (1:49.11) triumphed in the women's wheelchair race, adding to her 2007 win. David Weir won the men's wheelchair race to equal Tanni Grey-Thompson's record of six London Marathon victories. He crossed the line in a time of 1:32:23.

22 The Bahrain Grand Prix was won by current world drivers champion Sebastian Vettel to give him the lead in the drivers table and his team, Red Bull, the lead in the constructors table.

28 A week after Claire Squires died during the London Marathon whilst running on behalf of the Samaritans, an avalanche of donations propelled her expected £500 pledge to more than £1m.

30 Manchester City beat local rivals and Premiership leaders Manchester United 1-0 at the City of Manchester Stadium (aka the Etihad Stadium) to return to the top of the table on goal difference with both teams having two matches remaining. Sir Alex Ferguson had a furious row with Roberto Mancini as the match ended, clearly upset that the City manager spent large portions of the match vociferously barking orders to his team and castigating the officials.

May

1 Roy Hodgson, the 64-year-old West Bromwich Albion manager, became the England football boss, signing a four-year deal despite several of the players tweeting their preference for Spurs boss Harry Redknapp. The new manager, who has previously coached the Swiss, Finnish and United Arab Emirates national sides, would not be drawn on who will captain his team.
Seven-time world champion Stephen Hendry, 43, announced his retirement from snooker after a heavy 13-2 quarter-final defeat by Stephen Maguire at the World Championship at the Crucible in Sheffield. Stephen, who made a maximum 147 break during his first round match, apparently made the decision three months ago in order to spend more time with his family.

5 Chelsea beat Liverpool 2-1 in the FA Cup final at Wembley.
Camelot, ridden by J P O'Brien and trained by his father Aidan, won the 2,000 Guineas at Newmarket, the first English Classic of the season.

6 Trainer Aidan O'Brien completed the Guineas double by winning the 1,000 Guineas with his second string, Homecoming Queen, ridden by Ryan Moore, who won by nine lengths. O'Brien's hot favourite, Maybe, finished third.
Rory McIlroy regained his No 1 world golf ranking after losing in a play-off to American Rickie Fowler in the Wells Fargo Championship.

7 Ronnie O'Sullivan won his fourth world snooker championship, beating Ali Carter 18-11 at the Crucible, Sheffield.

8 Sprinter Dwain Chambers and cyclist David Miller were cleared to compete in this year's London Olympics after the Court of Arbitration (CAS) overruled a British Olympic life ban on drug offenders.

9 Atlético Madrid claimed a second Europa League title in three seasons with a commanding 3-0 win over Athletic Bilbao in Bucharest.
Hundreds of Atlético Madrid fans clashed with riot police after police prevented fans from celebrating their team's success at the Neptuno fountain in Madrid.

13 Manchester City won the Premier League title for the first time since 1968. The Blues beat their great rivals Manchester United on goal difference, both clubs ending on 89 points over the 38 games of the season. The stats however cannot tell of the agony that both Roberto Mancini, 47, and then Sir Alex Ferguson, 70, experienced in the dying moments as United beat Sunderland 1-0 away from home and actually finished the game as champions elect only for City to strike twice in injury time to complete a 3-2 home win over Queen's Park Rangers who played most of the second half with ten men after their skipper, Joey Barton was sent off after elbowing Carlos Tevez in the face. Barton then kneed Sergio Aguero in the back and attempted to head-butt Vincent Kompany on his way off the pitch. At the bottom end of the table Bolton, Blackburn and Wolves were relegated.

19 Chelsea beat Bayern Munich 4-3 on penalties in the Champions League final after the match ended 1-1 after normal time and no further goals were scored in extra time. Didier Drogba played a crucial part in the game, conceding a penalty and scoring the equaliser before slotting home the winning penalty. Chelsea goalkeeper Petr Cech also played an important role, saving a penalty in extra time before saving another three in the shoot-out.
Liverpool's David Price claimed the British and Commonwealth heavyweight titles after outclassing Sam Sexton before the referee stopped the fight in the fourth round after Sexton was sent crashing to the canvas.
Savannah Marshall celebrated her 21st birthday by being crowned Britain's first women's world boxing champion. The Hartlepool middleweight triumphed 17-15 over Azerbaijan's Elena Vystropova in Qinhuangdao.
The world's highest rated racehorse, Frankel, trained by Henry Cecil and ridden by Tom Queally, easily won his season opener the Group 1 Lockinge Stakes at Newbury.

20 Jessica Ennis beat the Olympic 100m hurdles champion Dawn Harper in a world class time of 12.75secs at the Great City Games in Manchester only to later have the race voided after organisers laid out nine hurdles instead of the mandatory 10.

21 Alastair Cook and Ian Bell restored order in a century stand which guided England to a five-wicket win over West Indies in the first Investec Test at Lord's after early wickets on the fourth day shifted momentum to the visitors.

23 Joey Barton, the QPR skipper, was banned for 12 games for being sent off and then bringing the game into disrepute during QPR's last match of the season against Manchester City.

26 Blonde Snapper (8-1), trained by Mark Wallis, won the £125,000 williamhill.com Greyhound Derby at Wimbledon.
Nottingham's Carl Froch delivered the performance of his career to destroy IBF world super-middleweight champion Lucian Bute in five rounds. The unbeaten Canadian was outclassed from the first bell before the referee stopped the fight, giving Froch his third world title.
Mark Cavendish missed out on a clean sweep of Grand Tour points jerseys by a single point at the Giro d'Italia. The pink jersey overall winner was Ryder Hesjedal (CAN) and the points winner Joaquim Rodríguez (ESP).
Roy Hodgson's first game in charge of England, a friendly against Norway in Oslo, ended in a 1–0 victory, the first win by an England side against Norway for 32 years

27 Jessica Ennis demolished Denise Lewis's 12-year-old British heptathlon record of 6,831 points with a score of 6,906 whilst winning at the Hypomeeting in Gotzis, Austria.

28 England swept to a nine-wicket victory over West Indies in the second Test at Trent Bridge to wrap up the series with a game to spare.
After the final play-off matches next year's Premiership will see West Ham United joined by Football League Championship winners Reading, and runners-up Southampton, replacing relegated Bolton Wanderers, Blackburn Rovers and Wolverhampton Wanderers.
Portsmouth (who were deducted ten points midway through the season for entering administration), Coventry City, and Doncaster Rovers were relegated from the Championship and replaced by Charlton Athletic, Sheffield Wednesday and Huddersfield Town. Swindon Town, Shrewsbury Town, Crawley Town and Crewe Alexandra were promoted to Football League One whilst Hereford United and Macclesfield Town were relegated to the Conference National. Fleetwood Town and York City were promoted to Football League Two.

31 Kevin Pietersen announced his retirement from one-day international cricket to concentrate on his Test match career.

June

1 Was, ridden by Seamie Heffernan and trained by Aidan O'Brien, won the Epsom Oaks.

2 England beat Belgium 1-0 in an international friendly at Wembley to maintain new manager Roy Hodgson's 100 per cent record.
Camelot, ridden by J P O'Brien and trained by his father Aidan, won the English Derby at Epsom by five lengths and remains on track to become the first colt since Nijinsky to win the Triple Crown. The win also means that Aidan O'Brien has won all four Classics run in Britain this season.

6 Andy Murray was beaten 6-4, 6-7, 6-3, 6-2 by Spaniard David Ferrer in the quarter-finals of the French Open in Paris.

8 Euro 2012 got underway with joint-hosts Poland drawing 1-1 with 2004 champions Greece.

9 Maria Sharapova won her first French Open title after beating Italian 21st seed Sara Errani 6-3 6-2 in the Roland Garros final. The Russian became the 10th woman to complete a career grand slam after she added the Paris title to her triumphs at Wimbledon (2004), U.S. Open (2006) and Australian Open (2008).

10 The WBO announced that Timothy Bradley's controversial split-decision win over Manny Pacquiao in Las Vegas the previous evening was to be reviewed by the World Boxing Organisation. One judge scored the world championship welterweight bout 115-113 to Pacquiao whilst the other two had the undefeated American ahead by the same score, prompting boos around the MGM Grand. It was a first defeat in seven years for Philippines' greatest fighter Pacquiao, who landed 94 more punches than Bradley.
The Republic of Ireland were beaten 3-1 by Croatia in their opening Euro 2012 encounter.
In one of dart's biggest shocks Robert Thornton of Scotland beat Phil Taylor 11-5 in the final of the UK Open.

11 England began their Euro 2012 campaign with a 1-1 draw against France in Donetsk, Ukraine.

13 Harry Redknapp agreed to leave Tottenham after a meeting with Spurs chairman Daniel Levy. A remarkable change of fortune in recent months has seen Redknapp vaunted as the next England manager before adverse results led to Roy Hodgson gaining the job. Despite Redknapp's fine record, billionaire owner Joe Lewis is thought to now want a younger manager.
Andy Murray's recent poor form continued with defeat at Queen's in his first grass court match of the year, 6-3, 6-7, 7-6 to Frenchman Nicolas Mahut.

15 England beat Sweden 3-2 in Kiev in their second group game of Euro 2012.

16 England beat the West Indies by 114 runs in the first One Day International, at the Ageas Bowl, Southampton.

17 American golfer Webb Simpson won the 112th US Open Championship in San Francisco, California.

Croatian Marin Cilic won the Aegon trophy at Queen's after Argentinian David Nalbandian (leading 7-6, 3-4) was disqualified for lashing out at an advertising box which then cut into line judge Andrew McDougall's shin, leaving the official with blood pouring from the wound.

18 Surrey cricketer Tom Maynard died after being hit by a London Underground District Line train on the line near Wimbledon Park Station in south London. The England Lions batsman was fleeing from police after being pulled over in his car for driving erratically.

19 England beat the West Indies by eight wickets in the second One Day International, at the Kia Oval, London.
Roy Hodgson's England team finished top of Group D after their 1-0 win over co-hosts Ukraine, and Sweden's shock 2-0 defeat of second place France.
The world's highest rated racehorse, Frankel, trained by Henry Cecil and ridden by Tom Queally, won the Queen Anne Stakes at Royal Ascot by eleven lengths at the prohibitive odds of 1-10. Many good judges now believe the unbeaten racehorse is an even better miler than the great Brigadier Gerard, who beat Mill Reef by three lengths in the 1971 2000 Guineas.

21 A header by Cristiano Ronaldo gave Portugal a place in the Euro 2012 semi-finals after they beat the Czech Republic 1-0 in their quarter-final in Warsaw.

22 Germany reached the semi-finals of the European Championships for a record seventh time by beating Greece 4-2.

23 Spain beat France 2-0 to book their place in the semi-finals of Euro 2012.
Australian wonder horse Black Caviar, ridden by Luke Nolen and trained by Peter Moody, won his 22nd consecutive race. The 18 August 2006 foal kept his unbeaten record in tact with a dramatic victory in the Diamond Jubilee Stakes at Royal Ascot after Nolen appeared to ease down on the mare and was almost caught on the line by French horse Moonlight Cloud. The world's second highest racehorse (after Frankel) was given a pat on the nose by the Queen in the unsaddling enclosure.
Dwain Chambers won the 100 metres at the British Olympic trials in Birmingham to seal his place in the Olympic team if he runs the 'A' qualifying time of 10.18secs during the European Championships in Helsinki next week.

24 Ireland's Paul Beecher won Hickstead's Carpetright Derby on Loughnatousa WB, beating Derby specialist William Funnell and Dorada in a jump-off, both riders jumping clear in the first round and Beecher going clear for the second time against the clock. Only 55 clear rounds have been jumped in the Derby's 51-year year history and Beecher, uniquely, achieved the 54th from pole position.
England lost on penalties in their quarter-final Euro 2012 clash with Italy after the game ended 0-0 after extra time despite the Italians dominating the match. Missed penalties by Ashley Young and Ashley Cole ultimately cost England a semi-final place.
Shara Proctor broke the British long jump record with a leap of 6.95m to gain victory at the Olympic trials.

25 The Wimbledon tennis championships got underway with Venus Williams losing on day one, 6-1, 6-3 to Russian Elena Vesnina.

28 Rafael Nadal was beaten 6-7, 6-4, 6-4, 2-6, 6-4, by 100th-ranked Lukas Rosol of the Czech Republic in the second round at Wimbledon, his earliest exit from a Grand slam event since 2005.

29 Heather Watson, the first British woman to reach the third round at Wimbledon since 2002, lost 6-0, 6-2 to Agnieszka Radwanska of Poland.
England cricketers beat Australia by 15 runs at Lord's in the first One Day International of the best-of-five series.
Robbie Grabarz became the first British man for 62 years to win the high jump at the European Championships. Grabarz jumped 2.31m in Helsinki to match the achievement of Alan Paterson in Brussels in 1950.

30 The Tour de France got underway with an eight kilometre prologue time trial won by Fabian Cancellara from tour favourite Bradley Wiggins.
Andy Murray beat Marcos Baghdatis 7-5, 3-6, 7-5, 6-1 in the third round of Wimbledon; the match on the closed roof of centre court finishing at 11.02pm.
Camelot, ridden by J P O'Brien and trained by his father Aidan, won the Irish Derby at the Curragh.

July

1 Spain beat Italy 4-0 in the Euro 2012 final in Kiev
England beat Australia by six wickets at The Oval to take a 2-0 lead in the One Day International series.

2 Mark Cavendish won his first stage of Le Tour 2012
Spanish driver Maria de Villota, 32, suffered head and facial injuries, including the loss of her right eye, during her first test run for the Marussia Formula One team at Duxford, Cambridgeshire.

6 Andy Murray became the first Brit in 74 years to reach a Wimbledon men's final as he beat France's Jo-Wilfried Tsonga 6-3, 6-4, 3-6, 7-5 in the semi-finals. The last British man to win the men's singles at Wimbledon was Fred Perry in 1936 but Bunny Austin lost in the final two years later to end the golden era of British tennis.

7 Jonathan Marray became the first Brit to win the Wimbledon men's doubles for 76 years after he and partner Frederik Nielsen of Denmark beat Romanian Horia Tecau and Sweden's Robert Lindstedt 4-6, 6-4, 7-6, 6-7, 6-3. The last successful British pair to win the doubles title were Raymond Tuckey and Pat Hughes in 1936. Frederik Nielsen is the grandson of Kurt Nielsen, who reached the singles finals of Wimbledon in 1953 (losing to Vic Seixas, having defeated Ken Rosewall in the quarterfinal) and 1955 (losing to Tony Trabert). Before this, he won the Boys' singles at Wimbledon in 1947 (defeating Sven Davidson). Besides his successes at Wimbledon, he won the Boys' singles at the French Open, and reached senior quarterfinals in the French Open (twice) and the US Open. With Althea Gibson, he won the US Open mixed doubles in 1957, thereby becoming the first Dane to have ever won a Grand Slam event as a senior. Serena Williams beat Agnieszka Radwanska 6-1 5-7 6-2 to claim her fifth Wimbledon singles title and later won the doubles with sister Venus, beating Czech pair Andrea Hlavackova and Lucie Hradecka 7-5 6-4.
After the abandonment of the third ODI against Australia normal service was resumed as England beat the Aussies by eight wickets at Chester-le-Street, Durham to take a winning 3-0 lead in the best-of-five series.
Bradley Wiggins took the Yellow Jersey in the Tour de France after finishing third to his Sky team-mate Chris Froome on the seventh stage.

8 Roger Federer beat Andy Murray 4-6, 7-5, 6-3, 6-4 to win his seventh Wimbledon singles title, giving him a share of the men's record along with William Renshaw and Pete Sampras and also returning him to the World No 1 spot. An emotional Murray was clearly drained by the match which started so well for him but after a rain-break early in the second set which caused the roof on Centre Court to be closed Federer began to dominate.
Red Bull driver Mark Webber won the British Grand Prix, overtaking Fernando Alonso on lap 48 of 52, to move within thirteen points of his Ferrari rival in the race for the Formula One championship.
Bradley Wiggins won his first-ever stage of the Tour de France with victory in the 26-mile time trial in a time of 51min 24sec; 35 seconds in front of fellow Team Sky member Chris Froome.

12 Scotsman David Millar notched his first stage win in Le Tour for nine years, becoming the fourth Team GB member to win a stage this year.

14 David Haye knocked out Dereck Chisora in the fifth round of their heavyweight grudge fight at Upton Park.

17 Just ten days before the start of the London Olympics the security company, G4S, charged with ensuring a smooth and safe Games, admitted they were having grave problems meeting the establishment figures budgeted, their chief executive Nick Buckles giving a limp response to criticism from the Commons home affairs select committee.

20 Mark Cavendish won his second stage of Le Tour 2012
Team GB footballers were outclassed in a 2-0 beating by Olympic favourites Brazil.

21 Bradley Wiggins won his second stage of the Tour de France with victory in the second time trial consolidating Team Sky's dominance at Le Tour. Chris Froome placed second to Wiggins to ensure the runner-up position to his team leader as the race ends in Paris tomorrow.

22 Mark Cavendish won the final stage of the Tour de France for the fourth year running as team-mate Bradley Wiggins completed the formality of victory in Paris; the first Englishman to win the world's most prestigious cycle race.
Fernando Alonso won the German Formula One Grand Prix at Hockenheim to increase his lead in the drivers' championship. Jenson Button finished third in the race but was promoted to second after Sebastian Vettel was docked 20 seconds for an illegal overtaking manoeuvre.
Ernie Els won the Open at Royal Lytham after Australian golfer Adam Scott blew a four-shot lead on the last four holes, bogeying them all to lose by a single shot.

23 South Africa beat England by an innings and 12 runs at the Oval

26 Welsh winger Craig Bellamy became the first British man to score in Team GB colours in 52 years during the 1-1 draw with Senegal at Old Trafford.

27 The Olympic opening ceremony was beamed to more than a billion viewers around the world. The Danny Boyle directed extravaganza focusing on aspects of British history from the Industrial Revolution to modern day included Kenneth Branagh as Isambard Kingdom Brunel

and Rowan Atkinson as Mr Bean hamming it up during a performance of Chariots of Fire. The Queen declared the Games open after playing a cameo role parachuting into the stadium (played by stuntman Gary Connery) with James Bond (Daniel Craig).

29 After the disappointment of Team GB failing to medal in the men's Olympic cycling road race Lizzie Armitstead won silver in the women's race, Great Britain's first medal of the Games.
In the swimming pool, defending champion Rebecca Adlington won the bronze medal in the 400m freestyle.
Lewis Hamilton won the Hungarian Formula One Grand Prix in Budapest

30 Great Britain won the bronze medal in the men's gymnastics team event.

31 The British team, including Zara Phillips, won the silver medal in the equestrian team event.

August

1 Great Britain collected its first gold medal of the London Games after Heather Stanning and Helen Glover won the coxless pairs, the first British female rowers to win an Olympic title. On the best day for Team GB to-date Bradley Wiggins also won gold, in equally impressive fashion, in the men's cycling time trial with team-mate Chris Froome taking the bronze. Wiggins' feat took him past Sir Steve Redgrave's total of six Olympic medals. Scottish swimmer Michael Jamieson, 23, secured silver in the 200m breastroke final and the men's coxed eight gained a bronze after a valiant attempt at overhauling the dominant German team but fading in the final 500m. On a more sour note, eight female badminton players were disqualified from the games. The players, from China, South Korea and Indonesia were charged with playing to lose to gain preferred opponents in the quarter-final draw.

2 Team GB won six more Olympic medals to rise to fifth in the league table. Tim Baillie and Etienne Stott claimed Britain's first ever gold in the canoe slalom C2 event at Lee Valley, with David Florence and Richard Hounslow taking silver. Dorset marksman Peter Wilson won Britain's fourth gold medal with victory in the double trap competition. After the disappointment of seeing the women's sprint team of Victoria Pendleton and Jessica Varnish disqualified for an infringement of the rules the men's sprint cycling team of Philip Hindes, Jason Kenny and Sir Chris Hoy twice broke the world record on their way to victory - a result that also saw Hoy equal Sir Steve Redgrave's British record of five Olympic titles. Earlier in the day, Britain won a rowing silver in the men's lightweight four at Eton Dorney and Gemma Gibbons gained a silver medal in the final of the 78kg judo competition, becoming Great Britain's first Olympic judo medallist since her coach Kate Howey also won silver 12 years ago.

3 Great Britain added three more gold medals taking their tally to eight. In the velodrome, Victoria Pendleton, 31, won the keirin event and Ed Clancy, Geraint Thomas, Peter Kennaugh and Steven Burke clocked three minutes 51.659 seconds to win the men's team pursuit in a world record time. Britain's eighth gold of the Games came in the women's double sculls with Katherine Grainger and Anna Watkins dominating the race from the start. British bronze medallists were Rebecca Adlington in the 800m freestyle, Alan Campbell in the single sculls, Karina Bryant in the +78kg judo event and George Nash & William Satch in the men's rowing pairs.

4 Team GB won three gold medals via Jessica Ennis in the heptathlon, Greg Rutherford in the long jump and Mo Farah in the 10,000m. Earlier in the day there was victory for the men's rowing four of Andy Triggs Hodge, Pete Reed, Tom James and Alex Gregory and the women's sculls pair of Katherine Copeland and Sophie Hosking plus the women's team pursuit cycling team of Dani King, Laura Trott and Joanna Rowsell who broke the world record on every ride in the competition culminating in a new mark of 3min 14.051sec. An emotional day also saw Zac Purchase and Mark Hunter gain silver in the lightweight men's double sculls although the British pair were inconsolable after the race as they led all the way only to be pipped on the line by the Danish pair. Team GB rose to third in the table with 14 golds, 7 silvers and 8 bronzes. On a momentous day in the pool Michael Phelps finished his career with an 18th Olympic gold, his 22nd medal, in the men's 4x100m medley relay final. The great American swimmer won four golds and two silvers at these Games and sits imperiously atop the all-time list of Olympic medallists.

5 Andy Murray added two medals to the impressive tally of Team GB, beating Roger Federer 6-2, 6-1, 6-4 in the singles final and less than an hour later partnering Laura Robson to a silver medal display narrowly losing the gold to Belarusian mixed doubles duo Victoria Azarenka and Max Mirnyi 10-8 in the champions tie-break after both couples won a set each. Ben Ainslie made it 16 Team GB golds after winning his fourth-consecutive Olympic sailing title in an epic battle at Weymouth, only taking the lead in the final race of the Finn class. Iain Percy and Andrew Simpson narrowly failed to defend the Star title they won in China four years ago, losing out on gold in the most agonising way imaginable, in the final few metres of the final leg. In the pommel horse discipline in the gymnastic arena Great Britain won two medals, a bronze by Max Whitlock and a silver by Louis Smith, who lost on countback to Hungary's Krisztian Berki after the two scored 16.066 for their flawless performances. On the athletics track Christine Ohuruogu was runner-up to American Sanya Richards-Ross in the 400m to narrowly fail to defend her title although running 49.7 secs, only the third time she has ever broken the 50-sec barrier. The only other two occasions were when she won World Championship gold in 2007 and her Olympic crown a year later. Ed Clancy won a bronze medal in the omnium after a magnificent final 1k time trial. Team GB maintained third place in the medals table with 16 golds, 11 silvers and 10 bronzes.

6 Great Britain won its first showjumping gold medal since 1952 with victory in the showjumping team event. Nick Skelton (Big Star), Ben Maher (Tripple X III), Scott Brash (Hello Sanctos) and Peter Charles (Vindicat Credit) gained victory over the Dutch team in a thrilling jump-off. The first three mentioned riders will be back in action at Greenwich Park for the individual competition. In the velodrome, Jason Kenny won gold in the men's sprint, defeating multiple world champion Gregory Bauge of France. Beth Tweddle ended her Olympic gymnastics career with a bronze medal in the uneven bars.

7 Team GB won four more Olympic gold medals via Laura Trott in the women's cycling omnium, Sir Chris Hoy in the men's keirin, Alistair Brownlee in the men's triathlon and Carl Hester, Laura Bechtolsheimer and Charlotte Dujardin in the team dressage competition. Victoria Pendleton bowed out of cycling with a silver medal in the women's sprint after being controversially disqualified in her first ride in the final for cycling out of her lane. Alistair Brownlee's brother, Jonathan Brownlee won bronze in the men's triathlon. Team GB's current medal total stands at 22 golds, 13 silvers and 13 bronzes.

9 After a blank Wednesday Team GB were back on track with gold medal victories by Jade Jones in the under-57kg featherweight Taekwondo category, Nicola Adams in the flyweight boxing final (the first woman ever to win gold for boxing), and Charlotte Dujardin in the dressage competition in which team-mate Laura Bechtolsheimer won bronze. On the day that Kenyan David Rushida broke the world record in the 800mts final in 1min 40.91secs, Usain Bolt confirmed his super superstar status by becoming the first man ever to successfully defend the 100mts and 200mts titles by again defeating his team-mate Yohan Blake in 19.32secs in a 200mt race which saw Jamaica make a clean sweep of the medals, Warren Weir taking the bronze.

10 Britain's sailing duos of Saskia Clark & Hannah Mills and Luke Patience & Stuart Bithell both took Olympic silver in the 470 class at Weymouth. There were also bronze medals for Anthony Ogogo in the middleweight boxing class, Lutalo Muhammad (replacement for the British and world No 1 Aaron Cook) in the under 80kg Taekwondo class, and the women's hockey team. Team GB's current medal total stands at 25 golds, 15 silvers and 17 bronzes.

11 Britain's gold rush continued with Olympic victories for canoeist Ed McKeever in the 200m K1 sprint, boxer Luke Campbell in the men's bantamweight (56kg) class, and distance runner Mo Farah in the 5,000mts.Team GB also secured bronze medals by Tom Daley in the 10m platform diving competition and Liam Heath & Jon Schofield in the K2 200m canoe sprint.

12 On the final day of Olympic competition Team GB gained eight more medals to finish their Games with 29 golds, 17 silvers and 19 bronzes, placing third in the table behind the USA (46, 29, 29) and China (38, 27, 22) but ahead of Russia (24, 35, 23). Super heavyweight boxer Anthony Joshua gained Britain's final gold and team-mate Fred Evans won silver in the welterweight class. Britain's final medal was won by Modern Pentathlete Samantha Murray who gained silver after passing two athletes during the final run/shoot stage.
Rory McIlroy won the USPGA title at Kiawah Island by eight shots.

24 Lance Armstrong was stripped of his seven Tour de France titles and given a lifetime ban by the United States Anti-Doping Agency (USADA). The US cyclist opted not to contest USADA drugs charges, saying he is tired of fighting the allegations. He strongly denies doping. The International Cycling Union, the world governing body, is yet to say if it intends to follow USADA's lead.

25 Warrington Wolves brought the Carnegie Challenge Cup back to the town for the third time in four years with a 35-18 defeat of Leeds Rhinos in rugby league's annual Wembley showpiece. Brett Hodgson became the fourth Australian to win the Lance Todd Trophy for man-of-the-match.

27 European captain Jose Maria Olazabal selected Ian Poulter and Belgian Nicolas Colsaerts as his wild cards for the 2012 Ryder Cup at Medinah, Chicago.

29 Andrew Strauss resigned as England cricket captain and was immediately replaced by Alastair Cook.

September

2 Jenson Button led from start to finish to win the Belgian Formula One GP at Spa.

5 England lost the fifth one day international against South Africa at Trent Bridge to tie the series 2-2 and hang on narrowly to their No 1 world ranking.

7 England began their qualifying campaign for the 2014 World Cup with a 5-0 defeat of Moldova. In other World Cup qualifiers Wales lost 2-0 to Belgium and Northern Ireland lost 2-0 to Russia while the Republic of Ireland beat Kazakhstan 2-1.

9 Great Britain finished third in the Paralympic medal table behind China and Russia. Team GB's 120 medals included 34 golds, 43 silvers and 43 bronzes. Wheelchair athlete David Weir completed a Grand Slam by winning the 800m, 1500m, 5000m and marathon.
Lewis Hamilton won the Italian Formula One GP at Monza.
Welshman Luke Rowe won the first stage of the Tour of Britain in Norfolk after Team Sky team-mate Mark Cavendish crashed with victory in sight.
Serena Williams came back from the brink of defeat to take her fourth US Open title, beating Victoria Azarenka of Belarus 6-2, 2-6, 7-5 in the final at Flushing Meadows.

10 Andy Murray became the first British man to win a tennis Grand Slam for 76 years, beating defending champion and world number two Novak Djokovic 7-6 (12-10) 7-5 2-6 3-6 6-2 at Flushing Meadows. The last British man to win a Grand Slam title was Fred Perry, who also won the US Open.

11 England drew 1-1 in their second Group H World Cup qualifier. In other qualifiers Wales were beaten 6-1 by Serbia and Scotland drew 1-1 with Macedonia, both in Group A, and Northern Ireland drew 1-1 with Luxembourg in Group F.

12 An independent panel chaired by the Bishop of Liverpool, James Jones, concluded that up to 41 of the 96 Liverpool fans who died during the Hillsborough disaster in 1989 might have been saved but for the failings of emergency services and public bodies. The report into the circumstances leading to the human crush which occurred during the semi-final FA Cup tie between Liverpool and Nottingham Forest football clubs on 15 April 1989 at the Hillsborough Stadium in Sheffield cleared Liverpool fans of any negligence and criticised police for allegedly covering up multiple failings.
England beat South Africa by 28 runs in the third and final Twenty20 international to draw the series 1-1

15 Camelot failed in his bid to become the first Triple Crown winner since 1970 as 25-1 shot Encke, ridden by Mickael Barzalona and trained by Mahmood Al Zarooni, was the surprise winner of the St Leger at Doncaster.

16 The Tour of Britain cycle race was won by Jonathan Tiernan-Locke, the first British winner since the present format began in 2004.

19 The British Horseracing Authority (BHA) announced that the Grand National will be run over 90 yards shorter from next April in an effort to slow down the field as it races to the first fence.

23 Sebastian Vettel won the Singapore Grand Prix after Lewis Hamilton failed to finish when leading the race.
England suffered a 90-run defeat at the hands of India in the World Twenty20 group stage in Colombo.
Chelsea captain John Terry announced his retirement from international football.

27 Chelsea star John Terry was given a four-match ban and fined £220,000 by the FA for a vile outburst aimed at black QPR player Anton Ferdinand

28 Lewis Hamilton announced he is to quit McLaren and join Mercedes as replacement for Michael Schumacher next year.

30 European golfers recovered from 10-6 down going into the final day singles to beat the USA by 14½-13½ in the Ryder Cup at Medinah Country Club, Chicago, Illinois. Martin Kaymer sank a five-foot putt on the 18th green to get his team to the 14 points needed to retain the trophy. Then a Tiger Woods bogey on the final green of the final match gifted Jose Maria Olazabal's side overall victory. The win matches the record recovery of Ben Crenshaw's US team in Brookline, Boston in 1999 and an emotional Olazabal paid a fitting tribute to his late friend Seve Ballesteros, the man who did so much to reinvigorate the competition and whose trademark navy blue and white the side wore on the final day in Chicago. Ian Poulter was in brilliant form all week and made it four wins out of four in typically indomitable fashion against Webb Simpson.

October

6 Australian Chris Holder was crowned speedway world champion after winning the Polish Grand Prix.

7 Solemia, ridden by Olivie Peslier and trained by Carlos Laffon-Parias, won the Prix de l'Arc de Triomphe at Longchamps.
A Marlon Samuels-inspired West Indies recovered from an awful start to beat Sri Lanka and win the World Twenty20 by 36 runs in Colombo.
Sebastian Vettel moved to within four points of leader Fernando Alonso by winning the Japanese Formula One Grand Prix at Suzuka.
Drew Brees made history when he threw a touchdown pass in his 48th consecutive game to break the 52-year-old NFL record set by Johnny Unitas. The New Orleans quarterback also led the Saints to their first win of the season, a 31-24 victory against San Diego, the team he began his career with.

12 England beat San Marino 5-0 at Wembley in World Cup Qualifier Group H. In other matches Wales beat Scotland 2-1 but the Republic of Ireland were beaten 6-1 by Germany in Dublin.

13 Audley Harrison was knocked out in 82 seconds by David Price in their British and Commonwealth heavyweight title showdown at the Liverpool Echo Arena.

14 Sebastian Vettel took a six-point lead in the drivers' championship after winning the Korean Grand Prix, beating Fernando Alonso into third place.
Novak Djokovic beat Andy Murray in three sets to win the Shanghai Masters.
Heather Watson saved four match points before beating Taiwan's Chang Kai-Chen 7-5, 5-7, 7-6 in the Japan Open final and thus become the first Briton to win a WTA singles title since 1988 when Sara Gomer won in Aptos, California.

15 Richard Hughes emulated Frankie Dettori by riding seven winners at one race meeting. Hughes was victorious on his first five rides at Windsor before Ever Fortune placed third in the sixth race. He then won on his final two rides, Mama Quilla bringing up the seven-timer.

16 England's World Cup qualifier against Poland in Warsaw was delayed a day in bizarre fashion after the roof of the stadium was not closed despite torrential rain. In other matches Northern Ireland drew 1-1 with Portugal in Porto, Wales were beaten 2-0 by Croatia, Scotland lost 2-0 to Belgium and the Republic of Ireland beat the Faroe Isles 4-1 in Torshavn.
Richard Hughes won the first two races at Leicester to bring his tally to nine wins from his last ten rides. The champion-elect had a third winner later in the meeting.
England Under-21 stars were embroiled in ugly scenes after the final whistle in an international against Serbia. Racist thugs made monkey chants at Danny Rose, who was subsequently sent off for reacting to the disgraceful abuse. Serbia skipper Slobodan Medojevic was also sent off after Connor Wickham scored the winning goal for England in injury time.

17 England drew 1-1 with Poland in the delayed World Cup group match.

19 Former England goalkeeper Chris Kirkland was shoved in the face by a Leeds Utd fan moments after the Sheffield Wednesday goalkeeper conceded a 79th minute equaliser.
Trenton Oldfield, 36, a protester who swam in front of the two crews during the Varsity Boat Race on April 7 was jailed for six months at Isleworth Crown Court.

20 Frankel, the world's greatest-ever racehorse, was retired to stud after his 14th consecutive victory, winning the Champion Stakes at Royal Ascot watched by the Queen.

24 Rower Alex Partridge and hockey player Hannah Macleod had their Olympic bronze medals stolen as they partied at a London nightclub.

27 Hannah Macleod, 28, received her bronze medal back after it was posted anonymously to the England Hockey head office at Bisham Abbey in Buckinghamshire.

28 After a controversial Premier League match at Stamford Bridge which ended 3-2 to Manchester United, match referee Mark Clattenburg stood accused (but subsequently cleared) of racially abusing two Chelsea players.
Sebastian Vettel won the Indian GP to consolidate his lead in the Drivers' Championship.
Casey Stoner won the Australian GP at Phillip Island for the sixth year in a row as Spain's Jorge Lorenzo secured his second MotoGP world championship, finishing second behind the Australian. Briton Cal Crutchlow claimed third, his second podium finish of the season.

29 Bradley Wiggins was awarded third place in the 2009 Tour de France after Lance Armstrong's result was wiped out of the record books. Swede Peter Eriksson was named as replacement for Charles van Commenee as new coach of UK Athletics.

November

4 Kimi Raikkonen won the Abu Dhabi Grand Prix from Fernando Alonso and Sebastian Vettel, who had been forced to start from the pit lane after his Red Bull was deemed to have had insufficient fuel in its tank after qualifying third.
7 Tour de France winner Bradley Wiggins was knocked off his bike and sustained bruised ribs while out on a training ride near his Eccleston home.
11 Britain's Nathan Cleverly retained his WBO light-heavyweight title with an eighth-round stoppage win over American Shawn Hawk in Los Angeles.
14 Sweden beat England 4-2 in a friendly international football match in Stockholm; all four Swedish goals scored by Zlatan Ibrahimovic - the last an overhead bicycle shot from outside the box.
17 Carl Froch retained his IBF world super-middleweight title with a third round stoppage of American Yusaf Mack in Nottingham.
19 India defeated England by nine wickets in the first Test at Ahmedabad with Kevin Pietersen failing twice with the bat on his recall to the England team.
21 Chelsea manager Roberto Di Matteo was sacked and replaced until the end of the season by Rafa Benitez.
24 Ricky Hatton was stopped by Vyacheslav Senchenko in round nine of his comeback fight at Manchester Arena.
25 Sebastian Vettel was crowned the youngest Formula One treble championship winner after finishing sixth behind Jenson Button in the Brazilian GP at Sao Paulo. Vettel ended the season on 281pts, three ahead of Fernando Alonso.
England rugby union captain Chris Robshaw controversially asked Owen Farrell to kick a penalty in the dying moments of an international match against South Africa. The three points resulted in a 15-16 loss.
26 England beat India by 10 wickets in the second Test at Mumbai, Kevin Pietersen being named man-of-the-match for his breath-taking innings of 186 from 233 balls.
30 Former England cricket star Freddie Flintoff, 34, made a successful debut as a professional heavyweight boxer, beating American Richard Dawson on points at the Manchester Arena after being knocked down in the second of the four rounds.

December

1 England beat the All Blacks 38-21 at Twickenham to go into the Six Nations as the favourites.
David Beckham played his final game for LA Galaxy in their 3-1 victory over Houston Dynamo.
3 Australian cricketer Ricky Ponting was dismissed for eight in his final Test innings as the hosts slipped to a 309-run defeat to South Africa in Perth.
5 Frankie Dettori, 41, was banned from race-riding for six months by French racing authority France Galop after the popular jockey tested positive for cocaine after a race in Paris in September.
6 Alastair Cook set a record for England Test centuries with his 23rd as the tourists assumed control of the third Test against India at Eden Gardens, Kolkata. The opener passed the mark of 22 held by Wally Hammond, Colin Cowdrey, Geoffrey Boycott and Kevin Pietersen.
Oxford beat Cambridge 26-19 in the annual rugby union Varsity match at Twickenham.
9 Manny Pacquiao was knocked out by Juan Manuel Márquez in the sixth round in Las Vegas to give the Mexican fighter his first victory over the Filipino boxer and politician - their three previous fights resulting in two wins for Pacquiao and a draw.
Barcelona striker Lionel Messi grabbed the opener at Real Betis to equal Gerd Muller's record of 85 goals in a calendar year. Nine minutes later Messi struck again to take his tally to 86 and help his side to a 2-1 victory.
England beat India by seven wickets in the third Test in Kolkata.
11 League Two Bradford defeated a full-strength Arsenal side on penalties in the quarter-final of the Capital One Cup after the match ended 1-1 in normal time.
15 Chelsea were beaten 1-0 by the Brazilian side Corinthians in the final of the Club World Cup in Yokohama, Japan.
16 Tour de France winner Bradley Wiggins was crowned BBC Sports Personality of the Year at the ExCel Centre in London. Heptathlete Jessica Ennis was runner-up and Andy Murray placed third.
Amir Khan stopped Carlos Molina in the 10th round at the Los Angeles Memorial Sports Arena to get his career back on track after two successive defeats.
17 England drew the fourth Test against India in Nagpur to win the four-match series 2-1; their first tour victory in India since 1984.
18 Following the recent closure of Hereford racecourse, Folkestone staged its last-ever horse racing meeting before the track becomes a housing development.
30 In the semi-final of the PDC World Darts Championship Michael van Gerwen threw 17 perfect darts to almost complete the first-ever successive nine-dart legs. The 23-year-old master threw 180 and 177 followed by two treble twenties and a double twelve before beginning the next leg with seven treble twenties, a treble nineteen and narrowly missing the double twelve. Despite losing the set Van Gerwen went on to win the match against James Wade 6-4.

Obituaries 2012

January

1 Gary Ablett, footballer, born November 19th 1965
Bob Anderson, Olympic fencer and stunt co-ordinator, born September 15th 1922
Kiro Gligorov, Serbian-born first President of the Republic of Macedonia, born May 3rd 1917
3 Josef Škvorecký, Czech writer, born September 27th 1924
Bob Weston, guitarist with Fleetwood Mac, born November 1st 1947
4 Harry Fowler, actor, born December 10th 1926
Eve Arnold, US photojournalist, born 21st April 1912
5 Hikaru Hayashi, Japanese composer, born October 22nd 1931
6 Bob Holness, South African-born television presenter, born November 12th 1928
7 Tony Blankley, English-born American political analyst, born January 21st 1948
8 Alexis Weissenberg, Bulgarian-born French pianist, born July 26th 1929
12 Reginald Hill, crime writer, born April 3rd 1936
13 Rauf Raif Denktaş, Cypriot barrister and the founding President of the Turkish Republic of Northern Cyprus, born January 27th 1924
17 Jimmy Castor, US saxophonist and singer, born June 23rd 1940.
20 Etta James, US jazz singer, born Jamesetta Hawkins, January 25th, 1938
21 Ernie Gregory, goalkeeper for West Ham United, born November 10th 1921.
24 Theo Angelopoulos, Greek filmmaker, screenwriter and film producer, born April 27th 1935.
25 Paavo Allan Engelbert Berglund, Finnish conductor, born April 14th 1929.
Colin Tarrant, actor, born June 14th 1952
29 Oscar Luigi Scalfaro, Italian politician, born September 9th 1918.

February

1 Angelo Dundee, US boxing trainer, born Angelo Mirena, August 30th 1921
John Harrison, Australian rower, born in 1924
3 Ben Gazzara, US actor, born Biagio Anthony Gazzarra, August 28th 1930
9 Josh Gifford, NH jockey and trainer, born August 3rd 1941

11 Whitney Elizabeth Houston, US singer, actress, producer, and model, born August 9th1963
12 David Kelly, Irish actor, born July 11th 1929
14 Dory Previn, US singer and poet, born Dorothy Veronica Langan, October 22nd 1925
15 James Whitaker, journalist, born October 4th 1940
18 Elizabeth Connell, South African soprano, born October 22nd 1946
22 (Hugh) Frank Carson, comedian, born November 6th 1926
Marie Colvin, US journalist, born January 12th 1956
28 Hal Roach, Irish comedian, born November 4th 1927
29 David Thomas 'Davy' Jones, pop singer and actor, born December 30th 1945

March

2 Norman St John-Stevas, Baron St John of Fawsley, politician, born May 18th 1929
3 Dave Charnley, lightweight boxing champion, born October 10th 1935
5 Philip Madoc, actor, born July 5th 1934
Robert Bernard Sherman , US songwriter, born December 19th 1925.
6 Gemma McCluskie, actress, born February 5th 1983
14 Pierre Schoendoerffer, French film director and war reporter, born May 5th 1928
15 Mervyn Davies, rugby union player, born December 9th 1946
17 Chaleo Yoovidhya, Thai businessman and co-creator of the Red Bull energy drink, born in 1922.
18 George Tupou V, the King of Tonga, born May 4th 1948.
20 Jim Stynes, Irish-born Australian rules football player, born April 23rd 1966
24 Jocky Wilson, darts champion, born March 22nd 1950
25 Hal E. "Hally" Chester, US film producer and child actor, born Harold Ribotsky, March 6th 1921

April

5 Bingu wa Mutharika, Malawian politician, born Brightson Webster Ryson Thom, February 24th 1934
Ferdinand Alexander Porsche, German industrial designer, born December 11th 1935
Bernard Noël "Banjo Barney" McKenna, Irish musician (Dubliners), born December 16th 1939
7 Myron Leon "Mike" Wallace, US journalist, game show host and actor, born May 9th 1918.
8 Jack Tramiel, Polish founder of Commodore International Computers, born December 13th 1928.
12 Andrew Love, US saxophonist, born November 21st 1941
16 Alan Hacker, clarinetist, born September 30th 1938
19 Levon Helm, US drummer, born May 26th 1940
20 Bert Weedon, guitarist, born May 10th 1920
26 Terry Spinks, 1956 Olympic flyweight boxing champion, born February 28th 1938
29 Amarillo Slim, US poker player, born Thomas Austin Preston, December 31st 1928

May

4 Adam 'MCA' Yauch, US pop star with the Beastie Boys, born August 5th 1964
8 Maurice Sendak, US writer and illustrator, born June 10th 1928
Frank Parr, Lancashire cricketer and jazz trombonist, born June 1st 1928
9 Vidal Sassoon, pioneering hairdresser who created the 'wedge', born January 17th 1928
14 Derek Hammond-Stroud, baritone opera singer, born January 10th 1926
Carlos Fuentes, Mexican novelist, born November 11th 1928
17 Donna Summer, US vocalist, born LaDonna Adrian Gaines, December 31st 1948
18 Alan Oakley, designer of the Raleigh Chopper, born April 27th 1927
20 Robin Hugh Gibb, singer and songwriter, born December 22nd 1949
Johnny Tapia, US boxer, born February 13th 1967
29 Arthel Lane "Doc" Watson, American guitarist and songwriter, born March 3rd 1923
Kaneto Shindo, Japanese film director, born April 22nd 1912
31 Paul Sussman, author, archaeologist and journalist, born July 11th 1966

June

2 Kathryn Joosten, US actress, born December 20th 1939
3 Andy Hamilton, Jamaican saxophonist, born March 26th 1918
Roy Francesco Salvadori, motor racing driver, born May 12th 1922
4 Herb Reed, US founder of The Platters, born August 7th 1928
5 Ray Bradbury, US science fiction writer, born August 22nd 1920
Barry Unsworth, Booker prize-winning novelist, born August 10th 1930
6 Nolan Miller, US cinematic costume designer, born January 8th 1933
7 Bob Welch US guitarist (formerly with Fleetwood Mac), born August 31st 1945
9 Abram Wilson, US jazz trumpeter, born August 30th 1973
John Maples, politician, born April 22nd 1943
11 Teófilo Stevenson Lawrence, Cuban boxer, born March 29th 1952
(Therese) Ann Rutherford, Canadian actress, born November 2nd 1917
12 Henry Hill, US mobster whose life story was documented in the film, Goodfellas, born June 11th 1943
Elinor Ostrom, US economist who became the first woman to win the Nobel Prize in Economics, born August 7th 1933
14 Lord (Peter) Archer of Sandwell, politician, born November 20th 1926
16 Susan Tyrrell, US actress, born March 18th 1945
18 Tom Maynard, cricketer, born March 25th 1989
Brian Hibbard, actor, born November 26th 1946
19 Richard Lynch, US actor, born February 12th 1936
Anthony Bate, actor, born August 31st 1927
26 Campbell Gillies, jockey, born June 27th 1990

July

4 Eric Sykes, comedian, writer and actor, born May 4th 1923
8 Ernest Borgnine, US actor, born Ermes Effron Borgnino, January 24th 1917
15 Celeste Holm, US actress, born April 29th 1917
16 Jon Lord, rock musician, born June 9th 1941
20 Alastair Burnet, newsreader, born July 12th 1928
Simon Ward, actor, born October 16th 1941
21 Angharad Rees, actress, born July 16th 1949
Don Wilson, cricketer, born August 7th 1937
23 Sally Ride, US astronaut, born May 26th 1951
24 Robert Ledley, US pioneer of electronic digital computers in medicine, born June 28th 1926
John Atta Mills, Ghanaian politician, born July 21st 1944

26 Mary Tamm, actress, born March 22nd 1950
27 Geoffrey Hughes, actor, born February 2nd 1944
Jack Taylor, football referee, born April 21st 1930
29 Chris Marker, French writer and film director, born July 29th 1921
30 Maeve Binchy (Snell), Irish novelist and playwright, born May 28th 1940
31 Gore Vidal, writer, born October 3rd 1925

August
1 Nigel Charnock, dancer and choreographer, born May 23rd 1960
2 Jimmy Jones, US singer, born June 2nd 1937
6 Marvin Hamlisch, US composer, born June 2nd 1944
(Alfred) Bernard Lovell, physicist and radio astronomer, born August 31st 1913
9 Mel Stuart, US film director, born September 2nd 1928
10 Phillippe Bugalski, French rally driver, born June 12th 1963
11 Sid Waddell, dart's commentator, born August 10th 1940
12 Alex C. Falconer, Labour Party politician, born April 1st 1940
Helen Gurley Brown, US editor-in-chief of Cosmopolitan (1965-97), born February 18th 1922
16 William Windom, US actor, born September 28th 1923
18 Scott McKenzie, US singer, born Philip Wallach Blondheim, January 10, 1939
19 Tony Scott, film director, born June 21st 1944
20 Dom Mintoff, Maltese politician, born August 6th 1916
Phyllis Diller, US comedienne, born July 17th 1917
23 Jerry Nelson, US puppeteer, born July 10th 1934
25 Neil Armstrong, US astronaut, born August 5th 1930
28 Rhodes Boyson, educator, author and politician, born May 11th 1925
31 Max Bygraves, entertainer, born Walter Bygraves, October 16th 1922

September
1 Hal David, US lyricist, born May 25th 1921
3 Sun Myung Moon, South Korean founder of the Unification Church, born February 25th 1920
Michael Clarke Duncan, US actor, born December 10th 1957
5 (John Lawrence), Lord Oaksey, television presenter and amateur jockey, born March 21st 1929
6 Terry Nutkins, naturalist, television presenter and author, born August 12th 1946
8 Pip Granger, author, born July 26th 1947
10 Winifred Roberts, violinist, born November 4th 1923
12 Derek Jameson, newspaper editor and radio & television presenter, born November 29th 1929
14 Louis Simpson, Jamaican poet, born March 27th 1923
15 Nevin Spence, rugby union player, born April 26th 1990
James "Sugar Boy" Crawford, US R&B musician, born October 12th 1934
18 Brian Woolnough, sports journalist, born September 30th 1948
19 Charles Richardson, gangster, born January 18th 1934
20 Tereska Torrès, French writer, born September 3rd 1920
23 Corrie Sanders, South African heavyweight boxing champion, born January 7th 1966
Jean Taittinger, French politician and Champagne producer, born January 25th 1923
25 (Howard) Andy Williams, US singer, born December 3rd 1927
John Bond, footballer and manager, born December 17th 1932
27 Herbert Lom, Czech actor, born Herbert Kuchačevič ze Schluderpacheru, September 11th 1917
29 Malcolm Wicks, Labour Party politician, born July 1st 1947

October
2 Big Jim Sullivan, guitarist, born James George Tomkins, February 14th 1941
6 Chadli Bendjedid, Algerian politician, born April 14th 1929
9 Michel Schwalbé, Polish-born violinist, born October 27th 1919
10 Alex Karras, US footballer, professional wrestler, and actor, born July 15th 1935
11 Helmut Haller, German footballer, born July 21st 1939
22 Mike Morris, television presenter, born June 26th 1946
24 Anita Björk, Swedish actress, born April 25th 1923
25 Emanuel Steward, US boxing trainer, born July 7th 1944
John Connelly, footballer, born July 18th 1938

November
5 Elliott Carter, US composer, born December 11 th 1908
6 Clive Dunn, actor, born January 9th 1920
9 Bill Tarmey, actor, born William Piddington, April 4th 1941
11 Rex Masterman Hunt, former Governor of the Falkland Islands, born June 29th 1926
13 Yao Defen, Chinese holder of title 'World's Tallest Woman' (2.33 m/7 ft 8 in), born July 15th 1972
16 William Turnbull, artist, born January 11th 1922
18 Kenny Morgans, footballer, born March 16th 1939
23 Larry Hagman, US actor, born September 21st 1931
24 Hector Camacho, Puerto Rican boxer, born May 24th 1962
25 Dave Sexton, football manager, born April 6th 1930

December
5 Dave Brubeck, US jazz pianist, born December 6th 1920
9 Norman Woodland, US inventor of the bar code, born September 6th 1921
Patrick Moore, astronomer and broadcaster, born March 4th 1923
(Dolores Janney) Jenni Rivera, US vocalist, born July 2nd 1969
11 Ravi Shankar, Indian sitar player, born April 7th 1920
14 Kenneth Kendall, Indian-born British newsreader, born August 7th 1924
24 Jack Klugman, US actor, born April 27th 1922
Charles, Durning, US actor, born February 28th 1923
26 Fontella Bass, US vocalist, born July 3rd 1940
Gerry Anderson, producer and inventor of supermarionation, born Gerald Abrahams, April 14th 1929
27 (Herbert) Norman Schwarzkopf, US Army general, born August 22nd 1934
29 Tony Greig, South African-born England cricketer, born October 6th 1946
William Rees-Mogg, former editor of The Times, born 14th July 1928

EDUCATION

Public Schools

	Founded
King's School, Canterbury, Kent	600
King's School, Rochester, Kent	604
St Peter's School, York	627
Sherborne School, Dorset*	705
St Alban's	948
King's School, Ely	973
Winchester	1382
Eton	1440
City of London	1442
Loughborough	1495
St Paul's	1509
Giggleswick School, N. Yorks	1512
Manchester Grammar	1515
Sedbergh School, Cumbria	1525
Bristol Grammar	1532
Berkhamsted, Herts	1541
Christ College, Brecon	1541
King's Worcester	1541
Bristol Cathedral	1542
Bradford Grammar School, West Yorkshire	1548
Bedford	1552
Leeds Grammar School	1552
Christ's Hospital, Horsham	1553
Tonbridge	1553
Shrewsbury	1552
Gresham's School, Holt, Norfolk	1555
Oundle, Northants	1556
Repton, Derby	1557
Merchant Taylors', Northwood	1560
Westminster	1560
Kingston	1561
Felsted, Dunmow, Essex	1564
Highgate	1565
Rugby	1567
Harrow	1571
Uppingham, Oakham	1584
Stonyhurst, RC, Clitheroe	1593
Wellingborough, Northants	1595
Trinity School, Croydon	1596
Whitgift School, Croydon	1596
Blundell's, Tiverton	1604
Downside, RC, Somerset	1607
Charterhouse, Godalming	1611
Douai, RC	1615
Dulwich College	1619
Merchant Taylors', Liverpool	1620
Haberdashers' Aske's, Herts	1690
Dame Allan's Boys', Newcastle upon Tyne	1705
Churcher's College, Petersfield	1722
Robert Gordon, Aberdeen	1729
James Allen's Girls' School	1741
Ampleforth, RC, North Yorkshire	1802
Wellington School, Somerset	1837
Cheltenham	1841
Marlborough College, Wiltshire	1843
Brighton College	1845
Radley College, Abingdon	1847
Lancing	1848
Hurstpierpoint, West Sussex	1849
Bradfield, Reading	1850
City of London Freemen's, Ashtead	1854
Cheadle Hulme, Cheshire	1855
Ardingly, West Sussex	1858
Oratory School, RC, Woodcote, Berks	1859
Wellington College, Crowthorne, Berks	1856
King's, Tynemouth	1860
Clifton, Bristol	1862
Haileybury, Hertford	1862
Cranleigh	1863
Fettes, Edinburgh	1870
Leys, Cambridge	1875
John Lyon, Harrow, Middlesex	1876
Alleyn's School	1882
Roedean	1885
Merchant Taylors' Girls, Liverpool	1888
Bedales, Petersfield	1893
Benenden, Cranbrook, Kent	1923
Canford, Wimborne	1923
Stowe, Buckinghamshire	1923
Gordonstoun, Elgin	1934
Millfield, Street, Somerset	1935

*Education at Sherborne was started by St Aldhelm when he became the first bishop of Sherborne in 705. However the school was linked with the Benedictine Abbey. The earliest known Master was Thomas Copeland in 1437. Edward VI refounded the school in 1550 on its present site.

NB: There are currently over 1,000 Independent Schools (Public Schools). The list here is not comprehensive, rather it is a cross-section of the better-known ones.

British Universities

	Founded
Oxford	1249
Cambridge	1284
St Andrew's	1413
Glasgow	1451
Aberdeen	1495
Edinburgh	1583
UMIST**	1824
Durham	1832
London	1836
Manchester**	1851
Newcastle Upon Tyne	1852
Wales, Cardiff	1893
Birmingham	1900
Liverpool	1903
Leeds	1904
Sheffield	1905
Queen's, Belfast	1908
Bristol	1909
Reading	1926
Nottingham	1948
Southampton	1952
Hull	1954
Exeter	1955
Leicester	1957
Sussex	1961
Keele	1962
East Anglia	1963
York	1963
Lancaster	1964
Essex	1964
Strathclyde, Glasgow	1964
Warwick, Coventry	1965
Kent	1965
Ulster	1965
Loughborough	1966
Heriot-Watt, Edinburgh	1966
Surrey, Guildford	1966
Bradford	1966
Bath	1966
Brunel, Uxbridge	1966
City	1966
Aston, Birmingham	1966
Stirling	1967
Dundee	1967
Salford	1967
Open	1969
Cranfield	1969
Buckingham	1976

**UMIST and the University of Manchester were merged in 2004.

British Universities: Former Polytechnics

	Founded
Leeds Metropolitan	1992
Kingston	1992
Huddersfield	1992
Hertfordshire	1992
Greenwich	1992
North London	1992
Wolverhampton	1992
Glamorgan	1992
Westminster	1992
West of England (Bristol)	1992
Paisley	1992
Plymouth	1992
Portsmouth	1992
Robert Gordon (Aberdeen)	1992
Sheffield Hallam	1992
South Bank	1992
Staffordshire	1992
Sunderland	1992
Teesside	1992
Thames Valley	1992
Northumbria at Newcastle	1992
Nottingham Trent	1992
Liverpool John Moores	1992
Manchester Metropolitan	1992
Middlesex	1992
Napier (Edinburgh)	1992
De Montfort (Leicester)	1992
Anglia Polytechnic (Chelmsford)	1992
Bournemouth	1992
Brighton	1992
Coventry	1992
Central England (Perry Barr)	1992
Central Lancashire (Preston)	1992
Oxford Brookes	1993
Derby	1993
Glasgow Caledonian	1993
East London	1993
Abertay Dundee	1994
Lincoln and Humberside	1996
Gloucestershire	2001
London Metropolitan	2002
Wales, Newport	2002
Bolton	2004
Arts, London	2004
Roehampton	2004
Bath Spa	2005
Canterbury Christ Church	2005
Chester	2005
Chichester	2005
Liverpool Hope	2005
Northampton	2005
Worcester	2005
Winchester	2005
Southampton Solent	2005
Bedfordshire	2006
Edge Hill	2006
York St John	2006
Queen Margaret	2007
Buckinghamshire New	2007
Imperial College	2007
Cumbria	2007
Aberystwyth	2007
Bangor	2007
Wales, Lampeter	2007
Wales, Swansea	2007
Swansea Metropolitan	2008
Glyndwr	2008

University of Cambridge

	Founded
Peterhouse	1284
Clare	1326
Pembroke	1347
Gonville and Caius	1348
Trinity Hall	1350
Corpus Christi	1352
King's	1441
Queens'	1448
St Catharine's	1473
Jesus	1496
Christ's	1505
St John's	1511
Magdalene	1542
Trinity	1546
Emmanuel	1584
Sidney Sussex	1596
Downing	1800
Homerton	1824
Girton	1869
Newnham	1871
Selwyn	1882
Hughes Hall	1885
St Edmund's	1896
Murray Edwards	1954
Churchill	1960
Darwin	1964
Lucy Cavendish	1965
Wolfson	1965
Clare Hall	1966
Fitzwilliam	1966
Robinson	1977

University of Oxford

	Founded
University	1249
Balliol	1263
Merton	1264
St Edmund Hall	1278
Exeter	1314
Oriel	1326
The Queen's	1340
New College	1379
Lincoln	1427
All Souls	1438
Magdalen	1458
Brasenose	1509
Corpus Christi	1517
Christ Church	1546
Trinity	1554
St John's	1555
Jesus	1571
Wadham	1612
Pembroke	1624
Worcester	1714
Harris Manchester	1786
Regent's Park*	1810
Keble	1868
Hertford	1874
Wycliffe Hall*	1877
Lady Margaret Hall	1878
Somerville	1879
St Hugh's	1886
Mansfield	1886
Campion Hall*	1896
St Benet's Hall*	1897
Greyfriars*	1910
Blackfriars*	1921
St Peter's	1929
Nuffield	1937
St Hilda's	1938
St Antony's	1950
St Anne's	1952
Linacre	1962
St Catherine's	1962
St Cross	1965
Templeton***	1965
Wolfson	1966
Green***	1979
Kellogg**	1990
St Stephen's House*	2003

*classified as Permanent Private Halls
**from 1990 to 1994 called Rewley House
***merged in 2008 to form Green Templeton

University of London: Colleges

Birkbeck College
British Institute in Paris
Courtauld Institute of Art
Goldsmith's College
Heythrop College
Institute of Cancer Research
Institute of Education
King's College London
London Business School
London School of Economics and Political Science
London School of Hygiene and Tropical Medicine
Queen Mary and Westfeld College
Royal Academy of Music
Royal Holloway and Bedford New College
Royal Veterinary College
School of Advanced Study
School of Oriental and African Studies
School of Pharmacy
St George's Hospital Medical School
University College London

University of Durham: Colleges

Collingwood
George Stephenson
Grey
Hatfield
John Snow
Josephine Butler
St Aidan's
St Chad's
St Cuthbert's Society
St Hild & St Bede
St John's
St Mary's
Trevelyan
University
Ushaw
Ustinov
Van Mildert

Miscellaneous Information

Academies – Established by Tony Blair in 2000, academies are all-ability state-funded schools established and managed by sponsors from a wide range of backgrounds. They are required to follow the National Curriculum in core subjects but have a specialism relative to their community and circumstances thereof.

A-Level – Consists of six units of assessment (three AS and three A2).

Baker Days – Part of the controversial education reform bill, during Kenneth Baker's tenancy as Education Minister 1986–89. His legislation on the in-service training days for teachers came to be known as Baker Days.

Cambridge College: Former Name – Murray Edwards was formerly called New Hall until 2008 – along with Newnham it is women only.

City Technology Colleges – Set up in the 1980s in an attempt to widen the choices of secondary education in disadvantaged urban areas. The Learning and Skills Act 2000 introduced a similar type of school, now known as 'Academy'.

Dulwich College – Founded by the English actor Edward Alleyn in 1619 but a distinct school from Alleyn's School, founded in 1882. Old Boys of Dulwich College are however known as Old Alleynians.

GCSE – General Certificate of Secondary Education.

GNVQ – General National Vocation Qualification (Further Education).

Gordonstoun – Founded by Kurt Hahn in 1934.

Grant-Maintained Schools – Came into being as a result of the 1988 Education Act which permits schools with more than 300 pupils to opt out of local authority control if the majority of parents wish to do so. Grant-maintained status was abolished in 1998 and now only CTC and Academy schools are directly funded by central government.

Independent Schools – Receive no grants from Public Funds and are funded by fees and contributions, and run by trusts.

Key Stages

Key Stage 1:	Reception	age 4 to 5
	Year 1	age 5 to 6
	Year 2	age 6 to 7
Key Stage 2:	Year 3	age 7 to 8
	Year 4	age 8 to 9
	Year 5	age 9 to 10
	Year 6	age 10 to 11
Key Stage 3:	Year 7	age 11 to 12
	Year 8	age 12 to 13
	Year 9	age 13 to 14
Key Stage 4:	Year 10	age 14 to 15
	Year 11	age 15 to 16
Key Stage 5:	Year 12	age 16 to 17
	Year 13	age 17 to 18

Lyceum school – Founded by Aristotle.

Mottoes – Eton – Floreat Etona (May Eton Flourish), Rugby – Orando Laborando (By Praying and by Working), Winchester – Manners Makyth Man, Ampleforth College – Dieu le Ward (God Protect Him), The Ridings, Calderdale – Together We Make the Difference.

National Curriculum – Under the 1988 Education Act the National Curriculum was set out in four Key Stages of a child's development. Key Stage 1 and 2 concerned 5–11-year-olds and stated that Core Subjects would include English, (Welsh in Welsh-speaking schools) Maths and Science; and the Foundation Subjects would be Design & Technology, Information Technology, History, Geography, Art, Music and PE. Key Stage 3 caters for 11–14-year-olds and states that a Modern Foreign Language must be included. Key

	Stage 4 concerns 14–16-year-olds. The Act states that the child must be tested at the end of each Key Stage i.e. 7, 11, and 14-years-old. 16-year-olds only require testing if staying in education. See also Key Stages.
Newnham College: 1st Male Fellow	Dr Rachel Padman (who had a sex change operation in 1982).
Ofsted	The Office for Standards in Education, Children's Services and Skills is responsible for inspecting the standards of both independent and state schools as well as local education authorities, child day care and childminding in England. Similar bodies exist in Scotland (HM Inspectorate of Education), Northern Ireland (The Education and Training Inspectorate) and Wales (Estyn). Ofsted's head office is in Holborn.
Parents Charter	Booklet informing parents about the education system.
Public Schools: Famous Founders	John Lyon (Harrow), Elizabeth I (Westminster), William of Wykeham (Winchester), Henry VI (Eton), Thomas Sutton (Charterhouse), Edward Alleyne (Dulwich College), Lawrence Sheriff (Rugby), John Colet (St Paul's), Edward VI (Shrewsbury).
Public Schools: Meaning	In recent years the term 'Public School' applies to those Independent Schools in membership of the Headmasters' and Headmistresses' Conference, the Governing Bodies Association or the Governing Bodies of Girl's Schools Association. Historically Public Schools were fee-paying private boarding schools, for pupils aged 13 years and above, which gained sufficient reputation to attract pupils from backgrounds of social worthiness. Public schools were contrasted with 'Private Schools' which were run for the profit of their proprietors. In Scotland, the term Public School refers to a free state school, open to all.
School Age Limits	In Great Britain schooling is compulsory between the ages of 5 and 16 (4 and 16 in Northern Ireland).
Scotvec	Scottish Vocational Education Council (Further Education).
St Andrews: Colleges	United College of St Salvator & St Leonard, College of St Mary.
Subfusc	Formal academic dress, especially at Oxford University.
UCAS	The Universities and Colleges Admissions Service acts as a clearing-house for those applying for admission to full-time first degree and first diploma courses at universities and other higher education institutions in the UK. UCAS was established in 1993 from the merger of the former Universities Central Council on Admissions (UCCA), the Polytechnics Central Admissions System (PCAS) and the Standing Conference on University Entrance (SCUE). UCAS is based in Cheltenham, Gloucestershire.
University: Most Students	Open University has the most registered students although London University has most on campus.

Famous People

Occupations: Former and Alternative

Joseph Addison (essayist) MP for Malmesbury (1708–19)
Aesop (fable writer) Phrygian slave
Prince Albert (husband of Queen Victoria) musician
Woody Allen (comic actor and director) jazz clarinet player
Idi Amin (Ugandan politician) British army sergeant
Kingsley Amis (writer) English lecturer at Swansea University
Clive Anderson (comedian and broadcaster) barrister
Andrew, St (Apostle) fisherman
Jennifer Aniston (actress) waitress and telemarketer
John Arlott (cricket commentator) policeman
Henry Armstrong (American boxer) Baptist minister
Paddy Ashdown (politician) Royal Marine
Isaac Asimov (science fiction writer) biochemist
Clement Attlee (British prime minister) lawyer and social worker
WH Auden (poet & essayist) stretcher bearer (Spanish Civil War)
Alfred Austin (poet) lawyer
Alan Ayckbourn (playwright) BBC Radio drama producer
Francis Bacon (philosopher) Lord Chancellor
Mily Balakirev (composer) railway official
Hastings Banda (Malawian politician) physician
Roger Bannister (athlete) doctor
Brendan Behan (author) painter & decorator and IRA member
Alexander Graham Bell (inventor) speech therapist to the deaf
Hilaire Belloc (poet and writer) Liberal MP
Arnold Bennett (novelist) solicitor's clerk
Cilla Black (entertainer) coat checker-In (Cavern Club, Liverpool)
RD Blackmore (novelist) lawyer
Alexander Borodin (composer) professor of chemistry
Jim Bowen (comedian) teacher
Susan Boyle (singer) trainee cook
Simon Brodkin (comedian) doctor
Danny Broome (television chef) professional ice hockey player
John Buchan (novelist) lawyer, publisher and MP for Scottish Universities (1927–35)
Robert Burns (poet) excise officer and farmer
Michael Caine (actor) Billingsgate fish porter
James Callaghan (British prime minister) civil servant (tax officer)
Geoff Capes (athlete) policeman
Lewis Carroll (writer) mathematics lecturer
Jimmy Carter (US president) peanut farmer
Joyce Cary (novelist) civil servant in Nigeria
Giacomo Casanova (Italian adventurer) librarian, spy and lottery director
Fidel Castro (Cuban President) film extra
Miguel Cervantes (novelist) professional soldier
Geoffrey Chaucer (poet) customs officer, MP and soldier
Claude Lorraine (artist) pastry cook
William Cobbett (writer) soldier and MP for Oldham (1832–5)
Edward Coke (lawyer) MP for Aldeburgh (1589)
Perry Como (singer) barber
Sean Connery (actor) coffin polisher and Royal Navy sailor
Billy Connolly (comedian and actor) shipyard worker
Gary Cooper (actor) photographer and stuntman
Tommy Cooper (comic magician) guardsman
Andres Courrèges (fashion designer) civil engineer
AJ Cronin (novelist) inspector of mines
César Cui (Russian composer) military engineer
Dante Alighieri (Italian poet) embassy official
Walter De La Mare (poet and novelist) oil company worker
Christopher Dean (figure skater) policeman
Dave Dee (pop singer) policeman
Daniel Defoe (writer) brickmaker and shopkeeper
Charles Dickens (writer) court stenographer and factory shoe black
Bruce Dickinson (rock singer) commercial airline pilot
Benjamin Disraeli (British prime minister) novelist
John Donne (poet) dean of St Paul's Cathedral (1621–31)
Sir Arthur Conan Doyle (writer) doctor (ophthalmologist)
John Boyd Dunlop (inventor) veterinary surgeon
Albrecht Dürer (painter and engraver) draughtsman
François Duvalier (president of Haiti) physician (hence 'Papa Doc')
John Dyer (poet and painter) lawyer
Clint Eastwood (actor) swimming instructor
Thomas Alva Edison (inventor) telegraph operator and newsboy
Albert Einstein (physicist) Patent Office clerk
TS Eliot (poet and dramatist) clerk with Lloyd's Bank
Juan Fangio (racing driver) bus driver
Michael Faraday (physicist) bookseller and laboratory technician
William Faulkner (novelist) postmaster
Kathleen Ferrier (contralto) telephone operator
Frank Finlay (actor) butcher
F Scott Fitzgerald (novelist) Hollywood scriptwriter
Ian Fleming (novelist) intelligence officer and journalist
Errol Flynn (actor) policeman (Tasmania)
Gerald Ford (US President) male model
George Foreman (boxer) minister
George Formby (entertainer) jockey
Benjamin Franklin (US statesman) printer and scientist
Frederick II, the Great (king of Prussia) musician
Billy Fury (singer) tugboat worker
Clark Gable (actor) lumberjack
Galileo Galilei (astronomer) doctor, mathematician and natural philosopher
Greta Garbo (actress) milliner's model
Graeme Garden (comic actor) doctor
Giuseppe Garibaldi (Italian patriot) candlemaker and privateer
James Garner (actor) swimsuit model
David Garrick (actor) wine merchant
Richard Gatling (US inventor) doctor
Paul Gauguin (artist) stockbroker and labourer on Panama Canal
Jean Genet (author) professional criminal and male prostitute
Edward Gibbon (historian) MP for Liskeard (1774–80)
William S Gilbert (librettist) barrister and cartoonist
Joseph Goebbels newspaper editor
Johann Goethe (poet and dramatist) fire chief, newspaper critic and Court Official
Sam Goldwyn (film producer) glove salesman
WG Grace (cricketer) doctor
Kenneth Grahame (writer) secretary to Bank of England
Cary Grant (actor) acrobat
Robert Graves (poet and novelist) professor of English (Cairo University)
Fulke Greville (poet) MP for Warwickshire
Zane Grey (writer) dentist
Terry Griffiths (snooker player) postman
Che Guevara (revolutionary leader) doctor
Gareth Hale (comedian) PE teacher
Thomas Hardy (writer) architect
Bob Harris (broadcaster) policeman
Russell Harty (broadcaster) teacher
Alex Harvey (musician) lion tamer
Teri Hatcher (actress) cheerleader
Nathaniel Hawthorne (writer) US consul in Liverpool (1853–7)
AP Herbert (writer) MP for Oxford University (1935–50)
William Herschel (astronomer) music teacher
Benny Hill (comedian) milkman
Harry Hill (comedian) doctor
Adolf Hitler (dictator) painter of postcards
Ho Chi Minh (Vietnamese politician) hotel worker and pastry cook
Bob Hope (comedian) boxer
Gerard Manley Hopkins (poet) classics professor (University College Dublin)

Bob Hoskins (actor) market porter, fire-eater, steeplejack and seaman
AE Housman (poet) classics teacher
Rod Hull (comedian) electrician
Gareth Hunt (actor) merchant seaman
Henryk Ibsen (dramatist) pharmacist
Julio Iglesias (vocalist) goalkeeper
Charles Ives (composer) insurance executive
David Jason (actor) electrician
Andrew Johnson (US president) tailor
Vinnie Jones (actor) footballer
James Prescott Joule (physicist) brewer
James Robertson Justice (actor) naturalist
Wassily Kandinsky (artist) lawyer
Harvey Keitel (actor) US marine
Charles Kingsley (author) Cambridge history professor
Alphonse de Lamartine (poet and historian) French foreign minister (1848)
Burt Lancaster (actor) circus acrobat
Eddie Large (comedian) electrician
Philip Larkin (poet) librarian (of Hull University)
Antoine Lavoisier (chemist) tax collector
Lee Kuan Yew (Singapore politician) barrister
Vladimir Lenin (Russian revolutionary) lawyer
Leopold I of Habsburg (Holy Roman Emperor) musician
Franz Liszt (musician) priest
Little Richard (musician) minister
Syd Little (comedian) decorator
Henry Wadsworth Longfellow (poet) Harvard lecturer
St Luke (New Testament evangelist) painter and physician
John Lydgate (poet) monk
Thomas Macaulay (author) lawyer and MP for Calne, Leeds, and Edinburgh
Harold MacMillan (British prime minister) publisher
Norman Mailer (writer) candidate for NY mayor (4th of 5)
André Malraux (writer) archaeologist & pilot in Spanish civil war
Thomas Malthus (economist) clergyman
Nelson Mandela (South African statesman) lawyer
Walter de la Mare (poet and novelist) Standard Oil Company employee
John Marston (dramatic poet) lawyer
Andrew Marvell (poet) MP for Hull (1659–78)
Karl Marx (political and economic theorist) journalist and editor
Marcello Mastroianni (actor) draughtsman and cashier
Quentin Matsys (Massys) (Flemish painter) blacksmith
St Matthew (apostle) tax collector
William Somerset Maugham (writer) surgeon and wartime spy
Herman Melville (writer) customs officer, bank clerk and adventurer
Gregor Mendel (biologist and botanist) monk
Jonathan Miller (stage director and author) doctor
John Mills (actor) toilet paper salesman
Robert Mitchum (actor) miner and professional boxer
Laura Moffatt (politician) nurse
Matt Monro (singer) bus driver
Roger Moore (actor) male model
Samuel Morse (inventor) artist
Arthur Mullard (actor) professional boxer
Benito Mussolini (politician) newspaper editor
Pol Pot (politician) teacher
Modest Mussorgsky (composer) civil servant
Dame Anna Neagle (actress) dance instructor
Jawaharlal Nehru (Indian statesman) lawyer
Thomas Newcomen (inventor) blacksmith
Bob Newhart (comedian) accountant
Paul Newman (actor) motor racing driver
Isaac Newton (scientist) warden of the Mint and MP
Harold Nicolson (author & critic) MP for West Leicester (1935-45)
David Niven (actor) army officer
Julius Nyerere (Tanzanian politician) teacher
Milton Obote (Ugandan politician) labourer, clerk and salesman
Sean O'Casey (playwright) building labourer
Tom O'Connor (comedian) teacher
Bruce Oldfield (musician) art teacher
George Orwell (novelist) policeman (Burma)
David Owen (politician) doctor
Norman Pace (comedian) PE teacher
Thomas Love Peacock (novelist and poet) chief examiner of East India Company
Peter I, the Great (Russian tsar) shipwright
St Peter (apostle) fisherman
François André Philidor (composer) chess master
Enoch Powell (politician) professor of Greek
Magnus Pyke (science broadcaster) nutritionist
Salvatore Quasimodo (poet) engineer
Edgar Quinet (writer) politician
François Rabelais (satirist) doctor and monk
Sir Walter Raleigh (explorer and navigator) MP for Devon (1585)
Charles Reade (writer) lawyer
Ray Reardon (snooker player) policeman and miner
Paul Revere (American patriot) silversmith
Arthur Rimbaud (poet) gun runner and merchant
Joan Rivers (comedian) fashion co-ordinator for Bond Stores
Auguste Rodin (sculptor) ornamental mason
Peter Roget (thesaurus writer) doctor
Leonard Rossiter (actor) insurance agent
Henri Rousseau (painter) customs officer
JK Rowling (novelist) teacher
Salman Rushdie (writer) actor and advertising copywriter
Willie Rushton (satirist) cartoonist
Sir Walter Scott (novelist and poet) lawyer
Steven Seagal (actor) martial artist
William Shakespeare (writer) actor
Richard Brinsley Sheridan (dramatist) MP for Stafford and Ilchester
Nevil Shute (writer) engineer (worked on RI00)
Sir Philip Sidney (poet) professional soldier
Norodom Sihanouk (Cambodian politician) musician
Delia Smith (cookery writer) hairdresser and Norwich City FC director
CP Snow (novelist) parliamentary sec (Ministry of technology) and physicist
Dave Spikey (comedian) haematologist
Benjamin Spock (paediatrician) Naval officer and olympic oarsman
Jerry Springer (talk-show host) lawyer
Joseph Stalin (Soviet leader) trainee monk
Freddie Starr (comedian) bricklayer
Sir Richard Steele (essayist) MP for Stockbridge (1713)
Tommy Steele (entertainer) merchant seaman
Laurence Sterne (novelist) clergyman
Wallace Stevens (poet) insurance company executive
Rod Stewart (singer) footballer (Brentford) and gravedigger
David Storey (writer) Rugby League professional
Jonathan Swift (writer) clergyman
Charles Talleyrand-Périgord (statesman) abbot
Jimmy Tarbuck (comedian) milkman
GP Taylor (novelist) Anglican priest
Pyotr Tchaikovsky (composer) civil servant
Shirley Temple (actress) US ambassador to Ghana
Valentina Tereshkova (astronaut) cotton mill worker
Margaret Thatcher (British prime minister) research chemist and barrister
John Thaw (actor) market porter
JRR Tolkien (writer) Oxford English professor
Leo Tolstoy (writer) army officer
Anthony Trollope (writer) Post Office worker
Harry S Truman (US president) haberdasher
Desmond Tutu (archbishop of Cape Town) schoolteacher
Liv Ullmann (actress) UNICEF ambassador
John Vanbrugh (playwright) architect
Vincent Van Gogh (artist) trainee priest

Jules Verne (writer) librettist
King Vidor (film director) cinema projectionist and cameraman
Kurt Vonnegut (writer) soldier
Lech Walesa (Polish politician) electrician
Lew Wallace (author) soldier
Bradley Walsh (comedian) footballer (Brentford)
George Washington (US president) British army colonel
Noah Webster (lexicographer) lawyer and teacher
Chaim Weizmann (Israeli statesman) biochemist
Orson Welles (actor and director) picador
HG Wells (writer) draper's assistant and teacher
Walt Whitman (poet) teacher and printer
William Wilberforce (philanthropist) MP for Hull and Yorkshire
Billy Wilder (film director) journalist and crime reporter
Tennessee Williams (playwright) poet, waiter and cinema usher
Ludwig Wittgenstein (philosopher) teacher, porter, gardener and engineer
Terry Wogan (broadcaster) bank clerk
Ermanno Wolf-Ferrari (composer) artist
William Wordsworth (poet) stamp distributor
Harry Worth (comic actor) miner
Sir Christopher Wren (architect) professor of astronomy
Tammy Wynette (singer) beautician
JR Wyss (writer and philosopher) Swiss national anthem writer
Yohji Yamamoto (fashion designer) lawyer
Boris Yeltsin (Russian president) construction company director
Andrew John Young (poet) clergyman
Brigham Young (Mormon leader) carpenter, painter and glazier
Lazarus Zamenhof (language inventor) oculist and philologist
Franco Zeffirelli (film director) actor and costume designer
Count Von Zeppelin (airship inventor) US Civil War soldier
Emile Zola (novelist) clerk in publishing house

Assassinations

681BC *Sennacherib of Assyria* Murdered by his two sons.
514BC *Hipparchus of Athens* Killed by Harmodius and Aristogeiton, two Athenians.
465BC *Xerxes I of Persia* Killed by members of his court, led by Artabanus.
336BC *Philip II of Macedon* Killed by Pausanias, a Spartan regent and general.
330BC *Darius III (Codomannus) of Persia* Slain by a satrap, Arterxes (Ardashir), whilst fleeing Alexander the Great.
44BC *Julius Caesar (Roman dictator)* Stabbed by Brutus, Cassius and others in the Senate.
41 *Caligula (Roman emperor)* Murdered by Cassius Chaerea, an officer of his guard.
54 *Claudius I (Roman Emperor)* Ate poisoned mushrooms served by his wife, Agrippina the Younger.
96 *Domitian (Roman dictator)* Stabbed in his bedroom by Stephanus, a freed slave.
192 *Commodus (Roman Emperor)* Strangled by wrestler Narcissus, at the behest of his mistress, Marcia.
978 *Edward the Martyr (King of England)* Murdered at Corfe Castle by his younger half-brother Ethelred's household, led by Elfthryth.
1057 *Macbeth (King of Scotland)* Killed by Malcolm III, Canmore, at Lumphanan (15 August).
1170 *Thomas à Becket* Killed by four knights, Fitzurse, Tracy, De Merville and Le Breton in Canterbury Cathedral.
1192 *Conrad, King of Jerusalem* Killed by members of the militant Islamic sect, the Assassins, who gave assassination their name.
1327 *Edward II of England* Murdered in Berkeley Castle possibly with a red-hot poker at the instigation of his wife, Isabella, and her lover Roger de Mortimer; possible perpetrators were De Gournay and Maltravers.
1437 *James I of Scotland* Murdered in court residence, a Dominican monastery, by assassins led by Sir Robert Graham.
1471 *Henry VI of England* Murdered in the Tower of London, possibly by Richard of Gloucester, the future Richard III.
1488 *James III of Scotland* Murdered following defeat of royal army at Sauchieburn by unknown.
1533 *Atahualpa (Last Inca ruler)* Strangled by Spanish forces under Francisco Pizarro.
1541 *Francisco Pizarro* Murdered at his home in Lima, possibly by Juan de Rada at the instigation of Diego de Almagro.
1567 *Henry, Lord Darnley (husband of Mary, Queen of Scots)* Strangled by Scottish nobles after explosion at Kirk O' Field, Edinburgh.
1584 *William the Silent (aka William of Orange)* Shot at Delft by Balthasar Gerard.
1589 *Henry III of France* Stabbed by Jacques Clément, a fanatical Dominican.
1610 *Henry IV of France* Murdered by François Ravaillac, a Catholic fanatic.
1628 *Duke of Buckingham* Stabbed at Portsmouth en route for La Rochelle by John Felton, a discontented subaltern.
1634 *Prince Wallenstein (German general)* Killed by Devereux.
1762 *Peter III, Tsar of Russia* Strangled in captivity by Count Aleksei Orlov, the lover of his wife and future empress, Catherine.
1793 *Jean Paul Marat (French Revolutionary)* Stabbed in his bath by Charlotte Corday.
1801 *Paul I of Russia* Strangled by army officers who had conspired to force his abdication.
1812 *Spencer Perceval (PM)* Shot while entering lobby of the House of Commons by John Bellingham, a bankrupt Liverpool broker.
1865 *Abraham Lincoln* Shot by actor John Wilkes Booth in Ford's Theater, Washington, while watching *Our American Cousin.*
1872 *Richard Burke, Earl of Mayo* Stabbed to death by Shere Ali, a convict, while inspecting the settlement at Port Blair on the Andaman Islands.
1881 *James A Garfield (US President)* Shot in a station by Charles Guiteau, a disappointed office-seeker.
Alexander II of Russia Died from injuries after a bomb was thrown near his palace by Nihilists, led by Sophia Perovskaya.
1882 *Lord Frederick Cavendish (Chief Secretary for Ireland)* Murdered by 'Irish invincibles' in Phoenix Park, Dublin.
1894 *Marie François Carnot (French President)* Stabbed by anarchist Cesare Giovanni Santo Caserio.
1897 *Antonio Cánovas del Castillo (Spanish Premier)* Shot by Italian anarchist Angiolillo at the bath of Santa Agueda, Vitoria.
1900 *Umberto I of Italy* Murdered by anarchist G Bresci in Monza.
1901 *William McKinley (US President)* Shot by anarchist Leon Czolgosz in Buffalo, NY.
1903 *Alexander Obrenovich (King of Serbia)* Murdered by military conspirators, along with his wife, Draga.
1913 *George I of Greece* Murdered by a Greek, Schinas, in Salonika.
1914 *Archduke Franz Ferdinand* Shot in a car by Gavrilo Princip in Sarajevo (28 June); the assassination helped to precipitate WWI.
Jean Jaurès (French Socialist) Shot by nationalist Raoul Villain in café.
1916 *Rasputin (Russian monk)* Killed and dumped in River Neva by group of nobles led by Prince Feliks Yusupov and Grand Duke Dimitry Pavlovich, revenging his influence over Tsarina Alexandra.
1922 *Michael Collins (Sinn Fein leader)* Killed in an ambush between Bandon and Macroom in the Irish Free State.
1923 *Pancho Villa (Mexican Revolutionary)* Assassinated on his ranch at Parral, Mexico (20 June).
1934 *Dr Engelbert Dollfuss (Austrian Chancellor)* Shot by Nazis in the Chancellery.

Sergey Mironovich Kirov (*Russian Communist*) Shot by Leonid Nikolayev at the Communist Party HQ (1 December); Stalin subsequently purged Leningrad of all suspected anti-Stalinists.
Alexander I of Yugoslavia (*King of the Serbs, Croats and Slovenes*) Murdered in Marseilles by a Macedonian terrorist.
1935 *Huey Long* (*US politician*) Murdered by Dr Carl Austin Weiss.
1940 *Leon Trotsky* (*exiled Russian leader*) Killed with an ice pick in Mexico by Ramón Mercader.
1942 *Reinhard Heydrich* (*second-in-command in the Nazi Secret Police*) Murdered by Czech resistance fighters.
1943 *Isoruku Yamamoto (Japanese Admiral)* Plane intercepted and shot down by US P-38 fighter squad after Japanese naval code was broken.
1948 *Mohandas Gandhi* (*Indian leader*) Shot by Hindu fanatic Nathuran Godse at Birla House, New Delhi.
Count Folke Bernadotte (*Swedish diplomat*) Murdered by Jewish extremists in ambush in Jerusalem.
1951 *Abdullah I of Jordan* Murdered by member of Jihad faction.
Liaquat Ali Khan (*Pakistani PM*) Murdered in Rawalpindi by fanatics advocating war with India.
1958 *Faisal II of Iraq* Murdered with his entire household during a military coup.
1959 *Solomon Bandaranaike* (*Sri Lankan statesman*) Murdered by Buddhist monk Talduwe Somarama.
Rafael Trujillo Molina (*Dominican Republic dictator*) Machine-gunned in car by assassins including General JT Diaz.
1963 *John F Kennedy* (*US President*) Shot while riding in open Lincoln Continental in Dallas, Texas, by rifleman Lee Harvey Oswald (22 Nov).
1965 *Malcolm X* (*Black Muslim leader*) Shot at political rally.
1966 *Hendrik Verwoerd* (*South African Premier*) Stabbed by parliamentary messenger Dimitri Tsafendas.
1968 *Martin Luther King* (*civil rights leader*) Shot on hotel balcony by James Earl Ray in Memphis, Tennessee.
Robert F Kennedy (*US Senator*) Shot by Jordanian Arab immigrant Sirhan Bishara Sirhan in the Hotel Ambassador, Los Angeles.
1975 *King Faisal of Saudi Arabia* Murdered by his nephew, Prince Faisal.
1976 *Christopher Ewart-Biggs* (*British Ambassador to Eire*) Car blown up by IRA landmine.
Georgi Markov (Bulgarian dissident) Infected with poisoned pellet on Westminster Bridge by Bulgarian agent.
1978 *Aldo Moro, former Italian PM* Kidnapped by Red Brigade and later found dead.
Wafizulah Amin (President of Afghanistan) Killed with his mistress in the presidential palace, Kabul, by KGB commandos.
1979 *Airey Neave, MP* Killed by IRA bomb in House of Commons car park.
Lord Mountbatten Killed by IRA bomb in sailing boat while fishing off County Sligo, Ireland.
Park Chung Hee (*South Korean President*) Shot in restaurant by chief of Korean Central Intelligence Agency.
1980 *John Lennon* (*former Beatle*) Shot by Mark Chapman outside his apartment in New York.
Oscar Romero (*Salvadorean RC Prelate*) Murdered by government troops.
1981 *Anwar Sadat* (*Egyptian President*) Shot by rebel soldier Khalid Ahmed Shawki and others while reviewing military parade.
Zia ur-Rahman (*Bangladeshi President*) Shot by military and replaced as President by Abdus Sattar.
1983 *Benigno Aquino* (*Filipino politician*) Shot in the head at Manila airport by a government-backed assassin.
1984 *Indira Gandhi* (*Indian PM*) Murdered by members of her Sikh bodyguard (Satwant and Beant Singh).
1986 *Olof Palme* (*Swedish PM*) Shot in Stockholm as he walked home from cinema by unknown hand.
1988 *General Zia ul-Haq* (*Pakistani leader*) Killed in air crash owing to sabotage.
1991 *Rajiv Gandhi* (*Former Indian PM*) Blown up during an election campaign by Thanu.
1992 *Muhammad Boudiaf* (*President of Algeria's High State Council*) Murdered during a speech.
1995 *Yitzhak Rabin* (*Israeli PM*) Murdered by Yigal Amir.
2002 *Pim Fortuyn (Dutch politician)* Shot six times whilst walking to his car in Hilversum. Six months after the shooting Volkert Van de Graaf confessed to the murder and was sentenced to 18 years in prison.
2003 Zoran Djindjic (*Serbian PM*) Shot in Belgrade by organised crime member.
2007 Benazir Bhutto (*Pakistani politician*) Shot by Al-Qaeda terrorists while leaving a campaign rally for the PPP in Rawalpindi.
2009 Joao Bernardo Vieira (*President of Guinea-Bissau*) Shot by soldiers in a revenge attack for the death of Army Chief of Staff Batista Tagme Na Waie.
2011 Burhanuddin Rabbani (*Former Afghan President*) Killed by a suicide bomber entering his home in Kabul.

Attempted Assassinations

Queen Beatrix of the Netherlands Karst Roeland Tates, a 38-year-old Dutchman, attempted to ram the Queen's bus at Apeldoorn, Netherlands on 30 April 2009. Tates later died of brain injuries.
Count Otto von Bismarck Attempts by Kulimann (1874) and Blind (1866).
Cassius Marcellus Clay (US Emancipationist and Senator) Shot point-blank during a speech in 1843 and used a Bowie knife to cut off the attacker's ear and nose and also cut out one of his eyes! Not to be confused with his illustrious namesake, who presumably would have dispatched the assailant with a swift left hook.
Queen Elizabeth I Numerous plots to replace Elizabeth on the throne by Mary Queen of Scots, notably the Ridolfi and Babington plots, but the only person to be put to death for an alleged direct attempt was Dr Lopez, her physician, in 1594.
Gerald Ford Assassination attempt by Lynette 'Squeaky' Fromme, member of Charles Manson's 'family' (1975).
Henry Frick Steel magnate who was shot and stabbed by anarchist Alexander Berkman (1892).
George III James Hadfield attempted assassination in 1800 but was acquitted due to insanity.
Hitler Bomb planted by Colonel Von Stauffenberg at his Wolf's Lair HQ in E Prussia in 1944 exploded but failed to kill him.
John Paul II Shot by Mehmet Ali Agca in 1981.
Lenin Assassination attempt by Fanny Kaplan in 1918 caused his health to go into steady decline.
Leopold II Gennaro Rubino made an attempt on the life of the Belgian king in 1902.
Napoleon III Felice Orsini attempted his assassination, but Napoleon eventually died of a gall bladder infection.
Prince of Wales Jean Baptiste Sipido made an attempt on the life of the future King Edward VII (1900).
Ronald Reagan Shot by John Hinckley in 1981.
Franklin Delano Roosevelt In 1933 he and Chicago mayor Anton Cermak were shot at by Giuseppe Zangara. Cermak was mortally wounded, whilst Roosevelt became President.

Theodore Roosevelt Attempt on life by John F Schrank, 14 October 1912. Despite being shot in the chest at a political rally managed to continue his speech for 90 minutes before seeking medical assistance.
William Henry Seward (US Senator) Survived an assassination attempt on 14 April 1865 (the same night Abraham Lincoln was shot) when Lewis Payne, an associate of John Wilkes Booth, broke into his bedroom and stabbed him repeatedly.
Shah of Persia Francois Salsou made an attempt on the life of the Shah in 1900.
Margaret Thatcher The IRA Grand Hotel bombing in Brighton (Oct 1984) was an attempt on her life.
Queen Victoria Attempts by Edward Oxford (1840), John William Bean (1842), John Francis (1842), William Hamilton (1849), Robert Pate (1850), Arthur O'Connor (1872) and Roderick Maclean (1882).
George Wallace Left paralysed after being shot by Arthur Bremer in 1972.
Andy Warhol Shot by Valerie Solanis, one of his starlets, in 1968.

Catchphrases and Slogans

NB: The list below shows a phrase and the most identifiable body to that phrase. In most cases the details are self-explanatory and where the phrase has actually been coined by a person then his information is given. Many phrases will be of doubtful origin and no attempt has been made to authenticate entries as original spoutings. To give Robert Walpole as an example from my list: the phrase 'every man has his price' is identified with the prime minister but the phrase was almost certainly used as a maxim centuries earlier, although impossible to research. Many more catchphrases associated with household products will be found in the TV Advert section.

a good idea . . . son Max Bygraves (as Archie Andrew's tutor in *Educating Archie*)
all human life is there News of the World (advertising slogan from a Henry James novel)
all done in the best possible taste Kenny Everett (in the guise of the leggy Miss Cupid Stunt)
a man of my cal-aye-ber Tony Hancock (originally coined in *Hancock's Half-Hour*)
am I bovvered Lauren Cooper the Teenager (Catherine Tate)
and now for something completely different John Cleese (in *Monty Python*)
and that's the way it is Walter Cronkite (in concluding his CBS TV *Evening News* programme)
and the next Tonight will be tomorrow night Cliff Michelmore (at the end of the nightly BBC magazine programme)
are you looking for a punch up the bracket? Tony Hancock (originally coined in *Hancock's Half-Hour*)
are you sitting comfortably ? Julia Lang (on BBC radio's *Listen with Mother*)
as it happens Jimmy Savile
ask the audience Chris Tarrant (in *Who Wants to be a Millionaire*)
as the art mistress said to the gardener Monica (Beryl Reid) as Archie Andrew's posh friend in *Educating Archie*
aw don't embarrass me Lenny the Lion (ventriloquist Terry Hall's creation)
awight at the back (sic) Michael Barrymore (at the start of many of his shows)
Ay, caramba! Bart Simpson in *The Simpsons*
beam me up, Scotty Attributed to Captain Kirk (William Shatner) in *Star Trek*
because it is there George Leigh Mallory (on being asked why he wanted to climb Mt Everest)
before you can say Jack Robinson Richard Brinsley Sheridan (in the Commons to avoid using a fellow MP's name)
before your very eyes Arthur Askey (from the name of his first television series as a proof of live TV)
be like dad, keep mum 1941 propaganda slogan advising civilians to not talk about war-related issues)
be prepared Pears' Soap usurped the slogan from the motto of the Boy Scout movement
Bernie, the bolt Bob Monkhouse (in the *Golden Shot*). Bernie's real name was Derek Young
better red than dead Bertrand Russell (in a 1958 article stating Communism was preferable over death)
bet you can't eat three Ian Botham (used in an advertising campaign for Shredded Wheat)
Beulah, peel me a grape Mae West (first said by the actress to a black maid in the film *I'm No Angel*)
Big Bang, the Nickname for the London Stock Exchange deregulation of 27 October 1986
Big Brother is watching you George Orwell in his novel *Nineteen Eighty-Four* first coined this cry for democracy
big-hearted Arthur, that's me Arthur Askey (introducing himself on radio's *Band Wagon*)
black is beautiful Stokely Carmichael (at a civil rights rally in Memphis in 1966)
black power Usually attributed to Stokely Carmichael after shooting of James Meredith in 1966
blonde bombshell Jean Harlow (not so much a catchphrase more a description and nickname)
book 'em Danno Steve McGarrett (Jack Lord) to Detective 'Danno' Williams in *Hawaii Five O*
boom, boom Billy Bennett (the comedian coined the phrase to underline the punchline of a gag). Basil Brush and Eric Morecambe usurped Billy Bennett's catchphrase in their acts
booyakasha! Sacha Baron Cohen in the guise of rapper Ali G.
born 1820, still going strong Johnnie Walker whisky slogan first used in 1908
British are coming, the Colin Welland (after collecting an Oscar for the film *Chariots of Fire*)
buck stops here, the Harry S Truman (from a sign on his desk in the Oval Office)
bumper bundle Coined by Jean Metcalfe whilst introducing *Two-Way Family Favourites.* The phrase denotes a large number of requests for the same record
can I do you now sir? Mrs Mopp (Dorothy Summers) in *ITMA* i.e. *It's That Man Again*
can we talk? Joan Rivers (interjection used by the comedienne to link her jokes)
can you hear me, mother ? Sandy Powell (coined in 1932, probably the first radio catchphrase that caught on)
carry on London Freddie Grisewood (at the end of BBC radio's *In Town Tonight*)
clap hands, here comes Charley Charlie Kunz (became the signature tune of the *American pianist*)
clunk, click, every trip Jimmy Savile (from a seat-belt campaign launched in 1971)
come on down *The Price is Right* (originated in America when the popular show began in 1957)
come up and see me sometime Mae West (originally said as 'Why don't you come up sometime and see me)
come with me to the Casbah Charles Boyer (attributed to the 1938 film *Algiers* although not in the final cut)
customer is always right, the H Gordon Selfridge (the American pioneer of the large department store)

daft as a brush Ken Platt (comedian who corrupted the northern phrase 'soft as a brush')
day war broke out, the Robb Wilton (after WWII the comedian substituted 'peace' for 'war')
dead as a door-nail From Langland's *Piers Plowman* (door-nail was a knob on which a knocker struck)
deal or no deal? Noel Edmonds in *Deal or No Deal?*
did you spot this week's deliberate mistake? Lionel Gamlin (from his BBC radio series *Monday Night at Seven*)
didn't he do well? Bruce Forsyth (at the end of the conveyor belt finale of the *Generation Game*)
dig for victory Sir Reginald Dorman Smith (slogan asking people to grow food during WWII)
disgusted . . . Tunbridge Wells Stock phrase used when the writer does not want to give their name
dodgy Norman Vaughan (the phrase was accompanied by a thumbs-down gesture)
doesn't it make you want to spit? Arthur Askey (from the radio show *Band Wagon*)
d'oh Homer Simpson in *The Simpsons*
don't forget the fruit gums mum Roger Musgrave (the copywriter coined the phrase for Rowntree's Fruit Gums)
don't have a cow, man! Bart Simpson in *The Simpsons*
don't spit, remember the Johnstown flood US admonition against spitting (citing the 1889 flood caused by a dam bursting)
don't touch me Julian Clary (said by the comedian when any contact is made on his person)
don't worry, be happy George Bush (unofficial campaign slogan used in the 1988 presidential election)
do you know the Bishop of Norwich? An allusion to a port drinker who is holding on to the bottle and not passing it round
Drinka Pinta Milka Day Bertrand Whitehead (the Executive Officer of the National Milk Publicity Council)
eat my shorts Bart Simpson in the cartoon series *The Simpsons*
economical with the truth Sir Robert Armstrong (whilst being cross-examined in 1986 regarding MI5 secrets)
elementary, my dear Watson Sherlock Holmes (attributed to him but not to be seen in Conan Doyle's writings)
eleventh commandment, the George Whyte-Melville (cites 'thou shalt not be found out' in his book *Holmby House*)
'er indoors Arthur Daley (George Cole) in the ITV series *Minder*
evening all George Dixon (Jack Warner) in *Dixon of Dock Green*
ever-open door, the Dr Barnardo's Homes (slogan used to describe the homes in the 1950s)
everybody out Paddy (Miriam Karlin) as the shop steward in the BBC's *The Rag Trade*
everybody wants to get into the act Jimmy Durante (subsequently changed to everybody wants to get in on the act)
every man has his price Often attributed to Robert Walpole
every picture tells a story Appears to originate in 1904 as a slogan for Doan's Backache and Kidney Pills. The slogan was accompanied by a picture of a person bent over with back pain
everything in the garden's lovely Marie Lloyd (from the title of one of her popular songs)
expletive deleted Made famous by the Watergate transcripts but a general US term in documents
exterminate . . . exterminate Daleks (in the BBC television series *Dr Who*)
eyes and ears of the world, the Slogan promoting the cinema newsreel, *Paramount News* 1927–57
fifty fifty Chris Tarrant (in *Who Wants to be a Millionaire*)
fleet's lit up, the Cdr Tommy Woodrooffe (the BBC radio commentator coined the phrase in 1937)
flippin' kids Tony Hancock (as Archie Andrew's tutor in *Educating Archie*)
Flying Fickle Finger of Fate Award, the Prize in a mock talent contest in Rowan and Martin's *Laugh In*
F. T. A. (Fuck The Army) Popular American graffiti used since 1960 among US Army recruits to express a dislike for orders especially in the Vietnam conflict. Protestants use F. T. P. to express their dislike for the Pope and N. Irish patriots use F. T. Q. for the Queen
fully paid-up member of the human race Kenneth Clarke (described as such by the *Observer* on 31 July 1988)
get out of that Eric Morecambe (whilst pressing his down-turned palm under Ernie Wise's chin)
gis a job Yosser Hughes (Bernard Hill) in *Boys from the Blackstuff*
give 'em the money Barney Wilfred Pickles (*Have a Go*) to Barney Colehan
give 'em the money Mabel Wilfred Pickles (to his wife Mabel in radio's *Have a Go*)
go ahead, make my day Harry Callahan (Clint Eastwood) originally in the 1983 film *Sudden Impact.* Ronald Reagan (in an address to the 1985 American Business Conference)
Godfrey Daniel WC Fields (used in place of 'God, damn you' to comply with the strict Hay's Code
gone for a Burton RAF expression of WWII denoting a presumed dead person had gone for a drink
good game, good game Bruce Forsyth (at the end of each round of the *Generation Game*)
good morning sir; was there something? Sam Costa (in the radio programme *Much Binding in the Marsh*)
goodnight children everywhere Uncle Mac (Derek McCulloch) in BBC radio's *Children's Hour*
goodnight, Mrs Calabash . . . wherever you are Jimmy Durante (when ending his radio and television appearances)
goody, goody gumdrops Humphrey Lestocq (presenter of BBC television's *Whirligig* in the 1950s)
greatest show on earth, the PT Barnum (describing the merger of his circus with Bailey's in 1881)
happy as a sandboy The phrase alludes to the happiness of the door-to-door sellers of sand during the nineteenth century. Sand was bought as an absorber of liquids and scourer
happy as Larry An Australian expression of delight referring to the boxer Larry Foley 1847–1917
hat-trick Originating in cricket parlance when the taker of 3 successive wickets would be awarded a new hat for his feat. The term is now used for any triple success
have a gorilla Neddie Seagoon (Harry Secombe) offering a cigarette in the *Goon Show*
haves and the have-nots Sancho Panza (in Miguel Cervantes' *Don Quixote*)
he can't fart and chew gum at the same time President Lyndon Johnson's insulting description of President Gerald Ford
he can't walk and chew gum at the same time Revision of Lyndon Johnson's words when Ford became President in 1974
Heinz the Bolt Jackie Rae (in television's the *Golden Shot*). Heinz later became Bernie the Bolt
hello folks Tommy Handley (eponymous hero of *It's That Man Again*)
hello folks and world Neddie Seagoon (Harry Secombe) in the *Goon Show*
hello, good evening, and welcome David Frost (coined in the *Frost Programme* but has become his stock greeting)
hello, it's me, Twinkletoes Bernard Bresslaw (as Archie Andrews' tutor in *Educating Archie*)
hello my darlings Charlie Drake (usual opening greeting of the diminutive funny man)
hello peeps Stavros (Harry Enfield)
hello playmates Arthur Askey (introducing himself on radio's *Band Waggon*)

hello possums Dame Edna Everage (Barry Humphries)
hello sailor Minnie Bannister (Spike Milligan) in the classic Goon's script *Tales of Men's Shirts.* The phrase has entered the language as a camp double-entendre
here and now, before your very eyes Arthur Askey (original catchphrase from the series *Before Your Very Eyes*)
here's another fine mess you've gotten me into Oliver Hardy (invariably to his long-suffering partner Stan Laurel)
here's a pretty kettle of fish Queen Mary (to Stanley Baldwin referring to the abdication crisis of 1936)
here's Johnny Ed McMahon (introduction to Johnny Carson on NBC's *Tonight show*)
here's looking at you kid Rick Blaine (Humphrey Bogart) in *Casablanca.* The phrase is used four times
here we are again Joey the Clown (Joseph Grimaldi) one of the oldest attributable catchphrases
he's fallen in the water Little Jim (Spike Milligan) in the *Goon Show*
he's loo-vely, Mrs Hoskins . . . . he's loo-oo-vely Ivy (Ted Ray) in the comedian's hit radio programme *Ray's a Laugh*
hi there pop pickers Alan Freeman (Australian disc-jockey) whilst presenting *Pick of the Pops*
how's about that then, guys and gals Jimmy Savile (phrase used by the disc-jockey after a particularly good record)
how tickled I am Ken Dodd (whilst usually shoving a tickling stick between his legs from behind)
how very dare you Derek Faye (Catherine Tate)
I am the greatest Muhammad Ali (Cassius Clay) usurped the phrase from wrestler Gorgeous George
I could do that Yosser Hughes (Bernard Hill) in *Boys from the Blackstuff*
I didn't get where I am today . . . CJ (John Barron) in *The Fall and Rise of Reginald Perrin*
I do not like this game Bluebottle (Peter Sellers) in the *Goon Show*
I don't mind if I do Colonel Chinstrap (Jack Train) in *ITMA* whenever a drink was offered him
if it ain't broke, why fix it? Bert Lance (President Carter's Director of the Office of Management and Budget) speaking on the subject of governmental reorganisation
if it's up there I'll give you the money myself Les Dennis (in *Family Fortunes*)
if you can't stand the heat, get out of the kitchen Harry S Truman (when he gave his reason for not standing in the 1952 elections). Truman himself was quoting Major-General Harry Vaughan
I got a horse Ras Prince Monolulu (Peter Carl McKay) racing pundit of the 1930s to the 1950s
I know nothing Sgt Schultz (John Banner) in *Hogan's Heroes*
I'll be leaving you now, sir Claud Snudge (Bill Fraser) in Granada Television's *Bootsie and Snudge*
illegitimi non carborundum General 'Vinegar Joe' Stilwell used this motto during WWII under the pretence that it meant 'don't let the bastards grind you down'
I'll give it foive Janice Nicholls; a member of the public who took part in *Thank Your Lucky Stars* Spin-a-Disc panel and became famous when she gave a maximum five
I'll give you the results in reverse order Eric Morley (giving *Miss World* results)
I love it when a plan comes together Hannibal (George Peppard) in *The A Team*
I'm a laydee Emily Howard (David Walliams) in the BBC television comedy, *Little Britain*
I'm a little worried about Jim Mrs Dale (in *Mrs Dale's Diary*)
I mean that most sincerely, friends Hughie Green (phrase usually accompanied by a clenched fist gesture)
I'm afraid that I was very, very drunk Rowley Birkin QC (Paul Whitehouse) in the BBC television comedy, *The Fast Show*
I'm a little bit werrrr, a little bit weyyyy! Chris Jackson (the geezer who'd nick anything) as played by Paul Whitehouse in the BBC comedy *The Fast Show*
I'm in charge Bruce Forsyth (whilst introducing the Beat the Clock section at the Palladium)
I'm not a number, I'm a free man The Prisoner (Patrick McGoohan) spoken in defiance of his number 6 nomenclature
I'm smarter than the average bear Yogi Bear (whilst constantly outwitting ranger John Smith in Jellystone Park)
I'm the only gay in the village Daffyd (Matt Lucas) in the BBC television comedy, *Little Britain*
in like Flynn Errol Flynn (alluding to his legendary bedroom prowess)
I only arsked (sic) Popeye Popplewell (Bernard Bresslaw) in *The Army Game*
I say, I say, I say Murray and Mooney; a famous double act of the 1930s in which Harry Mooney would utter the immortal words and Harry Murray would invariably reply with 'I don't wish to know that, kindly leave the stage'
I say, what a smasher Charlie Chester (from the BBC radio programme *Stand Easy*)
is she a friend of Dorothy ? An allusion to a homosexual (from Judy Garland's character in *The Wizard of Oz*). The phrase arose from Judy Garland's friendships within male homosexual circles
I thang you (sic) Arthur Askey (from the radio show *Band Waggon*)
I think the answer lies in the soil Arthur Fallowfield (Kenneth Williams) in *Beyond Our Ken*
I think we should be told Attributed to John Junor by *Private Eye* in a parody of his opinion column in the *Sunday Express.* Although the column invariably used the phrase it is doubtful whether Junor ever actually used the phrase himself
it'll play in Peoria Coined by John Ehrlichman during the Nixon election campaign of 1969. The phrase was an allusion to whether policies would appeal to 'Middle America'. Peoria is in Illinois and was chosen as it had four syllables and scanned well
it never rains, but it pours John Arbuthnot (the inventor of 'John Bull' coined this phrase in 1726)
it's goodnight from me . . . and it's goodnight from him Ronnie Barker and Ronnie Corbett (*The Two Ronnies*)
it's only a bloody game Magnus Magnusson would invariably say this to settle the nerves of contenders of *Mastermind*; of course, this ice-breaker was only for the ears of the audience and participants
it's the way I tell 'em Frank Carson (full phrase is 'you've heard them all before but it's the way I tell 'em')
it's turned out nice again George Formby (invariably opened his act with this phrase)
I've arrived, and to prove it, I'm here Max Bygraves (as Archie Andrews' tutor in *Educating Archie*)
I've found it, I've found the lost chord Jimmy Durante (whilst playing the piano he would feign this new discovery)
I've got a million of 'em Jimmy Durante (after telling a joke) Max Miller later used this phrase
I've got his pecker in my pocket Lyndon B Johnson (dates from his time as Senate Majority leader in Washington)
I've started so I'll finish Magnus Magnusson would say this if he had started asking a question on the BBC's *Mastermind* programme but the time had elapsed and the hooter sounded
I wanna tell you a story Max Bygraves (as Archie Andrew's tutor in *Educating Archie*)
I want me tea Grandma Grove (Nancy Roberts) who often made this demand in the *Grove Family*

I want to be alone Greta Garbo never actually spoke these words off-set although she was very reclusive. The most often quoted origin of these words on screen is in the 1932 film *Grand Hotel*, however she utters the immortal words in the earlier 1929 film *The Single Standard* but as it was a silent film it was subtitled

I won't take me coat off; I'm not stopping Ken Platt, the northern comedian's catchphrase was coined by Ronnie Taylor, producer of radio's *Variety Fanfare*, in 1951

jolly hockey sticks Monica (Beryl Reid) as Archie Andrews' posh friend in *Educating Archie*

just give me the facts, ma'am Joe Friday (Jack Webb) in *Dragnet*

just like that Tommy Cooper (sometimes the master comedian would say 'not like that, like that')

K-E-Y-N-S-H-A-M Horace Batchelor, the football pools export on Radio Luxembourg would always end his advert by spelling out his address in Bristol

Kilroy was here Phrase used in WWII to allude to the US Air Transport Command. The phrase is of doubtful origin but it is beloved of graffiti writers

kiss of death, the Stock phrase deriving from the kiss of betrayal given by Judas to Christ

lady bountiful George Farquhar coined the phrase from the name of a character in his 1707 work *The Beaux Stratagem* but phrase is now applied to a woman who is conspicuously generous to others less fortunate than herself

laugh and the world laughs with you From Ella Wheeler Wilcox poem 'Solitude', it continues 'weep and you weep alone'

left hand down a bit Leslie Phillips (in *The Navy Lark*) Jon Pertwee would reply 'left hand down it is, sir'

let's be careful out there Sgt Esterhaus (Michael Conrad) in *Hill Street Blues*

let's get outta here In a survey of stock film phrases this is the most often said in film history

life begins at forty William B Pitkin (Professor of Journalism at Columbia University in a 1932 book)

listening bank, the Midland Bank (advertising slogan used from 1980 onwards)

little of what you fancy does you good, a Marie Lloyd popularised the phrase in a song written by Fred W Leigh and George Arthurs. The phrase was invariably accompanied by a suggestive wink

Lloyd George knew my father Tommy Rhys Roberts, whose father did indeed know Lloyd George, popularised the phrase, which became a Welsh standard song, sung to the tune of 'Onward Christian Soldiers'

loadsamoney Harry Enfield character (first seen in *Friday Night Live*) who was a plasterer by trade

loook Alf Garnett (Warren Mitchell) in *Till Death Us Do Part*

love me, love my dog St Bernard of Clairvaux first espoused this philosophical metaphor, which meant in effect, you must love me warts and all. Incidentally St Bernard of Clairvaux is not the St Bernard (of Menthon) after whom the breed of Alpine dog is named

love you madly Duke Ellington often said 'We'd like you to know that the boys in the band all . . .'

man for all seasons, a Robert Bolt's title for his 1960 play about Sir Thomas More has entered the language to describe an adaptable, all-round accomplished person

man on the Clapham omnibus, the Lord Bowen first coined this phrase in 1903 when summing up a case. The phrase has entered the modern idiom to represent the ordinary man in the street

man they couldn't gag, the Peter Wilson (nickname of the *Daily Mirror* sports columnist)

man you love to hate, the Erich von Stroheim (epithet rather than catchphrase)

Martini . . . shaken not stirred James Bond (The line is first spoken in *Goldfinger* but does not appear in the books)

mean! moody! magnificent Jane Russell (epithet rather than catchphrase) first used as slogan for *The Outlaw*

mind how you go George Dixon (Jack Warner) in *Dixon of Dock Green*

mind my bike Jack Warner popularised this unlikely hit phrase on radio

moment of truth, the The phrase derives from a Spanish bullfighting term 'El momento de la verdad' in which the final sword thrust kills the animal

Mounties always get their man, the Unofficial motto of the Royal Canadian Mounted Police first coined by John J Healy, although the official motto since 1873 is 'Maintain the Right'

Mr Big Ian Fleming coined the phrase in his second novel *Live and Let Die* (1954). The character's name was Buonaparte Ignace Gallia, hence Mr Big. The phrase has come to mean any top man in an organisation

Mr Clean James Baker the American Secretary of State was given this epithet

Much Binding in the Marsh Not so much a catchphrase but this popular radio programme, that grew out of an edition of *Merry-Go-Round* and starred Kenneth Horne and Richard Murdoch, became the instigator of many catchphrases and a song of the same title

mum, mum, they're laughing at me Arthur English (whilst playing his cockney spiv character and unfurling his kipper tie)

my flabber has never been so gasted Frankie Howerd coined this ridiculous phrase that became an essential part of his act. He would say 'I'm flabbergasted, in fact my flabber has never been so gasted'

my name's Monica Beryl Reid (as Archie Andrew's posh friend in *Educating Archie*)

nah . . . Luton airport Lorraine Chase (in a famous advert for Campari)

never change / swap horses in midstream Abraham Lincoln is identified with the phrase in a citation of 1864

never knowingly undersold John Lewis Partnership (slogan) devised by John Spedan Lewis in 1920

nice 'ere innit Lorraine Chase (in a famous advert for Campari)

nice to see you, to see you nice Bruce Forsyth (originally from the *Generation Game* but often used in other shows)

night of the long knives, the Originally referred to the night of 2 July 1934 when Hitler, aided by Himmler's black-shirted SS, liquidated the leadership of the brown-shirted SA. The phrase has entered modern vernacular to mean a surprise bloodless purge, for example Harold Macmillan's wholesale reorganisation of his cabinet in 1962

nine days' wonder Possibly traced back to Geoffrey Chaucer and more recently alluding to the fact that a puppy is blind for the first nine days of its life. The phrase has come to mean anything of short-lived appeal

no such thing as a free lunch The Nobel Prize-winning economist Milton Friedman is identified with the saying and he wrote a book of this name, but the phrase dates back to the 19th century

not a lot Paul Daniels (usually before doing a trick he would say 'you're going to like this . . .')

not 'arf Alan Freeman would say this phrase out of context, which perhaps gave it appeal

not tonight, Josephine Napoleon I (attributed but never actually said)

now cut that out! Jack Benny

now that's magic Paul Daniels (after successfully performing a slick trick)

nudge nudge, wink wink, say no more squire Eric Idle (in *Monty Python*) showing suspect pictures to Terry Jones

often a bridesmaid, but never a bride Milton Feasley wrote this slogan for Listerine mouthwash in 1923

oh hello, I'm Julian, and this is my friend Sandy Hugh Paddick (referring to Kenneth Williams in *Round the Horne*) *old soldiers never die, they simply fade away* General Douglas MacArthur whilst addressing congress on 19 April 1951 after being dismissed by President Truman. The phrase originated much earlier

one foot in the grave Jonathan Swift in *Gulliver's Travels* (1726) made the phrase popular in connection with the Struldbruggs of Laputa

one small step for man Neil Armstrong's exact words when walking on the moon were 'That's one small step for a man, one giant leap for mankind'

only the names have been changed Narrator of the detective series *Dragnet* would continue . . . .'to protect the innocent'

on with the motley (vesti la giubba) From Leoncavallo's opera *I Pagliacci* relating to the fact that the clown must carry on despite a broken heart

on your bike Norman Tebbit, addressing the Conservative Party conference on 15 Oct 1981. He related how his father was brought up with unemployment but instead of rioting got on his bike and looked for work

ooh Betty Frank Spencer (Michael Crawford) in *Some Mothers do 'ave 'em*

ooh lovely! Sara Crowe in advert for Philadelphia cheese

ooh you are awful, but I like you Mandy (Dick Emery) accompanied by a slap on the interviewer's shoulder

oooo arr, me ol' pal, me ol' beauty Walter Gabriel (Chris Gittins) in the *Archers*

orft we jolly well go Jimmy Young (after finishing the link with Terry Wogan would utter these words)

pass The stock reply of contenders on the BBC's *Mastermind* programme to save time if the answer did not immediately spring to mind

pass the sick-bag, Alice John Junor (used in his *Sunday Express* column and parodied by *Private Eye*)

phone a friend Chris Tarrant (in *Who Wants to Be a Millionaire*)

pile it high, sell it cheap Sir John Cohen, founder of Tesco supermarkets, coined this phrase

play it again Sam attributed to Humphrey Bogart as Rick Blaine in *Casablanca*, although he never actually said these words

pop goes the weasel W R Mandale wrote the rhyme 'Up and down the City Road, In and out the Eagle, That's the way the money goes, Pop goes the weasel'. The meaning of the rhyme is uncertain but 'Pop' means to pawn

probably the best lager in the world Carlsberg (1973 advertising slogan voiced by Orson Welles)

public enemy No. 1 John Dillinger (Attorney General Homer Cummings gave this name to the murderer)

Queen Anne's dead Phrase of uncertain origin but used to put down someone who delights in telling you some very old news or what you knew already

quick and the dead, the from the New Testament 2 Timothy 4:1. The quick in this context meant the living

read my lips George Bush popularised this phrase in his acceptance speech for the Republican nomination on 19 August 1988. The rest of the line was 'no new taxes'

real thing, it's the Coca-Cola (advertising slogan dating from 1942)

refreshes the parts other beers cannot reach Heineken (advertising slogan for the lager)

respec' Sacha Baron Cohen in the guise of rapper Ali G

right monkey Al Read (the popular northern comedian also used 'cheeky monkey' in his act)

rock on, Tommy Bobby Ball (the comedian would often tug his braces at the same time)

Rodney, you plonker Del Boy (David Jason) to his younger brother in *Only Fools and Horses*

roses grow on you Norman Vaughan (advertising campaign for Roses Chocolates)

say goodnight Dick Dan Rowan (in *Rowan and Martin's Laugh In*) to his co-star Dick Martin

say goodnight Gracie George Burns (to his wife and co-star Gracie Allen)

say it with flowers Patrick O' Keefe, an advertising agent, coined the phrase in 1917

shame, shame Bruce Forsyth (usually accompanied by a cuddle from him)

she who must be obeyed Horace Rumpole (Leo McKern) referring to his wife in John Mortimer's *Rumpole of the Bailey.* The original expression came from Henry Rider Haggard's novel *She* and referred to the all-powerful Ayesha

short, fat, hairy legs Eric Morecambe (referring to Ernie Wise)

shut that door Larry Grayson (turning towards the wings and intimating a draught)

silly old moo Alf Garnett (Warren Mitchell) referring to Elsie, his wife, in *Till Death Us Do Part*

sit (sssit) Barbara Woodhouse (whilst demonstrating her methods of training dogs)

slow, slow, quick, quick, slow Victor Sylvester popularised this quickstep tempo in his radio and television series

smell my cheese you mother Alan Partridge (Steve Coogan) insulting the chief commissioning editor of BBC television

smile, you're on . . . *Candid Camera* (first coined by Allen Funt in the original American version)

sock it to me Judy Carne (in *Rowan and Martin's Laugh In*)

somebody up there likes me Rocky Graziano (world champion boxer had a film and book about him with this title)

some mothers do 'ave 'em Jimmy Clitheroe (corruption of the phrase 'don't some mothers have 'em')

somewhere to the right of Genghis Khan Arthur Scargill relating a political standpoint to John Mortimer

speak as you find, that's my motto Nola Purvis (Pat Coombs) in the radio series *Hello Playmates*

spend, spend, spend, I'm going to Viv Nicholson (after winning £152,000 on Littlewoods football pools in 1961)

stone me Tony Hancock (originally coined in *Hancock's Half-Hour*)

stop me and buy one Lionel and Charles Rodd came up with this slogan for Wall's ice-cream in 1923 although in those days it was for ice-cream tricycles rather than vans

stop messin' abaht (sic) Kenneth Williams (originally coined by Williams in *Hancock's Half-Hour*)

suck it and see Charlie Naughton of the Crazy Gang coined this phrase, which meant 'try it'

suit you sir! Ken and Kenneth the tailors in the BBC comedy series *The Fast Show*

sweet Fanny Adams The phrase originates from the murder of an eight-year-old child in 1867. Fanny Adams was the victim of Frederick Booth, a solicitor's clerk, who grotesquely mutilated her body. As these things tend to go, at around the same time, the Royal Navy issued tinned meat which sailors flippantly said probably contained the remains of the little girl. Fanny Adams became slang for mutton or stew and later any worthless item. In modern day vernacular 'Sweet F. A.' can also mean sweet fuck-all

swinging Norman Vaughan (the phrase was accompanied by a thumbs-up gesture)

ten, four Dan Matthews (Broderick Crawford) in the American detective series *Highway Patrol.* The phrase signified agreement and was always being bellowed into the radio

thank you music lovers Spike Jones, the American musician, would murder a classic piece of music along the same lines as Les Dawson or Eric Morecambe and then proceed to say . . .

that'll do nicely, sir American Express (advertising slogan originating in the late 1970s)

that's all folks Merry Melodies (Warner Brothers cartoons) written at the end of their cartoons

that's magic Paul Daniels (after completion of a successful trick or illusion)

that's well lush Stacey (Joanna Page) in *Gavin and Stacey*
the ranger ain't gonna like it Yogi Booboo bear (when Yogi bear had inventive ideas for stealing picker-nick baskets)
there's more Jimmy Cricket (whilst telling a joke in his act)
there's no answer to that Eric Morecambe (cleverly used if the quick-witted comedian was stuck for words)
thinking man's crumpet, the Frank Muir coined this phrase about television presenter Joan Bakewell
this is Funf speaking Funf the spy (in *ITMA*, i.e. *It's That Man Again*)
today is the first day of the rest of your life Charles Dederich (founder of anti-heroin centres in the USA)
too little, too late Professor Allan Nevins wrote this in an article in *Current History* (1935), referring to the Nazi menace in Germany and the lack of remedial action
T. T. F. N. (ta-ta for now) Mrs Mopp (Dorothy Summers) in *ITMA*. Jimmy Young adopted this phrase in his popular Radio Two morning show
turn on, tune in, drop out Dr Timothy Leary coined this pro drug phrase in 1967, although he himself suggests that he stole the phrase from Marshall McLuhan
unacceptable face of capitalism Edward Heath coined this phrase in 1973 when replying to a question from Jo Grimond in the House of Commons
up and under Eddie Waring (the much imitated rugby commentator was synonymous with the phrase)
very interesting, but stupid Arte Johnson (in *Rowan and Martin's Laugh In*) dressed as a German soldier and smoking a cigarette in a holder
wakey, wakey Billy Cotton (a fanfare of *Somebody Stole My Gal* would follow this cry)
walkies Barbara Woodhouse (whilst demonstrating her methods of training dogs)
weekend starts here, the *Ready Steady Go* (the Friday night pop show was always preceded by these words)
week is a long time in politics, a Harold Wilson (also deliberated that 48 hours was a long time in politics)
well, he would, wouldn't he? Mandy Rice-Davies (referring to Lord Astor's denial of involvement with her)
were you truly wafted here from paradise? Terry Howard wrote this Campari advert, which made Lorraine Chase a star
what a fucking liberty Joannie 'Nan' Taylor (Catherine Tate)
what do you think of it so far? Eric Morecambe would rhetorically ask this question whilst either performing one of Ernie's plays or during a lull between sketches. The stock reply by Eric himself was 'rubbish', which was often said through an inanimate object by way of him throwing his voice or saying it between clenched teeth
what's new pussycat? Warren Beatty (coined the phrase and had the film originally written for him)
what's occurring? Nessa (Ruth Jones) in *Gavin and Stacey*
what's on the table Mabel? Wilfred Pickles (to his wife Mabel in radio's *Have a Go*)
what's up, doc? Bugs Bunny originally said these words to his adversary Elmer J Fudd, a doctor, but eventually would say this as a form of greeting to almost everyone. The full phrase was 'er, what's up doc?' followed by a crunch on a carrot
when the going gets tough, the tough get going Joseph P Kennedy, the father of John F Kennedy, used this phrase in the bringing up of his sons, in an effort to help them through adversity
who dares wins, Rodney Del Boy (David Jason) in *Only Fools and Horses*
who loves ya, baby? Theo Kojak (Telly Savalas) in the popular American detective series, *Kojak*
wind of change, the Harold Macmillan used this phrase, written by Sir David Hunt, in describing the change of political standing in Africa in 1960
winter of discontent, the The phrase originates in the opening line of the eponymous Richard of Gloucester in Shakespeare's *Richard III*, however the term is now used as a description of the winter of 1978/79 when industrial action became rife due to the Labour Government's endeavours to curb pay rises
without hesitation, deviation or repetition *Just a Minute* (the popular radio panel game meant guests had to speak for a minute)
world's favourite airline, the British Airways slogan
wot, no Chad The phrase was very common in Britain during WWII and was accompanied by a depiction of a bald-headed man appearing over a wall and inquiring 'wot, no . . .' the blank being filled in by any commodity in short supply. Its origin is uncertain
yaroooo Billy Bunter (created by Frank Richards)
yeah, but no, but yeah, but Vicky Pollard (Matt Lucas) in the BBC television comedy, *Little Britain*
you ain't heard nothin' yet Al Jolson (the most often misquoted catchphrase of all. The line is from *The Jazz Singer*)
you ain't seen nothin' yet President Ronald Reagan used this phrase as a slogan during his 1984 re-election bid
you bet your sweet bippy Dick Martin (in *Rowan and Martin's Laugh In*) popular 1960s US comedy show
you cannot be serious John McEnroe (much caricatured phrase that the tennis player often said on court)
you can run but you can't hide Joe Louis (said of Billy Conn, a nifty heavyweight of the day who Louis knocked out)
you can't see the join Eric Morecambe (talking about Ernie Wise's fictitious wig)
you dirty old man Harold Steptoe (Harry H Corbett) addressing his father in *Steptoe and Son*
you dirty rat Cagney, James (dirty double-crossing rat were actual words in *Blonde Crazy* 1931)
you dirty rotten swine, you Bluebottle (Peter Sellers) in the *Goon Show*
you lucky people Tommy Trinder used this phrase whilst compering the *Sunday Night at the London Palladium* shows and it became his stock phrase identified with him
your starter for ten Bamber Gascoigne (an on the buzzer question to teams in *University Challenge*)
you too can have a body like mine Charles Atlas (slogan used for his mail-order body-building lessons)
you've never had it so good Harold MacMillan (actually said 'most of our people have never had it so good')

Causes of Death

Ace, Johnny Rhythm and blues act, died playing Russian roulette (1954).
Alexander the Great Died aged 32 after a prolonged banquet and drinking bout (323 BC).
Alkan, Charles-Henri Valentin French pianist and composer who died when bookshelf collapsed on him whilst reaching for the Talmud (1888).

Antony, Mark Roman triumvir, committed suicide by running onto his sword in 31 BC (misled by a false report of Cleopatra's death).
Archer, Fred English champion jockey, shot himself during an attack of typhoid (1886).
Astor, John Jacob American financier, went down in the *Titanic* in 1912.
Bach, Johann Sebastian German composer, suffered stroke following unsuccessful eye operation (1750).
Ballard, Florence Supremes vocalist, died of a heart attack aged 32 yrs 7 mths.
Barnett, Lady Isobel Committed suicide in her bathroom on 20 October 1980, one week after being found guilty of shoplifting.
Bartók, Bela Hungarian composer, died of leukaemia (1945).
Beethoven, Ludwig van German compuser, died of cirrhosis of the liver (lupus erythematosus is sometimes considered an alternative cause) (1827).
Belushi, John American actor, died of drug-related illness, aged 33 yrs 1 mth (1982).
Berbick, Trevor Former heavyweight boxing champion of the world, murdered in a churchyard in Kingston, Jamaica (28 October 2006).
Berg, Alban Austrian composer, died from infection from a septic insect bite (1935).
Berlioz, Hector French composer, died following brain haemorrhage (1869).
Billy the Kid Pseudonym of Henry McCarty, aka William H Bonney, American bandit, shot by sheriff Pat Garrett in 1881.
Bizet, Georges French composer, died of angina pectoris complicated by rheumatoid arthritis (1875).
Bolan, Marc T Rex singer, died in car crash aged 30 yrs 2 mths (1977).
Bonham, John Led Zeppelin member, died of alcohol poisoning, aged 32 yrs 3 mths (1980).
Brahms, Johannes German composer, died of liver cancer (1897).
Brooke, Rupert English poet, died of septicaemia, aged 27 yrs (1915).
Brown, Grace Murdered by Chester Gillett in 1906; formed basis for Theodore Dreiser's book *An American Tragedy.*
Calmette, Gaston Editor of *Le Figaro*, shot by Madame Caillaux, wife of the French Finance Minister, accusing her husband of fraud; she was later acquitted (1914).
Calvi, Roberto Italian banker, found hanging from scaffolding under Blackfriars Bridge (18 June 1982).
Carpenter, Karen American vocalist and drummer, died aged 32 yrs 11 mths from heart attack caused by anorexia nervosa (1983).
Castlereagh, Viscount British statesman, stabbed himself with a penknife (1822).
Chausson, Ernest French composer, died in a bicycle accident (1899).
Childers, Erskine Irish nationalist, was executed in 1922 by the Irish Free State authorities.
Chopin, Fryderyk Polish composer, died of pulmonary tuberculosis (1849).
Clarke, Ossie Fashion designer, murdered by his flatmate Diego Cogolato (7 August 1996).
Cleopatra Queen of Egypt, allegedly committed suicide by allowing an asp to bite her breast (30 BC).
Cline, Patsy Top American country singer, died in a plane crash aged 30 yrs 5 mths (1963).
Clive, Robert (of Plassey) English soldier, committed suicide (after several attempts) by shooting himself (1774).
Cobain, Kurt Lead singer of Nirvana, shot himself dead aged 27 yrs 1 mth (1994).
Cogan, Alma English singer, died of cancer aged 34 yrs 5 mths (1966).
Cooke, Sam American soul singer, shot dead aged 33 yrs 9 mths (1964).
Crane, Harold Hart American poet, committed suicide by leaping from a steamboat into the Caribbean (1932).
Davison, Emily Suffragette, threw herself under the King's horse in the 1913 Epsom Derby.
Dean, James American actor, died in a car crash in 1955, aged 24.
Debussy, Claude French composer, died of cancer of the rectum (1918).
Delius, Frederick English composer, died of syphilis in 1934.
Diana, Princess of Wales Died in Paris car crash (31 Aug 1997).
Dvorák, Antonín Czech composer, died of a brain haemorrhage (1904).
Eastman, George American inventor of the Kodak camera, shot himself in 1932.
Elgar, Edward English composer, died of a brain tumour in 1934.
Elliot, 'Mama' Cass American singer, died of a heart attack, aged 32 yrs 10 mths (1974).
Epstein, Brian Manager of the Beatles, died of a drugs overdose in 1967.
Fayed, Dodi Son of Harrods director, died in Paris car crash (31 Aug 1997).
Freud, Sigmund Austrian neurologist and founder of psychoanalysis, died of cancer in 1939.
Garland, Judy American entertainer, died of a drugs overdose in 1969.
Gately, Stephen Boyzone member, died of pulmonary oedema.
Genovese, Kitty Famous New York murder; nobody answered her calls for help.
Gershwin, George American composer, died of a brain tumour (1937).
Gibb, Andy Brother of the Bee Gees, died aged 30 of drug-related illness (1988).
Gibb, Maurice Member of the Bee Gees, died of a heart attack following an operation to clear an intestinal blockage. Maurice was born 22 December 1949 and died 12 January 2003.
Granados, Enrique Spanish composer, died when his ship SS *Sussex* was torpedoed by a German sub in the English Channel (1916).
Grieg, Edvard Norwegian composer, died from coronary artery disease with angina pectoris (1907).
Ham, Pete Badfinger member and co-writer of 'Without You', committed suicide after depression brought on possibly by royalty problems (1975).
Hancock, Tony Birmingham-born comedian, took a drug overdose in a Sydney hotel room in 1968.
Hannibal Carthaginian soldier, committed suicide by poison when the Romans demanded his surrender (182 BC).
Haydn, Franz Joseph Austrian composer, died of arteriosclerosis (1809).
Hemingway, Ernest American novelist, shot himself in the mouth in Ketchum, Idaho (1961).
Hendrix, Jimi American guitarist, suffocated in his own vomit after mixing drugs and alcohol aged 27 yrs 9 mths (1970).
Hickok, Wild Bill American gunfighter, shot from behind by Jack McCall whilst playing poker in 1876. Hickok's hand was a queen and 2 pair aces over eights (Dead man's hand).
Himmler, Heinrich German Nazi leader committed suicide with a cyanide phial concealed in his mouth (1945).
Holly, Buddy Rock and roll pioneer, died aged 22 yrs 5 months in a plane crash (with Ritchie Valens, 17 yrs 9 mths, and the Big Bopper, 29 yrs 4 mths) in 1959.
Houston, Whitney American vocalist, found unconscious in Suite 434 at the Beverly Hilton Hotel, California submerged in the bathtub. Toxicology results revealed Cocaine, Benadryl, Xanax, marijuana and Flexeril were in her system although her death was accidental.
Hull, Rod Comedian (with Emu puppet), died aged 63, after falling off his roof while trying to adjust his television aerial (18 March 1999).

Hutchence, Michael Lead singer with INXS, found hanging in a Sydney hotel room (21 Nov 1997).
Iliffe, Marc (Britain's Strongest Man 2002) Hanged himself in his gym in February 2003.
Ingram, Herbert English journalist, founder of the *Illustrated London News* and MP for Boston from 1856, drowned in a boat collision on Lake Michigan in 1860.
Ireton, Henry English Parliamentarian soldier, died of the plague in 1651.
Irving, Laurence Novelist son of actor Sir Henry Irving, drowned in the *Empress of Ireland* disaster in 1914.
James, Jesse Wild West robber, shot in the back of the head by Bob Ford (1882).
Jones, Brian Member of the Rolling Stones, drowned in a swimming pool (aged 27 yrs 4 mths) soon after leaving the group in 1969.
Joplin, Janis American folk singer, died aged 27 yrs 8 mths of heroin overdose (1970).
Klee, Paul Swiss artist, died of a heart attack (1940).
Koestler, Arthur and Cynthia Hungarian-born British author and his wife, committed suicide together in 1983 when he became terminally ill.
Leclair, Jean Marie French composer, stabbed in his own home, possibly by his wife (1764).
Liszt, Franz Hungarian composer, died of pneumonia (1886).
London, Jack American novelist, committed suicide by taking poison in 1916.
Lully, Jean-Baptiste French composer, died of gangrene and blood poisoning after he struck himself in the foot whilst conducting with a pointed cane (1687).
Lynott, Phil Thin Lizzy vocalist and guitarist, died of drug-related illness aged 34 yrs 4 mths (1986).
Markov, Georgi Bulgarian defector, famously murdered by the poison 'ricin' dispensed from the tip of an umbrella (1978).
Marten, Maria Mole-catcher's daughter, murdered by William Corder in May 1827 at the Red Barn at Polstead nr Ipswich.
Mendelssohn, Felix German composer, died of brain haemorrage (1847).
Milk, Harvey US gay rights activist and politician, killed alongside San Francisco Mayor, George Moscone, by ex-city employee Dan White (1978).
Mishima, Yukio Japanese writer, born Hiraoka Kimitake, committed Seppuku in 1970.
Monroe, Marilyn American model and actress, died from an overdose of sleeping pills in 1962.
Moon, Keith Who drummer, died of alcoholic poisoning aged 32 (in the same flat that Mama Cass died, owned by Harry Nilsson) in 1978.
Morrison, Jim Doors vocalist, died of drug related illness in 1971 (aged 27 yrs 6 mths); buried in Paris.
Mozart, Wolfgang Austrian composer died of heated military fever (nowadays usually considered to be Bright's Disease) (1791).
Murrell, Hilda Famous botanist (rose grower) and peace campaigner, found stabbed in a wood (1984) in suspicious circumstances as she was linked with documents about the sinking of the *General Belgrano.*
Niven, David English actor, died of motor neurone disease (1983).
Orton, Joe English dramatist, struck by hammer wielded by lover Kenneth Halliwell (1967), who subsequently committed suicide.
Owen, Wilfred English poet, killed on the bank of the Oise-Sambre Canal, nr Ors, one week before the armistice was signed in 1918.
Palach, Jan Czech philosophy student, set fire to himself in Jan 1969 in protest at the Russian invasion of Czechoslovakia the previous year.
Pasolini, Pier Paolo Italian writer and director, murdered, possibly as a result of a homosexual encounter, by Giuseppe Pelosi (1975).
Plath, Sylvia Poet wife of Ted Hughes, committed suicide by gassing herself (1963).
Pliny the Elder Roman writer, died in Stabiae (Castellamare) in AD 79 overcome by fumes from Vesuvius.
Presley, Elvis American singer, died of drug-related illnesses in 1977.
Prokofiev, Sergei Russian composer, died of brain haemorrage (1953).
Puccini, Giacomo Italian composer, died of throat cancer (1924).
Quisling, Vidkun Norwegian Fascist leader and puppet PM in occupied Norway, executed in May 1945.
Rachmaninov, Sergei Russian composer and pianist, died of malignant melanoma (1943).
Ravel, Maurice French composer, died of brain tumour (1937).
Redding, Otis Soul singer, died aged 26 yrs 3 mths in a plane crash (1967).
Relf, Keith Yardbirds musician, electrocuted himself, aged 33 yrs 1 mth (1976).
Rimsky-Korsakov, Nikolai Russian composer, died of coronary artery disease with angina pectoris (1908).
Riperton, Minnie American singer, died of cancer aged 31 yrs 8 mths (1979).
Rivett, Sandra Children's nanny, probably murdered by Lord Lucan in 1974 (convicted in absentia 19 June 1975).
Rizzio, David Italian courtier to Mary Queen of Scots, murdered by Scottish noblemen including the Earls of Morton and Lindsay, at the instigation of Lord Darnley (1566).
Robsart, Amy Wife of the Earl of Leicester (favourite of Elizabeth I), found dead at the bottom of a flight of stairs at Cumnor Place, Berkshire (1560).
Rossini, Gioacchino Italian composer, died of cancer of the rectum (1868).
Rothko, Mark Latvian-born American painter, committed suicide by slashing his wrists (1970).
Schubert, Franz Austrian composer, died of typhoid fever (1828).
Scriabin, Alexander Russian composer, died of an infection of a facial carbuncle (1915).
Shannon, Del American pop singer, shot himself whilst depressed (1990).
Siddall, Elizabeth Wife of Dante Gabriel Rossetti, took overdose of laudanum (1862).
Silkwood, Karen US nuclear activist, died in a car crash; her car was suspected to have been forced off the road (1973).
Stradella, Alessandro Italian composer, murdered by persons unknown (1682).
Swayze, Patrick American actor, died of pancreatic cancer.
Tchaikovsky, Piotr Russian composer, died of cholera in 1893.
Tone, Wolfe Irish nationalist, cut his throat with a penknife whilst awaiting hanging in Dublin (1798).
Tyler, Wat Leader of the Peasants' Revolt of 1381, wounded by William Walworth, Mayor of London and subsequently dragged from his hospital bed (St Bartholomew's) and beheaded.
Van Gogh, Vincent Dutch painter, shot himself whilst depressed (1890).
Versace, Gianni Murdered outside his Miami home (15 July 1997) by serial killer Andrew Cunanan, who committed suicide shortly afterwards.
Wagner, Richard German composer, died of coronary artery disease with angina pectoris (1883).
Wallace, William Scottish patriot, famously depicted in the film *Braveheart.* After being hanged, drawn and quartered by the British, his quarters were sent to Newcastle, Berwick, Stirling and Perth, as a reminder of his insurrection (1305).
Weber, Carl German composer, died of pulmonary tuberculosis and ulcerated larynx (1826).

Webern, Anton von Austrian composer, shot and killed by an American military policeman whilst out after curfew (1945).
Westbrook, Harriet First wife of the poet PB Shelley, committed suicide by drowning herself in the Serpentine, Hyde Park (1816).
Woolf, Virginia English novelist, drowned herself in the River Ouse, near her home at Rodmell in Sussex (1941).
Yamamoto, Isoruku Japanese admiral who directed the attack on Pearl Harbor; his plane was shot down over the Solomon Islands in 1943.
Zweig, Stefan Austrian-born British writer, committed suicide with his second wife in 1942.

NB: This section gives only a selective list; further death details may be found in other sections, eg Assassinations and Monarchs.

Countries of Birth

John Dalberg, 1st Baron Acton (Italy) English Historian
Joy Adamson (Austria) British Naturalist
Shmuel Yosef Agnon (Poland) Israeli Writer
Viscount Alanbrooke (France) British Soldier
Josef Albers (Germany) American Painter
Alexander Alekhine (Russia) French Chess master
Gubby Allen (Australia) English Cricketer
Peter Alliss (Germany) British Golfer
Lawrence Alma-Tadema (Holland) British Painter
Jeanette Altwegg (India) British Skating Gold Medallist
Leopold Amery (India) English Tory Politician
Lindsay Anderson (India) British Film Director
Peter André (England) Australian Singer
Mario Andretti (Italy) US Racing Driver
Natalie Appleton (Canada) British Singer
Nicole Appleton (Canada) British Singer
Edward Ardizzone (Vietnam) British Illustrator
Michael Arlen (Bulgaria) British Novelist
Pamela Armstrong (Borneo) British Newscaster
Paddy Ashdown (India) English Politician
Vladimir Ashkenazy (Russia) Icelandic Pianist
Frederick Ashton (Ecuador) English Choreographer
John Jacob Astor (Germany) American Financier
Nancy Astor (USA) British Politician
WH Auden (England) American Writer
John Audubon (Haiti) American Ornithologist
Frank Auerbach (Germany) British Artist
Charles Aznavour (Armenia) French Singer
Leo Baekland (Belgium) American Chemist
Bruce Bairnsfather (India) British Cartoonist
George Baker (Bulgaria) British Actor
JG Ballard (China) British Writer
Daniel Barenboim (Argentina) Israeli Pianist
Victor Barna (Hungary) British Table-Tennis Champion
John Barnes (Jamaica) English Footballer
Raymond Barre (Réunion) French Politician
Lord Beaverbrook (Canada) British Newspaper Magnate
Bee Gees (Isle of Man) Australian Pop Group
Menachem Begin (Poland [now Russia]) Israeli Statesman
Georg von Bekesy (Hungary) US Physiologist
Hilaire Belloc (France) British Writer
Saul Bellow (Canada) US Writer
Baruj Benacerraf (Venezuela) US Immunologist
Floella Benjamin (Trinidad) British TV Presenter
Jill Bennett (Straits Settlement, now Malaysia) British Actress
Irving Berlin (Russia) US Composer
Isaiah Berlin (Latvia) British Philosopher
Pete Best (India) British Musician
Hans A Bethe (Germany [Strasbourg, now France]) US Physicist
Lord Beveridge (India) British Economist
Zulfikar Ali Bhutto (India) Pakistani Statesman
Isla Blair (India) British Actress
George Blake (Netherlands) British Spy (for Soviet Union)
Nicolas Bloembergen (Netherlands) US Physicist
Paul Boateng (Ghana) British Politician
Andrew Bonar Law (Canada) English Prime Minister
Alan Bond (England) Australian Businessman
Daniel Bovet (Switzerland) Italian Pharmacologist
Anne Bradstreet (England) US Poet
Gyles Brandreth (West Germany) British Author and Politician
Frank Brangwyn (Belgium) Welsh Painter
Chris Brasher (British Guiana) British Athlete
Walter Houser Brattain (China) US Physicist
Alfred Brendel (Czechoslovakia) Austrian Pianist
Fenner Brockway (India) English Politician
Joseph Brodsky (Russia) US Poet
Ford Madox Brown (France) English Painter
Herbert C Brown (England) US Chemist
Yul Brynner (Russia) US Actor
Frances Hodgson Burnett (England) US Novelist
Terry Butcher (Singapore) English Footballer
Andrew Caddick (New Zealand) English Cricketer
Maria Callas (United States) Greek Soprano
Albert Camus (Algeria) French Writer
Jacques Canetti (Bulgaria) French Record Producer
Frank Capra (Sicily) US Film Director
Claudia Cardinale (Tunisia) Italian Actress
Barbara Carrera (Nicaragua) US Actress
Anna Carteret (India) British Actress
Gian Domenico Cassini (Genoa) French Astronomer
Marc Chagall (Russia) French Artist
Ernst Boris Chain (Germany) British Biochemist
William Chambers (Sweden) Scottish Architect
Philippe de Champaigne (Belgium) French Painter
Subrahmanyan Chandrasekhar (India [Lahore, now Pakistan]) US Astrophysicist
Louis Chevrolet (Switzerland) US Automobile Engineer
Erskine Childers (England) Irish Writer and Nationalist
Glynn Christian (New Zealand) British TV Broadcaster
Julie Christie (India) English Actress
Linford Christie (Jamaica) British Olympic Gold Medallist
Christo (Bulgaria) American Artist
Elizabeth Connell (South Africa) Irish Soprano
Joseph Conrad (Poland) English Novelist
Alistair Cooke (UK) American Journalist and Broadcaster
Harry H Corbett (Burma) English Actor
Carl Ferdinand Cori (Czechoslovakia) US Biochemist
Allan Cormack (South Africa) US Physicist
John Cornforth (Australia) British Chemist
Sir Michael Costa (Italy) British Conductor
André Frédéric Cournand (France) US Physicist
Cicely Courtneidge (Australia) English Actress
Colin Cowdrey (India) English Cricketer
Frederic Cowen (Jamaica) English Composer
Kid Creole (Canada) US Singer
Jason Crump (UK) Australian Sportsman
Cyril Cusack (South Africa) Irish Actor
György Cziffra (Hungary) French Pianist
Frank Damrosch (Germany) US Conductor
Walter Damrosch (Germany) US Conductor
Dana (Rosemary Scallon) (England) Irish Singer
Edward Dannreuther (Alsace) English Pianist
Edward De Bono (Malta) British Psychologist
Chris De Burgh (Argentina) British Singer
Christian R De Duve (England) Belgian Biochemist
Hans Dehmelt (Germany) US Physicist

Max Delbruck (Germany) US Biophysicist
Eamon De Valera (USA) Irish Politician
Ted Dexter (Italy) English Cricketer
Thomas Dolby (Egypt) British Musician
Gabrielle Drake (Pakistan) British Actress
Marcel Duchamp (France) American artist
Renato Dulbecco (Italy) American Biologist
George Du Maurier (France) English Writer
Lawrence and Gerald Durrell (India) English Writers
Sophie-Carmen Eckhardt-Gramatté (Russia) Canadian Composer
Glynn Edwards (Malaya) British Actor
Albert Einstein (Germany) Swiss physicist
Brian Elias (India) English Composer
Iso Elinson (Russia) British Pianist
TS Eliot (USA) British Poet
Mary Ellis (USA) English Soprano
Gloria Estefan (Cuba) American Singer
Eusebio (Mozambique) Portuguese Footballer
Enrico Fermi (Italy) US Nuclear Physicist
Edmond H Fischer (China) US Chemist
Bob Fitzsimmons (England) American Boxer
Errol Flynn (Tasmania) American Actor
CS Forester (Egypt) British Writer
Malcolm Forsyth (South Africa) Canadian Composer
Harry Freedman (Poland) Canadian Composer
Lucien Freud (Germany) British Artist
Marya Freund (Poland) French Soprano
Géza Frid (Hungary) Dutch Composer
Oskar Fried (Germany) Russian Conductor
Chris Froome (Kenya) British Cyclist
Fiona Fullerton British Actress
Henry Fuseli (Switzerland) British Painter
Dennis Gabor (Hungary) British Physicist
Ivan Galamian (Iran) US Violinist
Sandy Gall (Malaya) British Newsreader
Lamberto Gardelli (Italy) Swedish Conductor
Baron Francois Gérard (Italy) French Painter
Ivar Giaever (Norway) US Physicist
Mel Gibson (USA) Australian Actor
Werner Wolf Glaser (Germany) Swedish Composer
Vinko Globokar (France) Yugoslav Trombonist
Alma Gluck (Romania) American Soprano
Maria Goeppert-Mayer (Germany [Katowice, now Poland]) US Physicist
James Goldsmith (France) British Tycoon
Adam Lindsay Gordon (Azores) Australian Poet
Arshile Gorky (Armenia) US Painter
Bryan Gould (New Zealand) British Politician
Ragnar Granit (Finland) Swedish Physiologist
Bernie Grant (British Guiana) English Politician
Cary Grant (England) US Actor
El Greco (Crete (Candia)) Spanish Painter
Silvia Greenberg (Romania) Israeli Soprano
Tony Greig (South Africa) English Cricketer
André Grétry (Belgium) French Composer
Dulcie Grey (Malaya) British Actress
Frederick Grinke (Canada) British Violinist
Walter Gropius (Germany) US Architect
Georg Grosz (Germany) US Painter
Giovanni Guardi (Austria) Venetian Painter
Roger Guillemin (France) US Physiologist
Richard Hageman (Holland) US Composer
Thomas Duffus Hardy (Jamaica) English Archivist
Friedrich von Hayek (Austria) British Economist
Jascha Heifetz (Lithuania) US Violinist
László Heltay (Hungary) British Conductor
Victor Hely-Hutchinson (South Africa) English Composer
Audrey Hepburn (Belgium) American Actress
William Herschel (Germany) British Astronomer
David Low (New Zealand) British Political Cartoonist
Henry Luce (China) US Magazine Publisher
Gerhard Herzberg (Germany) Canadian Physical Chemist
Rudolf Hess (Egypt) German Politician
Victor Hess (Austria) US Physicist
Hermann Hesse (Germany) Swiss Novelist
Dorothy Hodgkin (Egypt) English Chemist
Roald Hoffmann (Poland) US Chemist
Adam Hollioake (Australia) English Cricketer
Ben Hollioake (Australia) England Cricketer
Bob Holness (South Africa) British Presenter
Gordon Honeycombe (India [now Pakistan]) British TV Presenter
Bob Hope (England) US Comedian
Harry Houdini (Hungary) US Escapologist
John Houseman (Hungary) US Actor / Director
Charles B Huggins (Canada) American Surgeon
William Morris Hughes (Wales) Australian Statesman
Olivia Hussey (Argentina) British Actress
Anjelica Huston (Ireland) American Actress
Alec Issigonis (Turkey) British Automobile Designer
Eddie Izzard (Yemen) English Comedian
Sid James (South Africa) British Actor
Karl Jaspers (Germany) Swiss Philosopher
Niels K Jerne (England) Danish Immunologist
Ruth Prawer Jhabvala (Germany) British Novelist
Alexander Johnson (England) American Philosopher
Boris Johnson (USA) British Politician
Dom Joly (Lebanon) British Comedian
Vasily Kandinsky (Russia) French Painter
Anna Karen (South Africa) British Actress
Boris Karloff (England) US Actor
Yousef Karsh (Turkey) Canadian Photographer
Kenneth Kendall (India) British TV Presenter
Har Gobind Khorana (India [Raipur, now Pakistan]) US Molecular Chemist
Nicole Kidman (Honolulu, Hawaii, USA) Australian Actress
Wilson Kipketer (Kenya) Danish Athlete
Rudyard Kipling (India) English Writer
Henry Kissinger (Germany) US Politician
Aaron Klug (Lithuania) British Biophysicist
Godfrey Kneller (Germany) British Artist
Arthur Koestler (Hungary) British Author
Oskar Kokoschka (Austria) British Artist
Tjalling Koopmans (Netherlands) US Economist
Alexander Korda (Hungary) British Film Producer
Alexis Korner (France) British Musician
Hans Adolf Krebs (Germany) British Biochemist
Polykarp Kusch (Germany) US Physicist
Simon Kuznets (Russia) US Economist
John Lang (Scotland) Australian Clergyman
Angela Lansbury (England) US Actress
Danny La Rue (Ireland) British Entertainer
Charles Laughton (England) US Actor
Stan Laurel (England) US Actor / Comedian
Sir Austen Layard (France) English Archaeologist
Bernard Leach (Hong Kong) English Potter
Vivien Leigh (India) British Actress
Peter Lely (Netherlands) British Painter
Philipp EA Lenard (Hungary) German Physicist
Wassily Leontief (Russia) US Economist
Doris Lessing (Persia [now Iran]) British Writer
Claude Lévi-Strauss (Belgium) French Anthropologist
W Arthur Lewis (St Lucia) British Economist
Wyndham Lewis (Canada) English Novelist / Painter
Eric Liddell (China) Scottish Athlete
Basil Liddell Hart (France) English Historian
Fritz A Lipmann (Germany) US Biochemist
David Lloyd George (England) Welsh Politician
Margaret Lockwood (India) British Actress
Frederick Loewe (Austria) US Composer
Peter Lorre (Hungary) US Actor

Bela Lugosi (Lugos Hungary [Lugos, now Romania]) US Actor
Jean-Baptiste Lully (Italy) French Composer
Joanna Lumley (Kashmir) British Actress
Salvador Luria (Italy) US Biologist
Rosa Luxemburg (Poland) German Revolutionary
Roddy McDowall (England) US Actor
John McEnroe (West Germany) US Tennis Player
Thomas McGee (Ireland) Canadian Writer
Patrick McGoohan (USA) British Actor
Shane MacGowan (England) Irish Musician
Donald McIntyre (New Zealand) English Bass-Baritone
Leo McKern (Australia) British Actor
Jean-Paul Marat (Switzerland) French Revolutionary
Ann-Margret (Sweden) US Actress
Raymond Massey (Canada) US Actor
William Somerset Maugham (France) British Writer
Robert Maxwell (Czechoslovakia) British Businesman
Jules Mazarin (Italy) French Prelate
Peter B Medawar (Brazil) British Zoologist
Golda Meir (Ukraine) Israeli Politician
Gian-Carlo Menotti (Italy) US Composer
Freddie Mercury (Zanzibar) British Singer
William Mervyn (Kenya) British Actor
Albert Michelson (Germany) US Physicist
Bette Midler (Hawaii [now US State]) US Singer
Ludwig Mies Van Der Rohe (Germany) USA Architect
Spike Milligan (India) British Comedian
Guy Mitchell (Yugoslavia) US Singer
Franco Modigliani (Italy) US Economist
Yves Montand (Italy) French Actor and Singer
Lola Montez (Eire) US Dancer
Benjamin Mottelson (USA) Danish Physicist
Vladimir Nabokov (Russia) US Novelist
Sam Neill (New Zealand) Australian Actor
Olivia Newton-John (UK) Australian Actress
Mike Nichols (Germany) US Film Director
Harold Nicolson (Persia [now Iran]) British Diplomat
Merle Oberon (India) British Actress
Severo Ochoa (Spain) US Biochemist
Jacques Offenbach (Germany) French Composer
Claes Oldenburg (Sweden) US Sculptor
Isaac Oliver (France) English Painter
Charles Chadwick Oman (India) English Historian
Lars Onsager (Norway) US Physical Chemist
Eugene Ormandy (Hungary) US Conductor
George Orwell (India) British Novelist
Thomas Paine (England) US Writer and Revolutionary
George Palade (Romania) US Biologist
Lili Palmer (Austria) French Actress
Adelina Patti (Spain) Italian Soprano
IM Pei (China) US Architect
Susan Penhaligon (Philippines) British Actress
Arno Penzias (Germany) US Astrophysicist
Max F Perutz (Austria) British Biochemist
Antoine Pevsner (Russia) French Painter
Harry Philby (Ceylon [Sri Lanka]) English Arabist and Explorer
Kim Philby (India) British Spy (for Soviet Union)
HRH Prince Philip (Greece) British Duke and Consort to the Queen
Camille Pissarro (West Indies [St Thomas]) French Painter
Sidney Poitier (Bahamas) US Actor
Roman Polanski (France) Polish Film-maker
Nyree Dawn Porter (New Zealand) British Actress
Vladimir Prelog (Bosnia) Swiss Chemist
Emeric Pressburger (Hungary) British Film Writer
Ilya Prigogine (Russia) Belgian Chemist
Victoria Principal (Japan) US Actress
Juliet Prowse (South Africa) US Dancer
Anthony Quinn (Mexico) US Actor
Peter Rachman (Poland) British Property Developer
Stamford Raffles (Jamaica [at sea]) English Colonial Administrator
Basil Rathbone (South Africa) British Actor
Cyril Regis (French Guiana) English Footballer
Elisabeth Rethberg (Germany) US Soprano
Cliff Richard (India) British Vocalist
Frederick Sleigh Roberts (India) English Soldier
Max Robertson (Bangladesh) British TV Presenter
Edward G Robinson (Romania) US Actor
Richard Rogers (Italy) English Architect
Ronald Ross (India) British Physician
Mark Rothko (Latvia) US Painter
Eero Saarinen (Finland) US Architect
Albert Sabin (Poland) American Physician
Andrew Sachs (Germany) British Actor
Nelly Leonie Sachs (Germany) Swedish Poet and Playwright
Yves Saint Laurent (Algeria) French Fashion Designer
Pamela Salem (India) British Actress
George Sanders (Russia) British Actor
Tessa Sanderson (Jamaica) British Olympic Gold Medallist
John Singer Sargent (Italy) US Painter
Andrew Schally (Poland) US Biochemist
Elsa Schiaparelli (Italy) French Fashion Designer
Shaun Scott (Canada) British Actor
Emilio Segre (Italy) US Physicist
Harry Selfridge (USA) British Merchant
Aloys Senefelder (Czechoslovakia) German Printer and Inventor
Robert Service (England) Canadian Poet
Yitzhak Shamir (Poland) Israeli Politician
William Bradford Shockley (England) US Physicist
Walter Sickert (Germany) English Artist
Claude Simon (Madagascar) French Novelist
Isaac Bashevis Singer (Poland) US Writer
Israel Singer (Poland) US Writer
Elaine Smith (Scotland) Australian Actress
Sydney Smith (New Zealand) British Poet
George Solti (Hungary) British Conductor
Basil Spence (India) Scottish Architect
Sheila Steafel (South Africa) British Actress
Brian Stein (South Africa) English Footballer
Max Steiner (Austria) US Composer
Edward Stourton (Nigeria) UK TV Presenter
Kiefer Sutherland (England) Canadian Actor
Robert Swinhoe (India) English Naturalist
Yves Tanguy (France) US Painter
Mother Teresa (Yugoslavia) Indian Roman Catholic Nun
WM Thackeray (India) British Author
Roy Thomson (Canada) British Newspaper Magnate
Angela Thorne (India [now Pakistan]) British Actress
Debbie Thrower (Kenya) British TV Presenter
Dmitri Tiomkin (Russia) US Composer
Richard Todd (Ireland) English Actor
JRR Tolkien (South Africa) English Novelist
Walter Trog (Canada) British Cartoonist
Liv Ullmann (Japan) Norwegian Actress
Rudolph Valentino (Italy) American Actor
Victor Vasarely (Hungary) French Painter
Hendrik Verwoerd (Holland) South African Politician
Colin Viljoen (South Africa) English Footballer
Selman A Waksman (Russia) US Biochemist
Hugh Walpole (New Zealand) British Novelist
Max Weber (Russia) US Painter
Vanessa-Mae (Singapore) British Violinist
Victor Weisz (Germany) British Political Cartoonist
Benjamin West (USA) English Painter
Alan Whicker (Egypt) British Broadcaster
Joseph Blanco White (Spain) English Poet
Patrick White (England) Australian Author
Terence Hanbury White (India) British Novelist

Roger Whittaker (Kenya) South African Singer
Bradley Wiggins (Belgium) British Cyclist
Eugene Paul Wigner (Hungary) US Physicist
Billy Wilder (Austria) US Film-maker
David Wilkie (Sri Lanka) Scottish Swimmer
John Williams (Australia) British Guitarist
Malcolm Williamson (Australia) British Composer
Bruce Willis (Germany) US Actor
Orde Wingate (India) British Soldier
William Wyler (Germany [Mulhausen, now France]) US Film-maker

Dying Words

Independence for ever **John Adams** *US President*
It is the last of Earth, I am content **John Quincy Adams** *US President*
See in what peace a Christian can die **Joseph Addison** *Essayist*
Kurt **Alfred Adler** *Psychologist*
If I feel in good form I shall take the difficult way up. If I do not, I shall take the easy one. I shall join you in an hour **Albert I** *King of Belgium*
I have had wealth, rank and power, but if these were all I had, how wretched I would be **Prince Albert** *Queen Victoria's Consort*
I have such sweet thoughts **Prince Albert** *Queen Victoria's Consort*
Is it not meningitis? **Louisa M Alcott** *American writer*
I am sweeping through the gates, washed in the blood of the lamb **Alexander II** *Russian Tsar*
Clasp my hand dear friend, I am dying **Vittorio Alfieri** *Italian Poet*
Haircut! **Albert Anastasia** *US gangster*
Give the boys a holiday **Anaxagoras** *Philosopher*
Monsieur, I beg your pardon. I did not do it on purpose **Marie Antoinette** *French Queen*
I see my God He calls me to Him **Antony of Padua** *Monk*
Wait till I have finished my problem **Archimedes** *Greek Mathematician*
May God forgive me for putting on any other **Benedict Arnold** *American Traitor*
I desire to die and be with Christ **Roger Ascham** *Elizabeth I's tutor*
Am I dying, or is this my birthday? **Nancy Astor** *British Politician*
Do you think I have played my part pretty well through the farce of life? **Augustus** *Roman Emperor*
The murder of the Queen has been represented to me as a deed; lawful and meritorious, I die a firm Catholic **Anthony Babington** *Plotter against Elizabeth I*
My name and memory I leave to men's charitable speeches, to foreign nations and to the next age **Francis Bacon** *Statesman and philosopher*
Oh God, here I go ... **Max Baer** *Heavyweight Boxer*
Let me have my own fidgets **Walter Bagehot** *Economist*
I can't sleep **JM Barrie** *Scottish Author*
I am a priest, fie, fie! All is gone **Cardinal Beaton** *Scottish prelate*
I am prepared to die for Christ and his Church **Thomas à Becket** *Archbishop of Canterbury*
Gloria Patri et Filio et Spiritu Sancto **Venerable St Bede** *Theologian and historian*
It is well, you have said the truth, it is indeed **Venerable St Bede** *Theologian and historian*
Now comes the mystery **Henry Ward Beecher** *US Clergyman*
Too bad, too bad! It's too late **Ludwig Van Beethoven** *Composer*
I shall hear in heaven **Ludwig van Beethoven** *Composer*
I thank God for having enabled me to meet my fate with so much fortitude and resignation **John Bellingham** *Assassin of Spencer Perceval*
One thousand greetings to Balakirev **Hector Berlioz** *Composer*
I want to live because there are a few things I want to do **Aneurin Bevan** *British Politician*
Who's there? **Billy the Kid** *American Outlaw*
I do not fear death **Thomas Blood** *Irish Adventurer*
My belief is rooted in hope **Léon Blum** *French Prime Minister*
I should never have switched from scotch to Martinis **Humphrey Bogart** *Film Actor*
It is a great consolation to a poet on the point of death that he has never written a line injurious to good morals **Nicolas Boileau** *French Poet*
The executioner is, I believe, very expert; and my neck is very slender **Anne Boleyn** *Queen Consort*
Take my baggage on board the frigate **Simon Bolivar** *Venezuelan Revolutionary*
Goodbye and God bless you, I'll see you again, tomorrow **Horatio Bottomley** *British Politician*
At least one knows that death will be easy **Bertold Brecht** *German Playwright*
puddle it, puddle it and puddle it again **James Brindley** *Engineer*
'tis enough – I shall need no more **James Brindley** *Engineer* (according to Josiah Wedgwood)
Take courage Charlotte, take courage **Anne Brontë** *Author*
If you will send for the doctor I will see him now **Emily Brontë** *Author*
Decay is inherent in all component things **Buddha (Prince Gautama Siddhartha)** *Founder of Buddhism*
I wish Johnny would come **Buffalo Bill** *American Frontiersman*
Well I think it is about time to go to bed now **Sir Redvers Buller** *Colonial Administrator*
World without end **John Bunyan** *Religious Writer*
With the best that was in me I have tried to write more happiness into the world **Frances Hodgson Burnett** *American Novelist*
Don't let the awkward squad fire over my grave **Robert Burns** *Scottish Poet*
I must sleep now **Lord George Byron** *English Poet*
Now I shall go to sleep **Lord George Byron** *English Poet*
Et tu, Brute **Julius Caesar** *Roman Statesman*
I am still alive! **Caligula** *Roman Emperor*
Spain and Portugal **George Canning** *British Prime Minister*
So this is death, well ... **Thomas Carlyle** *Historian and essayist*
Take away those pillows, I shall need them no more **Lewis Carroll** *Author*
Bankhead, let me fall into your arms. It is all over **Viscount Robert Castlereagh** *British statesman*
Stand by me, Tom, and we will die together **Robert Catesby** *Gunpowder Plotter*
Lord, into thy hands I commend my spirit **Catherine of Aragon** *Henry VIII's first wife*
Now I am master of myself **Marcus Porcius Cato (The Younger)** *Roman statesman*
Patriotism is not enough. I must have no hatred or bitterness towards anyone **Edith Cavell** *Nurse*
Italy is made – all is safe **Camillo Cavour** *Italian Patriot*
Pontier! Pontier! **Paul Cézanne** *French artist*
Approaching dissolution brings relief **Neville Chamberlain** *British Prime Minister*
Lord, into thy hands I commend my spirit **Charlemagne** *King of the Franks*
Remember **Charles I** *British King*
I have been a most unconscionable time a-dying, but I hope you will excuse it **Charles II** *English King*
Do not, do not let poor Nelly starve **Charles II** *English King*
Nurse, Nurse, what murder, what blood! Oh! I have done wrong, God pardon me **Charles IX** *French King*
I hope never again to commit a mortal sin, nor even a venial one, if I can help it **Charles VIII** *French King*
Give Dayrolles a chair **Philip Dormer Chesterfield** *English Statesman*

The issue now is clear, it is between light and darkness and everyone must choose his side **GK Chesterton** *British Essayist*

Glory to God for all things **St John Chrysostom** *Syrian Churchman*

Oh I'm so bored with it all **Winston Churchill** *British Prime Minister*

Strike **Marcus Tullius Cicero** *Roman Statesman*

Doctor, do you think it could have been the sausage? **Paul Claudel** *French writer*

I wish to be buried standing – facing Germany **Georges Clemenceau** *French Premier*

Thy kingdom come, thy will be done **Edward Coke** *English Jurist*

Honour these grey hairs young man **Admiral Gaspard Coligny** *French Huguenot Leader*

I am signing my death warrant **Michael Collins** *Irish Patriot*

Lord, into thy hands I commend my spirit **Christopher Columbus** *Italian Explorer*

What an irreparable loss **Auguste Comte** *French Philosopher*

My time has come to die **Confucius** *Chinese Philosopher*

You, Jess, I am better this morning. I can always get a rise out of you **Joseph Conrad** *British Author*

Now, O Lord, set thy servant free **Nicolas Copernicus** *Polish Astronomer*

That was the best ice-cream soda I ever tasted **Lou Costello** *American Comedian*

Goodnight my darlings, I'll see you tomorrow **Noël Coward** *British Playwright*

That unworthy hand! **Thomas Cranmer** *Archbishop of Canterbury*

My design is to make what haste I can to be gone **Oliver Cromwell** *Lord Protector of England*

That was a great game of golf, fellers **Bing Crosby** *American Singer*

Benteen – come on – big village – be quick – bring packs **George Custer** *US soldier*

Nurse, it was I that discovered that leeches had red blood **Georges Cuvier** *French naturalist*

Be sure you show the mob my head, it will be a long time before they see its like **Georges Danton** *French Revolutionary Leader*

I am not in the least afraid to die **Charles Darwin** *English Naturalist*

My fun days are over **James Dean** *American Film Star*

Lord, into thy hands I commend my spirit **Robert Devereux** *Earl of Essex*

The bullet hasn't been made that can kill me **Legs Diamond** *Gangster*

On the ground! **Charles Dickens** *Author*

The first step towards philosophy is incredulity **Denis Diderot** *French man of letters*

Dammit! put them back on. This is funny **Doc Holliday** *Gambler and gunfighter*

I have deserved a thousand deaths **John Dudley** *Duke of Northumberland*

Adieu my friends, I go on to glory **Isadora Duncan** *Dancer*

It is very beautiful over there **Thomas Alva Edison** *American Inventor*

Carry my bones before you on your march, for the rebels will not be able to endure the sight of me **Edward I** *King of England*

Trust in God and you need not fear **Jonathan Edwards** *American Philosopher*

All my possessions for a moment of time **Elizabeth I** *Queen of England*

I die for my king and for France **Louis Duke of Enghien** *French soldier*

Dear God! **Desiderius Erasmus** *Dutch Humanist*

Channel 5 is shit! **Adam Faith** *Singer and Actor*

Now I'll have eine kleine pause **Kathleen Ferrier** *Opera Singer*

On the whole, I'd rather be in Philadelphia **WC Fields** *American Comedian*

The nourishment is palatable **Millard Fillmore** *US President*

I've had a hell of a lot of fun and I've enjoyed every minute of it **Errol Flynn** *Actor*

I am a dead man, Lord have mercy upon me **Gaston de Foix** *French Soldier*

I suffer nothing, but I feel a sort of difficulty in living longer **Bernard Fontenelle** *French Author*

It don't signify, my dearest, dearest Liz **Charles James Fox** *English Statesman*

Never heed! The Lord's power is over all weakness and death **George Fox** *English Religious Leader*

We are all going to Heaven and Van Dyke is of the company **Thomas Gainsborough** *English landscape painter*

Yet it still moves **Galileo Galilei** *Astronomer*

Feed them when I am gone **Giuseppe Garibaldi** *Italian Patriot*

Wally, what is this? It is death, my boy. They have deceived me **George IV** *British King*

Bugger Bognor **George V** *British King*

How is the Empire? **George V** *British King*

Put your hands on my shoulders and don't struggle **WS Gilbert** *Librettist*

Let's do it **Gary Gilmore** *American Murderer*

Light, more light **Johann Wolfgang Goethe** *German poet and dramatist*

Where is the Mahdi? **Charles Gordon** *British general*

I want nobody distressed on my account **Ulysses S Grant** *American Soldier and Statesman*

It is done **Horace Greeley** *American Politician*

Lord, into thy hands I commend my spirit **Lady Jane Grey** *English Queen*

Well if it must be so **Edvard Grieg** *Composer*

I hope to see you on Tuesday at 10.30 am **Earl Douglas Haig** *British General*

I regret that I have but one life to give for my country **Nathan Hale** *American Soldier*

Remember, my Eliza, you are a Christian **Alexander Hamilton** *American Politician*

The rest is silence **Hamlet** *Shakespearean Character*

Let us now relieve the Romans of their fears by the death of a feeble old man **Hannibal** *Carthaginian Soldier*

That's good. Go on, read some more **Warren Harding** *US President*

Four sixes to beat **John Wesley Hardin** *American Outlaw*

I am about the extent of a tenth of a gnat's eyebrow better **Joel Chandler Harris** *American Author*

Cheer up, children, I'm all right **Franz Joseph Haydn** *Composer*

I know I'm going where Lucy is **Rutherford B Hayes** *US President*

Monks! Monks! Monks! **Henry VIII** *King of England*

One more summer and another winter **Hermann Hesse** *German Novelist*

Moderately, I am continuing to orbit **Richard Hillary** *English fighter pilot and writer*

And I wish myself the joy of your fellowship at Whitsuntide **Gustav Holst** *Composer*

I am tired of fighting. I guess this thing is going to get me **Harry Houdini** *Escapologist*

I'll tell that story on the golden floor **AE Housman** *Poet*

Texas, Texas, Margaret **Sam Houston** *Texan patriot*

I die a Queen, but I would rather die the wife of Culpepper **Catherine Howard** *Henry VIII's Fifth Wife*

God have mercy on my soul. Good people, I beg you pray for me. I see the black light **Victor Hugo** *French Poet*

Truth, truth **Anne Hyde** *Duchess of York*

Let us cross over the river and sit in the shade of the trees **Thomas Jackson** *US Civil War General*

It came with a lass and it will go with a lass **James V** *King of Scotland*

Do not hack me as you did my Lord Russell **James, Duke of Monmouth** *Charles II's illegitimate son*

That picture is crooked **Jesse James** *Train Robber*

Jesus Jesus Jesus, blessed be God **Joan of Arc** *French Patriot*

I commit my soul to God and my body to Saint Alstane **John** *King of England*

This is it, I'm going, I'm going **Al Jolson** *Singer*

Napoleon! Elba! Marie Louise! **Josephine** *French Empress*

Give me another horse, Howard! **Edmund Kean** *British Actor*

Such is life **Ned Kelly** *Australian Outlaw*

I wish to God you had heard them as I have heard them, and I praise God of that heavenly sound **John Knox** *Scottish Church Reformer*

Ah well, it is not the first time an innocent man has been condemned **Henri Landru** *French Murderer*

We shall this day light such a candle, by God's grace, in England, as I trust shall never be put out **Hugh Latimer** *Protestant Martyr*

I think it is time for morphine **DH Lawrence** *British Author*

Strike the tent **Robert E Lee** *Confederate General*

Now I have finished with all earthly business, and high time too **Franz Lehar** *Hungarian Composer*

Yes, yes, my dear child, now comes death. They won't think anything about it **Abraham Lincoln** *US President*

Tristan! **Franz Liszt** *Composer*

Jerusalem, Jerusalem **Louis IX** *French King*

Why weep you? Did you think I would live for ever? I thought dying was harder **Louis XIV** *French King*

Repeat those words, Monsieur Almoner, repeat them **Louis XV** *French King*

Frenchmen I Die guiltless of the crimes imputed to me. Pray God my blood falls not on France **Louis XVI** *French King*

I shall drink the cup to the last dregs **Louis XVI** *French King*

A king should die standing up **Louis XVIII** *French King*

Marty **Lucky Luciano** *US gangster*

Keep Paddy behind the big mixer **Alfred MacAlpine** *British building tycoon*

Lay on Macduff, and damned be him that first cries 'hold enough' **Macbeth** *Shakespearean Character*

Now all is over, let the piper play 'Return no More' **Rob Roy MacGregor** *Scottish Outlaw*

I love my country more than my soul **Niccolo Machiavelli** *Italian Statesman*

We are all going, we are all going ... oh dear! **William McKinley** *US President*

Mozart! **Gustav Mahler** *Composer*

Let's cool it, brothers **Malcolm X** *Black Muslim Leader*

I love the rain, I want the feeling of it on my face **Katherine Mansfield** *Writer*

Act in accordance with past principles **Mao Zedong** *Chinese Ruler*

Last words are for fools who haven't said enough **Karl Marx** *Philosopher*

My Lord, why do you not go on? I am not afraid to die **Mary II** *English Queen*

When I am dead and opened, you shall find Calais lying in my heart **Mary Tudor** *English Queen*

Thank you, Monsieur **Mata Hari** *Dutch Spy*

Dying is a very dull, dreary affair. My advice to you is to have nothing whatever to do with it **William Somerset Maugham** *British Writer*

Lotte! **Ferdinand-Joseph Maximilian** *Mexican Emperor*

I am crossing a beautiful wide river and the opposite shore is coming nearer and nearer **George Meade** *US Civil War General*

Ah, my God, I am dead **Catherine de Medici** *Florentine Ruler*

God bless Captain Vere **Herman Melville** *US Author*

Forgive some sinner and wink your eye at some homely girl **HL Mencken** *American Essayist*

Weary, very weary **Felix Mendelssohn** *Composer*

My soul I resign to God, my body to the Earth, My worldly goods to my next of kin **Michelangelo** *Italian sculptor and painter*

O Allah! Pardon my sins. Yes I come **Muhammad** *Founder of Islam*

For all my misfortunes, Malinche, I bear you no ill will **Montezuma II** *Aztec Emperor*

Commend your souls to God, for our bodies are the foe's **Simon de Montfort** *British Aristocrat*

See me safe up; for my coming down let me shift for myself **Thomas More** *English Statesman*

Did I not tell you I was writing this for myself **Wolfgang Amadeus Mozart** *Composer*

Put that bloody cigarette out **HH Munro** *British Author*

But, but, Mr Colonel ... **Benito Mussolini** *Italian Dictator*

France! Army! Head of the army! Josephine! **Napoleon I** *French Emperor*

I don't need anything more ... Poultices **Napoleon II** *Duke of Reichstadt*

Were you at Sedan? **Napoleon III** *French Emperor*

Thank God I have done my duty, kiss me, Hardy **Horatio Nelson** *British Naval commander*

What an artist the world is losing in me **Nero** *Roman Emperor*

I seem to have been only a boy playing on the seashore and diverting myself in now and then finding a smoother pebble or prettier shell than the ordinary whilst the great ocean of truth lay all undiscovered before me **Isaac Newton** *Scientist*

I am just going outside and I may be some time **Captain Lawrence Oates** *Explorer*

Die, my dear doctor, that's the last thing I shall do **Viscount Palmerston** *British Prime Minister*

Get my swan costume ready **Anna Pavlova** *Ballerina*

What is the scaffold? A short cut to Heaven **Charles Peace** *Murderer*

To be like Christ is to be a Christian **William Penn** *English Quaker*

Murder! **Spencer Perceval** *British Prime Minister*

Do not weep, do not grieve **Henri Pétain** *French Soldier*

Drink to me **Pablo Picasso** *Spanish Artist*

The hearse, the horse, the driver and – enough **Luigi Pirandello** *Italian Dramatist*

I think I could eat one of Bellamy's veal pies **William Pitt (the younger)** *British Prime Minister*

Oh my country, how I leave thee **William Pitt (the younger)** *British Prime Minister*

Lord help my soul **Edgar Allan Poe** *Writer*

I am dying, sir, of a hundred good symptoms **Alexander Pope** *Poet*

Turn up the lights, I don't want to go home in the dark **William Porter (O'Henry)** *US Short Story Writer*

I am going to sleep like you, but we shall all awake together and, I trust to everlasting happiness **Joseph Priestley** *Chemist*

My poor Elvira, my poor wife **Giacomo Puccini** *Composer*

Sister, sister, sister **Thomas de Quincey** *British Writer*

I could wish this tragic scene were over, but I hope to go through it with becoming dignity **James Quin** *Irish Actor*

Let down the curtain, the farce is over **François Rabelais** *French writer*

I am going to seek the great, perhaps **François Rabelais** *French writer*

It matters little how the head lies, so the heart be right **Walter Raleigh** *English Explorer and Statesman*

I look like a Moor **Maurice Ravel** *French Composer*

I know that all things on earth must have an end, and now I am come to mine **Joshua Reynolds** *English Artist*

Turn me over, Jack **Cecil Rhodes** *South African Statesman*

So little done, so much to do **Cecil Rhodes** *South African Statesman*

Take off his chains, give him a hundred shillings, and let him go **Richard I** *King of England*

Treason, treason! **Richard III** *King of England*

I have no enemies save those of the state **Cardinal Richelieu** *French Statesman*

Don't you think I'll be back? **Manfred von Richthofen** *German Air Ace*

O Liberty! What crimes are committed in thy name **Madame Marie Roland** *French Revolutionary*

I have a terrific headache **FD Roosevelt** *US President*

We are the first victims of American fascism **Ethel Rosenberg** *Alleged Atom Spy*

There is God! Yes, God Himself, who is opening his arms and inviting me to taste at last that eternal and unchanging joy that I had so long desired **Jean-Jacques Rousseau** *French Political Theorist*

You can keep the things of bronze and stone and give me one man to remember me just once a year **Damon Runyon** *American Writer*

The bitterness of death is now past **Lord William Russell** *English Whig Statesman*

Of all his victories, realms and riches, nothing remains to him but this **Saladin** *Sultan of Egypt and Syria*

I am leaving you with your worries, good luck **George Sanders** *British Film Star*

Ah, my children, you cannot cry for me so much as I have made you laugh **Paul Scarron** *French Writer*

Many things are growing plain and clear to my understanding. One look at the sun **Johann Von Schiller** *German Dramatist*

Here, here is my end **Franz Schubert** *Composer*

French Canadian bean soup. I want to pay. Let them leave me alone **Dutch Schultz** *New York Gangster*

God bless you all, I feel myself again **Sir Walter Scott** *British Novelist*

I can't live any longer with my nerves **Jean Seberg** *US Film Star*

They couldn't hit an elephant at this dist ... **John Sedgwick** *US General*

I am absolutely undone **Richard Brinsley Sheridan** *Irish Writer and Statesman*

I believe we must adjourn the meeting to some other place **Adam Smith** *Economist*

Let me go **Capt EJ Smith** *Captain of SS Titanic*

That's right Brother Taylor, parry them off as well as you can **Joseph Smith** *Mormon Martyr*

Crito, we owe a cock to Aesculapius; pay it and do not let it pass **Socrates** *Greek Philosopher*

Beautifully done **(Sir) Stanley Spencer** *British Artist*

Four o'clock. How strange, so that is time. Strange, enough! **Sir Henry Stanley** *Explorer*

I feel faint **Adlai Stevenson** *American Politician*

If this is dying, I don't think much of it **Lytton Strachey** *Biographer*

Put not your trust in princes **Thomas Strafford** *English Statesman*

Thy necessity is yet greater than mine **Philip Sydney** *British Soldier and Poet*

Lord, into thy hands I commend my spirit **Torquato Tasso** *Italian Poet*

How sweet it is to rest **John Taylor** *English Poet*

I have tried to do my duty, and am not afraid to die. I am ready **Zachary Taylor** *US President*

Brother warriors, we are about to enter an engagement from which I will not return. My body will remain on the field of battle **Tecumseh** *Indian Chief*

I have opened it **Lord Alfred Tennyson** *Poet*

Gentlemen of the jury, you may retire **Charles Tenterden** *Lord Chief Justice*

And my heart throbbed with an exquisite bliss **William Thackeray** *British Novelist*

To the health of the fair Critias **Theramenes** *Athenian Statesman*

I shall soon know the grand secret **Arthur Thistlewood** *English Conspirator*

I've had 18 straight whiskies, I think that's a record ... after 39 yrs this is all I've done **Dylan Thomas** *Poet*

I leave this world without a regret **Henry Thoreau** *American Essayist*

God bless ... God damn **James Thurber** *American humorist*

I'll be shot if I don't believe I'm dying **Edward Thurlow** *English Politician*

Oh look, see how the cherry blossoms fall mutely **Hideki Tojo** *Japanese Politician and Soldier*

The enemy have demanded a surrender and I have answered the summons with a cannon shot and our flag still waves proudly from the walls **W Barrett Travis** *Commander of the Alamo*

Now I stretch out my hand, and from the further shore I bid adieu to all who have cared to read any among the many words I have written **Anthony Trollope** *British Novelist*

I feel here that this time they have succeeded **Leon Trotsky** *Russian Leader*

The sun is God **JMW Turner** *British Artist*

Death, the only immortal, who treats us all alike, whose peace and whose refuge are for all, the soiled and the pure, the rich and the poor, the loved and unloved **Mark Twain** *American Novelist*

Lord forgive my sins. Especially my sins of omission **James Ussher** *Archbishop of Armagh*

I want the sunlight to greet me **Rudolph Valentino** *Film star*

I shall never get rid of this depression **Vincent Van Gogh** *Artist*

I suppose I am now becoming a God **Vespasian** *Roman Emperor*

Oh that peace may come **Victoria** *British Queen*

Do let me die in peace **Voltaire** *French Author and Philosopher*

I am fond of them, of the inferior beings of the abyss, of those who are full of longing **Richard Wagner** *Composer*

It is well, I die hard, but am not afraid to go **George Washington** *US President*

A last interview ... **Ethel Waters** *US Blues Singer*

Life, life, death, death, how curious it is **Daniel Webster** *American Statesman*

Go away, I'm all right **HG Wells** *Author*

I shall be satisfied with thy likeness – satisfied **Charles Wesley** *English Hymn Writer*

I am dying as I have lived: beyond my means **Oscar Wilde** *Dramatist*

Either this wallpaper goes or I do **Oscar Wilde** *Dramatist*

O my God, have mercy upon this poor people **William the Silent** *Stadholder of the Netherlands*

Edith **Woodrow Wilson** *US President*

I fear not this fire **George Wishart** *Scottish Reformer*

Give me back my youth **John Wolcot** *English Satirist*

What! do they run already? Then I die happy **James Wolfe** *English General*

Had I but served God as diligently as I have served the King, He would not have given me over in my grey hairs **Thomas Wolsey** *English Prelate*

Is that you Dora? **William Wordsworth** *Poet*

Mind your own business **Percy Wyndham-Lewis** *British artist*

Better fighting death than a slave's life **Emiliano Zapata** *Mexican Revolutionary*

Make my skin into drumheads for the Bohemian cause **John Ziska** *Bohemian Hussite Leader*

NB: This is an area of uncertainty and vagueness and cannot be said to be a true and exact glossary of last words. That is because quite often there would be some controversy over the reported words uttered before death by a solitary witness, and even when witnessed by many people there would often be a conflict of opinion, hence the need for double entries for various persons. It is thought, perhaps, that some of the more witty sayings were possibly the sort of thing that a particular person would have said and it is in the way of a tribute to a person that not too many questions would be asked. The point to remember about these last utterances is not so much the truth of the speech *per se*, but rather the fact that the words are universally identifiable with these people. Several persons have more than one entry for the reasons stated above.

First Names
(of people better known by other names)

Alvar Aalto – Hugo *Finnish Architect*
Patrick Abercrombie – Leslie *English Architect*
Pepper Anderson – Suzanne *TV character (Police Woman)*
Antonioni – Michelangelo *Film Director*
Corazon Aquino – Maria *Filipino President*
Yasser Arafat – Mohammed *Palestinian Resistance Leader*
Louis Armstrong – Daniel *Jazz Musician*
Cash Asmussen – Brian Keith *US Jockey*
Avon – Kerr *Blake 7 character*
Balakirev – Mily *Russian Composer*
Balzac – Honoré de *French Writer*
Banacek – Thomas *TV Character*
Batista – Fulgencio *Cuban President*
Baum – Lyman Frank *US Author*
Max Beerbohm – Henry *English Writer and Caricaturist*
Bix Beidebecke – Leon *Jazz Cornet Player*
Hilaire Belloc – Joseph *French-born Writer*
Arnold Bennett – Enoch *English Novelist*
Ingmar Bergman – Ernst *Film Director*
Busby Berkeley – William *Choreographer and Director*
Hector Berlioz – Louis *French Composer*
Ali Bhutto – Zulfikar *Pakistani Statesman*
John Biffen – William *English Politician*
Laurence Binyon – Robert *Poet*
Bizet – Georges Alexandre Césare Léopold *French Composer*
Blake – Roj *'Blake's 7' Character*
Boccaccio – Giovanni *Italian Writer*
Bodie and Doyle – William and Ray *TV Characters ('The Professionals')*
Bootsie (Pte 'excused boots' Bisley) – Montague *TV Character ('The Army Game')*
Gordon Brown – James *British Prime Minister*
Lord Byron – George *English Poet*
Calamity Jane – Martha *Wild West Heroine*
James Callaghan – Leonard *British Politician*
Callan – David *TV Character*
Hoss Cartwright – Eric *TV Western Hero ('Bonanza')*
Casanova – Giovanni Jacopo *Poet and Libertine*
Casey Jones – John Luther *TV Character based on Ballad*
Emmanuel Chabrier – Alexis *French Composer*
Paddy Chayevsky – Sidney *Playwright*
Chekov – Pavel *Star Trek Character*
Erskine Childers – Robert *Anglo-Irish Writer*
Colette – Sidonie *French Novelist*
Colin Cowdrey – Michael *English Cricketer*
Crane – Richard *TV Character*
Sonny Crockett – James *Miami Vice Character*
Cui – César *Russian Composer*
Robert Cummings – Charles *US Actor*
Bette Davis – Ruth *US Actress*
Tamasin Day-Lewis – Lydia *English Chef*
Debussy – Achille-Claude *French Composer*
Edgar Degas – Hilaire-Germain *French Artist*
Paul Delaroche – Hippolyte *French Painter*
Delibes – Léo *French Composer*
Delius – Frederick *English Composer*
Legs Diamond – Jack *Gangster*
Fats Domino – Antoine *US Vocalist*
Lonnie Donegan – Anthony *Skiffle Musician*
Donizetti – Gaetano *Italian Composer*
Duffy – Aimee *Welsh Singer*
Faye Dunaway – Dorothy *US Actress*
Dvorak – Antonin *Czech Composer*
Eddie 'the eagle' Edwards – Michael *British Skijumper*
Samantha Eggar – Victoria *US Actress*
Erasmus – Desiderius *Dutch Humanist*
Escoffier – Auguste *French Chef*
Max Faulkner – Herbert *English Golfer*
Corporal Fender – Sam *TV Character ('Bilko')*
Figgis – Roy *TV Character ('Only When I Laugh')*
Finlay, Dr – Alan (Bill Simpson) *TV Character*
Finlay, Dr – John (David Rintoul) *TV Character*
Private Fraser – James *'Dad's Army' Character*
Liam Gallagher – William *Pop Singer*
Paul Gauguin – Eugène *French Post-Impressionist*
Gigli – Beniamino *Italian Tenor*
Eric Gill – Arthur *English Sculptor*
Allen Ginsberg – Irwin *Poet*
Glinka – Mikhail *Russian Composer*
Glover – Archie *TV Character ('Only When I Laugh')*
Gluck – Christoph *German Composer*
Private Godfrey – Charles *'Dad's Army' Character*
Joseph Goebbels – Paul *Nazi Leader*
Pancho Gonzales – Richard *US Tennis Player*
Gounod – Charles *French Composer*
Goya – Francisco *Spanish Painter*
Ulysses S Grant – Hiram *US President*
Graham Greene – Henry *British Novelist*
Florence Griffith-Joyner – Delorez *US Athlete*
Brothers Grimm – Jacob and Wilhelm *Folktale collectors*
Che Guevara – Ernesto *Argentinian Revolutionary Leader*
Colonel Hall – John *TV Character ('Bilko')*
Mrs Hall – Nell *TV Character ('Bilko')*
Dashiell Hammett – Samuel *US Novelist*
Learned Hand – Billings *American Jurist*
Patsy Hendren – Elias *England Cricketer*
Barbara Hepworth – Jocelyn *English Sculptor*
William Herschel – Frederick *British Astronomer*
Rudolf Hess – Richard *Nazi Leader*
Patricia Highsmith – Mary *US Novelist*
Hinge and Bracket – Dr Evadne and Dame Hilda *comic duo*
Doc Holliday – John *Western gunfighter*
Holman Hunt – William *English Painter*
Honegger – Arthur *Swiss Composer*
Ron L Hubbard – Lafayette *SF Writer and Scientology Founder*
John Humphreys – Desmond *TV and Radio Presenter*
Lauren Hutton – Mary *US Actress*
Ivanhoe – Wilfred *Literary Character*
Jacuzzi – Candido *Inventor of luxury bath*
Storm Jameson – Margaret *British Novelist*
Janáček – Leoš *Czech Composer*
Jeeves – Reginald *PG Wodehouse character (named after Warwickshire Cricketer)*
Boris Johnson – Alexander *British politician*
Corporal Jones – Jack *'Dad's Army' Character*
Miss Jones – Ruth *TV Character ('Rising Damp')*
Khachaturian – Aram *Armenian Composer*
Rudyard Kipling – Joseph *Writer*
Evel Knievel – Robert *Stuntman*
Kookie – Gerald (Lloyd Kookson III) *TV Character ('77 Sunset Strip')*
Pixie Lott – Victoria *British Singer*
Lucky Luciano – Charles *Gangster*
Lugg – Magersfontein *Literary Character: Campion's Manservant*
Lytton Strachey – Giles *Biographer*
Harold Macmillan – Maurice *British Prime Minister*
Magnificent Evans – Plantagenet *TV Character*
Mr Magoo – Quincy *Cartoon Character*
Captain Mainwaring – George *Dad's Army Character*
Paul McCartney – James *Beatle*
Andie MacDowell – Rosalie *US Actress*
Campbell Menzies – Walter *MP and Former Athlete*
Mrs Merton – Dorothy *TV Character*
Mies Van Der Rohe – Ludwig *Architect*
Milhaud – Darius *French Composer*
Glen Miller – Alton *Bandleader*

Monteverdi – Claudio *Italian Composer*
Morse – Endeavour *Fictional detective*
Angela Mortimer – Florence *British Wimbledon Champion*
Mulder and Scully – Fox and Dana *TV Characters ('X Files')*
Brian Mulroney – Martin *Canadian Politician*
Murillo – Bartolomé *Spanish Painter*
Mussorgsky – Modest *Russian Composer*
Ogden Nash – Frederic *American Poet*
Birgit Nilsson – Märta *Swedish Soprano*
Captain Oates – Lawrence *Explorer*
Milton Obote – Apollo *Ugandan Politician*
Offenbach – Jacques *French Composer*
King Oliver – Joseph *American Cornet-player*
Ozzy Osbourne – John *British Rock Singer*
Palestrina – Giovanni *Italian Composer*
Captain Peacock – Stephen *TV Character*
Petrocelli – Tony *TV Character*
Brad Pitt – William *US Actor*
Graeme Pollock – Robert *South African Cricketer*
Jackson Pollock – Paul *American Action Painter*
Ponchielli – Amilcare *Italian Composer*
Potsie Weber – Warren *TV Character (Happy Days)*
Beatrix Potter – Helen *English Children's Writer*
Enoch Powell – John *British Politician*
Pressburger and Powell – Emeric and Michael *Film-makers*
Preston – Samuel *Singer with the Ordinary Boys*
Princip – Gavrilo *Assassin*
Prokofiev – Sergey *Russian Composer*
Puccini – Giacomo *Italian Composer*
Captain Pugwash – Horatio *TV Character*
Professor Quatermass – Bernard *TV Character*
Dan Quayle – James *US Vice-President*
Rachmaninoff – Sergey *Russian Composer*
Sonny Ramphal – Shridath *Secretary-General of the Commonwealth*
Ravel – Maurice *French Composer*
Django Reinhardt – Jean Baptiste *Belgian Guitarist*
Viv Richards – Isaac *West Indian Cricketer*
Cardinal Richelieu – Armand *French politician-prelate*
Rigsby – Rupert *TV Character ('Rising Damp')*
Rimsky-Korsakov – Nikolay *Russian Composer*
Sergeant Ritzik – Rupert *TV Character ('Bilko')*
Auguste Rodin – René-François *French Sculptor*
Rossini – Gioachino *Italian Composer*
Rostropovich – Mstislav *Russian Musician*
Mr Rumbold – Cuthbert *TV Character*
Salman Rushdie – Ahmed *British Novelist*
Anwar Sadat – Mohamed *Egyptian President*
Shelley – James *TV Character*
Phones (Sheridan) – George *TV Character ('Stingray')*
Shostakovich – Dmitry *Russian Composer*
Sibelius – Jean *Finnish Composer*
Mrs Slocombe – Betty *TV Character*
Smetana – Bedrich *Czech Composer*
Colonel Hannibal Smith – John *TV Character*
Snudge – Claude *TV Character ('Army Game')*
Leland Stanford – Amasa *US Railway Magnate*
Starsky and Hutch – David and Ken *TV policemen*
Nobby Stiles – Norbert *Footballer*
Michael Stipe – John *Vocalist*
Stockhausen – Karlheinz *German Composer*
August Strindberg – Johann *Swedish Playwright*
Sulu – *Hikaru 'Star Trek'* character
Booth Tarkington – Newton *US Author*
Tchaikovsky – Pyotr *Russian Composer*
Tinker – Edward Sexton *Blake's Assistant*
Daley Thompson – Francis *Athlete*
Wolfe Tone – Theobald *Irish Nationalist*
Topol – Chaim *Israeli Actor*
Uccello – Paolo *Florentine Painter*
Verdi – Giuseppe *Italian Composer*
Vivaldi – Antonio *Italian Composer*
Richard Wagner – Wilhelm *German Composer*
Private Walker – James *'Dad's Army' Character*
Dionne Warwick – Marie *US Singer*
Dr Watson – John *Literary Character*
Weber – Carl *German Composer*
Webern – Anton *Austrian Composer*
Orson Welles – George *Film-maker and Actor*
Andy Williams – Howard *US Singer*
Harold Wilson – James *British Prime Minister*
Debra Winger – Marie *US Actress*
Terry Wogan – Michael *Broadcaster*
Wolf-Ferrari – Ermanno *Italian Composer*
Roy Wood – Ulysses *Pop Musician*
Tiger Woods – Eldrick *US Golfer*
Virginia Woolf – Adeline *English Novelist*
Saint-Saens – Charles Camille *French Composer*
Vicario Sanchez – Arantxa *Tennis Player*
Savonarola – Girolamo *Italian Religious Reformer*
Leo Sayer – Gerard *Singer*
Schubert – Franz Peter *Austrian Composer*
Schumann – Robert *German Composer*
Paul Scofield – David *English Actor*
Scottie – Montgomery *'Star Trek' Character*
Norman Shaw – Richard *English Architect*

Firsts

Air hostess Ellen Church 1930
Airmail (GB) 9 Sept 1911
Airmail stickers 17 Aug 1918
Appendix operation
George Thomas Morton 1887
Athlete to use crouch start
Charles Sherrill 1888
Atom bomb
Alamogordo Air Base, New Mexico (16 July) 1945
Atom bomb (UK)
Monte Bello Islands off West Australia 1952
Atomic power station (large-scale)
Calder Hall, Cumbria 1956
Atomic research centre (UK)
Harwell in Berkshire 1946
Baronet Nicholas Bacon of Redgrove 1611
Bikini 24 June 1950
Blood transfusion
Montpellier University, France 1667
Boy Scout movement
Brownsea Island, Poole, Dorset 1907
Breakfast cereal (ready to eat)
Shredded Wheat 1893
Bus conductress Kate Barton 1909
Bus service (scheduled) Shillibeer's
Marylebone to Euston Rd Service 1829
Capital Gains Tax 6 April 1965
Car tax discs
On windowscreen from 1 Jan 1921
Casino (UK) Metropole in Brighton 1962
Catamaran
Experiment, built for Sir William Petty: adaptation from traditional Polynesian design 1662

Channel swim: both ways (UK)
Kevin Murphy (non-stop) in 35 hrs 10 mins 1970
Chelsea Flower Show
20–22 May by Royal Horticultural Society 1913
Christmas card John Calcott Horsley designed for Henry Cole 1843
Christmas speech of sovereign
Elizabeth II 1957
Christmas tree From German idea 1605
Circumnavigation of Earth
Juan Sebastian Del Cano in *Victoria* (Magellan killed en route) 1522
Circumnavigation of Earth: non-stop solo
Robin Knox-Johnston in *Suhaili* 1969
Club colours
Black, Red, Gold of I Zingari Cricket Club 1845
Coeducational school
Henry Morley opened Marine Terrace, Cheshire 1849
Comic *Comic Cuts* an 8-page weekly 1890
Comic strip in newspaper
Richard Outcault's 'Yellow Kid' 1897
Credit card Diners Club, New York 1950
Cremation (UK)
Honoretta Pratt 1769
Cub Scouts
Robertsbridge, Sussex (2 Feb) 1914
Daylight Saving (UK) Clocks put forward I hour 1916
Detective story Edgar Allan Poe's *The Murders in the Rue Morgue* 1841
Diet (scientifically planned)
Dr Harvey for undertaker William Banting 1862
Dinner jacket
Worn by G Lorillard,Tuxedo Park Country Club, NY 1886
Dresswear hire firm (UK)
Moss Bros of Covent Garden 1860
Driving tests (UK) Leslie Hore-Belisha instigated voluntary tests 1935
Duke (UK)
Edward, Duke of Cornwall 1337
Electric lamp J Lindsay developed but did not patent lamp 1835
Electric oven Installed Hotel Bernina, Samaden, Switzerland 1889
Electric power station
Central Power Station, Godalming, Surrey 1881
Escalator (UK)
Harrods Department Store 1898
Family allowance 15 June (5s per child) 1945
Film festival Hotel Excelsior Venice, Italy 1932
Fire brigade (UK)
Nicholas Barbon established in London 1684
Fixed penalty parking ticket (UK)
19 Sept 1961
Football: televised live (UK)
Wembley Cup Final 1938
Four-minute mile
Roger Bannister in 3: 59.4 (Oxford) 1954
Fruit machine
Liberty Bell designed by Charles Frey 1889
GCE 'O' and 'A' Levels
Introduced to replace School Certificate 1950
GCSE Introduced to replace CGE 'O' Level 1988
Girl Guide Allison Cargill 1908
Gold disc
Glen Miller's 'Chattanooga Choo Choo' 1941
Greetings card Designer W Harvey engraved by J Thompson 1829
Heart transplant
Christiaan Barnard, Groote Schuur Hospital 1967
Helicopter (free flight) Twin-rotor machine designed by Paul Cornu 1907

Hydrofoil (UK)
'Miranda III' by John Thornycroft 1909
Hydrogen bomb Detonated by USA at Eniwetok, Marshall Isles 1952
Indianapolis 500 Won by Ray Harroun (30 May) 1911
In-flight movie Conan Doyle's *The Lost World* 1925
Isle of Man TT Races
Won by Charles Collier on a Matchless 1907
Jazz band Led by Buddy Bolden, New Orleans 1900
Jukebox Installed at Palais Royal Saloon, San Francisco 1889
Life insurance policy Taken out by London Alderman Richard Martin 1583
Lighthouse (UK) Spurn Point, Yorkshire 1427
Lord Mayor's Show Instigated by Sir John Norman 1453
Loudspeaker Auxetophone by Horace Short 1900
Luncheon Vouchers (UK) 1 Jan 1955
Meteorological satellite Tiros I 1960
Miss World Contest 19 April 1951
Monarch to Abdicate: English Richard II 1399
MOT test 12 Sept 1960
Motorway Avus Autobahn, Germany 1921
Moving staircase (UK) Earls Court Station 1911
National park Yellowstone, Wyoming 1872
National park: GB Peak District 1950
National Savings stamps
On sale from 8 July 1918
Newspaper colour supplement (UK)
Sunday Times 1962
North Sea gas Piped ashore by BP 1967
Nuclear merchant vessel
Savannah (launched in New Jersey) 1962
Old age pensions
Bismarck introduced in Germany 1889
Old age pensions (UK)
Introduced on 1 Jan 1909
Old school tie Old Etonian, of narrow blue and broad black stripes 1900
Opera
Jacopo Peri's *Dafne*, libretto by Rinuccini 1597
Oral contraceptive (UK)
Marketed on 18 Aug (invented 1954) 1960
Parachute jump (aeroplane)
Albert Berry from a height of 1,500 feet 1912
Parachute jump (balloon) André-Jacques Garnerin from a height of 2,230 feet 1797
Parcel post Introduced on 1 Aug 1883
Parking meter (UK)
(America had them from 1935) 1958
Parking ticket (UK)
Dr Thomas Creighton was first victim 1960
Pedestrian crossing (UK)
Parliament Square, London 1926
Photo finish: horse race
Introduced by Ernest Marks, New Jersey 1888
Photographic process
Louis Daguerre first commercial success 1839
Pneumatic motor car tyres
Michelin fitted first tyre to a 4hp Daimler 1895
Policewoman
Mrs Alice Stebbins Wells of the LAPD 1910
Policewoman (UK) 27 Nov 1914
Postage stamp (adhesive)
James Chalmers of Dundee printed first 1834
Postage stamp (perforations)
Penny Red, issued in Feb 1854
Postal orders (UK)
Introduced on 1 Jan 1881
Postcard (UK) Introduced on 1 Oct 1870

Premium Bonds On sale from 1 Nov 1956
Prince of Wales: English
Edward of Caernarvon, later Edward II 1301
Prisoner of War camp
Norman X Depot, Stilton, for French PoWs 1797
Public library (UK)
Jerrom Goodwyn Library, Norwich 1608
Recorded delivery 1 Feb 1961
Registered letters
Introduced by GPO on 1 Jan 1878
Row across the Atlantic
Capt John Ridgway and Sgt Chay Blyth 1966
Row across the Atlantic (solo)
Tom McLean in 20 ft dory *Super Silver* 1969
Sex change operation George/Christine Jorgensen by Dr K Hamburger 1952
Space flight (manned)
Vostok I, piloted by Yuri Gagarin 1961
Space flight (by woman)
Vostok VI, piloted by Valentina Tereshkova 1963
Space walk
Aleksey Leonov, from *Voshkod II* 1965
Spacecraft on the Moon *Luna II* 1959
Spiritualist mediums
Margaretta and Kate Fox from New York 1848
Starting stalls: horse race (UK)
Newmarket on 8 July 1965
Tape recorder
Telagraphone by Valdemar Poulsen 1898
Telegrams (UK)
I shilling for 20 words (1st worldwide in 1843) 1870
Telephone directory (UK)
Published by London Telephone Co 1880
Telephone speaking clock (UK)
Aka TIM was voice of Ethel Cain for 20 yrs 1936
Television announcer (UK) Leslie Mitchell 1936
Television commercial, black and white (UK)
Gibbs SR Toothpaste 1955
Television commercial, colour (UK)
Birds Eye Peas 1969
Television licence (UK) Cost of £2 1946
Television communications satellite
Bell Telephone 'Telstar' 1962
Traffic lights Parliament Square, London 1868
Traffic lights: electric (UK) July 1926
Traffic lights: automatic (UK) 5 Nov 1927

Traffic wardens (UK)
15 Sept in London 1960
Train accident fatality
William Huskisson MP, run down by *Rocket* 1830
Traveller's cheques
Introduced on 1 Jan 1772
Underground railway (UK)
Metropolitan Line Paddington to Farringdon 1863
Underground railway (electric)
City branch of the Northern line 1890
Underground map
Albert Stanley, Lord Ashfield instigated 1908
Underground (Tube) train (automatic)
Central Line Woodford to Hainault 1964
Vending machine
So-called 'Honesty' tobacco boxes, 1d a go 1615
Vending machine (automatic)
Patented by Carl Ade in Germany 1867
Victoria Cross Mate Charles Lucas, for action aboard HMS *Hecla* 1854
Voting rights for women
New Zealand was 1st country to allow 1893
Finland 1st in Europe 1906
Windscreen wipers (mechanical)
Introduced in the USA 1916
Windscreen wipers (electrical)
The 'Berkshire', produced in the USA 1923
Woman cabinet minister (UK)
Margaret Bondfield, Minister of Labour 1929
Woman doctor (US) Elizabeth Blackwell 1849
Woman doctor (UK)
Elizabeth Garrett Anderson 1859
Woman MP (UK) Constance, Countess Markievicz, Sinn Fein MP 1918
Woman MP (to take seat)
Nancy Astor for Plymouth Sutton 1919
Woman novelist Lady Murasaki, Japan c1004
Woman novelist (UK) Aphra Behn 1687
Woman pilot Baronne Elise de la Roche 1909
Woman prime minister
Mrs Sirimavo Bandaranaike of Ceylon 1960
Women's Institute
Stoneycreek, Ontario, Canada 1897
Yellow lines restricting parking Laid in Slough 1956
Zebra crossing Trialled in 1949 but became law (31 Oct) 1951

NB: Although this topic of 'firsts' has been listed in the Famous People section, many of the entries relate to inanimate objects. This is purely a matter of expediency and is not an oversight on the part of the author.

Initials: Known by

WH Auden Wystan Hugh *British poet*
AJ Ayer Alfred Jules *English philosopher*
CPE Bach Carl Philipp Emanuel *German composer*
JC Bach Johann Christian *German composer*
JS Bach Johann Sebastian *German composer*
RM Ballantyne, Robert Michael *Scottish author*
JG Ballard James Graham *British writer*
JC Bamford Joseph Cyril *Founder of JCB Company*
BA Baracus Bad Attitude *Fictional TV character ('A Team')*
PT Barnum Phineas Taylor *US showman*
JM Barrie James Matthew *Scottish novelist*
HE Bates Herbert Ernest *English novelist*
CC Beck Clarence *US graphic artist*
AC Benson Arthur Christopher *English author and poet*
EF Benson Edward Frederic *English author*
EC Bentley Edmund Clerihew *English journalist and novelist*
RD Blackmore Richard Doddridge *English novelist*
PW Botha Pieter Willem *South African politician*
RA Butler Richard Austen *British politician*
AS Byatt Antonia Susan *English novelist and critic*
GK Chesterton Gilbert Keith *English novelist*
JM Coetzee John Maxwell *South African novelist*
GDH Cole George Douglas Howard *British economist*
AE Coppard Alfred Edgar *English poet and writer*
AJ Cronin Archibald Joseph *Scottish novelist*
ee cummings Edward Estlin *American writer and painter*
WH Davies William Henry *British poet*
JW De Forest John William *US novelist and historian*

FW De Klerk, Frederik Willem *South African politician*
RF Delderfield Ronald Frederick *English playwright*
EL Doctorow Edgar Lawrence *US novelist*
JP Donleavy James Patrick *Irish novelist*
TS Eliot Thomas Stearns *poet and dramatist*
JK Ewers John Keith *Australian writer*
JR Ewing John Ross *Fictional TV character ('Dallas')*
UA Fanthorpe Ursula Askham *British poet*
JG Farrell James Gordon *English novelist*
EH Fellowes Edmund Horace *English musicologist*
WC Fields William Claude *American comedy actor*
CS Forester Cecil Scott *British writer*
EM Forster Edward Morgan *English novelist*
AJ Foyt Anthony Joseph *US racing driver*
EA Freeman Edward Augustus *British historian*
CB Fry Charles Burgess *English sportsman*
JK Galbraith John Kenneth *economist*
TS Garp Technical Sergeant *John Irving character*
WS Gilbert William Schwenck *English operetta librettist*
KC Gillette King Camp *American inventor*
WE Gladstone William Ewart *British politician*
EW Godwin Edward William *English architect and designer*
HL Gold Horace Leonard *science fiction writer*
WG Grace William Gilbert *English cricketer*
DW Griffith David Wark *American film director*
AB Guthrie Alfred Bertram *US writer*
MC Hammer Master of Ceremonies *US rap artist*
WC Handy William Christopher *US Blues composer*
LP Hartley Leslie Poles *English author*
HJ Heinz Henry John *US food manufacturer*
WE Henley William Ernest *English poet and critic*
GA Henty George Alfred *English novelist*
AP Herbert Alan Patrick *English writer*
AD Hope Alec Derwent *Australian poet*
EW Hornung Ernest William *English writer*
AE Housman Alfred Edward *English poet*
EM Hull Edith Maude *British writer*
TE Hulme Thomas Ernest *British essayist and poet*

CLR James Cyril Lionel Robert *Trinidadian writer*
EL James Erika Leonard *English writer*
MR James Montague Rhodes *ghost story writer*
PD James Phyllis Dorothy *English writer*
WE Johns William Earl *English writer and aviator*
MM Kaye Mary Margaret *British writer*
HRF Keating Henry Raymond Fitzwalter *UK detective story writer*
AL Kennedy Alison Louise *British writer*
BB King Blues Boy *singer/guitarist*
WP Kinsella William Patrick *Canadian writer*
RB Kitaj Ronald Brooks *American painter*
LC Knight Lionel Charles *British critic and author*
RD Laing Ronald David *Scottish psychiatrist*
CJ Lamb Cara Jean *fictional TV character (LA Law)*
kd lang Kathryn Dawn *Canadian singer*
DH Lawrence David Herbert *English novelist*
TE Lawrence Thomas Edward *British soldier and writer*
FR Leavis Frank Raymond *English literary critic*
GH Lewes George Henry *British writer*
CS Lewis Clive Staples *Irish writer*
HP Lovecraft Howard Phillips *US science fiction writer*
LS Lowry Laurence Stephen *English artist*
HL Mencken Henry Louis *US journalist*
AA Michelson Albert Abraham *US physicist*
AA Milne Alan Alexander *children's writer*
LM Montgomery Lucy Maud *Canadian novelist*
CL Moore Catherine Lucille *US science fiction writer*
JP Morgan John Pierpoint *US financier*
JB Morton John Bingham *British journalist (Beachcomber)*
HH Munro Hector Hugh *English writer (Saki)*
VS Naipaul Vidiadhar Surajprasad *Trinidadian novelist*
RK Narayan Rasipuram Kirshnaswamy *Indian novelist*
PH Newby Percy Howard *British novelist*
TV Olsen Theodore Victor *US Westerns writer*
PJ O'Rourke Patrick John *US journalist*
CJ Parker Casey Jean *Fictional TV character ('Baywatch')*
SJ Perelman Sydney Joseph *US writer*
DBC Pierre Dirty But Clean *Australian novelist*
TF Powys Theodore Francis *British writer*

JB Priestley John Boynton *English novelist*
VS Pritchett Victor Sawdon *English writer*
JD Rockefeller John Davison *US businessman*
AV Roe Alliot Verdon *English aviation pioneer*
JK Rowling Joanne Kathleen *English children's writer*
JD Salinger Jerome David *US novelist*
EH Shepard Ernest Howard *English illustrator*
RC Sherriff Robert Cedric *English novelist*
NF Simpson Norman Frederick *British playwright*
OJ Simpson Orenthal James *US sportsman*
VP Singh Vishwanath Pratap *Indian politician*
CH Sisson Charles Hubert *British poet*
BF Skinner Burrhus Fredric *US psychologist*
EE 'Doc' Smith Edward Elmer *US science fiction writer*
WH Smith William Henry *English newsagent*
CP Snow Charles Percy *English novelist*
HM Stanley Henry Morton *journalist and explorer*
JIM Stewart John Innes Mackintosh *English writer*
JEB Stuart James Ewell Brown *Confederate general*
JM Synge John Millington *Irish dramatist*
AJP Taylor Alan John Percivale *English historian*
DM Thomas Donald Michael English writer
EP Thompson Edward Palmer *British historian*
EMW Tillyard Eustace Mandeville Wetenhall *British scholar and critic*
JRR Tolkien John Ronald Reuel *philologist and author*
PL Travers Pamela Lyndon *author of Mary Poppins*
AE Van Vogt Alfred Elton *science fiction writer*
CV Wedgwood Cicely Veronica *English historian*
HG Wells Herbert George *English novelist*
EB White Elwyn Brooks *US essayist and novelist*
TH White Terence Hanbury *English novelist*
JPR Williams John Peter Rhys *Welsh rugby player*
WD and HO Wills William Day and Henry Overton *tobacco manufacturers*
PG Wodehouse Pelham Grenville *English novelist*
FW Woolworth Frank Winfield *US businessman*
PC Wren Percy Christopher *English novelist*
WB Yeats William Butler *Irish poet*

Inventions and Discoveries

Adding machine *Blaise Pascal* 1642
Aeroplane (steam powered) *Clement Ader* 1886
Aeroplane *Wright Brothers* 1903
Aerosol *Erik Rotheim* 1926
Air pump *Otto Von Guericke* 1654
Airship (non-rigid) *Henri Giffard* 1852
Airship (rigid) *Ferdinand Von Zeppelin* 1900
Ambulance *Baron Dominique Jean Larrey* 1792
Anaesthesia *William Morton* 1846
Antiseptic surgery *Joseph Lister* 1867
Aqualung *Cousteau and Gagnan* 1943
Aspirin (synthesization) *Kolbe, Heinrich* 1859
Aspirin (intro into medicine) *H Dresser of Bayer AG* 1899
Assembly line *Samuel Colt* 1855
Atom bomb *Frisch, Bohr, Peierls* 1939
Baby incubator *Dr Alexandre Lion* 1891
Bakelite *Leo H Baekeland* 1907
Balloon *Montgolfier Brothers* 1783
Balloons: rubber *Michael Faraday* 1824
Balloons: toy *JG Ingram* 1847
Ball-point pen (patent) *John T Loud* 1888
Ball-point pen (mass-produced) *László Biro* 1938
Barbed wire (manufacture) *Joseph Glidden* 1874
Barbed wire (patent) *Lucien B Smith* 1867
Barometer *Evangelista Torricelli* 1643
Battery (electric) *Alessandro Volta* 1800
Bell (electric) *Joseph Henry* 1831
Betatron *Donald Kerst* 1940
Bicycle *Kirkpatrick MacMillan* 1839
Bicycle (spoked wheels) *James Starley* 1870
Bifocal Lens *Benjamin Franklin* 1780
Bikini *Louis Reard* 1946
Boy Scout movement Sir Robert Baden-Powell 1907
Bra (cantilevered) *Robard Howard Hughes* 1943
Breakfast cereal (ready to eat) *Henry D Perky* 1893
Bunsen burner *Robert Wilhelm Bunsen* 1855
Burglar alarm *Edwin T Holmes* 1858
Cable-car *W Ritter* 1866
Calculating clock *Wilhelm Schickard* 1623
Calculus *Leibniz and Newton* 1684
Canning *Nicholas Appert* 1795
Car (3 process wheel steam tractor) *Nicolas Cugnot* 1769
Car (petrol) *Karl Benz* 1885
Car speedometer *Thorpe and Salter* 1902
Carbon fibres *Courtaulds* 1964
Carbon paper *Ralph Wedgewood* 1806
Carburettor *Gottlieb Daimler* 1876
Carpet sweeper *Melville R Bissell* 1876
Cash register *James Ritty* 1879
Cats' eyes *Percy Shaw* 1933
Cellophane *Dr Jacques Brandenberger* 1908
Celluloid *Alexander Parkes* 1861
Cement (Portland) *Joseph Aspdin* 1824
Centigrade thermometer *Anders Celsius* 1742
Chewing gum (commercial) *John Curtis* 1848
Chocolate (solid) *François-Louis Cailler* 1819
Christmas card *Sir Henry Cole* 1843
Chronometer *John Harrison* 1735
Cinematography *Lumière brothers* 1895
Circulation of the blood *William Harvey* 1628
Clock (mechanical) *I-Hsing and Liang-Tsan* 725
Clock (quartz) *Warren Alvin Marrison* 1929
Cloud chamber *Charles Thomson Rees Wilson* 1927
Cluedo *Anthony Pratt* 1948
Coca-Cola *Dr John Pemberton* 1886
Coffee (instant) *Nestles* 1937
Gas meter *William Clegg* 1815
Compact disc *Philips and Sony* 1979
Computer *Charles Babbage* 1835
Computer (electronic) *Eckert and Mauchly* 1946
Concrete (reinforced) *François Hennebique* 1892
Condensed milk *Gail Borden* 1858
Condom *Gabriel Fallopius* 1560
Contact lens *Adolph E Fick* 1887
Contraceptive pill *Dr Gregory Pincus* 1950
Cordite *Dewar and Abel* 1905
Corrugated iron *Pierre Carpentier* 1853
Credit card *Ralph Scheider* 1950
Crossword puzzle *Arthur Wynne* 1913
Cyclotron *James Chadwick* 1935
DDT *Paul Muller* 1939
Decompression chamber *Robert H Davis* 1929
Disc brake *Dr F Lanchester* 1902
Diving suit *Andrew Becker* 1715
DNA structure *Francis Crick and James Watson* 1953
Dome (geodesic) *Richard Buckminster Fuller* 1945
Double-entry bookkeeping *Lucas Paciolus* 1495
Doughnut (with hole) *Hanson Gregory* 1847
Drill (electric) *Wilhelm Fein* 1895
Drill (pneumatic) *Germain Sommelier* 1861
Dry-cleaning *M Jolly-Bellin* 1849
Dynamite *Alfred Nobel* 1863
Dynamo *Hippolyte Pixii* 1832
Elastic bands *Stephen Perry* 1845
Electric chair *Harold Brown and EA Kenneally* 1890
Electric fan *Dr Schuyler Skaats* 1882
Electric flat iron *HW Seeley* 1882
Electric generator *Michael Faraday* 1831
Electric guitar *Rickenbacker, Barth and Beauchamp* 1931
Electric heating system *Dr W Leigh Burton* 1887
Electric lamp *Independently invented by Joseph, Swan and Thomas Alva Edison* 1879
Electric motor (AC) *Nikola Tesla* 1888
Electric motor (DC) *Zenobe Gramme* 1873
Electrocardiography *Willem Einthoven* 1903
Electromagnet *William Sturgeon* 1824
Electron *JJ Thomas* 1897
Electronic computer (dedicated) *Alan Turing* 1943
Electronic computer (general purpose) Eckert and John Mauchly 1946
Electronic computer (commercially available) *Eckert and Mauchly* 1951
Endoscope *Pierre Segalas* 1827
Equals sign (mathematics) *Robert Record* 1557
Escalator *Jesse W Reno* 1892
Esperanto *Dr Ludovic Zamenhof* 1887
Exclamation mark *J Day* 1553
Facsimile machine (Fax) *Arthur Korn* 1907
Ferrofluids *Ronald Rosensweig* 1968
Film (Moving outlines) *Louis Le Prince* 1885
Film (Musical sound) *Lee De Forest* 1923
Film (Talking) *Engl, Mussolle and Vogt* 1922
Fingerprint classification *Francis Galton* 1891
Fire extinguisher *M Fuches* 1734
Flying doctor service *KH Vincent Welsh* 1928
Foam rubber *John Boyd Dunlop* 1929
Food processor *Kenneth Wood* 1947
Fountain pen *Lewis Edson Waterman* 1884
Frozen food *Clarence Birdseye* 1930
Galvanometer *André-Marie Ampère* 1834
Gas fire *Philippe Lebon* 1799
Gas lighting *William Murdock* 1792

Gearbox (automatic) *Hermann Fottinger* 1910
Genetics *Gregor Mendel* 1865
Geodesic dome *Richard Buckminster Fuller* 1945
Gift coupons *Benjamin Talbert Babbit* 1865
Girl Guides *Robert and Agnes Baden-Powell* 1910
Glider *Sir George Cayley* 1853
Golliwog *Florence K Upton* 1895
Gramophone *Thomas Alva Edison* 1878
Gravitation, laws of *Isaac Newton* 1684
Gun cotton *Christian Friedrich Schønbein* 1845
Gyro-compass *Elmer Sperry* 1911
Gyroscope *Leon Foucault* 1852
Half-tone process *Carl Gustaf Wilhelm Carleman* 1871
Hearing aid (electric) *Miller Reese Hutchinson* 1901
Heart (artificial) *Vladimir Demikhov* 1937
Helicopter *Louis and Jacques Breguet* 1907
Holography *Dennis Gabor* 1947
Hovercraft *Christopher Cockerell* 1955
Hydrofoil *Comte de Lambert* 1897
Ice-cream cones *Italo Marcioni* 1896
Identikit *Hugh McDonald* 1959
Insulin *Frederick Grant Banting and Charles Herbert Best* 1921
Intelligence test (IQ) *Alfred Binet* 1896
Iron Lung *Philip Drinker* 1927
Jeans *Levi Strauss* 1850
Jet engine *Sir Frank Whittle* 1937
Jigsaw puzzle *John Spilsbury* 1767
Jukebox (pre-selective) *John C Dunton* 1905
Kaleidoscope *Sir David Brewster* 1816
Knitting machine *William Lee* 1589
Laser *Theodore Maiman* 1960
Lathe, screw-cutting *Henry Maudslay* 1800
Launderette *JF Cantrell* 1934
Lawn mower *Edwin Budding and John Ferrabee* 1830
Lie detector *John Larson* 1928
Lift (mechanical) *Elisha G Otis* 1852
Lightning conductor *Benjamin Franklin* 1752
Linoleum *Frederick Walton* 1860
Lithography *Aloys Senefelder* 1796
Locomotive *Richard Trevithick* 1804
Logarithms *John Napier* 1614
Loom, power *Edmund Cartwright* 1785
Loudspeaker *Horace Short* 1898
Loudspeaker (electric) *Miller Reece Hutchinson* 1906
Machine gun *James Puckle* 1718
Margarine *Hippolyte Mège-Mouriés* 1869
Maser *Charles H Townes* 1953
Match *Robert Boyle* 1680
Match (friction) *John Walker* 1826
Match (safety) *JE Lundstrom* 1855
Metronome *Dietrich Nikolaus Winkel* c1800
Microchip *Jack Saint Clair Kilby* 1958
Microphone *Alexander Graham Bell* 1876
Micro-processor *Moore and Hoff Noyce* 1971
Microscope *Zacharias Janssen* 1590
Microscope (electron) *EAF Ruska* 1933
Microwave oven *Percy Spencer* 1945
Miner's safety lamp *Sir Humphry Davy* 1816
Missile (air-to-air) *Herbert Wagner* 1943
Monopoly *Charles Darrow* 1931
Motor cycle *Gottlieb Daimler* 1885
Neon lamp *Georges Claude* 1910
Neptune (planet) *Johann Gottfried Galle* 1846
Neutron *James Chadwick* 1935
Non-stick pan *Marc Gregoir* 1954
Nylon *Wallace Carothers* 1937
Optical fibres *Navinder Kapany* 1955
Oven (electric) *Bernina Hotel, Switzerland* 1889
Roulette wheel *Blaise Pascal* 1647

Ozone *Christian Friedrich Schönbein* 1840
Pacemaker (implantable) *Wilson Greatbach* 1956
Paint (acrylic) *Reeves Ltd* 1964
Paint (fluorescent) *Joe and Bob Switzer* 1933
Paper *Tsai Lun* 105
Paper (from wood pulp) *Gottlob Keller* 1844
Paper clip *Johann Vaaler* 1900
Parachute *Jean-Pierre Blanchard* 1785
Parachute (patent) *André-Jacques Garnerin* 1802
Parking meter *Carlton Magee* 1935
Pasteurisation *Louis Pasteur* 1863
Pen (ball-point mass produced) *Laszlo Biro* 1938
Pen (ball-point patent) *John T Loud* 1888
Pen (fountain) *Lewis Waterman* 1884
Pencil (using pulverised graphite lead) *Nicolas Jacques Conté* 1795
Pendulum clock *Christiaan Huygens* 1656
Penicillin *Sir Alexander Fleming* 1928
Periodic table *Dmitri Mendelev* 1866
Photoelectric cell *Johann Phillip Elster and Hans F Geitel* 1896
Photographic lens *William H Wollaston* 1812
Photography (on pewter plate) *Joseph Nicéphore Niepce* 1826
Photography (on paper) *William Henry Fox Talbot* 1835
Photography (colour) *James Clerk Maxwell* 1861
Photography (on film) *John Carbutt* 1888
Pianoforte *Bartolomeo Cristofori* 1709
Pillar box (UK) *Anthony Trollope* 1851
Plastics *Alexander Parkes* 1852
Pluto (planet) *Clyde Tombaugh* 1930
Plutonium *GT Seaborg, JW Kennedy and AC Wahl* 1940
Pneumatic bicycle tyres *John Boyd Dunlop* 1887
Pneumatic tyres *RW Thompson.* 1845
Pocket calculator *Kilby, Tassell and Merryman* 1972
Polio vaccine (injection) *Jonas Salk* 1952
Polio vaccine (oral) *Albert Sabin* 1957
Polythene *RO Gibson* 1933
Potato crisps *George Crum* 1853
Pressure cooker *Denis Papin* 1679
Printing press (wooden) *Johann Gutenberg* 1455
Printing (rotary) *Richard Hoe* 1846
Propeller (boat, hand-operated) *David Bushnell* 1775
Propeller (ship) *Francis Smith* 1837
Propeller (ship), patent *Isambard Kingdom Brunel* 1844
Proton *Ernest Rutherford* 1920
Pyramid *Imhotep* 2650BC
Radar (application) *Taylor and Young* 1930
Radar (theory) *Nikola Tesla* 1900
Radar (UK) *Robert Watson-Watt* 1935
Radio telegraphy *Mahlon Loomis* 1864
Radio telegraphy (transatlantic) *Guglielmo Marconi* 1901
Radioactivity *Henri Becquerel* 1896
Rails (iron) *Abraham Darby* 1738
Railway airbrake *George Westinghouse* 1863
Railway (electric) *Ernst Siemens* 1878
Railway (underground) *Charles Pearson* 1843
Rayon *Joseph Swan* 1883
Razor (safety) *King Camp Gillette* 1895
Razor (electric) *Jacob Schick* 1931
Record (flat disc) *Emil Berliner* 1888
Record (LP) *Peter Goldmark* 1948
Refrigerator *James Harrison and Alexander Catlin Twinning* 1850
Revolver *Samuel Colt* 1835
Rickshaw *Jonathan Scobie* 1869
Roller skates *Joseph Merlin* 1760
Telescope (refractor) *Hans Lippershey* 1608

Rubber (latex foam) *Dunlop Rubber Co* 1928
Rubber (tyres) *Thomas Hancock* 1846
Rubber (vulcanised) *Charles Goodyear* 1841
Rubber (waterproof) *Charles Macintosh* 1823
Rubik cube *Erno Rubik* 1975
Safety pin *Walter Hunt* 1849
Scooter *Walter Lines* 1897
Scotch tape *Richard Drew* 1930
Scrabble *James Brunot* 1950
Sealing wax *Gerard Hermann* 1554
Seismographic scale *Charles Francis Richter* 1935
Self-starter motor (UK) *Charles F Kettering* 1911
Sewing machine *Thomas Saint* 1790
Shorthand *Marcus Tullius Tiro* 63BC
Shorthand (modern world) *Timothy Bright* 1588
Skyscraper *William Le Baron Jenny* 1882
Slide rule *William Oughtred* 1621
Snooker *Sir Neville Chamberlain* 1875
Spectacles *Salvino degli Armati and Alessandro delle Spina* c1280
Spinning frame *Richard Arkwright* 1769
Spinning jenny *James Hargreaves* 1764
Spinning mule *Samuel Crompton* 1779
Spirit level *JM Thévenot* 1666
Stamp (perforations) *Henry Archer* 1854
Stapler *Charles Henry Gould* 1868
Steam engine *Thomas Savery* 1698
Steam engine (condenser) *James Watt* 1765
Steam engine (piston) *Thomas Newcomen* 1712
Steamship *JC Perier* 1775
Steamturbine (ship's) *Charles Parsons* 1894
Steel production *Henry Bessemer* 1855
Steel (stainless) *Harry Brearley* 1913
Stereotype *William Ged* 1725
Stethoscope *René Laennec* 1816
Stopwatch *Jean Moyse* 1776
Submarine *Cornelius Jacobszoon Drebbel* 1620
Sun-tan cream *Eugene Schueller* 1936
Syringe (hypodermic) *Charles Gabriel Pravaz* 1835
Table tennis *James Gibb* 1890
Tampon *Earl Hass* 1830
Tank *Ernest Swinton* 1914
Tape recorder *Louis Blattner* 1929
Telegraph (electric) *George Louis Lesage* 1774
Telegraph *M Lammond* 1787
Telegraph code *Samuel Morse* 1837
Telephone *Antonio Meucci* 1849
Telephone (patent) *Alexander Graham Bell* 1876
Telephone switchboard *Almon B Strowger* 1889
Television (mechanical) *John Logie Baird* 1926
Tennis *Walter G Wingfield* 1873
Terylene *JR Whinfield and JT Dickson* 1941
Thermometer *Galileo Galilei* 1593
Thermometer (mercury) *Gabriel Fahrenheit* 1714
Thimble *Nicolas Van Benschoten* 1684
Toothbrush *William Addis* 1649
Top hat *John Hetherington* 1797
Torpedo (UK) *Robert Whitehead* 1866
Traffic lights *JP Knight* 1868
Traffic lights (automatic) *Alfred Benesch* 1914
Transformer *Michael Faraday* 1831
Transistor *John Bardeen, William Bradley Shockley and Walter Brattain* 1948
Travel agency *Thomas Cook* 1841
Travellers cheques *Robert Herries* 1772
Travellers cheques (commercial) *American Express* 1891
Tubercle bacillus *Robert Koch* 1882
Tuning fork *John Shore* 1711
Turbojet *Frank Whittle* 1928
Typewriter *Pellegrine Tarri* 1808
Typewriter (patent) *William Burt* 1829
Typewriter (mass produced) *Christopher Sholes* 1874
Ultrasonography (obstetric) *Ian Donald* 1979
Uranus *William Herschel* 1781
Vaccination *Edward Jenner* 1796
Vacuum cleaner (electric) *Hubert Cecil Booth* 1901
Vacuum cleaner (steam) *Ives McGaffrey* 1871
Vacuum flask *James Dewar* 1892
Vending machine *Percival Everitt* 1883
Ventilator *Théophile Guibal* 1858
Video recorder *Ampex Co* 1956
Videophone *American Telegraph and Telephone Co* 1927
Vulcanised rubber *Charles Goodyear* 1839
Washing machine (electric) *Hurley Machine Co* 1907
Watch *Bartholomew Manfredi* 1462
Watch (waterproof) *Rolex* 1927
Water closet *Sir John Harington* 1589
Welder (electric) *Elisha Thomson* 1877
Wheel *Mesopotamians* c3500BC
White road markings *Edward Norris Hines* 1911
Wire recorder (mechanical) *Valdemar Poulsen* 1898
Xerox copier *Chester Carlson* 1938
X-ray *Wilhelm Konrad Röntgen* 1895
Zip fastener *Whitcomb L Judson* 1891

Marriages: By Female Spouse

Diahnne Abbott	Actress	***Robert De Niro***	*Actor*
Paula Abdul (2)	Singer	***Emilio Estevez***	*Actor*
Victoria Adams	Spice girl	***David Beckham***	*Footballer*
Princess Adelaide of Saxe-Coburg Meiningen	German noblewoman	***William IV***	*British king*
Agrippina	Roman noblewomen	***Claudius***	*Roman emperor*
Caroline Aherne	Comedienne	***Peter Hook***	*Musician*
Pauline de Ahna	Soprano	***Richard Strauss***	*Composer*
Anouk Aimée (2)	Actress	***Albert Finney (5)***	*Actor*
Aisha	Muhammad's favourite wife	***Muhammad***	*Founder of Islam*
Maria Aitken	Actress	***Nigel Davenport***	*Actor*
Nadiya Aja (2)	Saudi tycoon's daughter	***Omar Sharif***	*Actor and bridge player*
Kitty Aldridge	Actress	***Mark Knopfler***	*Musician*
Princess Alexandra of Schlesung-Holstein-Sorderburg	Danish princess	***Edward VII***	*British king*
Princess Alexandra	British princess	***Angus Ogilvy***	*Businessman*
Alison Allen	TV producer	***Keith Allen***	*Actor*
Catherine Allen	Secretary	***Frankie Dettori***	*Jockey*

Gracie Allen	Comedienne	***George Burns***	*Comedian and actor*
Lorraine Allen (2)	Singer	***Xavier Cugat***	*Band leader*
June Allyson (2)	Actress	***Dick Powell***	*Actor*
Suzy Amis (5)	Actress	***James Cameron (2)***	*Film director*
Amphitrite	Greek mythical sea nymph	***Poseidon***	*Greek god of the Sea*
Gillian Anderson	Actress	***Clyde Klotz (1)***	*Art Director*
		Julian Ozanne (2)	*Photojournalist*
Loni Anderson (2)	Actress	***Burt Reynolds (3)***	*Actor*
Pamela Anderson	Actress (3)	***Tommy Lee (1)***	*Singer*
	Actress (1)	***Kid Rock (2)***	*Rap artist*
Nina Andreevskaya	Moscow socialite	***Wassily Kandinsky***	*Russian artist*
Ursula Andress (1)	Actress	***John Derek***	*Actor and director*
Julie Andrews	Actress/singer	***Blake Edwards (2)***	*Film director*
Marie Angel	Australian soprano	***David Freeman***	*Opera director*
Jennifer Aniston	Actress	***Brad Pitt***	*Actor*
Princess Anne	British princess	***Mark Phillips (1)***	*Equestrian rider*
		Tim Laurence (2)	*Naval Officer*
Princess Anne	Danish princess	***James I***	*British king*
Anne of Bohemia (1)	Emperor Charles IV's daughter	***Richard II***	*English king*
Queen Anne	British queen	***George of Denmark***	*Danish Prince*
Marie Antoinette	French princess	***Louis XVI***	*King of France*
Aphrodite	Greek goddess of Love	***Hephaestus***	*Greek god of fire*
Frances Appleton	Socialite	***Henry W Longfellow***	*US poet*
Natalie Appleton	Pop singer	***Liam Howlett***	*Musician*
Nicole Appleton (2)	Pop singer	***Liam Gallagher***	*Pop musician*
Ariadne	Mythical daughter of King Minos of Crete	***Dionysus***	*Greek god of wine*
Jean Armour	Socialite	***Robert Burns***	*Poet*
Patricia Arquette	Actress	***Nicholas Cage***	*Actor*
Debbie Ash (1)	Actress	***Eddie Kidd***	*Stunt motorcyclist*
Leslie Ash	Actress	***Lee Chapman***	*Footballer*
Jane Asher	Cook	***Gerald Scarfe***	*Cartoonist*
Edwina Ashley	Heiress and charity worker	***Louis Mountbatten***	*Naval commander*
Elizabeth Ashley	Actress (1)	***James Farentino (1)***	*Actor*
	Actress (2)	***George Peppard (2)***	*Actor*
Atalanta	Mythical Greek huntress	***Milanion***	*Mythical Greek athlete*
Rosalind Ayres	Actress	***Martin Jarvis***	*Actor*
Lauren Bacall	Actress (4)	***Humphrey Bogart (1)***	*Actor*
	Actress (3)	***Jason Robards (2)***	*Actor*
Barbara Bach (2)	Actress	***Ringo Starr***	*Musician*
Maria Barbara Bach (1)	Cousin of JS Bach	***JS Bach***	*Composer*
Enid Bagnold	Author	***Sir G Roderick Jones***	*MD of Reuters*
Lilian Bailey	American soprano	***George Henschel***	*Baritone*
Barbara Bain	Actress	***Martin Landau***	*Actor*
Shakira Baksh (2)	Actress and model	***Sir Michael Caine***	*Actor*
Jill Balcon	Actress	***Cecil Day-Lewis***	*Poet*
Caroline Balestier	Publishing heiress	***Rudyard Kipling***	*Novelist and poet*
Lucille Ball	Comedienne and actress	***Desi Arnaz***	*Musician and actor*
Zoe Ball	TV presenter	***Norman Cook***	*Musician*
Rose Bampton	Soprano	***Wilfred Pelletier***	*Conductor*
Anne Bancroft	Actress	***Mel Brooks***	*Actor/producer*
Glynis Barber	Actress	***Michael Brandon (2)***	*Actor*
Emma Bardac (2)	Socialite	***Claude Debussy***	*Composer*
Brigitte Bardot (1)	Actress	***Roger Vadim***	*Film director*
Margherita Barezzi (1)	Daughter of Verdi's sponsor	***Giuseppe Verdi***	*Composer*
Ellen Barkin	Actress	***Gabriel Byrne***	*Actor*
Nora Barnacle	Socialite	***James Joyce***	*Irish writer*
Pinkie Barnes	Table tennis international	***Sam Kydd***	*Actor*
Roseanne Barr	Actress	***Tom Arnold (2)***	*Actor*
	Actress	***Ben Thomas (3)***	*Actor*
Elizabeth Barrett	Poet	***Robert Browning***	*Poet*
Kim Basinger	Actress	***Alec Baldwin (2)***	*Actor*
Elizabeth Batts	Captain's wife	***James Cook***	*Seaman and explorer*
Stephanie Beacham	Actress	***John McEnery***	*Actor*
Priscilla Beaulieu	Actress	***Elvis Presley***	*Singer*
Mary Hayley Bell	Playwright	***John Mills***	*Actor*
Annette Bening	Actress	***Warren Beatty***	*Actor*
Jill Bennett	Actress	***John Osborne (1)***	*Playwright*
		Willis Hall (2)	
Veronica Bennett	Singer	***Phil Spector***	*Record producer*
Berengaria	Princess of Navarre	***Richard I***	*English king*
Candice Bergen (3)	Actress	***Louis Malle***	*Director*
Ingrid Bergman (2)	Actress	***Roberto Rossellini (2)***	*Director*
Halle Berry	US actress	***David Justice (1)***	*US baseball player*
		Eric Benét (2)	*US vocalist*
		Olivier Martinez (3)	*French actor*
Joy Beverley	Singer	***Billy Wright***	*Footballer*
Kathryn Bigelow (3)	Film director	***James Cameron***	*Film director*
Anne Birley (3)	Lady Annabel Vane-Tempest Stewart	***James Goldsmith***	*Tycoon*

Sophie Blake	Model & Presenter	***Scott Nicholls***	*Speedway rider*
Blanche of Lancaster (1)	English noblewoman	***John of Gaunt***	*English prince*
Melanie Blatt	Pop singer	***Stuart Zender***	*Musician*
Renate Blauel	Actress	***Elton John***	*Vocalist and composer*
Joan Blondell	Actress	***Dick Powell (1)***	*Actor*
		Mike Todd (2)	*Showman and film producer*
Claire Bloom	Actress (2)	***Rod Steiger (1)***	*Actor*
	Actress (2)	***Philip Roth (3)***	*Novelist*
Maureen Blott (2)	Actress	***Harry H Corbett***	*Actor*
Jean Boht	Actress	***Carl Davis***	*Composer*
Cherie Booth	Barrister	***Tony Blair***	*Politician*
Connie Booth	Actress	***John Cleese***	*Actor*
Catherine Boucher	Illiterate pauper	***William Blake***	*Poet and painter*
Boudicca	Queen of Iceni	***Prasutagus***	*King of Iceni*
Margaret Bourke-White	Photo-journalist	***Erskine Caldwell***	*US author*
Jacqueline Bouvier	Socialite	***John F Kennedy (1)***	*US president*
Elizabeth Bowen	Irish novelist	***Alan Charles Cameron***	*Businessman*
Marjory Bowes (1)	John Knox's 1st wife	***John Knox***	*Religious reformer*
Patti Boyd	Model	***George Harrison (1)***	*Musician*
		Eric Clapton (2)	*Musician*
Elizabeth Boyle	Socialite	***Edmund Spenser***	*English poet*
Philippa Braithewaite (2)	TV Producer	***Martin Clunes***	*Actor*
Sarah Brightman (2)	Singer	***Andrew Lloyd Webber (2)***	*Composer*
Cosima Von Bülow	Franz Liszt's daughter	***Hans von Bülow (1)***	*Conductor*
Christie Brinkley (2)	Model	***Billy Joel (2)***	*Singer*
May Britt	Actress	***Sammy Davis Jnr***	*Entertainer*
Vera May Brittain	Writer	***George Catlin***	*Professor of politics*
Charlotte Brontë	Writer	***Arthur Bell Nicholls***	*Curate*
Janet Brown	Impressionist	***Peter Butterworth***	*Actor*
Melanie Brown	Spice girl	***Jimmy Gulzar***	*Musician*
Coral Browne	Actress	***Vincent Price***	*Actor*
Jill Browne	Actress	***John Alderton (1)***	*Actor*
		Brian Wolfe (2)	*Theatre producer*
Anna Brueghel	Daughter of Jan Brueghel	***David Teniers the Younger***	*Flemish painter*
Sheila Buckley	Secretary	***John Stonehouse***	*Politician*
Cosima von Bülow (2)	Franz Liszt's daughter	***Richard Wagner***	*Composer*
Fanny Burney	English novelist	***General D'Arblay***	*French émigré*
Margaret Burr	Daughter of 4th Duke of Beaufort	***Thomas Gainsborough***	*English painter*
Irene Busch	Musician	***Rudolf Serkin***	*Pianist*
Danielle Bux (2)	Model	***Gary Lineker***	*Footballer*
Penny Calvert	Dancer	***Bruce Forsyth (1)***	*Entertainer*
		Peter Murray Hill (2)	*Actor and bookseller*
Dyan Cannon (4)	Actress	***Cary Grant***	*Actor*
Sarah Caplin	TV executive	***Nick Ross***	*Broadcaster*
Kate Capshaw (2)	Actress	***Steven Spielberg (2)***	*Director*
Mariah Carey	Singer	***Tommy Mottola***	*President of Sony Music*
Judy Carne	Actress	***Burt Reynolds***	*Actor*
Caroline of Ansbach	German noblewoman	***George II***	*British king*
Caroline of Brunswick	German noblewoman	***George IV***	*British king*
Caroline of Monaco	Princess	***Pierre Junot (1)***	*Businessman*
		Stefano Casiraghi (2)	*Businessman*
		Prince Ernst August (3)	*Hanoverian Prince*
Leslie Caron	Actress	***Peter Hall***	*Theatre director*
Theresa Carreño (1)	Pianist	***Eugène D'Albert***	*Composer and pianist*
June Carter	Singer	***Johnny Cash***	*Singer*
Martita Casals	Pablo Casals' widow	***Eugene Istomin***	*Pianist*
Carmen Castillo (1)	Singer	***Xavier Cugat***	*Bandleader*
Phoebe Cates	Actress	***Kevin Kline***	*Actor*
Princess Catherine	Valois princess	***Owen Tudor (1)***	*Grandfather of Henry VII*
Catherine I	Russian empress	***Peter the Great (2)***	*Russian Tsar*
Catherine II (the Great)	Russian empress	***Peter III***	*Russian Tsar*
Catherine de-Medici	Queen of France	***Henry II***	*French king*
Catherine of Braganza	Portuguese princess	***Charles II***	*English king*
Catherine of Valois	French princess	***Henry V (2)***	*English king*
Anna Cermakova	Socialite	***Antonin Dvorák***	*Composer*
Judith Chalmers	TV presenter	***Neil Durden-Smith***	*Sports commentator*
Alice Charigot	Socialite	***Pierre-Auguste Renoir***	*French painter*
Charlotte Sophia	German noblewoman	***George III***	*British king*
Charlotte Charpentier	Daughter of French émigré	***Walter Scott***	*Scottish novelist*
Cher	Actress/Singer	***Sonny Bono (1)***	*Actor and politician*
		Greg Allmann (2)	*Musician*
Helen Cherry	Actress	***Trevor Howard***	*Actor*
Chiang Ching (3)	Actress	***Mao Zedong***	*Chinese leader*
Agatha Christie	Writer	***Max Mallowan***	*Archaeologist*
Diane Cilento (1)	Actress	***Sean Connery***	*Actor*
Cleopatra VII	Queen of Egypt	***Ptolemy XIII (1)***	*Egyptian Ruler*
		Mark Antony (2)?	*Roman General*
Rosemary Clooney	Singer	***José Ferrer***	*Actor*
Clotilda	Queen of the Franks	***Clovis I***	*King of the Franks*

Clytemnestra	Mythical Queen of Mycenae	***Agamemnon***	*Mythical King of Mycenae*
Isabella Colbran (1)	Spanish soprano	***Gioacchino Rossini***	*Composer*
Venetia Collett-Barrett (1)	Actress	***Edward Woodward***	*Actor*
Joan Collins (1)	Actress	***Anthony Newley (1)***	*Actor and singer*
Pauline Collins (2)	Actress	***John Alderton***	*Actor*
Jane Colt (1)	Farmer's daughter	***Thomas More***	*Chancellor of England*
Shirley Conran	Authoress	***Terence Conran***	*Businessman*
Constance of Castile (2)	Castilian princess	***John of Gaunt***	*English prince*
Sarah Cook	Schoolgirl (13 when married)	***Musa Komeagac***	*Turkish waiter*
Rita Coolidge (2)	Singer	***Kris Kristofferson***	*Actor*
Dolores Costello	Actress	***John Barrymore***	*Actor*
Cicely Courtneidge	Actress	***Jack Hulbert***	*Actor*
Courtney Cox	Actress	***David Arquette***	*Actor*
Maureen Cox (1)	Childhood sweetheart	***Ringo Starr***	*Musician*
Charlotte Mary Craddock (1)	Socialite	***Henry Fielding***	*English novelist*
Jill Craigie	TV scriptwriter and author	***Michael Foot***	*Politician*
Gemma Craven (1)	Actress	***Frazer Hines***	*Actor*
Cindy Crawford	Supermodel	***Richard Gere***	*Actor*
Joan Crawford	Actress	***Douglas Fairbanks Jnr (2)***	*Actor*
Creusa	Mythical Roman character	***Aeneas***	*Mythical Trojan prince*
Cristina	Spanish Infanta	***Inaki Vrdangarin***	*Handball player*
Abigail Cruttenden (3)	Actress	***Sean Bean***	*Actor*
Penelope Cruz	Actress	***Javier Bardem***	*Actor*
Cynthia Curzon (1)	English noblewoman	***Oswald Mosley***	*Politician*
Sinead Cusack	Actress	***Jeremy Irons***	*Actor*
Martha Custis	Socialite	***George Washington***	*President of USA*
Sasha Czack (1)	Theatre usher	***Sylvester Stallone***	*Actor*
Lili Damita (1)	Socialite	***Errol Flynn***	*Actor*
Mary Daniel (2)	Maid	***Henry Fielding***	*English novelist*
Bebe Daniels	Radio comedienne	***Ben Lyon***	*Radio comedian*
Blythe Danner	Actress	***Bruce Paltrow***	*Director*
Joy Davidman	Poet	***CS Lewis***	*Author*
Geena Davis	Actress	***Renny Harlin (1)***	*Film director*
		Jeff Goldblum (2)	*Actor*
Lucy Davis	Actress	***Owain Yeoman***	*Actor*
Nancy Davis (2)	Actress	***Ronald Reagan***	*US president*
Sharron Davis	Swimmer	***Derek Redmond***	*Athlete*
Frances De La Tour	Actress	***Tom Kempinski***	*Playwright*
Isabel Dean	Actress	***William Fairchild***	*Playwright*
Sandra Dee	Actress	***Bobby Darin***	*Singer*
Judi Dench	Actress	***Michael Williams***	*Actor*
Catherine Deneuve (2)	Actress	***David Bailey***	*Photographer*
Bo Derek (3)	Actress	***John Derek***	*Actor and director*
Donna D'Errico	'Baywatch' actress	***Nikki Sixx***	*Motley Crue guitarist*
Félicité Desmousseaux	Actress	***César Franck***	*Composer*
Colleen Dewhurst	Socialite	***George C Scott***	*Actor*
Angie Dickinson (2)	Actress	***Burt Bacharach (2)***	*Composer*
Sandra Dickinson	Actress	***Peter Davison***	*Actor*
Marlene Dietrich	Actress	***Rudolf Seiber (1)***	*Production assistant*
Kitty Dobbs	Niece of Beatrice Webb	***Malcolm Muggeridge***	*Journalist*
Marika Dominczyk (2)	Actress	***Scott Foley (1)***	*Actor*
Hilda Doolittle	US poet	***Richard Aldington***	*Poet and novelist*
Diana Dors	Actress	***Alan Lake (3)***	*Actor*
		Dickie Dawson (2)	*US comedian*
Michele Dotrice (2)	Actress	***Edward Woodward***	*Actor*
Angela Douglas	Irish actress	***Kenneth More***	*Actor*
Lesley-Anne Down (2)	Actress	***William Friedkin (1)***	*Film director*
Margaret Drabble	Novelist	***Clive Swift (1)***	*Author*
		Michael Holroyd (2)	*Biographer*
Isadora Duncan (1)	Dancer	***Sergei Yessenin***	*Poet*
Jacqueline Du Pré	Cellist	***Daniel Barenboim***	*Pianist*
Otilie Dvorák	Daughter of Antonin Dvorák	***Josef Suk***	*Violinist*
Linda Eastman	Photographer	***Paul McCartney (2)***	*Musician*
Nora Eddington (3)	Actress	***Errol Flynn***	*Actor*
Martha Eggerth	Soprano	***Jan Kiepura***	*Tenor*
Anita Ekberg	Actress	***Anthony Steele***	*Actor*
Britt Ekland	Actress	***Peter Sellers (1)***	*Actor*
		Slim Jim Phantom McDonnell (2)	*Musician*
Eleanor of Aquitaine	French noblewoman	***Louis VII (1)***	*French king*
		Henry II	*English king*
Eleanor of Castile	Castilian princess	***Edward I***	*English king*
Eleanor of Provence	French noblewoman	***Henry III***	*English king*
George Eliot	Authoress	***John Walter Cross***	*Banker*
Elizabeth Bowes-Lyon	Earl of Strathmore's daughter	***George VI***	*British king*
Elizabeth of York	English princess	***Henry VII***	*English King*
Elizabeth Woodville	English noblewoman	***Edward IV***	*English King*
Jill Esmond (1)	Actress	***Laurence Olivier***	*Actor*
Eudoxia	Russian noblewoman	***Peter the Great (1)***	*Russian Tsar*
Dale Evans	Actress and singer	***Roy Rogers***	*Actor and singer*

Female spouse	Occupation	Male spouse	Occupation
Linda Evans (2)	Actress	***John Derek***	*Actor and director*
Chris Evert	Tennis player (1)	***John Lloyd (1)***	*Tennis player*
	Tennis player (1)	***Andy Mill (2)***	*Skier*
	Tennis player (2)	***Greg Norman (3)***	*Golfer*
Siobhan Fahey	Singer	***Dave Stewart***	*Musician*
Mia Farrow	Actress (3)	***Frank Sinatra (1)***	*Singer*
	Actress (3)	***André Previn (2)***	*Conductor*
Farrah Fawcett	Actress (2)	***Lee Majors (1)***	*Actor*
Gracie Fields	Singer	***Monty Banks***	*Film director*
Judy Finnegan	TV presenter	***Richard Madeley***	*TV presenter*
Donya Fiorentino	Model	***David Fincher (1)***	*Film director*
		Gary Oldman (2)	*Actor*
Carina Fitzalan-Howard (2)	Noblewoman	***David Frost***	*Broadcaster*
Carrie Fisher (2)	Actress	***Paul Simon***	*Singer and composer*
Isla Fisher	Actress	***Sacha Baron Cohen***	*Comedy actor*
Jennifer Flavin (3)	Model	***Sylvester Stallone***	*Actor*
Jane Fonda	Actress (3)	***Roger Vadim (1)***	*Film director*
	Actress (2)	***Tom Hayden (2)***	*Politician*
	Actress (3)	***Ted Turner (3)***	*Media Mogul*
Anna Ford	Broadcaster	***Mark Boxer***	*Cartoonist and journalist*
Margaret Forster	Author	***Hunter Davies***	*Author*
Helen Frankenthaler	US artist	***Robert Motherwell***	*US artist*
Lady Antonia Fraser (2)	Authoress	***Harold Pinter***	*Playwright*
Lynne Frederick	Actress	***Peter Sellers (1)***	*Actor*
		David Frost (2)	*Broadcaster*
Dido Freire (2)	Brazilian film-maker's daughter	***Jean Renoir***	*Film director*
Dawn French	Comedienne	***Lenny Henry***	*Comedian*
Valerie French	Actress	***Michael Pertwee***	*Actor*
Agnes Frey	Merchant's daughter	***Albrecht Dürer***	*German painter*
Edith Fricker	Socialite	***Robert Southey***	*Poet*
Sarah Fricker	Socialite	***Samuel Taylor Coleridge***	*Poet*
Sadie Frost	Actress	***Gary Kemp (1)***	*Actor and musician*
		Jude Law (2)	*Actor*
Fiona Fullerton (1)	Actress	***Simon MacCorkindale***	*Actor*
Magda Gabor (4)	Actress	***George Sanders (3)***	*Actor*
Zsa Zsa Gabor	Actress (2)	***Conrad Hilton (2)***	*Businessman*
	Actress (2)	***George Sanders (3)***	*Actor*
Myte Garcia	Belly dancer	***Prince (Symbol)***	*Singer*
Ava Gardner	Actress (2)	***Mickey Rooney (1)***	*Actor*
	Actress (5)	***Artie Shaw (2)***	*Bandleader*
	Actress (2)	***Frank Sinatra (3)***	*Singer*
Judy Garland	Actress	***Vincente Minnelli (2)***	*Film director*
		Sid Luft (3)	*Entertainer*
Jennifer Garner	Actress	***Scott Foley (1)***	*Actor*
		Ben Affleck (2)	*Actor*
Jane Garvey	Radio presenter	***Adrian Chiles***	*TV presenter*
Jill Gascoigne (1)	Actress	***Alfred Molina (2)***	*Actor*
Michelle Gayle	Actress and singer	***Mark Bright***	*Footballer*
Sarah Michelle Gellar	Actress	***Freddie Prinze Jnr***	*Actor*
Elvira Gemignani	Socialite	***Giacomo Puccini***	*Composer*
Susan George (2)	Actress	***Simon MacCorkindale***	*Actor*
Robin Givens (1)	Actress	***Mike Tyson (2)***	*Boxer*
Alma Gluck	Soprano	***Efrem Zimbalist***	*Violinist*
Liza Goddard	Actress	***Colin Baker (1)***	*Actor*
		Alvin Stardust (3)	*Pop singer*
Paulette Goddard	Actress (3)	***Charlie Chaplin (2)***	*Actor*
	Actress (3)	***Burgess Meredith (3)***	*Actor*
	Actress (3)	***Erich Maria Remarque (4)***	*Author*
Lady Godiva	Countess of Mercia	***Leofric***	*Earl of Mercia*
Beatrix Godwin	Widow of EW Godwin (architect)	***James McNeill Whistler***	*Artist*
Mary Godwin	Writer	***Percy Bysshe Shelley***	*Poet*
Jane Goldman	Writer	***Jonathan Ross***	*TV presenter*
Stephanie Goldner	Harpist	***Eugene Ormandy***	*Conductor*
Jemima Goldsmith	Heiress	***Imran Khan***	*Cricketer*
Betty Grable	Actress	***Jackie Coogan (1)***	*Actor*
		Harry James (2)	*Musician*
Dulcie Gray	Actress	***Michael Denison***	*Actor*
Effie Gray	Artist	***John Ruskin (1)***	*Art Critic*
		John Everett Millais (2)	*Artist*
Elspet Gray	Actress	***Brian Rix***	*Actor*
Alex Greaves	Jockey	***David Nicholls***	*Horseracing trainer*
Sarah Greene	TV presenter	***Mike Smith***	*TV presenter*
Debbie Greenwood	TV presenter (former Miss UK)	***Paul Coia***	*TV presenter*
Lady Jane Grey	English noblewoman	***Lord Guildford Dudley***	*English nobleman*
Lita Grey (2)	Actress	***Charlie Chaplin***	*Actor*
Melanie Griffith	Actress	***Don Johnson (1) + (3)***	*Actor*
		Antonio Banderas (4)	*Actor*
Tammie Grimes	Actress	***Christopher Plummer***	*Actor*

Diana Guinness (2)	Nancy Mitford's sister	***Oswald Mosley***	*Politician*
Nina Hagerup	Singer (Grieg's Cousin)	***Edvard Grieg***	*Composer*
Geneviève Halévy	Composer's daughter	***Georges Bizet***	*Composer*
Faten Hamama (1)	Actress	***Omar Sharif***	*Actor and bridge player*
Alana Hamilton (1)	Model	***Rod Stewart (2)***	*Singer*
Linda Hamilton (4)	Actress	***James Cameron (2)***	*Film director*
Sheila Hancock	Actress	***John Thaw (2)***	*Actor*
Sue Hanson	Actress	***Carl Wayne***	*Actor and Singer*
Harriet Harman	British politician	***Jack Dromey***	*Trade unionist*
Harmonia	Mythical daughter of Ares and Aphrodite	***Cadmus***	*Mythical founder of Thebes*
Mildred Harris (1)	Actress	***Charlie Chaplin***	*Actor*
Deborah Harry (common law)	Singer	***Chris Stein*** **(common law)**	*Guitarist*
Donna Hartley (3)	Athlete	***Bobby Knutt (1)***	*Actor and Comedian*
Teri Hatcher	Actress	***Jon Tenney***	*Actor*
Ann Hathaway	Farmer's daughter	***William Shakespeare***	*Playwright*
June Haver	Actress	***Fred MacMurray***	*Actor*
Jacquetta Hawkes	Archaeologist	***JB Priestley***	*Author*
Goldie Hawn	Actress	***Kurt Russell***	*Actor*
Anne Hayes (1)	Housewife	***Peter Sellers***	*Actor*
Rita Hayworth	Actress (2)	***Orson Welles (2)***	*Actor and director*
	Actress (2)	***Aly Khan (3)***	*Middle Eastern prince*
Patty Hearst	Heiress	***Bernard Shaw***	*Bodyguard*
Michelle Heaton	Singer	***Andy Scott-Lee***	*Singer*
Lillian Hellman	Playwright	***Dashiell Hammett***	*Author*
Heloise	Abelard's wife	***Peter Abelard***	*French philosopher*
Marie Helvin (3)	Model	***David Bailey***	*Photographer*
Anouska Hempel	Actress	***Mark Weinberg***	*Businessman*
Henrietta Maria	French princess	***Charles I***	*British king*
Natasha Henstridge	Canadian actress	**Damian Chapa (1)**	US actor/director
		Darius Danesh (2)	Scottish singer
Audrey Hepburn	Actress	***Mel Ferrer***	*Actor*
Barbara Hepworth	Sculptor	***John Skeaping (1)***	*Sculptor*
		Ben Nicholson (2)	*Artist*
Hera (3)	Sister of Zeus	***Zeus***	*Greek supreme god*
Lady Herries	Racehorse trainer	***Colin Cowdrey***	*Cricketer*
Irene Hervey	Actress	***Allan Jones***	*Singer and actor*
Eva Herzigova	Model	***Tico Torres***	*Pop musician (Bon Jovi)*
Andrée Heurschling (1)	Artist's model	***Jean Renoir***	*Film director*
Hildegarde	Queen of the Franks	***Charlemagne***	*King of the Franks*
Faith Hill	Country singer	***Tim McGraw***	*Country singer*
Melanie Hill (2)	Actress ('Bread')	***Sean Bean***	*Actor*
Tracy Hilton	Housewife	***Jim Davidson***	*Comedian*
Gill Hinchcliffe	TV Production assistant	***David Jason***	*Actor*
Liz Hobbs (2)	Waterskier	***Frazer Hines***	*Actor*
Valerie Hobson	Actress and dancer	***John Profumo (2)***	*Politician*
Chaatal Hochuli (1)	Swiss Heiress	***Ernst August***	*Prince of Hanover*
Catherine Hogarth	Newspaper magnate's daughter	***Charles Dickens***	*Author*
Alison Holloway	Presenter (3)	***Jim Davidson***	*Comedian*
Lauren Holly	Actress	***Jim Carrey***	*Actor*
Marilyn Horne	Mezzo-soprano	***Henry Lewis***	*Conductor*
Chantelle Houghton	*Big Brother* contestant	***Samuel Preston***	*Singer*
Whitney Houston	Singer	***Bobby Brown***	*Singer*
Elizabeth Jane Howard	Novelist	***Kingsley Amis***	*Novelist and poet*
Clementine Hozier	Charity worker	***Winston Churchill***	*Politician*
Mabel Hubbard	Deaf student	***Alexander Graham Bell***	*Inventor*
Benita Hume	Actress	***Ronald Colman (1)***	*Actor*
		George Sanders (2)	*Actor*
Kirsty Hume	Model	***Donovan Leitch***	*Actor*
Gayle Hunnicutt	Actress	***David Hemmings***	*Actor*
Rachel Hunter (2)	Model	***Rod Stewart***	*Singer*
Anjelica Huston	Actress and director	***Robert Graham***	*Sculptor*
Mary Hutchinson	Socialite	***William Wordsworth***	*Poet*
Barbara Hutton (2)	Actress	***Cary Grant***	*Actor*
Judy Huxtable (2)	Actress	***Peter Cook***	*Comedian and writer*
Anne Hyde (1)	Daughter of Earl of Clarendon	***James II***	*English King*
Georgie Hyde-Lees	Socialite	***WB Yeats***	*Poet*
Ildico	Consort of Attila	***Attila the Hun***	*Hunnish ruler*
Iman	Model	***David Bowie (2)***	*Singer/composer*
Jill Ireland	Actress (2)	***David McCallum (1)***	*Actor*
	Actress (2)	***Charles Bronson (2)***	*Actor*
Isabella	Daughter of Philip IV of France	***Edward II***	*English king*
Isabella of Angoulême (2)	French noblewoman	***John***	*King of England*
Isabelle (2)	Daughter of Charles VI of France	***Richard II***	*English king*
Hattie Jacques	Actress	***John Le Mesurier***	*Actor*
Debra James (1)	Hairdresser	***Sean Bean (1)***	*Actor*

Storm Jameson	Novelist	***Guy Chapman (2)***	*Historian*
Susan Jameson	Actress	***James Bolam***	*Actor*
Samantha Janus	Actress	***Mauro Mantovani***	*Actor*
Aino Järnefelt	General's daughter	***Jean Sibelius***	*Composer*
Zizi Jeanmaire	Dancer	***Roland Petit***	*Choreographer*
Cécile Jeanrenaud	Clergyman's daughter	***Felix Mendelssohn***	*Composer*
Ffion Jenkins	Ex-civil servant	***William Hague***	*Politician*
Jenny Jerome	Daughter of NY businessman	***Lord Randolph Churchill***	*Politician*
Jezebel	Queen of Israel	***Ahab***	*King of Israel*
Scarlett Johansson	Actress	***Ryan Reynolds***	*Actor*
Amy Johnson	Aviator	***Jim Mollison***	*Aviator*
Angelina Jolie	Actress	***Johnny Lee Miller (1)***	*Actor*
		Billy Bob Thornton (2)	*Actor*
Jennifer Jones	Actress	***Robert Walker (1)***	Actor
		David O'Selznick (2)	Director
Joséphine de Beauharnais	French noblewoman	***Napoleon I***	*French emperor*
Yootha Joyce	Actress	***Glyn Edwards***	*Actor*
Frida Kahlo	Painter	***Diego Rivera***	*Painter*
Kim Kardashian (1)	Television personality	***Kris Humphries (2)***	*Brooklyn Nets basketball pro*
Angelica Kauffmann	Swiss painter	***Antonio Zucchi***	*Venetian painter*
Ruby Keeler	Actress	***Al Jolson***	*Entertainer*
Maria Anna Keller	Hairdresser's daughter	***Franz Joseph Haydn***	*Composer*
Barbara Kelly	Actress and presenter	***Bernard Braden***	*Actor and presenter*
Margaret Kempson (1)	Housewife	***Denis Thatcher***	*Businessman*
Rachel Kempson	Actress	***Michael Redgrave***	*Actor*
Kay Kendall (3)	Actress	***Rex Harrison***	*Actor*
Suzy Kendall (1)	Actress	***Dudley Moore***	*Entertainer*
Cherly Kennedy	Actress	***Tom Courtenay***	*Actor*
Jacqueline Kennedy	Socialite	***Aristotle Onassis (2)***	*Businessman*
Patsy Kensit	Actress	***Jim Kerr (2)***	*Musician*
		Liam Gallagher (3)	*Pop musician*
Miranda Kerr	Australian model	***Orlando Bloom***	*Actor*
Nicole Kidman	Actress (2)	***Tom Cruise (1)***	*Actor*
	Actress (1)	***Keith Urban (2)***	*Country singer*
Carole King	Singer/composer	***Gerry Goffin***	*Composer*
Alex Kingston	Actress	***Ralph Fiennes (1)***	*Actor*
Heidi Klum	Supermodel	***Seal (2)***	*Musician*
Henrietta Knight	Racehorse trainer	***Terry Biddlecombe***	*Jockey*
Vivienne Knight (3)	Scriptwriter	***Patrick Campbell***	*Irish writer and wit*
Keira Knightley	Actress	***James Righton***	*Musician*
Gertrud Kolisch (2)	Musician	***Arnold Schoenberg***	*Composer*
Diana Krall	Musician	***Elvis Costello***	*Singer/songwriter*
Cleo Laine	Jazz singer	***John Dankworth (2)***	*Jazz musician*
Elsa Lanchester	Actress	***Charles Laughton***	*Actor*
Abbe Lane (3)	Singer	***Xavier Cugat***	*Bandleader*
Brogan Lane (3)	Actress	***Dudley Moore***	*Entertainer*
Hope Lange	Actress	***Alan J Pakula (2)***	*Film director*
Louise Lasser (2)	Actress	***Woody Allen***	*Actor/director*
Sue Lawley	Broadcaster	***Hugh Williams***	*TV magnate*
Nigella Lawson	Food writer	***John Diamond (1)***	*Journalist*
		Charles Saatchi (2)	*Advertising executive*
Evelyn Lear	Soprano	***Thomas Stewart***	*Baritone*
Kelly Le Brock	Actress	***Steven Seagal (2)***	*Actor*
Michelle Lee (2)	Actress and singer	***James Farentino***	*Actor*
Jane Leeves	Actress	***Marshall Coben***	*US television executive*
Janet Leigh	Actress	***Tony Curtis (3)***	*Actor*
Vivien Leigh (2)	Actress	***Laurence Olivier (2)***	*Actor*
Margaret Leighton	Actress	***Laurence Harvey (2)***	*Actor*
		Michael Wilding (3)	*Actor*
Rula Lenska (3)	Actress	***Dennis Waterman (2)***	*Actor*
Lotte Lenya	Actress/singer	***Kurt Weill (1)***	*Composer*
Kay Lenz	Actress	***David Cassidy***	*singer*
Tea Leoni	Actress	***David Duchovny (2)***	*Actor*
Lyubov Leonidovna (2)	Russian ballerina	***Marius Petipa***	*French choreographer*
Ginette Lery (2)	Secretary	***James Goldsmith***	*Tycoon*
Muriel Ling (1)	Model	***Harold Robbins***	*Writer*
Elizabeth Linley	Composer's daughter	***Richard Brinsley Sheridan***	*Irish dramatist*
Maureen Lipman	Actress	***Jack Rosenthal***	*Playwright*
Constance Lloyd	Socialite	***Oscar Wilde***	*Playwright/novelist*
Sue Lloyd	Actress	***Ronald Allen***	*Actor*
Lina Llubera	Spanish singer	***Sergei Prokofiev***	*Composer*
Heather Locklear (2)	Actress	***Tommy Lee***	*Singer*
Victoria Lockwood	Model	***Earl Charles Spencer***	*English nobleman*
Carole Lombard	Actress (2)	***William Powell (1)***	*Actor*
	Actress (3)	***Clark Gable (2)***	*Actor*
Claudine Longet	Actress	***Andy Williams***	*Singer*
Anita Lonsborough	Swimmer	***Hugh Porter***	*Cyclist*
Lydia Lopokova	Ballerina	***John Maynard Keynes***	*Economist*
Sophia Loren	Actress	***Carlo Ponti***	*Film producer*

Courtney Love	Actress/singer	***Kurt Cobain (2)***	*Musician (Nirvana)*
Sarah Lowndes	Poet	***Bob Dylan***	*Musician*
Lorna Luft	Singer	***Colin Freeman***	*Musical director*
Astrid Lundström (2)	Model	***Bill Wyman***	*Musician*
Linda Lusardi	Actress and model	***Sam Kane***	*Actor*
Emma Lyon	Blacksmith's daughter	***William Hamilton***	*Scottish diplomat*
Lulu	Singer	***Maurice Gibb***	*Singer*
Carol McGiffin	Radio DJ	***Chris Evans***	*Television presenter*
Cathy McGowan	Broadcaster	***Hywel Bennett***	*Actor*
Ali MacGraw	Actress	***Steve McQueen (2)***	*Actor*
Heather McIntyre	Actress and playwright	***William Hartnell***	*Actor*
Virginia McKenna	Actress	***Denholm Elliott (1)***	*Actor*
		Bill Travers (2)	*Actor*
Alison McNair	Doctor's daughter	***Donald Dewar (1)***	*British politician*
		Alexander AM Irvine (2)	*Lord Chancellor*
Kitty McShane	Music-hall artist	***Arthur Lucan***	*Music-hall artist*
Madonna	Singer and actress	***Sean Penn (1)***	*Actor*
		Guy Ritchie (2)	*Film director*
Justine Mahler	Sister of Gustav Mahler	***Arnold Rosé***	*Austrian violinist*
Madame de Maintenon	Louis XIV's 2nd wife	***Louis XIV***	*King of France*
Maria Malibran	Contralto	***Charles de Bériot***	*Violinist and composer*
Erika Mann	Writer	***WH Auden***	*Poet and essayist*
Jayne Mansfield	Actress	***Mickey Hargitay***	*Body-builder*
Katherine Mansfield	NZ writer	***George Bowden (1)***	*Businessman*
		John Middleton Murry	*Writer and critic*
Leslie Manville (1)	Actress	***Gary Oldman***	*Actor*
Margaret of Anjou	French noblewoman	***Henry VI***	*English king*
Princess Margaret	Elizabeth II's sister	***Anthony Armstrong Jones***	*Photographer*
Maria Theresa	Spanish princess	***Louis XIV***	*King of France*
Marie Louise	Austrian archduchess	***Napoleon I***	*French emperor*
Jean Marsh (1)	Actress	***Jon Pertwee***	*Actor*
Marion Marshall (2)	Actress	***Robert Wagner***	*Actor*
Barbara Marx (4)	Actress	***Frank Sinatra***	*Singer*
Mary II	British queen	***William III***	*British king*
Mary of Guise	French noblewoman	***James V***	*King of Scotland*
Mary of Modena (2)	Italian noblewoman	***James II***	*British king*
Mary of Teck	German noblewoman	***George V***	*British king*
Mary Stewart	Queen of Scots	***Francis II (1)***	*French Dauphin then king*
		Henry Darnley (2)	*English nobleman*
		Earl of Bothwell (3)	*Scottish nobleman*
Anna Massey	Actress	***Jeremy Brett***	*Actor*
Meg Matthews	Record company secretary	***Noel Gallagher***	*Pop musician*
Luisa Mattioli (2)	Housewife	***Roger Moore***	*Actor*
Sharon Maughan	Actress	***Trevor Eve***	*Actor*
Patricia Maynard (2)	Actress	***Dennis Waterman***	*Actor*
Patricia Medina	Actress	***Richard Greene***	*Actor*
Wilnelia Merced (3)	Beauty queen	***Bruce Forsyth***	*Entertainer*
Vivien Merchant (1)	Actress	***Harold Pinter***	*Playwright*
Melina Mercouri (2)	Actress	***Jules Dassin (2)***	*Film director*
Ethel Merman	Singer	***Ernest Borgnine (3)***	*Actor*
Messalina (3)	Roman noblewoman	***Nero***	*Roman emperor*
Jean Metcalfe	Broadcaster	***Cliff Michelmore***	*Broadcaster*
Metis (1)	Greek sea nymph	***Zeus***	*Greek supreme god*
Alice Middleton (2)	Widow of London mercer	***Thomas More***	*Chancellor of England*
Annabella Milbanke	Heiress	***Lord Byron***	*Poet*
Sarah Miles	Actress	***Robert Bolt***	*Playwright*
Antonina Miliukova	Pupil of Tchaikovsky	***Pyotr Tchaikovsky***	*Composer*
Rebecca Miller	Actress (Arthur Miller's daughter)	***Daniel Day-Lewis***	*Actor*
Elizabeth Minshull (3)	Milton's 3rd wife	***John Milton***	*Poet*
Marilyn Monroe	Actress	***Jim Dougherty (1)***	*Policeman*
		Joe Di Maggio (2)	*Baseball player*
		Arthur Miller (3)	*Playwright*
Margaret Montgomerie	Socialite	***James Boswell***	*Biographer*
Elizabeth Montgomery (3)	Actress	***Gig Young***	*Actor*
LM Montgomery	Canadian novelist	***Ewan Macdonald***	*Presbyterian minister*
Fanny Moody	English soprano	***Charles Manners***	*Irish bass and impresario*
Bel Mooney	Writer and broadcaster	***Jonathan Dimbleby***	*Broadcaster*
Demi Moore	Actress	***Bruce Willis***	*Actor*
Jeanne Moreau (1)	Actress	***William Friedkin (3)***	*Film director*
Anne Morrow	Writer	***Charles Lindbergh***	*Aviator*
Angela Mortimer	British Wimbledon champion	***John Barrett***	*Tennis commentator*
Carey Mulligan	Actress	***Marcus Mumford***	*Musician*
Iris Murdoch	Writer	***John Bayley***	*Professor of literature*
Patricia Neal	Actress	***Roald Dahl***	*Writer*
Nefertiti	Egyptian queen	***Akhenaton***	*Egyptian king*
Hildegarde Neil (2)	Actress	***Brian Blessed***	*Actor*
Wendy Neuss	Producer ('Star Trek')	***Patrick Stewart***	*Actor (StarTrek)*
Anne Nevill	English Noblewoman	***Richard III***	*English king*

Nanette Newman	Actress	***Bryan Forbes***	*Actor and director*
Sue Nicholls	Actress	***Mark Eden***	*Actor*
Mary Ellen Nicolls (1)	Daughter of Thomas Love Peacock	***George Meredith***	*English novelist*
Brigitte Nielsen (2)	Actress	***Sylvester Stallone***	*Actor*
Frances Nisbet	Doctor's widow	***Horatio Nelson***	*English naval hero*
Coleen Nolan	Singer	***Shane Richie***	*Comedian*
Catherine Nossenko (1)	Stravinsky's cousin	***Igor Stravinsky***	*Composer*
Kim Novak	Actress	***Richard Johnson (1)***	*Actor*
Jane Nugent	Secretary	***Edmund Burke***	*British statesman*
Louise Nurding	Pop singer	***Jamie Redknapp***	*Footballer*
Merle Oberon (2)	Actress	***Alexander Korda***	*Film director*
Octavia (1)	Roman noblewoman	***Nero***	*Roman emperor*
Octavia (1)	Emperor Augustus' sister	***Marc Antony***	*Roman general*
Georgia O'Keefe	US painter	***Alfred Stieglitz***	*US photographer*
Tamsin Olivier	Pub owner	***Simon Dutton***	*Actor*
Julia Trevelyan Oman	Designer	***Roy Strong***	*Writer and historian*
Tatum O'Neal	Actress	***John McEnroe***	*Tennis player*
Oona O'Neill (4)	Playwright's daughter	***Charlie Chaplin***	*Actor*
Yoko Ono (2)	Artist	***John Lennon (2)***	*Musician*
Dorothy Osborne	Daughter of governor of Guernsey	***William Temple***	*Diplomat and essayist*
Fanny Osbourne	Actress	***Robert Louis Stevenson***	*Author*
Ann Packer	Athlete	***Robbie Brightwell***	*Athlete*
Wendy Padbury	Actress	***Melvyn Hayes***	*Actor*
Geraldine Page	Actress	***Rip Torn***	*Actor*
Grace Palermo (5)	Socialite	***Harold Robbins***	*Writer*
Lilli Palmer (2)	Actress	***Rex Harrison (1)***	*Actor*
Gwyneth Paltrow	Actress	***Chris Martin***	*Musician*
Pandora	First woman of Greek myth	***Epimetheus***	*Titan*
May Pang	Authoress	***Tony Visconti***	*Record producer*
Vanessa Paradis	Singer	***Johnny Depp***	*Actor*
Euphrosyne Parepa	Soprano	***Karl Rosa***	*German conductor*
Mary Parker	Actress	***Harold French***	*Actor and theatre director*
Sarah Jessica Parker	Actress	***Matthew Broderick***	*Actor*
Isabel Patiño (1)	Bolivian tin magnate's daughter	***James Goldsmith***	*Tycoon*
Charlotte Payne-Townshend	Heiress	***George Bernard Shaw***	*Dramatist*
Olympie Pélissier (2)	Parisian hostess	***Gioacchino Rossini***	*Composer*
Penelope	Daughter of King Icarius of Sparta	***Odysseus***	*Mythical king of Ithaca*
Christine Perfect	Singer	***John McVie***	*Musician*
Rhea Perlman	Actress	***Danny DeVito***	*Actor*
Jean Peters	Actress	***Howard Hughes***	*Businessman*
Sandy Pflueger (2)	Equestrian rider	***Mark Phillips***	*Equestrian rider*
Maggie Philbin	TV presenter	***Keith Chegwin***	*TV presenter*
Philippa Hainault	Dutch noblewoman	***Edward III***	*English king*
Fiona Phillips	GMTV presenter	***Martin Frizell***	*GMTV presenter*
Michelle Phillips (2)	Actress and singer	***Dennis Hopper (2)***	*Actor*
Siân Phillips	Actress	***Peter O'Toole (2)***	*Actor*
Pat Phoenix (2)	Actress	***Anthony Booth (3)***	*Actor*
Edith Piaf	Singer	***Jacques Pills (1)***	*Singer*
		Théo Sarapo (2)	*Singer and actor*
Paloma Picasso	Beautician and businesswoman	***Rafael Lopez-Cambil***	*Argentinian playwright*
Evelyn Pickering	Pre-Raphaelite artist	***William Frend De Morgan***	*Pre-Raphaelite artist*
Mary Pickford (2)	Actress	***Douglas Fairbanks Snr***	*Actor*
Billie Piper (1)	Pop singer & actress	***Chris Evans (1)***	*Disc jockey*
		Laurence Fox (2)	*Actor*
Valerie Pitts	TV presenter	***Georg Solti***	*Conductor*
Minna Planer (1)	Opera singer and actress	***Richard Wagner (1)***	*Composer*
Sylvia Plath	Poet	***Ted Hughes***	*Poet*
Suzanne Pleshette	Actress	***Troy Donahue***	*Actor*
Joan Plowright (3)	Actress	***Laurence Olivier***	*Actor*
Pocahontas	Princess	***John Rolfe***	*English colonist*
Lily Pons	Soprano	***André Kostelanetz***	*Conductor*
Poppaea (2)	Roman noblewoman	***Nero***	*Roman emperor*
Elizabeth Porter	Schoolteacher	***Samuel Johnson***	*Writer and lexicographer*
Beatrix Potter	Author and illustrator	***William Heelis***	*Solicitor*
Eleanor Powell (3)	Actress	***Glenn Ford***	*Actor*
Mary Powell (1)	Royalist sympathiser	***John Milton***	*Poet*
Stefanie Powers	Actress	***Gary Lockwood***	*Actor*
Lisa-Marie Presley	Actress (1)	***Danny Keough (1)***	*Rock musician*
	Actress (1)	***Michael Jackson (2)***	*Entertainer*
	Actress (2)	***Nicolas Cage (3)***	*Actor*
Iris Pressagh (1)	Interior designer	***Billy Connolly (1)***	*Scottish comedian*
Kelly Preston	Actress	***John Travolta***	*Actor*
Soon-Yi Previn (3)	Personal assistant	***Woody Allen***	*Actor/director*
Katie Price	'Jordan'	***Peter André (1)***	*Singer*
		Alex Reid (2)	*Cage fighter*

		Kieran Hayler (3)	*Builder*
Libby Purves	Broadcaster	***Paul Heiney***	*Broadcaster*
Pyrrha	Daughter of Epimetheus and Pandora	***Deucalion***	*Son of Prometheus*
Miranda Quarry (3)	Actress	***Peter Sellers***	*Actor*
Gilda Radner	Psychotherapist	***Gene Wilder***	*Actor*
Anna Raeburn	Agony Aunt	***Nick Lilley***	*Businessman*
Gillian Raine (2)	Actress	***Leonard Rossiter***	*Actor*
Charlotte Rampling	Actress	***Jean-Michel Jarre***	*Musician*
Esther Rantzen	Broadcaster	***Desmond Wilcox***	*Producer*
Anthea Redfern (2)	Presenter	***Bruce Forsyth***	*Entertainer*
Vanessa Redgrave	Actress	***Franco Nero (1)***	*Actor*
		Tony Richardson (2)	*Film producer*
Amanda Redman	Actress	***Robert Glenister***	*Actor*
Alma Reville	Actress	***Alfred Hitchcock***	*Film director*
Debbie Reynolds (2)	Actress	***Eddie Fisher***	*Singer*
Ingeborg Rhosea (2)	Novelist	***Jon Pertwee***	*Actor*
Anneka Rice	TV presenter	***Nick Allott***	*Theatre producer*
Frieda von Richthofen	Socialite	***DH Lawrence***	*Writer*
Rachel Robards	Colonel's daughter	***Andrew Jackson***	*US president*
Amy Robbins	Student	***HG Wells***	*Author*
Margaret Roberts (2)	Politician	***Dennis Thatcher***	*Businessman*
Rachel Roberts (4)	Actress	***Rex Harrison***	*Actor*
Amy Robsart	Socialite	***Robert Dudley***	*Earl of Leicester*
Julie Rogers	Singer	***Michael Black***	*Theatrical agent*
Mimi Rogers (1)	Actress	***Tom Cruise***	*Actor*
Wenda Rogerson	Fashion model	***Norman Parkinson***	*Photographer*
Primula Rollo	Cipher clerk	***David Niven***	*Actor*
Micheline Roquebrune (2)	Artist	***Sean Connery***	*Actor*
Liberty Ross	Model/actress	**Rupert Sanders**	Film director
Isabella Rossellini	Actress (3)	***Martin Scorsese (2)***	*Director*
Jelka Rosen	Singer	***Frederick Delius***	*Composer*
Hannah Rothschild	Heiress	***Lord Rosebery***	*Scottish statesman*
Nicole Rothschild (4th)	Actress	***Dudley Moore***	*Entertainer*
Debbie Rowe (2)	Nurse	***Michael Jackson***	*Entertainer*
Gena Rowlands	Actress	***John Cassavetes***	*Actor*
Roxana	Queen of Macedon	***Alexander the Great***	*King of Macedon*
Meg Ryan (2)	Actress	***Dennis Quaid***	*Actor*
Sue Ryder	Philanthropist	***Leonard Cheshire***	*Philanthropist*
Vita Sackville-West	Poet and novelist	***Harold Nicolson***	*Diplomat*
Carol Bayer Sager (3)	Singer	***Burt Bacharach***	*Composer*
Jill St John	Actress	***Jack Jones (1)***	*Singer*
		Robert Wagner (2)	*Actor*
Beatrice Salkeld	Illustrator	***Brendan Behan***	*Irish writer*
Olga Samaroff (1)	Pianist	***Leopold Stokowski***	*Conductor*
Maria Elena Santiago	Secretary	***Buddy Holly***	*Musician*
Jennifer Saunders	Comedienne	***Ade Edmondson***	*Comedian*
Zelda Sayre	Socialite	***Francis Scott Fitzgerald***	*Novelist*
Prunella Scales	Actress	***Timothy West***	*Actor*
Alma Maria Schindler	Artist and musician	***Gustav Mahler (1)***	*Composer*
		Walter Gropius (2)	*Architect*
		Franz Werfel (3)	*Writer*
Elizabeth Schumann	German soprano	***Carl Alwin***	*German pianist/conductor*
Coretta Scott	Music graduate	***Martin Luther King***	*Civil rights leader*
Janette Scott (3)	Actress	***Mel Tormé (1)***	*Singer*
		Jackie Rae (3)	*TV presenter*
Lisa Scott-Lee	Singer	***Johnny Shentall***	*Singer*
Kyra Sedgwick	Actress	***Kevin Bacon***	*Actor*
Phyllis Sellick	Pianist	***Cyril Smith***	*Pianist*
Sandie Shaw	Singer	***Jeff Banks***	*Fashion designer*
Moira Shearer	Ballet dancer	***Ludovic Kennedy***	*Broadcaster*
Evgenia Shelepin (2)	Trotsky's secretary	***Arthur Ransome***	*Writer*
Dinah Sheridan	Actress	***Jimmy Hanley (2)***	*Entertainer*
		Sir John Davis (2)	*Rank chairman*
Brooke Shields	Actress	***André Agassi***	*Tennis player*
Pam Shriver (2)	Tennis player	***George Lazenby (2)***	*Actor*
Elizabeth Siddal	Model	***Dante Gabriel Rossetti***	*Poet and painter*
Simone Signoret	Actress	***Yves Montand (2)***	*Actor*
Sheila Sim	Actress	***Richard Attenborough***	*Actor*
Jean Simmons	Actress	***Stewart Granger***	*Actor*
Carly Simon	Singer	***James Taylor***	*Composer*
Wallis Simpson	American socialite	***Edward VIII***	*British king*
Carole Smillie	TV presenter	***Alex Knight***	*Restaurateur*
Anna Nicole Smith	Actress	***J Howard Marshall II***	*Oil tycoon*
Delia Smith	Cookery writer	***Michael Wynn Jones***	*Publisher*
Maggie Smith	Actress	***Robert Stephens***	*Actor*
Mandy Smith (3)	Model	***Bill Wyman***	*Rolling Stone*
Michelle Smith	Irish swimmer	***Erik De Bruin***	*Dutch discus thrower*
Harriet Smithson	Irish actress	***Hector Berlioz***	*Composer*
Wendy Snowden	Actress	***Peter Cook***	*Comedian and writer*
Sophia Dorothea	German noblewoman	***George I***	*British king*
Britney Spears (1)	Singer	***Kevin Federline (2)***	*Dancer*

Dorothy Squires (1)	Singer	***Roger Moore (2)***	*Actor*
Barbara Stanwick	Actress	***Robert Taylor***	*Actor*
Jann Stapp (6)	Businesswoman	***Harold Robbins***	*Writer*
Alison Steadman	Actress	***Mike Leigh***	*Dramatist*
Sheila Steafel (1)	Actress	***Harry H Corbett***	*Actor*
Mary Steenburgen	Actress	***Malcolm McDowell (1)***	*Actor*
		Ted Danson (2)	*Actor*
Gwen Stefani	Singer	***Gavin Rossdale***	*Musician*
Marion Stein	Musician	***7th Earl of Harewood (1)***	*English nobleman*
		Jeremy Thorpe (2)	*Politician*
Virginia Stephen	Novelist	***Leonard Woolf***	*Publisher and writer*
Pamela Stephenson	Actress and comedienne	***Nicholas Ball (1)***	*Actor*
		Billy Connolly (2)	*Scottish comedian*
Margaret Stewart (2)	Lord Ochiltree's daughter	***John Knox***	*Religious reformer*
Lara Stone	Supermodel	***David Walliams***	*Comedy actor*
Miriam Stoppard	TV presenter and journalist	***Christopher Hogg (2)***	*Industrialist*
Susan Stranks	Presenter	***Robin Ray***	*Broadcaster*
Barbra Streisand	Singer and actress	***Elliot Gould (1)***	*Actor*
		James Brolin (2)	*Actor*
Giuseppina Strepponi (2)	Soprano	***Giuseppe Verdi***	*Composer*
Imogen Stubbs (3)	Actress	***Trevor Nunn***	*Artistic director*
Una Stubbs	Actress	***Peter Gilmore (1)***	*Actor*
		Nicky Henson (2)	*Entertainer*
Trudie Styler (2)	Actress	***Sting***	*Singer*
Vera de Bosset Sudekeine (2)	Ballet dancer	***Igor Stravinsky***	*Composer*
Margaret Sullavan	Actress	***William Wyler***	*Film director*
Anna Beth Sully (1)	Actress	***Douglas Fairbanks Snr***	*Actor*
Mariya Surovshchikova (1)	Russian ballerina	***Marius Petipa***	*French choreographer*
Georgina Sutcliffe (4)	Actress	***Sean Bean (1)***	*Actor*
Joan Sutherland	Soprano	***Richard Bonynge***	*Conductor*
Janet Suzman (1)	Actress	***Trevor Nunn***	*Artistic director*
Gloria Swanson	Actress	***Wallace Beery***	*Actor*
Catherine Swynford (3)	Former mistress	***John of Gaunt***	*English Prince*
Jessica Tandy	Actress	***Jack Hawkins (1)***	*Actor*
		Hume Cronyn (2)	*Actor*
Sharon Tate (2)	Actress	***Roman Polanski***	*Director*
Christine Taylor	Actress	***Ben Stiller***	*Actor*
Elizabeth Taylor	Actress	***Nicky Hilton (1)***	*Hotelier*
		Michael Wilding (2)	*Actor*
		Mike Todd (3)	*Film producer*
		Eddie Fisher (4)	*Singer*
		Richard Burton(5 and 6)	*Actor*
		John Warner (7)	*Senator*
		Larry Fortensky (8)	*Builder*
Jessica Taylor	Singer	***Kevin Pietersen***	*Cricketer*
Sam Taylor-Wood	Film-maker and artist	***Jay Jopling***	*Art dealer*
Kiri Te Kanawa	Opera singer	***Desmond Park***	*Mining engineer*
Victoria Tennant	English actress	***Steve Martin***	*US actor*
Ellen Terry	English actress	***George Frederick Watts (1)***	*English painter*
		James Carew (2)	*US actor*
		Charlie Kelly (3)	*Actor*
Josephine Tewson (1)	Actress	***Leonard Rossiter***	*Actor*
Rosalie Texier (1)	Dressmaker	***Claude Debussy***	*Composer*
Themis (2)	Daughter of Gaia and Uranus	***Zeus***	*Greek supreme god*
Theodora	Actress	***Justinian***	*East Roman emperor*
Thetis	Mythical sea nymph (Nereid)	***Peleus***	*Mythical King of Phthia*
Emma Thompson	Actress	***Kenneth Branagh***	*Actor*
Elspeth Thomson	Socialite	***Kenneth Grahame***	*Children's writer*
Sybil Thorndike	Actress	***Lewis Casson***	*Actor and manager*
Hester Thrale	Writer	***Gabriel Piozzi***	*Musician*
Julia Thuillier	Socialite	***Walter Savage Landor***	*Writer*
Uma Thurman	Actress	***Gary Oldman (1)***	*Actor*
		Ethan Hawke (2)	*Actor*
Pauline Tiltson	Businesswoman	***John Prescott***	*British politician*
Ann Todd	Actress	***David Lean***	*Film director*
Mary Todd	Socialite	***Abraham Lincoln***	*US president*
Frances Tomelty (1)	Actress	***Sting***	*Singer*
Wanda Toscanini	Musician	***Vladimir Horowitz***	*Pianist*
Ludmilla Tourischeva	Gymnast	***Valeri Borzov***	*Athlete*
Marie Truffot	Socialite	***Camille Saint-Saëns***	*Composer*
Ivana Trump	Former wife of Donald Trump	***Ricardo Mazzucchelli (2)***	*Italian businessman*
Anthea Turner	TV presenter	***Peter Powell (1)***	*Disc jockey and producer*
		Grant Bovey (2)	*Businessman*
Cora Turner	Opera singer	***Hawley Crippen***	*Murderer*
Lana Turner	Actress	***Lex Barker (5)***	*Actor*
		Artie Shaw (1)	*Bandleader*
Martha Turner	Farmer's daughter	***John Clare***	*Poet*

Monica Turner (2)	Actress	***Mike Tyson (1)***	*Boxer*
Cheryl Tweedy	Singer	***Ashley Cole***	*Footballer*
Twiggy	Model and actress	***Leigh Lawson (2)***	*Actor*
Cathy Tyson	Actress	***Craig Charles***	*Actor*
Mary Ure	Actress	***John Osborne (1)***	*Playwright*
		Robert Shaw (2)	*Actor*
Saskia Uylenburgh	Burgomaster's daughter	***Rembrandt Van Rijn***	*Dutch painter*
Joanna Van Gyseghem (1)	Actress	***Ralph Bates***	*Actor*
Denise Van Outen	Entertainer	***Lee Mead***	*Singer*
Eva Marie Violetti	Viennese dancer	***David Garrick***	*Actor*
Galina Vishnevskaya	Soprano	***Mstislav Rostropovich***	*Cellist and conductor*
Carol Vorderman	TV presenter	***Paddy King***	*Businessman*
Marie Vulliamy (2)	Socialite	***George Meredith***	*English novelist*
Rebekah Wade	Newspaper editor	***Ross Kemp***	*Actor*
Lindsay Wagner	Actress	***Alan Rider (1)***	*Music publisher*
		Michael Brandon (2)	*Actor*
		Henry Kingi (3)	*Stuntman*
		Lawrence Mortoff (4)	*Producer*
Lillias Walker (2)	Actress	***Peter Vaughan***	*Actor*
Kay Walsh (2)	Actress	***David Lean (1)***	*Film director*
Lalla Ward (2)	Actress	***Tom Baker***	*Actor*
Rachel Ward	Actress	***Bryan Brown***	*Australian actor*
Sophie Ward	Actress	***Paul Hobson***	*Vet*
Sandra Warfield	Soprano	***James McCracken***	*Tenor*
Lavinia Warren	Circus performer	***Tom Thumb***	*Circus performer*
Jan Waters (2)	Actress	***Peter Gilmore (1)***	*Actor*
Ruby Wax	Comedienne	***Edward Bye***	*Producer*
Constance Weber	Singer	***Wolfgang Amadeus Mozart***	*Composer*
Denise Welch	Actress	***Tim Healy***	*Actor*
Tuesday Weld (2)	Actress	***Dudley Moore (2)***	*Entertainer*
Jane Baillie Welsh	Doctor's daughter	***Thomas Carlyle***	*Essayist*
Joanne Whalley	Actress	***Val Kilmer***	*Actor*
Billie Whitelaw (1)	Actress	***Peter Vaughan***	*Actor*
Clara Wieck	Pianist	***Robert Schumann***	*Composer*
Cynda Williams	Actress	***Billy Bob Thornton***	*Actor*
Esther Williams (4)	Actress	***Fernando Lamas (4)***	*Actor*
Penelope Wilton (4)	Actress	***Ian Holm***	*Actor*
Kate Winslet	Actress	***Jim Threapleton (1)***	*Director*
		Sam Mendes (2)	*Director*
		Ned Rocknroll (3)	*Businessman*
Shelley Winters	Actress	***Tony Franciosa (2)***	*Actor*
Reese Witherspoon	Actress	***Ryan Phillippe***	*Actor*
Natalie Wood	Actress	***Robert Wagner***	*Actor*
Victoria Wood	Comedienne	***Geoffrey Durham***	*Comedian*
Catherine Woodcock (2)	Commoner	***John Milton***	*Poet*
Catherine Woodville	Sister-in-law of Edward IV	***Henry Stafford***	*2nd Duke of Buckingham*
Joanne Woodward	Actress	***Paul Newman***	*Actor*
Helen Worth	Actress	***Michael Angelis***	*Actor*
Syreeta Wright	Singer	***Stevie Wonder***	*Musician*
Anna Magdalena Wülken (2)	Soprano	***JS Bach***	*Composer*
Tessa Wyatt	Actress	***Tony Blackburn***	*Disc jockey*
Jane Wyman (1)	Actress	***Ronald Reagan (3)***	*US president*
Patrice Wymore (2)	Actress	***Errol Flynn***	*Actor*
Xanthippe	Athenian	***Socrates***	*Philosopher*
Paula Yates	Broadcaster	***Bob Geldof***	*Singer*
Cecilia Young	Singer	***Thomas Arne***	*Composer*
Mathilde von Zemlinsky (1)	Musician	***Arnold Schoenberg***	*Composer*
Catherine Zeta Jones (2)	Actress	***Michael Douglas***	*Actor*
Marta Ziegler	Socialite	***Béla Bartók***	*Composer*
Anna Zimmerman	Housewife	***Charles Gounod***	*Composer*

Middle Names: Ordered by Surname

First Name	*Middle Name(s)*	*Surname*	
Charles	**Greely**	ABBOT	Astrophysicist
Diane	**Julie**	ABBOTT	Politician
Dean	**Gooderham**	ACHESON	American statesman
Joseph	**Randolf**	ACKERLEY	Author
Roy	**Claxton**	ACUFF	Country musician
Adam	**Llewellyn De Vere**	ADAMANT	Fictional TV character
John	**Bodkin**	ADAMS	Doctor and murder suspect
John	**Couch**	ADAMS	Astronomer
John	**Quincy**	ADAMS	US president
Marcus	**Algernon**	ADAMS	Photographer
Sarah	**Flower**	ADAMS	English poet

William	**Bridges**	ADAMS	Engineer
Wednesday	**Thursday**	ADDAMS	'Addams Family' character
Lawrence (Larry)	**Cecil**	ADLER	Musician
Vosdanig	**Manoog**	ADOIAN	Painter
Sade	**Folasade**	ADU	Singer
Spiro	**Theodore**	AGNEW	US vice-president
Shmuel	**Yosef**	AGNON	Israeli novelist
Henry	**Hinchcliffe**	AINLEY	Actor
George	**Biddell**	AIRY	Astronomer
Amos	**Bronson**	ALCOTT	Transcendentalist
Brian	**Wilson**	ALDISS	Science fiction writer
Thomas	**Bailey**	ALDRICH	Author
Thomas	**Massa**	ALSAGER	Newspaper manager
Luis	**Walter**	ALVAREZ	US physicist
Pamela	**Denise**	ANDERSON	Actress
Mario	**Gabriele**	ANDRETTI	Racing driver
Christian	**Boehmer**	ANFINSEN	US biochemist
Anders	**Jonas**	ANGSTROM	Physicist
Susan	**Brownell**	ANTHONY	Suffragette
Jeffrey	**Howard**	ARCHER	Author
George	**Augustus**	ARLISS	Actor
Klas	**Pontus**	ARNOLDSON	Swedish politician
Chester	**Alan**	ARTHUR	US president
Jeremy	**John Durham**	ASHDOWN	Politician
Arthur	**Bowden**	ASKEY	Comedian
Michael	**Terence**	ASPEL	Broadcaster
Herbert	**Henry**	ASQUITH	British prime minister
Miguel	**Angel**	ASTURIAS	Guatemalan poet
Richard	**Samuel**	ATTENBOROUGH	Actor
Wystan	**Hugh**	AUDEN	Poet
Alan	**Beresford**	B'STARD	TV character ('New Statesman')
Stephen	**Moulton**	BABCOCK	US agricultural chemist
Johann	**Christian**	BACH	Composer
Johann	**Sebastian**	BACH	Composer
Enid	**Algerine**	BAGNOLD	Author
Joan	**Dawson**	BAKEWELL	Broadcaster
Emily	**Greene**	BALCH	US social reformer
Michael	**Elias**	BALCON	Film producer
James	**Graham**	BALLARD	Author
Canaan	**Sodindo**	BANANA	Zimbabwean president
Hastings	**Kamuzu**	BANDA	Malawi politician
Iain	**Menzies**	BANKS	Author
Roger	**Gilbert**	BANNISTER	Athlete
Frederick	**Grant**	BANTING	Physiologist
Joseph	**Roland**	BARBERA	US animated cartoonist
Charles	**Glover**	BARKLA	English physicist
Christian	**Neethling**	BARNARD	Surgeon
Phineas	**Taylor**	BARNUM	Showman
James	**Matthew**	BARRIE	Author
Herbert	**Ernest**	BATES	Author
William	**Maddock**	BAYLISS	Physiologist
George	**Wells**	BEADLE	US biochemical geneticist
Henry	**Warren**	BEATY	Actor
Bill	**Blackledge**	BEAUMONT	Rugby Union player
Carl	**Lotus**	BECKER	US historian
Thomas	**Lovell**	BEDDOES	Poet and physiologist
Mary	**Hayley**	BELL	Playwright
Hilaire	**Pierre**	BELLOC	Writer
Peter	**Bradford**	BENCHLEY	Author
Enoch	**Arnold**	BENNETT	Author
Edward	**White**	BENSON	Archbishop of Canterbury
Edmund	**Clerihew**	BENTLEY	Writer
Ernst	**Ingmar**	BERGMAN	Film producer
Hans	**Albrecht**	BETHE	US physicist
Earl	**Derr**	BIGGERS	US novelist
Henry	**Rowley**	BISHOP	Composer
John	**Stuart**	BLACKIE	Scholar
Richard	**Doddridge**	BLACKMORE	Author
Anthony	**Charles Lynton**	BLAIR	Politician
Eric	**Arthur**	BLAIR	Author
Danny	**Dennio**	BLANCHFLOWER	Footballer
Tasker	**Howard**	BLISS	Soldier and statesman
Baruch	**Samuel**	BLUMBERG	US biochemist
James	**Hillier**	BLUNT	Singer/songwriter
Wilfrid	**Scawen**	BLUNT	Poet
Paul	**Yaw**	BOATENG	Politician
Dirk	**Niven**	BOGARDE	Actor
Humphrey	**De Forest**	BOGART	Actor
Robert	**Oxton**	BOLT	Playwright
Ian	**Terence**	BOTHAM	Cricketer
Virginia	**Hilda Brunette Maxwell**	BOTTOMLEY	Politician

Richard	**Southwell**	BOURKE	Earl of Mayo
David	**Hayward**	BOWIE	Musician and singer
Barbara	**Taylor**	BRADFORD	Novelist
Omar	**Nelson**	BRADLEY	US soldier
John	**Gerard**	BRAINE	Novelist
Kenneth	**Charles**	BRANAGH	Actor
Richard	**Charles Nicholas**	BRANSON	Entrepreneur
Walter	**Houser**	BRATTAIN	US physicist
John	**Cabell**	BRECKINRIDGE	US vice-president
Leonid	**Ilich**	BREZHNEV	USSR president
Robert	**Seymour**	BRIDGES	Poet
Charlie	**Dunbar**	BROAD	Philosopher
Rupert	**Chawner**	BROOKE	Poet
Norman	**Everard**	BROOKES	Tennis player
Spangler	**Arlington**	BROUGH	Actor
Henry	**Kirke**	BROWN	Sculptor
James	**Gordon**	BROWN	Politician
Charles	**Farrar**	BROWNE	Humorist and writer
Hablot	**Knight**	BROWNE	Illustrator
John	**Moses**	BROWNING	Gunsmith and inventor
Dave	**Warren**	BRUBECK	Jazz musician
William	**Cullen**	BRYANT	Poet
James	**McGill**	BUCHANAN	American economist
Pearl	**Sydenstricker**	BUCK	Author
Maria	**Esther**	BUENO	Tennis player
Ralph	**Johnson**	BUNCHE	American economist
Robert	**Wilhelm**	BUNSEN	Physicist
Billy	**George**	BUNTER	Fictional character
William	**Seward**	BURROUGHS	Author
George	**Herbert Walker**	BUSH	US president
Nicholas	**Murray**	BUTLER	US educationist
Reginald	**Cotterell**	BUTLER	Sculptor
Richard	**Austen**	BUTLER	Politician
Billy	**Edmund**	BUTLIN	Businessman
Betsy	**Cromer**	BYARS	Novelist
Richard	**Evelyn**	BYRD	Explorer
Harry	**Flood**	BYRD	Politician
George	**Gordon**	BYRON	Poet
James	**Branch**	CABELL	Novelist
George	**Washington**	CABLE	Novelist
Pedro	**Alvarez**	CABRAL	Navigator
James	**Mallahan**	CAIN	Writer
Michael	**Joseph**	CAINE	Actor
Aimo	**Kaarlo**	CAJANDER	Finnish politician
John	**Caldwell**	CALHOUN	US vice-president
James	**Leonard**	CALLAGHAN	British prime minister
Maria	**Meneghini**	CALLAS	Operatic soprano
Hugh	**Longbourne**	CALLENDAR	Physicist
Verney	**Lovett**	CAMERON	Explorer
Walter	**Chauncy**	CAMP	American footballer
Donald	**Malcolm**	CAMPBELL	Car and boat racer
John	**Franklin**	CANDY	Actor
Annie	**Jump**	CANNON	US astronomer
George	**Leonard**	CAREY	Archbishop
Chester	**Floyd**	CARLSON	US inventor
Ingvar	**Costa**	CARLSSON	Swedish politician
Jane	**Baillie**	CARLYLE	Wife of Thomas Carlyle
Ian	**Gillett**	CARMICHAEL	Actor
John	**Alden**	CARPENTER	Musician and businessman
John	**Dickson**	CARR	US detective writer
Willis	**Haviland**	CARRIER	US inventor
Johnnie	**William**	CARSON	US TV personality
William	**Hunter Fisher**	CARSON	Jockey
James	**Earl**	CARTER	US president
Barbara	**Hamilton**	CARTLAND	Writer
Hugh	**Maxwell**	CASSON	Architect
William	**Henry**	CAVENDISH-BENTINCK	British prime minister
Robert	**Arthur Talbot**	CECIL	British prime minister
Ernst	**Boris**	CHAIN	German biochemist
Arthur	**Neville**	CHAMBERLAIN	Politician
Charlie	**Spencer**	CHAPLIN	Comedy actor
Frank	**Michler**	CHAPMAN	Ornithologist
Greg	**Stephen**	CHAPPELL	Cricketer
Ian	**Michael**	CHAPPELL	Cricketer
Leslie	**Bowyer**	CHARTERIS	Author
Cornelius	**Crane**	CHASE	Actor
Anton	**Pavlovich**	CHEKHOV	Russian author
Geoffrey	**Leonard**	CHESHIRE	Philanthropist
Caryl	**Whittier**	CHESSMAN	Convict and author
Gilbert	**Keith**	CHESTERTON	Author
Robert	**Erskine**	CHILDERS	Writer

Jaques	**René**	CHIRAC	French prime minister
Martin	**Harcourt**	CHIVERS	Footballer
Walter	**Percy**	CHRYSLER	Automobile manufacturer
Winston	**Leonard Spencer**	CHURCHILL	British prime minister
Kenneth	**Mackenzie**	CLARK	Art historian
Arthur	**Charles**	CLARKE	Science fiction writer
Kenneth	**Harry**	CLARKE	Politician
Cassius	**Marcellus**	CLAY	Boxer
John	**Marwood**	CLEESE	Actor
Samuel	**Langhorne**	CLEMENS	Author
Stephen	**Grover**	CLEVELAND	US president
Edward	**Montgomery**	CLIFT	Actor
William	**Jefferson Blyth**	CLINTON	US president
Wells	**Wintemute**	COATES	Architect
Tyrus	**Raymond**	COBB	Baseball player
Samuel	**Franklin**	CODY	Aviator
William	**Frederick**	CODY	Showman
Sebastian	**Newbold**	COE	Athlete and politician
Frederick	**Donald**	COGGAN	Archbishop of Canterbury
Ferdinand	**Julius**	COHN	Botanist
Samuel	**Taylor**	COLERIDGE	Poet
Sidonie	**Gabrielle**	COLETTE	Author
William	**Gershom**	COLLINGWOOD	Artist
Charles	**Allston**	COLLINS	Artist
Joan	**Henrietta**	COLLINS	Actress
William	**Wilkie**	COLLINS	Novelist
Arthur	**Holly**	COMPTON	Physicist
Denis	**Charles Scott**	COMPTON	Cricketer
Maureen	**Catherine**	CONNOLLY	Tennis player
Jimmy	**Scott**	CONNORS	Tennis player
Joseph	**Teodor**	CONRAD	Author
Brian	**Rayner**	COOK	English baritone
Robin	**Finlayson**	COOK	Politician
Elizabeth	**Sprague**	COOLIDGE	American pianist
John	**Calvin**	COOLIDGE	US president
Leon	**Neil**	COOPER	US physicist
Alfred	**Edgar**	COPPARD	Writer
Ronnie	**Balfour**	CORBETT	Comedian
Carl	**Ferdinand**	CORI	American biochemist
John	**Warcup**	CORNFORTH	British chemist
Arthur	**Quiller**	COUCH	Man of letters
Noel	**Pierce**	COWARD	Actor and dramatist
Michael	**Colin**	COWDREY	Cricketer
William	**Randal**	CREMER	Nobel Laureate
Francis	**Harry Compton**	CRICK	Biologist
Hawley	**Harvey**	CRIPPEN	Murderer
Richard	**Stafford**	CRIPPS	Politician
Archibald	**Joseph**	CRONIN	Author
James	**Watson**	CRONIN	US physicist
Walter	**Leland**	CRONKITE	US broadcaster
Harry (Bing)	**Lillis**	CROSBY	Singer and actor
Ada	**Jemima**	CROSSLEY	Australian contralto
Irene	**Joliot**	CURIE	Nuclear physicist
Heber	**Doust**	CURTIS	US astronomer
Edward	**Sheriff**	CURTIS	US photographer
Glen	**Hammond**	CURTISS	US air pioneer
Henry	**Drysdale**	DAKIN	Chemist
Kenneth	**Mathieson**	DALGLISH	Footballer
Lawrence	**Bruno Nero**	DALLAGLIO	Rugby player
George	**Mifflin**	DALLAS	US vice-president
Clarence	**Seward**	DARROW	US Lawyer
Randall	**Thomas**	DAVIDSON	Archbishop of Canterbury
Dwight	**Filley**	DAVIS	Founder of Davis Cup
Miles	**Dewey**	DAVIS	Jazz musician
Charles	**Gates**	DAWES	US vice-president
Christian	**René**	DE DUVE	Belgian biochemist
Philip	**Ranulph**	DE GLANVILLE	Rugby Union player
Cecil	**Blount**	DE MILLE	Film director
James	**Byron**	DEAN	Actor
Eugene	**Victor**	DEBS	US politician
Claude	**Achille**	DEBUSSY	Composer
Len	**Cyril**	DEIGHTON	Novelist
Ronald	**Frederick**	DELDERFIELD	Author
Jacques	**Lucien Jean**	DELORS	European politician
Nigel	**Richard Patton**	DEMPSTER	Gossip columnist
Judi	**Olivia**	DENCH	Actress
Alfred	**Thompson**	DENNING	Law lord
Bruce	**MacLeish**	DERN	US actor
Donald	**Campbell**	DEWAR	British politician
Norman	**Colin**	DEXTER	Author
Edward (Ted)	**Ralph**	DEXTER	Cricketer

Thomas	**Frognall**	DIBDIN	Librarian
Philip	**Kindred**	DICK	US writer
Philip	**Kindred**	DICK	US science fiction writer
Charles	**John Huffam**	DICKENS	Author
Walt	**Elias**	DISNEY	Film producer
Henry	**Austin**	DOBSON	Poet
Kenneth	**Arthur**	DODD	Comedian
Basil	**Lewis**	D'OLIVEIRA	Cricketer
James	**Patrick**	DONLEAVY	Author
Alexander	**Frederick**	DOUGLAS-HOME	British prime minister
Hugh	**Caswell Tremenheere**	DOWDING	RAF chief
John	**Boyd**	DUNLOP	Inventor
Ronald	**Ossary**	DUNLOP	Irish painter
James	**Franciscus**	DURANTE	Entertainer
Gerald	**Malcolm**	DURRELL	Writer and naturalist
Lawrence	**George**	DURRELL	Novelist
Bob	**Alan**	DYLAN	Singer and composer
John	**Carew**	ECCLES	Australian neurophysiologist
John	**Presper**	ECKERT	American inventor
Gerald	**Maurice**	EDELMAN	US biochemist
Gertrude	**Caroline**	EDERLE	US swimmer
Thomas	**Alva**	EDISON	Inventor
Dwight	**David**	EISENHOWER	US president
Thomas	**Stearns**	ELIOT	Author
Edward ('Duke')	**Kennedy**	ELLINGTON	Pianist
Fred	**Handel**	ELLIOTT	'Coronation Street' character
Ralph	**Waldo**	EMERSON	US poet
John	**Franklin**	ENDERS	US bacteriologist
Chris	**Livingstone**	EUBANK	Boxer
Peter	**Carl**	FABERGÉ	Russian goldsmith
Gabriel	**Daniel**	FAHRENHEIT	Physicist
Charles	**Warren**	FAIRBANKS	US vice-president
Douglas	**Elton**	FAIRBANKS (Snr)	Actor
Nicholas	**Alexander**	FALDO	Golfer
Mia	**Villiers**	FARROW	Actress
Rainer	**Werner**	FASSBINDER	Film director
(Herbert) Max	**Gustavus**	FAULKNER	Golfer
Gabriel	**Urbain**	FAURÉ	Composer
William	**Claude**	FIELDS	Comedian and actor
Ranulph	**Twistleton-Wykeham**	FIENNES	Explorer
Robert	**Bannatyne**	FINLAY	Politician
Geoffrey	**Francis**	FISHER	Archbishop of Canterbury
Val	**Logsdon**	FITCH	US physicist
Augustus	**Henry**	FITZROY	British prime minister
Bob	**Prometheus**	FITZSIMMONS	Boxer
James	**Elroy**	FLECKER	Poet
Ian	**Lancaster**	FLEMING	English novelist
Jane	**Seymour**	FONDA	Actress
Michael	**Mackintosh**	FOOT	Politician
Gerald	**Rudolph**	FORD	US president
Cecil	**Scott**	FORESTER	Author
George	**Hoy**	FORMBY	Vocalist and musician
Edward	**Morgan**	FORSTER	Author
Bruce	**Joseph**	FORSYTH	Entertainer
Stephen	**Collins**	FOSTER	US songwriter
Michael J	**Andrew**	FOX	Actor
Clement	**Raphael**	FREUD	Liberal politician
Ragnar	**Kittil**	FRISCH	Norwegian economist
Kermit	**The**	FROG	Muppet
David	**Paradine**	FROST	Interviewer and presenter
Charles	**Burgess**	FRY	Sportsman
Stephen	**John**	FRY	Actor and author
Roy	**Broadbent**	FULLER	Poet
Hugh	**Todd Naylor**	GAITSKELL	Politician
Daniel	**Carleton**	GAJDUSEK	US virologist
Leopoldo	**Fortunato**	GALTIERI	Argentinian politician
Mohandas	**Karamchand**	GANDHI	Indian leader
James	**Abram**	GARFIELD	US president
John	**Nance**	GARNER	US vice-president
Elizabeth	**Cleghorn**	GASKELL	Writer
Herbert	**Spencer**	GASSER	US physiologist
Richard	**Jordan**	GATLING	Inventor
Richard	**Tiffany**	GERE	US actor
Ricky	**Dene**	GERVAIS	Comedian
Andrew	**Dewar**	GIBB	Scottish jurist
Lewis	**Grassic**	GIBBON	Novelist
Stella	**Dorothea**	GIBBONS	Writer
Mel	**Columcille**	GIBSON	Actor
Thomas	**Milner**	GIBSON	Politician
Arthur	**John**	GIELGUD	Actor
William	**Schwenck**	GILBERT	Librettist

Percy	**Carlyle**	GILCHRIST	Metallurgist
John	**Birks**	GILLESPIE	Jazz trumpeter
King	**Camp**	GILLETTE	Inventor
William	**Ewart**	GLADSTONE	British prime minister
Sheldon	**Lee**	GLASHOW	US physicist
John	**Herschel**	GLENN	US astronaut and politician
Robert	**Hutchings**	GODDARD	US rocket pioneer
William	**Gerald**	GOLDING	Novelist
Peter	**Carl**	GOLDMARK	Inventor
Barry	**Morris**	GOLDWATER	US politician
George	**Peabody**	GOOCH	Politician
Graham	**Alan**	GOOCH	Cricketer
Arthur	**Lehman**	GOODHART	US jurist
Benny	**David**	GOODMAN	US jazz clarinetist
Samuel	**Griswold**	GOODRICH	US publisher
Adam	**Lindsay**	GORDON	Australian poet
Cyrus	**Herzl**	GORDON	US Hebrew scholar
George	**Hamilton**	GORDON	British prime minister
Spencer	**Frederick**	GORE	Painter
Benjamin	**Apthorp**	GOULD	US astronomer
Charles	**François**	GOUNOD	Composer
Lawrence	**Burnett**	GOWING	Painter
Tiberius	**Sempronius**	GRACCHUS	Roman statesman
William	**Gilbert**	GRACE	Cricketer
Billy	**Franklin**	GRAHAM	US evangelist
Florence	**Nightingale**	GRAHAM	Beautician
Ulysses	**Simpson**	GRANT	US president
Milner	**Connorton**	GRAY	Graphic designer
Linda	**Esther**	GRAY	Scottish soprano
Lucinda	**Jane**	GREEN	Three-day eventer
Robson	**Golightly**	GREEN	Actor
Hugh	**Carleton**	GREENE	Journalist and broadcaster
Gordon	**Cuthbert**	GREENIDGE	Cricketer
William	**Wyndham**	GRENVILLE	British prime minister
Herbert	**Nigel**	GRESLEY	Locomotive engineer
Edvard	**Hagerup**	GRIEG	Norwegian composer
Christopher	**Murray**	GRIEVE	Poet
Walter	**Burley**	GRIFFIN	US architect
David	**Wark**	GRIFFITH	Film director
Angelina	**Emily**	GRIMKE	US feminist
Sarah	**Moore**	GRIMKE	US feminist
Friedrich	**Melchior**	GRIMM	Journalist
Jacob	**Ludwig Carl**	GRIMM	Folklorist
Wilhelm	**Carl**	GRIMM	Folklorist
Walter	**Adolph**	GROPIUS	Architect
Leroy	**Randle**	GRUMMAN	US aircraft pioneer
John	**Selwyn**	GUMMER	Politician
Johannes	**Gensfleisch**	GUTENBERG	German printer
Woodrow	**Wilson**	GUTHRIE	US folk singer
Franz	**Xaver**	HABERL	German musicologist
John	**Winthrop**	HACKETT	Soldier and academic
Gene	**Alden**	HACKMAN	Actor
Alfred	**Cort**	HADDON	Anthropologist
Henry	**Rider**	HAGGARD	Novelist
William	**Jefferson**	HAGUE	Politician
Alexander	**Meigs**	HAIG	US soldier
Thomas	**Chandler**	HALIBURTON	Canadian writer
Henry	**Wager**	HALLECK	US soldier
James	**Orchard**	HALLIWELL-PHILLIPPS	Shakespearean scholar
Dag	**Hjalmar Agne Carl**	HAMMARSKJÖLD	Swedish statesman
Robin	**Airling**	HANBURY-TENISON	Explorer
Tony	**Aloysius**	HANCOCK	TV character
Tony	**John**	HANCOCK	Comedy actor
George	**Frederick**	HANDEL	Composer
William	**Denby**	HANNA	US animated cartoonist
James	**Aloysius**	HANSOM	Designer
Warren	**Gamaliel**	HARDING	US president
Oliver	**Norville**	HARDY	Comedy actor
Thomas	**Duffus**	HARDY	Archivist
Thomas	**Masterman**	HARDY	Naval officer
Joel	**Chandler**	HARRIS	Author
William	**Henry**	HARRISON	US president
Leslie	**Poles**	HARTLEY	Author
Haldan	**Keffer**	HARTLINE	US physiologist
John	**Liptrot**	HATTON	Composer
Herbert	**Aaron**	HAUPTMAN	US physicist
Rutherford	**Birchard**	HAYES	US president
Seamus	**Justin**	HEANEY	Poet
Patricia	**Campbell**	HEARST	Heiress
Donald	**Olding**	HEBB	Canadian psychologist
Lillian	**Florence**	HELLMAN	US playwright

Ernest	**Millar**	HEMINGWAY	US novelist
Philip	**Showalter**	HENCH	US physician
Katharine	**Houghton**	HEPBURN	US actress
Jocelyn	**Barbara**	HEPWORTH	Sculptor
Georges	**Remi**	HERGÉ	Belgian cartoonist
Caroline	**Lucretia**	HERSCHEL	Astronomer
Alfred	**Day**	HERSHEY	US biologist
Michael	**Ray Dibdin**	HESELTINE	Politician
Philip	**Arnold**	HESELTINE	Composer
Emile	**William Ivanhoe**	HESKEY	Footballer
Alfred	**Hawthorne**	HILL	Comedian
Norman	**Graham**	HILL	Racing driver
Conrad	**Nicholson**	HILTON	Businessman
John (Jack)	**Berry**	HOBBS	English cricketer
Dorothy	**Crowfoot**	HODGKIN	Scientist
Dustin	**Lee**	HOFFMAN	Actor
Quintin	**McGarel**	HOGG	Politician
Edward	**Wheewall**	HOLDEN	Motor pioneer
Ben	**Caine**	HOLLIOAKE	English cricketer
Herbert	**Clark**	HOOVER	US president
John	**Edgar**	HOOVER	FBI director
Bob	**Leslie Townes**	HOPE	Comedian
Gerard	**Manley**	HOPKINS	Poet
Anthony	**Philip**	HOPKINS	Actor
Michael	**Murray**	HORDERN	Actor
Godfrey	**Newbold**	HOUNSFIELD	English electrical engineer
Alfred	**Edward**	HOUSMAN	Author
David	**Hunter**	HUBEL	US neurophysiologist
Charles	**Brenton**	HUGGINS	US surgeon
Howard	**Robard**	HUGHES	Businessman
Victor	**Marie**	HUGO	French writer
George	**Basil**	HUME	Cardinal
Johann	**Nepomuk**	HUMMEL	Austrian pianist
Hubert	**Horatio**	HUMPHREY	US vice-president
John	**Barry**	HUMPHRIES	Comedian and writer
Miller	**Reece**	HUTCHINSON	Inventor
Aldous	**Leonard**	HUXLEY	Novelist
Jeremy	**Israel**	ISAACS	Arts mogul
David	**Lewis**	JACOBS	Broadcaster
William	**Wymark**	JACOBS	Short story writer
Phyllis	**Dorothy**	JAMES	Authoress
James	**Hopwood**	JEANS	Physicist and astronomer
James	**Jackson**	JEFFRIES	Boxing champion
John	**Rushworth**	JELLICOE	Naval commander
Roy	**Harris**	JENKINS	Politician
Robert	**Banks**	JENKINSON	British prime minister
Niels	**Kai**	JERNE	Danish immunologist
Jerome	**Klapka**	JEROME	Author
Elton	**Hercules**	JOHN	Vocalist and composer
Alexander	**Boris De Pfeffel**	JOHNSON	Politician
Lyndon	**Baines**	JOHNSON	US president
Lionel	**Pigot**	JOHNSON	Poet
Richard	**Mentor**	JOHNSON	US vice-president
Joseph	**Eggleston**	JOHNSTON	US soldier
James	**Cellan**	JONES	Film director
Bobby	**Tyre**	JONES	US golfer
Michael	**Jeffrey**	JORDAN	US basketball player
James	**Prescott**	JOULE	Physicist
Carl	**Gustav**	JUNG	Swiss psychiatrist
Erik	**Axel**	KARLFELDT	Swedish poet
John	**Harvey**	KELLOGG	Inventor
Will	**Keith**	KELLOGG	Inventor
Gene	**Curran**	KELLY	Dancer
Edward	**Calvin**	KENDALL	US chemist
John	**Cowdery**	KENDREW	English biochemist
Edward	**Moore**	KENNEDY	US politician
John	**Fitzgerald**	KENNEDY	US president
Ludovic	**Coverley**	KENNEDY	Broadcaster
Nigel	**Paul**	KENNEDY	Violinist
Robert	**Francis**	KENNEDY	US politician
Søren	**Aabye**	KIERKEGAARD	Danish philosopher
William	**Rufus de Vane**	KING	US vice-president
Neil	**Gordon**	KINNOCK	Politician
Wilson	**Boit**	KIPKETER	Athlete
James	**Tiberius**	KIRK	Starship captain ('Star Trek')
Henry	**Alfred**	KISSINGER	USA statesman
Horatio	**Herbert**	KITCHENER	Irish soldier and statesman
Eartha	**Mae**	KITT	Singer
Nicholas	**Verity**	KNIGHT	Cricketer
Tjalling	**Charles**	KOOPMANS	US economist
Hans	**Adolf**	KREBS	British biochemist

Stanley	**Jasspon**	KUNITZ	US poet
Vladimir	**Petrovich**	KUTS	Russian athlete
Simon	**Smith**	KUZNETS	US economist
Fiorello	**Henry**	LA GUARDIA	US politician
René	**Théophile Hyacinthe**	LAENNEC	French physician
Selma	**Ottiliana Lovisa**	LAGERLOF	Swedish novelist
Carlos	**Saavedra**	LAMAS	Argentinian jurist
Willis	**Eugene**	LAMB	US physicist
Stephen	**Burton**	LANCASTER	Actor
Kenesaw	**Mountain**	LANDIS	Baseball commissioner
Walter	**Savage**	LANDOR	Writer
Henri	**Désiré**	LANDRU	French murderer
John	**Dunmore**	LANG	Clergyman
Harry	**Philmore**	LANGDON	US comedian
David	**Russell**	LANGE	New Zealand politician
Samuel	**Pierpont**	LANGLEY	US aeronautic pioneer
Cherilyn (Cher)	**Sarkisian**	LAPIERRE	Singer
Pierre	**Athanase**	LAROUSSE	French publisher
Hugh	**Callum**	LAURIE	Actor and comedian
Rodney	**George**	LAVER	Tennis player
Thomas	**Edward**	LAWRENCE	Author and soldier
David	**Herbert**	LAWRENCE	Author
Bill	**Morris**	LAWRY	Australian cricketer
Bernard	**Howell**	LEACH	English potter
Richard	**Erskine Frere**	LEAKEY	Palaeontologist and naturalist
Henrietta	**Swan**	LEAVITT	US astronomer
Christopher	**Carandini**	LEE	Actor
Vladimir	**Ilyich**	LENIN	Russian revolutionary
John	**Winston (then Ono)**	LENNON	Musician and composer
Henry	**Bernard**	LEVIN	Journalist and author
Harry	**Sinclair**	LEWIS	US novelist
Chris	**Clairmonte**	LEWIS	Cricketer
Clive	**Staples**	LEWIS	Author
John	**Spedan**	LEWIS	Businessman
Dennis	**Keith**	LILLEE	Australian cricketer
Charles	**Augustus**	LINDBERGH	US aviator
Gary	**Winston**	LINEKER	Footballer
Maureen	**Diane**	LIPMAN	Actress
William	**Nunn**	LIPSCOMB	US chemist
Penelope	**Margaret**	LIVELY	Writer
Harold	**Clayton**	LLOYD	US film comedian
Henry	**Cabot**	LODGE	US senator
Jack	**Griffith**	LONDON	US novelist
Francis	**Aungier**	LONGFORD	Prison reformer
Hendrik	**Antoon**	LORENTZ	Dutch physicist
Konrad	**Zacharias**	LORENZ	Austrian zoologist
Robert	**Hepler**	LOWE	Actor
Laurence	**Stephen**	LOWRY	Artist
Henry	**Robinson**	LUCE	US magazine publisher
Edwin	**Landseer**	LUTYENS	English architect
Humphrey	**Richard Adeane**	LYTTELTON	Musician
Thomas	**Babington**	MACAULAY	Author
George	**Brinton**	McCLELLAN	US soldier
Mark	**Hume**	McCORMACK	Promoter
James	**Ramsay**	MACDONALD	British prime minister
Rosalie	**Anderson**	MACDOWELL	Actress
Samora	**Moises**	MACHEL	Mozambican president
Donald	**Duart**	MACLEAN	English traitor
James	**Paul**	McCARTNEY	Musician and composer
Maurice	**Harold**	MACMILLAN	British prime minister
Robert	**Strange**	McNAMARA	Businessman and politician
Herman	**Cyril**	McNEILE	Author
Johann	**Nepomuk**	MAELZEL	German inventor
John	**Roy**	MAJOR	British prime minister
Nelson	**Rolihlahla**	MANDELA	South African president
Norman	**Washington**	MANLEY	Jamaican prime minister
Nigel	**Ernest James**	MANSELL	Racing driver
Ferdinand	**Edralin**	MARCOS	Filipino president
Bob	**Nesta**	MARLEY	Musician
Gabriel	**Garcia**	MARQUEZ	Columbian author
Jean	**Lyndsey Torren**	MARSH	Actress
George	**Catlett**	MARSHALL	American soldier and statesman
Jan	**Garrigue**	MASARYK	Czech statesman
Anna	**Raymond**	MASSEY	Actress
Daniel	**Raymond**	MASSEY	Actor
Marshall	**Bruce**	MATHERS III	Rap artist (aka Eminem)
William	**Somerset**	MAUGHAM	Author
Ian	**Robert**	MAXWELL	Businessman
Peter	**Barker Howard**	MAY	Cricketer
Michael	**Hugh**	MEACHER	Politician
Carlos	**Saul**	MENEM	Argentinian politician

Cliff	**Arthur**	MICHELMORE	Broadcaster
James	**Albert**	MICHENER	Author
Arthur	**Asher**	MILLER	US playwright
Alton	**Glenn**	MILLER	Bandleader
Jonathan	**Wolfe**	MILLER	Broadcaster
Alan	**Alexander**	MILNE	Author
Liza	**May**	MINNELLI	Singer
Walter	**Frederick (Fritz)**	MONDALE	US vice-president
Ernesto	**Teodoro**	MONETA	Italian journalist
Bernard	**Law**	MONTGOMERY	Field marshal
Brian	**Baden**	MOORE	Football commentator
Henry	**Spencer**	MOORE	Sculptor
Roger	**George**	MOORE	Actor
Sheridan	**Robert**	MORLEY	Author and broadcaster
George	**Ivan (Van)**	MORRISON	Singer and composer
Samuel	**Finley Breese**	MORSE	US inventor
John	**Cameron**	MORTON	Journalist
Levi	**Parsons**	MORTON	US vice-president
Oswald	**Ernald**	MOSLEY	British politician
Timothy	**Zakar**	MOSLEY	Rapper (Timbaland)
Benjamin	**Roy**	MOTTELSON	Danish physicist
Colin	**Berkeley**	MOYNIHAN	Politician
Robert	**Gabriel**	MUGABE	Zimbabwean president
Robert	**Sanderson**	MULLIKEN	American chemist
Hector	**Hugh**	MUNRO	Author
Keith	**Rupert**	MURDOCH	Businessman
Bartolomé	**Estebán**	MURILLO	Spanish painter
Edward	**Regan**	MURPHY	US comedian
John	**Middleton**	MURRY	Writer and critic
Maria	**Lurdes**	MUTOLA	Mozambique athlete
Frederic	**Ogden**	NASH	Poet
Pablo	**Neftali Reyes**	NERUDA	Poet
Marcus	**Cocceius**	NERVA	Roman emperor
Julia	**Babette Sarah**	NEUBERGER	Rabbi
George	**Eric**	NEWBY	Author
George	**Anthony**	NEWLEY	Actor and singer
Stavros	**Spyros**	NIARCHOS	Greek shipowner
Ben	**Lauder**	NICHOLSON	Abstract painter
Emma	**Harriet**	NICHOLSON	Politician
Jack	**William**	NICKLAUS	Golfer
Joseph	**Nicéphore**	NIEPCE	Inventor
Marshall	**Warren**	NIRENBERG	US biochemist
Richard	**Milhous**	NIXON	US president
Joshua	**Mqabuko Nyongolo**	NKOMO	Zimbabwean politician
Ronald	**Wreyford**	NORRISH	English chemist
Trevor	**Robert**	NUNN	Theatre director
Julius	**Kambarage**	NYERERE	Tanzanian president
Michael	**Vincent**	O'BRIEN	Racehorse trainer
Desmond	**Bernard**	O'CONNOR	Entertainer
David	**Feodorovich**	OISTRAKH	Violinist
James	**Trevor**	OLIVER	TV chef
Laurence	**Kerr**	OLIVIER	Actor
Aristotle	**Socrates**	ONASSIS	Shipping magnate
Eugene	**Gladstone**	O'NEILL	US playwright
Elisha	**Graves**	OTIS	Inventor
Peter	**Seamus**	O'TOOLE	Irish actor
George	**Emil**	PALADE	US biologist
Arnold	**Daniel**	PALMER	Golfer
Cyril	**Northcote**	PARKINSON	Political scientist
Eric	**Honeywood**	PARTRIDGE	Lexicographer
Linus	**Carl**	PAULING	Scientist
Thomas	**Love**	PEACOCK	Novelist and poet
Mervyn	**Laurence**	PEAKE	Author and artist
John	**Loughborough**	PEARSON	Architect
Lester	**Bowles**	PEARSON	Canadian politician
Eldred	**Gregory**	PECK	Actor
Richard	**Wayne**	PENNIMAN	Musician
Juan	**Domingo**	PERÓN	Argentinian president
Reginald	**Iolanthe**	PERRIN	TV character
Matthew	**Galbraith**	PERRY	US naval officer
Oliver	**Hazard**	PERRY	US naval officer
Publius	**Helvius**	PERTINAX	Roman emperor
Max	**Ferdinand**	PERUTZ	British biochemist
Henri	**Omer**	PÉTAIN	French statesman
Mary	**Elizabeth**	PETERS	Pentathlete
Roger	**Tory**	PETERSON	US ornithologist
Ulrich	**Bonnell**	PHILLIPS	US historian
River	**Jude**	PHOENIX	Actor
William	**Mervyn**	PICKWOAD	Actor
Lester	**Keith**	PIGGOTT	Jockey
Arthur	**Wing**	PINERO	Playwright

Jenny	**Susan**	PITMAN	Racehorse trainer
Gary	**Jim**	PLAYER	Golfer
Raymond	**Landry**	POINCARÉ	French statesman
John	**Marlan**	POINDEXTER	US naval officer
James	**Knox**	POLK	US president
Robert	**Graeme**	POLLOCK	Cricketer
Paul	**Jackson**	POLLOCK	US artist
William	**Sydney**	PORTER	Author
Michael	**Denzil Xavier**	PORTILLO	Politician
Dennis	**Christopher George**	POTTER	Playwright
Ezra	**Loomis**	POUND	Poet
Anthony	**Dymoke**	POWELL	English novelist
John	**Enoch**	POWELL	British politician
Austin	**Danger**	POWERS	Film character
John	**Leslie**	PRESCOTT	Politician
Elvis	**Aaron**	PRESLEY	American singer
Marthinus	**Wessels**	PRETORIUS	South African general
André	**George**	PREVIN	Conductor
John	**Boynton**	PRIESTLEY	Author
Archibald	**Philip**	PRIMROSE	British prime minister
James	**Leathes**	PRIOR	Politician
Victor	**Sawdon**	PRITCHETT	Writer and critic
Sergei	**Sergeyevich**	PROKOFIEV	Composer
Giacomo	**Antonio**	PUCCINI	Composer
Ana	**Fidelia**	QUIROT	Cuban athlete
Steve	**Russell**	RACE	Broadcaster
Sergey	**Vasilyevich**	RACHMANINOV	Composer
Thomas	**Stamford**	RAFFLES	Colonial administrator
Arthur	**Michael**	RAMSEY	Archbishop of Canterbury
Norman	**Foster**	RAMSEY	US physicist
John	**Crowe**	RANSOM	US poet and critic
Arthur	**Michell**	RANSOME	Author
Esther	**Louise**	RANTZEN	TV presenter
Claire	**Berenice**	RAYNER	Broadcaster
Ronald	**Wilson**	REAGAN	US president
Michael	**Scudamore**	REDGRAVE	Actor
Robert	**Oliver**	REED	British actor
Erich	**Maria**	REMARQUE	Author
Ruth	**Barbara**	RENDELL	Crime novelist
Dickinson	**Woodruff**	RICHARDS	US physician
Dorothy	**Miller**	RICHARDSON	English novelist
Eddie	**Vernon**	RICKENBACKER	Fighter pilot
Sally	**Kristen**	RIDE	US astronaut
Matthew	**Bunker**	RIDGWAY	US soldier
Nikolai	**Andreievich**	RIMSKY-KORSAKOV	Composer
Frederick	**Chapman**	ROBBINS	US physiologist
Frederick	**Sleigh**	ROBERTS	British soldier
Dale	**Lymoine**	ROBERTSON	US actor
James	**Logie**	ROBERTSON	Poet
Paul	**Bustill Le Roy**	ROBESON	Actor
Frederick	**John**	ROBINSON	British prime minister
Nelson	**Aldrich**	ROCKEFELLER	US vice-president
Anita	**Lucia**	RODDICK	Businesswoman
Edith	**Kermit**	ROOSEVELT	US First Lady
Franklin	**Delano**	ROOSEVELT	US president
Jack	**Morris**	ROSENTHAL	Playwright
Kenneth	**Ronald**	ROSEWALL	Tennis player
Liberty	**Lettice Lark**	ROSS	Model/actress
Mstislav	**Leopoldovich**	ROSTROPOVICH	Cellist
Philip	**Milton**	ROTH	Novelist
Meyer	**Amschel**	ROTHSCHILD	German financier
Francis	**Peyton**	ROUS	American pathologist
Robert	**Alexander**	RUNCIE	Archbishop of Canterbury
Ahmed	**Salman**	RUSHDIE	Author
Charles	**Taze**	RUSSELL	Religious leader
Gottlieb	**Eliel**	SAARINEN	Finnish–US architect
Nelly	**Leonie**	SACHS	Swedish poet and playwright
Jerome	**David**	SALINGER	Author
Jonas	**Edward**	SALK	Biologist
Seigfried	**Lorraine**	SASSOON	Poet
James	**Wilson Vincent**	SAVILE	Broadcaster
John	**Richard**	SCHLESINGER	Film director
Charles	**Monroe**	SCHULZ	US strip cartoonist
Harry	**Donald**	SECOMBE	Comedian and singer
Elzie	**Crisler**	SEGAR	US strip cartoonist
Harry	**Gordon**	SELFRIDGE	British merchant
David	**Oliver**	SELZNICK	US cinema mogul
Richard	**Bowdler**	SHARPE	Ornithologist
George	**Bernard**	SHAW	Author
Percy	**Bysshe**	SHELLEY	Poet
James	**Schoolcraft**	SHERMAN	US vice-president

William	**Tecumseh**	SHERMAN	General
William	**Bradford**	SHOCKLEY	US physicist
John	**Cody Fiddler**	SIMPSON	News reporter
Francis (Frank)	**Albert**	SINATRA	Singer
Upton	**Beall**	SINCLAIR	US novelist
Isaac	**Bashevis**	SINGER	Writer
Israel	**Joshua**	SINGER	Writer
Isaac	**Merritt**	SINGER	US inventor
Christopher	**Robert**	SMITH	British politician
Hamilton	**Othanel**	SMITH	US molecular biologist
Maggie	**Natalie**	SMITH	Actress
Sydney	**Goodsir**	SMITH	Poet
Samuel	**Jackson**	SNEAD	Golfer
Charles	**Percy**	SNOW	Author
Garfield	**St Auburn**	SOBERS	Cricketer
Robert	**Merton**	SOLOW	American economist
Aleksandr	**Isaevich**	SOLZHENITSYN	Author
Stephen	**Joshua**	SONDHEIM	Composer and lyricist
Donald	**Oliver**	SOPER	Methodist minister
Thomas	**Octave Murdoch**	SOPWITH	Aircraft designer
Charles	**Hamilton**	SORLEY	Poet
John	**Hanning**	SPEKE	Explorer
Basil	**Urwin**	SPENCE	Architect
Elmer	**Ambrose**	SPERRY	US inventor
Roger	**Wolcott**	SPERRY	US neuroscientist
Henry	**Morton**	STANLEY	Explorer and journalist
Edwin	**McMasters**	STANTON	US statesman
Publius	**Papinius**	STATIUS	Roman poet
George	**Ledyard**	STEBBINS	US botanist
David	**Martin Scott**	STEEL	Politician
William	**Howard**	STEIN	US biochemist
John	**Ernest**	STEINBECK	US novelist
Harold	**Kitchener**	STEPTOE	'Steptoe & Son' character
Patrick	**Christopher**	STEPTOE	Gynaecologist
Adlai	**Ewing**	STEVENSON	US politician
William	**Gladstone**	STEWART	TV broadcaster and producer
Richard	**Henry Simpson**	STILGOE	Songwriter and broadcaster
John	**Michael**	STIPE	US vocalist
Isidor	**Feinstein**	STONE	US journalist
Harlan	**Fiske**	STONE	US judge
William	**Wetmore**	STORY	Poet and sculptor
Rex	**Todhunter**	STOUT	US detective writer
Gavin	**Steel**	STRANG	Politician
Charles	**Sherwood**	STRATTON	Circus performer
Igor	**Fedorovich**	STRAVINSKY	Composer
Jack	**Whitaker**	STRAW	Politician
Meryl	**Mary Louise**	STREEP	Actress
Barbra	**Joan**	STREISAND	Singer
Arthur	**Seymour**	SULLIVAN	Composer
John	**Bird**	SUMNER	Archbishop of Canterbury
Frank	**Meadow**	SUTCLIFFE	Photographer
Joseph	**Wilson**	SWAN	Physicist
John	**Addington**	SYMONDS	Author
John	**Millington**	SYNGE	Author
William	**Howard**	TAFT	US president
Archibald	**Campbell**	TAIT	Archbishop of Canterbury
Abel	**Janszoon**	TASMAN	Navigator
Elizabeth	**Rosemond**	TAYLOR	Actress
Edward	**Lawrie**	TATUM	US biochemist
William	**Howson**	TAYLOR	Potter
Pyotr	**Ilyich**	TCHAIKOVSKY	Composer
Kiri	**Janette**	TE KANAWA	Opera Singer
Norman	**Beresford**	TEBBIT	Politician
George	**Philipp**	TELEMANN	Composer
Henry	**John**	TEMPLE	British prime minister
Ellen	**Alice**	TERRY	Actress
William	**Makepeace**	THACKERAY	Author
Margaret	**Hilda**	THATCHER	British prime minister
Anatole	**François**	THIBAULT	Author
Dylan	**Marlais**	THOMAS	Poet
Daley	**Francis Morgan**	THOMPSON	Athlete
John	**Taliaferro**	THOMPSON	US soldier and inventor
Hunter	**Stockton**	THOMPSON	US writer
George	**Paget**	THOMSON	English physicist
John	**Jeremy**	THORPE	Politician
James	**Grover**	THURBER	Humorist
Uma	**Karuna**	THURMAN	Actress
Louis	**Comfort**	TIFFANY	Glassmaker
Samuel	**Jones**	TILDEN	US politician
William	**Tatem**	TILDEN	US tennis player
Samuel	**Chao Chung**	TING	US physicist

Michael	**Kemp**	TIPPETT	Composer
Marcus	**Tullius**	TIRO	Inventor
Richard	**Palethorpe**	TODD	Actor
John	**Ronald Reuel**	TOLKIEN	Author
Theobald	**Wolfe**	TONE	Irish nationalist
Augustus	**Montague**	TOPLADY	Clergyman and hymnist
Donald	**Francis**	TOVEY	Pianist and composer
Charles	**Hard**	TOWNES	American physicist
Lee	**Buck**	TREVINO	American golfer
Rodney	**Charlton**	TROTTER	'Fools and Horses' character
Frederick (Freddy)	**Sewards**	TRUEMAN	Cricketer
Barry	**Emmanuel**	TUCKWELL	Australian musician
Alan	**Mathison**	TURING	Mathematician
Victor	**Witter**	TURNER	Anthropologist
Desmond	**Mpilo**	TUTU	South African prelate
William	**Marcy**	TWEED	US politician and criminal
Liv	**Rundgren**	TYLER	US actress
Liv	**Johanne**	ULLMANN	Norwegian actress
John	**Hoyer**	UPDIKE	Author
Leon	**Marcus**	URIS	US author
Peter	**Alexander**	USTINOV	Actor and writer
Louis	**Nicolas**	VAUQUELIN	Chemist
King	**Wallis**	VIDOR	Film director
Angelina	**Jolie**	VOIGHT	Actress
Sarah	**Virginia**	WADE	Tennis player
Thomas	**Griffiths**	WAINEWRIGHT	Art critic and murderer
Terence (Terry)	**Hardy**	WAITE	Religious adviser
Selman	**Abraham**	WAKSMAN	US biochemist
Alice	**Malsenior**	WALKER	US novelist
George	**Corley**	WALLACE	Governor of Alabama
Henry	**Agard**	WALLACE	US vice-president
Hugh	**Seymour**	WALPOLE	Novelist
William	**Turner**	WALTON	Composer
Arthur	**Sarsfield**	WARD	Author
Booker	**Taliaferro**	WASHINGTON	US educationist
Lewis	**Edson**	WATERMAN	Inventor
James	**Dewey**	WATSON	US biologist
Clifton	**Parmelee**	WEBB	Actor
Everton	**Decourcey**	WEEKES	West Indian cricketer
Caspar	**Willard**	WEINBERGER	US politician
Thomas	**Huckle**	WELLER	US physiologist
Alan	**Whipper**	WELLS	Athlete
Charles	**Watson**	WENTWORTH	British prime minister
Edith	**Newbold**	WHARTON	Author
Denis	**Yates**	WHEATLEY	Novelist
Alan	**Donald**	WHICKER	Broadcaster
Jimmy	**Warren**	WHITE	Snooker player
Joseph	**Blanco**	WHITE	English poet
Pearl	**Fay**	WHITE	US actress
Terence	**Hanbury**	WHITE	Novelist
William	**Hale**	WHITE	Writer
Alfred	**North**	WHITEHEAD	Philosopher and mathematician
Oscar	**Fingal O'Flahertie Wills**	WILDE	Playwright and novelist
Ralph	**Vaughan**	WILLIAMS	Composer
Bob	**Dylan**	WILLIS	Cricketer
Bob	**Primrose**	WILSON	Goalkeeper and broadcaster
James	**Harold**	WILSON	British prime minister
Robert	**Woodrow**	WILSON	US physicist
Thomas	**Woodrow**	WILSON	US president
Pelham	**Grenville**	WODEHOUSE	Author
Michael	**Terence**	WOGAN	Broadcaster
Thomas	**Clayton**	WOLFE	Novelist
Tom	**Kennerley**	WOLFE	Novelist
Arnold	**Whittaker**	WOLFENDALE	Astronomer
Comer	**Vann**	WOODWARD	US historian
Robert	**Burns**	WOODWARD	American chemist
Adeline	**Virginia**	WOOLF	Novelist
Frank	**Winfield**	WOOLWORTH	US businessman
Bertie	**Wilberforce**	WOOSTER	Fictional character
Frank	**Mortimer Magilinne**	WORRELL	Cricketer
Billy	**Ambrose**	WRIGHT	Footballer
Elinor	**Hoyt**	WYLIE	US author
Johann	**Rudolf**	WYSS	Swiss writer
Magdi	**Habib**	YACOUB	Surgeon
Charles	**Elwood**	YEAGER	US test pilot
William	**Butler**	YEATS	Author
Boris	**Nikolayevich**	YELTSIN	Russian president
Susannah	**Yolande**	YORK	Actress
Lazarus	**Ludwig**	ZAMENHOF	Inventor of Esperanto
Gianfranco	**Corsi**	ZEFFIRELLI	Film director
Mai	**Elizabeth**	ZETTERLING	Actress and director

Nicknames

Joseph Addison **Atticus**
Aeschylus **Father of Greek Tragedy**
Muhammed Ali **Louisville Lip**
Queen Anne **Brandy Nan**
Anne of Cleves **Flanders Mare**
Lord George Anson **Father of the Royal Navy**
Thomas Aquinas **Angelic Doctor**
Aristophanes **Father of Comedy**
Richard Arkwright **Father of the Factory System**
Henry Armstrong **Homicide Hank**
Louis Armstrong **Satchmo (Satchel Mouth)**
Charles Atlas **World's Most Perfectly Developed Man**
Attila the Hun **Scourge of God**
Aurelian (Roman emperor) **Restorer of the World**
Stephen Babcock **Father of Scientific Dairying**
Francis Bacon **Father of Inductive Philosophy**
Roger Bacon **Father of Philosophy**, **Admirable Doctor (Doctor Mirabilis)**
John Logie Baird **Father of Television**
Joan Bakewell **Thinking Man's Crumpet** (by Frank Muir)
Theda Bara **Vamp**
John Barbour **Father of Scottish Poetry**
Sir John Barnard **Father of London**
John Barrymore **Great Profile**
Sir Edmund Barton **Father of Australia**
Elyesa Bazna (spy) **Cicero**
Bill Beaumont **Amiable Geronimo**
Aphra Behn **Divine Astraea**
Alexander Graham Bell **Father of the Telephone**
John Bell **Father of Sunday Newspapers**
Jeremy Bentham **Father of Utilitarianism**
Lavrenti Beria **Himmler of Russia**
David Berkowitz **Son of Sam**
Irving Berlin **Father of Published Ragtime**
Tim Berners-Lee **Father of the Web**
Sarah Bernhard **Divine Sarah**
John Biddle **Father of English Unitarianism**
Clarence Birdseye **Father of Frozen Food**
Bismarck **Iron Chancellor**
Dr Greene Valadiman Black **Father of Modern Dentistry**
Simon Bolivar **Liberator**
Peter Bonetti **Cat**
Bononcini and Handel **Tweedle Dee and Tweedle Dum**
Jean Borotra **Bounding Basque**
James Boswell **Will O' the Wisp**
Clara Bow **It Girl**
Robert Boyle **Father of Chemistry**
Bessie Braddock **Workers' Champion**
William Bradford **Father of American History**
James Brindley **Father of Britain's Canals**
William Hill Brown **Father of the American Novel**
William Cullen Bryant **Father of American Poetry**
Martha Jane Burke **Calamity Jane**
Robert Burns **Bard of Ayrshire**
Richard Burton **The Voice**
George Bush **Wimp**
Francis X Bushman **Handsomest Man in the World**
David Bushnell **Father of the Submarine**
Caedmon **Father of English Song**
Cab Calloway **King of Hi de Ho**
Walter Chauncey Camp **Father of American Football**
Martha Jane Canary (Burke) **Calamity Jane**
Thomas Carlyle **Sage of Chelsea**
Primo Carnera **Ambling Alp**
Judy Carne **Sock-it-to-me-girl**
Georges Carpentier **Orchid Kid**
Jacques Cartier **Father of Canada**
John Cartwright **Father of Reform**
Johnny Cash **Man in Black**
Nicholas Catinat **Father Thoughtful**
William Caxton **Father of English Printing**
Sir George Cayley **Father of Aviation**
Craig Chalmers **Sponge**
Wilton Chamberlain **Wilt the Stilt**
Lon Chaney Snr **Man of a thousand Faces**
Charles I **Martyr King, Ahab of the Nation, Britain's Josiah, White King**
Charles II **Blackbird, Old Rowley, Merry Monarch**
Eddie Charlton **Steady Eddie**
Henri Charrière **Papillon**
Chris Chataway **Red Fox**
Geoffrey Chaucer **Father of English Poetry**
Cicero **Father of his Country**
Cassius Clay **Louisville Lip**
Georges Clemenceau **Tiger**
Daniel Cohn-Bendit **Danny the Red**
Mary Collier **The Washer-woman (Poet)**
Peter Cook **Cambridge Rapist**
John Calvin Coolidge **Silent Cal**
Jim Corbett **Gentleman Jim**
Paul Cotton **Poco**
Noël Coward **The Master**
Colin Cowdrey **Kipper**
Alexander Cozens **Father of English Watercolour**
Brigadier-General Alfred Critchley **Father of Greyhound Racing**
Oliver Cromwell **Old Noll, Nose Almighty, Old Ironsides**
Richard Cromwell **Tumbledown Dick**
Aleister Crowley **Wickedest Man in the World**
Duke of Cumberland **Butcher**
Laurie Cunningham **Black Pearl**
Edwina Currie **Vindaloo**
Clarence Darrow **Attorney for the Damned**
Freddie Davies (comedian) **Parrot Face**
William Henry Davies **Supertramp**
Steve Davis **Interesting**
William Morris Davis **Father of Geomorphology**
Eamon De Valera **Father of the Irish Republic**
Rodrigo de Vivar **El Cid**
Daniel Defoe **Father of Modern Prose Fiction**
Jack Dempsey (heavyweight) **Manassa Mauler, Nonpareil**
Joe Di Maggio **Yankee Clipper**
Mildred Didrikson **Babe**
Graham Dilley (cricketer) **Picca**
Tommy Docherty **Doc**
Antoine Domino **Fats**
General Abner Doubleday **Father of Baseball**
Antony Dowell and Antoinette Sibley **Golden Pair**
Jimmy Durante **Schnozzle**
Valentine Dyall **Man in Black**
Nelson Eddy and Jeanette MacDonald **America's Sweethearts**
Thomas Alva Edison **Wizard of Menlo Park**
Edmund II **Ironside**
Edward I **Longshanks**
Edward III **Father of English Commerce**
Edward V and brother Richard **Princes in the Tower**
Edward (son of Edward III) **Black Prince**
Eddie Edwards **Eagle**
George Edwards **Father of Ornithologists**
John Eley **The Cooking Canon**
Elizabeth I **Virgin Queen**
Elizabeth II **Brenda** (by *Private Eye*)
Elizabeth Stuart (of Bohemia) **Winter Queen**
Ernie Els **The Big Easy**
Eminem **The Real Slim Shady**
Empress Tzu Hsi **Old Buddha**

Arthur English **Prince of the Wide Boys**
Ethelred II **Unready**
Eusebio **Black Panther**
Eusebius of Caesarea **Father of Ecclesiastical History**
Derrick Evans **Mr Motivator**
Henry Fielding **Father of the English Novel**
Tom Finney **White Ghost**
Bob Fitzsimmons **Cornishman, Antipodean**
Florian Cloud de Bounevialle Armstrong **Dido**
George Formby Snr **Wigan Nightingale**
Tregonwell Frampton **Father of the English Turf**
Francis I of France **Father of Letters**
John Francome **Greatest Jockey** (by John McCririck)
Frederick I **Barbarossa**
Frederick II **Wonder of the World**
William Frederick **Great Elector (of Brandenburg)**
Alan Freeman **Fluff**
Tony Galento **Two Ton**
Gandhi **Mahatma ('Great Soul')**
Joel Garner **Big Bird**
George III **Farmer George**
George IV **Adonis of Fifty**
Cass Gilbert **Father of the Skyscraper**
Ian Gillis **Mycroft**
Bernard Gilpin **Father of the Poor**
Giotto Di Bondone **Father of Modern Art**
Thomas Girtin **Father of Modern Watercolour**
William Gladstone **Grand Old Man (GOM)**
Captain Sir John Hawley Glover **Father of the Hausas**
Major General Sir John Bagot Glubb **Father of the Chin, Glubb Pasha**
Sir James Goldsmith **Goldenballs** (by *Private Eye*)
Barry Goldwater **AuH2O**
Graham Gooch **Zap**
Benny Goodman **King of Swing**
Charles Goodnight **Father of the Cowboys**
Betty Grable **Million Dollar Legs**
Ulysses Simpson Grant **Uncle Sam**
Zachary Grey **Father of Modern Commentators**
Florence Griffith-Joyner **Flo Jo**
Sir Nicholas Grimshaw **Meccano Man**
Grock **King of Clowns**
Marvin Hagler **Marvellous (later became first name)**
Archie Hahn **Milwaukee Meteor**
John George Haigh **Acid Bath Murderer, Vampire Killer**
Handel and Bononcini **Tweedle Dum and Tweedle Dee**
WC Handy **Father of the Blues**
Harold I **Harefoot**
Russell Harty **Sooty**
Mark Hateley (footballer) **Attila**
Sir Christopher Hatton **Mutton, the Dancing Chancellor**
Franz Josef Haydn **Father of the Symphony**
Edward Heath **Grocer**
Henry I of England **Beauclerc**
Henry IV of France **Father of the People**
Henry V **Bluff Prince Hal**
Herodotus **Father of History**
Michael Heseltine **Tarzan, Veronica Lake, Action Man, Goldilocks**
Alex Higgins **Hurricane**
Jimmy Hill **Rabbi**
Bernard Hinault (cyclist) **Badger**
Hippocrates **Father of Medicine**
Bob Hite (Canned Heat) **Bear**
James Hogg **Ettrick Shepherd**
Michael Holding **Whispering Death**
John Philip Holland **Father of the Military Submarine**
Billie Holliday **Lady Day**
Homer **Father of Epic Poetry**
Thomas Hooker **Father of American Democracy**
Matthew Hopkins **Witchfinder General**
Lesley Hornby **Twiggy**
Geoffrey Howe **Mogadon Man**
Edmond Hoyle **Father of the Game of Whist**
George Hudson **Railway King**
Cordell Hull **Father of the United Nations**
Barbara Hutton **Poor Little Rich Girl**
Hypatia **Divine Pagan**
Thomas Ince **Father of Westerns**
Andrew Jackson **Old Hickory**
General Thomas Jackson **Stonewall (Battle of Bull Run)**
Joseph Holson Jagger **Man Who Broke the Bank at Monte Carlo**
James I **Wisest Fool in Christendom** (by Henry IV of France)
James II **King over the Water**
Thomas Jefferson **Moonshine Philosopher**
James J Jeffries **Boilermaker**
Edward Jenner **Father of Immunology**
William Le Baron Jenney **Father of the Skyscraper**
Gilbert Jessop (cricketer) **The Croucher**
Joan of Arc **Maid of Orleans**
Samuel Johnson **Great Cham**
Sir John Harvey Jones **Admiral**
Ben Jonson **Father of Poets**
Janis Joplin **Pearl**
Scott Joplin **Father of Ragtime**
William Joyce **Lord Haw Haw**
Alberto Juantorena **White Lightning**
Helen Kane **Boop a Doop Girl**
Nora Kaye **Duse of the Dance**
Buster Keaton **The Great Stone Face**
Joseph Keaton **Buster** (coined by Houdini)
Fanny Kemble **Anne of Swansea**
Rev Geoffrey Kennedy **Woodbine Willie**
Ludovic Kennedy **Uckers**
Admiral Sir Henry Keppel **Father of the Fleet**
Graham Kerr **Galloping Gourmet**
King John **Lackland**
Peter Kurten **Monster of Düsseldorf**
Henri Landru **Bluebeard**
Allen Lane **Father of Penguin Paperbacks**
Niki Lauda **Clockwork Mouse**
Rod Laver **Rockhampton Rocket**
Antoine Lavoisier **Father of Modern Chemistry**
Florence Lawrence **Biograph Girl**
Frances Lawrence (novelist) **Gidget**
John Lawrence **Noble Lord** (by John McCririck)
Major General Stringer Lawrence **Father of the Indian Army**
TE Lawrence **Lawrence of Arabia**
Jean-Baptiste Le Moyne **Father of Louisiana**
Jerry Lee Lewis **Killer**
Eric Liddell **Flying Scotsman**
Fred Lillywhite (cricketer) **Nonpareil Bowler**
Jenny Lind **Swedish Nightingale**
Charles Lindbergh **Lone Eagle**
David Lloyd George **Welsh Wizard**
Harry Longbaugh **Sundance Kid**
Lord Longford **Lord Porn**
Konrad Lorenz **Father of Ethology**
Lorenzo de' Medici **Father of Letters, The Magnificent**
Louis XII **Father of the People**
Louis XIV **Sun King**
Joe Louis **Brown Bomber**
Lord Lucan **Lucky**
Vera Lynn **Forces Sweetheart**
Ma Rainey **Mother of the Blues**
Mary McCauley **Molly Pitcher**
Derek McCulloch **Uncle Mac**
John McEnroe **Superbrat**
Barry McGuigan **Clones Cyclone**
Harold Macmillan **Supermac**
McPartlin and Donnelly **Ant and Dec**
James Madison **Father of the Constitution**
Mary Mallon **Typhoid Mary**
Rocky Marciano **Brockton Blockbuster**
Frances Marion **Swamp Fox**

Duchess of Marlborough **Mrs Freeman**
Duke of Marlborough (1st) **Anne's Great Captain**
Major William Martin (WW2 decoy) **Man Who Never Was**
Mary I **Bloody Mary**
Matilda **Empress Maud**
Stanley Matthews **Wizard of Dribble**
Colin Meads **Pine Tree**
Phil Mickelson **Lefty**
Bette Midler **Divine Miss M**
Henry Miller **Father of the Four Letter Word**
Joseph Miller **Father of Jests**
Max Miller **Cheekie Chappie**
Carmen Miranda **Brazilian Bombshell**
Thelonius Monk **High Priest of Bop**
Duke of Monmouth (James Scott) **Absalom**
Jean Monnet **Father of the Common Market**
Lady Mary Wortley Montague **Sappho**
Helen Wills Moody **Little Miss Poker Face**
Lewis Henry Morgan **Father of American Anthropology**
Jedediah Morse **Father of American Geography**
Charles Morton **Father of Variety, Champagne, Father of the Halls**
Lord Louis Mountbatten **Dickie**
Richard Murdoch **Stinker**
Lindley Murray **Father of English Grammar**
James Naismith **Father of Basketball**
Renaldo Nehemiah (athlete) **Skeets**
Jawaharlal Nehru **Pandit ('Wise Man')**
Donald Neilson (Nappey) **Black Panther**
Richard Neville (Earl of Warwick) **Kingmaker**
Marshal Ney **Bravest of the Brave**
Jack Nicklaus **Golden Bear**
Florence Nightingale **Lady with the Lamp**
Richard Nixon **Tricky Dicky**
Kwame Nkrumah **Showboy**
Greg Norman **Great White Shark**
Senator George Norris **Father of the 20th Amendment**
Paavo Nurmi **Flying Finn**
Lord John Oaksey **Noble Lord** (by John McCririck)
Ronald O'Bryan **Candy Man Killer**
Anita O'Day **Jezebel of Jazz**
Chris Old (cricketer) **Chilly**
Sir Henry Oliver **Father of Modern Navigation**
Christina Onassis **Thunderthighs**
Dr Robert Oppenheimer **Father of the Atom Bomb**
Count D'Orsay **Last of the Dandies**
Tessie O'Shea **Two-Ton Tessie**
Richard Fellow Outcault **Father of the Comic Strip**
Robert Owen **Father of British Socialism**
Jesse Owens **Ebony Antelope**
Bettie Page **Queen of Pinups**
Lord Palmerston **Pam**
Bonnie Parker **Suicide Sal**
Charlie Parker **Bird**
Archbishop Matthew Parker **Nosey Parker**
General George Patton **Old Blood and Guts**
Cynthia Payne **Madame Sin**
Pele **Black Pearl**
Vladimir Peniakoff (Belgian soldier) **Popski**
Sir Henry Percy **Hotspur**
Joseph Père **Grey Eminence**
William Perry **Refrigerator**
John Joseph Pershing **Black Jack**
Marius Petipa **Father of Classical Ballet**
Louis Philippe **Citizen King**
Edith Piaf **Little Sparrow**
Mary Pickford **America's Sweetheart**
William Pitt **Aeolus**
William Pitt the Elder **Great Commoner**
Gary Player **Man in Black**
John Playford **Father of British Music Publishing**
Edgar Allan Poe **Father of the Detective Story**
Alexander Pope **Wasp of Twickenham**
Elvis Presley **The Pelvis, The King**
Princess Michael of Kent **Princess Pushy**
Ferenc Puskas **Galloping Major**
Rufus Putnam **Father of Ohio**
Max Quartermann **Superhod**
Fabius Quintus **Cunctator (Delayer)**
Rabelais **Father of Ridicule**
Luise Rainer **Viennese Teardrop**
Sonny Ramadhin **Spin King**
Derek Randall (cricketer) **Arkle**
Maharajah Ranjit Singh **Lion of the Punjab**
Ranulf de Glanvill **Father of Jurisprudence**
John Ray **Father of English Natural History**
Johnny Ray **Prince of Wails**
Nancy Reagan **Smiling Mamba**
Ronald Reagan **Teflon President**
Ray Reardon **Dracula**
John Redwood **Vulcan**
John Reid **Father of American Golf**
John Rich **Father of Harlequins, Father of English Pantomime**
Richard I **Lionheart, Yea and Nay**
Richard de Beauchamp **Father of Courtesy**
Richard de Clare (2nd Earl of Pembroke) **Strongbow**
Richard Duke of York and Edward V **Princes in the Tower**
Samuel Richardson **Father of the English Novel**
Cardinal Richelieu **Red Eminence**
Manfred von Richthofen **Red Baron**
Eddie Rickenbacker **Ace of Aces**
Robespierre **Sea-Green Incorruptible**
George Robey **Prime Minister of Mirth**
Derek Robinson **Red Robbo**
Jimmie Charles Rodgers **Father of Country Music**
Steve Rogers **Captain America**
Erwin Rommel **Desert Fox**
Ken Rosewall **Muscles**
Stanley Rous **Father of English Football**
William Hepburn Russell **Father of the Pony Express**
Babe Ruth **Sultan of Swat**
Ernest Rutherford **Father of Nuclear Physics**
William Sacheverell **First Whig**
St Anthony **Father of Christian Monasticism**
St Ethelwold **Father of Monks**
St Thomas Aquinas **Father of Moral Philosophy**
Albert de Salvo **Boston Strangler**
Sir Malcolm Sargent **Flash Harry**
Sir Walter Scott **Wizard of the North, Great Unknown, Ariosto of the North, Old Peveril**
William Shakespeare **Swan of Avon, Bard of Avon**
Percy Bysshe Shelley **Ariel**
Ann Sheridan **Oomph Girl**
Manny Shinwell **Sinbad the Tailor**
Willie Shoemaker (jockey) **Shoe**
Antoinette Sibley and Anthony Dowell **Golden Pair**
Igor Sikorsky **Father of the Helicopter**
OJ Simpson **The Juice**
Frank Sinatra **The Voice**
Dennis Skinner **Beast of Bolsover**
Adam Smith **Father of Economics**
Bob Smith **Wolfman Jack**
William Smith **Father of English Geology**
Soeur Sourire **Singing Nun**
John Philip Sousa **March King**
Ursula Southiel **Old Mother Shipton**
Countess Spencer **Acid Raine**
John Spencer **Sniffer**
Bruce Springsteen **The Boss**
Craig Stadler (golfer) **Walrus**
Sylvester Stallone **Italian Stallion**
George Stephenson **Father of Railways**
Sir Rowland Stephenson **Father of Indian Railways**
Robert Franklin Stroud **Birdman of Alcatraz**

Charles Edward Stuart **Bonnie Prince Charlie, Young Pretender, Young Chevalier**
James Edward Stuart **Old Pretender, Old Chevalier**
Louis Sullivan (architect) **Father of Modernism**
Peter Sutcliffe **Yorkshire Ripper**
Thomas Tallis **Father of English Church Music**
James T Tanner **Father of Musical Comedy**
David Taylor (snooker player) **Silver Fox**
John Taylor **Water Poet**
Edward Teach **Blackbeard**
Norman Tebbit **Chingford Skinhead**
Temujin **Genghis Khan**
Alfred Lord Tennyson **Merlin**
Margaret Thatcher **Iron Lady, The Milk Snatcher, Attila the Hen**
Cliff Thorburn (snooker player) **Grinder**
William Tilden **Big Bill**
Timon (Athenian nobleman) **Misanthrope of Athens**
Thomas Tompion **Father of English Clockmaking**
Mel Tormé **Velvet Fog**
Charles Townshend **Turnip**
Hugh Montague Trenchard **Father of the RAF**
Lee Trevino **Super-Mex**
Richard Trevilthick **Father of the Locomotive**
Freddie Trueman **Fiery Fred**
Lyman Trumbell **Father of the 13th Amendment**
Sophie Tucker **Last of the Red Hot Mamas**
JMW Turner **Admiral Pugsy Booth, Blackbirdy**
Lana Turner **Sweater Girl**
William Turner (Dean of Wells) **Father of English Botany**
Christopher Tye **Father of the Anthem**
Frank Tyson (cricketer) **Typhoon**
Mike Tyson **Catskill Thunder**
Uganda **Pearl of Africa**
US Defense Dept **Foggy Bottom**
Rudolph Valentino **Pink Powder Puff**
Rudy Vallee **Vagabond Lover**
Venerable Bede **Father of English History**
Queen Victoria **Widow of Windsor**
Horace Walpole **Autocrat of Strawberry Hill**
Rosalind P Walter **Rosie the Riveter**
Izaak Walton **Father of Angling**
George Washington **Father of his Country**
Isaac Watts **Father of English Hymnody**
James Watt **Father of Steam**
John Wayne **Duke**
Josiah Wedgwood **Father of English Pottery**
Duke of Wellington **Iron Duke, Old Nosey, Achilles of England**
Jimmy White **Whirlwind**
William White (US writer) **Sage of Emporia**
Ann Widdecombe **Doris Karloff**
Bishop Samuel Wilberforce **Soapy Sam**
William Willett **Father of Daylight Saving**
William I **Conqueror**
William I of Orange **Silent**
William II **Rufus**
William IV **Silly Billy**
Esther Williams **Hollywood's Mermaid**
Walter Winchell **Father of the Gossip Column**
Orde Wingate **Robin Hood**
Sir Henry Wood **Old Timber**
Harry Wragg (jockey) **The Head Waiter**
Philemon Wright **Father of Ottawa**
Francis Xavier **Apostle of the Indies**

Traditional Occupations and Hobbies

This list of definitions includes some now-defunct traditional occupations alongside hobbies, pastimes, and colloquial names for certain types of worker. It also lists some lesser-known meanings for familiar professions.

Actuary Person employed to assess risks for insurance companies, a statistician
Alderman Senior member of a local council (until 1974)
Ale conner Inspector of beer and bread
Almoner Hospital social worker
Amanuensis Secretary employed to take dictation or copy manuscripts
Artificer Serviceman trained in mechanics
Bhishti (bheesty) Formerly a water carrier, in India
Bibliophile Collector of books
Bibliopole Dealer in rare books
Boatswain/bosun Petty officer on a merchant ship or warrant officer on a warship, responsible for maintenance
Bowyer Person who makes or sells archery bows
Broderer Person who embroiders
Bumbailiff Formerly, an officer employed to collect debts and arrest non-payers
Bursar Official in charge of finance in educational institutions
Campanologist Bell ringer
Cartographer Person who draws maps
Cartomancer Person who tells fortunes by use of playing cards
Cartophilist Collector of cigarette cards
Cartwright Maker of carts
Chandler Maker or seller of candles; grocer
Charcutier Pork butcher
Cobbler Shoemaker
Colporteur Hawker of books, especially bibles
Conchologist Collector of shells
Cooper Maker of barrels
Cordwainer Shoemaker, leather worker
Costermonger Fruit and vegetable salesman (formerly an apple vendor)
Couturier Person who designs, makes and sells fashion clothes for women
Coxswain Helmsman of a boat
Curator Person in charge of a collection, e.g. in a museum or library
Currier Person who grooms horses or curries leather
Deltiologist Picture-postcard collector
Didactics The art or science of teaching
Draper Person who sells cloth and cloth goods
Ecdysiast Striptease artist
Equerry Formerly, an officer in the royal household responsible for the horses
Farrier Person who shoes horses
Fletcher Maker of arrows
Founder Maker of bells and castings
Franklin Substantial landowner of free but not noble birth (Middle Ages)
Fromologist Person who collects cheese labels
Funambulist Tightrope walker
Gatherer Glass blower, and formerly a bookbinder
Glazier Person who fits windows, doors etc, with glass
Goliard Wandering scholar of 12th and 13th centuries, famed for riotous behaviour
Gombeen man An Irish moneylender
Gricer Person who seeks out and photographs unusual trains
Groom Person employed to clean and generally look after horses
Haberdasher Seller of sewing articles, e.g. buttons, needles, zips and ribbons
Haberdasher (USA) Men's clothes outfitter
Hack Run of the mill journalist
Hard hat Construction worker
Horner Person who made objects such as spoons and combs out of horn
Hosier Person who sells stockings

Houseman Junior doctor who is a member of the medical staff attached to a hospital
Ikebanist Practitioner of the Japanese decorative art of flower arranging
Intern North American equivalent to a houseman; it is also a US term for a student teacher
Ironmonger Dealer in hardware, eg nuts, bolts and locks, etc
Jobber Dealer in stocks and shares
Joiner Person skilled in making finished woodwork, eg windows, doors and stairs
Kamikaze Japanese pilot who performed suicide missions in World War II
Lepidopterist Butterfly and moth collector
Locum tenens Person who deputises for another in the same profession
Longshoreman American equivalent of a docker or stevedore
Lorimer/loriner Person who makes bits, spurs and other small metal objects
Matador Principal bullfighter
Mercer Textile dealer
Milliner Person who makes or sells women's hats
Millwright Engineer who designs, builds or repairs grain mills or mill machinery
Modiste Fashionable dressmaker or milliner
Navvy Labourer on a building site
Notary public Solicitor licensed to prepare legal documents
Numismatist Collector of coins and medals
Obstetrician Physician who specialises in childbirth
Ocularist Person who makes artificial eyes
Optometrist Person qualified to examine the eyes and prescribe lenses; also called optician or ophthalmologist
Origamist Person who folds paper into ornate figures and decorations
Paediatrician Physician who specialises in children and their diseases
Paramedic Person such as a laboratory technician who supplements the work of the medical profession
Pedagogue A teacher or educator
Pedant Archaic term for a teacher
Philatelist Stamp collector
Phillumenist Person who collects matchbox labels
Picador In bullfighting or horseman who lances the bull in early stages in order to weaken it
Pilot Person qualified to steer or guide a ship into or out of port
Potholer Cave and underground passage explorer
Prestidigitator Magician, especially one skilled in close sleight of hand
Publican In Roman times, a tax collector
Purser On a ship or plane, officer who keeps the accounts and attends to passenger welfare
Quantity surveyor Person who estimates the cost of the materials and labour necessary for a construction job
Radiographer/radiologist Person who takes X-rays
Recorder Barrister or solicitor of at least ten years, standing appointed to sit as a judge in the Crown Court
Registrar Hospital doctor, senior to a houseman but junior to a consultant
Roughneck Worker in an oil-drilling operation
Saddler Person who makes saddles, harnesses and other leather equipment for horses
Sandhog North American term for person who works in underground or underwater construction projects
Scrivener Formerly, a person who wrote out legal documents, a notary
Sempstress/seamstress Woman who sews and makes clothes
Sensei Japanese teacher of martial and other arts
Sexton Church helper responsible for church upkeep
Shaman Medicine man or witch doctor
Shipwright Artisan skilled in shipbuilding
Spelunker Cave explorer
Spodomancer Person who makes prophecies by divination of ashes
Stationer Person who sells stationery; formerly a publisher or bookseller
Steeplejack Person skilled in construction and felling of steeples, spires, chimneys and towers
Stenographer North American name for a shorthand typist
Stevedore Person employed to load or unload a ship
Stoker Person employed to tend a furnace, as on a steamship
Subaltern Army officer below the rank of captain, usually a second lieutenant
Tanner Person who tans skins and hides into leather
Timbrologist Stamp collector
Topiarist Person who shapes hedges into ornate shapes
Toreador Rank-and-file bullfighter
Turner Lathe operator
Upholsterer Person who upholsters furniture
Vexillologist Person who studies and collects information about flags
Vintner Wine merchant
Vulcanologist Person who studies volcanoes
Wainwright Maker of wagons, wains and carts
Wheelwright/wheeler Maker of wheels

Philosophers and Political Thinkers

Thales (c624–c545 BC) Greek natural philosopher and astronomer, born in Miletus, traditionally seen as the founder of European philosophy. Thales identified water as the basis of the universe and also predicted the solar eclipse that took place in 585 BC. He was included in the traditional canon of 'Seven Wise Men' and allegedly once fell into a well whilst looking at the stars.
Anaximander (c611–546 BC) Greek natural philosopher and astronomer, born in Miletus, and possibly a pupil of Thales. Anaximander is credited with producing the first maps. He was the second of the three great Milesian thinkers (the third was Anaximenes).
Pythagoras (c580– c500 BC) Greek philosopher and mathematician, born in Samos, Ionia. He established his ethico-political academy at Croton (now Crotona) in southern Italy. Famous for his theorem concerning properties of right-angled triangles.
Heraclitus (554–483 BC) Greek philosopher, born in Ephesus and nicknamed at various times 'the obscure' and 'the riddler'. Most famous doctrine is that everything is in a state of flux and that fire is the ultimate constituent of the world.
Confucius (551–479 BC) Chinese philosopher, born in what is now Shantung province. His birthday is celebrated on 28 September and is an official holiday in Taiwan ('Teacher's Day'). Although Confucius was not greatly revered in his lifetime, Confucianism, as expressed in his *Analects*, subsequently dominated Chinese life as both a religious and philosophical way of life.
Parmenides of Elea (510–483 BC) Greek philosopher from southern Italy and founder of the Eleatic school, which included his pupils Zeno and Melissus. His great work *On Nature* was written in hexameter verse.
Empedocles (c490–c430 BC) Greek philosopher, poet, statesman, religious teacher and physiologist, born in Acragas in Sicily. Held that the world is composed of 4 elements – air, fire, earth and water – governed by the opposing forces of love and discord. Heralded by his followers as a god, he allegedly died by leaping into the volcanic crater of Mount Etna whilst attempting to prove his divinity.
Socrates (469–399 BC) Athenian philosopher, held in such esteem that all earlier Greek philosophy is known as pre-Socratic. Little is known about him other than that he had an apparently shrewish wife, Xanthippe, and took part in military campaigns at Potidaea, Delium and Amphipolis. Socrates wrote nothing but was eulogised in the 'Dialogues' of his pupil, Plato. Socrates' approach was to question everything. He chose to pick holes in the deliberations of others and asked people to think for themselves. He was eventually charged with 'Impiety' and 'Corrupting the youth of Athens' and forced to die by drinking hemlock.
Democritus (c460–c370 BC) Greek philosopher, born in Abdera in Thrace and known as the 'laughing philosopher' because of his wry amusement at human foibles. A prolific writer, he is best known for the atomistic theory he developed from Leucippus.

Plato (c428–348 BC) Athenian philosopher who related the story of Socrates' trial in three of his *Dialogues*: the *Apology*, the *Crito* and the *Phaedo*. In c387 BC he founded the Academy, which became a famous establishment for philosophical, mathematical and scientific research. His writings comprise around 30 dialogues and a series of letters (only the 7th and 8th likely to be genuine). The dialogue *Symposium* is an allegory of the search for love, and the *Republic* an allegory of the search for justice. Plato was the teacher of Aristotle.

Aristotle (384–322 BC) Greek philosopher and scientist, born in Stagira, son of the court physician to the King of Macedon. Aristotle is one of the two most important philosophers of the ancient world, and one of the four or five most important of any time or place. For twenty years he was a member of Plato's Academy. When Plato died, Speusippus became head of the academy and Aristotle left Athens and became tutor to Alexander the Great (then aged 13). He returned to Athens in 335 BC and founded his 'Lyceum', so called from its proximity to the temple of Apollo Lyceius. The 'Aristotelian corpus' (1,462 pages of Greek text, including some spurious works) is probably derived from the lectures he gave in the Lyceum. Aristotle's followers became known as peripatetics (from his habit of walking around whilst lecturing). There is no doubt that many of the sub-categories of modern philosophy were formulated by Aristotle. Some areas in which Aristotle made a fundamental contribution in the expansion of philosophy as a science include logic, the study of nature, metaphysics, philosophy of mind, ethics and politics, and literary criticism and rhetorical theory. His works include the *Nicomachean Ethics, De Anima, Politics, Poetics, Metaphysics*, and the *Organon* (treatises on logic).

Epicurus (341–270 BC) Greek philosopher, born in Samos. His ethical philosophy was based on simple pleasures, friendship, and reflection. When Epicurus came to Athens in 306 BC he bought a house and established a school in the garden which became known as Ho Kepos (The Garden), where men and women of any background could attend. Like many of his predecessors he wrote treatises 'On Nature' but his best works were his ethical and theological dialogues, which made him a revered figure long after his death.

Lucretius (c99–55 BC) Roman philosopher and poet whose great works are his hexameter poem *De rerum natura* and his treatises attempting to separate philosophy from religion, which he denounced as the one great source of man's wickedness and misery. He was said to have died mad from the effects of a love potion administered by his wife, Lucilia.

Plotinus (c205–70) Born in Egypt of Roman parentage. His prolific writings were posthumously edited and arranged by his pupil, Porphyry, into six 'groups of nine books' or *Enneads*. These established the foundations of Neoplatonism, which combined Platonic with Pythagorean, Aristotelian and Stoic doctrines.

St Augustine of Hippo (354–430) Born in Tagaste in Numidia (modern Tunisia) of Roman descent, he was converted to Christianity in 386 and described his conversion in his most famous work *Confessions*. His other masterpiece was *The City of God*.

Roger Bacon (c1214–92) English philosopher and scientist, probably born near Ilchester, Somerset. His soubriquet 'Doctor Mirabilis' was gained because of his learning in magic and alchemy and he was the first European to describe the process for making gunpowder. Bacon held radical philosophical views and was imprisoned by Franciscans for some time because of his suspected heretical teachings.

St Thomas Aquinas (c1225–74) Italian Dominican philosopher and theologian, born in the castle of Roccasecca, near Aquino, Sicily. His early education was at the monastery of Monte Cassino and then the University of Naples. He was a pupil of the Dominican scholar, Albertus Magnus, at the University of Paris and from 1256 began teaching there himself. In 1259 he was appointed theological adviser to the papal Curia. His two major works are *Summa theologica* and *Summa contra gentiles*. Thomas was known as 'Doctor Angelicus' and canonised a saint in 1323 by Pope John XXII. Thomism was the standard teaching of the Dominican order.

John Duns Scotus (c1265–1308) Scottish scholastic philiosopher who became a Franciscan and was ordained a priest in St Andrew's Church, Northampton in 1291. He taught at Cologne, where he died and was buried. Duns Scotus was known by contemporaries as 'Doctor Subtilis' because of his extremely nuanced and technical resoning, but in the Renaissance the Scotists were dubbed 'Dunses' (hence the word 'dunce'). His important works include the *Opus Pariense* (Parisian Lectures), *Opus Oxiense* (Oxford Lectures, also known as the *Ordinatio*), *Tractatus de Primo Principio* and *Quaestiones Quodlibetales*.

William of Ockham (c1285–c1349) Philosopher, theologian and political writer, born in Ockham, Surrey. William entered the Franciscan order after studying theology at Oxford, although he failed to graduate, hence his nickname 'the Venerable Inceptor'. He was excommunicated by John XXII and fled to Bavaria where he died of the Black Death. His works greatly upset the papacy and included *Summa Logicae, Quodlibeta Septem* and commentaries on the sentences of Peter Lombard and Aristotle. His greatest philosophical contribution is 'Ockham's razor' or the 'Law of Parsimony', which states that entities are not to be multiplied beyond necessity. The principle was invoked previously by Durand de Saint-Pourçain but Ockham's frequent and sharp employment of the doctrine ensured that his name would be identified with the principle.

Nicholas of Cusa (1401–64) German philosopher, scientist and churchman, born in Cues, Trier. He studied at Heidelberg and Padua, was ordained in 1430 and subsequently became a papal diplomat and Cardinal. Nicholas stressed the incomplete nature of man's knowledge of God and the universe. His main philosophical work is *De Docta Ignorantia* (1440) but he was the precursor of Copernicus as regards his non-geocentric theories.

Niccolò Machiavelli (1469–1527) Italian political philosopher, statesman and writer, born in Florence. He rose to prominence after the demise of Savonarola's regime in 1498. He had a controversial career and was in and out of favour dependent on the political climate. His masterpiece, *The Prince*, was dedicated to Lorenzo de Medici and published 1532. This work epitomised his ethic of evil sometimes being necessary in order for good to prevail. Other works include *The Art of War*, and *Mandragola*, a comic play about seduction, as well as a discourse on Livy. He is buried in Santa Croce, Florence.

Giordano Bruno (1548–1600) Italian philosopher, born in Nola, nr Naples. Became a Dominican but came into conflict with the Inquisition due to his championing of Copernicus' heliocentricity theory, and his pantheistic views. He was eventually burned at the stake in Rome.

Sir Francis Bacon (1561–1626) English philosopher and statesman who became Viscount St Albans. He was a leading proponent of Empiricism and rejected Aristotelian deductive logic. His works include *The Advancement of Learning, Novum Organum* and *The New Atlantis*. Bacon was also a leading parliamentarian and his methodical and logical approach was not trusted by his uncle, Lord Burghley. An example of his political expediency was to try to convict his former friend, the Earl of Essex. He apparently died from hypothermia caused while carrying out food preservation experiments on chickens.

Thomas Hobbes (1588–1679) English political philosopher, born in Malmesbury (apparently prematurely, after his mother heard news of the approaching Spanish Armada). His first published work was a translation of Thucydides' *History* (1629); other works include *Elements of Law Natural and Politic* and his masterpiece *Leviathan* (1651), in which he argues that absolutist government is needed to ensure law and order. His later works, published in Holland, include *Behemoth: a History of the causes of the Civil Wars of England*.

René Descartes (1596–1650) French philosopher and mathematician, born near Tours in a town renamed Descartes in his honour. He is often called the father of modern philosophy. Descartes was in Germany with the army of the Duke of Bavaria when, on 10 November 1619 he had a visionary dream in a stove-heated room, which revealed a scientific postulate that would link all possible human knowledge together into an all-embracing wisdom. Most of his major works were published shortly after the death of his illegitimate daughter, Francine, in 1640, the most famous being the *Discourse on Method* which framed the basis for Cartesian philosophy, the phrase '*Cogito ergo sum*' (I think therefore I am) encapsulating his rational methodology. He died of pneumonia and his last words were supposedly 'So my soul a time for parting'. He was buried in Stockholm but was later moved to Saint-Germain-des-Prés, Paris.

Baruch Spinoza (1632–77) Dutch philosopher, born in Amsterdam. He was expelled from his Jewish community for heresy in 1656 and made a living grinding and polishing lenses (the glass dust was to cause his untimely death from consumption). His *Principia Philosophiae* was the only book published in his lifetime with his name on it. His main work, *Ethics*, was published posthumously. Spinoza is also known for his contributions to the development of an historical approach to the Bible.

John Locke (1632–74) English empiricist philosopher, born in Wrington, Somerset. Locke's *Essay Concerning Human Understanding* was the basis for the resurgence of Empiricism as an alternative to Cartesianism. He believed the mind at birth was a *tabula rasa*, as opposed to the Cartesian view that knowledge is derived from first principles.

Gottfried Wilhelm von Leibniz (1646–1716) German philosopher and mathematician, born in Leipzig. His optimism and faith in enlightenment and reason was satirised by Voltaire in *Candide* ('all is for the best in the best of all possible worlds'). His most famous work is the *Monadology*, in which he argues that the world is made up of an infinite number of units (monads), the highest of which is God. Apart from his philosophical essays, Leibniz also invented differential calculus, although the Royal Society formally declared Newton as its inventor in 1711 (nowadays both are credited).

Giovanni Vico (1668–1744) Italian philosopher, born in Naples. His major work, *Scienza Nuova* (The New Science), is concerned with the differences between scientific and historical explanation.

George Berkeley (1685–1753) Irish Anglican bishop and philosopher, born at Dysert Castle, Kilkenny. Bishop Berkeley was Dean of Derry and then Bishop of Cloyne; in between he tried to establish a college in the Bermudas but only got as far as Rhode Island. His celebrated claim that 'to be is to be perceived', whereby the contents of the material world are 'ideas' that only exist when they are perceived by a mind, is set out in his *Essay Towards a New Theory of Vision* and *A Treatise Concerning the Principles of Human Knowledge*. His other major work is *Three Dialogues Between Hylas and Philanous*.

David Hume (1711–76) Scottish philosopher and historian, born in Edinburgh. Hume's life was dogged in its early stages with fits of depression which he came to terms with whilst tutoring the insane nobleman, the Marquis of Annandale. His major works, *A Treatise of Human Nature* and *Dialogues Concerning Natural Religion* had a profound effect on Immanuel Kant and provoked the Idealists to counter Hume's scepticism. Hume was a friend of Rousseau but became embroiled in a famously bitter quarrel with him.

Jean-Jacques Rousseau (1712–78) French political philosopher, born in Geneva (his mother died in childbirth). He worked as a secretary and music copier in his early life. After a brief affair with Mme Louise de Warens he formed a lifelong liaison with Thérèse le Vasseur, with whom he had five children and eventually married in 1768. In 1762 he published his masterpiece *The Social Contract* which begins, 'Man is born free; and everywhere he is in chains.' His text, with its slogan 'Liberty, Equality, Fraternity', became the Bible of the French Revolution. At the invitation of David Hume, he lived at Wootton Hall near Ashbourne in Derbyshire. Here he began his *Confessions* but became increasingly paranoiac and returned to Paris where he completed the work. He became seriously insane and died in Ermenonville. His remains were placed alongside Voltaire's in the Panthéon in Paris.

Denis Diderot (1713–84) French philosopher and man of letters, born in Langres in Champagne, the son of a master cutler. He was a precursor of the Romanticists and was patronised by Catherine II, (the Great) of Russia. In 1743 he married Antoinette Champion, daughter of a linendraper, although his father disapproved. Diderot set out a philosophy of the arts and sciences which took the progress of civilisation to be a measure of mankind's moral improvement and perceived the Christian religion as morally harmful. From 1745 to 1772 Diderot served as chief editor of the *Encyclopédie*, one of the principal works of the Age of Enlightenment.

Immanuel Kant (1724–1804) German philosopher, born in Königsberg in Prussia (now Kaliningrad), the son of a saddler. He taught at the university and was known for his ordered way of life (locals allegedly set their watches by the time of his daily walks). Kant was a keen astronomer who predicted the existence of the planet Uranus before Herschel's discovery in 1781. Kant's most famous works, such as *Critique of Pure Reason* (1781), *Critique of Practical Reason* (1788) and *Critique of Judgement* (1790) were all pubished late in his life. Kant described his philosophy as 'transcendental' or 'critical' idealism.

Edmund Burke (1729–97) Irish philosopher and statesman, born in Dublin, and educated at a Quaker school and Trinity College. Burke's *Thoughts on the Present Discontents* and *Reflections on the French Revolution* were his masterpieces. Although a Whig all his life, Burke's political thought became, with Disraeli's, the philosophy of modern Conservatism.

Thomas Paine (1737–1809) Revolutionary philosopher and writer, born in Thetford, Norfolk, the son of a Quaker. He followed his father's trade as a corset maker before becoming, firstly a sailor, then a schoolmaster and ultimately an exciseman. It was during this period that he first showed his tendency to speak out against what he felt were injustices and was dismissed for disturbing the status quo by deriding the lack of pay increases. Benjamin Franklin helped him emigrate to America, where he settled in Philadelphia and became a radical journalist. He published a pamphlet *Common Sense* following the outbreak of the American Revolutionary War urging an immediate declaration of independence. He returned to England, after visiting France, and published *The Rights of Man* (1792) a reply to Burke's *Reflections on the French Revolution*. He was indicted for treason but fled to France whereupon he fell foul of Robespierre and was imprisoned but later freed on the grounds of his US citizenship (1795). His book *The Age of Reason* (1796) mostly written in prison, upset many of his American friends, including George Washington. He died alone and in poverty on his farm in New Rochelle, New York.

Jeremy Bentham (1748–1832) London-born philosopher, jurist and social reformer, best known as a proponent of Utilitarianism, as seen in his pioneering works *A Fragment on Government* (1776) and *Introduction to the Principles of Morals and Legislation* (1789), in which he argues that the proper objective of all conduct and legislation is 'the greatest happiness of the greatest number'. He developed 'hedonic calculus' to estimate the effects of different actions. Bentham became an honorary French citizen in 1792 and published treatises on social and penal reform. He also planned a special prison (Panopticon) and school (Chrestomathia), helped start the *Westminster Review* (1823) and founded University College, where his clothed skeleton is preserved.

Johann Fichte (1762–1814) German philosopher, born in Rammenau, Saxony, the son of a ribbon weaver. In 1793 Fichte married Johanna Maria Rahn and in the same year published two anonymous works, the most important being *Contribution to the Correction of the Public's Judgments Regarding the French Revolution*. He developed Kant's critical philosophy into a system of his own, which he named 'Theory of Science' (*Wissenschaftslehre*).

Georg Hegel (1770–1831) German Idealist philosopher, born in Stuttgart. After studying theology he became a lecturer at Jena but Napoleon's victory there in 1806 interrupted his career. Hegel worked temporarily as a newspaper editor at Bamberg and then headmaster of the gymnasium at Nuremberg. Hegel's first great work was *The Phenomenology of Mind* (1807), which describes the human mind's progression from mere consciousness through self-consciousness, reason, spirit and religion, to absolute knowledge. His second great work was *The Science of Logic* which gained him the chair at Heidelberg in 1816. Hegel's dialectic method of reasoning involved a sequence of thesis, antithesis and synthesis, and his doctrines influenced Karl Marx and contributed to the development of 'Modern Totalitarianism'. In 1818 he succeeded Fichte as professor in Berlin and remained there until his death from cholera.

Charles Fourier (1772–1837) French philosopher and social theorist, born in Besançon. He published a number of utopian socialist works including *The Social Destiny of Man; or, Theory of the Four Movements* (1857). Fourier argued for the existence of a natural social order corresponding to Newton's ordering of the physical universe, claiming that both evolved in eight ascending periods. In Harmony, the highest stage, human emotions would be freely expressed. Fournier declared that this stage could be attained by dividing society into phalanges, each comprising a commune approximately 1,800 people within which all property would be collectively owned. His other works include *Treatise on Domestic Agricultural Association* and *The New Industrial World*.

Friedrich Schelling (1775–1854) German idealist philosopher, born in Leonberg in Württemberg. His early work was influenced by Kant and Fichte, and included *On the Possibility and Form of Philosophy in General* and *Of the Ego as Principle of Philosophy* in which he discusses the theological concept of the 'Absolute'. Schelling's major work *System of Transcendental Idealism* was an attempt to unite his concept of nature having a spiritual separateness from man, with Fichte's philosophy that nature is merely a tool of man. Schelling spent time in Jena, where he replaced Fichte in his teaching post, and in 1803, married Caroline Schlegel, a leading German Romanticist. A disagreement with Hegel concerning the dispute with Fichte caused him to retreat to Munich. After the death of Caroline, he married her friend, Pauline Gotter.

Arthur Schopenhauer (1788–1860) German philosopher, born in Danzig, whose metaphysical doctrines of the will were in contrast to Hegelian idealism. He was strongly influenced firstly by Plato, and then by Immanuel Kant, and also became friendly with the playwright and poet Goethe, who invited his assistance with some problems concerning his 'Farbenlehre' (theory of colours). After finishing *On Vision and Colours*, Schopenhauer began his masterpiece, *The World as Will and Idea*, which expounds his pessimismistic and atheistic views. The premise being that man's nature as willing beings inevitably leads to suffering and such a life is worse than non-existence.

Auguste Comte (1798–1857) French philosopher and social theorist, born in Montpellier, and usually considered the founder of modern sociology and Positivism. Comte was nicknamed the 'Thinker' and was rebellious by nature. He was the first thinker to advocate the use of scientific procedures in the study of economics and politics. In a typical non conformist act he married a prostitute, Caroline Massin, in 1821. He then became increasingly depressed and mentally disturbed culminating in a suicide attempt in the Seine which seemed to bring him to his senses. His wife, however, resorted to her previous occupation and Comte formed an alliance with Clotilde de Vaux which lasted for two years until her death in 1846. Comte's major work was *The Positive Philosophy of Auguste Comte*, which became the bible for students of Positivism.

John Stuart Mill (1806–73) English philosopher and social reformer, born in London, the son of Scottish philosopher James Mill. He began publishing in *The Traveller* in 1822 and helped form the Utilitarian Society, which met in Jeremy Bentham's house, and he ultimately modified some of Bentham's doctrines. As with many philosophers, both before and after, Mill endured a phase of severe depression but in 1830 met and eventually married the bluestocking, Harriet Taylor, who influenced his future works. Mill's works include *System of Logic, On Liberty, Principles of Political Economy, Utilitarianism*, as well as a celebrated autobiography.

Søren Kierkegaard (1813–55) Danish philosopher, born in Copenhagen, the son of a Jewish merchant. Kierkegaard is considered the founder of Existentialism. His most famous work is probably *Either-Or*, in which he opposes Hegel by arguing the importance of individual choice. He was a convert to Christianity, although he fought against the formal structure of religion and believed that God and some special disciples were above moral laws as we know them. His other works include *The Concept of Irony, Christian Discourses, Fear of Trembling*, and *The Sickness Unto Death*.

Karl Marx (1818–1883) German social, political and economic theorist, born in Trier. His Jewish parents converted to Protestantism out of political expediency. Marx became the inspiration for international Communism. He studied at Bonn and then Berlin University, where he met the 'young Hegelians' who were chiefly concerned with the critique of religion. His doctoral dissertation was on 'The Difference between the Philosophies of Nature in Democritus and Epicurus'. Marx worked firstly as a journalist and then editor of the liberal Cologne paper *Rheinische Zeitung* but after the paper was suppressed by the government, Marx emigrated to Paris and became a communist. It was here that he first stated his belief that the proletariat must itself be the agent of revolutionary change in society, and wrote his first critique of capitalism, 'Economic and Philosophical Manuscripts of 1844' (not published until 1932). Marx had by now become friendly with Friedrich Engels and under political pressure they moved to Brussels, where they wrote *German Ideology* and the famous *Communist Manifesto* (1848) which ends with the Communist rallying cry: 'The workers have nothing to lose but their chains. They have a world to win. Workers of all lands, unite!' Marx moved to London in 1849 and wrote the first volume of his most famous work, *Das Kapital*, in 1867 (future volumes followed in 1884 and 1894) where he forecast the classless society. Marx is buried in Highgate cemetery, London.

Wilhelm Dilthey (1833–1911) German philosopher, born in Biebrich, Hesse. His central theme was the radical distinction between the natural sciences (*Naturwissenshaften*) and human sciences (*Geisteswissenschaften*). He also developed a theory of hermeneutics for the interpretation of historical texts and wrote biographies of Hegel, Lessing, Schleiermacher, and Goethe.

Friedrich Wilhelm Nietzsche (1844–1900) German philosopher, scholar and writer, born in Röcken, Saxony, son of a Lutheran pastor. He was seen by Nazi ideologists as a precursor of Nazism due to his doctrine of the superman (*Übermensch*) expounded in *Thus Spake Zarathustra* and *Beyond Good and Evil*. Nietzsche rejected Christianity by arguing that 'God is Dead'. His first work was *The Birth of Tragedy*, which compared Dionysian and Apollonian values, and was dedicated to Richard Wagner, whose operas he regarded as the true successors to Greek tragedy. Other works include *On the Genealogy of Morals, Beyond Good and Evil, Untimely Meditations* and his autobiography *Ecce Homo* (published posthumously in 1908).

Henri Bergson (1859–1941) French philosopher, born in Paris, son of a Polish Jewish musician and an English mother. Bergson claimed that time (which he calls duration), cannot be analysed as a set of moments, but is unitary. He claimed the same distribution between movement and the trajectory it covers. This became known as 'process philosophy'. He won the Nobel Prize for Literature in 1927. His major works include *Time and Freewill, Matter and Memory* and *Creative Evolution*.

Edmund Husserl (1859–1938) German philosopher, born in Prossnitz in the Austrian empire, of Jewish parentage. He studied mathematics at Berlin and psychology at Vienna, under Franz Brentano, a leading Aristotelian scholar. Husserl taught at Halle, Göttingen and Freiburg. He was the founder of the philosophical school of phenomenology which gave rise to Gestalt psychology. Works include *On the Goals and Problems of Metaphysics, Logical Investigations* (in which Husserl employed his Phenomenological methods) and *Ideas: General Introduction to Pure Phenomenology*.

Nishida Kitarō (1870–1945) Japanese philosopher, born near Kanazawa, Ishikawa, son of a school teacher. Nishida is considered Japan's first original modern philosopher and his work typifies Japanese attempts to absorb Western philosophy into the oriental spiritual tradition. His memoirs were entitled *A Certain Professor's Statement upon Retirement from Kyoto Imperial University, December 1928*.

Bertrand Russell (1872–1970) Philosopher, mathematician and author, born in Trelleck, Gwent, and brought up by his grandmother (the widow of the Liberal PM) following the death of both his parents in his youth. Russell was educated at Trinity College, Cambridge and became British Embassy attaché in Paris. He married Alys Pearsall Smith in 1895 and wrote his first book, *German Social Democracy*, soon after. Russell's first major philosophical work was *The Problems of Philosophy* (1912), which is often heralded as the perfect introduction for students of the subject. His pacifism caused the loss of his Trinity fellowship in 1916 and his imprisonment in 1918, after which he visited the Soviet Union and met Lenin, Trotsky and Gorky. He subsequently wrote *Theory and Practice of Bolshevism*. Russell's philosophy was now based on the premise that scientific knowledge was the only factual knowledge. His other major philosophical work was *A History of Western Philosophy*. Russell was also the co-author (with AN Whitehead) of *Principia Mathematica*.

Otto Neurath (1882–1945) Austrian socialist philosopher, economist and historian. Neurath was famous for creating the Isotype language for visual education. He was a founder member of the Vienna Circle.

György Lukács (1885–1971) Hungarian Marxist philosopher and critic, born in Budapest, of a wealthy Jewish family. Early works include *Soul and Form*, and *Theory of the Novel*. He joined the Hungarian Communist Party in 1918 but after the defeat of the uprising in 1919 travelled to Vienna and then Moscow. His major work on Marxism, *History and Class Consciousness* (1923), was condemned by the Russian Communist party as heretical.

Ludwig Wittgenstein (1889–1951) Austrian-born British philosopher, born in Vienna, son of an industrialist. Wittgenstein studied mechanical engineering at Berlin but became increasingly interested in mathematics and went to Cambridge to study under Bertrand Russell. He served in the Austrian army in WWI and was captured and held as a POW near Monte Cassino. Here he wrote *Tractatus Logico Philosophicus*, which expounded his 'picture theory' and the nature and limits of language whereby the deep truths of the nature of reality and representation cannot properly be said but can only be shown. Wittgenstein became a naturalised British citizen in 1938 and spent much of his time in Cambridge, although he worked as a porter in Guy's Hospital during World War II. Wittgenstein is undoubtedly one of the pre-eminent philosophers of the twentieth century.

Martin Heidegger (1889–1976) German philosopher, born in Messkirch in Baden, son of a Catholic sexton. He was appointed rector at Freiburg in 1933 and pledged support for Hitler in his inaugural address. His writings concern the predicament of human existence, the search for 'authenticity' and the distractions of Angst (anxiety). His major work, *Being and Time* (1927), although considered a masterpiece, is often misunderstood in philosophical circles due to its complexity. The essence of the work as a description of a fundamental ontology where he names the human entity 'Dasein' (the being) and argues that Dasein's own being is intrinsically temporal in an existential sense.

Rudolf Carnap (1891–1970) German-born US philosopher of Logical Positivism. He was a prominent member of the Vienna Circle and made significant contributions to logic, the philosophy of science, model theory and probability. He was viewed as an 'enfant terrible' in his early career but became one of the most respected philosophers of C20. Carnap was a great advocate of international languages.

Hans-Georg Gadamer (1900–2002) German philosopher, born in Marburg, Hesse. A pupil of Heidegger, his major work, *Truth and Method*, expounds his hermeneutic beliefs.

Karl Raimund Popper (1902–1994) Austrian-born British philosopher. Popper's greatest contributions are in philosophy of sciences and in political and social philosophy. His 'falsificationism' reverses the usual view that accumulated experience leads to scientific hypotheses. He was a member of the Vienna Circle.

Jean-Paul Sartre (1905–80) French philosopher, dramatist and novelist, born in Paris. He studied at the Sorbonne with Simone de Beauvoir, with whom he had a lifelong relationship. He taught philosophy at Le Havre, Paris and Berlin but joined the French army in 1939 and became a POW in 1941. On his release he became a key member of the French Resistance. In 1946, Sartre and De Beauvoir founded the avant-garde monthly *Les Temps Modernes* and Sartre began to develop his Existentialist doctrines. He declined the 1964 Nobel Prize for Literature and campaigned against American involvement in Vietnam. Sartre's major works were *Being and Nothingness* and his semi-autobiographical work *Nausea*, and a later more detailed autobiography, *Words* (*Les Mots*).

Maurice Merleau-Ponty (1908–61) French philosopher, born in Rochefort-sur-Mer, Charente-Maritime. Helped Sartre and De Beauvoir found *Les Temps Modernes* in 1945 but his philosophy was more akin to that of the German phenomenonologists Husserl and Heidegger. His major work was *The Phenomenology of Perception*.

Willard Quine (1908–2000) American philosopher, born in Akron, Ohio. He was professor of philosophy at Harvard from 1948 to 1978 and was much influenced by Carnap, the Vienna Circle and Empiricism. His major works include *Two Dogmas of Empiricism*, *Word and Object* and *The Roots of Reference*.

Sir Alfred Jules Ayer (1910–89) English philosopher, born in London. Ayer was educated at Eton and Oxford and served in the Welsh Guards in World War II before becoming a professor at University College London in 1947 and professor at Oxford in 1947. His major work, which was also his first, was *Language, Truth & Logic* (1936), which reflected the views of the Vienna Circle and established him a the leading English representative of logical positivism. It was dubbed 'The Young Man's book'. Ayer was knighted in 1970. His other major work was *The Problem of Knowledge*.

Albert Camus (1913–60) French writer, born in Mondovi, Algeria, son of a farm labourer. After studying philosophy at Algiers, Camus became an actor, schoolmaster, playwright and journalist before World War II, and subsequently became a French Resistance activist. He then became co-editor of the left-wing newspaper *Combat* and wrote his Existentialist novel *The Stranger*, and became identified with 'the absurd'. His other great work was *The Plague*, in which a plague-stricken city, Oran, symbolises man's isolation. He was awarded the 1957 Nobel Prize for Literature for having 'illuminated the problems of the human conscience in our times.' He died in a car accident.

Michel Foucault (1926–84) French philosopher, born in Poitiers. Foucault argued that social attitudes are manipulated by those in power, so that areas such as criminality, illness, sexuality and insanity have changing levels of acceptability dependent on the aims of those in positions of influence. His major works are *Madness and Civilization*, *The Order of Things*, and *The History of Sexuality*.

An Explanation of Some Philosophical Terms

Dialectics	The philosophy of metaphysical contradictions and their solutions.
Empiricism	The belief that all knowledge derives from experience and that the mind cannot postulate in advance.
Existentialism	Modern philosophical movement that stresses the importance of personal experience and responsibility and the demands that they make on the individual, who is seen as a free agent in a deterministic and seemingly meaningless universe. Although Jean-Paul Sartre is often accredited as being the first person to name himself an existentialist, the works of Søren Kiekegaard have retrospectively been attributed as existential.
Hermeneutics	The art of interpretation of human behaviour and social institutions. Originally the theory and method of interpreting the Bible and other theological texts but Wilhelm Dilthey extended it to the interpretation of all human acts.
Marxism	Broad term covering many different philosophical doctrines but ultimately relating to the various schools of thought flourishing since the death of Karl Marx in 1883. Western Marxism usually includes those thinkers that were influenced by the Hegelian idea of dialectics and who focused on the cultural as opposed to the economic aspects of capitalism.
Metaphysics	The branch of philosophy concerning first principles, especially of being and knowing. It is the study of the nature of reality and deals with such questions as the existence of God and the external world.
Nihilism	Philosophy of negation, rejection, or denial of some or all aspects of thought or life. An example would be moral nihilism, whereby any possibility of justifying or criticising moral judgements is rejected because morality is a cloak for egoistic self-seeking and therefore a sham. Nihilism is an extreme form of scepticism.
Ontology	The branch of metaphysics that deals with the nature of being.
Pascal's Wager	The postulate that it is better to wager that God does exist rather than on his non-existence.
Phenomenology	Movement founded by Husserl that concentrates on the detailed description of conscious experience without recourse to explanation, metaphysical assumptions or traditional philosophical questions.
Positivism	Extreme form of empiricism that rejects metaphysics and theology as seeking knowledge beyond the scope of experience and holds that experimental investigation and observation are the only sources of knowledge.
Scepticism	The view that we fail to know anything and the rejection of the postulate that some term of positive epistemic appraisal applies to our beliefs.
Solipsism	The extreme form of scepticism which denies the possibility of any knowledge other than of one's own existence.
Sophist	Pre-Socratic itinerant teacher of oratory and argument who was prepared to debate any matter however specious.
Stoicism	Philosophical system founded by Zeno of Citium (334–262 BC) in Athens c300 BC, viewing the world as permeated by rationality and divine planning. Moral goodness and happiness are achieved by replicating a perfect rationality in oneself, and by enacting one's own assigned role in the cosmic scheme of things.
Thomism	The name derives from Thomas Aquinas and relates to a body of philosophical and theological ideas that seek to articulate the intellectual content of Catholic Christianity.
Totalitarianism	Term adopted in the 1920s by the Italian Giovanni Gentile to describe the ideal fascist state. Totalitarianism has attracted the attention of philosophers because a number of classical philosophical systems have been suspected of harbouring totalitarian aspirations.
Vienna Circle	Group of thinkers drawn from the social and natural sciences who met regularly in Vienna between the two world wars to discuss philosophy. Its manifesto was published in 1929 *The Scientific Conception of the World: The Vienna Circle* by Carnap, Hahn and Neurath. The inner sanctum of the group organised by the physics professor Moritz Schlick in 1924, included Carnap, Neurath, Philip Frank, Kurt Gödel, and Edgar Zilsel. The likes of Ludwig Wittgenstein and Karl Popper often joined discussion groups. The public profile of the circle was provided by the Ernst Mach Society, but in 1934 the society was suspended for political reasons, and in 1936 Moritz Schlick was murdered. The circle disintegrated when many of its members were forced to leave Austria for racial and political reasons.

FAMOUS PEOPLE

Real Names: By Assumed Name

NB: This is not intended to be a comprehensive listing of pseudonyms but a selection of some of the best-known and most intriguing examples. It is an area that is surrounded with much uncertainty and potential for error. Generally the 'Assumed Name' is the more familiar, but not always (for instance when authors adopt a pen-name for a particular kind of writing). For people who have acquired titles, the title is given as the 'Assumed Name', although in such cases the 'Original Name' is of course equally valid.

Assumed Name		*Original Name*		
Abbot	Russ	***Roberts***	Russ	*Comedian*
Aberdeen	Earl of	***Gordon***	George Hamilton	*British Prime Minister*
AE		***Russell***	George William	*Irish Poet*
Agnon	Shmuel Yosef	***Czaczkes***	Shmuel Josef	*Israeli Novelist*
Aimée	Anouk	***Sorya***	Françoise	*Actress*
Albert	Eddie	***Heimberger***	Eddie	*US Actor*
Alda	Alan	***D'Abruzzo***	Alfonso	*Actor*
Aldington	Richard	***Godfree***	Edward	*English Poet*
Ali	Muhammad	***Clay***	Cassius Marcellus	*Boxer*
Ali G	–	***Cohen***	Sacha Baron	*Comedian*
Alkan	Charles-Valentin	***Morhange***	Charles-Valentin	*French Musician*
Allen	Dave	***O'Mahoney***	Tynian	*Comedian*
Allen	Woody	***Konigsberg***	Allen	*Actor and Director*
Amazon		***Davies***	Sharron	*Swimmer and TV Gladiator*
Anderson	Bronco Billy	***Arenson***	Max	*Entertainer*
Andrews	Julie	***Wells***	Julia	*Actress and Singer*
Aneka		***Sandeman***	Mary	*Pop singer*
Angel	Destiny	***Pointon***	Juliette	*'Captain Scarlet' Character*
Angel	Harmony	***Kwan***	Chan	*'Captain Scarlet' Character*
Angel	Melody	***Jones***	Magnolia	*'Captain Scarlet' Character*
Angel	Rhapsody	***Sims***	Diane	*'Captain Scarlet' Character*
Angel	Symphony	***Wainwright***	Karen	*'Captain Scarlet' Character*
Angelico	Fra	***di Pietro***	Guido di	*Artist*
Angelou	Maya	***Johnson***	Marguerite	*Poetess*
Ant	Adam	***Goddard***	Stuart	*Singer*
Apollinaire	Guillaume	***de Kostrowitzky***	Wilhelm Apollinaris	*French Poet*
Appleseed	Johnny	***Chapman***	John	*Missionary Nurseryman*
Arden	Elizabeth	***Graham***	Florence Nightingale	*Beautician*
Arden	Eve	***Quedens***	Eunice	*Actress*
Arlen	Michael	***Kouyoumdjian***	Dikran	*British Novelist*
Arliss	George	***Andrews***	Augustus George	*Actor*
Arness	James	***Aurness***	James	*US Actor*
Arnold	Edward	***Schneider***	Guenther	*Actor*
Arras	Leon	***Glover***	Brian	*Professional Wrestler*
Arthur	Beatrice	***Frankel***	Bernice	*US Actress*
Arthur	Jean	***Greene***	Gladys	*Actress*
Astaire	Fred	***Austerlitz***	Frederick	*Dancer and Actor*
Astor	Mary	***Langemanke***	Lucille	*Actress*
Ataturk	Kemal	***Kemal***	Mustafa	*Turkish Statesman*
Atheling	William	***Pound***	Ezra Loomis	*Poet*
Atlas	Charles	***Siciliano***	Angelo	*Athlete*
Atticus		***Addison***	Joseph	*Essayist and Politician*
Avery	Tex	***Bean***	Frederick	*Cartoonist*
Aznavour	Charles	***Aznavurjal***	Shahnovr	*Singer and Actor*
Bacall	Lauren	***Perske***	Betty Joan	*Actress*
Badger (Le Blaireau)		***Hinault***	Bernard	*Cyclist*
Badly Drawn Boy	–	***Gough***	Damon	*Singer and Songwriter*
Baker	Janet	***Abbott***	Janet	*Mezzo-soprano*
Balanchine	George	***Balanchivadze***	Georgi Melitonivich	*Choreographer*
Bancroft	Anne	***Italiano***	Anna Maria	*Actress*
Bara	Theda	***Goodman***	Theodosia	*Actress*
Bardot	Brigitte	***Javal***	Camille	*Actress*
Baron	David	***Pinter***	Harold	*Actor*
Barrie	Amanda	***Broadbent***	Shirley Ann	*Actress*
Barry	Gene	***Klass***	Eugene	*US Actor*
Barry	John	***Prendergast***	John Barry	*Musician*
Barry	Michael	***Bukht***	Michael	*Food Journalist*
Barrymore	Ethel	***Blythe***	Ethel	*Actress*
Barrymore	John	***Blythe***	John	*Actor*
Barrymore	Lionel	***Blythe***	Lionel	*Actor*
Bart	Black	***Bottom***	Charles	*Outlaw*
Bart	Lionel	***Begleiter***	Lionel	*Composer*
Basie	Count	***Basie***	William	*Musician*
Bassano	Jacopo	***Da Ponte***	Giacomo	*Italian Painter*
Batgirl		***Wilson***	Barbara	*Comic and Film Heroine*
Batman		***Wayne***	Bruce	*Comic and Film Hero*
Beachcomber	John	***Morton***	Cameron	*Newspaper Columnist*
Beaky		***Dymond***	John	*Guitarist*
Beatty	Warren	***Beaty***	Warren	*Actor*

Bedelia	Bonnie	***Culkin***	Bonnie	*Actress*
Beefheart	Captain	***Van Vliet***	Don	*Musician*
Beeton	Mrs	***Mayson***	Isabella	*Cookery Writer*
Bell	Acton	***Brontë***	Anne	*Novelist*
Bell	Currer	***Brontë***	Charlotte	*Novelist*
Bell	Ellis	***Brontë***	Emily	*Novelist*
Belle de Jour		***Magnanti***	Brooke	*Author*
Benatar	Pat	***Andrzejewski***	Pat	*Rock Singer*
Benedict	Dirk	***Niewoehner***	Dirk	*US Actor*
Ben-Gurion	David	***Green***	David	*Israeli Statesman*
Bennett	Harve	***Fischman***	Harve	*US TV Producer*
Bennett	Lennie	***Berry***	Mike	*Comedian*
Bennett	Tony	***Benevetto***	Anthony Dominic	*Vocalist*
Benny	Jack	***Kubelsky***	Benjamin	*Comedian*
Ben's Brother		***Hartman***	Jamie	*Musician*
Benton	Brook	***Peay***	Benjamin Franklin	*Singer/Songwriter*
Berkeley	Busby	***Enos***	William	*Choreographer*
Berlin	Irving	***Baline***	Israel	*Composer*
Bernhardt	Sarah	***Bernard***	Rosine	*Actress*
Berra	Yogi	***Berra***	Lawrence Peter	*Baseball Player*
Bickerstaffe	Isaac	***Steele***	Richard	*Author (shared -pen-name)*
Bickerstaffe	Isaac	***Swift***	Jonathan	*Author (shared -pen-name)*
B.I.G.	Notorious	***Wallace***	Christopher	*Pop Singer*
Big Show		***Wight***	Paul	*Professional Wrestler*
Bill	Buffalo	***Cody***	William	*Showman*
Billy the kid		***McCarty***	Henry	*Outlaw*
Blaby	Lord Lawson of	***Lawson***	Nigel	*Politician*
Captain Black		***Turner***	Conrad	*'Captain Scarlet' Character*
Black	Cilla	***White***	Priscilla	*Singer and TV Presenter*
Blackbeard		***Teach***	Edward	*Pirate*
Blake	Nicholas	***Day-Lewis***	Cecil	*Detective Writer*
Blondin	Charles	***Gravelet***	Jean François	*French Acrobat*
Bloodvessel	Buster	***Trendle***	Doug	*Singer*
Blue	Captain	***Svenson***	Adam	*TV Fictional Character*
Bluebeard		***Landru***	Henri	*French Murderer*
Blunt	James	***Blount***	James	*Singer/Songwriter*
Bly	Nellie	***Cochrane***	Elizabeth	*Aviator*
Blyton	Enid	***Walters***	Mrs Daryl	*Author*
Bogarde	Dirk	***Van Den Bogaerde***	Derek	*Actor*
Boilermaker		***Jeffries***	James Jackson	*Boxing Champion*
Bolan	Marc	***Feld***	Marc	*Musician*
Bono		***Hewson***	Paul	*Musician*
Big Bopper		***Richardson***	Jiles Perry (JP)	*Musician*
Bonney	William	***McCarthy***	Henry	*Outlaw Billy the Kid*
Boots	Little	***Hesketh***	Victoria	*Singer*
Borge	Victor	***Rosenbaum***	Borge	*Comic and Musician*
Bosch	Hieronymus	***Van Aken***	Jerome	*Dutch Painter*
Botticelli	Sandro	***Filipepi***	Alessandro	*Artist*
Bowen	Jim	***Whittaker***	James	*Comedian*
Bowie	David	***Jones***	David	*Musician*
Boyd	Stephen	***Millar***	William	*Actor*
Boyle	Katie	***Francabilla***	Marchesa Caterina de	*TV Presenter*
Boz		***Dickens***	Charles	*Author (occasional pen-name)*
Bracket	Hilda	***Fyffe***	Patrick	*Entertainer*
Brains		***Hackenbacker***	Hiram J	*'Thunderbirds' Character*
Brandt	Willy	***Frahm***	Karl Herbert	*German Chancellor*
Breen	Billy	***White***	William	*Comedian*
Brett	Jeremy	***Huggins***	Peter Jeremy	*Actor*
Bridie	James	***Mavor***	Osborne Henry	*Dramatist*
Britt	May	***Wilkens***	Maybritt	*Actress*
Bronson	Charles	***Buchinski***	Charles	*Actor*
Bronzino	il	***Mariano***	Agnolo di Cosimo	*Painter*
Brook	Kelly	***Parsons***	Kelly Ann	*Actress and Model*
Brooks	Albert	***Einstein***	Albert	*Actor*
Brooks	Elkie	***Bookbinder***	Elaine	*Singer*
Brooks	Mel	***Kaminsky***	Melvin	*Actor and Director*
Brown Bomber		***Louis***	Joe	*Boxer*
Bruce	Lenny	***Schweider***	Alfred	*Comedian*
Bryan	Dora	***Broadbent***	Dora	*Actress and Comedienne*
Brynner	Yul	***Khan Jnr***	Taidje	*Actor*
Buddha		***Siddhartha***	Gautama	*Founder of Buddhism*
Buntline	Ned	***Judson***	Edward Zane	*Inventor*
Burgess	Anthony	***Wilson***	Anthony	*Writer*
Burke	Betty	***Stuart***	Charles Edward	*Bonnie Prince Charlie*
Burns	George	***Birnbaum***	Nathan	*Comedian*
Burstyn	Ellen	***Gillorly***	Edna	*Actress*
Burton	Richard	***Jenkins***	Richard	*Actor*
Buttons	Red	***Schwatt***	Aaron	*Actor*
Bygraves	Max	***Bygraves***	Walter	*Entertainer*
Byrnes	Edd	***Breitenberger***	Edward	*Actor*
Cage	Nicolas	***Coppola***	Nicholas	*US Actor*
Cagliostro	Count	***Balsame***	Giuseppe	*Italian Adventurer*

Caine	Marti	***Stringer***	Lynne	*Comedienne and Singer*
Caine	Michael	***Micklewhite***	Maurice	*Actor*
Callas	Maria	***Kalageropoulos***	Cecilia	*Operatic Soprano*
Calvin	Jean	***Chauvin/Cauvin***	Jean	*French Theologian*
Canaletto		***Canale***	Giovanni Antonio	*Artist*
Cannon	Tommy	***Derbyshire***	Tommy	*Comedy Straight Man*
Cantor	Eddie	***Iskowitz***	Edward	*Comedian*
Capp	Al	***Caplin***	Alfred Gerald	*Cartoonist*
Caravaggio		***Merisi***	Michelangelo	*Artist*
Carlisle	Belinda	***Wunderman***	Leslie	*Vocalist*
Carlos 'the Jackal'		***Sánchez***	Illich Ramirez	*Revolutionary and Assassin*
Carne	Judy	***Botterill***	Joyce	*Actress*
Carr	Sally	***Young***	Sara	*Vocalist*
Carroll	Diahann	***Johnson***	Carol Diahann	*Actress*
Carroll	Lewis	***Dodgson***	Charles Lutwidge	*Author*
Carrott	Jasper	***Davis***	Robert	*Comedian*
Cassandra		***Connor***	William	*Journalist*
Cassidy	Butch	***Parker***	Robert LeRoy	*Outlaw Leader*
Cat		***Dibley***	Dwayne	*TV Character ('Red Dwarf')*
Cates	Phoebe	***Katz***	Phoebe	*Actress*
Cathcart	Helen	***Albert***	Harold	*Royal Biographer*
Chandler	Jeff	***Grossell***	Ira	*Actor*
Charisse	Cyd	***Finklea***	Tula Ellice	*Dancer*
Charles	Ray	***Robinson***	Ray Charles	*Singer*
Charteris	Leslie	***Yin***	Leslie Charles Bowyer	*Author*
Checker	Chubby	***Evans***	Ernest	*Singer*
Cher		***La Pierre***	Cherilyn Sarkisian	*Singer and Actress*
Chester	Charlie	***Manser***	Cecil	*Comedian*
Chico		***Slimani***	Yousseph	*Singer*
Child	Lee	***Grant***	Jim	*Thriller writer*
Chi-Minh	Ho	***Thann***	Nguyen Van	*Vietnamese Politician*
Chipmunk		***Fyffe***	Jahmaal Noel	*Grime MC*
Chopin	Kate	***O'Flaherty***	Katherine	*Author*
Cicero		***Tullius***	Marcus	*Roman Statesman*
Cid	El	***Vivár***	Rodrigo Díaz de	*Spanish Warrior*
Clair	René	***Chomette***	René Lucien	*Film Director*
Clapton	Eric	***Clapp***	Eric	*Guitarist and Singer*
Clarke	John	***Cromwell***	Richard	*Son of Oliver Cromwell*
Cliff	Jimmy	***Chambers***	James	*Singer*
Clift	Montgomery	***Montgomery***	Edward	*Actor*
Cobb	Lee J	***Jacob***	Lee	*Actor*
Coco		***Poliakov***	Nikolai	*Clown*
Colbert	Claudette	***Chauchoin***	Lily	*Actress*
Colbourne	Maurice	***Middleton***	Roger	*Actor*
Cole	Nat King	***Adams***	Nathaniel	*Singer*
Coltrane	Robbie	***McMillan***	Anthony Robert	*Actor and Comedian*
Como	Perry	***Perido***	Nick	*Singer*
Connery	Sean	***Connery***	Thomas	*Actor*
Conquest	Owen	***Hamilton***	Charles	*Author*
Conrad	Joseph	***Korzeniowski***	Jozef Teodor Konrad	*Author*
Cool James	Ladies Love	***Smith***	James Todd	*Rap Singer*
Cooper	Alice	***Furnier***	Vincent	*Singer*
Cooper	Gary	***Cooper***	Francis	*Actor*
Le Corbusier		***Jeanneret***	Charles Edouard	*Architect*
El Cordobes		***Perez***	Manuel Benitez	*Matador*
Corelli	Marie	***Mackay***	Mary	*English Novelist*
Corno di Bassetto		***Shaw***	George Bernard	*Author (as music critic)*
Correggio		***Allegri***	Antonio	*Artist*
Corvo	Baron	***Rolfe***	Frederick William	*Novelist*
Costello	Elvis	***McManus***	Declan	*Singer and Composer*
Costello	Lou	***Cristillo***	Louis	*Comedian*
Cougar	John	***Mellencamp***	John	*Vocalist*
Craddock	Fanny	***Primrose-Pechey***	Phyllis	*Television Cook*
Craig	Michael	***Gregson***	Michael	*Actor*
Cranach	Lucas	***Müller***	Lucas	*German Painter*
Craven	Sara	***Ashurst***	Anne	*Novelist*
Crawford	Joan	***Le Sueur***	Lucille	*Actress*
Crawford	Michael	***Dumbell-Smith***	Michael	*Actor and Singer*
Crazy Horse		***Witko***	Tasunko	*Sioux Indian Chief*
Creole	Kid	***Darnell Browder***	Thomas August	*Singer*
Creston	Paul	***Guttoveggio***	Joseph	*Musician*
Cricket	Jimmy	***Mulgrew***	James	*Comedian*
Crisp	Quentin	***Pratt***	Denis	*Writer*
Crompton	Richmal	***Lamburn***	Richmal	*Author*
Crosby	Bing	***Crosby***	Harry Lillis	*Singer and Actor*
Cruise	Tom	***Mapother***	Tom Cruise	*Actor*
Curie	Marie	***Sklodowska***	Manya	*Physicist*
Curtis	Chris	***Crummey***	Chris	*Pop Musician*
Curtis	Tony	***Schwartz***	Bernard	*Actor*
Cutpurse	Moll	***Frith***	Mary	*Pickpocket and Robber*

D'Ache	Caran	***Poire***	Emmanuel	*French Illustrator*
Daddy	Big	***Crabtree***	Shirley	*Wrestler*
D'Amato	Joe	***Massaccesi***	Aristide	*Film Director*
Dana		***Scallon (née Brown)***	Rosemary	*Singer and Politician*
Dane	Clemence	***Ashton***	Winifred	*English Dramatist*
Dappy		***Contostavlos***	Costadinos	*Rapper*
Darby	Kim	***Zerby***	Deborah	*Actress*
Darin	Bobby	***Cassotto***	Robert Walden	*Singer*
Darren	James	***Ercolani***	James	*US Actor*
Davis	Nancy	***Robbins***	Anne Frances	*Actress*
Davro	Bobby	***Nankeville***	Robert	*Comic Impressionist*
Dawes (He's a baby)	George	***Lucas***	Matt	*Comedian*
Dawn	Elizabeth	***Butterfield***	Sylvia	*Actress*
Dawson	Dickie	***Emm***	Colin	*Actor and Comedian*
Day	Doris	***Kappelhoff***	Doris Von	*Actress and Singer*
De Burgh	Chris	***Davison***	Christopher	*Vocalist*
De Carlo	Yvonne	***Middleton***	Peggy	*Actress*
De Paul	Lynsey	***Rubin***	Lynsey	*Singer*
De Quincey	Thomas	***Quincey***	Thomas	*Essayist*
De Valois	Ninette	***Stannus***	Edris	*Ballerina*
Dean	James	***Byron***	James	*Actor*
Dee	Dave	***Harman***	David	*Vocalist*
Dee	Kiki	***Matthews***	Pauline	*Singer*
Dee	Sandra	***Zuck***	Alexandra	*Actress*
Defoe	Daniel	***Foe***	Daniel	*Author*
Delfont	Bernard	***Winogradsky***	Boris	*Impresario*
Deneuve	Catherine	***Dorléac***	Catherine	*Actress*
Dennis	Les	***Heseltine***	Les	*Comedian*
Denver	John	***Deutschendorf Jnr***	Henry John	*Singer and Composer*
Derek	Bo	***Collins***	Cathleen	*Actress*
Derek	John	***Harris***	Derek	*Actor*
Desmousseaux	Félicité	***Saillot***	Félicité	*Actress*
Dickinson	Angie	***Brown***	Angeline	*Actress*
Dickinson	David	***Gulessarian***	David	*Antiques Dealer*
Dickson	Carter	***Carr***	John Dickson	*US Detective Writer*
Diddley	Bo	***Bates***	Otha Ellas	*Singer*
Diesel	Vin	***Vincent***	Mark	*Actor*
Dinesen	Isak	***Blixen***	Karen	*Writer*
Ding Ling		***Bingzhi***	Jiang	*Chinese Novelist*
Divine	Father	***Baker***	George	*Religious Leader*
Dixon	Franklin W	***Stratemeyer***	Edward	*Author*
DJ Quicksilver		***Terzi***	Orhan	*Turkish Pop Star*
Dolin	Anton	***Healey-Kay***	Patrick	*Choreographer*
Donovan		***Leitch***	Donovan	*Singer*
Dorsey	Gerry	***Dorsey***	Arnold	*Singer*
Douglas	Kirk	***Demsky***	Issur Danielovitch	*Actor*
Dover	Ben	***Honey***	Simon Lindsay	*Porn Star*
Downe	Bob	***Trevorrow***	Mark	*Australian Comedian*
Dozy		***Davies***	Trevor	*Bass Player*
Drake	Charlie	***Springall***	Charles	*Comedian*
Dylan	Bob	***Zimmerman***	Robert Alan	*Singer and Composer*
Dynamite	Miss	***McLean-Daley***	Niomi	*Singer*
Eden	Barbara	***Huffman***	Barbara	*US Actress*
Edge	The	***Evans***	Dave	*Musician*
Edwards	Jimmy	***O'Neill***	James	*Comedian and Actor*
Edwards	Vince	***Zoine***	Vincento	*US Actor*
Electra	Carmen	***Patrick***	Tata Leigh	*Actress*
Elia		***Lamb***	Charles	*Essayist*
Eliot	George	***Evans***	Mary Ann	*Novelist*
Ellis	Alexander John	***Sharpe***	Alexander John	*English Philologist*
Elytis	Odysseus	***Alepoudelis***	Odysseus	*Greek Poet*
Eminem		***Mathers III***	Marshall	*Rapper and Actor*
Erasmus	Desiderius	***Gheraerd***	Gheraerd	*Scholar*
Essex	David	***Cook***	David	*Singer and Actor*
Everage	Dame Edna	***Humphries***	Barry	*Comedian*
Everett	Kenny	***Cole***	Maurice	*Disc Jockey and Comedian*
Fabian		***Forte***	Fabiano	*Singer*
Fairbanks	Douglas	***Ullman***	Douglas	*Actor*
Faith	Adam	***Nelhams***	Terry	*Singer*
Fame	Georgie	***Powell***	Clive	*Musician*
Farrell	MJ	***Keane***	Molly	*Irish Novelist*
Fawn	Doctor	***Wilkie***	Edward	*'Captain Scarlet' Character*
Fenton	Shane	***Jewry***	Bernard	*Singer*
Fields	Gracie	***Stansfield***	Grace	*Actress and Singer*
Fields	WC	***Dukenfield***	William Claude	*Comedian and Actor*
50 Cent		***Jackson***	Curtis	*Rapper*
Finch	Peter	***Mitchell***	Ian	*Actor*
Fish		***Dick***	Derek	*Vocalist*
Fitzgerald	Barry	***Shields***	William	*Actor*
Fleming	Rhonda	***Louis***	Marilyn	*Actress*
Flying Scotsman		***Liddell***	Eric	*Athlete*

Flynn	Barbara	***McMurray***	Barbara	*Actress*
Fontaine	Joan	***De Havilland***	Joan	*Actress*
Fontayne	Fine Time	***Crossley***	Ian	*Actor*
Fonteyn	Margot	***Hookham***	Margaret	*Ballerina*
Ford	Gerald	***King***	Leslie	*US President*
Ford	John	***O'Fearna***	Sean	*Film Director*
Formby Jnr	George	***Booth***	George Hoy	*Music Hall Entertainer*
Formby Snr	George	***Booth***	James	*Music Hall Entertainer*
Forrest	Steve	***Andrews***	William Forrest	*US Actor*
Forsyth	Bruce	***Johnson***	Bruce	*Entertainer*
Foster	Jodie	***Munker***	Ariane	*US Actress*
Fox		***Baker***	Tammy Marie	*TV Gladiator*
Foxx	Jamie	***Bishop***	Eric	*Actor*
France	Anatole	***Thibault***	Anatole François	*Author*
Franciosa	Tony	***Papaceo***	Anthony	*Actor*
Francis	Connie	***Franconers***	Concetta	*Singer*
Francis of Assisi	Saint	***de Bernardone***	Giovanni	*Religious Leader*
Francisque		***Millet***	Jean-François	*Belgian Painter*
Freeze	Mr	***Fries***	Victor	*Fictional Super-Villain*
Fury	Billy	***Wycherly***	Ronald	*Vocalist*
Gabor	Dennis	***Dénes***	Gábor	*Physicist*
Gaga	Lady	***Germanotta***	Stefani	*Singer and Songwriter*
Garbo	Greta	***Gustaffsson***	Greta Louisa	*Actress*
Garcia	Andy	***Menendez***	Andres Arturo Garcia	*Actor*
Garland	Judy	***Gumm***	Frances	*Actress and Singer*
Garner	James	***Baumgartner***	James	*Actor*
Garrett	David	***Bengartz***	David	*Violinist*
Gaskell	Elizabeth	***Stevenson***	Elizabeth	*Writer*
Gayle	Crystal	***Gazzimos***	Brenda Gail	*Singer*
Gaynor	Gloria	***Fowles***	Gloria	*Singer*
Gee	Dustin	***Harrison***	Gerald	*Impressionist*
Genée	Adeline	***Jensen***	Anita	*Ballerina*
George	Boy	***O'Dowd***	George	*Singer*
Geraldo		***Bright***	Gerald	*Musician*
German	Edward	***Jones***	Edward	*English Composer*
Geronimo		***Goyathlay***		*Apache Indian Chief*
Giant Haystacks		***McMasters***	Luke	*Wrestler*
Gibbon	Lewis	***Mitchell***	James Leslie	*Novelist*
Giorgione		***Barbarelli***	Giorgio	*Artist*
Gish	Lillian	***Guiche***	Lilian	*Actress*
Glitter	Gary	***Gadd***	Paul	*Singer*
Gluck	Alma	***Fiersohn***	Reba	*American Soprano*
Goddard	Paulette	***Levy***	Marion	*Actress*
Gold		***Vander Walt***	Lize	*TV Gladiator*
Goldberg	Whoopi	***Johnson***	Caryn	*US Actress*
Goldsmith	Peter	***Priestley***	John Boynton	*Author*
Goldwyn	Sam	***Gelbfisz***	Samuel	*Film Producer*
Goodrich	William B	***Arbuckle***	Roscoe Conkling (Fatty)	*Actor*
Gordon	Richard	***Ostlere***	Gordon	*Doctor and Author*
Gorky	Arshile	***Adoian***	Vosdanig Manoog	*US Painter*
Gorky	Maxim	***Peshkov***	Max	*Author*
Gould	Elliott	***Goldstein***	Elliott	*Actor*
Grade	Lew	***Winogradsky***	Louis	*Impresario*
Granger	Stewart	***Stewart***	James	*Actor*
Grant	Cary	***Leach***	Archibald	*Actor*
Gray	Donald	***Tidbury***	Eldred	*South African Actor*
Grayson	Larry	***White***	William	*Comedian*
Graziano	Rocky	***Barbella***	Rocco	*Boxer*
El Greco		***Theotocopoulos***	Domenico	*Artist*
Green	Lt	***Griffiths***	Seymour	*TV Fictional Character*
Green	Lucinda	***Prior-Palmer***	Lucinda	*Three-Day Eventer*
Green	Peter	***Greenbaum***	Peter	*Musician*
Grey	Beryl	***Svenson***	Beryl	*Ballerina*
Grey	Captain	***Holden***	Bradley	*TV Fictional Character*
Gris	Juan	***González***	Juan Victoriano	*Cubist Painter*
Grock		***Wettach***	Adrien	*Clown*
Grünewald	Matthias	***Gothardt***	Mathis	*German Painter*
Guercino		***Barbieri***	Gian-Francesco	*Italian Painter*
H		***Watkins***	Ian	*Pop Singer*
Haliburton	Hugh	***Robertson***	James Logie	*Poet*
Hamilton	Clive	***Lewis***	CS	*British Writer*
Hamilton	Emma	***Lyon***	Emma	*Lord Nelson's Mistress*
Hammer	MC	***Burrell***	Stanley Kirk	*Rapper*
Harley	Steve	***Nice***	Stephen	*Pop Singer*
Harlow	Jean	***Carpentier***	Harlean	*Actress*
Hart	Emma	***Lyon***	Emma (Amy)	*Blacksmith's Daughter*
Harvey	Laurence	***Skikne***	Larushka Mischa	*Actor*
Haver	June	***Stovenour***	June	*Actress*
Hawk	Jeremy	***Lange***	Cedric	*Actor and TV Presenter*
Hawtrey	Charles	***Hartree***	George	*Actor*

FAMOUS PEOPLE

Hayden	Sterling	***Relyea***	Walter	*Actor*
Hayworth	Rita	***Cansino***	Marguerita	*Actress*
HD		***Doolittle***	Hilda	*Writer*
He-Man		***Adam***	Prince	*Fictional Superhero*
Headroom	Max	***Frewer***	Matt	*Fictional TV Character*
Hedley	Jack	***Hawkins***	Jack	*Actor*
Henderson	Mary	***Mavor***	Osborne Henry	*Dramatist*
Hepburn	Audrey	***Van Heemstra***	Edda Hepburn	*Actress*
Hepburn	Audrey	***Ruston***	Audrey	*Actress*
Herriot	James	***Wight***	James	*Vet and Author*
Hershey	Barbara	***Herzstein***	Barbara	*Actress*
Hershey	Barbara	***Seagull***	Barbara	*US Actress*
Hessling	Catherine	***Heurschling***	Andrée	*Jean Renoir's Wife (Actress)*
Heston	Charlton	***Carter***	Charlton	*Actor*
HHH (Triple H)	(Hunter Hearst Helmsley)	***Levesque***	Paul Michael	*Wrestler*
Higgins	Jack	***Patterson***	Henry	*Author*
Hill	Benny	***Hill***	Alfred Hawthorne	*Comedian*
Hill	Harry	***Hall***	Matthew	*Comedian*
Hinge	Evadne	***Logan***	George	*Entertainer*
Hirsel	Lord Home of the	***Douglas-Home***	Alec	*Prime Minister of Great Britain*
Hitler	Adolf	***Schicklgrüber***	Adolf	*Dictator*
Hobbema	Meindert	***Lubbertszoon***	Meyndert	*Dutch Painter*
Hoffa	Jimmy	***Riddle***	James	*US Union Leader*
Hogan	Hulk	***Bollea***	Terry	*Professional Wrestler and Actor*
Holden	William	***Beedle***	William	*Actor*
Holiday	Billie	***Fagan***	Eleanora	*Singer*
Holliday	Michael	***Milne***	Norman	*Singer*
Holly	Buddy	***Holley***	Charles Hardin	*Singer*
Hope	Anthony	***Hawkins***	Anthony	*Author*
Hope	Laura Lee	***Stratemeyer***	Edward	*Author*
Horowitz	Vladimir	***Gorowicz***	Vladimir	*Russian Pianist*
Houdini	Harry	***Weiss***	Ehrich	*Illusionist*
Houseman	John	***Haussman***	Jacques	*Actor*
Howard	Leslie	***Stainer***	Leslie	*Actor*
Howard	Thomas	***James***	Jesse	*American Outlaw*
Hudson	Rock	***Scherer Jnr***	Roy	*Actor*
Humperdinck	Engelbert	***Dorsey***	Arnold	*Singer*
Hunter		***Crossley***	James	*Gladiator*
Hunter	Tab	***Gellen***	Arthur	*Singer and Actor*
Hutton	Betty	***Thornburg***	Betty June	*US Comedy Actress*
I Spy	Big Chief	***Worrell***	Charles	*Author*
Ice Cube		***Jackson***	O'Shea	*Rapper and Actor*
Ice-T		***Marrow***	Tracy	*Rapper and Actor*
Innes	Michael	***Stewart***	John	*Author*
Irving	Henry	***Brodribb***	John Henry	*Actor*
Islam	Yusuf	***Stevens***	Cat	*Singer and Composer*
Ives	Burl	***Ivanhoe***	Burl	*Actor and Singer*
Ivy	Poison	***Isley***	Pamela	*Fictional Super-Villain*
Jack	Just	***Allsopp***	Jack	*Musician*
Jack	Wolfman	***Smith***	Robert	*Disc Jockey*
Jacques	Hattie	***Jaques***	Josephine	*Actress*
James	PD	***White***	PD	*Writer*
Jane	Calamity	***Canary***	Martha Jane	*Frontierswoman*
Janis	Byron	***Yanks***	Byron	*Musician*
Janssen	David	***Mayer***	David	*Actor*
Jason	David	***White***	David	*Actor*
Jayston	Michael	***James***	Michael	*Actor*
Jet		***Youdale***	Diane	*TV Gladiator*
Joan Collins' Fan Club		***Clary***	Julian	*Entertainer*
John	Elton Hercules	***Dwight***	Reginald Kenneth	*Singer and Composer*
John	Jilted	***Fellows***	Graham	*Pop Singer*
John Paul II	Pope	***Wojtyla***	Karol	*Pope*
Jolie	Angelina	***Voight***	Angelina	*Actress*
Jones	Tom	***Woodward***	Thomas	*Singer*
Jordan	Price	***Katie***		*Model*
Jordan	Louis	***Gendre***	Louis	*Actor*
Josh	Guru	***Walden***	Paul	*Acid House Performer*
Joyce	Yootha	***Needham***	Yootha	*Actress*
Julia	Raul	***Rafael Y Arcelos***	Raul	*Actor*
Kane		***Jacobs***	Glen	*Professional Wrestler*
Kane	Eden	***Sarstedt***	Richard	*Singer*
Kane Jeeves	Mahatma	***Dukenfield***	William Claude	*Comedian and Actor*
Karlin	Miriam	***Samuels***	Miriam	*Actress*
Karloff	Boris	***Pratt***	William Henry	*Actor*
Karno	Fred	***Westcott***	Fred	*Impresario*
Kaye	Danny	***Kaminsky***	David Daniel	*Entertainer*
Kaye	Nora	***Koreff***	Nora	*Ballerina*
Kaye	Tony	***Selvidge***	Anthony	*Musician*
Kazan	Elia	***Kazanjoglou***	Elia	*Film Director*

Keaton	Diane	***Hall***	Diane	*Actress*
Keaton	Michael	***Douglas***	Michael	*Actor (Batman Actor)*
Keene	Carolyn	***Stratemeyer***	Edward	*Author*
Kemp	Jeremy	***Walker***	Edmund	*Actor*
Kerr	Deborah	***Trimmler***	Deborah	*Actress*
Kesteven	Baroness Thatcher of	**Thatcher**	Margaret	*Prime Minister of Great*
Khan	Chaka	***Stephens***	Yvette Marie	*Singer*
Khashoggi	Soraya	***Daly***	Sandra	*Millionairess*
Kid Rock		***Ritchie***	Robert	*Rock Star*
King	Ben E	***Nelson***	Benjamin	*Singer*
King	Carol	***Klein***	Carole	*Singer*
King	David	***Kingshott***	David	*Comedian and Singer*
Kingsley	Ben	***Bhanji***	Krishna	*Actor*
Kit		***Hesketh-Harvey***	Kit	*Musical act 'Kit and*
Klenovsky	Paul	***Wood***	Henry	*English Conductor*
Kline	Patsy	***Hensley***	Virginia	*Singer*
Knickerbocker	Cholly	***Paul***	Maury	*NY Gossip Columnist*
Knickerbocker	Diedrich	***Irving***	Washington	*Author*
Knutt	Bobby	***Wass***	Robert	*Actor and Comedian*
Koresh	David	***Howell***	Vernon	*Branch Davidian Cult Leader*
La Rue	Danny	***Carroll***	Daniel	*Female Impersonator*
Ladd	Cheryl	***Stoppelmoor***	Cheryl	*Actress*
Laine	Denny	***Haynes***	Brian	*Guitarist*
Laine	Frankie	***Vecchio***	Frank Lo	*Vocalist*
Lamarr	Hedy	***Kiesler***	Hedwig	*Actress*
Lamarr	Mark	***Jones***	Mark	*Comedian*
Lamour	Dorothy	***Kaumeyer***	Dorothy Mary	*Actress*
Landis	Jerry	***Simon***	Paul	*Half of 50s Singing Duo 'Tom & Jerry'*
Landon	Michael	***Orowitz***	Eugene Maurice	*US Actor*
Lane	Carla	***Barrack***	Romana	*Scriptwriter*
Lanza	Mario	***Cocozza***	Alfredo	*Opera Singer*
Large	Eddie	***McGuinness***	Eddie	*Comedian*
Larrigan	Tex	***Ord***	Irene	*Author of Westerns*
Lassie (male)		***Pal (female)***		*Film Dog*
Laurel	Stan	***Jefferson***	Arthur Stanley	*Comedy Actor*
Laurie	Piper	***Jacobs***	Rosetta	*US Actress*
Laxness	Halldór	***Gudjonsson***	Halldór	*Icelandic Novelist*
Le Carré	John	***Cornwell***	David	*Author*
Le Duc Tho		***Dinh Khai***	Phan	*Vietnamese Politician*
Le Mesurier	John	***Halliley***	John Elton	*Actor*
Le Vell	Michael	***Turner***	Michael	*Corrie actor*
Lee	Alvin	***Barnes***	Graham	*Rock Guitarist*
Lee	Brenda	***Tarpley***	Brenda	*Vocalist*
Lee	Bruce	***Kam***	Lee Yuen	*Actor and Martial Artist*
Lee	Peggy	***Egstrom***	Norma	*Vocalist*
Leigh	Janet	***Morrison***	Jeanette	*Actress*
Leigh	Jennifer Jason	***Morrow***	Jennifer Lee	*Actress*
Leigh	Vivien	***Hartley***	Vivien	*Actress*
Lely	Peter	***Van der Faes***	Pieter	*Artist*
Lemmy		***Kilmister***	Ian	*Singer (Motorhead)*
Lenin	Vladimir Ilich	***Ulyanov***	Vladimir Ilich	*Russian Revolutionary*
Leno	Dan	***Calvin***	George	*English Comedian*
Lenya	Lotte	***Blamauer***	Karoline Wilhelmine	*Austrian Actress*
Lewis	Jerry	***Levitch***	Joseph	*Actor and Comedian*
Liberace		***Valentino***	Wladziu	*Pianist and Entertainer*
Lightning		***Williams***	Kim	*TV Gladiator*
Limahl		***Hamill***	Christopher	*Singer (Kajagoogoo)*
Little	Syd	***Mead***	Cyril	*Comedian*
Lloyd	Marie	***Wood***	Mathilda	*Actress*
Lom	Herbert	***Ze Schluderpacheru***	Herbert	*Actor*
Lombard	Carole	***Peters***	Jane	*Actress*
London	Jack	***Griffith***	John	*Author*
Lord	Jack	***Ryan***	John Joseph	*Actor*
Loren	Sophia	***Scicolone***	Sofia	*Actress*
Lorraine	Claude	***Gelée***	Claude	*Landscape Painter*
Lorre	Peter	***Loewenstein***	Laszlo	*Actor*
Lot	Parson	***Kingsley***	Charles	*Author*
Lottery	Lenny	***McGurran***	Aidan	*National Lottery Expert*
Louis	Joe	***Barrow***	Joseph	*Boxer*
Louis	Morris	***Bernstein***	Morris	*US Painter*
Lulu		***Lawrie***	Marie McLaughlin	*Singer*
Lynn	Vera	***Welch***	Vera	*Singer*
Mabuse	Jan	***Gossart***	Jan	*Flemish Painter*
MacBride	Maud	***Gonne***	Maud	*Irish Nationalist*
MacColl	Ewan	***Miller***	James	*Folk Singer*
MacDiarmid	Hugh	***Grieve***	Christopher Murray	*Poet*
Mack	Connie	***McGillicuddy***	Cornelius	*Baseball Player*
Maclaine	Shirley	***Beaty***	Shirley	*Actress*
Madonna		***Ciccone***	Madonna Louise	*Singer*
Magenta	Captain	***Donaghue***	Patrick	*Fictional TV Character*

Magnusson	Magnus	***Sigursteinnson***	Magnus	*Broadcaster*
Majors	Lee	***Yeary***	Harvey Lee	*Actor*
Malden	Karl	***Sekolovich***	Mladen	*Actor*
Mann	Manfred	***Lubowitz***	Michael	*Musician*
Mansfield	Jayne	***Palmer***	Vera Jane	*Actress*
Mansfield	Katherine	***Beauchamp***	Kathleen	*NZ Writer*
Manson	Charles	***Maddox***	No-Name	*Cult Leader*
Manson	Marilyn	***Warner***	Brian	*Pop Star*
March	Fredric	***Bickel***	Frederick	*Actor*
Margret	Ann	***Olsson***	Ann-Margret	*Actress*
Markham	Elizabeth	***Penrose***	Elizabeth	*Writer for Children*
Markham	Robert	***Amis***	Kingsley	*Novelist*
Markova	Alicia	***Marks***	Lilian Alice	*Ballerina*
Marks	Alfred	***Touchinsky***	Alfred	*Actor and Comedian*
Martin	Dean	***Crocetti***	Dino	*Actor*
Marvel	Captain	***Batson***	Billy	*Comics Hero*
Marvin	Hank	***Rankin***	Brian	*Guitarist*
Marx	Chico	***Marx***	Leonard	*Actor*
Marx	Groucho	***Marx***	Julius	*Actor*
Marx	Gummo	***Marx***	Milton	*Actor*
Marx	Harpo	***Marx***	Adolph	*Actor*
Marx	Zeppo	***Marx***	Herbert	*Actor*
Masaccio	di Simone Guidi	***de Giovanni***	Tommaso	*Florentine Painter*
Matthau	Walter	***Matuschanskavasky***	Walter	*Actor*
Maxwell	Robert	***Hoch***	Jan Ludvik	*Businessman*
Maynard	Bill	***William***	Walter	*Actor*
McBain	Ed	***Hunter***	Evan	*Writer*
McManus	Mick	***Matthews***	William	Professional Wrestler
McMasters	Luke	***Ruane***	Martin	*Wrestler*
Meatloaf		***Aday***	Marvin Lee	*Singer*
Meg	Mystic	***Lake***	Margaret	*TV Personality*
Meir	Golda	***Mabovitch***	Golda	*Israeli PM*
Melba	Dame Nellie	***Armstrong, née Mitchell***	Helen Porter	*Opera Singer*
Melbourne	Viscount	***Lamb***	William	*British Prime Minister*
Melmoth	Sebastian	***Wilde***	Oscar	*Author*
Mendelssohn	Felix	***Mendelssohn -Bartholdy***	Felix	*Composer*
Menken	Adah Isaacs	***Fuertes***	Dolores Adios	*American Actress and Poet*
Mennin	Peter	***Mennini***	Peter	*Musician*
Merchant	Vivien	***Thompson***	Ada	*Actress*
Mercury	Freddie	***Bulsara***	Frederick	*Singer*
Meredith	Burgess	***Burgess***	George	*Actor*
Merlin		***Tennyson***	Alfred Lord	*Poet*
Merman	Ethel	***Zimmerman***	Ethel	*Singer*
Merrion		***Francis***	Leigh	*Comedian*
Merton	Mrs	***Hook/Aherne***	Caroline	*Comedienne*
Merton	Paul	***Martin***	Paul	*Comedian*
Mervyn	William	***Pickwoad***	William	*Actor*
Michael	George	***Panayiotou***	Georgios	*Vocalist and Composer*
Michael of Kent	Princess	***von Reibnitz***	Marie	*Princess*
Milland	Ray	***Truscott-Jones***	Reginald	*Actor*
Miller	Max	***Sargent***	Thomas Henry	*Comedian*
Milligan	Spike	***Milligan***	Terence Alan	*Comedian and Writer*
Mistinguett		***Bourgeois***	Jeanne Marie	*French Dancer*
Mitchell	Cameron	***Mizell***	George	*Actor*
Mitchell	Guy	***Cernick***	Al	*Singer*
Mitchell	Joni	***Anderson***	Roberta Joan	*Singer and Composer*
Molière		***Poquelin***	Jean-Baptiste	*Playwright*
Molotov	Vyacheslav Mikhaylovich	***Skryabin***	Vyacheslav Mikhaylovich	*Russian Statesman*
Monroe	Marilyn	***Baker***	Norma Jean	*Actress*
Montand	Yves	***Levy***	Ivo	*Actor*
Montez	Lola	***Gilbert***	Maria Eliza (Délores)	*American Dancer*
Montgomery	George	***Letz***	George	*Actor*
Moody	Ron	***Moodnick***	Ronald	*Actor*
Moore	Archibald	***Wright***	Archibald	*Boxer*
Moore	Demi	***Guynes***	Demi	*Actress*
Moore	Julianne	***Smith***	Julie Anne	*US Actress*
Morecambe	Eric	***Bartholomew***	John Eric	*Comedian*
Morgan	Frank	***Wupperman***	Frank	*Actor*
Morrison	James	***Catchpole***	James	*Vocalist*
Morrison	Toni	***Wofford***	Chloe	*US Novelist*
Morrison	Van	***Morrison***	George Ivan	*Singer and Composer*
Moses	Grandma	***Robertson***	Anna Mary	*Artist*
Mostel	Zero	***Mostel***	Samuel Joel	*Actor*
Mycroft		***Gillis***	Ian	*'Brain of Britain'*
Nagasaki	Kendo	***Thornley***	Peter	*Professional Wrestler*
Naismith	Laurence	***Johnson***	Lawrence	*Actor*
Neagle	Anna	***Robertson***	Florence Marjorie	*Actress*
Negri	Pola	***Chalupek***	Appolonia	*Actress*

Nelly		***Haynes Jr***	Cornell	*Rapper*
Nelson	Baby Face	***Gillis***	Lester	*Gangster*
Nelson	Lee	***Brodkin***	Simon	*Comedian*
Nero		***Ahenobarbus***	Lucius Domitius	*Roman Emperor*
Nero	Franco	***Spartanero***	Franco	*Actor*
Newcastle	Duke of	***Pelham-Holles***	Thomas	*British Prime Minister*
Nichols	Mike	***Peschkowsky***	Michael	*American Film Director*
Nicole		***Skurnick***	Estelle	*'Renault Clio' Star of Advert*
Nolde	Emil	***Hansen***	Emil	*German Painter*
Novarra	Ramon	***Samaniegos***	Ramon	*Actor*
Novello	Ivor	***Davies***	David Ivor	*Composer*
Numan	Gary	***Webb***	Gary	*Vocalist and Composer*
Oakley	Annie	***Mozee***	Phoebe	*Frontierswoman*
Oberon	Merle	***Thompson***	Estelle	*Actress*
O'Brian	Patrick	***Russ***	Richard	*Novelist*
O'Brien	Flann	***O'Nolan***	Brian	*Irish Writer*
O'Brien	Hugh	***Krampke***	Hugh	*Actor*
O'Brien	Richard	***Smith***	Richard	*Actor*
Ochre	Captain	***Frazier***	Richard	*Fictional TV Character*
O'Connor	Frank	***O'Donovan***	Michael	*Irish Writer*
O'Day	Anita	***Colton***	Anita	US Jazz Singer
Offenbach	Jacques	***Eberst***	Jakob	*Composer*
O'Hara	Maureen	***Fitzsimmons***	Maureen	*Actress*
O'Henry		***Porter***	William Sydney	*Author*
Orlando	Tony	***Cassavitis***	Michael	*Vocalist*
Ormandy	Eugene	***Blau***	Jenö	*Musician*
Orwell	George	***Blair***	Eric Arthur	*Author*
O'Sullivan	Gilbert	***O'Sullivan***	Raymond	*Singer*
Ouida		***Ramée, de la***	Marie Louise	*English Author*
Page	Patti	***Fowler***	Clara Ann	*Singer*
Pollock	Mary	***Blyton***	Enid	*Children's Writer*
Palance	Jack	***Palaniuk***	Walter	*Actor*
Pallo	Jackie	***Gutteridge***	John	*Wrestler*
Palmer	Lilli	***Peiser***	Lilli	*Actress*
Panther		***Riley***	Helena	*TV Gladiator*
Parker	Cecil	***Schwabe***	Cecil	*Actor*
Parker	Dorothy	***Rothschild***	Dorothy	*Author*
Parley	Peter	***Goodrich***	Samuel	*US Publisher*
Parmigianino	Il	***Mazzola***	Girolamo Francesco Maria	*Italian Painter*
Pastry	Mr	***Hearne***	Richard	*Actor*
Patterson	Sir Les	***Humphries***	Barry	*Comedian*
Paycheck	Johnny	***Lytle***	Donald Eugene	*Country Singer*
Peel	John	***Ravenscroft***	John	*Disc Jockey*
Peerce	Jan	***Perelmuth***	Jacob Pincus	*Musician*
Pele		***do Nascimento***	Edson Arantes	*Footballer*
Pellow	Marti	***McLoughlin***	Mark	*Singer*
Penguin		***Cobblepot***	Oswald	*Batman Character*
Pennis	Dennis	***Kaye***	Paul	*Actor and Comedian*
Perkins	Elizabeth	***Pisperikos***	Elizabeth	*Actress*
Phillips	Lou Diamond	***Upchurch***	Lou	*Actor*
Phillips	Michelle	***Gilliam***	Holly	*Singer and Actress*
Phiz		***Browne***	Hablot Knight	*Illustrator*
Phoenix		***Young***	Sandy	*Gladiator*
Piaf	Edith	***Gassion***	Edith	*Singer*
Pickford	Mary	***Smith***	Gladys Mary	*Actress*
Pierre	DBC	***Finlay***	Peter Warren	*Australian Novelist*
Pindar	Peter	***Wolcot***	John	*Satirist*
Pink		***Moore***	Alicia	*Actress and Singer*
Pol Pot		***Sar***	Saloth	*Politician*
Pollock	Mary	***Blyton***	Enid	*Children's Writer*
Pop	Iggy	***Osterberg***	James Jewel	*Singer*
Porcupine	Peter	***Cobbett***	William	*Writer*
Powers	Stefanie	***Federkiewicz***	Stefania	*Actress*
Preston	Robert	***Meservey***	Robert	*Actor*
Price	Dennis	***Rose-Price***	Dennistoun Franklyn	*Actor*
Prince		***Nelson***	Prince Rogers	*Singer and Composer*
Proby	PJ	***Smith***	James Marcus	*Singer*
Pussyfoot		***Johnson***	William Eugene	*US Reformer*
Q		***Quiller-Couch***	Arthur	*Author and Anthologist*
Queen	Ellery	***Dannay***	Frederick	*Joint Authors*
		Lee	Manfred B	
Quentin	Caroline	***Jones***	Caroline	*Actress*
Quinn	Anthony	***Oaxaca***	Rudolph	*US Actor*
Quinten	Chris	***Bell***	Chris	*Actor*
Rafferty	Chips	***Goffage***	John	*Entertainer*
Raft	George	***Ranft***	George	*Actor*
Randall	Tony	***Rosenberg***	Leonard	*Actor*
Randi	Amazing	***Zwinge***	James Randall	*Magician*
Rascal	Dizzee	***Mills***	Dylan	*Rapper and Actor*
Raven	Paul	***Gadd***	Paul	*Vocalist*

Ray	Ted	***Olden***	Charles	*Comedian*
Reality	Maxim	***Palmer***	Keith	*MC*
Rebel		***Stoute***	Jenny	*TV Gladiator*
Red Cloud		***Iuta***	Mahpiua	*(Sioux) Chief*
Reed	Lou	***Firbank***	Louis	*Singer and Composer*
Reeves	Vic	***Moir***	Jim	*Comedian*
Regiomontanus		***Müller***	Johannes	*German Mathematician*
Remarque	Erich Maria	***Kramer***	Erich Maria	*Author*
Rendell	Ruth	***Grasemann***	Ruth	*Crime Novelist*
Rethberg	Elisabeth	***Sättler***	Elisabeth	*Musician*
Rhinehart	Luke	***Cockcroft***	George	*Author*
Richard	Cliff	***Webb***	Harold	*Singer*
Richard	Little	***Penniman***	Richard Wayne	*Singer*
Richards	Frank	***Hamilton***	Charles	*Author*
Rihanna		***Fenty***	Robyn Rihanna	*Singer and Model*
Rivers	Joan	***Molinsky***	Joan	*Comedienne*
Robbins	Harold	***Rubin***	Harold	*Author*
Robin		***Grayson***	Dick	*Comics Character*
Robinson	Edward G	***Goldenberg***	Emmanuel	*Actor*
Robinson	Ralph	***George III***		*British King (in Garden Periodicals)*
Robinson	Sugar Ray	***Smith***	Walker	*Boxer*
Rock		***Johnson***	Dwayne	*Actor and Wrestler*
Rocket		***Richards***	Pauline	*TV Gladiator*
Roddick	Anita	***Perilli***	Anita	*Founder of The Body Shop*
Rogers	Ginger	***McMath***	Virginia	*Actress and Dancer*
Rogers	Roy	***Slye***	Leonard	*Actor*
Rogers	Will	***Adair***	William Penn	*US Actor*
Rohmer	Sax	***Ward***	Arthur Sarsfield	*Author*
Rooney	Mickey	***Yule Jnr***	Joseph	*Actor*
Rose	Axl	***Bailey***	William	*Singer*
Rose Lee	Gypsy	***Hovick***	Rose Louise	*Entertainer*
Ross	Aircraftman John Hume	***Lawrence***	Thomas Edward	*Soldier and Author*
Ross	Barnaby	***Dannay*** / ***Lee***	Frederick / Manfred B	*Joint Authors*
Rotten	Johnny	***Lydon***	John	*Singer*
Rowland	Tiny	***Fuhrhop***	Roland	*Businessman*
Rowlands	John	***Stanley***	Henry Morton	*Explorer/Journalist*
Roy	Rob	***McGregor***	Robert	*Scottish Outlaw*
Ruffo	Titta	***Titta***	Ruffo	*Baritone*
Russell	Theresa	***Paup***	Theresa	*Actress*
Rutherford	Mark	***White***	William Hale	*Writer*
Ryder	Winona	***Horowitz***	Winona	*Actress*
Sable		***Merowitz***	Rena	*Professional Wrestler*
Sabrina		***Sykes***	Norma	*Model*
Sade		***Adu***	Helen Folasade	*Singer*
Sagan	Françoise	***Quoirez***	Françoise	*Novelist*
Saint-John Perse		***Léger***	Alexis Saint-Léger	*French Poet*
Saint-Laurent	Yves	***Mathieu***	Henri Donat	*French Designer*
Saki		***Monro***	Hector Hugh	*Writer*
Samaroff	Olga	***Hickenlooper***	Lucie	*Musician*
Sand	George	***Dudevant***	Amondine Lucie Dupin	*Writer*
Sapper		***McNeile***	Herman Cyril	*Author*
Sappho		***de Scudéry***	Madeleine	*French Novelist*
Saracen		***Lewis***	Mike	*TV Gladiator*
Sarandon	Susan	***Tomaling***	Susan	*Actress*
Sarapo	Théo	***Lamboukas***	Theophanis	*Greek Singer*
Savage	Lily	***O'Grady***	Paul	*Entertainer*
Saxon	John	***Orrico***	Carmen	*Actor*
Scarlet	Captain	***Metcalfe***	Paul	*Animated TV Character*
Schultz	Dutch	***Flegenheimer***	Arthur	*Gangster*
Scott	Randolph	***Crane***	Randolph	*Actor*
Seal		***Samuel***	Henry	*Singer*
Selassie	Hailie	***Makonnen***	Ras Tafari	*Ethiopian Emperor*
Sennett	Mack	***Sinnott***	Michael	*Film Producer*
Sensible	Captain	***Burns***	Ray	*Singer*
Dr Seuss		***Geisel***	Theodore Seuss	*Author*
Seymour	Jane	***Frankenberg***	Joyce	*Actress*
Shadow		***King***	Jefferson	*TV Gladiator*
Shaggy		***Burrell***	Orville Richard	*Pop Singer*
Shannon	Del	***Westover***	Charles	*Singer*
Sharif	Omar	***Shalhoub***	Michael	*Actor*
Shaw	Sandie	***Goodrich***	Sandra	*Singer*
Shaw	TE	***Lawrence***	Thomas Edward	*Soldier and Author (in Royal Tank Corps)*
Sheen	Martin	***Estevez***	Ramon	*Actor*
Shipton	Mother	***Southill/Southiel***	Ursula	*Prophetess*
Shirley	Anne	***O'Day***	Dawn	*Actress*
Shute	Neville	***Norway***	Neville	*Author*
Shuttleworth	John	***Fellows***	Graham	*Singer and Songwriter*

Sidebottom	Frank	***Sievey***	Chris	*Comedian*
Signoret	Simone	***Kaminker***	Henriette Charlotte	*Actress*
Sills	Beverly	***Silverman***	Belle	*Musician*
Silverheels	Jay	***Smith***	Harold J	*Actor*
Simmons	Gene	***Witz***	Chaim	*Rock Singer*
Simone	Nina	***Wayman***	Eunice	*Singer*
Sioux	Siouxsie	***Dallion***	Susan	*Singer*
Siren		***Paton***	Alison	*TV Gladiator*
Sitting Bull		***Iyotanka***	Tatanka	*Sioux Hunkpapa Chief*
Skinner	Frank	***Collins***	Chris	*Comedian*
Slater	Christian	***Hawkins***	Christian	*Actor*
Snoop Dogg		***Broadus***	Calvin	*Rapper*
Soul	David	***Solberg***	David	*Actor*
Spiderman		***Parker***	Peter	*Fictional Superhero*
Spikey	Dave	***Bramwell***	David	*Comedian*
Springfield	Dusty	***O'Brien***	Mary	*Singer*
Stack	Robert	***Modini***	Robert	*Actor*
Staff	Kathy	***Higginbottom***	Minnie	*Actress*
Stalin	Joseph	***Dzhugashvili***	Iosif Vissarionovich	*Russian Leader*
Stanislavsky		***Alexeyev Sergeivitch***	Konstantin	*Actor*
Stanley	Henry Morton	***Rowlands***	John	*Explorer*
Stanwyck	Barbara	***Stevens***	Ruby	*Actress*
Stardust	Alvin	***Jewry***	Bernard	*Singer*
Starr	Edwin	***Hatcher***	Charles	*Singer*
Starr	Freddie	***Fowell***	Frederick	*Comedian*
Starr	Ringo	***Starkey***	Richard	*Drummer and Composer*
Statto		***Loughran***	Angus	*TV Soccer Pundit*
Steele	Tommy	***Hicks***	Thomas	*Entertainer*
Stendhal		***Beyle***	Marie-Henri	*Author*
Stepniak		***Kravchinski***	Sergei Mikhailovich	*Russian Revolutionary*
Stevens	Cat	***Georgiou***	Stephen	*Singer*
Stevens	Connie	***Ingolia***	Concetta	*Actress*
Stevens	Inger	***Stengland***	Inger	*Actress*
Stevens	Shakin'	***Barrett***	Michael	*Singer*
Stewart	Ed	***Mainwaring***	Edward Stewart	*Disc Jockey*
Sting		***Sumner***	Gordon	*Vocalist and Musician*
Stone	Irving	***Tennenbaum***	Irving	*US Novelist*
Stone	Joss	***Stoker***	Joscelyn Eve	*Singer and Actress*
Stoppard	Miriam	***Stern***	Miriam	*Broadcaster*
Stoppard	Tom	***Straussler***	Thomas	*Dramatist*
Strange	Steve	***Harrington***	Steve	*Singer*
Stratas	Teresa	***Strataki***	Anastasia	*Soprano*
Strummer	Joe	***Mellor***	John	*Rock Star*
Sturges	Preston	***Biden***	Edmund Preston	*Writer and Director*
Styrene	Poly	***Elliot***	Marion	*Punk-Rock Singer*
Suggs		***McPherson***	Graham	*Singer (Madness)*
Sui Sin Far		***Eaton***	Edith	*Author*
Sumac	Yma	***Chavarri***	Emperatriz	*Musician*
Summer	Donna	***Gaines***	Donna Andrea	*Singer*
Summers	Ann	***Gold***	Jacqueline	*Businesswoman*
Sundance Kid		***Longabaugh***	Henry	*Outlaw*
Supergirl		***Danvers***	Linda	*Fictional Superhero*
Swanson	Gloria	***Svensson***	Gloria	*Actress*
Sylva	Carmen	***Elizabeth***	of Romania	*Queen of Romania*
T	T	***Tureaud***	Lawrence	*Actor*
Tanfucio	Neri	***Fucini***	Renato	*Italian Writer*
Tate	Catherine	***Ford***	Catherine	*Comedienne*
Tati	Jacques	***Tatischeff***	Jacques	*Actor*
Tauber	Richard	***Seiffert***	Ernst	*Austrian Tenor*
Taylor	Elizabeth	***Coles***	Elizabeth	*Novelist*
Taylor	Robert	***Brough***	Spangler	*Actor*
Tempah	Tinie	***Okogwu***	Patrick	*Rapper*
Tennant	David	***McDonald***	David	*Actor*
Tenzin Gyatso		***Tsering***	Lhamo Thondup	*14th Dalai Lama*
Terson	Peter	***Patterson***	Peter	*Playwright*
Theresa	Mother	***Bojaxhiu***	Agnes Gonxha	*Roman Catholic Nun*
Thomas	Terry	***Stevens***	Terry	*Comedy Actor*
Thumb	Tom	***Stratton***	Charles	*Circus Performer*
Tich		***Amey***	Ian	*Guitarist*
Tich	Little	***Relph***	Harry	*Comedian*
Tilley	Vesta	***Powles***	Matilda Alice	*Male Impersonator*
Tim	Tiny	***Khaury***	Herbert	*Singer*
Timbaland		***Mosley***	Timothy	*Rapper*
Tintoretto		***Robusti***	Jacopo	*Artist*
Titmarsh	Michael Angelo	***Thackeray***	William Makepeace	*Author*
Tito		***Broz***	Josip	*Yugoslav Leader*
Todd	Mike	***Goldenburger***	Avron	*Producer*
Tornado		***McIntosh***	David	*Television Gladiator*
Trog		***Fawkes***	Walter Ernest	*Cartoonist and Clarinettist*
Trotsky	Leon	***Bronstein***	Lev Davidovitch	*Russian Revolutionary*

Tucker	Richard	***Ticker***	Reuben	*Singer*
Tucker	Sophie	***Abruza***	Sophie	*Music Hall Singer*
Tuesday	Gayle	***Gilhooly***	Brenda	*Comedienne*
Tunes	MC	***Lockett***	Nicky	*Rapper*
Turner	Tina	***Bullock***	Annie Mae	*Singer*
Twain	Mark	***Clemens***	Samuel Langhorne	*Author*
Twain	Shania	***Edwards***	Eileen Regina	*Pop Singer*
Twiggy		***Hornby***	Leslie	*Model and Actress*
Twitty	Conway	***Jenkins***	Harold Lloyd	*Singer*
Tyler	Bonnie	***Sullivan (née Hopkins)***	Gaynor	*Singer*
Tyler	Steven	***Tallarico***	Stephen	*Rock Musician*
Ultimate Warrior		***Hellwig***	James	*Professional Wrestler*
Uncle Remus		***Harris***	Joel Chandler	*Author*
Undertaker		***Calloway***	Mark	*Wrestler*
Vadim	Roger	***Plemiannikov***	Roger Vadim	*Film Director*
Valens	Ritchie	***Valenzuela***	Ritchie	*Singer*
Valentino	Rudolph	***D'Antonguolla***	Rudolpho	*Actor*
Valli	Frankie	***Castellucio***	Frank	*Singer*
Van Damme	Jean-Claude	***Van Varenberg***	Jean-Claude	*Actor*
Vance	Tommy	***Hope-Weston***	Richard	*Disc Jockey*
Vangelis		***Papathanassiou***	Evangelos	*Musician*
Vanilla Ice		***Winkle***	Robert van	*Rapper and Actor*
Vaughan	Frankie	***Abelsohn***	Frank	*Singer*
Vaughan	Peter	***Ohm***	Peter	*Actor*
Vee	Bobby	***Velline***	Robert Thomas	*Singer*
Vegas	Johnny	***Pennington***	Michael	*Comedian*
Verdy	Violette	***Guillerm***	Nelly	*French Dancer*
Vernon	John	***Agopsowicz***	Adolphus	*US Actor*
Veronese	Paolo	***Caliari***	Paolo	*Venetian Painter*
Vicious	Sid	***Ritchie***	John	*Singer*
Villa	Pancho	***Arango***	Doroteo	*Mexican Patriot*
Villeneuve	Justin	***Davies***	Nigel	*Hair Stylist*
Vincent	Gene	***Craddock***	Eugene Vincent	*Singer*
Vine	Barbara	***Rendell***	Ruth	*Novelist*
Vinegar	Captain Hercules	***Fielding***	Henry	*Author*
Vivekananda	Swami	***Dutt***	Narendranath	*Hindu Missionary*
Voltaire		***Arouet***	François-Marie	*Philosopher*
Wall	Max	***Lorimer***	Maxwell George	*Actor and Comedian*
Ward	Artemus	***Browne***	Charles Farrar	*Writer and Humorist*
Warlock	Peter	***Heseltine***	Philip Arnold	*Composer*
Warner	Jack	***Waters***	Jack	*Actor*
Warner	Jack Leonard	***Eichelbaum***	Jack Leonard	*Film Mogul*
Warrior		***Aherne***	Michael	*TV Gladiator*
Warwick	Richard	***Winter***	Richard	*Actor*
Waters	Muddy	***Morganfield***	McKinley	*Singer*
Wayne	John	***Morrison***	Marion	*Actor*
Weathercock	Janus	***Wainewright***	Thomas Griffiths	*Art Critic and Murderer*
Webb	Clifton	***Hollenbeck***	Webb Parmalee	*Actor*
Weegee		***Fellig***	Arthur	*Photographer*
Welch	Bruce	***Cripps***	Bruce	*Guitarist*
Welch	Raquel	***Tejada***	Raquel	*Actress*
Weldon	Fay	***Birkinshaw***	Franklin	*Writer*
Wellthorpe	Edna	***Orton***	Joe	*Dramatist (as Fictional Letter Writer)*
West	Nigel	***Allason***	Rupert	*MP and Author*
West	Rebecca	***Fairfield***	Cicely Isabel	*Author*
Westmacott	Mary	***Christie***	Agatha	*Author (as Romantic Novelist)*
Wharton	Edith	***Jones***	Edith	*Author*
White	Colonel	***Gray***	Charles	*Fictional TV Character*
Widow		***Sisson***	Richard	*Musical act 'Kit and the Widow'*
Wilde	Kim	***Smith***	Kim	*Singer*
Wilde	Marty	***Smith***	Reginald	*Singer*
Wilder	Gene	***Silberman***	Jerome	*Actor*
Wiley		***Cowie***	Richard	*Rapper*
Wilton	Robb	***Smith***	Robert Wilton	*Comedian*
Windsor	Barbara	***Deeks***	Barbara	*Actress*
Winters	Bernie	***Weinstein***	Bernie	*Comedian*
Winters	Shelley	***Schrift***	Shirley	*Actress*
Wise	Ernie	***Wiseman***	Ernest	*Comedian*
Wolf	Howling	***Burnett***	Chester Arthur	*Singer and Composer*
Wonder	Stevie	***Judkins***	Steveland	*Singer and Composer*
Wood	Mrs Henry	***Price***	Ellen	*English Novelist*
Wood	Natalie	***Gurdin***	Natasha	*Actress*
Woodson	BJ	***James***	Frank	*American Outlaw*
Worth	Harry	***Illingworth***	Harry	*Comedian*
Wylie	Gerald	***Barker***	Ronnie	*Writer*
Wyman	Bill	***Perks***	William	*Musician*
Wyman	Jane	***Faulks***	Sarah Jane	*Actress*

Wymark	Patrick	***Cheeseman***	Patrick	*Actor*
Wynette	Tammy	***Pugh***	Wynette	*Singer*
Wyngarde	Peter	***Goldbert***	Cyril Louis	*Actor*
X	Malcolm	***Little***	Malcolm	*Civil Rights Leader*
Yates	Dornford	***Mercer***	Cecil William	*Novelist*
York	Michael	***Johnson***	Mike	*Actor*
York	Susannah	***Fletcher***	Susannah	*Actress*
Youens	Bernard	***Popley***	Bernard	*Actor*
Young	Gig	***Barr***	Byron	*Actor*
Young	Jimmy	***Young***	Leslie Ronald	*Broadcaster*
Zadora	Pia	***Schipani***	Pia	*Actress*
Zombie	Rob	***Cummings***	Robert Bartleh	*US Film Director*

Relationships

NB: The relationship given is that of the second column to the first.

Arthur Conan Doyle	EW Hornung	*Brother-in-law*
Stanley Baldwin	Rudyard Kipling	*Cousin*
Richard Briers	Terry-Thomas	*Cousin*
George Clooney	Miguel Ferrer	*Cousin*
Elizabeth I	Mary Queen of Scots	*Cousin*
King George V	Kaiser Wilhelm II	*Cousin*
Christopher Lee	Ian Fleming	*Cousin*
Patrick McNee	David Niven	*Cousin*
Kate Robbins	Paul McCartney	*Cousin*
Ginger Rogers	Rita Hayworth	*Cousin*
Franklin D Roosevelt	Theodore Roosevelt	*5th cousin*
Herbert H Asquith	Violet Bonham-Carter	*Daughter*
Ingrid Bergman	Isabella Rossellini	*Daughter*
Tony Booth (actor)	Cherie Blair	*Daughter*
Vera Brittain	Shirley Williams	*Daughter*
William Jennings Bryan	Ruth Rohde	*Daughter*
Jasper Carrott	Lucy Davis	*Daughter*
Blythe Danner	Gwyneth Paltrow	*Daughter*
Chris De Burgh	Rosanna Davidson (Miss World)	*Daughter*
Debbie Reynolds and Eddie Fisher	Carrie Fisher	*Daughter*
Judy Garland	Lorna Luft	*Daughter*
	Liza Minnelli	*Daughter*
Jeremy Hawk	Belinda Lang	*Daughter*
Goldie Hawn	Kate Hudson	*Daughter*
Tippi Hedren	Melanie Griffith	*Daughter*
Helios & Perse	Circe	*Daughter*
Thora Hird	Janette Scott	*Daughter*
Richard and Charlotte Hough	Deborah Moggach	*Daughter*
Roger Kemble	Sarah Siddons	*Daughter*
King Agenor and Queen Telephassa	Europa	*Daughter*
King Cepheus and Queen Cassiopeia	Andromeda	*Daughter*
King Priam and Queen Hecuba	Cassandra	*Daughter*
Phyllida Law	Sophie Thompson	*Daughter*
	Emma Thompson	*Daughter*
Lord Longford	Lady Antonia Fraser	*Daughter*
Mary of Guise and James V	Mary Queen of Scots	*Daughter*
Sharon Maughan	Alice Eve	*Daughter*
Arthur Miller	Rebecca Miller	*Daughter*
Thomas Moore	Margaret Roper	*Daughter*
Muhammad	Fatima	*Daughter*
Jawaharlal Nehru	Indira Gandhi	*Daughter*
Nanette Newman	Emma Forbes	*Daughter*
Tsar Nicholas II	Anastasia	*Daughter*
Oedipus and Jocasta	Antigone	*Daughter*
Christina Onassis	Athina Roussel	*Daughter*
Maureen O'Sullivan	Mia Farrow	*Daughter*
Diana Rigg	Rachael Stirling	*Daughter*
Kate Robbins	Emily Atack	*Daughter*
Ravi Shankar	Norah Jones	*Daughter*
Steven Tyler	Liv Tyler	*Daughter*
Jon Voight	Angelina Jolie	*Daughter*
Zeus and Leda	Helen and Clytemnestra	*Daughters*
Zeus and Metis	Athene	*Daughter*
Zeus and Themis	Clotho (one of the 3 Fates)	*Daughter*
Emmeline Pankhurst	Christabel and Sylvia	*Daughters*
James Fox	Billie Piper	*Daughter-in-law*
Aristotle Onassis	Athina Roussel	*Granddaughter*
Sigmund Freud	Clement and Lucian	*Grandsons*
Genghis Khan	Kublai Khan	*Grandson*
Herbert Beerbohm Tree	Oliver Reed	*Grandson*
Josiah Wedgwood	Charles Darwin	*Grandson*
Sigmund Freud	Emma (journalist) and Bella (fashion designer)	*Great-granddaughters*

FAMOUS PEOPLE

Queen Victoria	Queen Elizabeth II	*Great-great-grand-daughter*
Queen Victoria	Duke of Edinburgh	*Great-great-grandson*
Anna Neagle	Nicholas Hoult	*Great-Nephew*
Bonnie Bedelia	Macaulay Culkin	*Nephew*
Rosemary Clooney	George Clooney	*Nephew*
Francis Ford Coppola	Nicolas Cage	*Nephew*
Dick Francis	Leigh Francis	*Nephew*
Lucian Freud	Matthew (PR guru)	*Nephew*
Lord Salisbury	Arthur Balfour	*Nephew*
Carol Reed	Oliver Reed	*Nephew*
Ellen Terry	John Gielgud	*Nephew*
Circe	Medea	*Niece*
Sarah Siddons	Fanny Kemble	*Niece*
Echidna and Typhon	Cerberus, Chimaera, Hydra	*Offspring*
Poseidon and Medusa	Pegasus	*Offspring*
Dana Andrews	Steve Forrest	*Sibling*
Thomas Arne	Susanna Cibber	*Sibling*
Balarama	Krishna	*Sibling*
Warren Beatty	Shirley Maclaine	*Sibling*
David Broome	Liz Edgar	*Sibling*
Duggie Brown	Lynn Perrie	*Sibling*
Keith Chegwin	Janice Long	*Sibling*
Catherine Deneuve	Françoise Dorléac	*Sibling*
Margaret Drabble	AS Byatt	*Sibling*
Adila Fachiri (violinist)	Jelly Arányi (violinist)	*Sibling*
Joan Fontaine	Olivia de Havilland	*Sibling*
Lady Antonia Fraser	Rachel Billington	*Sibling*
Lucian Freud	Clement	*Sibling*
Crystal Gayle	Loretta Lynn	*Sibling*
Graham Greene	Hugh Carleton Greene	*Sibling*
Michael Hamburger (poet)	Paul Hamlyn (publisher)	*Sibling*
Hannibal	Hasdrubal	*Sibling*
Eden Kane	Peter and Robin Sarstedt	*Siblings*
John Kemble	Sarah Siddons	*Sibling*
Jimmy Logan	Annie Ross	*Sibling*
Lord Rothermere	Lord Northcliffe	*Sibling*
Paul McCartney	Mike McGear	*Sibling*
John Mills	Annette Mills	*Sibling*
Liza Minnelli	Lorna Luft	*Sibling*
Gary Oldman	Laila Morse	*Sibling*
Wendi Peters	Lindsey Dawson	*Sibling*
River Phoenix	Leaf, Rainbow, Summer, Liberty	*Siblings*
Brian Rix	Sheila Mercier	*Sibling*
Kate Robbins	Ted Robbins	*Sibling*
Eric Roberts	Julia Roberts	*Sibling*
Georhe Sanders	Tom Conway	*Sibling*
Julia Sawalha	Nadia Sawalha	*Sibling*
Talia Shire	Francis Ford Coppola	*Sibling*
Eric Sykes	Hattie Jacques	*Sibling (fictional)*
Tanita Tikaram	Ramon Tikaram	*Sibling*
Jack Warner	Elsie and Doris Waters	*Siblings*
Virginia Woolf	Vanessa Bell	*Sibling*
Aeacus and Endeis	Peleus	*Son*
Anu and Ki	Enki and Enlil	*Sons*
Ares and Aphrodite	Eros	*Son*
Atreus and Aerope	Agamemnon	*Son*
David Carradine and Barbara Hershey	Free (changed to Tom)	*Son*
Judith Chalmers and Neil Durden-Smith	Mark Durden-Smith	*Son*
Charles Martel	Pepin the Short	*Son*
Cleopatra and Julius Caesar	Caesarion (Ptolemy XV)	*Son*
Cecil Day-Lewis and Jill Balcon	Daniel Day-Lewis	*Son*
Elizabeth and Zacharias	John the Baptist	*Son*
Erebos and Nyx	Charon	*Son*
Eric the Red	Leif Eriksson	*Son*
Julia Foster	Ben Fogle	*Son*
Clement Freud	Matthew (PR guru)	*Son*
Indira Gandhi	Rajiv Gandhi	*Son*
Hamilcar	Hannibal	*Son*
Goldie Hawn	Oliver Hudson	*Son*
Helios and Clymene	Phaethon	*Son*
Iapetus and Clymene	Prometheus, Atlas, Epimetheus, Menoetius	*Sons*
Jenny Jerome	Winston Churchill	*Son*
Jupiter and Latona	Apollo	*Son*
Rosa Kaufman (pianist)	Boris Pasternak	*Son*
King Agenor and Queen Telephassa	Cadmus	*Son*
King Glaucus and Queen Eurynome	Bellerophon	*Son*
King Laius and Queen Jocasta	Oedipus	*Son*
Lulu	Jordan Frieda (actor)	*Son*
Mary Martin	Larry Hagman	*Son*
Mary Queen of Scots	James VI (Scotland) I (England)	*Son*
Marni Nixon	Andrew Gold	*Son*
Osiris and Nephthys	Anubis	*Son*
Norrie Paramour	John Paramour (golf director)	*Son*

Peleus and Thetis	Achilles	*Son*
Pepin the Short	Charlemagne	*Son*
Priam and Hecuba of Troy	Paris	*Son*
Martin Sheen	Emilio Estevez and Charlie Sheen	*Sons*
Ellen Terry and EW Godwin	Edward Gordon Craig	*Son*
Billy Two Rivers	Wayne Hemingway	*Son*
Suzanne Valadon	Maurice Utrillo	*Son*
Ian Wright	Bradley Wright-Phillips	*Son*
	Shaun Wright-Phillips	*Son (adopted)*
Zebedee	St John	*Son*
Zeus and Danaë	Perseus	*Son*
Zeus and Leda	Castor, Polydeuces	*Sons*
Zeus and Leto	Apollo	*Son*
Cecil B De Mille	Anthony Quinn	*Son-in-law*
Thora Hird	Mel Tormé	*Son-in-law*
Franz Liszt	Richard Wagner	*Son-in-law*
Thomas Mann	WH Auden	*Son-in-law*
Arthur Miller	Daniel Day Lewis	*Son-in-law*
Rupert Murdoch	Matthew Freud (PR guru)	*Son-in-law*
Eugene O'Neill	Charlie Chaplin	*Son-in-law*
Peter Vaughan	Gregor Fisher	*Son-in-law*

Crime and Punishment

Dr John Bodkin Adams (1899–1983) Physician who was tried in 1957 after one of his patients, Edith Morrell, died suspiciously. Like other elderly patients before her, Edith had made Adams a beneficiary of her will before dying by morphine overdose. On acquittal Adams was struck off but continued to treat private patients and was in fact reinstated by the General Medical Council in 1961. Whether he merely practised euthanasia or killed for personal gain will never be proven and the secret died with him.

Susan Barber (1956–) In May 1981 Susan Barber placed half a teaspoonful of weedkiller in her husband Michael's steak-and-kidney pie after he caught her in bed with her lover and threw him out of the window. Michael Barber was diagnosed with Goodpasture's syndrome, a rare nervous condition, but died shortly after. The cause of death was recorded as pneumonia and kidney failure. His wife gained £15,000 from her husband's pension fund and set up home with her defenestrated lover, Richard Collins. David Evans, the pathologist who conducted the post mortem, began to have a few doubts and sent organs from Barber's body to ICI, the manufacturers of the weedkiller Gramoxone, and sure enough, traces of the poison were detected. Barber and Collins were arrested in April 1982 and he was sentenced to two years imprisonment for conspiracy while Susan Barber was jailed for life.

Anne Bonny (1692–?) Irish pirate who lived in the early 18th century. Anne showed her fiery temper at an early age and is thought to have killed a servant girl with a case-knife. She was disinherited by her lawyer father and sailed to the Bahamas with her husband, the cause of the disinheritance. Bonny fell in with Captain John Rackham, the notorious Calico Jack, and sailed with him disguised as a man. Bizarrely enough another member of Jack's crew was Mary Read, who was also sailing under the guise of a man, and an amusing incident whereby Read tried to seduce Bonny proved to be the unveiling of both. In October 1720 Calico Jack's ship, *The Revenge*, was captured by a sloop on the orders of the governor of Jamaica and Jack was hung and Read and Bonny imprisoned. Mary Read died of a fever but Bonny managed to escape and her whereabouts remained a mystery.

Charles Bronson (1952–) Born Michael Gordon Peterson and first imprisoned in 1974 for robbing a jeweller of £35, but his aggressive behaviour has added an extra 25 years to his sentences and he has experienced only a total of 69 days of freedom since then. Bronson has shown some ability as a cartoonist and poet. He married Miss Saira Rehman in June 2001 at Woodhill Prison and Lord Longford was best man.

Burke and Hare William Burke (1792–1829) and William Hare (1790–c1860) met at Logue's lodging house, Edinburgh, in 1818. Sharing the same building was an army pensioner known as Old Donald, who died in 1827 owing Hare £4. Burke and Hare opened his coffin and substituted a sack of bark for his body and sold it for £7 10/- to Dr Robert Knox of Edinburgh's Anatomy School. Over the next 10 months Dr Knox became a regular customer of the pair, who at first produced a legitimate supply of corpses, but then began to create their own by foul means. Burke's common-law wife, Helen McDougal, or Hare's, Maggie Laird, would lure a victim back to the lodgings and then ply them with drink, Burke would then kneel on their chest, while stopping their breathing by placing his hands over their nose and mouth. This method became known as 'burking'. Victims included Mary Paterson, a local prostitute, and a local idiot called Daft Jamie, both of whose murders were suspected by Knox, who remained quiet. Eventually they slipped up by leaving the body of Margaret Docherty where other lodgers could find it. Hare and Laird escaped prosecution by turning King's evidence and the case against McDougal was unproven, but Burke was publicly hanged on 28 January 1829.

Capital punishment Relevant dates in the history of capital punishment in Britain are as follows: In 1868 public execution was abolished, Michael Barrett (26 May) being the last victim. On 13 July 1955 Ruth Ellis was the last woman to be hanged in Britain. On 13 August 1964 Peter Anthony Allen and Gwynne Owen Evans were the last victims of a British hanging. On 9 November 1965 the death penalty was suspended for a trial period of five years, but in December 1969 Parliament confirmed the permanent abolition.

Mary Ann Cotton (1832–73) District nurse from West Auckland, County Durham, who killed at least five people including her second husband Frederick, his two stepsons, and two lovers, a local excise officer named Quick-Manning and her lodger Joseph Natrass. She was suspected of killing many more, possibly 30. Her motive was invariably either to collect insurance money or to pave the way for a new liaison. Her chosen method of disposal was arsenic. She was eventually tried and sentenced to death in 1873. The hangman bungled the execution, causing her to take three and a half minutes to stop convulsing before dying at the rope's end.

Dr Hawley Harvey Crippen (1862–1910) Crippen, a patent medicine salesman and physician, poisoned his second wife, Cora Turner, a would-be music-hall artiste working under the name of Belle Elmore, after becoming infatuated with his young secretary Ethel Le Neve. After the murder at their home at 39 Hilltop Crescent, Islington, North London, Ethel, who was privy to the murder, became anxious of its detection so the couple fled to Canada aboard the SS *Montrose* under the names of Mr Robinson and his son (Ethel). The ship's captain became suspicious and contacted Scotland Yard by radio telegraphy and the couple were arrested. The case was famous for being the first example of a successful conviction by use of radio. Crippen was tried for murder at the Old Bailey on 18 October 1910, found guilty and hanged at Pentonville on 23 November. Neve was tried separately but ably defended by FE Smith and acquitted. She lived till 1967.

DNA DNA provides the building blocks of life – the unique gene code that makes us what we are. In 1985, Sir Alec Jeffreys developed the system, first discovered by Crick and Watson in 1953, so that police could take an individual's genetic 'fingerprint' to establish guilt. Colin Pitchfork was the first person to be convicted using DNA evidence when he was jailed for life in 1988 for murdering two schoolgirls. Pitchfork murdered 15-year-old Lynda Mann in 1983 in Narborough, Leicestershire. Three years later he killed Dawn Ashworth, also 15. A 17-year-old confessed to killing Dawn, but a DNA test proved his innocence, and the screening of 5,000 locals showed Pitchfork to be the culprit. DNA has also been used retrospectively, and James Hanratty, hanged for murdering civil servant Michael Gregston and raping and maiming his mistress, is the most famous example. Hanratty hijacked the couple in their car off the A6 in Berkshire, then attacked them near Bedford. He denied the crime, and family members battled for 40 years to prove his innocence, but his body was exhumed in 2001 and DNA tests proved his guilt.

Ruth Ellis (1927–55) Model and nightclub manageress, Ellis shot and killed her lover, racing driver David Blakely, outside the Magdala public house in Hampstead on Good Friday 1955. She was tried and convicted at the Old Bailey in June and hanged at Holloway prison on 13 July 1955, the last woman to be hanged in England.

Helen Duncan (1897–1956) Scottish medium, best known as the last person to be imprisoned under the British Witchcraft Act of 1735. Duncan was arrested in 1944 after a seance in Portsmouth in which she told a couple that their son, who was serving on HMS *Barham*, had appeared from the spirit world to let them know his ship had sunk. The 1941 sinking with the loss of over 800 lives had been kept secret to maintain wartime morale. She served nine months in Holloway Prison and there is a present campaign to grant her a pardon.

John George Haigh (1910–49) Whilst living in a small hotel in Kensington, Haigh became friendly with Olive Durand-Deacon, a wealthy 69-year-old widow, who told him of her ideas for the marketing of cosmetics. Haigh invited her to his factory in Crawley, West Sussex, where she was shot and her body disposed of in a vat of sulphuric acid. On 20 February 1949 he then presented himself at Chelsea police station and reported her missing. Police became suspicious and checked his factory where they found the murder weapon and Mrs Durand-Dickson's plastic dentures. Haigh made a statement admitting to eight other murders, including three members of a family called McSwann, a Dr and Mrs Henderson and three other people whose identities he had never established. He was tried at Lewes Crown Court in July 1949 and was executed at Wandsworth Prison on 10 August 1949.

Hangmen The most famous British public executioner was probably Albert Pierrepoint, who notched up 700 victims before his retirement. Albert died in 1982, leaving Syd Dernley as the last hangman to die since hanging was abolished. Dernley aided in the execution of 20 criminals between 1949 and 1953 but was removed from the register in 1954. He died in 1994. William Calcraft (1800–79) was the last to perform in public as hangings were held in prisons after 1868. James Berry (1852–1913) is probably the second most famous hangman after Albert Pierrepoint, although John Ellis became a celebrity after becoming the executioner of Dr Crippen and Sir Roger Casement. Ellis (1874–1926) was haunted by the aftermath of his career and eventually cut his own throat with a barber's razor. Other famous hangmen include Richard Arnett (1674–1728), Edward Dennis (1717–86), Jack Ketch, byname of John Ketch (d.1686), the Billington family, James (1847–1901), Thomas (1872–1902), William (1873–1934) and John (1880–1905), William Marwood (1820–83), George Smith (1805–74), Henry Pierrepoint (1874–1922) and Thomas Pierrepoint (1870–1954).

Jack the Ripper Unknown murderer of five prostitutes between August and November 1888 in Whitechapel, London. The five unfortunate victims were Mary Ann 'Polly' Nichols (42), Dark Annie Chapman (47), Elizabeth 'Long Liz' Stride (45), Catharine 'Kate Kelly' Eddowes (43) and Mary Jane Kelly (25). The inspector who initially investigated the murders was George Frederick Abberline (1843–1929).

William Kidd (1645–1701) Originally a respected sea captain in New York when hired by a Whig syndicate in 1695 as a government-commissioned privateer authorised to seize pirates, freebooters and sea-rovers in the name of the British government, Kidd decided to turn pirate himself. During an angry exchange with a crew member in 1697 he shot and killed his gunner, William Moore. On 9 May 1701 Kidd was found guilty of the murder of Moore and on five indictments of piracy. He was hanged immediately at Execution Dock, Wapping. Unfortunately for Kidd the rope broke the first time, he fell to the ground in his drunken state, and had to be strung up a a second time.

Kray Twins Reggie Kray (1933–2000) and his twin brother Ronnie (1933–95) established a grip on the criminal underworld in the 1960s through their protection rackets and frauds. They opened a club, the Double R, in Bow Road, east London, which soon became popular with a showbiz clientele. Ronnie, a closet homosexual, was the dominant twin, and earned the nickname 'The Colonel', Reggie had more of a business brain. In 1965 Reggie married Frances Shea, but she committed suicide in 1967. The Firm, as they became known, became increasingly involved in hostilities with Charlie Richardson's south London gang, and they arranged the escape from Dartmoor of Frank Mitchell, the so-called Mad Axeman, whose murder they subsequently ordered. On 8 March 1966 Ronnie Kray shot dead George Cornell, a Richardson henchman, in the Blind Beggar public house on the Mile End Road. Cornell's offence had been to call Ronnie 'a fat poof'. In October 1966 Reggie Kray fatally stabbed a small-time thief called Jack 'the Hat' McVitie in a borrowed flat in Stoke Newington. Jack's crime had apparently been to show disrespect to the boys by wearing Bermuda shorts in one of their clubs. Detective Superintendent Leonard 'Nipper' Read eventually established a case against the twins and they were brought to trial at the Old Bailey in January 1969, after a member of the 'Firm', Albert Donaghue, had turned Queen's evidence. They were acquitted of the Mitchell murder but were convicted of murdering Cornell and McVitie.

Lord Lucan (1934–?) John Bingham, the 7th Earl of Lucan, an inveterate gambler and merchant banker, inherited a quarter of a million pounds on the death of his father. By 1974 he was almost bankrupt. On the night of 7 November 1974 he killed Sandra Rivett, the nanny of his two children, in his house in Lower Belgrave Street, London, in mistake for his wife Veronica. After attacking his wife too, but failing to kill her, he drove to the house of his friend, Susan Maxwell-Scott, at Uckfield in Sussex. His car was discovered at Newhaven but he was never seen again. He was declared legally dead in October 1999.

Donald Merrett (1910–54) At the age of 17 Merrett murdered his mother for the price of a motor bicycle. Twenty-five years later, and now calling himself Ronald Chesney, he murdered his wife and her mother. The first murder was in 1927, and although he claimed she shot herself in the neck, it became apparent over the course of her surviving 15 days that he murdered her for money, as he repeatedly forged her cheques during this period. He was charged with murder and forgery after her death, but due to the defence testimony of the eminent pathologist Bernard Spilsbury, who was appearing for the only time as a defence witness, was acquitted and served only twelve months on the forgery charge.On his release Merrett changed his name to Ronald Chesney and lived a life of petty crime until in 1954 he called on his wife, whom he had married when first released from prison, and knocked her out with drink before drowning her in the bath. He also killed her mother, who had intercepted him on leaving the house. He flew back to Germany but had been seen at the scene of the crime, an old people's home in Ealing, and before Interpol could arrest him he shot himself in the head in a wood near Cologne. Before he died he confessed to his German girlfriend that his real name was Donald Merrett and that when he was 17 he had killed his mother.

Moors Murderers On 28 October 1965, Ian Brady, a 27-year-old stock-clerk, and Myra Hindley, a 23-year-old typist, were charged with the murder of ten-year-old Lesley Ann Downey at Chester Assizes. Lesley's body was found on Saddleworth Moor 13 days earlier. Police were subsequently alerted by a call from Hindley's brother-in-law, David Smith, who had witnessed the killing of 17-year-old Edward Evans with an axe. Police searched Brady's house and found Evans's body in a blanket. The police subsequently found a left-luggage ticket in Hindley's prayer book which led them to a suitcase containing tapes and pornographic photographs, one of which showed Hindley posing with a dog at what turned out to be the grave of a third murdered child, John Kilbride, aged 12. On 6 May, 1966, Brady was sentenced to three concurrent terms of life imprisonment for the murders of all three children while Hindley received two concurrent life sentences for the murders of Edward Evans and Lesley Ann Downey. Hindley died of lung cancer on 15 November 2002.

Donald Neilson (1936– 2011) Born Donald Nappey in Dewsbury, West Yorkshire, the diminutive builder changed the family name to Neilson after the birth of his daughter. Neilson began his criminal life as a house burglar before progressing to post office robberies and ultimately to murder, killing three post office workers in 1974. The media had by now dubbed Neilson 'The Black Panther' due to his dark clothing and speed of movement. In January 1975 Neilson kidnapped 17-year-old Lesley Whittle, the daughter of a transport magnate, from the family home in Highley, Shropshire and asked for a £50,000 ransom. Two months later, after a series of police bungles Lesley's body was found hanging from a wire at the bottom of a drainage shaft in Bathpool Park, Kidsgrove, Staffordshire. In December 1975 Neilson was apprehended by two policemen in Mansfield for acting suspiciously when passing their panda car. In his panic Neilson produced his sawn-off shotgun and entered the car and ordered the men to drive. The driver eventually swerved and ground to a halt outside The Junction Chip Shop in Rainworth where he managed to attract the attention of several men in the queue who helped to overpower Neilson. In July 1976, at Oxford Crown Court, Neilson was convicted of the kidnapping and murder of Lesley Whittle, and three weeks later he was convicted of the murders of two postmasters and the husband of a postmistress. In total Neilson received five life sentences plus 21 years for kidnapping Lesley Whittle, 10 years for blackmailing her mother and 10 years each for the burglary charges from which he stole guns and ammunition and for possessing a sawn off shotgun with intent to endanger life. All the sentences were to run concurrently. In 2008, Neilson was diagnosed with motor neurone disease and he died three years later.

Dennis Nilsen (1945-) Born in Fraserburgh, Aberdeenshire, to a Scottish mother and a Norwegian father (Olav Magnus Moksheim) who adopted the surname Nilsen. The so-called Muswell Hill Murderer began his working life as an army cook before briefly becoming a policeman and, from 1974, a civil servant in a jobcentre in Denmark Street, London. A homosexual, Nilsen committed the murders of 15 young men in London, between 1978 and 1983. The majority of Nilsen's victims were homeless or homosexual men whom he would typically meet on the streets or in bars and lure back to his home (firstly in Cricklewood but more infamously 23 Cranley Gardens, Muswell Hill) with an offer of refreshments or shelter. The victims were invariably strangled and drowned during the night (a method Nilsen thought most humane; hence his other nickname of the 'Kindly Killer'). He used his butchering skills to dismember the bodies (which were sometimes kept for months in various locations in his home). Nilsen later admitted to having engaged in sexual acts with the corpses. Nilsen sometimes flushed parts of his victims down the toilet which eventually led to his capture and arrest after Dyno-Rod were called out by neighbours for blocked pipes and found human remains in the system. Nilsen's trial began at the Old Bailey on 24 October 1983. He was convicted of six murders (several victims were unidentified) and two attempted murders and sentenced to life imprisonment on 4 November 1983. The Home Secretary later imposed a whole life tariff, which meant he would never be released.

Charles Peace (1832–79) Born in Manchester, the son of an animal trainer, Peace suffered an accident in childhood that left him crippled. To hide the loss of one finger he wore a false arm made of gutta-percha with a steel plate and a hook at the end of it. In 1876 he shot and killed a policeman whilst burgling a house. Two brothers were arrested for the murder and Peace attended the trial at which one of them, William Habron, was sentenced to death. Peace's next victim was a Mr Dyson, whose wife had formed a loose liaison with Peace, although it was to soon become a stalking situation. As a result of this murder, Peace became a wanted man and moved to London, where he rented a villa in Peckham. He now changed his name to John Ward and lived with his wife and his mistress, Susan Thompson, maintaining his lifestyle by a series of burglaries that he would attend in his pony and trap, carrying his tools in a violin case. He was eventually caught after wounding a policeman in Blackheath. He was sentenced to life imprisonment for wounding the policeman and then taken to Sheffield to stand trial for the murder of Arthur Dyson. On the way to Sheffield he managed to escape from the train, but was injured in the fall and was soon recaptured. He was tried for murder at Leeds assizes, found guilty and hanged by William Marwood after being refused a last drink. William Habron was released with a full pardon and awarded £1,000 compensation.

Peter Reyn-Bardt (1919–93) In May 1983 two peat-cutters working at Lindow Moss, near Wilmslow, Cheshire, dug up the skull of a middle-aged woman. Police reported the find to Peter Reyn-Bardt, a former executive with BOAC, whose wife Malika had disappeared in 1960, and under interrogation he confessed to her murder. He had strangled his wife, chopped up her body and buried the remains in the peat bog. He was tried and found guilty at Chester Crown Court and sentenced to life imprisonment. Subsequently the skull was sent to Oxford University for radiocarbon dating and was found to be dated *circa* 410 AD. The following year another skeleton was found in the bog with more obvious evidence of a violent death. However, this one turned out to be the remains of a man who had been killed in a ritualistic death circa 300 BC. The whereabouts of Mrs Reyn-Bardt's body remain a mystery.

Harold Shipman (1946–2004) Harold Frederick Shipman studied at Leeds University medical school and eventually achieved a mediocre degree. His mother had died of lung cancer in June 1963 and it is believed it was seeing her daily morphine administered by the local GP that led to his compulsion to set himself up as an angel of mercy, albeit in some cases for personal gain. Shipman married his fiancée Primrose and took up his first practice in 1974 at the age of 28 in the small Yorkshire town of Todmorden. In 1975 a suspicious receptionist, Marjorie Walker, noticed some peculiar entries in the controlled substances ledger of a local pharmacist whereby large quantities of pethidine, a morphine-based painkiller had been ordered by Dr Shipman. His explanation was that he was injecting the drug himself and he was fined £600 and booked into a drug rehabilitation centre without being struck off. In 1977 Shipman began working at the Donneybrook Medical Centre in Hyde, Manchester, and proceeded to rebuild his career. Despite doubts by several people over the years it was not until the death of Mrs Grundy, an 81-year-old former mayor of Hyde, on 24 June 1998, that questions were asked by Mrs Grundy's daughter Angela Woodruff, a solicitor by profession. Mrs Grundy had made a will in 1986 and lodged it with her daughter's law firm but now she was asked to believe that her mother had made another one without her knowledge and left £386,000 to Dr Shipman. Detective Superintendent Bernard Postles investigated and on reviewing the will came to the conclusion that Kathleen Grundy's signature had been forged and began to build a solid case against Shipman with the help of several interested parties who now came forward and expressed their own doubts about him. His trial began in October 1999 at Preston Crown Court and on 31 January 2000 Shipman was found guilty of 15 counts of murder. The Department of Health estimates that Shipman may have killed 236 patients between 1974 and 1998.

George Joseph Smith (1872–1915) Perpetrator of the Brides in the Bath Murders. In 1898 Smith married 19-year-old Beatrice Thornhill, his only legal wife. In 1910 he met and bigamously married Bessie Mundy in Weymouth calling himself Henry Williams. He eventually murdered Bessie by drowning her in a tin bath and attesting that she had a fit and drowned by misadventure. Smith subsequently gained from a trust fund set up in Bessie's name. He then bigamously married Alice Burnham in Southsea in November 1913 and then 'married' Margaret Lofty, a clergyman's daughter at Bath in 1914. In both cases he took his wives to the doctors before dispatching them, to show that they suffered from fits. A newspaper report of Margaret Lofty's death was seen by Alice Burnham's father, who alerted the police. The police soon realised that Smith was a murderer, and with the help of Bernard Spilsbury he was tried and found guilty, sentenced to death and hanged at Maidstone Prison on Friday 13 August 1915.

Peter Sutcliffe (1946–) Between 1975 and 1980 Sutcliffe murdered 13 women in the north of England. Many of his victims were prostitutes and were invariably banged over the head with a ball-pein hammer before being stabbed and mutilated. He was eventually caught during a routine check when he was found in a car with a prostitute. He asked the police if he could relieve himself and unknown to them at the time he hid his murder weapons behind an oil storage tank. The police ran a routine check on his car and found it had false plates. Sutcliffe was arrested and while in custody was found to be on the list of possible suspects. Sutcliffe, now nicknamed the Yorkshire Ripper, made a full confession and on 22 May 1981 was sentenced to life imprisonment. He began his sentence at Parkhurst but after being attacked was transferred to Broadmoor High Security Mental Institution, where he resides today. Sutcliffe often refers to himself as Peter William Coonan (his mother's maiden name).

Fashion and Dress

General Information

aba Loose gown worn in the Muslim world.

agal Fillet of two or three cords used to fasten a keffiyeh on the head.

Agnès B Born Agnès Troublé in Versailles, France, 1941, she worked as a junior editor on *Elle* magazine before opening her first boutique. Her style is characterised by precise tailoring, simple subdued colours, usually black, natural materials and casual looks. In 1987 she launched her 'Le B' perfume range and a maternity collection. More recently she founded a joint film production company with Harmony Korine called 'O'Salvation'.

aigrette Spray of gems worn on the head.

Alaia, Azzedine Tunisian designer who was a leading light throughout the 1980s but is experiencing a revival with his merger with Prada.

alb Long, white linen vestment with sleeves, usually worn by priests.

alpargata Light canvas shoe with a plaited fibre sole; an espadrille.

amice Rectangular piece of white linen worn by priests around the neck and shoulders under the alb, or formerly, on the head. Also a furred hood with long ends hanging down in front.

Amies, Sir Hardy (1909–2003) Queen's dressmaker for 50 years. Amies showed his first collection in 1946 and remained at the top of his profession until his death.

Armani, Giorgio Italian fashion designer based in Milan and New York. Armani opened his first fashion house in 1974 and, although well respected within his industry, rose to fame after dressing Richard Gere in the 1980 film *American Gigolo.*

Ashley, Laura Born in Merthyr Tydfil, South Wales (1925–85) as Laura Mountney. Married Bernard Ashley in 1949 and started a business manufacturing furnishing materials and wallpaper with patterns based upon document sources mainly from the 19th century. After giving up work to start a family she experimented with designing and making clothes, and this transformed the business into an international chain of boutiques, selling clothes, furnishing fabrics and wallpapers.

astrakhan wool Obtained from the Karakul breed of sheep.

babouche Turkish or oriental heelless slipper.

babushka Headscarf tied under the chin and worn by Russian peasant women.

Badgley Mischka American designers Mark Badgley and James Mischka. The duo are best known for their stellar beaded creations and 'aged look'. Their material is made in Italy and embroidered in Bombay, India.

balbriggan Knitted, unbleached cotton fabric, from which underwear is often made.

baldric Wide silk sash or leather belt worn over the opposite shoulder to the hip, for carrying a sword.

Balenciaga, Cristobal Spanish fashion designer (1895–1972) opened the House of Balenciaga in Paris, 1937, and retired in 1968.

Balmain, Pierre French fashion designer (1914–82) famous for his elegant simplicity. Immortalised by Peter Sarstedt in 'Where do you go to my lovely'.

Balmoral Can be a laced walking shoe, a woollen petticoat, a Scottish brimless hat, traditionally made of dark blue wool with a cockade and plume, a cloak, a jacket or mantle – all these styles set by Queen Victoria and Prince Albert in the 1850s and 60s.

bandanna Square of silk or cotton with spotted pattern, tied round the head or neck.

Banks, Jeff Born in Wales, 1943, became widely known in the mid 70s when he launched the 'Warehouse' chain. Presenter of the first dedicated television fashion programme, *The Clothes Show.* His first wife was singer Sandie Shaw.

banyan Loose-fitting shirt or jacket originally worn in India.

batiste Fine plain-weave cotton or linen fabric, used for shirts and dresses.

batwing sleeve Sleeve of a garment with a deep armhole and tight wrist.

bauchle General term for an old, worn shoe.

Bebe Top international brand name for designer shoes as in the name of their stores.

Belle and Bunty Label formed by Alice-Louise Shreeve &Hannah Coniam (née Roff). Their first collection, Go Wild, launched at the National Army Museum, made a huge impact. The label's name derives from the childhood nicknames of its founders.

Ben Sherman British clothing company founded in 1963 by Arthur Bernard Sugarman (1925–87). The shirts and accessories, sometimes sporting the RAF roundel, initially became the stock clothing for Mods but in the late 1960s were adopted by the skinhead subculture.

Benetton Fashion empire based in Treviso, Italy and identified with its sponsorship of rugby, basketball and volleyball but especially Formula One racing team.

Biba founder Barbara Hulanicki, born Warsaw, 1936.

biggin Plain, close-fitting cap, often tied under the chin, popular in 16th and 17th centuries based on coif-like caps worn by the Béguines lay sisters.

bijouterie Costume jewellery or trinkets, particularly finger-rings, from which the name derives.

bikini designer Louis Réard.

Bikkembergs, Dirk Born in Cologne, Germany, 1959, of Belgian extraction, first came to prominence as a shoe designer before establishing himself as a top ready-to-wear designer. Along with Ann Demeulemeester, Dirk Van Saene, Walter Van Beirendonck, Dries Van Noten, and Martin Margiela, one of the so-called Anvers 'Group of Six'.

billycock Any of several round-crowned brimmed hats of felt, named after William Coke, for whom it was first made in the 19th century.

biretta Stiff clerical cap with either three or four upright pieces projecting outwards from the centre to the edge, coloured black for priests, purple for bishops, red for cardinals and white for certain members of religious orders.

Blahnik, Manolo Born in the Canary Islands in 1942, of a Spanish mother and Czech father, Blahnik is a British-based designer of fashion shoes.

Bloomers Named after, and designed by Amelia Jenks Bloomer (1818–94), a New York campaigner for temperance and women's rights. Bloomers were originally the full-length Turkish trousers worn under a skirt in the 1850s, but evolved firstly into a knickerbock style, and made popular by lady cyclists in the 1890s, and subsequently into any loose-fitting ladies baggy undergarments.

boa Woman's long round scarf, usually of feathers or fur.

bodkin Blunt, large-eyed needle used for drawing tape through openwork, also a pin used in ancient times to fasten women's hair.

Body Shop founder Anita Roddick.

bolero Short jacket, just reaching the waist, as worn by men in Spain; also a woman's short, open jacket, with or without sleeves.

bonnet rouge Red cap worn by ardent supporters of the French Revolution.

Boudicca London-based label founded by Zowie Broach and Brian Kirkby. Named after the Queen of the Iceni who rebelled against the Romans in 61 AD.

bowler Hard felt hat with a rounded crown and a narrow curled brim, named after William Bowler in the US who designed it in 1850; in the US, a derby.

breeks Scottish name for breeches.

British warm Army officer's full-length, thick overcoat.

brogue (1) Rough shoe of untanned hide, formerly worn in Ireland but now having ornamental perforated bands and worn throughout the world.

brogue (2) Waterproof leggings with feet, used by anglers.

buckram Originally a fine cotton or linen fabric stiffened with size, later used in lining or stiffening clothes as well as bookbinding.

Bui, Barbara French fashion designer, born 1957, best known for her clean lines and offbeat femininity that combines various cultural and ethnic influences. Daughter of a French mother and Vietnamese father, Bui first came to prominence when opening her 'Kabuki' boutique in the 1980s with her actor husband William Halimi. In 1998 she started her 'BB Initials' line and more recently has started a line in designer shoes.

buibui Piece of black cloth worn as a shawl by Muslim women, especially on the North African coast.

bumfreezer Short jacket ; also a slang name for an Eton jacket.

Burberry Drapery business opened in Basingstoke, Hampshire, in 1856 by 21-year-old Thomas Burberry, producing waterproof garbardine raincoats. Since 1988 has enjoyed success with its youthful collections although appearing keen to distance itself from the so-called 'chav' culture. Famous for its trademark black, white and red pattern known as Haymarket Check.

burqa Head-to-toe garment worn by Muslim women (also spelled burka, burqua or burcka).

burlap Coarse fabric woven from jute or hemp.

burnous Arab or Moorish hooded cloak, now worn as a fashion accessory in the Western world.

busby Tall, fur helmet with a bag hanging from the top to the right side as worn by certain soldiers, usually hussars; it is also another name for a bearskin.

buskin Originally, a thick-soled boot worn by tragic actors in ancient Athenian theatre; now a half-boot.

bustle Pad or frame worn to puff out the back of a woman's skirt.

Busuuti Long garment with short sleeves and square neckline, as worn by Ugandan women.

cagoule Thin-hooded outer jacket, especially one that is windproof and waterproof, and worn by mountaineers and others following outdoor pursuits.

calash (also calèche) Woman's folding, hooped hood, worn in 18th century.

calico White or unbleached cotton fabric with no printed design (originally from 'Calicut, on the Malabar coast,' a town in India).

calotte Skullcap worn by Roman Catholic clergy.

cambric Originally a fine white linen fabric of the late Tudor and early Stuart period and imported from the French town of Cambrai. The lightness of the material made it popular as a decorative accompaniment to dress as ruffs, cuffs, bands and handkerchiefs. Modern cambric is made from high-quality American or Egyptian cotton and is identified with good-quality underwear.

camisole Woman's under-bodice with shoulder straps, originally designed as a cover for a corset.

capote Long cloak or soldier's coat, usually with a hood; also a kind of 19th-century bonnet.

capuchin Woman's cloak and hood resembling the dress of a Capuchin friar.

Cardin, Pierre Italian-born French fashion designer, born 1922, and known for his space age designs. In 1981 he purchased Maxim's restaurants.

casque Piece of armour to cover the head; a helmet.

castor Hat made of beaver fur.

Cerruti Founded in 1881 in Biella, Milan, by Antonio Cerruti as a fabric mill company, Cerruti became fashionable when Nino Cerruti, grandson of the founder developed the business into a ready-to-wear fashion house in 1957 when he opened 'Hitman' in Milan. In 1967 Nino opened 'Cerruti 1881', a men's couture house in the centre of Paris and soon established an international reputation. In 1976 Cerruti developed a women's ready-to-wear market and is now established in all aspects of haute couture.

cestus (1) Pugilist's gauntlet of bull's hide loaded or studded with metal.

cestus (2) Girdle, named after the girdle of Aphrodite.

chador/chuddar Large shawl or veil worn by Muslim or Hindu women that covers them from head to foot.

Chanel, Coco French fashion designer (1883–1971), worked as a milliner until 1912 and following service as a nurse during World War I, opened a couture house in Paris. Revolutionised women's fashions during the 1920s, her designs including the 'chemise' dress, the collarless cardigan jacket, and the 'little black dress'. Her designer perfume Chanel No. 5 became the ultimate status symbol. Chanel retired in 1938 but made a successful comeback in 1954 and her innovations such as the vogue for costume jewellery and the evening scarf have maintained their popularity.

Ch'ao-fu Pre-modern Chinese man's robe with long, close-fitting sleeves that terminated in the horse-hoof cuff introduced by the Manchus, and a closely-fitted neckband over which was worn a detached collar with wing-like tips that extended over the shoulders. The lower body consisted of a full, pleated skirt with a banded waist. Colours were dependent on rank.

chaplet Ornamental wreath of flowers or beads worn on the head. Also a precious metal circlet, possibly set with gems.

chaps protective leather trousers worn by American cowboys. The name comes from the Mexican 'chaparejos'.

chasuble Long, sleeveless outer vestment worn by a priest when celebrating Mass.

chemise Woman's loose-fitting undergarment or dress hanging straight from the shoulders.

cheongsam Woman's garment with high neck and slit skirt, worn in China.

chiffon (1) Light, diaphanous, plain-woven fabric of silk or nylon.

chiffon (2) Trimmings or other adornments on a woman's dress.

chi-fu Straight, kimono-sleeved robe, alternatively called lung-p'ao 'dragon robes', worn formally by both sexes in China under the Manchu empire.

chignon Arrangement of long hair in a roll or knot at the back of the head.

ch'ima Korean pleated skirt, as worn by women from the 15th century onward.

chintz Brightly patterned cotton fabric with glazed finish (from a Hindi word that indicates a spatter or stain).

chiton Long tunic worn in ancient Greece made of wool, linen or cotton.

chlamys Short woollen cloak worn mostly by men in Ancient Greece.

choga Loose Afghan garment with long sleeves.

chŏgori Traditional Korean jacket.

choli Short-sleeved blouse worn under a sari.

clinquant Imitation gold leaf worn as a fashion accessory.

cloche Woman's close-fitting bell-shaped hat.

Clothes Show BBC television programme that ran from 1985–8. Its presenters included Jeff Banks, Brenda Emmanus, Caryn Franklin, Tim Vincent and Margherita Taylor.

Coach Leading brand name in the field of luxury customised handbags for all occasions.

codpiece Bagged appendage to the fork of a man's breeches or close-fitting hose.

coif Close-fitting cap, worn under a veil in the Middle Ages or under a chainmail hood and tied under the chin with strings, now worn only by nuns.

coiffeur Professional hair-stylist.

coli Short-sleeved breast-length jacket, usually worn by Muslim women over a ghaghra.

Cook, Emma British designer, born 1975, who graduated from St Martins and like her classmates Stella McCartney and Alexander McQueen has become a leading light of the fashion industry. Formerly a consultant with Ghost, she is now freelance.

combinations One-piece woollen undergarment with long sleeves and legs; known in the USA as a union suit.

cote hardie Medieval close-fitting sleeved tunic, when worn by men long enough to cover the buttocks and belted around the hips; when worn by women, full-length and often unbelted..

cowl A cap or hood especially on a monk's habit.

Cox, Patrick Born in Canada, 1963, as a student he designed shoes for Vivian Westwood, Body Map and later for John Galliano. Cox introduced his own label 1987 and his fleurs-de-lys-logo is a sign of elegant fashion and quirky design.

cracowe Long pointed shoe named after the Polish city of Cracow (Kraków). It is thought that the marriage of Richard II of England to Anne of Bohemia in 1382 was responsible for the fashion in England.

cravat Scarf of silk or fine wool, worn round the neck, usually by men. Cravats were popularised by Croats in the French army during the Thirty Years' War and the name is a corruption of Croat.

crinoline In the 1830s a stiff fabric made of horsehair and cotton or linen thread, used for linings, hats and skirts. Later a petticoat with steel hoops worn under a skirt to make it stand out from the body in a bell-shape.

cuisse Piece of armour for the front of the thigh.

culottes Woman's breeches that hang like a skirt but have separate legs.

cymar (also simar, cimarra) Woman's loose gown, popular in the 17th and 18th centuries.

dalmatica Wide-sleeved, tunic-like vestment, open at the sides, worn by deacons and bishops. Originally worn by Roman noblemen from the 2nd century on and made of white Dalmatian wool.

damask Richly figured woven material, originally of silk, with a pattern visible on either side. It originated in Damascus in Syria.

dashiki Loose brightly coloured shirt worn in West Africa and also in the USA.

décolleté Low-cut neckline.

deerstalker Cloth cap, peaked in front and behind, with earflaps that are usually tied up on the top.

De La Renta, Oscar Born in the Dominican Republic, 1932, but became a naturalised American in the 1960s. He started his own company in 1965 with a reputation for opulent, ornately trimmed clothes, particularly evening dresses. In 1993 he became the first American to design for a French couture house, Pierre Balmain.

denim Originally serge de Nîmes (named from Nîmes, in France), now a twilled, hard-wearing, cotton fabric used for jeans.

dernier cri Latest fashion ('last cry').

dhoti Loincloth worn by male Hindus. The ends are passed between the legs and tucked in at the waist.

Dinnigan, Collette Born in South Africa to an Irish father and South African mother, she was brought up in New Zealand and after completing her education, emigrated to Australia. She started her own label in 1990 and in 1995 became the first Australian to have a full-scale ready-to-wear parade in Paris.

Dior, Christian French fashion designer (1905–57). Founded his fashion house in 1945 and achieved worldwide fame with his long-skirted 'New Look' of 1947. His later designs included the 'H' line and the 'A' line.

dirndl Dress in the style of an Alpine female peasant costume, with close-fitting bodice and full skirt.

Dolce & Gabbana Founded in Milan in 1982 by Domenico Dolce, a shy, bearded Sicilian, and the Venetian Stefano Gabbana. Throughout the 1990s they introduced menswear and a popular youth line. A further division of their operations created a White Line for day-to-day basics, and a Black Line for fantasy goods. In February 2005 they announced the end of their 19-year romantic liaison, although making clear the label is in no danger.

Dolly Varden Woman's large hat, named after a Dickens' character in *Barnaby Rudge*; also a flowered dress.

dolman (1) Long Turkish robe, open in the front and with narrow sleeves.

dolman (2) Hussar's jacket worn with the sleeves hanging loose.

dolman (3) Woman's mantle with dolman sleeves.

dolman sleeve Loose sleeve made in one piece with the body of a coat; it has a wide armhole but a tight wrist.

domino (1) Large, hooded cloak, worn with an eye mask at a masquerade.

domino (2) The eye mask worn at masquerades.

Donna Karan Born in New York as Donna Faske in 1948, she began her career as a designer for Anne Klein and subsequently took control on her death in 1974. Karan eventually began her own company with second husband Stephen Weis.

doublet Close-fitting body garment with or without sleeves and a short skirt, worn by men from medieval times to the 17th century.

duchesse Soft, heavy kind of satin; also a type of chaise longue.

dundreary Long sidewhiskers worn without a beard, named after Lord Dundreary, a character in Tom Taylor's comedy (1858).

dungaree Coarse cotton fabric used chiefly for work clothes - from a Hindi word.

durzi An Indian tailor.

Emanuels David, born 1952, and Elizabeth, born 1953, launched their label in 1975 but split up in the 1990s. Their most famous creation was the wedding dress of Diana, Princess of Wales. Co-authors of *Style for all Seasons.*

Erotokritos Cyprus-born, Paris-based fashion designer who launched his own label in 1994 and since his first Paris show in 1996 has built a reputation for chic yet casual clothing.

Eton jacket Waist-length jacket with a V-shaped back, open in the front, formerly worn by pupils of Eton College.

Etro Italian company that specialises in selling extraordinary crafted, brightly coloured paisley (Etro's hallmark), foulard and brocade ties and vests, as well as finely tailored suits. Gimno Etro is the head of the empire and his three sons, Ippolito, Jacopo and Kean, are directors.

Farhi, Nicole French-born Algerian designer known for her luxurious and sensual woman's collections. She opened her first store in 1983 as part of a Harvey Nichols and in 1984 opened a boutique in New York. Farhi's home shop is in Clifford Street London.

farjī Long, gown-like coat with short sleeves, made of wool or cotton (silk is forbidden to men by the Koran), as worn by Muslim priests or high officials.

farthingale Framework of hoops, or a hooped petticoat, used the 15th to 17th century to extend the skirts of a woman's dress.

Fendi Established in Rome, 1918, as a leather and fur workshop by Adele Casagrande (d. 1978). The named changed in 1925 when Adele married Edoardo Fendi. Since the death of Edoardo in 1954 the company has being run by his five daughters, Alda, Anna, Carla, Franca and Paola, although a controlling interest is now shared by Prada and Louis Vuitton. Karl Lagerfeld has designed the Fendi fur collection since 1962.

Ferré, Gianfranco Born in Legnano, Italy, 1944, he formed the Gianfranco Ferré company in 1978 with business partner Franco Mattioli. Unusually, Ferré has maintained a popularity in all aspects of the fashion industry, having had successful women's, men's and children's clothing lines and fragrances.

fez rimless felt or woollen cap, cylindrical in shape, usually red and with a tassel, usually worn by men in Muslim coutries and formerly the national head-dress of Turkey.

fichu Woman's small triangular shawl of lace for the shoulders and neck. Late 18th to late 19th century.

filibeg / philibeg Kilt worn by Scottish Highlanders.

finnesko Boot of reindeer skin with the hair on the outside.

forage cap Soldier's undress cap.

Ford, Tom Born in Texas 1962, he rose to prominence when taken on as Creative Director of Gucci and made an immediate impact. Ford is sometimes known as the 'It' Boy of the fashion world, or more recently the 'King of Cool'. He has often been targeted by animal rights activists for his refusal to stop using fur in his designs. His former womenswear director, Alessandra Facchinetti, took over his position at Gucci in 2004 before herself being replaced by Frida Giannini in 2005.

Franz Josef Long sidewhiskers, merging into a moustache, named in honour of the emperor of Austria.

frippery Originally old or second-hand clothes or tawdry adornment in dress; now means showy.

frog Decorative braided coat-fastening, originally forming part of military dress, consisting of a spindle-shaped button and a loop and a braided loop that retains it.

furisode Long-sleeved outer kimono traditionally worn by young, unmarried Japanese girls (married women wearing the short-sleeved kimono known as a kosode).

gabardine Raincoat made from a smooth, durable, twill-woven cloth of worsted or cotton; also a long loose cloak.

gaberdine Twill-weave worsted, cotton, or spun-rayon fabric.

Galliano, John British fashion designer currently head of the Dior fashion empire.

galligaskins Loose, wide breeches or hose, especially as worn by men in the 16th and 17th centuries; also the leather leggings worn in the 19th century.

gallus Trouser braces of a type worn in the USA, where braces are called suspenders.

galosh Originally a clog, or wooden sole attached to a shoe, but now an overshoe, usually made of rubber or plastic.

Garroudi, Pierre Born in Tehran, Iran, 1959, and educated in Paris. He moved to New York in 1986 and opened his own fashion house in 1993. His designs are daring and innovative and his shows are erotic, witty and provocative.

Gaultier, Jean-Paul French fashion designer, born 1952, and famous for designing Madonna's cone-bra for her 1990 Blond Ambition tour. Gaultier also hosted the television series *Eurotrash.*

georgette Thin silk or crêpe dress material, named after Georgette de la Plante, a French dressmaker.

gewgaw Worthless piece of frippery worn to be showy.

ghăghrā Open-fronted pleated skirt, as worn by Muslim women.

Ghost Tanya Sarne's 'Ghost' is well know for its trademark garment-dyed vintage-look viscose and ultra feminine garments. Its clothes are created by women for women.

Gibbs, Bill Scottish fashion designer (1943–88), launched his own label in 1971 in partnership with Kate Franklin. Inspired by the vast diversity and volume of ethnic costume as well as Scottish Highland dress. His signature motif was the bee (B for Bill).

Gibson girl Young woman typifying the fashionable ideal of around 1900, as represented in the work of Charles Dana Gibson (1867–1944) US artist.

gilet Waist-length, sleeveless garment, usually quilted and fastened up the front, designed to be worn over a blouse and often worn by cyclists and as part of a ballet dancer's costume. Gilet literally means waistcoat in French.

gingham Plain-woven cotton cloth, especially striped or checked (literally means 'striped' in Malay).

gipon Close-fitting padded tunic, buttoned down the front, the sleeves long enough to cover the knuckles, the neck round and low. Originally worn under medieval body armour.

Givenchy, Hubert Born in Beauvais, France, 1927, Hubert Givenchy opened his own house in 1952, producing ready-to-wear clothes under his Nouvelle Boutique label.

Gladstone bag A light portmanteau opening into two equal compartments and named after the British Prime Minister who carried such a bag.

Glengarry Brimless Scottish hat with a cleft down the centre and two ribbons hanging down the back, chiefly worn as part of Highland dress.

gorget (1) Collar-like piece of armour worn to protect the throat.

gorget (2) Part of a wimple worn by women to cover the neck and shoulders, especially in the late Middle Ages.

greave Piece of armour protecting the leg below the knee.

Gucci, Guccio Florentine fashion designer (1881–1953) opened his first shop in 1920, and became known for his leather craftsmanship and accessories. His four sons joined the firm and in 1953 the first overseas shop opened in New York. The empire has had several corporate identities and after Gucci's grandson Maurizio's (1949–95) presidency from 1989 to 1993, the company was sold to the multi-national Investcorp.

Guinness, Lulu British handbag designer, born Lucinda Jane Rivett-Carnac.

habergeon Sleeveless coat of mail.

haik Large cloak, usually white, worn by both sexes in North Africa.

hakama Very full men's trousers, as worn in Japan from the 7th century onwards.

Hartnell, Sir Norman (1901–78) Born in London and educated at Magdalene College, Cambridge. Started his own couturier business in 1923 and received the Royal Warrant in 1940. He was president of the Incorporated Society of London Fashion Designers (1946–56) and became famous for designing costumes for leading actresses of the day and Princess Elizabeth's Wedding and Coronation gowns.

hauberk Piece of defensive armour, for neck and shoulders at first, but soon developed into a long mail shirt or military tunic.

haute couture High fashion, literally 'high dressmaking'; collectively the leading dressmakers and fashion houses or their products.

Hermès Founded in 1837 by Thierry Hermès, the world-famous fashion house began life as a manufacturer of equestrian accessories such as saddles, riding boots and bridles. The present regime is headed by Jean-Louis Dumas, the fifth family successor to the Hermès empire.The current head designer is Martin Margiela, who has expanded the repertoire into his trademark camel coats and grunge apparel but the reputation of Hermès is built upon the success of their silk scarf and handbag market. The 'Kelly' bag, as popularised by Grace Kelly, is still a bestseller.

himation Outer garment worn over the left shoulder, and under the right, in ancient Greece.

hitatare The formal court dress of a Samurai.

hobble skirt Skirt so narrow at the hem as to impede walking; introduced before World War I

Holland Smooth hard-wearing linen fabric.

Homburg Man's felt hat with a narrow curled brim and a lengthwise dent in the crown.

houppelande Medieval tunic or gown worn by both sexes, with full sleeves and long train, belted at the waist. The collar was high, often with a dagged edge.

imperial Pointed tuft of whiskers on the chin, named in honour of Napoleon III (Emperor of France 1852–70).

isar Wide trousers, usually worn by Muslim men under the jãmah.

Jacobs, Marc Artistic director at Louis Vuitton since 1987 and now known as a leading designer in his own right. His colourful mat finishes in a 1960s style have become popular with celebrities and actress Winona Ryder was accused of shoplifting for Marc Jacob's designs.

Jacquard Method of weaving a design directly into the fabric instead of being printed or dyed on. The piece of apparatus used for this type of weave is called a Jacquard loom, after its French inventor Joseph M Jacquard (1752–1834).

jãmah Long-sleeved coat that reaches to, or below, the knees and has a belted waist; as worn by Muslim men.

jeans inventor Levi Strauss.

Jimmy Choo Born in 1961, his label was founded in 1996 in partnership with Tamara Yeardye and Sandra Choi, who is the Creative Director and designer of their popular fashion shoes which are affectionately known as 'Jimmys'.

Joseph Founded by Joseph Ettedgui, born 1935, a highly influential retailer who provides a showcase for top designers

Jon, Anand Indian fashion designer whose 'functional luxury' style is currently en vogue.

Juliet cap Small net ornamental cap worn by brides etc.

Jungle Jap shops Opened by Kenzo Takada in 1970.

juni hitoe Japanese noblewoman's full court costume meaning 'twelve layer' but possibly with more.

karaginu Outermost garment of the juni hitoe, consisting of a wide-sleeved jacket reaching only to the waist.

keffiyeh Bedouin Arab's kerchief or larger square of wool cotton or linen worn as a headdress and held in place by an agal.

kebaya (1) Light loose unisex tunic of a type worn in SE Asia.

kebaya (2) Short tight-fitting long-sleeved jacket, together with a sarong the traditional dress of Malay and Indonesian women.

Kenzo Popular name of Kenzo Takada, Kyoto-born fashion designer. He had small success in his home country before moving to Paris and producing freelance collections in 1964. His Jungle Jap shop built his reputation as an innovator and his creations blend Oriental and Western influences with traditional designs. Kenzo is also a trendsetter in the field of knitwear.

képi French military cap with a circular top and a horizontal peak.

Kidston, Cath English fashion designer (born 6 November 1958) famous for her home furnishings, floral patterns and Cath Kidston bags.

kimono A Japanese loose sashed ankle-length garment with wide sleeves. Literally means wear thing.

kirtle Old English name for a woman's skirt or dress; also the name of a man's tunic or coat, usually reaching to the knees.

Klein, Anne Native New Yorker Anne Klein, born 1923, made her name when setting up her company in 1968 and introducing a sporty element into US fashion. Following her death in 1974, Donna Karan and Louis Dell'Olio continued as co-designers and Dell'Olio remains the head designer and the overseer of the company's latest manifestation, Anne Klein II.

Klein, Calvin Born in New York, USA, in 1942. Opened his first store in 1968 in partnership with long-time friend and businessman Barry Schwartz. The simple but sophisticated style of his clothes soon gained him recognition and this became universal when actress Brooke Shields modelled his designer jeans in the late 1970s. Klein popularised designer men's underwear in 1982 and following the success of his fragrances, Obsession, Eternity and Escape, his CK One became the first of the unisex fragrances. In September 2003 Francisco Costa, a 34-year-old Brazilian fashion designer, took over as design director to bring an end to Klein's 30-year reign as head of his fashion empire.

knickerbockers Short, loose-fitting trousers gathered in at the knee or calf. Named after Diedrich Knickerbocker, fictitious author of a *History of New York* actually written by Washington Irving (1783–1859).

Lacroix, Christian Born in 1951, the French fashion designer opened the House of Lacroix in Paris, 1987, and specialises in ornate and frivolous designs.

Lagerfeld, Karl Born in 1939, Lagerfeld has been head of Chanel since 1983 and was previously chief designer of Chloe from 1963–84.

Lang, Helmut Born in Vienna, Austria, 1956, Lang has become a pioneer in many areas of the fashion industry. He is known for his use of techno fabrics, minimalism and deconstructionism. He sold his label to the Prada Group in November 2003 and resigned as creative director of his own brand in January 2005.

La Perla Founded by Ada Masotti in Italy, 1954, and known for high-quality and luxurious, intimate apparel. Pioneered the wearing of bodysuits as outerwear, and sleepwear as casual clothes.

Laroche, Guy French fashion designer (1923–89), born in La Rochelle. He worked in millinery, first in Paris, then New York, before returning to Paris to start his own company. By 1961 he was producing both couture and ready-to-wear clothes. From 1966 his designs included menswear.

leghorn Hat made of fine plaited straw.

leg-of-mutton sleeve Sleeve which is full and loose on the upper arm but close-fitting on the forearm.

lei Polynesian garland made of flowers, feathers or shells; often given as a symbol of affection.

leotard Close-fitting one-piece garment named after Jules Léotard, a French trapeze artist (1830–70).

Levi's Proprietary name for a type of blue denim jeans, produced by Levi Strauss as working clothes in the 1860s.

Liripipe / Liripoop In medieval times, the extended tail of a hood which could be as much as five or six feet long; also a medieval slang name for a shoelace.

Louis Vuitton Founded in 1854 by luggage manufacturer Louis Vuitton Malletier, the label has become the most imitated of all top fashion houses. The reputation was founded on their luxurious leather bags, often using exotic leathers such as alligator, ostrich and lizard.

mantelet / mantlet Women's short, loose, sleeveless cloak.

mantilla Light scarf, often made from black lace, worn over the head and shoulders, especially by Spanish women.

mantua Woman's loose gown of the 17th and 18th centuries. So spelled after an Italian city but originally from French manteau.

Marocain Dress fabric of ribbed crêpe.

McCartney, Stella Born in 1971, the daughter of Sir Paul McCartney, Stella was chief designer of the Chloe fashion house (1997–2001) before taking up an appointment with Gucci. She marrked Alasdhair Willis, the publisher of *Wallpaper* magazine, in August 2003.

McQueen, Alexander Born 1969, chief designer of the Givenchy fashion house between 1996 and 2001, and a contemporary of Emma Cook and Stella McCartney. Later founded the McQ label. He hanged himself on 11 February 2010, the day before his mother's funeral.

mignonette Light, fine, narrow lace used for trimming.

miniskirt Created by André Courrèges and popularised by Mary Quant.

Missoni Founded in Gallarate, Varese, Italy, 1953, by Ottavio Missoni and his wife Rosita (née Jelmeni). The Missoni label, created in 1958, is known for its fluidity and colour of its creations, which have an affinity to art.

mitra / mitre (1) Headband worn by women in ancient Greece.

mitra / mitre (2) Tall Asian head-dress, regarded by the Romans as effeminate when worn by men; the ceremonial turban of a high priest. Also the deeply-cleft head-dress worn in the Christian Church by a bishop or abbot, especially as a symbol of episcopal office, forming in outline the shape of a pointed arch, and often made of embroidered white linen or satin.

Miyake, Issey Japanese fashion designer born in Hiroshima in 1938. His distinctive style combines Eastern and Western influences in his loose-fitting garments which have a theatrical quality to them by the use of dramatic asymmetric outline and varied textures.

mo Women's pleated train, part of the formal court costume established in Japan by the time of the 8th century.

mob cap Large indoor cap covering all the hair, worn by women in 18th and 19th centuries.

moccasin Soft leather shoe, originally worn by Native Americans.

Monmouth Flat, round cap formerly worn by soldiers and sailors.

Montana, Claude Born 1949. Began his career in London with the Carnaby Street movement, where he designed jewellery made from large coloured stones embedded in papier mâché. On his return to Paris he became popular for his designer leather outfits and his 1976 show at the Angelina tea rooms in Paris caught the imagination of the fashion industry.

Montera / montero Spanish peaked travelling cap with a spherical crown and flaps for lowering over the ears;also the black hat worn by bullfighters.

muff Soft insulated covering, cylindrical, into which both hands may be thrusted at opposite ends to keep warm.

mutch Woman's or child's linen cap.

mutton chops Sidewhiskers narrow at the top and broad and rounded at the bottom.

muu-muu Woman's loose, brightly coloured dress from Hawaii.

Naga-Bakama Japanese formal undergarment made of a stiff red cloth and fastened high up under the breast and covering the feet at the front but extending out to a train at the back.

napery Household linen, especially table linen.

New Look Christian Dior's 1947 creation of women's dress with narrow shoulders and long, full skirts.

niqab similar to a burqa but with a full veil covering every part of the body except the eyes.

Norfolk jacket Man's loose belted sporting jacket with box pleats.

Nutter, Tommy Welsh fashion designer (1943–92), revolutionised menswear by introducing high fashion to Savile Row in 1969, funded by pop singer Cilla Black.

nylons Stockings or tights made from a synthetic polymeric amid. The process was invented by Wallace Carothers in the 1930s and named after New York and London.

Oldfield, Bruce Born in 1950, launched his own label in 1975. Famous for his pretty and glamorous evening wear. In 2008 he redesigned McDonald's staff uniform.

Oxfords Can be a type of shoe, shirt, or trousers (Oxford bags).

Ozbek, Rifat Turkish-born, 1953, British fashion designer who bizarrely first came to prominence for his extraordinary resemblance to Diana Vreeland. His transposing of ethnically inspired clothes into a modern context such as Indonesian Ikat patterns printed on slinky lycra tube skirts, and his opulent Oriental brocades woven into the English gentleman's tailcoats are trademark Ozbek creations.

Paddington Designer handbag produced by Chloé for their 2005 spring season. The soft, washed leather bag comes in chocolate brown, cream or tan and is distinguished by its brass padlock.

paji Traditional Korean trousers.

palisado During the reign of Elizabeth, women wore their hair turned back from the forehead over a pad or a wire known as a palisado.

palla Loose outer garment or outdoor wrap, usually worn by women in ancient Rome and Byzantium.

pallium (1) Man's large rectangular outdoor cloak worn in ancient Rome.

pallium (2) Woollen vestment conferred by the Pope on an archbishop, consisting of a narrow circular band worn round the shoulders with a short flap hanging from front and back.

Panama Hat made originally from the plaited leaves of the jipijapa plant of Ecuador.

pannier Framework, used to extend and support the skirt of a woman's dress in the late 17th and 18th centuries, and usually made from osier reeds or whalebone.

parure Matching set of jewels designed to be worn together.

pashmina A cashmere shawl made from pashm, the underfur of various Tibetan animals, but especially the goat.

patten Shoe or clog with a raised sole, or set on an iron ring, for walking over mud or on uneven ground.

pauldron Piece of shoulder armour.

pea-jacket Sailor's short, double-breasted overcoat of coarse dark blue cloth, also pilot or reefer jacket.

pelerine Woman's narrow cape with long, pointed ends in front (literally means 'pilgrim'); 18th and 19th century.

peplos Half- or full-length loose outer robe often two lengths of fabric pinned at the shoulders worn by women in ancient Greece.

perizoma Short pants worn by athletes in ancient Greece.

Perrin, Christina New York-based designer of Swedish extraction. Popular in the late 1990s for her silhouettes in distinctive fabrications, avant-garde use of leather and fur, and her unusual tailoring and richness of colour.

Persian lamb Silky, tightly curled fur of a breed of lamb called a Karakul, used in clothing.

peruke Kind of wig worn in Europe from 1660 to 1800. A skullcap covered with hair at first imitating the natural hair of the head, later often much more elaborate and imposing (also periwig, perruque).

petasos Low-crowned, wide-brimmed hat of ancient Greece, often with a cord which allowed it to be slung over the wearer's back when the weather permitted.

Petersham (1) Thick, corded, silk ribbon used for stiffening in dressmaking.

Petersham (2) A heavy overcoat or the rough cloth (usually dark blue) from which it was made.

petticoat Woman's undergarment, but also, in Elizabethan times, a small coat worn by men under the doublet.

Piccadilly Weepers Long sidewhiskers, worn without a beard.

pickelhaube German soldier's spiked helmet.

pileus Brimless, close-fitting felt cap, worn in ancient Greece; a similar cap was called a pilos.

pillbox A small cylindrical hat worn at the back of the head and popularised by Jacqueline Kennedy in the 1960s.

pinking shears Dressmaker's serrated shears for cutting a zigzag edge.

pith helmet Light sun-helmet made of the dried pith of the sola plant.

plus-fours Men's baggy knickerbockers reaching below the knee, now only worn for hunting or golf.

Poiret, Paul French couturier (1879–1944), the most fashionable dress designer of pre-war Paris, and designer of the hobble skirt.

poleyn Piece of armour for the knee.

poor boy Type of pullover.

Prada Since the mid 1990s there have been few status symbols as potent as the Prada-embossed silver triangle. Prada began life as a family-run leather goods business in Milan but enjoyed the patronage of a growing number of celebrities. The Prada empire has been run since 1978 by Patrizio Bertelli and his wife Miuccia Prada, the grand-daughter of the founder. In 1992 a youth-targeted 'Miu Miu' line was introduced as well as a 'Granello' and 'Prada Sport' range. Miuccia Prada has won critical praise for her innovative experiments in both fabric design and use of colour and her businessman husband equal praise for his shrewd purchasing of large share-holdings of rival operations such as Gucci, Lang, Alaia and Sander.

praetexta Toga with purple edge, worn by some Roman magistrates and pre-adult boys.

Proenza Schouler The label of the young New York duo Lazaro Hernandez and Jack McCollough. Their signature ideas encompass proportion (shrunken pea coats, pencil skirts), colour (army greens, browns, battleship greys), and silhouette (sleek, minimal). The label derives its name from the maiden names of the mothers of the founders.

p'u-fu Three-quarter-length coat worn by men and women in China over their ch'ao-fu or chi-fu.

puggaree (also pagari) Indian word for a full turban; also a pleated scarf around the crown of some hats, especially sun hats.

puttee (1) A strip of cloth wound round the leg from ankle to knee as a legging.

puttee (2) Leather-legging.

Quant, Mary Born in London, 1934, opened her first boutique in Chelsea in 1955, and married one of her partners, Alexander Plunket Greene. She was the inventor of the mini skirt in the 1960s and hot pants in the early 1970s.

Rabanne, Paco Born Francisco Rabaneda Cuervo in the Basque area of Spain in 1934, Rabanne's first collection in 1966 entitled 'Twelve Unwearable Dresses' set the scene for his unconventional career. He has designed in plastic, chain metal, fluorescent leather, ostrich feathers, aluminium, paper, laser discs, fibre optic wire, socks and doorknobs.

Ralph Lauren Born in the Bronx, NY in 1939 as Ralph Lifshitz, Lauren introduced the Polo label in 1967 and became popular following the 1974 film *The Great Gatsby* after many of his designs were worn.

reefer An overcoat, as worn in North America, often called a gaitor or reefer jacket.

rerebrace Piece of armour developed to cover the upper arm but later protecting to the shoulder and elbow.

Rhinegraves Late 17th-century breeches, loose at the knee and wide like shorts, often with frilly embellishments.

Rhodes, Zandra Born in 1940, first came to prominence when she opened the Fulham Road Clothes Shop in 1967. She is noted for her distinctive exotic designs in floating chiffons and silks.

roquelaure Man's knee-length cloak with a cape collar, fashionable in the 18th century.

ruff Decorative frill encircling the neck developed in mid-16th-century Spain and fashionable in Europe, in Jacobean and Elizabethan times. Also a frill around the sleave of a garment.

sabaton Piece of armour for the foot.

sabot Shoe made from a single block of wood; a clog or, in Holland, a klomp.

Saint-Laurent, Yves Born in Oran, Algeria, 1936, he studied in Paris and joined the House of Dior in 1955 after winning a Wool Secretariat design competition. On Dior's death in 1957 he took over the house. In 1962 he opened his own house and launched the first of his 160 Rive Gauche boutiques in 1966, selling ready-to-wear clothes, a trend that was soon copied by other fashion houses. Saint-Laurent also creates costumes for theatre, ballet, and films, and in 1985 was awarded a Best Fashion Design Oscar. He died in 2008.

Sander, Jill Born in Wesselburen, Germany, 1943, Sander is best known for her long, lean silhouettes. She has brought minimalism in fashion to an art form and superfluous buttons and zips have been banished. The Prada corporation presently own a large shareholding in the Sander fashion empire.

sand-shoe Light canvas shoe with a rubber sole; a plimsoll.

sari Traditional garment of Indian women, worn over a choli and an underskirt, consisting of a length of cotton, silk, or other cloth wrapped around the waist and draped over one shoulder.

sarong Traditional unisex skirt-like garment of the Malay archipelago, Java, and some Pacific islands, consisting of a long strip of cloth worn tucked round the waist or under the armpits by. Popularised by actress Dorothy Lamour in the 'Road' films.

sarong kebaya Traditional dress of Malay and Indonesian women, consisting of a sarong and a kebaya.

Schiaparelli, Elsa Italian fashion designer (1896–1973) born in Rome. After studying philosophy she worked as a film scriptwriter in America before venturing to Paris in 1920 and receiving her first order for a black sweater knitted with a white bow, ironically from an American store. Her following designs were innovative and sensational, and she was noted for her use of colour, including 'shocking pink', and also for her outrageous hats and use of zippers and buttons.

seersucker Material of linen or cotton with a puckered surface.

semmit An undervest, as worn in Scotland.

serge Durable woollen or worsted fabric.

shako Tall, cylindrical, military peaked cap worn with a plume or pompom.

Shilling, David Born in 1953, from the age of 12 he designed the extravagant headwear made famous by his mother Gertrude at Royal Ascot. Launched his own label in 1975. Author of *Thinking Rich – A Personal Guide to Luxury Living.*

shitagasane Kimono of white damask, worn under the ho, with an elongated train of up to 12 feet long.

sideburns Short sidewhiskers, originally called Burnsides, after US Union General Ambrose Everett Burnside (1824–81) who wore them.

Siemens, Crystal Canadian fashion designer who uses combinations of materials and colour to give an effect of light playing off the fabric.

Simons, Raf Born in Belgium, 1968, his first show was in Milan in 1995. Subsequent shows in Paris and New York have highlighted his influence by pop culture, particularly David Bowie, and are described by himself as fashion, youth culture, music and performance parades.

skinny rib Type of pullover.

Smith, Paul Nottinghamshire-born fashion designer knighted in 2000 for his longevity as a menswear icon. Born in 1946, Sir Paul has recently designed clothes for racing cyclists, he himself being an accomplished rider until an accident curtailed his career.

smock-frock Loose protective garment of coarse homepin linen or cotton reaching below the knees, traditionally worn by farm labourers before the machine age.

snood (1) Pouchlike hat, often of net, loosely holding a woman's hair at the back.

snood (2) Headband, formerly worn by young unmarried women in Scotland.

sokutai Japanese court costume, exclusively worn by the emperor, with a yellow outer robe (ho) patterned with hō-ō birds and kilin, and baggy white damask trousers (ue-no-hakama).

soup and fish Men's evening dress.

sou'wester Waterproof hat with a very broad rim behind, worn especially by seamen.

spat A short gaiter worn over the instep and reaching a little way above the ankle, worn to keep trousers or stockings clean, especially when riding. Spat is an abbreviation for Spatterdash, although nowadays a distinction is drawn between the fashion accessories.

spatterdash Long gaiter or legging of leather or cloth, worn to keep trousers or stockings clean.
Stetson Man's felt slouch hat with a broad brim and high crown, named after John Stetson (1830–1906), the hatter who designed it.
stock Long white scarf worn with formal riding dress.
stomacher Originally an ornamental 'V' or 'U' shaped piece of stiff material worn under a man's doublet to cover the chest and stomach. Later, an ornamental triangular panel filling the open front of a woman's dress, covering the breast and stomach, and often jewelled or embroidered.
suberakashi The elaborate coiffure worn as part of the juni-hitoe, consisting of a lacquered, gold-sprinkled comb surmounted by a gold-lacquered chrysanthemum crest.
Sui, Anna Born in Detroit, Michigan, USA, 1964, of Chinese extraction. Her baby-doll dresses of the early 1990s became in vogue with the inception of the grunge movement. Her designs are popular with pop musicians and models.
surplice Loose, white linen vestment with wide sleeves, reaching to the knees or feet and worn over a cassock by clergy and choristers at church services.
surtout Can be either a man's overcoat or a woman's hooded mantle.
tabard (1) Coarse outer garment formerly worn by the peasantry or by monks and foot-soldiers.
tabard (2) Short, open surcoat worn by a knight over his armour and emblazoned with armorial bearings.
taffeta Fine, lustrous silk with a crisp texture, used for making formal dresses.
tallith A shawl with fringed corners, traditionally worn by male jews whilst at prayer.
tam-o'-Shanter Scottish, brimless woollen cap, with a bobble in the centre, usually worn pulled down at one side.
tammy Glazed woollen or mixed fabric, used for linings or undergarments.
tarboosh Cap, similar to a fez, usually of red felt with a tassel at the top, worn by Muslim men either alone or as part of a turban.
tasset Piece of armour for the upper thigh.
tebenna Forerunner of the Roman toga, as worn in ancient Greece.
Temperley, Alice Born in Somerset, 1975. Launched fashion label, *Temperley London* in 2000. Best Young Designer of the Year Award in 2004 and MBE in 2011. Known for hand-finishes of lavish fabrics, her designs have been worn by royalty and Hollywood actresses.
tika dot Mark on the forehead of Hindu women, indicating caste, or worn by both sexes as an ornament.
tiki An amulet or figurine in the form of a carved representation of an ancestor, worn in some Polynesian cultures.
tippet (1) In Elizabethan times, a long streamer-like part to a sleeve or hood. Also a woman's fur cape for the shoulders, often consisting of the whole fur of a fox or marten.
tippet (2) The long stole worn by Anglican clergy during a service.
toga Loose, flowing outer garment worn by Roman citizens and made of a single piece of cloth covering the whole body except the right arm.
toga virilis White toga donned as a sign of manhood at the age of 14.
topi Hat, originally Indian but now a type of pith helmet.
toque (1) Woman's small, round, brimless hat, popular in Edwardian times.
top 10 fashion items In a poll of 3,500 shoppers carried out in Feb 2005 by Harvey Nichols, the miniskirt was voted Britain's favourite fashion item ever. The full top 10 were 1) Miniskirt 2) Jeans 3) Little black dress 4) Flares 5) Cowboy boots 6) Platform shoes 7) Poncho 8) Trainers 9) Combats 10) Trench coat.
toque (2) Hat with a small brim and pouched crown, popular in the 16th century.
toque (3) Canadian, close-fitting knitted hat, often with a tassel or pompom.
torchon Coarse bobbin lace with geometrical designs.
toreador pants Women's close-fitting, calf-length trousers.
trabea Roman toga ornamented with horizontal purple stripes, worn as a state robe by kings, consuls and other men of rank in ancient Rome.
tricorn Hat with the brim turned up on three sides.
trilby Soft felt hat with a narrow brim and indented crown, resembling that worn in the stage version of *Trilby* by the eponymous heroine of George Du Maurier's novel of 1894.
trousseau Clothes collected by a bride in preparation for her marriage.
turumagi Traditional Korean overcoat.
Tuscan straw Fine yellow wheat straw used for hats.
tutu Ballet dancer's skirt made up of layers of stiffened frills, very short and standing out from the legs.
tutulus Head-dress formed by plaiting the hair in a cone above the forehead, worn especially by a flamen and his wife.
tuxedo Dinner jacket, named after Tuxedo Park in New York, site of a country club where the garment was first worn.
tweed Rough-surfaced woollen cloth of varying texture, usually of mixed flecked colours, originally made in Scotland.
uchikake Outer kimono, fashionable in the Muromachi period (14th–16th centuries), sometimes with a short-sleeved kimono (kosode), but later (18th century) with a coloured sash (obi) around the waist and bunched at the back.
uwagi Outer kimono, of rich brocade, under which it is usual to wear a plain purple kimono and generally a third kimono-type robe known as itsutsu-ginu (usually having five bands of coloured silks attached at the sleeves, neckline and hem).
Valentino Popular name of Valentino Garavani, Italian fashion designer, born in Rome, 1933. He opened his first house in 1959 and achieved universal recognition following his Florence show in 1962.
vambrace Piece of armour for the arm, especially the forearm.
Van Dyke Broad, lace or linen collar or neckerchief, with an edge deeply cut into large points, and fashionable after the life of the painter (d. 1641) until the mid 18th century.
veldskoen Strong suede or leather shoe or boot of South African origin.
vent Opening or slit in a garment, especially in the lower edge of the back of a coat or skirt.
Versace, Donatella Born 1955. Took over as head of the Versace empire following the murder of her brother in 1997. Under the terms of Gianni Versace's will Donatella was left a 20% shareholding, her brother Santo having a 35% shareholding and her daughter Allegra a 45% holding.
Versace, Gianni Designer shot dead outside his Miami mansion by Andrew Cunanan (15 July 1997).
viyella A twilled fabric of cotton and wool, named from Via Gellia, a valley in Derbyshire where it was first made.
Vreeland, Diana Legendary fashion editor (1903–1989) of *Harper's Bazaar* and editor-in-chief of *Vogue.* Much parodied as the epitome of a fashion icon.
Watteau gown Loose gown, worn over a tight bodice, with long, vertical pleats falling from the shoulders to the ground, popular in the early 18th century and named after costumes depicted by the French artist.
Westwood, Vivienne Born in 1941, and first came to prominence in 1971 when she began a 13-year collaboration with Malcolm McLaren. She became the first British designer to show in Paris since Mary Quant when her 'Bufalo Collection', based on Peruvian women's fashion, caught the imagination in 1982. She was active in the punk rock fashion of the 1970s and the pioneer of the 'New Romantic' style of the early 1980s. Her designs have included leather bondage gear, latex lounge dresses, flesh-coloured body suits, slashed t-shirts and mink g-strings.
wide-awake Soft felt hat with a low crown and wide brim.
Williamson, Matthew Born 1971, and educated in London and known for his unique colour sense and exquisite embroidery and beading. His debut collection was in 1997 and his name is synonymous with 'The Karma Kit', a white leather clutch bag complete with leather flower, jasmine flower mist, a peppermint pulse-point balm, incense perfume and a pink travel candle.
wimple Piece of cloth draped around the head to frame the face, worn by women in the Middle Ages and still a part of the habit of some nuns.
winceyette Lightweight napped flannelette used for nightclothes.
windcheater Warm jacket, usually with a close-fitting knitted neck, cuffs and waistband.
Wong, Farida Dress designer who has carved a niche as a high-quality designer of ballroom gowns for both amateurs and professionals.

Worth, Charles Frederick (1826–95) English-born fashion designer often considered the Father of Haute Couture. Worth was the first designer to sew his label into garments.

Wrap dress inventor Diane von Furstenberg.

Xuly Bët Popular name of Kouyaté Lamine Badian, born in Bamako, Mali, 1962. His Xuly Bët (name means voyeur in his native Wolof dialect) label is identified with cheap and cheerful but quality goods, often recycled but always with an aesthetic quality. Very popular with the French youth culture.

Yamamoto, Yohji Born in Tokyo, 1943, he is the only Japanese fashion designer to be awarded the French Chevalier de l'Ordre des Arts et Lettres. Apart from his very successful clothing creations he also designs opera costumes and ballet sets.

yarmulka Skullcap worn by Jewish men.

yashmak Veil concealing the face, except the eyes, worn by some Muslim women when in public.

yukata Cotton kimono, worn by both men and women, formerly after bathing but now as outdoor wear on hot summer evenings.

Zoller, Amy Chicago-based fashion designer originally known for her minimalist silhouettes. Her reputation increased throughout the 1990s and she now has two shows a year in Chicago, Houston, New York and Los Angeles.

zucchetto Skullcap worn by Roman Catholic ecclesiastics: black for priests, purple for bishops, red for cardinals, and white for the Pope.

NB: This section is simply an A–Z of historical costume and dress, plus a few interesting snippets of additional information relating to designers and materials.

Other Fashion Designers

Christopher Bailey (b. 1971, West Yorkshire) Chief Creative Officer of Burberry.

Luella Bartley (b. 1974, Stratford Upon Avon) launched her label "Luella" in 1999 with a collection entitled "Daddy, I want a Pony".

Bill Blass (1922-2002) American fashion designer who had success in menswear and womenswear.

Jasper Conran (b. 1959) British designer, son of the designer, Sir Terence Conran, and the author, Shirley Conran. In 1994 he designed the wedding dress of Lady Sarah Armstrong-Jones. Jasper has also designed costumes and sets for fourteen ballet, opera and theatre productions.

Giles Deacon (b. 1969, Darlington, County Durham) best known for his playful designs and his collaboration with High Street retailer New Look.

Rudi Gernreich (1922-85) Austrian-born American fashion designer and gay activist most famous for designing the first topless swimsuit, which he called the "monokini".

Caroline Herrera (b. 1939, Caracas) US-based fashion designer best known for dressing First Ladies from Jacqueline Onassis to Michelle Obama.

Margaret Howell (b. 1946, Tadworth, Surrey) Jack Nicholson insisted on wearing his own Margaret Howell corduroy jacket for his role in The Shining.

Betty Jackson (b. 1949, Lancashire) London-based designer known for designing the costumes for Eddy and Patsy on the 1990s TV comedy *Absolutely Fabulous.*

Peter Jensen (b. 1969, Løgstør, Denmark) London-based mens and womenswear designer.

Betsey Johnson (b. 1942, Connecticut, USA) Known for her feminine and whimsical designs plus her performance of a cartwheel at the end of her fashion shows.

Michael Kors (b. Karl Anderson, Jr, 1959, New York City) Best known for designing classic American sportswear for women.

Julien MacDonald (b. 1971, Merthyr Tydfil, Wales) Appointed chief designer at Givenchy (Alexander McQueen's successor) in 2001.

Martin Margiela (b. 1957, Genk, Belgium) Creative director of the Hermès women's line (1997-2003).

Roland Mouret (b. 1969, Lourdes, France) Best known for his Moon dress made famous by Victoria Beckham.

Jean Muir (1928-95) London-based dressmaker developed the Jane & Jane brand before launching her own label.

Todd Oldham (b. 1961, Corpus Christi, Texas) In 1995, he produced a clothing line for *Batman Forever.*

Zac Posen (b. 1980, New York City) Became known for dress he designed for Naomi Campbell.

Agatha Ruiz de la Prada (b. 1960, Madrid) Spanish fashion designer and noblewoman (12th Marquise of Castelldosrius).

Emilio Pucci (1914-92) Florentine fashion designer, politician and noble(Marchese di Barsento). His company was known for its geometric prints in a kaleidoscope of colours.

John Rocha (b. 1953, Hong Kong) established himself with his Chinatown label in Dublin in the 1980.

Rebecca Taylor (b. 1969, New Zealand) New York-based fashion designer whose label was recently acquired by Kellwood Company.

Philip Treacy (b. 1967, Ballinasloe, County Galway) Irish milliner who designed the telephone-shaped headpiece for Lady Gaga.

British Designer of the Year

1984 Katharine Hamnett	1994 John Galliano	2004 Phoebe Philo
1985 Betty Jackson	1995 John Galliano	2005 Christopher Bailey
1986 Jasper Conran	1996 Alexander McQueen	2006 Giles Deacon
1987 John Galliano	1997 Alexander McQueen and John Galliano	2007 Stella McCartney
1988 Rifat Ozbek	1998 no ceremony	2008 Luella Bartley
1989 Workers for Freedom	1999 Hussein Chalayan	2009 Christopher Bailey
1990 Vivienne Westwood	2000 Hussein Chalayan	2010 Phoebe Philo
1991 Vivienne Westwood	2001 Alexander McQueen	2011 Sarah Burton
1992 Rifat Ozbek	2002 no ceremony	2012 Stella McCartney
1993 John Rocha	2003 Alexander McQueen	

Clothes Care Instructions

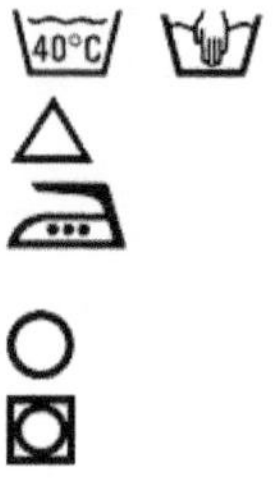

Most items of clothing have labels attached with care instructions.

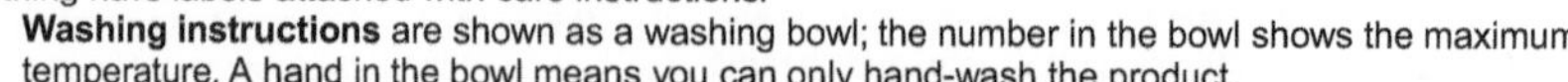

Washing instructions are shown as a washing bowl; the number in the bowl shows the maximum temperature. A hand in the bowl means you can only hand-wash the product.

Bleaching instructions are shown with a triangle: a cross over the triangle means do not wash with bleach.

Ironing instructions are shown by a picture of an iron. The dots on the iron show the maximum temperature at which it is safe to iron the product: three dots is very hot, one dot is cool. A cross over the iron means do not iron.

Dry-cleaning instructions: a circle symbol signifies that it is safe to dry-clean the product. The letter inside tells the dry-cleaners what method to use. A cross over the circle means do not dry- clean.

Tumble-drying instructions are shown by a square with a circle inside. The dots show the temperature at which it is safe to dry the product. A cross over the symbol means do not tumble dry.

Miss World Winners

1951	Kiki Haakonson, Sweden
1952	May Louise Flodin, Sweden
1953	Denise Perrier, France
1954	Antigone Costanda, Egypt
1955	Carmen Zubillaga, Venezuela
1956	Petra Schurmann, Germany
1957	Marita Lindahl, Finland
1958	Penelope Coelen, South Africa
1959	Corine Rottschafer, Holland
1960	Norma Cappagli, Argentina
1961	Rosemarie Frankland, United Kingdom
1962	Catharine Lodders, Holland
1963	Carole Crawford, Jamaica
1964	Ann Sidney, United Kingdom
1965	Lesley Langley, United Kingdom
1966	Reita Faria, India
1967	Madeiline Hartog Bel, Peru
1968	Penelope Plummer, Australia
1969	Eva Reuber Staier, Austria
1970	Jennifer Hosten, Grenada
1971	Lucia Petterle, Brazil
1972	Belinda Green, Australia
1973	Marjorie Wallace, USA
1974	Anneline Kriel, South Africa (Helen Morgan the original winner was disqualified for being a wife and having an illegitimate child.
1975	Wilnelia Merced, Puerto Rico
1976	Cindy Breakspeare, Jamaica
1977	Mary Stavin, Sweden
1978	Silvana Suarez, Argentina
1979	Gina Swainson, Bermuda
1980	Kimberly Santos, Guam
1981	Pilin Leon, Venezuela
1982	Mariasela Lebron, Dominican Republic
1983	Sarah Jane Hutt, United Kingdom
1984	Astrid Herrera, Venezuela
1985	Hofi Karlsdottir, Iceland
1986	Giselle Laronde, Trinidad
1987	Ulla Weigerstorfer, Austria
1988	Linda Petursdottir, Iceland
1989	Andeta Kreglicka, Poland
1990	Gina Marie Tolleson, USA
1991	Ninebeth Jiminez, Venezuela
1992	Julia Kourotchkina, Russia
1993	Lisa Hanna, Jamaica
1994	Aishwariya Rai, India
1995	Jacqueline Aquilera, Venezuela
1996	Irene Skliva, Greece
1997	Diana Hayden, India
1998	Linor Abargil, Israel
1999	Yukta Mookhey, India
2000	Priyanka Chopra, India
2001	Agbani Darego, Nigeria
2002	Azra Akin, Turkey
2003	Rosanna Davidson, Ireland
2004	Maria Garcia, Peru
2005	Unnur Vilhjalmsdottir, Iceland
2006	Tatana Kucharova, Czech Republic
2007	Zhang Zilin, China
2008	Ksenia Sukhinova, Russia
2009	Kaiane Aldorino, Gibraltar
2010	Alexandria Mills, USA
2011	Ivian Sarcos, Venezuela
2012	Yu Wenxia, China

British Hairdressers of the Year

1985	Trevor Sorbie
1986	Trevor Sorbie
1987	Irvine & Rita Rusk
1988	Anthony Mascolo
1989	John Frieda
1990	Anthony Mascolo
1991	Trevor Sorbie
1992	Trevor Sorbie
1993	Andrew Collinge
1994	Nicky Clarke
1995	Anthony Mascolo
1996	Charles Worthington
1997	Andrew Collinge
1998	Charles Worthington
1999	Umberto Giannini
2000	Mark Hill
2001	Beverly Cobella
2002	Beverly Cobella
2003	Mark Hill
2004	Antoinette Beenders
2005	Lisa Shepherd
2006	Andrew Barton
2007	Angelo Seminara
2008	Akin Konizi
2009	Akin Konizi
2010	Angelo Seminara
2011	Akin Konizi
2012	Angelo Seminara

Food and Drink

Dishes, Ingredients and Terms

Aemono Japanese term for a salad; 'dressed things'. A dress aemono may include fish, shellfish and seaweeds, poultry and cooked vegetables or may be made of only one ingredient
Agemono Japanese culinary term for something deep-fried
Aïoli Provençal sauce, mayonnaise, seasoned with garlic
Alboni sauce brown sauce with pine kernels and redcurrants, served with venison
Allumettes French, vegetables cut into matchstick-sized strips
Armoricaine in Breton fashion, with wine, brandy & tomato sauce
Angels on horseback oysters wrapped in bacon
Antipasto Italian term meaning 'before the meal', comparable to the French hors d'oeuvres
Artsoppa Swedish, dried pea soup with ham
Avgolemono Greek, sauce made with egg and lemon
Babka Polish bread similar to a fruit cake
Bagna cauda Italian sauce of garlic, anchovy and olive oil
Baklava Turkish/Greek filo (Phyllo) pastry filled with nuts (usually walnuts and almonds), honey flavoured
Balti (lit. bucket) Round-bottomed metal dish like a wok with two handles. Balti food is freshly prepared and healthy because the rapid stir-fry process retains the goodness of the food. Balti cooking is popular in Indian restaurants and particularly in the Midlands, Birmingham often being referred to as the Balti capital of Britain. Balti cooking originates from the Himalayan mountain region of Pakistani Kashmir, in Baltistan province
Bannock Scottish dish of oatmeal, soda and salt usually served with butter, honey or jam
Barquettes boat-shaped pastry moulds served with assorted fillings (lit. little boats)
Béarnaise French, egg yolk and butter sauce
Béchamel French, white sauce flavoured with onion
Bel Paese Creamy Italian cheese with a mild sweet flavour
Beurre, au French, cooked in butter
Bifteki Greek, hamburger patties
Bigarade French, orange-flavoured sauce served with duck
Biltong South African, dried meat
Bird's nest soup Chinese soup, contains saliva of swiftlet
Biryani Indian dish of pilau rice and meat or fish in spiced gravy
Bisque creamy soup usually made with sea food and enriched with cream or egg yolks
Black pudding sausage made of pig's blood and fat with oatmeal and seasoning
Blanquette French, meat stew made with white sauce
Blini Russian, stuffed pancake made with buckwheat flour and classically topped with sour cream and caviar
Blintz Jewish, pancakes stuffed with various sweet or savoury fillings, then fried
Bloater herring or sometimes a mackerel, that has been salted, smoked and cured (kipper is slit open, a bloater is not)
Blutwurst German, blood sausage
Boeuf bourguignon French beef dish in red wine sauce
Bombe spherical dessert dish consisting of an outer layer of ice cream or sherbet and a softer, inner layer of custard or mousse
Bonne femme French, in country style, or housewife style, homely, also sole poached in fish stock
Bordelaise Sauce of red wine, artichokes or shallots and marrow fat
Börek Turkish savoury pastry filled with spinach, eggs, pumpkin, cheese, meat or fruit
Borscht Russian, beetroot soup served with a sour cream garnish
Bouillabaisse French fish stew cooked in a highly flavoured stock with oil, spices and herbs
Bouillon French broth made by simmering meat, chicken, fish or vegetables in water (derives from 'to boil')
Bourride Provençal fish stew with aïoli sauce
Bratwurst German, fried sausage, usually pork
Bretonne, à la French, garnished with beans
Brochette, en French, on a skewer
Brouillé French, scrambled
Bruxelloise garnish for meat, composed of Brussel sprouts and pommes château, i.e. barrel-shaped potatoes, cooked in butter to a golden brown colour
Bubble and squeak Originally meat, cabbage and potatoes fried up as leftovers
Calamares Spanish fried squid or cuttlefish
Cannelloni Italian pasta stuffed with meat or cheese in cheese sauce
Cappelletti Italian pasta (meaning 'little hats') from Modena and traditionally served in broth.
Carpetbag steak Australian, thick cut of steak stuffed with oysters
Cassata Italian, ice cream dish of two types, cassata gelata and cassata siciliana. The siciliana is filled with ricotta cheese, the gelate with chopped nuts or candied fruit
Cassoulet French casserole with haricot beans, meat and vegetables
Ceviche South American dish of marinated raw fish
Chapatti Indian, bread pancake
Charlotte russe cold dessert made in a mould with sponge fingers enclosing a mash of whipped cream, lemon jelly and glacé cherries (literal meaning 'Russian Charlotte)
Charlotte: apple hot dessert of bread pudding with an apple filling
Charlotte: strawberry cold dessert similar to a Charlotte Russe but with a strawberry base
Chasseur French sauce of white wine, mushrooms and onions
Châteaubriand thick fillet steak
Chawan-mushi the most popular example of mushimono. Small pieces of poultry, fish or vegetables mixed with beaten eggs and dashi are steamed in a cup. Chawan-mushi literally means 'teacup steamed' and is the only Japanese dish to be eaten with a spoon
Chicken Kiev boned and flattened chicken breast wrapped around chilled butter lightly flavoured with chives, dipped in egg and breadcrumbs and fried
Chicken Marengo Italian fried chicken in a sauce of garlic, tomatoes and white wine supposedly named after Napoleonic battle when the owner of an inn was forced to use any food available to make a dish
Chicken Maryland Fried chicken served cold, iced or chilled
Chilli con carne Mexican minced beef with chilli and beans
Chop suey Originally a Cantonese dish that literally means 'bits and pieces' a way of dealing with leftovers by stir-frying; widely adopted in the USA under this Americanised name
Chorizo Spanish, spiced pork sausage
Chow mein Chinese-American fried noodles served with diced chicken, pork or seafood
Chowder fish or seafood thick soup or stew
Churro Spanish choux pastry fritter usually, served with a mug of chocolate
Ciabatta moist aerated Italian bread made from olive oil. Ciabatta literally means slipper (from the shape of the loaf)
Cocido Spanish, meat and vegetable stew
Cock-a-leekie Scottish, leek served onions and sometimes with prunes and chicken stew
Colbert French with lemon sauce, parsley and madeira
Colcannon Irish, potato and cabbage dish
Coleslaw Dutch and then American, shredded cabbage salad
Compôte dish of fruit cooked in a light sugar syrup and served hot or cold
Conchiglie Italian, pasta shaped like conch shells
Consommé French, clear soup
Coppa Italian, salted dried sausage made from neck or shoulder of pork
Coquilles Saint-Jacques French scallops
Coulibiac Russian, fish pie with buckwheat and chopped up hard-boiled eggs
Coulis French term meaning 'to strain' and often referring to a thin vegetable or fruit pureé

Couscous North African, steamed wheat mixed with semolina to form pasta-like pellets
Cranachan Scottish, dessert made from whipped cream, whisky, honey, raspberries and toasted oatmeal soaked overnight in whisky
Crécy, a la French, garnished with carrots
Crêpe suzette French, pancake with orange syrup and liqueur (Curacao)
Croque-monsieur French, toasted cheese sandwich with ham
Croûte, en French, in pastry
Cullen skink Scottish, traditional soup made from finnan haddock and potatoes. Cullen is the village on the coast of the Moray Firth where the recipe originated and skink refers to the stock or broth, usually fish stock, but water or milk is occasionally used. An onion is often added for enhancement of flavour and the soup is garnished with parsley
Cumberland sauce redcurrant-based sauce
Dashi the basic Japanese soup stock consisting of dried bonito (Katsuobushi) and giant kelp (Kombu)
Daube, en French, braised with vegetables in red wine and stock
Déglacer French, deglaze, to add wine, cream or stock to juices in a pan, thereby making a gravy
Dente al Italian, firm to the teeth
Devils on horseback stuffed prunes wrapped in bacon
Dhall general name for a variety of beans, peas and lentils used a staple in Indian cookery
Diablé French, devilled
Dolmades Greek/Turkish, vine leaves stuffed with meat and rice
Doner kebab Middle Eastern, a block of seasoned, sliced lamb roasted on a spit
Doré French, brushed with egg yolk
Dosa rice-based bread of southern India
Duchesse potatoes mashed in butter and egg shaped and then baked
Enchiladas Mexican, fried, stuffed pancakes cooked with chilli-flavoured sauce
Entrecôte steak cut from between two ribs
Espagnole French, brown sauce (fat and flour cooked in oven to light brown colour with stock added)
Falafel Middle Eastern, chickpea patties
Farci French, stuffed
Farfalle Italian, butterfly-shaped pasta
Fattoush Levantine, bread salad made from toasted or fried pieces of pita bread combined with mixed greens and other vegetables
Fettucine Italian, ribbon-shaped pasta
Filet mignon Henri IV French, steak dish served with potatoes, artichoke hearts and Béarnaise sauce
Financière French sauce made with Madeira and truffles
Florentine French, with spinach
Fluffernutter Massachusetts sandwich made with peanut butter and marshmallow creme, usually served on white bread
Focaccia a flat savoury Italian bread made with and usually seasoned with herbs
Fondue Swiss, melted cheese in white wine eaten with bread dips
Forestière French, with bacon, mushrooms and potatoes
Forno, à la from the oven
Fricassée French meat stew in white sauce
Frijoles Mexican beans
Frikadelle Swedish boiled meat ball
Fritto misto Italian, seafood fried in batter
Fusilli Italian, corkscrew-shaped pasta
Gado gado Indonesian, dish of vegetables in white sauce
Galantine chopped meat in calves-head jelly
Garni French, garnished
Gaspacho Spanish, cold vegetable soup
Glaze French, glossy finish produced by brushing food with beaten egg, milk, jelly or sugar syrup
Gnocchi Italian, savoury dumplings
Gougère French, savoury choux pastry with grated cheese mixed into the batter
Goulash Hungarian, paprika-flavoured meat stew
Granita Italian, water ice
Gratin, au French, browned with cheese and breadcrumbs
Gravlax Scandinavian, raw pickled salmon with mustard and dill sauce
Grecque, à la French, means ('Greek style'), cooked in oil and lemon juice (also an hors d'oeuvre with rice)
Guacamole Mexican, avocado dip
Gumbo stew with okra and rice
Haggis Scottish, sheep's stomach filled with offal, oatmeal, suet and seasoning
Halva Middle Eastern sesame seed, honey and almond sweet
Hoisin sauce sauce made from soya beans
Hollandaise French, sauce with egg yolk, vinegar, lemon juice and butter
Hot dog Frankfurter in bun
Hummus chickpea, garlic and sesame purée
Indienne, à la French, curried
Jardinière French, with garnish of fresh vegetables cut in julienne method
Julienne French, vegetables cut in fine strips
Kebab Turkish, lamb or mutton cooked on skewers (lit. on skewers)
Kedgeree Originally Indian, rice and bean dish adapted as breakfast dish by the British with flaked fish and hard-boiled eggs
Korma An Indian cooking instruction meaning 'to braise'
Kulfi Indian ice cream made with reduced milk and nuts
Larding threading strips of lard through lean meat to prevent dryness during roasting
Lasagne flat pasta dish with minced meat, tomatoes and white cheese sauce
Laulau Hawaiian, steamed pork and fish cooked in leaves
Liaison French, binding agent such as egg yolk or cream
Lobscouse fisherman's stew associated with Liverpool but similar dishes with similar names come from Denmark, Germany and Norway
Lumaconi Italian, pasta shaped like giant snails
Lyonnaise sauce with white wine and onions fried in butter
Macédoine French, mixture of fruit or vegetables cut into small pieces
Madeleine small sponge cake
Maître d'hotel French, sauce with butter, parsley, lemon and cayenne pepper (lit. headwaiter)
Marrons glacés French candied chestnuts
Melba sauce sauce made with fresh raspberries and served with peach melba
Melba toast thin toast named after opera singer Dame Nellie Melba by French chef Auguste Escoffier
Meringue baked pudding made with egg white and sugar
Meunière French, floured and cooked in butter with salt, pepper and lemon juice and garnished with parsley
Mez(z)e Selection of hot and cold dishes served as an hors d'oeuvres in Eastern Mediterranean regions
Miso a paste made from fermented soya beans and barley or rice malt, used in Japanese cookery
Mocha Arabian, a kind of coffee flavouring, often with chocolate
Mornay French, béchamel sauce with grated Parmesan cheese
Mortadella Italian, sausage from Bologna
Moussaka Greek, minced lamb, aubergine and tomato dish topped with cheese
Mulligatawny Indian, curried soup (means 'pepper water')
Mushimono Japanese culinary term for steamed dishes such as chicken, fish or vegetables, often treated with saké
Nabemono Japanese culinary term for one-pot dishes usually cooked at the table by the diners. Sukiyaki is a typical example of nabemono
Naan Wheatflour leavened bread, with yoghurt base, cooked in a clay tandoor
Nasi goreng Indonesian, meat and fried rice dish
Neige, à la French, white of egg beaten stiffly (literally means 'snow')
Nimono Japanese culinary term meaning 'to simmer'
Nori Japanese name for various edible seaweed often used to wrap sushi

Nougat French, sweet made from almonds and honey
Okashi Japanese culinary term for accompaniments to tea. Okashi can be made from various ingredients but usually based on sweet bean paste made with azuki bean
Orecchiette Italian, pasta from Puglia (literally means 'little ears')
Osso bucco Italian, braised knuckle of veal dish cooked with wine and tomatoes
Oysters Kilpatrick Australian, grilled oysters on bed of rock salt and topped with bacon
Paella Spanish, baked saffron rice with chicken, seafood and vegetables
Pancetta Italian cured belly of pork often used in pasta dressings. The name pancetta derives from the Italian for 'belly'
Panettone Italian, tall fat egg-rich cake studded with candied fruit and traditionally eaten at Christmas and Easter
Pappardelle Italian, ribbon-shaped pasta about an inch wide
Papillote, en French, cooked in a greased paper bag
Parata Indian flaky unleavened bread smeared with ghee and rolled and stuffed before frying
Parisienne French, with round, ball artichoke hearts or other vegetables, shaped potatoes and leeks
Parmentier potato, diced and fried in butter (named from Baron Parmentier, who first introduced potatoes into France)
Pâté de foie gras French goose liver pâté
Paupiette French, thin slice of meat, or fillet of fish, rolled around a savoury filling
Pavlova fruit, cream and meringue dessert (named after ballerina Anna Pavlova)
Paysanne, à la French, in peasant style
Peach melba dessert made of halved peaches and vanilla ice cream and topped with raspberry purée – named after opera singer Dame Nellie Melba by French chef Auguste Escoffier
Pecorino Italian, general name given to fresh, medium aged or matured cheeses made from sheep's milk. Fresh (*fresco*) Pecorino cheeses are soft and white with a mild, lemony flavour, such as Ricotta Salata. Their texture ranges from soft and moist to crumbly and granular
Penne Italian, quill-shaped pasta
Peperoni Italian, sweet peppers, also called capsicums
Périgueux sauce made with Madeira and truffles
Pesto Italian, sauce of basil, garlic, pine nuts and cheese.
Petit four French small cakes or crystallised fruit or sweets (literally means 'little oven').
Pilau/pilaf The cleaning of surface starch by means of simmering and steaming of rice to ensure separate grains
Piperade Basque tomatoes and peppers with egg beaten to a fluffy consistency
Pirozhki Russian, small pies with filling
Pissaladière French, pastry flan with onion, anchovy and black olives
Pizza Italian, flat-baked dough with various coverings (lit. pie)
Plat du jour French, dish of the day
Polenta Italian dish of maize, flour and water
Poivre, au French, with pepper
Pollo Italian, chicken
Polpetta Italian, meatball
Pomodori Italian, tomatoes
Poor Knights of Windsor eggy bread flavoured with cinnamon and sherry
Profiteroles choux pastry puffs, covered with chocolate, usually with cream filling
Prosciutto Italian, smoked ham
Provençale French, prepared with garlic, oil and often, tomatoes
Pumpernickel German, malted rye bread
Quesadilla Mexican cheese-based tortilla folded in half to form a crescent shape
Quiche lorraine French, savoury flan with egg, bacon and cheese filling
Radiatori Italian, pasta shaped like radiator grilles
Ragoût meat and vegetable stew
Raita Indian yoghurt-based cucumber salad
Ratatouille French, dish of aubergine, courgette, onions, peppers and tomatoes stewed in oil
Ravioli Italian, small pasta casings with stuffing
Red cooked braised in soy sauce and wine
Rijstafel Indonesian, a selection of dishes served with rice
Risotto Italian, rice dish cooked with stock
Rissole fried minced meat ball
Rogan josh Kashmiri, lamb curry with yoghurt
Rollmop German, raw herring with onion or gherkin pickled
Roti Indian, unleavened unsalted bread
Roux butter and flour cooked and constantly stirred until blended
Rum baba small sponge cake soaked in rum and syrup (invented by a Polish king: Stanislaus)
Ruote Italian, pasta shaped like wagon wheels
Sachertorte Austrian, chocolate sponge cake named after Sacher Hotel in Vienna
Salade niçoise tuna and anchovies
Saignant French, rare or underdone
Salmagundi English dish popular in 18th century and consisting of mixed salad items possibly with meat, eggs anchovies and onions
Salsa A spicy sauce especially served with Mexican food
Saltimbocca Italian, veal and ham dish
Sambal Indonesian spiced pickle
Samosa In Indian cuisine, small, crisp, flaky pastries, usually fried but may be baked. Samosas are stuffed with a variety of fillings such as cheese, egg, spiced minced meat, vegetables or sweets
Sashimi Japanese, raw fish
Satay Malaysian, grilled skewers of meat
Sauerkraut German, pickled cabbage
Scotch broth: cereal used barley
Scotch woodcock anchovies and eggs on toast
Searing browning meat rapidly with fierce heat to seal in the juices
Shiromono Generic Japanese culinary term describing all soups but thick soups in particular
Shish kebab Turkish, skewered meat pieces
Smörgasbord Swedish buffet including herring, seafood, cheese and crispbread
Smørrebrød Danish, open sandwich
Solyanka Russian, cucumber soup
Sorbet water ice, used to cleanse palate between courses
Soubise white sauce with onion or purée of onions and rice to accompany some cuts of meat
Soufflé French, dish of eggs whisked and baked
Soufflé cheese Parmesan and Gruyère are the two cheeses used traditionally
Steak à la tartare raw minced beef bound with egg into rissoles
Stollen German, fruit loaf
Stroganoff Russian, dish of thin strips of fillet of beef cooked in butter with sour cream and shallots
Strudel German, thin sheet of filled dough rolled up and baked (literally meaning 'eddy' or 'whirlpool')
Suimono Generic Japanese culinary term describing all clear soups
Sukiyaki Japanese dish of beef and vegetables in soy sauce
Sunomono Japanese culinary term meaning 'vinegared things' and referring to salad items given a vinegar dressing
Sushi Japanese, vinegared rice with fresh fish or other seafood
Syllabub dish dates from Elizabethan times. One definition claims that a favourite white wine in those days came from 'Sillery' in the Champagne region of France; the slang term for a bubbly drink was 'bub'; therefore the mixture of still wine and frothy cream became known as a 'syllabub'
Tabouli cracked wheat with lemon, parsley, tomato and mint
Taco Mexican, stuffed fried pancake
Tagliatelle Italian, ribbon-shaped pasta
Tamale Mexican dish of corn-based dough boiled in a leaf wrapper and filled with meats, cheeses, fruits, vegetables or chilies
Tandoori dish in a clay oven
Tapas Spanish small appetisers served in bars and varied according to season and locality
Taramasalata Greek, grey mullet smoked cod roe dip.

Tartare mayonnaise sauce mixed with hard-boiled egg yolks, onions or chives or herbs, capers and gherkins
Tempura Japanese, fish or vegetables deep-fried in batter
Teriyaki Japanese culinary term referring to a special glaze of soy sauce, saké, and mirin, applied to fish, meat or poultry when partly grilled
Terrine, en French, potted
Tikka Indian term referring to meat or poultry cooked on skewers
Tiramisu Italian dessert consisting of layers of sponge cake soaked in coffee and brandy or liqueur with powdered chocolate and mascarpone cheese. Tiramisu literally means 'pick-me-up'
Toad in the hole English sausage in batter
Tortillas Mexican, pancakes cooked on a griddle
Tournedos Rossini named after the composer by French chef Auguste Escoffier; thick round slices of fillet steak garnished with sliced sautéd truffles and foie gras
Tourtière Pie dish, for small pies
Tsukemono Japanese culinary term referring to various pickled vegetables and also for pickled umeboshi, a plum-like fruit
Tzatziki Greek, cucumber in yoghurt
Veal escalope veal fried in breadcrumbs
Velouté French, smooth white sauce with added white meat or fish stock
Vermicelli Italian, thin spaghetti (literally means 'little worms')
Vichyssoise potato and leek soup, usually cold
Vindaloo Indian, hot vinegary pork curry
Wai-Wai popular snack in Nepal, Sikkim and parts of West Bengal; a kind of noodle eaten raw or in soup. Unlike ordinary noodles, wai-wai is pre-cooked, flavoured, seasoned and fried before packaging
Waldorf salad American, celery, apples, mayonnaise and walnuts named after the Waldorf Astoria Hotel in New York City
Wellington English or Irish beef (or often any meat or fish) cooked in pastry
Welsh rarebit cheese on toast sometimes melted with mustard and with beer added
Wet Nelly traditional Liverpudlian dish of leftover cakes crushed onto an egg custard base
White sauce a roux with added milk used as a base for numerous sauces
Wiener schnitzel Austrian, breaded veal cutlet
Wonton Chinese, meat-filled dumplings
Yakimono Japanese culinary term for something grilled
Zensai Japanese culinary term for appetisers comparable to the French hors d'oeuvres
Zabaglione Italian dessert made from egg yolks with marsala and sugar
Zampone Italian, speciality sausage made from pig's leg stuffed with minced pork

Fruit and Vegetable Varieties

Apple Allington pippin, Api, Blanche d'hiver, Blenheim, Bramley, Braeburn Calville, Cortland, Costard, Cox's Orange Pippin, Discovery, Ellison's Orange, Faro, Flower of Kent, Fuji, Gala, Gillyflower, Gladstone, Golden Delicious, Granny Smith, Gravenstein, Idared, James Grieve, Jonathans, Laxton's Superb, McIntosh, Macoun, Mutsu, Newtown Pippin, Northern Spy, Pearmain Pippin, Reinette, Ribston Pippin, Rome Beauty, Russet, Star Kings, Wealthy, White Joaneting, White Transparent, Winesnap, Worcester, York Imperial.
Beetroot Cheltenham Green Top, Crimson Globe, Nutting's Red Globe.
Broad bean Bonny Lad, Bunyard's Exhibition, Express, Green Windsor, Red Epicure, Sutton, White Windsor.
Brussels sprout Bedford-Fillbasket, Bedford Winter Harvest, Cambridge No 5, Early Half Tall, Fortress, Huizer's Late, Peer Gynt, Predora, Welland, Wellington, Widgen.
Cabbage April, Christmas Drumhead, Derby Day, Durham Early, Golden Acre, Greyhound, Hargenger, Hispy, January King, June Star, Ormskirk, Quickstep, Rear Guard, Spivoy, Spring Hero, Velocity, Winnigstadt, Wivoy.
Carrot Autumn King, Early Giant, Favourite, Figaro, Regulus Imperial, St Valery.
Cauliflower Alpha, Canberra, Dominant, Nevada, Snow Cap, Snow Crown.
Cherry Amarelle, Bigarreau, Bing, Black Tartarian, Bradbourne Black, Cherokee, Coe's Transparent, Early Rivers, Griotte, Guigne, May Duke, Montmorency, Morello, Napoleon, Rainier, Stella, Van.
Cucumber Bushcrop, Conqueror, King of the Ridge, Pacer, Pepita, Stockwood Ridge, Telegraph, Tokyo Slicer.
Dates Asharasi, Barhi, Deglet Noor, Fardh, Gundila, Halawi, Hilali, Khadrawi, Khalas, Khustawi, Khidri, Medjool, Mactoum, Naghal, Yatimeh, Zahidi.
French bean Cordon, Loch Ness, Long Bow, Masterpiece, Remus, Sprite, Tendergreen.
Gooseberry Admiral Beattie, Alma, Aston Red, Australia, Bellona, Blucher, Broom Girl, Careless, Clayton, Cousin's Seedling, Criterion, Crown Bob, Dan's Mistake, Early Sulphur, Firbob, Freedom, Green Gem, Green Ocean, Guido, Gunner, Heart of Oak, Hero of the Nile, Howard's Lancer, Ironmonger, Jubilee, Keepsake, King of Trumps, Lancashire Lad, Leveller, London, Lord Derby, Lord Kitchener, Macherauch's Seedling, Marigold, Matchless, May Duke, Peru, Plunder, Queen of Hearts, Queen of Trumps, Sir George Brown, Speedwell, Sultan Juror, Surprise, Suter Johnny, Talford, Trumpeter, Whinham's Industry, White Eagle, White Lion, Whitesmith, Woodpecker,
Grape Alicante, Almeria, Barbera, Baresana, Barlinka, Cabernet Franc, Cabernet Sauvignon, Cardinal, Cassidy, Catawba, Chasselas, Cinsaut, Chardonnay, Concord, Delaware, Emporer, Gamay, Hermitage, Gewürztraminer, Grenache, Hanepoot, Irikara, Italia, Kishmishi, Madeleine Royale, Malaga, Malvasia, Merlot, Montefiascone, Muscat, Nebbiolo, Niagara, Palamino, Perlette, Pinot Blanc, Pinot Gris, Pinot Noir, Portugieser, Red Emporer, Regina, Ribier, Riesling, Sangiovese, Sémillon, Shiraz, Simone, Sultanina, Syrah, Thompson's Seedless, Tokay, Ugni Blanc, Viognier, Waltham Cross, Zinfandel.
Grapefruit Duncan, Marsh.
Leek Catalina, Early Market, Giant Winter-Wila, Lyon Prizetaker, Musselburgh, Royal Favourite, Walton Mammouth.
Lettuce Arctic King, Cos, Density, Fortune, Iceberg, Lakeland, Little Gem, Lobjoit's Green, Sabin, Saladin, Sigmaball, Stanstead Park, Paris White, Tom Thumb, Unrivalled, Webb's Wonder White.
Nut Acorn, Almond, Beech, Brazil, Breadnut, Calumpang, Candlenut, Chestnut, Cobnut, Coco de Mer, Coconut, Dika, Filbert, Gabon, Gingko, Gnetum, Groundnut, Hazelnut, Hickory, Illipe, Java Olive, Jojoba, Karaka, Kedrouvie, Kepayang, Kubuli, Macadamia, Madia, Manketti, Naras, Ngapi, Niger Seed, Okari, Olive, Oyster, Palm, Pecan, Pignut, Pili, Pine, Pistachio, Safflower, Sandalwood, Sapucaya, Sesame, Shea Butter, Souari, Sunflower, Walnut, Yeheb.
Onion Ailsa Craig, Autumn Queen, Bedfordshire Champion, Blood Red, Brunswick, Dobies Allrounder, Lancastrian, Marshall's Giant Fenglobe, North Holland Blood Red, Pearl Pickler, Ricardo, Southport Red Globe, Stuttgarter Giant, Sturon, Turbo.
Parsnip Improved Hollow Crown, The Student, Tender and True, White Gem.
Pea Feltham First, Histon Mini, Hurst Beagle, Hurst Green, Kelvedon Wonder, Little Marvel, Meteor, Onward, Semitar, Shaft.
Pear Abbé, Anjou, Bartlett, Beurré, Clapp Favourite, Conference, Doyenne du Comice, Glou Morceau, Jargonelle, Josephine de Malines, Kaiser, Louise Bonne der Jersey, Olivier de Serres, Passe Crasanne, Seckel, Wardens, Williams Bon Chrétien, Winter Nelis.
Plum Ambarella, Bokhara, Brazil, Burbank, Chrétien, Chickasaw, Czar, Davidson's, Denniston's Superb, Early Rivers, El Dorado, Greengage, Hog, Imperial Gage, Jew, Laxton's Cropper, Pershore, President, Prince's Gage, Red Gage, Santa Rosa, Victoria, Warwickshire Drooper, Washington.
Runner bean Butler, Kelvedon Marvel, Mergoles.

Yellow Champagne.

Potato Arran Pilot, Arran Victory, Blue, Catriona, Craig's Royal, Desiree, Edgecote Purple, Esteema, King Edward, Majestic, Maris Piper, May Queen, Pink Fir Apple, Romano, Vanessa, Whites, Wilja.

Raspberry Lloyd George, Newburgh, Norfolk Giant.

Rhubarb Brandy Carr Scarlet, Cawood Delight, Royal Albert, Stock Bridge Arrow.

Strawberry Baron Solemacher, Cambridge Vigour, Florence, Grandee, Hapil, Pegasus, Red Gauntlet.

Tomato Ailsa Craig, Alfresco, Alicante, Big Boy, Dombito, Early Girl, Eurocross, Golden Boy, Herald, Marmande, Minibel, Moneymaker, Piranto, Red Alert, Shirley, Tiny Tim, Supersonic.

Turnip Golden Ball, Green Globe, Model White, Veitch's Red Globe.

Fruit: Latin Names and Origin

English Name	*Species*	*Origin*
Apple	*Malus sylvestris*	Temperate regions
Apricot	*Prunus armeniaca*	Asia
Avocado	*Persea americana*	Central America
Banana	*Musa various species*	India/Asia
Bilberry	*Vaccinium myrtillus*	Europe/Asia
Blackberry	*Rubus fruticosus and other species*	Europe/Asia
Blackcurrant	*Ribes nigrum*	Europe/Asia/Africa
Blueberry	*Vaccinium various species*	Europe/USA
Breadfruit	*Artocarpus atilis*	Malaysia
Carambola	*Averrhoa carambola*	Asia
Cherry (sour)	*Prunus cerasus*	Temperate regions
Cherry (sweet)	*Prunus avium*	Temperate regions
Clementine	*Citrus reticulata*	Mediterranean
Coconut	*Cocos nucifera*	Pacific
Cranberry	*Oxycoccus macrocarpus*	North America
Damson	*Prunus institiia*	Temperate regions
Date	*Phoenix dactylifera*	Persian Gulf
Fig	*Ficus carica*	Asia
Gooseberry	*Ribes grossularia*	Europe
Grape	*Vitis vinifera*	Asia
Grapefruit	*Citrus paradisi*	West Indies
Greengage	*Prunus domestica*	Temperate regions
Kiwi fruit	*Actinidia deliciosa*	China
Kumquat	*Fortunella margarita*	China
Lemon	*Citrus limon*	Asia
Lime	*Citrus aurantifolia*	Asia
Loganberry	*Rubus loganobaccus*	America
Loquat	*Eriobotrya japorica*	China/Japan
Mandarin	*Citrus reticulata*	China
Mango	*Mangifera indica*	Asia
Medlar	*Mespilus germanica*	Europe/Asia
Mulberry	*Morus nigra*	Asia
Nectarine	*Prunus persica*	China
Olive	*Olea europaea*	East Mediterranean
Orange	*Citrus sinensis*	China
Passion fruit	*Passiflora edulis*	South America
Peach	*Prunus persica*	China
Pear	*Pyrus cummunis*	Middle East/Europe
Persimmon	*Diospyros kaki*	Far East
Pineapple	*Ananas comosus*	South America
Plum	*Prunus domestica*	Temperate regions
Pomegranate	*Punica granatum*	Persia
Pomelo	*Citrus grandis*	Asia
Quince	*Cydonia oblonga*	Persia
Raspberry	*Rubus idaeus*	Northern hemisphere
Redcurrant	*Ribes rubrum*	Worldwide
Rhubarb	*Rheum rharbararum*	Asia
Satsuma	*Citrus nobilis*	Japan
Strawberry	*Fragaria x ananassa*	Europe/Asia
Ugli fruit	*Citrus reticulata*	Jamaica
Watermelon	*Citrullus lanatus*	Africa
Whitecurrant	*Ribes rubrum*	Europe

Vegetables: Latin Names and Origin

English Name	*Species*	*Origin*
Artichoke, Chinese	*Stachys affinis*	China
Artichoke, globe	*Cynara scolymus*	Mediterranean
Artichoke, Jerusalem	*Helianthus tuberosus*	North America
Aubergine	*Solanum melongena*	Asia/Africa
Avocado	*Persea americana*	Central America
Bean sprout	*Vigna radiata Glycirve maximus*	China
Broad bean	*Vicia faba*	Africa/Europe
Kidney bean	*Phaseolus vulgaris*	America
Runner bean	*Phaseolus coccineus*	America
Soya bean	*Glycine soja*	East Asia
Beetroot	*Beta vulgaris*	Mediterranean
Broccoli	*Brassica oleracea*	Europe
Brussels sprout	*Brassica oleracea*	North Europe
Cabbage	*Brassica oleracea*	Europe/Asia
Celery	*Apium graveolens*	Europe/Africa/USA
Chick-pea	*Cicer arietinum*	West Asia
Chives	*Allium schoenoprasum*	Europe/USA
Courgette	*Cucurbita pepo*	Africa/S. America
Cucumber	*Cucumis sativus*	Uncertain
Fennel	*Foeniculum vulgare*	Italy
Garlic	*Allium sativum*	Uncertain
Gherkin	*Cucumis anguria*	Northern India
Kale	*Brassica oleracea acephala*	East Mediterranean
Kohlrabi	*Brassica oleracea caulorapa*	Asia
Leek	*Allium porrum*	Africa/Europe
Lettuce	*Lactuca sativa*	Middle East
Lettuce: lamb's tongue	*Valerianella locusta*	Europe
Mange-tout	*Pisum sativum saccharatum*	Near East
Mushroom	*Agaricus campestris*	Worldwide
Okra	*Hibiscus esculentus*	Africa
Onion	*Allium cepa*	Central Asia
Parsley	*Petroselinum crispum*	East Mediterranean
Parsnip	*Pastinaca sativa*	Europe
Pea	*Pisum sativum*	Asia/Europe
Pepper	*Capsicum annuum*	South America
Potato	*Solanum tuberosum*	South America
Pumpkin	*Cucurbita pepo*	South America
Radish	*Raphanus sativus*	China/Japan
Salsify	*Tragopogon porrifolius*	Europe
Sorrel	*Rumex acetosa*	Europe
Spinach	*Spinacia oleracea*	Persia
Squash, summer	*Cucurbita pepo*	America
Squash, winter	*Cucurbita maxima*	America
Swede	*Brassica napus*	Europe
Sweetcorn	*Zea mays*	Central & South America
Sweet potato	*Ipomaea batatas*	Central America
Tomato	*Lycopersicon esculentum*	South America
Turnip	*Brassica rapa*	Middle East
Water chestnut, Chinese	*Eleocharis dulcis*	China
Watercress	*Nasturtium officinale*	Europe/Asia
White cabbage	*Brassica oleracea capitata*	East Mediterranean
Yam	*Dioscorea various species*	Tropics

Spices: Latin Names and Origin

English Name	*Species*	*Origin*
Acitrón	*Echinocactus grandis*	Mexico
Agar wood	*Aquillaria agallocha*	Asia
Ajmud	*Trachyspermum roxburghianum*	Asia
Ajowan	*Trachyspermum ammi*	Asia
Alexanders	*Smyrnium olusatrum*	Mediterranean
Allspice	*Pimenta dioica*	West Indies
Angelica	*Angelica archangelica*	Europe
Anise	*Pimpinella anisum*	Mediterranean
Annatto	*Bixa orellana*	West Indies
Asafoetida	*Ferula assafoetida*	Asia
Ashanti pepper	*Piper guineense*	West Africa
Balm	*Melissa officinalis*	Mediterranean
Balsam	*Myroxylon balsamum*	Asia

Basil	*Ocimum basilicum*	Asia
Bay	*Laurus nobilis*	Mediterranean
Bergamot	*Monarda fistulosa*	Mexico
Bistort	*Polygonum bistorta*	Europe
Bitter berries	*Solanum aethiopicum*	North Africa
Black cumin	*Nigella sativa*	Asia
Borage	*Borago officinalis*	Mediterranean
Burnet	*Sanguisorba officinalis*	Europe
Calamint	*Calamintha sylvatica*	Europe
Caper	*Capparis spinosa*	Mediterranean
Caraway	*Carum carvi*	Europe/Asia
Cardamom	*Ellataria cardamomum*	Asia
Cassia	*Cinnamonum cassia*	Asia
Cayenne	*Capsicum frutescens*	America/Africa
Cherry laurel	*Laurocerasus officinalis*	Mediterranean
Chervil	*Anthriscus cerefolium*	Asia
Chinese keys	*Boesenbergia pandurata*	Asia
Cinnamon	*Cinnamomum zeylanicum*	Asia
Clary	*Salvia sclarea*	Europe
Cleavers	*Galium aparine*	Europe
Chilli pepper	*Capsicum annuum*	America
Cloves	*Syzygium aromaticum*	Moluccas
Coltsfoot (common)	*Tussilago farfara*	Europe
Coltsfoot (sweet)	*Petasites japonicus*	Japan
Comfrey	*Symphytum officinalis*	Europe
Coriander	*Coriandrum sativum*	Mediterranean
Corkwing	*Glehnia littoralis*	Asia
Costmary	*Tanacetum balsamita*	Asia
Costus	*Saussurea lappa*	Asia
Cowslip	*Primula veris*	Eurasia
Cubeb	*Piper cubeba*	Indonesia
Cumin seed	*Cuminum cyminum*	Mediterranean
Curry leaf	*Murraya koenigii*	India
Daun salam	*Syzygium polyanthum*	Indonesia
Dill	*Anethum graveolens*	Asia
Elecampane	*Inula helenium*	Europe
Epazote	*Chenopodium ambrosioides*	Mexico
Fennel	*Foeniculum vulgare*	Europe
Fenugreek	*Trigonella foenum-graecum*	India/Europe
Galingale/Galangal	*Alpinia galanga*	Asia
Garden mace	*Archillea decolorans*	Europe
Ginger	*Zingiber officinale*	Asia
Golden needles	*Hemerocallis fulva*	Asia
Grains of selim	*Xylopia aethiopica*	Africa
Ground Elder	*Aegopodium podagraria*	Europe
Guascas/huascas	*Galinsoga parviflora*	South America
Hedge garlic	*Alliaria petiolata*	Europe
Hogweed	*Heracleum sphondylium*	Eurasia
Horehound	*Marrubium vulgare*	Eurasia
Horseradish	*Armoracia rusticana*	Europe
Khus khus	*Vetiveria zizanioides*	Asia
Lemon grass	*Cymbopogon citratus*	Asia
Lemon verbena	*Lippia triphyllos*	Europe
Lime flowers	*Tilia platyphyllos*	Europe
Lovage	*Levisticum officinalis*	Europe
Mace	*Myristica fragrans*	Moluccas
Marjoram (sweet)	*Origanum majorana*	Mediterranean
Marjoram (wild)	*Origanum vulgare*	Europe
Mastic	*Pistacia lentiscus*	Mediterranean
Meadowsweet	*Filipendula ulmaria*	Northern Hemisphere
Melegueta pepper	*Aframomum melegueta*	Africa
Mint (water)	*Mentha aquatica*	Worldwide
Mint (wild)	*Mentha arvensis*	Asia
Mitsuba	*Cryptotaenia japonica*	Japan
Mugwort	*Artemisa vulgaris*	Northern Hemisphere
Mustard, black	*Brassica nigrar*	Worldwide
Mustard, white	*Sinapis aba*	Europe/Asia
Nasturtium	*Tropaeolum majus*	South America
Nutmeg	*Myristica fragrans*	Moluccas
Palilo	*Escobedia scabrifolio*	Peru
Paprika	*Capsicum annuum*	South America
Parsley	*Petroselenum crispum*	Mediterranean
Pennyroyal	*Mentha pulegium*	Asia
Pepper	*Piper nigrum*	India
Rau ram	*Polygonum odoratum*	Brazil
Rosemary	*Rosmarinus officinalis*	Mediterranean
Rue	*Ruta graveolens*	Mediterranean
Saffron	*Crocus sativus*	Eurasia
Sage	*Salvia officinalis*	Eurasia
Samphire (marsh)	*Salicornia europaea*	Europe
Samphire (rock)	*Crithmum maritmum*	Mediterranean

Sandalwood	*Santalum album*	India/Australia
Sansho	*Zanthoxylum piperitum*	Asia
Sarsaparilla	*Smilax officinalis*	America
Savory (summer)	*Satureja hortensis*	Mediterranean
Savory (winter)	*Satureja montana*	Mediterranean
Shado béni	*Eryngium foetidum*	Caribbean
Shiso	*Perilla frutescens*	Japan
Sichuan pepper	*Zanthoxylum silulans*	China
Smartweed	*Persicaria hydropiper*	Eurasia
Southernwood	*Artemisia abrotanum*	Europe
Spanish needles	*Bidens pilosa*	Worldwide
Spanish thyme	*Plectranthus amboinicus*	Uncertain
Spearmint	*Mentha spicata*	Mediterranean
Star anise	*Illicium verum*	China
Sweet cicely	*Myrrhis odorata*	Europe
Tansy	*Tanacetum vulgare*	Northern Hemisphere
Tarragon	*Artemisia dracunculus*	Eurasia
Thyme	*Thymus vulgaris*	Mediterranean
Turmeric	*Curcuma longa*	Asia
Vanilla	*Vanilla planifolia*	Central America
Vervain	*Verbena officinalis*	Europe
Wasabi	*Eutrema wasabi*	Japan
Water dropwort	*Oenanthe javanica*	Asia
Wintergreen	*Gaultheria procumbens*	North America
Woodruff	*Galium odoratum*	Eurasia
Wormwood (common)	*Artemisia absinthium*	Eurasia
Wormwood (Roman)	*Artemisia pontica*	Eurasia
Ylang-ylang	*Cananga odorata*	Asia
Zedoary	*Curcuma zedoaria*	Asia

Food: Miscellaneous Information

Abalone	shellfish
Aga: stoves from	Sweden (full name: Aktienbolagetgasackumalator)
Agurketid (Danish silly season)	literally means 'cucumber time': the season when they are served
Allspice: other name	pimento, Jamaican pepper
Associated with a place:	
Aberdeen	rowies (rolls) sausage
Arbroath	smokies
Bakewell	tart
Banbury	cake
Bath	bun, Oliver (biscuits)
Battenberg	cake
Berwick	cockles
Black Forest	gateau
Bologna	Bolognese sauce
Boston	baked beans, brown bread
Brussels	sprouts
Cayenne	pepper
Chelsea	bun
Cornish	pasty
Coventry	Godcakes
Cumberland	sausage, sauce
Denmark	pastries
Dublin	prawn
Dundee	cake
Eccles	cake
Frankfurt	sausage
Geneva	pudding
Genoa	fruit cake
Hamburg	hamburger
Hungary	goulash
Ireland	stew
Kendal	mint cake
Kiev	chicken
Lancashire	hot-pot
Lima	bean
Lorraine	quiche
Madeira	cake
Manchester	pudding
Maryland	chicken
Melton Mowbray	pork pie

Norway	lobster
Pontefract	liquorice cake
Selkirk	bannock (fruit cake)
Seville	orange
Siena	cake
Switzerland (Swiss)	roll
Tabasco	sauce
Vichy	Vichyssoise soup
Vienna	loaf
Wales (Welsh)	(rabbit) rarebit
Whitstable	oysters
Windsor	bean
Worcester	sauce
Yorkshire	pudding
Bagel	doughnut-shaped roll cooked in water, then baked
Bain-Marie	large pan of boiling water in which a smaller pan is placed to help the cooking process
Baking powder	bicarbonate of soda, cream of tartar and starch
Banana: cooking variety	plantain
Bombay duck	fish
Bouquet garni	parsley, thyme, bay leaf, used as flavouring in stews etc.
Brawn	pig's head (occasionally sheep or cow's head)
Brisling	small herring-like fish
Caboc cheese	soft, Scottish cheese rolled in toasted oatmeal
Caviar	roe of sturgeon
Cendrés cheeses	coated with ashes originally from vine roots, later from industrial charcoal
Champignon	French name for mushrooms, but usually refers to button mushrooms
Charcuterie	French name for pork products (and for a shop that sells these)
Chayote	Mexican vegetable related to the gourd family also called choko, christifine, custard marrow, militon
Cheeses: blue veined	Gorgonzola, bleu d' Auvergnes, bleu de Bresse, Roquefort, Stilton
Cheese: holes formed by	carbon dioxide gas produced by bacteria in the milk sugar
Cheese: agent used to curdle milk for	rennet (from calf's stomach)
Cheese: largest producer	USA
Cheese: unusual types	
Emmental	Swiss, cheese with bigger holes than Gruyère
Feta	Greek, salted, based on sheep or goat's milk.
Gorgonzola	made from ewe's milk with blue veins (named after village near Milan)
Mozzarella	originally made from buffalo milk
Parmesan	made from skimmed milk
Ricotta	sweet cottage cheese
Roquefort	made from ewe's milk
Sakura	Japanese, flavoured with mountain cherry leaves
Stilton	adds cream of one day to milk of next
Chef: 'Architect of French Cuisine'	Antonin Carême
Chewing gum: original base	chicle, the latex of the sapodilla tree
Cinnamon: from	bark of tree
Clementine: cross between	orange and tangerine
Coffee: source	pips of fruit (not beans)
Condensed milk: inventor	Gail Borden, US patent granted in 1856
Consumption: beer, most	Germany
Consumption: tea, most	Ireland
Consumption: wine, most	France consumes most wine overall but Portugal most per capita
Crab: how to tell if fresh	it should feel heavy but have no sound of water in it
Croissant	French, crescent-shaped roll
Croutons	toast pieces, fried in butter
Cuisses de grenouilles	frog's legs
Cuts of meat: beef neck	aka clod or sticking, it is usually used for stewing
beef sirloin	behind the neck (best beef for roasting)
beef topside	top of hind quarters of steer
Dariole (mould)	small and narrow with sloping sides used for setting creams and jellies or for steaming puddings
Denby Dale pie: created for	George III's recovery from an illness in 1788
Devon Garland cheese	layer of herbs pressed into the middle
Dredging	sprinkling with flour or icing sugar
E (European) numbers	code numbers used on food packaging which represent substances deemed safe by the EU
Edible grain crops: 9	wheat, barley, maize, oats, buckwheat, millet, rye, sorghum and rice
Eggs: brown or white more nutritious	no difference
Endive: English word for	chicory
Escargots	French, snails
Filbert: fruit of	hazel tree
Fines herbes	French, fresh chopped chives, chervil, parsley and tarragon but other fresh herbs may be added
Five-spice powder	Chinese, anise, pepper, cinnamon, cloves, fennel
Flageolet	a kind of haricot bean
Foodstuff: most extensively grown and eaten most generally by people	wheat (also used as animal fodder), rice

Fruit: nutrition	avocado is the most nutritious and cucumber the least
Gammon: part of pig from	thigh of legs (when salted and cured, this is ham)
Garam masala	mixed spices used in curry
Gas marks	Mark 1 – 275°F, Mark 2 – 300°F, Mark 3 – 325°F, Mark 4 – 350°F, Mark 5 – 375°F
Ghee	Indian clarified butter
Gohan	steamed rice
Grenadilla: aka	passion fruit
Grilling: Americans call	Broiling
Guinea pig: where eaten	Peru
Honey: nectar for 1 lb	from 2 million flowers
Huitres	oysters
Indian bread	poori, chapati, naan
Indian cinnamon tea	masala chai
Indian prawn dish	jhinga
Indian rice: most often used	Basmati (grown in the Himalayan foothills)
Indian-style chicken	murghi
Insect: most eaten	grasshopper
Instant potato: invented	Edward Asselberg (1941)
Kipper	split smoked herring
Langouste	crayfish
***Larousse Gastronomique:* original author**	Prosper Montagné
Licence: chefs require to prepare	fugu (puffer fish) in Japan, lethal if toxic parts are not completely removed
Loganberry	cross between a raspberry and a blackberry
Loquat: aka	Japanese medlar
Margarine: 1st ingredients	chopped sheep intestine, cow's udder, beef suet
Meat: cholesterol-free	kangaroo, possum
Milk: most protein	reindeer's milk contains three times as much protein as cow's milk
Milk: UHT; stands for	Ultra High Temperature
Miso	Japanese fermented soya bean paste
Mooli	long, parsnip-shaped vegetable, which tastes like radish
MSG	monosodium glutamate (used to intensify flavour)
Naan	Indian flat bread
Noisette	hazelnut (French)
Okra: called in Indian supermarkets	bhindi (aka ladies' fingers)
Omelette and a glass of wine, An	Elizabeth David book of the 1960s which challenged British eating habits
Onion family: smallest plant in	chive
Oranges: best for marmalade	Seville
Oysters: when to eat; saying	When there is an 'r' in the month
Palm trees: two fruits that grow on	coconuts and dates
Parboil	derived from old French for 'boiling thoroughly'; now means 'boiling preliminary to further cooking'
Pasteurisation: temperature	approx 63° C
Petits pois	small French green peas
Philadelphia Pepper Pot	thick stew of beef tripe, vegetables, pepper and other seasonings, attributed to Christopher Ludwick, baker general of the Continental Army during the American Revolutionary War. The stew is said to have kept the troops going during the harsh winter of 1777–1778 in Valley Forge
Pitta	Middle Eastern flat bread
Potato: poisonous parts	leaves and fruit (tubers eaten)
Prosciutto	Italian smoked ham
Prunes: made from	dried plums
Quargel cheese: from	Austria (sharp cheese, caraway-flavoured)
Quotations:	
Clement Attlee	The House of Lords is like a glass of champagne that has stood for 5 days.
James Beard	A gourmet who thinks of calories is like a tart who looks at her watch.
Paul Bocuse	Cuisine is like fireworks display, nothing remains. It is *une fête*, rapid, ephemeral.
Michel Bourdin	Cooking is a way of giving and making yourself desirable.
Mel Brooks	Where you eat is sacred.
George Burns	Actually, it only takes one drink to get me loaded. Trouble is, I can't remember if it's the thirteenth or the fourteenth.
Robert Byrne	Anybody who believes that the way to man's heart is through his stomach flunked geography.
Lord Byron	Let us have wine and women, mirth and laughter, Sermons and soda water the day after.
Titus Lucretius Carus	What is food to one man is bitter poison to others.
Malcolm de Chazal	Women eat when they talk, men talk when they eat.
Winston Churchill	[of champagne] In victory you deserve it, in defeat you need it.
Shirley Conran	Life is too short to stuff a mushroom.
Alexandre Dumas (Père)	Le Montrachet [a top Burgundy] should be drunk on the knees with head bared.
Edward VII	One not only drinks wine, one smells it, observes it, tastes it, sips it and – one talks about it.
William M Evarts	It was a brilliant affair – water flowed like champagne. (Description of a dinner given by teetotal President Rutherford B Hayes.)
Clifton Fadiman	Cheese – milk's leap towards immortality.
Sir Alexander Fleming	If penicillin can cure those who are ill, Spanish sherry can bring the dead back to life.
Clement Freud	If a bird says, 'Cluk bik bik bik bik' and 'Caw' you may kill it, eat it or ask Fortnums to pickle it in Napoleon brandy with wild strawberries. If it says, 'tweet' it is a dear and precious friend and you'd better lay off it if you want to remain a member of the Boodles.

Gail Greene	Great food is like great sex, the more you have the more you want.
Galileo	Wine is sunlight, held together by water.
Nubar Gulbenkian	The best number for a dinner party is two – myself and a damn good head waiter.
Philip W Haberman Jr	A gourmet is just a glutton with brains.
Ernest Hemingway	Wine is the most civilised thing in the world.
Horace	Wine is Life.
Jerome K Jerome	We drink one another's health and spoil our own.
Dr Johnson	Claret is the liquor for boys; port for men; but he who aspires to be a hero must drink brandy.
John Keats	Wine is only sweet to happy men.
Prue Leith	When you get to fifty-two food becomes more important than sex.
Joe E Lewis	A man is never drunk if he can lie on the floor without holding on.
Arnold Lobel	All's well that ends with a good meal.
Martin Luther	Who loves not women, wine and song, remains a fool his whole life long.
W Somerset Maugham	At a dinner party one should eat wisely but not too well, and talk well, but not too wisely.
George Mikes	On the Continent people have good food, in England people have good table manners.
Robert Morley	No man is lonely while eating spaghetti.
Napoleon	Champagne banishes etiquette.
Ogden Nash	Celery raw, develops the jaw; But celery stewed, Is more easily chewed.
Louis Pasteur	Wine is the most healthful and most hygienic of beverages. A meal without wine is like a day without sunshine.
St Paul	Use a little wine for thy stomach's sake.
Madame de Pompadour	Champagne is the only wine that leaves a woman beautiful after drinking it.
Anthony Powell	Dinner at Huntercombes' possessed only two dramatic features – the wine was a farce and the food a tragedy.
William Shakespeare	The food that to him now is as luscious as locusts, shall be to him shortly as bitter as coloquintida.
Robert Louis Stevenson	Wine is bottled poetry.
Jonathan Swift	I have been assured by a very knowing American of my acquaintance in London, that a young healthy child well nursed is at a year old a most delicious, nourishing and wholesome food, whether stewed, roasted, baked or boiled and I make no doubt that it will equally serve in a fricassee, or a ragout.
Raclette	Swiss mild cheese; also a dish made from it with potatoes, pickled onions and gherkins
Raisins: made from	dried grapes
Rambutan: aka	hairy lychee
Ramekin	small casserole dish
Ratafia	1. type of macaroon, small biscuit, 2. liqueur made from fruit juice and brandy, or essence of bitter almond
Restaurant guide: first European	Michelin 1900
Restaurant: first	Boulanger's, Paris (1765)
Sago	starch from the pith of a palm
Salami	Italian sausage flavoured with garlic (Latin for salted)
Sally Lunn: cake named after	legendary lady from Bath
Singin' hinny	Northumberland fruit loaf; it gets its name from the sound it makes as it cooks
Spam: name from	spiced ham – recently popularised again by Marguerite Patten's *Spam the Cookbook*
Spice: from same plant	nutmeg, mace
Spice: most expensive by weight	saffron
Stilton cheese	Became famous in the early 18th century, when it was sold in the Bell Inn, a coaching house on the Great North Road, at Stilton, Cambridgeshire. Stilton is a protected name and can only be made in the three counties of Derbyshire, Leicestershire and Nottinghamshire
Sweetbread from	pancreas
Tabasco: name from	Mexican state
Tapioca: source	root of cassava (manioc)
Tartrazine	azo dye that produces a yellow colour (E102)
Tava	concave cast-iron plate used for cooking bread
Tea: the Champagne of Tea	Darjeeling
Tea: country that produces most	India produces 30% of the world's tea crop annually
Tea: originally dried over burning ropes	lapsang souchong
Tea: spoon used for extracting floating tea leaves	mote spoon
Tea: weekly ration during WW2	2 oz per week
Terrine	pot used for pâté or savoury mixtures
Tofu	Japanese soya bean curd
Tripe	cow's, sheep's or other animal's stomach lining
Truffles: how found	detected by trained pigs in France; by dogs in N/W Italy
Turmeric: obtained from	rhizomes of curcuma plant
Ugli: fruit cross between	grapefruit, tangerine and orange
Vegetable: oldest known	broad bean (also called fava)
Wok	hemispherical pan used in Chinese stir-fry cookery
Worcester Sauce: origin	India
Yarg	Cornish cheese that is wrapped in nettles

Beers and Ales of the World

Beer	Brewery and/or place brewed
Abbot Ale	Greene King, Bury St Edmunds
Adnams	Suffolk
Alhambra	Spain
Almaza	Lebanon
Al-Sharq	Aleppo, Syria
Anchor	China
Antarctica	Brazil
Arkells Kingsdown	Swindon
Arran	Scotland
Asahi	Japan
Atom Splitter	Cambridge
Auld Rock	Scotland
Badger	Dorset
Balashi	Oranjestad, Aruba
Bali Hai	Java
Barada	Damascus, Syria
Barbar	Brussels, Belgium
Barena	Honduras
Bass	Burton-upon-Trent
Bateman's	Lincolnshire
Bavaria	Costa Rica
Beamish	Cork, Ireland
Beck's	Bremen, Germany
Belikin	Belize
Belvoir Melton Red	Leicestershire
Belvoir Old Dalby	Leicestershire
Bintang	Star, Indonesia
Birra Tirana	Albania
Bitter & Twisted	Scotland
Black Cat	Moorhouse's, Burnley
Black Sheep	Yorkshire
Blond Witch	Moorhouse's, Burnley
Blue Marlin	Mauritius
Bock	Einbeck, Germany
Bohemia	Mexico
Bolyarka	Veliko Tarnovo, Bulgaria
Brahma	São Paulo, Brazil
Brains	Cardiff
Brakspear	Oxfordshire
Brewdog	Aberdeenshire
Buckley's	Llanelli
Budweiser	USA
Budweiser Budvar	Czech Republic
Burton Bitter	Marstons, Burton-upon-Trent
Caffrey's	Belfast
Cains	Liverpool
Carling	London, Canada
Carlsberg	Copenhagen, Denmark
Carlton Draught	Australia
Carn Brea	Cornwall
Casablanca	Morocco
Cass	South Korea
Castle	South Africa
Caves	Lier, Belgium
Charles Wells' Bombardier	Bedfordshire
Chicha	Chile
Cocker Hoop	Jennings, Cockermouth
Coors	Colorado, USA
Corona	Mexico
Corsendonk	Antwerp, Belgium
Cotleigh	Somerset
Courage	Bermondsey, London
Cristal	Chile
Cruzcampo	Spain
Cumberland Ale	Jennings, Cockermouth
Dali	China
Delirium Tremens	Melle, Belgium
DeuS	Buggenhout, Belgium
Dodo	Réunion
Dorada	Spain
Dos Equis (XX)	Mexico
Double Diamond	England
Double Dragon	Llanelli
Efes	Turkey
Emu	Perth, Australia
Estrella	Spain
Felinfoel Stout	Llanelli
Fix	Greece
Foster's	Melbourne, Australia
Gaolers	Nottinghamshire
Golden Star	Eritrea
Goldstar	Israel
Gorkha	Nepal
Greene King IPA	Bury St Edmunds
Grimbergen	Belgium
Grolsch	Groenlo, Netherlands
Guinness	Dublin
Hahn	Sydney, Australia
Harp	Dundalk, Ireland
Heineken	Amsterdam, Netherlands
Hirter	Austria
Hite	South Korea
Hobson's Choice	Cambridgeshire
Holsten	Hamburg, Germany
Hue	Vietnam
Indio	Mexico
Jenlain	France
John Smith's	Tadcaster, North Yorkshire
Jupiler	Jupille, Belgium
Jurassic Ale	Dorset
Kalik	Nassau, Bahamas
Kamenitza	Plovdiv, Bulgaria
Karjala	Helsinki, Finland
Karlsberg	Homburg, Germany
Kingfisher	India
Kirin	Japan
Koff	Finland
Kotayk	Abovyan, Armenia
Kriek	Brussels, Belgium
Kronenbourg	Strasbourg, France
Kukko	Finland
La Zaragozana	Spain
Labatt	London, Canada
Ladybird Bio	India
Lapin Kulta	Tornio, Finland
Lasko	Slovenia
Latitude	Argyllshire, Scotland
Laurentina	Mozambique
Laziza	Lebanon
Little John's Myth	Nottinghamshire
Maccabee	Israel
Mackeson	Hythe, England
Mahou-San Miguel	Spain
Maiden's Magic	Nottinghamshire
Manica	Mozambique
Mariestads	Sweden
Marston's	Wolverhampton
McEwan's	Scotland
Medalla Light	Mayagüez, Puerto Rico
Miller	Milwaukee, USA
Molson	Montreal, Canada
Monkey Stout	Durham
Mosi	Lusaka, Zambia
Murphy's	Cork, Ireland
Mythos	Greece
Negra Modelo	Mexico
Ngok	Congo
Nile Special	Jinja, Uganda
Nimbus Blonde	Argyllshire, Scotland
OB	Oriental Brewery, South Korea
Old Empire	Marstons, Burton-upon-Trent
Old Engine Oil	Scotland
Old Peculier	North Yorkshire
Old Speckled Hen	Bury St Edmunds
Olivaria	Minsk, Belarus
Orion	Japan
Otaru	Japan
Ottakringer	Vienna, Austria
Pabst	Milwaukee, USA
Pacifico	Mazatlán, Mexico
Pedigree	Marstons, Burton-upon-Trent
Phoenix	Mauritius
Piddle Ales	Worcestershire

Beer	*Brewery and/or place brewed*
Port Royal	Honduras
Preta	Mozambique
Pride of Pendle	Moorhouse's, Burnley
Primus	Dem Rep of Congo
Pripps	Sweden
Quilmes	Buenos Aires, Argentina
Red Breast	Jennings, Cockermouth
Red MacGregor	Scotland
Red Stripe	Kingston, Jamaica
Reeb	China
Reina	Spain
Resolution	Marstons, Burton-upon-Trent
Ruddles County	Bury St Edmunds
Sahti	Finland
Salva Vida	Honduras
Samichlaus	Zürich, Switzerland
Schiehallion	Scotland
Schlitz	Milwaukee, USA
Schneider	Argentina
Shumensko	Bulgaria
Skol	Tetley's, England
SkullSplitter	Scotland
Sleeman	Guelph, Canada
Smithwick's	Kilkenny, Ireland
Sneck Lifter	Jennings, Cockermouth
Spéciale Flag	Morocco
Speight's	New Zealand
Spingo	Helston, Cornwall
Star	Ghana
Stella	Egypt
Stella Artois	Leuven, Belgium
Stiegl	Salzburg, Austria
Stolichno	Bulgaria

Beer	*Brewery and/or place brewed*
Stork	Morocco
Strela	Cape Verde
Suntory	Japan
Swan	Perth, Australia
Swan's Lake	Jennings, Cockermouth
Tafel	Namibia
Taybeh	Palestine
Tecate	Mexico
Tennent's Super	Glasgow
Tetley's	Leeds
Theakston	North Yorkshire
Three Horses	Antananarivo, Malaysia
Three Sisters	Scotland
Tiger	Singapore/Malaysia
Tom Fool	Jennings, Cockermouth
Tooheys	Sydney, Australia
Trumer Pils	Salzburg, Austria
Tsingtao	China
Tuborg	Copenhagen, Denmark
Tui	New Zealand
Tusker	Kenya
Tyskie	Tychy, Poland
Union	Slovenia
Victoria	Toluca, Mexico
Watney's Red Barrel	London, England
Wisby	Sweden
World's Biggest Liar	Jennings, Cockermouth
Worthington	Burton-upon-Trent
XXXX	Brisbane, Australia
Younger's Tartan	Scotland
Zambesi	Harare, Zimbabwe
Zywiec	Zywiec, Poland

Cocktails

Adonis dry sherry (2 parts), red vermouth (1 part), dash of orange bitters, twist of orange peel

Affinity scotch whisky (2 parts), dry vermouth (1 part), 2 dashes Angostura bitters

Afrodizzy white rum, banana liqueur, passion fruit juice, lemonade

Alaska gin (3 parts), yellow Chartreuse (1 part)

Alexander cognac (3 parts), crème de caçao (1 part) & cream (1 part)

Ambassador tequila (2 parts), sugar syrup (1 part), orange juice, slice of orange

American Beauty brandy, dry vermouth, white crème de menthe, port, orange juice, grenadine

Americano Campari, sweet vermouth, soda water, slice of orange

Angel Face dry gin (1/3), apricot brandy (1/3), calvados (1/3)

Angel's Kiss sloe gin, dark crème de caçao, prunelle liqueur, whipping cream

Atta Boy gin, dry vermouth, grenadine

Bacardi white rum (2 parts), lemon juice (1 part), a dash of grenadine

Bamboo dry sherry (1/2), dry vermouth (1/2), a dash of orange bitters

Bellini champagne, peach juice

Bentley calvados (1/2), Dubonnet (1/2)

Between the Sheets Cointreau, brandy, rum, lemon juice

Black Russian vodka, Kahlúa, cola

Black Velvet champagne, stout (equal measures)

Black Widow white rum, Kahlúa

Blarney Stone Irish whiskey, dry vermouth, green curaçao, orange bitters

Block and Fall cognac (2 parts), Cointreau (2 parts), calvados (1 part), anisette (1 part)

Bloody Mary vodka, tomato juice, lemon juice, Worcester sauce, salt and pepper

Blue Heaven white rum, blue curaçao, amaretto, lime juice, pineapple juice, sugar syrup

Blue Star gin, dry vermouth, blue curaçao, orange juice

Bobby Burns whisky, sweet vermouth, Benedictine

Bombay brandy (2 parts), dry vermouth (1 part), red vermouth (1 part), dash of pastis, 2 dashes curaçao

Boomerang Canadian Club whiskey, Swedish punch, dry vermouth, lemon, Angostura

Bosom Caresser brandy, orange curaçao, grenadine, egg yolk

Bronx gin, sweet vermouth, dry vermouth, orange juice

Brooklyn rye whiskey (2 parts), red vermouth (1 part), 1 dash of maraschino, 1 dash of Amer Picon

Bucks Fizz champagne, orange juice, grenadine (optional)

Butt Wobbler gin, calvados, dry vermouth, Pernod, lemonade

Buttock Clencher tequila, gin, melon liqueur, pineapple juice, lemonade

Caruso gin, dry vermouth, green crème de menthe

Casino dry gin (9 parts), maraschino (1 part), lemon juice (1 part), orange bitters (1)

Champagne Cocktail champagne, brandy

Champs-Elysées brandy, Chartreuse, lemon juice, Angostura

Cinderella pineapple juice, orange juice, lemon juice, soda water, sugar

Claridge dry gin (2 parts), dry vermouth (2 parts), apricot brandy (1 part), Cointreau (1)

Clover Club gin, grenadine, lime juice, egg white

Corcovado tequila, Drambuie, blue curaçao, Lemonade

Corpse Reviver brandy, sweet vermouth, calvados

Crème Puff crème de menthe, milk, soda water

Cuba Libre rum, lime juice, cola.

Czarina vodka (2 parts), dry vermouth (1 part), apricot brandy (1 part), dash of Angostura bitters

Daiquiri rum (4 parts), lemon juice (1 part), or lime juice, sugar

Dempsey calvados, gin, Pernod, grenadine

Depth Charge brandy, calvados, grenadine, lemon juice

Derby dry gin (55ml, 2oz), 2 dashes of peach bitters, 2 sprigs of fresh mint

Diki-Diki calvados (4 parts), Swedish punch (1 part), grapefruit juice (1 part)

Dirty Martini gin (4 parts), olive brine (1 part)

Double or Drop tequila, brandy, lime juice, honey

Dry Martini gin (4 parts),vermouth (1 part)

Duchess red vermouth (1 part), dry vermouth (1 part), pastis (1 part)
Earthquake whisky, gin, and Pernod
East-India brandy (6 parts), curaçao (1 part), orange juice (1 part)
Eclipse sloe gin, grenadine, gin, a cherry
El Presidente white rum (3 parts), curaçao (1 part), dry vermouth (1 part), dash of grenadine
Eve cognac, curaçao, caster sugar, Pernod, pink champagne
Fair and Warmer white rum, sweet vermouth, orange curaçao
Fallen Angel gin, lime juice, white crème de menthe, Angostura, lemonade
Floppy Dick brandy, dry vermouth, sweet vermouth, triple sec, vermouth
Flu Canadian Club whiskey, lemon juice, rock candy syrup, ginger brandy, Jamaican ginger
Fluffy Navel brandy, dry vermouth, sweet vermouth, triple sec, Pernod
Fourth Degree gin, sweet vermouth, dry vermouth, Pernod
Gibson gin (4 parts), vermouth (1 part), served with a cocktail onion
Gimlet gin, lime juice
Gin Fizz gin (4parts), lemon juice (2parts), sugar, soda water
Gin Sling gin, lemon juice, sugar (aka Pimm's No 1)
Gin Swizzle gin, soda water, lime juice, sugar syrup, Angostura
Glad Eye Pernod, crème de menthe
Grand Slam Swedish punch, sweet vermouth, dry vermouth
Grasshopper green crème de menthe, white crème de caçao, whipping cream
Green Dragon champagne, Midori
Harvey Wallbanger vodka (1 part), orange juice (2 parts), 2 teaspoons of Galliano (named after surfer, Tom Harvey)
Highball whisky, Angostura bitters, ginger ale
Hoopla brandy, Cointreau, dry vermouth, lemon juice
Hoots Mon whisky, sweet vermouth, dry vermouth
Horse's Neck brandy, Angostura, dry ginger ale
Hula Hula gin, orange juice, Cointreau
Hurricane rum, lime juice, passion fruit juice, orange juice, pineapple juice
Jägerbomb Jägermeister (German ginger lime 70-proof liqueur made with 56 herbs and spices) and Red Bull
Jelly Bean ouzo, blue curaçao, grenadine, lemonade, jelly beans
John Collins gin, lemon juice, spoonful of sugar, soda water
Jungle Juice Pisang Ambon, Mandarine Napoléon, gin, orange juice, sugar
Kicker Bacardi rum, calvados, sweet vermouth
Kir glass of white wine with a teaspoon of crème de cassis stirred in
Kir Royale glass of champagne with a teaspoon of crème de cassis stirred in
Knickerbocker gin, dry vermouth, sweet vermouth
Knock Out Punch gin, cider, Bénédictine, brandy, peach brandy, lemonade
Leap Year gin, Grand Marnier, sweet vermouth, lemon juice
Macaroni Pernod, sweet vermouth
Manhattan rye whiskey (2 parts), sweet vermouth (1 part), bitters, maraschino cherry
Named after a NY club and invented by Jenny Jerome (Winston Churchill's mother)
Margarita tequila (2 parts), lemon juice (1 part), curaçao (1 part), glass is salted
Mary Pickford white rum (1/2), natural pineapple juice (1/2), teaspoon grenadine, 6 dashes maraschino
Merry Widow gin, dry vermouth, Bénédictine, Pernod, Angostura
Mikado brandy (40 ml, 1 1/2oz), 2 drops curaçao, 2 drops crème de noyaux, 2 drops orange curaçao, 2 drops Orgeat, 2 drops Angostura bitters
Mint Julep bourbon, sugar syrup, sprigs of mint
Monkey Gland gin, orange juice, grenadine, 2 dashes of pastis
Monkey Wrench white rum, grapefruit juice, lemon juice
Morning Glory whisky, lemon juice, soda water, Angostura, sugar, egg white
Moscow Mule Smirnoff vodka, lime juice, dry ginger ale
Negroni red vermouth (1/3), Campari (1/3), dry gin (1/3)
Oh! Henry! whisky, Bénédictine, ginger ale
Old Fashioned bourbon, sugar cube, Angostura, 1/2 slice lemon, 1/2 slice orange, dash of soda water
Old Pal rye whiskey (1/3), dry vermouth (1/3), Campari (1/3)
Orange Blossom gin, orange juice, grenadine, orange bitters
Oriental rye whiskey (1/2), red vermouth (1/4), white curaçao (1/4), 2 teaspoons fresh lemon juice
Paradise gin, apricot brandy, orange juice
Parisian dry gin (2 parts), dry vermouth (2 parts), créme de cassis (1 part)
Parisian Blonde dark rum, triple sec, double cream, sugar syrup
Pimms 1–6 long drink with spirit base and fruit flavouring, bases as follows:
(1) gin (2) whisky (3) brandy (4) rum (5) rye whisky (6) vodka
Pina Colada rum, pineapple juice, coconut milk, whipping cream, sugar
Pink Elephant bourbon, lemon juice, grenadine, egg white
Pink Lady gin, grenadine, egg white
Planter's Punch lime juice (1 part), sugar syrup (2 parts), rum (3 parts), Ice (4 parts), 2 dashes Angostura
Planter's Punch Rhyme one of sour, two of sweet, three of strong, four of weak
Presto brandy, sweet vermouth, orange juice, Pernod
Princeton dry gin (2 parts), port (1 part), dash orange bitters, twist lemon peel
Prohibition dry vermouth, gin, apricot brandy, orange juice
Purple Cactus tequila, passion fruit juice, sweet sherry, grenadine
Rob Roy Scotch whisky, vermouth, Angostura bitters
Rolls Royce brandy, Cointreau, orange juice, egg white
Rose dry vermouth (2 parts), Kirsch (1 part), dash strawberry syrup
Rusty Nail whisky, Drambuie
Screwdriver vodka orange juice
Sensation gin, lemon juice, Maraschino, sprigs of mint
Sidecar brandy, Cointreau, lemon juice
Singapore Sling gin, Angostura bitters, lemon juice
Slow Comfortable Screw vodka, Southern Comfort, sloe gin, orange juice
Smoky Martini Gin with a splash of Scotch whisky, lemon peel
Snowball Advocaat, lime juice, lemonade
Sporran Free Drambuie, whisky, lemon juice, Angostura, soda water
Starboard Light crème de menthe (9 parts), brandy (1 part)
Stinger brandy, white crème de menthe
Tackety Boot whisky, Drambuie, sweet vermouth, dry vermouth, lemonade
Tequila Sunrise tequila, orange juice, grenadine
Third Degree gin, dry vermouth, Pernod
Third Rail white rum, brandy, calvados, Pernod
TNT tequila, Tia Maria, Mandarine Napoléon
Tom and Jerry rum, eggs, cinammon, sugar, cloves, allspice, soda, brandy, milk, nutmeg
Tom Collins gin (1 part), lemon juice (1 part), sugar syrup (1 teaspoon), soda water
Tonsil Teaser Grand Marnier, crème de banane, coffee liqueur, cream
Torpedo brandy, coffee liqueur, egg white
Triple Testosterone dark rum, white rum, triple sec, lime juice, Grenadine
Trouser Rouser whisky, mango juice, pineapple, lime juice, crème de banane, egg white
Wembley whiskey, dry vermouth, pineapple juice
Whisky Mac whisky, green ginger wine
White Lady gin, Cointreau, lemon juice
Whizz Bang whisky, dry vermouth, orange bitters, Absinthe, Grenadine
Za-Za Dubonnet (1/2), dry gin (1/2), dash Angostura bitters
Zombie white rum, dark rum, pineapple juice, sugar

Flavouring

Absinthe green alcoholic drink, technically a gin, originally having high wormwood content
Aki plum-flavoured alcoholic drink
Akvavit Scandinavian spirit made from potatoes and flavoured with caraway
Amaretto almond-flavoured alcoholic drink
Angostura bitters bitter aromatic tonic made from gentian and various spices, the true angostura bitters being obtained from the angostura bark
Arrack rice-based spirit with a coconut flavour from Eastern countries
Aurum orange-flavoured alcoholic drink (literal meaning 'gold'), based on Italian brandy
Ava Polynesian drink made from peppers
B & B Brandy and Bénédictine based liqueur
Beer barley, flavoured with hops and fermented with yeast
Brandy spirit distilled from the grape (literal meaning 'burnt wine'), Dutch 'brandewijn'
Calvados spirit distilled from apples grown in the Basse-Normandie region
Cassis blackcurrant-flavoured spirit
Chartreuse either of two liqueurs, green or yellow, with an orange flavour
Cider alcoholic drink made from the fermented juice of apples
Cointreau colourless liqueur with orange flavouring
Curaçao orange-flavoured liqueur originally made on the Caribbean island of that name
Drambuie Scottish liqueur made from whisky and heather honey (secret recipe given by Bonnie Prince Charlie to MacKinnon family in 1746)
Gin distilled grain flavoured with juniper berries
Grand Marnier French cognac-based liqueur with an orange flavour
Izarra Basque herb liqueur on an armagnac base that may be green or yellow (basque word for 'star')
Kahlúa Mexican coffee-flavoured liqueur
Kirsch brandy distilled from cherries, made principally in the Black Forest
Kriek-Lambic cherry-flavoured Belgian beer
Kumiss/Koumiss fermented mare's milk
Kümmel Dutch grain liqueur flavoured with cumin and aniseed
Kvass barley-flavoured East European drink distilled from stale bread
Lassi yoghurt-based drink served with either salt or sugar
Maraschino liqueur-flavoured with kernels of the marasca cherry and tasting of bitter almonds
Mastic aniseed-flavoured liquor which has additional flavour from mastic gum resin
Mead wine made by fermenting a solution of honey
Mirabelle plum-flavoured alcoholic drink
Ouzo Greek spirit with a strong aniseed flavour
Pastis aniseed-flavoured apéritif from France
Pernod aniseed-flavoured apéritif from France
Perry alcoholic drink made from the fermented juice of pears
Port sweet fortified dessert wine distilled from grapes
Pulque Mexican drink made from the juice of the maguey, a kind of agave plant, literal meaning 'decomposed', since it will only keep for a day
Raki/Rakee strong spirit distilled in Turkey and Yugoslavia and flavoured with aniseed
Retsina Greek wine flavoured with pine wood resin
Ricard aniseed-flavoured alcoholic drink
Rum spirit made from sugar cane and flavoured with molasses
Sake/Saki Japanese alcoholic drink made from fermented rice
Samshu Chinese alcoholic drink made from fermented rice
Sangria orange-flavoured Spanish red wine with cinnamon and cloves (literal meaning 'a bleeding')
Sherry fortified wine made from grapes, originally only made in Jerez and San Lucar, Spain
Shochu alcoholic drink flavoured by sweet potatoes
Slivovitz plum brandy from Eastern Europe, particularly Southern Slav regions
Southern Comfort peach and orange-flavoured liqueur with Bourbon base
Tequila Mexican drink made from the juice of the agave plant
Tia Maria coffee-flavoured liqueur from the West Indies
Tisane herbal infusion commonly with mint vervair or camomile. Literal meaning 'barley water'
Van der Hum South African Cape brandy liqueur with tangerine and a touch of rum. Literal meaning 'What's his name' or 'So and So'
Vodka alcoholic drink originating in Russia and distilled from either potato or grain
Whiskey Irish whiskey (spelt with an 'e' in Ireland); the same spelling is always used in the USA
Whisky (grain) spirit made by distilling various kinds of grain. Literal meaning 'water of life'
Whisky (malt) spirit made by distilling barley. Literal meaning 'water of life'
Wine alcoholic drink produced by fermenting grapes

Drink: General Information

Alcohol: coffee effect on	makes worse
Alcohol content of beers and wines	on average, beers contain 3 to 7% alcohol, whilst wines contain between 8 and 15%
Anjou rosé wine: from	Loire Valley
Asti Spumante: grape used	Muscat
Barbed wire	Australian term for lager, especially Castlemaine XXXX
Beer: highest alcohol content	barley wine
Bénédictine liqueur: distilled	Fécamp in Normandy (also in the UK, where the most popular distillery is in Blackburn because a Lancashire regiment was stationed at Fécamp during the First World War)
Bottle sizes: Bordeaux	Magnum (2 bottles), Marie-Jeanne (3), Double Magnum (4), Jéroboam (6), Impériale (8)
Bottle sizes: other wines	Magnum (2), Jeroboam (4), Rehoboam (6), Methuselah (8), Salmanazar (12), Balthazar (16), Nebuchadnezzar (20), Melchior (24)
Breweries, British: headquarters	Adnams – Suffolk; Badger – Dorset; Belhaven – Dunbar; Burtonwood – Warrington; Felinfoel – Llanelli; Greene King – Bury St Edmunds; Jennings – Cockermouth; King & Barnes – Horsham in Sussex; Marston's – Burton on Trent; Moorhouse's – Burnley; Morland – Abingdon; Rectory – Sussex; Wyre Piddle – Evesham, Worcs
Brewery: oldest in the world	Weihenstephan Brewery in Freising near Munich (founded 1040)
Budweiser: Advert	The famous three frogs named 'Bud', 'Weis' and 'Er' were created in the 1990s and their catchphrase was 'Whassup?'

Budweiser: Name dispute	Original Budweiser Bürgerbräu founded in 1785 in Budweis, Bohemia and began exporting to USA in 1871. A new company, Budvar, was established in Budweis in 1895 which also exported beer named Budweiser. The American Anheuser-Busch and the two Budweis-based breweries reached an agreement in 1911 that allowed the US brewery to use the brand only in the USA
Cap Bon wine: from	Tunisia
Champagne: designations	brut (very dry), demi-sec (sweet), extra-sec (medium dry), Sec (medium sweet)
Champagne grapes: 3 types	Pinot Noir, Pinot Meunier, Chardonnay
Champagne making: remuage	process of tilting the bottle and tapping it to help the sediment fall to the cork for subsequent removal, previously a manual process but now mechanical
Coca-Cola: original constituent	cocaine (until 1903)
Coffee: types	Blue Mountain, Bourbon, Caturra, Maragogype, Mocha, Mysore and Teaberry
Cru: French wine term	refers to the product of a growth from a single vineyard
Drink: drinking once could cause excommunication	chocolate (Central America in the 18th century)
Firkin of beer	9 gallons
French wine: only region to name its wines after the grape used	Alsace, eg. Riesling, Gewürztraminer and Muscat
Gin: former names	geneva (From French for juniper); Hollands (because the Dutch were the first to distil it)
Halbtrocken	any medium-dry German wine
Huckle-my-buff	Sussex drink of beer, eggs and brandy
Iced tea: inventor	Richard Blechynden (St Louis World Fair, 1904)
Iskra sparkling wine: from	Bulgaria (Iskra, meaning 'spark', is also from Russia)
Johnnie Walker Red Label: malt whisky used in blending of	Talisker, a single malt whisky from the Isle of Skye
Kvass	traditional Russian drink similar to beer made from rye flour mixed with sprouted barley
Mackeson: slogan	Looks good, tastes good, and by golly it does you good
Monbazillac wine: from	Bergerac region of France
Port: aka	'the Englishman's Wine', because it was originally produced by British traders settled there
Port: maturity	it can take 40 years for a vintage port to reach maturity
Port: name from	Oporto, Portugal
Prohibition in USA	Between 1920 and 1933
Rioja	Northern Spanish wine-producing region divided into Alta, Alavesa and Baja
Schlitz: slogan	The beer that made Milwaukee famous
Scotch whisky: matured in	oak casks (formerly in sherry butts, now in casks sprayed with sherry concentrate)
Sheeps dip: aka	single malt Scotch whisky
Sherry: name from	Jerez, Spain
Sherry: standard cask	butt (contains 108 gallons)
Sherry: standard glass	copita (Tulip shaped)
Sherry: types	fino (dry, pale, young wine); oloroso (darker, heavier and fuller); amontillado (fuller both in colour and body and made by ageing finos); Manzanilla (palest and driest of finos)
Solera system	tiered system of blending wines in the making of sherry
Sparkling wine: invented by	Dom Pérignon (1639–1715), a Benedictine monk from Hautvillers Abbey
Spätlese	German term for 'late picked' wine; the riper grapes make the wine sweeter
Spirit: best selling in the world	Bacardi
Stirrup cup	sloe gin is the traditional drink to take before hunting
Strega: liqueur from	Italy (literal meaning 'witch')
Table wine: Americans call	jug wine
Tea: bergamot-flavoured	Earl Grey
categories	black (fermented); green (unfermented); oolong (semi-fermented)
Chinese word for	cha
grades	orange pekoe (highest), pekoe, pekoe souchong, congou, pekoe dust, dust
Japanese ceremony	chanoyu
Original use	medicine
Used as currency	Siberia
Tetley: logo	In 2000 Tetley's dropped its traditional huntsman logo due to growing anti-hunt protests
Trocken	drier style of German wine
Tulip: glasses	best glass for serving cognac as balloon glass loses bouquet
Ullage	air gap between the cork and the wine, often found in very old wine; also refers to the space created in a wine barrel by evaporation
Vermouth: types	French has come to mean 'dry white', whilst Italian is 'sweet red'. The name Vermouth derives from the German word Wermut (wormwood).
VSOP	Very Special/Superior Old Pale: not more than 5 years old
Watney's	Brewers of the famous Party Four and Party Seven
Whisky: bourbon and rye contrast	bourbon comes from Kentucky, whilst rye comes from the USA and Canada; bourbon is aged in cold warehouses whilst rye is aged in heated rooms
Whisky: Johnnie Walker Black Label matured for	twelve years
Whisky: largest malt whisky distillery in the world	Suntory distillery at Hakushu, Japan
Whisky: meaning	water of life
Whisky: world's best-selling single-malt	Glenfiddich

Scottish whisky	
White Horse whisky: malt whisky used in blending of	Lagavulin
Wine: some famous Bordeaux districts	Entre-Deux-Mers, Graves, Margaux, Sauternes, St Emilion, Médoc, Pomerol
Wine: difference between English and British	English wine is made from grapes grown in England, British wine is made in Britain from concentrated grape juice imported from abroad and reconstituted with British water
Wine: difference between sweet & dry	sweet wine is taken from the vat before all the sugar is converted to alcohol by fermentation
Wine: grape colours	red and rosé wines made with red grapes; white wine may be made with red or white grapes
Wine labels: AC, control designation	Appellation Contrôlée (French quality-control designation)
Wine labels: Cava	found on Spanish sparkling wines (not quite as good as champagne), mostly from Catalonia
Wine labels: DOC, control designation	Denominazione di Origine Controllata (Italian quality-control designation)
Wine: Lacrima Christi	made on the south slopes of Mt Vesuvius, near Naples
Wine: length of cork denotes	the longer the cork, the longer period of time the wine is intended to be laid down for
Wine: louse that attacks vine roots of Vitis vinifera	*Phylloxera vastatrix* accidentally imported into Europe from the USA in the 1860s
Wine making: chapeau (hat)	refers to the layer of grape skins which rise to the surface during red wine fermentation
Wine making terms: must	unfermented grape juice seeds & skins; 1st stage in wine-making process or crushed grapes
Wine making: difference between red and white	skins of red grapes must be left in contact with the crushed grapes during fermentation, whilst the skins are removed before fermentation in production of white wine
Wine: marc	spirit distilled from grape skins and stalks
Wine: minimum alcohol content	7% (under EC laws)
Wine: off licence scale of sweetness	from 1 to 9: sweetest is 9 and driest is 1
Wine: origins	somewhere between the Black and Caspian seas, around 4000 BC
Wine producer: world's largest	Italy, in 8 years out of every 10, on average; otherwise France
Wine: rosé	basically white wine made from red grapes that causes it to be given a little colour and flavour by being left a short time with the skins
Wine: Sauternes, most expensive	Château Yquem
Wine: sparkling	sparkling wine is a wine which undergoes a second fermentation effervesces when poured
Wine: sparkling: production methods	méthode champenoise (bottle fermentation – method for best wines); cuve close; transfer system; transversage
Wine stored horizontally: reason	to keep cork in contact with the wine so that it does not shrink and admit air to the bottle
Wine: study of	oenology
Wine: some tasting terms:	
beefy	red wines high in alcohol, big, solid and chunky
buttery	refers to the soft, rich vanilla flavour imparted by new oak barrels
chewy	plenty of of tannin and a strong flavour
clean	no chemical or bacterial faults, and a straightforward, simple flavour
fat	heavy, perhaps clumsy
grapy	most common with Muscat, Gewürztraminer, and Müller-Thurgau, it denotes the flavour of the grape itself
green	unripe or tart
hard	red wines that have too much tannin
length	length of time and the way the flavour of wine continues to develop in the mouth after swallowing
prickly	refers to a wine with some residual gas left in it
stony	rather dull, empty dryness in either a red or white
tough	too much tannin
Wines: types:	
Amontillado	sherry
Amoroso	sherry
Asti Spumante	sparkling Italian wine from Muscat grape
Bull's Blood	Hungarian wine from Eger region
Chianti	Italian red wine from Tuscany
Claret	red Bordeaux wine (traditional English name for)
Fino	dry, light sherry
Hock	German Rhine wine (from the village called Hochheim)
Liebfraumilch	type of hock (blended wine from Rhine area)
Manzanilla	sherry (dry)
Marsala	Sicilian fortified wine
Moselle	German white wine
Oloroso	dark sherry
Retsina	Greek wine
Soave	white Italian wine
Tokay	Hungarian wine
Vinho Verde	white wine from the north of Portugal
Wine: vintage & non-vintage	vintage wine comes from a single harvest, whilst non-vintage is a blend of wines of more than one year
Wine: what it is	fermented juice of the grape; fermentation being a bio-chemical reaction in which sugar in grape juice is converted into ethyl alcohol and carbon dioxide gas
Wine: world's best seller	Lambrusco (especially popular in USA)
Zymurgy	the art or practice of fermentation in wine-making, brewing and distilling

GEOGRAPHY

British Overseas Territories

Anguilla – capital: The Valley
Bermuda (Somers Islands) – capital Hamilton
British Antarctic Territory – capital Rothera
British Indian Ocean Territory (Chagos Islands) – capital Diego Garcia
British Virgin Islands – capital Road Town
Cayman Islands – capital George Town
Falkland Islands – capital Stanley
Gibraltar – capital Gibraltar
Montserrat – capital Plymouth (de facto Brades)
Pitcairn Islands – capital Adamstown
St Helena and Dependencies – capital Jamestown (Ascension – capital Georgetown - and Tristan Da Cunha – capital Edinburgh of the Seven Seas)
South Georgia & South Sandwich Islands – capital King Edward Point
Sovereign Base (Akrotiri & Dhekelia areas of Cyprus) capital Episkopi
Turks and Caicos Islands – capital Cockburn Town on Grand Turk

Capitals: By Country

Country	*Capital*
Afghanistan	Kabul
Albania	Tirana
Algeria	Algiers
Andorra	Andorra La Vella
Angola	Luanda
Antigua and Barbuda	St John's
Argentina	Buenos Aires
Armenia	Yerevan
Australia	Canberra
Austria	Vienna
Azerbaijan	Baku
Bahamas	Nassau
Bahrain	Manama
Bangladesh	Dhaka
Barbados	Bridgetown
Belarus	Minsk
Belgium	Brussels
Belize	Belmopan
Benin	Porto Novo (*de facto* Cotonou)
Bhutan (aka Druk-Yul)	Thimphu
Bolivia	Sucre - judicial; La Paz - admin
Bosnia and Hercegovina	Sarajevo
Botswana	Gaborone
Brazil	Brasilia
Brunei	Bandar Seri Begawan
Bulgaria (Narodna Republic)	Sofia
Burkina Faso	Ouagadougou
Burundi	Bujumbura
Cambodia	Phnom Penh
Cameroon	Yaoundé
Canada	Ottawa
Cape Verde	Praia
Central African Republic	Bangui
Chad	N'Djamena
Chile	Santiago
China	Beijing (aka Peking)
Colombia	Bogotá
Comoros Islands	Moroni
Congo: Democratic Republic	Kinshasa
Congo: People's Republic	Brazzaville
Costa Rica	San José
Croatia	Zagreb
Cuba	Havana
Cyprus	Nicosia
Czech Republic	Prague
Denmark	Copenhagen
Djibouti	Djibouti
Dominica	Roseau
Dominican Republic	Santo Domingo
East Timor	Dili
Ecuador	Quito
Egypt	Cairo
El Salvador	San Salvador
England	London
Equatorial Guinea	Malabo
Eritrea	Asmara
Estonia	Tallinn
Ethiopia	Addis Ababa
Fiji	Suva
Finland	Helsinki
France	Paris
Gabon	Libreville
Gambia	Banjul
Georgia	Tbilisi
Germany	Berlin
Ghana	Accra
Greece	Athens
Grenada	St George's
Guatemala	Guatemala City
Guinea	Conakry
Guinea-Bissau	Bissau
Guyana	Georgetown
Haiti	Port-au-Prince
Honduras	Tegucigalpa
Hungary	Budapest
Iceland	Reykjavik
India (aka Bharat)	New Delhi
Indonesia	Jakarta
Iran	Tehran
Iraq	Baghdad
Ireland, Republic of	Dublin
Israel	Jerusalem
Italy	Rome
Ivory Coast	Yamoussoukro(*de facto* Abidjan)
Jamaica	Kingston
Japan	Tokyo
Jordan	Amman
Kazakhstan	Astana
Kenya	Nairobi
Kiribati	Bairiki on Tarawa Island
Kuwait	Kuwait
Kyrgyzstan	Bishkek
Laos	Vientiane
Latvia	Riga
Lebanon	Beirut
Lesotho	Maseru
Liberia	Monrovia
Libya	Tripoli
Liechtenstein	Vaduz
Lithuania	Vilnius
Luxembourg	Luxembourg
Macedonia	Skopje
Madagascar	Antananarivo
Malawi	Lilongwe
Malaysia	Kuala Lumpur
Maldives	Malé
Mali	Bamako
Malta	Valletta
Marshall Islands	Majuro
Mauritania	Nouakchott
Mauritius	Port Louis
Mexico	Mexico City
Moldova	Chisinau
Monaco	Monaco-Ville
Mongolia	Ulan Bator
Montenegro	Podgorica
Morocco	Rabat
Mozambique	Maputo
Myanmar (formerly Burma)	Naypyidaw
Namibia	Windhoek
Nauru	Yaren
Nepal	Kāthmāndu
Netherlands	Amsterdam
New Zealand	Wellington
Nicaragua	Managua
Niger	Niamey
Nigeria	Abuja
North Korea (aka Choson)	Pyongyang
Northern Ireland	Belfast
Norway	Oslo

SOME OTHER USEFUL CAPITALS

Country	Capital	Country	Capital
Oman	Muscat	South Korea	Seoul
Pakistan	Islamabad	South Sudan	Juba
Palau	Ngerulmud	Spain	Madrid
Panama	Panama City	Sri Lanka	Colombo
Papua New Guinea	Port Moresby	Sudan	Khartoum
Paraguay	Asunción	Suriname	Paramaribo
Peru	Lima	Swaziland	Mbabane
Philippines	Manila	Sweden	Stockholm
Poland	Warsaw	Switzerland	Berne
Portugal	Lisbon	Syria	Damascus
Qatar	Doha	Taiwan	Taipei
Romania	Bucharest	Tajikistan	Dushanbe
Russia	Moscow	Tanzania	Dodoma
Rwanda	Kigali	Thailand	Bangkok
St Kitts and Nevis	Basseterre	Togo	Lome
St Lucia	Castries	Tonga	Nuku'alofa
St Vincent and Grenadines	Kingstown	Trinidad and Tobago	Port of Spain
Samoa	Apia	Tunisia	Tunis
San Marino	San Marino	Turkey	Ankara
São Tomé and Príncipe	São Tomé	Turkmenistan	Ashkhabad
Saudi Arabia	Riyadh	Tuvalu	Fongafale (on Funafuti Isle)
Scotland	Edinburgh	Uganda	Kampala
Senegal	Dakar	Ukraine	Kiev
Serbia	Belgrade	United Arab Emirates	Abu Dhabi
Seychelles	Victoria	United States of America	Washington DC
Sierra Leone	Freetown	Uruguay	Montevideo
Singapore	Singapore	Uzbekistan	Tashkent
Slovakia	Bratislava	Vanuatu	Vila
Slovenia	Llubljana	Venezuela	Caracas
Solomon Islands	Honiara	Vietnam	Hanoi
Somalia	Mogadishu	Wales	Cardiff
South Africa	Pretoria - admin Capetown - legislative Bloemfontein - judicial	Yemen	Sana'a
		Zambia	Lusaka
		Zimbabwe	Harare

Some Other Useful Capitals

Area	Capital	Area	Capital
Abruzzi (Italy)	L'Aquila	Charente (France)	Angoulême
Alberta (Canada)	Edmonton	Charente-Maritime (France)	La Rochelle
Alderney (UK)	St Annes	Chechnya (Russia)	Grozny (aka Djohar)
Alsace (France)	Strasbourg	Chhattisgarh (India)	Raipur
American Samoa	Pago Pago	Corfu (Greece)	Corfu (Kerkyra)
Andalucia (Spain)	Seville	Corsica (France)	Ajaccio
Andaman & Nicobar Islands	Port Blair (India)	Côte-d'Or (France)	Dijon
Andhra Pradesh (India)	Hyderabad	Crete (Greece)	Heraklion
Appenzell (Swiss Canton)	Herisau	Dārfur (Sudan)	Al-Fāshir
Apulia (Italy)	Bari	Dordogne (France)	Périgueux
Aquitaine (France)	Bordeaux	East Flanders (Belgium)	Ghent
Aragón (Spain)	Zaragoza	Elba (Italy)	Portoferraio
Aruba (Netherlands)	Oranjestad	Emilia-Romagna (Italy)	Bologna
Arunāchal Pradesh (India)	Itānagar	Espirito Santo (Brazil)	Vitória
Assam (India)	Dispur	Extremadura (Spain)	Mérida
Asturias (Spain)	Oviedo	Finistère (France)	Quimper
Australian Capital Territory	Canberra	French Guiana	Cayenne
Auvergne (France)	Clermont-Ferrand	French Polynesia	Papeete
Azores (Portugal)	Ponta Delgada (admin)	Friesland (Netherlands)	Leeuwarden
Baden-Württemberg (Germany)	Stuttgart	Friuli-Venezia Giulia (Italy)	Trieste
Balearic Islands (Spain)	Palma de Mallorca	Fuerteventura (Spain)	Puerto del Rosario
Bali (Indonesia)	Denpasar	Galicia (Spain)	Santiago de Compostela
Balochistān (Pakistan)	Quetta	Gelderland (Netherlands)	Arnhem
Barbuda (Antigua)	Codrington	Goa (India)	Panaji
Basilicata (Italy)	Potenza	Gotland (Sweden)	Visby
Basque Country (Spain)	Vitoria Gasteiz	Gran Canaria (Spain)	Las Palmas
Bavaria (Germany)	Munich	Graubünden (Swiss Canton)	Chur
Bihar (India)	Patna	Greater Poland	Poznań
Bonaire (Netherlands)	Kralendijk	Greenland (Denmark)	Nuuk (aka Godthaab)
Bourgogne/Burgundy (France)	Dijon	Guadeloupe (France)	Basse-Terre
Brabant (Flemish)	Louvain (Leuven)	Guam (USA)	Hagåtña (aka Agana)
Brabant (Walloon)	Wavre	Guernsey (UK)	St Peter Port
Brandenburg (Germany)	Potsdam	Gujarāt (India)	Gāndhinagar
Bretagne/Brittany (France)	Rennes	Hainaut (Belgium)	Mons
British Columbia (Canada)	Victoria	Halland (Sweden)	Halmstad
Calabria (Italy)	Catanzaro	Haryana (India)	Chandigarh
Calvados (France)	Caen	Helmand (Afghanistan)	Lashkar Gah
Campania (Italy)	Naples	Hercegovina (Bosnia)	Mostar
Canary Islands (Spain)	Santa Cruz/Las Palmas	Hesse (Germany)	Wiesbaden
Cantabria (Spain)	Santander	Himāchal Pradesh (India)	Shimla
Castilla-La Mancha (Spain)	Toledo	Hokkaidō (Japan)	Sapporo
Castilla-León (Spain)	Valladolid	Hong Kong (China)	Central (aka Victoria)
Catalonia (Spain)	Barcelona	Hunan (China)	Changsha

Area	Capital
Île-de-France (France)	Paris
Isle of Man (UK)	Douglas
Jammu and Kashmir (India)	Srinagar-summer Jammu-winter
Jersey (UK)	St Helier
Jharkhand	Ranchi
Jura (Swiss canton)	Delémont
Karnataka	Bangalore
Kerala (India)	Trivandrum
Khyber Pakhtunkhwa	Peshawar (Pakistan)
Kosovo (Serbia?)	Pristina
KwaZulu-Natal (South Africa)	Pietermaritsburg
La Rioja (Spain)	Logrono
Lakshadweep Islands (India)	Kavaratti Island
Languedoc-Roussillon (France)	Montpellier
Lanzarote (Spain)	Arrecife
Lazio (Italy)	Rome
Liguria (Italy)	Genoa
Limburg (Belgium)	Hasselt
Limburg (Netherlands)	Maastricht
Limousin (France)	Limoges
Lombardy (Italy)	Milan
Lorraine (France)	Metz
Lower Saxony (Germany)	Hanover
Lower Silesian (Poland)	Wroclaw
Luxembourg (Belgium)	Arlon
Macedonia (Greece)	Thessaloniki
Madeira (Portugal)	Funchal
Madhya Pradesh (India)	Bhopal
Maharashtra (India)	Mumbai (Bombay)
Majorca (Spain)	Palma
Manipur (India)	Imphāl
Manitoba (Canada)	Winnipeg
Marche (Italy)	Ancona
Martinique (France)	Fort-de-France
Mayotte (France)	Mamoudzou
Mecklenburg-Vorpommern	Schwerin (Germany)
Meghalaya (India)	Shillong
Midi-Pyrénées (France)	Toulouse
Minorca (Spain)	Mahon
Mizoram (India)	Aizawl
Moluccas (Indonesia)	Ambon
Nāgāland (India)	Kohima
Navarre (Spain)	Pamplona
Netherlands Antilles	Willemstad
Nevis (St Kitts and Nevis)	Charlestown
New Brunswick (Canada)	Fredericton
New Caledonia (France)	Nouméa
New Providence (Bahamas)	Nassau
New South Wales	Sydney
Newfoundland (Canada)	St Johns
Nicobar Islands (India)	Car Nicobar
Norfolk Island (Australia)	Kingston
North Brabant (Netherlands)	's-Hertogenbosch
North Holland (Netherlands)	Haarlem
North Rhine–Westphalia	Düsseldorf (Germany)
Northern Territory (Australia)	Darwin
Northwest Territories (Canada)	Yellowknife
Nova Scotia (Canada)	Halifax
Nunavut (Canada)	Iqaluit
Odisha (aka Orissa)	Bhubaneswar (India)
Ontario (Canada)	Toronto
Orange Free State (South Africa)	Bloemfontein
Orkney Islands (UK)	Kirkwall
Pays de la Loire (France)	Nantes
Picardy (France)	Amiens
Piedmont (Italy)	Turin
Pomeranian (Poland)	Gdańsk
Saxony (Germany)	Dresden
Prince Edward Island (Canada)	Charlottetown
Puerto Rico (USA)	San Juan
Puglia (Italy)	Bari
Punjab (India)	Chandigarh
Punjab (Pakistan)	Lahore
Quebec (Canada)	Quebec
Queensland (Aus)	Brisbane
Rajasthan (India)	Jaipur
Réunion (France)	Saint-Denis
Rhineland-Palatinate	Mainz (Germany)
Rhodes (Greece)	Rhodes
Rhône-Alpes (France)	Lyon
Rift Valley (Kenya)	Nakuru
Saarland (Germany)	Saarbrücken
Saba (Netherlands)	The Bottom
Saint Barthélemy (France)	Gustavia
Saint Martin (France)	Marigot
Sardinia (Italy)	Cagliari
Saskatchewan (Canada)	Regina
Saxony-Anhalt (Germany)	Magdeburg
Schleswig-Holstein (Germany)	Kiel
Scilly Isles	Hugh Town
Seine-Maritime (France)	Rouen
Sicily (Italy)	Palermo
Sikkim (India)	Gangtok
Silesian (Poland)	Katowice
Sindh (Pakistan)	Karāchi
Sint Eustatius (Netherlands)	Oranjestad
Society Islands	Papeete
Somaliland (Somalia)	Hargeisa
South Australia	Adelaide
Styria (Austria)	Graz
Tahiti (France)	Papeete
Tamil Nadu (India)	Chennai (Madras)
Tasmania (Australia)	Hobart
Tenerife	Santa Cruz
Thuringia (Germany)	Erfurt
Tibet (China)	Lhasa
Tobago (Trinidad and Tobago)	Scarborough
Tripura (India)	Agartala
Tuscany (Italy)	Florence
Tyrol (Austria)	Innsbruck
Umbria (Italy)	Perugia
Uri (Swiss canton)	Altdorf
Uttar Pradesh (India)	Lucknow
Uttarakhand (India)	Dehradun
Värmland (Sweden)	Karlstad
Vaud (Swiss canton)	Lausanne
Victoria (Australia)	Melbourne
Virgin Islands (USA)	Charlotte Amalie
Wallis & Futuna Islands (France)	Mata-Utu
West Bengal (India)	Kolkata (Calcutta)
West Flanders (Belgium)	Bruges
Western Australia	Perth
Western Sahara	Laâyoune (El Aaiún)
Yukon Territory (Canada)	Whitehorse
Zeeland (Netherlands)	Middleburg

Capitals: Former

Aachen Holy Roman Empire
Aarau (Switzerland) Helvetic Republic
Abeokuta (Nigeria) Egba State
Aden South Yemen
Agra India
Akmola Kazakhstan
Alexandria Egypt
Amarapura Burma
Angkor Thom Cambodia
Antigua Guatemala Guatemala
Antioch Ancient Syria
Anuradhapura Ceylon
Arras Artois Province
Ashur (Assur) Assyria
Auch Gascony
Auckland New Zealand
Augusta Georgia, USA
Ava Burma
Ayutthaya (Ayuthia) Thailand
Babylon Babylonia
Baeza (Spain) Moorish Kingdom
Bakhchisarai Crimean Khans
Bamburgh Northumbria
Bastia Corsica
Belgrade Yugoslavia
Belize Belize
Bingerville Ivory Coast
Bucharest Wallachia
Calcutta India
Chan Chan Chimú Empire
Chania Crete
Ctesiphon Parthia

Cuzco Inca Empire
Danzig West Prussia
Dar Es Salaam Tanzania
Dawson Yukon
Entebbe Uganda
Fillmore Utah
Gondar Ethiopia
Gordium Phrygia
Grytviken South Georgia and South Sandwich Islands
Guthrie Oklahoma (USA)
Hague, The Netherlands
Hattusa Hittite Empire
Hué Annam
Jerusalem Palestine
Karachi Pakistan
Kaunas Lithuania
Koror Palau
Kracow Poland
Kyoto Japan
Kzyl-Orda Kazakhstan
Lagos Nigeria
Levuka Fiji
Livingstone Northern Rhodesia
Mandalay Burma
Maribo Lolland (Denmark)
Marrakesh Morocco
Melbourne Australia
Memphis Ancient Egypt
Mocha Yemen
M(o)ukden Manchuria
Nafplio Greece
Nanking China
Nara (Heijo-Kyo) Japan
New Haven Connecticut
New Orleans Louisiana (USA)
New York USA (1785–90)
Nineveh Assyria
Olomouc Moravia
Omaha Nebraska
Palio Horio (aka Chora) Alonissos (Greece)
Persepolis Persia
Perth Scotland
Philadelphia USA (1790–1800)
Quezon City Philippines
Rawalpindi Pakistan
Rio de Janeiro Brazil
Rovigno Istria
Saigon South Vietnam
St George Bermuda
St Mary's City Maryland (USA)
St Petersburg Russia
Sardis Lydia
Scodra Illyra
Sitka Alaska
Stettin Pomerania
Susa Elam (Persian Empire)
Sydney Australia
Tenochtitlán Aztec Empire
Thebes Ancient Egypt
Toledo Spain
Toulouse Languedoc
Trenton USA (1784–5)
Trondheim Norway
Trujillo Honduras
Turku Finland
Tyre Phoenicia
Vathy Ithaca
Wheeling West Virginia
Winchester England
Yangon (Rangoon) Myanmar
Yankton South Dakota
Yasodharapura Cambodia
Zanzibar Oman
Zomba Malawi

Continents

Continents	*Area (Sq Miles)*	*% of Earth's Land*	*Lowest Point*	*Estimated population mid-2000*
Asia	17,212,000	29.9	Dead Sea (-400 m)	3,879,000,000
Africa	11,668,599	20.3	Lake Assal (-156 m)	1,000,010,000
North America	9,540,000	16.5	Death Valley (-86 m)	528,720,588
South America	6,889,000	12.0	Valdés Peninsula (-40 m)	385,742,554
Antarctica	5,339,573	9.5	ice-covered (-2538 m)	No indigenous population
Europe	3,930,000	6.6	Caspian Sea (-28 m)	731,000,000
Australia	2,967,895	5.2	Lake Eyre (-16 m)	22,158,438

Deserts: World's Largest

Based on the definition of a desert as an area receiving less than 10 inches (250 mm) of precipitation per year, the world's largest desert is the continent of Antarctica at 13,829,430 sq km. The Arctic polar region at 13,726,937 sq km (5,300,000 sq miles) is therefore technically the second largest desert. The third largest desert after Antarctica and the Arctic, and the world's hottest desert, is the Sahara at more than 9,000,000 sq km (3,500,000 sq mi) and covers large parts of Algeria, Chad, Egypt, Libya, Mali, Mauritania, Morocco, Niger, Western Sahara, Sudan and Tunisia. The world's fourth largest desert at 2,330,000 sq km (900,000 sq miles) is the Arabian, which covers parts of Iraq, Jordan, Kuwait, Oman, Qatar, Saudi Arabia, United Arab Emirates and Yemen. Other deserts over 520,000 sq km (200,000 sq miles) include the Gobi (China and Mongolia) at 1,300,000 sq km (500,000 sq miles); the Kalahari (Angola, Botswana, Namibia and South Africa) at 900,000 sq km (360,000 sq miles); and the Patagonian Desert (Argentina and Chile) at 670,000 sq km (260,000 sq miles) although the desert region of Western Australia and surrounding area, sometimes called the Australian Desert (including the Great Victoria, Great Sandy, Tanami, Simpson, Gibson and Little Sandy Deserts) is collectively larger than the Gobi.

Earth's Extremes

coldest place	Plateau Station, Antarctica: annual average temperature -56.7°C
deepest canyon	Colca River Canyon, Peru: 3,625 m
driest place	Atacama Desert, Chile: rainfall negligible
greatest tides	Bay of Fundy, Nova Scotia: 16 m
highest waterfall	Angel, Venezuela: 3,212 ft (979 m)
hottest place	Dalol, Danakil Depression, Ethiopia: annual average temperature 35°C
largest canyon	Grand Canyon, Colorado River, Arizona: 466 km long and 183 m to 29 km wide, about 1.6 km deep
longest reef	Great Barrier Reef, Australia: 2,012 km
most predictable geyser	Old Faithful, Wyoming: annual average interval 69 to 78 minutes
wettest place	Mount Waialeale, Hawaii: annual average rainfall 16,800 mm

Major Earthquakes

	Richter scale	*Estimated deaths*	*Year*
Antioch, Turkey		250,000	526
Corinth, Greece		45,000	856
Shensi Province, China		830,000	1556
Catania, Italy		60,000	1693
Calcutta, India		300,000	1737
Lisbon, Portugal		60,000	1755
Calabria, Italy		50,000	1783
San Francisco	8.3	452	1906
Messina	7.5	83,000	1908
Avezzano, Italy	7.5	29,980	1915
Gansu, China	8.6	100,000	1920
Tokyo	8.3	140,000	1923
Nan-Shan, China	8.3	200,000	1927
Gansu, China	7.6	70,000	1932
Quetta, India	7.5	30,000	1935
Erzincan, Turkey	7.9	30,000	1939
Chillán, Chile	8.3	28,000	1939
USSR	7.3	110,000	1948
Assam, India	8.7	1,526	1950
Agadir, Morocco	5.8	12,000	1960
Valdivia, Chile	9.5	6,000	1960
Anchorage, Alaska	9.2	131	1964
Northern Peru	7.7	66,794	1970
Managua, Nicaragua	6.5	7,000	1971
Guatemala City	7.5	23,000	1976
Tangshan, China	8.2	242,000	1976
NE Iran	7.7	25,000	1978
El Asnam, Algeria	7.3	20,000	1980
Mexico	8.1	25,000	1985
Armenia, USSR	6.9	25,000	1988
San Francisco	7.1	300	1989
Roudhon, NW Iran	7.7	50,000	1990
Latur, India	6.5	9,748	1993
Kobe, Japan	7.2	5,500	1995
Neftegursk, Russia	7.5	1,989	1995
Qayen, NE Iran	7.1	4,000	1997
Ismit, Turkey	7.8	2,000+	1999
Gujarat, India	7.7	20,023	2001
Bam, Iran	6.6	26,271	2003
Indian Ocean	9.0	283,106	2004
Nias, Sumatra	8.7	1,300	2005
Pakistan	7.6	80,361	2005
Java (Indian Ocean)	6.3	5,782	2006
Sichuan, China	8.0	69,197	2006
Haiti	7.0	316,000	2010
Maule, Chile	8.8	525	2010
Eastern Japan	9.0	15,883	2011
Van Province, Turkey	7.2	604	2011

NB: The estimated deaths caused by these earthquakes are listed purely to indicate the devastation. It is very hard to draw accurate conclusions, as government statistics are in some instances based on bodies recovered. To give Tokyo 1923 as an example, the official death toll was 99,330, but that figure does not take into account the deaths caused by fire, famine, pestilence, and shock in the aftermath or the persons missing presumed dead.

European Capitals of Culture

1985	Athens
1986	Florence
1987	Amsterdam
1988	Berlin
1989	Paris
1990	Glasgow
1991	Dublin
1992	Madrid
1993	Antwerp
1994	Lisbon
1995	Luxembourg
1996	Copenhagen
1997	Thessaloniki
1998	Stockholm
1999	Weimar
2000	Avignon, Bergen, Bologna, Brussels, Helsinki, Krakow, Prague, Reykjavik, Santiago de Compostela (Spain)
2001	Rotterdam and Porto
2002	Bruges and Salamanca
2003	Graz
2004	Genoa and Lille
2005	Cork
2006	Patras
2007	Luxembourg and Sibiu (Romania)
2008	Liverpool and Stavanger (Norway)
2009	Vilnius and Linz
2010	Essen, Istanbul and Pécs (Hungary)
2011	Turku and Tallinn
2012	Guimarães (Portugal) and Maribor (Slovenia)
2013	Marseille and Košice (Slovakia)
2014	Umeå (Sweden) and Riga
2015	Mons (Belgium) and Plzeň (Czech Republic)

NB: Until 1999 the European Capitals of Culture were named European Cities of Culture.

General Information

anabranch Stream that leaves a river and re-enters it lower down, especially in Australia.

Antigua and Barbuda Spanish for 'Ancient' and 'Bearded'

Appalachian trail Public footpath that runs for over 2,000 miles between Mount Springer in Georgia and Mount Katahdin in Maine.

arroyo Dry channel in a semi-arid area that may be subject to flash flooding during seasonal downpours.

atmospheric layers Troposphere is the lowest layer, 11 miles thick at the equator. Stratosphere lies above the troposphere, contains most of the ozone layer. Mesosphere lies above the stratosphere and is often considered part of it. Thermosphere lies between the mesosphere and the exosphere reaching altitudes of 250 miles. Ionosphere is the area charged by the Sun's radiation, between 40 and 600 miles, and has 4 main layers: the D-layer (40–60 miles), E-layer (60–95 miles), F1 and F2-layers (95–250 miles). Exosphere is the outermost layer of the Earth's atmosphere.

berg Hot, dry north wind of Cape Province and Natal.

Bermuda: nine counties Devonshire, Hamilton, Paget, Pembroke, Sandys, Smith's, Southampton, Warwick, St George's

bise Cold, dry north wind prevalent in Switzerland and southern France.

bora Strong northerly wind that blows in the northern Adriatic.

brickfielder Hot, dry north wind of Australia.

bridge: longest by span Akashi-Kaikyo, Shikoku, Japan (6,528 ft).

building: tallest Burj Khalifa, Dubai (2,717 ft).

buran Snowstorm accompanied by high winds, chiefly prevalent in the Russian Steppes.

Cape Doctor Strong south-east wind which blows on the South African coast.

cataract A large, rushing waterfall, usually over a precipice.

Caver A gentle Hebridean breeze. Also spelt Kaver.

chinook Warm dry wind that blows in the Rocky Mountain region of North America.

clouds: classification *High cloud:* Cirrus – detached clouds resembling feathers, named from the Latin for 'lock of hair'. Cirrocumulus – rounded small clouds appearing in the form of grains or ripples. Cirrostratus – white veil of smooth fibrous ice crystals, often forming a halo of light.
Middle cloud: Altocumulus – grey or white clouds having rounded shapes, sometimes touching. Altostratus – flat, grey sheet cloud, often obscuring the Sun and often bringing drizzle. Nimbostratus – flat, shapeless clouds which are the main source of rain and snow.
Low Cloud: Cumulus – detached clouds that vary from small fleeces to large cauliflower shapes. Cumulonimbus – often anvil-shaped and noted for its accompaniment of thunder. Stratus – shapeless thin, grey cloud, often starting as fog. Stratocumulus – round-shaped patchy cloud often formed as Cumulus but thinning out.

coastline: longest Canada (152,100 miles).

coastline: shortest Monaco (3.5 miles).

continental extremities west–east–north–south *Africa* – Cape Vert, Senegal; Ras Hafun, Somalia; Cape Blanc, Tunisia; Cape Agulhas, South Africa. *Asia* – Cape Baba, Turkey; Cape Dezneva, Russia; Cape Celjuskin, Russia; Cape Piai, Malaysia. *Australia* – Steep Point; Cape Byron; Cape York; South East Point, Tasmania. *Europe* – Cape Roca, Portugal; Kara River; North Cape, Norway; Point Tarifa, Spain. *North America* – Cape Prince of Wales, Alaska; Cape Charles, Newfd; Boothia peninsula, NWT; SW Panama. *South America* – Punta Pariña, Peru; Cape Branco, Brazil; Punta Gallinas, Colombia; Cape Horn.
It should be noted that some countries are included in different continents from the country that administers them, e.g. Greenland is administered by Denmark, although part of North America.

cordillera System or group of parallel mountain ranges together with intervening plateaux, especially of the Andes and in Central America and Mexico.

dams: tallest Jinping-I Dam (1,001 ft) on the Yalong River in Liangshan, Sichuan, China, opened in 2013 is the tallest. The tallest in Europe is the Grande Dixence in Switzerland (935 ft).

depression: deepest Dead Sea (1,296 ft below sea level), Turfan Depression, China (505 ft), Qattara Depression, Egypt (436 ft).

desert: meaning From the Latin word *desertus* meaning 'abandoned'.

Diablo Northern Californian wind, sometimes gusting in excess of 60mph, due to high pressure over Nevada and lower pressure along the central Californian coast.

dictionary of places Gazetteer.

driest place on Earth Calama in the Atacama Desert, Chile, has no recorded rainfall.

Earth: composition The most abundant elements of the Earth's composition are iron (35.9%), oxygen (28.5%), magnesium and silicon (each about 15%). The most abundant elements of the Earth's crust are oxygen, silicon, and aluminium.

Earth: dimensions
Mass 5,974,000,000,000,000,000,000 metric tons.
Area 510,066,000 square kilometres.
Land 148,429,000 square kilometres (29.1%).
Water 361,637,000 square kilometres (70.9%).
Population 5,420,391,000 approximately.

Earth's layers Crust, mantle, core.

El Niño Destructive climatic phenomenon involving a periodic change of direction in the prevailing trade winds and ocean currents flowing from the Americas to Asia across the southern Pacific.

Elephanta Strong southerly or south-easterly wind which blows on the Malabar coast of India during September and October, marking the end of the monsoon season.

Etesian Dry north wind blowing over the Aegean and eastern Mediterranean during the summer months (aka Meltemi).

Euros Greek name for the rainy, stormy south-east wind.

Fö(e)hn Hot southerly wind on the northern slopes of the Alps.

footpaths Dales Way – runs for 81 miles from Ilkley in West Yorkshire to Bowness-on-Windermere. Icknield Way – most ancient road in Britain, 105 miles from Ridgeway to Peddars Way. Mid Shires Way – opened in 1994 covering 225 miles from Buckinghamshire to Greater Manchester. North Downs Way – stretches 141 miles from south-west of London (Farnham) to the Dover coast. Offa's Dyke – follows the English/Welsh border for 168 miles via the Wye Valley. Peddars Way – 94-mile stretch from Thetford to Cromer. Pembrokeshire Coastal Path – 186-mile stretch from Amroth on Carmarten Bay to west of Cardigan. Pennine Way – follows course of the Pennines from Edale in Derbyshire to Kirk Yetholm in the Borders. Ridgeway – runs 85 miles from Avebury to Ivinghoe Beacon. South Downs Way – 106-mile walk from Beachy Head to Winchester. South-west Coastal Path – runs 600 miles from Minehead in Somerset to Poole Harbour. West Highland Way – 95-mile route from Milngavie, near Glasgow to north of Fort William.

Fremantle Doctor Cooling sea breeze prevalent during the Western Australian summer.

fumarole Opening in or near a volcano through which hot vapours emerge.

ghibli Hot, dry southerly wind of Libya.

glacier types continental, mountain, piedmont.

grasslands Africa – savannah; Argentina/Paraguay – pampas; North America – prairies; Russia – Steppes.
In other South American countries the general term for a grassland is llanos. The Sahel of West Africa is a semi-arid transitional area between grassland and desert.

Great Lakes: mnemonic HOMES Huron, Ontario, Michigan, Erie, Superior

Green Line Boundary dividing Cyprus between Greek south and Turkish north since the 1974 Turkish invasion.

gregale Strong north-east wind blowing in the Mediterranean.

Gutenberg discontinuity The core–mantle boundary of the Earth.

haboob Violent and oppressive seasonal wind blowing in Sudan and causing fierce sand storms.

harmattan Parching dusty land-wind of the W African coast, blowing from the Sahara Desert.

helm Violent wind of the Lake District of England which often culminates in the formation of a cloud hanging over the mountain tops.

hypsography Description or mapping of the contours of the earth's surface.

isocheim Line on a map connecting places having the same average temperature in winter.

isohyet Line on a map connecting places having the same amount of rainfall in a given period.

Itaipu dam Joint project by Brazil and Paraguay on the River Parana. Largest hydro-electric dam in the world.

jungle: meaning From the Hindi *Jangal* meaning 'wilderness'.

Kanaks Native Melanesian population of the French overseas territory of New Caledonia.

Kashmir Territory in the north-west of the Indian subcontinent which has been the subject of rival claims by India and Pakistan and the cause of 2 wars between them in 1948 and 1965.

Kentish man Born in Kent west of the Medway (see Man of Kent)

khamsin Hot south or south-easterly wind occurring in Egypt for about 50 days in March, April and May.

Levant Area of the Mediterranean bordering Syria and the Lebanon.

lithosphere Rigid outer part of the earth consisting of the crust and upper mantle.

Maghreb Region of North Africa bordering the Mediterranean and comprising Morocco, Algeria, Tunisia and Libya.

man of Kent Born in Kent east of the Medway (see Kentish Man)

Mashriq Geographical region including Egypt, Sudan, Saudi Arabia, Yemen, Oman, Kuwait, UAE, Jordan, Lebanon, Syria and Iraq.

Medway towns Chatham, Gillingham, Rochester, Strood.

mistral Cold northerly wind that blows down the Rhône valley and southern France into the Mediterranean.

mofette Exhalation of vapour from a volcano. Sometimes used as an alternative name for the fumarole itself.

Moho Abbreviation for the Mohorovicic discontinuity, the boundary separating the earth's crust and mantle.

monsoon Seasonal wind of SW Asia and the Indian Ocean which brings heavy summer rain.

Øresund Bridge Longest road and rail bridge in Europe, connecting the Danish capital of Copenhagen and the Swedish city of Malmö. Its total length is 7,845m (25,738 ft). Opened in 2000.

pampero Strong cold SW wind in S. America blowing from the Andes towards the Atlantic.

peninsulas Arabian is the largest (1,250,000 sq miles); second largest is the Southern Indian (800,000 sq miles).

permafrost Term for ground that is permanently frozen (see tundra).

Pig Island Australian and NZ slang word for New Zealand.

puna Cold, dry wind of the Andes in Peru.

Punjab The five waters are the Jhelum, Chenab, Ravi, Sutleji and Beas; all tributaries of the Indus.

rock: types Igneous (formed through the cooling and solidification of magma or lava), sedimentary (formed by the deposition of material at the Earth's surface and within bodies of water), metamorphic (formed from the transformation of existing rock types due to heat).

Sargasso Sea Area of the North Atlantic, named after the 'Sargassum' seaweed that floats on the surface. The Sargasso lies south of Bermuda and is noted for having no land borders.

simoom Hot, suffocating wind of North Africa.

sirocco Hot, dusty wind blowing from North Africa across southern Europe via the Mediterranean. Called a léveche in Spain.

solano Hot, dusty south-easterly wind of mainland Spain.

Sumatra Violent wind in the Strait of Malacca and the Malay peninsula blowing from the direction of Sumatra.

taiga (cold forest) Coniferous forests of sub-Arctic North America and Eurasia bordered by tundra and steppes.

tectonic plates Regions of the Earth's crust that may be oceanic or continental, and relate to the activity within the Earth, creating new surface material, moving the plates against or underneath each other, changing their location over time, forming mountain ranges and causing earthquakes and volcanic activity.

temperature: highest recorded Al' Aziziyah, Libya, at 136 degrees Fahrenheit (58°C).

temperature: lowest recorded Vostock Station, Antarctica, at -129 degrees Fahrenheit (-89°C).

tombolo Narrow sand or shingle bar linking a small island with mainland.

tramontana Cold north wind in the Adriatic.

tundra Area south of the North Pole where the layers of soil are permanently frozen.

tunnels: longest vehicular Seikan Rail Tunnel, Japan (33.49 miles); Channel Tunnel, Cheriton, Kent – Sangatte, Calais (31.03 miles).

tunnels: longest non-vehicular Delaware Aqueduct, NY State (105 miles).

twilight: types Civil, nautical, astronomical (6, 12 and 18 degrees angle of the sun below the horizon).

typhoon Tropical storm in the western Pacific.

volcanic eruptions: famous Krakatoa (1883); Mont Pelée, Martinique (1902); Mount St Helens, Washington State (1980); Eyjafjallajökull (2010). This eruption caused closure of airspace throughout Europe.

volcano: classifications active, dormant, extinct.

volcano: highest Cotopaxi in Ecuador is the highest continuously active volcano (19,347 ft), although Guallatiri in Chile at 19,882 ft is the highest dormant and Aconcagua at 22,834 ft, and also in the Andes, is the highest extinct volcano (excluding underwater volcanoes).

volcano: largest Tamu Massif - an extinct volcano located in the Shatsky Rise about 1,600 km (990 mi) east of Japan. Its summit lies about 1,980 m (6,500 ft) below the surface of the ocean, and its base extends to a depth of about 6.4 km (4.0 mi). The volcano is about 4,460 metres (14,620 ft) tall and was previously thought to be a complex of volcanoes until September 2013.

Volcano Islands Three small volcanic islands, San Alexander (Kita-Iō) Iwo Jima (Iō) San Augustino (Minami-Iō), of the West Pacific between the Bonin Islands and the Mariana Islands. Japan has claimed the islands since 1891, apart from a brief USA administration from 1951 to 1968.

volcano: types Fissure and central.

williwaw Sudden, strong cold wind originally describing the squall through the Strait of Magellan but now describing any sudden strong wind of Alaska and Canada.

Willy-willy Tropical Australian cyclone, known by this name particularly in the south-west.

Zanzibar Principal islands are Zanzibar and Pemba islands. Joined with Tanganyika in 1964 to become Tanzania. Zanzibar's African population call themselves 'Shirazi' after the ancient Persian principality of Shîrāz, as traders from the Persian Gulf began to settle there after the 7th century.

zonda Hot dusty north wind of Argentina.

Geological Ages

Era	*Period*	*Epoch*	*Years ago (m)*	*Life forms*
Cenozoic		Holocene	0.01	
	Quaternary	Pleistocene	1.64	humans appeared
		Pliocene	5.2	
		Miocene	23.5	
	Tertiary	Oligocene	35.5	
		Eocene	56.5	
		Palaeocene	65	mammals flourished
Mesozoic	Cretaceous		146	heyday of dinosaurs
	Jurassic		208	first birds
	Triassic		245	first mammals and dinosaurs
Palaeozoic	Permian		290	reptiles expanded
	Carboniferous		363	first reptiles
	Devonian		409	first amphibians
	Silurian		439	first land plants
	Ordovician		510	first fish
	Cambrian		570	first fossils
Precambrian	Proterozoic		3500	earliest living things
	Archaean		4600	

Ice Ages: Years Before Present

Pleistocene	1.64m–10,000
Permo-Carboniferous	330–250m
Ordovician	440–430m
Varangian	615–570m
Sturtian	820–770m
Gnejsö	940–880m
Huronian	2700–1800m

Island Groups

Group	*Administered by*	*Sea Area*	*Main Islands*
Admiralty	Papua New Guinea	Pacific Ocean	Manus, Los Reyes, Rambutyo, Tong, Pak, Baluan. Lou Purdy Islands are a sub division of the Admiralty Islands.
Aeolian (aka Eolie)	Italy	Tyrrhenian Sea	Stromboli, Lipari, Vulcano, Salina, Filicudi, Panarea.
Åland	Finland	Gulf of Bothnia	Åland, Ahvenanmaa, Eckero, Lemland, Lumparland, Vardo.
Aleutian	Alaska, USA	Pacific Ocean	Andreanof, Adak, Amchitka, Atka, Attu, Fox, Kiska, Near, Rat, Seguam, Umnak, Unalaska, Unimak, Yunaska.
Alexander Archipelago	Alaska, USA	Gulf of Alaska	Baranof (chief city Sitka), Prince of Wales, Chichagof, Admiralty, Mitkof, Wrangell, Revillagigedo (chief city Ketchikan), Kupreanof, Zaremba, Kuiu, Kosciusko, Yakobi, Heceta.
Andaman (204 islands)	India	Bay of Bengal	North, Middle and South Andaman Islands (collectively known as Great Andaman).
Andreanof	Alaska, USA	Pacific Ocean	Kanaga, Great Sitkin, Amlia, Atka, Adak, Tanaga, Delarof. Andreanof Islands are a sub-division of the Aleutians.
Antilles, Greater	Various	Caribbean Sea	Cuba, Jamaica, Hispaniola, Puerto Rico.
Antilles, Lesser	Various	Caribbean Sea	Windward, Leeward, Netherlands Antilles.
Azores	Portugal	Atlantic Ocean	Flores, Corvo, Terceira, Graciosa, São Jorge, Faial, Pico, Santa Maria, Formigar, São Miguel.
Bahamas (700)	UK	Atlantic Ocean	Great Abaco, Acklins, Andros, Berry, Cay, New Providence, Grand Bahama, Inagua, Long, Mayaguana, Bimini, Cat, Exuma, Ragged, Crooked, Eleuthera. Nassau, the capital, is on New Providence and it was here that Columbus made his first landfall in the New World, 12 Oct 1492. Highest point: Mt Alvernia (formerly Como Hill), 206 ft, on Cat Island.
Balearic	Spain	Mediterranean	Ibiza, Majorca, Minorca, Formentera, Cabrera.
Banks	Vanuatu	Pacific Ocean	Vanua Lava, Santa Maria (Gaua), Mota, Mota Lava (Saddle).
Bay Islands	Honduras	Caribbean Sea	Utila, Roatan, Guanja.
Bermuda (181)	UK	Atlantic Ocean	Great Bermuda (aka Main), Boaz, Ireland, St David's, St George's, Somerset. All these inhabited islands are now joined by bridges.
Bismarck Archipelago	Papua New Guinea	Pacific Ocean	New Britain, New Ireland, Admiralty, Lavonga, New Hanover.
Bissagos	Guinea-Bissau	Atlantic Ocean	Orango, Formosa, Caravela, Roxa.
Canadian Arctic	Canada	Arctic Ocean	Baffin, Victoria, Queen Elizabeth, Banks.
Canaries	Spain	Atlantic Ocean	Tenerife, Gomera, Las Palmas, Lanzarote, Hierro, Fuerteventura, Gran Canaria.
Cape Verde Islands (10)	Cape Verde	Atlantic Ocean	Windward Islands: Barlavento, Santo Antão, São Vicente, São Nicolau, Boa Vista, Sal Sotavento, Santa Luzia. Leeward Islands: São Tiago, Maio Fogo, Brava.
Caroline (500+)	USA	Pacific Ocean	Yap, Ponape (Ascension or Pohnpei), Truk, Kusac, Belau (Palau).
Chagos	UK	Indian Ocean	Diego Garcia, Peros, Banhos, Salomon.
Channel	UK	English Channel	Jersey, Guernsey, Alderney, Sark, Herm.
Channel (Santa Barbara)	USA	Pacific Ocean	San Miguel, Santa Rosa, Santa Cruz, Anacapa, Santa Barbara, San Nicolas, Santa Catalina, San Clemente.
Chonos Archipelago	Chile	Pacific Ocean	Chaffers, Benjamin, James, Melchior, Victoria, Luz.
Commander	Russia	Bering Sea	Bering, Medny.
Comoros	Comoros	Mozambique Channel	Grande Comore, Anjouan, Mohéli, Mayotte.
Cook	New Zealand	Pacific Ocean	Rarotonga, Palmerston, Mangaia, Aitutaki.
Crozet	France	Indian Ocean	Île de la Possession, Îles des Pingouins, Îles des Apôtres.
Cyclades (220)	Greece	Aegean Sea	Andros, Mikonos, Milos, Naxos, Paros, Kithnos, Serifos, Siros, Tinos.
Denmark	Denmark	Baltic Sea	Zealand, Fyn, Lolland, Falster, Sjael/Langeland, Bornholm.
Desolation	France	Indian Ocean	Kerguelen, Grande Terre.
Dodecanese	Greece	Aegean Sea	Kasos, Karpathos, Rhodes, Samos, Khalki, Tilos, Simi, Astipalaia, Kalimnos, Leros, Patmos, Kos.
Egadi (Aegadi)	Italy	Mediterranean	Favignana, Levanzo, Marettimo.
Ellice	Tuvalu	Pacific Ocean	Funafuti, Nukefetau, Nukulailai, Nanumea.
Falkland (200)	UK	Atlantic Ocean	West Falkland, East Falkland, South Georgia, South Sandwich.
Farne (Staple)	UK	North Sea	House, Long Stone (lighthouse was the home of Grace Darling). St Cuthbert died on House (Inner Farne) in 687. Nowadays the group is a bird sanctuary and home for grey seals.
Faroe (17 inhabited)	Denmark	Atlantic Ocean	Stromo (Streymoy), Ostero (Eysturoy), Vågø (Vágar), Sando (Sandoy), Bordo (Bordhoy), Sudero (Sudhuroy).
Fiji	Fiji	Pacific Ocean	Viti Levu, Vanua Levu.
Frisian, East	Germany	North Sea	Borkum, Juist, Norderney, Langeoog, Spiekeroog, Wangerooge.
Frisian, North	Germany and Denmark	North Sea	Sylt, Fohr, Nordstrand, Pellworm, Amrum (German); Romo, Fano, Mando (Danish).
Frisian, West	Netherlands	North Sea	Texel, Vlieland, Terschelling, Ameland, Schiermonnikoog.
Galapagos (19)	Ecuador	Pacific Ocean	San Cristobal, Santa Cruz, Isabela, Floreana, Santiago, San Salvador, Rabida, Darwin, Wolf, Pinta, Marchena, Genovesa, Española, Santa Maria, Santa Fe, Pinzon, Fernandina, Baltra. Isabela (Albemarle) is largest, Santa Cruz (Indefatigable) is 2nd. Highest point is Mt Azul.
Gilbert	Kiribati	Pacific Ocean	Tarawa, Makin, Abaiang, Abemama, Tabiteuea, Nonouti, Beru.
Gotland	Sweden	Baltic Sea	Gotland, Faro, Karlso.
Great Britain	United Kingdom	Atlantic Ocean	Isle of Wight, Orkneys, Shetlands, Hebrides, Scillies, Skomer, Ramsey, Skokholm, Caldey, Holy, Lundy, Brownsea, Rat, Sully, Flat Holm, Horsey, Osea, Skerries, Bardsey, Hilbre, Little Eye, Read's, Calf of Man, Ailsa Crag, Craigleith, Fidra, Bass Rock, May, St Serfs (in Loch Leven).
Greater Sunda	Indonesia	South China Sea	Sumatra, Java, Borneo, Celebes (Sulawesi), Belitung. North-west Borneo is not under Indonesian administration.
Greenland	Denmark	Atlantic/Arctic	Greenland, Disko.
Hawaiian	USA	Pacific Ocean	Hawaii, Oahu, Maui, Lanai, Kauai, Molokai, Kahoolawe, Niihau.
Heard and McDonald	Australia	Indian Ocean	Heard, McDonald, Shag.
Hebrides, Inner	UK	Atlantic Ocean	Skye (chief town: Portree; home of the Cuillin Hills; also famous as the refuge of the Young Pretender in 1746), Raasay, Mull (chief town:

			Tobermory; contains Ben More at 3,171 ft); Eigg, Coll, Tiree, Iona, Staffa, Jura, Islay, Rum, Muck, Arran (containing Goat Fell at 2,868 ft), Colonsay and Oronsay.
Hebrides, Outer	UK	Atlantic Ocean	Lewis with Harris, North and South Uist, Benbecula, Baleshare, Barra, Bernera, Berneray, Eriskay, Grimsay, Scalpay, Vatersay.
Indonesia (17,508)	Indonesia	Pacific Ocean	Java, Sumatra, Kalimantan, Celebes, Lesser Sundas, Moluccas, Rian-Lingga Archipelago, Irian Jaya.
Ionian	Greece	Ionian Sea	Kerkira, Kefallinia, Zakinthos, Levkas.
Japan	Japan	Pacific Ocean	Hokkaido, Honshu, Shikoku, Kyushu, Ryuku.
Juan Fernandez	Chile	Pacific Ocean	Mas a Tierra (Nearer Land Island, aka Robinson Crusoe Island), Mas Afuera (Farther Out Island, aka Alexander Selkirk Island).
Kermadec	New Zealand	South Pacific	Raoul (Sunday), Macauley, Curtis. Highest point is Mt Mumukai at 1723 ft on Raoul Island.
Kuril (56)	Russia	Pacific Ocean	Shumsu, Iturup, Urup, Paramushir, Onekotan, Shiaskhotan, Kunashir, Shimushir, Shikotanto.
Lakshadweep	India	Arabian Sea	Amindivi, Laccadive, Minikoy (Maliku), Androth, Kavaratti.
Leeward Islands	Lesser Antilles	Caribbean Sea	Virgin Islands, Anguilla, Saint-Martin, St Christopher and Nevis, Antigua and Barbuda, Montserrat, Guadeloupe. Highest point is Mt Soufrière (on Guadeloupe) at 4813 ft.
Lesser Sunda	Indonesia/Timor	Indian Ocean	Bali, Lombok, Sumbawa, Sumba, Flores, Timor, Alor.
Line	Kiribati	Pacific Ocean	Christmas, Fanning, Washington.
Lipari	Italy	Tyrrhenian Sea	see Aeolian Islands.
Lofoten	Norway	Norwegian Sea	Hinney, Austvagey, Vestvagey, Moskenes.
Madeira	Portugal	Atlantic Ocean	Madeira, Ilha do Porto Santo, Ilhas Desertas, Ilhas Selvagens.
Malay Archipelago	Malaysia	Pacific/Indian	Borneo, Celebes, Java, Luzon, Mindanao, New Guinea, Sumatra.
Maldives	Maldives	Indian Ocean	Consisting of a double chain of twenty-six atolls, oriented north-south.
Malta	Malta	Mediterranean	Malta, Gozo, Comino.
Mariana	USA	Pacific Ocean	Saipan, Tinian, Rota, Pagan, Guguan.
Marquesas	France	Pacific Ocean	Nuku Hiva, Ua Pu, Ua Huka, Hiva Oa, Tahuata, Fatu Hiva, Eiao Hatutu.
Marshall	Marshall	Pacific Ocean	Bikini, Wotha, Kwajalein, Eniwetok, Maiura, Jalut, Rogelap.
Mascarenes	France/Mauritius	Indian Ocean	Réunion, Mauritius, Rodrigues.
Melanesia	Various	Pacific Ocean	Solomon Islands, Bismarck Archipelago, New Caledonia, Papua New Guinea, Fiji, Vanuatu.
Mentawai	Indonesia	Indian Ocean	Siberut, Sipura, Pagai, Utara (North Pagai), Pagai Selatan Utara and Pagai Selatan (South Pagai), aka Nassau Islands.
Micronesia	Various	Pacific Ocean	Caroline, Gilberts, Marianas, Marshalls, Guam, Kiribati, Nauru.
Moluccas (Maluku)	Indonesia	Pacific Ocean	Halmahera, Bacan, Sula, Obi, Moratai, Ternate.
Mussau	Papua New Guinea	Pacific Ocean	Mussau, Emira, Tench, Emira, Emananus, Tabalo.
Near	Alaska, USA	Pacific Ocean	Agattu, Semichi, Attu, Alaid, Nizki, Shemya. Near Islands are a sub division of the Aleutians.
New Hebrides	Vanuatu	Pacific Ocean	Espiritu Santo, Malekula, Efate, Ambrim, Eromanga, Tanna, Epi, Pentecost, Aurora.
New Siberian	Russia	Arctic Ocean	Kotelny, Faddeyevski.
Newfoundland	Canada	Atlantic Ocean	Prince Edward, Anticosti.
Nicobar	India	Bay of Bengal	Great Nicobar, Camorta with Nancowry, Car Nicobar, Teressa, Little Nicobar. Usually considered with the Andamans as a joint group.
Ninigo Islands	Papua New Guinea	Pacific Ocean	Manu, Aua, Wuvulu, Heina, Kaniet Islands, Hermit Islands.
Northeastern Aegean	Greece	Aegean Sea	Samos, Chios, Ikaria, Lesbos, Limnos, Samothraki, Thassos.
Northern Land	Russia	Arctic Ocean	Komsomolets, Bolshevik, October Revolution.
Norway	Vietnam	Gulf of Tonkin	aka Xuy Nong Chao.
Novaya Zemlya	Russia	Arctic Ocean	North and South Novaya Zemlya.
Orkney	UK	North Sea	Mainland, North and South Ronaldsay, Stronsay, Papa Westray, Hoy, Shapinsay, Rousay, Sanday, Burray, Eday, Flotta and Fara, Westray.
Palau	Palau	Pacific Ocean	Koror, Angaur, Babeldaob, Peleliu. The archipelago is also known as 'The Black Islands'.
Parry	NWT Canada	Arctic Ocean	Bathurst, Melville, Cornwallis, Devon.
Pelagian	Italy	Mediterranean	Lampedusa, Linosa, Lampione.
Philippines (7107)	Philippines	Pacific Ocean	Luzon, Mindanao, Samar, Palawan, Mindoro, Panay, Negros, Leyte, Masbate, Bohol, Cebu.
Phoenix	Kiribati	Pacific Ocean	Canton, Gardner, Phoenix, Sydney, Hull.
Polynesia	Various	Pacific Ocean	New Zealand, French Polynesia, Phoenix Islands, Hawaii, Line, Pitcairn, Tokelau, Tonga, Society, Easter, Samoa, Kiribati, Ellice, Cook.
Pribilof (Fur Seal)	Alaska, USA	Bering Sea	St Paul, St George, Walrus, Otter.
Prince Edward	South Africa	Indian Ocean	Prince Edward, Marion.
Queen Charlotte (150)	Canada	Pacific Ocean	Prince Rupert, Graham, Moresby, Louise, Lyell, Kunghit.
Queen Elizabeth	NWT Canada	Arctic Ocean	Ellesmere, Mackenzie King, Parry Islands, Zverdrup Islands.
Rat	Alaska, USA	Pacific Ocean	Kiska, Amchitka, Semisopochnoi, Little Sitkin, Little Kiska. Rat Islands are a subdivision of the Aleutians.
Safety (Iles du Salut)	French Guiana	Atlantic Ocean	Devil's Island (Ile du Diable), Royale, Saint-Joseph.
Santa Barbara	USA	Pacific Ocean	see Channel Islands.
São Tomé and Principe	São Tomé	Atlantic Ocean	São Tomé, Principe.
Saronic Gulf	Greece	Saronic Gulf	Aegina, Angistri, Hydra, Poros, Salamis, Spetses.
Scilly (150)	UK	English Channel	St Mary's, St Martin's, Tresco, St Agnes, Bryher.
Seychelles (115)	Seychelles	Indian Ocean	Praslin, La Digue, Silhouette, Mahé, Bird.
Shetland (100)	UK	North Sea	Mainland, Unst, Yell, Fetlar, Whalsay, Bressay, Muckle Roe, Trondra, West Burra, Housay, Fair Isle, East Burra.
Society	France	Pacific Ocean	Windward and Leeward, Tahiti.
Solomon	Solomon	Pacific Ocean	Choiseul, Guadalcanal, Malaita, New Georgia, San Cristobal, Santa Isabel, Vella Lavella, Kolombangara.
South Orkney	UK	Atlantic Ocean	Coronation, Signy, Laurie, Inaccessible.
South Shetland	UK	Atlantic Ocean	King George, Elephant, Clarence, Gibbs, Nelson, Livingstone, Greenwich, Snow.
Sporades (11)	Greece	Aegean Sea	Skiathos, Skopelos, Skyros, Alonissos (the four inhabited islands).
Sri Lanka	Sri Lanka	Indian Ocean	Mannar, Sri Lanka.
Taiwan	China	China Sea/Pacific	Taiwan, Lan Hsu, Lu Tao, Quemoy, Pescadores.
Tasmania	Australia	Tasman Sea	Tasmania, King, Flinders, Bruny.
Tierra Del Fuego	Arg/Chile	Pacific Ocean	Tierra Del Fuego, Isla de los Estados, Hoste, Navarino, Wollaston,

			Desolación, Santa Ines, Clarence, Dawson, Diego Ramirez.
Tres Marias	Mexico	Pacific Ocean	Maria Madre, Maria Magdalena, Maria Cleofas, San Juanito.
Tristan da Cunha	UK	Atlantic Ocean	Tristan da Cunha, Gough, Inaccessible, Nightingale.
Tuamotu Archipelago	France	Pacific Ocean	Makatea, Fakarava, Rangiroa, Anaa, Hao, Reao, Gambier, Duke of Gloucester.
Vesterålen	Norway	Norwegian Sea	Hinnoy, Langoya, Andoya, Hadseloy.
Virgin	USA	Caribbean Sea	St Croix, St Thomas, St John.
Virgin	UK	Caribbean Sea	Tortola, Virgin Gorda, Anegada, Jost Van Dyke.
Visayas (Bisayas)	Philippines	Philippine/ Sulu Sea	Bohol, Cebu, Leyte, Masbate, Negros, Panay, Samar.
Windward Islands	Lesser Antilles	Caribbean Sea	Dominica, Martinique, St Lucia, St Vincent, Grenada, Grenadines.
Zanzibar	Tanzania	Indian Ocean	Zanzibar, Tumbatu, Kwale.
Zemlya Frantsa-Iosifa	Russia	Arctic Ocean	Graham Bell, Wilczekland, Georgeland, Hooker, Zemlya Alexsandry, Ostrov Rudol'fa.

Islands

Island	*Area*	*Administered by*	*Sq Miles*
Adelaide	British Antarctic Territory	Great Britain	1,400
Admiralty	Alexander Archipelago	Alaska, USA	1,709
Alderney	English Channel Nearest of the Channel Islands to France	Great Britain	3
Alexander I	British Antarctic Territory Largest island in Antarctica	Great Britain	16,700
Andros	Atlantic Ocean	Bahamas	2,300
Andros	Aegean Sea The 2nd largest island of the Cyclades	Greece	145
Anticosti	Gulf of St Lawrence	Quebec, Canada	3,066
Ascension (Pohnpei)	Pacific Ocean Highest peak is Mt Totolom at 2,595 ft	Micronesia	129
Ascension	Atlantic Ocean	Great Britain	34
Bali	Indian Ocean	Indonesia	2,147
Bananal	Goiás State World's largest inland island	Brazil	7,720
Banks	Beaufort Sea	NWT, Canada	27,038
Bathurst	Timor Sea	NT Australia	1,000
Bathurst	Arctic Ocean	NWT Canada	6,194
Bioko	Gulf of Guinea	Equatorial Guinea	779
Bolshevik	Arctic Ocean	Russia	4,368
Bougainville	Solomon Sea Highest peaks Mt Balbi 9,000 ft, Mt Bagana 6,560 ft, Mt Takuan 7,358 ft	Papua New Guinea	3,880
Bouvet	South Atlantic	Norway	23
Cape Breton	Nova Scotia	Canada	3,981
Cebu	Bohol Sea	Philippines	1,703
Chatham Island	South Pacific Chief town is Waitangi	New Zealand	348
Chiloé	Pacific Ocean Chief town is Castro	Chile	3,241
Christmas	Indian Ocean Highest point is Murry Hill at 1,184 ft	Australia	52
Christmas (Kiritimati)	Pacific Ocean Largest island of purely coral formation in the world	Kiribati	150
Clipperton	Pacific Ocean	France	2
Coats	Northwest Territories	Canada	2,123
Cocos	Pacific Ocean	Costa Rica	9
Cornwallis	Northwest Territories	Canada	2,701
Corsica	Mediterranean Highest peak is Mont Cinto 8,890 ft	France	3,352
Crete	Mediterranean Highest peak is Mt Ida 8,058 ft	Greece	3,190
Cyprus	Mediterranean	Cyprus	3,572
Desolation Island	Indian Ocean aka Kerguélen Island	French Antarctica	2,239
Devon	Northwest Territories	Canada	21,331
Disko	Davis Strait	Greenland	3,312
East Falkland	South Atlantic Highest peak is Mt Usborne, 2,312 ft	Great Britain	2,550
Easter (Rapa Nui)	Pacific Ocean Famous for rongorongo hieroglyphs and stone statues in human form	Chile	63
Éfaté	Pacific Ocean aka Vaté or Sandwich; highest peak is Mt Macdonald, 2,123 ft	Vanuatu	353
Ellesmere	Northwest Territories	Canada	75,767
Euboea	Aegean Sea The 2nd largest island in Greece after Crete	Greece	1,412
Flores	Indian Ocean	Indonesia	5,500
Flores	Azores Highest peak is Morro Grande, 3,087 ft	Portugal	55
Fyn	Baltic Sea	Denmark	1,152
Gotland	Baltic	Sweden	1,212
Graham	British Columbia	Canada	2,456

Guernsey	English Channel The 2nd largest of the Channel Islands	Great Britain	24
Hai-nan	Kwangtung	China	12,962
Halmahera	Moluccas	Indonesia	6,865
Heard	Indian Ocean Highest peak is Mt Mawson on Big Ben Mountain at 9,005 ft	Australia	351
Hispaniola	Caribbean Offshore islands include Gonâve and Tortuga Island	Haiti/Dominican Republic	29,418
Holy Island (Lindisfarne)	North Sea St Aidan established church and monastery in 635 and the 7th-century Lindisfarne Gospels are now housed in the British Museum. Of the other Holy Islands, the most notable is the one off the coast of Anglesey	Great Britain	2
Hoste	Pacific Ocean	Chile	1,590
Ibiza	Mediterranean Highest point is La Atalaya at 1,558 ft	Spain	221
Iturup	Sea of Okhotsk	Russia	2,596
Iwo Jima	West Pacific Famous photo of marines raising the US flag over Mt Suribachi in Feb 1945	Japan	8
Jan Mayen	Greenland Sea Home of the Beerenberg volcano, 7,470 ft	Norway	144
Jersey	English Channel Largest and southernmost of the Channel Islands	Great Britain	44
Kangaroo	South Australia	Australia	1,680
Kiritimati	Pacific Ocean	Kiribati	see Christmas Islands
Kodiak	Gulf of Alaska	Alaska, USA	3,588
Kyushu	Pacific Kyushu means 'the nine provinces'	Japan	16,274
Lanzarote	Atlantic Ocean Easternmost of the Canary Islands	Spain	307
Leyte	Philippine Sea	Philippines	2,785
Lindisfarne	North Sea	Great Britain	see Holy Island
Long Island	New York	USA	1,723
Lundy	Bristol Channel	Great Britain	1
Mackenzie King	Northwest Territories	Canada	1,949
Mactan	Bohol Strait Ferdinand Magellan was killed here by Chief Lapulapu on 27 Apr 1521	Philippines	24
Majorca	Mediterranean	Spain	1,405
Man	Irish Sea	Great Britain	221
Mansel	Northwest Territories	Canada	1,228
Marajó	Atlantic Ocean	Brazil	15,500
Martinique	Caribbean Site of the Carbet Mountains: highest peaks Lacroix, 3,924 ft, Piquet, 3,806 ft; Dumauzé, 3,638 ft; Alma, 3,625 ft; Boucher, 3,510 ft	France	417
Melville	Timor Sea	NT Australia	2,240
Milne Land	Arctic Ocean	Greenland	1,400
Minorca	Mediterranean The 2nd largest of the Balearics	Spain	258
Náxos	Aegean Sea Largest island of the Cyclades, highest peak Mt Zeus at 3,377 ft	Greece	165
Negros	Philippine Sea	Philippines	4,905
New Britain	Bismarck Archipelago	Papua New Guinea	14,100
New Caledonia	Coral Sea	France	6,467
New Ireland	Bismarck Archipelago	Papua New Guinea	3,340
Norfolk	Pacific Ocean	Australia	13
Norway	Beaufort Sea	NWT, Canada	13
Palawan	South China Sea	Philippines	4,550
Panay	Sulu Sea	Philippines	4,446
Pitcairn	Pacific Ocean	Great Britain	2
Pohnpei	Pacific Ocean	Micronesia	see Ascension
Prince Charles	Foxe Basin	NWT, Canada	3,676
Prince Edward	Gulf of St Lawrence	Canada	2,184
Prince of Wales	Alexander Archipelago Islands of the same name in Canada and Australia	Alaska, USA	2,731
Puerto Rico	Caribbean	USA	3,435
Réunion	Indian Ocean	France	970
Riesco	Pacific Ocean	Chile	1,973
Roosevelt	East River	NY City, USA	1
Roosevelt	Ross Sea	NZ Antarctica	2,900
St Helena	South Atlantic Peaks include Mt Actaeon at 2,685 ft and Diana Peak at 2,700 ft	Great Britain	47
St Lawrence	Bering Sea	Alaska, USA	1,780
Samar	Philippine Sea	Philippines	5,050
Santa Catalina	Pacific Ocean One of the Channel Islands, highest peak Mt Orizaba at 2,130 ft	USA	74
Sardinia	Mediterranean	Italy	9,194

Sark	English Channel Sark's area includes Brechou	Great Britain	2
Seram (Ceram)	West Pacific Highest point is Mt Binaiyi 9,905 ft	Indonesia	6,621
Shikoku	Pacific Ocean	Japan	7,261
Sicily	Mediterranean	Italy	9,830
Socotra	Indian Ocean	Yemen	1,400
Somerset	Northwest Territories	Canada	9,570
South Georgia	Falklands Islands	Great Britain	1,450
Southampton	Hudson Bay	NWT, Canada	15,913
Spitsbergen	Barents Sea	Norway	15,075
Stewart Island	Pacific Ocean Third largest NZ island after North and South	New Zealand	674
Sumbawa	Indian Ocean	Indonesia	5,965
Taiwan (Formosa)	Pacific Ocean	Taiwan (Formosa)	13,851
Tasmania	Indian Ocean Other islands in the Tasmanian state include Bruny, King, Flinders and Macquarie	Australia	24,868
Tenerife	Atlantic Ocean Largest of the Canary Islands	Spain	795
Timor	Indian Ocean	Indonesia/Timor	11,883
Traill	Greenland Sea	Greenland	1,300
Vancouver	Pacific Ocean	BC, Canada	12,079
Vanua Levu	Pacific Ocean	Fiji	2,137
Viti Levu	Pacific Ocean	Fiji	4,011
Wellington	Pacific Ocean	Chile	2,549
West Falkland	South Atlantic	Great Britain	1,750
Wight	English Channel Largest British island outside the mainland	Great Britain	147
Wrangel	Chukchi Sea	Russia	2,800
Yap	Pacific Ocean Highest peak is Mt Tabiwol at 5682	USA Micronesia	21
Zealand (Sjaelland)	Baltic Sea	Denmark	2,713
Zemlya Aleksandry	Franz Josef Land	Russia	1,080
Zemlya Georga	Franz Josef Land	Russia	1,120

Islands: World's Largest

		Area (Sq Miles)	*Location*
1	Greenland	840,000	Arctic Ocean
2	New Guinea	306,000	Western Pacific
3	Borneo	280,100	Western Pacific
4	Madagascar	226,658	Indian Ocean
5	Baffin Island	195,928	Arctic Ocean
6	Sumatra	165,000	Indian Ocean
7	Honshu	87,805	North Pacific
8	Great Britain	84,186	North Atlantic
9	Victoria Island	83,897	Arctic Ocean
10	Ellesmere Island	75,767	Arctic Ocean
11	Celebes (Sulawesi)	69,000	Indian Ocean
12	South Island (NZ)	58,305	South Pacific
13	Java	48,900	Indian Ocean
14	Cuba	44,218	North Atlantic
15	North Island (NZ)	44,035	South Pacific
16	Newfoundland	42,030	North Atlantic
17	Luzon	40,880	West Pacific
18	Iceland	39,770	North Atlantic
19	Mindanao	36,775	West Pacific
20	Ireland	31,839	North Atlantic
21	Hokkaido	30,077	North Pacific
22	Hispaniola	29,418	North Atlantic
23	Sakhalin	28,597	North Pacific
24	Tasmania	26,383	South Pacific
25	Sri Lanka	25,332	Indian Ocean

NB: What is the largest island in the world? This is the subject of constant frustration to the more enlightened quiz player. In fact, the answer is very simple when one understands that the dictionary defines an island as a body of land, smaller than a continent, that is wholly surrounded by water. The dictionary defines Australia as the smallest continent and consequently, although it is surrounded by water, it clearly should not be included in geographical listings of islands. If an island was to be considered any area of land wholly surrounded by water then the whole of mainland Eurasia would in fact be far larger than Australia!

Lakes: World's Largest

		Location	*Area Sq Miles*	*Details*
1	Caspian Sea	Russia, Kazakhstan, Turkmenistan, Azerbaijan, Iran	143,552	classed as a brackish lake; although salinity rises to 32% in the Kara-Bogaz-Gol Gulf, it is negligible around the Volga area
2	Superior	Canada, USA	31,795	often considered the largest freshwater lake in the world, although the Caspian Sea is freshwater in parts; the largest of the Great Lakes of North America

3	Victoria	Uganda, Tanzania, Kenya	26,834	aka Victoria Nyanza, the chief reservoir of the Nile
4	Huron	Canada, USA	23,011	one of the Great Lakes, often considered as a single entity with Lake Michigan
5	Michigan	USA	22,394	one of the Great Lakes, often considered as a single entity with Lake Huron
6	Aral Sea	Uzbekistan, Kazakhstan	15,444	the largest true salt lake in the world, although its area has been diminished
7	Tanganyika	Dem Rep of Congo, Tanzania, Zambia, Burundi	12,703	at 410 miles it is the longest true freshwater lake in the world and at 4,710ft the second deepest in the world
8	Great Bear	Northwest Territories (Canada)	12,279	lying astride the Arctic Circle, it is the largest lake wholly in Canada
9	Baikal	Russia	11,776	world's deepest lake at 5,314 ft
10	Malawi	Malawi, Tanzania, Mozambique	11,429	aka Lake Nyasa (which means 'lake')
11	Great Slave	Northwest Territories (Canada)	11,031	links the Mackenzie River to the Slave River
12	Erie	Canada, USA	9,910	one of the 5 Great Lakes of North America
13	Winnipeg	Manitoba (Canada)	9,417	named from the Cree Indian words for 'muddy water'
14	Ontario	Canada, USA	7,550	smallest of the Great Lakes of North America
15	Balkhash	Kazakhstan	7,115	shallow salt lake whose area has varied considerably over the years
16	Chad	Cameroon, Chad, Niger, Nigeria	6,875	freshwater lake whose area varies from about 4,000 to 10,000 sq miles
17	Ladoga (Ladozhskoye)	Russia	6,835	largest lake in Europe, situated near the Gulf of Finland; there is also a small lake in Indiana, USA, of the same name
18	Maracaibo	Venezuela	5,150	large brackish inlet of the Caribbean Sea, lying in the Maracaibo Basin
19	Bangweulu	Zambia	3,800	Bangweulu is Bantu for 'large water'
20	Onega	Russia	3,753	2nd-largest lake in Europe, situated between Lake Ladoga and the White Sea
21	Eyre	South Australia	3,600	dry for most of the year
22	Volta	Ghana	3,283	artificial lake
23	Titicaca	Peru, Bolivia	3,200	highest navigable lake in the world at 12,500 ft above sea level
24	Nicaragua	Nicaragua	3,190	freshwater lake, the largest lake of Central America
25	Athabasca	Saskatchewan, Alberta (Canada)	3,064	explored by Samuel Hearne in 1771, who named it 'Lake of the Hills'
26	Reindeer	Saskatchewan, Manitoba	2,568	the Reindeer River links the lake to the Churchill River
27	Tonle Sap	Cambodia	2,525	linked to the Mekong by the Tonle Sap River
28	Rudolf	Ethiopia, Kenya	2,473	known as Lake Turkana in Kenya
29	Issyk Kul	Kyrgyzstan	2,408	salt lake
30	Torrens	South Australia	2,230	dry for most of the year
31	Albert	Uganda, Dem Rep of Congo	2,160	aka Albert Nyanza and since 1973 Lake Mobuto Sese Seko
32	Vänern	Sweden	2,156	largest lake in Sweden and a major source of hydroelectric power
33	Urmia	Iran	2,150	salt lake
34	Netilling	Northwest Territories (Canada)	2,140	situated in Baffin Island
35	Winnipegosis	Manitoba (Canada)	2,075	situated north of Lake Manitoba and west of Lake Winnipeg
36	Kariba	Zambia, Zimbabwe	2,000	artificial lake formed by the damming of the Zambesi River
37	Mweru	Zambia, Dem Rep of Congo	1,900	Mweru is the Bantu word for 'lake'
38	Nipigon	Ontario (Canada)	1,872	Nipigon is the Indian word for 'deep, clear water'
39	Gairdner	South Australia	1,845	dry for most of the year
40	Manitoba	Manitoba (Canada)	1,799	lies south of lakes Winnipeg and Winnipegosis
41	Koko Nor	Tsinghai (China)	1,770	salt lake, aka Ch'ing Hai or Tsing Hai
42	Taymyr	Russia	1,760	freshwater lake
43	Kyoga	Uganda	1,710	freshwater lake
44	Great Salt	Utah (USA)	1,700	salt lake that has varied from about 2,400 sq miles in 1873 to 950 sq miles in 1963 depending on the level of evaporation and the flow of the surrounding rivers; largest salt lake in the Western Hemisphere
	Iso Saimaa	Finland	1,700	largest lake in Finland
46	Kharka (Hsing-K'ai)	Russia, China	1,690	freshwater lake
47	Lake of the Woods	Canada, USA	1,679	situated where the provinces of Ontario and Manitoba and the US State of Minnesota meet
48	Dubawnt	Northwest Territories (Canada)	1,480	freshwater lake
49	Van	Turkey	1,434	salt lake
50	Tana	Ethiopia	1,418	freshwater lake
51	Peipus	Estonia, Russia	1,400	freshwater lake
52	P'o-yang	Kiangsi (China)	1,383	freshwater lake
53	Uvs	Mongolia	1,300	salt lake
54	Amadjuak	Northwest Territories (Canada)	1,203	freshwater lake
55	Tung-t-'ing	Hunan (China)	1,089	freshwater lake
56	Kivu	Rwanda, Dem Rep of Congo	1,040	freshwater lake
57	Wollaston	Saskatchewan (Canada)	1,035	freshwater lake
58	Alakol	Kazakhstan	1,025	salt lake
59	Hövsgöl	Mongolia	1,012	freshwater lake
60	Illamna	Alaska (USA)	1,000	freshwater lake
	Poopó	Bolivia	1,000	salt lake
	Rukwa	Tanzania	1,000	salt lake
	Chilwa	Malawi, Mozambique	1,000	salt lake
64	Edward (Idi Amin Dada)	Uganda, Dem Rep of Congo	970	freshwater lake
65	Chany	Russia	960	salt lake
66	Tangra (T'ang-ku-la-yu-mu)	Tibet, China	950	salt lake
67	T'ai	Chekiang, Kiangsu (China)	936	freshwater lake
68	Mistassini	Quebec (Canada)	902	freshwater lake
69	Frome	South Australia	900	dry for most of the year
70	Hu-lun	Inner Mongolia	894	freshwater lake
71	Leopold II (Mai-Ndombe)	Dem Rep of Congo	890	freshwater lake
72	Nueltin	Northwest Territories, Manitoba (Canada)	880	freshwater lake
73	Southern Indian	Manitoba (Canada)	868	freshwater lake
74	Buenos Aires	Chile, Argentina	865	freshwater lake
75	Michikamau	Newfoundland (Canada)	784	freshwater lake
76	Lama	Russia	772	freshwater lake
77	Lop Nor (Lo-pu)	Sinkiang (China)	770	dry for most of the year

Rank	Name	Location	Area	Notes
78	Hung-tse	Anhwei, Kiangsu (China)	757	freshwater lake
79	Hamar	Iraq	750	freshwater lake
80	Na-mu (Nam)	Tibet, China	741	salt lake
81	Vättern	Finland	738	freshwater lake
82	Baker	Northwest Territories (Canada)	729	freshwater lake
83	Ch'i-lin (Zilling)	Tibet, China	720	salt lake
84	Chiquita	Argentina	714	salt lake
85	Okeechobee	Florida (USA)	700	freshwater lake
86	Martre	Northwest Territories (Canada)	686	freshwater lake
87	Har Us	Mongolia	680	freshwater lake
88	Williston	British Columbia (Canada)	641	freshwater lake
89	Seul	Ontario (Canada)	640	freshwater lake
90	Pontchartrain	Louisiana (USA)	625	considered a tidal lagoon - connected to the Gulf of Mexico by the Rigolets
91	Tengiz	Kazakhstan	614	salt lake
92	Tuz	Turkey	580	salt lake
	Po-ssu-t'eng (Baghrash)	Sinkiang (China)	580	freshwater lake
94	Yathkyed	Northwest Territories (Canada)	559	freshwater lake
95	Claire	Alberta (Canada)	555	freshwater lake
96	Cree	Saskatchewan (Canada)	554	freshwater lake
97	Argentino	Argentina	546	freshwater lake
	Ronge	Saskatchewan (Canada)	546	freshwater lake
99	Hyargas	Mongolia	543	salt lake
100	Eau Claire	Quebec (Canada)	534	freshwater lake
101	Moose	Manitoba (Canada)	528	freshwater lake
102	Sevan	Armenia	525	freshwater lake
103	Cedar	Manitoba (Canada)	522	freshwater lake
104	Kasba	Northwest Territories (Canada)	518	freshwater lake
105	Bienville	Quebec (Canada)	482	freshwater lake
106	Island	Manitoba (Canada)	472	freshwater lake
107	St Clair	Canada, USA	460	freshwater lake
108	Becharof	Alaska (USA)	458	freshwater lake
109	Lesser Slave	Alberta (Canada)	451	freshwater lake
	Red	Minnesota (USA)	451	freshwater lake
111	Abaya	Ethiopia	448	freshwater lake
112	Gods	Manitoba (Canada)	444	freshwater lake
113	Toba	Sumatra (Indonesia)	440	freshwater lake
	Mälaren	Sweden	440	freshwater lake
115	Champlain	Canada, USA	435	freshwater lake
116	Aberdeen	Northwest Territories (Canada)	425	freshwater lake
	Stefanie	Ethiopia	425	salt lake
118	Päyänne	Finland	421	freshwater lake
119	Viedma	Argentina	420	freshwater lake
120	Chapala	Mexico	417	freshwater lake
	Napaktulik	Northwest Territories (Canada)	417	freshwater lake
122	Mackay	Northwest Territories (Canada)	410	freshwater lake
123	Managua	Nicaragua	402	freshwater lake
124	Eyasi	Tanzania	400	salt lake
125	Dead Sea	Israel, Jordan	394	salt lake; the lowest body of water on Earth at 1,388 ft below sea level
126	San Martin (O'Higgins)	Argentina, Chile	391	freshwater lake
127	Saint-Jean	Quebec (Canada)	387	freshwater lake
128	Wei-shan	Kiangsu, Shantung (China)	386	freshwater lake
	Ebi	Sinkiang (China)	386	salt lake
	Inari	Finland	386	freshwater lake
131	Limen	Russia	379	freshwater lake
132	Pipmuacan	Quebec (Canada)	378	freshwater lake
133	Garry	Northwest Territories (Canada)	377	freshwater lake
134	Contwoyto	Northwest Territories (Canada)	370	freshwater lake
135	Abitibi	Ontario (Canada)	360	freshwater lake
	Rainy	Canada, USA	360	freshwater lake
137	Bay	Luzon (Philippines)	356	salt lake
138	Hottah	Northwest Territories (Canada)	354	freshwater lake
139	Natron	Tanzania	350	salt lake
140	Oulu	Finland	348	freshwater lake
141	Salton Sea	California (USA)	340	salt lake
	P'u-mo (Pomo)	Tibet, China	340	freshwater lake
	Amadeus	Northern Territories (Australia)	340	dry for most of the year
144	Llanquihue	Chile	330	freshwater lake
145	Pielinen	Finland	328	freshwater lake
146	Aylmer	Northwest Territories (Canada)	327	freshwater lake
147	Eskimo North	Northwest Territories (Canada)	324	freshwater lake
148	Nipissing	Ontario (Canada)	321	freshwater lake
149	Teshekpuk	Alaska (USA)	315	freshwater lake
150	Imandra	Russia	314	freshwater lake
151	Terinam (Cha-jih-nan-mu)	Tibet, China	313	freshwater lake
152	Colhué Huapi	Argentina	310	freshwater lake
153	Yamdrok (Yang-cho-yung)	Tibet, China	309	freshwater lake
	Ch'ao	Anhwei (China)	309	freshwater lake
155	Nonacho	Northwest Territories (Canada)	303	freshwater lake
156	Abe	Djibouti, Ethiopia	300	salt lake
	Peter Pond	Saskatchewan (Canada)	300	freshwater lake
	Seletyteniz	Kazakhstan	300	freshwater lake
159	Atlin	British Columbia, Yukon (Canada)	299	freshwater lake

160	Minto	Quebec (Canada)	294	freshwater lake
161	Cross	Manitoba (Canada)	292	freshwater lake

Other Notable Lakes	*Location*	*Area Sq Miles*	*Details*
Bala (Llyn Tegid)	Gwynedd, Wales	1.69	deepest lake in Wales (125 ft)
Balaton	Hungary	230.96	largest lake of central Europe
Bassenthwaite Water	Cumbria, England	2.06	Lake District lake
Bitter Lakes	Suez Canal	219.86	named for its high concentrations of sodium sulphate, as opposed to alkali lakes which contain sodium carbonate
Coniston	Cumbria, England	1.89	famous for the water speed exploits of both Malcolm and his son Donald Campbell
Constance (Bodensee)	Switzerland, Germany, Austria	209.69	forms part of the River Rhine; first flight of the Zeppelin (2 July 1900) was from a floating hangar on Lake Constance
Crater	Oregon (USA)	28.14	deepest lake in USA (1,932 ft)
Derwent Water	Cumbria, England	2.06	Lake District lake
Ellesmere	South Island (New Zealand)	69.76	brackish lake
Geneva (Lac Léman)	Switzerland, France	225.19	lake is formed by the Rhône River
Lomond	Strathclyde Region, Scotland	27.46	largest lake of mainland Britain
Mead	Arizona, Nevada	229.84	reservoir of Hoover Dam formed by the damming of the Colorado River, it forms, with Lake Powell, the extremities of the Grand Canyon National Park
Menteith	Central Region, Scotland	1.48	the only true Scottish lake, as all the others are lochs. The lake contains 3 islands including Inchmahome, the temporary hideaway of the young Mary, Queen of Scots after the Battle of Pinkie in 1547
Mono	California	87.62	devoid of any life due to its high alkalinity
Morar	Highlands, Scotland	10.33	deepest lake in Great Britain (1,0172)
Neagh	Northern Ireland	147.39	largest lake in British Isles; borders all 6 counties bar Co Fermanagh
Ness	Highlands, Scotland	21.87	famous for its monster legend
Ohrid	Albania, Former Yugoslav Rep of Macedonia	134.49	deepest lake in the Balkans (938 ft)
Seneca	New York (USA)	67.44	largest and deepest (618 ft) of the Finger Lakes
Tahoe	California, Nevada (USA)	193.79	freshwater lake
Tiberias (Sea of Galilee)	Israel	64.34	Old Testament name 'Kinneret', later 'Gennesaret'
Ullswater	Cumbria, England	3.44	the 2nd largest lake in England
Vyrnwy	Powys, Wales	1.75	largest lake in Wales
Wastwater	Cumbria, England	1.12	deepest lake in England (260 ft)
Windermere	Cumbria, England	5.69	largest lake in England. Henry Segrave died on this lake in 1930 while attempting a water speed record
Zurich	Zurich (Switzerland)	34.11	freshwater lake

Mountains

10 Highest	*Height (ft)*	*Height (m)*	*Range*	*First Climbed*	*By*	*Country*
Everest	29,029	8,848	Himalaya	29 May 1953	Hillary (NZ) and Tenzing Norgay	Nepal/Tibet
K2 (Chogori)	28,251	8,611	Karakorum	31 July 1954	Compagnoni and Lacedelli (Italian)	Pakistan
Kanchenjunga	28,169	8,586	Himalaya	25 May 1955	Charles Evans (British)	Nepal/Sikkim
Lhotse	27,940	8,516	Himalaya	18 May 1956	Luchsinger and Reiss (Swiss)	Nepal/Tibet
Makalu 1	27,762	8,462	Himalaya	15 May 1955	Couzy and Terray (French)	Nepal/Tibet
Cho Oyu	26,906	8,201	Himalaya	19 Oct 1954	Tichy and Jochler (Austrian)	Nepal/Tibet
Dhaulagiri 1	26,795	8,167	Himalaya	13 May 1960	Max Eiselin (Swiss)	Nepal
Manaslu 1 (Kutang)	26,760	8,156	Himalaya	9 May 1956	Japanese expeditions	Nepal
Nanga Parbat (Diamir)	26,660	8,124	Himalaya	3 Jul 1953	Hermann Buhl (Austrian)	Pakistan
Annapurna 1	26,546	8,091	Himalaya	3 Jun 1950	Herzog and Lachenal (French)	Nepal

Highest Subsidiary Peaks	*Height (ft)*	*Height (m)*	*Range*	*First climbed*
Everest South Summit	28,707	8,750	Himalaya	26 May 1953
Lhotse (Zemu gap peak)	27,591	8,410	Himalaya	unclimbed
Kanchenjunga West	27,894	8,502	Himalaya	14 May 1973
Kanchenjunga South Peak	27,848	8,488	Himalaya	19 May 1978
Kanchenjunga Middle Peak	27,806	8,475	Himalaya	22 May 1978

Highest Continental Peaks	*Height (ft)*	*Height (m)*	*Range*	*General Info*
Lhotse Shar	27,504	8,383	Himalaya	12 May 1970
Africa – Kilimanjaro (Kibo peak)	19,331	5,892	Monarch	dormant Tanzanian volcano 1st climbed: Meyer & Purtscheller 1889
Antarctica – Vinson Massif	16,864	5,140	Ellsworth	first climbed in 1966
Asia – Everest	29,029	8,848	Himalaya	29 May 1953 Hillary (NZ) and Tenzing Norgay
Europe, East – Elbrus	18,510	5,642	Caucasus	extinct volcano, first climbed in 1874
Europe, West – Mt Blanc	15,781	4,810	Alps	first climbed by Jacques Balmat in 1786
North America – Mt McKinley	20,320	6,194	Alaska Range	known to local Indians as Denali and 1st climbed on 7 June 1913 by Stuck and Karstens, although smaller North Peak was climbed by Taylor and Anderson in 1910
Mainland USA – Whitney	14,494	4,418	Sierra Nevada	first climbed by AH Johnson, CD Begole, J Lucas in 1873
South America – Aconcagua	22,834	6,960	Andes	first climbed by Matthias Zurbriggen in 1897
Australia – Kosciusko	7,316	2,228	Great Dividing	named by Paul Strzelecki in 1840 in honour of Polish patriot

Mountain Ranges: Longest

	Miles	Kilometres	High Point	Height (ft)
Andes	4,500	7,240	Aconcagua (Arg)	22,834
Rockies (Western America)	3,000	4,827	Mt Elbert (US)	14,433
Himalaya–Karakorum–Hindu Kush	2,400	3,861	Everest (China/Nepal)	29,029
Great Dividing Range (Aus)	2,250	3,620	Kosciusko	7,316
Trans-Antarctic Mts	2,200	3,540	Vinson	16,863
Brazilian Atlantic Coast Range	1,900	3,057	Bandeira	9,482
West Sumatran–Javan Range	1,800	2,896	Kerintji	12,484
Aleutian Range (Alaska)	1,600	2,574	Shishaldin	9,387
Tien Shan (Kyrgyzstan/China)	1,400	2,252	Pik Pobeda	24,406
Central New Guinea Range	1,250	2,011	Jayakusumu (Ngga Pulu)	16,503
Altai Mountains (Russia/Mongolia)	1,250	2,011	Gora Belukha	14,783
Urals (Russia)	1,250	2,011	Gora Narodnaya	6,214
Kamchatka (Russia)	1,200	1,930	Klyuchevskaya Sopka	15,910
Atlas (North Africa)	1,200	1,930	Jebel Toubkal (Morocco)	13,665
Verkhoyansk (Russia)	1,000	1,609	Gora Mas Khaya	9,708
Western Ghats (India)	1,000	1,609	Anai Madi	8,841
Sierra Madre Oriental (Mexico)	950	1,528	Orizaba (Citlaltépetl)	18,490
Zagros (Iran)	950	1,528	Zard Kuh	14,921
Scandinavian Range (Nor/Swed)	950	1,528	Galdhopiggen (Nor)	8,098
Semien Mountains (Ethiopia)	900	1,448	Ras Dashen	14,928
Sierra Madre Occidental (Mexico)	900	1,448	Nevado de Colima	13,993
Malagasy Range (Madagascar)	850	1,367	Tsaratanana	9,465
Drakensberg (S Africa)	800	1,287	Thabana Ntlenyana	11,425
Chersky Range (Russia)	800	1,287	Gora Pobeda (Mt Victory)	10,325
Caucasus (Geor/Rus/Azer)	750	1,206	Elbrus, West Peak	18,510
Alaska Range	700	1,126	McKinley, South Peak	20,320
Assam–Burma Range	700	1,126	Hkakabo Razi	19,296
Cascades (USA/Canada)	700	1,126	Rainier (US)	14,410
Crocker Range (Borneo)	700	1,126	Kinabalu (Mal)	13,455
Apennines (Italy)	700	1,126	Corno Grande	9,617
Appalachians (Eastern USA)	700	1,126	Mt Mitchell	6,684
Alps	650	1,045	Mt Blanc (Fr)	15,771
Elburz Mountains (Iran)	560	900	Mt Damavand	18,386
Allegheny Mountains (USA)	500	800	Spruce Knob	4,862
Pyrenees (France/Spain)	270	434	Mt Aneto (Spa)	11,178
Jura (France/Switzerland)	225	360	Crêt de la Neige (Fr)	5,636

NB: A definition of a mountain is an upward projection of the Earth's surface with an altitude of at least 600 m (about 1,968 ft), often having a rocky surface.
Mountains that are not part of a designated range, e.g. Kilimanjaro, are known as monarchs.

The list of mountains and ranges that follows is a fair representation of the major peaks and systems in the world, but more information can be found in the World Geographical Gazetteer (see below). The list also contains details of the major volcanic mountains. A few general terms are listed below.

The highest points of various countries can be difficult to determine and in some cases controversial. To give India as an example, K2 could be considered its highest mountain as it lies in a territory disputed since 1947. Nanda Devi is the highest peak wholly within the boundaries of India, but Kanchenjunga, although on the border with Nepal, would lay claim to being considered most worthy of the title.

GPS systems have enabled more accurate height readings, meaning some alterations of heights since the last edition.

Mountain Ranges: General

Name	Area	Details
Absaroka Range	USA	Situated in north-western Wyoming and southern Montana, highest point is Francs Peak
Adirondacks	USA	Situated in north-eastern New York state, highest peak being Mt Marcy
Aleutian Range	USA	Stretching across southern Alaska and north Pacific islands, highest peak being Shishaldin
Allegheny Mountains	USA	Part of the Appalachians extending south-southwestward for more than 500 miles from north-central Pennsylvania to south-western Virginia
Alps	Central Europe	Extending about 650 miles from the Gulf of Genoa in the south-west to Vienna in the north-east. Highest peak is Mont Blanc
Altai Mountains	Central Asia	Running in a southeast–northwest direction from the Gobi desert to the West Siberian Plain, through Chinese, Mongolian and Soviet territory. Highest peak is Belukha
Amambai Mountains	Brazil–Paraguay	Situated in western Mato Grosso do Sul state of Brazil, and eastern Paraguay
Andes	South America	Stretching the length of the South American continent from Lake Maracaibo in the north to the Tierra del Fuego archipelago in the south
Apennine Range	Italy	The backbone of peninsular Italy extending from the Colle di Cadibona, close to the maritime Alps in the north-west, as far as the Egadi Islands to the west of Sicily
Appalachians	USA	Extending from the Gaspé Peninsula in Quebec through eastern United States southward to central Alabama
Apuseni Range	Romania	Subgroup of the Western Carpathians, lying north of the Mures River in north-western Romania
Arāvalli Range	India	Situated in northern India and running north-easterly for 350 miles through Rājasthān state. Highest point is Guru Sikhar on Mount Abu
Armorican Massif	France	Flattened erosional upland encompassing the western French départements of Finistère, Côtes-du-Nord, Morbihan, and Ille-et-Vilaine and parts of Manche, Orne, Mayenne, Maine-et-Loire, Loire-Atlantique, and Vendée. Highest mountain in the Massif is Avaloirs, in Orne at 1,368 ft
Atherton Tableland	Australia	Also called the Atherton Plateau, part of the Great Dividing Range
Name	Area	Details
Athos Range	Antarctica	Located in West Antarctica, joining the Lambert Glacier
Atlas	North Africa	Running north-east to south-west through the three countries of the Maghrib i.e. Morocco,

		Algeria, and Tunisia, the highest point Jebel Toubkal being in Morocco
Australian Alps	Australia	Part of the Great Dividing Range, occupying the south-easternmost corner of Australia, in eastern Victoria and south-eastern New South Wales
Balkan Mountains	Bulgaria	Extending from the Timok Valley near the Yugoslav border and stretching eastward towards the Black Sea, highest point is Botev Peak
Baranya Mountains	Hungary	See Mecsek Mountains
Beartooth Range	USA	North-eastern spur of the Absarokas, highest point is Granite Peak
Berkshire Hills	USA	Part of the Appalachians in western Massachusetts, Mt Greylock highest point in the state
Black Mountain Range	Bhutan	Southern spur of the Assam Himalayas
Black Mountains	Wales	Situated in east Dyfed and west Powys, highest peak being Carmarthen Van
Black Mountains	Wales	Situated in east Gwent, highest peak being Waun Fach
Black Mountains	USA	Situated in Yancey County in western North Carolina, extending from the Blue Ridge Mountains
Blue Ridge Mountains	USA	Part of the Appalachians extending south-west from Carlisle, Pennsylvania, through Maryland, Virginia, N. Carolina, South Carolina, to Mt Oglethorpe in Georgia
Brecon Beacons	Wales	Red sandstone mountains
Cader Idris	Wales	Situated in Gwynedd, highest point is Pen-y-Gader (Cader Idris means 'chair of Idris')
Caribou Mountains	Canada	Subdivision of the Columbia Mountains in British Columbia, highest peak is Mt Sir Wilfrid Laurier
Carpathians	East Europe	Crescent-shaped continuation of the Alps running through parts of The Czech Republic, Poland, Hungary, Romania, and the Ukraine, highest peak being Mt Gerlach (Gerlachovsky Stit)
Cascades	USA–Canada	Extending 700 miles from Lassen Peak in northern California, through Oregon and Washington to the Fraser River in southern British Columbia
Catskills	USA	Dissected segment of the Allegheny Plateau, and part of the Appalachians, lying mainly in Greene and Ulster counties of south-eastern New York. Highest point is Slide Mountain
Caucasus	East Europe	Situated between the Black Sea and the Caspian Sea on the border of Russia, Georgia and Azerbaijan, highest point being Mt Elbrus
Cheviots	England	Range of rounded hills, mainly in Northumberland, forming the border between England and Scotland, highest point is Cheviot Peak
Chilterns	England	Range of chalk hills stretching 40 miles north-east from the Thames near Reading, highest point is Coombe Hill
Columbia Mountains	Canada – USA	Major mountain group of British Columbia that includes the Selkirk, Monashee, Cariboo, and Purcell ranges.
Dângrêk Mountains	Asia	Situated between Thailand and Cambodia
Darling Range	Australia	Situated on the south-west coast of Western Australia, highest peaks: Mts Cooke, Solus & Dale
Dartmoor	England	Area of high moorland in Devon, highest peak being High Willhays
Dauphiné Alps	France	Western spur of the Cottian Alps in south-eastern France
Dolomites	Italy	Eastern section of the northern Italian Alps, named after the 18th-century French geologist, Dieudonné Dolomieu, highest peak being Marmolada
Dome Rock Mountains	USA	Situated in western Arizona in the Sonoran Desert region near the California border
Drakensberg	South Africa	Extends from north-eastern Transvaal, through Lesotho, to south-eastern Cape Province, highest peak being Mt Thabana Ntlenyana
Durack Range	Australia	Situated in northern Western Australia, forming the eastern edge of the Kimberley Plateau
Elburz Mountains	Iran	Situated in northern Iran, highest point Mt Damāvand
Exmoor	England	Area of high moorland on the border of Somerset and Devon, highest point: Dunkery Beacon
Fan Si Pan Mountains	Vietnam	Situated in northern Vietnam, the highest peak is Mt Fan Si Pan
Flinders Range	Australia	Situated in eastern South Australia between Lake Torrens & Lake Frome, highest peak: St Mary
Gawler Ranges	Australia	Situated in South Australia, the eastern sector is known as the Middleback Ranges; the highest peak is Mount Bluff
Ghāts	India	Two ranges, East and West, forming the eastern and western edges of the Deccan Plateau of peninsular India. Ghāts means 'river landing stairs'
Golan Heights	Middle East	Situated in south-western Syria, overlooking the upper Jordan Valley, occupied by Israel since 1967 and unilaterally annexed in 1981
Grampians	Scotland	Dividing the Highlands and Lowlands, and including Ben Nevis, highest peak in the UK, the Cairngorms & Schiehallion
Great Dividing Range	Australia	Parallels the coasts of Queensland, New South Wales, and Victoria
Great Smoky Mountains	USA	Western segment of the Appalachian Mountains between Asheville, North Carolina and Knoxville, Tennessee; they are sometimes considered part of the Unaka Mountains
Great Western Mountains	Australia	Situated in central Tasmania, highest peak is Ironstone Mountain
Hamersley Range	Australia	Situated in the Pilbara region, north-western Western Australia, highest peak Mt Bruce
Himalayas	Central Asia	Extends in a south-easterly arc from Nanga Parbat peak in Jammu and Kashmir, to Namcha Barwa peak in Tibet, it contains 9 of the 14 highest peaks in the world and touches India, China, Nepal, Sikkim, and Bhutan
Hindu Kush	Central Asia	Stretches 1000 miles from the Pakistan/Chinese border in the east to a south-westerly point in Afghanistan; highest point is Tirich Mir
Jura Mountains	Central Europe	Situated on the Franco-Swiss border from the Rhône River to the Rhine
Karakoram Range	Central Asia	Northern extension of the Himalayas stretching from easternmost Afghanistan south-eastward into Jammu and Kashmir, highest peak being K2
Kibara Mountains	Zaïre	Reaching heights of 6,070 ft and situated in the Upemba National Park
King Leopold Ranges	Australia	Situated in northern Western Australia, forming the south-western edge of the Kimberley Plateau, highest peak is Mt Ord at just over 3,000 ft
Kipengere Range	Tanzania	Situated north of Lake Malawi
Kunlun Mountains	China	Extends from Pamirs due east along the coast of Sinkiang to the Sino-Tibetan range of Tsinghai
Kwanto Range	Japan	Aka Kantō-sammyaku, situated on Honshu, the northern range is known as the Chichibu Mts
Kyrenia Mountains	Cyprus	Extending 100 miles east to west from Cape St Andreas to Cape Kormakiti, highest point being Mt Kyparissovouno
Lofty Range	Australia	Situated on the Tropic of Capricorn in Western Australia
MacDonnell Ranges	Australia	Situated in south central Northern Territory, west of Alice Springs; Mt Ziel being the highest peak
Malverns	England	Granite ridge of Hereford and Worcester, high point being Worcester Beacon
Mealy Mountains	Canada	Situated south of Lake Melville in the Labrador peninsula of Newfoundland
Mecsek Mountains	Hungary	Aka Baranya Mts, situated in Baranya (Megye) county, southern Hungary. Highest peak: Zengõ
Monashee	Canada	Major subdivision of the Columbia Mountains in British Columbia
Mount Lofty Ranges	Australia	Situated in South Australia as a continuation of the Flinders range, highest point is Mt Byron
North Yolla Bolly	USA	California mountain range
Ore Mountains	East Europe	Situated on the border of Czech Republic and Eastern Germany highest peak: Klinovec (4080 ft)
Name	*Area*	*Details*
Ozark Mountains	USA	Extends south-westward from St Louis, Missouri to Arkansas River, highest point: Taum Sauk
Pamirs	Tajikistan	Often called 'The Roof of the World', highest point Communism Peak

Pare Range	Tanzania	Situated near the border with Kenya
Parecis Range	Brazil	Situated near the border with Bolivia
Peak District	England	Hill area in Derbyshire, forming the southern end of the Pennines, highest peak: Kinder Scout
Pennines	England	Range of limestone hills with a footpath stretching from Edale in Derbyshire to Kirk Yetholm in the Borders, highest point is Cross Fell
Pisgah Range	Jordan	Situated north-east of the Dead Sea, the ridge includes Mt Nebo
Przhevalsky Range	Central Asia	Extension of the Kunlun Mountains, highest peak being Wu-Lu-k'o-mu-shih Ling
Purcell Range	Canada – USA	Major subdivision of the Columbia Mountains extending from British Columbia into northern Idaho
Queen Alexandra Range	Antarctica	Situated in the Ross Dependency (NZ admin), highest point Mt Kirkpatrick
Queen Elizabeth Range	Antarctica	Situated in the Ross Dependency (NZ admin), highest point Mt Miller
Queen Maud Range	Antarctica	Situated in the Ross Dependency (NZ admin), a subdivision of the Transarctic Mountains
Rhodope Mountains	Balkan Peninsula	Situated mainly in Bulgaria, but extends into Macedonia, Greece, and Turkey, highest point being Golyam Perelik
Ring of Fire	Pacific	Not a mountain range but a colloquial name for the band of volcanoes that circle the Pacific and erupt frequently
Rockies	USA – Canada	Extending from British Columbia to New Mexico, highest peak is Mt Elbert
Ruwenzori Range	Zaire – Uganda	Highest mountain in the range is Mt Stanley, the highest peak being Margherita
Salt Range	Pakistan	Situated between the valleys of the Indus and Jhelum rivers of the northern Punjab, highest point being Mt Sakesar
San Bernardino Mountains	USA	Segment of the Pacific coast Ranges of southern California extending from Cajon Pass to Gorgonio Pass, highest point being San Gorgonio
San Francisco Peaks	USA	Three summits, Humphreys, Agassiz, and Fremont, on the ridge of an eroded volcano, 10 miles north of Flagstaff in north central Arizona
San Gabriel Mountains	USA	Segment of the Pacific coast Ranges of southern California extending from Newhall Pass to Cajon Pass, highest point being Mt San Antonio
San Jacinto Mountains	USA	Segment of the Pacific Coast Ranges of southern California extending from Gorgonio Pass to Santa Rosa Mountains
Sangre de Cristo Mountains	USA	Segment of the southern Rockies, extending south-eastward for about 250 miles, from Poncha Pass in south Colorado to north central New Mexico, highest point being Blanca Peak
Santa Marta Mountains	Colombia	Part of the Andes of northern Colombia, highest point Pico Cristóbal Colón is also the highest peak in Colombia
Sarykol Range	Central Asia	Borders Tajikistan and China, highest point being Mt Lyavirdyr
Sawatch Range	USA	Segment of the southern Rocky Mountains in central Colorado stretching from the Eagle River to Saguache, highest point being Mt Elbert
Selkirk Mountains	Canada – USA	Major subdivision of the Columbia Mountains extending for 200 miles from British Columbia into northern Idaho and Montana, highest peak is Mt Sir Stanford
Sentinel Range	Antarctica	Located in West Antarctica, joining the Heritage Range, making up the Ellsworth Mountain Range, contains the Continent's highest peak, Vinson Massif
Sierra Madre	Mexico	Includes the 3 ranges, Sierra Madre Occidental, Sierra Madre Oriental, and Sierra Madre del Sur
Sierra Madre de Chiapas	Mexico	Aka Sierra de Soconusco, and extending to the south-east along the Pacific Coast from the Isthmus of Tehuantepec to the Guatemalan border
Sierra Nevada	Spain	Highest division of the Penibético Mountain System of south-eastern Spain, highest point being Cerro de Mulhacén
Sierra Nevada Range	USA	Extending for more than 250 miles along the eastern edge of California, from the Mojave Desert in the south to the Cascades in the north, highest peak is Mt Whitney
Southern Alps	New Zealand	Situated on South Island and extending from Haast Pass, north-eastwards to Arthur's Pass, highest point being Mt Cook
Sperrin Mountains	N. Ireland	Situated 20 miles south-east of Londonderry, major peaks include, Mullaclogher, Sawel, and Mullaghaneany
St Elias Range	Canada	Situated in south-western Yukon Territory near the Pacific coast, highest peak is Mt Logan
Tatras	East Europe	Situated along the Slovak–Polish border, it is the highest range of the Central Carpathians, high point being Mt Gerlach
Transylvanian Alps	Romania	Aka Southern Carpathians, the section of the Carpathians between the Prahova River Valley and the gap between the Timis and Cerna rivers, highest point Mt Moldoveanu
Uinta Mountains	USA	Mountain range in N.E. Utah, part of the Rocky Mountains, the highest point being Kings Peak
Unaka Mountains	USA	Extending from south-west Virginia, along the Tennessee-North Carolina border, into northern Georgia. Unaka means 'white' in Cherokee
Urals	Russia	Extending from the Arctic Ocean to northern Kazakhstan, forming part of the boundary between Europe and Asia, highest peak Mt Narodnaya
Velikonda Range	India	Situated in Andhra Pradesh state of southern India
Virunga Range	Central Africa	Also spelled Birunga, and also called M'Fumbiro Mountains. The range straddles Zaire, Rwanda and Uganda, although, the highest peak, Karisimbi, borders Zaire & Rwanda
Vosges Mountains	France	Extending west of the Rhine River Valley in the Haut-Rhin, Bas-Rhin, and Vosges départements of eastern France; highest point Ballon de Guebwiller
White Mountains	USA	Segment of the Appalachians extending across New Hampshire and into western Maine, highest point is Mt Washington
Wilhelmina Gebergte	Suriname	Forming part of South America's granitic Precambrian Guiana Shield, highest point: Juliana Top
Wilson's Promontory	Australia	Not a range of mountains as such but the southernmost point of the Australian mainland, in Victoria; it is a mountainous area, highest point being Mt Latrobe
Wind River Range	USA	Situated in the central Rocky Mountains, west central Wyoming, the highest peak: Gannett Peak
Wrangell Mountains	USA	Part of the Pacific Coast Range, extending south in south-eastern Alaska for 100 miles from the Copper River to the St Elias Mountains near the Yukon border; highest point: Mt Blackburn
Yablonovy Range	Russia	Situated in the Transbaikalia region of Chita and Buryat, highest point being Mt Kusotuy
Zagros Mountains	Iran	Situated in south-west Iran, extending north-west to south-east from the Sirvān (Diyala) river to Shirāz, the highest peak being Zard Kuh
Zambales Mountains	Philippines	Situated in the south-western part of northern Luzon, from Lingayen Gulf in the north to the entrance to Manila Bay in the south, highest point being High Peak
Zeravshan Range	Tadzhik – Uzbek	Extends 230 miles as an east-west parallel to the Turkistan Range, highest point: Chimtorga

Mountain Passes, Valleys and Gorges

Arthur's	the lowest pass (3,038 ft) of the Southern Alps, west-central South Island, New Zealand, the Otira Tunnel crosses the Alps at this point
Berthoud	situated in the Front Range of the central Rocky Mountains at an altitude of 11,315 ft
Bran	situated to the west of Predeal Pass and linking Brasov to Cimpulung between the Bucegi Massif and the Fagaras Mountains, Romania
Brenner	lying on the Italian–Austrian border and at 4,498 ft one of the lowest Alpine passes
Cameron	situated in the extreme southerly end of the Medicine Bow Mountains in Colorado at an altitude of 10,285 ft
Great Saint Bernard	lying on the Italian–Swiss border and at 8,100 ft one of the highest Alpine passes
Gumal	situated between the Khyber pass and Bolān pass and connects Ghazni in eastern Afghanistan with Tānk and Dera Ismāil Khān in Pakistan
Iron Gate	last gorge of the Djerdap gorge system on the Danube River, dividing the Carpathian and Balkan mountains and forming part of the boundary between Yugoslavia and Romania. The gorge is two miles long and 530 ft wide
Katára	situated in Pindus Mountains of northern Greece and southern Albania (known as Métsovo) at an altitude of 5,593 ft
Khyber	connecting Kābul, Afghanistan, with Peshāwar, Pakistan. The pass reaches 3,518 ft at its highest point
Kicking Horse	situated on the Alberta–British Columbia border, the highest point on the Canadian Pacific Railway at 5,338 ft
Little Saint Bernard	at 7,178 ft one of the highest passes of the French Alps. The road across the pass links France and Italy
Lolo	situated in the Bitterroot Range along the Idaho–Montana border at an altitude of 5,236 ft
Loveland	situated in the Front Range of the central Rocky Mountains at an altitude of 11,990 ft.
Marias	situated in the Lewis Range of the northern Rockies at an elevation of 5,216 ft
Pajares	railway pass through the Cantabrian Mountains of northern Spain linking Oviedo and León at an altitude of 4,524 ft
Pele	cuts through the Black Mountain Range of the Assam Himalayas at an altitude of 11,055 ft
Plöcken (Passo di Monte Croce)	situated at an elevation of 4,462 ft in the Carnic Alps on the Austrian–Italian border
Predeal	links the city of Brasov and the Birsei Depression to the north with the city of Ploiesti and the Danube Plain to the south, across the Transylvanian Alps (Southern Carpathians)
Predel	separates the Julian Alps at the Italian–Slovenian border at an altitude of 3,793 ft
Radstädter Tauern	situated in the Niedere Tauern Range at an elevation of 5,705 ft
Saint Gothard	a 16-mile-long pass situated in the Lepontine Alps of southern Switzerland. The pass has an altitude of 6,916 ft ; the nine-mile-long St Gothard railway tunnel underneath the pass links Italy and Switzerland via Milan and Luzern; the ten-mile long St Gothard road tunnel links Göschenen and Airolo
Simplon	situated in the southern Swiss Alps at an altitude of 6,581 ft; the Simplon railway tunnel cuts through beneath the pass and connects Brig, Switzerland and Iselle, Italy
Uspallata	situated in the Andes, at 12,500 ft, connecting Mendoza, Argentina and Santiago, Chile

Mountains (General)

Name	*Area*	*Height (ft)*	*Details*
Abu (Guru Sikhar)	India	5,650	highest mountain in the Arāvalli range of northern India
Aconcagua	Argentina	22,834	highest peak in the Andes and in the Western Hemisphere, first climbed in 1897
Adam's Peak	Sri Lanka	7,360	situated in south-western Sri Lanka, 11 miles north-east of Ratnapura; famous for its footprint (5 ft 4 ins x 2 ft 6 ins) revered as the Buddha's, Adam's or Siva's, dependent on faith.
Agel	France/Monaco	3,766	situated on the border between France and Monaco, the highest point is in France but Chemin des Révoires peak is in Monaco
Alverstone	North America	14,565	situated in the St Elias Mountains, on the Yukon/Alaska border, and first climbed in 1951
Ampato	Peru	20,702	situated in the Andes, first climbed in 1972
Anai Mudi	India	8,842	situated in Kottayam district, eastern Kerala state, SW India, in the Western Ghāts, highest point of peninsular India
Annapurna	Nepal	26,546	first peak above 26,000 ft to be climbed to the summit, on 3 June 1950, by Maurice Herzog and Louis Lachenal
Apo	Philippines	9,690	volcanic mountain, the highest point of the Philippines, part of the Cordillera Central
Aragats	Armenia	13,418	highest point in both Armenia, and the Little Caucasus range
Ararat (Agri Dagi)	Turkey	16,854	extinct volcano, highest peak in Turkey. Little Ararat (Kucuk Agri Dagi) rises to 12,782 ft
Aspiring	New Zealand	9,932	situated in the Southern Alps of west central South Island, first climbed in 1909 by Major Bernard Head
Athos	Greece	6,670	situated in northern Greece, it is also the site of a semi-autonomous republic of Greek Orthodox monks
Backbone	USA	3,360	highest point in Maryland
Baden-Powell	USA	9,389	twin peak, with North Baldy, and situated in the San Gabriel Mountains
Bagzan	Niger	6,630	situated in the south central Air Mountains, aka Mont Idoukal-n-Taghès
Baker	USA	10,778	volcano situated in the Cascade range in Washington
Ballon de Guebwiller	France	4,672	highest peak of the Vosges Mountains
Bandeira	Brazil	9,482	situated on the border of Espirito Santo and Minas Gerais states, eastern Brazil; until Neblina peak was discovered in 1962 Bandeira was the highest known peak in Brazil
Batu	Ethiopia	14,130	situated in the Eastern Highlands between the Genale and Shebele rivers
Bear	USA	14,831	situated in the Wrangell Mountains, first climbed in 1951
Belukha	Russia	14,783	highest peak in the Altai Mountain range
Ben Macdui	Scotland	4,296	highest peak of the Cairngorms and the second highest mountain in the British Isles
Ben Nevis	Scotland	4,409	highest mountain of the British Isles
Betling Sib	India	3,280	highest peak of the Tripura Hills of north-eastern India
Big Black Mountain	USA	4,150	highest peak of Kentucky
Blackburn	USA	16,523	highest point in Alaska's Wrangell Mountains, first climbed in 1912
Blanc	France/Italy	15,781	highest peak in the Alps
Blanca Peak	USA	14,345	highest peak in the Sangre de Cristo Mountains of Colorado/New Mexico
Blue Mountain Peak	Jamaica	7,402	highest peak of the Blue Mountains in eastern Jamaica
Bluff	Australia	1,550	highest peak of the Gawler ranges of South Australia
Bolivar	Venezuela	16,342	situated in the Sierra Nevada National Park of Mérida and Barinas states, north-western Venezuela; Pico Bolivar (Columna) is marginally higher than Humboldt and Bonpland and is the highest peak in Venezuela: the cable-car running from Mérida to nearby Pico Espejo (Mirror Peak), 15,600 ft, is thought to be the highest in the world
Bona	USA	16,421	situated in the Wrangell Mountains, first climbed in 1930
Botev Peak	Bulgaria	7,795	highest point in the Balkan Mountain range

Name	Area	Height (ft)	Details
Boundary Peak	USA	13,140	highest point in Nevada
Brandberg	Namibia	8,550	located in Damaraland in the Namib Desert: the highest peak is known as Königstein
Brasstown Bald	USA	4,784	highest point in Georgia, part of the Unaka range of the Blue Ridge
Brown	USA	14,530	situated in the Alaska range
Bruce	Australia	4,056	highest peak in the Hamersley range, and the highest in Western Australia
Bukit Maxwell	Malaysia	3,399	situated in Taiping, West Malaysia, and formerly called Mazwells Hill
Byron	Australia	3,058	highest point of the Mount Lofty ranges of South Australia
Carmarthen Van	Wales	2,632	highest peak of the Black Mountains of east Dyfed
Carn Mairg	Scotland	3,087	highest peak of the Monadhliath Mountains in the Highlands between Loch Ness and the River Spey; aka Grey Hills
Carrantuohill	Ireland	3,406	highest point of Macgillicuddy's Reeks in County Kerry and highest mountain in Ireland
Chances Peak	Montserrat	3,002	situated east of the capital Plymouth in the Soufrière Hills
Cheaha	USA	2,407	highest point in Alabama
Cheviot Peak	England	2,676	highest point of the Cheviots of northern England
Chimborazo	Ecuador	20,561	extinct volcano in the Andes of central Ecuador
Chimtorga	Tajik/Uzbek	18,009	highest point of the Zeravshan range
Chiriqui	Panama	11,398	highest peak in Panama; aka Volcán Barú
Churchill	USA	15,638	situated in the Wrangell Mountains
Cleveland	USA–Canada	10,479	highest peak of the Lewis range in the northern Rockies
Clingman's Dome	USA	6,643	highest point in Tennessee, situated in the Great Smoky Mountains National Park
Cloud Peak	USA	13,165	highest peak of the Bighorn Mountains in the northern Rocky Mountains, southern Montana
Communism Peak	Tajikistan	24,590	highest point of the Pamirs (and Tajikistan), known since 1998 as Ismoil Somoni Peak
Cook	New Zealand	12,316	situated in the Southern Alps, the highest peak of New Zealand
Cooke	Australia	1,910	highest peak in the Darling range of Western Australia
Coombe Hill	England	825	highest peak of the Chilterns
Corn Ddu	Wales	2,863	twin peak, with Pen-y-Fan, of the Brecon Beacons
Cotopaxi	Ecuador	19,347	active volcano situated in the Andes, last eruption in 1975
Crêt de la Neige	France	5,636	situated in the French segment of the Jura Mountains
Cristóbal Colón	Colombia	18,701	situated in the Santa Marta Mountains and is the highest peak in Colombia, although since remeasuring is disputed with Pico Simón Bolivar
Cross Fell	England	2,930	highest peak in the Pennines
Curcubăta Marc	Romania	6,063	highest peak of the Bihor Massif in the Apuneni Mountains
Dandenong	Australia	2,077	highest peak in the Dandenong range of southern Victoria
Davis	USA	3,213	highest point in Pennsylvania, part of the Allegheny Mountains
Dhaulagiri	Nepal	26,795	Himalayan mountain; name means 'White Mountain2 in Sanskrit
Djebel Chélia	Algeria	7,638	situated in the Aurès range of Northern Algeria
Doda Betta	India	8,652	highest peak in Tamil Nādu state, south-eastern India, and 2nd highest in the Western Ghāts
Dom Mountain	Indonesia	4,396	situated on the island of New Guinea, there is also a Dom Peak in the Apennines
Dome Fuji Peak	Antarctica	12,487	situated on Queen Maud Land
Dome Mountain	Canada	896	situated south of Lake Melville in Newfoundland
Dufourspitze	Switzerland	15,203	highest peak in Switzerland, in the Monte Rosa Massif
Dunkery Beacon	England	1,750	highest peak of Exmoor, on the border of Somerset and Devon
Eagle	USA	2,300	highest peak in Minnesota
Ebal	Palestine	3,084	situated in the West Bank just north of Mt Gerizim
Edith	USA	9,504	highest peak of the Big Belt Mountains, a segment of the northern Rocky Mountains
Egmont	New Zealand	8,260	extinct volcano on the Taranaki peninsula of North Island
Eiger	Switzerland	13,026	first climbed in 1858 by Charles Barrington and Christian Almer. The 6,000 ft North Face was first climbed in July 1938 by Heinrich Harrer, Fritz Kasparek, Anderl Heckmair and Ludwig Vorg; the difficulty of this climb earned the Eiger Nordwand many nicknames, including 'The White Spider', 'The White Cobra' and 'Murder Wall'
El Capitan	USA	3,604	highest peak in Yosemite National Park, central California. Part of Sierra Nevada range
El Misti	Ecuador	19,233	volcano situated in the Ecuadorean Andes; last eruption in 1878
Elbert	USA	14,433	situated in the Sawatch range of the Rockies, highest point in Colorado and the Rockies
Elbright Road	USA	442	situated in New Castle County, the highest point in Delaware
Elbrus	Russia	18,510	highest peak in the Caucasus and highest in Russia, just north of the Georgia border
Elgon	Kenya/Uganda	14,140	extinct volcano on the Kenya/Uganda border, first climbed by Sir Frederick Jackson and Ernest Gedge in 1890, highest peak is Wagagai
Encuolo	Ethiopia	14,144	situated in the Eastern Highlands north of the Shebele river
Erebus	Antarctica	12,448	volcano on Ross Island, discovered by Sir James Ross in 1841 and named after his ship
Estrela	Portugal	6,539	situated in the Serra da Estrela range it is the highest point of mainland Portugal (Mount Pico, in the Azores, is higher).
Etna	Italy	10,855	situated on the island of Sicily, this volcano, the highest in Europe, had a major eruption in 1669 when 20,000 people were killed and the city of Catania was devastated
Evans	USA	14,264	highest peak of the Front range in the central Rocky Mountains
Everest	Nepal/Tibet	29,029	highest point on Earth, named after George Everest, Surveyor General of India (1830–43), called Peak XV until 1865; Dalai Lama 1st gave permission to climb in 1920 and Sir John Hunt led the 1953 successful expedition; Dougal Haston and Doug Scott in 1976 became the first British climbers; Reinhold Messner was the first to make a successful climb without oxygen; Junko Tabei of Japan became the first woman to climb Everest on 16 May 1975; Alison Hargreaves became first woman to climb Everest without oxygen but died soon after on K2; Everest is aka Goddess Mother of the World (Chomolungma in Tibetan language)
Fairweather	North America	15,299	situated in the St Elias Mountains, on British Columbia/Alaska border; first climbed in 1931
Fan Si Pan	Vietnam	10,308	highest peak in Vietnam
Fanthams Peak	New Zealand	6,438	extinct volcano on the Taranaki peninsula of North Island
Fichtelberg	Germany	3,983	highest peak on the German side of the Ore Mountains
Finsteraarhorn	Switzerland	14,022	highest peak of the Bernese Alps
Foraker	USA	17,400	situated in the Alaska range, and first climbed in 1934
Francs Peak	USA	13,140	highest peak of the Absaroka range of the northern Rocky Mountains in northwestern Wyoming and southern Montana
Fremont Peak	USA	13,730	situated in the Wind River range of Wyoming
Galtymore	Ireland	3,018	highest peak of the Galty Mountains of Western Ireland
Gangkhar Puensum	China	24,836	situated on, or close to, the border with Bhutan and its exact location is disputed
Gannett Peak	USA	13,763	highest peak in the Wind River range and also the highest peak in Wyoming

Name	*Area*	*Height (ft)*	*Details*
Gerizim (Jabal At-Tur)	Palestine	2,890	Since 1967 has been part of the West Bank of Judaea and Samaria, under Israeli administration, it is twinned with Mt Ebal, which is just north of Gerizim
Gerlach	Slovakia	8,711	situated in Tatra segment of the Carpathian Mountains; the highest peak of the Carpathians
Glittertinden	Norway	8,110	situated in the Jotunheimen (Giant's Home) Mountain and although twelve feet higher than Galdhopiggen the peak is a 65 ft thick permanent, glacial ice cap
Golyam Perelik	Balkans	7,188	highest peak in the Rhodope Mountains
Goodsir	Canada	11,683	situated in the Yoho National Park of eastern British Columbia
Grandfather	USA	5,964	situated in North Carolina, part of the Blue Ridge Mountains
Granite Peak	USA	12,799	highest peak in Montana, part of the Beartooth range
Greylock	USA	3,491	situated in the Berkshire Hills, the highest point in Massachusetts
Guadalupe Peak	USA	8,749	highest point in Texas
Guge	Ethiopia	13,790	situated west of Lake Abaya
Guru Sikhar	India	5,650	See Mt Abu
Hagen	New Guinea	12,392	situated in the Central Highlands of New Guinea Island, Papua New Guinea
Harney Peak	USA	7,242	highest peak in South Dakota situated in the Black Hills
Hartz Mountain	Australia	4,111	highest peak of the Hartz Mountain range in Southern Tasmania
Harvard	USA	14,420	situated in the Sawatch Mountains, a segment of the Rockies running through Colorado
Hermon	Syria/Lebanon	9,232	aka Jabal ash-Shaikh, and situated west of Damascus, Hermon means 'Forbidden Place'. The southern elevation (7,336 ft) is controlled by Israel.
High Peak	Philippines	6,683	highest peak of the Zambales Mountains
High Point	USA	1,803	highest peak in New Jersey
High Willhays	England	2,039	highest peak in the Dartmoor National Park of Devon
Hochgolling	Austria	9,393	highest peak of the Niedere Tauern range of the Eastern Alps
Hood	USA	11,235	situated in the Cascade range, highest peak in Oregon
Huascarán	Peru	22,205	extinct volcano in west Peru, in the Peruvian Andes, highest peak in Peru
Hubbard	North America	15,015	situated in the St Elias Mountains, on the Yukon/Alaska border, and first climbed in 1951
Humphrey's Peak	USA	12,633	one of the three San Francisco Peaks, the highest peak in Arizona
Hunter	USA	14,573	situated in the Alaska range
Ida	Crete	8,058	highest peak on the island at 2,456m, it is just three metres higher than Mt Pachnes
Illampu	Bolivia	20,892	located in the Cordillera Real, in the Andean Range, east of Lake Titicaca
Illimani	Bolivia	21,122	highest mountain in the Cordillera Real, just south of La Paz
Ingleborough	England	2,376	one of the so called Three Peaks of the Yorkshire Dales National Park
Ironstone	Australia	4,736	highest peak of the Great Western Mountains in Tasmania
Ismoil Somoni Peak	Tajikistan	24,590	formerly known as Stalin Peak (1933–62) and Communism Peak (1962–98)
Isto	USA	9,058	highest peak of the Brooks range in the northern Rocky Mountains near the Canadian border
Iztaccíhuatl	Mexico	17,159	dormant volcano which last erupted in 1868, situated on the México-Puebla state line in central Mexico, 10 miles north of its twin, Popocatépetl
Jerimoth Hill	USA	812	highest peak in Rhode Island, less than a mile from the Connecticut border
Juliana Top	Suriname	4,199	highest peak of the Wilhelmina Gebergte range of central Suriname
Jungfrau	Switzerland	13,642	situated in the Bernese Alps 11 miles south-east of Interlaken; first climbed by two Swiss brothers, Rudolf and Hieronymus Meyer, in 1811
K2	Pakistan	28,250	situated in the Karakorum range in the Himalayas, on the western side of the Indian/Pakistani line of control in Jammu and Kashmir, first climbed by Compagnoni and Lacedelli in 1954 K2 is also known as Mt Godwin Austen, Dapsang, and Chogori
Kanchenjunga	Nepal/India	28,169	on the border of Nepal and Sikkim, the 3rd highest mountain in the world was first climbed in 1955, although Charles Evans stopped short of the summit in deference to Sikkimese religious beliefs; Kanchenjunga means 'Five Treasuries of the Great Snow' (Sikkim)
Karisimbi	Rwanda	14,787	highest peak of the Virunga range – part of mountain in the Democratic Republic of Congo
Katahdin	USA	5,268	highest peak in Maine
Kellerwand	Austria	9,121	highest peak of the Carnic Alps
Kennedy Peak	Myanmar	2,704	situated on the Tropic of Cancer near the Indian border
Kennesaw	USA	551	situated in Atlanta, Georgia
Kenya (Batian Peak)	Kenya	17,057	extinct volcano, first climbed in 1899 by Halford and Mackinder of Great Britain
Kerintji	Indonesia	12,484	highest peak in the West Sumatran/Java range
Khan Tengri	Kazakhstan	22,999	situated on the border with Kyrgyzstan
Kilimanjaro	Tanzania	19,331	Volcanic mountain near Kenyan border, the Kibo peak being the highest point in Tanzania and probably the only snow-covered point on the equator; the other main peak is Mawenzi
Kimpõ	Japan	8,514	situated in the Chichibu Mountains, the northern extension of the Kwanto range
Kinabalu	Malaysia	13,455	highest peak in Malay Archipelago (on Borneo), formerly known as St Peter's Mount
Kinder Scout	England	2,088	highest point in the Peak District
King	Canada	16,972	situated in the St Elias Mountains, Yukon Territory, and first climbed in 1952
Kings Peak	USA	13,528	highest point in Utah, situated in the Uintas range
Kirkpatrick	Antarctica	14,856	highest point of the Queen Alexandra range
Klinovec	Czech Republic	4,080	highest peak in the Ore Mountains
Klyuchevskaya Sopka	Russia	15,584	highest active volcano in Asia, situated in Kamchatka Peninsula
Kompasberg	South Africa	8,215	highest peak of the Sneeuberg (Snow Mountain) range in central Cape Province
Kosciusko	Australia	7,316	situated in the Snowy Mountains of New South Wales, the highest peak of mainland Australia (but see Mawson's Peak)
Krakatoa	Indonesia	2,667	famous for the eruption of 1883 when 163 villages were destroyed and 36,417 people were killed. Despite the title of the 1968 film, Krakatoa is actually west of Java
Kriván	East Europe	8,182	one of the highest peaks of the High Tatras on the Poland/Slovakia border
Kusotuy	Russia	5,512	highest point of the Yablonovy range
Kyparissovouno	Cyprus	3,360	highest point of the Kyrenia Mountains
La Dôle	Switzerland	5,545	situated in the Swiss segment of the Jura Mountains
Lascar	Chile	18,508	Volcano situated in the Chilean Andes, last eruption in 1969
Lassen	USA	10,457	Volcano situated in the Cascade range in California
Latrobe	Australia	2,475	highest point of Wilson's Promontory in southern Victoria
Le Reculet	France	5,633	situated in the French segment of the Jura Mountains
Les Écrins	France	13,461	highest peak of the Dauphiné Alps
Lhotse (E)	Nepal/Tibet	27,940	situated just south of Everest, to which it is joined by a 25,000 ft ridge; The 'E' of its original name stands for Everest
Llullaillaco	S America	22,058	Dormant volcano situated in the Andes on the Argentina/Chile border, last eruption in 1877
Logan	Yukon	19,550	2nd highest peak in North America, first climbed in 1925 by MacCarthy and Lambert; mountains with the same name in Quebec, Arizona and Washington

Name	*Area*	*Height (ft)*	*Details*
Lomnicky	East Europe	8,635	one of the highest peaks of the High Tatras on the Poland/Slovakia border
Lozère	France	5,584	highest peak of the Cévennes range of southern France
Lucania	Canada	17,146	situated in the St Elias Mountains, Yukon Territory, and first climbed in 1937
Lugnaquilla	Ireland	3,039	highest peak of the Wicklow Mountains
Lyavirdyr	Tajikistan	20,837	highest point of the Sarykol range
Magazine	USA	2,753	highest peak in Arkansas
Mansfield	USA	4,393	highest point in Vermont
Marcy	USA	5,344	highest peak of the Adirondacks, and the highest peak of New York state
Mariveles	Philippines	4,659	Most southerly peak of the Zambales Mountains, lying opposite Manila Bay
Markham	Antarctica	14,272	highest point of the Queen Elizabeth range
Marmolada	Italy	10,964	highest peak in the Dolomites
Mary's Peak	USA	4,097	South-west of Corvallis, the highest point of the Oregon Coastal range
Massive	USA	14,421	situated in the Sawatch Mountains, a segment of the Rockies running through Colorado
Matterhorn	Switzerland/Italy	14,691	First climbed 14 Jul 1865 by British explorer Edward Whymper, although the Italian ridge was scaled 3 days later by Giovanni Carrel; Matterhorn was named after the Swiss city of Zermatt; Italian name is Monte Cervino
Mauna Kea	USA	13,796	Dormant volcano situated on Hawaii Island, the highest point in Hawaii state, in fact, its 32,000 ft height from the seafloor makes it the world's highest peak from base to tip
Mauna Loa	USA	13,678	situated on Hawaii Island, the actual height of the volcano from its base on the seafloor is second only to Mauna Kea; last erupted in 1988
Mawson Peak	Australia	9,006	situated on Heard Island in the Southern Ocean, this is the 3rd highest mountain on Australian territory (see Mt McClintock & Mt Menzies)
McClintock	Australia	11,457	situated in the Britannia Range in Australian Antarctic Territory, this is the highest mountain on Australian territory
McIntyre	USA	5,114	situated in the Adirondack range of New York state; highest peak is Algonquin
McKinley	USA	20,320	situated in the Alaska range, and first climbed in 1913, the highest peak of North America
Menzies	Australia	11,007	situated on the south side of Fisher Glacier in the Australian Antarctic Territory, this is the 2nd highest mountain on Australian territory
Mercedario	Argentina	22,211	situated in the Andes, first climbed in 1934
Meru	Tanzania	14,980	located near the Kenyan border, south-west of Kilimanjaro
Mikeno	Dem Rep Congo	14,557	situated in the Virunga Mountains (some peaks being in Rwanda)
Miller	Antarctica	13,646	situated in the Queen Elizabeth range
Mitchell	USA	6,684	highest point in North Carolina, situated in the Black Mountains, part of the Blue Ridge Mountains; highest peak east of the Mississippi
Moldoveanu	Romania	8,346	situated in the Transylvanian Alps, the highest peak in Romania
Mönch	Switzerland	13,448	flanked by the Eiger and Jungfrau in the Bernese Alps
Mount Darwin	Zimbabwe	4,951	situated in northern Zimbabwe, locals call it Pfura, meaning 'rhinoceros'
Mount Obama	Antigua	1,319	highest point of the south-western Shekerly Mountains. Named after Barack Obama and known as Boggy Peak prior to August 2009
Muchinga	Zambia	7,350	Although this is the highest named peak in Zambia the actual highest point is an unnamed location in Mafinga Hills at 2,329 m (7,641 ft)
Mulhacén	Spain	11,421	situated in the Sierra Nevadas of southern Spain, highest mountain of the Iberian Peninsula
Nanda Devi	India	25,643	situated in the Uttar Pradesh segment of the Himalayas; the highest mountain wholly in India
Nanga (Naked) Parbat	Kashmir	26,660	often regarded as the first major peak of the western Himalayas; the local name is Diamir (King of the Mountains)
Neblina	Brazil	9,823	situated in the Serra Tapirapeó, Amazonas state, highest peak in Brazil
Nebo	Jordan	2,631	highest point of the Pisgah Ridge, from which Moses viewed the Promised Land
Nimba	Ivory Coast	5,748	straddles Guinea & Liberia; highest peak in the range is known locally as Mt Richard-Molard
North Baldy	USA	9,131	Twin peak, with Mt Baden-Powell, situated in San Gabriel Mountains of southern California
Ojos del Salado	S America	22,615	Although the mountain straddles the Chile/Argentina border, the highest peak is totally in Chile. First climbed in 1937, it is also the highest active volcano in the world (previously designated as dormant but it started to 'steam' in 1981 and has recently produced vents)
Olga	Australia	3,507	situated in Uluru National Park, Mt Olga is the most westerly of Australia's 3 giant tors, the others being Ayers Rock at 2,845 ft and Mt Conner
Orizaba (Citlaltépetl)	Mexico	18,490	dormant volcano situated in Altiplano de Mexico, last erupted in 1687
Pelée	Martinique	4,582	In 1902 the town of St Pierre was destroyed by this volcano's eruption, which killed all 26,000 inhabitants, except for a prisoner who survived in the thick-walled prison
Pen-y-Fan	Wales	2,906	highest point of the Brecon Beacons
Pen-y-Gader	Wales	2,927	highest point of the Cader Idris range
Pen-y-Ghent	England	2,278	one of the so called Three Peaks of the Yorkshire Dales National Park
Pico Bette	Libya	7,438	located in the Tibesti Mountains in southern Libya near the border with Chad. Aka Bikku Bitti
Pinátubo	Philippines	5,723	situated in Luzon, this volcano last erupted in 1991, when 847 people were killed – the most lethal eruption of the 20th century
Pissis	Argentina	22,241	situated in the Andes, first climbed in 1937
Popocatépetl	Mexico	17,930	volcano which last erupted in 1997, the first eruption since 1802, although it does emit large clouds of smoke periodically; known locally as Nahuatl (smoking mountain)
Poroshiri	Japan	6,732	highest peak of the Hidaka–Sammyaku range on Hokkaido
Profitis	Greece	1,857	volcanic mountain on the island of Thera in the Cyclades, the highest point on the island
Punta Pora	Paraguay	2,296	second-highest peak in Paraguay
Puy de Sancy	France	6,184	highest peak of the Massif Central
Rainier	USA	14,410	dormant volcano, highest peak of the Cascade range and also the highest peak in Washington state, first climbed in 1870
Ramlo	Ethiopia	6,988	situated inland of the Red Sea coast, north of Djibouti
Revelstoke	Canada	6,375	situated in the Selkirk Mountains of south-eastern British Columbia
Rock Creek Butte	USA	9,105	highest peak of Blue Mountains, situated on Elkhorn Ridge on Oregon/Washington border
Rogers	USA	5,729	highest point in Virginia, part of the Blue Ridge Mountains
Rosa	Switzerland/Italy	15,203	situated SE of Zermatt, often identified with Dufourspitze, although Monte Rosa has many other named peaks
Round	Australia	5,300	highest peak of the New England range, NSW
Ruapehu	New Zealand	9,177	active volcano and highest point on North Island
Rushmore	South Dakota	6,040	situated in the Black Hills, and famous for its carved faces (60 ft high) of Washington, Lincoln, Jefferson and Roosevelt, executed by Gutzon Borglum between 1927 and 1941
St Helens	USA	8,360	volcano in Washington state (Cascades); erupted in 1980 after lying dormant from 1857

Name	Area	Height (ft)	Details
St Mary	Australia	3,825	highest peak in the Flinders ranges
Sajama	Bolivia	21,463	situated in the Andes, first climbed in 1939, the highest peak of Bolivia
Sakesar	Pakistan	4,992	highest peak of the Salt range in the northern Punjab
San Antonio	USA	10,080	Nicknamed 'Old Baldy'; the highest peak of the San Gabriel Mountains of southern California
San Bernardino	USA	10,630	situated in the San Bernardino Mountains of southern California
San Gorgonio	USA	11,502	situated in the San Bernardino Mountains, highest point in southern California
San Jacinto Peak	USA	10,804	highest point of the San Jacinto Mountains of southern California
San Pedro	Chile	20,339	volcano situated in the Chilean Andes, last eruption in 1960
Sanford	USA	16,237	situated in the Wrangell Mountains of south-eastern Alaska, first climbed in 1938
Sassafras	USA	3,560	highest point in South Carolina, part of the Blue Ridge Mountains
Scafell	England	3,162	south-west of Scafell Pike, the 2nd-highest peak in England
Scafell Pike	England	3,210	situated in the Lake District of Cumbria, highest point in England
Scott Peak	USA	11,394	highest peak of the Bitterroot range in the northern Rocky Mountains, Idaho
Shasta	USA	14,162	extinct volcano situated in the Cascade range of northern California
Shirane	Japan	10,472	highest mountain of the Japanese Alps, on Honshu island; highest peak named Ontake
Shishaldin	USA	9,387	volcanic mountain in the Unimak Islands, the highest point in the Aleutian range of Alaska
Sierra Blanca	USA	12,003	highest peak of the Sacramento Mountains in the southern Rockies
Sinai	Egypt	7,497	situated on Sinai Peninsula, under Israeli administration from Six-Day War of 1967 to 1979 when it was returned to Egypt; God gave Moses the Ten Commandments here
Sir James McBrien	Canada	9,061	highest peak of the Mackenzie Mountains in the Yukon Territory
Sir Sanford	Canada	11,590	highest peak of the Selkirk Mountains
Sir Wilfrid Laurier	Canada	11,299	highest peak of the Cariboo range of British Columbia
Slide	USA	4,204	highest point of the Catskill Mountains
Slieve Donard	N Ireland	2,796	highest peak of the Mourne Mountains
Snaefell	Isle of Man	2,034	highest peak of the Isle of Man
Snowdon	Wales	3,560	situated in Snowdonia National Park, Clwyd and Gwynedd, highest peak in Wales
Solomon's Throne	Pakistan	18,481	situated in the Sulaimân range of central Pakistan
Spruce Knob	USA	4,862	highest point in West Virginia, part of the Allegheny Mountains
Stanley	Dem Rep Congo/ Uganda	16,763	highest mountain in the Ruwenzori range (highest peak named after Queen Margherita of Italy), first climbed in 1906 by Luigi Abruzzi
Steele	Canada	16,644	situated in the St Elias Mountains, Yukon Territory, and first climbed in 1935
Sugar Loaf	Brazil	1,325	overlooking the entrance of Guanabara Bay, south-eastern Brazil
Sunflower	USA	4,039	highest point in Kansas, situated south-east near the Colorado border
Table (Tafelberg)	South Africa	3,563	Flat-topped mountain overlooking Cape Town and Table Bay; the highest peak is Maclear's Beacon, subsidiary peaks include Lion's Head (2,195 ft) and Devil's Peak (3,281 ft)
Tahan	Malaysia	7,175	situated in Taman Negara National Park, West Malaysia
Tahat	Algeria	9,852	situated in the Hoggar Massif of the southern Saharan Atlas mountains
Talo	Ethiopia	14,478	situated in central Ethiopia in the Gojam Massif
Tambora	Indonesia	9,350	situated on Sumbawa and famous for its eruption of 1815 when over 90,000 people perished
Tapuaenuku	New Zealand	9,465	highest peak of the Kaikoura range on South Island
Tata Mailau	East Timor	9,720	highest peak of East Timor, aka Mt Ramelau
Taum Sauk	USA	1,772	highest peak of the Ozark Mountains, and highest point in Missouri
Teide	Spain	12,190	volcanic mountain situated on the island of Tenerife in the Canaries, last erupted in 1909
Tendre	Switzerland	5,550	situated in the Swiss segment of the Jura Mountains
Thabana Ntlenyana	Lesotho	11,425	highest peak in the Drakensberg Mountains
Thera	Greece	1,960	southernmost island of the Cyclades group, aka Santorini, and famous for its volcanic eruption *c*1550 BC which possibly gave rise to the legend of the lost city of Atlantis
Timpanogos	USA	12,008	highest peak of the Wasatch range in the south central Rocky Mountains
Tirich Mir	Pakistan	25,230	highest peak in the Hindu Kush range, lying 155 miles north of Peshawar
Titano	San Marino	2,424	highest peak and dominant feature of San Marino
Toluca	Mexico	4,577	volcano situated in Mexico state, central Mexico near Toluca, the crater partly filled by a lake
Triglav	Slovenia	9,396	highest peak of the Julian Alps of Slovenia, first climbed in 1778
Tsiafajavona	Madagascar	8,671	situated in the Ankaratra Mountain region, 2nd-highest peak of Madagascar
Tupungato	S. America	22,310	situated in the Andes, on the Argentina/Chile border, first climbed in 1897
Tyree	Antarctica	16,289	situated in the Sentinel range of the Ellsworth Mountains, first climbed in 1967
Vancouver	North America	15,700	situated in the St Elias Mountains, on the Yukon/Alaska border, and first climbed in 1949
Veleta	Spain	11,128	situated in the Sierra Nevadas of southern Spain, 2nd highest mountain of mainland Spain
Vesuvius	Italy	4,198	volcano situated in the Bay of Naples, first major eruption in AD 79 and the last in 1944
Victoria	Myanmar	10,150	highest peak of the Arakan Yoma range separating Myanmar from the Indian subcontinent
Victory Peak	Kyrgyzstan	24,406	situated on the border with China, it is the highest peak in the Tian Shan range, known in Russian as Pik Pobedy and locally as Jengish Chokosu
Vikhren	Bulgaria	9,564	situated in the Rhodope Mountains; second-highest peak in Bulgaria
Vinson Massif	Antarctica	16,864	situated in the Sentinel range of the Ellsworth Mountains, first climbed in 1966
Waddington	Canada	13,104	highest peak of the Coast Mountains of British Columbia
Walsh	Canada	14,780	situated in the St Elias Mountains, Yukon Territory, and first climbed in 1941
Warren	USA	13,720	situated in the Wind River range of Wyoming
Washington	USA	6,288	highest peak in Presidential range of the White Mountains, highest peak in New Hampshire
Waun Fach	Wales	2,660	highest peak of the Black Mountains of east Gwent
Wheeler Peak	USA	13,161	situated in the Sangre de Cristo Mountains, the highest point in New Mexico
Whernside	England	2,416	one of the so-called Three Peaks of the Yorkshire Dales National Park
White Butte	USA	3,506	highest peak in North Dakota
Whiteface	USA	4,865	situated in the Adirondacks of New York
Whitney	USA	14,494	highest peak of Sierra Nevada range in California and the highest peak of the 48 coterminous United States of America
Wilson	USA	5,710	situated in the San Gabriel Mountains of southern California
Wood	Canada	15,886	situated in the St Elias Mountains, Yukon Territory, and first climbed in 1941
Woodroffe	Australia	4,724	highest peak of South Australia, situated in the Musgrave ranges
Worcester Beacon	England	1,395	highest peak of the Malverns
Wrangell	USA	14,163	situated in the Wrangell Mountains of south-eastern Alaska
Wu-t'ai	China	10,033	situated in north-east Shansi Province, the name meaning 'five terraces'
Yes Tor	England	2,028	situated in the Dartmoor National Park of Devon, and twinned with High Willhays
Zengö	Hungary	2,237	highest peak of the Mecsek Mountains of southern Hungary
Ziel	Australia	4,954	highest peak of the MacDonnell ranges of Australia
Zomba	Malawi	6,846	highest point of the Zomba Massif in southern Malawi
Zugspitze	Germany	9,721	part of the Wettersteingebirge in the Bavarian Alps, lying on the Austrian border.

Oceans

	Area (Sq Miles)	% of Earth's Water	Deepest Point
Pacific	64,186,300	46.0	Challenger Deep
Atlantic	33,420,000	23.9	Milwaukee Deep
Indian	28,350,500	20.3	Planet Deep
Arctic	5,105,700	3.6	Eurasia Basin

British Place Names: Meanings of Suffixes and Prefixes

Name	Meaning
aber	river mouth
ac	oak or acorn
agh	field
aig	nook or creek
aird	height
ald	old
alt	brook
alt	steep place
an	terminal diminutive
ard	height
ath	ford
auch	field
auchter	summit
avon	river
ax	water
ay	island
bal	village or town
balloch	pass
bally	village or town
ban	white or fair
bar	point or projecting height
beath	birch tree
beck	brook
bedd	grave
beg	little
ben	mountain
bere	barley
blair	plain
borough	fortified place
bourne	stream
brae	promontory
bre	promontory
brogh	fortified place
bruach	slope or brae
bryn	ridge
burg	fortified place
burn	brook
bury	fortified place
by	village
caer	camp or fortified place
cairn	pile of stones
cambus	crooked
carn	pile of stones
carrick	cliff
caster	walled camp
cefn	ridge
cester	walled camp
cheap	market
chester	walled camp
chipping	market place
clach	stone
clere	hill
clon	meadow
coe	narrow
coln	colony
combe	grassy hollow
cote	mud cottage
craig	rock or cliff
crick	cliff
croe	sheepfold
croft	enclosure
cwm	grassy valley
dal	dale
dal	field
dar	water
dean	wooded vale
dearg	red
del	dale
den	wooded vale
dene	wooded vale

Name	Meaning
der	water
dhu	black
don	hill or water
dor	water
dour	water
drom	ridge
drum	ridge
dum	fortress
dun	hill (England)
dun	fortress (Scotland + Ireland
dur	water
dwfr	water
dyke	ditch
ea	island
eccles	church
egles	church
ennis	island
esk	water
ex	water
ey	island
fell	mountain
field	clearing
fin	white or fair
fleet	river
force	waterfall
ford	shallow river crossing
gair	short
garth	enclosure
gate	passage
ghyll	ravine
gill	ravine
glen	narrow valley
ham	home or enclosure
hampton	home farm or village
hanger	wood on hillside
haugh	meadow between hills
hause	pass or col
hay	hedge
head	headland or hill
hithe	haven
holme	river island
holt	small wood
hoo	heel of land
hurst	thick wood on a hill
inch	island
ing	meadow
ing	son of
ing	people of
innis	island
inver	river mouth
keld	spring
ken	head
kil	church
kirk	church
knock	knoll
knoll	hill top
kyle	strait
lade	river mouth
law	rising ground
lea	meadow
leck	field of corpses
lee	meadow
leigh	woodland glade or meadow
ley	woodland glade or meadow
linn	waterfall
lis	enclosure
litch	field of corpses
llan	church
llech	smooth cliff
llwyd	grey or hoary
llwyn	wood

Name	Meaning
llyn	lake
loch	lake
lough	lake
low	rising ground or mound
lynn	waterfall
madah	wolf
madan	fair
maen	stone
magh	plain
mawr	great
mere	lake or marsh
mickle	great or much
minster	monastic establishment
moor	lake or marsh
mor	great
moss	bog
mull	headland
nant	brook or valley
ness	promontory
ock	water
oke	water
or	river or sea shore
pen	hill or headland
pike	mountain summit
pont	bridge
port	harbour
pwil	pool
rath	round earthwork
rhos	moor
rhyd	ford
rigg	ridge
ross	promontory
royd	ridded of trees
scar	cliff
seat	cultivated place or dwelling
set	settlement
sex	Saxon
shan	mountain
shaw	shady place
shot	protruding land
shott	protruding land
slievh	mountain
staple	store or market
stead	place or holding
stock	palisaded place
stoke	palisaded place
stow	holy place or enclosure
strat	roman road
strath	broad valley
tam	wide
thorpe	farm or village
thwaite	clearing
tober	well
toft	enclosure
ton	farm or town
tor	rocky hill
tre	dwelling or small town
tree	post, cross or crucifix
try	dwelling
twistle	boundary
ty	house
ux	water
wald	wood
walt	wood
weald	wood
wich	marshy meadow
wick	village or farm
win	plain
wold	wood
worth	protected enclosure
ystrad	vale

British Place Names: Meanings

Name	*Meaning*
Accrington	Acorn Farm
Crawley	Crows Wood
Croydon	Saffron Valley
Cumbernauld	Meeting of the Streams
Cumbria	Fellow Countrymen
Derby	Deer Village
Derwent	Oak River
Devizes	Boundaries
Diss	Ditch
Ely	Eel
Epping	Look-out Place
Falkirk	Speckled Church
Gateshead	Goat's Head
Gatwick	Goat Farm
Harlow	Army Mound
Harrogate	Heap of Stones Road
Harwich	Military Settlement
Hendon	High Hill
Hythe	Landing Place
Kesteven	Wood Meeting Place
Lampeter	St Peter's Church
Leatherhead	Grey Ford
Lerwick	Mud Bay
Lichfield	Open Land by the Grey Forest
Llanfair-Pwllgwyngyllgogerychwyrndrobwillantysiliogogogoch	St Mary's Church in the hollow of the White Hazel
Lundy	Puffin (Norse meaning)
Malpas	Bad Step
March	Boundary
Margate	Sea Gate
Matlock	Assembly Oak
Melrose	Bare Moor
Menai	Carrying
Merton	Farm by a Pool
Morecambe	Curved Sea
Morpeth	Murder Path
Moulton	Mule's Settlement
Neasden	Nose-shaped Hill
Neath	Shining One
Nottingham	Home of Snot's People
Oundle	Non-sharing Ones
Pontypridd	Bridge by the Earthen House
Powys	Provincial
Prestatyn	Priest's Village
Preston	Priest's Village
Prestwick	Priest's Outlying Farm
Purbeck	Bittern's Beak
Purley	Pear-Tree Wood
Ramsey	Land of Wild Garlic
Ramsgate	Raven's Gap
Redhill	Red Slope
Reigate	Doe Gate
Renfrew	Current Point
Rhondda	Noisy One
Ribble	Tearing One
Rievaulx	Rye Valley
Salford	Willow-Tree Ford
Selby	Village by the Willows
Sherborne	Bright Stream
Skye	Wing
Snaefell	Snow Mountains
Soho	Hunting Cry (named after)
Solihull	Muddy Hill
Staines	Stone
Stevenage	Place at the firm Oak
Stranraer	Fat Peninsula
Streatham	Home by a Roman Road
Surrey	Southern District
Sussex	South Saxons
Sutton	Southern Farm
Swindon	Pig Hill
Tay	Silent One
Tees	Seething One
Tenby	Little Fort
Tintagel	Throat Fort
Tobermory	St Mary's Well
Tranmere	Cranes
Tresco	Elder-Tree Farm
Tring	Tree-covered Hillside
Trossachs	Transverse Hills
Unst	Abode of Eagles

World Place Names: Meanings

Name	*Meaning*
Aachen	Water Springs
Acapulco	Place where the Reeds Grow
Accra	Ant
Aceldama	Field of Blood
Acropolis	Citadel
Addis Ababa	New Flower
Africa	People of the Dusty Land
Agadir	Wall
Agulhas, Cape	Needle
Ajaccio	Resting Place
Alamo	Cottonwood
Alaska	Great Land
Amritsar	Immortal Lake
Anatolia	Sunrise East
Angostura	Strait Narrows
Anguilla	Eel
Annapurna	Abundant Food
Antananarivo	City of a Thousand
Antofagasta	Hidden Copper
Antrim	One House
Antwerp	Wharfside
Appenzell	Abbot's Cell
Aquitaine	Water Land
Arabia	Tent Dweller
Aral Sea	Island Sea
Aran Islands	Kidney Islands
Ararat	Mountain of Sorrow
Ardennes	Land of Forests
Argentina	Land of Silver
Arizona	Dry Region
Arnhem	Sand Homestead
Asturias	Rock Water
Atacama	Black Duck
Australia	Southern Land
Austria	Eastern Borderland
Azores	Goshawks
Babylon	Gate of the Gods
Baden	Baths
Baghdad	Gift of God
Bahrain	Two Seas
Baku	Windward
Bangkok (see Krung Thep)	Region of Olive Trees
Bangui	Rapids
Banjui	Rope Matting
Barbados	Bearded
Basse-Terre	Low Land
Baton Rouge	Red Stick
Beijing	Northern Capital
Beirut	The Wells
Belfast	Mouth of the Sandbank
Belgrade	White City
Belorussia	White Russia
Bern	Bear
Bethany	House of Poverty
Bethlehem	House of Bread
Bethphage	House of Figs
Betws-y-Coed	Chapel in the Woods
Bhutan (see Druk Yul)	End of Tibet
Bihar	Monastery
Bikini	Surface Coconut
Bizerta	Stable Flowing Through
Bloemfontein	Fountain of Flowers
Boise	Wooded
Bosporus	Oxford
Brindisi	Deer
Brno	Clay
Bruges	Bridge
Brussels	Marsh Room
Bulawayo	Place of the Massacre
Bulgaria	Mixed Race
Burkina Faso	Land of the Worthy Men

Name	Meaning
Cairo	The Fort
Calvary	Skull
Cambrai	Crayfish
Canada	Camp
Canberra	Meeting Place
Carlow	Four Lakes
Carmel	Garden
Carthage	New Town
Casablanca	White House
Cayman Islands	Alligator
Ceylon	Lion
Chattanooga	Rock Rising to a Point
Chicago	Garlic Place
Chittagong	White Village
Clonmel	Meadow of Honey
Comoros	Moon
Conakry	Over the Water
Coney Island	Rabbit Island
Copenhagen	Merchant's Port
Cork	Marsh
Costa Dorada	Gold Coast
Costa Rica	Rich Coast
Cotonou	Dead Person Lagoon
Cotopaxi	Shining Mountain
Cyprus	Copper
Dahomey	On the Stomach of Dan
Dalmatia	Young Animal
Danube	River of Sheep
Dar es Salaam	House of Peace
Darjeeling	Diamond Island (literal) aka Place of the Thunderbolt
Davos	Behind
Deauville	Damp Plain
Dijon	Divine
Djibouti	Plate
Dnieper	Far River
Dodecanese	Twelve Islands
Dominica	Lord's Day
Donegal	Fort of Foreigners
Drakensberg	Dragon Mountain
Druk Yul (see Bhutan)	Land of the Dragon
Dublin	Black Pool
Dubrovnik	Oak Forest
Dumbarton	Fort of the Britons
Dunkirk	Dune Church
Dunsinane	Hill of the Teat
Dushanbe	Monday
Egypt	Temple of Soul Ptah
Eindhoven	End Property
Ephesus	Overseer
Eritrea	Red
Ethiopia	Burnt Appearance
Faeroes	Islands of Sheep
Fair Isle	Islands of Sheep
Formosa	Beautiful
Franche-Comté	Free County
Fray Bentos	Brother Benedict
Galapagos	Giant Tortoise
Gallipoli	Beautiful Town
Galway	Stony
Gangtok	Hill Summit
Geelong	Marshy Place
Gelderland	Yellow Mountain
Georgia	Fertile Earth/Tilled Land
Ghent	Confluence
Gibraltar	Mountain of Tariq
Grasse	Fat
Graubunden	Grey League
Graz	Small Fort
Greece	Venerable
Gretna	Gravel Hill
Groningen	Green
Grozny	Awesome
Guadalajara	River of Stones
Guadalupe	River Wolf
Guatemala	Land of the Eagle
Haarlem	Height Silt
Haiphong	Sea Room
Haiti	Mountain Land/Nest
Hanoi	Inside the River
Hanover	High Bank
Harbin	Place Where Fish is Dried
Harfleur	High Estuary
Harlech	Beautiful Rock
Harz	Forest
Hawaii	Place of the Gods

Name	Meaning
Hebron	To Unite
Hekla	Cloak
Hokkaido	North Sea Province
Holm	Island
Honshu	Main District
Huang Hai	Yellow Sea
Huang Ho	Yellow River
Hunan	South of the Lake
Hyderabad	Lion Town
Ibadan	Worship
Ibiza	Island of Perfumes
Inchon	Virtue River
Iona	Yew Tree
Irian Jaya	Cloud-Covered Victory
Jaffa	Beautiful
Japan	Sun Origin
Jericho	Moon Month
Johore	To Tie
Kanchenjunga	Five Treasures of the Snow
Kara Kum	Black Sands
Katmandu	Wooden Temples
Kattegat	Boat Way
Kawasaki	River Cape
Kazan	Cauldron
Khartoum	End of Elephant's Trunk
Kildare	Church of the Oak
Kilimanjaro	Mountain of the God of Cold
Killarney	Church of the Sloes
Kobe	House of God
Koblenz	Confluence
Kosovo	Blackbird
Kronstadt	Crown City
Krung Thep (see Bangkok)	City of Angels
Kuala Lumpur	Mouth of the Muddy River
Kyushu	Nine Provinces
Kyzyl Kum	Red Sand
Labrador	Labourer
Lagos	Lakes
Las Vegas	Meadows
Latakia	People Ruler
Lebanon	White
Leipzig	Lime Tree
Leitrim	Grey Ridge
Lesbos	Wooded
Levant	Rising
Lhasa	City of the Gods
Liepaja	Lime Tree
Limburg	Lime-Tree Fortress
Limerick	Bare Area of Ground
Limoges	Elm-Tree Village
Limpopo	Crocodile River
Linkoping	Flax Market
Linz	Lime Tree
Lisburn	Fort of the Gamblers
Lodz	Boat
Lofoten	Fox Foot
Lombardy	Long Beards/Axes
Longjumeau	New Market
Los Angeles	City of Angels
Luanda	Tax
Luxembourg	Little Fort
Machu Picchu	Old Man Peak
Malaga	Queen
Malmo	Mineral Island
Managua	Rain Spirit
Manama	Place of Rest/Dreams
Mandalay	Circle
Marathan	Fennel
Marianske Lazne	Mary's Springs
Marmara	Marble
Marrakesh	Fortified
Massachusetts	People of the Big Hill
Mato Grosso	Dense Forest
Matsuyama	Pine Mountain
Mayo	Plain of the Yew Tree
Meath	Middle
Mecca	Ruined/Sanctuary
Mechelen	Meeting Place
Medina	The City
Melanesia	Black Islands
Memphis	His Beauty
Mesopotamia	Between the Rivers
Monaghan	Little Thickets
Monte Carlo	Charles's Mountain
Montenegro	Black Mountain

Name	*Meaning*
Montreal	Royal Mountain
Morocco	Far West
Munich	Monk
Munster	Monastery
Muscat	Hidden
Myanmar	The Strong
Nairobi	Marsh
Nanking	Southern Capital
Narvik	Narrow Bay
Natal	Christmas
N'Djamena	Resting Place
Negev	South
Nepal	Fly Down
Netherlands	Lower Land
Neuchâtel	New Castle
Neustria	New Western Kingdom
Nevada	Snowy
New York (named after)	Future James II
Newry	Yew Tree
Nicosia	Victory
Nijmegen	New Market
Nîmes	Sanctuary
Norrkoping	Northern Trading Place
Nova Scotia	New Scotland
Nullarbor	No Trees
Oahu	Place of Assembly
Omaha	Those Who Live Upstream on the River
Omsk	Calm
Orinoco	Place of Paddling
Oruro	Black and White
Osnabrück	Current Bridge
Pacific	Calm
Padua	Pine
Pagalu	Father Cockerel
Pakistan	Land of the Pure
Palermo	Safe Anchorage
Palestine	Land of the Philistines
Pamplona	Pompey's City
Panmunjom	Floor Gate Shop
Papeete	Water Basket
Pemba	Green Island
Peshawar	Frontier Town
Petra	Rock
Philadelphia	Brotherly Love
Philippines (named after)	Philip II of Spain
Phnom Penh	Mountain of Plenty
Picardy	Pike
Piedmont	Foot of the Mountain
Plovdiv	Philip's Town
Po	Pines
Pomerania	By the Sea
Pompeii	Five
Pont-L'Évêque	Bishop's Bridge
Popocatepetl	Smoking Mountain
Port Louis (named after)	Louis XV of France
Portugal	Warm Harbour
Potomac	Where Goods are Brought in
Potsdam (Germany)	Under the Oaks
Prague	Threshold
Praia	Beach
Prince Edward Isle	Father of Queen Victoria (named after)
Puerto Rico	Rich Harbour
Punjab	Five Waters
Punta Arenas	Sandy Point
Pusan	Pot Mountain
Pyongyang	Flat Land
Quebec	Place Where Waters Narrow
Quemoy	Golden Gate
Rajasthan	Land of Kings
Reykjavik	Bay of Smoke
Rio de Janeiro	River of January
Rio Muni	Silent River
Riyadh	Gardens
Robben Island	Seal Island
Roncesvalles	Bramble Valley

Name	*Meaning*
Roquefort	Strong Rock
Roscoff	Hill of the Blacksmith
Roubaix	Horse Stream
Rub-al-Khali	Empty Quarter
Ryukyu	Ball of Precious Stones
'sHertogenbosch	Duke's Wood
Sahara	Desert
Sakhalin	Black River
Samos	Dune
Santo Domingo	Holy Sunday
Sapporo	Pavillion of Banknotes
Saratov	Yellow Mountain
Sarayevo	Palace
Saskatchewan	Rapid Flowing River
Saskatoon	Fruit of Tree of Many Branches
Schaffhausen	Sheep House
Shaba	Copper
Shikoku	Four Provinces
Shiraz	Good Grape
Sichuan	Four Rivers
Sierra Leone	Lion Mountains
Sierra Madre	Mother Range
Sierra Nevada	Snowy Mountains
Sikkim	Summit
Singapore	Lion House
Smolensk	Tar
Society Islands (after)	Royal Society
Solferino	Sulphur
Soweto (acronym)	South Western Townships
Sporades	Disseminated
Sri Lanka	Island of the Blessed
Srinagar	City of Happiness
Stromboli	Round
Stuttgart	Mares Garden
Sudan	Land of the Blacks
Sulawesi	Spear Iron
Surabaya	Hero Danger
Tabor	Navel
Taipei	Northern Taiwan
Taiwan	Terrace Bay
Tegucigalpa	Silver Mountain
Tehran	Level
Tel Aviv	Hill Spring
Temirtau	Mountain of Iron
Teplice	Warm
Texas	Friends
Thailand	Free People
Tigris	Arrow
Timor	East
Tiruchchirappalli	Town of the Sacred Rock
Tokyo	Eastern Capital
Topeka	A Good Place to Dig Potatoes
Transylvania	Beyond the Forest
Trieste	Trade Market
Trinidad	Trinity
Tripoli	Three Towns
Tsushima	Pair of Horses
Turku	Market Place
Tuscany (named after)	Etruscans
Tuvalu	Eight Standing Together
Tyre	Stone
Ukraine	Border Country
Ulan Bator	Town of the Red Hero
Ulm	Marsh
Utah	Mountain Men
Uttar Pradesh	North State
Xinjiang	New Frontier
Yucatan	Massacre
Zagreb	Beyond the Bank
Zamora	Emerald
Zanzibar	Black Coast
Zermatt	At the Pasture
Zhengzhou	Solemn Region
Zimbabwe	House of Stones

Places: Alternative Names

Aachen	Aix-La-Chapelle
Almaty	Alma-Ata
Banaba	Ocean Island
Bangkok	Krung Thep
Bavaria	Bayern
Belarus	Belorussia
Belfast	Athens of Ireland
Bermuda	Somers Islands
Bhutan	Druk Yul
Bioko	Fernando Po
Bogotá	Santa Fé de Bogotá
Boston	Athens of the New World
Bulgaria	Narodna Republic
Burma	Myanmar

Cairo	Al-Qãhirah
China	Cathay
Christiansted	Bassin
Cordoba	Athens of the West
Croagh Patrick, Mt	Reek
East Timor	Timor-Leste
Edinburgh	Athens of the North
Egypt	Misr
Florence	Firenze
Gambier Islands	Mangareva Islands
Godthaab	Nuuk
Golgotha	Calvary
Gravelly Hill Interchange	Spaghetti Junction
Grenada	Isle of Spice
Istanbul	Stamboul
Japan	Nihon – Nippon
K2	Godwin Austen
Korea	Choson
Lake Constance	Bodensee
Lake Geneva	Lac Léman
Lake Gennesaret	Sea of Galilee
Lake Tiberias	Sea of Galilee
Le Havre	Newhaven
Lhasa	Forbidden City
Liberec	Reichenburg
Lindisfarne	Holy Island
Livorno	Leghorn
London	The Smoke
Lushun	Port Arthur
Macao	Aomin
Munich	München
New Orleans	The Big Easy
New York	The Big Apple
New Zealand	Pig Island
Niue	Savage Island
Osaka	Venice of Japan
Peking	Beijing – Celestial City
Persian Gulf	Arabian Gulf
Regensburg	Ratisbon
Rio Grande	Rio Bravo
Rome	Eternal City
Sousse	Susa
Sweden	Sverige
Switzerland	Confederation of Helvetia
Sydney	The Big Smoke
Thessaloníki	Salonika
Turin	Torino
Victoria (Mt)	Tomaniivi (Fiji)

Places: Former Names

Albany (NY)	Fort Orange
Almaty	Zailiyskoye (1854–55), Verny (1855–1921)
Alvernia (Mt)	Como Hill (Bahamas)
Annapolis	Providence, Town of Proctor's, Town at the Severn, Anne Arundel Town
Astana	Akmola
Bangladesh	East Bengal (until 1947), East Pakistan (1947-70)
Belize	British Honduras (until 1973)
Benin	Dahomey (until 1975)
Bermuda	Somers Islands
Bioko	Macias Nguema Biyogo (1973–79)
Black Sea	The Euxine
Bodrum	Halicarnassus
Bolivia	Upper Peru
Botswana	Bechuanaland (until 1966)
Bujumbura	Usumbura
Burkina Faso	Upper Volta (until 1984)
Burundi	Urundi
Cambodia	Kampuchea, Khmer Empire
Canada	New France
Cape Horn	Elizabetha
Central African Republic	Ubanghi Shari
Congo, Dem	Zaïre, Belgian Congo, Congo
Dardanelles	Hellespont
Djakarta	Sunda Kelapa
Djibouti	French Somaliland
Donetsk	Stalino
Duarte (Mt)	Trujillo (Dominican Republic)
Dunaujváros	Sztalinvaros (Hungary)
Dushanbe	Stalinabad
East Timor	Portuguese Timor
Edirne	Adrianople
Equatorial Guinea	Spanish Guinea
Ethiopia	Abyssinia
Frunze	Pishpek
Ghana	Gold Coast
Grenada	Conception
Guinea	French Guinea
Guinea-Bissau	Portuguese Guinea
Guyana	British Guiana
Harare	Salisbury
Hawaii	Sandwich Islands
Ho Chi Minh City	Saigon
Indonesia	Dutch East Indies
Iran	Persia
Iraq	Mesopotamia
Istanbul	Constantinople, Byzantium
Izmir	Smyrna
Iznik	Niacaea
Jordan	Transjordan
Kathmandu	Manju-Patan
Katowice	Stalinogrod
Kinshasa	Léopoldville (until 1966)
Kiribati	Gilbert Islands
Klagenfurt	Chlagenvurt
Klondyke	River of Fish
Kota Kinabalu	Jesselton
Kyrgyzstan	Khirgizia
Ladoga	Neva
Ladysmith	Windsor
Lahore	Lava
Lahti	Bay (Finland)
Le Mans	Cenomannis
Le Puy	Podium
Leningrad	St Petersburg (1703–1914 and 1991 to present), Petrograd (1914–24)
Lesotho	Basutoland
Malawi	Nyasaland
Mali	French Sudan
Maputo	Lourenço Marques
Marianske Lazne	Marienbad
Mariupol	Zhdanov
Marseille	Ville-sans-Nom
Mauritius	Île de France
Micronesia	Caroline Islands
Moldova	Moldavia, Bessarabia
Mongolian People's Republic	Outer Mongolia
Montreal	Ville Marie
Myanmar	Burma
Namibia	South West Africa
N'Djamena	Fort-Lamy
New Britain	Neu-Pommern
New York	New Amsterdam (1625–64)
Novokuznetsk	Stalinsk
Novomoskovsk	Stalinogorsk
Nuuk	Godthaab
Olympia	Smithfield
Oman	Muscat and Oman
Oslo	Kristiania
Ottawa	Bytown
Palm Beach	Palm City
Palm Springs	Agua Caliente
Palmyra	Tadmor
Pittsburgh	Fort Duquesne
Podgorica	Titograd (1946-92)
Prince Edward Island	Île Saint-Jean
Princeton	Stony Brook
Puerto Rico	San Juan (Puerto Rico was then capital)
Réunion	Île Bonaparte; Île Bourbon; Île Mascareigne
Richmond (Eng)	Sheen
Seychelles	Seven Sisters
Shaba	Katanga
Shenyang	Mukden
Sofia	Serdica
Sousse	Hadrumetum
Sparta	Lacedaemonia
Sri Lanka	Ceylon, Serendip
Stepanakert	Khankendy
Suriname	Dutch Guiana
Tahiti	King George III Island, Nouvelle-Cythère
Taiwan	Formosa
Tanzania	Tanganyika
Tasmania	Van Diemen's Land

Thailand	Siam
Tiruchchirappalli	Trichinopoly
Tokyo	Edo
Tomanivi	Victoria (mountain in Fiji)
Toronto	York
Troy	Ilium
Tuvalu	Ellice Islands
Ubangi-Shari	French Equatorial Africa
Ulyanovsk	Simbirsk
Uskudar	Scutari
United Arab Emirates	Trucial States
Vanuatu	New Hebrides
Volgograd	Tsaritsyn (1589–1925) Stalingrad (1925–61)
Western Sahara	Spanish Sahara
Yangon	Rangoon
Yemen	Aden
Zambia	Northern Rhodesia
Zanzibar	Shirazi
Zimbabwe	Southern Rhodesia (1911–64) Rhodesia (1964–79) Zimbabwe Rhodesia (1979–80)

Rivers: World's Longest

		Source	*Length (miles)*	*Course and Outflow*
1	Nile	Kagera River, Burundi	4,145	Tanzania/Uganda/South Sudan/Sudan/Egypt to eastern Mediterranean.
2	Amazon	Apurimac River, Peru	4,007	Colombia to Brazil to South Atlantic (Canal do Sul).
3	Mississippi-Missouri	Jefferson (Red Rock) River, Montana	3,710	N and S Dakota/Nebraska/Iowa/Missouri/ Kansas/Illinois/Kentucky/Tennessee/ Arkansas/Mississippi/Louisiana to Gulf of Mexico. Although the Missouri is a tributary of the Mississippi, it is also an extension via Lake Itasca (see individual entries), so the system is made up of the total length of the Missouri and 1,395 miles of the Mississippi.
4	Yenisey	Selenga River, Mongolia	3,442	Flows due north through central Russia to the Kara Sea.
5	Yangtze	Kunlun Mts, China	3,436	Flows in easterly course across China to the East China Sea near Shanghai.
6	Yellow River	Qinghai, China	3,395	Flows north of Yangtze in easterly course to the Yellow Sea. Aka Huang Ho
7	Ob'-Irtysh	Altai Mts, Russia	3,361	Northern course touching Kazakhstan and through Russia to Kara Sea.
8	Paraná	Paranáiba and Grande confluence, Brazil	3,032	Flows south via Paraguay border and Argentina into confluence with River Uruguay to the Rio de la Plata (River Plate) estuary in the South Atlantic near Buenos Aires. The system is aka Rio de la Plata-Paraná.
9	Zaïre (Congo)	Chambeshi River, Zambia	2,920	Called Lualaba Dem Rep of Congo. Runs along border into Atlantic at Angola.
10	Amur-Argun	China	2,782	See individual entries of the 2 rivers.
11	Lena	Kirenga River, Siberia	2,734	Russia and northward to Laptev Sea in the Arctic Ocean.
12	Mackenzie-Peace	Finlay/Parsnip confluence, BC	2,635	Flows east to Alberta then north via NWT to Beaufort Sea. The system is linked by the Slave River between Lake Athabasca and the Great Slave Lake.
13	Mekong	Lants'ang, Tibet	2,600	China/Burma/Laos/Thailand/Cambodia/Vietnam to South China Sea.
14	Niger	Loma Mts, Guinea	2,590	Flows through Mali, Niger and along Benin border into Nigeria before discharging into the Gulf of Guinea in the Atlantic.
15	Murray-Darling	New England Plateau, NSW/Queensland	2,330	See individual entries of the 2 rivers.
16	Zambesi	Kalene Hill, Zambia	2,200	Flows south across Angola and western Zambia, then north-eastward forming the border between Zambia and Zimbabwe, and finally south-eastward across Mozambique to its delta on the Indian Ocean.
17	Volga	Valdai Hills, nr Moscow	2,193	Flows generally south-eastward to discharge into the Caspian Sea in Russia. The Volga is considered the longest river in Europe as the longer Russian rivers flow east of the Urals which are considered the boundary into Asia.
18	Madeira	Mamoré and Beni Rivers, Bolivia	2,082	Joins Amazon 90 miles east of Manaus - the 2nd longest tributary in the world.
19	Jurua	Puerto Portillo, Peru	2,040	Flows east and north into Brazil before joining the Amazon south of Fonte Boa.
20	Purus	Loreto Department, Peru	1,995	Flows northeast to Brazil; joins Amazon near Manaus (Solimões River).

NB: A usual definition of a river might be 'a freshwater channelled body of water that flows from its source into another river, a lake, the sea, or an inland desert', in which case the Missouri and Mississippi Rivers would make the above listing as separate entries. However, the table above includes the system as a whole and both the rivers are dealt with individually below. The alphabetic listing is for ease of reference, as in many of the sections, but is in no way an attempt to be fully comprehensive; it is merely a useful gazetteer of some interesting rivers.

Rivers: Other Notable

	Source	*Length (miles)*	*Course and Outflow*
Achelous (Akhelóös)	Pindus Mountains	140	Divides Aetolia from Acarnania and discharges into the Ionian Sea.
Amu Darya (Oxus)	Eastern Pamirs	1,578	Follows Afghanistan/Tajikistan border and then Turkmenistan/Uzbekistan border before discharging into the Aral Sea. The source of the Amu Darya is often thought to be the confluence of the Vakhsh and Pyandzh rivers but in fact its longest headstream is the Daryā-ye Vākhjir in the Eastern Pamirs.
Amur	Russia/China	1,755	Tatar Strait of the Pacific Ocean.
Argun	Khingan range, China	1,007	Joins Amur at the confluence of the Shilka.
Arkansas	Sawatch range of Rockies	1,459	Flows southeast to Mississippi at Arkansas City via Kansas and Oklahoma.
Arno	Monte Falterona, Tuscan Apennines	150	Flows west via Florence & Pisa to the Ligurian Sea area of the Mediterranean.
Athabasca	Columbia Icefield, Canadian Rockies	765	Forms the southernmost part of the Mackenzie River system in northern Alberta and discharges into Lake Athabasca.
Avon	Devizes, Wiltshire	48	Aka Hampshire Avon or East Avon, flows generally south via Salisbury to the English Channel at Christchurch Harbour.
Avon (Lower)	Cotswolds	75	Aka Bristol Avon, flows through Gloucester, Wiltshire, & Avon before entering Bristol Channel via Severn estuary, at Avonmouth, the ocean port of Bristol.
Avon (Upper)	Naseby, Leicester/Northants border	96	Aka Warwickshire Avon, flows southwest via Northants, Leics, Warwickshire, and Hereford & Worcs before joining the Severn at Tewkesbury, Gloucs.
Axe	Beaminster, Dorset	24	Flows west to form boundary between Dorset and Somerset before reaching Axminster in Devon and entering the English Channel south of Axmouth.

Bann	Co Down, NI	76	Longest river of Northern Ireland; flows into the Atlantic Ocean.
Black	Yunnan Province, China	498	Flows southeast into Vietnam parallel to Red River, which it joins near Hanoi.
Black	Ozark Mountains, Missouri	280	Flows south-eastward to Poplar Bluff, Missouri, and then flows south-west before entering the White River near Newport, Arkansas.
Black Volta (Mouhoun)	Bobo Dioulasso, Burkina Faso	720	Flows along the border of Burkina Faso and Côte D'Ivoire with Ghana before discharging into Lake Volta in northern Ghana.
Boyne	Bog of Allen, Co Kildare	70	Flows north-east to enter the Irish Sea just south of Drogheda.
Brahmaputra	Tibetan Himalayas	1,800	Confluence with the Ganges as the Jamuna and into the Bay of Bengal in Bangladesh.
Bug	Western Ukraine	516	Flows into Poland via Brest in Belarus and discharges into the Vistula just south of Warsaw.
Camel	Davidstow, Cornwall	30	Generally flows northward into the Celtic Sea at Padstow.
Cher	North-west Massif Central, France	217	Flows north across the Combrailles Plateau, eventually reaching the Loire at Cinq-Mars-la-Pile.
Cimarron	Capulin Mt Monument, New Mexico	698	Flows east past Black Mesa peak in Oklahoma and into Kansas via Colorado before re-entering Oklahoma and discharging into Arkansas River near Tulsa.
Clyde	Lowther Hills, Strathclyde	98	Flows north-westerly into the Firth of Clyde.
Colorado	Rockies, Colorado	1,450	Flows south-west to the Gulf of California.
Colorado	Grande and Barrancas confluence	530	Flows south-eastward across Patagonia and into the Atlantic Ocean south of Bahia Blanca.
Columbia	Rockies, British Columbia	1,243	Flows south through central Washington to the Oregon border and then due west before discharging into the Pacific Ocean.
Danube	Black Forest, Germany	1,775	Flows through Germany, Austria, Slovakia, Hungary, Croatia, Serbia, Bulgaria, Romania, Moldova, and into the Black Sea in the Ukraine.
Darling	New England Plateau, NSW Queensland	1,702	Follows the NSW/Queensland border into NSW to join the Murray at Wentworth on the Victoria border. Longest river of Australia.
Dee	Cairngorms	87	Famous for its salmon, the Dee flows east to the North Sea at Aberdeen. The 17-mile stretch between Braemar and Ballater is known as 'Royal Deeside' because Balmoral Castle is a popular holiday retreat of the Royal Family.
Dee	Snowdonia National Park	70	Flows via Lake Bala and then north-east to Corwen and eastward past Llangollen before travelling north to Chester and out to the Irish Sea at Flint.
Dee	Dumfries and Galloway	50	Flows south and enters the Solway Firth at Kircudbright.
Delaware	Schoharie County, New York	405	Flows along the New York/ Pennsylvania, New Jersey/ Pennsylvania, and Delaware/ New Jersey borders before discharging into Delaware Bay.
Demerara	Central Guyana	215	Flows northward to the Atlantic Ocean at Georgetown.
Derwent	Tasmania	107	Flows south-east to the Tasman Sea.
Derwent	Peak District	60	Flows south-east through Derby to the River Trent.
Derwent	Fylingdales Moor	57	Flows south joining the Ouse just west of the Humber estuary.
Derwent	Borrowdale Fells, Cumbria	34	Flows north and west to the Irish Sea.
Dnestr	Carpathian Mountains	877	Flows south from Ukraine into Moldova before emptying into the Black Sea.
Dnieper (Dnepr)	Valdai Hills, Smolensk	1,367	Flows through Russia, Belarus and the Ukraine into the Black Sea.
Don	Novomoskovsk, Russia	1,224	Flows south and discharges into the Gulf of Taganrog in the Sea of Azov.
Don	Grampians	78	Flows south-eastward into the North Sea at the Bridge of Don.
Douro	Sierra de Urbión, Spain	556	Flows across Spain and northern Portugal to Atlantic Ocean at Foz do Douro.
Dunajec	Tatra Mountains, Slovak/Polish border	156	Flows north-east across Poland into the Vistula.
Ebro	Fontibre, Cantabrian Mts	565	Longest river in Spain. Flows in a south-easterly direction via Zaragosa and into the Balearic Sea area of the Mediterranean.
Eden	Lake District Fells	90	Flows north-westward to the Irish Sea at the Solway Firth inlet.
Elbe	Czech/Polish border	724	Flows west through Czech Republic (where it is known as the Labe) then north westerly east of Prague through Germany to discharge into the North Sea.
Euphrates	South-west Turkey	1,700	Flows in south-easterly direction through Syria and Iraq to the Persian Gulf.
Exe	The Chains, Somerset	60	Flows south across Devon and into the English Channel at Exmouth.
Forth	Ben Lomond	65	Flows eastward into the Firth of Forth, near Kincardine.
Frome	Evershot, Dorset	40	Flows eastward into Poole Harbour at Wareham.
Gambia	Guinea Republic	700	Flows westwards via the Gambia into the Atlantic Ocean.
Ganges	Indian Himalayas	1,553	Confluence with the Brahmaputra as the Jamuna and into the Bay of Bengal in Bangladesh.
Garonne	Spanish Pyrenees	357	Flows north-east to Toulouse then north-west to the Bay of Biscay via the Gironde estuary.
Great Ouse	Brackley, Northants	150	Flows through Buckinghamshire, Bedfordshire and Cambridgeshire before discharging into the North Sea at the Wash.
Hudson	Lake Tear of Clouds, New York State	315	Flows south-eastward to Corinth in Saratoga County and then north-eastwards to Hudson Falls before travelling south to New York Bay.
Hunter	Mt Royal Range, New South Wales	287	Flows south-west through Glenbawn Reservoir before entering the Tasman Sea at Newcastle.
Iguaçu	Serra do Mar, Brazil	808	Flows west to join the Paraná at border of Argentina, Brazil and Paraguay.
Indus	Tibet	1,790	Runs through Pakistan north to south and discharges into the Arabian Sea.
Irrawaddy	Northern Myanmar	1,337	Flows south through Mandalay and west of Yangon into the Andaman Sea.
Isar	Karwendelgebirge, Innsbruck, Austria	183	Flows into Germany at Scharnitz Pass then after travelling through Munich enters the Danube.
James	Jackson and Cowpasture confluence, Virginia	340	Flows in an easterly direction, crossing the Blue Ridge Mountains near Lynchburg and continuing past Richmond into the southern end of Chesapeake Bay at the Hampton Roads.
Jordan	Mount Hermon, Syria	223	Lowest river in the world, flows south across Israel and into Jordan before draining into the Dead Sea. The distance between the Sea of Galilee and the Dead Sea is approximately 100 miles and yet the Jordan's length is double that distance due to its meandering course. The Jordan became the cease-fire line during the Israeli–Jordanian hostilities.
Jumna (Yamuna)	Jamnotri, Himalayas	855	Flows from Uttar Pradesh along the border with Haryãna and then via Delhi to the Agra Canal before joining the Ganges at its most sacred point.
Liffey	Wicklow Mountains	50	Flows through Co Wicklow, Kildare and Dublin before entering the Irish Sea at Dublin Bay.
Limpopo	Witwatersrand, South Africa	1,100	Rises as the Crocodile River and flows in an arc first north-east and then east, forming the border between Transvaal and Botswana and then Transvaal and Zimbabwe before veering south-east into Mozambique and into the Indian Ocean north of Maputo. It becomes the Limpopo at the Crocodile's confluence

			with the Marico on the Transvaal/Botswana border.
Loire	Southern Massif Central	634	Longest river in France. Flows north and west towards the Brittany peninsula, where it discharges into the Bay of Biscay in the Atlantic Ocean.
Mackenzie	Great Slave Lake, Canada	1,060	Flows through the North West Territory and into Beaufort Sea in Arctic Ocean.
Magdalena	Colombian Andes	930	Flows northward to the Caribbean Sea.
Manzanares	El Pardo Reservoir, Madrid	42	Minor river that discharges into a canal system south of Madrid, it is notable only for being the river on which Madrid stands (at over 2,100 ft the highest capital of Europe).
Marañón	Peruvian Andes	879	Flows northwest from northeast Peru before receiving the Huallaga River and combining with the Ucayali River, to form the Amazon.
Marne	Langres, Plateau de Langres, France	326	Flows north-northwest past Chaumont and Saint- Dizier, then turns west-northwest to Epernay before veering south of Paris and discharging into the Seine at Charenton.
Medina	St Catherine's Downs	13	Flows from the south of the Isle of Wight to its northern outflow into the Solent.
Medway	East Grinstead, West Sussex	70	Follows the Sussex/Kent boundary to Ashurst before turning north-east to the Thames at the Sheerness delta.
Merrimack	White Mts, New Hampshire	110	Flows south into Massachusetts before veering north to empty into Atlantic.
Mersey	Confluence of Goyt, Etherow, Tame	70	Flows eastward to the Irwell and the Manchester Ship Canal.
Meuse	Pouilly, Plateau de Langres, France	590	Flowing north through Belgium and the Netherlands to the North Sea.
Mississippi	Lake Itasca, Minnesota	2,348	Gulf of Mexico.
Missouri (Big Muddy)	Beaverhead Co, Montana	2,315	Joins Mississippi 10 miles north of St Louis; the longest tributary in the world.
Motagua	Chichicastenango	250	Longest river in Guatemala, flowing east-north-east into the Gulf of Honduras.
Murray	Snowy Mts, NSW	1,609	Flows along the boundary of NSW and Victoria, bends south at Morgan, South Australia, and discharges into the Indian Ocean at Encounter Bay in the Great Australian Bight.
Negro	Eastern Colombia	1,400	Major tributary of the Amazon that follows the Colombian/Venezuelan border and into Brazil to join the Amazon at the Solimões confluence.
Negro	Bagé, Brazil	500	Flows south-west into Uruguay before joining the Uruguay River at Soriano.
Negro	Chilean Andes	400	Flows south-eastward across northern Patagonia and discharges into the Atlantic Ocean south-east of Viedma and Carmen de Patagones.
Neisse (Nysa)	Sudeten Mountains	157	Forms part of the German/Polish frontier before joining the Oder River. There is another Neisse also rising in the Sudeten Mountains but totally in Poland.
Nene	Northants/Leics	102	Flows north-easterly via Peterborough to the North Sea in the Wash.
Oder	Oder Mountains, Czechoslovakia	531	Flows north-east then north when it picks up the Neisse and flows into the Baltic Sea.
Ohio	Allegheny and Monongahela, Pittsburgh	981	Flows north-west out of Pennsylvania then south- westward, forming boundaries between Ohio/Kentucky, Indiana/Kentucky, and Illinois/Kentucky before joining the Mississippi at Cairo, Illinois.
Omo	Ethiopian Highlands	290	Flows south across Ethiopia before emptying into Lake Rudolf on the Ethiopia/Sudan border.
Orange	Sinqu River, Lesotho	1,300	Flows west along the Orange Free State/Cape Province border through Upington and along the southern border of Namibia before discharging into the Atlantic Ocean at Alexander Bay.
Orinoco	Venezuela–Brazil border	1,700	Flows in a northern arc forming the boundary between Venezuela and Colombia before veering north-eastward across Venezuela and into the Atlantic Ocean near Trinidad.
Ouse	Swale and Ure Confluence	57	Flows south-east to the Humber estuary.
Parramatta	Sydney	15	Meaning 'plenty of eels'. Flows through Sydney and into Port Jackson on the Tasman Sea.
Patuca	Guayape and Guayambre confluence	200	Flows from north-eastern Honduras and crosses the Mosquito Coast before discharging into the Caribbean at Patuca Point.
Peace	Finlay River, BC, Canada	1,195	Slave River in Wood Buffalo National Park.
Pechora	Northern Urals	1,124	Flows south and then west and north across Russia before emptying into the Barents Sea.
Pecos	Mora County, New Mexico	735	Flows into Texas and empties into the Rio Grande at the Amistad National Recreation Area.
Piddle	Alton Pancras, Dorset	21	Aka the Trent, and flowing south-eastward to Poole Harbour.
Po	Monte Viso Mts, Cottian Alps	405	Longest river in Italy. Flows eastwards in its upper course then northward through Turin and finally eastward to its delta on the Gulf of Venice in the Adriatic area of the Mediterranean.
Potomac	Appalachian Mts, West Virginia	383	Forms boundary between Maryland and Virginia via Washington DC and into Chesapeake Bay.
Red River	New Mexican Plains	1,270	Flows south-eastward through Texas, Oklahoma and Louisiana and into the Gulf of Mexico via the Mississippi River near Baton Rouge.
Red River (Hong)	Yunnan Province, SW China	750	Principal river of northern Vietnam, flowing south-east across the Tonkin region through Hanoi before discharging into the Gulf of Tonkin.
Red Volta	NW of Ouagadougou, Burkina Faso	200	Flows south-south-east to join the White Volta near the Gambaga scarp, northern Ghana.
Rhine	Swiss Alps	865	Forms the boundary between Switzerland, Liechtenstein and Germany and then runs north, bordering France and Germany and finally north-westward towards the North Sea via the Netherlands.
Rhône	Swiss Alps	505	Flows into Lake Geneva and then through France, merging with the Saône at Lyons, before entering the Mediterranean west of Marseille in Golfe du Lion.
Ribble	Gayle and Cam confluence, Yorkshire	75	Flows south into Lancashire after rounding Whernside, at 2,419 ft the highest peak in the Yorkshire Dales National Park; on entering Preston it flows due west towards the Irish Sea near Lytham St Annes.
Rio Grande	Rockies, Colorado	1,885	Forms the boundary between Texas and Mexico before discharging into the Gulf of Mexico. The Rio Grande is known in Mexico as the Rio Bravo.
Salween	Eastern Tibet	1,500	Flows east and south through China and forms the border between Myanmar and Thailand before emptying into the Gulf of Martaban
São Francisco	Serra da Canastra, Minais Gerais, Brazil	1,811	Longest river totally in Brazil flows in a north- easterly direction to the Atlantic.
Sava	Triglav Mts, Slovenia	584	Flows south-east through Slovenia and Croatia and follows border of Bosnia & Herzegovina to discharge into the Danube at Belgrade.
Scheldt	Northern France	270	Flows north and north-east through western Belgium to Antwerp, then north-

			west to the North Sea in the Netherlands.
Seine	Langres Plateau, nr Dijon	485	Flows north-westerly through Paris before emptying into the English Channel near Le Havre.
Severn	Finger Lakes, Ontario	610	Flows north-east through Severn Lake to Hudson Bay.
Severn (Hafren)	Plynlimon, Northern Powys	220	Flows south via Shropshire, Worcestershire, Gloucestershire, and into Bristol Channel in the Atlantic Ocean. It is the longest river in Britain.
Shannon	Tiltinbane Mts, Co Cavan	240	Flows through Leitrim and boundaries of Roscommon, Longford, Westmeath, Offaly, Galway, Tipperary, Clare, Limerick, and discharges into the Atlantic Ocean at Loop Head, Co Clare.
Shenandoah	Virginia	370	Flows north to meet the Potomac at Harper's Ferry.
Spey	Corrieyairack Forest	107	Flows north-east across Highlands into the North Sea, east of the Moray Firth.
Spree	Lusatian Mts, Germany	250	Rising near the Czech/Polish border, the Spree flows north through Berlin and into the Havel River, a tributary of the Elbe, at Spandau.
St Lawrence	St Louis River, Minnesota	1,945	Gulf of St Lawrence in Quebec. (The St Lawrence proper is 760 miles in length as the remainder runs from its source via Great Lakes, except Lake Michigan.)
Stour	East Cambridgeshire	47	Flows eastward through East Anglia, forming most of the Suffolk/Essex boundary, and discharges into the North Sea at Harwich.
Stour (Dorset)	Stourhead, Wiltshire	51	Flows south-eastward through Blandford Forum and into the English Channel at Christchurch Harbour.
Stour (Great)	South of Ashford	40	Aka Kentish Stour, flows through the Weald, past Ashford to Canterbury and Sandwich and into the English Channel.
Suir	Devil's Bit Mountains	114	Flows south across Co Tipperary through Thurles before discharging into Waterford Harbour.
Susquehanna	Otsego Lake, New York State	444	Flows south through Pennsylvania and into Chesapeake Bay in Maryland.
Sutlej (Zaradros)	Lan-ka Ts'o, SW Tibet	900	Longest of the Punjab's 'Five Rivers', flowing into India and Pakistan, where it joins the Chenãb River, west of Bahãwalpur.
Swan	Corrigin, Western Australia	224	Rises as the Avon and flows through Perth to the Indian Ocean at Fremantle.
Syr Darya	Naryn and Karadarya confluence	1,374	The Syr Darya is 1,876 miles long including the 500 miles of the Naryn. On leaving the Fergana Valley the river flows north-west via Kyrgyzstan and into the Aral Sea at Kazakhstan.
Taff	Brecon Beacons	38	Flows southwards through Merthyr Tydfil, Pontypridd and finally Cardiff.
Tagus	Sierra de Albarracin, Spain	626	Flows west into Portugal before discharging into Atlantic Ocean near Lisbon.
Tamar	Woolley, Morwenstow	61	Flows south along the border between Devon and Cornwall and into the English Channel at Plymouth Sound.
Tay	Ben Lui, southern Grampians	117	Longest river in Scotland flows out to the Firth of Tay in the North Sea.
Tees	Cross Fell, Pennines	70	Flows eastwards defining the boundary of Cumbria and Durham then into Cleveland, passing via Stockton and Middlesbrough and into the North Sea.
Teifi	Strata Florida, Cambrian Mts	56	Famous for the many castle ruins along its banks, the Teifi flows south-west through Lampeter and Cenarth Falls, where salmon can be seen climbing the artificial ladder up the falls, before discharging into Cardigan Bay.
Test	Overton, nr Basingstoke, Hants	40	Famous trout river that flows southward into Southampton Water, the last 16 miles between Romsey and Southampton Water are famous for their salmon.
Thames	Cotswolds, Gloucs	215	Flows east into North Sea at Tilbury. Tributaries include the Churn, Coln, Mole, Windrush, Evenlode, Cherwell, Ock, Thame, Kennett, Loddon, Colne & Wey.
Tiber (Tevere)	Monte Fumaiolo, Apennines	252	Flows in a southerly direction through the city of Rome and into the Tyrrhenian Sea area of the Mediterranean near Ostia Antica.
Tigris	South-west Turkey	1,180	Flows south into Iraq, through Baghdad and joins Euphrates before discharging into the Persian Gulf between Iraq and Iran.
Towy (Tywi)	Rhandirmwyn, Cambrian Mts	65	The longest river wholly in Wales, although since the damming of its main headwater in 1972 to form Llyn Brianne Reservoir it is shorter than before.
Trent	Pennines, Staffordshire	170	Historically the boundary between north and south England, running south-east through the Potteries and Stoke-on-Trent, then north-east via Burton-on-Trent and Nottingham before entering the North Sea by the Humber estuary.
Tweed	Peebles	96	Flows easterly into the North Sea.
Tyne	Peel Fell, near Kielder, Northumberland	62	Flows east along the Northumberland/Co Durham border before discharging into the North Sea at the Tyne estuary in Tynemouth, near Newcastle.
Urubamba	Peruvian Andes	450	Flows northward to meet the Apurimac to become the Ucayali.
Uruguay	Southern Brazil	990	Flows west through Brazil and then south-west forming the Argentina/Brazil border before veering southward to form the Argentina/Uruguay border and discharging into the Rio de la Plata estuary at its confluence with the Paraná.
Usk	Black Mountain, Brecon Beacons	57	Flows generally south via Abergavenny and into the Bristol Channel at Newport.
Vistula (Wisła)	Beskidy Mts, Poland	664	Longest river of Poland, flows northwards via Kracow and Warsaw before entering the Baltic Sea on the Gulf of Gdansk; it is the longest river that empties into the Baltic Sea.
Vltava (Moldau)	South-west Bohemia	270	Longest river of the Czech Republic, flows north through Prague before discharging into the Elbe (Labe) at Melnik, just north of Prague.
Volta	Black and White Voltas	1,000	The extension of the Black and White Voltas through Lake Volta, discharging into the Gulf of Guinea in Ghana, near the Togo border.
Wear	Weardale, Co Durham	65	Flows south-east towards Bishop Auckland then north-east to Durham before discharging into the North Sea at Sunderland.
White Volta (Nakambe)	Ouagadougou, Burkina Faso	400	Flows generally southward into Lake Volta in northern Ghana.
Witham	Leicestershire	80	Flows through Lincoln and then south-east into the North Sea at the Wash.
Wye	Plynlimon, Northern Powys	130	Rises within 2 miles of the Severn and flows south-west into England at Hay before travelling through Hereford and back into Wales just south of Monmouth and finally through Tintern and Chepstow to discharge into the Bristol Channel at the Severn estuary.
Yare	Norfolk Broads	55	Flows through the middle of Broadland into Yarmouth and the North Sea; its tributary the Wensum flows through Norwich City.
Yarqon	Rosh ha-'Ayin	16	Flows westward north of Tel Aviv via the Plain of Sharon to the Mediterranean.
Yarra	Mt Matlock, Victoria	153	Flows west to Melbourne and discharges into Hobson's Bay, at the head of Port Phillip Bay.
Yellowstone	Yount Peak, Wyoming	671	Flows northeasterly via the Yellowstone National Park into Montana before joining the Missouri River on the border of Montana and North Dakota.
Yukon	Tagish Lake, Yukon-BC	1,875	Flows north into Alaska and discharges into the Bering Sea at Norton Sound.
Zaradros (Sutlej)	Lan-ka Ts'o, SW Tibet	900	Longest of the Punjab's 'Five Rivers', flowing into India and Pakistan where it joins the Chenãb River, west of Bahãwalpur.
Zeravshan	Eastern Turkestan Range	545	Flows west through Tajikistan and south-eastern Uzbekistan to Chardzhou.

Seas of the World

	Details	*Sq Miles*	*Ocean*
Adriatic	arm of the Mediterranean between Italy, Slovenia, Croatia, Montenegro, Albania, and Bosnia and Hercegovina	50,590	inland
Aegean	arm of the Mediterranean between Greece and Turkey; Crete is its southern boundary	83,000	inland
Andaman	bounded by Myanmar, Thailand, Malay Peninsula, Sumatra and the Andaman and Nicobar Islands	218,100	Indian
Arabian	bounded to the east by India, to the north by Pakistan and Iran and to the west by the Arabian Peninsula and the Horn of Africa	1,490,000	Indian
Arafura	situated between the north coast of Australia, the Gulf of Carpentaria and the south coast of New Guinea, it lies east of the Timor Sea, from which it is separated by the Torres Strait	250,000	Pacific
Azov	inland sea north of the Black Sea between Ukraine and Russia	15,000	inland
Baltic	bordered by Norway, Sweden, Denmark, Germany, Poland, Lithuania, Latvia, Estonia, Russia and Finland	147,500	Atlantic
Banda	bounded by the Moluccas and Lesser Sunda Islands	180,000	Pacific
Barents	formerly known as the Murmean Sea, bounded by the Russian and Norwegian mainlands to the south, Franz Josef Land to the north, the Norwegian and Greenland seas to the west, Spitsbergen to the north-west and the Novaya Zemlya archipelago to the east	542,000	Arctic
Beaufort	situated north of Alaska and Canada	184,000	Arctic
Bering	separates the Asian and North American continents and contains St Lawrence Island, St Matthew Island, Nunivak Island and the Pribilof Islands and the northern border of the Aleutians	875,750	Pacific
Bismarck	lies north of the Solomon Sea off the north-east coast of Papua New Guinea	15,000	Pacific
Black	inland sea lying between Turkey, Bulgaria, Romania, Moldova, Ukraine, Russia and Georgia	196,100	inland
Caribbean	deepest sea in the world, average depth about 8,0002 and maximum depth 30,2492	971,400	Atlantic
Celebes (Sulawesi)	bounded to the north by the Sulu Sea, to the east by the Sangi Islands, to the south by Celebes and to the west by Borneo	110,000	Pacific
Chukchi	situated north of the Bering Sea separating Alaska and Russia	225,000	Arctic
Coral	lies off the east coast of Australia north of the Tasman Sea	1,886,000	Pacific
East China	bounded by South Korea, Japan, Taiwan and China	256,600	Pacific
East Siberian	lying between the Laptev Sea and the Chukchi Sea	361,000	Arctic
English Channel	separates the southern coast of England from the northern coast of France; the French call the Channel 'La Manche' (the sleeve) and its minimum width of 21 miles lies between Dover and Calais	34,700	Atlantic
Flores	situated between the Lesser Sunda Islands to the south and Sulawesi (Celebes) Island to the north	93,000	Pacific
Greenland	borders Greenland to the west, Iceland and the Norwegian Sea to the south and the Arctic Ocean to the north	465,000	Arctic
Ionian	arm of the Mediterranean between Greece to the east, Sicily to the south-west and the Italian mainland to the west	49,500	inland
Irish	bounded by Scotland on the north, England on the east, Wales on the south and Ireland on the west	34,200	Atlantic
Japan	northern extension of the East China Sea, bounded by Japan and Sakhalin Island to the east and by Korea and Russia to the west	391,100	Pacific
Java	bounded by Borneo to the north and Java to the south	167,000	Pacific
Kara	situated off the northern coast of Russia between the Barents Sea and the Laptev Sea	340,000	Arctic
Laccadive	bordering the south-west coast of mainland India, Lakshadweep Islands and the Maldives	209,000	Indian
Laptev	until 1935 known as the Siberian Sea, lying between the Kara Sea and East Siberian Sea	276,000	Arctic
Ligurian	arm of the Mediterranean between the north-west coast of Italy and Corsica to the south	9,800	inland
Mediterranean	largest inland sea in the world, linked to the Atlantic in the west by the Strait of Gibraltar; it encompasses many named sea areas	966,500	inland
Molucca	merges with the Ceram Sea to the south-east and the Banda Sea to the south	77,000	Pacific
North	extends southward from the Norwegian Sea between Norway and the UK, connecting the Skagerrak with the English Channel	164,900	Atlantic
Norwegian	bordered by the Greenland and Barents seas, Norwegian mainland, Shetland and Faeroe islands, Icelandic mainland, Jan Mayen Island, North Sea and Atlantic Ocean	712,000	Atlantic
Okhotsk	bounded by the east Russian mainland, Japan and the Kuril Islands	537,500	Pacific
Philippine	lying east of the Philippines and Japan, its southern boundary includes the Caroline Islands, its western boundary includes Guam, and the northern boundary by the Volcano Islands to the north-east and Honshu to the north-west	400,000	Pacific
Red	inland sea extending from Suez in Egypt to the Strait of Bāb el-Mandeb in the south, it washes the shores of Egypt, Sudan, Eritrea, Ethiopia, Djibouti, Saudi Arabia and Yemen	174,900	inland
Savu	situated in the Lesser Sunda Islands between Timor and Sumba Islands	41,000	Pacific
Sea of Marmara (Propontis)	inland sea separating parts of Asian Turkey from European Turkey	4,429	inland
Solomon	lies north of the Coral Sea off the east coast of New Guinea	280,000	Pacific
South China	bounded by the Malay Peninsula, Taiwan, Philippines, Borneo, China and Vietnam	1,148,500	Pacific
Sulu	situated in the Philippine Islands north of the Celebes Sea	100,000	Pacific
Tasman	situated between the south-east coast of Australia and New Zealand	900,000	Pacific

Timor	lies south-west of the Arafura Sea off the north-west coast of Australia	235,000	Indian
Tyrrhenian	bounded by Sicily and the Italian mainland to the east and Corsica and Sardinia to the west	51,000	inland
White	lying south of the Barents Sea off the north-west coast of Russia	35,000	Arctic
Yellow	lying between the People's Republic of China to the north and west, and Korea to the east	113,500	Pacific
Zuiderzee (Southern Sea)	inlet of the North Sea washing the shores of the Netherlands	2,000	Atlantic

NB: The areas given for the above seas, as well as the following gulfs, straits and bays, are as produced by the latest world statistics, which are open to interpretation because it is not always clear at what point the waters merge. Most lists of seas only include those recognised by the International Hydrographic Bureau, and this is a controversial area as, although the reasoning is that seas not recognised are either parts of larger seas or oceans, in fact many of the seas that are recognised – e.g. the Caribbean – are also part of larger sea areas. Surely the Panama Canal links the Atlantic to the Pacific and not merely the Caribbean to the Pacific! The criterion used by the Bureau appears to be that a sea must be surrounded by large areas of land to enable it to be separately identifiable from the oceans but, apart from the inland seas noted above, all other seas are purely geographical markings. In order not to be too controversial I have given the best judgements possible of the areas usually considered as seas by cartographers in the list above, but have remained true to tradition when listing the seas by size elsewhere in this section. This will mean that although the South China Sea will be listed as the world's largest sea in the relevant section, this is inconsistent with the above table which shows the Coral Sea as the largest. If the question is asked, 'What is the largest sea in the world?' then the safe answer would be the South China Sea, which is part of the much larger Malay Sea, no longer recognised by the Bureau, but one has to be aware that large sea areas such as the Coral Sea and Arafura Sea are, rather ambiguously, classed as parts of oceans.

Seas: World's Largest

		Area (Sq Miles)
1	South China	1,148,500
2	Caribbean	971,400
3	Mediterranean	966,500
4	Bering	875,750
5	Gulf of Mexico	582,100
6	Okhotsk	537,500
7	Sea of Japan	391,100
8	Hudson Bay	281,900
9	East China	256,600
10	Andaman	218,100
11	Black	196,100
12	Red	174,900

NB: The Malay Sea, which embraced the South China Sea and the Strait of Malacca, is no longer recognised by the International Hydrographic Bureau. Similarly, many other large seas (e.g. the Coral and the Arafura) would normally be included in the list but are also not recognised by the Bureau.

Straits of the World

Bass	Named by English navigator Matthew Flinders after the surgeon-explorer George Bass, the strait is 180 miles in length with an area of 28,950 sq mi; it separates the Tasman Sea area of the Pacific from the Indian Ocean. Technically it is the Tasman Sea that separates Victoria from Tasmania, but the whole of the northern coast of Tasmania borders the waters of the Bass Strait.
Belle Isle	Links the Atlantic to the Gulf of St Lawrence between Newfoundland and Labrador; it is 90 miles long.
Bosporus	Links the Black Sea and the Sea of Marmara, and separates part of Asian Turkey from European Turkey. The strait is 19 miles in length. Aka Bosphorus
Cabot	A 60-mile-long channel linking the Gulf of St Lawrence to the Atlantic between Newfoundland and Nova Scotia.
Cook	Links the Tasman Sea to the South Pacific between North Island and South Island, New Zealand. The Cook Strait is 14 miles wide at its narrowest point.
Dardanelles	Formerly called the Hellespont, they are 38 miles long and link the Aegean Sea with the Sea of Marmara.
Davis	Links Baffin Bay and the Labrador Sea between Greenland and Baffin Island, part of the Northwest Passage linking the Atlantic to the Pacific, it is approximately 400 miles long and wide.
Denmark	Links the Greenland Sea to the North Atlantic between Greenland and Iceland. The British battleship Hood was sunk by the German battleship Bismarck in the strait on 24 May 1941.
Dover	Links the English Channel (Fr. La Manche) to the North Sea. Its width is approximately 20 miles. The French refer to this stretch of water as the Pas-de-Calais.
Florida	Links the Gulf of Mexico and the Atlantic between Florida and Cuba; it is 110 miles in length. The Spanish explorer Ponce de León was the first European to navigate the strait, in 1513.
Foveaux	Links the Tasman Sea to the South Pacific between South Island and Stewart Island, New Zealand.
Gibraltar	Links the Mediterranean Sea to the Atlantic Ocean. The western extreme is 27 miles wide between the capes of Trafalgar and Spartel and the eastern extreme is 14 miles wide between the Rock of Gibraltar (Pillars of Hercules) and Mount Hacho. The length of the strait is 36 miles and it is also known as Fretum Herculeum.
Hormuz	Links the Persian Gulf to the Gulf of Oman between Iran and the Arabian Peninsula.
Hudson	Links Hudson Bay and the Labrador Sea between Baffin Island and Quebec and is approximately 500 miles in length.
Johore	The northern arm of the Singapore Strait between Singapore Island and Johor State, Malaysia, it is 30 miles in length.
Kattegat	Links the Baltic to the North Sea (Skagerrak inlet) and separates Denmark and Sweden; it is 137 miles in length.
Magellan	Links the Atlantic and Pacific Oceans, between the mainland southern tip of South America and Tierra del Fuego. It is 350 miles in length.
Makassar	Links the Celebes Sea to the Java Sea between Borneo and Celebes; it stretches for approximately 500 miles.

Malacca	Links the Andaman Sea to the South China Sea between Sumatra and the Malay Peninsula; it is 500 miles in length and has an area of 25,000 sq miles.
Messina	Links the Tyrrhenian Sea and the Ionian Sea between Sicily and mainland Italy; it is 20 miles in length and ranges from 2 to 10 miles in width.
North Channel	Links the Irish Sea and the North Atlantic Ocean and washes the shores of Northern Ireland and Scotland. The minimum width of 13 miles lies between the Mull of Kintyre and Torr Head; it is 52 miles long.
Otranto	Links the Adriatic Sea and the Ionian Sea between Albania and Italy. Capo d'Otranto is the most easterly point in Italy and from that point the width of the strait is 40 miles.
St George's Channel	Links the Irish Sea to the Celtic Sea in the North Atlantic, its minimum width of 47 miles lies between Carnsore Point, near Rosslare, Ireland and St David's Head in Dyfed, Wales. It is 100 miles in length.
Singapore	Links the Strait of Malacca and the South China Sea between Singapore Island and the Riau Islands of Indonesia; it is 65 miles in length and 10 miles in width.
Taiwan (Formosa)	Links the South China Sea and the East China Sea between Fukien Province of China and Taiwan; its former name of Formosa means 'beautiful' in Portuguese.
Torres	Links the Coral Sea and the Arafura Sea between New Guinea to the north and Cape York Peninsula, Queensland, Australia, to the south. It is about 80 miles wide between these points. The many islands in the Torres Strait may be remnants of a land bridge that once linked Asia and Australia.
Yucatán Channel	Although not actually called a strait, it links the Gulf of Mexico and the Caribbean Sea between Cuba and Mexico, and is 135 miles in length.

Towns and Cities on Rivers

Aberdeen	Dee and Don
Adelaide	Torrens
Albuquerque	Rio Grande
Alexandria	Nile
Alloa	Forth
Amsterdam	Amstel
Anstruther	Forth
Antwerp	Scheldt
Astrakhan	Caspian Sea
Augusta	Savannah
Aviemore	Spey
Avignon	Rhône
Babylon	Euphrates
Baghdad	Tigris
Baku	Caspian Sea
Balmoral	Dee
Bamako, Mali	Niger
Bangkok	Chao Phraya
Bangui	Ubangi
Basel	Rhine
Basra	Shatt al Arab
Bath	Bristol Avon
Baton Rouge	Mississippi
Bedford	Great Ouse
Belfast	Lagan
Belgrade	Danube, Sava
Benares	Ganges
Berlin	Spree
Berne	Aare
Berwick	Tweed
Birkenhead	Mersey
Blandford Forum	Dorset Stour
Bonn	Rhine and Seig
Bootle	Mersey
Bordeaux	Garonne
Bowness	Forth
Bratislava	Danube
Brecon	Usk
Bremen	Weser
Brest, Belarus	Bug
Brighouse	Calder
Bristol	Bristol Avon
Brussels	Senne
Bucharest	Danube tributary: Dimbovita
Buckhaven	Forth
Buckingham	Ouse
Budapest	Danube
Buenos Aires	Rio de la Plata
Buffalo	Lake Erie
Cairo	Nile (Rosetta and Damietta)
Calcutta	Hoogly
Cambridge	Cam (aka Granta)
Canterbury	Stour
Cardiff	Taff
Carlisle	Eden
Carmarthen	Towy
Chester	Dee
Chicago	Lake Michigan
Chichester	Lavant
Chongqing	Yangzi
Cincinnati	Ohio
Cockermouth	Derwent and Cocker
Colchester	Colne
Coldstream	Tweed
Coleraine	Bann
Cologne	Rhine
Concord, NH	Merrimack
Cork	Lee
Cowes	Medina
Delft	Schie
Derby	Derwent
Derry	Foyle
Detroit	Lake St Clair
Dewsbury	Calder
Doncaster	Don
Dorchester	Frome
Dorking	Mole
Dresden	Elbe
Dublin	Liffey
Dumbarton	Clyde
Dumfries	Nith
Dundee	Tay
Dunoon	Clyde
Durham	Wear
Düsseldorf	Rhine
Edinburgh	Forth, Firth of
Ennis	Fergus
Enniskillen	Erne
Evesham	Warwickshire Avon
Exeter	Exe
Falmouth	Fa
Florence	Arno
Frankfurt am Main	Main
Frankfurt an der Oder	Oder
Fremantle	Swan
Geneva	Rhône
Geneva	Lake Geneva
Gillingham	Medway
Glasgow	Clyde
Gloucester	Severn
Godalming	Wey
Grantchester	Granta
Grantham	Witham
Gravesend	Thames
Greenock	Clyde
Grenoble	Isère
Grimsby	Humber
Guangzhou	Zhujiang
Guildford	Wey
Hamburg	Elbe
Hanoi	Song-Koi (Red)
Harrogate	Nidd
Harwich	Stour
Haverfordwest	Cleddau
Hawick	Teviot and Slitrig
Heidelberg	Neckar
Helensburgh	Clyde
Hereford	Wye
Hertford	Lea
Ho Chi-Minh City	Saigon
Hull	Humber
Huntingdon	Ouse
Hyderabad	Indus
Ilkley	Wharfe
Indianapolis	White
Inverness	Ness
Ipswich	Orwell
Jarrow	Tyne
Kathmandu	Vishnumati
Kelso	Tweed and Teviot
Khartoum	White and Blue Nile
Kidderminster	Stour
Kiev	Dnieper
Kilkenny	Nore
Kilmarnock	Irvine
King's Lynn	Great Ouse
Lahore	Ravi
Lancaster	Lune
Langholm	Esk
Le Havre	Seine
Leamington Spa	Warwickshire Avon
Leeds	Aire
Leicester	Soar
Leipzig	Pleisse, Parthe, Elster
Lima	Rimac
Limerick	Shannon
Limoges	Vienne
Lincoln	Witham
Linz	Danube
Lisbon	Tagus
Lisburn	Lagan
Littlehampton	Arun
Liverpool	Mersey
London	Thames
Loughborough	Soar
Louisville	Ohio
Luton	Lea
Lyons	Rhône and Saône
Madrid	Manzanares
Maidstone	Medway
Maldon	Blackwater
Mallow	Blackwater
Manchester	Irwell
Manchester, NH	Merrimack
Mandalay	Irrawaddy
Maputo	Delagoa Bay
Marlow	Thames
Melbourne	Yarra
Melrose	Tweed
Middlesbrough	Tees
Midhurst	Rother
Milan	Olono
Mold	Alyn
Montreal	St Lawrence and Ottawa
Morpeth	Wansbeck
Moscow	Moskva
Munich	Isar
Nantes	Loire
Nantwich	Weaver
Nashville	Cumberland
New Delhi	Jumna
New Orleans	Mississippi Gulf of Mexico
New York	Hudson
Newbury	Kennet
Newcastle	Tyne
Newport (Gwent)	Usk
Newport (I of W)	Medina

Niamey, Niger	Niger	**Rome**	Tiber	**Taunton**	Tone
Northampton	Nene	**Rotterdam**	Rhine, Maas, Scheldt	**Tewkesbury**	Severn, Warwickshire Avon
Norwich	Wensum	**Rugby**	Warwickshire Avon	**Thebes (Egypt)**	Nile
Nottingham	Trent	**Rye**	Rother	**Tidmarsh**	Pang
Nuneaton	Anker	**Salisbury**	Hampshire Avon and Wily	**Tintern Abbey**	Wye
Omdurman	Nile	**São Paulo**	Tiete	**Tipperary**	Ara
Oporto	Douro	**Seoul**	Han	**Tiverton**	Exe
Orléans	Loire	**Shanghai**	Hwangpu	**Tokyo**	Sumida and Tama
Oxford	Thames (Isis and Cherwell)	**Sheffield**	Don, and Sheaf	**Tonbridge**	Medway
Pangbourne	Thames	**Shoreham-by-Sea**	Adur	**Totnes**	Dart
Paris	Seine	**Shrewsbury**	Severn	**Turin**	Po
Patna	Ganges	**Sligo**	Garavogue	**Vienna**	Danube
Peebles	Tweed	**Southampton**	Test, and Itchen	**Wakefield**	Calder
Perth, Australia	Swan	**Southend-on-Sea**	Thames	**Wareham**	Frome
Perth, Scotland	Tay	**Spalding**	Welland	**Warsaw**	Vistula
Peterborough	Nene	**St Albans**	Ver	**Warwick**	Warwickshire Avon
Philadelphia	Delaware	**St Ives (Cambs)**	Ouse	**Washington DC**	Potomac
Phnom Penh	Mekong	**St Louis**	Mississippi	**Waterford**	Suir
Pisa	Arno	**St Petersburg**	Neva	**Whalley**	Calder
Pittsburgh	Ohio	**Stafford**	Sow	**Whitby**	Esk
Plock	Vistula	**Stoke**	Trent	**Wimborne**	Stour and Allen
Prague	Vltava	**Strabane**	Mourne	**Winchester**	Itchen
Preston	Ribble	**Strasbourg**	Ill	**Windsor**	Thames
Quebec	St Lawrence, St Charles	**Stratford**	Warwickshire Avon	**Worcester**	Severn
Reading	Thames and Kennet	**Stuttgart**	Neckar	**Wuhan**	Han and Yangzi
Richmond	Swale (Yorkshire)	**Sunderland**	Wear	**Yonkers**	Hudson
Richmond	James (Virginia)	**Swansea**	Tawe	**York**	Ouse
Ripon	Ure			**Zagreb**	Sava
Rochester	Medway			**Zurich**	Limmat

Trenches: Deepest

Trench	*Deepest Point*
Marianas Trench (Pacific)	Challenger Deep 35,840 ft
Puerto Rico Trench (Atlantic)	Milwaukee Deep 28,232 ft
Java Trench (Indian)	Planet Deep 23,376 ft
Eurasia Basin (Arctic)	Eurasia Basin 17,880 ft

Waterways

Aden Links the Red Sea to the Arabian Sea and borders Yemen to the north and Somalia to the south. The gulf is 920 miles in length and has an area of 205,000 sq miles.

Alaska Inlet of the North Pacific on the south coast of Alaska, and bordered by Kodiak Island to the west and Cape Spencer to the east, it has an area of 592,000 sq miles.

Alphonse XIII Canal Opened in 1926 and runs for 53 miles, linking Seville to the Atlantic via the Gulf of Cadiz.

Angel Falls Situated in the Guiana Highlands in Bolivar state, south-eastern Venezuela, on the Rio Churún, a tributary of the Caroni. At 3,212 ft the falls are the highest in the world.

Aqaba North-eastern arm of the Red Sea between Saudi Arabia and the Sinai Peninsula. The gulf is 100 miles in length.

Baffin Bay Inlet of the North Atlantic with an area of 266,000 sq miles, situated between Greenland and Baffin Island.

Bengal, Bay of Inlet of the Indian Ocean bordering India, Myanmar, Sri Lanka, and the Andaman and Nicobar Islands; it occupies an area of 839,000 sq miles.

Biscay, Bay of Inlet of the North Atlantic bordering northern Spain and south-west France; it has an area of 86,000 sq miles.

Biscayne Bay Inlet of the Atlantic in south-eastern Florida; it is 40 miles in length and between 2 and 10 miles in width.

Bothnia Northern arm of the Baltic between Sweden on the west and Finland on the east.

Boyoma Falls Formerly called the Stanley Falls; situated on the Lualaba River in the Democratic Republic of Congo, it has a drop of 200 ft and is the world's greatest waterfall by volume of water.

Bridgewater Canal Opened in 1761 and named after Francis Egerton, 3rd Duke of Bridgewater. The canal was built by James Brindley and originally ran for 10 miles, carrying barges over the Irwell at Barton; it was extended to Liverpool in 1776, joining the Mersey at Runcorn.

Bristol Channel Inlet of the Atlantic between South Wales and the English counties of Somerset, Devon and Cornwall.

Caledonian Canal Built by Thomas Telford in 1803–21 and opened in 1822, it has 29 locks and links the east and west coasts of Scotland via the lakes of the Great Glen.

California Aka Sea of Cortés and situated in northwestern Mexico, it is 750 miles in length and has an area of 62,000 sq miles.

Carpentaria Inlet of the Arafura Sea indenting the north-eastern coast of Australia. The gulf has an area of 120,000 sq miles.

Cauldron Snout Situated on the River Tees, Cumbria/Durham border, the highest waterfall in England (200 ft).

Churchill Falls Discovered in 1839 by John McLean and known as the Grand Falls until 1965, when they were renamed in honour of Winston Churchill. Situated on the Churchill River, in west Labrador, Newfoundland, the falls have a drop of 245 ft.

Corinth Inlet of the Ionian Sea separating the Peloponnese from mainland Greece.

Delagoa Bay Situated on the south-east coast of Mozambique, it is 19 miles in length and 16 miles wide.

Eas a' Chuàl Aluinn Situated in Sutherland in the Scottish Highlands in Glas Bheinn, the highest waterfall in the British Isles (658 ft).

False Bay Inlet of the Atlantic, south of Cape Town, South Africa.

Finland Eastern arm of the Baltic between Finland to the north, Estonia to the south, and Russia to the east.

Florida Bay Triangular-shaped body of water at the southern tip of mainland Florida stretching from Cape Sable in the west, Key Largo in the east and Long Key in the south.

Fundy, Bay of Inlet of the Atlantic between New Brunswick and Nova Scotia; it stretches for 94 miles.

Genoa Inlet of the Ligurian Sea stretching eastwards for 90 miles around the north-west coast of Italy from Imperia to La Spezia.

Grand Canal Waterway that splits the city of Venice from St Mark's Cathedral to Sta Chiara church; it is 2.1 miles in length.

Grand Canal (China) Often considered a river system rather than a canal system, but much of its 1,107 miles is artificial waterway made by damming rivers and lakes. Nowadays it is treated in the same fashion as the St Lawrence Seaway and not included in lists of canals. It runs from Beijing to Hangzhou, was opened in AD 610 and has been regularly reconstructed ever since.

Grand Union Canal Before 1929 was known as the Grand Junction Canal but was enlarged by amalgamating several canals and is now a main line between London and Birmingham and has several forks, the largest connecting to Leicester. The main sideshoots of the system are the Regent's Canal (Little Venice), the Paddington Arm to Brentford, the Aylesbury Arm, the Northampton Arm, and the Erewash Canal, which extends to the Leicester branch.

Great Australian Bight Inlet of the Indian Ocean extending eastwards from West Cape, Western Australia, to South-West Cape, Tasmania.

Guinea Inlet of the Atlantic washing the coasts of Liberia (Grain Coast), Côte D'Ivoire (Ivory), Ghana (Gold), Togo (Slave), Benin (Slave), Nigeria (Slave), Equatorial Guinea, Gabon, and Cameroon (Bight of Bonny).

Hauraki (North Wind) Inlet of the South Pacific indenting eastern North Island, New Zealand, covering an area of 884 sq miles.

Houston Canal Shipping channel running through Houston, Texas, into Galveston Bay and ultimately the Gulf of Mexico after a journey of 56.7 miles. The Houston Canal has no locks.

Hudson Bay Inland sea bordering Manitoba, Ontario, Quebec, and Northwest Territories; it has an area of 281,900 sq miles and contains Belcher Islands, Mansel Island, Coats Island and Southampton Island. The southern section has an inlet between Ontario and Quebec (James Bay).

Islands, Bay of Situated in the north of North Island, New Zealand, it has a shoreline of 500 miles.

James Bay Southern extension of the larger Hudson Bay; it is 275 miles in length and 135 miles in width and contains many islands the largest being, Akimiski.

Khone Falls Situated on the Mekong River, Laos, on the border with Cambodia, it has a drop of 45 ft and is the world's second greatest waterfall by volume.

Kiel Canal (North Sea) Stretches for 60.9 miles and links the North Sea (at the mouth of the Elbe) to Kiel Harbour on the Baltic.

Love Canal Not a canal at all nowadays but an area of Niagara Falls, New York, which, in 1978, was the scene of the worst environmental disaster involving chemical wastes in US history. The area, which had become a dumping ground for nuclear waste, has become a byword for similar areas.

Manchester Ship Canal Opened in 1894 and runs for 39.7 miles linking Manchester to the Irish Sea.

Mexico, Gulf of Large body of water occupying an area of 582,000 square miles situated on the southeast coast of North America and connected to the Atlantic Ocean by the Straits of Florida and to the Caribbean Sea by the Yucatan Channel.

Mozambique Channel Channel of the Indian Ocean between Madagascar and Mozambique which stretches for about 1,000 miles.

Niagara Falls Situated on the Niagara River, the falls are divided into two cataracts divided by Goat Island. The larger cataract is called the Horseshoe Falls with its drop of 1622 and crest line of 2,600 ft; the smaller is called the American Falls with its drop of 167 ft but much smaller crest line of 1,000 ft across. Niagara Falls is the world's third greatest waterfall by volume of water.

Oman Northwestern arm of the Arabian Sea between Oman and Iran, it is 350 miles in length and is linked to the Persian Gulf via the Strait of Hormuz.

Panama Canal Connecting the Atlantic and Pacific oceans and stretching for 50.71 miles, the canal was begun by Ferdinand de Lesseps in 1879, but numerous difficulties caused its cancellation until the Hay-Bunau-Varilla Treaty of 1903 between Panama and the USA granted the United States the building rights. The engineer, John F Stevens, drafted the final plan in 1906 but was succeeded as chief engineer by George Washington Goethals in 1907. The canal opened on 15 August 1914, and under the Carter-Torrijos Treaty of 1977 was officially handed back to Panama on 31 December 1999 by US President Bill Clinton. The 6 locks are the Gatún Locks (a set of three), Pedro Miguel Lock and Miraflores Locks (a set of two) . The Caribbean entrance is at Limón Bay and its southern entrance is in the Bay of Panama. Vessels cannot navigate the waters under their own power.

Persian Gulf Shallow body of water between the Arabian Peninsula and Iran. The surface area of this inlet of the Indian Ocean is approximately 88,800 square miles.

Pistyll-y-Llyn Situated on the Powys/Dyfed border, at 240 ft the highest waterfall in Wales.

Port Phillip Bay Inlet of Bass Strait on the south central coast of Victoria, Australia. Its entrance is known as 'the Rip'.

Powerscourt Falls Situated in the River Dargle, Co Wicklow, the highest waterfall in Ireland (350 ft).

Prince William Sound Inlet of the Gulf of Alaska with Hinchinbrook and Montague islands at its entrance.

Princess Charlotte Bay Inlet of the Coral Sea off the coast of Queensland; named after the daughter of George IV, it is bounded by Cape Melville to the east and Claremont Point to the west.

Ribbon Falls Situated in the Yosemite National Park, California.

Riga Inlet of the Baltic bounded by the northern coast of Latvia and the western coast of Estonia, it has an area of 7,000 sq miles.

Saint Lawrence Truly, a sea area of 91,800 sq miles with borders on Quebec, Newfoundland, Nova Scotia and New Brunswick; and containing Prince Edward Island.

Saint Lawrence Seaway Stretching from the Atlantic Ocean to the western end of the Great Lakes, the seaway was begun in August 1954, completed in April 1959 and measures 2,342 miles in length. It is a series of nearly 60 canals, of which the Welland is the longest.

Saint Vincent Inlet of the Indian Ocean on the south-east coast of South Australia, it is 90 miles in length.

Saronic (Aegina) Inlet of the Aegean Sea lying east of the Gulf of Corinth from which it is separated by the Corinth Canal.

Skagerrak Arm of the North Sea between Norway and the Jutland peninsula of Denmark on the south.

Spencer Inlet of the Great Australian Bight between the Eyre and Yorke peninsulas of South Australia, it contains many small islands including Gambier, Thistle, Sir Joseph Banks, and Neptune.

Suez North-western arm of the Red Sea between Africa and the Sinai Peninsula, it is 195 miles in length and its most northerly point at Suez marks the beginning of the Suez Canal.

Suez Canal The first fact to determine about the Suez Canal is its length, a subject that is one of the most frequently asked quiz questions. It is officially 100.6 miles long, but many reputable sources will have it listed anywhere between 100 and 105 miles; this difference is mainly due to alterations to accommodate larger vessels. The canal was built by Ferdinand de Lesseps (1805–94) and opened in 1869; its extremities are Port Said at the northern end and Suez to the south; it links two broad areas of sea, the Mediterranean and the Red Sea (via the Gulf of Suez), and is therefore technically, like many canals, a strait. It has no locks.

Sutherland Falls Situated in the Arthur River near Milford Sound, Otago, South Island, New Zealand; at 1,904 ft the fifth-highest waterfall in the world.

Tadjoura Situated at the western end of the Gulf of Aden around the port of Djibouti. The gulf is 50 miles in length.

Taranto Arm of the Ionian Sea in southern Italy between Cape Santa Maria di Leuca and Cape Colonne, forming the hollow in front of the 'boot' of Italy.

Thailand (Siam) Bordering Thailand, Cambodia, and South Vietnam, the gulf is 350 miles wide and 450 miles in length.

Thérmai Inlet of the Aegean Sea in north eastern Greece between Macedonia, Thessaly, and the Chalcidice Peninsula.

Tonkin Inlet of the South China Sea bounded by China, Hainan Island, and North Vietnam. The gulf is 300 miles in length and 150 miles in width.

Tugela Falls Situated in the Tugela River, Natal, South Africa; at 3,110 ft the second highest cataract in the world.

Utigård Falls Situated in the Jostedal Glacier, Nesdale, Norway, the highest of the many great waterfalls of Norway and with a total drop of 2,625 ft the third highest in the world.

Victoria Falls Truly breathtaking waterfall on the Zambesi River on the border between Zambia and Zimbabwe, its drop is 355 ft and it is known locally as 'The Smoke That Thunders'.

Volga–Don Shipping Canal Runs from Kalach on the Tsimlyansk Reservoir on the Don 62.2 miles to Krasnoarmeysk on the Volga; it was completed in 1952 and joins the Black Sea to the Caspian Sea.

Welland Canal Completed in 1932 and now part of the St Lawrence Seaway, it is 27.6 miles in length and is situated in southern Ontario between Lake Erie to the south and Lake Ontario to the north; it was built as an alternative route through the River Niagara because of the impassable falls.

White Sea–Baltic Canal Longest ship canal in the world (141 miles), between Povenets and Belomorsk in Russia; it has 19 locks and was opened in 1933 as the Stalin Canal.

Yosemite Falls Situated in Yosemite National Park, central California, USA. The Upper Yosemite Fall drops 1,430 ft and the Lower Falls 320 ft with the cascades between making a total drop of 2,425 ft.

Definitions of Waterways

bay a wide semicircular indentation of a shoreline, especially between two headlands or peninsulas.

canal an artificial waterway constructed for navigational aid, irrigation, or hydro-electric power.

lake a body of water, either freshwater or salt, completely surrounded by land.

ocean very large stretch of sea, especially one of the 4 main oceans of the world, i.e. Pacific, Atlantic, Indian, Arctic. The Antarctic Ocean is made up of the southern extremities of the Atlantic, Pacific and Indian Oceans.

river see definition in relevant section.

sea a mass of salt water that may be part of one of the Earth's oceans or part of a larger sea area.

strait a narrow channel of the sea, bordered by land and linking two larger sea areas. It is often confusing to think of a strait as connecting waters, as opposed to land, because it is usually the land boundaries of the strait that are better known. To give a typical example, most people realise that the Bass Strait lies between mainland Australia and Tasmania, but few will know that the strait links the Tasman Sea area of the Pacific and the Indian Ocean.

Sea Areas

Weather forecasts are broadcast on a regular basis for the Shipping Forecast Areas around the British coast and neighbouring countries. It should be noted that the areas on the map are the boundaries set by Britain and are not universally accepted by other countries who have their own boundary limits and names. German Bight was previously called Heligoland until 1956 and FitzRoy (named after the Met office founder and HMS *Beagle* captain, Admiral Robert FitzRoy) was called Finisterre until 2002.

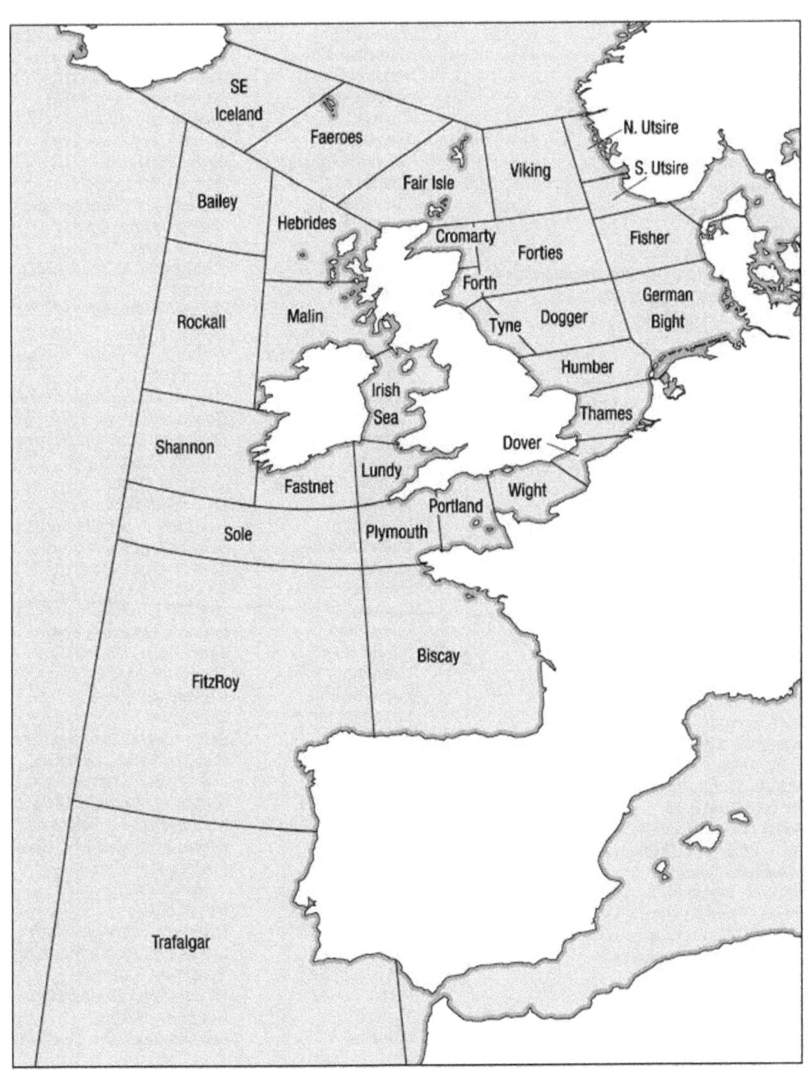

G
E
O
G
R
A
P
H
Y

Beaufort Scale

0	Calm	3	Gentle breeze	6	Strong breeze	9	Strong gale
1	Light air	4	Moderate breeze	7	Moderate gale	10	Whole gale
2	Light breeze	5	Fresh breeze	8	Fresh gale	11	Storm
						12	Hurricane

Devised in 1805 by Francis Beaufort. Force 13 to 17 were added in 1955 by the US Weather Bureau but are seldom used

Roman Place Names of Britain

Roman Name	*British Name*
Abone	*Sea Mills, Avon*
Aballava	*Burgh by Sands, Cumbria*
Ad Ansam	*Higham, Suffolk*
Ad Pontem	*East Stoke, Nottinghamshire*
Aesica	*Great Chesters, Northumberland*
Ageloco	*Littleborough, Lancashire*
Alabum	*Llandovery, Dyfed*
Alauna	*Maryport, Cumbria* *Ardoch, Tayside* *Watercrook, Cumbria*
Albion	*England*
Anderitum	*Pevensey, East Sussex*
Aquae Arnemetiae	*Buxton, Derbyshire*
Aquae Sulis	*Bath, Avon*
Arbeia	*South Shields, Tyne & Wear*
Ardotalia	*Melandra Castle, Derbyshire*
Ariconium	*Weston-under-Penyard, Hereford & Worcestershire*
Banna	*Birdoswald, Cumbria*
Bannaventa	*Whilton Lodge, Northamptonshire*
Bannovalum	*Horncastle, Lincolnshire*
Bibra	*Beckfoot, Cumbria*
Blatobulgium	*Birrens, Dumfries and Galloway*
Bovio	*Holt, Cheshire*
Bovivum	*Tilston, Cheshire*
Branodunum	*Brancaster, Norfolk*
Bravoniacum	*Kirkby Thore, Cumbria*
Bravonium	*Leintwardine, Hereford & Worcestershire*
Bremenium	*High Rochester, Northumberland*
Bremetenacum	*Ribchester, Lancashire*
Bremia	*Llanio, Dyfed*
Brocavum	*Brougham, Cumbria*
Brocolitia	*Carrawburgh, Northumberland*
Burrium	*Usk, Gwent*
Caesarea	*Jersey* and *Sark* (possibly)
Caesaromagus	*Chelmsford, Essex*
Calacum	*Burrow in Lonsdale, Lancashire*
Calcaria	*Tadcaster, North Yorkshire*
Caledonia	*Scotland*
Calleva Atrebatum	*Silchester, Hampshire*
Camboglanna	*Castlefields, Cumbria*
Camboritum	*Lackford, Suffolk*
Cambria	*Wales*
Camulodunum	*Colchester, Essex* *Slack, West Yorkshire*
Canonium	*Kelvedon, Essex*
Canovium	*Caerhun, Gwynedd*
Castra Exploratorum	*Netherby, Cumbria*
Cataractonium	*Catterick, North Yorkshire*
Causennis	*Saltersford, Lincolnshire*
Cecucmum	*Y Gaer, Powys*
Cilurnum	*Chesters, Northumberland*
Clausentum	*Bitterne, Hampshire*
Combretovium	*Baylham House, Suffolk*
Concangis	*Chester-le-Street, Durham*
Concavata	*Drumburgh, Cumbria*
Condate	*Northwich, Cheshire*
Condercum	*Benwell, Tyne & Wear*
Coria	*Corbridge, Northumberland*
Corinium Dobunnorum	*Cirencester, Gloucestershire*
Crococalana	*Brough, Nottinghamshire*
Cunetio	*Mildenhall, Wiltshire*
Danum	*Doncaster, South Yorkshire*
Delgovicia	*Millington, East Yorkshire*
Derventio	*Malton, North Yorkshire* *Littlechester, Derbyshire* *Papcastle, Cumbria*
Deva	*Chester, Cheshire*
Dubris	*Dover, Kent*
Dunum	*Hod Hill, Dorset*
Durnovaria	*Dorchester, Dorset*
Durobrivae	*Rochester, Kent* *Water Newton, Cambridgeshire*
Durocobrivis	*Dunstable, Bedfordshire*
Durocornovium	*Wanborough, Wilts*
Duroliponte	*Cambridge, Cambs*
Durovernum Cantiacorum	*Canterbury, Kent*
Durovigutum	*Godmanchester, Cambridgeshire*
Eboracum	*York, North Yorkshire*
Epiacum	*Whitley Castle, Northumberland*
Esmeduna	*Liverpool*
Fanumcocium	*Bewcastle, Cumbria*
Gabrosentum	*Moresby, Cumbria*
Galava	*Ambleside, Cumbria*
Gariannum	*Burgh Castle, Norfolk*
Gernemuta magna	*Great Yarmouth*
Glanibanta	*Ambleside, Cumbria*
Glevum	*Gloucester, Gloucestershire*
Gobanneum	*Abergavenny, Gwent*
Granta	*Cambridge*
Habitancum	*Risingham, Northumberland*
Hibernia	*Ireland*
Isca	*Caerleon, Gwent*
Isca Dumnoniorum	*Exeter, Devon*
Isurium Brigantum	*Aldborough, North Yorkshire*
Itunocelum	*Ravenglass, Cumbria*
Lactodurum	*Towcester, Northamptonshire*
Lagentium	*Castleford, West Yorkshire*
Launa	*Learchild, Northumberland*
Lavatris	*Bowes, Durham*
(Portus) Lemanis	*Lympne, Kent*
Letocetum	*Wall, Staffordshire*
Leucarum	*Loughor, West Glamorgan*
Leucomagus	*East Anton, Hampshire*
Levobrinta	*Forden Gear, Powys*
Lindinis	*Ilchester, Somerset*
Lindum	*Lincoln, Lincolnshire*
Londinium	*London, Greater London*
Longovicium	*Lanchester, Durham*
Luentinum	*Pumsaint, Dyfed*
Luguvalium	*Carlisle, Cumbria*
Lunecastrum	*Lancaster*
Magiovinium	*Dropshort, Buckinghamshire*
Magis	*Burrow Walls, Cumbria*
Maglona	*Old Carlisle, Cumbria*
Magna	*Carvoran, Northumberland*
Magnis	*Kenchester, Herefordshire*
Maia	*Bowness-on-Solway, Cumbria*
Mamucium/ Mancunium	*Manchester, Greater Manchester*
Manavia	*Isle of Man*
Manduessedum	*Mancetter, Warwickshire*
Margidunum	*Castle Hill, Nottinghamshire*
Mediobogdum	*Hardknott, Cumbria*
Mediolanum	*Whitchurch, Shropshire*
Mona	*Isle of Anglesey*
Morbium	*Piercebridge, Co. Durham*

Roman Name	*British Name*
Moridunum	*Carmarthen, Dyfed* *Seaton, Devon*
Navio	*Brough, Derbyshire*
Nemeto Statio	*North Tawton, Devon*
Nidum	*Neath, West Glamorgan*
Noviomagus	*Crayford, Greater London*
Noviomagus Regnorum	*Chichester, West Sussex*
Olenacum	*Elslack, North Yorkshire*
Onnum	*Halton, Northumberland*
Orcades Insulae	*Orkney Islands*
Othona	*Bradwell-on-Sea, Essex*
Pennocrucium	*Water Eaton, Staffordshire*
Petuarea	*Brough on Humber, Humberside*
Pons Aelius	*Newcastle, Tyne & Wear*
Pontes	*Staines, Surrey*
Portus Ardaoni	*Portchester, Hants (also Portus Ardurni)*
Portus Dubris	*Dover, Kent*
Ranatis/Tanatus	*Thanet*
Ratae Corieltavorum	*Leicester, Leicestershire*
Regodunum	*Castleshaw, Greater Manchester*
Regulbium	*Reculver, Kent*
Riduna	*Alderney, Channel Islands*
Rutupiae	*Richborough, Kent*
Salinae	*Droitwich, Worcestershire* *Middlewich, Cheshire*
Sarnia	*Guernsey*
Segedunum	*Wallsend, Tyne & Wear*
Segelocum	*Littleborough, Nottinghamshire*
Segontium	*Caernarfon, Gwynedd*

Roman Name	*British Name*
Sorviodunum	*Old Sarum, Wiltshire*
Sullon Iacis	*Brockley Hill, Greater London*
Trimontium	*Newstead, Borders*
Tripontium	*Cave's Inn, Warwickshire*
Uxacona	*Redhill, Shropshire*
Uxelodunum	*Stanwix, Cumbria*
Vagniacis	*Springhead, Kent*
Varis	*St Asaph, Clwyd*
Vectis	*Isle of Wight*
Veluniate	*Carriden, Falkirkshire*
Venonis	*High Cross, Leicestershire*
Venta Belgarum	*Winchester, Hampshire*
Venta Icenorum	*Caistor St Edmund, Norfolk*
Venta Silurum	*Caerwent, Gwent*
Verbeia	*Ilkley, West Yorkshire*
Vercovicium	*Housesteads, Northumberland*
Verlucio	*Sandy Lane, Wiltshire*
Vernemetum	*Willoughby, Nottinghamshire*
Verteris	*Brough, Cumbria*
Verulamium	*St Albans, Hertfordshire*
Vigornia	*Worcester*
Vindobala	*Rudchester, Northumberland*
Vindocladia	*Badbury, Dorset*
Vindolanda	*Chesterholm, Northumberland*
Vindomora	*Ebchester, Durham*
Vinovia	*Binchester, Durham*
Viroconium Cornoviorum	*Wroxeter, Shropshire*
Virosidum	*Brough-by-Bainbridge, North Yorkshire*
Voreda	*Old Penrith, Cumbria*

NB The above are sites of Roman cities during their occupation in the first four centuries AD. A few of the situations are doubtful and alternatives are given in areas of uncertainty.

Roman Place Names of the World

Roman Name	*British Name*
Abbatis Cella (Abbot's Cell)	*Appenzell*
Aegyptus	*Egypt*
Africa	*Libya / Tunisia*
Aquincum	*Budapest*
Arabia Felix	*Arabia*
Arabona	*Gyor*
Arenacum	*Arnhem*
Ariminum	*Rimini*
Augusta Taurinorum	*Turin*
Aurelianum	*Orléans*
Caesarea Augusta	*Zaragoza*
Caesaria	*Jersey*
Caesaria Maritima	*Palestine*
Candia	*Crete*
Cibinium	*Sibiu*
Crassus	*Grasse*
Curicum	*Krk*
Dacia	*Romania*
Fiscamnum	*Fécamp*
Fretum Herculaneum	*Gibraltar (Strait of)*
Gades	*Cadiz*
Gallia	*France*
Germania	*Germany*
Graecia	*Greece*
Helvetia	*Switzerland*
Hibernia	*Ireland*
Hispania	*Spain*

Roman Name	*British Name*
Italia	*Italy*
Portus Veneris	*Port-Vendres*
Langobardus	*Lombardy*
Lausodunum	*Lausanne*
Limonum	*Poitiers*
Lugdunum	*Lyon*
Lusitania	*Portugal*
Lutetia	*Paris*
Massilia	*Marseilles*
Matisco	*Macon*
Mauretania	*Morocco*
Mediolanum	*Milan*
Noviomagus	*Longjumeau*
Noviomagus	*Nijmegen*
Olisipo	*Lisbon*
Patavium	*Padua*
Pinciacum	*Poissy*
Portus Cale	*Oporto*
Praenestum	*Palestrina*
Puteoli	*Pozzuoli*
Sexantaprista	*Ruse*
Sparnacum	*Epernay*
Trajectum Castrum	*Utrecht*
Turicum	*Zurich*
Vapincum	Gap
Vasconia	*Gascony*
Vindobona	*Vienna*

World Table: Geographical Gazetteer

Country	GMT	Currency	Split into 100	UN Member	Common-wealth	Europe	Official Languages	Highest Point (ft)	Area Sq Km	Area Sq Miles	Population
Afghanistan	+4.5	afghani	puls	1946			Pashto, Dari Persian	Noshaq (24,581)	652,230	251,827	31,108,077
Albania	+1	lek	qindarka	1955			Albanian	Korab (9,068)	28,748	11,100	3,011,405
Algeria	+1	dinar	centimes	1962			Arabic, Berber, French	Tahat (9,852)	2,381,741	919,591	38,087,812
Andorra	+1	euro	cents	1993			Catalan, French, Spanish	Coma Pedrosa (9,656)	468	181	85,293
Angola	+1	kwanza	lweis	1976			Portuguese	Serra Moco (8,596)	1,246,700	481,351	18,565,269
Antigua and Barbuda	-4	East Caribbean $	cents	1981	1981		English	Mount Obama (1,319)	442	171	90,156
Argentina	-3	peso	centavo	1945			Spanish	Aconcagua (22,834)	2,766,889	1,068,297	42,610,981
Armenia	+4	dram	luma	1992			Armenian	Aragats (13,418)	29271	11,302	2,974,184
Australia	+8–+11	dollar	cents	1945	1931		English	Kosciusko (7,316)	7,686,848	2,967,895	22,262,501
Austria	+1	euro	cents	1955		1995	German	Grossglockner (12,462)	83,849	32,374	8,221,646
Azerbaijan	+4	manat	gopik	1992			Azeri	Bazardüzü (14,652)	86,600	33,436	9,590,159
Bahamas	-5	dollar	cents	1973	1973		English	Alvernia (on Cat Island) (206)	13,935	5,380	319,031
Bahrain	+3	dinar	fils (1,000)	1971			Arabic	Jabal ad-Dukhan (440)	765	295	1,281,332
Bangladesh	+6	taka	poisha	1974	1972		Bengali	Saka Haphong (3,451)	147,570	56,977	163,654,860
Barbados	-4	dollar	cents	1966	1966		English	Hillaby (1,115)	430	166	288,725
Belarus	+2	rouble	kopeks	1945			Belarussian	Dzerzhinsky (1,135)	207,600	80,154	9,625,888
Belgium	+1	euro	cents	1945		1958	Dutch, French, German	Botrange (2,277)	30,513	11,781	10,444,268
Belize	-6	dollar	cents	1981	1981		English	Doyle's Delight (3,688)	22,965	8,867	334,297
Benin	+1	franc	centimes	1960			French, Fon, Adja, Yoruba	Sokbaro (2,159)	112,622	43,484	9,877,292
Bermuda	-4	dollar	cents				English	Town Hill (250)	53	20	69,467
Bhutan	+6	ngultrum	chetrum	1971			Dzongkha, Bumthangka	Gangkhar Puensum (24,836)	38,394	14,824	725,296
Bolivia	-4	boliviano	centavos	1945			Spanish, Quechua, Amyara	Nevado Sajama (21,463)	1,098,581	424,163	10,461,053
Bosnia-Hercegovina	+1	marka	fening	1992			Bosnian	Maglic (7,830)	51,129	19,741	3,875,723
Botswana	-2	pula	thebes	1966	1966		Setswana, English	Otse (4,891)	581,730	224,606	2,127,825
Brazil	-2–-5	real	centavos	1945			Portuguese	Pico da Neblina (9,823)	8,511,965	3,286,473	201,009,622
Brunei	+8	dollar	sen	1984	1984		Malay, English	Bukit Pagon (6,070)	5,765	2,226	415,717
Bulgaria	+2	lev	stotinki	1955		2007	Bulgarian	Musala (9,596)	110,912	42,823	6,981,642
Burkina Faso	0	franc	centimes	1960			French, Mossi	Tenakourou (2,457)	274,200	105,869	17,812,961
Burundi	+2	franc	centimes	1962			Rundi, French, Swahili	Heha (8,809)	27,834	10,747	10,888,321
Cambodia	+7	riel	sen	1955			Khmer, French	Phnom Aural (5,938)	181,035	69,898	15,205,539
Cameroon	+1	franc	centimes	1960	1995		French, English	Cameroon (13,255)	475,442	183,568	20,549,221
Canada	-4–-8	dollar	cents	1945	1931		English, French	Logan (19,550)	9,976,185	3,851,809	34,568,211
Cape Verde	-1	escudo	centavos	1975			Portuguese, Crioulo	Mount Fogo (9,281)	4,033	1,557	531,046
Central African Rep	+1	franc	centimes	1960			French, Sangho	Ngaoui (4,659)	622,984	240,534	5,166,510
Chad	+1	franc	centimes	1960			French, Arabic	Emi Koussi (11,302)	1,284,000	495,753	11,193,452
Chile	-3–-5	peso	centavos	1945			Spanish	Ojos del Salado (22,615)	756,945	292,257	17,216,945
China	+8	renmimbi-yuan	jiāo	1945			Mandarin Chinese	Everest (29,029)	9,596,961	3,705,390	1,349,585,838
Colombia	-5	peso	centavos	1945			Spanish	Pico Cristobal Colon (18,701)	1,141,748	440,829	45,745,783
Comoros	+3	franc	centimes	1975			French, Arabic, Comoran	Kartala (7,746)	2,171	838	752,288
Congo, Dem Rep of	+1–+2	franc	centimes	1960			French, Lingala, Kiswahili	Stanley (Ngaliema) (16,763)	2,345,409	905,563	75,507,308
Congo, Rep of	+1	franc	centimes	1960			French	Mont Nabeba (3,346)	342,000	132,046	4,492,689
Costa Rica	-6	colon	centimos	1945			Spanish	Chirripo (12,533)	50,700	19,575	4,695,942

Country	GMT	Currency	Split into 100	UN Member	Common-wealth	Europe	Official Languages	Highest Point (ft)	Area Sq Km	Area Sq Miles	Population
Croatia	+1	kuna	lipas	1993			Croatian	Dinara (6,007)	56,538	21,829	4,475,611
Cuba	-5	peso	centavos	1945			Spanish	Pico Turquino (6,467)	110,861	42,803	11,061,886
Cyprus	+2	euro	cents	1960	1961	2004	Greek, Turkish	Olympus (6,401)	9,251	3,572	1,155,403
Czech Republic	+1	koruna	haléru	1993		2004	Czech, Slovak	Snezka (5,256)	78,644	30,364	10,162,921
Denmark	+1	krone	ore	1945		1973	Danish	Møllehøj (561)	43,069	16,629	5,556,452
Djibouti	+3	franc	centimes	1977			French, Arabic, Afar, Somali	Mousa Ali (6,654)	22,000	8,494	792,198
Dominica	-4	East Caribbean $	cents	1978	1978		English	Morne Diablotins (4,747)	748	289	73,286
Dominican Republic	-4	peso	centavos	1945			Spanish	Pico Duarte (10,164)	48,734	18,816	10,219,630
East Timor	+9	US dollar	cents	2002			Portuguese	Tata Mailau (9,720)	14,874	5,743	1,172,390
Ecuador	-5	US dollar	cents	1945			Spanish	Chimborazo (20,561)	283,561	109,483	15,439,429
Egypt	+2	pound	piastres	1945			Arabic	Jebel Katherina (8,651)	1,001,449	386,660	85,294,388
El Salvador	-6	US dollar	cents	1945			Spanish	Cerro El Pital (8,957)	21,041	8,124	6,108,590
Equatorial Guinea	+1	franc (was epkwele)	centimes	1968			Spanish	Pico Basilé (9,878)	28,051	10,831	704,001
Eritrea	+3	nafka	cents	1993			English, Arabic	Emba Soira (9,902)	121,320	46,842	6,233,682
Estonia	+2	euro	cents	1991		2004	Estonian	Munamagi (1,042)	45,125	17,423	1,266,375
Ethiopia	+3	birr	cents	1945			Amharic, Galla, Somali	Ras Dashen (14,928)	1,128,221	435,607	93,877,025
Falkland Islands	-3	pound	pennies	1945	1931	1973	English	Mt. Usborne (2,312)	12,713	4,700	3,140
Fiji	+12	dollar	cents	1970	1970		English, Fijian	Tomaniivi (4,341)	18,274	7,056	896,758
Finland	+2	euro	cents	1955		1995	Finnish, Swedish	Haltiatunturi (4,344)	338,000	130,502	5,266,114
France	+1	euro	cents	1945		1958	French	Blanc (15,781)	547,026	211,207	65,951,611
Gabon	+1	franc	centimes	1960			French, Fang, Eshira, Mbete	Bengoué (3,510)	267,667	103,346	1,640,286
Gambia	0	dalasi	butut	1965	1965		English	Red Rock (173)	11,295	4,361	1,883,051
Georgia	+4	lari	tetri	1992			Georgian, Russian, Armenian	Shichara (17,060)	69,700	26,911	4,555,911
Germany	+1	euro	cents	1973		1958	German	Zugspitze (9,721)	357,050	137,857	81,147,265
Ghana	0	cedi	pesewas	1957	1957		English, Asante, Ewe, Fante	Afadjato (2,877)	238,537	92,099	25,199,609
Gibraltar	+1	pound	pennies	1945	1931	1973	English	Rock of Gibraltar (1,398)	6.8	2.6	29,111
Greece	+2	euro	cents	1945		1981	Greek	Olympus (9,577)	131,944	50,944	10,772,967
Greenland	+0–4	krone	ore				Greenlandic, Danish	Gunnbjorns Field (12,139)	2,175,600	840,000	57,714
Grenada	-4	East Caribbean $	cents	1974	1974		English	St Catherine (2,756)	344	133	109,590
Guatemala	-6	quetzal	centavos	1945			Spanish	Tajumulco (13,881)	108,889	42,042	14,373,472
Guinea	0	franc	centimes	1958			French	Nimba (5,748)	245,857	94,925	11,176,026
Guinea-Bissau	0	franc	centimes	1974			Portuguese, Creole, Fulani	unnamed location (984)	36,125	13,948	1,660,870
Guyana	-4	dollar	cents	1966	1966		English, Hindu, Urdu	Roraima (9,094)	214,969	83,000	739,903
Haiti	-5	gourde	centimes	1945			French, Creole	Pic La Selle (8,793)	27,750	10,714	9,893,934
Honduras	-6	lempira	centavos	1945			Spanish	Cerro Las Minas (9,400)	112,088	43,277	8,448,465
Hong Kong	+8	dollar	cents				Chinese, English	Tai Mo Shan (3,143)	1,071	414	7,182,724
Hungary	+1	forint	filler	1955		2004	Magyar	Kekes (3,330)	93,030	35,919	9,939,470
Iceland	0	krona	aurar	1946			Icelandic	Hvannadalshnukur (6,923)	103,000	39,768	315,281
India	+5.5	rupee	paisa	1945	1947		Hindi, English	Kanchenjunga (28,169)	3,287,590	1,269,340	1,220,800,359
Indonesia	+7–+9	rupiah	sen	1950			Bahasa Indonesia	Puncak Jaya (16,020)	1,904,569	735,355	251,160,124
Iran	+3.5	rial	dinars	1945			Farsi	Qolleh-ye Damavand (18,386)	1,648,000	636,293	79,853,900
Iraq	+3	dinar	fils-1000	1945			Arabic	Cheekha Dar (11,847)	434,924	167,924	31,858,481
Ireland	0	euro	cents	1955	left 1949	1973	Irish, English	Carrantuohill (3,406)	70,283	27,136	4,775,982

Country	GMT	Currency	Split into 100	UN Member	Common-wealth	Europe	Official Languages	Highest Point (ft)	Area Sq Km	Area Sq Miles	Population
Israel	+2	Shekel	Agorot	1949			Hebrew, Arabic	Meron (3,963)	20,770	8,019	7,707,042
Italy	+1	euro	cents	1955		1958	Italian	Blanc (15,781)	301,225	116,303	61,482,297
Ivory Coast	0	franc	centimes	1960			French	Nimba (5,748)	322,463	124,503	22,400,835
Jamaica	-5	dollar	cents	1962	1962		English	Blue Mountain Peak (7,402)	10,991	4,244	2,909,714
Japan	+9	yen	sen	1956			Japanese	Fuji (12,388)	369,792	142,777	127,253,075
Jordan	+2	dinar	fils–1,000	1955			Arabic	Jabal Umm ad Dami (6,083)	97,740	37,737	6,482,081
Kazakhstan	+4–+6	tenge	tiyn	1992			Kazakh, Russian	Khan-Tengri Peak (22,999)	2,717,300	1,049,151	17,736,896
Kenya	+3	shilling	cents	1963	1963		Swahili, English, Kikuyu	Kenya (17,057)	582,646	224,960	44,037,656
Kiribati	+12–+13	Australian $	cents	1979	1979		English, Kiribati (Gilbertese)	Banaba Peak (265)	728	281	103,248
Korea, North (Chosun)	+9	won	chon	1991			Korean	Pektu San (9,003)	120,538	46,540	24,720,407
Korea, South	+9	won	jeon	1991			Korean	Halla-san (6,398)	98,477	38,022	48,955,203
Kuwait	+3	dinar	fils–1000	1963			Arabic	Ash-Shaqaya (951)	17,818	6,880	2,695,316
Kyrgyzstan	+6	som	tyiyn	1992			Kirghiz, Russian	Victory Peak (24,406) (Pik Pobedy/Jengish Chokusu)	198,500	76,641	5,548,042
Laos	+7	kip	at	1955			Lao, French	Phou Bia (9252)	231,800	89,498	6,695,166
Latvia	+2	lat	santims	1991		2004	Latvian	Gaizinkalns (1,024)	63,935	24,685	2,178,443
Lebanon	+2	pound	piastres	1945			Arabic	Qurnat as-Sawda (10131)	10,400	4,015	4,131,583
Lesotho	+2	loti	lisente	1966	1966		Sesotho, English	Thabana Ntlenyana (11425)	30,355	11,720	1,936,181
Liberia	0	dollar	cents	1945			English	Mount Wuteve (4,724)	111,369	43,000	3,989,703
Libya	+1	dinar	dirhams-1000	1955			Arabic	Pico Bette (7,438)	1,759,540	679,359	6,002,347
Liechtenstein	+1	Swiss franc	rappen/ centimes	1993			German	Grauspitze (8,526)	158	61	37,009
Lithuania	+2	litas	centas	1991		2004	Lithuanian	Aukstojas Hill (965)	65,200	25,174	3,515,858
Luxembourg	+1	euro	cents	1945		1958	French, German, Letzeburgesch	Kneiff (1,837)	2,586	998	514,862
Macedonia	+1	denar	denis	1993			Macedonian, Albanian	Korab (9,068)	25,713	9,928	2,087,171
Madagascar	+3	ariary	iraimbilanjas–5	1960			Malagasy, French	Maromokotro (9436)	587,041	226,657	22,599,098
Malawi	+2	kwacha	tambala	1964	1964		English, Chichewa	Mlanje Sapitwa (9843)	118,484	45,747	16,777,547
Malaysia	+8	ringgit	sen	1957	1957		Malay, Chinese, English	Kinabalu (13455)	329,749	127,316	29,628,392
Maldives	+5	rufiyaa	laaris	1965	1982		Divehi	no land above 8ft	298	115	393,988
Mali	0	franc	centimes	1960			French, Bambara, Fulani	Hombori Tondo (3789)	1,240,000	478,764	15,968,882
Malta	+1	euro	cents	1964	1964	2004	Maltese, English, Italian	Ta'Dmejrek (830)	246	95	411,277
Marshall Islands	+12	US dollar	cents	1991			Marshallese, English	no land above 20ft	181	70	69,747
Mauritania	0	ouguiya	khoums–5	1961			Arabic, French, Hassaniya	Kediet Ijill (3,002)	1,030,700	397,954	3,437,610
Mauritius	+4	rupee	cents	1968	1968		English	Black River Mountain (2,711)	2,045	790	1,322,238
Mexico	-6/-8	peso	centavos	1945			Spanish	Orizaba (18,490)	1,972,547	761,601	116,220,947
Moldova	+2	leu	bani	1992			Moldovan, Russian	Balaneshty (1,409)	33,700	13,012	3,619,925
Monaco	+1	euro	cents	1992			French	Chemin de Revoires (533)	1.9	0.73	30,500
Mongolia	+8	tugrik	möngö	1961			Khalkha Mongolian	Khüiten Peak (14,350)	1,565,000	604,247	3,226,516
Montenegro	+1	euro	cents	2006			Montenegrin	Zla Kolata (8,314)	13,812	5,019	653,474
Morocco	0	dirham	centimes	1956			Arabic, French, Berber	Jebel Toubkal (13,665)	446,550	172,413	32,649,130
Mozambique	+2	metical	centavos	1975	1995		Portuguese	Monte Binga (7,992)	801,590	309,494	24,096,669
Myanmar (Burma)	+6.5	kyat	pyas	1948			Burmese, English	Hkakabo Razi (19,295)	676,552	261,217	55,167,330
Namibia	+2	Namibian $	cents	1990	1990		Afrikaans, English	Brandberg (8,550)	824,292	318,259	2,182,852
Nauru	+12	Australian $	cents	1968	1968		English	Command Ridge (233)	21	8	9,434
Nepal	+5.75	rupee	paisa	1955			Nepali	Everest (29,029)	140,747	54,342	30,430,267

Country	GMT	Currency	Split into 100	UN Member	Common-wealth	Europe	Official Languages	Highest Point (ft)	Area Sq Km	Area Sq Miles	Population
Netherlands	+1	euro	cents	1945		1958	Dutch	Vaalserberg (1,053)	40,844	15,770	16,805,037
New Zealand	+13	dollar	cents	1945	1931		English, Maori	Cook (12,316)	268,867	103,810	4,365,113
Nicaragua	-6	cordoba	centavos	1945			Spanish	Pico Mogoton (6,913)	130,000	50,193	5,788,531
Niger	+1	franc	centimes	1960			French, Hausa, Tuareg	Mont Bagzan (6,630)	1,267,000	489,189	16,899,327
Nigeria	+1	naira	kobo	1960	1960		English, Hausa, Ibo, Yoruba	Chappal Waddi (7,940)	923,768	356,667	174,507,539
Norway	+1	krone	ore	1945			Norwegian	Galdhopiggen (8,098)	386,958	149,405	4,722,701
Oman	+4	rial omani	baizas–1000	1971			Arabic	Jabal ash Sham (10,089)	212,457	82,030	3,154,134
Pakistan	+5	rupee	paisa	1947	1947		Urdu	K2 (aka Godwin Austen) (28,251)	883,254	341,025	193,238,868
Palau	+9	US dollar	cents	1994			Palauan, English	Ngerchelchauus (794)	459	177	21,108
Panama	-5	balboa	centesimos	1945			Spanish	Chiriqui (aka Barú) (11,398)	77,082	29,761	3,559,408
Papua New Guinea	+10	kina	toea	1975	1975		English, Pidgin, Moru	Wilhelm (14,790)	461,691	178,259	6,431,902
Paraguay	-3	guarani	céntimos	1945			Spanish, Guarani	Cerro Pero (2,762)	406,752	157,047	6,623,252
Peru	-5	new sol	cents	1945			Spanish, Quechua	Huascaran (22,205)	1,285,216	496,222	29,849,303
Philippines	+8	peso	centavos	1945			Filipino, English	Apo (9,690)	300,000	115,830	105,720,644
Poland	+1	zloty	groszy	1945		2004	Polish	Rysy (8,199)	312,677	120,725	38,383,809
Portugal	0	euro	cents	1955		1986	Portuguese	Pico (7,713)	88,880	34,317	10,707,924
Qatar	+3	riyal	dirhams	1971			Arabic	Qurayn Abual Bawl (338)	11,000	4,247	2,042,444
Romania	+2	leu	bani	1955		2007	Romanian	Moldoveanu (8,346)	237,500	91,699	21,790,479
Russia	+3–+12	rouble	kopeks	1991			Russian	Elbrus (18,510)	17,075,400	6,592,819	142,500,482
Rwanda	+2	franc	centimes	1962	2009		French, Kinyarwanda	Karisimbi (14,787)	26,338	10,169	12,012,589
St Kitts and Nevis	-4	East Caribbean $	cents	1983	1983		English	Liamuiga Nevis (3,792)	269	104	51,134
St Lucia	-4	East Caribbean $	cents	1979	1979		English	Gimie (3,117)	616	238	162,781
St Vincent	-4	East Caribbean $	cents	1980	1979		English	Soufrière (4,048)	388	150	103,220
Samoa	+13	tala	sene	1976	1970		Samoan, English	Mauga Silisli (6,094)	1,714	662	195,476
San Marino	+1	euro	cents	1992			Italian	Titano (2,424)	61	24	32,448
São Tomé	0	dobra	centavos	1975			Portuguese	Pico de São Tomé (6,640)	964	372	186,817
Saudi Arabia	+3	riyal	halalah	1945			Arabic	Jabal Sawda (9,843)	2,149,640	829,977	26,939,583
Senegal	0	franc	centimes	1960			French,Wolof, Fulani	Unnamed (1,906)	196,192	75,750	13,300,410
Serbia	+1	dinar	paras	2000			Serbian	Daravica (8,714)	88,361	34,116	7,243,007
Seychelles	+4	rupee	cents	1976	1976		Creole, English, French	Seychellois (2,969)	456	176	90,846
Sierra Leone	0	leone	cents	1961	1961		English, Krio, Mende	Bintimani (6,390)	71,740	27,699	5,612,685
Singapore	+8	dollar	cents	1965	1965		Malay, Chinese, Tamil, English	Bukit Timah (537)	639	247	5,460,302
Slovakia	+1	euro	cents	1993		2004	Slovak, Hungarian, Czech	Gerlachovsky (8,711)	49,035	18,932	5,488,339
Slovenia	+1	euro	cents	1993		2004	Slovene, Hungarian	Triglav (9,396)	20,251	7,819	1,992,690
Solomon Islands	+11	dollar	cents	1978	1978		English, Pidgin	Popomanaseu (7,661)	28,446	10,983	597,248
Somalia	+3	shilling	cents	1960			Somali, Arabic, English	Shimbiris (8,038)	637,657	246,200	10,251,568
South Africa	+2	rand	cents	1945	1931		Afrikaans, English, Xhosa, Zulu	Mafadi (11,300)	1,221,031	471,441	48,601,098
South Sudan	+3	pound	piasters	2011			English, Arabic, Dinka	Kinyeti (10,456)	619,745	239,285	11,090,104
Spain	+1	euro	cents	1955		1986	Spanish	Teide (12,190)	504,782	194,897	47,370,542
Sri Lanka	+5.5	rupee	cents	1955	1948		Sinhalese, Tamil	Pidurutalagala (8,292)	65,610	25,332	21,675,648
Sudan	+3	pound	qirsh	1956			Arabic	Deriba Caldera (9,980)	1,886,068	728,215	34,847,910
Suriname	-3	dollar	cents	1975			Dutch, Hindustani, Sranang Tongo	Julianatop (4,199)	163,265	63,037	566,846
Swaziland	+2	lilangeni	cents	1968	1968		English, Swazi	Emlembe (6,113)	17,363	6,704	1,403,362

Country	GMT	Currency	Split into 100	UN Member	Common-wealth	Europe	Official Languages	Highest Point (ft)	Area Sq Km	Area Sq Miles	Population
Sweden	+1	krona	ore	1946		1995	Swedish, Finnish	Kebnekaise (6,903)	449,964	173,731	9,119,423
Switzerland	+1	Swiss franc	centimes/ rappen	2002			German, French, Italian, Romansch	Dufourspitze (15,203)	41,293	15,943	7,996,026
Syria	+2	pound	piastres	1945			Arabic, Kurdish, Armenian	Jabal ash–Shaikh (Hermon) (9,232)	185,180	71,498	22,457,336
Taiwan	+8	dollar	cents	1945			Mandarin Chinese	Yu Shan (Morrison/Jade) (12,966)	35,742	13,800	23,299,716
Tajikistan	+5	somoni	dirams	1992			Tajik, Uzbek, Russian	Ismoil Somoni Peak (24,590)	143,100	55,251	7,910,041
Tanzania	+3	shilling	cents	1964	1961		English, Kiswahili	Kilimanjaro (19,331)	945,087	364,898	48,261,942
Thailand	+7	baht	satang	1946			Thai	Doi Inthanon (8,415)	514,000	198,456	67,448,120
Togo	0	franc	centimes	1960			French, Ewe, Kabiye	Baumann (3,235) aka Agou	56,785	21,925	7,154,237
Tonga	+13	pa'anga	seniti	1999	1970		Tongan, English	Kao (3,380)	699	270	106,322
Trinidad and Tobago	-4	dollar	cents	1962	1962		English, Hindi, French, Spanish	Cerro Aripo (3,085)	4,828	1864	1,225,225
Tunisia	+1	dinar	millemes–1,000	1956			Arabic, French	Djebel Chambi (5,066)	164,150	63,378	10,835,873
Turkey	+2	lira	kurus	1945			Turkish	Buyuk Agridagi (Ararat) (16,854)	814,578	314,509	80,694,485
Turkmenistan	+5	manat	tenge	1992			Turkmenian, Russian, Uzbek	Gora Ayrybaba (10,299)	488,100	188,456	5,113,040
Tuvalu	+12	dollar	cents	2000	1978		Tuvaluan, English	no land above 15ft	16	6	10,698
Uganda	+3	shilling	cents	1962	1962		English, Swahili, Luganda	Stanley (16,763)	236,036	91,134	34,758,809
Ukraine	+2	hryvna	kopiykas	1945			Ukrainian, Russian	Hoverla (6,760)	603,700	233,089	44,573,205
United Arab Emirates	+4	dirham	fils	1971			Arabic	Jabal Bil Ays (6,266)	83,600	32,278	5,473,972
United Kingdom	0	pound	pence	1945	1931	1973	English	Ben Nevis (4,409)	240,883	93,005	63,395,574
USA	-5/–-10	dollar	cents	1945			English	McKinley (20,320)	9,158,960	3,536,278	316,668,567
Uruguay	-3	peso	centesimos	1945			Spanish	Cerro Catedral (1,686)	176,215	68,037	3,324,460
Uzbekistan	+5	sum	tiyin	1992			Uzbek, Russian, Tajik	Khazret Sultan (15,233)	447,400	172,741	28,661,637
Vanuatu	+11	vatu	centimes	1981	1980		Bislama, French, English	Tabwebesana (6,158)	12,190	4,707	261,565
Vatican City	+1	euro	cents				Italian, Latin, Polish	none	0.44	0.17	839
Venezuela	-4	bolivar	centimos	1945			Spanish	La Pico Columna (Bolivar) (16,342)	912,050	352,143	28,459,085
Vietnam	+7	dong (=10 Hao)	xu	1977			Vietnamese	Fan si Pan (10,308)	329,556	127,242	92,477,857
Yemen	+3	riyal	fils	1947			Arabic	Jabalan Nabi Shu'ayb (12,028)	527,969	203,849	25,408,288
Zambia	+2	kwacha	ngwee	1964	1964		English, Bemba, Nyanja	Muchinga (7,350)	752,614	290,585	14,222,233
Zimbabwe	+2	dollar	cents	1980			English, Sindebele, Chishona	Nyangani (8,503)	390,580	150,803	13,182,908

NB: Of the 54 Commonwealth members, 16 have Queen Elizabeth II as head of state, 33 are republics and five have their own monarchies. Pakistan left the Commonwealth in 1972 but rejoined in 1989, but was suspended on 18 October 1999. Zimbabwe was suspended on 20 March 2002. In December 2003 the suspension was extended indefinitely and the Zimbabwean government responded by announcing the country was leaving the Commonwealth for good. Fiji's membership has been suspended since 8 December 2006. The areas given are land areas.

NB: The Serbian population estimate does not include the disputed area of Kosovo.

Country	International Car Registration	Drives	International Civil Aircraft Markings	Type of government	President	Religion	National Day	Internet TLD	IDD Codes from UK	IDD Codes to UK
Afghanistan	AFG	right	YA	republic	Hamid Karzai	Sunni-Islam	19 Aug	.af	0093	0044
Albania	AL	right	ZA	republic	Bujar Nishani	Islam	28 Nov	.al	00355	0044
Algeria	DZ	right	7T	republic	Abelaziz Bouteflika	Sunni-Islam	1 Nov	.dz	00213	0044
Andorra	AND	right	C3	unicameral co-principality	Antoni Marti (PM)	RC	8 Sept	.ad	00376	0044
Angola	ANG	right	D2	republic	José Eduardo dos Santos	Christianity	11 Nov	.ao	00244	0044
Antigua and Barbuda	AG	left	V2	constitutional monarchy	Baldwin Spencer (PM)	Christianity	1 Nov	.ag	001268	01144
Argentina	RA	right	LQ, and LV	republic	Christina Fernández de Kirchner	RC	25 May	.ar	0054	0044
Armenia	ARM	right	EK	republic	Serzh Sargsyan	Christianity	21 Sept	.am	00374	81044
Australia	AUS	left	VH	federal parliamentary state	Julia Gillard (PM)	Christianity	26 Jan	.au	0061	001144
Austria	A	right	OE	republic	Heinz Fischer	RC	26 Oct	.at	0043	0044
Azerbaijan	AZ	right	4K	republic	Ilham Aliyev	Shia-Islam	28 May	.az	00994	81044
Bahamas	BS	left	C6	constitutional monarchy	Perry Christie (PM)	Christianity	10 July	.bs	001242	01144
Bahrain	BRN	right	A9C	constitutional monarchy	King Hamad bin Isa Al Khalifah	Islam	16 Dec	.bh	00973	044
Bangladesh	BD	left	S2	republic	Abdul Hamid	Sunni-Islam	26 Mar	.bd	00880	0044
Barbados	BDS	left	8P	constitutional monarchy	Freundel Stuart (PM)	Christianity	30 Nov	.bb	001246	01144
Belarus	BY	right	EW	republic	Alexander Lukashenko	RC	27 July	.by	00375	81044
Belgium	B	right	00	constitutional monarchy	King Philippe	RC	21 July	.be	0032	0044
Belize	BZ	right	V3	constitutional monarchy	Dean Barrow (PM)	Christianity	21 Sept	.bz	00501	01144
Benin	DY	right	TY	republic	Yayi Boni	RC	30 Nov	.bj	00229	0044
Bermuda	VQ-B	left	VP-B	British colony	Craig Cannonier (PM)	Christianity	24 May	.bm	001441	01144
Bhutan	BHT	left	A5	constitutional monarchy	King Jigme Wangchuck	Buddhism	17 Dec	.bt	00975	0044
Bolivia	BOL	right	CP	republic	Evo Morales	RC	6 Aug	.bo	00591	0044
Bosnia-Hercegovina	E7	right	T9	republic	Zeljko Komsic	Islam	1 Mar	.ba	00396	9944
Botswana	RB	left	A2	republic	Ian Khama	Christianity	30 Sept	.bw	00267	0044
Brazil	BR	right	PP, and PT	republic	Dilma Rousseff	RC	7 Sept	.br	0055	0044
Brunei	BRU	left	V8	monarchy (sultanate)	Sultan Hassanol Bolkiah	Islam	23 Feb	.bn	00673	0144
Bulgaria	BG	right	LZ	republic	Rosen Plevneliev	Christianity	3 Mar	.bg	00359	0044
Burkina Faso	BF	right	XT	republic	Blaise Compaoré	Islam	11 Dec	.bf	00226	0044
Burundi	BU	right	9U	republic	Pierre Nkurunziza	Christianity	1 July	.bi	00257	9044
Cambodia	K	right	XU	republic	King Norodom Sihamoni	Buddhism	9 Nov	.kh	00855	0044
Cameroon	CAM	right	TJ	republic	Paul Biya	Christianity	20 May	.cm	00237	0044
Canada	CDN	right	C	federal parliamentary state	Stephen Harper (PM)	Christianity	1 July	.ca	001	01144
Cape Verde	D4	right	D4	republic	Jorge Carlos Fonseca	RC	5 July	.cv	00238	044
Central African Rep	RCA	right	TL	republic	Michel Djotodia	Christianity	1 Dec	.cf	00236	0044
Chad	TCH	right	TT	republic	Idriss Déby	Islam	13 Apr	.td	00235	0044
Chile	RCH	right	CC	republic	Sebastián Piñera	RC	18 Sept	.cl	0056	0044
China	RC	right	B	people's republic	Xi Jinping	Buddhism	1 Oct	.cn	0086	0044
Colombia	CO	right	HK	republic	Juan Manuel Santos	RC	20 July	.co	0057	9044
Comoros	D6	right	D6	republic	Ikililou Dhoinine	Islam	6 July	.km	00269	1044
Congo, Dem Rep of	CD	right	9Q	republic	Joseph Kabila	RC	24 Nov	.cd	00243	0044
Congo, Rep of	RCB	right	TN	republic	Denis Sassou Nguesso	RC	15 Aug	.cg	00242	0044
Costa Rica	CR	right	TI	republic	Laura Chinchilla	RC	15 Sept	.cr	00506	0044
Croatia	HR	right	9A	republic	Ivo Josipovic	RC	30 May	.hr	00385	9944
Cuba	C	right	CU	republic	Raúl Castro	RC	1 Jan	.cu	0053	11944
Cyprus	CY	left	5B	republic	Nicos Anastasiades	Greek Orthodox	1 Oct	.cy	00357	0044
Czech Republic	CZ	right	OK	republic	Miloš Zeman	RC	28 Oct	.cz	00420	0044
Denmark	DK	right	OY	constitutional monarchy	Queen Margrethe II	Evangelical Lutheran	5 June	.dk	0045	0044
Djibouti	DJI	right	J2	republic	Ismail Omar Guelleh	Islam	27 June	.dj	00253	0044
Dominica	WD	left	J7	republic	Eliud Williams	RC	3 Nov	.dm	00767	01144
Dominican Republic	DOM	right	HI	republic	Danilo Medina	RC	27 Feb	.do	001809	01144
East Timor	RI	left	PK	republic	Taur Matan Ruak	RC	20 May	.tl	00670	00144
Ecuador	EC	right	HC	republic	Rafael Correa	RC	10 Aug	.ec	00593	0144

Country	International Car Registration	Drives	International Civil Aircraft Markings	Type of government	President	Religion	National Day	Internet TLD	IDD Codes from UK	IDD Codes to UK
Egypt	ET	right	SU	republic	Adly Mansour (acting)	Islam	23 July	.eg	0020	0044
El Salvador	ES	right	YS	republic	Mauricio Funes	RC	15 Sept	.sv	00503	0044
Equatorial Guinea	EQ	right	3C	republic	Teodoro Obiang	RC	12 Oct	.gq	00240	1944
Eritrea	ER	right	E3	republic	Isaias Afewerki	Islam/Christianity	24 May	.er	00291	operator
Estonia	EST	right	ES	republic	Toomas Hendrik Ilves	Lutheran	24 Feb	.ee	00372	80044
Ethiopia	ETH	right	ET	republic	Girma Wolde-Giorgis	Christianity	28 May	.et	00251	0044
Falkland Islands			VP-F	UK overseas territory	Nigel Haywood (Governor)	Christianity	14 June	.fk	00500	0144
Fiji	FJI	left	DQ	republic	Epeli Nailatikau	Christianity	10 Oct	.fj	00679	0544
Finland	FIN	right	OH	republic	Sauli Niinistö	Evangelical Lutheran	6 Dec	.fi	00358	99044
France	F	right	F	republic	François Hollande	RC	14 July	.fr	0033	0044
Gabon	GAB	right	TR	republic	Ali Bongo Ondimba	RC	17 Aug	.ga	00241	0044
Gambia	WAG	right	C5	republic	Yahya Jammeh	Islam	18 Feb	.gm	00220	0044
Georgia	GE	right	4L	republic	Mikheil Saakashvili	Christianity	26 May	.ge	00995	81044
Germany	D	right	D	republic	Angela Merkel (Chancellor)	Christianity	3 Oct	.de	0049	0044
Ghana	GH	right	9G	republic	John Dramani Mahama	Christianity	6 Mar	.gh	00233	0044
Gibraltar	GBZ	right	VR-G	UK overseas territory	Sir Adrian Johns (Governor)	Christianity	10 Sept	.gi	00350	0044
Greece	GR	right	SX	republic	Karolos Papoulias	Greek Orthodox	25 Mar	.gr	0030	0044
Greenland	KN	right	OY	constitutional monarchy	Queen Margrethe II	Evangelical Lutheran	21 June	.gl	00299	00944
Grenada	WG	left	J3	constitutional monarchy	Keith Mitchell (PM)	Christianity	7 Feb	.gd	001809	01144
Guatemala	GCA	right	TG	republic	Otto Pérez Molina	RC	15 Sept	.gt	00502	0044
Guinea	RG	right	3X	republic	Alpha Condé	Islam	2 Oct	.gn	00224	0044
Guinea-Bissau	GW, RGB	right	J5	republic	Manuel Serifo Nhamadjo	Islam	24 Sept	.gw	00245	operator
Guyana	GUY	left	8R	republic	Bharrat Jagdeo	Christianity	26 May	.gy	00592	00144
Haiti	RH	right	HH	republic	Michel Martelly	RC	1 Jan	.ht	00509	operator
Honduras	HN	right	HR	republic	Porfirio Lobo Sosa	RC	15 Sept	.hn	00504	0044
Hong Kong	HK	left	B-H	territory of China	Leung Chun-Ying (CE)	Buddhism	29 Aug	.hk	00852	00144
Hungary	H	right	HA	republic	János Áder	RC	15 Mar	.hu	0036	0044
Iceland	IS	right	TF	republic	Ólafur Ragnar Grímsson	Evangelical Lutheran	17 June	.is	00354	0044
India	IND	left	VT	republic	Pranab Mukherjee	Hinduism	26 Jan	.in	0091	0044
Indonesia	RI	left	PK	republic	Susilo Bambang Yudhoyono	Islam	17 Aug	.id	0062	00144
Iran	IR	right	EP	republic	Mahmoud Ahmadinejad	Islam	11 Feb	.ir	0098	0044
Iraq	IRQ	right	YI	republic	Jalal Talabani	Islam	17 July	.iq	00964	0044
Ireland	IRL	left	EI, and EJ	republic	Michael D. Higgins, Enda Kenny (Taoiseach)	RC	17 Mar	.ie	00353	0044
Israel	IL	right	4X	republic	Shimon Peres, Benjamin Netanyahu (PM)	Judaism	14 May	.il	00972	0044
Italy	I	right	I	republic	Giorgio Napolitano, Enrico Letta (PM)	RC	2 June	.it	0039	0044
Ivory Coast	CI	right	TU	republic	Laurent Gbagbo	Islam	7 Dec	.ci	00225	0044
Jamaica	JA	left	6Y	constitutional monarchy	Portia Simpson-Miller (PM)	Christianity	Aug 1st	.jm	001879	01144
Japan	J	left	JA	constitutional monarchy	Emperor Akihito	Shintoism	23 Dec	.jp	0081	00144
Jordan	HKJ	right	JY	Hashemite kingdom	King Abdullah II	Islam	25 May	.jo	00962	0044
Kazakhstan	KZ	right	UN	republic	Nursultan Nazarbayev	Islam	16 Dec	.kz	007	81044
Kenya	EAK	left	5Y	republic	Uhuru Kenyatta	Christianity	12 Dec	.ke	00254	00044
Kiribati	KIR	left	T3	republic	Anote Tong	Christianity	12 July	.ki	00686	0044
Korea, North	P	right	P	democratic people's republic	Kim Il-sung	Buddhism	8 Sept	.kp	00850	01044
Korea, South	ROK	right	HL	republic	Park Geun-hye	Christianity	15 Aug	.kr	0082	00144
Kuwait	KWT	right	9K	constitutional monarchy	Emir Sabah Al-Ahmad Al-Jaber Al-Sabah	Islam	25 Feb	.kw	00965	0044
Kyrgyzstan	KS	right	EX	republic	Almazbek Atambayev	Islam	31 Aug	.kg	00996	81044
Laos	LAO	right	RDPL	republic	Lt Gen. Choummaly Sayasone	Buddhism	2 Dec	.la	00856	operator
Latvia	LV	right	YL	republic	Andris Bērziņš	Lutheran	18 Nov	.lv	00371	81044

Country	International Car Registration	Drives	International Civil Aircraft Markings	Type of government	President	Religion	National Day	Internet TLD	IDD Codes from UK	IDD Codes to UK
Lebanon	RL	right	OD	republic	Michel Suleiman	Islam	22 Nov	.lb	00961	0044
Lesotho	LS	left	7P	constitutional monarchy	King Letsie III	RC	4 Oct	.ls	00266	0044
Liberia	LB	right	A8	republic	Ellen Johnson Sirleaf	Christianity	26 July	.lr	00231	0044
Libya	LAR	right	5A	republic	Ali Zeidan (PM)	Islam	1 Sept	.ly	00218	0044
Liechtenstein	FL	right	HB	principality	Prince Hans-Adam II	RC	15 Aug	.li	0041	0044
Lithuania	LT	right	LY	republic	Dalia Grybauskaite	RC	16 Feb	.lt	00370	81044
Luxembourg	L	right	LX	grand duchy	Grand Duke Henri Guillaume	RC	23 June	.lu	00352	0044
Macedonia	MK	right	Z3	republic	Gjorge Ivanov	Christianity	18 Sept	.mk	00389	9944
Madagascar	RM	right	5R	republic	Albert Camille Vital (PM)	Christianity	26 June	.mg	00261	0044
Malawi	MW	left	7Q	republic	Joyce Banda	Christianity	6 July	.mw	00265	10144
Malaysia	MAL	left	9M	constitutional monarchy	Najib Tun Razak (PM)	Islam	31 Aug	.my	0060	0044
Maldives	MV	left	8Q	republic	Mohammed Waheed Hassan	Islam	26 July	.mv	00960	0044
Mali	RMM	right	TZ	republic	Dioncounda Traoré	Islam	22 Sept	.ml	00223	0044
Malta	M	left	9H	republic	George Abela	RC	31 Mar	.mt	00356	0044
Marshall Islands	MH	right	V7	republic	Christopher Loeak	Christianity	21 Oct	.mh	00692	01244
Mauritania	RIM	right	5T	republic	Mohamed Ould Abdel Aziz	Islam	28 Nov	.mr	00222	0044
Mauritius	MS	left	3B	republic	Kailash Purryag	Hinduism	12 Mar	.mu	00230	0044
Mexico	MEX	right	XA, XB, XC	republic	Enrique Peña Nieto	RC	16 Sept	.mx	0052	9844
Micronesia	FSM	left	V6	federal states		none			00691	01144
Moldova	MD	right	ER	republic	Nicolae Timofti	Eastern Orthodox	27 Aug	.md	00373	81044
Monaco	MC	right	3A	principality	Prince Albert II	RC	19 Nov	.mc	0037793	0044
Mongolia	MGL	right	JU	republic	Tsakhiagiin Elbegdorj	Buddhism	11 July	.mn	00976	operator
Montenegro	MNE	right	40	republic	Filip Vujanovic	Christianity	13 July	.me	00381	9944
Morocco	MA	right	CN	kingdom	King Mohammed VI	Islam	3 Mar	.ma	00212	0044
Mozambique	MOC	left	C9	republic	Armando Guebuza	RC	25 June	.mz	00258	0044
Myanmar (Burma)	BUR	right	XY, XZ	military regime	Thein Sein	Buddhism	4 Jan	.mm	0095	044
Namibia	NAM	left	V5	republic	Hifikepunye Pohamba	Lutheran	21 Mar	.na	00264	0944
Nauru	NAU	left	C2	republic	Baron Waqa	Christianity	31 Jan	.nr	00674	0044
Nepal	NEP	left	9N	republic	Ram Baran Yadav	Hinduism	18 Feb	.np	00977	0044
Netherlands	NL	right	PH	kingdom	HM King Willem-Alexander	RC	30 April	.nl	0031	0044
New Zealand	NZ	left	ZK	constitutional monarchy	John Key (PM)	Christianity	6 Feb	.nz	0064	0044
Nicaragua	NIC	right	YN	republic	Daniel Ortega	RC	15 Sept	.ni	00505	0044
Niger	RN	right	5U	republic	Mahamadou Issoufou	Islam	18 Dec	.ne	00227	0044
Nigeria	WAN	right	5N	republic	Goodluck Jonathan	Islam	1 Oct	.ng	00234	00944
Norway	N	right	LN	constitutional monarchy	King Harald V	Christianity	17 May	.no	0047	09544
Oman	OM	right	A40	Sultanate	Sultan Qaboos bin Said al Said	Islam	18 Nov	.om	00968	0044
Pakistan	PK	left	AP	republic	Asif Zardari	Islam	23 Mar & 14 Aug	.pk	0092	0044
Palau		right	T8A	democratic republic	Tommy Remengesau	Christianity	1 Oct	.pw	00680	01144
Panama	PA	right	HP	republic	Ricardo Martinelli	RC	3 Nov	.pa	00507	0044
Papua New Guinea	PNG	left	P2	constitutional monarchy	Peter O'Neill (PM)	RC	16 Sept	.pg	00675	0544
Paraguay	PY	right	ZP	republic	Federico Franco	RC	15 May	.py	00595	00244
Peru	PE	right	OB	republic	Ollanta Humala	RC	28 July	.pe	0051	0044
Philippines	RP	right	RP	republic	Benigno Aquino III	RC	12 June	.ph	0063	0044
Poland	PL	right	SP	republic	Bronisław Komorowski	RC	3 May	.pl	0048	0044
Portugal	P	right	CS	republic	Aníbal Cavaco Silva	RC	10 June	.pt	00351	0044
Qatar	QA	right	A7	constitutional monarchy	Emir HH Sheikh Hamad bin Khalifa Al Thani	Islam	3 Sept	.qa	00974	044
Romania	RO	right	YR	republic	Traian Basescu	Eastern Orthodox	1 Dec	.ro	0040	0044
Russia	RUS	right	RA	republic	Vladimir Putin, D. Medvedev (PM)	Russian Orthodox	12 June	.ru	007	81044
Rwanda	RWA	right	9XR	republic	Paul Kagame	RC	1 July	.rw	00250	0044
St Kitts and Nevis	SCN	left	V4	constitutional monarchy	Dr Denzil Douglas (PM)	Christianity	19 Sept	.kn	001869	operator

Country	International Car Registration	Drives	International Civil Aircraft Markings	Type of government	President	Religion	National Day	Internet TLD	IDD Codes from UK	IDD Codes to UK
St Lucia	WL	left	J6	constitutional monarchy	Kenny Anthony (PM)	Christianity	22 Feb	.lc	001758	044
St Vincent	WV	left	J8	constitutional monarchy	Ralph Gonsalves (PM)	Christianity	27 Oct	.vc	001809	0044
Samoa	WS	right	5W	republic	Tufuga Efi	Christianity	1 June	.ws	00685	144
San Marino	RSM	right	T7	serene republic	Antonella Mularoni &Denis Amici (Captains Regent)	RC	3 Sept	.sm	00378	0044
São Tomé	STP	right	S9	republic	Manuel Pinto da Costa	RC	12 July	.st	00239	0044
Saudi Arabia	SA	right	HZ	kingdom	King Abdullah bin Abdul Aziz	Islam	23 Sept	.sa	00966	0044
Senegal	SN	right	6V	republic	Macky Sall	Islam	4 Apr	.sn	00221	0044
Serbia	SRB	right	YU	republic	Tomislav Nikolić	Eastern Orthodox	15 Feb	.rs	00381	9944
Seychelles	SY	left	S7	republic	James Michel	RC	5 June	.sc	00248	044
Sierra Leone	WAL	right	9L	republic	Ernest Bai Koroma	Islam	27 Apr	.sl	00232	044
Singapore	SGP	left	9V	republic	Tony Tan Keng Yam	Buddhism	9 Aug	.sg	0065	00544
Slovakia	SK	right	OM	republic	Ivan Gasparovic	RC	1 Jan	.sk	0042	0044
Slovenia	SLO	right	S5	republic	Borut Pahor	RC	25 June	.si	00386	0044
Solomon Islands	SOL	left	H4	constitutional monarchy	Gordon Darcy Lilo (PM)	Christianity	7 July	.sb	00677	0044
Somalia	SO	right	6O	republic	Hassan Sheikh Mohamud	Islam	1 July	.so	00252	operator
South Africa	ZA	left	ZS	republic	Jacob Zuma	Christianity	27 April	.za	0027	0944
South Sudan		right		republic	Salva Kiir Mayardit	Animism/Christianity	9 July	.ss	00211	0044
Spain	E	right	EC	kingdom	King Juan Carlos I	RC	12 Oct	.es	0034	0744
Sri Lanka	CL	left	4R	republic	Mahinda Rajapaksa	Buddhism	4 Feb	.lk	0094	0044
Sudan	SUD	right	ST	republic	Omar al-Bashir	Islam	1 Jan	.sd	00249	0044
Suriname	SME	left	PZ	republic	Dési Bouterse	Christianity	25 Nov	.sr	00597	00144
Swaziland	SD	left	3D	kingdom	King Mswati III	Christianity	6 Sept	.sz	00268	0044
Sweden	S	right	SE	constitutional monarchy	King Carl XVI Gustaf	Lutheran	6 June	.se	0046	00744
Switzerland	CH	right	HB	republic	rotating seven-man council	RC	1 Aug	.ch	0041	0044
Syria	SYR	right	YK	republic	Bashir al-Assad	Islam	17 Apr	.sy	00963	0044
Taiwan	RC	right	B	republic	Ma Ying-jeou	Buddhism	10 Oct	.tw	00886	00244
Tajikistan	TJ	right	EY	republic	Emomalii Rahmon	Islam	9 Sept	.tj	007	81044
Tanzania	EAT/EAZ	left	5H	republic	Jakaya Kikwete	Christianity	26 Apr	.tz	00255	0044
Thailand	T	left	HS	constitutional monarchy	King Bhumibol Adulyadej (Rama IX)	Buddhism	5 Dec	.th	0066	00144
Togo	TG	right	5V	republic	Faure Gnassingbé	Christianity	13 Jan	.tg	00228	0044
Tonga	TO	left	A3	constitutional monarchy	King Aho□eitu Tupou VI	Christianity	4 June	.to	00676	0044
Trinidad and Tobago	TT	left	9Y	republic	George Maxwell Richards	Christianity	31 Aug	.tt	001868	01144
Tunisia	TN	right	TS	republic	Moncef Marzouki	Islam	20 Mar	.tn	00216	0044
Turkey	TR	right	TC	republic	Abdullah Gül	Islam	29 Oct	.tr	0090	0044
Turkmenistan	TM	right	EZ	republic	Gurbanguly Berdimuhamedow	Islam	27 Oct	.tm	00993	81044
Tuvalu	TUV	left	T2	constitutional monarchy	Willy Telavi (PM)	Protestantism	1 Oct	.tv	00688	0044
Uganda	EAU	left	5X	republic	Yoweri Museveni	Christianity	9 Oct	.ug	00256	0044
Ukraine	UA	right	UR	republic	Viktor Yanukovych	RC	24 Aug	.ua	00380	81044
UAE	UAE	right	A6	federal monarchy	Sheikh Khalifa Bin Zayed Al Nahyan	Islam	2 Dec	.ae	00971	0044
UK	GB	left	G	constitutional monarchy	David Cameron (PM)	Christianity		.uk		
USA	USA	right	N	republic	Barack Obama	Christianity	4 July	.us	001	01144
Uruguay	ROU	right	CX	republic	José Mujica	RC	25 Aug	.uy	00598	0044
Uzbekistan	UZ	right	UK	republic	Islam Karimov	Islam	1 Sept	.uz	007	81044
Vanuatu	VA	right	YJ	republic	Iolu Abil	Christianity	30 July	.vu	00678	0044
Vatican City	V	right	HV	state	Pope Francis	RC	22 Oct	.va	003966982	0044
Venezuela	YV	right	YV	republic	Nicolás Maduro	RC	5 July	.ve	0058	0044
Vietnam	VN	right	VN	republic	Tr□ng Tấn Sang	Buddhism	2 Sept	.vn	0084	0044
Yemen	YAR	right	7O	republic	Abd Rabbuh Mansur Hadi	Islam	22 May	.ye	00967	0044
Zambia	Z	left	9J	republic	Michael Sata	Christianity	24 Oct	.zm	00260	0044
Zimbabwe	ZW	left	Z	republic	Robert Mugabe, Morgan Tsvangirai (PM)	Christianity	18 Apr	.zw	00263	11044

National Anthems

Country	National Anthem
Afghanistan	Soroud-e-Melli First line: As long as the earth and heavens exist
Albania	The Flag that in Battle United Us
Algeria	Qassaman (The Pledge) First line: We swear by the lightning that destroys
Andorra	Great Charlemagne, My Father
Angola	Angola Avante
Antigua and Barbuda	Fair Antigua and Barbuda
Argentina	Hear, Oh Mortals, the Sacred Cry of Liberty
Armenia	Mer Hayrenik (Our Fatherland)
Australia	Advance Australia Fair
Austria	Land of Mountains, Land on the River (possibly from Mozart's 'Little Masonic Cantata')
Bahamas	March on, Bahamaland
Bahrain	Bahrainona (Our Bahrain)
Bangladesh	Amar Sonar Bangla First line: My golden Bengal, I love you
Barbados	In Plenty and in Time of Need
Belarus	My Belarusy (We, the Belarusians)
Belgium	La Brabançonne
Belize	O Land of the Free
Benin	The New Dawn
Bolivia	Oh Bolivia, Our Long-Felt Desires First line: Bolivians, propitious fate has crowned our hopes
Bosnia and Hercegovina	First line: You're the Light of the Soul
Botswana	Fatshe Leno La Rona First line: Blessed be this noble land
Brazil	From Peaceful Ypiranga's Banks
Brunei	O God, Long Live Our Majesty the Sultan
Bulgaria	Mila Rodino (Dear Motherland) First line: Stara Planina's Peaks Proudly Rise
Burkina Faso	Une Seule Nuit (One Single Night) First line: Against the Humiliating Bars, a Thousand Years Ago
Burundi	Dear Burundi, O Pleasant Land
Cambodia	Nokoreach (Royal Kingdom)
Cameroon	O Cameroon Thou Cradle of Our Forefathers
Canada	O Canada, Our Home and Native Land
Cape Verde	Cântico da Liberdade (Song of Freedom)
Chile	Chorus: Dulce Patria, Recibe Los Votos (Sweet Fatherland accept the vows)
China	March of the Volunteers
Colombia	Oh Gloria Inmarcesible (Oh, unfading glory)
Comoros	The Union of the Great Islands
Congo, Dem	Debout Congolais (Arise Congolese)
Congo, Rep	La Congolaise (The Congolese)
Costa Rica	Noble homeland, your beautiful flag
Croatia	Our Beautiful Homeland
Cuba	To Battle, Men of Bayamo

Country	National Anthem
Cyprus	Ode to Freedom
Czech Rep	Where is my Motherland
Denmark	There is a Lovely Country
Dominica	Isle of Beauty
Dominican Rep	Brave men of Quisqueya, Let Us Raise Our Song
East Timor	Patria Patria (Fatherland, fatherland)
Ecuador	Salve, Oh Patria (We Salute You, Our Fatherland)
Egypt	Biladi (My Country)
El Salvador	Let Us Proudly Hail the Fatherland
Equatorial Guinea	Let Us Tread the Path
Estonia	My Fatherland
Ethiopia	March Forward, Dear Mother Ethiopia
Fiji	Meda Dau Doka (God bless Fiji)
Finland	Maamme Suomi (Our Land, Finland)
France	La Marseillaise (The Song of Marseille)
Gabon	Uni dans la Concorde
Gambia, The	For The Gambia, Our Homeland
Georgia	Tavisupleba (Freedom)
Germany	Unity and Justice and Freedom
Ghana	God bless our Homeland, Ghana
Greece	Hymn to Freedom (longest – 158 verses)
Guatemala	Happy Guatemala
Guinea	Liberté (Liberty) - First line: People of Africa
Guyana	Dear land of Guyana
Haiti	La Dessalinienne
Honduras	Your Flag is a Heavenly Light
Hungary	God Bless the Hungarians
Iceland	O God of Our Country
India	Jana-gana-mana (Hail the ruler of all minds)
Indonesia	Indonesia, Our Native Land
Iran	Sorood-e Jomhoori-e Eslami
Iraq	Mawtini (My Homeland)
Ireland	Amhrán na bhFiann (The Soldier's Song)
Israel	Hatikvah (The Hope)
Italy	Inno di Mameli (aka Song of the Italians)
Ivory Coast	L'Abidjanaise (Song of Abidjan)
Jamaica	First line: Jamaica, Land We Love
Japan	Kimi ga yo Wa (May Your Peaceful Reign Last Long) First line: The reign of our emperor (lyrics date C9 melody added C19)
Jordan	Long Live the King
Kazakhstan	First line: Sky of golden sun
Kenya	Ee Mungu nguvu yetu (Oh God of all creation)
Kiribati	Stand up, Kiribati
Korea, North	Shine Bright O Dawn on This Land So Fair
Korea, South	Aegukka (Patriotic Song)
Kyrgyzstan	First line: High mountains, valleys and fields
Laos	First line: For the whole of time the Lao people glorified their Fatherland
Latvia	God Bless Latvia

Country	*National Anthem*
Lebanon	First line: All of us! For our Country
Lesotho	Lesotho, land of our fathers
Liberia	All Hail, Liberia, Hail
Liechtenstein	High on the Rhine
Lithuania	First line: Lithuania, Our Homeland
Luxembourg	Our Homeland
Macedonia	Today over Macedonia
Madagascar	Oh, Beloved Land of our Ancestors
Malawi	O God Bless our Land of Malawi
Malaysia	Negara-Ku (My Country)
Maldives	First line: We salute you in this national unity
Mali	A ton appel, Mali (at your call Mali)
Malta	L-Innu Malti
Mauritania	First line: Be a helper for God
Mauritius	Glory to Thee, Motherland
Mexico	First line: Mexicans, the War Cry
Moldova	Limba noastră (Our Language)
Monaco	Hymne Monégasque - First line: Forever, in our land
Mongolia	First line: Our unwavering independent nation
Montenegro	Oh, the Bright Dawn of May
Morocco	Hymn of the Sharif
Mozambique	Lovely Homeland (Patria Amada)
Myanmar	Kaba Ma Kyei (Till the End of the World)
Nepal	Hundreds of Flowers
Netherlands	Wilhelmus (oldest in the world dating from 1574)
New Zealand	God Defend New Zealand/God Save the Queen
Nicaragua	Hail, Nicaragua
Niger	La Nigérienne (The Nigerien)
Nigeria	Arise, O Compatriots
Norway	Yes, We Love This Country
Oman	First line: O Lord, protect our Sultan
Pakistan	First line: Blessed be the sacred land
Palau	Belau Rekid (Our Palau)
Panama	Himno Istmeño (Hymn of the Isthmus)
Papua New Guinea	Arise, All You Sons of This Land
Paraguay	Paraguayans, Republic or Death
Peru	First line: We Are Free
Philippines	Bayang Magiliw (Beloved Land)
	First line: Beloved land, pearl of the Orient
	Aka Lupang Hinirang (Chosen Land)
Poland	Poland Has Not Yet Been Destroyed
Portugal	A Portuguesa
Romania	Deşteaptă-te, române! (Awaken Thee, Romanian)
Russia	First line: Russia – our sacred homeland
Rwanda	Rwanda Nziza (Beautiful Rwanda)
St Kitts and Nevis	O Land of Beauty
St Lucia	Sons and Daughters of Saint Lucia
St Vincent	St Vincent, Land So Beautiful
Samoa	The Banner of Freedom

Country	*National Anthem*
San Marino	Unofficial lyrics: O ancient Republic
São Tomé	Independência total (Total Independence)
Saudi Arabia	As-Salam Al Malaki (The Royal Salute)
Senegal	Everyone Strum Your Koras, Strike the Balafons
Serbia	God of Justice
Seychelles	Koste Seselwa (Seychelles Unite)
Sierra Leone	High We Exalt Thee, Realm of the Free
Singapore	Majulah Singapura
Slovakia	Storm over the Tatras
Slovenia	Zdravljica (A Toast)
	First line: The vintage, friends, is over
Solomon Islands	God Bless our Solomon Islands
South Africa	The Call of South Africa, and God Bless South Africa
South Sudan	South Sudan Oyee!
Spain	Marcha Real Española (no lyrics)
Sri Lanka	Sri Lanka Matha (Mother Sri Lanka)
Sudan	We Are the Army of God
Swaziland	O Lord our God of the Swazi
Sweden	Thou Ancient, Thou Freeborn
Switzerland	First line: When the morning skies grow red
Syria	Defenders of the Homeland
Tajikistan	Surudi Milli
Tanzania	God Bless Africa
Thailand	Pleng Chart
Togo	Land of our forefathers
Tonga	Oh Almighty God Above
Trinidad and Tobago	Forged from the Love of Liberty
Tunisia	Humata Al Hima
	First line: Immortal and precious the blood we have shed
Turkey	The Independence March
	First line: Be not afraid! Our flag will never fade
Turkmenistan	First line: I am ready to give life for native hearth
Tuvalu	Tuvalu for the Almighty
Uganda	Oh, Uganda - First line: Pearl of Africa
U. A. E.	Ishy Biladi (Long Live my Nation)
UK	God Save the Queen
Ukraine	Ukraine's Glory Has Not Perished
Uruguay	Easterners, the Fatherland or Death
USA	The Star-Spangled Banner
Uzbekistan	First line: My sunny free land
Vanuatu	First line: Yumi, yumi, yumi i glat blong tale se, yumi, yumi, yumi i man blong Vanuatu (We, we, we are glad to tell, we, we we are the people of Vanuatu)
Venezuela	Glory to the Brave People
Vietnam	Soldiers of Vietnam, We Are Advancing
Yemen	First line: Repeat, O World My Song
Zambia	Stand and Sing of Zambia, Proud and Free
Zimbabwe	Blessed be the Country of Zimbabwe

History

Chronicles of World History

AD 1 The accepted year of Jesus' birth as calculated by Dionysius Exiguus in AD 525. (The more probable date is now considered to be 4 or possibly 6 BC.)
The King of the Trinovantes tribe, in Southern England, Addedomarus, dies and is succeeded by Dubnovellaunus.

2 Lucius Caesar (the 1st grandson of Augustus) dies.

3 The future Roman Emperor Galba is born.

4 Gaius Caesar (2nd grandson of Augustus) dies leaving Tiberius, the Emperor's newly adopted grandson, as heir.

5 Romans defeat the Lombard tribes on the lower Elbe.

6 Chinese initiate 'Civil Service' examinations for prospective politicians.

7 Ovid works on his masterpiece, *Metamorphoses.*

8 Ovid is exiled to Tomis (now Constanta, in present-day Romania) by the Emperor Augustus for reasons unknown.

9 Germans under Arminius wipe out 3 Roman legions in the Teutoburg Forest. Titus Livius (Livy), from Padua, completes his 142-volume *History of Rome.*

10 Cunobelinus (Cymbeline) rules over most of southern England from his HQ at Camulodunum (Colchester).

12 Gaius Caesar (later nicknamed Caligula, meaning 'little boots') is born.

13 Tiberius is appointed his successor by Augustus.

14 Death of Augustus. His adopted son Agrippa Postumus is immediately executed, and Tiberius becomes emperor.

15 The law of 'Maiestas', making it a crime to harm the interests of Rome, and therefore of the Emperor, is brought back by Tiberius to ensure that his sovereign power is not undermined.

16 An attempt to overthrow Tiberius is thwarted when a slave of Agrippa Postumus, named Clemens, is killed.

17 The poet Ovid dies in exile. Livy dies in Patavium (Padua).

18 In China, the usurper Emperor Wang Mang's forces fail to subdue the rebel band known as the Red Eyebrows at Shandong.

19 Tiberius' nephew Germanicus is poisoned in Syria, possibly by Gnaeus Calpurnius Piso, the governor of Syria.

20 Piso commits suicide during his trial.

21 A revolt by the Gallic tribes, the Treveri and the Aedui, is put down by Gaius Silius.

22 Wang Mang is defeated and killed, during a revolt by followers of the Han regime.

23 Drusus, the son of Tiberius, is poisoned by Lucius Aelius Sejanus, commander of the Praetorian Guard.

24 Tacfarinas, king of the Numidians, is killed by the Romans after a 7-year revolt.

25 Tiberius retires to Capri on the advice of the increasingly dominating Sejanus. Buddha is represented in human form for the first time at Gandhara.

26 Pontius Pilate becomes the 5th Roman procurator of Judaea and Samaria.

27 Tiberius leaves Rome and settles on Capri.

29 Agrippina, widow of Germanicus, is arrested on the orders of Tiberius.

30 Jesus of Nazareth is crucified at Golgotha. Dionysius Exiguus, the inventor of the Christian calendar, wrongly dated the birth of Jesus according to the Roman system, i.e. 754 years after the founding of Rome.

31 Sejanus is executed by Tiberius when the extent of his plotting emerges.

32 In Rome, interest rates rocket as a result of a currency shortage. The Emperor Otho is born.

35 Tiberius makes Caligula and Tiberius Gemellus heirs to his private estate.

36 The future Emperor Nerva is born.

37 Tiberius dies at Misenum and is succeeded by Gaius Caesar (Caligula). The Emperor Nero is born.

38 Drusilla, beloved sister and consort of Caligula, dies, and is deified.

39 Caligula puts down a conspiracy by the governor of higher Germany, Gaetulicus.

40 King Ptolemy of Mauretania is assassinated by order of Caligula.

41 Caligula declares himself a god and is assassinated shortly afterwards. Claudius succeeds him.

42 Cunobelinus, ruler of most of Southern England, dies.

43 The Romans, on the orders of Claudius, invade Britain.

44 James becomes the first Christian apostle to be martyred.

45 The philosopher Philo dies.

46 The kingdom of Thrace becomes a province of Rome.

47 Messalina, wife of the Emperor Claudius, is acquiring a reputation as a sexual profligate.

48 Emperor Guang Wudi re-establishes Chinese domination of the people of inner Mongolia. Claudius has Messalina executed for infidelity.

49 Claudius expels Jewish Christians from Rome.

50 Claudius adopts his stepson Nero.

51 Caractacus, son of Cunobelinus, is captured by the Romans at Ludlow.

52 The future Emperor Domitian is born.

53 Nero marries his stepsister Octavia.

54 Claudius dies after eating poisoned mushrooms administered by the Empress Agrippina. Nero succeeds him.

55 Britannicus, son of Claudius, dies, possibly poisoned by Nero.

57 Paul is arrested at Caesarea and held for trial.

58 Paul writes an epistle to the Romans.

59 Nero has his mother, Agrippina, killed.

60 Mark, a disciple of Jesus, chronicles the life of his master, from baptism by his cousin, John, to his eventual death.

61 During a rebellion led by Queen Boudicca of the Iceni, the Trinovantes and Iceni tribes sack Roman Colchester, St Albans and London. Boudicca commits suicide after defeat by Suetonius Paulinus.

62 Paul is put under 'house arrest' in Rome.

63 The Armenian throne is returned to Tiridates after the peace of Rhandeia.

64 Paul of Tarsus is executed, as is Peter the apostle. Fire destroys over half of the city of Rome.

65 Nero's pregnant wife dies after being kicked by him.

66 The courtier Gaius Petronius is accused of treason and has to commit suicide.

67 The Jews rise up against the Romans.

68 Nero commits suicide to end the Julio-Claudian line of Roman Emperors. He is succeeded by Servius Sulpicius Galba.

69 The year of 4 Roman emperors, Galba, Vitellius, Otho and Vespasian.

70 Vespasian's son, Titus, sacks Jerusalem, destroying most of the 3rd Temple; only the 'Wailing Wall' is left standing.

71 The 'Arch of Titus', in celebration of the sacking of Jerusalem, is erected in Rome.

73 Chinese forces under General Ban Chao gain control over the 'Oasis' states. After a two-year siege, the fortress of Masada in Judea falls to the Romans.

74 Vespasian institutes 'Latin Rights' which give inhabitants of towns identical civil rights to 'Citizens' except for holding public office.

75 Vespasian completes his Temple of Peace in Rome.

76 Johanan Ben Zakkai re-establishes the Sanhedrin, the Jewish religious court.

77 Gnaeus Julius Agricola arrives in Britain to complete the conquest.

78 Vima Kadphises, the Kushan king, who rules India from Benares, sends a delegation to Rome to arrange a surprise attack on the Parthians.
79 Vesuvius erupts, destroying Pompeii and the neighbouring towns of Herculaneum and Stabiae. Pliny the Elder is one of the victims. Vespasian dies, and his son Titus succeeds him.
80 The apostle Luke begins to write his gospel. The Colosseum is opened in Rome.
81 Titus dies of the plague and is succeeded by his brother, Titus Flavius Domitianus (Domitian). Domitian consecrates the triumphal arch to celebrate Titus's victory over the Jews.
82 Spanish poet Marcus Valerius Martialis (Martial) begins his *Epigrams.*
83 Agricola defeats the Caledonians at Mount Graupius.
84 Agricola is called back to Rome.
85 Domitian appoints himself censor for life, thereby giving himself complete control of the composition of the Senate.
86 The future Emperor Antoninus is born.
87 The Romans suffer a serious setback in the Dacian War.
88 The revolt of Saturninus, governor of Upper Germany, leads to Domitian declaring that only one legion is to be quartered in each Roman camp, to prevent any local commander from gaining excessive influence over troops.
89 Domitian is forced to sign a peace treaty with the Dacian king, Decebalus.
90 Domitian begins the persecution and execution of opponents.
91 Chinese general Ban Chao defeats the Indian Kushans.
92 The Iazyges, a nomadic tribe, invade Dacia. Domitian leads his soldiers in person and succeeds in repelling them.
94 General Ban Chao completes his conquest of the Tarim basin.
95 Malaria appears in rural areas around Rome.
96 Emperor Domitian is stabbed to death by plotters led by his wife, Domitia. Senator Marcus Cocceius Nerva succeeds him.
97 Emperor Nerva recalls General Marcus Ulpius Trajanus (Trajan) from Upper Germany and adopts him.
98 Emperor Nerva dies, and is succeeded by Trajan.
99 Julius Frontinus, a former governor of Britain, surveys and describes the aqueducts of Rome in his capacity as superintendent of Rome's water supply.
100 The Sun and Moon pyramids are begun at Teotihuacán in Mexico.
101 Trajan invades Dacia (in present-day Romania), fearing the increasing dominance of Decebalus.
102 Sarmizegethusa, capital of Dacia, is taken by Trajan; Decebalus agrees to become a Roman ally.
104 Martial dies at Bibilis, in Spain.
105 Tsai Lun, a Chinese eunuch, invents a kind of paper made from tree bark, hemp and rags.
106 Dacia becomes a Roman province after King Decebalus and his chiefs commit suicide.
110 Pliny the Younger is appointed governor of Bithynia. Juvenal publishes his first book of *Satires* in Rome, highlighting corruption, vice and the unjust treatment of the poor.
114 Trajan's Column and Basilica are built. Armenia is annexed to the Roman Empire.
115 Mesopotamia is occupied by the Romans.
116 Assyria is annexed to the Roman Empire.
117 Trajan dies and is succeeded by Publius Aelius Hadrianus (Hadrian). Cornelius Tacitus, the celebrated historian, dies.
120 Construction of the Pantheon in Rome is begun.
122 Construction of Hadrian's Wall is begun.
123 Emperor Hadrian meets the king of Parthia, thus averting war.
125 Plague and famine in North Africa.
128 The Greek physician Galen is born.
130 Hadrian's Wall is completed.
132 The Jewish population of Jerusalem revolts over the construction of a shrine to Jupiter on the site of the Temple.
135 The Romans retake and demolish Jerusalem; Jewish leader Simon Bar-Kokhba killed near Caesarea; diaspora begins.
138 Hadrian dies and is succeeded by his recently adopted son Antonius Pius.
139 The Romans advance northwards under governor Quintus Lollius Urbicus from Hadrian's Wall to the Clyde–Forth line.
142 Construction of the Antonine Wall is begun.
154 Brigantian revolt in Pennines put down by governor Julius Verus, but troops withdrawn from Caledonia as a result.
155 Partial destruction by indigenous Picts of the Antonine Wall.
161 Antonius dies and is succeeded by his adopted son Marcus Annius Verus (Marcus Aurelius).
163 Antonine Wall abandoned.
167 Barbarians attack Rome, but are repelled by Marcus Aurelius. The Marcomanni and Quadi cross the Danube into Roman territory.
168 The Marcomanni, who have occupied North-western Italy, are conquered by Marcus Aurelius.
169 The Marcomanni revolt, but the revolt is crushed.
174 The Germanic Quadi tribe defeated by Marcus Aurelius.
175 Avidius Cassius encourages the legions in Asia to revolt, but is assassinated and his head sent to Marcus Aurelius.
177 Persecution of Christians recommences in Rome; they adopt the fish symbol as an emblem of their faith.
180 Marcus Aurelius dies and is succeeded by his son Commodus.
185 Mass mutiny of the Roman army in Britain eventually quelled by newly appointed governor Publius Helvius Pertinax.
192 Commodus murdered by his mistress and chamberlain, who found their names on an execution list.
193 Pertinax is chosen as emperor by the senate, but his strict rule leads to his assassination. Didius Julianus becomes emperor after an auction but has already been deposed and killed by the time that Septimius Severus, the Pannonian legate, invades Rome and is declared emperor.
197 Clodius Albinus, the British legate, revolts, but is defeated and killed by Severus at Lyons.
200 Japanese empress, Jingu, sends a fleet to invade Korea, which surrenders on sight of it.
205 Plotinus, founder of Neoplatonism, is born.
209 Roman legions under Severus and Caracalla march against the Caledonii, advancing as far as Aberdeen; forts built on Firths of Forth and Tay.
211 Septimus Severus dies at York; he is succeeded by his sons Caracalla and Geta.
212 Caracalla murders Geta and slaughters thousands of his brother's supporters. He extends Roman citizenship to all free inhabitants of the Empire by the Edict of Caracalla.
215 Manes, who develops the dualist philosophy known as Manichaeism, is born in southern Mesopotamia.
216 Britannia is divided into two provinces – Upper Britain (south and west) and Lower Britain (north).
217 Caracalla is murdered by his officers, and is succeeded by Macrinus.
218 Macrinus is defeated in battle near Antioch and executed. He is succeeded by Varius Avitus Bassianus, who takes the name Heliogabalus.
220 Fall of the Han Dynasty in China, which splits into a number of smaller states.
222 Heliogabalus is murdered by the Praetorian Guard. His cousin and adopted son Bassianus succeeds him, taking the name Severus Alexander.
225 Southern India breaks up into several kingdoms with the end of the Andgra dynasty.
226 The rebel prince Ardashir takes control of Persia, founding the Sassanid dynasty.
234 Severus Alexander decrees that bread, rather than grain, be given to Rome's poor.
235 The Alemanni invade Gaul, but are bought off by Severus Alexander. As a result, he is murdered by his army, who proclaim Maximinus as Emperor.

238 The African provinces set up Gordianus I, a descendant of Trajan, as Emperor. Gordianus commits suicide when his son is killed by supporters of Maximinus, but when Maximinus is assassinated by the Praetorian Guard, Gordianus' grandson, Gordianus III, becomes emperor.
244 Gordianus III defeats the Persians at Resaena, but soon after is murdered during a mutiny by Marcus Philippus, who replaces him and makes peace with the Persians.
248 Games are held to celebrate Rome's millennium.
249 Decius usurps the throne from Philippus, who is killed. The Goths cross the River Danube and lay waste several Roman provinces.
250 Decius initiates further persecution of Christians.
251 Decius dies in battle against the Goths; his successor Gallus bribes the Goths to return from whence they came.
253 Aemilian revolts against Gallus, who dies by the hand of his own troops. Aemilian dies and Valerianus becomes Emperor.
254 Origen, one of the leading Christian scholars, dies.
255 Plague sweeps across Europe.
257 The Goths move into the Black Sea area.
258 The Alemanni and Suevi invade Northern Italy, but are repulsed at Milan.
260 Valerianus seized by the Persians and dies in captivity; his son Gallienus succeeds him.
267 Prince Odenathus of Palmyra assassinated with Gallienus' complicity.
268 Gallienus murdered by his own troops at Milan. Claudius II becomes emperor.
269 The Goths invade the Balkans, sacking Athens, Sparta and Corinth, but are defeated in battle by Claudius II.
270 Claudius II dies. His brother Quintillus succeeds him, but commits suicide when his troops desert him. Aurelian becomes emperor.
271 Aurelian ejects the Alemanni from Italy, and rebuilds the walls of Rome.
272 Aurelian conquers the kingdom of Palmyra.
274 A rebellion at Châlons is put down by Aurelian, who returns to Rome in triumph.
275 The Romans pull back to the Danube and Rhine, which are established as the Empire's frontier. Aurelian is assassinated by his officers, and Tacitus succeeds him as emperor.
276 Tacitus killed by his own troops after defeating the Goths in Asia Minor. His brother Florianus succeeds, only to be killed also. Marcus Aurelius Probus becomes Emperor. Mani is crucified on the grounds of heresy.
282 The Franks and Alemanni invade Gaul, but are repulsed by Probus, who is killed by his troops in Egypt. Marcus Aurelius Carus replaces him.
283 Marcus Aurelius Carus dies, to be succeeded by his son Numerianus.
284 Numerianus is assassinated, to be replaced by Diocletian.
285 Diocletian partitions the Empire – he rules in the East, to counter the barbarian threat there, while Maximian is appointed to run the Western portion.
286 Carausius, commander of the Channel fleet, revolts and seizes Britain, where construction begins on a series of forts to guard the south-eastern coast (the Saxon Shore forts).
290 Construction begins on the amphitheatre in Verona.
291 Persian King Vahram II kills the Manichaean Sisih.
293 Carausius murdered by Allectus, his finance minister, who seizes power in Britain. Britannia is divided into four provinces – Britannia Prima (capital Cirencester), Britannia Secunda (York), Flavia Caesariensis (Lincoln) and Maxima Caesariensis (London).
296 Allectus defeated and killed by Constantius Chlorus in battle near Silchester.
300 Diocletian builds a palace at Ragusa (later Dubrovnik).
301 Christianity proclaimed the state religion in Armenia.
303 The notary Genesius is martyred. Diocletian begins a general persecution of Christians.
304 The Kingdom of Cheng Han is founded in Sichuan.
305 Diocletian and his co-ruler Maximian abdicate and are succeeded by Galerius and Constantius Chlorus respectively.
306 Constantius Chlorus dies near York. His son Constantine is proclaimed Emperor, but Galerius raises Severus instead.
307 Severus dies; Galerius raises Licinius to co-Emperor.
308 Maxentius, son of Maximian, becomes despot in Rome.
311 Galerius attempts to expel Maxentius, but is defeated and dies soon after.
312 Constantine defeats Maxentius, his rival Western emperor, at the Milvian Bridge.
313 Christianity tolerated in the Roman Empire by the Edict of Milan.
316 The Xiongnu, later identified with the Huns, invade China.
323 Constantine and Licinius at war; Constantine victorious.
324 Licinius executed; Constantine becomes sole ruler. Christianity declared the official religion of the Roman Empire.
325 Council of Nicaea declares Christ and God are of the same substance – 'consubstantial'.
330 Constantinople (formerly Byzantium; known today as Istanbul) is dedicated as the new capital of the Roman Empire.
335 Church of the Holy Sepulchre consecrated in Jerusalem.
337 Constantine I dies, not long after taking Christian baptism; he is succeeded by his three sons, Constantine II, Constantius II and Constans.
338 Jewish calendar reformed by establishing variable year lengths.
340 Constantine II killed at Aquileia fighting Constans; Empire splits into East under Constantius II and West under Constans.
350 Constans murdered by General Magnentius in a coup.
352 Magnentius is defeated by Constantius II at Mursa in Mesopotamia.
353 Magnentius commits suicide. Constantius II reunites Empire.
356 All pagan temples in the Roman Empire ordered closed by Constantius II.
360 Lo-tsun founds the Caves of the Thousand Buddhas in Gansu, China. The Huns invade Europe for the first time.
361 Constantius II dies, and is succeeded by his pagan cousin Julian.
363 Julian dies in battle against the Persians; Jovian, captain of the Imperial Bodyguard, succeeds to the throne.
364 Jovian cedes Armenia to Shah Shapur II of Persia, and dies on his return. Valentinian I becomes emperor, and appoints his brother Valens to rule in the Eastern half.
367 Picts, Scots, Angles and Saxons invade Britain in a joint attack, later known as the 'Barbarian Conspiracy'..
369 Theodosius, a Roman general, re-establishes order in Britain.
372 Buddhism reaches Korea from China.
375 Valentinian I dies. His 4-year-old son Valentinian II nominally succeeds him in the West but his older half-brother Gratian has effective control.
376 The Huns invade Russia and defeat the Visigoths. From now on, tribes pushed westward by the Huns press harder into the Roman Empire.
378 Visigoths defeat and kill the Emperor Valens at the battle of Adrianople.
379 Gratian's general, Theodosius becomes Emperor in the East.
382 Visigoths settled as Foederati (military allies) in the Balkans by Theodosius.
383 Magnus Maximus mutinies against Gratian, who is assassinated. Magnus rules in Britain, Gaul and Spain.
386 Hymn singing introduced by St Ambrose, Bishop of Milan.
388 Magnus Maximus invades Italy, to be defeated by Theodosius and murdered. Valentinian II established in power in the West.
391 The library at Alexandria is destroyed in a fire started by a Christian mob seeking to eradicate non-Christian works.
392 The Frankish general Arbogast organises the assassination of Valentinian II and replaces him with a puppet emperor, Eugenius.
394 Eugenius defeated and killed by Theodosius, who reunites the Empire. Arbogast commits suicide.
395 Theodosius dies, and the Roman Empire splits in two for good. His son Arcadius rules in the East, Honorius in the West.
396 Alaric the Visigoth invades Greece.

397 Stilicho, regent to Honorius, ejects the Visigoths from Greece and crushes a rebellion in North Africa.
401 The Visigoths invade Northern Italy.
402 Visigoths halted by Stilicho at the battle of Pollentia.
405 The Colosseum closed by Honorius.
406 Stilicho halts barbarian invasion of Italy. Vandals under Gunderic invade Gaul.
407 Roman troops depart Britain under the pretender Constantine III; Britain left to fend for itself.
408 Stilicho is murdered on Honorius' orders. Arcadius dies. His son Theodosius II becomes emperor in Constantinople.
409 The Vandals cross the Pyrenees and enter Spain.
410 Visigoths under Alaric sack Rome. Alaric dies shortly afterwards; his brother Ataulf takes command.
411 Constantine III defeated and executed by troops loyal to Honorius. Pelagius calls on St Augustine at Hippo but Augustine refuses to see him.
412 The Visigoths enter Gaul from Italy and establish a kingdom there.
415 Neoplatonist philosopher Hypatia is killed in Alexandria by a Christian mob who scraped her to death with oyster shells.
416 Vandal kingdom of Spain falls to the Visigoths.
418 Franks enter Gaul and settle.
420 Nanjing becomes the capital of northern China once more. Eastern Qin state in China is overthrown by its general Liu Yu, who founds the Liu Song state. St Jerome dies.
422 Theodosius II makes peace with Shah Varahran of Persia, and agrees an annual tribute with the Huns.
423 Death of Honorius, emperor of the West.
425 Constantinople University founded.
426 Yash Kukhmol arrives from Teotihuacán in Copán, founding a Mayan dynasty.
427 Korean capital moved to Pyongyang by King Changsu.
429 Vandals invade Africa, led by King Gaiseric. The British, led by Bishop Germanus, defeat barbarian invaders (the 'Alleluia Victory').
430 Cunedda, chief of the Gododdin, moves at the Welsh King Vortigern's behest from Scotland to Gwynedd, whose royal house he thereby founds.
431 Council of Ephesus deposes Patriarch Nestorius of Constantinople for his belief that Jesus had two natures, one human and one divine.
432 Saint Patrick sent as a missionary to Ireland.
433 Attila becomes co-ruler of the Huns.
439 Carthage taken by Gaiseric's Vandals, who make it their capital.
440 The town of Ys in Armorica (later Brittany) is submerged in a great flood. The Vandals invade Sicily.
441 Britain invaded by Angles, Saxons and Jutes.
443 The Alemanni settle in Alsace.
444 The wheelbarrow developed in China.
446 Britain told to fend for itself when it appeals to Rome for help against barbarian invaders.
450 Theodosius II dies, to be succeeded by Marcian, who refuses to continue paying tribute to the Huns to prevent them from attacking.
451 Huns defeated at battle of Châlons by Romans and Visigoths under Flavius Aetius.
452 Venice founded by refugees from the Huns.
453 Death of Attila on his wedding night.
455 The Vandals sack Rome.
457 Marcian dies, to be succeeded by Leo I.
460 Roman fleet destroyed by the Vandals off Cartagena.
461 Severus III becomes Western emperor.
466 Theodoric II of the Visigoths killed by his brother Euric, who succeeds him.
467 Anthemius elected Western emperor at Leo I's behest; they mount a joint expedition against the Vandals in North Africa.
468 The Vandals successfully repulse the Roman invasion.
471 Goths and Eastern Romans clash due to a feud caused by the failure of the expedition against the Vandals.
472 Ricimer the Visigoth captures Anthemius, and appoints Olybrius in his stead. Both Ricimer and Olybrius subsequently die; Gundobad the Burgundian takes control.
473 Gundobad names Glycerinus Western emperor, but he is deposed by Julius Nepos, a protégé of Leo I.
474 Leo I dies, to be succeeded by his son-in-law Zeno.
475 Orestes deposes Julius Nepos and makes his son Romulus Augustulus Western emperor.
476 Romulus Augustulus deposed by Odoacer at Ravenna; Western Roman Empire ends.
477 Sussex founded by Aelle, who lands with his sons at Selsey.
478 Shinto shrines appear in Japan.
481 At the age of 15, Clovis I succeeds his father Childeric I as king of the Franks.
484 Armenia revolts successfully against the Persians led by Vahan Mamikonian. Freedom of religious worship was restored to them by the Treaty of Nvarsag.
486 Clovis defeats governor Syragius at Soissons and takes control of Northern Gaul.
488 The Ostrogoths, led by Theodoric and prompted by Zeno, invade Italy, now ruled by Odoacer.
491 Zeno dies, to be succeeded by Anastasius, who marries his widow. The South Saxons under Aelle capture Pevensey Castle.
493 Odoacer surrenders to Theodoric at Ravenna after a siege, and is murdered by him. Theodoric founds the Ostrogoth kingdom of Italy.
495 Cerdic, founder of Wessex, lands near Southampton.
496 Clovis defeats the Alemanni near Strasbourg, and converts to Christianity, being baptised by Bishop Remigius of Rheims.
500 The Marcomanni invade Bavaria from Bohemia, which is settled by the Czechs. Incense is added to Christian services to cover the smell of unwashed worshippers.
502 King Gundobad of Burgundy issues a legal code that establishes equality before the law for Burgundians and Romans.
507 Clovis defeats the Visigoths, killing King Alaric II at Vouillé, near Poitiers, and goes on to conquer Southern Gaul.
508 The Ostrogoths under Theodoric conquer Provence and Septimania.
511 Death of Clovis. His kingdom of Francia is divided into four to provide kingdoms for his four sons.
516 The British comprehensively defeat the Saxons at Mons Badonicus.
517 Emperor Wudi introduces Buddhism to central China.
518 Emperor Anastasius I dies, to be succeeded by Justin I, chief of the imperial guard, who entrusts much imperial policy to his nephew Justinian.
519 Eastern and Western Churches reconciled.
520 Priscian codifies Latin grammar with his long treatise, the *Institutiones Grammaticae.*
522 The philosopher and statesman Boethius arrested on a charge of conspiring against Theodoric.
523 King Thrasamund of the Vandals dies and is succeeded by Hilderic.
524 Boethius writes *The Consolation of Philosophy* and is executed shortly after.
525 Yemen invaded by Abyssinians under Caleb. Dionysius Exiguus wrongly sets the date of Christ's birth as 25 December in the 753rd year of Rome.
526 Theodoric the Ostrogoth dies, and is succeeded by his 10-year-old grandson Athalaric.
527 Death of Justin I; his nephew Justinian succeeds him.
528 Hun King Grod converted to Christianity and was killed. The Korean state of Silla officially recognised Buddhism.
529 Benedict of Nursia founds the monastery of Monte Cassino. Justinian closes the non-Christian Academy at Athens.
530 The great Byzantine general Belisarius defeats the Persians at Dara. King Hilderic of the Vandals dies, to be succeeded by Gelimer.
531 Chosroes I becomes Shah of Persia. The Franks conquer Thuringia.
532 Burgundy invaded by the Franks.

533 Belisarius conquers the Vandal kingdom of North Africa, reclaiming it for Byzantium.
534 Toledo made capital of the Visigoth kingdom of Spain. Malta captured by the Byzantine army.
535 Belisarius invades and captures Sicily, and moves into Southern Italy.
536 Belisarius takes Rome from the Ostrogoths.
537 Arthur and Medrault fall at the battle of Camlann.
539 Witigis, leader of the Ostrogoths, is captured by Belisarius at Ravenna. Belisarius recalled to Constantinople.
540 Totila, an Ostrogoth leader, expels the Byzantines from Italy. The Roman statesman and author Cassiodorus founds the monastery at Vivarium in Calabria and retires there.
541 Totila succeeds to the Ostrogothic throne on the death of his uncle Hildebad. The bubonic 'Plague of Justinian' pandemic starts in Constantinople.
542 The Welsh monk Gildas writes *De Excidio et Conquestu Britanniae*, a history of the Roman conquest and Anglo-Saxon invasion of Britain.
543 Justinian condemns the writings of Origen.
546 Totila captures Rome. Audoin establishes a new Lombard kingdom in Austria.
547 The Plague of Justinian reaches Britain. The Angle king Ida accedes to the throne of Bernicia, in north-east England.
549 The last games are held in Rome.
550 The Toltecs overrun Teotihuacán. St David converts the Welsh.
551 The Byzantines defeat an Ostrogothic fleet in a naval battle.
552 Totila killed at Taginae fighting the Byzantines under Narses. Justinian sends missionaries to China to smuggle silkworms out. Buddhism arrives in Japan from Korea.
553 Rome and Naples annexed by Narses for Byzantium.
554 Narses appointed Exarch of Italy.
558 Reunification of Francia by Chlothar I after the death of his brother Childebert I.
559 The Bulgars attack Constantinople, but are repelled by Belisarius.
560 Aethelbert I becomes king of Kent. Ceawlin becomes king of Wessex.
561 Death of Chlothar I – Francia again split in four by his sons. Battle of the Books ultimately results in the exile of Columeille to Iona in 563.
563 Foundation of monastery on Iona by Columcille (Saint Columba).
565 St Columba subdues a monster on Loch Ness. Belisarius dies. Justinian I dies, and is succeeded by his nephew Justin II.
567 With the death of Charibert, Francia reorganised into Austrasia in the east, Neustria in the west and Burgundy in the south.
568 Alboin founds a Lombard kingdom in Northern and Central Italy.
570 Muhammad born in Mecca. The Persians take the Yemen from the Abyssinians.
571 Foundation of the kingdom of East Anglia.
572 War breaks out between Persia and Byzantium.
573 Sigebert of Austrasia attacks Chilperic of Neustria over the murder of Galswintha, sister of Sigebert's wife Brunhilda.
574 Aidan ordained king of the Argyll Scots by St Columba.
575 King Sigebert assassinated on the orders of Chilperic's wife and former mistress Fredegunde; Brunhilda seeks revenge.
577 Celtic kings Commail, Condidan and Farinmail killed at the battle of Dyrham (Deorham) by West Saxons under Cuthwine and Ceawlin.
578 Death of Justin II, to be succeeded by Tiberius II.
579 Death of Shah Chosroes of Persia.
581 China's Sui dynasty founded by Emperor Wendi (Yang Jian). H
582 Death of Tiberius II, to be succeeded by his son-in-law Maurice. I
583 Wendi moves into the new city of Chang'an, soon to become the world's largest city. S
584 Death of Chilperic of Neustria, who is succeeded by his son Chlothar II. T
585 King Leovigild of the Visigoths puts down a revolt by his son Hermenegild, whom he kills, and proceeds to conquer the rest of the Iberian peninsula. O R
586 King Leovigild dies, leaving the Visigothic throne to his son Recared. Disputes in Japan between Shinto and Buddhist adherents. Y
587 The Visigoths convert from Arianism to Catholicism. The first Buddhist monastery is built in Japan.
588 Shah Hormizd of Persia deposed and murdered after defeats by Byzantines; replaced by his son Chosroes II.
589 Wendi defeats the Chen at Jian-Kang and reunites China. Chosroes II deposed in Persia, fleeing to Constantinople.
590 Gregory I the Great becomes Pope and undertakes reforms in Rome, as well as helping to expel the plague from the city.
591 Maurice helps restore Chosroes II to the Persian throne in return for territorial concessions.
592 Ceawlin of Wessex deposed by Ceol. The Bretwaldaship (overlordship) of the English peoples south of the Humber passes to Aethelbert of Kent.
593 Aethelfrith succeeds Hussa as King of the Bernicians.
594 The 'Plague of Justinian' pandemic comes to an end. Gregory of Tours dies.
596 St Augustine dispatched by Pope Gregory to convert Britain.
597 Saint Augustine arrives in Kent, converts King Aethelbert and founds the archdiocese of Canterbury.
600 Tibet begins to develop into a unitary state.
602 Emperor Maurice killed and replaced by Phocas.
603 Battle of Catraeth (Catterick): Aethelfrith of Northumbria defeats a coalition of British from Lothian, North Wales and North West England.
604 The Japanese code of Prince Shotoku Taishi demands the veneration of Buddha, his priests and his laws. Aethelfrith unites Bernicia and Deira to create the kingdom of Northumbria.
606 Harsha of Thanesar founds an empire in Northern India, the last indigenous ruler to do so for several centuries.
607 Horyuji temple and hospital, the oldest surviving wooden building in the world, constructed in Japan.
609 Consecration of the Pantheon in Rome.
610 Emperor Phocas deposed and killed by Heraclius. Muhammad has a vision of the angel Gabriel on Mount Hira.
611 Death of Ceolwulf of Wessex, succeeded by Cynegils.
612 Harsha of Thanesar takes the title of Emperor of the Five Indies. St Gall founds the hermitage, later a monastery of St Gallen in Switzerland.
613 Francia reunited under Chlothar II after his conquest of Austrasia.
614 Chlothar II issues the *Edictum Chlotacharii*, which defines the rights of kings, nobles and Church within Francia.
615 Jerusalem sacked by the Persians, who take the 'True Cross' as booty.
616 Aethelbert of Kent dies; Raedwald of East Anglia becomes Bretwalda; he kills Aethelfrith of Northumbria at the River Idle, replacing him by the exiled Edwin.
618 Sui dynasty replaced by the Tang.
619 Publication of the *Suan-Ching*, textbooks for use in public examinations in China.
620 Chosroes II takes Rhodes, thus restoring the Persian Empire to the extent it reached under Darius I.
622 In July Muhammad flees from Mecca to Medina (the hegira, from which the Islamic calendar year 1 is dated).
623 Samo, a Frankish merchant, frees Slav tribes in Carinthia from Avar overlordship and becomes their ruler.
625 Death of Raedwald; Edwin of Northumbria becomes Bretwalda.
626 Chinese Emperor Gaozu abdicates in favour of his son Taizong.
627 The Byzantines decisively defeat the Persians at Nineveh.
628 Chosroes II murdered by his son Kavadh II, who succeeds him.
629 Chlothar II dies, to be succeeded by his son Dagobert I. Emperor Heraclius recovers Jerusalem from the Persians.

630 Mecca falls to Muhammad who writes letters on the principles of Islam to various rulers.

632 Death of Muhammad; Abu Bakr chosen as Caliph. Edwin of Northumbria killed by Mercian/Welsh forces at Hatfield. They proceed to ravage the kingdom, which splits back in two.

634 Abu Bakr dies; Umar becomes Caliph. Oswald re-establishes the kingdom of Northumbria and becomes Bretwalda.

635 Islamic forces take Damascus, which becomes the capital of the Caliphate. Harsha invades the land of the Chalukyas, but is repulsed.

638 Jerusalem falls to Islamic forces under Umar.

639 Dagobert I of Francia dies; the kingdom is split again.

641 Great Library at Alexandria destroyed in a fire. Oswald of Northumbria dies in battle at Maserfelth (near Oswestry) fighting King Penda of Mercia; he is succeeded in Bernicia by Oswy. Persia is conquered and made subject to the Caliphate.

644 Byzantine forces capture Alexandria, which revolted against Islamic rule, but the Arabs retake it. Caliph Umar dies, to be succeeded by Uthman.

646 The Taikwa reform in Japan establishes centralised government under Imperial control.

647 Harsha of Thanesar dies, and his Northern Indian empire fragments as a result.

649 Cyprus falls to Islamic forces.

650 The Bulgarian Empire, then in Southern Russia, conquered by the Khazars.

652 Arabs come to an agreement with the Nubians, establishing Aswan as the southern limit of the Caliphate in Egypt.

653 The Visigothic king Recesswinth of Spain draws up a legal code for his domains, the *Liber ludicorium.*

654 Penda of Mercia, Aethelhere of East Anglia and various other royals are killed in the battle of the River Winwaed by Oswy of Bernicia, who re-establishes Northumbria.

655 A Byzantine fleet led by Constans II defeated at Lycia by an Arab fleet.

656 Caliph Uthman is murdered in Medina. Muhammad's son-in-law Ali replaces him. Grimoald attempts to usurp the throne of Austrasia after the death of Clovis II.

657 Mercia released from Northumbrian rulership; Wulfhere son of Penda becomes king.

661 Ali deposed and murdered; the Umayyad dynasty, founded by Muawiya, assumes the Caliphate at Damascus.

664 The English Church adopts the Roman liturgy in preference to the Irish at the Synod of Whitby.

668 Emperor Constans II dies mysteriously in his bath at Syracuse.

669 Theodore of Tarsus ordained Archbishop of Canterbury, and proceeds to reform the English Church.

670 Death of Oswy of Northumbria, the last Bretwalda; his son Ecgfrith succeeds him.

671 The weapon Greek fire – an inflammable liquid that could be propelled through bronze tubes – invented by Kallinikos of Byzantium.

672 The see of Canterbury given authority over the church in England by the Synod of Hertford.

674 The Arabs penetrate as far as the Indus.

678 After several years' siege, the Arabs fail to take Constantinople and establish a 30-year peace with the Byzantine Empire.

680 Caliph Yaezid puts down a revolt by Hussain, son of Ali, who is killed.

682 Islamic forces overrun Tripoli, Carthage and Tangiers, expelling the Byzantines from North Africa.

685 Ecgfrith of Northumbria falls in battle against the Picts at Nechtanesmere; he is succeeded by Aldfrith.

687 Pepin II of Hérstal defeats his foes at Tertry and gains effective control of all of Francia. He and his successors rule as 'mayors of the palace', holding real power under figurehead Merovingian kings.

688 Caedwalla of Wessex resigns the kingship and goes on pilgrimage to Rome, succeeded by Ine.

689 Justinian II defeats Slavic forces in Thrace, and deports many of them to Anatolia.

690 Wihtred becomes King of Kent.

692 Berhtwald becomes the first native Archbishop of Canterbury; the Irish church accepts the authority of Rome at the Synod of Tara.

694 King Ine codifies the laws of Wessex.

695 Emperor Justinian II deposed by his officers, who cut off his nose and exile him; he is replaced by Leontius.

696 Paoluccio Anafesto is appointed the first doge of Venice.

697 Carthage destroyed by the Arabs.

698 Emperor Leontius deposed and replaced by Tiberius III.

700 The Agilofings, dukes of Bavaria, make Ratisbon their capital.

701 The Japanese emperor passes a law making him the sole proprietor of land in the country.

705 Justinian II restored as emperor.

709 Deaths of bishops Aldhelm of Sherborne, who converted Wessex, and St Wilfrid of Hexham.

710 Nara established as the capital of Japan.

711 Fall of the Visigothic kingdom in Spain to the invading Arab and Moorish forces after the defeat and death of King Roderick; only Asturias remains a Christian kingdom. Justinian II murdered by Philip Bardanes, who takes the throne as Philippicus.

712 The Arabs take Samarkand, where they discover the art of making paper, and Sind.

713 Emperor Philippicus deposed and replaced by Anastasius II.

714 Death of Pepin II in Francia. His son, Charles Martel, begins to unify the Frankish kingdom.

715 Winfrith, the future St Boniface, begins his missionary work among the Germans.

716 Emperor Anastasius II deposed; he is replaced by Theodosius III. Aethelbald becomes king of Mercia, succeeding Ceolred.

717 Theodosius III deposed by Leo III. The Arabs besiege Constantinople. Omar II becomes caliph and grants a tax exemption to true believers.

718 Constantinople fights off the Arab siege; Greek fire is spectacularly used to decimate the Arab fleet.

720 The Arabs conquer Sardinia and cross the Pyrenees, taking Narbonne.

722 St Boniface made the first bishop among the Germans.

725 The heathen Oak of Thor felled by St Boniface.

726 Ine of Wessex dies on pilgrimage in Rome; succeeded by Aethelheard.

730 Emperor Leo III excommunicated by Pope Gregory II over his iconoclastic policies, which forbid making images of Christ, the Virgin Mary or the saints.

731 Bede completes his *Ecclesiastical History of the English People.*

732 Charles Martel defeats the Arabs at the battle of Tours (or Poitiers), their furthest incursion into Europe.

735 Burgundy conquered by Charles Martel. The Venerable Bede dies.

737 Death of King Theuderic IV of Francia.

739 Bishoprics at Passau, Ratisbon and Salzburg founded by St Boniface. Charles Martel and his Lombard allies expel the Moors and Arabs from Provence.

741 Death of Charles Martel, who divides his mayoralty between his sons Carloman in Neustria and Pepin in Austrasia.

743 Childeric III becomes king of Francia after a six-year interregnum.

744 Swabia added to territory of Francia.

746 Constantine V retakes Cyprus from the Arabs. Carloman retires to a monastery, leaving Pepin as mayor of all of Francia.

748 The first printed newspaper published in what is now Beijing.

749 The Neighing Stallion sculpted out of fire-clay in China. As-saffah establishes Abbasid rule in Baghdad.

750 Umayyad Caliph Marwan II deposed and killed by the Abbasids, descended from the Prophet's uncle.

751 Childeric III, last Merovingian monarch, replaced as king by Pepin III the Short, who founds the Carolingian dynasty.

754 Pepin III assists Pope Stephen III against the Lombards.

756 Abd-al-Rahman establishes the Umayyad Emirate of Cordoba.

757 Offa succeeds Aethelbald as king of Mercia after the latter's murder.

758 King Edbriht of Northumbria abdicates to become a monk, succeeded by his son Osulf.

759 Narbonne retaken from the Moors by Frankish troops.

760 Turkish empire founded by a Tartar tribe in Armenia.

762 Caliph Mansur founds Baghdad as capital of the Abbasid Caliphate.
765 China invaded by a Tibetan army.
768 Pepin III dies; Francia is split between his sons Charles (later Charlemagne) and Carloman.
770 Death of the poet Tu Fu.
771 Carloman dies; kingdom reunited under Charlemagne.
772 Charlemagne invades and subdues Saxony.
773 Charlemagne invades and subdues Lombardy.
774 Charlemagne confims the Donation of Pepin, a grant of lands made by his father to Pope Stephen II in 757, which creates the Papal States.
775 Tibet and China confirm a boundary agreement.
776 Kent gains temporary independence from Mercia as a result of winning the battle of Otford.
778 Roland, Lord of the Breton Marches, killed by Basques at Roncesvalles as Charlemagne's army withdraws from a venture in Spain.
779 Offa defeats Cynewulf of Wessex near Benson and becomes de facto ruler of England.
780 On the death of her husband, Leo IV, the Empress Irene becomes Regent of the Byzantine Empire and restores Image Worship.
781 Nestorian Christians in China develop monasteries.
782 Charlemagne executes 4,500 Saxon hostages at Verdun and annexes Saxony.
783 Widukind leads a Saxon revolt against Frankish rule.
784 Work commences on Offa's Dyke.
785 Widukind submits to Charlemagne and is baptised.
786 Harun al-Rashid becomes Caliph, succeeding his brother al-Hadi.
787 First Viking raid on England, near Wareham.
788 Charlemagne annexes Bavaria, deposing Duke Tassilo.
789 Frankish ports closed to English merchants due to a dispute between Charlemagne and Offa.
790 Irish monks sail to Iceland in skin-frame vessels.
792 Offa has King Aethelbert of East Anglia beheaded, and annexes his kingdom.
793 Lindisfarne and Jarrow sacked by the Vikings.
794 The Japanese capital moves from Nara to Heian (later known as Kyoto).
795 First Viking attacks on Ireland.
796 Death of Offa brings his son Ecgfrith to the throne. He dies soon after, and Cenwulf succeeds him.
797 Empress Irene of Byzantium deposes and blinds her son Constantine VI.
798 Revolt in Kent against Mercian rule subdued by King Cenwulf, who blinds the Kentish royal leader Eadbert and cuts off his hands.
799 Charlemagne captures and destroys Fiume.
800 Charlemagne crowned Holy Roman Emperor on Christmas Day. The Book of Kells (Four Gospels) is transcribed by Celtic monks.
802 Empress Irene deposed by her finance minister Nicephorus; Egbert succeds Brihtric as king of Wessex.
803 The Bulgarians free themselves from Tartar overlordship.
804 Charlemagne finally defeats the Saxons.
805 The Japanese Buddhist priest Saicho brings tea to Japan.
807 Monastery founded by Cellach of Iona at Kells.
808 Foundation of Fez, in Morocco, as a tent colony.
809 Death of Harun al-Rashid, succeeded by his son al-Amin.
810 Musa al-Khwarazmi writes a book on equations, introducing the Hindu numerals now known as Arabic.
812 Byzantine Empire recognises Charlemagne as emperor in the West.
813 Al-Mamun murders and succeeds his brother Caliph al-Amin.
814 Death of Charlemagne. His son Louis the Pious succeeds him.
815 Cornwall conquered by Egbert of Wessex.
817 Louis the Pious partitions the Holy Roman Empire amongst his sons and makes Lothair, his eldest son, co-emperor.
819 Conchobar becomes High King of Ireland.
821 Tibetan independence from China ratified by treaty at Chang'an.
825 Egbert of Wessex defeats Beornred of Mercia at Ellandun, near Swindon, and briefly controls all England.
826 Islamic pirates capture Crete and use it as a base for raids in the Aegean. Nominoë becomes Count of Brittany.
827 Sicily invaded by Arab forces.
829 Louis the Pious invests his son Charles the Bald with the dukedom of Swabia, upsetting the status quo.
830 The Great Moravian Empire founded by Prince Moimir.
831 Anskar is created bishop of Hamburg, with responsibility for converting Scandinavia.
832 Emperor Theophilus issues an edict banning the worship of images.
833 Louis the Pious defeated by his elder sons at Colmar and imprisoned.
834 Louis the Pious restored to his throne by loyalists; his eldest son Lothair retires to his Italian sub-kingdom.
838 The Arabs sack Marseilles and also cross to Southern Italy.
839 Egbert of Wessex dies, and is succeeded by his son Aethelwulf.
840 Death of Louis the Pious. The Holy Roman Empire splits into three, but the new emperor, Lothair, seeks to conquer his brothers' portions.
841 Lothair defeated by his brothers Louis the German and Charles the Bald at Fontenoy, thus frustrating his imperial plans. The Vikings found the city of Dublin in Ireland.
842 Emperor Theophilus dies, and is succeeded by his son Michael III. Under the regency of his mother, Theodora, image worship is restored.
843 Treaty of Verdun establishes the territories of the three remaining sons of Louis the Pious, thus dividing for good the lands of the Holy Roman Empire. Kenneth MacAlpin, king of Dalriada since 840, unites the Picts and Scots into a single kingdom (Alba), the forerunner of Scotland.
845 Buddhism suppressed in China by Emperor Wu Tsung.
846 Rome is attacked and badly damaged by Arab forces.
847 Al-Mutawakkil succeeds his brother al-Wathiq as caliph.
849 Birth of Alfred the Great of Wessex, at Wantage.
850 Rurik the Norseman becomes the ruler of Kiev.
851 The Vikings sack London and Canterbury, but are halted in their depredations by Aethelwulf of Wessex and his son Aethelbald at Aclea.
852 Muhammad I succeeds to the Emirate of Cordoba on the death of his father Abdul-Rahman II.
853 Kudawara Kudanari, the first major Japanese painter, dies.
855 Holy Roman Emperor Lothair I dies; his portion of the empire is divided amongst his three sons; Louis II succeeds his father as Emperor.
856 Aethelbald replaces Aethelwulf as king in Wessex, Kent, Surrey and Sussex. Vikings burn Paris.
857 Ergotism epidemics, caused by poisoned grain, begin to appear in Europe.
858 Death of Aethelwulf of Wessex. Aethelbald becomes sole king of Wessex but grants his brother Aethelbert an under-kingship.
859 Norse marauders enter the Mediterranean and cause havoc.
860 Aethelbald of Wessex dies, to be succeeded by his brother Aethelbert.
861 Cologne, Paris, Aix-la-Chapelle, Toulouse and Worms sacked by Viking raiders.
862 Novgorod, capital of Kiev Rus, founded by Rurik. Constantine succeeds his uncle as King of the Picts.
863 The Cyrillic alphabet is developed by Cyril and his brother Methodius in Moravia.
864 King Boris I of Bulgaria converts to Christianity.

865 Ivar the Boneless and his brother Halfdan arrive in England in an attempt to conquer the country. Aethelbert of Wessex dies; his brother Aethelred I succeeds him.
867 Basil I, the Macedonian, murders Michael III and becomes Byzantine emperor.
868 Ahmad ibn Tulun establishes the Tulunid dynasty in Egypt.
869 Malta captured by Islamic forces.
870 Martyrdom of King (later St) Edmund of East Anglia at the hands of the Vikings.
871 Vikings defeated by Wessex at Ashdown but victorious at Reading, Basing, Merton and Wilton. Alfred succeeds Aethelred I as king of Wessex.
874 The Vikings begin to colonise Iceland. Burgred, last independent English king of Mercia, forced to abdicate by the Vikings, who replace him with their puppet Ceolwulf II.
875 Holy Roman Emperor Louis II dies; his uncle Charles the Bald establishes himself as his successor.
876 Louis the German dies; his portion of the Holy Roman Empire is divided amongst his three sons.
877 Charles the Bald dies; he is succeeded as French king by his son Louis II the Stammerer. The imperial throne is left unfilled. Aed (of the White Flowers) succeeds his brother Constantine I as King of the Picts.
878 Alfred, after a period in hiding at Athelney, decisively defeats the Vikings at Edington, Wiltshire, and preserves Wessex as an English kingdom.
879 The treaty of Wedmore establishes the Danelaw in parts of England: Danish laws and customs will prevail there. Louis II dies; his sons Louis III and Carloman jointly succeed him.
880 Southern Italy reconquered from the Arabs by the Byzantine Emperor Basil.
881 Charles III, king of Swabia, crowned Holy Roman Emperor.
882 Louis III of France dies; his brother Carloman reigns alone. Kiev replaces Novgorod as capital of Kiev Rus under Oleg.
883 The Zenj rebellion of African slaves in Chaldea, which has lasted fourteen years, finally suppressed by al-Muwaffiq, brother of Caliph al-Mu'tamid.
884 Carloman of France dies while hunting. Emperor Charles III the Fat takes control, temporarily reuniting most of the Holy Roman Empire.
885 Ashot IV, Prince of Armenia, assumes the title King Ashot I.
886 Paris besieged by Vikings, who are paid off by Charles the Fat. London retaken by Alfred, who gives it and English Mercia to his son-in-law Aethelred.
887 Charles III deposed as emperor at Tribur; the Carolingian Empire falls apart.
888 Odo Count of Paris elected king of France; Berengar I of Friuli, grandson of Louis the Pious, becomes king of Italy. Rudolf I becomes king of a reformed Burgundy.
889 Donald II succeeds his cousin Eochaid as king of Scotland. Guido of Spoleto replaces Berengar I as king of Italy.
890 Alfred the Great establishes an English navy and militia. Harald I Finehair defeats his opponents at Hafursfjord and claims the sovereignty of Norway.
891 Guido of Spoleto crowned first non-Carolingian Holy Roman Emperor. Arnulf of Germany drives the Vikings from his country.
892 Caliph al-Mu'tamid dies; he is succeeded by his nephew al-Mu'tadid. The Vikings launch another invasion attempt on England.
893 The Vikings are decisively defeated by Alfred's son, Edward the Elder, at Farnham. Asser writes his life of Alfred.
894 Guido of Spoleto dies; his son Lambert succeeds him in Italy and as Emperor. Svatopluk I of Moravia, who has created the greater Moravian kingdom dies; his sons Moimir I and Svatopluk II jointly succeed him.
895 The Magyars, expelled from southern Russia, move under Arpad into Hungary.
896 By request of Pope Formosus, Arnulf of Germany replaces Lambert of Spoleto as Holy Roman Emperor, re-establishing Carolingian rule. Alfred defeats the Vikings at sea and ends their threat.
897 Pope Formosus' body is exhumed, dressed in papal vestments and tried for perjury; found guilty, it has three fingers cut off and is thrown into the Tiber.
898 Odo of France dies. The Carolingian pretender Charles III the Simple replaces him. Lambert of Spoleto dies and Berengar I reclaims the Italian crown.
899 Alfred the Great dies, and his son Edward succeeds him. Emperor Arnulf dies, and is succeeded in Germany by his son Louis III the Child.
900 Gunbjorn discovers Greenland. The Arab physician al-Razi identifies measles, smallpox, plague, consumption and rabies. Constantine II succeeds Donald II as King of the Picts, the area now known as Alba.
901 Louis III of Provence, grandson of Emperor Louis II, crowned Holy Roman Emperor. Edward the Elder takes the title 'King of the Angles and Saxons'.
902 With the fall of Taormina to the Arabs, Sicily is lost to Byzantium.
903 Pope Leo V is deposed after one month as Pontiff by Christopher, who lasts a year.
904 Leo of Tripoli commands an Arab fleet that sacks Thessalonica. The election of Pope Sergius III leads to a period of pornocracy in the Vatican.
905 Emperor Louis III surprised and blinded by insurgents, leading to his deposition from the imperial throne. Sancho I of Navarre succeeds his brother Fortun Garces and makes the county a kingdom. Shaiban succeeds his nephew Harun as king of Egypt, but is deposed shortly after; the Tulunid dynasty falls as a result.
906 Annam gains independence from China.
907 Fall of the Tang dynasty following conquest by Khitan Mongols. The Later Liang Dynasty under Taizu replaces it. The Magyars invade and destroy the Moravian empire of Moimir I, who perishes in the invasion.
909 The Fatimid dynasty is founded in Tunisia when al-Mahdi claims the caliphate.
910 The Byzantine Emperor Leo VI is forced to pay tribute to the Magyars. The kingdom of Asturias is renamed the kingdom of León its new capital. The Abbey of Cluny is founded.
911 Normandy established as a Norse province by the treaty of Saint-Clair-sur-Epte; Hrolf (Rollo) becomes duke. Louis III of Germany dies, the Carolingians die out and Conrad I of Franconia is elected king in his place.
912 Abdul-Rahman III succeeds his grandfather Abdullah as emir of Cordoba. The Byzantine Emperor Leo VI dies; his brother Alexander II succeeds him.
913 Emperor Alexander II dies; his nephew Constantine VII, still a child, succeeds him. Byzantium refuses to pay its tribute to Symeon of Bulgaria, who calls himself Emperor of the Romans but fails to take Constantinople.
914 With the death of Pope Lando, no Pope until John Paul I in 1978 will take a name that has not been used by a Pope before, starting with Lando's successor, John X.
915 Berengar I of Italy is crowned Holy Roman Emperor, the last Carolingian to hold the title.
916 Essex taken from the Vikings by king Edward the Elder.
917 Symeon of Bulgaria overruns Thrace and now controls the Balkans.
918 Deaths of Conrad I of Germany and Lady Aethelflaed of the Mercians. The latter acknowledge Edward the Elder as their king; he now controls all England south of the Humber.
919 Henry the Fowler, duke of Saxony, elected king of Germany. Ragnald the Viking seizes York, and makes himself king.
920 Edward the Elder acknowledged as overlord by the kings of Scotland, York and Strathclyde.
921 Sitric Caoch of Dublin succeeds Ragnald as king of York.
922 Charles III of France deposed by his barons, who elect Robert Capet, duke of Francia, king in his place; Charles raises an army to contest this.
923 Robert of France killed at the battle of Soissons, but Charles III is defeated and imprisoned; Duke Rudolf of Burgundy, Robert's son-in-law, is elected by the barons as king. Fall of the Later Liang dynasty in China, Li Cunxu of the Later Tang replacing Modi as emperor, taking the name Zhuengzong.
924 Edward the Elder of Wessex and England dies; his son Athelstan is hailed king in Mercia but Wessex disputes the succession. Symeon of Bulgaria unsuccessfully attacks Constantinople. Emperor Berengar, king of Italy, dies; the Imperial crown falls into abeyance.

925 Athelstan crowned king of England, having finally been accepted by Wessex. Henry the Fowler conquers Lorraine.
926 Symeon of Bulgaria defeated by Croat allies of the Byzantine Empire. Hugh of Arles becomes king of Italy after Rudolf II of Burgundy resigns the throne.
927 Symeon of Bulgaria dies. His son Peter succeeds him and signs a peace treaty with the Byzantines. Sitric of York dies. He is succeeded by his brother Guthfrith who is forced to flee when Athelstan conquers York and Southern Northumbria. The kings of Scotland and Strathclyde acknowledge Athelstan as their overlord.
928 Cornwall subdued by Athelstan, who sets the River Tamar as its boundary.
929 Duke Wenceslas of Bohemia murdered by non-Christians led by his brother Boleslav I, who succeeds him. Charles III of France dies, leaving Rudolf II as sole king. Emir Abdul-Rahman III of Corboba proclaims himself caliph.
930 The Black Stone stolen from the Kaaba in Mecca by the Carmathians, a Muslim sect.
931 Rameiro II succeeds his brother Alfonso IV as king of León.
932 William Longsword succeeds his father Rollo as duke of Normandy.
933 Henry the Fowler defeats Magyar raiders at the battle of Merseburg.
934 Scotland invaded by Athelstan, whose fleet ravages the coast as far as Caithness.
936 Louis IV (d'Outremer) returns from exile in England to be king of France after the death of Duke Rudolf of Burgundy. Henry the Fowler dies, and is succeeded by his son Otto I. The Tang dynasty falls in China; Shi Jing-tang of the Later Jin replaces Feidi as emperor, taking the name Gaozu.
937 Athelstan defeats a coalition of his foes at Brunanburh (whereabouts unknown), cementing his power in Britain. King Rudolf of Burgundy dies, his son Conrad succeeding him.
938 Yenching (later Peking and Beijing) founded as a Khitan capital.
939 Athelstan dies, and is succeeded by his half-brother Edmund (the Elder). Olaf Guthricson retakes York for the Vikings. Otto I defeats Eberhard of Franconia and his ducal allies at Andernach, confirming his monarchical authority in Germany.
940 Olaf of York invades the Midlands. By the treaty of Leicester much of the old Danelaw is ceded to him.
941 Igor of Kiev attacks Constantinople by way of the River Dnieper and the Black Sea, but his fleet is destroyed by Greek fire. Olaf of York dies; his cousin Olaf Sitricsson succeeds him.
942 Richard the Old succeeds his father William Longsword as duke of Normandy after the latter's murder by Arnold I of Flanders. The Five Boroughs of Derby, Leicester, Lincoln, Nottingham and Stamford are recovered by Edmund the Elder. Erik Bloodaxe succeeds his father Harald I Finehair as king of Norway on the latter's abdication at the age of 80. Hywel Dda (the Good) succeeds to the Welsh throne.
943 Constantine II of Scotland abdicates and retires to a monastery, his son Malcolm I succeeds him. Byzantine troops recover the Mandylion.
944 Edmund the Elder recovers York, expelling Ragnald Guthricson, who had usurped the throne from his cousin Olaf the previous year.
945 Igor of Kiev dies; he is succeeded by his wife Olga. Mozambique attacked by Indonesians. Imad ibn-Buwayhid conquers Baghdad, keeping Caliph al-Mustaqfi as a figurehead. Louis IV taken prisoner by Hugh the Great, duke of France.
946 Caliph al-Mustaqfi deposed and blinded by the Buwayhids; his cousin al-Muti replaces him. Edmund the Elder and Otto I act in support of Louis IV, who is freed. Edmund the Elder assassinated at Pucklechurch; his brother Eadred succeeds him.
947 Eric Bloodaxe deposed as king of Norway by his brother Haakon I due to his violence. He flees to England where Wulfstan of York makes him king of that city. Hugh of Arles dies; his son Lothair of Arles succeeds him as king of Italy. The Later Jin dynasty falls in China, Emperor Chudi being replaced by Gaozu of the Later Han.
948 Eadred ravages Northumbria in response to their crowning of Eric Bloodaxe, who is forced to flee.
949 Olaf Sitricsson is invited to return as king of York.
950 Hywel Dda, prince of Deheubarth and Gwynedd and creator of a Welsh law code, dies; Gwynedd and Deheubarth separate. Mixcoatl, Toltec emperor, is assassinated and deified as a result; Lothair of Arles dies; Italy ruled jointly by Berengar II of Ivrea and his son Adalbert.
951 The Later Han dynasty falls in China; Emperor Yindi is replaced by Guo Wei of the Later Zhou, who takes the name Taizu.
952 Eric Bloodaxe returns to York and resumes the kingship.
954 Louis IV of France dies; his son Lothair succeeds him. Eric Bloodaxe forced to flee from York and is killed soon after; Eadred now rules all England.
955 Otto I decisively defeats the Magyars at the battle of Lechfeld. Eadred of England dies; his nephew Eadwig succeeds him.
956 St Dunstan, abbot of Glastonbury, exiled from England after a quarrel with King Eadwig.
957 Mercia and Northumbria rebel against Eadwig and choose his younger brother Edgar as their king.
959 Eadwig of Wessex dies; his brother Edgar the Peaceable succeeds him and reunites the kingdom of England. Emperor Constantine VII dies, his son Romanus II succeeds him.
960 Northern Song dynasty established by Zhao Kuangyin, who takes the name Taizu, replacing Gongdi of the Later Zhou. The kingdom of Poland created by King Mieszko I, who founds the Piast dynasty.
961 A Byzantine fleet commanded by Nicephorus Phocas recaptures Crete from the Arabs. Caliph Abdul-Rahman III of Cordoba dies; his son al-Hakam II succeeds him.
962 Otto I of Germany is crowned Holy Roman Emperor, re-establishing that title. Indulf, King of the Scots, is killed fighting Vikings near Cullen and is succeeded by Dub, son of Malcolm I.
963 The Byzantine Emperor Romanus II is poisoned by his wife Theophano, who marries Nicephorus Phocas, elevating him to the imperial crown.
965 Cyprus recaptured from the Arabs by Byzantine forces. Al-Mutannabi, the Arab poet, is murdered by bandits.
966 Sancho I of León dies; he is succeeded by his son Ramiro III. King Dub of Scotland dies; he is succeeded by his third cousin Culen. Poland's first historically documented ruler, Prince Mieszkol, is baptised, adopting Catholic Christianity as the nation's new official religion.
967 Duke Boleslav I of Bohemia dies; he is succeeded by his son Boleslav II.
968 Dinh Tien-Hoang De becomes king of North Vietnam, founding the Dinh dynasty.
969 Byzantine Emperor Nicephorus II Phocas murdered by his wife's lover, John Tzimisces, who rules in his stead. Cairo founded by the Fatimids, who have conquered Egypt.
970 Garcia II of Navarre dies, and is succeeded by his son Sancho II.
971 Culen of Scotland dies; he is succeeded by his third cousin Kenneth II. St Swithin reinterred inside Winchester Cathedral; 40 days of rain follow.
972 Boris II of Bulgaria forced to abdicate by the invading Byzantines, ending the Krum dynasty's reign in that country.
973 Holy Roman Emperor Otto I dies; he is succeeded by his son Otto II. Edgar of England crowned king at Bath.
975 Edgar dies, and is succeeded by his son Edward. Modern arithmetical notation introduced into Europe by the Arabs.
976 Byzantine Emperor John I Tzimisces dies; succeeded by Basil II, son of Romanus II. Leopold I of the house of Babenberg made Margrave of Austria. Caliph al-Hakam II of Cordoba dies; his son Hisham II succeeds him. Samuel makes himself Tsar of Bulgaria. Duke Henry the Quarrelsome of Bavaria deposed by Otto II.
978 Edward (the Martyr) assassinated at Corfe and succeeded by his half-brother Aethelred II (Unraed). Mohammad ibn abi-Amir al-Mansur, regent of Cordoba, takes effective control of the Caliphate there.
979 Dinh Tien-Hoang De of Dai Vet (Vietnam) dies; succeeded by his son Dinh De-Toan.
980 Le Dai-Hanh Hoang-De usurps the Dai Vet throne from Dinh De-Toan, establishing the Earlier Le Dynasty. Vladimir of Novgorod seizes Kiev from his brother Yaropolk I.
981 León made tributary to the Caliphate of Cordoba. Italy invaded by Arabs; Otto II marches against them but the Byzantines offer them support.
982 Otto II defeated by a combination of Byzantine and Arab forces at Basientello. Eric the Red settles in Greenland.
983 Emperor Otto II dies, his three-year-old son Otto III succeeds him.
984 Henry the Quarrelsome seizes Otto III in an attempt to make himself regent, but is thwarted by Otto II's widow Theophano of Byzantium.

985 Henry the Quarrelsome returned to the dukedom of Bavaria. Harald I Bluetooth of Denmark dies, and is succeeded by his son Sweyn I Forkbeard. Otto-William, a Carolingian prince, establishes the county of Burgundy.
986 Lothair of France dies, he is succeeded by his son Louis V. Sultan Sabuk-Tigan of Ghazni invades India. Bjarni Herjolfsson sights the coast of Labrador.
987 Louis V dies; the Carolingians are replaced as kings of France by the Capetians, when Hugh I is crowned King.
988 Vladimir of Kiev converts to Christianity, marries Anne, sister of Emperor Basil II, and sets about converting his subjects.
989 Emperor Basil II, with the aid of Russian troops, defeats Anatolian insurgents led by Bardas Phocas.
990 William IV of Aquitaine dies; succeeded by his son William V. Ghanaian forces take Awdaghost and establish the king of Ghana as the most powerful ruler in non-Islamic Africa.
991 Norsemen raid England led by Olaf Tryggvesson, defeating English forces under Ealdorman Byrhtnoth at Maldon; they are paid to leave by Danegeld.
992 Mieszko I of Poland dies, and is succeeded by his son Boleslav I the Brave, who invades Pomerania to gain access to the Baltic.
993 Khitan Mongols annex Korea.
994 Sweyn of Denmark, assisted by Olaf Tryggvesson, raids England, unsuccessfully besieges London and is paid off by Aethelred II. Olaf Tryggvesson converts to Christianity.
995 Syria retaken by the Byzantine Empire. Olaf Tryggvesson succeeds to the throne of Norway, and forcibly attempts to convert his subjects to Christianity. Kenneth II dies and is succeeded by Constantine III, who himself subsequently dies and is succeeded by Kenneth III, son of Dub.
996 Otto III crowned Holy Roman Emperor by his cousin Pope Gregory V. Hugh I of France dies, and is succeeded by his son Robert II. Richard I the Old, Duke of Normandy dies; succeeded by his son Richard II the Good. Emperor Basil II defeats the Bulgarians and recovers Greece.
997 Duke Geza of Hungary dies; succeeded by his son Stephen I. Sultan Sabuk-Tagin of Ghazni, in modern Afghanistan, dies; succeeded by his son Ismail.
998 Sultan Ismail of Ghazni dies; succeeded by his brother Mahmud.
999 Boleslav I of Poland conquers Silesia. Gerbert of Aurillac becomes Pope, taking the name Sylvester II; he is the first French Pope. Brian Boru conquers Dublin from the Norse settlers.
1000 Ceylon conquered by King Rajaraja of the Cholas. Stephen I of Hungary becomes king with Papal approval. Olaf Tryggvesson commits suicide after his defeat by the kings of Denmark and Sweden at the naval battle of Svolder; Erik Jarl of Lade replaces him as king of Norway.
1002 Emperor Otto III dies of malaria; succeeded by his cousin Henry II. Al-Mansur, chief minister of Cordoba dies, the Caliphate begins to decline. Aethelred II marries Emma, sister of Richard II of Normandy, and orders the massacre of Danish settlers in southern England.
1003 King Sweyn of Denmark raids England in revenge for the massacre of his countrymen, exacting tribute from Aethelred.
1004 China pays tribute to the Khitan Mongols as the result of a peace treaty. Emperor Henry II defeats Ardoin of Lombardy and is crowned king of that country.
1005 Kenneth III of Scotland is killed in battle against his cousin Malcolm II, who succeeds him.
1006 Islamic settlers arrive in north-western India. Mount Metrop erupts in Java, killing King Dharmawangs.
1007 Danegeld of £36,000 paid by Aethelred II to protect England from raids for two years.
1008 Sultan Mahmud of Ghazni defeats Hindu forces at Peshawar and expands his realms.
1009 Caliph al-Hakim of Egypt sacks the Church of the Holy Sepulchre in Jerusalem. Caliph Hisham II of Cordoba deposed by his cousin Muhammad II, who is deposed in his turn by his cousin Suleiman.
1010 The 'Peace of God' established in France by Robert II. Danish forces under Thorkell the Tall defeat the East Anglians at Ringmere. Muhammad II regains the caliphate of Cordoba from Suleiman, but is ousted again, this time by a returning Hisham II.
1011 Canterbury taken by the Danes, who capture Archbishop Alphege.
1012 Danegeld of £48,000 paid to the Danes, who nevertheless kill Alphege before they leave. Thorkell the Tall defects to the English. Persecution of heretics in Germany commences.
1013 Sweyn Forkbeard conquers England, helped by Thorkell, who redefects. Aethelred II flees to Normandy. Hisham II of Cordoba dies, and is succeeded by Suleiman.
1014 Sweyn dies, and Aethelred returns from exile. Brian Boru wins the battle of Clontarf but is killed. Emperor Basil II seizes Western Bulgaria and blinds the resisting native army.
1015 Olaf II succeeds Eric as king of Norway and establishes its independence from Denmark. Cnut invades England and Wessex submits to him.
1016 Aethelred II dies, succession disputed between his son Edmund Ironside and Cnut. Cnut wins the battle of Ashingdon; Edmund allowed to reign in Wessex but dies shortly afterwards.
1017 Cnut divides England into four earldoms, Wessex, East Anglia, Mercia and Northumbria, for administrative purposes.
1018 The treaty of Bautzen ends the war between Germany and Poland. Macedonia regained by the Byzantines after the submission of the Bulgarians.
1019 Yaroslav I the Wise succeeds his brother Sviatopolk I as prince of Kiev. Cnut becomes king of Denmark on the death of his brother Harald II.
1020 Corsica annexed by Pisa. Faroes, Shetlands and Orkneys recognise Olaf II of Norway as king. Godwin becomes earl of Wessex.
1021 Emperor Basil II invades Armenia. An epidemic of St Vitus' Dance sweeps Europe.
1022 Emperor Henry II defeats a Byzantine army in Southern Italy. The Synod of Pavia decrees celibacy for higher clergy.
1023 Abdul-Rahman V becomes caliph of Cordoba, replacing the Hammudid al-Qasim of Malaga.
1024 Emperor Henry II dies. He is succeeded by his second cousin twice removed, Conrad II of Franconia. Boleslav I of Poland is crowned king of that country.
1025 Emperor Basil II dies, and is succeeded by his brother Constantine VIII. Boleslav I of Poland dies and is succeeded by his son Mieszko II and reverts to the title of prince.
1026 Cnut thwarts a combined Norwegian and Swedish attack at the sea battle of the Holy River. Guido d'Arezzo introduces solmisation in music.
1027 Robert I the Devil becomes duke of Normandy on the death of his brother Richard III.
1028 Cnut conquers Norway and sends his son Sweyn to rule it. Emperor Constantine VIII dies, succeeded by his daughter Zoë. Romanus III becomes co-emperor upon marrying her. Sancho III of Navarre conquers Castile.
1030 Olaf II of Norway attempts to win back his throne, but is defeated and killed by Cnut's forces at Stiklestad. Sultan Mahmud of Ghazni dies, and is succeeded by his son Muhammad.
1031 Muhammad of Ghazni deposed and blinded by his brother Masud I. Caliph Hisham III deposed, ending the Umayyad Caliphate of Cordoba, which fragments. Robert II the Pious of France dies; succeeded by his son Henry I.
1032 Rudolf III of Burgundy dies without an heir, and Conrad II unites the kingdom with the Empire.
1033 Mieszko II of Poland defeated by combined German and Russian forces and his realm forced to become a fief of the Empire. Castile granted independence from Navarre.
1034 Empress Zoe murders Romanus III and marries Michael IV, who becomes co-Emperor. Mieszko of Poland dies; his son Kasimir I succeeds him but the country plunges into civil war. Malcolm II of Scotland dies, and is succeeded by his grandson Duncan I.
1035 Duke Robert the Magnificent of Normandy dies on pilgrimage to Jerusalem. His illegitimate son William (the future 'Conqueror') succeeds, sparking a succession dispute. Sancho III of Navarre dies, and is succeeded in Navarre by his son Garcia IV and in Castile by his son Ferdinand I. Cnut dies. Harthacnut succeeds him in Denmark and England, but his brother Harold seizes England for himself. Magnus I the Good, son of Olaf II, regains Norwegian independence, defeating Sweyn.
1036 Alfred, son of Aethelred II, returns to England but is murdered by Godwin of Wessex. Harold I (Harefoot) proclaimed Regent of England.
1037 Harold I proclaimed king of England. Ferdinand I of Castile conquers León, deposing Vermudo III. The Islamic philosopher and physician Avicenna dies.

1038 King Stephen of Hungary dies, and is succeeded by his nephew by marriage Peter Orseolo.
1039 Emperor Conrad II dies, succeeded by his son Henry III. Gruffydd ap Llywelyn, prince of Gwynedd, defeats an English invading force on the River Severn.
1040 Macbeth defeats and kills King Duncan of Scotland and assumes the crown. Harold I dies; Harthacnut successfully claims the English crown by right of succession.
1041 Samuel Aba usurps the Hungarian throne from Peter Orseolo. Co-Emperor Michael IV dies; his nephew Michael V fills the breach.
1042 Harthacnut dies; his half-brother Edward the Confessor is elected king whilst Magnus of Norway takes Denmark. Michael V imprisons the Empress Zoë, but a rebellion blinds him, locks him in a monastery and frees Zoë, who marries Constantine IX and makes him co-Emperor.
1043 Samuel Aba of Hungary invades Bavaria, where he is countered by Emperor Henry III. Coventry Abbey founded by Leofric of Mercia.
1044 Emperor Henry III defeats Samuel Aba's Hungarians and restores Peter Orseolo to his throne. Anawrata founds the Pagan dynasty in Burma.
1045 The deposed Pope Benedict IX retakes the throne from Sylvester III by force, and then sells it to Gregory VI.
1046 Peter Orseolo of Hungary deposed by his second cousin Andras I. Emperor Henry III forces Gregory VI to abdicate on grounds of simony, ratifies the depositions of his two predecessors and installs Clement II at the Synod of Rome.
1047 Norman rebels defeated at Val-ès-Dunes by Duke William, who thus lies secure in his rule. King Magnus dies. Sweyn II, a nephew of Cnut, succeeds him in Denmark, whilst Harald III Hardrada, Magnus' uncle, succeeds him in Norway.
1048 Last Viking raid on south-east England, the raiders flee to Flanders, which is attacked by Edward the Confessor and Emperor Henry III.
1049 Leo IX elected Pope after the death of Damasus II.
1050 Empress Zoë dies, her older sister Theodora succeeding her. Robert of Jumièges becomes Archbishop of Canterbury.
1051 Earl Godwin of Wessex rebels unsuccessfully against Edward the Confessor, he and his family flee to Flanders.
1052 Earl Godwin and his family return to power in England. Stigand uncanonically becomes Archbishop of Canterbury as Archbishop Robert is forced to flee. Pisa takes Sardinia from the Arabs.
1053 Robert Guiscard defeats Papal forces at Civitate, capturing Leo IX, before taking Benevento from the Byzantines and founding a Norman state in Southern Italy. Godwin of Wessex dies, his son Harold succeeding him as earl.
1054 Final schism between Roman Catholic and Orthodox churches. Henry I of France invades Normandy and is defeated at Mortemer. Macbeth defeated by Malcolm Canmore and Earl Siward of Northumbria at Dunsinane.
1055 Seljuk Turks led by Togril-Beg enter Baghdad to liberate the Abbasid Caliphate from Shiite control; Togril-Beg makes himself the Caliph's temporal master. Co-Emperor Constantine IX dies, Theodora reigns alone. Earl Siward of Northumbria dies, and is succeeded by Tostig Godwinson, brother of the future King Harold II of England.
1056 Emperor Henry III dies, succeeded by his son Henry IV. Empress Theodora dies, ending the reign of the Macedonian dynasty in Byzantium. Michael VI succeeds her.
1057 Macbeth killed by Malcolm III Canmore at Lumphanan, but is succeeded by his stepson Lulach. Isaac Comnenus overthrows Emperor Michael VI.
1058 Lulach killed by Malcolm III Canmore, who becomes king of Scotland. Prince Kasimir I of Poland dies; succeeded by his son Boleslav II.
1059 By the treaty of Melfi Robert Guiscard becomes Duke of Apulia and Sicily and swears fealty to the Papacy. Emperor Isaac Comnenus abdicates in favour of Constantine X.
1060 Andras I of Hungary deposed by his brother Bela I. Henry I of France dies; succeeded by his son Philip I.
1061 Northumbria raided by Malcolm III of Scotland. Duke Spitihnev II of Bohemia dies, succeeded by his brother Vratislav II.
1062 By the Coup d'Etat of Kaiserswerth, Emperor Henry IV seized by Archbishop Anno of Cologne, who takes power in Germany alongside Archbishop Adalbert of Bremen.
1063 Gwynedd conquered by Earls Harold and Tostig; Prince Gruffydd killed by his own men. Bela I of Hungary dies, succeeded by his nephew Salomon, son of deposed king Andras. Alp Arslan succeeds his uncle Togril-Beg as sultan of the Seljuk Turks.
1064 Belgrade seized by the Hungarians from Byzantium. Armenia conquered by Alp Arslan.
1065 Ferdinand I of Castile and León dies; succeeded by his sons Sancho II in Castile and Alfonso VI in León. Westminster Abbey is consecrated.
1066 Death of Edward the Confessor causes succession dispute in England. Harold II Godwinson chosen king, defeats and kills Harald Hardrada at Stamford Bridge but is defeated and killed at Hastings by William of Normandy, who becomes king.
1067 Emperor Constantine X dies; his widow marries Romanus IV Diogenes, who becomes Emperor. Boleslav II of Poland captures Kiev. El Cid founds the world's first leper hospital in Castile.
1068 Earls Edwin and Morcar rebel against William I, but are defeated in York.
1069 Northumbrians and Mercians rebel, with Danish help, against William I, but the risings are put down and William devastates Northumbria ('the harrying of the North').
1070 The Order of the Knights of St John founded in Jerusalem by Amalfian merchants. Sweyn II of Denmark attacks England, but is bought off by William I, who puts down the revolt of Hereward the Wake.
1071 Robert Guiscard captures Bari, thus expelling the Byzantines from Italy. Byzantine forces heavily defeated at Manzikert under Alp Arslan, by Seljuk Turks who capture Emperor Romanus. When released he is blinded by the Byzantines, who select Michael VII as Emperor, and dies soon after. The Seljuqs now control Asia Minor.
1072 Sancho II of Castile murdered at the siege of Zamora whilst fighting Navarrese forces. He is succeeded by his brother Alfonso VI of León. Palermo taken by Robert and Roger Guiscard. Alp Arslan murdered by a captive while campaigning in Transoxiana; his son Malik Shah becomes sultan.
1073 Hildebrand of Soana elected Pope, taking the title Gregory VII.
1074 Salomon of Hungary deposed by his cousin Geza I. Robert Guiscard excommunicated by Gregory VII, who also excommunicates all married priests.
1075 Malik Shah subdues Syria and Palestine. Gregory VII bans simony and declares the Pope to be absolute sovereign of the Church.
1076 German bishops at the Synod of Worms declare Gregory VII deposed and Henry IV demands Gregory's abdication. Gregory excommunicates the bishops and Henry, whom he declares deposed. Thus the 'Investiture Contest' begins between Emperor and Pope, over the right of the Emperor to appoint bishops, who hold secular as well as spiritual power.
1077 When Henry IV does penance at Canossa to Gregory VII, the Germans declare him deposed and elect Rudolf of Swabia as anti-king. Geza I of Hungary dies, and is succeeded by his brother Ladislas I.
1078 Emperor Michael VII abdicates; Nicephorus III elected in his place.
1079 King Boleslav II of Poland excommunicated by Bishop (later Saint) Stanislas of Cracow, who is assassinated on Boleslav's orders. Gregory VII excommunicates Boleslav, who is deposed by a revolt by his nobles and succeeded by his brother Vladislav I Herman, who reverts to the title Prince.
1080 Anti-king Rudolf of Swabia defeated and killed by Henry IV's forces. Gregory VII again excommunicates and deposes Henry IV, who then seeks to depose Gregory, replacing him with the Archbishop of Ravenna as Clement III.
1081 Emperor Nicephorus III abdicates in favour of Alexius I Comnenus. Emperor Henry IV invades Italy seeking to establish Clement III as Pope.
1082 Bishop Odo, Earl of Kent, revolts against his half-brother William I, but is stripped of his earldom and imprisoned.
1083 The Kiyowara family revolt in northern Japan; Yoshiiye Minamoto sent to quell the rebellion.
1084 The Synod of Rome deposes Gregory VII and recognises Clement III, but Henry IV and Clement III are forced to withdraw when Robert Guiscard advances in support of Gregory from Southern Italy.
1085 Toledo taken from the Arabs by Alfonso VI of Castile. Pope Gregory VII dies at Salerno. Robert Guiscard dies, and is succeeded as duke of Apulia by his son Roger Borsa. William I commissions the Domesday Book.
1086 Islamic rule in Southern Spain rejuvenated by the Almoravids of Morocco, who defeat Alfonso VI of Castile at Zallaka. The Domesday Book is compiled. Cnut IV of Denmark dies, ending an invasion threat to England. His brother Olaf IV succeeds him.

1087 William I dies of an injury sustained at the siege of Mantes, and is succeeded by his sons Robert in Normandy and William II Rufus in England.

1088 Urban II elected Pope, but only partially recognised. Bishop Odo and various Norman barons in England rebel against William II, but the revolt is crushed.

1089 Archbishop Lanfranc of Canterbury dies, but no successor is chosen, so William II can enjoy the revenues of the see.

1090 Count Roger Guiscard of Sicily captures Malta from the Arabs.

1091 William II of England and Robert of Normandy make their peace by the treaty of Caen. Malcolm III of Scotland invades Northumbria, but is repulsed by William and Robert and acknowledges William as his overlord.

1092 The Seljuk vizier Nizam al-Malik assassinated by the Ismailite sect, the Hashishin (Assassins). King Vratislav of Bohemia dies. He is succeeded for a short while by his brother Conrad and then his son Bretislav II, who reverts to the title Duke. William II takes Cumberland from the Scots and refounds Carlisle as his north-western outpost.

1093 William II falls gravely ill and appoints St Anselm to the see of Canterbury, recovering soon after. Malcolm III invades Northumbria again but is killed near Alnwick; his wife Margaret dies 4 days later. He is succeeded by his brother Donald III Bane.

1094 Rodrigo Diaz de Vivar, El Cid, takes Valencia from the Moors. Donald Bane is deposed from the Scottish throne by his nephew Duncan II, who dies after six months. Donald Bane returns to the throne.

1095 Ladislas I of Hungary conquers Croatia and Dalmatia but dies soon after, and is succeeded by his nephew Koloman. Olaf IV of Denmark dies, and is succeeded by his brother Erik I. First Crusade launched by Pope Urban II at the council of Clermont, aiming to take Jerusalem and the Holy Land from the Seljuk Turks.

1096 Peter the Hermit preaches the crusade in France and Germany, assembling a rag-tag force which goes East. Germans such as Ermich of Leiningen take advantage of crusade hysteria to persecute Jews in the Holy Roman Empire. Robert of Normandy leases his duchy to William II in order to go on crusade.

1097 Peter the Hermit's crusaders massacred near Nicaea in Asia Minor by Seljuk Turks, but the main crusading force wins major victories both there and at Dorylaeum. Donald Bane of Scotland deposed with William II's help, and replaced by his nephew Edgar.

1098 Robert de Molesme founds the monastery of Cîteaux, and thereby the Cistercian order. Magnus III of Norway seizes the Orkneys, Hebrides and Isle of Man. Crusaders take Antioch after a lengthy siege.

1099 Jerusalem captured by the crusaders; Godfrey of Bouillon becomes Advocate of the Holy Sepulchre. El Cid dies at Cuenca after defeat by the Almoravids.

1100 Godfrey of Bouillon dies, and his brother Baldwin succeeds him and founds the Kingdom of Jerusalem. William II of England dies whilst hunting, and is succeeded by his brother Henry I.

1101 Robert of Normandy invades England to take the throne from brother Henry, but is bought off by the treaty of Alton. Roger d'Hauteville, count of Sicily, dies; succeeded by his son Simon.

1102 Vladislav I of Poland abdicates, and is succeeded after a power struggle by his son Boleslav III. Alfonso VI of Castile raises the year-long siege of Valencia.

1103 Magnus III of Norway invades Ireland, but is killed in battle; his son Eysten I succeeds him. Bohemund of Otranto ransomed from captivity by the Danishmend Emir.

1104 Acre taken by crusaders under Baldwin I of Jerusalem. Mount Hekla in Iceland erupts violently.

1105 Emperor Henry IV is captured by his son Henry and is forced to abdicate in favour of him; when he breaks the terms of his abdication he is imprisoned.

1106 Henry IV escapes from prison but dies whilst raising an army against his son, who succeeds him. Henry of England defeats Robert of Normandy at Tinchebrai, dispossessing Robert of his duchy and imprisoning him.

1107 King Edgar of Scotland dies, and his succeeded by his brother Alexander I.

1108 Philip I of France dies, and is succeeded by his son Louis VI. Bohemund of Otranto defeated by the Emperor Alexius at Durazzo.

1109 Boleslav III of Poland defeats Emperor Henry V at Hundsfeld. Crusaders led by Raymond of St Gilles take Tripoli and Beirut; Raymond founds the County of Tripoli.

1110 The earliest known miracle play performed at Dunstable.

1111 Henry V crowned emperor under duress by Pope Paschal II. Bohemund of Otranto dies, and is succeeded as prince of Antioch by his nephew Tancred. Count Roger of Apulia dies; his son William II succeeds him.

1112 Emperor Henry V excommunicated. Tancred of Antioch dies, and is succeeded by his nephew Roger of Salerno. Henry of Burgundy, count of Portugal, dies, and is succeeded by his son Alfonso I.

1113 Pisa conquers the Balearic Islands. Sviatopolk of Kiev dies, and is succeeded by his cousin Vladimir II Monomach. The Knights Hospitaller resolve to defend the Holy Land.

1114 Pipe rolls introduced by Bishop Roger of Salisbury as a means of recording Exchequer accounts.

1115 St Bernard founds a monastery at Clairvaux and becomes its first abbot. The Juchens create the Chinese state of Jin under their chieftain Aguda.

1116 Coloman of Hungary dies; succeeded by his son Stephen II.

1117 St Magnus, earl of Orkney, murdered on the island of Egilsay on the orders of his cousin Earl Haakon.

1118 The Knights Templar founded in Jerusalem by Hugh de Payens. Emperor Alexius I dies, and is succeeded by his son John II. Baldwin I of Jerusalem dies, and is succeeded by his great-nephew Baldwin II. Alfonso I of Aragon takes Zaragoza from the Almoravids and makes it his capital.

1119 Count Baldwin VII of Flanders dies; succeeded by his cousin Charles the Good. Crusading armies are heavily defeated at the Field of Blood in Syria. Roger of Antioch is killed.

1120 Prince William, heir and only legitimate son of Henry I, drowns in the wreck of the *White Ship*.

1121 Peter Abelard's teachings on the Trinity condemned at the Synod of Soissons.

1122 Emperor John II wipes out the Pecheneg Turks in the Balkans. The Investiture Question is finally settled with the Concordat of Worms; Emperor Henry V renounces the right of investiture.

1123 Emperor John II defeats the Serbs in the Balkans. Marriage of priests banned by the First Lateran Council. The Augustinian canon Rahere founds St Bartholomew's Hospital in London.

1124 Emperor John II defeats the Hungarians. Alexander I of Scotland dies; succeeded by his brother David I.

1125 Emperor Henry V dies, leaving no successor; Lothair of Saxony is elected to succeed him. Morocco conquered by the Almohads.

1126 Emperor Lothair III makes his son-in-law, Henry X the Proud, duke of Bavaria, succeeding Henry's father, Henry IX. Chinese Emperor Huizong dies after being captured by the Jin; his son Qinzong succeeds him.

1127 The Jin overrun Northern China and Emperor Qinzong perishes; his brother Gaozong flees south and establishes the Southern Song dynasty. Count William III of Apulia dies, Roger of Sicily claims overlordship, but the inhabitants appeal to the Pope for protection. Roger is excommunicated.

1128 Count Charles the Good of Flanders is murdered; Louis VI attempts to impose Robert of Normandy on the county but the inhabitants install Thierry of Alsace, a cousin of Charles. The Templars gain papal recognition; St Bernard draws up their rule. Alfonso I of Portugal defeats Alfonso VII of Castile at São Mamede and shakes off Castilian overlordship. Pope Honorius accepts Roger of Sicily's claim to Apulia and invests him as count.

1129 First Cistercian abbey founded in England, at Waverley. Henry of Blois becomes Bishop of Winchester. Count Fulk V of Anjou resigns the county to his son Geoffrey and goes to Jerusalem to marry Melisande, heiress to King Baldwin II.

1130 Pope Honorius II dies. Innocent II is elected to succeed him but the election is disputed and an antipope, Anacletus II, is also elected. Innocent II flees to France, where he is championed by St Bernard, while Anacletus is backed by Roger II of Sicily, whom he crowns king of that country.

1131 Baldwin II of Jerusalem dies, and is succeeded by his son-in-law Fulk V. Rievaulx Abbey founded.

1132 Fountains Abbey founded.

1133 Lothair III crowned Emperor by Innocent II in the Lateran while the antipope Anacletus II is established in St Peter's. St Bartholomew's Fair founded in London.

1134 Emperor Lothair makes Albert the Bear margrave of Brandenburg and head of the North March.
1135 Henry I of England dies of a surfeit of lampreys; although he made his barons swear that his daughter Matilda would succeed him, his nephew Stephen of Blois engineers his own coronation as king.
1136 Emperor Lothair takes Apulia from Roger II of Sicily. Peter Abelard writes his *Historia calamitatum mearum.*
1137 Louis VI of France dies, and is succeeded by his son Louis VII. Gruffydd ap Cynan, prince of Gwynedd, dies, and is succeeded by his son Owain Gwynedd. Emperor Lothair III dies.
1138 Conrad III of Hohenstaufen elected emperor to succeed Lothair III. When Boleslav III of Poland dies, his country is divided amongst his four sons. David I of Scotland invades England in support of Matilda but is defeated at the battle of the Standard.
1139 The Second Lateran Council ends the schism in the Church. Innocent II is now universally recognised as Pope. Alfonso I crowned king of Portugal. Matilda lands at Arundel, staking her claim to the English throne; anarchy breaks out in the country.
1140 Prince Sobeslav I of Bohemia dies, and is succeeded by his son Vladislav II. Peter Abelard is condemned for heresy at the council of Sens, on a motion railroaded through by St Bernard.
1141 Stephen of England taken prisoner after defeat at Lincoln. Matilda proclaimed queen, but her high-handed behaviour alienates many, in particular London. Stephen is released in exchange for Robert, earl of Gloucester, and Matilda is forced back on the defensive.
1142 The duchy of Bavaria is conferred by Conrad III on Margrave Henry II of Austria. Peter Abelard dies, worn out by the Church's ill-treatment.
1143 Emperor John II of Byzantium dies, and is succeeded by his son Manuel I. Fulk V of Jerusalem dies; his son Baldwin III succeeds him.
1144 Geoffrey of Anjou subdues Normandy and is proclaimed duke. Imad-ud-Din Zangi, sultan of Mosul, captures Edessa, in eastern Turkey, causing alarm in Outremer and in Western Europe.
1145 Arnold of Brescia establishes a republic in Rome; the newly-crowned Pope Eugenius III is forced to flee. St Bernard takes the lead in proclaiming the Second Crusade, to avenge the fall of Edessa.
1146 Zangi of Mosul is murdered, and succeeded by his formidable son Nur-ud-Din, who consolidates the conquest of Edessa.
1147 The Second Crusade collapses in chaos as the crusaders attack Damascus, an ally of Jerusalem, thus alienating it. Lisbon however is taken from the Moors by King Alfonso of Portugal. Matilda leaves England; her son Henry is left to carry on the fight, though only fourteen.
1148 Sugar brought back from the Middle East by returning crusaders.
1149 Raymond of Poitiers, prince of Antioch, killed by Nur-ud-Din.
1150 The University of Paris is founded. *The Black Book of Carmarthen*, an anthology of ancient Welsh poetry, is compiled.
1151 Geoffrey of Anjou dies, and is succeeded in Anjou, Normandy and associated domains by his son Henry. Fire and plague insurance policies are developed in Iceland.
1152 Emperor Conrad III dies and is succeeded by his nephew Frederick I Barbarossa. Louis VII divorces Eleanor of Aquitaine, who promptly marries Henry of Anjou.
1153 David I of Scotland dies; succeeded by his grandson Malcolm IV. Ascalon falls to Baldwin III of Jerusalem. St Bernard of Clairvaux dies. The Treaty of Wallingford brings the English anarchy to an end by recognising Henry of Anjou as Stephen's heir.
1154 Roger II of Sicily dies; succeeded by his son William I. Damascus surrenders to Nur-ud-Din, who now controls most of Syria. Stephen of England dies and is succeeded by Henry, who now rules half of France as well as England. On the death of Anastasius IV, Nicholas Breakspear is elected Pope, taking the name Adrian IV.
1155 Ireland bestowed on Henry II by Pope Adrian IV. Adrian IV restores papal authority in Rome. Arnold of Brescia is hanged as a heretic by Emperor Frederick. St Berthold founds the Carmelite order of monks.
1156 Austria made a duchy with special status by Emperor Frederick. William I of Sicily recovers Bari from the Greeks and makes his peace with Rome.
1157 Erik IX of Sweden conquers and forcibly converts Finland. Alfonso VII of Castile dies; he is succeeded by his sons Sancho III in Castile and Ferdinand II in León.
1158 Prince Vladislav of Bohemia elevated to king by Emperor Frederick. Sancho III of Castile dies, and is succeeded by his infant son Alfonso VIII.
1159 Pope Adrian IV dies, and is succeeded by Alexander III. John of Salisbury writes the *Policraticus*, a treatise on government.
1160 Emperor Frederick, incensed by witnessing the inhabitants of Crema dismembering their prisoners during his siege, hurls his own prisoners over the walls before entering and destroying the city.
1161 Edward the Confessor is canonised.
1162 Emperor Frederick destroys Milan. Thomas Becket is chosen as Archbishop of Canterbury. Danegeld – by now just a general tax – is collected in England for the final time.
1163 The Welsh rebel against Henry II, but the revolt is suppressed and Prince Rhys ap Gruffydd is imprisoned. Henry II and Thomas Becket quarrel over the Church's status vis-à-vis the monarch.
1164 Legal rights of Church and State codified by Henry II at the council of Clarendon; Becket rejects the code and is forced to flee after he is condemned at the council of Northampton. Héloïse dies and is buried next to Abelard.
1165 Emperor Manuel allies with Venice against Emperor Frederick. Malcolm IV of Scotland dies, and is succeeded by his brother William the Lion. Charlemagne is canonised.
1166 *The Song of Cnut* written down by a monk of Ely. The erection of jails in all English counties ordered by the Assize of Clarendon. William I of Sicily dies, and is succeeded by his son William II.
1167 Oxford University is created when English students are barred from attending Paris.
1168 Milan is rebuilt. Prince Andrei I Bogoliubsky of Vladimir-Suzdal sacks Kiev and assumes the title Grand Prince.
1169 Saladin becomes vizier to the Fatimid caliph al-'Adid of Cairo, effectively controlling Egypt. Norman-Welsh barons land at Wexford supporting King Dermot of Leinster's efforts to regain his throne.
1170 Henry II has his son Henry crowned joint-king (the 'Young King'). Richard Strongbow, earl of Pembroke, takes Waterford and marries Dermot of Leinster's daughter. Thomas Becket returns to Canterbury, but is murdered four weeks later.
1171 Dermot of Leinster dies, and is succeeded by his son-in-law Richard Strongbow, who is forced to accept Henry II as his overlord when Henry crosses to Ireland. Saladin abolishes the Fatimid caliphate and rules Egypt himself.
1172 Henry II receives homage from the Irish at Cashel, but his wife Eleanor raises Aquitaine against him, forcing him to seek a reconciliation with Pope Alexander at Avranches.
1173 Henry II's wife and sons revolt against him, supported by William the Lion of Scotland and Louis VII of France. Eleanor of Aquitaine is captured and imprisoned. Thomas Becket is canonised.
1174 Henry II does public penance for Becket's murder and subdues the revolt against him. Nur-ud-Din dies and a fight for power in the Arab world ensues. Saladin takes Damascus. Amalric I of Jerusalem dies, and is succeeded by his leper son Baldwin IV.
1175 By the treaty of Windsor Rory O'Connor recognised as High King of Ireland under Henry II's overlordship.
1176 The Lombard League defeats Emperor Frederick at Legnano. The first eisteddfod is held at Cardigan Castle. Construction of the first stone London Bridge begins.
1177 Baldwin IV of Jerusalem defeats Saladin at Ramleh. Angkor Wat, capital of the Khmer empire, falls to Champa invaders.
1178 Construction starts on the bridge at Avignon.
1179 The Waldensians, Roman Catholic reformers are forbidden to preach by the Pope without the permission of bishops. The Third Lateran Council rules that popes will henceforth be elected by a two-thirds majority of the College of Cardinals.
1180 Louis VII of France dies, and is succeeded by his son Philip Augustus. Emperor Manuel I dies, and is succeeded by his son Alexius II. Henry II reforms the English coinage.
1181 Pope Alexander III dies; Lucius III succeeds him.
1182 Valdemar I of Denmark dies, and is succeeded by his son Cnut VI. Revolts in Byzantium force Emperor Alexius II to make his father's cousin Andronicus co-Emperor.
1183 Emperor Alexius II murdered, and replaced by his co-emperor, Andronicus I. Emperor Frederick, the Pope and the Lombard League make the Peace of Constance. Saladin takes Aleppo. Henry the 'Young King', rebellious son of Henry II of England, dies.

1184 Cyprus gains freedom from Byzantium. Giorgi III of Georgia dies, and is succeeded by his daughter Thamar. Glastonbury Abbey burns down.
1185 Emperor Andronicus I killed by rioters and succeeded by Isaac II Angelus. Bulgarians under Peter and Ivan Asen revolt against Byzantium. Saladin takes Mosul. Prince John sent to govern Ireland, antagonises the local lords and is recalled.
1186 Emperor Frederick marries his son Henry to Constance, heiress of Sicily, and has him crowned Caesar. Baldwin V of Jerusalem dies. The crown passes to Guy of Lusignan.
1187 Saladin defeats a crusader army at Hattin and takes Jerusalem. The Punjab conquered by the Ghaznavid Mohammad of Ghur. Bulgaria becomes independent under Ivan Asen.
1188 The Third Crusade is proclaimed; to this end the first general tax, the Saladin Tithe, is levied in France. Henry II quarrels with his son Richard and Philip II of France over his French lands and the succession.
1189 Henry II dies, and is succeeded by his son Richard, whose coronation is accompanied by a massacre of Jews. William II of Sicily dies; his bastard cousin Tancred takes the throne.
1190 Emperor Frederick I Barbarossa drowns in Cilicia whilst on crusade, he is succeeded by his son Henry VI. The Jews in York are massacred, but the city is fined.
1191 Richard I conquers Cyprus from the Byzantines and sells it to the Templars, before capturing Acre. Philip II returns to France after falling ill. Richard defeats Saladin at Arsuf. The Order of Germanic Hospitallers is founded at Acre. Zen Buddhism is introduced to Japan.
1192 Richard I, realizing he cannot win in Palestine, makes a truce with Saladin, ending the Third Crusade. On his return home, he is captured and imprisoned by Leopold, duke of Austria. Sultan Muhammad of Ghur captures Delhi, which becomes the Muslim capital in India. Yoritomo Minamoto becomes the first shogun (warlord) of Japan, effectively ruling under a figurehead emperor.
1193 Richard I is handed over to Holy Roman Emperor Henry VI, who demands ransom for his release. Prince John takes the opportunity to foment rebellion whilst Hubert Walter, archbishop of Canterbury, raises the sum. Saladin dies, and is succeeded in Cairo by his son Imad-ud-Din, whilst his relatives rule elsewhere in Arabia.
1194 The Yellow River changes course. Spitsbergen discovered by Norsemen. Richard I is freed after the ransom is paid, returns to England briefly to put down John's rebellion and leaves the country permanently for France. Emperor Henry VI conquers Sicily, deposing William III, son of Tancred. Prince Dafydd of Gwynedd is forced to abdicate, and is succeeded by his nephew Llywelyn ap Iorwerth the Great.
1195 Emperor Isaac II deposed, blinded and imprisoned by his brother Alexius III.
1196 Alfonso II of Aragon dies, and is succeeded by his son Pedro II. Bela III of Hungary dies; his son Imre succeeds him.
1197 Emperor Henry VI dies, sparking a succession dispute. Peter Asen of Bulgaria is murdered, and succeeded by his brother Kalojan. Prince Rhys of Deheubarth dies, and is succeeded by his son Gruffydd.
1198 Pope Celestine III dies. He is succeeded by Innocent III, who excommunicates Philip II of France for repudiating his wife Ingeborg of Denmark. Two rival emperors are established: Philip of Swabia, brother of Henry VI, and Otto, Duke of Saxony.
1199 Richard I dies after an injury at the siege of Chalus. He is succeeded by his brother John, although Philip II goes to war in France in support of John's nephew Arthur of Brittany. The Declaration of Speyer gives the German princes the right to elect their king.
1200 John of England and Philip II of France make peace at Le Goulet, with John confirmed in the Angevin lands in France under Philip's overlordship. Llywelyn the Great seizes Anglesey.
1201 The St Gotthard Pass is opened in Switzerland.
1202 The Fourth Crusade is proclaimed by Innocent III, with leadership given to Count Boniface III of Montferrat. The crusaders get into debt with Venice, whose doge, Enrico Dandolo, persuades them to take Zara for Venice. For this the crusaders are excommunicated by Innocent III.
1203 John murders his nephew, Arthur of Brittany, causing his French possessions to revolt. Crusaders and Venetians agree to help Isaac II regain the Byzantine throne from Alexius III, and are successful.
1204 Emperor Isaac II and his son Alexius IV deposed by Alexius V Ducas. The crusaders conquer Constantinople, and Alexius V flees to Morea, where he is captured and executed. Baldwin of Flanders is elected emperor, but the Byzantine empire disintegrates as relatives of the former ruling families set up independent states. Eleanor of Aquitaine dies. Normandy is captured by Philip Augustus.
1205 The Duchy of Athens is founded by Othon de la Roche. William of Champlitte founds the Principate of Achaea. Emperor Baldwin is defeated and executed by Kalojan of Bulgaria at Adrianople; he is succeeded by his brother Henry. Ladislas III of Hungary deposed by his uncle Andras II.
1206 The Mongol leader Temujin is proclaimed Genghis Khan at Karakorum. Qutb-ud-Din Aibak kills Sultan Muhammad and founds the Sultanate of Delhi. Theodore I Lascaris elected Legitimist Emperor at Nicaea.
1207 Marco I Sanudo founds the duchy of Naxos. Boniface of Montferrat, king of Thessalonica dies, and is succeeded by his son Demetrius.
1208 Philip of Swabia, pretender to the Holy Roman Empire, murdered by Otto of Wittelsbach, who is elected to succeed him and betrothed to his daughter. England placed under interdict by Innocent III. The Albigensian Crusade is proclaimed by Innocent III against Cathar heretics in Languedoc.
1209 The Albigensian fortress of Carcassonne is brutally taken by crusaders under Simon de Montfort. Otto of Wittelsbach crowned Emperor Otto IV in Rome. King John is excommunicated by Innocent III. Cambridge University founded by students leaving Oxford due to town and gown clashes.
1210 The order of the Friars Minor, founded by Francis of Assisi, approved by Innocent III. *Tristan und Isolde* written by Gottfried von Strassburg.
1211 Genghis Khan invades China. Sancho I of Portugal dies, and is succeeded by his son Alfonso II. Emperor Otto deposed by the German princes.
1212 Frederick II elected king by the German princes. Alfonso VIII of Castile decisively defeats the Moors at Las Navas de Tolosa. Stephen of Cloyes leads the Children's Crusade to its doom: many of the children who sail from Marseilles for the Holy Land end up in slavery.
1213 King John submits to the Papacy. Simon de Montfort invades Aragon, defeating the Aragonese at Muret and killing Pedro II, whose infant son James I is put into the care of the Templars.
1214 King John, Otto IV and other lords form alliance against Philip Augustus, who defeats the allied troops at Bouvines, Flanders. William the Lion of Scotland dies, and is succeeded by his son Alexander II.
1215 A revolt by barons in England leads to the signing under duress by King John of Magna Carta; rebel barons later capture Rochester Castle but John retakes it. Frederick II crowned emperor at Aachen. St Dominic founds the Dominican Order.
1216 Baronial revolts against King John gather force and the Dauphin Louis is invited to become king of England. John loses his baggage in the Wash and dies at Newark; he is succeeded by his son Henry III, with William Marshal, earl of Pembroke, proclaimed Regent. Pope Innocent III dies, and is succeeded by Honorius III.
1217 William Marshal defeats baronial rebels at Lincoln; the French fleet is later defeated off Sandwich and Prince Louis sues for peace. Henry III established as unchallenged king of England. The Fifth Crusade is launched under the leadership of John de Brienne.
1218 Persia overrun by Genghis Khan's Mongols. Deposed Emperor Otto IV dies, leaving Frederick II unchallenged. The Dannebrog is adopted as the flag of Denmark.
1219 Sultan Ka'us I of Rum dies, and is succeeded by his brother Kubadh I. Robert succeeds his mother Yolande as emperor in Constantinople. William Marshal dies.
1220 The Dresden Boys' choir founded. Building commences on Salisbury and Amiens cathedrals.
1221 Samarkand sacked by Genghis Khan. The Fifth Crusade ends in failure.
1222 University of Oxford establishes St George's Day, 23 April, as national holiday of England.
1223 Philip Augustus of France dies, and is succeeded by his son Louis VIII. Russians defeated by the Mongols at Kalka River. Alfonso II of Portugal dies, and is succeeded by his son Sancho II.
1224 The Jodo Shin (True Pure Land) sect founded in Japan by Shinran Shonin. Poitou and Gascony, possessions of Henry III of England, invaded by Louis VIII of France.
1225 Magna Carta is reissued in definitive form.
1226 Louis VIII of France dies, and is succeeded by his son Louis IX. St Francis of Assisi dies. The Teutonic Knights are commissioned to conquer and convert Prussia.

1227 Genghis Khan dies; his empire is divided among his three sons. Pope Honorius III dies, and is succeeded by Gregory IX. Frederick II embarks upon crusade, but is forced back by illness and excommunicated by Gregory IX for temporizing.
1228 Frederick II embarks upon crusade whilst Pope Gregory IX invades his realm. Francis of Assisi canonised.
1229 Frederick II reaches an agreement with Sultan Malik-al-Kamil, gaining Jerusalem, Bethlehem, Nazareth and an access corridor from Acre with a 15-year truce, and has himself crowned king of Jerusalem in Jerusalem. Returning from Palestine, Frederick defeats his enemies in Italy. The Balearic Islands conquered by Aragon.
1230 Frederick II and Pope Gregory IX reach an agreement at San Germano and Frederick's excommunication is lifted. Alfonso IX of León; dies his son Ferdinand III of Castile unites the two kingdoms.
1231 The Japanese shogun Fujiwara Yoritsune forbids the selling of children into slavery. Frederick II founds a medical school at Salerno.
1232 Muhammad I al-Ghalib comes to power in Granada, founding the Nasrid dynasty. Anthony of Padua canonised a year after his death.
1233 Pope Gregory IX founds the Papal Inquisition for the suppression of heresy and entrusts it to the Dominicans. The earl of Pembroke, aided by Llywelyn of Wales, leads a baronial revolt against Henry III.
1234 The earl of Pembroke is murdered in Ireland defending his Leinster estates against royalist attacks. Henry III and Llywelyn of Wales make peace.
1235 The Jin state in China falls to the Great Khan Ogedei's Mongols. Andras II of Hungary dies, and is succeeded by his son Bela IV.
1236 Alexander Nevsky succeeds to the Grand Duchy of Novgorod.
1237 The Mongols, led by Subutai and Ogedei, invade Russia, capture Moscow and devastate Poland.
1238 Moorish Valencia surrenders to James I of Aragon.
1239 Emperor Frederick II excommunicated again by Gregory IX.
1240 Prince Llywelyn of Gwynedd dies, and is succeeded by his son Dafydd. Richard of Cornwall and his brother-in-law Simon de Montfort lead a crusade to the Holy Land. The Mongol leader Batu, a grandson of Genghis Khan, takes and destroys Kiev.
1241 The Mongols advance into Eastern Europe, routing the Germans at Liegnitz in Silesia, but the death of Khan Ogedei saves Europe from invasion. Pope Gregory IX dies, and is succeeded by Celestine IV, who dies after seventeen days as Pontiff.
1242 Batu establishes the Golden Horde Mongols at Sarai on the Volga. Alexander Nevsky defeats the Teutonic Knights on the frozen Lake Peipus.
1243 Innocent IV elected Pope after an eighteen-month delay due to quarrels with Emperor Frederick II.
1244 Pasha Khwarazmi of Egypt recaptures Jerusalem for the Arabs. The Cathar stronghold of Montségur falls to Catholic besiegers and a mass execution of the defenders takes place outside.
1245 The Council of Lyon declares Frederick II deposed, causing civil war in Germany. Sancho II of Portugal deposed by Pope Innocent IV, who offers the throne to Sancho's brother Alfonso III.
1246 Landgrave Henry Raspe of Thuringia is elected German king. He defeats Frederick II's son Conrad at Nidda but is driven out of Thuringia by Conrad and Duke Otto II of Bavaria. Duke Frederick II of Austria dies; Emperor Frederick II seizes his duchy.
1247 Buda founded by Bela IV of Hungary to replace Pest, destroyed by the Mongols. With the demise of Henry of Thuringia, William II of Holland is elected anti-king in Germany.
1248 Louis IX of France sets off on the Seventh Crusade. Rhodes taken from the Byzantines by the Genoese. Moorish Seville falls after a two-year siege to Ferdinand III of Castile.
1249 The crusaders land in Egypt and take Damietta. Alexander II of Scotland dies, and is succeeded by his son Alexander III.
1250 Louis IX of France captured by Caliph Turan Shah of Egypt at the battle of Fariskur but released after paying ransom. The Mamluks depose and kill Turan Shah; Musa, a cousin of Turan Shah, becomes Caliph but rules in name only. Emperor Frederick II dies, and is succeeded by his son Conrad IV.
1251 Ottokar, margrave of Moravia, elected duke of Austria.
1252 Ferdinand III of Castile dies; his son Alfonso X succeeds him. Duke Andrei II of Vladimir deposed by the Great Khan Mongka in favour of his younger brother Alexander Nevsky.
1253 Wenceslas I of Bohemia dies, and is succeeded by his son Ottokar II, duke of Austria. The Buddhist monk Nichiren founds his own sect in Japan.
1254 Pope Innocent IV offers the Sicilian throne to Edmund, son of Henry III, who accepts on his behalf. Louis IX of France returns from crusade. Emperor Conrad IV dies. The succession of his infant son Conradin is blocked by opponents of the Hohenstaufens.
1255 Prince Llywelyn of Gwynedd ousts his brother Owen from joint rulership of the Principality.
1256 Venice and Genoa go to war. The order of Augustinian Hermits is founded. Hulagu, a grandson of Genghis Khan, conquers Persia.
1257 Richard, earl of Cornwall, is crowned German King (formally 'King of the Romans') in Aachen, but his election is disputed by Alfonso X of Castile.
1258 Hulagu Khan conquers Baghdad, killing Caliph al-Musta'sim and bringing the Abbasid Caliphate to an end. The Provisions of Oxford establish a form of parliamentary government in England. Manfred, regent of Sicily, crowns himself king, deposing his nephew Conradin, and is excommunicated by Pope Alexander IV.
1259 By the treaty of Paris Henry III gives up his claim to Normandy, Anjou and Poitou, and does homage for Gascony and Aquitaine to Louis IX.
1260 The Mamluk Baibars I becomes sultan in Egypt and defeats the Mongols at Ain Jalut in Palestine, saving Egypt from invasion and turning the tide of Mongol attacks. Kublai Khan comes to power in China.
1261 The Greeks reconquer Constantinople, driving the Latin Emperor Baldwin II from the city. The Nicaean Emperor Michael VIII Palaeologus succeeds him.
1262 Haakon IV of Norway unites Greenland and Iceland with his kingdom. Cadiz taken from the Moors.
1263 Alexander III of Scotland defeats Haakon IV of Norway at Largs and takes the Hebrides. Haakon dies on his way home and is succeeded by his son Magnus VI.
1264 Civil war erupts in England between Henry III and a baronial alliance led by Simon de Montfort; de Montfort defeats and captures Henry at Lewes, becoming de facto ruler of England.
1265 Charles of Anjou granted crusading privileges to conquer Sicily by Pope Clement IV. Simon de Montfort summons parliament, but is defeated and killed at Evesham by Prince Edward, who has escaped from imprisonment.
1266 Charles of Anjou defeats and kills Manfred of Sicily at Benevento and becomes king of Sicily. The Hebrides and the Isle of Man granted to Scotland by Norway under the terms of the Treaty of Perth.
1267 Llewelyn of Gwynedd, recognised as Prince of Wales by the treaty of Montgomery, pays homage to Henry III.
1268 Sultan Baibars captures Jaffa and Antioch. Conradin attempts to reclaim Sicily from Charles of Anjou, but is captured and executed. Pope Clement IV dies; the Papacy is left vacant.
1269 Louis IX of France orders Jews in his country to wear a purple wheel on their clothing.
1270 Louis IX of France dies in Tunisia whilst leading the Eighth Crusade; he is succeeded by his son Philip III. The poet Tannhäuser dies.
1271 Pope Gregory X elected to the three-years-vacant papal throne. Marco Polo accompanies his father and uncle to the Far East. Prince Edward of England sails to Acre as part of the short-lived Ninth Crusade.
1272 Richard of Cornwall, king of the Romans, dies. Henry III of England dies, and is succeeded by his son Edward I, who is on crusade. Robert the Bruce is born at Turnberry.
1273 Rudolf, count of Habsburg, elected German king and Holy Roman Emperor.
1274 Thomas Aquinas dies, leaving unfinished his *Summa Theologiae*. Kublai Khan sends an invasion fleet to Japan, but it is destroyed by a typhoon.
1275 Moses de León completes the Jewish mystical text the *Zohar*. Prince Llywelyn of Wales refuses homage to Edward I.
1276 Pope Gregory dies, followed by his successors Innocent V and Hadrian V; John XXI becomes 4th Pope of the year. Ottokar of Bohemia outlawed by Rudolf of Habsburg, but submits to him and is allowed to keep Bohemia and Moravia.
1277 Roger Bacon imprisoned for heresy. Sultan Baibars I of Egypt dies, and is succeeded by his son Baraka Khan. Llywelyn of Gwynedd forced to submit to Edward I by the treaty of Conway.

1278 Ottokar of Bohemia defeated and killed by Rudolf of Habsburg at Dürnkrut. He is succeeded by his son Wenceslas II. The glass mirror is invented.
1279 Alfonso III of Portugal dies near Macao, and is succeeded by his son Diniz. Kublai Khan defeats the Southern Song dynasty in a sea battle and reunites China under the rule of his Yuan dynasty.
1280 Magnus VI of Norway dies; his son Erik II succeeds him.
1281 When Kublai Khan sends a second invasion fleet to Japan it is again decimated by a typhoon, which the Japanese call *kamikaze*, divine wind.
1282 When his younger brother David starts a rebellion against Edward I, Llywelyn of Gwynedd is forced to take part, but is killed near Builth. His brother succeeds him. In the Sicilian Vespers, Sicilian nobles revolt against Charles of Anjou, who flees whilst his countrymen are massacred. Pedro III of Aragon is offered the Sicilian crown and arrives to accept it.
1283 Prussia subdued by the Teutonic Knights. Edward I conquers Wales. Prince David of Gwynedd is surrendered by his men and executed by Edward.
1284 Kublai Khan invades Vietnam, but his army is destroyed by local guerrillas. Edward I settles Welsh affairs by the Statute of Rhuddlan and arranges for his son Edward to be born in Caernarfon castle.
1285 Charles of Anjou, king of Naples, dies whilst preparing to invade Sicily, succeeded by his son Charles II. Philip III of France dies, and is succeeded by his son Philip IV the Fair. Pedro III of Aragon and Sicily dies, to be succeeded in Aragon by his son Alfonso III and in Sicily by his son James.
1286 Alexander III of Scotland dies on a night ride; his heir is his granddaughter Margaret, the Maid of Norway.
1287 Kublai Khan invades Burma.
1288 Charles II of Naples is released from custody in Aragon on the condition that he accepts Aragonese rule in Sicily.
1289 Tripoli falls to Egyptian forces. Block printing is introduced to Europe at Ravenna.
1290 Edward I expels the Jews from England. Richard of Haldingham draws the *Mappa Mundi.* Margaret of Norway dies whilst on board ship to Scotland; the throne is vacant.
1291 Acre falls to Egyptian forces, ending crusader interest in Outremer. The Knights Hospitallers settle in Cyprus. Rudolf of Habsburg dies. The cantons of Uri, Schwyz and Unterwalden form the Everlasting League, the beginnings of Switzerland.
1292 Adolf, count of Nassau, elected German king. Edward I grants the Scottish throne to John de Balliol.
1293 Kublai Khan sends an expedition to take Java, but it fails.
1294 Philip IV of France confiscates Gascony; Edward I declares war but preparations are disrupted by revolt in Wales. Kublai Khan dies, and is succeeded by his grandson Temür.
1295 A Welsh revolt collapses after defeat at Maes Moydog. Scotland, resentful of a summons to help Edward I, forms the Auld Alliance with France. The Model Parliament convenes at Westminster.
1296 The Genoese defeat the Venetian fleet at Curzola; Marco Polo is amongst those captured. Edward I invades Scotland, forces John de Balliol to abdicate and takes the Stone of Scone, where Scottish kings are crowned, to Westminster. The arms of Scotland are torn from John's surcoat, hence the abiding name of 'Toom Tabard'.
1297 William Wallace leads a Scottish revolt against Edward I, defeating the English at Stirling Bridge and invading Northumberland and Cumberland. Giant moas become extinct on New Zealand's North Island.
1298 Adolf of Nassau is dethroned by his electors and killed at the battle of Göllheim; Albrecht of Austria, son of Rudolf of Habsburg, replaces him as German king. Edward I invades Scotland, defeating the Scots at Falkirk; Wallace flees abroad.
1299 Osman I, first of the Ottomans, becomes sultan of Turkey.
1300 Arnaud de Villeneuve distils brandy at Montpellier. Edward I invades Scotland again, but makes a truce after a Papal appeal to withdraw. Henry of Great Poland is deposed; Wenceslas II of Bohemia is elected to succeed him.
1301 Andras III of Hungary dies, ending the rule of the Arpad dynasty. Wenceslas II of Bohemia becomes king in his stead, but civil war breaks out. Edward I makes his son Edward Prince of Wales.
1302 The Black faction drive the Whites from Florence; Dante is exiled as a result. The Estates-General of France meet for the first time. Flemish burghers defeat the French at the battle of the Spurs.
1303 Philip IV of France sends Guillaume de Nogaret to capture Pope Boniface VIII and bring him to face trial in France. De Nogaret is thwarted by the Roman citizens, but Boniface dies a virtual prisoner and a broken man in the Vatican shortly after.
1304 The Scottish barons submit to Edward I at St Andrews whilst Stirling Castle only submits after a siege.
1305 Bertrand de Got, Archbishop of Bordeaux, elected Pope as Clement V. Wenceslas II of Bohemia, Poland and Hungary dies. He is succeeded in Bohemia and Poland by his son Wenceslas III, but in Hungary by Otto III of Bavaria. William Wallace is captured, tried and executed by the English.
1306 Wenceslas III of Bohemia and Poland is murdered. Albrecht of Austria invests his son Rudolf with Bohemia whilst Ladislas IV of Kujavia succeeds in Poland. Jews expelled from France. Rhodes purchased by the Knights Hospitallers. Robert Bruce murders John Comyn and is subsequently crowned king of Scots at Scone. The English invade Scotland and force Bruce to flee.
1307 Edward I of England dies, and is succeeded by his son Edward II, who creates Piers Gaveston earl of Cornwall. Philip IV seizes the property of the Knights Templar in France so as to replenish his treasury, but some of the Templar treasure is hidden away.
1308 The Templars are suppressed in England. Parliament forces Edward II to banish Piers Gaveston, who is created Lieutenant in Ireland. Albrecht of Austria is murdered on orders of his nephew John; Henry IV of Luxembourg is elected his successor.
1309 Clement V moves the Papacy to Avignon, thus beginning The 'Babylonian Captivity'.
1310 Parliament forces Edward II to appoint 21 Lords Ordainers to reform the government. A Council of Ten is appointed to rule Venice.
1311 The English Parliament orders baronial consent to appointments by Edward II. Robert Bruce raids Northumberland.
1312 The Knights Templar are abolished in France. Lyons is incorporated into France by the treaty of Vienne. Piers Gaveston is captured by barons and executed.
1313 Perth, Roxburgh, Edinburgh and the Isle of Man taken by the Scots, who besiege Stirling Castle. Emperor Henry VII dies.
1314 Jacques de Molay, Grand Master of the Knights Templar, is burned as a heretic; he curses Philip IV and Pope Clement V at the stake, both of whom die before the year is out. Edward II invades Scotland, but is routed at Bannockburn. Louis X succeeds his father Philip. Louis of Bavaria is elected German king, but a faction elects his rival Frederick of Austria as anti-king; civil war breaks out in Germany.
1315 Edward Bruce, Robert's brother, is offered the High Kingship of Ireland; he sails to Ireland and defeats the Earl of Ulster near Connor.
1316 Edward Bruce, is crowned high king of Ireland. Louis X of France dies. He is briefly succeeded by his son Jean I, who dies soon after his father, and then by his brother Philip V. John XXII elected Pope after a two year hiatus.
1317 The Salic Law is adopted by the French royal family: from now on females and descendants of the female line may not inherit the crown or other titles.
1318 Edward Bruce is killed in the battle of Faughart.
1319 Scots raid into England, defeating an army at the battle of Myton-in-Swaledale; a truce is subsequently made between the English and Scots.
1320 Vladislav IV is crowned king of Poland. The Declaration of Arbroath asserts Scots independence and loyalty to Robert Bruce. Tughluq Shah I founds the Tughluq dynasty as rulers of the sultanate of Delhi, overthrowing Khusraw Shah of the Khalji dynasty.
1321 Parliament forces Edward II to banish his close supporters Hugh Despenser and his son, but he recalls them and raises an army. Dante Alighieri dies.
1322 Philip V of France dies, and is succeeded by his brother Charles IV. Edward II defeats his cousin Thomas, earl of Lancaster, at Boroughbridge; Lancaster is executed and Edward's opponents punished. Frederick of Austria defeated and taken prisoner by Louis of Bavaria at the battle of Mühldorf.
1323 Thomas Aquinas is canonised.
1324 Marco Polo dies. Charles IV of France invades Gascony.
1325 Tughluq Shah I of Delhi is murdered by his son Muhammad Shah I, who replaces him as Sultan. Louis of Bavaria accepts Frederick of Austria as co-regent of Germany, but the move is unsuccessful.

1326 Osman I of Turkey dies; his son Orkhan succeeds him. Queen Isabella of England and her lover Roger Mortimer invade England; Edward II is captured and the Despensers executed.

1327 Edward II is forced to abdicate in favour of his son Edward III, and is murdered 8 months later in Berkeley Castle. Munich is devastated by fire.

1328 Charles IV of France dies, and is succeeded by his cousin Philip VI, first of the Valois dynasty. Robert Bruce is recognised as king of the Scots by the treaty of Northampton; Pope John XXII also recognises him.

1329 Robert Bruce dies of leprosy; he is succeeded by his son David II.

1330 Frederick of Austria dies; by the treaty of Hagenau Louis of Bavaria is recognised as emperor by the Habsburg faction. Edward III takes control of government in England, capturing and executing Roger Mortimer.

1331 Stephen Urosh III of Serbia is overthrown and murdered by his son Stephen Urosh IV Dushan, who replaces him as king.

1332 Lucerne joins the Swiss League. Edward Balliol invades Scotland, defeating loyalist forces at Dupplin Moor, and is crowned king, but is then defeated by loyalists and flees to England.

1333 Vladislav IV of Poland dies, and is succeeded by his son Casimir III the Great. Edward III and Edward Balliol besiege Berwick and defeat a relieving force at Halidon Hill. The Isle of Man is seized by England.The Black Death pandemic – a combination of bubonic and pneumonic plague passed on by fleas from infected rats – emerges in China.

1334 Casimir III of Poland encourages Jewish immigration. David II of Scotland flees to France and loyalist revolts break out. Berwick ceded to England by Edward Balliol. Pope John XXII dies, and is succeeded by Benedict XII.

1335 Emperor Andronicus III conquers Thessaly.

1336 Alfonso IV of Aragon dies, and is succeeded by his son Pedro IV. The Vijayanagar Empire is founded in southern India by Harihara I of the Yadava dynasty.

1337 Edward III claims the throne of France, thus precipitating the Hundred Years War.

1338 The French initiate hostilities against England, burning Portsmouth and Southampton. Edward III and Emperor Louis IV enter into an alliance. The university of Pisa is founded. Ashikaga Takaufi founds the Ashikaga shogunate.

1339 Venice conquers Treviso, thus gaining its first mainland possession.

1340 Waldemar IV, youngest son of the deposed Christopher II, ascends the Danish throne, ending eight years of anarchy. The English win a decisive naval victory over the French at Sluys.

1341 David II returns to Scotland, forcing the withdrawal of Edward Balliol. Emperor Andronicus III dies, and is succeeded by his 9-year-old son John V. When John's guardian, John Cantacuzene, attempts to set himself up as emperor, civil war erupts.

1342 Edward III conquers most of Brittany. Charles Robert, king of Hungary dies, and is succeeded by his son Louis I the Great.

1343 The Peruzzi banking house of Florence collapses as Edward III defaults on his loan repayments. The Black Death spreads amongst the Tartars in the Crimea.

1344 The Bardi banking house in Florence collapses. The Yellow River floods 16,000 square km of China and changes its course. Alfonso XI of Castile conquers Algeciras from the Moors.

1345 Stephen Urosh IV Dushan proclaims himself emperor of the Serbs and prepares to attack Byzantium.

1346 The French annihilated at Crécy by English bowmen. John of Luxembourg perishes in the battle, and is succeeded by his son Charles I, who is subsequently crowned German king. Scottish forces under David II invade England but are routed at Neville's Cross with David II taken prisoner.

1347 John Cantacuzene is victorious in the Byzantine civil war and reigns, nominally as co-emperor with John V, as John VI. Cola di Rienzi overthrows the Roman plutocracy, but attracts the enmity of Pope Clement VI and is forced to abdicate. Calais surrenders to Edward III after an 11-month siege. Emperor Louis IV dies during a bear hunt, and is succeeded by his rival Charles I of Luxembourg. The Black Death reaches the Black Sea, Sicily and Marseilles.

1348 The Black Death sweeps across Europe and has entered England by summer. Despite Pope Clement VI absolving them of blame, Jews are blamed in areas of France, Germany and Switzerland for the plague pandemic and are persecuted. Many leave for Poland and Russia which are more tolerant. Edward III founds the Order of the Garter.

1349 The Black Death reaches Scotland, Ireland and Poland. A flagellant movement appears as a response to the plague pandemic, but it is denounced and suppressed by Clement VI.

1350 Philip VI of France dies, and is succeeded by his son Jean II. Alfonso XI of Castile dies of the plague whilst besieging Gibraltar, and is succeeded by his son Pedro I the Cruel. Cola di Rienzi appears in Prague, where he is imprisoned by Charles of Luxembourg.

1351 Zurich joins the Swiss League. Florence and Milan go to war over Tuscany. The Statute of Labourers fixes wage rates and restricts movement of labourers in England, as a result of Black Death depopulation and the economic strain of war.

1352 Glarus and Zug join the Swiss League. The Black Death penetrates Russia. Cola di Rienzi is sentenced to death at Avignon, but is saved when Clement VI dies and his successor Innocent VI pardons him.

1353 Bern joins the Swiss League. Giovanni Boccaccio completes *The Decameron.*

1354 The Ottoman Turks take Gallipoli. Innocent VI grants Cola di Rienzi the title Senator and sends him to Rome, but he is killed in a riot within two months. The Genoese defeat a Venetian fleet at Sapienza.

1355 Stephen Urosh IV Dushan of Serbia dies, and is succeeded by his son Stephen Urosh V. The St Scholastica's Day riots in Oxford last three days, with many students killed in 'town and gown' clashes.

1356 Jean II of France captured by the English at the battle of Poitiers, where the Black Prince Edward Prince of Wales, gains a crushing victory. Edward Balliol, a King of Scotland in name only for more than 20 years, officially abdicates.

1357 Parisian merchants, led by Etienne Marcel and Robert le Coq, revolt against the dauphin's administration. David II of Scotland ransomed by the treaty of Berwick.

1358 French peasants revolt in the Jacquerie uprising in the Beauvais but it is suppressed with English assistance. Etienne Marcel is assassinated in Paris by a supporter of the dauphin.

1359 Revolutionaries in red hats storm Bruges in an unsuccessful attempt to overthrow the patrician government. Ivan II of Muscovy dies, and is succeeded by his son Dimitri Donskoy.

1360 England and France sign the treaty of Brétigny, which gives England territorial gains and stipulates the payment of a ransom for Jean II. When the ransom cannot be raised Jean II voluntarily goes back into captivity. Sultan Orkhan of Turkey dies, and is succeeded by Murad I.

1361 Murad I takes Adrianople and makes it the Ottoman capital. The Black Death reappears in England and France.

1362 The Black Prince is appointed ruler of Aquitaine. William Langland writes *Piers Plowman*, a much-heralded Middle English allegorical narrative poem.

1363 Tughlug Timur, shah in Turkestan, dies; he is succeeded by his son Ilyas Khoja, establishing Zungarian Chaghatai rule.

1364 Jean II of France dies in captivity in England, and is succeeded by his son Charles V.

1365 By the Statute of Praemunire the English parliament repudiates Papal overlordship of the country and forbids appeals to the Papal court.

1366 Amadeus of Savoy takes Gallipoli as part of his crusade against the Turks. Pedro the Cruel of Castile is deposed in favour of his half-brother Henry of Trastamara.

1367 Pedro I of Portugal dies and is succeeded by his son Ferdinand. The Black Prince invades Castile in support of Pedro the Cruel, defeating Castilian and French forces at Najera and restoring Pedro's crown.

1368 Chinese Yuan Emperor Shundi is deposed by the Ming Zhu Yuanzhang, who takes the throne with the name Hongwu.

1369 Pedro the Cruel of Castile offends the Black Prince, who abandons him. Besieged by Henry of Trastamara at Montiel, Pedro is defeated and killed by Henry who replaces him as king. France declares war on England and confiscates English lands in the country.

1370 The Mongol ruler Timur the Lame (Tamburlaine) takes the throne of Samarkand. The Black Prince sacks Limoges. Casimir III of Poland dies in a hunting accident; the last Piast king, he is succeeded by his nephew Louis of Anjou, the king of Hungary.

1371 David II of Scotland dies; he is succeeded by his nephew Robert II, the first of the Stuarts. Sultan Murad I wins the battle of Chernomen – Macedonia, Bulgaria and the Byzantines are forced to admit his suzerainty.

1372 The English defeated by Castilian forces at sea off La Rochelle, which falls, along with Poitou, to the French.

1373 Brandenburg annexed by Emperor Charles IV from Otto V of Bavaria, and is given to his son Wenceslas to rule.

1374 A mysterious dancing craze affects Aix-La-Chapelle, when the inhabitants inexplicably dance themselves to exhaustion.

1375 England and France sign the truce of Bruges – English possessions in France much reduced as a result. The Mamluks take Sis from the Armenian King León V, ending Armenian independence.

1376 Edward, the Black Prince, dies. The Good Parliament is convened; Sir Peter de la Mare is chosen Speaker for the House of Commons.

1377 Pope Gregory XI returns the Papacy to Rome. Edward III dies, and is succeeded by his grandson Richard II; John of Gaunt becomes Regent. The French raid Sussex and Kent, burning Rye and Hastings. Sir Thomas Hungerford becomes the first official holder of the title Speaker of the House of Commons.

1378 Pope Gregory XI dies. Urban VI is elected his successor but tries to reform the College of Cardinals, leading the French Cardinals to create Robert of Geneva Pope Clement VII at Anagni. He moves his Curia to Avignon and the Great Schism begins. Emperor Charles IV dies, and is succeeded by his son Wenceslas.

1379 Henry II of Castile dies, and is succeeded by his son Juan I.

1380 St Catherine of Siena dies. Charles V of France dies, and is succeeded by his son Charles VI the Mad. Dmitri III Donskoi, prince of Moscow, defeats the Mongols at Kulikovo.

1381 Wat Tyler and John Ball lead the Peasants' Revolt in England. Archbishop Sudbury is murdered outside the Tower by a mob but Tyler is stabbed to death by William Walworth, mayor of London, on meeting Richard II at Smithfield. Ball is executed and the rising is suppressed. Venice defeats Genoa in the war of Chioggia.

1382 The religious reformer John Wycliffe is condemned by Archbishop William Courtenay and barred from teaching at Oxford. Louis of Anjou, king of Hungary and Poland, dies, and is succeeded by his daughters Mary in Hungary and Jadwiga in Poland.

1383 The Bishop of Norwich leads the 'Norwich Crusade' to Flanders in support of Pope Urban VI, but is repulsed and impeached at home by Chancellor Michael de la Pole. Ferdinand of Portugal dies, and is succeeded by his daughter Beatrix.

1384 Juan I of Castile marries Beatrix of Portugal, but the Portuguese resist his claim to their throne. John Wycliffe dies.

1385 Scottish forces, aided by the French, raid Northumbria. Portuguese forces defeat Juan of Castile at the battle of Aljubarrota; João of Aviz, an illegitimate son of Pedro I, takes the kingship.

1386 England and Portugal sign the treaty of Windsor, sealed by the marriage of João I with John of Gaunt's daughter Philippa. Jadwiga of Poland marries Jagiello of Lithuania, who takes the name Vladislav V. Leopold III of Styria and Tyrol defeated and killed by the Swiss at the battle of Sempach; his 4 sons jointly succeed him.

1387 Olaf V of Denmark and Norway dies, and is succeeded by his mother Margaret I. Sigismund of Luxembourg, margrave of Brandenburg, marries Mary of Hungary, becoming king. Geoffrey Chaucer begins *The Canterbury Tales* – a story of 29 pilgrims and their host, Harry Bailey, who set out from the Tabard Inn, Southwark, to visit the shrine of St Thomas Becket of Canterbury Cathedral. The pilgrims agree to tell four stones each, the best one, as chosen by the host, being rewarded with a supper paid for by the remaining pilgrims.

1388 At the battle of Otterburn (Chevy Chase) the Scots under the earl of Douglas defeat and capture Henry 'Hotspur' Percy, though Douglas himself is killed.

1389 Margaret I of Denmark and Norway is offered the Swedish throne, invades and defeats King Albert II of Mecklenburg at Falköping, and thereby unites the Scandinavian thrones. Sultan Murad I defeats a Serb-led coalition at Kosovo and conquers Serbia. Murad is subsequently assassinated by the Serb noble Lazar, who is captured and put to death by Murad's son and successor Bayazid I.

1390 Byzantine Emperor John V is deposed by his grandson John VII, but his son Manuel restores him to the throne. Robert II of Scotland dies, and is succeeded by his son Robert III. Juan I of Castile dies, and is succeeded by his son Henry III.

1391 Emperor John V dies, and is succeeded by his son Manuel II. Jews persecuted in Andalusia and Barcelona, as scapegoats for plague. Gedun Truppa is the first Dalai Lama in Tibet.

1392 Charles VI of France suffers his first fit of madness. Yi Songgye founds the Yi Dynasty in Korea, supplanting the Koryo Dynasty and making Kyongsong (later known as Seoul) the capital.

1393 Bulgaria subdued by Sultan Bayazid I. Timur the Lame takes Baghdad. Emperor Wenceslas IV tortures and murders St John of Nepomuk in Prague.

1394 Emperor Wenceslas taken prisoner by his cousin Jobst of Moravia. Anti-Pope Clement VII dies, and is replaced by Benedict XXIII. Richard II goes to Ireland and sets the limit of the territory later known as 'The Pale'.

1395 Richard II receives the submission of 80 Irish chiefs and returns to England. Albert of Mecklenburg renounces the Swedish throne, confirming Margaret of Denmark as queen.

1396 England and France agree a 28-year truce. Sigismund of Hungary leads a Crusade to Nicopolis, where his army is routed by the Ottoman Turks. Gian Galeazzo Visconti buys the title Duke of Milan from Emperor Wenceslas.

1397 Scandinavian nobles assembled in the Union of Kalmar officially recognise the union of Denmark, Norway and Sweden under Queen Margaret. Sultan Bayazid besieges Constantinople but withdraws when Timur the Lame appears in his lands.

1398 Richard II orders a duel to settle the dispute between John of Gaunt's son Henry Bolingbroke and the duke of Norfolk; he then intercedes and banishes the pair. Timur the Lame conquers and sacks Delhi.

1399 John of Gaunt dies. Richard II confiscates the Lancastrian inheritance of Gaunt. Bolingbroke returns from exile, engineers the deposition of Richard II, and is crowned Henry IV in his stead.

1400 Richard II murdered in Pontefract Castle. Emperor Wenceslas is deposed for drunkenness and incompetence; Rupert III of the Palatinate elected to replace him. Owain Glyndwr attacks Lord Grey of Ruthin, proclaims himself prince of Wales and engineers a revolt in the Principality. Chaucer dies before completion of the *Canterbury Tales*; 22 finished and two unfinished stories were later published but the winner of the aforementioned prize (see entry 1387) was not revealed.

1401 Baghdad and Damascus fall to Timur the Lame.

1402 Sultan Bayazid defeated and captured by Timur the Lame at the battle of Ankara; Bayazid is forced to become Timur's footstool while his favourite wife Despina is made a naked waitress. Duke Gian Galeazzo Visconti of Milan dies whilst besieging Florence, and is succeeded by his son Giovanni Maria. The earl of Northumberland and his son Hotspur capture the earl of Douglas at the battle of Homildon Hill.

1403 Sultan Bayazid dies in captivity at Timur's camp; his sons Suleiman and Muhammad dispute the succession. The Doge of Venice imposes quarantine as an attempt to ward off the Black Death. The earl of Northumberland rebels against Henry IV but is defeated at Shrewsbury, where his son Hotspur perishes.

1404 Owain Glyndwr holds a Welsh parliament at Dolgellau.

1405 Timur the Lame dies, and is succeeded by his sons Miran Shah and Shah Rukh and by Miran Shah's son Khalil Sultan in his domains. Owain Glyndwr is defeated at Grosmont by John Talbot and at Usk by Henry, Prince of Wales. Richard Scrope, Archbishop of York, leads a revolt against Henry IV, but the rebellion collapses and Scrope is executed.

1406 Robert III of Scotland sends his son James to France for safety, fearing his brother Albany, but James is captured by the English at sea and imprisoned. Robert III dies and Albany becomes regent as James is kept captive.

1407 Louis, duke of Orléans, is assassinated on the orders of John the Fearless, duke of Burgundy, causing a feud between Burgundian and Armagnac followers in France.

1408 The last threat to Henry IV in England is extinguished by the Sheriff of Yorkshire's victory at Bramham Moor; the earl of Northumberland dies in the battle.

1409 Henry, prince of Wales, captures Harlech castle, kills Edmund Mortimer and subdues the Welsh revolt. In an attempt to end the Great Schism a conclave of cardinals announces that both Gregory XII and Benedict XIII are deposed, and elects Alexander V in their stead. Both Gregory and Benedict refuse to accept this election, and there are now three contending popes. Dalmatia recovered by Venice.

1410 Anti-Pope Alexander V dies and John XXIII replaces him as the third pope. Emperor Rupert dies. Sigismund of Hungary, brother of the deposed Wenceslas, is elected to succeed him. The Teutonic Knights are decisively defeated by a Polish-Lithuanian force at Tannenberg.

1411 Portugal and Castile make peace. Poland and the Teutonic Knights make the Peace of Thorn.

1412 Duke Giovanni Visconti of Milan is assassinated, and succeeded by his brother Filippo Maria of Pavia. Margaret of Denmark, Sweden and Norway dies, and is succeeded by her great-nephew Erik of Pomerania.

1413 Henry IV of England dies; his son Henry V succeeds him. Civil war amongst the Ottomans ends when Muhammad I defeats and kills his brother Musa outside Constantinople.

1414 The Lollards, radical religious reformers, under Sir John Oldcastle, revolt against Henry V, but are suppressed. The Council of Constance is convened by John XXIII at the instigation of Sigismund of Hungary, in an attempt to end the Great Schism.

1415 The Council of Constance deposes John XXIII and accepts the abdication of Gregory XII, but Benedict XIII refuses to abdicate. Jan Hus is burnt for heresy, causing outrage in Bohemia. Henry V goes to war with France after the failure of negotiations to marry Catherine of Valois, and gains a crushing victory at Agincourt.

1416 Jerome of Prague, a follower of Hus, is burned for heresy. The Venetians defeat the Ottomans in the Dardanelles.

1417 Caen falls to Henry V. Oddo, Colonna is elected Pope, taking the name Martin V, and the Great Schism comes to an end, although Benedict XIII and a small number of clerics hold out.

1418 Madeira discovered by Portuguese explorers under the aegis of Henry the Navigator. John the Fearless of Burgundy takes control of the French government, but the Dauphin Charles sets up a rival administration at Bourges.

1419 Rouen, and subsequently Normandy fall to Henry V. Hussites rebel in Bohemia, defenestrating Catholic councillors in Prague. John the Fearless of Burgundy is assassinated by Armagnacs supporting Dauphin Charles, driving his successor Philip the Good to an alliance with England.

1420 The Anglo-Burgundian alliance makes the treaty of Troyes with Charles VI of France; Henry is made Charles' heir and marries his daughter Catherine. Chinese Emperor Yongle moves his capital to Dadu and renames it Beijing ('northern capital').

1421 Sultan Muhammad I dies, and is succeeded by his son Murad II. Florence buys the city of Livorno. The Zuider Zee is formed by an irruption of the North Sea; 100,000 perish in the process.

1422 Henry V dies, and is succeeded by his nine month-old son Henry VI. Charles VI of France dies and his son Charles VII declares himself king, but Henry VI is proclaimed king by Protector Bedford in the Anglo-Burgundian areas in accordance with the treaty of Troyes.

1423 Thessalonica is purchased from the Byzantines by Venice in an attempt to prevent the Ottomans taking it. James I of Scotland is freed from captivity by the treaty of London on payment of a ransom.

1424 Chinese Emperor Yongle dies and is succeeded by his son Hongxi. James I returns to Scotland and takes up government from his uncle Albany. The English defeat Charles VII at Verneuil.

1425 James I of Scotland executes his uncle Albany and his family. Emperor Manuel II dies, and is succeeded by his son John VIII. Le Mans falls to the English. Henry the Navigator takes the Canary Islands from Castile.

1426 Venice and Milan go to war.

1427 Yeshak of Ethiopia attempts to form an anti-Islamic alliance with Aragon and France.

1428 By the terms of the Treaty of Delft, Duke Phillip of Burgundy is made governor of Hainault, Holland and Zeeland and heir to Jacqueline of Bavaria, Countess of these lands.

1429 French lose to the English at Rouvray (battle of the Herrings) but under the leadership of Jeanne d'Arc relieve Orleans and are victorious at Patay, where Talbot is captured. Charles VII is crowned at Rheims.

1430 Thessalonica falls to the Ottomans of Murad II. Jeanne d'Arc is captured by the Burgundians at Compiègne and sold to the English, who imprison her at Rouen.

1431 A Lollard conspiracy led by 'Jack Sharp' is crushed by the duke of Gloucester. Jeanne d'Arc is burned as a witch at Rouen.

1432 The Azores are discovered by the Portuguese sailor Gonzalo Cabral. Sultan Murad II takes Albania.

1433 Lucca defeats Florence. Timbuktu falls to the Tuaregs. João I of Portugal dies, and is succeeded by his son Duarte. Duke Phillip of Burgundy forces Jacqueline of Bavaria to abdicate in Hainault, Holland and Zeeland after she had incited a failed revolt against him.

1434 The Khmer move their capital from Angkor to Phnom Penh. Cosimo de Medici is recalled from exile to rule Florence. Vladislav V of Poland dies, and is succeeded by his son Vladislav VI. Jan Van Eyck paints Giovanni Arnolfini and his wife.

1435 The Riksdag of Sweden meets for the first time and makes Engelbrecht Engelbrechtson regent for the ineffectual King Erik. Alfonso V of Aragon attempts to capture Naples, thus reuniting Naples and Sicily under one crown but is captured and later released. France and Burgundy are reconciled by the peace of Arras.

1436 The Compact of Iglau ends the Hussite wars in Bohemia and Emperor Sigismund is acknowledged king. Paris falls to the French. The Scots fail to capture Roxburgh Castle.

1437 James I of Scotland is murdered at Perth by Sir Robert Graham, who is executed for the deed. James II succeeds his father. Emperor Sigismund dies, and is succeeded by his son-in-law Albrecht II of Habsburg.

1438 Pahacutec founds the Inca dynasty in Peru. Erik of Denmark, Norway and Sweden flees from rebellions to Gotland, where he takes up piracy.

1439 Serbia falls to Sultan Murad II. The Council of Florence ratifies the union of Roman and Byzantine churches under Rome's primacy. German King Albrecht II dies, leaving his wife pregnant.

1440 Frederick III of Styria is elected German king. Ladislas Posthumus is born and succeeds his late father Albrecht in Austria and Bohemia; in Hungary Vladislav VI of Poland is invited to be king. Eton College is founded by Henry VI.

1441 The Churches of Rome and Ethiopia sign an act of union. The Portuguese sell Africans as slaves in Lisbon: from this the slave trade will develop.

1442 Eleanor Cobham, duchess of Gloucester, is divorced and imprisoned on charge of attempting to kill Henry VI by sorcery.

1443 The Ottomans defeated by the Hungarian hero Janos Hunyadi at Nish; George Castriota, governor of Albania, takes advantage of this defeat by declaring his province independent.

1444 Christians and Ottomans declare a truce at Adrianople and George Brankovich is restored to his principality of Serbia; Hungarians break the truce but are defeated at Varna; Vladislav VI of Poland perishes there and Ladislas Posthumus succeeds to the Hungarian throne.

1445 Cape Verde discovered by Diniz Diaz of Portugal. Copenhagen becomes the capital of Denmark.

1446 Corinth falls to the Ottomans. Janos Hunyadi is elected regent of Hungary for Ladislas.

1447 Casimir of Lithuania, a brother of the late Vladislav VI, is elected king of Poland. Milan becomes a republic on the death of Filippo Maria Visconti. Shah Rukh, Lord of Turkestan dies, and is succeeded by his son Ulugh Beg.

1448 With the death of Christopher of Bavaria, king of Sweden, Denmark and Norway, the Union of Kalmar dissolves. Christian of Oldenburg reigns in Denmark and Norway whilst Karl Knutsen is elected king of Sweden. Sultan Murad defeats the Hungarians under Janos Hunyadi at the second battle of Kosovo. Emperor John VIII dies, and is succeeded by his brother Constantine XI.

1449 Ulugh Beg, Lord of Turkestan, is executed by his son Abd al-Latif, who also puts his brother Abd al-Aziz to death. The Timurid provinces in Turkestan fragment as a result, and Babur ibn Baisonqur, a nephew of Ulugh Beg, takes power in Khurasan.

1450 Abd al-Latif dies; his cousin Abdullah Mirza succeeds him as Lord of Turkestan. Francesco Sforza overthrows the republic in Milan and makes himself duke. Normandy reconquered by France. Jack Cade leads a revolt in Kent and Sussex; it fails and Cade is killed, but Henry VI is forced to flee for safety to Kenilworth for a while.

1451 Gascony reconquered by the French. Sultan Murad II dies, and is succeeded by his son Muhammad II.

1452 Borso of Este is created duke of Modena by Emperor Frederick III. James II of Scotland murders the earl of Douglas at Stirling. John Talbot leads an expedition to Gascony and reconquers much of it.

1453 Constantinople falls to the Ottoman Sultan Muhammad II; Emperor Constantine XI perishes in the fighting and the Byzantine Empire is no more. The French win a decisive victory over the English at Castillon, where Talbot dies. Gascony is reconquered and the English hold only Calais in France. The Hundred Years War is thus brought to an end. Henry VI has a bout of insanity.

1454 The duke of York is appointed protector during Henry VI's incapacity. The Peace of Lodi is reached between Venice and Milan and their allies. Venice signs a treaty with Sultan Muhammad II.

1455 Henry VI recovers his sanity and dismisses the duke of York from the post of Protector. The Wars of the Roses begin when York and the earl of Warwick raise an army and defeat and capture Henry VI at St Albans. York is made Constable of England but pro-Lancastrian riots break out. Johannes Gutenberg produces the first printed Bible, using the movable metal type that he started to perfect in the 1450s.

1456 The Ottomans capture Athens but are repulsed from Belgrade by Janos Hunyadi, who dies soon after from plague. Vlad III the Impaler retakes the Wallachian throne from Vladislav II.

1457 Karl VIII of Sweden is driven out and replaced by Christian I of Denmark. Laszlo Hunyadi, son of Janos, is arrested and beheaded in Buda, sparking outrage in Hungary; Ladislas Posthumus is forced to flee to Prague, where he dies suddenly. Emperor Frederick III succeeds in Austria; George Podiebrad, leader of the Hussites, is elected king in Bohemia.

1458 Matthias Corvinus, second son of Janos Hunyadi, is elected king of Hungary. Alfonso V of Aragon dies, and is succeeded in Aragon and Sicily by his brother Juan II and in Naples by his bastard son Ferdinand.

1459 Civil war is renewed in England. The Yorkists are victorious at Blore Heath but defeated at Ludford Bridge. The Irish come out in support of the Yorkists.

1460 Henry VI defeated and captured by the Yorkists at Northampton; the duke of York is named heir to Henry but dies at the battle of Wakefield, where the Lancastrians are victorious. James II of Scotland dies when a cannon misfires at Roxburgh, and is succeeded by his son James III. Henry the Navigator dies.

1461 Yorkists victorious at Mortimer's Cross, where Owen Tudor is captured and executed, but defeated at St Albans. Henry VI is rescued by the Lancastrians. Edward of York deposes Henry VI and crushes the Lancastrians at Towton; Henry VI and his family flee to Scotland. Charles VII of France dies, and is succeeded by his son Louis XI. Trebizond falls to the Ottomans.

1462 Vlad III the Impaler of Wallachia is deposed and replaced by his pro-Turkish brother Radu III. Prince Vasili of Moscow dies, and is succeeded by his son Ivan III the Great.

1463 Bosnia conquered by the Ottomans, who go to war with the Venetians. England, France and Burgundy sign the Truce of Hesdin, the latter two recognizing Edward IV of York as king of England.

1464 Yorkists victorious at Hedgeley Moor and Hexham, and gain control of Northern England. Louis XI of France founds the *Poste Royale*. Cosimo de Medici dies, and is succeeded by his son Piero I.

1465 Henry VI captured in Ribblesdale and imprisoned in the Tower. Louis XI of France defeated by a coalition of royal dukes at Montlhéry and is forced to sign the treaty of Conflans.

1466 The Medicis form an alliance with the Vatican to finance alum mining in the Papal States. George Podiebrad, king of Bohemia, excommunicated by Pope Paul II.

1467 Philip the Good of Burgundy dies, and is succeeded by his son Charles the Bold.

1468 Zara Ya'kob Constantine of Ethiopia dies, and is succeeded by his son Ba'eda Maryam I. James III of Scotland contracts to marry Margaret, daughter of Christian of Denmark; the Orkneys and Shetlands are pledged as security for her dowry.

1469 Rebellion develops in England against Edward IV and the power of his wife's family. Edward is imprisoned after his army deserts him at Olney, and is released with a promise to appease the rebels. Piero de Medici dies; his sons Lorenzo the Magnificent and Giuliano succeed him. Ferdinand, heir to the throne of Aragon, marries Isabella, heiress of Castile.

1470 Portuguese seafarers reach the Gold Coast. Edward IV defeats a rebel army at Empingham, but Warwick and the Lancastrians reach an accord and invade, forcing Edward to flee to Burgundy. Henry VI is restored to the throne.

1471 Edward IV returns to England, defeats and kills Warwick at Barnet and then decisively defeats the Lancastrians at Tewkesbury, where Edward Prince of Wales perishes. Henry VI is murdered in the Tower. Louis XI of France and Charles the Bold of Burgundy go to war.

1472 Lopo Gonçalves is the first European to cross the Equator. Ivan III of Moscow marries Zoe, niece of Emperor Constantine XI, thus attempting to transfer imperial lustre to himself.

1473 Charles the Bold of Burgundy occupies Lorraine and Alsace. Cyprus falls under Venetian rule.

1474 The Union of Constance is formed against Charles the Bold of Burgundy, who makes an anti-French alliance, via the treaty of London, with Edward IV. Henry IV of Castile dies, and is succeeded by his half-sister Isabella and her husband Ferdinand, son of Juan II of Aragon.

1475 Edward IV invades France but is let down by his absent ally Charles the Bold and goes on to sign a 7-year truce with Louis XI via the treaty of Picquigny.

1476 Charles the Bold makes war on the Swiss, but is defeated at Granson, and later at Morat. Duke Galeazzo Sforza of Milan is assassinated by republicans, but is succeeded by his son Gian Galeazzo. William Caxton establishes the first English printing press.

1477 Edward IV bans early forms of skittles and cricket due to their interference with archery practice. Charles the Bold of Burgundy dies fighting the Swiss at the battle of Nancy; his state implodes and is effectively shared between Louis XI and Charles' son-in-law Maximilian, son of Emperor Frederick III.

1478 The duke of Clarence is drowned in a butt of Malmsey while imprisoned in the Tower of London. Novgorod subdued by Ivan the Great of Muscovy. Isabella of Castile unleashes the Inquisition on Jewish converts. Pope Sixtus VI and the Pazzi family plot to assassinate the Medicis; Giuliano is killed but Lorenzo escapes and decimates the Pazzis in revenge.

1479 Juan II of Aragon dies. His son Ferdinand succeeds him and the thrones of Castile and Aragon are thus united. The treaty of Constantinople ends the war between Venice and the Ottoman Empire.

1480 Ivan III frees Muscovy from Tartar domination. Duke René of Anjou dies; his domains, including Provence, are annexed by Louis XI. Otranto is taken by the Ottomans.

1481 Sultan Muhammad II dies, and is succeeded by his son Bayazid II. Alfonso V of Portugal dies, and is succeeded by his son João II.

1482 Venice goes to war with Ferrara. Louis XI and the Habsburgs make the Peace of Arras, partitioning the Burgundian domains.

1483 Edward IV dies, and is succeeded by his son Edward V, who disappears along with his brother Richard in the Tower. Their uncle Richard assumes the kingship. Louis XI of France dies, and is succeeded by his son Charles VIII. The Dominican Tomás de Torquemada takes control of the Spanish Inquisition.

1484 Diogo Cão discovers the mouth of the River Congo. Pope Innocent VIII issues the bull *Summis Desiderantes* against witchcraft.

1485 Emperor Frederick III expelled from Vienna by Matthias Corvinus of Hungary. Henry Tudor invades England against Richard III, defeats and kills him at Bosworth Field, and takes the throne. Caxton publishes Malory's *Morte d'Arthur.*

1486 Matthias Corvinus devises a law code for Hungary. Henry VII marries Elizabeth of York and unites the houses of Lancaster and York. Krämer and Spränger publish the *Malleus Maleficarum* attacking witches and witchcraft.

1487 Lambert Simnel leads revolt against Henry VII, claiming to be Edward IV's nephew, but is defeated at Stoke and sent to work in the royal kitchens. Bartholomew Diaz sails around the Cape of Good Hope, which he names the Cape of Storms.

1488 James III of Scotland is murdered; his son James IV succeeds him. Duke Francis of Brittany dies, and is succeeded by his daughter Anne. Johann Widmann develops the use of the symbols (+), (&), and (-). Bartholomew Diaz returns to Lisbon, where João II gives the Cape of Good Hope its name.

1489 Typhus is brought to Aragon by soldiers returning from Cyprus. Catherine Cornaro of Cyprus is forced to sell her kingdom to Venice. Henry VII signs the anti-French treaty of Redon with Brittany.

1490 Matthias Corvinus of Hungary dies without an heir, and is succeeded by Ladislas of Bohemia.

1491 Perkin Warbeck claims to be Richard, duke of York, and rallies support for his cause in France and Ireland. Charles VIII of France annexes Brittany by forcing Anne of Brittany to marry him.

1492 Granada, the last Moorish city, conquered by Ferdinand and Isabella; Spain effectively one country. Lorenzo the Magnificent of Florence dies, and is succeeded by his son Piero II. Casimir IV of Poland and Lithuania dies, and is succeeded by his sons John Albert in Poland and Alexander in Lithuania. Rodrigo Borgia elected Pope as Alexander VI. Henry VII invades France and is bought off by Charles VIII under the treaty of Étaples, with compensation for Brittany's annexation and the expulsion of Warbeck. Jews in Spain are ordered to convert or quit the country. Christopher Columbus discovers Cuba and Hispaniola.

1493 Columbus returns home from the Indies, and is sent back as governor of the new lands by Isabella of Castile, discovering Dominica. Pope Alexander VI publishes the bull *Inter Cetera Divina* dividing the New World between Spain and Portugal. Emperor Frederick III dies, and is succeeded by his son Maximilian I.

1494 Emperor Maximilian I recognises Warbeck as king of England. Spain and Portugal divide the New World by the treaty of Tordesillas. Charles VIII of France invades Italy, deposes Piero de Medici in Florence and takes Rome. Duke Gian Galeazzo of Milan dies, probably poisoned by his uncle Lodovico, who succeeds him.

1495 Charles VIII of France expels Alfonso II of Naples and is crowned king of the state, but is forced to retreat by Alfonso's son Ferdinand II, who assumes the kingship. Syphilis strikes the state and the French soldiers are badly affected by it. The Diet of Worms is established to modernise the Holy Roman Empire. João II of Portugal dies, and is succeeded by his cousin Manuel the Fortunate. Warbeck received by James IV of Scotland. A dry-dock is built in Portsmouth, establishing the dockyard there.

1496 Henry VII commissions John Cabot to search for new lands. The Canary Islands conquered by Spain. Ferdinand II of Naples dies, and is succeeded by his uncle Frederick IV. James IV invades Northumberland in support of Warbeck. Manuel I of Portugal expels the Jews from his country.

1497 John and Sebastian Cabot reach Labrador and Newfoundland. The Cornish rebel against taxation but are defeated at Blackheath; Warbeck lands in Cornwall but is captured. John of Denmark defeats the Swedish at Brunkeberg and revives the Union of Kalmar. Savonarola stages a bonfire of vanities in Florence. Vasco da Gama rounds the Cape of Good Hope and gives Natal its name as he discovers it on Christmas Day.

1498 Charles VIII of France dies, and is succeeded by his second cousin once removed Louis XII, duke of Orléans. Savonarola burned at the stake for heresy. Vasco da Gama reaches Malindi in East Africa and then Calicut in India. Columbus embarks on a third voyage, discovering Trinidad and the Orinoco River.

1499 Louis XII of France divorces his wife Jeanne and marries Anne of Brittany to keep the duchy in French hands. Emperor Maximilian and the Swiss go to war; by the Peace of Basel, Swiss independence is granted. Venice and the Ottomans go to war; the Venetian fleet is defeated at Sapienza. Montenegro falls to the Ottomans. Louis XII takes Milan, forcing Ludovico Sforza to flee to the Tyrol. Perkin Warbeck is executed.

1500 Ludovico Sforza recaptures Milan, but the French return and capture Sforza on retaking the city. Pedro Cabral discovers Brazil when blown off course en route for India.

1501 Lithuania invaded by Ivan III of Moscow. Basel and Schaffhausen admitted to the Swiss Confederation. Frederick IV of Naples dies; Pope Alexander VI declares Louis XII Frederick's successor. Ismail I, sheikh of Ardabil, defeats Shah Alwand of Persia at Shurur and establishes Safavid rule in the country. Emperor Maximilian I recognises the French conquests in Italy by the Peace of Trent.

1502 St Helena discovered by João de Nova. Arthur, Prince of Wales, dies at Ludlow. His brother, Henry, becomes Prince of Wales and heir to the throne.

1503 Louis XII of France abandons his claim to the Neapolitan throne after his alliance with Ferdinand of Aragon collapses. Gonzalo de Cordoba defeats a French army and enters Naples. James IV of Scotland marries Margaret Tudor, daughter of Henry VII. Pope Alexander VI dies, and is succeeded briefly by Pius III, and then by Julius II.

1504 Albert of Bavaria defeats Rupert, son of the Elector Palatine in the Bavarian War, during which at Landshut the Frankonian knight Götz von Berlichingen loses his right hand and has it replaced by one of iron. Michelangelo's statue of *David* is put on display in Florence.

1505 Ivan III of Muscovy dies, and is succeeded by his son Vasili III.

1506 Niccolò Machiavelli forms a Florentine militia, the first national army established in Italy. Christopher Columbus dies. 4,000 Jews perish in a riot in Lisbon. Philip the Handsome, son of the Emperor Maximilian and husband of the de jure Castilian Queen Juana (Joanna) dies, sending his wife mad.

1507 Cesare Borgia dies whilst besieging Viana, in Spain.

1508 Juan Ponce de León colonises Puerto Rico. Pope Julius II confirms that the German King will automatically become Holy Roman Emperor. Michelangelo starts painting the ceiling of the Sistine Chapel.

1509 Francisco de Almeida destroys a Muslim fleet at the battle of Diu, guaranteeing Portuguese control of the spice trade. Pope Julius II excommunicates the Venetian Republic, which is defeated by the French at Agnadello. Henry VII dies, and is succeeded by his son Henry VIII.

1510 Afonso de Albuquerque seizes Goa for Portugal. Sir Richard Empson and Edmund Dudley beheaded by Henry VIII for their unpopular fiscal policies under his father.

1511 Portuguese forces under Albuquerque seize Malacca, the centre of the spice trade. Julius II forms the Holy League with Venice to drive the French from Italy and enlists the support of Ferdinand of Aragon and Henry VIII.

1512 Forces of the Holy League are defeated by the French at Ravenna, but the French are then driven from Milan; Massimiliano Sforza, son of the deposed Duke Ludovico, becomes duke. Sultan Bayazid dies mysteriously after being deposed by his Janissaries; his son Selim I the Grim succeeds him.

1513 Juan Ponce de León discovers Florida. John of Denmark dies, and is succeeded by his son Christian II, who is rejected by the Swedes. Pope Julius II dies, and is succeeded by Leo X. Henry VIII invades France, where he and Emperor Maximilian are successful in the battle of Guinegatte (the Spurs). James IV of Scotland takes advantage of the English in France to invade, but his army is routed at Flodden and James is killed, to be succeeded by his infant son James V.

1514 The *Henry Grace a Dieu*, the largest warship in the world, is launched in England. Thomas Wolsey becomes Archbishop of York. The Ottoman Sultan Selim invades Persia and routs the Persian army at Chaldiran.

1515 Louis XII of France dies, and is succeeded by his son-in-law François I, who defeats the Swiss and Venetians at Marignano and takes Milan. Thomas Wolsey becomes a cardinal, giving him precedence over the Archbishop of Canterbury.

1516 Ferdinand II of Aragon dies, and is succeeded on the Spanish throne by his grandson Charles I. Pope Leo X and François I of France sign the Concordat of Bologna, giving France freedom in ecclesiastical appointments. Sultan Selim I defeats the Mamluks at Marjdabik and takes Syria. Thomas More publishes *Utopia*.

1517 Egypt falls to the Ottoman Turks, to whom the Sharif of Mecca submits, leaving Arabia under Ottoman control. Martin Luther nails 95 theses to the door of Wittenberg Cathedral attacking the sale of indulgences.

1518 Huldrych Zwingli forces the expulsion from Zurich of Barnardin Samson, a Franciscan seller of indulgences. Wolsey negotiates the Peace of London between England, France, the Holy Roman Empire, Spain and the Papacy; they agree to crusade against the Turks.

1519 Emperor Maximilian dies, and is succeeded by his grandson Charles V (I of Spain). Vasco de Balboa is beheaded in Panama as he loses the power struggle amongst the Spanish in Central America. Hernán Cortés enters Tenochtitlán, the Aztec capital, and is received by Emperor Montezuma, whom he takes prisoner.

1520 Christian II of Denmark invades Sweden and is successful at Tiveden and Uppsala before taking Stockholm; despite proclaiming an amnesty he executes numerous leading Swedes. Henry VIII and François I meet at the Field of the Cloth of Gold near Calais. Cortés driven from Tenochtitlán by Cuauhtemoc. Sultan Selim I dies, and is succeeded by his son Suleiman I the Magnificent. Ferdinand Magellan sails through the Strait of Magellan and names the Pacific.

1521 Martin Luther is interrogated by the Diet of Worms; refusing to recant he is put in the castle of Wartburg for his own protection by Frederick of Saxony and begins a German translation of the Bible. Ferdinand Magellan dies in a skirmish in the Philippines. Cortés overthrows the Aztec empire; Montezuma II dies in the fighting. Sultan Suleiman I takes Belgrade. Henry VIII is awarded the title 'Defender of the Faith' by Leo X for an anti-Lutheran work.

1522 Luther returns to Wittenberg and initiates church services in German. Sultan Suleiman takes Rhodes from the Knights of St John. Juan Sebastiano del Cano returns home after finishing Magellan's circumnavigation of the world.

1523 Christian II of Denmark deposed by his nobles for cruelty and replaced by his uncle Frederick I. Gustavus Vasa takes advantage of the situation to be crowned king of Sweden. Sir Thomas More elected Speaker of the House of Commons. Zwingli publishes his 67 Articles in Zurich.

1524 Giovanni da Verrazano discovers New York Bay, naming Manhattan Angoulême. Denmark confirms Swedish independence by the treaty of Malmö. Shah Ismail I of Persia dies, and is succeeded by his son Tahmasp I.

1525 Emperor Charles V defeats François I of France at Pavia, imprisons him and establishes control over Italy. Albert von Brandenburg, Grand Master of the Teutonic Knights, makes himself duke of Prussia. A peasants' revolt in Germany is suppressed, and its leader Thomas Müntzer executed. Cardinal Wolsey gives Hampton Court to Henry VIII.

1526 François I of France signs the treaty of Madrid, ceding various lands to Charles V, but renounces it because the terms were extorted from him, and allies himself with Sultan Suleiman, who defeats and kills Louis II of Hungary at the battle of Mohacs. Ferdinand, brother of Emperor Charles V is chosen to succeed Louis II in Hungary and Bohemia, but the Hungarians elect John Zapolya as king. Zahir-ud-Din Babur defeats Sultan Ibrahim Lodi of Delhi at Panipat, takes Agra and founds the Mughal Empire.

1527 The Mughal Emperor Babur defeats Rajput forces at Kanvaha. England and France ally via the treaty of Westminster. Imperial troops sack Rome; Pope Clement VII is imprisoned in the Castel Sant' Angelo. Holbein paints Thomas More and his family.

1528 The physician and alchemist Paracelsus is forced from Basel due to his unorthodox medical opinions and treatments.
1529 François I of France and Emperor Charles V make peace via the treaty of Cambrai. Suleiman the Magnificent takes Buda and besieges Vienna but fails to take it. Cardinal Wolsey falls from power due to his inability to secure a divorce for Henry VIII from Catherine of Aragon. Sir Thomas More replaces him as Lord Chancellor, the first layman to hold the post.
1530 The Knights of St John are settled in Malta by Emperor Charles V. Melanchthon prepares the *Confession of Augsburg* as a statement of faith for the German Protestant princes, who form the Schmalkaldic League against Emperor Charles V. Cardinal Wolsey is arrested for treason, but dies whilst on his way to trial. The Mughal Emperor Babur dies, and is succeeded by his son Humayun.
1531 Lisbon is destroyed by an earthquake. The Catholic Swiss Cantons attack and defeat Zurich in the battle of Kappel; Zwingli dies in the fighting.
1532 The English clergy recognise Henry VIII as Supreme Head of the Church. Sultan Suleiman invades Hungary. The Inca chief Atahualpa seized by Pizarro, who reintroduces horses to South America. François Rabelais publishes *Pantagruel.* Thomas Cromwell becomes Henry VIII's chief minister.
1533 Henry VIII divorces Catherine of Aragon and marries Anne Boleyn with the sanction of Thomas Cranmer, newly appointed archbishop of Canterbury; this leads to Henry's excommunication. Pizarro executes Atahualpa by strangling and causes the downfall of the Incas. Holbein paints *The Ambassadors.* Vasili III of Moscow dies, and is succeeded by his son Ivan IV the Terrible.
1534 John of Leiden sets up the radical Protestant Anabaptist kingdom of Zion at Münster. Jacques Cartier sails for the New World by command of François I and reaches the Gulf of St Lawrence. Ignatius Loyola founds the Society of Jesus (Jesuits). The Act of Supremacy marks the final break between England and Rome, comfirming Henry VIII as Supreme Head of the Church of England.
1535 Jacques Cartier sails up the St Lawrence to Montreal. Thomas Cromwell is appointed Vicar-General to investigate religious houses in England. Francis of Waldeck retakes Münster from the Anabaptists. John Fisher, Bishop of Rochester, and Sir Thomas More executed for refusing to take an oath supporting Henry VIII's acts. Emperor Charles V conquers Tunis, defeating the pirate leader Khair ad-Din. Duke Francesco Sforza of Milan dies; the duchy reverts to Emperor Charles V.
1536 John of Leiden is executed in Münster. The Anabaptist Jacob Hutter is burned at the stake. Dissolution of the monasteries commences in England, leading to a rising under Robert Aske (the Pilgrimage of Grace). Henry VIII executes Anne Boleyn on the grounds of adultery and marries Jane Seymour. Wales is formally united with England. William Tyndale is executed for heresy.
1537 Pope Paul III prohibits enslavement of New World natives and excommunicates Catholic slave traders. Robert Aske is received by Henry VIII and Cromwell, but is later executed for treason. Jane Seymour dies after bearing the future Edward VI.
1538 Pope Paul III allies with Charles V and the Venetians in a Holy League against the Ottoman Empire, but the combined Venetian, Genoese and papal fleet is defeated at Prevesa by the Ottomans.
1539 Charles V and François I make peace with the treaty of Toledo. The Six Articles are passed in England, enforcing Catholic orthodoxy. Dissolution of the monasteries ends; the abbots of Reading, Colchester and Glastonbury are executed in the process.
1540 Henry VIII marries Anne of Cleves but quickly repudiates her. The marriage is annulled and he marries Catherine Howard. Thomas Cromwell falls from grace over the Cleves marriage and is executed. The Jesuits are recognised by Pope Paul III. The Norse colony of Greenland comes to an end, with the last colonist discovered dead outside his hut with a dagger in his hand.
1541 John Calvin sets up a theocratic government in Geneva. Henry VIII is accepted by the Irish Parliament as king of Ireland and head of the Irish Church.
1542 Henry VIII executes Catherine Howard for adultery. Pope Paul III establishes the Universal Inquisition to repress the Reformation. James V of Scotland raids Cumberland, but is defeated badly at Solway Moss. He dies soon after and is succeeded by his six-day-old daughter, Mary.
1543 Pope Paul III establishes an index of prohibited books. The Spanish Inquisition commences burning Protestants at the stake. Henry VIII marries Catherine Parr. Copernicus publishes his *De revolutionibus orbium coelestrium*, stating his belief that the planets orbit a stationary Sun.
1544 Henry VIII captures Boulogne, but subsequently retires from France when his ally Charles V and François I make peace with the treaty of Crépy-en-Valois.
1545 The *Mary Rose* capsizes off Portsmouth. Charles V and Suleiman the Magnificent make a truce with the treaty of Adrianople. The Council of Trent meets, in an attempt by the Catholic church to establish a Counter-Reformation.
1546 England and France make peace with the treaty of Ardres, by which England holds Boulogne for eight years before returning it to France. The Paris printer Etienne Dolet is executed for heresy and blasphemy as a result of publishing humanist works by the likes of Erasmus.
1547 Ivan IV the Terrible of Moscow crowned Tsar of Russia. Henry VIII dies, and is succeeded by his nine-year-old-son Edward VI. François I laughs on receiving news of Henry's death, develops a fever and dies, to be succeeded by his son Henri II. John Knox is captured at St Andrews and sent to work on a French galley. Protector Somerset, ruling on behalf of his nephew Edward, invades Scotland and defeats the Scots at Pinkie.
1548 Francis Xavier founds a Jesuit mission in Japan. Sigismund I of Poland dies, and is succeeded by his son Sigismund II Augustus. Catherine Parr, now married to her fourth husband, Thomas Seymour, gives birth to her only child, Mary, but dies six days later at Sudeley Castle.
1549 Ivan IV summons the first Russian national assembly. The Protestant Book of Common Prayer is imposed in England, leading to risings in Devon and Cornwall. Robert Kett leads a revolt in Norfolk against land enclosures, but is defeated at Dussindale.
1550 England makes peace with France and Scotland by the treaty of Boulogne; Boulogne is returned to France and John Knox released from galley labour. Cricket is first referred to.
1551 Henri II of France disavows the Council of Trent and renews the war against Charles V. The Ottomans attack Malta, but are repulsed and take Tripoli instead.
1552 The duke of Somerset is executed. Tsar Ivan IV takes Kazan and attacks Astrakhan. The second Book of Common Prayer is introduced.
1553 Richard Chancellor opens a trade route to Moscow via the White Sea and Archangel. Edward VI dies, and is succeeded by his Catholic half-sister Mary, despite the duke of Northumberland's efforts to install Lady Jane Grey, his daughter-in-law, as a Protestant queen. Northumberland is later executed.
1554 Sir Thomas Wyatt leads revolt from Kent over Mary I's proposed marriage to Philip of Spain, but is defeated and executed. Lady Jane Grey is also executed, whilst Mary's half-sister Elizabeth is imprisoned in the Tower.
1555 Pope Julius III dies, his successor Marcellus II dies after a month, and Paul IV succeeds. Paul walls in Rome's Jewish quarter, creating a ghetto. John Knox returns to Scotland. Tobacco is brought to Europe from America. Mary I persecutes Protestants; Latimer and Ridley are burned at the stake in Oxford. Charles V hands sovereignty of the Netherlands to his son Philip.
1556 Thomas Cranmer is dismissed as Archbishop of Canterbury and burned at the stake. Emperor Charles V abdicates; his brother Ferdinand succeeds him as Emperor whilst his son Philip II succeeds in Spain. Indian Mughal emperor Humayun dies after falling from his library roof, and is succeeded by his son Jalal-ud-Din Akbar I.
1557 Tsar Ivan IV invades Poland. Macao founded by the Portuguese, whose King João III dies, and is succeeded by his grandson Sebastian. The Spanish drive the French from Italy after victory at the battle of St Quentin.
1558 Calais, England's last continental possession, falls to the French. Mary I dies, and is succeeded by her half-sister Elizabeth. William Cecil becomes Secretary of State. John Knox writes his *First Blast of the Trumpet Against the Monstrous Regiment of Women.*
1559 Christian III of Denmark dies, and is succeeded by his son Frederick II; Christian's imprisoned predecessor Christian II also dies.The Act of Supremacy restores the Church of England. The war between England, Spain and France is ended by the treaty of Cateau-Cambrésis. Henri II of France dies after a jousting accident, and is succeeded by his son François II.
1560 The treaty of Berwick is made between England and the Protestant Scottish lords against the French, whose troops are forced to return home; the Scots Parliament approves Knox's Calvinistic Confession of Faith. Louis de Bourbon organises the Huguenot Conspiracy of Amboise against the Catholic Guises, but is thwarted by the Dowager Queen Catherine de Medici. François II of France dies, and is succeeded by his brother Charles IX.
1561 Philip II declares Madrid the capital of Spain. Persecution of French Huguenots suspended by the Edict of Orléans. Flemish Calvinist refugees settle in England. St Paul's Cathedral damaged by fire after a lightning strike.

1562 The duc de Guise orders the massacre of Huguenots at Vassy, thus precipitating the Wars of Religion in France. The English establish the 39 Articles of Religion.

1563 The duc de Guise is murdered by a Huguenot; Catherine de Medici is left in charge of the Catholic faction and grants limited toleration to the Huguenots by the Peace of Amboise, ending the First War of Religion. John Foxe's *Book of Martyrs* is published. The Council of Trent comes to an end. The English establish the 39 Articles of religion, defining Anglican doctrine.

1564 England and France make peace by the treaty of Troyes: in return for 220,000 crowns Elizabeth renounces claim to Calais. Emperor Ferdinand I dies, and is succeeded by his son Maximilian II.

1565 The Ottomans besiege Malta, but 700 Knights of St John under Jean de La Valette hold them off for 4 months before Spanish troops relieve them and force the Ottomans to withdraw. Mary Queen of Scots marries her cousin Henry, Lord Darnley.

1566 Mary Queen of Scots' secretary, David Rizzio, is murdered at Holyrood. Calvinists riot in the Netherlands and petition the Regent, Margaret of Palma, to abolish the Inquisition. Suleiman the Magnificent dies, and is succeeded by his son Selim II.

1567 Lord Darnley is murdered at Kirk o'Field; the earl of Bothwell, who is believed to have ordered the assassination, marries Mary Queen of Scots. The earl of Morton discovers the possibly fabricated Casket Letters incriminating Bothwell and Mary; the Scots Lords rebel against Mary, imprison her in Lochleven Castle and force her abdication in favour of her son James VI, with Moray as Regent. Philip II sends the duke of Alba to eliminate Protestant resistance in the Netherlands, where he begins a reign of terror. Regent Margaret resigns.

1568 The Second War of Religion in France is ended by the treaty of Longjumeau. Mary Queen of Scots escapes Lochleven, raises an army, but is defeated by Moray at Langside and flees to England. Alba beheads Counts Egmont and Hoorn in Brussels for opposing the Inquisition and confiscates the estates of those who failed to attend the Council of Blood. Erik XIV of Sweden is deposed due to mental illness and replaced by his brother John III. The first modern Eisteddfod is held at Caerwys.

1569 Elizabeth orders Mary of Scots' detention in Tutbury Castle and imprisons the duke of Norfolk, who seeks to marry Mary. Catholics under the duc d'Anjou defeat Huguenot forces at Jarnac. Mercator publishes his map of the world and establishes his projection. The Union of Lublin unites Poland and Lithuania. Catholic earls of Northumberland and Westmorland revolt, seize Durham, but are forced to flee by Baron Hunsdon. Cosimo de Medici is made the Grand duke of Tuscany by Pope Pius V.

1570 Regent Moray is assassinated; the earl of Lennox takes over the regency. Elizabeth I is excommunicated. The third War of Religion is ended by the Peace of St Germain-en-Laye. Tsar Ivan IV establishes a reign of terror in Great Novgorod and violently purges his government in Moscow. Denmark recognises Swedish independence by the Peace of Stettin.

1571 Pope Pius V establishes the anti-Turkish Maritime League with Spain, Venice, Malta and Genoa; its fleet gains a decisive victory over the Turks at Lepanto. Roberto di Ridolfi plots to free Mary Queen of Scots and depose Elizabeth I, but the plots are exposed and fail. Sir Thomas Gresham's bourse is chartered as the Royal Exchange. Regent Lennox is murdered at Stirling; the earl of Mar replaces him.

1572 The duke of Norfolk is executed for treason in assisting the Ridolfi plot. Sigismund II of Poland dies without an heir; the Polish estates declare the crown elective. Catherine de Medici organises the Massacre of St Bartholomew's Day against the Huguenots; Admiral Gaspard de Coligny is disembowelled and defenestrated while still living. 3,000 Protestants die; Pope Gregory XIII congratulates Catherine. The fourth War of Religion commences. Regent Mar dies, replaced by the earl of Morton.

1573 The Peace of Constantinople ends the war between Venice and the Turks. Poland elects Henri, duc d'Anjou as king. The Edict of Boulogne ends the fourth War of Religion. Francis Walsingham is appointed Elizabeth's Secretary of State.

1574 The fifth War of Religion breaks out. Charles IX of France dies, and is succeeded by his brother Henri III, who abandons the Polish throne. Juan Fernandez discovers the Juan Fernandez Islands. Sultan Selim II dies after a fall in his bath, succeeded by his son Murad III.

1575 Dutch rebels fail to reach agreement with the Spanish Governor-General Requesens at Breda. The duc de Guise defeats the Huguenots at Dormans. Stephen Bathory of Transylvania is elected king of Poland.

1576 The Peace of Chastenoy ends the fifth War of Religion, but grants so many concessions to the Huguenots that the French Catholics ally with Philip II; Henri III outlaws Protestantism to appease them. Spanish troops rampage in the Netherlands, sacking Antwerp; the Pacification of Ghent allies the Lowland provinces in a pact for independence as a result. Emperor Maximilian II dies, and is succeeded by his son Rudolf II. Shah Tahmasp is murdered, and succeeded by his son Ismail II. The Theatre, England's first playhouse, is opened by Richard Burbage in Shoreditch.

1577 The sixth War of Religion breaks out; Catholic forces are victorious but to curb the power of the Holy League Henri III grants the Huguenots terms via the Peace of Bergerac. Don John of Austria arrives to take up the Governorship of the Netherlands, but his Perpetual Edict is rejected by William the Silent, who enters Brussels in triumph. Francis Drake sets out on a circumnavigation of the world.

1578 Alessandro Farnese, duke of Parma, sent with an army to the Netherlands, where he defeats the Dutch at Gemblours and succeeds as governor on the death of Don John. Shah Isma'il II dies, and is succeeded by his brother Muhammad Kundabanda. King Sebastian of Portugal invades Morocco, but perishes along with most of his army at Al Kasr al Kebir, although the king of Fez is also killed. A cult develops around the dead king and four pretenders appear, who are all executed. Sebastian's great-uncle Henry succeeds him.

1579 The Union of Arras unites the Walloons of the Netherlands whilst the Dutch provinces unite under the Union of Utrecht and sign a military alliance with England. Francis Drake lands in California and claims English sovereignty over the area he calls 'New Albion'.

1580 The seventh War of Religion breaks out in France, but is ended by the treaty of Fleix. The Spanish invade Portugal led by the duke of Alva, defeat the Portuguese at Alcantara and conquer the country. Francis Drake completes a circumnavigation of the world.

1581 Stephen Bathory of Poland invades Russia. William the Silent appoints François, duc d'Alençon, king of the Netherlands. Tsar Ivan the Terrible kills his heir with his own hands. The Jesuit Edmund Campion is arrested, tortured, tried and executed.

1582 Tsar Ivan the Terrible makes peace with Poland and Sweden with the Peace of Jam-Zapolski and abandons Livonia and Estonia to Poland. James VI of Scotland kidnapped by pro-English nobles at Ruthven. Pope Gregory XIII introduces the Gregorian calendar, devised by Aloysius Lilius.

1583 James VI of Scotland escapes from his captors after 10 months. Humphrey Gilbert founds a colonial settlement in Newfoundland at St John's, but drowns on the return journey. Plots against Elizabeth I by John Somerville and Francis Throckmorton are foiled.

1584 Walter Raleigh founds a colony on Roanoke Island, Virginia. Tsar Ivan the Terrible dies, and is succeeded by his son Feodor I. François, duc d'Alencon dies, leaving Henri III with no direct heir; Henri of Navarre becomes nearest male heir. William the Silent is assassinated at Delft by Balthazar Gérard, but his son Maurice of Nassau continues the struggle against Spain.

1585 The Eighth War of Religion (the War of the Three Henris) breaks out in France as the Holy League under Henri, duc de Guise, attempt to stop Henri of Navarre from succeeding to the throne. The Netherlands are taken under English protection by the treaty of Nonsuch and a force under the earl of Leicester is sent to assist them.

1586 Kashmir annexed by the Emperor Akbar. Francis Drake raids Spanish New World colonies and rescues the survivors from the failed Roanoke settlement. Anglo-Dutch forces defeat the Spanish at Zutphen but Sir Philip Sidney dies as a result of a wound sustained there. Sir Anthony Babington plots against Elizabeth I, but Walsingham uncovers the plot and Babington is executed. Mary Queen of Scots is tried for her involvement and sentenced to death. Stephen Bathory of Poland dies.

1587 Mary Queen of Scots executed at Fotheringhay Castle. Sir Francis Drake raids Cadiz, 'singeing the king of Spain's beard' and disrupting preparations for the Armada. Sir Christopher Hatton is appointed Lord Chancellor. Poland elects Sigismund, son of John of Sweden, as king. Henri of Navarre defeats the Catholic League at Coutras.

1588 Frederick II of Denmark dies, and is succeeded by his son Christian IV. Henri, duc de Guise, enters Paris and forces Henri III to flee. The Spanish Armada sails for England under the duke of Medina Sidonia, but is defeated by the English and the weather. Although the tonnage of the 2 fleets was similar the Spanish lost nearly half of their 130 ships and the English none. Henri III arranges for Guise's assassination.

1589 The Russian Orthodox Church makes itself independent of Constantinople. Henri III of France is assassinated at St Cloud by Jacques Clément, a Dominican monk; he nominates Henri of Navarre as his successor, who founds the Bourbon line and defeats the Catholic League at Arques. The Rev. William Lee invents the first knitting machine, whilst Sir John Harington invents the Ajax, a flushing toilet.

1590 Shah Akbar conquers Orissa. Shah Abbas of Persia and Sultan Murad make peace, with Georgia, Azerbaijan and other provinces passing to the Turks. The Catholic League proclaim the cardinal Charles de Bourbon king of France; he dies soon after whilst Henri IV defeats them at Ivry. Edmund Spenser writes the first three books of *The Faerie Queene*. Shakespeare writes the *Henry VI* trilogy.

1591 The Tsarevich Dmitri is murdered, probably on order of the Regent Boris Godunov. Sir Richard Grenville dies after his ship, *Revenge*, battles a Spanish squadron single-handed for 15 hours.

1592 Galileo Galilei is forced to move from Pisa to Padua after publishing his results on falling weights. The Japanese warlord Hideyoshi invades Korea and takes Seoul and Pyongyang. John III of Sweden dies, and is succeeded by his son Sigismund, king of Poland. Trinity College, Dublin, is founded by Queen Elizabeth. It is the oldest university in Ireland.

1593 The Chinese enter Korea and force Hideyoshi to retreat to the south coast. Christopher Marlowe is stabbed to death in Deptford by Ingram Frizer during a tavern brawl. Henri IV converts to Catholicism to win over his subjects (saying 'Paris is well worth a mass'). Salisbury Cathedral's organist strikes the Dean in a fit of rage and is dismissed from his post.

1594 Henri IV enters Paris and grants Huguenots freedom of worship by the Edict of St Germain-en-Laye. John Lancaster returns to Britain after sailing to the East Indies and establishes a spice trade. The philosopher Giordano Bruno is seized by the Vatican for espousing the Copernican theory of the Solar System.

1595 Sultan Murad III dies, and is succeeded by his son Muhammad III. Henri IV drives the Spanish from Burgundy after victory at Fontaine-Française. Spanish forces attack Cornwall, burning Penzance and Mousehole. Francis Drake and John Hawkins leave Plymouth to raid Panama; Hawkins dies en route near Puerto Rico.

1596 Francis Drake dies of dysentery off Panama. The tomato is introduced to England. The Catholic League submit to Henri IV, ending the Wars of Religion. Willem Barents discovers Spitsbergen. The English sack Cadiz whilst Spain captures Calais. The Ottomans defeat the Hungarians at Erlau and Keresztes.

1597 Philip II sends a second Armada to England, but it is scattered by storms and fails. Transylvania ceded to Emperor Rudolf II by Sigmund Bathory.

1598 Tsar Feodor I dies; his brother-in-law Boris Godunov seizes the throne and forces the national assembly to accept him. Henri IV of France grants rights to Huguenots by the Edict of Nantes. France and Spain make peace by the treaty of Vervins. Philip II of Spain dies, and is succeeded by his son Philip III.

1599 The Globe Theatre is built in London. The earl of Essex is made Lord Lieutenant of Ireland, but after signing an unauthorised truce with the earl of Tyrone returns to England and is arrested by Elizabeth I. The Swedish Diet deposes Sigismund III and makes Karl of Sodermanlund, uncle of Sigismund, regent for Sigismund's younger brother John.

1600 The East India Company is founded. Giordano Bruno is burned at the stake for heresy in Rome due to his support for the Copernican system. Ieyasu Tokugawa defeats his rivals at Sekigahara and takes control of Japan, moving the capital from Kyoto to Edo (Tokyo); the shipwrecked English mariner Will Adams becomes an adviser to him. Will Kemp morris-dances from London to Norwich.

1601 The earl of Essex leads a revolt against Elizabeth I, which fails and Essex is executed for treason. Moghul Emperor Akbar the Great annexes Berar, Ahmadnagar and Khandesh. A Spanish army lands in Ireland to support Tyrone's revolt.

1602 The Spaniards in Ireland surrender to Mountjoy at Kinsale. The Dutch East India Company is founded. Emperor Rudolf II suppresses the Moravian Brethren.

1603 Elizabeth I dies, her cousin twice removed; James VI of Scotland, succeeds her. Tyrone submits to Mountjoy in Ireland, where James proclaims an amnesty. Walter Raleigh attempts to put Arabella Stuart on the throne rather than James, and is imprisoned for treason. Ieyasu founds the Tokugawa Shogunate in Japan. Sultan Muhammad III dies, and is succeeded by his son Ahmed I.

1604 The Hampton Court Conference convenes to discuss religious matters, and commissions an English translation of the Bible. Regent Karl becomes king of Sweden after his nephew John renounces the throne. England and Spain make peace. Ostend falls to the Spanish after a three-year siege.

1605 Tsar Boris Godunov dies; his son Feodor II succeeds him but is assassinated. A pretender, Dmitri, who claims to be a son of Ivan the Terrible, enters Moscow and is crowned Tsar. Akbar the Great dies, and is succeeded by his son Jahangir. Shogun Ieyasu retires in favour of his son Hidetada. Robert Catesby leads a plot to assassinate James I, but the plot fails and Guy Fawkes is caught red-handed under the House of Lords. Miguel de Cervantes publishes part one of *Don Quixote*.

1606 Tsar Dmitri is assassinated by the boyar (noble) Vasili Shuisky, who is elected Tsar. The Virginia Company is set up and 120 colonists leave London, led by Captain Christopher Newport. Shakespeare's *Macbeth* and *King Lear* are first performed.

1607 The English Parliament rejects the union of England and Scotland. Jamestown, Virginia is founded by Christopher Newport, who returns to England leaving Captain James Smith in charge; captured by the Algonquin, Smith's life is saved by the chief's daughter Pocahontas.

1608 Tsar Vasili Shuisky is defeated by a second 'False Dmitri', who advances on Moscow. Frederick IV of the Palatinate organises a Protestant Union in Germany. Emperor Rudolf II is forced to cede Hungary, Austria and Moravia to his brother Matthias. The Jesuit state of Paraguay is established.

1609 Philip III of Spain signs a 12-year truce with the Dutch, effectively recognising their independence. Duke Maximilian of Bavaria organises a Catholic League to oppose the Protestant Union in Germany. John-William of Jülich-Cleves dies without an heir; Brandenburg and Neuburg quarrel over the territory. James I begins settling Protestants in Ulster.

1610 Galileo observes four moons orbiting Jupiter. Henri IV of France is assassinated by François Ravaillac; he is succeeded by his son Louis XIII. The Jamestown colonists abandon their settlement, but on meeting a ship of new settlers return and try again. Tsar Vasili Shuisky is deposed by Sigismund III of Poland and abducted to Warsaw; Vladislav, Sigismund's son, is offered the throne. Frederick IV of the Palatinate dies, and is succeeded by his son Frederick V.

1611 Henry Hudson is marooned by mutineers whilst searching for the North-west Passage and is never heard of again. Denmark declares war on Sweden. Emperor Rudolf II is forced to resign the Bohemian crown in favour of his brother Matthias. Karl IX of Sweden dies, and is succeeded by his son Gustavus II Adolphus.

1612 Emperor Rudolf II dies, and is succeeded as Holy Roman Emperor by his brother Matthias. Prince Dmitri Pojarsky forces the Polish in Moscow to surrender, thwarting Vladislav of Poland's claim for the throne. Henry, prince of Wales, dies of typhoid.

1613 Sweden and Denmark make the Peace of Knärod; Sweden gives up Finland. Mikhail Romanov, son of the Patriarch of Moscow, is elected Tsar by the boyars. The Globe Theatre burns down during a performance of Shakespeare's *Henry VIII*.

1614 Pocahontas marries John Rolfe, a settler. The 'Addled Parliament' meets, but is dissolved after clashes with James I over finance. The French parliament, the Estates-General convene, but is dismissed by the duc de Richelieu. The Virginian colonists resist French colonial attempts in Maine and Nova Scotia. Jülich-Cleves is divided between Brandenburg and Neuburg by the treaty of Xanten. John Napier publishes a book of logarithms.

1615 The Moluccas seized from the Portuguese by the Dutch, whilst the English defeat a Portuguese fleet off Bombay. Osaka falls to the Tokugawa shogunate. Lady Arabella Stuart starves herself to death in the Tower of London.

1616 Baffin Bay discovered by William Baffin. Francis Beaumont and Miguel de Cervantes die. William Shakespeare dies on his 52nd birthday. Manchurian Tartars invade China. Walter Raleigh is released from the Tower to search for El Dorado. James I sells peerages to raise funds. Maximilian of Tyrol and Archduke Albert renounce their claims to the Imperial throne in favour of Ferdinand of Styria. Galileo is arrested for heresy.

1617 Russia and Sweden make the Peace of Stolbovo; Novgorod is returned to Russia but Karelia is ceded to Sweden. Pocahontas is received by James I at court, but dies of smallpox soon after. Sultan Ahmad I dies, and is succeeded by his brother Mustafa I.

1618 Richelieu is exiled to Avignon after conspiring with the Queen Mother. Bohemian rebels throw the regents, Jaroslav von Martinitz and William Slawata, out of the Hradcany Palace in the Defenestration of Prague, an act which precipitates the Thirty Years War, as rebels led by Heinrich von Thurn advance on Austria and an Imperial army is raised to face them. Duke Albert Frederick of Prussia dies, his duchy passes to John Sigismund of Brandenburg. Francis Bacon is made Lord Chancellor. Walter Raleigh returns from his fruitless expedition to South America, and is executed by James I for treason to appease the Spaniards. Sultan Mustafa I is declared unfit to rule and is replaced by his nephew Osman II.

1619 Emperor Matthias dies. His cousin Ferdinand II of Styria succeeds him, but is deposed by the Bohemian Diet in favour of Frederick V of the Palatinate. A Bohemian army under Count von Thurn besieges Vienna, but is forced to withdraw. Louis XIII recalls Richelieu to subdue a revolt by Marie de Medici; the treaty of Angoulême ends the conflict. William Harvey establishes the circulation of the blood.

1620 Gustavus Adolphus of Sweden occupies Livonia after declaring war on Poland. The Pilgrim Fathers depart from Plymouth to America; the *Speedwell* is forced to turn back but the *Mayflower* arrives at Cape Cod; the settlement is called New Plymouth. Count Von Tilly leads a Catholic Union army to victory in the battle of the White Mountain against Frederick of Bohemia, who is deposed; the Bohemian revolt is suppressed by Emperor Frederick. Oliver Cromwell is denounced for playing cricket.

1621 Frederick V of the Palatinate is placed under Imperial Ban and his electorate invaded. The Huguenots rebel against Louis XIII. Philip III of Spain dies, and is succeeded by his son Philip IV, who resumes the war with the Netherlands. Count Olivares becomes chief minister of Spain. The Dutch West India Company is founded. Francis Bacon is impeached by Parliament for corruption, but is pardoned by James I.

1622 Richelieu is created a cardinal by Louis XIII, who makes peace with the Huguenots by reaffirming the Edict of Nantes. Count von Tilly is defeated at Wiesloch, but defeats Baden at Wimpfen and Brunswick at Höchst. Sultan Osman II is murdered by his Janissaries after planning to reform them and Mustafa I is restored to the throne.

1623 Abbas I of Persia takes Baghdad and Mosul from the Ottomans. Sultan Mustafa I is removed again from the throne and replaced by his nephew Murad IV. Count von Tilly defeats Brunswick at Stadtlohn and advances on Westphalia. Shogun Hidetada abdicates in favour of his son Iemitsu. Velázquez is appointed Court Painter to Philip IV of Spain. The First Folio of Shakespeare's plays is published.

1624 Cardinal Richelieu is made the chief minister of Louis XIII of France.

1625 James I dies, and is succeeded by his son Charles I. Sir William Courteen establishes a settlement on Barbados. Henri duc de Rohan leads a Huguenot rebellion against Louis XIII. Emperor Ferdinand II makes Wallenstein general of the Imperial forces and duke of Friedland. Breda falls to the Spanish after an eleven-month siege. Count von Tilly invades Saxony.

1626 Peter Minuit buys Manhattan from the Wappinger Confederacy for 60 guilders, founding New Amsterdam. The French colonise Madagascar. Louis XIII and the Huguenots make the Peace of La Rochelle. Wallenstein defeats a Protestant army at the Bridge of Dessau. The Duchy of Urbino is bequeathed to the Pope.

1627 Pirates attack Reykjavik. The Huguenots rise again; Richelieu besieges La Rochelle, which the duke of Buckingham tries but fails to relieve. Imperial forces conquer Silesia, Brunswick, Mecklenburg, Schleswig, Holstein and Jutland, forcing Christian IV of Denmark to retire from the war. Shah Jahangir dies, and is succeeded by his grandson Dawar Bakhsh.

1628 Wallenstein obtains the Duchy of Mecklenburg, assumes the title Admiral of the Baltic, but fails to take Stralsund. Shah Dawar Bahsh is removed from the throne by his uncle Shah Jahan I. Gustavus Adolphus enters the Thirty Years War. The duke of Buckingham is assassinated by John Felton at Portsmouth. La Rochelle capitulates to Louis XIII. Ignatius Loyola is canonised.

1629 Shah Abbas of Persia dies, and is succeeded by his grandson Safi I. Charles I dissolves Parliament and assumes direct rule. Emperor Ferdinand II issues the Edict of Restitution, restoring Church estates and permitting freedom of worship only to adherents of the Confession of Augsburg, which the Catholic League ruthlessly enforces. Christian IV of Denmark regains his lands by the Peace of Lübeck, on condition he refrains from intervening in Imperial affairs. Sweden and Poland make the Peace of Altmark. Bethlen Gabor of Transylvania dies, and is succeeded by his wife Catherine of Brandenburg.

1630 Gustavus Adolphus invades Germany whilst Emperor Ferdinand II dismisses Wallenstein and replaces him with Tilly. Boston founded by John Winthrop. Sultan Murad IV defeats the Persians and captures Hamadan. Anglo-French hostilities are ended by the treaty of Madrid. George Rakoczy I is elected prince of Transylvania on the death of Stephen Bethlen.

1631 Richelieu and the German Protestant princes ally with Gustavus Adolphus against Emperor Ferdinand II. Urbino is annexed by the Papacy. Tilly brutally sacks Magdeburg, burns Halle and invades Saxony, but is defeated by Gustavus Adolphus at the battle of Breitenfeld. Gustavus Adolphus takes Frankfurt-am-Oder, Würzburg and Mainz. Wallenstein is reappointed by Emperor Ferdinand II.

1632 Gustavus Adolphus defeats Tilly, who is mortally wounded, at the Lech and takes Munich. At the battle of Lützen he defeats Walenstein but is killed in action. His daughter Christina succeeds him on the Swedish throne. Shah Jehan orders the destruction of Hindu temples. Charles I issues a charter for the colony of Maryland under the governorship of Lord Baltimore. The first coffee shop opens in London. Sigismund III of Poland dies, and is succeeded by his son Vladislav IV.

1633 Wallenstein defeats Bernard of Saxe-Weimar and a Swedish army at Steinau and occupies Bohemia. Galileo is forced by the Inquisition to abjure the theories of Copernicus.

1634 The Oberammergau Passion Play is enacted for the first time. Russia and Poland make peace via the treaty of Polianovska; Vladislav VII renounces his claim to Russia. Emperor Ferdinand II relieves Wallenstein of command, replacing him with Matthias Gallas. Wallenstein is assassinated soon after, whilst Imperial troops defeat the Swedes at Nördlingen and conquer Württemberg and Franconia.

1635 Cardinal Richelieu founds the Académie Française. Emperor Ferdinand II settles differences with Elector John George of Saxony via the Peace of Prague, after France and Sweden formally ally against him, formally bringing France into the Thirty Years War. Sweden and Poland agree a 20-year truce via the treaty of Stuhmsdorf. France and Saxe-Weimar ally by the treaty of St Germain-en-Laye. The first General Post Office in England opens in Bishopsgate, London.

1636 Persia and the Ottoman Empire make peace. Olivares invades Picardy. Swedish troops defeat the Saxons at the battle of Wittstock. Harvard College is founded in Cambridge, Massachusetts.

1637 Emperor Ferdinand II dies, and is succeeded by his son Ferdinand III. Bogislav XIV of Pomerania dies without an heir; his lands are divided between Sweden and Prussia. The Dutch under Frederick Henry of Orange recapture Breda.

1638 The Scottish Covenant is drawn up and signed, forcing Charles I to withdraw Laud's liturgy in Scotland. Bernhard of Saxe-Weimar takes Freiburg and Breisach. Sultan Murad IV retakes Baghdad from the Persians. Torture is abolished in England.

1639 The First Bishops' War erupts in Scotland between the Covenanters and Charles I. Peace comes by the Pacification of Berwick, and Charles I grants the Scots a General Assembly and Parliament, which he dissolves at the end of the year. Dutch admiral Maarten Tromp destroys a Spanish fleet in the decisive battle of the Downs.

1640 Catalonia revolts against Spanish taxes and control. Sultan Murad IV dies, and is succeeded by his brother Ibrahim. Charles I is forced to reconvene Parliament but the 'Short Parliament' refuses to authorise any taxes and is dissolved.The Scots revolt in the Second Bishops' War, defeating the English at Newburn. Thomas Wentworth is created earl of Strafford. The Great Council of Peers summoned by Charles I concludes the treaty of Ripon, paying off the Scots, and insists on the election of Parliament. The 'Long Parliament', is duly elected. João of Braganza is elected king of Portugal, which breaks free from Spain, but Spain refuses to recognise this. Elector George William of Brandenburg dies, and is succeeded by his son Frederick William, the 'Great Elector'. Strafford and Laud are impeached.

1641 Tsar Michael I forbids the sale and use of tobacco, yet makes the substance a State monopoly. Strafford is executed. Parliament abolishes the Star Chamber. Parliament sends the Grand Remonstrance to Charles I, who is infuriated. The comte de Soissons plots against Louis XIII, but Jean d'Orléans, the king's brother, exposes him. The Irish Catholics revolt.

1642 Charles I enters the House of Commons to arrest Hampden, Pym, Holles, Haselrig and Strode for treason, but the quintet have been warned and take refuge in the City of London. Charles I flees London, rejects Parliament's 19 Propositions and raises his standard in Nottingham, triggering the Civil War. Rupert of the Rhine defeats the Parliamentarians at Powick Bridge and Edgehill. Blaise Pascal invents an adding machine. Cardinal Richelieu dies; Cardinal Mazarin replaces him as first minister of France. Abel Tasman discovers Van Diemen's Land (Tasmania) and New Zealand.

1643 Evangelista Torricelli develops the barometer. Parliamentarians under Fairfax take Leeds. Cromwell is victorious at Grantham, but Hampden is defeated and killed at Chalgrove Field. Louis XIII of France dies, and is succeeded by his son Louis XIV. French troops defeat a combined Spanish, Italian, Dutch and Flemish army at the battle of Rocroi. Royalists are victorious at Roundway Down and take Bristol, but are defeated at Gloucester, Newbury and Winceby. John Pym dies of cancer. Olivares falls from power in Spain.

1644 Ming Emperor Chongzhen commits suicide as Peking falls to the bandit Li Zicheng, thus ending his dynasty's rule. Li proclaims himself emperor, but is driven out by the Manchus, who found the Qing dynasty with Shunzhi as Emperor. John Milton writes his pamphlet the *Areopagitica*, on press freedom. The Scottish Covenanters join the Civil War on the Parliamentarian side. After a Royalist victory at Cropredy Bridge, Cromwell heavily defeats Prince Rupert at Marston Moor and takes York. Scottish royalists under Montrose defeat the Covenanters at Tippermuir, Charles captures Fowey, whilst the second battle of Newbury is indecisive.

1645 Archbishop Laud is executed. Montrose defeats the Covenanters at Inverlochy. The Ottomans and Venice war over Crete. Armistice talks between Charles I and Parliament fail at Uxbridge. John Lilburne publicizes Leveller ideas. Swedish troops defeat the Imperial army at Jankau and take Moravia. The Dutch occupy St Helena. Parliament creates the New Model Army under Fairfax and Cromwell which decisively defeats the royalists at Naseby. Tsar Michael I dies, and is succeeded by his son Alexei. The French defeat the Bavarians at Nördlingen. Prince Rupert surrenders Bristol, incurring his uncle's wrath. Covenanters rout Montrose at Philiphaugh.

1646 The Swedes take Prague, and in concert with the French invade Bavaria. Royalist armies in Exeter and Oxford capitulate to Parliamentarians; Charles surrenders to the Covenanters at Southwell. Held in Newcastle, Charles fails to reach agreement with Parliament and tries, but fails, to escape.

1647 George Fox founds the 'Friends of the Truth', later to become the Quakers. Matthew Hopkins, the 'Witchfinder General', is found guilty of witchcraft himself and hanged. Bear baiting and folk dancing are banned in England. The Scots hand over Charles I to Parliament in return for £400,000. Stadtholder Frederick Henry of Holland dies, and is succeeded by his son William II. Naples revolts against Spanish rule. Bavaria and Cologne state their neutrality in the Thirty Years War by the treaty of Ulm, but Emperor Ferdinand III gains their support. Mainz and Hesse withdraw from the fray.

1648 Parliament loses patience with Charles I after he makes a secret treaty with the Scots, who rebel along with the Welsh. Spain reasserts its rule over Naples. Ukrainians under Bogdan Chmielnicki lead a pogrom of Jews in a bid to establish independence from Poland. Sultan Ibrahim is deposed and killed by his Janissaries for lifting the siege of Heraklion, and is succeeded by his son Muhammad IV. The Second Civil War is short-lived, Cromwell defeating the Scots at Preston, and Colonel Thomas Pride purges Parliament to ensure Charles I is put on trial. The Fronde riots break out in Paris asserting the rights of the Paris Parlement (Parliament). The Peace of Westphalia ends the Thirty Years War, but is condemned by Pope Innocent X.

1649 Charles I is tried by Parliament and executed; Parliament abolishes the monarchy and the House of Lords, proclaiming a 'Commonwealth'. The War of the Fronde is ended by the treaty of Rueil; however a second Fronde uprising breaks out. The Levellers and Diggers are suppressed. Royalists rebel in Ireland; Cromwell sacks Drogheda and Wexford.

1650 Mazarin allies himself with the leaders of the first Fronde, and imprisons the leaders of the second. René Descartes dies whilst in the service of Queen Christina. Montrose leads a Scottish uprising against Parliament but is defeated at Carbisdale, betrayed by Neil McLeod and hanged. Archbishop James Ussher calculates that the Earth was created in 4004 BC. Charles II arrives in Scotland. Cromwell invades Scotland and is victorious at Dunbar. Stadtholder William II dies of smallpox, leaving a posthumously born heir, William III. The Holy Roman Empire and Sweden reach an accord with the treaty of Nuremberg.

1651 Charles II is crowned at Scone and invades England but is defeated by Cromwell at Worcester, evades capture and flees to France. Thomas Hobbes publishes *Leviathan*, and John Playford *The English Dancing Master*. Paris Parlement votes for the release of the Great Condér, leader of the Fronde, forcing Mazarin from the country, but he returns with an army to suppress the rebellion. Shogun Iemitsu dies, and is succeeded by his son Ietsuna, who quickly suppresses two rebellions.

1652 Jan Van Riebeck founds Cape Town. The Great Condé defeats a royalist army at Bléneau and is welcomed in Paris, where a rebel government is formed; however, the government quarrels with the Parisian middle class, which lets Louis XIV into the city. Parliament publishes the reconciliatory Act of Pardon and Oblivion. Admiral Robert Blake defeats Maarten Tromp off Dover, and England and Holland go to war, but Blake is defeated off Dungeness.

1653 The pirate Zheng Chenkong ravages the Chinese coast in his war with the Manchus. Mazarin returns to Paris and suppresses the Fronde. Lorenzo Tonti devises the Tontine system of life insurance. The English fleet defeats the Dutch off Portland, North Foreland and Texel. Cromwell dissolves the Long Parliament, and after the unsuccessful Barebones Parliament is made Lord Protector. Izaak Walton publishes *The Compleat Angler.*

1654 The treaty of Westminster ends the Anglo-Dutch War. Queen Christina of Sweden abdicates, and is succeeded by her cousin Karl X. Bogdan Chmielnicki swears allegiance to Russia, which goes to war with Poland, taking Smolensk.

1655 Colonel Penruddock leads a rising against Cromwell in Wiltshire, which is suppressed. The English under Vice-Admiral Penn take Jamaica from the Spanish. Karl X of Sweden invades Poland, precipitating the first Northern War. Elector Frederick William of Brandenburg invades Prussia. Cromwell divides England into 11 districts, each governed by a major-general.

1656 Sweden and Prussia ally by the treaty of Königsberg, whilst Denmark, Russia and the Holy Roman Empire declare war on Sweden. Spain declares war on Britain. Sweden defeats Poland at the battle of Warsaw. Baruch Spinoza is excommunicated for heresy. João IV of Portugal dies, and is succeeded by his son Alfonso VI. Cromwell readmits Jews into England.

1657 Christiaan Huygens develops the pendulum clock. Cromwell rejects an offer of the crown and establishes a nominated House of Lords. Emperor Ferdinand dies, and is succeeded by his son Leopold I. Admiral Blake destroys a Spanish treasure fleet at Santa Cruz. Brandenburg allies with Poland against Sweden by the treaty of Bromberg.

1658 The stage coach service is established in England. Jan Swammerdam observes red blood cells for the first time. The treaty of Roskilde ends the first Northern War, but Charles X of Sweden starts a second by unsuccessfully attacking Copenhagen. An Anglo-French force defeats the Spanish at the battle of the Dunes and England acquires Dunkirk. Shah Jahan I is imprisoned by his son Aurangzeb Alamgir I, who replaces him as Mughal emperor. Oliver Cromwell dies; his son Richard becomes Lord Protector.

1659 Elector Frederick William of Brandenburg drives the Swedes from Prussia. Richard Cromwell resigns as Lord Protector; conflict between army and Parliament leads to a state of near-anarchy. France and Spain make the Peace of the Pyrenees.

1660 General Monck, commanding general in Scotland, leads his troops to London to call for a new Parliament, which meets and votes for the restoration of the monarchy under Charles II. Karl X of Sweden dies, and is succeeded by his son Karl XI. Charles II makes the Declaration of Breda promising religious toleration and returns to England. The Peace of Oliva ends the hostilities between Sweden, Poland, Brandenburg and the Holy Roman Empire. Denmark reaches peace with and cedes Skania to Sweden by the treaty of Copenhagen. The Royal Society for the Promotion of Natural Knowledge is founded. George Racoczy II of Transylvania dies in battle against the Turks.

1661 Michael Apafi I is elected to replace the deceased George Racoczy III as Prince of Transylvania. Chinese living within 10 miles of the coast are ordered to move inland in an attempt to deter pirate Zheng Chenkong. Cardinal Mazarin dies, letting Louis XIV begin personal rule. The Cavalier Parliament meets in England. The Peace of Kardis between Sweden and Russia finally ends the second Northern War. Tangier and Bombay are ceded to England by Portugal in a treaty of alliance.

1662 France and Holland ally against England. The revised Prayer Book is imposed on Anglicans. The Royal Society is granted a Royal Charter by Charles II. Dunkirk is sold to France by Charles II for £400,000.

1663 The Theatre Royal, Drury Lane, opens with a performance of John Fletcher's *The Humorous Lieutenant.* Colbert founds the Académie des Inscriptions et Belles Lettres in Paris. The Ottomans declare war on the Holy Roman Empire and invade Hungary. Colbert makes New France into a colony with Quebec as the capital.

1664 France and Saxony make an alliance. The Conventicle Act bans unauthorised religious meetings of more than 5 people in England, in an attempt to suppress nonconformism. Austrian troops defeat the Turks at St Gotthard on the Raab River and make the Truce of Vasvar. New Amsterdam under Peter Stuyvesant surrenders to the English, who rename it New York.

1665 The Great Plague hits London. The second Anglo-Dutch War opens; the Dutch are defeated off Lowestoft. Anglo-Portuguese forces defeat the Spanish at Villaviciosa and Montes Claros, securing Portuguese independence. Philip IV of Spain dies, and is succeeded by his son Charles II.

1666 Louis XIV founds a French Academy of Sciences. Holland allies with Brandenburg, Brunswick and Denmark to secure its safety, whilst France declares war on England. The English and Dutch fleets meet in the inconclusive Four Days Battle before an English victory at Orford Ness. London is ravaged by a Great Fire starting in Pudding Lane.

1667 Russia and Poland make peace with the treaty of Andrusovo, ending their 13-year war; Kiev, Smolensk and the Eastern Ukraine are ceded to Russia. John Milton's *Paradise Lost* is published. French troops invade Flanders and Hainault, starting the War of Devolution. The Dutch sail up the Medway to Chatham, sinking several ships and taking the English flagship back to Holland. England, Holland and France make peace by the treaty of Breda. The Medway débâcle leads to the fall of Clarendon, and the Cabal administration under Clifford, Arlington, Buckingham, Ashley and Lauderdale is formed. (Cabal is a mnemonic for its members but the word does not derive from them.) The Regent Pedro banishes Alfonso VI of Portugal to the Azores.

1668 England, Holland and Sweden ally by the treaty of the Hague. John Dryden is appointed the first Poet Laureate. Spain recognises Portuguese independence by the treaty of Lisbon. The War of Devolution is ended by the Peace of Aix-La-Chapelle, whilst Louis XIV and Emperor Leopold I reach an agreement over future partition of Spanish realms. John Kasimir of Poland abdicates.

1669 The Lithuanian Michael Wisniowecki is elected king of Poland. The Mughal Aurangzeb bans Hinduism in India and destroys Hindu temples, leading to widespread revolts. Crete falls to the Ottomans. The Hanseatic League holds its last meeting. Antonio Stradivari makes his first violin. Samuel Pepys ceases writing his diary.

1670 Frederick III of Denmark dies, and is succeeded by his son Christian V. The Ukrainian Cossacks rebel against Polish rule, but are suppressed by Jan Sobieski. Gabriel Mouton, a French clergyman, proposes the establishment of decimal measurements. France and Bavaria make a defensive alliance, whilst Charles II makes the secret treaty of Dover with Louis XIV, pledging anti-Dutch collaboration and conversion to Roman Catholicism at an appropriate moment.

1671 The buccaneer Henry Morgan captures Panama City, is tried for piracy but pardoned and knighted by Charles II and later becomes Deputy Governor of Jamaica. The Ottomans declare war on Poland. The Don Cossacks under Stenka Razin revolt, but their rising is quelled and Razin executed. Milton publishes *Paradise Regained* and Aphra Behn *The Forced Marriage.*

1672 The Russian serfs rebel. Charles II issues the Declaration of Indulgence. Louis XIV declares war on the Dutch and sends his troops in; an English fleet defeats the Dutch at Southwold Bay. The Dutch Grand Pensionary Jan de Witt and his brother Cornelius are murdered by a mob, after William III of Orange has been appointed to the revived office of Stadtholder and put in charge of the Dutch army.

1673 Parliament forces Charles II to revoke the Declaration of Indulgence and instead passes the Test Act. Brandenburg pledges to refuse assistance to enemies of France by the treaty of Vossen, whilst Leopold I declares war on France. Michael Wisniowecki of Poland dies; the next day Jan Sobieski defeats the Ottomans at Khorzim.

1674 France devastates the Palatinate whilst Spain deters the anti-French coalition. Jan Sobieski is elected king of Poland. England and Holland make peace by the the treaty of Westminster. The bandit Sivaji Bhonsala founds a Marāthā state as independent from the Mughal Empire.

1675 France recovers Alsace after victory at Turkheim. Sweden goes to war with Denmark and Brandenburg, but is defeated by the latter at Fehrbellin. The Royal Greenwich Observatory is founded, with John Flamsteed as first Astronomer Royal.

1676 Tsar Alexis dies, and is succeeded by his son Feodor III. Jan Sobieski of Poland makes peace with the Ottomans under the treaty of Zuravno, ceding the Polish Ukraine. The Swedes defeat the Danes at Lunden.

1677 The Dutch are defeated by the French at Cassel, but with the Danes defeat a Swedish fleet at Öland. Jean Racine's tragedy *Phèdre* is first performed. Edmund Halley returns from St Helena, having catalogued the Southern Night Sky.

1678 France captures Ghent and Ypres. Russia joins the war against Sweden. France, Spain and Holland make the peace of Nijmegen; Holland regains its lost territories. False allegations made by Titus Oates and others of a 'Popish Plot' to kill Charles II lead to severe anti-Catholic measures. Hungarians under Emeric Tokolyi rebel against Imperial rule. Brandenburg takes Stralsund from the Swedes. The factional terms Whig and Tory enter use in Parliament.

1679 The Cavalier Parliament is dissolved. Archbishop Sharp of St Andrews murdered by Covenanters, whose rising is defeated by Monmouth at Bothwell Brig. Louis XIV forces the Peace of St Germain-en-Laye on Sweden and Brandenburg; the latter relinquishes its conquests. Sweden and Denmark make peace by the treaty of Lund. Henry Purcell is appointed organist of Westminster Abbey.

1680 Sivaji Bhonsala dies, and is succeeded by his son Sambhaji I, but Emperor Aurangzeb attempts to reconquer the Marathas. Shogun Ietsuna dies, and is succeeded by his brother Tsunayoshi.

1681 Charles II grants Pennsylvania as a nonconformist colony to William Penn. Emperor Kangxi suppresses the Rebellion of the Three Feudatories. France annexes Strasbourg. Bank cheques are issued for the first time in England.

1682 Louis XIV moves his court to Versailles. The Chelsea Hospital is founded. La Salle reaches the mouth of the Mississippi, names the surrounding area 'Louisiana' claiming it for France. Tsar Feodor III of Russia dies. His sister Sophia becomes regent for her younger brothers, Ivan V, who is mentally defective, and her half-brother Peter I, and seeks to kill Peter's supporters as a threat to her position.

1683 By the League of The Hague, Spain and the Holy Roman Empire join Holland and Sweden in an anti-French coalition. The Rye House Plot against Charles II and James, duke of York is unmasked; Lord William Russell and Algernon Sidney are executed for their roles in the plot and the earl of Essex commits suicide. Alfonso VI of Portugal dies, and is succeeded by his brother Pedro II. Ottomans besiege Vienna, but are forced to withdraw by Jan Sobieski of Poland and Charles, duke of Lorraine. China captures Formosa (Taiwan).

1684 The Japanese poet Saikaku composes 23,500 verses in 24 hours. The Holy Roman Empire, Poland and Venice form the Holy League of Linz against the Turks. Jews are expelled from Bordeaux.

1685 Charles II dies, and is succeeded by his brother James II, but his illegitimate son the duke of Monmouth leads an uprising which ends in defeat at Sedgemoor. Monmouth is beheaded and Judge Jeffreys conducts the 'Bloody Assizes' against Monmouth's followers. Louis XIV revokes the Edict of Nantes, forcing Huguenots to flee abroad and damaging the French economy.

1686 The Institut de Saint Louis is founded by Madame de Maintenon to educate the daughters of poor gentlefolk; the curriculum includes cookery; graduates are given a blue ribbon – the *cordon bleu.* The League of Augsburg is formed against Louis XIV by the Holy Roman Empire, Spain, Sweden, Saxony, Bavaria and the Palatinate. Buda is liberated from the Ottomans, whilst Russia declares war on them.

1687 Shogun Sunayoshi forbids the killing of animals in Japan. James II proclaims freedom of worship and receives the Papal Nuncio. Ottomans defeated by Charles of Lorraine at Mohács who expell them from Hungary, they lose the Greek Peloponnese and Athens to the Venetians. Sultan Muhammad IV is deposed by his Janissaries and replaced by his brother Suleiman III. Newton's *Principia* is published.

1688 Elector Frederick William of Brandenburg dies, and is succeeded by his son Frederick III. An heir to James II is born. To forestall a Catholic succession William of Orange is invited to replace James, which he does in the 'Glorious Revolution'. James II flees to exile in France. The Ottomans surrender Belgrade to the Austrians. France invades the Palatinate. A marine insurance society is founded in Edward Lloyd's Coffee House in London.

1689 Natal becomes a Dutch colony. Louis XIV declares war on Britain whilst James II arrives in Ireland and besieges Londonderry. A Jacobite rising in Scotland defeats a Covenanter army at Killiecrankie before being defeated at Dunkeld. Regent Sophia is deposed in Russia after conspiring to abduct Peter I, who is established as tsar. The Declaration of Rights is proclaimed in England.

1690 Marlborough captures Cork and Kinsale from Jacobite supporters. Spain and Savoy join the League of Augsburg, which is defeated at Fleurus. The French defeat an Anglo-Dutch fleet off Beachy Head and burn Teignmouth. William III defeats James II at the battle of the Boyne, forcing James back to France. Calcutta is founded by the East India Company. The Ottomans retake Transylvania, Serbia, Belgrade and Bulgaria.

1691 The first directory of addresses is published in Paris. Sultan Suleiman III dies, and is succeeded by his brother Ahmad II, whose reign starts poorly with defeat at Slankamen and expulsion from Hungary. The Irish Jacobites are defeated at Aughrim and pacified by the treaty of Limerick.

1692 The Campbells massacre the MacDonalds at Glencoe. Marlborough is briefly imprisoned for suspected treasonable contact with James II. The Salem witch trials commence. The English defeat a French invasion fleet at La Hogue, but an Anglo-Dutch army is defeated at Steenkirk. Ernst Augustus of Brunswick is made Elector of Hanover.

1693 William III borrows £1 million, instigating the National Debt. French fleet defeats an Anglo-Dutch one at Cape St Vincent and Lagos; French armies are also successful at Neerwinden and Marsaglia.

1694 William Paterson leads the founding of the Bank of England, with Sir John Houblon as its first Governor. Shah Suleiman I of Persia dies, and is succeeded by his son Husain I. Mary II of England dies.

1695 Princess Anne returns to court to act as hostess for her brother-in-law William III. Sultan Ahmad II dies, and is succeeded by his nephew Mustafa II. William Paterson helps found the Bank of Scotland. Peter the Great besieges Azov, but is forced to withdraw by the Turks with heavy losses. William III takes Namur.

1696 Jan Sobieski of Poland dies. Peter the Great takes Azov and conquers Kamchatka. The Window Tax is introduced in England, whilst John Locke and Isaac Newton reform the coinage.

1697 Peter the Great travels incognito from Russia to study European ways of life. Karl XI of Sweden dies, and is succeeded by his son Karl XII. Elector Frederick-Augustus I of Saxony is elected king of Poland, taking the title Augustus II. France, Britain, Spain and the Holy Roman Empire make peace by the treaty of Ryswick. Eugene of Savoy heavily defeats the Turks at Zenta.

1698 Elector Ernst Augustus of Hanover dies, and is succeeded by his son George. Leopold of Anhalt-Dessau introduces goose-stepping to the Prussian army. Whitehall Palace is largely destroyed by fire. The Streltzy, elite musketeer regiments, revolt in Moscow, but the rising is quelled.

1699 Turkey signs the Peace of Karlowitz with Austria, to which it cedes Hungary, Croatia and Transylvania. Turkey also cedes its portion of the Ukraine to Poland, and Morea and Dalmatia to Venice. Christian V of Denmark dies, and is succeeded by his son Frederick IV. Denmark, Russia, Poland and Saxony sign the treaty of Preobrazhenskoe to carve up the Swedish Empire. William Dampier explores the western Australian coast. Henry Winstanley builds the first Eddystone Lighthouse.

1700 The German Protestant states adopt the Gregorian calendar. The Great Northern War opens with concerted attacks on Sweden; Saxony invades Livonia and Denmark invades Schleswig, but Sweden invades Zeeland, forces the Danes from the war by the treaty of Travendal, and defeats Russia at Narva. The duke of Gloucester dies, leaving no direct Stuart heir after Princess Anne (James Stuart being unacceptable). Charles II of Spain dies, the Habsburg line ends with him and the throne goes to Philip V, grandson of Louis XIV.

1701 Elector Frederick of Brandenburg makes himself king of Prussia; Emperor Leopold acquiesces in return for military aid. The War of the Spanish Succession opens; England, Holland and Savoy join the Holy Roman Empire in the Grand Alliance. Karl XII of Sweden invades Poland. Eugene of Savoy defeats the French at Carpi and Chiara. Antoine Cadillac founds Detroit. The Act of Settlement provides for the succession in England to pass to Electress Sophia of Hanover after Princess Anne. Jethro Tull develops the seed drill.

1702 William III dies, and is succeeded in England by his sister-in-law Anne, whilst in Holland the Stadtholdership is put into abeyance. The *Daily Courant* becomes London's first daily newspaper. Karl XII of Sweden takes Warsaw and Cracow. Marlborough captures Venlo, Roermond and Liège, and is raised from an earl to a Duke. Protestant peasants, the Camisards, revolt in the Cévennes.

1703 The Swedish defeat the Russians at Pulutsk. Marlborough takes Cologne and Bonn. Peter the Great founds St Petersburg. The Grand Alliance proclaims Archduke Charles of Austria king of Spain. Portugal joins the Grand Alliance and signs the Methuen treaty with England. The Eddystone Lighthouse is destroyed as a great storm hits Southern England.

1704 Sweden secures the deposition of Augustus II of Poland in favour of Stanislas Leszczynski. Gibraltar is captured by the English, who defeat a relieving force at Velez Malaga. Marlborough and Eugene of Savoy heavily defeat the French at Blenheim. Beau Nash becomes Master of Ceremonies at Bath.

1705 Edmund Halley predicts the return in 1758 of the comet that will bear his name. Emperor Leopold dies, and is succeeded by his son Joseph I. Peter the Great's westernization provokes revolts in Astrakhan. Barcelona falls to the Grand Alliance.

1706 Karl XII of Sweden defeats a Russo-Saxon army at Fraustadt. Marlborough defeats the French at Ramillies; Brussels, Antwerp, Ghent and Ostend quickly capitulate to him. Archduke Charles is installed in Madrid, but is driven out after 3 months by Philip V of Spain. Eugene of Savoy defeats the French at Turin and drives them from Lombardy. Augustus II of Poland abdicates, recognizing his usurper Stanislas I.

1707 Emperor Aurangzeb dies, and is succeeded by his son A'zam Shah, whose death soon after puts his brother Bahadur Shah I on the throne. A French army under the duke of Berwick defeats an Anglo-Portuguese force at Almanza. England and Scotland formally unite with the Act of Union. Prussia and Sweden sign a Perpetual Alliance. Admiral Sir Cloudesley Shovell's squadron runs aground in the Scillies, only one man survives. Fortnum & Mason's opens in Piccadilly.

1708 Marlborough and Eugene of Savoy defeat the French at Oudenarde; Marlborough subsequently captures Lille. Minorca captured by the British. The East India Company and the New East India Company merge. The Sikh guru Govind Singh is assassinated by order of the Mughal Bahadur Shah. Karl XII of Sweden invades the Ukraine.

1709 The *Tatler* is launched by Richard Steele and Joseph Addison. Tsar Peter defeats Karl XII of Sweden at Poltava, forcing Karl to take refuge in Anatolia and breaking Sweden's power. Augustus II takes advantage of this by driving Stanislas I from Poland and regaining the throne. Marlborough and Eugene of Savoy take Tournai and Mons and defeat the French at Malplaquet. Abraham Darby develops coke-fuelled iron smelting at Coalbrookdale.

1710 Stanhope is victorious at Almenara and Saragossa but is defeated and captured at Brihuega. Handel is appointed Kapellmeister to Elector George of Hanover. Christopher Wren completes St Paul's Cathedral.

1711 Addison and Steele launch the *Spectator.* Queen Anne establishes Ascot racecourse. Emperor Joseph I dies, and is succeeded by his brother Charles VI, who guarantees a Hungarian constitution by the Peace of Szathmar. Russia and Turkey sign the treaty of Pruth; Tsar Peter is forced to return Azov to the Turks. Rio de Janeiro is captured by the French. The South Sea Company is established. Marlborough is dismissed from command and replaced by Ormonde.

1712 Civil war breaks out in Switzerland; the Protestant cantons are victorious at Villmergen and peace is re-established by the treaty of Aarau. The Mughal Emperor Bahadur Shah I dies; his sons quarrel over the succession.

1713 Farrukhsiyar, grandson of Bahadur Shah, establishes himself as Mughal emperor. Karl XII of Sweden is taken prisoner by the Ottomans at Bender in Moravia. Frederick I of Prussia dies and is succeeded by his son Frederick William I. The treaties of Utrecht end the War of the Spanish Succession, with Philip V allowed to keep the throne, establishing the Bourbon dynasty in the country; the thrones of France and Spain are never to be united. Emperor Charles VI does not sign. Charles VI issues the Pragmatic Sanction, allowing female succession in Habsburg domains. Shogun Ienobu dies, and is succeeded by his infant son Ietsugu.

1714 The Board of Longitude promises a £20,000 reward for anybody who can discover a method of divining longitude. Russia gains control of Finland after victory at the battle of Storkyro. Charles VI makes peace with France at Rastatt and Baden. Queen Anne dies, and is succeeded by her second cousin George I, as his mother Sophia had died shortly before. Karl XII of Sweden is released by the Turks.

1715 Louis XIV dies, and is succeeded by his great-grandson Louis XV. Mir Vais, chief of Kandahar, dies; his son Mir Maahmoud succeeds him, but is assassinated by his uncle Mir Abdullah who takes power. The earl of Mar leads a Jacobite rising in Scotland; the Old Pretender James lands at Peterhead to support the rising, but his supporters are defeated at Sheriffmuir and Preston.

1716 The Old Pretender returns to France as the '15 rebellion fizzles out. Shogun Ietsugu dies aged seven and is succeeded by Yoshimune, a distant relation. Eugene of Savoy defeats the Ottomans at Peterwardein; Emperor Charles VI joins the war and Temesvar, the last Ottoman possession in Hungary, falls. The Tsarevich Alexei flees Russia and places himself under the protection of Charles VI.

1717 The Grand Lodge of the Freemasons is established at the Goose and Gridiron Tavern, Covent Garden. School attendance is made compulsory in Prussia. Lhasa is occupied by Mongols. Eugene of Savoy defeats the Ottomans at Belgrade.

1718 Edward Teach, Blackbeard, is killed in a fight in North Carolina. The first English banknotes are issued. Philip V of Spain sends troops into Sicily; the Quadruple Alliance of the Empire, France, England and Holland is formed to counter him. Tsarevich Alexei is killed by order of Peter the Great and his friends executed. Karl XII is killed at Fredriksten during an expedition into Norway, and is succeeded by his sister Ulrika.

1719 Liechtenstein becomes an independent principality under Count Hans von Liechtenstein, who has bought the territory. Herat rebels against Shah Hussein, and defeats an army sent to subdue the area. Sweden and Hanover make the Peace of Stockholm. The Mughal emperor Farrukhsiyar dies, creating a succession dispute which is eventually resolved when his cousin Muhammad ascends the throne.

1720 The Great Northern War is brought to an end as Sweden makes peace with her neighbours. Ulrika of Sweden abdicates in favour of her husband Frederick of Hesse. A plague outbreak in Marseille is the final time the Black Death pandemic strikes. The South Sea Company collapses (South Sea Bubble), as does John Law's Mississippi Company, bringing ruin to many. China makes Tibet a protectorate.

1721 A revolt in Formosa is suppressed by China. A regular postal service is established between London and New England. John Aislabie, Chancellor of the Exchequer, is dismissed and imprisoned for fraud. Robert Walpole is appointed First Lord of the Treasury by George I, becoming the first prime minister. Sweden and Russia sign the treaty of Nystadt; Russia gains Estonia. Peter the Great is proclaimed Emperor of All the Russias.

1722 Mir Mahmoud of Kandahar conquers Afghanistan, defeats the Persians at Gulnabad, and takes Isfahan. Shah Hussein abdicates in favour of his son Tahmasp, but Mahmoud proclaims himself Shah. Russia and the Ottoman Empire exploit the situation and invade; the Russians withdraw after an outbreak of ergotism. Hungary rejects Emperor Charles' Pragmatic Sanction. Jacob Roggeveen discovers Rapa Nui, naming it Easter Island.

1723 Louis XV of France attains his majority, ending the Regency period. Britain and Prussia sign the treaty of Charlottenburg, arranging marriages between the two royal houses.

1724 Philip V of Spain abdicates in favour of his son Luis, who dies some months after, and Philip returns to the throne. Russia and the Ottoman Empire make a treaty for the dismemberment of Persia, where Mir Mahmoud goes insane.

1725 Tsar Peter the Great dies, and is succeeded by his widow Catherine I. The Pragmatic Sanction is guaranteed by the treaty of Vienna. Tabriz falls to the Ottomans. Mir Mahmoud kills 39 Persian princes; the surviving nobles elect his cousin Ashraf to replace the insane Shah, who is murdered on order of Ashraf. The treaty of Hanover allies Britain, Prussia and France against Austria and Spain.

1726 Voltaire is exiled in England. General George Wade commences a programme of road-building in Scotland. Montevideo is founded. Cardinal Fleury becomes chief minister to Louis XV.

1727 Spain besieges Gibraltar, but does not formally declare war on Britain. Shah Ashraf defeats an Ottoman army and the two powers make peace. Catherine I of Russia dies, and is succeeded by Peter II, a grandson of Peter I. George I dies of apoplexy, and is succeeded by his son George II.

1728 The Kiakhta treaty sets the border and terms of trade between China and Russia. Spain abandons its siege of Gibraltar when the Convention of the Prado settles a truce with Britain. Roman Catholics are disenfranchised in Ireland. Vitus Bering discovers the Bering Strait. The Empire and Prussia make the treaty of Berlin. A Freemasons' Lodge is founded in Madrid, but is quickly suppressed by the Inquisition.

1729 Emperor Yongzheng bans opium smoking in China. Corsica temporarily becomes independent of Genoa. France, Britain and Spain end hostilities with the treaty of Seville. Charles Wesley founds the Holy Club at Oxford with his brother John and George Whitehead.

1730 Peter II of Russia dies of smallpox; his cousin Anne takes power in a coup. Shah Ashraf is murdered after defeat near Shiraz; Tahmasp II returns to power. Viscount Townshend improves crop husbandry with the use of turnips after leaving Walpole's government. Crown Prince Frederick of Prussia is imprisoned at Küstrin after attempting to flee to England. Sultan Ahmad III is deposed, and replaced by his nephew Mahmud I. Frederick IV of Denmark dies, and is succeeded by his son Christian VI.

1731 John Hadley invents the reflecting quadrant. Shah Tahmasp is defeated by the Ottomans at Arijan and sues for peace, ceding large tracts of land to the Ottomans. Tahmasp is imprisoned by his brother-in-law Nadir Kuli and his infant son Abbas III set up as Shah. The Holy Roman Empire makes the treaty of Vienna with Britain, Holland and Spain, securing support for the Pragmatic Sanction.

1732 Genoa regains control of Corsica.

1733 James Oglethorpe establishes a colony at Savannah, founding the state of Georgia. John Kay invents a flying shuttle loom. Augustus II of Poland dies; France persuades Polish nobles to restore Stanislas I but Austria and Russia demand that Augustus' son, Frederick Augustus of Saxony, succeed his father. In the War of the Polish Succession, they invade Poland.

1734 Persia and the Ottoman Empire go to war. France and Spain defeat Austrian armies in Naples and Parma. Danzig falls to the invading Russian army, but Stanislas I escapes to Prussia.

1735 William Pitt is elected MP for Old Sarum. The treaty of Vienna ends the War of the Polish Succession, and Augustus III is established on the Polish throne. Russia allies with the Persian Nadir Kuli against the Ottoman Empire; Nadir defeats the Ottomans at Baghavand and takes Tiflis. John Harrison develops his chronometer. Linnaeus publishes *Systema naturae*, the origin of modern classification of plants and animals.

1736 Shah Abbas III dies, and Nadir Kuli succeeds him. Claudius Aymond performs the first successful appendectomy. Freemasonry is condemned by Pope Clement XII. Statutes against witchcraft are repealed in England. Emperor Yongzheng dies, and is succeeded by his son Qianlong.

1737 Benjamin Franklin creates the Philadelphia police force, the first of its kind. The Licensing Act orders all plays to submit to the Lord Chamberlain's censorship. Gian Gastone di Medici dies, last of his line. The Grand Duchy of Tuscany passes to Francis of Lorraine, whilst Lorraine passes to Stanislas I of Poland as a reward for renouncing his claim to the Polish throne.

1738 Orsova falls to the Ottomans, who drive the Imperial troops back to Belgrade. Jean H.L. Orry imposes the corvée, compulsory labour, to construct roads in France. John and Charles Wesley form the Methodist Society.

1739 Dick Turpin is hanged at York. Shah Nadir of Persia sacks Delhi, drastically diminishing Mughal power in India. Nadir seizes the Koh-i-Noor diamond. Emperor Charles VI makes peace with the Ottomans by the treaty of Belgrade, ceding the city to the Ottomans. England and Spain go to war (the War of Jenkins' Ear) over alleged Spanish transgressions. Porto Bello in Panama is seized by Admiral Vernon.

1740 Frederick William I of Prussia dies, and is succeeded by his son Frederick II the Great, who invades Silesia. Emperor Charles VI dies; he is succeeded in his kingdoms by his daughter Maria Theresa, but Saxony, Bavaria and Spain dispute her right to succeed and the War of the Austrian Succession begins. Tsarina Anna dies, and is succeeded by her infant great-nephew Ivan VI.

1741 Frederick the Great defeats the Austrians at Mollwitz and captures Brieg, Neisse, Glatz and Olmütz before the British mediate. Prague is occupied by a French, Bavarian and Saxon army. Elizabeth, daughter of Peter the Great, deposes Tsar Ivan VI and rules herself.

1742 Anders Celsius develops the centigrade thermometer system. Elector Charles Albert of Bavaria is elected to the vacant title of Holy Roman Emperor. Robert Walpole resigns as Prime Minister, replaced by the earl of Wilmington. Prussia defeats the Austrians at Chotusitz, before signing treaty of Berlin with Austria, gaining upper and lower Silesia. Britain and Prussia sign the treaty of Westminster, safeguarding Hanover.

1743 George II leads a multinational Pragmatic Army to victory over the French at Dettingen. Pogroms of Jews occur in Russia. Persia and the Ottoman Empire go to war. Austria and Saxony ally, whilst Bavaria is conquered by Austria.

1744 Frederick the Great invades Saxony and Bohemia, taking Prague before being driven back to Saxony. Maria Theresa launches a series of pogroms in Moravia and Bohemia against the Jews.

1745 Emperor Charles VII dies. Francis of Lorraine, grand duke of Tuscany and husband of Maria Theresa, is elected the new Emperor. The French defeat an army led by the duke of Cumberland at Fontenoy and advance into the Austrian Netherlands. The Prussians defeat the Austrians and Saxons at Hohenfriedberg and the Austrians at Soor. Charles Edward Stuart lands on Eriskay, proclaiming his father king. He gains support from various Scottish clans, takes Edinburgh and is victorious at Prestonpans, but loses his nerve on reaching Derby and withdraws.

1746 The retreating Jacobites are victorious at Falkirk but are routed by Cumberland at Culloden. The Young Pretender escapes, and helped by Flora MacDonald reaches Skye, from where he returns to France. Cumberland severely represses the Scots, and the wearing of tartan is outlawed. Canaletto moves to England. Philip V of Spain dies, and is succeeded by his son Ferdinand VI. France defeats Austria at Raucoux and takes the Austrian Netherlands.

1747 The Republic of the United Provinces is overthrown by the French and William IV of Orange-Nassau resumes the post of Stadtholder. Prussia and Sweden form a defensive alliance. The French defeat an Anglo-Dutch army at Laufeld. Shah Nadir is murdered in Afghanistan; his nephew Adil succeeds him whilst Ahmed Shah Durrani takes advantage of the situation to establish an independent Afghanistan. Lord Lovat is beheaded for Jacobitism on Tower Hill, the last man to be executed there.

1748 The treaty of Aix-la-Chapelle ends the War of the Austrian Succession with a stalemate peace. This gives general recognition to the Pragmatic Sanction and the Prussian conquest of Silesia.

1749 Thomas Chippendale opens a workshop. Admiral Anson reforms the Royal Navy. Henry Fielding publishes *Tom Jones*. Henry Fielding and his brother John found the Bow Street Runners.

1750 Thomas Gray's 'Elegy Written in a Country Churchyard' is written in Stoke Poges. The Jockey Club is founded in the Star and Garter Coffee House, Pall Mall. JS Bach dies. João V of Portugal dies, and is succeeded by his son Jose I, who appoints the marquis of Pombal as his chief minister. Pombal strips the Inquisition of its power.

1751 China invades Tibet. Robert Clive seizes Arcot from the French. Stadtholder William IV dies, and is succeeded by his infant son William V. Britain adopts January 1 as the beginning of the New Year, instead of 25 March.

1752 Britain adopts the Gregorian calendar system; 11 days disappear from September. Benjamin Franklin invents the lightning conductor. Ahmed Shah of Afghanistan takes Lahore. Spain and the Holy Roman Empire sign the treaty of Aranjuez.

1753 Sir Hans Sloane dies; his legacy of books and collections are used to found the British Museum and British Library. The Marriage Act forbids unlicensed weddings in Britain. The Jewish Naturalisation Act seeks to remove disabilities for Jews in Britain, but the hostility it engenders leads to its repeal.

1754 The Royal and Ancient Golf Club is founded at St Andrews, and codifies the rules of the sport. William Cookworthy pioneers English porcelain production. The first iron-rolling mill is built, in Fareham, Hampshire. In North America the Albany Convention is convened by several colonies and the Iroquois to form a joint defence against the French, who defeat two expeditions led by George Washington. The Convention agrees to Franklin's proposal for the union of the 13 colonies. Sultan Mahmud I dies while dismounting from his horse, and is succeeded by his brother Osman III.

1755 Casanova is imprisoned in Venice for spying. Pasquale de Paoli is elected general in Corsica, and leads a revolt against Genoa. In North America, General Braddock is killed in the battle of the Wilderness, as the French rout a British expedition, but the French are subsequently defeated at Lake George. Lisbon is devastated by an earthquake and tidal wave; 30,000 die.

1756 A porcelain factory is founded at Sèvres. John Smeaton builds a new Eddystone Lighthouse. England and Prussia ally by the treaty of Westminster. Minorca surrenders to Franco-Spanish forces after Admiral Byng breaks off a naval action. Britain declares war on France, but Montcalm drives the British from the Great Lakes. Siraj-ud-Daula, a French ally, seizes Calcutta, imprisoning 146 Britons in a small guardroom (Black Hole of Calcutta); according to English propaganda, only 23 emerge alive the next morning. Seven Years War erupts as Prussia invades Saxony, which has allied with France, Austria, Russia and Sweden against it.

1757 John Campbell invents the sextant. Ahmed Shah of Afghanistan takes Delhi and the Punjab. Robert Clive recovers Calcutta and defeats Siraj-ud-Daula at Plassey. For his role in losing Minorca, Admiral Byng is shot 'pour encourager les autres' at Portsmouth. Frederick the Great defeats the Austrians at Prague, but is defeated at Kolin before further victories at Rossback and Leuthen. Cumberland is routed by the French at Hastenbeck and is forced by the Convention of Klosterzeven to surrender Hanover to them. Sultan Osman III dies, and is succeeded by his cousin Mustafa III.

1758 Britain promises assistance to Prussia by the treaty of London. Samuel Johnson founds *The Idler.* Clive becomes governor of Bengal. An English army fighting for Frederick II of Prussia defeats the French at Krefeld, and Frederick crushes the Russians at Zorndorf but is defeated by the Austrians at Hochkirch. Fort Duquesne is captured from the French by George Washington and John Forbes and renamed Pittsburgh.

1759 Handel dies. Guadeloupe is captured by the British. Samuel Johnson publishes *Rasselas.* The French defeat Brunswick at Brunswick, but are defeated by an Anglo-Prussian army at Minden. Ferdinand VI of Spain dies, and is succeeded by his half-brother Charles III. Frederick the Great is defeated by an Austro-Russian army at Kunersdorf. General Wolfe defeats Montcalm on the Plains of Abraham outside Quebec; both generals die in battle. Quebec falls to the British. Admiral Hawke destroys a French squadron off Quiberon.

1760 Earl Ferrers is hanged at Tyburn, the last peer to be executed in Britain. Austria defeats Prussia at Landshut, but is defeated at Liegnitz. Amherst captures Montreal. Russian troops capture and burn Berlin. George II dies, and is succeeded by his grandson George III. Prussia defeats the Austrians at Torgau. John Harrison develops his H-4 chronometer.

1761 Ahmed Shah of Afghanistan defeats the Marathas at Panipat. Pondicherry, the French base in southern India, falls to Sir Eyre Coote. France and Spain invade Portugal; Portugal asks for British help. Spain and the Bourbon Italian states ally with France against Britain.

1762 Tsarina Elizabeth dies, and is succeeded by her nephew Peter III who withdraws from the Seven Years War and returns Pomerania to Prussia. St Vincent, Martinique Grenada and St Lucia seized by the British under Rodney. Jean-Jacques Rousseau writes the *Social Contract.* Sweden and Prussia ally by the treaty of Hamburg. Peter is assassinated on behalf of his wife, who succeeds him as Catherine II. John Stuart, Earl of Bute, becomes the first Scottish Prime Minister and the first Tory to hold the office.

1763 The treaty of Paris ends the Seven Years War. Spain cedes Florida to Britain. The *Almanach de Gotha* is first published. Augustus III of Poland and Saxony dies; he is succeeded in Saxony only by his son Frederick-Christian, who also dies, and is succeeded by his son Frederick-Augustus III.

1764 James Hargreaves invents the spinning jenny. Stanislas Poniatowski is elected to the vacant Polish throne. Hyder Ali takes Mysore. Sir Hector Monro defeats the Nawab of Oudh at Buxar, and takes control of Bengal. Ex-Tsar Ivan VI is murdered in prison.

1765 Frederick the Great founds the Bank of Prussia. The Stamp Act imposes taxation on the American colonists, much to their disgust. Emperor Francis I dies, and is succeeded by his son Joseph II. The auto-da-fé is abolished in Lisbon.

1766 On the death of ex-king Stanislas, duke of Lorraine, the duchy reverts to France. The Stamp Act is repealed, but the Declaratory Act affirms the right of Parliament to tax the American colonists. Frederick V of Denmark dies, and is succeeded by his son Christian VII.

1767 Siam is invaded by the Burmese. Nevil Maskelyne, the Astronomer Royal, issues the first Nautical Almanac. Clive leaves India.

1768 The Royal Academy of Arts is founded, with Joshua Reynolds as the first president. The first edition of the *Encyclopaedia Britannica* is published. The Gurkha king Prithvi Naryan Shah makes Nepal a unitary kingdom. Corsica is bought by the French from Genoa. Austria renounces all claims to Silesia.

1769 Austria occupies the Lvov and Zips regions of Poland. Frederick the Great and Emperor Joseph II meet at Neisse to discuss the partition of Poland. Richard Arkwright develops the spinning frame. James Watt patents a steam engine. Josiah Wedgwood opens his pottery works at Etruria. Wellington, Napoleon, Ney and Soult are born.

1770 Joseph Cugnot constructs a steam-powered road vehicle in France. Lord North replaces Grafton as prime minister. The 'Boston Massacre', a brawl between civilians and troops, leaves 3 dead. All taxes, bar that on tea, on the American colonists are repealed. An Anglo-Spanish dispute over the Falklands is resolved by French mediation. Captain James Cook lands at Botany Bay, Australia. A Russian fleet defeats the Ottomans at the battle of Chesme.

1771 The Crimea is conquered by Russian Cossacks. Duke Charles-Emmanuel III of Savoy abolishes serfdom. Adolphus Frederick of Sweden dies, and is succeeded by his son Gustav III. The Marathas drive the Afghans from Delhi.

1772 The Danish nobility rebel against Count Johann von Struensee, who has held absolute power for a year, torturing and beheading him. George III secures the passage of the Royal Marriages Act to control whom the royal family may marry. Russia, Prussia and Austria perform the first partition of Poland. Gustav III of Sweden re-establishes absolute monarchy. Carl Wilhelm Scheele discovers oxygen (Priestley discovers it independently in 1774); Daniel Rutherford, Joseph Priestley, Henry Cavendish and Carl Wilhelm Scheele independently discover nitrogen.

1773 Emperor Joseph II expels the Jesuits, prompting Pope Clement XIV to dissolve the order. Tea is thrown into the sea in the protest known as the Boston Tea Party as a protest against the tea duty. The first Stock Exchange opens in London. Captain Cook enters the Antarctic Circle. Denmark cedes Oldenburg to Russia. Thomas Pritchard constructs the Ironbridge at Coalbrookdale.

1774 The Coercive Acts against Massachusetts include closing the port of Boston. Lord North is robbed by a highwayman at Chiswick. Louis XV of France dies, and is succeeded by his grandson Louis XVI. Sultan Mustafa III dies, and is succeeded by his brother Abdul-Hamid I. Russia acquires the northern Black Sea coast by the treaty of Kuchuk-Kainardji with Turkey. Joseph Priestley discovers oxygen. Austria occupies Bukovina. The Continental Congress, comprising all the America colonies bar Georgia, convenes, deciding to ban imports from and exports to Britain.

1775 Paul Revere rides to Lexington to warn of British troop movements. The American War of Independence opens. The colonists win victories at Concord, Fort Ticonderoga and Crown Point. The Second Continental Congress convenes and John Hancock is elected its president. The British defeat the rebels at Bunker Hill.

1776 Adam Smith publishes *The Wealth of Nations.* The St Leger is first run (founded by Colonel Barry St Leger). Grigori Potemkin organises a Russian Black Sea Fleet. Russia and Denmark sign the treaty of Copenhagen. The American colonists issue the Declaration of Independence. After defeat at Long Island and on Lake Champlain they score a major victory at Trenton.

1777 Spain and Portugal settle their differences over their South American colonies. The Americans are victorious at Princeton, Ridgefield and Bennington, but lose at the Brandywine and Germantown before victory at Bemis Heights provokes Burgoyne to surrender at Saratoga. Elector Maximilian III of Bavaria dies; with no direct heir, the Electorship passes to Count Karl Theodor of the Palatine.

1778 Joseph Bramah patents an improved water closet. Captain Cook discovers and names the Sandwich Islands. France signs treaties of alliance with the United States. Frederick the Great opens the War of the Bavarian Succession by invading Bohemia. The British take Savannah.

1779 Samuel Crompton develops the spinning mule. Captain Cook is killed by natives in Hawaii. The Oaks is first run (named after the house at Epsom leased by the 12th earl of Derby). Warren Hastings sends British troops against the Marathas. The Peace of Teschen settles the War of the Bavarian Succession. British troops are defeated at Baton Rouge by an augmented American army. Spain declares war on Britain.

1780 Admiral Rodney defeats the Spanish off Cape St Vincent. Lord George Gordon whips up anti-Catholic hysteria in London into the Gordon riots. The Americans are defeated at Camden, but are victorious at Kings Mountain. Emperor Joseph II abolishes serfdom in Bohemia and Hungary. Maria Theresa dies, and is succeeded in Habsburg territories by her son Emperor Joseph. The Derby is first run. Peruvian Indians rebel against Spanish rule, led by the Inca descendant Tupac Amaru, who is executed next year as the revolt is suppressed.

1781 William Herschel discovers Uranus. Warren Hastings plunders the treasure of the Nabob of Oudh. Emperor Joseph II grants religious tolerance in the Holy Roman Empire and abolishes serfdom in Austria. General Cornwallis surrenders to the Americans at Yorktown, ending British military operations in America.

1782 Spain captures Minorca from Britain, and completes the conquest of Florida. Lord North resigns as prime minister, and is succeeded by Rockingham; on his death Shelburne replaces him, and Pitt the Younger becomes chancellor of the exchequer. Admiral Rodney defeats the French at the battle of the Saints. Rama I founds the Chakri dynasty as kings of Siam, ruling from Bangkok. The *Royal George* sinks off Portsmouth, with the loss of 800 men.

1783 Shelburne resigns as prime minister, succeeded by Portland, whose government falls; Pitt the Younger becomes prime minister at the age of 24. Henry Cort develops a method of puddling iron. The treaty of Versailles recognises American Independence and cedes Florida to Spain. The Montgolfier brothers make the first balloon flight at Annonay. Potemkin annexes the Crimea for Russia.

1784 Turkey is forced to accept the Russian annexation of the Crimea by the treaty of Constantinople. John Wesley draws up his 'Deed of Declaration', providing for the continuance of the Methodist movement. A revolt in Transylvania persuades Emperor Joseph II to suspend the Hungarian constitution. The East India Company is put under government control.

1785 Jean Blanchard and John Jeffries cross the English Channel by balloon. *The Daily Universal Register*, later renamed *The Times*, is founded. The prince of Wales secretly weds Maria Fitzherbert. Warren Hastings resigns as governor-general of India. The Diamond Necklace affair discredits Marie Antoinette and leads to the arrest of Cardinal de Rohan. Austria and Holland settle their differences by the treaty of Fontainebleau.

1786 Jacques Balmat and Michel-Gabriel Paccard make the first ascent of Mont Blanc. Penang is ceded by the Rajah of Kedah to Britain. Frederick the Great of Prussia dies, and is succeeded by his nephew Frederick William II.

1787 The Marylebone Cricket Club is founded, and Thomas Lord opens his first cricket ground. Warren Hastings is impeached by Edmund Burke. George Washington chairs a Constitutional Convention in America which draws up the constitution. Russia and Turkey go to war. Delaware, Pennsylvania and New Jersey are the first states to join the union of the United States.

1788 William Symington develops a workable steamboat. The First Fleet lands convicts at Botany Bay and Sydney is founded to house them. The trial for corruption of Warren Hastings begins. Gustavus III of Sweden invades Russian Finland. Louis XVI is persuaded to summon the Estates-General in France. George III suffers a bout of mental illness.

1789 Sultan Abdul Hamid I is poisoned and succeeded by his nephew Selim III. George Washington is elected the first president of the United States. A mutiny takes place, led by Fletcher Christian, on HMS *Bounty*; Christian and the mutineers settle on Pitcairn Island; Captain Bligh, set adrift, navigates across 3,600 miles of ocean to Timor. George III recovers from his illness. The Estates-General meet at Versailles; the Third Estate declares itself a National Assembly and swears not to dissolve until a constitution is granted. The Paris mob storm the Bastille, starting a revolution. Feudalism is abolished in France. The National Assembly issues the Declaration of the Rights of Man. Louis XVI and his family are forced to go to Paris as the mob attacks Versailles. Belgrade and Bucharest are taken by Austria.

1790 Emperor Joseph II dies, and is succeeded by his brother Leopold II. Louis XVI accepts a revolutionary constitution. Philadelphia becomes the American capital. Alexander Hamilton founds Washington DC.

1791 Marie Harel develops Camembert cheese. The *Observer* begins publication. Boswell's *Life of Johnson* and Tom Paine's *Rights of Man* are published. John Wesley dies. The Canada Constitutional Act splits Canada into Upper and Lower Canada, with legislatures in Ontario and Quebec. Louis XVI flees Paris, but is captured at Varennes and forced to return. Mozart's *The Magic Flute* is 1st performed. The Bill of Rights, consisting of the first ten amendments to the American constitution, is codified.

1792 Denmark abjures slavery. The Democratic Republican and Federalist parties are founded in America. Russia and Turkey make the Peace of Jassy. Cornwallis defeats Tipu Sultan of Mysore at Seringapatam and takes half of Mysore. Emperor Leopold II dies, and is succeeded by his son Francis II. Gustavus III of Sweden is assassinated in Stockholm Opera House, and is succeeded by his son Gustavus IV. Prussia and Austria ally against France, which declares war on them and Sardinia. Prussia takes Verdun but the French are victorious at Valmy and conquer the Austrian Netherlands. The Paris mob storms the Tuileries; the Swiss Guard fire on them. Louis XVI is imprisoned in the Temple and the National Convention abolishes the monarchy. The Jacobins seize power and the guillotine is put into use.

1793 Louis XVI is executed, as are his cousin Philippe Égalité, duke of Orléans, and Queen Marie Antoinette. France declares war on Britain, Holland and Spain, which join the First Coalition against France. The Vendée rises against republican excesses, but a rebel army is routed at Savenay. America declares its neutrality, unable to decide which side to back. The Committee of Public Safety take power; Robespierre heads a government which embarks on the Reign of Terror. Prussia and Russia perform the Second Partition of Poland, seizing half of Poland's territory. Marat is murdered by Charlotte Corday. Toulon is occupied by the British, but recaptured by a force including Napoleon.

1794 King Kamehameha of Polynesia cedes Hawaii to George III, but the cession is not ratified. Shah Lutf Ali of Persia is defeated and killed by Agha Muhammad, who founds the Qajar dynasty. Kosciusko leads a rising of Polish patriots, which is suppressed by the Russians. The Reign of Terror reaches a height as Danton and Desmoulins are executed. Habeas Corpus is suspended in Britain. Admiral Howe defeats the French fleet on the 'Glorious First of June', but the French have revenge at Charleroi and Fleurus. Robespierre holds the Festival of the Supreme Being; Thermidorean moderates stage a coup – Robespierre and St Just are executed and the Jacobin Club closed.

1795 The French capture the Dutch fleet in the River Texel; Stadtholder William V is forced to flee to England and the French form the Batavian republic in the Netherlands. Prussia makes peace with France by the treaty of Basel. The Speenhamland magistrates devise a new form of poor relief. Warren Hastings is acquitted. The Chouan uprising occurs in Brittany. Cape Town and Trincomalee are taken by the British. The Directory, led by Barras, comes to power in France. Austria, Prussia, and Russia perform the Third Partition of Poland; Stanislas II is forced to abdicate as his country ceases to exist.

1796 Colombo is taken by the British, establishing British control over Ceylon. Emperor Qianlong abdicates, and is succeeded by his son Jiaqing. Napoleon leads an army into Italy; it defeats the Austrians at Millesimo, Lodi and Arcol and establishes the Lombard Republic. François Babeuf leads a conspiracy to overthrow the Directory, but it fails. Edward Jenner discovers a vaccine against smallpox. Elba is captured by Britain. Robert Burns dies aged 37. Spain and Britain go to war. Tsarina Catherine the Great dies, and is succeeded by her son Paul I.

1797 Napoleon defeats the Austrians at Rivoli, seizes Mantua, and founds the Ligurian republic in Genoa and the Cisalpine Republic. Trinidad and St Lucia are taken by the British from the French. Admiral Jervis defeats the Spanish at Cape St Vincent. French troops are landed at Fishguard, but are quickly captured. The first £1 banknotes are issued. John Adams succeeds George Washington as American President. The Royal Navy suffers mutinies at the Nore and Spithead, but defeats a Franco-Dutch fleet at Camperdown. Barras thwarts a royalist reaction by the coup d'état of Fructidor. By the Peace of Campo Formio, the Austrian Netherlands are annexed by France whilst Venice and its territories are passed to Austria; Venice thus loses its independence. Frederick William II of Prussia dies, and is succeeded by his son Frederick William III.

1798 Thomas Malthus produces his *Essay on the Principles of Population*. Coleridge and Wordsworth publish *Lyrical Ballads*. Napoleon captures Rome, proclaiming the Roman Republic and forcing Pope Pius VI into custody at Valence. The Helvetic Republic, encouraged by the French, is proclaimed in Bern. Napoleon then captures Malta en route to Egypt, where he defeats the Mamluks at the battle of the Pyramids, but Nelson destroys his fleet at the battle of the Nile. Irish rebels are defeated at Vinegar Hill, whilst French troops landing in support are forced to surrender at Ballinamuck. The Irish nationalist Wolfe Tone is captured, condemned, but commits suicide. Ferdinand IV of Naples enters Rome, but is driven out by the French and Naples overrun. Income Tax is introduced in Britain.

1799 Napoleon invades Syria, but is repulsed by Sir Sidney Smith at Acre. The Rosetta Stone is discovered. Britain and Hyderabad share Mysore after Tipu Sultan is killed at Seringapatam. The Second Coalition against France is organised by Pitt. Russian troops defeat the French at Zurich, but are eventually driven out; after victory at Cassano they overthrow the Cisalpine Republic. Napoleon defeats an Anglo-Turkish army at Aboukir. On 18 Brumaire Napoleon overthrows the Directory and becomes First Consul.

1800 The American capital is transferred from Philadelphia to Washington DC. The French defeat the Turks at Heliopolis. Austrian troops starve Genoa into submission, but are defeated at Marengo, giving Napoleon control of Italy. Malta is captured by the British.

1801 Great Britain and Ireland unite. France adopts a metric system of weights and measures. The Bank of France is founded. Austria and France make the peace of Lunéville, which destroys the viability of the Holy Roman Empire. Thomas Jefferson becomes American president. Pitt the Younger resigns as prime minister over Catholic Emancipation, and is replaced by Addington. Tsar Paul I is assassinated, succeeded by his son Alexander I. Nelson defeats the Danish fleet at Copenhagen (after the famous incident of him turning a blind eye to Parker's orders). The French troops in Egypt surrender to the English.

1802 William Cobbett founds the *Political Register*. The *Charlotte Dundas*, the world's first steamship, is built by William Symington. Madame Tussaud mounts her first waxworks exhibition in London. Napoleon becomes president of the Italian Republic, which has superseded the Cisalpine Republic. Britain and France make peace by the treaty of Amiens. Napoleon creates the Légion d'Honneur, is made First Consul for life and annexes Piedmont, Parma and Piacenza.

1803 The Swiss cantons regain their independence by the Act of Mediation. Henry Shrapnel develops an explosive shell. The United States purchase the Louisiana territory – over 800,000 sq. miles of land west of the Mississippi – from France. Thomas Telford commences building the Caledonian Canal. France and Britain resume hostilities; France occupies Hanover. Arthur Wellesley (the future duke of Wellington) leads British troops to victory against Sindhia of Gwalior in the Second Maratha War.

1804 Richard Trevithick develops a steam locomotive. The duc d'Enghien is executed for plotting a Bourbon restoration. The Code Napoleon comes into force. Addington is forced to resign by Pitt the Younger, who replaces him. Napoleon is proclaimed Emperor of the French, crowning himself in the presence of Pope Pius VII. A revolt forces the French to withdraw from Haiti. Former US treasury secretary Alexander Hamilton is killed in a duel with Vice-President Aaron Burr.

1805 Francis Beaufort devises the Beaufort Scale. Mungo Park explores the Upper Niger. Muhammad Ali is proclaimed Pasha of Egypt. Napoleon crowns himself king of Italy in Milan wih the old Lombard crown. Austria, Russia, Sweden and Britain form the Third Coalition against France. The British fleet is victorious at Trafalgar over a Franco-Spanish fleet, but Nelson is mortally wounded. On the same day Napoleon defeats an Austro-Russian army at Ulm, and is subsequently victorious at Austerlitz. France and Austria make peace by the treaty of Pressburg; Austria is forced to yield the Tyrol and her Italian possessions whilst Bavaria and Württemberg become kingdoms and Baden a grand duchy.

1806 Britain occupies the Cape of Good Hope. Pitt the Younger dies; Grenville forms a coalition, the 'Ministry of All the Talents', to replace him. Britain establishes a blockade of the European coastline; Napoleon retaliates by the Berlin Decree establishing the Continental System to bar European ports to British ships. Napoleon makes his brothers Joseph and Louis kings of Naples and Holland respectively. France organises the Confederation of the Rhine; the Holy Roman Empire thus ceases to exist and Francis II is merely Emperor of Austria. Prussia joins the Third Coalition. Napoleon defeats the Prussians at Jena and Auerstadt and enters Berlin. Saxony becomes a kingdom by the Peace of Posen.

1807 Charles and Mary Lamb's *Tales from Shakespeare* is published; Charles is guardian to his sister, who stabbed their mother during a bout of insanity. Slavery is prohibited in Britain. Sultan Selim III is deposed by his Janissaries and succeeded by his cousin Mustapha IV. HMS *Leopard* takes deserters from USS *Chesapeake*, enraging the Americans. Napoleon meets Tsar Alexander at Tilsit and makes the peace by the treaty of Tilsit. Napoleon makes his brother Jerome king of Westphalia. Copenhagen is bombarded by the British. Baron von Stein becomes Prussian prime minister and emancipates the serfs there. France invades Portugal, which has refused to join the Continental System; the Portuguese royal family flees to Brazil.

1808 French troops under Murat invade Spain. Charles IV of Spain abdicates in favour of his son Ferdinand VII, but Napoleon orders Murat to force Joseph Bonaparte upon them. Spanish resistance puts Joseph to flight, but Napoleon takes Madrid and restores him. Grand Vizier Bairakdar attempts to restore Sultan Selim III, who is strangled by the janissaries. Bairakdar deposes and murders Sultan Mustafa IV, replacing him with his brother Mahmud II. Murat replaces Joseph as king of Naples.

1809 Sir John Moore is mortally wounded as British troops evacuate Corunna. Gustavus IV of Sweden is captured in a coup; the Duke of Sudermania forms a government and Gustavus is forced to abdicate. Gustavus IV's uncle Karl XIII eventually succeeds him. Britain and the Sikhs make a pact of friendship by the treaty of Amritsar. Napoleon annexes the Papal States, taking Pope Pius VII prisoner, and to further his dynastic ambitions, divorces Josephine. Wellington defeats Soult at Oporto and Jourdan at Talavera. Napoleon is defeated by the Austrians at Aspern, but is victorious at Wagram and makes peace with Austria by the treaty of Schönbrunn. Canning, British foreign secretary, and Castlereagh, war minister, fight a duel on Putney Heath and resign from office. Metternich becomes Austrian minister of foreign affairs. Austria joins the Continental System.

1810 Napoleon marries Marie Louise of Austria. Andreas Hofer leads an Austrian rebellion, but is executed at Mantua. Napoleon annexes Holland when his brother Louis abdicates, and later annexes Hanover and various German ports. Jean Bernadotte is invited to become heir to the Swedish throne as Karl XIII has no children. The Krupp steel works open in Essen.

1811 George III descends into madness and the prince of Wales is declared Regent. Belgrade is seized by the Russians. Pasha Muhammad Ali massacres the Mamluks at Cairo. Luddism erupts in the Midlands. Wellington defeats the French at Fuentes de Onoro and Albuera. Francisco de Miranda declares Venezuelan independence; Paraguay follows suit. William Harrison defeats the Shawnee at Tippecanoe.

1812 In Spain, Wellington takes Ciudad Rodrigo and Badajoz, defeats Marmont at Salamanca and enters Madrid. Prime minister Spencer Perceval is assassinated by John Bellingham, and is succeeded by the earl of Liverpool. America declares war on Britain. Napoleon leads his Grand Army into Russia. Britain, Russia and Sweden ally via the treaty of Örebro. De Miranda is made dictator of Venezuela after an earthquake, but is captured by the Spanish. After victory at Smolensk and an inconclusive outcome at Borodino Napoleon takes an evacuated Moscow, which is then burned down by Russian saboteurs. He orders a retreat, and has to suffer terrible losses in crossing the River Berezina. General Claude Malet attempts to depose Napoleon in his absence, but is executed as the conspiracy fails.

1813 The locomotive 'Puffing Billy' is developed by William Hedley. Prussia declares war on France, but is defeated, along with Russia, by Napoleon at Lützen, Bautzen and Wurschen. Wellington defeats Jourdan at Vittoria and crosses into France. Simon Bolívar becomes dictator of Venezuela. Austria declares war on France. Prusso-Russian troops defeat Napoleon at Grossbeeren and Wahlstatt, but are defeated at Dresden before further victory at Dennewitz. An Austro-Prusso-Russian army defeats Napoleon at Leipzig, and drives him back across Germany. Mexico declares independence from Spain. The French are expelled from Holland.

1814 Denmark cedes Heligoland to Britain by the treaty of Kiel. Murat deserts Napoleon and joins the Allies, who inflict defeats on Napoleon at La Rothière, Laon, Arcis and Fère-Champenoise before entering Paris. Wellington defeats the French at Toulouse. Napoleon abdicates, is banished to Elba, and is granted its sovereignty. Louis XVIII returns from exile. Ferdinand VII returns to the Spanish throne. The Austrian Netherlands and Holland unite to form the kingdom of the Netherlands. The White House is burned down by British troops.The Cape of Good Hope becomes a British colony. The Congress of Vienna opens. The treaty of Ghent ends hostilities between Britain and America.

1815 Napoleon returns from Elba, forcing Louis XVIII to flee to Ghent. His forces under Ney are victorious at Quatre Bras, but Wellington defeats him at Waterloo. After surrendering to the British, he is exiled to St Helena. Louis XVIII returns, Ney is executed and Murat deposed from Naples; he is executed when trying to regain his throne. Spanish troops reconquer Venezuela, forcing Bolívar to flee. To protect domestic growers against cheaper imports, the Corn Laws are passed in Britain. The treaty of Vienna draws up a new political map of Europe: Norway is passed to Denmark, the Rhineland to Prussia, Poland to Russia and various monarchs restored to their thrones.

1816 Argentina declares itself independent, as does Brazil under the Portuguese prince João, who succeeds to the Portuguese throne on the death of his mother Maria I, but remains in Brazil. The first Diet of the German Confederation opens in Frankfurt. Cobbett's *Political Register* increases its radical influence after a price cut to 2d.

1817 José de San Martín and Bernardo O'Higgins defeat the Spanish at Chacabuco and establish an independent Chile. The last major Luddite attack takes place in Loughborough. The 'Blanketeers' march from Manchester to protest against the suspension of the Habeas Corpus Act, but are halted at Stockport; there are similar riots elsewhere. Bolivar reestablishes an independent Venezuela. The Ottomans grant partial autonomy to the Serbs.

1818 The Rajput states and Indore come under British control by the treaty of Mundosir. Karl XIII of Sweden dies, and is succeeded by Bernadotte, who takes the name Karl XIV. The American-Canadian border is defined along the 49th parallel. James Blundell performs the first successful blood transfusion. At the Congress of Aix-la-Chapelle, the victorious allies agree to withdraw their troops from France, which has paid the war indemnity imposed in 1815.

1819 Stamford Raffles founds the city of Singapore. The United States take over Florida from Spain. The reactionary Karlsbad Decrees are promulgated in Germany. The Peterloo Massacre kills 11 people in Manchester, when yeomen attack a reformist crowd. The reactionary Six Acts are passed in England. Simon Bolivar becomes president of the newly independent Colombia.

1820 Liberia is founded for the repatriation of American Negroes. There are revolts in Spain, where Ferdinand VII is forced to restore the constitution of 1812, and in Portugal, demanding a constitution. George III dies, and is succeeded by his son George IV. The duc de Berry, heir to the French throne, is assassinated; a son, the comte de Chambord, is born posthumously. At the Congress of Troppau, Prussia, Austria and Russia discuss concerted action against revolutionary movements with Britain and France. The Cato Street Conspiracy to murder British cabinet ministers is discovered and its leaders executed. Keats publishes *Lamia, Isabella, The Eve of St Agnes and other Poems.*

1821 A Carbonarist uprising in Naples is put down by the Austrians, sanctioned by the Congress of Laibach. Bolívar defeats the Spanish at Carabobo, ensuring Venezuelan independence. Peru declares independence under José de San Martín. El Salvador, Honduras, Costa Rica, Guatemala and Panama follow suit. Greeks start an insurgence against the Ottomans in an attempt to gain independence. Victor Emmanuel of Piedmont is forced to abdicate in favour of his more liberal brother Charles Felix. The Austrians intervene, defeating the Piedmontese at Novara and reasserting control over the country.

1822 Viceroy Wellesley is attacked by Orangemen in Dublin in the 'Bottle Riots'. The Ottomans capture Chios and massacre its inhabitants. Agostín de Itúrbide is declared emperor of Mexico. A Greek flotilla burns an Ottoman fleet, bringing further reprisals. British foreign secretary Castlereagh commits suicide. Regent Pedro, son of João VI of Portugal, declares Brazil independent.

1823 Michael Faraday succeeds in liquefying chlorine. Emperor Agostín de Itúrbide is forced to abdicate as Mexico declares itself a republic. *The Lancet* is first published. A revolt in Spain is quelled with French assistance. President Monroe issues the Monroe Doctrine, closing the Americas to European colonialism.

1824 The RNLI is founded. The First Burmese War between Britain and Burma commences; Rangoon is taken by the British. Lord Byron dies at Missolonghi whilst assisting the Greeks. Beethoven's 9th Symphony is first performed. Louis XVIII of France dies, and is succeeded by his brother Charles X.

1825 Ferdinand I of the Two Sicilies dies, and is succeeded by his son Francis I. John Quincy Adams is elected American president by the House of Representatives after none of the four candidates gains a majority in the election. Bolivia under Jose de Sucre declares independence from Peru, and Uruguay, with Argentine support, from Brazil. The Stockton–Darlington railway opens, the first passenger-carrying line. The Erie Canal links the Hudson River to the Great Lakes and the American Midwest. Tsar Alexander I dies, and is succeeded by his brother Nicholas I, who is confronted by the Decembrist revolt of officers, which he puts down.

1826 The First Burmese War is ended by the treaty of Yandabo. João VI of Portugal dies, and is succeeded by his son Pedro IV, who abdicates in favour of his daughter Maria II and remains in Brazil. Persia and Russia go to war; the Russians are victorious at Ganja. Stamford Raffles founds the Royal Zoological Society in London.

1827 Peru secedes from Colombia. Count Kapodistrias is elected president of Greece as Britain, France and Russia sign the treaty of London pledging support for the Greeks; an allied fleet crushes an Ottoman and Egyptian fleet at Navarino. Russia defeats Persia and takes Yerevan.

1828 Wellington becomes prime minister. Russia makes peace with Persia by the treaty of Turkmanchai, and subsequently declares war on the Ottomans. Maria II of Portugal is deposed by her uncle, the Regent Dom Miguel, and flees to England as civil war breaks out. The treaty of Rio de Janeiro confirms Uruguayan independence. Thomas Arnold becomes headmaster of Rugby School.

1829 The Catholic Emancipation Act is passed in Britain. Wellington fights a duel with the earl of Winchelsea. The Metropolitan Police is founded by Robert Peel. The first Boat Race takes place at Henley. The London Protocol establishes Greek independence; the treaty of Adrianople ends Russo-Turkish hostilities. Stephenson's *Rocket* wins the Rainhill Trials. Slavery is abolished in Mexico.

1830 Joseph Smith founds the Church of Jesus Christ of Latter-Day Saints. The Swing riots, caused by the introduction of threshing machines and rural unemployment, start in Kent and spread west and north. George IV dies, and is succeeded by his brother William IV. Algeria is conquered by France, but an uprising in Paris forces Charles X to abdicate in favour of his grandson, however Louis-Philippe, duc d'Orléans, usurps the throne. Belgium secedes from the Kingdom of the Netherlands. Wellington is ousted as prime minister after a general election, and replaced by earl Grey.

1831 Independence agitations in Italy are quelled by Austrian troops. Pedro I of Brazil abdicates, and is succeeded by his son Pedro II. A Polish revolt is put down after Russian troops are victorious at Ostroleka. Leopold of Saxe-Coburg is elected king of the Belgians. Charles Felix of Piedmont dies, and is succeeded by his distant relation Charles Albert. The Greek President Kapodistrias is assassinated. Faraday invents the dynamo. The defeat of Grey's Reform Bill in the Lords causes anti-clerical agitation. Mazzini founds Young Italy.

1832 The First Reform Act is passed, doubling the franchise. Otto of Bavaria is elected king of Greece.

1833 Britain annexes the Falkland Islands. The Convention of Kutahya passes control of Syria to Muhammad Ali of Egypt. Slavery is abolished in the British Empire. Ferdinand VII of Spain dies, and is succeeded by his infant daughter Isabella II. Santa Anna becomes President of Mexico whilst civil war looms in the country.

1834 The Zollverein customs union comes into operation in Germany. The Spanish Inquisition is abolished. To protect their constitutions, Portugal and Spain form a Quadruple Alliance with France and Britain. Don Carlos attempts to usurp the Spanish throne from his niece Isabella II, plunging the country into civil war, whilst in Portugal Dom Miguel is forced to flee as troops led by his brother Pedro restore Maria II to her throne. For forming a trade union, the Tolpuddle Martyrs are arrested and transported to Australia. Fire destroys the Houses of Parliament.

1835 Francis II of Austria dies, and is succeeded by his son Ferdinand I. Juan de Rosas becomes dictator of Argentina. The Boers begin the 'Great Trek'. Texas attempts to secede from Mexico.

1836 Santa Anna takes the Alamo at San Antonio; Davy Crockett and Jim Bowie are killed. Sam Houston defeats and captures Santa Anna at San Jacinto; Texas gains independence with Houston as president. Louis Napoleon Bonaparte attempts a revolt at Strasbourg, and is banished to America.

1837 William IV dies, and is succeeded in England by his niece Victoria and in Hanover by his brother Ernst Augustus, duke of Cumberland, who promptly cancels the constitution of 1833 there. Brunel launches the *Great Western.* Births, marriages and deaths are officially registered in England and Wales. Isaac Pitman develops shorthand. French Canadians revolt against British rule.

1838 Chopin begins his liaison with George Sand. Richard Cobden establishes the Anti-Corn Law League. The 'People's Charter' is published. Grace Darling assists in the rescue from the wreck of the *Forfarshire.* The First Afghan War begins; the British capture Kabul and imprison the Emir Dost Muhammad. The Boers defeat the Zulus at Blood River.

1839 The Rebecca Riots against the Poor Law Amendment Act take place in Wales (rioters disguise themselves as women). Goodyear discovers how to vulcanise rubber. Argentina and Uruguay go to war. The Ottomans invade Syria but are defeated by Ibrahim Pasha at Nezib. The treaty of London guarantees Belgian independence and neutrality. Sultan Mahmud II is poisoned, and succeeded by his son Abdul Mejid. Chinese attempts to stop the importation of opium lead to the Opium War with Britain. Frederick VI of Denmark dies, and is succeeded by his nephew, Christian VIII. Bradshaw's provides first railway timetables.

1840 The Maoris cede sovereignty of New Zealand to England by the treaty of Waitangi. Rowland Hill introduces the Penny Post. Frederick William III of Prussia dies, and is succeeded by his son Frederick William IV. Britain, Austria, Prussia and Russia ally against Muhammad Ali of Egypt by the treaty of London; after Beirut and Acre are captured, Muhammad agrees to return Syria to Ottoman rule. Lower and Upper Canada are united under a single legislature. Rafael Carrera becomes dictator of Guatemala. Louis Napoleon Bonaparte is imprisoned at Ham after another attempt to foment revolt fails. William I of Holland abdicates, and is succeeded by his son William II.

1841 Hong Kong is taken by the British. William Harrison dies after catching cold giving his inaugural address as US president, and is succeeded by John Tyler. Thomas Cook arranges his first excursion, to a temperance meeting. The Straits Convention closes the Bosporus to warships. Carlos Lopez becomes President of Paraguay. The first issue of *Punch* is published.

1842 Crawford W Long performs the first operation under anaesthesia. British troops in Afghanistan are massacred. The second Chartist petition is rejected. Civil war erupts in Uruguay. The Webster-Ashburton treaty defines the US–Canadian border. The treaty of Nanking ends the Opium War; Hong Kong is ceded to Britain. Alexander Karageorgevich deposes Michael Obrenovich as prince of Serbia. Marx meets Engels. Britain withdraws from Afghanistan.

1843 The Thames Tunnel opens, first underwater tunnel in the world. Brunel launches the *Great Britain.* Sind is conquered by General Charles Napier. Hawaii becomes independent, with recognition from France and Britain.

1844 George Williams founds the YMCA. Karl XIV of Sweden dies, and is succeeded by his son Oscar I. The Factory Act fixes maximum workdays of 6½ hours for children, 12 hours for women. Samuel Morse transmits his first telegraph message. The Dominican Republic gains independence from Haiti. The Co-operative movement is founded in Rochdale.

1845 The Irish famine begins as the potato crop fails. Henry Newman converts to Catholicism. Sir John Franklin sets out with the *Erebus* and *Terror* to find the North-West Passage. British incursions in the Punjab and Kashmir cause the Anglo-Sikh War. The Sonderbund is formed when 7 Catholic cantons secede from the Confederation in Switzerland.

1846 The Anglo-Sikh War is ended by the treaty of Lahore. Cracow is annexed by Austria. Louis Napoleon Bonaparte escapes from prison and moves to London. The treaty of Washington settles the Oregon–Canada border along the 49th Parallel. America goes to war with Mexico after failing to purchase New Mexico; after victories at Palo Alto and Resaca de la Palma New Mexico is annexed by the United States. Peel repeals the Corn Laws, fatally splitting his party and forcing him to resign as prime minister; Lord John Russell replaces him. Charles Dickens founds the *Daily News*.

1847 Mexican troops under Santa Anna are defeated by the Americans at Buena Vista and Cerro Gordo. Liberia is proclaimed an independent republic. The Catholic cantons refuse to dissolve the Sonderbund, precipitating war in Switzerland.

1848 Christian VIII of Denmark dies, and is succeeded by his son Frederick III. Gold is discovered in California. The treaty of Guadalupe Hidalgo ends the conflict between America and Mexico, which is forced to yield its lands north of the Rio Grande. Marx and Engels publish the *Communist Manifesto*. Paris erupts in revolt, forcing Louis Philippe to abdicate. The Second French Republic is formed; a workers' revolt is put down (the June Days) and Louis Napoleon Bonaparte is elected President. The revolution in France inspires a wave of revolts across Europe: Metternich falls in Austria; Milan, Parma, Venice, Hungary and the Czechs revolt against Austrian dominion; liberals rise across Germany, creating a National Assembly; Rome rises against Papal war, forcing Pope Pius IX to flee to Gaeta. Piedmont declares war on Austria, but after victories at Goito and Pastrengo is defeated by Radetzky at Custozza. Windischgrätz suppresses the Czech rising; nevertheless, Emperor Ferdinand I is forced to abdicate in favour of his nephew Franz Josef. The Second Anglo-Sikh war breaks out. The third Chartist petition is presented amid a meeting which collapses in farce, and is rejected. Switzerland becomes a federal union. The Pre-Raphaelite Brotherhood is founded.

1849 The Sikhs are defeated by the British at Chillianwalla and forced to surrender at Rawalpindi; the Punjab is annexed by Britain. A Roman republic under Mazzini is formed, but French, Austrian, Spanish, Neapolitan and Tuscan troops capture Rome and restore Pope Pius IX. Radetzsky defeats the Piedmontese at Novara. Charles Albert of Piedmont abdicates in favour of his son Victor Emmanuel II and the Peace of Milan ends hostilities. The German National Assembly elects Frederick William IV 'Emperor of the Germans', but he refuses the title and the Assembly collapses in chaos. Hungary proclaims independence under Kossuth, but Russian troops invade and are victorious at Temesvar; Kossuth flees and Hungary returns to Austrian rule. Venice submits to the Austrians.

1850 Palmerston blockades Piraeus over the Don Pacifico Affair, forcing the Greeks to comply with his wishes, but is censured in parliament. Prussia and Denmark reach an accord on Schleswig-Holstein by the treaty of Berlin. Hong Xiuquan leads the Taiping rebellion in China. Count Camillo Cavour becomes chief minister of Piedmont.

1851 Danilo II succeeds Peter II in Montenegro and makes the state a principality. The Great Exhibition is held in Hyde Park. The Americas Cup yacht race is first held around the Isle of Wight. The Australian Gold Rush begins. Louis Napoleon Bonaparte stages a coup d'état in France.

1852 Juan Manuel de Rosas, Argentine dictator, is forced to flee after defeat by insurgents with Uruguayan and Brazilian help at Caseros. The Second Burmese War breaks out between Britain and Burma. Louis Napoleon Bonaparte proclaims the Second Empire, crowning himself Napoleon III.

1853 Pegu is taken by Britain as the Second Burmese War ends. Shogun Ieyoshi dies, and is succeeded by his son Iesada, who opens two Japanese ports to foreign trade. Russia invades the Ottoman Danubian principalities and destroys the Turkish fleet at Sinope. Maria II of Portugal dies, and is succeeded by her son Pedro V.

1854 The Convention of Bloemfontein leaves the Orange Free State free for the Boers and withdraws the British south of the Orange River. America makes the treaty of Kanagawa with Japan over trade and the Elgin treaty with Britain over Canadian trade. Britain and France declare war on Russia in support of Turkey and are victorious at the Alma, Balaklava (where the Charge of the Light Brigade takes place), and Inkerman, before besieging Sebastopol.

1855 Piedmont joins the anti-Russian alliance in the Crimean War by the treaty of Turin. Aberdeen resigns as prime minister over the conduct of the war, and is replaced by Palmerston.Tsar Nicholas I dies, and is succeeded by his son Alexander II. Britain and Afghanistan sign the anti-Persian treaty of Peshawar. The *Daily Telegraph* is first published. Sebastopol falls to the allied armies.

1856 The Victoria Cross is instituted. Britain annexes Oudh and establishes Natal as a Crown Colony. The Crimean War is ended by the treaty of Paris; the integrity of the Ottoman Empire is recognised and the Black Sea demiltitarised. The Chinese board the *Arrow* off Canton over suspected piracy; British ships bombard Canton in response. Marthinius Pretorius establishes the Transvaal republic. Henry Bessemer introduces his steel-making converter.

1857 Britain forces Afghani independence on the Persians by the treaty of Paris. The Sepoys in Meerut revolt, sparking a general Indian Mutiny; the inhabitants of Cawnpore are massacred and Lucknow besieged for six months. Garibaldi forms the Italian National Association. British and French forces occupy Canton.

1858 Felice Orsini attempts to assassinate Napoleon III, causing Anglo-French tension and turning Napoleon's mind towards Italy; he has secret meetings at Plombières with Cavour. Anglo-Chinese hostilities are ended by the treaty of Tianjin. The Indian Mutiny is suppressed; the East India Company is wound up and its powers transferred to the British crown. Frederick William IV is declared insane; his brother William is made Regent. Alexander Karageorgevich is deposed by the Serbian Diet and replaced by Milos Obrenovich. France launches *La Gloire*, a naval vessel partially clad in iron.

1859 Piedmont traps Austria into war, and backed by Napoleon III is victorious at Magenta and Solferino. Ferdinand of the Two Sicilies dies, and is succeeded by his son Francis II. Napoleon III and Franz Josef of Austria make the Peace of Villafranca; Lombardy is passed to Piedmont. John Brown raids Harpers Ferry. Darwin publishes the *Origin of Species*. Queensland is established as a separate colony with Brisbane as its capital.

1860 Piedmont cedes Nice and Savoy to France by the treaty of Turin. Plebiscites in the Italian duchies favour union with Piedmont. Garibaldi and his 1,000 redshirts sail from Genoa to Sicily, take the island and then progress to Naples, where he proclaims Victor Emmanuel II of Piedmont king of Italy. Piedmontese troops invade the Papal States en route to the Two Sicilies, which Garibaldi hands to Victor Emmanuel II; Garibaldi retires to Caprera. South Carolina secedes from the Union in protest at the election of Abraham Lincoln as president. The Second Maori War breaks out in New Zealand. Richard Cobden negotiates an Anglo-French trade treaty. Anglo-French forces bombard Sinho, occupy the Tagu forts, defeat the Chinese army at Ba Lizhao and burn the Summer Palace in Peking in retaliation for Chinese treaty breaches and cruelty to captives; the treaty of Peking forces further concessions on the Chinese.

1861 Frederick William IV of Prussia dies and is succeeded by his brother Wilhelm I. Tsar Alexander II emancipates the Russian serfs. The kingdom of Italy is proclaimed, with its capital at Florence, as Rome refuses to join. The Confederate States of America are proclaimed at the Congress of Montgomery and go to war with the Union by bombarding Fort Sumter: the Civil War begins. The Confederates are victorious at Bull Run. Prince Albert dies. With the commissioning into the Royal Navy of the iron-hulled HMS *Warrior*, all other naval vessels are rendered effectively obsolete.

1862 In America the Union launches the ironclad USS *Monitor*, which fights the Confederate ironclad *Merrimack* to a draw in Hampton Roads.The battle of Shiloh is a bloody draw, whilst the Confederates are subsequently victorious at the second battle of Bull Run and Fredericksburg. Napoleon III sends French troops to establish a Catholic empire in Mexico, forcing the withdrawal of British and Spanish troops; the French are heavily defeated at Puebla. Bismarck is appointed prime minister of Prussia. A military revolt forces Otto I of Greece to abdicate and return to Bavaria.

1863 The first underground railway, from Farringdon Street to Paddington, is opened. The Greeks elect Prince Alfred of Britain as their new king, but he is forced to reject the position; William of Denmark is elected instead, taking the title George I. The Confederates are victorious at Chancellorsville, but are routed at Gettysburg, which proves a turning point. The Union has further victories at Vicksburg and Chattanooga but is defeated at Chickamauga. Lincoln gives the Gettysburg Address at the dedication of the cemetery there. Mexico City falls to the French, who invite Archduke Maximilian of Austria to become emperor of the country. Japan closes its ports and expels foreign traders, prompting Britain to bombard Kagoshima. Frederick VII of Denmark dies, and is succeeded by his nephew Christian IX, who incorporates Schleswig into the country after German pressure on the area. The English Football Association is founded.

1864 Austrian and Prussian troops invade Schleswig-Holstein, defeating the Danes at Düppel. A conference in London fails to settle the dispute, and Prussia and Austria force Denmark to cede the area by the treaty of Vienna. Archduke Maximilian accepts the Mexican crown. Brazil invades Uruguay after a dispute with Paraguay. The Taiping Rebellion is suppressed, with help from General Gordon's troops; Hong Xiuquan commits suicide. Ulysses S Grant takes command of the Union army. In the Wilderness campaign in Virginia, the Union loses 60,000 of an army of over 100,000, the Confederacy 20,000 of its 60,000 men. Sherman takes Atlanta and Savannah as his Union army marches through Georgia. General George Thomas wipes out a Confederate army under JB Hood at Nashville.

1865 The Confederate states surrender to the Unionists at Appomattox; five days later Abraham Lincoln is assassinated by John Wilkes Booth. William Booth founds the Christian Revival Association (later the Salvation Army). Edward Whymper climbs the Matterhorn. Joseph Lister's use of carbolic acid founds modern antiseptic surgery. Lord Palmerston dies in office, and is succeeded as prime minister by Lord John Russell. Leopold I of Belgium dies, and is succeeded by his son Leopold II. The Thirteenth Amendment abolishes slavery in the US.

1866 Prince Alexander of Romania is dethroned and replaced by Carol I of Hohenzollern. Bismarck, with Italian assistance, engineers war against Austria and allied German states, defeating the Austrians at Sadowa, although the Italians are defeated at Custozza and the naval battle of Lissa. The Peace of Prague gives Prussia Hanover, Hesse, Nassau, Frankfurt and Holstein. Shogun Iemochi dies, and is succeeded by his kinsman Yoshinobu. The treaty of Vienna cedes Venetia to Italy.

1867 The Ausgleich creates the Dual Monarchy of Austria-Hungary. Alaska is sold by Russia to America. The Dominion of Canada is created. Emperor Maximilian of Mexico surrenders to insurgents after the French abandon him and is executed. Prussia forms the North German Confederation. The Second Reform Act doubles the British electorate. Garibaldi marches on Rome, but is defeated by a Franco-Papal army at Mentana and taken prisoner. The Queensberry Rules on boxing are drawn up.

1868 The Shogunate is abolished in Japan; by the Meiji Restoration power passes to Emperor Matsuhito. Disraeli becomes prime minister, but is defeated in a general election by Gladstone, who replaces him. Prince Michael of Serbia is assassinated, succeeded by his kinsman Milan II Isabella II of Spain is deposed after a revolution in Spain. The first Trades Union Congress meets in Manchester. The last public hangings in England take place.

1869 The first Nihilist Congress meets in Basel. The *Cutty Sark* is launched. Napoleon III reintroduces a parliamentary system into France. The Suez Canal is opened.

1870 Papal infallibility is proclaimed. Isabella II of Spain abdicates in favour of her son Alfonso XII but the throne is offered to Leopold of Hohenzollern, who is forced to decline it after French protests. These protests are edited by Bismarck into the 'Ems telegram' and used to foment war between France and Prussia. After a French victory at Saarbrücken, Prussia is victorious at Weissenberg, Wörth, Mars-la-Tour, Gravelotte and Sedan. Napoleon III surrenders and abdicates as Paris revolts and proclaims the Third Republic. Paris is besieged by the Prussians. Italian troops enter Rome and absorb it into the kingdom; it is made the capital. Amadeus of Savoy accepts the Spanish throne.

1871 Wilhelm I of Prussia is proclaimed emperor of a federal Germany at Versailles. Paris surrenders to the Prussians. The leftist Commune takes power there, and is repressed with the loss of 20,000 lives. The Convention of London abolishes the demilitarization of the Black Sea. Britain and America settle differences by the treaty of Washington. France and Germany make the Peace of Frankfurt; Alsace-Lorraine is ceded to Germany and an indemnity paid by France. Stanley meets Livingstone at Ujiji (now in Tanzania). Bank holidays are introduced.

1872 Wanderers win the first FA Cup final. Don Carlos invades Spain, but is routed at Oroquista and forced to withdraw. The secret ballot is introduced in Britain. Germany, Austria-Hungary and Russia form the Three Emperors League. The *Marie Celeste* is found deserted.

1873 A Spanish republic is proclaimed and Amadeus I forced to abdicate. Sultan Bargash Sayyid closes the slave markets in Zanzibar. The cities of Buda and Pest are united to form the Hungarian capital. WC Wingfield invents Sphairistike (lawn tennis).

1874 Disraeli defeats Gladstone in the General Election. Japan invades Formosa, and withdraws on payment of compensation by China. Fiji is annexed by Britain. Alfonso XII of Spain proclaims his reign at Sandhurst.

1875 Bismarck foments tension between Germany and France ('Is War in Sight?' article in the *Berlin Post*). Bosnia-Herzegovina revolts against Turkish rule. Matthew Webb swims the English Channel. Disraeli arranges the purchase of shares in the Suez Canal. Sir Joseph Bazalgette completes the London sewerage system. The MCC codifies the rules of lawn tennis.

1876 Korea becomes independent from China. Alexander Graham Bell patents the telephone. Bulgaria rises against Turkey, but is savagely repressed, drawing Gladstone out of retirement. Queen Victoria is proclaimed Empress of India and is officially inaugurated in January 1877. Sultan Abdul Aziz is deposed in favour of his nephew Murad V and commits suicide; Murad is himself deposed in favour of his brother Abdul Hamid II. General Custer is defeated and killed by the Sioux at the battle of Little Big Horn. Serbia and Montenegro declare war on Turkey, but the Serbs are routed at Alexinatz. Wild Bill Hickok is shot dead.

1877 Rutherford B Hayes is elected American president after an electoral commission decides in his favour. Russia declares war on Turkey and takes Kars and Plevna. Britain warns Russia off taking Constantinople. Serbia also declares war on Turkey. Australia beats England in the first cricket Test match. The first Lawn Tennis Championships are held at Wimbledon.

1878 Victor Emmanuel II of Italy dies, and is succeeded by his son Umberto I. Russia takes Adrianople; the Turks capitulate and sign the treaty of San Stefano, in which Bulgarian, Romanian and Serbian independence is fully established. The provisions are unacceptable to other European powers; differences are resolved at the Congress of Berlin, where the San Stefano provisons are reduced in scale.

1879 The Irish Land League is founded. Britain goes to war with the Zulus, who massacre the British at Isandhlwana but are held at Rorke's Drift and defeated at Ulundi. Their king Cetewayo is captured and deported and the Zulu wars end; the Prince Imperial, heir of Napoleon III, is a casualty. Britain occupies the Khyber Pass by the treaty of Gandamak with Afghanistan and invades when the legation in Kabul is massacred, taking the city and deposing Emir Yakub. Khedive Ismail of Egypt is deposed in favour of his son Tewfik. The Tay Bridge collapses in a storm; 78 lives are lost as a train crossing the bridge falls into the river.

1880 Andrew Carnegie presents Dunfermline with a free library. Gladstone defeats Disraeli in the General Election. Tahiti is annexed by France. Morocco gains independence. Captain Boycott is ostracised by his tenants in County Mayo. Paul Kruger declares the Transvaal an independent republic.

1881 Boers repulse the British at Laing's Neck and defeat them at Majuba Hill; peace is made by the treaty of Pretoria, which recognises an independent Transvaal as the South African Republic. James Garfield is inaugurated as American president but is shot and fatally wounded soon after. Tsar Alexander II is assassinated; he is succeeded by his son Alexander III, who responds by introducing repressive measures. Tunisia is made a French protectorate.

1882 Prince Milan II of Serbia declares himself king. The Hague Convention establishes a three-mile limit for territorial waters. The Fenians assassinate two British ministers in Phoenix Park, Dublin. Nationalist riots in Egypt led by Arabi Pasha lead to the British fleet bombarding Alexandria; Sir Garnet Wolseley defeats Arabi at Tel-el-Kebir and occupies Cairo.

1883 Paul Kruger becomes president of the South African Republic. Krakatoa erupts in spectacular fashion. Khedive Tewfik appoints a British agent to assist his government; Sir Evelyn Baring takes up the post. The Orient Express makes its first run. The Mahdi stirs up a revolt in Sudan and defeats an Anglo-Egyptian army at El Obeid.

1884 The Fabian Society is established. General Gordon reaches Khartoum intent on evacuating the city but decides to stay. China declares war on France after the latter bombards Formosa as a reprisal for China's refusal to acknowledge a French protectorate over Indo-China. The Third Reform Act is passed in Britain.

1885 Wolseley defeats the Mahdi's followers at Abu Klea but reaches Khartoum two days after its fall and Gordon's death. Wolseley is forced to withdraw and the news helps contribute to the fall of Gladstone's government. The Congo becomes the personal possession of Leopold II of Belgium. Germany annexes Tanganyika and Zanzibar. The Mahdi dies, but his successor Abdullah el Tasshi gains control over Sudan. Alfonso XII of Spain dies; his pregnant widow Maria Christina becomes regent.

1886 General Boulanger becomes French war minister. Gladstone's conversion to Irish Home Rule splits the Liberals; Joseph Chamberlain leads the Liberal Unionists into partnership with the Conservatives. Alfonso XIII of Spain is born king. France banishes the Bonaparte and Orléans families. Prince Alexander of Bulgaria abdicates after a coup. Randolph Churchill resigns as chancellor in a fit of pique and destroys his political career in the process. The discovery of gold in Transvaal transforms the politics of southern Africa.

1887 The First Colonial Conference opens in London. Germany and Russia make the secret Reinsurance Treaty. Zululand is annexed by Britain. Ferdinand of Saxe-Coburg is elected prince of Bulgaria. Italy and Abyssinia go to war; the Italians are routed at Dogali. Macao is ceded to Portugal.

1888 Kaiser Wilhelm I dies; his son Frederick III succeeds him, but dies soon after and is succeeded by his son Wilhelm II. Brazil frees its slaves. The Jack the Ripper murders take place in London. The first beauty contest is held in Spa, Belgium. The Suez Canal Convention, guaranteeing freedom of access to the canal, is signed in Constantinople.

1889 Urged by his supporters to stage a coup d'état, Boulanger refuses and flees abroad. Crown Prince Rudolf of Austria shoots his mistress and commits suicide at Mayerling. Milan II of Serbia abdicates in favour of his son Alexander II. Gustave Eiffel completes the Eiffel Tower for the Paris Exhibition. The first Pan-American Conference meets in Washington. The Brazilian army deposes King Pedro II and installs General Manuel de Fonseca as president.

1890 The Forth Railway Bridge opens. Kaiser Wilhelm forces Bismarck's resignation as Chancellor. Social insurance is introduced in Switzerland. Heligoland is exchanged for the German colonies of Zanzibar and Pemba by Britain. The first Japanese elections are held. William III of Holland dies, and is succeeded by his daughter Wilhelmina. Luxembourg separates from the Netherlands under Duke Adolf of Nassau. Sitting Bull is captured and killed; American troops massacre 200 Sioux at Wounded Knee.

1891 WL Judson invents the zip. President Fonseca of Brazil is ousted in favour of Vice-President Floriano Peixoto.

1892 Khedive Tewfik of Egypt dies, and is succeeded by his son Abbas II. Lizzie Borden murders her parents. Gladstone forms his fourth administration at the age of 82 after victory in the general election.

1893 The Independent Labour Party is founded in Bradford. Natal is granted self-government. The Matabele rise against the British South Africa Company, but Jameson crushes the revolt and takes Bulawayo, forcing King Lobengula into exile. Gladstone's Irish Home Rule Bill is defeated in the House of Lords. Transvaal annexes Swaziland.

1894 The Manchester Ship Canal is opened. Gladstone resigns from office, and is replaced as prime minister by Lord Rosebery. Uganda becomes a British protectorate. The Ottomans massacre thousands of Armenians in suppressing a revolt. President Carnot of France is assassinated by an Italian anarchist at Lyon. Korea and Japan declare war on China. Albert Dreyfus is arrested on a treason charge; convicted, he is imprisoned on Devil's Island.

1895 The treaty of Shimonoseki ends the Sino-Japanese War after the Japanese crush the Chinese at Wei hai wei; Formosa and Port Arthur are ceded to Japan but returned in exchange for an indemnity. Italy invades Abyssinia, but is defeated at Amba Alagi. The British South Africa Company's land south of the Zambezi is renamed Rhodesia. Premier Stamboulov of Bulgaria is assassinated. The Kiel Canal is opened. Wilhelm Röntgen discovers X-rays. The first public film show takes place. Jameson raids Transvaal, but fails to foment a rebellion against its Boer rulers.

1896 Jameson is captured by the Boers at Doorn Kop. Kaiser Wilhelm sends the Kruger Telegram, inflaming Anglo-German relations. Becquerel discovers radioactivity in uranium. Italy is defeated by the Abyssinians at Adowa and withdraws by the treaty of Addis Ababa. The first modern Olympic Games are held in Athens. Shah Nasir-ud-Din of Persia is assassinated; he is succeeded by his son Muzaffir-ud-Din. Marconi patents wireless telegraphy. Kitchener leads an Anglo-Egyptian force into the Sudan. Over 50,000 Armenians are massacred by the Turks.

1897 Crete proclaims union with Greece, prompting a war between Greece and Turkey; the Turks are victorious and the island stays under Turkish hands by the treaty of Constantinople. Hawaii is annexed by the United States. The first Zionist Congress meets in Basel.

1898 Zola publishes 'J'accuse' over the Dreyfus affair, proved to have been fabricated by anti-Semitic army officers. The USS *Maine* explodes in Havana harbour, Spanish involvement is suspected, and war breaks out between America and Spain; the Spanish fleet in Manila Bay is destroyed and the Americans are successful at San Juan and Santiago Bay; peace is made by the treaty of Paris, by which Spain cedes Cuba, Puerto Rico, Guam and the Philippines in return for $20m. Empress Elizabeth of Austria is murdered by an Italian anarchist. Kitchener defeats the Sudanese at Omdurman, retakes Khartoum and advances to Fashoda, where he discovers a French force which is ordered to withdraw after the British government protests to the French.

1899 The First Hague Peace Conference meets. Dreyfus is pardoned by presidential decree after being found guilty again in a second trial prompted by public opinion. Transvaal declares war on Britain; the Orange Free State allies with Transvaal. The Boers besiege Kimberley, Mafeking and Ladysmith and are victorious at Stormberg, Magersfontein and Colenso.

1900 The Boers are victorious at Spion Kop, but Kimberley, Ladysmith and Mafeking are relieved and Bloemfontein, Johannesburg and Pretoria are taken by the British, who annex the Orange Free State and Transvaal. Kruger flees to Germany but is refused an audience by Kaiser Wilhelm II. The Labour Representation Committee is established, with Ramsay MacDonald as secretary. The Boxer Rebellion against foreign influence in China breaks out; the German ambassador is murdered and the foreign legations in Beijing besieged, but are subsequently relieved. The first Zeppelin airship takes to the air. Umberto I of Italy is assassinated by an anarchist; his son Victor Emmanuel III succeeds him.

1901 The Commonwealth of Australia is created. The Boers begin guerrilla warfare against the British. The first British submarine, *Holland I*, is launched. Queen Victoria dies, and is succeeded by her son Edward VII. US President William McKinley is assassinated by an anarchist; Vice-President Theodore Roosevelt succeeds him. The Boxer Rebellion is ended by the Peace of Beijing. The first Nobel Prizes are awarded. Marconi, who is in Newfoundland receives a wireless message from Cornwall.

1902 Britain allies with Japan. St Pierre, Martinique, is destroyed by the eruption of Mount Pelée. The treaty of Vereeniging ends the Boer War with British sovereignty imposed. Trotsky escapes from prison in Siberia and flees to London, where he meets Lenin. The Order of Merit is established.

1903 King Alexander I and Queen Draga of Serbia are assassinated by supporters of the rival Karageorgevich dynasty, whose heir Peter I ascends the throne in their place. The first Tour de France takes place. The Russian Social Democratic Party splits into Mensheviks and Bolsheviks at its London conference. The Wright Brothers perform the first successful powered flight. Newgate is pulled down and replaced by the Central Criminal Court (Old Bailey).

1904 The wireless distress signal CQD is adopted. The Japanese attack the Russians in Port Arthur, setting off war between the two countries; the Japanese are subsequently victorious at Liaoyang. Britain and France ally by the 'Entente Cordiale'. The Rolls-Royce motor company is founded. Vycheslav Plehve, Russian minister of the interior, is assassinated. The British enter Tibet by imposing the treaty of Lhasa; they aim to safeguard it from Russian penetration. The Russian fleet attacks Hull trawlers off the Dogger Bank, mistaking them for Japanese warships; the French mediate between Britain and Russia and the matter is resolved.

1905 Port Arthur surrenders to the Japanese; the resulting protests in St Petersburg are brutally crushed (Bloody Sunday); revolts flare up in Russia as a result, exacerbated by defeats at Mukden and the Tsushima Strait, where the navy is annihilated; the battleship *Potemkin* mutinies; the Russo-Japanese war is ended by the treaty of Portsmouth, a Soviet is established in St Petersburg and Tsar Nicholas II issues a liberal policy (the October Manifesto). Crete revolts against Turkish rule. Kaiser Wilhelm II visits Tangier, where he emphasizes German interests, to the alarm of other countries. Norway separates from Sweden; Prince Charles of Denmark is elected king, taking the name Haakon VII. The Conservative Party splits over tariff reform; Balfour resigns as PM as a result and Campbell-Bannerman replaces him. A failed political plot to remove Campbell-Bannerman is hatched by H. H. Asquith, Sir Edward Grey and R B Haldane at Grey's Scottish retreat of Relugas. Albert Einstein publishes his special theory of relativity. Sinn Fein ('We Ourselves') is established.

1906 The Liberals gain a landslide victory in the General Election. HMS *Dreadnought* is launched in Britain, making all other warships outdated and precipitating a naval arms race. The Algeciras Conference settles the Moroccan question and defuses European tension. San Francisco is hit by a severe earthquake. The Duma meets in Russia, but it is too liberal for the Tsar's liking and is dissolved. As the Tsar's control is re-established over the country, he backtracks on his liberal reforms. Dreyfus is rehabilitated in France and awarded the Légion d'Honneur. South Sinai is ceded to Egypt by the Turks under British pressure. Transvaal and the Orange River colonies are granted self-government.

1907 France and Japan reach agreement on an 'open door' policy in China. The Second Hague Peace Conference meets. Emperor Ko-jong of Korea is forced to abdicate by the Japanese, who establish a protectorate over the country with his son Sun-jong as a figurehead emperor. Britain and Russia reach an entente, forming the Triple Entente with France as a counterweight to the Triple Alliance of Germany, Italy and Austria-Hungary. New Zealand becomes a dominion.

1908 Carlos I of Portugal and his heir are assassinated; his younger son Manuel II succeeds him. The Young Turks revolt at Resina before gaining a majority in the new Ottoman parliament and introducing reforms. The first Ford Model T is sold. Bulgaria declares independence;

Prince Ferdinand assumes the title of Tsar. Austria annexes Bosnia-Herzegovina, to international consternation. Crete declares union with Greece again.

1909 Turkey and Serbia are forced to accept the Austrian annexation of Bosnia-Herzegovina. Sultan Abdul Hamid II is deposed by the Young Turks in favour of his brother Muhammad V. Shah Muhammad Ali of Persia is deposed in favour of his son Ahmad by Ali Kuli Khan. Louis Blériot crosses the English Channel by aeroplane. The House of Lords rejects Lloyd-George's 'People's Budget', causing a constitutional crisis; Asquith calls a general election.

1910 Liberals and Tories tie in a General Election; Asquith's government depends on Labour and Irish Nationalist votes. Premier Boutros Ghali of Egypt is assassinated by a nationalist fanatic, whilst Islamic agitation increases. Edward VII dies, and is succeeded by his son George V, who inherits a constitutional crisis. South Africa becomes a dominion. Japan annexes Korea. Montenegro declares itself a kingdom under Nicholas I. Manuel II of Portugal is deposed by a revolution which declares Portugal a republic headed by Teofilo Braga. A second election produces another hung parliament.

1911 Electric escalators are installed for the first time at Earl's Court Station. Germany sends the gunboat *Panther* to Agadir, creating another international crisis. The Parliament Bill is passed by the Lords, under duress, settling the constitutional crisis. Italy declares war on Turkey as it attempts to invade Tripolitania (Libya). Sun Yat-sen leads a revolution overthrowing the Manchu monarchy in China and establishing a republic, with himself as its first president. The Mexican Civil War is ended by the establishment in power of the revolutionary, Francisco Madero. Roald Amundsen becomes the first man to reach the South Pole.

1912 The *Titanic* sinks on its maiden voyage, with the loss of over 1,500 lives. It becomes the first ship to use the newly adopted SOS distress signal. Emperor Meiji (Mutsuhito) of Japan dies, and is succeeded by his son Yoshihito. The treaty of Lausanne makes peace between Italy and Turkey, and accepts Italy's conquest of Tripolitania. The first Balkan War takes place when Serbia, Montenegro and Bulgaria declare war on Turkey, whose remaining European possessions are overrun.

1913 Greece joins the anti-Turkish alliance in the Balkans. George I of Greece is assassinated; his son Constantine I succeeds him. The great powers force the treaty of London on the combatants, which leaves none of them satisfied. Suffragette Emily Davison throws herself under the king's horse at the Derby. A Second Balkan War, precipitated by Bulgaria, erupts, with Serbia, Greece, Russia and Turkey against the country; this war is resolved by the treaty of Bucharest but tensions still simmer.

1914 Archduke Franz Ferdinand of Austria is assassinated by a Serb extremist in Sarajevo. Austria seeks to punish Serbia, but merely succeeds in dragging most of Europe into World War I. The British Expeditionary Force lands to support the French. Russia invades Germany, but is repulsed at Tannenberg and defeated at the Masurian Lakes. Germany invades Belgium and France, but is held at the Marne. The First battle of Ypres is a bloody draw and the trench system of warfare emerges on the Western Front. The British fleet is defeated by the Germans at Coronel but victorious at the Falkland Islands. Ireland is pushed to the brink of civil war over Home Rule, but the onset of war diverts attention away from the crisis. The Panama Canal opens.

1915 Germany uses poison gas for the first time at the Second battle of Ypres. The British attempt to surprise Turkey at Gallipoli, but are repulsed. German U-boat sinks the *Lusitania*, causing international outrage. Italy is enticed on to the Entente side in the war by the secret treaty of London and attacks Austria, but fails to advance. Edith Cavell is shot after accusations that she helped Allied soldiers escape from Brussels.

1916 The Mexican revolutionary Pancho Villa raids New Mexico. Germany and France fight a bloody draw over Verdun, which remains in French hands. Irish republicans stage the Easter Rising in Dublin, but the coup fails and the leaders are executed. American troops act as peacekeepers in the Dominican Republic. The British and German fleets fight the battle of Jutland, which proves indecisive but the German fleet withdraws to Kiel and remains there. Allied troops mount a major offensive on the Somme, which gains them some ground after 5 months of bloody battle. Emperor Franz Joseph of Austria dies, and is succeeded by his great-nephew Charles I. The Russian monk Rasputin is assassinated by a group of nobles concerned about his influence at court. Einstein publishes his general theory of relativity.

1917 The Orders of the Companions of Honour and of the British Empire are established. America, Cuba and China enter the war on the Allied side. The Allies are victorious at Arras and Passchendaele, although with much loss of life at the latter. Constantine I of Greece abdicates in favour of his son Alexander I. Mata Hari is executed as a spy. The Balfour Declaration over a Jewish homeland in Palestine is issued. Tanks are used for the first time with any effect at Cambrai. Troops mutiny in Russia; the worsening situation prompts Tsar Nicholas II to abdicate in favour of his brother Grand Duke Michael, who refuses the throne and the Tsardom collapses. A provisional government is set up, but fails to manage the war any better. Revolts against it in July are suppressed, as is Brusilov's coup attempt. However, the Bolsheviks succeed in a coup in November, forcing prime minister Kerensky to flee. Lenin is established in power.

1918 In Britain, a Representation of the People Act gives the vote to all men over 21 and all women over 30. Russia withdraws from the war by making the treaty of Brest-Litovsk with Germany; Finland, Poland and the Baltic States are given independence. A coalition of Bolshevik opponents declare war on them, starting civil war in Russia. The Bolsheviks murder the Tsar and his family. A German offensive is successful on the Western Front, but the Allies regroup and push them back, being victorious at the marne and Amiens. Ferdinand I of Bulgaria abdicates in favour of his son Boris III. The Austro-Hungarian Empire collapses; Emperor Charles I abdicates and the Empire becomes several republics. Allied forces remove the Turks from the Middle East. The Czechs declare independence under Tomas Masaryk. The German navy mutinies. Kaiser Wilhelm II abdicates; Germany becomes a republic. An armistice is signed ending action in World War I. The kingdom of Yugoslavia, under Peter I of Serbia, is proclaimed. A Spanish Influenza pandemic begins.

1919 The Eighteenth Amendment is passed, establishing Prohibition in America. The Allies convene in Paris to settle the world map after World War I; the treaties of Versailles with Germany, Saint-Germain with Austria and Neuilly with Bulgaria are imposed. The Bolsheviks establish the Third International. The League of Nations is founded. Alcock and Brown become the first men to fly the Atlantic. The German fleet is scuttled in Scapa Flow. In India, British troops kill 379 demonstrators in the Amritsar Massacre. Austria exiles the Habsburgs.

1920 Irish republicans begin guerrilla war against continued British rule. President Venustiano Carranza of Mexico is assassinated; he is succeeded by Adolfo de la Huerta. The treaties of Trianon with Hungary and Sèvres with Turkey are imposed. The International Court of Justice is established at The Hague. The Little Entente of Czechoslovakia and Yugoslavia (joined next year by Romania) is formed. King Alexander I of Greece dies; his father Constantine I resumes the throne.

1921 The first All-India parliament is opened in Delhi. Reza Khan Pahlevi organises a coup d'etat in Persia. Ex-Emperor Charles fails to regain the Hungarian throne. The Bolsheviks are victors in the Russian Civil War, but the economy is ruined, forcing Lenin to adopt the New Economic Policy. The Allied Reparations Commission levies compensation of £6,650m on Germany. Britain and Irish republicans reach an accord; Northern Ireland is granted its own parliament with Sir James Craig as prime minister. Spanish troops in Morocco are annihilated by Berber rebels, at Anual. Faisal I is elected king of Iraq after a plebiscite. Eduardo Iradier, prime minister of Spain is assassinated by an anarchist. Takashi Hara, prime minister of Japan, is assassinated.

1922 The treaties of Washington establish a Pacific status quo. The Irish Free State is established, but the IRA declares civil war against the government in Dublin and assassinates Prime Minister Michael Collins. The kingdom of Egypt is established under Fuad I. Mustafa Kemal evicts the Greeks from Smyrna. The Arabs in Palestine reject the British mandate. Constantine I of Greece abdicates again, in favour of his son George II. The Conservatives withdraw from the coalition government, bringing down Lloyd George. Bonar Law becomes prime minister. Mussolini leads the Fascists in a March on Rome and succeeds in forming a government. Mustafa Kemal proclaims Turkey a republic; Sultan Muhammad VI is deposed; his cousin Abdul-Majid II maintains the title Caliph. Howard Carter opens Tutankhamun's tomb. The BBC begins its radio broadcasts. The Union of Soviet Socialist Republics (USSR) is formed.

1923 The French occupy the Ruhr after the Germans default on reparations. Prime minister Stamboliski of Bulgaria is removed from office by a coup and shot while trying to escape. The treaty of Lausanne resolves the war between Greece and Turkey. President Warren Harding of America dies in office, and is succeeded by his laconic Vice-President Calvin Coolidge. Germany is hit by hyper-inflation. Primo de Rivera establishes a dictatorship in Spain with the approval of Alfonso XIII. Mustafa Kemal moves the Turkish capital to Ankara. Hitler mounts the 'Beer Hall Putsch'; it fails and he is imprisoned. The Greek army deposes George II.

1924 Venizelos becomes prime minister of Greece. Lenin dies; a triumvirate of Stalin, Kamenev and Zinoviev replaces him in power. After a general election produces a hung parliament, Ramsay MacDonald forms the first Labour government in Britain; he is defeated in a subsequent election, in which the Conservatives are helped by the forged Zinoviev Letter. Kemal abolishes the Caliphate and exiles the Ottomans from Turkey.

1925 Norway renames its capital Oslo and annexes Spitsbergen. Sun Yat-sen dies; Chiang Kai-shek is appointed his replacement by the Guomindang (Chinese Nationalist Party). Hindenburg is elected president of Germany. Hitler sets up the SS (Schutzstaffel) as his personal bodyguard. Reza Khan Pahlavi deposes Shah Ahmad of Persia and ascends the throne himself. The Locarno treaties are signed, guaranteeing the common borders of Belgium, France and Germany, and demilitarizing the Rhineland.

1926 Abdul-Aziz II Ibn Saud of Najd becomes king of the Hijaz. The General Strike, in support of the miners, is called in Britain, but fails to achieve much. Pilsudski stages a coup d'état in Poland. Lebanon is proclaimed a republic. Stalin forces the banishment of Trotsky and Zinoviev from Moscow as he assumes control of Russia. Emperor Yoshihito of Japan dies, and is succeeded by his son Hirohito. John Logie Baird develops television.

1927 Charles Lindbergh makes the first solo flight across the Atlantic. Trotsky is expelled from the Communist Party. Ferdinand I of Romania dies, and is succeeded by his infant nephew Michael.

1928 In Britain, all women receive the vote. The anti-war Kellogg-Briand Pact is signed. Albania becomes a kingdom under Ahmed Bey Zogu, who takes the title Zog I. The first Five Year Plan is outlined by Stalin. Chiang Kai-shek is formally elected president of China.

1929 Alexander I of Yugoslavia suppresses the constitution and proclaims a dictatorship. Italy and the Vatican make the Lateran Treaties, establishing an independent Vatican City. The St Valentine's Day Massacre of gangsters occurs in Chicago. Labour wins a general election for the first time and Ramsay MacDonald returns to office as prime minister. The Wall Street Crash leads to a collapse of share prices and the onset of severe economic depression in America.

1930 France starts work on the Maginot Line of defences. Primo de Rivera resigns office through ill health and dies soon after. Brüning forms a right-wing coalition government in Germany. Haile Selassie becomes king of Abyssinia. Carol II of Romania replaces his young son Michael as King. President Leguia of Peru is forced from office by a military coup. José Uriburu leads a military coup in Argentina. The R101 airship crashes and burns. Getulio Vargas leads a revolution in Brazil and is named President. The Youth Hostels Association is founded.

1931 Oswald Mosley leaves the Labour Party and forms the short-lived New Party. Alfonso XIII of Spain abdicates and leaves the country. The Credit-Anstalt bank of Austria collapses, creating a financial crisis in central Europe. The Invergordon mutiny over pay cuts occurs. Japan occupies Manchuria. MacDonald forms a National Government to deal with the deteriorating economic situation, but the Labour Party mostly splits from him. The Statute of Westminster defines dominion statutes and creates the Commonwealth.

1932 Gandhi is arrested after the Indian National Congress is declared illegal. President Doumer of France is assassinated by a Russian émigré. The Nazis win the German general election, but refuse to serve under President Hindenburg's nominee as Chancellor, Von Papen, who is later forced to resign. Iraq ceases to be a British mandate. Mosley founds the British Union of Fascists. Franklin D Roosevelt defeats President Hoover in a landslide victory in the American presidential elections.

1933 Hitler is appointed German Chancellor. Prohibition is abolished in America. The Reichstag, Germany's parliament, building burns down; Communists are blamed. Chancellor Dollfuss of Austria rules by decree, provoking riots from Austrian Nazis. The first German concentration camps are opened. Hitler takes dictatorial powers; systematic persecution of Jews begins; the Gestapo is founded. Nadir Shah of Afghanistan is assassinated, succeeded by his son Muhammad Zahir Shah.

1934 Hitler purges the Nazi party in the 'Night of the Long Knives'. Austrian Nazis assassinate Dollfuss in a failed putsch; Schuschnigg becomes chancellor. Hitler becomes German president on the death of Hindenburg. The USSR joins the League of Nations. King Alexander of Yugoslavia is assassinated together with the French foreign minister, Louis Barthou, at Marseille by a Croat revolutionary based in Hungary; he is succeeded by his son Peter II. Mao Zedong leads the Chinese Communists on the Long March. Sergei Kirov is assassinated in Leningrad, giving Stalin a pretext to purge the Russian Communists of his opponents.

1935 The Saar is returned to Germany after a plebiscite; Hitler repudiates the Versailles treaty and passes the Nuremberg decrees against Jews. Persia is renamed Iran by order of the Shah. Alcoholics Anonymous is established. Japan withdraws from the League of Nations. Italy invades Abyssinia; the League of Nations imposes sanctions against Italy but the Anglo-French Hoare–Laval plan proposes partial acquiescence in the conquest. George II of Greece returns to his throne. The US creates the Commonwealth of the Philippines, a step towards Filipino independence.

1936 George V dies, his son Edward VIII succeeds him but abdicates in favour of his brother George VI after falling in love with Wallis Simpson. The Japanese army attempts a coup, but fails. Germany reoccupies the Rhineland. King Fuad of Egypt dies, and is succeeded by his son Farouk. Italy completes its conquest of Abyssinia. Spanish generals, led by Franco, revolt against the Republican government; this leads to civil war. Television broadcasts start in Britain. 200 marchers walk from Jarrow to London to protest against unemployment in the North East.

1937 Guernica is destroyed by aircraft of the German Condor Legion assisting Franco's rebels. The Peel Commission on Palestine proposes partition into Arab and Jewish states with a British mandate for Jerusalem and Bethlehem. Amelia Earhart disappears on a Pacific flight. Japan invades China, surprising the Chinese at the Marco Polo Bridge and capturing Beijing, Nanjing, Tianjin and Shanghai; the Chinese government moves to Chongqing. The legitimate Spanish government moves to Barcelona. Italy withdraws from the League of Nations.

1938 Austria is forced to unite with Germany (the Anschluss). Continuing his Great Purge of all potential opposition, Stalin tries and executes former colleagues including Buthasin, Rykor and Yagoda. The Sudeten Germans demand secession from Czechoslovakia; Britain and France appease Hitler at Munich and allow this, to much public disgust. Britain drops the Peel proposals on Palestine, prompting terrorist attacks in the area. Hungary annexes southern Slovakia. The anti-Jewish Kristallnacht takes place in Germany. Kemal Ataturk dies, and is succeeded as Turkish president by Ismet Inonu.

1939 Germany occupies the rump Czech lands and places Slovakia under protection. Franco's insurgents capture Madrid and are victorious in the Spanish Civil War. Italy invades Albania. Hungary and Spain quit the League of Nations. Germany and Russia conclude a non-aggression pact and carve up Poland between themselves. Poland is invaded by the two countries; Britain and France, who have pledged to guarantee Poland, declare war on Germany as a result. A German u-Boat sinks HMS *Royal Oak* in Scapa Flow. Russia invades Finland and the Baltic States and is expelled from the League of Nations. The *Graf Spee* is scuttled after losing the battle of the River Plate.

1940 Finland and Russia make peace. Germany invades Norway, Denmark, Benelux and France. Churchill replaces Chamberlain as prime minister. Allied troops are evacuated at Dunkirk. Italy declares war on Britain and France. The puppet Vichy France is established. The British destroy the French fleet at Mers-el-Kebir to prevent it falling into Vichy hands. The Home Guard is founded. A German aerial assault on Britain is repulsed (the Battle of Britain). Trotsky is assassinated in Mexico, possibly on Stalin's orders. Germany, Italy and Japan form the 'Axis'.

1941 British troops help the Abyssinians expel the Italians; Haile Selassie is restored to his throne. The pro-Nazi Regent Paul of Yugoslavia is deposed; Germany invades the country. Germany invades Russia. Reich Marshal Hermann Göring instructs Reinhard Heydrich, deputy chief of the SS, 'to carry out the final solution of the Jewish question'. Iran is invaded by Britain and Russia; Reza Shah abdicates in favour of his pro-Allied son Muhammad Reza. Mass deportations begin to death camps such as Auschwitz, Chelmno and Treblinka. Japan bombs Pearl Harbor and invades the Philippines; America thereby enters the war. Hong Kong falls to the Japanese.

1942 The Japanese take the Philippines, Dutch East Indies, Singapore and Burma, but lose the naval battles of the Coral Sea and Midway to the Americans. Two Czech resistance men sent from Britain assassinate Reinhard Heydrich; the Nazis burn Lidice as revenge. Rommel, after taking Tobruk, is defeated at El Alamein and forced to retreat across North Africa. The battle of Stalingrad begins.

1943 Churchill, Roosevelt and De Gaulle meet at Casablanca. The Germans surrender at Stalingrad and are driven back West. Guadal canal falls to the US. Allied aircraft destroy a Japanese convoy at the Bismarck Sea. The Warsaw Ghetto is attacked by the Germans, falls after a siege, and survivors are deported to concentration camps. The Allies drive the Germans from North Africa and cross into Sicily and Italy. The Soviets score a major victory at Kursk in the largest-ever tank battle. Mussolini is forced to resign and Badoglio replaces him. Italy signs an armistice with the Allies, but the Germans keep up the fight in the country. Churchill, Stalin and Roosevelt meet at Tehran.

1944 The Allies land at Anzio and take Rome. Leningrad is relieved by the Russians. The Solomon and Marshall Islands fall to the Americans, who defeat the Japanese at the Philippine Sea. The D-Day landings provide the springboard for the reconquest of France. Iceland gains independence from Denmark. Warsaw rises against the Germans. Guam falls to the Americans. The Russians enter Romania, Czechoslovakia, Bulgaria and Hungary. Stauffenberg leads a failed attempt on Hitler's life; Rommel is implicated and forced to commit suicide. The Germans fight back at the battle of the Bulge. North Burma is retaken by the British. Raoul Wallenberg (1912-47), Sweden's special envoy during the Red Army's Siege of Budapest, saved tens of thousands of lives by issuing protective passports to Hungarian Jews.

1945 The Allies enter Germany. The Americans take the Philippines and Okinawa. The League of Arab States is founded. FD Roosevelt dies, and is succeeded as American president by Truman. Mussolini is killed by partisans. Hitler commits suicide. Burma is recaptured by the British. Germany surrenders to the Allies. Churchill, Truman and Stalin meet at Potsdam to consider the future. Attlee replaces Churchill after a Labour landslide at the general election. America drops atomic bombs on Hiroshima and Nagasaki and Japan surrenders. Ho Chi Minh declares Vietnam an independent republic. The United Nations is founded. The Nuremberg trials commence. Peter II of Yugoslavia is deposed by the Communists.

1946 The United Nations convenes in London, as the League of Nations is formally wound up. Jewish terrorism recommences in Palestine. Juan Perón becomes president of Argentina. Mao Zedong proclaims war against the Guomindang regime in China. Victor Emmanuel III of Italy abdicates in favour of his son Umberto II, who is exiled when a referendum votes to abolish the monarchy. Transjordan becomes an independent state under King Abdullah. Bulgaria votes to abolish its monarchy and becomes a communist state. The Fourth Republic is established in France.

1947 The Dead Sea Scrolls are discovered. Mount Hekla erupts in Iceland. The Palestine question is passed to the United Nations for resolution after British partition proposals are rejected there. United Nations partition proposals are rejected by the Arabs. George II of Greece dies, and is succeeded by his brother Paul I. India, Pakistan and Burma become independent states. Michael of Romania is forced to abdicate by the communists.

1948 Gandhi is assassinated by a Hindu fundamentalist. The communists mount a coup in Czechoslovakia. The British leave Palestine once their mandate expires; Ben Gurion proclaims the state of Israel, which is immediately attacked by its Arab neighbours but fights them off. The Russians blockade West Berlin; the Allies respond by an airlift. Apartheid laws are passed in South Africa. Wilhelmina of Holland abdicates in favour of her daughter Juliana. Nehru sends Indian troops to force Hyderabad to join India, and the Nizam gives way under force.

1949 NATO is created. The Republic of Ireland is proclaimed. The Council of Europe is created. West and East Germany are created. Transjordan is renamed Jordan. The Chinese communists drive the Guomindang from China; it takes refuge on Formosa. Mao Zedong becomes the head of state of China. Indonesia is granted independence; Sukarno is elected president.

1950 North Korea invades South Korea, but the United Nations sends troops to defend it; when North Korea is forced to withdraw, China sends troops to assist it. Leopold III of Belgium returns from exile, but decides to abdicate after protests against him. China invades Tibet.

1951 MacArthur is replaced as UN commander in Korea, as the war develops into stalemate. The spies Burgess and Maclean flee to Moscow. King Abdullah of Jordan is assassinated, and is succeeded by his son Talal. Japan is granted independence after military occupation. A general election makes Churchill prime minister again.

1952 George VI dies, and is succeeded by his daughter Elizabeth II. Kenyatta heads the Mau Mau resistance to drive the British from Kenya. General Naguib leads a coup in Egypt; King Farouk is forced to abdicate in favour of his infant son Fa'ad II. King Talal of Jordan is deposed after being declared unfit to rule and is succeeded by his son Hussein. Britain produces an atomic bomb. America develops the H-bomb.

1953 Stalin dies; Malenkov succeeds to his posts; Khrushchev is appointed First Secretary. Hillary and Tensing achieve the first successful ascent of Mount Everest. A republic is proclaimed in Egypt and Naguib is granted dictatorial powers. The combatants in the Korean War sign an armistice at Panmunjon, ending the active war. The Federation of Rhodesia and Nyasaland is established.

1954 The Vietnamese communists defeat the French at Dien Bien Phu and occupy Hanoi. Alfredo Stroessner is elected president of Paraguay on the death of President Lopez. Vietnam is split into two at a conference in Geneva. SEATO is established. Rebellion breaks out in French Algeria. Colonel Nasser seizes power in Egypt from General Naguib. Laos gains independence from France. Britain's Roger Bannister runs the first sub 4-minute mile, at Iffley Road, Oxford.

1955 Malenkov resigns in Russia, and is replaced by Bulganin. Churchill resigns as prime minister, and is replaced by Eden. The Warsaw Pact is established as a communist counterweight to NATO. Austrian independence is restored by the Vienna Treaty. Juan Perón is ousted by a military coup in Argentina.

1956 The first Eurovision Song Contest is won by Switzerland. Sudan and Tunisia become independent republics. Morocco becomes an independent kingdom. Archbishop Makarios and Cypriot Enosis (union with Greece) agitators are deported to the Seychelles. Nasser nationalizes the Suez Canal. Imre Nagy is returned to power in Hungary after demonstrations, but proves too independent for Russia. Israel invades the Sinai, encouraged by Britain and France, who send troops to the Suez Canal to 'protect' it. Under international pressure, they withdraw when UN forces arrive. Russian troops are sent to Hungary; Nagy is seized and executed.

1957 Eden resigns as prime minister after the Suez fiasco, and is succeeded by Harold Macmillan. Ghana is granted independence. The European Economic Community is established by the treaty of Rome. Russia launches Sputnik I, the first space satellite. Mao Zedong decrees the disastrous Great Leap Forward in Chinese agriculture and rural industry.

1958 Egypt and Sudan unite as the United Arab Republic under Nasser. Khrushchev ousts Bulganin as Chairman of the Council of Ministers in Russia and has effective control of the government. The Fourth Republic in France collapses through the ramifications of the Algerian crisis; De Gaulle forms a government, establishes the Fifth Republic and is elected president. General Kassem stages a coup in Iraq, assassinating King Faisal, his son and the premier and taking power.

1959 Fidel Castro ousts President Batista from Cuba and creates a communist state there. The Dalai Lama is forced to flee Tibet as China represses the indigenous population. Mao Zedong resigns as China's head of state in favour of Liu Shaoqi, but remains in power as chairman of the communists. Singapore gains independence under prime minister Lee Kuan Yew. Cyprus is granted independence; Archbishop Makarios is elected president.

1960 The South African police fire on a protest in Sharpeville, killing 69. Gary Powers is shot down over Russia, causing US/Russian tension. Belgium grants independence to the Congo. Mrs Bandaranaike becomes prime minister in Ceylon, the first woman anywhere to hold such a post.

1961 Yuri Gagarin is launched into space in *Vostok 1*. Cuban rebels, assisted by America, land at the Bay of Pigs, but are repulsed by the Cuban army. South Africa leaves the Commonwealth. The Berlin Wall is constructed. UN Secretary-General Dag Hammarskjöld is killed in a plane crash in the Congo; U Thant is elected as his successor.

1962 Algeria is granted independence by France. Former SS administrator Adolf Eichmann is hanged by Israel for war crimes. Russia attempts to send arms to Cuba and establish a missile base there; President Kennedy blockades the island and forces Khrushchev to withdraw; for a few days the spectre of nuclear war looms large.

1963 Kim Philby flees to Moscow after his espionage activities are uncovered. The Profumo crisis develops in Britain, weakening Macmillan's government. Doctor Beeching's report initiates harsh cuts in the British railway system. The nuclear submarine USS *Thresher* sinks. A nuclear test ban treaty is signed by the US, USSR and Britain. Martin Luther King makes his 'I have a dream' speech. Macmillan resigns through ill health, and is replaced by Alec Douglas-Home. A military coup succeeds in South Vietnam. President Kennedy is assassinated; his assumed killer Lee Harvey Oswald is shot dead days later by Jack Ruby.

1964 Fighting breaks out in Cyprus between the Greek and Turkish communities; Greece refuses direct talks while the UN sends peacekeeping troops. King Paul of Greece dies, and is succeeded by his son Constantine II. Ian Smith becomes prime minister of Southern Rhodesia. Nelson Mandela, found guilty in the Rivonia treason trial, is sentenced to life imprisonment. Nyasaland gains independence as Malawi. America escalates operations against North Vietnam. Malta gains independence. Khrushchev is ousted from power in the USSR; Brezhnev and Kosygin take over. Northern Rhodesia becomes independent as Zambia.

1965 Nicolae Ceausescu becomes premier of Romania. In reprisals after a failed communist coup, the Indonesian army kills half a million people. Rhodesia declares independence from Britain; sanctions are imposed on it as an illegal state. General Mobutu takes power in the Belgian Congo in a coup.

1966 Mrs Gandhi becomes prime minister of India. France withdraws from NATO. England win the football World Cup, defeating West Germany 4–2. South African prime minister Hendrik Verwoerd is assassinated, replaced by Vorster. Harold Wilson and Ian Smith discuss the Rhodesia affair on HMS *Tiger*, but the talks come to nothing.

1967 A military coup in Greece removes Constantine II from the throne; he is forced to flee as a counter-coup fails. Arab nations invade Israel, but Israel forces them back and captures Sinai, the West Bank and the Golan Heights in the Six Days War. Colour television begins in Britain. Jerusalem is proclaimed a united city under Israeli rule. General de Gaulle encourages the secession of Quebec whilst on a visit there, causing a diplomatic storm. Che Guevara is captured and shot in Bolivia. South Yemen gains independence.

1968 The communists begin the Tet Offensive in Vietnam. America commits the My Lai Massacre. Martin Luther King and Robert Kennedy are assassinated. Alexander Dubcek comes to power in Czechoslovakia, but his liberalization policies are unpopular in Russia, which sends in troops to re-establish a government more to its liking. Dubcek is arrested. Student riots in Paris destabilise the government, but de Gaulle uses his personal authority to reestablish effective government.

1969 Yasser Arafat is elected chairman of the PLO. General de Gaulle resigns as President of France, and is replaced by Georges Pompidou. America begins to withdraw troops from Vietnam. America lands men on the moon. Civil unrest in Northern Ireland spills over into fighting and terrorism; troops are sent to maintain order. Colonel Gaddafi deposes King Idris of Libya and assumes power.

1970 The Nigerian civil war ends with the capitulation of Biafra. Brazil win the football World Cup with the best team ever according to the popular press. The Portuguese dictator Salazar dies, and is succeeded as premier by Marcello Caetano. King Hussein of Jordan and Pope Paul VI survive assassination attempts. Salvador Allende is elected President of Chile. President Nasser of Egypt dies, and is succeeded by Anwar Sadat. The Japanese novelist Yukio Mishima commits suicide after failing to launch a military coup to purge the disgrace of defeat in 1945.

1971 Idi Amin seizes power in Uganda. The Vietnam war spreads into Laos and Cambodia. Decimal coinage is introduced in Britain. President François Duvalier of Haiti dies, and is succeeded by his son Jean-Claude (Baby Doc). Internment is introduced in Northern Ireland. The Congo is renamed Zaïre by President Mobutu. East Pakistan gains independence as Bangladesh.

1972 The Bloody Sunday shootings take place in Londonderry. President Nixon's visit to China initiates US-Chinese détente. Direct rule is imposed in Northern Ireland. Ceylon becomes the republic of Sri Lanka. The Democratic headquarters in the Watergate building, Washington are burgled; President Nixon is implicated, but is re-elected for a 2nd term. Palestinian terrorists seize and kill Israeli athletes at the Munich Olympics. Idi Amin expels Asians from Uganda.

1973 Britain, Ireland and Denmark join the EEC. A ceasefire is proclaimed in the Vietnam War, but fighting still continues in the area. The Cod War between Britain and Iceland develops. General Pinochet ousts President Allende of Chile in a violent coup, in which Allende perishes. Egypt and Syria attack Israel in the Yom Kippur War, but Israel repulses them. Vice-President Spiro Agnew of America resigns over income tax evasion; Gerald Ford replaces him. Arab oil producers embargo shipments to the West, which supports Israel in the war, causing an energy crisis. A coal strike in Britain forces the government to declare a three-day working week.

1974 After a coup in Portugal, Portuguese Guinea gains independence as Guinea-Bissau. Chancellor Willy Brandt of West Germany resigns when one of his aides is unmasked as an East German spy. Cypriot rebels overthrow Archbishop Makarios; Turkish forces invade Cyprus and occupy much of the north. The military junta in Greece resigns and a civilian government under Karamanlis is restored. President Nixon is forced to resign as a result of the Watergate affair; Gerald Ford replaces him and grants a pardon.

1975 North Vietnam overruns South Vietnam; America withdraws and Vietnam is reunited under a communist leadership. Portugal grants independence to Angola and Mozambique. Eritrean secessionists begin a guerrilla war in Ethiopia. King Faisal of Saudi Arabia is assassinated by his nephew Prince Faisal, who is beheaded for murder; the King's brother Khalid succeeds him. Chiang Kai-Shek dies, and is succeeded as President of Taiwan by Yan Jiangan. The Khmer Rouge declare Year Zero in Cambodia and embark on a programme of mass executions. General Franco dies; the country reverts to a monarchy under Juan Carlos I, grandson of Alfonso XIII.

1976 Chou En-lai and Mao Zedong die in China; the 'Gang of Four' attempt to take over but are arrested. Spain withdraws from Spanish Sahara, which is promptly seized by Morocco; Mauritania also takes a portion. Concorde enters regular passenger service. Harold Wilson resigns as prime minister and is succeeded by James Callaghan. Palestinian terrorists hijack an Air France plance, but Israeli commandos storm it at Entebbe.

1977 President Bante of Ethiopia and 10 aides are killed in a gun battle in a council meeting in Addis Ababa; Colonel Mengistu fills the void. Two Boeing 747s collide on the runway at Tenerife; 577 die. Deng Xiaoping assumes power in China. President Sadat of Egypt visits Israel. Jean Bedel Bokassa crowns himself Emperor of the Central African Empire (Republic) in an extravagant ceremony.

1978 Secessionist rebels, backed by Angola, Cuba and Russia, invade Katanga in Zaïre, but are repulsed with American help. Red Brigade terrorists abduct and kill former Italian premier Aldo Moro. Communists seize control in South Yemen, and assassinate the President of North Yemen. Pope Paul VI dies, as does his successor John Paul I after 33 days; Karol Wojtyla is elected the first non-Italian Pope for 455 years and takes the name John Paul II. The first transatlantic balloon crossing is made. In Nicaragua the Sandinista guerrillas begin a campaign of violence against President Somoza. Israel and Egypt sign the Camp David accords. The Shah of Iran imposes martial law to curb dissent.

1979 The Khmer Rouge are overthrown in Cambodia. The Shah of Iran flees to Egypt and an Islamic fundamentalist regime under Ayatollah Khomeini is established; when the seriously ill Shah is allowed into America, extremists seize the American embassy in Tehran. Former prime minister Bhutto of Pakistan is hanged by the regime of General Zia. Margaret Thatcher comes to power in Britain. Saddam Hussein comes to power in Iraq, replacing Hassan al-Bakr. The Sandinistas overthrow Somoza and establish a junta in Nicaragua. Lord Mountbatten is assassinated by the IRA. Emperor Bokassa is deposed and the Central African Republic restored. Soviet troops enter Afghanistan, supposedly at the request of the government there, igniting civil war.

1980 Zimbabwe gains independence; Robert Mugabe comes to power. Queen Juliana of Holland abdicates in favour of her daughter Beatrix. President Tito of Yugoslavia dies, leaving a power vacuum. The SAS retake the Iranian Embassy, which had been taken by opponents of the Islamic regime. Mount St Helens erupts. The Moscow Olympic Games are boycotted by America and other countries in protest over Afghanistan. Solidarity is formed by shipyard workers in Gdansk. Iran and Iraq go to war.

1981 Ronald Reagan becomes US president. Iran releases the American Embassy hostages. The Space Shuttle makes its maiden space flight. Pope John Paul II is wounded in an assassination attempt in Rome by an extremist Turk. Several attacks on Iranian government officials leave many of the government dead, but it survives. President Sadat of Egypt is assassinated by extremists; Hosni Mubarak replaces him. Jerry Rawlings takes power in Ghana after a coup.

1982 Argentina invades the Falklands, but Britain sends a task force and retakes them; the military junta in Argentina falls as a result of this defeat. Israel withdraws from Sinai, but becomes enmeshed in Lebanon by trying to subdue the PLO's activities there. The Lebanese President Bashir Gemayel is assassinated; his brother Amin succeeds him. Leonid Brezhnev dies; Yuri Andropov replaces him as Soviet leader. The *Mary Rose* is raised.

1983 Benigno Aquino is killed on returning to the Philippines in a government conspiracy to muzzle opposition. The Soviets shoot down a Boeing 747 that had strayed into Soviet airspace off Sakhalin. A coup in Grenada leaves prime minister Maurice Bishop and most of his cabinet dead; America sends troops in to restore order, to some anger in Britain.

1984 Yuri Andropov dies; Konstantin Chernenko replaces him as Soviet leader. Sikh extremists occupy the Golden Temple at Amritsar; over 200 die when Mrs Gandhi sends troops in to clear them. York Minster catches fire shortly after the modernist David Jenkins is enthroned as bishop of Durham. Britain agrees to hand Hong Kong back to China in 1997 on the expiration of the lease on the New Territories. Sikhs in revenge organise the assassination of Mrs Gandhi; her son Rajiv succeeds her as prime minister.

1985 Uruguay returns to civilian rule under President Sanguinetti. Chernenko dies; Mikhail Gorbachev succeeds him as Soviet leader and undertakes policies of openness (Glasnost) and reform (Perestroika). Brazil returns to civilian rule under President José Sarney. Enver Hoxha dies, and is succeeded by Ramiz Alia as President of Albania. A military coup removes Milton Obote from power in Uganda. The army, under General Babangida, takes power in Nigeria. The cruise liner *Achille Lauro* is hijacked by Palestinian guerrillas. RMS *Titanic* is located off Newfoundland.

1986 All 7 crew die when the space shuttle *Challenger* explodes shortly after take-off. President Jean-Claude Duvalier of Haiti resigns and flees to Paris after revolts against his regime. The government of President Marcos of the Philippines falls; Cory Aquino is elected his successor. Prime minister Olof Palme of Sweden is mysteriously assassinated. America bombs Libya in reprisal for Libyan-sponsored terrorist actions. The nuclear power station in Chernobyl, Ukraine, suffers meltdown and explodes. The London Stock Exchange is computerised in the 'big bang'.

1987 Terry Waite is taken hostage in Lebanon whilst seeking to free others. *The Herald of Free Enterprise* capsizes outside Zeebrugge. A great storm crosses southern England, causing much damage. Boris Yeltsin is dismissed in Moscow for complaining at the slow pace of reform. An escalator catches fire at King's Cross; 31 die in the ensuing conflagration. America and Russia sign a nuclear weapons reduction treaty.

1988 The USSR begins withdrawal from Afghanistan. Iran and Iraq end their 8-year war. Iraq gasses dissident Kurds. General Zia of Pakistan is killed in a plane crash. Benazir Bhutto is subsequently elected prime minister of Pakistan. A terrorist bomb brings down a Pan-Am 747 over Lockerbie. USS *Vincennes* mistakenly shoots down an Iranian Airbus.

1989 Emperor Hirohito of Japan dies, and is succeeded by his son, Akihito. Alfredo Stroessner, dictator of Paraguay, is overthrown. General Noriega is defeated in the Panama general elections but ignores the result, causing the Americans to send in troops to remove him. Ayatollah Khomeini dies and Hojatolislam Rafsanjani becomes president of Iran. Communist governments collapse in Poland, Hungary, Czechoslovakia and Romania. The Berlin Wall comes down. President Ceausescu is executed in Romania.

1990 Nelson Mandela is released from prison. Lithuania secedes from the USSR, which sends troops in an attempt to bring it to heel. East and West Germany are reunited. Iraq invades and annexes Kuwait. Sanctions are imposed by the UN, which sends troops to expel Iraq. The premiership of Mrs Thatcher collapses; John Major is elected to replace her.

1991 Somali rebels overthrow President Barre. The UN force expels Iraq from Kuwait, but leaves Saddam Hussein in power in Iraq. Rajiv Gandhi is assassinated by Tamil extremists while campaigning in the Indian general election. Croatia and Slovenia declare independence from Yugoslavia; Serbs and Croats begin a series of ethnic wars. Hard-line Communists attempt to overthrow President Gorbachev, but fail, and communism in Russia collapses. The Baltic states are granted independence. Gorbachev resigns as Russian president and Boris Yeltsin is elected his successor. The USSR dissolves into its constituent parts.

1992 Algerian general elections are declared void when Islamic fundamentalists win; the latter begin a terrorist campaign. The sovereignty of Bosnia-Herzegovina is recognised by the EC and US, but Bosnian Serbs declare independence under Radovan Karadzic, and a vicious civil war develops; 'ethnic cleansing' kills thousands of Albanians and displaces hundreds of thousands. Hindu militants destroy the mosque at Ayodhya.

1993 Czechoslovakia splits into the Czech Republic and Slovakia. Israel and the PLO sign a peace accord. Cultists led by David Koresh kill American government officials at Waco and commit suicide after being besieged. President Premadasa of Sri Lanka is killed by a Tamil terrorist. The Russian communists rebel against President Yeltsin, but the revolt is quelled.

1994 Nelson Mandela is elected President of South Africa. The US invades Haiti. Jordan and Israel sign a peace treaty. Russia invades Chechnya. John Smith dies of a heart attack and Margaret Beckett becomes temporary leader of the Labour Party, before giving way to Tony Blair.

1995 The World Trade Organization is founded. The Russians take the Chechen capital, Grozny; resistance continues elsewhere, but peace is agreed. Prime minister Yitzhak Rabin of Israel is assassinated by a Jewish fanatic; Shimon Peres succeeds him.

1996 Yasser Arafat is elected first president of Palestine. Benjamin Netanyahu defeats Shimon Peres in the Israeli general election; his hardline policies set back the peace process.

1997 Deng Xiaoping dies; Jiang Zemin takes power in China. Hong Kong is passed to China. Diana, Princess of Wales, is killed in a car crash. Labour wins a landslide victory in the general election; Tony Blair becomes prime minister. President Mobutu is overthrown in Zaïre, which the new government renames the Democratic Republic of Congo. The treaty of Amsterdam, providing for further European integration, is signed. Mother Teresa of Calcutta dies in her adopted city, aged 87. Jenny Shipley is sworn in as New Zealand's first woman prime minister. William Hague replaces John Major as leader of the Conservative Party.

1998 Frank Sinatra dies following a long illness. Frenchman Benoit Lecomte becomes the first man to swim the Atlantic; his 3,716-mile swim from Cape Cod to Quiberon, takes 72 days. Gerhard Schröder, the Social Democrat leader, replaces Christian Democrat leader Helmut Kohl as German Chancellor.

1999 Bill Clinton is impeached but cleared of high crimes and misdemeanours. The Australian people vote to 're-elect' the Queen as their Head of State. Cardinal Basil Hume, Archbishop of Westminster dies.

2000 General Augusto Pinochet, who was to stand trial in Britain for human rights violations, is allowed home to Santiago, Chile, following medical opinion that he is not fit enough to face the ordeal. Pope
John Paul II makes an historic visit to the Holy Land and begins it by standing on Mount Nebo in Jordan, the peak from where Moses is said to have seen the Promised Land. The Right Reverend Lord (Donald) Coggan, Archbishop of Canterbury, 1974–80, dies.

2001 North America is subjected to a devastating series of terrorist attacks. American Airlines flight AA11, a Boeing 767 from Boston, is hijacked en route to Los Angeles and crashes into the World Trade Center North Tower at 8.58am (1.58pm BST), killing all 92 on board. United Airlines flight UA175, a Boeing 767 from Boston, is also hijacked en route to Los Angeles and crashes into the World Trade Center South Tower at 9.16am (2.16pm BST), killing all 65 on board. American Airlines flight AA77, a Boeing 757, is hijacked en route from Washington to Los Angeles and crashes into the Pentagon at 9.43am (2.43pm BST), killing 64 on board. United Airlines flight UA93, a Boeing 757 from Newark to San Francisco, targeted on Camp David, crashes at 10.30am (3.30pm BST), 80 miles south-east of Pittsburgh, killing 45 on board. Thousands more are killed in the buildings and on the streets below. The terrorist group al-Qa'ida and its leader Osama bin Laden are thought to be responsible for the atrocities.

2002 Her Majesty Queen Elizabeth the Queen Mother dies, aged 101. Switzerland joins the United Nations. HRH Princess Margaret dies. Ireland adopts the euro as its new currency.

2003 Iain Duncan Smith loses a confidence vote and is forced to resign as leader of the Conservative Party; he is temporarily replaced by Michael Howard.

2004 An underwater earthquake registering 9.0 on the Richter scale devastates the Indian Ocean. The tsunami crashes into the coasts of Sri Lanka, southern India, Indonesia, Thailand and Malaysia, with its epicentre west of Sumatra. The official death toll is 283,106.

2005 Pope John Paul II dies peacefully at the Vatican. The Prince of Wales marries Camilla Parker Bowles in a civil wedding at Windsor's Guildhall. Hurricane Katrina devastates New Orleans and Mississippi, killing thousands. David Cameron defeats David Davis to become leader of the Conservative Party.

2006 Former Iraqi dictator Saddam Hussein is executed for his crimes against humanity.

2007 Benazir Bhutto, the former prime minister of Pakistan, is assassinated on leaving an election rally in Rawalpindi. Tony Blair stands down as prime minister and is replaced by Gordon Brown.

2008 Barack Obama, 47, becomes the first African-American US president.

2009 Two sappers from 38 Regiment Royal Engineers are the first soldiers to be killed in Northern Ireland for 12 years.

2010 An earthquake in Haiti kills an estimated 316,000 people.

2011 An earthquake in New Zealand claims 185 victims and is followed by a superquake in Japan that kills 15,883 people. Al-Qaeda leader Osama bin Laden and Libyan dictator Colonel Muammar Gaddafi are both killed within months of each other.

2012 Bradley Wiggins becomes the first Englishman to win the Tour de France cycle race.

2013 Cardinal Jorge Mario Bergoglio, the archbishop of Buenos Aires, becomes the first non-European to be elected Pope for almost 1,300 years and the first-ever member of the Jesuit order. The bespectacled 76-year-old Argentinian prelate, who became the 266th incumbent, decides to take the name Francis I as his Papal nomenclature. In Egypt, the military remove President Mohamed Morsi from power in a coup d'état and install an interim government. King Albert II, 79, abdicates as King of Belgium and is succeeded by his eldest son Philippe, 53. The Italian-born Paola Ruffo di Calabria is replaced by Countess Mathilde d'Udekem d'Acoz, the first Belgian-born Queen of the Belgians.

NB. The chronology above is a brief cross-section of British and world events of the last two thousand years. Some of the data will inevitably be duplicated in other sections but it is useful to be reminded of the order of events relative to other happenings of the day.

In a book that endeavours to seek the truth it seems incongruous to chronicle prehistorical events which by definition must be open to some doubt, even with all the latest DNA and radiocarbon dating techniques. The approach adopted is to give a brief overview of the order of events that are likely to be of interest to the reader and to chronicle other events, although still open to interpretation, of a more definite nature.

Every schoolchild learns to classify prehistory into Stone Age, Bronze Age and Iron Age but it is very difficult to be pedantic and say when one age started and another ended. In fact, of course the Stone and Bronze ages never really ended anyway. The Paleolithic Period or Old Stone Age is deemed to have commenced over two million years ago with evidence of the use of rudimentary chipped stone tools, probably by a distant relative of modern man. Fossil remains of this precursor of *Homo sapiens* were found at Olduvai Gorge, Tanzania, in 1964 and variously assigned the names *Homo habilis*, *Australopithecus africanus*, or *Australopithecus robustus*, although the latter two names are often applied to an even older relative of modern man thought to have existed millions of years earlier. Fossil remains of Peking Man and Java Man suggested another forerunner of modern man, *Homo erectus*, dated from over a million years ago until 300,000 years ago. From about 300,000 BC other species of early man evolved and were given the general name of *Homo sapiens*. In 1856 the remains of a species of *Homo sapiens* was discovered in the Neander Valley in Germany and dated between 200,000 BC and 30,000 BC. The species of *Homo sapiens* that archaeologists and prehistorians call 'Modern Man' appears to date from circa 38,000 BC. The period from the identification of 'Modern Man' to the end of the Old Stone Age was characterised by the production of Paleolithic cave drawings, the oldest of which, the Chauvet paintings of southeast France, were discovered in 1994 and dated circa 29,000 BC, making them circa 15,000 years older than the Lascaux paintings, Dordogne. This period also saw the beginning of organised tool-making industries beginning with the Aurignacian Culture and developing via the Gravettian (Périgordian), Solutrean, and Magdalenian Culures to the Azilian industry which specialised in microlith tools for catching fish, birds and small mammals as the big game of the last ice age disappeared.

The next classification of prehistory is the Neolithic Period or New Stone Age, characterised by stone tools shaped by polishing or grinding. This period of our history corresponds to the geological Holocene Epoch circa 8,000 BC, the most recent interval of the Earth's geological history. This period also corresponds to the end of the last ice age. In circa 10,400 BC a major climatic warming occurred, the Bolling interstadial, which lasted for approximately 400 years and this was followed by the Allerod interstadial between circa 9,800 BC and circa 9,000 BC. This intermittent global warming became constant in circa 8,000 BC and can be classified as the end of the last ice age, which began around the same time as the emergence of 'Modern Man', and the beginning of the New Stone Age. The first free-standing stone buildings were built during the Neolithic Period, the oldest of which is Cgantija, a temple on the edge of the Xaghra plateau in the middle of the Maltese island of Gozo, circa 3,600 BC. The most recent archaeological find attributed to the Neolithic Period was the ice-man 'Otzi', discovered in the Otzal Alps on the Austrian–Italian border at an altitude of 3,210 metres, in 1991. Modern technology has established 'Otzi's size, looks, apparel and enabled a reconstruction in the Museum of Archaeology in Bolzano, Italy, the country that claimed him. The consensus opinion is that 'Otzi' lived circa 3,300 BC. It is very difficult to approximate the beginning of the Bronze Age as there was a long period of quasi-copper-based tools being produced. This period is referred to as the Chalcolithic (Copper-Stone) Age and even this period was precursed by the use of pure copper in Anatolia by 6,500 BC. The speculative classification of a Bronze Age perhaps can be dated to circa 3,000 BC, when it is established that the Greeks first added tin to copper, although this practice only became widespread a thousand years later. The last technological and cultural period in our classification is the Iron Age, which once again is very difficult to give a definite date of identification as there was a long period of overlapping with the Bronze Age. There is evidence of sparse use of iron in the Middle East as early as 3,000 BC, but it did not replace bronze as a superior metal until circa 1,200 BC.

5508 The year of creation as adopted in Constantinople in 7th century and used by the Eastern Orthodox Church for 1,000 years.
5490 The year of creation as calculated by early Christians in Syria.
4004 James Ussher's 17th-century postulate as being the date of the creation of the universe.
3150 Egypt is united under Menes, the first king of the First Dynasty, and the first prehistoric human whose name we know. Sumerians invent a primitive writing system.
3100 Stonehenge is laid out.
3000 Egyptians pioneer the use of hieroglyphs.
2650 Pyramid of Zoser at Saqqara is built by Imhotep.
2566 The Great Pyramid of Khufu (aka Cheops), at Giza, is built and stands 480 feet high.
2500 A mysterious cult of 'Beaker folk' spreads throughout Europe, warriors being buried with their ornate cups.
2100 In Mesopotamia the first code of law is devised by Ur-Nammu and his son, Shulgi.
1700 Abraham, a prince of Ur, moves to Canaan and founds a religion.
1650 Jewish religion is developed by Abraham's grandson, Jacob.
1349 The young Pharaoh, Tutankhamun, is buried at Thebes.
1237 Ramesses II of Egypt dies and is succeeded by his son Merneptah.
1198 Ramesses III rallies the Egyptians against Mediterranean invaders known as 'Sea Peoples'.
1193 King Priam's city of Troy falls to the Greeks under Agamemnon.
1025 Samuel anoints Saul as king of Hebron.
1012 Saul and his son, Jonathan, are killed at the battle of Mount Gilboa, and succeeded by David.
1005 Jerusalem falls to King David who is anointed King of Judea by Samuel.
1000 The Rig Veda (Hindu hymns) are written.
990 Absalom, 3rd son of King David, kills Amnon in revenge for the rape of his sister, Tamar, and is banished by David.
978 Absalom leads a rebellion but is killed by David's nephew, Joab.
961 David dies and is succeeded by his son, Solomon, who executes Joab for killing Absalom.
922 Solomon is succeeded by his son, Rehoboam, but 10 northern tribes establish Israel, with Jeroboam as king.
850 In Babylon an epic poem 'When on High' is dedicated to the great god, Marduk.
800 The Vedas are written.
776 The first Olympic Games are held in Olympia, Greece.
753 Rome is founded by Romulus and Remus.
750 *Iliad* and *Odyssey* become popular in Greece. Etruscans settle in Tuscany from the Middle East.
722 Israel's capital since 879 BC, the Hill of Samaria, falls to Assyrian forces.
721 The 27,000 Israelites are taken off by the Assyrians and become known as 'The Lost Tribes of Israel'.
658 Byzantium is founded by Greek colonists from Megara.
630 *The Shi Jing* (*Book of Songs*), an early book of Chinese poems is written.
629 King Ashurbanipal of Assyria dies, leaving a library of over 25,000 books.
621 The Athenian lawgiver Draco issues a code of laws that makes almost every offence punishable by death.
597 Jerusalem falls to Nebuchadnezzar II, who exiles Jews in what becomes known as 'The Babylonian Captivity'.
586 The transportation of Judaeans to Babylon, known as the Babylon Exile or Captivity.
582 The first Pythian games are held.
563 Siddhartha Gautama (Buddha) is born.
550 The Temple of Artemis is built at Ephesus in Turkey.
551 Kung Fu-tse (Confucius) is born.
538 Cyrus allows the Jews to return to Jerusalem, thus ending the Babylonian Exile.
528 Buddhism is founded in India.
509 Tarquinius Superbus, King of Rome, is overthrown and Rome becomes a republic.
490 Battle of Marathon gives Athens victory over the Persians.
483 Siddhartha Gavtama (Budda) dies.
480 Battle of Thermopylae gives the Persians, under Xerxes, victory over the Spartans and Thespians, under Leonidas. Battle of Salamis gives the Greeks (400 ships) victory over the Persians (1,000 ships).
456 Aeschylus dies after writing 90 plays, of which only 7 are to survive.
356 The Temple of Artemis, built by Croesus, king of Lydia, is burned by a madman, Herostratus.
354 Mausoleum at Halicarnassus is built.
336 Alexander the Great succeeds his father on the Macedonian throne.
323 Alexander the Great dies, aged 32, in Babylon.
276 First Syrian War begins.
265 Archimedes invents his 'Archimedean Screw' for raising irrigation water.

264 The First Punic War between Rome and Carthage begins.
237 Hamilcar Barca leads a Carthaginian army in an invasion of Spain.
228 Hamilcar Barca is killed and his command in Spain passes to his son-in-law Hasdrubal.
221 Hasdrubal is assassinated and his command passes to Hannibal, the 26-year-old son of Hamilcar Barca.
220 The Flaminian Way between Rome and Rimini is completed.
218 The second Punic War begins.
217 Battle of Lake Trasimene in Umbria gives Hannibal victory over Gaius Flaminius and 16,000 Romans.
216 Battle of Cannae gives Hannibal a resounding victory over the Romans.
190 Battle of Magenta, near Smyrna, gives Rome a victory over Antiochus III of Syria.
183 Hannibal poisons himself.
160 Judas Maccabaeus is killed, his brother, Jonathan is destined to make Judaea a largely independent state.
149 Romans invade North Africa and besiege Carthage.
135 Rome's first Slave War begins.
102 Julius Caesar is born. (It is possible he was born up to 2 years later.)
83 Mark Antony is born.
73 Third Slave War breaks out under the leadership of Spartacus, a Thracian slave. Herod the Great is born.
63 Cicero, a Roman Consul, unmasks a conspiracy led by Catiline, the former governor of Africa.
60 The first Roman Triumvirate is formed by Julius Caesar, Pompey, and Crassus.
55 Julius Caesar's first invasion of Britain.
54 Julius Caesar's second invasion of Britain; Cassivellaunus agrees to pay tribute.
52 Gang warfare in Rome between supporters of Clodius and Milo results in the death of Clodius in a brawl.
49 Julius Caesar leads his legions across the Rubicon into Italy to begin the civil war.
47 Julius Caesar leads his legions across Asia Minor where he defeats Pharnaces III, King of Pontus, near Zela. announcing his victory in the dispatch 'Veni, Vidi, Vici' (I came, I saw, I conquered).
45 Julian calendar introduced by Sosigenes.
44 Julius Caesar is assassinated on the Ides of March.
43 The second Roman Triumvirate is formed by Octavian, Mark Antony, and Marcus Lepidus.
Cicero is beheaded on the orders of Mark Antony.
42 Brutus and Cassius are defeated at Philippi in Macedonia; Cassius orders his shield-bearer to cut his throat, while Brutus runs on to the sword of his friend, Strato.
41 Mark Antony meets Cleopatra at Tarsus and as Julius Caesar had before him, he forms an alliance.
37 Herod the Great becomes King of Judea.
31 Battle of Actium gives victory to Octavian but Cleopatra escapes to Egypt.
30 Mark Antony commits suicide and Cleopatra follows soon after; her son, Caesarion is murdered. Egypt becomes a Roman province.
27 Augustus becomes the first Roman Emperor after changing his name from Octavian.

Modern History

Agent Orange Notorious herbicide used by the US military machine in Vietnam in the 1960s and 1970s; its active ingredient 245-T was also used in weedkillers and caused devastation.

A6 Murder Michael Gregsten and Valerie Storie were shot in their car in a lay-by off the A6 between Luton and Bedford in August 1961. Storie, who survived the shooting, picked out James Hanratty at an identity parade, which led to his hanging in April 1962. Journalist Paul Foot has campaigned on behalf of Hanratty pointing out that Peter Alphon confessed to the murder.

Balfour Declaration A milestone on the way to establishing the state of Israel. Arthur Balfour the former Conservative PM, served as foreign secretary in 1916–19, and in November 1917 wrote to Lord Rothschild, leader of the British Jewish community, to the effect that Britain favoured a national home for the Jewish people provided that it did not prejudice the civil and religious rights of existing non-Jewish communities in Palestine.

Barlow Clowes Fraudulent investment company, details of which came to light in 1988. Elizabeth Barlow disappeared but Peter Clowes was sentenced to 10 years imprisonment in 1992. The government at first refused to pay compensation, but the Ombudsman found maladministration by the Department of Trade and Industry so £150 m was provided.

Beveridge Report Report laying down the framework for the development of the Welfare State. Published in 1942 and accepted by the coalition government in 1944, it became operational in 1948.

Big Bang Transformation of the London Stock Exchange in October 1986 which reflected the advent of global stock and bond trading networks and of round-the-clock trading. It also abolished the different categories of stockbrokers and jobbers.

Birmingham Six Patrick Hill, Richard McIlkenny, John Walker, William Power, Gerard Hunter and Hugh Callaghan wrongly imprisoned for IRA activities following the bombing of 2 public houses in Birmingham in November 1974. Their convictions were quashed in the Appeal Court in March 1991.

Bloody Sunday A day of serious conflict in the Bogside area of Londonderry on 30 January 1972 when the security forces opened fire on a civil rights march, killing 13 civilians.

Blue Streak British rocket which in the 1950s was expected to provide a nuclear delivery capability independent of US technological expertise; abandoned in 1960 in favour of the US Skybolt missile.

Bridgewater Four Michael and Vincent Hickey, James Robinson and Patrick Molloy were convicted of killing newspaper delivery boy Carl Bridgewater at Yew Tree Farm in Staffordshire, largely because of a confession made by Molloy, who died in prison in 1981. The remaining 3 were released on 20 February 1997 after evidence of police corruption.

Chiltern Hundreds British MPs cannot resign directly, but they may not hold an office of profit under the crown. The solution is to apply for the stewardship of various crown sinecures, of which the Chiltern Hundreds is the best-known.

Citizens' Charter Government charter instigated by John Major in 1991 with the intention of improving standards of public services in the UK.

Cod War A series of disputes between UK and Iceland in the 1960s over fishing rights.

Cuban Missile Crisis US hostility towards the Cuban revolution, together with Castro's open espousal of communism, had brought Cuba into a close relationship with USSR. Following the US-sponsored Bay of Pigs invasion, Castro requested Soviet atomic weaponry to improve their defences. When US reconnaissance spotted missile sites being built, President Kennedy declared a blockade, on 22 October 1961. For several days a confrontation of superpowers appeared likely, but the Russians backed off, and the blockade ended on 20 November.

Dikko Affair UK customs found the exiled Nigerian politician Umari Dikko drugged in a crate at Stansted airport in July 1984. Three Israelis and a Nigerian diplomat concealed in another crate were charged with kidnapping and administering drugs.

Doomsday Clock Picture of a clock, the hands of which indicate the time estimated to remain before nuclear war (midnight), which has been printed in every issue of the *Bulletin of Atomic Scientists* since its founding in 1945. It stood at 11.58 during the cold war but was put back to 11.50 in 1989.

Echo 1 First US communications satellite; a large aluminium-coated balloon that reflected radio signals. Launched on 12 August 1960 by NASA as part of the US effort to close the satellite telecommunications lead achieved by the USSR with the Sputnik.

Elgin Marbles Sculptures from the Parthenon obtained cheaply from the occupying Turks by the British Ambassador Lord Elgin in 1801 and later sold to the British Museum. The continuing Greek campaign for their return was spearheaded by Melina Mercouri as Minister for Culture and the injustice is often highlighted by the well-known television producer and quiz show host, William G Stewart.

Fourth Estate Term used in modern times to describe the power of the press. The Middle Ages divided society into 3 estates: nobility, church and commons.

Fourth Man Anthony Blunt was given this epithet when revealed as a spy in 1979 following the defections to the USSR of the spies Burgess and Maclean in 1951 and Kim Philby in 1963.

Gaza Strip A 146-sq-mile area of land bordered by the Mediterranean, Israel and Egypt, captured by Israel from Egypt during the Six-Day War of 1967 and inhabited by 700,000 people, mostly stateless Palestinians living in refugee camps.

General Strike Staged by the TUC from 3 to 13 May 1926 in an unsuccessful attempt to support coalminers. The strike provoked retaliatory legislation against trade unions.

Geneva Summit 1985 First of a series of bilateral superpower summit meetings held in the later 1980s involving Mikhail Gorbachev and Ronald Reagan (followed by George Bush).

Golan Heights Range of strategic hills in south-west Syria overlooking northern Israel, captured by Israel from Syria in the Six-Day War of 1967.

Gold Standard Economic system in which a country's paper currency is supported by gold, anyone having the right to demand from the national bank the same amount of gold as the face value of a banknote. Britain was on the gold standard from 1821 to 1914, partly returned to it in 1925 as a result of Churchill's wishes, but finally abandoned it in 1931 under the chancellorship of Philip Snowden.

Great Leap Forward Campaign undertaken by Mao Zedong between 1957 and 1960 to organise China's vast population into large-scale rural communes and local manufacturing units, to meet the country's economic problems.

Guildford Four Patrick Armstrong, Gerard Conlon, Carole Richardson and Paul Hill were sentenced to life imprisonment in 1975 for the murder of 7 people in 1974 after the bombing of 2 public houses in Guildford and 1 in Woolwich. They were released on appeal in 1989 after police evidence was found to be misleading.

Herald of Free Enterprise British car ferry owned by Townsend Thoresen which overturned and sank off the Belgian port of Zeebrugge on 6 March 1987 with the loss of 193 lives after the bow doors were left open.

Heysel Stadium Disaster Death of 39 Belgian and Italian spectators on 29 May 1985 at the final of the European Cup football competition between Liverpool and Juventus in Belgium's Heysel Stadium when visiting British fans caused a wall and safety barriers to collapse.

Hiroshima Southern Japanese city destroyed on 6 August 1945 by the first atomic bomb, nicknamed Little Boy and dropped from the US B-29 bomber *Enola Gay*.

Hiss Case Legal case which typified US anti-communist paranoia. On 29 January 1950 Alger Hiss, accused by Whittaker Chambers of being a communist during the 1930s while working for the US State Department, was given a 5-year prison term.

Ho Chi Minh Trail Network of concealed tracks through eastern Laos developed during the early stages of the Vietnam War as a supply route for North Vietnamese and Viet Cong forces in South Vietnam.

Holt Drowning Disappearance and presumed death of Australian PM and Liberal Party leader Harold Holt while swimming at Portsea near Melbourne on 17 December 1967.

Human Shield After Iraq's occupation of Kuwait in August 1990 Saddam Hussein used Western nationals captured there as a defence against possible action by the opposing coalition forces during operation Desert Shield.

100 Flowers Bloom Political slogan adopted by Mao Zedong (Mao Tse-tung) in 1956 and launched as a movement in February 1957 to allow more free speech in Communist China. The high level of strikes that followed caused Mao to retract his original statement and suggested that the campaign was a means of identifying reactionary elements.

Hungarian Uprising Popular uprising against Soviet domination in 1956 when after 4 days of demonstrations in Budapest, on 24 October the former communist PM, Imre Nagy, formed a revolutionary multi-party government and proclaimed Hungary's withdrawal from the Warsaw Pact. The Soviet Union crushed the uprising and Janos Kadar took over as head of a pro-Soviet regime and supervised the normalisation policy. Nagy was executed by the new government in 1958.

Hutton Report In September 2002 the Government published a dossier about alleged Iraqi weapons of mass destruction, including claims they could be deployed within 45 minutes. In May 2003 the BBC *Today* programme's Andrew Gilligan claimed Downing Street 'sexed up' the dossier. On 17 July 2003 Dr David Kelly, the Government scientist at the centre of the controversy, was found dead in an Oxfordshire wood. In August 2003 Lord Hutton began six weeks of hearings about the circumstances around Dr Kelly's death. In January 2004 the Hutton Report found that Dr Kelly had killed himself. It fully exonerated the Government but was scathing in its criticism of the BBC. Gavyn Davies, Chairman of Governors of the BBC, resigned in the wake of Lord Hutton's report.

In Place of Strife Document published by the Labour government of the UK on 17 January 1969 setting out its policy for controlling industrial relations through legal sanctions.

Intifada (Arabic: 'shaking off') Palestinian mass popular uprising in the Gaza Strip and West Bank which started in December 1987 with demonstrations, strikes and violent confrontation between Palestinian youths and Israeli occupying forces. Israel responded with an iron-fist approach which included beatings and deportations.

Iranian Embassy Siege Storming of the Iranian embassy in London by the SAS after it was seized on 30 April 1980 by Iranian dissidents seeking to draw attention to the plight of the Arab minority in Iran and demanding the release of 91 of their comrades imprisoned in Khuzestan.

Iron Curtain Frontier dividing the Eastern Europe of the communist bloc from the capitalist West. Winston Churchill popularised the phrase, using it in a 1946 speech at Westminster College, Fulton, Missouri when he said: 'From Stettin in the Baltic to Trieste in the Adriatic, an iron curtain has descended across the continent'. Joseph Goebbels has been credited with inventing the term.

ITT Scandal Scandal involving the activities of International Telephone and Telegraph in the USA and overseas. The scandal broke in 1972 when a plan to nationalise the Chilean Telephone Company (Chitelco) was sabotaged; ITT's collusion with the CIA culminated in the 1973 coup which overthrew the Allende government.

JAL Air Disaster World's worst air crash involving a single aircraft: a Boeing 747 on a Japan Airlines flight from Tokyo to Osaka crashed in mountainous terrain near Tokyo on 12 August 1985 and killed 520 of the 524 passengers and crew.

Jamahiriya Term coined by Colonel Gaddafi, who in 1977 changed the name of Libya to 'Socialist People's Libyan Arab Jamahiriya'. The word means 'State of the masses'.

Jonestown Massacre Mass death of 913 children, men and women at Jonestown, in the Guyana jungle, on 29 November 1978. The Rev. Jim Jones, founder of the People's Temple in Indianapolis in 1957, had set up a commune in Guyana in 1977. After murdering investigators, he led and apparently enforced a mass suicide using cyanide.

Khaki Election General election of October 1900, called by Salisbury's Conservative-Unionist government, and named after the new khaki uniform worn by the British army in the Boer war.

Korean War War in 1950–3 between communist North Korea (supported by the USSR and China) and South Korea (supported by the USA and UN).

Lame-Duck President Term used to describe an outgoing US president between the elections in November and the beginning of the new president's term on 20 January the following year.

Lancaster House Agreement UK Foreign and Commonwealth Secretary Lord Carrington brokered this agreement which ended UDI and heralded the independence of Zimbabwe. It was signed on 21 December 1979 by former Rhodesian leader Ian Smith, PM Bishop Abel Muzorewa, Robert Mugabe and Joshua Nkomo, as well as by Carrington and Sir Ian Gilmour representing the British delegation. Lord Soames became governor during the transitional period.

LDC Least Developed Country, a category used by the UN to describe many of its poorer member states. According to UN estimates, over 500 million people lived in LDCs in 1990.

Limehouse Declaration Political statement issued on 25 January 1981 by four senior members of the British Labour Party, Roy Jenkins, David Owen, William Rodgers and Shirley Williams, who became popularly known as the gang of four, effectively launching the Social Democratic Party (SDP).

Lockerbie Scottish town on which a Pan Am airliner PA103 en route from London to New York crashed after a mid-air explosion on 21 December 1988, killing all 259 passengers and crew as well as 11 townspeople. Two Libyans went on trial in Holland in 2000, accused of organising the bombing. Abdelbaset Ali Mohamed Al Megrahi was found guilty and sentenced to life but Al Amin Khalifa Fhimah was freed due to lack of evidence.

Lockheed Scandal Political scandal which emerged in Japan in 1976, involving the acceptance of bribes by Kakuei Tanaka, PM 1972–4, from the Lockheed Aircraft Corporation.

Long March The 6,000-mile journey undertaken in 1934–5 by forces of the Chinese Communist Party from Jiangxi province to Yan'an in north Shaanxi to avoid encirclement by the forces of the nationalist Guomindang.

Los Angeles Riots Major disturbances which occurred in LA between 29 April and 4 May 1992 involving widespread destruction and ethnic violence that brought 58 deaths. The riots were sparked off when an all-white jury acquitted 4 white police officers who had been filmed beating black motorist Rodney King in March 1991.

Maastricht Netherlands town where the 12 EU member states met in December 1991 for the summit that concluded the treaty on European Union. They returned on 7 Feb 1992 for the formal signing of what became the Maastricht Treaty, which was an accord on European political union and on EMU (European Monetary Union).

MAD Mutually Assured Destruction, which would result from a full-scale nuclear war between the superpowers according to the theorists of deterrence by the 'balance of terror'.

Markov Affair Controversy associated with the death in London on 15 September 1978 of Georgi Markov, a Bulgarian journalist employed by the BBC World Service, who was injected with the poison ricin from a specially adapted umbrella by an agent of the Bulgarian security service.

Marshall Plan Plan to assist the economic recovery of post-war Europe, proposed by US Secretary of State George Marshall in June 1947. The scheme offered US funding to European countries (eventually over $12 billion) if they co-operated with each other in drafting recovery programmes.

Mason-Dixon Line Boundary between the US states of Maryland and Pennsylvania which marks the border between former slave states of the south and northern states where slavery was illegal.

McCarthyism Anti-communist hysteria endemic in the USA in the early 1950s, built upon a foundation established by the House Committee on Un-American Activities. Senator Joseph McCarthy of Wisconsin made a speech in Wheeling, West Virginia, in February 1952 which began the series of anti-communist witch hunts.

Messina Conference June 1955 meeting between the foreign ministers of Belgium, France, Italy, Luxembourg, Netherlands and West Germany which led to the Rome Treaty of March 1957.

Mildenhall Treasure Hoard of Roman silver of the 4th century AD, discovered during ploughing in Suffolk in 1942. The main item of value is the 'Great Dish'.

Montgomery Bus Boycott Year-long boycott of the public transport system in Montgomery, Alabama, which provided a key early victory for the US civil rights movement. It began on 5 December 1955, after a black woman, Rosa Parks, was arrested for refusing to give up her seat on a bus to a white passenger.

Montreal Protocol Agreement signed in September 1987 by 24 countries which undertook to halve their CFC production by 1999. The protocol aims to reduce damage to the ozone layer.

Moro Affair Circumstances surrounding the kidnapping on 16 March 1978 of Aldo Moro, president of the Italian Christian Democratic Party, by the left-wing Brigate Rosse, and his assassination on 9 May after the government refused to meet the kidnappers' demands.

Nagasaki Target city on 9 August 1945 of the second atomic bomb which caused the Japanese surrender in World War II.

Normalisation Sinister name for the programme aimed at stabilising communist rule in Czechoslovakia after the suppression of the 1968 Prague Spring. Under Gustav Husak, Normalisation featured a purge of tens of thousands of politically unreliable professionals and communist party members as well as an end to freedom of speech.

Orange Revolution Series of protests in Ukraine between November 2004 and January 2005, following accusations that the run-off vote for the presidential election between Viktor Yushchenko and Viktor Yanukovych was rigged by the authorities in favour of the latter. After a revote was ordered by Ukraine's Supreme Court, Yushchenko was declared the winner. Ironically, Yanukovych succeeded Yushchenko in 2010.

Pairing Convention whereby pairs of MPs, one each from the government and opposition sides, agree that if one is unable to be present to vote, the other will abstain.

Peacock Throne Metaphor for the pre-1979 Iranian monarchy and a reference to the throne used by the two Pahlavi shahs at their coronations. The original Peacock Throne was stolen by the Iranian conqueror Nadir Shah during a raid on the Mughal bastion, the Red Fort, in Delhi in 1793.

Perestroika Restructuring, slogan adopted by Soviet leader Mikhail Gorbachev in late 1986 to denote his policies of pragmatic reform.

***Pieds Noirs* (Black Feet)** Term used to describe white French settlers resident in France's North African colonies, especially Algeria, and who returned to France after decolonisation in the 1960s.

Ponting Affair Trial and acquittal of Clive Ponting in the UK in 1985 under the 1911 Official Secrets Act. Ponting, a high-flying civil servant in the MOD, was accused of leaking classified information to Labour MP Tam Dalyell, relating to the sinking of the Argentinian cruiser *Belgrano* during the 1982 Falklands War.

Potsdam Conference held from 17 July to 2 August 1945 between the USSR, UK and USA, the Big Three allied powers of World War II, to decide the treatment of defeated Germany.

Poulson Affair The events leading to the resignation on 18 July 1972 of Reginald Maudling as home secretary in the UK Conservative Cabinet. John Poulson was an architect who built up a major international practice in the 1960s and increased his standing through contacts with influential politicians. By the early 1970s he faced bankruptcy and was subsequently charged with corruption relating to bribes given to national and local politicians aimed at winning contracts. Poulson was sentenced to 7 years whilst Maudling, who had been chaiman of the Poulson company, resigned.

Prague Spring In January 1968, the newly elected First Secretary of the Communist Party of Czechoslovakia, Alexander Dubček attempted to decentralise administrative authority and loosen restrictions on the media, speech and travel. This continued until 21 August when the Soviet Union and all members of the Warsaw Pact, with the notable exception of Romania, invaded the country to halt the reforms. Jan Palach, 20, a Czech student of history and political economy at Charles University, committed suicide by self-immolation as a political protest against the end of the Prague Spring in January 1969. See also Normalisation and Velvet Revolution.

Profumo Affair Scandal leading to the resignation in 1963 of John Profumo as secretary of state for war in the UK Conservative Cabinet. Profumo had formed a liaison with Christine Keeler, who simultaneously was having a relationship with a Soviet military attaché in London, Eugene Ivanov.

Rivers of Blood Controversial speech made by UK Conservative MP Enoch Powell on 20 April 1968 in which he warned of what he saw as the social and economic consequences of continued immigration into the UK of black people from the Commonwealth. Powell compared himself to a Roman in Virgil's Aeneid who had a vision of the River Tiber foaming with blood.

Roe v Wade The landmark 1973 Supreme Court decision which made abortion legal in the USA.

Rosenbergs US couple, Julius and Ethel, who were executed in Sing Sing prison in 1953 for having allegedly supplied the Soviet Union with atomic bomb secrets.

San Francisco Conference International conference held April–June 1945 after which participants signed the UN charter. The conference was attended by 47 fully independent states as well as Byelorussia and Ukraine, which were Soviet constituents, and India and the Philippines, which had not at that stage achieved full independence.

Scarman Report Serious racial disturbances in South-East London in April 1981 led to Lord Scarman carrying out a thorough public inquiry, whose findings were published in November.

Schuman Plan Proposal advanced by French foreign minister Robert Schuman on 9 May 1950 which formed the European Coal and Steel Community.

Seles stabbing Tennis player Monica Seles was stabbed by a crazed fan of her rival, Steffi Graf, during a match in Hamburg on 30 April 1993.

Sellafield Site on the west coast of England, in Cumbria, run by British Nuclear Fuels. The first nuclear power station opened here, at Calder Hall, in 1956. At that time the area was known as Windscale, but on 10 October 1957 an atomic pile overheated, causing a near-catastrophe and some long-term fatalities. To protect the image of the industry the name of the site was changed.

Sharpeville Massacre In this South African township 50 miles from Johannesburg on 21 March 1960 the police killed 69 peaceful demonstrators protesting against the Pass Laws. The UN subsequently called for the abandonment of apartheid.

Six-Day War Threatened by a build-up of hostile Arab forces, between 5 and 10 July 1967 Israel attacked Egypt, Jordan and Syria and occupied the Sinai peninsula, the Gaza Strip, East Jerusalem, the West Bank and the Golan Heights, before declaring a ceasefire.

Social Contract Informal agreement between the UK Labour government and the TUC in the mid-1970s aiming to balance wage restraint against a loosening of legal restrictions on trade unions.

Spin Doctor In politics, a public relations expert working behind the scenes to have the media interpret events from the viewpoint favoured by a particular individual, faction of party.

Stockholm Syndrome Psychological condition in which hostages grow to empathise with their captors' political or personal convictions. The term derives from a bank robbery in Stockholm in 1973 when several people taken as hostages lent their support to the robbers.

Suez Crisis Middle East crisis precipitated by the nationalisation of the mainly British and French-owned Suez Canal by Egyptian President Gamal Abdel Nasser on 26 July 1956. Nasser acted after the USA had reneged on a commitment to help finance the construction of the Aswan High Dam. Israel invaded on 29 October; acting in collusion, French and British forces intervened a week later, under guise of keeping the peace. By March 1957, all 3 had withdrawn under strong UN pressure.

Sutton Hoo Ship Burial Anglo-Saxon treasure unearthed in 1939 at Sutton Hoo in Suffolk and believed to have been the tomb of an Anglo-Saxon king buried about 625, possibly Raedwald. Mrs Pretty, who owned the land and hence the treasure, kindly donated the find to the British Museum.

TD Gaelic for Teachta Dála, a member of the Irish Dáil or lower house of parliament.

Territorial Waters The offshore area in which a coastal state claims sovereign jurisdiction, save for the customary rights of freedom of navigation for merchant shipping. At present 12 miles is the accepted boundary of territorial waters, with a few exceptions, mostly in Africa and Central and South America.

Third Man Kim Philby, a UK journalist and former intelligence officer who defected to the Soviet Union in January 1963, was given this epithet after the earlier defections of Guy Burgess and Donald Maclean in 1951.

***Tiger* Talks** Negotiations held aboard HMS *Tiger* off Gibraltar on 2–4 December 1966 between Harold Wilson and Ian Smith, which failed to end Rhodesian UDI.

Trident Multiple-warhead submarine-launched nuclear missile with a range of 4,500 miles, introduced in 1979 by the US Navy in refitted Poseidon submarines, and in larger *Ohio*-class submarines first delivered in 1981. A more powerful Trident 2 missile was introduced in 1990.

Union Carbide Disaster In December 1984 a leak of toxic gas from Union Carbide pesticide plant near Bhopal, India, killed 2,500 and injured 200,000.

Vatican II The 2nd Vatican Council (the first was in 1869-70), which met in 4 sessions between 11 October 1962 and 8 December 1965. Launched by Pope John XXIII, it was concluded by his successor Pope Paul VI. Vatican II was the 21st Ecumenical Council in the history of the Roman Catholic Church and brought a reformist, liberalising outlook to existing dogma.

Velvet Revolution Term coined by Czech economist and politician Rita Klímová for the non-violent demonstrations that took place in November and December 1989 against the single-party government of the Communist Party of Czechoslovakia, which ultimately saw its collapse and the subsequent conversion to a parliamentary republic. Czech playwright Václav Havel became the last president of Czechoslovakia (1989–1992) and the first president of the Czech Republic (1993–2003). Slovakians refer to the uprising as the 'Gentle Revolution'. See also Prague Spring.

Vietnam War The 1954–75 war between North and South Vietnam, the latter assisted from 1961 by the USA. The war resulted in victory for the North and the union of the two Vietnams in 1976.

Vincennes On 3 July 1988 the US warship *Vincennes*, serving in the Persian Gulf, mistook an Iran Air A3000 Airbus for an attacking bomber and shot it down, costing 290 civilian lives.

Waco Siege A 51-day siege of the HQ of the Branch Davidian religious cult near Waco, Texas, began on 28 February 1993 and ended on 19 April when the FBI stormed the compound and fire broke out, killing its leader David Koresh and 70 of its members.

Warnock Report UK report published in July 1984 on bio-ethics as well as the social and legal implications of recent and potential developments in the field of human-assisted reproduction. Chaired by Dame Mary Warnock, the committee recommended that certain forms of infertility treatment should be viewed as ethically acceptable.

Warren Commission Chaired by the head of the US Supreme Court, Chief Justice Earl Warren, the Commission investigated circumstances surrounding the assassination of President JF Kennedy in Dallas on 22 November 1963. The Commission's report concluded on 22 September 1964 that Lee Harvey Oswald had been solely responsible for the killing.

West Bank Territory of Palestine west of the River Jordan, claimed from 1949 to 1988 as part of Jordan, but occupied by Israel since the Six-Day War of 1967. The territory, excluding East Jerusalem, is widely referred to within Israel by its biblical names, Judea and Samaria, and is considered part of Eretz Israel. In September 1993 Israeli forces withdrew from the West Bank but the territory is still disputed by many Israelis.

Winter of Discontent Time of industrial unrest in the UK over the severe winter of 1978–9.

Wolfenden Report Report of the UK Committee on Homosexual Offences and Prostitution, chaired by Sir John Wolfenden, which recommended in particular the decriminalisation of homosexual acts between consenting adult males and an increase in penalties for soliciting by prostitutes. The landmark report published on 4 September 1957 led to the Street Offences Act of 1959 and to the Sexual Offences Act of 1967.

Year Zero Slogan adopted by the Khmer Rouge to denote the start of their 4-year period of rule in Cambodia in April 1975.

Yom Kippur War On 6 October 1973 Syria and Egypt mounted a surprise attack on Israel as it observed Yom Kippur (the Jewish Day of Atonement), aiming to regain territory lost during the Six-Day War of 1967. Although Israel was caught off guard initially, by 24 October the Israelis were advancing on Cairo and Damascus and a ceasefire was declared, restoring the status quo.

Zeebrugge Disaster see *Herald of Free Enterprise*.

Language

Derivation of Popular Phrases

Phrase	*Meaning*	*Derivation*
A1	the highest quality	Lloyd's Register of Shipping use an alphanumeric code in classifying ships for insurance purposes. The state of a ship's hull is designated by letters and that of the anchors, cables and other moveable parts by figures. A1 therefore denotes vessels of the highest quality.
above board	honest and open	Phrase which originated in the gaming community. If card players kept their hands above the table (board) they could be seen to be playing fairly.
according to Hoyle	according to the highest authority in a particular field	English writer Edmond Hoyle (1672–1769) wrote books on the rules and customs of backgammon (1743) and chess (1761), but was best known for his definitive treatise on whist (1742) and it is from this that the phrase derives.
Aga saga	a type of popular novel set in middle England, populated by the middle classes	Phrase coined in the 1990s, referring to novels about the lives of people who have a high standard of living and live in the English countryside; the type indeed that might own Aga cookers. The works of Joanna Trollope are often spoken of as Aga sagas. Contrast **kitchen sink**.
argy-bargy	wrangle or verbal dispute	Corruption of a Scottish dialect phrase *argle-bargle*, first recorded in 1887. It is itself a composite word deriving from 'argue' and 'haggle'.
back to square one	back to the beginning	Phrase thought to have derived from early BBC radio broadcasts of football. Lance Sieveking, the producer of the first broadcast on 22 January 1927, used a grid system of eight numbered squares to explain to listeners where the action was taking place on the pitch. The squares were designated square one and two, defence, square three, four, five and six, midfield, square seven and eight, attack. A thwarted attack and punt downfield may well have been referred to as 'back to square one' during these commentaries.
baker's dozen	thirteen	In the Middle Ages in England there were severe penalties for anyone who gave short weight. Bakers were often uneducated and unable to count. To guard against miscounting 12 as 11 they habitually gave 13 loaves when selling a dozen. The 13th loaf was known as the 'vantage loaf'.
balaclava	close-fitting woollen hood that covers the head and neck	Named after Balaclava, the Black Sea port on the Crimea made famous by the battle that took place there (25 October 1854).
bandy words	to argue fervently	Bandy is a ferocious Irish game in which the ball is played to and fro with sticks. In John Webster's *The White Devil* (1612), the term was applied to tennis, at that date probably real tennis: 'He had been bandying at tennis'.
barmy army	a raucous and undisciplined group	Coined in the UK and most often used as an ironic nickname for the travelling supporters of the English cricket team. Barmy, or balmy, means crazy; barm is the froth made by fermenting yeast. Barmy people are those that froth at the mouth, like rabid dogs.
battle royal	a fierce contest	Phrase derived from cockfighting contests, where 16 birds were often engaged in fights to the death, the surviving eight then contesting the quarter-finals and so on until only one bird remained.
bed of roses, a	a situation of ease and pleasure	First mention of this phrase was in the third verse of Christopher Marlowe's poem 'The Passionate Shepherd To His Love' (1599): 'There will I make thee beds of roses And a thousand fragrant posies'.
bee in your bonnet, to have a	to be preoccupied or obsessed with an idea	Phrase became popular after a verse in Robert Herrick's poem 'Mad Maid's Song' (1648): 'For pity, sir, find out that bee Which bore my love away. I'll seek him in your bonnet brave'.
bee's knees, the	excellent – the highest quality	Phrase first coined in America in 1922 and which is merely a catchy sounding rhyme, often corrupted to 'the business'. Another similar expression of the day was 'the mutt's nuts', which itself was corrupted to 'the dog's bollocks'.
below the belt	unfair or cowardly	The Marquis of Queensberry formulated rules for boxing in 1867 which disallowed hitting below the belt.
below the salt	common or lowly	In medieval England, nobility sat at a high table and commoners at lower trestle tables. Salt was expensive and only the nobs were provided with it. Hence the peasantry were below the salt.
belt and braces	careful – not taking chances	Using both belt and braces is a double insurance against having your trousers fall down.
berk	a stupid person	Rhyming slang derivation: Berkshire Hunt – cunt.
beware of Greeks bearing gifts	be on your guard against trickery	An allusion to the incident in Virgil's *Aeneid* where the Greeks tricked their way into Troy by hiding in a huge wooden horse, apparently offered as a gift, before springing out at night and taking the city.
beyond the pale	unacceptable; outside agreed standards of decency	The 'pale' derives from paling, meaning fence. In the United Kingdom the Pale was the region of Dublin under English rule; areas outside this zone were considered unsafe and uncivilised.
bigwig	an important person	From the large, imposing wigs worn by the aristocracy from the 17th century.
blacklist	to exclude a person from an activity due to unsuitability	Errant students in early British universities had their names placed in black books as a form of disgrace. As a noun the phrase refers to the list itself.
blinking idiot	a stupid person	Mild expletive first coined in Shakespeare's *The Merchant of Venice* (1596–7), Act 2 Scene 9. After the Prince of Aragon decides to open the silver casket in an attempt to win the hand of Portia, within is but a portrait of a 'blinking idiot'.

blot on the landscape	something that spoils the view or ruins a previously comfortable situation	TE Lawrence first coined the phrase in a letter of 1912. The phrase was further popularised by Tom Sharpe's 1975 novel of that name, where Blott was the name of the leading character.
bluestocking	formerly, a learned woman who dispensed with traditional feminism	This phrase originally described a group of intellectuals under the patronage of Elizabeth Montagu in London around 1750. Benjamin Stillingfleet, a prominent member, was in the habit of wearing blue stockings and James Boswell further popularised the group by describing Stillingfleet in his *Life of Johnson* (1791).
Bob's your uncle	used to imply that an intended task or mission is as good as completed	Piers Brendon, in *Eminent Edwardians* (1979), suggests the origin as being the unexpected promotion of Arthur Balfour as Chief Secretary for Ireland by his uncle Robert Arthur Talbot Gascoyne-Cecil, 3rd Marquis of Salisbury, the Prime Minister.
booby prize	a consolation prize given to the loser (the booby) in a contest or game	Booby has been in use meaning dunce since at least the late 15th century.
booby trap	a concealed trap for the unaware	See **booby prize** above. This form of trap would quite easily catch a person of low intelligence.
Boxing Day	public holiday on the day after Christmas Day	St Stephen's Day became known as Boxing Day via the tradition whereby casual offerings left in the church-box were counted on Christmas Day and distributed to the poor the next day. A similar practice of giving tradesmen a gratuity or 'Christmas Box' is still followed.
boycott, to	to ostracise	Captain Boycott (1832–97) was an unforgiving and harsh English land agent for the Earl of Erse in County Mayo in the late 19th century. He would dispossess tenants for the slightest arrears and was reviled by all. Charles Parnell of the Irish Land League advised tenants to treat Boycott and his type as lepers; hence the phrase.
brown goods	large electrical goods usually found in the lounge	Marketing term for consumer goods such as televisions, radios and videos, traditionally finished in brown colours.
bunny boiler	an obsessive and dangerous female, in pursuit of a lover who has spurned her	From the 1987 film *Fatal Attraction*. The plot concerns a woman scorned (played by Glenn Close) who obsessively pursues her ex-lover (played by Michael Douglas). The phrase comes from the plot device where the woman boils the man's daughter's pet rabbit.
by hook or by crook	by any means possible	Derives from Cromwell's attempt to capture the city of Waterford. He is reported as saying he would take the city 'by hook or by crook'. Hook is the headland on the Wexford side and Crook is the name of the Waterford side.
cardigan	woollen sweater with buttons down the front	Named after James Thomas Brudenell, 7th Earl of Cardigan (1797–1868) who wore such a garment during his service in the Crimean War to ward off the severe cold.
caviare to the general	of no interest to the average man	Derives from Shakespeare's *Hamlet* (1601), Act 2 Scene 2; the 'general' cited is the general public and the phrase refers to the notion that such a novel delicacy was not for the edification of the common man.
chav	streetwise youngster who loves designer labels	Expression which became fashionable in southern England in 2004 and is thought to be a corruption of 'chavi', the Romany word for a child. The chav society have their own sign language of derogatory terms and are usually seen sporting hooded tops and baseball caps. (Other terms associated with youth culture and fashion, but deriving from the USA, include bling or bling-bling, breakbeat and phat.)
cold enough to freeze the balls off a brass monkey	extremely cold	A brass monkey was the name given to the tray on which cannon balls were stacked aboard Royal Navy warships of the early 19th century. In severe cold weather the brass would contract and the balls would topple off the top of the pile.
disgusted, Tunbridge Wells	reference to a critical correspondent without specifying name	The reference to Tunbridge Wells has no significance other than that it was originally the name of a character played by Wallas Eaton in the radio comedy series *Take it From Here* from 1953.
doolally	out of one's mind	Named after Deolali, a town near Bombay with a sanatorium where many British soldiers were detained before being shipped home. The term became military slang for a crazy person circa 1925.
dressed up like a dog's dinner	describes something that is messy	Derives from the description in 2 Kings where Jezebel adorned herself before being defenestrated and eaten by dogs. This phrase often has the word 'breakfast' substituted for 'dinner'.
eat crow	to be forced to do something humiliating	Term dates back to the War of 1812 where a New England soldier entered British lines and shot a crow. An unarmed British officer feigned interest in the American's firearm and, when allowed to examine it, turned the gun on the soldier and forced him to take a bite of the crow.
eat humble pie	to be humiliated	Expression derives from tradition of offering the unappealing parts of a hunted deer, the numbles (entrails, later corrupted to umbles) to those of inferior rank or standing
feather in one's cap	an achievement to be proud of	Dates from the Battle of Crécy (1346) when Edward, the Black Prince, was awarded the crest of three ostrich feathers of King John of Bohemia; these became the symbol of every subsequent Prince of Wales.
fifth column	an organised body working for the enemy within a country at war	Originally coined by Emilio Mola Vidal, a Nationalist general during the Spanish Civil War (1936–9). As four of his army columns moved on Madrid, the general referred to his militant supporters within the capital as his 'fifth column', intent on undermining the loyalist government from within.
flash in the pan	short-lived success before ultimate failure	Derives from the propensity of the old flintlock pistols to misfire. A hammer strikes a flint, producing a spark which explodes the charge. The powder in the chamber, named the pan, often flashed but failed to ignite the charge.
fourth estate	the press	General usage of the term dates back to 1828 when Thomas Macaulay wrote of the House of Commons, 'The gallery in which the reporters sit has become the fourth estate of the realm'. The established three estates were the House of Lords, divided into the Lords Spiritual and the Lords Temporal, and the House of Commons.
full monty, the	the whole thing	There have been suggestions that the expression derives from the somewhat large breakfasts enjoyed by Field Marshal Montgomery, but it is more likely to be a reference to the famous men's tailor Montague Burton whose standard outfit was a two-piece suit, but who offered as an optional extra a waistcoat and a second pair of trousers. Paying the extra was going for the full Monty. The feature film of the 1990s

		gave the word a very different meaning, making an allusion to the fact that a group of male strippers would 'go all the way' if the price were right.
gamp	an umbrella	Nickname derives from Dickens' character Sarah Gamp in *Martin Chuzzlewit*, who always carried a large umbrella.
get out of the wrong side of bed	to start the day in a foul mood	An early 16th-century phrase arising from the tradition that it was unlucky to place the left foot on the ground before the right when getting out of bed.
get the sack	to be dismissed from a job	Dates from circa 1825, in the days when tradesmen owned their tools and gave the sack or bag in which they carried them to the employer to mind for them. When dismissed from his job, the employee's sack would be returned to him by the employer.
gone for a Burton	person or object that is missing	The most probable source is from RAF slang where to go for a Burton meant to have 'bought it', an allusion to buying a beer from the famous Burton-on-Trent brewery. Another possible derivation, also RAF slang, is from the fact that a Blackpool billiard hall over a Montague Burton tailor shop was used as a Morse code instruction centre. The phrase was used to describe failure on the course.
Gordon Bennett!	an exclamation of surprise – one of the many euphemisms that avoid the use of the word God	James Gordon Bennett II (1841–1918), editor-in-chief of the *New York Herald,* was the man who sent Henry Morton Stanley in search of David Livingstone in Africa. He was also an adventurer and one of his many reported exploits was an incident where he flew an aeroplane through an open barn. The surprised onlookers were supposed to have said 'That was Gordon Bennett!'
grockle	a tourist	This supposedly Devonshire dialect word for a tourist, particularly one from north of the Watford Gap, was popularised in the 1962 film *The System*, which was set in the Devon resort of Torquay, although its exact origin is disputed. One idea is that it derives from the resemblance between the famous clown named 'Grock' and a red-faced tourist with a knotted handkerchief on his head. The other, more probable derivation is simply from a cartoon strip of the time in the *Dandy* comic entitled 'Danny and his Grockle', the grockle being a dragon-like creature.
gung ho	over-eager and undisciplined	From the Chinese *kung* and *ho*, meaning 'work together'.
hat-trick	in a sporting context, to score three times or take three wickets	In early cricket, a bowler taking three wickets with three successive balls was entitled to a new hat at the expense of the club.
Hobson's choice	no choice at all	Thomas Hobson (1544–1631) was a coachman and hirer of horses in Cambridge. The phrase derives from Hobson's insistence that the customer could hire any horse they liked, as long as it was the one nearest the door!
hoist with one's own petard	ruined by one's own devices against others	Derives from Shakespeare's *Hamlet* (1601), Act 3 Scene 3. A petard was an explosive device used to break through walls.
Hooray Henry	loud, upper-class man with extravagant manners	Phrase coined by Jim Godbolt in 1951 in reference to the upper-class contingent attracted to a jazz club at 100 Oxford Street, London, where Humphrey Lyttelton played trumpet. The term itself derives from a character in Damon Runyon's 'Tight Shoes' (1936).
hwyl	to put body and soul into something	Welsh word that has various meanings but in the patriotic sense has come to mean to approach a task with vigour and energy: 'Put some hwyl into it' .
jam tomorrow	a promise which is never likely to be kept	From Lewis Carroll's *Through the Looking Glass and What Alice Found There* (1871), in which The White Queen offers Alice 'Jam to-morrow and jam yesterday – but never jam today'. Socialist circles often used it to ridicule the capitalist system as offering the same empty promise.
kiss the Blarney Stone	to have a way with words	In 1602 it is said that Cormac Macarthy was to surrender Blarney Castle, near Cork, as a declaration of his loyalty to Elizabeth I, but his prevarication gave cause for the Queen to exclaim 'Odds bodikins, more Blarney talk.'
kitchen sink	descriptive of dramas that reflect ordinary life	Phrase coined in the 1950s to describe dramas centred on the unsatisfactory nature of the UK's class system and working-class life. John Osborne was a leading exponent of such plays and when Shelagh Delaney's novel *A Taste of Honey* was made into a feature film in 1961, the term became a stock phrase to describe any drama form dealing with domestic reality. Contrast **Aga saga**.
knuckle down	to apply oneself to an exacting task	Phrase derives from about 1740, when a game of marbles commenced with the knuckle being placed on the ground in order to shoot.
lager lout	alliterative name for a person with a propensity for drunken violence	Phrase coined by Simon Walters, the political correspondent of *The Sun*, in 1988, and used to describe football hooligans and other drunken, unruly young males.
lame duck	person or thing that is disabled or ineffectual	Phrase used from about 1761, deriving from defaulters on the London Stock Exchange who were seen to waddle out of Exchange Alley like the proverbial lame duck.
left-footer	a Roman Catholic	Irish phrase referring to an agricultural labourer's tendency to use his left foot when making the initial thrust of his spade into the ground, the assumption being that most Irish labourers are Catholics.
let the cat out of the bag	disclose a secret	Phrase derives from the mid-18th century when a crowd would be shown a pig at a country fair and the vendor would then place the animal in a bag before sale, only for the unsuspecting purchaser to find it had been substituted by a less valuable cat!
living dog is better than a dead lion, a	even a wretched existence is better than no existence while hope remains	Ecclesiastes 9:4 expresses this philosophical idiom and the sentiment is fairly evident. While a person lives they have hope of salvation and can know death but when dead they know nothing.
mad as a hatter	completely and utterly crazy	Phrase deriving from the character in Lewis Carroll's *Alice's Adventures in Wonderland* (1865), who was decidedly eccentric in his mannerisms. The related phrase 'mad as a March hare' dates from the early 16th century; Carroll based his character of the March Hare on this phrase.
man on the Clapham omnibus	the ordinary person in the street	Legal term first used by Lord Bowen in 1903 when summing-up in a case of negligence, his exact words being: 'We must ask ourselves what the man on the Clapham omnibus would think.'
mind your ps and qs	be cautious and careful	The ps and qs in question relate to pints and quarts and refer to an innkeeper's custom of chalking up a customer's tally on the slate.

Mrs Grundy	a censorious person	The name derives from Thomas Morton's play *Speed the Plough* (1798) in which a character would often show disapproval by saying 'What will Mrs Grundy say?' In the 19th century Mrs Ormiston Chant was an actual campaigner against vulgarity in the music hall and in the 20th century her equivalent was Mrs Mary Whitehouse.
Morton's Fork	the dictate that no man is spared taxes on the premise that the rich have obvious wealth while the ostensibly poor must therefore save	John Morton (1420–1500) was Archbishop of Canterbury (1486–1500) but it was in his position as Lord Chancellor from 1487 that the phrase derives. In order to raise revenue during the reign of Henry VII, Morton propounded the theory that became known as Morton's Fork in order to ensure that no man was excluded from paying taxes.
namby-pamby	weak and insipid	The phrase derives from the nickname of Ambrose Phillips (died 1749) whose pastoral verse was criticised for its insipidity. Fellow poet Henry Carey is thought to have first used this derogatory name in 1726.
nine days' wonder	something with short-lived appeal	Phrase deriving from the proverb 'A wonder lasts nine days, and then the puppy's eyes are open', an allusion to the fact that a puppy is born blind and innocent but then its eyes are opened to the world.
no room to swing a cat	a small confined space	The 'cat' referred to was not a feline at all, but a flail-like whip used to punish sailors in the British Navy from the 17th century.
Old Bill	policeman	Term deriving from the cartoon character invented by British Army Captain Bruce Bairnsfather (1888–1959) during his convalescence from shell-shock during WWI. The name was used as a nickname for policemen from the outbreak of WWII.
on tenterhooks	in a state of anxious suspense	Phrase derived from the process of cleaning woollen cloth after weaving. To prevent shrinkage the cloth was placed in a wooden frame called a tenter and was stretched by fixing hooks. The word tenter in this sense comes from the Latin *tendere* (to stretch). First use of the phrase was in Tobias Smollett's *Roderick Random* (1748).
page three girl	a topless photographic model	Phrase derived from a feature that began in *The Sun* newspaper on 17 November 1970 when the then editor Larry Lamb introduced topless pin-ups to page three. The term is now used generically for any such nude model or for describing any overtly beautiful woman.
pass the buck	to shift responsibility to another	Phrase derived from the game of poker where a marker, known as a buck, is placed in front of the dealer as a reminder of who the dealer is.
pathetic fallacy	attribution of human feelings to inanimate objects in nature	Literary term coined by John Ruskin in *Modern Painters*, vol. 3 part 4 (1856) where he gives examples of the attribution of emotions to inanimate objects in poetry, e.g.: 'The spendthrift crocus bursting through the mould, naked and shivering, with his cup of gold'.
Peeping Tom	a voyeur	Derived from the name of Tom the Tailor, who was struck blind when he peeped at Lady Godiva (wife of Leofric, Earl of Mercia & Lord of Coventry) as she rode naked through the streets of Coventry to excuse her husband's tenants from his exactions. The legend was recorded by Roger of Wendover (d. 1236) in his *Flores Historiarum*, although the addition of Tom to the legend was made during the reign of Charles II.
pommy	Australian slang term for British immigrants	Term first coined in Sydney, Australia, in 1912. DH Lawrence described its derivation in his novel *Kangaroo* (1923) as corrupted rhyming slang: pomegranate – immigrant. Other more popular derivations such as Prisoner of Mother England (POME) bear no semblance of truth.
quiz	set of questions to test knowledge	Came into use in 1782 when Mr Daly, a Dublin theatre manager, made a wager that he could introduce a new word into the language within 24 hours. This he achieved by scrawling the word 'quiz' all over the walls of Dublin. Its meaning was given as 'an odd, or eccentric person' – as many quiz players are, of course! The present sense of the word came into common usage in the 1860s.
real McCoy	the genuine article	Phrase derived from the name of middleweight boxing champion Charles 'Kid' McCoy who had two ways of fighting; occasionally lacklustre, on his day he was unbeatable in the middleweight division, taking the world title on the retirement of Bob Fitzsimmons in 1897.
red letter day	a special day	High days and holidays used to be marked in red on church calendars. Dates from the Reformation.
red tape	bureaucratic rules	Legal documents were traditionally bound with red tape.
rob Peter to pay Paul	use money allocated to one project to complete another without any overall benefit	Westminster Abbey is dedicated to St Peter. In 1540 Henry VIII had designated the Abbey a cathedral with its own bishop and diocese. However, when the bishopric was dissolved in 1550 and the church made a second cathedral in the diocese of London, some lands belonging to the church were exchanged or sold off. Some of this money was used for the repair of (old) St Paul's cathedral, hence robbing St Peter's church to pay for St Paul's cathedral.
sandwich	two slices of bread filled with any foodstuff	Coined by John Montagu, 4th Earl of Sandwich (1718–92), an avid gambler who disliked leaving the gaming tables and so sent out for snacks to be brought to him while playing. Sandwiches are still supplied at the tables of many gaming clubs.
scot free	get away with something without penalty	Phrase deriving from a medieval tax called 'scot and lot'. The scot is a Scandinavian word for a contribution and the lot was a shortened version of allotment. A person able to circumvent the rules for payment was said to have got off scot free. The 1832 Reform Act dispensed with the tax.
snob	person who behaves condescendingly to those perceived as of lower class	Term first used in the late 18th century as slang for a cobbler. Although cobblers were perceived as being from humble origins, the term later became attached to those who looked down on such honest craftsmen.
splice the mainbrace	to have an alcoholic drink	The mainbrace is the rope which controls the movement of sails aboard ship and the phrase compares the degree of difficulty in gaining an extra rum ration from the Royal Navy with that of controlling the mainbrace.
spoonerism	the transposition of parts of words	The Reverend William Spooner (1844–1930), warden of New College, Oxford, was famous for muddling his words and the phrase entered common usage by 1885. The classic example of a spoonerism is 'Sir, you have tasted two whole worms, you have hissed all my mystery lectures and have been caught fighting a liar in the quad; you will leave Oxford by the next town drain', although this is thought to be apocryphal. If the good reverend had been a film fan, perhaps he would have liked *Shaving Ryan's Privates*!

spud	colloquial name for a potato	Name given to the implement used to dig a potato out of the ground, first coined in the diary of Samuel Pepys in 1667. The Irish people immediately used this expression for the humble potato, although Murphy remains another popular term. People with the surname Murphy are invariably nicknamed Spud.
square meal	a hearty meal	In the Royal Navy sailors traditionally received their meals on a square plate.
stool pigeon	a police informer	Hunters traditionally used decoy pigeons fixed to posts (stools) to lure their quarry. The term was later adopted to describe people who helped the police by luring criminals into police traps. It later came to mean anyone who helped the police by informing on others.
tell it to the Marines	exclamation of disbelief	The phrase derives from the fact that marines were perceived as being neither one thing or the other as they operated on land and sea; hence they were classed as second-rate and stupid, and open to believe a tall story. In fact, of course, marines are among the brightest and toughest of servicemen.
thin blue line	defensive barrier of policemen	A line of policemen, particularly those holding back a surging crowd. More recent adaptation of the **thin red line**.
thin end of the wedge	something small and seemingly unimportant that conceals the bigger picture	The phrase was first coined in the mid 1800s and alluded to the narrow wedge inserted into a log for splitting wood.
thin red line	defensive barrier formed by soldiers	According to jingoistic folklore in the UK, a small group of British soldiers (who wore red jackets) were enough to hold back a mob of warlike foreigners.
third degree, the	close interrogation	In a masonic lodge there are three ranks or degrees: the first is called Entered Apprentice, the second Fellowcraft, and the third is Master Mason. When a candidate receives the third degree in a Masonic lodge, he is subjected to activities that include an interrogation and are more physically challenging than those entailed in the first two degrees.
throw one's hat into the ring	show an intention to join an enterprise	Phrase derived from early 18th century prize-fights when it was traditional to throw one's hat into the ring when making a challenge to the resident fighter.
Tin Pan Alley	centre of musical creativity	The area around Denmark Street, off Charing Cross Road, was known as Tin Pan Alley by 1934, although the name itself was used as early as 1908 to refer to a similar area of musical activity in Manhattan, New York, where the noise of countless pianos being tinkled sounded like the crashing of tin pans.
turn the tables	achieve a reversal of fortune	Phrase derived from the quick reversal of fortunes experienced while playing backgammon. The gameboard is divided into four quarters, two being designated the inner table and two the outer table. An errant throw of the dice can quickly change a position from a favourable to a precarious one.
Walter Plinge	an actor's alternative name	Mr Plinge was said to be a stage-struck pub landlord working near the Theatre Royal, Drury Lane, in the 19th century and in homage to his enthusiasm actors would use his name in programmes when playing two parts. Sometimes the name was used for a fictional character to boost the cast list and at other times because of uncertainty of final casting. The American equivalent is George Spelvin.
whipping boy	a scapegoat punished for the inadequacies of others	It used to be the practice in some cultures that the nobility could not be touched. When they committed a crime that warranted physical punishment it was therefore delegated to an unfortunate victim – the whipping boy. Barnaby Fitzpatrick stood as whipping boy for Edward VI and Mungo Murray for Charles I before they were crowned. This seemingly outlandish practice was in reality a means to instil a sense of justice and righteousness in future monarchs; it was hoped they would behave appropriately in the knowledge that an innocent bystander might be punished on their behalf.
white bread	pertaining to white middle classes in the USA. Something that is more trouble than it is worth	Derogatory term that refers to the supposed bland and uninteresting nature of white middle-class culture in the USA, brown wholemeal bread being more exciting and generally beneficial.
white elephant	Something that is more trouble than its worth	White (albino) elephants were regarded as holy in ancient times in Thailand and other Asian countries. To keep a white elephant was a very expensive task, since you had to provide the elephant with special food, and provide access for people who wanted to come and worship it. If a king became dissatisfied with a subordinate, he would sometimes give him a white elephant in order to ruin him.
white goods	large electrical kitchen goods	Marketing term used to describe large household appliances such as refrigerators, microwaves and cookers which are often finished in white enamel. The term is also used to describe household linen such as sheets, towels and tablecloths.
white knight	an organisation that comes to the aid of another during a hostile takeover	Making an analogy to the bygone age of chivalry, the phrase became common at the Stock Exchange by 1981. The knight would rescue a targeted company by offering to acquire it far above the pursuer's value and generally under better terms.
wooden spoon, receive the	to finish last in a competition	In the University of Cambridge, England, the scholar whose name stood last of all on the printed list of honours, at the Bachelors' Commencement in January, was scoffingly said to gain the wooden spoon. Eventually an actual wooden spoon was presented to the person placed last in the mathematical tripos.

LANGUAGE

Foreign Words and Phrases

ab initio (L.) from the beginning
à bon marché (Fr.) a good bargain, cheap (lit. at a good market)
a cappella (It.) without instrumental accompaniment (lit. in chapel style)
à cheval (Fr.) on horseback (also denotes two roulette numbers)
achtung (Ger.) look out, beware, take heed (lit. attention)
ad astra (L.) to the stars
ad hoc (L.) for this special purpose (lit. to this)
ad libitum (L.) at pleasure
ad rem (L.) to the purpose, to the point (lit. to the matter)
Agnus Dei (L.) lamb of God
à la carte (Fr.) each dish priced separately (lit. according to the menu)
à la mode (Fr.) according to custom or fashion
al dente (It.) firm when bitten (lit. to the teeth)
al fresco (It.) in the open air (lit. in the fresh)
alloi kamon, alloi onanto (Gr.) some toil, others reap the advantage

Alma Mater (L.) applied to former school, university, or college, (lit. fostering or bounteous mother)
alter ego (L.) other self
amor vincit omnia (L.) love conquers all
Angst (Ger.) anxiety
annus mirabilis (L.) a remarkable year (lit. year of wonder)
Anschauung (Ger.) point of view (lit. looking around)
Anschluss (Ger.) joining together
ante bellum (L.) before the war
a priori (L.) from cause to effect (lit. from the previous)
à propos (Fr.) to the purpose
auberge (Fr.) inn, tavern
au courant (Fr.) fully acquainted with (lit. in the current)
Aufklärung (Ger.) clarification, enlightenment
auf Wiedersehen (Ger.) till we meet again
au pair (Fr.) home-help from a foreign country (lit. on an equal basis)
au revoir (Fr.) till we meet again
auto-da-fé (Port.) act of faith
avant-garde (Fr.) progressive or radical artists and thinkers (lit. vanguard)
bain-marie (Fr.) a double saucepan (lit. bath of Maria)
baksheesh (Pers.) gratuity or tip (lit. a present)
banzai (Jap.) a Japanese battle-cry (lit. 10,000 years)
barrio (Sp.) district, suburb (lit. open country)
bas bleu (Fr.) literary woman, blue-stocking worker (lit. under blue)
batik (Malay) cloth dyeing method using wax, the cloth itself, (lit. painted)
bête noire (Fr.) a bugbear, pet aversion (lit. black beast)
bibelot (Fr.) trinket, curio, knick-knack (lit. small book)
bidet (Fr.) bestridable bath (lit. small horse)
Bildungsroman (Ger.) novel concerning early development of its central figure, (lit. education novel)
billet-doux (Fr.) love letter (lit. sweet note)
Blitzkrieg (Ger.) intense military attack (lit. lightning war)
Boche (Fr.) French slang for a German soldier (lit. rascal)
bois brûlé (Fr.) French-Canadian Indian (lit. burnt wood)
bona fide (L.) with good faith
bona-roba (It.) prostitute, wench (lit. good dress)
bona vacantia (L.) goods without any apparent owner and to which the Crown has the rights (lit. ownerless goods)
bonheur du jour (Fr.) small writing-table (lit. happiness of the day)
bonhomie (Fr.) good-nature (lit. good man)
bon mot (Fr.) witty remark (lit. good word)
bonsai (Jap.) miniature tree in a pot (lit. bowl growing)
bourgeois (Fr.) middle-class person (lit. town dweller)
cacoethes (Gr) bad habit, mania (lit. evil habit)
carabiniere (It.) member of Italian police force
carpe diem (L.) seize the day
carte blanche (Fr.) freedom of action, card hand with no court cards (lit. blank card)
caveat emptor (L.) let the buyer beware
cave canem (L.) beware of the dog
cela va sans dire (Fr.) needless to say, that goes without saying
c'est la vie (Fr.) that's life
ceteris paribus (L.) other things being equal
cinquecento (Fr.) classical style of art of the 16th century (lit. five hundred)
cire perdue (Fr.) bronze casting using wax technique (lit. lost wax)
cogito, ergo sum (L.) I think, therefore I am
compos mentis (L.) sound of mind
corpus delicti (L.) body or substance of a crime
corregidor (Sp.) chief magistrate of a Spanish town (lit. to correct)
corrida (Sp.) a bullfight (lit. corral)
corrigenda (L.) things to be corrected
coup de foudre (Fr.) love at first sight, sudden event (lit. flash of lightning)
coup de grâce (Fr.) action that puts an end to something, (lit. stroke of mercy)
coup d'état (Fr.) sudden and violent change of government, (lit. stroke of state)
cri de coeur (Fr.) heartfelt appeal or protest (lit. cry from the heart)
cru (Fr.) French vineyard (lit. growth)
cucullus non facit monachum (L.) the cowl does not make the monk
cui bono (L.) to whose benefit
cul-de-sac (Fr.) road with one end blocked off, dead end (lit. bottom of the bag)
cum grano salis (L.) with a grain of salt
curriculum vitae (L.) course of life
dacha (Rus.) Russian country villa (lit. gift)
de facto (L.) in fact
déjà vu (Fr.) already seen
de jure (L.) by right (lit. from the law)
de profundis (L.) out of the depths
de rigueur (Fr.) required by etiquette (lit. of strictness)
Dei gratia (L.) by God's grace
Deo volente (L.) God willing
dernier cri (Fr.) latest fashion, last word (lit. last cry)
de trop (Fr.) superfluous, not wanted (lit. too much)
die dulci fruere (L.) have a nice day
Doppelgänger (Ger.) wraith, look-a-like (lit. double goer)
dos-à-dos (Fr.) a seat on which the users sit back to back, (lit. back to back)
dramatis personae (L.) cast of a play
duce (It.) leader
duende (Sp.) Imp, goblin, ghost
Dummkopf (Ger.) dumb-head
e pluribus unum (L.) one out of many
Ecce Homo (L.) artistic representation of Christ crowned with thorns. From the words of Pontius Pilate to his accusers, (lit. behold the man)
echt (Ger.) real, genuine, authentic
effendi (Turk.) mister (lit. master)
emeritus (L.) honourably retired (lit. meritorious)
ersatz (Ger.) replacement, substitute, imitation
esprit de corps (Fr.) pride in belonging to a group (lit. spirit of a body)
eureka (Gr.) I have found it
ex cathedra (L.) with authority
ex officio (L.) by virtue of his office (lit. out of duty)
fabricati diem (L.) make my day
fac ut gaudeam (L.) make my day
fait accompli (Fr.) thing already done (lit. accomplished fact)
fartlek (Swed.) interval athletics training (lit. speed play)
fatwa (Arab.) a legal decision
faux pas (Fr.) social blunder, indiscretion (lit. false step)
Fidei Defensor (L.) defender of the faith
flagrante delicto (L.) in the act of a crime
floreat (L.) let it flourish
force de frappe (Fr.) French nuclear deterrent (lit. striking force)
Führer (Ger.) leader
Gastarbeiter (Ger) person with temporary permission to work, in a foreign country (lit. guest-worker)
Gauleiter (Ger.) district leader
gestalt (Ger.) organised whole in which each part affects every other part (lit. shape)
Gesundheit (Ger.) your health (lit. healthy sound)
glasnost (Rus.) openness
Götterdämmerung (Ger.) In German mythology the final destruction of the world (lit. twilight of the gods)
goût (Fr.) taste, artistic discernment
gravitas (L.) solemn demeanour
gringo (Sp.) term used by Latin-Americans for foreigners, (lit. foreigner)
gulag (Rus.) labour camp
habeas corpus (L.) a writ to produce a prisoner before a court, (lit. you should have the body)
haiku (Jap.) amusement verse
hajj (Arab.) pilgrimage
Hakenkreuz (Ger.) swastika (lit. hooked cross)
halal (Arab.) cooked according to Muslim law (lit. lawful)
haute couture (Fr.) high fashion (lit. high dressmaking)
haute cuisine (Fr.) high-class cooking
haute école (Fr.) classic style of riding (lit. high school)
hic et nunc (L.) here and now
hic et ubique (L.) here and everywhere
hic jacet (L.) here lies
hic sepultus (L.) here buried
hoi polloi (Gr.) common people or rabble (lit. the many)
hominis est errare (L.) to err is human
homme d'affaires (Fr.) businessman
homme d'esprit (Fr.) man of wit or genius
honi soit qui mal y pense (Fr.) shamed be he who thinks evil

honores mutant mores (L.) honours change manners
hors de combat (Fr.) disabled or injured (lit. out of the fight)
hors d'oeuvre (Fr.) savoury appetiser (lit. out of the course)
Ibidem (L.) in the same place
Ich dien (Ger.) I serve
id est (L.) that is
ignorantia juris neminem excusat (L.) ignorance of the law excuses no one
illegitimi non carborundum (L.) don't let the bastards grind you down
in camera (L.) in secret (Lit. in the chamber)
incunabulum (L.) book printed before 1501 (lit. from cradle), original Latin meaning was 'swaddling clothes'
in extremis (L.) at the point of death (lit. in the last)
in flagrante delicto (L.) in the act of a crime or red-handed, (lit. with the crime still ablaze), sometimes written 'flagrante delicto'
infra dig(nitatem) (L.) beneath one's dignity
in loco parentis (L.) in place of a parent
in petto (It.) when a cardinal is selected by the pope but not yet anounced (lit. in the breast)
inshallah (Arab.) equivalent to the term 'touch wood' (lit. if Allah wills)
inter alia (L.) among other things
intra vires (L.) within the powers of
in utero (L.) before birth (lit. in the womb)
in vino veritas (L.) drunken people often speak the truth, (lit. in wine, truth)
in vitro (L.) in a test tube (lit. in glass)
ipso facto (L.) by the fact itself
jacquerie (Fr.) a peasants' revolt as in France in 1358 (lit. peasant)
j'adoube (Fr.) I adjust (chess term)
je ne sais quoi (Fr.) indefinable quality (lit. I know not what)
jeune premier (fem. -ière) (Fr.) juvenile lead in musical play or theatrical production (lit. first youth)
jeunesse dorée (Fr.) rich and fashionable young people (lit. gilded youth)
jihad (Arab.) a Muslim holy war (lit. conflict)
joie de vivre (Fr.) joy of living
Jugendstil (Ger.) art nouveau (lit. youth style)
Junker (Ger.) class of Prussian land-owning aristocracy (lit. young lord)
juste milieu (Fr.) happy medium or golden mean (lit. the right mean or the right course)
kamikaze (Jap.) Japanese suicide pilots in WWII (lit. divine wind)
Kapellmeister (Ger.) person in charge of an orchestra (lit. chapel master)
karaoke (Jap.) Japanese entertainment of singing to backing tapes, (lit. empty orchestra)
Katzenjammer (Ger.) colloquial term for a hangover (lit. cat's wailing)
kia ora (Maori) good luck (lit. be well)
kibbutz (Heb.) Jewish community in Israel (lit. gathering)
kibitzer (Yid.) person who gives unwanted advice especially at a card game, (lit. lapwing or plover)
kitsch (Ger.) worthless art
kolkhoz (Rus.) Russian collective farm
kulak (Rus.) land-owning peasant (lit. fist)
Kulturkampf (Ger.) culture struggle
la dolce vita (It.) the sweet life
laissez-faire (Fr.) unrestricted commerce (lit. allow to do)
Langlauf (Ger.) cross-country skiing (lit. long run)
lapsus calami (L.) slip of the pen
lapsus linguae (L.) slip of the tongue
lares et penates (L.) household goods
l'chaim (Heb.) a Jewish toast (lit. to life)
Lebensraum (Ger.) territory needed by a state for its natural development, (lit. living space)
Lederhosen (Ger.) leather trousers
lèse-majesté (Fr.) high treason (lit. injured majesty)
lex scripta (L.) written law
lex talionis (L.) law of retaliation (lit. such law)
litterae humaniores (L.) name given to study of classics at Oxford University (lit. more humane letters)
locum tenens (L.) a deputy (lit. place held)
locus classicus (L.) authoritive and oft-quoted passage from a standard text (lit. classical place)
lycée (Fr.) in France, a state secondary school (lit. pupil)
magnum opus (L.) a great work of art or literature
maharishi (Hin.) Hindu teacher of religion (lit. great sage)
mahatma (Sans.) Brahman sage (lit. great soul)
maillot (Fr.) tights worn for balet or gymnastics (lit. swaddling clothes)
mal de mer (Fr.) seasickness
mañana (Sp.) tomorrow
manqué (Fr.) unfulfilled potential (lit. having missed)
maven (Yid.) a connoisseur (lit. understanding)
mazel tov (Heb.) congratulations or good luck (lit. good star)
mea culpa (L.) by my own fault
memento mori (L.) reminder of death
mene, mene, tekel, upharsin (Aram.) words that appeared on the wall during Belshazzar's Feast (lit. numbered, numbered, weighed, divided)
mens rea (L.) criminal intent (lit. guilty mind)
modus operandi (L.) method of working
mot juste (Fr.) appropriate word
multum in parvo (L.) much in little
mutatis mutandis (L.) with required changes
né(e) (Fr.) born
ne plus ultra (L.) extreme perfection (lit. not more beyond)
nil desperandum (L.) never despair (lit. nothing to be despaired)
nisi (L.) coming into effect unless otherwise stated (lit. unless)
noblesse oblige (Fr.) obligation of nobility or privileged to be honourable (lit. nobility obliges)
nom de guerre (Fr.) an assumed name (lit. name of war)
nom de plume (Fr.) pen-name
non sequitur (L.) statement that has no relevance to what went before (lit. it does not follow)
nota bene (L.) note well
nuit blanche (Fr.) sleepless night (lit. white night)
Nunc Dimittis (L.) the Canticle of Simeon (Luke 2:29–32), (lit. now depart)
obiter dictum (L.) said in passing
objet d'art (Fr.) small object of artistic worth (lit. object of art)
objet trouvé (Fr.) ordinary object seen from an artistic viewpoint, (lit. found object)
oeuvre (Fr.) total output of an artist or writer
om mani padme hum (Sans.) Tibetan Buddhists' meditational chant. Aka Shadakshari mantra (lit. hail, jewel in the lotus)
omnia vincit amor (L.) love conquers all
panem et circenses (L.) bread and circuses (written by Juvenal of the loves of the typical Roman citizen)
parador (Sp.) Inn or tavern
par avion (Fr.) by airmail (lit. by air)
parvenu (Fr.) an upstart or social climber (lit. to attain)
paterfamilias (L.) male head of a household (lit. father of the family)
patois (Fr.) dialect
pax vobiscum (L.) peace be with you
per ardua ad astra (L.) through adversity to the stars
perestroika (Rus.) reconstruction
per se (L.) In itself
persona non grata (L.) unacceptable person
petit bourgeois (Fr.) lower middle-class
petit four (Fr.) small rich, sweet cakes, usually with icing (lit. little oven)
petit mal (Fr.) mild form of epilepsy with short bouts of unconsciousness (lit. little illness)
pied à terre (Fr.) temporary lodging (lit. foot to the ground)
pince-nez (Fr.) spectacles without ear-pieces (lit. pinch nose)
pinxit (L.) an inscription found after an artist's name on a painting (lit. painted)
pis aller (Fr.) a compromise or last resort (lit. the worst going)
plongeur (Fr.) washer-up (lit. plunger)
poco a poco (It.) little by little
poilu (Fr.) French equivalent of 'Tommy', an infantryman (lit. hairy)
posada (Sp.) an inn in a Spanish-speaking country (lit. place for stopping)
pose plastique (Fr.) theatrical presentation of the motionless nude female form (lit. flexible pose)
post meridiem (L.) after midday
pousse-café (Fr.) small glass of spirits especially brandy or a liqueur (lit. push-coffee)
prêt-à-porter (Fr.) ready to wear or off the peg
prima donna (It.) leading female operatic star (lit. first lady)
prima facie (L.) at first sight (lit. first face)
primus inter pares (L.) first among equals
pro tempore (L.) for the time being

quattrocento (It.) the 15th century especially in relation to Italian arts (lit. four hundred) short for milquattrocento '1400'
que será será (Sp.) whatever will be will be
quidnunc (L.) person eager to learn news or scandal, a gossipmonger, (lit. what now)
quid pro quo (L.) one thing for another
qui tacet consentit (L.) silence implies consent
quod erat demonstrandum (L.) which was to be demonstrated
quod vide (L.) usually seen as qv after a word treated more fully elsewhere (lit. which see)
raison d'être (Fr.) reason for being
rapporteur (Fr.) person appointed by a committee to prepare reports of meetings, (lit. reporter)
Realpolitik (Ger.) ruthlessly realistic and opportunist approach to statesmanship
repéchage (Fr.) heat of a contest in which eliminated contestants compete again (lit. fishing out again)
requiescat in pace (L.) rest in peace
res ipsa loquitur (L.) the thing speaks for itself
rien ne va plus (Fr.) roulette term meaning no more bets are to be placed (lit. nothing further goes)
Risorgimento (It.) the 19th century movement for the political unification of Italy (lit. to rise again)
roman à clef (Fr.) novel in which real people are depicted under disguised names (lit. novel with a key)
sang-froid (Fr.) composure in the face of danger (lit. cold blood)
sanpaku (Jap.) visibility of the white of the eye below the iris and on both sides (lit. three white)
sansculotte (Fr.) low-class Republican during the French Revolution (lit. without knee breeches)
sans souci (Fr.) without cares
sasquatch America's equivalent of the abominable snowman, aka big foot
satyagraha (Sans.) a policy of non-violent resistance to British rule in India, (lit. truth pertinacity)
savoir-faire (Fr.) knowing how to act
sayonara (Jap.) goodbye
Schadenfreude (Ger.) delighting in another's misfortune (lit. harm joy)
schlock (Yid.) cheap or shoddy (lit. damaged merchandise)
schmaltz (Yid.) sentimentality (lit. melted fat)
schmuck (Yid.) contemptible person (lit. penis)
schweinhund (Ger.) term of abuse (lit. pig dog)
seicento (It.) the 17th century especially in relation to Italian arts (lit. six hundred) short for milseicento '1600'
semper eadem (L.) always the same (motto of Elizabeth I and Anne Boleyn)
semper fidelis (L.) always faithful
semper ubi sub ubi (L.) always wear underwear (Latin scholar's joke)
seppuku (Jap.) the correct term in Japan for hara-kiri, which is a colloquialism (lit. cut open the stomach)
shiatsu (Jap.) acupuncture using fingers instead of needles (lit. finger pressure)
shmatte (Yid.) shabbiness especially of clothes (lit. rag)
sic (L.) bracketed insert in a text to indicate questionable word is correct (lit. thus or so)
sic transit gloria mundi (L.) thus passes the glory of the world
Sieg Heil (Ger.) Nazi salute accompanied by the raising of the right arm (lit. hail to victory)
sine die (L.) without a fixed date (lit. without a day)
sine prole (L.) without offspring
sine qua non (L.) an essential condition or requirement (lit. without which not)
son et lumière (Fr.) entertainment staged at night to set off a building artistically (lit. sound and light)
sotto voce (It.) musical term 'In an undertone' (lit. under voice)
soupçon (Fr.) trace, hint, small amount (lit. suspicion)
sputnik (Rus.) unmanned artificial Earth satellite (lit. travelling companion)
stet (L.) literary mark in proofing meaning correction should be ignored (lit. let it stand)
Sturm und Drang (Ger.) late 18th century German literary style (lit. storm and stress)
subbotnik (Rus.) voluntary Saturday work to assist economy (lit. Saturday)
sub judice (L.) under consideration of a judge
sub poena (L.) writ compelling a court attendance (lit. under a penalty)
sub rosa (L.) in secret (lit. under the rose)
summa cum laude (L.) with the highest praise
table d'hôte (Fr.) fixed-price meal with set courses (lit. host's table)
tabula rasa (L.) clean slate (lit. scraped table)
tai chi (Chin.) Chinese system of callisthenics (lit. great fist)
tempus fugit (L.) time flies
terra firma (L.) firm ground
tête-bêche (Fr.) double-headed stamp (lit. head to double-head)
tot homines, quot sententiae (L.) so many men, so many minds
tour de force (Fr.) masterly accomplishment (lit. show of strength)
trecento (It.) the 14th century especially in relation to Italian arts (lit. three hundred) short for miltrecento '1300'
tricoteuse (Fr.) woman who knitted at executions during French Revolution (lit. knitter)
trompe l'oeil (Fr.) appearance of reality in art (lit. deceives the eye)
ultra vires (L.) beyond the powers of
urbi et orbi (L.) to the city and the world
veni, vidi, vici (L.) I came, I saw, I conquered
verbum sat sapienti (L.) a word is enough for a wise man
victor ludorum (L.) overall winner of a competition (lit. winner of the games)
videlicet (L.) namely
vis-à-vis (Fr.) in relation to (lit. face to face)
viva voce (L.) orally (lit. with the living voice)
vox populi (L.) voice of the people
Wanderjahr (Ger.) wonder year
Wehrmacht (Ger.) German forces 1921–45 (lit. defence force)
Wunderkind (Ger.) a highly talented child (lit. wonder child)
yordim (Heb.) emigrants from the state of Israel
Zaibatsu (Jap.) family business conglomerate (lit. wealthy clique)
Zeitgeist (Ger.) spirit of the times

Cockney Rhyming Slang

Cockney–Standard

Abergavenny	penny
Adam and Eve	believe
airs and graces	faces; braces; Epsom Races
alderman's nail	tail
alligator	later
almond rocks	socks
Alphonse	ponce
Andy Cain	rain
Anna Maria	fire
'apenny dip	ship
apple fritter	bitter (beer)
apples and pears	stairs
April fools	stools; tools; football pools
April showers	flowers
Aristotle	bottle
army and navy	gravy
artful dodger	lodger
Auntie Ella	umbrella
Auntie Nellie	belly
babbling brook	cook; crook
bacon and eggs	legs
ball of chalk	walk
balloon car	saloon bar
band in the box	pox
band of hope	soap
Barnaby Rudge	judge
Barnet Fair	hair
bat and wicket	ticket
Bath bun	son; sun
battle-cruiser	boozer
bazaar	bar (pub)
bear's paw	saw
Beecham's Pill	bill; still (photo)
bees and honey	money

beggar my neighbour	on the labour (dole)
bird lime	time
biscuits and cheese	knees
bladder of lard	card
boat race	face
Bob Squash	wash
Bo-Peep	sleep
boracic lint	skint
bottle and glass	arse
bow and arrow	sparrow
bread and butter	gutter
bread and cheese	sneeze
Bristol Cities	titties
Brussels sprouts	scouts
bubble and squeak	beak (magistrate); Greek
bucket and pail	jail
bull and cow	row
burnt cinder	window
Burton-on-Trent	rent
bushel and peck	neck
Bushey Park	lark
butcher's hook	look
Cain and Abel	table
canal boat	tote
Cape of Good Hope	soap
Captain Cook	book
carving knife	wife
cash and carried	married
cat and mouse	house
Chalk Farm	arm
cheerful giver	liver
Cherry Hogg	dog
Chevy Chase	face
china plate	mate
chop sticks	six
clickety click	sixty-six
cobbler's awls	balls
cock linnet	minute
cockroach	coach
cock sparrow	barrow
cocoa	say so
Conan Doyle	boil
country cousin	dozen
crust of bread	head
cuddle and kiss	miss
currant bun	son; sun; *The Sun*
custard and jelly	telly
cuts and scratches	matches
daffydown dilly	silly
Daily Mail	tale
daisy roots	boots
dickory dock	clock
dicky bird	word
Dicky Dirt	shirt
dig in the grave	shave
ding dong	song
ding dong bell	hell
dinky doo	twenty-two
Doctor Crippen	dripping
dog and bone	phone
do me goods	Woods (Woodbines)
Duchess of Fife	wife
Duke of York	chalk; cork; fork
dustbin lids	kids
early hours	flowers
earwig	twig (understand)
eighteen pence	sense
elephant's trunk	drunk
field of wheat	street
fife and drum	bum
fine and dandy	brandy
fisherman's daughter	water
flowery dell	cell
four by two	Jew
frog and toad	road
front wheel skid	yid
garden gate	magistrate
gay and frisky	whisky
German bands	hands
ginger beer	queer; engineer
Glasgow Rangers	strangers
God forbids	kids
goose's neck	cheque
Gordon and Gotch	watch
grasshopper	copper
greengages	wages
Hampstead Heath	teeth
Hampton Wick	prick
Harry Randall	candle
Harvey Nichols	pickles
hearts of oak	broke
hit and miss	kiss; piss
holy friar	liar
iron hoof	pouf
iron tank	bank
Isle of Wight	right
I suppose	nose
Jack and Jill	hill; bill; till
jackdaw	jaw
Jack Jones	alone
Jack Tar	bar
Jack the Ripper	kipper
jam jar	car
Jerry O'Gorman	Mormon
Jimmy Riddle	piddle
Jim Skinner	dinner
Joanna	piano
Johnnie Horner	corner
Kate and Sydney	steak and kidney
Kate Karney	army
Khyber Pass	arse
kidney punch	lunch
la-di-dah	car
Lilian Gish	fish
Lilley and Skinner	dinner; beginner
linen draper	paper
lion's lair	chair
loaf of bread	head
loop the loop	soup
Lord Lovell	shovel
Lord Mayor	swear
lousy brown	Rose and Crown
Lucy Locket	pocket
macaroni	pony
Marie Corelli	telly
Mickey Mouse	house
mince pies	eyes
Molly Malone	phone
monkeys' tails	nails
Mother Hubbard	cupboard
mother's ruin	gin
Mrs Chant	aunt
Mutt and Jeff	deaf
nanny goat	boat; tote; coat
near and far	bar; car
needle and pin	gin
Nervo and Knox	pox; goggle box
Newington Butts	guts
Noah's ark	park; nark
north and south	mouth
oily rag	fag
old pot and pan	old man
Oliver Twist	fist
on the floor	poor
orchestra stalls	balls
Owen Nares	chairs
Oxford scholar	dollar
peas in the pot	hot
pen and ink	stink
piccolo and flute	suit
pig's ear	beer
pimple and blotch	scotch
pitch and toss	boss
plates of meat	feet
pleasure and pain	rain
potatoes in the mould	cold
rabbit and pork	talk
read and write	fight
Richard the Third	bird
Rory O'More	door

Rosy Lee	tea	tea pot lid	yid; quid; kid
round the houses	trousers	tiddly wink	drink
rub-a-dub-dub	pub	tit for tat	hat
Salford Docks	rocks	Tod Sloan	(on one's) own
salmon and trout	stout	Tom and Dick	sick
sausage and mash	cash; crash	Tommy Tucker	supper
Scapa Flow	go	Tom Thumb	rum
Scotch pegs	legs	trouble and strife	wife
Sexton Blake	cake; fake	two and eight	state
skin and blister	sister	Uncle Bert	shirt
sky rocket	pocket	Uncle Fred	bread
sorry and sad	bad	Uncle Ned	bed
stammer and stutter	butter	weasel and stoat	coat
stand at ease	cheese	weeping willow	pillow
tea leaf	thief	whistle and flute	suit
		you and me	tea

Greek Alphabet

Α	α	alpha	Ν	ν	nu
Β	β	beta	Ξ	ξ	xi
Γ	γ	gamma	Ο	ο	omicron
Δ	δ	delta	Π	π	pi
Ε	ε	epsilon	Ρ	ρ	rho
Ζ	ζ	zeta	Σ	σ	sigma (ς - word final position)
Η	η	eta	Τ	τ	tau
Θ	θ	theta	Υ	υ	upsilon
Ι	ι	iota	Φ	φ	phi
Κ	κ	kappa	Χ	χ	chi
Λ	λ	lambda	Ψ	ψ	psi
Μ	μ	mu	Ω	ω	omega

Hebrew Alphabet

NB There are 22 letters in the alef-bet and Hebrew script is written from right to left, alef being the first letter and tav the last. Khaf/Kaf (1), mem (2), nun (1), Fe/Pei (1) and tzadei (1) are variant characters used at the end of a word.

Americanisms

English word	*American equivalent*	*English word*	*American equivalent*
A (film rating)	M (Mature film rating)	Alf Garnett	Archie Bunker
AA (film rating)	R (Restricted film rating)	Alsatian	German Shepherd
accumulator bet	parlay	aluminium	aluminum
Akela	Den Mother	anorak	parka

English word	*American equivalent*
approved school	reform school
Armistice Day	Veteran's Day
articulated lorry	trailer truck
aubergine	eggplant
autumn	fall
avocado	alligator pear
baby's liquid feed	formula
baby's dummy	pacifier
bag	sack
baking tray	cookie sheet
bank account	checking account
bank holiday	legal holiday
bank note	bill
bed (folding)	murphy bed
beggar	pan handler
big wheel	ferris wheel
biscuit	cookie
Black Maria	patrol wagon
blue-eyed boy (pet)	fair-haired boy (pet)
bottom drawer	hope chest
bowler hat	derby
box room	lumber room
braces	suspenders
broad bean	Lima bean
budgerigar	parakeet
bullseye	zinger
bum	fanny
bum-bag	fanny pack
by-law	ordinance
camp bed	cot
candy floss	cotton candy
car bonnet	hood
car boot	trunk
car park	parking lot
caravan site	trailer park
caretaker	janitor
cashier	teller
casserole	pot roast
catapult	slingshot
cattle grid	Texas gate
chat	confab
cheat	gyp
chemist's shop	drug store
cheque	check
chest of drawers	bureau
chick-pea	garbanzo bean
chimney	smokestack
chips	french fries
chiropodist	podiatrist
cigar box	humidor
city centre	down town
class/form	grade
commis waiter	bus boy
complimentary ticket	Annie Oakley
condom	rubber
convict	yardbird
coriander	cilantro
cos lettuce	romaine lettuce
courgette	zucchini
cravat	Ascot
cream cracker	soda cracker
crisps	chips
cupboard	closet
current account	checking account
curriculum vitae	résumé
curtains	drapes
curtains (net)	sheers/underdrapes
death duties	estate tax
dinner jacket	tuxedo
directory inquiries	information
district	precinct
docker	longshoreman
double cream	whipping cream
drainpipe	downspout
draughts	checkers
drawing pin	thumb tack
dress circle	mezzanine/loge
dressing gown	bathrobe

English word	*American equivalent*
dual carriageway	divided highway
dustbin	garbage pail
earth wire	ground wire
eiderdown	comforter
elastic band	rubber band
estate agent	realtor
estate car	station wagon
Europe	yarrup
evening classes	night school
fan light	transom
fill in (a form)	fill out (a form)
fire hydrant	fire plug
firework	firecracker
flannel	wash cloth
flat (leased or owned)	apartment
flat (owned)	condominium
flatterer	apple polisher
flautist	flutist
flex	wire
flick knife	switchblade
floor	deck
flyover	overpass
foot and mouth	hoof and mouth
foyer	lobby
frying pan	skillet
full stop	period
funny bone	crazy bone
garage	bodyshop
garden	yard
gardening	yard work
gear lever	gearshift
girl guide	girl scout
glow worm	lightning bug
goods van (train)	box car
goods wagon (train)	freight car
gossip	scuttle butt
got	gotten
greaseproof paper	wax paper
green fingers	green thumb
grill	broil
gundog	birddog
guttering	eavestrough
haberdashery	notions
handbag	pocketbook; purse
hash (symbol)	octothorpe
hat (woollen)	toque
Heath Robinson	Rube Goldberg
hire purchase	instalment plan
hob	burner
homeless woman	bag lady
hot dog	weenie
housewife	homemaker
housing estate	sub-division
hymen	cherry
ice lolly	popsicle
icing sugar	confectionery sugar; powdered sugar
ignorant person	redneck
illegal immigrant	wet-back
income support	relief
influenza	grippe
jam	jelly
jelly	jello
jemmy	jimmy
jug	pitcher
jumble sale	rummage sale
knacker's yard	glue factory
ladder (in stockings)	run (in tights)
ladybird	ladybug
lame	gimpy
lantern	jacklight
lay-by	pull-off
level crossing	grade crossing
lift	elevator
limited (company)	incorporated (inc)
lodger	roomer
long jump	broad jump
lorry	truck
lovebite	hickey

English word	*American equivalent*
lucky dip	grab bag
maize	corn
megaphone	bullhorn
men's outfitter	haberdasher
merry-go-round	carousel
minced meat	hamburger meat; ground meat
money paid illicitly	kickback
motorway	throughway; freeway expressway; superhighway
mudguard (car)	fender
music-hall	vaudeville
muslin	cheesecloth
Naafi	PX (Post Exchange)
nappy	diaper
non-alcoholic drink	root beer
notepad	scratchpad
noughts & crosses	tic tac toe
offal	variety meat
okra	gumbo
open air stands	bleachers
oven	range
oven gloves	pot holders
packed lunch	sack lunch
pageboy (hotel)	bellhop
paraffin	kerosene
patience (card game)	solitaire
paunch (spare tyre)	bay window
pavement	sidewalk
pedestrian crossing	crosswalk
pelmet	valance
Perspex (trade name)	Plexiglas
persuade	buffalo
petrol	gas
petrol station	filling station
pharmacist	druggist
phone-in	call-in
pimple	zit
plaster (medical dressing)	Band-Aid
plus fours	knickers
police patrol car	prowl car
policeman (uniformed)	patrolman
porter	bellhop
post code	zip code
pouffe	hassock
primary school	grade school
public convenience	comfort station
public school	private school
pushchair	stroller
queue	line
quilt	comforter
railway porter	redcap
receptionist	desk clerk
reef knot	square knot
refrigerator	icebox
reserve price	upset price
residential area	uptown
revision (for exams)	review
riding whip	quirt
ring doughnut	cruller
road	pavement
rosé wines	blush wines
rota	roster
roundabout	traffic circle
rubbish	garbage
sack	fire
sailor (US navy)	bluey jacket
saloon car	sedan
salt beef	corned beef
sandpit	sand box
sausages	links

English word	*American equivalent*
scarf	neckerchief
season ticket	commuter ticket
second-hand	pre-owned
self-catering	cook-in
semi-detached	duplex
short-hand typist	stenographer
short trousers	knee pants
sideboards	sideburns
skipping rope	jumping rope
skirting board	base board; mopboard
smoked salmon	lox
smoking jacket	lounge jacket
sofa	davenport
solicitor	attorney
sorbet	sherbet
spanner	wrench
spare room	glory hole
stalls	orchestra seats
state school	public school
states on Gulf of Mexico	Gulf States
stiletto heels	spike heels
stock	inventory
streaming (in schools)	tracking
string	cord
striptease artist	peeler
suitcase	valise
surgical spirit	rubbing alcohol
swede	rutabaga
sweet potato	yam
sweets	candy
Swiss roll	jelly roll
tallboy	highboy
tap	faucet
telephone box	phone booth
television	boot tube
tennis shoes	sneakers
ticket (free)	Annie Oakley
tie-pin	stick-pin
tobacconist's shop	cigar store
toilet (domestic)	restroom
toilet (outdoor)	out-house
torch	flashlight
tornado	twister
training camp (military)	boot camp
tram	streetcar
trilby	fedora
trousers	pants
truncheon	nightstick
turn-ups (trousers)	cuffs
U (Universal film rating)	G (General film rating)
underground (tube)	subway
underpants	shorts
undertaker	mortician
up to you	down to you
US marine	leatherneck
use hindsight after the event	second-guess
verruca	plantar wart
vest	undershirt
VIP address book	blue book
waistcoat	vest
waiter (apprentice)	bus boy
walk with style	sashay
wallet	billfold
washing up bowl	dishpan
wedding ring	wedding band
wet paint	fresh paint
wheelbarrow	pushcart
wholemeal biscuit	graham cracker
windscreen	windshield
zed (z)	zee

Forenames: Meanings

Aaron high mountain/bright
Abdullah servant of God
Abel breath
Adam red earth
Abelard resolute
Abigail father rejoices
Abner father of light
Cordelia jewel of the sea
Abraham father on high/father of many
Absalom father of peace
Ada noble/happy/prosperous
Hans (variant of John)

Adolph noble wolf
Adrian dark one of the Adriatic
Aesop burnt faced
Agatha good
Agnes lamb/chaste
Ahab uncle
Ajax eagle
Akram excellent
Alan harmony/handsome
Alaric ruler of all
Alastair form of Alexander
Albert nobly bright
Alexander defender of men
Alfred elf/wise counsellor
Algernon bearded
Ali protected by God/the greatest
Alison of noble kind
Alma apple/nourishing/loving
Amadeus lover of God
Amanda fit to be loved
Ambrose immortal
Amelia hard-working
Amos burden
Amy beloved
Andrea female form of Andrew
Andrew manly
Angela messenger/angel
Anita grace, mercy
Anne English form of Hannah
Anthea flowery
Anthony inestimable
April name of a month
Arnold eagle power
Arthur bear/stone/valorous
Audrey noble strength
Aziz famous
Barbara strange/foreign land
Barry fair-headed/spear
Baruch blessed
Basil royal/kingly
Beatrice bringer of joy
Belinda beautiful and pretty
Benjamin son of my right hand
Berenice one who brings victory
Bernard brave bear
Bertram glorious raven
Beth pet form of Elizabeth
Betty pet form of Elizabeth
Bill pet form of William
Bipin forest
Bjorn bear
Bob pet form of Robert
Boris fighter
Brandon broom-covered hill
Brenda burning/a flame
Brian hill/strength
Bronwyn white breasted
Bud brother
Byron from the cottage
Carl man/husbandman
Cameron crooked nose/awesome
Carmen garden/song
Carol female form of Charles
Casper treasure
Catherine pure
Cecilia blind
Charles man/husbandman
Cher beloved
Christine anointed
Christopher carrier of Christ
Claire bright/shining
Colette victorious
Colin form of Nicholas
Lucille light

Craig rock
Cressida golden
Cyril lord
Damian to tame
Daniel God is my judge
Danielle female form of Daniel
Darius wealthy
Darren beloved
David beloved/friend
Dean valley/leader
Deborah bee/eloquent
Declan man of prayer
Dennis of Dionysus (Greek God of wine)
Derek gifted ruler (form of Theodonic)
Dermot free man
Derry red-haired
Diane divine
Donald world ruler
Donna lady
Donovan dark warrior
Doris gift of the sea
Dorothy gift of God
Douglas from the dark water
Dudley of the people's meadows
Eamon rich protector
Ebenezer stone of help
Edward prosperous guardian
Eileen Irish form of Helen
Eldridge wise ruler
Elijah Jehovah is my God
Elizabeth my God is bountiful
Elvis all wise
Emily industrious
Emma all-embracing
Emmanuel God with us
Enoch dedicated
Eric ruler of all
Erasmus lovable
Esther star
Ethan firm/strong
Eugenie well born
Evelyn pleasant
Ezekiel God will strengthen
Ezra helper
Felipe lover of horses
Felix fortunate
Ferdinand adventuresome
Fidel faithful
Finlay fair hero
Floyd grey-haired
Frank Frenchman/freeman
Franklin freeholder
Frederick peaceful ruler
Gabriel God is my strength
Gail pet form of Abigail
Gareth gentle/firm spear
Garth protector
Gary spear/form of Gareth
Gavin hawk
Gemma gem
Geoffrey peaceful ruler/God's peace
George husbandman/farmer
Gerard bold spear
Graham warlike person
Gregory on the watch
Griselda grey battle maid
Gudrun God secret
Gulliver glutton
Guy lovely
Habib beloved
Hamish (variant of Jacob)
Hanif believer
Hannah grace/favour
Pamela all honey

Harold leader of armies
Harry pet form of Henry
Hayley hay-meadow
Hector steadfast
Helen bright/shining one
Henry household ruler
Hermione well-born lady
Hilary joyful
Hilda battle maid
Hiram most noble
Homer pledge
Horace keeper of the hours
Hortense gardener
Howard guardian
Hubert bright minded
Hugh heart/mind
Humphrey warrior peace
Ian Scottish form of John
Ichabod departed glory
Ida work
Imran strong
Ira watchful
Irene peace
Iris rainbow
Irvin handsome/fair
Isaac he will laugh
Isaiah God is salvation
Ishmael God will hear
Ivan his favour
Jacqueline female form of James
James one who takes by the heel
Jane female form of John
Jared descending
Jason to heal
Javier owner of a new horse
Jed hard
Jemima dove
Jennifer fair
Jeremy Jehovah exalts/appointed by God
Jess wealthy
Jessica God beholds
Jethro superabundance
Jezebel domination
Joab God is the father
Joachim God will judge
Joan helper
John Jehovah has been gracious
Jonathan Jehovah's gift
Joseph Jehovah adds
Joyce joyful
Julie descended from Jove/youthful
Julian descended from Jove/youthful
Karen from Katarina/pure
Katarina (form of Catherine)
Keir dark skinned
Keith of the forest
Kelly warlike one
Kenneth handsome; fair one or fire sprung
Kevin handsome at birth
Lakisha woman
Latoya Antonia
Laura bay/laurel
Leah gazelle
Lee of the meadow
Leila night
Leonard strong lion
Leslie of the grey, fortress
Letitia joy
Lilith of the night
Linda pretty
Lindsay pool on the island
Lloyd grey
Loretta pure
Stacey resurrection

Lyn cascade
Madhur sweet
Madison warrior's son
Magnus great
Malcolm dove
Mandy much loved
Marcus war-like
Margaret pearl
Mario war-like
Mark Mars (god of war)
Martin Mars (god of war)
Marvin sea friend
Mary 'bitterness' or wished-for child
Matilda battle maiden
Matthew gift of the Lord
Maureen little Mary
Maurice dark-skinned
Melissa bee/honey
Merill famous
Michael like the Lord
Miranda fit to be wondered at
Moses saved
Nadia hope
Nancy pet form of Anne
Natalie birthday of the Lord
Neil champion
Nicholas victory of the people
Noah rest/comfort
Omar first son
Patricia noble
Paul small
Peter stone/rock
Philip lover of horses
Quentin fifth born child
Rachel ewe
Randolph edge wolf/house wolf
Raphael God has healed
Raymond counsel for the defence/wise protection
Rebecca noose/one who brings peace
Rhoda rose
Richard strong ruler
Robert bright fame
Roger famous spear
Rolf swift wolf
Ronald counsel/power
Ronan little seal
Rowan red
Roxane dawn
Ruth vision of beauty/compassion
Samuel heard/name of God
Sarah princess
Saskia protector of the universe
Sean (form of John)
Sebastian revered
Sharon the plain
Shirley bright clearing
Simon listening attentively
Stephen crown
Stuart steward
Susan lily
Sylvia forest
Teresa woman of Theresia/reaper
Theodoric gifted ruler
Thomas twin
Tiffany manifestation of God
Timothy honouring God
Tracy pet form of Teresa
Trevor big village/prudent
Tristan the noisy one
Ursula she bear
Vera faith/truth
Victoria victory
Vincent conquer
Virgil flourishing
Virginia maiden
Vladimir possess peace
Walter ruling people
Wayne wagon maker
William helmet of resolution
Xavier bright
Yuri farmer
Yusuf one chosen by God
Zachariah God's remembrance
Zadok just
Zia enlightened
Zoe life

LITERATURE

Autobiographies: By Title

Title	Author
Absolutely Mahvelous	Billy Crystal
Absolutely Now	Lynn Franks
Accidental MP, An	Martin Bell
Actor and His Time, An	John Gielgud
Acts of Defiance	Jack Ashley
Acts of Faith	Adam Faith
Against Goliath	David Steel
Against the Grain	Boris Yeltsin
Alderman's Tale, The	Don Mosey
All Above Board	Wilfrid Brambell
All Creatures Great and Small	James Herriott
Alliss in Wonderland	Peter Alliss
All My Yesterdays	Edward G Robinson
All Those Tomorrows	Mai Zetterling
Almost a Gentleman (1991)	John Osborne
Along My Line	Gilbert Harding
Also Known as Shirley (1987)	Shelley Winters
Always Playing	Nigel Kennedy
An Actor's Life for Me	Lilian Gish
An American Comedy	Harold Lloyd
Animal Days	Desmond Morris
Another Part of the Wood (1974)	Kenneth Clark
Anything for a Quiet Life	Jack Hawkins
Apple Sauce	Michael Wilding
Arias and Raspberries	Sir Harry Secombe
As I Am	Trisha Goddard
As I Remember Them (1962)	Eddie Cantor
As I Walked Out One Midsummer's Morning	Laurie Lee (1929)
As It Happened (1954)	Clement, Attlee
As It Happens (1975)	Jimmy Savile
As It Seemed to Me	John Cole
Astronomer by Chance	Bernard Lovell
At My Mother's Knee	Paul O'Grady
Backward Glance, A	Edith Wharton
Banjaxed	Terry Wogan
Bardot, Deneuve, and Fonda	Roger Vadim
Barefaced Lies and Boogie Woogie Boasts	Jools Holland
Battling for Peace	Shimon Peres
Beam Ends (1934)	Errol Flynn
Beating Time	Antony Hopkins (conductor)
Before I Forget	James Mason
Before the Dawn	Gerry Adams
Beginning	Kenneth Branagh
Being Jordan	Katie Price
Being Myself	Martina Navratilova
Beneath the Underdog	Charlie Mingus
Best of Times, Worst of Times	Shelley Winters
Better Class of Person, A (1981)	John Osborne
Beware, Dobermans, Donkeys and Ducks	Alexandra Basted
Blessings in Disguise (1985)	Alec Guinness
Bonus of Laughter, The	Leslie Crowther
Born Lucky	John Francome
Born to Believe (1953)	Lord Longford
Bound for Glory	Woody Guthrie
Boy	Roald Dahl
Bring on the Empty Horses	David Niven
British Picture, A (1985)	Ken Russell
Buried Day, The	Cecil Day Lewis
By Myself	Lauren Bacall
Can You Have It All	Nicola Horlick
Caught in the Act (1986)	Richard Todd
Change Lobsters and Dance	Lili Palmer
Changing	Liv Ullmann
Child of My Love	Sue Ryder
Choices	Liv Ullmann
Chronicles of Wasted Time	Malcolm Muggeridge
Cider With Rosie (1959)	Laurie Lee
Citizen Jane	Jane Fonda
Cleared for Take Off (1996)	Dirk Bogarde
Clear Water Stream, A (1958)	Henry Williamson
Closing Ranks (1997)	Dirk Bogarde
Coal Miner's Daughter, The	Loretta Lynn
Coming Attraction (1988)	Terence Stamp
Confessions	Jean-Jacques Rousseau
Confessions of an Actor	John Barrymore
Confessions of an Actor	Laurence Olivier
Confessions of an English Opium-Eater	Thomas De Quincey
Courting Triumph	Virginia Wade
Crying with Laughter	Bob Monkhouse
Cuban Rebel Girls (1959)	Errol Flynn
Dancing in the Light (1985)	Shirley MacLaine
Dancing in the Moonlight	Ronnie Barker
Dear Me	Peter Ustinov
Diet for Life	Lynn Redgrave
Don't Fall off the Mountain	Shirley MacLaine (1970)
Don't Laugh at Me	Norman Wisdom
Door Marked Summer, The	Michael Bentine
Double Feature (1989)	Terence Stamp
Drums under the Window (1945)	Sean O' Casey
Duke, The	David Nicholson
Ecstasy and Me	Hedy Lamarr
Ed Wynn's Son	Keenan Wynn
80 Not Out	Patrick Moore
Eternal Male, The	Omar Sharif
Evening All	Ted Willis
Every Other Inch a Lady	Beatrice Lilley
Every Shot I Take	Davis Love III
Eye of the Tiger	Frank Bruno
Facing the Music	Jane Torvill & Christopher Dean
Falling towards England	Clive James
Farce about Face	Brian Rix
Final Dress (1983)	John Houseman
Fire over England (1994)	Ken Russell
First Interval	Donald Wolfit
Five Lives (1964)	Lord Longford
For Dogs and Angels	Chili Boucher
Free House, A	Walter Sickert
From a Bundle of Rags	Jim Bowen
Front and Center (1980)	John Houseman
Full Monty, The	Jim Davidson
Fun in a Chinese Laundry	Josef von Sternberg
Funny Kind of Love, A	Sian Lloyd
Future Indefinite (1954)	Noel Coward
Gay Illiterate, The (1944)	Louella Parsons
Gift of Joy, A (1965)	Helen Hayes
Girl Power	Spice Girls
Glorious Uncertainty	Jenny Pitman
Good Vibrations	Jacqueline Gold (Ann Summers)
Good Vibrations	Evelyn Glennie
Goodbye to All That	Robert Graves
Goodness Had Nothing to Do with It	Mae West (1959)
Good, the Bad and the Bubbly,	George Best
Grace Abounding	John Bunyan
Grain of Wheat (1974)	Lord Longford
Grand Inquisitor	Robin Day
Greatest Game of All, The (1969)	Jack Nicklaus
Great Meadow (1992)	Dirk Bogarde
Great Morning (1947)	Osbert Sitwell
Halfway Through the Door	Alan Arkin
Happy Go Lucky (1959)	Kenneth More
Happy Hooker, The	Xaviera Hollander
Haunted Life, A	Anthony Perkins
Have Tux Will Travel (1958)	Bob Hope
Here Lies	Eric Ambler
His Eye Is on the Sparrow	Ethel Waters
Hitting across the Line	Viv Richards
Hollywood in a Suitcase (1980)	Sammy Davis Jnr
Hons and Rebels	Jessica Mitford
Hundred Different Lives, A	Raymond Massey
I Can't Stay Long (1975)	Laurie Lee
I.E. (1965)	Mickey Rooney
I Knock at the Door (1939)	Sean O' Casey
I Know Why the Caged Bird Sings	Maya Angelou
I Like What I Know	Vincent Price

Title	Author
I'm Still Here	Yvonne De Carlo
I'm Still Here (1989)	Eartha Kitt
In and Out of Character	Basil Rathbone
In Camera (1989)	Richard Todd
In Darkness and Light	Anthony Hopkins
Inishfallen Fare Thee Well	Sean O' Casey (1949)
In My Father's Court	Isaac Bashevis Singer
In My Mind's Eye (1983)	Michael Redgrave
In Search of History: A Personal Adventure	Theodore H White
Inside the Third Reich	Albert Speer
Intermission	Anne Baxter
I Owe Russia $2000 (1963)	Bob Hope
I Paid Hitler	Baron Von Thyssen
I Reach for the Stars	Barbara Cartland
I Search for Rainbows (1967)	Barbara Cartland
I Seek the Miraculous (1978)	Barbara Cartland
I Was Born Greek	Melina Mercouri
Is It Me	Terry Wogan
Isthmus Years, The (1943)	Barbara Cartland
It Doesn't Take a Hero	Norman Schwarzkopf
It's All in the Playing (1987)	Shirley MacLaine
It's Been Fun (1949)	Anna Neagle
It's Me, O Lord! (1957)	AE Coppard
Jack of All Trades	Jack Warner
Jacob's Ladder	David Jacob
Jump Jockeys Don't Cry	Sharron Murgatroyd
Just a Job	Norman Collier
Just Resting	Leo McKern
Just Williams	Kenneth Williams
Keeping It Real	Jodie Marsh
Kentish Lad, A	Frank Muir
King's Story, A (1951)	Duke of Windsor
Kink	Dave Davies
Knock Wood	Candice Bergen
Last Christmas Show, The	Bob Hope (1976)
Laugh Is on Me, The	Phil Silvers
Laughter in the Next Room	Osbert Sitwell (1948)
Leaving a Doll's House	Claire Bloom
Left Hand: Right Hand	Osbert Sitwell (1944)
Let's Get through Wednesday	Reginald Bosanquet
Let the Chips Fall	Rudy Vallee
Life for Life's Sake	Richard Aldington
Life in Movies, A	Michael Powell
Life in Movies, A	Fred Zinneman
Life Is a Banquet	Rosalind Russell
Life Is Too Short (1991)	Mickey Rooney
Life Lines (1989)	Jill Ireland
Life of an American Workman,	Walter Percy Chrysler
Life on Film (1971)	Mary Astor
Life, Sex and ESP (1975)	Mae West
Life Wish (1987)	Jill Ireland
Limelight and After	Claire Bloom
Little Clown, The	Reg Varney
Little Girl Lost	Drew Barrymore
Little Wilson and Big God	Anthony Burgess (1987)
Lonely Life, The (1962)	Bette Davis
Long Banana Skin, The	Michael Bentine
Long Walk to Freedom	Nelson Mandela
Lorenzo Goes to Hollywood	Edward Arnold
Losing My Virginity	Sir Richard Branson
Love Is a Many-Splendoured Thing	Han Suyin
Love Is an Uphill Thing	Jimmy Savile (1975)
Man Who Listens to Horses,	Monty Roberts
Martha, Jane and Me	Mavis Nicholson
Mask or Face (1958)	Michael Redgrave
Master of None	Gilbert Harding
Me	Katherine Hepburn
Mein Kampf	Adolf Hitler
Memoirs of an Unfit Mother	Anne Robinson
Memoirs of a Professional Cad	George Sanders
Memories	Ethel Barrymore
Middle of My Century, The	Shelley Winters (1989)
Mingled Chime, A	Thomas Beecham
Minnie the Moocher and Me	Cab Calloway
Mirror in My House (1956)	Sean O' Casey
Moab Is My Washpot	Stephen Fry
Moment of War, A	Laurie Lee
Moon's a Balloon, The	David Niven

Title	Author
More or Less (1978)	Kenneth More
Mother Goddam (1975)	Bette Davis
Movies, Mr Griffith and Me, The	Lilian Gish
Mr Nice	Howard Marks
Musician at Large	Steve Race
Must the Show Go On?	Les Dennis
My American Journey	Colin Powell
My Days and Dreams	Edward Carpenter
My Double Life	Sarah Bernhardt
My Early Life (1981)	Ronald Reagan
My Life	Richard Wagner
My Life Line	Lady Isobel Barnett
My Life, My Way	Cliff Richard
My Lucky Stars: A Hollywood Memory (1989)	Shirley Maclaine
My Many Lives	Lotte Lehmann
My Name Escapes Me (1996)	Alec Guinness
My Story (1959)	Mary Astor
My Ten Years in the Studios	George Arliss (1940)
My Time	Bradley Wiggins
My Turn	Nancy Reagan
My Wicked Wicked Ways (1955)	Errol Flynn
Naked Civil Servant, The	Quentin Crisp
Nice One Cyril	Cyril Fletcher
Noa-Noa	Paul Gauguin
No Bed of Roses	Joan De Havilland
No Bells on Sunday	Rachel Roberts
Noble Essences (1950)	Osbert Sitwell
No Minor Chords	André Previn
Nostalgia Isn't What It Used to Be	Simone Signoret
Nothing's Impossible	Brian Blessed
Not the Whole Truth	Patrick Lichfield
Now and Forever	Bernie Nolan
Now and Then	Roy Castle
Oak and the Calf, The	Alexander Solzhenitsyn
Odd Man Out	Ronnie Biggs
Odd Woman Out	Muriel Box
On and Off the Fairway (1979)	Jack Nicklaus
On and Off the Lee	Dorothy Hamill
One Day at a Time	Bernie Winters
One Hump or Two	Frank Worthington
One Man Tango	Anthony Quinn
One Small Footprint (1980)	Molly Weir
On My Way to the Club	Ludovic Kennedy
On Reflection (1969)	Helen Hayes
On the Other Hand	Fay Wray
On the Stage (1926)	George Arliss
Ooh! What a Lovely Pair	Ant and Dec
Open Book, An	John Huston
Opening Up	Mike Atherton
Ordeal	Linda Lovelace
Orderly Man, An (1983)	Dirk Bogarde
Original Sin, The	Anthony Quinn
Other Half, The (1977)	Kenneth Clark
Other Side of the Street, The	Jean Alexander
Outline	Paul Nash
Out of Africa	Isak Dinesen / Karen Blixen
Out on a Limb	Heather Mills
Out on a Limb (1983)	Shirley MacLaine
Peacework (1991)	Spike Milligan
People	Edgar Wallace
Pictures in the Hallway (1942)	Sean O' Casey
Please Don't Hate Me	Dmitri Tiomkin
Poet in the Family, A	Dannie Abse
Point of View, A	Barry Took
Polly Wants a Zebra	Michael Aspel
Postillion Struck by Lightning,	Dirk Bogarde (1977)
Precious Little Sleep	Wayne Sleep
Present Indicative (1937)	Noël Coward
Prick up Your Ears	Joe Orton
Prima Donna's Progress, A	Joan Sutherland
Quite Contrary	Mary Whitehouse
Ragman's Son, The	Kirk Douglas
Rebel with a Cause	Hans Eysenck
Reluctant Jester, The	Michael Bentine
Road to Hollywood (1977)	Bob Hope
Roamin' in the Gloaming	Sir Harry Lauder
Roar of the Crowd	Gentleman Jim Corbett
Runthrough (1972)	John Houseman

Title	Author
Scarlet Tree, The (1946)	Osbert Sitwell
Screening History	Gore Vidal
Second Act	Joan Collins
Self Consciousness	John Updike
Self Portrait	Gene Tierney
Shelley (1980)	Shelley Winters
Shoes Were for Sunday	Molly Weir (1970)
Shooting the Actor	Simon Callow
Short Walk from Harrods, A	Dirk Bogarde (1994)
Silver and Gold	Norman Hartnell
Snakes and Ladders	Dirk Bogarde (1978)
Some Other Rainbow	John McCarthy and Jill Morrell
Sound of Laughter, The	Peter Kay
Spend Spend Spend	Vivian Nicholson
Stamp Album (1987)	Terence Stamp
Stand By Your Man	Tammy Wynette
Stare Back and Smile	Joanna Lumley
Steps in Time	Fred Astaire
Still Dancing	Lew Grade
Still on My Way to Hollywood	Ernie Wise
Story of a Bad Man	Thomas Aldrich
Story of a Soul, The	Thérèse of Lisieux
Straight Man, The	Nicholas Parsons
Straight Shooting	Robert Stack
Suite in Four Movements	Eric Coates
Summoned by Bells	John Betjeman
Sunday Night at Seven	Jack Benny
Sunset and Evening Star (1955)	Sean O'Casey
Surprised by Joy	CS Lewis
Take It Like a Man	Boy George
Take My Life (1957)	Eddie Cantor
Taken on Trust	Terry Waite
Tall, Dark and Gruesome	Christopher Lee
Tell It to Louella (1962)	Louella Parsons
Testament of Youth	Vera Brittain
Testing Times	Graham Gooch
Thanks for Nothing	Jack Dee
There's Always Tomorrow	Anna Neagle (1974)
There's Lovely	Johnny Morris
Things I Had to Learn, The	Loretta Young
Those Twentieth Century Blues	Michael Tippett
Thursday's Child	Eartha Kitt
Time and Chance	James Callaghan
Time to Declare	David Owen
To Hell and Back	Niki Lauda
To Hell and Back	Audie Murphy
To Keep the Ball Rolling	Anthony Powell
Travelling Player	Michael York
Tree Is a Tree, A	King Vidor
Twenty Questions	Norman Hackforth
Twice Over Lightly (1981)	Helen Hayes
Two-Way Story	Cliff Michelmore & Jean Metcalfe
Unreliable Memoirs	Clive James
Up from Slavery	Booker T Washington
Up in the Clouds, Gentlemen Please	John Mills
Up the Ladder to Obscurity	David Lodge
Up the Years from Bloomsbury	George Arliss (1927)
Vanished World, The	HE Bates (1969)
Vie d'Henri Brulard, La	Stendhal
Voyage (1978)	Sterling Hayden
Walking in the Shade	Doris Lessing
Walking Tall	Simon Weston
Wanderer (1963)	Sterling Hayden
Way I See It, The (1959)	Eddie Cantor
Wet Flanders Plain, The	Henry Williamson (1929)
What Falls Away	Mia Farrow
What's It All About	Michael Caine
When I Was Young	Raymond Massey
Where Have All the Bullets Gone (1985)	Spike Milligan
Where's Harry	Harry Carpenter
Where's the Rest of Me	Ronald Reagan
White Slave	Marco Pierre White
Why Me (1989)	Sammy Davis Jnr
Will This Do	Auberon Waugh
With Nails	Richard E Grant
Words	Jean-Paul Sartre
World Elsewhere, A	Michael Hordern
World of Yesterday, The	Stefan Zweig
World Within World	Stephen Spender
Years of Opportunity, The	Barbara Cartland (1947)
Yes I Can (1966)	Sammy Davis Jnr
Yo Yo Man, The	Bill Maynard
You Can Get There from Here (1975)	Shirley MacLaine
Yours Indubitably	Robertson Hare
You've Had Your Time (1990)	Anthony Burgess
Zero to Hero	Frank Bruno

NB: Dates are only provided when authors listed have more than one volume of autobiography or in instances where an author's identity may need clarification.

First Lines of Books and Poems

Adams, Douglas *The Hitch Hiker's Guide to the Galaxy* Far out in the uncharted backwaters of the unfashionable end of the Western Spiral arm of the Galaxy lies a small unregarded yellow sun.

Adams, Douglas *The Restaurant at the End of the Universe* There is a theory which states that if anyone discovers exactly what the Universe is for and why it is here, it will instantly disappear and be replaced by something even more bizarre and inexplicable.

Adams, Richard *Watership Down* The primroses were over.

Adams, Richard *Shardik* Even in the dry heat of summer's end, the great forest was never silent.

Agee, James *A Death in the Family* We are talking now of summer evenings in Knoxville, Tennessee in the time that I lived there so successfully disguised to myself as a child.

Albom, Mitch *The Five People You Meet in Heaven* This is a story about a man named Eddie and it begins at the end, with Eddie dying in the sun.

Alcott, Louisa May *Good Wives* In order that we may start afresh and go to Meg's wedding with free minds, it will be well to begin with a little gossip about the Marches.

Alcott, Louisa May *Little Men* Please, sir, is this Plumfield? asked a ragged boy of the man who opened the great gate at which the omnibus left him.

Alcott, Louisa May *Little Women* Christmas won't be Christmas without any presents, grumbled Jo, lying on the rug.

Angelou, Maya *I Know Why the Caged Bird Sings* When I was three and Bailey was four, we had arrived in the musty little town.

Arnold, Matthew 'Dover Beach' The sea is calm tonight. The tide is full, the moon lies fair.

Ashford, Daisy *The Young Visiters* Mr Salteena was an elderly man of 42 and was fond of asking peaple (sic) to stay with him.

Asimov, Isaac *Foundation* His name was Gaal Dornick and he was just a country boy who had never seen Trantor before.

Asimov, Isaac *I, Robot* I looked at my notes and I didn't like them. I'd spent three days at U.S. Robots and might as well have spent them at home with the Encyclopedia Tellurica.

Atwater, Richard & Florence *Mr. Popper's Penguins* It was an afternoon in late September. In the pleasant city of Stillwater, Mr. Popper, the house painter, was going home from work.

Atwood, Margaret *The Blind Assassin* Ten days after the war ended, my sister Laura drove a car off a bridge.

Atwood, Margaret *Cat's Eye* Time is not a line but a dimension, like the dimensions of space.

Auden, WH *Night Mail* This is the Night Mail crossing the border, bringing the cheque and the postal order.

Austen, Jane *Emma* Emma Woodhouse, handsome, clever, and rich, with a comfortable home and happy disposition, seemed to unite some of the best blessings of existence.

Austen, Jane *Mansfield Park* About thirty years ago, Miss Maria Ward of Huntingdon with only seven thousand pounds had the good luck to captivate Sir Thomas Bertram.

Austen, Jane *Northanger Abbey* No one who had ever seen Catherine Morland in her infancy would have supposed her born to be an heroine.
Austen, Jane *Persuasion* Sir Walter Elliot, of Kellynch Hall, in Somersetshire, was a man who, for his own amusement, never took up any book but the Baronetage . . .
Austen, Jane *Pride and Prejudice* It is a truth universally acknowledged, that a single man in possession of a good fortune, must be in want of a wife.
Austen, Jane *Sense and Sensibility* The family of Dashwood has long been settled in Sussex.
Baldwin, James *Go Tell It on the Mountain* Everyone had always said that John would be a preacher when he grew up, just like his father.
Ballard, JG *Crash* Vaughan died yesterday in his last car-crash.
Banks, Iain *The Crow Road* It was the day my grandmother exploded.
Banks, Lynne Reid *The Indian in the Cupboard* It was not that Omri didn't appreciate Patrick's birthday present to him.
Barrie, JM *Peter Pan* All children, except one, grow up.
Barth, John *Giles Goat-Boy* George is my name; my deeds have been heard of in Tower Hall, and my childhood has been chronicled in the *Journal of Experimental Psychology.*
Barth, John *The Sot-Weed Factor* In the last years of the seventeenth century there was to be found among the fops & fools of the London coffee-houses one rangy, gangling flitch called Ebenezer Cooke, more ambitious than talented, and yet more talented than prudent.
Baum, Frank *The Wonderful Wizard of Oz* Dorothy lived in the midst of the great Kansas prairies, with Uncle Henry, who was a farmer, and Aunt Em, who was the farmer's wife.
Beckett, Samuel *Company* A voice comes to one in the dark.
Beckett, Samuel *Murphy* The sun shone, having no alternative, on the nothing new.
Bellow, Saul *The Adventures of Augie March* I am an American, Chicago born—Chicago, that somber city.
Bellow, Saul *Herzog* If I am out of my mind, it's all right with me thought Moses Herzog.
Bellow, Saul *Humboldt's Gift* The book of ballads published by Von Humboldt Fleisher in the Thirties was an immediate hit.
Bemelmans, Ludwig *Madeline* In an old house in Paris that was covered with vines lived 12 little girls in two straight lines.
Benchley, Peter *Jaws* The great fish moved silently through the night water, propelled by short sweeps of its crescent tail.
Berryman, John *Homage to Mistress Bradstreet* The Governor your husband lived so long.
Bester, Alfred *The Stars My Destination* This was a Golden Age, a time of high adventure, rich living, and hard dying . . . but nobody thought so.
Betjeman, John 'A Subaltern's Love-Song' Miss J. Hunter Dunn, Miss J. Hunter Dunn, Furnish'd and burnish'd by Aldershot sun.
Blake, William 'Tyger!' Tyger! Tyger! burning bright In the forests of the night, What immortal hand or eye Could frame thy fearful symmetry?
Blatty, William Peter *The Exorcist* Like the brief doomed flare of exploding suns that registers dimly on blind men's eyes, the beginning of the horror passed almost unnoticed.
Böll, Heinrich *The Clown* It was dark by the time I reached Bonn, and I forced myself not to succumb to the series of mechanical actions which had taken hold of me in five years of travelling back and forth.
Boyle, T Coraghessan *The Road to Wellville* Dr. John Harvey Kellogg, inventor of the cornflake and peanut butter, not to mention caramel-cereal coffee, Bromose, Nuttolene and some seventy-five other gastronomically correct foods, paused to level his gaze on the heavyset women in front of him.
Bradbury, Ray *Fahrenheit 451* It was a pleasure to burn.
Bradley, Marion Zimmer *Mists of Avalon* Even in high summer, Tintagel was a haunted place; Igraine, Lady of Duke Gorlois, looked out over the sea from the headland.
Braine, John *Life at the Top* She woke me up by lifting my eyelids; then she slipped under the bed clothes beside me and lay there smiling.
Brautigan, Richard *A Confederate General from Big Sur* When I first heard about Big Sur I didn't know that it was a member of the Confederate States of America.
Camus, Albert *The Stranger* Mother died today. Or perhaps it

Brontë, Anne *Agnes Grey* All true histories contain instruction, though in some, the treasure may be hard to find, and when found, so trivial in quantity that the dry shrivelled kernel scarcely compensates for the trouble of cracking the nut.
Brontë, Anne *The Tenant of Wildfell Hall* You must go back with me to the autumn of 1827.
Brontë, Charlotte *Jane Eyre* There was no possibility of taking a walk that day.
Brontë, Charlotte *The Professor* The other day, in looking over my papers, I found in my desk the following copy of a letter.
Brontë, Charlotte *Villette* My Godmother lived in a handsome house in the clean and ancient town of Bretton.
Brontë, Emily *Wuthering Heights* 1801 – I have just returned from a visit to my landlord.
Brooke, Rupert 'The Soldier' If I should die, think only this of me: That there's some corner of a foreign field That is forever England.
Brown, Dan *Angels & Demons* High atop the steps of the Pyramid of Giza a young woman laughed and called down to him.
Brown, Dan *The Da Vinci Code* Robert Langdon awoke slowly.
Brown, Dan *Deception Point* Toulos Restaurant, adjacent to Capitol Hill, boasts a politically incorrect menu of baby veal and horse carpaccio ...
Brown, Dan *Digital Fortress* They were in the Smoky Mountains at their favorite bed-and-breakfast.
Brown, Margaret Wise *Goodnight Moon* In the great green room, there was a telephone and a red balloon.
Brown, Rita Mae *Rubyfruit Jungle* No one remembers her beginnings.
Brown, Rita Mae *Venus Envy* Dying's not so bad. At least I won't have to answer the telephone.
Browning, Elizabeth Barrett 'How Do I Love Thee' How do I love thee? Let me count the ways. .
Browning, Robert 'Childe Roland to the Dark Tower Came' My first thought was, he lied in every word.
Browning, Robert 'Home-Thoughts: from Abroad' Oh, to be in England now that April's there . . .
Buchan, John *The Thirty-Nine Steps* I returned from the city about three o'clock on that May afternoon, pretty well disgusted with life.
Buck, Pearl *The Good Earth* It was Wang Lung's marriage day.
Bulwer-Lytton, Edward *Paul Clifford* It was a dark and stormy night and the rain fell in torrents – except at occasional intervals, when it was checked by a violent gust of wind which swept up the streets (for it is in London that our scene lies), rattling along the housetops, and fiercely agitating the scanty flame of the lamps...
Bunyan, John *The Pilgrim's Progress* As I walked through the wilderness of this world, I lighted on a certain place where was a Den, and I laid me down in that place to sleep: and, as I slept, I dreamed a dream.
Burgess, Anthony *A Clockwork Orange* What's it going to be then, eh?
Burgess, Anthony *Earthly Powers* It was the afternoon of my eighty-first birthday and I was in bed with my catamite when Ali announced that the Archbishop had come to see me.
Burnett, Frances Hodgson *A Little Princess* Once on a dark winter's day, when the yellow fog hung so thick and heavy in the streets of London that the lamps were lighted and the shop windows blazed with gas as they do at night, an odd-looking little girl sat in a cab with her father and was driven rather slowly through the big thoroughfares.
Burnett, Frances Hodgson *The Secret Garden* When Mary Lennox was sent to Misselthwaite Manor to live with her uncle everybody said she was the most disagreeable-looking child ever seen.
Burns, Robert 'A Red Red Rose' O my luve's like a red, red rose, That's newly sprung in June.
Burns, Robert 'To a Field Mouse' Wee, sleekit, cow'rin', tim'rous beastie, O what a panic's in thy breastie.
Butler, Samuel *The Way of All Flesh* When I was a small boy at the beginning of the century I remember an old man who wore knee-breeches and worsted stockings, and used to hobble about the street of our village with the help of a stick.
Byron, Lord 'She Walks in Beauty' She walks in beauty, like the night Of cloudless climes and starry skies.
Caldwell, Taylor *Great Lion of God* He is very ugly, said his mother.

was yesterday, I don't know.

Capote, Truman *Breakfast at Tiffany's* I am always drawn back to the places where I have lived, the houses & their neighborhoods.

Capote, Truman *In Cold Blood* The village of Holcomb stands on the high wheat plains of western Kansas, a lonesome area that other Kansans call 'out there'.

Carey, Peter *Jack Maggs* It was a Saturday night when the man with the red waistcoat arrived in London.

Carroll, Lewis *Alice's Adventures in Wonderland* Alice was beginning to get very tired of sitting by her sister on the bank, and of having nothing to do: once or twice she had peeped into the book her sister was reading, but it had no pictures or conversations in it, 'and what is the use of a book, thought Alice 'without pictures or conversation?'

Carroll, Lewis *Through the Looking Glass and What Alice Found There;* One thing was certain, that the *white* kitten had had nothing to do with it – it was the black kitten's fault entirely.

Castaneda, Carlos *The Teachings of Don Juan* My notes on my first session with don Juan are dated June 23,1961.

Cather, Willa *My Ántonia* I first heard of Ántonia on what seemed to me an interminable journey across the great midland plains of North America.

Cervantes, Miguel de *Don Quixote* At a village of La Mancha, whose name I do not wish to remember, there lived a little while ago one of those gentlemen who are wont to keep a lance in the rack, an old buckler, a lean horse and a swift greyhound.

Chandler, Raymond *The Big Sleep* It was about eleven o'clock in the morning, mid-October, with the sun not shining and a look of hard wet rain in the clearness of the foothills.

Chang, Jung *Wild Swans* At the age of fifteen my grandmother became the concubine of a warlord general.

Chaucer, Geoffrey *The Canterbury Tales* Whan that Aprill with his shoures soote The droghte of March hath perced to the roote.

Chesterton, GK *The Man Who Was Thursday* The suburb of Saffron Park lay on the sunset side of London, as red and ragged as a cloud of sunset.

Chesterton, GK *The Donkey* When fishes flew and forests walked and figs grew upon thorn.

Chesterton, GK *The Napoleon of Notting Hill* The human race, to which so many of my readers belong . . .

Chopin, Kate *The Awakening* A green and yellow parrot, which hung in a cage outside the door, kept repeating over and over: 'Allez vous-en! Allez vous-en ! Sapristi ! That's all right !'

Christie, Agatha *The Mirror Crack'd* Miss Jane Marple was sitting by her window.

Clarke, Arthur C *Childhood's End* The Volcano that had reared Taratua up from the Pacific depths had been sleeping now for half a million years. Yet in a little while, thought Reinhold, the island would be bathed in fires fiercer than any that had attended its birth.

Clarke, Arthur C *The City and the Stars* Like a glowing jewel, the city lay upon the breast of the desert. Once it had known change and alteration, but now time passed it by. Night and day fled across the desert's face, but in Diaspar it was always afternoon, and darkness never came.

Clarke, Arthur C *2001: A Space Odyssey* The drought had lasted now for ten million years, and the reign of the terrible lizards had long since ended.

Cleland, John *Fanny Hill* Madam, I sit down to give you an undeniable proof of my considering your desires as indispensable orders.

Coelho, Paulo *The Alchemist* The boy's name was Santiago.

Coetzee, JM *Disgrace* For a man of his age, fifty-two, divorced, he has, to his mind, solved the problem of sex rather well.

Collins, Wilkie *The Moonstone* In the first part of Robinson Crusoe, at page one hundred and twenty-nine, you will find it thus written: 'Now I saw, though too late, the Folly of beginning a Work before we count the Cost, and before we judge rightly of our own strength to go through with it.'

Collins, Wilkie *The Woman in White* This is the story of what a Woman's patience can endure, and what a Man's resolution can achieve.

Condon, Richard *Prizzi's Honor* Corrado Prizzi's granddaughter was being married before the baroque altar of Santa Grazia de Traghetto, the lucky church of the Prizzi family.

Conrad, Joseph *Heart of Darkness* Nellie, a cruising yawl, swung to her anchor without a flutter of sails, and was at rest.

Dickens, Charles *Little Dorrit* Thirty years ago, Marseilles lay

Conrad, Joseph *Lord Jim* He was an inch, perhaps two, under six feet, powerfully built, and he advanced straight at you with a slight stoop of the shoulders, head forward, and a fixed from-under stare which made you think of a charging bull.

Conrad, Joseph *Nostromo* In the time of Spanish rule, and for many years afterwards, the town of Sulaco – the luxuriant beauty of the orange gardens bears witness to its antiquity – had never been commercially anything more important than a coasting port with a fairly large local trade in ox-hides and indigo.

Conrad, Joseph *An Outcast of the Islands* When he stepped off the straight and narrow path of his peculiar honesty, it was with an inward assertion of unflinching resolve.

Conrad, Joseph *The Secret Agent* Mr Verloc, going out in the morning, left his shop nominally in charge of his brother-in-law.

Coolidge, Susan *What Katy Did Next* The September sun was glinting cheerfully into a pretty bedroom furnished with blue.

Cooper, James Fenimore *The Last of the Mohicans* It was a feature peculiar to the colonial wars of North America, that the toils and dangers of the wilderness were to be encountered before the adverse hosts could meet.

Crane, Stephen *The Red Badge of Courage* The cold passed reluctantly from the earth, and the retiring fogs revealed an army stretched out on the hills, resting.

Dahl, Roald *Charlie and the Chocolate Factory* These two very old people are the father and mother of Mr. Bucket.

Dante, Alighieri *Divine Comedy* Midway along the path of life.

Davies, Robertson *The Cunning Man* Should I have taken the false teeth?

Davies, WH 'Leisure' What is this life if, full of care, We have no time to stand and stare?

De Bernieres, Louis *Captain Corelli's Mandolin* Dr Iannis had enjoyed a satisfactory day in which none of his patients had died or got any worse.

Defoe, Daniel *Robinson Crusoe* I was born in the year 1632, in the city of York, of a good family, though not of that country, my father being a foreigner of Bremen, who settled first at Hull. He got a good estate by merchandise, and leaving off his trade lived afterward at York, from whence he had married my mother, whose relations were named Robinson, a good family in that country, and from whom I was called Robinson Kreutznear.

Deighton, Len *Catch a Falling Spy* Smell that air, said Major Mann.

Deighton, Len *The Ipcress File* They came through on the hot line at about half past two in the afternoon.

De La Mare, Walter 'The Listeners' 'Is there anybody there?' said the Traveller, Knocking on the moonlit door.

Dick, Philip K *Do Androids Dream of Electric Sheep?* A merry little surge of electricity piped by automatic alarm from the mood organ beside his bed awakened Rick Deckard.

Dickens, Charles *Barnaby Rudge* In the year 1775, there stood upon the borders of Epping Forest, at a distance of about twelve miles from London – measuring the Standard in Cornhill, or rather from the spot on or near to which the Standard used to be in days of yore – a house of public entertainment called the Maypole; which fact was demonstrated to all such travellers as could neither read nor write (and at that time a vast number both of travellers and stay-at-homes were in this condition) by the emblem reared on the roadside over and against the house, which, if not of those goodly proportions that Maypoles were wont to present in olden times, was a fair young ash, thirty feet in height, and straight as any arrow that ever English yeoman drew.

Dickens, Charles *Bleak House* London. Michaelmas term lately over, and the Lord Chancellor sitting in Lincoln's Inn Hall.

Dickens, Charles *A Christmas Carol* Marley was dead, to begin with. There is no doubt whatever about that.

Dickens, Charles *David Copperfield* Whether I shall turn out to be the hero of my own life, or whether that station will be held by anybody else, these pages must show.

Dickens, Charles *Dombey and Son* Dombey sat in the corner of the darkened room in the great armchair by the bedside, and Son lay tucked up in a warm little basket bedstead, carefully disposed on a low settee immediately in front of the fire and close to it, as if his constitution were analogous to that of a muffin, and it was essential to toast him brown while he was very new.

Dickens, Charles *Great Expectations* My father's family name being Pirrip, and my christian name Philip, my infant tongue could make of both names nothing longer or more explicit than Pip.

Dickens, Charles *Hard Times* Now, what I want is Facts.

burning in the sun, one day.

Dickens, Charles *Martin Chuzzlewit* As no lady or gentleman, with any claims to polite breeding, can possibly sympathise with the Chuzzlewit Family without being first assured of the extreme antiquity of the race, it is a great satisfaction to know that it undoubtedly descended in a direct line from Adam and Eve; and was, in the very earliest times, closely connected with the agricultural interest.

Dickens, Charles *The Mystery of Edwin Drood* An ancient English Cathedral Tower?

Dickens, Charles *Nicholas Nickleby* There once lived, in a sequestered part of the county of Devonshire, one Mr Godfrey Nickleby: a worthy gentleman, who, taking it into his head rather late in life that he must get married, and not being young enough or rich enough to aspire to the hand of a lady of fortune, had wedded an old flame out of mere attachment, who in her turn had taken him for the same reason.

Dickens, Charles *The Old Curiosity Shop* Night is generally my time for walking.

Dickens, Charles *Oliver Twist* Among other public buildings in a certain town, which for many reasons it will be prudent to refrain from mentioning, and to which I will assign no fictitious name, there is one anciently common to most towns, great or small – to wit, a workhouse; and in this workhouse was born, on a day and date which I need not trouble myself to repeat, inasmuch as it can be of no possible consequence to the reader, in this stage of the business at all events, the item of mortality whose name is prefixed to the head of this chapter.

Dickens, Charles *Our Mutual Friend* In these times of ours, though concerning the exact year there is no need to be precise, a boat of dirty and disreputable appearance, with two figures in it, floated on the Thames, between Southwark Bridge which is of iron, and London Bridge which is of stone, as an autumn evening was closing in.

Dickens, Charles *Pickwick Papers* The first ray of light which illumines the gloom, and converts into a dazzling brilliancy that obscurity in which the earlier history of the public career of the immortal Pickwick would appear to be involved, is derived from the perusal of the following entry in the transactions of the Pickwick Club, which the editor of these papers feels the highest pleasure in laying before his readers as a proof of the careful attention, indefatigable assiduity, and nice discrimination, with which his search among the multifarious documents confided to him has been conducted.

Dickens, Charles *A Tale of Two Cities* It was the best of times, it was the worst of times, it was the age of wisdom, it was the age of foolishness, it was the epoch of belief, it was the epoch of incredulity, it was the season of Light, it was the season of Darkness, it was the spring of hope, it was the winter of despair, we had everything before us, we had nothing before us, we were all going direct to Heaven, we were all going direct the other way – in short, the period was so.

Dickinson, Emily untitled poem I heard a Fly buzz – when I died . . .

Doctorow, EL *Ragtime* In 1902 Father built a house at the crest of the Broadview Avenue hill in New Rochelle, New York.

Dos Passos, John *1919* Oh the infantree the infantree With the dirt behind their ears

ARMIES CLASH AT VERDUN IN GLOBE'S GREATEST BATTLE
150,000 MEN AND WOMEN PARADE

but another question and a very important one is raised.

Dostoevsky, Fyodor *The Brothers Karamazov* Alexey Fyodorovitch Karamazov was the third son of Fyodor Pavlovitch Karamazov, a landowner well known in our district in his own day, and still remembered among us owing to his gloomy and tragic death, which happened thirteen years ago, and which I shall describe in its proper place.

Dostoevsky, Fyodor *Crime and Punishment* On an exceptionally hot evening early in July a young man came out of the garret in which he lodged in S. Place and walked slowly, as though in hesitation, towards K. bridge.

Doyle, Sir Arthur Conan *The Hound of the Baskervilles* Mr. Sherlock Holmes, who was usually very late in the mornings, save upon those not infrequent occasions when he was up all night, was seated at the breakfast table.

Dryden, John *Absalom and Achitophel* In pious times, ere priestcraft did begin . . .

Du Maurier, Daphne *The King's General* September 1653. The last of summer. The first chill winds of autumn.

Du Maurier, Daphne *Rebecca* Last night I dreamt I went to Manderley again.

Dumas, Alexandre *The Count of Monte Cristo* On the 24th of February, 1815, the lookout of Notre Dame de la Garde signalled the three-master, the *Pharaon*, from Smyrna, Trieste, and Naples. As usual, a pilot put off immediately, and rounding the Chateau d'If, got on board the vessel between Cape Morgion and the Isle of Rion.

Dumas, Alexandre *The Three Musketeers* On the first Monday of the month of April, 1625, the town of Meung, in which the author of The Romance of the Rose was born, appeared to be in a perfect state of revolution as if the Huguenots had just made a second Rochelle of it.

Eco, Umberto *The Name of the Rose* In the beginning was the Word, and the Word was with God, and the Word was God. (Also the first line of the Gospel of John)

Eliot, George *Middlemarch* Miss Brooke had that kind of beauty which seems to be thrown into relief by poor dress.

Eliot, George *The Mill on the Floss* A wide plain, where the broadening Floss hurries on between its green banks to the sea, and the loving tide, rushing to meet it, checks its passage with an impetuous embrace.

Eliot, George *Silas Marner* In the days when the spinning-wheels hummed busily in the farmhouses – and even great ladies, clothed in silk and thread-lace, had their toy spinning-wheels of polished oak – there might be seen in districts far away among the lanes, or deep in the bosom of the hills, certain pallid undersized men, who, by the side of the brawny country-folk, looked like the remnants of a disinherited race.

Eliot, TS *East Coker* In my beginning is my end.

Eliot, TS 'The Love Song of J. Alfred Prufrock' Let us go then, you and I . . .

Ellis, Bret Easton *American Psycho* ABANDON ALL HOPE YE WHO ENTER HERE is scrawled in blood-red lettering on the side of the Chemical Bank . . .

Ellison, Ralph *Invisible Man* I am an invisible man.

Farmer, Philip Jose *To Your Scattered Bodies Go* His wife had held him in her arms as if she could keep death away from him. He had cried out, 'My God, I am a dead man!'

Faulkner, William *Absalom, Absalom!* From a little after two o'clock until almost sundown of the long still hot weary dead September afternoon they sat in what Miss Coldfield still called the office . . .

Faulkner, William *Go Down, Moses* Isaac McCaslin, 'Uncle Ike', past seventy and nearer eighty than he ever corroborated any more, a widower now and uncle to half a country and father to one.

Faulkner, William *Sanctuary* From behind the screen of bushes which surrounded the spring, Popeye watched the man drinking.

Faulkner, William *The Sound and the Fury* Through the fence, between the curling flower spaces, I could see them hitting.

Federman, Raymond *Double or Nothing* Once upon a time two or three weeks ago, a rather stubborn and determined middle-aged man decided to record for posterity, exactly as it happened, word by word and step by step, the story of another man.

Fielding, Henry *Tom Jones* An author ought to consider himself not as a gentleman who gives a private or eleemosynary treat.

Fitzgerald, F Scott *The Great Gatsby* In my younger and more vulnerable years my father gave me some advice that I've been turning over in my mind ever since.

Flaubert, Gustave *Madame Bovary* We were in the study-hall when the headmaster entered, followed by a new boy not yet in school uniform and by the handyman carrying a large desk.

Fleming, Ian *Chitty-Chitty-Bang-Bang* Most motorcars are conglomerations (this is a long word for bundles) of steel and wire and rubber and plastic, and electricity and oil and gasoline and water, and the toffee papers you pushed down the crack in the back seat last Sunday.

Fleming, Ian *Goldfinger* James Bond, with two double bourbons inside him, sat back in the final departure lounge of Miami Airport and thought about life and death.

Ford, Ford Madox *The Good Soldier* This is the saddest story I have ever heard.

Forster, EM *A Passage to India* Except for the Marabar Caves – and they are twenty miles off – the city of Chandrapore presents nothing extraordinary.

Forsyth, Frederick *The Odessa File* Everybody seems to

remember what they were doing on November 22nd 1963, when Kennedy was shot.

Fowles, John *The French Lieutenant's Woman* An easterly is the most disagreeable wind in Lyme Bay – Lyme Bay being that largest byte from the underside of England's outstretched southwestern leg – and a person of curiousity could at once have deduced several strong probabilities about the pair who began to walk down the quay at Lyme Regis, the small but ancient eponym of the inbite, one incisively sharp and blustery morning in the late March of 1867.

Gallico, Paul *The Poseidon Adventure* At seven o'clock, the morning of the 26th of December, the S.S. *Poseidon*, 81,000 tons, homeward bound for Lisbon after a month-long Christmas cruise to African and South American ports, suddenly found herself in the midst of an unaccountable swell, 400 miles south-west of the Azores, and began to roll like a pig.

Galsworthy, John *The Man of Property* Those privileged to be present at a family festival of the Forsythes have seen that charming and instructive sight – an upper middle class family in full plumage.

Gardner, John *Grendel* The old ram stands looking down over rockslides, stupidly triumphant.

Gibson, William *Neuromancer* The sky above the port was the color of television, tuned to a dead channel.

Gide, André *The Fruits of the Earth* Do not hope, Nathaniel, to find God here or there – but everywhere.

Gipson, Fred *Old Yeller* We called him Old Yeller.

Golding, William *Lord of the Flies* The boy with fair hair lowered himself down the last few feet of rock and began to pick his way towards the lagoon.

Golding, William *The Princess Bride* This is my favorite book in all the world, though I have never read it.

Goldman, William *Marathon Man* Everytime he drove through Yorkville, Rosenbaum got angry, just on general principles.

Goldsmith, Oliver 'Elegy on the Death of a Mad Dog' Good people all, of every sort, Give ear unto my song.

Grahame, Kenneth *The Wind in the Willows* The Mole had been working very hard all the morning, spring-cleaning his little home.

Grass, Günter *The Tin Drum* Granted: I am an inmate of a mental hospital; my keeper is watching me, he never lets me out of his sight; there's a peephole in the door, and my keeper's eye is the shade of brown that can never see through a blue-eyed type like me.

Graves, Robert *I, Claudius* I, Tiberius Claudius Drusus Nero Germanicus This-that-and-the-other (for I shall not trouble you yet with all my titles) who was once, and not so long ago either, known to my friends and relatives and associates as 'Claudius the Idiot', or 'That Claudius', or 'Claudius the Stammerer', or 'Clau-Clau-Claudius' or at best as 'Poor Uncle Claudius', am now about to write this strange history of my life; starting from my earliest childhood and continuing year by year until I reach the fateful point of change where, some eight years ago, at the age of fifty-one, I suddenly found myself caught in what I may call the 'golden predicament' from which I have never since become disentangled.

Gray, Thomas 'Elegy Written in a Country Churchyard' The curfew tolls the knell of parting day . . .

Gray, Thomas 'The Progress of Poesy' Awake, Aeolian lyre, awake

Greene, Graham *The End of the Affair* A story has no beginning or end; arbitrarily one chooses that moment of experience from which to look back or from which to look ahead

Greene, Graham *The Power and the Glory* Mr Tench went out to look for his ether cylinder, into the blazing Mexican sun.

Greene, Graham *The Quiet American* After dinner I sat and waited for Pyle in my room over the rue Catinat: he had said, 'I'll be with you at latest by ten,' and when midnight had struck I couldn't stay quiet any longer and went down into the street.

Guterson, David *Snow Falling on Cedars* The accused man, Kabuo Miyamoto, sat proudly upright with a rigid grace.

Ha Jin *Waiting* Every summer Lin Kong returned to Goose Village to divorce his wife, Shuyu.

Haddon, Mark *The Curious Incident of the Dog in the Night-Time* It was 7 minutes after midnight. The dog was lying on the grass in the middle of the lawn in front of Mrs Shears' house.

Haggard, H Rider *King Solomon's Mines* It is a curious thing that at my age, fifty-five last birthday, I should find myself taking up a pen to try and write a history.

language that is no longer mine the snow is qanik –

Haggard, H Rider *She* There are some events of which each circumstance and surrounding detail seem to be graven on the memory in such a fashion that we cannot forget them.

Hailey, Arthur *Airport* At half-past six on a Friday evening in January, Lincoln International Airport, Illinois, was functioning, though with difficulty.

Haley, Alex *Roots* Early in the spring of 1750, in the village of Juffure, four days upriver from the coast of Gambia, West Africa, a manchild was born to Omoro and Binta Kinte.

Hammett, Dashiell *The Maltese Falcon* Samuel Spade's jaw was long and bony, his chin a jutting 'V' under the more flexible 'V' of his mouth.

Hammett, Dashiell *The Thin Man* I was leaning against a bar in a speak-easy on Fifty-second Street, waiting for Nora to finish her Christmas shopping, when a girl got up from the table where she had been sitting.

Hardy, Thomas *Far from the Madding Crowd* When Farmer Oak smiled, the corners of his mouth spread till they were within an unimportant distance of his ears, his eyes were reduced to chinks, and diverging wrinkles appeared round them, extending upon his countenance like the rays in a rudimentary sketch of the rising sun.

Hardy, Thomas *Jude the Obscure* The schoolmaster was leaving the village, and everybody seemed sorry.

Hardy, Thomas *The Mayor of Casterbridge* One evening of late summer, before the nineteenth century had reached one-third of its span, a young man and woman, the latter carrying a child, were approaching the large village of Weydon-Priors, in Upper Wessex, on foot.

Hardy, Thomas *Tess of the D'Urbervilles* On an evening in the latter part of May a middle-aged man was walking homeward from Shaston to the village of Marlott, in the adjoining Vale of Blakemore or Blackmoor.

Harris, Robert *Fatherland* Thick cloud had pressed down on Berlin all night and now it was lingering into what passed for morning.

Hartley, LP *The Go-Between* The past is a foreign country, they do things differently there.

Hawthorne, Nathaniel *The House of the Seven Gables* Halfway down a bystreet of one of our New England towns stands a rusty wooden house, with seven acutely peaked gables, facing towards various points of the compass, and a huge, clustered chimney in the midst.

Hawthorne, Nathaniel *The Scarlet Letter* A throng of bearded men, in sad-colored garments and gray, steeple-crowned hats, intermixed with women, some wearing hoods, and others bareheaded, was assembled in front of a wooden edifice, the door of which was heavily timbered with oak, and studded with iron spikes.

Heinlein, Robert *The Moon Is a Harsh Mistress* I see in *Lunaya Pravda* that Luna City Council has passed on first reading a bill to examine, license, inspect – and tax – public food vendors operating inside municipal pressure.

Heinlein, Robert *Stranger in a Strange Land* Once upon a time there was a Martian named Valentine Michael Smith.

Heller, Joseph *Catch-22* It was love at first sight.

Heller, Joseph *Something Happened* I get the willies when I see closed doors.

Hemans, Felicia 'Casabianca' The boy stood on the burning deck, Whence all but he had fled.

Hemingway, Ernest *The Old Man and the Sea* He was an old man who fished alone in a skiff in the Gulf stream and he had gone 84 days now without taking a fish.

Hemingway, Ernest *The Sun Also Rises* Robert Cohn was once middleweight boxing champion of Princeton.

Herrick, Robert 'To the Virgins, to Make Much of Time' Gather ye rosebuds while ye may, Old Time is still a-flying.

Hesse, Hermann *Siddhartha* In the shade of the house, in the sunshine on the river bank by the boats, in the shade of the sallow wood and the fig tree, Siddharta, the handsome Brahmin's son, grew up with his friend Govinda.

Higgins, Colin *Harold and Maude* Harold Chasen stepped up on the chair and placed the noose about his neck.

Hoban, Russell *Riddley Walker* On my naming day when I come 12 I gone front spear and kilt a wyld boar he parbly ben the las wyld pig on the Bundel.

Høeg, Peter *Miss Smilla's Feeling for Snow* It's freezing – an extraordinary 0° fahrenheit – and it's snowing, and in the

Homer *The Odyssey* By now the other warriors, those that had escaped head-long ruin by sea or in a battle, were safely home.

Hopkins, Gerard Manley 'The Wreck of the Deutschland' Thou mastering me . . .

Hughes, Thomas *Tom Brown's Schooldays* The Browns have been illustrious by the pen of Thackeray and the pencil of Doyle.

Hugo, Victor *The Hunchback of Notre-Dame* It was three hundred forty-eight years, six months, and nineteen days ago today that the citizens of Paris were awakened by the pealing of all the bells in the triple precincts of the City, the University, and the Town.

Hugo, Victor *Les Misérables* In 1815, M. Charles-François-Bienvenu Myriel was Bishop of D—.

Hurston, Zora Neale *Their Eyes Were Watching God* Ships at a distance have every man's wish on board.

Huxley, Aldous *Brave New World* A squat gray building of only thirty-four stories. Over the main entrance the words CENTRAL LONDON HATCHERY AND CONDITIONING CENTRE, and in a shield the World State's motto, Community, Identity, Stability.

Huxley, Aldous *Crome Yellow* Along this particular stretch of line, no express had ever passed.

Irving, John *The Hotel New Hampshire* The summer my father bought the bear, none of us was born – we weren't even conceived: not Frank, the oldest; not Fanny, the loudest; not me, the next; and not the youngest of us, Lilly and Egg.

Irving, John *A Prayer for Owen Meany* I am doomed to remember a boy with a wrecked voice – not because of his voice, or because he was the smallest person I ever knew, or even because he was the instrument of my mother's death, but because he is the reason I believe in God; I am a Christian because of Owen Meany.

Irving, John *The World According to Garp* Garp's mother, Jenny Fields, was arrested in Boston in 1942 for wounding a man in a movie theater.

Jacques, Brian *Redwall* Mathias cut a comical figure as he hobbled his way along the cloisters, with his large sandals flip-flopping and his tail peeping from beneath the baggy folds of an oversized novice's habit.

James, EL *Fifty Shades of Grey* I scowl with frustration at myself in the mirror. Damn my hair – it just won't behave, and damn Katherine Kavanagh for being ill and subjecting me to this ordeal.

James, Henry *The Turn of the Screw* The story had held us, round the fire, sufficiently breathless, but except the obvious remark that it was gruesome, as, on Christmas Eve in an old house, a strange tale should essentially be, I remember no comment uttered till somebody happened to say that it was the only case he had met in which such a visitation had fallen on a child.

James, Henry *The Wings of the Dove* She waited, Kate Croy, for her father to come in, but he kept her unconscionably, and there were moments at which she showed herself, in the glass over the mantel, a face positively pale with the irritation that had brought her to the point of going away without sight of him.

Jong, Erica *Fear of Flying* There were 117 psychoanalysts on the Pan Am flight to Vienna and I'd been treated by at least six of them.

Jonson, Ben 'To Celia' Drink to me only with thine eyes: and I will pledge with mine.

Joyce, James *Dubliners* There was no hope for him this time: it was the third stroke.

Joyce, James *Finnegan's Wake* Riverrun, past Eve and Adam's, from swerve of shore to bend of bay . . .

Joyce, James *Portrait of the Artist as a Young Man* Once upon a time and a very good time it was there was a moocow coming down along the road and this moocow that was coming down along the road met a nicens little boy named baby tuckoo.

Joyce, James *Ulysses* Stately plump Buck Mulligan came from the stairhead, bearing a bowl of lather on which a mirror and a razor lay crossed.

Juster, Norton *The Phantom Tollbooth* There was a boy named Milo who didn't know what to do with himself . . .

Kafka, Franz 'Metamorphosis' As Gregor Samsa awoke one morning from uneasy dreams, he found himself transformed into a giant insect.

Kafka, Franz *The Castle* It was late in the evening when K. arrived.

Kafka, Franz *The Trial* Someone must have been telling lies

Le Carré, John *The Russia House* In a broad Moscow street about Joseph K, for without having done anything wrong he was arrested one fine morning.

Keats, John 'La Belle Dame Sans Merci' Oh, What can ail thee, knight at arms Alone and palely loitering.

Keats, John *Hyperion* Deep in the shady sadness of a vale . . .

Keats, John 'On First Looking into Chapman's Homer' Much have I travell'd in the realms of gold, And many goodly states and kingdoms seen.

Keats, John 'To Autumn' Season of mists and mellow fruitfulness, close bosom-friend of the maturing sun.

Kennedy, William *Quinn's Book* I, Daniel Quinn, neither the first nor the last of a line of such Quinn's, set eyes on Maud the wondrous on a late December day in 1849 on the banks of the river of the aristocrats and paupers, just as the great courtesan Magdalena Colón, also known as La Última, a woman whose presence turned men into spitting, masturbating pigs, boarded a skiff to carry her across the river's icy water from Albany to Greenbush, her first stop en route to the city of Troy, a community of iron, where later that evening she was scheduled to enact, yet again, her role as the lascivious Lais, that fabled prostitute who spurned Demosthenes' gold and yielded free to Diogenes, the virtuous, impecunious tub-dweller.

Kidd, Sue *The Secret Life of Bees* At night I would lie in bed and watch the show, how bees squeezed through the cracks of my bedroom wall...

King, Stephen *Carrie* Nobody was really surprised when it happened, not really, not on the subconscious level where savage things grow.

King, Stephen *Cujo* Not so long ago, a monster came to the small town of Castle Rock, Maine.

Kingsolver, Barbara *The Bean Trees* I have been afraid of putting air in a tire ever since I saw a tractor tire blow up and throw Newt Hardbines's father over the top of the Standard Oil sign.

Kingsolver, Barbara *Pigs in Heaven* Women on their own run in Alice's family.

Kipling, Rudyard 'Gunga Din' You may talk o'gin and beer, when you're quartered safe out 'ere.

Kipling, Rudyard 'If' If you can keep your head when all about you are losing theirs and blaming it on you.

Kipling, Rudyard *The Jungle Book* It was seven o'clock of a very warm evening in the Seeonee hills when Father Wolf woke up from his day's rest, scratched himself, yawned, and spread out his paws one after the other to get rid of the sleepy feeling in their tips.

Kipling, Rudyard *Kim* He sat in defiance of municipal orders, astride the gun of Zam-Zammeh on her brick platform opposite the old Ajaibgher – the Wonder House, as the natives called the Lahore Museum.

Kipling, Rudyard *Stalky and Co* In summer all right-minded boys built huts in the furze-hill behind the College – little lairs whittled out of the heart of the prickly bushes, full of stumps, odd root-ends, and spikes, but, since they were strictly forbidden, palaces of delight.

Knowles, John *A Separate Peace* I went back to the Devon School not long ago, and found it looking oddly newer than when I was a student there fifteen years before.

Kosinski, Jerzy *The Painted Bird* In the first weeks of World War II, in the fall of 1939, a six year old boy from a large city in Eastern Europe was sent by his parents, like thousands of other children, to the shelter of a distant village.

Kundera, Milan *The Unbearable Lightness of Being* The idea of eternal return is a mysterious one, and Nietzsche has often perplexed other philosophers with it: to think that everything recurs as we once experienced it, and that the recurrence itself recurs ad infinitum! What does this mad myth signify?

L'Engle, Madeline *A Wrinkle In Time* It was a dark and stormy night.

Lawrence, DH *Lady Chatterley's Lover* Ours is essentially a tragic age, so we refuse to take it tragically.

Lawrence, DH *Sons and Lovers* 'The Bottoms' succeeded to 'Hell Row'.

Lawrence, DH *Women In Love* Ursula and Gudrun Brangwen sat one morning in the window-bay of their father's house in Beldover, working and talking.

Le Carré, John *The Honourable Schoolboy* Afterwards, in the dusty little corners where London's secret servants drink together, there was argument about where the Dolphin case history should really begin.

not two hundred yards from the Leningrad station, on the upper floor of an ornate and hideous hotel built by Stalin in the style known to Muscovites as Empire During the Plague, the British Council's first ever audio fair for the teaching of the English language and the spread of British culture was grinding to its excruciating end.

Le Carré, John *The Spy Who Came in from the Cold* The American handed Leamas another cup of coffee and said, 'Why don't you go back and sleep? We can ring you if he shows up.'

Le Carré, John *Tinker, Tailor, Soldier, Spy* The truth is, if old Major Dover hadn't dropped dead at Taunton races Jim would never have come to Thursgood's at all.

Lee, Harper *To Kill a Mockingbird* When he was nearly thirteen, my brother Jem got his arm badly broken at the elbow.

Le Guin, Ursula *The Dispossessed* There was a wall.

Le Guin, Ursula *The Left Hand of Darkness* I'll make my report as if I told a story, for I was taught as a child on my homeworld that Truth is a matter of the imagination.

Leroux, Gaston *The Phantom of the Opera* It was the evening on which MM. Debienne and Poligny, the managers of the Opera, were giving a last gala performance to mark their retirement.

Levin, Ira *Rosemary's Baby* Rosemary and Guy Woodhouse had signed a lease on a five-room apartment in a geometric white house on First Avenue when they received word, from a woman named Mrs. Cortez, that a four-room apartment in Bramford had become available.

Lewis, CS *The Lion, the Witch and the Wardrobe* Once there were four children whose names were Peter, Susan, Edmond, and Lucy.

Lewis, CS *Surprised By Joy* I was born in the winter of 1898 at Belfast, the son of a solicitor and of a clergyman's daughter.

Lewis, CS *The Voyage of the Dawn Treader* There was a boy called Eustace Clarence Scrubb, and he almost deserved it.

Lewis, Sinclair *Babbitt* The tower of Zenith aspired above the morning mist; austere towers of steel and cement and limestone, sturdy as cliffs and delicate as silver rods.

Lewis, Sinclair *Elmer Gantry* Elmer Gantry was drunk. He was eloquently drunk, lovingly and pugnaciously drunk.

Lewis, Sinclair *Main Street* This is America – a town of a few thousand, in a region of wheat and corn and dairies and little groves. The town is, in our tale, called 'Gopher Prairie, Minnesota.' But its Main Street is the continuation of Main Streets everywhere.

Lodge, David *Changing Places* High, high above the North Pole, on the first day of 1969, two professors of English Literature approached each other at a combined velocity of 1200 miles per hour.

London, Jack *The Call of the Wild* Buck did not read the newspapers or he would have known that trouble was brewing.

Longfellow, Henry Wadsworth *The Song of Hiawatha* Should you ask me, whence these stories?

Longfellow, Henry Wadsworth 'The Village Blacksmith' Under a spreading chestnut tree The village smithy stands.

Lovecraft, HP *The Call Of Cthulhu* The most merciful thing in the world, I think, is the inability of the human mind to correlate all its contents.

Ludlum, Robert *The Bourne Identity* The trawler plunged into the angry swells of the dark furious sea like an awkward animal . .

Macaulay, Rose *The Towers of Trebizond* 'Take my camel dear', said my aunt Dot, as she climbed down from this animal on her return from High Mass.

McCarthy, Cormac *All the Pretty Horses* The candleflame and the image of the candleflame caught in the pierglass twisted and righted when he entered the hall . . .

McCloskey, Robert *Make Way for Ducklings* Mr. and Mrs. Mallard were looking for a place to live.

McCullers, Carson *The Heart Is a Lonely Hunter* In the town there were two mutes, and they were always together.

McCullough, Colleen *The First Man in Rome* Having no personal commitment to either of the new consuls, Gaius Julius Caesar and his son simply tacked themselves onto the procession which started nearest to their own house, the procession of the senior consul, Marcus Minucius Rufus.

McCullough, Colleen *The Thorn Birds* On December 8th, 1915, Meggie Cleary had her fourth birthday.

McCullough, Colleen *Caesar's Women* Brutus, I don't like the look of your skin. Come here to the light, please.

Morrison, Toni *Paradise* They shoot the white girl first.

MacDonald, Betty *Mrs. Piggle Wiggle* I expect I might as well begin by telling you about Mrs. Piggle-Wiggle.

McEwan, Ian *Enduring Love* The beginning is simple to mark.

McKenna, Richard *The Sand Pebbles* Hello, ship, Jake Holman said under his breath.

McMillan, Terry *Waiting to Exhale* Right now I'm supposed to be all geeked up because I'm getting ready for a New Year's Eve party that some guy named Lionel invited me to.

McMurtry, Larry *Terms of Endearment* The success of a marriage invariably depends on the woman, Mrs. Greenway said.

Malamud, Bernard *The Fixer* From the small crossed window of his room above the stable in the brickyard, Yakov Bok saw people in their long overcoats running somewhere early that morning, everybody in the same direction.

Mann, Thomas *Buddenbrooks* And – and – what comes next? Oh, yes, yes, what the dickens does come next? C'est la question, ma très chère demoiselle! Frau Consul Buddenbrooks shot a glance at her husband and came to the rescue of her daughter.

Marks, Leo 'Code Poem for the French Resistance' The life that I have is all that I have, And the life that I have is yours.

Márquez, Gabriel García *Love in the Time of Cholera* It was inevitable: the scent of bitter almonds always reminded him of the fate of unrequited love.

Márquez, Gabriel García *One Hundred Years of Solitude* Many years later, as he faced the firing squad, Colonel Aureliano Buendía was to remember that distant afternoon when his father took him to discover ice.

Martel, Yann *Life of Pi* My suffering left me sad and gloomy.

Marvell, Andrew 'To His Coy Mistress' Had we but world enough, and time, This coyness, Lady, were no crime.

Masefield, John 'Sea-Fever' I must go down to the seas again, to the lonely sea and the sky, And all I ask is a tall ship and a star to steer her by . . .

Matheson, Richard *I Am Legend* On those cloudy days, Robert Neville was never sure when sunset came . . .

Maugham, W Somerset *Of Human Bondage* The day broke grey and dull.

Maugham, W Somerset *The Razor's Edge* I have never begun a novel with more misgiving.

Melville, Herman *Billy Budd* In the time before steamships, or then more frequently than now, a stroller along the docks of any considerable sea-port would occasionally have his attention arrested by a group of bronzed mariners, man-of-war's men or merchant-sailors in holiday attire ashore on liberty.

Melville, Herman *Moby-Dick* Call me Ishmael.

Metalious, Grace *Peyton Place* Indian summer is like a woman. Ripe, hotly passionate, but fickle, she comes and goes as she pleases so that one is never sure whether she will come at all, nor for how long she will stay.

Michener, James A *The Source* On Tuesday the freighter steamed through the Straits of Gibraltar and for five days plowed eastward through the Mediterranean, past islands and peninsulas rich in history, so that on Saturday night the steward advised Dr. Cullinane, 'If you wish an early sight of the Holy Land you must be up at dawn.'

Miller, Henry *Tropic of Cancer* I am living at the Villa Borghese. There is not a crumb of dirt anywhere nor a chair misplaced. We are alone here and we are dead.

Miller Jr, Walter *A Canticle for Leibowitz* Brother Francis Gerard of Utah might never have discovered the blessed documents, had it not been for the pilgrim with girded loins who had appeared during that young novice's Lenten fast in the desert.

Milton, John *Lycidas* Yet once more, O ye laurels, and once more, Ye myrtles brown, with ivy never sere.

Milton, John 'On His Blindness' When I consider how my light is spent, Ere half my days, in this dark world and wide.

Milton, John *Paradise Lost* Of man's first disobedience, and the fruit Of that forbidden tree, whose mortal taste Brought death into the world, and all our woe, With loss of Eden.

Mitchell, Margaret *Gone with the Wind* Scarlett O'Hara was not beautiful, but men seldom realized it when caught by her charm as the Tarleton twins were.

Montgomery, Lucy Maud *Anne of Green Gables* Mrs. Rachel Lynde lived just where the Avonlea main road dipped down into a little hollow.

Morrison, Toni *Beloved* 124 was spiteful.

Morrison, Toni *Sula* In that place, where they tore the night shade and blackberry patches from their roots to make room for the Medallion City Golf Course, there was once a neighborhood.
Nabokov, Vladimir *Lolita* Lolita, light of my life, fire of my loins.
Naylor, Gloria *The Women of Brewster Place* Brewster Place was the bastard child of several clandestine meetings between the alderman of the sixth district and the managing director of the Unico Realty Company.
Niven, Larry *Ringworld* In the night time heat of Beirut in one of a row of general address transfer booths, Louis Wu flicked into reality.
Norton, Mary *The Borrowers* It was Mrs May who first told me about them.
Oates, Joyce Carol *Because It Is Bitter, and Because It Is My Heart* Little Red Garlock, sixteen years old, skull smashed soft as a rotted pumpkin and body dumped into the Cassadaga River near the foot of Pitt Street, must not have sunk as deep as he'd been intended to sink, or floated as far.
Oates, Joyce Carol *Bellefleur* It was many years ago in that dark, chaotic, unfathomable pool of time before Germaine's birth (nearly twelve months before her birth), on a night in late September stirred by innumerable frenzied winds, like spirits contending with one another.
Oates, Joyce Carol *Expensive People* I was a child murderer.
O'Connor, Flannery *The Violent Bear It Away* Francis Marion Tarwater's uncle had been dead for only half a day when the boy got too drunk to finish digging his grave.
Orwell, George *1984* It was a bright cold day in April, and the clocks were striking thirteen.
Ovid *Metamorphoses* My purpose is to tell of bodies which have been transformed into shapes of a different kind.
Owen, Wilfred 'Anthem for Doomed Youth' What passing-bells for these who die as cattle?
Pasternak, Boris *Doctor Zhivago* On they went, singing 'Rest Eternal,' and whenever they stopped, their feet, the horses, and the gusts of wind seemed to carry on their singing.
Paterson, Katherine *Bridge to Terabitha* Ba-room, ba-room, ba-room, baripity, baripity, baripity, baripity – Good.
Piercy, Marge *Small Change* Beth was looking in the mirror of her mother's vanity.
Pierre, DBC *Vernon God Little* It's hot as hell in Martirio . . .
Piper, Watty *The Little Engine That Could* Chug, chug, chug. Puff, puff, puff. Ding-dong, ding-dong.
Plath, Sylvia *The Bell Jar* It was a queer, sultry summer, the summer they electrocuted the Rosenbergs, and I didn't know what I was doing in New York.
Poe, Edgar Allan *The Raven* Once upon a midnight dreary, as I pondered weak and weary . . .
Pohl, Frederik *Gateway* My name is Robinette Broadhead, in spite of which I am male.
Pope, Alexander *The Dunciad* The Mighty Mother, and her Son, who brings The Smithfield muses to the ear of kings, I sing.
Porter, Katherine Anne *Ship of Fools* August, 1931 – The port town of Veracruz is a little purgatory between land and sea.
Portis, Charles *True Grit* People do not give it credence that a fourteen-year-old girl could leave home and go off in the wintertime to avenge her father's blood.
Potok, Chaim *The Chosen* For the first fifteen years of our lives, Danny and I lived within five blocks of each other and neither of us knew of the other's existence.
Proust, Marcel *In Search of Lost Time* For a long time I went to bed early.
Pullman, Philip *Northern Lights* Lyra and her daemon moved through the darkening hall.
Puzo, Mario *The Godfather* Amerigo Bonasera sat in New York Criminal Court Number 3 and waited for justice; vengeance on the men who had so cruelly hurt his daughter.
Pynchon, Thomas *The Crying of Lot 49* One summer afternoon Mrs. Oedipa Maas came home from a Tupperware party whose hostess had put perhaps too much kirsch in the fondue.
Pynchon, Thomas *Gravity's Rainbow* A screaming comes across the sky.
Rand, Ayn *Atlas Shrugged* Who is John Galt?.
Remarque, Erich Maria *All Quiet on the Western Front* We are five miles behind the front.
Renault, Mary *The King Must Die* The Citadel of Troizen, where the Palace stands, was built by giants before anyone remembers.
Simak, Clifford *City* Gramp Stevens sat in a lawn chair,
Rey, HA *Curious George* This is George. He lived in Africa.
Rhys, Jean *Wide Sargasso Sea* They say when trouble comes close ranks, and so the white people did.
Robbins, Tom *Even Cowgirls Get the Blues* Amoebae leave no fossils.
Robbins, Tom *Jitterbug Perfume* The beet is the most intense of vegetables.
Robbins, Tom *Still Life with Woodpecker* In the last quarter of the twentieth century, at a time when Western civilization was declining too rapidly for comfort and yet too slowly to be exciting, much of the world sat on the edge of an increasingly expensive theater seat, waiting – with various combinations of dread, hope, and ennui – for something momentous to occur.
Robinson, Marilynne *Housekeeping* My name is Ruth. I grew up with my sister, Lucille, under the care of my grandmother,.
Rölvaag, OE *Giants in the Earth* Bright, clear sky over a plain so wide that the rim of the heavens cut down on it around the entire horizon.
Roth, Philip *Portnoy's Complaint* She was so deeply imbedded in my consciousness that for the first year of school I seemed to have believed that each of my teachers was my mother in disguise.
Rowling, JK *The Casual Vacancy* Barry Fairbrother did not want to go out to dinner.
Rowling, JK *The Cuckoo's Calling* The buzz in the street was like the humming of flies. NB written under pseudonym Robert Galbraith
Rowling, JK *Harry Potter and the Philosopher's Stone* Mr and Mrs Dursley, of number four Privet Drive, were proud to say that they were perfectly normal, thank you very much.
Rushdie, Salman *Midnight's Children* I was born in the city of Bombay . . . once upon a time.
Rushdie, Salman *The Satanic Verses* To be born again, sang Gibreel Farishta tumbling from the heavens, 'first you have to die'.
Sabatini, Raphael *Scaramouche* He was born with a gift of laughter and a sense that the world was mad.
Salinger, JD *The Catcher in the Rye* If you really want to hear about it, the first thing you'll probably want to know is where I was born, and what my lousy childhood was like.
Schaefer, Jack *Shane* He rode into our valley in the summer of '89.
Scott, Paul *The Day of the Scorpion* Ex-Chief Minister Mohammed Ali Kasim was arrested at his home in Ranpur at 5am on August 9th 1942 by a senior English police officer who arrived in a car, with a motorcycle escort, two armed guards and a warrant for his detention under the Defence of India Rules.
Scott, Sir Walter *Old Mortality* 'Most Readers,' says the Manuscript of Mr Pattieson, 'must have witnessed with delight the joyous burst which attends the dismissing of a village-school on a fine summer evening.'
Sebold, Alice *The Lovely Bones* My name was Salmon, like the fish; first name, Susie.
Segal, Erich *Love Story* What can you say about a 25 year old girl who died?
Selden, George *The Cricket in Times Square* A mouse was looking at Mario. The mouse's name was Tucker.
Service, Robert *The Shooting of Dan McGrew* A bunch of the boys were whooping it up in the Malamute saloon.
Sewell, Anna *Black Beauty* The first place that I can well remember was a large pleasant meadow with a pond of clear water in it.
Sharpe, Tom *The Midden* It was Timothy Bright's ambition to make a fortune.
Shaw, Irwin *Rich Man, Poor Man* Mr. Donnelly, the track coach, ended the day's practice early because Henry Fuller's father came down to the high-school field to tell Henry that they had just got a telegram from Washington announcing that Henry's brother had been killed in action in Germany.
Shelley, Mary *Frankenstein* You will rejoice to hear that no disaster has accompanied the commencement of an enterprise which you have regarded with such evil forebodings.
Shelley, Percy Bysshe 'Ozymandias of Egypt' I met a traveller from an antique land . . .
Sholokhov, Mikhail *And Quiet Flows the Don* The Melekhov farm was right at the end of the Tatarsk village.
Shute, Nevil *On the Beach* Lt Commander Peter Holmes of the Royal Australian Navy woke soon after dawn.

watching the mower at work, feeling the warm, soft sunshine seep into his bones.

Simak, Clifford *Way Station* The noise was ended now. The smoke drifted like thin gray wisps of fog above the tortured earth and the shattered fences.

Sims, George R *In the Workhouse – Christmas Day* It is Christmas Day in the Workhouse.

Singer, Isaac Bashevis *Shosha* I was brought up on three dead languages – Hebrew, Aramaic, and Yiddish (some consider the last not a language at all) – and in a culture that developed in Babylon: the Talmud.

Smith, Betty *A Tree Grows in Brooklyn* Serene was a word you could put to Brooklyn, New York.

Smith, Dodie *I Capture the Castle* I write this sitting in the kitchen sink.

Smith, Dodie *101 Dalmatians* Not long ago, there lived in London a young married couple of Dalmatian dogs named Pongo and Misses Pongo.

Solzhenitsyn, Alexander *The Gulag Archipelago* How do people get to this clandestine Archipelago?

Sontag, Susan *Death Kit* Diddy the Good was taking a business trip.

Spencer, Scott *Endless Love* When I was seventeen and in full obedience to my heart's most urgent commands, I stepped far from the pathway of normal life and in a moment's time ruined everything I loved – I loved so deeply, and when the love was interrupted, when the incorporeal body of love shank back in terror and my own body was locked away, it was hard for others to believe that a life so new could suffer so irrevocably.

Spenser, Edmund *The Faerie Queene* A Gentle Knight was pricking on the plaine.

Steinbeck, John *Cannery Row* Cannery Row in Monterey in California is a poem, a stink, a grating noise, a quality of light, a tone, a habit, a nostalgia, a dream.

Steinbeck, John *The Grapes of Wrath* To the red country and part of the gray country of Oklahoma, the last rains came gently, and they did not cut the scarred earth.

Steinbeck, John *Of Mice and Men* A few miles south of Soledad, the Salinas River drops in close to the hill-side bank and runs deep and green.

Steinbeck, John *The Pearl* Kino awakened in the near dark.

Sterne, Laurence *Tristram Shandy* I wish either my father or my mother, or indeed both of them, as they were in duty both equally bound to it, had minded what they were about when they begot me.

Stevenson, Robert Louis *The Strange Case of Dr Jekyll and Mr Hyde* Mr. Utterson the lawyer was a man of a rugged countenance, that was never lighted by a smile; cold, scanty and embarrassed.

Stevenson, Robert Louis *Kidnapped* I will begin the story of my adventures with a certain morning early in the month of June, the year of grace 1751, when I took the key for the last time out of the door of my father's house.

Stevenson, Robert Louis *Treasure Island* Squire Trelawney, Dr. Livesey, and the rest of these gentlemen having asked me to write down the whole particulars about Treasure Island.

Stevenson, RL & L Osbourne *The Wrong Box* How very little does the amateur, dwelling at home at ease, comprehend the labours and perils of the author.

Stewart, Mary *The Crystal Cave* I am an old man now, but then I was already past my prime when Arthur was crowned King.

Stoker, Bram *Dracula* 3 May. Bistritz. – Left Munich at 8:35 P.M., on 1st May, arriving at Vienna early next morning; should have arrived at 6:46, but the train was an hour late. Buda-Pesth seems a wonderful place, from the glimpse which I got from the train and the little I could walk through the streets.

Stone, Irving *Lust for Life* Monsieur Van Gogh, it's time to wake up.

Stout, Rex *The Hand in Glove* It was not surprising that Sylvia Raffray, on that Saturday in September, had occasion for discourse with various men, none of them utterly ordinary, and with one remarkable young woman; it was not surprising that all this happened without any special effort on Sylvia's part, for she was rich, personable to an extreme, an orphan, and six months short of twenty-one years.

Stowe, Harriet Beecher *Uncle Tom's Cabin* Late in the afternoon of a chilly day in February, two gentlemen were sitting

clinging to them.

alone over their wine, in a well-furnished dining parlour, in the town of P——, in Kentucky.

Sturgeon, Theodore *More Than Human* The idiot lived in a black and gray world, punctuated by the white lightning of hunger and the flickering of fear.

Styron, William *The Confessions of Nat Turner* To the public – The late insurrection in Southampton has greatly excited the public mind and led to a thousand idle, exaggerated and mischievous reports.

Sukenick, Ronald *Blown Away* Psychics can see the color of time it's blue.

Swift, Jonathan *Gulliver's Travels* My father had a small estate in Nottinghamshire; I was the third of five sons.

Tan, Amy *The Hundred Secret Senses* My sister Kwan believes she has yin eyes.

Tan, Amy *The Joy Luck Club* My father asked me to be the fourth corner at the Joy Luck Club.

Thackeray, William M *Vanity Fair* While the present century was in its teens, and on one sunshiny morning in June, there drove up to the great iron gate of Miss Pinkerton's academy for young ladies, on Chiswick Mall, a large family coach, with two fat horses in blazing harness, driven by a fat coachman in a three cornered hat and wig, at the rate of four miles an hour.

Theroux, Paul *The Mosquito Coast* We drove past Tiny Polski's mansion house to the main road, and then the five miles into Northampton, Father talking the whole way about savages and the awfulness of America – how it got turned into a dope-taking, door-locking, ulcerated danger zone of rabid scavengers and criminal millionaires and moral sneaks.

Thomas, Dylan *Under Milk Wood* To begin at the beginning, It is spring, moonless night in the small town, starless and bible-black . . .

Thompson, Flora *Lark Rise to Candleford* The hamlet stood on a gentle rise in the flat, wheat-growing north-east corner of Oxfordshire.

Thompson, Hunter S *Fear and Loathing in Las Vegas* We were somewhere around Barstow on the edge of the desert when the drugs began to take hold.

Thoreau, Henry David *Walden* When I wrote the following pages, or rather the bulk of them, I lived alone, in the woods, a mile from any neighbor, in a house which I had built myself, on the shore of Walden Pond, in Concord, Massachusetts, and earned my living by the labor of my hands only.

Thurber, James *The Thirteen Clocks* Once upon a time, in a gloomy castle on a lonely hill, where there were thirteen clocks that wouldn't go, there lived a cold, aggressive Duke, and his niece, the Princess Saralinda.

Tolkien, JRR *The Hobbit* In a hole in the ground there lived a hobbit.

Tolstoy, Leo *Anna Karenina* All happy families are alike, but an unhappy family is unhappy after its own fashion.

Tolstoy, Leo *War and Peace* Well, Prince, so Genoa and Lucca are now just family estates of the Buonapartes.

Travers, PL *Mary Poppins* If you want to find Cherry Tree Lane all you have to do is ask a policeman at the crossroads.

Twain, Mark *The Adventures of Huckleberry Finn* You don't know about me, without you have read a book by the name of *The Adventures of Tom Sawyer*, but that ain't no matter.

Twain, Mark *The Adventures of Tom Sawyer* TOM!

Tyler, Anne *Breathing Lessons* Maggie and Ira Moran had to go to a funeral in Deer Lick, Pennsylvania.

Undset, Sigrid *Kristin Lavransdatter* When the lands and goods of Ivar Gjesling the younger, of Sundbu, were divided after his death in 1306, his lands in Sil of Gudbrandsdal fell to his daughter Ragnfrid and her husband Lavrans Björngulfsön.

Updike, John *Rabbit at Rest* Standing amid the tan, excited post-Christmas crowd at the Southwest Florida Regional Airport, Rabbit Angstrom has a funny sudden feeling that what he has come to meet, what's floating in unseen about to land, is not his son Nelson and daughter-in-law Pru and their two children but something more ominous and intimately his: his own death, shaped vaguely like an airplane.

Updike, John *Rabbit Is Rich* Running out of gas, Rabbit Angstrom thinks as he stands behind the summer-dusty windows of the Springer Motors display.

Updike, John *Rabbit Redux* Men emerge pale from the little printing plant at four sharp, ghosts for an instant, blinking, until the outdoor light overcomes the look of constant indoor light

Updike, John *Rabbit, Run* Boys are playing basketball around a telephone pole with a backboard bolted to it.

Uris, Leon *Exodus* The airplane plip-plopped down the runway to a halt before the big sign: WELCOME TO CYPRUS.

Verne, Jules *Around the World in 80 Days* Mr Phileas Fogg lived, in 1872, at No. 7, Savile Row, Burlington Gardens, the house in which Sheridan died in 1814.

Vidal, Gore *Creation* I am blind. But I am not deaf. Becuase of the incompleteness of my misfortune, I was obliged yesterday to listen for nearly six hours to a self-styled historian whose account of what the Athenians call 'the Persian Wars' was nonsense of a sort that were I less old and more privileged, I would have risen in my seat at the Odeon and scandalized all Athens by answering him.

Vidal, Gore *Lincoln* Elihu B. Washburne opened his gold watch.

Vidal, Gore *Myra Breckinridge* I am Myra Breckinridge whom no man will ever possess.

Virgil *Aeneid* I sing of arms and the man.

Voltaire *Candide* In the country of Westphalia, in the castle of the most noble Baron of Thunder-ten-tronckh, lived a youth whom Nature had endowed with a most sweet disposition.

Vonnegut, Kurt *Breakfast of Champions* This is a tale of a meeting of two lonesome, skinny, fairly old white men on a planet which was dying fast.

Vonnegut, Kurt *Cat's Cradle* Call me Jonah.

Vonnegut, Kurt *Slapstick* To whom it may concern: It is springtime.

Vonnegut, Kurt *Slaughterhouse-Five* All this happened, more or less.

Walker, Alice *The Color Purple* You better not never tell nobody but God.

Walker, Alice *Possessing the Secret of Joy* I did not realize for a long time that I was dead.

Waller, Robert *The Bridges of Madison County* On the morning of August 8, 1965, Robert Kincaid locked the door to his small two-room apartment on the third floor of a rambling house in Bellingham, Washington.

Warren, Robert Penn *A Place To Come To* I was the only boy, or girl either, in the public school in the town of Dugton, Claxford County, Alabama, whose father had ever got killed in the middle of the night standing up in the front of his wagon to piss on the hindquarters of one of a span of mules and, being drunk, pitching forward on his head, still hanging onto his dong, and hitting the pike in such a position and condition that both the left front and left rear wheels of the wagon rolled, with perfect precision, over his unconscious neck, his having passed out being, no doubt, the reason he took the fatal plunge in the first place.

Warren, Robert Penn *All the King's Men* To get there you follow Highway 58 . . .

Waugh, Evelyn *Brideshead Revisited* When I reached C Company lines, which were at the top of the hill, I paused and looked back at the camp, just coming into full view before me through the grey mist of early morning.

Wells, HG *The Invisible Man* The stranger came early in February, one wintry day, through a biting wind and a driving snow . . .

Waugh, Evelyn *Scoop* While still a young man, John Courteney Boot had, as his publisher proclaimed, 'achieved an assured and enviable position in contemporary letters'.

Wells, HG *The Island of Doctor Moreau* I do not propose to add anything to what has already been written concerning the loss of the 'Lady Vain'.

Wells, HG *The Time Machine* The Time Traveller (for so it will be convenient to speak of him) was expounding a recondite matter to us.

Wells, HG *The War of the Worlds* No one would have believed in the last years of the nineteenth century that this world was being watched keenly and closely by intelligences greater than man's and yet as mortal as his own; that as men busied themselves about their various concerns they were scrutinised and studied, perhaps almost as narrowly as a man with a microscope might scrutinise the transient creatures that swarm and multiply in a drop of water.

Welsh, Irvine *Trainspotting* The sweat wis lashing oafay Sick Boy; he wis trembling.

Welty, Eudora *The Optimist's Daughter* A nurse held the door open for them. Judge McKelva going first, then his daughter Laurel, then his wife Fay, they walked into the windowless room where the doctor would make his examination.

Wharton, Edith *Ethan Frome* I had the story, bit by bit, from various people, and, as generally happens in such cases, each time it was a different story.

White, EB *Charlotte's Web* Where's Papa going with that ax? said Fern to her mother as they were setting the table for breakfast.

White, EB *Stuart Little* When Mrs. Frederick C. Little's second son arrived, everybody noticed that he was not much bigger than a mouse.

Wibberley, Leonard *The Mouse That Roared* The Duchy of Grand Fenwick lies in a precipitous fold of the northern Alps and embraces in its tumbling landscape portions of three valleys, a river, one complete mountain with an elevation of two thousand feet and a castle.

Wilde, Oscar *The Ballad of Reading Gaol* He did not wear his scarlet coat.

Wilde, Oscar *The Picture of Dorian Gray* The studio was filled with the rich odour of roses, and when the light summer wind stirred amidst the trees of the garden there came through the open door the heavy scent of the lilac, or the more delicate perfume of the pink-flowering thorn.

Wilder, Thornton *The Bridge of San Luis Rey* On Friday noon, July the twentieth, 1714, the finest bridge in all Peru broke and precipitated five travelers into the gulf below.

Wolfe, Thomas *You Can't Go Home Again* It was the hour of twilight on a soft spring day toward the end of April in the year of Our Lord 1929, and George Webber leaned his elbows on the sill of his back window and looked out at what he could see of New York.

Wolfe, Thomas *Look Homeward, Angel* A destiny that leads the English to the Dutch is strange enough; but one that leads from Epsom into Pennsylvania, and thence into the hills that shut in Altamont over the proud coral cry of the cock, and the soft stone smile of the angel, is touched by that dark miracle of chance which makes new magic in a dusty world.

Woolf, Virginia *Orlando* He – for there could be no doubt of his sex, though the fashion of the time did something to disguise it – was in the act of slicing at the head of a Moor which swung from the rafters.

Wordsworth, William *The Prelude* Oh there is blessing in this gentle breeze.

Wouk, Herman *The Winds of War* Commander Victor Henry rode a taxi-cab home from the Navy building on Constitution Avenue, in a gusty gray March rainstorm that matched his mood.

Wright, Richard *Native Son* Brrrrrrriiiiiiiiiiiiiiiiiiiiiinng! An alarm clock clanged in the dark and silent room. A bed spring creaked. A woman's voice sang out impatiently. 'Bigger, shut that thing off!'

Wyndham, John *The Day of the Triffids* When a day that you happen to know is Wednesday starts off by sounding like Sunday, there is something seriously wrong somewhere.

Wyss, Johann *The Swiss Family Robinson* For many days we had been tempest-tossed.

Yeats, WB 'When You are Old' When you are old and grey and full of sleep, And nodding by the fire, take down this book . . .

Zelazny, Roger *Lord of Light* His followers called him Mahasamatman and said he was a god. He preferred to drop the Maha- and the -atman, however, and called himself Sam.

NB: This is another section where it is only possible to list a good cross-section of works rather than a fully comprehensive catalogue. It is hoped that many of the better-known openings are included, as well as some more obscure but interesting ones. In the cases of works written in a foreign language and translated into English, the wording will vary according to the translator.

Closing Words of Books and Poems

Arnold, Matthew 'Dover Beach' Swept with confused alarms of struggle and flight, where ignorant armies clash by night.
Arnold, Matthew 'The Scholar Gipsy' Shy traffickers, the dark Iberians come, And on the beach undid his corded bales.
Asimov, Isaac *I Robot* She died last month at the age of Eighty Two.
Austen, Jane *Emma* But, in spite of these deficiencies, the wishes, the hopes, the confidence, the predictions of the small band of true friends who witnessed the ceremony, were fully answered in the perfect happiness of the union.
Austen, Jane *Lady Susan* I confess that I can pity only Miss Manwaring, who coming to town and putting herself to an expense in clothes, which impoverished her for two years, on purpose to secure him, was defrauded of her due by a woman ten years older than herself.
Austen, Jane *Mansfield Park* Fanny had never been able to approach but with some painful sensation of restraint or alarm, soon grew as dear to her heart, and as thoroughly perfect in her eyes, as everything else within the view and patronage of Mansfield Park had long been.
Austen, Jane *Northanger Abbey* I leave it to be settled by whomsoever it may concern, whether the tendency of this work be altogether to recommend parental tyranny or reward filial disobedience.
Austen, Jane *Persuasion* She gloried in being a sailor's wife, but she must pay the tax of quick alarm for belonging to that profession which is, if possible, more distinguished in its domestic virtues than in its national importance.
Austen, Jane *Pride and Prejudice* And they were both ever sensible of the warmest gratitude towards the persons who, by bringing her into Derbyshire, had been the means of uniting them.
Austen, Jane *Sanditon* It was impossible not to feel him hardly used; to be obliged to stand back in his own house and see the best place by the first constantly occupied by Sir Harry Denham.
Austen, Jane *Sense and Sensibility* Between Barton and Delaford, there was that constant communication which strong family affection would naturally dictate; and among the merits and the happiness of Elinor and Marianne, let it not be ranked as the least considerable, that though sisters and living almost within sight of each other, they could live without disagreement between themselves, or producing coolness between their husbands.
Austen, Jane *The Watsons* Emma was of course un-influenced, except to greater esteem for Elizabeth, by such representations – and the visitors departed without her.
Bellow, Saul *Henderson the Rain King* I guess I felt it was my turn now to move, and so went running – leaping, leaping, pounding, and tingling over the pure white lining of the gray Arctic silence.
Bennett, Arnold *Clayhanger* He braced himself to the exquisite burden to life.
Bennett, Arnold *The Old Wives' Tale* She glanced at the soup plate, and, on the chance that it might after all contain something worth inspection, she awkwardly balanced on her old legs and went to it again.
Brontë, Anne *Agnes Grey* And now I think I have said sufficient.
Brontë, Anne *The Tenant of Wildfell Hall* Till then, farewell, Gilbert Markham Staningley, June 10th 1847.
Brontë, Charlotte *Jane Eyre* Amen; even so come, Lord Jesus.
Brontë, Charlotte *The Professor* Papa, Come!
Brontë, Charlotte *Villette* Madame Walravens fulfilled her ninetieth year before she died. Farewell.
Brontë, Emily *Wuthering Heights* I lingered around them under that benign sky; watched the moths fluttering among the heath and harebells, listening to the soft wind breathing through the grass, and wondered how anyone could ever imagine unquiet slumbers for the sleepers in that quiet earth.
Buchan, John *The Thirty-Nine Steps* But I had done my best service, I think, before I put on khaki.
Carey, Peter *Jack Maggs* Affectionately Inscribed to Percival Clarence Buckle, A man of letters, A patron of the arts.
Carroll, Lewis *Alice's Adventures in Wonderland* And how she would feel with all their simple sorrows, and find a pleasure in all their simple joys, remembering her own child-life, and the happy summer days.
Carroll, Lewis *Through the Looking Glass* But the provoking kitten only began on the other paw, and pretended it hadn't heard the question. Which do *you* think it was?
Cervantes, Miguel de *Don Quixote* Farewell.
Clarke, Arthur C *2001* But he would think of something.
Cleland, John *Fanny Hill* I shall see you soon, and in the meantime think candidly of me, and believe me ever, madam, Yours, etc, etc, etc.
Collins, Wilkie *The Moonstone* Who can tell?
Conrad, Joseph *Lord Jim* While he waves his hand sadly at his butterflies.
Conrad, Joseph *An Outcast of the Islands* And Almayer, who stood waiting, with a smile of tipsy attention on his lips, heard no other answer.
Cookson, Catherine *The Maltese Angel* Oh, let me cry. Let me cry, my love.
Cookson, Catherine *The Year of the Virgins* Listen to me, Flo Coulson, your mother loves me. Do you hear that? Your mother loves me. Everything comes to him who waits. Your mother loves me.
Cooper, James Fenimore *The Pioneers* Who are opening the way for the march of the Nation across the Continent.
Defoe, Daniel *Robinson Crusoe* And here, resolving to harass myself no more, I am preparing for a longer journey than all these, having lived 72 years, a life of infinite variety, and learn'd sufficiently to know the value of retirement, and the blessing of ending our days in peace.
Dickens, Charles *David Copperfield* Oh Agnes, Oh my soul, so may thy face be by me when I close my life indeed; so may I, when realities are melting from me like the shadows which I now dismiss, still find thee near me, pointing upward!
Dickens, Charles *Great Expectations* I took her hand in mine, and we went out of the ruined place; and, as the morning mists had risen long ago when I first left the forge, so, the evening mists were rising now, and in all the broad expanse of tranquil light they showed to me, I saw the shadow of no parting from her.
Dickens, Charles *Oliver Twist* These, and a thousand looks and smiles, and turns of thought and speech – I would fain recall them every one.
Dickens, Charles *Oliver Twist (supplementary)* I believe it none the less because that nook is in a church, and she was weak and erring.
Dickens, Charles *A Tale of Two Cities* It is a far, far better thing that I do, than I have ever done: it is a far, far better rest that I go to, than I have ever known.
Dostoevsky, Fyodor *Crime and Punishment* That might be the subject of a new story, but our present story is ended.
Doyle, Arthur Conan *The Hound of the Baskervilles* We can stop at Mancini's for a little dinner on the way.
Dumas, Alexander *The Three Musketeers* The opinion of those who thought themselves the best informed was that he was boarded and lodged in some royal castle at the expense of his generous eminence.
Fielding, Henry *Tom Jones* Who doth not most gratefully bless the day when Mr Jones was married to Sophia.
Greene, Graham *Brighton Rock* She walked rapidly in the thin June sunlight towards the worst horror of all.
Harris, Robert *Fatherland* Then he tugged the gun from his waistband, checked to make sure it was loaded and moved towards the silent trees.
Hartley, LP *Eustace and Hilda* But the cold crept onwards and he did not wake.
Heller, Joseph *Catch-22* The knife came down missing him by inches, and he took off.
Hughes, Thomas *Tom Brown's School Days* We can come to the knowledge of him in whom alone, the love and the tenderness, and the purity, and the strength, the courage, and the wisdom of all these, dwell for ever and ever in perfect fullness.
Huxley, Aldous *Crome Yellow* He climbed into the hearse.
Le Carré, John *The Honourable Schoolboy* And nor does Guillam, for George's sake.
Le Carré, John *The Russia House* It's going to be alright Harry, he assured me as he showed me off the premises. Tell them that. Spying is waiting.
Lewis, CS *The Lion, The Witch and The Wardrobe* But if the Professor was right it was only the beginning of the adventures of Narnia.
Lewis, Sinclair *Arrowsmith* We'll plug along on it for two or three years, and maybe we'll get something permanent – and probably we'll fail!
Longfellow, Henry Wadsworth 'The Village Blacksmith' Thus on its sounding anvil shaped Each burning deed and thought.

Longfellow, Henry Wadsworth 'The Wreck of the Hesperus' Christ saves us all from a death like this, on the reef of Norman's woe.
Lowry, Malcolm *Under the Volcano* Somebody threw a dead dog after him down the ravine.
Martel, Yann *Life of Pi* Very few castaways can claim to have survived so long at sea as Mr Patel, and none in the company of an adult Bengal tiger.
Marvell, Andrew 'To His Coy Mistress' Thus though we cannot make our Sun, stand still, yet we will make him run.
McEwan, Ian *Enduring Love* So now, Rachael said. Tell Leo as well. Say it again slowly, that thing about the river.
Melville, Herman *Billy Budd* I am sleepy, and the oozy weeds about me twist.
Milton, John *On His Blindness* They also serve who only stand and wait.
Mitchell, Margaret *Gone With the Wind* After all, Tomorrow is another day.
O'Brien, Flann *At Swim-Two-Birds* He went home one evening and drank three cups of tea with three lumps of sugar in each, cut his jugular with a razor three times and scrawled with a dying hand on a picture of his wife, goodbye, goodbye, goodbye.
Scott, Paul *The Day of the Scorpion* She closed her eyes as perhaps Susan was doing, even now, and after a while felt the quietness of her own happiness and grace welling up inside her; and smiled, ignoring the rain that seemed to be falling on her face.
Service, Robert 'The Shooting of Dan McGrew' The woman that kissed him and pinched his poke, was the lady that's known as Lou.
Sewell, Anna *Black Beauty* I am still in the orchard at Birtwick standing with my old friends under the apple trees.
Shaw, Irwin *The Young Lions* Because he knew he had to deliver Noah Ackerman, personally, to Captain Green.
Solzhenitsyn, Alexander *One Day in the Life of Ivan Denisovich* The three extra days were because of the leap years.
Steel, Danielle *Kaleidoscope* He held her tightly in his arms and she knew he was telling the truth. 'Everything's going to be all right now.'
Steel, Danielle *Star* Home at last. Together.
Swift, Jonathan *Gulliver's Travels* And therefore, I here entreat those who have any tincture of this absurd vice, that they will not presume to appear in my sight.
Thompson, Flora *Lark Rise to Candleford* They were spun of love and kinship and cherished memories.
Tolstoy, Leo *War and Peace* In the present case, it is an essential to surmount a consciousness of an unreal freedom and to recognise a dependence not perceived by our senses.
Tremain, Rose *Restoration* Before I have grown too frail to climb the stairs – I shall bring you back.
Twain, Mark *The Adventures of Tom Sawyer* And if I git to be a reg'lar ripper of a robber, and everybody talking 'bout it, I reckon she'll be proud she snaked me in out of the wet.
Waugh, Evelyn *Brideshead Revisited* 'You're looking unusually cheerful today,' said the second-in-command.
Wilde, Oscar *The Ballad of Reading Gaol* The coward does it with a kiss, The brave man with a sword.
Wood, Mrs Henry *East Lynne* Oh Barbara, never forget – never forget that the only way to ensure peace in the end, is to strive always to be doing right, unselfishly, under God.
Wyndham, John *The Day of the Triffids* Until we have wiped the last one of them from the face of the land they have usurped.

Index of Books (in title order)

(* denotes author's first book)

Book	*Author*
Aaron's Rod	DH Lawrence
The Abbot	Walter Scott
Absalom, Absalom!	William Faulkner
The Absentee	Maria Edgeworth
The Acid House	Irvine Welsh
The Actual	Saul Bellow
*Adam Bede**	George Eliot
Adolphe	Benjamin Constant
The Adventures of Huckleberry Finn	Mark Twain
The Adventures of Peregrine Pickle	Tobias Smollett
The Adventures of Sherlock Holmes	Arthur Conan Doyle
The Aeneid	Virgil
The Affair	Lee Child
Affliction	Fay Weldon
The African Queen	CS Forester
*Afternoon Men**	Anthony Powell
The Age of Innocence	Edith Wharton
The Age of Reason	Thomas Paine
*Agnes Grey**	Anne Brontë
The Agony and the Ecstasy	Irving Stone
Airframe	Michael Crichton
Airport	Arthur Hailey
The Alexandria Quartet	Lawrence Durrell
Alias Grace	Margaret Atwood
Alice's Adventures in Wonderland	Lewis Carroll
Allan Quatermain	Henry Rider Haggard
All Quiet on the Western Front	Erich Maria Remarque
*All the Conspirators**	Christopher Isherwood
*Almayer's Folly**	Joseph Conrad
Alphabats	Paul Sellers
Altered States	Anita Brookner
The Ambassadors	Henry James
Amelia	Henry Fielding
An American Dream	Norman Mailer
American Pastoral	Philip Roth
American Psycho	Brett Easton Ellis
Amsterdam	Ian McEwan
An American Tragedy	Theodore Dreiser
An Evil Cradling	Brian Keenan
And Quiet Flows the Don	Mikhail Sholokhov
Angel Pavement	JB Priestley
Angela's Ashes	Frank McCourt
Angels & Demons	Dan Brown
Animal Farm	George Orwell
Anna Karenina	Leo Tolstoy
Anna of the Five Towns	Arnold Bennett
*Anne of Green Gables**	LM Montgomery
Antic Hay	Aldous Huxley
Any Old Iron	Anthony Burgess
Appassionata	Jilly Cooper
Armageddon	Leon Uris
Around the World in 80 Days	Jules Verne
As I Lay Dying	William Faulkner
*At Mrs Lippincote's**	Elizabeth Taylor
Atlas Shrugged	Ayn Rand
Atonement	Ian McEwan
August 1914	Alexander Solzhenitsyn
The Awakening	Kate Chopin
An Awfully Big Adventure	Beryl Bainbridge
Bad Luck and Trouble	Lee Child
The Bad Place	Dean R Koontz
The Ballad of Peckham Rye	Muriel Spark
The Ballad of the Sad Café	Carson McCullers
Bambi	Felix Salten
Barchester Towers	Anthony Trollope
Barnaby Rudge	Charles Dickens
Baron Münchhausen	RE Raspe
Bartimaeus Trilogy	Jonathan Stroud
The Battle of the Books	Jonathan Swift
The Beach	Alex Garland

Book	Author
*Cover Her Face**	PD James
Cranford	Mrs Elizabeth Gaskell
Credo	Melvyn Bragg
Crime and Punishment	Fyodor Dostoyevsky
The Crocodile Bird	Ruth Rendell
Crome Yellow	Aldous Huxley
Cross of St George	Alexander Kent
The Cruel Sea	Nicholas Monsarrat
Cry, the Beloved Country	Alan Paton
A Cure for Cancer	Michael Moorcock
Curtain	Agatha Christie
Daisy Miller	Henry James
*Dame's Delight**	Margaret Forster
A Dance to the Music of Time (12 volumes)	Anthony Powell
Dangerous Davies	Leslie Thomas
Dangerous Love	Ben Okri
*The Dangling Man**	Saul Bellow
Daniel Deronda	George Eliot
*Dark Carnival**	Ray Bradbury
*The Dark Frontier**	Eric Ambler
Darkness at Noon	Arthur Koestler
Dark Shadows Falling	Joe Simpson
The Darling Buds of May	HE Bates
David Copperfield	Charles Dickens
The Da Vinci Code	Dan Brown
The Day of the Jackal	Frederick Forsyth
The Day of the Locust	Nathanael West
*The Day of the Triffids**	John Wyndham
A Dead Cert	Dick Francis
Dead Man Walking	Sister Helen Prejean
Dead Souls	Nikolai Gogol
Death Comes for the Archbishop	Willa Cather
Death in the Afternoon	Ernest Hemingway
Death in Venice	Thomas Mann
Death Is Now My Neighbour	Colin Dexter
The Decameron	Giovanni Boccaccio
Deception Point	Dan Brown
*Decline and Fall**	Evelyn Waugh
The Decline and Fall of the Roman Empire	Edward Gibbon
Deliverance	James Dickey
Demon Seed	Dean Koontz
Denis Duval (unfinished)	WM Thackeray
The Descent of Man	Charles Darwin
*Desperate Remedies**	Thomas Hardy
Desperation	Stephen King
Devil May Care	Sebastian Faulks
The Devil Rides Out	Dennis Wheatley
The Devils of Loudun	Aldous Huxley
The Dharma Bums	Jack Kerouac
Diana: Her New Life	Andrew Morton
The Diary of a Madman	Nikolai Gogol
The Diary of Anne Frank	Anne Frank
The Diary of a Nobody	George and Weedon Grossmith
Die Trying	Lee Child
*Digital Fortress**	Dan Brown
Discworld	Terry Pratchett
Doctor Doolittle	Hugh Lofting
Doctor Faustus	Thomas Mann
Doctor Kildare	Max Brand
Doctor Sax	Jack Kerouac
Doctor Zhivago	Boris Pasternak
*The Dog It Was That Died**	Alan Coren
The Dogs of War	Frederick Forsyth
Dog Years	Günther Grass
Don Quixote	Miguel Cervantes
The Doors of Perception	Aldous Huxley
Double Act	Jacqueline Wilson
Double Indemnity	James M Cain
Down Among the Women	Fay Weldon
Down and Out in Paris and London	George Orwell
Dracula	Bram Stoker
Dracula Unbound	Brian Aldiss
The Dream Life of Balso Snell	Nathanael West
*The Dream Merchants**	Harold Robbins

Book	Author
The Dressmaker	Beryl Bainbridge
*The Drowned World**	JG Ballard
The Dubliners	James Joyce
Dune	Frank Herbert
Dying Light	Stuart MacBride
Eagle Has Landed	Jack Higgins
Earthly Powers	Anthony Burgess
East of Eden	John Steinbeck
*Eating People Is Wrong**	Malcolm Bradbury
Eats, Shoots & Leaves	Lynne Truss
Echo Burning	Lee Child
Eclipse	Stephenie Meyer
Ecstasy	Irvine Welsh
The Eleventh Commandment	Jeffrey Archer
Emily	Jilly Cooper
Eminent Victorians	Lytton Strachey
Emma	Jane Austen
Empire of the Sun	JG Ballard
The End of Alice	AM Homes
Enduring Love	Ian McEwan
Enemies of the System	Brian Aldiss
The Enemy	Lee Child
The English Assassin	Michael Moorcock
English Journey	Beryl Bainbridge
The English Patient	Michael Ondaatje
Erewhon	Samuel Butler
Esther Waters	George Moore
Ethan Frome	Edith Wharton
Eugene Onegin	Alexander Pushkin
*Evelina**	Fanny Burney
Evening Class	Maeve Binchy
Evening in Byzantium	Irwin Shaw
Every Man for Himself	Beryl Bainbridge
Excalibur	Bernard Cornwell
The Executioner's Song	Norman Mailer
Executive Orders	Tom Clancy
Exodus	Leon Uris
The Exorcist	William Peter Blatty
The Expedition of Humphrey Clinker	Tobias Smollett
Eyeless in Gaza	Aldous Huxley
Eye of the Tiger	Wilbur Smith
Fahrenheit 451	Ray Bradbury
Fair Stood the Wind for France	HE Bates
A Fairytale of New York	JP Donleavy
Faith	Len Deighton
'The Fall of the House of Usher'	Edgar Allan Poe
Fame Is the Spur	Howard Spring
Famous Five	Enid Blyton
Fanfarlo	Charles Baudelaire
Fanny Hill	John Cleland
*Fanshawe**	Nathaniel Hawthorne
Fantastic Beasts and Where to Find Them	JK Rowling
Farewell, My Lovely	Raymond Chandler
A Farewell to Arms	Ernest Hemingway
Far from the Madding Crowd	Thomas Hardy
The Fatal Englishman	Sebastian Faulks
Father Brown stories	GK Chesterton
Fathers and Sons	Ivan Turgenev
*The Fat Woman's Joke**	Fay Weldon
Fear and Loathing in Las Vegas	Hunter S Thompson
Fear Is the Key	Alistair MacLean
Fear of Flying	Erica Jong
Feet of Clay	Terry Pratchett
Felix Holt	George Eliot
Felix in the Underworld	John Mortimer
*Fever Pitch**	Nick Hornby
The Fiend's Delight	Ambrose Bierce
Fifty Years of Europe	Jan Morris
Filthy Lucre	Beryl Bainbridge
The Final Programme	Michael Moorcock
Finnegans Wake	James Joyce
First Among Equals	Jeffrey Archer
The First Circle	Alexander Solzhenitsyn
*First Love, Last Rites**	Ian McEwan

Book	Author
The Hunchback of Notre Dame	Victor Hugo
Huntingtower	John Buchan
Ice Station Zebra	Alistair Maclean
I, Claudius	Robert Graves
Icon	Frederick Forsyth
The Idiot	Fyodor Dostoyevsky
If This Is A Man	Primo Levi
I Hear Voices	Paul Ableman
Immediate Action	Andy McNab
The Immigrants	Howard Fast
In a Free State	VS Naipaul
In Camera	Jean-Paul Sartre
Incognita, or Love and Duty Reconciled*	William Congreve
Inside Mr Enderby	Anthony Burgess
Insomnia	Stephen King
In the Beauty of the Lilies	John Updike
The Invisible Man	HG Wells
The Ipcress File*	Len Deighton
I, Robot	Isaac Asimov
Island in the Sun	Alec Waugh
It	Stephen King
I, The Jury	Mickey Spillane
Ivanhoe	Walter Scott
The Jacaranda Tree	HE Bates
J'Accuse (letter)	Émile Zola
Jacob's Room	Virginia Woolf
Jake's Thing	Kingsley Amis
Jamaica Inn	Daphne Du Maurier
James and the Giant Peach	Roald Dahl
James Bond series	Ian Fleming
The James Bond Dossier	Robert Markham
Jane Eyre	Charlotte Brontë
Jaws	Peter Benchley
Jennie	Paul Gallico
Jigsaw*	Barbara Cartland
Jonathan Livingston Seagull	Richard Bach
Jorrocks's Jaunts and Jollities	Robert Smith Surtees
Joseph Andrews	Henry Fielding
A Journal of the Plague Year	Daniel Defoe
Journal to Stella	Jonathan Swift
Journey to the Centre of the Earth	Jules Verne
Jude the Obscure	Thomas Hardy
Jumping the Queue	Mary Wesley
The Jungle	Upton Sinclair
Junk	Melvin Burgess
Jurassic Park	Michael Crichton
Just Above My Head	James Baldwin
Justine	Marquis de Sade
Just Like a Woman	Jill Gascoigne
Just William	Richmal Crompton
Kaleidoscope	Stefan Zweig
Kangaroo	DH Lawrence
Kate Hannigan*	Catherine Cookson
Kenilworth	Walter Scott
A Kestrel for a Knave	Barry Hines
The Keys of the Kingdom	AJ Cronin
The Keys to the Street	Ruth Rendell
Kidnapped	Robert Louis Stevenson
Killing Floor*	Lee Child
King Rat	James Clavell
King Solomon's Mines	Henry Rider Haggard
King Solomon's Ring	Konrad Lorenz
A Kiss Before Dying	Ira Levin
The Kraken Wakes	John Wyndham
Lace	Shirley Conran
La Chartreuse de Parme	Stendhal
Lady Chatterley's Lover	DH Lawrence
The Lady in the Lake	Raymond Chandler
The Lady of the Camellias	Alexander Dumas (Fils)
The Lark	Edith Nesbit
Lark Rise to Candleford	Flora Thompson
The Last Continent	Terry Pratchett
The Last Days of Pompeii	Edward Bulwer-Lytton
The Last Enemy	Richard Hillary
The Last Juror	John Grisham
The Last of the Mohicans	James Fenimore Cooper
Last Orders	Graham Swift

Book	Author
The Last Testament of Oscar Wilde	Peter Ackroyd
The Last Tycoon	F Scott Fitzgerald
La Symphonie Pastorale	André Gide
Leather-Stocking stories	James Fenimore Cooper
The Legend of Sleepy Hollow	Washington Irving
Le Rouge et le Noir	Stendhal
Les Misérables	Victor Hugo
The Liar	Stephen Fry
The Life and Loves of a She-Devil	Fay Weldon
Life at the Top	John Braine
The Life of Charlotte Brontë	Mrs Elizabeth Gaskell
Light a Penny Candle*	Maeve Binchy
The Light That Failed	Rudyard Kipling
Lily Hart	Charlotte Brontë
The Lion and the Unicorn	George Orwell
The Lion, the Witch and the Wardrobe	CS Lewis
Little Book of Calm	Paul Wilson
Little Dorritt	Charles Dickens
The Little Drummer Girl	John Le Carré
Little Lord Fauntleroy	Frances Hodgson Burnett
Little Men	Louisa May Alcott
The Little Minister	JM Barrie
Little Red Riding Hood	Charles Perrault
Little Women	Louisa May Alcott
Liza of Lambeth*	William Somerset Maugham
Lola Rose	Jacqueline Wilson
Lolita	Vladimir Nabokov
London: The Novel	Edward Rutherfurd
The Loneliness of the Long-Distance Runner	Alan Sillitoe
The Long and the Short and the Tall	Willis Hall
Long Walk to Freedom	Nelson Mandela
Longitude	Dava Sobel
Looking for Mr Goodbar	Judith Rossner
The Looking-Glass War	John Le Carré
The Loom of Youth*	Alec Waugh
Lord Jim	Joseph Conrad
Lord of the Flies*	William Golding
The Lord of the Rings (Trilogy)	JRR Tolkien
Lorna Doone	RD Blackmore
Lost Continent: Travels in Small Town America	Bill Bryson
Lost Horizon	James Hilton
The Lost World of the Kalahari	Laurens Van Der Post
The Lost World	Michael Crichton
The Lost World	Arthur Conan Doyle
Love in a Cold Climate	Nancy Mitford
Love in Another Town	Barbara Taylor Bradford
Love in the Time of Cholera	Gabriel García Márquez
Love on the Dole	Walter Greenwood
Love Story	Eric Segal
The L-Shaped Room	Lynne Reid Banks
The Luck of Barry Lyndon	WM Thackeray
Lucky Jim*	Kingsley Amis
Lust for Life	Irving Stone
The Macdermots of Ballycloran*	Anthony Trollope
Madame Bovary	Gustave Flaubert
Mad Cows	Kathy Lette
Made in America	Bill Bryson
The Magic Mountain	Thomas Mann
The Magus	John Fowles
The Maid of Buttermere	Melvyn Bragg
Maigret	Georges Simenon
Making History	Stephen Fry
The Maltese Falcon	Dashiell Hammett
The Man from the North*	Arnold Bennett
A Man Lay Dead*	Ngaio Marsh
The Man Who Listens to Horses	Monty Roberts
Man Who Was Thursday	GK Chesterton
The Man Who Watched the Trains Go By	Georges Simenon
Manhattan Transfer	John Dos Passos

Book	Author
Mansfield Park	Jane Austen
The Martian	George Du Maurier
*Martin Chuzzlewit**	Charles Dickens
*Mary Barton**	Elizabeth Gaskell
The Mary Deare	Ralph Hammond Innes
Mary Poppins	PL Travers
The Mask of Dimitrios	Eric Ambler
Maskerade	Terry Pratchett
Master and Commander	Patrick O'Brian
The Master and Margarita	Mikhail Bulgakov
Matilda	Roald Dahl
The Mayor of Casterbridge	Thomas Hardy
Meet the Tiger	Leslie Charteris
Melincourt	Thomas Love Peacock
Memoirs of a Fox-Hunting Man	Siegfried Sassoon
The Memory Game	Nicci French
Men Are from Mars, Women Are from Venus	John Gray
Men at Arms	Terry Pratchett
Message from Malaga	Helen MacInnes
The Metamorphosis	Franz Kafka
Metroland	Julian Barnes
The Midden	Tom Sharpe
Midnight Cowboy	James Herlihy
Midnight's Children	Salman Rushdie
The Midwich Cuckoos	John Wyndham
Miguel Street	VS Naipaul
Mildred Pierce	James M Cain
The Mill on the Floss	George Eliot
Miss Lonelyhearts	Nathanael West
Moby-Dick	Herman Melville
Moll Flanders	Daniel Defoe
A Month in the Country	Ivan Turgenev
The Moon and Sixpence	William Somerset Maugham
The Moonstone	Wilkie Collins
The Moor's Last Sigh	Salman Rushdie
Mort	Terry Pratchett
Le Morte D'Arthur	Thomas Malory
Mother	Maxim Gorky
Mother, Can You Hear Me?	Margaret Forster
Mother Goose	Charles Perrault
Mother Goose Treasury	Raymond Briggs
Mourning Doves	Helen Forrester
Mr Men	Roger Hargreaves
Mr Midshipman Easy	Capt. Frederick Marryat
Mr Nice	Howard Marks
Mr Norris Changes Trains	Christopher Isherwood
Mrs Dalloway	Virginia Woolf
Mr Sponge's Sporting Tour	Robert Smith Surtees
Murder Must Advertise	Dorothy L Sayers
The Murder of Roger Ackroyd	Agatha Christie
'The Murders in the Rue Morgue'	Edgar Allan Poe
My Cousin Rachel	Daphne Du Maurier
My Family and Other Animals	Gerald Durrell
My Son, My Son	Howard Spring
The Mysterious Affair at Styles	Agatha Christie
The Mystery of Edwin Drood	Charles Dickens
*The Mystic Masseur**	VS Naipaul
My Universities	Maxim Gorky
*The Naked and the Dead**	Norman Mailer
The Naked Lunch	William Burroughs
The Name of the Rose	Umberto Eco
Nana	Émile Zola
The Napoleon of Notting Hill	GK Chesterton
National Velvet	Enid Bagnold
Nausea	Jean-Paul Sartre
Neither Here Nor There	Bill Bryson
Never Love a Stranger	Harold Robbins
The New Machiavelli	HG Wells
New Moon	Stephenie Meyer
Next of Kin	Joanna Trollope
Nexus	Henry Miller
Nicholas Nickleby	Charles Dickens
The Nigger of the Narcissus	Joseph Conrad
Night and Day	Virginia Woolf
The Night Manager	John Le Carré

Book	Author
Nightmare Abbey	Thomas Love Peacock
Night Train	Martin Amis
The Nine Billion Names of God	Arthur C Clarke
The Nine Tailors	Dorothy L Sayers
Nineteen Eighty-Four	George Orwell
Noble House	James Clavell
Noddy	Enid Blyton
Non-Stop	Brian Aldiss
North and South	Mrs Elizabeth Gaskell
Northanger Abbey	Jane Austen
Nostromo	Joseph Conrad
*Not a Penny More, Not a Penny Less**	Jeffrey Archer
Notes From a Small Island	Bill Bryson
Now We Are Six	AA Milne
The Oak and the Calf	Alexander Solzhenitsyn
Oblomov	Ivan Goncharov
The Odessa File	Frederick Forsyth
An Occurrence at Owl Creek Bridge	Bierce Ambrose
Of Human Bondage	William Somerset Maugham
Of Mice and Men	John Steinbeck
O, How the Wheel Becomes It!	Anthony Powell
The Old Curiosity Shop	Charles Dickens
The Old Devils	Kingsley Amis
The Old Man and the Sea	Ernest Hemingway
Old Peter's Russian Tales	Arthur Ransome
The Old Wives' Tale	Arnold Bennett
Oliver Twist	Charles Dickens
The Once and Future King	TH White
On the Road	Jack Kerouac
*One Day in the Life of Ivan Denisovich**	Alexander Solzhenitsyn
One Fat Englishman	Kingsley Amis
One Hundred Years of Solitude	Gabriel Garcia Márquez
One Shot	Lee Child
One-Upmanship	Stephen Potter
On the Beach	Nevil Shute
Only When I Larf	Len Deighton
O Pioneers!	Willa Cather
The Origin of Species	Charles Darwin
Oroonoko	Aphra Behn
*Other Voices, Other Rooms**	Truman Capote
Our Game	John Le Carré
Our Man in Havana	Graham Greene
Our Mutual Friend	Charles Dickens
An Outcast of the Islands	Joseph Conrad
Out of the Silent Planet	CS Lewis
The Outsider	Albert Camus
*Outskirts**	Hanif Kureishi
The Overcoat	Nikolai Gogol
Overture to Death	Ngaio Marsh
Paddy Clarke Ha Ha Ha	Roddy Doyle
The Pallisers	Anthony Trollope
Pamela	Samuel Richardson
Pandora's Diamond	Julia Stephenson
Pantagruel	François Rabelais
Papillon	Henri Charrière
Paradise Postponed	John Mortimer
A Parliamentary Affair	Edwina Currie
The Partner	John Grisham
A Passage to India	EM Forster
*The Passionate Elopement**	Compton Mackenzie
Payment Deferred	CS Forester
The Pelican Brief	John Grisham
The Pen and the Sword	Michael Foot
Pendennis	WM Thackeray
Perfume	Patrick Susskind
Perry Mason (series)	Erle Stanley Gardner
Persuader	Lee Child
Persuasion	Jane Austen
*Peter Camenzind**	Herman Hesse
Peter Simple	Capt. Frederick Marryat
Peyton Place	Grace Metalious
The Physiology of Taste	Anthelme Brillat-Savarin
The Pickwick Papers	Charles Dickens
The Picturegoers	David Lodge

Book	*Author*
The Picture of Dorian Gray	Oscar Wilde
Picture This	Joseph Heller
*Pied Piper of Lovers**	Lawrence Durrell
The Pilgrim's Progress	John Bunyan
Pincher Martin	William Golding
Piracy	Michael Arlen
'The Pit and the Pendulum'	Edgar Allan Poe
The Plague	Albert Camus
Planet of the Apes	Pierre Boulle
*Player Piano**	Kurt Vonnegut
Ploughman of the Moon	Robert Service
The Plumed Serpent	DH Lawrence
Point Counter Point	Aldous Huxley
Poldark	Winston Graham
Popcorn	Ben Elton
Porky	Deborah Moggach
Porterhouse Blue	Tom Sharpe
Portnoy's Complaint	Philip Roth
The Portrait of a Lady	Henry James
Portrait of the Artist as a Young Dog	Dylan Thomas
Portrait of the Artist as a Young Man	James Joyce
The Poseidon Adventure	Paul Gallico
Possession	AS Byatt
The Postman Always Rings Twice	James M Cain
The Power and the Glory	Graham Greene
Prater Violet	Christopher Isherwood
A Prayer for Owen Meany	John Irving
*Precaution**	James Fenimore Cooper
Prelude	Katherine Mansfield
*Prelude to Space**	Arthur C Clarke
The President's Daughter	Jack Higgins
Prester John	John Buchan
Pretend You Don't See Her	Mary Higgins Clark
Pride and Prejudice	Jane Austen
The Prime of Miss Jean Brodie	Muriel Spark
Prime Time	Joan Collins
The Prince	Niccolò Machiavelli
Princess Daisy	Judith Krantz
Princess in Love	Anna Pasternak
The Prisoner of Zenda	Anthony Hope
The Professor	Charlotte Brontë
Promiscuities	Naomi Wolf
Prozac Nation	Elizabeth Wurtzel
Psychology, the Science of Mind and Behaviour	Richard D Gross
Public Good	Thomas Paine
Puss in Boots	Charles Perrault
A Question of Proof	Rex Stout
A Question of Upbringing (first of *A Dance to the Music of Time*)	Anthony Powell
Quidditch Through the Ages	JK Rowling
A Quiet Drink	Deborah Moggach
Quo Vadis	Henry Sienkiewicz
Rabbit Tetralogy	John Updike
The Radiant Way	Margaret Drabble
Raffles	EW Hornung
The Ragged Trousered Philanthropists	Robert Tressell
The Ragman's Daughter	Alan Sillitoe
The Railway Children	Edith Nesbit
The Rainbow	DH Lawrence
The Rainmaker	John Grisham
Raj Quartet	Paul Scott
The Rats	James Herbert
The Razor's Edge	William Somerset Maugham
Rebecca	Daphne Du Maurier
The Red Badge of Courage	Stephen Crane
The Remains of the Day	Kazuo Ishiguro
Remembrance Day	Brian Aldiss
Remembrance of Things Past (novel cycle in 7 parts)	Marcel Proust
*Remote Control**	Andy McNab
The Return of the Native	Thomas Hardy
The Rhinemann Exchange	Robert Ludlum

Book	*Author*
Riceyman Steps	Arnold Bennett
Riders of the Purple Sage	Zane Grey
Right Ho, Jeeves	PG Wodehouse
The Rights of Man	Thomas Paine
Ring of Bright Water	Gavin Maxwell
*Riotous Assembly**	Tom Sharpe
Rip Van Winkle	Washington Irving
Rites of Passage	William Golding
Road Rage	Ruth Rendell
The Roads to Freedom (Trilogy)	Jean-Paul Sartre
The Road to Wigan Pier	George Orwell
Robinson Crusoe	Daniel Defoe
Rob Roy	Walter Scott
Rockets Galore	Compton Mackenzie
The Adventures of Roderick Random	Tobias Smollett
Rogue Justice	Geoffrey Household
Rogue Male	Geoffrey Household
Romola	George Eliot
Rookwood	William Harrison Ainsworth
Room at the Top	John Braine
A Room with a View	EM Forster
Rosemary's Baby	Ira Levin
Runaway Jury	John Grisham
Rupert of Hentzau	Anthony Hope
Rural Rides	William Cobbett
The Sailor Who Fell from Grace with the Sea	Yukio Mishima
The Saint	Leslie Charteris
Salammbô	Gustave Flaubert
Salar the Salmon	Henry Williamson
Salmagundi	Washington Irving
Sard Harker	John Masefield
The Satanic Verses	Salman Rushdie
Saturday	Ian McEwan
*Saturday Night and Sunday Morning**	Alan Sillitoe
Say Cheese and Die Again!	RL Stine
The Scarlatti Inheritance	Robert Ludlum
The Scarlet Letter	Nathaniel Hawthorne
The Scarlet Pimpernel	Baroness Orczy
The Screwtape Letters	CS Lewis
The Sea, The Sea	Iris Murdoch
Sea-Wolf	Jack London
The Second Sex	Simone de Beauvoir
*Secret Diary of Adrian Mole Aged 13¾**	Sue Townsend
The Secret Garden	Frances Hodgson Burnett
The Secret Life of Walter Mitty	James Thurber
The Secret Seven	Enid Blyton
The Seed and the Sower	Laurens Van Der Post
Seesaw	Deborah Moggach
Seize the Day	Saul Bellow
The Selfish Gene	Richard Dawkins
*Sense and Sensibility**	Jane Austen
The Sentinel	Arthur C Clarke
Seventh Avenue	Norman Bogner
79 Park Avenue	Harold Robbins
Shadow Baby	Margaret Forster
*Shadow of a Sun**	AS Byatt
Sharpe's Devil	Bernard Cornwell
She	Henry Rider Haggard
The Shipping News	E Annie Proulx
Shogun	James Clavell
A Short History of Nearly Everything	Bill Bryson
Shout at the Devil	Wilbur Smith
The Sign of Four	Arthur Conan Doyle
Silas Marner	George Eliot
The Silence of the Lambs	Thomas Harris
The Silmarillion	JRR Tolkien
The Simisola	Ruth Rendell
Sins	Judith Gould
Sir Charles Grandison	Samuel Richardson
61 Hours	Lee Child
Slaughterhouse-Five	Kurt Vonnegut
Sleepers	Lorenzo Carcaterra
The Sleeping Beauty	Charles Perrault
Small Is Beautiful	Ernst Schumacher

Book	Author
Vanity Fair: A Novel Without a Hero	WM Thackeray
Vathek	William Beckford
Vicar of Wakefield	Oliver Goldsmith
Vicky Angel	Jacqueline Wilson
Victory	John Williams
Villette	Charlotte Brontë
The Virginians	WM Thackeray
*The Virgin Soldiers**	Leslie Thomas
*A Vision of Battlements**	Anthony Burgess
Visitors	Anita Brookner
*Vivien Grey**	Benjamin Disraeli
*The Voyage Out**	Virginia Woolf
Waiting For Sunrise	William Boyd
Walden, or Life in the Woods	Henry Thoreau
A Wanted Man	Lee Child
War and Peace	Leo Tolstoy
The Warden	Anthony Trollope
The War of the Worlds	HG Wells
Washington Square	Henry James
The Wasp Factory	Iain Banks
The Water-Babies	Charles Kingsley
Watership Down	Richard Adams
Waverley	Walter Scott
The Way of All Flesh	Samuel Butler
*A Weekend with Claud**	Beryl Bainbridge
Weir of Hermiston	Robert Louis Stevenson
The Well of Loneliness	Radcliffe Hall
Westward Ho!	Charles Kingsley
What America Means to Me	Pearl Buck
What Did You Do in the War, Mummy	Mavis Nicholson
What Katy Did	Susan Coolidge
What's Become of Waring?	Anthony Powell
What's Bred in the Bone	Robertson Davies
Wheels	Arthur Hailey
When Eight Bells Toll	Alistair Maclean
*When the Lion Feeds**	Wilbur Smith
When the Wind Blows	Raymond Briggs
Where Eagles Dare	Alistair Maclean
Whisky Galore	Compton Mackenzie
The White Company	Arthur Conan Doyle
White Eagles Over Serbia	Lawrence Durrell
White Fang	Jack London
The White Hotel	DM Thomas
*The White Peacock**	DH Lawrence
Whose Body?	Dorothy L Sayers
A Wide Field	Günther Grass
Wild Swans	Jung Chang
Wilhelm Meister's Apprenticeship	Johann Goethe
Wilhelm Meister's Travels	Johann Goethe
Wilt	Tom Sharpe
The Wind in the Willows	Kenneth Grahame
A Window in Thrums	JM Barrie
The Winds of War	Herman Wouk
Winnie-the-Pooh	AA Milne
Winnie-the-Pooh: Now We Are Six	AA Milne
Winsome Winnie	Stephen Leacock
The Witches of Eastwick	John Updike
The Witching Hour	Anne Rice
With These Hands	Pam Ayers
Witness for the Prosecution	Agatha Christie
The Woman in White	Wilkie Collins
The Woman Who Walked into Doors	Roddy Doyle
Women in Love	DH Lawrence
The Wonderful Adventures of	Selma Lagerlöf *Nils*
Worrals of the WAAF	Capt. WE Johns
Worst Fears	Fay Weldon
A Wreath of Roses	Elizabeth Taylor
Wreckers Must Breathe	Ralph Hammond Innes
Wuthering Heights	Emily Brontë
The X Files	Les Martin
A Year in Cricklewood	Alan Coren
A Year in Provence	Peter Mayle
Year of the Tiger	Jack Higgins
*You Must Be Sisters**	Deborah Moggach
The Young Fur Traders	RM Ballantyne
*The Young Man**	Stephen Potter
Youth	Leo Tolstoy
Zen and the Art of Motorcycle Maintenance	Robert Pirsig

NB: The list above is a good cross-section of popular works, but by no means comprehensive. Many popular books are included and some interesting less-known works. For ease of reference, the list is re-sorted below by author.

Books: General Information

The Admirable Crichton Master: Lord Loam. Ship: *The Bluebell.*

Alexandria Quartet *Justine, Balthazar, Mountolive, Clea* (who had her right hand cut off to save her from drowning after it was pinned underwater by a harpoon gun).

Alice in Wonderland In the croquet game, the mallets were flamingoes and the balls were hedgehogs.

The Anglo-Saxon Chronicle Early record in English of events in England from the arrival of Christianity to 1154, surviving in seven manuscripts and begun about 890, possibly by Alfred the Great. Entries include the arrival of Hengist and Horsa, the story of Cynewulf and Cyneheard, and Alfred's last series of Danish wars. One famous passage is a poem about the battle of Brunanburh (937). The chronicle was expanded and continued, particularly in the late 16th and early 17th century.

Animal Farm The manor farm was owned by Mr Jones, Napoleon the pig became the leader, Boxer was the horse.

Anna Karenina Anna's death: She threw herself under a train.

Anne of Green Gables Prince Edward Island was the setting for Anne Shirley's adventures.

Antic Hay Title from a line in *Edward II* by Christopher Marlowe.

Around the World in 80 Days Central character is Phileas Fogg and his valet is Passepartout. They start and finish at the Reform Club in London. The Indian Widow is Aouda.

Baedeker Books Named after Karl Baedeker of Essen (1801–59), who started the issue of the famous guidebooks in Koblenz. The tradition was continued by his son Fritz, who transferred the business to Leipzig. The term 'Baedeker raids' was applied to the deliberate bombing in WWII of provincial cities of great historic and cultural significance, such as Bath, Exeter and Norwich.

Bartimaeus Trilogy *The Amulet of Samarkand, The Golem's Eye, Ptolemy's Gate.*

Bildungsroman (lit. education novel) Novels portraying a person's formative years, a favourite genre with German authors. *Agathon* (1766) is considered the first example, but Goethe's *Wilhelm Meister's Apprenticeship* (1796) is outstanding.

Bleak House Court case was Jarndyce *v* Jarndyce, the rag and bone man was Krook (who died of spontaneous combustion).

Book of the Century *Lord of the Rings* was voted Book of the Century in a survey of 25,000 people carried out in 1997 by Channel 4 and Waterstone's.

Bookshop First WH Smith: Euston Station.

The Borrowers The Names: Pod, Homily, Arrietty.

Bradshaw's Railway Guide First published in 1839 in the form of Railway Time Tables by George Bradshaw (1801–53), a Quaker printer and engraver. These developed into Bradshaw's Monthly Railway Guide in 1841 and continued to be published until May 1961.

Brave New World Title from Shakespeare's *The Tempest*

The Brothers Karamazov Alyosha, Dmitry, Ivan, Smolykov.

Cakes and Ale Title from a line in *Twelfth Night* by William Shakespeare.

The Call of the Wild Dog's name Buck.

Candide Dr Pangloss's famous quote: 'All is for the best in the best of possible worlds.'

Canterbury Tales The pilgrims met at the Tabard Inn, Southwark. The host on the pilgrimage was Harry Bailly. The summoner's tale tells of a corrupt mendicant friar who is tricked into accepting a donation of a fart.

Catch-22 Set in Pianosa in the Mediterranean. Captain Yossarian had the predicament. Kid Sampson died: cut in half by a low-flying aircraft. Catch-22 is the predicament faced by US bomber crews: You don't have to fly any more missions if you're crazy, but if you ask to be grounded you prove you're not crazy.

The Catcher in the Rye Central character Holden Caulfield.

Children's Laureate Position awarded in the United Kingdom once every two years to a distinguished writer or illustrator of children's books. Quentin Blake became the first in 1999. Subsequent holders: Anne Fine (2001-03), Michael Morpurgo (2003-05), Jacqueline Wilson (2005-07), Michael Rosen (2007-09), Anthony Browne (2009-11), Julia Donaldson (2011-13), Malorie Blackman (2013-15).

Clayhanger Trilogy *Clayhanger, Hilda, Lessways, These Twain.* A fourth novel, *The Roll Call*, is loosely connected to the trilogy.

Cold Comfort Farm Cows' names: *Aimless, Feckless, Graceless, Pointless.*

The Corridors of Power War Minister was Roger Quaife.

The Count of Monte Cristo The Count was Edmond Dantès, imprisoned in Château d'If - inherited a fortune left by Abbé Faria.

Crime and Punishment Crime: murder of a female pawnbroker. Criminal: Raskolnikov. Investigating Inspector: Petrovitch.

David Copperfield Headmaster of Salem House School: Mr Creakle. Aunt: Betsy Trotwood. Wives: Dora Spenlow and Agnes Wickfield.

Death in Venice Gustav von Aschenbach dies of cholera.

Dickens Only novel with female narrator: *Bleak House.*

Doctor Zhivago Title character: Dr Yuri Zhivago. Wife: Tania Gromeko. Lover: Lara Antipova.

Dombey and Son Captain Cuttle's famous quote: 'When found, make a note of.'

Don Quixote Horse: Rosinante. Squire: Sancho Panza. Lady: Dulcinea.

East of Eden Based on the story of Cain and Abel.

Emma Emma Woodhouse marries Mr Knightley.

Every Man For Himself Story of the *Titanic* disaster told by Morgan, a well connected young man.

Fair Stood the Wind for France Title from 'Ballad of Agincourt' by Michael Drayton.

Far from the Madding Crowd Bathsheba Everdene marries Sergeant Troy and Gabriel Oak. Title from 'Elegy Written in a Country Church-yard' by Thomas Gray.

Feet of Clay Main character Commander Sir Samuel Vimes, head of Ankh-Morpork City Guard.

Fictional lands Ambrosia *(Billy Liar)*, Vulgaria *(Chitty Chitty Bang Bang).*

Finnegans Wake Central character is Humphrey Chimpden Earwicker, a publican; the action takes place during one night.

Forsyte Saga Trilogy *A Man of Property, In Chancery, To Let.*

For Whom the Bell Tolls Title from a sermon by John Donne.

Foundation Trilogy *Foundation, Foundation and Empire,* Second *Foundation.*

Gargantua and Pantagruel Published under name 'Alcofri bas Nasier' (anagram of François Rabelais).

George Smiley First appeared in *Call for the Dead.*

Glass of Blessings (Barbara Pym) Title from 'The Pulley' by George Herbert.

Gone with the Wind Scarlett O'Hara marries Charles Hamilton, Frank Kennedy, Rhett Butler.

Gothic Novel: 1st *The Castle of Otranto* by Horace Walpole (1764).

Grapes of Wrath The Joad family – Tom, Al, Noah, Ruthie, Winfield and Rosasharn leave Oklahoma for California.

Gravity's Rainbow Central character Tyrone Slothrop.

The Great Gatsby Jay Gatsby loves Daisy Buchanan, cousin of narrator Nick Carraway.

Gulliver's Travels Horses: Houyhnyms. Humans: Yahoos. Lands visited: Lilliput, Brobdingnag, Laputa, Blefuscu. Subtitle: 'Travels into Several Remote Nations of the World'.

Hardy's last novel *Jude the Obscure.*

Harleian Manuscripts Collection of manuscripts made by Robert Harley, first earl of Oxford (1661–1724). It consisted of over 50,000 books, 350,000 pamphlets, and 7,000 manuscripts of biblical texts and other historical data. The manuscripts were bought by Parliament in 1753 and placed in the British Museum. They are now housed in the British Library.

Harry Potter Books Illustrated by Mary Grandpré. First in the series titled *Harry Potter and the Sorcerer's Stone* in the USA.

Heavy Metal Phrase coined by William Burroughs in *The Naked Lunch.*

Helliconia Trilogy *Helliconia Spring, Helliconia Summer, Helliconia Winter.*

The History Man Title character Howard Kirk.

Hitch Hiker's 'Trilogy' *The Hitch Hiker's Guide to the Galaxy*; *The Restaurant at the End of the Universe*; *Life, the Universe and Everything*; *So Long, and Thanks for All the Fish*; *Mostly Harmless.* A sixth book in the 'Trilogy', entitled *And Another Thing*, was written by Artemis Fowl author Eoin Colfer after the death of Adams.

Hoax *Nat Tate: An American Artist 1928-1960* (1998) by William Boyd. Nat Tate, a combination of the names of the National Gallery and the Tate Gallery, was supposedly an abstract expressionist who destroyed 99% of his work and leapt to his death from the Staten Island ferry. His body was never found. Gore Vidal and David Bowie (who read excerpts from the biography) were in on the hoax which fooled much of the art world.

Howard's End House owners Mr and Mrs Wilcox.

Incunabula Books printed before 1501 (means 'swaddling clothes').

Interior Monologue Extended representation in prose or verse of a character's unspoken thoughts, memories and impressions, rendered as if directly overheard by the reader without the intervention of a summarising narrator.

Ivanhoe Love interest: Lady Rowena.

James Bond books not by Fleming *Colonel Sun* and *The James Bond Dossier* by Kingsley Amis, writing as Robert Markham. *Devil May Care* by Sebastian Faulks.

Jane Eyre Mr Rochester lives at Thornfield Hall. Jane's school is Lowood. Jane's bullying cousin is John Reed. Her home until aged 10 is Gateshead Hall. Dedicated to William Makepeace Thackeray.

The Jewel in the Crown First novel in the Raj Quartet. Plot revolves around the alleged rape in the Bibighar Gardens of Daphne Manners.

Jude the Obscure Jude Fawley aspires to go to Christminster (Oxford), but fails to get into Sarcophagus College.

Kidnapped Central character is David Balfour. His friend is the Jacobite Alan Breck. The ship that is meant to take David to the Carolina is the *Covenant.*

Kipps Central character Arthur Kipps. Occupation: draper's assistant.

The Last Tycoon Allegedly based on the Hollywood film producer Irving Thalberg.

Leather-Stocking stories Hero: Natty Bumppo, also called 'Hawkeye', 'Pathfinder' and 'Deerslayer'. The Last of the Mohicans was Uncas and his father was Chingachgook.

Lee Child novels Hero: Jack Reacher, a former American military policeman.

Little Lord Fauntleroy Title character: Cedric Errol.

Little Women They are the March sisters: Amy, Beth, Jo and Meg.

Lolita Title character: Dolores Haze.

The Longest Journey (EM Forster) Title from *Epipsychidion* by Percy Bysshe Shelley.

Look Homeward, Angel (Thomas Wolfe) from *Lycidas* by John Milton.

The Lord of the Rings Setting: Middle Earth. Hobbit: Bilbo Baggins. Bilbo's nephew: Frodo. Maker of the One Ring: Sauron. Sauron's land: Mordor. Wizard: Gandalf. Gandalf's horse: Shadowfax. Books in the trilogy: *The Fellowship of the Ring, The Two Towers, The Return of the King.*

Madame Bovary Title character née Emma Rouault.

Mansfield Park Heroine Fanny Price.

The Mayor of Casterbridge Mayor: First Michael Henchard then Donald Farfrae. Setting: Wessex. 'Casterbridge' is Dorchester. Henchard sells his wife and daughter for five guineas.

The Memory Game Nicci Gerrard and Sean French are co-writers.

The Mill on the Floss Central characters: Tom and Maggie Tulliver. Setting: Dorlcote Mill.

Mirror Crack'd From Side to Side (Agatha Christie) Title from 'The Lady of Shalott' by Alfred Lord Tennyson.

Moby Dick Captain: Ahab. Narrator: Ishmael. Ship: *Pequod.*

The Moon and Sixpence Inspired by the life of Paul Gauguin.

The Moonstone Title is the name of a diamond.

Morse Christian name Endeavour (revealed in *Death Is Now My Neighbour*).

Mort Main character, Mort, is Death's hopelessly inept teenage apprentice.

***Mr Weston's Good Wine* (TF Powys)** Title from *Emma*, by Jane Austen.

My Son, My Son Original title *Oh Absalom.*

Nicholas Nickleby Nicholas marries Madeline Bray. School: Dotheboys Hall. Schoolmaster: Wackford Squeers. Friend: Smike.

The Nine Tailors Are church bells that cause Geoffrey Deacon's death.

Nineteen Eighty-Four Hero: Winston Smith. His lover: Julia (junior member of the anti-Sex League). Britain depicted as Airstrip One (part of Oceania).

Northanger Abbey Heroine Catherine Morland.

Our Mutual Friend Title character: John Harmon. Marries: Bella Wilfe. Villain: Silas Wegg the peg-leg.

Pale Fire (Nabokov) Title from *Timon of Athens* by William Shakespeare.

A Passage to India Setting: Chandrapore. Central characters: Dr Aziz and Cyril Fielding. Aziz accused of rape by Adela Quested.

Peter Rabbit's father Killed and made into a pie by Mrs McGregor.

The Pickwick Papers Cricket match*:* All-Muggleton *v* Dingley Dell.

The Pilgrim's Progress Hero: Christian. Castle: Doubting. Giant: Despair. Goal: Celestial City.

The Portrait of a Lady Title character Isabel Archer.

Power and the Glory Set in Mexico.

The Prime of Miss Jean Brodie Art teacher*:* Teddy Lloyd.

The Prince and the Pauper Title characters – Prince: Edward, Prince of Wales, later Edward VI; Pauper: Tom Canty.

Prison: authors in

Jeffrey Archer spent two years in various prisons (including Belmarsh, Wayland, North Sea Camp and Lincoln) for perjury. On his release he published three volumes of prison diaries.

Brendan Behan for IRA activities.

William Blake in Chichester for fighting with a soldier.

John Bunyan in Bedford gaol for preaching without a licence.

Daniel Defoe after writing *The Shortest Way with Dissenters* (a satire on High Church attitudes to religious nonconformism).

John Donne in the Fleet for marrying Anne Moore (a minor) in 1576. Hence his comment: 'John Donne – Anne Donne – Undone.'

Fyodor Dostoyevsky was condemned to death for belonging to a revolutionary organisation but was reprieved and served 4 years hard labour in Siberia.

Ben Jonson was imprisoned for killing Gabriel Spenser, but after pleading benefit of clergy was merely branded on the left thumb.

Ezra Pound was charged with treason for delivering radio broadcasts on behalf of the Axis powers during WWII, but was found unfit to plead and instead imprisoned in an asylum.

Alexander Solzhenitsyn spent 8 years in a prison camp for criticising Stalin's conduct of the war against Nazi Germany.

Oscar Wilde was imprisoned for 2 years in Reading Gaol for homosexual offences. He wrote *De Profundis* while incarcerated, not *The Ballad of Reading Gaol.*

The Prisoner of Zenda Title character: King Rudolf. Kingdom: Ruritania. Imprisoned by: Duke Michael.

Quentin Durward Marries Isabelle de Croye.

Rabbit Tetralogy *Rabbit, Run*; *Rabbit Redux*; *Rabbit Is Rich*; *Rabbit at Rest.*

The Railway Children Names*:* Peter, Phyllis, Roberta.

The Raj Quartet *The Jewel in the Crown, The Day of the Scorpion, A Division of the Spoils, The Towers of Silence.*

The Red and The Black (Stendhal's *Le Rouge et le Noir*). Colours symbolise respectively the Army and the Church.

The Red Badge of Courage Set in the American Civil War.

Rip Van Winkle Set in the Catskill Mountains. Rip sleeps for 20 years.

Room 101 In Orwell's *Nineteen Eighty-Four*, this room contained rats used to help interrogate Winston Smith, as they were his great fear.

The Scarlet Letter Central character: Hester Prynne. The Scarlet Letter: A for Adultery.

The Scarlet Pimpernel Title character*:* Sir Percy Blakeney.

Scriblerus Club Literary group including Swift, Pope, Gay, Arbuthnot and Thomas Parnell, which met from January to July 1714 to 'ridicule all the false tastes in learning'. Martinos Scriblerus was a pseudonym occasionally used by Pope.

The Seed and the Sower Filmed as *Merry Christmas Mr Lawrence.*

Sense and Sensibility Characters who represent these quallities*:* Sense – Elinor Dashwood. Sensibility – Marianne Dashwood.

Sherlock Holmes Landlady*:* Mrs Hudson.

Shogun Central character*:* John Blackthorne.

Slaughterhouse-Five Hero*:* Billy Pilgrim.

Sons and Lovers Son*:* Paul Morel.

The Sound and the Fury Title from: *Macbeth* by William Shakespeare. Family: Benjy, Caddy, Jason and Quentin Compson.

Spanish Civil War Served as stretcher bearer*:* WH Auden (for the Republicans).

The Spy Who Came in from the Cold Title character*:* Leamas.

Stammered Somerset Maugham.

Steppenwolf Central character*:* Harry Haller.

Stream of Consciousness Term coined in William James's (1842–1910) *Principles of Psychology* (1890) and used to describe the continuity of impressions and thoughts in the human mind. The literary sense of the term was introduced in 1918 by May Sinclair (1863–1946) in a review of early volumes of Dorothy Richardson's (1873–1957) novel sequence *Pilgrimage* (1915–38) and is a method for representing the aforementioned psychological principle in unpunctuated or fragmentary forms of interior monologue.

The Sun Also Rises Source of the term*:* 'The Lost Generation'.

Swiss Family Robinson Johann David Wyss wrote the story and his son Johann Rudolf completed and edited it. The Robinsons' names: Fritz, Ernest, Franz and Jack.

Sword of Honour Trilogy *Men at Arms, Officers and Gentlemen, Unconditional Surrender.*

The Tailor of Panama Tailor: Harry Pendel.

The Tale of Two Cities Cities: Paris and London. Sentenced to guillotine: Charles Darnay. Sacrificed himself in Darnay's place: Sydney Carton.

1066 and All That Full title: 1066 and All That: A Memorable History of England, comprising all the parts you can remember, including 103 Good Things, 5 Bad Kings and 2 Genuine Dates. The whimsical reworking of the history of England was written by W. C. Sellar and R. J. Yeatman and illustrated by John Reynolds and first appeared serially in *Punch* magazine and was published in book form by Methuen & Co. Ltd. in 1930.

Tender Is the Night Title from 'Ode to a Nightingale' by John Keats. Main character: Dick Diver.

Tess of the D'Urbervilles Tess marries Angel Clare.

The Thirty-Nine Steps Hannay's servant*:* Paddock.

Three Men in a Boat Title characters: George, Harris, Jerome himself, not forgetting Montmorency (the dog).

Thrums Name given in JM Barrie to disguise Kirriemuir, his home town.

The Tin Drum Hero*:* Oskar Matzerath (a dwarf).

Tobacco Road Sharecropper: Jeeter Lester. Jeeter's wife: Ada.

Tom Jones Tom's wife: Sophia Western. Her servant: Mrs Honour.

The Trial Central character*:* Joseph K.

The Turn of the Screw Children: Miles and Flora. Ghosts: Miss Jessel and Peter Quint.

2001: A Space Odyssey Book based on the film of the same name.

Ulysses Central characters: Leopold and Molly Bloom and Stephen Daedalus. Set during 18 hours in Dublin on 16 June 1904.

Uncle Tom's Cabin Slave owner*:* Simon Legree.

Unnatural Exposure Plot*:* Bodies are being dumped in rubbish and bin men demand stress counselling.

Vanity Fair Central character: Becky Sharp marries: Rawdon Crawley. Becky's friend: Amelia Sedley. she marries: (1) George Osborne; (2) Captain Dobbin. School: Miss Pinkerton's. Illustrated by: WM Thackeray.

Victory (John Williams) Set during Tony Blair's campaign for the 1997 election (pictures by Tom Stoddart).

Villette Villette is a city based on Brussels.

The Water-Babies Set in Vendale.

Watership Down Rabbits Bigwig, Fiver, General Woundwort, Hazel.

The Well of Loneliness Originally banned for lesbian content.

Westward Ho! Hero: Amyas Leigh. His love: Rose of Torridge.

What Katy Did Heroine's full name*:* Katy Carr.

Whisky Galore Setting*:* Great and Little Todday.

Whitbread Awards: Man and Wife Michael Frayn and Claire Tomalin became the first married couple to win Whitbread Awards, in 2003.

White Fang offspring of a wolf-dog and a dog.

WH Smith *The End of Alice*, banned for its content of child abuse

Wind in the Willows Characters: Badger, Mole, Toad, Water Rat.

Winnie-the-Pooh Title character: Edward (Pooh). Boy: Christopher Robin. Donkey: Eeyore. Elephant: Heffalump. Kidnapped baby: Roo (kangaroo). Illustrator: EH Shepard.

Woman publishers Virago (run by women for women).

Women in Love Gudrun Brangwen and Gerald Crich were based on Katherine Mansfield and John Middleton Murry.

Wuthering Heights Narrated by Mr Lockwood and Nelly Deane.

Wyss, Johann Rudolf Wrote the Swiss National Anthem 'Rufst du mein Vaterland'.

Zuleika Dobson (Max Beerbohm) Servant: Mélisande.

Jane Austen's Characters (of her six completed novels)

Jane Austen was born in 1775 and died at Winchester, aged 42, in the summer of 1817, having lived a quiet, uneventful life. One of eight children, she lived in the rectory at Steventon until she was 16, when her family moved to Bath. Her father died in 1805 and she remained unmarried, spending the rest of her life with her mother and sister, Cassandra, initially in Southampton, then in Chawton in Hampshire. She was well-read and her favourite writer, Dr Johnson, is quoted in several of her works.

***Emma*: Completed in 1815 and published in 1816. The novel was dedicated to the Prince Regent. The Churchills' estate in Yorkshire is Enscombe, the Bateses lived in Highbury and the Woodhouse residence was in Hartfield, Highbury.**

Abbot, Misses The two Abbots (first names unknown), students at Mrs Goddard's school.

Abdy, John Son of Old John, ostler and head man at the Crown.

Abdy, Old John For 27 years clerk to the late Reverend Bates.

Bates, Miss Hetty Daughter of Reverend Bates and Mrs Bates, sister to Miss Jane Bates, aunt to Jane Fairfax. The town chatterbox, but has a sweet and kind nature and is loved by all though being neither married, rich nor pretty. She is insulted by Emma at Box Hill and true to her nature takes no offence, but this teaches Emma a valuable lesson.

Bates, Miss Jane Youngest daughter of Reverend Bates and Mrs Bates, sister to Miss Hetty Bates. Married Lieutenant Fairfax, who died in battle; Jane herself died soon after giving birth to Jane Fairfax.

Bates, Mrs Old, deaf widowed mother of Miss Jane Bates and Miss Hetty Bates.

Bates, Reverend Father to Miss Jane Bates and Miss Hetty Bates.

Bickerton, Miss Betty Parlour border at Mrs Goddard's school. She and Harriet are attacked by gypsies while out walking and Miss Bickerton flees, leaving Harriet to fend for herself.

Bird, Mrs Friend of Augusta Hawkins.

Bragge, Mr Cousin of Mr Suckling.

Bragge, Mrs Cousin of Mr Suckling. Mrs Elton offers Jane Fairfax a position with Mrs Bragge.

Braithwaite family Friends of Mr and Mrs Churchill.

Brown, Mrs Friend of Augusta Hawkins.

Campbells Colonel and Mrs Campbell and their daughter. Friends of Lieutenant Fairfax and patron of Jane Fairfax. Miss Campbell marries Mr Dixon and Jane then leaves to become a governess.

Churchill, Frank Foppish son of Captain Weston and Miss Churchill, adopted by his aunt and uncle, Mr and Mrs Churchill of Enscombe. Meets Jane Fairfax in Weymouth and enters into a secret engagement. A charming and attractive man who flirts with Emma to allay suspicion of his secret, but eventually agrees to marry Jane.

Churchill, Miss Mr Churchill's sister. Married Captain Weston and had a son, Frank Weston Churchill.

Churchill, Mr and Mrs Of Enscombe in Yorkshire, although also having a home in Richmond. The aunt and uncle of Frank Weston Churchill, whom they fostered when Miss Churchill/Weston died. Mrs Churchill died in Richmond and Mr Churchill allows Frank to marry Jane Fairfax.

Coles Mr and Mrs Cole are nouveaux riches and although they have 'been settled some years in Highbury', Emma continues to think of them as inferior until they hold a party and she is dismayed to find all her friends are going.

Cooper, Mrs James Friend of Augusta Hawkins.

Cox family Lower-class family in Highbury although William was a lawyer, as was his father. They are friends of the Bateses and the Eltons.

Dixon, Mr Of Balycraig, Ireland. Once saved Jane Fairfax from drowning and Emma imagines they are in love. Frank Churchill teased Jane with the name 'Dixon'. Mr Dixon marries Miss Campbell.

Elton, Mr Philip Vicar of Highbury who falls in love with Emma, although she wants him to marry Harriet. He is offended at this suggestion and leaves Highbury. He meets Miss Augusta Hawkins while staying at the White Hart in Bath and marries her. On his return to Highbury he is now smug and resentful and he and his new wife never miss a chance to slight Emma.

Fairfax, Jane Orphaned daughter of Lieutenant Fairfax and Miss Jane Bates. Niece of Miss Hetty Bates. Meets Frank Churchill in Weymouth and becomes engaged secretly. She is then employed by Mrs Smallridge as governess. Disliked by Emma Woodhouse initially although for no good reason at all, she eventually marries Frank.

Fairfax, Lieutenant Father of Jane Fairfax and husband of Jane Bates. He died in battle soon after his daughter was born.

Farmer Mitchell Provides Mr Weston with umbrellas.

Ford, Mrs Highbury shopkeeper.

Gilberts The two Gilberts, Mrs and Miss, are Highbury residents mentioned in chapter 29.

Goddard, Mrs Owner of school for girls in Highbury at which Harriet Smith attends. Harriet boards with Mrs Goddard.

Graham, Mr Friend of Mr John Knightley.

Green, Mr Friend of Augusta Hawkins at Bath.

Hannah Servant at Randalls, the nearby estate of Hartfield. She is the daughter of James the Hartfield coachman.

Harry Servant at Donwell Abbey.

Hawkins, Miss Augusta Sister of Selina. A conceited social climber who meets Mr Elton at Bath and marries him. She shares a mutual dislike of Emma. Refers to her husband as Mr E of 'Caro Sposo'.

Hawkins, Miss Selina Sister to Augusta. She marries Mr Suckling.

Hodges, Mrs Housekeeper at Donwell Abbey.

Hughes family Residents of Highbury.

James The trusted coachman for the Woodhouse family at Hartfield.

Jeffereys, Miss see Partridge, Miss Clara.

Knightley, Bella and Emma Daughters of Isabella Woodhouse and John Knightley. Nieces of Emma Woodhouse.

Knightley, George Son of Isabella Woodhouse and John Knightley. Nephew of Emma Woodhouse.

Knightley, Henry Oldest son of Isabella Woodhouse and John Knightley. Nephew of Emma Woodhouse.

Knightley, Isabella Daughter of Henry Woodhouse and shares his concern about illness. Her mother died when she was about 12 years old. She is about seven years older than her sister Emma. She is married to Mr John Knightley and lives in London.

Knightley, Master John Youngest son of Isabella Woodhouse and John Knightley. Nephew of Emma Woodhouse.

Knightley, Mr George Brother of John Knightley. A kind and honest man who was not scared to point out Emma's shortcomings. George is also the most attractive man in the novel and eventually marries Emma.

Knightley, Mr John Of Brunswick Square. George Knightley's brother. Married to Isabella Woodhouse.

Larkins, William Mr Knightley's property manager; the manager of Donwell Abbey.

Martin family Of Abbey Mill Farm. Mr and Mrs Martin and their son Robert and daughters Elizabeth (and one other). Harriet stays with them and forms a friendship with Robert. Emma persuades her that the Martins are socially inferior and there is a period of difficulty before Harriet comes to her senses and marries Robert.

Martin, Elizabeth Sister of Robert Martin who breaks the ice between her brother and Harriet Smith, thus allowing them to marry.

Martin, Robert Promises Harriet Smith to read two books, *Romance of the Forest* by Anne Radcliffe and *The Children of the Abbey* by Regina Maria Roche. He eventually marries Harriet after being turned down initially.

Milmans Now Mrs Bird and Mrs James Cooper.

Nash, Miss Head teacher at Mrs Goddard's school who sang the praises of Mr Elton.

Otways Highbury residents referred to in chapter 46.

Partridge, Miss Clara Friend of Mrs Elton. Sometimes called Miss Jeffereys.

Patty Maid to Mrs and Miss Bates.

Perry, Mr Apothecary at Highbury.

Perry, Mrs Wife of the apothecary at Highbury. They have several children.

Prince, Miss Teacher at Mrs Goddard's school.

Richardson, Miss Teacher at Mrs Goddard's school.

Saunders, John Miss Bates considers taking her mother's spectacles to him to fix.

Serle Cook at Hartfield.

Smallridge, Mrs Friend of Sucklings and Bragges, offered Jane Fairfax a governess position.

Smith, Harriet A boarder at Mrs Goddard's. Her favourite book is *The Vicar of Wakefield* and she is delighted that Robert Martin has read it. Her keepsake box has the words 'most precious treasures' written on the silver tissue wrapping. After refusing Robert Martin's proposal of marriage and then having several romantic adventures, she eventually sees sense and marries him.

Stokes, Mrs Referred to by Emma in chapters 29 and 38 at the Crown Inn at Highbury.

Suckling, Mr Of Maple Grove, near Bristol. A rich and cultured man who marries Selina Hawkins, the sister of Mrs Elton. He is often mentioned by Mrs Elton in the hope of elevating herself.

Taylor, Anne Governess to Emma at Hartfield, where she was employed for 16 years. She marries Mr Weston at the start of the novel. A kind and friendly woman who was more of a friend than a teacher to Emma.

Tom Servant at Randalls.

Tupman Upstart who settled near the Suckling home of Maple Grove.

Wallis, Mrs Bakes apples for Miss Bates.

Weston, Captain Mr Of Randalls near Hartfield. Frank Churchill is his son from his first marriage. His second marriage is to Miss Anne Taylor. He is a good friend of Emma's.

Wingfield, Mr Isabella Knightley's apothecary in London.

Woodhouse, Emma Daughter of Henry Woodhouse and sister to Isabella Knightley. Her mother died when she was about five years old. She is the central character of the novel. She is nearly 21 years old and is beautiful, clever and rich, with true hazel eyes, and according to Mrs Weston 'is the picture of grown-up health'. She is however a snob; she befriends Harriet Smith with intention to improve her and invents various romantic liaisons for her. She is also a gossip and invents an affair between Jane Fairfax and Mr Dixon, before insulting Miss Bates at Box Hill and being rebuked by George Knightley. This causes a re-examination of her previous conduct. She changes her ways and is rewarded by marrying George.

Woodhouse, Mr Henry Of Hartfield, Highbury. Father of Isabella Knightley and Emma Woodhouse. A chronic hypochondriac whose favourite dish was 'gruel, gruel, gruel'.

Wright Housekeeper at the vicarage.

***Mansfield Park*: Completed in 1813 and first published in 1814. Often cited as the least romantic of Austen's novels but acutely socially aware, focusing as it does on the slave trade and the British aristocracy's propensity to exploit their social inferiors.**

Anderson, Miss Younger sister of Charles Anderson. Described as Miss Anderson of the Aylmers, of Twickenham.

Anderson, Mr Charles Friend of Tom Bertram.

Aylmers Reside in Twickenham. Maria Rushworth (née Bertram) stays with them and Charles Crawford visits.

Baddeley Sir Thomas Bertram's butler.

Bertram, Edmund Younger son of Sir Thomas and Lady Bertram. As he is not the heir to Mansfield Park, he is groomed to be a clergyman. He is good-natured and is the only Bertram to show kindness to Fanny Price. He is initially smitten with Mary Crawford before turning his attentions towards Fanny Price and eventually marrying her.

Bertram, Julia The Bertrams' younger daughter. Shares her sister's temperament and personality although, as she is younger and less beautiful, she is not so self-assured. She tends to follow Maria around and upon her sister's elopement she runs away with Yates, her brother Tom's friend.

Bertram, Lady Maria Née Ward (sister to Mrs Norris and Mrs Frances Price). She is the wife of Sir Thomas, mother to the Bertram children and aunt to Fanny Price. She is neurotic, lazy and an incorrigible hypochondriac who values attractiveness over other, more lasting qualities.

Bertram, Maria The Bertrams' older daughter. Vain and arrogant of manner, she treats Fanny Price badly and marries the equally odious Mr Rushworth for his wealth.

Bertram, Sir Thomas Baronet and Member of Parliament. Married to Maria Ward. They have four children: Tom, Edmund, Maria and Julia. He takes on Fanny Price, the child of his sister-in-law who has fallen on difficult times. Sir Thomas is a stern but kind man. He is also the owner of Mansfield Park. The novel tells of the departure of Sir Thomas to the West Indies and the moral decline of his household into a series of inappropriate relationships and forbidden theatricals. Sir Thomas owns slaves on his plantations in the Caribbean but a series of disasters ensue to show him the error of his ways.

Bertram, Tom The Bertrams' older son and heir to Mansfield Park. He is a hard-drinking party-goer who gets into debt, for which Edmund suffers. His lifestyle eventually catches up with him and he nearly dies from an illness caused by his excessive drinking.

Crawford, Admiral Uncle of Henry and Mary Crawford, whom he brings up after their parents die. His wife dies, and his mistress moves in with him. Uses his influence to help William Price secure his lieutenant's commission.

Crawford, Henry Brother of Mary Crawford. He is an attractive but unprincipled man who initially woos Fanny Price; both Maria and Julia Bertram fall under his spell too. Maria marries but Henry runs off with her, although their relationship ends badly.

Crawford, Mary Sister of Henry Crawford. Mary is as passionate as her brother and equally lacking in principle. She is a free spirit; Edmund Bertram falls in love with her and nearly proposes.

Ellis Maid of the Bertrams, attends Maria and Julia.

Grant, Dr 45 years old. Succeeds Mr Norris as Rector of Mansfield. Brother-in-law to Henry and Mary Crawford. Made Dean of Westminister, but dies there in a fit of apoplexy brought on after three large dinners.

Grant, Mrs Half-sister of Henry and Mary Crawford. Wife of Dr Grant, the second parson at Mansfield. She lives in the Rectory but after her husband dies she lives with Mary Crawford.

Harding, Mr Old friend of Sir Thomas Bertram. Warns of, and later informs him of Maria (Bertram) Rushworth's and Henry Crawford's elopement. His attempts to prevent a scandal are thwarted by the elder Mrs Rushworth.

Holford, Mrs Acquaintance of Tom Bertram. It is at her house that he is embarrassed by Miss Anderson.

Jackson, Christopher Carpenter who is prevented from profiting from the dismantling of the stage and scenery during the amateur theatricals episode.

Jackson, Dick Son of Christopher. Prevented from profiting from the dismantling of the stage and scenery. Mentioned in chapter 15.

Lee, Miss Governess to Maria and Julia Bertram, and to Fanny Price.

Nanny Mrs Norris's servant and chief counsellor.

Norris, Mrs Oldest of the three Ward sisters. She married a clergyman and settled at Mansfield Parsonage until widowed and moving to a smaller house. She has no children and is an officious busybody, always endeavouring to derive glory from her association with the Bertram family. She is cruel to Fanny Price, whom she is always reminding of her 'place' in the family.

Norris, Reverend Friend of Sir Thomas Bertram, marrying his sister-in-law Miss Ward. Sir Thomas gives him a living at Mansfield, later becomes ill and dies.

Price, Betsy Youngest child of Lieutenant and Frances Price. Fanny's youngest sister is five years old.

Price, Charles Youngest son of Lieutenant and Frances Price. Fanny's youngest brother is eight years old.

Price, Fanny Central character of the novel. Oldest daughter of Lieutenant and Mrs Fanny Price. Her parents, unable to support nine children, send her off to live with her aunt Lady Maria Bertram and her rich husband Sir Thomas Bertram, at Mansfield Park. She falls in love and marries her cousin Edmund Bertram, although first subject to proposals from the slick Henry Crawford.

Price, Mary Daughter of Lieutenant and Frances Price. Is about four years old when Fanny leaves home, but dies a few years later. Gives Susan a silver knife.

Price, Mr Officer in the Marines, who was prone to a drink or two. After 11 years he was disabled from active service and lived in Portsmouth. He married Frances Ward, their children being: William, Fanny, Mary (deceased), Susan, John and Richard, Tom, Charles, and Betsy.

Price, Mrs Frances Youngest of three Ward sisters (Lady Maria Bertram and Mrs Norris being the other two). She married Lieutenant Price of the Marines to disoblige her family, causing a rift with Mrs Norris. Lives in Portsmouth with her disabled husband. Children: William, Fanny, Mary (deceased), Susan, John, Richard, Tom, Charles, Sam and Betsy.

Price, Susan Third daughter of Lieutenant and Frances Price. Fanny's younger sister is 14 years old when she moves to Mansfield Park, where she takes Fanny's place as Lady Bertram's companion.

Price, Tom Son of Lieutenant and Frances Price. Nine years old. Fanny helped care for him before her departure to Mansfield Park.

Price, William Oldest child of Lieutenant and Frances Price, and favourite brother of Fanny. Joins the Royal Navy, serves as midshipman with Captain Marshall. In his attempt to woo Fanny, Henry Crawford arranges a promotion to second lieutenant for William.

Ravenshaw, Lord Owner of Ecclesford in Cornwall where a large house party is held, and *Lovers' Vows* is staged (called off upon the death of his grandmother).

Rebecca The Prices' slovenly and lazy upper servant.

Repton, Mr Humphrey A landscape gardener and improver of estates. Mr Rushworth considers hiring him, at the rate of five guineas a day. Humphrey Repton was of course a notable real-life landscapist of the day.

Rushworth, Mr Wealthy landowner but thoroughly idiotic and lacking in personality. He marries Maria Bertram.

Sneyd, Mr Tom Bertram's friend who lives in Ramsgate with Mrs Sneyd his mother, and his two sisters.

Sneyd, Mrs Mother of Mr, Miss and Augusta Sneyd.

Stornoway, Lady Née Ross. Former intimate friend of Mary Crawford, although the two have not been close for thre years. Is attracted to Henry Crawford. Later jilts a young officer in the Blues and marries Lord Stornoway.

Stornoway, Lord Husband of Lady Stornoway.

Yates, Mr Friend of Tom Bertram, who proposes the amateur theatricals at Mansfield Park. He shows an interest in Julia Bertram and eventually elopes with her.

***Northanger Abbey*: Published posthumously in 1818, it is the shortest of Austen's six major works. The novel was completed in 1799 and pokes fun at the existing fashion for the Gothic novel typified in the works of Ann Radcliffe, particularly *The Mysteries of Udolpho*. The novel was originally called *Susan* but Austen renamed the heroine and the book.**

Northanger Abbey is the home of the Tilney family in Bath.

Alice In chapter 28 Eleanor asks Catherine to write to her 'Direct to me at Lord Longtown's, and, I must ask it, under cover to Alice.'

Allen, Mr and Mrs Mr and Mrs Allen live in Fullerton. They are older and wealthier than the Morlands and treat Catherine Morland as a daughter. They invite Catherine to go to Bath with them. Mr Allen spends most of his time playing cards in Bath while his wife splashes her time either shopping, knitting or talking to Mrs Thorpe.

Andrews, Miss A friend of Isabella Thorpe, described in chapter 6 as 'a sweet girl, one of the sweetest creatures in the world'. She is a great fan of Gothic novels and appears to have read them all.

Hughes, Mrs A lady who is a member of Henry and Eleanor's party at the ball in the Upper Rooms, Bath.

Hunt, Captain An admirer of Isabella Thorpe. Mentioned in chapter 6: 'I told Captain Hunt, at one of our assemblies this winter, that if he was to ask me to tease me all night, I would dance with him unless he would allow Miss Andrews to be as beautiful as an angel.'

Morland, Catherine The 17-year-old heroine of the novel. Having spent her formative years in her family's modest home in Fullerton reading Gothic novels, she lets her imagination run riot when she stays with the Tilney family at Northanger Abbey. She believes General Tilney murdered his wife and although she has a kind and intelligent nature, it becomes apparent that her inexperience makes her a bad reader of people. After overcoming the embarrassment of suspecting his father of murder, Catherine is eventually betrothed to Henry.

Morland, George One of Catherine Morland's youngest siblings, a child of six.

Morland, Harriet The youngest in the Morland family, a four-year-old girl who vies with little George in being the first to welcome Catherine home from her adventures.

Morland, James Catherine Morland's oldest brother who is a fellow student of John Thorpe at Oxford University. He is a good-natured but inexperienced young man, who becomes engaged to Isabella Thorpe but breaks it off when she begins to flirt with Frederick Tilney.

Morland, Mr Father of the Morland clan. He was a clergyman in Fullerton and appears briefly at the beginning and end of the novel.

Morland, Mrs Wife of the clergyman. A sensible soul, who does not insist on her daughters being accomplished in spite of incapacity or distaste.

Morland, Richard The heroine's second oldest brother – a young man who would apparently have to do without cravats if he were entirely dependent on the love-sick Catherine for that article of dress.

Morland, Sarah (Sally) Catherine Morland's 16-year-old sister who, being a young lady of common gentility, has naturally altered her name as far as she can, from Sally to Sarah.

Skinner, Dr Mentioned in chapter 8 as having stayed with his family at the pump rooms in Bath for some three months.

Thorpe, Anne One of Mrs Thorpe's two younger daughters. Although not as beautiful as Isabella, she does very well by pretending to be as handsome, imitating her air, and dressing in the same style.

Thorpe, Edward One of three sons of Mrs Thorpe. He attended Merchant Taylors.

Thorpe, Isabella One of three daughters of Mrs Thorpe and sister of John Thorpe. She is beautiful but shallow and as such a perfect friend for Catherine Morland. She is a master of artifice and is able to charm all and sundry, but eventually Catherine sees her for the malicious gossip she is, as do her romantic interests James Morland and Frederick Tilney.

Thorpe, John The arrogant and boastful brother of Isabella Thorpe, and the would-be suitor of Catherine Morland. He attended Oxford University.

Thorpe, Mrs A former schoolfellow and intimate of Mrs Allen's. She is the widowed mother of Isabella and their natures are similar.

Thorpe, William Another young Thorpe sibling. This one is at sea, but like his more academic brothers, and according to his mother (in chapter 6), he too is apparently beloved and respected by all who know him!

Tilney, Eleanor Henry's younger sister. A shy, quiet young woman who shares her brother's interest in reading.

Tilney, Frederick A dashing captain in the 12th Light Dragoons, oldest brother of Henry and Eleanor. He flirts with Isabella

Thorpe, which leads her to break off her engagement to James Morland, but then abandons her in Bath.

Tilney, General The authoritarian father of Henry, Frederick and Eleanor. A widower who takes great pride in his home, Northanger Abbey, which he refurbished himself. He is material and as such is concerned that his children marry well. He is also gruff and overbearing which makes Catherine Morland think poorly of him, to the extent of suspecting him of murder.

Tilney, Henry The hero of the novel. A 26-year-old parson in the village of Woodston. He is intelligent, witty and charming, and nurtures Catherine through her fantasies. Her true nature shines through in the end and Henry falls in love with her.

***Persuasion*: Completed in 1816 during her second phase of writing. As in the case of *Northanger Abbey*, *Persuasion* was published posthumously by Austen's brother Henry in 1818.**

Benwick, Captain Formerly first lieutenant of the *Laconia*. He was engaged to Fanny Harville, who died the preceding summer while he was at sea. Later attracted to Anne Elliot, he falls in love with and becomes engaged to Louisa Musgrove. Captain Benwick is a sensitive man who loves poetry.

Brand, Admiral Brother of Captain Frederick Wentworth. Disliked by Mrs Croft because he 'got away some of my best men' (as relayed by Admiral Croft). He has the curacy of Monksford, but later moves out of the county, marries and has a parish in Shropshire.

Brigden, Captain A friend of Admiral Croft, mentioned in chapter 18.

Carteret, Miss Daughter of Lady Dalrymple: 'So plain and so awkward, that she would never had been tolerated in Camden Place but for her birth'.

Clay, Mrs Penelope Elizabeth Elliot's gold-digging friend. Both Anne and Lady Russell are concerned about her romantic designs on Sir Walter while staying at Bath. She is a divorcee with two children.

Croft, Admiral Sir Walter is persuaded to lease Kellynch Hall to the admiral and his wife.

Croft, Mrs Sophia Wife of Admiral Croft.

Dalrymple, Lady An Irish viscountess. Mother of the Honourable Miss Carteret and cousin of Sir Walter Elliot. She takes a house for three months at Laura Place, Bath, and Sir Walter writes to her in the hope of patching up old wounds.

Dalrymple, Viscount Husband of Viscountess Dalrymple. His death before the beginning of the novel has caused some friction between the Dalrymples and the Elliots as Sir Walter did not send a letter of condolence to the viscountess due to his own life-threatening illness.

Drew, Sir Archibald Friend of Admiral Croft who mistook Anne Elliot for the Admiral's wife while walking the streets of Bath. He has a grandson, mentioned in chapter 18.

Durands Visitors to Bath, mentioned in chapter 21.

Elliot, Anne The central character of the novel. Two years younger than her sister, Elizabeth. Both Elizabeth and her father Sir Walter show her little affection but she is the favourite of Lady Russell, who convinced her to break her engagement with Captain Wentworth eight years ago when she was 19, due to his limited funds. Anne visits her sister, Mary, at Uppercross, and is very loving to her two children, Charles and Walter. Anne meets Captain Wentworth on the street. They exchange pleasantries and then deeper thoughts and feelings, realise they are in love and are eventually married.

Elliot, Elizabeth Oldest daughter of Sir Walter Elliot. She is 29 at the beginning of the novel and runs the house, Kellynch Hall. Sir Walter, Mrs Clay and she go to reside in Bath while the unwanted Anne goes to visit her hypochondriacal sister Mary at the Musgroves' residence, Uppercross.

Elliot, Lady Elizabeth Wife of Sir Walter and mother of Elizabeth, Anne and Mary. She died 14 years before the novel begins. Lady Elliot was the daughter of James Stevenson of South Park, Gloucester.

Elliot, Mary Youngest daughter of Sir Walter. Married to Charles Musgrove. They live at Uppercross with their two children. Mary is a hypochondriac.

Elliot, Mrs Granddaughter of a butcher, daughter of a glazier. Her wealth attracts William Walter Elliot who marries her. She dies after an unhappy marriage.

Elliot, Sir Walter Of Kellynch Hall, Somersetshire. Baronet. Sir Walter is 54 years old at the beginning of the novel. His wife, Elizabeth, died 14 years before the novel begins. Father of Elizabeth, Anne and Mary. To manage his debts he is forced to leave Kellynch Hall and move to more humble quarters at Camden Place, Bath.

Elliot, Sir Walter The Second Elliot, grandfather of Mr William Elliot.

Elliot, William Walter Grandson and presumed heir of Sir Walter Elliot (the Second). Recently widowed, he begins to have designs on Anne Elliot, causing Captain Wentworth to feel jealous pangs. Mrs Smith informs Anne of Elliot's true and despicable nature. He is the nephew of the first Sir Walter.

Frankland, Mrs Friend of Lady Russell. Visitor to Bath.

Harville, Captain Resident of Lyme. Friend of Captain Frederick Wentworth. Mr and Mrs Harville have three children.

Harville, Mrs Wife of Captain Harville. Anne looks upon their union as an example of a happy marriage.

Hayter, Charles Oldest son of the Hayters. Non-resident curate. Has an understanding with, and marries his cousin, Henrietta Musgrove, after securing a church living.

Hayter, Mr Henry Owner of Winthrop. Husband of Mrs Musgrove's sister. They have a son, Charles, and two daughters.

Hayter, Mrs Mrs Musgrove's sister. Wife of Henry and mother of a son, Charles, and two daughters.

Jeeves Servant of the Crofts who drove their carriage.

Jemima Servant of the Musgroves at Uppercross.

Musgrove, Charles Elder son of Charles and Mary Musgrove (née Elliot).

Musgrove, Charles Oldest child of Charles and Mary Musgrove. Married to Mary Elliot. They live at Uppercross with their two children, Charles (little) and Walter.

Musgrove, Mr Charles The elder Charles Musgrove is the owner of Uppercross Hall, Somerset. Second only to Sir Walter Elliot in the neighbourhood. His children include Charles, Richard (Dick), Henrietta, Louisa, Mary, and several younger ones, Harry being the youngest son.

Musgrove, Louisa Second daughter of Charles (elder) and Mrs Musgrove, 19 years old.

Musgrove, Mary Youngest daughter of Sir Walter Elliot. Marries Charles Musgrove (the younger) after he is refused by her sister Anne. Mother of Charles and Walter. She is a hypochondriac.

Musgrove, Mrs Mary Wife of the elder Charles Musgrove. Always had a special connection with Captain Frederick Wentworth as he was the commander in charge of her late son, Dick.

Musgrove, Richard Dick Musgrove is the good-for-nothing but now deceased son of the elder Charles Musgrove and Mary Musgrove.

Musgrove, Walter Younger son of Charles and Mary Musgrove (née Elliot), aged two at the beginning of the novel.

Rooke, Nurse Sister of Mrs Smith's landlady.

Russell, Lady Wife of the late Sir Henry Russell. She was the close friend of Lady Elliot and continues to support her daughters after Lady Elliot's death. She is Anne's godmother and treats her with more affection than other members of the Elliot family.

Russell, Sir Henry Lady Russell's late husband.

Shepherd, Mr Trusted family advisor of the Elliots. Helps Lady Russell draw up a plan for ways that Sir Walter Elliot can save money.

Smith, Mrs Née Hamilton. Friend of Anne Elliot at school. Later Anne finds her again in Bath, widowed, impoverished and crippled, and helps her after finding out that it was Mr William Walter Elliot who put her into debt and refused to help her after her husband died.

Speed, Mrs Landlady at Mrs Smith's lodgings in Bath.

Wallis, Colonel Friend of Mr Elliot, 'a highly respectable man, perfectly the gentleman'.

Wentworth, Captain Brother of Edward Wentworth and Sophia Croft. Captain Frederick Wentworth has been in love with Anne Elliot but Lady Russell persuaded Anne to break off the relationship due to his limited means. Eventually Lady Russell concedes she was wrong in her judgement of him and, now in a healthier financial position, he lets Anne know of his feelings for her in a letter and finally marries her.

Wentworth, Edward Brother of Captain Frederick Wentworth and Sophia Croft. He has the curacy of Monksford but later moves out of the county, marries and has a parish in Shropshire.

***Pride & Prejudice*: Completed in 1797, under the title *First Impressions*, and published in 1813. The imaginary places mentioned in the novel include Longbourn, Herts (residence of the Bennets), Netherfield Park, Herts (residence of the Bingleys), Pemberley, Derbyshire (residence of Fitzwilliam**

Darcy).

Annesley, Mrs Companion to Miss Georgiana Darcy. A genteel, agreeable looking woman.

Bennet, Catherine (Kitty) The fourth Bennet sister. Kitty tends to follow Lydia's lead in whatever she does.

Bennet, Elizabeth Second oldest of the five Bennet sisters and the central character of the novel. She is quick-witted, intelligent, bold and attractive (with particularly fine eyes). She prides herself on being a good judge of character but in reality her vanity often clouds her judgement. After a stormy relationship she eventually marries Mr Fitzwilliam Darcy. Jane Austen called Elizabeth 'as delightful a creature as ever appeared in print'.

Bennet, Jane Oldest of the five Bennet sisters and foil to Elizabeth's more rash deliberations. Jane is the model of the perfect older sister: beautiful, kind and loving, with unerring good sense. Marries Charles Bingley at the end of the novel.

Bennet, Lydia The youngest of the Bennet sisters and the favourite of her mother, whose frivolous nature she mirrors. Elopes with George Wickham despite his involvement with Mary King.

Bennet, Mary The third Bennet sister, who is described as 'the only plain one in the family'. Annoys Elizabeth with her unaccomplished singing in front of Mr Darcy.

Bennet, Mr Father of the five Bennet sisters, and long-suffering husband of a foolish woman. A kindly, intelligent man who settles for an easy life to the cost of his youngest daughter's honour.

Bennet, Mrs Mother of the five Bennet sisters. A shrewish woman who is intent on marrying off her five daughters.

Bingley, Charles The amiable and good-tempered man who rents Netherfield Park at the beginning of the novel. Father of Caroline and Louisa Hurst. He marries Jane Bennet by the end of the book and moves out of the neighbourhood.

Bingley, Miss Caroline Charles Bingley's unmarried sister. She is arrogant and superficial but unlike Darcy has no redeeming virtues, always ridiculing the poor manners of the Bennet children.

Carter, Captain Member of the regiment in Meryton.

Chamberlayne, Mr Member of the regiment in Meryton.

Collins, Rev. William Clergyman and Mr Bennet's cousin who is in line to inherit Longbourn when Mr Bennet dies. A rather comical fellow, prone to making long rambling speeches on nothing but what he feels will elevate him in the esteem of the listener.

Darcy, Georgiana Fitzwilliam Darcy's younger sister who has all of her brother's virtues but none of his aloofness.

Darcy, Lady Anne Born Lady Anne Fitzwilliam; Lady Catherine de Bourgh's sister and Mr Darcy's mother.

Darcy, Mr (the elder) Fitzwilliam Darcy's father, who died approximately five years before the novel begins.

Darcy, Mr Fitzwilliam Wealthy aristocrat and owner of Pemberley. At the beginning of the novel he is very conscious of class difference but falls in love with Elizabeth Bennet because she refuses to treat him as anything but an equal. He begins to judge people by their character rather than their social standing. He eventually marries Elizabeth.

Dawson Lady Catherine's maid.

De Bourgh, Anne Lady Catherine's sickly daughter who is pampered by her mother.

De Bourgh, Catherine Mr Collins' patron and Mr Darcy's aunt. Extremely wealthy and aristocratic, she likes the world to know of her superior standing. Her shallowness helps Darcy to mend his ways.

De Bourgh, Sir Lewis Lady Catherine's late husband.

Denny, Captain A member of the regiment in Meryton and friend of George Wickham.

Fitzwilliam, Colonel Mr Darcy's cousin who accompanies Elizabeth Bennet during her stay with the Collinses and confides to her that he must marry for money as he is a second son.

Forster, Colonel Head of the regiment stationed at Meryton. A decent man who suffers great guilt when Lydia Bennet elopes with George Wickham.

Forster, Harriet Colonel Forster's wife who befriends Lydia Bennet and invites her to spend the summer with them in Brighton, from where Lydia elopes with Wickham.

Gardiner, Mr Edward Brother of Mrs Bennet who works as a merchant and, unlike the aristocrats who live off the interest of their land, is seen as of inferior class. Darcy eventually overcomes his prejudice towards the working class by perceiving the decency of Mr Gardiner.

Gardiner, Mrs Mr Gardiner's wife who tends to act as a mother-figure for Elizabeth and Jane Bennet. She brings Jane to London with her in order to ease her heartbreak over Bingley's failure to return to Netherfield. She also gives good counsel to Elizabeth with regard to Wickham's intentions.

Gouldings, The Residents of Haye-Park. Only William Goulding is mentioned: 'we overtook William Goulding in his curricle', chapter 51.

Grantley, Miss An acquaintance of Miss Caroline Bingley.

Haggerston, Mr Mr Gardiner's attorney.

Harrington, Harriet Acquaintance of Mrs Forster and Lydia Bennet in Brighton.

Harrington, Miss 'Pen' Acquaintance of Mrs Forster and Lydia Bennet in Brighton.

Hill, Mrs Housekeeper at Longbourn.

Hurst, Mr Husband of Charles Bingley's sister Louisa. Does nothing but eat and play cards.

Hurst, Mrs Louisa Charles Bingley's married sister who has a similarly abhorrent nature to her unmarried sister.

Jenkinson, Mrs Anne de Bourgh's companion.

John Both Collinses and Gardiners have a servant named John.

Jones, Mr The apothecary at Meryton.

King, Miss Mary Heiress to 10,000 pounds who was courted by Wickham.

Long, Mrs The Bennets' neighbour who has two nieces.

Lucas, Charlotte Elizabeth's friend who is intent on marrying for security and avails herself of the intentions of the Reverend Collins.

Lucas, Lady Sir William's wife and mother of Charlotte and Maria.

Lucas, Maria Charlotte Lucas's younger sister who travels with her father and Elizabeth Bennet when visiting Charlotte.

Lucas, Sir William Friend and neighbour of the Bennets who loves nothing better than to talk of his knighthood.

Metcalfe, Lady Acquaintance of Lady Catherine.

Morris, Mr The man who shows Netherfield Park to Mr Bingley.

Nicholls, Mrs The housekeeper at Netherfield.

Philips, Mr The husband of Mrs Bennet's sister. An attorney in Meryton.

Philips, Mrs Mrs Bennet's sister who lives in Meryton (where the soldiers are based) and consequently is often visited by the Bennet sisters.

Pope, Miss Governess in Lady Metcalf's family.

Pratt, Mr Member of the regiment at Meryton.

Reynolds, Mrs Housekeeper at Pemberley.

Richard, Mr An employee of Mr Philips – Lydia mentions that he will join the regiment if her uncle lets him go.

Robinson, Mr Man who, at the Assembly Ball, asked Mr Bingley which girl he thought the handsomest.

Sarah A maid.

Stone, Mr Mr Gardiner's clerk.

Watson, Miss A resident of Meryton whom the soldiers visited.

Webbs, The Miss Acquaintances of Lady Catherine.

Wickham, George An officer in the regiment stationed at Meryton. Initially favoured by Elizabeth Bennet to be a good and amiable man but events contrive to show his true character to be deceitful and mercenary. After forming a liaison with Mary King, he eventually elopes with Lydia Bennet.

Wickham, Old Mr Father of George and steward to the late Mr Darcy.

Younge, Mrs Former governess of Georgiana Darcy who informs Darcy of the whereabouts of Wickham and Lydia.

***Sense and Sensibility*: Written in 1797 and published in 1811, her first published novel was financed by Austen herself after both *Northanger Abbey* and *Pride and Prejudice* were rejected by a publisher. Her brother Henry and sister Cassandra were instrumental in convincing Austen to publish the novel, originally entitled *Elinor and Marianne*.**

Betsy Dashwoods' servant at Norland Park and Barton Park.

Betty Mrs Jennings' maid.

Brandon, Colonel Of Delaford in Dorsetshire. A 35-year-old former military officer who was stationed in India. His stern exterior hides a soft heart. Marries Marianne Dashwood and becomes less stern.

Careys A family in Newton, near Barton Park. Friends of the Middletons.

Cartwright Mrs Jennings' servant, mentioned in chapter 26.

Clarke, Mrs An 'intimate acquaintance' of Mrs Jennings.

Courtland, Lord Friend of Robert Ferrars. Robert disapproves of all three of his building plans, and suggests a cottage instead.

Dashwood, Elinor At 19 the oldest and wisest of the daughters of

Mrs Dashwood and Henry, often sacrificing her own happiness in order to maintain the family's status quo. Marries Edward Ferrers and lives at Delaford where she is eventually joined by Marianne and the colonel.

Dashwood, Fanny Daughter of Mrs Ferrars, sister of Edward and Robert Ferrars, married John Dashwood and has a more miserly temperament even than he.

Dashwood, Harry John & Fanny Dashwood's spoilt four-year-old.

Dashwood, Henry Of Stanhill and Norland Park, Sussex. By his first wife he had one son, John; by his second, three daughters, Elinor, Marianne and Margaret. He dies at the beginning of the novel, leaving his son his estate and ensuring his daughters are forced to accept an invitation from Sir John Middleton to Barton Cottage.

Dashwood, John Son of Henry Dashwood. Mean and miserly to his three half-sisters. Married to Fanny Ferrars, with one son, Harry, four years old.

Dashwood, Margaret Henry and Mrs Dashwood's youngest daughter. At 13 years old she is at a difficult age and although she aspires to Marianne's romantic inclinations her sounder sense prevails.

Dashwood, Marianne Henry and Mrs Dashwood's second daughter. Two years younger than Elinor and lacking her discretion and calm. After falling and hurting her ankle is carried home by the rakish Willoughby who shares her love of the arts. Willoughby lets her down in love, and she eventually marries Colonel Brandon and lives happily at Delaford.

Dashwood, Mrs Mother of Elinor, Marianne and Margaret. She is close to her daughters but hopes to see them married off.

Davies, Dr Discussed in chapter 32 as a possible beau of Anne Steele.

Dennison, Mrs Mrs Dennison mistakes Elinor and Marianne for their brother's guests in chapter 36.

Donavan, Mr Apothecary who attends Charlotte Palmer's baby in chapter 37.

Elliott, Lady Elliott's wife who can't entertain for want of space.

Elliott, Sir Robert Ferrars' friend who lives in a cottage near Dartford.

Ellisons Miss Grey's guardians.

Ferrars, Edward The 23-year-old brother of Fanny but with a very different nature. Shy and retiring with a kind heart, he eventually marries Elinor Dashwood.

Ferrars, Mrs Of Park Street. Mother of Edward, Robert and Fanny. A bad-tempered woman who ironically disowns her benevolent son, Edward.

Ferrars, Robert Edward's brother and husband of Lucy Steele. Arrogant of manner but beloved of his mother.

Godby, Miss Told Miss Sparks that nobody in their senses could expect Mr Ferrars to give up a woman like Miss Morton, chapter 38.

Grey, Sophia John Willoughby's wife, whom he married in preference to Marianne Dashwood as she was wealthier.

Harris, Dr Helps to cure Marianne Dashwood during her illness at Cleveland.

Henshawe, Biddy Aunt of Miss Grey who 'married a very wealthy man'.

Jennings, Mrs Of Berkeley-street, a jolly but vulgar widow who makes endless jokes about potential suitors for Elinor and Marianne. The mother of Lady Mary Middleton and Charlotte Palmer.

Middleton, Anna-Maria Sir John Middleton's daughter, about three years old.

Middleton, John Sir John Middleton's son, about six years old.

Middleton, Lady Mary Daughter of Mrs Jennings, sister of Charlotte Palmer, and wife of Sir John Middleton. A vain and proper woman who does not share her husband's gregarious nature.

Middleton, Sir John Owner of Barton Park in Devonshire, and as such, the Dashwoods' landlord. A gregarious man who is forever inviting the Dashwoods to his neighbouring property, Barton Cottage. Married to Mary Jennings.

Middleton, William Sir John Middleton's son.

Morton, Miss Only daughter of Lord Morton. She was first supposed to marry Edward Ferrars, then his brother Robert, but ends up with neither.

old Gibson Former resident of East Kingham Farm, the property 'immediately adjoining' Norland Park, who is alluded to in chapter 33.

Palmer, Charlotte Daughter of Mrs Jennings. Married to Thomas Palmer; forever apologising for her husband's ill manners to all and sundry and seemingly blind to his shortcomings.

Palmer, Thomas Of Cleveland in Somerset, and Hanover Square. Married Charlotte Jennings. Very disagreeable nature.

Pratt, Mr Of Longstaple, uncle of the Steeles.

Richardson, Mrs Friend of Anne Steele, appearing in chapter 38.

Robert, Sir Edward and Robert Ferrars' and Fanny Dashwood's uncle.

Rose, Mr One of Anne Steele's beaus; clerk to Mr Simpson in Exeter, mentioned in chapter 21.

Sharpe, Martha Friend of Anne Steele who shared her habit of eavesdropping as portrayed in chapter 38.

Simpson, Mr Exeter resident; employer of Mr Rose, mentioned in chapter 21.

Smith, Mrs Of Allenham Court in Devonshire. Willoughby's aunt, who does not appear in the novel but disinherits her nephew and sends him to London when she hears of the plight of Miss Williams.

Sparks, Miss Referred to in gossip with Miss Godby about Mr Ferrars' giving up of Lucy Steele as being quite reasonable, in chapter 38.

Steele, Anne (Nancy) Sister of Lucy Steele, nearly 30 years old and 'never succeeded in catching the Doctor'. A distant cousin of Mrs Jennings who becomes a guest at Barton Cottage and gains the approval of Lady Middleton through flattery towards her and her children.

Steele, Lucy Anne Steele's younger sister, Mr Pratt's niece. Marginally smarter than her sister and a bit of an opportunist. Marries Robert Ferrars.

Taylor, Mrs Mrs Jennings' friend and the main source for news about Miss Grey.

Thomas Dashwoods' servant at Norland Park and Barton Park.

Walker, Miss Acquaintance of Mrs Taylor, mentioned in chapter 30.

Westons Friends of Mrs Jennings in London, mentioned in chapter 20.

Williams, Eliza Colonel Brandon's adopted daughter of a woman he once held in great affection. She does not appear in the novel, but her seduction by Willoughby, and eventual abandonment by him, are integral to the plot.

Willoughby, John Of Combe Magna in Somerset; 25-year-old, roguish young man who loves art and literature but is ultimately reckless and deceitful. Husband of Sophia Grey whom he married for money after disappointing Marianne Dashwood.

Charles Dickens's Characters (the novels)

Barnaby Rudge*: fifth published novel (1841), originally as serial in weekly magazine *Master Humphrey's Clock

Benjamin Member of the Prentice Knights with Simon Tappertit.

Chester, Edward Son of John, eventually overcomes the opposition of his father and marries Emma Haredale. The couple relocate to the West Indies.

Chester, Sir John Father of Edward, tries to prevent Edward's marriage to Emma Haredale. Becomes a member of Parliament. Killed in a duel by Emma's uncle Geoffrey.

Cobb, Tom Friend of John Willet at the Maypole Inn.

Daisy, Solomon Clerk and bell-ringer at the parish church in Chigwell. Friend of John Willet at the Maypole Inn. Daisy tells the story of Reuben Haredale's murder.

Dennis, Ned Executioner at Tyburn, becomes involved in the Gordon Riots and is executed.

Fielding, Sir John Blind half-brother of novelist Henry Fielding. Magistrate at Bow Street. Dickens has him at the scene of the Gordon Riots when, in fact, Fielding was on his deathbed at the time of the riots.

Gashford Lord George Gordon's hypocritical secretary. He urges the rioters to exact revenge on Geoffrey Haredale, who had exposed his treacherous ways. He abandons Lord Gordon when the riots are suppressed by soldiers and becomes a government spy.

Gordon, Lord George 1751–93 Historical figure and leader of the Gordon (anti-Catholic) Riots of 1780.

Grip Barnaby Rudge's pet raven, who carried his head on one side and seemed to embody the spirit of all-knowingness with his sound unwitting advice.

Grueby, John Loyal servant of Lord George Gordon who tries to isolate Gordon from the rioters when the protest turns to violence.

Haredale, Emma Daughter of the murdered Reuben and niece of Geoffrey. She eventually marries Edward Chester.

Haredale, Geoffrey Brother of the murdered Reuben and uncle of Emma. Suspected of being responsible for the murder of his brother, he spends his life in pursuit of the real killer. A Catholic, his house is burned in the Gordon Riots. He fights a duel with Sir John Chester.

Haredale, Reuben Brother of Geoffrey, father of Emma. Murdered before the story begins.

Hugh Ostler at the Maypole. Joins the rioters in London and is later hanged. Revealed to be the son of Sir John Chester.

Langdale Kindly vintner and distiller in Holborn based on an historical figure. The Catholic Langdale shelters Geoffrey Haredale from the rioters. His home and warehouse are burned in the riots, his stores of spirits are consumed by the mob.

Miggs, Miss Maid in the Varden household. Comically allies with Martha Varden against her husband. Miggs aids the rioters when they attempt to capture Gabriel. She is discharged after the riots and becomes a jailer in a women's prison.

Parkes, Phil Friend of John Willet at the Maypole Inn.

Philips Constable who the Lord Mayor of London suggests might help to protect Langdale during the Gordon Riots.

Rudge, Barnaby Main character, a simple but good-hearted boy who unwittingly gets involved in the Gordon Riots when he falls into bad company. He is later arrested and sentenced to death but gains reprieve through the help of Gabriel Varden.

Rudge, Barnaby Sr Father of Barnaby and husband of Mary. He was the Steward at the Warren and murdered his employer, Reuben Haredale. He went into hiding after the murder and resurfaces years later trying to extort money from his wife. He is finally captured by Geoffrey Haredale.

Rudge, Mary Barnaby's mother, goes to great lengths to keep Barnaby away from his father who has murdered Reuben Haredale.

Stagg Blind member of the Prentice Knights with Simon Tappertit. He joins Barnaby Rudge Sr trying to extort money from Mary Rudge. Killed when he tries to run from officers arresting Hugh, Barnaby, and Rudge Sr.

Tappertit, Simon Locksmith Gabriel Varden's apprentice, who is in love with Gabriel's daughter, Dolly. He becomes a leader of the rioters during the Gordon Riots and during the fighting loses his slender legs, long his pride and joy.

Varden, Dolly Daughter of Gabriel and Martha, friend of Emma Haredale, loved by Joe Willet, whom she eventually marries.

Varden, Gabriel Honest locksmith and owner of the Golden Key where Simon Tappertit is apprenticed. Father of Dolly and long-suffering husband of Martha. He is a friend of Barnaby's mother and, after the Gordon Riots, helps clear Barnaby's name.

Varden, Martha Overbearing wife of Gabriel, mother of Dolly. A woman of 'uncertain temper' and a fanatical Protestant, her fanaticism is tempered after the riots when she witnesses the heroics of her husband.

Willet, Joe Son of John who resents his father's treatment of him. He joins the army and loses an arm in the American Revolution. Later he marries Dolly Varden. The couple become proprietors of the rebuilt Maypole Inn.

Willet, John Proprietor of the Maypole Inn and father of Joe. Father and son quarrel when John treats the adult Joe as a child and Joe leaves, joining the army. John witnesses the destruction of the Maypole by the rioters. He is later reconciled with his son.

***Bleak House*: ninth novel published in 20 monthly parts between March 1852 and September 1853**

Badger, Bayham Doctor, cousin of Kenge, to whom Richard Carstone is apprenticed. Badger's wife Laura talks incessantly about her two former husbands, Captain Swosser and Professor Dingo.

Bagnet Family Musical, military family headed by Matthew, an old army friend of George Rouncewell. Bagnet's wife, the old girl, knows Matthew so well that he always calls upon her to supply his opinion. The Bagnet children, Quebec, Malta and Woolwich, are named after the bases where the family have been stationed. Matthew is guarantor to George's loan from Smallweed. When Smallweed calls in the debt George is forced to deliver a document Smallweed needs to help Tulkinghorn learn Lady Dedlock's secret.

Barbary, Miss Godmother who raises Esther Summerson. Later found to be Esther's aunt, the sister of Lady Dedlock.

Bogsby, James George 'Highly respectable' landlord of the Sol's Arms.

Boodle, Lord Politician who attends Sir Leicester Dedlock's social gatherings. Like Buffy he speculates on governmental machinations, including Coodle, Doodle and so on through the alphabet up to Quoodle.

Boythorn, Lawrence Friend of John Jarndyce whom Dickens based on writer Walter Savage Landor (1775-1864)

Bucket, Inspector Detective in charge of finding Tulkinghorn's murderer. After Lady Dedlock's disappearance Sir Leicester hires Bucket to find her. He later uncovers the will that is instrumental in clearing up the Jarndyce and Jarndyce Chancery case.

Buffy, the Right Hon. William MP who attends Sir Leicester Dedlock's social gatherings. Like Lord Boodle he speculates on governmental machinations, including Cuffy, Duffy and so on through the alphabet up to Puffy.

Carstone, Richard Ward of John Jarndyce and a party to the case of Jarndyce and Jarndyce. He marries Ada Clare and later dies when his health declines as the estate he hopes to acquire is consumed in court costs.

Chadband, Reverend Typical Dickensian hypocritical reverend, admonishing Jo in the spirit while he starves. Marries the former Mrs Rachael.

Clare, Ada Ward of John Jarndyce, friend of Esther Summerson, cousin of Richard Carstone, whom she marries but is soon widowed.

Darby Police constable on duty in Tom-all-Alone's, who accompanies Inspector Bucket and Mr Snagsby

Dedlock, Lady Honoria Wife of Sir Leicester Dedlock and, unknown to her husband, mother of Esther Summerson. A tainted woman who lives a life of lies. When Tulkinghorn, the family lawyer, learns the secret she runs away and is found dead by Esther at the gates of the cemetery in which Esther's father, Captain Hawdon, lies buried.

Dedlock, Sir Leicester Husband of Lady Dedlock, a baronet who is 20 years older than his wayward wife. Owner of Chesney Wold, and guardian of the status quo.

Dedlock, Volumnia Poor relation of Sir Leicester Dedlock. 'Rouged and necklaced' hanger-on at Chesney Wold.

Dingo, Professor Mrs Bayham Badger's second husband, who was said to have been 'of European reputation'.

Doyce, Daniel Smith and engineer who has perfected the ultimate invention, involving a very curious secret process, but is constantly thwarted by the government in his attempt to get it developed. The invention goes unexplained.

Flite, Miss A slightly mad old woman who is a regular attendant at the court of Chancery, expecting to receive a favourable judgement in a case that no one is sure has ever existed.

Gridley Known as the 'Man from Shropshire' and another casualty of Chancery.

Grub, Mr President of the Umbugology and Ditchwaterisics session at the second meeting of the Mudfog Association.

Grubble, Mr Landlord of the Dedlock Arms, who never wore a coat except at church. His wife was a beautiful woman who broke her ankle but it never healed.

Guppy, William Clerk for Kenge and Carboy. Proposes marriage to Esther Summerson, which she refuses. Guppy is involved in the investigation of Lady Dedlock's secret.

Hawdon, Captain *See* Nemo.

Hortense, Mademoiselle Lady Dedlock's French maid. She is dismissed in favour of Rosa and aids Tulkinghorn in discovering Lady Dedlock's secret. When Tulkinghorn spurns her she murders him. Hortense is based on Mrs Manning, a murderer whose execution Dickens witnessed in 1849.

Jarndyce, John Owner of Bleak House and party in the Chancery suit of Jarndyce and Jarndyce. He adopts Esther Summerson, who becomes close friends with John's cousins, Ada Clare and Richard Carstone. John hates the lawsuit which has gone on for so long with no end in sight. Richard, however, becomes totally consumed by the case, hoping it will make him his fortune. This obsession causes Carstone and Jarndyce to suffer a falling out. Jarndyce falls in love with Esther and asked her to marry him, but although she originally consents, she subsequently falls in love with Allan Woodcourt.

Jellyby, Caroline (Caddy) Neglected daughter of Mrs Jellyby and acts as her personal secretary ('I'm pen and ink to ma'). Caddy leaves home and marries Prince Turveydrop.

Jellyby, Mrs Mrs Jellyby is involved in many causes and charities but neglects her large family. Dickens modelled Mrs Jellyby on Caroline Chisholm.
Jellyby, Peepy Little brother of Caddy and son of Mrs Jellyby whose clothes were either too big or too small.
Jenny Brickmaker's wife, befriended by Esther Summerson after Jenny's child dies. Later exchanges coats with Lady Dedlock, throwing Bucket off in his pursuit of Lady Dedlock as she flees following the revealing of her secret.
Jo The crossing sweeper. When Jo shows Lady Dedlock the haunts of Captain Hawdon, lawyer Tulkinghorn has Jo kept moving from place to place. He befriends Esther Summerson at Bleak House and communicates smallpox to Charlie, and then Esther. Jo later dies at George's Shooting Gallery.
Jobling, Tony (Weevle) Friend of Guppy who takes Nemo's room at Krook's after Nemo's death. Jobling and Guppy discover the spectacular death of Krook and are temporary celebrities, drinking for free at the Sol's Arms.
Kenge Solicitor for John Jarndyce in the firm Kenge and Carboy. Known as 'Conversation Kenge'.
Krook Drunken and illiterate proprietor of a rag and bottle shop. Known as the 'Lord Chancellor', Krook collects court documents. A will instrumental in the Jarndyce and Jarndyce court case is found among his holdings by Mr Smallweed, who inherits Krook's possessions following his demise by spontaneous combustion. Krook is Mrs Smallweed's brother.
Lord Chancellor A high legal figure in the Court of Chancery (of course).
Mooney Beadle who is summoned to Krook's home on Hawdon's (Nemo's) death and gives evidence at the inquest.
Neckett, Charlotte (Charley) Daughter of sheriff's officer Neckett. When her father dies Charley cares for her two younger siblings, Emma and Tom. Charley becomes Esther Summerson's maid, nursing Esther through smallpox. She later marries a miller.
Neckett, Mr Sheriff's officer who arrests debtors and delivers them to Coavin's sponging house (temporary debtor's prison). Thus Skimpole gives Neckett the nickname 'Coavinses'. Neckett dies leaving three orphans: Charlotte (Charley), Emma and Tom.
Nemo Alias of Captain Hawdon (Nemo is Latin for 'nobody'). Nemo is doing some law copying for Snagsby and is a boarder in Krook's rag and bottle shop when he dies of an opium overdose. He is later found to be the former lover of Lady Dedlock and the father of Esther Summerson.
Pardiggle, Mrs Associate of Mrs Jellyby in her charitable works.
Quale, Mr Part of Mrs Jellyby's circle of friends, although interested in Caddy Jellyby. Eventually weds Miss Wisk.
Rachael, Mrs Esther Summerson's nurse. Later marries Reverend Chadband.
Rosa Personal maid to Lady Dedlock after Hortense is dismissed. Marries Mrs Rouncewell's grandson.
Rouncewell, George Son of the Dedlock's housekeeper Mrs Rouncewell. George ran away to join the army and cut himself off from his mother. After leaving the army he buys a shooting gallery in London with money borrowed from Smallweed. Smallweed pressures George to give over examples of Captain Hawdon's handwriting in order to help Tulkinghorn learn Lady Dedlock's secret. Charged with the murder of Tulkinghorn by Bucket, later George is exonerated of the crime and is reunited with his mother.
Rouncewell, Mrs Longtime housekeeper of Chesney Wold, home of Sir Leicester Dedlock. Mother of George and another son, who is an important ironmaster in northern England.
Skimpole, Harold Friend of John Jarndyce who claims he is a mere child who understands nothing of money, and through this smooth act manages to have everyone else pay his way through life. Dickens modelled Skimpole on Leigh Hunt.
Smallweed, Mr Joshua Grandfather Smallweed is a usurer to whom Rouncewell owes money. Smallweed uses this leverage to obtain from George a sample of Nemo's handwriting in an attempt to help Tulkinghorn learn Lady Dedlock's secret. Also in the Smallweed family are grandmother – Krook's sister, at whom grandfather throws cushions when she mentions money – and the twin grandchildren, Bartholomew and Judy.
Snagsby Law stationer near Chancery Lane who hires Nemo to do some copy work. Snagsby's wife is a zealous supporter of Rev. Chadband.
Squod, Phil George Rouncewell's ugly little assistant at the shooting gallery. Formerly a travelling tinker.
Summerson, Esther Principal character in the story and one of the narrators. She is brought up an orphan by her aunt, Miss Barbary. On her aunt's death she is adopted by John Jarndyce and becomes companions to his wards, Ada Clare and Richard Carstone. It is revealed that Esther is the illegitimate daughter of Captain Hawdon and Lady Dedlock. John Jarndyce falls in love with her and asks her to marry him. She consents out of respect for Jarndyce, but during the engagement she falls in love with Allan Woodcourt.
Tangle, Mr Barrister who is the leading living authority on the case of Jarndyce v Jarndyce having read nothing else since his schooldays.
Tulkinghorn, Mr Family lawyer to the Dedlocks. When he finds out Lady Dedlock's secret past, and tries to gain from it, he is murdered by Lady Dedlock's former maid, Hortense.
Turveydrop, Mr Owner of a dance academy on Newman Street and a 'model of deportment'.
Turveydrop, Prince Son of Mr Turveydrop, owner of a dance academy. Prince, named for the Prince Regent, gives dancing lessons and supports his father.
Vholes Richard Carstone's solicitor in Symond's Inn, recommended by Skimpole, who lures Richard deeper into the Chancery case that will ultimately lead to Richard's despair and death.
Wisk, Miss Feminist who eventually accepts Mr Quale as her husband.
Woodcourt, Allan A young surgeon who falls in love with Esther Summerson before going away as ship's doctor to India. On his return to England he learns that Esther is engaged to John Jarndyce. When Jarndyce learns that Esther is in love with Woodcourt he releases her to marry him.

***A Christmas Carol*: Christmas book published December 1843 by Chapman and Hall; illustrated by John Leech; too short to be classified as a novel and perhaps more correctly categorised as a novella**

Belle Scrooge's former fiancée, whom he had forgotten until reminded by the Ghost of Christmas Past.
Cratchit, Bob Long-suffering clerk of Ebenezer Scrooge and father of Tiny Tim. Bob endures his employer's mistreatment until Scrooge, reformed by the visit of the three spirits, raises his salary and vows to help his struggling family.
Cratchit, Caroline Wife of Bob and mother of four children, Peter, Belinda, Martha and the youngest, Tiny Tim.
Cratchit, Tiny Tim Crippled son of Bob Cratchit. The forecast of Tim's death by the Ghosts of Christmas Present and Future is instrumental in Scrooge's reformation, after which Tim is afforded proper medical attention and is cured.
Dilber, Mrs A laundress whom Ebenezer Scrooge meets in his vision of Christmas Future, selling his belongings after his death.
Fan Scrooge's sister, mother of his nephew Fred. She has died before the story begins, but lives again in the 'shadows' shown to Scrooge by the Ghost of Christmas Past.
Fezziwig, Mr Scrooge was apprenticed to 'Old Fezziwig' after he left school. Scrooge visits his old employer with the Ghost of Christmas Past and is reminded of what a kind, generous man he was.
Fezziwig, Mrs Wife of the merchant 'Old Fezziwig'.
Fred Ebenezer Scrooge's nephew who is ignored in his invitation to Scrooge to attend Christmas dinner, but the Ghost of Christmas Present shows Fred saying some good-natured things about his uncle.
Ghost of Christmas Future Shows Scrooge the demise of Tiny Tim and of himself, leading to Scrooge's reformation.
Ghost of Christmas Past Shows Scrooge his lonely and difficult childhood and gradual decline into the miser he will become.
Ghost of Christmas Present Shows Scrooge the joy that Christmas brings, both at the poor household of the Cratchits and at the home of his nephew Fred.
Joe A fence (seller of stolen goods).
Marley, Jacob Scrooge's former partner, who died seven Christmas Eves ago. Jacob, in life, was a penny-pinching miser like Scrooge and is suffering for it in the afterlife. His ghost comes to haunt Scrooge, hoping to change Scrooge's life and therefore help him to avoid Marley's fate.
Scrooge, Ebenezer Probably Dickens' best-known character, the miserly Scrooge, with his familiar cry of 'Bah, Humbug!', is visited by the ghost of his former partner, Jacob Marley, who sends three more spirits in hopes of reforming Scrooge's heartless and penny-pinching ways. It is a tough assignment for them and he fights the inevitable, but he is eventually transformed into a benevolent humanitarian.

Topper, Mr A bachelor who is a guest at Fred's Christmas dinner.
Wilkins, Dick Scrooge's fellow apprentice at Mr Fezziwig's.

***David Copperfield*: eighth novel published in 20 monthly parts between May 1849 and November 1850**

Babley, Richard *See* Mr Dick.
Bailey, Captain Army officer who makes David Copperfield jealous by dancing with the eldest Miss Larkins.
Barkis A carrier between Blunderstone and Yarmouth. He marries Clara Peggotty. Famous quote: 'Barkis is willing', denoting his desire to marry Peggotty.
Charley The 'dreadful old man' who owns a marine shop at Chatham. David Copperfield sells his jacket to Charley for eighteen pence.
Chestle, Mr Elderly Kentish hop-grower, who marries the eldest Miss Larkins.
Chillip, Doctor Attends Mrs Copperfield at David's birth.
Copperfield, Clara Mother of David Copperfield. A widow when David is born, she later is lured into marriage by Edward Murdstone, who destroys her spirit. She dies along with her newborn son while David is away at school.
Copperfield, David Main character and narrator of the story, modelled after Dickens's life. Begins life with his widowed mother and their maid, Peggotty. When his mother marries Mr Murdstone his life becomes miserable. He is sent to Creakle's school, where he meets Steerforth and Traddles. After the death of his mother he goes to work at Murdstone and Grinby and is lodged with the Micawbers. David runs away to live with his aunt Betsey Trotwood in Dover. He marries Dora Spenlow and then Agnes Wickfield.
Creakle, Mr Severe headmaster of Salem House Academy, where David first goes to school. He was based on William Jones, headmaster of Wellington Academy, which Dickens attended from 1825 to 1827.
Creakle, Mrs Mr Creakle's wife (unnamed). They have a daughter (unnamed also) who attracts David and Steerforth.
Crewler, Reverend Horace A curate in Devonshire. Father of Sophy Crewler.
Crewler, Sophy Daughter of the Reverend Horace Crewler and fiancée of Tommy Traddles.
Crupp, Mrs David Copperfield's brandy-loving landlady at the Adelphi.
Dartle, Rosa Companion to Mrs Steerforth, possessively attached to Steerforth, who has marked her face when a child by throwing a hammer in a fit of temper. Rosa hates Little Em'ly for running away with Steerforth.
Demple, George A doctor's son and fellow pupil of David Copperfield at Salem House.
Dick, Mr Kite-making, memoir-writing companion to Betsey Trotwood, who gives good advice but is not all there. Mr Dick's real name was Richard Babley but he was always referred to as plain Mr Dick. His insight is uncanny and he becomes a friend of David's.
Em'ly, Little Mr Peggotty's niece and David's childhood friend. She is later engaged to Ham but is lured away by the charms of Steerforth. Mr Peggotty is heartbroken and searches for her, finally finding her when Steerforth tires of her and she leaves him. She later emigrates to Australia with her uncle.
Endell, Martha A girl whose ruin foreshadows Little Em'ly's and helps to prevent her falling into the same trap. She eventually emigrates to Australia with Little Em'ly, Mr Peggotty and Mrs Gummidge.
Fibbitson, Mrs Elderly inmate of the almshouses where Mrs Mell lives.
Gummidge, Mrs Widow of Mr Peggotty's former partner in a boat concern, who had died very poor. She lives with Mr Peggotty and later emigrates to Australia with him.
Heep, Uriah A hypocritical clerk of Mr Wickfield's who is continually citing his humbleness. He deviously plots to ruin Wickfield but is later undone by Mr Wilkins Micawber. On their first meeting, David describes him as 'a red-haired person – a youth of fifteen, as I take it now, but looking much older – whose hair was cropped as close as the closest stubble; who had hardly any eyebrows, and no eyelashes'.
Jip Dora Spenlow's pet spaniel, whose name was short for Gypsy. He dies at David Copperfield's feet at the very moment of Dora's death.
Joram Assistant to Mr Omer in his capacity as the Yarmouth undertaker, who, after marrying Omer's daughter, Minnie, becomes a partner in the business.
Jorkins, Mr Partner of Francis Spenlow in the firm of proctors where David Copperfield is articled. Jorkins is largely unseen, although Spenlow finds it expedient to refer to his opinion to justify his own conduct.
Kidgerbury, Mrs Domestic help of David and Dora, described as 'the oldest inhabitant of Kentish Town who went out charring'.
Larkins Family Mr Larkins and his two daughters, the youngest Miss Larkins and the eldest Miss Larkins. The eldest Miss Larkins would be about 30 years old when David, as a young 17-year-old, had a crush on her.
Littimer Manservant to Steerforth, involved in the concealment of the elopement of Steerforth and Emily. He is later guilty of embezzlement and is captured with the help of Miss Mowcher. David says of him: 'I believe there never existed in his station a more respectable-looking man. He was taciturn, soft-footed, very quiet in his manner, deferential, observant, always at hand when wanted, and never near when not wanted; but his great claim to consideration was his respectability'.
Maldon, Jack Annie Strong's cousin, who goes to India; he may have been dishonourable in his intentions to Annie without her reciprocating.
Mealy Potatoes Boy who works at Murdstone and Grinby's warehouse, whose name derived from the complexion of his skin.
Mell, Charles Assistant schoolmaster at Salem House Academy. David Copperfield befriends Mell and finds that his mother lives in an almshouse, which he innocently relates to Steerforth. Steerforth uses this information to discredit Mell and have him dismissed. Mell later emigrates to Australia and becomes headmaster at Colonial Salem House Grammar School in Port Middlebay.
Micawber, Emma Long-suffering wife of Mr Micawber, whom she swears she will never leave despite his financial difficulties. David describes her as 'a thin and faded lady, not at all young, with a baby at her breast. This baby was one of twins; and I may remark here that I hardly ever, in all my experience of the family, saw both the twins detached from Mrs Micawber at the same time. One of them was always taking refreshment'.
Micawber, Wilkins David lodges at his home. Always in debt and waiting for 'something to turn up', he ends up in debtor's prison. On his release he has various occupations but is eventually employed at Mr Wickfield's office, where he exposes the deeds of Uriah Heep. In gratitude for this his debts are paid and he emigrates to Australia, where he prospers. Famous quote: 'Annual income £20, annual expenditure £19 19/6, result, happiness. Annual income £20, annual expenditure £20 0/6d, result, misery'.
Mills, Julia Friend and confidante of Dora Spenlow and David's go-between during his courtship with Dora. She later goes to live in India.
Mowcher, Miss Steerforth's friend; a dwarf who sells cosmetics; his relations with her give the reader insight into the pity that dominates Steerforth's character (which includes self-pity).
Murdstone, Edward Second husband of Clara Copperfield whom David dislikes. He is a stern disciplinarian with a violent nature, who sends David off to Salem House School and later consigns him to the warehouse of Murdstone and Grinby.
Murdstone, Jane The equally stern sister of Edward Murdstone who moves in with David and his mother after her marriage to Murdstone.
Omer, Minnie Daughter of Mr Omer, who marries his foreman, Joram.
Omer, Mr Draper, tailor, haberdasher and furnisher, who resided in Yarmouth and arranged the funeral of Clara Murdstone and her baby son.
Peggotty, Clara David's devoted nurse and sister to Daniel Peggotty. After the death of David's mother she is discharged and marries Barkis. When Barkis dies she goes to live with David and Betsey Trotwood.
Peggotty, Daniel Crotchety fisherman brother of Clara. He lives in an overturned boat on the beach at Yarmouth with Little Em'ly, Ham and Mrs Gummidge. When Em'ly abandons them to elope with Steerforth, Daniel vows to find her. Steerforth later leaves Em'ly and she is reunited with Daniel. At the end of the novel Daniel, Em'ly and Mrs Gummidge resettle in Australia.
Peggotty, Ham Orphaned nephew of Daniel Peggotty and fiancé of Little Em'ly. A fisherman and boatbuilder. He drowns trying to rescue Steerforth. 'He was a huge, strong fellow of six feet high, broad in proportion, and round-shouldered; but with a simpering boy's face and curly light hair that gave him quite a sheepish look.'

Shepherd, Miss Boarder at Misses Nettingall's educational establishment and a brief early romantic fixation of young David Copperfield.
Spenlow, Dora Daughter of David's employer, Francis Spenlow. She and David are married and David tries to teach her to keep house, but she has no head for it. She becomes ill with an unspecified illness and dies young.
Spenlow, Francis Proctor at Doctor's Commons where David is apprenticed. David says of him: 'He was a little light-haired gentleman, with undeniable boots, and the stiffest of white cravats and shirt-collars. He was buttoned up mighty trim and tight, and must have taken a great deal of pains with his whiskers, which were accurately curled.'
Steerforth, James Friend of David, whom he often calls 'Daisy', at the Salem House school where his engaging charm makes him everyone's favourite. David later runs into him again in London and he accompanies David on a trip to Yarmouth, where he charms Little Em'ly into eloping with him. They go abroad and Steerforth soon tires of Em'ly and deserts her. He is later drowned in a shipwreck where Ham Peggotty, from whom Steerforth stole Em'ly away, dies trying to save him.
Strong, Annie Young wife of Dr Strong who has a strong affiliation to Jack Maldon.
Strong, Dr David's teacher who is writing a dictionary; his wife is much younger and David's observance of their relationship shapes his early doubts about marriage.
Tiffey, Mr Chief clerk at Spenlow and Jorkins, who tells David Copperfield of Mr Spenlow's accidental death.
Tipp Carman at Murdstone and Grinby's, who addressed David Copperfield as 'David' whereas the other workers referred to him as 'the little gent' or 'the young Suffolker'.
Topsawyer According to a story told to David Copperfield at the inn in Yarmouth, Topsawyer ordered a glass of ale like that ordered by David, drank it and fell dead.
Traddles, Tommy Downtrodden pupil with David Copperfield and Steerforth at Salem House. David's best friend and best man at David's wedding to Dora Spenlow. He later becomes a lawyer and marries Sophy Crewler.
Trotwood, Betsey David Copperfield's great aunt. David runs away from London, when he is installed at Murdstone and Grinby's warehouse, and goes to Dover to live with Betsey. She helps David get a start in life and, when she loses her fortune, goes to London to live with David.
Wickfield, Agnes Childhood friend of David Copperfield and daughter of Betsey Trotwood's lawyer. Becomes David's wife after the death of Dora.
Wickfield, Mr Father of Agnes and lawyer to Betsey Trotwood. His overindulgence of wine causes him to be vulnerable to the schemes of Uriah Heep, who becomes his partner and attempts to ruin him.
Yawler Friend of Tommy Traddles at Salem House 'with his nose on one side'.

***Dombey and Son*: seventh novel, published in monthly parts by Bradbury and Evans, from October 1846 to April 1848**
Bagstock, Joe Dombey's friend who sets him up with Edith Granger.
Blimber, Cornelia Prim and proper daughter of Dr and Mrs Blimber.
Blimber, Dr Pompous and pedantic headmaster of the school in Brighton where Paul Dombey was a pupil.
Blimber, Mrs Proud and devoted wife of Dr Blimber who feigned learnedness.
Bokum, Mrs Widow, and 'dearest friend' of Mrs MacStinger. She kept a close eye on Captain Bunsby on his way to his wedding to Mrs MacStinger in case he attempted escape.
Briggs One of Paul Dombey's fellow pupils at Doctor Blimber's school.
Brogley, Mr The 'sworn broker and appraiser' who took possession of The Wooden Midshipman after Solomon Gills fell into debt.
Brown, Conversation Acquaintance of Cousin Feenix, who was a 'four-bottle man at the Treasury Board'.
Brown, Good Mrs An ugly old rag and bone vendor and mother of Alice Marwood (Brown). She kidnaps Florence Dombey and steals her clothes.
Bunsby, Captain Jack Commander of the *Cautious Clara* and friend of Captain Cuttle, who marries Mrs MacStinger.
Burgess and Co. Mr Toots's tailors, who were 'fash'nable but very dear'.
Carker, Harriet Takes pity on Alice Marwood, who at first shuns her when she finds out that she is James Carker's sister but eventually becomes her friend. Harriet marries Mr Morfin.
Carker, James Manager at Dombey and Son who is employed to convey messages to Edith but not content with seducing her also contrives to bring the firm to ruin. Blessed with a set of extremely white teeth, he is the brother of John and Harriet Carker. He is eventually killed under a train whilst in flight from Dombey.
Carker, John Referred to as Carker the Junior, due to his lowly position, although in actual fact is older than James by nearly three years. John stole money from the firm but was kept on by Dombey, although his brother never lets him forget the indiscretion. John is devoted to his sister Harriet.
Chick, Louisa Sister of Paul Dombey Snr and friend to Mrs Tox. Her famous quote is 'make an effort'.
Chick, Mr Husband of Louisa Chick and therefore Mr Dombey's brother-in-law.
Cuttle, Captain Seafaring friend of Sol Gills, whose shop he cares for when Sol goes in search of his lost nephew, Walter Gay. His famous quote is 'When found, make a note of'.
Daws, Mary Young kitchen-maid in Paul Dombey's household.
Diogenes Dog owned by the Blimber family originally but given to Florence Dombey by Toots, with the Blimbers' blessing.
Dombey, Florence Neglected daughter of Paul Dombey and sister of little Paul, whom she nurses in his illness. She marries Walter Gay and eventually cares for her bankrupt and invalid father.
Dombey, Paul Jnr The long-hoped-for heir to the house of Dombey and Son. His mother dies at his birth, leaving him a frail and sickly child. His father sends him to Brighton in the care of Mrs Pipchin, hoping the sea air will bolster his failing health. He lives only six years.
Dombey, Paul Snr Powerful head of the House of Dombey shipping firm. He wants a son and when a daughter (Florence) is born he despises her. His second child, a son (Paul), is weak and sickly and dies a child. Paul's first wife dies with the birth of Paul Jnr and he remarries.
Feenix, Cousin Referred to as 'Cousin' although in actuality a Lord. He is nephew to Cleopatra Skewton.
Flowers Cleopatra Skewton's personal maid.
Game Chicken, The Pugilist employed by Mr Toots in the 'cultivation of those gentle arts which refine and humanise existence'.
Gay, Walter Sol Gill's nephew, he is employed in the house of Dombey and Son. When Walter befriends Florence Dombey her father is displeased and sends him to the firm's branch in Barbados. The ship in which he sails is lost and Sol goes to search for him.
Gills, Solomon Uncle of Walter Gay and owner of a ship's chandler shop called 'The Wooden Midshipman'. When Walter's ship is lost at sea Solomon goes in search of him, leaving the care of the shop to his friend, Captain Cuttle.
Glubb, Old Old, crab-faced man who influences Paul Dombey with his stories of fish and sea monsters.
Granger, Colonel First husband of Edith Granger.
Granger, Edith Paul Dombey's second wife is the widow of Colonel Granger and the daughter of Mrs Skewton. She marries Dombey but does not love him. She later elopes with John Carker, a manager at Dombey's firm, to punish her husband.
Howler, the Rev. Melchisedech Officiates at the wedding of Captain Bunsby and Mrs MacStinger.
MacStinger, Mrs Captain Cuttle's irascible landlady, who is a widow with three children: Charles (known as Chowley), Juliana and Alexander.
Marwood, Alice Good Mrs Brown's daughter, who was John Carker's mistress and Edith's cousin.
Morfin, Mr The assistant manager of Dombey and Son who marries Harriet Carker.
Nipper, Susan Florence's companion who speaks her mind and later marries Mr Toots.
Pankey, Miss Young lady who is the only other boarder at Mrs Pipchin's when Paul Dombey lives there.
Perch, Mr Timid messenger in the firm of Dombey and Son.
Pipchin, Mrs Keeper of 'an infantine Boarding House of a very select description' in Brighton.
Rob the Grinder Robin Toodle, who has a miscreant youth then works at first for Captain Cuttle and then James Carker.
Skewton, Cleopatra Mother of Edith Granger. She dies after having a stroke.
Toodle, Mr Husband of Polly Toodle and father of Rob the

Grinder. He is a stoker on the railway and later an engine driver.

Toodle, Polly Little Paul Dombey's nurse, known in the Dombey household as Richards, dismissed when she takes Paul to visit her family in a poorer section of London. She re-enters the story when Captain Cuttle asks her to look after Sol Gill's Shop 'The Wooden Midshipman'.

Toots, Mr A student at Dr Blimber's school who loves Florence but marries Susan.

Tox, Lucretia Close friend of Mrs Chick, Paul Dombey Snr's sister. She has hopes to marry Paul Snr after his first wife dies. Paul marries Mrs Granger instead, breaking Miss Tox's heart, but she stays loyal to him through later hardships.

Withers Mrs Skewton's page, who pushes her around in her wheelchair.

***Great Expectations*: thirteenth novel published in 36 weekly parts in 1860 / 1861**

Avenger, The Pip's name for Pepper, a servant boy hired by him. Pip has such a hard time finding things to keep him busy 'that I sometimes sent him to Hyde Park Corner to see what o'clock it was.'

Barley, Clara Herbert Pocket's secret sweetheart. She is secret because Herbert knows his mother would say she is below his 'station'. She's actually a sweet, fairy-like girl who takes care of her dying drunk of a father.

Barley, Old Bill Clara's father, an unseen 'sad old rascal' who used to be a ship's purser.

Biddy A kind, intelligent girl Pip's age who works for Mr Wopsle's great aunt at the school. Later, she comes to work for Joe, taking care of Mrs Joe Gargery. She loves Pip but he ignores her as his expectations are realised. When Pip eventually realises he loves her too it is too late as she has married Joe.

Black Bill A prisoner Wemmick recognises in Newgate Prison 'behind the cistern' when he takes Pip on a visit to the prison.

Brandley, Mrs Friend of Miss Havisham, whom Estella boarded with at Richmond.

Camilla Ageing relative of Miss Havisham who doesn't have an inch of love for the woman but is greedy for her money. She buzzes around Miss Havisham like a sycophantic fly. Matthew Pocket's sister.

Compeyson Con man who deceives Miss Havisham to get her money and then leaves her at the altar. He is an accomplice of Magwitch in the original prison break. He later exposes Magwitch and accidentally drowns when Magwitch is recaptured.

Drummle, Bentley Pip's fellow student at Matthew Pocket's. He marries Estella for her money and abuses her. He is killed when kicked by a horse that he has mistreated.

Estella Pip meets Estella at Satis House and falls in love with her, but she is cruel to him. Pip goes to London and becomes a gentleman and continues to adore Estella, but she warns him that she is incapable of love. She later marries Bentley Drummle, who mistreats her and she leaves him. Drummle dies and Estella and Pip meet two years later and vow to remain together.

Gargery, Joe Blacksmith, friend and adoptive father to Pip. Joe is also the husband of Pip's sister, Georgiana Mary, who mistreats him as badly as she does Pip. After his wife's death Joe comes to London and nurses Pip through an illness. Later he marries Pip's friend Biddy.

Gargery, Mrs Joe Wife of Joe Gargery and sister of Pip; a bitter, angry woman who brings up Pip 'by hand' – that is, she whips him whenever she can, often employing 'the tickler'. She is ultimately beaten to death by Orlick.

Georgiana Ageing relative of Miss Havisham.

Handel Herbert Pocket's affectionate name for Pip.

Havisham, Miss A very rich and grim old woman who lives in seclusion at Satis House. She is the adopted mother of Estella, whom she teaches to break men's hearts to avenge her own misfortune at being left at the altar by Compeyson years before. She continues to wear her wedding dress and even keeps the mouldy wedding cake. Pip goes to Miss Havisham's to play and meets and falls in love with Estella. Pip believes Miss Havisham is his secret benefactor as he goes to London and becomes a gentleman. She dies in a house fire.

Hubble, Mr and Mrs Simple, silly folks from Pip's village. Mr Hubble is a wheelwright.

Jaggers Lawyer who serves Miss Havisham and Magwitch, as he specialises in getting convicts light sentences. It is through Jaggers that Pip receives the benefits of the great expectations that he assumes are from Miss Havisham but in reality are from the convict Magwitch.

Magwitch, Abel A convict whom Pip helps in the marshes after his escape from the prison ship. He is recaptured and transported to Australia, where he gains a fortune which he secretly uses to increase Pip's 'expectations'. He secretly returns to England as Provis and confronts Pip with the secret source of his good fortune. Magwitch is recaptured and dies before he can be executed. Magwitch is also the father of Estella.

Molly Jaggers' housekeeper, Magwitch's wife and Estella's mother.

Orlick, Dolge Joe Gargery's journeyman blacksmith, he quarrels with Mrs Joe and later attacks her, leaving her with injuries of which she later dies. He falls in with a bad lot and tries to murder Pip.

Pip (Philip Pirrip) The narrator as well as the protagonist of the story. Pip is an orphan being raised by his sister, Mrs Joe Gargery, and her husband, Joe Gargery, a blacksmith.

Pocket, Herbert Pip goes to London and meets Herbert, who he discovers is the 'pale young gentleman' with whom he fought at Miss Havisham's as a child. Pip and Herbert become best friends and share chambers at Barnard's Inn and at the Temple. Herbert helps teach Pip 'city manners'. Pip helps Herbert become a partner in the firm of Clarriker and Co., which enables Pocket to marry Clara Barley.

Pocket, Matthew Father of Herbert and cousin of Miss Havisham. He is the only one of Miss Havisham's relatives who speaks honestly of her and has been banished from her presence. Matthew is Pip's tutor in London. He has no control over his large family and has a habit of pulling himself up by his hair in frustration. Pip tells Miss Havisham of Matthew's good character and she leaves him 4,000 pounds in her will. Matthew's wife, Belinda, is obsessed with social position, having been the daughter of a knight.

Pocket, Sarah Ageing relative of Miss Havisham.

Pumblechook, Uncle Joe's uncle, a well-to-do corn-chandler in the village. He considers himself upper-class and is actually a bombastic fool: 'A large hard-breathing middle-aged slow man, with a mouth like a fish, dull staring eyes, and sandy hair standing upright on his head, so that he looked as if he had just been all but choked'.

Raymond, Cousin Ageing relative of Miss Havisham.

Skiffins, Miss Very partial to the Aged Wemmick and eventually marries John Wemmick at a church in Camberwell Green.

Startop Student and boarder of Matthew Pocket. He is a good friend of Pip's.

Trabb Tailor who makes Pip a new suit of clothes before he goes to London, also in charge of the mourners at Pip's sister's funeral.

Trabb's Boy Assistant to Trabb, the tailor, who terrorises Pip. He later leads Herbert to the limekiln to rescue Pip from Orlick.

Wemmick, John Jagger's confidential clerk, friend of Pip (in private) who lives in a delightfully strange house with 'an aged parent'. 'A dry man, rather short in stature, with a square wooden face, whose expression seemed to have been imperfectly chipped out with a dull-edged chisel.'

Wemmick, 'The Aged' Wemmick's elderly, and quite deaf, relative (commonly held to be Wemmick's father, but not described as such by Dickens). The Aged lives with Wemmick in his castle and is quite happy when you nod at him.

Whimple, Mrs Landlady of the house where Old Barley and his daughter Clara had lodgings.

Wopsle's Great-Aunt A 'ridiculous old lady' who runs the so-called school in town out of a cottage.

Wopsle, Mr Parish clerk, friend of the Gargerys. He aspires to enter the Church and preach in the pulpit but instead becomes an actor with the stage name of Waldengarver. Pip sees him perform *Hamlet* in London.

***Hard Times*: tenth novel, written for *Household Words* from April to August 1854**

Bitzer A student in Gradgrind's school of hard facts. Later a light porter in Bounderby's bank.

Blackpool, Stephen A worker in Bounderby's mill. His wife is a drunk and he befriends Rachael, but falls out with his employer and leaves to look for work elsewhere. He is accused of robbing the bank, and before his name is cleared he falls down a well and dies. Later he is cleared with the discovery that the robbery was committed by young Tom Gradgrind.

Bounderby, Josiah Coketown Banker, mill owner and 'self-made man', abandoned as a child. His story is exposed as a sham when Mrs Pegler, his loving mother whom he has discarded, is found. Bounderby marries his friend Gradgrind's daughter Louisa and later discards her.

Childers, EWB Young man who is an equestrian in Sleary's Circus. He marries Sleary's daughter Josephine and has a son, who at three years old is, according to Sleary, 'The Little Wonder of Thcolathtic Equitation'.

Gordon, Emma Tightrope-walker, who comforts Sissy Jupe when her father vanishes.

Gradgrind, Adam Smith and Malthus The two youngest sons of Thomas Gradgrind, named by their father after famous political economists.

Gradgrind, Louisa Oldest daughter of Thomas and like him a victim of utilitarianism. She marries Bounderby, whom she doesn't love. She later leaves her husband and returns to her father.

Gradgrind, Mrs Wife of Thomas and mother of their five children.

Gradgrind, Thomas A mill owner retired from business and father of Louisa and Tom. He runs a school and emphasises the importance of facts and figures over fancy to his students and his children. By the end of the story he learns that facts and figures must be tempered by love and forbearance.

Gradgrind, Tom Son of Thomas, nicknamed 'The Whelp' by Harthouse. He is employed at Bounderby's bank, from which he later steals; the blame is set on Stephen Blackpool. He finally leaves the country with the aid of Sleary and his circus troupe.

Harthouse, James A Parliamentary candidate visiting Coketown, he befriends Tom Gradgrind in an attempt to seduce his sister Louisa, who is in an unhappy marriage to Bounderby. As a result of the attempted seduction Louisa runs home to her father, refuses to return to her husband, and is later disowned by him.

Jupe, Cecilia (Sissy) Daughter of Signor Jupe, a clown in Sleary's Circus, who is deserted by her father and taken in by Gradgrind. She befriends Louisa.

Kidderminster Small boy with an old face, who played the part of Childers's infant son in 'his daring vaulting act as the Wild Huntsman of the North American Prairies'.

M'Choakumchild Schoolmaster in Gradgrind's school where fancy and imagination are discouraged in favour of hard facts.

Merrylegs Signor Jupe's highly trained performing dog which makes its way to Sleary's Circus at Chester following Jupe's disappearance and dies at Sleary's feet.

Pegler, Mrs Revealed at the end of the story to be Bounderby's loving mother, exposing as a sham his claim to be a 'self-made man', who raised himself in the streets.

Rachael Friend of Stephen Blackpool, who loves her but cannot gain release from his drunken wife. She defends Stephen when he is accused of theft from the bank.

Slackbridge Rabble-rousing trade union delegate who persuades the Coketown millworkers to shun Stephen Blackpool.

Sladdery, Mr Fashionable London librarian who boasts of having a high connection.

Sleary Proprietor of Sleary's Circus. Speaks with a lisp ('People mutht be amuthed'). He helps Tom Gradgrind escape abroad after the bank robbery.

Sparsit, Mrs Housekeeper of Bounderby with aristocratic connections. She is a busybody, causing dissension between Bounderby and his wife Louisa Gradgrind.

***Little Dorrit*: eleventh novel, published in 1857**

Bangham, Mrs Charwoman and messenger at the Marshalsea Prison who attended Mrs Dorrit at the birth of Amy.

Barnacle, Tite A senior official in the Circumlocution Office, where everything goes round in circles, and nothing ever gets done.

Barroneau, Madame The widow whom Rigaud married and was accused of murdering, although his version of events is that she leapt over a cliff-top after a violent quarrel.

Casby, Christopher Formerly town-agent to Tite Barnacle. His benevolent appearance leads to him being referred to as the 'last of the Patriarchs'. Father of Flora Finchina.

Charlotte The 'false young friend' of Miss Wade when they were schoolgirls.

Chivery, John and Young John The two sons of the turnkey at the Marshalsea. John Chivery was dubbed the 'sentimental son' whilst Young John loves Amy Dorrit and assists in finding her father's fortune.

Chivery, Mr and Mrs John John Chivery was a turnkey at the Marshalsea Prison who never opened his mouth 'without occasion'. His wife ran a tobacconist shop.

Clennam, Arthur Returns to England from abroad, where he has spent years with his father in the family business. On his father's death he falls out with his mother and gives up his share of the business. He befriends Amy Dorrit at the Marshalsea and becomes business partner to Daniel Doyce. After losing everything in a banking scam by Merdle he is himself imprisoned in the Marshalsea. His health fails and Amy cares for him in the prison. The novel ends with Arthur and Amy's marriage.

Clennam, Mrs Invalid mother of Arthur, with whom she has a falling-out over the family business. She avoids a blackmail scheme by Rigaud/Blandois when her tumbledown house tumbles down on him.

Dawes, Mary Nurse in the poor nobleman's household where Miss Wade was employed as a governess.

Dorrit, Amy Title character, daughter of William Dorrit, born in the Marshalsea debtors' prison. She works for Mrs Clennam and befriends Arthur. Her father inherits a fortune and they leave the prison and travel abroad. After her father's death she discovers that the fortune has been lost in a banking scam. She nurses Arthur in the Marshalsea when his fortune is lost in the same banking scam, and eventually marries him.

Dorrit, Edward (Tip) Ne'er-do-well brother of Amy Dorrit and son of Edward Dorrit.

Dorrit, Fanny Sister of Amy. A dancer with social aspirations, Fanny marries Mr Sparkler, stepson of Mr Merdle. Fanny and Sparkler lose everything in the Merdle banking scam.

Dorrit, Frederick Brother of William, uncle of Fanny, Edward and Amy. He plays clarionet in a small-time theatre. He is due an inheritance but the knowledge is kept from him by the intrigues of Mrs Clennam.

Dorrit, William Father of Amy, Fanny and Edward, and long-time inmate of the Marshalsea debtors' prison. He inherits an estate and leaves the prison, travelling in style with his daughters. After his death Amy learns that his fortune has been lost in the Merdle banking scam.

Doyce, Daniel Inventor of an unspecified mechanical wonder which he is unable to get a patent for in the Circumlocution Office. He enters a partnership with Arthur Clennam, who loses the firm's money in the Merdle scandal. Doyce later sells the invention abroad and returns to liberate Arthur from the Marshalsea.

Finching, Flora Former sweetheart of Arthur Clennam who reappears 20 years later, 'grown to be very broad, and short of breath'. Dickens modelled the character of Flora after his own early sweetheart, Maria Beadnell, who reappears later in Dickens's life but not quite the way he remembered her.

Flintwinch, Ephraim Brother of Jeremiah whose looks are almost identical.

Flintwinch, Jeremiah Mrs Clennam's clerk to whom her son Arthur relinquishes his share of the family business.

Flintwinch, Mrs Jeremiah, née Affery Wife of Mrs Clennam's clerk who sees the evil doings of the house in dreams.

Gowan, Henry Arthur Clennam first meets him when Gowan is idly tossing stones into the Thames. The always affable Henry marries Pet Meagles.

Haggage, Doctor Prisoner who attends at the birth of Amy Dorrit.

Jenkinson Messenger in the Circumlocution Office.

Lion Henry Gowan's Newfoundland dog, who dies by poison probably administered by Blandois.

Maggy Simple-minded granddaughter of Mrs Bangham.

Meagles, Mr and Mrs Kind-hearted retired banker Mr Meagles, his wife and daughter Minnie 'Pet', befriend Arthur Clennam, Amy Dorrit and Daniel Doyce. The Meagleses adopt Tattycoram from the Foundling Hospital.

Merdle, Mr and Mrs Mr Merdle is an unscrupulous banker. Investing in his enterprises ruins the Dorrits, Arthur Clennam and others. Merdle commits suicide when his fraud is uncovered. Mrs Merdle is the mother of Mr Sparkler by a previous marriage.

Mr F's Aunt Companion to Flora Finching (aunt to her late husband) and one of the funniest characters in Dickens. Dickens describes her as 'an amazing little old woman, with a face like a staring wooden doll too cheap for expression, and a stiff yellow wig perched unevenly on the top of her head, as if the child who owned the doll had driven a tack through it anywhere, so that it only got fastened on'. She has a great propensity for uttering totally nonsensical barbs.

Pancks Clerk and rent collector for Mr Casby. He assists in finding William Dorrit's fortune. A comical character who does everything 'with a puff and a snort'.

Plornish, Mr A simple, good-natured plasterer.

Rigaud/Blandois Villain of the novel. Rigaud attempts to blackmail Mrs Clennam and has her house fall and crush him for his efforts.

Slingo Dealer in horses who vowed to give Tip Dorrit 'a berth' on his release from the Marshalsea.

Sparkler, Mr Edmund Son of Mrs Merdle by her first marriage. Edmund is one of the Lords of the Circumlocution Office and marries Fanny Dorrit.

Tattycoram/Harriet Beadle Adopted by the Meagleses from the Foundling Hospital, Harriet is given the name Tattycoram and is maid to the Meagleses daughter, Pet. She exhibits fits of temper and is counselled by Mr Meagles to 'count five and twenty'.

Wade, Miss Dark figure who lures Tattycoram away from the kind-hearted Meagles.

Wobbler, Mr Member of the Secretarial Department of the Circumlocution Office.

Martin Chuzzlewit*: sixth novel published in 1843–4 as *The Life and Adventures of Martin Chuzzlewit

Bailey, Christopher Impish 'small boy with a large red head, and no nose to speak of' who worked as boot-boy and porter at Mrs Todgers's Commercial Boarding House.

Brick, Jefferson War correspondent on the *New York Rowdy Journal*.

Buffum, Oscar One of the deputation who arranges the 'le-vee' in honour of Elijah Pogram at the National Hotel in an American town.

Bullamy Porter at the offices of Montague Tigg's fraudulent Anglo-Bengalee Disinterested Loan and Assurance Company. Following Tigg's murder Bullamy and Crimple make off with the firm's money.

Chiggle An 'immortal' American sculptor who made a statue of Elijah Pogram.

Choke, General Cyrus American swindler, who introduces Martin Chuzzlewit to Scadder.

Chollop, Major Hannibal American 'worshipper of freedom', who meets Martin Chuzzlewit and Mark Tapley in Eden.

Chuzzlewit, Jonas Son of Anthony Chuzzlewit, he kills his father to gain his inheritance, marries Mercy Pecksniff and, through his cruelty, breaks her spirit. He murders Tigg and, on the way to prison, kills himself.

Chuzzlewit, Martin Grandson of Martin Sr. He has a falling-out with his grandfather over his love for Mary Graham. Becomes a pupil of Pecksniff who, because of pressure from the grandfather, throws young Martin out.

Chuzzlewit, Old Martin Grandfather of Martin, cousin of Pecksniff, brother of Anthony, uncle of Jonas. Martin is suspicious of his hypocritical relatives, chiefly Pecksniff, whose hypocrisy Martin exposes and is reconciled with his grandson, young Martin.

Crimple, David Officer at the offices of Montague Tigg's Anglo-Bengalee Disinterested Loan and Assurance Company. He and Bullamy steal the firm's money after Tigg's murder.

Diver, Colonel Editor of the *New York Rowdy Journal*.

Dunkle, Doctor Ginery A 'gentleman of great poetical elements' who acts as the spokesman of the committee that welcomes Elijah Pogram.

Fips, Mr Lawyer in Austin Friars, who was secretly commissioned by Old Martin to employ Tom Pinch to arrange and catalogue books at £100 per year.

Gamp, Sarah A midwife, nurse and 'layer-out' of the dead. She is a fixture in the story and appears to be much more concerned with her own creature comforts than those of her patients.

Gill, Mrs Client of Mrs Gamp, who could calculate exactly when the birth of her babies was due.

Graham, Mary Mary cares for old Martin Chuzzlewit with the knowledge that she will not profit from Martin's wealth after his death. Chuzzlewit's grandson Martin falls in love with Mary, which displeases his grandfather, who disinherits young Martin but eventually gives them his blessing to marry.

Harris, Mrs Sarah Gamp's alluded-to but unseen friend. Betsey Prig expresses disbelief as to her existence.

Hominy, Mrs Pretentious so-called philosopher and authoress whom Martin Chuzzlewit meets in America.

Izzard, Mr Member of the committee that welcomes Elijah Pogram.

Jinkins, Mr Boarder at Mrs Todgers's who, although talking of splendid things, was a fish-salesman's book-keeper.

Jobling, Doctor John Doctor who attended Anthony Chuzzlewit and Lewsome and who became the medical officer of the Anglo-Bengalee Disinterested Loan and Life Assurance Company.

Kedgick, Captain Landlord of the National Hotel in an American town.

Kettle, La Fayette Secretary of the Watertoast Association, whom Martin Chuzzlewit encounters on his travels to Eden.

Lewsome Young surgeon attended by Doctor Jobling and nursed by Sarah Gamp during a serious illness.

Lupin, Mrs Landlady of the Blue Dragon who eventually marries Mark Tapley.

Mould, Mr Undertaker whose countenance often belied the seriousness of his job.

Nadgett Inquiry agent employed at a salary of £1 per week by Tigg's fraudulent company. Discovers Jonas Chuzzlewit's intention to poison Anthony Chuzzlewit and later Jonas's guilt in the murder of Tigg, by fishing his blood-stained clothes from the river.

Pecksniff, Seth Sanctimonious surveyor and architect, and one of the biggest hypocrites in fiction. A cousin of old Martin Chuzzlewit and the father of Mercy and Charity.

Pinch, Tom Devoted admirer and assistant to Pecksniff. A kindly, sweet-tempered fellow, completely blind to Pecksniff's hypocrisy despite a multitude of evidence of it. He finally becomes aware of Pecksniff's true character and is dismissed.

Pogram, Hon. Elijah American Congressman who meets Martin Chuzzlewit on a steamboat on the way back from Eden.

Prig, Mrs Betsey Nurse who is a friend and colleague of Sarah Gamp and who comically doubts the existence of Mrs Harris.

Scadder, Zephania Agent of the Eden Land Corporation who is introduced to Martin Chuzzlewit by Cyrus Choke.

Tacker Chief mourner for Mr Mould the undertaker.

Tamaroo Slow-witted old woman who replaced Young Bailey at Todgers's.

Tapley, Mark Ostler at the Blue Dragon Inn and servant to young Martin Chuzzlewit. He accompanies Martin to America and later marries Mrs Lupin, the Blue Dragon's landlady. The inn is renamed The Jolly Tapley.

Tigg, Montague Disreputable adventurer, who changes his name to Tigg Montague. Tigg discovers the murderous intentions of Jonas Chuzzlewit via his agent, Nadgett, and is killed by Jonas.

Todgers, Mrs Proprietor of a Commercial Boarding House in London in which she welcomes Charity and Mercy Pecksniff despite her rule of only receiving gentlemen boarders.

Wolf, Mr One of Montague Tigg's guests at a dinner attended by Jonas Chuzzlewit.

***The Mystery of Edwin Drood*: fifteenth novel unfinished at Dickens's death in 1870**

Bazzard Clerk to Hiram Grewgious who writes an unproduced tragedy, 'The Thorn of Anxiety'. Grewgious admits that Bazzard has a strange power over him.

Billickin, Mrs London landlady of Rosa Bud and her chaperone, Miss Twinkleton. She insists on using the title 'Billickin' in business matters, fearing being taken advantage of because she is a woman. Mrs Billickin and Miss Twinkleton take a comical dislike for one another.

Brobity, Miss The owner of a school in Cloisterham. Miss Brobity married Mr Sapsea.

Bud, Rosa Betrothed to Edwin Drood in childhood, they later agree that they cannot marry. Edwin disappears and John Jasper declares his love for Rosa. In terror she flees to London to her guardian, Grewgious. 'The pet pupil of the Nuns' House is Miss Rosa Bud, of course called Rosebud; wonderfully pretty, wonderfully childish, wonderfully whimsical'.

Chinaman, Jack Keeper of a London opium den in competition with Princess Puffer's den.

Crisparkle, Septimus Minor canon of Cloisterham Cathedral. 'Mr Crisparkle, Minor Canon, early riser, musical, classical, cheerful, kind, good-natured, social, contented, and boy-like'. He takes Neville Landless as a pupil and helps Neville flee to London when suspicion is cast on him for the disappearance of Edwin Drood.

Datchery, Dick Mysterious visitor to Cloisterham whose 'white head was unusually large, and his shock of white hair was unusually thick and ample'. Datchery keeps an eye on John Jasper after the disappearance of Edwin Drood. The true identity of Datchery is one of the most contested points of the uncompleted mystery.It is widely believed that Datchery is one of the characters in the book in disguise; most likely candidates include Neville, Bazzard, Tartar, Grewgious, Helena, or even Edwin Drood himself.

Deputy (Winks) Boy hired by Durdles to throw stones at him when he is wandering drunk at night. 'Sometimes the stones hit him, and sometimes they miss him, but Durdles seems indifferent to either fortune. The hideous small boy, on the contrary, whenever he hits Durdles, blows a whistle of triumph through a jagged gap, convenient for the purpose in the front of his mouth, where half his teeth are wanting; and whenever he misses him, yelps out "Mulled agin!"'

Drood, Edwin He is an orphan and had been betrothed by his father to Rosa Bud since early childhood. Later Edwin and Rosa rebel against the arrangement. Rosa is also wooed by Edwin's uncle John Jasper. Edwin turns up missing and his watch is found in the river. Jasper hints suspicion of Neville Landless in the disappearance when the novel stops short with the death of Dickens in 1870.

Durdles Drunken stonemason who engraves tombstones for Cloisterham Cathedral. John Jasper is interested in Durdles's ability to tap on the tombs and discover their contents. Durdles hires Deputy to throw stones at him when he catches him wandering about drunk at night. No man is better known in Cloisterham.

Giggles, Miss Pupil at Miss Twinkleton's school who is described as 'so deficient in sentiment' that she professes to pull faces at any young man paying homage.

Grewgious, Hiram Guardian of Rosa Bud. He is upset at John Jasper's advances to Rosa and finds her lodging in London at an apartment owned by Mrs Billickin. He later investigates the disappearance of Edwin Drood and is suspicious of Jasper. 'An angular man with no conversational powers' is how he describes himself.

Honeythunder, Luke Loud, overbearing philanthropist and guardian of Neville and Helena Landless.

Jasper, John Uncle of Edwin Drood who has an opium habit. He cares for his nephew but harbours secret feelings for Edwin's fiancée Rosa Bud. Edwin disappears and the story ends prematurely with Dickens's death, but many believe that it was Jasper who killed Edwin Drood. 'Mr Jasper is a dark man of some six-and-twenty, with thick, lustrous, well-arranged black hair and whiskers. He looks older than he is, as dark men often do. His voice is deep and good, his face and figure are good, his manner is a little sombre.' He is said to be capable of mesmerism.

Landless, Helena Twin sister of Neville who, as the story ends prematurely, is falling in love with Canon Crisparkle.

Landless, Neville Twin brother of Helena. He and his sister are brought to Cloisterham by their guardian, Mr Honeythunder. Neville is attracted to Rosa Bud and, being set up by Jasper, quarrels with Edwin Drood. After Drood's disappearance Jasper casts blame on Neville, who has no alibi and flees to London with his sister.

Puffer, Princess Old hag who runs the London opium den that John Jasper frequents.

Sapsea, Thomas Pompous auctioneer turned mayor of Cloisterham. 'The purest Jackass in Cloisterham.'

Tartar Retired navy man and friend of Crisparkle. He befriends Neville in London and works with Grewgious and Crisparkle in protecting Neville from John Jasper.

Tisher, Mrs Miss Twinkleton's assistant at the school for girls at Nun's House.

Tope, Mr Chief verger and showman of Cloisterham Cathedral. His wife acts as John Jasper's housekeeper.

Twinkleton, Miss Principal of a school for girls at Nun's House in Cloisterham (Cloisterham was based on Rochester) where Rosa Bud and Helena Landless attend. She is assisted by Mrs Tisher. Miss Twinkleton later becomes Rosa's chaperone in London.

Nicholas Nickleby*: third published novel (1839) as *The Life and Adventures of Nicholas Nickleby

Alphonse Mrs Wititterly's page whose appearance belied his name.

Bolder Pupil at Dotheboys Hall whose father was 'two pound ten short' in the payment of his fees.

Bonney, Mr The promoter of The United Metropolitan Hot Muffin and Crumpet Baking and Punctual Delivery Company.

Bravassa, Miss Beautiful actress in Mr Crummles's company.

Bray, Madeline Cares for her selfish invalid father who tries to sell her in marriage to his creditor Arthur Gride, assisted by Ralph Nickleby. Her father dies and the scheme is exposed. She marries Nicholas at the end of the story.

Bray, Walter Father of Madeline whose sudden death on the morning of his daughter's sham of a wedding day prevents the marriage.

Brooker, Mr Ralph Nickleby's former clerk, who took charge of his employer's son and named him Smike. On returning to England following an eight-year sentence of transportation he reveals Smike's real identity.

Browdie, John Bluff Yorkshire corn factor and stalwart friend of Nicholas Nickleby and Smike. He marries Matilda Price.

Browndock, Miss Mr Nickleby's cousin's sister-in-law.

Bulph, Mr Pilot in whose house the Crummleses live when they visit Portsmouth.

Cheeryble Brothers Charles and Edwin (Ned). Benevolent businessmen who employ and befriend Nicholas Nickleby and his family.

Cheeryble, Frank Nephew of the Cheeryble twins, who marries Kate Nickleby.

Chowser, Colonel Disreputable acquaintance of Ralph Nickleby. He was a Colonel 'of the Militia . . . and the race-courses'.

Crummles, Mr Vincent Manager of a touring acting company who hires Nicholas Nickleby and Smike and becomes their friend.

Dibabs, Jane Former acquaintance of Mrs Nickleby, who cites her as an example of a woman who 'married a man who was a great deal older than herself'.

Dick Blind blackbird owned by Tim Linkinwater and kept in the Cheeryble Brothers' counting-house.

Folair, Mr Pantomimist in Mr Crummles's touring company.

Gallanbile, Mr MP who seeks a cook through the General Agency Office which Nicholas also uses.

Gride, Arthur Old miserly character who tries to buy a marriage to Madeline Bray with the help of her father.

Grudden, Mrs General helper at the Crummles's touring company who could turn her hand to anything.

Hawk, Sir Mulberry Friend of Ralph Nickleby who has lecherous designs on Kate and assaults her. Hawk is a man of fashion and a gambler. He shoots and kills Lord Frederick Verisopht in a duel.

Kenwigs Family Mr Kenwigs was a turner in ivory and he and his family lodged in the same house as Newman Noggs.

Knag, Miss Madame Mantalini's forewoman who ultimately becomes the proprietor of the business.

Knag, Mortimer Brother of Miss Knag, who works as an ornamental stationer and small circulating library keeper in a street off the Tottenham Court Road.

La Creevy, Miss Miniature painter in the Strand. The Nicklebys lease lodging from her briefly and she becomes their faithful friend. In the end she marries the Cheeryble Brothers' old clerk, Tim Linkinwater.

Ledbrook, Miss Actress in Mr Crummles's touring company and a friend of Miss Snevellici.

Lillyvick, Mr Collector of water rates, and Mrs Kenwig's uncle, who marries Henrietta Petowker.

Linkinwater, Tim Faithful clerk to the Cheeryble Brothers and friend of the Nicklebys. He marries Miss La Creevy.

Mantalini, Madame Milliner and dressmaker who employs Kate Nickleby. Her business is ruined by her husband's extravagances and is transferred to Miss Knag.

Mantalini, Mr Husband of Madame Mantalini who ultimately separates from her and becomes bankrupt and imprisoned where he is taken by a laundress to turn a mangle in a cellar. 'My life is one demd horrid grind.'

Nickleby, Kate Sister of Nicholas. She is placed by her uncle, Ralph Nickleby, with Madame Mantalini. She is the object of the undesirable attentions of some of the evil-minded clients of her uncle, who is using her to his advantage.

Nickleby, Mrs Mother of Nicholas and Kate. Absent-minded and self-absorbed, she continues to 'put on airs' even in the reduced situation of her family after the financial ruin and death of her husband. The character is heavily drawn from Dickens's mother.

Nickleby, Nicholas Brother to Kate, nephew of Ralph, and the principal character of the story. Hoping to provide support for his mother and sister after the death of his father, he turns to his uncle Ralph for assistance.

Nickleby, Ralph Uncle to Nicholas and Kate (and later we find, father of Smike). A rich and miserly moneylender who feigns to help his late brother's family but, in reality, tries to humiliate Nicholas and use Kate to his own advantage.

Noggs, Newman Once a well-to-do gentleman but he squanders his money and is reduced to serving Ralph Nickleby as clerk. He befriends Nicholas and eventually helps him escape the designs of Ralph.

Petowker, Miss Henrietta Actress at the Theatre Royal, Drury Lane, who meets Mr Lillyvick at the Kenwigs' home and marries him.

Price, Matilda Miller's daughter, who marries John Browdie.

Pupker, Sir Matthew The chairman of The United Metropolitan

Hot Muffin and Crumpet Baking and Punctual Delivery Company.

Sliderskew, Peg Arthur Gride's housekeeper who steals a box of documents from her master, including a will relating to Madeline Bray's inheritance. Peg is apprehended for the theft and sentenced to transportation.

Smike Abandoned at Dotheboys Hall in the care of the evil Squeers, Smike is mistreated for years before being rescued by Nicholas. He later dies from the treatment he received as a child. After his death it is discovered that he was Ralph Nickleby's son.

Snevellici, Miss Actress in Mr Crummles's touring company and a friend of Miss Ledbrook.

Squeers, Wackford Proprietor of Dotheboys Hall, he took in boys who were not wanted by their families and mistreated them. Nicholas Nickleby becomes his assistant master but sees the way he treats his charges, gives him a sound thrashing, and leaves.

Timberry, Snittle Actor who presides at Vincent Crummles's farewell dinner before the family leaves for America.

Tix, Tom Broker who takes possession of the Mantalinis' business.

Verisopht, Lord Frederick Young nobleman in Ralph Nickleby's circle who is killed in a duel with Sir Mulberry Hawk.

Wititterly, Henry and Julia Married couple living in Cadogan Place, Sloane Street. Kate Nickleby was employed briefly as Mrs Wititterly's companion.

Wrymug, Mrs A 'genteel female' who is a client at the General Agency Office.

***The Old Curiosity Shop*: fourth published novel in 1841**

Barbara 'Little servant-girl', 'very tidy, modest and demure, but very pretty too'.

Brass, Sally Sister and partner of Quilp's unscrupulous attorney, Sampson Brass. She is the mother of the Marchioness, the below-stairs maid.

Brass, Sampson 'An attorney of no good repute', Brass served as Daniel Quilp's lawyer. He helps Quilp get the Curiosity Shop from Nell's grandfather and when he tries to help Quilp frame Kit Nubbles he is undone with the help of his clerk Dick Swiveller.

Cheggs, Mr and Miss Friends of Sophy Wackles, the sweetheart of Dick Swiveller. Mr Cheggs is a market gardener, who eventually marries Sophy, much to the chagrin of Dick.

Codlin and Short Proprietors of a travelling Punch and Judy show that Nell and her grandfather meet on their travels through the English countryside.

Edwards, Miss Student-teacher at Miss Monflathers' Boarding and Day Establishment who lodged for nothing but also received no pay.

Foxey Revered father of Sally and Sampson Brass. His maxim was 'always suspect everybody'.

Grinder, Mr A travelling entertainer who followed behind a couple in Highland dress on stilts, with a drum on his back.

Jarley, Mrs Proprietor of a travelling waxworks who employs Nell and her grandfather. When the grandfather schemes to steal from Mrs Jarley, in order to support a gambling habit, Nell persuades him that they should take to the road again.

Jiniwin, Mrs Mrs Quilp's mother, who has many unsuccessful verbal run-ins with Daniel Quilp.

Monflathers, Miss Head of the Boarding and Day Establishment in the town where Mrs Jarley sets up her waxwork exhibition.

Nell's Grandfather Owner of the Old Curiosity Shop. He has a secret gambling habit, hoping to make a fortune for his granddaughter. He borrows money to gamble from Quilp. When he cannot pay he takes Nell and escapes London to the country. When Nell dies he is heart-broken.

Nubbles, Kit Kit is shop boy at the Curiosity Shop owned by Nell's grandfather.

Quilp, Daniel An evil dwarf who lends money to Nell's grandfather who gambles it away and flees London with Nell in an attempt to avoid Quilp. Quilp attempts to find the pair as they travel through the country. Later Quilp is pursued by the police and, lost in the fog, he drowns in the Thames.

Single Gentleman, The Mysterious lodger of the Brasses who is trying to find Nell and her grandfather. He is revealed to be the brother of the grandfather and finds the pair shortly before his brother's death.

Slum, Mr Tallish gentleman who composes verses to advertise products for a fee.

Sweet William Travelling conjuror met by Little Nell and her grandfather at the Jolly Sandboys.

Swiveller, Dick Friend of Fred Trent who has designs to marry Fred's sister Nell Trent but is encouraged to wait until Nell has inherited her grandfather's money. When Nell and her grandfather leave London Swiveller is befriended by Quilp, who helps him gain employment.

The Marchioness Dick Swiveller's nickname for the little servant kept locked below stairs by the Brasses. Swiveller later marries her.

Trent, Fred Nell's brother, a gambler, would like to get his hands on his grandfather's money through his friend Dick Swiveller.

Trent, Nelly Known as Little Nell, she is the principal character in the story. She lives with her grandfather, when he falls into the clutches of Daniel Quilp she helps him escape London. The hardships endured during their wanderings are too much for the delicate Nell.

Wackles, Sophy First love of Dick Swiveller. Swiveller reluctantly leaves her and enters into a scheme, hatched by Nell's brother Fred Trent, to marry Nell and inherit the grandfather's money. Sophy marries Cheggs, a market gardener.

Whisker Self-willed pony who, from being the most obstinate and opinionated pony on the face of the earth, was, in Kit Nubbles's hands, the meekest and most tractable of animals.

***Oliver Twist*: second published novel, originally in *Bentley's Miscellany* between February 1837 and April 1839 in 24 monthly instalments**

Artful Dodger, The *See* Jack Dawkins.

Bates, Charley Member of Fagin's band of thieves. He mends his ways after Fagin is captured.

Bedwin, Mrs A 'motherly old lady' who is Mr Brownlow's housekeeper.

Betsy (Bet) Prostitute and friend of Nancy. Goes mad after identifying Nancy's body.

Blathers Bow Street Runner (London policeman) who, along with Duff, investigates the attempted robbery of the Maylie home.

Brittles Despite being over 30 years old, described as a 'lad of all work' residing at Mrs Maylie's.

Brownlow, Mr Adopts Oliver after he is charged with pickpocketing. He later establishes Oliver's true identity.

Bull's-eye Bill Sikes's white shaggy dog who falls to his death at the same time as Sikes accidentally hangs himself on Jacob's Island, Bermondsey.

Bumble, Mr Beadle at the workhouse where Oliver is born. He mistreats the residents in his care and becomes the symbol of Dickens's distaste for the workhouse system. Bumble names the foundling Twist due to his coming next alphabetically after the last 'Swabble'. In fact he says the next one will be 'Unwin' and then 'Vilkins'. He marries Mrs Corney and later is disgraced and becomes a resident in the same workhouse. Famous quote when told by Mr Brownlow that the law supposes that your wife acts under your directions: 'If the law supposes that, then the law is a ass . . . a idiot.'

Charlotte Maidservant to Mr and Mrs Sowerberry. She is very partial to Noah Claypole, whom she feeds with oysters.

Chickweed, Conkey According to Blathers, he was a publican who carried out a fake burglary on himself, althought the crime was detected by Jem Spyers.

Chitling, Tom Member of Fagin's gang and Betsy's sweetheart.

Claypole, Noah Assistant at Sowerberry's with whom Oliver fights. Noah later joins Fagin's band and spies on Nancy. After Fagin's capture he testifies against him and becomes an informer for the police.

Corney, Mrs Matron of the workhouse where Oliver is born. She marries Bumble, making him miserable. The Bumbles are disgraced and end up as paupers in the workhouse they once ruled over.

Dawkins, Jack The most successful and interesting of Fagin's thieves. He shows Oliver the ropes of the pickpocket game and is later captured and sentenced to transportation. Dawkins is better known as The Artful Dodger.

Duff Bow Street Runner (London policeman) who, along with Blathers, investigates the attempted robbery of the Maylie home.

Fagin A crafty old Jew who runs a thieves' school near Field Lane in Saffron Hill. Oliver falls in with Fagin's band when he runs away from the workhouse. When Fagin attempts to help Monks destroy Oliver's reputation he is arrested and executed at Newgate.

Fleming, Agnes Mother of Oliver, whom she gives birth to out of wedlock with Edwin Leeford and subsequently dies at the workhouse. Agnes is also the sister of Rose Maylie.

Gamfield, Mr Cruel chimney sweep who does not let the safety of his sweeps concern him. 'Even if they've stuck in a chimbley, roasting their feet makes 'em struggle to hextricate themselves.'

Grimwig, Mr Cantankerous friend of Mr Brownlow. Quote: 'I'll eat my head!'

Kags Robber who was in the house on Jacob's Island when Bill Sikes sought refuge there.

Leeford, Edward Villainous son of Edwin and half-brother of Oliver Twist who plots with Fagin to corrupt Oliver, in which case Leeford will inherit all of their father's property. After the plan is foiled Leeford is forced to emigrate to America, where he dies in prison. Leeford is referred to as Monks.

Leeford, Edwin Father of Oliver, whom he has fathered out of wedlock with Agnes Fleming. Also father of Edward (Monks) from a previous marriage. Edwin has died before the story begins.

Losberne, Dr Impetuous doctor who treats Oliver and Rose in illness. A friend of the Maylie family.

Mann, Mrs Matron of a workhouse farm where Oliver is raised until he is nine years old.

Maylie, Harry Son of Mrs Maylie, he marries Rose.

Maylie, Mrs Mother of Harry and the adopted mother of Rose.

Maylie, Rose A poor girl adopted by Mrs Maylie. She and Mr Brownlow endeavour to help Oliver through Nancy. When Nancy's conversation with Rose on London Bridge is overheard by Claypole, Nancy is murdered by Sikes. She later marries Harry.

Monks *See* Edward Leeford.

Nancy Prostitute and member of Fagin's band of thieves. Befriends Oliver and is eventually murdered by Sikes trying to help Oliver escape Fagin's clutches.

Sally, Old Old hag present at Oliver's birth. She steals the locket and ring from Oliver's mother as she lies dying.

Sikes, Bill A vicious thief working on the fringes of Fagin's band of pickpockets. He uses Oliver in an attempt to burgle the Brownlow home. When Nancy tries to help Oliver she is found out by Fagin who relates the information to Sikes. He murders Nancy, and later hangs himself by accident while trying to escape a hue-and-cry.

Slout Master of the workhouse where Oliver was born, replaced by Mr Bumble following his death.

Sowerberry, Mr Undertaker to whom Oliver is apprenticed. Oliver is mistreated and runs away to London.

Spyers, Jem Bow Street Runner who detected the deception of Conkey Chickweed's fake burglary.

Twist, Oliver Principal character in the story. He is born in a workhouse, where he is mistreated by Bumble, the beadle (quote: 'Please sir, may I have some more?'). He is apprenticed to Sowerberry, the undertaker, and runs away to London where he falls in with Fagin.

***Our Mutual Friend*: fourteenth novel, published in 1865**

Blight Mortimer Lightwood's office boy, often referred to as 'young Blight'.

Blogg, Mr Beadle who permits Betty Higden to adopt Sloppy

Boffin, Mrs Henrietta Noddy Boffin's wife, who, unlike her husband, enjoyed the good life.

Boffin, Nicodemus John Harmon's servant. When John's son is supposed drowned, Boffin and his wife inherit the Harmon fortune, for a time.

Boots and Brewer Guests at the Veneerings' social gatherings.

Dolls, Mr Father of Jenny Wren, whose real name is Cleaver but is called Mr Dolls by Eugene Wrayburn.

Gliddery, Bob Pot-boy at the Six Jolly Fellowship Porters.

Goody, Mrs The Reverend Mr Milvey suggests that the Boffins adopt her grandchild but his wife disagrees, as she is an 'inconvenient woman, who drank eleven cups of tea the previous Christmas, and grumbled all the time'.

Handford, Julius Alias taken by John Harmon in order to investigate his own supposed drowning.

Harmon, John Son of a wealthy dust contractor and heir to his fortune if he agrees to marry Bella Wilfer. He is away from England when his father dies, and on the way home he is supposed drowned in a case of mistaken identity.

Headstone, Bradley A schoolteacher and master of the boys department of a school on the borders of Kent and Surrey. He becomes obsessed with Lizzie Hexam. Lizzie wants nothing to do with him and he becomes jealous.

Hexam, Charley Brother of Lizzie and son of Gaffer, who becomes Bradley Headstone's pupil.

Hexam, Gaffer Waterman, father of Lizzie, who plies the Thames looking for dead bodies. He finds a body thought to be John Harmon, the central character in the story.

Hexam, Lizzie Daughter of waterman Gaffer Hexam and sister of Charley. She is opposed to her father's business of combing the Thames looking for drowned bodies but is true to him. When her father drowns she goes to live with Jenny Wren. Eventually she marries Eugene Wrayburn.

Higden, Betty Almost 80 years old but still very active. She keeps 'a Minding School' for children.

Kibble, Jacob Fellow-passenger with John Harmon on the voyage from the Cape to London.

Lightwood, Mortimer A lawyer, too lazy to take on much work, and friend of Eugene Wrayburn. His only clients are the Boffins, which puts him in the middle of much of the story.

Milvey, Mrs Margaretta Wife of the Reverend Milvey and mother of their six children.

Milvey, the Reverend Frank The Boffins' clergyman, whom they consult when they decide to adopt an orphan.

Potterson, Miss Abbey Proprietor of the Six Jolly Fellowship Porters, on the Thames.

Riah 'An old Jewish man, in an ancient coat, long of skirt and wide of pocket' who fronts a money-lending business. He befriends Lizzie Hexam and Jenny Wren.

Riderhood, Rogue Waterman and former partner of Gaffer Hexam who tries to pin blame on Gaffer for the Harmon murder to gain a reward. Riderhood later becomes a lock-keeper and tries to blackmail Bradley Headstone after Bradley tries to murder Eugene Wrayburn.

Rokesmith, John Alias used by John Harmon when he is employed as secretary to the Boffins.

Sloppy Orphan boy adopted by Betty Higden and given the job of turning the mangle at her Minding School.

Tootle, Tom Gentleman who tells Miss Abbey Potterson that a man has been run down in a wherry, by a foreign steamer, on the Thames. The man turns out to be Rogue Riderhood.

Veneering, Hamilton & Anastasia High society couple at whose frequent dinner parties the story of John Harmon is discovered. Hamilton buys his way into Parliament and is later bankrupt and the couple flee to France.

Venus, Mr Taxidermist and dealer in bones and skeletons who owned a 'little dark greasy' shop in Clerkenwell.

Wegg, Silas Rascally street vendor hired by Mr Boffin to read to him. Wegg is illiterate and makes the stories up as he goes along. After installing himself in the Boffin household he goes about trying to get a piece of the Boffin fortune.

Wilfer, Bella Girl specified in old Harmon's will as the one that his son John should marry in order to gain his inheritance. When John disappears and is presumed drowned she is left 'a widow without ever being married'. She leaves her home and goes to live with the Boffins.

Williams, William Regular customer of Miss Abbey Potterson at the Six Jolly Fellowship Porters.

Wrayburn, Eugene Lawyer and friend of Mortimer Lightwood. 'If there is a word in the dictionary under any letter from A to Z that i abominate, it is energy.' He becomes interested in the Harmon case and meets Lizzie Hexam and falls in love with her. She loves him also but tries to distance herself from him because they come from different classes of society.

Wren, Jenny aka Fanny Cleaver Crippled dolls' dressmaker with whom Lizzie Hexam lives after the death of her father. She helps Lizzie escape London when pursued by Headstone and Wrayburn.

Pickwick Papers:* first published novel and serialised between April 1836 and November 1837 as *The Posthumous Papers of the Pickwick Club

Allen, Arabella Sister of Benjamin, who attempted to marry her to his friend Bob Sawyer. Arabella eventually marries Nathaniel Winkle.

Allen, Benjamin Medical student and close friend of Bob Sawyer.

Bagman, The Appears twice in the novel, first at the Peacock, Eatanswill, and then at the Bush Inn, Bristol, reciting a story on each occasion: 'The Bagman's Story' and 'The Bagman's Uncle'.

Bantam, Angelo Cyrus Master of Ceremonies at Bath.

Bardell, Mrs Martha Mr Pickwick's landlady in Goswell Street.

Betsy Mrs Raddle's dirty and slipshod maid.

Bladud, Prince Legendary founder of Bath, the subject of 'The True Legend of Prince Bladud' that Mr Pickwick reads in his bedroom.

Boffer A Stock Exchange broker, on whose probable methods and timing of committing suicide Wilkins Flasher and Frank

Simmery placed bets.

Boldwig, Captain 'Little fierce man in a stiff black neckerchief and blue surtout', who discovered Mr Pickwick asleep in a wheelbarrow on his land.

Bolo, Miss Mr Pickwick's whist partner whilst at Bath, who 'went straight home in a flood of tears, and a sedan chair' due to his bad play.

Brooks Pieman who could 'make pies out o' anything' including cats. He lodged at Sam Weller's.

Brown The Muggleton shoemaker, whose name on Rachael Wardle's shoes, which had been left with Sam Weller for cleaning, showed Mr Wardle that she was staying at the White Hart.

Budger, Mrs Elderly widow with whom Mr Jingle dances at the Rochester ball, in Mr Winkle's dress-suit, to the jealous fury of Doctor Slammer, who consequently challenges the unfortunate Winkle to a duel.

Bulder, Colonel Head of the Rochester garrison who attends the charity ball also attended by the Pickwick-ians. Bulder also commands the military review at Chatham when Mr Pickwick gets in the way.

Bullman Plaintiff in the case discussed by Dodson and Fogg's clerks in the hearing of Mr Pickwick and Sam Weller.

Burton, Thomas Member of the Brick Lane Branch of the United Grand Junction Ebenezer Temperance Association. 'Purveyor of cat's meat to the Lord Mayor and Sheriffs, and several members of the Common Council.'

Buzfuz, Sergeant Bullying counsel for Mrs Bardell, who is a wicked caricature of a type of histrionic advocate frequently encountered in those days.

Charley Dishevelled, red-headed pot-boy at the Magpie and Stump where Mr Pickwick and Sam Weller go in search of Mr Lowten.

Cripps, Tom Errand-boy to Benjamin Allen and Bob Sawyer.

Crookey Servant at Namby's sponging-house.

Dodson and Fogg Mrs Bardell's attorneys who commit her to prison for non-payment of their costs.

Dowler, Mr and Mrs Army officer and his wife who travelled with Mr Pickwick to Bath.

Dumkins, Mr A formidable cricketer who played for the All-Muggleton club.

Fizkin, Horatio Buff candidate in the Eatanswill election, who was defeated by the Honourable Samuel Slumkey.

Flasher, Wilkins A Stock Exchange broker who, with Frank Simmery, placed bets on Boffer's probable methods and timing of committing suicide.

Groffin, Thomas Chemist, who attempts, unsuccessfully, to be excused jury duty in the case of Bardell v Pickwick.

Grub, Gabriel Subject of 'The Story of the Goblins who stole a Sexton' as told by Mr Wardle.

Grundy, Mr Gentleman who refuses to oblige the company with a song at the Magpie and Stump where Mr Pickwick and Sam Weller have arranged to meet Mr Lowten.

Harris Greengrocer in whose shop the Bath footmen hold their party.

Humm, Mr Anthony President of the Brick Lane Branch of the United Grand Junction Ebenezer Temperance Association.

Hunt Head gardener to Captain Boldwig, who is receiving orders from his master when the appearance of Mr Pickwick asleep in a wheelbarrow on his land is brought to the attention of Boldwig.

Isaac A 'shabby man in black leggings' who accompanies Mr Jackson when he arrests Mrs Bardell.

Jackson, Mr Dodson and Fogg's clerk who arrests Mrs Bardell and serves the Pickwickians with subpoenas to attend the trial.

Jingle, Alfred A wandering rascal who befriends Mr Pickwick and accompanies the group to the Wardle home at Dingley Dell. He entices Miss Rachael to elope with him and is run down and bought off by Rachael's brother. Pickwick eventually exposes Jingle, who uses the alias of Charles Fitz-Marshall when tricking Pickwick into thinking he is planning another elopement.

Jinkins, Mr Suitor of the widow in 'The Bagman's Story'.

Jinks, Mr Dishevelled-looking clerk who worked for Mr Nupkins as the magistrate's adviser.

Lowten, Mr Mr Perker's clerk who first meets Mr Pickwick after singing a comic song at the Magpie and Stump.

Muzzle Mr Nupkins's footman who challenges Job Trotter to a fight over the affections of the cook.

Namby, Mr Sheriff's deputy of Bell Alley, Coleman Street, who arrests Mr Pickwick at the suit of Mrs Bardell.

Nupkins, Mr George Magistrate in attendance on the Pickwickian expedition to Ipswich.

Perker, Mr Mr Wardle's lawyer at Gray's Inn, who looks after Mr Pickwick's interests in the case of Bardell v Pickwick.

Pickwick, Samuel Founder and Chairman of the Pickwick Club. Pickwick, along with his friends Tupman, Snodgrass and Winkle and his servant Sam Weller, travel around England in search of adventure. Pickwick is one of Dickens's most loved characters.

Porkenham Family Close friends of the Nupkins family. George Nupkins is horrified at the possibility that they might know the true identity of Captain Fitz-Marshall.

Roker, Tom Turnkey at the Fleet, who shows Mr Pickwick his accommodation for the next three months.

Samba, Quanko Bowler in the West Indies cricket match described by Alfred Jingle at Dingley Dell. He apparently bowled Jingle out but never recovered from his exertions and died.

Sawyer, Bob Medical student and close friend of Benjamin Allen. 'Sawyer, late Nockemorf', who eventually gains a medical appointment in India.

Simmery, Frank A Stock Exchange broker, who, with Wilkins Flasher, placed bets on Boffer's probable methods and timing of committing suicide.

Skimpin, Mr Sergeant Buzfuz's assistant during the trial of Bardell v Pickwick.

Slammer, Dr Surgeon who is infuriated when Alfred Jingle, wearing Nathaniel Winkle's coat, dances with Mrs Budger, and consequently challenges Winkle to a duel, but discovers the mistaken identity before any damage is done.

Slasher, Dr Surgeon at St Bartholomew's Hospital, who was said to be the best operator alive. 'Took a boy's leg out of the socket last week, boy ate five apples and a gingerbread cake exactly two minutes after it was all over, boy said that he wouldn't lie there to be made game of and he'd tell his mother if they didn't begin.'

Slumkey, the Hon. Samuel Blue candidate in the Eatanswill election, who defeated Horatio Fizkin.

Slurk, Mr Editor of the *Eatanswill Independent* who has a furious quarrel with a rival editor.

Snodgrass, Augustus A member of the Pickwick Club and party to the adventures of Pickwick's travels. He falls in love with Emily Wardle and marries her at the end of the story.

Snubbin, Sergeant Mr Pickwick's counsel for defence in the trial of Bardell v Pickwick, who proves out of his depth against the redoubtable Sergeant Buzfuz.

Struggles, Mr Extremely passionate but unsuccessful bowler for the Dingley Dell cricket team.

Trotter, Job Servant to Alfred Jingles who has a couple of run-ins with Sam Weller, who takes a dislike to him, not least because he has a habit of calling him Mr Walker.

Trundle, Mr Partner of Isabel Wardle in a game of cards and ultimately becomes her partner in marriage.

Tupman, Tracy A member of the Pickwick Club, and travelling companion to Mr Pickwick in the story's adventures.

Upwitch, Richard Greengrocer who was a jury member in the trial of Bardell v Pickwick.

Wardle, Emily Daughter of Mr Wardle and niece of Rachael, who marries Augustus Snodgrass.

Wardle, Isabella Daughter of Mr Wardle and niece of Rachael, who marries Mr Trundle.

Wardle, Mr Yeoman farmer and owner of Manor Farm at Dingley Dell. Pickwick and his friends visit Manor Farm frequently. Wardle's daughter marries Pickwickian Augustus Snodgrass. Jingle tries to elope with Miss Rachael, Wardle's sister, but is caught and bought off.

Wardle, Rachael Sister of Mr Wardle who was persuaded to elope by Mr Jingle but is accosted by Mr Pickwick at the White Hart Inn and Jingle is bought off for £120.

Weller, Sam Mr Pickwick's servant is one of the most popular characters in Dickens's works. He counsels his master with Cockney wisdom and is thoroughly devoted to Pickwick. Sam has an unfortunate habit of transposing Ws and Vs to comical effect.

Weller, Tony Samuel's father, Tony Weller, is equally entertaining, also having the same unfortunate habit of transposing Ws and Vs to comical effect.

Whiffers, Mr Footman who resigns at the 'swarry' at Bath because the requirement for him to eat cold meat was a manly outrage.

Wicks, Mr One of Dodson and Fogg's clerks.

Wildspark, Tom Tony Weller's example of the importance of an alibi 'Ve got Tom Vildspark off that 'ere manslaughter, with a alleybi, ven all the bigvigs to a man said as nothing couldn't save him.'

Wilkins Gardener to Captain Boldwig, who brings to the attention of his master the appearance of Mr Pickwick asleep in a wheelbarrow on his land.

Winkle, Nathaniel Member of the Pickwick Club and travelling companion to Pickwick and his friends. He marries Arabella Allen, which upsets his father. Later Winkle's father comes to London and sees his daughter-in-law for himself, and is reconciled to the marriage.

Wugsby, Mrs Colonel One of the ladies that Mr Pickwick plays cards with at Bath.

***A Tale of Two Cities*: twelfth novel, serialised in *All the Year Round* in weekly parts from April to November 1859**

Carton, Sydney Lawyer who is able to get a charge of treason reversed for Charles Darnay due to a strong physical resemblance. He later takes Darnay's place at the guillotine. Quote: 'It is a far, far better thing I do than I have ever done.'

Cruncher, Jerry Messenger for Tellson's Bank who moonlights as a grave robber.

Darnay, Charles Nephew of Marquis St Evrémonde. He is tried for treason in London and is acquitted due to his resemblance to Sydney Carton. He marries Lucie Manette, daughter of Dr Manette. He returns to Paris to help a friend imprisoned there and is arrested once more.

Defarge, Ernest Husband of Madame Defarge and keeper of a wine shop in Paris. He is a leader among the revolutionaries.

Defarge, Madame Thérèse Wife of wine-shop keeper Ernest Defarge, and a leader among the revolutionaries. She records enemies of the Republic in her knitting. She accidentally shoots herself dead in a struggle with Miss Pross in Paris.

Foulon, Joseph-François Unscrupulous financier of the ancien régime who is seized by a mob and decapitated.

Gabelle, Théophile Postmaster in the village of St Evrémonde who is arrested when the French Revolution begins. Dickens named the character after the salt tax imposed in the pre-revolutionary days.

Jacques Name by which several of the French revolutionaries are known. Defarge is 'Jacques Four'.

Lorry, Jarvis A clerk in Tellson's bank who is instrumental in bringing Dr Manette, who is imprisoned in Paris, back to England. He returns to Paris to look after the bank's interest after the Revolution starts and while there helps Lucie and Charles Darnay in their predicament.

Manette, Dr Alexandre A prisoner in the Bastille in Paris for eighteen years. He is released and accompanies his daughter, Lucie, and Jarvis Lorry to England. He returns to Paris after the outbreak of the Revolution and, as a former prisoner, is able to secure Darnay's release.

Manette, Lucie Daughter of Dr Manette. She is taken to Paris by Jarvis Lorry when her father is released from prison. She marries Charles Darnay but is adored from afar by Sydney Carton, who feels unfit for her. Darnay and Lucie have a daughter, also named Lucie. When Darnay is imprisoned in Paris by the revolutionaries Carton takes his place at the guillotine, thereby fulfilling his promise to help Lucie.

Pross, Miss Lucie Manette's loyal maid. In the end of the novel she struggles with Madame Defarge and Defarge is killed in the scuffle.

Pross, Solomon/John Barsad Miss Pross's brother, who sneaks Carton into the prison to trade places with Darnay.

Stryver, Mr Solicitor friend of Sydney Carton who helps to defend Charley Darnay from the charges of treason.

'Vengeance, The' Fiery woman friend of Madame Defarge who regularly attended the executions at the guillotine.

The Pilgrim's Progress by John Bunyan

To give the religious allegory its full title, *The Pilgrim's Progress: From this World to That Which is to Come.* The story begins with a man having a dream, in which he sees a troubled man carrying a book. This, we shortly learn, is **Christian**, the pilgrim of the title. Christian first meets **Evangelist**, who gives him a parchment roll on which is written 'Flee from the wrath to come' and tells him to go to the **wicket-gate** via the **shining light**. Christian sets out on a wondrous journey towards heaven and salvation. His neighbours **Obstinate** and **Pliable** attempt to bring him back to his abandoned family, living in what Christian describes as **the city of destruction**, but to no avail, and Pliable decides to accompany him on his journey. On their way Christian falls into a slough (called Despond) and Pliable readily abandons him. Fortunately **Help** is at hand who plucks him out of the **slough of Despond** and he continues on his way, next meeting **Mr Worldly Wiseman** (who lives in the town of **Carnal Policy**). Christian tells Mr Worldly Wiseman of his great burden since reading the book; he is advised to go to the town of **Morality** and talk to **Legality** or **Civility**, and thus ease his burden.

The town is at the top of an ever-steepening hill which begins to breathe fire. Christian begins to quake with fear but comes upon Evangelist, who reminds him of his righteous path to the wicket-gate. On reaching his destination Christian reads the words 'knock and it shall be open to you' over the gate, and on knocking he meets **Goodwill** and tells him he is going to Mount Zion to be delivered from the wrath to come. Goodwill tells Christian of the nearby castle lorded over by Beelzebub and how Christian should take joy in his burden until it is time to relinquish it. He also tells him to knock on the door of the **Translator**, who will guide him. The Translator shows Christian into a dark room with an iron cage, inside which a man is locked. The man was once a respected professor but is now in despair as he has hardened his heart against God.

Christian next comes to the wall called **Salvation** and then ascends towards a cross with a sepulchre beneath it. The sight of the cross causes his burden to drop from his back, and he is moved to tears. He then sees three **Shining Ones**, the first saying to him 'Thy sins be forgiven thee.' The second strips him of his rags and clothes him in finery, while the third places a mark on his forehead and gives him a roll with a seal on it, which is to be given in at the **Celestial Gate**. Christian then meets **Simple**, **Sloth** and **Presumption**, who are in fetters but seemingly oblivious to their predicament. Further on he meets **Formalist** and **Hypocrisy**, born in the land of **Vainglory**. On approaching a hill with three ways

Christian decides to take the steepest route, called **Difficulty**, while Formalist and Hypocrisy take the other two ways, **Danger** and **Destruction**. Danger leads one to a dark wood while Destruction causes the other to fall into an abyss and to be seen no more. Christian sleeps in an arbour midway up the hill Difficulty; while asleep he loses his roll, and he wakes to hear a voice telling him to 'go to the ant thy sluggard, consider her ways and be wise'. He goes further up the hill and meets two more men, **Timorous** and **Mistrust**, who warn him of the lions in his path. He then realises he has lost his roll and goes back to the arbour, where he retrieves it with joy.

Christian travels onwards to **The Palace Beautiful** and spies the two lions, but goes on unharmed. He meets the porter of the house, **Watchful**, who asks him his name. Christian tells him but also informs him his name was once **Graceless**. Watchful calls for the damsel, **Discretion**, who introduces Christian to her sisters **Prudence**, **Piety** and **Charity**. Christian tells them he has a wife and four small children but explains that he could not avail of them to join him in his pilgrimage. Christian sleeps at the Palace in a chamber called **Peace**. The next day the damsels tell Christian of **Immanuel's Land** and **The Delectable Mountains** and they arm him with **proof** in case of assaults, so he may continue his journey in safety. Before Christian leaves, Watchful tells him that **Faithful**, a friend and fellow pilgrim, had passed some time before. Christian departs with some bread, wine and raisins, and in the **Valley of Humiliation** meets the hideous monster **Apollyon**. Christian wants to turn back but knows he has no armour for his back so does not want to turn it. Apollyon has scales like a fish, feet like a bear, wings like a dragon and a mouth like a lion, from which smoke and fire bellow.

Christian is alarmed that Apollyon knows of his struggle but warns him that he feels protected by the **Lord of the Hill**. Apollyon aims flaming darts at Christian but his shield protects him somewhat, although he is wounded all over his body. The battle lasts half a day before, in desperation, Christian waves his sword and smites at the mighty Apollyon, defying him to kill him so he might rise again. With this Apollyon flies away, never to be seen again.

Christian is given some leaves from a hand from the **Tree of Life** and his wounds are healed. He travels onwards through the **Valley of the Shadow of Death** with his sword in hand. His journey is hazardous, with quagmires and ditches all around, the dark gloom and terrible cries of fear adding to his perilous state. Through the midst of the valley he encounters dragons, hobgoblins and satyrs, but keeps the faith and eventually comes to an ascent at the end of the valley. Here he meets his old friend and townsman Faithful, who relays to him his adventurous journey. Faithful missed falling into the slough of Despond but had to resist the temptress named **Wanton**.

The pilgrims journey on to the town of Vanity and find at the town a fair named **Vanity Fair**, named from the fair colour of the town. Legion, Beelzebub and Apollyon set up the fair 5,000 years before. To reach the **Celestial City** the pilgrims have to venture through the wretched town and are set upon by the townsfolk and caged in chains. They are asked what they want to buy at the fair and they answer '**truth**'. Faithful is brought before the judge **Lord Hategood** and three witnesses – **Envy**, **Gainglory** and **Superstition**, all three being worshippers of Beelzebub – are called to give evidence against him. The jury are **Mr Blindman** (the foreman), **Mr No Good**, **Mr Malice**, **Mr Love Lust**, **Mr Live Loose**, **Mr Heady**, **Mr High Mind**, **Mr Liar**, **Mr Enmity**, **Mr Cruelty**, **Mr Hate Light** and **Mr Implacable** (sometimes known as **Mr No Satisfying**). Faithful is found guilty, scourged and pierced with swords and knives and then burnt. On his death he is transported by chariot unto the Celestial Gate. Christian is saved by divine intervention and flees, accompanied by another friend, **Hopeful**, who appears after the death of Faithful.

They meet a man called **By-ends** (though he does not tell them his name) from a town called **Fair Speech**. By-ends tells of his friends, **Lord Turnabout**, **Lord Time-Server**, **Lord Fair Speech**, **Mr Smooth Man**, **Mr Facing Both Ways**, **Mr Anything** and **Mr Two Tongues**, the Parson of the manor. He also speaks of his wife, **Madam Feigning's daughter**. The pilgrims fail to persuade By-ends to mend his ways, so they refuse his company and continue their journey ahead of the unrepentant sinner. They turn to see three men following By-ends, **Mr Hold The World**, **Mr Money Love** and **Mr Save All**, all being former school friends of By-ends and all being taught by **Mr Gripe Man**, a school teacher in **Love Gain**, a marketing town in the county of **Coveting** in the north. The four men debate their self-satisfying version of the scriptures and then catch up with the pilgrims to proffer the view that it is virtuous to make use of religion for monetary profit. Christian is furious and cites many biblical verses in an attempt to teach the men the error of their ways, before again setting off ahead of them and coming to a luxurious plain called **Ease**.

On the other side of the plain is a hill called **Lucre** and in that hill lies a silver mine, about which many have been killed by the uncertain ground surrounding its entrance. A man named **Demas** is beckoning travellers into the mine but the pilgrims resist. Demas says he is the son of Abraham, but Christian knows **Gehazi** to be his great-grandfather and Judas his father. By-Ends and his friends do of course answer the call of Demas and are heard of no more. The pilgrims now venture upon a pillar in the form of a woman; on her head is written 'Remember Lot's Wife', and they know it to be the wretched woman who looked back with a covetous heart when fleeing Sodom. Further on they come to what King David called 'The River of God' and John 'The River of the Water of Life'. They drink the water and eat the fruit on the trees in the nearby **By-path** meadow and are revitalised. After some days they journey onwards and meet a man named **Vain Confidence**, who tells them a certain path leads to the Celestial Gate. So they follow him, but alas, Vain Confidence falls into a deep pit in the gathering gloom. The pilgrims sleep.

Not far from where they lie is a castle called **Doubting Castle**; its owner's name is **Giant Despair** and it is on his property that they lie. He awakes them and imprisons them in a dark and dank dungeon within his castle for four days (Wednesday morning to Saturday night) without food or drink. **Diffidence**, the wife of the giant, instructs him to beat the pilgrims, and when she realises they are still alive tells him to instruct the pilgrims to take their own lives as their plight is hopeless. The pilgrims ask the giant to let them go, angering him so that he rushes towards them to kill them. But he has a fit and loses the use of his hand. When their predicament is almost unbearable, they pray. Christian then remembers he has a key called **Promise** in his coat pocket next to his heart; this key will surely open any lock in Doubting Castle. As they make their escape the giant stirs but fortunately for them has another of his fits, and they arrive back safely on the **King's Highway**. The pilgrims erect a pillar, engraving on it the words 'Over these steps is the way to Doubting Castle, which is kept by Giant Despair, who despises the King of the Celestial Country and seeks to destroy His holy Pilgrims'.

They next approach the **Delectable Mountains** (sometimes called the **Delightful Mountains**), on top of which are shepherds feeding their flocks. The shepherds tell the pilgrims that the mountains were once part of 'Immanuel's Land' and that he laid down his life for all who lived here. The pilgrims then ask how far it is to the Celestial City and are told, 'Too far but for those who get there.' The shepherds, whose names are **Knowledge**, **Experience**, **Watchfulness** and **Sincerity**, take the pilgrims to a hill called **Error**; there at the bottom of the hill are the dead bodies of several who have fallen by the wayside. They then take them to another hill called **Caution**, where they see men who had been blinded by Giant Despair roaming aimlessly among the dead. The shepherds then lead them to another place in a valley where there is a door in the side of a hill. On opening the door, the pilgrims hear cries of torment amid a dark smoky atmosphere and smell the scent of burning sulphur. The shepherds tell them it is the entrance to hell. The shepherds then take them to the top of a high hill called **Clear** and give them a lens through which they may look to see the gates of the city, but the memory of the blind wanderers makes their hands shake and they are unable to see clearly. When they depart on their way the first shepherd gives them a map of the **Way**, another warns them to beware of the **Flatterer**, the third tells them to take heed not to sleep on the **Enchanted Ground** and the fourth bids them God speed.

And so the man awakes from his dream. After a while he sleeps and dreams again.

He sees the pilgrims descending the mountain along the Highway toward the city. On the left side is the country of **Conceit** and on a little crooked lane they meet a lad named **Ignorance** who is also trying to get to the Celestial City, but knows not how. He has lost his way, missing the **Narrow Gate** and coming in by the **Crooked Path**. They next meet **Little Faith**; he has been set upon by three hoodlums, **Faint Heart**, **Mistrust** and **Guilt**, who stole his money but left him with his certificate to hand in at the Celestial Gate. Little Faith did not wear the **Proven Armour** and his journey has been blighted by this apparent loss. Christian and Hopeful then come to a fork in the road and know not which way to go. They meet a man with dark flesh and white robe who tells them to follow him as he knows the way, but only serves to get them entangled in a great net. Fortunately a Shining One frees them after scolding them for following a 'Flatterer' (a false apostle masquerading as an angel of light) and for not reading their maps. Next they come upon a man named **Atheist** with his back to Mount Zion. Atheist laughs at the pilgrims and tells them assuredly there is no Celestial City, for he has been searching for it for 20 years.

The pilgrims then come across the Enchanted Ground and feel drowsy in the sleep-inducing atmosphere, but stay awake by telling each other of their conversion. Over the Enchanted Ground is the country of **Beulah**, whose air is sweet and pleasant. In this country the sun shines night and day, fresh flowers appear daily, and turtle-doves are plentiful. The reflection of the sun on the city is so extremely glorious, with the streets paved with gold and all manner of jewels, that the pilgrims cannot look directly upon it. Upon the bank of a river they see two **Shining Men** who say, 'We are ministering spirits sent to serve those who will inherit salvation.' The two Shining Men go on to tell the pilgrims they have but two more difficulties to experience before entering the Celestial City.

Presently they come to a deep river without a bridge. The pilgrims ask the Shining Men if there is another way and are told, 'Yes, but only Enoch and Elijah have ever been permitted to tread that path.' They are further told that the water will be as deep or as shallow as faith permits. Christian enters with great trepidation and the water begins to cover his head. He cries out to Hopeful, who has found shallower water. Christian thinks the Lord has forsaken him, but Hopeful reminds him that his faith is merely being tried, and with that they find dry land.

The two Shining Men then accompany the pilgrims in their final hardship, up a very steep hill, higher than the clouds, but they make great haste as their mortal clothes are left behind in the river. When they approach the gate a **Heavenly Host** come out to meet them and trumpeters form a heavenly cross around them as if to protect them on the last stretch of their journey. Now when they come up to the gate, written over it in letters of gold are the words 'Blessed are those who wash their robes, that they may have the right to the tree of life and may go through the gates to the city'. At the gate Enoch, Moses, Elijah and other prophets can clearly be seen. The pilgrims give in their certificates and are given harps and crowns, experiencing more joy than the narrator is able to set in print. On looking back one can see Ignorance approach the gate, but he has no certificate and is taken to the door at the side of the hill. And thus the man awakes from his dream.

The Pilgrim's Progress (part two)

This book tells of the pilgrimage of **Christiana** (Christian's wife); her four sons, **Matthew** (the eldest), **Samuel**, **Joseph** and **James**; and Christiana's friend, **Mercy**. The theme is the conversion of Christiana, which begins with her sorrow at the loss of her husband and the guilt she feels on abandoning him to his lonely pilgrimage. In a dream she sees Christian in paradise and on awakening prays for Mercy. The next morning she is visited by **Secret**, who tells her of Christian and his paradise. She is also visited by her neighbours **Timorous** and Mercy, the first making her excuses as to why she should not trace her husband's steps, the second deciding to accompany her 'a little of the way'.

And thus another epic journey to the Celestial City begins. The old familiar places are visited in the aftermath of Christian's pilgrimage and a whole host of new characters are met, including **Mr Skill** (who heals Matthew, who ate green plums from Beelzebub's orchard, and is given pills to be taken three at a time with tears of repentance), **Mr Great Heart** (their guide), **Mr Mnason** (a Cyprusian), **Grace** (Mr Mnason's daughter who eventually marries Samuel), **Martha** (Mr Mnason's daughter who eventually marries Joseph), and **Mr Valiant-For-Truth** (a noble pilgrim from **Dark Land** who has fought **Wild Head**, **Inconsiderate** and **Pragmatic** in the course of his journey to the Celestial City). The pilgrimage ends with first Christiana, then **Mr About To Fall**, **Mr Feeble Mind**, **Mr Despondency**, **Mr Honest**, Mr Valiant-For-Truth and **Mr Standfast**, all crossing the river into the Celestial City, followed at some distance by the four children. The book contains the ever-popular hymn 'He Who Would Valiant Be'.

Plays and Playwrights

(* denotes playwright's first play)

Playwright	*Play*
Aeschylus	*Oresteia Trilogy*
(*c.* 525–456 BC)	*The Persians*
	Prometheus Bound
	Seven Against Thebes
	Suppliants
Edward Albee	*The American Dream*
(1928–)	*At Home at the Zoo*
	A Delicate Balance
	Knock! Knock! Who's There!?
	Me, Myself and I
	Three Tall Women
	Tiny Alice
	Who's Afraid of Virginia Woolf?
	The Zoo Story
Maxwell Anderson	*Anne of the Thousand Days*
(1888–1959)	
Jean Anouilh	*Antigone*
(1910–87)	*Becket*
	Eurydice
	The Lark (L'Alouette)
	*L'Hermine**
	L'Invitation au Château
	Thieves' Carnival
	Waltz of the Toreadors
John Arden	*All Fall Down**
(1930–)	*Ironhand*
	Live Like Pigs
	Serjeant Musgrave's Dance
	Vandaleur's Folly
	The Workhouse Donkey
Aristophanes	*The Acharnians*
(c448–388 BC)	*The Birds*
	Clouds
	Ecclesiazusae
	The Frogs
	The Knights
	Lysistrata
	The Peace
	Plutus
	Thesmophoriazusae
	The Wasps
W H Auden	*The Ascent of F6*
(1907–73)	*The Dance of Death*
Alan Ayckbourn	*Absent Friends*
(1939–)	*Absurd Person Singular*
	Awaking Beauty
	Bedroom Farce
	Boy Who Fell into a Book
	By Jeeves
	Callisto 5
	A Chorus of Disapproval
	Comic Potential
	Communicating Doors
	Damsels in Distress
	Drowning on Dry Land
	How the Other Half Loves
	If I Were You
	Improbable Fiction
	Jeeves
	Joking Apart
	Just Between Ourselves
	Life and Beth
	Living Together
	Man of the Moment
	Miss Yesterday
	*Mr Whatnot**
	My Wonderful Day
	The Norman Conquests
	Private Fears in Public Places
	Relatively Speaking
	Round and Round the Garden
	Season's Greetings
	Sisterly Feelings
	A Small Family Business
	Snake in the Grass
	Sugar Daddies
	Table Manners
	Ten Times Table
	Things that Go Bump
	Time and Time Again
	Time of My Life
	Way Upstream
	Woman in Mind
J M Barrie	*The Admirable Crichton*
(1860–1937)	*The Boy David (last)*
	Dear Brutus
	Mary Knows
	Peter Pan
	Quality Street
	*Walker, London**
	What Every Woman Knows
H E Bates	*The Last Bread*
(1905–74)	
Pierre Beaumarchais	*The Barber of Seville*
(1732–99)	*Eugénie**
	The Marriage of Figaro
Samuel Beckett	*Breath*
(1906–89)	*Endgame*
	Happy Days
	Ill Seen Ill Said
	Not I
	Waiting for Godot

Playwright	Play
Brendan Behan (1923–64)	*The Hostage* *The Quare Fellow**
Aphra Behn (1640–89)	*The Feigned Courtizans* *The Forced Marriage* *The Rover*
Alan Bennett (1934–)	*An Englishman Abroad* *Forty Years On** *Getting On* *Habeas Corpus* *The Habit of Art* *The History Boys* *Kafka's Dick* *The Madness of George III* *The Old Country* *On the Margin* (1st TV play) *A Question of Attribution* *Talking Heads*
Alan Bleasdale (1946–)	*Are You Lonesome Tonight?* *Boys from the Blackstuff* *Having a Ball* *It's a Madhouse* *Jake's Progress* *The Monocled Mutineer* *No More Sitting on the Old School Bench** *On the Ledge*
Edward Bond (1934–)	*Early Morning* *Narrow Road to the Deep North* *The Pope's Wedding**
Dion Boucicault (*c.* 1820–90)	*The Colleen Bawn* *The Corsican Brothers* *London Assurance* (written under name of Lee Morton) *The Octoroon* *The Shaughraun*
Bertolt Brecht (1898–1956)	*Baal* *The Caucasian Chalk Circle* *Drums in the Night** *Fear and Misery in the Third Reich* *The Good Woman of Setzuan* *Mother Courage* *The Preventable Rise of Arturo Ui* *The Threepenny Opera*
Abe Burrows (1910–85)	*Cactus Flower*
Jim Cartwright (1958–)	*Bed* *Hard Fruit* *The Rise and Fall of Little Voice* *Road**
Anton Chekhov (1860–1904)	*The Bear* *The Cherry Orchard* *Ivanov** *The Island of Sakhalin* *The Seagull* *The Three Sisters* *Uncle Vanya* *The Wood Demon*
Caryl Churchill (1938–)	*The Ants** *Cloud Nine* *Drunk Enough to Say I Love You* *Fen* *Icecream* *Light Shining in Buckinghamshire* *Lives of the Great Poisoners* *A Number* *Serious Money* *Seven Jewish Children* *Softcops* *Top Girls*
Jean Cocteau (1889–1963)	*L'Aigle à deux têtes* *Les Mariés de la Tour Eiffel* *Orpheus* *Ladies' Tailor** *Pig in a Poke*
William Congreve (1670–1729)	*The Double Dealer* *Love for Love* *The Mourning Bride* *The Old Bachelor** *The Way of the World*
Pierre Corneille (1606–84)	*Andromède* *Le Cid* *Cinna* *Clitandre* *La Galerie du Palais* *Horace* *The Liar (Le Menteur)* *Mélite** *La Mort de Pompée* *Nicomède* *Polyeucte* *Pulchérie* *Rodogune* *Théodore* *La Veuve*
Noël Coward (1899–1973)	*Bitter Sweet* *Blithe Spirit* *Cavalcade* *Design for Living* *Easy Virtue* *Fallen Angels* *Hay Fever* *I'll Leave it to You** *Nude with Violin* *Peace in Our Time* *Post Mortem* *Present Laughter* *Private Lives* *Relative Values* *This Happy Breed* *The Vortex*
John Dryden (1631–1700)	*All for Love* *The Indian Emperor* *Marriage à-la-Mode* *The Rival Ladies* *The State of Innocence*
Alexander Dumas (Fils) (1824–95)	*Camille*
T S Eliot (1888–1965)	*The Cocktail Party* *The Confidential Clerk* *The Elder Statesman* *The Family Reunion* *Murder in the Cathedral* *The Rock* *Sweeney Agonistes**
Ben Elton (1959–)	*Blast from the Past* *Gasping** *Popcorn* *Silly Cow*
George Etherege (*c.* 1635–92)	*The Comical Revenge, or Love in a Tub* *The Man of Mode, or Sir Fopling Flutter* *She Would If She Could*
Euripides (*c.* 484–406 BC)	*Alcestis** *Andromache* *The Bacchae* *Electra* *Hecuba* *Helen* *Hippolytus* *Ion* *Iphigenia in Aulis* *Iphigenia in Tauris* *Medea* *The Phoenician Women* *The Trojan Women*
George Farquhar (*c.* 1677–1707)	*The Beaux' Stratagem* *The Constant Couple* *Love and a Bottle** *The Recruiting Officer*
Georges Feydeau (1862–1921)	*An Absolute Turkey* *A Flea in her Ear* *Hotel Paradiso*
Eduardo de Filippo (1900–84)	*Filumena* *La Grande Magia* *Saturday, Sunday, Monday*
Alistair Foot and Anthony Marriot	*No Sex Please, We're British*

Playwright	*Play*
John Ford	*The Broken Heart*
(*c.* 1586–1640)	*The Lady's Trial*
	The Lover's Melancholy
	Perkin Warbeck
	'Tis Pity She's a Whore
Dario Fo	*The Accidental Death of an*
(1926–)	*Anarchist*
Michael Frayn	*Alphabetical Order*
(1933–)	*Benefactors*
	Clouds
	Copenhagen
	Democracy
	Donkeys' Years
	Here
	Look, Look
	Make and Break
	Noises Off
	The Sandboy
	*The Two of Us**
Brian Friel	*Dancing at Lughnasa*
(1929–)	*The Enemy Within*
	Faith Healer
	The Freedom of the City
	The Home Place
	Molly Sweeney
	Philadelphia, Here I Come!
	Translations
	Wonderful Tennessee
Christopher Fry	*The Boy With a Cart*
(1907–2005)	*Curtmantle*
	The Lady's Not for Burning
	A Phoenix Too Frequent
	Thursday's Child
	The Tower
	Venus Observed
John Galsworthy	*The Silver Box*
(1867–1933)	*The Skin Game*
Jean Genet	*The Balcony*
(1910–86)	*The Maids*
	The Screens
John Godber	*April in Paris*
(1956–)	*Big Trouble in the Little*
	Bedroom
	Bouncers
	Funny Turns
	Happy Families
	Happy Jack
	Lucky Sods
	Next Best Thing
	The Office Party
	On a Night Like This
	On the Piste
	Our House
	Salt of the Earth
	September in the Rain
	Shakers
	Teechers
	Up 'N' Under
Johann W von Goethe	*Götz von Berlichingen*
(1749–1832)	*Die Mitschuldigen*
	Egmont
	Erwin und Elmire
	Faust (Parts I & II)
	Iphigenie auf Tauris
	Torquato Tasso
Nikolai Gogol	*The Inspector General*
(1809–52)	
William Golding	*The Brass Butterfly*
(1911–93)	
Oliver Goldsmith	*She Stoops to Conquer*
(1728–74)	
Maxim Gorky	*The Lower Depths*
(1868–1936)	
Harley Granville Barker	*The Madras House*
(1877–1946)	*The Marrying of Ann Leete*
	The Voysey Inheritance
	Waste

Playwright	*Play*
Simon Gray	*Butley*
(1936–2008)	*Cell Mates*
	The Common Pursuit
	Dog Days
	Dutch Uncle
	Hidden Laughter
	The Idiot
	Japes
	The Late Middle Classes
	Life Support
	Molly
	Old Masters
	Otherwise Engaged
	Plaintiffs and Defendants
	Quartermaine's Terms
	The Rear
	Simply Disconnected
	Sleeping Dog
	Spoiled
	Stagestruck
	Two Sundays
	*Wise Child**
John Guare	*The House of Blue Leaves*
(1938–)	*Landscape of the Body*
Patrick Hamilton	*Six Degrees of Separation*
(1904–62)	*Gaslight* (aka: *Angel Street)*
Christopher Hampton	*Rope* (US title: *Rope's End)*
(1946–)	*After Mercer*
	Les Liaisons Dangereuses
	The Philanthropist
	Savages
	The Talking Cure
	Total Eclipse
	Treats
	*When Did You Last See My Mother?**
David Hare	*The Absence of War*
(1947–)	*Gethsemane*
	Knuckle
	Licking Hitler (TV play)
	Man Above Men (TV play)
	Murmuring Judges
	The Power of Yes
	Racing Demon
	The Secret Rapture
	*Slag**
Richard Harris	*The Business of Murder*
(1934–)	*Dead Guilty*
	The Maintenance Man
	Outside Edge
	Stepping Out
Harold Harwood	*The Grain of Mustard Seed*
(1874–1959)	
Ronald Harwood	*After the Lions*
(1934–)	*Another Time*
	*Country Matters**
	The Dresser
	An English Tragedy
	Goodbye Kiss
	The Handyman
	Mahler's Conversion
	Poison Pen
	Reflected Glory
	Taking Sides
Victor Hugo	*Angelo*
(1802–85)	*Cromwell*
	Hernani
	Lucrèce Borgia
	Marie Tudor
	Marion Delorme
	Le Roi s'amuse
	Ruy Blas
Henrik Ibsen	*Catiline**
(1828–1906)	*A Doll's House*
	An Enemy of the People
	Ghosts
	Hedda Gabler
	John Gabriel Borkman
	Love's Comedy

Playwright	*Play*
	The Master Builder *Peer Gynt* *The Wild Duck*
Eugène Ionesco (1912–94)	*The Bald Prima Donna* *Rhinoceros* *The Lesson*
Alfred Jarry (1873–1907)	*Ubu Roi*
Terry Johnson (1955–)	*Dead Funny* *Hitchcock Blonde* *Hysteria* *Imagine Drowning* *Insignificance* *Unsuitable for Adults*
Ben Jonson (1572–1637)	*The Alchemist* *Bartholomew Fair* *Catiline* *Cynthia's Revels* *Every Man in His Humour* *Every Man Out of His Humour* *The Poetaster* *The Sad Shepherd* (unfinished) *Sejanus* *The Silent Woman* *Volpone*
Tom Kempinski (1938–)	*Duet for One* *Separation*
Joseph Kesselring (1902–67)	*Arsenic and Old Lace*
Thomas Kyd (1558–94)	*The Spanish Tragedy*
Mike Leigh (1943–)	*Abigail's Party* *Babies Grow Old* *Big Basil* *The Box Play** *Greek Tragedy* *Individual Fruit Pies* *My Parents Have Gone to Carlisle* *Nuts in May* *Two Thousand Years*
Alain-René Lesage (1668–1747)	*Turcaret*
Ira Levin (1929–2007)	*Deathtrap* *Veronica's Room*
Frederick Lonsdale (1881–1954)	*Aren't We All?* *Canaries Sometimes Sing* *The Last of Mrs Cheyney* *On Approval*
Federico García Lorca (1898–1936)	*Blood Wedding* *The House of Bernarda Alba* *Yerma*
Compton Mackenzie (1883–1972)	*The Gentleman in Grey*
Maurice Maeterlinck (1862–1949)	*The Blue Bird* *La Princesse Maleine* *Mary Magdalene* *Pelléas et Mélisande*
David Mamet (1947–)	*American Buffalo* *Boston Marriage* *The Cryptogram* *Duck Variations* *Glengarry Glen Ross* *A Life in the Theater* *Oleanna* *Sexual Perversity in Chicago* *The Shawl* *Speed-the-Plow*
Christopher Marlowe (1564–93)	*Doctor Faustus* *Edward II* *The Jew of Malta* *The Massacre at Paris* *Tamburlaine the Great*
Conor McPherson (1971–)	*Dublin Carol* *The Weir*
Thomas Middleton (*c.* 1570–1627)	*Blurt* *The Changeling* (with William Rowley) *A Game at Chess* *Master Constable* *The Spanish Gypsy* (with William Rowley) *Women Beware Women*
Arthur Miller (1915–2005)	*After the Fall* *All My Sons** *Broken Glass* *The Crucible* *Danger: Memory!* *Death of a Salesman* *The Last Yankee* *The Man Who Had All the Luck* *The Price* *The Ride Down Mount Morgan* *A View from the Bridge*
Molière (1622–1673)	*The Blue-Stockings* *Le Bourgeois Gentilhomme* *The Impostor* *Le Malade Imaginaire* *Le Misanthrope* *The Miser* *The School for Wives* *Tartuffe*
Nicholas Monsarrat (1910–79)	*The Visitors*
John Mortimer (1923–2009)	*The Dock Brief* *A Voyage Round My Father*
Peter Nichols (1927–)	*Ben Spray* *Born in the Gardens* *Chez Nous* *Daddy Kiss It Better* *A Day in the Death of Joe Egg** *Forget-Me-Not Lane* *The Freeway* *The Heart of the Country* *The National Health* *Nicholodeon* *Passion Play* *A Piece of My Mind* *Poppy* *Privates on Parade* *So Long Life* *Walk on the Grass* (first TV play) *When the Wind Blows*
Edna O'Brien (1932–)	*Flesh and Blood* *Madame Bovary* *Our Father* *Virginia*
Sean O'Casey (1880–1964)	*The Bishop's Bonfire* *Cockadoodle Dandy* *Juno and the Paycock* *The Plough and the Stars* *The Shadow of a Gunman* *The Silver Tassie*
Clifford Odets (1906–63)	*Awake and Sing!* *Golden Boy* *Till the Day I Die* *Waiting for Lefty*
Eugene O'Neill (1888–1953)	*Ah, Wilderness* *Anna Christie* *Beyond the Horizon* *Desire under the Elms* *The Emperor Jones* *The Great God Brown* *The Hairy Ape* *The Iceman Cometh* *Lazarus Laughed* *Long Day's Journey into Night* *Marco Millions* *Mourning Becomes Electra* *Strange Interlude* *A Touch of the Poet* *The Web**
Joe Orton (1933–67)	*Entertaining Mr Sloane** *The Erpingham Camp* *Loot* *The Ruffian on the Stair* *What the Butler Saw*
John Osborne (1929–94)	*The Entertainer* *Epitaph for George Dillon*

Playwright	Play
	The Hotel in Amsterdam
	Inadmissible Evidence
	Jill and Jack (TV play)
	Look Back in Anger
	Luther
	A Patriot for Me
	West of Suez (TV play)
Arthur Wing Pinero (1855–1934)	*The Cabinet Minister*
	Dandy Dick
	The Gay Lord Quex
	His House in Order
	The Magistrate
	Mid-Channel
	The Profligate
	The Schoolmistress
	The Second Mrs Tanqueray
	The Squire
	Trelawny of the 'Wells'
	*£200 a Year**
Harold Pinter (1930–2008)	*Ashes to Ashes*
	Betrayal
	The Birthday Party
	The Caretaker
	The Homecoming
	Hothouse
	Moonlight
	No Man's Land
	One for the Road
	Other Places
	*The Room**
Luigi Pirandello (1867–1936)	*Come Tu Mi Vuoi*
	Enrico IV
	Six Characters in Search of an Author
Sylvia Plath (1932–63)	*Three Women*
J B Priestley (1894–1984)	*Dangerous Corner**
	I Have Been Here Before
	An Inspector Calls
	Laburnum Grove
	The Linden Tree
	Time and the Conways
	When We Are Married
Alexander Pushkin (1799–1837)	*Boris Godunov*
Jean Racine (1639–99)	*Alexandre le Grand*
	Andromaque
	Athalie
	Bajazet
	Bérénice
	Britannicus
	Esther
	Iphigénie
	La Thébaïde, ou Les Frères ennemis
	Mithridate
	Phèdre
Terence Rattigan (1911–77)	*Adventure Story*
	The Browning Version
	Cause Célèbre
	The Deep Blue Sea
	Flare Path
	French Without Tears
	Harlequinade
	Ross
	Separate Tables
	The Winslow Boy
Edmond Rostand (1868–1918)	*Chantecler*
	Cyrano de Bergerac
William Rowley (*c.* 1585–1642)	*A New Wonder: A Woman Never Vext*
Willy Russell (1947–)	*Blind Scouse Trilogy**
	Blood Brothers
	Boy with Transistor Radio
	Breezeblock Park
	Educating Rita
	Hoovering the Moon
	I Read the News Today (radio)
	John, Paul, George Ringo . . . and Bert
	King of the Castle (TV play)
	One for the Road
	Our Day Out
	Shirley Valentine
	Stags and Hens
Jean-Paul Sartre (1905–80)	*In Camera*
	The Condemned of Altona
James Saunders (1925–2004)	*The Ark**
	Bodies
	Making It Better
	Next Time I'll Sing to You
	Retreat
	A Scent of Flowers
Friedrich von Schiller (1759–1805)	*Demetrius* (unfinished)
	Don Carlos
	The Maid of Orleans
	Maria Stuart
	*The Robbers**
	Wallenstein Trilogy
	William Tell
Anthony Shaffer (1926–2001)	*The Case of the Oily Levantine*
	Murderer
	Sleuth
Peter Shaffer (1926–)	*Amadeus*
	Black Comedy
	Equus
	*Five-Finger Exercise**
	The Gift of the Gorgon
	Lettice and Lovage
	The Private Ear
	The Public Eye
	The Royal Hunt of the Sun
	Yonadab
George Bernard Shaw (1856–1950)	*Androcles and the Lion*
	Arms and the Man
	Back to Methuselah
	Caesar and Cleopatra
	Candida
	Captain Brassbound's Conversion
	The Devil's Disciple
	The Doctor's Dilemma
	Getting Married
	Heartbreak House
	John Bull's Other Island
	Major Barbara
	Man and Superman
	The Millionairess
	Mrs Warren's Profession
	Pygmalion
	Saint Joan
	Widowers' Houses
	You Never Can Tell
Sam Shepard (1943–)	*Buried Child*
	*Cowboys**
	The Curse of the Starving Class
	Dog and Rocking Chair
	Eyes for Consuela
	Fool for Love
	A Lie of the Mind
	The Rock Garden
	Simpatico
	The Tooth of Crime
	True West
Richard Brinsley Sheridan (1751–1816)	*The Critic*
	Jupiter
	The Rivals
	St Patrick's Day
	The School for Scandal
R C Sherriff (1896–1975)	*Home at Seven*
	*Journey's End**
Alan Sillitoe (1928–) and Ruth Fainlight (1931–)	*All Citizens Are Soldiers*
Neil Simon (1927–)	*Barefoot in the Park*
	Biloxi Blues
	California Suite
	*Come Blow Your Horn**
	The Dinner Party
	45 Seconds from Broadway
	The Gingerbread Lady
	The Good Doctor

Playwright	*Play*
	Last of the Red Hot Lovers
	Little Me
	Lost in Yonkers
	The Odd Couple
	Plaza Suite
	The Prisoner of Second Avenue
	Promises, Promises
	Rose's Dilemma
	The Sunshine Boys
	Sweet Charity
	They're Playing Our Song
Sophocles (*c.* 496–405 BC)	*Ajax*
	Antigone
	Electra
	Ichneutae
	Oedipus at Colonus
	Oedipus Rex
	Philoctetes
	Trachiniae
Tom Stoppard (1937–)	*After Magritte*
	Albert's Bridge (radio)
	Dirty Linen
	The Dissolution of Dominic Boot (radio)
	Enter a Free Man
	Indian Ink
	The Invention of Love
	Jumpers
	M is for Moon Among OtherThings (radio)
	Night and Day
	Professional Foul (TV play)
	The Real Inspector Hound
	Rosencrantz and Guildenstern Are Dead
	Separate Peace (first TV play)
	Squaring the Circle (TV play)
	Travesties
	*A Walk on the Water**
Tom Stoppard and André Previn (1929–)	*Every Good Boy Deserves Favour*
David Storey (1933–)	*The Changing Room*
	The Contractor
	Cromwell
	Early Days
	The Farm
	Home
	In Celebration
	Life Class
	The March on Russia
	Mother's Day
	*The Restoration of Arnold Middleton**
	Sisters
	This Sporting Life
August Strindberg (1849–1912)	*The Creditors*
	The Dance of Death
	A Dream Play
	The Father
	Master Olof
	Miss Julie
	To Damascus
J M Synge (1871–1909)	*In the Shadow of the Glen*
	The Playboy of the Western World
	Riders to the Sea
	The Tinker's Wedding
	The Well of the Saints
Peter Terson (1932–)	*Zigger Zagger*
Brandon Thomas (1856–1914)	*Charley's Aunt*
Dylan Thomas (1914–53)	*Under Milk Wood*
John Vanbrugh (1664–1726)	*The Confederacy*
	The Provok'd Husband
	The Provok'd Wife
	(both above completed by Colley Cibber)
	The Relapse, or Virtue in Danger
John Webster (1580–1625)	*The Devil's Law Case*
	The Duchess of Malfi
	The White Devil
Frank Wedekind (1864–1918)	*Earth Spirit*
	Pandora's Box
	Spring Awakening
Arnold Wesker (1932–)	*Annie Wobbler*
	Chicken Soup With Barley
	Chips With Everything
	I'm Talking About Jerusalem
	The Kitchen
	Roots
Peter Whelan (1931–)	*The Accrington Pals**
	The Bright and Bold Design
	Clay
	Divine Right
	The Herbal Bed
	Nativity
	A Russian in the Woods
	The School of Night
	Shakespeare Country
Hugh Whitemore (1936–)	*The Best of Friends*
	Breaking the Code
	It's Ralph
	Pack of Lies
	*Stevie**
Oscar Wilde (1854–1900)	*The Duchess of Padua*
	An Ideal Husband
	The Importance of Being Ernest
	Lady Windermere's Fan
	Salome
	A Woman of No Importance
Thornton Wilder (1897–1975)	*The Angel that Troubled the Waters*
	The Long Christmas Dinner
	The Matchmaker
	Our Town
	The Skin of Our Teeth
	The Trumpet Shall Sound
Tennessee Williams (1911–83)	*Battle of Angels**
	Camino Real
	Cat on a Hot Tin Roof
	The Glass Menagerie
	The Night of the Iguana
	The Rose Tattoo
	A Streetcar Named Desire
	Suddenly Last Summer
	Sweet Bird of Youth
William Wycherley (1640–1716)	*The Country Wife*
	The Gentleman Dancing Master
	The Plain Dealer

Theatre: General Information

After the Fall Central character: Quentin. Former wife: Maggie (modelled on Marilyn Monroe).

Arms and the Man Setting: Bulgaria. Family: Petkoffs.

Banned by Lord Chamberlain *Early Morning* by Edward Bond (1968) was the last play to be banned by the Lord Chamberlain, whose office was abolished on 26 Sept. 1968.

The Birthday Party Party for: Stanley. Boarding house owners: Meg and Petey.

The Blue Bird Children: Mytyl and Tyltyl.

Broadway theatre named after Neil Simon is the only living American playwright to be so honoured.

Camille Central character Marguerite Gautier.

Candida Candida's husband: Reverend Morell. Poet: Marchbanks.

The Caretaker Title character Davies.

Cat on a Hot Tin Roof Title character: Maggie Pollitt. Husband: Brick. Location: St Louis.

Cell Mates Took over from Stephen Fry: Simon Ward.

Charley's Aunt Title character: Donna Lucia d'Alvadores. Charley's surname: Wykeham.

Chips with Everything Setting: RAF.
Comedy Meaning: Revel-song.
Comedy of Intrigue Founder: Sir George Etherege.
Death of a Salesman Salesman: Willie Loman.
Doll's House Doll's name: Nora. Nora's husband: Torvald Helmer.
Entertainer Title character Archie Rice.
Equus Psychiatrist: Dysart. Stableboy: Alan Strang.
The Gingerbread Lady Filmed as: *Only When I Laugh.*
The Glass Menagerie Family: Wingfields.
Hedda Gabler Husband: Professor George Tessman.
The Iceman Cometh Salesman: Hickey. Setting: Harry Hope's saloon (NY).
The Importance of Being Ernest Title character: Jack Worthing (real name Ernest Moncrieff). Governess: Miss Prism. Jack found in handbag at station. Left in baby's place: novel. Algernon Moncrieff's fictional friend: Bunbury.
In Camera Setting: Hell. Characters: Garcin, Estelle, Inez.
The Inspector General Impostor: Khlestakov.
Japanese theatre Two main types: Nō (lit: talent) was developed in the 14th century from a court dance and the acrobatics of the sarugaku troupes. Kabuki (lit: singing and dancing art) was developed in the 17th century and was originally only performed by women. The costumes worn come from the Edo period (1603–1868).
The Jew of Malta Title character: Barabas.
Journey's End Setting: First World War.
Jumpers Professor: George Moore. George's Wife: Dotty.
Juno and the Paycock Paycock: Jack Boyle.
Killed by Tortoise Aeschylus was allegedly killed when an eagle dropped a tortoise on his head.
Killed fellow actor in duel Ben Jonson.
Le Bourgeois Gentilhomme Title character: Monsieur Jourdain.
Lady Windermere's Fan Mother: Mrs Erlynne.
The Lady's Not for Burning Setting: Cool Clary.
Famous Lines Brazil, where the nuts come from (*Charley's Aunt*).
He is the very pineapple of politeness (Mrs Malaprop in *The Rivals*).
Heav'n has no rage, like love to hatred burn'd,
Nor Hell a fury, like a woman scorned (*The Mourning Bride*).
Music hath charms to soothe a savage breast (*The Mourning Bride*).
Our civil community is founded on the pestiferous soil of falsehood (Dr Stockman in *An Enemy of the People*).
Very flat, Norfolk (*Private Lives*).
The Long Day's Journey into Night Family: Tyrones.
Look Back in Anger Central character: Jimmy Porter. Jimmy's wife: Alison.
Lyceum Managed by Sir Henry Irving 1878–99.
The Maids Title characters: Claire and Solange.
Le Misanthrope Title character: Alceste.
The Miser Lead character: Harpagon.
Mourning Becomes Electra Based on the Oresteia Trilogy by Aeschylus.
Norman Conquests *Table Manners, Round and Round the Garden, Living Together.*
Oresteia Trilogy (Aeschylus) *Agamemnon, Choephoroe* (*The Libation-Bearers*), *Eumenides.*
Peter Pan Children: John, Michael and Wendy Darling. Hook educated at Eton. Dog: Nana.
Phèdre Based on *Hippolytus* by Euripides.
The Playboy of the Western World Title character: Christie Mahon.
Prison Written in: *Our Lady of the Flowers* by Jean Genet.
Private Lives Written for Gertrude Lawrence.
Pushkin's 'Little Tragedies' *Mozart and Salieri, The Covetous Knight, The Stone Guest, The Feast during the Plague.*
Pygmalion Professor: Henry Higgins. Flowergirl: Eliza Doolittle. Higgins home: Wimpole St. Scandal over: use of the word 'bloody'.
The Quare Fellow Set in a Dublin prison.
The Rivals Rivals: Captain Absolute (Ensign Beverley) and Sir Lucius O'Trigger (Bob Acres). Setting: Bath. Lady: Lydia Languish. Her Aunt: Mrs Malaprop.
Roots Central character: Beatie Bryant. Setting: Norfolk.
Seagull Central characters: Irina, Nina, Trigorin the novelist.
Second Mrs Tanqueray Title character: Paula Ray.
She Stoops to Conquer Central character: Marlow. Marlow's love: Miss Hardcastle.
State of Innocence Based on *Paradise Lost* by John Milton.
A Streetcar Named Desire Central character: Blanche Du Bois. Blanche's sister: Stella. Stella's husband: Stanley Kowalsky. Setting: New Orleans.
***Sturm und Drang* (Storm and Stress)** German literary movement that preceded Romanticism, taking its name from the play by Max Klinger *Der Wirrwarr, oder Sturm und Drang.*
Subtitle *Man and Superman* 'A Comedy and a Philosophy'.
Theatre of Cruelty Name given by Antonin Artaud to his use of lighting effects, screams and oversized puppets to induce audience reaction, as in *Les Cenci.*
Theatre of Fact Aka Documentary Theatre: a German movement founded in the early 1960s by Rolf Hochuth, Peter Weiss and Heinar Kipphardt, highlighting the political propaganda of post-Second World War Germany.
Theatre of the Absurd Name given to the pessimistic vision of humanity struggling vainly to find a purpose as depicted in works by Beckett (*Waiting for Godot*), Ionesco (*The Bald Soprano*), and such diverse dramatists as Jean Genet, Arthur Adamov and Harold Pinter.
The Three Sisters Title characters: Irina, Masha, Olga.
Tragedy Meaning: goat-song.
Travesties Setting: Zurich.
Volpone Servant: Mosca.
Waiting for Godot Tramps: Vladimir (Didi), Estragon (Gogo).
Waiting for Lefty Title character: Lefty Costello.
Wallenstein Trilogy *Wallensteins Lager, Die Piccolomini, Wallensteins Tod.*
The Way of the World Central characters: Mirabell, Millamant, Lady Wishford.
Wesker Trilogy *Chicken Soup with Barley, Roots, I'm Talking About Jerusalem.*
What the Butler Saw Setting: Psychiatrist's clinic.
The Winslow Boy Based on Archer–Shee case.

Theatres of the British Isles

(excluding London, see separate section; English unless stated otherwise)

Aberdeen, Capitol (Sco)
Aberdeen, His Majesty's Theatre (Sco)
Aberdeen, Music Hall (Sco)
Aldeburgh, Snape Maltings
Alnwick, Playhouse
Andover, Cricklade Theatre
Andover, Winton Studio Theatre
Armagh, The Marketplace Theatre (Ire)
Averham, Robin Hood Theatre
Aylesbury, Limelight Theatre
Barnstaple, Queens Theatre
Basildon, Towngate Theatre
Basingstoke, The Anvil
Basingstoke, Haymarket
Bath, Rondo Studio Theatre
Bath, Theatre Royal
Belfast, The Grand Opera House (Ire)
Belfast, Group Theatre (Ire)
Belfast, Lyric Theatre (Ire)
Belfast, Waterfront (Ire)
Bexhill, De La Warr Pavilion
Birmingham, Alexandra
Birmingham, Crescent
Birmingham, Hippodrome
Birmingham, Repertory Theatre
Birmingham, Symphony Hall
Blackburn, King George's Hall
Blackburn, Opera House
Blackpool, Grand Theatre
Blackpool, Opera House
Bolton, Albert Hall
Bolton, Octagon
Bournemouth, Pavilion Theatre
Bradford, Alhambra Theatre
Bradford, St George's Hall
Brighton, Brighton Centre
Brighton, Dome
Brighton, Gardner Arts Centre
Brighton, Komedia Theatre

Brighton, Theatre Royal
Bristol, Colston Hall
Bristol, Hippodrome
Bristol, Old Vic Theatre
Bristol, Theatre Royal
(oldest in Britain: built 1766)
Bromley, Churchill Theatre
Bury St Edmunds, Theatre Royal
Buxton, Opera House
Cambridge, ADC Theatre
Cambridge, Arts Theatre
Cambridge, Corn Exchange
Canterbury, Gulbenkian Theatre
Canterbury, Marlowe Theatre
Cardiff, New Theatre (Wal)
Cardiff, St David's Hall (Wal)
Cardiff, Sherman Theatre (Wal)
Carlisle, Sands Centre
Carshalton, Charles Cryer Studio Theatre
Chatham, Theatre Royal
Cheltenham, Everyman Theatre
Cheltenham, Playhouse Theatre
Chester, Gateway Theatre
Chesterfield, Pomegranate Theatre
Chichester, Festival Theatre
Chichester, Minerva Studio
Cockermouth, Kirkgate Centre
Colchester, Mercury Theatre
Coleraine, Riverside Theatre (Ire)
Cork, Cork Opera House (Ire)
Cork, Everyman Palace Theatre (Ire)
Cork, Granary Theatre (Ire)
Cork, Half Moon Theatre (Ire)
Cork, Savoy Theatre (Ire)
Coventry, Belgrade Theatre
Coventry, Warwick Arts Centre
Crawley, The Hawth
Crewe, Lyceum
Croydon, Fairfield Hall & Ashcroft Theatre
Croydon, Warehouse Theatre
Darlington, Civic Theatre – Arts Centre
Derby, Assembly Rooms
Derby, Playhouse Theatre
Dublin, Abbey Theatre (Ire)
Dublin, Andrews Theatre (Ire)
Dublin, Dublin Gate Theatre (Ire)
Dublin, Gaiety Theatre (Ire)
Dublin, Olympia Theatre (Ire)
Dublin, Peacock Theatre (Ire)
Dublin, Tivoli Theatre (Ire)
Dumfries, Theatre Royal (Sco)
Eastbourne, Congress Theatre
Eastbourne, Devonshire Park Theatre
Eastbourne, Winter Garden
Edinburgh, Festival Theatre (Sco)
Edinburgh, Gilded Balloon (Sco)
Edinburgh, King's Theatre (Sco)
Edinburgh, Playhouse (Sco)
Edinburgh, Royal Lyceum Theatre (Sco)
Edinburgh, Traverse (Sco)
Eltham, Bob Hope Theatre
Exeter, Northcott Theatre
Felixstowe, Spa Pavilion Theatre
Galway, Blackbox Theatre (Ire)
Galway, Druid Theatre (Ire)
Glasgow, Citizens Theatre (Sco)
Glasgow, Pavilion Theatre (Sco)
Glasgow, Royal Concert Hall (Sco)
Glasgow, Theatre Royal (Sco)
Glasgow, Tramway (Sco)
Glasgow, Tron Theatre (Sco)
Glyndebourne, Opera House
Grimsby, Auditorium
Great Yarmouth, Britannia Theatre
Great Yarmouth, New Wellington Theatre
Great Yarmouth, St George's Theatre
Guildford, Civic Theatre
Guildford, Yvonne Arnaud Theatre
Halifax, Victoria Theatre
Hanley, The Royal
Hastings, The Stables
Hastings, White Rock Theatre
High Wycombe, Wycombe Swan Theatre
Hitchin, The Queen Mother Theatre
Hornchurch, Queen's Theatre
Harrogate, Harrogate Theatre
Huddersfield, Lawrence Batley Theatre
Hull, Donald Roy Theatre
Hull, Hull Arena
Hull, Hull City Hall
Hull, Hull Truck Theatre
Ifield, Barn Theatre
Ilford, Kenneth More Theatre
Ilfracombe, The Landmark Theatre
Inverness, Eden Court Theatre (Sco)
Isle of Man, Gaiety Theatre
Ipswich, Corn Exchange
Ipswich, New Wolsey Theatre
Ipswich, Regent Theatre
Ipswich, Sir John Mills Theatre
Keswick, Theatre By The Lake
Lancaster, Dukes Playhouse
Lancaster, Grand Theatre
Lancaster, Nuffield Theatre
Leeds, City Varieties
Leeds, Grand Theatre
Leeds, West Yorkshire Playhouse
Leicester, De Montfort Hall
Leicester, Haymarket Theatre
Leicester, Phoenix Arts
Liverpool, Empire
Liverpool, Everyman Theatre
Liverpool, Neptune Theatre
Liverpool, Playhouse
Liverpool, Royal Court Theatre
Liverpool, Royal Phillharmonic Hall
Liverpool, St George's Hall
Llandudno, North Wales Theatre (Wal)
Manchester, Apollo
Manchester, Bridgewater Hall
Manchester, Contact Theatre
Manchester, Library Theatre
Manchester, Lowry Centre
Manchester, Palace Theatre-Opera House
Manchester, Royal Exchange Theatre
Mansfield, Palace Theatre
Milton Keynes, Milton Keynes Theatre
Mold, Theatre Clwyd (Wal)
Mull, Little Theatre (Sco)
Newark, Palace Theatre
Newbury, Corn Exchange
Newbury, Watermill Theatre
Newcastle, Opera House
Newcastle, Playhouse
Newcastle, Theatre Royal
Newcastle-under-Lyme, New Vic Theatre
Northampton, Derngate Theatre
Northampton, Royal Theatre
Norwich, The Maddermarket
Norwich, Playhouse
Norwich, Theatre Royal
Nottingham, Lace Market Theatre
Nottingham, Playhouse
Nottingham, Royal Centre
Nottingham, Theatre Royal
Oldham, Coliseum Theatre
Oldham, Sixth Form College Theatre
Oxford, Apollo Theatre
Oxford, Old Fire Station
Oxford, Playhouse Theatre
Perth, Perth Theatre (Sco)
Peterborough, Key Theatre
Pitlochry, Festival Theatre (Sco)
Plymouth, Drum Theatre
Plymouth, Mayflower
Plymouth, Theatre Royal
Poole, The Lighthouse
Porthcurno (Cornwall), Minack (open-air)
Portsmouth, Guildhall
Portsmouth, New Theatre Royal
Preston, Guildhall & Charter Theatre
Reading, The Hexagon
Reading, The Mill at Sonning
Redhill, Harlequin
Rhyl, Pavilion Theatre (Wal)
St Helens, Theatre Royal
Salford, The Lowry
Salisbury, Playhouse
Scarborough, Futurist Theatre
Scarborough, Spa Theatre
Scarborough, Stephen Joseph Theatre
Sheffield, City Hall
Sheffield, Crucible
Sheffield, Lyceum
Sligo, Hawk's Well Theatre (Ire)
South Shields, Custom House
Southampton, The Gantry
Southampton, The Mayflower
Southampton, The Nuffield Theatre
Southsea, Kings Theatre
Stevenage, Gordon Craig Theatre
Stoke-on-Trent, New Victoria Theatre
Stoke-on-Trent, The Royal
Stoke-on-Trent, Victoria Hall
Stratford-upon-Avon, The Other Place
Stratford-upon-Avon, Royal Shakespeare Theatre
Stratford-upon-Avon, Swan Theatre
Sunderland, Empire Theatre
Swansea, Grand Theatre (Wal)
Swindon, Wyvern Theatre
Tamworth, Arts Centre
Taunton, Brewhouse Theatre
Tewkesbury, Roses Theatre
Torquay, Princess Theatre
Truro, Hall For Cornwall
Wakefield, Theatre Royal & Opera House
Warrington, Parr Hall
Watford, Palace Theatre
Wavendon, The Stables
Wellingborough, The Castle
Weymouth, Pavilion
Winchester, Theatre Royal
Windsor, Theatre Royal
Woking, Ambassadors / New Victoria
Wolverhampton, Arena
Wolverhampton, Grand Theatre
Worcester, Swan Theatre
Worthing, Connaught Theatre
Worthing, Northbrook Theatre
Worthing, Pavilion Theatre
Wythenshaw, Forum Theatre
York, Barbican
York, Grand Opera House
York, Theatre Royal

Poetry: By Poet

Peter Ackroyd	*Country Life*
(1949–)	*London Lickpenny*
	Ouch
Anna Akhmatova	*Anno Domini*
(1889–66)	*White Flock*
Matthew Arnold	*Dover Beach*
(1822–88)	*Empedocles on Etna*
	The Forsaken Merman
	The Scholar Gypsy
	Sohrab and Rustum
	The Strayed Reveller
	Thyrsis
	Tristram and Iseult
Margaret Atwood	*The Circle Game*
(1939–)	*The Door*
W H Auden	*In the Secular Night*
(1907–73)	*About the House*
	The Age of Anxiety
	Another Time
	City Without Walls
	The Double Man
	Homage to Clio
	In Memory of W.B. Yeats
	Look, Stranger!
	Miss Gee
	New Year Letter
	Night Mail
	On This Island
	The Orators
	Paid on Both Sides
	The Shield of Achilles
	Spain
	Stop All the Clocks
Richard Harris Barham	*The Ingoldsby Legends*
(1788–1845)	*The Jackdaw of Rheims*
Charles Baudelaire	*Les Fleurs du mal*
(1821–67)	
Hilaire Belloc	*The Bad Child's Book of Beasts*
(1870–1953)	*Cautionary Tales*
	Matilda
John Betjeman	*Continual Dew*
(1906–84)	*Death in Leamington*
	A Few Late Chrysanthemums
	Highland Low
	The Metropolitan Railway
	Mount Zion
	New Bats in Old Belfries
	A Nip in the Air
	Old Lights for New Chancels
	A Subaltern's Love Song
Laurence Binyon	*For the Fallen*
(1869–1943)	*Tristram's End*
William Blake	*Jerusalem*
(1757–1827)	*Milton*
	The Sick Rose
	Songs of Experience
	Songs of Innocence
	The Tyger
Aleksandr Blok	*Nocturnal Hours*
(1880–1921)	*The Rose and the Cross*
	The Scythians
	Songs About the Lady Fair
	The Twelve
Edmund Blunden	*Almswomen*
(1896–1974)	*Bonadventure*
	Pastorals
	Undertones of War
	The Waggoner
Wilfrid Scawen Blunt	*The Old Squire*
(1840–1922)	
Gordon Bottomley	*Poems of Thirty Years*
(1874–1948)	*To Ironfounders and Others*
Robert Bridges	*Eros and Psyche*
(1844–1930)	*The Growth of Love*
	London Snow
	October
	Prometheus the Firegiver
	The Spirit of Man
	The Testament of Beauty
Emily Brontë	*Gondal*
(1818–48)	*Last Lines*
	Plead for Me
	Remembrance
	To Imagination
Rupert Brooke	*1914*
(1887–1915)	*The Old Vicarage, Grantchester*
	The Soldier
Elizabeth Barrett	*Aurora Leigh*
Browning	*The Battle of Marathon*
(1806–61)	*Casa Guidi Windows*
	The Cry of the Children
	How Do I Love Thee?
	Poems before Congress
	The Seraphim
	Sonnets from the Portuguese
Robert Browning	*Andrea del Sarto*
(1812–89)	*Bells and Pomegranates*
	Childe Roland to the Dark Tower Came
	Fra Lippo Lippi
	Home Thoughts From Abroad
	Home-Thoughts, from the Sea
	How They Brought the Good News from Ghent to Aix
	Men and Women
	My Last Duchess
	Paracelsus
	Pauline
	The Pied Piper of Hamelin
	Pippa Passes
	Rabbi Ben Ezra
	The Ring and the Book
	Soliloquy of the Spanish Cloister
	Sordello
John Bunyan	*The Pilgrim*
(1628–88)	
Robert Burns	*Address to a Mouse*
(1759–96)	*Auld Lang Syne*
	Comin' Through the Rye
	The Cotter's Saturday Night
	Death and Doctor Hornbook
	Despondency
	Desolate and Pale Moonlight
	Epistle to Davie
	Ae Fond Kiss
	For a' that and a' that
	Halloween
	The Holy Fair
	Holy Willie's Prayer
	The Jolly Beggars
	Kilmarnock Poems
	The Lament
	A Red, Red Rose
	Scots Musical Museum
	Tam O'Shanter
	To a Field Mouse
	The Twa Herds
Samuel Butler	*Hudibras*
(1612–80)	
Lord Byron	*Beppo*
(1788–1824)	*Childe Harold's Pilgrimage*
	The Destruction of Sennacherib
	Don Juan
	Hours of Idleness
	Lara
	The Prisoner of Chillon
	She Walks in Beauty
	The Siege of Corinth
	The Vision of Judgment
	We'll Go No More A-Roving
Luis de Camoes	*The Lusiads*
(1524–1580)	*Rimas*
Roy Campbell	*The Flaming Terrapin*
(1901–1957)	*Flowering Rifle*
	Soldier's Reply to the Poet
	The Wayzgoose
Thomas Campbell	*Gertrude of Wyoming*
(1777–1844)	
Lewis Carroll	*The Hunting of the Snark*
(1832–98)	*Jabberwocky*
	Phantasmagoria and other Poems
	The Walrus and the Carpenter
Sydney Carter	*Lord of the Dance*
(1915–2004)	
Charles Causley	*Farewell, Aggie Weston*
(1917–2003)	*Figure of 8*
	RIJP
	Survivor's Leave
	Underneath the Water

Union Street
The Young Man of Cury

Thomas Chatterton (1752–70)
The Rowley Poems

Geoffrey Chaucer (*c.* 1343–1400)
The Canterbury Tales
Troilus and Criseyde

G K Chesterton (1874–1936)
The Donkey
Greybeards at Play
The Wild Knight

John Clare (1793–1864)
First Love
The Rural Muse
The Shepherd's Calendar
Village Minstrel

Samuel Taylor Coleridge (1772–1834)
The Ancient Mariner
Christabel
Dejection: An ode
Kubla Khan
Ode to France
The Rime of the Ancient Mariner

William Cory (1823–92)
Heraclitus
Ionica

William Cowper (1731–1800)
John Gilpin
The Task

George Crabbe (1754–1832)
The Borough
The Village

Hart Crane (1899–1932)
The Bridge
White Buildings

Dante Alighieri (1265–1321)
Banquet
Canzoniere
The Divine Comedy

W H Davies (1871–1940)
Leisure
Money
School's Out
A Soul's Destroyer

Emily Dickinson (1830–86)
A Bird Came Down the Walk
A Narrow Fellow in the Grass
Parting

Austin Dobson (1840–1921)
At the Sign of the Lyre
A Fancy From Fontenelle
Proverbs in Porcelain
Vignettes in Rhyme

John Donne (*c.* 1572–1631)
Anniversaries
The Canonization
The Exstasie
The Good-Morrow
Metempsychosis
A Nocturnall upon St Lucies Day
Song
The Sun Rising
A Valediction: Forbidding Mourning

Ernest Dowson (1867–1900)
Decorations
Non Sum Qualis Eram
Vitae Sumina Brevis

John Dryden (1631–1700)
Absalom and Achitophel
Alexander's Feast
Annus Mirabilis: The Year of Wonders, 1666
Astræ Redux
Fables, Ancient and Modern
The Hind and the Panther
The Medal
Religio Laici
A Song for St Cecilia's Day
Sylvia the Fair

T S Eliot (1888–1965)
Ash Wednesday
Four Quartets
Gerontion
The Hollow Men
The Journey of the Magi
The Love Song of J. Alfred Prufrock
The Waste Land

Ralph Waldo Emerson (1803–82)
Brahma
Give All to Love
May–Day
The Problem

William Empson (1906–84)
The Gathering Storm

Quintus Ennius (239–169 BC)
Annales

Gavin Ewart (1916–95)
Poets

Edward Fitzgerald (1809–83)
The Rubaiyat of Omar Khayyam (translation from Persian)

James Elroy Flecker (1884–1915)
The Bridge of Fire
The Golden Journey to Samarkand
The Old Ships

Robert Lee Frost (1874–1963)
After Apple-Picking
Birches
A Boy's Will
The Death of the Hired Man
Dust of Snow
Fire and Ice
A Further Range
The Gift Outright
A Lone Striker
Mountain Interval
Mowing
Neither Out Far Nor In Deep
New Hampshire
North of Boston
The Oven Bird
Pan With Us
The Silken Tent
Steeple Bush
Stopping by Woods on a Snowy Evening
The Tuft of Flowers
West-Running Brook
A Witness Tree

Jean Genet (1910–86)
Chant Secret

Allen Ginsberg (1926–97)
Empty Mirror
*Howl**
Kaddish
Planet News
Reality Sandwiches

Johann Wolfgang von Goethe (1749–1832)
Erlkönig
Kennst du das Land
Roman Elegies

Oliver Goldsmith (1728–74)
The Deserted Village
Elegy on the Death of a Mad Dog
The Traveller

Robert Graves (1895–1985)
Fairies and Fusiliers
Over the Brazier
A Slice of Wedding Cake

Thomas Gray (1716–71)
The Bard
The Descent of Odin
Elegy Written in a Country Churchyard
The Fatal Sisters
Ode on a Distant Prospect of Eton College
The Progress of Poesy

Graham Greene (1904–91)
Bubbling April

Julian Grenfell (1888–1915)
Into Battle

William Hamilton (1665–1751)
Last Dying Words of Bonny Heck

William Hamilton (1704–54)
The Braes of Yarrow

Thomas Hardy (1840–1928)
The Darkling Thrush
The Dynasts
Wessex Poems
Winter Words

Seamus Heaney (1929–2013)
Beowulf (translation)
Field Work
Death of a Naturalist
District and Circle
Door into the Dark
Electric Light
Haw Lantern
Seeing Things
The Spirit Level (collection)
Sweeney's Flight

Felicia Hemans (1793–1835)
Casabianca
The Landing of the Pilgrim Fathers

William Henley (1849–1903)
England, My England
For England's Sake
Hawthorn and Lavender
In Hospital
Invictus
A Song of Speed
Song of the Sword

Robert Herrick (1591–1674)
Cherry-Ripe
Delight in Disorder
To the Virgins, To Make Much of Time
Upon Julia's Clothes

Friedrich Hölderlin (1770–1843)
Friedensfeier (Celebration of Peace)

Homer (8th century BC)
The Iliad
The Odyssey

Thomas Hood (1799–1845)
Autumn, Ode to
The Dream of Eugene Aram
Faithless Sally Brown
Lycus the Centaur
National Tales
Ruth

	The Song of the Shirt
	Tim Turpin
	Whims and Oddities
Gerard Manley Hopkins	*Felix Randal*
(1844–89)	*Pied Beauty*
	The Windhover
	The Wreck of the Deutschland
A E Housman	*Epitaph on an Army of Mercenaries*
(1859–1936)	*Fancy's Knell*
	Last Poems
	More Poems
	A Shropshire Lad
Ted Hughes	*Birthday Letters (collection)*
(1930–98)	*Cave Birds*
	Crow
	The Hawk in the Rain
	Lupercal
	Moortown
	The Remains of Elmet
	Wodwo
Victor Hugo	*Les Châtiments*
(1802–85)	*Les Contemplations*
James Leigh Hunt	*Abou Ben Adhem*
(1784–1859)	*Jenny Kissed Me*
	Juvenilia
	The Nile
Henrik Ibsen	*Brand*
(1828–1906)	
Elizabeth Jennings	*The Animals' Arrival*
(1926–2001)	*Lucidities*
	One Flesh
	Relationships
	Song for a Birth or a Death
	A Way of Looking
Samuel Johnson	*London*
(1709–84)	*The Vanity of Human Wishes*
Ben Jonson	*Drink to Me Only With Thine Eyes*
(1572–1637)	*To Celia*
John Keats	*Endymion*
(1795–1821)	*The Eve of St Agnes*
	Grecian Urn, Ode on a
	Hymn to Pan
	Hyperion
	Isabella or the Pot of Basil
	La Belle Dame Sans Merci
	Lamia
	Ode on Melancholy
	Ode to a Nightingale
	On First Looking into Chapman's Homer
	Ode to Psyche
	To Autumn
Rudyard Kipling	*The Ballad of East and West*
(1865–1936)	*Barrack-Room Ballads*
	The Betrothed
	Cities and Thrones and Powers
	The Female of the Species
	The Gods of the Copybook Headings
	Gunga Din
	If
	Mandalay
	The Way Through the Woods
	The White Man's Burden
Walter Savage Landor	*Gebir*
(1775–1864)	*Rose Aylmer*
William Langland	*Piers Plowman*
(*c.* 1322–1400)	
Philip Larkin	*Church Going*
(1922–85)	*High Windows*
	The North Ship
	This Be the Verse
	The Whitsun Weddings
Emma Lazarus	*Admetus*
(1849–87)	*By the Waters of Babylon*
	The New Colossus
Edward Lear	*The Jumblies*
(1812–88)	*The Owl and the Pussycat*
	The Pobble Who Has No Toes
Laurie Lee	*April Rise*
(1914–97)	*The Bloom of Candles*
	My Many–Coated Man
	The Sun My Monument
Cecil Day Lewis	*Beechen Vigil*
(1904–72)	*Overtures to Death*
C S Lewis(1898–1963)	*Dymer*
Henry Wadsworth Longfellow	*The Belfry of Bruges*
(1807–82)	*The Courtship of Miles Standish*
	Evangeline
	Excelsior
	Kalevala
	The Golden Legend
	The Song of Hiawatha
	Paul Revere's Ride
	The Skeleton in Armour
	The Village Blacksmith
	Voices of the Night
	Wayside Inn, Tales of a
	The Wreck of the Hesperus
Federico García Lorca	*Canciones*
(1898–1936)	*Romancero Gitano*
Richard Lovelace	*To Althea*
(1618–57)	*To Lucasta, On Going to the Wars*
Hugh MacDiarmid	*A Drunk Man Looks at the Thistle*
(1892–1978)	*Sangschaw*
Louis MacNeice	*Autumn Sequel*
(1907–63)	*Bagpipe Music*
	Blind Fireworks
	The Burning Perch
	Solstices
Stéphane Mallarmé	*L'Après-midi d'un Faune*
(1842–98)	
Osip Mandelstam Kamen	*Stone*
(1891–1938)	*Tristia*
Walter de la Mare	*The Listeners*
(1873–1956)	*O Lovely England*
	Peacock Pie
	Silver
	Songs of Childhood
	The Veil
Leo Marks (1920–2001)	*Code Poem for the French Resistance*
Christopher Marlowe	*Come Live With Me and Be My Love*
(1564–93)	*Hero and Leander* (unfinished)
	The Passionate Shepherd to His Love
Andrew Marvell	*The Definition of Love*
(1621–78)	*The Garden*
	An Horatian Ode
	To His Coy Mistress
John Masefield	*Cargoes*
(1878–1967)	*Dauber*
	The Everlasting Mercy
	Gallipoli
	Nan
	Reynard the Fox
	Sea Fever
	Shakespeare
	The Widow in the Bye-Street
Vladimir Mayakovsky	*The Backbone Flute*
(1894–1930)	*A Cloud in Trousers*
	150,000,000
John McCrae	*In Flanders Fields*
(1872–1918)	
William McGonagall	*Poetic Gems*
(1830–1902)	*The Tay Bridge Disaster*
Alice Meynell	*Renouncement*
(1847–1922)	*The Shepherdess*
John Milton	*At a Solemn Music*
(1608–74)	*Comus*
	De Doctrina Christiana
	Il Penseroso
	L'Allegro
	Let Us with a Gladsome Mind
	Lycidas
	Nativity Ode
	On His Blindness
	On the Late Massacre in Piedmont
	Paradise Lost
	Paradise Regained
	Samson Agonistes
E G Moll	*Returned Soldier*
(1900–93)	
Clement Moore	*A Visit from St Nicholas*
(1779–1863)	
Thomas Moore	*Irish Melodies*
(1779–1852)	*Lalla Rookh*
	The Last Rose of Summer
	The Light of Other Days
Pete Morgan	*August Light*
(1939–)	*My Enemies Have Sweet Voices*
Edwin Muir	*Chorus of the Newly Dead*
(1887–1959)	*The Confirmation*
	Journeys and Places
	The Labyrinth
Ogden Nash	*Bed Riddance*
(1902–71)	*I'm a Stranger Here Myself*
	Versus

Henry Newbolt (1862–1938)	*The Death of Admiral Blake* *Drake's Drum* *The Island Race* *Songs of the Sea*
Cardinal J H Newman (1801–90)	*The Dream of Gerontius*
Alfred Noyes (1880–1958)	*Drake* *The Flower of Old Japan* *The Forest of Wild Thyme* *Forty Singing Seamen* *The Highwayman* *The Torchbearers*
Arthur O'Shaughnessy (1844–81)	*An Epic of Women* *Lays of France* *Music and Moonlight* *Ode (We Are The Music-Makers)* *Songs of a Worker*
Wilfred Owen (1893–1918)	*Anthem For Doomed Youth* *Disabled* *Dulce et Decorum Est*
Francis Palgrave (1824–97)	*Idylls and Songs*
Boris Pasternak (1890–1960)	*Above the Barriers* *Lieutenant Shmidt*
Coventry Patmore (1823–96)	*Amelia* *The Toys* *The Unknown Eros* *The Victories of Love*
George Peele (1556–96)	*A Farewell to Arms*
Sylvia Plath (1932–63)	*Ariel* *The Colossus* *Crossing the Water* *A Winter Ship* *Winter Trees*
Edgar Allan Poe (1809–49)	*Annabel Lee* *The Bells* *Eureka* *Israfel* *Lenore* *The Raven* *Tamerlane* *To My Mother*
Alexander Pope (1688–1744)	*The Dunciad* *Eloisa to Abelard* *An Epistle to Doctor Arbuthnot* *An Essay on Man* *Of the Use of Riches* *The Rape of the Lock* *Windsor Forest*
Ezra Pound (1885–1972)	*A Lume Spento* *The Cantos* *Exultations* *Homage to Sextus Propertius* *Hugh Selwyn Mauberley* *If This Be Treason* *Pisan Cantos* *Quia Pauper Amavi* *Umbra*
John Pudney (1909–77)	*For Johnny*
Alexander Pushkin (1799–1837)	*The Bronze Horseman* *Egyptian Nights* *Eugene Onegin* *Poltava* *The Prisoner of the Caucasus* *The Robber Brothers* *Ruslan and Lyudmilla* *Tzigani*
Francis Quarles (1592–1644)	*Argalus and Parthenia* *Divine Fancies*
Manuel Quintana (1772–1857)	*Al combate de Trafalgar*
Rainer Maria Rilke (1875–1926)	*Die Sonnette an Orpheus*
Arthur Rimbaud (1854–91)	*Le Bateau ivre (The Drunken Boat)* *Les Illuminations*
Pierre de Ronsard (1524–85)	*Amours* *Le Bocage*
Isaac Rosenberg (1890–1918)	*On Receiving News of the War* *Trench Poems*
Christina Rossetti (1830–94)	*A Birthday* *Goblin Market* *A Pageant* *The Prince's Progress* *Remember* *Uphill*
Dante Gabriel Rossetti (1828–82)	*The Blessed Damozel* *The House of Life* *The King's Tragedy* *The White Ship*
Siegfried Sassoon (1886–1967)	*Aftermath* *Attack* *Counter-Attack* *Everyone Sang* *The Old Huntsman*
Alan Seeger (1888–1916)	*Rendezvous*
Robert Service (1874–1958)	*Rhymes of a Rolling Stone* *The Shooting of Dan McGrew*
William Shakespeare (1564–1616)	*Let Me Not to the Marriage of True Minds* (Sonnet 116) *Shall I Compare Thee to a Summer's Day* (Sonnet 18)
P B Shelley and Elizabeth Shelley	*Original Poetry by Victor and Cazire*
Percy Bysshe Shelley (1792–1822)	*Adonais* *Alastor* *Epipsychidion* *Hellas* *Julian and Maddalo* *Love's Philosophy* *To Naples* *Ode to the West Wind* *Ozymandias of Egypt* *Prometheus Unbound* *Queen Mab* *To a Skylark* *To Liberty* *The Witch of Atlas*
Sir Philip Sidney (1554–86)	*Arcadia* *Astrophel and Stella*
Alan Sillitoe (1928–)	*Marmalade Jim at the Farm* *The Rats and Other Poems* *Snow on the North Side of Lucifer* *Storm* *Sun Before Departure* *Tides and Stone Walls*
Stevie Smith (1902–71)	*Not Waving But Drowning*
Charles Hamilton Sorley (1895–1915)	*All the Hills and Vales Along* *Marlborough*
Robert Southey (1774–1843)	*The Battle of Blenheim* *Bishop Bruno* *Bishop Hatto* *The Inchcape Rock* *The Old Man's Comforts*
Muriel Spark (1918–2006)	*The Fanfarlo*
Edmund Spenser (*c.* 1552–99)	*The Faerie Queene* *Mother Hubberds Tale* *The Shepheardes Calender*
James Stephens (1882–1950)	*The Crock of Gold* *In the Poppy Field* *Insurrections*
Robert Louis Stevenson (1850–94)	*A Child's Garden of Verses* *A London Sabbath Morn* *Underwoods* *The Vagabond* *The Woodman*
John Still (1543–1608)	*Jolly Good Ale and Old*
Rabindranath Tagore (1861–1941)	*The Crescent Moon* *Gitanjali* *The Golden Boat* *Manasi*
Ann Taylor (1782–1866) Jane Taylor(1783–1824)	*Twinkle Twinkle Little Star*
Alfred, Lord Tennyson (1809–92)	*The Charge of the Light Brigade* *Crossing the Bar* *Idylls of the King* *In Memoriam* *The Lady of Shalott* *Locksley Hall* *The Lotos-Eaters* *Maud* *Oenone* *The Princess* *The Revenge* *Rizpah* *Timbuctoo* *To Virgil* *Ulysses*

William Makepeace Thackeray (1811–63)	*The Sorrows of Werther*
Dylan Thomas (1914–53)	*After the Funeral*
	Altarwise by Owl-Light
	And Death Shall Have No Dominion
	Deaths and Entrances
	Do Not Go Gentle into That Good Night
	Especially When the October Wind
	In Country Sleep
	In the White Giant's Thigh
	I See the Boys of Summer
	Light Breaks Where No Sun Shines
	Over Sir John's Hill
	Poem in October
	We Lying by Seasand
Edward Thomas (1878–1917)	*Adlestrop*
Henry David Thoreau (1817–62)	*Independence*
	Smoke
Rose Thorpe (1850–1939)	*Curfew Must Not Ring Tonight*
John Updike (1932–)	*The Carpentered Hen and Other Tame Creatures*
Paul Valéry	*La Jeune Parque* (1871–1945)
Edward de Vere 17th Earl of Oxford (1550–1604)	*What Cunning Can Express*
Emile Verhaeren (1855–1916)	*Les Débâcles*
	Les Flamandes
	La Multiple Splendeur
Paul Verlaine (1844–96)	*La Bonne Chanson*
	Fêtes Galantes
	Sagesse
François Villon (1431–1463)	*Ballade des pendus*
	Le Grand Testament
	Le Petit Testament
Virgil (70–19 BC)	*The Aeneid*
	The Bucolics
	The Georgics (or Art of Husbandry)
Vincent Voiture (1597–1648)	*Vers de Société*
Voltaire (1694–1778)	*La Henriade*
Walt Whitman (1819–92)	*Drum-Taps*
	Leaves of Grass
	O Captain! My Captain!
	Song of Myself
	When Lilacs Last in the Dooryard Bloom'd
John Greenleaf Whittier (1807–92)	*At Sundown*
	Barbara Frietchie
	The Battle Autumn of 1862
	In War Time
	Laus deo
	Snow-bound
Oscar Wilde (1854–1900)	*The Ballad of Reading Gaol*
	Ravenna
	To Milton
Tennessee Williams (1911–83)	*The Summer Belvedere*
	In the Winter of Cities
William Wordsworth (1770–1850)	*The Affliction of Margaret*
	The Borderers
	To the Cuckoo
	Daffodils
	Ode to Duty
	The Excursion
	Guilt and Sorrow
	Intimations of Immortality
	I Wandered Lonely as a Cloud
	The Lucy Poems
	My Heart Leaps Up
	Nutting
	The Prelude
	Resolution and Independence
	She Was a Phantom of Delight
	The Solitary Reaper
	Tintern Abbey
	Upon Westminster Bridge
	Vaudracour and Julia
W B Yeats (1865–1939)	*Brown Penny*
	Byzantium
	Ego Dominus Tuus
	He Wishes For the Cloths of Heaven
	An Irish Airman Foresees His Death
	The Lake Isle of Innisfree
	Sailing to Byzantium
	When You Are Old
Sergey Yesenin (1895–1925)	*The Black Man*
	Confessions of a Hooligan
	Desolate and Pale Moonlight
	Moscow of the Taverns
Yevgeny Yevtushenko (1933–)	*Babi Yar*
	Heavy Soils
	Ivan the Terrible
	A Wave of the Hand
	Zima Junction

Poetry: General Information

alexandrine Iambic or trochaic hexameter (line of 12 syllables or 6 feet) with, usually, a caesura (break) at the 6th syllable.

allegory Narrative or description in prose or verse with an underlying meaning or moral message as in *The Faerie Queene* or *The Pilgrim's Progress*.

apocope Omission of the final letter, syllable or sound of a word, e.g. the poetic use of th' instead of the.

assonance Use of the same or similar vowel sounds close together for the sake of euphony, memorability or emotional effect, e.g. 'And deep asleep he seemed'.

asylum, committed to John Clare from 1837 until his death.

W H Auden Friend and collaborator: Christopher Isherwood.

The Ballad of Reading Gaol Famous extract: 'And all men kill the thing they love, by all let this be heard, Some do it with a bitter look, Some with a flattering word. The coward does it with a kiss, The brave man with a sword!'

ballade Poem of three eight-line stanzas, rhyming ababbcbc, and one four-line *envoi* (final stanza) rhyming bcbc, with a refrain at the end of each of its four sections. François Villon was a great exponent of the ballade in French, Hilaire Belloc in English.

Bastille Imprisoned for a year in 1717: Voltaire (François Marie Arouet).

bathos Anticlimax or sudden descent, intended or not, from the sublime to the commonplace, e.g. the last 2 lines of Tennyson's *Enoch Arden*: 'And when they buried him the little port, Had seldom seen a costlier funeral.'

Beat Poets Lawrence Ferlinghetti, Allen Ginsberg, Jack Kerouac, Gregory Corso.

Belloc Many of his works illustrated by G K Chesterton.

The Betrothed Extract: A woman is only a woman, but a good cigar is a Smoke.

epigram Pointed, witty saying or verse that may be aphoristic,

Elizabeth Barrett Browning Pet name: She was affectionately known as 'My Little Portuguese' by her husband Robert Browning.

Brunanburh Poem in Old English, included in four manuscripts of the *Anglo-Saxon Chronicle* under the year 937 and dealing with the battle of that name.

catachresis Misuse or incorrect application of a word, e.g. 'chronic' to mean 'severe', or 'refute' to mean 'deny'.

Christian Poet First English: Caedmon.

Clerihew Comic biographical poem in the form of a quatrain with lines of various length, rhyming aabb, named after its inventor Edmund Clerihew Bentley (1875–1956). Example: The Art of Biography is different from Geography. Geography is about maps, Biography is about chaps.

dithyramb Song or poem in honour of Dionysus.

The Donkey Describes itself as 'the devil's walking parody On all four-footed things'.

Dover Beach First lines 'The sea is calm tonight The tide is full.'

duels Ben Jonson killed fellow actor Gabriel Spencer. To defend his wife's honour, Alexander challenged and was killed by Baron d'Anthès.

Dymer C S Lewis published this work under the name of Clive Hamilton.

Elegy Written in a Country Churchyard Opening: 'The curfew tolls the knell of parting day, The lowing herd wind slowly o'er the lea . . .' Extract: 'Far from the madding crowd's ignoble strife . . .'

elision Suppression of a vowel or syllable in verse for the sake of metrical correctness, e.g. 'ta'en' (one syllable) replacing 'taken' (two).

enjambement Running-on of one line of verse into another without a grammatical break, e.g.: 'Nay, but this dotage of our general's / O'erflows the measure . . . ' (*Antony and Cleopatra*).

sarcastic, complimentary or amusing.

euphuism Highly elaborate prose style as found in John Lyly's *Euphues* (1580).

The Exeter Book Important manuscript containing Old English poetry, copied about 940 and given by Bishop Leofric (d. 1072) to Exeter Cathedral. The best-known poems include *The Wanderer, The Seafarer, Widsith, The Ruin, Wulf and Eadwacer, The Wife's Lament, The Husband's Message* and *Resignation.*

***Four Quartets* (T S Eliot)** *Burnt Norton, East Coker, The Dry Salvages, Little Gidding.*

The Four Boileau, La Fontaine, Molière, Racine.

Georgian Poets Writing during the reign of *George V*: Lascelles Abercrombie, Hilaire Belloc, Rupert Brooke, W H Davies, Ernest Dowson, John Drinkwater, James Elroy Flecker, Robert Graves, Ralph Hodgson, John Masefield, Walter de la Mare, Harold Monro, Siegfried Sassoon, Sir John Squire, Edward Thomas.

Gertrude of Wyoming Poem by Thomas Campbell in Spenserian stanzas, published 1809. Describes the destruction of the settlement of Wyoming in Pennsylvania by a force of Indians.

The Golden Treasury of best songs and Lyrical poems in the English language Editor: Francis Palgrave edited the classic book of poetic works (1861) with the help of his friend Tennyson, but controversially omitted all of William Blake's poems.

Griffin Poetry Prize Inaugurated in 2001 in Canada. $40,000 awarded to best Canadian collection and $40,000 to best international collection.

haiku Japanese verse form of seventeen syllables in three lines of five, seven and five syllables, encapsulating an idea, image or mood.

Home-Thoughts, From Abroad Opening: 'Oh, to be in England Now that April's there . . .'

Imagism Poetic movement and theory (1909–17) which emphasised direct treatment of subject-matter, concreteness, extreme economy of language and the rhythm of phrases rather than the rhythm of regular metres. Poets include Richard Aldington, HD, F S Flint, James Joyce, Amy Lowell and Ezra Pound.

Keats's epitaph By himself: 'Here lies one whose name was writ in water.'

Kubla Khan Sacred river: Alph.

Lake Poets Wordsworth, Coleridge and Southey.

Leisure Opening: 'What is this life if, full of care, We have no time to stand and stare?'

limerick Five-line nonsense verse popularised by Edward Lear and following a rhyming scheme of aabba. Example: There was a young lady of Wilts Who walked up to Scotland on stilts When they said it was shocking To show so much stocking She answered 'Then what about kilts?'

The Listeners First line: '"Is there anybody there?" said the traveller . . .'

Maud Classic lines: 'Come into the garden, Maud, For the black bat, night, has flown . . .'

Metaphysical Poets A group of English poets of the 17th century, who include John Donne, George Herbert, Henry Vaughan, Richard Crashaw and Andrew Marvell (term first used by Samuel Johnson, possibly influenced by a phrase of Dryden's).

metre Measure of lines of verse which in English is basically accentual, determined by stress, each group of syllables, usually two or three, forms a metrical unit called a foot.

Milton called Athens 'Mother of arts and eloquence'.

The New Colossus Lines from this sonnet, inscribed on the Statue of Liberty: 'Give me your tired, your poor, Your huddled masses, yearning to breathe free, The wretched refuse of your teeming shore. Send these, the homeless, tempest-tost to me, I lift my lamp beside the golden door'.

Night Mail Opening: 'This is the Night Mail crossing the Border, Bringing the cheque and the postal order.'

Ode on a Distant Prospect of Eton College Extract: 'Ye distant spires, ye antique towers . . .'

Ode to Autumn Opening: 'Season of mists and mellow fruitfulness, Close bosom-friend of the maturing sun'.

Old English poem, 1st *Beowulf* (probably composed orally in the 8th century; written down in 10th century).

The Old Vicarage, Grantchester Details: Contains German and Greek lines (Jeffrey Archer purchased the property).

On his Blindness First line: 'When I consider how my light is spent'.

Ozymandias First line: 'I met a traveller from an antique land . . .'

pathetic fallacy The ascription of human emotions to non-human objects and phenomena, e.g. 'the cruel sea'.

Pléiade, La Group of seven French poets and writers of the 16th century, led by Pierre de Ronsard. The name was taken from that given by the Alexandrian critics to seven tragic poets of the reign of Ptolemy III Philadelphus (285–246 BC). The other six members of La Pléiade were Joachim du Bellay, Jean-Antoine de Baif, Jean Dorat, Rémy Belleau, Etienne Jodelle and Pontis de Tyard.

Poet Laureate Deposed: John Dryden, who became a Catholic in 1685 and was deposed in 1689 after the Glorious Revolution. Longest in office: Alfred, Lord Tennyson (1850–92).

Pott's disease Suffered by Alexander Pope, who was only 4 ft 6 ins tall.

prisoner poets François Villon – for his various criminal activities. James Leigh Hunt: 2 years (1813–15) for libelling the Prince Regent. Jean Genet: for theft, male prostitution, and other crimes. Richard Lovelace: in 1642, for being a Royalist.

The Rape of the Lock Two Catholic families quarrel after a male member of one steals a lock of hair from a female member of the other.

***Sally Brown* (Thomas Hood)** Extract: 'They went and told the sexton, and The sexton toll'd the bell'.

Sea Fever Opening: 'I must go down to the seas again, to the lonely sea and the sky, And all I ask is a tall ship and a star to steer her by'

Shall I compare thee to a summer's day Next lines: 'Thou art more lovely and more temperate. Rough winds do shake the darling buds of May, And summer's lease hath all too short a date . . .'

The Soldier First line: 'If I should die think only this of me'.

***Song* (John Donne)** First line: 'Go and catch a falling star . . .'

Songs of Childhood Published by Walter de la Mare using the pseudonym Walter Ramal.

sonnets Three basic types: Spenserian, Shakespearian and Petrarchan.

Spasmodic School Term coined by William Aytoun (1813–65) in his *Firmilian, or The Student of Badajoz* (1854) as an attack on the intensely melodramatic poems of such as P J Bailey, J W Marston, S T Dobell and Alexander Smith.

Spenserian stanza Eight iambic pentameters followed by one iambic hexameter, rhyming ababbcbcc.

spondee Metrical foot consisting of two long or stressed syllables.

The Star-Spangled Banner By Francis Scott Key (1779–1843). First line: 'Oh say can you see by the dawn's early light . . .'

Stella (from *Astrophel and Stella*) Thought to be Penelope Devereux.

A Subaltern's Love-song Beloved: Miss Joan Hunter Dunn. Towns mentioned: Aldershot and Camberley. Car mentioned: Hillman.

Tennyson quotes 'In the Spring a young man's fancy lightly turns to thoughts of love.'
'Man is the hunter; woman is his game . . .'
''Tis better to have loved and lost Than never to have loved at all.'

tercet Three-line stanza, particularly as used in terza rima.

terza rima Verse-form of three-line stanzas rhyming aba, bcb, cdc, and so on, usually iambic pentameters, e.g. *Ode to the West Wind.*

To a Field Mouse Opening: 'Wee, sleekit, cow'rin', tim'rous beastie, O what a panic's in thy breastie ! Extract: 'The best laid schemes o' mice an' men. Gang aft a-gley.'

To a Skylark Opening: 'Hail to thee, blithe Spirit'!

To the Virgins, To Make Much of Time First line: 'Gather ye rosebuds while ye may . . .'

Transcendentalists A mid 19th-century New England movement of writers, poets and philosophers who believed in the unity of all creation, the innate goodness of man and the supremacy of insight over logic and experience. Notable adherents were Ralph Waldo Emerson and Henry David Thoreau.

Upon Westminster Bridge Opening: 'Earth has not anything to show more fair . . .'

The Village Blacksmith Opening: Under the spreading chestnut tree The village smithy stands . . .'

A Visit from St Nicholas Opening: ''Twas the night before Christmas . . .'

Whitbread Literary Award Winners

	Category	Title	Author
1971	Novel	*The Destiny Waltz*	Gerda Charles
	Biography	*Henrik Ibsen*	Michael Meyer
	Poetry	*Mercia Hymns*	Geoffrey Hill
1972	Novel	*The Bird of Night*	Susan Hill
	Biography	*Trollope*	James Pope-Hennessy
	Children's book	*The Diddakoi*	Rumer Godden

1973	Novel	*The Chip-Chip Gatherers*	Shiva Naipaul
	Biography	*CB: A Life of Sir Henry Campbell-Bannerman*	John Wilson
	Children's book	*The Butterfly Ball & the Grasshopper's Feast*	Alan Aldridge and William Plomer
1974	Novel	*The Sacred and Profane Love Machine*	Iris Murdoch
	Biography	*Poor Dean Brendan*	Andrew Boyle
	Children's book (joint)	*How Tom Beat Captain Najork and His Hired Sportsmen*	Russell Hoban and Quentin Blake
		The Emperor's Winding Sheet	Jill Paton Walsh
1975	Novel	*Docherty*	William McIlvanney
	Autobiography	*In Our Infancy*	Helen Corke
	First book	*The Improbable Puritan: A Life of Bulstrode Whitelocke*	Ruth Spalding
1976	Novel	*The Children of Dynmouth*	William Trevor
	Biography	*Elizabeth Gaskell*	Winifred Gerin
	Children's book	*A Stitch in Time*	Penelope Lively
1977	Novel	*Injury Time*	Beryl Bainbridge
	Biography	*Mary Curzon*	Nigel Nicolson
	Children's book	*No End to Yesterday*	Shelagh Macdonald
1978	Novel	*Picture Palace*	Paul Theroux
	Biography	*Lloyd George: The People's Champion*	John Grigg
	Children's book	*The Battle of Bubble and Squeak*	Philippa Pearce
1979	Novel	*The Old Jest*	Jennifer Johnston
	Autobiography	*About Time*	Penelope Mortimer
	Children's novel	*Tulku*	Peter Dickinson
1980	Novel & Book of the Year	*How Far Can You Go?*	David Lodge
	Biography	*On the Edge of Paradise: A.C. Benson the Diarist*	David Newsome
	Children's novel	*John Diamond*	Leon Garfield
1981	Novel	*Silver's City*	Maurice Leitch
	Biography	*Monty: The Making of a General*	Nigel Hamilton
	Children's novel	*The Hollow Land*	Jane Gardam
	First novel	*A Good Man in Africa*	William Boyd
1982	Novel	*Young Shoulders*	John Wain
	Biography	*Bismarck*	Edward Crankshaw
	Children's novel	*The Song of Pentecost*	W J Corbett
	First novel	*On the Black Hill*	Bruce Chatwin
1983	Novel	*Fools of Fortune*	William Trevor
	Biography	*Vita*	Victoria Glendinning
	(joint)	*King George V*	Kenneth Rose
	Children's novel	*The Witches*	Roald Dahl
	First novel	*Flying to Nowhere*	John Fuller
1984	Novel	*Kruger's Alp*	Christopher Hope
	Biography	*T.S. Eliot*	Peter Ackroyd
	Children's novel	*The Queen of the Pharisees' Children*	Barbara Willard
	First novel	*A Parish of Rich Women*	James Buchan
	Short story	*Tomorrow is Our Permanent Address*	Diane Rowe
1985	Novel	*Hawksmoor*	Peter Ackroyd
	Biography	*Hugh Dalton*	Ben Pimlott
	Children's novel	*The Nature of the Beast*	Janni Howker
	First novel	*Oranges Are Not the Only Fruit*	Jeanette Winterson
	Poetry & Book of the year	*Elegies*	Douglas Dunn
1986	Novel & Book of the Year	*An Artist of the Floating World*	Kazuo Ishiguro
	Biography	*Gilbert White*	Richard Mabey
	Children's novel	*The Coal House*	Andrew Taylor
	First novel	*Continent*	Jim Crace
	Poetry	*Stet*	Peter Reading
1987	Novel	*The Child in Time*	Ian McEwan
	Biography & Book of the Year	*Under the Eye of the Clock*	Christopher Nolan
	First novel	*The Other Garden*	Francis Wyndham
	Poetry	*The Haw Lantern*	Seamus Heaney
1988	Novel	*The Satanic Verses*	Salman Rushdie
	Biography	*Tolstoy*	A N Wilson
	Children's novel	*Awaiting Developments*	Judy Allen
	First novel & Book of the Year	*The Comforts of Madness*	Paul Sayer
	Poetry	*The Automatic Oracle*	Peter Porter
1989	Novel	*The Chymical Wedding*	Lindsay Clarke
	Biography and Book of theYear	*Coleridge: Early Visions*	Richard Holmes
	Children's novel	*Why Weeps the Brogan?*	Hugh Scott
	First novel	*Gerontius*	James Hamilton
	Poetry	*Shibboleth*	Michael Donaghy
1990	Novel & Book of the Year	*Hopeful Monsters*	Nicholas Mosley
	Biography	*A.A. Milne: His Life*	Ann Thwaite
	Children's novel	*A.K.*	Peter Dickinson
	First novel	*The Buddha of Suburbia*	Hanif Kureishi
	Poetry	*Daddy, Daddy*	Paul Durcan
1991	Novel	*The Queen of the Tambourine*	Jane Gardam
	Biography & Book of the Year	*A Life of Picasso*	John Richardson
	Children's novel	*Harvey Angell*	Diana Hendry
	First novel	*Alma Cogan*	Gordon Burn
	Poetry	*Gorse Fires*	Michael Longley
1992	Novel	*Poor Things*	Alasdair Gray
	Biography	*Trollope*	Victoria Glendinning
	Children's novel	*The Great Elephant Chase*	Gillian Cross
	First novel & Book of the Year	*Swing Hammer Swing!*	Jeff Torrington
	Poetry	*The Gaze of the Gorgon*	Tony Harrison

1993	Novel & Book of the Year	*Theory of War*	Joan Brady
	Biography	*Philip Larkin*	Andrew Motion
	Children's novel	*Flour Babies*	Anne Fine
	First novel	*Saving Agnes*	Rachel Cusk
	Poetry	*Mean Time*	Carol Ann Duffy
1994	Novel & Book of the Year	*Felicia's Journey*	William Trevor
	Biography	*The Married Man*	Brenda Maddox
	Children's novel	*Gold Dust*	Geraldine McCaughrean
	First novel	*The Longest Memory*	Fred D'Aguiar
	Poetry	*Out of Danger*	James Fenton
1995	Novel	*The Moor's Last Sigh*	Salman Rushdie
	Biography	*Gladstone*	Roy Jenkins
	Children's novel	*The Wreck of the Zanzibar*	Michael Morpurgo
	First novel & Book of the Year	*Behind the Scenes at the Museum*	Kate Atkinson
	Poetry	*Gunpowder*	Bernard O'Donoghue
1996	Novel	*Every Man for Himself*	Beryl Bainbridge
	Biography	*Thomas Cranmer: A Life*	Diarmaid MacCulloch
	First novel	*The Debt to Pleasure*	John Lancaster
	Poetry & Book of the Year	*The Spirit Level*	Seamus Heaney
	Children's Book of the Year	*The Tulip Touch*	Anne Fine
1997	Novel	*Quarantine*	Jim Crace
	Biography	*Victor Hugo*	Graham Robb
	First novel	*The Ventriloquist's Tale*	Pauline Melville
	Poetry & Book of the Year	*Tales from Ovid*	Ted Hughes
	Children's Book of the Year	*Aquila*	Andrew Norriss
1998	Novel	*Leading the Cheers*	Justin Cartwright
	Biography	*Georgiana, Duchess of Devonshire*	Amanda Foreman
	First novel	*The Last King of Scotland*	Giles Foden
	Children's Book of the Year	*Skellig*	David Almond
	Poetry & Book of the Year	*Birthday Letters*	Ted Hughes
1999	Novel	*Music and Silence*	Rose Tremain
	Biography	*Berlioz: Servitude and Greatness*	David Cairns
	First novel	*White City Bloc*	Tim Lott
	Children's Book of the Year	*Harry Potter and the Prisoner of Azkaban*	J K Rowling
	Poetry & Book of the Year	*Beowulf*	Seamus Heaney
2000	Novel & Book of the Year	*English Passengers*	Mathew Kneale
	Biography	*Bad Blood: A memoir*	Lorna Sage
	First novel	*White Teeth*	Zadie Smith
	Children's Book of the Year	*Coram Bay*	Jamila Gavin
	Poetry	*The Asylum Dance*	John Burnside
2001	Novel	*Twelve Bar Blues*	Patrick Neate
	Biography	*Selkirk's Island*	Diana Souhami
	First novel	*Something Like A House*	Sid Smith
	Children's Book & Book of the Year	*The Amber Spyglass*	Philip Pullman
	Poetry	*Bunny*	Selima Hill
2002	Novel	*Spies*	Michael Frayn
	Biography & Book of the Year	*Samuel Pepys: The Unequalled Self*	Claire Tomalin
	First Novel	*The Song of Names*	Norman Lebrecht
	Children's Book of the Year	*Saffy's Angel*	Hilary McKay
	Poetry	*The Ice Age*	Paul Farley
2003	Novel & Book of the Year	*The Curious Incident of the Dog in the Night-Time*	Mark Haddon
	Biography	*Orwell: The Life*	D J Taylor
	First Novel	*Vernon God Little*	D B C Pierre
	Children's Book of the Year	*The Fire-Eaters*	David Almond
	Poetry	*Landing Light*	Don Paterson
2004	Novel & Book of the Year	*Small Island*	Andrea Levy
	Biography	*My Heart Is My Own: The Life of Mary Queen of Scots*	John Guy
	First Novel	*Eve Green*	Susan Fletcher
	Children's Book of the Year	*Not the End of the World*	Geraldine McCaughrean
	Poetry	*Corpus*	Michael Symmons
2005	Novel	*the accidental*	Ali Smith
	Biography & Book of the Year	*Matisse: The Master*	Hilary Spurling
	First Novel	*The Harmony Silk Factory*	Tash Aw
	Children's Book of the Year	*The New Policeman*	Kate Thompson
	Poetry	*Cold Calls*	Christopher Logue
2006	Novel	*Restless*	William Boyd
	Biography	*Keeping Mum*	Brian Thompson
	First Novel & Book of the Year	*The Tenderness of Wolves*	Stef Penney
	Children's Book of the Year	*Set in Stone*	Linda Newbery
	Poetry	*Letter to Patience*	John Haynes
2007	Novel & Book of the Year	*Day*	A L Kennedy
	Biography	*Young Stalin*	Simon Sebag Montefiore
	First Novel	*What Was Lost*	Catherine O'Flynn
	Children's Book of the Year	*The Bower Bird*	Ann Kelley
	Poetry	*Tilt*	Jean Sprackland
2008	Novel & Book of the Year	*The Secret Scripture*	Sebastian Barry
	Biography	*Somewhere Towards the End*	Diana Athill
	First Novel	*The Outcast*	Sadie Jones
	Children's Book of the Year	*Just Henry*	Michelle Magorian
	Poetry	*The Broken Word*	Adam Foulds
2009	Novel	*Brooklyn*	Colm Tóibin
	Biography	*The Strangest Man: The Hidden Life of Paul Dirac*	Graham Farmelo
	First Novel	*Beauty*	Raphael Selbourne

	Children's Book of the Year	*The Ask and the Answer*	Patrick Ness
	Poetry & Book of the Year	*A Scattering*	Christopher Reid
2010	Novel	*The Hand That First Held Mine*	Maggie O'Farrell
	Biography	*The Hare with Amber Eyes*	Edmund de Waal
	First Novel	*Witness the Night*	Kishwar Desai
	Children's Book of the Year	*Out of Shadows*	Jason Wallace
	Poetry & Book of the Year	*Of Mutability*	Jo Shapcott
2011	Novel & Book of the Year	*Pure*	Andrew Miller
	Biography	*Now All Roads Lead to France: The Last Years of Edward Thomas*	Matthew Hollis
	First Novel	*Tiny Sunbirds Far Away*	Christie Watson
	Children's Book of the Year	*Blood Red Road*	Moira Young
	Poetry	*The Bees*	Carol Ann Duffy
2012	Novel & Book of the Year	*Bring up the Bodies*	Hilary Mantel
	Biography	*Dotter of Her Father's Eyes*	Mary & Bryan Talbot
	First Novel	*The Innocents*	Francesca Segal
	Children's Book of the Year	*Maggot Moon*	Sally Gardner
	Poetry	*The Overhaul*	Kathleen Jamie
	Short Story	*Millie and Bird*	Avril Joy

NB: From 2006 the awards are sponsored by Costa

Pulitzer Prize for Fiction

Year	Book	Author
1918	*His Family*	Ernest Poole
1919	*The Magnificent Ambersons*	Booth Tarkington
1920	No Award	
1921	*The Age of Innocence*	Edith Wharton
1922	*Alice Adams*	Booth Tarkington
1923	*One of Ours*	Willa Cather
1924	*The Able McLaughlins*	Margaret Wilson
1925	*So Big*	Edna Ferber
1926	*Arrowsmith*	Sinclair Lewis
1927	*Early Autumn*	Louis Bromfield
1928	*The Bridge at San Luis Rey*	Thornton Wilder
1929	*Scarlet Sister Mary*	Julia Peterkin
1930	*Laughing Boy*	Oliver LaFarge
1931	*Years of Grace*	Margaret Ayer Barnes
1932	*The Good Earth*	Pearl S Buck
1933	*The Store*	T S Stribling
1934	*Lamb in his Bosom*	Caroline Miller
1935	*Now in November*	Josephine Winslow Johnson
1936	*Honey in the Horn*	Harold L Davis
1937	*Gone with the Wind*	Margaret Mitchell
1938	*The Late George Apley*	John Phillips Marquand
1939	*The Yearling*	Marjorie Kinnan Rawlings
1940	*The Grapes of Wrath*	John Steinbeck
1941	No Award	
1942	*In This Our Life*	Ellen Glasgow
1943	*Dragon's Teeth*	Upton Sinclair
1944	*Journey in the Dark*	Martin Flavin
1945	*A Bell for Adano*	John Hersey
1946	No Award	
1947	*All the King's Men*	Robert Penn Warren
1948	*Tales of the South Pacific*	James A Michener
1949	*Guard of Honor*	James Gould Cozzens
1950	*The Way West*	A B Guthrie Jr
1951	*The Town*	Conrad Richter
1952	*The Caine Mutiny*	Herman Wouk
1953	*The Old Man and the Sea*	Ernest Hemingway
1954	No Award	
1955	*A Fable*	William Faulkner
1956	*Andersonville*	Mackinlay Kantor
1957	No Award	
1958	*A Death in the Family*	James Agee
1959	*The Travels of Jamie McPheeters*	Robert Lewis Taylor
1960	*Advise and Consent*	Allen Drury
1961	*To Kill a Mockingbird*	Harper Lee
1962	*The Edge of Sadness*	Edwin O'Connor
1963	*The Reivers*	William Faulkner
1964	No Award	
1965	*The Keepers of the House*	Shirley Ann Grau
1966	*Collected Stories of Katherine Anne Porter*	Katherine Anne Porter
1967	*The Fixer*	Bernard Malamud
1968	*The Confessions of Nat Turner*	William Styron
1969	*House Made of Dawn*	N Scott Momaday
1970	*Collected Stories*	Jean Stafford
1971	No Award	
1972	*Angle of Repose*	Wallace Stegner
1973	*The Optimist's Daughter*	Eudora Welty
1974	No Award	
1975	*The Killer Angels*	Michael Shaara
1976	*Humboldt's Gift*	Saul Bellow
1977	No Award	
1978	*Elbow Room*	James Alan McPherson
1979	*The Stories of John Cheever*	John Cheever
1980	*The Executioner's Song*	Norman Mailer
1981	*A Confederacy of Dunces*	John Kennedy Toole
1982	*Rabbit is Rich*	John Updike
1983	*The Color Purple*	Alice Walker
1984	*Ironweed*	William Kennedy
1985	*Foreign Affairs*	Alison Lurie
1986	*Lonesome Dove*	Larry McMurty
1987	*A Summons to Memphis*	Peter Taylor
1988	*Beloved*	Toni Morrison
1989	*Breathing Lessons*	Anne Tyler
1990	*The Mambo Kings Play Songs of Love*	Oscar Hijuelos
1991	*Rabbit at Rest*	John Updike
1992	*A Thousand Acres*	Jane Smiley
1993	*A Good Scent from a Strange Mountain*	Robert Olen Butler
1994	*The Shipping News*	E Annie Proulx
1995	*The Stone Diaries*	Carol Shields
1996	*Independence Day*	Richard Ford
1997	*Martin Dressler: Tale of an American Dreamer*	Steven Millhauser
1998	*American Pastoral*	Philip Roth
1999	*The Hours*	Michael Cunningham
2000	*Interpreteur of Maladies*	Jhumpa Lahiri
2001	*The Amazing Adventures of Kavalier & Clay*	Michael Chabon
2002	*Empire Falls*	Richard Russo
2003	*Middlesex*	Jeffrey Eugenides
2004	*The Known World*	Edward P Jones
2005	*Gilead*	Marilynne Robinson
2006	*March*	Geraldine Brooks
2007	*The Road*	Cormac McCarthy
2008	*The Brief Wondrous Life of Oscar Wao*	Junot Diaz
2009	*Olive Kitteridge*	Elizabeth Strout
2010	*Tinkers*	Paul Harding
2011	*A Visit From the Goon Squad*	Jennifer Egan
2012	Not Awarded	
2013	*The Orphan Master's Son*	Adam Johnson

Booker Prize for Fiction

Year	Book	Author
1969	*Something to Answer For*	P H Newby
1970	*The Elected Member*	Bernice Rubens
1971	*In a Free State*	V S Naipaul
1972	*G*	John Berger
1973	*The Siege of Krishnapur*	J G Farrell
1974	*The Conservationist*	Nadine Gordimer
	Holiday	Stanley Middleton (joint)
1975	*Heat and Dust*	Ruth Prawer Jhabvala
1976	*Saville*	David Storey
1977	*Staying On*	Paul Scott
1978	*The Sea, The Sea*	Iris Murdoch
1979	*Offshore*	Penelope Fitzgerald
1980	*Rites of Passage*	William Golding
1981	*Midnight's Children*	Salman Rushdie
1982	*Schindler's Ark*	Thomas Keneally
1983	*The Life and Times of Michael K*	J M Coetzee
1984	*Hotel Du Lac*	Anita Brookner
1985	*The Bone People*	Keri Hulme
1986	*The Old Devils*	Kingsley Amis
1987	*Moon Tiger*	Penelope Lively
1988	*Oscar and Lucinda*	Peter Carey
1989	*The Remains of the Day*	Kazuo Ishiguro
1990	*Possession*	A S Byatt
1991	*The Famished Road*	Ben Okri
1992	*Sacred Hunger*	Barry Unsworth
	The English Patient	Michael Ondaatje (joint)
1993	*Paddy Clarke Ha Ha Ha*	Roddy Doyle
1994	*How Late it Was, How Late*	James Kelman
1995	*The Ghost Road*	Pat Barker
1996	*Last Orders*	Graham Swift
1997	*The God of Small Things*	Arundhati Roy
1998	*Amsterdam*	Ian McEwan
1999	*Disgrace*	J M Coetzee
2000	*The Blind Assassin*	Margaret Atwood
2001	*True History of the Kelly Gang*	Peter Carey
2002	*Life of Pi*	Yann Martel
2003	*Vernon God Little*	D B C Pierre
2004	*The Line of Beauty*	Alan Hollinghurst
2005	*The Sea*	John Banville
2006	*The Inheritance of Loss*	Kiran Desai
2007	*The Gathering*	Anne Enright
2008	*The White Tiger*	Aravind Adiga
2009	*Wolf Hall*	Hilary Mantel
2010	*The Finkler Question*	Howard Jacobson
2011	*The Sense of an Ending*	Julian Barnes
2012	*Bring Up the Bodies*	Hilary Mantel

NB: The Man Booker Prize is awarded for a novel by a citizen of the UK, Eire, South Africa, or any Commonwealth country, with the proviso that it was first published in Britain. In 1971 the Booker switched from being a retrospective prize to one given in the year of publication, with the award moving from April to November. This meant a whole year of fiction slipped though the net. In May 2010 a 'lost' Booker Prize was awarded posthumously to J G Farrell for his 1970 novel *Troubles*.

Orange Prize for Fiction

The Orange Award was launched in January 1996 and is restricted to female novelists. As well as the annual prize of £30,000 the winner receives a bronze figurine created by Griznel Niven known as the 'Betsie'. In 2005 the 'Orange of Oranges' was awarded to Andrea Levy for *Small Island.* From 2013 the award is to be known as The Baileys Women's Prize for Fiction.

Winners	Year	Title
Helen Dunmore	1996	*A Spell of Winter*
Anne Michaels	1997	*Fugitive Pieces*
Carol Shields	1998	*Larry's Party*
Suzanne Berne	1999	*A Crime in the Neighbourhood*
Linda Grant	2000	*When I Lived in Modern Times*
Kate Grenville	2001	*The Idea of Perfection*
Ann Patchett	2002	*Bel Canto*
Valerie Martin	2003	*Property*
Andrea Levy	2004	*Small Island*
Lionel Shriver	2005	*We Need to Talk About Kevin*
Zadie Smith	2006	*On Beauty*
Chimamanda Ngozi Adichie	2007	*Half of a Yellow Sun*
Rose Tremain	2008	*The Road Home*
Marilynne Robinson	2009	*Home*
Barbara Kingsolver	2010	*The Lacuna*
Téa Obreht	2011	*The Tiger's Wife*
Madeline Miller	2012	*The Song of Achilles*
A.M. Homes	2013	*May We Be Forgiven*

LITERATURE

Fictional Literary Characters

(except Austen, Dickens and Shakespeare)

Captain Absolute	*The Rivals*
Captain Ahab	*Moby-Dick*
Roderick Alleyn	created by Ngaio Marsh
Charlie Allnutt	*The African Queen*
Squire Allworthy	*Tom Jones*
Andy Capp	drawn by Reg Smythe
Andy Pandy	created by Maria Bird
Harry Angstrom	the Rabbit Tetralogy
Lara Antipova	*Doctor Zhivago*
Aouda	*Around the World in 80 Days*
John Appleby	created by Michael Innes
Isobel Archer	*The Portrait of a Lady*
Jack Aubrey	*Master and Commander* (and others)
Steve Austin	*Cyborg* (by Martin Caidin)
Ayesha	*She*
Dr Aziz	*A Passage to India*
Babar	created by Jean de Brunhoff
Badger	*The Wind in the Willows*
Bilbo Baggins	*The Hobbit, Lord of the Rings*
David Balfour	*Kidnapped*
The Baron (John Mannering)	created by Anthony Morton (John Creasey)
Oliver Barrett IV	*Love Story*
Bastable Family	*The Treasure-Seekers* (by E Nesbit)
Batman	created by Bob Kane
Dr Jim Bayliss	*All My Sons*
Bazarov	*Fathers and Sons*
Belinda	*The Rape of the Lock*
Inspector Bertozzo	*Accidental Death of an Anarchist*
Margot Beste-Chetwynde	*Decline and Fall*
Big Daddy	*Cat on a Hot Tin Roof*
Bigwig (rabbit)	*Watership Down*
Ernie Bilko	created by Nat Hiken

John Blackthorne	*Shogun*
Modesty Blaise	created by Peter O'Donnell
Sir Percy Blakeney	*The Scarlet Pimpernel*
Colonel Blimp	created by David Low
Leopold Bloom	*Ulysses*
Prince Andrey Bolkonsky	*War and Peace*
James Bond	created by Ian Fleming
Bosinney	*The Forsyte Saga*
Boxer the Horse	*Animal Farm*
Jack Boyle	*Juno and the Paycock*
Lady Bracknell	*The Importance of Being Ernest*
Ben Braddock	*The Graduate*
Alan Breck	*Kidnapped*
Brer Rabbit	the Uncle Remus stories
Dorothea Brooke	*Middlemarch*
Father Brown	created by G K Chesterton
Pinkie Brown	*Brighton Rock*
Beatrice Bryant	*Roots*
Daisy Buchanan	*The Great Gatsby*
Charlie Bucket	*Charlie and the Chocolate Factory*
Buck (the Dog)	*The Call of the Wild*
Natty Bumppo	the Leatherstocking stories
Albert Campion	created by Margery Allingham
Tom Canty	*The Prince and the Pauper*
Sir Danvers Carew	*Dr Jekyll and Mr Hyde*
William Carey	*Of Human Bondage*
Katy Carr	*What Katy Did*
Captain Cat	*Under Milk Wood*
Anne Catherick	*The Woman in White*
Catherine	*The Bell*
Holden Caulfield	*The Catcher in the Rye*
Jenny Cavillieri	*Love Story*
Professor Challenger	*The Lost World*
Canon Chasuble	*The Importance of Being Ernest*
Chauntecleer (the hen)	*Nun's Priest's Tale*
Jack Chesney	*Charley's Aunt*
Harvey Cheyne	*Captains Courageous*
Chichikov	*Dead Souls*
Chingachgook	the Leatherstocking stories
Mr Charles Chipping	*Goodbye, Mr Chips*
Petty Officer Claggart	*Billy Budd*
Angel Clare	*Tess of the D'Urbervilles*
Eric Claudin	*The Phantom of the Opera*
Darius Clayhanger (printer)	*Clayhanger*
Clegg	*The Collector*
Robert James Colley	*Rites of Passage*
Compson family	*The Sound and the Fury* and *Absalom, Absalom!*
Hugh Conway	*Lost Horizon*
Alex Cross	*Along Came a Spider (1st)*
Guy Crouchback	*Men at Arms*
Lenina Crowne	*Brave New World*
Isabelle de Croye	*Quentin Durward*
Sergeant Cuff	*The Moonstone*
Curdie (miner)	*The Princess and the Goblin*
Stephen Daedalus	*Ulysses*
Adam Dalgleish	created by P D James
Edmond Dantès	*Count of Monte Christo*
Mrs Danvers	*Rebecca*
Dapper	*The Alchemist*
Anne Deever	*All My Sons*
Danny Deever	*Barrack-Room Ballads*
Maxim De Winter	*Rebecca*
Dick Diver	*Tender Is the Night*
James Dixon	*Lucky Jim*
Captain Dobbin	*Vanity Fair*
Eliza Doolittle	*Pygmalion*
Paul Drake	created by Erle Stanley Gardner
Abel Drugger	*The Alchemist*
Blanche Du Bois	*A Streetcar Named Desire*
Lady Dulcinea	*Don Quixote*
Auguste Dupin	created by Edgar Allan Poe
Albus Dumbledore	Harry Potter books
Dudley Dursley	Harry Potter books
Catherine Earnshaw	*Wuthering Heights*
Humphrey Chimpden Earwicker	*Finnegans Wake*
Eeyore	*Winnie-the-Pooh*
Montague Egg	created by Dorothy L Sayers
Mrs Erlynne	*Lady Windermere's Fan*
Cedric Errol	*Little Lord Fauntleroy*
Esmeralda	*The Hunchback of Notre Dame*
Estragon	*Waiting for Godot*
Etienne	*Germinal*
Bathsheba Everdene	*Far from the Madding Crowd*
Face	*The Alchemist*
Jude Fawley	*Jude the Obscure*
Gervase Fenn	created by Edmund Crispin
Cyril Fielding	*A Passage to India*
Fiver	*Watership Down*
Pegeen Flaherty	*The Playboy of the Western World*
Flashman	*Tom Brown's Schooldays*
Henry Fleming	*The Red Badge of Courage*
Phileas Fogg	*Around the World in 80 Days*
Fossil family	*Ballet Shoes* (Noel Streatfeild)
Frodo	*The Lord of the Rings*
Archdeacon Frollo	*The Hunchback of Notre Dame*
Gandalf	*The Lord of the Rings*
James Gatz (Jay Gatsby)	*The Great Gatsby*
Marguerite Gautier	*Camille*
Gerard	*The Cloister and the Hearth*
Inspector Ghote	created by H R F Keating
Roderick Glossop (psychiatrist)	the Jeeves stories
Anthony Gloster (shipowner)	*The Mary Gloster* (Kipling)
Holly Golightly	*Breakfast at Tiffany's*
Gollum	*The Lord of the Rings*
Hermione Granger	Harry Potter books
Cordelia Gray	created by P D James
Grendel	*Beowulf*
Jack Grey	*Pale Fire*
Joan Griffin	*The Invisible Man*
Clyde Griffiths	*An American Tragedy*
Captain Grimes	*Decline and Fall*
Tania Gromeko	*Doctor Zhivago*
Gunga Din	created by Rudyard Kipling
Tod Hackett	*The Day of the Locust*
Harry Haller	*Steppenwolf*
Basil Hallward	*The Picture of Dorian Gray*
Charles Hamilton	*Gone With the Wind*
Richard Hannay	*The Thirty-Nine Steps*
Miss Hardcastle	*She Stoops to Conquer*
Hawkeye	the Leatherstocking stories
Bill Haydon (spy)	*Tinker, Tailor, Soldier, Spy*
Dolores Haze	*Lolita*
Hazel (rabbit)	*Watership Down*
Nora Helmer	*A Doll's House*
Michael Henchard	*The Mayor of Casterbridge*
Frederic Henry	*A Farewell to Arms*
Hickey	*The Iceman Cometh*
Henry Higgins	*Pygmalion*
Charles Highway	*The Rachel Papers*
Bridget Hitler	*Young Adolf* by Beryl Bainbridge
Captain Hook	*Peter Pan*
Houyhnhnms (horses)	*Gulliver's Travels*
Humbert Humbert	*Lolita*
Humpty Dumpty	*Through the Looking Glass*
Injun Joe	*Tom Sawyer*
Mrs Jessel	*The Turn of the Screw*
Tom Joad	*The Grapes of Wrath*
Jocasta	*Oedipus the King*
Victoria Jones	*Bhowani Junction* (John Masters)
Robert Jordan	*For Whom the Bell Tolls*
Monsieur Jourdain	*Le Bourgeois Gentilhomme*
Joseph K	*The Trial*
Alyosha Karamazov	*The Brothers Karamazov*
Dmitri Karamazov	*The Brothers Karamazov*
Ivan Karamazov	*The Brothers Karamazov*
Chris Keller	*All My Sons*
Frank Kennedy	*Gone With the Wind*
Khlestakov	*The Inspector General*
Kipps (draper's assistant)	*Kipps*
Howard Kirk	*The History Man*
Joseph Knecht	*The Glass Bead Game* (aka *Magister Ludi*)
Kostoglotov	*Cancer Ward*
Stanley Kowalsky	*A Streetcar Named Desire*
Lydia Languish	*The Rivals*
Leamas	*The Spy Who Came in from the Cold*
Simon Legree	*Uncle Tom's Cabin*
Amyas Leigh	*Westward Ho!*
Jeeter Lester	*Tobacco Road*
Adrian Leverkühn (composer)	*Doctor Faustus*
Levin	*Anna Karenina*
Ligia	*Quo Vadis?*
Teddy Lloyd	*The Prime of Miss Jean Brodie*
Lord Loam	*The Admirable Crichton*
Willy Loman	*Death of a Salesman*
Lovewit	*The Alchemist*

Frank Lubey	*All My Sons*
Lucky	*Waiting for Godot*
Tertius Lydgate (surgeon)	*Middlemarch*
Lt Macaulay	*Bhowani Junction* (John Masters)
Christie Mahon	*The Playboy of the Western World*
Major Major	*Catch-22*
Mrs Malaprop	*The Rivals*
Draco Malfoy	Harry Potter books
Captain Charles Mallison	*Lost Horizon*
Daphne Manners	*The Jewel in the Crown*
Stephen Maturin	created by Patrick O'Brian
Oskar Matzerath	*The Tin Drum*
Oliver Mellors	*Lady Chatterley's Lover*
Merrylegs (pony)	*Black Beauty*
Messala	*Ben Hur*
Duke Michael	*The Prisoner of Zenda*
Mildew	*Fungus the Bogeyman*
Millamant	*The Way of the World*
George Milton	*Of Mice and Men*
Minnehaha	*Hiawatha*
Mirabell	*The Way of the World*
Mold	*Fungus the Bogeyman*
Mole	*The Wind in the Willows*
Algernon Moncrieff	*The Importance of Being Ernest*
Montmorency (the dog)	*Three Men in a Boat*
Dr Monygham	*Nostromo*
Paul Morel	*Sons and Lovers*
Dean Moriarty	*On the Road*
Mother's Younger Brother	*Ragtime* (E L Doctorow)
Mowgli	*The Jungle Book*
Matthew Mugg (catsmeat man)	*Doctor Dolittle*
Prince Myshkin	*The Idiot*
Mytyl	*The Blue Bird*
Nana	*Peter Pan*
Napoleon the Pig	*Animal Farm*
Nawab of Satipur	*Heat and Dust* (Ruth Prawer Jhabvala)
Nayland-Smith	*Fu Manchu*
Captain Nemo	*Twenty Thousand Leagues Under the Sea*
Norah Nesbit	*Of Human Bondage*
Gabriel Oak	*Far from the Madding Crowd*
Kitty Oblonsky	*Anna Karenina*
Julia O'Brien	*Nineteen Eighty-Four*
Mrs Ogmore-Pritchard	*Under Milk Wood*
O-Lan	*The Good Earth*
Oompa Loompas	*Charlie and the Chocolate Factory*
George Osborne	*Vanity Fair*
Doctor Pangloss	*Candide*
Panurge	*Gargantua and Pantagruel*
Sancho Panza	*Don Quixote*
Passepartout	*Around the World in 80 Days*
Paul Pennyfeather	*Decline and Fall*
Pertelote (the cock)	*The Nun's Priest's Tale*
Ronald Osprey Petrefact	*Ancestral Vices* (Tom Sharpe)
Petrovitch	*Crime and Punishment*
Alexander Petrovsky	*Russian Hide-and-Seek* (Kingsley Amis)
Aunt Peturia	Harry Potter books
Phaedrus	*Zen and the Art of Motorcycle Maintenance*
Piggy	*Lord of the Flies*
Billy Pilgrim	*Slaughterhouse-Five*
Captain Pissani	*Accidental Death of an Anarchist*
Maggie Pollitt	*Cat on a Hot Tin Roof*
Polynesia (parrot)	*Doctor Dolittle*
Ernest Pontifex	*The Way of All Flesh*
Jimmy Porter	*Look Back in Anger*
Claude (Mustard) Pott	created by P G Wodehouse
Harry Potter	Harry Potter books
Pozzo	*Waiting for Godot*
Ford Prefect	*The Hitchhiker's Guide to the Galaxy*
Private Prewitt	*From Here to Eternity*
Dr Primrose	*The Vicar of Wakefield*
Miss Prism	*The Importance of Being Ernest*
Dr Proudie	*Barchester Towers*
Mrs Proudie	*Barchester Towers*
Hester Prynne	*The Scarlet Letter*
Pushmi-Pullyu (two-headed llama)	*Doctor Dolittle*
Roger Quaife	*The Corridors of Power*
Quasimodo	*The Hunchback of Notre Dame*
Queen of Hearts	*Alice's Adventures in Wonderland*
Adela Quested	*A Passage to India*
Quint	*The Turn of the Screw*

Ralph	*Lord of the Flies*
Elwin Ransome	*Perelandra* by C S Lewis
Raskolnikov	*Crime and Punishment*
Paul Ray	*The Second Mrs Tanqueray*
Red Queen	*Through the Looking Glass*
Ignatius J Reilly	*Confederacy of Dunces* (John K Toole)
Archie Rice	*The Entertainer*
Rico Bandello	*Little Caesar* (W R Burnett)
John Ridd	*Lorna Doone*
Sir Colenso Ridgeon	*The Doctor's Dilemma*
Rikki Tikki Tavi	*The Jungle Book*
Christopher Robin	*Winnie-the-Pooh*
Fanny Robin	*Far from the Madding Crowd*
Mr Rochester	*Jane Eyre*
Mildred Rodgers	*Of Human Bondage*
Rose of Torridge	*Westward Ho!*
Emma Rouault	*Madame Bovary*
Lady Rowena	*Ivanhoe*
Roxane	*Cyrano de Bergerac*
Nicholas Rubashov	*Darkness at Noon*
King Rudolf	*The Prisoner of Zenda*
Captain Charles Ryder	*Brideshead Revisited*
Iris Aroon St Charles	*Good Behaviour* (Molly Keane)
Sauron	*The Lord of the Rings*
Rose Sayer	*The African Queen*
Scamper	*The Secret Seven*
Basil Seal	*Black Mischief*
Amelia Sedley	*Vanity Fair*
John Francis Shade	*Pale Fire*
Shadowfax (horse)	*The Lord of the Rings*
Shalimar	*The Arabian Nights*
Becky Sharp	*Vanity Fair*
Anne Shirley	*Anne of Green Gables*
Napoleon Bonaparte Simpson	*The Spectacles* (Edgar Allan Poe)
Saleem Sinai	*Midnight's Children*
Dr Slop	*Tristram Shandy*
Obadiah Slope	*Barchester Towers*
Tyrone Slothrop	*Gravity's Rainbow*
Lennie Small	*Of Mice and Men*
Pavel Smedyakov	*The Brothers Karamazov*
George Smiley	created by John le Carré
Smith	*Loneliness of the Long Distance Runner*
Winston Smith	*Nineteen Eighty-Four*
Lady Sneerwell	*The School for Scandal*
Julian Sorel	*The Red and the Black*
Bertie Stanhope	*Barchester Towers*
Steerpike	*Titus Groan*
Alan Strang	*Equus*
Subtle	*The Alchemist*
Joseph Surface	*The School for Scandal*
Svengali	*Trilby*
Tadzio	*Death in Venice*
John Tanner	*Man and Superman*
Tatiana	*Eugene Onegin*
Lady Teazle	*The School for Scandal*
Professor George Tessman	*Hedda Gabler*
Becky Thatcher	*Tom Sawyer*
Timmy	*The Famous Five*
Tinker Bell	*Peter Pan*
Tiresias	*Oedipus the King*
Toad	*The Wind in the Willows*
Uncle Toby	*Tristram Shandy*
Kenneth Marchal Toomey	*Earthly Powers*
Topsy	*Uncle Tom's Cabin*
Rev. John Treherne	*The Admirable Crichton*
Trigorin	*The Seagull*
Trilby (artist's model)	*Trilby*
Disko Troop	*Captains Courageous*
Sergeant Troy	*Far from the Madding Crowd*
Maggie Tulliver	*The Mill on the Floss*
Tom Tulliver	*The Mill on the Floss*
Tweedledum and Tweedledee	*Through the Looking Glass*
Tyltyl	*The Blue Bird*
Uncas	the Leatherstocking stories
Andrew Undershaft (arms maker)	*Major Barbara*
Jean Valjean	*Les Misérables*
Piet van der Valk	created by Nicolas Freeling
Harriet Vane	created by Dorothy L Sayers
Uncle Vernon	Harry Potter books
Vladimir	*Waiting for Godot*
Gustav Von Aschenbach	*Death in Venice*
Voldemort	Harry Potter books

Count Vronsky	*Anna Karenina*
Alice Walker	*The Color Purple*
The Walrus and the Carpenter	*Through the Looking Glass*
Wang Lung	*The Good Earth*
Water Rat	*The Wind in the Willows*
Ronald Weasley	Harry Potter books
Sophia Western	*Tom Jones*
Reg Wexford	created by Ruth Rendell
Ann Whitefield	*Man and Superman*
White Queen	*Through the Looking Glass*
Ashley Wilkes	*Gone With the Wind*
Aaron Winthrop	*Silas Marner*
Willy Nilly	*Under Milk Wood*
Willy Wonka	*Charlie and the Chocolate Factory*
Nero Wolfe	created by Rex Stout
Ernest Wooley	*The Admirable Crichton*
Wormold	*Our Man in Havana*
Jack Worthing	*The Importance of Being Ernest*
General Woundwort (rabbit)	*Watership Down*
Charles Wykeham	*Charley's Aunt*
Yahoos (humans)	*Gulliver's Travels*
Mary Yellan	*Jamaica Inn*
Captain Yossarian	*Catch-22*
Falther Zossima	*The Brothers Karamazov*

Chaucer's Canterbury Pilgrims

1 The Knight's Tale
2 The Miller's Tale
3 The Reeve's Tale
4 The Cook's Tale
5 The Man of Law's Tale
6 The Wife of Bath's Tale
7 The Friar's Tale
8 The Summoner's Tale
9 The Clerk's Tale
10 The Merchant's Tale
11 The Squire's Tale
12 The Franklin's Tale
13 The Physician's Tale
14 The Pardoner's Tale
15 The Shipman's Tale
16 The Prioress's Tale
17 Chaucer's Tale of Sir Thopas
18 Chaucer's Tale of Melibeus
19 The Monk's Tale
20 The Nun's Priest's Tale
21 The Second Nun's Tale
22 The Canon's Yeoman's Tale
23 The Manciple's Tale
24 The Parson's Tale

NB: The Canterbury Tales was an unfinished collection of tales told in the course of a pilgrimage to Thomas Becket's shrine at Canterbury. In addition to the 22 story-tellers listed above, the party included a dyer, weaver, arrowmaker, haberdasher, carpenter, ploughman and guidesman, making a total of 29. Chaucer himself may be included as a pilgrim to give a definitive total of 30.

Mr Men and Little Misses

Mr Men

1 Mr Bounce is round and yellow and very cuddly. He is forever turning somersaults while landing on his head.
2 Mr Brave proves that looks can be deceiving, bespectacled and yellow-looking but utterly fearless.
3 Mr Bump is always having accidents of all sorts, and so is always wrapped in bandages from his latest injury.
4 Mr Busy always has something to do, and like Mr Rush this blue character simply cannot relax.
5 Mr Chatterbox never ever stops talking, not even for a moment. It is impossible to get a word in edgeways.
6 Mr Cheeky is extremely rude. When he meets people in the street he insults them unashamedly. (Not one of the original 43 characters but introduced in 2001 as a result of a nationwide competition to celebrate the 30th anniversary of their birth. Gemma Almond, 8, from Shropshire won the competition.)
7 Mr Cheerful is always looking on the bright side of life and is there to cheer you up when you are down.
8 Mr Christmas was not one of the original 43 Mr Men books but was created for a Christmas special.
9 Mr Clever is wide-eyed and bespectacled, and of course knows absolutely everything.
10 Mr Clumsy means well but really is very clumsy indeed, so don't let him near Mr Bump's children.
11 Mr Daydream is in a world of his own most of the time, his imagination running rife.
12 Mr Dizzy lives in a land where pigs and elephants are clever, and he just can't get his head around it all.
13 Mr Forgetful is big and blue and egg-shaped and very very absent-minded.
14 Mr Funny lives in a teapot-shaped house, and drives a shoe-shaped car. He is a practical joker par excellence.
15 Mr Fussy likes things to be neat and tidy, and even irons his shoelaces. He is green and fastidious.
16 Mr Greedy is the greediest person alive. When he comes to visit, make sure there's no food lying around!
17 Mr Grumble is never content. On a lovely day he hates the hot sun, and when it snows he's too cold!
18 Mr Grumpy is always in a bad mood, no matter what. He can't stand it when other people have fun.
19 Mr Happy lives in Happyland where everyone and everything is always happy. Big and yellow with a grin to match.
20 Mr Impossible really can do the impossible! Mauve in colour, there is nothing up his sleeve!
21 Mr Jelly is scared of everything and anything. The quivering red blob is also known as Mr Nervous.
22 Mr Lazy likes nothing more than to do absolutely nothing. He'll laze about in the sun all day if he can.
23 Mr Mean is not very nice really. He's tall and slim but with short arms and long pockets.
24 Mr Messy needs to get his act together. His garden is overgrown and his washing up is never done.
25 Mr Mischief is a bigger practical joker than Mr Fun. He is always sniggering over his latest prank.
26 Mr Muddle just can't get things right, so if you meet him in the morning, he'll say 'Good Afternoon!'
27 Mr Noisy is always shouting. He's utterly incapable of talking quietly.
28 Mr Nonsense looks like a clown and acts like one, his big red nose protruding from a nonsensical grin.
29 Mr Nosey is incapable of minding his own business. His long green nose is taller than himself.
30 Mr Perfect is as his name implies. He has a perfect house with a perfect garden and his lawn is always perfect.
31 Mr Quiet can't stand noisy people or places. Unfortunately he lives in Loudland and it's very trying for him.
32 Mr Rush is always in a hurry and this mauve, triangular-faced flash is heading for a fall unless he slows down.
33 Mr Silly is just plain daft! Even his large red hat is pulled down over his eyes so he cannot see properly.
34 Mr Skinny is long, yellow and as skinny as a rake – literally! Perhaps he should help Mr Messy with his garden!
35 Mr Slow is in no hurry. His moustachioed face gives him a distinguished look . . . but don't rush him!
36 Mr Small really is very tiny, his little red features barely discernible unless you are looking down!
37 Mr Sneeze lives in Coldland, and always has a cold and a very red nose and a blue face from all his sneezing.
38 Mr Snow is the personification of all the snowmen you have ever made in wintertime.
39 Mr Strong can lift entire buildings. He eats a lot of eggs, too, to keep his strength up. He is Big and Square.
40 Mr Tall is as tall as a cliff. He has very long legs, so he can walk a long way very very quickly.
41 Mr Tickle likes to tickle people but his long arms can make breakfast while lying in bed! He was the first Mr Man.

42 Mr Topsy-Turvy reads books upside-down and has a clock that goes anti-clockwise. He greets people he meets by saying 'Morning Good' and he also wears his hat upside-down.
43 Mr Uppity is an outrageous snob, although his black topper makes him look rather distinguished and dapper.
44 Mr Worry is always deep in thought, with a deep frown upon his round blue face.
45 Mr Wrong just can't get things right. He can't even choose a pair of gloves of the same colour!

Little Misses

1 Little Miss Bossy can't stop ordering people around and shouting at them. When she says jump you jump.
2 Little Miss Brainy is the female counterpart of Mr Clever.
3 Little Miss Busy is always busy cleaning the house, shopping, gardening, cooking. She never stops!
4 Little Miss Chatterbox is the female counterpart of Mr Chatterbox and is equally talkative.
5 Little Miss Contrary is always deep in thought but will never agree about anything!
6 Little Miss Curious cannot help but have an inquiring mind.
7 Little Miss Dotty lives in nonsenseland, where Mr Silly and Mr Nonsense live, and she is equally dotty.
8 Little Miss Fickle changes her mind constantly and who knows what or where the mood takes her.
9 Little Miss Fun is a party animal! She's always ready to go out and have fun somewhere.
10 Little Miss Giggles can't stop giggling. She giggles so much that when she's around, everyone else starts too!
11 Little Miss Greedy is as greedy as Mr Greedy. In the earliest books she was also called Little Miss Plump.
12 Little Miss Helpful tries her hardest to be as helpful as she possibly can be. She really does try . . . so hard!
13 Little Miss Late is never on time and punctuality is certainly not her byword.
14 Little Miss Lucky doesn't seem quite as lucky as her name implies, but things always come out all right in the end.
15 Little Miss Magic can do magic! I suppose Mr Impossible would be her male equivalent.
16 Little Miss Naughty is very naughty and her naughty ways do not make her very many friends!
17 Little Miss Neat can't stand any sort of mess. She is bespectacled, round and green.
18 Little Miss Quick doesn't hang around at all, and whatever she does she does it very quickly indeed.
19 Little Miss Scatterbrain is very absent-minded and her male equivalent would be Mr Forgetful.
20 Little Miss Shy is very unassuming and would rather be left alone so I won't embarrass her any longer.
21 Little Miss Somersault has very long legs and is very gymnastic. She is forever turning somersaults.
22 Little Miss Splendid looks a little aloof but is quite splendid really although a little prim and proper.
23 Little Miss Star is round and blue with lovely green shoes. She is a real star through and through.
24 Little Miss Stubborn will not listen. No matter how silly her ideas are she is determined to follow them through.
25 Little Miss Sunshine is a vision in yellow and her beaming smile is sure to cheer the hardest heart.
26 Little MissTidy is not green like Little Miss Neat but yellow, and she doesn't wear glasses either.
27 Little Miss Tiny is very small indeed. In fact she is smaller than Mr Small!
28 Little Miss Trouble cannot help but find trouble. She is the female equivalent of Mr Mischief.
29 Little Miss Twins do everything in pairs, and say things twice twice. They live in Twoland. The Little Miss Twins were inspired by Roger Hargreaves's twin daughters.
30 Little Miss Wise is the person to consult if you want some sound advice, as she is very wise indeed.

Note

Mr Men and Little Misses received six new friends 15 years after the death of their creator Roger Hargreaves. His son penned the tales of Mr Cool, Mr Rude, Mr Good, Little Miss Bad, Little Miss Scary and Little Miss Whoops. Adam Hargreaves took over the running of the Mr Men empire after his father died of a stroke in 1988 at the age of 53. Adam had been the original inspiration for the books when he asked his father what a tickle looked like. The result was Mr Tickle, the first in a series which went on to sell over 100 million copies worldwide. The first four new books were published in April 2003 and two others in September 2003. The books were written by Adam, but he still credited his father as author to keep his father's memory alive. Four further new books, *Mr Birthday* (2006), *Little Miss Birthday* (2007), *Mr Nobody* (2010) and *Little Miss Princess* (2011) have since been added plus various special edition characters such as *Mr Birthday, Little Miss Birthday* and *Little Miss Christmas*

Poets Laureate

John Dryden (1668-88)
Thomas Shadwell (1688–92)
Nahum Tate (1692–1715)
Nicholas Rowe (1715–18)
Laurence Eusden (1718–30)
Colley Cibber (1730–57)
William Whitehead (1757–85)
Thomas Warton (1785–90)
Henry James Pye (1790–1813)
Robert Southey (1813–43)
William Wordsworth (1843–50)
Alfred, Lord Tennyson (1850–92)
Alfred Austin (1896–1913)
Robert Bridges (1913–30)
John Masefield (1930–67)
Cecil Day-Lewis (1968–72)
Sir John Betjeman (1972–84)
Ted Hughes (1984–1998)
Andrew Motion (1999–2009)
Carol Ann Duffy (2009–)

NB: Ben Jonson was the first to be granted a pension as poet, to James I (1616), and in 1630 Charles I added an annual butt of canary wine, which was discontinued by Henry Pye who preferred money. Sir William Davenant succeeded Jonson but the position was only made official in 1668. William Whitehead appointed after Thomas Gray declined the honour. Similarly Alfred, Lord Tennyson became laureate after Samuel Rogers declined.

Servants (and Masters)

Lugg	Campion
Bunter	Lord Peter Wimsey
Miss Lemon	Poirot
Mrs Hudson	Sherlock Holmes
Reginald Jeeves	Bertie Wooster
Launcelot Gobbo	Shylock
Passepartout	Phileas Fogg
Sancho Panza	Don Quixote
Mélisande	Zuleika Dobson
Mrs Bird	Brown Family (*Paddington Bear*)
Paddock	Richard Hannay
Françoise	Marcel Family (*Remembrance of Things Past*)
Anatole	Aunt Dahlia (Jeeves stories)
Mary Ann	White Rabbit
Eurycleia	Ulysses
Feers	Madame Ranevsky (*Cherry Orchard*)
Mrs Honour	Sophia Western (*Tom Jones*)
Corporal Trim	Uncle Toby (*Tristram Shandy*)

London

Theatres

Name	*Address*	*Post*	*Details*
Adelphi	Strand	WC2	Opened by John Scott in 1806 and originally called the Sans Pareil. First performance on 17 November 1806, *The Rout,* recitations by Miss Jane M Scott. Present auditorium built in 1930.
Albery	St Martin's Lane	WC2	Designed in 1903 by W G R Sprague and called the New Theatre till 1923. In July 2006 Cameron Mackintosh renamed the theatre the Noel Coward Theatre.
Aldwych	Aldwych	WC2	Designed 1905 by W G R Sprague. Home of Ben Travers farces 1925–33.
Almeida	Almeida St	N1	Fringe theatre situated in Islington.
Ambassadors	West St	WC2	Designed in 1913 by W G R Sprague. Ivor Novello made debut here in *Deburau.*
Apollo	Shaftesbury Ave	W1	Designed in 1901 by Lewen Sharp.
Apollo Victoria	Victoria	SW1	Opened in 1930 as a cinema; theatre since 1979.
Arts	Great Newport St	WC2	Opened in 1927 as an avant-garde theatre challenging the censorial constraints of the Lord Chamberlain's Office.
Barbican (and Pit)	Silk St	EC2	Opened in 1982, since when the London Symphony Orchestra has been in residence at Barbican Hall. Also home of the Royal Shakespeare Company.
Bloomsbury	Gordon St	WC1	Fringe theatre that shows a wide spectrum of work.
Bridewell	Bride Lane	EC4	Fringe theatre.
Bush	Shepherd's Bush	W12	Fringe theatre founded in 1972.
Cambridge	Earlham St	WC2	Designed in 1930.
Charing Cross	Off Villiers St	SW1	Situated underneath Charing Cross arches – formerly the (New) Players Theatre.
Coliseum	St Martin's Lane	WC2	Largest theatre in the West End, seating nearly 2,500. Interior designed in 1904 by Frank Matcham. Home of the English National Opera since 1968.
Criterion	Piccadilly	W1	Designed in 1874 by Thomas Verity.
Dominion	Tottenham	WC1	Built 1929 by William and T R Millburn.
Donmar Warehouse	Earlham St	WC2	A 250-seat subsidised (not for profit) theatre. Sam Mendes was artistic director between 1990 and 2002
Drury Lane Theatre Royal	Catherine St	WC2	Designed in 1812 by Benjamin Wyatt.
Duchess	Catherine St	WC2	Designed in 1929 by Ewen Barr.
Duke of York's	St Martin's Lane	WC2	Designed by Walter Emden in 1892 and called the Trafalgar Square till 1895.
Fortune	Russell St	WC2	Designed in 1924 by Ernest Schaufelberg.
Gaiety	Strand	WC2	Opened in 1868 and had England's first electric lighting system in 1878.
Garrick	Charing Cross Rd	WC2	Designed by Walter Emden and C J Phipps in 1889.
Gate (Prince Albert Pub)	Pembridge Rd	W11	Reputation for high-quality productions of neglected European classics.
Gielgud	Shaftesbury Ave	W1	Designed 1906 by W G R Sprague. Originally the Hick's Theatre: then the Globe (1909–95).
Greenwich	Crooms Hill	SE10	Open since 1969 in reconstructed Victorian music hall.
Hackney Empire	Mare St	E8	Designed by Frank Matcham (1854–1920), was most famous music hall at turn of last century. After being used as television studio and bingo hall, it has reverted to its music-hall roots since its refurbishment and reopening in 2002. The Bullion Room and the Acorn (seating 60) are two small auditoriums within the complex. Has gained a fine reputation for giving young black talent a chance to express itself.
Hampstead Theatre Club	Swiss Cottage	NW3	Fringe theatre founded in a Scout hall in Hampstead Village in 1959, but presently situated at Eton Avenue, Swiss Cottage.
Harold Pinter	Panton St	SW1	Designed in 1881 by Thomas Verity. Formerly the Comedy Theatre.
Her Majesty's	Haymarket	SW1	Original theatre designed by Sir John Vanbrugh in 1705; present theatre by CJ Phipps in 1896.
Jerwood Downstairs	Sloane Square	SW3	Previously known as the Royal Court Downstairs.
Jerwood Upstairs	Sloane Square	SW3	Previously known as the Royal Court Upstairs.
King's Head	Upper St	N1	Founded as a pub theatre in 1970.
Leicester Square	Leicester Square	WC2	Opened in November 2001, the brainchild of Adam Kenwright. Was specifically designed to show the musical Taboo, based on the life of pop singer Boy George. Formerly call The Venue.
Lyceum	Wellington St	WC2	Designed by James Payne in 1771.
Lyric	King St Hammersmith	W6	Designed in 1979. Usually performances of planned short-season runs.
Lyric	Shaftesbury Ave	W1	Designed in 1888 by C J Phipps.
Mayfair	Mayfair Hotel	W1	Part of the hotel complex.
Menier	Southwark St	SE1	Opened in 2004 - 180 seat off-West End theatre – full name Menier Chocolate Factory
Mermaid	Puddle Dock	EC4	Founded in 1959 by Sir Bernard Miles.
New End	New End	NW3	Fringe theatre.
New London	Drury Lane	WC2	Designed in 1973 by Paul Turkovic.
Noël Coward	St Martins Lane	WC2	Formerly the Albany Theatre, renamed in July 2006 by Cameron Mackintosh.
Novello	Aldwych	WC2	Designed 1905 by W G R Sprague. Formerly the Strand Theatre.
Old Vic	Waterloo Rd	SE1	Designed 1818 by Rudolf Cabanel. Currently owned by the Old Vic Theatre Trust 2000 Ltd.
Palace	Cambridge Circus	WC2	Built by T E Collcutt and G H Holloway, opened in 1891 as The Royal English Opera House showing Sir Arthur Sullivan's *Ivanhoe.*
Palladium	Argyll St	WC1	Opened in 1910 as a music hall.
Peacock	Portugal St	WC2	Part of Sadler's Wells group, providing a major West End home for world class dance.
Phoenix	Charing Cross Rd	WC2	Designed by Giles Gilbert Scott and Bertie Crewe and opened in 1930.
Piccadilly	Denman St	W1	Designed in 1928 by Bertie Crewe and Edward Stone.
Playhouse	Northumberland Ave	WC2	Designed by Sefton Parry in 1882.
Prince Edward	Old Compton St	W1	Opened in 1930.
Prince of Wales	Coventry St	W1	Designed 1937 by Robert Cromie.
Queen's	Shaftesbury Ave	W1	Interior designed 1907 by W G R Sprague, new exterior redesigned by Bryan Westwood and Hugh Casson after bomb damage in 1940, reopened 1959.
Regent's Park	Regent's Park	NW1	Founded in 1932. Stages annual productions of *A Midsummer Night's Dream.* Open air theatre.
Royal National Theatre	South Bank	SE1	Designed by Denys Lasdun, opened 1976. Three auditoriums, the Olivier (large and open-spaced), the Lyttelton (proscenium arched) and the Cottesloe (small but flexible).
Royal Opera	Bow St	WC2	Designed by Edward Shepherd in 1732. Redesigned by E M Barry in 1858 and called The Covent Garden Opera Company. Renamed the Royal Opera House in 1968.

Sadler's Wells	Rosebery Ave	EC1	Opened in 1683 by Thomas Sadler. A studio theatre, the Lilian Baylis, was opened in 1998.
Savoy	Strand	WC2	Designed in 1881 by C J Phipps and financed by Richard D'Oyly Carte for the production of Gilbert and Sullivan Operas. First public building to be lit by electricity, although the Gaiety Theatre had experimented in 1878.
Shaftesbury	Shaftesbury Ave	WC1	Designed in 1911 by Bertie Crewe.
Shakespeare's Globe	Southwark	SE1	Sam Wanamaker's dream of a theatre for all was opened in 1997 with Mark Rylance playing Henry V.
Soho	Dean St	W1D	Opened in 2000 - 140 seat auditorium, 85/100 seat studio – comedy, cabaret and new plays.
St James	Palace St	SW1	Opened September 2012 with Sandi Toksvig's *Bully Boy.* 312 seat theatre and 100 seat studio.
St Martin's	West St	WC2	Designed in 1916 by W G R Sprague.
Theatre Royal, Haymarket	Haymarket	SW1	Built in 1821 by John Nash.
Theatre Royal, Stratford	Gerry Raffles Square	E15	Built in 1884 by James George Buckle.
Trafalgar Studios	Whitehall	SW1	Built in 1930 to the design of E A Stone. Formerly named the Whitehall Theatre, and known for its farces. Renamed 2004.
Tricycle	Kilburn High Rd	NW6	Fringe theatre opened in 1980.
Unicorn	Tooley St	SE1	Presently a travelling company following the closure of its theatre in Great Newport Street.
Vaudeville	Strand	WC2	Designed by C J Phipps 1870.
Victoria Palace	Victoria St	SW1	Designed in 1911 by Frank Matcham.
Westminster	Palace St	SW1	Possibly the nearest theatre to Buckingham Palace before it burnt down on 27 June 2002.
Wyndham's	Charing Cross Rd	WC2	Designed by W G R Sprague and opened in 1899.
Young Vic	The Cut	SE1	Built in 1970.

NB: Notable London fringe theatres (and pubs) not listed above include Half Moon, Old Red Lion, Orange Tree, Bird's Nest, Landor, Hen & Chickens, Pentameters, Albany, Etcetera, Oval House, Pleasance, Richmond (The Green) and Riverside Studios.

Statues

Site	*Person(s) Depicted*
Albert Hall (SW7)	*Prince Albert* by Joseph Durham (1863).
Bank of England (EC2)	Stone statues of *Sir John Soane* by Sir William Reid Dick (1937) and *King William III* by Sir Henry Cheere (1735).
Banqueting House, Whitehall (SW1)	Lead bust of *Charles I* by unknown sculptor.
Belgrave Square (SW1)	Bronze of *Simon Bolivar* by Hugo Daini (1974).
Birdcage Walk (SW1)	Bronze of *Field Marshal Earl Alexander of Tunis* by James Butler (1985).
Bloomsbury Square, (WC1)	*Charles James Fox* by Richard Westmacott (1816).
Cannon St (EC4)	Bronze mask of *Winston Churchill* by Frank Dobson (1959) over the entrance to Bracken House.
Carey St / Serle St (WC2)	Stone figure of *Sir Thomas More* by Robert Smith (1866).
Carlton Gardens (SW1)	Bronze of *General Charles de Gaulle* and *George VI* by William McMillan.
Cavendish Square (W1)	Bronze of *William George Bentinck* by Thomas Campbell (1851).
Charing Cross Rd (WC2)	Bronze of *Sir Henry Irving* by Thomas Brock (1910) by the St Martin's Place side of the National Portrait Gallery.
Chelsea Embankment (SW3)	Bronze of *Thomas Carlyle* by Sir Joseph Boehm (1882); seated bronze of *Sir Thomas More* by L Cubitt Bevis (1969).
Chelsea Hospital (SW3)	*Bronze of King Charles II in Roman Costume*, by Grinling Gibbons (1676).
Chiswick House (W4)	Stone figure of *Inigo Jones* by John Rysbrack (1729).
City Rd (EC1)	*John Wesley* by John Adams-Acton (1891).
Cockspur St (SW1)	Bronze equestrian of *George III* by Matthew Cotes Wyatt.
Commercial Rd (E1)	Bronze of *Clement Attlee* by Frank Forster (1988) outside Limehouse Library.
Cornhill (No 32) EC3	Mahogany carving of *The Brontë sisters in Conversation with William Makepeace Thackeray* by Walter Gilbert (1939).
Crystal Palace Park (SE19)	Marble bust of *Sir Joseph Paxton* by W F Woodington (1869).
Downing St (SW1)	*Mountbatten* outside Foreign Office.
Euston Station (NW1)	Bronze of *Robert Stephenson* by Baron Marochetti (1871).
Festival Hall (SE1)	Bronze of *Frederic Chopin*, beside the Festival Hall, by B Kubica (1975).
Fleet St (EC4)	Stone of *Elizabeth I* by William Kerwin (1586) over the vestry porch of St Dunstan in the West. This is the oldest statue of a monarch in London and, in fact, the oldest outdoor statue of any kind.
Fleet St (Nos 143–4) EC4	Stone of *Mary, Queen of Scots*, placed by an admirer, Sir John Tollemache Sinclair (1880).
Greenwich Park (SE10)	Samuel Nixon's Foggit Tor granite of *William IV*, erected in King William IV St in 1844 and moved to present site in 1938.
Grosvenor Gardens (SW1)	Bronze equestrian of *Marechal Foch* by G. Mallisard (1930).
Grosvenor Square (W1)	Bronze of *F.D. Roosevelt* by Sir William Reid Dick; bronze of *General Dwight D. Eisenhower* by Robert Dean (1989).
Guildhall (EC2)	Limewood carvings of mythical giants, *Gog and Magog*, by David Evans, replacing those burned in 1940.
Hamilton Gardens (W1)	Bronze of *George Gordon Byron* by Richard Belt (1880).
Hanover Square (W1)	Bronze of *William Pitt the Younger* by Francis Chantrey (1831).
Highgate Cemetery (N6)	Bronze of *Karl Marx* by Laurence Bradshaw (1956).
Holborn Circus (EC1)	Equestrian bronze of *Prince Albert* by Charles Bacon (1874).
Horse Guards Parade (SW1)	Bronze of *Field Marshal Earl Kitchener* by John Tweed (1926); bronze equestrian of *Field Marshal Viscount Wolseley* by Sir William Goscombe John (1920).
Houses of Parliament (SW1)	Equestrian bronze of *Richard I* in Old Palace Yard by Carlo Marochetti (1861); bronze of *Oliver Cromwell* outside Westminster Hall by Sir Hamo Thornycroft (1899). Statue of *George VI* stands opposite the *Richard I* outside the grounds and was sculpted by William Reid Dick (1947).
Hyde Park Corner (SW1)	Bronze of *The Duke of Wellington* on his horse, Copenhagen, by J E Boehm (1888).
Kensington Gardens (SW7)	Bronze of *Sir Winston and Lady Churchill* by Oscar Nemon (1981) situated near Hyde Park Gate; seated statue of *Queen Victoria* by her daughter, Princess Louise (1893); Albert Memorial designed by George Gilbert Scott, with seated statue of Albert begun by Baron Marochetti and completed in 1876 by John Foley.
Kensington Palace (W8)	Bronze of *William III* by Heinrich Baucke (1907) presented by Kaiser Wilhelm II to his uncle, Edward VII.
King Charles Street (SW1)	Bronze figure of *Robert Clive* by John Tweed (1912).
King Edward Street (EC1)	Granite figure of *Sir Rowland Hill*, founder of the Penny Post, by R Onslow Ford (1881).
Leicester Square: Centre (WC2)	Marble of *William Shakespeare* by Giovanni Fontana (1874); bronze of *Charlie Chaplin* by John Doubleday (unveiled by Ralph Richardson in 1981).

Leicester Square: Gates (WC2)	Memorial gates, to *John Hunter* by Thomas Woolner, *Isaac Newton* by William Calder Marshall, *Joshua Reynolds* by Henry Weekes (all 1874) and *William Hogarth* by Joseph Durham (1875), all of whom have commemorative busts.
The Mall (near Admiralty Arch, SW1)	Bronze of *Captain James Cook* by Sir Thomas Brock (1914). Seated marble statue of Queen Victoria by Sir Thomas Brock (1911).
Marylebone Rd (NW1)	Bronze of *John Fitzgerald Kennedy* by Jacques Lipchitz (1965).
Millbank (SW1)	Bronze of *Sir John Everett Millais* by Sir Thomas Brock (1904).
Old Bailey (EC4)	Gilt of *Justice* by F W Pomeroy (1907).
Park Crescent (W1)	Bronze of *Edward Augustus, Duke of Kent* (Queen Victoria's father) by S S Gahagen (1827).
Park Lane (W1)	*Achilles* (20 ft bronze cast in 1822 by Sir Richard Westmacott) 'Erected by the women of England to Arthur, Duke of Wellington and his brave companions in arms'.
Parliament Square (SW1)	Bronzes of *George Canning*, in a toga, by Richard Westmacott (1832); *Sir Robert Peel* by Matthew Noble (1876); *Field Marshal Jan Christian Smuts* by Jacob Epstein (1958); *Abraham Lincoln* (copy of the statue by Augustus Saint-Gaudens in Chicago); *Winston Churchill* by Ivor Roberts Jones (1973); *Benjamin Disraeli* by Mario Raggi (1883); *Lord Palmerston* by Thomas Woolner (1876).
Piccadilly Circus (W1)	*Shaftesbury Memorial Fountain*, better known as *Eros* although Alfred Gilbert's 1893 aluminium statue in fact depicts *The Angel of Christian Charity*, in honour of Lord Shaftesbury himself.
Pimlico Gardens (SW1)	Stone of *William Huskisson* in a Roman toga, by John Gibson (1836).
Prudential Assurance (Holborn EC1)	Cupronised plaster bust of *Charles Dickens* by Percy Fitzgerald (1907).
Red Lion Square (WC1)	Bronze bust of *Bertrand Russell* by Marcelle Quinton (1980).
Royal Exchange (EC2)	Equestrian bronze of *Wellington* begun by Francis Chantrey & completed by Henry Weekes (1844); and stone figure of *Richard Whittington* by J E Carew (1845).
Royal Geographical Society Kensington Gore (SW7)	Bronzes of *David Livingstone* by T B Huxley-Jones (1953) & *Sir Ernest Shackleton* by C Sarjeant Jagger (1932).
St Bartholomew's Hospital (EC1)	Stone figure of *Henry VIII*, the founder, by Francis Bird (1702) stands over the gateway.
St Giles Cripplegate	Memorial statue of *John Milton* by Montford (1904).
St James's Square (SW1)	*William III*, equestrian bronze by John Bacon the Elder (1808).
St Martin's Place (WC2)	Marble statue of *Edith Cavell* by Sir George Frampton (1920). Famous inscription reads: 'Patriotism is not enough. I must have no hatred or bitterness for anyone.'
St Thomas's Hospital (SE1)	Statue of *Sir Robert Clayton*, the hospital's benefactor. The only outdoor stone statue by Grinling Gibbons.
Savoy Place (WC2)	Bronze of *Michael Faraday* by J H Foley (1889) situated outside the Institution of Electrical Engineers.
Soho Square (W1)	Stone statue of *King Charles II* by Caius Gabriel Cibber once owned by W S Gilbert.
Somerset House, Strand (WC2)	Baroque fountain in bronze, including a figure of *King George III* by John Bacon the Elder (1788).
South Africa House (Trafalgar Square)	Large stone figure of *Bartholomew Diaz* by Coert Steynberg (1934).
South Square, Gray's Inn (WC1)	*Francis Bacon* by F W Pomeroy (1912).
Strand (WC2)	Bronzes of *Air Chief Marshal Lord Dowding* and *Sir Arthur 'Bomber' Harris* by Faith Winter (1988) opposite St Clement Danes, the RAF church, *William Gladstone* by Sir Hamo Thorneycroft (1905) and *Dr Samuel Johnson* by Percy Fitzgerald (1910).
Tavistock Square (WC1)	Bronze of *Mahatma Gandhi* by Fredda Brilliant (unveiled by Harold Wilson in 1968).
Tooting Broadway (SW17)	Bronze of *King Edward VII* by L F Roselieb (1911).
Trafalgar Square (WC2)	Bronzes outside National Gallery of *George Washington* by Jean-Antoine Houdon and *James II* in Roman dress by Grinling Gibbons; *Sir Henry Havelock* by William Behnes (1861); bronze equestrians of *George IV* by Sir Francis Chantrey (1834) and *Charles I* by Hubert Le Sueur (1633); *Nelson's column* (1702 23), with statue of Nelson by E H Bailey (1843) and Landseer's lions cast in 1868 from guns recovered from the wreck of the *Royal George*. On the north wall of the Square are bronze busts of Admirals *Lord Beatty* by William McMillan (1984), *Lord Cunningham*, by Franta Belsky (1967) and *Lord Jellicoe* by Sir Charles Wheeler (1948).
University College London (WC1)	Bronze tablet and medallion of *Richard Trevithick* by L S Merrifield (1933).
Victoria Embankment (WC2)	*Isambard Kingdom Brunel* by Carlo Marochetti (1877); *Cleopatra's Needle* (68 ½').
Victoria Embankment Gardens (WC2)	Bronzes of *John Stuart Mill* by Thomas Woolner (1878); *Robert Burns* by Sir John Steel (1884); *Sir Arthur Sullivan* by W Goscombe John (1903), with a mourning female on the plinth; *Robert Raikes* by Sir Thomas Brock (1880).
Victoria Tower Gardens, Westminster (SW1)	*Burghers of Calais* by Rodin, copy (installed 1915) of original in Calais, created1895. Emmeline and Christabel Pankhurst by A G Walker (1930).
Waterloo Place (SW1)	*Duke of York Column* memorial to Frederick, 2nd son of George III, statue by Sir Richard Westmacott 1834; bronze equestrian of *King Edward VII* by Sir Bertram Mackennal (1922); bronze of *Captain Robert Falcon Scott* by Lady Scott (1915); *Florence Nightingale* by Arthur George (A G) Walker.
Westminster Bridge (SE1)	Thomas Thornycroft's *Boadicea* at the north-eastern end.
Whitehall (SW1)	Bronzes of *Sir Walter Raleigh* by William McMillan (1959); *Field Marshal Montgomery of Alamein* by Oscar Nemon (unveiled by Queen Mother in 1980); *Field Marshal the Viscount Alanbrooke* and *Field Marshal the Viscount Slim*, both by Ivor Roberts Jones.
Woodford Green (E18)	Bronze of *Winston Churchill* by David McFall (unveiled by Field Marshal Montgomery in October 1959).
Woolwich, Royal Arsenal (SE18)	Stone figure of *Wellington* by Thomas Milnes (1848).

Bridges

From East to West	*Type*	*Opened*	
Queen Elizabeth II	Road	1991	Clockwise route of M25; the Dartford Tunnel is the anti-clockwise route.
Tower	Road	1894	Built by John Wolfe-Barry to a design by Sir Horace Jones, the furthest bridge downstream in London.
London	Road	1831	Rebuilt by John Rennie but moved to Lake Havasu City, Arizona, in 1967; new bridge opened by Queen Elizabeth II, 16 March 1973.
Alexandra	Rail	1866	Cannon St in the north to Clink St in the south.
Southwark	Road	1819	Built by John Rennie; rebuilt 1921.
Millennium	Foot	2000	Built by an amalgamation of Norman Foster, Anthony Caro and Ove Enge. Links St Paul's Cathedral and the Tate Modern.
Blackfriars	Rail	1864	Upper Thames St in the north to Southwark St in the south.
Blackfriars	Road	1769	Rebuilt 1869 and widened 1910.
Waterloo	Road	1817	Built by John Rennie but rebuilt by LCC between 1937 and 1944 to plans of Sir Giles Gilbert Scott, opened by Herbert Morrison 1945.

Hungerford	Rail & Foot	1863	Suspension bridge built by Brunel 1845 but rebuilt 1863 as Rail & Foot bridge designed by Sir John Hawkshaw.
Westminster	Road	1750	Leads from Westminster Abbey and Houses of Parliament to the former County Hall and St Thomas' Hospital. The bridge was rebuilt in 1862.
Lambeth	Road	1862	Leads from Millbank in the north to Lambeth Palace. Rebuilt in 1932.
Vauxhall	Road	1816	Leads from Millbank in the north to Kennington Lane. Rebuilt in 1906.
Grosvenor	Rail	1860	Rebuilt 1967.
Chelsea	Road	1934	Built 1858 but rebuilt as suspension bridge 1934 and widened 1937.
Albert	Road	1873	Restructured by Sir Joseph Bazalgette in 1884 and strengthened 1973.
Battersea	Road	1772	Built of wood by Henry Holland and rebuilt by Bazalgette 1890.
Battersea	Rail	1863	Properly called the Cremorne Bridge.
Wandsworth	Road	1873	Rebuilt 1940.
Putney	Rail	1889	Also known as Fulham Rail Bridge.
Putney	Road	1729	Rebuilt by Bazalgette 1886.
Hammersmith	Road	1827	Rebuilt by Bazalgette 1887 and the first London suspension bridge.
Barnes	Rail & Foot	1849	Restructured 1893.
Chiswick	Road	1933	Built by Sir Herbert Baker and Alfred Dryland.
Kew	Rail	1869	Carries the North London Line and District Line.
Kew	Road	1759	Rebuilt and renamed The King Edward VII Bridge 1903.
Richmond Lock	Foot	1894	Opened by the Duke and Duchess of York.
Twickenham	Road	1933	Designed by Maxwell Ayrton.
Richmond	Rail	1848	Restructured 1908.
Richmond	Road	1777	Widened 1937.
Teddington Lock	Foot	1889	Designed by G Pooley.
Kingston	Rail	1863	Carries the Kingston–Richmond loop line.
Kingston	Road	1828	Widened 1914.
Hampton Court	Road	1753	Replaced by iron bridge 1865 and rebuilt 1933.

Postal Areas

E1	Whitechapel
E2	Bethnal Green
E3	Bow
E4	Chingford
E5	Clapton
E6	East Ham
E7	Forest Gate
E8	Hackney
E9	Homerton
E10	Leyton
E11	Leytonstone
E12	Manor Park
E13	Plaistow
E14	Poplar
E15	Stratford
E16	Victoria Docks
E17	Walthamstow
E18	South Woodford
N1	Islington
N2	East Finchley
N3	Finchley (Church End)
N4	Finsbury Park
N5	Highbury
N6	Highgate
N7	Holloway
N8	Hornsey
N9	Lower Edmonton
N10	Muswell Hill
N11	New Southgate
N12	North Finchley
N13	Palmers Green
N14	Southgate
N15	South Tottenham
N16	Stoke Newington
N17	Tottenham
N18	Upper Edmonton
N19	Upper Holloway
N20	Whetstone
N21	Winchmore Hill
N22	Wood Green
SW1	Belgravia
SW2	Brixton
SW3	Chelsea
SW4	Clapham
SW5	Earls Court
SW6	Fulham
SW7	South Kensington
SW8	South Lambeth
SW9	Stockwell
SW10	West Brompton
SW11	Battersea
SW12	Balham
SW13	Barnes
SW14	Mortlake
SW15	Putney
SW16	Streatham
SW17	Tooting
SW18	Wandsworth
SW19	Wimbledon
SW20	West Wimbledon
W1	Mayfair
W2	Paddington
W3	Acton
W4	Chiswick
W5	Ealing
W6	Hammersmith
W7	Hanwell
W8	Kensington
W9	Maida Vale
W10	North Kensington
W11	Notting Hill
W12	Shepherds Bush
W13	West Ealing
W14	West Kensington
WC1	Bloomsbury
WC2	St James
EC1	Finsbury
EC2	City
EC3	Spitalfields
EC4	Fleet St
SE1	Southwark
SE2	Abbey Wood
SE3	Blackheath
SE4	Brockley
SE5	Camberwell
SE6	Catford
SE7	Charlton
SE8	Deptford
SE9	Eltham
SE10	Greenwich
SE12	Lee
SE13	Lewisham
SE14	New Cross
SE15	Peckham
SE16	Rotherhithe
SE17	Walworth
SE18	Woolwich
SE19	Norwood
SE20	Anerley
SE21	Dulwich
SE22	East Dulwich
SE23	Forest Hill
SE24	Herne Hill
SE25	South Norwood
SE26	Sydenham
SE27	West Norwood

SE28	Thamesmead
NW1	Camden Town
NW2	Cricklewood
NW3	Hampstead
NW4	Hendon
NW5	Kentish Town
NW6	Kilburn
NW7	Mill Hill
NW8	Marylebone
NW9	Kingsbury
NW10	Willesden
NW11	Golders Green

General Information

Admiralty Arch (SW1) Built in 1910 to the design of Sir Aston Webb (who also designed the façade of Buckingham Palace) and consisting of 3 identical arches. Situated where the Mall leads into Trafalgar Square.

Alexandra Palace (N22) Sited in Muswell Hill and built in 1875 by Meeson and Johnson.

Alsop, William Designer of North Greenwich Jubilee Line Station.

Art galleries Tate Gallery, Millbank; Tate Modern, Bankside; National Gallery, Trafalgar Square; National Portrait Gallery, St Martin's Place; Wallace Collection, W1; Courtauld Institute, Strand; Sir John Soane's Museum, Lincoln's Inn Fields; William Morris Gallery, Forest Rd, E17; Queen's Gallery in Buckingham Palace; Dulwich Picture Gallery built by Sir John Soane 1811–13, England's oldest public art gallery.

Banqueting House Designed by Inigo Jones in 1622 and the only part of Whitehall Palace still standing.

***Belfast*, HMS (SE1)** Built in 1939 and situated at Symon's Wharf in Vine Lane, this 11,000-ton cruiser, the largest ever built was opened to the public in 1971.

Big Ben Housed in St Stephen's Tower within the Houses of Parliament (Palace of Westminster) Big Ben, weighing in at 13.5 tons, is the name of the large bell housed in the clock tower and named after, either Benjamin Caunt, a popular boxer of the day (1858), or more likely Sir Benjamin Hall, the Chief Commissioner of Works. The clock tower is now officially called the Elizabeth Tower, after being renamed in 2012 to celebrate the Diamond Jubilee of Elizabeth II.

Billingsgate Market (EC3) Fish market in Lower Thames St, in use for over 7 centuries, which closed on 16 Jan 1982.

Billingsgate Market (E14) Opened on the Isle of Dogs 3 days after the original market closed.

Birdcage Walk (SW1) Here stood the aviary of James I.

Birkbeck College (WC1) Founded in 1823 as the London mechanics' Institution. Took its present name in 1907 and became part of the University of London in 1920. Situated in Malet Street.

Bishop of London, first St Mellitus, c. AD 604.

Blackfriars Bridge Roberto Calvi, an Italian banker, found hanging beneath it on 19 June 1982.

Blue Plaques William Ewart had the idea of using these to commemorate famous people, and Lord Byron was the first to have a plaque conferred on the house where he was born in Holles St, Westminster.

British Library Formed in 1973 from the amalgamation of the British Museum Library, National Central Library and National Lending Library. Now situated at St Pancras.

British Museum (WC1) Founded in 1753, initially to house the collection of Hans Sloane (1660–1753), it was opened to the public in 1759 at Montague House. The present museum was built on the same site in 1823–47 to a design of Robert Smirke. The ethnographical department of the museum is called The Museum of Mankind. Among the best known of the museum's treasures are the Elgin Marbles, Portland Vase, Mildenhall Treasure, Rosetta Stone, Sutton Hoo, Lewis Chessman, and the Lindow Man. Recent millennium renovations include the museum's inner courtyard, hidden from the public for 150 years being turned into the '*Great Court*' covered with a spectacular glass and steel roof designed by Norman Foster.

British Telecom Tower Designed by Eric Bedford and stands 5802 high with a 402 mast giving an overall height of 6202. Originally called the Post Office Tower and nowadays simply the Telecom Tower.

***Burghers of Calais* replica** Sited in Victoria Tower Gardens.

Canary Wharf Tower Designed by Cesar Pelli and at 850 feet exceeds the British Telecom Tower as Britain's tallest structure. Officially called No. 1 Canada Square.

Centre of London Charing Cross is now used as the point for measuring distances to other places.

Charing Cross Station (WC2) Situated just off the Strand and designed by Sir John Hawkshaw in 1864.

Clink Street (SE1) Site of the Bishop of Winchester's London estate and synonymous with the name of his Ecclesiastical prison.

city guilds, The Water Conservators being the latest set up in 2000.

Clubs Boodle's; Brooks's; Carlton; White's (all situated in St James's St, SW1); Beefsteak; Garrick; Pratt's (all the waiters are called George); Reform (Pall Mall), Athenaeum, Portland, Savile, Travellers, Groucho.

Coal Tax Christopher Wren's 50 new churches were paid for by a tax on coal entering London.

Cockneys Must be born within the sound of the church bells of St Mary le Bow.

Concert halls: famous Barbican Hall; Royal Festival Hall & Queen Elizabeth Hall; Royal Albert Hall; Wigmore Hall; London Coliseum; Royal Opera House.

Congestion charge From 17 February 2003 motorists driving into central London paid £5 (Now £10 as at July 2013) for the privilege!

Courtauld Institute of Art Owned by the University of London and situated at Somerset House on the Strand.

Covent Garden Market (WC2) London's main wholesale fruit, flower and vegetable market. Congestion in Central London caused its closure in 1974 after 340 years trading. The New Covent Garden Market was opened immediately at the former railway yard at Nine Elms, Battersea.

Denmark St Aka Tin Pan Alley; home of the music publishing industry.

Docklands Light Railway Opened in 1987 and now extended from the Isle of Dogs to Bank.

Drainage system Designed by Joseph Bazalgette between 1859 and 1875 and still serving as the basis of London's sewage system.

Eel Pie Island, Twickenham Joined to the mainland by an old rickety concrete bridge, about 32 wide. Made famous in the 1960s when the Rolling Stones played a concert there.

Football clubs: oldest Fulham (formed in 1879); Leyton Orient (1881); Spurs (1882); QPR (1885); Millwall (1885); Arsenal (1886); Brentford (1889); Wimbledon (1889); West Ham (1900); Chelsea (1905); Crystal Palace (1905); Charlton (1905).

Fringe theatres (not listed in main table) Arcola; Artsdepot; Barons Court; Blue Elephant; Brockley Jack; Bull; Camden People's; Chelsea; Chicken Shed; Clapham Common; Diorama; Etcetera; Finborough; Hanover Grand; Hen and Chickens; Hoxton Hall; Jackson's Lane; Laban; Little Angel; Millfield Arts; North Garden; Oval House; Pentameters; Pleasance; Questors; Roundhouse; Shaw; Southwark Playhouse; Stratford Circus; Tabard; Theatre 503; Tristan Bates; Union; Warehouse; Waterman's; White Bear.

Fulham Palace Official residence of the Bishop of London until 1973.

Gherkin, The Popular name of the Swiss Re Building at 30 St Mary Axe in the City. Designed by Foster and Partners and opened in 2004, the 591 ft (180 m) high 40-floor skyscraper has quickly become one of the most recognisable and iconic buildings in Britain.

Greater London Consists of 31 boroughs and the cities of Westminster and London.

Greater London Council Created in 1965, but abolished in 1986. Originally called the London County Council, formed 1889.

Greenwich Palace (SE10) Built by Humphrey Deele of Gloucester in 1426 and now the site of the Royal Naval Hospital.

Gun salutes A salute of 62 guns is fired at the Tower of London on the birthdays of HRH Prince Philip, HM Queen Elizabeth, the Queen Mother and HM the Queen, who also has a 62-gun salute on accession and coronation day. A 42-gun salute is fired at the Tower of London and Hyde Park on other state occasions, e.g. opening and dissolution of Parliament, the birth of a royal infant, or a royal procession through London.

Hampton Court Maze Constructed for William and Mary (1690).

Highgate Hill Dick Whittington supposedly 'turned' here and became Lord Mayor.

Hyde Park Corner (SW1) Historic entrance to London from the west via the tollgate through Kensington and Knightsbridge.

Imperial War Museum Opened in 1920, and since 1935 occupying the remaining part of the old Bethlehem Royal Hospital, opened in 1815.

Livery Companies Craft guilds set up to promote the various trades of London. The Weavers are the oldest established guild whilst the Mercers are thought of as the senior guild. At present there are 102

Lloyd's of London Insurance underwriting corporation functional since the late 17th century, housed since 1986 in a headquarters designed by Richard Rogers.

London Eye Situated on the South Bank between the Hungerford and Westminster bridges. The British Airways London Eye is administered by the Tussauds Group. The diameter of the wheel is 135 metres (450 feet) and the architects were David Marks and Julia Barfield. The eye is also known as The Millennium Wheel.

London Gazette Henry Muddiman started it in 1665. It is published on Tuesdays and Fridays, as the official organ of Britain's government. It was known as the *Oxford Gazette* for the first 23 bulletins.

London Stone Now set in the wall of the Bank of China, Cannon St, and possibly once used by the Romans as a measuring point.

Marble Arch Designed by John Nash to commemorate Nelson's victories, erected on side of Buckingham Palace in 1827, moved to Hyde Park in 1851.

Marylebone Road Site of Madame Tussaud's and the Planetarium.

May Day Parade Traditional parade through Hyde Park.

Mayor Ken Livingstone (as at February 2007).

Monument (EC2) Contains 311 steps and commemorates the nearby spot in Pudding Lane where the Great Fire started in 1666. Designed by Christopher Wren, the total height is 202 feet.

Museum: Childhood Situated in Bethnal Green. Administered by the Victoria and Albert Museum, opened in 1872.

Museum of London (EC2) Opened in 1976 and illustrating the history of London from prehistoric times to the present day.

Museum: Wellington Apsley House, Hyde Park Corner. Administered by the Victoria and Albert Museum.

National History Museum (SW7) Situated near the V & A Museum in Cromwell Rd and opened in 1881 to a design of Alfred Waterhouse. Merged with the Ecological Museum in 1985.

National Maritime Museum (SE10) Founded in 1932.

New Scotland Yard (SW1) Metropolitan Police HQ situated near Victoria Street since 1967. The previous Scotland Yard building on the North Bank near Westminster Bridge was completed by Norman Shaw in 1890, after the original building at the top of Whitehall was damaged by a Fenian bomb in 1884.

O2 Arena Multi-purpose indoor arena located in Drawdock Road, North Greenwich SE10 0BB – with a capacity of 20,000.

Oldest club White's, founded 1693.

Oldest theatre The Theatre Royal, Drury Lane, its present auditorium being built in 1812.

Palace of Westminster (SW1) The first palace was built for Edward the Confessor, not completed till 1858, but after the fire of 1834 its replacement was designed to become the home of both Houses of Parliament. Charles Barry's design was preferred to 96 other entrants, and he brought in Augustus Pugin to provide the Gothic interiors. The House of Commons was rebuilt by Giles Gilbert Scott after the bombing of 1941. St Stephen's Tower tops the Commons building, whilst the Victoria Tower stands at the southern end, at the other extreme from Big Ben.

Parks (central London) Green, Hyde, Regent's, St James's, Kensington Gardens.

Pelicans Live in St James's Park.

Peter Pan Statue in Kensington Gardens sculpted by George Frampton in 1912.

Petticoat Lane (E1) East London's long-established Sunday market (8am to 2pm) on Middlesex Street. Originally called Hog Lane Market in the 15th century. Given the name Petticoat Lane around 1600 because of its clothes stalls.

Piccadilly Circus Junction of Haymarket, Regent St, Piccadilly, Shaftesbury Avenue, Coventry Street.

Planetarium Opened in 1958 in Marylebone Rd, next to Madame Tussaud's.

Pool of London A reach of Thames consisting of two parts: the Lower running from Limekiln Creek to Cherry Garden Pier, and the Upper, from Cherry Garden Pier to London Bridge. Tower Bridge divides the two.

Queen's House, Greenwich Started by Inigo Jones during the reign of James I, as a gift to his wife Anne of Denmark; eventually completed in 1640. Now the centrepiece of the National Maritime Museum.

Ratcliff Highway Murders Seven victims were murdered in 2 incidents on this street in present-day Stepney in Dec. 1811. John Williams, a lodger at the Pear Tree public house, was arrested but hanged himself before his trial. The incident was a spur to the eventual forming of the Metropolitan Police in 1829.

Richard II Oldest painting of an English monarch from life (late 14th century), in Westminster Abbey.

Roman Gates of London Wall Aldgate; Aldersgate; Bishopsgate; Cripplegate; Ludgate; Newgate.

(to Chelsea Bridge); Chelsea (to Battersea Bridge); Battersea (to

Royal Academy Founded by Joshua Reynolds in 1768, and originally site at Somerset House. Established in 1868 at Burlington House. Piccadilly Sackler Galleries added in 1990 by Norman Foster.

Royal Courts of Justice Designed by George Street in 1868 and situated on the north side of the Strand, the courts hear civil cases and criminal appeals. Opened by Queen Victoria in 1882 the Supreme Court is made up of the High Court, Court of Appeal and Crown Court. The High Court has 3 divisions: Queen's Bench, Family and Chancery. There are over 150 judges in the Royal Courts of Justice, a corridor known as the Chicken Run, and a recent wing named after St Thomas More. A tributary of the River Fleet is reputed to run under the building.

Royal Exchange (EC3) Founded by Thomas Gresham in 1566 as the 'Bourse' and proclaimed the Royal Exchange by Elizabeth I in 1570. First building destroyed in the Great Fire in 1666; second burned down in 1838; third completed 1842.

Royal National Theatre Building on the South Bank opened in 1976 and designed by Denys Lasdun. Lyttelton was 1st of the 3 auditoria to open, followed by the Olivier and Cottesloe.

Science Museum (SW7) Originally housed in the Victoria and Albert Museum but moved into its own building, across Exhibition Road, in 1913. The museum is the world's pre-eminent museum of science, medicine and technology. The Wellcome Wing, designed by Richard MacCormac, was opened in 2000 in partnership with the Wellcome Trust, Science Museum, and the Heritage Lottery Fund.

St James's Palace (SW1) Built by Henry VIII.

St Paul's Cathedral The new St Paul's Cathedral was built by Sir Christopher Wren between 1675 and 1710. The frescoes depicting the life of St Paul, above the Whispering Gallery on the underside of the dome are by James Thornhill. In the lower part of the south-west tower stands William Kempster's Geometrical Staircase and the clock room in the upper part houses Great Tom, the largest of three bells. The original St Paul's was built in 604 in the reign of St Ethelbert of Kent, the first Christian king in England, only to be destroyed by fire soon after. Two more rebuildings took place, culminating in the destruction by the Great Fire of 1666, when the only monument to survive was that of John Donne, the poet, who had been Dean of St Paul's for the last 10 years of his life. From pavement to the top of the cross on the tower of the dome, St Paul's is 365 feet high.

Shard, The 95-storey skyscraper opened in February 2013 and situated at 32 London Bridge Street, Southwark. The glass-clad pyramidal tower has 72 habitable floors, with a viewing gallery and open-air observation deck. See entry for Renzo Piano in the Architect section.

Silent Change Annual ceremony to admit the new Lord Mayor.

Smithfield Market (EC1) London's largest meat market which, although in decline, employs its own police force.

Somerset House Designed by Sir William Chambers in the late 18th century and situated on the Strand.

Stock Exchange (EC2) The new Stock Exchange opened in June 1973, replacing a building opened in 1888.

Strawberry Hill Horace Walpole's Twickenham residence, built in 1748 and much extended, which is now the Roman Catholic St Mary's College of Higher Education.

10 Downing St: postal code SW1A 2AA

Thames No native name is known before Julius Caesar called the river 'Tamesis'. After Kent it is the oldest place name in England. Since 1996 it has been controlled by the Environment Agency.

Thames Embankments Victoria Embankment on the north side of the river, running from Westminster to Blackfriars, the Albert Embankment on the south side from Westminster Bridge to Vauxhall, and the Chelsea Embankment, from Chelsea Bridge to Battersea Bridge were constructed by Sir J W Bazalgette.

Thames tunnels The first tunnel under the Thames, completed in 1843, and linking Wapping and Rotherhithe, was called the 'Thames Tunnel' and is still in existence as a railway tunnel. The oldest road tunnel is the old Blackwall, opened in 1897; other road tunnels include the new Blackwall (1967), Rotherhithe (1908), and Dartford (1963 and 1980). The only foot tunnel still in existence runs from Greenwich to the Isle of Dogs.

Thames reaches Starting from the mouth and proceeding upriver, the reaches are: Sea Reach (Yantlet Creek to West Blyth Buoy); Lower Hope (to Coalhouse Point); Gravesend (to Tilburyness); Northfleet Hope (to Broadness); St Clement's or Fiddlers' (to Stoneness); Long (to Dartford Creek); Erith Rands (to Coalharbour Point); Erith (to Jenningtree Point); Halfway (to Crossness); Barking (to Tripcock Point); Gallions (to Woolwich Hoba Wharf); Woolwich (to Lyle Park); Bugsby's (to Blackwell Point); Blackwall (to Dudgeon's Dock); Greenwich (to Deptford Creek); Limehouse (to Limekiln Creek); Lower Pool (to Cherry Garden Pier); Upper Pool (to London Bridge); London Bridge to Westminster Bridge and Westminster Bridge to Vauxhall Bridge (both nameless); Nine Elms

Westminster Abbey: Nave At the end of the Nave, just in front of

Wandsworth Bridge); Wandsworth (to Putney Bridge); Barn Elms (to Hammersmith Bridge); Chiswick (to Chiswick Ferry); Corney (to Barnes Railway Bridge); and Mortlake (to Kew Bridge).

Theatre: largest Coliseum.

Tower of London: first foundation White Tower built by Gundul, bishop of Rochester, between 1078 and 1098.

Tower of London: Crown Jewels first housed During reign of Henry III.

Tower of London: last beheading Simon Fraser, Lord Lovat, in 1747. Last execution: Joseph Jacobs (15 Aug 1941).

Tower of London: last Monarch to occupy James I.

Tower of London: Towers Beauchamp; Bell; Bloody; Bowyer; Brick; Broad Arrow; Byward; Constable; Cradle; Devereux; Develin; Flint; Lanthorn; Martin; Middle; Salt; St Thomas's; Wakefield; Wardrobe (no longer standing); Well, White (the oldest).

Underground First stretch of underground electric railway between City and Stockwell opened in 1890.

John Fowler and Sir Benjamin Baker engineered the work.

Other British Underground systems in Glasgow, Liverpool, and Newcastle.

Metropolitan Railway, using steam locomotives, opened in 1863 and ran from Paddington to Farringdon St. Harry Beck (1902–74) redesigned the map in 1931 and his use of straight lines and a colour-coding system for the different lines is still in use.

Underground Map Albert Stanley, Lord Ashfield, issued first map in 1908. The present colour-coded map was implemented in 1933 from a design by Harry Beck.

Unknown Warrior's Tomb Westminster Abbey.

Victoria and Albert Museum (SW7) The national museum of fine and applied art and design. Founded in 1852, and moved to its present site in 1857, being known then as the South Kensington Museum. The building was designed by Aston Webb and given its current name in 1899.

Wallace Collection Art collection in Hertford House, Manchester Square, W1. Most famous work: *The Laughing Cavalier.*

Wardour St Once used as a term to denote the British film industry.

Westminster Abbey: founder St Edward the Confessor.

the Great West Door, is a memorial to Winston Churchill and nearby is the grave of the Unknown Warrior, commemorating those who were killed in WW1. The graves and memorials in the Nave include those of David Livingstone, David Lloyd George, Clement Attlee, Ramsay MacDonald, Isaac Newton, Lord and Lady Baden-Powell and F D Roosevelt.

Westminster Abbey: Poets' Corner Graves and memorials of most of the major English poets and some writers and musicians. The foremost tomb is that of Geoffrey Chaucer, the first to be buried there, and the foremost memorial is that of William Shakespeare. Among the 20th-century poets commemorated are W H Auden, Dylan Thomas and T S Eliot. Gerard Manley Hopkins (1844–89), although buried in Glasnevin Cemetery, Dublin, has a commemorative plaque. Samuel Johnson, Charles Dickens and G F Handel are also buried there, and Oscar Wilde has been commemorated on floor and window.

Westminster Abbey: Royal Tombs Elizabeth I; Mary I; Edward the Confessor; Henry VII; James I; Edward VI; George II; Henry III; Edward I; Edward III; Richard II; Henry V; Anne; Charles II; William III; Mary II and Mary Stewart; Queen of Scotland and France.

Westminster Abbey: Tomb of Elizabeth & Mary Latin inscription on their tomb reads: 'Consorts both in throne and grave, here sleep we two sisters, Elizabeth and Mary, in the hope of one resurrection.'

Westminster Cathedral (SW1) Roman Catholic Cathedral in Francis St, SW1, built of brick and Portland stone, to the design of John Francis Bentley and completed in 1903.

Westminster Hall Built by William Rufus between 1097 and 1099, home of the Royal Courts of Justice till they moved to the Strand in 1882, and incorporated in the Houses of Parliament.

White Lodge Built in 1727–8 in Richmond Park and formerly a royal residence, it is now the Royal Ballet School.

Whitehall Palace Tudor Palace much used by Henry VIII (died there in 1547) but William III found the river air exacerbated his asthma so transferred the royal residence to Kensington Palace. Only the Banqueting House, a later addition, survived the fire that destroyed the palace in 1698.

Zoo Founded by Sir Stamford Raffles; opened in 1828 after his death. Aviary designed by Lord Snowdon and opened in 1965.

MEDICINE

Medical Discoveries

Discovery	*Date*	*Discoverer*	*Nationality*
adrenal gland: function of	1856	Alfred Vulpian	French
adrenalin	1901	Jokichi Takamine	Japanese
AIDS	1981	Lost Angeles scientists	American
antisepsis	1865	Joseph Lister	British
blood circulation	1628	William Harvey	British
blood groups	1901	Karl Landsteiner	Austrian
chloroform	1847	James Simpson	British
chromosomes	1888	Thomas Morgan	American
corpuscles, red	1684	Antoni van Leeuwenhoek	Dutch
cortisone	1934	Edward Kendall	American
diabetes, cause of	1901	Eugene Opic	American
diphtheria bacillus	1884	Edwin Klebs and Friedrich Löffler	German
DNA, structure of	1953	Francis Crick and James Watson	British/American
Down's Syndrome, cause of	1959	Dr Jerome, Lejeune	French
electro-encephalogram	1929	Hans Berger	German
endorphins	1975	Hughes, Guillemin	American
enzymes	1833	Anselme Payen, Jean-François Persoz	French
ether as anaesthetic	1846	William Morton	American
heparin	1915	Jay McLean	American
heredity	1865	Gregor Mendel	Austrian
HIV virus, isolated	1983	Luc Montagnier (among others)	French
insulin, isolated	1921	F G Banting, C H Best, J J R McLeod	Canadian
interferon	1957	A Isaacs, J Lindemann	UK/Swiss
leprosy bacillus	1869	Gerhard Hansen	Norwegian
microbes	1762	M A Plenciz	Austrian
morphine	1805	Friedrich Sertürner	German
nitrous oxide	1776	Joseph Priestley	British
nucleic acid	1869	J F Miescher	Swiss
penicillin	1928	Alexander Fleming	British
protozoa	1675	Antoni van Leeuwenhoek	Dutch
rabies vaccination	1885	Louis Pasteur	French
Rhesus factor	1939	Karl Landsteiner, A S Wiener	Austrian
scurvy, treatment of	1740	James Lind	British
sleeping sickness transmission	1895	David Bruce	British
smallpox vaccination	1796	Edward Jenner	British
streptomycin	1943	Selman Waksman	American
tomography	1915	André Bocage	French
tuberculosis bacillus	1882	Robert Koch	German
typhus bacillus	1880	Karl Eberth	German
vitamin A	1913	E McCollum, M Davis, T Osborne, L Mendel	American
vitamin B	1913	Casimir Funk	Polish
vitamin B1 (thiamin)	1897	Christiaan Eijkman	Dutch
vitamin B2 (riboflavin)	1933	R Kuhn, A von Szent-Gyorgi, J Wagner-Jauregg	Austrian/ Hungarian/ Austrian
vitamin B3 (niacin)	1937	Madden, Strong, Wooley, Elvehjem	British/American
vitamin B5	1933	R J Williams	American
vitamin B6	1936	Birch, A von Szent-Gyorgi	US/Hungarian
vitamin B9 (folic acid)	1938	Day	British
vitamin B12	1937	G R Minot, W P Murphy	British
vitamin C (isolated)	1928	A von Szent-Gyorgi	Hungarian
vitamin D (isolated)	1924	Steenbock, Hess, Weinstock	German
vitamin E	1923	H M Evans, Bishop	American
vitamin K1	1934	Carl Peter Henrik Dam	Danish
vitamins, necessity of	1906	Sir Frederick Hopkins	British
X-rays	1892	Heinrich Hertz	German
X-rays, properties of	1895	Wilhelm Röntgen	German
yellow fever, mosquito transmission	1881	Ronald Ross	British

Bones in the Human Body

skull	
occipital	1
parietal – 1 pair	2
sphenoid	1
ethmoid	1
inferior nasal conchae – 1 pair	2
frontal – 1 pair fused	1
nasal – 1 pair	2
lacrimal – 1 pair	2
temporal – 1 pair	2
maxilla – 1 pair	2
zygomatic – 1 pair	2
vomer	1
palatine – 1 pair	2
mandible – 1 pair fused	1
	22

arms		
upper arm:	humerus – 1 pair	2
lower arm:	radius –1 pair	2
	ulna – 1 pair	2
carpus:	scaphoid – 1 pair	2
	lunate – 1 pair	2
	triquetral – 1 pair	2
	pisiform – 1 pair	2

trapezium – 1 pair		2
	trapezoid – 1 pair	2
	capitate – 1 pair	2
	hamate – 1 pair	2
metacarpals – 5 pairs		10
phalanges:	1st digit – 2 pairs	4
	2nd digit – 3 pairs	6
	3rd digit – 3 pairs	6
	4th digit – 3 pairs	6
	5th digit – 3 pairs	6
		60

hip bones (pelvic girdle)

ilium fused with ischium and pubis – 1 pair	2

ears

malleus	2
incus	2
stapes	2
	6

vertebrae

cervical	7
thoracic	12
lumbar	5
sacral – 5 fused to form sacrum	1
coccyx – fused joint	1
	26

ribs

true ribs – 7 pairs	14
false ribs – 5 pairs (2 floaters)	10
	24

Sternum	1

throat

hyoid	1

pectoral girdle

clavicle – 1 pair	2
scapula – 1 pair	2
	4

legs

upper leg:	femur – 1 pair	2
	patella – 1 pair	2
lower leg:	tibia – 1 pair	2
	fibula – 1 pair	2
tarsus:	talus – 1 pair	2
	calcaneus – 1 pair	2
	navicular – 1 pair	2
	medial cuneiform – 1 pair	2
	intermediate cuneiform – 1 pair	2
	lateral cuneiform – 1 pair	2
	cuboid – 1 pair	2
metatarsals – 5 pairs		10
phalanges	1st digit – 2 pairs	4
	2nd digit – 3 pairs	6
	3rd digit – 3 pairs	6
	4th digit – 3 pairs	6
	5th digit – 3 pairs	6
		60

Total

skull	22
arms	60
hips	2
ears	6
vertebrae	26
ribs	24
sternum	1
throat	1
pectoral girdle	4
legs	60
	206

General Information

abdomen contains most of the digestive system. It is the biggest cavity in the body, extending from underneath the diaphragm to the groin area and bounded at the back of the body by the spine, and round its upper sides by the ribs. The abdomen contains the alimentary canal, liver, spleen, kidneys and pancreas.

acid in stomach hydrochloric.

acupuncture Traditional acupuncture is based on the principle that our health is dependent on the -balanced functioning of the body's motivating energy, known as Qi (ch'i). This Qi flows throughout the body, but is concentrated in channels beneath the skin, known as meridians. The aim of treatment is to restore the balance between the equal and opposite qualities of Qi, namely the Yin and Yang.

The Human body is composed of 12 meridians that mirror themselves on the left and right side of the body. Each of these meridians contains / is a part of muscles, tendons, ligaments and a surrounding facia that stretches all along the meridian, a bit like a string of sausages. From childhood there were times when we felt that powerful emotions would overwhelm us. We learnt to suppress these overwhelming emotions by contracting muscles within us. These contractions become habitual and are thought to have an effect on the body structure affecting bone alignment in the joints, spine and cranium. When the body structure is distorted (extremely common) nerves can get pinched or stretched, internal body organs become distorted, hormonal glands under- or overproduce, joints can wear out quicker, and various muscles and tendons may become shortened or overstretched. Stress is the most common cause of this distortion, but there are other common factors that will also affect our health and well-being. These include diet, drugs and lack of appropriate exercise.

Acupuncture treats the body as a whole – the physical, mental (emotional) & psychic (spirit) levels, not only the disease or ailment. It is an ancient art of healing developed over thousands of years and works by stimulating the Qi and eliminating all toxins from the body. This is achieved by stimulation of specific energy points. Acupuncture can be done without needle – laser, electro-acupuncture, finger pressure (shiatsu) or ultrasound. It is not a substitute for conventional medicine but acts to compliment it. It paired organs. Though the pericardium has no separate

was popularised in the Western world in 1972 following Richard Nixon's visit to China and his championing of its benefits.

There are hundreds of acupuncture points throughout the body, but here is a list of the main 12 meridians:

(1) the Lung Channel of Hand, (2) the Large Intestine Channel of Hand, (3) the Stomach Channel of Foot, (4) the Spleen Channel of Foot, (5) the Heart Channel of Hand, (6) the Small Intestine Channel of Hand, (7) the Urinary Bladder Channel of Foot, (8) the Kidney Channel of Foot, (9) the Pericardium Channel of Hand, (10) the Triple Burner Channel of Hand, (11) the Gall Bladder Channel of Foot, (12) the Liver Channel of Foot. Notes: The lungs (Yin) and large intestine (Yang) are paired organs. Their opening is the nose, and they govern skin and hair. The main function of the large intestine is the metabolism of water and the passing of water. The spleen (Yin) and the stomach (Yang) are paired organs. Their opening is the mouth and they control the flesh and the limbs.The spleen is the main organ of digestion. Its function is to transport nutrients and regulate the blood (keep it within the channels). It is responsible for the transformation of food into nourishment. The stomach receives food while the spleen transports nutrients. The stomach moves things downward while the spleen moves things upward.

The heart (Yin) and the small intestine (Yang) are paired organs. Their point of entry is the tongue. They control the blood vessels and are reflected in the face. The heart governs the blood vessels and is responsible for moving blood through them. It also stores the spirit, and is the organ usually associated with mental processes.The major function of the small intestine is to separate waste material from the nutritious elements in food. The nutritious elements are then distributed throughout the body and the waste is sent on to the large intestine. The kidneys (Yin) and the urinary bladder (Yang) are paired organs. Their opening is the urethra. They control the bones, marrow, and brain, and their health is reflected in the hair of the head. The kidneys store Original Essence (Yuan Jing) and are therefore responsible for growth, development, and reproductive functions. They play the primary role in water metabolism and control the body's liquids, and also hold the body's most basic Yin and Yang. The main function of the urinary bladder is to transform fluids into urine and excrete it from the body. The pericardium (Yin) and the triple burner (Yang) are physiological functions, it is generally mentioned with regard to the delirium induced by high fevers. The triple burner is regarded as 'having a name but no form' but is considered to be an organ that coordinates all the functions of water metabolism.

The liver (Yin) and the gall bladder (Yang) are considered paired organs. Their point of entry is the eyes. They control the sinews (muscles and joints), and their health is reflected in the finger and toe nails. The main task of the liver is spreading and regulating Qi throughout the entire body. Its unique character is flowing and free, so depression or frustration can disturb its functioning. In addition, the liver is responsible for storing blood when the body is at rest. This characteristic, together with its control over the lower abdomen, makes it the most critical organ in terms of women's menstrual cycle and sexuality. The main function of the gall bladder is storing and excreting the bile produced by the liver.

adrenal glands glands that produce adrenalin, which prepares the body for stress by increasing heart rate and blood pressure. They also produce cortisone, which has a variety of metabolic effects.

allergy term used by Clemens von Pirquet (1874–1929) in 1906 following his observations of the skin reaction to his test for tuberculosis.

allopathy treatment of disease by conventional means – i.e. with drugs having opposite effects to the symptoms (opposite of homoeopathy).

Alzheimer's disease serious disorder of the brain manifesting itself in premature senility. Named after the German neurologist Alois Alzheimer (1864–1915), who first identified it.

analeptic drug restores and invigorates.

anaphylaxis an extreme, often life-threatening reaction to an antigen, e.g. to a bee sting, due to hypersensitivity.

anaplasty medical name for plastic surgery.

anatomy Science of the bodily structure of animals and plants.

angioplasty surgical technique for restoring normal blood flow through an artery by means of laser therapy or insertion of a balloon into the narrowed section.

artery tubular thick-walled muscular vessel that conveys oxygenated blood from the heart, the largest being the aorta.

Asperger's syndrome mild variant of autism diagnosed in 1994. Sufferers may have extraordinary compensating talents, e.g. musical prodigy Joseph Erber (born 1984).

axilla anatomical name for the armpit.

biology the study of living organisms.

blepharitis inflammation of the eyelids.

blood: circulation time 23 seconds on average.

blood content in body varies slightly, but average man has 12 pts (5.6 litres) and woman 7 pts (3.3 litres), making the average 9 pints in general. An approximate calculation for adults is 60 millilitres per kilogram of body weight.

blood groups A, B, AB, O. Blood groups may also be divided into Rhesus negative and positive. The most common group is O, which is universally given, and AB can receive from any group.

blood pressure: readings systolic is highest blood pressure reading; diastolic is lowest. Abnormally high or low conditions are called hypertension and hypotension respectively.

body build classification system is called somatotype and consists of: ectomorph (tall), endomorph (fat), mesomorph (muscular).

bones consist of collagen, calcium phosphate and inorganic salts, mainly hydroxyapatite. Smallest is the stapes and the largest the femur. The only non-connected bone is the hyoid in the throat.

bradycardia abnormally slow heart action.

brain the brain contains 10,000 million nerve cells, each of which has a potential 25,000 inter-connections with other cells. Average weight of the brain is 3lb (1.4 kg). The left side is the rational side.

calcaneus heel bone.

cells the smallest cell in the human body is the male sperm, the largest is the female ovum.

central nervous system brain and spinal cord (vertebrates).

Chinese restaurant syndrome monosodium glutamate intolerance

cholangiography X-ray examination of the bile ducts used to locate obstructions.

cholecystography X-ray examination of the gall bladder used to detect the presence of gall stones.

chromosomes 23 pairs in the human body, the female having two X sex chromosomes while the male has one XY pair. They carry the gene sequence and, therefore, full genetic blueprint.

collagen protein of great tensile strength present in bones, cartilage, tendons, ligaments and the skin.

colostrum mother's first breast-product after a birth before milk flow begins. Contains antibodies that bring important immunities.

comedo medical name for a blackhead.

conjunctivitis aka pink eye.

cornea convex transparent membrane that forms the forward covering of the eyeball; it is the only part of the body devoid of blood supply.

couéism form of auto-suggestion propagated by Emile Coué (1857–1926). A key phrase was: 'Every day, and in every way, I am becoming better and better.'

coxa (aka innominate bone) hip bone or joint (contrast ilium).

Crohn's disease chronic inflammatory disease of the intestines, especially the colon and ileum, causing ulcers and fistulae. Named after B B Crohn, US pathologist (1874–1983).

crural of the leg.

cubital of the forearm.

dentine calcified tissue of tooth.

diaphragm dome-shaped muscular partition that separates the abdominal and thoracic cavities.

disease: most widespread tooth and gum disease.

Down's syndrome: cause extra chromosome (three number 21s instead of the usual two, hence the medical name, Trisomy 21).

Economo's disease trypanosomiasis (sleeping sickness).

English disease aka bronchitis.

enuresis Involuntary urination.

epiglottis cartilaginous flap that covers the entrance to the larynx during swallowing, preventing food from entering the trachea.

epilepsy: categories petit mal, grand mal, psychomotor.

epistaxis a nose bleed.

erysipelas aka St Anthony's Fire.

erythrocyte red blood cell containing the pigment haemoglobin. Transports oxygen and carbon dioxide to and from the tissues.

eye chart, standard Snellen chart.

gall bladder muscular membranous sac; its function is to store and concentrate bile, a fluid that is received from the liver and is important in digestion. In humans, it is situated on the underside of the liver and is pear-shaped and expendable, with a capacity of about 1.7 fluid ounces (50 ml).

gland: largest the liver.

glandular fever viral disease causing swelling of the lymph glands and prolonged lassitude. Aka infectious mononucleosis.

Government Chief Medical Officer Professor Dame Sally Davies

Graves disease exophthalmic goitre with characteristic swelling of the neck and protrusion of the eyes, resulting from an overactive thyroid gland.

haemoglobin red oxygen-carrying protein containing iron and present in the red blood cells of vertebrates.

haemophilia male-only disease that prevents the blood from clotting. Women may be carriers. Aka Royal Disease.

hallux big toe.

hardest substance in body tooth enamel.

Harefield Britain's leading hospital for heart and heart-and-lung operations, situated 20 miles west of London.

hemicrania migraine.

hernia the projection of an organ through the lining of the cavity in which it is normally situated. The two most common forms of hernia are femoral (upper thigh) and inguinal (groin).

heroin: made from morphine, an opium derivative.

herpes zoster shingles, an acute painful inflammation of the nerve ganglia, with a skin eruption, often forming a girdle around the waist, and caused by the same virus as chickenpox.

homoeopathy treatment of disease by minute doses of drugs that in a healthy person would produce symptoms of the disease.

hormones: female sex oestrogen and progesterone.

hospice movement: founder Dame Cicely Saunders.

housemaid's knee inflammation and swelling of the bursa in front of the kneecap, often caused by continual kneeling on hard surfaces. Aka prepatellar bursitis.

humerus bone extending from the shoulder to the elbow.

humours obsolete name for the four chief fluids of the body, i.e. blood, phlegm, yellow bile and black bile, that were once thought to determine a person's physical and mental qualities. Aka cardinal humours.

Hurler's syndrome defect in metabolism resulting in mental retardation, a protruding abdomen and bone deformities, including an abnormally large head. Aka gargoylism.

hypermetropia the condition of having long sight.

illium bone forming the upper part of each half of the human pelvis (contrast coxa).

inferiority complex named by Alfred Adler.

innominate bone (aka coxa) bone formed from the fusion of the ilium, ischium and pubis, aka the hip bone.

insulin: gland that produces pancreas (in cells called the islets of Langerhans).

interferon proteins made by cells in response to virus infection.

iridology diagnosis by examination of the iris of the eye (used mainly in alternative medicine).

iris the coloured muscular diaphragm that surrounds and controls the size of the pupil.

jaw bones maxilla (upper jaw), mandible (lower jaw).

joints: lubricating fluid synovial fluid.

keloid/cheloid overgrown scar tissue.

kidney organ that maintains water balance and expels metabolic wastes. The kidneys consist of two series of specialised tubules that empty into two collecting ducts, the Wolffian ducts. The two kidneys are positioned on the back wall of the abdomen.

kissing disease glandular fever.

kyphosis excessive outward curvature of the thoracic spine causing hunching of the back.

larynx cartilaginous and muscular hollow organ forming part of the air passage to the lungs. Aka Adam's apple, voice-box.

Lassa fever acute and often fatal febrile viral haemorrhagic disease of tropical Africa, named from the village in Nigeria where first reported.

Legionnaires' disease form of bacterial pneumonia first identified after an outbreak at an American Legion meeting in Philadelphia in 1976 and spread by water droplets through air-conditioning systems and similar devices.

leucocyte colourless amoeboid cell of blood and lymph, containing a nucleus and important in fighting disease. Aka white blood cell/white corpuscle.

leucoderma (aka vitiligo) skin condition characterized by loss of melanin pigmentation.

leucoma a white opacity in the cornea of the eye.

leucotomy surgical cutting of white nerve fibres within the brain, especially prefrontal lobotomy.

leukaemia malignant disease in which the bone marrow and other blood-forming organs produce too many leucocytes.

ligament short band of tough flexible fibrous connective tissue linking bones together.

ligature tie or bandage used in surgery for a bleeding artery.

lingua the tongue.

lipids organic compounds that are esters of fatty acids and are found in blood, cell membranes and elsewhere.

lithotomy surgical removal of a calculus (stony secretion) from the bladder or urinary tract.

lithotripsy removal of a calculus from the bladder or urinary tract by means of ultrasound techniques that shatter the stone so that fragments passs naturally from the body.

liver largest organ in the human body, composed of a spongy mass of wedge-shaped lobes that has numerous metabolic and secretory functions. It is tucked beneath the diaphragm, protected from damage by the lower ribs of the right side. Its average weight is 3 to 4 lb (1.36 to 1.81 kg).

liver: functions production of bile to emulsify fat in the bowel. Reception of all the products of food absorption and the subsequent release as energy sources. Carbohydrates are stored as glycogen, and the liver uses insulin from the pancreas to control the body's glucose level. Purification of blood. Production of proteins needed for blood clotting.

liver transplants: hospital Addenbrooke's Hospital near Cambridge was the pioneer.

lordosis inward curvature of the spine.

lungs the 700 million air sacs are called alveoli, and the right lung is heavier than the left.

lunula crescent-shaped white area at the base of the fingernail.

Lyme disease form of arthritis caused by spirochaete bacteria transmitted by ticks. Named after a town in Connecticut, USA, where an outbreak occurred in 1975.

Mantoux test intradermal tuberculin test named after French physician Charles Mantoux 1877–1947.

mastoid process conical prominence on the temporal bone behind the ear, to which muscles are attached.

Ménière's syndrome inner ear disorder characterised by ringing in ear, dizziness and impaired hearing.

miner's disease pneumoconiosis (caused by inhalation of coal dust).

mnemonic for nerves in the superorbital tissue: Lazy French Tarts Lie Naked In Anticipation (Lacrimal, Frontal, Trochlear, Lateral, Nasociliary, Internal, Abduceris).

mons pubis rounded mass of fatty tissue lying over the joint of the pubic bones.

mons veneris rounded mass of fatty tissue on a woman's abdomen above the vulva (Latin: Mount of Venus).

Moorfields (London EC1) Britain's leading hospital specialising in eye injuries.

MRSA general term for a group of bacteria that are penicillin-resistant. It particularly attacks the infirm and is prevalent in hospital environments among patients with open wounds.

Munchausen's syndrome medical name for feigned symptoms brought on with a view to gaining admission into hospital.

Munchausen's syndrome by proxy mental condition in which a person seeks attention by inducing illness in another person, especially a child. Named after R E Raspe's literary hero.

muscae volitantes moving black specks seen before the eyes, caused by opaque fragments floating in the vitreous humour ('floaters') or a defect in the lens.

muscle: not attached at both ends tongue.

muscles: smile or frown debate although smiling is more beneficial to one's wellbeing, frowning uses more muscles.

myeloid tissue term for bone marrow, found in the spinal cord and elsewhere.

myopia short-sightedness.

naevus birthmark in the form of a raised red patch on the skin.

nosology branch of medical science dealing with the classification of diseases.

obstetrics of or relating to childbirth and associated processes.

oedema condition characterised by an excess of watery fluid collecting in the cavities or tissues of the body. Aka dropsy.

oesophagus part of the alimentary canal between the pharynx and the stomach. Aka gullet.

olfactory of or relating to the sense of smell.

organs: largest the skin is the largest and heaviest organ of the human body, but the largest and heaviest organ within the human body is the liver.

Paget's cancer cancer of the nipple and surrounding tissue. Named after Sir James Paget (1814–99) the English surgeon and pathologist who described this disease.

Paget's disease chronic disease of the bones characterised by inflammation and deformation. Aka *osteitis deformans.*

pancreas gland secreting the hormone insulin, which regulates glucose levels in the body. Deficiency of insulin causes diabetes mellitus (sugar diabetes). The pancreas lies across the upper part of the abdomen, in front of the spine and on top of the aorta and the vena cava (the body's main artery and vein). The basic structures in the pancreas are the acini, collections of secreting cells round the blind end of a small duct. Among the acini are small groups of cells called the 'islets of Langerhans'. These constitute the whole 'other life' of the pancreas as an endocrine organ secreting the insulin required by the body to control its sugar level. The pancreas also has an exocrine gland which produces essential alkali in the form of sodium bicarbonate to neutralise the acidic content of the stomach.

pathology study of causes and nature of diseases.

phlebitis inflammation of a vein.

phlegm: medical name sputum.

plasma clear yellowish fluid portion of blood or lymph in which the corpuscles and cells are suspended.

prescription charge from 1 April 2013 £7.85p.

purkinje effect As light intensity decreases red objects are perceived to fade faster than blue objects of similar brightness.

radius outer and slightly shorter of the two bones of the forearm.

retina light-sensitive portion of the eyeball.

retrovir brand name of zidovudine (AZT), used in treating HIV and AIDS.

rubella German measles.

rubeola medical name for measles.
Scalene muscles a group of three pairs of muscles in the neck.
Schick test identifies susceptibility to diphtheria.
sclera the white part of the eye.
sex change operation: first George (Christine) Jorgensen (1952).
Siamese twins: called after most famous conjoined twins to survive into adulthood: Chang and Eng (1811–74), born in Siam.
singultus hiccup.
skin accounts for 16% of the body's weight and has an average surface area of 2,800 sq in (18,000 sq cm); as such, it is the largest and heaviest organ of the human body.
spleen main function is to act as a filter for the blood and to make antibodies. It lies just below the diaphragm at the top of the left-hand side of the abdomen. It is normally about 5 inches (13 cm) long and weighs about ½ lb (240 g) and lies along the line of the 10th rib.
Stockholm syndrome psychological term for process of bonding between hostage and captors.
Stoke Mandeville Britain's leading hospital for the treatment of spinal injuries.
stomach capacity about 2–2½ pints (0.94–1.18 litres).
stomatology study of mouth diseases.
strabismus medical name for a squint.
syncope technical name for a faint.
talipes club foot.
talus the ankle bone.
teeth By the age of 2–3 a child will usually have a complete set of 20 deciduous (milk) teeth. A full set of 32 permanent teeth develops after the age of six. The front four teeth in each jaw are called incisors, the next two are the canines (eyeteeth), the next four are premolars (the hindmost being the third molar or wisdom teeth), the outer teeth are called molars.
teeth: mnemonic 4 canines ('dogs' 4 letters)
8 incisors (8 letters in word)
8 premolars (8 letters in word)
12 molars (remaining teeth)
C is before I and M in alphabet and premolar implies that they come before molars.
tendon cord of strong fibrous tissue attaching a muscle to a bone.
testes two glands that produce sperms and the male hormone testosterone.
test tube baby: first Louise Brown in 1978 (doctors were Steptoe and Edwards).
thalassotherapy ancient medical treatment of lying in sea water.
thorax anatomical name for the chest.
thyroid gland situated in the neck in front of the windpipe. Controls the metabolism.
tincture medicinal extract in a solution of alcohol.
tongue medical name lingua. Studding the tongue are many small projections called papillae. Inside these are some 9,000 taste buds which respond to four tastes i.e. sweet, sour, salt and bitter.
Tourette's syndrome neurological disorder characterised by tics, involuntary vocalisation, and in some cases the compulsive utterance of obscenities. The syndrome is named after French neurologist Gilles de la Tourette.
trachea the windpipe.
trachoma contagious disease of the eye with inflamed granulation on the inner surface of the lids, caused by chlamydiae.
trench foot medical condition prevalent throughout the First World War caused by standing around in cold, wet and unsanitary conditions and in severe cases resulting in amputation of the feet.
trismus variety of tetanus with tonic spasms of the jaw muscles causing the mouth to remain tightly closed. Aka lockjaw.
ulna inner and longer of the two bones of the forearm.
urticaria hives or nettle rash.
varicella chickenpox.
variola smallpox.
vascular relating to blood vessels.
venereal disease: most common gonorrhea.
vitiligo (aka leucoderma) skin disease characterised by loss of melanin pigmentation.
vitamin term coined by Casimir Funk (1884–1967) in 1911 for the unidentified substances present in food that could prevent the diseases scurvy, beriberi and pellagra.
Wasserman test: used for testing for syphilis.
white death tuberculosis.
yellow fever tropical virus disease with fever and jaundice, transmitted by the mosquito and often fatal.

Phobias

abluto	bathing
acaro	itching
acero	sourness
achulo	darkness
acro	heights
aero	air
agateo	insanity
aglio	pain
agora	open spaces
agra	sexual abuse
agrizoo	wild animals
agyro	crossing roads
aichuro	points
ailuro	cats
akoustico	sound
albuminuro	kidney disease
alektoro	chickens
algo	pain
allium	garlic
allodoxa	opinions
amaka	carriages
amatho	dust
amaxo	vehicles
ambulo	walking
amycho	being scratched
anable	looking up
ancrao	wind
andro	men
anemo	wind
angino	narrowness
anglo	England and the English
angro	anger
ankylo	immobility
anthro	flowers
anthropo	man
antlo	flood
anupta	staying single
apeiro	infinity
aphenphosm	being touched
api	bees
apotemno	amputation
arachibutyro	peanut butter
arachno	spiders
astheno	weakness
astra	lightning
ataxio	disorder
ate	ruin
atelo	imperfection
athazagora	being forgotten
atychi	failure
aulo	flute
aurora	Northern Lights
automyso	being dirty
bacilli	microbes
ballisto	missiles
baro	gravity
baso	walking
batho	depth
batracho	reptiles
belone	needles
blenno	slime
bromidrosi	body odour
bronto	thunder
bufono	toads
caco	ugliness
caino	novelty
caligyne	beautiful women
carcino	cancer
cardio	heart condition
carno	meat
catapeda	jumping
cathiso	sitting
catoptro	mirrors
chaeto	hair
cheima	cold
chero	cheerfulness
chiono	snow
chirapto	being touched
chrometo	money
chromo	colour
chrono	duration
chronometro	clocks
cibo	food
crystallo	crystals
claustro	closed spaces
clino	going to bed
cnido	stings
coimetro	cemeteries
coito	sexual intercourse
cometo	comets
consecotaleo	chopsticks
coprastaso	constipation
copro	faeces
coulro	clowns
cremno	precipices
cryo	ice, frost
cymo	sea swell
cyno	dogs
cyprido	venereal disease

deipno dining
demo crowds
demono demons
dendro trees
dermato skin
dermatosio skin disease
dextro objects on one's right
didaskaleino school
dike justice
dipso drinking
domato houses
dora fur
doxo expressing opinions
dromo crossing streets
dysmorpho deformity
eisoptro mirror
electro electricity
eleuthero freedom
emeto vomiting
enete pins
entomo insects
eoso dawn
ephibi teenagers
epistemo knowledge
eremo solitude
ergasio surgery
erythro blushing
frigo being cold
gallo France and the French
gato cats
gameto marriage
gelio laughter
genio chins
geno sex
genu knees
gephyro crossing bridges
geuma taste
gnosio knowledge
grapho writing
gymno nudity
gyno women
hade Hell
haemato blood
halo speaking
hamartio sin
haphe being touched
hapto touch
harpaxo robbers
hedono pleasure
helmintho worms
hexakosioihexekontahexa No. 666
hiero sacred things
hippo horses
hippopotomonstrosesquippedalio long words
hodo travel
homichlo fog
homo homosexuals
horme shock
hyalinopygo glass bottoms
hydro water
hygro dampness
hypegia responsibility
hypno sleep
hypso high places
iatro doctors
ideo ideas
io rust
ithyphallo erect penis
kakorraphia failure
katagelo ridicule
keno void
keraunothneto fall of man-made satellites
kineso motion
kineto motion
klepto stealing
kolpo genitalia
koni dust
kopo fatigue
koumpouno buttons
kristallo ice
kyno rabies
kypho stooping
lachano vegetables
lalo stuttering
leuko white
levo objects on one's left
limno lakes
linono string
litica lawsuits
logo words
lutra otters
lysso insanity
maieusio pregnancy
mania insanity
mastigo flogging
mechano machinery
medomalacu losing erection
melano black
melo music
merintho being bound
metallo metals
metathesio changes
meteoro meteors
metro poetry
mono being alone
motte moths
musico music
muso mice
myrmeco ants
myso dirt or contamination
myxo slime
nebula fog
necro corpses
negro black people
nelo glass
neo newness
nepho clouds
nosema illness
noso disease
nosocome hospitals
nosto returning home
noverca stepmother
nycto darkness
ochlo crowds
ocho vehicles
odonto teeth
oeno wine
oiko home
olfacto smell
ombro rain
ommeta eyes
omphalo navels
oneiro dreams
ophidio snakes
opto opening eyes
ornitho birds
osmo odours
osphresio body odours
ostracono shellfish
ourano Heaven
paedo children or dolls
pago ice
pantho suffering
panto everything
paralipo neglect of duty
paraskavedekatria Friday the 13th
partheno girls
patho disease
patroio heredity
peccato sinning
pediculo lice
pedio dolls
pelado bald people
penia poverty
phago swallowing
phasmo ghosts
phengo daylight
philema kissing
phobo fears
phono speaking aloud or noise
photo light
phronemo thinking
phthisio tuberculosis
phyllo leaves
pnigero smothering
pocresco gaining weight
pogono beards
poine punishment
poly many things
potamo rivers
poto alcohol
psellismo stuttering
pteromerhano flying
pterono feathers
pupa puppets
pyro fire
ranida frogs
rhabdo being beaten
rhyti wrinkles
russo Russia
rypo soiling
samhaino Halloween
satano Satan
scelero burglars
scio shadows
scoliono school
scopo being stared at
scoto darkness
seia flash
sela flashes
selacho sharks
sesquipedalo long words
sidero stars
siderodromo travelling by train
sino China
sito food
socera parents-in-law
sopho learning
soterio dependence on others
sperma germs
spermato semen
sphekso wasps
staso standing
stygio hell
symmetro symmetry
syngeneso relatives
syphilo syphilis
tacho speed
tapho graves and being buried alive
terato monsters
terdeka the number 13
texto fabrics
thaaso sitting
thalasso sea
thanato death
theo God
thermo heat
thixo touching
toco childbirth
toxi poison
traumato injury
tremo trembling
trichopatho hair
triskaideka the number 13
trypano injections
vesti clothes
virginiti rape
vitrico step father
wicca witchcraft
xantho yellow
xeno foreigners
xyro razors
zelo jealousy
zoo animals

MILITARY

Operations: Military and Social

Accolade Unfulfilled 1943 plan for capture of Rhodes and other Aegean islands.

Acrobat Original name for Operation Torch and the name used in the 1943 film *Tunisian Victory*, it was the planned British operation to advance from Cyrenaica to Tripoli, 1941.

Adlertag (Eagle Day) Start of main German air offensive on 13 August 1940, which led to the Adlerangriff (German plan for Battle of Britain).

A Go Japanese plan for a counterattack against possible US recapture of the Marianas during 1944.

Alaric First German codename for their possible military takeover in Italy.

Allied Force Began on 24 March 1999 when United States military forces, acting with Nato allies, commenced air strikes against Serbian military targets in the former Yugoslavia. The multinational force was tasked by Nato to bring an end to crimes committed by the Federal Republic of Yugoslavia against ethnic Albanians in the southern province of Kosovo. On 20 June 1999 Operation Allied Force was officially terminated. This was in response to the departure of all FRY military and police forces from Kosovo in compliance with the Military Technical Agreement, which was signed by the Commander of KFOR and representatives of the FRY Government on 9 June 1940.

Alpen Veilchen (Alpine Violet) Proposed plan for Italians to break out from Albania into Greece. Cancelled 19 January 1940.

Anakim First Allied plan for amphibious reconquest of Burma, abandoned in 1943.

Anton German occupation of Vichy France on 11 November 1942, first codenamed Attila.

Anvil Original codename for Allied landing on the French coast between Toulon and Cannes, later changed to Dragoon.

Aphrodite American scheme to load surplus bombers with explosives and fly them to the south coast of Britain, where the two-man crew would bail out and another plane would guide the plane to crash into a V-1 site. Joe Kennedy, elder brother of JFK, was blown up on a test run over Norfolk.

Apostle I Allied return to Norway on 10 May 1945.

Arcadia Codename for the conference between Churchill and F.D. Roosevelt in Washington, 22 December 1941–14 January 1942.

Aufbau Ost Prior to Barbarossa, this was the German buildup in the east.

Autumn Mist (Herbstnebel) Codename for the Ardennes Offensive (Battle of the Bulge) in 1944.

Avalanche US and British forces landing in the Gulf of Salerno causing the Germans to withdraw to the Gustav Line across the peninsula north of Naples, 9–19 September 1943.

Avonmouth Failed Allied expedition to Narvik May–June 1940.

Axis (Achse) Originally called 'Alaric', the disarming of the Italian army after their surrender to the Germans on 8 September 1943.

Babylon 7 June 1981, destruction of Osirak nuclear reactor in Iraq by Israeli F16s.

Badr 6 October 1973, Arab assault in Yom Kippur War.

Bagration Successful Soviet offensive in the central part of the German-occupied Russian Front, 23 June–29 August 1944.

Barbarossa German invasion of the USSR on 22 June 1941, supported by Romanian troops.

Battleaxe 15 June 1941, the first British offensive into 'Hellfire' (Halfaya) Pass, which failed to recapture Tobruk.

Baytown British landing at Reggio, 3 September 1943, and advance into the south-west Italian mainland, reaching Auletta on 19 September and Potenza on 20 September.

Bernhard Failed German plan to flood Britain with forged money during the Second World War, by means of an air drop, and thereby ruin the British economy.

Bigot Security classification for Normandy landing planning documents.

Birdcage Airborne leaflet drop on POW camps in the Far East announcing Japanese surrender.

Blackbuck 1 1 May 1982, bombing of Port Stanley runway by a Vulcan bomber.

Blackcock XII British Corps attack at Roermond, southeast Holland, 16–26 January 1945.

Black (Schwarz) The German occupation of Italy in 1943.

Blue Book Following an unexplained UFO sighting in Roswell, New Mexico, in 1947 the US Air Force set up a study group code-named Project Sign. Of the 147 reported sightings all but 12 were explained. A further rush of sightings prompted the set up of Project Grudge on 11 February 1949. The USAF attempted to explain every UFO sighting but of the 273 official sightings, 231 were classed as unidentified. In March 1952 Project Grudge went public as Project Blue Book and for the next 17 years remained the USAF's official UFO Study Program. Investigations ceased in 1969 as the US government advised the USAF that the project was no longer justifiable.

Bluecoat Normandy Operation of 30 July 1944, which concerned the initial British diversionary breakout from their American boundary, followed by the US 3rd Army, under Patton, breaking through the German defences at Avranches, the gateway from Normandy into Brittany.

Bodenplatte Luftwaffe offensive operation against Allied airfields in north-western Europe during December 1944.

Bodyguard Overall codename for multiple Allied deception tactics in 1944, but usually associated with the diversionary operation to deceive the Germans into thinking that the invasion was to be Kent-based and aimed at the Pas de Calais. Originally codenamed Jael.

Bolero The build up of US troops in the UK in 1942.

Bolo During Vietnam War, an ambush operation by American F-4 fighters, flying like bombers, which knocked out 7 North Vietnamese Migs in one go.

Brassard Allied amphibious landings launched from Corsica on Elba, 17 June 1944.

Brevity 15 May 1941, the first British offensive into Hellfire Pass.

Buckshot Planned British attack in Libya, May 1942.

Bumblebee Anti-burglary device instigated by the Metropolitan Police on 1 June 1993 and sponsored by Yellow Pages. Bumblebee has several aspects to its 'sting'. The aim is to target known burglars in an effort to 'fight back' against criminals. In 1995 the Bumblebee Imaging System was implemented whereby stolen property recovered by the police can be matched against photographs supplied by the victim. Bumblebee has also run a campaign to make people aware that covert police patrols are carried out at car boot sales. Another key factor in Bumblebee operations is the personalisation of belongings. The increase in computer and mobile phone companies having tracing methods has meant their products are no longer worth stealing.

Cartwheel Phase One US troops recapture important islands in the Solomon Island Group from 1 July to 25 November 1943.

Cartwheel Phase Two US and Australian forces invasion of north-east New Guinea from 4 Sept 1943 to 23 March 1944.

Catapult 3 July 1940, British naval attack on French fleet at Mers-el-Kebir, destroying or damaging most of its ships to prevent them from falling into German or Italian hands.

Catherine British plan for forcing a passage into the Baltic to aid Poland, before the country's invasion by Germany and the Soviet Union in September 1939.

Cedar Falls The US clearance of Vietcong from Iron Triangle, Vietnam, in 1967.

Centaur Crackdown on Britain's 'black economy' by Customs and Excise from 1985 onwards. Lester Piggott was a famous catch.

Cerberus Channel dash of the German ships *Scharnhorst*, *Prinz Eugen* and *Gneisenau* from Brest to Germany in February 1942.

Chariot 27–28 March 1942, British Commando raid on St Nazaire to destroy the Normandie Dock.

Charnwood Normandy operation of 7 July 1944: attack north of Caen following a massive RAF bombardment.

Chastise British bombers led by Wing-Commander Guy Gibson attacked three dams in the Ruhr region of Germany in May 1943, using the spinning or 'bouncing' bombs designed by Barnes Wallis. Two dams were breached. Aka the Dambusters' Raid.

Cheshire British equivalent of Operation 'Provide Promise', i.e. the RAF flights into Sarajevo.

Chicken Little Abortive attempt to predict time and place of Skylab's return to Earth in 1979.

Chromite 15 September 1950, General MacArthur's successful amphibious landing at Inchon during the Korean War.

Clean Hands Launched by Milan magistrates in February 1992 to halt corruption in the city, especially collusion between the Mafia and the Christian Democratic Party.

Cobra Allied Normandy USAAF breakout of July 25 1944, following massive bombardment by USAAF.

Cockade Part of Allied deception plan to convince Germans that invasion of Europe would be anywhere but Normandy in summer of 1944. Brittany, northern Norway and the Pas de Calais were false objectives.

Colossus First British airborne operation (unsuccessful), Tragino viaduct, Campagne, Italy, on 10 February 1941.

Compass 9 December 1940, British 8th Army attack at Sidi Barrani, Egypt, which began the destruction of the Italian 10th Army.

Corkscrew Allied operations against the Mediterranean island of Pantelleria in June 1943.

Coronet Proposed US invasion of Japanese island of Honshu in March 1946 overtaken by Japanese surrender the year before.

Corporate British recapture of the Falklands in May/June 1982.

Countryman Investigation into alleged corruption in the Metropolitan Police.

Cromwell Not an operation but a British codeword for 'Invasion Imminent' used from 1940.

Crossbow Operation using fighters, anti-aircraft batteries and barrage balloons against German V-1 flying bombs in 1944, and later to bomb the V-2 rocket launch sites.

Crusader The 8th Army's first offensive (as 8th Army) in Libya, 18 November to 12 December 1941.

Culverin Allied plan for recapture of northern Sumatra in 1943 – never carried out.

Deliberate Force Nato's air campaign against Bosnian Serbs from 30 August to 14 Sepember 1995.

Deny Flight UN denial of Bosnian airspace to warring parties, began on 12 April 1993. On 28 February 1994 four Bosnian Serb warplanes violating the no-fly zone were shot down by Nato aircraft. This was the first military engagement ever undertaken by the UN/NATO Alliance.

Desert Sabre Official name for the ground war in the Persian Gulf Jan–Feb 1991. US media often used the term 'Desert Sword'.

Desert Shield US-led multinational force, whose establishment was formally announced on 9 November 1990 and whose aim was to secure the withdrawal of Iraqi troops from Kuwait.

Desert Storm Air offensive launched by US-led allied forces on the night of 17 January 1991 against targets in Iraq and Iraqi-occupied Kuwait. The campaign lasted until 27 February 1991.

Detachment US capture of the Japanese island of Iwo Jima from 19 February to 1 March 1945.

Diadem Allied offensive that began on 11 May 1944, and broke the German Gustav Line, capturing Rome on 4 June 1944.

Dickens The 3rd Battle of Cassino, Italy, 15 March 1944. The original codename was Bradman, a cricket reference.

Diver British anti-V-1 measures.

Downfall Projected Allied invasion of mainland Japan, planned for 1 November 1945 and never carried out.

Dragoon Launched on 15 August 1944; Allied invasion of southern France, subsequent to Operation Anvil. When the US 7th Army and the French 1st Army landed on the French Riviera the Americans drove through the Alps to take Grenoble, while the French took Marseilles and advanced up the Rhône valley to rejoin the Americans near Lyons and move northeastward into Alsace in September 1944.

Dracula Liberation of Rangoon completed on 3 May1945.

Dynamo Evacuation of Anglo-French forces from Dunkirk, 26 May to 4 June 1940.

Eclipse Proposed dropping of Allied airborne army on Berlin in April 1945.

Edelweiss German Army Group A's operations against Baku area of the Caucasus during the summer of 1942.

Eisenhammer Planned Luftwaffe attack on Soviet power stations during February 1945.

El Dorado Canyon 14 April 1986, 24 USAF F-111 bombers attacked Tripoli in reprisal raid.

Epsom Normandy operation in the last 5 days of June 1944, a british move to outflank Caen from the West.

Eureka Codename for the Tehran conference of November 1943 between Churchill, Roosevelt and Stalin.

Exporter British and Free French invasion of Vichy-ruled Lebanon and Syria from 8 June to 12 July 1941.

Felix Proposed German plan to capture Gibraltar and the Canary and Cape Verde Islands with Spanish aid in November 1940. Spain's neutrality ruled it out.

Firebrand Allied occupation of Corsica, largely by Free French forces, from September to October 1943.

Flash Codename for attempt on Hitler's life in March 1943 when a bomb placed in his plane by Fabian von Schlabrendorff failed to explode.

Flintlock US invasion of Marshall Islands and Kwajalein Atoll from 31 January to 7 February 1944.

Forager US invasion of the Marianas between J11 and 26 June 1944.

Fortitude, North and South Deception campaigns to suggest that invasion of Northern Europe would be directed at either Norway or the Pas de Calais in 1944.

Freeborn 8th Army provision for withdrawal to Egyptian frontier in 1941.

Frequent Wind US evacuation of Saigon, Vietnam, in April 1975.

Fritz Initial plan for German invasion of the Soviet Union in December 1940, precursor of Barbarossa.

Fuller Attempt to prevent the German warships *Scharnhorst* and *Gneisenau* escaping from Brest in December 1943.

Full Flow Greatest UK exercise since 1945 involving transfer of 57,000 troops from UK to Germany for Lionheart/Cold Fire exercises; began 3 September 1984.

Galvanic US occupation of Tarawa, Makin and Apamama, in the Gilbert Islands, on 20–21 November 1943.

Gemsbock Anti-partisan drive in Greece, July 1944.

Gomorrah RAF fire-storm raid on Hamburg, 25 July 1943, when anti-radar chaff, codenamed 'Window', was used for the first time.

Goodwood Normandy offensive of 18 July 1944: an attack by the British Second Army south-east of Caen following massive bombardment by RAF.

Granby British contribution to the Gulf War from Operation Desert Storm to the ceasefire on 11 April 1991.

Granite US offensive operations in the Central Pacific, beginning March 1944.

Grapeshot Allied attack on German-occupied northern Italy in 1944.

Grenade Operation that linked Lieutenant General William Simpson's 9th US Army to the Canadian offensive against the lower Rhine (Operation Veritable) in February 1945.

Gymnast Proposed British landings in Tunisia and Algeria in 1941, superseded by Torch.

Hammer Proposed Allied attack on Trondheim, central Norway, April 1940, abandoned as impracticable.

Hercules Proposed German airborne invasion of Malta in the spring of 1942 involving airborne and sea landings. The operation was cancelled.

Herrick Codename under which all British operations in the War in Afghanistan have been conducted since 2002 (see Operation Veritas).

Horrido German anti-partisan drive in Yugoslavia - spring 1944.

Husky US and British troops landing in Sicily on 10 July 1943; total occupation achieved by 17 August 1943.

Icarus Proposed German invasion of Iceland in 1940; not carried out.

Iceberg US capture of Okinawa from 1 April to 22 June 1945.

I Go Japanese codename for naval counter-offensive in the Pacific during April 1943.

I - Go Sakusen Japanese air offensive in south-west Pacific, 7 to 16 April 1945 (aka Operation A).

Iltis German anti-partisan drive in Greece during March 1944.

Infatuate Allied operation to capture Walcheren Island in the Scheldt estuary on 1–18 November 1944.

Irma Media term for the airlift of 40 people injured in the war in Bosnia-Herzegovina to hospitals in the UK, Sweden and Italy in August 1993. Named after Irma Hadzimuratovic, a wounded 5-year-old whose plight was given huge media coverage after Prime Minister John Major arranged for her flight out of Sarajevo.

Ironclad British occupation of Diego Suarez, Madagascar, 8 May 1942.
Isabella (Ilona) Abortive German plans to occupy Atlantic coasts of Spain and Portugal in 1941.
Jericho RAF Mosquito raid on Amiens jail to release Resistance prisoners, 18 February 1944.
Joint Guardian In the aftermath of Operation Allied Force the Joint Guardian operation continues to pursue the ultimate goal of a peaceful multi-ethnic and democratic Kosovo. The original five-point plan of Allied Force was to stop the Serb offensive, force a Serb withdrawal, establish democratic self-government in Kosovo, allow a Nato-led peacekeeping force and to allow the safe return of Kosovar Albanian refugees.
Jubilee Disastrous Anglo-Canadian amphibious raid on Dieppe on 19 August 1942.
Junction City Only US para assault of Vietnam War, 22 February–14 May 1967.
Jupiter Projected Allied invasion of northern Norway in 1942; not carried out.
Just Cause Code name for the US military invasion of Panama between 20 December 1989 and 13 February 1990. It saw the first operational use of the stealth bomber.
Ka Go Japanese reinforcement of Guadalcanal in August 1942 resulting in the battle of the Eastern Solomons.
Kathleen A German-planned invasion of Ireland in the summer of 1940, with the support of the IRA. Preparing work on this plan was made by the IRA themselves, but aborted.
Konstantin German operation to seize control of Italian-controlled Balkans during September 1943.
Koralle German anti-partisan drive in Greece during July 1944.
Kreuzoller German anti-partisan drive in Greece - August 1944.
Kugelblitz German anti-partisan drive in Yugoslavia late 1943.
Kutuzov Soviet counter-offensive in the Kursk salient of July 1943.
Leopard German assault on the island of Leros, Greece, in 1943.
Lightfoot General Montgomery's plan for the breakthrough phase of the 2nd Battle of El Alamein, 23 October 1942. It failed to break the German defences.
Lila German operation to seize the French fleet at Toulon. They found the fleet scuttled on 27 November 1942.
Limerick British attack in Libya, June 1942.
Linebacker II The 1972 Christmas bombing offensive against North Vietnam by US B-52 bombers.
Little Saturn Soviet offensive against the German relief forces trying to break through to the encircled 6th Army at Stalingrad, launched on 16 December 1942.
Lumberjack Advances by US First Army to the Rhine at Cologne and by US Third Army further south in February 1945.
Lustre British transfer of forces from Western Desert to Greece in March 1941.
Luttich German attempt to cut off the Americans breaking out of Normandy by attacking at Mortain 17 August 1944.
Magic Name given to the overall US Intelligence programme before and during the Second World War devoted to breaking Japanese codes.
Magic Carpet Airlift of some 50,000 Jews from Yemen to Israel in the late 1940s and early 1950s.
Magician Codename for the Metropolitan Police Flying Squad operation to foil the world's biggest armed robbery at the Millennium Dome in London. Armed with smoke bombs, ammonia and a nail gun, the gang crashed into the building in a stolen JCB. Their aim was to steal the DeBeers Millennium Diamonds, worth between £200 and £350 million. The police had known about the attempted robbery for months and duly arrested the five robbers on 7 November 2000. The men were sentenced on 18 February 2002; two received 18 years, two 15 years and one five years.
Magnet Codename for the arrival of US forces in Northern Ireland in February 1942.
Mailfist Planned Allied recapture of Singapore, in 1945.
Manhattan District Cover name for the USA's atomic bomb project begun in June 1942.
Mannah Dropping of food supplies to occupied Holland by RAF in April and May 1945. Also codename for British intervention in the Greek civil war in October 1944.
Marita German assault on Yugoslavia and Greece in May 1941.
Maritime Monitor Royal Navy blockade of Serbia.
Market Garden The disastrous Allied airborne attack near Arnhem on 17 September 1944 which failed to link up with the British Second Army. Market was the airborne operation in which Allied paratroops were to seize key river crossings in advance of Second Army's tanks. Garden was the ground phase.
Menace Failed Anglo-Free French attempt to capture Vichy Dakar in West Africa with help from De Gaulle in September 1940.
Mercury German airborne assault on Crete in May 1941.
Midsummer Night's Dream Probing attack by Rommel in Libya, 14 September 1941.
Millennium RAF Bomber Command's 30/31 May 1942, 1,000-bomber raid on Cologne.
Mincemeat Aka The Man Who Never Was. Precursor of Operation Husky, whereby the aim was to deceive the German general staff into believing the proposed Allied attack on Sicily was, in fact, to be on Sardinia and Corsica in the west and the Greek mainland in the east. The deception was the plan of two relatively junior officers, Squadron Leader Sir Archibald Cholmondley and intelligence officer Lt Cmdr Ewen Montagu. It was Cholmondley who first suggested planting a series of subtle clues on a dead body and ensuring the Germans would be privy to this information, and it was Montagu who gave the plan its feasibility. The dead body, whose true identity was never revealed, was given the name of Captain (acting major) William Martin of the Royal Marines, and his mode of death was a plane crash at sea off the Spanish coast, where the Abwehr (German Intelligence) was known to be very active. The plan was a total success and 'Husky' gave the Allies control of the Mediterranean.
Mongoose Operation launched by President John F Kennedy and his brother Robert Kennedy, the Attorney-General, in December 1961, with the aim of overthrowing Fidel Castro of Cuba.
Moonlight Sonata German air-raid on Coventry on 14 and 15 November 1940.
Moses Secret airlift of Ethiopian Jews, or Falashas, to Israel from refugee camps in Sudan 1984–5.
Musketeer Anglo-French assault on Suez on 5 November 1956, first ever use of helicopters in amphibious landing.
Myth Soviet investigation into the death of Hitler in 1946, with aim of ensuring that he was in fact dead.
Neptun German anti-partisan drive, Greece 1944.
Neptune Naval side of Operation Overlord, involving 7,000 Allied ships.
No Ball Air attacks on German rocket-launching sites in 1944–5.
Noble Eagle American military operation to eliminate terrorist networks around the world. The ongoing assault on terrorism was launched in response to the terrorist attack on the World Trade Center on 11 September 2001. More than 35,000 military reservists were activated in the first year to support homeland defence as part of the campaign.
Nordlicht (Northern Lights) German operation against Leningrad during the summer of 1942.
Nordwind German counter-attack in Alsace (west of Strasbourg) in January 1945.
Oak Rescue of former prime minister Benito Mussolini from captivity in the Abruzzi mountains on 12 September 1943 by a small German force under Otto Skorzeny.
Olive Allied attack on the Gothic Line, Italy, in August 1944.
Olympic Proposed Allied plan to invade Kyushu in October 1945, precursor of projected Operation Downfall, the assault on Japan itself.
Ore The ongoing investigation into paedophilia via the Internet. The police have been able to track down downloaders of child pornography, via their credit card details, and specifically target those that have regular contact with children. So far the operation has unmasked over a thousand offenders in the UK, many of whom live a middle-class suburban lifestyle ranging from businessmen to pop musicians.
Overcast US plan launched in July 1945 to spirit German weapon scientists away from Europe to work in US laboratories.
Overlord Code name for the Allied invasion of Normandy in 1944. Originally planned for May, the day finally chosen was 5 June but the operation was delayed 24 hours by bad weather.
Panther German anti-partisan drive in Yugoslavia in early 1944.

Paperclip American project authorised by Harry S Truman in September 1946 whereby a selection of German scientists was brought to America to work on behalf of the US Government during the 'Cold War' following the end of the Second World War.

Paraquat British recapture of South Georgia on 25 April 1982.

Peace for Galilee Codename for Israel's full-scale invasion of Lebanon in June 1982, launched with aim of eradicating the PLO from Lebanon.

Pedestal British convoy to supply Malta in August 1942, involving 2 battleships (*Nelson* and *Rodney*), 3 aircraft carriers (*Victorious* and *Eagle* were sunk and *Indomitable* damaged), 2 ferry carriers (*Argus* and *Furious* carrying Spitfires), to Malta, 14 merchantmen (9 sunk, 5 arrived, including tanker, *Ohio* which was literally dragged into Malta sandwiched between 2 destroyers.

Pegasus 15 April 1968, relief by US and South Vietnamese forces of Khe Sanh combat base, Vietnam, besieged since mid-January.

Plan Blue (Fall Blau) Originally, the name given to a 1938 study from the Luftwaffe about aerial warfare in England, but more commonly the German offensive in southern Russia in the spring of 1942. Aka 'Case Blue'.

Plan Green (Fall Grün) In 1937 the plan to attack and occupy Czechoslovakia, which was executed without resistance in May 1938, after the Munich conference. In 1940 it was the name given to the plan for a frontal attack on the Maginot Line, later called Fall Braun.

Plan Red (Fall Rot) In 1935 Fall Rot was a study to defend against a surprise attack by France while defending the borders against Czechoslovakia and Poland. The 1937 version of Fall Rot included offensive operations against Czechoslovakia with the aim of preventing a prolonged two-front war. In 1940 it was the second part of the western campaign; after the destruction of the British Expeditionary Force and the northern army of France, it was, with Fall Braun, the attack on the rest of the French army, which was still entrenched in the Maginot Line.

Plan White (Fall Weiss) German invasion of Poland in September 1939. Aka 'Case White'.

Plan Yellow (Fall Gelb) German assault in the Low Countries and France launched on10 May 1940. Aka 'Case Yellow'.

Platinum Part of 'Barbarossa' comprising operations towards Murmansk in the north.

Plunder Montgomery's crossing of the Rhine at the head of the 21st Army Group on 23 March 1945.

Pointblank Bombing campaign against German military, industrial and economic targets from May 1943.

Polar Bear German assault on the island of Kos, Greece, in 1943.

Provide Assistance Codename for the US relief operation launched on 23 July1994 to deliver humanitarian relief to Rwandan refugees in Zaïre, prompted by an outbreak of cholera, aka Operation Support Hope.

Provide Comfort Code name for an emergency relief programme announced by Western allied forces on 16 April 1991, for the besieged Kurdish population of northern Iraq.

Provide Promise USAF flights into Sarajevo during conflict. Began on 2 July 1992 with 21 nations forming a coalition to resupply a war-ravaged Sarajevo. The longest humanitarian airlift in history ended on 9 January 1996.

Puma Proposed British operation to seize Canary Islands in 1941.

Punishment German air attacks on Yugoslav capital of Belgrade from 6 to 8 April 1941.

Quadrant Codename of the Quebec conference of August 1943, attended by Churchill and Roosevelt.

Rankin Allied plans for return to European continent. Rankin A involved possible return in advance of scheduled Normandy invasion, B was response in case of German withdrawal from France or Norway, C in case of German surrender.

Ratweek RAF and Yugoslav partisans launch attacks on roads and railways intending to prevent German withdrawal from Yugoslavia, September 1944.

Reckless US action against Hollandia, New Guinea - April 1944.

Regenbogen (Rainbow) Scuttling of German U-boats at the end of the Second World War. 231 scuttled during May 1945.

Restore Hope Codename given to the December 1992 deployment of a US-led 35,000-strong multinational force in Somalia to ensure the safe delivery of international aid to Somalis who were starving as a result of the year-long civil war.

Rhine Exercise The one and only cruise of the German battleship *Bismarck* from19 to 27 May 1941, when she sank in the Bay of Biscay.

Rhubarb RAF Fighter Command sweeps over the English Channel and occupied French coastline from late 1940 onwards.

Richard German plan for intervention in Spain in the event of a Republican victory in the Civil War.

Ring Soviet operation to destroy encircled German 6th Army at Stalingrad in January 1943.

Rösselsprung (Knight's Move) German attack on Tito's HQ, Hvar, Yugoslavia, 25 May 1944.

Rolling Thunder Programme of sustained US bombing of North Vietnam mounted by administration of President Lyndon Johnson, March 1965–November 1968.

Rosario Argentine invasion of the Falklands on 3 April 1982.

Roundup Allied plan to land in France between the Somme and the Seine (Dieppe and Le Havre) in spring 1943 by 30 US and 18 British divisions; replaced by Overlord.

Rumpelkammer (Junk Room) German V1 campaign against UK 1944–5.

Rumyantsev Soviet counter-offensive following Operation Citadel, August 1943, mounted at southern end of the Kursk salient.

Salmon Trap Abortive German plan to cut Murmansk railway in 1942.

Sandstone Codename for the US Army's nuclear testing series of 1948.

Schneesturm (Snowstorm) German anti-partisan drive in Yugoslavia late 1943.

Scorcher British occupation of Crete after withdrawal from Greece, May–June 1941.

Sea-Lion Proposed German invasion of England in 1940.

Sextant Cairo conference held just before and after the British–Soviet–US Tehran conference. At Cairo were US, British and Chinese heads of state, November and December 1943.

Sharp Guard Nato-WEU restriction on shipping to the Federal Republic of Yugoslavia in 1994.

Sheepskin Invasion of Anguilla in March 1969 by 300 British troops and 50 police to restore British rule from St Kitts-Nevis.

Shingle Amphibious landing at Anzio, 22 Jan 1944, sealed off by Germans until Operation Diadem broke through the Gustav Line.

Sho Go (Victory) Japanese defence plan in the summer of 1944, embracing several plans which could be put into effect once the axis of Allied advance became clear. Plan 1 provided for the defence of the Philippines, Plan 2 for the defence of Formosa and the Ryukyus, Plan 3 for the defence of Japan itself, Plan 4 for the defence of the Kuriles and Hokkaido. After Plan 1 was triggered, the Battle of Leyte Gulf ensued.

Shrapnel Abortive British plan of 1940 to seize the Cape Verde Islands in the event of Spain entering the war on Germany's side and threatening Gibraltar.

Sickle Cover name for the build-up of the US Eighth Air Force in Britain from 1942.

Slapstick British landing at Taranto on the heel of Italy and advance along the coast towards the German Gustav Line 9 September–30 November 1943.

Sledgehammer Proposed British–American contingency plan to invade Normandy and Brittany in Autumn 1942 if the Soviet Union appeared about to collapse.

Source British midget submarine attack on German battleship *Tirpitz*, 22 September 1943.

Spring Canadian breakout in Normandy July 1944, coordinated with Operations Goodwood and Cobra.

Starfish British deception plan early in the Second World War to simulate the effects of marker incendiaries dropped by bombers, and lure German bombers away from real targets.

Starkey Allied invasion practice in English Channel, September 1943, part of the Cockade deception plan.

Starvation US naval operation, launched in March 1945, to mine Japan's home waters.commenced March.

Steinadler German anti-partisan drive in Greece in July 1944.

Steinbock (Ibex) Luftwaffe bombing attacks on Britain in the spring of 1944.

Stosser German parachute operations during the Ardennes Offensive in 1944.

Strangle Air attacks destroying German communications in Italy before Operation Diadem in March 1944.
Student The German occupation of Rome in 1943.
Sunrise Secret negotiations with the German command in Italy for surrender of German forces in May 1945.
Supercharge I British break-out in the 2nd Battle of El Alamein 2–4 November 1942.
Super-Gymnast Plan for an Allied landing in north-west Africa in 1942, which evolved into Operation Torch.
Symbol Anglo–US Casablanca Conference 14–23 Jan 1943.
Taxable RAF drop window off the Pas de Calais, as diversion for D-Day, 5–6 June 1944.
Telic Codename for the 2003 Invasion of Iraq.
Terminal Allied conference at Potsdam 16 July to 2 August 1945.
Thunderbolt 3 July 1976, Israeli commando raid to release hostages of hijacked Palestinian terrorists to Entebbe. Thunderbolt was also codename in the Second World War for Luftwaffe cover for 'Cerberus'.
Thunderclap Plan favoured by 'Bomber' Harris for an all-out bombing assault on Germany, as a war winning *coup de grâce*, applied in particular to the bombing of Dresden in February 1945.
Tidal Wave USAAF bombing of the oil refineries at Ploesti, Romania, 1 August 1943.
Tiger British fast convoy loaded with war material which passed the length of the Mediterranean during May 1941, bringing tanks and fighter planes to the 8th Army in Egypt.
Torch Final codename for Allied landings in north-west Africa, 8 November 1942.
Totalize Normandy Operation of 7 Aug 1944, concerning Canadian attack towards Falaise, Normandy, aiming to link with US forces closing in from the south to trap German troops concentrated southward in the 'Falaise pocket'.
Tractable Canadian follow-up attack towards Falaise of 14 August 1944, an extension of Totalize.
Trident Anglo–American summit conference, Washington 12–25 May 1943. Operation Trident is also the name of a Metropolitan Police initiative begun in March 1998 to end a spate of shootings among the black communities in London.
Turquoise Codename for French military operation in Rwanda launched on 23 June 1994 following the death in a plane crash of President Juvenal Habyarimana and the violence that followed.
Typhoon (Taifun) German push to capture Moscow, September–December 1941.
U Go Japanese drive on India, from Burma in March 1944.
UNOSOM II The aftermath of Operation Restore Hope in Somalia in 1994.
Uphold Democracy 19 September 1994, USA ousting of Haitian Junta in favour of exiled President Jean-Bertrand Aristide.
Uranus Soviet attack which trapped the Germans 6th Army in Stalingrad, November 1942.
Urgent Fury Codename for the military invasion of the Caribbean island of Grenada in October 1983 by 7,000 US Marines in order to rescue medical students embroiled in political chaos following the murder of PM Maurice Bishop by hardline Stalinists.
Valkyrie Codeword for anti-Nazi uprising planned to follow the failed assassination attempt on Adolf Hitler by Claus von Stauffenberg on 20 July 1944.
Varsity Airborne assault that accompanied Montgomery's crossing of the Rhine on 24 March 1945.
Velvet Unrealised offer made late in 1942, to base 20 Anglo–American air force squadrons in Soviet Caucasus.
Vengeance Assassination of Admiral Yamamoto, Japanese naval commander in chief, by American P-38 fighters on 18 April 1943.
Veritable Opening of the Allied Rhineland campaign on 8 February 1945 with Canadians driving south from Nijmegen in the Netherlands to capture land between the Rhine and Maas and so clear German troops from the west bank of the Upper Rhine.
Veritas Codename used for British military operations against the Taliban government of Afghanistan in 2001 (see Operation Herrick).
Vittles US name for Berlin Airlift, 26 June 1948 to 30 Sept 1949.
Vulcan Final Allied offensive in Tunisia, 6 May 1943.
Warden RAF flights over northern Iraq, post Gulf War.
Watch on the Rhine German counter-offensive in the Ardennes commencing 16 December 1944, aka the Battle of the Bulge.
Watchtower 7 August 1942, US capture of airstrip on Guadalcanal and the naval and seaplane base Tulagi in Solomon Isles, leading to a 6-month campaign to expel the Japanese from Guadalcanal.
Weiss 1 and 2 German anti-partisan drive in Bosnia, Feb 1943.
Weser Exercise The German invasion of Norway in April 1940.
Wilfred Proposed British plan to mine neutral Norwegian waters in April 1940, which was --
pre-empted by German invasion of Norway, though not before one minefield was laid.
Winter Storm General Von Manstein's unsuccessful operation to relieve Germany's encircled 6th Army at Stalingrad, December 1942.
Wolf German anti-partisan drive in Yugoslavia in the spring of 1944.
Yewtree Metropolitan Police investigation into alleged sexual abuse, instigated in October 2012 after allegations against the then recently deceased Jimmy Savile and other celebrities.
Zeppelin Abortive German plot to assassinate Stalin in July 1944.
Zipper Projected British assault on Japanese-occupied Malaya in 1945, which was pre-empted by their surrender.
Zitadelle German attack that led to the Battle of Kursk (central Russia) in July 1943, the largest tank battle in history.
Zorba Codename for the ongoing investigation into Freemasonry within the Police Force.

General Information

aerobatics team: RAF Red Arrows.
army: European country without one Liechtenstein.
army: largest China.
bugle calls Reveille (1st), Last Post (2nd last), Lights Out (Last)
concentration camp: first British in the Boer War.
decorations: highest UK civilian George Cross.
decorations: highest UK military Victoria Cross.
Foreign Legion Founded by King Louis-Philippe (1831) as an aid to controlling French colonial possessions. The Legion's unofficial motto is *Legio Patria Nostra* (The Legion is Our Fatherland). Its monthly magazine is *Képi Blanc* (White Kepi). Its HQ was in Sidi Ben Abbas (Algeria) but is now in Aubagne, near Marseilles.
guards regiments Grenadiers, Coldstream, Scots, Irish, Welsh.
home guard: original name Local Defence Volunteers.
Household Cavalry regiments Life Guards, Blues and Royals.
Marines: attached to Admiralty (although classified as soldiers). The Royal Marines were founded in 1664.
Monty's double Clifford James.
National Service Commencing in 1949, initially for men between ages of 18 & 26 and for an 18-month term (increased to 2 years in 1950); abolished in 1960. Last recruits passed out in 1962.
Officer Training School: Army Sandhurst.
Officer Training School: Navy Dartmouth.
Officer Training School: RAF Cranwell.
Parachute Regiment: nickname Red Devils.
private army: only force allowed in UK Duke of Atholl Highlanders.
RAF: formed Initially the Royal Flying Corps formed 13 May (1912) but amalgamated with the Royal Naval Air Service on 1 April 1918 to form the RAF.
salutes Queen's Birthday 62 guns, opening of Parliament 42 guns.
SAS (Special Air Service): Founder David Stirling.
Special Forces equivalents Delta Force (US), SAS and SBS (Britain), Spetznaz (Russia).
US Air Force Academy (Colorado Springs) Founded in 1954 and is the Officer Training School for the US Air Force.
US Marines: founded 1775.
US Military Academy (West Point) Founded in 1802 and is the Officer Training School for the US Army.
US Naval Academy (Annapolis) Founded in 1845 and is the Officer Training School for the US Navy and Marine Corps.

Comparative Ranks in the Armed Forces

OFFICERS		
Royal Navy	**Army**	**RAF**
Admiral of the Fleet	Field Marshal	Marshal of the Royal Air Force
Admiral	General	Air Chief Marshal
Vice-Admiral	Lieutenant-General	Air Marshal
Rear-Admiral	Major-General	Air Vice-Marshal
Commodore	Brigadier	Air Commodore
Captain	Colonel	Group Captain
Commander	Lieutenant-Colonel	Wing Commander
Lt-Commander	Major	Squadron Leader
Lieutenant	Captain	Flight Lieutenant
Sub-Lieutenant	Lieutenant	Flying Officer
Acting Sub-Lieutenant	Second Lieutenant	Pilot Officer
NONCOMMISSIONED OFFICERS		
Warrant Officer	Warrant Officer Class 1	Warrant Officer
Chief Petty Officer	Warrant Officer Class 2	Flight Sergeant
Petty Officer	Staff Sergeant	Chief Technician
Leading Hand	Sergeant	Sergeant
Rating	Corporal	Corporal
	Lance-Corporal	Junior Technician
	Private	Aircraftman

Battles

Battle	*War*	*Date*	*Details*
Aachen	Second World War	21 Oct. 1944	Eight-day battle culminating in Allies capturing first major German city in the war.
Abensberg	Napoleonic Wars	20 Apr. 1809	French and Bavarians under Napoleon defeat Austrians under Archduke Charles.
Aberdeen	English Civil War	13 Sept. 1644	Royalists under marquis of Montrose defeated the Covenanters under Lord Burleigh.
Aboukir Bay/Nile	French Revolutionary	1 Aug. 1798	Nelson destroyed 11 French ships in harbour, Wars nullifying Napoleon's Egyptian land successes.
Abraham, Plains	Seven Years' War	13 Sept. 1759	British secured Quebec; British and French leaders' James Wolfe and Marquis de Montcalm, were killed.
Actium	Second Triumvirate War	2 Sept. 31 BC	Octavian defeated Antony and Cleopatra on a promontory in Acarnania, Greece.
Adrianople	Roman/Visigoth War	9 Aug. AD 378	The Visigoth Fritigern defeated Romans led by Emperor Valens.
Adowa/Adwa	Italian Invasion of Ethiopia	1 Mar. 1896	King Menelik II's decisive defeat of General Baratieri forced Treaty of Addis Ababa on Italy, October 1896.
Adwalton Moor	English Civil War	30 June 1643	Royalists under the earl of Newcastle defeated Lord Fairfax's parliamentarians.
Aegospotami	Peloponnesian War	405 BC	The final battle of the Peloponnesian War in which the fleets of the two Greek rival powers fought a sea battle in the Hellespont and the Spartan leader Lysander using better tactics eventually defeated the Athenians under Conon.
Agincourt	Hundred Years' War	25 Oct. 1415	Henry V's archers laid foundations for defeat of French, under Constable Charles d'Albret.
Alamo	Texan/Mexican War	6 Mar. 1836	Col. Travis, Jim Bowie and Davy Crockett were among 183 Texans killed by Santa Anna's Mexican troops.
Åland	Great Northern War	July 1714	Russian fleet under Apraksin and Peter the Great defeated the Swedes under Ehrenskjold.
Alarcos	Spanish/Muslim Wars	18 July 1195	Moors under Yakub el Mansur defeated Spaniards under Alfonso VIII of Castile.
Aleppo	Tatar Invasion of Syria	11 Nov. 1400	Tatars under Tamerlane defeated Turks under the Syrian Emirs.
Alesia	Gallic Wars	c. 52 BC	Romans under Julius Caesar defeated Gauls under Vercingetorix.
Alexandria	British invasion of Egypt	21 Mar. 1801	British under Sir Ralph Abercromby (killed) defeated French under General Menou.
Algeciras Bay	French Revolutionary Wars	8 July 1801	Two sea battles between British under Saumarez and French under Linois; the first was indecisive but the second won a victory for Saumarez.
Alicante	War of Spanish Succession	29 June 1706	Admiral Sir George Byng commanded a fleet of 5 ships that attacked the city walls causing severe damage.
Aliwal	First Anglo-Sikh War	28 Jan. 1846	General Sir Harry Smith led a joint British/Indian force to victory against Sikhs.
Alkmaar	Eighty Years' War	8 Oct. 1573	Siege was laid, 21 August 1573, by 1,000 Spaniards but Dutch defended successfully.
Alma	Crimean War	20 Sept. 1854	Indecisive battle between Russian and joint British/French/Turkish army.
Alnwick	Anglo-Scottish Wars	13 Nov. 1093	Malcolm Canmore, king of Scotland, and his son Edward were slain.
Alsen	Schleswig-Holstein War	29 June 1864	In this last engagement of the war, the Prussians defeated the Danes.
Amphipolis	Peloponnesian War	422 BC	Indecisive attempt by the Athenians under Cleon to recapture Amphipolis from the Spartans.
Ankara	Ottoman Wars	20th July 1402	Mongols under Tamerlane defeated Ottomans under sultan Bayezid I.

Antietam	US Civil War	17 Sept. 1862	Decisive battle that halted the Confederates in their advance on Maryland.
Antioch	First Crusade	3 June 1098	Siege started on 21 October 1097; Saracens held out against crusaders for 7 months.
Antwerp	Eighty Years' War	4 Nov. 1576	Known as the Spanish Fury; Sancho d'Avila's Spaniards slaughtered 8,000 Walloons.
Anzio	Second World War	22 Jan. 1944	A surprise landing near Rome by nearly 50,000 British/American troops.
Appomattox	US Civil War	9 Apr. 1865	Confederate army was surrounded in the Court House and Lee surrendered to Grant.
Arausio	Teutonic Wars	105 BC	Germanic tribes defeated Romans under Quintus Servilius Caepio and Gnaeus Mallius Maximus.
Arbela	Alexander's Asiatic Wars	1 Oct. 331 BC	Macedonians defeated Persians under Darius, making Alexander master of Asia.
Arcot	Carnatic War	Aug. 1751	Robert Clive captured fortress and held it for 7 weeks, delaying French advance in India.
Ardennes	Second World War	16 Dec. 1944	Aka Battle of the Bulge (coined by Churchill), the last German offensive on the Western Front. Allies prevailed; the battle officially ended on 25 January 1945.
Armada	Anglo-Spanish War	July 1588	Spanish Armada of 130 ships defeated by English fleet of 197, under Lord Howard.
Arnhem	Second World War	17 Sept. 1944	While airborne US troops secured bridges over Maas and Waal, British Arnhem landing severely de
Arques	French Religious Wars	21 Sept. 1589	Henry of Navarre, later King Henry IV, led Huguenots to victory against Catholic League.
Arsuf	Third Crusade	7 Sept. 1191	King Richard I gained notable tactical victory against the Saracens.
Ascalon/Ashqelon	First Crusade	19 Aug. 1099	Crusaders under Godefroi de Bouillon gained a victory against Saracens under Kilidj Arslan.
Ashdown	Danish invasion of Britain	8 Jan. 871	King Ethelred of Wessex aided by Alfred the Great defeated the Danes.
Ashingdon	Danish invasion of Britain	18 Oct. 1016	Canute of Denmark defeated Edmund Ironside, which led to him becoming King.
Aspern	Napoleonic Wars	22 May 1809	French retreated to the island of Lobau in the Danube; they had few supplies and Napoleon rejected his generals' advice to retreat. Napoleon's first defeat, by an Austrian army.
Aughrim	War of English Succession	12 July 1691	William III's army led by Godert de Ginkel scattered a Jacobite army in Galway.
Auldearn	English Civil War	9 May 1645	Royalists under marquis of Montrose defeated Covenanters nr Nairn.
Austerlitz	Napoleonic Wars	2 Dec. 1805	Aka Battle of the Three Emperors (Russian, French, Austrian). Napoleon defeated Kutuzov.
Bãhãdurpur	Mughal Civil War	24 Feb 1658	Conflict between the four sons of Shãh Jehan, Mughal emperor of India, over the succession. The shah's second son, Shujã, set himself up as the governor of Bengal but was defeated in battle by the son of Dãrã Shikoh, the eldest son of Shah Jehan. The third son, Aurangzeb, later executed his nephew, Sulaymãn Shikoh.
Balaclava	Crimean War	25 Oct. 1854	Allied victory over the Russians, but disastrous charge of British Light Brigade prompted General Bosquet to say 'This is not war.'
Ball's Bluff	US Civil War	21 Oct. 1861	Confederates under Gen Evans defeated Union army under Gen Stone.
Baltimore	War of 1812	11 Sept. 1814	British under Gen Ross (killed) defeated Americans under Gen Winder.
Bannockburn	Scottish Independence	24 June 1314	Robert the Bruce defeated English invaders under King Edward II.
Barãri Ghãt	Afghan-Marãthã War	9 Jan. 1760	Afghan army under Ahmad Shãh Durrãni defeated the Marãthãs under Dattãji Sindhia (died).
Barnet	Wars of the Roses	14 Apr. 1471	Yorkists under King Edward IV defeated Lancastrians under earl of Warwick (killed).
Beachy Head	War of English Succession	29–30 June 1690	English and Dutch under Lord Torrington defeated by French under Tourville.
Belleau Wood	First World War	6 June 1918	First major US – German clash of the war, a hard-won victory by General Bundy over Ludendorff.
Bellevue	Franco-Prussian War	18 Oct. 1870	Marshal Bazaine was driven back from Metz by Germans.
Berwick	Scottish Independence	28 Mar. 1296	Edward I's troops killed thousands after John de Balliol's refusal to supply men for Gascon War.
Beymaroo	First British-Afghan War	23 Nov.1841	General Elphinstone allowed only 1 gun for Brigadier Shelton to dislodge Afghans.
Bismarck	Second World War	27 May 1941	After sinking the cruiser *Hood*, Lutjens' battleship was sunk near Brest by British torpedo planes and warships.
Blenheim	War of Spanish Succession	13 Aug. 1704	Duke of Marlborough and Eugene of Savoy defeated French under Marshal Tallard in Bavarian town.
Blood River	Afrikaner-Zulu War	16 Dec. 1838	Zulus under King Dingaan (Dingane) were routed by the Boers.
Blore Heath	Wars of the Roses	23 Sept. 1459	Yorkists under earl of Salisbury dispersed Lancastrians under Audley.
Borodino	Napoleonic Wars	7 Sept. 1812	Napoleon paved the way for his triumphant march on Moscow by defeating Kutuzov.
Bosworth Field	Wars of the Roses	21 Aug. 1485	Henry, Duke of Richmond, later Henry VII, defeated and killed Richard III to end wars.
Boudicca	Roman invasion of Britain	AD 61	Suetonius routed Queen Boudicca of the Iceni, who took poison on the battlefield.
Boyne	War of English Succession	1 July 1690	Decisive battle of the war; William III defeated James II.
Brandywine	US War of Independence	11 Sept. 1777	British under General Howe forced George Washington's troops to retreat.

Breitenfeld	Thirty Years' War	17 Sept. 1631	First major Protestant victory of the war, in which the Roman Catholic Habsburg emperor Ferdinand II and the Catholic League under Johan Isaclaes Graf von Tilly were defeated by the Swedish-Saxon army under King Gustavus II Adolphus of Sweden.
Brill	Eighty Years' War	1 Apr. 1572	De La Marck's *Wetergeuzen* (sea beggars) took Dutch port from Spain to gain first Dutch victory of war.
Britain	Second World War	June 1940 –Apr. 1941	German air raids intended to prepare for invasion of Britain but repulsed by RAF
Bronkhurst Spruit	First Boer War	20 Dec. 1880	Opening engagement of the war, a British columnof 259 was ambushed and defeated.
Bull Run (Manassas) (First)	US Civil War	21July 1861	Beauregard defeated McDowell's Union army, Confederate General Jackson gained nickname 'Stonewall'.
Bull Run (Manassas) (Second)	US Civil War	29–30 Aug. 1862	Confederates Lee and Jackson routed troops under General Pope.
Bunker Hill	US War of Independence	17 June 1775	British troops under Howe gained Breed's Hill and Bunker Hill but suffered heavy losses.
Burgos	Peninsular War	19 Sept.–22 Oct. 1812 10–12 June 1813	Duke of Wellington twice laid siege to Burgos. The first attempt against the French garrison was disastrous and 2,000 Allied troops were killed, while the French lost 600. In a second, decisive attempt the city was captured within two days.
Burlington Heights	War of 1812	5 May 1813	British under Col. Proctor attacked by Clay but gained the day.
Bussaco	Peninsular War	27 Sept. 1810	Wellington defeated pursuing French army under Marshals Masséna and Ney.
Buxar/Baksar	British/Bengal War	23 Oct.1764	Major Munro's victory over a confederation of Indian pirates gave the East India Company control of Bengal and Bihar.
Cadiz	Anglo-Spanish War	29 Apr. 1587	Drake destroyed over 100 ships in his famous singeing of the Spanish king's beard.
Caer Caradoc	Roman invasion of Britain	AD 50	Romans under Ostorius Scapula defeated Caratacus, king of the British tribe of Trinovantes.
Calais	Anglo-French Wars	6 Jan. 1558	Last English stronghold in France lost, causing Mary I to say 'When I am dead and opened, you shall find Calais will be writ on my heart'.
Cambodia	Vietnamese invasion	7 Jan. 1979	Vietnamese army captured Phnom Penh and formed People's Republic of Kampuchea.
Cambrai	First World War	20 Nov.– 7 Dec. 1917	Brig.-Gen. Elles led world's first massed tank attack: dramatic breakthrough but soon reversed.
Camden	US War of Independence	16 Aug. 1780	British under Cornwallis defeated Americans under General Gates.
Camperdown	French Revolutionary Wars	11 Oct.1797	British fleet under Duncan intercepted and routed a Dutch convoy on its way to support a French invasion of Ireland.
Campo Santo	War of Austrian Succession	8 Feb. 1743	Indecisive battle between Spaniards under Mortemar and Imperialists under Count Traum.
Camulodunum	Second Roman invasion of Britain	c. AD 43	Romans under Emperor Claudius accepted surrender of local tribes after defeat on the Medway.
Cannae	Second Punic War	3 Aug. 216 BC	Hannibal gained a devastating victory over Romans under Varro due to superior cavalry.
Cape Matapan	Second World War	28 Mar. 1941	Small British fleet sank six or seven Italian ships off Cape Matapan, Greece (aka Cape Tainaron).
Cape St Vincent	French Revolutionary Wars	14 Feb. 1797	Spaniards were totally defeated by fleet of Sir John Jervis, who was made earl of St Vincent.
Caporetto	First World War	24 Oct. – 4 Nov. 1917	Austro-German offensive on the River Isonzo causing capture of 300,000 Italians.
Carabobo	Latin American Wars	24 June 1921	South American rebels under Antonio Simon Bolivar defeated Spanish royalists under General La Torre.
Carbisdale	English Civil War	27 Apr. 1650	Marquis of Montrose captured by parliamentary force and executed the following month.
Carchemish	Syrian War	605 BC	Babylonian troops led by Crown Prince Nebuchadrezzar II captured Carchemish from the Egyptians.
Carlisle	Jacobite Rebellion of '45	9 Nov. 1745	Young Pretender, Charles Edward Stuart, Bonny Prince Charlie, defeated duke of Cumberland.
Carrhae	Roman/Mesopotamia War	53 BC	Romans under Marcus Licinius Crassus (killed) invaded Mesopotamia but were defeated by the Parthians.
Carrical	Seven Years' War	2 Aug. 1758	British under Admiral Pocock defeated French under Comte d'Ache but with few gains.
Cartagena	War of Austrian Succession	9 Mar. 1741	Port blockaded by British under Admiral Vernon but extensive losses forced his withdrawal.
Cassino	Second World War	Jan./May 1944	Fierce and protracted battle during which Allies blew up the Benedictine monastery, 15 February, believing it to be German-occupied.
Castillon	Hundred Years' War	17 July 1453	John Talbot, earl of Shrewsbury, was killed, and the English lost Gascony, in the last battle of the war.
Cedar Creek	US Civil War	19 Oct. 1864	Union General Sheridan defeated Confederates under General Early.
Cedar Mountain	US Civil War	9 Aug. 1862	Union Corps under Banks attacked Confederates under Jackson but forced to withdraw.
Cerignola	Franco-Spanish Wars	28 Apr. 1503	Spanish under Cordoba defeated French troops under Louis XII.
Chaeronea	Philippan Campaigns	338 BC	Macedonians under Philip II defeated the joint Theban/Athenian army.
Chaldiran	Ottoman Wars	23 Aug.1514	Ottomans under Sultan Selim I defeated Safavid army under Shah Esma'il northeast of Lake Van.

Châlons	Attila Conquests	451 AD	Aka Battle of the Catalaunian Plains. Joint force of Romans and Visigoths defeated the Huns under Attila.
Chevy Chase	Scottish Independence	15 Aug. 1388	Aka Otterburn. Henry Percy's (Hotspurs) superior forces were soundly beaten by Scots.
Chickahominy	US Civil War	3 June 1864	General Lee's Confederates soundly repulsed Union attacks under Grant.
Chippenham	Danish Invasion of Britain	Jan. 878	Danes under Guthrum attacked King Alfred on12th Night; he was forced to hide at Athelney.
Chongju	Russo-Japanese War	Apr. 1904	First land battle of war; Cossacks were driven back with few losses.
Chorillos	Peruvian-Chilean War	13 Jan. 1861	Chileans comprehensively defeated Peruvians.
Christianople	Danish-Swedish Wars	Autumn 1611	First military exploit of the 16-year-old King Gustavus Adolphus of Sweden was a total success.
Chrysler's Farm	War of 1812	11 Nov. 1813	British under Colonel Morrison defeated Americans under General Boyd.
Ciudad Rodrigo	Peninsular War	8 Jan. 1812	Decisive battle 54 miles south-west of Salamanca. Wellington ordered an assault on the border fortress that eventually succeeded, but 600 Allied troops were killed, including General Robert Craufurd.
Cold Harbour	US Civil War	3 June 1864	Grant's frontal attack on entrenched Confederate forces repulsed but counter-assault was disastrously defeated by Lee.
Colenso	Second Boer War	15 Dec. 1899	Sir Redvers Buller's first move to relieve Ladysmith repelled by Gen. Botha.
Copenhagen	French Revolutionary Wars	2 Apr. 1801	Nelson turned his blind eye to Admiral Hyde Parker's signal to retire and gained the day.
Coral Sea	Second World War	8 May 1942	Naval conflict fought mainly by aircraft from carriers. US carrier *Lexington* lost, but Japanese withdrew.
Coronel	First World War	1 Nov. 1914	Von Spee's *Scharnhorst* and *Gneisenau* sank the British ships *Monmouth* and *Good Hope*.
Corunna	Peninsular War	16 Jan. 1809	French under Marshal Soult defeated by British under Sir John Moore (killed).
Crécy	Hundred Years' War	26 Aug. 1346	Edward III's archers and cannon defeated French under Philip VI.
Cropredy Bridge	English Civil War	29 June 1644	Royalists under Charles I defeated Sir William Waller's parliamentarians near Banbury.
Cross Keys	US Civil War	8 June 1862	Confederates under Ewell fought successful rearguard action against Fremonts' Federals.
Cuba	Castro Revolt	26 July 1953	Fidel and Raul Castro led unsuccessful raid on armoury at Santiago and were imprisoned.
Culloden	Jacobite Rebellion of '45	16 Apr. 1746	Aka Drumossie Moor. Duke of Cumberland earned epithet 'Butcher' for treatment of Jacobite Rebels after his crushing victory.
Custoza (First)	Italian War of Independence	24 July 1848	Crushing defeat for the forces of Charles Albert, king of Sardinia -Piedmont by the Austrian veteran Field Marshal Joseph Radetzky.
Custoza (Second)	Italian War of Independence	24 June 1866	An 80,000-man Austrian army under Archduke Albert defeated a 120,000-man Italian army under Victor Emmanuel II.
Cyprus	Turkish Invasion	20 July 1974	Turkey invaded northern Cyprus and established a beachhead around Kyrenia.
D-Day	Second World War	6 June 1944	The launching of Operation Overlord, the Allied Invasion of Normandy, was a major turning point of the war.
Dettingen	War of Austrian Succession	27 June 1743	Anglo-Austrian-German victory over French; the last occasion that a British sovereign (George II) led his troops into battle.
Diamond Hill	Second Boer War	11 June 1900	Lord Roberts attacked General Botha near Pretoria and drove him from his position.
Dien Bien Phu	French-Vietnamese War	13 Mar.– 7 May 1954	General Giap's siege and capture of key stronghold ended French power in Indochina and caused the partition of Vietnam.
Dieppe	Second World War	19 Aug. 1942	Daytime Allied raid testing German Atlantic defences; 2nd Canadian Division suffered terrible losses.
Dingaan's Day	Afrikaner-Zulu War	16 Dec. 1838	Zulus under Dingaan were routed by the Transvaal Boers.
Dominica	US War of Independence	12 Apr. 1782	Aka Battle of Les Saintes. Admiral Rodney defeated French fleet, preserved British hold on Jamaica.
Dorylaeum	First Crusade	1 July 1097	Victory for Crusaders under Bohemond and Raymond of Toulouse over Seljuk Turks.
Douro	Peninsular War	12 May 1809	Wellington crossed the Douro and drove Marshal Soult's French troops out of Oporto.
Dover	Anglo-Dutch Wars	29 Nov. 1652	Dutch fleet under van Tromp victorious over Admiral Blake's English fleet at Dover and at Dungeness shortly after.
Dresden	Napoleonic Wars	26 Aug. 1813	Napoleon victorious over Russians, Prussians and Austrians.
Dunkirk	Second World War	27 May – 4 June 1940	Almost 340,000 French and British troops ferried across the Channel to England.
Ebro River	Spanish Civil War	July–Nov. 1938	General Franco's Nationalists won a counter-offensive against Republicans under Modesto.
Edgecote	Wars of the Roses	26 July 1469	Lancastrian victory over Yorkists under the earl of Pembroke.
Edgehill	English Civil War	24 Oct. 1642	Indecisive first battle of Civil War between Charles I and parliamentarians under earl of Essex.
El Alamein	Second World War	Oct.–Nov. 1942	Montgomery's 8th Army drove Germans out of Egypt.
Elands River	Second Boer War	4 Aug. 1900	Australians under Col. Hore held out under fire until relieved by Kitchener.
Empingham	Wars of the Roses	12 Mar. 1470	Aka Losecoat Field. King Edward IV routed Sir Robert Welles's rebels.
Entholm	Northern Wars	11 June 1676	Swedes were defeated by Danish fleet under Admiral van Tromp.
Erbach	French Revolutionary Wars	15 May 1800	French under Sainte-Suzanne held out against Austrians under General Baron Kray.
Evesham	Second Barons' War	4 Aug. 1265	Prince Edward defeated the Barons, killed Simon de Montfort and restored Henry III.
Eylau	Napoleonic Wars	7–8 Feb. 1807	Indecisive battle between French troops under Napoleon and a joint Russian and Prussian army under Leonty Leontyevich Bennigsen.

Falkirk (First)	Scottish Independence	22 July 1298	English under Edward I defeated Scots under Sir William Wallace, who became a fugitive.
Falkirk (Second)	Jacobite Rebellion of '45	17 Jan. 1746	Jacobite army under Charles Edward Stuart (Young Pretender) defeated royalist forces under Henry Hawley.
Falkland Islands	First World War	8 Dec. 1914	Sturdee's squadron sank most of German Pacific squadron under von Spee (died).
Falkland Islands	British-Argentine War	2 Apr. 1982	Argentinian armed forces under General Galtieri invaded Falklands. On 3 April South Georgia was taken and on 5 April Rear Admiral Sandy Woodward led the task force to free islands. On 2 May the *General Belgrano* was sunk by the sub *Conqueror*, and on 4 May the destroyer *Sheffield* was hit, and sank on 10 May. On 21 May 5,000 troops under Major-Gen. Jeremy Moore went ashore at Port San Carlos, and Argentinian surrender terms were eventually signed on 14 June, 10 weeks and 3 days after invasion.
Ferrybridge	Wars of the Roses	28 Mar. 1461	Lancastrians under Clifford defeated Yorkists under Fitzwalter (killed).
Fisher's Hill	US Civil War	22 Sept. 1864	Union force under Sheridan defeated Confederates under General Early.
Five Forks	US Civil War	1 Apr.1865	Sheridan and Warren defeated Pickett's Confederates causing Lee's withdrawal from Richmond and surrender at Appomattox on 9 April.
Flodden	Anglo-Scottish Wars	9 Sept. 1513	English under the earl of Surrey (Thomas Howard) defeated Scots under James IV (killed).
Fontenoy	War of Austrian Succession	11 May 1745	French under Marshal de Saxe repulsed duke of Cumberland's abortive drive to relieve Tournai.
Formigny	Hundred Years' War	15 Apr. 1450	French under the comte de Clermont defeated English under Kyrielle, restoring Normandy to France.
Fort Frontenac	Seven Years' War	27 Aug. 1758	Colonel Bradstreet defeated French under Noyan, who lost control of Lake Ontario.
Gebora	Peninsular War	19 Feb. 1811	Spanish under Mendizabal were routed by French under Marshal Soult.
Gettysburg	US Civil War	1–3 July 1863	Greatest battle of the war between Meade's army of the Potomac and Lee's army of Virginia. Only a narrow Union victory, but it stopped Lee's invasion of the North.
Gibraltar	War of Spanish Succession	24 July 1704	British and Dutch fleet under Sir George Rooke defeated Spanish under marquis de Salinas and took Gibraltar.
Gitschin	Seven Weeks' War	29 June 1866	Prussians under Prince Frederick Charles defeated Austrians and Saxons under Clam-Gallas.
Glorious 1st of June	French Revolutionary Wars	1 June1794	Aka Ushant. British under Lord Howe defeated French and sank the *Vengeur.*
Golden Spurs	Flemish War	11 July 1302	Aka Courtrai. Untrained Flemish guild workers defeated French cavalry in Flanders and took their spurs as a trophy of their victory.
Graf Spee	Second World War	17 Dec. 1939	The pride of the German fleet, the pocket battle ship *Graf Spee* was scuttled by Captain Hans Langsdorf after being harried by three British cruisers *Achilles*, *Ajax* and *Exeter* and forced into Montevideo harbour. The Uruguayan government ordered the ship to sea but, rather than face a certain defeat, Hitler himself ordered the scuttling and Langsdorf shot himself.
Granada	Moorish Wars	Jan. 1492	Moors under Boabdil were defeated and the city came under Catholic rule of Ferdinand II of Aragon and Isabella I of Castille.
Grant's Hill	Seven Years' War	14 Sept. 1758	Major Grant with 800 Highlanders defeated by French under de Ligneris at Fort Duquesne.
Gravelines	Franco-Spanish Wars	13 July 1558	Spanish under comte d'Egmont, backed by an English fleet, defeated French under Marshal de Thermes.
Guadalajara	Spanish Civil War	8 Mar. 1937	Republicans defeated Nationalists under Franco and Italian Fascists under General Roatta.
Guadalcanal	Second World War	Aug. 1942– Jan. 1943	Americans eventually gained victory over Japanese after 5 months' fighting on land and sea.
Guadeloupe	French Revolutionary Wars	3 July 1794	Sir John Jervis captured island but it was recaptured by the French on 10 December.
Guilford Courthouse	US War of Independence	15 Mar. 1781	British under Lord Cornwallis defeated Americans under General Greene.
Halidon Hill	Scottish Independence	19 July 1333	English troops under Edward III defeated Scottish forces attempting to relieve Berwick-upon-Tweed.
Han Ko/Hangö	Great Northern War	4–6 Aug. 1714	Peter the Great commanded a fleet against Swedes, the first major Russian victory at sea.
Harfleur	Hundred Years' War	Aug.–Sept. 1415	English under Henry V defeated the French troops after a 6-week siege of the port.
Harpers Ferry	US Civil War	15 Sept. 1862	Confederates under General Thomas Stonewall Jackson forced Union garrison to surrender.
Hastings	Norman Conquest	14 Oct. 1066	Aka Battle of Senlac Hill. Harold II of England (killed) defeated by William, duke of Normandy.
Hedgeley Moor	Wars of the Roses	25 Apr. 1464	Yorkist Lord Montagu routed Lancastrians under Margaret of Anjou and Ralph Percy (killed).
Heligoland	Napoleonic Wars	31 Aug. 1807	British squadron under Admiral Thomas Russell captured island from Danes.
Heligoland Bight	First World War	28 Aug. 1914	Admiral Beatty's battle cruiser *Lion* sank the German cruisers *Mainz* and *Koln.*
Heliopolis	French Revolutionary Wars	20 Mar. 1800	Turks in Egypt under Ibrahim Bey routed by French under Gen. Kléber.
Herrings	Hundred Years War	12 Feb. 1429	Sir John Fastolfe defeated the comte de Clermont at Rouvray.
Hexham	Wars of the Roses	15 May 1464	Yorkists under Lord Montagu defeated and executed duke of Somerset.
Homildon Hill	Scottish Independence	14 Sept. 1402	English troops under Sir Henry Percy (Hotspur) defeated the Scots under the 4th earl of Douglas.

Hydaspes	Alexander's Asiatic Wars	326 BC	Fourth and last pitched battle fought by Alexander the Great during his Asiatic Campaign. Despite overwhelming numerical superiority of the Persian army led by Porus, and the 200 elephants that Porus had at his disposal, Alexander's tactical genius won the day.
Hyderabad	Conquest of Sind	24 Mar. 1843	British under Sir Charles Napier defeated Baluchis under Shir Mohammed.
Ilipa	Second Punic War	206 BC	Romans under Publius Cornelius Scipio (Africanus) defeated Carthaginians under Hasdrubal. Gisco and Mago in the Spanish town near Seville.
Imola	French Revolutionary Wars	3 Feb. 1797	French and Italian troops under Marshal Victor defeated Papal troops under General Colli.
Imphal	Second World War	29 Mar. 1944	Japanese troops besieged the city of Imphal in Assam, north-east India.
Inchon	Korean War	15 Sept. 1950	Amphibious landing by General Almond's X Corps drove the North Korean troops inland and seized Kimpo airfield.
Ingogo River	First Boer War	8 Feb. 1881	Boers defeated a small British column of 5 companies, 4 guns and a mounted force.
Inhlobane Mountain	Zulu War	28 Mar. 1879	British force of 1,300 under Cols Buller and Russell defeated by Zulus.
Inkerman	Crimean War	5 Nov. 1854	Russians under Prince Menshikov defeated by Franco-British troops under Raglan.
Ipsus	Macedonian-Egyptian War	301 BC	The combined forces of Lysimachus king of Thrace and Seleucus I Nicator of Babylon defeated the Macedonian army under Antigonus (killed) and his son Demetrius.
Isandhlwana	Zulu War	22 Jan. 1879	Six companies of 24th Regiment under Col. Durnford overwhelmed by Zulus under Matyana.
Issus	Alexander's Asiatic War	333 BC	Alexander the Great defeated Persians under King Darius.
Ivry	French Religious Wars	14 Mar. 1590	Henry IV's Huguenots defeated Catholic League under duc de Mayenne.
Iwo Jima	Second World War	19 Feb. 1945	General Schmidt's US V Amphibious Corps assaulted and secured the small island (8 sq miles) by 26 March.
Jajau	Mughal Civil War	12 June 1707	Family conflict to decide the successor to the Mughal emperor Aurangzeb; eventually his eldest surviving son Bahādur Shāh succeeded after a bloody battle with his brother Azam Shāh.
Jarnac	French Religious Wars	13 Mar. 1569	Catholics under the duke of Anjou defeated Huguenots under the prince de Condé.
Jena	Napoleonic Wars	14 Oct. 1806	Napoleon defeated the prince of Hohenlohe's Prussian army.
Jutland	First World War	31 May 1916	(Aka Skagerrak) Only major clash betwen British and German fleets in the war. British lost two ships, but German High Seas fleet did not seek battle thereafter.
Kadesh	Egyptian/Hittite War	1299 BC	Seeking to recapture the Syrian city of Kadesh, Ramses II engaged the Hittite leader Muwatallis without success and was forced to retreat; the Hittites moving southward into Damascus.
Kambula	Zulu War	29 Mar. 1879	British under Colonel Wood defeated Zulus under Cetewayo.
Karbalā	Muslim Wars	10 Oct. 680	Husayn ibn Ali, grandson of the Prophet Muhammad was defeated and killed by an army sent by the Umayyad Caliph Yazid I.
Karnāl	Mughal Civil Wars	24 Feb. 1739	Persian forces under Nāder Shāh defeated the Mughals under Emperor Muhammad Shāh.
Kemendine	First Burma War	10 June 1824	British under Sir Archibald Campbell defeated Burmese troops.
Khartoum	British-Sudan Campaign	26 Jan. 1885	General Gordon killed defending the city against the Mahdi after Beresford's troops were delayed.
Killiecrankie	Jacobite Rising	27 July 1689	Highland Jacobites under 'Bonny' Dundee defeated William III's troops under General Mackay, but Dundee's death undid the victory.
Kilsyth	English Civil War	15 Aug. 1645	Royalists under marquis of Montrose defeated Covenanters under General Baillie.
Kimberley	Second Boer War	15 Oct. 1899	Gen. French relieved town on 15 Feb. 1900 from Boer siege led by General Cronje.
Kioge	Northern War	July 1677	Danish fleet under Admiral Juel defeated Swedes under Admiral Horn.
Kissingen	Seven Weeks War	10 July 1866	Prussians under Gen Falkstein defeated Bavarians under Gen Zoller.
Kiu-lien-Cheng	Russo-Japanese War	1 May 1904	Japanese under Marshal Kuroki defeated Russians under General Sassulitch.
Königgrätz	Seven Weeks War	3 July 1866	Aka Battle of Sadowa. Decisive battle of the conflict in which Helmuth von Moltke's Prussian army defeated the Austrian army led by General Benedek, which led to Austria's exclusion from a Prussian-dominated Germany. The war was formally concluded on 23 August 1866 by the Treaty of Prague. Bismarck's alliance with Italy meant Venetia was ceded to the Italians.
Kosovo	Byzantine Wars	June 1389	Battle fought at Kosovo Polje (Field of Blackbirds) between Serbs under Prince Lazar and Turks under Sultan Murad I, who gained victory.
Kursk Salient	Second World War	5–13 July 1943	Largest tank battle of the war, in which Russians smashed massive German offensive.
Ladysmith	Second Boer War	2 Nov. 1899	Sir George White defended against Boers until Redvers Buller relieved town 27 Feb. 1900.
Laings Nek	First Boer War	28 Jan. 1881	British under Gen Colley repulsed by Boers.
Lake Erie	War of 1812	10 Sept. 1813	Master Commandant Oliver Hazard Perry's fleet of 9 ships engaged 6 British warships under Captain Robert Heriot Barclay and although having to transfer from his flagship *Lawrence* to its sister ship *Niagara*, Perry sailed directly into the British line and firing broadsides as he went eventually forced the British to surrender.
Lake Trasimeno	Second Punic War	217 BC	The Carthaginian General Hannibal defeated the Roman army under Gaius Flaminius (killed) on the north shore of the Italian lake.

Landau	War of Spanish Succession	29 July 1702	French under de Melac lost the fortress to Prince Louis of Baden.
Langport	English Civil War	10 July 1645	Parliamentarians under Thomas Fairfax defeated Royalists under Lord Goring.
Langside	Anti-Marian Uprising	13 May 1568	Mary Queen of Scots's army was defeated by earl of Moray; Mary escaped to England.
Lansdowne	English Civil War	5 July 1643	Royalists under Sir Ralph Hopton defeated parliamentarians under Sir William Waller.
La Rochelle	Hundred Years' War	1372	A Castilian fleet under Bocanegra, acting in support of the French, defeated the English under Pembroke.
Lauffeld	War of Austrian Succession	2 July 1747	French under Marshal Saxe defeated allied Austrian and British army under Cumberland.
Leck	Thirty Years' War	5 Apr. 1632	Gustavus Adolphus's Swedish/German army defeated Imperialists under Tilly (mortally wounded).
Leghorn	Anglo-Dutch Wars	31 Mar. 1653	Admiral Van Gelen (killed) destroyed 6 English ships commanded by Commodore Appleton.
Leipzig	Napoleonic Wars	16–19 Oct. 1813	Napoleon defeated, and forced into decisive retreat, by Coalition of Blücher, Schwarzenberg and Bernadotte.
Le Mans	Franco-Prussian War	10–11 Jan. 1871	French under Chanzy were completely routed by Germans under Prince Frederick Charles.
Leningrad	Second World War	15 Jan. 1944	Russians relieved the 30-month blockade of city after 5 days' fighting.
Lepanto	Cyprus War	7 Oct. 1571	Last major battle using oared ships brought decisive victory for the Holy League fleet under Don John of Austria over Ottoman Turks.
Leuctra	Boeotian-Athenian War	371 BC	Boeotian army under Epaminondas defeated a Spartan army under King Cleombrotus.
Lewes	English Barons' War	14 May 1264	Simon de Montfort defeated Henry III and Prince Edward and signed the Mise of Lewes.
Lexington	US War of Independence	19 Apr. 1775	First battle of the war resulted in minor victory for British troops under Lt-Col. Francis Smith.
Leyte Gulf	Second World War	24–26 Oct. 1944	Biggest ever naval battle. United States defeated Japanese comprehensively, losing 6 ships to Japan's 28.
Liaoyang	Russo-Japanese War	25 Aug.–3 Sept. 1904	Japanese army under Marshal Oyama forced Russians under General Kuropatkin to retreat.
Lille	War of Spanish Succession	12 Aug. 1708	French under Marshal de Boufflers surrendered to Prince Eugene on 25 Oct. 1708.
Lindley	Second Boer War	27 May 1900	Colonel Spragge surrendered to superior Boer force.
Little Bighorn	Sioux Rising	25 June 1876	Col. Custer (killed) and his 7th US Cavalry wiped out by Sioux and Cheyenne warriors under Sitting Bull.
Loudoun Hill	Scottish Independence	10 May 1307	Robert the Bruce defeated earl of Pembroke's cavalry by his spearmen's steadfastness.
Lucknow	Indian Mutiny	June–Nov. 1857	Siege relieved by General Sir Colin Campbell.
Lundy's Lane	War of 1812	25 July 1814	Americans under General Brown unsuccessfully attacked British under Sir George Drummond.
Lützen	Thirty Years' War	16 Nov. 1632	Indecisive battle in which Gustavus II Adolphus of Sweden lost his life while engaging the Habsburg forces of Albrecht von Wallenstein.
Madrid	Spanish Civil War	7 Nov. 1936	Nationalists under General Mola attacked the Republican forces of General Miaja causing the government to flee to Valencia.
Mafeking	Second Boer War	Oct. 1899	Colonel Baden-Powell resisted Boers under General Cronje in siege not raised until 17 May 1900.
Magdeburg	Thirty Years' War	Mar. 1631	Imperialists under Field Marshal Tilly besieged the city and von Falkenberg was killed.
Magenta	Italian Independence Wars	4 June 1859	French under General MacMahon defeated Austrians under Marshal Gyulai.
Majuba Hill	First Boer War	27 Feb. 1881	Boers under General Joubert defeated British under Sir George Colley (killed).
Maldon	Danish Invasion of Britain	AD 991	Danish army under Tryggvason defeated Anglo- Saxons under Brithnoth.
Malplaquet	War of Spanish Succession	11 Sept. 1709	German and British forces under Marlborough defeated French under Villars in costly victory.
Malvern Hill	US Civil War	1 July 1862	Union repelled fierce Confederate attacks during 7 days' battle.
Mantineia	Peloponnesian War	418 BC	Spartan forces under King Agis defeated the Athenians.
Manzikert	Anatolian Wars	AD 1071	Byzantines under the emperor Romanus IV Diogenes were defeated by the Seljuq Turks led by Sultan Alp-Arslan.
Marathon	Persian-Greek Wars	Sept. 490 BC	Athenians under Miltiades, 10,000 in number, defeated 50,000 Persians.
Marengo	French Revolutionary Wars	14 June 1800	Napoleon with aid of General Desaix (killed) defeated Austrians under General Mélas.
Margate	Hundred Years' War	24 Mar. 1387	Earls of Arundel and Nottingham repelled invasion threat from Franco-Castilian force.
Marne	First World War	6–9 Sept. 1914 and July 1918	Two bloody battles. In both cases the Germans were forced to retreat.
Marston Moor	English Civil War	2 July 1644	Prince Rupert's royalists defeated by Cromwell's Ironsides under Fairfax and Manchester.
Medellín	Peninsular War	28 Mar. 1809	French under Marshal Victor defeated Spanish under Cuesta.
Medway	Second invasion of Britain	c. AD 43	Romans under Emperor Claudius defeated Britons under Caratacus and his brother Togodumnus (died)
Megiddo	Palestinian War	c.1468 BC	Palestinian town of Megiddo captured by Egyptian king Thutmosis III.
Metauro River	Second Punic War	207 BC	Romans under Marcus Livius Salinator and Claudius Nero defeated Carthaginians under Hasdrubal (died), the brother of Hannibal.
Midway	Second World War	3–6 June 1942	In battle fought mainly by aircraft, Japanese attack on US base repelled, US carrier *Yorktown* lost, but 4 Japanese carriers sunk.

Missolonghi (First)	Greek War of Independence	Jan. 1823	The Ottomans were forced to withdraw after failing to take the key fortress of Missolonghi (Mesolóngion).
Missolonghi (Second)	Greek War of Independence	23 Apr. 1826	Joint Turkish/Egyptian forces under Ibrahim Pasha defeated a small Greek garrison under Mavrocordatos.
Mohács	Ottoman Wars	29 Aug. 1526	Turks under Suleyman I defeated Hungarians under Louis II.
Molinos del Rey	Peninsular War	21 Dec. 1808	French under General St Cyr defeated Spanish under Reding.
Monongahela	French-Indian War	9 July 1755	British army under General Edward Braddock was routed by the joint French and Indian forces under Captain Daniel de Beaujeu and, after his death, by Captain Jean Dumas. The survivors of the battle near Fort Duquesne (Pittsburgh) included George Washington.
Mons Lactarius	Ostrogoth War	AD 553	Byzantine General Narses defeated the Goths under Teias (died), near Naples, Italy.
Morat	Swiss-Burgundy War	22 June 1476	Victory for the Swiss Confederation over the Burgundians under Charles the Bold.
Morgarten	Swiss War of Independence	15 Nov. 1315	Swiss Confederation's first military success against the Austrians under Leopold I.
Mortimer's Cross	Wars of the Roses	2 Feb. 1461	Edward, duke of York, defeated Lancastrians under earls of Pembroke and Wiltshire.
Mukden	Russo-Japanese War	19 Feb.–10 Mar. 1905	Russian stronghold in Manchuria that finally fell to the Japanese.
Munda	Roman Civil War	45 BC	Decisive battle of the Roman Civil War when Julius Caesar conclusively defeated the Pompeians.
Mylae	First Punic War	260 BC	Romans destroyed 50 Carthaginian ships.
Näfels	Swiss War of Independence	9 Apr. 1388	Victory for the newly formed Swiss Confederation in its struggle against Habsburg overlordship. Albert III of Austria advanced with an army against Glarus, a district that had adhered to the confederacy in 1352 but had been restored to the Habsburgs in 1355.The rebels, reinforced by troops from Schwyz, at first repelled the attack but then made a successful counter-attack on the heights of Näfels.
Nahāvand	Arabian Wars	AD 642	Arab forces under Nu'mān defeated Sāsānian troops under Firuzan.
Nancy	Swiss-Burgundy War	1477	Victory for the Swiss Confederation over the Burgundians under Charles the Bold (died).
Nanjing	Chinese Civil War	22 Apr. 1949	Communists captured Chiang Kai-shek's Nationalist capital, enabling communists under Mao Zedong to take control of China.
Naseby	English Civil War	14 June 1645	Parliamentarians under Fairfax routed Prince Rupert's royalists.
Nashville	US Civil War	15–16 Dec. 1864	Union army under General Thomas defeated Confederates under General Hood.
Navarino	Greek War of Independence	20 Oct. 1827	Last action between wooden ships. Britain, France and Russia defeated Turks and Egyptians.
Nemea	Corinthian War	394 BC	After the victory of Sparta in the Peloponnesian War against Athens it maintained its military superiority against a coalition of troops from Thebes, Corinth, Athens and Argos, largely due to their skill in hoplite warfare (use of heavy infantry).
Neva River	Swedish Holy War	15 July 1240	Novgorod army under Prince Alexander Yaroslavich defeated the Swedes under earl Birger on the banks of the Neva. Yaroslavich was given the name Nevsky in honour of his victory.
Neville's Cross	Anglo-Scottish Wars	17 Oct. 1346	Scots under David II routed by Henry de Percy and Ralph de Neville.
Newbury (First)	English Civil War	20 Sept. 1643	Charles I failed to prevent the parliamentarians under the earl of Essex from marching to London.
Newbury (Second)	English Civil War	27 Oct. 1644	Charles I's inconclusive encounter with parliamentary force under the earl of Manchester spurred formation of the New Model Army.
New Orleans	War of 1812	Jan. 1815	Andrew Jackson defeated English force under General Sir Edward Pakenham (killed).
New Orleans	US Civil War	16 Apr. 1862	Union fleet under Commodore Farragut bombarded Forts Jackson and forced surrender of city.
Niagara	Seven Years' War	June 1759	British under General Prideaux (killed) besieged the Canadian fort and William Johnson successfully repulsed Ligneris.
Nicopolis	Ottoman Wars	25 Sept. 1396	Turks under Sultan Bayezid I defeated a Christian Allied army under Sigismund, king of Hungary.
Nile/Aboukir Bay	French Revolutionary Wars	1–2 Aug. 1798	French fleet destroyed and Admiral Brueys killed by Nelson, checking Napoleon's plans in Middle East.
Nong Sa Rai	Thai War of Independence	1593	The final battle between the Thai troops under Prince Naresuen and Burmese troops under King Nanda Bayin - Burmese Crown Prince was slain by Naresuen and Thai independence was safe for 150 yrs.
Nördlingen	Thirty Years' War	5–6 Sept. 1634	Decisive victory for the Holy Roman Empire and Spain under Matthias Gallas over Swedish army led by Gustav Karlsson Horn and Bernhard of Saxe-Weimar, which led to the dissolution of the Heilbronn alliance and forced Cardinal Richelieu to bring France into the war.
Northampton	Wars of the Roses	10 July 1460	Earl of March, later Edward IV, routed the Lancastrians, captured Henry VI and executed supporters, including Buckingham and Shrewsbury.
Novara	Italian War of Independence	23 Mar. 1849	Austrian troops under Marshal Joseph Radetzky routed Piedmontese army.
Okinawa	Second World War	1 Apr.–21 June 1945	US amphibious landing met fierce and protracted resistance inland, losing over 7,000 men to Japan's 100,000 killed. US and Japanese commanders Bruckner and Ushiima.
Omdurman	British-Sudan	2 Sept. 1898	General Kitchener destroyed the Mahdi's army. Campaigns last full-scale cavalry charge by 21st Lancers,including Winston Churchill.
Opequan	US Civil War	19 Sept. 1864	Confederates under General Early defeated by General Sheridan and Lt-Col. George Custer.

Oporto	Peninsular War	28 Mar. 1809	French under Marshal Soult defeated Portuguese under Lima and Pareiras.
Orléans	Hundred Years' War	12 Oct. 1428–8 May 1429	Decisive siege in which English were forced to withdraw after Joan of Arc captured key siege forts.
Oswego	Seven Years' War	11 Aug. 1756	French under marquis of Montcalm took English fort held by Col. Mercer (killed).
Otterburn	Scottish Independence	15 Aug. 1388	Aka Chevy Chase. Scots under earls Douglas (killed) and Murray defeated Henry Percy (Hotspur).
Oudenarde	War of Spanish Succession	11 July 1708	British and Imperialists under Marlborough and Prince Eugene defeated French under Ventome and Burgundy.
Palo Alto	Mexican War	8 May 1846	First clash of the Mexican War in which the Americans under General Zachary Taylor defeated the Mexican army under General Mariano Arista.
Panipat (First)	Indian Wars	21 Apr. 1526	Mughal chief Bābur defeated Sultan Ibrāhim Lodo of Delhi (died).
Panipat (Second)	Indian Wars	5 Nov. 1556	Bayram Khān, the guardian of Mughal emperor Akbar, defeated the Hindu General Hemu.
Panipat (Third)	Indian Wars	14 Jan. 1761	Afghan chief Ahmad Shāh Durrāni defeated the Marāthā army under the Bhāo Sahib.
Parma	War of Polish Succession	29 June 1734	French under Marshal de Coigny defeated Imperialists under Count Claudius de Mercy (killed).
Passchendaele	First World War	30 Oct. 1917	Aka 3rd Battle of Ypres. Canadian 3rd and 4th Division and British pushed back Germans but suffered heavy casualties.
Patay	Hundred Years War	18 June 1429	French under Joan of Arc and duc d'Alençon defeated English under Talbot and Fastolfe.
Pea Ridge	US Civil War	6–8 Mar. 1862	Aka Elk Horn Tavern. First key Union victory west of Mississippi. Confederate General Ben McCulloch killed.
Pearl Harbor	Second World War	7 Dec. 1941	Japanese carrier-based planes attacked US Pacific fleet without declaring war, sank 19 ships. USA forced into the war.
Pharsalus	Roman Civil War	48 BC	Julius Caesar defeated the much larger force of Pompey. Caesar, who had only minor losses, exclaimed 'Hoc voluerunt' ('They would have it so').
Philippi	Brutus' Rebellion	42 BC	Republicans under Brutus & Cassius (both committed suicide) defeated by Octavian and Mark Antony, exposing Rome to autocratic rule.
Pichincha	Latin-American Wars	24 May 1822	South American rebels under Antonio José de Sucre overcame Spanish royalists.
Pinkie Cleugh	Anglo-Scottish Wars	10 Sept. 1547	Scots under the earls of Arran and Huntly defeated by English under Protector Somerset.
Plains of Abraham	Seven Years' War	13 Sept. 1759	French under Montcalm defeated by Wolfe and lost Quebec. Both generals killed.
Plassey	Seven Years' War	23 June 1757	British under Robert Clive defeated nawab of Bengal and assured East India Company's rule there.
Poitiers	Hundred Years' War	19 Sept. 1356	English archers under Edward the Black Prince defeated French under King John II.
Plataea	Persian-Greek Wars	479 BC	Greeks under Pausanias won a decisive victory over the Persians under Mardonius.
Port Arthur	Sino-Japanese War	21 Nov. 1894	(Now Lushun.) Japanese defeated Chinese with very few casualties.
Port Arthur	Russo-Japanese War	8 Feb. 1904	Japanese fleet attacked Russian squadron without declaring war. Japan won the port after almost a year's fighting (treaty of Portsmouth).
Preston	English Civil War	17–19 Aug. 1648	Cromwell's Roundheads defeated royalists under duke of Hamilton and Sir Marmaduke Langdale, ending the Second Civil War.
Preston	Jacobite Rebellion 1715	13 Nov. 1715	General Will Thomas's royalists defeated Jacobites under Thomas Forster.
Prestonpans	Jacobite Rebellion 1745	21 Sept. 1745	Aka Gladsmuir. Jacobites under Young Pretender Charles Edward Stuart defeated royalists in a 10-minute battle.
Princeton	US War of Independence	3 Jan. 1777	Americans under George Washington defeated British under Cornwallis.
Pydna	Third Macedonian War	22 June 168 BC	Romans under Lucius Aemilius Paullus defeated the Macedonians under king Perseus.
Pyramids	French Revolutionary Wars	21 July 1798	Napoleon defeated Mamelukes under Murad Bey and went on to occupy Cairo.
Quatre Bras	Napoleon's Hundred Days	16 June 1815	Marshal Ney engaged Wellington, causing his withdrawal to Waterloo.
Quebec	Seven Years' War	27 June 1759	First of two battles of war, which decided the future of Canada.
Queenston Heights	War of 1812	13 Oct. 1812	British in Canada under General Brock (killed) defeated Americans under General Van Rensselaer.
Quiberon Bay	Seven Years' War	20 Nov. 1759	British fleet under Admiral Hawke defeated French under Marshal de Conflans.
Radcot Bridge	Richard II's Barons' War	20 Dec. 1387	Earl of Derby, later Henry IV, defeated Richard II's supporter Robert de Vere, earl of Oxford.
Ramillies	War of Spanish Succession	23 May 1706	British and Imperialists under Marlborough defeated French under Villeroi.
Rieti	Italian War of Independence	7 Mar. 1821	Austrians defeated Pepe's Neapolitans, entered Naples and reinstated Ferdinand IV on the throne.
Rio Salado		30 Oct. 1340	Castilian forces under Alfonso XI and Portuguese forces under Alfonso IV defeated Muslim Marinids of North Africa.
River Plate	Second World War	13 Dec. 1939	The battle in Uruguayan waters between British and German warships ended on 17 December with the scuttling of the German pocket battleship *Graf Spee*

Roanoke Island	US Civil War	7 Feb. 1862	Union General Burnside defeated Confederates under General Wise.
Rocroi	Thirty Years War	19 May 1643	French army under the Duc d'Enghien (later known as the Great Condé) routed a Spanish army under Don Francisco de Melo, ending the Spanish ascendancy in Europe.
Rorke's Drift	Zulu-British War	22 Jan. 1879	Lts Chard and Bromhead led a company from 24th Regiment to repulse numerically far superior Zulu attack. 11 VCs awarded.
Ruhr Pocket	Second World Warl	1 Apr. 1945	US 9th Army surrounded remnants of Field Marshal Model's Army Group B, causing mass surrender and Model's suicide.
Sadowa	Seven Weeks' War	3 July 1866	See Königgrätz.
Sahagun	Peninsular War	21 Dec. 1808	Decisive British cavalry victory over the French 133 miles north-east of Salamanca. Henry Paget (Lord Uxbridge) led the 15th Hussars against General Debelle's cavalry fleeing from the 10th Hussars under General Slade. Debelle mistook the British cavalry for inferior Spanish troops and engaged them in battle. Debelle and half his men escaped but left behind at least 120 killed and more than 160 captured. Paget lost two men.
St Albans (First)	Wars of the Roses	22 May 1455	First battle in these wars. Duke of York defeated Lancastrians. Henry VI captured. Northumberland and Somerset killed.
St Albans (Second)	Wars of the Roses	17 Feb. 1461	Lancastrians under Margaret of Anjou defeated Yorkists and released Henry VI.
Saintes	US War of Independence	12 Apr. 1782	British under Admiral Sir George Rodney gained a decisive naval victory in the West Indies over a French fleet under the Comte de Grasse.
Salamanca	Peninsular War	22 July 1812	Wellington's Allied army defeated Marshal Auguste Marmont's force, the main French army in Spain.
Salamis (First)	Persian-Greek Wars	480 BC	Greeks under Themistocles won a naval victory over the Persians under Xerxes.
Salamis (Second)	Macedonian-Egyptian War	306 BC	Demetrius I Poliorcetes of Macedonia won a naval encounter with the Egyptians under Ptolemy I.
Salerno	Second World War	Sept. 1943	In Allied amphibious landing, 5th Army reinforced by US 82nd Airborne and British 7th Armoured took port and entered Naples by 1 October
Samaria	Palestinian War	722 BC	The capital of the Hebrew kingdom of Israel was destroyed by the Assyrians under Sargon II.
Samugarh	Mughal Civil War	29 May 1658	Decisive battle of the struggle for the Mughal throne between Aurangzeb and Murād Bakhsh, the third and fourth sons of Shah Jehan, on the one side, and the eldest son, Dārā Shikoh, on the other. Aurangzeb triumphed and began his long rule as emperor.
San Jacinto	Texan Rising	21 Apr. 1836	General Houston defeated Mexicans under Santa Anna, which led to admission of Texas to the United States in 1845.
Santa Cruz (First)	Anglo-Spanish Wars	1657	British fleet under Robert Blake destroyed the harboured Spanish fleet.
Santa Cruz (Second)	Anglo-Spanish Wars	1797	Horatio Nelson lost his right arm during his unsuccessful assault on the Tenerife port.
Saratoga (First)	US War of Independence	19 Sept. 1777	Aka Battle of Freeman's Farm. British army under General Burgoyne unsuccessfully attempted to gain access to Albany.
Saratoga (Second)	US War of Independence	7 Oct. 1777	Aka Battle of Bemis Heights or Second Battle of Freeman's Farm. General Burgoyne's continued engagement of American troops was thwarted by General Benedict Arnold.
Saratoga (Third)	US War of Independence	17 Oct. 1777	Decisive battle of the war whereby the British army under General Burgoyne was defeated by the Americans under Gates; the outcome encouraged the French into the war.
Sauchie Burn	Barons' Rebellion	18 June 1488	James III of Scotland (killed) defeated by rebel barons under the earl of Angus.
Sedan	Franco-Prussian War	1 Sept.1870	General von Moltke's German Army defeated French, Emperor Napoleon III surrendered, French Second Empire fell.
Sedgemoor	Monmouth's Rebellion	6 July 1685	Royal troops under the earl of Feversham defeated James, duke of Monmouth.
Selby	English Civil War	11 Apr. 1644	Sir Thomas Fairfax defeated royalists under Col. John Bellasis.
Seringapatam	Fourth Mysore War	1799	British army under Richard Wellesley defeated the Indians under Tipu Sultan (died).
Sevastopol	Crimean War	Sept. 1854–Sept. 1855	Successful Allied siege of Russian naval base.
Seven Days battle	US Civil War	26 June–2 July 1862	Confederates under General Lee staved off Union campaign to capture Richmond after a week-long series of battles.
Sevenoaks	Cade's Rebellion	18 June 1450	Rebels under Jack Cade defeated royal troops under Sir Humphrey Stafford (died).
Shanghai	Sino-Japanese War	8 Aug. 1937	Chinese defended port for 3 months before succumbing to Japanese.
Shannon and Chesapeake	War of 1812	1 June 1813	British frigate *Shannon* under Capt. Broke captured US frigate *Chesapeake* under Captain Lawrence (killed).
Sheerness	Anglo-Dutch Wars	7 June 1667	Dutch fleet under Admiral de Ruyter sailed up the Medway to Upnor Castle and sank 7 ships.
Sheriffmuir	Jacobite Rebellion 1715	13 Nov. 1715	Indecisive battle between 10,000 Jacobite rebels under the earl of Mar and 3,300 loyalist Scots under the duke of Argyll.
Shiloh	US Civil War	6–7 Apr. 1862	Major engagement with even casualties, but Confederates under General Johnston (killed) eventually left the field to Grant's Federal troops.
Shirogawa	Satsuma Rebellion	24 Sept. 1876	Imperial army under Prince Taruhito defeated rebels under Takamori Saigo (killed).
Shrewsbury	Percy's Rebellion	21 July 1403	Royalists under Henry IV defeated Henry Percy (Hotspur - killed).
Six Day War	Israeli–Arab War	5–10 June 1967	Victory over United Arab Republic, Syria and Jordan brought Israel control of Golan Heights, West Bank, Gaza Strip, Sinai Peninsula and the Old City of Jerusalem.

Sluys	Hundred Years' War	24 June 1340	English archers under Edward III defeated French in the Zwyn estuary in the main naval engagement of the war.
Solferino	Italian War of Independence	24 June 1859	Indecisive but bloody battle that led to the peace of Villafranca and the Austrian loss of Lombardy to Italy.
Solway Moss	Anglo-Scottish Wars	25 Nov. 1542	Scots under Oliver Sinclair were routed by English under Thomas Dacre and John Musgrave.
Somme	First World War	1 July–19 Nov. 1916	Franco-British offensive cost over 1 million casualties, made small territory gains. First tank attack of war on 15 Sept. In 1918 Germans made the Somme target for their last offensive.
Stamford Bridge	Norse Invasion of Britain	25 Sept. 1066	English under Harold II defeated Norsemen under Harold Hardrada and Tostig (both killed).
Stirling Bridge	Scottish Independence	11 Sept. 1297	Scots under Sir William Wallace defeated the invading English under the earl of Surrey.
Stoke	Lambert Simnel's Rebellion	16 June 1487	Royal troops under Henry VII defeated rebels under John de la Pole, earl of Lincoln.
Talavera	Peninsular War	28 July 1809	Arthur Wellesley was made Viscount Wellington after defeating the French under King Joseph Bonaparte and Marchand Jourdan.
Tālikota	Muslim Wars	Jan. 1565	Muslim sultans of Bijāpur, Bidar, Ahmadnagar, and Golconda defeated the forces of the Hindu raja of Vijayanagar.
Tearless Battle	Spartan Wars	368 BC	Arcadians attempted to cut off Spartan army under Archidamus but no Spartans were killed.
Tel-el-Kebir	Egyptian Revolt	13 Sept. 1882	Sir Garnet Wolseley defeated Egyptian nationalists under Arabi Pasha.
Teutoburg Forest	German-Roman War	AD 9	The Germanic Cherusci tribe, led by the young German prince Arminius, ambushed and slaughtered the Roman army under General Quinctilius Varus (committed suicide).
Tewkesbury	Wars of the Roses	4 May 1471	Yorkists under Edward IV defeated Lancastrians under Queen Margaret and Somerset. Prince Edward, son of Henry VI (killed).
Thapsus	Roman Civil War	6 Feb. 46 BC	Romans under Julius Caesar slaughtered the troops of Quintus Metellus Scipio, the father-in-law of Pompey the Great, and within weeks had conquered the rest of Roman Africa.
Thermopylae	Third Persian Invasion	19 Aug. 480 BC	Spartans and Thespians under Leonidas defeated by Persians under Xerxes.
Thorn	Great Northern War	22 Sept. 1702	Swedes under Charles XII defeated Poles and elected Stanislas Leszczynski king of Poland.
Tinchebrai	Norman Civil War	28 Sept. 1106	English under Henry I defeated his brother duke Robert of Normandy, annexing Normandy.
Toulon	French Revolutionary Wars	Aug.–Dec. 1793	Notable for being the engagement that earned Napoleon Bonaparte his reputation as a military tactician when he forced the withdrawal of the Anglo-Spanish fleet.
Tours/Poitiers	Muslim Invasion of France	10 Oct. 732	Franks under Charles Martel defeated Saracens under Abderrahman Ibn Abdillah (killed), halting the Moorish conquest of Europe.
Towton	Wars of the Roses	29 Mar. 1461	Edward IV defeated Lancastrians under Henry VI and was crowned on 28 June.
Trafalgar	Napoleonic Wars	21 Oct. 1805	British fleet under Nelson (died) and Collingwood defeated Spanish and French under Villeneuve, losing no ships and capturing half of the enemy's.
Trenton	US War of Independence	26 Dec. 1776	Notable as the first success of George Washington in open warfare.
Tsushima Strait	Russo-Japanese War	27–28 May 1905	Admiral Togo routed Russian fleet under Rozlidestrenski, making first use of naval radio.
Ulm	Napoleonic Wars	20 Oct. 1805	Napoleon defeated Austrians under General Baron Mack von Leiberich (court-martialled).
Ulundi	Zulu-British War	4 July 1879	Final battle of the Anglo-Zulu War, in which Cetshwayo (Cetewayo) was defeated and taken prisoner.
Ushant			See Glorious 1st of June.
Valmy	French Revolutionary Wars	20 Sept. 1792	French under Dumouriez and Kellerman defeated Prussians under Duke of Brunswick.
Verdun	First World War	21 Feb.–20 Dec. 1916	German General von Falkenhayn's war of attrition against French, with combined casualties of over 650,000 and no conclusive outcome.
Vienna	Ottoman Wars	July–Sept. 1683	The Siege of Vienna by the Turks against the Habsburg Holy Roman Emperor Leopold I. On 12 September a combined force led by John III Sobieski defeated the Turks.
Vinegar Hill	Irish Rebellion	21 June 1798	Irish loyalists under General Lake defeated Catholic rebels under Father Murphy.
Virginia Capes	US War of Independence	5 Sept. 1781	French naval victory over a British fleet under Admiral Thomas Graves near Chesapeake Bay.
Vitoria	Peninsular War	21 June 1813	British under Wellington defeated French and expelled Joseph Bonaparte from Spain.
Vyborg	Russo-Finnish War	24 Apr. 1918	General Mannerheim's Finnish White Army defeated Bolsheviks.
Wakefield	Wars of the Roses	30 Dec. 1460	Lancastrians under Somerset defeated Yorkists under Richard of York (killed).
Wandiwāsh	Seven Years' War	22 Jan. 1760	British under Sir Eyre Coote defeated French under Comte de Lally in what was the decisive battle in the Anglo-French conflict in southern India.
Warburg	Seven Years' War	31 July 1760	French under Chevalier du Muy forced to retire by Prussian/British force
Warsaw	Polish-Soviet War	13–25 Aug. 1920	Polish forces commanded by Jósef Pilsudski destroyed Russian forces under Mikhail Tukhachevski ensuring Western Europe was free of Soviet threat for the next 20 years.
Waterloo	Napoleon's Hundred Days	18 June 1815	Wellington aided by Prussians under Blücher defeated Napoleon, who abdicated on 22 June.

Worcester	English Civil War	3 Sept. 1651	Last pitched battle of civil war in which Cromwell defeated royalists under Charles II.
Yarmuk River	Palestinian Wars	20 Aug. 636	Arabian army under Khālid ibn al-Walid defeated a Byzantine army under Theodorus.
Yom Kippur	Israeli-Arab War	6–24 Oct. 1973	Syrian and Egyptian surprise offensive along Golan Heights and Suez Canal defeated after heavy fighting.
Yorktown	US War of Independence	19 Oct. 1781	General Cornwallis forced to surrender to US and French troops, ending war.
Ypres (First)	First World War	14 Oct.1914	General von Falkenhayn's push to reach ports of Calais and Dunkirk halted by the British Expeditionary Force under Sir John French.
Ypres (Second)	First World War	22 Apr.– late May 1915	General Falkenhayn used lethal chlorine gas for the first time, causing many Allied deaths and advancing about 3 miles.
Ypres (Third)	First World War		See Passchendaele.
Zama	Second Punic War	202 BC	Carthaginians under Hannibal were defeated by Romans under Scipio Africanus in final battle of this war.
Zenta	Ottoman Wars	11 Sept. 1697	Ottoman army under Sultan Mustafa II was engaged by an Austrian army under Prince Eugene of Savoy while crossing the Tisza river and comprehensively defeated.
Zutphen	Dutch War of Independence	22 Sept. 1586	Spanish victory over English force under Leicester notable for the death of Sir Philip Sidney.

The Victoria Cross

The VC was introduced at the behest of Queen Victoria on 29 January 1856 in order to reward acts of extreme courage during the Crimean War. It is the highest military decoration and has been awarded 1,356 times to 1,353 individual recipients. The first awards ceremony was held on 26 June 1857 when the Queen invested 62 of the 111 Crimean recipients in a ceremony in Hyde Park.

Three people have been awarded the VC and Bar, the bar representing a second award of the VC: British Royal Army Medical Corps doctors Noel Chavasse and Arthur Martin-Leake, for rescuing wounded under fire; and New Zealand infantryman Charles Upham, for two combat actions during the Second World War.

The largest number of VCs awarded for actions on a single day was 24 at the Second Relief of Lucknow and the largest number awarded in a single action was 11 at Rorke's Drift.

An Irishman, Surgeon General William Manley, remains the sole recipient of both the Victoria Cross and the Iron Cross. His VC was awarded for his actions during the Waikato-Hauhau Maori War, on 29 April 1864, while the Iron Cross was awarded for tending the wounded during the Franco-Prussian War of 1870–1.

New Zealand Flying Officer Lloyd Trigg is the only man ever awarded a VC on evidence provided solely by the enemy. The recommendation was made by the captain of the German U-boat *U-468* sunk by Trigg's aircraft.

In 1921 the Victoria Cross was given to the American Unknown Soldier of the First World War.

Queen Victoria laid a Victoria Cross beneath the foundation stone of Netley military hospital in 1856. When the hospital was demolished in 1966, 'The Netley VC' was retrieved and is now on display in the Army Medical Services Museum, Mytchett, near Aldershot.

At time of writing (July 2013), there are only five living holders of the VC – three British (John Alexander Cruickshank, William Speakman, Johnson Beharry), one Australian (Keith Payne), and one Gurkha (Rambahadur Limbu). Since 2002, the annuity paid to them by the British government is £1,495 per year.

The decoration itself is a bronze cross pattée, bearing the crown of Saint Edward surmounted by a lion, with the inscription 'For Valour'. The ribbon is crimson.

British businessman Lord Ashcroft has amassed a collection of 162 VCs since 1986 and recently acquired the VC and Bar of Captain Noel Chavasse from St Peter's College, Oxford for almost £1.5 million. The collection is currently on display at the Imperial War Museum.

The following table lists the Victoria Cross recipients by campaign – with names or other items of note alongside.

Crimean War (1854–6) Charles Lucas 1st recipient for action on 21 June 1854	111
Anglo-Persian War (1856–7) John Malcolmson, Arthur Moore, John Wood	3
Indian Mutiny (1857–9) 24 at the Relief of Lucknow on 16 November 1857	182
Taranaki Maori War, New Zealand (1860–1) John Lucas and William Odgers	2
Third China War (1860–2) All at Taku Forts, China, 21 August 1860	7
T'ai P'ing Rebellion (1851–64) George Hinckley (Eng) 9 October 1862	1
Umbeyla Campaign (1863) George Fosbery (Eng) and Henry Pitcher (Eng)	2
Shimonoseki Expedition, Japan (1864) Duncan Boyes later committed suicide	3
Waikato-Hauhau Maori War, NZ (1863–6) William Hanley later received Iron Cross	13
Bhutan War (1864–5) James Dundas (Sco) and William Trevor (Eng)	2
Danville, Quebec (1866) Timothy O'Hea (Ire) Only VC awarded not under fire	1
The Gambia (1st) (1866) Samuel Hodge (W. Indies) The first black award-winner	1
Andaman Islands Expedition (1867) All at Little Andaman, 7 May 1867	5
Abyssinian War (1867–8) Irishmen James Bergin and Michael Magner at Magdala	2
Looshai Expedition, India (1872) Donald Macintyre (Sco) 4 January 1872	1
Anglo-Ashanti Wars (1874) Mark Bell, Edric Gifford, Sam McGaw, Reg Sartorius	4
Perak War – Malaya (1875–6) George Channer (Eng) 20 December 1875	1
Baluchistan Campaign (1877) Andrew Scott (Eng) 26 July 1877	1
Ninth Cape Frontier War (1877–8) Hans Moore (Ire) 29 December 1877	1
Zulu War (1879) 11 for the defence of Rorke's Drift on 22 January 1879	23
Second Afghan War (1878–80) Euston Sartorius was the brother of Reginald	16
Second Naga Hills Expedition (1879–80) Richard Ridgeway (Ire) 22 November 1879	1
First Boer War (1880–1) The First Boer War is also known as the Transvaal War	6
Basuto War, Lesotho (1879–81) The Basuto War is also known as the Gun War	6

Occupation of Egypt (1882) Frederick Corbett, William Edwards, Israel Harding	3
British Rule in Burma (1888–9) John Crimmin and Ferdinand Le Quesne	2
Hunza-Naga Campaign, India (1891) Fenton Aylmer, Guy Boisragon, John Smith	3
Manipur Expedition, India (1891) Charles Grant (Sco) captured Thobal near Manipur	1
The Gambia (2nd) (1892) William Gordon (W. Indies) 13 March 1892	1
Kachin Hills Expedition, Burma (1892–3) Owen Lloyd (Ire) 6 January 1893	1
Chitral Expedition, India (1895) Harry Whitchurch (Eng) 3 March 1895	1
Matabeleland Rebellion, Rhodesia (1896) Frank Baxter and Herbert Henderson	2
Mashona Rebellion, Rhodesia (1896–7) Randolph Nesbitt (SA) 19 June 1896	1
Occupation of Crete (1898) William Maillard (Eng) 6 September 1898	1
Malakand Frontier War, India (1897–8) Edmond Costello (Eng) 26 July 1897	1
Mohmand Campaign, India (1897–8) James Colvin, James Smith, Thomas Watson	3
Tirah Campaign, India (1897–8) The Afridi tribe rebellion in the Khyber Pass	7
Boxer Rising, China (1900) Basil Guy (Eng) and Lewis Halliday (Eng)	2
Mahdist War, Sudan (1881–99) Arthur Wilson later became First Sea Lord	10
Third Ashanti Expedition (1900–1) John Mackenzie and Charles Melliss	2
Somaliland Expeditions (1902–5) HQ of Malawi army named after Alexander Cobbe	6
Second Boer War (1899–1902) Arthur Martin-Leake awarded Bar in First World War	78
Kano-Sokoto Expedition, Nigeria (1903) Wallace Wright later MP for Tavistock	1
Armed Mission to Tibet (1903–4) John Grant (Eng) 6 July 1904	1
First World War (1914–18) Albert Ball posthumous VC, Noel Chavasse VC & Bar	628
North Russia Relief Force (1919) Arthur Sullivan later fell and died in Birdcage Walk	5
Arab Revolt, Mesopotamia (1920) George Henderson (Sco) 24 July 1920	1
Waziristan Campaign, India (1919–21) Henry Andrews, William Kenny, Ishar Singh	3
Mohmand Campaign (2nd), India (1935) Godfrey Meynell (Eng) 29 September 1935	1
Second World War (1939–45) Leonard Cheshire and Charles Upham most famous	182
Korean War (1950–3) Bill Speakman first to receive VC from Queen Elizabeth II	4
Malaysia-Indonesia Confrontation (1963–6) Rambahadur Limbu (Nep) 21 Nov 1965	1
Vietnam War (1959–75) All four are Australian only Keith Payne still living	4
Falklands War (1982) Lt-Col Herbert 'H' Jones and Sgt Ian McKay	2
Operation Telic (Invasion of Iraq) (2004) Lance Corporal Johnson Gideon Beharry	1
Afghan War (2001–present) Corporal Bryan Budd and Lance Corporal James Ashworth	2

Music: Classical

Opera: Précis of Plots

Aida (Verdi, 1871) Aida, a captive Ethiopian princess, is servant to the Egyptian princess Amneris. Both are in love with General Radamès, who loves Aida. Radamès goes to war against the Ethiopians, defeats them and is given Amneris's hand in marriage, but Radames is suspected of having betrayed his country in trying to help Aida and sentenced to death. Aida conceals herself in the tomb where both of them are buried alive, while above them, Amneris prays.

Albert Herring (Britten, 1946) Lady Billows, the self-appointed guardian of public morals in the small Suffolk town of Loxford, with the help of Florence Pike, who keeps a list of miscreants and misdemeanours, and a committee of local worthies is resolved to find a worthy candidate to occupy the position of May Queen. It is eventually decided that no girl is virtuous enough but that Albert Herring, the retarded, only son of Mrs Herring, who keeps the greengrocer's, should be made May King. Sid, the butcher's boy, suggests that Albert should break free from his mother's control, and with the help of Nancy, from the baker's, resolves to help things along. The crowning of the new May King is duly carried out, Sid, however, has laced Albert's lemonade with rum. After the ceremony Albert, now uninhibited, makes a break for freedom. The next morning his mother is distraught at his absence and is joined by others, lamenting what might well be his early death. Albert re-appears, however, free at last, thanks to Sid and Nancy.

The Barber of Seville (Rossini, 1816) Count Almaviva, aided by his barber Figaro, is pursuing Rosina. Her guardian, Bartolo, who wants to marry her himself, tries to stop them but is unsuccessful, and Rosina marries the count.

The Bartered Bride (Smetana, 1866) Marenka loves Jenik, whose parents want to marry her to the halfwit son of Micha. Jenik is offered money to give her up, and accepts on condition she marries Micha's eldest son. This turns out to be Jenik himself; Marenka can marry him after all.

Billy Budd (Britten, 1951) Set on HMS Indomitable in 1797, during the French wars, the drama involves the relationship between Edward Fairfax Vere and the innocent seaman Billy Budd who is in conflict with Claggart, the evil master-at-arms, who resolves to destroy him. Struck by Billy Budd, Claggart is killed and Captain Vere, who is aware of Billy Budd's innate goodness but compelled by duty to sentence him to death.

Bluebeard's Castle (Bartók, 1911) Newly married to Duke Bluebeard, Judith opens a series of doors, revealing, behind the seventh, Bluebeard's three former wives, representing the morning, noon and evening of his life: Judith represents night. Bluebeard dresses her in the crown and robes from the third door, the Treasury, and she passes with the others through the seventh door, leaving Bluebeard to solitude and the coming eternal darkness.

La Bohème (Puccini, 1896) Mimi, who is consumptive, falls in love with a Bohemian poet, Rodolfo, and for a while they live together, but constant quarrels drive them apart. Then Rodolfo's friends discover that Mimi is dying and bring her to him, but it is too late and she dies in his arms.

Carmen (Bizet, 1875) The soldier Don José deserts the army to follow the gypsy girl Carmen, who leaves him for the toreador Escamillo. Mad with jealousy, Don José follows her to the bullring and kills her.

Cavalleria Rusticana (Mascagni, 1890) Brokenhearted because her lover, Turiddu, has abandoned her for another woman, Santuzza tells the other woman's husband what is going on. He kills Turiddu in a duel.

The Coronation of Poppaea (Monteverdi, 1643) Emperor Nero resolves to marry his mistress Poppaea. One by one, he murders everyone who stands in their way until Poppaea is crowned empress.

Così fan tutte (Mozart, 1790) The sisters Fiordiligi and Dorabella swear to be faithful to their lovers Ferrando and Guglielmo, so to try their fidelity the latter pretend to go off to the wars. But they return in disguise and each proceeds to make advances to the other's girl, who both respond. The men then reveal their disguise, but forgive their wayward sweethearts, and both couples are reunited.

Cox and Box (Sullivan, 1866) Arthur Sullivan's first operetta deals with the comic activities of a landlord who lets the same room to two lodgers, alternating, unknown to them, by day and night.

Don Giovanni (Mozart, 1787) Foiled in his attempts to seduce Donna Anna, the libertine Don Giovanni (aka Don Juan) kills her father, the Commendatore. Anna and her fiancé Don Ottavio vow to avenge him. They are joined by Donna Elvira, another former victim of the Don. In a gesture of defiance, Don Giovanni has confronted a statue of the Commendatore and invited him to dinner. The Commendatore duly accepts, arrives at the Don's house and drags him down to hell.

Eugene Onegin (Tchaikovsky, 1879) Tatyana, young and open-hearted, falls in love with the worldly Eugene Onegin and confesses her feelings, but he rejects her. Years later they meet again and this time he falls in love with her, but by now she is married and, though still attracted to him, sends him away for ever.

Falstaff (Verdi, 1892) Shakespeare's fat knight, Sir John Falstaff, is simultaneously wooing two wives of Windsor, Mistress Ford and Mistress Page, who discover what he is up to and contrive to pay him back, but Falstaff eventually takes it in good part anqkld the opera finishes with a happy ending for a young couple involved in the plotting – Nannetta Ford and her lover, Fenton.

Faust (Gounod, 1859) Faust has been given back his youth by the devil, Mephistopheles, so he can pursue the beautiful Marguerite. They fall in love and she has a child, but Faust then deserts her. She kills the child and is condemned to death. Faust returns to save her, but he is too late, and she dies and is borne to heaven.

Fidelio (Beethoven, 1805) When Florestan is unjustly imprisoned, his wife Leonora disguises herself as a young man called Fidelio and gets a job inside the prison, from where she succeeds in getting him freed.

The Flying Dutchman (Wagner, 1843) A Dutch sea captain has been condemned by the Devil to sail the seas for ever, unless he can find a woman who will love him until death. Once in every seven years he is allowed to land in search of her. He meets Senta, who declares her love for him, but leaves her owing to a misunderstanding, whereupon she throws herself into the sea and drowns, thus freeing him.

Gloriana (Britten, 1953) The libretto was based on Lytton Strachey's *Elizabeth and Essex* and concerns the decline of Essex in the affections of Queen Elizabeth. The opening act tells of a fight between Essex and Lord Montjoy at the court of Elizabeth. They are rebuked, but the rebellious nature of Essex is recognised by the Queen. Essex is appointed Deputy of Ireland and given the charge of subduing Tyrone, but fails miserably. On his return to England the disgraced Essex rebels and is arrested as a traitor. At his trial at Whitehall, Essex is given a death sentence, which is eventually signed by Elizabeth after an injudicious word from Lady Rich.The final act depicts the Queen reflecting on her life to the audience.

Lakmé (Delibes, 1882) In British India the young English officer Gérald falls in love with Lakmé, daughter of the Brahmin priest Nilakantha, who harbours feelings of hatred towards the British. Nilakantha is angry at the pollution of his land by the intruder and sets his daughter to attract the man by her singing. This she does, and when Gérald, in the market-place, rushes forward to help her as she faints, Nilakantha stabs him. Gérald is tended in the forest in secret by Hadji, a servant loyal to Lakmé, who aids him in his task. She goes to bring water from the sacred spring to confirm their love, but Frédéric appears, reminding Gérald of his duty. He resolves to obey and Lakmé poisons herself, leaving Gérald, as she dies, to drink the sacred water that would have united them.

Lohengrin (Wagner, 1850) The heroine, Elsa, falsely accused, will lose her life if she cannot find a champion. When one appears (Lohengrin, a knight searching for the Holy Grail), he agrees to defend her so long as she never asks his name. Eventually they marry, but an enemy dupes her into asking her husband's name. Now she has broken her vow and he leaves her for ever.

Lucia di Lammermoor (Donizetti, 1835) Lucy Ashton is in love with Edgar, but is tricked by her brother into marrying someone else. On her wedding night she goes mad and kills her husband. When he learns of her subsequent death, Edgar kills himself.

Madame Butterfly (Puccini, 1904) The American naval Lieutenant Pinkerton has married the innocent Japanese girl Cio-Cio-San. He regards the arrangements as only temporary and leaves her when the time comes, but she loves him and longs for his return. When he does, with an American wife, Butterfly promises to give him their child and then kills herself.

The Magic Flute (Mozart, 1791) This is a contest between Good (the high priest Sarastro) and Evil (the Queen of the Night). Prince Tamino falls in love with the Queen of the Night's daughter, Pamina, and has to undergo many tests and temptations, helped by a gift of a magic flute, before he conquers Evil and wins the hand of his beloved.

Manon (Massenet, 1884) Manon Lescaut and the Chevalier Des Grieux fall in love and run away together, but she prefers luxury to poverty and leaves him for a rich man. She is eventually deported for being a prostitute. Des Grieux follows her, but she is overwhelmed by her suffering and dies in his arms.

The Marriage of Figaro (Mozart, 1786) Figaro, barber to the womanising Count Almaviva, is about to be married to Susanna, the countess's maid, but discovers the count has designs on her. Figaro, Susanna, the countess and her page Cherubino hatch a plot to unmask the count, and all ends happily with the wedding of Figaro and Susanna.

The Mastersingers of Nuremberg (Wagner, 1868) The Mastersingers of Nuremberg are to hold a song contest, the prize being the hand of Eva. The knight Walther arrives, falls in love with Eva and decides to compete, coached by Hans Sachs the cobbler. Although his rival Beckmesser does his best to discredit him, he wins both the contest and Eva.

Norma (Bellini,1831) The Druid priestess Norma has had two children by the Roman general Pollione, who has now fallen in love with a younger priestess, Adalgisa. Norma incites a Gallo-Roman war, Pollione is captured and sentenced to death, and they both go to be sacrificed together.

Otello (Verdi, 1887) Otello, the Moor of Venice, is tricked by the evil Iago into believing his wife, Desdemona, has been unfaithful to him. In a fit of jealousy he kills her, learns the truth, then kills himself.

I Pagliacci (Leoncavallo, 1893) A troupe of strolling players enact a real-life drama. The clown, Canio, does not know that his wife, Nedda, is having an affair with Silvio, a villager, although he is suspicious. At that night's performance, in which Canio plays a jealous husband, reality gets the better of him, the play becomes a real quarrel, and he stabs both Nedda and Silvio to death.

The Pearl Fishers (Bizet, 1863) Pearl fishers Zurga and Nadir have long loved the priestess, Leila, but have vowed not to let this destroy their friendship. Then Leila arrives to conduct a religious ceremony, and she and Nadir confess their love. They are discovered and sentenced to death. Zurga helps them escape but loses his own life as a result.

Peter Grimes (Britten, 1945) The lone fisherman, Peter Grimes, is an outsider in the East Coast fishing community where he lives. Already under suspicion after the mysterious death of his young apprentice, when a second boy dies unaccountably, Grimes is forced to take to sea and drowns himself.

Rigoletto (Verdi, 1851) The hunchback jester Rigoletto has helped his master, the Duke of Mantua, to seduce the daughter of the courtier Monterone, who curses him. The duke believes that Rigoletto has a mistress (actually his daughter), Gilda, and seduces her. In revenge, Rigoletto plots to have the duke murdered, but the plot misfires and Gilda is killed instead. The curse has been fulfilled.

The Ring Cycle (Wagner, 1876) *The Rhinegold*: The magic Rhinegold is at the bottom of the River Rhine, guarded by the Rhinemaidens. Alberich, the wicked dwarf, steals it and makes a ring from it to become all-powerful. Meanwhile, the god Wotan is looking for money to pay for his castle of Valhalla and plots to steal the gold. He tricks Alberich into parting with it, but it is cursed and results in a death. *The Valkyrie*: Wotan has fathered nine warrior-maidens, the Valkyries; his favourite is Brünnhilde. He also has a son and a daughter, Siegmund and Sieglinde, who were separated at birth. In a storm, Siegmund takes shelter in a hut where Sieglinde lives with her husband Hunding. The two fall in love and run away but are pursued by Hunding, who kills Siegmund. Brünnhilde carries Siegmund off to Valhalla in defiance of her father, who condemns her to sleep in a ring of fire until a hero comes to rescue her. *Siegfried*: Sieglinde has died giving birth to a son, Siegfried, who has been brought up by the dwarf Mime in the hope that he will one day get the Ring back. With the help of Wotan and Brünnhilde, Siegfried is led to the magic rock where he awakes Brünnhilde and they fall in love. *Twilight of the Gods*: Siegfried has taken the Ring from the dragon that was guarding it and now gives it to Brünnhilde while he goes in search of further adventure. He reaches the Hall of the Gibichungs, who hope to marry him to their sister Gutrune. Although Brünnhilde comes with the Ring to rescue him, he is killed. Brünnhilde builds a funeral pyre for him and climbs on to it herself. The Rhinemaidens arrive in a flood and snatch back the Ring, while Valhalla is consumed in flames. It is the end of the gods.

Der Rosenkavalier (Strauss, 1911) The young Count Octavian is having an affair with an older woman, the Marschallin, although she knows it cannot last. Octavian is sent to bear a silver rose as a symbol of the forthcoming marriage of the beautiful young Sophie von Faninal to a much older man, Baron Ochs. The two young people fall in love, their elders realise that it is better to let them go, and Octavian and Sophie face a future together.

Ruslan and Lyudmila (Glinka, 1842) Svyetozar is hosting a wedding celebration for his daughter Lyudmila, who is betrothed to the knight Ruslan. The bard Bayan sings but foretells ill fortune for the newly-weds. A thunderclap followed by total darkness interrupts the festivities. Light returns but Lyudmila has disappeared. Lyudmila's former suitors search in vain. Ruslan encounters the wise magician Finn, who tells him of Lyudmila's abduction by the evil dwarf Chernomor. Ruslan acquires a magic sword and challenges Chernomor to a duel. The dwarf casts a sleeping spell on Lyudmila before encountering Ruslan, who defeats him by cutting off his beard, the source of power. Ruslan awakens Lyudmila with a magic ring.

The Tales of Hoffmann (Offenbach, 1881) The poet Hoffmann relates the stories of the three loves of his life, all destroyed by the same evil genius. First, there is Olympia, who, he does not realize until too late, is only a mechanical doll. Then the courtesan Giulietta, who leaves him for another, and finally Antonia, a pure young girl who knows she will die if she tries to sing but is tricked into doing so. The story of loss is about to be repeated with the opera singer Stella, and Hoffmann is left alone to drown his sorrows in beer.

The Thieving Magpie (Rossini, 1817) Ninetta hopes to marry Giannetto, returning from the war. She tries to shelter her father Fernando Villabella, who has deserted from the army, and is troubled by the attentions of the mayor, Gottardo. A missing spoon and the evidence of Isacco, the pedlar, who has bought a piece of silver from Ninetta to raise money for her father, lead to her accusation and imprisonment. She is tried and found guilty, to be saved from death at the last minute by the discovery of the thief, the thieving magpie of the title.

Tosca (Puccini, 1900) The opera singer Floria Tosca is loved by the political agitator Cavaradossi and desired by the evil police chief Scarpia. Cavaradossi is arrested, but Scarpia promises Tosca he will free him if she agrees to give herself to him. She kills Scarpia, but he has tricked her and Cavaradossi is shot, whereupon Tosca throws herself to her death from the prison battlements.

La Traviata (The Fallen Woman) (Verdi, 1853) Violetta, a courtesan, has fallen in love with a young aristocrat, Alfredo, but Alfredo's father begs her to break off the relationship as it will bring disgrace to his family, and she goes back to her old life. Alfredo confronts and denounces her, but she is dying of consumption, and when, too late, he returns to her side, she dies in his arms.

Tristan und Isolde (Wagner, 1865) Isolde is to be married to King Mark of Cornwall and his nephew Tristan is sent to fetch her, but the two fall in love. After the wedding they meet, but they are discovered and Tristan is wounded. Isolde comes to him as he dies, then herself falls lifeless over his body.

Il Trovatore (The Troubadour) (Verdi, 1853) Leonora is being serenaded by a mysterious troubador, regarded as a rival by Count di Luna, who is in love with her. The troubador turns out to be Manrico, apparently the son of the gypsy Azucena. But Azucena explains that years ago, in revenge for the agony of seeing her mother burned to death, she threw the Count's abducted baby brother into the flames – but by mistake threw her own baby instead. Manrico and Leonora run away but are pursued by the Count, who imprisons Manrico. Leonora agrees to marry the Count as the price of Manrico's freedom, but then kills herself. The Count executes Manrico, then is told by Azucena that he has killed his own brother.

Turandot (Busoni, 1917) The cruel Chinese princess Turandot will marry only if a suitor prince can solve her three riddles. If he cannot, he will die. An unknown prince answers the riddles correctly but tells her that if she can discover his name by morning, he will agree to die. Turandot tortures the slave girl Liu, who knows the name but will not reveal it, and Liu eventually dies. The prince tells Turandot his name. It is 'Love,' and she accepts him as her husband.

Wozzeck (Berg, 1922) Wozzeck is shaving the Captain, who tells him to go slower and makes fun of him, particularly over the matter of his illegitimate child. Wozzeck's common-law wife, Marie, is seduced by a Drum Major. Wozzeck enters, suspicious of the earrings that the Drum Major has given, which she claims to have found in the street. In the guard-room Wozzeck fights with the boasting Drum Major. In the half-light of evening Marie and Wozzeck walk together along a forest path. He talks of fidelity and love and stabs her. Wozzeck drinks to forget, his blood-stained hands noticed by Margret, Marie's neighbour. Wozzeck returns to the forest path, looking for his knife. Stumbling against Marie's body, he finally goes mad, wading into the forest pool, where he drowns. The Doctor and the Captain pass by, unconcerned.

NB: The above is only a small selection of operas but offers a flavour of the moods and emotions that can be explored in others.

Composers

(Chronological order)

Name	*Principal works*	*Details*
Hildegard of Bingen 1098–1179	Church music departing from traditional plainsong style	Saint and abbess
Pérotin *c.* 1160–*c.* 1205	Christmas and St Stephen's Day graduals (1198, 1199)	aka Perotinus Magnus; maître de chapelle at Notre Dame; exponent of *ars antiqua*
Adam de la Halle *c.* 1250–?1306	*Le jeu de Robin et de Marion* anticipated the genre of opéra comique	Aka Adam the Hunchback; born Arras, France and died in Naples; court musician of the Comte d'Artois
Machaut, Guillaume de *c.* 1300–*c.*1377	*Messe de Notre Dame* (for four violins); *Voir Dit* (Tale of Truth), collection of ballads; 23 motets	Born and died in Reims; leading French composer of free-flowing *ars nova* style of 14th century; canon of Reims Cathedral
Landini, Francesco *c.* 1325–1397	Various madrigals; over 140 ballads	Born and died in Florence; blinded in youth from smallpox; noted for 'Landini Cadence' in which sixth degree octave is inserted between leading note and octave
Dunstable, John *c.* 1390–1453	Masses and motets	Aka Dunstaple; internationally renowned in his day
Du Fay, Guillaume *c.* 1400–1474	8 masses; 87 motets; 59 French chansons	Composed earliest requiem mass; possibly originated Fauxbourdon style; canon of Cambrai
Ockeghem, Johannes *c.* 1430–1495	14 masses; 10 motets; 20 chansons	Born Flanders and died Tours; composer to 3 successive French kings: Charles VII, Louis XI, Charles VIII
Josquin des Prés *c.* 1445–1521	18 masses; 100 motets	Born Picardy and died Hainault; Luther called him 'Master of the Notes'
Isaac, Heinrich *c.* 1450–1517	36 masses; 'Innsbruck I Must Leave You' (song) reworked by J.S. Bach and Brahms	Born Brabant and died Florence; taught in household of Medici family
Taverner, John *c.* 1490–1545	8 masses (inc. *Westron Wynde*); other church music	Occasionally alleged to have given up music to persecute Catholics under Thomas Cromwell; subject of opera by Peter Maxwell Davies
Cabezón, Antonio de *c.* 1510–1566	'El Caballero variation'	Born Burgos and died Madrid; blind from birth
Tallis, Thomas *c.* 1510–1585	'Spem in alium nunquam habui' (In no other is my Hope) (motet)	Elizabeth I granted monopoly of sheet music to Tallis and William Byrd
Gabrieli, Andrea *c.* 1510–1586	7 masses and numerous motets	Born and died in Venice
Palestrina, Giovanni 1525–1594	Over 100 masses and 250 motets, including *Stabat Mater*	Took his name from his birthplace; lost his family in Italian plague
Lassus, Orlande 1532–1594	Wrote some 2,000 madrigals, motets, chansons, canzonas, masses, lieder, etc.	Born at Mons, died at Munich; preceded Palestrina as chapelmaster of Papal Church of St John Lateran, Rome

Name	*Principal works*	*Details*
Byrd, William 1543–1623	Prolific composer and pioneer of madrigals but also composed motets, masses and music for organ and virginals, his most famous work being the collection of 42 virginal pieces *My Lady Nevells Book*	Pupil of Thomas Tallis and favoured by Queen Elizabeth despite being a Catholic; granted monopoly of all sheet music in England along with Tallis
Victoria Tomás Luis de 1548–1611	Composed in a similar style to that of Palestrina but distinguished by his use of Spanish melody. His total output consisted of church music including the motets *Vexilla Regis* and *Magnum Mysterium*, the acclaimed *Officium Hebdonadae Sanctae*, and the Requiem Mass composed at the death of Empress Maria	Spanish composer, born in Avila; studied for priesthood in Rome and in 1576 became chaplain to the widowed Empress Maria, sister of Philip II, returning with her to Madrid in 1583 to the convent of the Descalzas Reales, where he remained as choirmaster until his death
Morley, Thomas 1557–1602	Father of the English madrigal who edited the collection *The Triumphs of Oriana*; his last work was *The First Book of Ayres*	Pupil of Byrd who became organist at St Paul's Cathedral and Gentleman of the Chapel Royal in 1592
Sweelinck, Jan Piterszoon 1562–1621	Wrote over 250 vocal works and 70 for keyboard. His fantasias were the first example of fully worked-out fugues. He founded the North German school which later included Diderik Buxtehude and J S Bach	Dutch composer, organist and harpsichordist. Succeeded his father as organist of the Oude Kerk (old church). Amsterdam in 1580, a position he held until his death
Bull, John *c.* 1562–1628	Although Bull's reputation was as a performer rather than a composer, he, along with William Byrd and Orlando Gibbons, published the first book of keyboard music in England, the aptly named *Parthenia* (Maidenhood), 1611. his other works include the virginal pieces *Walsingham* and *God Save the King*, although the attribution of our present National Anthem to Bull is perhaps not from this piece but a later untitled work	English musician. Appointed organist in the Queen's Chapel in 1586 and became the first music lecturer at Gresham College in 1597, and organist to James I in 1607. His Catholicism led him to flee England in 1613 to become organist of the Chapel Royal, Brussels and in 1615 became organist at Antwerp Cathedral, where he remained until his death
Dowland, John 1562–1626	Published 87 songs as well as *Lachrimae* (1604), 21 dance pieces containing 7 pavanes, all beginning with the theme of Dowland's song 'Flow my tears'	Lutenist and singer/songwriter for the king of Denmark (1598–1606) and Lord Howard de Walden (1606–12) as well as Anne of Denmark and Charles I
Monteverdi, Claudio 1567–1643	First opera *La Favola d'Orfeo* (1607) is earliest opera in the regular repertoire; last opera: *L'Incoronazione di Poppea* (1642); many operas lost; other works listed in tables	Son of a barber/surgeon who wed the singer Claudia Cattaneo; he was a pupil of Ingegneri and was patronised by the duke of Mantua; took holy orders for a short time
Gibbons, Orlando 1583–1625	Composer of madrigals, e.g. 'The Silver Swan', and anthems, e.g. 'This is the Record of John'; also contributed to the first book of keyboard music printed in England, *Parthenia*	Organist of Chapel Royal from 1604 and Westminster Abbey from 1623
Frescobaldi, Girolamo 1583–1643	In 1612 he published 12 fantasias, and in 1624 a collection of 10 ricercari, five canzoni and 11 capriccios. Frescobaldi was a strong influence of the German Baroque school through the work of his pupils Froberger and Tunder	Italian virtuoso organist, born in Ferrara. Became organist at St Peter's, Rome, where 30,000 people are said to have attended his first performance
Schütz, Heinrich 1585–1672	*Christmas Oratorio*; settings of the Passion	German composer and organist who studied law and was one of Bach's influences
Froberger, Johann Jakob 1616–67	Froberger was the first important German composer for the harpsichord and a leading light of early Baroque music	German composer, born in Stuttgart. He became a court organist in Vienna, 1637, and later that year travelled to Rome to study under Frescobaldi
Lully, Jean-Baptiste 1632–1687	Composed 20 operas and ballets, including *Alceste* (1684), *Psyché* (1678), *Roland* (1685), *Armide et Rénaud* (1686), *Achille et Polixène* (posthumous collaboration with Colasse) and *Le Bourgeois Gentilhomme* (collaboration with Molière)	Italian-born but took French nationality in 1661; from 1664 collaborated with Molière in series of comedy-ballets which were forerunners of French opera; danced role of the Mufti in *Le Bourgeois Gentilhomme*; died accidentally by stabbing himself in the foot with long pole used to conduct (wound turned gangrenous)
Buxtehude, Diderik *c.* 1637–1707	20 cantatas, of which the cycle of seven Membra Jesu Nostri, are the most famous. He also wrote toccatas, preludes, fugues and chaconnes. Most of his harpsichord music has been lost	Danish organist and composer. Handel visited him in 1703 and In 1705 J S Bach was known to have walked the 200 miles from Arnstadt to hear him play

Name	*Principal works*	*Details*
Blow, John 1649–1708	Wrote over 100 anthems and 13 services but best known work was masque *Venus and Adonis* (1682)	One of the first choirboys of Chapel Royal after Restoration and organist at Westminster Abbey (1668–79), preceding Henry Purcell
Corelli, Arcangelo 1653–1713	First composition: Sonata for Violin and Lute. 60 sonatas (48 trio and 12 solo) 12 Concerti Grossi (published posthumously) the most famous being his *Christmas Concerto*	Italian violinist, conductor and composer. From 1687 he was under the patronage of Cardinal Pamphili. Corelli was a skilled conductor and is often thought of as a pioneer of modern orchestral direction
Purcell, Henry 1659–1695	Only opera *Dido and Aeneas* (1683); fantasias for strings (1680); 'My Heart is Inditing' for Coronation of James II (1685); semi-operas include *The Fairy Queen*, *King Arthur*, *The Tempest* and the unfinished *The Indian Queen*	Succeeded Matthew Locke as composer to the king's violins and John Blow as organist of Westminster Abbey (1679); in 1682 became one of the three organists of the Chapel Royal
Scarlatti, Alessandro 1660–1725	First of 115 operas *Gli Equivoci*; his greatest considered to be *Mitridate Eupatore* (1707); only comic opera *Il Trionfo dell'Onore* (1718); last opera *La Griselda* (1721)	Founder of Neapolitan School of composers; father of Domenico Scarlatti
Couperin, François 1668–1733	Composed 230 harpsichord pieces, also chamber music	Wrote textbook *The Art of Touching the Keyboard*; known as 'Couperin the Great' on account of quantity of musicians in the family
Vivaldi, Antonio 1678–1741	First opera *Ottone in Villa* (1713); first Venetian opera *Orlando Finto Pazzo*; best known opera *Orlando Furioso* (1727); most famous work *The Four Seasons* (1725); most famous oratorio *Juditha Triumphans* (1716)	Nicknamed the Red Priest after taking holy orders in 1703; taught violin at Ospedale della Pietà, an orphanage, from 1703; died and buried in a pauper's grave in Vienna; Peter Ryom catalogued works, Leipzig, 1974 with prefix RV (Ryom Verzeichnis)
Telemann, Georg Philipp 1681–1767	Often considered the most prolific of all composers with 600 overtures and 44 passions to his name as well as 40 operas (best known being *Pimpinone*, 1725)	German composer and organist who had no formal training but studied Lully and André Campra; appointed Kantor at the Thomaskirche, Leipzig, in preference to J S Bach
Bach, Johann Sebastian 1685–1750	Orchestral and keyboard works include: *Brandenburg Concertos (Nos 1–6)* (1717); *The Well-Tempered Klavier* (48 preludes and fugues); *Goldberg Variations* (30 variations on original theme); English suites and French suites, as well as the unfinished *Die Kunst der Fuge* (The Art of Fugue); famous oratorios include *St John Passion*, *St Matthew Passion* and *Christmas Oratorio*	Born Eisenach and died in Leipzig; orphaned at age of 10 and lived with elder brother at Ohrdruf;married his cousin Maria Barbara Bach in 1707 and afterher death in 1720 married Anna Magdalena Wilcken (December 1721); almost totally blind during last year of life; Wagner described his work as 'The most stupendous miracle in all music'; catalogues have BWV nos (Bach Werke Verzeichnis)
Scarlatti, Domenico 1685–1757	About 550 harpsicord sonatas; also operas and oratorios	Long-time friend of Handel; powerful influence on modern keyboard technique
Handel, George Frederick 1685–1759	First opera *Almira* (1705) and last *Deidamia* (1740); other notable operas include *Agrippina* (1709), *Rinaldo* (1711), *Teseo* (1712), *Radamisto* (1720), *Tamerlano* (1724), *Orlando* (1733), *Ariodante* (1735), *Alcina* (1735), Berenice (1737), *Serse* (1738); orchestral works include *Water Music* (1717) and *Music for Royal Fireworks* (1749) played in Green Park to mark the Peace of Aix-la-Chapelle; oratorios include *Esther* (1732), *Athalia* (1733), *Alexander's Feast* (1736), *Israel in Egypt* (1739), *Messiah* (1741), *Judas Maccabaeus* (1746); church music includes *Dettingen Te Deum* (1743), *Chandos Anthems* (1718), *Zadok the Priest* (1737); other famous work is 5th Harpsichord Suite, nicknamed *The Harmonious Blacksmith* (1720)	Born in Halle and died in London; son of a barber/surgeon; studied law until his father died; became English citizen in 1726; received pension of £200 p.a. for life from Queen Anne (1712), which was increased to £600 by King George I for whom he wrote his famous *Water Music* suite in 1717; blind for last 7 years of his life and aided by his agent and friend, John Christopher Smith

Name	*Principal works*	*Details*
Arne, Thomas Augustine 1710–1778	First opera was *Rosamond* (1733); composed settings for Shakespeare songs including 'Under the Greenwood Tree', 'Where the Bee Sucks' and 'Blow Blow thou Winter Wind'; most famous work is 'Rule Britannia', originally written for *The Masque of Alfred*	Born and died in London; son of an upholsterer and educated at Eton; his sister was famous actress Mrs Cibber; son Michael wrote 'The Lass with a delicate air'; married a singer, Cecilia Young (1736)
Boyce, William 1711–1779	Most famously associated with the song 'Heart of Oak', composed in 1759 for pantomime *Harlequin's Invasion* to words by David Garrick; 8 symphonies and 12 overtures	Master of the King's Musick from 1755
Gluck, Christoph Willibald 1714–1787	First opera *Artaserse* (1741); best known opera is *Orfeo et Eurydice* (1762); other operas include *La Clemenza di Tito* (1752), *Alceste* (1767) and *Armide* (1777); his best-known ballet is *Don Juan* (1761); opera comiques include *The Pilgrimage to Mecca*	Born Erasbach, Germany and died in Vienna; German composer under patronage of Prince Lobkowitz in his formative years; in 1754 Empress Maria Theresa appointed him opera Kapellmeister to court theatre in Vienna
Haydn, Franz Joseph 1732–1809	Composed 104 numbered symphonies; Symphony in D Major No 96 is called the 'Miracle' because it was thought that after its first performance the audience flocking to applaud him escaped injury when a chandelier fell on their empty seats. In fact, this incident occurred on 2 February 1795 while his 102nd Symphony was playing; composed 20 operas, the first *La Canterina* 1766 and the last *Orfeo ed Euridice* (1791); other works include numerous masses, cantatas, sonatas, oratorios, concertos and chamber music	Austrian-born son of a farmer-wheelwright; precocious talent as a child; from 1761 was patronised by Prince Paul Esterházy, working as Vice-Kapellmeister at Eisenstadt, Hungary; mutual admiration for Mozart influenced his work from 1781; Beethoven was his pupil for a short period; regarded as the father of the symphony only because of his prolific output; his works are often given Hob nos., after Anthony van Hoboken (1887–1983), who catalogued them
Cimarosa, Domenico 1749–1801	First of 65 operas was *Le Stravaganze del Conti* (1772); best known opera *The Secret Marriage* (1792); other operas include *Artaserse* (1784), *Penelope* (1795) and *L'Apprensivo Raggirato* (1798); also wrote 30 keyboard sonatas	Court composer to Catherine II of Russia; in 1791 succeeded Salieri as Kapellmeister to Leopold II in Vienna; sentenced to death in 1799 for supporting French Republican army but reprieved on condition he left Naples
Mozart, Wolfgang Amadeus 1756–1791	First opera was *Apollo et Hyacinthus* (1767); other operas include *Bastien und Bastienne* (1768), *Idomeneo* (1780), *The Marriage of Figaro* (1786), *Don Giovanni* (1787), *Così fan tutte* (1789), *Die Zauberflöte* (The Magic Flute) (1791); last opera *La Clemenza di Tito* (1791); of the 41 symphonies the last 3 were composed in a matter of a few weeks; also wrote numerous orchestral pieces and concertos for both piano and violin as well as horn concertos, string quartets, 40 songs and many sonatas; *Eine kleine Nachtmusik* (1787) is a popular orchestral piece, being theme tune for *Brain of Britain* quiz	Born in Salzburg and died in Vienna; Johannes Chrysostomus Wolfgangus Theophilus was baptismal name; son of Leopold, Vice-Kapellmeister to Prince Archbishop of Salzburg; sister was Maria Anna (Nannerl; 1751–1829); in Rome in 1769 he heard Allegri's *Miserere* and wrote it out from memory; married Constance Weber in August 1782; his *Requiem Mass* for Count von Walsegg was completed after his death by Franz Süssmayr; work was catalogued by Ludwig von Köchel, an Austrian botanist and mineralogist
Beethoven, Ludwig van 1770–1827	Only opera *Fidelio* (1805) was originally called *Leonora*; nine complete symphonies, but Dr Barry Cooper, a music lecturer at Aberdeen University, has pieced together, from sketches, a 10th Symphony by making projections of existing themes; composed 32 piano sonatas, including No. 14 in C sharp minor (*Moonlight*) and No. 15 in D major (*Pastoral*); best-known piano concerto was No. 5 (*Emperor*); numerous songs, sonatas and masses; one violin concerto	Born in Bonn and buried in Central Friedhof, Vienna; father was court singer to the elector of Cologne; dedicated his 3rd Symphony to Napoleon but retracted it on hearing he had made himself emperor; learned he was going deaf in 1798; mystery cloaks identity of his 'Immortal Beloved', although Antonie Brentano is a candidate as he dedicated his *Diabelli Variations* to her; freedom of Vienna bestowed on him in 1815
Paganini, Niccolò 1782–1840	Six violin concertos remain but various others lost; composed many variations on existing works, such as *God Save the King*, an aria from *La Cenerentola* and *Witches' Dance*, based on an air by Süssmayr; popular work is *Variations on a Theme of Rossini* and *24 Caprices*; also wrote 12 sonatas for violin and guitar	Born in Genoa, died of cancer of the larynx in Nice; regarded as greatest genius of the violin; successful gambler who owned a casino and lent money to struggling musicians, e.g. Berlioz; Mephistophelean looks fostered stories of satanic powers
Weber, Carl Maria 1786–1826	First of 9 operas *Das Waldmädchen* (1800); other operas include *Silvana* (1810), *Abu Hassan* (1811), *Der Freischütz* (1821) and his final opera *Oberon* (1826).	Born Eutin, Germany; died of TB while staying with Sir George Smart in his Great Portland St home and re-buried in Dresden in 1844

Name	Principal works	Details
Meyerbeer, Giacomo 1791–1864	First opera *Jephtas Gelübde* (1812). Other notable operas include *Robert le Diable* (1831), *Les Huguenots* (1836), *Le Prophète* (1940), *L'Etoile du Nord* (1854) and *L'Africaine* (1864). Also wrote oratario, marches, songs, and church music	German operatic composer, born in Berlin and originally named Jakob Liebmann Beer. He was a child prodigy pianist, playing a Mozart concerto at the age of 11. Meyerbeer's pageant-like operas were attacked by the anti-Semitism of Wagner
Rossini, Gioachino Antonio 1792–1868	First of 35 operas was *Demetrio e Polibio* (1806); best-known operas include *Tancredi* (1813), *Otello* (1816), *Elizabeth of England* (1815), *La Gazza Ladra*, *Cinderella* (1817) and his last opera *William Tell* (1829); also composed cantatas, sonatas and orchestral works although retired completely from opera as a result of neurasthenia; late works include *Petite Messe Solennelle* and a variety of pieces he called 'Sins of my Old Age'; notable prodigy: 6 string sonatas date from his early teens	Born Pesaro in Italy, died in Paris; buried in Père Lachaise cemetery, but reinterred in Florence in 1887; son of a trumpeter and a singer; married soprano Isabella Colbran (1821) and then after divorcing her, Olympe Pélissier; court composer to Charles X of France in 1825; famous for his 'Samedi Soirs' performances; a gourmand:Tournedos Rossini is named after him; nicknamed Monsieur Crescendo
Schubert, Franz Peter 1797–1828	Wrote 9 numbered symphonies although 7th and 8th were unfinished, as were some unnumbered ones; first opera *Des Teufels Lustschloss* (1814); prolific output included over 600 songs of which 144 were written in 1815 (8 in one day); some popular songs include 'Death and the Maiden (1817), the *Winterreise* (Winter Journey) song cycle (1827) and settings of Shakespearean songs, e.g. 'Who is Sylvia?' and 'Hark, Hark the Lark', also notable Goethe settings; of his oratorios, *Lazarus* (1820), his setting of psalm 23, is best known, although 'Wanderier Fantasy' is popular; unusually did not compose any concertos	Born and died in Vienna, buried near to Beethoven at Währing, and later exhumed and reburied in the Central Cemetery of Vienna; father was schoolmaster and his first teacher; the celebrated baritone Michael Vogl sang many of his lieder; Schubert was a torchbearer at Beethoven's funeral in 1827; his works were catalogued by Otto Deutsch
Donizetti, Gaetano 1797–1848	First opera *Il Pigmalione* (1816); other operas include *Enrico di Borgogna* (1818), *Zoraide di Grenate* (1822), *Ann Boleyn* (1830), *Lucretia Borgia* (1833), *Lucia di Lammermoor* (1835), *Mary Stuart* (1835), *Roberto Devereux* (1837), *Don Pasquale* (1843) and (last) *Dom Sébastien* (1843); also wrote church music, string quartets and symphonies	Born and died in Bergamo; joined the Austrian army and composed in his spare time until 1822 when he left and became full-time composer; became insane in later life due to syphilis
Bellini, Vincenzo 1801–1835	First opera *Adelson e Salvini* (1825); others include *The Sleepwalker* (1831), *Norma* (1831) and, last opera, *I Puritani* (1835)	Born in Catania, Sicily, died in Puteaux, near Paris, reinterred in Catania 1876; studied under Niccolò Zingarelli in Naples
Berlioz, Hector 1803–1869	Operas: *Benvenuto Cellini* (1837), *Les Troyens* (1858) and *Béatrice et Bénédict* (1862); famous orchestral works include *Waverley* (1828), *King Lear* (1831), *Le Corsaire* (1831), *Rob Roy* (1832), *Harold in Italy* (1834), *Symphonie Funèbre et Triomphale* (1840); best known work is *Symphony Fantastique* (1830); famous dramatic cantata is *The Damnation of Faust*	Born Grenoble and died in Paris; son of a provincial doctor but dropped out of medical school for a music career; married Irish actress Harriet Smithson (1833); Paganini paid him 20,000 francs for *Harold in Italy*; formed liaison with singer Marie Recio (1841)
Strauss the Elder, Johann 1804–1849	Composed 251 works of which 152 were waltzes; *Radetzky March* (1848), named after an Austrian field-marshal, easily his best known work	Born and died (scarlet fever) in Vienna
Glinka, Mikhail 1804–1857	Two operas *Life for the Tsar* (1836) – aka Ivan Susanin – and *Ruslan and Lyudmila* (1842); orchestral works include *Kamarinskaya* (1848) and *Night in Madrid* (1848)	Born in Smolensk and died in Berlin; first Russian composer to be recognised outside Russia; worked in Communications Ministry 1824–8
Mendelssohn, Felix 1809–1847	Twelve early string symphonies, also 5 mature symphonies and concertos (e.g. for violin); dramatic works include *Midsummer Night's Dream* and the unfinished opera *Lorelei*; best known oratorios *Elijah* (1846) and *St Paul* (1836); hymns include 'Hear My Prayer' (1844), which contains the section 'O for the Wings of a Dove'	Born Hamburg and died in Leipzig, probably due to overwork and blow of sister's death; grandson of philosopher Moses Mendelssohn; wrote *Hebrides Overture* (aka *Fingal's Cave*) after visit to Britain in 1829; eldest sister was Fanny, a piano virtuoso; at 12 became friend of the 72-year-old Goethe
Chopin, Frédéric 1810–1849	Piano works include the 'Funeral March' Sonata (1837), *Krakowiak Rondo* (1828) and *Là ci darem variations*; famous for his nocturnes, preludes, mazurks, études, written for solo piano; Waltz in D flat, known as the Minute Waltz	Born in Zelazowa Wola, Poland, of French father and Polish mother, died in Paris; all works involve a piano; though a piano virtuoso, gave only about 30 public performances; lover of novelist George Sand (1837–47)

Name	*Principal works*	*Details*
Schumann, Robert 1810–1856	Only opera *Genoveva* (1849); incidental music to Byron's verse-drama *Manfred* 1849; 4 symphonies, songs and song-cycles, and numerous piano pieces, including *Abegg Variations* (dedicated to Meta Abegg and written using notes of her surname in 1830)	Born in Zwickau and died in Endenich; studied law at Leipzig and Heidelberg; married Clara Wieck in 1840; attempted suicide in 1854 by throwing himself in the Rhine and was committed to an asylum
Liszt, Franz 1811–1886	One opera *Don Sanche* (1825) in collaboration with Ferdinando Paer; 2 symphonies *Faust* (1857) and *Dante* (1856); piano works include 19 composed 'Hungarian Rhapsodies', 1846–85, *Années de pèlerinage* (1848–77) and concertos; symphonic poems include *Les Préludes* (1848), *Orpheus* (1854), *Prometheus* (1850) and *Hamlet* (1858); also composed numerous études, songs and oratorios	Born Raiding in Hungary, died Bayreuth; child prodigy who gave first piano recital aged 9; lived with Countess Marie d'Agoult from 1833 and had 3 children, one of whom, Cosima, first married Hans Bülow and then Wagner; Kapellmeister at Weiner court 1848–59, and championed Wagner and Berlioz; in 1865 he took minor orders and became Abbé Liszt
Wagner, Richard 1813–1883	Composed only 1 symphony, in C (1832); first opera *Die Feen* (The Fairies 1834) although he did compose earlier work *Die Hochzeit* but destroyed it; other operas include *Rienzi*, *The Flying Dutchman*, *Lohengrin*, *Tannhäuser*, *Der Ring des Nibelungen*, *The Mastersingers of Nuremberg* and *Parsifal* (his last); the opera *Tristan und Isolde* reflected his emotional turmoil over Mathilde Wesendonck; orchestral works include overture based on 'Rule, Britannia', *Faust* overture, *Siegfried Idyll* and concert overture *Polonia*; also composed *7 Songs From Goethe's Faust*, as well as many books on music; pioneer of the Leitmotiv	Born Leipzig and died in Venice, buried at Wahnfried; attended school in Dresden and Thomasschule in Leipzig; married actress Minna Planer in 1836 but had affair with Mathilde Wesendonck; King Ludwig of Bavaria became his patron; Minna died in 1866 and he started affair with Cosima, wife of Hans Bülow, who bore him 2 daughters (Isolde and Eva); Cosima's marriage was annulled in 1869 and she gave birth to Wagner's son, Siegfried; Wagner and Cosima were married in 1870
Verdi, Giuseppe 1813–1901	First opera *Oberto, Conte di San Bonifacio* (1838) although an earlier one, *Rocester*, is lost; other operas include *Nabucco* (1841), *Ernani* (1843), *Attila* (1846), *Macbeth* (1847), *Luisa Miller* (1849), *Stiffelio* (1850), *Rigoletto* (1851), *Il Trovatore* (1852), *Otello* (1886) and *Falstaff* (1892); Verdi's *Requiem* composed in memory of poet Manzoni and played at funeral of Diana, Princess of Wales (1997)	Born Parma, died in Milan leaving bulk of his money to a home he had founded for elderly musicians; innkeeper's son first taught by local organist Antonio Barezzi, a wholesaler whose daughter he married; between 1838 and 1840 his wife and 2 children died; married soprano, Giuseppina Strepponi in 1859; in 1860, after Italian independence from Austria, elected deputy in first National Parliament
Gounod, Charles 1818–1893	First opera *Sapho* (1851); best known *Faust* (1859); 3 symphonies and various oratorios and cantatas; also *Funeral March of a Marionette* (1872)	Born in Paris, died in St Cloud; won Grand Prix de Rome in 1839; studied for priesthood but chose a life in music
Offenbach, Jacques 1819–1880	First opera *Die Rheinnixen* (1864); only grand opera *The Tales of Hoffmann* (1881); only ballet *Le Papillon* (1860); operettas include *Orpheus in the Underworld* (1858), *La Belle Hélène* (1864) and *Daphnis et Chloé* (1860)	Born in Deutz, near Cologne, and died in Paris; son of a cantor in Cologne synagogue; surname Offenbach came from the name of family's home town
Bruckner, Anton 1824–1896	Ten symphonies, last unfinished; masses in D Minor (1864), E Minor (1869) and F Minor (1872) as well as cantatas and chamber music; many works edited by composer and others, and exist in various versions	Born in Ansfelden, died in Vienna; known internationally as a virtuoso organist; first (unnumbered) symphony written in his late thirties
Smetana, Bedrich 1824–1884	First opera *The Brandenburgers in Bohemia* (1863); other operas include *The Bartered Bride* (1866), *The Secret* (1878), *The Kiss* (1876) and *Two Widows* (1874); cycle of 6 symphonic poems, *Má Vlast* (My Country 1874–9)	Born in Litomysl, died in Prague; regarded as founder of Czech music; active in founding national opera house; venereal disease caused deafness and later insanity
Strauss the Younger, Johann 1825–1899	Composed nearly 400 waltzes of which the best known include *Blue Danube*, *Tales from the Vienna Woods* (1868), *Roses From the South* (1880) and *Emperor Waltz* (1888); most famous operetta *Die Fledermaus* (The Bat 1874); also composed various polkas and an unfinished ballet, *Cinderella* (completed by Joseph Bayer)	Born and died in Vienna; worked as a bank clerk in early career; known as the Waltz King; in 1848 revolution supported opposite side to his father
Borodin, Alexander 1833–1887	Only opera *Prince Igor* left unfinished and completed by Rimsky-Korsakov and Alexander Glazunov; 3 symphonies, the 3rd completed by Glazunov; 2 string quartets; tone poem *In The Steppes of Central Asia*; music used in Forrest and Wright's musical *Kismet*	Born and died in St Petersburg; illegitimate son of Russian prince; doctor and professor of chemistry; feminist who founded a school of medicine for women

Name	*Principal works*	*Details*
Brahms, Johannes 1833–1897	Four symphonies and 4 concertos; orchestral works include *Tragic Overture* (1880), *Academic Festival Overture* (1880) and *Variations on a Theme by Haydn* (1873); key choral works, *German Requiem* (1866) and Schickalslied (1871); no operas, but nearly 200 songs as well as chamber music, organ works and piano works, including *Variations on a Theme by Paganini* (1866)	Born in Hamburg, died in Vienna; son of professional double-bass player; hailed as genius by Schumann in essay 'New Paths' 1853 and succeeded him as teacher to Princess Friederike of Lippe-Detmold
Saint–Saëns, Camille 1835–1921	First opera *La Princesse Jaune* (1872); most famous opera *Samson and Delilah* (1868); 3 symphonies (2 other symphonies were withdrawn); symphonic poems include *Danse Macabre* (1874); popular orchestral piece *Carnival of the Animals* (1886), its performance forbidden in the composer's lifetime (movement 13, 'The Swan', most popular piece); also composed *Variations on a Theme of Beethoven* (1874) and *Polonaise* for 2 pianos; various oratorios and masses include Psalm 150 (1907); 5 piano concertos, No. 2 best known	Born in Paris and died in Algiers; symphony No. 3 dedicated to Liszt's memory; wrote coronation march for Edward VII, 1902; *Carnival of the Animals* in 14 movements i.e. 'Royal March of the Lion', 'Hens & Cocks', 'Wild Asses', 'Tortoises', 'The Elephant', 'Kangaroos', 'Aquarium', 'Persons with Long Ears', 'Cuckoo in the Depths of Woods', 'Aviary', 'Pianists', 'Fossils', 'The Swan', 'Finale'; the tortoises are represented by the can-can in slow motion, the 'Dance of the Sylphs' on double-basses for the elephant and the fossils is a parody of *Danse Macabre*
Bizet, Georges 1838–1875	First opera *Le Docteur Miracle* (1856); last and most famous opera *Carmen* (1874); one symphony; orchestral suite *L'Arlésienne*	Born in Paris, died in Bougival; entered Paris Conservatory at age 9; Won Grand Prix de Rome in 1857
Mussorgsky, Modest 1839–1881	First opera *Salammbô* (unfinished); *Boris Godunov* (1869) only completed opera. piano works *Pictures at an Exhibition*; orchestral *A Night on the Bare Mountain*	Born in Karevo, Pskov, died in St Petersburg; one of the Russian 5 or Mighty Handful (the others: Balakirev, Cui, Borodin, Rimsky-Korsakov)
Tchaikovsky, Pyotr 1840–1893	First opera *Voyevoda* (1868); others include *Eugene Onegin* (1879) and *The Queen of Spades* (1890); last opera *Yolanta* (1891); 3 ballets *Swan Lake* (1876), *Sleeping Beauty* (1889) and *Nutcracker* (1892); other works include 6 symphonies, 2 piano concertos, a violin concerto, a number of tone poems including *Romeo and Juliet* and *Italian Caprice*, as well as an unnumbered *Manfred Symphony* (1885); *Rococo Variations* for cello and orchestra	Born in Votkinsk, died in St Petersburg of cholera, although may have taken poison to avoid a homosexual scandal; read law in St Petersburg and became civil servant; married Antonina Miliukova 1877 but left her a month later and attempted suicide in his guilt; Countess Nadezhda von Meck was his patron although they never met (it is said that he crossed the street once to avoid a meeting).
Dvořák, Antonín 1841–1904	Opera *Alfred* (1870); best-known *Rusalka* (1900); last opera *Armida* (1903); 9 symphonies, including No. 9 in E Minor, *From the New World*; and other cello concertos	Born in Nelahozeves, Bohemia, died in Prague; son of a village butcher; joined National Theatre of Prague as viola player in 1866
Sullivan, Arthur 1842–1900	Only grand opera *Ivanhoe* (1890); composed tune for hymn 'Onward Christian Soldiers'; 14 operettas in collaboration with W.S. Gilbert; songs include 'The Lost Chord'; first operetta *Cox and Box* (1866, librettist Burnand); last operetta *The Emerald Isle* left unfinished (completed by Edward German to Basil Hood's libretto); oratorios include *The Prodigal Son* (1869); cantatas include *Kenilworth* (1864); composed a symphony in E (the 'Irish'); incidental music to various Shakespeare plays	Born in Lambeth and died, appropriately, on St Cecilia's Day, at Westminster; son of Irish bandmaster at Sandhurst; first to win Mendelssohn Scholarship of the Royal Academy of Music, 1856; knighted in 1883; *Thespis* in 1871 was 1st collaboration with Gilbert; Savoy Theatre, opened during run of *Patience*, specialized in Gilbert and Sullivan; the two fell out during a run of *The Gondoliers* supposedly over a choice of carpet for the theatre; they were reconciled for *Utopia Ltd* and *The Grand Duke* (1896)
Grieg, Edvard 1843–1907	Orchestral works include *Peer Gynt Suite* (1875), *Lyric Suite* (1904) and *Holberg Suite* (1884); wrote *Norwegian Dances* (4 hands) and numerous songs for piano; 1 symphony, 1 piano concerto	Born and died in Bergen; married his cousin, soprano Nina Hagerup, in 1867 when he also founded the Norwegian Academy of Music; Ibsen commissioned incidental music to *Peer Gynt*
Rimsky-Korsakov, Nikolay 1844–1908	First opera *The Maid of Pskov* (aka: *Ivan the Terrible*) 1872; last opera (of 14) *The Golden Cockerel* (1907); 3 symphonies – first major Russian symphonies; famous orchestral works include *Spanish Caprice* (1887) and *Sheherazade* (1888)	Born in Tikhvin, died in Lyubensk; navy cadet as child, hoping to become a sailor; slow movement of 1st Symphony written off Gravesend; wrote 1st opera whilst serving as a naval lieutenant; edited *100 Russian Folk-Songs* 1877

Name	*Principal works*	*Details*
Janáček, Leoš 1854–1928	First opera *Sárka* (1888); others *Jenůfa* (1904) and *From the House of the Dead* (1930: his last); Glagolitic Mass; rhapsody *Taras Bulba*; 2 string quartets; song-cycle *Diary of One Who Disappeared*	Born in Moravia, died in Moravská, Ostrava; Czech composer who had his success late in life; inspired by an affair with Kamila Stösslova
Elgar, Edward 1857–1934	Composed 2 symphonies and an unfinished 3rd; cantata, *The Dream of Gerontius* (1900); orchestral works *Pomp and Circumstance* marches (1901–30), *Enigma Variations* (1899); Violin Concerto in B Minor (1910); Cello Concerto in E Minor (1919); unfinished opera *The Spanish Lady*	Born in Broadheath, Worcestershire, died in Worcester; son of an organist and music shop proprietor in Worcester; married General's daughter Caroline Roberts who died in 1920; knighted in 1904 as first English composer of International repute since Purcell
Puccini, Giacomo 1858–1924	First opera *Le Villi* (The Willis) 1883; best-known opera *Manon Lescaut* (1893), *La Bohème* (1896), *Tosca* (1900), *Madame Butterfly* (1904), *Turandot* (unfinished, but completed by Franco Alfano)	Born in Lucca, Italy, died in Brussels; came from a long line of church musicians
Mahler, Gustav 1860–1911	Ten symphonies (one unfinished, completed by Deryck Cooke, 1st 8 of which Mahler conducted first performances); song symphony *Song of the Earth* (1909); song-cycle *Kindertotenlieder* (1904); cantata *Das Klagende Lied* (1880); only opera was completion of Weber's *The Three Pintos*	Born Kalist, Bohemia, d. Vienna; brilliant conductor who headed Hamburg Opera from 1891; then Vienna State Opera, NY Met Opera, NY Philharmonic; converted from Judaism to Roman Catholicism 1897; married musician Alma Schindler in 1902
Debussy, Achille-Claude 1862–1918	Most famous opera *Pelléas et Mélisande*; orchestral works *Prélude à l'après-midi d'un Faune* (1894); *La Mer* (1905); *Nocturnes* (1899)	Born St Germain-en-Laye, d. (cancer) Paris; won Prix de Rome in 1884 with cantata *L'Enfant prodigue*; influenced by Javanese gamelan music as well as by impressionist painters; married Lily Texier 1899 but left her 5 years later for singer, Emma Bardac and married her in 1908; part of *La Mer* written in Eastbourne
Delius, Frederick 1862–1934	First opera *Irmelin* (1892); last opera *Fennimore and Gerda* (1910); others *The Magic Fountain* (1895), *Koanga* (1897), *A Village Romeo and Juliet* (1901), and *Margot-la-Rouge* (1902); orchestral pieces *Brigg Fair* (1907), *On Hearing the First Cuckoo in Spring* (1912); choral works *Sea Drift* (1909), *A Mass of Life* (1909); various Norwegian songs, as well as concertos, piano pieces and melodramas	Born in Bradford, Yorkshire, died in Grez-sur-Loing; reinterred in May 1935 at Limpsfield, Surrey; until 1904 composed under name of Fritz Delius; influenced by lasting friendship with Grieg; married Jelka Rosen 1903 and lived near Fontainebleau; became blind (probably due to syphilis) and continued composing helped by a young Yorkshire musician, Eric Fenby
Szymanowski, Karol 1882–1937	Operas *Hagith* (1913), *King Roger* (1924); 4 symphonies, 2 violin concertos, 2 ballets; voices and orchestra *Love Songs of Hafiz* (1911), *Stabat Mater* (1926); violin and piano, *Myths* (1915); also songs	Born in Tymoslowska, Ukraine, died in Lausanne; leading figure at turn of century in composer's association 'Young Poland in Music'; later influenced both by Stravinsky and by folk music of Tatra Mountains
Strauss, Richard 1864–1949	First of 15 operas *Guntram* (1893); others *Salome* (1905), *Electra* (1909), *Der Rosenkavalier* (1911), *Die Frau ohne Schatten* (1919); last opera *Capriccio* (1941); ballets include *Josephslegende* (1914); tone poems include *Till Eulenspiegel*, *Don Quixote* and *Also sprach Zarathustra*	Born in Munich, died in Garmisch-Partenkirchen; son of a horn player in Munich Court Orchestra; married soprano Pauline de Ahna, 1894; became Austrian citizen in 1947
Dukas, Paul 1865–1935	One opera *Ariane et Barbe-Bleu* (1906); 1 ballet *La Péri* (1912); most famous work, symphonic poem *The Sorcerer's Apprentice* (1897); 1 symphony, 1 piano sonata	Born and died in Paris; never prolific, he burned at least 15 years of unpublished work before he died; helped Saint-Saëns complete Guiraud's opera *Frédégonde*
Sibelius, Jean 1865–1957	Tone poem *Finlandia* became voice of his country; others *En Saga* (1901), *The Swan of Tuonela* (1893); 7 symphonies, 1 violin concerto	Born in Hämeenlinna (Tavastehus), died in Järvenpää; received State pension for life in 1897 to free him to compose; 5th Symphony written on his 50th birthday; did not compose for the last 27 years of his life
Nielsen, Karl 1865–1931	Six symphonies for violin, flute and clarinet; concertos, string quartets, piano music, songs; operas: *Saul and David* (1902), *Maskarade* (1906)	Born in Nøotre-Lyndelse, Denmark, died in Copenhagen; wife a sculptor; developed 'progressive tonality' in which a work may change its key as it develops; in 5th symphony, sidedrummer is instructed to improvise so as to halt progress of orchestra

Name	Principal works	Details
Satie, Erik 1866–1925	Three ballets *Parade* (1917), *Mercure*, and *Relâche* (1924). Parade was scored for typewriters, airplane propellers, sirens, ticker-tape, steamship whistle and lottery wheel. A marionette opera *Geneviève de Brabant* (1899). Piano pieces, include *Trois morceaux en forme de poire* (Three pear-shaped pieces) a work for four hands (1903) and *Gymnopédies* (1888) a trio of piano pieces Nos 1 and 3 orchestrated by Debussy and No. 2 by Roland-Manuel.	French composer and pianist, born in Honfleur, of a French father and Scottish mother. In 1893, he had a stormy affair with the artist Suzanne Valadon but lived as a recluse for some . years Satie parodied the orthodoxy and stiffness of established music using whimsical titles and musical directions. He was a major influence on many French composers including Debussy, Ravel and 'Les Six'
Vaughan Williams, Ralph 1872–1958	First opera *Hugh the Drover* (1914); last *The Pilgrim's Progress* (1951); orchestral works *In the Fen Country* (1904), *Fantasia on a Theme by Thomas Tallis* (1910); 9 symphonies, also concertos, ballets, songs and chamber music	Born in Down Ampney, Gloucestershire, died in London; lived in Dorking in Surrey 1929–53
Rachmaninoff, Sergei 1873–1943	Three symphonies; 4 piano concertos, notably the 2nd in C minor; *Rhapsody on a Theme of Paganini* (1934) for piano and orchestra; many piano pieces; first opera *Aleko* (1892), last *Monna Vanna* (1907)	Born in Semyonovo, Starorussky, died in Beverly Hills; virtuoso pianist; became US citizen in 1943; lifelong friend of the celebrated bass Chaliapin; underwent hypnosis when experiencing creative block – 2nd piano concerto dedicated to hypnotist
Holst, Gustav 1874–1934	Best known for orchestral suite *The Planets* (1918); also for orchestra: *Egdon Heath* (1927), *Book Green Suite* (1933); first opera *Savitri* (1908), last opera *The Wandering Scholar* (1930)	Born in Cheltenham, died in London; worked as trombonist for Carl Rosa Opera (1898–1900); learned Sanskrit to translate hymns from *Rig Veda*
Schoenberg, Arnold 1874–1951	First opera (the monodrama): *Erwartung* (1909), last *Moses und Aron* (19051) other significant works include: *Gurrelieder*, *Pierrot Lunaire*, *A Survivor from Warsaw* and *Verklarte Nacht*	Revolutionised music to reach atonality and serialism; had a phobia about the number 13, and 'Moses und Aron' is spelled thus so as to only have 12 letters; teacher of Webern and Berg; became a US citizen in 1941
Ives, Charles 1874–1954	Four symphonies and the so-called first orchestral set (New England Symphony); 'Universe' Symphony was never completed in his lifetime but Johnny Reinhard completed it and performed it in 1996; also wrote the song 'Shall We Gather at the River'	Born in Danbury, Connecticut, died in New York; wrote symphony while at Yale; formed his own insurance company (1907); 3rd symphony won Pulitzer Prize (1947)
Ravel, Maurice 1875–1937	Operas: *L'Heure Espagnole* (1907), *L'Enfant et les Sortilèges* (1925); ballets: *Daphnis et Chloé* (1911), *Boléro* (1928); 2 piano concertos (written simultaneously); also for piano: *Pavane pour une infante défunte* (1899), *Le Tombeau de Couperin* (1917); chamber music	Born in Ciboure, died in Paris; orchestrated Mussorgsky's *Pictures at an Exhibition*; repeated failure to win Prix de Rome led to resignation of director of Paris Conservatoire, which awards it
Respighi, Ottorino 1879–1936	Roman trilogy of symphonic poems: *Pines of Rome*, *Fountains of Rome*, *Roman Festivals*; also *Three Botticelli Pictures*; concertos and operas	Born in Bologna, died in Rome; studied under Rimsky-Korsakov in St Petersburg and Max Binch in Berlin
Bridge, Frank 1879–1941	One opera: *The Christmas Rose* (1929). Orchestral suite *The Sea* (1911) String Quartets: *Sir Roger de Coverley* (1922), *Scherzo Phantastick* (1901), and *Sally in our Alley* (1916)	Born in Brighton, died in Eastbourne; English composer, conductor, violist and violinist. In 1927 taught the 14-year-old Benjamin Britten. Conducted the New Symphony Orchestra from its inception at Covent Garden. Best known for his string quartets
Ireland, John 1879–1962	Orchestral prelude *The Forgotten Rite* (1913). Symphonic rhapsody *Mai-Dun* (1921); the title refers to the prehistoric Dorset fortification, Maiden Castle. Comic overture *Satyricon* 1946). Tone poem *Sea Fever* (1913)	English composer and pianist, born in Bowden, Cheshire, and died in Washington, West Sussex. Established his reputation with his Violin Sonata in A (1917) but is best remembered for his settings of poems by Hardy, Housman and Masefield
Bartók, Béla 1881–1945	*Music for Strings, Percussion and Celesta* (1936); *Concerto for Orchestra* (1943); only opera *Duke Bluebeard's Castle* (1911); ballets: *The Wooden Prince* (1911) and *The Miraculous Mandarin* (1919); 3 piano concertos; 2 violin concertos; 6 string quartets	Born in Nagyszentmiklós, Hungary (now Romania), died (leukaemia) in New York; dedicated collector of Hungarian and other East European folk music; anti-Nazi who emigrated to USA in 1940

Name	*Principal works*	*Details*
Kodály, Zoltán 1882–1967	Three operas *Háry János* (1926), *Spinning Room* (1932), and *Czinka Panna* (1948). Choral and orchestral work *Psalmus Hungaricus* (1923) was based on text of Psalm 55 and commissioned for the 50th anniversary of the union of Buda and Pest. Two sets of Hungarian dances for orchestra *Marosszék Dances* (1930) and *Dances of Galánta* (1933)	Hungarian composer born in Kecskemét and died in Budapest. Wrote collections of folksongs with Béla Bartók between 1906 and 1921, although these were not published until 1951 as *Corpus Musicae Popularis Hungariae.* He carried out reforms in musical education and developed an evolutionary system of training and sight-singing
Stravinsky, Igor 1882–1971	Ballets include *The Firebird* (1910), *Petrushka* (1911), *The Rite of Spring* (1913), *Agon* (1953); first opera *The Nightingale* (1909), last *The Rake's Progress* (1951); important works in all the major forms include *Symphony of Psalms* (1930), *Ebony Concerto* (1946), *Septet* (1953), *Threni* (1958)	Born Oranienbaum, died New York; most influential classical composer of 20th century; became French citizen 1934, American 1945; first performance of *The Rite of Spring* in Paris caused famous riot by unattuned listeners
Webern, Anton 1883–1945	String quartet (1938); *Variations* for orchestra (1940); 3 cantatas; 1 symphony	Studied under Schoenberg and became rigorous exponent of serial music; born in Vienna, died in Mittersill after being shot accidentally by American sentry
Bax, Arnold 1883–1953	One ballet *Between Dusk and Dawn* (1917); seven symphonies. orchestral tone poem *Tintagel* (1919) first performed 1920; other orchestral works include *November Woods* (1917) and *Mourning Song* (1946)	Born in Streatham and died in Cork; English composer and pianist; master of the Kings/Queens; Music 1942–53. Knighted in 1937. His autobiography *Farewell My Youth* (1943) is an acclaimed work
Varèse, Edgard 1883–1965	Orchestral works include *Amériques* (1921), *Octandre* (1923) *Intégrales* (1925), *Arcana* (1927) and *Ionisation* (1931). Known for his experimental use of instrument combinations and unconventional percussion. His *Désert* (1954) employs tape-recorded sound; concentrated on electronic music later	French composer and conductor, born in Paris and died in New York. Became an American citizen in 1926. He organised the international Composers' Guild in 1921 and co-founded the Pan-American Association of Composers in 1927
Berg, Alban 1885–1935	Two operas, *Wozzeck* (1922) and *Lulu* (1935); *Lyric Suite* for string quartet (1926); violin concerto (1935)	Born and died in Vienna (insect bite); quit civil servant career to compose; *Lulu* completed by Friedrich Cerha, many years after Berg's death, due to reluctance of his widow
Prokofiev, Sergey 1891–1953	Seven symphonies, also concerti and string quartets; symphonic tale *Peter and the Wolf* (1936); ballets include *The Buffoon* (1920), *Age of Steel* (1926), *Romeo and Juliet* (1936); operas include *The Gambler* (1917), *Love for Three Oranges* (1919), *War and Peace* (1943)	Born Sontsovka, died in Moscow; lived in Paris 1920–33; wrote film scores, e.g. *Lieutenant Kijé* and *Alexander Nevsky*; died on the same day as Stalin
Bliss, Arthur 1891–1975	First opera *The Olympians* (1949); last opera *Tobias and the Angel* (1960); first ballet *Checkmate* (1937); last ballet *The Lady of Shalott* (1958); first symphony: *Colour Symphony*	Born and died in London; wrote music for Korda's film based on H G Wells's *Things to Come*; knighted in 1950; became master of the Queen's Musick in 1953
Howells, Herbert 1892–1983	Two piano concertos. Church music includes a complete service for King's College, Cambridge (the Collegium Regale) and settings of the Magnificat and Nunc Dimittis for the choirs of St John's College, Cambridge and various cathedrals	Born in Lydney, Gloucestershire and died in London. Ralph Vaughan Williams was a close friend and mentor. Diagnosed with Graves' disease in 1915 and subsequently became the first person in Britain to receive radium treatment
Hindemith, Paul 1895–1963	Operas include *Murder, the Hope of Women* (1919), *Mathis der Maler* (1935), *The Long Christmas Dinner* (1960); ballets: *Der Dämon* (1922), *Noblissima Visione* (1938), *Hérodiade* (1944); several symphonies; a wealth of string quartets and sonatas	Born in Hannau, died in Frankfurt; married Gertrud Rottenberg in 1924; satirical opera *News of the Day* (1929) featured soprano singing in her bath; founded a music school in Ankara; associated with Gebrauchmusik ('utility' music, written for some social purpose)
Gershwin, George 1898–1937	First 'hit' song was 'Swanee' (1919); 1 opera: *Porgy and Bess*; *Rhapsody in Blue* for piano, jazz band and orchestra (1924); tone poem for *An American in Paris* (1928)	Born in Brooklyn, NY, died in Beverly Hills, California; turned pro musician aged 14; many collaborations with his elder brother, lyricist Ira Gershwin
Poulenc, Francis 1899–1963	First opera: *Les Mamelles de Tirésias* (1944), last *La Voix Humaine* (1958); ballet *Les Riches* (1923); solo piano works, concertos, sonatas and many songs; church music including *Gloria* and *Stabat Mater*	Born and died in Paris; had independent income (related to family in Rhône-Poulenc pharmaceuticals); longtime companion of baritone Pierre Bernac

Name	Principal works	Details
Copland, Aaron 1900–1990	First ballet *Grohg* (1925); others *Billy the Kid* (1938), *Rodeo* (1942), *Appalachian Spring* (1944); 5 symphonies; orchestral work *El Salon Mexico* (1936); only opera *The Tender Land* (1954)	Born in Brooklyn, NY, died in New York; symphony finale based on *Fanfare for the Common Man*
Walton, William 1902–1983	Two symphonies; 4 concertos; oratorio *Belshazzar's Feast* (1931); 2 operas *Troilus and Cressida* (1954) and *The Bear* (1967); first ballet *The First Shoot* (1935)	Born in Oldham, died in Forio d'Ischia; son of choirmaster and singing teacher; wrote *Façade* to accompany Edith Sitwell; film scores include *First of the Few* and *Henry V*
Tippett, Michael 1905–1998	First opera *The Midsummer Marriage* (1955), also *The Knot Garden* (1969), *The Ice Break* (1976), last *New Year* (1989); 4 symphonies, 5 string quartets, concertos etc.; oratorio *A Child of Our Time* includes negro spirituals	Born and died in London; wrote own libretti; committed pacifist – acted as page-turner for Britten and Pears while imprisoned in Wormwood Scrubs as conscientious objector
Shostakovich, Dmitry 1906–1975	Fifteen symphonies, 15 string quartets, 6 concertos; piano preludes; first opera *The Nose* (1928); first ballet *The Age of Gold* (1930)	Born in St Petersburg, died in Moscow; twice severely criticised for formalism by Stalinist regime; fire fighter in Nazi siege of Leningrad 1941; wrote much film music
Messiaen, Olivier 1908–1992	One symphony *Turangalîla* (premiered by Bernstein, 1948); *L'Ascension* for orchestra (1935); much organ music; 1 opera *St Francis of Assisi*	Born in Avignon, died in Paris; many works inspired by birdsong; *Quartet for the End of Time* (1941) written and premiered in POW camp
Carter, Elliott 1908–	Ballets *Pocahontas* (1939), *The Minotaur* (1947); concertos and symphonic works; many sonatas; *Night Fantasies* for piano (1980); 3 string quartets	Born in New York; encouraged by Ives; studied under Nadia Boulanger in Paris 1932–5
Barber, Samuel 1910–1981	Three operas and three symphonies; two ballets *Medea* (1946), revised as *Cave of the Heart* in 1947, and *Souvenirs* (1952); tone poem *Knoxville: Summer of 1915* (1947)	American composer and pianist; born in West Chester, Pennsylvania, and died in New York. Reputation made with his tone poem based on Arnold's 'Dover Beach' (1931)
Britten, Benjamin 1913–1976	First opera *Paul Bunyan* (1941); others include *Peter Grimes* (1945), *Billy Budd* (1951), *The Turn of the Screw* (1954) and last *Death in Venice* (1973); *Variations on a Theme of Frank Bridge* for string orchestra (1937); *War Requiem* for choir and orchestra (1961); only ballet *The Prince of the Pagodas* (1956)	Born at Lowestoft on St Cecilia's Day (22 Nov.) and died at Aldeburgh; lifelong friendship with Peter Pears; founded Aldeburgh Festival in 1948; became Lord Britten of Aldeburgh in 1976; first composer to be created life peer
Lutoslawski, Witold 1913–1994	Four symphonies; *Concerto for Orchestra* (1954); concertos for violin, cello, etc.; *Venetian Games* for orchestra (1961)	Warsaw café pianist in Second World War; regularly wrote controlled aleatory music, leaving certain things to chance; refused to write opera as could not see why people should sing rather than talk
Bernstein, Leonard 1918–1990	Three symphonies, 1 violin concerto (called *Serenade*); operas, *Trouble in Tahiti*, later became part of *A Quiet Place*; musicals: *On the Town*, *West Side Story*, *Candide*	Born in Lawrence, Massachusetts, died in New York; celebrated conductor and teacher; wrote film music for *On the Waterfront* (1954)
Simpson, Robert 1921–1997	11 symphonies; two piano sonatas *Variations and Finale on a Theme of Haydn* (1948) and *Variations and Finale on a Theme of Beethoven* (1990)	English composer, musicologist and author; on BBC music staff 1951–80. Wrote books on several composers, including Carl Nielsen, Anton Bruckner and Jean Sibelius
Arnold, Malcolm 1921–2006	Nine symphonies; ballets: *Homage to the Queen* (1953), *Rinaldo and Armida* (1955) and *Electra* (1963); concert overture *Beckus the Dandipratt* (1948)	Born in Northampton; English composer, trumpeter, and conductor. Like Richard Rodney Bennett composed several film scores including *The Bridge on the River Kwai*; knighted in 1993
Boulez, Pierre 1925–	*Le Marteau sans Maître* for voice and chamber orchestra (1957); *Pli Selon Pli* for voice and orchestra (1962); *Eclats/Multiples* (1976)	Born in Montbrison; leader of French 12-tone music school; once suggested burning down opera houses, but now conducts in them regularly; continually revises a small number of works
Ligeti, György 1923–2006	Opera *Le Grand Macabre* (1978), *Kammerkonzert* (1970); 2 string quartets, piano études; various orchestral works	Born in Discöszentmáron; left Hungary in 1956; music used in film *2001*, though he only found out when he went to see it; one work is for 100 metronomes

Name	*Principal works*	*Details*
Berio, Luciano 1925–2003	Orchestral music; many pieces for voice and various instruments include *Circles* (1960); operas include *La Veria Storia* (1982); most famous work *Sinfonia* (1969)	Exponent of serial and electronic music; one movement of *Sinfonia* mixes a movement of Mahler's *Resurrection* with much other music and spoken text
Henze, Hans Werner 1926–2012	Ten symphonies; prolific in most musical forms; first opera *Das Wundertheater* (1949), others include *The Bassarids* (1965), *The English Cat* (1983), *Venus and Adonis* (1997); *Phaedra* (2007)	Born Gütersloh; d. Dresden. German master of atonal, aleatory and conventional techniques; much influenced by Italy, living there for some years; many works have left-wing inspiration
Stockhausen, Karlheinz 1928–2007	Many works for varying ensembles, e.g. *Gruppen* for 3 orchestras and *Stimmung* for singers and tape; piano pieces, also electronic music; ongoing operatic project: *Licht* (cycle of 7 operas each linked to a day of the week)	Born in Mödrath, near Cologne; studied under Frank Martin, Messiaen and Milhaud; experimental works include a string quartet for players in helicopters
Rautavaara, Einojuhani 1928–	Operas include *Vincent* (based on Van Gogh); latest opera *Rasputin* (2003); 8 symphonies, concertos, etc.	Born in Helsinki; a number of works invoke angels; *Cantus Arcticus* is a concerto for birds (recorded) and orchestra
Sondheim, Stephen 1930–	First musical *Saturday Night* (1957, but premiered in 1998); also *A Funny Thing Happened on the Way to the Forum* (1962), *Company* (1970), *A Little Night Music* (1973), *Pacific Overtures* (1976), *Sweeney Todd* (1979), *Passion* (1995), *Bounce* (2003), *Road Show* (2008)	Born in New York; writes lyrics and music; wrote lyrics for *West Side Story* and *Gypsy*; writes film scores, plays and film scripts; works often presented by opera companies
Górecki, Henryk 1933–	Three symphonies – the 3rd (*Symphony of Sorrowful Songs*) catapulted him to fame; also 2 string quartets, *Lerchenmusik, Kleines Requiem für ein Polka*, etc.	Born in Czernice, Poland; earlier work in a much more modern style; now exploring medieval influences
Maxwell Davies, Peter 1934–	Eight symphonies as of 2009; 10 Strathclyde Concertos for Scottish Chamber Orchestra, among other concertos; first opera *Taverner* (1970), latest *The Doctor of Myddfai* (1996); other works include the tone poem *Mavis in Las Vegas* and *Mr Emmet Takes a Walk*. Recent works include *Naxos Quartet No. 6* (2005) and *Military March* (2005)	Born in Salford, very prolific; lives in Orkney (since 1970), many works inspired by Orcadian writer George Mackay Brown; surname is really Davies; universally known as Max; his 8th symphony, 'Antarctic Symphony' was composed after visiting the Antarctic peninsula between 20 December 1997 and 8 January 1998. His works are catalogued by his manager Judy Arnold and are therefore known by 'J' numbers
Birtwistle, Harrison 1934–	First opera *Punch and Judy* (1967), latest *The Minotaur* (2008); and one ballet: *Pulsefield* (1977); *Pulse Shadow* (1996) for soprano, ensemble and strings	Born in Accrington; *Panic* (concertante work for saxophone and drum kit) commissioned for last night of centenary Prom season 1995; co-founded Pierrot Players with Maxwell Davies; knighted in 1998
Schnittke, Alfred 1934–1998	Eight symphonies, several concerti, including concerti grossi; first opera *Life with an Idiot* (1992), *The Eleventh Commandment* (1962), latest *Gesualdo* (1994); ballets include *Peer Gynt* (1986); also *Faust* cantata	Born in Engels, USSR, died in Hamburg; Russian-born of German origin; name linked to 'polystylism', where many styles of music appear in one piece; symphony No. 5 is also Concerto Grosso No. 4
Pärt, Arvo 1935–	Four symphonies, plus concerti; choral works include *St John's Passion* (1982), *Miserere* (1989) and *Berlin Mass* (1991)	Born in Paide, Estonia; emigrated to West Berlin in 1982; his early works were influenced by Shostakovich but developed his own austere style. Specialises in religious texts
Bennett, Richard Rodney 1936–	Five operas: *The Ledge* (1961), *The Midnight Thief* (1964), *The Mines of Sulphur* (1965), *Penny for a Song* (1966), *Victory* (1969); ballets: *Jazz Calendar* (1964) and *Isadora* (1981); setting of poems by Kathleen Raine for soprano, chorus and orchestra *Spells* (1974). Three symphonies	Born in Broadstairs, Kent; English composer and pianist educated at the Royal Academy of Music and in Paris under Pierre Boulez; ventured into the jazz field with his 1964 ballet *Jazz Calendar*, and followed this with *Jazz Pastoral* (1969); knighted in 1998. Lived in New York since 1979
Tavener, John 1944–	Operas include *Thérèse* (1979), *Mary of Egypt* (1992); many works for various instrumental groupings; *The Whale* (1967) was in the first ever concert by London Sinfonietta; cello and strings piece *The Protecting Veil* (1987); choral work: *We Shall See Him as He Is* (1990), *Song for Athene* (sung at the funeral of Diana, Princess of Wales)	Born in London; recent work pervaded by religious sentiment of Russian Orthodox Church which he joined in 1977; claims descent from John Taverner. He was knighted in 2000

Name	Principal works	Details
Adams, John 1947–	First operas *Nixon in China* (1987), *The Death of Klinghoffer* (1991). Ballets include *Shaker Loops* (1978), *Grand Pianola Music* (1982) and *The Chairman Dances* (1985). Most famous orchestral work: *Harmonium* (1981)	Born in Worcester, Massachusetts. Originally known as a minimalist but more recently has broadened his style and has consequently emerged as one of the best-known and most often performed American composers
Dillon, James 1950–	His major works include choral and vocal music including the cycle *L'évolution du vol* (1993) and the opera *Philomela* (2004), the orchestral works *helle Nacht* (1987), *ignis noster* (1992), *Via Sacra* (2000), and *La navette* (2001), as well as a violin concerto for Thomas Zehetmair (2000) and the piano concerto *Andromeda* (2006) for his wife, Noriko Kawai.	Born in Glasgow, Scotland. composer who is often regarded as belonging to the New Complexity school. Although studying art and design, linguistics, piano, acoustics, Indian rhythm, mathematics and computer music, is a self-taught composer. From 1982-2000, he worked on the *Nine Rivers* cycle, a 3-hour work for voices, strings, percussion, live electronics and computer-generated tape. The epic work was first performed in full in Glasgow, November 2010
Martland, Steven 1959–	Most famous orchestral work to date *Babi Yar* (1983); ensemble piece *Remembering Lennon* (1981)	English composer born in Liverpool; professed aim 'to return music to the streets'. His trademark flat-top haircut and Bermuda shorts, and his touring 'band' give him popular appeal to a wider audience
Turnage, Mark-Anthony	Two widely performed operas. *Greek,* first performed in 1988 at the Munich Biennale, is based on Steven Berkoff's adaptation of Oedipus the King. *The Silver Tassie*, first performed in 2000, is based on the play by Seán O'Casey. Also composed numerous orchestral and chamber works. His most recent opera, Anna Nicole, based on the life of American model, actress, and television personality Anna Nicole Smith (born Vickie Lynn Hogan, 1967-2007) premiered on 17 February 2011 at the Royal Opera House, London with Dutch soprano Eva-Maria Westbroek as Anna.	Born in Corringham, Essex. In 1990 he was appointed the first Radcliffe Composer in Association with the City of Birmingham Symphony Orchestra. In 2006, Turnage became co-composer in-residence of the Chicago Symphony Orchestra. Has been strongly influenced by jazz, in particular the work of Miles Davis.
Adès, Thomas 1971–	*Chamber Symphony* (1990) first performed in 1993; *Five Eliot Landscapes* (1990); *The Origin of the Harp* (1994); *The Premises Are Alarmed* (1996) for the opening of the Bridgewater Hall in which the Halle was conducted by Kent Nagano; *Powder Her Face* (1995) Chamber Opera; *Asyla* (1997)	English composer and pianist; second in piano section of the BBC Young Musician of the Year in 1989; graduated from Cambridge in 1992 with a double-starred first and established himself as a leading light both as a virtuoso and composer; Made his Proms debut in 1998 and the following year conducted the BBC Symphony Orchestra in the London premiere of *Asyla*

Operatic Characters (by opera)

Opera	*Composer*	*Character*	*Role*
Aida	Verdi	Aida	Ethiopian princess
		Amneris	Egyptian princess
		Amonasro	Aida's father (King of Ethiopia)
		Ramfis	High priest
		Rhadames	Captain of the Guard
Albert Herring	Britten	Albert Herring	Greengrocer's assistant
		Lady Bellows	Elderly autocrat
		Mr Gedge	Vicar
		Mr Upfold	Mayor
		Nancy	Baker's assistant
		Sid	Butcher's assistant
Alceste	Gluck	Admetus	Alceste's husband
		Alceste	Wife of Admetus
L'Amico Fritz	Mascagni	David	Rabbi
Andrea Chénier	Giordano	Charles Gérard	Revolutionary leader
		Comtesse de Coigny	Madeleine's mother
		Dumas	President of the tribunal
		Incredible	Spy
		Madeleine de Coigny	In love with Andrea Chénier
		Madelon	Old woman
		Mathieu	Waiter
		Roucher	Andrea's friend
Arlecchino	Busoni	Matteo del Sarto	Tailor
The Barber of Seville	Rossini	Almaviva	Count
		Ambrogio	Bartolo's servant
		Bartolo	Rosina's guardian
		Basilio	Singing teacher
		Berta	Housekeeper
		Figaro	Barber
		Fiorello	Servant
		Rosina	Dr Bartolo's ward
The Bartered Bride	Smetana	Esmerelda	Dancer
		Jenik	Micha's son
		Kathinka	Marenka's mother
		Kecal	Marriage broker
		Marenka	In love with Jenik
		Micha	Jenik's father
		Muff	Comedian
		Vasek	Micha's second son
The Beggar's Opera	Pepusch	Ben Budge	Highwayman
		Betty Doxy	Lady of the town
		Dolly Trull	Lady of the town
		Filch	Pickpocket
		Harry Paddington	Highwayman
		Jemmy Twitcher	Highwayman
		Jenny Diver	Lady of the night
		Lockit	Jailer
		Lucy Lockit	Jailer's daughter
		Macheath	Highwayman
		Mat of the Mint	Highwayman
		Miss Vixen	Lady of the town
		Molly Brazen	Lady of the town
		Mrs Coaxer	Lady of the town
		Mrs Trapes	Tally woman
		Nimming Ned	Highwayman
		Peachum	Fence
		Polly Peachum	Peachum's daughter, Macheath's wife
		Suky Tawdry	Lady of the town
Billy Budd	Britten	Arthur Jones	Seaman
		Billy Budd	Seaman and stammerer
		Captain Vere	Ship's captain
		Claggart	Master-at-arms
		Dansker	Seaman
		Donald	Seaman
		Mr Redburn	First lieutenant
		Red Whiskers	Impressed seaman
La Bohème	Puccini	Alcindoro	Musetta's escort
		Benoît	Landlord
		Colline	Philosopher
		Marcello	Painter
		Mimi	Seamstress
		Musetta	In love with Marcello
		Parpignol	Toy Vendor
		Rodolfo	Poet
Boris Godunov	Mussorgsky	Feodor	Son of Boris Godunov
		Grigorij	False Dimitri
		Kruschev	Boyar
		Marina Mnishek	Daughter of Voyevode Sandomir
		Missail	Vagrant
		Pimen	Hermit
		Rangoni	Jesuit
		Varlaam	Vagrant
		Xenia	Boris Godunov's daughter

Opera	*Composer*	*Character*	*Role*
Capriccio	Richard Strauss	Claison	Actress
		Flamand	Musician
		Olivier	Poet
Cardillac	Hindemith	Cardillac	Goldsmith
Carmen	Bizet	Carmen	Gypsy
		Don José	Corporal in the Guard
		El Dancairo	Smuggler
		El Remondado	Smuggler
		Escamillo	Bullfighter
		Frasquita	Gypsy
		Lillas Pastia	Innkeeper
		Mercedes	Gypsy
		Micaela	Village girl
		Morales	Officer of the Guard
		Zuniga	Captain of the Guard
Cavalleria Rusticana	Mascagni	Alfio	Teamster
		Lola	Alfio's wife
		Mama Lucia	Turiddu's mother
		Santuzza	In love with Turiddu
		Turiddu	Soldier
La Cenerentola	Rossini	Alidoro	Philosopher and magician
		Angelina	Don Magnifico's stepdaughter, Cinderella
		Clorinda & Thisbe	Don Magnifico's daughters
		Dandini	Valet
		Don Magnifico	Baron of Montflagon
		Don Ramiro	Prince of Salerno
La Clemenza di Tito	Mozart	Annius	Patrician
		Publius	Captain of Praetorian Guard
		Titus	Emperor of Rome
		Vitellia	Daughter of deposed emperor
Der Corregidor	Wolf	Frasquita	Tio Lucas' wife
		Juan Lopez	Mayor
		Manuela	Maid
		Repela	Valet to magistrate
		Tio Lucas	Miller
		Tonuelo	Court messenger
Così fan tutte	Mozart	Despina	Maid
		Don Alfonso	Don
		Dorabella	Fiordiligi's sister
		Ferrando	Dorabella's fiancé
		Fiordiligi	Dorabella's sister
		Guglielmo	Fiordiligi's fiancé
La Dame Blanche	Boieldieu	Dickson	Tenant of the White Lady
		Georges Brown	English officer
		Jenny	Dickson's wife
		MacIrton	Justice of the Peace
		Marguerite	Servant
Dido and Aeneas	Purcell	Aeneas	Trojan general
		Belinda	Lady-in-waiting
		Dido	Queen of Carthage
Don Carlos	Verdi	Don Carlos	Heir to Spanish throne
		Principessa Eboli	Lady in waiting
Don Giovanni	Mozart	Commendatore	Donna Anna's father
		Donna Anna	Don Ottavio's fiancée
		Donna Elvira	Lady from Burgos
		Leporello	Servant
		Masetto	Peasant
		Zerlina	Engaged to Matteo
Don Pasquale	Donizetti	Dr Malatesta	Don Pasquale's friend
		Ernesto	Don Pasquale's nephew
		Norina	Widow
Duke Bluebeard's Castle	Bartók	Judith	Bluebeard's last wife
Elektra	Richard Strauss	Aegisth	Klytemnestra's lover
		Chrysothemis	Elektra's sister
		Elektra	Agamemnon's daughter
		Orest	Elektra's brother
Emperor Jones	Gruenberg	Brutus Jones	Escaped convict, tribal leader
Ernani	Verdi	Don Carlos	King of Castile
		Elvira	Ernani's beloved
		Jago	Silva's squire
Eugene Onegin	Tchaikovsky	Filipievna	Nurse
		Prince Gremin	General
		Larina	Tatyana's mother
		Lenski	Olga's fiancé
		Olga	Tatiana's sister
		Tatiana	In love with Eugene
Falstaff	Verdi	Alice Ford	Citizen of Windsor
		Fenton	In love with Nanetta
		Frank Ford	Alice's husband
		Nanetta	Ford's daughter
Faust	Gounod	Marguérite	Beloved of Faust
		Martha Schwerlein	Marguérite's neighbour
La Favorita	Donizetti	Alfonso XI	King of Castile
		Balthazar	Superior of the monastery
		Leonara di Gusman	King's mistress

Opera	*Composer*	*Character*	*Role*
Fedora	Giordano	Cirillo	Coachman
		Désiré	Valet
		Dimitri	Groom
		Grech	Policeman
		Lorek	Surgeon
		Loris Ipanov	Count
		Nicola	Footman
Fidelio	Beethoven	Don Pizarro	Prison governor
		Florestan	Spanish nobleman
		Jacquino	Rocco's assistant
		Leonora	Florestan's wife
		Marcellina	Rocco's daughter
		Rocco	Chief jailer
Die Fledermaus	Johann Strauss II	Adele	Eisenstein's maid
		Dr Blind	Eisenstein's attorney
		Dr Falke	Eisenstein's friend
		Frank	Prison governor
		Frosch	Jailer
		Orlovsky	Rich Russian
		Rosalinda	Eisenstein's wife
The Flying Dutchman	Wagner	Daland	Sea captain
		Senta	Daland's daughter
Die Frau ohne Schatten	Richard Strauss	Barak	Dyer
		One-Arm	Barak's brother
		One-Eye	Barak's brother
La Gioconda	Ponchielli	Barnaba	Spy
		Enzo	Sea captain
		La Gioconda	Street singer, Enzo's love
The Girl of the Golden West		Ashby	Wells-Fargo agent
		Billy Jackrabbit	Red Indian
		Dick Johnson	alias Ramerrez, a bandit
		Happy, Trim	Miners
		Jack Rance	Sheriff
		Jake Wallace	Minstrel
		Joe, Larkens	Miners
		Minnie	Barmaid
		Nick	Bartender
		Wowkle	Billy's squaw
Hänsel and Gretel	Humperdinck	Gertrude	Mother of Hansel and Gretel
		Peter	Father of Hansel and Gretel
Háry János	Kodály	Abraham	Innkeeper
		Estrella	Lady-in-waiting
		Ilka	Háry's fiancée
		Marie-Louise	Napoleon's second wife
		Marzci	Marie's coachman
		Melusine	Countess
Hugh the Drover	Vaughan Williams	Aunt Jane	Sister of the constable
		John the Butcher	Mary's fiancé
		Mary	Constable's daughter
Idomeneo	Mozart	Arbace	Idomeneo's confidante
		Elettra	Greek princess
		Idamente	Idomeneo's son
		Idomeneo	King of Crete
		Ilia	Trojan princess
Intermezzo	Richard Strauss	Christine	Storch's wife
		Justizrat	Storch's friend
		Kammersänger	Storch's friend
		Robert Storch	Musical conductor
The Jewels of the Madonna	Wolf-Ferrari	Gennaro	Blacksmith
		Maliella	Gennaro's adopted sister
		Rafaele	Leader of the Camorra
Le Jongleur de Notre Dame	Massenet	Boniface	Cook
Jonny Spielt Auf (Jonny Plays on)	Krenek	Daniello & Jonny	Artists
		Max	Composer
		Yvonne	Chambermaid
Lakmé	Delibes	Gérald	English officer
		Hadji	Nilakantha's servant
		Lakmé	Nilakantha's daughter
		Mallika	Lakmé's slave
		Nilakantha	Brahmin priest
		Rose	An English lady
Lohengrin		Godfrey	Elsa's brother
		Lohengrin	Parsifal's son
		Ortrud	Wife of Frederick
		Telramund	Count of Brabant
The Love for Three Oranges	Prokofiev	Celio	Magician
		Farfarello	A devil
		Fata Morgana	Witch
		King of Clubs	Ruler of the kingdom
		Leandro	King of Spades and prime minister
		Linette, Nicoletta	Princesses hidden in an orange
		Ninetta	Princess hidden in an orange
		Pantaloon	King's friend
		Prince	Hypochondriac
		Princess Clarissa	King's niece

Opera	Composer	Character	Role
Lucia di Lammermoor	Donizetti	Alice/Alisa	Lucia's companion
		Arthur Bucklaw/Arturo	Lord
		Henry Ashton/Enrico	Lord of Lammermoor
		Edgar/Edgardo	Edgar of Ravenswood
		Norman/Normando	Follower of Ashton
		Raymond/Raimondo	Chaplain, Lucy's tutor
Lucrezia Borgia	Donizetti	Alfonso d'Este	Duke of Ferrara, Lucrezia's third husband
		Gennaro	Venetian nobleman, Lucrezia's son
		Gubetta	Servant to Lucrezia
		Lucrezia Borgia	Duchess of Ferrara
		Maffio Orsini	Lucrezia's enemy
		Rustighello	Alfonso's henchman
		Vitellozzo	Nobleman, Gennaro's friend
Lulu	Berg	Alwa	Writer
		Dr Schön	Editor
		Lulu	Prostitute
		Prince	Traveller in Africa
Madame Butterfly	Puccini	The Bonze	Priest
		Cio-Cio-San	A geisha, Pinkerton's wife
		Goro	Marriage broker
		Kate	Pinkerton's American wife
		Lt Pinkerton	Lieutenant in US Navy
		Sharpless	US consul in Nagasaki
		Suzuki	Servant
		Trouble	Cio-Cio-San's child
		Yamadori	Rich Japanese
The Magic Flute	Mozart	Monostatos	Servant
		Pamina	Daughter of Queen of the Night
		Papagena	Destined to be Papageno's wife
		Papageno	Bird catcher
		Sarastro	High priest
Manon	Massenet	Chevalier des Grieux	Manon's love
		Comte des Grieux	Chevalier's father
		de Bretigny	A nobleman
		Lescaut	A gambler
		Manon	Lescaut's cousin
The Marriage of Figaro	Mozart	Almaviva	Count
		Antonio	Gardener
		Barbarina	Antonio's daughter
		Cherubino	Page
		Don Basilio	Organist
		Don Curzio	Lawyer
		Figaro	Servant to Almaviva
		Marcellina	Housekeeper
		Susanna	Maid
A Masked Ball	Verdi	Amelia	Riccardo's love, wife of Renato
		Oscar	Riccardo's page
		Renato	Riccardo's secretary
		Riccardo	Governor of Louisiana
		Silvano	A young sailor
		Ulrica	Fortune teller
The Mastersingers of Nuremberg	Wagner	Augustin Moser	Mastersinger and tailor
		Balthasar Zorn	Mastersinger and pewterer
		Sixtus Beckmesser	Mastersinger and town clerk
		Conrad Nachtigall	Mastersinger and bucklemaker
		David	Hans Sachs's apprentice
		Eva	Pogner's daughter
		Fritz Kothner	Mastersinger and baker
		Hans Foltz	Mastersinger and coppersmith
		Hans Sachs	Mastersinger and cobbler
		Hans Schwarz	Mastersinger and stocking weaver
		Hermann Ortel	Mastersinger and soap boiler
		Kunz Vogelgesang	Mastersinger and furrier
		Magdalena	Nurse
		Ulrich Eisslinger	Mastersinger and grocer
		Veit Pogner	Mastersinger and goldsmith (Eva's father)
		Walter von Stolzing	Franconian knight
Mathis der Maler	Hindemith	Albrecht von Brandenburg	Archbishop of Mainz
		Mathis	Painter (Grünewald)
		Riedinger	Rich Lutheran
		Truchsess von Waldburg	Leader of the army
		Ursula	Riedinger's daughter
		Wolfgang Capito	Councillor
The Mother of Us All	Thomson	Susan B Anthony	American suffragette
Nabucco	Verdi	Abdallo	Nabucco's officer
		Abigaille	Nabucco's adopted daughter
		Fenena	Nabucco's daughter
		Nabucco	Nebuchadnezzar, King of Babylon
		Zaccaria	High Priest of Jerusalem
Norma	Bellini	Adalgisa	Temple virgin
		Clotilde	Norma's friend
		Flavio	Centurion
		Norma	Druid priestess
		Oroveso	Norma's father
		Pollione	Proconsul of Rome

Opera	Composer	Character	Role
Oberon	Weber	Abdullah	Pirate
		Babekan	Saracen prince
		Charlemagne	Emperor of the Franks
		Fatima	Reiza's companion
		Haroun al Rashid	Calif of Baghdad
		Namouna	Fatima's grandmother
		Reiza	Haroun el Rashid's daughter
Oedipus Rex	Stravinsky	Creon	Jocasta's brother
		Jocasta	Wife of Oedipus
		Oedipus	King of Thebes
		Tiresias	Blind soothsayer
Orfeo et Euridice	Gluck	Amor	God of love
		Euridice	Orfeo's wife
		Orfeo	Singer poet
I Pagliacci	Leoncavallo	Beppe	Harlequin
		Canio	Pagliaccio (clown)
		Nedda	Canio's wife
		Silvio	In love with Nedda
Palestrina	Pfitzner	Avosmediano	Bishop of Cadiz
		Ighino	Palestrina's son
		Lucretia	Palestrina's wife
		Palestrina	Composer
Parsifal	Wagner	Amfortas	King of the Grail
		King Titurel	Father of Amfortas
		Klingsor	Magician
		Kundry	Bewitched woman
		Parsifal	Knight of the Holy Grail
Pelléas et Mélisande	Debussy	Geneviève	Mother of Pelléas
		Golaud	Arkel's grandson
		Mélisande	Golaud's wife
		Pelléas	Arkel's grandson
		Yniold	Golaud's son
Peter Grimes	Britten	Bob Boles	Fisherman
		Ellen Orford	Schoolteacher
		John	Peter's apprentice
		Ned Keene	Apothecary
		Peter Grimes	Fisherman
The Pilgrim's Progress	Vaughan Williams	Apollyon	Fallen angel
		Mistrust, Obstinate	Neighbours
		Pilgrim	Pilgrim
		Pliable	Neighbour
		Timorous	Neighbour
		Watchful	Porter
The Poisoned Kiss	Vaughan Williams	Amaryllus	Empress's son
		Angelica	Tormentilla's maid
		Dipsacus	Magician
		Gallanthus	Amaryllus's sister
		Hob	Servant of Dipsacus
		Lob	Assistant of Dipsacus
		Tormentilla	Daughter of Dipsacus
Porgy and Bess	Gershwin	Bess	Porgy's mistress, formerly Crown's
		Clara	Jake's wife
		Crown	Stevedore
		Frazier	Catfish Row 'lawyer'
		Jake	Fisherman
		Jim	Cotton picker
		Lily	Strawberry woman
		Maria	Cookshop keeper
		Mr Archdale	White man
		Peter	Honey-man
		Porgy	A crippled beggar
		Sportin' Life	Dope dealer
Prince Igor	Borodin	Eroshka	Gudok player
		Gzak	Polovtsian Khan
		Jaroslavna	Prince Igor's wife
		Kontchak	Polovtsian Khan
		Kontchakovna	Kontchak's daughter
		Ovlour	Polovtsian traitor
		Prince Igor	Prince of Seversk
		Vladimir Igorevitch	Igor's son
		Vladimir Yaroslavovitch	Yaroslavna's brother
The Rake's Progress	Stravinsky	Baba the Turk	Bearded lady
		Tom Rakewell	The Rake
		Trulove	Anne's father
The Rape of Lucretia	Britten	Bianca	Nurse
		Collatinus	Soldier
		Junius	Roman general
		Lucia	Lucretia's attendant
		Lucretia	Wife of Collatinus
Rienzi	Wagner	Adriano	Colonna's son
		Baroncelli	Roman citizen
		Cola Rienzi	Papal legate
		Irene	Rienzi's sister
		Paolo Orsini	Patrician
		Raimondo	Papal legate

Opera	*Composer*	*Character*	*Role*
Rigoletto	Verdi	Cavaliere Marullo	Courtier
		Duke of Mantua	Nobleman
		Gilda	Rigoletto's daughter
		Maddalena	Sparafucile's sister
		Matteo Borsa	Courtier
		Rigoletto	Gilda's father, a jester
Der Ring des Nibelungen	Wagner	Alberich	Nibelung dwarf
		Brünnhilde	Valkyrie
		Donner	Norse god
		Erda	Earth goddess
		Fafner & Fasolt	Giants, builders of Valhalla
		Flosshilde	Rhinemaiden
		Freia	Goddess of youth and beauty
		Fricka	Wotan's wife
		Froh	Norse god
		Gerhilde	Valkyrie
		Grimgerde	Valkyrie
		Gunther	Hagen's half-brother
		Gutrune	Gunther's sister
		Helmwige	Valkyrie
		Hunding	Siegmund's enemy
		Loge	Norse god
		Mime	A Nibelung
		Ortlinde	Valkyrie
		Rossweisse	Valkyrie
		Siegfried	Son of Siegmund and Sieglunde
		Sieglunde	Siegmund's twin sister
		Siegmund	Mortal son of Wotan
		Waltraute	Valkyrie
		Wellgunde	Rhine maiden
		Woglinde	Rhine maiden
		Wotan	Norse god
La Rondine	Puccini	Bianca	Magda's friend
		Crébillon	Perichaud's friend
		Lisette	Magda's maid
		Magda	Salon owner, Rambaldo's mistress
		Périchaud	Rambaldo's friend
		Prunier	Poet
		Rambaldo	Banker
		Ruggero	Son of Rambaldo's childhood friend
		Suzy	Magda's friend
		Yvette	Magda's friend
Der Rosenkavalier	Richard Strauss	Annina	Valzacchi's partner
		Baron Ochs	Sophie's would-be suitor
		Faninal	Sophie's father
		Mahomet	Negro page
		Marianne	Sophie's duenna
		Marschallin	Princess
		Octavian	Bearer of the Rose
		Sophie	Daughter of Faninal
		Valzacchi	Scandalmonger
Ruddigore	Sullivan	Mad Margaret	Mad woman
Ruslan and Lyudmila	Glinka	Bayan	Bard
		Chernomor	An evil dwarf
		Farlaf	Warrior
		Finn	Wizard
		Gorislava	Ratmir's lover
		Lyudmila	a noblewoman
		Naina	Witch
		Ratmir	Knight, suitor to Lyudmila
		Ruslan	Suitor to Lyudmila
		Svyetozer	Lyudmila's father
Salome	Richard Strauss	Herod	Ruler of Galilee
		Herodias	Herod's wife
		John the Baptist	Jewish prophet
		Narraboth	Captain of the Guard
		Salome	Daughter of Herodias
Samson et Dalila	Saint-Saëns	Abimielech	Satrap of Gaza
The Secret Marriage	Cimarosa	Carolina	Geronimo's daughter
		Elisetta	Geronimo's older daughter
		Fidalma	Geronimo's sister
		Geronimo	Citizen of Bologna
		Paolino	Carolina's secret husband
The Sleepwalker (La Sonnambula)	Bellini	Amina	The sleepwalking girl
		Elvino	Farmer
Il Tabarro	Puccini	Giorgetta	Michele's wife
		Luigi	Stevedore, Giorgetta's lover
		Michele	Barge owner
		Talpa	Stevedore
		Tinca	Stevedore
The Tales of Hoffmann	Offenbach	Chochenille	Spalanzani's servant
		Coppelius	Scientist
		Dapertutto	Sorcerer
		Dr Miracle	Doctor
		Frantz	Crespel's servant

Opera	Composer	Character	Role
The Tales of Hoffmann (continued)	Offenbach	Hermann	Student
		Hoffmann	Poet
		Lindorf	Councillor of Nuremberg
		Luther	Innkeeper
		Nathanael	Student
		Nicklaus	Hoffmann's friend
		Olympia	Mechanical doll
		Pittichinaccio	Giulietta's admirer
		Spalanzani	Inventor
		Stella	Opera singer
Tannhäuser	Wagner	Biterolf	Knight
		Elisabeth	Hermann's niece
		Hermann	Landgrave of Thuringia
		Reinmar von Zweter	Knight
		Tannhäuser	Knight
		Venus	Supernatural seductress
		Walther von der Vogelweide	Knight
		Wolfram	Knight
Tosca	Puccini	Baron Scarpia	Chief of Police
		Cavaradossi	Painter
		Cesare Angelotti	Escaped political prisoner
		Mario Cavaradossi	Painter
		Tosca	Singer
La Traviata	Verdi	Alfredo Germont	Violetta's lover (a singer)
		Annina	Violetta's confidante
		Douphol	Baron
		Violetta Valery	Courtesan
Tristan und Isolde	Wagner	Brangäne	Isolde's maid
		Isolde	Irish princess
		King Marke	King of Cornwall
		Kurvenal	Tristan's retainer
		Melot	Courtier
		Tristan	Cornish knight
The Trojans (Les Troyens)	Berlioz	Andromaque	Hector's widow
		Chorèbe	Cassandra's lover
		Hylas	Trojan sailor
		Iopas	Poet
		Narbal	Dido's minister
		Panthée	Priest
		Polyxène	Priam's daughter
		Priam	King of Troy
Il Trovatore	Verdi	Azucena	Gypsy woman
		Count de Luna	Count of Aragon
		Ferrando	Captain of the Guard
		Manrico	Troubadour
		Leonora	Beloved of Manrico
The Tsar Has His Photograph Taken	Weill	Angèle	Photographer
Turandot	Busoni	Adelma	Turandot's slave
		Barak	Servant
		Calaf	Suitor to Turandot
		Pantalone	Minister
		Queen Mother of Samarkand	Negress
Turandot	Puccini	Calaf	Suitor to Turandot
		Emperor Altoum	Turandot's father
		Liù	Slave girl
		Pang	Lord of Provisions
		Ping	Chinese Grand Chancellor
		Pong	Lord of the Imperial Kitchen
		Princess Turandot	Daughter of Altoum
A Village Romeo and Juliet	Delius	The Dark Fiddler	Real owner of land
		Manz	Farmer
		Marti	Farmer
		Sali	Manz's daughter
		Vreli	Marti's daughter
Wozzeck	Berg	Marie	Prostitute
		Wozzeck	Soldier
The Wreckers	Smyth	Lawrence	Lighthouse keeper
Zazà	Leoncavallo	Bussy	Journalist
		Cascart	Music-hall performer
		Duclou	Stage manager
		Mme Dufresne	Milio's wife
		Lartigen	Monologist
		Marco	Dufresne's butler
		Marlardot	Music-hall owner
		Michelin	Journalist
		Milio Dufresne	Zaza's lover
		Natalia	Zazà's maid
		Toto	Dufresne's child
		Zazà	Music-hall singer

Operas and Operettas

Operas and operettas	*Composer*	*First performance*	*Librettist*	*General information*
Adriana Lecouvreur	Francesco Cilea	1902 Milan	Colautti	Enrico Caruso in the tenor role of Maurizio at debut
L'Africaine	Giacomo Meyerbeer	1865 Paris	Scribe	Based on fictitious events in the life of Vasco da Gama
Ägyptische Helena	Richard Strauss	1928 Dresden	Hofmannsthal	English title: *The Egyptian Helen*
Aida	Giuseppe Verdi	1871 Cairo	Ghislanzoni	Not written to celebrate opening of Suez Canal
Ainadamar	Osvaldo Golijov	2005 Santa Fe, New Mexico	David Henry Hwang	Story of Federico García Lorca and his lover, Catalan actress Margarita Xirgu
Akhnaten	Philip Glass	1984 Stuttgart	Glass	Dick Riddell, Bob Israel & Shalom Goldman helped with libretto
Albert Herring	Benjamin Britten	1947 Glyndebourne	Crozier	1st work written for the English Opera Group
Alceste	Christoph Gluck	1767 Vienna	Calzabigi	Based on the play *Alcestis* by Euripides.
Aleko	Sergei Rachmaninov	1892 Moscow	Nemirovich-Danchenko	Adaptation of the poem *The Gypsies* by Alexander Pushkin
Alfred	Thomas Arne	1740 London	Thomson and Mallet	Contains song 'Rule, Britannia'
Alice in Wonderland	Unsuk Chin (b. 1961)	2007 Munich	David Henry Hwang	Chin's first opera in which she also contributed towards the libretto
Almira	George Frederick Handel	1705 Hamburg	Feustking	Handel's first opera
Alzira	Giuseppe Verdi	1845 Naples	Cammarano	Based on the play *Alzire, ou les Américains* by Voltaire.
Amahl and the Night Visitors	Gian Carlo Menotti	1951 New York	Menotti	First opera written for TV
Amelia	Daron Hagen	2010 Seattle	Gardner McFall	Based on a story by Stephen Wadsworth
Amelia Goes to the Ball	Gian Carlo Menotti	1937 Philadelphia	Menotti	Composed in 1936 when Menotti was twenty-three.
L'Amico Fritz	Pietro Mascagni	1891 Rome	Daspuro	Based on novel *L'ami Fritz* by Émile Erckmann & Pierre-Alexandre Chatrian.
Amleto (Hamlet)	Franco Faccio	1865 Genoa	Boito	Revised for La Scala production 12 February 1871 – its last performance
Andrea Chénier	Umberto Giordano	1896 Milan	Illica	Based on the life of the French poet (1762-1794) executed during French Revolution.
Aniara	Karl-Birger Blomdahl	1959 Stockholm	Lindegren	Based on the poem *Aniara* by Harry Martinson
Anne Boleyn	Gaetano Donizetti	1830 Milan	Romani	Jane Seymour/Anne Boleyn duet "Sul suo capo aggravi un Dio" operatic masterpiece
Antar	Gabriel Dupont	1921 Paris	Dupont	First performed after Dupont's death in a grandiose and exotically dark production
Antony and Cleopatra	Samuel Barber	1966 New York (Met)	Zeffirelli and Barber	Premiere on 16 September was also the opening of the Metropolitan Opera House
Arabella	Richard Strauss	1933 Dresden	Hofmannsthal	The composer's sixth and last operatic collaboration with the librettist
Ariadne auf Naxos	Richard Strauss	1916 Vienna	Hofmannsthal	Developed from a thirty-minute divertissement Strauss first performed in 1912.
Ariane et Barbe-bleu	Paul Dukas	1907 Paris	Maeterlinck	English translation: Ariadne and Bluebeard
Arlecchino (Harlequin)	Ferruccio Busoni	1917 Zurich	Busoni	Unusual in that the title role of Arlecchino is primarily a speaking role
Armide	Christoph Gluck	1777 Paris	Quinault	Gluck's own favourite among his works
Artaxerxes	Thomas Arne	1762 London	Metastasio	The first English opera seria
At the Boar's Head	Gustav Holst	1925 Manchester	Holst	Based on Shakespeare's *Henry IV, Part 1* and *Henry IV, Part 2.*
The Barber of Seville	Giovanni Paisiello	1782 St Petersburg	Petrosellini	Libretto differs from Sterbini's by emphasising the love story rather than the comedy
The Barber of Seville	Gioachino Rossini	1816 Rome	Sterbini	Based on Beaumarchais comedy
The Bartered Bride	Bedrich Smetana	1866 Prague	Sabina	Notable for folksongs and Bohemian dance forms such as the polka and furiant
The Bassarids	Hans Werner Henze	1966 Salzburg	Auden and Kallman	Constructed like a classical symphony in four 'movements'
The Bear	William Walton	1967 Aldeburgh	Dehn and Walton	Based on the play of the same title by Anton Chekhov
Beatrice Cenci	Berthold Goldschmidt	1988 London	Esslin	Prizewinner in Festival of Britain Competition 1951
Béatrice et Bénédict	Hector Berlioz	1862 Baden-Baden	Berlioz	Based on Shakespeare's *Much Ado About Nothing.*
The Beautiful Galathea	Franz von Suppe	1865 Vienna	Henrion and von Suppe	Poly Henrion was the pseudonym of Leonhard Kohl von Kohlenegg
The Beggar's Opera	Christoph Pepusch	1728 London	Gay	Pepusch merely provided incidental music to John Gay's ballad opera
Belfagor	Ottorino Respighi	1923 Milan	Claudio Gaustalla	Based on the comedy *Belfagor* of Ercole Luigi Morselli
Belisario	Gaetano Donizetti	1836 Venice	Cammarano	Based on the life of Belisarius the 6th century Byzantine Empire
La Belle Hélène	Jacques Offenbach	1864 Paris	Meilhac and Halévy	Opéra bouffe parodying Helen's elopement with Paris, which set off the Trojan War
The Bells of Corneville	Robert Planquette	1877 Paris and New York	Clairville and Gabet	Aka *Les cloches de Corneville*, or in English as *The Chimes of Normandy*
Benvenuto Cellini	Hector Berlioz	1838 Paris	Wailly and Barbier	Based on the memoirs of the Florentine sculptor Benvenuto Cellini
Berenice	George Frederick Handel	1737 London	Salvi	Originally entitled *Berenice, regina d'Egitto* (Berenice, Queen of Egypt)
Billy Budd	Benjamin Britten	1951 London	E.M Forster and Crozier	Only men in the cast
The Black Mask	Krzysztof Penderecki	1986 Salzburg	Kupfer and Penderecki	Based on the Gerhart Hauptmann play of the same title
Blond Eckbert	Judith Weir	1994 London	Weir	Based on short story Der blonde Eckbert by German Romantic writer Ludwig Tieck
Bluebeard's Castle	Béla Bartók	1918 Budapest	Béla Balázs	Bartók's only opera

Operas and operettas	*Composer*	*First performance*		*Librettist*	*General information*
Boccaccio	Franz von Suppé	1879	Vienna	Walzel and Génée	Based on Giovanni Boccaccio's *The Decameron*
La Bohème	Ruggiero Leoncavallo	1897	Venice	Leoncavallo	Based on *Scènes de la vie de bohème* by Henri Murger.
La Bohème	Giacomo Puccini	1896	Turin	Giacosa and Illica	Although Leoncavallo's version is rarely seen Puccini's masterpiece remains popular
The Bohemian Girl	Michael Balfe	1843	London	Bunn	Title translates as *La Bohème*, though not the same story
Boris Godunov	Modeste Mussorgsky	1874	St Petersburg	Mussorgsky	Mussorgsky's only completed opera
Boulevard Solitude	Hans Werner Henze	1952	Hanover	Grete Weil	A modern telling of François Prévost's *Manon Lescaut*
Die Brautwahl	Ferruccio Busoni	1912	Hamburg	Busoni	Based on a short story by E.T.A. Hoffmann. English title: The Bridal Choice
The Burning Fiery Furnace	Benjamin Britten	1966	Orford	William Plomer	One of three Parables for Church Performances composed by Britten
The Caliph of Baghdad	François Boieldieu	1800	Paris	Saint-Just	Opéra comique in one act
La Calisto	Pietro Francesco Cavalli	1651	Venice	Faustini	Based on the mythological story of Callisto
La Campana Sommersa	Ottorino Respighi	1927	Hamburg	Guastalla	Title translates as *The Submerged Bell*
Candide	Leonard Bernstein	1956	Boston	Hellmann	Based on the play *Die versunkene Glocke* by German author Gerhart Hauptmann
El Capitán	John Philip Sousa	1896	Boston	Klein	Lyrics by Charles Klein and Tom Frost
Capriccio	Richard Strauss	1942	Munich	Krauss and Strauss	Subtitled "A Conversation Piece for Music".
I Capuleti e i Montecchi	Vincenzo Bellini	1830	Venice	Romani	The Capulets and the Montagues, i.e. Romeo and Juliet
Cardillac	Paul Hindemith	1926	Dresden	Ferdinand Lion	Based on the short story *Das Fräulein von Scuderi* by E.T.A. Hoffmann
Caritas	Robert Saxton	1991	Wakefield	Wesker	Robert Saxton was born in London in 1953 and started composing at the age of six
Carmen	Georges Bizet	1875	Paris	Meilhac and Halévy	Carmen dies by stabbing (at the hands of Don José)
Castor and Pollux	Jean-Philippe Rameau	1737	Paris	Bernard	Based on the stories concerning the mythological twins
The Catiline Conspiracy	Iain Hamilton	1974	Stirling	Hamilton	Iain Hamilton (born Glasgow, 6 June 1922; died London, 21 July 2000)
Cavalleria Rusticana	Pietro Mascagni	1890	Rome	Menasci and Targioni-Tozzetti	Often performed in a double-bill with I Pagliacci by Ruggero Leoncavallo.
Cendrillon (Cinderella)	Nicolò Isouard	1810	Paris	Étienne	opéra comique with spoken dialogue between the musical numbers
Cendrillon (Cinderella)	Jules Massenet	1899	Paris	Henry Cain	Based on Perrault's 1698 version of the Cinderella fairy tale
La Cenerentola (Cinderella)	Gioachino Rossini	1817	Rome	Ferretti	Best-known version of the fairy tale by Charles Perrault
Chérubin	Jules Massenet	1905	Monte Carlo	Henry Cain and Francis de Croisset	The story of Cherubino after the marriage of Figaro
Cheryomushki	Dmitry Shostakovich	1959	Moscow	Mass and Chervinsky	Shostakovich's only operetta
The Chocolate Soldier	Oscar Straus	1908	Vienna	Jacobson and Bernauer	Based on G B Shaw's play *Arms and the Man*
Christmas Eve	Nikolay Rimsky-Korsakov	1895	St Petersburg	Rimsky-Korsakov	Based on Gogol story
Le Cid	Jules Massenet	1885	Paris	D'Ennery, Gallet and Blau	Based on the play of the same name by Pierre Corneille
La Clemenza di Tito	Wolfgang Amadeus Mozart	1791	Prague	Metastasio	Mozart's last opera
Comedy on the Bridge	Bohuslav Martinu	1937	Prague (Radio)	Martinu	Originally a radio opera
La Commedia	Louis Andriessen	2008	Amsterdam	Andriessen	Film opera with texts by Dante and Vondel and from the Old Testament
Conchita	Riccardo Zandonai	1911	Milan	Vaucaire and Zangarini	Based on Pierre Louÿs's 1898 novel *La Femme et le pantin*
Confessions of a Justified Sinner	Thomas Wilson	1976	York	John Currie	Based on the novel by James Hogg
The Consul	Gian Carlo Menotti	1950	Philadelphia	Menotti	The Consul represents bureaucratic red tape
Le Coq d'Or	Nikolay Rimsky-Korsakov	1909	Moscow	Belsky	Rimsky-Korsakov's 14th and last opera
The Coronation of Poppaea	Claudio Monteverdi	1643	Venice	Busenello	Monteverdi's last opera
Der Corregidor (The Magistrate)	Hugo Wolf	1896	Mannheim	Mayreder	Based on *The Three-Cornered Hat* by Alarcón
Il Corsaro	Giuseppe Verdi	1848	Trieste	Piave	Based on Byron's poem *The Corsair*
Così fan tutte	Wolfgang Amadeus Mozart	1790	Vienna	da Ponte	Role of Fiordiligi long regarded as unsingable
The Count of Luxemburg	Franz Lehár	1909	Vienna	Wilner and Bodanzky	German title: *Der Graf von Luxemburg*
Cox and Box	Arthur Sullivan	1867	London	Burnand	Based on the 1847 farce *Box and Cox* by John Maddison Morton
The Cunning Little Vixen	Leoš Janáček	1924	Brno	Janácek	Incorporates Moravian folk music and rhythms within its composition.
Curlew River	Benjamin Britten	1964	Orford	Plomer	A church parable
Dafne	Jacopo Peri	1598	Florence	Rinuccini	Generally regarded to be the earliest opera
Dalibor	Bedrich Smetana	1868	Prague	Spindler	Translation of German text by Joseph Wenzig
La Dame Blanche (White Lady)	François Boieldieu	1825	Paris	Scribe	Based on Scott's *The Monastery* and *Guy Mannering*
Danton's Death	Gottfried Von Einem	1947	Salzburg	Blacher and Von Einem	Based on drama by Büchner
Daphne	Richard Strauss	1938	Dresden	Gregor	Subtitled "Bucolic Tragedy in One Act".
Dardanus	Jean-Philipe Rameau	1739	Paris	De La Bruyère	Rameau replaced Jean-Baptiste Lully as the dominant composer of French opera
The Daughter of the Regiment	Gaetano Donizetti	1840	Paris	Saint-Georges and Bayard	Written while the composer was living in Paris
David	Darius Milhaud	1954	Jerusalem	Lunel	Milhaud was a member of Les Six
Day of Peace (Friedenstag)	Richard Strauss	1938	Munich	Gregor	The opera thematically expresses anti-war sentiments
Dead Man Walking	Jake Heggie	2000	San Francisco	Terrence McNally	Based on the book of the same name by Sister Helen Prejean

Operas and operettas	*Composer*	*First performance*		*Librettist*	*General information*
Death in Venice	Benjamin Britten	1973	Aldeburgh	Myfanwy Piper	Britten's last opera
Debora e Jaële	Ildebrando Pizzetti	1922	Milan	Pizzetti	Based on the story of Deborah and Jael from the Book of Judges in the Bible
Deidamia	George Frederick Handel	1741	London	Rolli	Handel's last opera
The Deserted Island	Franz Joseph Haydn	1779	Eszterháza	Metastasio	Also the title of an opera by G Scarlatti
Les Deux Journées (The Two Days)	Luigi Cherubini	1800	Paris	Bouilly	Known in Britain as *The Water Carrier*
Les Dialogues des Carmélites	Francis Poulenc	1957	Milan	Lavery	Paris and San Francisco performances followed its debut almost immediately
Dido and Aeneas	Henry Purcell	1689	Chelsea	Nahum Tate	Frst performance at Josias Priest's girls' school in London
A Dinner Engagement	Lennox Berkeley	1954	Aldeburgh	Paul Dehn	Opera in Two Scenes
Doctor Atomic	John Adams	2005	San Francisco	Peter Sellars	Reflects on angst of those at Los Alamos, New Mexico during Manhattan Project
Doctor Miracle	Georges Bizet	1857	Paris	Battu and Halévy	Joint winner of the Offenbach Prize with Lecocq
Doctor Miracle	Charles Lecocq	1857	Paris	Battu and Halévy	Joint winner of the Offenbach Prize with Bizet
The Doctor of Myddfai	Peter Maxwell Davies	1996	Cardiff	Pountney	Adapted from an ancient Welsh legend which inspired *The Lady of the Lake*
Doktor Faust	Ferruccio Busoni	1925	Dresden	Busoni	Completed after Busoni's death by Jarnach
Dollar Princess	Leo Fall	1907	Vienna	Willner and Grünbaum	Musical in three acts
Don Carlos	Giuseppe Verdi	1867	Paris	Méry and Du Locle	Also known as *Don Carlo*
Don Giovanni	Wolfgang Amadeus Mozart	1787	Prague	Da Ponte	Based on Bertati's *Don Juan* (1775)
Don Pasquale	Gaetano Donizetti	1843	Paris and London	Ruffini	Donizetti was music director for Emperor Ferdinand I of Austria
Don Quixote	Jules Massenet	1910	Monte Carlo	Henry Cain	Based on novel by Miguel de Cervantes
The Duenna	Roberto Gerhard	1949	BBC Radio	Gerhard and Hassall	Based on Sheridan work
The Duenna	Sergey Prokofiev	1946	Leningrad	Prokofiev and Mendelson	Based on Sheridan work
Duke Bluebeard's Castle	Béla Bartók	1918	Budapest	Béla Balázs	Based on the French literary tale *La Barbe bleue* by Charles Perrault
Duke of Alba	Gaetano Donizetti	1882	Rome	Scribe	Completed by Salvi
The Dwarf (Der Zwerg)	Alexander Zemlinsky	1922	Cologne	G C Klaren	Based on Oscar Wilde's *The Birthday of the Infanta*
Edgar	Giacomo Puccini	1889	Milan	Fontana	Based on the play in verse *The Cup and the Lips* by Alfred de Musset
Einstein on the Beach	Philip Glass	1976	Avignon	Knowles, Childs, Johnson	Composed in collaboration with Robert Wilson
Electrification of the Soviet Union	Nigel Osborne	1987	Glyndebourne	Craig Raine	Based on Pasternak's 'Last Summer' and 'Spectorsky'
Elegy for Young Lovers	Hans Werne Henze	1961	Schwetzingen	Auden and Kallman	First performance in English at Glyndebourne
Elektra	Richard Strauss	1909	Dresden	Hofmannsthal	First of many collaborations between Strauss and Hofmannsthal
L'Elisir d'Amore	Gaetano Donizetti	1832	Milan	Romani	English title: *The Elixir of Love*
Elizabeth, Queen of England	Gioachino Rossini	1815	Naples	Giovanni Schmidt	Based on Sophia Lee's novel *The Recess*
The Emerald Isle	Arthur Sullivan	1901	London (Savoy)	Basil Hood	Posthumous comic opera completed by Edward German
The Emperor Jones	Louis Gruenberg	1933	New York	Gruenberg	Adapted by the composer from Eugene O'Neill's 1920 play of the same name
L'Enfant et les Sortilèges	Maurice Ravel	1925	Monte Carlo	Colette	English title: *The Child and the Spells*
The English Cat	Hans Werner Henze	1983	Schwetzingen	Edward Bond	Based on *The heartbreak of an English cat* by Honoré de Balzac
Ernani	Giuseppe Verdi	1844	Venice	Piave	Based on Victor Hugo's play *Hernani*
Esclarmonde	Jules Massenet	1889	Paris	Blau and de Gramont	American soprano Sibyl Sanderson made her debut in the title role for its opening
L'Étoile (The Star)	Emmanuel Chabrier	1877	Paris	Leterrier and Vanloo	Score was rewritten by Ivan Caryll for an adaptation at the Savoy Theatre in 1899
L'Étoile du Nord (The North Star)	Giacomo Meyerbeer	1854	Paris	Eugene Scribe	Notable feature of the opera is the triple march in the finale to the second act
Eugene Onegin	Pyotr Tchaikovsky	1879	Moscow	Shilovsky and Tchaikovsky	Based on Alexander Pushkin's novel in verse of the same name
Euryanthe	Carl Maria Weber	1823	Vienna	Helmina von Chézy	Rarely performed as the libretto is deemed weak
The Excursions of Mr Brouček	Leoš Janáček	1920	Prague	Janáček	Full title: *The Excursions of Mr. Brouček to the Moon and to the 15th Century*
The Fair Maid of Perth	Georges Bizet	1867	Paris	St George and Adenis	Based on Sir Walter Scott's play of the same name
The Faithful Shepherd	George Frederick Handel	1712	London	Rossi	Based on Guarini's play
The Fall of the House of Usher	Claude Debussy	1977	New Haven	Debussy	Based on Edgar Allan Poe work but left unfinished and reconstructed by W Harwood
Falstaff	Giuseppe Verdi	1893	Milan	Boito	Verdi's last opera
Fanny Robin	Edward Harper	1975	Edinburgh	Harper	Based on Wessex poems and *Far From the Madding Crowd*
Faust	Ludwig Spohr	1816	Prague	J K Bernard	Not based on Goethe's Faust
Faust	Charles Gounod	1859	Paris	Barbier and Carré	Based on Carré's *Faust et Marguerite* and Goethe's *Faust*
La Favola d'Orfeo	Claudio Monteverdi	1607	Mantua	Alessandro Striggio	Tells the story of Orpheus' descent to Hades in search of Eurydice
La Favorite	Gaetano Donizetti	1840	Paris	Royer and Vaëz	Based on the play *Le comte de Comminges* by Baculard d'Arnaud
Fedora	Umberto Giordano	1898	Milan	Colautti	Based on Sardou's play of the same name
Die Feen (The Fairies)	Richard Wagner	1888	Munich	Wagner	Wagner's first opera
Fennimore and Gerda	Frederick Delius	1919	Frankfurt	Delius	Delius's 6th and last opera
Der Ferne Klang	Franz Schreker	1912	Frankfurt	Franz Schreker	English title: *The Distant Sound*
La Fiamma	Ottorino Respighi	1934	Rome	Claudio Guastalla	Based on Hans Wiers-Jenssen's 1908 play *Anne Pedersdotter, The Witch*
Fidelio, or the Triumph of Married Love	Ludwig van Beethoven	1805	Vienna	Josef Sonnleithner	Beethoven's only opera
Fidelity Rewarded	Franz Joseph Haydn	1781	Esterháza, Hungary	G Lorenzi	Plot revolves around the worship of Roman Goddess Diana by people of Cumae

Operas and operettas	*Composer*	*First performance*		*Librettist*	*General information*
The Fiery Angel	Sergey Prokofiev	1954	Paris	Prokofiev	Prokofiev's Symphony No. 3 uses themes from this opera
La Finta Giardiniera (The Feigned Garden Girl)	Wolfgang Amadeus Mozart	1775	Munich	Uncertain	Mozart's first significant opera
Die Fledermaus (The Bat)	Johann Strauss II	1874	Vienna	Haffner and Genée	Strauss conducted the orchestra for its debut
The Flying Dutchman	Richard Wagner	1843	Dresden	Wagner	Opera in 3 acts although often played in one
Die Frau ohne Schatten	Richard Strauss	1919	Vienna	Hofmannsthal	English title: *The Woman without a Shadow*
*Friday from Light**	Karlheinz Stockhausen	1996	Leipzig	Stockhausen	5th of 7 to be completed for opera cycle *Light: The Seven Days of the Week*
From One Day to the Next	Arnold Schoenberg	1930	Frankfurt	Max Blonda	Max Blonda was Gertrud Schoenberg
From the House of the Dead	Leoš Janáček	1930	Brno	Janáček	Based on Dostoyevsky's novel
The Gambler	Sergey Prokofiev	1929	Brussels	Prokofiev	Based on Dostoyevsky's short story
The Gamblers	Dmitry Shostakovich	1978	Leningrad	Shostakovich	Unfinished opera completed by Krzysztof Meyer
Gawain	Harrison Birtwistle	1991	London	David Harsent	Based on the Middle English romance *Sir Gawain and the Green Knight*
Genoveva	Robert Schumann	1850	Leipzig	Reinick and Schumann	Also the name of an opera by Detlev Müller-Siemens
Gesualdo	Alfred Schnittke	1994	Vienna	Bletschacher	Based on life of the composer Gesualdo
Der Gewaltige Hahnrei	Berthold Goldschmidt	1992	Berlin	Goldschmidt	Composed in 1930
Gianni Schicchi	Giacomo Puccini	1918	New York	Forzano	The third part of Puccini's *Il Trittico*
La Gioconda	Amilcare Ponchielli	1876	Milan	'Tobia Gorrio' (Arrigo Boito)	Contains the ballet *Dance of the Hours* (Act 3)
Un Giorno di Regno	Giuseppe Verdi	1840	Milan	Romani	Lit. *A One-Day Reign* but usually translated into English as *King for a Day*
The Girl of the Golden West (La Fanciulla del West)	Giacomo Puccini	1910	New York (Met)	Civinini and Zangarini	Based on Belasco's play *The Girl of the Golden West*
Giuditta	Franz Lehár	1934	Vienna	Knepler and Löhner	Lehár's only opera
Gloriana	Benjamin Britten	1953	London	W Plomer	Commissioned for coronation of Elizabeth II
The Golden Gate	Conrad Cumming	2010	New York	Vikram Seth	Libretto from the novel in verse by Vikram Seth, adapted by the composer
Golem	Nicolae Bretan	1924	Cluj (Romania)	Bretan	Based on the legend of the Golem as expressed in a drama by Illés Kaczér
Golem	John Casken	1989	London	Casken and Audi	Based on the Jewish legend of Golem
Golem	Larry Sitsky	1993	Sydney	Larry Sitsky	Sitsky is currently writing a series of operas based on the stories of Enid Blyton
The Gondoliers	Arthur Sullivan	1889	London	W S Gilbert	Aka: 'The King of Barataria'
Götterdämmerung (The Twilight of the Gods)	Richard Wagner	1876	Bayreuth	Wagner	Final opera in his tetralogy *Der Ring des Nibelungen*
The Government Inspector	Werner Egk	1957	Schwetzingen	Egk	Based on Gogol's story
The Grand Duke	Arthur Sullivan	1896	London and Berlin	W S Gilbert	Aka: 'The Statutory Duel'
Grande Duchesse de Gérolstein	Jacques Offenbach	1867	Paris	Meilhac and Halévy	Premiered with French soprano Hortense Schneider in the title role
The Grand Macabre	György Ligeti	1978	Stockholm	Meschke	Based on the 1934 play, *La balade du grand macabre*, by Michel De Ghelderode
The Grapes of Wrath	Ricky Ian Gordon	2007	Minnesota	Michael Korie	Based on John Steinbeck's 1939 novel of the same name
Greek	Mark-Anthony Turnage	1988	Munich	Turnage and Jonathan Moore	Based on Berkoff's play *Greek*
The Greek Passion	Bohuslav Martinů	1961	Zurich	Martinů and Kazantzakis	Based on Kazantzakis novel *Christ Recrucified*
Griséldis	Jules Massenet	1901	Paris	Silvestre and Morand	Based on a story in Boccaccio's *Decameron*
The Growing Castle	Malcolm Williamson	1968	Dynevor	Williamson	Based on Strindberg's dream play
Guntram	Richard Strauss	1894	Weimar	Strauss	Strauss's first opera
Gwendoline	Emmanuel Chabrier	1886	Brussels	Catulle Mendès	Gwendoline was Chabrier's attempt to write a serious opera in the style of Wagner
The Gypsy Baron (Zigeunerbaron)	Johann Strauss II	1885	Vienna	Ignaz Schnitzer	Based on *Sáffi* by Mór Jókai.
Halka	Stanislaw Moniuszko	1848	Vilnius	Wolski	Polish story of the tragic love of the highlander girl Halka, for the noble Janusz
Hamlet (3 acts)	Humphrey Searle	1968	Hamburg	Searle	Other operas on the subject by Scarlatti, Gasparini, Mercadante, Grandi, Szokolay
Hamlet (5 acts)	Ambroise Thomas	1868	Paris	Barbier and Carré	Based on French adaptation by Dumas, père, and Meurice of Shakespeare's play
The Handmaid's Tale	Poul Ruders	2000	Copenhagen	Paul Bentley	Based on the novel of the same name written by Canadian author Margaret Atwood
Hans Heiling	Heinrich Marschner	1833	Berlin	Devrient	Librettist Eduard Devrient also sang the title role at the première
Hänsel and Gretel	Engelbert Humperdinck	1893	Weimar	Adelheid Wette	Based on the story by the Brothers Grimm
The Happy Prince	Malcolm Williamson	1965	Farnham	Williamson	Allegorical children's opera based on story of the same name by Oscar Wilde
Harmony of the World	Paul Hindemith	1957	Munich	Hindemith	Based on life of Johann Kepler
Henry VIII	Camille Saint-Saëns	1883	Paris	Détroyat and Silvestre	Based on *The schism in England* by Pedro Calderón de la Barca.
Hérodiade	Jules Massenet	1881	Brussels	Millet and Grémont	Based on the novella *Hérodias* (1877) by Gustave Flaubert.
L'Heure Espagnole	Maurice Ravel	1911	Paris	Franc-Nohain	English title: *The Spanish Time/Hour*
Higglety Pigglety Pop!	Oliver Knussen	1985	Glyndebourne	Knussen and Sendak	Children's opera based on Sendak's book of the same name
Hin und Zurück (There and Back)	Paul Hindemith	1927	Baden Baden	Marcellus Schiffer	The work lasts for just 12 minutes

Operas and operettas	*Composer*	*First performance*	*Librettist*	*General information*
HMS Pinafore	Arthur Sullivan	1878 London	W S Gilbert	Aka: 'The Lass That Loved a Sailor'
The Horseman	Aulis Sallinen	1975 Savonlinna, Finland	Paavo Haavikko	Aulis Sallinen was born 9 April 1935 in Salmi, Finland
Hugh the Drover	Ralph Vaughan Williams	1924 London	Harold Child	Aka: 'Love in the Stocks'
Les Huguenots	Giacomo Meyerbeer	1836 Paris	Scribe and Deschamps	Story culminates in the historical St. Bartholomew's Day Massacre in 1572
The Ice Break	Michael Tippett	1977 Covent Garden	Tippett	Conductor for the first performance was Colin Davis, the dedicatee of the opera
Idomeneo, King of Crete	Wolfgang Amadeus Mozart	1781 Munich	G B Varesco	Richard Strauss worked on a revised version, which premiered in 1930
Imeneo	George Frederick Handel	1740 London	Handel	The Italian-language libretto was adapted from Silvio Stampiglia's *Imeneo*
The Immortal Hour	Rutland Boughton	1914 Glastonbury	Boughton	Fairy tale based on the works of Fiona MacLeod, pseudonym of William Sharp
Importance of Being Earnest	Mario Castelnuovo-Tedesco	1975 New York	Castelnuovo-Tedesco	Gerald Barry recently revived the opera based on the Oscar Wilde play
L'Incoronazione di Poppea	Claudio Monteverdi	1642 Venice	Giovanni Busenello	Story of how Poppaea, mistress of Nero, is crowned empress
The Indian Queen	Henry Purcell	1695 London	Dryden and R Howard	Concerns Mexican–Peruvian rivalry
Inès de Castro	James MacMillan	1996 Edinburgh	Clifford	Story of the exhumed and declared lawful wife of King Peter I of Portugal
L'Infedeltà delusa	Franz Joseph Haydn	1773 Eszterháza, Hungary	Marco Coltellini	English title: *Deceit Outwitted*
Intermezzo	Richard Strauss	1924 Dresden	Strauss	Two main characters portrayed are Strauss and his wife
Into the Little Hill	George Benjamin	2006 Paris	Martin Crimp	Received its London premiere at the Royal Opera House in February 2009
Intolleranza	Luigi Nono	1961 Venice	Nono	Based on idea by Angelo Maria Ripellino, using texts and poetry by Julius Fučík
The Invisible City of Kitezh	Nikolay Rimsky-Korsakov	1907 St Petersburg	Vladimir Belsky	Story of the city which became invisible when attacked by the Tatars
Iolanthe	Arthur Sullivan	1882 London and New York	W S Gilbert	Aka: 'The Peer and the Peri'
Iphigénie en Aulide	Christoph Gluck	1774 Paris	Du Roullet	Based on Jean Racine's tragedy *Iphigénie*
Iphigénie en Tauride	Christoph Gluck	1778 Paris	Nicolas Guillard	Based on the play *Iphigenia in Tauris* by the ancient Greek dramatist Euripides
Iris	Pietro Mascagni	1898 Rome	Luigi Illica	Notable arias: *Apri la tua finestra* and the *Hymn to the Sun* (*Inno al Sole*)
Irish Legend	Werner Egk	1955 Salzburg	Egk	Based on W B Yeats's 'Countess Cathleen'
Irmelin	Frederick Delius	1953 Oxford	Delius	Thomas Beecham was conductor for first performance
The Italian Girl in Algiers	Gioachino Rossini	1813 Venice	Anelli	Libretto taken from Mosca's opera of the same name
Ivan IV	Georges Bizet	1951 Bordeaux	F H Leroy and H Trianon	Originally written for Gounod
Ivanhoe	Arthur Sullivan	1891 London	J Sturgis	Based on Sir Walter Scott's novel
The Jacobin	Antonin Dvorák	1889 Prague	M Cervinková-Riegrová	Marie Červinková-Riegrová based characters on story by Alois Jirásek
Jenůfa	Leoš Janáček	1904 Brno	Janáček	Retains title of 'Her Foster-Daughter' in Czech Republic
Jérusalem	Giuseppe Verdi	1847 Paris	Royer and Vaëz	Adaptation of Verdi's 1843 Italian opera, *I Lombardi alla prima crociata*
The Jewels of the Madonna	Ermanno Wolf-Ferrari	1911 Berlin	Golisciani and Zangarini	First performance under the title *Der Schmuck der Madonna*
The Jewess (La Juive)	Fromental Halévy	1835 Paris	Scribe	Story of an impossible love between a Christian man and a Jewish woman
Joan of Arc	Giuseppe Verdi	1845 Milan	Temistocle Solera	Based on the play *Die Jungfrau von Orleans* by Friedrich von Schiller
Le Jongleur de Notre Dame	Jules Massenet	1902 Monte Carlo	Maurice Léna	Based on the story of the same name by Anatole France
Jonny Spielt Auf	Ernst Krenek	1927 Leipzig	Krenek	English title: *Jonny Strikes Up*. The plot is about a jazz violinist.
The Journey to Rheims	Gioachino Rossini	1825 Paris	Balocchi	Full title: *The Journey to Rheims or Inn of the Golden Lily*
Judith	Arthur Honegger	1925 Monte Carlo	René Morax	Libretto about Judith killing the Assyrian enemy Holofernes with his own sword
Judith	Eugene Goossens	1929 London and Philadelphia	Arnold Bennett	Joan Sutherland made her operatic début in the title role
Judith	Alexander Serov	1863 St Petersburg	Serov	Based on the story of Judith from the Old Testament Apocrypha
Juha	Aarre Merikanto	1958 Finland	Aino Ackté	Based on the 1911 novel of the same name by Juhani Aho
Julien	Gustave Charpentier	1913 Paris	Charpentier	Sequel to *Louise*
Julietta	Bohuslav Martinu	1938 Prague	Bohuslav Martinu	Based on play *Juliette, or The Key of Dreams* by French author Georges Neveux
Julius Caesar in Egypt	George Frederick Handel	1724 London	N F Haym	Numerous other operas on the theme of Julius Caesar
The Jumping Frog of Calaveras County	Lukas Foss	1950 Indiana	J Karsavina	Based on Mark Twain story
Der Junge Lord (The Young Lord)	Hans Werner Henze	1965 Berlin	Ingeborg Bachmann	Based on Wilhelm Hauff's *The Ape as Man* from 'The Sheik of Alexandria'
K	Philippe Manoury	2000 Paris	Manoury	Based on Franz Kafka's *The Trial*
Der Kaiser von Atlantis	Viktor Ullmann	1943 Terezin	Kien	Premiere in Terezin prison camp banned
Kashchey the Immortal	Nikolay Rimsky-Korsakov	1902 Moscow	Rimsky-Korsakov	Based on a Russian fairy tale about Koschei the Deathless, an evil, ugly old wizard
Kate and the Devil	Antonin Dvorák	1899 Prague	Adolf Wenig	Based on a farce by Josef Kajetán Tyl
Katerina Izmaylova	Dmitry Shostakovich	1934 Moscow	A Preys and Shostakovich	Revision of *Lady Macbeth of the Mtsensk District*
Die Kathrin	Erich Korngold	1939 Stockholm	Korngold	Based on Heinrich Edward Jakob's novel *The Maid of Aachen*
Katya Kabanova	Leoš Janáček	1921 Brno	Janácek	Based on Ostrovsky's play *The Storm*
Khovanshchina (The Khovansky Affair)	Modest Mussorgsky	1886 St Petersburg	V Stasov and Mussorgsky	Completed by Rimsky-Korsakov
King Arthur, or the British Worthy	Henry Purcell	1691 London	Dryden	Semi-opera, but in reality a play with extensive music
The King Goes Forth to France	Aulis Sallinen	1984 Savonlinna	P Haavikko	Story of a prince & prime minister fleeing to France after ice age threatens England
Hippolyte et Aricie	Jean-Philippe Rameau	1733 Paris	Abbé Pellegrin	Based on Racine's tragedy *Phèdre.*
Historia von D. Johann Fausten	Alfred Schnittke	1995 Hamburg	Morgener and Schnittke	The Russian composer Schnittke had a stroke during composition of the opera
The King of Lahore	Jules Massenet	1877 Paris	Louis Gallet	Love story of Sita priestess of Indra and Alim, King of Lahore
The King of Ys	Édouard-Victor-Antoine Lalo	1888 Paris	Édouard Blau	Based on the old Breton legend of the drowned city of Ys

Operas and operettas	*Composer*	*First performance*	*Librettist*	*General information*
King Priam	Michael Tippett	1962 Coventry	Tippett	Based on Homer's *Iliad*
King Roger	Karol Szymanowski	1926 Warsaw	J Iwaszkiewicz	Szymanowski helped his cousin Jarosław Iwaszkiewicz with the libretto
The King's Children	Engelbert Humperdinck	1897 Munich and London	Ernst Rosmer	Rosmer the pseudonym of Else Bernstein-Porges
The Kiss	Bedrich Smetana	1876 Prague	E Krásnohorská	Based on story by Joanna Muzakova
Die Kluge (The Clever Girl)	Carl Orff	1943 Frankfurt	Orff	Aka *The Wise Woman*
The Knot Garden	Michael Tippett	1970 Covent Garden	Tippett	Shakespeare's *The Tempest* is a central theme of the opera
Koanga	Frederick Delius	1904 Elberfeld	C F Keary	Based on G W Gable's novel *The Grandissimes*
König Hirsch (King Stag)	Hans Werner Henze	1956 Berlin	Heinz von Cramer	Based on a fable by Carlo Gozzi
Lady Macbeth of Mtsensk District	Dmitry Shostakovich	1963 Leningrad	A Preys and Shostakovich	See *Katerina Izmaylova*
Lakmé	Léo Delibes	1883 Paris and Chicago	Gondinet and Gille	"The Flower Duet" is often used in adverts
The Lambton Worm	Robert Sherlaw Johnson	1978 Oxford	Anne Ridler	Based on County Durham legend of Sir John Lambton and his battle with a worm
The Land of Smiles	Franz Lehár	1923 Vienna	L Herzer and F Löhner	Title refers to the Chinese custom of smiling, whatever happens in life
The Last Temptations	Joonas Kokkonen	1975 Helsinki	L Kokkonen	Based on life of Finnish evangelist Paavo Ruotsalainen
Lear	Aribert Reimann	1978 Munich	Claus Henneberg	Based on Shakespeare's tragedy *King Lear*
The Legend of Tsar Sultan	Nikolay Rimsky-Korsakov	1900 Moscow	Belsky	Based on Pushkin poem; contains 'The Flight of the Bumble Bee'
Leonora, or Married Love	Pierre Gaveaux	1798 Paris	J N Bouilly	Beethoven's only opera was a reworking with libretto by Joseph Sonnleithner
Let's Make An Opera	Benjamin Britten	1949 Aldeburgh	Eric Crozier	The Little Sweep, opus 45, is the second part of the stage production
Das Liebesverbot	Richard Wagner	1836 Magdeburg	Wagner	Based on Shakespeare's *Measure for Measure*
Life for the Tsar	Mikhail Glinka	1836 St Petersburg	Baron Egor Rosen	Libretto helpers: Nestor Kukolnik, Vladimir Sollogub and Vasily Zhukovsky
Life with an Idiot	Alfred Schnittke	1992 Amsterdam	Erofeyev	An allegory of Soviet oppression
The Light Cavalry	Franz von Suppé	1866 Vienna	C Costa	The *Light Cavalry Overture* remains popular distinct from the opera
The Lighthouse	Peter Maxwell Davies	1980 Edinburgh	Davies	The scenario was inspired by a true story of a deserted lighthouse
Linda di Chamounix	Gaetano Donizetti	1842 Vienna	Gaetano Rossi	Set in Chamonix in the French Alps 1760
The Lodger	Phyllis Tate	1960 London	David Franklin	The lodger's identity is revealed as Jack the Ripper
Lodoïska	Luigi Cherubini	1791 Paris	Fillette-Loraux	Based on Jean-Baptiste Louvet de Couvrai's, *Les amours du chevalier de Faublas*
Lohengrin	Richard Wagner	1850 Weimar	Wagner	Liszt was the conductor at the first performance
I Lombardi	Giuseppe Verdi	1843 Milan	Solera	See entry for *Jérusalem*
The Long Christmas Dinner	Paul Hindemith	1963 New York	Thornton Wilder	The opera depicts 90 years in the history of the mid-western Bayard family
Louise	Gustave Charpentier	1900 Paris	Charpentier	Contribution to libretto by Saint-Pol-Roux, a symbolist poet
The Love for Three Oranges	Sergey Prokofiev	1921 Chicago	Prokofiev	Ultimately based on Giambattista Basile's fairy tale of the same name
The Love of Danae	Richard Strauss	1952 Salzburg	Joseph Gregor	Based on *Danae, or The Marriage of Convenience*, by Hugo Hofmannsthal
The Love of the Three Kings	Italo Montemezzi	1913 La Scala	Benelli	Italian title: *L'amore dei tre re*
Love from Afar	Kaija Saariaho	2000 Salzburg	Amin Maalouf	French title: *L'amour de loin*
Lowland (Tiefland)	Eugen D'Albert	1903 Prague	Rudolph Lothar	Based on the 1896 Catalan play *Terra baixa* by Àngel Guimerà
Lucia di Lammermoor	Gaetano Donizetti	1835 Naples	Cammarano	Based on Scott's novel *Bride of Lammermoor* (1819)
Lucio Silla	Wolfgang Amadeus Mozart	1772 Milan	Giovanni de Gamerra	Story of Lucius Cornelius Sulla, dictator of Rome
Lucrezia Borgia	Gaetano Donizetti	1833 Milan	Felice Romani	Based on the play by Victor Hugo
Luisa Miller	Giuseppe Verdi	1849 Naples	Salvadore Cammarano	Based on the play *Kabale und Liebe (Intrigue and Love)* by Friedrich von Schiller
Lulu	Alban Berg	1937 Zurich	Berg	Based on Frank Wedekind's plays *Earth Spirit* (1895) and *Pandora's Box* (1904)
Macbeth	Giuseppe Verdi	1847 Florence	Francesco Maria Piave	Based on William Shakespeare's play
Macbeth	Ernest Bloch	1910 Paris	Edmond Fleg	Based on William Shakespeare's play
Macbeth	Lawrance Collingwood	1934 London	Collingwood	Based on William Shakespeare's play
Madame Angot's Daughter	Charles Lecocq	1872 Brussels	Clairville, Siraudin and Koning	The French libretto was by Clairville, Paul Siraudin and Victor Koning
Madame Butterfly	Giacomo Puccini	1904 Milan	Giacosa and Illica	Based on Belasco's play
Madame Sans-Gêne	Umberto Giordano	1915 New York and Turin	Renato Simoni	Libretto taken from Victorien Sardou and Emile Moreau's play of same name
Maddalena	Sergey Prokofiev	1978 Manchester	Prokofiev	Completed by Edward Downes based on Oscar Wilde play *A Florentine Tragedy*
The Magic Flute	Wolfgang Amadeus Mozart	1791 Vienna	Emanuel Schikaneder	Work is in the form of a Singspiel (both singing and spoken dialogue)
The Magic Fountain	Frederick Delius	1977 London	Jutta Bell and Delius	Set in 16th century Florida
The Magic Island (Die Zauberinsel)	Heinrich Sutermeister	1942 Dresden	Sutermeister	Based on Shakespeare's *The Tempest*
The Maid of Orleans	Pyotr Tchaikovsky	1881 St Petersburg	Tchaikovsky	Dedicated to conductor Eduard Nápravník
The Maid of Pskov	Nikolay Rimsky-Korsakov	1873 St Petersburg	Rimsky-Korsakov	Based on the drama of the same name by Lev Mei
The Makropulos Affair	Leoš Janáček	1926 Brno	Janáček	Based on Karel Čapek's play
Les Mamelles de Tirésias	Francis Poulenc	1947 Paris	Poulenc	Based on Apollinaire play
Manon	Jules Massenet	1884 Paris	Meilhac and Gille	Based on Prévost's novel *Manon Lescaut*
Manon Lescaut	Giacomo Puccini	1893 Turin	Puccini, Leoncavallo,	Libretto contributors: Giuseppe Giacosa, Domenico Oliva, Luigi Illica, Marco Praga
Margot la Rouge	Frederick Delius	1981 BBC Radio	Rosenval	Composed 1902

Operas and operettas	*Composer*	*First performance*		*Librettist*	*General information*
Maria di Rohan	Gaetano Donizetti	1843	Vienna	Cammarano	Based on Lockroy and Edmond Badon's *Un duel sous le cardinal de Richelieu*
Maria Golovin	Gian Carlo Menotti	1958	Brussels and New York	Menotti	Story of romantic meeting between a blind recluse named Donato and title character
Maria Stuarda	Gaetano Donizetti	1835	Milan	G Bardari	Based on Schiller's play
Maritana	Vincent Wallace	1845	London	Edward Fitzball	William Vincent Wallace (1812-65) was an Irish composer and musician
Marouf	Henri Rabaud	1914	Paris	Népoty	Based on a tale from the Arabian Nights about a Cairo cobbler
The Marriage	Bohuslav Martinu	1954	Hamburg	Martinu	First airing was on American television (NBC) in 1953
The Marriage	Modest Mussorgsky	1917	Petrograd	Mussorgsky	Unfinished opera based on Nikolai Gogol's comedy *Marriage (Zhenitba)*
The Marriage of Figaro	Wolfgang Amadeus Mozart	1786	Vienna	Da Ponte	Based on Beaumarchais play
Martha, or Richmond Fair	Friedrich von Flotow	1847	Vienna	Friedrich Riese	Based on a story by Jules-Henri Vernoy de Saint-Georges
The Martyrdom of St Magnus	Peter Maxwell Davies	1977	Kirkwall	Davies	First performance, St Magnus Cathedral, Kirkwall, Orkney
Mary of Egypt	John Tavener	1992	Aldeburgh	Mother Thekla	Story of the prostitute-saint of Alexandria
Mary, Queen of Scots	Thea Musgrave	1977	Edinburgh	Musgrave	Also the name of a ballet by John McCabe
The Mask of Orpheus	Harrison Birtwistle	1986	London	Peter Zinovieff	*The Mask of Orpheus* explores the Orpheus myth in a number of directions at once
Maskarade	Carl Nielsen	1906	Copenhagen	Vilhelm Andersen	Based on the comedy of the same name by Ludvig Holberg.
A Masked Ball	Giuseppe Verdi	1859	Rome	Antonio Somma	Italian title: *Un ballo in maschera*
I Masnadieri (The Robbers)	Giuseppe Verdi	1847	London	Andrea Maffei	Based on *Die Räuber* by Friedrich von Schiller.
Master Peter's Puppet Show	Manuel de Falla	1923	Seville	Falla	Based on incident in Cervantes' *Don Quixote*
The Mastersingers of Nuremberg	Richard Wagner	1868	Munich	Wagner	Usually takes four and a half hours to perform
Mathis der Maler (Matthias the Painter)	Paul Hindemith	1938	Zurich	Hindemith	Based on life of Matthias Grünewald
Mavra	Igor Stravinsky	1922	Paris	Boris Kochno	Based on Aleksandr Pushkin's *The Little House in Kolomna*
May Night	Nikolay Rimsky-Korsakov	1880	St Petersburg	Rimsky-Korsakov	Based on Gogol story
Mazeppa	Pyotr Tchaikovsky	1884	Moscow	Victor Burenin	Based on Pushkin's poem *Poltava*
Medea (Médée)	Luigi Cherubini	1797	Paris	F B Hoffman	Based on Euripides' tragedy of *Medea* and Pierre Corneille's play *Médée*
The Medium	Gian Carlo Menotti	1946	Columbia University	Menotti	Menotti directed a film version in 1951
Mephistopheles	Arrigo Boito	1868	Milan	Boito	Based on Goethe's *Faust*
Merrie England	Edward German	1902	London (Savoy)	Basil Hood	Story concerns love and rivalries at the court of Queen Elizabeth I
The Merry Widow	Franz Lehár	1905	Vienna	V Léon and L Stein	Widow's name is Hanna Glawari
The Merry Wives of Windsor	Otto Nicolai	1849	Berlin	S H Mosenthal	Based on Shakespeare's play
The Midsummer Marriage	Michael Tippett	1955	London	Tippett	Based on Mozart's *The Magic Flute*
A Midsummer Night's Dream	Benjamin Britten	1960	Aldeburgh	Pears and Britten	Based on Shakespeare's play
Mignon	Ambroise Thomas	1866	Paris	Barbier and Carré	Based on Goethe's novel *Wilhelm Meisters Lehrjahre*
The Mikado	Arthur Sullivan	1885	London	W S Gilbert	Aka: *The Town of Titipu*
The Mines of Sulphur	Richard Rodney Bennett	1965	London	Beverley Cross	One of the most successful first full-length operas ever produced
Mireille	Charles Gounod	1864	London and Paris	Michel Carré	The vocal score is dedicated to George V of Hanover
The Miserly Knight	Sergei Rachmaninov	1906	Moscow	Rachmaninov	Based on Alexander Pushkin's drama of the same name
Miss Donnithorne's Maggot	Peter Maxwell Davies	1974	Adelaide	Randolph Stow	Opera is usually performed in 32 minutes
Miss Julie	Ned Rorem	1965	New York	Kenward Elmslie	Based on Strindberg's play
Miss Julie	William Alwyn	1976	Broadcast	Alwyn	Other version by Rorem and Bibalo
Mitridate, Rè di Ponto	Wolfgang Amadeus Mozart	1770	Milan	V A Cigna-Santi	Based on Giuseppe Parini's Italian translation of Jean Racine's play *Mithridate*
Mlada	Nikolay Rimsky-Korsakov	1892	St Petersburg	Viktor Krylov	An opera-ballet in four acts
Moby Dick	Jake Heggie	2010	Dallas	Gene Scheer	Based on Herman Melville's novel *Moby-Dick*
*Monday From Light**	Karlheinz Stockhausen	1988	Milan	Stockhausen	3rd of 7 composed for the opera cycle *Light: The Seven Days of the Week*
Monsieur Beaucaire	André Messager	1919	Birmingham	Lonsdale and Ross	Based on Booth Tarkington's story
The Moon (Der Mond)	Carl Orff	1939	Munich	Orff	Based on a Brothers Grimm fairy tale
Moses in Egypt	Gioachino Rossini	1818	Naples	A L Tottola	Based on a 1760 play by Francesco Ringhieri, *L'Osiride*
Moses und Aron	Arnold Schoenberg	1954	Hamburg	Schoenberg	Follows the Book of Exodus
The Mother (Matka)	Alois Hába	1931	Munich	Hába	Opera is written in prose
The Mother of Us All	Virgil Thomson	1947	New York	Stein	Gertrude Stein and Virgil Thomson are characters
Mozart and Salieri	Nikolay Rimsky-Korsakov	1898	Moscow	Rimsky-Korsakov	Libretto taken almost verbatim from Pushkin's 1830 verse drama of same name
La Muette de Portici	Daniel Auber	1828	Paris	Scribe and Delavigne	Aka: *Masaniello*
Nabucco (Nebuchadnezzar)	Giuseppe Verdi	1842	Milan	T Solera	Based on Biblical story and 1836 play by Auguste Anicet-Bourgeois & Francis Cornue
La Navarraise	Jules Massenet	1894	Covent Garden	Jules Claretie and Henri Cain	Based on Claretie's short story *La Cigarette*
Nelson	Lennox Berkeley	1953	London	Alan Pryce-Jones	Story of the love affair of Horatio Nelson and Emma, Lady Hamilton
Nero (Nerone)	Arrigo Boito	1924	Milan	Boito	Unfinished - ends with the Great Fire of Rome
Nero (Nerone)	Pietro Mascagni	1935	Milan	Targioni-Tozzetti	Based on the play *Nerone* by Pietro Cossa

Operas and operettas	*Composer*	*First performance*		*Librettist*	*General information*
Neues vom Tage	Paul Hindemith	1929	Berlin	Marcellus Schiffer	English title: *News of the Day*
New Year	Michael Tippett	1989	Houston	Tippett	Choreographer of original production was noted American dancer Bill T. Jones
A Night at the Chinese Opera	Judith Weir	1987	Cheltenham	Weir	Weir's first full-scale opera
The Night Bell	Gaetano Donizetti	1836	Naples	Donizetti	Italian title: *Il campanello di notte*
A Night in Paris	Frederick Delius	1982	London	Rosenval	Aka Margot-la-Rouge – unpublished opera broadcast in studio by BBC
A Night in Venice	Johann Strauss II	1883	Berlin	F Zell (Camillo Walzel) and Richard Génée	German title: *Eine Nacht in Venedig*
The Nightingale (Le Rossignol)	Igor Stravinsky	1914	Paris and London	Stravinsky and S Mitusov	Based on the tale of *The Nightingale* by Hans Christian Andersen
Nixon in China	John Adams	1987	Houston	Alice Goodman	Inspired by U.S. President Richard Nixon's visit to China in 1972
Norma	Vincenzo Bellini	1831	Milan	Romani	Based on *Norma, or The Infanticide* by Alexandre Soumet.
The Nose	Dmitry Shostakovich	1930	Leningrad	Zamyatin, Yunin, Preys	Based on Gogol story. Shostakovich wrote part of libretto
Notre Dame	Franz Schmidt	1914	Vienna	Leopold Wilk and Schmidt	Based loosely on the novel *The Hunchback of Notre-Dame* by Victor Hugo.
Noye's Fludde	Benjamin Britten	1958	Aldeburgh	Britten	Based on Chester miracle play
Oberon, or the Elf-King's Oath	Carl Maria Weber	1826	Covent Garden	J R Planché	Based on a German poem, *Oberon*, by Christoph Martin Wieland
L' Oca del Cairo	Wolfgang Amadeus Mozart	1860	Frankfurt	Varesco	Unfinished *opera buffa*
Oedipus	George Enescu	1936	Paris	E Fleg	Covers the entire story of Oedipus' life, from birth to death
Oedipus Rex	Igor Stravinsky	1927	Paris	J Cocteau	From Sophocles
The Olympians	Arthur Bliss	1949	London	J B Priestley	Based on characters of Roman mythology
The Opera Ball	Richard Heuberger	1898	Vienna	Léon and Waldeberg	Contains the aria 'Geh'n wir in's Chambre séparée'
The Oracle	Franco Leoni	1905	Covent Garden	C Zanoni	Based on story *The Cat and the Cherub* by C B Fernald
Orfeo ed Euridice	Christoph Gluck	1762	Vienna	Calzabigi	Most popular of Gluck's works
Orlando	George Frederick Handel	1733	London	Anon	Based on Ariosto's 16th-century poem, *Orlando Furioso*
Orlando Furioso	Antonio Vivaldi	1727	Venice	Grazio Braccioli	Based on the poem of the same name by Ludovico Ariosto
Orlando Paladino	Franz Joseph Haydn	1782	Eszterháza, Hungary	Nunziano Porta	Based on another libretto, Le pazzie d'Orlando, by Carlo Francesco Badini
Orpheus & Euridice	Ricky Ian Gordon	2005	New York	Gordon	Retelling of the story from classical mythology
Orpheus in the Underworld	Jacques Offenbach	1858	Paris	Crémieux and Halévy	*Infernal Galop* is famous outside classical circles as the music for the "can-can"
Osud (Fate)	Leoš Janáček	1958	Brno	Janáček	Janáček and Fedora Bartosová
Otello	Giuseppe Verdi	1887	Milan	Boito	Based on Shakespeare's play
Ottone	George Frederick Handel	1723	London	Nicola Haym	From the libretto by Stefano Benedetto Pallavicino for Antonio Lotti's opera *Teofane*
Our Man in Havana	Malcolm Williamson	1963	London	Sidney Gilliat	Based on Graham Greene's novel
Our Town	Ned Rorem	2006	Indiana	J. D. McClatchy	First opera to be adapted from the Thornton Wilder play of the same name
Padmâvatî	Albert Roussel	1923	Paris	L Laloy	Opera-ballet
I Pagliacci	Ruggiero Leoncavallo	1892	Milan	Leoncavallo	Famous aria 'Vesti la giubba' ('On with the motley') refers to clown's attire
Palestrina	Hans Pfitzner	1917	Munich	Pfitzner	Based on a legend about the Renaissance musician Giovanni Pierluigi da Palestrina
Paradise Lost	Krzysztof Penderecki	1978	Chicago	Christopher Fry	Based on Milton's poem
Paris and Helen	Christoph Gluck	1770	Vienna	Ranieri de Calzabigi	Story of events between Judgment of Paris and flight of Paris and Helen to Troy
Parisian Life (La Vie Parisienne)	Jacques Offenbach	1866	Paris	Meilhac and Halévy	Offenbach's first full-length piece to portray contemporary Parisian life
Parsifal	Richard Wagner	1882	Bayreuth	Wagner	Wagner's last opera
Partenope	George Frederick Handel	1730	London	Silvio Stampiglia	Handel's first unserious opera since the much earlier *Agrippina*
Patience	Arthur Sullivan	1881	London	W S Gilbert	Aka: *Bunthorne's Bride*
Paul Bunyan	Benjamin Britten	1941	New York	W H Auden	Music covers a variety of American styles, including folk songs, blues and hymns
The Pearl Fishers	Georges Bizet	1863	Paris	Cormon and Carré	Action set in Ceylon (Sri Lanka)
Penelope	Rolf Liebermann	1954	Salzburg	H Strobel	Based on the story of Ulysses' wife in Homer's *Odyssey*
Pénélope	Gabriel Fauré	1913	Monte Carlo and Paris	René Fauchois	Based on Homer's *Odyssey*
A Penny For a Song	Richard Rodney Bennett	1967	London	Colin Graham	Light-hearted political satire
The Perfect Fool	Gustav Holst	1923	Covent Garden	Holst	Holst originally asked Clifford Bax to write the libretto, but Bax declined
Peter Grimes	Benjamin Britten	1945	London	Montagu Slater	Based on George Crabbe's poem 'The Borough'
Peter Schmoll and his Neighbours	Carl Maria Weber	1803	Augsburg	Joseph Türk	Written when the composer was 15-years-old
The Pilgrim's Progress	Ralph Vaughan Williams	1951	Covent Garden	Vaughan Williams	Christian's name in Bunyan's novel is changed to Pilgrim
The Pirate	Vincenzo Bellini	1827	Milan	Romani	Based on the tragic play Bertram, or The Castle of St Aldobrando by Charles Maturin
The Pirates	Stephen Storace	1792	London	James Cobb	Performed for King George III at the King's Theatre, London on 16 May 1794
The Pirates of Penzance	Arthur Sullivan	1879	New York	W S Gilbert	Aka: *The Slave of Duty*
The Poacher or the Voice of Nature	Albert Lortzing	1842	Leipzig	Lortzing	Based on the comedy *Der Rehbock, oder Die schuldlosen Schuldbewussten*
The Poisoned Kiss	Ralph Vaughan Williams	1936	London and Cambridge	Evelyn Sharp	Aka: *The Empress and the Necromancer*
Polly	Christoph Pepusch	1777	London	John Gay	Sequel to Gay's *The Beggar's Opera*
Porgy and Bess	George Gershwin	1935	New York	DuBose Heyward	Lyrics by DuBose Heyward and Ira Gershwin

Operas and operettas	Composer	First performance		Librettist	General information
Powder her Face	Thomas Adès	1995	Cheltenham	Philip Hensher	Shown on British television on Christmas Day 1999
Il Prigioniero (The Prisoner)	Luigi Dallapiccola	1949	Italy	Dallapiccola	Set in Zaragoza, Spain in the second half of the Sixteenth Century
Prima Donna	Arthur Benjamin	1949	London	Cedric Cliffe	Set in Italy, mid-18th century
Prima Donna	Rufus Wainwright	2009	Manchester	Bernadette Colomine	New York-born Canadian singer/composer Rufus McGarrigle Wainwright (b. 1973)
Prima la Musica e Poe le Parole	Antonio Salieri	1786	Vienna	Casti	First performed in double bill with Mozart's *Der Schauspieldirektor*
Prince Igor	Alexander Borodin	1890	St Petersburg	Borodin	Completed by Rimsky-Korsakov and Glazunov
The Prince of Homburg	Hans Werner Henze	1960	Hamburg	Ingeborg Bachmann	Based on the 1811 play, *Prinz Friedrich von Homburg* by Heinrich von Kleist
Princess Ida	Arthur Sullivan	1884	London and Boston	W S Gilbert	Aka: *Castle Adamant*
The Prodigal Son	Benjamin Britten	1968	Orford	Plomer	A church parable
Le Prophète	Giacomo Meyerbeer	1849	Paris	Eugène Scribe	Set in Dordrecht and Münster during the religious wars of the 16th century
Punch and Judy	Harrison Birtwistle	1968	Aldeburgh	Stephen Pruslin	Based on the puppet figures of the same names
Purgatory	Gordon Crosse	1966	Cheltenham	W B Yeats	One-act setting of the play by William Butler Yeats
I Puritani (di Scozia)	Vincenzo Bellini	1835	London and Paris	C Pepoli	Bellini's last opera
I Quattro Rusteghi (The Four Rustics)	Ermanno Wolf-Ferrari	1906	Munich	Sugano and Pizzolato	Four curmudgeonly husbands vainly attempt to keep their women in order
The Queen of Sheba	Károly Goldmark	1875	Vienna	S H Mosenthal	Based on the Biblical mention of the visit of the Queen of Sheba to Solomon
The Queen of Spades (Pique Dame)	Pyotr Tchaikovsky	1890	St Petersburg	Modest Tchaikovsky	Based on Pushkin story. Famous line "Three, seven, ace! Three, seven, queen!".
Quiet Flows the Don	Ivan Dzerzhinsky	1935	Leningrad	Dzerzhinsky	Based on the epic novel in four volumes by Michail Aleksandrovich Sholokhov
A Quiet Place	Leonard Bernstein	1983	Houston	S Wadsworth	Revised in 3 acts incorporating Bernstein's *Trouble in Tahiti*
Radamisto	George Frederick Handel	1720	London	Nicola Haym	Based on *L'amor tirannico, o Zenobia* (Domenico Lalli) and *Zenobia* (Matteo Noris)
The Rajah's Diamond	Alun Hoddinott	1979	BBC TV	Myfanwy Piper	Starred Geraint Evans and featured the BBC National Orchestra of Wales
The Rake's Progress	Igor Stravinsky	1951	Venice	Chester Kallman and W H Auden	Based on the 8 paintings and engravings *A Rake's Progress* by William Hogarth
The Rape of Lucretia	Benjamin Britten	1946	Glyndebourne	Ronald Duncan	Based on André Obey's play *Le Viol de Lucrèce*
The Red Line	Aulis Sallinen	1978	Helsinki	Sallinen	Finnish title: *Punainen viiva*
Regina	Marc Blitzstein	1949	New Haven	Blitzstein	Based on Lillian Hellman's play *The Little Foxes*
Il Rè Pastore (The Shepherd King)	Wolfgang Amadeus Mozart	1775	Salzburg	Metastasio	Libretto based on a work by Torquato Tasso called *Aminta*
Resurrection	Peter Maxwell Davies	1987	Darmstadt	Maxwell Davies	Besides the protagonist, represented by a dummy, there are 23 roles
Das Rheingold (The Rhine Gold)	Richard Wagner	1869	Munich	Wagner	Became the prologue to the *The Ring* cycle
Richard the Lionhearted	André Grétry	1784	Paris	M J Sedaine	Based on a legend about King Richard I of England's captivity in Austria
Richard III	Giorgio Battistelli (b. 1953)	2005	Antwerp	Ian Burton	Based on Shakespeare play
Riders to the Sea	Ralph Vaughan Williams	1937	London	J M Synge	Faithful setting of Synge's play
Rienzi	Richard Wagner	1842	Dresden	Wagner	Based on Bulwer-Lytton's novel
Rigoletto	Giuseppe Verdi	1851	Venice	Piave	Based on Hugo's play *Le Roi s'Amuse*
Rinaldo	George Frederick Handel	1711	London	Rossi	Handel's first opera in England
Der Ring des Nibelungen	Richard Wagner	1876	Bayreuth	Wagner	Cycle of four epic operas based on characters from Norse sagas and Nibelungenlied
Der Ring des Polykrates	Erich Korngold	1916	Hamburg	Leo Feld	The libretto was reworked by the composer's father Julius Korngold
The Rise and Fall of the City of Mahagonny	Kurt Weill	1930	Leipzig	Brecht	The Alabama Song has English lyrics
The Rising of the Moon	Nicholas Maw	1970	Glyndebourne	Beverley Cross	The title comes from the Irish patriotic song of the same name
Il Ritorno d'Ulisse in Patria	Claudio Monteverdi	1640	Venice	G Badoaro	English title: *Ulysses' Return to His Native Land*
Robert Devereux, Earl of Essex	Gaetano Donizetti	1837	Naples	Cammarano	Story of the fallen favourite of Elizabeth I of England
Robert the Devil	Giacomo Meyerbeer	1831	Paris	Scribe and Delavigne	Has only superficial connection to the medieval legend of Robert the Devil
Rodelinda	George Frederick Handel	1725	London	Nicola Haym	Based on an earlier libretto by Antonio Salvi
Le Roi l'a dit	Léo Delibes	1873	Paris	Edmond Gondinet	Set during the reign of Louis XIV
Le Roi malgré lui	Emmanuel Chabrier	1887	Paris	De Najac and Buroni	English title: *King in Spite of Himself* or *The reluctant king*
Romeo and Juliet	Charles Gounod	1867	Paris	Barbier and Carré	Notable for 4 duets for main characters and waltz song "Je veux vivre" for soprano
Romeo and Juliet	Heinrich Sutermeister	1940	Dresden	Sutermeister	Based on Shakespeare's play
La Rondine (The Swallow)	Giacomo Puccini	1917	Monte Carlo	Giuseppe Adami	Adapted from a German libretto by Alfred Lillner and Heinze Reichart
Der Rosenkavalier	Richard Strauss	1911	Dresden	Hofmannsthal	English title: *The Knight of the Rose*
The Royal Hunt of the Sun	Iain Hamilton	1977	London	Hamilton	Based on Peter Shaffer's play
Ruddigore	Arthur Sullivan	1887	London and New York	W S Gilbert	Aka: *The Witch's Curse*
Rusalka	Alexander Dargomyzhsky	1856	St Petersburg	Dargomyzhsky	Adapted by the composer from Pushkin's dramatic poem of the same name.
Rusalka	Antonin Dvorák	1901	Prague	J Kvapil	Based on the fairy tales of Karel Jaromír Erben and Božena Němcová.
Ruslan and Lyudmila	Mikhail Glinka	1842	St Petersburg	Shirkov and Bakhturin	Based on Pushkin's poem
Ruth	Lennox Berkeley	1956	London	Crozier	Chamber opera set in three scenes
Sadko	Nikolay Rimsky-Korsakov	1898	Moscow	Rimsky-Korsakov,	Libretto by Rimsky-Korsakoff with help from Vladimir Belsky and Vladimir Stasov

Operas and operettas	*Composer*	*First performance*	*Librettist*	*General information*
St François d'Assise	Olivier Messiaen	1983 Paris	Messiaen	Messiaen's only opera
The Saint of Bleecker Street	Gian Carlo Menotti	1954 New York	Menotti	Set in the intensely Catholic Little Italy of New York City in 1954
Salome	Antoine Mariotte	1908 Lyons	Oscar Wilde	Based on Oscar Wilde's play
Salome	Richard Strauss	1905 Dresden	Hedwig Lachmann	Based on Wilde's play
Samson et Dalila	Camille Saint-Saëns	1877 Weimar	Lemaire	Based on the Biblical tale of Samson and Delilah
Sapho	Jules Massenet	1897 Paris	Cain and Bernède	Based on the novel of the same name by Alphonse Daudet
Sárka	Zdeněk Fibich	1897 Prague	Schulzová	Bohemian legend of Šárka which appears in 14th-century Czech literature
Sárka	Leoš Janáček	1925 Brno	Zeyer	First performance in honour of the composer's 70th birthday
*Saturday from Light**	Karlheinz Stockhausen	1984 Milan	Stockhausen	2nd of 7 to be composed for the opera cycle *Light: The Seven Days of the Week*
Saul and David	Carl Nielsen	1902 Copenhagen	Christiansen	Tells the Biblical story of Saul's jealousy of the young David,
Der Schauspieldirektor (The Impresario)	Wolfgang Amadeus Mozart	1786 Vienna	G Stephanie	Mozart wrote the opera as his entry in a musical competition
Schwanda the Bagpiper	Jaromir Weinberger	1927 Prague	Kares and Brod	Based on *The Bagpiper of Strakonice* by Josef Kajetán Tyl
Die Schweigsame Frau	Richard Strauss	1935 Dresden	Stefan Zweig	Translates as 'The Silent Woman'
The Secret	Bedřich Smetana	1878 Prague	Krásnohorská	Czech title: *Tajemství*
The Secret Marriage	Domenico Cimarosa	1792 Vienna	G Bertati	Italian title: *Il matrimonio segreto*
Semele	John Eccles	1964 Oxford	Congreve	Based on Ovid's *Metamorphoses*
Semele	George Frederick Handel	1744 London	Congreve	Includes aria 'Where'er you walk'
Semiramide	Gioachino Rossini	1823 Venice	G Rossi	Many other operas based on Voltaire's *Sémiramis*
Semyon Kotko	Sergey Prokofiev	1940 Moscow	Prokofiev	Based on Valentin Katayev's 1937 novel *I, Son of Working People*
The Short Life	Manuel De Falla	1913 Nice	Fernández Shaw	Italian title: La Vida Breve
The Sicilian Vespers	Giuseppe Verdi	1855 Paris	Scribe and Duveyrier	Italian title: *Les vêpres Siciliennes*
The Siege of Corinth	Gioachino Rossini	1826 Paris	Balocchi and Soumet	Rossini's first French opera
Siegfried	Richard Wagner	1876 Bayreuth	Wagner	Third part of *Der Ring das Nibelungen*
Sigurd	Ernest Reyer	1884 Brussels and London	Du Locle and Blau	Based on the Nibelungenlied and the Eddas
The Silken Ladder	Gioachino Rossini	1812 Venice	G M Foppa	Italian title: *La scala di seta*
Simon Boccanegra	Giuseppe Verdi	1857 Venice	Piave and Montanelli	Based on the play *Simón Bocanegra* (1843) by Antonio García Gutiérrez
Sir John in Love	Ralph Vaughan Williams	1929 London	Vaughan Williams	'Greensleeves' is sung by Mistress Ford in Act 3
The Sleepwalker	Vincenzo Bellini	1831 Milan and London	Romani	Italian title: *La Sonnambula*
The Small Venetian Square	Ermanno Wolf-Ferrari	1936 Milan	Ghisalberti	Aka *Il campiello* (The Little Square)
The Snow Maiden (Snegurochka)	Nikolay Rimsky-Korsakov	1882 St Petersburg	Rimsky-Korsakov	Based on the play of the same name by Alexander Ostrovsky
Die Soldaten (The Soldiers)	Bernd Alois Zimmermann	1965 Cologne	Zimmermann	Dedicated to Austrian conductor Hans Rosbaud
Son and Stranger	Felix Mendelssohn	1851 Leipzig	Klingemann	German title: *Die Heimkehr aus der Fremde*
The Sorcerer	Arthur Sullivan	1877 London	W S Gilbert	Based on a Christmas story, *An Elixir of Love* by Gilbert
Sorochintsy Fair	Modest Mussorgsky	1913 Moscow	Mussorgsky	Unfinished opera based on Gogol story
The Spanish Lady	Edward Elgar	Never performed	Elgar	Incomplete. Based on Jonson's *The Devil Is an Ass*
Stiffelio	Giuseppe Verdi	1850 Trieste	Piave	Based on *Le pasteur, ou L'évangile et le foyer* by ouvestre and Bourgeois
The Stone Guest	Alexander Dargomyzhsky	1872 St Petersburg	Pushkin	Same story as *Don Giovanni*
The Story of a Real Man	Sergey Prokofiev	1948 Leningrad	Mira Mendelson and Prokofiev	Based on the novel of the same name by Boris Polevoy
La Straniera	Vincenzo Bellini	1829 Milan	Romani	English title: *The Stranger Woman*
*Sunday from Light**	Karlheinz Stockhausen	2011 Cologne	Stockhausen	7th of 7 to be composed for opera cycle *Light: The Seven Days of the Week*
Suor Angelica (Sister Angelica)	Giacomo Puccini	1918 New York	Forzano	The second part of Puccini's Il *Trittico*
Susanna's Secret	Ermanno Wolf-Ferrari	1909 Munich	Zangarini and Golisciani	Secret is that Susanna smokes
Il Tabarro (The Cloak)	Giacomo Puccini	1918 New York	Adami	The first part of Puccini's *Il Trittico*
A Tale of Two Cities	Arthur Benjamin	1957 London	Cedric Cliffe	Based on the Dickens' novel
The Tales of Hoffmann	Jacques Offenbach	1881 Paris	Barbier and Carré	Three acts: Olympia, Antonia and Giulietta ('Barcarolle' in Act 3)
Tamerlane (Tamerlano)	George Frederick Handel	1724 London	N F Haym	Composed in the space of 20 days in July 1724
The Taming of the Shrew	Hermann Goetz	1874 Mannheim	J V Widmann	Based on Shakespeare's play
Tancredi	Gioachino Rossini	1813 Venice	Rossi	Based on Voltaire's play *Tancrède* (1759)
Tannhäuser	Richard Wagner	1845 Dresden	Wagner	Full title: *Tannhäuser and the Singing Contest on the Wartburg*
Taras Bulba	Arturo Berutti	1895 Buenos Aires	Berutti	Loosely based on Nikolai Gogol's short novel of the same name
Taverner	Peter Maxwell Davies	1972 Covent Garden	Maxwell Davies	Based on the life of the 16th-century English composer John Taverner
The Telephone	Gian Carlo Menotti	1947 New York	Menotti	Comic opera first presented on a double bill with Menotti's *The Medium*
The Tempest	Thomas Adès	2004 London	Meredith Oakes	Based on Shakespeare's play
The Tempest (Der Sturm)	Frank Martin	1956 Vienna	Martin	Based on Shakespeare's play
The Tender Land	Aaron Copland	1954 New York	H Everett	Librettist Horace Everett real name was Erik Johns
Thaïs	Jules Massenet	1894 Paris	L Gallet	Based on Anatole France novel (1890)

Operas and operettas	*Composer*	*First performance*		*Librettist*	*General information*
Theseus (Teseo)	George Frederick Handel	1713	London	N F Haym	Only Handel opera that is in five acts
Thespis	Arthur Sullivan	1871	London	W S Gilbert	Aka: *The Gods Grown Old*
The Thieving Magpie	Gioachino Rossini	1817	Milan	Gherardini	Italian title: *La Gazza Ladra*
The Threepenny Opera	Kurt Weill	1928	Berlin	Brecht	Based on *The Beggar's Opera* by John Gay and Christoph Pepusch
*Thursday from Light**	Karlheinz Stockhausen	1981	Milan	Stockhausen	1st of 7 to be composed for opera cycle *Light: The Seven Days of the Week*
Tom Jones	Edward German	1907	London and Manchester	Thompson and Courtneidge	Based on Henry Fielding's 1749 novel, *The History of Tom Jones, a Foundling*
Tom Jones	Stephen Oliver	1976	Snape	Oliver	Oliver died of AIDS-related complications in London 1992
Tom Jones	François Philidor	1765	Paris	Poinsinet and Davesne	Libretto revised by Michel-Jean Sedaine in 1766
Tosca	Giacomo Puccini	1900	London and Rome	Giacosa and Illica	Based on Sardou's play
Die Tote Stadt (The Dead City)	Erich Korngold	1920	Hamburg and Cologne	Paul Schott	Paul Schott is the pseudonym for Erich Korngold and his father Julius Korngold
The Travelling Companion	Charles Villiers Stanford	1925	Liverpool	Henry Newbolt	Stanford's last opera
La Traviata (The Fallen Woman)	Giuseppe Verdi	1853	Venice	Piave	Based on Dumas fils' novel *Lady of the Camellias* collaboration
The Trial (Der Prozess)	Gottfried von Einem	1953	Salzburg	Blacher and H von Cramer	From Franz Kafka's novel
Trial by Jury	Arthur Sullivan	1875	London	W S Gilbert	Only grand opera produced by Gilbert and Sullivan
Tristan und Isolde	Richard Wagner	1865	Munich	Wagner	Hans von Bülow was the conductor at premiere
Troilus and Cressida	William Walton	1954	Covent Garden	Christopher Hassall	Based on Chaucer's story, as opposed to Shakespeare's
The Trojans (Les Troyens)	Hector Berlioz	1863	Paris	Berlioz	Based on Virgil's epic poem the *Aeneid*
Trouble in Tahiti	Leonard Bernstein	1952	New York	Bernstein	A one-act opera in seven scenes
Il Trovatore (The Troubadour)	Giuseppe Verdi	1853	Rome	Cammarano and Bardare	Fourth act completed by Bardare, after death of Cammarano
The Tsarevich (Der Zarewitsch)	Franz Lehár	1927	Berlin	Reichart and Jenbach	Based on the play of the same name by Polish author Gabriela Zapolska
The Tsar Has His Photograph Taken	Kurt Weill	1928	Leipzig	Georg Kaiser	Opera buffa in one act
The Tsar's Bride	Nikolay Rimsky-Korsakov	1899	Moscow	L A Mey	Adaptation of L A Mey's play, extra scene by Tumenev
*Tuesday from Light**	Karlheinz Stockhausen	1977	Tokyo	Stockhausen	4th of 7 to be completed for opera cycle *Light: The Seven Days of the Week*
Turandot	Ferruccio Busoni	1917	Zurich	Busoni	Based on Gozzi's play
Turandot (unfinished)	Giacomo Puccini	1926	Milan	Adami and Simoni	Final scene completed by Franco Alfano
Il Turco in Italia	Gioachino Rossini	1814	Milan	Romani	Opera buffa influenced by Mozart's *Cosi fan tutte*
The Turn of the Screw	Benjamin Britten	1954	Venice and London	Myfanwy Piper	Based on Henry James's story
The Twin Brothers	Franz Schubert	1820	Vienna	G von Hofmann	one-act Singspiel (German title: Die Zwillingsbrüder)
The Two Widows	Bedrich Smetana	1874	Prague	Emanuel Züngel	Libretto based on Jean Pierre Felicien Mallefille's one-act play *Les deux veuves*
Ulisse	Luigi Dallapiccola	1968	Berlin	Dallapiccola	Based on Homer
Ulysses	Reinhard Keiser	1722	Copenhagen	F M Lersner	Popular German composer based in Hamburg. He wrote over 100 operas
Ulysses	John C Smith	1733	London	S Humphreys	Based on Homer
Utopia Limited	Arthur Sullivan	1893	London	W S Gilbert	Aka: *The Flowers of Progress*
Vakula the Smith	Pyotr Tchaikovsky	1876	St Petersburg	Y Polonsky	Based on Gogol's story *Christmas Eve*
The Valkyrie (Die Walküre)	Richard Wagner	1870	Munich	Wagner	The Valkyrie is Brünnhilde
The Vampire	Heinrich Marschner	1828	Leipzig	W A Wohlbrück	Based on John Polidori's story 'The Vampyre'
Vanessa	Samuel Barber	1958	New York	Menotti	Based on Dinesen's *Seven Gothic Tales*
Venus and Adonis	John Blow	1683	London	Anon	Written for the court of King Charles II
La Vera Constanza (True Constancy)	Franz Joseph Haydn	1779	Eszterháza	F Puttini	Story explores the troubles of a sentimental heroine abandoned by a mad lover
Véronique	André Messager	1898	Paris	Vanloo and Duval	Messager's most enduring operatic work
Das Verratene Meer (The Sea Betrayed)	Hans Werner Henze	1990	Berlin	Treichel	Based on Yukio Mishima's novel *The Sailor Who Fell from Grace with the Sea*
La Vestale	Gaspare Spontini	1807	Paris	De Jouy	Spontini's patron, the Empress Josephine helped to produce the opera
Victory	Richard Rodney Bennett	1970	Covent Garden	Beverley Cross	Based on Joseph Conrad's novel
A Village Romeo and Juliet	Frederick Delius	1907	Berlin	Delius	Frederick's wife, Jelka helped him write the libretto
Le Villi	Giacomo Puccini	1884	Milan	F Fontana	Le Villi (The Willis or The Fairies) is an opera-ballet in two acts
Violanta	Erich Korngold	1916	Munich	Hans Müller-Einigen	Korngold's second opera was written when he was only seventeen years old.
The Violins of Saint-Jacques	Malcolm Williamson	1966	London	William Chappell	Based on the novel of the same name by Patrick Leigh Fermor
The Visit of the Old Lady	Gottfried von Einem	1971	Vienna	Dürrenmatt	Based on the play of the same name by the Swiss dramatist Friedrich Dürrenmatt
The Voice of Ariadne	Thea Musgrave	1974	Snape Maltings	A Elguera	Chamber opera in three acts
La Voix Humaine (The Human Voice)	Francis Poulenc	1959	Paris	Cocteau	Poulenc wrote the opera for French soprano Denise Duval
Waiting for the Barbarians	Philip Glass	2005	Erfurt, Germany	Christopher Hampton	Based on the 1980 novel by South African-born author John M. Coetzee
La Wally	Alfredo Catalani	1892	Milan	Illica	Wally is short for the girl's name Wallburga.
The Wandering Scholar	Gustav Holst	1934	Liverpool	Clifford Bax	Based on the book *The Wandering Scholars* by Helen Waddell.
War and Peace	Sergey Prokofiev	1944	Moscow	Mira Mendelson and Prokofiev	Prokofiev spent 11 years on this opera
Wat Tyler	Alan Bush	1974	Sadler's Wells	Nancy Bush	Composer Michael Nyman (b. 1947) was pupil of Bush at Royal Academy of Music
We Come to the River	Hans Werner Henze	1976	London	Edward Bond	Notable for its large cast of 111 roles

Operas and operettas	*Composer*	*First performance*		*Librettist*	*General information*
The Wedding of the Camacho	Felix Mendelssohn	1827	Berlin	F Voight	Based on an episode in *Don Quixote*
*Wednesday from Light**	Karlheinz Stockhausen	2012	Birmingham	Stockhausen	6th of 7 to be composed for opera cycle *Light: The Seven Days of the Week*
Werther	Jules Massenet	1892	Vienna	Blau, Milliet, Hartmann	Based on Goethe's novel *The Sorrows of Young Werther*
Where the Wild Things Are	Oliver Knussen	1980	Brussels	Maurice Sendak	The lead role of Max the Wolf-Boy often performed by female soprano
William Tell	Gioachino Rossini	1829	Paris	De Jouy and Bis	André Grétry and B A Weber composed operas on same subject
The World on the Moon	Franz Joseph Haydn	1777	Eszterháza	Goldoni	Opera buffa first performed at Eszterháza, Hungary
Wozzeck	Alban Berg	1925	Berlin	Berg	Berg's first opera - composed between 1914 and 1922
The Wreckers	Ethel Smyth	1906	Leipzig	Henry Brewster	First performed under the title of *Strandrecht* (Beach rights)
Das Wunder der Heliane	Erich Korngold	1927	Hamburg	Müller	English translation: The Miracle of Heliane
Wuthering Heights	Bernard Herrmann	1982	Portland, Oregon	Lucille Fletcher	The librettist was Herrmann's first wife
Xerxes (Serse)	George Frederick Handel	1738	London	Stampiglia	Opening aria *Ombra mai fu* (Never was a shade) became operatic classic
Yan Tan Tethera	Harrison Birtwistle	1986	London	T Harrison	Yan Tan Tethera is a sheep counting rhyme used by shepherds in Northern England
The Yeomen of the Guard	Arthur Sullivan	1888	London and NY	W S Gilbert	Aka: *The Merryman and his Maid*
Yolanta (Iolanta)	Pyotr Tchaikovsky	1892	St Petersburg	M Tchaikovsky	The libretto was written by the composer's brother Modest
Young Caesar	Lou Harrison	2007	San Francisco	Robert Gordon	Purported love affair between Julius Caesar and King Nicomedes IV of Bithynia
Zampa, or the Marble Bride	Ferdinand Hérold	1831	Paris	Mélesville	The overture is a staple of orchestral repertoire.
Zar und Zimmermann	Albert Lortzing	1837	Leipzig	Lortzing	English translation: *Tsar and Carpenter*
Zazà	Ruggiero Leoncavallo	1900	Milan	Leoncavallo	Première conducted by Arturo Toscanini

*The original German titles for the opera cycle *Light: The Seven Days of the Week* (*Licht: die sieben Tage der Woche*) are *Monday from Light (Montag aus Licht), Tuesday from Light (Dienstag aus Licht), Wednesday from Light (Mittwoch aus Licht), Thursday from Light (Donnerstag aus Licht), Friday from Light (Freitag aus Licht), Saturday from Light (Samstag aus Licht)* and *Sunday from Light (Sonntag aus Licht).*
Wednesday and Sunday were first produced after the composer's death. Light (*Licht)* consists of 29 hours of music and the theme is unification of religion, science and philosophy within a mythological setting.
Not only is each of the seven operas a self-sufficient work, but so are the individual acts, scenes, and, in some cases - part scenes.
Each day of the cycle is also assigned a principal colour, as well as one or more secondary colours as follows: Monday (dedicated to Eve – principal colour bright green and secondary colours opal and silver), Tuesday (principal colour red), Wednesday (principal colour bright yellow), Thursday (dedicated to Michael – principal colour bright blue), Friday (principal colour orange), Saturday (dedicated to Lucifer - principal colour black) and Sunday (principal colour gold).

Operatic Suicides and Deaths

Character	*Opera*	*Composer*	*Method*
Aida	*Aida*	Verdi	Hides herself in vault in which her lover is immured to share his death.
Andrey	*Khovanshchina*	Mussorgsky	Climbs a funeral pyre and perishes in the flames.
Brünnhilde	*Götterdämmerung*	Wagner	Rides her horse Grane on to Siegfried's funeral pyre.
Carmen	*Carmen*	Bizet	Stabbed by Don José.
Cio-Cio-San	*Madame Butterfly*	Puccini	Commits hara-kiri.
Cleopatra	*Antony and Cleopatra*	Barber	Presses an asp to her bosom.
Dido	*Dido and Aeneas*	Purcell	Stabs herself and mounts a funeral pyre.
Edgardo	*Lucia di Lammermoor*	Donizetti	Stabs himself with a dagger at Lucia's tomb.
Ernani	*Ernani*	Verdi	Stabs himself in fulfilment of a pledge to die when his enemy, Silva, sounds his horn.
Fenella	*La Muette de Portici*	Auber	Throws herself into the sea when she learns that her brother Masaniello has been killed.
Gioconda	*La Gioconda*	Ponchielli	Stabs herself to frustrate the lust of the spy Barnaba.
Gwendoline	*Gwendoline*	Chabrier	Stabs herself to join her Danish lover, Harald, in death.
Herman	*Queen of Spades (Pique Dame)*	Tchaikovsky	Stabs himself when he sees the ghost of an old countess whose death he has caused.
Iris	*Iris*	Mascagni	Throws herself into a sewer after unjustly being accused of becoming a geisha.
Katerina Ismailova	*Lady Macbeth of Mtsensk District*	Shostakovich	Drowns herself in a river en route to a Siberian prison camp.
La Wally	*La Wally*	Catalani	Throws herself from a precipice during an avalanche in the Alps.
Lakmé	*Lakmé*	Delibes	Poisons herself with the juice of an exotic flower when she loses her lover, Gerald.
Leonora	*Il Trovatore*	Verdi	Takes poison from a ring and swallows it rather than submit to the Count di Luna.
Liù	*Turandot*	Puccini	Stabs herself rather than reveal under torture the name of the Unknown Prince, Calaf.
Magda Sorel	*The Consul*	Menotti	Seals her kitchen and turns on the gas.
Manfredo	*The Love of Three Kings*	Montemezzi	Deliberately kisses the poisoned lips of his murdered wife Fiora in her tomb.
Marfa	*Khovanshchina*	Mussorgsky	Climbs a funeral pyre and perishes in the flames.
Margared	*Le Roi d'Ys*	Lalo	Leaps from precipice in remorse for aiding enemies to open dikes that protect city from sea.
Mizgir	*The Snow Maiden (Snegurochka)*	Rimsky-Korsakov	Flings himself into a lake when his beloved Snow Maiden is melted by a ray of sunlight.
Otello	*Otello*	Verdi	Stabs himself with a dagger following his murder of Desdemona.
Pollione	*Norma*	Bellini	Joins the Druid priestess on her funeral pyre.
Salome	*Hérodiade*	Massenet	Stabs herself upon learning that John the Baptist has been executed.
Selika	*L'Africaine*	Meyerbeer	Inhales the perfume of the manchinel tree, deadly to all who breathe it.
Seneca	*L'Incoronazione di Poppea*	Monteverdi	Opens his veins in the bath at the command of Emperor Nero.
Sister Angelica	*Suor Angelica*	Puccini	Swallows a poisonous potion she has concocted from the herbs in her convent's garden.
Tosca	*Tosca*	Puccini	Leaps to her death from parapet of the castle of Sant' Angelo in Rome after her lover is shot.
Violetta	*La Traviata*	Verdi	Dies of consumption.
Werther	*Werther*	Massenet	Shoots himself with a pistol.
Wozzeck	*Wozzeck*	Berg	Stabs his wife then walks into a pond and drowns.

Opera: General Information

aria (air) Solo vocal piece in A-B-A form.

bleeding chunks Operatic extracts played out of context. Term coined by Sir Donald Tovey.

burletta A comic operetta.

Camerata Society of 16th-century Florentine poets and musicians who developed opera.

canon Counterpoint in which one melodic strand gives the rule to another.

cantata Musical setting of a text, often religious, consisting of arias and choruses interspersed with recitatives.

canticle Bible hymn, other than a psalm, used in church liturgy.

cantor 1) Leading singer in a synagogue. 2) Director of music in Lutheran Church.

caoine (pronounced 'keen') Irish funeral song accompanied by wailing.

castrato Male soprano or contralto whose voice was preserved by castration before puberty.

'Catalogue Aria' Nickname for Leporello's aria in Act 1 Scene 2 of Mozart's *Don Giovanni* in which he recounts to Donna Elvira a list of his master Don Giovanni's conquests.

coloratura Word applied both to a florid virtuoso aria and to the voice required for such a passage.

Don Giovanni: conquests Italian 640, German 231, French 100, Turkish 91, Spanish 1003 = 2,065 (according to Leporello, although in the opera he has none).

English National Opera Assumed name in 1974, six years after moving into Coliseum in St Martin's Lane from previous London HQ at Sadler's Wells, Rosebery Avenue.

Gilbert and Sullivan: row over Librettist and composer fell out over choice of carpet for the Savoy.

Gluck and Piccinni war Divided Paris into French and Italian opera fans in the 1770s.

grand opera Opera on a large scale, usually entirely sung.

intermezzo Instrumental interlude used in course of an opera or play. Term also used for short opera performed between the acts of a larger one.

La Scala, Milan Built in 1778 and named after Regina della Scala, wife of a Duke of Milan. The opera house (lit. the staircase) opened on 3 August 1778 with operas of Salieri.

The Legend of Tsar Saltan Orchestral interlude 'The Flight of the Bumble Bee' appears in Act 3.

leitmotif (leading theme) Recurring theme written for a specific character or event in opera or television and film music.

libretto The words of any vocal piece such as an oratorio, but particularly the text of an opera.

'Love-Death' Wagner's name given to love duet in Act 2 of *Tristan und Isolde*, although more generally regarded as Isolde's aria at end of Act 3.

Mastersingers: 13 See operatic characters - Walther von Stolzing was an unemployed Mastersinger and Franconian knight

Moody-Manners Opera Co Touring opera company formed in 1898 by Charles Manners and his wife Fanny Moody; disbanded in 1916.

***opera buffa* (Fr. *opera bouffe*)** Comic opera; the opposite of *opera seria.*

opéra-comique 1) Second opera house of Paris; originally opened 1715; has a history of name changes and re-location; it is currently known as Salle Favart. 2) Term describing opera with spoken dialogue.

operetta Light opera, sometimes of a comic nature.

overture Introductory music for an opera, oratorio or ballet.

Paris Opéra (Académie de Musique) Latest building opened in 1875 and commonly known as Garnier or Salle Garnier, after its architect. After the opening of the Opéra Bastille in 1990, the Garnier Opéra is now used mainly for ballet. The term Paris Opéra is now used to mean the Garnier and the Bastille.

pasticcio/pastiche Opera in which each act is by a different composer. Although these terms are often used synonymously, pastiche describes a work written in the style of another period or manner.

patter song Rapid, sometimes tongue-twisting song often found in comic opera and now in pop music.

polo Andalusian folk song accompanied with dance and performed in 3/8 with syncopations and vocal coloraturas on words, e.g. 'Ole' and 'Ay', as performed in several operas.

prima donna (first lady) Most important female singer in an opera.

prologue Introductory piece that presents the background for an opera.

Puccini: unfinished opera *Turandot* (completed by Franco Alfano).

Singspiel German light opera with spoken dialogue.

soubrette Soprano comedienne.

surtitle A printed translation of part of the text of an opera, usually projected on a screen above the stage. This innovation was first used on 21 January 1983 by the Canadian Opera company for *Electra.*

travesti Term used to describe operatic roles whereby character parts are sung by the opposite gender, e.g. Cherubino in *The Marriage of Figaro* or Prince Orlofsky in *Die Fledermaus.* Such parts are often called breeches or trouser-roles.

Turandot: three riddles What is born each night and dies each dawn ... hope. What flickers red and is warm like a flame, yet is not fire ... blood. What is like ice but burns ... Turandot.

TV opera: first *Amahl and the Night Visitors* (Magi) by Menotti (1951).

Valkyries Brünnhilde, Gerhilde, Grimgerde, Helmwige, Ortlinde, Rossweise, Schwertleite, Siegrune, Waltraute.

Venice Opera House Teatro La Fenice, opened in 1792 and destroyed by fire 1836, rebuilt 1837 but damaged again in 1996.

voice registers Chest, head and middle voice; so called because the notes seem to come from these areas.

Hymns, Anthems, Songs and Ballads

Abide With Me Henry Francis Lyte.

America the Beautiful Katherine Lee Bates (words); Samuel Augustus Ward (music).

America (My Country 'tis of Thee) Samuel Francis Smith (tune of 'God Save the Queen').

Annie Laurie William Douglas. First line: Maxwelton's braes are bonnie, where early fa's the dew.

Auld Lang Syne Robert Burns.

Battle Hymn of the Republic Julia Ward Howe. First line: Mine eyes have seen the glory of the coming of the Lord (tune of 'John Brown's body')

Beer Barrel Polka (Roll out the barrel) Tune by Jaromir Vejvoda.

Caller Herrin' Tune by Nathaniel Gow blends fishwives' cry with bells of St Andrew's Church; words by Lady Nairne.

Calm Sea and Prosperous Voyage J W Goethe.

The Campbells are Coming Anon.

Columbia, the Gem of the Ocean Thomas à Becket (1808–90).

Eternal Father, Strong To Save William Whiting (words); J B Dykes (music); aka 'The Navy's Hymn'. First line, 'O thou who bidd'st the ocean deep'.

Evening Hymn Purcell (music); Fuller (words). First line, 'Now that the sun hath veiled his light'.

The Flowers that Bloom in the Springtime W S Gilbert (words); Arthur Sullivan (music).

For the Fallen 3rd movement of Elgar's choral work *Spirit of England* with words by Laurence Binyon.

Funiculì Funiculà Luigi Denza's song composed for the opening of the Naples funicular railway in 1880.

General William Booth Enters into Heaven Ives (music); Vachel Lindsay (words).

Girl I Left Behind Me, The Played in the British Army on occasions of departure and sometimes known as 'Brighton Camp'.

God Bless the Prince of Wales Henry Brinley Richards (music); Ceiriog Hughes (words).

God Preserve the Emperor Francis (Emperor's Hymn) Lorenz Haschka (words); Haydn (music); known as 'Austria' in hymn-books and became Austrian anthem. The German anthem 'Deutschland über Alles' adopted the tune.

Greensleeves Old English tune mentioned by Shakespeare in *The Merry Wives of Windsor* and tune used by Holst in *St Paul's Suite* and by Busoni in *Turandot.* Attribution to Henry VIII doubtful

Habañera Cuban song and dance of African origins: popular in Spain. Famous example is the habañera in Bizet's *Carmen.*

Happy Birthday to You Composed in USA by Mildred Hill and published by Clayton F Summy as 'Good Morning to All'.

Hark, the Herald Angels Sing Words by Charles Wesley.

Hear My Prayer Hymn by Mendelssohn containing section 'O for the wings of a dove'.

Heart of Oak Written by actor David Garrick in 1759 to music by William Boyce. It was a topical song from the pantomime *Harlequin's Invasion* and commemorated the British victories at Minden, Quiberon Bay and Quebec.

Home, Sweet Home Henry Bishop composed the music (1821) and the words were by J H Payne.

Internationale Socialist song composed by P Degeyter to words by Eugène Pottier; it was the official anthem of Communist Russia until 1 January 1944 and often confused with 'The Red Flag'.

Jerusalem Music by Hubert Parry (1916); words by William Blake.

Jubilate Psalm 100 (Anglican service), alternative to Benedictus; set to music by various composers.

Keel Row Quoted by Debussy in the 3rd movement of his *Images.* This song, of unknown origin, first appeared in a collection of favourite Scots tunes and is principally identified with the North-east of England.

keen (caoine) Irish funeral song with wailing. Represented in Vaughan Williams's opera *Riders to the Sea.*

Land of Hope and Glory Finale of Elgar's *Coronation Ode* with words by A C Benson. The tune adapts the melody of the trio section of *Pomp and Circumstance March* No. 1 in D.

Land of My Fathers (Hen Wlad fy Nhadau) National anthem of Wales (words by Evan James; music by his son James); originally called 'Glan Rhondda'.

Lass of Richmond Hill James Hook (music); L McNally (words). The song refers to Richmond in Yorkshire.

Last Rose of Summer, The Adaption of R A Millihin's 'The Groves of Barley' by Thomas Moore (1779-1852), famously heard in Friedrich von Flotow's opera *Martha.*

Let Us Garlands Bring Song-cycle by Gerald Finzi to words by Shakespeare, first performed in 1942 for the 70th birthday of Vaughan Williams. The five songs are 1) 'Come Away Death', 2) 'Who Is Sylvia?' 3) 'Fear No More the Heat O' the Sun', 4) 'O Mistress Mine', 5) 'It Was a Lover and His Lass'.

Lilliburlero Song of unknown origin, which is the tune of Northern Ireland's 'Orange' party, set to different words as 'Protestant Boys'.

Lincoln, the Great Commoner Song by Charles Ives; words by Edwin Markham.

Londonderry Air Irish folk tune first published in the Petrie collection of 1855, the most famous words being those of 'Danny Boy' by F E Weatherly.

The Lost Chord Song by Arthur Sullivan composed in 1877 in sorrow at his brother's death.

Magnificat Canticle of the Virgin Mary, 'My Soul Doth Magnify the Lord', as it appears in St Luke's Gospel. Latin name is the first word of the Vulgate translation, i.e. Magnificat anima mea Dominum.

La Marseillaise French national anthem, words and music by Claude Rouget de Lisle; written in 1792 under the title 'War Song for the Rhine Army'. Famously quoted in Tchaikovsky's *1812 Overture.*

Nearer, My God, to Thee Hymn existing in British and American versions, both set to verses by Sarah Flower Adams. The English version was composed by John Dykes, and the American version is sung to the tune 'Bethany,' by Lowell Mason.

O Canada! Canadian national anthem; originally a hymn in honour of St John the Baptist; music composed by Calixa Lavallée in 1880.

O Come All Ye Faithful John Francis Wade wrote both the words and music in the early 1740s.

O God, Our Help in Ages Past Based on Psalm 90 by Isaac Watts to a tune by William Croft, this hymn is particularly associated with Remembrance Day services.

Old Folks at Home By Stephen Foster. First line: 'Way down upon the Swanee River, far, far away'.

Onward, Christian Soldiers Reverend Sabine Baring-Gould published the words in 1868 and Arthur Sullivan the music in 1871.

***Pammelia* (All Honey)** First collection of rounds, catches and canons published in England, by T Ravenscroft in 1609.

Rock of Ages, Cleft For Me Hymn; words by Reverend Augustus Montague Toplady; music by Richard Redhead.

Rule, Britannia! Music by Thomas Arne to words of James Thomson and first played in *The Masque of Alfred* at Maidenhead on 1 August 1740.

St Anne English hymn possibly composed by William Croft. It is usually sung to the words 'O God, Our Help in Ages Past'.

Seven Gypsy Songs Dvořák (music), Heyduk (words). 1) 'My Song Resounds', 2) 'My Triangle is Singing', 3) 'Silent the Woods', 4) 'Songs My Mother Taught Me', 5) 'Sound the Fiddle', 6) 'Clean Cotton Clothes', 7) 'To the Heights of Tatra'.

Sheep May Safely Graze Air by J S Bach subsequently arranged by several composers, notably William Walton in *The Wise Virgins.*

Simple Gifts Shaker hymn composed by Joseph Brackett (1848) and quoted by Copland in *Appalachian Spring.*

Song of Destiny (Schicksalslied) Brahms (music); Hölderlin (words)

Song of the Fates (Gesang der Farzen) Brahms (music); Goethe (words)

The Star-Spangled Banner National anthem of USA. Words by Francis Scott Key (1814), written during the war of 1812, and music adapted from John Stafford Smith's *Anacreon in Heaven.*

Sumer is Icumen In (Summer is coming in) Dating from *c.* 1240 and often quoted as the oldest extant canon. Aka 'The Reading Rota' as the author is thought to have been John of Fornsete, a monk of Reading Abbey.

Tea for Two Song by Vincent Youmans, written for *No, No, Nanette* (1925). An orchestral version by Shostakovich (1928) was given the name 'Tahiti Trot'.

'Tis the Last Rose of Summer Old Irish air originally called 'Castle Hyde'.

While Shepherds Watched Their Flocks Words by Nahum Tate.

Ballets

Name	*Music by*	*Choreographer*	*First performance*	
The Age of Gold	Dmitry Shostakovich	Kaplan and Vaynonen	1930	Leningrad
Agon	Igor Stravinsky	Balanchine	1957	Los Angeles
El Amor brujo (Love the Magician)	Manuel de Falla	Falla (as pantomime)	1915	Madrid
		La Argentinita (as ballet in 1931)		
Apollo Musagetes (Apollo, Leader of the Muses)	Igor Stravinsky	Bolm	1928	Washington
		Balanchine	1928	Paris
Appalachian Spring	Aaron Copland	Martha Graham	1944	Washington
L'Après-midi d'un faune	Claude Debussy	Nijinsky	1912	Paris
		Robbins	1946	New York
Bacchus and Ariadne	Albert Roussel	Lifar	1931	Paris
La Bayadère	Léon Minkus	Petipa	1877	St Petersburg
Les Biches	Francis Poulenc	Nijinskaya	1924	Monte Carlo
Billy the Kid	Aaron Copland	Loring	1938	Chicago
Boléro	Maurice Ravel	Nijinskaya	1928	Paris
The Bolt	Dmitry Shostakovich	Lopokov	1931	Leningrad
La Boutique Fantastique	Ottorino Respighi (arr. of Rossini's music)	Massine	1919	London
The Box of Toys	Claude Debussy	André Hellé	1919	Paris
Caroline Mathilde	Peter Maxwell Davies	Flindt	1991	Amsterdam
Checkmate	Arthur Bliss	de Valois	1937	Paris
Cinderella	Sergey Prokofiev	Ashton	1948	Moscow
Coppélia	Léo Delibes	Saint-Léon	1870	Paris
La Création du Monde	Darius Milhaud	Börlin	1923	Paris
The Creatures of Prometheus	Ludwig van Beethoven	Viganò	1801	Vienna
		Ashton	1970	Bonn
Daphnis et Chloé	Maurice Ravel	Fokine	1912	Paris
		Ashton	1957	London
Les Deux Pigeons	André Messager	Mérante	1886	Paris
Don Quixote	Léon Minkus	Petipa	1869	St Petersburg
Edward II	John McCabe	Bintley	1996	Stuttgart
Façade	William Walton	Ashton	1931	London
The Fairy's Kiss	Igor Stravinsky	Nijinskaya	1928	Paris
		MacMillan	1980	London
Fall River Legend	Morton Gould	de Mille	1948	New York
Fancy Free	Leonard Bernstein	Robbins	1944	New York
Le Festin de l'araignée (Spider's Banquet)	Albert Roussel	Staats	1913	Paris
La Fille mal gardée (The Unchaperoned Girl)	John Lanchbery (arr. of Ferdinand Hérold's music)	Ashton	1960	London
Firebird	Igor Stravinsky	Fokine	1910	Paris
The Four Temperaments	Paul Hindemith	Balanchine	1946	New York
Gaîté Parisienne	Manuel Rosenthal (arr. of Offenbach's music)	Massine	1938	Monte Carlo
Gayane	Aram Khachaturian	Anisimova	1942	Leningrad
Giselle, or the Wilis	Adolphe Adam	Coralli and Perrot	1841	Paris
		Petipa	1884	St Petersburg
The Good-Humoured Ladies	Domenico Scarlatti (arr. by Tommasini)	Massine	1917	Rome
The Haunted Ballroom	Geoffrey Toye	de Valois	1934	London
Homage to the Queen	Malcolm Arnold	Ashton	1953	London
Horoscope	Constant Lambert	Ashton	1938	London
Jeux (Games)	Claude Debussy	Nijinsky	1913	Paris
Josephslegende (Legend of Joseph)	Richard Strauss	Fokine	1914	London and Paris
Madame Chrysanthème	Alan Rawsthorne	Ashton	1955	London
Les Mariés de la Tour Eiffel	Les Six (excluding Durey)	Börlin	1921	Paris
Miracle in the Gorbals	Arthur Bliss	Helpmann	1944	London

Name	Music by	Choreographer	First performance	
Miss Julie	Andrzej Panufnik	MacMillan	1970	Stuttgart
Nobilissima Visione	Paul Hindemith	Massine	1938	Monte Carlo
Nutcracker	Pyotr Tchaikovsky	Ivanov	1892	St Petersburg
Ondine (Undine)	Hans Werner Henze	Ashton	1958	London
Orpheus	Igor Stravinsky	Balanchine	1948	New York
Parade	Erik Satie	Massine	1917	Paris
Le Pas d'Acier	Sergey Prokofiev	Massine	1927	Paris
Paul Bunyan	William Bergsma	Ballet for puppets	1939	San Francisco
Peer Gynt	Alfred Schnittke	Neumeier	1986	Hamburg
The Peri	Paul Dukas	Clustine	1912	Paris
Perséphone	Igor Stravinsky	Jooss	1934	Paris
		Ashton	1962	London
Les Petits Riens	Wolfgang Amadeus Mozart	Jean Noverre	1778	Paris
Petrushka	Igor Stravinsky	Fokine	1911	Paris
Pineapple Poll	Arthur Sullivan (arr. by Mackerras)	Cranko	1951	Sadler's Wells
The Prince of the Pagodas	Benjamin Britten	Cranko	1957	Covent Garden
		MacMillan	1995	London
The Prodigal Son	Sergey Prokofiev	Balanchine	1929	Paris
Pulcinella	Igor Stravinsky	Massine	1920	Paris
The Rake's Progress	Gavin Gordon	de Valois	1935	London
Raymonda	Alexander Glazunov	Petipa	1898	Paris
The Rite of Spring	Igor Stravinsky	Nijinsky	1913	London and Paris
		MacMillan	1962	London
Rodeo	Aaron Copland	de Mille	1942	New York
Romeo and Juliet	Sergey Prokofiev	Psota	1938	Brno
		MacMillan	1965	London
Salome	Peter Maxwell Davies	Flindt	1978	Copenhagen
The Sanguine Fan	Edward Elgar	Hynd (1976 revival)	1917	London
Scaramouche	Jean Sibelius	Walbom	1922	Copenhagen
Scheherazade	Nikolay Rimsky-Korsakov	Fokine	1910	Paris
Schlagobers (Whipped Cream)	Richard Strauss	Kröller	1924	Vienna and Breslau
The Seven Deadly Sins	Kurt Weill	Balanchine	1933	Paris
The Sleeping Beauty	Pyotr Tchaikovsky	Petipa	1890	St Petersburg
The Song of the Earth	Gustav Mahler	MacMillan	1965	London
Spartacus	Aram Khachaturian	Jacobson	1956	Leningrad
Le Spectre de la Rose	Carl Maria Weber	Fokine	1911	Monte Carlo
The Stone Flower	Sergey Prokofiev	Lavrovsky	1954	Moscow
Swan Lake	Pyotr Tchaikovsky	Reisinger	1877	Moscow
		Petipa and Ivanov	1895	St Petersburg
Les Sylphides	Frederic Chopin	Mérante	1876	Paris
Sylvia, ou La Nymph de Diane	Léo Delibes	Fokine	1907	St Petersburg
		Ashton	1952	London
The Tales of Hoffmann	Jacques Offenbach (arr. Lanchbery)	Darrell	1973	London
The Three-Cornered Hat	Manuel de Falla	Massine	1919	London
Tiresias	Constant Lambert	Ashton	1951	London
The Triumph of Neptune	Lord Berners	Balanchine	1926	London
La Ventana	Holm Lumbye	Bournonville	1854	Copenhagen
A Wedding Bouquet	Lord Berners	Ashton	1936	London
The Wedding (Les Noces)	Igor Stravinsky	Nijinskaya	1923	Paris
The Wise Virgins	William Walton	Ashton	1940	Sadler's Wells
The Wooden Prince	Bela Bartók	Balázs	1917	Budapest

NB: Where ballets have been re-choreographed, both original and better-known modern versions are listed.

Ballet: General Information

ballet: first *Balet Comique de la Royne* (Paris 1581), produced by violinist Balthasar de Beaujoyeux.

Ballets Russes Founded in Paris in 1909 by Serge Diaghilev (Mikhail Fokine was his choreographer).

ballet terms Jeté – leap from one foot to another; arabesque – one leg raised behind and arms extended; entrechat – leap while striking heels together; pirouette – rapid whirling round on the point of one foot.

Bolshoi Theatre (Great Theatre) Oldest theatre in Moscow, originally called the Petrovsky, built by Maddox (1780), home of the Bolshoi Ballet.

classic ballet: first *Le Bourgeois Gentilhomme* (1670).

comédie-ballet French musico-dramatic entertainment devised by Molière and Lully in the late 17th century.

corps de ballet The ballet troupe excluding the principal dancers.

Dance Theatre of Harlem Founded by Arthur Mitchell (1968) as the first black classical ballet company.

defections from USSR Mikhail Baryshnikov while dancing with the Kirov in Toronto (1974); Natalia Makarova while dancing with the Kirov in London (1972); Rudolf Nureyev while dancing with the Kirov in Paris (1961).

***La Fille mal gardée* (*The Unchaperoned Girl*)** Adaptation of a work based on French songs and airs originally produced in Bordeaux 1789.

Marie Taglioni (1804–1884) First ballerina to dance on points and to wear a tutu.

professional ballet dancer: first female La Fontaine in Lully's *Le Triomphe de l'Amour* at the Paris Opera House 1681.

Pulcinella Scenes and costumes by Picasso.

ritual dances: four dances (*The Midsummer Marriage*) 'The Earth in Autumn', 'Waters in Winter', 'Air in Spring', 'Fire in Summer'.

Ritual Fire Dance From Falla's *El Amor brujo* (*Love the Magician*).

Royal Ballet Founded in 1931 by Dame Ninette de Valois, initially as a merger of the Old Vic and Sadler's Wells theatres both owned by Lilian Baylis. The current name was bestowed by Royal Charter in 1956 on the former Sadler's Wells Ballet, Covent Garden. The Birmingham Royal Ballet was the touring company for some time but is now independent of the Royal Ballet. Darcey Bussell spent her whole career at the Royal Ballet although another illustrious dancer, the late Dame Margot Fonteyn, is the Prima ballerina assoluta.

Le Spectre de la Rose Weber's *Invitation to the Dance* used as musical score.

Dance Types

allemande German dance, moderately paced in 4/4 rhythm, and performed in a cheerful fashion.
anglaise English country dance in quick duple metre.
apache French dance, often violent, imitating a Parisian gangster and his girlfriend.
badinage Playful dance or dance movement of a suite.
beguine Sensuous Latin ballroom dance originating in the Caribbean and danced to a bolero rhythm.
bergamasque (bergomask) Peasant dance of Bergamo, Italy, resembling a tarantella.
black bottom Popular dance of the late 1920s, originally in North America, involving lively rotation of the hips.
bolero Spanish dance in triple rhythm, said to have been invented in Cadiz around 1780.
bossa-nova Brazilian variation of the samba.
bourrée French dance, in quadruple time, performed in a lively style very like the gavotte.
branle French country dance of the 15th century characterised by a swaying motion and performed in a linked circle.
break dance Energetic solo dance frequently involving spinning on the floor on the back or head; originating in the USA in the 1980s.
cachucha Andalusian dance in triple metre similar to a bolero, for solo dancer.
cakewalk Popularised in the 1890s when black slaves parodied the white method of dance, a cake being awarded to best dancers.
calinda Negro dance, which was basis for an orchestral dance-interlude by Delius in his second opera *Koanga.*
calypso West Indian folk dance but better known in its sung form.
canaries Old 17th-century dance similar to a gigue and so called because it imitated Canary Island rituals.
can-can Boisterous Parisian dance of quadrille pattern originating in Algeria in the 1830s.
carmagnole Round dance, popular in the French Revolutionary period.
cha-cha-cha Cuban dance developed from the mambo in 1950s.
chaconne Slow and dignified dance, probably originating in Spain.
Charleston Fast foxtrot named after Charleston, South Carolina, and popularised in New York in 1922.
conga Latin American dance of three steps and kick to the side, performed in chain with hands on the next person's hips.
cotillon Lively French formation dance of the 18th century similar to a quadrille.
courante From the French meaning 'running', a courante is moderate to lively in pace, with shifting rhythms.
csárdás Hungarian dance in two sections: 1) Slow and melancholy, 2) quick and lively.
cushion dance Dance where one partner dropped a cushion before the other, who then knelt on it and bestowed a kiss on the bearer.
danse champêtre French rustic dance performed in the open air.
divertissement Dance or ballet with or without lyric, included in an opera or play to add variety.
ezcudantza Basque festival dance for two performers with accompaniment of pipe and tabor.
fandango Old Spanish courtship dance in triple time.
farandole French line dance in 6/8 time usually to the accompaniment of galoubet and tambourin.
flamenco Spanish dance with lively toe and heel steps, usually accompanied by guitar and castanets.
foxtrot Dance in quadruple time combining short and long steps in various sequences, originated in USA in the early 20th century.
funk Style of popular dance music of US black origin, popularised by singers such as James Brown. The staccato body movements follow the heavy syncopation of the music.
galliard Spirited dance popular in Tudor times, performed in a gay, rollicking manner, in triple time.
galop (galopade) Mid-19th-century dance with lively rhythm, executed with hopping movements.
gavotte French dance in 4/4 time, starting on the third beat of bar.
gigue Formal dance for two in the 16th and 17th centuries; derived from the jig and usually with violin accompaniment.
gitana Spanish gypsy dance.
gopak Lively Russian folk dance in duple time.
guajira Spanish dance with alternating rhythm between 6/8 and 3/4.
guaracha Spanish and Mexican folk dance in two sections, one in triple time and the other in duple. Dancer usually plays guitar.
habañera Cuban dance named after the city of Havana. Performed in 2/4 time.
halling Norwegian dance possibly originating in the Hallingdal. It is a frantic dance accompanied by Hardanger fiddle and other violins.
hanacca Moravian dance in simple triple time; a sort of quick polonaise.
haute danse Old term for a dance where feet are lifted, as opposed to *basse danse* in which they stay close to the floor.
hay Traditional country dance for two or more partners, with interweaving steps.
hob-and-nob Scottish country dance (1745) tune developed into 'The Campbells are Coming'.
hopak (gopak) Ukrainian folk dance, once for men only but later danced by couples. Steps are improvised but in 2/4 time.
hornpipe Lively English sailors' dance in 4/4 time.
jabo/jaleo Spanish dance for solo performer in a slow triple rhythm.
jarabe Spanish tap dance.
jig Lively British folk dance, usually in 6/8 time.
jitterbug Energetic dance, popular in the 1940s, performed chiefly to swing music.
jive Lively and jerky dance performed to jazz and, later, to rock and roll, popular in the 1940s and 1950s. Nowadays a generic term for any lively dance.
joropo Latin dance in rapid 3/4 time.
jota Spanish dance in rapid triple time with castanets and accompanied by guitar and voice.
krakoviak Polish dance from Krakow district, in lively 2/4 time.
kujawiak Polish dance for two, slower variant of the mazurka.
lambada Fast erotic Brazilian dance in which couples frequently touch hips. (lit: A beating)
lancer Quadrille for 8 or 16 pairs, popular in 19th-century England.
Ländler Traditional couple dance of Bavaria and Alpine Austria which greatly influenced the evolution of the waltz.
lezginka Dance of the Lezghins, a Muslim tribe on the Iran border.
loure French dance, similar to a gigue but slower and graver, usually with bagpipe accompaniment.
malagueña Spanish dance from Málaga and Murcia, similar to fandango and exported to Mexico by Spanish settlers.
mambo Latin American ballroom dance.
matelotte Dutch sailors' dance similar to hornpipe but danced in clogs, with arms interlinked behind the dancers' backs.
maxixe Brazilian dance, precursor of the tango.
mazurka Polish national dance in triple time.
merengue Latin American ballroom dance.
minuet Stately court dance of 17th century in triple time. The style was adopted by classical composers in suites and overtures, and as third movement of symphonies and quartets.
morris English folk dance for men with accompaniment of fiddle, tabor, pipe, concertina and accordion, long associated with Whitsuntide. The dancers wear bells on their knees and often represent characters, e.g. the Fool or the Queen of the May.
musette Dance with a drone bass accompaniment.
nachtanz (after-dance) Term applied to the second of the two dance tunes which were commonly paired from the 15th to 16th centuries, i.e. pavane and salliard, sarabande and gigue, and passamezzo and salfarello.
new Jack swing Type of funk dance, often with rap.
paso doble Spanish dance with double steps in rapid 2/4 time.
passacaglia Almost indistinguishable from the chaconne in its slow triple-time steps.
passamezzo Italian dance of the 16th and 17th centuries, similar to pavane but faster and less serious.
passepied Lively minuet of Breton origin in triple time and popular in the 17th century.
pavane Slow, stately dance of Spanish origin, often danced in conjunction with the galliard.
polka Bohemian dance, popular in 19th century and comprising three steps and a hop in fast duple time.
polonaise Polish dance in 3/4 time performed as a march in a ceremonial style.
polska Scandinavian dance in simple triple time that derives from the Mazurka and dates from the union of the Polish and Swedish crowns (1587).
quadrille Square dance in five movements, for four or more couples.
quick-step Fast version of the foxtrot. Also a lively march in 2/4, also known as a quick march.
rant Old English 17th-century dance of the jig variety, originating in the north of England and Scotland.
redowa Bohemian dance resembling the Polish mazurka.

rigaudon (rigadoon) Light and graceful dance performed in 4/4 time and in a lively spirit, originating in Provence.

rondeña Fandango of southern Spain, named after Ronda in Andalusia.

rueda Spanish round dance in quintuple time, popular in Castile.

rumba Cuban dance in 8/8 time, originating in the 1920s and extending into the jazz age and into ballroom dancing.

running set English folk dance still popular in the Appalachian mountains of America.

salsa Latin American dance style combining Latin rhythms with rock.

saltarello Traditional Italian dance usually in compound duple time and as the name suggests incorporates a series of jumps and leaps.

samba Lively, modern ballroom dance from Brazil, developed from the maxixe. The samba was popularized in Britain in the 1940s and 1950s by Edmundo Ros.

saraband(e) Originating in 17th century Spain and performed in slow, dignified triple metre.

sardana National dance of Catalonia performed to the accompaniment of the fluvial.

schottische (Scottish) A 19th-century German dance resembling a slow polka. Introduced to England in 1848 and known as the 'German polka'.

seguidilla Andalusian national dance in fast triple metre.

Sir Roger de Coverley English country dance of uncertain origin.

springer Norwegian folk dance in 3/4 time.

Strathspey Scottish dance, slower than a reel, in 4/4 time using the Scotch snap rhythm.

tango Faster version of habañera, originating in Argentina *c.* 1900; characterised by long gliding steps and sudden pauses.

tarantella Neapolitan peasant dance in 6/8 time.

tirana Spanish song/dance in 6/8 time, usually to guitar accompaniment; popular in Andalusia.

torch Dance (Fackeltanz) More often a torchlight procession to music, usually performed at weddings.

trepak Quick Russian dance in 2/4 time, most often associated with Cossacks.

veleta (valeta) Ballroom dance in triple-time. (Lit. weather-vane)

verbunkos Hungarian soldiers' dance used in the late 18th century to attract recruits for the army.

volta Lively Italian dance resembling a galliard and popular in the 16th and 17th centuries. Aslo known as lavolta. Britten's *Gloriana* includes a volta.

waltz Developed from the ländler around 1800 and performed in triple time whilst couples spin around the dance floor.

zamba Argentinian scarf dance (originated in Peru) in 6/8 time.

zapateado Spanish dance in triple time, characterised by rhythmic heel stamping.

zortziko Basque folk dance in 5/4 time, similar to the rueda.

zydeco Style of popular dance music that mixes cajun and Afro-Caribbean with rhythm and blues.

Organ Stops

Two types are flue pipes and reed pipes. Pipes may vary from 32 feet in length to less than an inch, giving the organ a range of nine octaves, larger than any other instrument. Below are listed some common stops minus numerical ones such as Fifteenth, Nineteenth and Forty-third.

Aeolina
Amoroso
Bassoon
Bible-Regal
Bird Whistle
Block-flute
Bombarde
Bourdon
Canary
Carillon
Celesta
Cello
Clarabella
Clarinet Flute
Clarion
Corno di Bassetto
Corno Dolce
Cornopean
Cor-Oboe
Cremona
Crumhorn
Cuckoo
Cymbel
Diapason
Diaphone
Doppelflöte
Dulciana Mixture
Echo Gamba
Fernflöte (Distant Flute)
Flageolet
Flûte à Pavillon
Furniture
Gamba
Gedackt
Gemshorn
Grave Mixture
Harmonic Bass
Harmonic Flute
Harmonic Piccolo
Harp
Hautboy
Hummel
Italian Principal
Jubal
Keen Strings
Keraulophon
Kerophone
Kleine Mixture
Koppel
Largo
Larigot
Magnaton
Marimba
Melodia
Melophone
Mixture Stop
Musette
Night Horn
Nightingale
Oboe
Octavin
Oiseau
Ottavina
Parade Drum
Parforce
Phoneuma
Piano
Piccolo
Plein Jeu
Point-Flute
Portunal
Quadragesima
Quincena
Quint
Racket
Rain
Reed Flute
Resultant
Sackbut
Salicional
Scarf
Serpent
Thunder
Tibia
Tympani
Ucceli
Unda Maris (Wave of the Sea)
Untersatz
Vidula
Viola di Samba
Vox Angelica
Vox Humana
Wald Quint
Woodland Flute
Xylophone
Zauberflöte
Ziflot
Zimbelstern
Zünk

Ballet Dancers and Choreographers

Alvin Ailey Jr (1931–89)
Alicia Alonso (1921–)
Frederick Ashton (1904–88)
George Balanchine (1904–83)
Mikhail Baryshnikov (1948–)
Maurice Béjart (1927–2007)
Svetlana Beriosova (1932–98)
David Bintley (1957–)
Carlo de Blaisis (1795–1878)
August Bournonville (1805–79)
Darcy Bussell (1969–)
Maria Anna de Camargo (1710–70)
Enrico Cecchetti (1850–1928)
Harold Christensen (1904–89)
Lew Christensen (1909–84)
John Cranko (1927–73)
Birgit Cullberg (1908–99)
Merce Cunningham (1919– 2009)
Patrick Delcroix (1963–)
Agnes De Mille (1905–93)
Charles-Louis Didelot (1797–1837)
Anton Dolin (1904–83)
Anthony Dowell (1943–)
Nacho Duato (1957–)
Isadora Duncan (1878–1927)
Thomas Edur (1969––)
Mats Elk (1945–)
Garth Fagan (1940–)
Suzanne Farrell (1945–)
Mikhail Fokine (1880–1942)
Margot Fonteyn (1919–91)
William Forsythe (1949–)
Loie Fuller (1862–1928)
Martha Graham (1894–1991)
Beryl Grey (1927–)
Carlotta Grisi (1819–99)
Sylvie Guillem (1965–)
Hanya Holm (1893–1992)
Doris Humphrey (1895–1958)
Kurt Jooss (1901–79)
Tamara Karsavina (1885–1978)
Gelsey Kirkland (1952–)
Jirì Kylàn (1947–)
Rudolf von Laban (1879–1958)
Serge Lifar (1905–86)
Paul Lightfoot (1966–)
Anya Linden (1933–)
Kenneth MacMillan (1929–1992)
Natalia Makarova (1940–)
Hans van Manen (1932–)
Alicia Markova (1910–2004)
Léonide Massine (1896–1979)
Mikhail Mordkin (1880–1944)
Bronislava Nijinska (1891–1972)
Vaclav Nijinsky (1890–1950)
Alwin Nikolais (1910–93)
Rudolf Nureyev (1939–93)
Gideon Obarzanek (1966–)
Agnes Oaks (1970–)
Anna Pavlova (1885–1931)
Marius Petipa (1818–1910)
Roland Petit (1924– 2011)
Maya Plisetskya (1925–)
Sergei Polunin (1989-)
Jerome Robbins (1918–98)
Marie Sallé (1707–56)
Amanda Schull (1978–)
Antoinette Sibley (1939–)
Maria Taglioni (1808–84)
Glen Tetley (1926–2007)
Twyla Tharp (1941–)
Antony Tudor (1908–87)
Galina Ulanova (1910–98)
Ninette de Valois (1898–2001)
Auguste Vestris (1760–1842)
Gaetano Vestris (1729–1808)
Charles Weidman (1901–75)
Mary Wigman (1886–1973)

Orchestral Positions
(can vary with conductor's preference)

Section	*Position*
First violins	Left of conductor and to the right of second violins
Second violins	Left of first violins and in front but slightly left of conductor
Cellos	Right of conductor and to the left of the violas
Violas	Right of cellos and in front but slightly right of the conductor
Double basses	Behind the violas and cellos
Trumpets	Behind the double basses and double bassoons
Horns	Behind the clarinets and bassoons
Harp	Behind the bass clarinet and in front of percussion
Piccolo	Left of second violin and in front of bass clarinet
Flutes	Left of piccolo and in front of clarinets
Cor anglais	Right of double basses and back of violas
Oboes	Right of cor anglais and left of the flutes
Bassoons	Behind the oboes and in front of the horns
Double bassoon	Behind the cor anglais and in front of the trumpets
Clarinets	Behind the flutes and in front of the horns
Bass clarinet	Behind the piccolo and to the left of second violins
Percussion	Behind the harp and to the right of timpani
Timpani	Behind the horns and between percussion and trombones
Trombones	Behind horns and trumpets
Tuba	Behind trumpets and to the left of trombones

NB: All positions are viewed relative to the section and not the front.

Master of the King's/Queen's Music

1625	Nicholas Lanier
1666	Louis Grabu
1674	Nicholas Staggins
1700	John Eccles
1735	Maurice Greene
1755	William Boyce
1779	John Stanley
1786	William Parsons
1817	William Shield
1834	Christian Kramer
1848	George Frederick Anderson
1870	William George Cusins
1893	Walter Parratt
1924	Edward Elgar
1934	Walford Davies
1942	Arnold Bax
1953	Arthur Bliss
1975	Malcolm Williamson (died 2 March 2003)
2004	Peter Maxwell Davies

Classical Works

Abegg Variations	Robert Schumann
Academic Festival Overture	Johannes Brahms
An Alpine Symphony	Richard Strauss
Also sprach Zarathustra (Thus Spake Zoroaster)	Richard Strauss
Alto Rhapsody	Johannes Brahams
The Apostles (oratorio)	Edward Elgar
Appassionata Sonata	Ludwig van Beethoven
Archduke Trio	Ludwig van Beethoven
Ariana a Naxos (cantata)	Franz Joseph Haydn
The Art of Fugue	Johann Sebastian Bach
Asrael (symphony)	Josef Suk
Aurora's Wedding	Pyotr Tchaikovsky
Bergomask Suite	Claude Debussy
Brandenburg Concertos	Johann Sebastian Bach
El Capitán (march)	John Philip Sousa
Capriccio Espagnol	Nikolay Rimsky-Korsakov
Carmina Burana (part 1 of *Trionfi* trilogy)	Carl Orff
Carnaval	Robert Schumann
Carnival	Antonín Dvořák
The Carnival of Animals	Camille Saint-Saëns
Catulli Carmina (cantata)	Carl Orff
Caucasian Sketches	Mikhail Ippolitov-Ivanov
Celtic Requiem	John Tavener
Chagall Windows	John McCabe
Chamber Symphony (name of two works)	Arnold Schoenberg
Chandos Anthems	George Frederick Handel
A Child of Our Time	Sir Michael Tippett
The Childhood of Christ	Hector Berlioz
Children's Corner	Claude Debussy
A Children's Overture	Roger Quilter
Christmas Oratorio	Johann Sebastian Bach
Clair de Lune	Claude Debussy
The Cloud Messenger	Gustav Holst
Cockaigne (In London Town)	Edward Elgar
Colonel Bogey	Kenneth Alford
Colour Symphony	Arthur Bliss
Concertino Pastorale	John Ireland
Construction in Metal (name of three works)	John Cage
Coronation Mass	Wolfgang Amadeus Mozart
Coronation Ode	Edward Elgar
The Creation	Franz Joseph Haydn
Crown Imperial	William Walton
The Crown of India	Edward Elgar
The Crucifixion	John Stainer
The Curlew (song cycle)	Peter Warlock
The Damnation of Faust	Hector Berlioz
Dance of Death (Totentanz)	Franz Liszt
Danse Macabre	Camille Saint-Saëns
Dante Symphony	Franz Liszt
Davidde Penitente	Wolfgang Amadeus Mozart
Death and the Maiden	Franz Schubert
Death and Transfiguration	Richard Strauss
The Death of Cleopatra	Hector Berlioz
Deborah	George Frederick Handel
Diabelli Variations	Ludwig van Beethoven
The Dream of Gerontius	Edward Elgar
Ebony Concerto	Igor Stravinsky
Éclats (Fragments)	Pierre Boulez
Egdon Heath	Gustav Holst
Eight Songs for a Mad King	Peter Maxwell Davies
Eine Kleine Nachtmusik (A Little Night Music)	Wolfgang Amadeus Mozart
Elegy For JFK	Igor Stravinsky
Elijah Oratorio	Felix Mendelssohn
Emperor March	Richard Wagner

Emperor Waltz	Johann Strauss II
The Enclosed Garden	Gabriel Fauré
L'Enfant prodigue (cantata)	Claude Debussy
An English Suite	Parry, Hubert
España	Emmanuel Chabrier
Esther	George Frederick Handel
Façade	William Walton
The Fair Melusina	Felix Mendelssohn
Fanfare for the Common Man	Aaron Copland
Fantasia on a Theme by Thomas Tallis	Ralph Vaughan Williams
Fantasia on a Theme of Handel	Michael Tippett
Fantasia on Christmas Carols	Ralph Vaughan Williams
Fantasia on Greensleeves	Ralph Vaughan Williams
Faust Overture	Richard Wagner
Fêtes galantes	Claude Debussy
Finlandia	Jean Sibelius
Fireworks	Igor Stravinsky
Fireworks Music	George Frederick Handel
Five Tudor Portraits	Ralph Vaughan Williams
The Flight of the Bumble Bee	Nikolay Rimsky-Korsakov
Four Last Songs	Richard Strauss
Four Sea Interludes	Benjamin Britten
The Four Seasons	Antonio Vivaldi
Four Serious Songs	Johannes Brahms
French Suites	Johann Sebastian Bach
Froissart	Edward Elgar
From Stone to Thorn	Peter Maxwell Davies
From the Diary of Virginia Woolf	Dominick Argento
Funeral March of a Marionette	Charles Gounod
The Garden of Fand	Arnold Bax
Gaspard de la Nuit	Maurice Ravel
A German Requiem	Johannes Brahms
The Girl With the Flaxen Hair	Claude Debussy
Gold and Silver (waltz)	Franz Lehár
The Golden Spinning Wheel	Antonín Dvořák
Golliwogg's Cakewalk	Claude Debussy
Good Friday Music	Richard Wagner
Gymnopédies	Erik Satie
Gypsy Songs (Zigeunerlieder)	Johannes Brahms
Habañera	Maurice Ravel
Hail to the Chief	James Sanderson
Hamlet (fantasy overture)	Pyotr Tchaikovsky
Hamlet (symphonic poem)	Franz Liszt
Harold in Italy	Hector Berlioz
L'Heure Espagnole (The Spanish Hour)	Maurice Ravel
Hiawatha	Samuel Coleridge-Taylor
Hodie (On This Day)	Ralph Vaughan Williams
Holberg Suite	Edvard Grieg
The Holy Boy	John Ireland
Holy Sonnets of John Donne	Benjamin Britten
L'Horizon chimérique	Gabriel Fauré
Hungarian Dances	Johannes Brahms
Hungarian Rhapsodies	Franz Liszt
The Hymn of Jesus	Gustav Holst
Hymn of Paradise	Herbert Howells
Hymn to St Magnus	Peter Maxwell Davies
Hymns from the Rig Veda	Gustav Holst
Iberia	Isaac Albéniz
Imaginary Landscape	John Cage
In a Summer Garden	Frederick Delius
Indian Diary	Ferruccio Busoni
Indian Fantasy	Ferruccio Busoni
In Honour of the City	George Dyson
In Honour of the City of London	William Walton
In the Faery Hills	Arnold Bax
In the South	Edward Elgar
In the Steppes of Central Asia	Alexander Borodin
Invitation to the Dance	Carl Maria Weber
In Windsor Forest	Ralph Vaughan Williams
Irish Symphony	Hamilton Harty
Islamey	Mily Balakirev
The Island of Joy	Claude Debussy
The Isle of the Dead	Sergei Rachmaninov
Israel in Egypt	George Frederick Handel
Israel Symphony	Ernest Bloch
Italian Caprice	Pyotr Tchaikovsky
Italian Serenade	Hugo Wolf
Jacob's Ladder	Arnold Schoenberg
Jamaican Rumba	Arthur Benjamin
Jeux d'Eau (Fountains)	Maurice Ravel
Jeux d'Enfants (Children's Games)	Georges Bizet
Joan of Arc at the Stake (oratorio)	Arthur Honegger
Joan of Arc at the Stake (concert aria)	Franz Liszt
Johannesburg Festival Overture	William Walton
Joshua	George Frederick Handel
Judas Maccabaeus	George Frederick Handel
Judith (oratorio)	Thomas Arne (1761)
Judith (oratorio)	Hubert Parry (1888)
Judith Triumphant	Antonio Vivaldi
Kakadu Variations	Ludwig van Beethoven
Kamarinskaya (Wedding Song)	Mikhail Glinka
Karelia Suite	Jean Sibelius
Kinderscenen (Scenes From Childhood)	Robert Schumann
King David	Arthur Honegger
The Kingdom (oratorio)	Edward Elgar
King of Prussia Quartets	Wolfgang Amadeus Mozart
King Stephen	Ludwig van Beethoven
Kontakte (Contacts)	Karlheinz Stockhausen
Lachrimae	John Dowland
Lachrymae	Benjamin Britten
Lady in the Dark	Kurt Weill
The Lady of Shalott	Maurice Jacobson
The Lady of Shalott	PhyllisTate
Lady Radnor's Suite	Hubert Parry
Land of the Mountain and the Flood	Hamish MacCunn
The Lark Ascending	Ralph Vaughan Williams
The Last Sleep of the Virgin	Jules Massenet
Late Swallows	Frederick Delius
Lazarus (oratorio)	Franz Schubert
The Legend of St Elizabeth	Franz Liszt
Lélio, or the Return to Life	Hector Berlioz
Lie Strewn the White Flocks (pastoral)	Arthur Bliss
Lieutenant Kijé	Sergey Prokofiev
The Light of Life	Edward Elgar
A Lincoln Portrait	Aaron Copland
Little Suite	Claude Debussy
Little Symphony	Charles Gounod
A London Overture	John Ireland
A London Symphony	Ralph Vaughan Williams
The Love Feast of the Apostles	Richard Wagner
Love-Dreams (Liebesträume)	Franz Liszt
Love-Song Waltzes	Johannes Brahms
The Magic Island	William Alwyn
Makrokosmos	George Crumb
Mantra	Karlheinz Stockhausen
The Mask of Time	Michael Tippett
Mass of Christ the King	Malcolm Williamson
A Mass of Life	Frederick Delius
Má Vlast (My Country)	Bedřich Smetana
Mazeppa	Franz Liszt
Memento Vitae (Memory of Life)	Thea Musgrave
Mephisto Waltzes	Franz Liszt
La Mer (The Sea)	Claude Debussy
Messiah (oratorio)	George Frederick Handel
Metamorphosen	Richard Strauss
A Midsummer Night's Dream (1826)	Felix Mendelssohn
A Midsummer Night's Dream	Carl Orff (1939)
Mikrokosmos	Béla Bartók
The Miraculous Mandarin	Béla Bartók
Mládí (Youth)	Leoš Janáček
Moby Dick (cantata)	Bernard Herrmann

Moby Dick (concertato)	Peter Mennin
Moby Dick (symphonic poem)	Douglas Moore
Morning Heroes	Arthur Bliss
Mother Goose Suite	Maurice Ravel
Name Day (Namensfeier)	Ludwig van Beethoven
Natural Histories	Maurice Ravel
New England Holidays	Charles Ives
Night and Dreams	Franz Schubert
Night on the Bare Mountain	Modest Mussorgsky
Noble and Sentimental Waltzes	Maurice Ravel
The Noonday Witch	Antonín Dvořák
Norfolk Rhapsody	Ralph Vaughan Williams
North Country Sketches	Frederick Delius
Nursery Suite	Edward Elgar
The Oceanides	Jean Sibelius
Ode For St Cecilia's Day	Henry Purcell (1683–92)
Ode For St Cecilia's Day	George Frederick Handel (1739)
Ode For St Cecilia's Day	Hubert Parry (1889)
Ode to Death	Gustav Holst
Ode to Napoleon Bonaparte	Arnold Schoenberg
Odyssey	Nicholas Maw
Oiseaux Exotiques	Olivier Messiaen
Omar Khayyám	Granville Bantock
On Hearing the First Cuckoo in Spring	Frederick Delius
Orb and Sceptre March	William Walton
Organ Solo Mass	Wolfgang Amadeus Mozart
Orpheus	Franz Liszt
Othello	Antonín Dvorák
An Oxford Elegy	Ralph Vaughan Williams
Pacific 231	Arthur Honegger
Pan and Syrinx	Carl Nielsen
Papillons (Butterflies)	Robert Schumann
Paradise Lost (cantata)	Christopher Steel
Pavane	Gabriel Fauré
Pavane For a Dead Infanta	Maurice Ravel
Peacock Variations	Zoltán Kodály
Peasant Cantata	Johann Sebastian Bach
Peer Gynt	Edvard Grieg
Pelléas et Mélisande	Gabriel Fauré
Pelléas et Mélisande	Arnold Schoenberg
Pelléas et Mélisande	Jean Sibelius
Peter and the Wolf	Sergey Prokofiev
Phaëton	Camille Saint-Saëns
Phoebus and Pan	Johann Sebastian Bach
Pierrot Lunaire	Arnold Schoenberg
Pines of Rome	Ottorino Respighi
The Planets	Gustav Holst
The Pleasure Dome of Kubla Khan	Charles Griffes
Poet & Peasant Overture	Franz von Suppé
Pohjola's Daughter	Jean Sibelius
Polovtsian Dances	Alexander Borodin
Portsmouth Point	William Walton
Prélude à l'Après-midi d'un faune	Claude Debussy
Préludes	Claude Debussy
Les Préludes	Ferencz Liszt
Procession	Karlheinz Stockhausen
The Prodigal Son	Benjamin Britten
The Prodigal Son	Claude Debussy
The Prodigal Son (oratorio)	Arthur Sullivan
Prometheus	Franz Liszt
Queen Mary's Funeral Music	Henry Purcell
Quiet City	Aaron Copland
Radetzky March	Johann Strauss the Elder
Raft of the Medusa, The	Hans Werner Henze
Rakastava (The Lover)	Jean Sibelius
Ramifications	György Ligeti
Rapsodie Espagnole	Franz Liszt
Rapsodie Espagnole (including *Habañera*)	Maurice Ravel
Renard (The Fox)	Igor Stravinsky
Rhapsody in Blue	George Gershwin
Rhapsody on a Theme of Paganini	Sergei Rachmaninov
Roman Festivals	Ottorino Respighi
Romeo and Juliet (fantasy overture)	Pyotr Tchaikovsky
Romeo and Juliet (symphony)	Hector Berlioz
Roses From the South	Johann Strauss II
Le Rouet d'Omphale	Camille Saint-Saëns
Rugby	Arthur Honegger
Ruins of Athens	Ludwig van Beethoven
Rule, Britannia! (from the masque *Alfred*)	Thomas Arne
Running Set	Ralph Vaughan Williams
Russian Easter Festival Overture	Nikolay Rimsky-Korsakov
Rustic Wedding	Károly Goldmark
Rustle of Spring	Christian Sinding
St Anthony Variations	Johannes Brahms
St John Passion	Johann Sebastian Bach
St Ludmila	Antonín Dvořák
St Matthew Passion	Johann Sebastian Bach
St Nicolas	Benjamin Britten
St Paul	Felix Mendelssohn
St Paul's Suite	Gustav Holst
St Thomas Wake	Peter Maxwell Davies
Samson (oratorio)	George Frederick Handel
Sarnia	John Ireland
Satyricon	John Ireland
Scapino	William Walton
Scaramouche	Darius Milhaud
Scenes from the Bavarian Highlands	Edward Elgar
Scenes From the Saga of King Olaf	Edward Elgar
Scottish Fantasy	Max Bruch
Scythian Suite	Sergey Prokofiev
The Sea	Frank Bridge
Sea Drift	Frederick Delius
Sea Fever	John Ireland
Sea Pictures	Edward Elgar
The Seasons	Franz Joseph Haydn
Serenade for Tenor, Horn and Strings	Benjamin Britten
Severn Suite	Edward Elgar
Sheherazade	Nikolay Rimsky-Korsakov (1889)
Shéhérazade	Maurice Ravel (1904)
Shepherd Fennel's Dance	Balfour Gardiner
Shylock	Gabriel Fauré
Siegfried Idyll	Richard Wagner
Simple Symphony	Benjamin Britten
Slavonic Dances	Antonín Dvořák
Slavonic Rhapsodies	Antonín Dvořák
The Soldier's Tale	Igor Stravinsky
A Song for the Lord Mayor's Table	William Walton
The Song of Sorrow	Gustav Mahler
The Song of the Earth	Gustav Mahler
Song of the Flea	Modest Mussorgsky
Song of the High Hills	Frederick Delius
Song of the Young Boys	Karlheinz Stockhausen
Songs Without Words	Felix Mendelssohn
Songs and Dances of Death	Modest Mussorgsky
Songs My Mother Taught Me	Antonín Dvořák
Songs of Travel	Ralph Vaughan Williams
The Sorcerer's Apprentice (based on Goethe poem)	Paul Dukas
The Spectre's Bride	Antonín Dvořák
The Spirit of England	Edward Elgar
Spitfire Prelude and Fugue	William Walton
A Spring Symphony	Benjamin Britten
Spring (Printemps)	Claude Debussy
The Starlight Express	Edward Elgar
La Stravaganza (The Extraordinary)	Antonio Vivaldi
Street Corner	Alan Rawsthorne
Such a Day, Such a Night	Francis Poulenc
Suite bergamasque	Claude Debussy
Summer Night on the River	Frederick Delius
Summer's Last Will and Testament	Constant Lambert
The Swan of Tuonela	Jean Sibelius
Swan Song	Franz Schubert
The Swan-Turner	Paul Hindemith
Symphonia Domestica	Richard Strauss
Symphonic Dances	Sergei Rachmaninov

Symphonic Metamorphosis of Themes by Weber	Paul Hindemith
Symphonie Espagnole	Édouard-Victor-Antoine Lalo
Symphonie Fantastique	Hector Berlioz
Symphonie Funèbre et Triomphale	Hector Berlioz
Symphonies of Wind Instruments	Igor Stravinsky
Symphony in Three Movements	Igor Stravinsky
Symphony of Psalms	Igor Stravinsky
Syrinx	Claude Debussy
Tahiti Trot	Dmitry Shostakovich
Tales from the Vienna Woods	Johann Strauss II
Tam O'Shanter	Malcolm Arnold
Taras Bulba	Leoš Janáček
The Tempest	Pyotr Tchaikovsky (1873)
The Tempest	Jean Sibelius (1925)
Theodora	George Frederick Handel
Three Pear-Shaped Pieces	Erik Satie
Three Places in New England	Charles Ives
Three Screaming Popes	Mark-Anthony Turnage
Till Eulenspiegel	Richard Strauss
Tintagel	Arnold Bax
To the Children	Sergei Rachmaninov
The Tomb of Couperin	Maurice Ravel
Tragic Overture	Johannes Brahms
Transcendental Studies	Franz Liszt
Turandot	Carl Maria Weber
Tzigane (Gypsy)	Maurice Ravel
Ultimos Ritos (Last Rites)	John Tavener
Ulysses (cantata)	Mátyás Seiber
The Unanswered Question	Charles Ives
Universal Prayer	Andrzej Panufnik
Vallée d'Obermann (Obermann Valley)	Franz Liszt
La Valse (The Waltz)	Maurice Ravel
Valse Triste (Sad Waltz)	Jean Sibelius
Variations on a Rococo Theme	Pyotr Tchaikovsky
Variations on a Theme by Haydn	Johannes Brahms
Variations on a Theme of Frank Bridge	Benjamin Britten
Variations on a Theme of Hindemith	William Walton
Venetian Games	Witold Lutoslawski
A Vision of Aeroplanes	Ralph Vaughan Williams
The Vision of Judgement	Peter Racine Fricker
The Vision of St Augustine	Michael Tippett
Visions Fugitives (Fleeting Visions)	Sergey Prokofiev
The Wand of Youth	Edward Elgar
War Requiem	Benjamin Britten
The Wasps	Ralph Vaughan Williams
Water Music	George Frederick Handel
The Water Sprite	Antonín Dvořák
Wedding Day at Troldhaugen	Edvard Grieg
Welles Raises Kane	Bernard Herrmann
The Whale	John Tavener
The White Peacock	Charles Griffes
Wine	Alban Berg
Winterreise (Winter Journey)	Franz Schubert
The Wood Dove	Antonín Dvořák
The Young Person's Guide to the Orchestra	Benjamin Britten
Zyklus (Cycle)	Karlheinz Stockhausen

Musical Instructions

a cappella In chapel style - unaccompanied

accarezzevole Caressingly.

accelerando Becoming faster.

ad libitum At will, improvised.

adagietto Not quite as slow as adagio.

adagio At ease. Slow tempo between largo (slower) and andante (faster).

adagissimo Very slow.

addolorato Sorrowfully.

à demi-jeu With half the power.

à demi-voix With half the voice, whispered.

affábile Gently, pleasingly.

afflito Sorrowfully, mournfully, sadly.

affrettando Hurrying.

allegramente Brightly, gaily.

allegretto Moderately quick.

allegro Quick.

ancora Repeat, again.

andante Moving along, flowing (slowish but not slow).

andantino Diminutive of andante although nowadays usually means a little faster.

arcato Bowed.

arpeggio Playing of the notes of a chord individually in quick succession.

ballabile In a dance style.

bariolage Rapid alternation of open and stopped strings in violin playing.

barré Playing a chord on the guitar with finger across all strings raising their pitch equally.

bisbigliando Both hands playing adjacent strings of harp repeatedly pianissimo.

bouche fermée Closed-mouth singing, i.e. humming.

brio Vigour, spirit.

calando Diminishing gradually – softer and slower.

calcando Quickening gradually (literally, trampling).

col legno With the wood; using the stick part of the bow to strike the string.

common time 4/4 metre.

comodo Leisurely, moderate speed.

con brio With vigour.

con fuoco With fire; using force and speed.

con lancio With verve.

con sordini Muted (see **gedämpft)**

coperti Covered; relates to drums being muted by being covered with a cloth.

crescendo Becoming louder.

da capo From the beginning (literally, from the head).

dal segno From the sign, meaning return to the sign and repeat.

diminuendo Becoming quieter.

diminution Opposite of augmentation, i.e shortening of the time-values of notes of melodic parts.

dolce Sweet, with an implication of 'soft'.

forte Loudly.

fortissimo Very loudly.

gedämpft (damped) Therefore muted for strings and horns; muffled for drums; soft-pedalled for piano.

giocoso Merry, playful.

grazioso Graceful.

jeté (flung) Bowing technique whereby the upper bow is bounced on the string.

larghetto Slow tempo, faster than largo.

largo Broad, slow tempo.

legato Smoothly, with no breaks between successive notes.

lento Slow.

maestoso Majestically or stately.

martelé (hammered) Playing the violin with short strokes never lifting bow from strings.

mezza voce Subdued tone between piano and forte (literally, middle voice).

morendo Dying away, fading.

muta Direction to change keys, frequently found in timpani and horn parts.

piacere (pleasure) At the performer's discretion.

pianissimo (pp) Very soft.

pianississimo (ppp) Very, very soft.

piano (p) Soft.

pianoforte Soft-loud.

pizzicato (pinched) Plucking the string.

poco a poco Little by little, gradually.

portamento Carrying of the sound from one note to another (very legato).

portato Between staccato and legato.

prestissimo Very fast; the fastest tempo.

presto Fast.

rake On guitar, dragging the pick across muted strings in an arpeggiated fashion.

rallentando Becoming gradually slower.

ritardando Delaying, becoming slower.

rubato (robbed) Freely slowing down and speeding up the tempo without changing the basic pulse.

saltato (saltando) Bounce the bow lightly on the string. Aka **spiccato (detached)**

scherzando (scherzhaft) Playfully.

scherzo Piece in a lively tempo; 'joke'.

sostenuto Sustained.

sotto voce Under the voice (quiet and soft)

stringendo Tightening, increasing the tension by hurrying the tempo.

strophic Describes a song that has identical music in each verse.

subito Suddenly, at once.

sul ponticello Play stringed instrument with the bow as near as possible to the bridge.

sul tasto Instruction to take the bow over the fingerboard. Means 'on the fingerboard'. Aka **sur la touche**

susurrando Whispering, murmuring.

tacet Stop playing and be silent.

tutti (all) Instruction for the whole orchestra to play.

una corda The use of the soft pedal which causes the hammers of a piano to strike only one string per note instead of three.

vibrato Rapid alteration of pitch or intensity of a note to impart 'expression'.

vivace Vivacious, i.e. fast and lively.

Names and Nicknames of Symphonies (by composer)

Alwyn's Symphony No. 5	*Hydriotaphia*
Beethoven's Symphony No. 3 in E flat major	*Eroica*
Beethoven's Symphony No. 3 in E flat Op. 55 (2nd movement)	*Funeral March*
Beethoven's Symphony No. 5 in C minor Op. 67	*Fate*
Beethoven's Symphony No. 6 in F major	*Pastoral*
Beethoven's Symphony No. 9 in D minor Op. 125	*Choral*
Beethoven's Symphony No. 9 in D Op. 125 (4th movement)	*Ode to Joy*
Bernstein's Symphony No. 1	*Jeremiah*
Bernstein's Symphony No. 2	*The Age of Anxiety*
Bernstein's Symphony No. 3	*Kaddish*
Berwald's Symphony No. 1	*Sérieuse*
Berwald's Symphony No. 2	*Capricieuse*
Berwald's Symphony No. 3 in C major	*Singulière*
Bloch's 'Epic Rhapsody' Symphony (1926)	*America*
Bloch's Symphony (1916)	*Israel*
Brian's Symphony No. 1 in D minor	*Gothic*
Brian's Symphony No. 4	*Das Siegeslied*
Britten's Op. 68 dedicated to Rostropovich	*Cello Symphony*
Britten's Symphony Op. 20	*Sinfonia da Requiem*
Britten's Symphony Op. 4	*Simple*
Bruckner's Symphony in F minor	*Study*
Bruckner's Symphony No. 0 in D minor	*Die Nullte*
Bruckner's Symphony No. 3 in D minor	*Wagner*
Bruckner's Symphony No. 4 in E flat major	*Romantic*
Bruckner's Symphony No. 7	*Apocalyptic*
Dutilleux's Symphony No. 3	*Le Double*
Dvořák's Symphony No. 1 in C minor Op. 3	*The Bells of Zlonice*
Dvořák's Symphony No. 5 (No. 9) in E minor (2nd movement)	*Largo*
Dvořák's Symphony No. 9 (formerly No. 5) in E minor	*From the New World*
Glière's No. 3	*Ilya Murometz*
Goldmark's Symphony Op. 26	*Rustic Wedding*
Gubaildulina's Symphony (1986)	*Stimmen Verstummen*
Hanson's Symphony No. 1 in E minor Op. 21	*Nordic*
Hanson's Symphony No. 2 Op. 30	*Romantic*
Hanson's Symphony No. 4 Op. 34	*Requiem*
Hanson's Symphony No. 7	*Sea*
Haydn's Symphony No. 6 in D	*Le Matin (Morning)*
Haydn's Symphony No. 7 in C	*Le Midi (Noon)*
Haydn's Symphony No. 8 in G	*Le Soir (Evening)*
Haydn's Symphony No. 8 in G (4th movement)	*Tempest*
Haydn's Symphony No. 22 in E flat	*The Philosopher*
Haydn's Symphony No. 26 in D minor	*Christmas*
Haydn's Symphony No. 26 in D minor	*Lamentation*
Haydn's Symphony No. 30 in C	*Alleluiasymphonie*
Haydn's Symphony No. 31 in D	*Horn Signal*
Haydn's Symphony No. 43 in E flat	*Mercury*
Haydn's Symphony No. 44 in E minor	*Trauer (Mourning)*
Haydn's Symphony No. 45 in F sharp minor	*Farewell (Abschied)*
Haydn's Symphony No. 47 in G	*Palindrome*
Haydn's Symphony No. 48 in C	*Maria Theresia*
Haydn's Symphony No. 49 in F minor	*La Passione*
Haydn's Symphony No. 53 in D	*Imperial*
Haydn's Symphony No. 55 in E flat	*Schoolmaster*
Haydn's Symphony No. 59 in A	*Fire*
Haydn's Symphony No. 60 in C major	*The Distraught Man*
Haydn's Symphony No. 63 in C major	*La Roxolane*
Haydn's Symphony No. 64 in A	*Tempora Mutantur*
Haydn's Symphony No. 69 in C	*Laudon*
Haydn's Symphony No. 73 in D	*The Hunt (La Chasse)*
Haydn's Symphonies Nos 82–87	*Paris Symphonies*
Haydn's Symphony No. 82 in C	*The Bear (L'Ours)*
Haydn's Symphony No. 83 in G minor	*The Hen (La Poule)*
Haydn's Symphony No. 85 in B flat	*La Reine (The Queen)*
Haydn's Symphony No. 92 in G	*Oxford*
Haydn's Symphonies Nos 93–104	*London Symphonies*
Haydn's Symphonies Nos 93–104	*Salomon Symphonies*
Haydn's Symphony No. 94 in G major	*Surprise*
Haydn's Symphony No. 96 in D	*Miracle*
Haydn's Symphony No. 100 in G	*Military*
Haydn's Symphony No. 101 in D	*Clock*
Haydn's Symphony No. 103 in E flat	*Drumroll*
Haydn's Symphony No. 104 in D	*London*
Haydn's Symphony No. 104 in D	*Salomon*
Hindemith's Symphony (1934)	*Mathis der Maler*
Hindemith's Symphony (1946)	*Serena*
Hindemith's Symphony (1958)	*Pittsburgh*
Holmboe's Symphony No. 3	*Sinfonia Rustica*
Holmboe's Symphony No. 4	*Sinfonia Sacra*
Holmboe's Symphony No. 8	*Sinfonia Boreale*
Honegger's Symphony No. 3	*Liturgique*

Honegger's Symphony No. 4	*Deliciae Basiliensis*
Honegger's Symphony No. 5	*Di Tre Re*
Hovahness' Symphony No. 2 Op. 132	*Mysterious Mountain*
Ives's 1st movement of his 'New England Holidays'	*Washington's Birthday*
Ives's 2nd movement of his 'New England Holidays'	*Decoration Day*
Ives's 3rd movement of his 'New England Holidays'	*Fourth of July*
Ives's 4th movement of his 'New England Holidays'	*Thanksgiving Day*
Ives's Symphony No. 3	*The Camp Meeting*
Ives's Symphony No. 4, 2nd movement; fantasy piece for piano	*Celestial Railroad*
Ives's Symphony (1904–13)	*Holidays*
Ives's Symphony (1904–13)	*New England Holidays*
Kanchell's Symphony No. 4	*Michelangelo*
Kernis's Symphony No. 1	*Waves*
Khachaturian's Symphony No. 2 in A minor	*The Bell*
MacMillan's Symphony (1997)	*Vigil*
Mahler's Symphony No. 1 in D major	*Titan*
Mahler's Symphony No. 2 in C minor	*Resurrection*
Mahler's Symphony No. 8 in E flat major	*Symphony of a Thousand*
Malipiero's Symphony No. 1	*Four Seasons*
Malipiero's Symphony No. 2	*Sinfonia Elegiaca*
Martinu's Symphony No. 6	*Fantaisies*
Mathias's Symphony No. 2	*Summer Music*
Mendelssohn's Symphony No. 2 in B flat Op. 52	*Lobgesang (Hymn of Praise)*
Mendelssohn's Symphony No. 3 in A minor Op. 56	*Scotch (Scottish)*
Mendelssohn's Symphony No. 4 in A major Op. 90	*Italian*
Mendelssohn's Symphony No. 5 in D minor	*Reformation*
Mozart's Symphony No. 25 in G minor, K183	*Little G Minor*
Mozart's Symphony No. 31 in D, K297	*Paris*
Mozart's Symphony No. 35 in D, K385	*Haffner*
Mozart's Symphony No. 36 in C, K425	*Linz*
Mozart's Symphony No. 38 in D, K504	*Prague*
Mozart's Symphony No. 40 in G minor, K550	*Great G Minor*
Mozart's Symphony No. 41 in C major, K551	*Jupiter*
Nielsen's Symphony No. 2 in C minor Op. 16	*The Four Temperaments*
Nielsen's Symphony No. 3	*Espansiva (Expansive)*
Nielsen's Symphony No. 4, Op. 29	*The Inextinguishable*
Nielsen's Symphony No. 6	*Simple*
Panufnik's Symphony No. 1	*Sinfonia Rustica*
Panufnik's Symphony No. 2	*Sinfonia Elegiaca*
Panufnik's Symphony No. 3	*Sinfonia Sacra*
Panufnik's Symphony No. 5	*Sinfonia di Sfere*
Panufnik's Symphony No. 6	*Sinfonia Mistica*
Panufnik's Symphony No. 8	*Sinfonia Votiva*
Prokofiev's Symphony No. 1 in D Op. 25	*Classical*
Rimsky-Korsakov's Symphony No. 2 Op. 9 (Oriental Suite)	*Antar*
Rubbra's Symphony No. 9	*Resurrection*
Rubbra's Symphony No. 9	*Sinfonia Sacra*
Saint-Saëns's Symphony No. 3 in C minor	*Organ*
Sallinen's Symphony No. 5	*Washington Mosaics*
Sallinen's Symphony No. 6	*From a New Zealand Diary*
Sallinen's Symphony No. 7	*Dreams of Gandalf*
Schnittke's Symphony No. 2	*St Florian*
Schubert's Symphony No. 4 in C minor	*Tragic*
Schubert's Symphony No. 6 in C major	*Little C Major*
Schubert's Symphony No. 8 in B minor	*Unfinished*
Schubert's Symphony No. 9 in C major	*Great C Major*
Schubert's Symphony No. 9 in C major, D944	*Heavenly Length*
Schubert's Symphony No. 1 in B flat Op. 38	*Spring*
Schubert's Symphony No. 3 in E flat major Op. 97	*Rhenish*
Scriabin's Symphony No. 3 in C minor Op. 43	*The Divine Poem*
Shostakovich's Symphony No. 2 in B major Op. 14	*October*
Shostakovich's Symphony No. 3 in E flat Op. 20	*First of May*
Shostakovich's Symphony No. 7 in C major Op. 60	*Leningrad*
Shostakovich's Symphony No. 11 in G minor Op. 103	*The Year 1905*
Shostakovich's Symphony No. 12 in D minor Op. 112	*The Year 1917*
Shostakovich's Symphony No. 12 in D minor Op. 12	*To the Memory of Lenin*
Shostakovich's Symphony No. 13 in B flat minor Op. 113	*Babi Yar*
Smetana's Symphony in E	*Festive/Triumph*
Spohr's Symphony No. 9 in B minor	*Seasons*
Stanford's Symphony No. 3 in F minor Op. 28	*Irish*
Suk's Symphony No. 2 in C minor Op. 27	*Asrael*
Sullivan's Symphony in E minor	*Irish*
Szymanowski's Symphony No. 3	*Song in the Night*
Tchaikovsky's Symphony No. 1 in G minor Op. 13	*Winter Daydreams*
Tchaikovsky's Symphony No. 2 in C minor Op. 17	*Little Russian/Ukrainian*
Tchaikovsky's Symphony No. 3 in D Op. 29	*Polish*
Tchaikovsky's Symphony No. 4 in F minor Op. 36	*Fate*
Tchaikovsky's Symphony No. 6 in B minor Op. 74	*Pathétique*
Vaughan Williams's Symphony No. 1 in C	*Sea*
Vaughan Williams's Symphony No. 2	*London*
Vaughan Williams's Symphony No. 3	*Pastoral*
Vaughan Williams's Symphony No. 7	*Antarctica*

Nicknames of Classical Works

Actus Tragicus — Bach's church cantata No. 106 ('God's time is the best')
Adieux Sonata — Beethoven's Piano Sonata No. 26 in E flat major, which he called 'The Farewell'
African — Saint-Saën's Piano Concerto No. 5
Air on the G String — Wilhelmj's arrangement of Bach Suite for Orchestra No. 3 in D (2nd movement)
American Quartet — Dvorák's String Quartet in F Op. 96
Andante Cantabile — Tchaikovsky's String Quartet No. 1 in D Op. 11 (2nd movement)
Appassionata Sonata — Beethoven's Piano Sonata No. 23 in F minor Op. 57
Archduke Trio — Beethoven's Piano Trio in B flat Op. 97, dedicated to Archduke Rudolf of Austria
Arpeggione — Schubert's Sonata in A minor for cello and piano
Basle Concerto — Stravinsky's Concerto in D for strings
Battle Symphony — Beethoven's orchestral work 'Wellington's Victory' Op. 91
The Bell — Haydn's String Quartet in D minor Op. 76 No. 2
The Bird — Haydn's String Quartet in C Op. 33 No. 3
The Black Mass — Scriabin's Piano Sonata No. 9 in F Op. 68
Black-key Étude — Chopin's Étude in G flat major for piano Op. 10 No. 5
Brandenburg Concertos — Bach's 6 concertos for various instruments, BWV 1046–1051
Bridal Chorus — Wagner's chorus from Act 3 of *Lohengrin*
Butterfly — Chopin's Étude in G flat for piano Op. 25 No. 9
Cat Waltz — Chopin's Waltz in F for piano Op. 34 No. 3
Cat's Fugue — Scarlatti's Fugue in G minor for harpsichord
La Chasse — Haydn's String Quartet in B flat Op. 1 No. 1
Chopsticks — Anonymous quick waltz tune for piano, first published in London 1877
Coffee Cantata — Bach's Cantata No. 211
Colas Breugnon — Kabalevsky's opera *The Craftsman of Clamecy*
Concord Sonata — Ives's Piano Sonata No. 2
Contemplation of Nothing Serious — Ives's orchestral piece *Central Park in the Dark in the Good Old Summertime*
Coronation Concerto — Mozart's Piano Concerto No. 26 in D, K537
The Cuckoo and the Nightingale — Handel's second set of six concertos for organ and orchestra
Dance Before the Golden Calf — Schoenberg's climax of Act 2 of his opera *Moses und Aron*
Dance of the Blessed Spirits — Gluck's slow dance in Act 2 of *Orfeo ed Euridice*, noted for its flute solo
Dance of the Comedians — Smetana's dance episode in Act 3 of *The Bartered Bride*, featuring clowns
Dance of the Hours — Episode, frequently played separately, in Act 3 of Ponchielli's *La Gioconda* and representing the conflict between darkness and light
Dance of the Seven Veils — Dance episode during Strauss's opera *Salome*
Dance of the Sylphs — Berlioz's orchestral episode during *La Damnation de Faust*, which forms part of Faust's dream on the banks of the Elbe
Dance of the Tumblers — Rimsky-Korsakov's episode during *The Snow Maiden* in which acrobats dance for the Tsar Berendey
Dead March in Saul — Handel's Funeral March from the oratorio *Saul*
Death and the Maiden — Schubert's String Quartet No. 14 in D minor
Dettingen Te Deum — Handel's *Te Deum* in D
Devil's Trill — Tartini's Violin Sonata in G minor
Diabelli Variations — Beethoven's 33 variations on a waltz by Diabelli in C for piano Op. 120
The Difficult Decision — Beethoven's String Quartet in F Op. 135 (4th movement)
Dissonance Quartet — Mozart's String Quartet No. 19 in C major, K465
Dog Waltz — Chopin's Waltz in D flat for piano Op. 64 No. 1
Dominicus Mass — Mozart's Mass in C, K66
Donkey Quartet — Haydn's String Quartet in D minor Op. 76 No. 2
Dorian Toccata and Fugue — Bach Toccata and Fugue in D minor for organ, BWV 538
A Dream — Haydn's String Quartet in F Op. 50 No. 5 (2nd movement)
Dumbarton Oaks — Stravinsky's Concerto in E flat for chamber ensemble
Dumky Trio — Dvořák's Piano Trio in E minor Op. 90
Ebony — Stravinsky's Concerto for clarinet and jazz band
Edward — Brahms's Ballade in D minor for piano Op. 10 No. 1
Eine Kleine Nachtmusik — Mozart's Divertimento in G for strings, K525
Eine Kleine Trauermusik — Schubert's Nonet in E flat minor for wind instuments
Elegy — Massenet's orchestral selection in E minor from his opera *Les Érinnyes*
Elvira Madigan — Mozart's Piano Concerto No. 21 in C
Emperor Concerto — Beethoven's Piano Concerto No. 5 in E flat major Op. 73
Emperor Quartet — Haydn's String Quartet in C major Op. 76 No. 3
English Suites — Bach's 6 Suites for harpsichord, BWV 806-811
Erdödy Quartets — Haydn's 6 String Quartets
Eroica Variations — Beethoven's 15 Variations and fugue on an Original Theme in E flat major Op. 76 Nos 75–80 for piano
Eyeglass Duo — Beethoven's Duo in E flat for viola and cello
Fall of Warsaw — Chopin's Étude in C minor for piano Op. 10 No. 12
Il Favorito — Vivaldi's Violin Concerto in E minor Op. 11 No. 2
Fiddle Fugue — Bach's Fugue in D minor for organ, BWV 539
Fifths — Haydn's String Quartet in D minor Op. 76 No. 2
Fingal's Cave — Mendelssohn's Overture for orchestra Op. 26, originally named *The Lonely Island*
The Forty-eight — Bach's *Well-Tempered Clavier*
The Four Seasons — Vivaldi's 4 Violin Concertos Op. 8 Nos 1–4
The Four Temperaments — Hindemith's Theme and Variations for string and piano: melancholic, sanguine, phlegmatic, choleric
French Suites — Bach's 6 Suites for harpsichord, BWV 812–817
The Frog — Haydn's String Quartet in D Op. 50 No. 6
From My Life — Smetana's String Quartets No. 1 in E minor (especially) and No. 2 in D minor
Funeral Anthem — Handel's anthem in G minor, *The Ways of Zion Do Mourn*
Funeral March — Chopin's Piano Sonata No. 2 in B flat minor Op. 35 (3rd movement)
Funeral March — Beethoven's Piano Sonata No. 12 in A flat Op. 26 (3rd movement)
Für Elise — Beethoven's Bagatelle in A minor for piano
Il Gardellino — Vivaldi's Flute Concerto in D Op. 10 No. 3
Gassenhauer Trio — Beethoven's Trio in B flat for clarinet, cello and piano Op. 11
German Suites — Bach's set of 6 keyboard partitas
Ghost Trio — Beethoven's Piano Trio in D major Op. 70 No. 1
The Girl With Enamel Eyes — Delibes 3-act ballet *Coppelia*

Goldberg Variations	Bach's Aria with Diverse Variations for harpsichord, BWV 988
Golden Sonata	Purcell's Sonata in F for two violins, viola da gamba and organ
Grand Duo	Schubert's Sonata in C major for piano (4 hands)
Grande Valse Brillante	Chopin's Waltz in E flat for piano Op. 18
Grazer Fantasie	Schubert's Fantasy in C for piano
Great Fugue	Beethoven's Fugue in B flat major for String Quartet Op. 133
Great Organ Mass	Haydn's Mass in E flat, Hob. XXII:4
Grief	Chopin's Étude in E for piano Op. 10 No. 3
Gypsy Rondo	Haydn's Piano Trio in G, Hob. XV:25 (3rd movement)
Haffner Serenade	Mozart's Suite in D major for orchestra, K250
Hallelujah Chorus	Handel's Chorus in D from his oratorio *Messiah*, No. 44
Hallelujah Concerto	Handel's Organ Concerto in B flat Op. 106
Hammerklavier	Beethoven's Piano Sonata No. 29 in B flat major Op. 106
Handel Variations	Brahms's Variations and Fugue on a Theme by Handel in B flat for Piano
Handel's Largo	Handel's aria 'Ombre mai fù', from his opera *Serse* (*Xerxes*)
Harmonious Blacksmith	Handel's Harpsichord Suite No. 5 in E (4th movement) Air with 5 variations
Harmonious Inspiration	Vivaldi's 12 concertos for various instruments Op. 3
Harmony Mass	Haydn's Mass No. 12 in B flat, H XXII:14
Harp Étude	Chopin's Étude in A flat for piano Op. 25 No. 1
Harp Quartet	Beethoven's String Quartet in E flat major Op. 74
Haydn Quartets	Mozart's 6 String Quartets Op. 10, K387–465
Haydn Variations	Brahms's Variations on a Theme by Joseph Haydn in B flat
The Hebrides	Mendelssohn's Overture for orchestra Op. 26
Heiliger Dankgesang	Beethoven's String Quartet in A minor Op. 132 (3rd movement)
Heiligmesse	Haydn's Mass in B flat, Hob. XXII:10
Hexenmenuet	Haydn's String Quartet in D minor Op. 76 No. 2 (3rd movement)
Hoffmeister Quartet	Mozart's String Quartet in D, K499
Hornpipe (aka *Lark*)	Haydn's String Quartet in D Op. 64 No. 5
Hornpipe Concerto	Handel's Concerto Grosso in B minor Op. 6, No. 12
Horn Trio	Brahms's Trio in E flat for violin, horn and piano Op. 40
Horseman (aka *The Rider*)	Haydn's String Quartet in G minor Op. 74 No. 3
Housatonic at Stockbridge	Ives's 'Three Places in New England' (3rd movement)
Humoresque	Dvořák's piano piece in G flat Op. 101 No. 7
Hunt Cantata	Bach Cantata 208 'Was mir behagt, ist nur die munter Jagd!'
The Hunt	Mozart's String Quartet No. 17 in B flat, K458
The Hunt	Haydn's String Quartet in B flat Op. 1 No. 1
Imperial Mass	Haydn's Mass No. 9 in D minor, Hob. XXII:11
Italian Concerto	Bach's Concerto for solo harpsichord, BWV 971
Jesu, Joy of Man's Desiring	Bach's chorale prelude from Cantata 147, 'Herz und Mund und Tat und Leben'
Jeunehomme Concerto	Mozart's Piano Concerto in E flat Op. 33 No. 2
Jig Fugue	Bach's Fugue in G for organ, BWV 577
The Joke	Haydn's String Quartet in E flat Op. 33 No. 2
Jungfernquartette	Haydn's 6 String Quartets Op. 33
Kaiser (aka *Emperor*)	Haydn's String Quartet in C Op. 76 No. 3
Kamennoi-Ostrov	Rubinstein's piece for piano in F sharp No. 22
Kettledrum Mass (*Paukenmesse*)	Haydn's Mass No. 7 in C major, Hob. XXII:9
Kreutzer Sonata	Beethoven's Violin Sonata No. 9 in A major Op. 47
Kreutzer Sonata Quartet	Janáček's String Quartet No. 1
Lark (aka *Hornpipe*)	Haydn's String Quartet in D Op. 64 No. 5
Late Quartets	Beethoven's String Quartets Op. 127, 130–133 and 135
Liebestraum	Liszt's Nocturne in A flat for piano; No. 3 of 3 of that title
Little Fugue in G Minor	Bach's Fugue for organ, BWV 578
Little Organ Mass	Haydn's Mass in B flat No. 5, Hob. XXII:7
Lobkowitz Quartets	Haydn's 2 String Quartets Op. 77 Nos 81–82
La Malinconia	Beethoven's String Quartet in B flat Op. 18 No. 6 (4th movement)
Manzoni Requiem	Verdi's *Requiem*, in memory of poet Alessandro Manzoni
Marche Militaire	Schubert's March in D for piano duet Op. 51 No. 1
Mariazell Mass	Haydn's Mass in C, Hob. XXII:8
Mass in Time of War	Haydn's Mass No. 7 in C, Hob. XXII:9
Mazeppa Études	Liszt's Transcendental Études for piano No. 4
Meditation	Massenet's selection in D for violin and orchestra from the opera *Thaïs*
Melody in F	Rubinstein's Piano Piece No. 1 of 2 melodies Op. 3
Military Polonaise	Chopin's Polonaise in A for piano Op. 40 No. 1
Minuet in G	Beethoven's 6 Minuets, WoO 10 No. 2
Minuet in G	Paderewski's Minuet for piano Op. 14 No. 1
Minuet in G	Bach's 'Notebook for Anna Magdalena Bach', 1st selection
Minute Waltz	Chopin's Waltz in D flat for piano Op. 64 No. 1
Missa Solemnis	Beethoven's Mass in D Op. 123
Moonlight Sonata	Beethoven's Piano Sonata No. 14 in C sharp minor Op. 27 No. 2
The Mount of Olives	Beethoven's Oratorio *Christ on the Mount of Olives* Op. 85
Mozartiana	Tchaikovsky's Suite No. 4 for orchestra
A Musical Joke	Mozart's Divertimento in F for chamber ensemble, K522
Muss es sein? Es muss sein! Es muss sein!	Beethoven's String Quartet in F major Op. 135 (4th movement)
Nelson Mass	Haydn's Mass No. 9 in D minor, Hob. XXII:11
New England	Ives's first orchestral set
Nicolai Mass	Haydn's Mass in G, Hob. XXII:6
Organ Solo Mass	Mozart's Mass in C, K259
Paganini Études	Liszt's 6 Études for piano on themes of Paganini
Paganini Variations	Brahms's *Variations on a Theme of Paganini* in A minor for piano
Pastoral Sonata	Beethoven's Piano Sonata No. 15 in D major Op. 28
Pastoral Symphony	Handel's interlude from his oratorio *Messiah*, No. 13
Pathétique	Beethoven's Piano Sonata No. 8 in C minor Op. 13
Paukenmesse (*Kettledrum Mass*)	Haydn's Mass in C major, Hob. XXII:9
Peasant Cantata	Bach's Cantata 212 'Mer hahn en neue Oberkeet'
Pomp and Circumstance	Elgar's March in D major, from a set of 5 with that title, Op. 39 No. 1
Posthorn Serenade	Mozart's Serenade in D for orchestra, K320

Prelude in C	Bach's *Well-Tempered Clavier* Volume I, 1st selection
Prelude in C sharp minor	Rachmaninoff's Prelude for piano, Op. 3 No. 2
Prussian Quartets	Mozart's 3 String Quartets, K575, 589, 590
Prussian Quartets	Haydn's 6 String Quartets Op. 50 Nos 1–6
Quartetto Serioso	Beethoven's String Quartet in F minor Op. 95
Quartettsatz	Schubert's String Quartet No. 12 in C minor
Quintenquartett	Haydn's String Quartet in D minor Op. 76 No. 2
Rage over a Lost Penny	Beethoven's Rondo a Capriccio in G for piano Op. 129
Raindrop Prelude	Chopin's Prelude in D flat for piano Op. 28 No. 15
Rain Sonata	Brahms's Violin Sonata No. 1 in G Op. 78
Ratswahl Cantata	Bach's Cantata 71, 'Gott ist mein König'
Razor Quartet	Haydn's String Quartet in F minor Op. 55 No. 2
Razumovsky Quartets	Beethoven's 3 String Quartets Op. 59
Recitative	Haydn's String Quartet in G Op. 17 No. 5
Reliquie Sonata	Schubert's Piano Sonata No. 13 in C
Rêve Angélique	Rubinstein's piano piece in F sharp No. 22 from Kamennoi-Ostrov
Revolutionary Étude	Chopin's Étude in C minor for piano Op. 10 No. 12
The Rider (aka *Horseman*)	Haydn's String Quartet in G minor Op. 74 No. 3
Rondo a Capriccio	Beethoven's Piano Sonata in G Op. 129
Rondo alla Turca	Mozart's Piano Sonata in A, K331 (3rd movement)
Russian Quartets	Haydn's 6 String Quartets Op. 33 Nos 1–6
Russian Quartets	Beethoven's 3 String Quartets Op. 59
St Anne Fugue	Bach's Fugue in E flat for organ, BWV 552
St Anthony Chorale	Haydn's Divertimento in B flat for wind, instruments II:46 (2nd movement)
St Cecilia Mass	Haydn's Mass in C, XXII:5
St Joseph Mass	Haydn's Mass in E flat, Hob. XXII:4
Gli Scherzi	Haydn's 6 String Quartets Op. 33 Nos 37–42
Scherzoso	Beethoven's String Quartet in B flat Op. 130
Schübler Chorales	Bach's 6 Chorale Preludes for organ, BWV 645–50
Serenade	Haydn's String Quartet in F Op. 3 No. 5
Sheep May Safely Graze	Bach's Cantata 208, 'Was mir behagt ist nur die muntre Jagd'
Shepherd Boy Étude	Chopin's Étude in A flat for piano Op. 25 No. 1
Six-Four-Time Mass	Haydn's Mass in G, Hob. XXII:6
Solemn Vespers	Mozart's *Vesperae Solennes de Confessore* in C, K339
Sonata Facile	Mozart's Piano Sonata in C, K545
Sonata quasi una Fantasia	Beethoven's Piano Sonata No. 13 in E flat and No. 14 in C sharp minor
Spatzenmesse	Mozart's Mass in G, K220
Spaur Mass	Mozart's Mass in C, K258
Spring Sonata	Beethoven's Violin and Piano Sonata No. 5 in F Op. 24
Spring Song	Mendelssohn's 'Lied ohne Worte' (Song Without Words)
La Stravaganza	Vivaldi's 12 Violin Concertos Op. 4
Street Song Trio	Beethoven's Trio in B flat for clarinet, cello and piano Op. 11
Sun Quartets	Haydn's 6 String Quartets Op. 20 Nos 1–6
Sunrise Quartet	Haydn's String Quartet in B flat Op. 76 No. 4
Swedish Rhapsody	Alfvén's *Midsommarvaka* for orchestra Op. 19
Tempest	Beethoven's Piano Sonata No. 17 in D
Theresia Mass	Haydn's Mass No. 10 in B flat, Hob. XXII:12
Three Places in New England	Ives's first orchestral set
Timpani Mass	Haydn's Mass in C, Hob. XXII:9
To the Memory of an Angel	Berg's Violin Concerto
The Torrent	Chopin's Étude in C sharp Minor for piano Op. 10 No. 4
Tost Quartets	Haydn's 12 String Quartets Op. 54, 55, and 64
Trauer-Ode	Bach's Cantata 198, 'Lass, Fürstin, lass noch einen Strahl'
Ein Traum	Haydn's String Quartet in F Op. 50 No. 5 (2nd movement)
Triangle Concerto	Liszt's Piano Concerto No. 1 in E flat
Triple Concerto	Beethoven's Concerto in C for piano, violin and cello Op. 56
Tristesse	Chopin's Étude in E for piano Op. 10 No. 3
Trout Quintet	Schubert's Quintet in A for piano, violin, viola, cello and double bass
Trumpet Tune	Purcell's harpsichord piece in C
Trumpet Voluntary	Jeremiah Clarke's instrumental piece in D
Turkish March	Beethoven's incidental music to *The Ruins of Athens* for orchestra
Turkish Rondo	Mozart's Piano Sonata in A, K331 (3rd movement)
Twinkle Twinkle Variations	Mozart's Variation on 'Ah, vous dirai-je, maman' in C for piano
Two-Cello Quintet	Schubert's String Quintet in C Op. 163
Utrecht Jubilate	Handel's Jubilate in D
Utrecht Te Deum	Handel's Te Deum in D
Villanelle	Chopin's Étude in G flat for piano Op. 25 No. 9
Voces Intimae (*Friendly Voices*)	Sibelius' String Quartet in D minor Op. 56
Waisenhausmesse	Mozart's Mass in C minor, K139
Waldstein	Beethoven's Piano Sonata No. 21 in C major Op. 53
Wedding March	Mendelssohn's incidental music to *A Midsummer Night's Dream* for orchestra Op. 61 (9th movement)
Wedge Fugue	Bach's Fugue in E minor for organ
The White Mass	Scriabin's Piano Sonata No. 7 in F sharp Op. 64
Wind-Band Mass	Haydn's Mass No. 12 in B flat, Hob. XXII:14
Winter Wind Étude	Chopin's Etude in A minor for piano Op. 25 No. 11
Witches' Minuet	Haydn's String Quartet in D minor Op. 76 No. 2 (3rd movement)
WTC	Bach's *Well-Tempered Clavier*

General Information

acciaccatura A short grace note played simultaneously with the principal note and released immediately.

Aldeburgh Festival Founded by Benjamin Britten in 1948, held in Aldeburgh, Suffolk, with concert hall, the Maltings, at nearby Snape.

Amati family Violin makers in Cremona, 16th–18th century. Nicola Amati taught Stradivari and Guarneri.

arpeggio Chord spread, i.e. notes played one after the other as on the harp.

Ars Antiqua (Old Art) Refers to music of 12th and 13th centuries derived from the school of Paris.

Ars Nova (New Art) Style of music developed in 14th-century France and Italy. Term coined by Philippe de Vitry.

attempted suicide: Debussy's wife Rosalie 'Lily' Texier shot herself during a bout of depression.

attempted suicide: Tchaikovsky Walked into the freezing River Neva at dead of night following his disastrous marriage in 1877.

Aurora's Wedding Divertissement of last act of *Sleeping Beauty*, sometimes performed separately.

bagatelle Short, plain composition especially for pianoforte e.g. Für Elise.

Baroque Musical era roughly from 1600 to around 1750.

Battle Symphony Beethoven's orchestral work *Wellington's Victory* Op. 91 (includes 'Rule, Britannia!' and 'God Save the King').

berceuse Lullaby.

Boehm system Theobald Boehm (1794–1881) devised an acoustically superior system of placing and sizing the holes in the flute, and of using the keys to cover them, now universally used.

Bond Popular all-girl classical combo created by Mike Batt. Its four members are Elspeth Hanson (1st violin), Eos Chater (2nd violin), Tania Davis (viola) and Gay-Yee Westerhoff (cello), Tania is a native Australian, Eos is Welsh and Gay-Yee and Elspeth are English.

Boosey and Hawkes Ltd London music publishers (merged 1930).

Boston Symphony Orchestra Founded in October 1881 by Henry Lee Higginson.

Brahms: personal motto *Frei aber Froh* (free but happy). He used the initial letters as the thematic structure of his 3rd Symphony.

Brandenburg Concertos Bach's 6 Concerti Grossi dedicated to Christian Ludwig, Margrave of Brandenburg.

brindisi Drinking song usually accompanying a toast.

Canterbury degrees (Lambeth degrees) Music degrees conferred traditionally by the Archbishop of Canterbury.

capriccio Musical work with original and unexpected effects.

Carnegie Hall Largest concert-hall in New York, designed by W B Tuthill and opened in 1891.

cataloguers of works Schubert – Deutsch; Haydn – Hoboken; Scarlatti – Kirkpatrick (Longo numbers are also still used); Mozart – Köchel; Vivaldi – Ryom (Pincherle & Fanna also catalogued works); J S Bach – Schmieder (used initials BWV: Bach-Werke-Verzeichnis); Liszt – both R and S numbers; Nielsen – FS (Fog and Schousboe); Frank Bridge – H numbers; Holmboe – Rapoport (M for Meta numbers, after Holmboe's wife); Bartók – Sz numbers; Beethoven – Kinsky (used WoO numbers for works without an opus) and Hess (used Hn numbers for other works); Purcell – Zimmerman; Handel – Baselt (HMV numbers); Dvorak – Burghauser; Donizetti – Inzaghi; Chopin – Brown.

catch Type of round where words may sound comical when sung. A catch club was formed in London in 1761.

chamber music Term coined by Charles Burney in 1805 to describe music not intended for the church, theatre or public concert room, but now applied to ensemble music written for small groups, such as string quartets.

Cheltenham Festival Music festival started in 1945 as Festival of British Contemporary Music but since 1969 drawing music from international sources.

J. & W. Chester Ltd Music publishers founded in Brighton (1874) and specialising in Russian and other foreign composers.

Chetham's School of Music Founded in 1656, by a bequest from Humphrey Chetham (1580–1653), situated in Long Millgate, Manchester; Chetham's is Britain's only full-scale music school for children, with over 280 boys and girls aged 8–18.

Chicago Symphony Orchestra Founded in 1891 by Theodore Thomas; it is the third oldest orchestra in USA.

children: most born to one composer Twenty to J S Bach.

Children's Corner Six piano pieces dedicated by Debussy to his daughter: 1) Dr Gradus ad Parnassum, 2) Jimbo's Lullaby, 3) Serenade for the Doll, 4) Snow is Dancing, 5) The Little Shepherd, 6) Golliwogg's Cakewalk.

clam Playing a wrong note in a performance.

Classical Period Ranges from late 18th to the early 19th century.

Colour Symphony (Arthur Bliss): movements The four movements: *Purple*, *Red*, *Blue* and *Green*.

Composers' Guild of Great Britain Founded in 1944 to protect the rights of composers; affiliated to the Society of Authors. First president was Vaughan Williams.

concerto Work, usually in three movements, which contrasts and integrates a solo instrument with the orchestra.

conductor with 36 names Louis Julien (1812–60) was sponsored at his baptism by 36 members of the local philharmonic society.

coronach (corranach) Funeral dirge of Ireland and Highland Scotland.

Crossover Chart Established in 1996 and includes popular light classical pieces.

deaf composers Beethoven, Fauré, Smetana.

deaf percussionist Evelyn Glennie.

Diabelli Variations Beethoven's Thirty-Three Variations on a Waltz by Diabelli.

Dido's Lament Aria from Act 3 of Purcell's *Dido and Aeneas*, played annually at Remembrance Day service at the Cenotaph and beginning with the words 'When I am laid in earth'.

The Divine Poem Scriabin's Symphony No. 3 in C minor Op. 43 (three movements entitled *Struggles*, *Delights* and *Divine Play*).

Dvořák: son-in-law Josef Suk.

Early Music Consort Founded by David Munrow in 1967 to perform Renaissance and medieval music on original instruments.

Edinburgh Festival Founded in 1947 with Rudolf Bing as director. Three-week festival of music held in August–September now teems with other arts and entertainments.

***Eighteen-Twelve* (1812)** Concert overture Op. 49 by Tchaikovsky commemorating the defeat of Napoleon's Grande Armée on its retreat from Moscow. It incorporates 'La Marseillaise'.

English Chamber Orchestra Founded in 1948 as the Goldsbrough Orchestra (after its founder); present name adopted in 1960.

English Folk Dance and Song Society Amalgamation in 1932 of Folk Song Society (founded 1898) and English Folk Dance Society (founded 1911); HQ in Cecil Sharp House, London, NW1 7AY.

***Enigma Variations*: musical portraits** 1) Lady Elgar (C.A.E.); 2) Hew Steuart-Powell (H.D.S.-P.); 3) RB Townshend (R.B.T.); 4) W. Meath Baker (W.M.B.); 5) Richard P. Arnold (R.P.A.); 6) Isabel Fitton (Ysobel); 7) A. Troyte Griffith (Troyte); 8) Winifred Norbury (W.N.); 9) AJ Jaeger (Nimrod); 10) Dora Penny (Dorabella); 11) GR Sinclair (G.R.S.); 12) Basil Nevinson (B.G.N.); 13) Lady Mary Lygon; 14) Elgar (E.D.U.).

***Estampes* (*Engravings*)** Three piano pieces by Debussy: *Pagodas*, *Evening in Granada*, and *Gardens in the Rain*.

étude (study) Composition intended to test and extend the performer's technique.

eurhythmics Method invented by Émile Jaques-Dalcroze (1865–1950) for expressing rhythmical aspect of music through gymnastic exercises.

Faust Symphony (Liszt) Movements portray three characters: *Faust*, *Gretchen* and *Mephistopheles*.

Fireworks Music Handel wrote the music to celebrate the Peace of Aix-La-Chapelle (1749); first played in Green Park, London.

First Post British Army bugle call, a summons back to the barracks, sounded at 9.30 p.m.

The Five (aka The Mighty Handful) Russian composers Balakirev, Borodin, Cui, Mussorgsky and Rimsky-Korsakov.

Frankfurt Group English composers who were pupils of Iwan Knorr in the 1890s; they were Norman O'Neill, Roger Quilter, Cyril Scott and Balfour Gardiner.

funeral marches Famous ones include the 3rd movement of Chopin's 2nd piano sonata; Handel's Dead March in *Saul*; 2nd movement of Beethoven's *Eroica*; Siegfried's Funeral March from Wagner's *Götterdämmerung*.

Gagliano family 18th-century family of violin-makers from Naples. Key members: Alessandro, his sons, Niccolò and Gennaro, and grandsons Ferdinando and Giuseppe.

gamelan A kind of orchestra widespread in south-east Asia, especially Indonesia, whose range of percussion includes gongs, drums, marimbas and chimes.

Gebrauchsmusik (utility music) Term associated in the 1920s with works by Hindemith, Weill and Krenek, influenced by Brecht and designed for social and educational purposes.

Gesamtkunstwerk Wagner's term for a dramatic work in which drama, music, poetry, song and painting would be united into a single artistic whole.

glee Vocal music for three or four parts, unaccompanied and homophonic, popular in late 18th- and early 19th-century England.

Goldberg Variations J S Bach's 30 variations on a theme for two-manual harpsichord.

Grove, Sir George English music writer (1820–1900) who, after training as a civil engineer, turned to musical studies and compiled *Grove's Dictionary of Music and Musicians*, then published in 4 volumes, now expanded into 20.

Guarneri Quartet American string quartet formed in 1964 in Vermont. Members are Arnold Steinhardt and John Dally (violins), Michael Tree (viola) and Peter Wiley (cello), who replaced founding member David Soyer in 2000.

Hail to the Chief March traditionally played at formal American events to announce the arrival of the President, first used at the inauguration of Martin Van Buren in 1837. The words, from Sir Walter Scott's *Lady of the Lake,* are no longer used. Derived from an old Gaelic tune, the melody was adapted by English composer, James Sanderson (1769–1841) for a scene in Scott's play.

hairpins Nickname for the signs < (crescendo) and > (diminuendo).

Hallé Orchestra Founded in 1857 by Charles Hallé and based in Manchester. Sir John Barbirolli was the principal conductor from 1943 to his death in 1970. Kent Nagano has been the conductor since 1992.

Haydn's Symphony No. 45 Haydn directed his musicians to gradually leave the stage during the last movement, hence the nickname 'Farewell'.

Henry Wood: pseudonym Paul Klenovsky was the cryptic name (Klen means maple tree) under which Wood transcribed for orchestra Bach's Toccata and Fugue in D minor.

Hexameron Six variations for piano on a march from Bellini's *I Puritani*, each written by a different composer/pianist, i.e. Liszt, Pixis, Herz, Thalberg, Czerny and Chopin, each of whom played his variation at the first performance of the work in a charity concert in Paris in 1837 (first of the super groups one might say!). Liszt later added orchestral accompaniments and played whole series at recitals.

humoresque Humorous or capricious instrumental piece. Famous examples are by Dvorák and Schumann.

Images Title used by Debussy for two works: 1) *Images* for Orchestra, including *Gigues, Ibéria* and *Rondes de Printemps*; 2) two sets for solo piano: *Reflets dans l'eau, Hommage à Rameau, Movement, Cloches à travers les feuilles, Et la lune descend sur le temple qui fut* and *Poissons d'or.*

Jena Symphony A work found by Fritz Stein in 1909 in Jena, Germany, and linked until 1957 with Beethoven; it turned out that Friedrich Witt was the composer.

La Jeune France (Young France) Group of four French composers (Yves Baudrier, André Jolivet, Daniel Lesur and Olivier Messiaen) who resolved in Paris in 1936 to carry out 'a return to the human' in composition.

jubilate Hymn of praise, usually based on Psalm 100 (in Roman Catholic Psalter, Psalm 99).

Juilliard Quartet Founded by William Schuman in New York in 1946; the line-up as at October 2009 is Nick Eanet and Ronald Copes (violins), Samuel Rhodes (viola) and Joel Krosnick (cello).

K numbers Named after the cataloguers of two composers: Mozart – Ludwig von Köchel; Scarlatti – Ralph Kirkpatrick.

karaoke (empty orchestra) Singing along with recorded accompaniment.

Kneller Hall Headquarters, founded in 1857 at Twickenham, Middlesex, of Royal Military School of Music.

La Scala (The Staircase) Milan opera house built in 1778 on the site of a church founded in the 18th century by Regina della Scala, wife of a Duke of Milan.

Last Post British Army bugle call sounded at 10 p.m. that ends the day. It is customary to play the Last Post at military funerals.

Leeds Piano Competition Established in 1963 by Fanny Waterman and Marion Thorpe and held triennially. The first winner was Michael Roll, and many placed pianists have won international reputations, notably Peter Donohoe, who was placed sixth in 1981.

Leitmotiv Term first used by A W Ambrose (*c.*1865) in an article about Wagner's operas and Liszt's symphonic poems; it was later used by F W Jähns, to denote a short and recurrent musical figure standing for an idea or character.

Les Six Term coined by Henri Collet in 1920 to describe the avant-garde French composers Georges Auric (1899–1983), Louis Durey (1888–1979), Arthur Honegger (1892–1955), Darius Milhaud (1892–1974), Francis Poulenc (1899–1963) and Germaine Tailleferre (1892–1983).

Leventritt Competition International competition alternately for pianists and violinists, established in 1939 by Leventritt Foundation, New York. Winner's prize consists of engagements with prominent orchestras and offer of recording contract.

Lincoln Center for the Performing Arts New York arts centre consisting of Metropolitan Opera House, Avery Fisher Hall, Juilliard School and various theatres and societies.

London Philharmonic Orchestra Founded by Sir Thomas Beecham in 1932.

London Symphony Orchestra Founded by players who seceded from Henry Wood's Queen's Hall orchestra in 1904 and run by its own members ever since.

Má Vlast Cycle of 6 symphonic poems by Smetana: 1) *The High Citadel* (*Vysehrad*); 2) *River Moldau* (*Vltava*); 3) *Sàrka*; 4) *From Bohemia's Meadows and Forests* (*Z Ceskych Luhu a Haju*); 5) *Tabor*; 6) *Blánik* (*The Valhalla of the Hussite heroes*).

madrigal Song form for two or more voices developed in 13th- and 14th-century Italy, most often secular and unaccompanied; revived and enhanced during the Renaissance into an expressive, polyphonic form introduced into Elizabethan England.

Manchester School Name given to group of composers (Maxwell Davies, Harrison Birtwistle, Alexander Goehr and John Ogdon) taught in Manchester by Richard Hall in the late 1950s.

masque Courtly entertainment that evolved in 17th-century England, incorporating music, acting and spectacular costumes and scenery.

Mighty Handful (aka The Five) Alternative name for 'The Five' (coined by Vladimir Stasov).

minimalism Style of music that developed in the 1960s, involving repetition of short musical motifs in simple harmonic idiom. Prominent members include Philip Glass, Steve Reich and Terry Riley.

minuet Movement (usually the 3rd) in sonatas and symphonies of the classical period, derived from the dance of the same name.

Miserere Psalm 51 (50 in Roman Catholic Psalter) set to music by various composers.

most prolific composer Georg Philipp Telemann is often assigned this title; among his output are over 600 overtures, 44 Passions, 40 operas and numerous other works.

motet Choral composition, generally on a sacred text.

motif Short melodic pattern or idea that runs throughout a piece.

***Mourning Music* (*Trauermusik*)** Paul Hindemith work composed within hours of the death of George V in 1936.

Mozart: wrote down on first hearing Gregorio Allegri's *Miserere* was supposedly sacrosanct to the Vatican; Mozart went to a service there and went home and wrote it down from memory, thereby risking excommunication. It is however very likely that Mozart had heard the piece on at least one occasion prior to his visit to Rome.

Mozart's Piano Concerto No. 21 in C Given nickname of 'Elvira Madigan' in 1967 because it was the theme tune of the film of that name.

Mozart's Piano Concerto No. 26 in D Given nickname of 'Coronation' because it was played at King Leopold II of Prussia's coronation.

Mozart's String Quartets 14–19 Dedicated to Haydn with the words 'I send my six sons to you'.

Mozart: work falsely attributed to *Adélaïde* violin concerto. In 1977 Marius Casadesus admitted he composed it.

musical epochs Medieval 600–1425; Renaissance 1425–1600; Baroque 1600–1750; Classical 1750–1825; Romantic 1820–80; Post-Romantic 1880–1910; Modern since 1910; some historians also identify a Nationalist epoch 1860–1910 and an Impressionist epoch 1890–1920.

musique concrète Music composed by manipulating recorded sounds, especially natural sounds rather than electronic.

National Gallery Recitals During the Second World War Dame Myra Hess founded and directed a series of lunchtime recitals, which became very popular and helped to sustain morale.

New Symphony Orchestra London orchestra founded by Sir Thomas Beecham in 1905 and became Royal Albert Hall Orchestra in 1920 and later disbanded.

New York Philharmonic Orchestra Oldest US symphony orchestra, founded in 1842 as Philharmonic Society of New York; merged with New York Symphony Orchestra in 1928 to become Philharmonic Symphony Orchestra of New York; now known as the NYPO.

nocturne Night-piece, serenade.

notes of the scale: English to Italian A=la, B=si, C=do, D=re, E=mi, F=fa, G=sol.

octet A group of 8 musicians, or a piece of music written for such a group. A string octet is usually a double string quartet.

opus (work) Opus numbers are used to designate the order in which a given composer's works were written or published.

oratorio Musical setting for voices and orchestra of a text based on the Scriptures or an epic theme. Could be described as an opera without staging, scenery or costumes.

Parthenia Title of the first book of keyboard music printed in England (1611), collecting pieces by William Byrd, John Bull and Orlando Gibbons.

pastorale Either a musical play based on a rustic subject, or a composition with rustic overtones.

Performing Right Society Society of composers, authors, and music publishers founded in Britain in 1914 to collect royalties for non-dramatic public performance and broadcasting of members' works.

Philharmonia Orchestra English symphony orchestra founded in 1945 by Walter Legge.

piano quartet Piano, violin, viola and cello.

piano quintet Usually string quartet plus piano.

piano trio Piano, violin, and cello.

Pictures at an Exhibition Mussorgsky's versions in music of 10 pictures displayed at a memorial exhibition for Russian artist Victor Hartmann: 1) *The Gnome*; 2) *The Old Castle*; 3) *Tuileries*; 4) *Bydlo* (a farm cart); 5) *Unhatched Chickens*; 6) *Samuel Goldenberg and Shmuyle*; 7) *Market-Place at Limoges*; 8) *Catacombs*; 9) *Baba-Yaga (The Hut on Fowl's Legs)*; 10) *The Great Gate of Kiev*.

Pierrot Players Instrument ensemble founded in 1967 by Maxwell Davies and Harrison Birtwistle, regrouped to form the Fires of London in 1970 before disbanding in 1987.

Pomp and Circumstance Elgar's title (taken from Act 3 of *Othello*) for his set of five marches for symphony orchestra, the first of which was the basis for 'Land of Hope and Glory' (words by A C Benson).

Pre-classical Term applied to composers such as C P E Bach who are considered to be later than baroque and leading to the 'Classical' style of Haydn and Mozart.

Promenade Concerts Although promenade concerts (at which listeners could saunter around) were put on in London as early as 1838, it was not until 1895 that they became a regular annual feature when Robert Newman began a series at Queen's Hall with Henry Wood as conductor. Wood's name became synonymous with the Proms, and after his death in 1944, Malcolm Sargent became principal conductor (1948–67). Royal Albert Hall became venue in 1941 on the destruction of Queen's Hall.

Proms: centenary 1995; Harrison Birtwistle composed *Panic*.

Queen's Hall Once London's chief concert hall, situated in Langham Place, opened in 1893 and destroyed by fire in 1941, following a Nazi bombing raid.

rāga Indian musical form that represents a mood, concept or occasion by one of many patterns of notes presented as an ascending and descending scale used as a basis for improvisation.

Ring Cycle Full title *Der Ring des Nibelungen* (*The Ring of the Nibelung*). Often referred to as the tetralogy although Wagner himself called the first opera, *Das Rheingold*, the prologue. After it comes *Die Walküre* (*The Valkyrie*), followed by *Siegfried* and finally, *Götterdämmerung* (*Twilight of the Gods*).

Royal Academy of Music Founded in London in 1822 and situated in Tenterden Street but moved to Marylebone Road in 1912. The RAM has about 700 students and 150 staff.

Royal College of Music Founded in 1882 but moved to its present site at Prince Consort Road, South Kensington in 1894.

Royal Philharmonic Orchestra Founded in 1946 by Sir Thomas Beecham, who was principal conductor until his death in 1961.

St Louis Symphony Orchestra Founded in March 1881, the second oldest symphony orchestra in the USA.

Scottish Chamber Orchestra Founded in 1974 with headquarters in Queen's Hall, Edinburgh.

septet Make-up varies, but typical format would be violin, viola, French horn, clarinet, bassoon, cello and double bass.

sextet String sextet usually two each of violins, violas and cellos.

sonata Instrumental composition usually in three or four movements for unaccompanied piano or, more rarely, for another stringed instrument with piano accompaniment.

stanza One of a number of sections of a song, two or more lines long, characterised by a common metre, rhyme and number of lines.

string quartet Violins (1st and 2nd), viola and cello.

string quintet String quartet with added viola or cello.

string trio Violin, viola and cello.

Sturm und Drang (Storm and Stress) Term applied to a period (*c.*1760–80) of great emotional intensity in German literature and music. Musically, it is particularly associated with F J Haydn's works around the time of his Symphonies 40–59.

Suite bergamasque Piano suite by Debussy, its 4 movements: *Prélude, Menuet, Clair de Lune*, and *Passepied*.

symphonic structure In the Classical model, 4 movements: 1) a fast sonata; 2) a slow movement; 3) a minuet scherzo; 4) a fast movement, mostly a rondo.

Tchaikovsky Piano Competition Quadrennial competition first held in Moscow in 1954. Famous winners include Van Cliburn, John Ogdon, Vladimir Ashkenazy.

Three Bs Bach, Beethoven, Brahms (coined by Hans von Bülow).

Three Choirs Festival Annual meeting that rotates among the 3 cathedral choirs of Gloucester, Hereford and Worcester, held almost continuous since the early 18th century.

tonic sol-fa System of sight-singing and notation devised by Sarah Ann Glover in England in the 1840s, though much the same system had been introduced in the USA by D Sower in 1832.

toy symphony Term for a symphony in which toy instruments are used as well as strings and piano; the most popular example is a work by Leopold Mozart, with toy instruments now thought to have been added by Michael Haydn.

train wreck Colloquial term for what happens when the parts in an ensemble collide because the musicians are not playing together.

The Triumphs of Oriana Collection of 5- and 6-part English madrigals by 24 composers assembled by Thomas Morley in 1601 in honour of Elizabeth I.

trumpet voluntary Piece that imitates a trumpet but is, in fact, played using a similar sounding organ stop. The best known version is a transcription by Henry Wood of a piece originally ascribed to Purcell but now credited to Jeremiah Clarke. He called it 'The Prince of Denmark's March', but Wood's title has superseded Clarke's.

Tuning of Strings Cello: C, G, D, A (octave lower than the viola). Violin: G, D, A, E. Double-bass: E, A, D, G. Banjo: 4 strings C, G, D, A; 5 strings G, D, G, B, D. Viola: C, G, D, A (5th lower than violin).

Tweedledum and Tweedledee Name coined by John Byrom (1692–1763) to satirise the public feuding between composers G F Handel and G Bononcini.

violinists: known for revealing garments Vanessa Mae, Anne-Sophie Mutter, Linda Lampenius.

Wagner's patron Ludwig II, King of Bavaria (1845–86).

The Walk to the Paradise Garden Intermezzo before concluding scene of Delius's opera *A Village Romeo and Juliet*. The Paradise Garden is actually a public house.

Wedding March Played at the end of Act 4 of Mendelssohn's *Midsummer Night's Dream* and traditionally used on exit from the church. The Bridal Chorus from *Lohengrin* commonly announces the entry.

Wigmore Hall London concert hall in Wigmore Street, opened in 1901 as Bechstein Hall.

WoO Werk ohne Op. zahl (work without opus number): system of cataloguing used where a composer's work lacks opus numbers.

woodwind quintet Usually flute, clarinet, oboe, French horn and bassoon.

Musical Instruments

accordion Invented by Friedrich Buschmann of Berlin in 1822.

Aeolian harp Box and strings that sound when hit by a current of air.

aeolina Mouth organ.

angelica Instrument of the lute family with 16 or 17 strings.

arpeggione Six-stringed cello invented by G Staufer of Vienna in 1823. Aka *guitare d'amour*.

aulos Double-reed wind instrument of ancient Greece.

autoharp Zither on which chord keys are pressed by one hand and strings strummed by the other.

Bach trumpet Valveless trumpet in either C or D.

backfall Part of an organ that connects the rods to the keyboard.

bagpipes Ancient instrument popular throughout the world but particularly identified with Scotland. The Scottish Highland bagpipe has two tenor drones and a bass drone, tuned an octave apart. The chanter is the pipe that plays the tune. Versions of the bagpipe around the world include the Bulgarian *gaida*, the *cornemuse* of France and Belgium, the *gaita* of northwestern Spain and the Irish Uilleann pipes.

balalaika Russian three-stringed instrument of the lute family with a triangular belly and moveable frets on the arm. The balalaika was developed in the 18th century from the *domra*.

bamboula West Indian tambourine.

bandoneon Argentinian variant of the accordion.

baritone horn Brass instrument in B flat, related to the euphonium with a smaller bore and 3 valves.

baryton Stringed instrument similar to viola da gamba but with sympathetic strings. Played by Prince Esterházy (Haydn's patron); it has made a revival in recent years.

Basque drum Tambourine.

bassanello Shawm-like woodwind instrument, no longer played.

bassoon Bass member of the double-reed oboe family, pitched in C.

bell lyra Type of portable glockenspiel.

bissex Twelve-string guitar invented in 1770 by Vanhecke.

bodhran Irish frame drum played with a double-ended stick.

bombard Alto-pitched shawm.

bombardon Form of bass tuba with 3 piston valves.

boobams Percussion instrument consisting of bamboo tubes.
bottleneck Tube that fits over a finger on the fretting hand used for slide-guitar playing.
bouzouki Greek fretted string instrument with a long neck and 4 sets of strings.
cabaca/cabasa Latin American percussion instrument, around or pear-shaped gourd covered with beads and fitted with a handle.
calliope Literally meaning 'beautiful-voiced' after the Muse of epic poetry; US name for a steam-driven organ.
campanelle Glockenspiel.
canale Psaltery.
canntaireachd Ancient Highland bagpipe notation, using syllables to represent a group of notes.
carillon Alternative name for glockenspiel, so called by Handel in 1739 when he first used the instrument in *Saul*.
castanets Twin cup-shaped clappers; name derives from the Spanish *castaña*, chestnut wood.
celesta Small keyboard instrument patented by Auguste Mustel in 1886 and famously used in Tchaikovsky's 'Dance of the Sugar Plum Fairy'.
cello: full name Violoncello.
cembalo Short for clavicembalo, the Italian word for harpsichord.
cetera Zither.
chalumeau Forerunner of the clarinet with 6 to 8 finger-holes.
chanterelle The E string on a violin, or the highest string on any instrument in the violin or lute family.
charivari Cacophonous, extemporised music produced with any household utensil or object that will make a noise.
chitarrone Lute similar to a theorbo but longer.
choke cymbal: aka High-hat cymbal.
chromatic harp Harp built by Pleyel in 1897; equipped with a string for every semitone, it needed no pedals.
cimbalom Form of dulcimer native to Hungary, made up of a box on which strings are hit with mallets.
cittern A 15th-century forerunner of the lute with metal strings tuned in pairs and plucked.
clapper Striker in the middle of a bell.
clarinet Single-reed woodwind instrument developed by J C Denner of Nuremberg in the late 17th century.
clàrsach Ancient small Celtic harp having brass strings instead of gut or nylon ones.
clavecin Harpsichord.
claves Cuban percussion instruments consisting of round wooden sticks that are stuck together.
clavichord/clarichord Small keyboard instrument invented in 14th century. Aka manichord or chekker.
colascione European version of oriental long-necked lute popular in the Tudor period.
colophony Bow rosin (named after Colophon in Asia Minor, the source of the best rosin).
concertina Invented by Charles Wheatstone in 1829 as the 'Symphonium'. Similar to accordion but no keyboard.
console Operational part of organ **cor anglais** French for English horn, but in fact an alto oboe; invented by Ferlandis of Bergamo.
cor de chasse Hunting horn developed in France in 17th century.
cornopean Late 19th-century brass instrument similar to a trumpet.
crembalum Type of Jew's harp.
crook Tube inserted into a brass instrument to lengthen its tube and change its pitch.
crotales Ancient Greek percussion instrument in form of a rattle or clapper.
crumhorn Early and widely used Renaissance double-reed instrument. Name means 'curved horn'.
crwth Welsh medieval instrument with 6 strings, a bowed lyre.
cuckoo Two-note wind instrument imitating the bird.
damper Felt piece that damps the vibration of the string on a piano until the key is depressed.
didjeridu (didgeridoo) Native Australian wind instrument, which allows player to breathe through nose while playing.
digitorium Small keyboard machine usually having 5 keys, which are sprung more severely than usual so as to strengthen fingers. Invented by Myer Marks in the mid-19th century.
domra Type of early balalaika with a round body and two or three metal strings tuned a fourth apart.
double bass: aka Bull-fiddle, doghouse.
Dudelsack German form of bagpipe.
dulcimer Ancient instrument with wire strings stretching over a shallow box which are struck with rods.
dulcitone Instrument similar to celesta but with steel tuning forks instead of steel plates.
duplex-coupler piano Invented by Emanuel Moór in 1921; has 2 keyboards, upper tuned an octave higher.
electronde Electronic instrument invented by Martin Taubman in 1933, like the theramin but can create staccato effect.
embouchure Mouthpiece of a brass instrument.
emicon Electric instrument invented in USA in 1931 and producing notes from air in graded chromatic scale.
English flute: aka Recorder.
English horn Alto oboe, pitched a 5th lower and having a conical shape and bulbous bell.
euphonium Tenor tuba in B flat. Also name of instrument made of glass plates and rods by Ernst Chladni in 1790.
fagotto Bassoon.
fipple Mouthpiece for all wind instruments.
flageolet Small type of recorder.
flexatone Patented in 1922 and consisting of a flexible metal sheet suspended in a wire frame with handle. Shaking produces a tremolo sound.
flugelhorn Brass instrument in the cornet family but with a wider bore and larger bell.
flûte à bec (beak flute) Type of recorder.
French harp Harmonica.
French horn Coiled brass wind intrument extending to 11ft when uncoiled with a bell of 14in diameter. Early form supposedly introduced to the orchestra by Lully; modern form uses valves introduced in the 1820s.
frog On bowed instruments, the end of the bow that is held in the hand. Aka nut.
Geigenwerk Type of hurdy-gurdy invented in Nuremberg in 1575 by Hans Haiden.
gekkin Japanese instrument with circular body like banjo but with 9 frets and 4 strings tuned in pairs.
gemshorn Type of flute made of horn, not used since 16th century. Aka chamois horn.
gittern Medieval ancestor of guitar.
glockenspiel (lit. bell play) Musical instrument consisting of hanging metal bars, which are struck with a hammer.
gong Ancient percussion instrument first found in China, a metal disc generally with upturned edges, usually with indefinite pitch but sometimes tuned.
grelots Little bells, e.g. sleigh bells, used as percussion.
gusla One-stringed bowed instrument long popular in Slavonic cultures.
gusli Ancient Russian instrument of the zither family.
harmonica Mouth organ with metal reeds, first produced by Friedrich Buschman of Berlin in 1821 as the 'Mundäoline'. The two main types of harmonicas are the chromatic and the diatonic. The chromatic harmonica is preferred by blues players such as Bob Dylan and Neil Young. The diatonic harmonica has a wider range and more suited to the virtuoso such as Larry Adler.
harmonium Small portable reed organ perfected by Alexandre Debain of Paris in the early 1840s.
harp Forty-seven-stringed instrument whose modern orchestral version with a pedal mechanism was developed by Sébastien Érard.
harpsichord Wing-shaped keyboard instrument in which the strings are mechanically plucked rather that struck with a hammer.
hautbois French name for oboe, (lit. 'high wood').
Hawaiian guitar Ukulele (also nickname of steel guitar) introduced by the Portuguese.
heckelphone Double-reed, baritone oboe with a conical bore and bulbous bell.
helicon Tuba with a circular construction that can be wrapped around the body for marching bands.
hellertion Electric instrument developed in Frankfurt in 1936 by Bruno Helberger and Peter Lertes, similar to Theremin but with a range of 6 octaves.
hitschiriki Japanese instrument like a bamboo flute with 7 finger-holes and 2 thumb-holes.
hityokin Japanese vertical flute made of bamboo.
hornpipe Wind instrument with a single reed and a cow's horn fitted on the end.
hummel Swedish zither.
hurdy-gurdy Medieval instrument resembling a viol but whose sound is produced by friction of hand-cranked wooden wheel on strings that could be stopped by keys.
huruk Hourglass-shaped Indian drum.
hydraulis Ancient instrument, aka water organ, supposedly invented in Greece by Ktesibios in the 3rd century BC.
idiophone Term used for instrument whose own material makes a characteristic sound such as castanets, gongs, bells, etc.
Irish harp Small harp played while held in the lap.

Japanese fiddle One-stringed instrument played by street performers.

Jew's harp Folk instrument consisting of a metal frame that contains a flexible strip of metal. The frame is held between the player's teeth while the metal strip is twanged.

kazoo Short tube open at both ends, with a vibrating membrane in between, played by humming into it; a kind of mirliton.

kin Japanese string instrument, a small koto.

kithara Ancient but sophisticated Greek lyre, which is finger plucked.

klavier Keyboard instrument (with strings).

knollhorn Soft-sounding herald horn from the mid-western region of the US.

Korean temple block Oriental addition to the 20th-century dance-band drummer's equipment, constituting a skull-shaped hollow block of wood, in several sizes, and struck with a drumstick.

koto Japanese instrument resembling a zither, with 7 to 13 silk strings plucked by the fingers.

lira A 16th-century string instrument with drones, played with a bow.

loure French bagpipe.

lute Ancient musical instrument with a pear-shaped belly and a long, fretted fingerboard and played like a modern guitar.

lutherie The art of making string instruments – not only lutes, but also guitars and the violin family.

luthier One who practises lutherie.

lyra (lyre) Ancient Greek instrument with a 4-sided frame, encompassing strings attached from a soundbox to a crossbar. Played like a harp.

machete Portuguese 4-string folk guitar.

mandocello Bass mandolin.

mandola/mandora Small, early precursor of the lute and mandolin with 9 frets and up to 6 strings.

mandolin Instrument in the lute family, fretted and with 8 wire strings tuned in four pairs, G, D, A, E.

maracas Latin American percussion instrument consisting of two seed-filled gourds, which are shaken by handles.

mardakion Accordion-like instrument from the mid-west US.

marimba African percussion instrument introduced to Latin America, a deeper pitched version of the xylophone with metal resonators.

m'bira African 'thumb piano' made up of a number of metal or cane tongues held in position with a bar attached to a box or board. The free ends are twanged with the thumbs.

mellophone Variation of the French horn constructed for marching.

melodeon Related to the concertina, with 10 treble keys on the right, bellows and 4 bass keys on the left.

metallophone Percussion instrument consisting of tuned metal bars arranged in single or double rows.

mirliton Instrument containing a membrane to modify a sound made when the player hums or sings into or against it.

monochord Musical instrument with one string, used for determining the ratios of musical intervals.

Moog synthesizer Earliest commercial, voltage-controlled synthesizer, invented by Robert Moog in 1965.

mouth organ The term covers many instruments with metal reeds but nowadays is synonymous with the harmonica.

musetta Bellows-operated French bagpipe popular in the court of Louis XIV.

mute Device usually conical in shape, that muffles a brass instrument's sound.

nightingale Toy instrument used in by Scarlatti in an oratorio by Scarlatti and by Leopold Mozart in his *Toy Symphony*.

nose flute Originating in Polynesia, a bamboo flute blown through the nostrils.

nut On bowed instruments, device fitted on to the end of the bow that is held in the hand, and used to adjust the bow's tension.

oboe Double-reed woodwind instrument with a conical bore in C and a natural scale of D.

oboe d'amore Slightly bigger than the normal oboe, with a pear-shaped bell, and pitched a minor third lower.

ocarina (little goose) Small, round, wind instrument with finger holes, and made out of clay or porcelain; so named by Giuseppe Donati in mid-1800s; aka sweet potato.

oliphant Small medieval horn made from an elephant's tusk.

ondes Martenot Electronic keyboard instrument developed by Maurice Martenot in the 1920s; shaped like a spinet.

ophicleide Large, brass, keyed bass bugle played in the upright position, developed from the serpent (name is Greek for 'serpent with keys') but displaced by the bass tuba.

panharmonicon Mechanical orchestra invented by Johann Maelzel in 1805; inspiration of Beethoven's *Battle Symphony*.

panpipes (aka syrinx) Ancient wind instrument consisting of several pipes of graduated lengths bound together.

pegbox Box at the end of the neck on string instruments into which the pegs that adjust the strings are inserted.

phagotum Type of bellows-blown bagpipe invented by Canon Afranio of Ferrara in the early 1500s.

pianoforte Full name of the piano, with 88 keys, first made in Florence around 1700 by Bartolomeo Cristofori; name is Italian for soft-loud.

pianola Player piano manufactured in the early 1900s by the Aeolian Corporation; the first of the kind was the Welte-Mignon.

piccolo Small flute that sounds an octave higher than written (piccolo in C) or, less often, a minor ninth higher than written (piccolo in D flat).

point Tip of the bow of a string instrument.

poliphant Thirty-seven-stringed instrument of early 17th century; a cross between harp, lute and theorbo.

posthorn Cylindrical, valveless straight horn used by coachmen and mailcarriers to announce arrival.

psaltery Ancient string instrument, similar to the dulcimer.

purfling Decorative strip inlaid around edges of a string instrument.

pyiba Pear-shaped, four-stringed, ancient Chinese lute.

racket Double-reed instrument consisting of short, thick cylinder of wood drilled along its length with a bore-holes connected into a single air channel.

raspa Cuban percussion instrument made out of gourd with notches that are scraped with a stick.

ratamacue Drum rudiment consisting of an alternating-hand sticking pattern.

ratchet/rattle Percussion instrument with a cogwheel that strikes one or more metal or wooden projections when twirled.

rebab An ancient North African and Middle Eastern short-necked fiddle with two strings.

rebec Small, pear-shaped, medieval bowed instrument, a development of the Arab rebab, with a short neck and three to five strings.

recorder End-blown wooden flute without keys, with a tapering bore.

reed(s) Clarinet is a single-reed instrument; oboe and bassoon are double-reed.

regal Portable reed organ of the 16th century.

Rhodes piano Electric piano developed by Harold Rhodes.

rhythmicon Keyboard percussion instrument using photoelectric cell and devised by Lev Theremin and Henry Cowell in 1931.

rosin Block of hardened tree resin that is rubbed across the bow hairs to enhance the friction.

rote (rotta) Lyre-type instrument from the Middle Ages.

sackbut Renaissance name for the slide trombone, which then had a smaller bell and narrower bore.

saddle On guitar, a thin strip of ivory, bone or plastic set into the bridge.

saltbox Charivari instrument used by flipping the lid and beating the side with a rolling pin or spoon.

samisen Flat-backed, long-necked lute from Japan with a skin-covered belly and three silk strings.

sarangi Northern Indian fiddle with short, thick neck and 3 to 4 bowed strings plus sympathetic strings.

sarod Indian instrument usually having 6 main strings and 12 to 15 sympathetic strings.

sarrusophone Double-reed woodwind instrument related to the oboe but made of brass, invented by French bandleader Sarrus in 1856.

saxophone Single-reed family of instruments, usually metal but sometimes plastic, invented by Adolphe Sax around 1840 and patented in 1846.

scordatura Changing the tuning of one or more strings from their standard pitch.

scroll Ornamental curled portion at the end of the pegbox on instruments of the violin family.

Scruggs picking Banjo finger-picking style developed by Earl Scruggs, using the thumb and two fingers.

serpent S-curved wooden horn with a conical bore, finger holes and a cup-shaped mouthpiece.

seven-string guitar Has an extra, high A string.

shakuhachi End-blown bamboo flute from Japan.

shawm Family of high-pitched, double-reed woodwind instruments of the Middle Ages; precursors of the oboe.

sheng Chinese mouth organ made up of wind chamber fitted with pipes with reeds that vibrate.

shofar Ancient Hebrew ceremonial wind instrument made of a ram's horn.

simandl bow For string basses; a bow configured to be held with the palm up.

sistrum Ancient percussion instrument made up of metal disc rattles threaded on rods.
sitar Long-necked Indian lute with moveable arched frets, a gourd resonator close to the pegboard, and 3 to 7 strings, below which are sympathetic strings, often as many as 12. Made popular in the West by Ravi Shankar.
skirl On bagpipe, the sounds made by the upper pipes.
sousaphone Tuba that encircles the body and made specifically for John Philip Sousa's band.
spinet Small Renaissance keyboard instrument with a plucking action like a harpsichord.
steel drums Made out of various-sized oil drums, with deeply incised patterns with different pitches.
stick, Chapman Electric 10-stringed (5 bass and 5 guitar) instrument that utilises tapping technique on strings.
swell Mechanical device on some keyboard instruments for adjusting the volume of sound.
switch Percussion instrument, made up of wires bound at one end, that is struck against the hand.
sympathetic string String that vibrates in an instrument without being plucked in response to the vibrations of strings that are plucked, or to a percussion impact.
tablas Asymmetrical pair of conical, tuned, wooden Indian drums, beaten with the hands.
tabor Earliest form of the snare drum, which evolved into a military instrument.
talon The nut end of the bow used to play string instruments.
tambour Type of drum.
tambourine Percussion instrument of Arab origin consisting of a small, shallow, circular drum with metal discs inserted into its frame. The discs are known as jingles.
tambur(a) Long-necked, round-bodied lute. Indian tamburas have 4 strings, drones and a moveable ivory bridge to adjust pitch; Balkan tamburas are fretted.
tam-tam Large, flat, thin metal saucer suspended on a frame and struck with a soft beater.
theorbo Sixteenth-century arch-lute with numerous stopped and unstopped strings attached to separate pegbox.
Theremin Electronic instrument developed by Lev Theremin (1920); the hands do not touch the instrument but produce oscillations when they move around the antenna.
ti tzu Chinese flute with 6 finger-holes and a 7th hole covered with thin membrane whose vibration dictates the tone.
timbrel Ancient Middle Eastern tambourine, and its medieval European descendant.
tin whistle High-pitched, end-blown Irish flute with 6 holes, made out of metal.
tonette Wood or plastic end-blown flute with finger-holes.
tremolo arm Device that changes the pitch of the strings by moving the bridge with a type of spring action.
trombone Brass instrument, larger than a trumpet, and with a sliding tube to extend notes.
trumpet Brass wind instrument consisting of a long tubular central piece with a cup-shaped mouth-piece and wide, bell-shaped base. A trumpet has three valves.
tuba Bass instrument patented by W Wieprecht and Moritz in Berlin (1835).
tubular bells Percussion instrument in the form of suspended tubes, tuned to the diatonic scale, and struck with a hammer.
tuning-fork Two-pronged metal instrument invented in 1711 by the trumpeter John Shore. The pure tone that it emits when set vibrating helps to give the pitch to singers or instruments.
uilleann pipes Irish bagpipes worked by bellows held under one arm.
ukelele (ukulele) Four-stringed instrument developed in Hawaii in the 1870s from a kind of Portugese guitar
upright piano Piano in which strings are vertical. John Isaac Hawkins of Philadelphia first built iron-framed uprights in 1800.
vibraphone (vibes) Xylophone with metal bars and a wide vibrato effect produced by electrically operated fans.
vihuela Six-string Spanish instrument of the 1600s that looks like a guitar but is tuned as a lute.
vina Indian stringed instrument, those from northern India having a long stick-like unfretted fingerboard resting on two resonating gourds, those from southern India having a much broader fingerboard and a wooden body in place of one of the gourds.
viola da braccio Tenor viol played under the arm.
viola da gamba Bass viol played between the knees.
viola d'amore Unfretted tenor instrument with 7 strings and 7 to 14 sympathetic strings.
violin Treble stringed instrument with 4 strings tuned to G, D, A, E.
violoncello Tenor stringed instrument of the violin family, played between the knees, using bass clef, with 4 strings tuned to C, G, D, A.
virginal Small, soft-sounding harpsichord of the 16th and 17th centuries, with one string to a note.
Wagner tuba Invented by Richard Wagner specifically for his *Ring Cycle*; look is more of a horn than a tuba.
whammy bar Another name for tremolo arm.
woodwind Recorders, flutes, clarinets, saxophones, oboes, piccolos, cor anglais and bassoons (lowest pitch).
xylophone (lit. wood sound) Percussion instrument consisting of graduated, tuned wooden bars which are struck with a hammer.
xylorimba Combination of xylophone and marimba.
zither Family of plucked string instruments including the dulcimer, hummel, koto, autoharp and psaltery, where the (up to 45) strings run the entire length of a flat body.

Famous Musicians

Bassoonists
Archie Camden
John Hebden
D Kern Holoman
Jacques Hotteterre
Edwin James
John Lampe
William Waterhouse

Cellists
Hugo Becker
Luigi Boccherini
Anner Bylsma
Pablo Casals
Gaspar Cassadó
Mischel Cherniavsky
Myung-Wha Chung
Robert Cohen
Christopher Coin
Karl Davidoff
Jean Louis Dufort
Jean Pierre Dufort
Jacqueline Du Pré
Maurice Eisenberg
Emanuel Feuermann
Amaryllis Fleming
Pierre Fournier
Auguste Franchomme
Carl Fuchs
Karine Georgian
Georg Goltermann
Bernard Greenhouse
Natalia Gutman
Lynn Harrell
Beatrice Harrison
Nicola Haym
John Hebden
Thomas Igloi
Steven Isserlis
Giuseppe Maria Jacchini
Ivor James
Antonio Janigro
Hans Kindler
Ralph Kirshbaum
Anton Kraft
Nicolaus Kraft
Robert Lindley
Julian Lloyd Webber
Martin Lovett
Antonio Lysy
Yo-Yo Ma
Enrico Mainardi
Mischa Maisky
António Meneses
Howard Mitchell
May Mukle
André Navarra
Charles Neate
Zara Nelsova
Arto Noras
Vladimir Orloff
Siegfried Palm
Stephen Paxton
Boris Pergamenschikov
Gregor Piatigorsky
Alfredo Piatti
Anthony Pini
William Pleeth
David Popper
Julius Rietz
Bernhard Romberg
Leonard Rose
Mstislav Rostropovich
Milos Sádlo
Felix Salmond
Samuil Samosud
Heinrich Schiff
Johann Schlick
Georg Schnéevoigt
Mátyás Seiber
Adrien François Servais
Raphael Sommer
William Henry Squire
János Starker
Guilhermina Suggia
Paul Tortelier
Arturo Toscanini
Christopher Van Kampen
Alfred Wallenstein
Raphael Wallfisch
Moray Welsh
August Wenzinger
Gay-Yee Westerhoff
Hanus Wihan

Clarinettists
John Adams
Heinrich Bärmann
Jack Brymer
Louis Cahuzac
Benny Goodman
Woody Herman
Janet Hilton
Emma Johnson
Reginald Kell
Thea King
Hyacinth Klosé
Henry Lewis
Richard Mühlfeld
Gervase de Peyer
Artie Shaw
Anton Stadler
Richard Stolzman
Morton Subotnick
Frederick Thurston
Bernard Walton

Double Bass
Giovanni Bottesini
Ida Carroll

Eugene Cruft
Domenico Dragonetti
Barry Guy
Gary Karr
Franz Kotzwara
Serge Koussevitzky

Flautists
Richard Adeney
Bruno Bartoletti
Michel Blavet
Theobald Boehm
Giulio Briccialdi
Franz Doppler
Karl Doppler
Louis François Fleury
James Galway
Severino Gazzelloni
Geoffrey Gilbert
Dave Heath
Hans-Joachim Koellreutter
Hans-Martin Linde
Johann Bernhard Logier
Edward McGuire
Susan Milan
Gareth Morris
Marcel Moyse
Aurèle Nicolet
Johann Quantz
Jean-Pierre Rampal
Elaine Shaffer
Fritz Spiegl
Adolf Terschak
David Van Vactor

French Horn
Hermann Baumann
Aubrey Brain
Dennis Brain
Alan Civil
Anthony Halstead
David Pyatt
Barry Tuckwell

Guitarists
Julian Bream
Leo Brouwer
Cornelius Cardew
Ferdinando Carulli
Tommy Emmanuel
Mauro Giuliani
Peter Katona
Zoltan Katona
Miguel Llobet
Carlos Montoya
Gaspar Sanz
Andrés Segovia
Philip Selby
Fernando Sor
Francisco Tárrega
Jason Vieaux
John Williams
Narciso Yepes

Harpists
Osian Ellis
Félix Godefroid
Marie Goossens
Sidonie Goossens
Alphonse Hasselmans
Ursula Holliger
Alfred Holý
Maria Korchinska
Johann Krumpholtz
François Naderman
Elias Parish-Alvars
John Parry
Nansi Richards
Marisa Robles
Carlos Salzédo
Marcel Tournier
Nicanor Zabaleta

Horns
Johannes Amon
David Amram
Adolph Borsdorf
Alan Civil
Louis-François Dauprat
John Denison
Heinrich Domnich
Anton Joseph Hampel
Maurice Handford
Ifor James
Ignaz Leutgeb
Giovanni Punto
Timothy Reynish
Franz Joseph Strauss
Barry Tuckwell

Mouth Organists
Larry Adler
Tommy Reilly

Oboists
Evelyn Barbirolli (née Rothwell)
Neil Black
Janet Craxton
John Cruft
Johann Fischer
Leon Goossens
Heinz Holliger
John Lancie
Ludwig August Lebrun
Charles Mackerras
Jean-Claude Malgoire
Friedrich Ramm
Ray Still
Edo de Waart

Organists
Herbert Andrews
Jennifer Bate
Jonathan Battishill
William Best
E Power Biggs
John Birch
John Blitheman
John Blow
Léon Boëllmann
Georg Böhm
Kevin Bowyer
John Dykes Bower
Ernest Bullock
Charles Burney
John Camidge
Matthew Camidge
Thomas Camidge
Melville Cook
George Cunningham
Carlo Curley
John Danby
Thurston Dart
Christopher Dearnley
William Done
Maurice Dupré
Hermann Finck
Grattan Flood
Virgil Fox
Alfred Gaul
Nicolas Gigault
Eugène Gigout
Johann Goldberg
John Goss
Alan Gray
Nicolas de Grigny
Douglas Guest
George Guest
Christopher Herrick
Edward Hopkins
Karl Friedrich Horn
Francis Jackson
Geraint Jones
Johann Kerll
Jacob Kirckman
Leonhard Kleber
Carlmann Kolb
Johann Krebs
Jean Langlais
Philip Ledger
Edwin Lemare
Henry Ley
Gaston Litaize
Charles Lloyd
Vincent Lübeck
David Lumsden
André Marchal
Louis Marchand
Giovanni Martini
Olivier Messiaen
Georg Monn
James Nares
Edward Naylor
Martin Neary
Sydney Nicholson
Thomas Noble
Vincent Novello
Herbert Oakeley
Boris Ord
Johann Pachelbel
Jane Parker-Smith
Peter Pears
Simon Preston
Daniel Purcell
Henry Purcell
James Pyne
Helmuth Rilling
Edward Rimbault
Alec Robertson
Douglas Robinson
Lionel Rogg
Cyril Rootham
Barry Rose
Bernard Rose
Francisco de Salinas
Sir Malcolm Sargent
Heinrich Scheidemann
Samuel Scheidt
Albert Schweitzer
John Scott
George Sinclair
Johann Staden
Paul Steinitz
Leopold Stokowski
Karl Straube
Herbert Sumsion
Richard Terry
George Thalben-Ball
David Titterington
Thomas Trotter
David Tudor
Franz Tunder
Denis Vaughan
Louis Vierne
Helmut Walcha
William Walond
Henry Watson
Gillian Weir
Charles Wesley
Allan Wicks
Charles-Marie Widor
David Willcocks
Charles Lee Williams
Malcolm Williamson
Arthur Wills
Philipp Wolfrum
Leslie Woodgate
Henry Wood
Klaus Wunderlich
Pietro Alessandro Yon
Pietro Ziani

Percussionists
James Blades
Evelyn Glennie
Stomu Yamashita

Pianists
Jacques Abram
Joaquin Achucarro
Thomas Ades
Daniel Adni
Roy Agnew
Martha Argerich
Vladimir Ashkenazy
Stefan Askenase
Victor Babin
Gina Bachauer
Paul Badura-Skoda
Daniel Barenboim
Hans Barth
Ethel Bartlett
Harold Bauer
Malcolm Bilson
Christian Blackshaw
Marc Blitzstein
Michel Block
Susan Bradshaw
Alfred Brendel
Yefim Bronfman
Bruno Canino
Teresa Carreño
Jean Casadesus
Robert Marcel Casadesus
Yihan Chen
Shura Cherkassky
Aldo Ciccolini
Van Cliburn
Harriet Cohen
Elizabeth Coolidge
Imogen Cooper
Joseph Cooper
Alfred Cortot
Johann Cramer
Paul Crossley
Clifford Curzon
Karl Czerny
György Cziffra
Michel Dalberto
Edward Dannreuther
Bella Davidovich
Peter Donohoe
Ania Dorfmann
Barry Douglas
Karl Engel
John Field
Margaret Fingerhut
Rudolf Firkusny
Annie Fischer
Edwin Fischer
Leon Fleisher
Myers Foggin
Andor Foldes
Hubert Foss
Ian Fountain
Fou Ts'ong
Philip Fowke
Homero Francesch
Samson François
Peter Frankl
Justus Frantz
Géza Frid
Ignaz Friedman
Benjamin Frith
Liza Fuchsova
Ossip Gabrilowitsch
Irwin Gage
Andrei Gavrilov
Walter Gieseking
Emil Gilels
Arabella Goddard
Leopold Godowsky
Anthony Goldstone
Richard Goode
Glenn Gould
Gary Graffman
Percy Grainger
Arthur de Greef
Gordon Green
Horacio Gutiérrez
Monique Haas
Ingrid Haebler
Charles Hallé
Mark Hambourg
Paul Hamburger
Iain Hamilton
Clara Haskil
Claude Helffer
Clifton Helliwell
Myra Hess
Rolf Hind
Alfred Hipkins
Ludwig Hoffman
Vladimir Horowitz
Colin Horsley

Louis Horst
Mieczyslaw Horszowski
Stephen Hough
Andrew Imbrie
John Ireland
Edward Isaacs
Leonard Isaacs
Michael Isador
Martin Isepp
Eugene Istomin
Paul Jacobs
Byron Janis
Grant Johannesen
Graham Johnson
Geneviève Joy
Eileen Joyce
Terence Judd
Jeffrey Kahane
Joseph Kalichstein
Friedrich Kalkbrenner
William Kapell
Jean-Rodolphe Kars
Julius Katchen
Peter Katin
Mindru Katz
Wilhelm Kempff
John Kirkpatrick
Evgeny Kissin
Bernhard Klee
Walter Klien
Karl Klindworth
Zoltán Kocsis
Alfons Kontarsky
Aloys Kontarsky
Lili Kraus
Katia Labèque
Marielle Labèque
Frederic Lamond
Lang Lang
Alicia de Larrocha
Philip Ledger
Lee Pui Ming
Yvonne Lefébure
Theodor Leschetizky
Oscar Levant
Raymond Lewenthal
Paul Lewis
Hans Leygraf
Josef Lhévinne
Rosina Lhévinne
John Lill
Eugene List
Kathleen Long
Marguérite Long
Alessandro Longo
Yvonne Loriod
Radu Lupu
Moura Lympany
Alexei Lyubimov
Joanna McGregor
Witold Malcuzynski
Leopold Mannes
Tobias Matthay
Denis Matthews
Florence May
Fanny Mendelssohn
Hephzibah Menuhin
Frank Merrick
Noel Mewton-Wood
Nina Milkina
Benno Moiseiwitsch
Federico Mompou
David Money
Stephen Montague
Gerald Moore
Angus Morrison
Ignaz Moscheles
Charles Neate
Marc Neikrug
Ivor Newton
Joaquin Nin
David Owen Norris
Lev Oborin
Noriko Ogawa
John Ogdon
Garrick Ohlsson
Mercedes Olivera
Georges Onslow
Ursula Oppens
Rafael Orozco
Leslie Orrey
Cristina Ortiz
George Osborne
Cécile Ousset
Vladimir Ovchinikov
Vladimir de Pachmann
Ignacy Jan Paderewski
Kun Woo Paik
Maria von Paradis (blind)
Jon Kimura Parker
Eric Parkin
Geoffrey Parsons
Güher Pekinel
Süher Pekinel
Leonard Pennario
Murray Perahia
Vlado Perlemuter
Egon Petri
Nikolai Petrov
Isidor Philipp
Maria-João Pires
Johann Peter Pixis
Artur Pizarro
Barbara von Ployer
Ivo Pogorelich
Maurizio Pollini
Jean-Bernard Pommier
Viktoria Postnikova
Leff Pouishnoff
Ferdinand Praeger
André Previn
Stephen Pruslin
Gwenneth Pryor
Anne Queffélec
Qin Chuan
Ruth Railton
Thomas Rajna
Dezsö Ránki
Clarence Raybould
Julius Reubke
Robert Riefling
Ferdinand Ries
Bernard Roberts
Rae Robertson
Pascal Rogé
Michael Roll
Martin Roscoe
Charles Rosen
Moriz Rosenthal
Mstislav Rostropovich
Anton Rubinstein
Arthur Rubinstein
Nikolay Rubinstein
Mikhail Rudy
Christian Rummel
Walter Rummel
Harold Rutland
Vasily Safonov
Harold Samuel
György Sándor
Jesús Maria Sanromá
Vasily Sapellnikov
Sir Malcolm Sargent
Irene Scharrer
Xaver Scharwenka
Ernest Schelling
Heinrich Schenker
Andras Schiff
Allan Schiller
Artur Schnabel
Karl Ulrich Schnabel
Irina Schnittke
Clara Schumann
Phyllis Sellick
Yitkin Seow
Peter Serkin
Rudolf Serkin
Shulamith Shafir
William Shakespeare
Howard Shelley
Maxim Shostakovich
Béla Siki
Constantin Silvestri
Abbey Simon
Leonard Slatkin
Jan Smeterlin
Cyril Smith
Ronald Smith
Yonty Solomon
Georg Solti
Peter Stadlen
Bernhard Stavenhagen
Wilhelm Stenhammar
Ronald Stevenson
Soulima Stravinsky
Walter Susskind
Roberto Szidon
Carl Tausig
André Tchaikowsky
Boris Tchaikovsky
Alec Templeton
Sigismond Thalberg
Jean-Yves Thibaudet
Tian Jiang
Michael Tilson Thomas
Martino Tirimo
Donald Tovey
Valerie Tryon
Norman Tucker
David Tudor
Rosalyn Tureck
Mitsuko Uchida
Nick Van Bloss
Sergio Varella-Cid
Tamás Vásáry
Bálint Vazsonyi
Isabelle Vengerova
Adela Verne
Mathilde Verne
Roger Vignoles
Ricardo Viñes
Lucille Wallace
Peter Wallfisch
Fanny Waterman
Sydney Watson
André Watts
Daniel Wayenberg
Joseph Weingarten
Erik Werba
Jósef Wieniawski
Earl Wild
David Wilde
Malcolm Williamson
Paul Wittgenstein
Roger Woodward
Enloc Wu
Friedrich Wührer
Marie Wurm
Jürg Wyttenbach
Théophile Ysaye
Yuja Wang
Carlo Zecchi
Géza Zichy
Alexander Ziloti
Krystian Zimerman
Jan Zimmer
Agnes Zimmermann

Trumpeters
Maurice André
Malcolm Arnold
Alison Balsom
Ernest Hall
Håkan Hardenberger
Philip Jones
Humphrey Lyttelton
Johann Petzold
Gerard Schwarz
Crispian Steel-Perkins
Edward Tarr
John Wilbraham

Tuba
Eleazar de Carvalho

Violists
Yuri Bashmet
Tania Davis
Paul Doktor
Watson Forbes
Rivka Golani
Karel Hába
Nobuko Imai
Allan Pettersson
Jean Pougnet
William Primrose
Frederick Riddle
Hermann Ritter
Jordi Savall
Peter Schidlof
Bernard Shore
Lionel Tertis
Walter Trampler
Efrem Zimbalist

Violinists
Joseph Achron
Delphin Alard
Pierre Amoyal
Jelly Arányi
Alexandre-Joseph Artôt
Thomas Baltzar
John Banister
Angel Barrios
Richard Barth
Yuri Bashmet
Rudolf Baumgartner
Hugh Bean
Paul Beard
Boris Belkin
Joshua Bell
Nicola Benedetti
Norbert Brainin
George Bridgetower
Adolph Brodsky
Ole Bull
Alfredo Campoli
John Carrodus
Marius Casadesus
Arthur Catterall
Eos Chater
Levon Chilingiran
Kyung-Wha Chung
Raymond Cohen
Béla Dekany
Gioconda De Vito
Augustine Dumay
Haylie Ecker
John Ella
Mischa Elman
Devy Erlih
Adila Fachiri
Carlo Farina
Alfonso Ferrabosco
Christian Ferras
Michael Festing
Carl Flesch
Giovanni Fontana
Zino Francescatti
Miriam Fried
Joseph Fuchs
Mayumi Fujikawa
Ivan Galamian
David Garrett
Saschko Gawriloff
André Gertler
Rivka Golani
Szymon Goldberg
Stephane Grappelli
Hyam Greenbaum
Sidney Griller
Frederick Grinke
Ida Haendel
Marie Hall
Jascha Heifetz
Joseph Hellmesberger
Willy Hess
Ulf Hoelscher
Karl Hoffmann
Ralph Holmes
Henry Holst
Yuzuko Horigome
Jenö Hubay
Bronislaw Huberman
Monica Huggett
Shizuka Ishikawa
Feliks Janiewicz
Joseph Joachim

Leila Josefowicz
Joseph Kaminski
Mark Kaplan
Louis Kaufman
Hans Keller
Nigel Kennedy
Willem Kes
Isabelle van Keulen
Young-Uck Kim
Pawel Kochánski
Leonid Kogan
Franz Kotzwara
Fritz Kreisler
Gidon Kremer
Rodolphe Kreutzer
Wenzel Krumpholtz
Oleg Krysa
Jan Kubelik
Sigiswald Kuijken
Georg Kulenkampff
Franz Lamotte
Linda Lampenius
Jaime Laredo
Cho-Liang Lin
Tasmin Little
Alan Loveday
Mark Lubotsky
Anne Macnaghten
Vanessa Mae
André Mangeot
Mantovani
Alessandro Marcello
Silvia Marcovici
Johanna Martzy
Joseph Massart
Nicola Matteis
Eduard Melkus
Isolde Menges
Yehudi Menuhin
Goto Midori
Stoika Milanova
Nathan Milstein
Shlomo Mintz
Lydia Mordkovitch
Viktoria Mullova
Charles Munch
Anne-Sophie Mutter
Pietro Nardini
Yfrah Neaman
Wilma Neruda
Ginette Neveu
Sigmund Nissel
David Oistrakh
Igor Oistrakh
Raphael Oleg
Frantisek Ondncek
Igor Ozim
Niccolò Paganini
Manoug Parikian
György Pauk
Edith Peinemann
Itzhak Perlman
George Frederic Pinto
Adolf Pollitzer
Jean Pougnet
Maud Powell
William Primrose
Gaetano Pugnani
Giovanni Punto
Michael Rabin
John Ravenscroft
Ede Reményi
Vadim Repin
Ruggiero Ricci
Franz Anton Ries
Hubert Ries
Alexander Ritter
Andreas Jakob Romberg
Arnold Rosé
Carl Rosiers
Max Rostal
Christian Rummel
George Saint-George
Prosper Sainton
Johann Peter Salomon
Albert Sammons
Eugene Sarbu
Emile Sauret
Rosario Scalero
Anton Schindler
Alexander Schneider
Wolfgang Schneiderhan
Jaap Schröder
Franz Schubert
Ignaz Schuppanzigh
Otakar Sevcik
Emily Shinner
Oscar Shumsky
Joseph Silverstein
Dmitry Sitkovetzky
Camillo Sivori
Nikolay Sokoloff
Paolo Spagnoletti
Albert Spalding
Theodore Spiering
Johann Wenzel Stamitz
Simon Standage
Isaac Stern
Julius Stern
Frederick Stock
George Stratton
Josef Suk
Zoltán Székely
Henryk Szeryng
Josef Szigeti
Gabor Takács-Nagy
Václav Talich
Giuseppe Tartini
Vilmos Tátrai
Charles Taylor
Arve Tellefsen
Emil Telmányi
Henri Temianka
Klaus Tennstedt
Carlo Tessarini
Jacques Thibaud
César Thomson
Luigi Tomasini
Giuseppe Torelli
Yan Pascal Tortelier
Roman Totenberg
Berthold Tours
Chrétien Urhan
Tibór Varga
Sándor Végh
Maxim Vengerov
Henri Verbrugghen
Henri Vieuxtemps
H. Waldo Warner
Joseph Miroslav Weber
Henryk Wieniawski
Wanda Wilkomirska
Marie Wilson
Michael Zacharewitsch
Christian Zacharias
Zvi Zeitlin
Jakob Zeugheer
Efrem Zimbalist
Frank Peter Zimmermann
Louis Zimmermann
Yossi Zivoni
Olive Zorian
Pinchas Zukerman
Paul Zukofsky

Famous Singers

Sopranos
Aïno Ackté
Roberta Alexander
Jeannine Altmeyer
Elly Ameling
Marie Angel
Sheila Armstrong
Martina Arroyo
Florence Austral
Lilian Bailey
Isobel Baillie
Josephine Barstow
Kathleen Battle
Hildegard Behrens
Elizabeth Billington
Judith Blegen
Hannelore Bode
Barbara Bonney
Lucrezia Bori
Inge Borkh
Sarah Brightman
Gré Brouwenstijn
Norma Burrowes
Montserrat Caballé
Teresa Cahill
Maria Callas
Emma Calvé
Maria Caniglia
Maria Caradori-Allan
Margherita Carosio
Katharina Cavalieri
Maria Cebotari
Maria Chiara
Charlotte Church
Gina Cigna
Mimi Coertse
Isabella Colbran
Elizabeth Connell
Mary Costa
Régine Crespin
Joan Cross
Lella Cuberli
Maud Cunitz
Toti Dal Monte
Suzanne Danco
Barbara Daniels
Gloria Davy
Anne Dawson
Lynne Dawson
Lisa Della Casa
Joséphine De Reszke
Emmy Destinn
Libuse Domaninska
Helen Donath
Dorothy Dorow
Dorothy Dow
Elizabeth Duparc
Denise Duval
Noël Eadie
Jean Eaglen
Emma Eames
Florence Easton
Christiane Eda-Pierre
Mary Ellis
Anne Evans
Carole Farley
Geraldine Farrar
Eileen Farrell
Helen Field
Sylvia Fischer
Kirsten Flagstad
Mirella Freni
Elizabeth Fretwell
Marya Freund
Marta Fuchs
Johanna Gadski
Amelita Galli-Curci
Mary Garden
Lesley Garrett
Catherine Gayer
Mechthild Gessendorf
Sona Ghazarian
Christel Goltz
Jill Gomez
Linda Esther Gray
Silvia Greenberg
Giulia Grisi
Reri Grist
Edita Gruberova
Nora Gruhn
Elisabeth Grümmer
Hilde Gueden
Nancy Gustafson
Marie Gutheil-Schoder
Alison Hagley
Joan Hammond
Heather Harper
Eiddwen Harrhy
Kathryn Harries
Elizabeth Harwood
Minnie Hauk
Cynthia Haymon
Lorna Haywood
Frieda Hempel
Elvira de Hidalgo
Judith Howarth
Karen Huffstodt
Rita Hunter
Maria Ivogün
Gundula Janowitz
Maria Jeritza
Sumi Jo
Eva Johannson
Gwyneth Jones
Ava June
Sena Jurinac
Raina Kabaivanska
Kiri Te Kanawa
Julie Kaufmann
Adelaide Kemble
Barbra Kemp
Yvonne Kenny
Adele Kern
Emma Kirkby
Dorothy Kirsten
Katharina Klafsky
Anny Konetzni
Hilde Konetzni
Annelies Kupper
Selma Kurz
Dora Labbette
Aloysia Lange
Nanny Larsén-Todsen
Magda Laszló
Marjorie Lawrence
Evelyn Lear
Lilli Lehmann
Liza Lehmann
Lotte Lehmann
Frida Leider
Adèle Leigh
Hellen Lemmens
Tiana Lemnitz
Mary Lewis
Miriam Licette
Caterina Ligendza
Jenny Lind
Berit Lindholm
Wilma Lipp
Pilar Lorengar
Victoria de Los Angeles
Felicity Lott
Germaine Lubin
Pauline Lucca
Sylvia McNair
Catherine Malfitano
Mathilde Mallinger
Blanche Marchesi
Lois Marshall
Margaret Marshall
Eva Marton
Valerie Masterson
Amalie Materna
Edith Mathis
Karita Mattila
Johanna Meier
Nellie Melba
Janine Micheau
Julia Migenes
Zinka Milanov
Anna von Mildenburg
Audrey Mildmay

Aprile Millo
Nelly Miricioiu
Martha Mödl
Anna Moffo
Fanny Moody
Grace Moore
Elsie Morison
Edda Moser
Maria Müller
Yuriy Mynenko
Carol Neblett
Judith Nelson
Anna Netrebko
Mignon Nevada
Agnes Nicholls
Birgit Nilsson
Christine Nilsson
Alda Noni
Elizabeth Norberg
Lillian Nordica
Jessye Norman
Clara Novello
Jarmila Novotná
Magda Olivero
Elaine Padmore
Felicity Palmer
Euphrosyne Parepa
Anne Pashley
Giuditta Pasta
Adelina Patti
Rose Pauly
Fanny Persiani
Roberta Peters
Helga Pilarczyk
Rosalind Plowright
Deborah Polaski
Lily Pons
Rosa Ponselle
Lucia Popp
Leontyne Price
Margaret Price
Yvonne Printemps
Ana Pusar
Ashley Putnam
Louisa Pyne
Rosa Raisa
Hildegard Ranczak
Judith Raskin
Aulikki Rautawaara
Delia Reinhardt
Maria Reining
Elisabeth Rethberg
Esther Réthy
Katia Ricciarelli
Margaret Ritchie
Faye Robinson
Joan Rodgers
Amanda Roocroft
Annaliese Rothenberger
Hermine Rudersdorff
Leonie Rysanek
Hilde Sadek
Sibyl Sanderson
Sylvia Sass
Bidú Sayão
Marianne Schech
Erna Schlüter
Elisabeth Schumann
Vera Schwarz
Elisabeth Schwarzkopf
Graziella Sciutti
Renata Scotto
Nadine Secunde
Irmgard Seefried
Meta Seinemeyer
Marcella Sembrich
Luciana Serra
Ellen Shade
Ekaterina Shcherbachenko
Honor Sheppard
Margaret Sheridan
Amy Shuard
Margarethe Siems
Anja Silja
Dorothy Silk
Beverly Sills
Jeannette Sinclair
Victoria Sladen
Oda Slobodskaya
Elisabeth Söderström
Henriette Sontag
Elena Souliotis
Maria Stader
Eleanor Steber
Hanny Steffek
Sophie Stehle
Anna Steiger
Teresa Stich-Randall
Lilian Stiles Allen
Teresa Stolz
Anna Storace
Rosina Storchio
Teresa Stratas
Rita Streich
Cheryl Studer
Rosa Sucher
Elsie Suddaby
Susan Sunderland
Joan Sutherland
Helena Tattermuschová
Renata Tebaldi
Giusto Tenducci (male)
Milka Ternina
Margarete Teschemacher
Eva Tetrazzini
Luisa Tetrazzini
Maggie Teyte
Thérèse Tietjens
Pauline Tinsley
Anna Tomowa-Sintow
Helen Traubel
Carrie Tubb
Eva Turner
Dawn Upshaw
Viorica Ursuleac
Leontina Vaduva
Benita Valente
Anita Välkki
Ninon Vallin
Carol Vaness
Julia Varady
Astrid Varnay
Elizabeth Vaughan
Galina Vishnevskaya
Deborah Voigt
Jennifer Vyvyan
Johanna Wagner
Yoko Watanabe
Claire Watson
Janice Watson
Lilian Watson
Aloysia Weber
Gillian Webster
Lucie Weidt
Ljuba Welitsch
Ruth Welting
Catherine Wilson
Marie Wittich
Sophie Wyss
Rachel Yakar
Mara Zampieri
Ruth Ziesak
Teresa Zylis-Gara

Mezzo-sopranos
Janet Baker
Agnes Baltsa
Cecilia Bartoli
Teresa Berganza
Faustina Bordoni
Olga Borodina
Marianne Brandt
Marie Brema
Grace Bumbry
Sally Burgess
Majorano Caffarelli
Sarah Jane Cahier
Susanna Cibber
Katherine Ciesinski
Cynthi Clarey
Sarah Connolly
Girolamo Crescentini
Claire Croiza
Janice De Gaetani
Astra Desmond
Joyce DiDonato
Oralia Dominguez
Nancy Evans
Maria Ewing
Brigitte Fassbaender
Linda Finnie
Muriel Forster
Elena Gerhardt
Rita Gorr
Bernadette Greevy
Giuditta Grisi
Barbara Hendricks
Jane Henschel
Alfreda Hodgson
Grace Hoffman
Elisabeth Höngen
Marilyn Horne
Anne Howells
Eirian James
Katherine Jenkins
Della Jones
Fiona Kimm
Louise Kirkby-Lunn
Gillian Knight
Nadezda Kniplová
Kathleen Kuhlmann
Lotte Lenya
Marjana Lipovsek
Martha Lipton
Jean Madeira
Maria Malibran
Mathilde Marchesi
Waltraud Meier
Susanne Mentzer
Kerstin Meyer
Yvonne Minton
Diana Montague
Ann Murray
Hyacinth Nicholls
Elena Obraztsova
Maria Olczewska
Anne Sofie von Otter
Rosa Papier
Anna Pollak
Florence Quivar
Eva Randová
Nell Rankin
Regina Resnik
Anna Reynolds
Jean Rigby
Vera Rozsa
Trudeliese Schmidt
Hanna Schwarz
Constance Shacklock
Mitsuko Shirai
Giulietta Simionato
Monica Sinclair
Doris Soffel
Frederica von Stade
Risë Stevens
Ebe Stignani
Conchita Supervia
Gladys Swarthout
Klara Takács
Blanche Thebom
Kerstin Thorborg
Jennie Tourel
Zélia Trebelli
Tatiana Troyanos
Lucia Valentini-Terrani
Josephine Veasey
Shirley Verrett
Pauline Viardot-Garcia
Sieglinde Wagner
Edyth Walker
Sarah Walker
Carolyn Watkinson
Lucie Weidt
Eugenia Zareska
Delores Ziegler

Counter-tenors
James Bowman
Michael Chance
Alfred Deller
Jochen Kowalski
Andreas Scholl

Contraltos
Muriel Brunskill
Clara Butt
Giovanni Carestini
Kathleen Ferrier
Birgit Finnilä
Maureen Forrester
Louise Homer
Mary Jarred
Sigrid Onegin
Norma Procter
Gladys Ripley
Charlotte Sainton-Dolby
Ernestine Schumann-Heink
Antoinette Sterling
Caroline Unger
Lucia Elizabeth Vestris
Mary Wakefield
Helen Watts

Baritones
Thomas Allen
Carlos Álvarez
Pasquale Amato
Ettore Bastianini
Pierre Bernac
John Brownlee
Sesto Bruscantini
Renato Bruson
Delme Bryn-Jones
Renato Capecchi
Piero Cappuccilli
Clive Carey
Ulrik Cold
Brian Cooke
Peter Dawson
Giuseppe De Luca
Willi Domgraf-Fassbänder
Geraint Evans
Keith Falkner
David Ffrangcon-Davies
Dietrich Fischer-Dieskau
Lucien Fugère
Peter Glossop
Tito Gobbi
John Goss
Franz Grundheber
Hakan Hagegard
Derek Hammond-Stroud
Thomas Hampson
Percy Heming
Thomas Hemsley
Roy Henderson
George Henschel
Jason Howard
Neil Howlett
Gerhard Hüsch
Dmitri Hvorostovsky
Jorma Hynninen
Richard Jackson
Herbert Janssen
Phillip Joll
Dimitri Kharitonov
Peter Knapp
Otakar Kraus
Tom Krause
Jean-Louis Lassalle
Sergei Leiferkus
François Le Roux
George London
Benjamin Luxon
Donald McIntyre
James Maddalena
Victor Maurel
Donald Maxwell
Michael Maybrick
Yury Mazurok
Robert Merrill
Johannes Messchaert
Dennis Noble
John Noble
Alan Opie
Rolando Panerai

Charles Panzéra
Kostas Paskalis
Antonio Pini-Corsi
Juan Pons
Hermann Prey
Gino Quilico
Louis Quilico
Frederick Ranalow
John Rawnsley
Theodor Reichmann
Maurice Renaud
Marko Rothmüller
Titta Ruffo
Kennerley Rumford
Karel Salomon
Mario Sammarco
Charles Santley
Heinrich Schlusnus
Andreas Schmidt
Paul Schöffler
Antonio Scotti
William Shimell
John Shirley-Quirk
Paolo Silveri
Knut Skram
Russell Smythe
Gérard Souzay
Oley Speaks
Mariano Stabile
Thomas Stewart
Richard Stilwell
Julius Stockhausen
Jonathan Summers
Giuseppe Taddei
Carlo Tagliabue
Antonio Tamburini
Lawrence Tibbett
Alan Titus
Hermann Uhde
Theodor Uppman
Giuseppe Valdengo
Anton Van Rooy
Ramón Vinay
Michael Vogl
Eberhard Wächter
Ian Wallace
Jess Walters
William Warfield
Leonard Warren
Bernd Weikl
Willard White
Clarence Whitehill
David Wilson-Johnson
Ingvar Wixell
Ekkerhard Wlaschiha
Gregory Yurisich
Giorgio Zancanaro

Tenors
Valentin Adamberger
John Aler
John Alexander
Luigi Alva
Max Alvary
Francisco Araiza
John Beard
Karl Beck
Kim Begley
Carlo Bergonzi
Jussi Björling
Beno Blachut
Rockwell Blake
Alfie Boe
Dino Borgioli
Stuart Burrows
José Carreras
Enrico Caruso
Richard Cassilly
Graham Clark
John Coates
Vinson Cole
Peter Cornelius
Jean Cox
Charles Craig
Richard Crooks
Hugues Cuénod
Arthur Davies
Ben Davies
Ryland Davies
Tudor Davies
Mario Del Monaco
François Delsarte
Fernando De Lucia
Gregory Dempsey
Jean De Reszke
Anton Dermota
Plácido Domingo
Nigel Douglas
Ronald Dowd
Warren Ellsworth
Poul Elming
Gervase Elwes
Karl Erb
Bruce Ford
Paul Frey
Manuel del Garcia
Nicolai Gedda
Giuseppe Giacomelli
Beniamino Gigli
Reiner Goldberg
Karl Graun
Donald Grobe
Jerry Hadley
Ben Heppner
Martyn Hill
Joseph Hislop
Werner Hollweg
Hans Hopf
Walter Hyde
Hermann Jadlowker
Neil Jenkins
Siegfried Jerusalem
Edward Johnson
Parry Jones
Manfred Jung
Michael Kelly
Jan Kiepura
Waldemar Kmentt
Heinrich Knote
Alfredo Kraus
Werner Krenn
David Kuebler
Charles Kullman
Gary Lakes
Philip Langridge
Mario Lanza
Giacomo Lauri-Volpi
Jeffrey Lawton
Richard Leech
Keith Lewis
Richard Lewis
Luis Lima
Edward Lloyd
Max Lorenz
Giordano Lucà
Veriano Lucheti
John McCormack
James McCracken
Giovanni Mario
Giovanni Martinelli
Yury Marusin
Helmut Melchert
Lauritz Melchior
Chris Merritt
Thomas Moser
Frank Mullings
Heddle Nash
Angelo Neumann
Albert Niemann
Adolphe Nourrit
Karl Oestvig
Alexander Oliver
Joseph O'Mara
Juan Oncina
Dennis O'Neill
Ian Partridge
Julius Patzak
Luciano Pavarotti
Peter Pears
Jan Peerce
Aureliano Pertile
Alfred Piccaver
Paul Potts
Vilém Pribyl
Josef Protschka
Anton Raaff
Torsten Ralf
Thomas Randle
Sims Reeves
Alberto Remedios
David Rendall
Kenneth Riegel
Anthony Rolfe Johnson
Vladimir Rosing
Helge Roswaenge
Robert Rounseville
Giovanni-Battista Rubini
Thomas Salignac
Giovanni-Battista Sbriglia
Benedikt Schack
Aksel Schiotz
Tito Schipa
Erik Schmedes
Ludwig Schnorr
Rudolf Schock
Peter Schreier
Peter Seiffert
William Shakespeare
George Shirley
Léopold Simoneau
Leo Slezak
Fritz Soot
Gerhard Stolze
Ian Storey
Kurt Streit
Ludwig Suthaus
Set Svanholm
Ferruccio Tagliavini
Francesco Tamagno
Enrico Tamberlik
Richard Tauber
John Templeton
Jess Thomas
Joseph Tichatschek
Richard Tucker
Fritz Uhl
Ragnar Ulfung
Georg Unger
Gerhard Unger
Jon Vickers
Ramón Vinay
Heinrich Vogl
Joseph Ward
Russell Watson
Spas Wenkoff
Walter Widdop
Steuart Wilson
Gösta Winbergh
Wolfgang Windgassen
Hermann Winkelmann
Hermann Winkler
Ludwig Wüllner
Fritz Wunderlich
Alexander Young
Heinz Zednik
Giovanni Zenatello
Ivo Zidek

Castrato
Domenico Annibali Majorano
Caffarelli
Girolano Crescentini
Carlo Farinelli
Gaetano Guadagni
Domenico Mustafa
Senesino

Bass
Donald Adams
Paul Bender
Kurt Böhme
Kim Borg
Fyodor Chaliapin
Boris Christoff
Henry Cooke
Stafford Dean
Otto Edelmann
Signor Foli
David Franklin
Gottlob Frick
Manuel Garcia
Nicolai Ghiaurov
Nicola Ghiuselev
Josef Greindl
Paul Hillier
Robert Holl
Gwynne Howell
Marcel Journet
Manfred Jungwirth
Alexander Kipnis
Paul Knüpfer
Luigi Lablache
Charles Manners
Josef von Manowarda
Jan Martinik
Kurt Moll
Paolo Montarsolo
Yevgeny Nesterenko
Robert Newman
Siegmund Nimsgern
Ezio Pinza
Pol Plançon
Paul Plishka
Robert Radford
Ruggero Raimondi
Karl Ridderbusch
Michael Rippon
Paul Robeson
Forbes Robinson
Nicola Rossi-Lemeni
Joseph Rouleau
Kurt Rydl
Matti Salminen
Manfred Schenk
Andrew Shore
Cesare Siepi
Hans Sotin
Roger Soyer
Horace Stevens
Fyodor Stravinsky
Mihály Székely
Italo Tajo
Martti Talvela
Bryn Terfel
David Thomas
John Tomlinson
Richard Van Allan
José Van Dam
Norman Walker
Gustavus Waltz
David Ward
Ludwig Weber
Nicola Zaccaria

Conductors

Claudio Abbado
Komei Abe
Hermann Abendroth
Maurice Abravanel
Byron Adams
John Adams
Kurt Adler
Peter Adler
Yuri Ahronovitch
Gerd Albrecht
John Alldis
Antonio Almeida
Marin Alsop
Petr Altricher
Carl Alwin
Gilbert Amy
Karel Ancerl
Géza Anda
Karsten Andersen
Martin André
Volkmar Andreae
Paul Angerer
Enrique Arbós
Richard Armstrong
Vladimir Ashkenazy
David Atherton
Moshe Atzmon
Daniel Barenboim
Thomas Beecham
Jiri Belohlavek
Richard Bernas
Leonard Bernstein
Henry Bishop
Stanley Black
Richard Blackford
Nadia Boulanger
Pierre Boulez
Adrian Boult
Martyn Brabbins
Joly Braga-Santos
Nicholas Braithewaite
Warwick Braithwaite
Max Bruch
Hans Bülow
Fritz Busch
Ferruccio Busoni
Basil Cameron
Philip Cannon
Guido Cantelli
André Caplet
Franco Capuana
John Carewe
Mosco Carner
Jean-Claude Casadesus
Fritz Cassirer
Aldo Ceccato
Zdenek Chalabala
Harry Christophers
Myung-Whun Chung
Nicholas Cleobury
Stephen Cleobury
André Cluytens
Albert Coates
James Conlon
Emil Cooper
Michael Costa
Robert Craft
John Crosby
Edric Cundell
William Cusins
Henryk Czyz
Frank Damrosch
Leopold Damrosch
Walter Damrosch
Paul Daniel
Oskar Danon
Stephen Darlington
Dennis Russell Davies
Andrew Davis
Colin Davis
Jacques Delacôte
Norman Del Mar
Gaetano Delogu
John DeMain
Neville Dilkes
Christoph von Dohnányi
Antal Dorati
Clive Douglas
Edward Downes
Sian Edwards
Mark Elder
Karl Elmendorff
Alberto Erede
Mark Ermler
Franco Faccio
Bryan Fairfax
Charles Farncombe
Robert Farnon
Vladimir Fedoseyev
Frederick Fennell
Arthur Fiedler
Max Fiedler
Adam Fischer
Ivan Fischer
Anatole Fistoulari
Grzegorz Fitelberg
Claus Peter Flor
Lawrence Foster
Myer Fredman
Ferenc Fricsay
Oskar Fried
Lionel Friend
Janos Fürst
Wilhelm Furtwängler
Piero Gamba
John Eliot Gardiner
Valery Gergiev
Alexander Gibson
Michael Gielen
Carlo Maria Giulini
Jane Glover
Daniel Godfrey
Walter Goehr
Georg Göhler
Vladimir Golschmann
Reginald Goodall
Roy Goodman
Ron Goodwin
Eugene Goossens (Belg.)
Eugene Goossens (Fr.)
Eugene Goossens (GB)
Hans Graf
Michael Graubart
Noah Greenberg
Bohumil Gregor
Charles Groves
Hermann Grunebaum
Marco Guidarini
Karl Haas
Robert Haas
François Habeneck
Alan Hacker
Hartmut Haenchen
Bernard Haitink
Charles Hallé
Louis Halsey
Simon Halsey
Maurice Handford
Vernon Handley
Nikolaus Harnoncourt
Trevor Harvey
László Heltay
Philippe Herreweghe
Bernard Herrmann
Alfred Hertz
Leslie Heward
Richard Hickox
Alfred Hill
Jun'ichi Hirokami
Irwin Hoffman
Christopher Hogwood
Heinrich Hollreiser
Imogen Holst
Bo Holten
Anthony Hopkins
John Hopkins
Jascha Horenstein
Milan Horvat
Anthony Hose
Elgar Howarth
Owain Arwel Hughes
Donald Hunt
George Hurst
Eliahu Inbal
Michiyoshi Inoue
Ernest Irving
Robert Irving
José Iturbi
Hiroyuki Iwaki
René Jacobs
Reginald Jacques
Jussi Jalas
Marek Janowski
Arvid Jansons
Mariss Jansons
Neeme Järvi
Paavo Järvi
Graeme Jenkins
Newell Jenkins
Eugen Jochum
Jullien Joly
Simon Joly
Enrique Jordá
Armin Jordan
James Judd
Louis Julien
Jürgen Jürgens
Robert Kajanus
Okko Kamu
Herbert von Karajan
Jacek Kasprzyk
Bernard Keeffe
Christopher Keene
Joseph Keilberth
Rudolf Kempe
Paul van Kempen
István Kertész
Willem Kes
Hans Kindler
Robert King
Bernhard Klee
Carlos Kleiber
Erich Kleiber
Otto Klemperer
Paul Kletzki
Berislav Klobucar
Hans Knappertsbusch
Kazuhiro Koizumi
Kyril Kondrashin
Franz Konwitschny
Kazimierz Kord
Zdenek Kosler
André Kostelanetz
Serge Koussevitzky
Jiri Kout
Karel Kovarovic
Clemens Krauss
Yakov Kreizberg
Jan Krenz
Henry Krips
Josef Krips
Jaroslav Krombholc
Karl Krueger
Rafael Kubelik
Gustav Kuhn
Efrem Kurtz
Franz Lachner
Charles Lamoureux
Michael Lankester
Joseph Lanner
Lars-Erik Larsson
Eduard Lassen
Ashley Lawrence
Alexander Lazarev
Philip Ledger
Michel Legrand
György Lehel
Erich Leinsdorf
Lawrence Leonard
Raymond Leppard
Hermann Levi
James Levine
Anthony Lewis
Henry Lewis
András Ligeti
Andrew Litton
Grant Llewellyn
David Lloyd-Jones
James Lockhart
Alain Lombard
Jesus Lopez-Cobos
James Loughran
Ferdinand Löwe
John Lubbock
Leighton Lucas
Leopold Ludwig
Alexandre Luigini
Peter Maag
Lorin Maazel
Zdenek Macal
Denis McCaldin
Nicholas McGegan
Charles Mackerras
Ernest MacMillan
Fritz Mahler
Gustav Mahler
Jerzy Maksymiuk
Jean-Claude Malgoire
Nikolay Malko
Luigi Mancinelli
August Manns
Mantovani
Gino Marinuzi
Neville Marriner
Odaline de la Martinez
Jean Martinon
Giuseppe Martucci
Diego Masson
Kurt Masur
Eduardo Mata
Lovro von Matacic
Muir Mathieson
John Mauceri
Peter Maxwell Davies
Zubin Mehta
Willem Mengelberg
Herbert Menges
Howard Mitchell
Bernardino Molinari
Francesco Molinari-Pradelli
Pierre Monteux
Kenneth Montgomery
Rudolf Moralt
Wyn Morris
Felix Mottl
Evgeny Mravinsky
Karl Muck
Michael Mudie
Leopoldo Mugnone
Charles Munch
Karl Münchinger
Riccardo Muti
Kent Nagano
Garcia Navarro
Boyd Neel
John Nelson
Woldemar Nelsson
Frantisek Neumann
Václav Neumann
Roy Newsome
Harry Newstone
Arthur Nikisch
Roger Norrington
David Oistrakh
Sakari Oramo
Eugene Ormandy
Tadaaki Otaka
Willem van Otterloo
Seiji Ozawa
Ettore Panizza
Paul Paray
Alain Paris
Andrew Parrott
Jules-Étienne Pasdeloup
Giuseppe Patanè

Bernhard Paumgartner
Emil Paur
Wilfrid Pelletier
Murray Perahia
Libor Pesek
Zoltán Peskó
Trevor Pinnock
Percy Pitt
Michel Plasson
Giorgio Polacco
Egon Pollak
John Poole
Frederik Prausnitz
Georges Prêtre
André Previn
Fernando Previtali
Brian Priestman
Klaus Pringsheim
John Pritchard
Felix Prohaska
Eve Queler
Peter Raabe
Ruth Railton
Karl Rankl
Simon Rattle
Clarence Raybould
Ernest Read
Hans Redlich
Leopold Reichwein
Fritz Reiner
Edouard van Remoortel
Timothy Reynish
Hans Richter
Karl Anton Rickenbacher
Kathleen Riddick
Hugo Rignold
Helmuth Rilling
Carlo Rizzi
James Robertson
Christopher Robinson
Stanford Robinson
Arthur Rodzinski
Landon Ronald
Karl Rosa
Hans Rosbaud
Albert Rosen
Joseph Rosenstock
Antoni Ros Marbá
Mario Rossi
Mstislav Rostropovich
Walter Rothwell
Tony Rowe
Witold Rowicki
Gennady Rozhdestvensky
Julius Rudel
Max Rudolf
Christian Rummel
Donald Runnicles
John Rutter

Paul Sacher
Vasily Safonov
Karel Salomon
Esa-Pekka Salonen
Samuil Samosud
Kurt Sanderling
Nello Santi
Gabriele Santini
Nino Sanzogno
Jukka-Pekka Saraste
Sir Malcolm Sargent
Wolfgang Sawallisch
Franz Schalk
Xaver Scharwenka
Hermann Scherchen
Heinrich Schiff
Anton Schindler
Thomas Schippers
Erich Schmid
Ole Schmidt
Hans Schmidt-Isserstedt
Georg Schnéevoigt
Alexander Schneider
Max Schönherr
Michael Schonwandt
Hans-Hubert Schönzeler
Peter Schreier
Ernst von Schuch
Ignaz Schuppanzigh
Carl Schuricht
Gerard Schwarz
Rudolf Schwarz
Claudio Scimone
Christopher Seaman
Uri Segal
Leif Segerstam
Karel Sejna
Jerzy Semkow
Tullio Serafin
Robert Shaw
Howard Shelley
Maxim Shostakovich
Oscar Shumsky
Joseph Silverstein
Constantin Silvestri
Geoffrey Simon
Yury Simonov
Vassily Sinaisky
George Sinclair
Dmitri Sitkovetsky
Stanislaw Skrowaczewski
Leonard Slatkin
Nicolas Slonimsky
Alexander Smallens
George Smart
Váslav Smetácek
Nicholas Smith
Ethel Smyth
Nikolay Sokoloff

Georg Solti
Marc Soustrot
Theodore Spiering
Peter Stadlen
Simon Standage
Bernhard Stavenhagen
Erwin Stein
Fritz Stein
Horst Stein
Emil Steinbach
Fritz Steinbach
Pinchas Steinberg
William Steinberg
Markus Stenz
Fritz Stiedry
Frederick Stock
Leopold Stokowski
Josef Stransky
George Stratton
Karl Straube
Eduard Strauss I
Eduard Strauss II
Richard Strauss
Igor Stravinsky
Simon Streatfeild
Wolfgang Stresemann
Frank van der Stucken
Otmar Suitner
Walter Susskind
Yevgeny Svetlanov
Hans Swarowsky
Ward Swingle
Tadeusz Sygietynski
Georg Szell
Eugen Szenkar
Michel Tabachnik
Anu Tali
Václav Talich
Egisto Tango
Jeffrey Tate
Vilem Tausky
Pyotr Tchaikovsky
Yuri Temirkanov
Klaus Tennstedt
Richard Terry
Christian Thielemann
Michael Tilson Thomas
Theodore Thomas
Bryden Thomson
Heinz Tietjen
Martino Tirimo
Paul Tortelier
Yan Pascal Tortelier
Arturo Toscanini
Geoffrey Toye
Barry Tuckwell
Rosalyn Tureck
Martin Turnovsky
Erik Tuxen

Heinz Unger
Eduard Van Beinum
André Vandernoot
Osmo Vanska
Silvio Varviso
Tamás Vásáry
Denis Vaughan
Sándor Végh
Henri Verbrugghen
Gilbert Vinter
Jaroslav Vogel
Hans Vonk
Edo de Waart
Roger Wagner
Siegfried Wagner
Alfred Wallenstein
Bruno Walter
Günter Wand
Volker Wangenheim
Guy Warrack
Akeo Watanabe
Sydney Watson
Joseph Miroslav Weber
Martin Wegelius
Bruno Weil
Felix Weingartner
George Weldon
Walter Weller
Franz Welser-Möst
August Wenzinger
Ian Whyte
Günther Wich
Allan Wicks
Mark Wigglesworth
David Wilde
Stephen Wilkinson
Jósef Wilkomirski
David Willcocks
Malcolm Williamson
Antoni Wit
Albert Wolff
Hugh Wolff
Henry Wood
David Wooldridge
Barry Wordsworth
Franz Wüllner
Jürg Wyttenbach
Arvid Yansons
Simone Young
Eugène Ysaye
Takuo Yuasa
Lothar Zagrosek
Carlo Zecchi
Hans Zender
Jakob Zeugheer
Alexander Ziloti
David Zinman
Pinchas Zukerman
Paul Zukofsky
Herman Zump

Music: Pop

Show and Film Songs: By Show or Film

Show/Film	***Song***
After Midnight	Mona Lisa
A Hard Day's Night	All My Loving
	Can't Buy Me Love
	She Loves You
Aladdin and His Wonderful Lamp	Genie With the Light Brown Lamp
Alexander's Ragtime Band	Alexander's Ragtime Band
	All Alone
	Blue Skies
	Everybody's Doing It
	What'll I Do
All This and World War II	With a Little Help from My Friends
Allegro (show)	A Fellow Needs a Girl
	The Gentleman Is a Dope
American Gigolo	Call Me
Americana	Brother, Can You Spare a Dime
Americana (show)	Sunny Disposish
An American in Paris	By Strauss
	Embraceable You
	I Got Rhythm
	I'll Build a Stairway to Paradise
	Liza
	Nice Work If You Can Get It
	Our Love Is Here to Stay
	S'Wonderful
Anchor's Aweigh	The Charm of You
And the Angels Sing	It Could Happen to You
Annie Get Your Gun	Anything You Can Do
	Doin' What Comes Naturally
	I Got the Sun in the Morning
	There's No Business Like Show Business
Anything Goes	All Through the Night
	Blow, Gabriel, Blow
	I Get a Kick out of You
	It's d'Lovely
	You're the Top
Anything Goes (show)	The Gipsy in Me
April in Paris	April in Paris
April Showers	April Showers
	Carolina in the Morning
Aspects of Love (show)	Love Changes Everything
Atlantic City	Ain't Misbehavin'
At Long Last Love	At Long Last Love
At the Circus	Lydia the Tattooed Lady
Avenue Q (show)	Everyone's a Little Bit Racist
	Fantasies Come True
	If You Were Gay
	I'm Not Wearing Underwear Today
	The Internet is for Porn
	It Sucks to Be Me
	My Girlfriend Who Lives in Canada
	School for Monsters
	There is Life Outside Your Apartment
	There's a Fine Fine Line
	What Do You Do with a BA in English
Babes in Arms	Ida, Sweet as Apple Cider
	Where or When
Babes in Arms (show)	I Wish I Were in Love Again
	Johnny One Note
	The Lady Is a Tramp
	My Funny Valentine
Back to the Future	The Power of Love

Show/Film	***Song***
Bambi	Little April Shower
The Band Wagon	That's Entertainment
The Barkleys of Broadway	They Can't Take That Away from Me
	Shoes With Wings On
Beaches	Wind beneath My Wings
Beau James	Someone to Watch over Me
Because You're Mine	All the Things You Are
The Belle of New York	Baby Doll
Bells Are Ringing	Just in Time
The Benny Goodman Story	Avalon
	On the Sunny Side of the Street
Best Foot Forward	Buckle Down, Winsocki
The Best Things in Life Are Free	The Best Things in Life are Free
	The Birth of the Blues
	Broken Hearted
	Button Up Your Overcoat
	If I Had a Talking Picture of You
	Life is Just a Bowl of Cherries
	Lucky in Love
	My Sin
	Sonny Boy
	Together
	You're the Cream in My Coffee
The Best Years of Our Lives	Among My Souvenirs
Beverly Hills Cop	The Heat Is On
The Big Beat	As I Love You
The Big Broadcast	Marta
	Minnie the Moocher
	Where the Blue of the Night
The Big Broadcast of 1936	Goodnight, Sweetheart
The Big Broadcast of 1938	Thanks for the Memory
Birth of the Blues	Blues in the Night
	By the Light of the Silvery Moon
Bitter-Sweet	Dear Little Cafe
	I'll See You Again
	To-Kay
The Blackboard Jungle	Rock around the Clock
Black Joy	When Will I See You Again?
Black Vanities (show)	Let's Be Buddies
Black Velvet (show)	Most Gentlemen Don't Like Love
The Blue Angel	Falling in Love Again
Blue Hawaii	Can't Help Falling in Love
The Blue Paradise	Auf Wiederseh'n
Blue Skies	Always
	Blue Skies
	Puttin' on the Ritz
	White Christmas
Bonnie and Clyde	Foggy Mountain Breakdown
Born Free	Born Free (1966)
Born to Dance	I've Got You under My Skin
Both Ends of the Candle	April in Paris
	Avalon
	Bill
	Can't Help Loving Dat Man
	Do Do Do
	Don't Ever Leave Me
	I've Got a Crush on You
	The Man I Love
	On the Sunny Side of the Street
	Someone to Watch Over Me
The Boy Friend	All I Do is Dream of You
	I Could Be Happy With You
	Nicer in Nice
	Perfect Young Ladies

Show/Film	***Song***
The Boy Friend (continued)	The Riviera
	Safety in Numbers
	Won't You Charleston With Me?
The Boys from Syracuse	Falling in Love with Love
	Sing for Your Supper
	This Can't Be Love
Breakfast at Tiffany's	Moon River (1961)
Bridge on the River Kwai	Colonel Bogey March
	The River Kwai March
Brigadoon	Almost Like Being in Love
Bright Eyes	On the Good Ship Lollipop
Broadway	Alabamy Bound
Broadway (show)	Yes, Sir, That's My Baby
Broadway Gondolier	Lulu's Back in Town
Broadway Melody of 1936	All I Do Is Dream of You
Broadway Melody of 1938	You Made Me Love You
Broadway Melody of 1940	Begin the Beguine
	I Concentrate on You
	I've Got My Eyes on You
Broadway Rhythm	All the Things You Are
	Irresistible You
	Somebody Loves Me
Buck Privates	Boogie Woogie Bugle Boy
	I'll Be with You in Apple Blossom Time
Butch Cassidy and the Sundance Kid	Raindrops Keep Falling On My Head
The Caddy	That's Amore
Calamity Jane	The Black Hills of Dakota
	The Deadwood Stage
	Secret Love
Call Me Madam	It's a Lovely Day Today
Call of the Canyon	Boots and Saddle
Camelot	How to Handle a Woman
	If Ever I Would Leave You
Can-Can	C'est Magnifique
	I Love Paris
	It's All Right with Me
	Just One of Those Things
	Let's Do It (Let's Fall in Love)
Careless Lady	All of Me
Carmen Jones	Beat Out Dat Rhythm on a Drum
	Dat's Love
Carousel	If I Loved You
	June Is Busting Out All Over
	Mister Snow
	You'll Never Walk Alone
Casablanca	As Time Goes By
Casbah	For Every Man There's Woman
Casino Royale	The Look of Love
Cats	Bustopher Jones
	Mr Mistofolees
	Memory
Chasing Rainbows	Happy Days Are Here Again
Chess (show)	I Know Him So Well
	One Night in Bangkok
Christmas Holiday	Always
Chu Chin Chow	Any Time's Kissing Time
Cinderella	Bibbidi-Bobbidi-Boo
Cinderella (show)	Do I Love You BecauseYou're Beautiful?
The Cockeyed World	You're the Cream in My Coffee
College Rhythm	Stay as Sweet as You Are
Company	Another Hundred People
	Getting Married Today
	Marry Me a Little
	Side By Side By Side
A Connecticut Yankee	My Heart Stood Still
	Thou Swell

Show/Film	***Song***
A Connecticut Yankee (show)	To Keep My Love Alive
Convoy	Don't It Make My Brown Eyes Blue
Cooley High	Dancing in the Street
	Road Runner
Countess from Hong Kong	This Is My Song
Cover Girl	Long Ago and Far Away
Cuban Pete	The Breeze and I
Curly Top	Animal Crackers in My Soup
Damn Yankees (show)	Whatever Lola Wants
A Damsel in Distress	A Foggy Day
	Nice Work If You Can Get It
A Day at the Races	All God's Chillun Got Rhythm
Days of Wine and Roses	Days of Wine and Roses
Deep in My Heart	Auf Wiederseh'n
	When I Grow Too Old to Dream
Deliverance	Duelling Banjos
The Desert Song	French Military Marching Song
	The Riff Song
Destry Rides Again	The Boys in the Backroom
The Diamond Horseshoe	The More I See You
Dirty Dancing	Time of My Life (1987)
Doctor Dolittle	Talk to the Animals
Doctor No	The James Bond Theme
The Dolly Sisters	Carolina in the Morning
	Give Me the Moonlight
	I'm Always Chasing Rainbows
Don't Fence Me In	Don't Fence Me In
Don't Knock the Rock	Tutti Frutti
Down Dakota Way	Candy Kisses
Dr Zhivago	Lara's Theme (somewhere my love)
DuBarry Was a Lady	Do I Love You, Do I
	Friendship
	I'm Getting Sentimental over You
DuBarry Was a Lady (show)	Well, Did You Evah?
Easter Parade	A Couple of Swells
	Everybody's Doing It
	I Love a Piano
The Eddie Cantor Story	Bye Bye Blackbird
	Ida, Sweet as Apple Cider
	Yes Sir, That's My Baby
	You Must Have Been a Beautiful Baby
The Eddie Duchin Story	April Showers
	Brazil
	Just One of Those Things
	On the Sunny Side of the Street
	Stardust
	What Is This Thing Called Love?
	The Man I Love
The Emperor Waltz	Kiss in Your Eyes
Evergreen	Dancing on the Ceiling
	Over My Shoulder
Everybody's Welcome (show)	As Time Goes By
Evita	Don't Cry For Me, Argentina
	Oh, What a Circus
Evita (show)	Another Suitcase in Another Hall
The Exorcist	Tubular Bells
The Fabulous Dorseys	Everybody's Doing It
Fame	Fame
Feather Your Nest	Leaning on a Lamp Post
Fiddler on the Roof	Sunrise, Sunset
	If I Were a Rich Man
Finian's Rainbow	How Are Things in Glocca Morra?
The Firefly	The Donkey Serenade
Five Easy Pieces	D.I.V.O.R.C.E.
The Five Pennies	Won't You Come Home Bill Bailey
Flashdance	Flashdance – What a Feeling
The Fleet's In	I Remember You

Show/Film	Song
The Fleet's Lit Up (show)	It's d'Lovely
Flower Drum Song	You Are Beautiful
Follow the Band	Ain't Misbehavin'
Follow The Boys	I'll See You in My Dreams
Follow the Fleet	Let's Face the Music and Dance
Follow Through	Button Up Your Overcoat
Footloose	Let's Hear It for the Boy
For Me and My Gal	Oh, You Beautiful Doll
The French Doll (show)	Please Do It Again
Funny Face	Clap Yo' Hands
	How Long Has This Been Going On
	My One and Only
	S'Wonderful
Funny Girl	Don't Rain on My Parade
	Second-Hand Rose
Funny Lady	Clap Hands, Here Comes Charley
The Gay Divorcee	The Continental
	I've Got You on My Mind
	Night and Day
Gentlemen Marry Brunettes	Have You Met Miss Jones
	I Wanna Be Loved by You
	I've Got Five Dollars
	My Funny Valentine
	Ain't Misbehavin'
Gentlemen Prefer Blondes	Diamonds Are a Girl's Best Friend
George White's Scandals	Life Is Just a Bowl of Cherries
George White's Scandals of 1922 (show)	I'll Build a Stairway To Paradise
George White's Scandals of 1924 (show)	Somebody Loves Me
George White's Scandals of 1945	Liza
George White's Scandals (show)	The Black Bottom
G.I. Blues	Wooden Heart
Gigi	Gigi (1958)
	Night They Invented Champagne
	Thank Heaven for Little Girls
The Girl Can't Help It	Be-Bop-A-Lula
Girl Crazy	Bidin' My Time
	But Not for Me
	Embraceable You
	Fascinating Rhythm
	I Got Rhythm
The Girl He Left Behind	Brazil
Girls! Girls! Girls!	Return to Sender
The Glenn Miller Story	At Last
	Basin Street Blues
	Bidin' My Time
	Chattanooga Choo Choo
	In the Mood
Glorifying the American Girl	Baby Face
	Blue Skies
The Glorious Days (show)	Swanee
Godspell	Day by Day
Going My Way	Swingin' on a Star
Going Places	Jeepers Creepers
Gold Diggers of 1933	We're in the Money
Gold Diggers of 1935	Lullaby of Broadway
The Goldwyn Follies	Love Walked In
	Our Love Is Here to Stay
Gone with the Wind	Tara's Theme
Good Boy (show)	I Wanna Be Loved by You
Good News	The Best Things in Life Are Free
	Lucky in Love
	Varsity Drag
Grease	Blue Moon
	Hopelessly Devoted to You
	Summer Nights
	You're the One That I Want
The Great American Broadcast	Alabamy Bound
	If I Didn't Care
The Great Schnozzle	Inka Dinka Doo
Gulliver's Travels	It's A Hap-Hap-Happy Day
Guys and Dolls	Adelaide
	If I Were a Bell
	Luck Be a Lady Tonight
	Sit Down You're Rocking the Boat
Guys and Dolls (show)	Bushel and a Peck
Gypsy	Everything's Coming Up Roses
Hair	Ain't Got No – Got Life
	Aquarius
	Good Morning Starshine
Half a Sixpence (show)	Flash Bang Wallop
Hands across the Water	Cool Water
Hans Christian Andersen	Anywhere I Wander
	The Ugly Duckling
Hard to Get	You Must Have Been a Beautiful Baby
The Harvey Girls	On the Atchison, Topeka and Santa Fe
Has Anybody Seen My Gal?	Five Foot Two, Eyes of Blue
	When the Red Red Robin
Heads Up	Ship Without a Sail
Hello, 'Frisco, Hello	You'll Never Know
Hellzapoppin	Watch the Birdie
Help!	Help
Here Comes Elmer	Straighten Up and Fly Right
Here Comes the Band	Roll Along, Prairie Moon
Here Comes the Groom	In the Cool, Cool, Cool of the Evening
Here Come the Waves	That Old Black Magic
	Ac-cent-tchu-ate the Positive
Here Is My Heart	June in January
	With Every Breath I Take
Her Kind of Man	It Had to Be You
Her Soldier Boy (show)	Pack Up Your Troubles in Your Old Kit Bag
Hey Boy! Hey Girl!	Fever
Hi Diddle Diddle (show)	Miss Otis Regrets
High Noon	High Noon (1952)
High Society	I Love You, Samantha
	True Love
	Well, Did You Evah?
	Who Wants to Be a Millionaire?
High Time	The Second Time Around
High, Wide and Handsome	Can I Forget You
	The Folks Who Live on the Hill
Hi Neighbour	Deep in the Heart of Texas
Hold That Ghost	Me and My Shadow
Hole in the Head	High Hopes (1959)
Holiday Inn	Be Careful, It's My Heart
	Happy Holiday
	White Christmas
Hollywood Canteen	Don't Fence Me In
Hollywood Revue of 1929	Singin' in the Rain
Hot Chocolates (show)	Ain't Misbehavin'
Hullo America	Give Me the Moonlight
Hullo Tango (show)	Get Out and Get Under
Idiot's Delight	Puttin' on the Ritz
If I Had My Way	April Played the Fiddle
I'll Cry Tomorrow	I'm Sitting on Top of the World
	When the Red Red Robin
I'll Get By	You Make Me Feel So Young
I'll See You in My Dreams	Carolina in the Morning
	I'll See You in My Dreams
	It Had to Be You
I Married an Angel	Spring Is Here
Incendiary Blonde	Ida, Sweet as Apple Cider
	It Had to Be You

Show/Film	Song
Indian Territory	Chattanoogie Shoeshine Boy
Innocents of Paris	Louise
Irene	Alice Blue Gown
Is Everybody Happy	On the Sunny Side of the Street
Istanbul	When I Fall in Love
It's Trad, Dad	Beale Street Blues
I Wonder Who's Kissing Her Now	I Wonder Who's Kissing Her Now
Jailhouse Rock	Baby I Don't Care
The James Dean Story	Let Me Be Loved
Jazz on a Summer's Day	Tea for Two
The Jazz Singer	Blue Skies
	I'm Looking Over a Four-Leaf Clover
Jericho	Short'nin' Bread
Jesus Christ Superstar	I Don't Know How to Love Him
Jewel of the Nile	When the Going Gets Tough
Jigsaw (show)	Swanee
John, Paul, George, Ringo and Bert	Help
	Here Comes the Sun
	Lucy in the Sky with Diamonds
The Joker Is Wild	All the Way
Jolson Sings Again	April Showers
	Baby Face
	California, Here I Come
	Carolina in the Morning
	I'm Looking Over a Four-Leaf Clover
	Sonny Boy
	Swanee
	You Made Me Love You
The Jolson Story	After the Ball
	The Anniversary Song
	April Showers
	Avalon
	By the Light of the Silvery Moon
	California, Here I Come
	I'm Sitting on Top of the World
	Liza
	Swanee
	When the Red Red Robin
	You Made Me Love You
Jubilee (show)	Begin the Beguine
	Just One of Those Things
Jumbo	Little Girl Blue
	The Most Beautiful Girl in the World
	My Romance
	This Can't Be Love
Karate Kid II	The Glory of Love
The King and I	Getting to Know You
	The March of the Siamese Children
	Hello, Young Lovers
	I Whistle a Happy Tune
	Shall We Dance?
	We Kiss in the Shadow
The King of Jazz	Rhapsody in Blue
Kismet	And This Is My Beloved
	Baubles, Bangles and Beads
	Stranger in Paradise
Kiss Me, Kate	Always True to You in My Fashion
	I Hate Men
	So in Love
	Too Darn Hot
	Why Can't You Behave?
	Wunderbar
Kiss Them for Me	Blue Moon
	I've Got a Gal in Kalamazoo
Knickerbocker Holiday	September Song
Lady, Be Good!	Fascinating Rhythm
	The Last Time I Saw Paris
	Oh, Lady Be Good

Show/Film	Song
Lady, Be Good (show)	So Am I
Lady in the Dark	Jenny
Lady on a Train	Night and Day
Lady Sings the Blues	All of Me
	The Man I Love
	Our Love Is Here to Stay
Las Vegas Story	My Resistance Is Low
Latin Quarter (show)	C'est Si Bon
Leave It to Me (show)	Get Out of Town
	Most Gentlemen Don't Like Love
Les Misérables	Empty Chairs at Empty Tables
	God on High
Les Girls	Ça C'est l'Amour
Let's Make Love	My Heart Belongs to Daddy
Lilacs in the Spring	We'll Gather Lilacs
Lillian Russell	After the Ball
Little Jesse James (show)	I Love You (Archer and Thompson)
Little Nellie Kelly	Singin' in the Rain
A Little Night Music (show)	Send in the Clowns
Looking for Love	Be My Love
Love, Honour and Behave	Bei Mir Bist Du Schön
Love Is a Many-Splendored Thing	Love is a Many- Splendored Thing
Lovely to Look At	I Won't Dance
	Smoke Gets in Your Eyes
Love Me Or Leave Me	I'm Sitting on Top of the World
	You Made Me Love You
Love Me Tonight	Isn't It Romantic?
	Mimi
Love Never Dies (show)	The Coney Island Waltz
	Gustave! Gustave!
	Mother Did You Watch?
	Once Upon Another Time
Lovers and Other Strangers	For All We Know
Love Thy Neighbour	My Heart Belongs to Daddy
Lucky Boy	California, Here I Come
Lullaby of Broadway	Just One of Those Things
	Somebody Loves Me
	Lullaby of Broadway
Mad Dogs and Englishmen	Delta Lady
The Magic Christian	Come and Get It
Mahogany	Do You Know Where You're Going To?
Make It Snappy (show)	The Sheik of Araby
A Man Could Get Killed	Strangers in the Night
Man from the Folies Bergere	Rhythm of the Rain
The Man I Love	Bill
	Liza
	The Man I Love
Man of La Mancha	The Impossible Dream
The Man Who Knew Too Much	Que Sera, Sera
Mary Poppins	Chim Chim Cheree
	Feed the Birds
	Jolly Holiday
	Let's Go Fly a Kite
	A Spoonful of Sugar
	Supercalifragilisticexpialidocious
Mary Poppins (show)	Practically Perfect
M.A.S.H.	Suicide Is Painless
Mayfair and Montmartre (show)	Please Do it Again
Me and My Girl	The Lambeth Walk
	Leaning on a Lamp Post
Meet Danny Wilson	All of Me
	I've Got a Crush on You
	That Old Black Magic
	When You're Smiling
Meet Me in St Louis	Have Yourself a Merry Little Christmas
	The Trolley Song

Show/Film	*Song*
Meet the People	I Like to Recognise the Tune
Mexican Hayride	I Love You (Porter)
Midnight Cowboy	Everybody's Talkin'
Mississippi	It's Easy to Remember
Monkey Business	When I Take My Sugar to Tea
Moonlight in Havana	I Wonder Who's Kissing Her Now
Moon over Miami	You Started Something
Mother Wore Tights	Burlington Bertie from Bow
Music Man	Seventy-Six Trombones
	Till There Was You
My Dream Is Yours	You Must Have Been a Beautiful Baby
My Fair Lady	Get Me to the Church On Time
	I Could Have Danced All Night
	I've Grown Accustomed to Her Face
	On the Street Where You Live
	With a Little Bit of Luck
	Wouldn't It Be Loverly
My Man	Second-Hand Rose
Nancy Goes to Rio	Embraceable You
Neptune's Daughter	Baby It's Cold Outside
Never on Sunday	Never on Sunday
New Faces	C'est Si Bon
The New Moon	Wanting You
Night and Day	Begin the Beguine
	Do I Love You, Do I
	I Get a Kick out of You
	In the Still of the Night
	I've Got You under My Skin
	Just One of Those Things
	Let's Do It (Let's Fall in Love)
	Miss Otis Regrets
	My Heart Belongs to Daddy
	Night and Day
	What Is This Thing Called Love
	You're the Top
A Night in Casablanca	Who's Sorry Now?
The Night Is Young	When I Grow Too Old to Dream
No, No, Nanette	I Want To Be Happy
	Tea for Two
Nymph Errant (show)	Experiment
	The Physician
Octopussy	All Time High
An Officer and a Gentleman	Up Where We Belong
Of Thee I Sing (show)	Love Is Sweeping the Country
Oh Kay (show)	Clap Yo' Hands
	Do Do Do
	Maybe
Oh, Look (show)	I'm Always Chasing Rainbows
Oh, You Beautiful Doll	Oh You Beautiful Doll
Oklahoma!	I Cain't Say No
	Oh What a Beautiful Morning
	Out of My Dreams
	People Will Say We're in Love
	The Surrey With the Fringe On Top
Oliver	As Long As He Needs Me
	Consider Yourself
	I'd Do Anything
One Minute to Zero	When I Fall in Love
One Night of Love	Indian Love Call
On Her Majesty's Secret Service	All the Time in the World
On Moonlight Bay	I'm Forever Blowing Bubbles
On Stage Everybody	Straighten Up and Fly Right
On the Sunny Side of the Street	On the Sunny Side of the Street
On the Town	New York, New York
On Your Toes	Slaughter on Tenth Avenue
On Your Toes (show)	There's a Small Hotel
	You Took Advantage of Me

Show/Film	*Song*
Orchestra Wives	At Last
	I've Got a Gal in Kalamazoo
Painting the Clouds with Sunshine	The Birth of the Blues
	We're in the Money
	With a Song in My Heart
Paint Your Wagon	I Talk to the Trees
	They Call the Wind Maria
	Wanderin' Star
The Pajama Game	Hernando's Hideaway
The Paleface	Buttons and Bows
Pal Joey	Bewitched, Bothered & Bewildered
	I Could Write a Book
	I Didn't Know What Time It Was
	The Lady is a Tramp
	My Funny Valentine
	There's a Small Hotel
Panama Hattie	Just One of Those Things
	Let's Be Buddies
Papa's Delicate Condition	Call Me Irresponsible
Paramount on Parade	Come Back to Sorrento
	Sweeping the Clouds Away
Pardon My Rhythm	I'll See You in My Dreams
Pardon My Sarong	Do I Worry
Paris	Among My Souvenirs
Paris (show)	Let's Do it (Let's Fall in Love)
Paris Holiday	April in Paris
	The Last Time I Saw Paris
Pat Garrett and Billy the Kid	Knockin' on Heaven's Door
Pepe	Mimi
	September Song
Perchance to Dream (show)	We'll Gather Lilacs
Performance	Memo to Turner
The Perils of Pauline	I Wish I Didn't Love You So
Pete Kelly's Blues	Bye Bye Blackbird
	Somebody Loves Me
Phantom of the Opera (show)	All I Ask of You
	Music of the Night
Pickwick (show)	If I Ruled the World
Pinocchio	Hi-Diddle-Dee-Dee (An Actor's Life For Me)
	When You Wish upon a Star
The Pirate	Be a Clown
Play It Cool	Once upon a Dream
The Pleasure Seekers (show)	Get Out and Get Under
Porgy and Bess	I Got Plenty of Nuttin'
	It Ain't Necessarily So
	Summertime
Present Arms	You Took Advantage of Me
The Prime of Miss Jean Brodie	Jean
Prince for Tonight (show)	I Wonder Who's Kissing Her Now
Privilege	I've Been a Bad Bad Boy
The Producers (flop play 'Funny Boy' – a musical version of Hamlet)	Along Came Bialy
	In Old Bavaria
	Keep It Gay
	The King of Broadway
	Springtime for Hitler
Promises, Promises (show)	I'll Never Fall in Love Again
Province Town Follies (show)	Red Sails in the Sunset
Puttin' on the Ritz	Puttin' on the Ritz
Radio Stars on Parade	That Old Black Magic
Rain or Shine	Happy Days Are Here Again
Rainbow Round My Shoulder	Bye Bye Blackbird
Red Hot and Blue (show)	It's d'Lovely
Reveille with Beverley	Night and Day
Rhapsody in Blue	Bidin' My Time
	Clap Yo' Hands
	Embraceable You
	Fascinating Rhythm
	I Got Rhythm

Show/Film	***Song***
Rhapsody in Blue (continued)	I'll Build a Stairway to Paradise
	Liza
	Love Walked In
	The Man I Love
	Oh, Lady Be Good
	Please Do It Again
	Rhapsody in Blue
	Somebody Loves Me
	Someone to Watch over Me
	Swanee
	S'Wonderful
Rhythm on the River	Ain't It a Shame about Mame
Road House	Again
Road to Morocco	Ain't Got a Dime to My Name
	Moonlight Becomes You
Road to Rio	But Beautiful
Road to Utopia	Put It There, Pal
	Welcome to My Dream
Roberta	I Won't Dance
	Smoke Gets in Your Eyes
Rock around the Clock	Only You
	Rock around the Clock
Rocky III	Eye of the Tiger
Romance in the Dark	The Nearness of You
Roman Scandals	Keep Young and Beautiful
Rosalie	In the Still of the Night
Rosalie (show)	How Long Has This Been Going On
Rose Marie	Indian Love Call
Rose of Washington Square	California, Here I Come
Sadie McKee	All I Do Is Dream of You
Sailors Three	All Over the Place
St Louis Blues	Beale Street Blues
Salad Days	Cleopatra
	We're Looking for a Piano
Saludos Amigos	Brazil
Sanders of the River	The Canoe Song
The Sandpiper	The Shadow of Your Smile
Satchmo the Great	Mack the Knife
Saturday Night Fever	Staying Alive
September Affair	September Song
Sergeant Pepper's Lonely Hearts Club Band	With a Little Help from My Friends
Serious Charge	Living Doll
Set to Music (show)	Mad about the Boy
Seven Brides for Seven Brothers	Bless Yore Beautiful Hide
The Seven Hills of Rome	Arriverderci Darling
	Jezebel
	Memories are Made of This
Seven Lively Arts (show)	Ev'ry Time We Say Goodbye
Shaft	Shaft (1971)
Shall We Dance?	Beginner's Luck
	Let's Call the Whole Thing Off
	Slap That Bass
	They All Laughed
	They Can't take that away from Me
She Loves Me Not	Love in Bloom
Shipyard Sally	Wish Me Luck As You Wave Me Goodbye
The Shocking Miss Pilgrim	For You, for Me, for Everyone
Show Boat	Bill
	Can't Help Loving Dat Man
	Make Believe
	Ol' Man River
	Why Do I Love You?
Show Business	Alabamy Bound
	It Had to Be You
Show Girl (show)	Liza
The Show Is On (show)	By Strauss

Show/Film	***Song***
Silk Stockings	All of You
Sinbad (show)	Swanee
Sincerely Yours	Embraceable You
	The Man I Love
	Swanee
	Tea for Two
Since You Went Away	Together
The Singing Fool	I'm Sitting on Top of the World
	Sonny Boy
The Singing Hill	Blueberry Hill
The Singing Nun	Dominique
Singin' in the Rain	All I Do Is Dream of You
	Singin' in the Rain
Singin' in the Rain (show)	Be a Clown
	Fascinating Rhythm
Sleepy Lagoon	By the Sleepy Lagoon
Snow White and the Seven Dwarfs	Some Day My Prince Will Come
	Whistle While You Work
So Dear to My Heart	Lavender Blue
Somebody Loves Me	Somebody Loves Me
Some Like It Hot	Down among the Sheltering Palms
	Sweet Georgia Brown
	I Wanna Be Loved by You
Something to Shout About	You'd Be So Nice to Come Home to
Song of Norway	Strange Music
Song of the South	Zip-a-dee-doo-dah
Son of Paleface	Buttons and Bows
The Sound of Music	Climb Ev'ry Mountain
	Do-Re-Mi
	Edelweiss
	My Favourite Things
South Pacific	Bali Ha'i
	A Cock-Eyed Optimist
	Happy Talk
	I'm Gonna Wash That Man Right Out of My Hair
	I'm in Love with a Wonderful Guy
	Some Enchanted Evening
	There Is Nothing Like A Dame
	This Nearly Was Mine
	Younger Than Springtime
Spring Is Here	With a Song in My Heart
Springtime in the Rockies	Chattanooga Choo Choo
The Spy Who Loved Me	Nobody Does It Better
Star	Burlington Bertie from Bow
	Do Do Do
	Jenny
	The Physician
	Someone to Watch over Me
Stardust	With a Little Help from My Friends
	You've Lost That Lovin' Feelin'
A Star Is Born	Evergreen
	The Black Bottom
	Swanee
	You Took Advantage of Me
Starlift	Liza
	S'Wonderful
	What Is This Thing Called Love?
Star Spangled Rhythm	That Old Black Magic
State Fair	Isn't It Kinda Fun
	It Might As Well Be Spring
	That's For Me
The Sting	The Entertainer
The Stooge	Louise
Stop Flirting (show)	I'll Build a Stairway to Paradise
Stop the World – I Want To Get Off	What Kind of Fool Am I?
	Gonna Build a Mountain
Stormy Weather	Ain't Misbehavin'

Show/Film	***Song***
The Story of Vernon and Irene Castle	Hello, Hello, Who's Your Lady Friend?
	Oh, You Beautiful Doll
Strike Up the Band (show)	I've Got a Crush on You
	Soon
The Strip	Ain't Misbehavin'
	Basin Street Blues
The Stud	Emotions
The Student Prince	The Drinking Song
Summer Holiday	Bachelor Boy
The Sun Also Rises	I Love You
Sunbonnet Sue	By the Light of the Silvery Moon
Sunny	Two Little Blue Birds
Sunny Side of the Street	I Get a Kick Out of You
Sunny Side Up	If I Had a Talking Picture of You
Sunset Boulevard	Charmaine
Sun Valley Serenade	At Last
	Chattanooga Choo Choo
	In the Mood
Swanee River	Beautiful Dreamer
Sweet Adeline	Don't Ever Leave Me
Sweet Adeline (show)	Why Was I Born?
Sweet and Low (show)	Cheerful Little Earful
Sweet Charity	Big Spender
	Rhythm of Life
Swing Parade of 1946	On the Sunny Side of the Street
Swing Time	The Way You Look Tonight
Swingtime Johnny	Boogie Woogie Bugle Boy
Syncopation	You Made Me Love You
Take a Chance	It's Only a Paper Moon
Tea for Two	Do Do Do
	Here in My Arms
	I Want to Be Happy
	Tea for Two
Thank Your Lucky Stars	I'm Riding for a Fall
That Certain Feeling	That Certain Feeling
That Midnight Kiss	Down among the Sheltering Palms
That Night in Rio	Chica Chica Boom Chic
	I Yi Yi Yi Yi I Like You Very Much
That Summer	Because the Night
There's No Business Like Show Business	Alexander's Ragtime Band
	There's No Business Like Show Business
	After You Get What You Want You Don't Want It
These Foolish Things (show)	Music, Maestro, Please
This Could Be the Night	I've Got You under My Skin
	Blue Moon
This Is the Life	With a Song in My Heart
This Time for Keeps	Inka Dinka Doo
The Thomas Crown Affair	Windmills of Your Mind
Thoroughly Modern Millie	Baby Face
	Please Do It Again
Thousands Cheer	Honeysuckle Rose
Three Coins in the Fountain	Three Coins in the Fountain
Three for the Show	I've Got a Crush on You
	Someone to Watch over Me
Three Little Girls in Blue	You Make Me Feel So Young
Three Little Words	I Wanna Be Loved by You
	Who's Sorry Now?
Threepenny Opera (show)	Mack the Knife
Till the Clouds Roll By	Long Ago and Far Away
	All the Things You Are
	Can't Help Loving Dat Man
	I Won't Dance
	The Last Time I Saw Paris
	Make Believe
	Ol' Man River
	Smoke Gets in Your Eyes

Show/Film	***Song***
Time	She's So Beautiful
The Time, the Place and the Girl	I Wonder Who's Kissing Her Now
Tin Pan Alley	Honeysuckle Rose
	The Sheik of Araby
Tip-Toes (show)	Looking for a Boy
	Sweet and Lowdown
	That Certain Feeling
Tip Top (show)	Feather Your Nest
The Toast of New Orleans	Be My Love
To Have and Have Not	Hong Kong Blues
Tommy	I'm Free
	Pinball Wizard
Too Many Girls	I Didn't Know What Time It Was
Too Many Girls (show)	I Like to Recognize the Tune
Too Young to Know	It's Only a Paper Moon
Top Gun	Take My Breath Away
Top Hat	Cheek to Cheek
	Isn't This a Lovely Day
Torch Song	Blue Moon
A Trip to Chinatown (show)	After the Ball
Trouble in Store	Don't Laugh at Me
Two for the Show	How High the Moon?
Two for Tonight	From the Top of Your Head
Two Girls and a Sailor	Inka Dinka Doo
Two Weeks with Love	By the Light of the Silvery Moon
Up in Central Park	Close As Pages in a Book
The Vagabond King	Only a Rose
	Some Day
Variety Jubilee	Keep the Home Fires Burning
	A Little of What You Fancy
Waikiki Wedding	Sweet Leilani
Wait Till the Sun Shines, Nellie	Pack Up Your Troubles in Your Old Kit Bag
Wake Up and Dream	What Is This Thing Called Love?
Wake Up and Dream (show)	Let's Do It (Let's Fall in Love)
The Wall	Another Brick in the Wall
Watership Down	Bright Eyes
Way Out West	Trail of the Lonesome Pine
The Way We Were	The Way We Were
Wedding Bells	How Could You Believe Me?
Weekend Pass	All or Nothing at All
We're Not Dressing	Love Thy Neighbour
West Side Story	America
	I Feel Pretty
	Maria
	Something's Coming
	Somewhere
	Tonight
Wharf Angel	Oh, You Beautiful Doll
	You Made Me Love You
What Lola Wants	Whatever Lola Wants
What's Cooking?	Woodchoppers' Ball
White Christmas	Blue Skies
	White Christmas
White Nights	Say You, Say Me
Whoopee	My Baby Just Cares for Me
The Wicked Lady	Love Steals Your Heart
Will o' the Whispers (show)	The Man I Love,
With a Song in My Heart	California, Here I Come
	Deep in the Heart of Texas
	Embraceable You
	Tea for Two
	Alabamy Bound
	Blue Moon
	With a Song in My Heart
The Wizard of Oz	Ding Dong the Witch Is Dead
	Over the Rainbow
Woman in Red	I Just Called to Say I Love You
Wonderful Life	On the Beach

Show/Film	*Song*
Woodstock	Dance to the Music
	With a Little Help from My Friends
Words and Music	Slaughter on Tenth Avenue
	Blue Moon
	I Wish I Were in Love Again
	Johnny One Note
	The Lady Is a Tramp
	Mountain Greenery
	My Heart Stood Still
	There's a Small Hotel
	This Can't Be Love
	Thou Swell
	Where or When
	Where's That Rainbow?
	With a Song in My Heart
Words and Music (show)	Mad about the Boy
The World Is Full of Married Men	Right Back Where We Started From
Yellow Submarine	All You Need Is Love
	Eleanor Rigby
	With a Little Help from My Friends
Yesterday's Heroes	Hold the Line
You Can't Have Everything	Afraid to Dream
You Never Know (show)	At Long Last Love
Young at Heart	Just One of Those Things
	The Man I Love
	Someone to Watch over Me
Young Man of Music	With a Song in My Heart
You're My Everything	Ain't She Sweet?
	California, Here I Come
You Were Meant for Me	Ain't Misbehavin'
	Ain't She Sweet?
	Goodnight, Sweetheart
Ziegfeld Follies of 1921 (show)	Second-Hand Rose
The Ziegfeld Girl	I'm Always Chasing Rainbows
	You Stepped Out of a Dream
Zorba the Greek	Zorba's Dance

Dubbed Singing Voice of Well-Known Actors

Actor	*Voice and film*
Ann Blyth	Gogi Grant (Both Ends of the Candle)
Audrey Hepburn	Marni Nixon (My Fair Lady)
Christopher Plummer	Bill Lee (Sound of Music)
Cyd Charisse	India Adams (The Band Wagon)
Deborah Kerr	Marni Nixon (King and I)
Diahann Carroll	Bernice Peterson (Carmen Jones)
Dorothy Dandridge	Marilyn Horne (Carmen Jones)
Edmund Purdom	Mario Lanza (The Student Prince)
Franco Nero	Gene Merlina (Camelot)
Harry Belafonte	LeVerne Hutcherson (Carmen Jones)
Jean Seberg	Anita Gordon (Paint Your Wagon)
Jeanne Crain	Anita Ellis (Gentlemen Marry Brunettes)
Joan Leslie	Louanne Hogan (Rhapsody in Blue)
Joe Adams	Marvin Hayes (Carmen Jones)
John Kerr	Bill Lee (South Pacific)
Juanita Hall	Muriel Smith (South Pacific)
Larry Parks	Al Jolson (The Jolson Story)
Lucille Bremer	Trudy Erwin (Till the Clouds Roll By)
Natalie Wood	Marni Nixon (West Side Story)
Ned Beatty	Vernon Midgley (Hear My Song)
Peter O'Toole	Simon Gilbert (Man of La Mancha)
Richard Beymer	Jim Bryant (West Side Story)
Rita Moreno	Leona Gordon (King and I)
Rita Moreno	Betty Wand (West Side Story)
Rossano Brazzi	Giorgio Tozi (South Pacific)
Sophia Loren	Renata Tebaldi (Aida)
Susan Hayward	Jane Froman (With a Song in My Heart)
Vera-Ellen	Carole Richards (Call Me Madam)

Theme Songs or Signature Tunes

Song/Tune	*Artiste*
Back to Those Happy Days	Herman Darewski
Be My Love	Mario Lanza
Because of You	Tony Bennett
Begin the Beguine	Leslie (Hutch) Hutchinson
Bei Mir Bist Du Schön	Andrews Sisters
Bewitched Bothered and Bewildered	Bill Snyder
Bill	Helen Morgan
Blue Flame (opening theme)	Woody Herman
Bugle Call Rag	Harry Roy
Ciribiribin	Harry James
Clap Hands Here Comes Charlie	Charlie Kunz
Cocktails for Two	Carl Brisson
Coquette	Guy Lombardo
Cry	Johnnie Ray
Cuban Love Song	Edmundo Ros
Dancing Time	Oscar Rabin
Darling, Je Vous Aime Beaucoup	Hildegarde
Dear Old Southland	Layton and Johnstone
Deep Forest	Earl Hines
Dinah	Dinah Shore
Don't Laugh at Me	Norman Wisdom
Dream	The Pied Pipers
Dream Along with Me	Perry Como
Everybody Loves Somebody	Dean Martin
Give Me the Moonlight	Frankie Vaughan
Give My Regards to Broadway	George M Cohan
Goodbye (closing theme)	Benny Goodman
Goodnight	Cavan O'Connor
Goodnight, Sweetheart (closing theme)	Ray Noble
Here's to the Next Time	Henry Hall
How High the Moon	Les Paul and Mary Ford
Hurry on Down	Nellie Lutcher
Ida, Sweet as Apple Cider	Eddie Cantor
I Do Like to Be Beside the Seaside	Reginald Dixon
I Don't Care	Eva Tanguay
If I Didn't Care	Ink Spots
I Got Rhythm	Ethel Merman
I'll See You Again	Noël Coward
I'll See You in My Dreams	Tony Martin
I Love a Lassie	Harry Lauder
I'm Getting Sentimental Over You	Tommy Dorsey
Inka Dinka Doo	Jimmy Durante
In the Mood	Joe Loss
I Used to Sigh for the Silvery Moon	G H Elliott (Chocolate-coloured Coon)

Song/Tune	Artiste
J'Attendrai	Jean Sablon
Just an Old-Fashioned Girl	Eartha Kitt
Just Like a Melody from Out of the Sky	Jay Wilbur
La Mer	Charles Trenet
Leaning on a Lamp Post	George Formby
Let's Dance (opening theme)	Benny Goodman
Life Is Nothing without Music	Fred Hartley
Louise	Maurice Chevalier
Love in Bloom	Jack Benny
Love Is Like a Violin	Ken Dodd
Lullaby of Broadway	George Shearing
Makin' Whoopee	Eddie Cantor
Mañana Is Soon Enough For Me	Peggy Lee
Marigold	Billy Mayerl
Marta	Arthur Tracy (The Street Singer)
Minnie the Moocher	Cab Calloway
Moonlight Serenade	Glenn Miller
Mother Machree	John MacCormack
Music, Maestro, Please	Harry Leader
My Blue Heaven	Gene Austin
My Heart Belongs to Daddy	Mary Martin
My Mammy	Al Jolson
My Time Is Your Time	Rudy Vallee
Near You	Francis Craig
Nightmare	Artie Shaw
Oh Monah	Lew Stone
O Mein Papa	Eddie Calvert
One O'Clock Jump	Count Basie
On the Air	Carroll Gibbons
Over the Rainbow	Judy Garland
Paper Doll	Mills Brothers
Rags, Bottles or Bones	Syd Walker
Red Sails in the Sunset	Suzette Tarri
Rhapsody in Blue	Paul Whiteman
Rose of Washington Square	Fanny Brice
Sally	Gracie Fields
Say It With Music	Jack Payne
Sentimental Journey	Les Brown
She's My Lovely	Billy Ternent
Shine On Harvest Moon	Nora Bayes
Skyliner	Charlie Barnet
Sleepy Serenade	Cyril Stapleton
Smoke Rings	Glen Gray
Some of These Days	Sophie Tucker
Somebody Stole My Gal	Billy Cotton
So Rare (closing theme)	Jimmy Dorsey
So Tired	Russ Morgan
Speak to Me of Love	Lucienne Boyer
Stage Coach	Eric Winstone
Stormy Weather	Lena Horne
Straighten Up and Fly Right	Nat King Cole
Sugar Blues	Clyde McCoy
Summertime	Bob Crosby
Sunrise Serenade	Frankie Carle
Sweet and Lovely	Russ Columbo
Take Me to Your Heart Again	Edith Piaf
Take the 'A' Train	Duke Ellington
Tenderly	Rosemary Clooney
Thanks for the Memory	Bob Hope
That Old Black Magic	Stanley Black
	Billy Daniels
That's What I Like about the South	Phil Harris
The Dicky Bird Hop	Ronald Gourlay
The Donkey Serenade	Monte Rey
The Jolly Brothers	Albert Whelan
The Sweetest Music This Side of Heaven	Maurice Winnick
The Very Thought of You (opening theme)	Ray Noble
The Wheel of Fortune	Kay Starr
Tumbling Tumbleweeds	Sons of the Pioneers
We'll Be Together Again	Frankie Laine
What's New	Billy Butterfield
When Day Is Done	Ambrose
When It's Sleepy Time Down South	Louis Armstrong
When My Baby Smiles At Me	Ted Lewis
When the Moon Comes Over the Mountain	Kate Smith
When You're Smiling	George Elrick
Where the Blue of the Night	Bing Crosby
Whispering	Roy Fox
Woodchoppers' Ball	Woody Herman
You're Dancing on My Heart	Victor Sylvester
Yours	Vera Lynn

NB: The theme tunes or signature tunes above are the ones the people themselves considered to be so, and not always the one most readily identifiable with the artist. For example, few would consider 'Yours' to be more identifiable with Vera Lynn than 'The White Cliffs of Dover'. Similarly, 'Take Me To Your Heart Again' is certainly not the most famous Edith Piaf song.

It is probably a good idea at this stage to lay to rest once and for all the most common source of frustration for quiz players on the topic of signature tunes, i.e. is Glenn Miller's signature tune 'In the Mood' or 'Moonlight Serenade'? The problem arises because 'In the Mood' was one of Glenn Miller's most popular tunes and was featured in both Sun Valley Serenade and The Glenn Miller Story; however, Glenn Miller himself composed 'Moonlight Serenade' and always considered this to be his signature tune. Joe Loss did in fact record 'In the Mood' and subsequently adopted it as his signature.

TV and Radio Theme Tunes

Programme	Tune (and/or composer)
Absolutely Fabulous	'This Wheel's on Fire' by Julie Driscoll
Angel	Theme tune performed by Darling Violetta
The Archers	'Barwick Green' from My Native Heath suite written in 1922 by Arthur Wood
Auf Wiedersehen Pet	'That's Living Alright' sung by Joe Fagin
The Avengers	Theme by Laurie Johnson
Big Brother	Theme tune by Element Four (aka Paul Oakenfold and Andy Gray)
Billy Cotton Band Show	'Somebody Stole My Gal'
Blake's 7	Music by Dudley Simpson
Blue Peter	'Barnacle Bill the Sailor' by Robison and Luther (famous adaptation by Mike Oldfield)
Bonanza	Music by David Rose
Bootsie and Snudge	'Pop Goes the Weasel'
Brain of Britain	Mozart's Eine kleine Nachtmusik
Buffy the Vampire Slayer	Theme written and performed by rock band Nerf Herder
Captain Pugwash	'Hornblower' (played on the accordion by Tommy Edmondson)
Crossroads	Theme by Tony Hatch and later adapted by Paul McCartney

Programme	*Tune (and/or composer)*
Dad's Army	'Who Do You Think You're Kidding, Mr Hitler?' sung by Bud Flanagan
Danger Man	Music by Edwin Astley
Desert Island Discs	'By the Sleepy Lagoon' by Eric Coates
Doctor Kildare	'Three Stars Will Shine Tonight' (vocal version by Richard Chamberlain)
Dr Who	Theme by Ron Grainer
The Dukes of Hazzard	Theme tune by Waylon Jennings
EastEnders	Theme tune by Simon May
EastEnders: vocal version	'Anyone Can Fall in Love' sung by Anita Dobson
Equaliser	Theme tune by Stewart Copeland
Friends	'I'll Be There For You' by Rembrandts
Grand Prix	BBC – 'The Chain' by Fleetwood Mac
Great Antiques Hunt	Theme tune by the Brodsky Quartet
Harry's Game	Theme by Clannad
Have Gun, Will Travel	'The Ballad of the Paladin'
Hawaii Five O	Music by Morton Stevens
Horse of the Year Show	Mozart's 'A Musical Joke'
Howards Way	Theme tune by Simon May
Howards Way: vocal version	'Always There' by Marti Webb
I'm Sorry I'll Read That Again	'The Angus Prune Tune'
Inspector Morse	Theme tune by Barrington Pheloung
Ironside	Theme by Quincy Jones
Jason King	Theme by Laurie Johnson
Juke Box Jury	'Hit and Miss' by John Barry
Just a Minute	Minute Waltz by Chopin
The Killing Game	'Tom Hark' by the Piranhas
Kojak	Theme by Billy Goldenberg
Life and Times of David Lloyd George	'Chi Mai' by Ennio Morricone
Light of Experience	Theme by Doina De Jale
The Lone Ranger	William Tell Overture by Rossini
M.A.S.H.	'Suicide Is Painless' by Mash
Mastermind	'Approaching Menace' by Neil Richardson
Match of the Day	Drum Majorette
Miami Vice	'Miami Vice Theme' and 'Crockett's Theme' (both by Jan Hammer)
Minder	'I Could Be So Good For You' by Pat Waterman and Gerard Kenny
Mission Impossible	Theme by Lalo Schifrin
Mistral's Daughter	'Only Love' (sung by Nana Mouskouri)
Monty Python's Flying Circus	'Liberty Bell' by John Paul Souza
Moonlighting	'Moonlighting Theme' by Al Jarreau
Neighbours	Theme by Tony Hatch
Noddy	Paul K Joyce
No Honestly	'No Honestly' by Lynsey de Paul
Onedin Line	Spartacus by Khatchaturian
One Foot in the Grave	Composed and sung by Eric Idle
Owen MD	'Sleepy Shores' by Johnny Pearson
Perry Mason	Theme by Fred Steiner
The Persuaders	Music by John Barry
The Prisoner	Music by Ron Grainer
Prisoner Cell Block H	'On the Inside' sung by Lynne Hamilton
Protectors	'Avenues and Alleyways' by Tony Christie
Randall and Hopkirk (Deceased)	Music by Edwin Astley
Rawhide	Theme sung by Frankie Laine
Ready Steady Go!	'Wipe Out' (The Surfaris); '5-4-3-2-1' (Manfred Mann)
The Saint	Music by Edwin Astley
The Seven Faces of Woman	'She' (sung by Charles Aznavour)
The Sky at Night	At the Castle Gate by Sibelius (from Pelléas et Mélisande)
The Snowman	'Walking in the Air' sung by Aled Jones
South Bank Show	Variations on a Theme of Paganini by Julian Lloyd Webber
Star Trek	Music by Alexander Courage
Stingray	'Aquamarina' (sung by Garry Miller)
Supergran	Theme composed and sung by Billy Connolly
Test Match Special	'Soul Limbo' by Booker T & The MGs
That Was the Week That Was	Sung by Millicent Martin
The Third Man	'Harry Lime Theme' by Anton Karas
Tinker, Tailor, Soldier, Spy	Nunc Dimittis, arranged by Geoffrey Burgon
Top of the Pops	'Yellow Pearl' by Phil Lynott (co-written by Lynott and Ray Davies); 'Whole Lotta Love' by CCS (instrumental version of Led Zeppelin song); 'The Wizard' by Paul Hardcastle; 'Get Out of That' by Tony Gibber
Top Secret	'Sucu Sucu'
Two-Way Family Favourites	'With a Song in My Heart' by Richard Rodgers
Van Der Valk	'Eye Level' by Simon Park
What the Papers Say	From the Cornish Dances by Malcolm Arnold
X Files	Music by Mark Snow
Yes Honestly	'Yes Honestly' by Georgie Fame
Z Cars	'Theme from Z Cars' aka 'Johnny Todd' by the Johnny Keating Orchestra

Eurovision Song Contest Winners

Year	*Song*	*Country (and Singer)*	*UK Entry*	*UK Posn*
1956	Refrain	Switzerland (Lys Assia)	No entry	
1957	Net Als Toen	Holland (Corry Brokken)	All (Patricia Breden)	6th
1958	Dors, Mon Amour	France (André Claveau)	No entry	
1959	Een Beetje	Holland (Teddy Scholten)	Sing Little Birdie (Pearl Carr and Teddy Johnson)	2nd
1960	Tom Pillibi	France (Jacqueline Boyer)	Looking High, High, High (Bryan Johnson)	2nd
1961	Nous, les Amoureux	Luxembourg (Jean-Claude Pascal)	Are You Sure (Allisons)	2nd
1962	Un Premier Amour	France (Isabelle Aubret)	Ring-a-ding Girl (Ronnie Carroll)	4th
1963	Dansevise	Denmark (Grethe Jorgen Ingmann)	Say Wonderful Things (Ronnie Carroll)	4th
1964	Non Ho L'Eta (This Is My Prayer)	Italy (Gigliola Cinquetti)	I Say the Little Things (Matt Monro)	2nd

Year	*Song*	*Country (and Singer)*	*UK Entry*	*UK Posn*
1965	Poupée de Cire, Poupée de Son	Luxembourg (France Gall)	I Belong (Kathy Kirby)	2nd
1966	Merci Chérie	Austria (Udo Jurgens)	A Man without Love (Kenneth McKellar)	7th
1967	Puppet on a String	UK (Sandie Shaw)	Puppet on a String	1st
1968	La La La	Spain (Massiel)	Congratulations (Cliff Richard)	2nd
1969	Viva Cantando	Spain (Salome)	Boom Bang-A-Bang	1st
	Boom Bang-A-Bang	UK (Lulu)		
	De Troubadour	Holland (Lennie Kuhr)		
	Un Jour Un Enfant	France (Frida Boccara)		
1970	All Kinds of Everything	Ireland (Dana)	Knock Knock (Mary Hopkin)	2nd
1971	Un Banc, Un Arbre, Une Rue	Monaco (Séverine)	Jack in the Box (Clodagh Rodgers)	4th
1972	Après Toi (Come What May)	Luxembourg (Vicky Leandros)	Beg, Steal or Borrow (New Seekers)	2nd
1973	Tu Te Reconnaîtras (Wonderful Dream)	Luxembourg (Anne-Marie David)	Power to all our Friends (Cliff Richard)	3rd
1974	Waterloo	Sweden (Abba)	Long Live Love (Olivia Newton-John)	4th
1975	Ding A Dong	Holland (Teach In)	Let Me Be the One (Shadows)	2nd
1976	Save Your Kisses for Me	UK (Brotherhood of Man)	Save Your Kisses For Me	1st
1977	L'Oiseau et L'Enfant	France (Marie Myriam)	Rock Bottom (Lynsey de Paul)	2nd
1978	A-ba-ni-bi	Israel (Izhar Cohen and the Alpha-Beta)	The Bad Old Days (Coco)	11th
1979	Hallelujah	Israel (Milk and Honey featuring Gali Atari)	Mary Ann (Black Lace)	7th
1980	What's Another Year?	Ireland (Johnny Logan)	Love Enough for Two (Prima Donna)	3rd
1981	Making Your Mind Up	UK (Buck's Fizz)	Making Your Mind Up	1st
1982	Ein Bisschen Frieden (A Little Peace)	Germany (Nicole)	One Step Further (Bardo)	7th
1983	Si la Vie Est Cadeau	Luxembourg (Corinne Hermes)	I'm Never Giving Up (Sweet Dreams)	6th
1984	Diggi loo-Diggi Ley	Sweden (Herreys)	Love Games (Belle and the Devotions)	7th
1985	La Det Swinge (Let it Swing)	Norway (Bobbysocks)	Love Is (Vikki)	4th
1986	J'aime la Vie	Belgium (Sandra Kim)	Runner in the Night (Ryder)	7th
1987	Hold Me Now	Ireland (Johnny Logan)	Only the Light (Rikki)	13th
1988	Ne Partez Pas Sans Moi	Switzerland (Celine Dion)	Go (Scott Fitzgerald)	2nd
1989	Rock Me	Yugoslavia (Riva)	Why Do I Always Get It Wrong (Live Report)	2nd
1990	Insieme:1992	Italy (Toto Cutugno)	Give a Little Love Back to the World (Emma)	6th
1991	Fångad Av En Stormvind	Sweden (Carola)	A Message to Your Heart (Samantha Janus)	10th
1992	Why Me?	Ireland (Linda Martin)	One Step Out of Time (Michael Ball)	2nd
1993	In Your Eyes	Ireland (Niamh Kavanagh)	Better the Devil You Know (Sonia)	2nd
1994	Rock 'n' Roll Kids	Ireland (Paul Harrington and Charlie McGettigan)	We Will Be Free - Lonely Symphony (Frances Ruffelle)	10th
1995	Nocturne	Norway (Secret Garden)	Love City Groove (Love City Groove)	10th
1996	The Voice	Ireland (Eimear Quinn)	Just a Little Bit (Gina G)	8th
1997	Love Shine a Light	UK (Katrina and the Waves)	Love Shine a Light	1st
1998	Diva	Israel (Dana International)	Where Are You? (Imaani)	2nd
1999	Take Me to Your Heaven	Sweden (Charlotte Nilsson)	Say It Again (Precious)	12th
2000	Fly on the Wings of Love	Denmark (Olsen Brothers)	Don't Play That Song Again (Nikki French)	16th
2001	Everybody	Estonia (Tanel Pader and Dave Benton)	No Dream Impossible (Lindsay Dracass)	15th
2002	I Wanna	Latvia (Marija Naumova)	Come Back (Jessica Garlick)	3rd equal
2003	Every Way That I Can	Turkey (Sertab Erener)	Cry Baby (Jemini)	Last
2004	Wild Dances	Ukraine (Ruslana)	Hold onto Our Love (James Fox)	16th
2005	My Number One	Greece (Helena Paparizou)	Touch My Fire (Javine Hylton)	22nd
2006	Hard Rock Hallelujah	Finland (Lordi)	Teenage Life (Daz Sampson)	18th
2007	Molitva	Serbia (Marija Serifovic)	Flying the Flag (Scooch)	23rd
2008	Believe	Russia (Dima Bilan)	Even If (Andy Abraham)	25th
2009	Fairytale	Norway (Alexander Rybak)	It's My Time (Jade Ewen)	5th

Year	Song	Country (and Singer)	UK Entry	UK Posn
2010	Satellite	Germany (Lena Meyer-Landrut)	That Sounds Good to Me (Josh Dubovie)	Last
2011	Running Scared	Azerbaijan (Ell & Nikki)	I Can (Blue)	11th
2012	Euphoria	Sweden (Loreen)	Love Will Set You Free (Englebert Humperdinck)	25th
2013	Only Teardrops	Denmark (Emmelie de Forest)	Believe in Me (Bonnie Tyler)	19th

Classical-based Pop Tunes

Baubles, Bangles and Beads Adapted from the String Quartet in D major by Alexander Borodin

Beat Out Dat Rhythm on a Drum Based on 'The Gypsy Song' from the opera Carmen by Georges Bizet

Can Can (Bad Manners) Adapted from Orpheus in the Underworld by Jacques Offenbach

Can't Help Falling in Love Based on Plaisir d'Amour by Giovanni Martini

Capstick Comes Home Based on Dvorák's Symphony No. 9 in E minor (2nd movement, Largo)

Danny Boy Lyrics by Frederick Weatherly (1848–1929) and based on 'The Londonderry Air'

Dat's Love Based on 'Habañera' from the opera Carmen by Georges Bizet

Fanfare for the Common Man (ELP) Based on Aaron Copland's orchestral piece of the same name

Hello Muddah, Hello Fadduh Adapted from 'Dance of the Hours', Act 3 of La Gioconda by Amilcare Ponchielli

Hot Diggity Adapted from España (Spanish Rhapsody) by Emmanuel Chabrier

I Believe in Father Christmas Adapted from the Lieutenant Kijé Suite, Op. 60 by Sergei Prokofiev

I'd Climb the Highest Mountain Based on Humoresque Opus 101 No. 7 by Antonín Dvořák

If I Had Words Adapted from the 3rd movement of Symphony No. 3 Op. 78 by Charles Camille Saint-Saëns

If You Are But a Dream Adapted from Romance in E flat by Anton Rubinstein

I'm Always Chasing Rainbows Adapted from Fantaisie Impromptu in C sharp minor Op. 66 by Frederic Chopin

In An Eighteenth-century Drawing Room Adapted from Piano Sonata No. 3 in C by Wolfgang Amadeus Mozart

Joybringer Adapted from the 4th movement of The Planets Suite Op. 32 by Gustav Holst ('Jupiter – Bringer of Jollity')

Kiss in Your Eyes Adapted from Une Chambre séparée by Richard Heuberger

Lamp Is Low Adapted from Pavane pour une infante défunte by Maurice Ravel

Land of Hope and Glory Based on Pomp and Circumstance March No. 1 by Edward Elgar

Like I Do Adapted from 'Dance of the Hours', Act 3 of La Gioconda by Amilcare Ponchielli

Moon Love Based on the 2nd movement of Tchaikovsky's Symphony No. 5

More Than Love Adapted from the 2nd movement of the Sonata for Piano No. 8 in C minor, Op. 13 by Ludwig van Beethoven

My Reverie Based on Debussy's Rêverie

Narcissus Adapted from the Water Scenes Suite, Op. 13 No. 4 by Ethelbert Nevin

Nut Rocker Adapted from the March from Casse-noisette Suite, Op. 71 by Tchaikovsky

On the Isle of May Based on Tchaikovsky's Andante Cantabile

Our Love Based on Tchaikovsky's Romeo and Juliet Overture

Question and Answer Adapted from Petite Suite de Concert, Op. 77 by Samuel Coleridge-Taylor

River Kwai March Based on 'Colonel Bogey March' by Kenneth Alford

Rodrigo's Concerto An arrangement of the 2nd movement of the Concerto for Guitar and Orchestra in D major by Joaquin Rodrigo

Sabre Dance Adapted from Gayaneh Ballet by Aram Khatchaturian

So Deep Is the Night Adapted from Etude in E minor, Op. 10 No. 3 by Frédéric Chopin

Song of India Adapted from Chanson indoue by Nikolai Rimsky-Korsakov

The Story of a Starry Night Based on the 1st movement of Symphony No. 6 by Tchaikovsky

Strange Music Adapted from Wedding-Day in Troldhaugen by Edvard Grieg

Stranger in Paradise Adapted from a theme of the Polovtsian Dances by Alexander Borodin

Suddenly (Tony Bennett) Adapted from Une Chambre Séparée by Richard Heuberger

Surrender (Elvis Presley) Adapted from 'Torna A Surriento' by Ernesto De Curtis

The Things I Love Based on Melodie in E flat major, Op. 42 No 3 by Tchaikovsky

Till the End of Time Based on Chopin's Polonaise No. 6 in A flat for piano

Toccata and Fugue (Vanessa Mae) Variation of a Toccata and Fugue by Johann Sebastian Bach

Under the Lilac Bough From the musical Lilac Time, based on various pieces of music of Franz Schubert

Wagon Wheels Adapted from the 2nd movement of Dvorak's Symphony No. 9 in E minor

Wild Horses Based on 'Wilder Reiter' by Robert Schumann

Wooden Heart Adapted from the German folk song 'Muss I denn'

Composers of Pop Songs and Tunes

Song	Composer
Alexander's Ragtime Band	Irving Berlin
Alfie	Burt Bacharach and Hal David
All along the Watchtower	Bob Dylan
All of You	Cole Porter
All the Young Dudes	David Bowie
Alternate Title	Mickey Dolenz
Always Something There To Remind Me	Burt Bacharach and Hal David
And I Love You So	Don McLean
Anything You Can Do	Irving Berlin
Automatically Sunshine	William 'Smokey' Robinson
Baby I Don't Care	Leiber and Stoller
Bad To Me	Lennon and McCartney
Batdance	Prince
Beautiful Dreamer	Stephen Foster
Begin the Beguine	Cole Porter
Boat That I Row, The	Neil Diamond
Born Free	Don Black and John Barry
Bright Eyes	Mike Batt
Bring it on Home to Me	Sam Cooke
Brown Eyed Handsome Man	Chuck Berry
Carnival Is Over	Tom Springfield
Chain Reaction	Bee Gees
Chantilly Lace	J P Richardson (The Big Bopper)
Cheek to Cheek	Irving Berlin
Close to You	Burt Bacharach and Hal David
Come and Get It	Paul McCartney

Song	*Composer*
A Couple of Swells	Irving Berlin
Cupid	Sam Cooke
Dancing in the Street	Marvyn Gaye and William Stevenson
Dancing on a Saturday Night	Barry Blue and Lynsey De Paul
The Day I Met Marie	Hank Marvin
Dick-A-Dum Dum (Kings Road)	Jim Dale
Do They Know It's Christmas?	Bob Geldof and Midge Ure
Do You Know Where You're Going To?	Gerry Goffin and Michael Masser
Do You Love Me	Berry Gordy Jr
Do You Want To Know a Secret	Lennon and McCartney
Doctorin' the Tardis	Gary Glitter, Ron Grainer, Chapman and Chinn
Doin' What Comes Naturally	Irving Berlin
Don't Cry Out Loud	Carole Bayer Sager and Peter Allen
Don't Give Up On Us	Tony Macaulay
Don't Sleep in the Subway	Tony Hatch and Jackie Trent
Easter Parade	Irving Berlin
Eloise	Paul Ryan
Fascinating Rhythm	George and Ira Gershwin
First Cut Is the Deepest	Cat Stevens
Floy Joy	William 'Smokey Robinson'
For the Good Times	Kris Kristofferson
Genie with the Light Brown Lamp	Marvin, Welch, Bennett, Rostill (Shadows)
Georgy Girl	Jim Dale and Tom Springfield
Giving It All Away	Leo Sayer and David Courtney
Goldfinger	Tony Newley, John Barry and Leslie Bricusse
Goodbye	Lennon and McCartney
Goodbye (Mary Hopkin)	Lennon and McCartney
Got to Get You into My Life	Lennon and McCartney
Grease	Barry Gibb
A Groovy Kind of Love	Carole Bayer Sager and Tony Wine
Halfway to Paradise	Gerry Goffin and Carole King
Happy Holiday	Irving Berlin
A Hard Rain's Gonna Fall	Bob Dylan
Have I Told You Lately	Van Morrison
Help Me Make It through The Night	Kris Kristofferson
Hey, Good Looking	Hank Williams
Hopelessly Devoted to You	John Farrar
The Hustle	Van McCoy
I Don't Wanna Fight	Lulu
I Don't Want to Talk About it	Cat Stevens and Danny Whitten
If Not for You	Bob Dylan
I Get a Kick Out of You	Cole Porter
I Got Plenty of Nuttin'	George and Ira Gershwin
I Got Rhythm	George and Ira Gershwin
I Got the Sun in the Morning	Irving Berlin
I Just Don't Know What to do with Myself	Burt Bacharach and Hal David
I'll Keep You Satisfied	Lennon and McCartney
I'll Never Fall in Love Again	Burt Bacharach and Hal David
I'll Never Fall in Love Again (Tom Jones)	Lonnie Donegan and Jimmie Currie
I Love You, Samantha	Cole Porter
I'm a Believer	Neil Diamond
I'm a Tiger	Marty Wilde and Ronnie Scott
I'm into Something Good	Gerry Goffin and Carole King

Song	*Composer*
I Say a Little Prayer	Burt Bacharach and Hal David
I Shot the Sheriff	Bob Marley
Isn't This a Lovely Day	Irving Berlin
It Doesn't Matter Anymore	Paul Anka
It Don't Mean a Thing	Duke Ellington and Irving Mills
It Might as Well Rain until September	Gerry Goffin and Carole King
It's All in the Game	Charles Dawes and Carl Sigman
I've Got You under My Skin	Cole Porter
I Wanna Be Your Man	Lennon and McCartney
I Will Drink the Wine	Paul Ryan
Jackie Wilson Said	Van Morrison
Jambalaya	Hank Williams
The James Bond Theme	Monty Norman
Just Like a Woman	Bob Dylan
Killing Me Softly with His Song	Charles Fox and Norman Gimbel
Knockin' on Heaven's Door	Bob Dylan
Lady	Lionel Richie
The Lady is a Tramp	Rodgers and Hart
Leaning on a Lamp Post	Noel Gay
Leavin' on a Jet Plane	John Denver
Legend of the Glass Mountain	Nino Rota
Let's Call the Whole Thing Off	George and Ira Gershwin
Let's Do It (Let's Fall in Love)	Cole Porter
Let's Face the Music and Dance	Irving Berlin
Little Bit Me, Little Bit You	Neil Diamond
Living Doll	Lionel Bart
The Locomotion	Gerry Goffin and Carole King
Love and Marriage	Sammy Cahn and Jimmy Van Heusen
MacArthur Park	Jim Webb
Mack the Knife	Weill, Brecht, Blitzstein
Mad about the Boy	Noël Coward
Mad Dogs and Englishmen	Noël Coward
Magic Moments	Burt Bacharach and Hal David
Mama Told Me Not to Come	Randy Newman
The Man Who Sold the World	David Bowie
The March of the Siamese Children	Richard Rodgers
Mighty Quinn	Bob Dylan
Miss Otis Regrets	Cole Porter
Mr Tambourine Man	Bob Dylan
Money (That's What I Want)	Berry Gordy Jr and Janie Bradford
Mrs Brown You've Got a Lovely Daughter	Trevor Peacock
My Guy	William 'Smokey' Robinson
My Heart Belongs to Daddy	Cole Porter
My Resistance Is Low	Hoagy Carmichael and Harold Adamson
Needles and Pins	Sonny Bono and Jack Nitzche
A Nice Cup Of Tea	A P Herbert
Night and Day	Cole Porter
Nothing Compares 2 U	Prince
Oh, Carol	Neil Sedaka and Howard Greenfield
Oh No, Not My Baby	Gerry Goffin and Carole King
Photograph	Ringo Starr and George Harrison
Pink Cadillac	Bruce Springsteen
The Purple People Eater	Sheb Wooley
Puttin' on the Ritz	Irving Berlin
Rhapsody in Blue	George Gershwin
River Kwai March	Malcolm Arnold

Song	Composer
Roamin' in the Gloamin'	Harry Lauder
Rocket Man	Elton John and Bernie Taupin
Roll Over Beethoven	Chuck Berry
Running Bear	J P Richardson (The Big Bopper)
Saving All My Love for You	Gerry Goffin and Michael Masser
September Song	Maxwell Anderson and Kurt Weill
Simon Smith and His Amazing Dancing Bear	Randy Newman
Something's Gotten Hold of My Heart	Roger Cook and Roger Greenaway
Something Tells Me	Roger Cook and Roger Greenaway
Sophisticated Lady	Duke Ellington, Irving Mills and Mitchell Parish
Step Inside Love	Lennon and McCartney
The Stripper	David Rose
S'Wonderful	George and Ira Gershwin
Take Five	Paul Desmond and Lola Brubeck
Take Good Care of My Baby	Gerry Goffin and Carole King
Tara's Theme	Max Steiner
Tears of a Clown	Smokey Robinson, Stevie Wonder, Henry Cosby
This Guy's in Love With You	Burt Bacharach and Hal David
This is My Song	Charlie Chaplin
This Wheel's on Fire	Bob Dylan and Rick Danko
Throw Down A Line	Hank B Marvin
To Keep My Love Alive	Rodgers and Hart
To Know Him is To Love Him	Phil Spector
To Love Somebody	Barry and Robin Gibb
Too Darn Hot	Cole Porter
Trains and Boats and Planes	Burt Bacharach and Hal David
True Love	Cole Porter

Song	Composer
Twenty-Four Hours from Tulsa	Burt Bacharach and Hal David
Twisting the Night Away	Sam Cooke
Up on the Roof	Gerry Goffin and Carole King
Up Where We Belong	Buffy St Marie, Jack Nitzche, William Jennings
We Are the World	Michael Jackson and Lionel Richie
Well, Did You Evah?	Cole Porter
What'll I Do	Irving Berlin
What's New, Pussycat?	Burt Bacharach and Hal David
When I'm Dead and Gone	Gallagher and Lyle
When I Need You	Carole Bayer Sager and Albert Hammond
Wherever I Lay My Hat	Marvin Gaye and Norman Whitfield
A Whiter Shade of Pale	Keith Reid, Matt Fisher, Gary Brooker
Who Wants to Be a Millionaire	Cole Porter
Wichita Lineman	Jim Webb
Wild Thing	Chip Taylor
Wild World	Cat Stevens
Will You Love Me Tomorrow	Gerry Goffin and Carole King
A Winter's Tale	Mike Batt
Wired for Sound	B A Robertson and Alan Tarney
Without You	Peter Ham and Tony Evans (Badfinger)
Woman in Love	Barry and Robin Gibb
Woodstock	Joni Mitchell
A World Without Love	Lennon and McCartney
Wunderbar	Cole Porter
You Make Me Feel So Young	Mack Gordon and Joseph Myrow
Your Cheating Heart	Hank Williams
You're the One That I Want	John Farrar
You're the Top	Cole Porter
You've Got Your Troubles	Roger Cook and Roger Greenaway

Derivations of Names

Group	Derivation	Where from
Abba (1972)	The initials of of its members' Christian names	Sweden/Norway
Adam and the Ants (1977)	Adopted his surname as collective name for his group of four	London
A-Ha (1982)	Keyboardist Mags Furuholmen chose name as it was a universally accepted expression	Norway
Alice Cooper (1965)	Spelt out by a ouija board	USA
America (1967)	Met at London school; all 3 members were sons of US Air Force officers stationed in UK	USA
Archies (1967)	Named after a popular CBS cartoon series based on John Goldwater comic book characters	USA
Art of Noise (1983)	The name of an Italian futurist manifesto	UK
Aswad (1983)	Arabic for 'Black'	UK
Bachman-Turner Overdrive (1973)	Added name of a trucking magazine, Overdrive, to those of its founding members	Canada
Bad Company (1973)	From a Jeff Bridges film	UK
Bangles (1981)	Forced to change name from the Bangs because of existing band	Los Angeles
Bauhaus (1980)	Named after the German art movement	UK
Bay City Rollers (1970)	Chosen by sticking pin in map of USA and pricking Bay City	UK
Bee Gees (1959)	From the initials of their founder Barry Gibb. There is no substance to the myth that a racetrack promoter (Bill Goode) and a DJ (Bill Gates) inspired the name	Australia
B-52's	Southern US nickname for a bouffant hairstyle adopted by its female members	Georgia
Blondie (1975)	Lead singer's hair colour	New York
Boney M (1975)	Named after an Aboriginal televiision detective	West Indies
Boomtown Rats (1978)	Originally Nightlife Thugs; changed name to phrase in Woody Guthrie biography Bound For Glory	Dublin
Bread (1968)	Chosen after they were stuck behind a Wonder Bread truck in a traffic jam	Los Angeles
Buffalo Springfield (1966)	A make of steamroller	California
Canned Heat (1966)	From 1928 song by Mississipi bluesman Tommy Johnson, 'Canned Heat Blues'	Los Angeles
Captain And Tennille (1971)	Mike Love of the Beach Boys called Daryl Dragon 'Captain Keyboards' and the name stuck; other member Toni Tennille	San Francisco
CCS (1970)	Collective Consciousness Society, a collaboration between Alexis Korner, Mickie Most and John Cameron	UK
Clannad (1981)	Gaelic for 'Family'	Ireland
Commodores (1968)	Random choice from dictionary (nearly called the Commodes, so they say)	USA
Cream (1966)	Thought themselves the best so named themselves accordingly	UK
Creedence Clearwater Revival (1968)	Creedence was a friend of the band and Clearwater came from a beer commercial	USA
Crystals (1961)	After Crystal Bates, daughter of their first songwriter, Leroy Bates	USA
Cult (1982)	Originally called Southern Death Cult, taken from a newspaper headline	UK
Cure (1976)	Originally called the Easy Cure, a stock phrase of the day	Crawley
Damned (1976)	From the Dracula-style fancy dress worn by lead singer Dave Vanian	UK
Deacon Blue (1987)	From a Steely Dan record	UK
Dead Kennedys (1978)	Name was designed to shock, as it refers to the Kennedy brothers John and Robert	San Francisco
Deep Purple (1968)	Chosen as a contrast to Vanilla Fudge, on whom they based their early music	UK
Def Leppard (1977)	Corruption of Deaf Leopard, proposed by band's lead singer Joe Elliott	Sheffield
Depeche Mode (1980)	From a French fashion magazine, meaning 'Fast Fashion'	UK
Devo (1972)	From video Truth about De-evolution, award winner at Ann Arbor Film Festival	Akron, Ohio
Dexy's Midnight Runners (1978)	Slang term for the pep pill Dexedrine	Birmingham
Dire Straits (1977)	From the financial plight of the group when formed	UK
Doobie Brothers (1970)	After 'doobie' the Californian nickname for a marijuana cigarette	San Jose, California
Doors (1965)	From Aldous Huxley book The Doors of Perception (Huxley took title from Blake work)	Los Angeles
Dr Feelgood (1971)	From 1962 US hit 'Doctor Feel-Good' by bluesman Piano Red	UK

Group	Derivation	Where from
Dr Hook (1968)	Prompted by the eye patch (as in Captain Hook) worn by lead singer Ray Sawyer	New Jersey
Duran Duran (1978)	First gig was at Barbarella's in Birmingham so used a name from the Jane Fonda film	Birmingham
Earth, Wind and Fire (1969)	Singer and drummer Maurice White named band after 3 of the ancient elements	USA
The Easybeats	From a BBC Light programme pop show hosted by Brian Matthew	USA
Echo and the Bunnymen (1977)	Echo was the nickname for their drum machine, which was replaced by Pete de Freitas	Liverpool
Eurythmics (1977)	Named in 1980 after 'Rhythm Gymnastics' style devised by Emile Jaques-Dalcroze	UK
Everything But the Girl (1982)	Took their name from a local furniture store	Hull
Faces (1969)	Steve Marriot left the Small Faces to form Humble Pie and the 'Small' was dropped	London
Fairport Convention (1967)	After the house, 'Fairport', in which its guitarist Simon Nicol lived in Muswell Hill	London
Faith No More (1980)	After a greyhound on which they had a bet	Los Angeles
Fifth Dimension (1966)	Originally called Versatiles changed name to reflect being beyond the 4th dimension	Los Angeles
Fine Young Cannibals (1984)	From the Robert Wagner/Natalie Wood film All the Fine Young Cannibals	UK
Fixx (1980)	Originally called the Portraits but changed it to Fix then to Fixx because of drug slur	UK
Fleetwood Mac (1967)	From 2 members, drummer Mick Fleetwood and bassist John McVie	UK
Flock of Seagulls (1979)	From cult novel by Richard Bach, Jonathan Livingstone Seagull (1970)	Liverpool
Frankie Goes to Hollywood (1980)	Headline in Variety magazine about Sinatra moving from Las Vegas to Hollywood	Liverpool
G4 (2004)	All four members are graduates of the Guildhall School of Music. Name derives from Guildhall and the number in the band	UK
Genesis (1965)	Originally Garden Wall; Jonathan King renamed them in 1967 as they were being 'born'	London
Grateful Dead (1963)	Said to come from an Egyptian prayer book	San Francisco
Guess Who (1965)	Forerunner of Bachman-Turner Overdrive; name based on British band The Who	Canada
Guns N' Roses (1985)	Combination of former guitarist Tracii Guns and the lead singer's assumed name	Los Angeles
Harpers Bizarre (1963)	Variation on the magazine Harper's Bazaar (Harper's and Queen)	San Francisco
Headgirl (1981)	Motorhead and Girlschool united for one-hit wonder 'The St Valentine's Day Massacre'	UK
Heaven 17 (1980)	Named after a group in Anthony Burgess's novel A Clockwork Orange	Sheffield
Herman's Hermits (1961)	The Herman was derived from Sherman, the flying squirrel in Rocky and Bullwinkle Show	Manchester
Hollies (1962)	Tribute to Buddy Holly	Manchester
Hot Chocolate (1969)	Named by an agent from the Apple record company as a pun on their colour and style	London
Human League (1977)	From a science-fiction computer game	Sheffield
Humble Pie (1969)	Superstars Frampton and Marriott named band to contrast with their pop idol status	London
Icehouse (1980)	Originally Flowers; changed name to that of their 1st album so as not to clash with existing group	Sydney
INXS (1977)	Originally called Farriss Brothers after 3 members but changed to a pun on In Excess	Australia
Iron Maiden (1976)	From a medieval instrument of torture	London
Jam (1972)	Thought up by Paul Weller's sister at the breakfast table: 'We've had the Bread and we've had the Marmalade, so let's have the Jam'	Woking
Jefferson Airplane (1965)	Hippie jargon for a paper match split at one end to hold a reefer; subsequently changed name to Jefferson Starship (1974) then Starship (1985)	San Francisco
Jesus and Mary Chain (1983)	After Alan McGee's club in London, where they performed early hits	Scotland
Jethro Tull (1967)	From the famous agriculturist, author of Horse Hoeing Husbandry	Blackpool
Joy Division (1977)	Nazi slang term for a military brothel	UK
Judas Priest (1973)	From Bob Dylan song, 'Ballad of Frankie Lee and Judas Priest'	Birmingham
Kaiser Chiefs (2003)	Named after a successful South African football team	Leeds
Kajagoogoo (1983)	Supposedly from original surname of film director Elia Kazan 'Kazanjoglou'	UK
Kasabian (1999)	From Linda Kasabian, a former member of Charles Manson's 'Family'	Leicester
KC and the Sunshine Band (1973)	Named after founder Harry Wayne Casey	Florida
Kinks (1963)	Named by pop impresario Larry Page, based on 'Kinky,' a vogue word of swinging London	London

Group	Derivation	Where from
Kooks (2004)	From a track on David Bowie's Hunky Dory album	UK
Kraftwerk (1970)	German for power plant referring to their electronic synthesisers	Düsseldorf
Level 42 (1980)	From the answer to the meaning of life in Douglas Adams's The Hitch Hiker's Guide to the Galaxy	UK
Lovin' Spoonful (1965)	From a line in a song by bluesman John Hurt	USA/Canada
Lynyrd Skynyrd (1966)	Named after the gym teacher who had expelled them from school	Jacksonville, Florida
Madness (1976)	From a Prince Buster song	UK
Mamas and the Papas (1965)	Named from 2 married couples in group, John and Michelle Phillips and Cass Elliot and John Hendricks	New York
Manhattan Transfer (1969)	From novel by Jon Dos Passos	New York
McFly (2002)	Named after the schoolboy hero of the film Back to the Future	UK
Men at Work (1979)	From road sign 'Danger Men at Work'	Melbourne
Metallica (1981)	Adopted a name to suit their particular type of rock music	Los Angeles
Mindbenders (1965)	The name of a Dirk Bogarde film	UK
Mothers of Invention (1965)	Originally called the Muthers but changed to echo proverb 'necessity is the . . .'	Los Angeles
Motley Crue (1981)	Play on phrase motley crew, which was an apt name for their bizarre appearance	USA
Motorhead (1975)	Song written by Ian 'Lemmy' Kilminster for Hawkwind, group he was sacked from	UK
Mott the Hoople (1968)	From an obscure novel by Willard Manus published in 1967	Hereford
Move (1966)	From the 5 members various moves from their prior bands	Birmingham
New Kids on the Block (1984)	Named by manager Maurice Starr as a white equivalent to his other band, New Edition	Massachusetts
New Order (1980)	After suicide of Ian Curtis, Joy Division became New Order, which was also a Nazi term	UK
Oasis (1991)	Originally called The Rain (after a 1966 Beatles B-side). Liam took the name Oasis from Oasis Leisure Centre, Swindon on an Inspiral Carpets tour poster	Manchester
Pet Shop Boys (1981)	Named by its members for friends who worked in an Ealing pet shop	London
Pink Floyd (1965)	Named as tribute to bluesmen Pink Anderson and Floyd Council	London
Planxty (1972)	From an Irish folk dance	Ireland
Platters (1953)	Black American group took their name from the slang term for gramophone records	Los Angeles
Poco (1968)	Originally called Pogo after a comic strip but forced to amend it when creator objected	Los Angeles
Pogues (1983)	Original name was Pogue Mahone ('Kiss my arse'); changed after BBC banned them	UK/Ireland
Pretenders (1978)	Named by Chrissie Hynde after a Platters hit, 'The Great Pretender'	UK/USA
Pretty Things (1963)	After the Bo Diddley hit 'Pretty Thing'	Sidcup, Kent
Procul Harum (1967)	Originally called the Paramounts, said to have been renamed after someone's cat	Southend, Essex
Psychedelic Furs (1977)	From Velvet Underground hit 'Venus in Furs'	London
R.E.M. (1980)	Although an abbreviation for rapid eye movement, the name was arbitrarily arrived at	Athens, Georgia
REO Speedwagon (1967)	From an early make of fire engine, Ransom E. Olds Speedwagon	Champaign, Illinois
Righteous Brothers (1962)	Originally called Paramours; took their name from the slang for excellent performers	Anaheim, California
Rolling Stones (1962)	From the Muddy Waters song 'Rolling Stone'	London
Ronettes (1959)	From the nickname of Veronica Bennett (Ronnie), one of the founder members	New York
Roxy Music (1971)	Based on the Roxy cinema chain	London
Run DMC (1982)	Nicknames of their 2 lead singers, Joseph 'Run' Simmons and Darryl 'D' McDaniels	New York
Scissor Sisters (1999)	From the interlocking sexual position of lesbians	New York
Scritti Politti (1977)	Based on the Italian phrase for 'political writings'	Leeds
Searchers (1961)	Named after the John Wayne film	Liverpool
Selecter (1979)	From the 'B' side of their debut single 'Gangsters', written by Noel Davies	Coventry
Sex Pistols (1975)	Malcolm McLaren named them after his boutique 'Sex' and Shakespeare character	London
Shadows (1959)	Originally called the Drifters; Jet Harris changed name in a Ruislip pub in 1959	London
Shakatak (1980)	From a local boutique	London
Shakespears Sister (1989)	From a Smiths' song (spelt wrongly)	UK

Group	Derivation	Where from
Shalamar (1977)	Named after the Shalimar Gardens near Lahore in Pakistan	Los Angeles
Shirelles (1957)	Name based on their lead singer Shirley Owens	Passaic, New Jersey
Showaddywaddy (1973)	From 'Bop bop showaddywaddy' backing of 'Little Darlin' by the Diamonds	Leicester
Simple Minds (1977)	Self-deprecatory name adopted during the Punk era	Glasgow
Simply Red (1985)	Named after the red hair of its lead singer Mick Hucknall	Manchester
Slade (1969)	Originally Ambrose Slade among other names, shortened to Slade in 1969	Wolverhampton
Smiths (1982)	Suggests the anonymity its members are said to have sought	Manchester
Soft Cell (1979)	Pun on 'soft sell', a term used for selling by inducement	Leeds
Soft Machine (1966)	After the William Burroughs novel of 1961	Canterbury
Spandau Ballet (1979)	Name derived from 2 contrasting words as an oxymoron to give effect	London
Split Enz (1972)	Originally called Split Ends after hair that has split, but changed spelling in 1975	Auckland, NZ
Squeeze (1974)	From a Velvet Underground album	London
Starsailor (2000)	Named after the 1970 album by Tim Buckley	Chorley/Wigan
Steeleye Span (1969)	Name adopted from the traditional Lincolnshire ballad 'Horkston Grange'	UK
Steely Dan (1972)	Name of steam-powered dildo in novel The Naked Lunch by William Burroughs	Los Angeles
Steppenwolf (1968)	From the Herman Hesse novel	USA/Canada
Stone Roses (1980)	Originally played as Patrol and English Rose; chose similar name to Rolling Stones	Manchester
Stranglers (1974)	Originally the Guildford Strangler; shortened name when gaining following	Guildford
Strawbs (1967)	Originally the Strawberry Hill Boys, from the area of London they were from	London
Supertramp (1969)	From the W H Davies book Autobiography of a Super-tramp	London
Supremes (1959)	Originally called the Primettes as they supported the Primes (Temptations)	Detroit
Sweet (1966)	Originally called Wainwright's Gentlemen then Sweetshop	UK
Swinging Blue Jeans (1958)	Originally called Bluegenes; changed name on gaining sponsorship from jeans company	Liverpool
Take That (1994)	From the caption beside a Madonna poster	UK
Talking Heads (1975)	From the television jargon for a kind of static presentation	New York
Teardrop Explodes (1978)	From a caption in a Marvel science fiction comic	Liverpool
Tears for Fears (1981)	From Arthur Janov's book on primal therapy Prisoners of Pain	UK
Ten cc (10cc) (1972)	Named by Jonathan King, because the average male semen ejaculation was 9 cc	Manchester
Ten Thousand Maniacs (1981)	Name resulted from mishearing of film title 12,000 Maniacs	Jamestown, New York
Ten Years After (1965)	Originally called Jaybirds changed name in 1966 on 10th anniversary of rock 'n' roll	Nottingham
The The (1980)	Parody of the many rock groups whose name begins with 'The'	London
Thin Lizzy (1969)	From 'Tin Lizzy,' colloquial name for an old car	Dublin
Thompson Twins (1977)	From the characters in the Tintin cartoons by Hergé	Sheffield
Three Dog Night (1968)	Australian expression for a cold night when 3 dogs are needed to keep warm	USA
Ting Tings (2006)	Named after a waitress colleague of singer Katie White's at a Chinese restaurant	Salford
Toto (1978)	Corruption of real name of lead singer, Toteaux, to give the name of dog in The Wizard of Oz	Los Angeles
T'Pau (1986)	Carol Decker named group from the high priestess of Vulcan, a character in Star Trek	London
U2 (1977)	Said to be suggestive of the words 'You too'	Dublin
UB40 (1978)	From designation of Unemployment Benefit form	Birmingham
Ultravox (1976)	Name means 'beyond the voice', but may also refer to founder John Foxx	London
Velvet Underground (1965)	From the title of a pornographic publication	London
Wet Wet Wet (1986)	From a lyric on a Scritti Politti record	UK
X (1977)	From group's lead singer Exene Cervenka, nicknamed X	Los Angeles
XTC (1977)	Suggests 'ecstasy', but last 2 letters are initials of their drummer Terry Chambers	Swindon
Yardbirds (1963)	From the jazzman Charlie Parker, nicknamed Yardbird	Kingston-upon-Thames
Yazoo (1982)	From an early blues record label	UK

UK Number One Singles

(The following is a list of every No. 1 record from the inception of the charts until the beginning of October 2013)

	Artist	Song	Date
1	Al Martino	Here In My Heart	14 Nov 1952
2	Jo Stafford	You Belong To Me	16 Jan 1953
3	Kay Starr	Comes A-Long A-Love	23 Jan 1953
4	Eddie Fisher	Outside Of Heaven	30 Jan 1953
5	Perry Como	Don't Let The Stars Get In Your Eyes	6 Feb 1953
6	Guy Mitchell	She Wears Red Feathers	13 Mar 1953
7	Stargazers	Broken Wings	10 Apr 1953
8	Lita Roza	(How Much Is) That Doggie In The Window	17 Apr 1953
9	Frankie Laine	I Believe	24 Apr 1953
10	Eddie Fisher	I'm Walking Behind You	26 June 1953
11	Mantovani	Song from 'The Moulin Rouge'	14 Aug 1953
12	Guy Mitchell	Look At That Girl	11 Sept 1953
13	Frankie Laine	Hey Joe	23 Oct 1953
14	David Whitfield	Answer Me	6 Nov 1953
15	Frankie Laine	Answer Me	13 Nov 1953
16	Eddie Calvert	Oh Mein Papa	8 Jan 1954
17	Stargazers	I See The Moon	12 Mar 1954
18	Doris Day	Secret Love	16 Apr 1954
19	Johnnie Ray	Such A Night	30 Apr 1954
20	David Whitfield	Cara Mia	2 July 1954
21	Kitty Kallen	Little Things Mean A Lot	10 Sept 1954
22	Frank Sinatra	Three Coins In The Fountain	17 Sept 1954
23	Don Cornell	Hold My Hand	8 Oct 1954
24	Vera Lynn	My Son My Son	5 Nov 1954
25	Rosemary Clooney	This Ole House	26 Nov 1954
26	Winifred Atwell	Let's Have Another Party	3 Dec 1954
27	Dickie Valentine	Finger Of Suspicion	7 Jan 1955
28	Rosemary Clooney	Mambo Italiano	14 Jan 1955
29	Ruby Murray	Softly, Softly	18 Feb 1955
30	Tennessee Ernie Ford	Give Me Your Word	11 Mar 1955
31	Perez 'Prez' Prado & His Orchestra	Cherry Pink And Apple Blossom White	29 Apr 1955
32	Tony Bennett	Stranger In Paradise	13 May 1955
33	Eddie Calvert	Cherry Pink And Apple Blossom White	27 May 1955
34	Jimmy Young	Unchained Melody	24 June 1955
35	Alma Cogan	Dreamboat	15 July 1955
36	Slim Whitman	Rose Marie	29 July 1955
37	Jimmy Young	The Man From Laramie	14 Oct 1955
38	Johnston Brothers	Hernando's Hideaway	11 Nov 1955
39	Bill Haley & His Comets	Rock Around The Clock	25 Nov 1955
40	Dickie Valentine	Christmas Alphabet	16 Dec 1955
41	Tennessee Ernie Ford	Sixteen Tons	20 Jan 1956
42	Dean Martin	Memories Are Made Of This	17 Feb 1956
43	Dream Weavers	It's Almost Tomorrow	16 Mar 1956
44	Kay Starr	Rock And Roll Waltz	30 Mar 1956
45	Winifred Atwell	Poor People Of Paris	13 Apr 1956
46	Ronnie Hilton	No Other Love	4 May 1956
47	Pat Boone	I'll Be Home	15 June 1956
48	Frankie Lymon & The Teenagers	Why Do Fools Fall in Love	20 July 1956
49	Doris Day	Whatever Will Be Will Be (Que Sera, Sera)	10 Aug 1956
50	Anne Shelton	Lay Down Your Arms	21 Sept 1956
51	Frankie Laine	A Woman In Love	19 Oct 1956
52	Johnnie Ray	Just Walking In The Rain	16 Nov 1956
53	Guy Mitchell	Singing The Blues	4 Jan 1957
54	Tommy Steele	Singing The Blues	11 Jan 1957
55	Frankie Vaughan	The Garden Of Eden	25 Jan 1957
56	Tab Hunter	Young Love	22 Feb 1957
57	Lonnie Donegan	Cumberland Gap	12 Apr 1957
58	Guy Mitchell	Rock-A-Billy	17 May 1957
59	Andy Williams	Butterfly	24 May 1957
60	Johnnie Ray	Yes Tonight Josephine	7 June 1957
61	Lonnie Donegan	Puttin' On The Style / Gamblin' Man	28 June 1957
62	Elvis Presley	All Shook Up	12 July 1957
63	Paul Anka	Diana	30 Aug 1957
64	The Crickets	That'll Be The Day	1 Nov 1957
65	Harry Belafonte	Mary's Boy Child	22 Nov 1957
66	Jerry Lee Lewis	Great Balls Of Fire	10 Jan 1958
67	Elvis Presley	Jailhouse Rock	24 Jan 1958
68	Michael Holliday	The Story Of My Life	14 Feb 1958
69	Perry Como	Magic Moments	28 Feb 1958
70	Marvin Rainwater	Whole Lotta Woman	25 Apr 1958
71	Connie Francis	Who's Sorry Now	16 May 1958
72	Vic Damone	On The Street Where You Live	27 June 1958
73	Everly Brothers	All I Have To Do Is Dream / Claudette	4 July 1958

	Artist	Song	Date
74	Kalin Twins	When	22 Aug 1958
75	Connie Francis	Carolina Moon / Stupid Cupid	26 Sept 1958
76	Tommy Edwards	All In The Game	7 Nov 1958
77	Lord Rockingham's XI	Hoots Mon	28 Nov 1958
78	Conway Twitty	It's Only Make Believe	19 Dec 1958
79	Jane Morgan	The Day The Rains Came	23 Jan 1959
80	Elvis Presley	I Got Stung / One Night	30 Jan 1959
81	Shirley Bassey	As I Love You	20 Feb 1959
82	The Platters	Smoke Gets In Your Eyes	20 Mar 1959
83	Russ Conway	Side Saddle	27 Mar 1959
84	Buddy Holly	It Doesn't Matter Anymore	24 Apr 1959
85	Elvis Presley	A Fool Such As I / I Need Your Love Tonight	15 May 1959
86	Russ Conway	Roulette	19 June 1959
87	Bobby Darin	Dream Lover	3 July 1959
88	Cliff Richard	Living Doll	31 July 1959
89	Craig Douglas	Only Sixteen	11 Sept 1959
90	Jerry Keller	Here Comes Summer	9 Oct 1959
91	Bobby Darin	Mack The Knife	16 Oct 1959
92	Cliff Richard	Travellin' Light	30 Oct 1959
93	Adam Faith	What Do You Want	4 Dec 1959
94	Emile Ford & The Checkmates	What Do You Want To Make Those Eyes At Me For	18 Dec 1959
95	Michael Holliday	Starry Eyed	29 Jan 1960
96	Anthony Newley	Why	5 Feb 1960
97	Adam Faith	Poor Me	10 Mar 1960
98	Johnny Preston	Running Bear	17 Mar 1960
99	Lonnie Donegan	My Old Man's A Dustman	31 Mar 1960
100	Anthony Newley	Do You Mind	28 Apr 1960
101	Everly Brothers	Cathy's Clown	5 May 1960
102	Eddie Cochran	Three Steps To Heaven	23 June 1960
103	Jimmy Jones	Good Timin'	7 July 1960
104	Cliff Richard	Please Don't Tease	28 July 1960
105	Johnny Kidd & The Pirates	Shakin' All Over	4 Aug 1960
106	Shadows	Apache	25 Aug 1960
107	Ricky Valance	Tell Laura I Love Her	29 Sept 1960
108	Roy Orbison	Only The Lonely	20 Oct 1960
109	Elvis Presley	It's Now Or Never	3 Nov 1960
110	Cliff Richard	I Love You	29 Dec 1960
111	Johnny Tillotson	Poetry In Motion	12 Jan 1961
112	Elvis Presley	Are You Lonesome Tonight	26 Jan 1961
113	Petula Clark	Sailor	23 Feb 1961
114	Everly Brothers	Walk Right Back / Ebony Eyes	2 Mar 1961
115	Elvis Presley	Wooden Heart	23 Mar 1961
116	The Marcels	Blue Moon	4 May 1961
117	Floyd Cramer	On The Rebound	18 May 1961
118	The Temperance Seven	You're Driving Me Crazy	25 May 1961
119	Elvis Presley	Surrender	1 June 1961
120	Del Shannon	Runaway	29 June 1961
121	Everly Brothers	Temptation	20 July 1961
122	Eden Kane	Well I Ask You	3 Aug 1961
123	Helen Shapiro	You Don't Know	10 Aug 1961
124	John Leyton	Johnny Remember Me	31 Aug 1961
125	Shirley Bassey	Reach For The Stars / Climb Ev'ry Mountain	21 Sept 1961
126	Shadows	Kon Tiki	5 Oct 1961
127	The Highwaymen	Michael	12 Oct 1961
128	Helen Shapiro	Walkin' Back To Happiness	19 Oct 1961
129	Elvis Presley	His Latest Flame	9 Nov 1961
130	Frankie Vaughan	Tower Of Strength	7 Dec 1961
131	Danny Williams	Moon River	28 Dec 1961
132	Cliff Richard	The Young Ones	11 Jan 1962
133	Elvis Presley	Can't Help Falling In Love / Rock-A-Hula Baby	22 Feb 1962
134	Shadows	Wonderful Land	22 Mar 1962
135	B Bumble & The Stingers	Nut Rocker	17 May 1962
136	Elvis Presley	Good Luck Charm	24 May 1962
137	Mike Sarne with Wendy Richard	Come Outside	28 June 1962
138	Ray Charles	I Can't Stop Loving You	12 July 1962
139	Frank Ifield	I Remember You	26 July 1962
140	Elvis Presley	She's Not You	13 Sept 1962
141	Tornados	Telstar	4 Oct 1962
142	Frank Ifield	Lovesick Blues	8 Nov 1962
143	Elvis Presley	Return To Sender	13 Dec 1962
144	Cliff Richard	The Next Time / Bachelor Boy	3 Jan 1963
145	Shadows	Dance On	24 Jan 1963
146	Jet Harris & Tony Meehan	Diamonds	31 Jan 1963
147	Frank Ifield	Wayward Wind	21 Feb 1963
148	Cliff Richard	Summer Holiday	14 Mar 1963
149	Shadows	Foot Tapper	29 Mar 1963
150	Gerry & The Pacemakers	How Do You Do It?	11 Apr 1963
151	Beatles	From Me To You	2 May 1963
152	Gerry & The Pacemakers	I Like It	20 June 1963
153	Frank Ifield	Confessin' (That I Love You)	18 July 1963

	Artist	Song	Date
154	Elvis Presley	(You're The) Devil In Disguise	1 Aug 1963
155	Searchers	Sweets For My Sweet	8 Aug 1963
156	Billy J Kramer & The Dakotas	Bad To Me	22 Aug 1963
157	Beatles	She Loves You	12 Sept 1963
158	Brian Poole & The Tremeloes	Do You Love Me	10 Oct 1963
159	Gerry & The Pacemakers	You'll Never Walk Alone	31 Oct 1963
160	Beatles	I Want To Hold Your Hand	12 Dec 1963
161	Dave Clark Five	Glad All Over	16 Jan 1964
162	Searchers	Needles And Pins	30 Jan 1964
163	Bachelors	Diane	20 Feb 1964
164	Cilla Black	Anyone Who Had A Heart	27 Feb 1964
165	Billy J Kramer & The Dakotas	Little Children	19 Mar 1964
166	Beatles	Can't Buy Me Love	2 Apr 1964
167	Peter & Gordon	A World Without Love	23 Apr 1964
168	Searchers	Don't Throw Your Love Away	7 May 1964
169	Four Pennies	Juliet	21 May 1964
170	Cilla Black	You're My World	28 May 1964
171	Roy Orbison	It's Over	25 June 1964
172	Animals	The House Of The Rising Sun	9 July 1964
173	Rolling Stones	It's All Over Now	16 July 1964
174	Beatles	A Hard Day's Night	23 July 1964
175	Manfred Mann	Do Wah Diddy Diddy	13 Aug 1964
176	Honeycombs	Have I The Right	27 Aug 1964
177	Kinks	You Really Got Me	10 Sept 1964
178	Herman's Hermits	I'm Into Something Good	24 Sept 1964
179	Roy Orbison	Oh Pretty Woman	8 Oct 1964
180	Sandie Shaw	(There's) Always Something There To Remind Me	22 Oct 1964
181	Supremes	Baby Love	19 Nov 1964
182	Rolling Stones	Little Red Rooster	3 Dec 1964
183	Beatles	I Feel Fine	10 Dec 1964
184	Georgie Fame & The Blue Flames	Yeah Yeah	14 Jan 1965
185	Moody Blues	Go Now!	28 Jan 1965
186	Righteous Brothers	You've Lost That Loving Feeling	4 Feb 1965
187	Kinks	Tired Of Waiting For You	18 Feb 1965
188	Seekers	I'll Never Find Another You	25 Feb 1965
189	Tom Jones	It's Not Unusual	11 Mar 1965
190	Rolling Stones	The Last Time	18 Mar 1965
191	Unit Four Plus Two	Concrete And Clay	8 Apr 1965
192	Cliff Richard	The Minute You're Gone	15 Apr 1965
193	Beatles	Ticket To Ride	22 Apr 1965
194	Roger Miller	King Of The Road	13 May 1965
195	Jackie Trent	Where Are You Now (My Love)	20 May 1965
196	Sandie Shaw	Long Live Love	27 May 1965
197	Elvis Presley	Crying In The Chapel	17 June 1965
198	Hollies	I'm Alive	24 June 1965
199	Byrds	Mr Tambourine Man	22 July 1965
200	Beatles	Help!	5 Aug 1965
201	Sonny & Cher	I Got You Babe	26 Aug 1965
202	Rolling Stones	(I Can't Get No) Satisfaction	9 Sept 1965
203	Walker Brothers	Make It Easy On Yourself	23 Sept 1965
204	Ken Dodd	Tears	30 Sept 1965
205	Rolling Stones	Get Off Of My Cloud	4 Nov 1965
206	Seekers	The Carnival Is Over	25 Nov 1965
207	Beatles	Day Tripper / We Can Work It Out	16 Dec 1965
208	Spencer Davis Group	Keep On Running	20 Jan 1966
209	Overlanders	Michelle	27 Jan 1966
210	Nancy Sinatra	These Boots Are Made For Walking	17 Feb 1966
211	Walker Brothers	The Sun Ain't Gonna Shine Anymore	17 Mar 1966
212	Spencer Davis Group	Somebody Help Me	14 Apr 1966
213	Dusty Springfield	You Don't Have To Say You Love Me	28 Apr 1966
214	Manfred Mann	Pretty Flamingo	5 May 1966
215	Rolling Stones	Paint It Black	26 May 1966
216	Frank Sinatra	Strangers In The Night	2 June 1966
217	Beatles	Paperback Writer	23 June 1966
218	Kinks	Sunny Afternoon	7 July 1966
219	Georgie Fame & The Blue Flames	Getaway	21 July 1966
220	Chris Farlowe	Out Of Time	28 July 1966
221	Troggs	With A Girl Like You	4 Aug 1966
222	Beatles	Yellow Submarine / Eleanor Rigby	18 Aug 1966
223	Small Faces	All Or Nothing	15 Sept 1966
224	Jim Reeves	Distant Drums	22 Sept 1966
225	Four Tops	Reach Out I'll Be There	27 Oct 1966
226	Beach Boys	Good Vibrations	17 Nov 1966
227	Tom Jones	Green Green Grass Of Home	1 Dec 1966
228	Monkees	I'm A Believer	19 Jan 1967
229	Petula Clark	This Is My Song	16 Feb 1967
230	Engelbert Humperdinck	Release Me	2 Mar 1967
231	Frank Sinatra & Nancy Sinatra	Somethin' Stupid	13 Apr 1967
232	Sandie Shaw	Puppet On A String	27 Apr 1967
233	Tremeloes	Silence Is Golden	18 May 1967

	Artist	Song	Date
234	Procol Harum	A Whiter Shade Of Pale	8 June 1967
235	Beatles	All You Need Is Love	19 July 1967
236	Scott McKenzie	San Francisco (Be Sure To Wear Some Flowers In Your Hair)	9 Aug 1967
237	Engelbert Humperdinck	The Last Waltz	6 Sept 1967
238	Bee Gees	Massachusetts	11 Oct 1967
239	Foundations	Baby Now That I've Found You	8 Nov 1967
240	Long John Baldry	Let The Heartaches Begin	22 Nov 1967
241	Beatles	Hello Goodbye	6 Dec 1967
242	Georgie Fame	The Ballad Of Bonnie And Clyde	24 Jan 1968
243	Love Affair	Everlasting Love	31 Jan 1968
244	Manfred Mann	The Mighty Quinn	14 Feb 1968
245	Esther & Abi Ofarim	Cinderella Rockefella	28 Feb 1968
246	Dave Dee, Dozy, Beaky, Mick & Tich	Legend Of Xanadu	20 Mar 1968
247	Beatles	Lady Madonna	27 Mar 1968
248	Cliff Richard	Congratulations	10 Apr 1968
249	Louis Armstrong	What A Wonderful World / Cabaret	24 Apr 1968
250	Union Gap featuring Gary Puckett	Young Girl	22 May 1968
251	Rolling Stones	Jumpin' Jack Flash	19 June 1968
252	Equals	Baby Come Back	3 July 1968
253	Des O'Connor	I Pretend	24 July 1968
254	Tommy James & The Shondells	Mony Mony	31 July 1968
255	Crazy World of Arthur Brown	Fire	14 Aug 1968
256	Beach Boys	Do It Again	28 Aug 1968
257	Bee Gees	I've Gotta Get A Message To You	4 Sept 1968
258	Beatles	Hey Jude	11 Sept 1968
259	Mary Hopkin	Those Were The Days	25 Sept 1968
260	Joe Cocker	With A Little Help From My Friends	6 Nov 1968
261	Hugo Montenegro Orchestra	The Good The Bad And The Ugly	13 Nov 1968
262	Scaffold	Lily The Pink	11 Dec 1968
263	Marmalade	Ob-La-Di Ob-La-Da	1 Jan 1969
264	Fleetwood Mac	Albatross	29 Jan 1969
265	Move	Blackberry Way	5 Feb 1969
266	Amen Corner	(If Paradise Is) Half As Nice	12 Feb 1969
267	Peter Sarstedt	Where Do You Go To My Lovely?	26 Feb 1969
268	Marvin Gaye	I Heard It Through The Grapevine	26 Mar 1969
269	Desmond Dekker & The Aces	Israelites	16 Apr 1969
270	Beatles	Get Back	23 Apr 1969
271	Tommy Roe	Dizzy	4 June 1969
272	Beatles	The Ballad Of John And Yoko	11 June 1969
273	Thunderclap Newman	Something In The Air	2 July 1969
274	Rolling Stones	Honky Tonk Women	23 July 1969
275	Zager & Evans	In The Year 2525 (Exordium And Terminus)	30 Aug 1969
276	Creedence Clearwater Revival	Bad Moon Rising	20 Sept 1969
277	Jane Birkin & Serge Gainsbourg	Je T'Aime ... Moi Non Plus	11 Oct 1969
278	Bobbie Gentry	I'll Never Fall In Love Again	18 Oct 1969
279	Archies	Sugar Sugar	25 Oct 1969
280	Rolf Harris	Two Little Boys	20 Dec 1969
281	Edison Lighthouse	Love Grows (Where My Rosemary Goes)	31 Jan 1970
282	Lee Marvin	Wand'rin' Star	7 Mar 1970
283	Simon & Garfunkel	Bridge Over Troubled Water	28 Mar 1970
284	Dana	All Kinds Of Everything	18 Apr 1970
285	Norman Greenbaum	Spirit In The Sky	2 May 1970
286	England World Cup Squad	Back Home	16 May 1970
287	Christie	Yellow River	6 June 1970
288	Mungo Jerry	In The Summertime	13 June 1970
289	Elvis Presley	The Wonder Of You	1 Aug 1970
290	Smokey Robinson & The Miracles	Tears Of A Clown	12 Sept 1970
291	Freda Payne	Band Of Gold	19 Sept 1970
292	Matthews Southern Comfort	Woodstock	31 Oct 1970
293	Jimi Hendrix	Voodoo Chile	21 Nov 1970
294	Dave Edmunds	I Hear You Knocking	28 Nov 1970
295	Clive Dunn	Grandad	9 Jan 1971
296	George Harrison	My Sweet Lord	30 Jan 1971
297	Mungo Jerry	Baby Jump	6 Mar 1971
298	T Rex	Hot Love	20 Mar 1971
299	Dave & Ansil Collins	Double Barrel	1 May 1971
300	Dawn	Knock Three Times	15 May 1971
301	Middle Of The Road	Chirpy Chirpy Cheep Cheep	19 June 1971
302	T Rex	Get It On	24 July 1971
303	Diana Ross	I'm Still Waiting	21 Aug 1971
304	Tams	Hey Girl Don't Bother Me	18 Sept 1971
305	Rod Stewart	Maggie May	9 Oct 1971
306	Slade	Coz I Luv You	13 Nov 1971
307	Benny Hill	Ernie (The Fastest Milkman In The West)	11 Dec 1971
308	New Seekers	I'd Like To Teach The World To Sing (In Perfect Harmony)	8 Jan 1972
309	T Rex	Telegram Sam	5 Feb 1972
310	Chicory Tip	Son Of My Father	19 Feb 1972
311	Nilsson	Without You	11 Mar 1972

	Artist	Song	Date
312	The Pipes & Drums & Military Band of The Royal Scots Dragoon Guards	Amazing Grace	15 Apr 1972
313	T Rex	Metal Guru	20 May 1972
314	Don McLean	Vincent	17 June 1972
315	Slade	Take Me Bak 'Ome	1 July 1972
316	Donny Osmond	Puppy Love	8 July 1972
317	Alice Cooper	School's Out	12 Aug 1972
318	Rod Stewart	You Wear It Well	2 Sept 1972
319	Slade	Mama Weer All Crazee Now	9 Sept 1972
320	David Cassidy	How Can I Be Sure	30 Sept 1972
321	Lieutenant Pigeon	Mouldy Old Dough	14 Oct 1972
322	Gilbert O'Sullivan	Clair	11 Nov 1972
323	Chuck Berry	My Ding-A-Ling	25 Nov 1972
324	Little Jimmy Osmond	Long Haired Lover From Liverpool	23 Dec 1972
325	Sweet	Blockbuster	27 Jan 1973
326	Slade	Cum On Feel The Noize	3 Mar 1973
327	Donny Osmond	The Twelfth Of Never	31 Mar 1973
328	Gilbert O'Sullivan	Get Down	7 Apr 1973
329	Dawn featuring Tony Orlando	Tie A Yellow Ribbon Round The Old Oak Tree	21 Apr 1973
330	Wizzard	See My Baby Jive	19 May 1973
331	Suzi Quatro	Can The Can	16 June 1973
332	10CC	Rubber Bullets	23 June 1973
333	Slade	Skweeze Me Pleeze Me	30 June 1973
334	Peters & Lee	Welcome Home	21 July 1973
335	Gary Glitter	I'm The Leader Of The Gang (I Am)	28 July 1973
336	Donny Osmond	Young Love	25 Aug 1973
337	Wizzard	Angel Fingers	22 Sept 1973
338	Simon Park Orchestra	Eye Level	29 Sept 1973
339	David Cassidy	Daydreamer / The Puppy Song	27 Oct 1973
340	Gary Glitter	I Love You Love Me Love	17 Nov 1973
341	Slade	Merry Xmas Everybody	15 Dec 1973
342	New Seekers	You Won't Find Another Fool Like Me	19 Jan 1974
343	Mud	Tiger Feet	26 Jan 1974
344	Suzi Quatro	Devil Gate Drive	23 Feb 1974
345	Alvin Stardust	Jealous Mind	9 Mar 1974
346	Paper Lace	Billy Don't Be A Hero	16 Mar 1974
347	Terry Jacks	Seasons In The Sun	6 Apr 1974
348	Abba	Waterloo	4 May 1974
349	Rubettes	Sugar Baby Love	18 May 1974
350	Ray Stevens	The Streak	15 June 1974
351	Gary Glitter	Always Yours	22 June 1974
352	Charles Aznavour	She	29 June 1974
353	George McCrae	Rock Your Baby	27 July 1974
354	Three Degrees	When Will I See You Again	17 Aug 1974
355	Osmonds	Love Me For A Reason	31 Aug 1974
356	Carl Douglas	Kung Fu Fighting	21 Sept 1974
357	John Denver	Annie's Song	12 Oct 1974
358	Sweet Sensation	Sad Sweet Dreamer	19 Oct 1974
359	Ken Boothe	Everything I Own	26 Oct 1974
360	David Essex	Gonna Make You A Star	16 Nov 1974
361	Barry White	You're The First, The Last, My Everything	7 Dec 1974
362	Mud	Lonely This Christmas	21 Dec 1974
363	Status Quo	Down Down	18 Jan 1975
364	Tymes	Ms Grace	25 Jan 1975
365	Pilot	January	1 Feb 1975
366	Steve Harley & Cockney Rebel	Make Me Smile (Come Up And See Me)	22 Feb 1975
367	Telly Savalas	If	8 Mar 1975
368	Bay City Rollers	Bye Bye Baby	22 Mar 1975
369	Mud	Oh Boy	3 May 1975
370	Tammy Wynette	Stand By Your Man	17 May 1975
371	Windsor Davies & Don Estelle	Whispering Grass	7 June 1975
372	10CC	I'm Not In Love	28 June 1975
373	Johnny Nash	Tears On My Pillow	12 July 1975
374	Bay City Rollers	Give A Little Love	19 July 1975
375	Typically Tropical	Barbados	9 Aug 1975
376	Stylistics	Can't Give You Anything (But My Love)	16 Aug 1975
377	Rod Stewart	Sailing	6 Sept 1975
378	David Essex	Hold Me Close	4 Oct 1975
379	Art Garfunkel	I Only Have Eyes For You	25 Oct 1975
380	David Bowie	Space Oddity	8 Nov 1975
381	Billy Connolly	D.I.V.O.R.C.E.	22 Nov 1975
382	Queen	Bohemian Rhapsody	29 Nov 1975
383	Abba	Mamma Mia	31 Jan 1976
384	Slik	Forever And Ever	14 Feb 1976
385	Four Seasons	December '63 (Oh, What A Night)	21 Feb 1976
386	Tina Charles	I Love To Love (But My Baby Loves To Dance)	6 Mar 1976
387	Brotherhood Of Man	Save Your Kisses For Me	27 Mar 1976
388	Abba	Fernando	8 May 1976
389	J J Barrie	No Charge	5 June 1976
390	Wurzels	Combine Harvester (Brand New Key)	12 June 1976

	Artist	Song	Date
391	Real Thing	You To Me Are Everything	26 June 1976
392	Demis Roussos	The Roussos Phenomenon EP (main track: Forever And Ever)	17 July 1976
393	Elton John & Kiki Dee	Don't Go Breaking My Heart	24 July 1976
394	Abba	Dancing Queen	4 Sept 1976
395	Pussycat	Mississippi	16 Oct 1976
396	Chicago	If You Leave Me Now	13 Nov 1976
397	Showaddywaddy	Under The Moon Of Love	4 Dec 1976
398	Johnny Mathis	When A Child Is Born (Soleado)	25 Dec 1976
399	David Soul	Don't Give Up On Us	15 Jan 1977
400	Julie Covington	Don't Cry For Me Argentina	12 Feb 1977
401	Leo Sayer	When I Need You	19 Feb 1977
402	Manhattan Transfer	Chanson D'Amour	12 Mar 1977
403	Abba	Knowing Me Knowing You	2 Apr 1977
404	Deniece Williams	Free	7 May 1977
405	Rod Stewart	I Don't Want To Talk About It / First Cut Is The Deepest	21 May 1977
406	Kenny Rogers	Lucille	18 June 1977
407	Jacksons	Show You The Way To Go	25 June 1977
408	Hot Chocolate	So You Win Again	2 July 1977
409	Donna Summer	I Feel Love	23 July 1977
410	Brotherhood Of Man	Angelo	20 Aug 1977
411	Floaters	Float On	27 Aug 1977
412	Elvis Presley	Way Down	3 Sept 1977
413	David Soul	Silver Lady	8 Oct 1977
414	Baccara	Yes Sir I Can Boogie	29 Oct 1977
415	Abba	The Name Of The Game	5 Nov 1977
416	Wings	Mull Of Kintyre / Girls' School	3 Dec 1977
417	Althia & Donna	Up Town Top Ranking	4 Feb 1978
418	Brotherhood Of Man	Figaro	11 Feb 1978
419	Abba	Take A Chance On Me	18 Feb 1978
420	Kate Bush	Wuthering Heights	11 Mar 1978
421	Brian & Michael	Matchstalk Men And Matchstalk Cats And Dogs	8 Apr 1978
422	Bee Gees	Night Fever	29 Apr 1978
423	Boney M	Rivers Of Babylon / Brown Girl In The Ring	13 May 1978
424	John Travolta & Olivia Newton John	You're The One That I Want	17 June 1978
425	Commodores	Three Times A Lady	19 Aug 1978
426	10CC	Dreadlock Holiday	23 Sept 1978
427	John Travolta & Olivia Newton John	Summer Nights	30 Sept 1978
428	Boomtown Rats	Rat Trap	18 Nov 1978
429	Rod Stewart	Da Ya Think I'm Sexy	2 Dec 1978
430	Boney M	Mary's Boy Child / Oh My Lord	9 Dec 1978
431	Village People	Y.M.C.A.	6 Jan 1979
432	Ian Dury & The Blockheads	Hit Me With Your Rhythm Stick	27 Jan 1979
433	Blondie	Heart Of Glass	3 Feb 1979
434	Bee Gees	Tragedy	3 Mar 1979
435	Gloria Gaynor	I Will Survive	17 Mar 1979
436	Art Garfunkel	Bright Eyes	14 Apr 1979
437	Blondie	Sunday Girl	26 May 1979
438	Anita Ward	Ring My Bell	16 June 1979
439	Tubeway Army	Are 'Friends' Electric	30 June 1979
440	Boomtown Rats	I Don't Like Mondays	28 July 1979
441	Cliff Richard	We Don't Talk Anymore	25 Aug 1979
442	Gary Numan	Cars	22 Sept 1979
443	Police	Message In A Bottle	29 Sept 1979
444	Buggles	Video Killed The Radio Star	20 Oct 1979
445	Lena Martell	One Day At A Time	27 Oct 1979
446	Dr Hook	When You're In Love With A Beautiful Woman	17 Nov 1979
447	Police	Walking On The Moon	8 Dec 1979
448	Pink Floyd	Another Brick In The Wall	15 Dec 1979
449	Pretenders	Brass In Pocket	19 Jan 1980
450	Specials	The Special AKA Live EP (main track: Too Much Too Young)	2 Feb 1980
451	Kenny Rogers	Coward Of The County	16 Feb 1980
452	Blondie	Atomic	1 Mar 1980
453	Fern Kinney	Together We Are Beautiful	15 Mar 1980
454	Jam	Going Underground / Dreams Of Children	22 Mar 1980
455	Detroit Spinners	Working My Way Back To You / Forgive Me Girl	12 Apr 1980
456	Blondie	Call Me	26 Apr 1980
457	Dexy's Midnight Runners	Geno	3 May 1980
458	Johnny Logan	What's Another Year	17 May 1980
459	MASH	Suicide Is Painless (Theme from M*A*S*H)	31 May 1980
460	Don McLean	Crying	21 June 1980
461	Olivia Newton John & Electric Light Orchestra	Xanadu	12 July 1980
462	Odyssey	Use It Up And Wear It Out	26 July 1980
463	Abba	The Winner Takes It All	9 Aug 1980
464	David Bowie	Ashes To Ashes	23 Aug 1980
465	Jam	Start	6 Sept 1980
466	Kelly Marie	Feels Like I'm In Love	13 Sept 1980

	Artist	Song	Date
467	Police	Don't Stand So Close To Me	27 Sept 1980
468	Barbra Streisand	Woman In Love	25 Oct 1980
469	Blondie	The Tide Is High	15 Nov 1980
470	Abba	Super Trouper	29 Nov 1980
471	John Lennon	(Just Like) Starting Over	20 Dec 1980
472	St Winifred's School Choir	There's No One Quite Like Grandma	27 Dec 1980
473	John Lennon	Imagine	10 Jan 1981
474	John Lennon	Woman	7 Feb 1981
475	Joe Dolce Music Theatre	Shaddap You Face	21 Feb 1981
476	Roxy Music	Jealous Guy	14 Mar 1981
477	Shakin' Stevens	This Ole House	28 Mar 1981
478	Bucks Fizz	Making Your Mind Up	18 Apr 1981
479	Adam & The Ants	Stand And Deliver	9 May 1981
480	Smokey Robinson	Being With You	13 June 1981
481	Michael Jackson	One Day In Your Life	27 June 1981
482	Specials	Ghost Town	11 July 1981
483	Shakin' Stevens	Green Door	1 Aug 1981
484	Aneka	Japanese Boy	29 Aug 1981
485	Soft Cell	Tainted Love	5 Sept 1981
486	Adam & The Ants	Prince Charming	19 Sept 1981
487	Dave Stewart & Barbara Gaskin	It's My Party	17 Oct 1981
488	Police	Every Little Thing She Does Is Magic	14 Nov 1981
489	Queen & David Bowie	Under Pressure	21 Nov 1981
490	Julio Iglesias	Begin The Beguine (Volver A Empezar)	5 Dec 1981
491	Human League	Don't You Want Me	12 Dec 1981
492	Bucks Fizz	Land Of Make Believe	16 Jan 1982
493	Shakin' Stevens	Oh Julie	30 Jan 1982
494	Kraftwerk	The Model / Computer Love	6 Feb 1982
495	Jam	Town Called Malice / Precious	13 Feb 1982
496	Tight Fit	The Lion Sleeps Tonight	6 Mar 1982
497	Goombay Dance Band	Seven Tears	27 Mar 1982
498	Bucks Fizz	My Camera Never Lies	17 Apr 1982
499	Paul McCartney & Stevie Wonder	Ebony And Ivory	24 Apr 1982
500	Nicole	A Little Peace	15 May 1982
501	Madness	House Of Fun	29 May 1982
502	Adam Ant	Goody Two Shoes	12 June 1982
503	Charlene	I've Never Been To Me	26 June 1982
504	Captain Sensible	Happy Talk	3 July 1982
505	Irene Cara	Fame	17 July 1982
506	Dexy's Midnight Runners	Come On Eileen	7 Aug 1982
507	Survivor	Eye Of The Tiger	4 Sept 1982
508	Musical Youth	Pass The Dutchie	2 Oct 1982
509	Culture Club	Do You Really Want To Hurt Me	23 Oct 1982
510	Eddy Grant	I Don't Wanna Dance	13 Nov 1982
511	Jam	Beat Surrender	4 Dec 1982
512	Renee & Renato	Save Your Love	18 Dec 1982
513	Phil Collins	You Can't Hurry Love	15 Jan 1983
514	Men At Work	Down Under	29 Jan 1983
515	Kajagoogoo	Too Shy	19 Feb 1983
516	Michael Jackson	Billie Jean	5 Mar 1983
517	Bonnie Tyler	Total Eclipse Of The Heart	12 Mar 1983
518	Duran Duran	Is There Something I Should Know	26 Mar 1983
519	David Bowie	Let's Dance	9 Apr 1983
520	Spandau Ballet	True	30 Apr 1983
521	New Edition	Candy Girl	28 May 1983
522	Police	Every Breath You Take	4 June 1983
523	Rod Stewart	Baby Jane	2 July 1983
524	Paul Young	Wherever I Lay My Hat	23 July 1983
525	K C & The Sunshine Band	Give It Up	13 Aug 1983
526	UB40	Red Red Wine	3 Sept 1983
527	Culture Club	Karma Chameleon	24 Sept 1983
528	Billy Joel	Uptown Girl	5 Nov 1983
529	Flying Pickets	Only You	10 Dec 1983
530	Paul McCartney	Pipes Of Peace	14 Jan 1984
531	Frankie Goes To Hollywood	Relax	28 Jan 1984
532	Nena	99 Red Balloons	3 Mar 1984
533	Lionel Richie	Hello	24 Mar 1984
534	Duran Duran	The Reflex	5 May 1984
535	Wham!	Wake Me Up Before You Go-Go	2 June 1984
536	Frankie Goes To Hollywood	Two Tribes	16 June 1984
537	George Michael	Careless Whisper	18 Aug 1984
538	Stevie Wonder	I Just Called To Say I Love You	8 Sept 1984
539	Wham!	Freedom	20 Oct 1984
540	Chaka Khan	I Feel For You	10 Nov 1984
541	Jim Diamond	I Should Have Known Better	1 Dec 1984
542	Frankie Goes To Hollywood	The Power Of Love	8 Dec 1984
543	Band Aid**	Do They Know It's Christmas	15 Dec 1984
544	Foreigner	I Want To Know What Love Is	19 Jan 1985
545	Elaine Paige & Barbara Dickson	I Know Him So Well	9 Feb 1985
546	Dead Or Alive	You Spin Me Round (Like A Record)	9 Mar 1985

	Artist	Song	Date
547	Philip Bailey & Phil Collins	Easy Lover	23 Mar 1985
548	USA For Africa	We Are The World	20 Apr 1985
549	Phyllis Nelson	Move Closer	4 May 1985
550	Paul Hardcastle	19	11 May 1985
551	Crowd	You'll Never Walk Alone	15 June 1985
552	Sister Sledge	Frankie	29 June 1985
553	Eurythmics	There Must Be An Angel (Playing With My Heart)	27 July 1985
554	Madonna	Into The Groove	3 Aug 1985
555	UB40 & Chrissie Hynde	I Got You Babe	31 Aug 1985
556	David Bowie & Mick Jagger	Dancing in the Street	7 Sept 1985
557	Midge Ure	If I Was	5 Oct 1985
558	Jennifer Rush	The Power Of Love	12 Oct 1985
559	Feargal Sharkey	A Good Heart	16 Nov 1985
560	Wham!	I'm Your Man	30 Nov 1985
561	Whitney Houston	Saving All My Love For You	14 Dec 1985
562	Shakin' Stevens	Merry Christmas Everyone	28 Dec 1985
563	Pet Shop Boys	West End Girls	11 Jan 1986
564	A-Ha	The Sun Always Shines On TV	25 Jan 1986
565	Billy Ocean	When The Going Gets Tough, The Tough Get Going	8 Feb 1986
566	Diana Ross	Chain Reaction	8 Mar 1986
567	Cliff Richard & The Young Ones	Living Doll	29 Mar 1986
568	George Michael	A Different Corner	19 Apr 1986
569	Falco	Rock Me Amadeus	10 May 1986
570	Spitting Image	The Chicken Song	17 May 1986
571	Doctor & The Medics	Spirit In The Sky	7 June 1986
572	Wham!	The Edge Of Heaven	28 June 1986
573	Madonna	Papa Don't Preach	12 July 1986
574	Chris De Burgh	The Lady In Red	2 Aug 1986
575	Boris Gardiner	I Want To Wake Up With You	23 Aug 1986
576	Communards	Don't Leave Me This Way	13 Sept 1986
577	Madonna	True Blue	11 Oct 1986
578	Nick Berry	Every Loser Wins	18 Oct 1986
579	Berlin	Take My Breath Away	8 Nov 1986
580	Europe	The Final Countdown	6 Dec 1986
581	Housemartins	Caravan Of Love	20 Dec 1986
582	Jackie Wilson	Reet Petite	27 Dec 1986
583	Steve 'Silk' Hurley	Jack Your Body	24 Jan 1987
584	George Michael & Aretha Franklin	I Knew You Were Waiting (For Me)	7 Feb 1987
585	Ben E King	Stand By Me	21 Feb 1987
586	Boy George	Everything I Own	14 Mar 1987
587	Mel & Kim	Respectable	28 Mar 1987
588	Ferry Aid	Let It Be	4 Apr 1987
589	Madonna	La Isla Bonita	25 Apr 1987
590	Starship	Nothing's Gonna Stop Us Now	9 May 1987
591	Whitney Houston	I Wanna Dance With Somebody (Who Loves Me)	6 June 1987
592	The Firm	Star Trekkin'	20 June 1987
593	Pet Shop Boys	It's A Sin	4 July 1987
594	Madonna	Who's That Girl	25 July 1987
595	Los Lobos	La Bamba	1 Aug 1987
596	Michael Jackson	I Just Can't Stop Loving You	15 Aug 1987
597	Rick Astley	Never Gonna Give You Up	29 Aug 1987
598	M/A/R/R/S	Pump Up The Volume / Anitina (The First Time I See She Dance)	3 Oct 1987
599	Bee Gees	You Win Again	17 Oct 1987
600	T'Pau	China In Your Hand	14 Nov 1987
601	Pet Shop Boys	Always On My Mind	19 Dec 1987
602	Belinda Carlisle	Heaven Is A Place On Earth	16 Jan 1988
603	Tiffany	I Think We're Alone Now	30 Jan 1988
604	Kylie Minogue	I Should Be So Lucky	20 Feb 1988
605	Aswad	Don't Turn Around	26 Mar 1988
606	Pet Shop Boys	Heart	9 Apr 1988
607	S'Express	Theme from S'Express	30 Apr 1988
608	Fairground Attraction	Perfect	14 May 1988
609	Wet Wet Wet / Billy Bragg with Cara Tivey	With A Little Help From My Friends / She's Leaving Home	21 May 1988
610	Timelords	Doctorin' The Tardis	18 June 1988
611	Bros	I Owe You Nothing	25 June 1988
612	Glenn Medeiros	Nothing's Gonna Change My Love For You	9 July 1988
613	Yazz & The Plastic Population	The Only Way Is Up	6 Aug 1988
614	Phil Collins	A Groovy Kind Of Love	10 Sept 1988
615	Hollies	He Ain't Heavy He's My Brother	24 Sept 1988
616	U2	Desire	8 Oct 1988
617	Whitney Houston	One Moment In Time	15 Oct 1988
618	Enya	Orinoco Flow (Sail Away)	29 Oct 1988
619	Robin Beck	The First Time	19 Nov 1988
620	Cliff Richard	Mistletoe & Wine	10 Dec 1988
621	Kylie Minogue & Jason Donovan	Especially For You	7 Jan 1989
622	Marc Almond with Gene Pitney	Something's Gotten Hold Of My Heart	28 Jan 1989
623	Simple Minds	Belfast Child	25 Feb 1989
624	Jason Donovan	Too Many Broken Hearts	11 Mar 1989

	Artist	Song	Date
625	Madonna	Like A Prayer	25 Mar 1989
626	Bangles	Eternal Flame	15 Apr 1989
627	Kylie Minogue	Hand On Your Heart	13 May 1989
628	Gerry Marsden, Paul McCartney, Holly Johnson & The Christians	Ferry 'Cross The Mersey	20 May 1989
629	Jason Donovan	Sealed With A Kiss	10 June 1989
630	Soul II Soul (ft Caron Wheeler)	Back To Life	24 June 1989
631	Sonia	You'll Never Stop Me Loving You	22 July 1989
632	Jive Bunny & The Mastermixers	Swing The Mood	5 Aug 1989
633	Black Box	Ride On Time	9 Sept 1989
634	Jive Bunny & The Mastermixers	That's What I Like	21 Oct 1989
635	Lisa Stansfield	All Around The World	11 Nov 1989
636	New Kids On The Block	You Got It (The Right Stuff)	25 Nov 1989
637	Jive Bunny & The Mastermixers	Let's Party	16 Dec 1989
638	Band Aid II**	Do They Know It's Christmas	23 Dec 1989
639	New Kids On The Block	Hangin' Tough	16 Jan 1990
640	Kylie Minogue	Tears On My Pillow	27 Jan 1990
641	Sinead O'Connor	Nothing Compares 2 U	3 Feb 1990
642	Beats International	Dub Be Good To Me	3 Mar 1990
643	Snap	The Power	31 Mar 1990
644	Madonna	Vogue	14 Apr 1990
645	Adamski	Killer	12 May 1990
646	EnglandNewOrder	World In Motion	9 June 1990
647	Elton John	Sacrifice / Healing Hands	23 June 1990
648	Partners In Kryme	Turtle Power	28 July 1990
649	Bombalurina	Itsy Bitsy Teeny Weeny Yellow Polka Dot Bikini	25 Aug 1990
650	Steve Miller Band	The Joker	15 Sept 1990
651	Maria McKee	Show Me Heaven	29 Sept 1990
652	Beautiful South	A Little Time	27 Oct 1990
653	Righteous Brothers	Unchained Melody	3 Nov 1990
654	Vanilla Ice	Ice Ice Baby	1 Dec 1990
655	Cliff Richard	Saviour's Day	22 Dec 1990
656	Iron Maiden	Bring Your Daughter To The Slaughter	5 Jan 1991
657	Enigma	Sadness Part 1	19 Jan 1991
658	Queen	Innuendo	26 Jan 1991
659	KLF	3AM Eternal	2 Feb 1991
660	Simpsons	Do The Bartman	16 Feb 1991
661	Clash	Should I Stay Or Should I Go	9 Mar 1991
662	Hale & Pace	The Stonk	23 Mar 1991
663	Chesney Hawkes	The One And Only	30 Mar 1991
664	Cher	Shoop Shoop Song (It's In His Kiss)	4 May 1991
665	Color Me Badd	I Wanna Sex You Up	8 June 1991
666	Jason Donovan	Any Dream Will Do	29 June 1991
667	Bryan Adams	(Everything I Do) I Do It For You	13 July 1991
668	U2	The Fly	2 Nov 1991
669	Vic Reeves & The Wonder Stuff	Dizzy	9 Nov 1991
670	Michael Jackson	Black Or White	23 Nov 1991
671	George Michael & Elton John	Don't Let The Sun Go Down On Me	7 Dec 1991
672	Queen	Bohemian Rhapsody / These Are The Days Of Our Lives	21 Dec 1991
673	Wet Wet Wet	Goodnight Girl	25 Jan 1992
674	Shakespears Sister	Stay	22 Feb 1992
675	Right Said Fred	Deeply Dippy	18 Apr 1992
676	KWS	Please Don't Go / Game Boy	9 May 1992
677	Erasure	Abba-esque EP	13 June 1992
678	Jimmy Nail	Ain't No Doubt	18 July 1992
679	Snap	Rhythm Is A Dancer	8 Aug 1992
680	Shamen	Ebeneezer Goode	19 Sept 1992
681	Tasmin Archer	Sleeping Satellite	17 Oct 1992
682	Boyz II Men	End Of The Road	31 Oct 1992
683	Charles & Eddie	Would I Lie To You	21 Nov 1992
684	Whitney Houston	I Will Always Love You	5 Dec 1992
685	2 Unlimited	No Limit	13 Feb 1993
686	Shaggy	Oh Carolina	20 Mar 1993
687	Bluebells	Young At Heart	3 Apr 1993
688	George Michael & Queen with Lisa Stansfield	Five Live (EP)	1 May 1993
689	Ace Of Base	All That She Wants	22 May 1993
690	UB40	(I Can't Help) Falling In Love With You	12 June 1993
691	Gabrielle	Dreams	26 June 1993
692	Take That	Pray	17 July 1993
693	Freddie Mercury	Living On My Own	14 Aug 1993
694	Culture Beat	Mr Vain	28 Aug 1993
695	Jazzy Jeff & The Fresh Prince (Will Smith)	Boom! Shake The Room	25 Sept 1993
696	Take That (ft Lulu)	Relight My Fire	9 Oct 1993
697	Meat Loaf	I'd Do Anything For Love (But I Won't Do That)	23 Oct 1993
698	Mr Blobby	Mr Blobby	11 Dec 1993
699	Take That	Babe	18 Dec 1993

	Artist	Song	Date
700	Chaka Demus & Pliers	Twist & Shout	8 Jan 1994
701	D:Ream	Things Can Only Get Better	22 Jan 1994
702	Mariah Carey	Without You	19 Feb 1994
703	Doop	Doop	19 Mar 1994
704	Take That	Everything Changes	9 Apr 1994
705	Prince	The Most Beautiful Girl In The World	23 Apr 1994
706	Tony Di Bart	The Real Thing	7 May 1994
707	Stiltskin	Inside	14 May 1994
708	Manchester United 1994 Football Squad	Come On You Reds	21 May 1994
709	Wet Wet Wet	Love Is All Around	4 June 1994
710	Whigfield	Saturday Night	17 Sept 1994
711	Take That	Sure	15 Oct 1994
712	Pato Banton (with Robin & Ali Campbell)	Baby Come Back	29 Oct 1994
713	Baby D	Let Me Be Your Fantasy	26 Nov 1994
714	East 17	Stay Another Day	10 Dec 1994
715	Rednex	Cotton Eye Joe	14 Jan 1995
716	Celine Dion	Think Twice	4 Feb 1995
717	Cher, Chrissie Hynde, Neneh Cherry & Eric Clapton	Love Can Build A Bridge	25 Mar 1995
718	Outhere Brothers	Don't Stop (Wiggle Wiggle)	1 Apr 1995
719	Take That	Back For Good	8 Apr 1995
720	Oasis	Some Might Say	6 May 1995
721	Livin' Joy	Dreamer	13 May 1995
722	Robson Green & Jerome Flynn	Unchained Melody / White Cliffs Of Dover	20 May 1995
723	Outhere Brothers	Boom Boom Boom	8 July 1995
724	Take That	Never Forget	5 Aug 1995
725	Blur	Country House	26 Aug 1995
726	Michael Jackson	You Are Not Alone	9 Sept 1995
727	Shaggy	Boombastic	23 Sept 1995
728	Simply Red	Fairground	30 Sept 1995
729	Coolio featuring LV	Gangsta's Paradise	28 Oct 1995
730	Robson & Jerome	I Believe / Up On The Roof	11 Nov 1995
731	Michael Jackson	Earth Song	9 Dec 1995
732	George Michael	Jesus To A Child	20 Jan 1996
733	Babylon Zoo	Spaceman	27 Jan 1996
734	Oasis	Don't Look Back In Anger	2 Mar 1996
735	Take That	How Deep Is Your Love	9 Mar 1996
736	Prodigy	Firestarter	30 Mar 1996
737	Mark Morrison	Return Of The Mack	20 Apr 1996
738	George Michael	Fastlove	4 May 1996
739	Gina G	Ooh Aah ... Just A Little Bit	25 May 1996
740	Baddiel, Skinner & Lightning Seeds	Three Lions	1 June 1996
741	Fugees	Killing Me Softly	8 June 1996
742	Gary Barlow	Forever Love	20 July 1996
743	Spice Girls	Wannabe	27 July 1996
744	Peter Andre	Flava	14 Sept 1996
745	Fugees	Ready Or Not	21 Sept 1996
746	Deep Blue Something	Breakfast At Tiffany's	5 Oct 1996
747	Chemical Brothers	Setting Sun	12 Oct 1996
748	Boyzone	Words	19 Oct 1996
749	Spice Girls	Say You'll Be There	26 Oct 1996
750	Robson & Jerome	What Becomes Of The Broken Hearted / Saturday Night At The Movies / You'll Never Walk Alone	9 Nov 1996
751	Prodigy	Breathe	23 Nov 1996
752	Peter Andre	I Feel You	7 Dec 1996
753	Boyzone	A Different Beat	14 Dec 1996
754	Dunblane	Knockin' On Heaven's Door / Throw These Guns Away	21 Dec 1996
755	Spice Girls	2 Become 1	28 Dec 1996
756	Tori Amos	Professional Widow (It's Got To Be Big)	18 Jan 1997
757	White Town	Your Woman	25 Jan 1997
758	Blur	Beetlebum	1 Feb 1997
759	LL Cool J	Ain't Nobody	8 Feb 1997
760	U2	Discotheque	15 Feb 1997
761	No Doubt	Don't Speak	22 Feb 1997
762	Spice Girls	Mama / Who Do You Think You Are	15 Mar 1997
763	Chemical Brothers	Block Rockin' Beats	5 Apr 1997
764	R Kelly	I Believe I Can Fly	12 Apr 1997
765	Michael Jackson	Blood On The Dance Floor	3 May 1997
766	Gary Barlow	Love Won't Wait	10 May 1997
767	Olive	You're Not Alone	17 May 1997
768	Eternal (ft Bebe Winans)	I Wanna Be The One	31 May 1997
769	Hanson	MmmBop	7 June 1997
770	Puff Daddy & Faith Evans	I'll Be Missing You	28 June 1997
771	Oasis	D'You Know What I Mean	19 July 1997
772	Will Smith	Men In Black	16 Aug 1997
773	Verve	The Drugs Don't Work	13 Sept 1997
774	Elton John	Candle In The Wind '97 / Something About The Way You Look Tonight	20 Sept 1997

	Artist	Song	Date
775	Spice Girls	Spice Up Your Life	25 Oct 1997
776	Aqua	Barbie Girl	1 Nov 1997
777	Various Artists*	Perfect Day	29 Nov 1997
778	Teletubbies	Teletubbies Say Eh-oh!	13 Dec 1997
779	Spice Girls	Too Much	27 Dec 1997
780	All Saints	Never Ever	17 Jan 1998
781	Oasis	All Around The World	24 Jan 1998
782	Usher	You Make Me Wanna ...	31 Jan 1998
783	Aqua	Doctor Jones	7 Feb 1998
784	Celine Dion	My Heart Will Go On	21 Feb 1998
785	Cornershop	Brimful Of Asha	28 Feb 1998
786	Madonna	Frozen	7 Mar 1998
787	Run DMC vs Jason Nevins	It's Like That	21 Mar 1998
788	Boyzone	All That I Need	2 May 1998
789	All Saints	Under The Bridge / Lady Marmalade	9 May 1998
790	Aqua	Turn Back Time	16 May 1998
791	Tamperer featuring Maya	Feel It	30 May 1998
792	B*Witched	C'est La Vie	6 June 1998
793	Baddiel, Skinner & Lightning Seeds	Three Lions '98	20 June 1998
794	Billie	Because We Want To	11 July 1998
795	Another Level	Freak Me	18 July 1998
796	Jamiroquai	Deeper Underground	25 July 1998
797	Spice Girls	Viva Forever	1 Aug 1998
798	Boyzone	No Matter What	15 Aug 1998
799	Manic Street Preachers	If You Tolerate This Your Children Will Be Next	5 Sept 1998
800	All Saints	Bootie Call	12 Sept 1998
801	Robbie Williams	Millennium	19 Sept 1998
802	Melanie B (ft Missy Elliott)	I Want You Back	26 Sept 1998
803	B*Witched	Rollercoaster	3 Oct 1998
804	Billie	Girlfriend	17 Oct 1998
805	Spacedust	Gym And Tonic	24 Oct 1998
806	Cher	Believe	31 Oct 1998
807	B*Witched	To You I Belong	19 Dec 1998
808	Spice Girls	Goodbye	26 Dec 1998
809	Chef	Chocolate Salty Balls (PS I Love You)	2 Jan 1999
810	Steps	Heartbeat / Tragedy	9 Jan 1999
811	Fatboy Slim	Praise You	16 Jan 1999
812	911	A Little Bit More	23 Jan 1999
813	Offspring	Pretty Fly (For A White Guy)	30 Jan 1999
814	Armand van Helden ft Duane Harden	You Don't Know Me	6 Feb 1999
815	Blondie	Maria	13 Feb 1999
816	Lenny Kravitz	Fly Away	20 Feb 1999
817	Britney Spears	Baby One More Time	27 Feb 1999
818	Boyzone	When The Going Gets Tough	13 Mar 1999
819	B*Witched	Blame It On The Weatherman	27 Mar 1999
820	Mr Oizo	Flat Beat	3 Apr 1999
821	Martine McCutcheon	Perfect Moment	17 Apr 1999
822	Westlife	Swear It Again	1 May 1999
823	Backstreet Boys	I Want It That Way	15 May 1999
824	Boyzone	You Needed Me	22 May 1999
825	Shanks & Bigfoot	Sweet Like Chocolate	29 May 1999
826	Baz Luhrmann	Everybody's Free (To Wear Sunscreen)	12 June 1999
827	S Club 7	Bring It All Back	19 June 1999
828	Vengaboys	Boom Boom Boom Boom	26 June 1999
829	ATB	9PM (Till I Come)	3 July 1999
830	Ricky Martin	Livin' La Vida Loca	17 July 1999
831	Ronan Keating	When You Say Nothing At All	7 Aug 1999
832	Westlife	If I Let You Go	21 Aug 1999
833	Geri Halliwell	Mi Chico Latino	28 Aug 1999
834	Lou Bega	Mambo No 5	4 Sept 1999
835	Vengaboys	We're Going To Ibiza	18 Sept 1999
836	Eiffel 65	Blue (Da Ba Dee)	25 Sept 1999
837	Christina Aguilera	Genie In A Bottle	16 Oct 1999
838	Westlife	Flying Without Wings	30 Oct 1999
839	Five	Keep On Movin'	6 Nov 1999
840	Geri Halliwell	Lift Me Up	13 Nov 1999
841	Robbie Williams	She's The One / It's Only Us	20 Nov 1999
842	Wamdue Project	King Of My Castle	27 Nov 1999
843	Cliff Richard	Millennium Prayer	4 Dec 1999
844	Westlife	I Have A Dream / Seasons In The Sun	25 Dec 1999
845	Manic Street Preachers	The Masses Against The Classes	22 Jan 2000
846	Britney Spears	Born To Make You Happy	29 Jan 2000
847	Gabrielle	Rise	5 Feb 2000
848	Oasis	Go Let It Out	19 Feb 2000
849	All Saints	Pure Shores	26 Feb 2000
850	Madonna	American Pie	11 Mar 2000
851	Chicane featuring Bryan Adams	Don't Give Up	18 Mar 2000
852	Geri Halliwell	Bag It Up	25 Mar 2000
853	Melanie C with Lisa 'Left Eye' Lopes	Never Be The Same Again	1 Apr 2000
854	Westlife	Fool Again	8 Apr 2000

	Artist	Song	Date
855	Craig David	Fill Me In	15 Apr 2000
856	Fragma	Toca's Miracle	22 Apr 2000
857	Oxide & Neutrino	Bound 4 Da Reload (Casualty)	6 May 2000
858	Britney Spears	Oops! ... I Did It Again	13 May 2000
859	Madison Avenue	Don't Call Me Baby	20 May 2000
860	Billie Piper	Day & Night	27 May 2000
861	Sonique	It Feels So Good	3 June 2000
862	Black Legend	You See The Trouble With Me	24 June 2000
863	Kylie Minogue	Spinning Around	1 July 2000
864	Eminem	Real Slim Shady	8 July 2000
865	Corrs	Breathless	15 July 2000
866	Ronan Keating	Life Is A Rollercoaster	22 July 2000
867	Five and Queen	We Will Rock You	29 July 2000
868	Craig David	7 Days	5 Aug 2000
869	Robbie Williams	Rock DJ	12 Aug 2000
870	Melanie C	I Turn To You	19 Aug 2000
871	Spiller	Groovejet (If This Ain't Love)	26 Aug 2000
872	Madonna	Music	2 Sept 2000
873	A1	Take On Me	9 Sept 2000
874	Modjo	Lady (Hear Me Tonight)	16 Sept 2000
875	Mariah Carey & Westlife	Against All Odds	30 Sept 2000
876	All Saints	Black Coffee	14 Oct 2000
877	U2	Beautiful Day	21 Oct 2000
878	Steps	Stomp	28 Oct 2000
879	Spice Girls	Holler / Let Love Lead The Way	4 Nov 2000
880	Westlife	My Love	11 Nov 2000
881	A1	Same Old Brand New You	18 Nov 2000
882	LeAnn Rimes	Can't Fight The Moonlight	25 Nov 2000
883	Destiny's Child	Independent Women Part 1	2 Dec 2000
884	S Club 7	Never Had A Dream Come True	9 Dec 2000
885	Eminem	Stan	16 Dec 2000
886	Bob The Builder	Can We Fix It	23 Dec 2000
887	Rui Da Silva (ft Cassandra)	Touch Me	13 Jan 2001
888	Jennifer Lopez	Love Don't Cost A Thing	20 Jan 2001
889	Limp Bizkit	Rollin'	27 Jan 2001
890	Atomic Kitten	Whole Again	10 Feb 2001
891	Shaggy (ft Rikrok)	It Wasn't Me	10 Mar 2001
892	Westlife	Uptown Girl	17 Mar 2001
893	Hear'Say	Pure And Simple	24 Mar 2001
894	Emma Bunton	What Took You So Long	14 Apr 2001
895	Destiny's Child	Survivor	28 Apr 2001
896	S Club 7	Don't Stop Movin'	5 May 2001
897	Geri Halliwell	It's Raining Men	12 May 2001
898	DJ Pied Piper	Do You Really Like It	2 June 2001
899	Shaggy (ft Rayvon)	Angel	9 June 2001
900	Christina Aguilera with Lil' Kim, Mya & Pink	Lady Marmalade	30 June 2001
901	Hear'Say	The Way To Your Love	7 July 2001
902	Roger Sanchez	Another Chance	14 July 2001
903	Robbie Williams	Eternity / The Road To Mandalay	21 July 2001
904	Atomic Kitten	Eternal Flame	4 Aug 2001
905	So Solid Crew	21 Seconds	18 Aug 2001
906	Five	Let's Dance	25 Aug 2001
907	Blue	Too Close	8 Sept 2001
908	Bob The Builder	Mambo No 5	15 Sept 2001
909	DJ Otzi	Hey Baby	22 Sept 2001
910	Kylie Minogue	Can't Get You Out Of My Head	29 Sept 2001
911	Afroman	Because I Got High	27 Oct 2001
912	Westlife	Queen of My Heart	17 Nov 2001
913	Blue	If You Come Back	24 Nov 2001
914	S Club 7	Have You Ever	1 Dec 2001
915	Daniel Bedingfield	Gotta Get Thru This	8 Dec 2001
916	Robbie Williams & Nicole Kidman	Somethin' Stupid	22 Dec 2001
917	Aaliyah	More Than A Woman	19 Jan 2002
918	George Harrison	My Sweet Lord	26 Jan 2002
919	Enrique Iglesias	Hero	2 Feb 2002
920	Westlife	World Of Our Own	2 Mar 2002
921	Will Young	Anything Is Possible / Evergreen	9 Mar 2002
922	Gareth Gates	Unchained Melody	30 Mar 2002
923	Oasis	The Hindu Times	27 Apr 2002
924	Sugababes	Freak Like Me	4 May 2002
925	Holly Valance	Kiss Kiss	11 May 2002
926	Ronan Keating	If Tomorrow Never Comes	18 May 2002
927	Liberty X	Just A Little	25 May 2002
928	Eminem	Without Me	1 June 2002
929	Will Young	Light My Fire	8 June 2002
930	Elvis vs JXL	A Little Less Conversation	22 June 2002
931	Gareth Gates	Anyone Of Us (Stupid Mistake)	20 July 2002
932	Darius	Colourblind	10 Aug 2002
933	Sugababes	Round Round	24 Aug 2002

	Artist	Song	Date
934	Blazin' Squad	Crossroads	31 Aug 2002
935	Atomic Kitten	The Tide Is High (Get The Feeling)	7 Sept 2002
936	Pink	Just Like A Pill	28 Sept 2002
937	Will Young & Gareth Gates	The Long And Winding Road / Suspicious Minds	5 Oct 2002
938	Las Ketchup	The Ketchup Song (Asereje)	19 Oct 2002
939	Nelly (ft Kelly Rowland)	Dilemma	26 Oct 2002
940	DJ Sammy & Yanou featuring Do	Heaven	9 Nov 2002
941	Westlife	Unbreakable	16 Nov 2002
942	Christina Aguilera	Dirrty	23 Nov 2002
943	Daniel Bedingfield	If You're Not The One	7 Dec 2002
944	Eminem	Lose Yourself	14 Dec 2002
945	Blue (ft Elton John)	Sorry Seems To Be The Hardest Word	21 Dec 2002
946	Girls Aloud	Sound Of The Underground	28 Dec 2002
947	David Sneddon	Stop Living The Lie	25 Jan 2003
948	Tatu	All The Things She Said	8 Feb 2003
949	Christina Aguilera	Beautiful	8 Mar 2003
950	Gareth Gates	Spirit In The Sky	22 Mar 2003
951	Room 5 (ft Oliver Cheatham)	Make Luv	5 Apr 2003
952	Busted	You Said No	3 May 2003
953	Tomcraft	Loneliness	10 May 2003
954	R Kelly	Ignition	17 May 2003
955	Evanescence	Bring Me To Life	14 June 2003
956	Beyonce	Crazy In Love	12 July 2003
957	Daniel Bedingfield	Never Gonna Leave Your Side	2 Aug 2003
958	Blu Cantrell (ft Sean Paul)	Breathe	9 Aug 2003
959	Elton John	Are You Ready For Love?	6 Sept 2003
960	Black Eyed Peas	Where Is The Love?	13 Sept 2003
961	Sugababes	Hole In The Head	25 Oct 2003
962	Fatman Scoop	Be Faithful	1 Nov 2003
963	Kylie Minogue	Slow	15 Nov 2003
964	Busted	Crashed The Wedding	22 Nov 2003
965	Westlife	Mandy	29 Nov 2003
966	Will Young	Leave Right Now	6 Dec 2003
967	Kelly & Ozzy Osbourne	Changes	20 Dec 2003
968	Michael Andrews (ft Gary Jules)	Mad World	27 Dec 2003
969	Michelle McManus	All This Time	17 Jan 2004
970	LMC vs U2	Take Me To The Clouds Above	7 Feb 2004
971	Sam & Mark	With A Little Help From My Friends / Measure Of A Man	21 Feb 2004
972	Busted	Who's David	28 Feb 2004
973	Peter Andre	Mysterious Girl	6 Mar 2004
974	Britney Spears	Toxic	13 Mar 2004
975	DJ Casper	Cha Cha Slide	20 Mar 2004
976	Usher	Yeah	27 Mar 2004
977	McFly	Five Colours In Her Hair	10 Apr 2004
978	Eamon	F**k It (I Don't Want You Back)	24 Apr 2004
979	Frankee	F.U.R.B. (F U Right Back)	22 May 2004
980	Mario Winans (ft Enya & P Diddy)	I Don't Wanna Know	12 June 2004
981	Britney Spears	Everytime	26 June 2004
982	McFly	Obviously	3 July 2004
983	Usher	Burn	10 July 2004
984	Shapeshifters	Lola's Theme	24 July 2004
985	The Streets	Dry Your Eyes	31 July 2004
986	Busted	Thunderbirds / 3AM	7 Aug 2004
987	3 Of A Kind	Babycakes	21 Aug 2004
988	Natasha Bedingfield	These Words	28 Aug 2004
989	Nelly	My Place / Flap Your Wings	11 Sept 2004
990	Brian McFadden	Real To Me	18 Sept 2004
991	Eric Prydz	Call On Me	25 Sept 2004
992	Robbie Williams	Radio	16 Oct 2004
993	Ja Rule (ft R Kelly & Ashanti)	Wonderful	6 Nov 2004
994	Eminem	Just Lose It	13 Nov 2004
995	U2	Vertigo	20 Nov 2004
996	Girls Aloud	I'll Stand By You	27 Nov 2004
997	Band Aid 20**	Do They Know It's Christmas	11 Dec 2004
998	Steve Brookstein	Against All Odds	8 Jan 2005
999	Elvis Presley	Jailhouse Rock	15 Jan 2005
1000	Elvis Presley	I Got Stung / One Night	22 Jan 2005
1001	Ciara (ft Petey Pablo)	Goodies	29 Jan 2005
1002	Elvis Presley	It's Now Or Never	5 Feb 2005
1003	Eminem	Like Toy Soldiers	12 Feb 2005
1004	U2	Sometimes You Can't Make It On Your Own	19 Feb 2005
1005	Jennifer Lopez	Get Right	26 Feb 2005
1006	Nelly (ft Tim McGraw)	Over And Over	5 Mar 2005
1007	Stereophonics	Dakota	12 Mar 2005
1008	McFly	All About You / You've Got A Friend	19 Mar 2005
1009	Tony Christie (ft Peter Kay)	(Is This The Way To) Amarillo	26 Mar 2005
1010	Akon	Lonely	8 May 2005
1011	Oasis	Lyla	22 May 2005
1012	Crazy Frog	Axel F	5 June 2005

	Artist	Song	Date
1013	2Pac (ft Elton John)	Ghetto Gospel	26 June 2005
1014	James Blunt	You're Beautiful	17 July 2005
1015	McFly	I'll Be OK	21 Aug 2005
1016	Oasis	The Importance Of Being Idle	28 Aug 2005
1017	Gorillaz	Dare	4 Sep 2005
1018	Pussycat Dolls (ft Busta Rhymes)	Don't Cha	11 Sep 2005
1019	Sugababes	Push The Button	2 Oct 2005
1020	Arctic Monkeys	I Bet You Look Good On The Dancefloor	23 Oct 2005
1021	Westlife	You Raise Me Up	30 Oct 2005
1022	Madonna	Hung Up	13 Nov 2005
1023	Pussycat Dolls	Stickwitu	4 Dec 2005
1024	Nizlopi	JCB Song	18 Dec 2005
1025	Shayne Ward	That's My Goal	25 Dec 2005
1026	Arctic Monkeys	When The Sun Goes Down	22 Jan 2006
1027	Notorious BIG (ft Diddy, Nelly, Jagged Edge & Avery Storm)	Nasty Girl	29 Jan 2006
1028	Meck (ft Leo Sayer)	Thunder In My Heart Again	12 Feb 2006
1029	Madonna	Sorry	26 Feb 2006
1030	Chico	It's Chico Time	5 Mar 2006
1031	Orson	No Tomorrow	19 Mar 2006
1032	Ne-Yo	So Sick	25 Mar 2006
1033	Gnarls Barkley	Crazy	2 Apr 2006
1034	Sandi Thom	I Wish I Was A Punk Rocker (With Flowers In My Hair)	4 June 2006
1035	Nelly Furtado	Maneater	11 June 2006
1036	Shakira (ft Wyclef Jean)	Hips Don't Lie	2 July 2006
1037	Lily Allen	Smile	9 July 2006
1038	McFly	Don't Stop Me Now / Please Please	23 July 2006
1039	Shakira (ft Wyclef Jean)	Hips Don't Lie	30 July 2006
1040	Beyonce (ft Jay-Z)	Deja Vu	27 Aug 2006
1041	Justin Timberlake	Sexyback	3 Sept 2006
1042	Scissor Sisters	I Don't Feel Like Dancin'	10 Sep 2006
1043	Razorlight	America	8 Oct 2006
1044	My Chemical Romance	Welcome To The Black Parade	15 Oct 2006
1045	McFly	Star Girl	29 Oct 2006
1046	Fedde Le Grande	Put Your Hands Up For Detroit	5 Nov 2006
1047	Westlife	The Rose	12 Nov 2006
1048	Akon (ft Eminem)	Smack That	19 Nov 2006
1049	Take That	Patience	26 Nov 2006
1050	Leona Lewis	A Moment Like This	24 Dec 2006
1051	Mika	Grace Kelly	21 Jan 2007
1052	Kaiser Chiefs	Ruby	25 Feb 2007
1053	Take That	Shine	4 Mar 2007
1054	Sugababes vs Girls Aloud	Walk This Way	18 Mar 2007
1055	Proclaimers (ft Brian Potter & Andy Pipkin)	I'm Gonna Be (500 Miles)	25 Mar 2007
1056	Timbaland / Nelly Furtado / Justin Timberlake	Give It To Me	15 Apr 2007
1057	Beyonce & Shakira	Beautiful Liar	22 Apr 2007
1058	McFly	Baby's Coming Back / Transylvania	13 May 2007
1059	Rihanna (ft Jay-Z)	Umbrella	20 May 2007
1060	Timbaland (ft Keri Hilson & DOE)	The Way I Are	29 July 2007
1061	Robyn with Kleerup	With Every Heartbeat	12 Aug 2007
1062	Kanye West	Stronger	19 Aug 2007
1063	Sean Kingston	Beautiful Girls	2 Sept 2007
1064	Sugababes	About You Now	30 Sept 2007
1065	Leona Lewis	Bleeding Love	28 Oct 2007
1066	Katie Melua & Eva Cassidy	What A Wonderful World	16 Dec 2007
1067	Leon Jackson	When You Believe	23 Dec 2007
1068	Basshunter (ft DJ Mental, Theo's Bazzheadz & Seb Westwood	Now You're Gone	13 Jan 2008
1069	Duffy	Mercy	17 Feb 2008
1070	Estelle (ft Kanye West)	American Boy	23 Mar 2008
1071	Madonna (ft Justin Timberlake & Timbaland)	4 Minutes	20 Apr 2008
1072	Ting Tings	That's Not My Name	18 May 2008
1073	Rihanna	Take A Bow	25 May 2008
1074	Mint Royale	Singin' In The Rain	8 June 2008
1075	Coldplay	Viva La Vida	22 June 2008
1076	Ne-Yo	Closer	29 June 2008
1077	Dizzee Rascal (ft Calvin Harris & Chrome)	Dance Wiv Me	6 July 2008
1078	Kid Rock	All Summer Long	3 Aug 2008
1079	Katy Perry	I Kissed A Girl	10 Aug 2008
1080	Kings of Leon	Sex On Fire	14 Sept 2008
1081	P!nk	So What	5 Oct 2008
1082	Girls Aloud	The Promise	26 Oct 2008
1083	X Factor Finalists 2008	Hero	2 Nov 2008
1084	Beyoncé	If I Were A Boy	23 Nov 2008
1085	Take That	Greatest Day	30 Nov 2008

	Artist	Song	Date
1086	Leona Lewis	Run	7 Dec 2008
1087	Alexandra Burke	Hallelujah	21 Dec 2008
1088	Lady Gaga (ft Colby O'Donis)	Just Dance	11 Jan 2009
1089	Lily Allen	The Fear	1 Feb 2009
1090	Kelly Clarkson	My Life Would Suck Without You	1 Mar 2009
1091	Flo Rida (ft Ke$ha)	Right Round	8 Mar 2009
1092	Vanessa Jenkins & Bryn West ft Sir Tom Jones & Robin Gibb	Islands In The Stream	15 Mar 2009
1093	Lady Gaga	Poker Face	22 Mar 2009
1094	Calvin Harris	I'm Not Alone	12 Apr 2009
1095	Tinchy Stryder (ft N-Dubz)	Number 1	26 Apr 2009
1096	Black Eyed Peas	Boom Boom Pow	17 May 2009
1097	Dizzee Rascal & Armand Van Helden	Bonkers	24 May 2009
1098	Black Eyed Peas	Boom Boom Pow	7 June 2009
1099	Pixie Lott	Mama Do (Uh Oh, Uh Oh)	14 June 2009
1100	David Guetta (ft Kelly Rowland)	When Love Takes Over	21 June 2009
1101	La Roux	Bulletproof	28 June 2009
1102	Cascada	Evacuate The Dancefloor	5 July 2009
1103	JLS	Beat Again	19 July 2009
1104	Black Eyed Peas	I Gotta Feeling	2 Aug 2009
1105	Tinchy Stryder (ft Amelle)	Never Leave You	9 Aug 2009
1106	Black Eyed Peas	I Gotta Feeling	16 Aug 2009
1107	David Guetta (ft Akon)	Sexy Bitch / Sexy Chick	23 Aug 2009
1108	Dizzee Rascal	Holiday	30 Aug 2009
1109	Jay-Z (ft Rihanna & Kanye West)	Run This Town	6 Sept 2009
1110	Pixie Lott	Boys And Girls	13 Sept 2009
1111	Taio Cruz	Break Your Heart	20 Sept 2009
1112	Chipmunk (ft Dayo Olatunji)	Oopsy Daisy	11 Oct 2009
1113	Alexandra Burke (ft Flo Rida)	Bad Boys	18 Oct 2009
1114	Cheryl Cole	Fight For This Love	25 Oct 2009
1115	JLS	Everybody In Love	8 Nov 2009
1116	Black Eyed Peas	Meet Me Halfway	15 Nov 2009
1117	X Factor Finalists 2009	You Are Not Alone	22 Nov 2009
1118	Peter Kay's Animated All Star Band	The Official BBC Children In Need Medley	29 Nov 2009
1119	Lady Gaga	Bad Romance	13 Dec 2009
1120	Rage Against The Machine	Killing In The Name	20 Dec 2009
1121	Joe McElderry	The Climb	27 Dec 2009
1122	Lady Gaga	Bad Romance	3 Jan 2010
1123	Iyaz	Replay	10 Jan 2010
1124	Owl City	Fireflies	24 Jan 2010
1125	Helping Haiti	Everybody Hurts	14 Feb 2010
1126	Jason Derülo	In My Head	28 Feb 2010
1127	Tinie Tempah	Pass Out	7 Mar 2010
1128	Lady Gaga (ft Beyonce)	Telephone	28 Mar 2010
1129	Scouting for Girls	This Ain't a Love Song	11 Apr 2010
1130	Usher (ft Will I Am)	OMG	25 Apr 2010
1131	Diana Vickers	Once	2 May 2010
1132	Roll Deep	Good Times	9 May 2010
1133	BoB (ft Bruno Mars)	Nothin' On You	30 May 2010
1134	Dizzee Rascal	Dirtee Disco	6 June 2010
1135	David Guetta (ft Chris Willis)	Getting' Over You	13 June 2010
1136	Dizzee Rascal (ft James Corden)	Shout	20 June 2010
1137	Katy Perry (ft Snoop Dogg)	California Gurls	4 July 2010
1138	JLS	The Club Is Alive	18 July 2010
1139	B.o.B (ft Hayley Williams)	Airplanes	25 July 2010
1140	Yolanda Be Cool vs D Cup	We No Speak Americano	1 Aug 2010
1141	Wanted	All Time Low	8 Aug 2010
1142	Ne-Yo	Beautiful Monster	15 Aug 2010
1143	Flo Rida (ft David Guetta)	Club Can't Handle Me	22 Aug 2010
1144	Roll Deep	Green Light	29 Aug 2010
1145	Taio Cruz	Dynamite	5 Sept 2010
1146	Olly Murs	Please Don't Let Me Go	12 Sept 2010
1147	Alexandra Burke (ft Laza Morgan)	Start Without You	19 Sept 2010
1148	Bruno Mars	Just the Way You Are	3 Oct 2010
1149	Tinie Tempah (ft Eric Turner)	Written in the Stars	10 Oct 2010
1150	Cee Lo Green	Forget You	17 Oct 2010
1151	Cheryl Cole	Promise This	7 Nov 2010
1152	Rihanna	Only Girl (In the World)	14 Nov 2010
1153	JLS	Love You More	28 Nov 2010
1154	The X Factor Finalists 2010	Heroes	5 Dec 2010
1155	The Black Eyed Peas	The Time (Dirty Bit)	19 Dec 2010
1156	Matt Cardle	When We Collide	26 Dec 2010
1157	Rihanna (ft Drake)	What's My Name?	16 Jan 2011
1158	Bruno Mars	Grenade	23 Jan 2011
1159	Ke$ha	We R Who We R	6 Feb 2011
1160	Jessie J (ft B.o.B)	Price Tag	13 Feb 2011
1161	Adele	Someone Like You	27 Feb 2011
1162	Nicole Scherzinger	Don't Hold Your Breath	27 Mar 2011
1163	Adele	Someone Like You	3 Apr 2011
1164	Jennifer Lopez (ft Pitbull)	On the Floor	10 Apr 2011

	Artist	Song	Date
1165	LMFAO (ft Lauren Bennett & GoonRock)	Party Rock Anthem	24 Apr 2011
1166	Bruno Mars	The Lazy Song	22 May 2011
1167	Pitbull (ft Ne-Yo, Afrojack & Nayer)	Give Me Everything	29 May 2011
1168	Example	Changed the Way You Kiss Me	19 June 2011
1169	Jason Derülo	Don't Wanna Go Home	3 July 2011
1170	DJ Fresh (ft Sian Evans)	Louder	17 July 2011
1171	The Wanted	Glad You Came	24 July 2011
1172	JLS (ft Dev)	She Makes Me Wanna	7 Aug 2011
1173	Cher Lloyd	Swagger Jagger	14 Aug 2011
1174	Nero	Promises	21 Aug 2011
1175	Wretch 32 (ft Josh Kumra)	Don't Go	28 Aug 2011
1176	Olly Murs (ft Rizzle Kicks)	Heart Skips a Beat	4 Sept 2011
1177	Example	Stay Awake	11 Sept 2011
1178	Pixie Lott	All About Tonight	18 Sept 2011
1179	One Direction	What Makes You Beautiful	25 Sept 2011
1180	Dappy	No Regrets	2 Oct 2011
1181	Sak Noel	Loca People	9 Oct 2011
1182	Rihanna (ft Calvin Harris)	We Found Love	16 Oct 2011
1183	Professor Green (ft Emeli Sandé)	Read All About It	6 Nov 2011
1184	Rihanna (ft Calvin Harris)	We Found Love	20 Nov 2011
1185	The X Factor Finalists 2011	Wishing On a Star	11 Dec 2011
1186	Olly Murs	Dance with Me Tonight	18 Dec 2011
1187	Little Mix	Cannonball	25 Dec 2011
1188	Military Wives with Gareth Malone	Wherever You Are	1 Jan 2012
1189	Coldplay	Paradise	8 Jan 2012
1190	Flo Rida	Good Feeling	15 Jan 2012
1191	Jessie J	Domino	22 Jan 2012
1192	Cover Drive	Twilight	5 Feb 2012
1193	David Guetta (ft Sia)	Titanium	12 Feb 2012
1194	Gotye (ft Kimbra)	Somebody That I Used to Know	19 Feb 2012
1195	DJ Fresh (ft Rita Ora)	Hot Right Now	26 Feb 2012
1196	Gotye (ft Kimbra)	Somebody That I Used to Know	4 Mar 2012
1197	Katy Perry	Part of Me	1 Apr 2012
1198	Chris Brown	Turn Up the Music	8 Apr 2012
1199	Carly Rae Jepsen	Call Me Maybe	15 Apr 2012
1200	Tulisa	Young	13 May 2012
1201	Rita Ora (ft Tinie Tempah)	R.I.P.	20 May 2012
1202	Fun (ft Janelle Monáe)	We Are Young	3 June 2012
1203	Rudimental (ft John Newman)	Feel the Love	10 June 2012
1204	Gary Barlow and the Commonwealth Band featuring Military Wives	Sing	17 June 2012
1205	Cheryl	Call My Name	24 June 2012
1206	Maroon 5 (ft Wiz Khalifa)	Payphone	1 July 2012
1207	will.i.am (ft Eva Simons)	This is Love	8 July 2012
1208	Maroon 5 (ft Wiz Khalifa)	Payphone	15 July 2012
1209	Florence and the Machine	Spectrum (Say My Name)	22 July 2012
1210	Wiley (ft Ms D)	Heatwave	12 Aug 2012
1211	Rita Ora	How We Do (Party)	26 Aug 2012
1212	Sam and the Womp	Bom Bom	2 Sept 2012
1213	Little Mix	Wings	9 Sept 2012
1214	Ne-Yo	Let Me Love You (Until You Learn to Love Yourself)	16 Sept 2012
1215	The Script (ft will.i.am)	Hall of Fame	23 Sept 2012
1216	Psy	Gangnam Style	7 Oct 2012
1217	Rihanna	Diamonds	14 Oct 2012
1218	Swedish House Mafia ft John Martin	Don't You Worry Child	21 Oct 2012
1219	Calvin Harris (ft Florence Welch)	Sweet Nothing	28 Oct 2012
1220	Labrinth (ft Emeli Sandé)	Beneath Your Beautiful	4 Nov 2012
1221	Robbie Williams	Candy	11 Nov 2012
1222	One Direction	Little Things	25 Nov 2012
1223	Olly Murs (ft Flo Rida)	Troublemaker	2 Dec 2012
1224	Gabrielle Aplin	The Power of Love	16 Dec 2012
1225	James Arthur	Impossible	23 Dec 2012
1226	The Justice Collective	He Ain't Heavy, He's My Brother	30 Dec 2012
1227	James Arthur	Impossible	6 Jan 2013
1228	will.i.am (ft Britney Spears)	Scream & Shout	20 Jan 2013
1229	Bingo Players ft Far East Movement	Get Up (Rattle)	3 Feb 2013
1230	Macklemore & Ryan Lewis ft Wanz	Thrift Shop	17 Feb 2013
1231	Avicii vs. Nicky Romero	I Could Be the One	24 Feb 2013
1232	One Direction	One Way or Another (Teenage Kicks)	3 Mar 2013
1233	Justin Timberlake	Mirrors	10 Mar 2013
1234	The Saturdays (ft Sean Paul)	What About Us	31 Mar 2013
1235	PJ & Duncan	Let's Get Ready to Rhumble	7 Apr 2013
1236	Duke Dumont (ft A*M*E)	Need U (100%)	14 Apr 2013
1237	Rudimental (ft Ella Eyre)	Waiting All Night	28 Apr 2013
1238	Daft Punk (ft Pharrell Williams)	Get Lucky	5 May 2013
1239	Naughty Boy (ft Sam Smith)	La La La	2 June 2013
1240	Robin Thicke (ft T.I. & Pharrell)	Blurred Lines	9 June 2013
1241	Icona Pop (ft Charli XCX)	I Love it	7 July 2013
1242	John Newman	Love Me Again	14 July 2013

	Artist	Song	Date
1243	Robin Thicke (ft T.I. & Pharrell)	Blurred Lines	21 July 2013
1244	Avicii	Wake Me Up	28 July 2013
1245	Miley Cyrus	We Can't Stop	18 Aug 2013
1246	Ellie Goulding	Burn	25 Aug 2013
1247	Katy Perry	Roar	15 Sept 2013
1248	Jason Derulo (ft 2 Chainz)	Talk Dirty	29 Sept 2013

*The artists on the 777th No. 1, 'Perfect Day', were the BBC Symphony Orchestra with Andrew Davis, Thomas Allen, Brett Anderson (Suede), Laurie Anderson, Joan Armatrading, Bono (U2), David Bowie, Boyzone, Brodsky Quartet, Ian Broudie (Lightning Seeds), Burning Spear, Robert Cray, Evan Dando (Lemonheads), Dr John, Gabrielle, Lesley Garrett, Emmylou Harris, Huey Morgan (Fun Lovin' Criminals), Elton John, Tom Jones, Shane McGowan, Courtney Pine, Lou Reed, Skye (Morcheeba), Heather Small (M People), Suzanne Vega, Visual Ministry Orchestra, Sheona White, Tammy Wynette.

**The artists on Band Aid were Keren Woodward, Sarah Dallin, Siobhan Fahey (Bananarama); Bob Geldof, Johnny Fingers, Simon Crowe, Pete Briquette (Boomtown Rats); David Bowie; Phil Collins; Boy George, Jon Moss (Culture Club); Simon Le Bon, Nick Rhodes, Andy Taylor, John Taylor, Roger Taylor (Duran Duran); Holly Johnson (Frankie Goes to Hollywood); Martin Ware, Glenn Gregory (Heaven 17); Robert 'Kool' Bell, James Taylor, Dennis Thomas (Kool and the Gang); Marilyn; Paul McCartney; George Michael; Jody Watley (Shalimar); Tony Hadley, John Keeble, Gary Kemp, Martin Kemp, Steve Norman (Spandau Ballet); Francis Rossi, Rick Parfitt (Status Quo); Sting; Adam Clayton, Bono (U2); Midge Ure, Chris Cross (Ultravox); Paul Weller; Paul Young.

The artists on Band Aid II were Bananarama, Big Fun, Bros, Cathy Dennis, D Mob, Jason Donovan, Kevin Godley, Glen Goldsmith, Kylie Minogue, The Pasadenas, Chris Rea, Cliff Richard, Jimmy Somerville, Sonia, Lisa Stansfield, Technotronic, Wet Wet Wet.

The artists on Band Aid 20 were Damon Albarn (made the tea); Tim Wheeler (Ash); Daniel Bedingfield; Natasha Bedingfield; James Bourne, Mattie Jay, Charlie Simpson (Busted); Chris Martin (Coldplay); Ed Graham, Dan Hawkins, Justin Hawkins, Frankie Poullain (The Darkness); Dido; Ms Dynamite; Grant Nichols (Feeder); Bob Geldof; Neil Hannon (The Divine Comedy); Jamelia; Tom Chaplin, Richard Hughes, Tim Rice-Oxley (Keane); Beverley Knight; Lemar; Shaznay Lewis; Paul McCartney; Madonna; Katie Melua; Roisin Murphy (Moloko); Skye (Morcheeba); Jonny Greenwood, Thom Yorke (Radiohead); Dizzee Rascal; Richard Colburn, Gary Lightbody, Mark McClell, John Quinn (Snow Patrol); Rachel Stevens; Joss Stone; Keisha Buchanan, Mutya Buena, Heidi Range (The Sugababes); Danny Goffey (Supergrass); Ben Carrigan, Connor Deasy, Kevin Horan, Padraic MacMahon, Daniel Ryan (The Thrills); Andy Dunlop, Fran Healy, Dougie Payne, Neil Primrose (Travis); Olly Knights, Gail Paradjanian (Turin Brakes); Bono, The Edge (U2); Midge Ure; Robbie Williams; Will Young.

The featured artists in the original recording with their lyrics are as follows: (**Paul Young**) It's Christmas time, There's no need to be afraid. At Christmas time, We let in light and we banish shade (**Boy George**) And in our world of plenty We can spread a smile of joy, Throw your arms around the world at Christmas time (George Michael) But say a prayer, Pray for the other ones, At Christmas time it's hard (**Simon Le Bon**) But when you're having fun, There's a world outside your window (**Sting**) And it's a world of dread and fear, Where the only water flowing is (**Bono** joins in) The bitter sting of fears, And the Christmas bells that are ringing, Are clanging chimes of doom (**Bono** only) Well, tonight thank God it's them instead of you (**All**) And there won't be snow in Africa this Christmas time, The greatest gift they'll get this year is life, Where nothing ever grows, No rain or river flows, Do they know it's Christmas time at all? Feed the world, Let them know it's Christmas time, Feed the world, Do they know it's Christmas time at all? (**Paul Young**) Here's to you raise a glass for everyone, Here's to them underneath the burning sun, Do they know it's Christmas time at all? (**All**) chorus repeat.

The official BBC Children in Need Medley performed by Peter Kay's Animated All Star Band consisted of the following songs, in order: 'Can You Feel It' (The Jacksons), 'Don't Stop' (Fleetwood Mac/Status Quo), 'Jai Ho' (A R Rahman & The Pussycat Dolls), 'Tubthumping' (Chumbawamba), 'Never Forget' (Take That), 'Hey Jude' (The Beatles), 'One Day Like This' (Elbow).

The artists performing 'Everybody Hurts' as Helping Haiti in order of appearance: Leona Lewis, Rod Stewart, Mariah Carey, Cheryl Cole, Mika, Michael Bublé, Joe McElderry, Miley Cyrus, James Blunt, Gary Barlow, Mark Owen, Jon Bon Jovi, James Morrison, Alexandra Burke, Jason Orange, Susan Boyle, JLS, Shane Filan, Mark Feehily, Kylie Minogue, Robbie Williams, Kian Egan, Nicky Byrne.

The artists performing 'He Ain't Heavy, He's My Brother' as The Justice Collective included Melanie C, Robbie Williams, Paul Heaton, Paloma Faith, Paul McCartney, Gerry Marsden, Kenny Dalglish, Alan Hansen, Rebecca Ferguson and Beverley Knight - for various charities associated with the Hillsborough disaster.

Christmas No. 1s

1952 Here in My Heart – Al Martino
1953 Answer Me – Frankie Laine
1954 Let's Have Another Party – Winifred Atwell
1955 The Christmas Alphabet – Dickie Valentine.
1956 Just Walkin' in the Rain – Johnnie Ray
1957 Mary's Boy Child – Harry Belafonte
1958 It's Only Make Believe – Conway Twitty
1959 What Do You Want to Make Those Eyes at Me For – Emile Ford and the Checkmates
1960 I Love You – Cliff Richard and the Shadows
1961 Moon River – Danny Williams
1962 Return to Sender – Elvis Presley
1963 I Want to Hold Your Hand – Beatles
1964 I Feel Fine – Beatles
1965 Day Tripper/We Can Work It Out – Beatles
1966 Green Green Grass of Home – Tom Jones
1967 Hello Goodbye – Beatles
1968 Lily the Pink – Scaffold
1969 Two Little Boys – Rolf Harris
1970 I Hear You Knockin' – Dave Edmunds
1971 Ernie – Benny Hill
1972 Long Haired Lover from Liverpool-Little Jimmy Osmond
1973 Merry Xmas Everybody – Slade
1974 Lonely This Christmas – Mud
1975 Bohemian Rhapsody – Queen
1976 When a Child Is Born – Johnny Mathis
1977 Mull of Kintyre/Girls' School – Wings
1978 Mary's Boy Child – Boney M
1979 Another Brick in the Wall – Pink Floyd
1980 There's No One Quite Like Grandma – St Winifred's School Choir
1981 Don't You Want Me – Human League
1982 Save Your Love – Renee and Renato
1983 Only You – Flying Pickets
1984 Do They Know It's Christmas – Band Aid
1985 Merry Christmas Everyone – Shakin' Stevens
1986 Reet Petite – Jackie Wilson
1987 Always on My Mind – Pet Shop Boys
1988 Mistletoe and Wine – Cliff Richard
1989 Do They Know It's Christmas? – Band Aid II
1990 Saviour's Day – Cliff Richard
1991 Bohemian Rhapsody / These Are the Days of Our Lives – Queen
1992 I Will Always Love You – Whitney Houston
1993 Mr. Blobby – Mr. Blobby
1994 Stay Another Day – East 17
1995 Earth Song – Michael Jackson
1996 2 Become 1 – Spice Girls
1997 Too Much – Spice Girls
1998 Goodbye – Spice Girls
1999 I Have a Dream/Seasons in the Sun – Westlife
2000 Can We Fix It – Bob The Builder
2001 Somethin' Stupid – Robbie Williams and Nicole Kidman
2002 Sound Of The Underground – Girls Aloud
2003 Mad World – Michael Andrews featuring Gary Jules
2004 Do They Know It's Christmas? – Band Aid 20
2005 That's My Goal – Shayne Ward
2006 A Moment Like This – Leona Lewis
2007 When You Believe – Leon Jackson
2008 Hallelujah – Alexandra Burke
2009 Killing In the Name – Rage Against the Machine
2010 When We Collide – Matt Cardle
2011 Wherever You Are – Military Wives & Gareth Malone
2012 He Ain't Heavy, He's My Brother - Justice Collective

LPs

Title	*Group/Artiste*
Abacab	Genesis
Abbey Road	Beatles
Accelerate (1)	R.E.M.
According to My Heart	Jim Reeves
Achtung Baby	U2
Actually	Pet Shop Boys
Adrenalize	Def Leppard
Aerial	Kate Bush
Affection	Lisa Stansfield
Afterburner	ZZ Top
Aftermath	Rolling Stones
The Age of Consent	Bronski Beat
The Age of the Understatement (1)	Last Shadow Puppets
Agent Provocateur	Foreigner
Aja	Steely Dan
Aladdin Sane	David Bowie
Album of the Year	Faith No More
Alf	Alison Moyet
All Change	Cast
All the Lost Souls (1)	James Blunt
All Things Must Pass	George Harrison
Amarantine	Enya
Ancient Heart	Tanita Tikaram
Andromeda Heights	Prefab Sprout
An End Has A Start (1)	Editors
Another Time, Another Place	Bryan Ferry
Anthem	Toyah
The Anvil	Visage
Appetite for Destruction	Guns 'N' Roses
Are You Experienced?	Jimi Hendrix Experience
Are You Gonna Go My Way	Lenny Kravitz
Argus	Wishbone Ash
Armed Forces	Elvis Costello
Arrival	Abba
Astral Weeks	Van Morrison
Atlantic Crossing	Rod Stewart
Atom Heart Mother	Pink Floyd
Attack of the Grey Lantern	Mansun
Auberge	Chris Rea
Autobahn	Kraftwerk
Automatic for the People	R.E.M.
Avalon	Roxy Music
Babylon and On	Squeeze
Back Home (1)	Westlife
Back in Black	AC/DC
Back to Basics	Christina Aguilera
Back to Bedlam	James Blunt
Back to Front (1)	Gilbert O'Sullivan (1972)
Back to Front (1)	Lionel Richie (1992)
Bad	Michael Jackson
Bagsy Me	Wannadies
Band of Gypsies	Jimi Hendrix
Band on the Run	Wings
Batman	Prince
Bat Out Of Hell	Meat Loaf
Beautiful World	Take That
Because of the Times (1)	Kings of Leon
Before the Rain	Eternal
Beggars Banquet	Rolling Stones
Be Here Now (1)	Oasis
Behind the Mask	Fleetwood Mac
The Best Damn Thing (1)	Avril Lavigne
Big Bang	We've Got a Fuzzbox and We're Gonna Use it
Big River	Jimmy Nail
Billion Dollar Babies	Alice Cooper
Black Ice (1)	AC/DC
Black Tie White Noise	David Bowie
Blast	Holly Johnson
Blonde on Blonde	Bob Dylan
Blondes Have More Fun	Rod Stewart
Blood on the Dance Floor (1)	Michael Jackson
Blood Sugar Sex Magik	Red Hot Chili Peppers
Bloody Tourists	10cc
Blue for You	Status Quo
Blue Is the Colour	Beautiful South

Title	*Group/Artiste*
Blue Sky on Mars	Matthew Sweet
Bookends	Simon and Garfunkel
Both Sides	Phil Collins
Boys and Girls	Bryan Ferry
Brand New Eyes (1)	Paramore
Breakfast In America	Supertramp
Breathless	Kenny G
Bridge of Spies	T'Pau
Bridge Over Troubled Water	Simon and Garfunkel
British Steel	Judas Priest
Brothers in Arms	Dire Straits
Buddah and the Chocolate Box	Cat Stevens
Bullet in a Bible	Green Day
Bursting at the Seams	Strawbs
Business as Usual	Men at Work
Cafe Bleu	Style Council
Call off the Search	Katie Melua
Can't Slow Down	Lionel Richie
Captain Fantastic and the Brown Dirt Cowboy	Elton John
Captain Paralytic and the Brown Ale Cowboy	Mike Harding
Caribou	Elton John
Carry On up the Charts	Beautiful South
Catch Bull at Four	Cat Stevens
Celebration (1)	Madonna
Change (1)	Sugababes
China Town	Thin Lizzy
Chorus	Erasure
Circle of One	Oleta Adams
The Circus	Erasure
The Circus (1)	Take That
Cloud Nine	George Harrison
Collection (1)	Travelling Wilburys
Colour	Christians
The Colour and the Shape	Foo Fighters
Colour By Numbers	Culture Club
The Colour of My Love	Celine Dion
Come On Over	Shania Twain
Coming Up	Suede
Communiqué	Dire Straits
Confessions on a Dance Floor	Madonna
Connected	Stereo MCs
Conscience	Womack and Womack
Conversation Peace	Stevie Wonder
Cosmo's Factory	Creedence Clearwater Revival
Cracked Rear View	Hootie and the Blowfish
Crazy Love (1)	Michael Buble
Crazy You	G.U.N.
Cricklewood Green	Ten Years After
Crime of the Century	Supertramp
Crocodiles	Echo and the Bunnymen
Cross of Changes	Enigma
Crossroads	Tracy Chapman
Cuts Both Ways	Gloria Estefan
Dancin' in the Key of Life	Steve Arrington
Dangerous	Michael Jackson
Dare	Human League
Dark Side of the Moon	Pink Floyd
Day & Age (1)	Killers
A Day at the Races	Queen
Daydream	Mariah Carey
Days of Future Passed	Moody Blues
Death Magnetic (1)	Metallica
Demon Days	Gorillaz
Destination Anywhere	Jon Bon Jovi
Destiny	Gloria Estefan
Devil Without a Cause	Kid Rock
Diamond Dogs	David Bowie
Diamond Life	Sade
A Different Beat	Boyzone
Different Class	Pulp
Dig Out Your Soul (1)	Oasis
Dig Your Own Hole	Chemical Brothers
Discovery	Electric Light Orchestra
Disraeli Gears	Cream

Title	*Group/Artiste*
Diva	Annie Lennox
The Division Bell	Pink Floyd
Dizzy Heights	Lightning Seeds
Do It Yourself	The Seahorses
Don't Be Cruel	Bobby Brown
Don't Believe the Truth	Oasis
Don't Shoot Me, I'm Only the Piano Player	Elton John
Dookie	Green Day
Double Fantasy	John Lennon
Down Drury Lane to Memory Lane	One Hundred and One Strings
Down in Albion	Babyshambles
Drag	kd lang
Dreamland	Robert Miles
Dreams Are Nothin' More Than Wishes	David Cassidy
Dr Feelgood	Motley Crue
Duke	Genesis
Eat to the Beat	Blondie
Echo (1)	Leona Lewis
Echoes Silence Patience & Grace (1)	Foo Fighters
Electric Ladyland	Jimi Hendrix Experience
Electric Warrior	T Rex
Elegantly Wasted	INXS
The Element of Freedom (1)	Alicia Keys
Eliminator	ZZ Top
Emergency on Planet Earth	Jamiroquai
Emotional Rescue	Rolling Stones
Employment	Kaiser Chiefs
Endless Flight	Leo Sayer
English Settlement	X-Ray Specs
Enjoy Yourself	Kylie Minogue
Every Good Boy Deserves Favour	Moody Blues
Every Picture Tells a Story	Rod Stewart
Everybody Else Is Doing it, So Why Can't We	Cranberries
Everything Changes	Take That
Everything Must Go	Manic Street Preachers
Exile on Main Street	Rolling Stones
Extra Virgin	Olive
Eyes Open	Snow Patrol
Façades	Sad Cafe
Face to Face	Westlife
Face Value	Phil Collins
Falling Into You	Celine Dion
The Fame (1)	Lady Gaga
Fantastic!	Wham!
Faster Than the Speed of Night	Bonnie Tyler
The Fat of the Land (1)	Prodigy
Favourite Worst Nightmare (1)	Artic Monkeys
Fear of the Dark	Iron Maiden
Fever In Fever Out	Luscious Jackson
The Final Cut	Pink Floyd
Fireball	Deep Purple
First Impressions of Earth	The Strokes
Flaming Pie (1)	Paul McCartney
Flesh and Blood	Roxy Music
Flowers in the Dirt	Paul McCartney
Flying Colours	Chris De Burgh
Fog on the Tyne	Lindisfarne
Foreign Affair	Tina Turner
Forever	Damage
Forever Changes	Love
Forth (1)	Verve
461 Ocean Boulevard	Eric Clapton
Four Symbols	Led Zeppelin
Foxtrot	Genesis
Fresh	Gina G
Fresh Cream	Cream
From the Cradle	Eric Clapton
Funhouse (1)	Pink
The Game	Queen
Germ Free Adolescents	X-Ray Spex
Ghost in the Machine	Police
The Gift	Jam

Title	*Group/Artiste*
Give Me the Reason	Luther Vandross
Glittering Prize	Simple Minds
Goat's Head Soup	Rolling Stones
Going for the One	Yes
Going to a Go-Go	Smokey Robinson & the Miracles
Gold Blade	Hometurf
Goodbye	Cream
Goodbye Cruel World	Elvis Costello
Goodbye Yellow Brick Road	Elton John
Good Girl Gone Bad (1)	Rihanna
Goodnight Vienna	Ringo Starr
Graceland	Paul Simon
Graduation (1)	Kanye West
Graffiti Bridge	Prince
A Grand Don't Come For Free	The Streets
The Great Escape	Blur
Great Expectations	Tasmin Archer
The Great Rock 'N' Roll Swindle	Sex Pistols
Guilty	Barbra Streisand
Handbuilt by Robots (1)	Newton Faulkner
Happy Nation	Ace of Base
Hard Candy (1)	Madonna
Harvest	Neil Young
Headquarters	Monkees
The Healing Game	Van Morrison
Hearsay	Alexander O'Neal
Heaven and Hell	Vangelis
Heavy Soul (1)	Paul Weller
Hedgehog Sandwich	Not the 9 O'Clock News Cast
Hello	Status Quo
Help!	Beatles
Here I Stand (1)	Usher
Hergest Ridge	Mike Oldfield
High on the Happy Side	Wet Wet Wet
Highway 61 Revisited	Bob Dylan
History – Past Present and Future Book	Michael Jackson
Hit	Wannadies
Home Before Dark (1)	Neil Diamond
Hopes and Fears	Keane
Horses	Patti Smith
Hotel California	Eagles
Hot Rats	Frank Zappa
Hounds of Love	Kate Bush
Houses of the Holy	Led Zeppelin
Human Racing	Nik Kershaw
Human's Lib	Howard Jones
Human Touch	Bruce Springsteen
Humbug (1)	Arctic Monkeys
Hunky Dory	David Bowie
Hunting High and Low	A-Ha
The Hurting	Tears for Fears
Hypnotised	Undertones
Hysteria (1)	Def Leppard
Hysteria (3)	Human League
I Am	Earth Wind and Fire
Icky Thump (1)	White Stripes
I Do Not Want What I Haven't Got	Sinead O'Connor
I Dreamed a Dream (1)	Susan Boyle
If the Beatles Had Read Hunter . . . The Singles	Wonder Stuff
The Immaculate Collection	Madonna
In Blue	Corrs
In It for the Money	Supergrass
Innervisions	Stevie Wonder
An Innocent Man	Billy Joel
The Innocents	Erasure
Innuendo	Queen
In Rainbows (1)	Radiohead
Intensive Care	Robbie Williams
Invaders Must Die (1)	Prodigy
In Search of the Lost Chord	Moody Blues
In Square Circle	Stevie Wonder
In Through the Out Door	Led Zeppelin
Into the Gap	Thompson Twins
Invaders Must Die (1)	Prodigy
Invisible Touch	Genesis
I Say I Say I Say	Erasure

Title	*Group/Artiste*
I Should Coco	Supergrass
It Doesn't Matter Anymore	Supernaturals
It's Better to Travel	Swing Out Sister
It's Great When You're ... Straight Yeah!	Black Grape
It's Not Me It's You (1)	Lily Allen
It Won't Be Soon Before Long (1)	Maroon 5
I've Been Expecting You	Robbie Williams
Jagged Little Pill	Alanis Morissette
Jam	Little Angels
John Wesley Harding	Bob Dylan
Join With Us (1)	Feeling
Jollification	Lightning Seeds
The Joshua Tree	U2
Journey Through the Secret Life of Plants	Stevie Wonder
Journey to the Centre of the Earth	Rick Wakeman
Ju Ju	Siouxsie and the Banshees
Jumping All Over the World (1)	Scooter
Junction Seven	Steve Winwood
K	Kula Shaker
Kaleidoscope	Siouxsie and the Banshees
Kavana	Kavana
Keep the Faith	Bon Jovi
Kimono My House	Sparks
Kings of the Wild Frontier	Adam Ant
Konk (1)	Kooks
Koo Koo	Debbie Harry
L	Steve Hillage
Labour of Love	UB40
La Passione	Chris Rea
Ladies and Gentlemen	George Michael
The Last Waltz	The Band
L.A. Woman	Doors
Legend	Bob Marley and the Wailers
Let It Bleed	Rolling Stones
Let's Talk About Love	Celine Dion
The Lexicon of Love	ABC
Lie	Charles Manson
Life	Simply Red
Life After Death	Notorious B.I.G.
Life Thru a Lens	Robbie Williams
Lights (1)	Ellie Goulding
Lil' Darlin'	Thomas Ribeiro
The Lion and the Cobra	Sinead O'Connor
Little Creatures	Talking Heads
Live at the BBC	Beatles
Live in the City of Light	Simple Minds
Liverpool	Frankie Goes to Hollywood
Living in Oz	Rick Springfield
Living in the Material World	George Harrison
Living in the Past	Jethro Tull
The Lone Ranger	Suggs
Long Road Out of Eden	Eagles
Love	Beatles
Love at the Greek	Neil Diamond
Love de Luxe	Sade
Love Hurts	Cher
Love Is the Answer (1)	Barbra Streisand
Love over Gold	Dire Straits
Lovesexy	Prince
Lungs (1)	Florence & The Machine
Machine Head	Deep Purple
Mad Dogs and Englishmen	Joe Cocker
Made in Heaven	Queen
Made of Bricks (1)	Kate Nash
Magic (1)	Bruce Springsteen
Magic and Medicine (1)	Coral
Make It Big	Wham!
Makin' Movies	Dire Straits
Manifesto	Roxy Music
The Man Who	Travis
Meat is Murder	Smiths
Meaty, Beaty, Big and Bouncy	Who
Medusa	Annie Lennox
Middle of Nowhere (1)	Hanson
Millennium	Backstreet Boys

Title	*Group/Artiste*
Minutes to Midnight (1)	Linkin Park
The Miracle	Queen
Mirror Ball	Neil Young
Misplaced Childhood	Marillion
Missing ... Presumed Having a Good Time	Notting Hillbillies
Mondo Bongo	Boomtown Rats
Monster	R.E.M.
The More Things Change	Machine Head
Morning Glory	Oasis
Mother Nature Calls	Cast
Mr Fantasy	Traffic
Mr Wonderful	Fleetwood Mac
Mud Slide Slim and the Blue Horizon	James Taylor
Music Box	Mariah Carey
Music for the Jilted Generation	Prodigy
Music from Big Pink	The Band
My Aim Is True	Elvis Costello
Naked	Talking Heads
Nashville Skyline	Bob Dylan
Natural	Peter Andre
Never a Dull Moment	Rod Stewart
Never for Ever	Kate Bush
Nevermind	Nirvana
Never Mind the Bollocks Here's the Sex Pistols	Sex Pistols
New Boots and Panties!!	Ian Dury & the Blockheads
A New Flame	Simply Red
New Jersey	Bon Jovi
A New World Record	Electric Light Orchestra
A Night at the Opera	Queen
Night Birds	Shakatak
Night Flight to Venus	Boney M
Nightfreak and the Sons of Becker	Coral
A Night on the Town	Rod Stewart
Night Owl	Gerry Rafferty
Nine Lives	Aerosmith
19 (1)	Adele
1982	Status Quo
Nobody Else	Take That
A Nod's as Good as a Wink To a Blind Horse	Faces
No Fences	Garth Brooks
No Jacket Required	Phil Collins
No More Heroes	Stranglers
No Need to Argue	Cranberries
No Parlez	Paul Young
No Sleep till Hammersmith	Motorhead
No Strings Attached	'N Sync
Nothing Like the Sun	Sting
The Number of the Beast	Iron Maiden
Ocean Drive	Lighthouse Family
Oceans of Fantasy	Boney M
Odds and Sods	Who
Off the Wall	Michael Jackson
Ogden's Nut Gone Flake	Small Faces
OK Computer (1)	Radiohead
Old New Borrowed and Blue	Slade
Older	George Michael
On an Island	David Gilmour
Once Upon a Star	Bay City Rollers
Once Upon a Time	Simple Minds
Once Upon a Time in the West (1)	Hard-Fi
One Chance (1)	Paul Potts
One Hot Minute	Red Hot Chili Peppers
On Every Street	Dire Straits
Only By the Night (1)	Kings of Leon
Only Human	Dina Carroll
Only Yesterday	Carpenters
On the Level	Status Quo
On the Threshold of a Dream	Moody Blues
Ooh-La-La	Faces
Open Road (1)	Gary Barlow
Original Pirate Material	The Streets
Our Favourite Shop	Style Council
Out of Control (1)	Girls Aloud

Title	Group/Artiste
Out of Time	R.E.M.
Outlandos d'Amour	Police
Overcome (1)	Alexandra Burke
Oxygene	Jean-Michel Jarre
Parallel Lines	Blondie
Paranoid	Black Sabbath
Parklife	Blur
Pastpresent	Clannad
Pearl	Janis Joplin
Pearls	Elkie Brooks
Perfect Symmetry (1)	Keane
Pet Sounds	Beach Boys
Phuq	Wildhearts
Physical Graffiti	Led Zeppelin
Picture This	Wet Wet Wet
Piece By Piece	Katie Melua
Pieces of You	Jewel
Pills 'N' Thrills and Bellyaches	Happy Mondays
Pin-Ups	David Bowie
Piper at the Gates of Dawn	Pink Floyd
Pisces, Aquarius, Capricorn and Jones Ltd	Monkees
Play (1)	Moby
The Pleasure Principle	Gary Numan
Pocketful of Kryptonite	Spin Doctors
Pop	U2
Popped in Souled Out	Wet Wet Wet
Porcupine	Echo and the Bunnymen
Pornography	Cure
Postcard	Mary Hopkin
Pot Luck	Elvis Presley
Presence	Led Zeppelin
Private Collection	Cliff Richard
Private Dancer	Tina Turner
The Promise (1)	Il Divo
Promises and Lies	UB40
Prophets, Seers and Sages	T Rex
Protection	Massive Attack
Pull the Pin (1)	Stereophonics
Pulse	Pink Floyd
Pump	Aerosmith
Pump Up the Jam	Technotronic
Push	Bros
A Question of Balance	Moody Blues
Quick Step and Side Kick	Thompson Twins
Rage	T'Pau
Rage in Eden	Ultravox
Ram	Paul and Linda McCartney
Rattle and Hum	U2
The Raw and the Cooked	Fine Young Cannibals
Ready for the Weekend (1)	Calvin Harris
Real Things	2 Unlimited
Reality Killed the Video Star	Robbie Williams
Red River Valley	Slim Whitman
Regatta de Blanc	Police
Relapse (1)	Eminem
Reload	Tom Jones
Reminiscing	Buddy Holly and the Crickets
Replicas	Tubeway Army
Republic	New Order
The Resistance (1)	Muse
Return of the Space Cowboy	Jamiroquai
Return to Fantasy	Uriah Heep
Revenge	Eurythmics
Revolver	Beatles
Rhythm of the Saints	Paul Simon
The Riddle	Nik Kershaw
Rising from the East	Bally Sagoo
Rockferry (1)	Duffy
Roping the Wind	Garth Brooks
Rubber Soul	Beatles
Rumours	Fleetwood Mac
Rum, Sodomy and the Lash	Pogues
Runaway Horses	Belinda Carlisle
Said and Done	Boyzone
Saturday Night	Zhane
Savage	Eurythmics
Scary Monsters and Super Creeps	David Bowie

Title	Group/Artiste
Script for a Jester's Tear	Marillion
The Secret of Association	Paul Young
The Seeds of Love	Tears for Fears
Sensational	Michelle Gayle
Sentimental Journey	Ringo Starr
Sergeant Pepper's Lonely Hearts Club Band	Beatles
Seven and the Ragged Tiger	Duran Duran
Seventh Son of a Seventh Son	Iron Maiden
Share My World	Mary J. Blige
Shaved Fish	John Lennon
Shelter	Brand New Heavies
Shepherd Moons	Enya
She's So Unusual	Cyndi Lauper
She's the Boss	Mick Jagger
Silk and Steel	Five Star
Singles	Alison Moyet
The Six Wives of Henry VIII	Rick Wakeman
Sleeping with the Past	Elton John
Sleep Through the Static (1)	Jack Johnson
The Slider	T Rex
Slippery When Wet	Bon Jovi
Slowhand	Eric Clapton
Smiler	Rod Stewart
The Smoker You Drink The Player You Get	Joe Walsh
So	Peter Gabriel
So Far So Good	Bryan Adams
Solitude Standing	Suzanne Vega
So Long So Wrong	Alison Krauss and Union Station
Some Friendly	Charlatans
So Much for the City	The Thrills
Song Bird	Eva Cassidy
The Song Remains the Same	Led Zeppelin
Songs About Jane	Maroon 5
Songs For My Mother (1)	Ronan Keating
Songs in the Key of Life	Stevie Wonder
Songs of Faith and Devotion	Depeche Mode
The Soul Cages	Sting
Soul Provider	Michael Bolton
Sound of Lies	Jayhawks
Sparkle in the Rain	Simple Minds
Spartacus	Farm
Speak and Spell	Depeche Mode
Spellbound	Paula Abdul
Spirit (1)	Leona Lewis
Spirits Having Flown	Bee Gees
Sports Car	Judie Tzuke
Stadium Arcadium	Red Hot Chili Peppers
Standing Stone	Paul McCartney
Stand Up	Jethro Tull
Stanley Road	Paul Weller
Staring at the Sun	U2
Stars	Simply Red
Station to Station	David Bowie
Stay on These Roads	A-Ha
Steel Wheels	Rolling Stones
Steeltown	Big Country
Step by Step	New Kids on the Block
Sticky Fingers	Rolling Stones
Still Crazy after All These Years	Paul Simon
Still Waters	Bee Gees
Stop the Clocks	Oasis
Stranded	Roxy Music
The Stranger	Billy Joel
Street Fighting Years	Simple Minds
String of Hits	Shadows
Stripped	Rolling Stones
Stupidity	Dr Feelgood
Sunny Side Up (1)	Paolo Nutini
Supernatural	Santana
Surrealistic Pillow	Jefferson Airplane
Sweet Baby James	James Taylor
Symbol	Prince
Synchronicity	Police
Take Two	Robson and Jerome
Tales from Topographic Oceans	Yes
Talk On Corners	Corrs

Title	Group/Artiste
Talking Back to the Night	Steve Winwood
Talking Book	Stevie Wonder
Talking with the Taxman about Poetry	Billy Bragg
Tango in the Night	Fleetwood Mac
Tanx	T Rex
Tapestry	Carole King
A Tapestry of Dreams	Charles Aznavour
Take Me Home	One Direction
Tarkus	Emerson, Lake and Palmer
Tears and Laughter	Johnny Mathis
Tease Me	Chaka Demus and Pliers
Teaser and the Firecat	Cat Stevens
Technique	New Order
Telekon	Gary Numan
Tell Me on a Sunday	Marti Webb
Tellin' Stories	The Charlatans
10	Wet Wet Wet
Ten	Pearl Jam
Ten Good Reasons	Jason Donovan
Tennis	Chris Rea
The Man and His Music	Sam Cooke
This Is the Life (1)	Amy MacDonald
3 Words (1)	Cheryl Cole
Thriller	Michael Jackson
Through the Barricades	Spandau Ballet
Thunder and Lightning	Thin Lizzy
Time for Healing	Sounds of Blackness
Timeless	Sarah Brightman
To Lose My Life (1)	White Lies
To the Extreme	Vanilla Ice
To the Faithful Departed	Cranberries
Together Through Life (1)	Bob Dylan
Touch	Eurythmics
Tragic Kingdom	No Doubt
Transformer	Lou Reed
Travelling without Moving	Jamiroquai
The Trick To Life (1)	Hoosiers
Trout Mask Replica	Captain Beefheart and his Magic Band
True Stories	Talking Heads
Tubular Bells	Mike Oldfield
Tuesday Night Music Club	Sheryl Crow
Tug of War	Paul McCartney
Tunnel of Love	Bruce Springsteen
Turn Back the Clock	Johnny Hates Jazz
Turn It Upside Down	Spin Doctors
Tusk	Fleetwood Mac
12 Gold Bars	Status Quo
21	Adele
21st Century Breakdown (1)	Green Day
21 Today	Cliff Richard
U.F. Orb	Orb
22 Dreams (1)	Paul Weller
Ultra	Depeche Mode
Under the Iron Sea	Keane
Under the Pink	Tori Amos
Undiscovered	James Morrison
The Unforgettable Fire	U2
Universal Soldier	Donovan

Title	Group/Artiste
Up	Right Said Fred
Up All Night	One Direction
Upstairs at Eric's	Yazoo
Urban Hymns (1)	Verve
Use Your Illusion	Guns 'N' Roses
Vauxhall and I	Morrissey
Very	Pet Shop Boys
Viva Hate	Morrissey
Voice of Love	Diana Ross
Voices from the Holy Land	Aled Jones
Voodo Lounge	Rolling Stones
Voulez-Vous	Abba
Wake Up!	Boo Radleys
Waking Up the Neighbours	Bryan Adams
Walking Wounded	Everything But the Girl
Walthamstow	East 17
Wanted	Yazz
War	U2
Water Sign	Chris Rea
Watermark	Enya
We All Had Doctors' Papers	Max Boyce
We Are the Night (1)	Chemical Brothers
We Can Make It	Peters and Lee
We Can't Dance	Genesis
We'll Live And Die in These Towns (1)	Enemy
We'll Meet Again (1)	Vera Lynn
We Started Nothing (1)	Ting Tings
We Too Are One	Eurythmics
Welcome to the Pleasuredome	Frankie Goes to Hollywood
Welcome to Wherever You Are	INXS
West Ryder Pauper Lunatic Asylum (1)	Kasabian
Whatever People Say I am, That's What I'm Not	Arctic Monkeys
Whatever You Want	Status Quo
When the World Knows Your Name	Deacon Blue
Where We Belong	Boyzone
Whipped Cream and Other Delights	Herb Alpert and the Tijuana Brass
White Feathers	Kajagoogoo
White on Blonde	Texas
The Whole Story	Kate Bush
Wicked Game	Chris Isaak
Wild!	Erasure
Wild Wood	Paul Weller
Wish	Cure
Wish You Were Here	Pink Floyd
Women and Captain First	Captain Sensible
Words of Love	Buddy Holly and the Crickets
Working On a Dream (1)	Bruce Springsteen
Wu-Tang Forever	Wu-Tang Clan
You and Me Both	Yazoo
Young Americans	David Bowie
Your Secret Love	Luther Vandross
You Showed Me	Lightning Seeds
Youthquake	Dead or Alive
Zenyatta Mondatta	Police
Zooropa	U2

Nationalities of Pop Groups and Soloists

Abba Sweden and Norway
AC/DC UK and Australia
Adamski UK
Air Supply UK and Australia
Alphabeat Denmark
Alphaville Germany
Aneka UK
Angry Anderson Australia
Anthrax USA
Aphrodite's Child Greece
Aqua Denmark
Babyshambles UK
Baccara Spain
Basia Poland
Belle Stars UK
Black Box Italy
Boney M Jamaica, Antilles, Montserrat
Boris Gardiner Jamaica
Cappella Italy
Cardigans Sweden
Catatonia Wales
Champs Boys France
Chicory Tip UK
Coral UK
Crowded House Australia and NZ
Curved Air UK
Cutting Crew UK and Canada
Danny Mirror Holland
Darts UK
Deee-Lite USA, Russia and Japan
Del Amitri UK
Eddy Grant Guyana
Edmund Hockridge Canada
Emile Ford UK
Enigma Germany and Romania
Enya Ireland
Europe Sweden
Father Abraham Holland
Fleetwood Mac UK and USA
Foreigner UK and USA
Fox UK and USA
FPI Project Italy

Franz Ferdinand Scotland
Funkadelic USA
Gallagher and Lyle UK
Gibson Brothers Martinique
Go-Gos USA
Golden Earring Holland
Greyhound Jamaica
Guess Who Canada
Hawkwind UK (German dancer)
Helmut Zacharias Germany
Hothouse Flowers Ireland
Human Resource Holland
Icehouse New Zealand
Incognito UK and France
Inner Circle Jamaica
Jam and Spoon Germany
Jam Machine Italy
Jam Tronik Germany
Jan Hammer Czechoslovakia
John Farnham Australia
John Parr UK
John Paul Young Australia
JT and the Big Family Italy
Kaoma France
Keane UK
Kraftwerk Germany
Lobo (70s band) USA
Lobo (80s band) Holland
Mai Tai Holland
Manfred Mann South Africa
M/A/R/R/S UK
Martha and the Muffins Canada
Martika USA
McFly UK
Men at Work Australia
Men Without Hats Canada
Mental As Anything Australia
Metallica USA and Denmark
Mezzoforte Iceland
Midnight Oil Australia
Milk and Honey Israel
Millie Jamaica
Milli Vanilli France and Germany
Mixmaster Italy
Modern Talking Germany
Mouth and MacNeal Holland
New Seekers UK
Norman Greenbaum USA
Opus Austria
Ottawan France
Pasadenas UK
Patsy Gallant Canada
Peppers France
Percy Faith Canada
Perez Prado Cuba
Plastic Bertrand Belgium
Poppy Family Canada
Praga Khan Belgium
Prefab Sprout UK
Pseudo Echo Australia
Python Lee Jackson Australia
Razorlight England and Sweden
Rob 'N' Raz (featuring Leila K) Sweden
Roxette Sweden
Rozalla Zimbabwe
Rush Canada
Shocking Blue Holland
Silver Convention Germany and USA
Snap Germany and USA
Soeur Sourire (Singing Nun) Belgium
Spagna Italy
Split Enz New Zealand and UK
Starlight Italy
Starsound Holland
Stereophonics Wales
Sweet People France
Sylvia Sweden
Teach-In Holland
Technotronic Belgium
Ten Sharp Holland
Third World Jamaica
Thomas Dolby UK
Thompson Twins New Zealand and UK
Thrills Ireland
2 Unlimited Holland
Vanessa Paradis France
Van Halen Holland and USA
Whigfield Denmark
Wigan's Chosen Few USA
Wombats UK
Yello Switzerland
Zucchero Italy
Zutons UK

Composition of Pop Groups

A1
Ben Adams
Christian Ingebrigtsen
Paul Marazzi
Mark Read

ABBA
Benny Andersson
Agnetha Fältskog
Anni-Frid Lyngstad
Björn Ulvaeus
Swedish group except for the Norwegian brunette Anni-Frid Lyngstad

ABC
Martin Fry – Vocals
Mark Lickley – Bass
Dave Robinson – Drums
Steve Singleton – Saxophone
Mark White – Guitar

AC/DC
Dave Evans – Vocals (left 1977)
Mark Evans – Bass
Brian Johnson – Vocals (replaced Bon Scott)
Phil Rudd – Drums (Left in 1982)
Bon Scott – Vocals (previously drums, died 1980)
Chris Slade
Cliff Williams (replaced Dave Evans)
Simon Wright (replaced Phil Rudd)
Angus Young – Lead Guitar
Malcolm Young – Guitar

Ace of Base
Jonas 'Joker' Berggren
Jenny Berggren
Linn Berggren
Ulf 'Buddha' Ekberg

Adam and the Ants
Matthew Ashman – Guitar and Piano
Melanie Blatt
Dave Barbe 'Barbarossa' – Drums
Johnny Bivouac – Guitar
Stuart Goddard (Adam) – Lead Vocals and Guitar
Jordan – Vocals
Andy Warren – Bass

Aerosmith
Jimmy Crespo – Guitar (joined after Whitfield left)
Rick Dufay – Guitar (joined after Whitfield left)
Tom Hamilton – Bass
Joey Kramer – Drums
Joe Perry – Guitar
Ray Tabano – Guitar (replaced by Brad Whitfield)
Steve Tyler – Lead Vocals
Brad Whitfield – Guitar (left in 1980)

A-Ha
Magne Furuholmen – Keyboards, Guitar, Backing Vocals
Morten Harket – Lead Vocals
Paul Waaktaar-Savoy – Guitar and Backing Vocals

Airforce
Ginger Baker – Drums and Percussion
Graham Bond – Saxophone
Rick Grech – Bass and Violin
Jeanette Jacobs – Vocals
Remi Kabaka – Percussion
Denny Laine – Guitar
Steve Winwood – Guitar, Keyboards and Vocals
Chris Wood – Saxophone and Flute

Alarm, The
Eddie MacDonald – Guitar and Vocals
Mike Peters – Bass and Vocals
Dave Sharp – Guitar and Vocals
Mark Taylor – Keyboards
Nigel Twist – Drums

All Saints
Natalie Appleton
Nicole Appleton
Robert Henrit – Drums and Percussion

Shaznay Lewis

Alphabat
Anders B – Guitar
Stine Bramsen – Vocals
Troels Hansen – Drums
Rasmus Nagel – Keyboards
Anders Reinholdt – Bass
Anders SG – Vocals

Altered Images
Michael 'Tich' Anderson – Drums
Caesar – Guitar
Claire Grogan – Vocals
Tony McDaid – Guitar
Johnny McElhone – Bass

Amazulu
Sharon Bailey – Percussion
Lesley Beach – Saxophone
Debbie Evans – Drums
Clare Henny – Bass
Rose Minor – Vocals
Margo Sagov – Guitar

Amen Corner
Dennis Bryon – Drums
Andy Fairweather Lowe – Guitar and Lead Vocals
Alan Jones – Saxophone
Neil Jones – Guitar
Mike Smith – Saxophone
Clive Taylor – Bass
Blue Weaver – Guitar

Animals
Vic Briggs – Bass
George Bruno – Keyboards and Vocals
Eric Burdon – Vocals
Charles 'Chas' Chandler – Bass
Luke Francis – Guitar and Vocals
Barry Jenkins – Drums and Percussion
Danny McCullough – Bass, Guitar and Vocals
Zoot Money – Organ
Alan Price – Piano and Vocals
Dave Rowberry – Organ
Andy Somers – Guitar
John Steele – Drums
Hilton Valentine – Guitar
John Weider – Guitar, Violin and Bass

Another Level
Mark Baron
Dane Bowers
Bobak Kianoush
Wayne Williams

Aphrodite's Child
Silver Koulouris – Guitar and Percussion
Vangelis Papathanassiou – Keyboards, Flute and Vocals
Demis Roussos – Vocals
Lucas Sideras – Drums and Vocals

Aqua
René Dif – Bald-headed Vocalist Claus Noreen
Lene Nystrom – Lead Vocalist
Soren Rasted
Danish group except for Nystrom, who is Norwegian

Arctic Monkeys
Jamie Cook – Guitar and Vocals
Matt Helders – Drums
Nick O'Malley – Bass
Alex Turner – Vocals and Guitar
Glyn Jones – Vocals (replaced by Turner)
Andy Nicholson – Bass (replaced by O'Malley)

Argent
Rod Argent – Keyboards and Vocals
Russ Ballard – Guitar, Piano and Vocals
Jim Grimaldi – Guitar
Jim Rodford – Bass and Vocals
John Verity – Guitar and Vocals

Art of Noise
Anne Dudley – Keyboards
JJ Jeczalik – Keyboards

Ash
Mark Hamilton – Bass
Charlotte Hatherly – Guitar
Rick 'Rock' McMurray – Drums
Tim Wheeler – Vocals, Guitar

Asia
Geoff Downes – Keyboards
Steve Howe – Guitar
Greg Lake – Vocals and Bass
Mandy Meyer – Guitar
Carl Palmer – Drums
John Payne – Vocals and Bass
Al Pitrelli – Guitar
John Wetton – Vocals and Bass

Aswad
Donnal Benjamin – Guitar and Vocals
Brinsley Forde – Guitar and Vocals
Tony Gadd – Bass
Angus 'Drummie Zeb' Gaye – Drums
Donald 'Dee' Griffiths – Guitar
Courtney Hemmings – Keyboards
Bunny McKenzie – Harmonica and Vocals
Candy McKenzie – Vocals
George 'Ras' Oban – Bass
Tony Robinson – Bass and Keyboards

Atomic Kitten
Jenny Frost
Natasha Hamilton
Liz McLarnon
Kerry McFadden (née Katona) – replaced by Jenny Frost

Atomic Rooster
Steve Bolton – Guitar
John Cann – Guitar and Vocals
Vincent Crane – Keyboards and Vocals
Chris Farlowe – Vocals
Pete Frenchy – Vocals
Paul Hammond – Drums and Percussion
Johnny Mandala – Guitar
Carl Palmer – Drums and Percussion
Ric Parnell – Drums and Percussion

Average White Band
Roger Ball – Keyboards and Saxophone
Malcolm Duncan – Saxophone
Alan Gorrie – Vocals
Robbie Mcintosh – Drums and Percussion
Onnie Mcintyre – Guitar and Vocals
Hamish Stuart – Bass, Guitar and Vocals

Aztec Camera
Roddy Frame – Guitar and Vocals
Dave Mulholland – Drums
Campbell Owens – Bass

B-52s, The
Fred Schneider – Keyboards and Vocals
Kate Pierson – Organ and Vocals
Keith Strickland – Drums
Cindy Wilson – Guitar and Vocals
Ricky Wilson – Guitar

Babyshambles
Gemma Clarke – Drums (left in 2005)
Pete Doherty – Guitar and Vocals
Adam Ficek – Drums (replaced Gemma Clarke)
Drew McConnell – Bass
Patrick Walden – Guitar

Bachelors
Con and Declan Cluskey
John Stokes

Backstreet Boys
Nick Carter
Howie Dorough
Brian Littrell
AJ McLean
Kevin Richardson

Bad Manners
Buster Bloodvessel – Vocals
Louis Cook – Guitar and Vocals
Dave Farren – Bass
Paul Hyman – Trumpet
Chris Kane – Tenor Sax
Andrew Marson – Alto Sax
Alan Sayag – Harmonica and Vocals
Martin Stewart – Keyboards
Brian Tuitt – Drums

Badfinger
Tom Evans – Bass, Guitar and Vocals
Mike Gibbons – Drums
Pete Ham – Vocals
Joey Molland – Guitar and Vocals

Bananarama
Sarah Dallin
Siobhan Fahey (left 1987 and formed Shakespears Sister)
Jacquie O'Sullivan (1988–1991)
Keren Woodward

Band, The
Rick Danko – Bass and Vocals
Levon Helm – Drums, Keyboards and Vocals
Garth Hudson – Accordion, Keyboards and Saxophone
Richard Manuel – Harmonica, Drums, Sax, Organ and Vocals
Robbie Robertson – Guitar, Keyboards and Vocals

Band of Gypsies, The
Billy Cox – Bass
Jimi Hendrix – Guitar and Vocals
Buddy Miles – Drums

Bangles, The
Lyne Elklnad – Guitar, Vocals (replaced by Susanna Hoffs)
Susanna Hoffs – Vocals, Rhythm Guitar
Amanda Mills – Vocals, Bass (replaced by Annette Zilinkas
Debbi Peterson – Vocals, Drums
Vicki Peterson – Vocals, Lead Guitar
Michael 'Mickis' Steele – Bass and Vocals
Annette Zilinkas – Bass, Harmonica

Bardot
Belinda Chapple
Sophie Monk
Sally Polyhronas
Katie Underwood (left in May 2001)
Tiffany Wood
Winners of the Australian 'Popstars', disbanded in May 2002

Barron Knights, The
Barron Anthony – Vocals
Butch Baker – Guitar and Vocals
Dave Ballinger – Drums
Duke D'Mond – Vocals
Peanuts Langford – Guitar and Vocals

Bay City Rollers
Eric Faulkner – Guitar, Mandolin and Vocals
Alan Longmuir – Accordion, Bass, Piano and Vocals
Derek Longmuir – Drums and Percussion
Les McKeown – Guitar and Lead Vocals
Ian Mitchell – Guitar and Vocals
Stuart Wood – Bass, Guitar, Piano and Vocals

Beach Boys
Glen Campbell – Guitar and Vocals
Blondie Chapman
Ricky Fataar
Al Jardine – Rhythm Guitar and Vocals
Bruce Johnstone
Mike Love – Lead Vocals
David Marks
John Stamos
Brian Wilson – Vocals, Keyboard and Bass
Carl Wilson – Vocals and Guitar
Dennis Wilson – Drums

Beastie Boys
Michael Diamond
Adam Horowitz
Adam Yauch

Beatles, The
Pete Best – Drums
George Harrison – Lead Guitar and Vocals
John Lennon – Vocals, Guitar, Harmonica and Piano
Paul McCartney – Vocals, Bass, Guitar and Piano
Ringo Starr – Drums
Stu Sutcliffe – Guitar and Vocals
Brian Epstein – Manager (died in 1967)

Beautiful South
Jacqui Abbot – Vocals
Briana Corrigan – Vocals (replaced by Jacqui Abbot in 1994)
Paul Heaton – Vocals
David Hemmingway – Drums
David Rotheray – Guitar
David Stead – Drums
Sean Welch – Bass

Bee Gees
Barry Gibb
Maurice Gibb (died 12 Jan 2003)
Robin Gibb (died 20 May 2012)

Bellamy Brothers, The
David Bellamy – Vocals
Howard Bellamy – Vocals
Richard Bennett – Guitar
King Errison – Percussion
Alan Estes – Drums
Emory Gordy – Bass

B*witched
Lindsay Armaou
Edele Lynch
Keavy Lynch
Sinead O'Carroll

Big Brother and the Holding Company
Peter Albin – Bass and Vocals
Sam Andrew – Guitar and Vocals
David Getz – Drums and Vocals
James Gurley – Guitar and Vocals
Janis Joplin – Lead Vocals

Big Country
Stuart Adamson – Lead Vocals and Guitar (died 2001)
Pat Ahern – Drums
Mark Brzezicki – Drums
Tony Butler – Bass and Vocals
Bruce Watson – Guitar and Vocals

Björn Again
Benny Anderwear
Agnetha Falstart
Frida Longstokin
Bjorn Volvo-us
Australian tribute-band backed by Ola Drumkitt and Rutger Sonofagunn

Black Box
Daniele Davoli – Lead Vocals
Mirko Limoni
Valeno Semplici

Black Eyed Peas
Will.ia.m (born William Adams)
apl.de.ap (born Allan Pineda)
Fergie (born Stacy Ann Ferguson)
Taboo (born Jaime Gomez)
Duncan James

Dante Santiago (1992–95)
Kim Hill (1995–2000)

Black Sabbath
Vinnie Apice – Drums
Terry 'Geezer' Butler – Bass
Ian Gillan – Vocals
Glen Hughes – Vocals
Tony Iommi – Guitar
Ronnie James – Vocals (replaced by Ian Gillan)
Geoff Nicols – Keyboards
Ozzy Osbourne – Vocals and Harmonica (replaced by James)
Cozy Powell – Drums
Eric Singer – Drums
Dave Spitz – Bass
Rick Wakeman – Keyboard
Bill Ward – Drums

Blazin' Squad
DJ Tommy B
Flava
MC Freek
Kenzie
Krazy
Melo-D
Reepa
Rocky B
Spike-E
Strider

Blind Faith
Ginger Baker – Drums
Eric Clapton – Lead Guitar
Rick Grech – Bass and Violin
Steve Winwood – Vocals

Bloc Party
Russell Lissack – Lead Guitar
George Moakes – Bass
Kele Okereke – Vocals and Guitar
Matt Tong – Drums

Blodwyn Pig
Mick Abrahams – Guitar and Vocals
Ron Berg – Drums and Percussion
Jack Lancaster – Cornet, Saxophone and Violin
Andy Pile – Bass

Blondie
Clement Burke – Drums
Paul Carbonara – Guitar
James Destri – Keyboard
Leigh Foxx – Bass
Debbie Harry – Lead Vocals
Nigel Harrison – Bass
Frank Infante – Guitar
Chris Stein – Guitar

Blood, Sweat and Tears
Dave Bergeron – Trombone and Tuba
David Clayton-Thomas – Vocals
Bobby Colomby – Drums
Jim Fielder – Bass
Jerry Hyman – Trombone
Steve Katz – Guitar, Harmonica and Vocals
Tom Klatka – Trumpet
Al Kooper – Guitar, Keyboards and Vocals
Jerry La Croix – Saxophone and Vocals
Fred Lipsius – Saxophone and Piano
Ron McLure – Bass
Dick Nalligan – Keyboards
Alan Rubin – Trumpet
Lou Soloff – Trumpet
William Tillman – Saxophone
George Wadenius – Guitar
Larry Willis – Keyboards
Chuck Winfield – Trumpet

Blue
Anthony Costa
Lee Ryan
Simon Webbe

Blur
Damon Albarn – Lead Vocals and Keyboards
Graham Coxon – Guitar
Alex James – Bass
Dave Rowntree – Drums

Bon Jovi
Jon Bon Jovi – Lead Vocals and Guitar
Richie Sambora – Lead Guitar
Dave Bryan – Keyboardist
Tico Torres – Drums
Alec John Such – Bass (replaced by Hugh McDonald)
Hugh McDonald – Bass

Boney M
Marcia Barrett
Bobby Farrell
Liz Mitchell
Maisie Williams

Bonzo Dog Doo-Dah Band
Vernon Dudley Bowhay-Nowell – Percussion
Glen Colson – Drums
Neil Innes – Guitar, Piano and Vocals
Rodney Slater – Saxophone
Larry 'Legs' Smith – Drums
Roger Ruskin Spear – Percussion, Saxophone, Trumpet
Sam Spoons – Acoustic Bass and Percussion
Vivian Stanshall – Lead Vocals and Various Instruments

Boomtown Rats
Pete Briquette – Bass and Vocals
Gerry Cott – Guitar
Simon Crowe – Drums and Vocals
Johnny Fingers – Keyboards
Bob Geldof – Lead Vocals
Gary Roberts – Guitar and Vocals

Bow Wow Wow
Matthew Ashman – Guitar and Vocals
Dave Barbe 'Barbarossa' – Drums
Leigh Gorman – Bass and Vocals
Annabella Lu-Win – Lead Vocals

Boyz II Men
Mike McCaryl
Nathan Morris
Wanya Morris
Shawn Stockman

Boyzone
Keith Duffy
Stephen Gately
Mikey Graham
Ronan Keating
Shane Lynch

Bread
Mike Botts – Drums and Percussion
David Gates – Lead Vocals, Guitar, Keyboards, Violin, Bass
James Griffin – Guitar, Keyboards and Vocals
Larry Knechtel – Harmonica (replaced Rob Royer)
Rob Royer – Vocals, Guitar and Keyboards

British Sea Power
Hamilton (Neil Wilkinson) – Bass
Noble (Martin Noble) – Guitar and Keyboards
Wood (Matthew Wood) – Drums
Yan (Scott Wilkinson) – Vocals and Guitar

Bronski Beat
Steve Bronski – Keyboards
John Foster – Vocals (replaced Jimmy Somerville in 1986)
Jimmy Somerville – Lead Vocals
Larry Steinbeck – Keyboards

Bros
Matt Goss
Luke Goss
Craig Logan

Brotherhood of Man
Tony Burrows (founder member left before Eurovision)
Sue Glover (founder member left before Eurovision)
Johnny Goodison (founder member left before Eurovision)
Roger Greenaway (founder member left before Eurovision)
Martin Lee (Eurovision winner)
Sunny Leslie (founder member left before Eurovision success)
Lee Sheriden (Eurovision winner)
Nicky Stevens (Eurovision winner)
Sandra Stevens (Eurovision winner)
Russell Stone (founder member left before Eurovision)
Tony Burrows was also lead singer with The Ivy League, White Plains, Flowerpot Men, Pipkins and Edison Lighthouse

Bucks Fizz
Jay Aston
Cheryl Baker
Bobby G (real name Robert Gubby)
Mike Nolan
Shelley Preston (replaced Jay Aston in 1985)
David Van Day (ex Dollar) replaced Mike Nolan in 1995 but then formed another version of the band with Nolan, whilst Bobby G continued as the only founder member of his version. When Nolan left after a dispute with Van Day, Bobby G sued for improper use of name and although it was originally found in favour of Van Day in 2001 the verdict was set aside out of court in 2002 and Bobby G was given the proprietary use of the group's name whilst the other version was then called David Van Day's Bucks Fizz.

Buffalo Springfield
Richie Furay – Guitar and Vocals
Doug Hastings – Vocals
Dewey Martin – Drums
Jim Messina – Bass and Vocals
Bruce Palmer – Bass
Stephen Stills – Guitar and Piano
Neil Young – Guitar and Vocals

Buggles
Geoff Downes – Keyboards
Trevor Horn – Vocals and Various Instruments

Busted
Charlie Simpson
Matt Jay
James Bourne

Buzzcocks
Garth Davies – Bass
Howard Deveto – Vocals
Steve Diggle – Bass and Guitar
Steve Garvey – Bass
John Maher – Drums
Pete Shelley – Guitar and Vocals

Byrds, The
Skip Battin
Gene Clark (co-founder but left in 1966 and died in 1991)
Michael Clarke – Drums (founding member, died in 1993)
David Crosby – Guitar and Vocals (founding member)
John Guerin
Chris Hillman – Bass and Mandolin (founding member)
Kevin Kelley
Roger McGuinn – Lead Vocals and Guitar (founding member)
Gene Parsons – Drums (replaced David Crosby)
Gram Parsons – Guitar
Clarence White – Guitar
John York
Two of the five founding members have now died, but the other three get together with various combinations of the above-named musicians to perform as The Byrds, although the last gig by the original five was in 1991.

Calling, The
Alex Band – Lead Vocals
Aaron Kamin – Guitar
Billy Mohler – Bass
Nate Wood – Drums
Sean Woolstenhulme – Guitar

Captain and Tennille
Daryl Dragon – Keyboards
Toni Tennille – Lead Vocals

Carpenters, The
Karen Carpenter – Vocals and Drums
Richard Carpenter – Vocals and Piano

Catatonia
Paul Jones – Bass
Dafydd Ieuan – Drums (left 1995 to join Super Furry Animals)
Cerys Matthews – Lead Vocals
Clancy Pegg – Keyboard (left in 1995)
Owen Powell – Guitar (joined after Ieuan and Pegg left)
Aled Richards – Drums (replaced Dafydd Ieuan)
Mark Roberts – Guitar

CCS (Collective Consciousness Society)
Alexis Korner – Vocals, Guitar
Peter Thorup – Vocals
Various guest musicians including
Tony Carr – Drums
Herbie Flowers – Bass
Henry Lowther – Trumpet

Chairmen of the Board
General Norman Johnson – Lead Vocals
Ken Knox – Saxophone
Danny Woods – Vocals

Charlatans
John Baker – Guitar
Martin Blunt – Bass (nervous breakdown after Baker left)
Jon Brookes – Drums
Tim Burgess – Lead Vocals
Mark Collins – Guitar (replaced John Baker)
Rob Collins – Organ (died in a car crash 23 July 1996)
Tony Rogers – Keyboards

Chemical Brothers
Tom Rowlands
Ed Simons

Chic
Bernard Edwards – Bass (died 1996)
Nile Rodgers – Guitar

Chicago
DaWane Bailey (joined temporarily between 1991 and 1993)
Peter Cetera – Vocals & Bass (founding member left 1985)
Bill Champlin – Keyboards (joined in 1982)
Donnie Dacus – Guitar (replaced Kath after shooting accident)
Marty Grebb – Saxophone and Guitars (briefly played in 1981)
Keith Howland – Guitars (joined in 1995)
Tris Imboden – Drums (replaced Danny Seraphine in 1991)
Terry Kath – Guitar and Vocals (founding member died 1978)
Robert Lamm – Keyboard and Vocals (founding member)
Lee Loughnane – Trumpet and Percussion (founding member)
Laudir De Oliveira – Congas, Bongos and Percussion (1974–82)
James Pankow – Trombone (founding member)
Walter Parazaider (Walt Perry) – Saxophone (founding member)
Chris Pinnick – Guitar (replaced Dacus in 1980, left in 1981)
Jason Scheff – (replaced Peter Cetera in 1985)
Danny Seraphine – Drums and Percussion (founding member)
Steven Stills – Guitar (replaced by Chris Pinnick)
Originally named Chicago Transit Authority when having their first hit 'I'm a Man' but forced to change it after being threatened with legal action by Mayor Richard Daley.

Clash, The
Terry Chimes – Drums (replaced by Topper Headon in 1977)
Topper Headon – Drums
Mick Jones – Guitar and Vocals
Paul Simonon – Bass
Joe Strummer – Lead Vocals and Guitar (died December 2002)

Cliff Richard and The Shadows
Cliff Richard – Vocals
See separate entry for The Shadows

Coldcut
Matt Black
Jonathan Moore

Coldplay
Guy Berryman – Bass
Jon Buckland – Guitar
Will Champion – Drums
Chris Martin – Lead Vocals, Keyboard

Commodores, The
William King – Trumpet
Ronald LaPread – Bass
Thomas McClary – Guitar
JD Nicholas – (formerly of Heatwave, replaced Lionel Richie)
Walter 'Clyde' Orange – Drums
Lionel Richie – Lead Vocals, Piano and Saxophone
Milan Williams – Keyboards

Communards
Richard Coles – Keyboard
Jimmy Somerville – Vocals

Coral, The
Paul Duffy – Bass and Saxophone
Nick Power – Keyboards and Vocals
Bill Ryder-Jones – Guitar and Trumpet
Ian Skelly – Drums
James Skelly – Lead Vocals
Lee Southall – Guitar and Vocals

Corrs, The
Andrea Corr – Lead Vocals
Caroline Corr – Drums and Vocals
Jim Corr – Guitar and Keyboard
Sharon Corr – Violin and Vocals

Courteeners, The
Michael Campbell – Drums and Vocals
Mark Cuppello – Bass
Liam Fray – Guitar and Lead Vocals
Daniel Conan Moores – Guitar

Cranberries
Mike Hogan – Bass
Noel Hogan – Guitarist (main song writer)
Feargal Lawler – Drums
Dolores O'Riordan – Lead Vocals

Cream
Peter 'Ginger' Baker – Drums
Jack Bruce – Bass and Vocals
Eric Clapton – Guitar and Vocals

Crickets
Jerry Allison – Drums
Sonny Curtis – Guitar and Vocals (joined in circa 1961)
Buddy Holly – Guitar and Lead Vocals
Joe B Mauldin – Bass
Niki Sullivan – Rhythm Guitar (founding member left in 1958)

Crowded House
Neil Finn (New Zealander founding member)
Tim Finn (songwriting brother of Neil joined band 1989–91)
Mark Hart – Guitarist (American joined in 1993)
Paul Hester – Drums (Australian founding member)
Craig Hooper – Guitar (founding member 1985–6)
Nick Seymour – Bass (Australian founding member)
Formed in 1985 as the Mullanes (founder Neil Finn's middle name) but became Crowded House in 1986. Disbanded 1996.

Culture Club
Mikey Craig – Bass
Boy George – Lead Vocals
Rob Hay – Guitar
Jon Moss – Drums
Nick Semper – Bass (founding member)

Cure, The
Andy Anderson – Drums
Perry Bamonte – Guitar
Jason Cooper – Drums
Michael Dempsey – Bass
Simon Gallup – Bass
Roger O'Donnell – Keyboards
Robert Smith – Guitar and Vocals
Porl Thompson – Guitar
Phil Thornalley – Bass
Lol Tolhurst – Keyboards
Boris Williams – Drums

Cutting Crew
Martin 'Frosty' Beedle – Drummer
Nick Van Eede – Lead Vocals
Colin Farley – Bass
Kevin MacMichael – Guitar

Damned, The
Brian James – Guitar
Rat Scabies – Drums
Captain Sensible – Bass
Dave Vanian – Vocals

Dave Clark Five
Dave Clark – Drums
Lenny Davidson Guitar
Rick Huxley – Guitar
Denis Payton – Saxophone
Mike Smith – Keyboards and Lead Vocals

Dave Dee, Dozy, Beaky, Mick and Tich
Ian Amey (Tich) – Guitar
Trevor Davies (Dozy) – Bass
John Dymond (Beaky) – Guitar
David Harman (Dave Dee) – Vocals
Michael Wilson (Mick) – Drums

Dawn
Telma Hopkins
Tony Orlando
Pam Vincent
Joyce Vincent-Wilson

Deacon Blue
Guy Barker – Trumpet
Pete Beachill – Trombone
Dave Bishop – Baritone Saxophone
Stuart Elliot – Bodhran
Mark Feltham – Harmonica
Simon Gardener – Trumpet
Graham Kelling – Guitar (founding member)
Lorraine Mcintosh – Vocals (founding member)
James Prime – Piano
Ricky Ross – Vocals (founding member)
Neil Sidwell – Trombone
Jamie Talbot – Baritone Saxophone
Phil Todd – Tenor Saxophone
Ewen Vernal – Bass
Douglas Vipond – Drums (founding member)
Chris White – Tenor Saxophone
Gavin Wright – Fiddle
Husband and wife team of Ricky Ross and Lorraine Mcintosh played with various artists on LPs and the above are mostly session musicians.

Deep Purple
Don Airey – Keyboards (joined in 2002)
Ritchie Blackmore – Guitar (founder left 1975 returned 1989–92)
Tommy Bolin – Guitar and Vocals (replaced Blackmore 1975)
David Coverdale – Guitar and Vocals (replaced Gillan 1973–6)
Rod Evans – Vocals (founding member)
Ian Gillan – Vocals (replaced Evans 1969 left, returned 1994)
Roger Glover – Bass (replaced Nick Semper in June 1969)
Glenn Hughes – Bass (replaced Roger Glover in 1973)
John Lord – Keyboards (founding member)
Steve Morse – Guitar (joined in 1994)
Ian Paice – Drums (founding member)
Joe Satriani – Guitar (1993–4)

Joe Lyn Turner – Vocals (1989–92)
Founded in 1968 as Roundabout but changed name in April to Deep Purple

Def Leppard
Richard Allen – Drums (lost left arm in car accident)
Vivian Campbell – Guitar (replaced Steve Clark)
Steve Clark – Guitar joined in 1977, died 1991)
Phil Cohen – Guitar (replaced Pete Willis)
Joe Elliott – Vocals (joined in 1977)
Rick Savage – Bass
Pete Willis – Guitar (fired from the band for alcoholism)

Depeche Mode
Vince Clarke – Synthesiser (replaced by Wilder in 1982)
Andy Fletcher – Keyboard and Backing Vocals
David Gahan – Lead Vocals
Martin Gore – Guitar, Keyboard and Backing Vocals
Alan Wilder – Keyboard, Piano and Drums (left in 1995)

Destiny's Child
Beyonce Knowles
Kelly Rowland
Michelle Williams

Dexy's Midnight Runners
Kevin 'Billy' Adams – Guitar and Banjo
Kevin 'Al' Archer – Keyboards and Vocals (founding member)
Mickey Billingham – Keyboards
Geoff Blythe – Tenor Saxophone
Steve Brennan – Violin
Andy 'Stoker' Growcott – Drums (replaced Bobby Junlor)
Bobby Junior – Drums
Giorgio Kilkenny – Bass (replaced Steve Wynn)
Andy Leek – Keyboards
Roger MacDuff – Violin
Brian Maurice – Alto Saxophone
Helen O'Hara – Violin
Jim Paterson – Trombone
Kevin Rowlands – Lead Vocals (founding member)
Peter Saunders – Alto Saxophone
Seb Shelton – Drums
Paul Speare – Tenor Saxophone
Steve 'Babyface' Spooner – Alto Sax (replaced Saunders)
Mick Talbot – Keyboards
Pete Williams – Bass
Steve Wynn – Bass

Dire Straits
John Illsley – Bass
Dave Knopfler – Guitar
Mark Knopfler – Lead Vocals and Guitar
Pick Withers – Drums

Dirty Pretty Things
Carl Barât – Vocals and Guitar
Didz Hammond – Bass
Gary Powell – Drums
Anthony Rossomando – Guitar

Dollar
Thereze Bazar
David Van Day

Doobie Brothers
Mike Hossack – Drums
Tom Johnston – Guitar
Keith Knudsen – Drums and Vocals
Michael McDonald – Vocals
John McFee – Guitar and Violin
Patrick Simmons – Guitar and Vocals

Doves
Jimi Goodwin – Bass and vocals
Andy Williams – Drums
Jez Williams – Guitar
(Martin Roman Rebelski is touring keyboard player)

Drifters
Willie Ferbie
Eric Troyer – Keyboards and Backing Vocals
Colin Walker – Cello
Ben E King
Rudy Lewis (died in 1964)
Clyde McPhatter (founder died in 1972)
Johnny Moore (died 1998)
Bill Pinkney (only living founding member in 1953)
Charlie Thomas
Andrew Thrasher
Gearhardt Thrasher
Since 1958 Pinkney has used the name The Original Drifters to differentiate themselves from a British group that became The Shadows

Duran Duran
Simon Le Bon – Lead Vocals
Nick Rhodes – Keyboards
Andy Taylor – Guitar
John Taylor – Bass
Roger Taylor – Drums

Eagles
Dan Felder – Guitar and Lead Vocals
Glenn Frey – Guitar, Piano, Keyboard and Vocals
Don Henley – Drums
Timothy B Schmit – Bass
Joe Walsh – Guitar, Organ and Vocals

Earth, Wind and Fire
Philip Bailey – Drums and Vocals (founding member)
Ronald Bautista – Guitar and Vocals
Michael Beal – Guitar and Harmonica
Leslie Drayton – Trumpet
Larry Dunn – Keyboards
Sonny Emory – Drums
Wade Flemons – Backing Vocals
John Graham – Guitar
Yackov Ben Israel – Conga and Percussion
Ralph Johnson – Drums
Ronnie Laws – Saxophone and Flute
Al McKay – Rhythm Guitar (founding member)
Sheldon Reynolds – Backing Vocals
Sherry Scot – Backing Vocals
Alexander Thomas – Trombone
Chet Washington – Tenor Saxophone
Fred White – Drums and Percussion
Maurice White – Drums and Vocals (founder 1970)
Verdine White – Bass
Don Whitehead – Keyboards and Backing Vocals
Andrew Woolfolk – Saxophone
Band's name derived from the astrological signs of the three founding members

East 17
Terry Caldwell – Vocals
Brian Harvey – Lead Singer
John Hendy – Vocals
Tony Mortimer – Keyboards

Elbow
Guy Garvey – Guitar and Vocals
Richard Jupp – Drums
Craig Potter – Keyboards
Mark Potter – Guitar
Pete Turner – Bass

Electric Light Orchestra
Michael De Albuquerque – Bass and Cello
Phil Bates – Guitar and Backing Vocals
Bev Bevan – Drums, Percussion and Backing Vocals
Louis Clark – Keyboards and Backing Vocals
Mike Edwards – Cello
Melvyn Gale – Cello
Wilf Gibson – Violin
Kelly Groucutt – Bass and Backing Vocals
Pete Haycock – Bass and Backing Vocals
Parthenon Huxley – Guitar and Backing Vocals
Mik Kaminski – Violin
Neil Lockwood – Backing Vocals
Jeff Lynne – Guitar, Keyboards and Vocals
Hugh McDowell – Cello
Richard Tandy – Piano, Harmonica and Backing Vocals

Roy Wood – Guitar, Banjo, Sitar and Vocals

EMF
James Atkin – Lead Vocals
Derry Brownson – Keyboards
Mark Decloedt – Drums
Ian Dench – Guitar and Keyboards
Zac Foley – Bass

En Vogue
Terry Ellis
Cindy Herron-Braggs
Maxine Jones
Dawn Robinson (left in 1995)

Erasure
Andy Bell
Vince Clarke

eScala
Nastasya Hodges – Cello
Izzy Johnston – Violin
Chantal Leverton – Viola
Victoria Lyon – Violin

Eternal
Easther Bennett
Vernette Bennett
Kelle Bryan
Louise Redknapp (née Nurding)

Eurythmics
Annie Lennox
Dave Stewart

Faces, The
Kenney Jones – Drums
Ronnie Lane – Bass
Ian McLagan – Keyboards
Rod Stewart – Lead Vocals
Ronnie Wood – Guitar and Backing Vocals
Following Marriott's defection to form Humble Pie in 1969, Ron Wood and Rod Stewart were brought in and the Small Faces became The Faces

Fairground Attraction
Roy Dodds – Drums
Simon Edwards – Bass
Mark Nevin – Guitar
Eddi Reader – Lead Vocals

Feeder
Taka Hirose – Bass
Jon Lee – Drums
Grant Nicholas – Vocals, Guitar

Feeling, The
Ciaran Jeremiah – Keyboards
Kevin Jeremiah – Guitar
Richard Jones – Bass
Dan Gillespie Sells – Guitar and Vocals
Paul Stewart – Drums

Fine Young Cannibals
Andy Cox – Guitar
Roland Gift – Lead Vocals
David Steele – Bass

Five
Richard Abidin Breen 'Abs'
Jason Brown 'J'
Sean Conlon
Ritchie Neville
Scott Robinson

Five Star
Delroy, Deniece, Doris, Lorraine and Stedman Pearson – all five members brothers and sisters from Romford.

Fleetwood Mac
Lindsey Buckingham – Vocals and Guitar (joined in 1974)
Mick Fleetwood – Drums
Peter Green – Guitar
Christine McVie née Perfect – Keyboards and Vocals
John McVie – Bass
Stevie Nicks – Vocals

Florence and the Machine
Robert Ackroyd – Guitar
Christopher Lloyd Hayden – Drums
Tom Monger – Harp
Isabella Summers – Keyboards
Florence Welch – Lead Vocals

Foo Fighters
William Goldsmith – Drums
Dave Grohl – Vocals and Guitar
Nate Mendel – Bass
Pat Smear – Guitar

Foreigner
Thom Gimbel – Saxophone, Guitar
Lou Gramm – Lead Vocals
Jeff Jacobs – Piano, Vocals
Mick Jones – Guitar, Piano, Vocals
Mark Schulman – Drums
Bruce Turgon – Bass

Four Tops
Renaldo Benson
Abdul Fakir
Lawrence Payton
Levi Stubbs

Frankie Goes to Hollywood
Peter Gill – Drums
Holly Johnson – Lead Vocals
Nasher Nash – Guitar
Mark O'Toole – Bass
Paul Rutherford – Vocals

Frankie Lymon and the Teenagers
Sherman Garnet – Vocals
Frankie Lymon – Vocals
James Merchant – Vocals
Joe Negroni – Vocals
Herman Santiago – Vocals

Franz Ferdinand
Robert Hardy – Bass
Alexander Kapranos – Guitar and Vocals
Nicholas McCarthy – Guitar
Paul Thomson – Drums

Fray, The
Joe King – Guitar and Vocals
Dan Lavery – Touring Bass Player
Isaac Slade – Piano and Vocals
Dave Welsh – Guitar
Ben Wysocki – Drums

Free
Andy Fraser – Bass
Simon Kirke – Drums
Paul Kossoff – Guitar
Paul Rodgers – Vocals

Fugees
Lauryn 'L' Hill
Wyclef 'Clef' Jean
Prakazrel 'Pras' Michel

Fun Boy Three
Lynval Golding – Guitar and Vocals
Terry Hall – Vocals
Neville Staples – Vocals

Fun Lovin' Criminals
Steve 'O' Borovini – Drums (left 1999 replaced by Jayson)
Maxwell 'Mackie' Jayson – Drums
Brian 'Fast, Fisty, etc' Leiser – Guitar
Huey 'DiFontaine' Morgan – Lead Vocals and Guitar

G4
Jonathan Ansell
Mike Christie
Matt Stiff
Ben Thapa

Genesis
Tony Banks – Keyboard
Phil Collins – Drums (joined in 1970, left in 1996)
Peter Gabriel – Lead Vocals (left in 1975)
Steve Hackett – Guitar (joined in 1970, left in 1977)
Anthony Philips – Guitar (left in 1970)
Mike Rutherford – Bass
John Silver – Drums (replaced by Collins)
Chris Stewart – Drums (replaced by John Silver)
Ray Wilson – Drums (replaced Phil Collins)

Gerry and the Pacemakers
Les Chadwick – Bass
Arthur Mack – Piano (replaced by Les Maguire)
Les Maguire – Piano
Freddie Marsden – Drums
Gerry Marsden – Lead Vocals and Guitar

Girls Aloud
Nadine Coyle
Sarah Harding
Nicola Roberts
Cheryl Tweedy
Kimberley Walsh
Girl group formed through ITV's *Popstars: The Rivals*

Gladys Knight and the Pips
William Guest – Vocals
Gladys Knight – Lead Vocals
Merald Knight – Vocals
Edward Patten – Vocals

Glasvegas
James Allan – Vocals and Guitar
Rab Allan – Lead Guitar
Paul Donoghue – Bass
Caroline McKay – Drums

Go West
Peter Cox – Vocals
Richard Drummie – Guitar, Keyboards and Vocals

Gorillaz
Paula Cracker – Guitar (replaced by Noodle)
Del – (the blue phantom in the 'Clint Eastwood' and 'Rock the House' videos)
Russel Hobbs – Drums
Murdoc Niccals – Bass
Noodle – Guitar, Vocals
2D – Vocals, Keyboards

Guillemots
Fyfe Dangerfield – Keyboard, Guitar and Vocals
Aristazabal Hawkes – Double Bass and Vocals
McLord Magrão – Guitar and Bass
Greig Stewart – Drums

Green Day
Billie Joe Armstrong – Vocals and Guitar
Tre Cool – Drums
Mike Dirnt – Bass
John Kiffmeyer – Drums (replaced by Tre Cool)

Guns 'N' Roses
Steven Adler – Drums (replaced by Matt Sorum)
Duff 'Rose' McKagan – Bass
Dizzy Read – Keyboard (added in 1990)
Axl Rose – Lead Vocals
Slash – Guitar
Matt Sorum – Drums
Izzy Stradlin – Guitar

Happy Mondays
Bez – Percussion
Paul Davis – Keyboards
Mark 'Cow' Day – Guitar
Paul Ryder – Bass
Shaun Ryder – Vocals
Gary Whelan – Drums

Hawkwind
Dave Brock – Guitar and Vocals
Robert Calvert – Vocals
Ian 'Lemmy' Kilmister – Lead Vocals and Bass
Stacia – Dancer
Nik Turner – Saxophone and Flute
Memorable for Lemmy's vocals on 'Silver Machine' and the nude gyrations of six-foot dancer Stacia

Hear'Say
Danny Foster
Mylenne Klass
Kim Marsh (left in 2001 and was replaced by Shentall)
Suzanne Shaw
Johnny Shentall
Noel Sullivan

Heaven 17
Glenn Gregory – Vocals
Ian Craig Marsh – Keyboards (previously in Human League)
Martin Ware – Keyboards (previously in Human League)
Carol Kenyon was the uncredited vocalist on 'Temptation'

Hollies, The
Bernard Calvert – Bass (replaced Eric Haydock in 1966)
Alan Clarke – Lead Vocals (founding member)
Bobby Elliott – Drums (replaced Rathbone in 1963)
Eric Haydock – Bass (founding member 1962–6)
Tony Hicks – Guitar
Graham Nash – Guitar and Vocals (founder 1962–8, and 1983)
Don Rathbone – Drums (founding member 1962–3)
Mikael Rikfors – Lead Vocals (replaced Alan Clarke 1971–3)
Terry Sylvester – Guitar and Vocals (replaced Nash in 1968)
Founded in 1962

Hot Chocolate
Franklyn De Allie – Guitar
Errol Brown – Lead Vocals
Tony Connor – Drums
Larry Ferguson – Pianist
Harvey Hinsley – Guitar
Ian King – Drums (replaced by Tony Connor)
Patrick Olive – Percussionist
Tony Wilson – Bass (left in 1976)

Housemartins, The
Stan Cullimore – Bass
Norman Cook – Guitar
Paul Heaton – Vocals and Guitar (later formed Beautiful South)
David Hemmingway – Drums (later formed Beautiful South)
Ted Key – Guitar (replaced by Norman 'Fat Boy Slim' Cook)
Hugh Whitaker – Drums (replaced by David Hemmingway)

Hue and Cry
Greg Kane
Pat Kane

Huey Lewis and the News
Mario Cipollina – Bass
Johnny Colla – Guitar and Saxophone
Bill Gibson – Drums
Chris Hayes – Guitar
Sean Hopper – Keyboards
Huey Lewis – Lead Vocals

Human League, The
Ian Burden (joined in 1981)
Jo Callis – Synthesiser (joined in 1981)
Joanne Catherall
Ian Craig Marsh (left in 1980 to form Heaven 17)
Philip Oakley

Susan Anne Sulley
Martyn Ware (left in 1980 to form Heaven 17)
Adrian Wright – Synthesiser

Humble Pie
Dave 'Clem' Clempson – Guitar and Vocals (replaced Frampton)
Dave 'Bucket' Colwell (member of Humble Pie 2000)
Peter Frampton – Guitar and Vocals (left in 1971)
Steve Marriott – Guitar and Lead Vocals
Zoot Money – Keyboards (member of Humble Pie 2000)
Greg Ridley – Bass and Vocals
Jerry Shirley – Drums
Bob Tench – Guitar (member of Humble Pie 2000)

Il Divo
Urs Buhler – Tenor (Swiss)
Sebastien Izambard (French)
Carlos Marin – Baritone (Spanish)
David Miller – Tenor (American)

Ink Spots
Jerry Daniels (founding member)
Charles Fuqua (founding member)
Orville 'Hoppy' Jones (founding member)
Bill Kenny (replaced Jerry Daniels in 1936)
Jim 'Mr inkspots' Nabbie (replaced Kenny 1945, died 1992)
Ivory 'Deek' Watson (founding member)
Founded in 1932

Inspiral Carpets
Clint Boon – Organ
Craig Gill – Drums
Stephen Holt – Vocals
Graham Lambert – Guitar
David Swift – Bass

INXS
Michael Hutchence – Lead Vocals (died in 1997)
Garry Beers – Bass, Vocals
Andrew Farriss – Keyboard
Jon Farriss – Drums
Tim Farriss – Guitar
Kirk Pengilly – Guitar, Saxophone and Vocals

Isley Brothers
Ernie Isley – Drums, Guitar and Percussion
Marvin Isley – Bass and Percussion
O'Kelly Isley – Vocals
Ronald Isley – Vocals
Rudolph Isley – Vocals
Chris Jasper – Drums and Keyboards

Jackson Five
Jackie Jackson (born Sigmund Jackson)
Jermaine Jackson – Bass and Lead Vocals
Marlon Jackson
Michael Jackson – Lead Vocals
Randy Jackson – (replaced Jermaine 1976)
Tito Jackson (born Toriano Jackson) – Guitar

Jam, The
Rick Buckler – Drums (replaced David Waller in 1978)
Bruce Foxton – Bass
David Waller – Drums
Paul Weller – Vocals, Guitar

James
Tim Booth – Vocals
Saul Davies – Violin (added 1990)
Andy Diagram – Trumpet (added 1990)
Paul Gilbertson – Guitar
Jim Glennie – Bass
Larry Gott – Guitar (replaced Paul Gilbertson 1985)
Mark Hunter – Keyboard (added 1990)
Michael Kulas – Guitar (added 1999)
Adrian Oxaal – Guitar (added 1997)
David Baynton-Power – Drums (replaced Gavan Whelan 1990)
Gavan Whelan – Drums

Jamiroquai
Wallis Buchanan – Vibraphone
Nick Fyffe – (replaced Stuart Zender)
J (Jason) K (Kay) – Lead Vocals
Derrick McKenzie – Drums
Toby Smith – Keyboard
Stuart Zender – Bass (left October 1998)

Jethro Tull
Mick Abrahams – Guitar and Vocals
Ian Anderson – Flute, Guitar, Mandolin, Saxophone and Vocals
Barriemore Barlow – Drums (replaced Clive Bunker in 1971)
Clive Bunker – Drums
Glen Cornick – Bass
Martin Barre – Flute and Guitar
John Evan – Keyboards
John Glascock – Bass and Vocals (replaced Hammond, 1976)
Jeffrey Hammond – Bass (replaced Glen Cornick in 1971)
David Palmer – Keyboard

JLS (Jack the Lad Swing)
Jonathan 'JB' Gill
Marvin Humes
Aston Merrygold
Oritsé Williams

Joy Division
Ian Curtis – Vocals and Guitar
Peter Hook – Bass and Vocals
Stephen Morris – Drums and Percussion
Bernard Sumner – Guitar and Keyboards

Kaiser Chiefs
Nick 'Peanuts' Baines – Keyboards
Nick Hodgson – Drums and Vocals
Simon Rix – Bass
Andrew 'Whitey' White – Guitar
Ricky Wilson – Lead Vocals

Kasabian
Chris Edwards – Bass
Ash Hannis – Drums (replaced by Ian Matthews)
Chris Karloff – Guitar and Keyboards (replaced by Jay Meyler)
Tom Meigham – Vocals
Sergio Pizzorno – Guitar and Vocals

Keane
Tom Chaplin – Vocals
Richard Hughes – Drums
Tim Rice-Oxley – Keyboards

King Crimson
Robert Fripp – Guitar and Mellotron
Michael Giles – Drums and Vocals
Greg Lake – Bass and Vocals
Ian McDonald – Flute, Keyboards and Saxophone

Kings of Leon
Caleb Followill – Lead Vocals and Guitar
Jared Followill – Bass
Matthew Followill – Lead Guitar
Nathan Followill – Drums

Kinks, The
Mick Avory – Drums
John Beecham – Trombone and Tuba
Laurie Brown – Vocals
Mike Cotton – Trumpet
John Dalton – Bass (left in 1976)
Dave Davies – Guitar, Vocals
Raymond Douglas Davies – Vocals, Guitar, Piano
John Gosling – Keyboards
Alan Holmes – Saxophone and Clarinet
Davy Jones – Saxophone and Clarinet
Peter Quaife – Bass (left in 1969 and replaced by Dalton)

Kiss
Peter Criss – Drums and Vocals
Ace Frehley – Guitar and Vocals
Gene Simmons – Bass and Vocals
Paul Stanley – Guitar

Kooks, The
Paul Garrad – Drums
Hugh Harris – Guitar
Dan Logan – Bass (replaced Max Rafferty in 2008)
Luke Pritchard – Vocals and Guitar

Kool & The Gang
Clifford Adams – Trombone
Robert 'Kool' Bell – Bass
Robert 'The Captain' Bell – Keyboards and Saxophone
Gary Brown – Vocals
'Funky' George Brown – Drums
Skip Martin – Vocals
Odeen Mays – Vocals
Robert 'Spike' Mickens – Trumpet
Michael Ray – Trumpet
Pharoah Sanders
Charles 'Calydes' Smith – Guitar
James 'JT' Taylor – Vocals (joined in 1979, left after Toon)
Dennis 'DT' Thomas – Saxophone
Leon Thomas
Earl Toon Jnr – Vocals (left and Taylor became front man)

Kraftwerk
Klaus Dinger
Wolfgang Flur – Electronic Drums
Thomas Homann (left the band)
Ralf Hutter – Organ
Eberhardt Khranemann – Bass (left the band)
Klaus Roeder – Guitar, Violin, Keyboards
Michael Rother – Guitar
Florian Schneider – Woodwind

Kula Shaker
Alonza Bevan – Bass
Jay Darlington – Keyboard
Crispian Mills – Lead Vocals
Paul Winterhart – Drums

Last Shadow Puppets, The
Miles Kane – Guitar and Vocals
Alex Turner – Guitar and Vocals

Led Zeppelin
Jason Bonham – Drums (replaced his father in 1980)
John 'Bonzo' Bonham – Drums (died in 1980)
John Paul Jones – Bass
Jimmy Page – Lead Guitar
Robert Plant – Lead Vocals
Jimmy Page decided to reform the Yardbirds under the name of the New Yardbirds. Keith Moon commented that it would go down like a lead balloon, in fact, a Le(a)d Zeppelin.

Level 42
Boon Gould – Guitar
Phil Gould – Drums
Mark King – Bass and Vocals
Mark Lindup – Keyboards and Vocals

Libertines, The
Carl Barat – Vocals
Pete Doherty – Vocals and Guitar (fired in 2004)
John Hassall – Bass
Gary Powell – Drums
Anthony Rossomando – Guitar (replaced Doherty)

Liberty X
Michelle Heaton
Tony Lundon
Kevin Simm
Jessica Taylor
Kelli Young

Lighthouse Family, The
Tunde Baiyewu – Lead Vocals
Paul Tucker – Keyboards

Lightning Seeds
Ian Broudie – Lead Vocals and Guitar
Martyn Campbell – Bass
Paul Hemmings – Guitar
Ali Kane – Keyboards (replaced by Angie Pollock in 1996)
Angie Pollock – Keyboards
Mat Priest – Drums
Chris Sharrock – Drums (replaced by Mat Priest in 1996)

Limp Bizkit
Wes Borland – Guitar
Fred Durst – Lead Vocals
DJ Lethal (joined in 1996)
John Otto – Drums
Sam Rivers – Bass

Lonestar
Michael Britt – Guitar and Vocals
Richie McDonald – Lead Vocals
Keech Rainwater – Drums
Dean Sams – Keyboard and Vocals

Love Affair
Maurice Bacon – Drums
Rex Brayley – Guitar
Steve Ellis – Vocals
Morgan Fisher – Organ
Lynton Guest – Organ
Mick Jackson – Bass
A less well-known US band had the same name

Lynyrd Skynyrd
Bob Burns – Drums
Allen Collins – Guitar
Steve Gaines – Guitar
Ed King – Guitar
Billy Powell – Keyboards
Gary Rossington – Guitar
Leon Williams – Bass
Ronnie Van Zant – Vocals

M People
Paul Heard
Mike Pickering
Heather Small

Madcon
Critical (Yosef Wolde-Mariam)
Kapricon (Tshawe Baqwa)

Madness
Mike 'Barso' Barson – Keyboards
Mark 'Bedders' Bedford – Bass
Chris 'Chrissy Boy' Foreman – Guitar
Graham 'Suggs' McPherson – Lead Vocals
Carl 'Chas' Smash – Trumpet and Backing Vocals
Lee 'Kix' Thompson – Saxophone and Vocals
Daniel 'Woody' Woodgate – Drums and Percussion

Magic Band, The
Captain Beefheart – Vocals and Harmonica
John 'Drumbo' French – Drums and Vocals
Gary Lucas – Guitar
Rockette Morton (Mark Boston) – Bass
Zoot Horn Rollo (Bill Harkleroad) – Guitar
Denny 'Feelers Rebo' Walley – Guitar

Mamas and the Papas
Denny Doherty – Vocals
Mama Cass Elliot – Vocals
John Phillips – Guitar and Vocals
Michelle Phillips – Vocals

Manfred Mann
Michael D'Abo – Lead Vocals (replaced Paul Jones in 1966)
Mike Hugg – Drums and Percussion
Paul Jones – Lead Vocals
Tom McGuinness – Bass
Manfred Mann – Keyboards
Mike Vickers – Guitar

Manhattan Transfer
Tim Hauser
Laurel Masse
Alan Paul
Janis Siegel

Manic Street Preachers
James Dean Bradfield – Lead Vocals, Lead and Rhythm Guitar
Richey Edwards – Rhythm Guitar (went missing in 1995)
Sean Moore – Drums
Nicky Wire – Bass

Marillion
Fish – Vocals (left in 1988)
Steve Hogarth – Vocals (replaced Fish in 1989)
Mark Kelly – Keyboards
Ian Mosley – Drums
Mick Pointer – Drums
Steve Rothery – Guitar
Pete Trewavas – Bass

Marmalade
William 'Junior' Campbell – Guitar and Vocals (founding member)
Raymond Duffy – Drums (founding member)
Patrick Fairley – Guitar (founding member)
Dean Ford – Lead Vocals (founding member)
Graham Knight – Bass and Vocals (founding member)
Alan Whitehead – Drums (replaced Duffy in late 1966)
Founded in 1966 having previously been named Dean Ford and the Gaylords

Martha Reeves and the Vandellas
Rosalind Ashford, Betty Kelly, Lois Reeves
Martha Reeves, Sandra Tilley, Gloria Williams

McFly
Tom Fletcher – Guitar and Vocals
Danny Jones – Guitar and Vocals
Harry Judd – Drums
Dougie Poynter – Bass and Vocals

Middle of the Road
Phil Anderson – Guitar and Vocals
Ken Andrew – Drums and Vocals (founding member)
Eric Campbell-Lewis – Guitar (founding member)
Ian Campbell-Lewis – Guitar (founding member)
Sally Carr – Lead Vocals (founding member)
Shug Devun – Keyboards
Derek Hall – Guitar and Vocals
Neil Henderson – Bass and Vocals
Kenny McKay – Guitar and Vocals
Pat Monaghan – Guitar and Vocals

Mindbenders
Wayne Fontana – Lead Vocals
Graham Gouldman – Guitar
Paul Hancox – Drums
James O'Neill – Guitar
Eric Stewart – Guitar, Piano and Vocals

Mis-Teeq
Alesha Dixon
Su-Elise Nash
Sabrina Washington

Monkees, The
Mickey Dolenz – Drums and Vocals
Davy Jones – Tambourine and Vocals
Mike Nesmith – Guitar and Vocals
Peter Tork – Bass and Vocals

Moody Blues
Graeme Edge – Drums and Vocals (founder member)
Justin Hayward – Guitar and Vocals (replaced Laine)
Denny Laine – Guitar and Vocals (founder member left, 1966)
John Lodge – Bass, Cello, Guitar and Vocals
Mike Pinder – Keyboards and Vocals (founder member)
Ray Thomas – Reeds and Vocals (founder member)
Clint Warwick – Guitar (founder member left in 1966)

Motorhead
Phil Campbell – Guitar
Mikkey Dee – Drums
Ian 'Lemmy' Kilmister – Lead Vocals and Bass

Mott the Hoople
Dale Griffin – Drums and Vocals
Ian Hunter – Piano, Guitar and Lead Vocals
Mick Ralphs – Guitar and Vocals
Overend Watts – Bass and Vocals

Move, The
Bev Bevan – Drums
Trevor Burton – Guitar and Vocals
Chris Kefford – Bass
Jeff Lynn – Guitar and Vocals
Rick Pride – Bass and Vocals
Carl Wayne – Guitar and Vocals
Roy Wood – Guitar, Banjo, Sitar and Vocals

Mud
Rob Davis
Les Gray
Dave Mount
Ray Stiles

Mugwumps
Denny Doherty – Vocals
Cass Elliot – Vocals
James Hendricks – Vocals
Zal Yanovsky – Guitar and Vocals

Mungo Jerry
Mike Cole – Bass
Ray Dorset – Vocals, Guitar
Colin Earl – Piano, Vocals
Paul King – Banjo, Guitar, Vocals

My Chemical Romance
Bob Bryar – Drums
Frank Iero – Guitar
Matt Pelissier – Drums (replaced by Bryar)
Ray Toro – Lead Guitar
Gerard Way – Lead Vocals
Mikey Way – Bass

N-Dubz
Dino 'Dappy' Contostavlos
Tula 'Tulisa' Contostavlos
Richard 'Fazer' Rawson

'N Sync
Lance Bass
JC Chasez
Joey Fatone
Chris Kirkpatrick
Justin Timberlake

Nazareth
Pete Agnew – Bass (founding member)
Manny Charlton – Guitar (founding member)
Zal Cleminson – Guitar (1979–81)
Ronnie Leahy – Keyboards
John Locke – Keyboards (replaced Zal Cleminson)
Dan McCafferty – Vocals (founding member)
Jimmy Murrison – Guitar
Bill Rankin – Guitar and Keyboards (replaced Locke in 1981)
Darrell Sweet – Drummer (founding member)

N*E*R*D
Shay Haley
Chad Hugo
Pharrell Williams

New Christy Minstrels, The
Karen Black (better known nowadays as an actress)
Bob Buchanan
Gene Clark (left to join The Byrds)
Barry McGuire – Lead Vocals
Larry Ramos

Kenny Rogers – Vocals (1966–7)
Mike Settle (left 1967 to start First Edition with Rogers)
Randy Sparks (founder of the group)

New Kids on the Block
Jonathan Knight
Jordan Knight
Joe McIntyre
Donnie Wahlberg
Danny Wood

New Order
Phil Cunningham – Guitar & Synthesiser (replaced Gilbert 2005)
Gillian Gilbert – Guitar and Keyboards
Peter Hook – Bass and Vocals
Stephen Morris – Drums and Percussion
Bernard Sumner – Guitar and Keyboards

New Seekers
Chris Barrington – Bass (founding member left in 1970)
Peter Doyle (joined in 1970)
Eve Graham (founding member)
Sally Graham (founding member left in 1970)
Laurie Heath – Guitar (founding member left in 1970)
Marty Kristian (founding member)
Paul Layton (joined in 1970)
Peter Oliver (replaced Peter Doyle in 1973)
Lyn Paul (joined in 1970)
Keith Potger (founder but only played on one LP)

Nice, The
Brian 'Blinky' Davison – Drums
Keith Emerson – Keyboards
Lee Jackson – Bass
David O'List – Guitar and Vocals

Nickelback
Chad Kroeger – Vocals and Guitar
Mike Kroeger – Guitar
Ryan Peake – Guitar and Vocals
Ryan Vikedal – Bass

911
Lee Brennan
Jimmy Constable
Simon 'Spike' Dawbarn

Nirvana
Kurt Cobain – Lead Vocals and Guitar (died in 1994)
David Grohl – Drums and Vocals
Chris Novoselic – Bass and Vocals

Noisettes
Jamie Morrison – Drums
Shingai Shoniwa – Vocals and Bass
Dan Smith – Guitar

Oasis
Gem Archer – Guitar (replaced Paul Arthurs in 1999)
Paul 'Bonehead' Arthurs – Rhythm Guitar
Andy Bell – Bass (replaced Paul McGuigan)
Liam Gallagher – Vocals
Noel Gallagher – Vocals and Guitar
Tony McCarroll – Drums
Paul 'Guigsy' McGuigan – Bass
Alan White – Drums (replaced Tony McCarroll in 1994)

Ocean Colour Scene
Steve Craddock – Lead Guitar, Keyboards and Vocals
Simon Fowler – Lead Vocals, Guitar and Harmonica
Oscar Harrison – Drums and Vocals
Damon Minchela – Bass

O'Jays
Bill Isles, Eddie Levert, Bobby Massey, William Powell
Walter Williams - Formed in 1958 as the Mascots and became the O'Jays in honour of Cleveland DJ Eddie O'Jay

One Direction
Niall Horan
Zayn Malik
Liam Payne
Harry Styles
Louis Tomlinson

Orchestral Manoeuvres in the Dark (OMD)
Malcolm Holmes – Keyboards
Dave Hughes – Drums and Percussion
Paul Humphreys – Keyboards
Andy McCluskey – Bass and Vocals

Osmonds, The
Donny Osmond
Alan Osmond
Little Jimmy Osmond
Wayne Osmond
Jay Osmond
Merrill Osmond

Pet Shop Boys
Chris Lowe
Neil Tennant – Lead Vocals

Peter, Paul and Mary
Paul Stookey – Guitar and Vocals
Mary Travers – Vocals
Peter Yarrow – Guitar and Vocals

Pink Floyd
Syd Barrett – Guitar and Vocals
Dave Gilmour – Guitar and Vocals
Nick Mason – Drums and Percussion
Roger Waters – Bass, Piano and Percussion
Rick Wright – Keyboards

Plastic Ono Band
Eric Clapton – Guitar
John Lennon – Vocals, Guitar and Piano
Yoko Ono – Vocals
Ringo Starr – Drums
Klaus Voorman – Bass
Alan White – Drums

Platters
Alex Hodge
David Lynch (died in 1981)
Herb Reed
Paul Robi (died in 1989)
Zola Taylor
Sonny Turner
Tony Williams (died in 1992)
Managed by Sam 'Buck' Ram

Pogues, The
James Fearnley – Piano Accordion and Guitar
Jim Finer – Banjo and Mandolin
Darryl Hunt – Bass
Shane MacGowan – Lead Vocals (replaced by Joe Strummer)
Cait O'Riordan – Bass (replaced by Darryl Hunt)
Andrew Ranken – Drums
Peter 'Spidey' Stacy – Tin Whistle
Joe Strummer – Lead Vocals
Terry Woods

Police
Stewart Copeland – Drums
Sting (Gordon Sumner) – Lead Vocals and Bass
Andy Summers – Guitar

Pretenders, The
Martin Chambers – Drums
Pete Farndon – Bass (left 1982, died 1983)
Malcolm Foster – Bass (added 1983)
James Honeyman-Scott – Guitar (died in 1982)
Chrissie Hynde – Lead Vocals
Robbie McIntosh – Guitar (added 1983)

Proclaimers
Charlie and Craig Reid

Procol Harum
Gary Brooker – Piano and Lead Vocals
Alan Cartwright – Bass
Chris Copping – Bass and Organ
Matthew Fisher – Guitar and Organ
Mick Grabham – Guitar
Bobby Harrison – Drums and Percussion
David Knights – Bass
Ray Royer – Guitar
Peter Solley – Organ
Robin Trower – Guitar and Vocals
BJ Wilson – Drums and Percussion

Prodigy
Graham 'Gizz' Butt – Guitar
Keith Flint – Lead Vocals
Liam Howlett – Keyboards
Alison 'Alli' MacInnes – Guitar
Sharky – Dancer and Backing Vocals
Leeroy Thornhill – Dancer
MC Maxim Reality (born Keith Palmer)

Public Image Ltd
Keith Levine – Guitar
John Lydon (Johnny Rotten) – Lead Vocals
Jim Walker – Drums
Jah Wobble – Bass

Pulp
Jarvis Cocker – Lead Vocals and Guitar
Peter Dalton – Keyboard
Wayne Furniss – Drums
Jamie Pinchbeck – Bass

Pussycat Dolls, The
Carmit Bachar – Dance, Vocals
Ashley Roberts – Dance, Vocals
Nicole Scherzinger – Lead Vocals
Jessica Sutta – Dance, Vocals
Melody Thornton – Vocals
Kimberley Wyatt – Dance, Vocals
Former members include: Cyia Batten, Carmen Electra, Nadine Ellis, Erica Gudis, Kaya Jones, Rebecca Pickering, Rachel Sterling

Quarrymen, The
George Harrison – Lead Guitar and Vocals
John Lennon – Rhythm Guitar and Vocals
Paul McCartney – Bass and Vocals
Pete Best – Drums
Formed 1958 and became The Silver Beatles in 1959 when Tony Sheridan joined them. Whatever became of them?

Queen
John Deacon – Bass
Brian May – Guitar and Vocals
Freddie Mercury (born Freddie Bulsara) – Vocals and Keyboard
Roger Taylor – Drums

Q-Tips, The
Stewart Blandmer – Saxophone and Vocals
Steve Farr – Saxophone and Vocals
Tony Hughes – Trumpet
Mick Pearl – Bass
Garth Watt Roy – Guitar and Vocals
Barry Watts – Drums
Paul Young – Guitar and Lead Vocals

Radiohead
Johnny Greenwood – Lead Guitar
Colin Greenwood – Bass
Ed O'Brien – Rhythm Guitar
Phil Selway – Drums
Thom Yorke – Lead Vocals and Rhythm Guitar

Rainbow
Don Airey – Keyboards (replaced David Stone)
Jimmy Bain – Bass (replaced Craig Gruber)
Ritchie Blackmore – Guitar
Graham Bonnet – Vocals (replaced Ronnie James Dio)
Tony Carey – Keyboards (replaced Mickey Lee Soule)
Mark Clarke – Bass (replaced Jimmy Bain)
Bob Daisley – Bass (replaced Mark Clarke)
Ronnie James Dio – Vocals
Gary Driscoll – Drums
Roger Glover – Bass (replaced Bob Daisley)
Craig Gruber – Bass
Cozy Powell – Drums (replaced Gary Driscoll)
Mickey Lee Soule – Keyboards
David Stone – Keyboards (replaced Tony Carey)

Rascals, The
Joe Edwards – Bass
Miles Kane – Vocals and Guitar
Greg Mighall – Drums

Razorlight
Björn Agren – Guitar
Johnny Borrell – Vocals and Guitar
Andy Burrows – Drums
Carl Dalemo – Bass
Christian Smith Pancorvo – Drums (replaced by Burrows)

Red Hot Chili Peppers, The
Flea (Michael Balzary) – Trumpet, Bass (founding member)
John Frusciante – (replaced Duane 'Blackbird' McKnight)
Jack Irons – Drums (left to form What Is This)
Anthony Kiedis – Vocals (founding member)
Duane 'Blackbird' McKnight – Guitar (replaced Hillel Slovak)
Arik Marshall – Guitar (replaced John Frusciante)
Cliff Martinez – Bass
Dave Navarro – (replaced Jesse Tobias)
DH Peligro – Drums (formerly with Dead Kennedys)
Jack Sherman – Guitar
Hillel Slovak – Guitar (died 25 June 1988)
Chad Smith – Drums (replaced DH Peligro)
Jesse Tobias – Guitar (replaced Arik Marshall)
The Red Hot Chili Peppers were once known as Tony Flow and the Miraculously Majestic Masters of Mayhem

REM
Bill Berry – Drums (left in 1996)
Peter Buck – Lead Guitar, Mandolin and Banjo
Mike Mills – Bass, Keyboard
Michael Stipe – Lead Vocals and Guitar

Righteous Brothers
Bobby Hatfield
Bill Medley
Jimmy Walker (replaced Bill Medley in 1968)

Right Said Fred
Fred Fairbrass
Richard Fairbrass
Rob Manzoli

Rolling Stones, The
Mick Jagger – Lead Vocals
Brian Jones – Guitar (died in 1969)
Darryl Jones – Bass (joined in 1994)
Keith 'The Human Riff' Richards – Guitar
Ian Stewart – Piano (died 12 December 1985)
Mick Taylor – Guitar (1969–74)
Charlie Watts – Drums
Ron Wood – Bass (joined in 1975)
Bill Wyman – Bass (left in 1992)
Andrew Loog Oldham – Manager

Ronettes
Estelle Bennett
Veronica 'Ronnie' Bennett
Nedra Talley

Roxette
Marie Fredriksson – Vocals
Per Gessle – Guitar and Vocals

Roxy Music
Roger Bunn – Guitar
Brian Eno – Synthesiser
Bryan Ferry – Lead Vocals and Keyboards
John Gustafson – Bass (replaced Sal Maida)
Eddie Jobson – Keyboards
Rik Kenton – Bass (replaced Graham Simpson)

Andy MacKay – Saxophone
Sal Maida – Bass (replaced John Porter)
Phil Manzanera – Guitar
David O'List – Guitar
John Porter – Bass (replaced Rik Kenton)
Graham Simpson – Bass
David Skinner – Keyboards
Paul Thompson – Drums
Gary Tibbs – Bass (replaced John Wetton)
John Wetton – Bass

Rutles, The
Dirk McQuickly (Eric Idle)
Ron Nasty (Neil Innes)
Stig O'Hara (Ricky Fataar)
Barry Wom (John Halsey)
Leggy Mountbatten (Terence Bayler) – Manager
Spoof group invented by Eric Idle and Gary Weiss and modelled on The Beatles. Had a minor hit in actuality with 'I Must Be In Love'

S Club
Tina Barrett
Paul Cattermole (left 2002)
Jon Lee
Bradley McIntosh
Jo O'Meara
Hannah Spearritt
Rachel Stevens
Formerly known as S Club 7 until Paul Cattermole left

S Club Juniors
Aaron, Calvin, Daisy, Frankie, Hannah, Jay, Rochelle, Stacey

Saint Etienne
Sarah Cracknell – Vocals
Bob Stanley – Keyboards and Xylophone
Pete Wiggs – Keyboards

Salt-N-Pepa
Sandra 'Pepa' Denton
DJ Pamela Green
Cheryl 'Salt' James
DJ Dee Dee 'Spinderella' Roper (replaced Pamela Green)

Saturdays, The
Una Healy
Mollie King
Frankie Sandford
Vanessa White
Rochelle Wiseman

Savage Garden
Darren Hayes – Lead Vocals
Daniel Jones – Guitar

Scaffold
John Gorman,Mike McGear, Roger McGough

Scissor Sisters
Babydaddy (Scott Hoffman) – Bass and Keyboards
Paddy Boom (Patrick Seacor) – Drums
Del Marquis (Derek Gruen) – Guitar
Ana Matronic (Ana Lynch) – Vocals
Jake Shears (Jason Sellards) – Lead Vocals

Searchers, The
Chris Curtis
Tony Jackson
John McNally
Mike Pinder

Seekers
Judith Durham – Vocal
Athol Guy – Bass
Keith Potger – Guitar
Bruce Woodley – Guitar

Sex Pistols
Paul Cook – Drums
Steve Jones – Guitar
Glen Matlock – Bass (replaced by Sid Vicious in 1977)
Wally Nightingale – Lead Vocals
Jonny Rotten – Vocals
Sid Vicious – Bass (died in 1979)
Malcolm McLaren – Manager
Reformed in 1996 for the 'Filthy Lucre' tour

Shadows, The
Brian Bennett – Drums (founding member)
Warren Bennett – Guitar and Keyboards (son of Brian)
John Farrar – Bass Guitar (replaced Alan Tarney in 1977)
Mo Foster – Bass (classed as an honorary Shadow)
Mark Griffiths – Bass (replaced Alan Jones in 1987)
Cliff Hall – Piano (from 1978 an honorary Shadow)
Jet Harris – Bass (replaced by Brian Locking in 1962)
Alan Hawkshaw – Piano and Keyboards (joined 1968)
Alan Jones – Bass (from 1977 an honorary Shadow)
Brian 'Licorice' Locking – Bass (left for religious reasons 1964)
Ben Marvin – Guitar (son of Hank)
Hank Marvin – Lead Guitar
Tony Meehan – Drums (replaced by Brian Bennett in 1961)
John Rostill – Bass Guitar (joined 1964, died in 1973)
Alan Tarney – Bass Guitar and Piano (1973–7)
Bruce Welch – Rhythm Guitar

Shakespears Sister
Marcella Detroit
Siobhan Fahey

Shalamar
Jeffrey Daniel
Howard Hewett
Jody Watley

Shamen, The
Colin Angus
Derek McKenzie (replaced by William Sinnott)
Keith McKenzie
William Sinnott (drowned in 1991)
Peter Stephenson
Richard 'Mr C' West

Simply Red
Tony Bowers – Bass
Mick 'Red' Hucknall – Lead Vocals
Chris Joyce – Drums
Tim Kellett – Brass, Keyboards
Fritz McIntyre – Keyboards
Sylvan Richardson – Guitar

Slade
Dave Hill – Lead Guitar and Backing Vocals
Noddy Holder – Lead Vocals and Guitar
Jim Lea – Bass and Violin
Don Powell – Drums

Small Faces
Kenney Jones – Drums
Ronnie Lane – Bass
Ian McLagan – Keyboards
Steve Marriott – Vocals and Guitar
Following Marriott's defection to form Humble Pie in 1969, Ron Wood and Rod Stewart were brought in and the Small Faces became The Faces

Smashing Pumpkins
Jimmy Chamberlin – Drums
Billy Corgan – Lead Vocals and Guitar
James Iha – Lead Guitar
Melissa Auf Der Maur – Bass
D'Arcy Wretzky – Bass (replaced by Melissa Auf Der Maur)

Smiths
Mike Joyce – Drums
Johnny Marr – Guitar
Stephen Morrissey – Vocals
Andy Rourke – Bass

Smokey Robinson and the Miracles
Bill Griffin – Vocals
Pete Moore – Vocals
Smokey Robinson – Lead Vocals
Bobby Rogers – Vocals
Ronny White – Vocals

So Solid Crew
Harvey
Lisa
Romeo
Band is reputed to have at least 30 transient -members

Soft Cell
Marc Almond – Lead Vocals
Dave Ball – Synthesiser

Spandau Ballet
Tony Hadley – Lead Vocals
John Keeble – Drums
Gary Kemp – Guitar
Martin Kemp – Bass
Steve Norman – Guitar, Saxophone and Percussion
Steve Dagger – Manager

Spencer Davis Group
Spencer Davis – Guitar and Vocals (founding member)
Ray Fenwick – Guitar (replaced Phil Sawyer)
Eddie Hardin – Keyboards (replaced Phil Sawyer)
Phil Sawyer – Guitar and Keyboards
(joined 1967 after Steve Winwood left)
Muff Winwood – Bass (founding member left in 1967)
Steve Winwood – Vocals, Guitar and Piano (founding member)
Peter York – Drums (founding member)
Steve Winwood left in 1967 to form Traffic

Spice Girls
Victoria Beckham (née Adams) 'Posh Spice'
Melanie 'B' Brown 'Scary Spice'
Emma Bunton 'Baby Spice'
Melanie 'C' Chisholm 'Sporty Spice'
Geri Halliwell 'Ginger Spice' (left the group in 1999)

Spinal Tap
Joe 'Mama' Bessemer – Drums (replaced Mick Shrimpton)
Peter James Bond (replaced Childs, spontaneously combusted)
Eric 'Stumpy Joe' Childs – Drums (died in 1974 after choking)
Ian Faith – Manager (replaced Hampton)
Glyn Hampton – Manager (left in 1975)
Ross MacLochness – Keyboards (replaced Denny Upham)
John 'Stumpy' Pepys – Drums (died in gardening accident 1969)
Jeanine Pettibone – Manager (replaced Ian Faith)
Ronnie Pudding – Bass
David St Hubbins (Michael McKean)
Viv Savage – Keyboards (replaced MacLochness)
Mick Shrimpton – Drums (replaced Bond but suffered same fate)
Ric Shrimpton – Drums (played in the 1992 revival group)
Derek Smalls (Harry Shearer) – Bass
Nigel Tufnel (Christopher Guest)
Denny Upham – Keyboards
CJ Vanston – Keyboards (played in the 1992 revival group)
Fictitious group played by McKean, Guest and Shearer in the 1984 satirical film *This Is Spinal Tap*, although spawning minor hits such as 'Bitch School' and 'The Majesty of Rock'.

Squeeze
Paul Carrack – Keyboards and Vocals
Chris Difford – Guitar and Vocals
Paul Gunn – Drums (replaced by Gilson Lavis)
Jools Holland – Keyboards and Vocals
Gilson Lavis – Drums
Glenn Tilbrook – Guitar and Vocals
Miles Copeland – Manager (in the early days)

Starsailor
Ben Byrne – Drums
James Stelfox – Bass
James Walsh – Vocals and Guitar
Barry Westhead – Keyboards

Status Quo
John Coghlan – Drums
Alan Lancaster – Bass
Roy Lynes – Keyboards
Rick Parfitt – Guitar and Vocals
Francis Rossi – Guitar and Vocals
The above are the five founding members, although various other musicians have played with the Quo over the years

Steps
Lee Latchford-Evans
Claire Richards
Lisa Scott-Lee
Faye Tozer
Ian 'H' Watkins

Stereophonics
Stuart Cable – Drummer
Kelly Jones – Lead Vocals and Guitar
Richard Jones – Bass

Stone Roses
Ian Brown – Vocals
Andy Couzens – Guitar
Pete Garner – Bass (replaced by Gary 'Mani' Mounfield)
Gary 'Mani' Mounfield – Bass
John Squire – Guitar
Simon Wolstencroft – Drums (replaced by Alan 'Reni' Wren)
Alan 'Reni' Wren – Drums

Stranglers, The
Jet Black – Drums
Jean-Jacques Burnel – Bass and Vocals
Hugh Cornwell – Guitar and Vocals
Dave Greenfield – Keyboards

Streets, The
Mike Skinner

Strokes, The
Julian Casablancas – Lead Vocals
Nikolai Fraiture – Bass
Albert Hammond Jr – Guitar
Fabrizio Moretti – Drums
Nick Valensi – Guitar

Suede
Brett Anderson – Lead Vocalist
Bernard Butler – Guitar (replaced by Richard Oakes)
Neil Codling – Keyboard, Vocals
Justine Frischmann – Guitar (left)
Simon Gilbert – Drums
Richard Oakes – Guitar
Mat Osman – Bass

Sugababes, The
Amelle Berrabah (replaced Buena)
Keisha Buchanan
Mutya Buena
Siobhan Donaghy (left in 2001)
Heidi Range (replaced Donaghy)

Super Furry Animals
Huw 'Bunf' Bunford – Guitar and Vocals
Cian Ciaran – Keyboards
Dafydd Ieuan – Drums
Guto Pryce – Bass
Gruff Rhys – Lead Vocals and Guitar

Supergrass
Gaz Coombes – Lead Vocals and Guitar
Danny Goffey – Drums
Micky Quinn – Bass

Supertramp
Rick Davies – Keyboards, Harmonica and Vocals
Mark Hart – Keyboards and Vocals
John Helliwell – Keyboards and Saxophones
Cliff Hugo – Bass
Bob Sjebenberg – Drums

Jesse Sjebenberg – Keyboards, Guitar, Percussion and Vocals
Dougie Thompson – Bass
Lee Thornburg – Trumpet and Trombone
Carl Verheyen – Guitar and Vocals

Supremes
Florence Ballard
Cindy Birdsong
Diana Ross
Jean Terrell (joined after Ross left)
Mary Wilson (replaced by Birdsong on becoming Supremes)
Jean Terrell (joined after Ross left)
Originally called Primettes

Sweet
Brian Connolly – Vocals (founding member, died in 1997)
Steve Priest – Bass (founding member)
Andy Scott – Guitar
Mick Stewart – Guitar
Frank Torpey – Guitar (founding member)
Mick Tucker – Drums (founding member)
Phil Wainman – Drums

Take That
Gary Barlow – Lead Vocals, Piano and Composer
Howard Donald
Jason Orange
Mark Owen
Robbie Williams (left in 1995 but rejoined in 2010)
Disbanded in February 1996, reformed (without Williams) 2005

Talking Heads
David Byrne – Guitar and Lead Vocals
Chris Frantz – Drums
Jerry Harrison – Guitar, Keyboards and Vocals
Martina Weymouth – Bass

Tears For Fears
Oleta Adams – Vocals
Roland Orzabal – Guitar, Keyboards and Vocals (founder)
Curt Smith – Bass and Vocals (founding member)
Ian Stanley – Keyboards
Basically a duo that became a one-man band when
Curt Smith left in 1991

Temptations
Dennis Edwards
Mel Franklin
Eddie Kendricks
David Ruffin
Otis Williams
Paul Williams

10CC
Lol Creme – Guitar and Keyboards
Kevin Godley – Drums, Percussion and Vocals
Graham Gouldman – Bass, Guitar and Vocals
Eric Stewart – Guitar, Piano and Vocals

Ten Years After
Chick Churchill – Keyboards
Alvin Lee – Guitar and Vocals
Ric Lee – Drums and Percussions
Leo Lyons – Bass

Texas
Eddie Campbell – Keyboards
Richard Hynde – Drums
Stuart Kerr – Drums
Johnny McElhone – Bass
Ally McErlaine – Guitar
Tony McGovern – Guitar
Sharleen Spiteri – Lead Vocals and Guitar
Mykey Wilson – Drums

Them
Jim Armstrong – Sitar, Guitar and Drums
Peter Bardens – Organ
Ray Elliot – Organ, Flute, Saxophone
Billy Harrison – Guitar
David Harvey – Drums
Alan Henderson – Bass
John McAuley – Drums, Harmonica and Vocals
Ray Ken McPowell – Vocals
Van Morrison – Harmonica, Tenor Saxophone and Vocals

Them Crooked Vultures
Dave Grohl – Drums
Josh Homme – Guitar and Vocals
John Paul Jones – Bass and Keyboard

Thin Lizzy
Eric Bell – Guitar (founding member 1970–74)
Brian Downey – Drums (founding member 1970–83)
John DuCann – Guitar (January to April 1974)
Dave Flett – Guitar (1979–80)
Andy Gee – Guitar (January to April 1974)
Scott Gorham – Guitar (1974–83)
Phil Lynott – Bass and Vocals (founding member, died 1986)
Gary Moore – Guitar (January to April 1974 and 1977–9)
Mark Nauseef – Drums (1978–9)
Brian 'Robbo' Robertson – Guitar and Vocals (1974–8)
Midge Ure – Guitar (1979–80)
Darren Wharton – Keyboards (1980-83)
Snowy White – Guitar (1980–82)
Eric Wrixon – Keyboards (founding member, 1970)

Thompson Twins
Tom Bailey – Synthesiser and Vocals
Chris Bell – Drums
Alannah Currie – Percussion, Saxophone and Vocals
Joe Leeway – Percussion
John Roog – Guitar
Matthew Seligman – Bass
Pete Todd – Guitar

Three Degrees
Sheila Ferguson
Valerie Holiday
Fayette Pinkney

Three Dog Night
Michael Allsup – Guitar
Jimmy Greenspoon – Keyboards
Danny Hutton – Vocals
Chuck Negren – Vocals
Joe Schermie – Bass
Floyd Sneed – Drums and Percussion
Cory Wells – Vocals

Thrills, The
Ben Carrigan – Drums
Conor Deasy – Vocals
Kevin Horan – Keyboards
Patraic McMahon – Bass
Daniel Ryan – Guitar

Thunderclap Newman
Speedy Keen – Drums, Guitar and Vocals
Jimmy McCulloch – Guitar
Andy Newman – Keyboards

Ting Tings
Jules De Martino – Drums and Guitar
Katie White – Vocals and Guitar

TLC
Lisa 'Left-eye' Lopes (died in 2002)
Rozonda 'Chilli' Thomas
Tionne 'T-Boz' Watkins

Toploader
Julian Deane – Lead Guitar and Vocals
Rob Green – Drums
Dan Hipgrave – Rhythm and Acoustic Guitar
Matt Knight – Bass
Joseph Washbourn – Lead Vocals, Piano and Organ

T'Pau
Tim Burgess – Drums
Michael Chetwood – Keyboards
Carol Decker – Vocals
Paul Jackson – Bass

Ron Rogers – Guitar
Taj Wyzgowski – Guitar

Traffic
Reebop Kwaku Baah – Percussion
Barry Beckett – Keyboards
Jim Capaldi – Drums, Percussion and Vocals
Jim Gordon – Drums
Rick Grech – Bass and Violin
Roger Hawkins – Drums
David Hood – Bass
Dave Mason – Bass, Guitar, Sitar and Vocals
Steve Winwood – Lead Vocals, Guitar and Keyboard
Chris Wood – Flute, Organ, Percussion, Saxophone, Vocals)

Travelling Wilburys
Bob Dylan
George Harrison
Jeff Lynne
Roy Orbison
Tom Petty

Travis
Andy Dunlop – Lead Guitar
Fran Healey – Lead Vocals and Guitar
Douglas Payne – Bass
Neil Primrose – Drums

Tremeloes, The
Alan Blakely – Guitar
Dave Munden – Drums
Len 'Chip' Hawkes – Bass and Vocals
Rick West – Guitar
Formed 1959 and began life as backing group to Brian Poole. Signed by Decca in preference to The Beatles, who auditioned on the same day. When Poole went solo in 1966 they became equally -successful in their own right.

T Rex
Miller Anderson – Guitar
Marc Bolan – Guitar and Vocals (died 1977)
Steve Currie – Bass
Dino Dines – Keyboards
Mickey Finn – Drums and Percussion
Herbie Flowers – Bass
Jack Green – Guitar
Gloria Jones – Vocals and Clarinet
Bill Legend – Drums
Dave Lutton – Drums
Tony Newman – Drums
Tyrone Scott – Keyboards
Steve 'Peregrine' Took – Percussion (replaced by Finn in 1969)
Tony Visconti
Formed in 1968 as Tyrannosaurus Rex but shortened to T Rex by the time of their first number one, 'Hot Love', in 1971

Troggs
Ronnie Bond – Drums and Percussion
Chris Britton – Guitar
Reg Presley – Lead Vocals
Peter Staples – Bass

2 Unlimited
Anita Doth (stage name of Anita Dells)
Ray Slijngaard

U2
Adam Clayton
Dave 'The Edge' Evans
Paul 'Bono' Hewson
Larry Mullen Jr

UB40
Astro – Trumpet, Vocals
James Brown – Drums
Ali Campbell – Lead Vocals
Robin Campbell – Guitar and Vocals
Earl Falconer – Bass and Vocals
Norman Hassan – Percussion and Vocals
Martin Meredith – Saxophone and Keyboards
Laurence Parry – Trumpet and Trombone
Brian Travers – Saxophone and Horn
Michael Virtue – Keyboards

Velvet Revolver
Dave Kushner – Guitar
Duff McKagan – Bass
Slash – Lead Guitar
Matt Sorum – Drums
Scott Weiland – Vocals (left in 2008)

Velvet Underground
Willie 'Loco' Alexander – (replaced Lou Reed)
John Cale – Vocals and various stringed instruments
Sterling Morrison – Guitar
Nico – Occasional Lead Singer (died 1988)
Lou Reed – Lead Vocals, Keyboards, Guitar
Maureen Tucker – Vocals, Guitar and Drums
Doug Yule – Vocals and Bass (replaced John Cale)

Vengaboys
DJ Dansky
DJ Delmundo
Denice
Kim
Robin
Roy
Yorick (replaced Robin in 1999)
Formed by Spanish DJs Dansky and Delmundo but the four singer / dancers from Hungary, Trinidad, Brazil and Holland became the live performers. Vengaboys became the first Netherlands-based act to score six successive Top 5 singles.

Verve
Richard Ashcroft – Lead Vocals and Guitar
Simon Jones – Bass
Nick McCable – Lead Guitar
Peter Salisbury – Drums
Simon Tang – Guitars, Keyboard

Village People
Eric Anzalone – Biker (replaced Glenn Hughes)
Alexander Briley – G.I.
David Hodo – Construction Worker
Glenn Hughes – Biker
Jeff Olson – Cowboy
Felipe Rose – Indian
Victor Willis – Cop (replaced by Ray Simpson)

Visage
Rusty Egan – Founding Member
Sandrine Gouriou – Present Member
Rosie Harris – Present Member
Steve Strange – Founding and present member
Ross Tregenza – Present Member
Midge Ure – Founding Member
Seven Young – Present Member

Vixen
Janet 'Patricia' Gardner – Vocals
Laurie Hedlund – Drums
Tamara Ivanov – Rhythm Guitar
Pia Koko – Bass
Jan 'Lynn' Kuehnemund – Lead Guitar and Founder
Sharon 'Share' Pederson – Bass (replaced Pia Koko)
Maxine Petrucci – Bass (replaced Share Pederson)
Roxy Petrucci – Drums (replaced Laurie Hedlund)
Rana Ross – Bass (replaced Maxine Petrucci)
Gina Stile – Rhythm Guitar (replaced Tamara Ivanov)

Wailers
Aston Barrett – Bass, Guitar and Percussion
Carlton Barrett – Drums and Percussion
Tyrone Downie – Bass, Keyboards and Percussion
Bob Marley – Guitar, Percussion and Lead Vocals (died in 1981)
Alvin Patterson – Percussion
Earl Smith – Guitar and Percussion
I-Threes – Marcia Griffiths, Rita Marley, Judy Mowati
I-Threes were a vocal trio that backed Marley

Walker Brothers
Scott Engel (assumed the name Scott Walker)
Gary Leeds – Drums
John Maus – Guitar and Vocals

Was (Not Was)
Don Fagenson
David Weiss

Weather Girls
Izora Redman
Martha Wash

Weezer
Brian Bell – Guitar and Vocals
Rivers Cuomo – Lead Vocals and Rhythm Guitar
Matt Sharp – Bass and Vocals
Patrick Wilson – Drums

Westlife
Nicky Byrne
Klan Egan – Piano
Mark Feehily
Shane Filan – Lead Vocals
Bryan McFadden
Only act to reach No 1 with their first 7 releases, all entered at the top, and only band to have 4 number ones in a single year.

Wet Wet Wet
Graeme Clark – Bass and Vocals
Tom Cunningham – Drums
Neil Mitchell – Keyboard and Vocals
Marti Pellow (born Mark McLoughlin) – Lead Vocals

Wham!
George Michael
Andrew Ridgeley

Whitesnake
Tommy Aldridge – Drums
Richard Bailey – Keyboards
Vivian Campbell – Guitar
Denny Carmassi – Drums
David Coverdale – Guitar and Vocals
Warren DeMartini – Guitar
David Dowle – Drums
Aynsley Dumber – Drums
Mel Galley – Guitar
Colin Hodgkinson – Bass
Brian Johnston – Keyboards
Jon Lord – Keyboards
Bernie Marsden – Guitar
Micky Moody – Guitar
Neil Murray – Bass
Ian Paice – Drums
Cozy Powell – Drums
Guy 'Starka' Pratt
Rudy Sarzo – Bass
Rick Serrate – Keyboards
Pete Solley – Keyboards
John Sykes – Guitar
Brett Tuggle – Keyboards
Steve Vai – Guitar
Adrian Vandenberg – Guitar

White Stripes, The
Jack White – Lead Vocals, Guitar and Piano
Meg White – Drums and Vocals

Who, The
Roger Daltrey – Lead Vocals
John Entwistle – Bass, Vocals, Piano and Brass (died in 2002)
Kenny Jones – Drums (replaced Keith Moon)
Keith Moon – Drums and Percussion (died in 1978)
Pete Townshend – Guitar, Organ, Synthesizer and Vocals

Wings
Geoff Britton – Drums
Joe English – Vocals, Drums (1975–6 replaced Sewell)
Denny Laine – Vocals, Keyboards, Guitar
Linda McCartney – Vocals, Keyboard (died in 1998)
Paul McCartney – Vocals, Piano, Bass
Jimmy McCulloch – Guitar and Vocals
Denny Sewell – Drums, Percussion and Vocals (1971–5)

Wizzard
Mike Burney – Saxophone
Charlie Grima – Drums and Percussion
Bill Hunt – Keyboards
Hugh McDowell – Cello
Nick Pentelow – Saxophone
Rick Price – Bass and Vocals
Keith Smart – Drums
Roy Wood – Guitar and Vocals

Wombats, The
Dan Haggis – Drums
Matthew Murphy – Vocals, Guitar, Keyboards
Tord Øverland-Knudsen – Bass

Wu Tang Clan
Genius, Ghostface Killah, Inspectah Deck, Masta Killa, Method Man, Ol' Dirty Bastard, Raekwon, RZA, U-God

X-Ray Spex
Jak 'Airport' Stafford – Guitar
Paul Dean – Bass
Glyn Johns – Saxophone
Paul 'BP' Hurding – Drums
Lora Logic and Steve 'Rudi' Thompson – Saxophones
Poly Styrene – Vocals

Yardbirds
Jeff Beck – Lead Guitar (replaced Eric Clapton in 1965)
Eric Clapton – Lead Guitar (replaced Top Topham in 1963)
Chris Dreja – Guitar (became bass after Samwell-Smith left)
Jim McCarty – Drums
Jimmy Page – Lead Guitar (replaced Samwell-Smith in 1966)
Keith Relf – Lead Vocals and Harmonica
Paul Samwell-Smith – Bass
Anthony 'Top' Topham – Lead Guitar

Yazoo
Vince Clarke – Drum Machine, Guitar and Keyboards
Alison 'Alf' Moyet – Vocals

Yes
Jon Anderson – Vocals (left briefly in 1980 but rejoined 1983)
Peter Banks – Guitar
Bill Bruford – Drums
Geoff Downes – Keyboards (replaced Rick Wakeman 1980)
Trevor Horn – Guitar and Vocals (replaced Anderson in 1980)
Steve Howe – Guitar (replaced Peter Banks in 1970)
Tony Kaye – Organ (1968–71 and then rejoined in 1983)
Patrick Moraz – Keyboards (replaced Rick Wakeman 1974)
Trevor Rabin – Guitar joined in 1983)
Chris Squire – Bass (remained with the band throughout)
Rick Wakeman – Keyboards (1971–4, rejoined 1976–80)
Alan White – Drums (replaced Bill Bruford in 1972)

Young Knives, The
Oliver Askew – Drums
Henry Dartnell – Vocals, Guitar
Thomas 'House of Lords' Dartnall – Vocals, Bass

Zombies
Rod Argent – Clarinet, Keyboards, Violin and Vocals
Paul Atkinson – Guitar, Violin and Harmonica
Colin Blunstone – Guitar, Percussion and Vocals
Hugh Grundy – Drums
Chris White – Bass and Vocals

Zutons, The
Boyan Chowdhury – Guitar
Abi Harding – Saxophone
David McCabe – Vocals
Sean Payne – Drums
Russell Pritchard – Bass

ZZ Top
Frank Beard – Drums (ironically only clean-shaven member)
Billy Gibbons – Vocals, Guitar
Dusty Hill – Bass

General Information

album charts: first No. 1 *South Pacific, Original Soundtrack.*

album charts: started 1958.

album cover: famous designers Peter Blake (Sgt Peppers), Klaus Voorman (Revolver) and Storm Thorgerson (Dark Side of the Moon).

best-selling UK single 'Candle in the Wind '97' (by Elton John)

B sides: famous 'I Talk to the Trees' by Clint Eastwood, B side of 'Wand'rin Star'; 'I Do it For You' by Fatima Mansions, B side of 'Theme from Mash' by Manic Street Preachers.

bongo player on 'Apache' Cliff Richard.

Booker T. and the M.G.s MG stands for Memphis Group.

charts: symbol indicating rise or fall Bullet.

Crowd: 'Ferry 'Cross the Mersey' Christians, Holly Johnson, Paul McCartney, Gerry Marsden and Stock Aitken Waterman.

David Bowie First TV appearance on *Gadzooks! It's All Happening* in 1965 with the Manish Boys. Other groups he formed included King Bees, Kon-Rads, Feathers, Hype, and the Lower Third.

Demis Roussos *Phenomenon* EP: Tracks 'Forever and Ever', 'Sing an Ode To Love', 'So Dreamy', 'My Friend the Wind'.

download chart 'Flying Without Wings' by Westlife was No. 1 in the first official download chart, announced on BBC Radio 1 on 1 September 2004.

Gorillaz Virtual band created by Damon Albarn & Jamie Hewlett.

Madonna: father of children Carlos Leon, actor and personal trainer, Guy Ritchie, film director (husband).

Monkees Advertisement in the Los Angeles *Daily Vanity* in September 1965 by Bob Rafelson and Bert Schneider led to the formation of the band. Of the 437 hopefuls who were auditioned, Stephen Stills, Charles Manson and Danny Hutton (later of Three Dog Night) were among those turned down.

most weeks on LP charts *Bat Out of Hell*

No. 1 in LP charts throughout year *South Pacific, Original Soundtrack* (1959).

pop star thrown off plane in Germany Keith Flint of Prodigy.

single charts: started 14 November 1952 (12 records).

single: wrong name on label 'Elizabethan Reggae' by Boris Gardiner originally had 'Byron Lee' on label.

Spice Girls: No. 1s Four of the five original members have had solo No. 1s, although Victoria Beckham's highest chart entry is at number two.

That's What Friends Are For Dionne Warwick and Friends featuring Elton John, Stevie Wonder and Gladys Knight.

1000th No. 1 'One Night' / 'I Got Stung' double A-side for Elvis Presley. Also became his 20th No. 1.

Top of the Pops: theme tunes 'Whole Lotta Love' (CCS), 'Yellow Pearl' (Phil Lynott), 'The Wizard' (Paul Hardcastle), 'Get out of That' (Tony Gibber).

Vice-President of USA wrote: No. 1 Hit Charles Dawes adapted his 'Melodie' with Carl Sigman, which became 'It's all in the game'.

Vince Clarke: bands involved with Depeche Mode, Yazoo (with Alison Moyet) and Erasure (with Andy Bell).

Previous Names of Groups

The Alarm Toilets, 17
Alphabeat Sodastar
America Daze
Applejacks Jaguars, Crestas
Badfinger Iveys
Bangles Supersonic Bangs, The Bangs
Bauhaus Bauhaus 1919
Beach Boys Carl and the Passions
Beatles Silver Beatles, Quarrymen, Beatals, Beat Brothers
Black Eyed Peas Atban Klann
Black Sabbath Earth
Boomtown Rats Nightlife Thugs
Boyz II Men Unique Attraction
The Christians Natural High
The Commodores Mighty Mystics
The Cult Southern Death Cult
Culture Club In Praise of Lemmings, Sex Gang Children
The Cure The Easy Cure
Deep Purple Roundabout
Depeche Mode Composition of Sound
Dire Straits Cafe Racers
Doobie Brothers Pud
Dr Hook Chocolate Papers
Eurythmics The Catch, Tourists
Faces Quiet Melon, Small Faces
Family Farinas
Fifth Dimension Versatiles
The Fixx Portraits, The Fix
The Fourmost Blue Jays, Four Jays
The Four Seasons Variatones, Four Lovers
The Four Tops Four Aims
Frankie Goes to Hollywood Hollycaust
Freddie and the Dreamers Kingfishers
Genesis Garden Wall
Gerry and the Pacemakers Mars Bars
The Grateful Dead Warlocks
Herman's Hermits Heartbeats
Hollies Fourtones, Deltas
Human League Dead Daughters, Future
Icehouse Flowers
INXS Farriss Brothers
JLS UFO (Unique Famous Outrageous)
Joy Division Warsaw
Led Zeppelin New Yardbirds, Birmingham Water Buffalo Society
Madness The Invaders
Mamas and the Papas The New Journeymen, Mugwumps
Manfred Mann Mann-Hugg Blues Brothers
Marillion Silmarillion
The Mission Sisters of Mercy
Mothers of Invention Muthers, Mothers
Mott the Hoople Silence
New Order Joy Division
Orchestral Manoeuvres in the Dark (OMD) VCL XL
Pogo Poco
Pogues Pogue Mahone
Procol Harum Paramounts
Righteous Brothers Paramours
Shadows Drifters
Simon and Garfunkel Tom and Jerry
Simply Red Frantic Elevators
Slade Ambrose Slade, 'N' Betweens
Sonny and Cher Caesar and Cleo
Spice Girls Touch (without Emma Bunton)
Split Enz Split Ends
Starsailor Waterface
Starship Jefferson Airplane, Jefferson Starship
Status Quo Spectres, Traffic Jam
Stone Roses Patrol, English Rose
Stranglers Guildford Stranglers
Strawbs Strawberry Hill Boys
Supremes Primettes
Sweet Wainwright's Gentlemen, Sweetshop
Swinging Blue Jeans Bluegenes
Talking Heads Portable Crushers, Vague Dots
Ten Years After Jaybirds
T Rex Tyrannosaurus Rex
Ultravox Zips, Innocents, London Soundtrack, Fire of London
Wham Executive (Paul Ridgeley and David Mortimer in line-up)
The Who High Numbers
The Young Knives Simple Pastoral Existence

Mythology and Legend

Deities

Role	*Greek*	*Roman*	*Egyptian*	*Norse*	*Sumerian*
Principal god	Zeus	Jupiter	Am(m)on	Odin	An
Principal goddess	Hera	Juno	Mut	Frigg	Inanna
Messenger of the gods	Hermes	Mercury	Thoth	Hermod	Uncertain
God of agriculture	Cronus	Saturn	Osiris	Frey	Emesh
Goddess of agriculture	Demeter	Ceres	Renenutet	Rindr	Nisaba
Goddess of childbirth	Eileithyia	Juno	Apet	Uncertain	Ninhursaga
Goddess of the dawn	Eos	Aurora	Uncertain	Uncertain	Anahita
God of the dead	Thanatos	Mors	Anubis	Odin	Nergal
Goddess of death	Hecate	Libitina	Nephthys	Hel	Uncertain
God of destruction	Ares	Mars	Seth	Uncertain	Uncertain
God of dreams	Morpheus	Morpheus	Uncertain	Uncertain	Uncertain
God of the Earth	Aesculapius	Aesculapius	Geb	Uncertain	Uncertain
Goddess of the Earth	Gaia	Tellus	Maat	Nerthus	Ki
God of fertility	Priapus	Faunus	Ing	Frey	Ninurta
Goddess of fertility	Artemis	Diana	Bastet	Gefjon	Inanna
God of fire	Hephaestus	Vulcan	Ptah	Loki	Gerra
Goddess of flowers	Hestia	Flora	Qudshu	Nanna	Uncertain
Goddess of health	Hygeia	Salus	Meresger	Eir	Nininsina Dazimus
Goddess of the hearth	Hestia	Vesta	Uncertain	Sigyn	Uncertain
God of heaven	Zeus	Jupiter	Ptah	Uncertain	An
Goddess of the hunt	Artemis	Diana	Neith	Skadi	Uncertain
Goddess of justice	Themis	Uncertain	Maat	Forseti (god)	Uncertain
God of love	Eros	Cupid	Uncertain	Baldur	Uncertain
Goddess of love	Aphrodite	Venus	Hathor	Freyja	Inanna
Goddess of magic	Hecate	Uncertain	Isis	Uncertain	Uncertain
God of marriage	Hymen	Hymen	Bes	Uncertain	Uncertain
God of the Moon	Apollo	Apollo	Neferhotep	Uncertain	Nanna
Goddess of the Moon	Selene	Luna	Isis	Mani	Ningal
Goddess of motherhood	Rhea	Ops	Taweret	Uncertain	Uncertain
God of music	Apollo	Apollo	Uncertain	Bragi	Uncertain
Goddess of night	Nyx	Uncertain	Nephthys	Nott	Uncertain
Goddess of peace	Irene	Pax	Uncertain	Eir	Uncertain
God of poetry	Apollo	Apollo	Thoth	Odin/Bragi	Uncertain
Goddess of the rainbow	Iris	Uncertain	Uncertain	Uncertain	Uncertain
God of the sea	Poseidon	Neptune	Nun	Aegir/Njord	Apsu
Goddess of the sea	Amphitrite	Salacia	Tefenet	Ran	Nammu
God of the sky	Uranus	Jupiter	Uncertain	Odin	An
Goddess of the sky	Hera	Juno	Nut	Uncertain	Inanna
God of sleep	Hypnos	Somnus	Uncertain	Uncertain	Uncertain
Goddess of spring	Persephone	Proserpine	Renpet	Uncertain	Ninkasi
God of the sun	Helios	Sol	Ra (Re)	Sol	Utu
God of thunder	Hephaestus	Jupiter	Seth	Thor	Adad
Goddess of truth	Themis	Justitia	Maat	Uncertain	Uncertain
God of the Underworld	Pluto/Hades	Orcus/Dis	Osiris	Villi	Endugukka
Goddess of the Underworld	Hecate	Proserpine	Hathor	Hel	Ereshkigal
Goddess of victory	Nike	Victoria	Apet	Uncertain	Uncertain
God of war	Ares	Mars	Seth	Tyr/Odin	Ninurta
Goddess of war	Athene	Minerva	Sekhmet	Uncertain	Inanna
God of water	Ganymede	Uncertain	Hapi	Uncertain	Enki
God of wine	Dionysus	Bacchus/Liber	Bes	Uncertain	Uncertain
God of wisdom	Apollo	Apollo	Thoth	Odin	Enki
Goddess of wisdom	Athene	Minerva	Neith	Snotra	Hea
God of woods	Pan	Silvanus	Min	Uncertain	Ashnan
Goddess of youth	Hebe	Juventas	Renpet	Uncertain	Uncertain

Deities of Other Mythologies

Role	***Babylonian***	***Hindu***	***Phoenician***	***Celtic***	***Aztec***
King of the gods	Marduk	Indra	Kumarbi/El	Dagda	Tezcatlipoca
God of agriculture	Tammuz	Sita	Telepinu	Amaethon	Centeotl
Goddess of childbirth	Uncertain	Shashti	Ashtaroth	Brigit	Chihuacoatl
Goddess of the dawn	Aja	Ushas	Shachar	Uncertain	Uncertain
God of the Dead	Uncertain	Yama	Mot	Dagda	Mictlantecuhtli
Goddess of death	Uncertain	Kali	Uncertain	Morrígan	Mictlantecuhtli
God of destruction	Uncertain	Shiva	Uncertain	Balor	Itzlacoliuhqui
God of the Earth	Apsu	Uncertain	Uncertain	Dagda	Ometecuhtli
Goddess of the Earth	Tiamat	Pitthivi	Beruth	Danu	Coatlicue
God of fertility	Hadad	Dyaus	Baal	Cernunnos	Tlaloc
Goddess of fertility	Ishtar	Prithivi	Anath/Astarte	Danu	Chalchiuhtlicue
God of fire	Uncertain	Agni	Uncertain	Belenus	Xiuhtecuhtli

Role	*Babylonian*	*Hindu*	*Phoenician*	*Celtic*	*Aztec*
Goddess of flowers	Uncertain	Uncertain	Uncertain	Olwen	Xochiquetzal
God of heaven	Apsu	Dyaus	Anu	Uncertain	Ometeotl
Goddess of the hunt	Uncertain	Minakshi	Uncertain	Abnoba	Uncertain
God of love	Uncertain	Kama	Uncertain	Angus	Huehuecoyotl
Goddess of love	Ishtar	Rati	Astarte	Aine	Xochiquetzal
Goddess of magic/witchcraft	Uncertain	Dursa	Kamrusepa	Bodhbh	Malinalxochi
God of the Moon	Sin	Chandra	Yarikh	Uncertain	Uncertain
Goddess of the Moon	Anunitu	Candi	Nikkal	Arianrhod	Coyolxauhqui
Goddess of motherhood	Nintur	Devi	Hannahanna	Danu	Chalchiuhtlicue
God of music	Uncertain	Uncertain	Uncertain	Maponus	Macuilxochitl
Goddess of night	Uncertain	Ratri	Shalim	Uncertain	Itzlacoliuhqui
God of poetry	Uncertain	Uncertain	Uncertain	Ogma	Huitzilopochtli
God of the sea	Uncertain	Varuna	Yamm	Manannan	Uncertain
Goddess of the sea	Tiamat	Uncertain	Asherat	Don	Chalchiuhtlicue
God of the sky	Anu	Dyaus	Teshub	Camulus	Tlaloc
Goddess of the sky	Tiamat	Aditi	Shapash	Don	Uncertain
God of the sun	Shamash	Surya	Nergal	Lug	Tonatiuh
God of thunder	Hadad	Indra	Taru	Taranis	Tlaloc
God of war	Uncertain	Karttikeya	Astabis	Uncertain	Huitzilopochtli
Goddess of war	Ishtar	Durga	Astarte	Morrígan	Clhvacoatl
God of water	Ea	Varuna	Uncertain	Nechtan	Tlaloc
God of wine	Uncertain	Uncertain	Uncertain	Uncertain	Tepoztecatl
God of wisdom	Ea	Ganes(h)a	Uncertain	Uncertain	Uncertain
Goddess of wisdom	Uncertain	Uncertain	Uncertain	Sul	Uncertain

NB: There are a number of points that should be borne in mind when studying the above tables.

First, it should be remembered that in many instances there would be more than one representation of a god for a particular subject. For example, as well as Aegir, both Njord and Vili are often described as Norse gods of the sea. In all cases I have listed the main god who is usually identified with the subject.

Second, there is often a transposition of gods in some mythologies, and in particular the Middle East should be treated with some care. Babylonian mythology is often called Assyrian, Akkadian or Persian, while Phoenician can also be called Hittite as well as Assyrian and Akkadian.

Third, where there is controversy over an entry or there is no god who represents a subject, the word 'Uncertain' has been entered; this does not mean, for instance, that there was no Egyptian god of love but merely that there is not a single god who unequivocally fits the criteria of being both universally accepted and identifiable.

Groups

Muses (9)	*Of*	*Literal meaning*	*Pleiades* (7)	*against Thebes* (7)	*Sages of India* (7)	*Hills of Rome* (7)
Thalia	Comedy	Good cheer	Maia	Polynices	Atri	Capitoline (can)
Clio	History	Fame	Taygete	Tydeus	Bharadvaja	Quirinal (queen)
Melpomene	Tragedy	Singing	Elektra	Adrastus	Gautama	Viminal (victoria)
Urania	Astronomy	Celestial	Alkyone	Capaneus	Jamadagni	Esquiline (Eat)
Polyhymnia	Song and mime	Many songs	Asterope	Hippomedon	Kashyapa	Caelian (cold)
Erato	Love poetry	Lovely	Kelaino	Parthenopaeus	Vashista	Aventine (apple)
Euterpe	Lyric poetry	Joy	Merope	Amphiarus	Visvamitra	Palatine (pie)
Calliope	Epic poetry	Beautiful voice				
Terpsichore	Dance	Joyful dance				

Furies (Erinyes or Eumenides)	*Graces (Charites)*	*Fates (Moerae)*	*Gorgons (3)*
Tisiphone (avenger of murder)	Euphrosyne (jollity)	Clotho (spun the thread of life)	Medusa
Alecto (relentless)	Aglaia (splendid/bright one)	Atropos (cut off the thread)	Euryale
Megaera (resentful)	Thaleia (good cheer)	Lachesis (measured the thread)	Stheno
Useful mnemonic: Furies aren't TAMe	Useful mnemonic: Say Grace before you EAT	Useful mnemonic: CALl the fates in time of trouble	Useful mnemonic: Medusa's hair was a MESs

Twelve Labours of Heracles

Killing of the Nemean lion Heracles beat the lion senseless and throttled it; he then skinned the lion with its own claws and donned the pelt to render himself invulnerable.

Killing of the Lernaean Hydra Iolaus cauterised the neck of the Hydra to prevent the two new heads growing each time that Heracles chopped off one of its nine heads.

Capture of the Hind on Mt Ceryneia Heracles chased the Hind for a year, for its golden horns and bronze hoofs. He blamed Eurystheus for its capture so as not to bring the wrath of Artemis on himself.

Capture of the Boar of Mt Erymanthus Heracles returned with the Boar to Tiryns, and Eurystheus hid in an urn at its sight.

Cleansing of the Augean stables Heracles cleaned the stables, which had not been cleaned in 30 years, by diverting the rivers Alpheus and Peneus through them.

Killing of the Birds of Lake Stymphalos Heracles scared them from the trees with bronze castanets and shot them with arrows.

Capture of the Cretan Bull Heracles captured the Bull and returned it to Greece.

Capture of the Mares of Diomedes Heracles slew Diomedes, fed him to the Mares and tamed them.

Capture of the Girdle of Hippolyte Heracles slew the queen of the Amazons and took the Girdle for Eurystheus' daughter.

Capture of Geryon's Cattle Heracles slew Geryon and returned to Greece with the Cattle.

Capture of the Apples of the Hesperides Heracles slew Ladon, the dragon that guarded the tree tended by the Hesperides, and took the Golden Apples (later returned by Athene).

Capture of Cerberus Heracles entered the underworld to capture the 3-headed dog.

General Information

Abderus Friend of Heracles in whose care Heracles left the mares of Diomedes. The horses ate him and Heracles founded a town in Thrace in his honour.
Abnoba The goddess of the hunt in the mythology of Gaul. Identified with the Roman Diana.
Acheloüs Greek river god, the son of Oceanus and Tethys.
Achilles Greek hero, born in Thessaly, son of Peleus and the goddess Thetis. When he was a baby his mother dipped him in the Styx, making him invulnerable save for his right heel, by which she held him.
Actaeon Greek hero, grandson of Cadmus, changed into a stag by Artemis and killed by his own hounds because he spied her bathing.
Admetus In Greek mythology the king of Pherae in Thessaly. Apollo served him for a year and introduced him to Alcestis.
Adonis Syrian god, the son of Myrrha and her father Cinyras. He was born from the bark of a tree and brought up by Persephone and forced to spend a third of his time with her and a third with Aphrodite. He was mortally wounded by a wild boar sent by a hostile god or goddess.
Aeacus Son of Zeus and Aegina and king of the Myrmidones. The Myrmidones were originally ants, transformed into men by Zeus at the request of Aeacus. He had two sons, Peleus and Telamon, by his wife Endeis and was also the father of Phocus by a Nereid. Aeacus was one of the three judges of the Underworld.
Aeëtes In Greek mythology, the king of Colchis and possessor of the Golden Fleece sought by Jason.
Aegeus Greek king of Athens and father of Theseus by Aethra, daughter of Pittheus, king of Troezen. Aethra brought Theseus up secretly at her father's court, during which time Aegeus married Medea. When Theseus finally returned to his father's court, Medea fled. Before Theseus went to slay the Minotaur he and Aegeus agreed that he would hoist a white sail when returning to Athens to signal his success. On returning, Theseus forgot to do this and Aegeus, seeing a black sail on his son's ship, supposed him dead and, in grief, threw himself into the sea, henceforth called the Aegean.
Aegisthus In Greek mythology the seducer of Clytemnestra, the wife of his cousin Agamemnon, whom the two lovers conspired to kill. Agamemnon's son Orestes avenged the assassination by killing Aegisthus and Clytemnestra.
Aeneas Trojan hero, son of Aphrodite and Anchises, bravest of the Trojans after Hector and, according to some Roman lines of mythology, the founder of Rome. Aeneas was the lover of Dido, queen of Carthage.
Aeneid Virgil's unfinished epic poem in 12 volumes recounting the deeds of Aeneas, supposed ancestor of Emperor Augustus of Rome. The epic begins after the fall of Troy and ends with the defeat of Turnus the Rutulian prince and the subsequent marriage of Aeneas and Lavinia, the Latin princess.
Aeolus Greek god of the winds and son of Poseidon who gave Odysseus a sack containing all the winds.
Aesculapius Roman god of medicine. Greek -counterpart is Asclepius.
Aesir Norse race of warlike gods, who lived in Asgard. They included Odin, Thor, Tyr, Baldur and Frigg (see Vanir).
Aetolus Conqueror of Aetolia. The son of Endymion, king of Elis, he was banished across the Corinthian Gulf after accidentally killing Apis in a chariot race.
Agamemnon Greek king of Argos, murdered by his wife Clytemnestra.
Aganippe Fountain at the foot of Mt Helicon, sacred to the Muses, who are sometimes called the Aganippides.
Ajax (the greater) Greek hero, a giant of a man, the son of Telamon. Killed himself in fury at not receiving Achille's armour after his death.
Ajax (the lesser) Greek hero, son of Oileus. Raped King Priam's daughter Cassandra on the altar of Athene.
Alcestis Greek heroine who saved her husband Admetus by offering her own life.
Alcheringa According to Australian aboriginal mythology, the Golden Age when the first ancestors were created.
Alcides Another name for Heracles, whose grand-father was reputed to be Alcaeus.
Alcmene Wife of Amphitrion, son of Alcaeus. Alcmene mothered Heracles by Zeus in the guise of her husband. Married Rhadamanthus after Amphitrion's death.
Alphito Greek barley goddess of Argos.
Amalthea She-goat. Zeus broke off one of Amalthea's horns to make the Cornucopia (Horn of Plenty).
Amazons Warrior women of Greek mythology who removed a breast to give free play to bow arm.
Amphitrion In Greek mythology king of Tiryns and husband of Alcmene.
Amphitrite Daughter of Nereus, leader of the Nereids. Mothered Triton by Poseidon.
Anchises According to Greek and Roman mytho-logy, the Trojan father of Aeneas by Aphrodite.
Androcles Roman slave who aided and befriended a lion that later saved his life when he was thrown to the lions for attempting to escape.
Andromache In Greek mythology, the wife of Hector and slave of Neoptolemus.
Andromeda According to Greek mythology, daughter of king Cepheus and queen Cassiopeia; she was rescued by Perseus from a sea-monster and subsequently married him.
Angels Nine choirs divided into three ranks: Seraphim, Cherubim and Thrones; Dominions, Powers and Virtues; Principalities, Archangels and Angels.
Antaeus Libyan giant, son of Poseidon and Ge, who was an invincible wrestler until Hercules – realising he drew his strength from his mother, Earth – held him in the air and squeezed him to death.
Antigone In Greek mythology the daughter of Oedipus and Jocasta and sister of Ismene.
Anubis Egyptian god who guides souls to the world beyond. Often depicted with the head of a jackal.
Aphrodite Greek goddess of love and beauty and wife of Hephaestus.
Apis In Egyptian mythology, the sacred bull of Memphis, seen as an incarnation of Osiris.
Apollo Greek and Roman god of prophecy, music, youth, archery and healing, and son of Zeus and Leto (Jupiter and Latona in Roman myth).
Arachne According to Greek mythology, a weaver from Lydia who was changed into a spider by Athena.
Ares Greek god of war, son of Zeus and Hera and lover of Aphrodite.
Arethusa Greek goddess of springs and fountains.
Argo The 50-oared longship which carried Jason and the Argonauts to Colchis in their quest for the Golden Fleece.
Argonauts The band of heroes chosen by Jason to man the Argo and sail in search of the Golden Fleece. The Argonauts included Argus, Atalanta, Calais, Castor and Polydeuces, Heracles, Meleager, Orpheus, Peleus, Telamon and Zetes.
Argus (1) Greek watchman with 100 eyes who watched over Io but was killed by Hermes. His eyes were placed in the peacock's tail by Hera. (2) The faithful hound of Odysseus/Ulysses. (3) The builder of the *Argo*.
Ariadne In Greek mythology, the daughter of King Minos of Crete and wife of Dionysus after Theseus abandoned her.
Arjuna The Hindu god of dawn and charioteer of the sun, often identified with the Greek and Roman goddesses Eos and Aurora. Arjuna was also known as Rumra (lit. rosy).
Artemis Greek goddess of fertility and the hunt, daughter of Zeus and Leto and twin sister of Apollo.
Arthur Legendary British king, son of Uther Pendragon and Igraine, said to have lived in the 6th century. He was born in Tintagel and buried in Glastonbury; Arthur's court was at Camelot (Winchester, according to Malory's *Morte d'Arthur*).
Aruru One of the names of the Sumerian goddess of childbirth, Ninhursaga (lit. germ loosener).
Asclepius Greek god of healing.
Asgard In Norse mythology the realm of the gods in heaven and connected to the earth by the rainbow bridge, Bifrost, which was guarded by Heimdall.
Ask In Norse myhtology the ash tree from which man was hewn.
Asphodel, Plain of That part of Hades reserved for the great proportion of the dead. There they continued a shadowy existence in continuance of their former lives since they were bodiless. Contrast Elysium and Tartarus.
Ataentsic According to Iroquois and Huron mythology, the first woman and ancestor of the human race.
Atalanta Greek heroine who refused to marry any man unless he could beat her in a foot race. Milanion became her husband after

Aphrodite helped him defeat her. Atalanta was the sole female Argonaut.
Aten Egyptian god; took the form of a solar disc.
Athene According to Greek mythology, the daughter of Zeus and Metis who sprang from her father's head fully armed. Among her titles was Parthenos (Virgin), from which the Parthenon was named.
Atlas Titan that bears up the earth. Son of Iapetus and Clymene and brother of Prometheus.
Attis Greek god of vegetation.
Autolycus Son of Hermes and Chione and grand-father of Odysseus.
Baba Yaga Witch or ogress in Slav mythology.
Bacchae Female followers of the cult of Bacchus or Dionysus.
Bacchus Roman mythological counterpart of the Greek Dionysus, god of wine and ecstasy.
Baldur Norse favourite of the gods and son of Odin and Frigg. Baldur was invulnerable to everything except mistletoe, and Loki tricked the blind god Hoder into throwing a mistletoe dart that killed him.
Balmung Siegfried's sword, according to the *Nibelungenlied.*
Basilisk Greek monster also called a Cockatrice, that killed with a stare.
Bastet According to Egyptian mythology, the cat-headed goddess of fertility, love and sex.
Befana Good fairy of Italian children who is supposed to fill their stockings with toys on Twelfth Night.
Belenus The Celtic god of healing and light, referred to as 'The Shining One'. He was in charge of the welfare of sheep and cattle. His wife is the goddess Belisama; they are often compared to the Roman Apollo and Minerva.
Bellerophon Greek hero who tamed Pegasus and killed the Chimera.
Bellona Greek goddess of war.
Beowulf Norse warrior prince who killed the man-eating monster Grendel in a wrestling match.
Bifrost In Norse mythology, the rainbow bridge that led from Asgard to Earth. Literally means quivering path.
Biton and Cleobis Sons of a priestess of Hera in Argos who drew their mother's chariot several miles to the goddess's temple when no oxen could be found.
Bor (Burr) Norse god who married the giantess Bestla. She bore him three sons, Odin, Villi and Vé.
Boreas Greek god of the north wind.
Bragi Norse god of poetry and music, son of Odin.
Briareus One of the Hecatoncheires. Aka Aegaeon.
Brigit Celtic goddess of the poetic arts, childbirth and divination.
Bunyip In Australian aboriginal mythology, monster who was the source of evil.
Cadmus In Greek mythology, the son of Agenor, king of Phoenicia and grandson of Poseidon. When Zeus carried off his sister Europa, he went to look for her but was told by the Delphic oracle to relinquish the search and to follow a magical cow. Where the cow lay down he was to found a city, the future city of Thebes. Cadmus married Harmonia.
Caishen Chinese god of wealth.
Calais Twin brother of Zetes. The winged sons of Boreas and Oreithyia, they accompanied the Argonauts and drove off the Harpies.
Calchas Renegade Trojan seer who helped the Greeks at Troy and foretold that Troy would not fall without Achilles' presence and that the sacrifice of Iphigenia was necessary to secure a favourable wind.
Callisto Daughter of Lycaon, who became one of Artemis's huntresses. She bore Arcas to Zeus, who sought to conceal their affair from his wife Hera by turning Callisto into a bear.
Calypso (Hidden) Nymph of the island of Ogygia who tended Odysseus there for 8 years until Zeus ordered him home to Ithaca.
Cassandra Greek heroine given the gift of prophecy by Apollo with the proviso that, although telling the truth, she would not be believed.
Cassiopeia Wife of Cepheus and mother of Andromeda.
Castor and Pollux Roman counterpart of Castor and Polydeuces.
Castor and Polydeuces Aka the Dioscuri, sons of Zeus and Leda. Castor was an expert horseman and Polydeuces was the best boxer in Greece. Some versions have the mortal Castor as son of Tyndareus (Leda lay with both Zeus and Tyndareus). They were transformed into the Gemini constellation
Centaur In Greek mythology the hybrid offspring of Centaurus, son of Ixion, and the mares of Mt Pelion in Thessaly.
Cepheus In Greek mythology, the husband of Cassiopeia and father of Andromeda.
Cerberus According to Greek mythology, the three-headed dog that guards the entrance to the Underworld. Offspring of Echidna and Typhon.
Chac Maya god of rain and lightening.
Chaos In Greek creation myth, Chaos was the infinite space existing before creation, from which Ge (the Earth) sprang.
Charon According to Greek mythology, the ferryman of the underworld. Offspring of Erebos and Nyx. Greeks to this day place a coin in the mouth of corpses to pay for the ferry charge.
Charybdis Greek mythological monster resembling a giant whirlpool which infested the Strait of Messina together with Scylla.
Chimera Greek monster with the head of lion, the body of a goat and the tail of a serpent. Offspring of Echidna and Typhon.
Chiron Centaur who was untypically wise and civilised. When Chiron died he became the constellation Sagittarius.
Circe Greek sorceress who turned Odysseus's men into swine. Daughter of Helios and Perse.
Clytemnestra Greek twin sister of Helen and wife of Agamemnon.
Conán the Bald According to Celtic mythology, a warrior and follower of the hero Finn Mac Cumhall. Conán was the son of Morna and brother of Goll.
Conchobar Celtic king of Ulster and illegitimate son of Nessa, queen of Ulster, and the druid Cathbhadh.
Consus Roman god of seed sowing.
Cressida According to Greek mythology, she deserted Troilus, a Trojan prince, for Diomedes.
Cretan bull Magnificent white bull sent by Poseidon to Minos for sacrifice. Minos's wife Pasiphaë so admired the bull that she had Daedalus construct a hollow cow for her to get inside and mate with the bull – that was how she came to bear the Minotaur. The bull was captured by Heracles, freed by Eurystheus and finally recaptured by Theseus at Marathon and sacrificed to Athene.
Croesus Last king of Lydia, famous for his vast wealth.
Cronus Greek god of agriculture and father of Zeus.
Cuchulainn In Celtic mythology the legendary Irish hero, called the 'Hound of Culann' because, having accidentally slain the watchdog of the smith, Culann, he subsequently took the animal's place as penance. He was brought up in the court of King Conchobar of Ulster, whose kingdom he defended against all invaders. Cuchulainn's parents were the sun god Lug, and Dechtire, the wife of an Ulster chieftain. Although Cuchulainn was a handsome youth, in battle he would turn into a frenzied monster, with one eye receding into his head while the other stood out huge and red on his cheek. Cuchulainn's wife was Emer, daughter of the chieftain Forgall. Women continued to fall in love with Cuchulainn after his marriage, and his eventual death was as a result of rebuffing the war goddess Morrigan, who assaulted him with innumerable foes.
Cupay In the mythology of the Peruvian Inca people, the god of death. He is sometimes known as Supay.
Cybele Greek goddess of the earth and lover of Attis.
Cyclops One-eyed giants descended from Gaia and Uranus. Polyphemus is most famous for his capture of Odysseus, who blinded him.
Daedalus In Greek mythology the greatest of mortal craftsmen who made wings out of wax and feathers for himself and his son Icarus to escape imprisonment in the Cretan labyrinth. However, Icarus flew too near the sun and fell to his death when the wax melted.
Damocles Member of the court of Dionysius I, tyrant of Syracuse. Cicero tells how the tyrant had him eat a sumptuous dinner while a sword was suspended by a hair over his head, to show him the limits of rank and power.
Danu (Dana) The Celtic earth-mother goddess, also identified with fertility, wisdom and the wind. In Welsh versions she is known as Don and is associated with the air and the sea.
Daphne Greek heroine turned into a laurel bush to evade Apollo.
Daphnis Son of Hermes and a nymph. The originator of pastoral poetry.
Deianeira Greek princess, the daughter of King Oenus and Queen Althaea of Aetolia, and the second wife of Heracles, whom she killed by mistake when she smeared his garment with a centaur's poisonous blood, thinking it was a love charm.
Deidamia Maiden who fell in love with Achilles and bore him Neoptolemus.

Deirdre According to Irish legend, she killed herself after being forced to marry King Conchobar.
Delphi Site of Apollo's Dorian shrine and oracle, the most famous centre of his worship.
Deucalion Greek hero, son of Prometheus, who repopulated the earth with his wife Pyrrha after Zeus's flood.
Devi (Mahadevi) In Hindu mythology the wife of S(h)iva. Originally there were several goddesses acknowledged as the wives of S(h)iva by different Hindu castes, but eventually they merged into the one manifestation, Devi. Other forms of Devi include, Bhairavi, Chandi, Durga, Gauri (Jagadgauri), Jaganmata, Kali, Parvati, Sati and Uma.
Dian-Cecht The Celtic god of medicine and healing, and the grandfather of the sun god Lug.
Dido Greek heroine, daughter of the King of Tyre, who founded Carthage. Virgil told of her suicide when abandoned by her lover, Aeneas.
Dioscuri (sons of Zeus) Zeus had intercourse with Leda in the form of a swan and she produced two eggs. From one came Castor and Clytemnestra and from the other came Polydeuces and Helen.
Draupnir Odin's magic ring.
Dryad In classical mythology a tree-nymph, sometimes called a hamadryad, which was supposed to die when the tree died. Oak trees were usually favoured by dryads.
Durga In Hindu mytholog a fierce form of Devi who was born fully grown and beautiful; she was immediately armed by the gods and sent forth against the buffalo demon Mahisha. Although blessed with beautiful golden skin, Durga had a fixed, menacing expression and rode upon a tiger. In each of her 10 hands she held one of the god's weapons, i.e. Agni's flaming dart, Indra's thunderbolt, Kubera's club, Shesha's garland of snakes, S(h)iva's trident, Surya's quiver and arrow, Varuna's conch shell, Vayu's bow, Vishnu's discus and Yama's iron rod.
Echidna In Greek mythology, she was the offspring of the earth goddess Gaia and her brother Tartarus. Echidna had the upper body of a nymph and the lower body of a serpent.
Echo Greek nymph who pined away till she was only a voice for the love of Narcissus.
Edda Norse collection of mythological and heroic lays. Also the title of a manual of mythology compiled by the Icelandic historian Snorri Sturluson (1178–1241).
Egeria Roman goddess of fountains and childbirth.
Electra Daughter of Agamemnon and Clytemnestra, and sister of Orestes and Iphegenia.
Electryon Son of Perseus and Andromeda, king of Mycenae and father of Alcmene, the wife of Amphitrion.
Elysian Fields (Elysium) Greek mythological paradise to which the great and virtuous went after death.
Embla In Norse mythology the elm tree from which woman was hewn.
Endymion King of Elis who was visited by Selene while sleeping in a cave and forced into an endless sleep so she could admire his beauty.
Enlil In Sumerian mythology one of the triad of creator-gods with Enki and An.
Epeius Cowardly son of Panopeus who built the Trojan horse.
Epigoni Greek sons of the 7 against Thebes who succeeded in destroying the city.
Epimetheus In Greek mythology, the brother of Prometheus and husband of Pandora.
Epona Roman goddess of horses.
Erebus (Darkness) Son of Chaos and father of Aether and Hemera by Night, his sister.
Eros (Desire) Greek god of love, the offspring of Aphrodite and Ares.
Eshmun The Phoenician god of healing, identified with the Greek Asclepius and Roman Aesculapius.
Europa According to Greek mythology, the daughter of King Agenor and Queen Telephassa of Phoenicia. Zeus wooed Europa as a bull and had intercourse with her in the guise of an eagle. She bore him three sons: Minos, Rhadamanthus and Sarpedon. Europa married the Cretan king Asterius.
Eurus South-east wind, son of Astraeus and Eos.
Eurydice Greek dryad, wife of Orpheus. She was lost forever after Orpheus looked back to make sure she was following as he led her out of Hades.
Eurystheus King of the Argolid region of the Peloponnese, son of King Sthenelus and Queen Nicippe of Mycenae. Heracles was sentenced to serve him for 12 years as penance for killing his wife, Megara. Eurystheus subsequently set him the twelve labours.
Fafnir In Germanic mythology a dragon who guarded the Nibelung hoard of treasure.
Fauna Roman goddess of fertility.
Faunus Roman god of crops, herds and woodlands.
Fenrir In Norse mythology a monstrous wolf who was the offspring of Loki.
Ferghus Irish hero of superhuman size and strength. King of Ulster before Conchobar, Ferghus was the lover of Nessa, the mother of Conchobar.
Feronia Roman goddess of spring flowers.
Fides Roman god of honesty.
Finn mac Cumhal Irish hero who possessed the gift of foresight when biting his thumb.
Fintan In Irish mythology the salmon of knowledge, which Finn mac Cumhal tasted accidentally. He burned his thumb on the flesh as he turned it on a spit. Once he sucked the thumb he became a sage.
Fjorgyn Norse goddess, mother of Thor.
Fortuna Roman goddess of chance and fate.
Frey Norse god of fertility.
Freyja Norse goddess of love, twin sister of Frey.
Frigg Norse goddess of fertility, wife of Odin.
Ganesha Hindu god depicted with the head of an elephant; the offspring of Parvati, the wife of S(h)iva.
Ganymede Greek god of rain and cupbearer to the gods; the son of King Tros of Troy.
Garang The first man according to the Dinka people of the Sudan.
Genius Roman protective god, one for every individual, group and State.
Geryon Three-bodied monster living on the island of Erythia who owned cattle guarded by Eurytion.
Gilgamesh Sumerian king of Uruk, son of the goddess Ninsun and a mortal. His story is told in the Gilgamesh epic, the oldest extant work of literature (*c.* 2000 BC), which tells of his search for the secret of eternal life.
Gimli In Norse mythology the highest heavenly abode that was not consumed in Ragnarok.
Ginnungagap In Norse mythology the 'Yawning Gap' or primeval emptiness, which held all the potential energy of creation.
Glaucus (1) King of Corinth, son of Sisyphus and Merope and father of Bellerophon. He fed his horses on human flesh but Aphrodite caused them to devour Glaucus himself because he mocked her.
Glaucus (2) Grandson of Bellerophon who fought for the Trojans and was slain by Ajax.
Glaucus (3) Son of Minos and Pasiphaë who was drowned in a barrel of honey.
Glaucus (4) Boeotian fisherman who pursued Scylla and was turned into a sea god on eating a magic herb.
Golden Age Concept of the Greek poet Hesiod, who listed Golden, Silver, Bronze and Iron as the four ages of man in his *Works and Days.*
Golden Bough A gift Aeneas had to take to Proserpina before he could enter the underworld.
Golden Fleece Fleece of the golden ram of Colchis, kept by King Aeëtes of Colchis and guarded by an unsleeping dragon.
Gorgons Three sisters – Eurydale, Medusa and Scheno – offspring of Phorcys and Ceto. Medusa was the mortal sister killed by Perseus. The Gorgons were the sisters of the Graiae.
Götterdämmerung Literally means 'Twilight of the Gods'; in Germanic mythology the equivalent of the Norse final battle, Ragnarok.
Graces Daughters of Zeus and the sea nymph Eurynome.
Graiae In Greek mythology, three sisters who had one eye and one tooth between them; sisters of the Gorgons.
Great Mother of the Gods Oriental and Greco-Roman deity, known as Cybele in Latin literature. Her full Roman name was Mater Deum Magna Idaea (Great Idaean Mother of the Gods). Her Phrygian name was Agdistis or Dindymus.
Griffin Greek monster with lion's body and eagle's head and wings.
Gula In Babylonian mythology the goddess of healing corresponding to the Sumerian Bau.
Hades In Greek mythology the son of Cronus and Rhea, and brother of Zeus and Poseidon. The three brothers drew lots for their realms and Hades drew the underworld. Although this nether world was not originally given a name, it became known by the name of its chief god Hades (unseen). The god Hades was also known as Pluto (rich), and the Roman equivalent was Dis or

Orcus. The realm of Hades can be sub-divided into Elysium, Tartarus and the Plain of Asphodel.

Hamadryad See Dryad.

Hanuman In Indian mythology the monkey that became the most loyal companion of Rama and his consort Sita.

Harpies Greek spirits with heads of women and bodies of birds.

Hebe Greek goddess of youth and spring, daughter of Zeus and Hera, and wife of Heracles after his death.

Hecate Greek goddess of the underworld and daughter of Coeus and Phoebe.

Hector According to Greek mythology, the bravest Trojan and son of Priam; the brother of Paris and husband of Andromache. Killed by Achilles.

Hecuba Wife of King Priam of Troy and mother of Hector, Paris, Troilus and Cassandra.

Heimdall Norse god, and guardian of the bridge, Bifrost. Born of nine mothers.

Hekatoncheires (100 hands) In Greek mythology, the name of three giants with 100 hands and 50 heads each: Briareus, Cottus and Gyges. They were the offspring of Gaia and Uranus.

Helen Greek heroine, daughter of Zeus and Leda, sister of Clytemnestra and Castor and Pollux.

Hephaestus Son of Zeus and Hera who was thrown from Olympia by his mother and landed in the sea. Hephaestus made the armour for Achilles.

Hera Greek goddess of marriage and childbirth and queen of the gods.

Heracles Greek hero who performed the Twelve Labours of Eurystheus. Offspring of Zeus and Alcmene.

Hercules Roman equivalent of Heracles.

Hermaphroditus Son of Hermes and Aphrodite. Salmacis embraced him so closely that they became fused as one, with a woman's breasts and a man's genitals.

Hermes Son of Zeus and Maia. Hermes invented the lyre soon after birth.

Hermione Daughter of Helen and Menelaus.

Hermod Norse god, son of Odin.

Hero Greek high priestess and lover of Leander, who swam the Hellespont every night to see her but was eventually drowned causing Hero to throw herself in the sea.

Hesperides In Greek mythology, the daughters of the evening star who guarded the Golden Apples together with the dragon Ladon.

Hindu myth and religion Of all the world's leading mythologies, by far the most complex and expansive are Hindu beliefs. Even the term 'mythology' does not sit easily with a body of culture that is still revered today. It is beyond the scope of this work to trace the roots of Hindu beliefs and philosophy with its many tributaries, which themselves form a whole, separate strata of mythology. Many of the gods have personifications under differing names, and others have re-incarnations (avatars), which may bring with them a whole new substrata of mythology. Hindu mythology does not lend itself to fall comfortably within the table of comparative gods, indeed, the choice of Indra as principal god, or king of the gods, can only be loosely adhered to as a comparative to Zeus or Jupiter. Hindu mythology can be further divided into pre-Vedic, late-Vedic, post-Vedic, pre-Aryan post-Aryan and Classical, all of which has its own version of the creation. In the late-Vedic period, *c.*1200 BC, Brahma might have been considered the most important Hindu god, but he was gradually eclipsed by Vishnu and S(h)iva. Strict adherence to the Veda would place Prajapati (Lord of Creatures) as the creator god. In another version, the Prajapatis are the 10 'mind-born' children of Brahma. The -traditional Trimurti of Brahma, Vishnu and S(h)iva, would be considered the most important Hindu gods, but it is true to say that Indra is the equivalent of Zeus in Greek mythology or Jupiter in Roman.

Hippolyte Queen of the Amazons and sister of Antiope.

Hoder Blind Norse god who killed Baldur.

Horus Egyptian god of light with a falcon's head, son of Osiris and Isis.

Huitzilopochtli Chief Aztec god, linked with the sun, fire, war and human sacrifice.

Hyacinthus Peloponnesian youth loved by Apollo who was killed when the jealous Zephyrus diverted a discus to hit him.

Hydra Greek monster usually depicted with 9 heads; slain by Heracles.

Hyperion Greek Titan, son of Uranus and Gaia.

Iapetus Greek Titan, father of Prometheus and Atlas, grandfather of Deucalion.

Icarus Son of Daedalus; he flew too near the sun while escaping from Crete and fell into the Aegean Sea and drowned.

Idavold In Norse mythology the playground of the gods.

Idomeneus King of Crete who contributed 100 ships to the expedition against Troy.

Idunn Norse goddess of the golden apples of youth, wife of Bragi.

Iliad Homer's epic poem on the siege of Troy.

Imhotep The Egyptian god of medicine and healing.

Io Greek heroine turned into a heifer by Zeus to save her from the wrath of Hera.

Iphigenia Daughter of Agamemnon and Clytemnestra, sacrificed by her father at Aulis to gain a favourable wind for the Greek fleet sailing to Troy.

Isis Egyptian goddess of magic and mother of Horus.

Ismene Daughter of Oedipus and Jocasta. She followed her father and her sister, Antigone, into exile.

Isthmian Games Quadrennial games held at Corinth in honour of Poseidon.

Ithaca Island home of Odysseus, one of the Ionian Islands.

Ixion Greek king of Thessaly who was the first to murder a kinsman, his father-in-law; he was bound to a wheel of fire in Tartarus for trying to rape Hera.

Janus Roman god of entrances, travel and the dawn, depicted as a man with two faces.

Jason Son of Aeson, the Aeolian King of Iolcos. Aeson's half-brother Pelias usurped the throne and Queen Alcimede was forced to smuggle her son to safety, entrusting him to the care of Chiron, the centaur. Jason returned to Iolcos to regain his father's kingdom and was told by Pelias that he would step down in return for the golden fleece of a ram, which hung from a tree in Colchis, and was guarded by a dragon. Jason engaged Argus to build a large galley for the journey and successfully attained his goal with the help of some legendary Greek heroes. During his adventures he married the sorceress Medea, but whether he ever attained the throne of Iolcos is doubtful. Jason eventually died when the decaying prow of the Argo fell on him.

Jimmu-tenno Legendary first Emperor of Japan, aka Kamu-yamato-iware-biko.

Jocasta Wife of King Laius and mother of Oedipus.

Jotunheim In Norse mythology the land of the race of giants, said to lie among the roots of Yggdrasil.

Jumala Finnish supreme god.

Juno Roman goddess of marriage, childbirth and light, and queen of the gods.

Jupiter Originally a Roman sky god, but then regarded by the Romans as *Dies Pater* (Father Day), and later still became the Roman equivalent of Zeus.

Kama Hindu god of love and pleasure.

Khnum Egyptian goddess of creation.

Khonsou Egyptian god, son of Ammon.

Kvasir Norse god of wisdom.

Laertes King of Ithaca and father of Odysseus by Anticleia.

Lakshmi In Hindu mythology, also known as Sri, attained importance as the consort of Vishnu under each of his incarnations; when he became Rama she was faithful Sita, and when he became Krishna she became his wife, Rukmini.

Lamia In Greek mythology a beautiful queen of Libya who became a child-eating demon. Sometimes depicted with a serpent's tail, Lamia was the daughter of King Belus of Egypt, making her the granddaughter of Poseidon and Lybie. Through unification with Zeus she was the mother of Herophile, a noted sibyl.

Lapithes Mythological race that fought a famous war with the centaurs.

Lares Roman gods of the house and fertility.

Leander Mythical youth of Abydos who drowned while swimming the Hellespont to meet Hero.

Leda Seduced by Zeus in the form of a swan and gave birth to Helen and Polydeuces in one egg and Castor and Clytemnestra in another. Other versions record that Helen and Polydeuces were children of Zeus and that Castor and Clytemnestra were children of her husband, Tyndareus.

Leviathan Sea monster mentioned in the book of Job, resembling a crocodile.

Liber Pater Roman god of agriculture and human fertility.

Libitina Roman goddess of funeral rites.

Lilith Demonic first wife of Adam in Hebrew mytholgy.

Lohengrin In Germanic legend, the son of Parsifal.

Loki Norse god of mischief.

Lorelei In German mythology a siren said to dwell on a rock at the

edge of the Rhine, south of Koblenz, who lures boatmen to destruction.
Lud(d) Mythical king of Britain whose temple in Roman London was near St Paul's Cathedral. Ludd was also the name of a Celtic god of the sea.
Llyr (Lir) A Celtic god of waters and the sea; father of Manannan.
Maat Egyptian goddess of sterility, truth and justice.
Mabinogion A collection of stories written in Welsh in medieval times, the principal source of ancient Welsh and British myths.
Macha In Celtic mythology a collective name for the trinity of war goddesses Macha, Morrígan and Nemain. As an individual, Macha was sometimes known as Dana (crow) or Badb (raven).
Mahabharata Sanskrit verse epic composed between 400 BC and AD 400. It relates a dynastic feud between the Pandavas and their cousins the Kauravas, respectively gods and demons.
Maia Roman goddess of fertility.
Manasa Serpent goddess of Hindu mythology.
Manitou Supreme deity of the Algonquian people of North America.
Manticore A fabulous monster with the body of a lion, the head of a man, porcupine's quills, and the tail or sting of a scorpion.
Marduk Supreme god of Babylon.
Mazda Persian god of wisdom.
Medea In Greek mythology a princess of Colchis and powerful sorceress; deserted by Jason after helping him to steal the Golden Fleece, she killed their two children.
Megara Daughter of King Creon of Thebes and first wife of Heracles, who killed her in a fit of madness caused by the goddess Hera.
Megingjord Name of Thor's belt, which magnifies his strength.
Meleager In Greek mythology the heir of King Oeneus of Calydon. The Fates appeared to his mother, Althaea, when he was seven days old, they pointed to a burning stick in the fireplace and told her that her son's life would last as long as the stick would burn. Althaea snatched the stick from the fire and hid it away. His father incurred the wrath of Artemis and she sent a wild boar to Calydon to ravage his crops. Meleager offered the boar's pelt and tusks to anyone who could deliver the death blow. Many of his fellow Argonauts joined the hunt, including Atalanta, who he was besotted by. Although Meleager himself delivered the final death thrust, he gave the pelt to Atalanta, which upset his two uncles. In a rage he killed them both, and his mother, seeing the corpses of her brothers, threw the stick into the fire, and Meleager's life drained away
Menelaus King of Sparta, younger brother of Agamemnon and husband of Helen.
Merope A Pleiad and wife of Sisyphus.
Metis In Greek mythology the daughter of Oceanus and Tethys and first wife of Zeus.
Mictlan Aztec land of the dead.
Midas Mythical king of Phygian. In one story, Apollo burdens him with ass's ears for fudging badly in a music contest. In another, he receives but manages to shed the gift of turning all he touches to gold.
Midgard In Norse mythology the dwelling place of mankind, formed from the body of the giant Ymir and linked to Asgard by Bifrost, the rainbow bridge.
Milo Champion wrestler in Greek mythology.
Mimir Norse giant who guarded the well of wisdom near the roots of Yggdrasil.
Minos In Greek mythology the son of Europa and Zeus and brother to Sarpedon and Rhadamanthys. Following a dispute with his two brothers, Minos succeeded to the throne of Crete. The issue of the succession was decided when, having prayed for a divine sign, Poseidon sent Minos a magnificent bull from the sea. However, because Minos neglected to sacrifice the bull, Poseidon cursed him, causing his wife, Pasiphaë, to fall madly in love with the creature. With the help of the craftsman Daedalus, Pasiphaë was able to satisfy her lust by hiding in a decoy cow. The offspring of this union was the Minotaur, a monster with the head of a bull but the body of a man. Minos commissioned Daedalus to construct a labyrinth to house the Minotaur, and each year 9 boys and 9 girls were brought from Athens as food for the monster. One year the Greek hero Theseus was chosen for sacrifice and slew the Minotaur with the help of Minos's daughter Ariadne, who supplied him with a thread to enable him to retrace his steps after the slaying. King Minos -followed Daedalus to Sicily with his mind set on revenge, but Daedalus was warned of his presence and arranged for boiling oil to kill the king when he took a bath at Kamikos.
Minotaur Greek monster, son of Pasiphaë and a bull, kept in a labyrinth on Crete by King Minos.
Mithra(s) Persian god of light, justice and war.
Mjollnir Thor's hammer, said to cause lightning.
Mnemosyne Greek Titan who was the mother of all the Muses.
Morrígan Irish war goddess whose name means phantom queen; also the collective name of the trinity of war goddesses Macha, Morrígan and Nemain.
Muses Sacred to Mount Helicon, the nine daughters of Zeus and Mnemosyne are the personification of knowledge and the arts.
Myrmidons People of Aegina, created by Zeus for King Aeacus; some of them fought for Achilles at Troy.
Myth The term was first used by the Greek historian Herodotus (*c.*484 BC – *c.*420 BC) to describe a body of knowledge or beliefs that have no foundation in fact and so must be distinguished from history although recorded fact can take mythical proportions due to historical interpretation.
Nabu (Nebo) In Babylonian mythology, son of Marduk, and the scribe and herald of the gods.
Naiads Freshwater nymphs in Greek mythology.
Nanna Norse goddess, wife of Baldur.
Narcissus Greek hero whom Nemesis caused to fall in love with his own reflection.
Nataraja Title of the Hindu god S(h)iva, meaning lord of the dance.
Nehallenia Norse goddess of plenty.
Nemesis Greek goddess of destiny, the daughter of Oceanus.
Nereids Fifty beautiful sea nymphs, the daughters of Nereus and Doris, of whom the most famous were Amphitrite and Thetis.
Nereus Greek god of the sea.
Nessus Greek centaur whose blood caused the death of his killer, Heracles.
Nestor King of Pylos and only one of Neleus's 12 sons spared by Heracles. The oldest of the Greeks at Troy and the only one to return home without mishap.
Nibelung In German legend, any of the race of dwarfs who possessed a treasure hoard stolen by Siegfried.
Nibelungenlied Heroic epic of unknown authorship written in the early 13th centruy and based on German history and legend.
Niflheim In Norse mythology the abode of the dead, sometimes identified with hell.
Niobe In Greek mythology, queen of Thebes, wife of King Amphion and daughter of Tantalus and Dione.
Njord Norse god, father of Frey and Freyja.
Norns Norse goddesses of destiny: Urdr – the past, Verdandi – the present, and Skuld – the future.
Notus Greek mythology. South-west wind known to the Romans as Auster. Son of Astraeus and Eos.
Numa Pompilius Legendary second King of Rome who succeeded Romulus.
Nun In Egyptian mythology, the dark primeval ocean of chaos, which existed before the first gods.
Nymph Any one of a class of mythological, youthful female divinities inhabiting woods, springs, mountains or the sea. Although nymphs were not immortal, their life span was usually several thousand years.
Oceanid(e)s Greek sea-nymphs, daughters of Oceanus and Tethys.
Oceanus Greek god of the River Oceanus and son of Gaia and Uranus.
Odysseus (aka Ulysses) Greek hero, the son of Laertes and Anticlea, king and queen of Ithaca, a key figure in Homer's *Iliad* and central in the *Odyssey.*
Oedipus (swollen foot) Greek hero, king of Thebes, who inadvertently killed his father and married his mother.
Oisin In Celtic mythology, a warrior and poet, son of Finn mac Cumhall and Sadb.
Ops Roman goddess of the harvest, and consort of Saturn.
Oread A Greek mountain-nymph.
Orestes In Greek mythology the king of Argos and Sparta, son of Agamemnon and Clytemnestra.
Orion In Greek mythology a giant hunter, son of Poseidon and Euryale.
Orpheus Greek musician and poet, son of King Oeagrus of Thrace and Calliope. He married Eurydice, failed to rescue her from Hades after she was killed by a snake, and was finally torn to pieces by the women of Thrace.
Osiris Egyptian god of vegetation, brother of Seth and husband of Isis.
Otr Norse otter god.

Otus and Ephialtes Twin sons of Iphimedeia and Poseidon.
Pales Roman goddess of flocks.
Palladium Mythical statue of Athene given to Dardanus by Zeus to ensure the protection of Troy.
Pan Greek god of male sexuality, herds and woods.
Pandora In Greek mythology the first woman on earth. When her dowry box was opened it released all the world's ill and retained only hope.
Paris A prince of Troy, the son of Priam. He abducted Helen, the wife of Menelaus, so causing the Trojan War.
Parvati In Hindu mythology Parvati (the mountaineer) was one of the forms of Devi and as such, the mother of the elephant-headed god of wisdom, Ganes(h)a. Parvati became the golden-skinned Gauri.
Pasiphaë In Greek mythology the daughter of Helios and mother of the Minotaur.
Patroclus Greek warrior who, while wearing Achilles' armour, was killed by Hector during the siege of Troy.
Pegasus Greek winged horse that sprang from the body of Medusa after her death.
Pelasgus The first man, according to one version of the Greek creation myth.
Peleus In Greek mythology the King of Phythia in Thessaly. He married Thetis and fathered Achilles.
Penates Roman gods of food and drink.
Penelope The wife of Odysseus. During his long absence after the Trojan war, she tricked the suitors who were plaguing her to marry by unravelling a shroud every night, having promised to make her decision when she had finished weaving it.
Persephone Greek goddess of the underworld, corn and the spring.
Perse Daughter of Oceanus and wife of Helios, to whom she bore Circe, Pasiphaë, Aeëtes and Perses.
Perses (1) Son of Perseus and Andromeda. Said to have given his name to Persia.
Perses (2) Son of Helios and Perse and father of Hecate.
Perseus Greek hero, son of Zeus and Danaë; he slew the Gorgon Medusa and married Andromeda.
Phaeton Greek hero, son of Helios and Clymene. Killed by a thunderbolt from Zeus after losing control of the sun-chariot and endangering the safety of the world. Phaeton's body fell into the river Eridanus (Po).
Philoctetes Greek hero who killed Paris.
Pleiades The 7 daughters of Atlas and Pleione, born on Mount Cyllene. They are the sisters of Calypso, Hyas, the Hyades, and the Hesperides and are nymphs in the train of Artemis, and together with the seven Hyades were called the Atlantides, Dodonides, or Nysiades - nursemaids and teachers to the infant Bacchus.
Plutus Greek god of wealth.
Polybus In Greek mythology the king of Corinth, husband of Merope and adoptive father of Oedipus.
Pomona Roman goddess of fruit trees.
Portunus Roman god of husbands and harbours.
Poseidon Greek god of the sea and earthquakes.
Priam In Greek mythology the king of Troy, son of King Laomedon and Queen Strymo.
Priapus Son of Dionysus and Aphrodite, a fertility god, often portrayed with a grotesquely large phallus.
Procrustes (Stretcher) In Greek mythology an innkeeper who killed travellers on the road between Athens and Eleusis by lopping or stretching their bodies to fit his bed. Theseus killed him by decapi-tation.
Prometheus In Greek mythology a Titan, sometimes credited with making mankind out of clay. Because he stole fire from the gods and gave it to man, Zeus bound him to a rock for an eagle to peck out his liver, which always regrew because Prometheus was immortal.
Proserpine Roman goddess of the Underworld, corn and the spring.
Proteus Sea god, the son of Oceanus and Tethys. Proteus was a seer but would take any form to avoid questioning.
Psyche In Greek mythology the soul, often portrayed as a butterfly. Personified as a woman, she fell in love with Eros and suffered many ordeals before they were united.
Ptah Egyptian god of creation.
Pygmalion In Greek mythology the king of Cyprus who fell in love with Aphrodite and, because she would not lie with him, made an ivory image of her and laid it in his bed. Aphrodite brought the statue to life as Galatea.
Pyrrha Daughter of Epimetheus and Pandora and wife of Deucalion with whom she repopulated the earth after the flood.
Quetzalcoatl Toltec and Aztec god of vegetation and the wind, sometimes depicted as a bearded man wearing a mask, sometimes as a feathered serpent..
Quirinus Roman god of war, after whom a hill of Rome was named.
Ragnarok Final destruction of the Norse gods in a battle to the death with evil.
Ramayana One of the two great Sanskrit verse epics (along with the *Mahabharata*) dating back to the 3rd century BC, the story of Prince Rama, his struggle for the throne of Ajodhya, and his war with the demon Ravana to rescue his abducted wife Sita, with Hanuman's help
Remus See Romulus and Remus.
Rhadamanthus Son of Europa and Zeus and brother to Minos and Sarpedon. After death he became a judge in the underworld.
Rhea Greek goddess of motherhood; sister and wife of Cronus.
Rhesus Thracian king who helped the Trojans but was slain by Odysseus.
Rhiannon In Welsh Celtic mythology, the daughter of the King of the Otherworld and wife of Pwyll, prince of Dyfed.
Romulus and Remus Twin sons of Mars, and legendary founders of Rome.
Round Table In Arthurian legend the great table of Camelot that seated King Arthur's knights. The Siege Perilous (dangerous seat) remained vacant because only the bringer of the Holy Grail could use it without coming to harm.
Rumina Roman goddess of nursing mothers.
Sarpedon In Greek mythology the son of Europa and Zeus and brother to Minos and Rhadamanthus.
Satyr A Greek mythological creature, part man, part goat; the satyrs were followers of Dionysus.
Scaean (Left-Hand) Gate Situated in the walls of Troy; the spot where Achilles fell.
Scylla Greek sea monster; originally the daughter of Poseidon, she was turned into a monster by Amphitrite. In Strait of Messina located opposite Charybdis and depicted as snake with 6 heads that lived in a cave.
Sekmet Egyptian goddess of power and battle, depicted with the head of a lioness.
Selene Greek goddess of the moon, daughter of Hyperion and Thea; she was most notably the lover of Endymion.
Semiramis In Assyrian mythology the wife of Ninus and co-founder with him of Nineveh.
Set(h) Egyptian god of evil.
Seven against Thebes Greek champions who failed to overthrow Eteocles from his Kingship.
Seven Kings of Rome Romulus (753–715 BC), Numa Pompilius (715–673 BC), Tullius Hostilius (673–642 BC), Ancus Marcius (642–616 BC), Tarquin the Elder (616–579 BC), Servius Tullius (579–534 BC), Tarquinius Superbus (Proud Tarquin) (534–510 BC).
Seven Sages of India aka Saptarishi, the seven rishis who are extolled at many places in the Vedas and Hindu literature.
Shu Egyptian god of Air.
Sibyl Roman prophetess.
Sibylline Books Roman tradition tells how a sibyl offered Tarquinius Priscus 9 prophetic books which he refused to buy at the price. She destroyed three and he still refused them; she burned three more and he took the remaining three at the price demanded for the nine. Special priests kept them and they were consulted only when the Senate authorised it in time of need. In 83 BC the originals were destroyed by fire. The original books instructed the Romans to convey the sacred stone of Cybele to Rome.
Sif Norse goddess, wife of Thor.
Sigmund In Germanic legend the son of Volsung who won the divine sword Gram by extracting it from a tree trunk.
Sigurd In Germanic legend the son of Sigmund and Hjordis and owner of the horse, Grani.
Sigyn Norse goddess, wife of Loki.
Silvanus Roman god of trees and forests.
Siren In Homer's *Odyssey* one of a group of creatures, half woman and half bird, who lure sailors to their death by their singing. Odysseus and the Argonauts withstood their fatal charms, the latter because Orpheus outsang them.
Sisyphus In Greek mythology a Corinthian king -destined in Hades to roll a large stone up a hill for evermore, only for it to keep rolling back when it reaches the top.
Skadi In Norse mythology the wife of Njord.

Skan Lakota god embodying the sky.
Sleipnir Odin's 8-legged horse.
Sobek Egyptian crocodile god.
Soma In Hindu mythology an intoxicating drink. Soma was also an early god of the moon.
Spartoi (sown men) Sprang up fully armed when Cadmus sowed the dragon's teeth and killed each other until five remained: Echion, Udaeus, Chthonius, Hyperenor and Pelorus.
Sphinx Greek monster with a woman's head and lion's body.
Stentor Greek herald during the Trojan War, famous for his very loud voice.
Stymphalian birds In Greek mythology a flock of man-eating birds, which infested Lake Stymphalos in Arcadia. Killed by Heracles.
Surabhi In Indian mythology a divine cow of plenty.
Syrinx Greek nymph of Arcadia. She was pursued by Pan, who made the first pan-pipes from her embodiment, as turning into a bed of reeds was the only way she could escape him.
Tantalus Greek mythological king of Sipylos in Lydia, who stole the food of the gods and was condemned to stand thirsty and hungry forever in a pool that receded when he bent down to drink, beneath fruit trees whose branches retreated when he reached to pick their fruit.
Tarpeian Rock Named after Tarpeia, the traitor daughter of the keeper of the Roman citadel. Became the rock from which Roman traitors were thrown.
Tartarus That part of Hades reserved for those that offended the gods during their lifetime.
Taweret Egyptian protector goddess of women and children, often depicted as part crocodile, part lion and part hippopotamus.
Telamon Son of Aeacus and brother of Peleus; Telamon fathered Ajax by Periboea.
Telemachus Greek hero, son of Odysseus and Penelope.
Tenes Son of Apollo who gave his name to the Greek island of Tenedos.
Themis Daughter of Ge and Uranus and sister of Cronus. The wife of Zeus before Hera.
Theseus Mythical Greek hero, king of Athens and son of King Aegeus and Queen Aethra; it was Theseus who defeated the Minotaur in its labyrinth home in Crete.
Thetis Greek goddess and mother of Achilles.
Thunderbird Totem figure of Native Americans from the north-west. Aka Skyamsen.
Tiresias Legendary blind prophet of Thebes who had been both male and female and estimated that women had 9 times more pleasure during intercourse than men.
Titans In the first generation of twelve Titans, the males were Oceanus, Hyperion, Coeus, Cronus, Crius, and Iapetus and the females Mnemosyne, Tethys, Theia, Phoebe, Rhea, and Themis. The second generation of Titans consisted of Hyperion's children Eos, Helios, and Selene; Coeus's daughters Leto and Asteria; Iapetus's children Atlas, Prometheus, Epimetheus, and Menoetius; Oceanus' daughter Metis; and Crius's sons Astraeus, Pallas, and Perses.
Tonalpohualli Aztec sacred calendar consisting of 260 days which were divided into 20 weeks of 13 days.
Trimurti Trinity of Hindu gods: Brahma(n) the Creator, Vishnu the Preserver and S(h)iva the Destroyer.
Tristan and Isolde Celtic legend. Tristan was a harpist and Isolde was the daughter of the king of Ireland. They drank a love potion together by mistake and fell irretrievably in love.
Triton Son of Poseidon and Amphitrite. He was a merman, the upper half human, the lower half fish. Triton used a conch shell trumpet to calm the waves.
Troilus In Greek mythology, the young son of Priam, slain by Achilles. His romance with Cressida is a medieval invention.
Ull Norse god and stepson of Thor.
Underworld Rivers The five rivers of the Greek underworld (where souls went after death) are Cocytus (wailing), Lethe (forgetfulness), Acheron (grief), Styx (hate) and Phlegethon (fire). Useful mnemonic: CLASP
Valhalla In Norse mythology the great hall of Odin in Asgard, where warriors who died as heroes in battle dwelled eternally.
Valkyries Norse warrior handmaidens to Odin.
Vanir Norse race of benevolent gods including Njörd, Frey and Freyja. The Vanir warred with the Aesir and were eventually absorbed into their number.
Varuna In Hindu mythology, the upholder of heaven and earth and often associated with Surya as the creator of the sun. In post-Vedic mythology he became god of the seas and rivers.
Vertumnus Roman god of fertility.
Vestal virgins College of priestesses of the Roman cult of Vesta, the hearth goddess. Originally four of them; later 6 (generally considered as the number); and finally 7.
Vidar Norse god, a son of Odin and slayer of the wolf Fenir.
Vishnu's Incarnations The 10 avatars of Vishnu are 1. Matsya, 2. Kurma, 3. Varaha, 4. Narasinha, 5. Vamana 6. Paras(h)urama, 7. Ramachandra (Rama), 8. Krishna, 9. Buddha, 10. Kalki.
Völund In Norse mythology, a smith and artificer and king of the elves. In Germanic legends he appears as Wieland; in English folklore as Wayland Smith.
Völuspá First and best known poem of the Edda, telling the story of the creation of the world and its coming end.
Wyvern Mythical beast with a dragon's head, a -serpent's tail and a body with wings and two legs.
Yggdrasil In Norse mythology, the ash tree that binds the heavens, earth and the underworld with its roots and branches. It shelters the remnants of humanity when Ragnarok destroys the gods and sets the world on fire.
Ymir The first being and forefather of all the Norse giants. Slain by Odin, who made the earth from his flesh, the water from his blood and the sky from his skull.
Zephyrus West Wind, the son of Astraeus and Eus and father of Xanthus and Balius, the talking horses of Achilles. Roman counterpart was Favonius.
Zetes Twin of Calais; winged sons of Boreas and Oreithyia- they accompanied the Argonauts and drove off the Harpies.

Zeus's Conquests

The supreme god of the Greek parthenon took many forms in his amorous pursuit of goddesses, nymphs and humans. See a few below.

Conquest	*Form*	*Offspring*	Conquest	*Form*	*Offspring*
Alcmene	Amphitryon	Heracles	Io	Cloud	Epaphos
Antiope	Satyr	Amphion & Zetheus	Leda	Swan	Helen, Pollux
Danaë	Shower of gold	Perseus	Leto	Quail	Apollo and Artemis
Demeter	Himself	Persephone	Maia	Himself	Hermes
Europa	Bull and eagle	Minos, Sarpedon	Mnemosyne	Himself	Muses
Eurynome	Himself	Graces	Semele	Mortal	Dionysus

Famous Horses of Myth and History

Name	*Owner*	*Owner's identity*	*Name*	*Owner*	*Owner's identity*
Aethenoth	Lady Godiva	Anglo-Saxon noblewoman	Aethon	Helios	Greek sun god
Arvak	Sol	Norse maiden	Aeton	Pluto	Greek god
Abaster	Pluto	Greek god	Al Borak	Mohammed	Founder of Islam
Abatos	Pluto	Greek god	Alfana	Gradasso	Literary creation
Abraxa	Aurora	Roman goddess	Alsvid	Sol	Norse maiden
Actaeon	Helios	Greek sun god	Amethea	Helios	Greek sun god

Name	*Owner*	*Owner's identity*
Arion	Hercules	Mythological hero
Arundel	Bevis of Hampton	Literary creation
Babieca	El Cid	Spanish hero
Balios	Achilles	Greek hero
Barbary Roan	Richard II	English king
Bayard	Renaud de Montauban	Legendary Frankish knight
Black Agnes	Mary Queen of Scots	Scottish queen
Black Bess	Dick Turpin	Literary creation
Brigliadoro	Orlando	Legendary character
Bronte	Helios	Greek sun god
Bucephalus	Alexander the Great	Macedonian ruler
Carman	Chevalier de Bayard	French knight
Celer	Lucius Verus	Roman emperor
Cerus	Adrastus	Mythological king of Argos
Champion	Gene Autry	TV cowboy
Comanche	US cavalry	Only survivor Little Big Horn
Copenhagen	Duke of Wellington	Soldier and statesman
Cyllaros	Castor and Pollux	Roman mythological twins
Dapple	Sancho Panza	Literary character
Diablo	Cisco Kid	Literary creation
Dinos	Diomedes	Mythological king of Argos
Doublet	Princess Anne	Royal Olympian
Eos	Aurora	Roman goddess
Erythreos	Helios	Greek sun god
Ethon	Hector	Trojan hero
Fadda (mule)	Mohammed	Founder of Islam
Ferrant d'Espagne	Oliver	Legendary Frankish knight
Foxhunter	Col Harry Llewellyn	Olympic champion
Galathe	Hector	Trojan hero
Grani	Siegfried	German legend
Gringolet	Sir Gawain	Arthurian Knight
Grizzle	Dr Syntax	Literary creation
Gulltoppr	Heimdall	Norse god
Haizum	Gabriel	Archangel
Harpagus	Castor and Pollux	Roman mythological twins
Hercules	The Steptoes	TV creation
Hippocampus	Neptune	Roman god
Hrimfaxi	Nott	Horse of Night (Norse myth)
Incitatus	Caligula	Roman emperor
Kantanka	Prince Gautama	The Buddha
Lampon	Diomedes	Mythological king of Argos
Lampos	Helios	Greek sun god
Lamri	King Arthur	Legendary Anglo-Saxon king
Marengo	Napoleon	French emperor
Marocco	Mr Banks	Elizabethan horseman
Marsala	Garibaldi	Italian patriot
Nonios	Pluto	Greek god
Pegasus	Bellerophon	Greek hero
Phaeton	Aurora	Roman goddess
Phallus	Heraclius	Byzantine emperor
Phlegon	Helios	Greek sun god
Phrenicos	Hiero of Syracuse	Winner of 73rd olympiad
Podarge	Hector	Trojan hero
Purocis	Helios	Greek sun god
Ronald	Lord Cardigan	British soldier
Rosabelle	Mary Queen of Scots	Scottish queen
Rosinante	Don Quixote	Literary creation
Savoy	Charles VIII	French king
Scout	Tonto	TV creation
Sefton	British Army	Bomb victim
Shadowfax	Gandalf	Wizard in *Lord of the Rings*
Shibdiz	Chosroes II	Persian ruler
Silver	Lone Ranger	TV creation
Skinfaxi	Dagr	Horse of Day (Norse myth)
Sleipnir	Odin	Norse supreme god
Sorrel	William III	British king
Strymon	Xerxes	Persian king
Tachebrune	Ogier the Dane	Hero of chansons de geste
Tony	Tom Mix	Film cowboy
Topper	Hopalong Cassidy	Film cowboy
Trebizond	Guarinos	French knight Roncesvalles
Trigger	Roy Rogers	TV cowboy
White Surrey	Richard III	English king
Xanthus	Achilles	Greek hero

Famous Dogs (Fact and Fiction)

Name	*Owner or details*
Argos	Ulysses
Asta	*Thin Man* series
Blondie	Hitler
Boatswain	Lord Byron (Newfoundland)
Boot	Old English sheepdog *Perishers* (cartoon strip)
Bounce	Alexander Pope
Boy	Prince Rupert's dog, killed at Marston Moor
Bran	Finn mac Cumhal
Brutus	Landseer's greyhound (invader of the larder)
Bullseye	Bill Sykes in *Oliver Twist*
Cabal (Cavall)	King Arthur's favourite hound
Cerberus	Three-headed dog that guards Hades
Checkers	Richard Nixon
Crab	Launce in *Two Gentlemen of Verona*
Daisy	Blondie
Dash	Charles Lamb
Diamond	Isaac Newton
Dougal	Character in *Magic Roundabout*
Dragon	Aubry of Montdidier
Flash	*Dukes of Hazzard*
Fluffy	Three-headed dog that guarded the Philosopher's Stone in Harry Potter
Flush	Elizabeth Barrett Browning
Freeway	Jonathan and Jennifer Hart
Gargittios	One of Geryon's dogs slain by Hercules
Geist	Matthew Arnold's dachshund
Gelert	Prince Llewellyn's greyhound
Giallo	Walter Savage Landor
Gnasher	Dennis the Menace
Goofy	Disney cartoon dog
Greyfriars Bobby	Watched over owner's grave for 14 years (Skye terrier)
Hamlet	Sir Walter Scott's black greyhound
Hodain	Tristan (Hodain aka Leon)
Kaiser	Matthew Arnold's dachshund
Lady	Poodle owned by Walt Disney
Laika	Fox terrier that was the first dog in space
Lassie	Actually a female dog named Pal
Luath	Cuchulainn (Robbie Burns also owned a Luath)
Lufra	Douglas's hound in Scott's *Lady of the Lake*
Maida	Sir Walter Scott's deerhound
Mathe	Richard II's greyhound
Montmorency	Three Men in a Boat
Nana	Darling family (*Peter Pan*)
Nigger	Guy Gibson
Nipper	Fox terrier logo for His Master's Voice (HMV)
Olaf	Snoopy's brother
Orthos	One of Geryon's dogs slain by Hercules
Paddy	Harold Wilson
Pearl	Beryl the Peril
Perdita	*101 Dalmations*
Peritas	Alexander the Great
Petra	*Blue Peter* (Shep was also a famous dog)
Pickles	Found the World Cup
Pluto	Disney cartoon dog
Pongo	*101 Dalmations*
Rin Tin Tin	Died in Jean Harlow's arms (German Shepherd)
Robot	Discovered Lascaux cave paintings in 1940
Rufus	Sir Winston Churchill's poodle
Sandy	Little Orphan Annie
Scamper	Secret Seven
Sceolang	Finn mac Cumhal
Snoopy	Beagle in *Peanuts* (cartoon strip)
Snowy	Tintin
Spike	Snoopy's brother
Spottie	*The Woodentops*
Strelka	Survived an orbital space mission
Theron	Roderick the Goth
Thisbe	Marie Antoinette
Timmy	Famous Five member
Toby	Punch
Toto	Cairn terrier owned by Dorothy in *Wizard of Oz*
Well'ard	*EastEnders.* Dog's real name is Kyte
Won Ton Ton	Saved Hollywood in 1976 film

NATURE

Living Creatures (except birds)

aardvark nocturnal mammal, inhabiting the grasslands of Africa south of the Sahara and feeding on ants and termites. It is the sole member of its family (Orycteropodidae) and order (Tubulidentata). Research by British, Chinese and South African scientists in 2003 reveals that the aardvark has the greatest number of features in common with other mammals, which makes it the closest living relative of our common ancestor. The aardvark is also called an ant bear. Sp.: *Orycteropus afer.*

aardwolf nocturnal mammal, inhabiting the plains of east and southern Africa, feeding on termites and insect larvae. Family: Hyaenidae (Hyenas) and Order: Carnivora. Sp.: *Proteles cristatus.*

abalone gastropod mollusc with a shallow, ear-shaped shell lined with mother-of-pearl. Gen.: *Haliotis.*

albacore long-finned tunny fish. Sp.: *Thunnus alalunga.*

alewife fish of the north-west Atlantic related to the herring. Sp.: *Alosa pseudoharengus.*

alligator either of two crocodilian reptiles of the family Alligatoridae (alligators and caymans) and distinguished from true crocodiles by their shorter and broader snouts. The American alligator (*Alligator mississippiensis*), the larger of the two species, can grow to a length of almost 6 metres, and the Chinese alligator (*Alligator sinensis*) to about a -quarter of that length.

alpaca South American herbivore mammal of the Andes with long shaggy hair, related to the llama. Sp.: *Lama pacos.*

anchovy small marine food fish of the herring family. Sp.: *Engraulis encrasicholus.*

ant small social insect of the order Hymenoptera, typically living in organised colonies of winged males (drones), wingless sterile females (workers) and fertile females (queens). The body of an ant has three segments, i.e. head, abdomen and thorax. Family: Formicidae.

ant: Amazon ant which captures pupae of other ant species to raise as slaves. Gen.: *Polyergus.*

antelope bovid mammals of Africa and Asia that include bushbucks, elands, gnus, gazelles, impalas, springboks, dik-diks, blackbucks, oryxes, gerenuks and nilgai. Antelopes have unbranched horns, which they do not shed. Family: Boridae.

ape primates characterised by long arms and the absence of a tail. Great apes are the chimpanzee, gorilla and orang-utan (Family: Pongidae). Lesser apes are the various gibbons (Family: Hylobatidae).

argalis large Asiatic wild sheep with massive horns. Sp.: *Ovis ammon.*

armadillo nocturnal insect-eating but generally omnivorous edentate mammal native to the southern USA and Central and S. America, with large claws for digging and a body covered in bony plates, often rolling itself into a ball when threatened. They range from 3- to as many as 13-banded. Burmeister's and pink fairy armadillos are endangered species. Family: Dasypodidae.

axolotl aquatic newt-like salamander from Mexico, which in natural conditions retains its larval form for life but is able to breed. Name means 'water servant'. Sp.: *Ambystoma mexicanum.*

aye-aye nocturnal arboreal prosimian primate of Madagascar related to the lemurs. Sp.: *Daubentonia madagascariensis.*

babirusa wild hog with upturned tusks native to the Malay archipelago. Sp.: *Babyrousa babyrussa.*

baboon primate of the family Cercopithecidae, characterised by its fox-like muzzle and long tail. Gen.: *Papio.*

badger (American) stout-bodied carnivore with greyish to reddish coat and black facial stripes. Sp.: *Taxidea taxus.*

badger (Eurasian) stout-bodied carnivore with greyish coat and black and white facial stripes. All badgers are members of the family Mustelidae. Sp.: *Meles meles.*

badger (honey) aka ratel. Musteline mammal inhabiting wooded regions of Africa and Asia. Sp.: *Mellivora capensis.*

bandicoot any small, agile terrestrial marsupial of the family Peramelidae of Australia and New Guinea. Bandicoots typically have long, pointed muzzles, large ears and long tails, and feed mainly on small invertebrates.

bandicoot rat large, dark brown, burrowing rat of the family Muridae, order Rodentia, of India and Sri Lanka, sometimes known as a mole rat. The bandicoot rat makes a grunting noise similar to that of a pig. Sp.: *Bandicota indica.*

barnacle small marine crustacean of the subclass Cirripedia that, as an adult, lives head-down attached to rocks or the bottom of the hull of a ship.

barnacle: goose common barnacle found worldwide, living attached by a stalk to driftwood. Gen.: *Lepas.*

basking shark large slow-moving shark of the family Cetorhinidae, prone to swimming or floating at the surface with its mouth agape. The basking shark is the second largest shark after the whale shark, growing up to 14 metres in length. Sp.: *Cetorhinus maximus.*

bear large plantigrade, omnivorous mammal of the family Ursidae, order Carnivora. The smallest species is the Malaysian sun bear (*Helarctos malayanus*), and the largest is the Kodiak bear (*Ursus arctos middendorffi*).

beluga large kind of Russian sturgeon from which caviar is obtained. Sp.: *Huso huso.*

bib light brown European marine gadoid food fish. Aka pout. Sp.: *Gadus luscus.*

binturong arboreal civet of southern. Asia with a shaggy black coat and a prehensile tail. Sp.: *Arctictis binturong.*

bison: American ox-like grazing mammal with short-haired body and longer, darker hair on its head. Aka plains buffalo. Sp.: *Bison bison.*

black widow any venomous spider of the family Theridiidae, inhabiting warm climates throughout the world. The venom of the spider causes sharp pain and some muscle cramping but is usually only temporary and never fatal. The female is characterised by its dark colour and red hourglass marking on its abdomen. The males are rarely seen as they are often eaten by the female after mating. Black widows are known as button spiders in South Africa, redbacks in Australia and katipos in New Zealand. Gen.: *Latrodectus.*

bobcat small Northern American lynx with a spotted, reddish-brown coat and a short tail. Sp.: *Felis rufus.*

bonito one of several small, tuna-like marine food fishes of the family Scombridae (tunnies and mackerels) inhabiting warm Atlantic and Pacific waters. Gen.: *Sarda.*

boomslang venomous tree-snake native to sub-Saharan Africa. Sp.: *Dispholidus typus.*

brachiosaurus herbivorous dinosaurs, probably the largest land animals ever known (80 tons+). Gen.: *Brachiosaurus.*

brandling red earthworm with rings of a brighter colour, which is often found in manure and used as fishing bait. Sp.: *Eisenia foetida.*

brown recluse North American venomous spider with a dark brown body about 3 centimetres long with a distinct violin-shaped design on its back. Sp.: *Loxosceles reclusa.*

buffalo (African) large, black, sparsely haired animal weighing up to 700kg. Sp.: *Syncerus caffer.*

buffalo (Indian) aka water buffalo or carabao. South-east Asian domestic beast of burden weighing up to 1200kg. Sp.: *Bubalus bubalis.*

bullfrog large frog native to North America and Mexico and known for its loud croak. Sp.: *Rana cateseiana.*

bumble-bee large social bee with a loud hum. Aka humble-bee. Gen.: *Bombus.*

bummalo small fish of south Asian coasts, dried and used as food, especially Bombay duck. Sp.: *Harpodon nehereus.*

bush baby small nocturnal tree-dwelling African primate with very large eyes. Aka galago. Six species of the family Lorisidae.

cacomistle raccoon-like animal of North America with a dark ringed tail. Sp.: *Bassariscus sumichrasti.*

callop gold-coloured freshwater fish of Australia. Aka golden perch. Sp.: *Plectroplites ambiguus.*

camel: Arabian camel with one hump native to the deserts of North Africa and the Near East (aka dromedary). Sp.: *Camelus dromedarius.*

camel: Bactrian camel with two humps native to central Asia. Sp.: *Camelus bactrianus.*

capelin small smeltlike fish of the North Atlantic used as food and as bait for catching cod. Sp.: *Mallotus villosus.*

capuchin monkey of the family Cebidae, characterised by its head hair suggestive of a cowl. Gen.: *Cebus.*

capybara very large, semi-aquatic rodent (up to 65 kg) native to South America east of the Andes. Sp.: *Hydrochoerus hydrochaeris.*

caracal lynx native to Norht Africa and south-west. Asia. Sp.: *Felis caracal.*

caribou large deer of Arctic regions of North America, having large branched antlers in the male and female, the only species of deer to do so. The caribou is known as a reindeer in Eurasia. Sp.: *Rangifer tarandus.*

carpenter ant large ant which bores into wood to nest. Gen.: *Camponotus.*

cat: domestic small feline mammal often kept as household pet. The cat is thought to have originated in Egypt. Unusual breeds include the Angora, which is usually deaf, the Manx, which is tailless, and the Siamese, which has blue eyes. Cats move in the same way as the camel and giraffe, i.e. by moving first the front and back legs on one side, then the front and back legs on the other side. Most cats have 18 toes, 5 on the front foot and 4 on the back. Sp.: *Felis domesticus.*

cat: wild feline mammal living in the wild. Sp.: *Felis silvestris.*

cattle dairy breeds include Ayrshire, Danish Red, Friesian, Guernsey, Jersey and Kerry. Beef cattle include Aberdeen Angus, Blonde d'Aquitaine, Blue Grey, Charolais, Chianina, Devon, Galloway, Hereford, Highland, Limousin, Lincoln Red, Luing, Maine-Anjou, Shorthorn and Sussex. Dual-purpose breeds include Dexter, Meuse-Rhine-Ijssel, Red Poll, Dairy Shorthorn, Simmental, South Devon and Welsh Black. Gen.: *Bos.*

cavy any small South American rodent of the family Caviidae, especially of the genus *Cavia.*

cayman (caiman) reptile of the family Alligatoridae (alligators and caymans), inhabiting riverbanks of Central and South America.

centipede carnivorous arthropod, having a body of between 14 and 190 segments, each bearing one pair of legs. The common house centipede, order Scutigerida, is 25 millimetres (1 inch) long with a black striped body and 15 pairs of legs. Class: Chilopoda.

chamois agile goat-antelope native to the mountains of Europe and Asia. Sp.: *Rupicapra rupicapra.*

cheese-fly small black fly that breeds in cheese. Sp.: *Piophila casei.*

cheetah fastest-running feline with a leopard-like spotted coat and non-retractable claws. Sp.: *Acinonyx jubatus.*

chigger tropical flea of which females burrow under people's skin, causing painful sores. Aka chigoe, sand flea and jigger. Sp.: *Tunga penetrans.*

chimpanzee tailless primate of the family Pongidae, inhabiting forests and savannahs of tropical west and central Africa. The two species are the common chimpanzee (*Pan troglodytes*) and the pygmy chimpanzee (*Pan paniscus*).

chinchilla small South American rodent of the family Chinchillidae, which is bred in captivity for its soft grey fur. Chinchillas resemble long-tailed rabbits, although their ears are smaller. Sp.: *Chinchilla laniger.*

Chinese water deer along with the musk deer, one of only two species of deer that do not have antlers. Sp.: *Hyfropotes inermis.*

chipmunk North American ground squirrel having alternate light and dark stripes running down the body. Gen.: *Tamias.*

cicada any of 1,500 varieties of winged-insects of the order Homoptera. The dog-day cicada of the genus *Tibicen*, is typically 3 centimetres long with greenish head and wings, acting as a canopy over its abdomen and thorax. The so-called periodic cicadas of the genus *Magicicada*, including the 17-year and 13-year cicadas, are darker in colour and have red eyes.

civet cat-like mammals of Africa and Southern Asia with spotted fur, noted for the powerful-smelling fluid from their anal glands from which they bear their name. Family: Viverridae.

clouded leopard large spotted arboreal cat of South-east Asia. Sp.: *Neofelis nebulosa.*

coati raccoon-like, omnivorous mammals of Central and South America with a long flexible snout and a long, usually ringed, tail. Gen.: *Nasua* and *Nasuella.*

coelacanth primitive lobe-finned fish of the Indian Ocean, thought to be many millions of years extinct until a living specimen was caught in 1938. Sp.: *Latimeria chalumnae.*

colugo see flying lemur.

coral any of a variety of invertebrate marine organisms of the phylum Cnidaria, class Anthozoa, characterised by having spikey, leathery or stonelike skeletons. Stony coral, of the order Madreporaria, form reefs and islands. Red coral, of the genus *Corallium*, also known as precious coral, is used to make ornaments and jewellery.

cougar see puma.

coyote aka prairie wolf. Predatory canine mammal of North America, smaller than the wolf. Sp.: *Canis latrans.*

crane-fly large two-winged flies with very long legs. Aka daddy-long-legs or leatherjacket. Family: Tipulidae.

crayfish small lobster-like freshwater crustacean. Aka spiny lobster. Gen.: *Astacus.*

cribo large, non-venomous American snake. Aka indigo snake or gopher snake. Sp.: *Drymarchon corais.*

crocodile any reptile of the family Crocodilidae, typically having a broad head, tapering snout, massive jaws, and a thick outer covering of boney scales. The salt water crocodile may grow up to 7 metres long and is the world's largest reptile. The sex of a crocodile is decided during incubation: a male is born if the egg is maintained at a constant 31.6 ° Celsius; hotter or colder and the sex is female. Gen.: *Crocodilus.*

crown of thorns starfish that feeds on coral polyps and has increasingly threatened Australia's Great Barrier Reef. The species can grow up to 50 centimetres, has numerous red spines and may have up to 19 arms. Sp.: *Acanthaster planci.*

dace freshwater fish related to the carp. Sp.: *Leuciscus leuciscus.*

death's-head hawk-moth Large dark hawk-moth with yellowish underwings and skull-like markings on the back of the thorax. Sp.: *Acherontia atropos.*

death-watch beetle small beetle which makes a sound like a watch ticking, once supposed to portend death, and whose larva bores in dead wood. Sp.: *Xestobium rufovillosum.*

deer any ruminant quadruped of the family Cervidae, distinguished in the male by the presence of deciduous branching horns or antlers, and in the young by the presence of spots. The furry covering of the newly formed antlers is given the name velvet.

devil's coach-horse large rove beetle. Sp.: *Ocypus olens.*

devil's darning needle alternative name for a dragonfly or damselfly. Order: Odonata.

dhole fierce canine pack-hunting mammal of the forests of central and South-east Asia. Sp.: *Cuon alpinus.*

dik-dik dwarf antelope native to Africa. Gen.: *Madoqua.*

dingo wild dog of the family Canidae, generally light brown in colour with long muzzle and bushy tail. The dingo, also known as the warrigal, can be found throughout mainland Australia and Tasmania. It is a scavenging carnivore and has a distinct howl but does not bark. Sp.: *Canis dingo.*

diplodocus four-legged plant-eating dinosaur with the longest known tail of all dinosaurs (11 metres). Gen.: *Diplodocus.*

dog domesticated carnivorous mammal. Sp.: *Canis familiaris.*

dolphin any of various marine cetacean mammals of the family Delphinidae, which are typically larger than porpoises but smaller than whales. The common dolphin is *Delphinus delphis.*

dolphin: bottle-nosed inhabiting all the world's oceans and named after its beak-like snout, which is shaped like a bottle and gives the impression of having a permanent smile. Sp.: *Tursiops truncatus.*

dormouse: common nocturnal squirrel-like rodent with bushy tail. Sp.: *Muscardinus avellanarius.*

dormouse (edible) aka fat dormouse. Largest of the dormice, once prized as food by the Romans. Sp.: *Glis glis.*

douroucouli monkey of South America having large, staring eyes. Aka night monkey or owl monkey. Sp.: *Aotus trivirgatus.*

dragonet Any scaleless, spiny marine fish of the family Callionymidae, the males of which are brightly coloured.

dragonfly predatory insect of the suborder Anisoptera, order Odonata, having a large head and eyes, long slender body and two pairs of iridescent wings, which may have a span in excess of 15 centimetres. Sp.: *Libellula forensis.* Alternative names of the dragonfly include devil's darning needle and devil's arrow.

drosophila small fruit fly used extensively in genetic research because of its large chromosomes, numerous varieties and rapid rate of reproduction. Gen.: *Drosophila.*

duck-billed platypus amphibious egg-laying mammal of eastern Australia, having dense fur, a broad flat bill and tail and webbed feet. The platypus and echidna are the only two members of the order Monotremata, i.e. mammals that lay eggs. The male has a toxic horny spur on both hind legs, the venom of which is powerful enough to kill a dog and cause excruciating pain to humans. An excellent swimmer, the platypus has a buoyant body so always swims in a downward tract and is capable of being submerged for up to 10 minutes if resting. Sp.: *Ornithorhynchus anatinus.*

dugong large marine mammal of the order Sirenia, closely related to the manatee; the sole extant member of the family Dugongidae. The dugong is shorter than the manatee and darker skinned but has the same body shape. Manatees inhabit the waters of the Caribbean, South America and West Africa, while the dugongs are found in East African and Australian waters. Like the manatee, the dugong is also sometimes called a sea cow because of its grass-eating habits. Sightings of dugongs and manatees by early explorers gave rise to the mythology of mermaids and sirens. Sp.: *Dugong dugon.*

duiker mostly forest-dwelling African antelopes having a crest of long hair between their horns. Gen.: *Cephalophus* and *Sylvicapra.*

eagle ray large ray with long pointed pectoral fins. Family: Myliobatidae.

earth worm any of various species of ground worms of the phylum Annelida, class Oligochaeta, especially members of the genera *Lumbricus, Allolobophora* and *Eisenia.*

echidna egg-laying insectivorous mammals native to Australia and New Guinea, with a covering of spines, a long snout and long claws. Aka spiny anteater. Family: Tachyglossidae.

eel teleost fish having long, snake-like body, smooth slimy skin and reduced fins. Gen.: *Anguilla.*

eland antelope native to Africa, having spirally twisted horns. The giant eland is the largest of living antelopes. Gen.: *Taurotragus.*

elephant: African larger of the two species of elephant. Sp.: *Loxodonta africana.*

elephant: Indian smaller of the two species of elephant. Gen.: *Elephas maximus.*

emperor moth large moth related to the silk moths with eye-spots on all four wings. Sp.: *Saturnia pavonia.*

eyra reddish-brown variety of jaguarondi. Sp.: *Felis yagouaroundi.*

fallfish freshwater fish of North America resembling the chub. Sp.: *Semotilus corporalis.*

fallow deer small deer having a white-spotted reddish-brown coat in the summer. Sp.: *Dama dama.*

false gavial (gharial) Southeast Asian reptile of the family Crocodilidae with long straight snout, giving the impression of being a gavial. Sp.: *Tomistoma schlegeli.*

fennec smallest fox, native to North Africa and Arabia, having large pointed ears. Sp.: *Vulpes zerda.*

fer-de-lance large, highly venomous pit viper of tropical South America and the West Indies. Sp.: *Bothrops atrox.*

ferret domesticated albino variety of the polecat, bred for hunting rats and rabbits. Sp.: *Mustela putorius.*

fly member of the insect order Diptera, containing over 85,000 species divided into the suborders Nematocera (midges, gnats, crane flies and mosquitoes), Brachycera (bee flies, robber flies and horse flies) and Cyclorrhapha (house flies, fruit flies, blow flies, and leafminers). Dipterans are distinguished from other insects (such as dragonflies and mayflies) by their wing structure, the so-called 'true' flies being characterised by the use of only one pair of wings for flight, the second pair becoming fixed and being used for balance. The smallest two-winged flies are midges, and the largest are robber flies of the family Asilidae, which can attain lengths of up to 8 centimetres.

flying fish warm-water fish with wing-like pectoral fins for gliding through the air. Family: Exocoetidae.

flying fox fruitbats with fox-like heads, largest species with wingspan approaching 2 metres. Family: Pteropodidae.

flying lemur either of two lemur-like mammals of South-east Asia, having a membrane between the fore and hind limbs for gliding from tree to tree. Aka colugo. Gen.: *Cynocephalus.*

flying lizard long-tailed lizard of S.E. Asia with elongated ribs supporting membranes for gliding. Gen.: *Draco.*

flying squirrel any squirrel with skin joining the fore and hind limbs for gliding from tree to tree. Gen.: *Aeromys, Belomys, Eupetdurus, Glaucomys, Hylopetes, Petaurista, Petinomys, Pteromys, Pteromyscus, Trogopterus.*

fox various members of the dog family, Canidae, typically small in stature with a bushy tail known as a brush. They include the African Sand, Bat-eared, Bengal, Black, Blanford's, Brant, Chama, Corsac, Hoary, Indian, Kit, Pale, Rüppell's, Samson, Sand, Silver, Steppe, Swift and Tibetan Sand. Gen.: *Vulpes, Dusicyon, Alopex, Otocyon.*

frog several families of the order Anura, mainly insectivorous amphibians having a short, tailless body with long hind legs for hopping. The European common frog is Sp.: *Rana temporaria.*

furniture beetle beetle whose larvae bore into wood and are known as 'woodworm'. Sp.: *Anobium punctatum.*

galago see bush baby.

galliwasp West Indian lizard. Sp.: *Diploglossus monotropis.*

garfish marine fish having long, beak-like jaws with sharp teeth. Aka needlefish. Family: Belonidae.

gavial (gharial) long-snouted reptile of the order Crocodilia, and the only species of the family Gavialidae. The gavial inhabits the rivers of northern India and grows to a length of up to 5 metres. Sp.: *Gavialis gangeticus.*

gazelle antelope of Asia or Africa. Gen.: *Gazella, Antilope, Antidoreas, Procapra, Ammodoreas, Litocranius.*

gecko nocturnal lizards found in warm climes, with adhesive feet for climbing purposes, the only lizards with voices. Family: Gekkonidae.

gelada brownish baboon with a bare red patch on its chest, native to Ethiopia. Sp.: *Theropithecus gelada.*

gemsbok large antelope of south-west and east Africa. Sp.: *Oryx gazella.*

genet (genette) cat-like mammal native to Africa and Southern Europe with spotted fur and a long, ringed, bushy tail. Gen.: *Genetta.*

gerbil various genera of mouse-like desert rodents. The species often kept as a pet is *Meriones unguiculatus*, the Mongolian gerbil.

gerenuk antelope native to east Africa, with a very long neck and small head. Sp.: *Litocranius walleri.*

giant anteater edentate (toothless) mammal of Central and South America with long snout used for feeding on termites. Sp.: *Myrmecophaga tridactyla.*

gila monster venomous lizard of southwest USA and northwestern Mexico. The gila monster is stout-bodied with black and pink markings and grows to about 45 centimetres (18 inches). Sp.: *Heloderma suspectum.*

giraffe ruminant mammal of Africa with a long neck and forelegs and a skin of dark patches separated by lighter lines. It is the tallest living animal (over 5 metres). Sp.: *Giraffa camelopardalis.*

gnu two antelope species of the genus *Connochaetes*, native to southern Africa, Kenya, Tanzania and Zambia, with a large, erect head and brown stripes on the neck and shoulders. Aka wildebeest.

goat males are called rams or billies and females are does or nannies. Domesticated breeds include Angora, Kashmir, Nubian, Saanen and Toggenburg. Sp.: *Capra hircus.*

goldfish freshwater cyprinid fish of eastern Europe and Asia, especially China. Sp.: *Carassius auratus.*

gopher burrowing rodents of the family Geomyidae native to North America, having food pouches on the cheeks. Aka pocket gopher.

gopher tortoise tortoise native to southern USA, that excavates tunnels to shelter from the sun. Gen.: *Gopherus.*

gorilla largest anthropoid ape, native to central Africa. Sp.: *Gorilla gorilla.*

gourami large freshwater fish native to South-east Asia. Aka labyrinth fish. Sp.: *Osphronemus goramy.*

grampus dolphin with a blunt snout and long, pointed black flippers. Aka Risso's dolphin. Sp.: *Grampus griseus.*

grasshopper any orthopterous insect of the families Acrididae (short-horned grasshoppers) and Tettigoniidae (long-horned grasshoppers). The grasshopper frequents semi-arid regions and grasslands. Many species are green in colour, although some are brownish-grey with red or yellow markings. The upper hind legs of a grasshopper are elongated, and the males tend to produce a buzzing sound by rubbing the femur against its wings. The young of a grasshopper is called a nymph.

grayling silver-grey freshwater fish with a long, high dorsal fin. Gen.: *Thymallus.*

grayling butterfly having wings with grey undersides and bright eye-spots on the upper side. Sp.: *Hipparchia semele.*

greenbottle fly of the genus *Lucilia* - lays eggs in the flesh of sheep.

grunion slender Californian silverside fish, which spawns on beaches. Sp.: *Leuresthes tenuis.*

gudgeon: common small European freshwater fish, often used as bait. Sp.: *Gobio gobio.*

guinea pig domesticated Southern American cavy kept as a pet or for research in biology. Sp.: *Cavia porcellus.*

haddock edible marine fish of the north Atlantic, similar to cod but smaller. Sp.: *Melanogrammus aeglefinus.*

hairstreak species of butterfly of the family Lycaenidae, distinguished by the hair-like markings on the underside of their wings. Usually brown or grey in colour but occasionally red and black. Gen.: *Callophrys.*

hamadryas large, powerful monkey of the plains and open-rock areas of southern Arabia and northeast Africa. Aka sacred baboon or Arabian baboon. Sp.: *Papio hamadryas.*

hamster: common Eurasian rodent of the subfamily Cricetinae, having a short tail and large cheek pouches for storing food. Sp.: *Cricetus cricetus.*

hamster: golden Eurasian rodent of the subfamily Cricetinae, having a short tail and large cheek pouches for storing food and often kept as a pet or as a laboratory animal. Sp.: *Mesocricetus auratus.*

hanuman Indian langur venerated by Hindus. Aka wanderoo. Sp.: *Semnopithecus entellus.*

hare larger than a rabbit, with longer ears, its habitat is called a form. Sp.: *Lepus europaeus.*

harp seal earless seal of the family Phocidae, found in the North Atlantic and Arctic oceans. The typical male is golden-grey with dark markings on its back and face and can grow up to 2 metres long and weigh in excess of 200 kilograms (440 pounds). A young harp seal is variously named bedlamer, beater or greyback, depending on its age and development. Sp.: *Pagophilus groenlandicus.*

hartebeest large African antelope with ringed horns bent back at the tips. Gen.: *Alcelaphus.*

harvest mouse small mouse with a prehensile tail, which nests in the stalks of growing grain. Sp.: *Micromys minutus.*

hedgehog Old World mammal of the order Insectivora with spiny back and very small tail. The common western European species is *Erinaceus europaeus.*

hellbender large, brownish-grey North American salamander measuring up to 75 centimetres in length, with a flat head, short stout legs and a wrinkled fold of skin down its sides. Sp.: *Cryptobranchus alleganiensis.*

hercules beetle large South American beetle with two horns extending from its head. Sp.: *Dynastes hercules.*

herring soft-finned fish of northern seas with elongated scaled body and smooth head. Sp.: *Clupea harengus.*

horned toad South-east Asian toads with horn-shaped extensions over the eyes. Family: Pelobatidae.

horned toad American lizard covered with spiny scales. Gen.: *Phrynosoma.*

hornet large wasp with brown and yellow striped body, capable of inflicting a severe sting. Sp.: *Vespa crabro.*

horseshoe bat bat of the Old World with a horseshoe-shaped ridge on the nose. Family: Rhinolophidae.

horseshoe crab large marine arthropod with a horseshoe-shaped shell and a long tail-spine. Gen.: *Limulus.*

house mouse very common grey mouse, which scavenges around human dwellings. Often kept as pets or used in laboratory experiments. Sp.: *Mus musculus.*

housefly fly of the family Muscidae, breeding in decaying organic matter and often entering houses. Sp.: *Musca domestica.*

hyena (spotted) long-legged, carnivorous, dog-like mammal of Africa. Aka laughing hyena. Sp.: *Crocuta crocuta.*

ibex wild goat of mountainous areas of Europe, north Africa and Asia, with a beard and thick, curved, ridged horns. Sp.: *Capra ibex.*

iguanodon large, herbivorous, long-tailed bipedal dinosaur of the Cretaceous period. Gen.: *Iguanodon.*

impala medium-size antelope of South and East Africa capable of long high jumps. Sp.: *Aepyceros melampus.*

indigo snake see cribo.

jackal four species of African or South Asian canine mammals of the genus *Canis.*

jackrabbit North American hare with long hind legs and large ears. The white-tailed jackrabbit is *Lepus townsendii.*

jaguar large feline mammal of south-west USA and Central and South America, similar to the leopard but with a shorter tail and larger spots on its coat. Sp.: *Panthera onca.*

jaguarondi North and South American small grey cat with short legs and long tail. Sp.: *Felis yagouaroundi.*

jellyfish marine coelenterate of the class Scyphozoa having an umbrella-shaped, jelly-like body and stinging tentacles.

kalong fruit-eating bat. Aka flying fox. Sp.: *Pteropus edulis.*

kangaroo any of up to 50 species of Australasian marsupial mammals of the family Macropodidae. Kangaroos may grow to a height in excess of 2.5 metres and leap a distance of over 13 metres in a single bound at a speed of 50 km per hour.

katipo venomous spider of New Zealand, usually black with a red or orange stripe on its abdomen. Sp.: *Latrodectus katipo.*

katydid orthopterous insect of the family Tettigoniidae (long-horned grasshopper). The katydid is usually coloured green and lives among the foliage of North American trees. Its name derives from the cry of 'katydid, katy didn't' which is heard throughout the night and produced by the insect rubbing its wings together.

kiang wild ass of a race native to Tibet with a thick furry coat, a subspecies of the Asiatic ass, *Equus hemionus.*

killer whale actually a kind of dolphin, with a black back, white belly and prominent dorsal fin. Sp.: *Orcinus orca.*

king cobra world's largest venomous snake (up to 5.5 metres), found from southern China to the Philippines and Indonesia. Aka hamadryad. Sp.: *Ophiophagus hannah.*

kinkajou nocturnal fruit-eating mammal of Central and South America, with a prehensile tail and a very long tail. Sp.: *Potos flavus.*

kissing gourami small, brightly coloured freshwater fish, a popular aquarium pet. Sp.: *Helostoma temminckii.*

koala slow-moving, arboreal marsupial of eastern Australia, having grey fur and feeding on eucalyptus leaves and bark. The koala is also known as a koala bear, although not related to the Ursidae family. It is the only animal apart from humans with unique fingerprints. Sp.: *Phascolarctos cinereus.*

kolinsky Siberian and Asian weasel with a rich brown coat. Sp.: *Mustela sibirica.*

Komodo dragon predatory lizard native to the East Indies, largest of all surviving lizards, reaching over 3 metres long. Sp.: *Varanus komodoensis.*

kouprey rare grey ox, native to forests in Indo-China. Sp.: *Bos sauveli.*

krait any venomous snake of the Asiatic genus *Bungarus.*

lamprey mostly parasitic, eel-like fish of the family Petromyzontidae, without scales, paired fins or jaws, but having a sucker mouth with horny teeth and a rough tongue.

land crab crab that lives in burrows inland and migrates in large numbers to the sea to breed. Sp.: *Cardisoma guanhumi.*

langur any of various agile arboreal Old World monkeys of the family Cercopithecidae.

laughing hyena see hyena (spotted).

leafcutter ant ant of tropical America, which cuts pieces from leaves to cultivate fungus. Gen.: *Atta.*

leafcutter bee solitary bee, which lines its nest with leaf fragments. Family: Megachilidae.

lemon shark member of the shark family Carcharhinidae breeding in western Atlantic waters. Have a short, blunt, rounded nose and feed on bony fish and molluscs. They grow up to 3.3 metres long.

lemon sole flatfish of the plaice family. Sp.: *Microstomus kitt.*

lemur any Madagascan prosimian primate of the family Lemuridae.

leopard large African or Asian feline mammal with either a black-spotted yellowish fawn or all-black coat. Aka panther. Sp.: *Panthera pardus.*

limpet marine gastropod mollusc with a shallow conical shell and a broad muscular foot that sticks tightly to rocks. The common limpet is *Patella vulgata.*

lion large predatory feline mammal of Africa and north-west India, often called the king of beasts. Sp.: *Panthera leo.*

llama South American ruminant related to the camel, kept as a beast of burden and for its soft woolly fleece. Sp.: *Lama glama.*

loach small, edible freshwater fish of the family Cobitidae.

locust orthopterous insect of the family Acrididae (short-horned grasshopper), which is prone to multiply quickly and migrate long distances in destructive swarms billions strong.

loris: slender and slow small slow-moving nocturnal tree-dwelling primates with small ears and a very short tail. The slender loris, *Loris tardigradus*, is found in southern India. The slow loris, *Nycticebus coucang*, is found in south-west Asia and the East Indies.

louse wingless insect parasitic on a wide range of birds and mammals. Those that infest the human hair and skin and transmit various diseases are *Pediculus humanus.*

lynx short-tailed cat inhabiting forests of Europe, Asia and North America. The lynx is distinguished by its tufted ears, hairy soles, broad short head and mottled fur. Sp.: *Felis lynx.*

macaque medium-sized monkey of the Old World genus *Macaca*, including the rhesus monkey and barbary ape, typically having a rather long face with cheek pouches.

mackerel (common) North Atlantic marine fish with a greenish-blue body, used for food. Sp.: *Scomber scombrus.*

magpie moth white geometrid moth with black and yellow markings whose caterpillars feed on fruit bushes. Sp.: *Abraxas grossulariata.*

Malayan stink badger aka teledu or skunk badger. Strong-smelling dark coat is key feature. Sp.: *Mydaus javanensis.*

mamba any venomous African snake of the genus *Dendroaspis*, especially the green and black mambas, *Dendroaspis angusticeps* and *Dendroaspis polylepis.*

mammoth large, extinct elephant of the Pleistocene period. Gen.: *Mammuthus.*

mammoth (woolly) large extinct elephant of the Pleistocene period having a hairy coat and long tusks. Sp.: *Mammuthus primigenius.*

manatee large, aquatic, plant-eating, sirenian mammal with paddle-like forelimbs, no hind limbs and a powerful tail. Aka sea cow. Gen.: *Trichechus.*

mandrill large West African baboon, the adult of which has a brilliantly coloured face and blue-coloured buttocks. Sp.: *Papio sphinx.*

mangabey various small long-tailed West and Central African monkeys of the genus *Cercocebus.* Named after a region of Madagascar.

marbled white whitish butterfly with black markings. Sp.: *Melanargia galathea.*

margay small wild Central and South American cat. Sp.: *Felis wiedii.*

markhor large, spiral-horned wild goat of Central Asia. Sp.: *Capra falconeri.*

marmoset tropical American monkeys having a long silky coat and a bushy tail. Gen.: *Callithrix.*

marmot burrowing, hibernating rodents of the squirrel family with a heavy-set body and short bushy tail, living in colonies in Europe, Asia and the Americas. Gen.: *Marmota.*

marten any weasel-like carnivore of the genus *Martes*, having valuable fur.

massasauga small North American rattlesnake named from corruption of Mississagi River, Ontario. Sp.: *Sistrurus catenatus.*

mastodon extinct, elephant-like proboscidean mammal common in the Miocene period. Gen.: *Mammut.*

mayfly insects with an acquatic nymph and a fragile-winged adult, which lives only briefly in spring. Aka green drake. Order: Ephemeroptera.

meadow brown common brown butterfly with eye-spots on the upper wing. Sp.: *Maniola jurtina.*

megaloceros giant deer whose antlers had a 3.5 metre span; it lived in Eurasia during the last Ice Age. Gen.: *Megaloceros.*

megalosaurus flesh-eating dinosaur, the first to receive a scientific name. Gen.: *Megalosaurus.*

Mexican bearded lizard related to the gila monster and inhabiting the same territory, the Mexican bearded lizard is similar in colour but grows to about 80 centimetres (32 inches). Together they are the only species of poisonous lizards. Sp.: *Heloderma horridum.*

miller's thumb small, spiny, freshwater fish with a large head. Aka bullhead. Sp.: *Cottus gobio.*

millipede herbivorous arthropod of the class Diplopoda, which can have up to 200 pairs of legs.

mink: American semi-aquatic musteline mammal having slightly webbed feet, often hunted for their valuable fur. Sp.: *Mustela vison.*

mink: European slightly smaller version of the American mink. Sp.: *Mustela lutreola.*

mite small parasitic arachnid of the order Acarina, similar to ticks but distinguished by the lack of a sensory pit, known as Haller's organ, on the end segment of the first of four pairs of legs.

mola (ocean sunfish, headfish) large grey heavy ocean fish with short body, flattened sideways. Aka Sp.: *Mola mola.*

mole small burrowing mammals of the order Insectivora, family Talpidae, found in Europe, Asia and North America. The British mole is *Talpa europaeus.*

mongoose small predatory mammals of Africa, southern Europe and Asia, having long tail and brindled coat. Two sub-families: Galidinae and Herpestinae.

monkey any of numerous primates of a group including the families Cebidae (capuchins), Callithricidae (marmosets and tamarins) and Cercopithecidae (baboons and macaques), especially any of the long-tailed varieties.

moonfish see opah.

moose North American elk. Sp.: *Alces alces.*

mouf(f)lon wild mountain sheep of South Europe. Sp.: *Ovis musimon.*

mud puppy large, grey, neotenous aquatic salamander of eastern USA with conspicuous red feathery gills. Sp.: *Necturus maculosus.*

mudskipper any small goby of the family Periophthalmidae, found along the coasts of the Indian and Pacific oceans, able to leave the water and scramble over mud.

mulloway large Australian marine fish used as food. Sp.: *Argyrosomos hololepidotus.*

muntjac any small deer of the genus *Muntiacus*, native to South-east Asia, the male having tusks and small antlers.

musk deer three species of small Asian deer of the genus *Moschus*, having no antlers and in the male having long protruding canine teeth. The musk gland of the male is valued for its use in perfume and medicines.

musk ox large goat-antelope native to North America with a thick, shaggy coat and small, curved horns. Sp.: *Ovibos moschatus.*

muskellunge large North American pike particularly inhabiting the Great Lakes. Aka maskinonge. Sp.: *Esox masquinongy.*

muskrat large aquatic rodent of the vole tribe, native to North America, having a musky smell. Aka musquash. Gen.: *Ondata zibethicus.*

narwhal small Arctic whale, the male of which has a long, straight, spirally twisted tusk developed from one of its teeth. Sp.: *Monodon monoceros.*

natterjack toad of western Eurasia with a bright yellow stripe down its back and moving by running not hopping. Sp.: *Bufo calamita.*

newt any of more than 40 species of tailed amphibian of the order Urodela and family Salamandridae. Aquatic newts have smooth moist skins, while terrestrial species have rough skin and are known as efts. British newts are of the genera *Triturus* (tritons), the most common being the smooth newt (*Triturus vulgaris*).

nilgai large short-horned Indian antelope. Sp.: *Boselaphus tragocamelus.*

Norway lobster small European lobster or scampi. Aka Dublin Bay prawn. Sp.: *Nephrops norvegicus.*

numbat small western Australian termite-eating marsupial with a bushy tail and black and white striped back. Sp.: *Myrmecobius fasciatus.*

nurse shark Atlantic and Caribbean shark of the family Orectolobidae. Yellow-brown or grey-brown in colour and growing up to 4.2 metres, they are the most common hazard to divers although rarely fatally as their teeth are relatively small. Sp.: *Ginglymostoma cirratum.*

ocelot medium-size cat native to the Americas, having a deep yellow or orange coat with black striped and spotted markings. Sp.: *Felis pardalis.*

octopus any cephalopod mollusc of the order Octopoda, varying in size from 1 centimetre to almost 6 metres, with an armspan of almost 9 metres. Octopuses (or octopi) have 8 tentacles and eject an inky fluid when attacked. The largest species is the North Pacific octopus (*Octopus dofleini*) and the smallest is the Californian octopus (*Octopus micropyrsus*).The common octopus (*Octopus vulgaris*) reaches an average size of 1 metre. The octopus has the most complex brain of any invertebrate, having both long-term and short-term memories.

opah large, rare, deep-sea fish having a silver-blue back with white spots and crimson fins. Aka moonfish. Sp.: *Lampris guttatus.*

opossum any mainly tree-living marsupial of the family Didelphidae, native to North and South America, and having a prehensile tail and hind feet with an opposable thumb.

orang-utan large, red, long-haired, tree-living ape native to Borneo and Sumatra. Aka wild man of the woods. Sp.: *Pongo pygmaeus.*

orfe freshwater cyprinid fish of Europe that occurs in two colour varieties i.e. golden and silver. Orfes are often called goldfish. Sp.: *Idus idus.*

oribi small African grazing antelope having reddish-fawn back and white underparts. Sp.: *Ourebia ourebi.*

oryx large African antelope having long straight nearly upright horns. Gen.: *Oryx.*

otter freshwater carnivorous mammals of Europe, Asia, Africa and the Americas, with smooth fur and webbed feet. Sub-family Lutrinae.

ounce see snow leopard.

paddlefish primitive bony fish of the Mississippi and Yangtze rivers, leaden grey, with a long flat snout. Sp.: *Polyodon spathula* and *Psephurus gladius*

paddymelon (pademelon) small wallaby of coastal scrubby regions of Australia. Gen.: *Thylogale.*

painted lady orange-red butterfly with black and white spots. Sp.: *Cynthia cardui.*

panda: giant large, rare, bear-like mammal native to certain mountain bamboo forests of China, having characteristic black and white markings. Sp.: *Ailuropoda melanoleuca.*

panda: red Himalayan raccoon-like mammal with reddish-brown fur and a long, bushy tail. Sp.: *Ailurus fulgens.*

pangolin various mammal species native to Asia and Africa covered with overlapping horny scales and having a small head with elongated snout and tongue, with which they feed on ants, and a tapering tail. Aka scaly anteater. Gen.: *Manus.*

peacock butterfly butterfly with eye-like markings on its wings. Sp.: *Inachis io.*

pearl-oyster any of various marine bivalve molluscs of the genus *Pinctada*, bearing pearls.

peccary three species of American, wild, pig-like mammals of the family Tayassuidae. Sp.: *Tayassu tajacu, Tayassu pecari* and *Catagonus wagneri.*

Père David's deer large, slender-antlered deer, named after Father A David, French missionary and naturalist (d. 1900). Sp.: *Elaphurus davidiensis.*

phalanger any of various species of Australasian marsupial mammals of the family Phalangeridae, also known as possums on the Australian mainland and Tasmania.

plaice European flatfish having a brown back with orange spots and a white underside, much used for food. Sp.: *Pleuronectes platessa.*

polar bear white carnivorous bear of coastal regions of the North Pole. Sp.: *Ursus maritimus.*

polecat (European) small, brownish-black, fetid flesh-eating mammal of the weasel family. Sp.: *Mustela putorius.*

porpoise any of various marine cetacean mammals of the families Delphinidae and Phocoenidae, which are typically smaller than dolphins and with chubbier shape and blunter snout. Sp.: *Phocoena phocoena.*

possum any member of the Phalangeridae family of marsupial mammals native to Australasia. Possums are tree-dwellers. The brush-tailed possum (*Trichosurus vulpecula*) is the most common marsupial in Australia.

potto short-tailed prosimian primate, of the family Lorisidae, having vertebral spines protruding through its neck. The potto is often confused with the kinkajou, as it is a slow-moving, nocturnal, arboreal mammal.

prawn any of various marine decapod crustaceans of the genera *Palaemon* and *Penaeus*, similar to shrimps but having two pairs of pincers.

pterodactyl extinct flying reptile of the late Jurassic, having membranous wings supported on an elongated 4th digit. Gen.: *Pterodactylus.*

puma largest American feline mammal, resembling a lion. It is the best jumper of the cat family. Aka cougar or mountain lion. Sp.: *Felis concolor.*

pygmy white-toothed shrew smallest member of the mouse-like, long-snouted mammals of the family Soricidae. Sp.: *Suncus etruseus.*

quokka small marsupial resembling a wallaby, primarily inhabiting Rottnest Island off the coast of Perth, Western Australia. Sp.: *Setonix brachyurus.*

rabbit burrowing leporid mammal which is smaller than a hare and has much shorter ears. The European rabbit is *Oryctolagus cuniculus.*

raccoon omnivorous mammal of the genus *Procyon* occupying diverse habitats in North and South America. It has a pointed muzzle, long tail and greyish-black fur with black bands around the tail and across the face. The common raccoon of North America is *Procyon lotor.*

ratel see badger (honey).

red deer forest-dweller of Europe and western to central Asia. Males are called harts and females, hinds. Harts with 12 tines are known as 'Royal' and one with 14 tines is a 'Wilson'. Sp.: *Cervus elaphus.*

reindeer see caribou.

ring-tailed lemur rock-dwelling lemur with elongated hind legs and a long tail with brown and white ringed markings. Sp.: *Lemur catta.*

Rocky Mountain goat massive, yellowish-white goat-antelope inhabiting mountains in western North America. Sp.: *Oreamnos americanus.*

roe deer small, graceful woodland deer of Eurasia, the males having small antlers and a reddish-brown summer coat. Sp.: *Capreolus capreolus.*

sable marten of northern Asian and Japanese forests, with dark brown luxuriant fur. Sp.: *Martes zibellina.*

sabre-toothed tiger extinct, lion-size mammal of the cat family (only distantly related to the tiger) with long, curved, upper canine teeth. Aka sabre-toothed cat. Gen.: *Smilodon.*

salamander any tailed amphibian of the order Urodela that most commonly inhabit freshwater and damp woodlands. Salamanders resemble lizards but are related to newts in the family Salamandridae, and can be aquatic, semi-aquatic, or terrestrial. They are generally very small (10–15 centimetres) but giant salamanders may attain a length of up to 180 centimetres. The semi-aquatic Chinese giant salamander (*Andrias davidianus*) grows in excess of 1 metre but the largest salamander is the Japanese giant salamander (*Andrias japonicus*).

sand lizard small, green-grey-brown Eurasian lizard with long clawed digits. Sp.: *Lacerta agilis.*

scorpion arachnid of the order Scorpionida, having an elongated body and a segmented, upwardly curving tail that is tipped with a venomous stinger. During mating the male and female perform a courtship dance and after copulation the female often devours the male.

seal: eared carnivorous pinniped (paddle-footed) aquatic mammal of the family Otariidae, which comes to shore to breed. Eared seals swim by 'rowing' with their front flippers and can turn their hindflippers forward to walk on land.

seal: elephant large seal, the male having an inflatable snout. Aka sea elephant. Gen.: *Mirounga.*

seal: true carnivorous pinniped (paddle-footed) aquatic mammal of the family Phocidae, which comes to shore to breed. They are earless, swim with their hindflippers, and hump along on land, unable to use their hindflippers as support.

sea lion any of five species of eared seal of the South Atlantic and Pacific. The Californian sea lion (*Zalophus californianus*) is the species trained for circus performances.

sea squirt any small primitive marine animal of the class Ascidiacea, having a sac-like body with openings through which water enters and leaves. Sea squirts are sedentary and sessile and can be found on coral reefs, pier pilings, ships' hulls, rocks and seashells. Peculiarly, they can be found on the backs of some species of crabs, while other species of crabs may dwell inside the cavities of a sea squirt.

serval slender feline mammal of the African savanna, having an orange-brown coat with black spots, large ears and long legs. Sp.: *Felis serval.*

shark any of the cartilaginous fish of the class Chondrichthyes with pointed snouts extending over a crescent-shaped mouth. Sharks do not have a swim bladder. There are more than 200 living species of shark including the hammerhead, mako, thresher, bull, bonnethead and Greenland. See also separate entries.

sheep any of various bovid mammals having ribbed horns and a narrow face. Domesticated breeds, genus *Ovis*, include Border Leicester, Cheviot, Clun Forest, Cobb 101, Cotswold, Dartmoor, Devon Longwool, Dorset Down, Dorset Horn, Exmoor Horned, Hampshire, Herdwick, Ile-de-France, Karakul, Kerry Hill, Leicester, Lincoln, The Lonk, Masham, Merino, Oxford, Rambouillet, Romney, Roscommon, Ryeland, Scottish Blackface, Shropshire, Southdown, Suffolk, Swaledale, Welsh Mountain, Wensleydale and Wiltshire Horned.

shrew small, mouse-like, long-snouted mammals of the order Insectivora, family Soricidae. The European common shrew is *Sorex araneus.* Aka shrewmouse.

shrew: elephant small, insect-eating mammals native to Africa, having a long snout and long hind limbs Family: Macroscelididae.

shrimp any of various marine decapod crustaceans of the genus *Crangon*, having a slender flattened body, long tail and a single pair of pincers. Although large shrimps in excess of 5 millimetres are sometimes called prawns, this is misleading as a prawn is a distinct species with two sets of pincers. The two most important shrimps are the common shrimp (*Crangon vulgaris*) and the edible shrimp (*Peneus setiferus*).

skunk American musteline mammals of the sub-family Mephitinae, typically having a black and white coat and bushy tail.They eject a foul-smelling fluid from the anal gland when attacked. The familiar striped skunk is *Mephitis mephitis.*

slender-tailed meerkat see suricate.

sloth shaggy-coated, arboreal edentate mammals of Central and South America that hang upside down by their arms. Three-toed sloths, genus *Bradypus*; two-toed sloths, genus *Choloepus.*

slow worm Eurasian legless lizard with brownish-grey, snake-like body. Sp.: *Anguis fragilis.*

snake (grass) non-venomous European snake having brownish-green body. Sp.: *Natrix natrix.*

snow leopard large, feline, mammal of mountainous regions of central Asia, having a long, pale brown coat marked with black rosettes. Aka ounce. Sp.: *Panthera uncia.*

solenodon rare, shrew-like, nocturnal mammal of the West Indies, having a long hairless tail and an elongated snout. Cuban species, *Solenodon cubanus*; Hispaniola species, *Solenodon paradoxus.*

spectacled bear solitary South American species of the family Ursidae and inhabiting mountainous terrain, which gives it an alternative name of Andean bear. It grows up to 180 centimetres long (6 feet) and has a dark brown coat, with whitish markings around its eyes and facial circumference. Sp.: *Tremarctos ornatus.*

sponge any member of primitive multicellular aquatic animals of the phylum Porifera, which have porous, baglike bodies with a skeleton of hard spicules or elastic fibres. The dried skeleton of sponges are procured for commercial purposes as bathroom sponges because of their ability to hold water.

squirrel (grey) grey-furred squirrel native to eastern North America but found worldwide. Sp.: *Sciurus carolinensis.*

squirrel (red) reddish-brown squirrel inhabiting woodlands of Europe and Asia. Sp.: *Sciurus vulgaris.*

starfish any echinoderm of the classes Asteroidea (sea stars) and Ophiuroidea (brittle stars), typically having a flat body and 5 tentacles, although some species may have many more.

stoat small, long-bodied carnivorous mammal of the weasel family having reddish-brown upper parts and a black-tipped tail and in northern areas turning white in winter, when it is known as ermine. Sp.: *Mustela erminea.*

sturgeon primitive bony fish of temperate waters of the northern hemisphere, valued as a source of caviar and isinglass. Lake sturgeons can live to well over 100 years old. Family: Acipenseridae.

sugar glider Australian possum that glides from tree to tree by means of a fold of skin that joins its front and hind legs. The sugar glider is also known as the flying possum or flying phalanger. Sp.: *Petaurus breviceps.*

suricate southern African mongoose which has a lemur-like face. Aka slender-tailed meerkat. Sp.: *Suricata suricatta.*

swallowtail butterfly member of the subfamily Papilioninae, order Lepidoptera. Swallowtails are found worldwide and are named for the tail-like extensions of their hindwings. Gen.: *Papilio.*

taipan large highly venomous snake of north-east Australia, dark brown with a creamy-coloured head. Sp.: *Oxyuranus scutellatus.*

tapeworm any of various parasitic flatworms of the order Cestoda, which attack the liver and digestive tract of vertebrates.

tapir four species of forest-dwelling perissodactyl mammals of South and Central America and South-east Asia, having an elongated snout, three-toed hind legs and four-toed forelegs. Genus *Tapirus.*

tarpon large, silvery, game fish of warm Atlantic waters, having a compressed, scaled body. *Tarpon atlanticus* is the best-known species.

Tasmanian devil small, ferocious, carnivorous marsupial having black fur with pale markings, strong jaws and short legs. Aka ursine dasyure. Sp.: *Sarcophilus harrisi.*

Tasmanian wolf see thylacine.

tayra large, arboreal, musteline mammal of Central and South America, having a dark brown body and paler head. Sp.: *Eira barbata.*

teledu see Malayan stink badger.

tenrec: tailless small mammal of Madagascar (but largest insectivore), resembling a hedgehog or shrew. Sp.: *Tenrec ecaudatus.*

termite whitish, ant-like insect of the order Isoptera. The two main species are 'ground' termites and 'drywood' termites. Termites feed on cellulose, which is found in wood and wood products. They are social insects, and a typical colony would include workers, soldiers, winged reproductives, and a king and queen. The alternative name for a termite is 'white ant', although there are subtle differences between the body shape of an ant and a termite. An ant has a tapered abdomen, while that of a termite is straight. The ant also has bent antennae whereas the termite's are straight. The winged reproductives are similar to flying ants, although their double wings are even in size while the ant's double wings are uneven in size.

terrapin web-footed chelonian reptile that lives on land or in fresh water. Family: Emydidae.

thylacine presumed extinct, dog-like carnivorous marsupial of Tasmania, having greyish-brown fur with dark vertical stripes on the back. Aka Tasmanian wolf. Sp.: *Thylacinus cynocephalus.*

tick small parasitic arachnid of the families Ixodidae and Nuttalliellidae (hard ticks) and Argasidae (soft ticks). Ticks dwell on the skin of warm-blooded animals and feed on the blood and tissues of their hosts.

tiger large Asian feline mammal with yellowy coat and black stripes. Sp.: *Panthera tigris.*

tiger shark large voracious shark of the family Carcharhinidae. Possess a reputation as a man-eater, but although undoubtedly capable of eating almost anything, in actuality they swim away from divers. Tiger sharks grow up to a length of 7.3 metres and have commercial use as a source of leather and liver oil. Sp.: *Galeocerdo cuvier.*

timber rattlesnake heavy-bodied snake with a broad head that is distinct from its narrow neck. The rattlesnake inhabits the prairies of North America, where it feeds on a variety of small mammals, which are killed by its venomous bite. Humans are not under threat from rattlesnakes as 60 per cent of all bites are dry, and even venomous bites rarely cause more than temporary discomfort. The rattlesnake is generally golden-brown with black markings except for the head, which is plain brown, and its rattler, at the tip of its tail, which is dark black. Sp.: *Crotalus horridus.*

toad anuran amphibian, secreting a poisonous fluid, similar to frogs but more terrestrial, having drier, warty skin. The Eurasian common toad is *Bufo bufo.*

tokay large (35 cm) grey gecko with orange and deep blue spots, of South-east Asia. Sp.: *Gekko gecko.*

tortoise herbivorous chelonian reptile found in warm regions worldwide except Australia. Family: Testudinidae.

tree frog arboreal frog of the family Hylidae, with sucker-like pads to aid in climbing. Tree frogs are also known as tree toads.

triceratops rhinoceros-like herbivorous dinosaur of the Cretaceous period, up to 9 metres long, having three horns and a short armoured neck frill. Gen.: *Triceratops.*

turtle aquatic chelonian reptiles with a flattened shell and flipper-like limbs for swimming. Several families of the order Chelonia.

Tyrannosaurus rex 14 metres long, 6 metres tall, flesh-eating dinosaur with relatively small 2-fingered hands. Gen.: *Tyrannosaurus.*

unau aka Linné's two-toed sloth. Sp.: *Choloepus didactylus.*

vervet small, yellowish-grey, African, long-tailed monkey. Sp.: *Cercopithecus aethiops.*

vicuña South American mammal of the high Andes related to the llama, with fine silky wool. Sp.: *Vicugna vicugna.*

viscacha large South American burrowing rodent related to the chinchillas. Gen.: *Lagidium* and *Lagostomus.*

vole (field) small, rodent of the family Cricetidae with stocky body, short tail and small ears. Sp.: *Microtus agrestis.*

vole (water) large amphibious vole of Eurasian river banks. Sp.: *Arvicola terrestris.*

wallaby (hare) small rodent-like herbivorous marsupial of Australia and New Guinea, family Macropodidae. Gen.: *Lagorchestes.*

wallaby (rock) herbivorous marsupial of Australia and New Guinea, resembling a small kangaroo, of the family Macropodidae. Gen.: *Protemnodon.*

walrus large, tusked, aquatic mammal of the Arctic, a bottom feeder – mainly on molluscs – related to the eared seals. Its family, Odobenidae, has only one species: *Odobenus rosmarus.*

wapiti big North American deer, which is now considered as a larger race of the red deer. Sp.: *Cervus canadensis.*

warble fly any of various flies of the genus *Hypoderma*, whose larvae infest the skin of cattle and horses.

warthog African wild pig with a large head, warty lumps on its face and large curved tusks. Sp.: *Phacochoerus aethiopicus.*

wasp stinging insect of the order Hymenoptera, with black and yellow stripes and a very thin waist.

water moccasin (cottonmouth) poisonous, semi-aquatic pit viper of south-eastern USA. Sp.: *Agkistrodon piscivorus.*

water opossum semi-aquatic tropical American opossum with dark-banded grey fur. Aka yapok. Sp.: *Chironectes minimus.*

weasel (European common) small, brown and white carnivorous mammal with a slender body, related to the stoat. Gen.: *Mustela nivalis.*

whale any of the larger marine mammals of the order Cetacea, having a streamlined body and horizontal tail, and breathing air through a blowhole on the head. Gen.: *Cetacea.*

whale shark large, tropical whale-like shark feeding close to the surface, mainly on plankton. It is however the world's largest living fish, attaining a maximum length of 16.9 metres. Sp.: *Rhincodon typus.*

white admiral mottled brown butterfly with a white splashed band down its wings. Sp.: *Limenitis camilla.*

wildcat wild cat of Eurasia and Africa with a grey and black coat and a bushy tail. Sp.: *Felis silvestris.*

wildebeest see gnu.

wisent the European bison. Sp.: *Bison bonasus.*

witch North Atlantic flatfish resembling the lemon sole. Sp.: *Glyptocephalus cynoglossus.*

wobbegong (spotted) carpet shark of the family Orectolobidae, inhabiting Australian waters and having a richly patterned brown and white skin. Sp.: *Orectolobus maculatus.*

wolf (grey) wild, flesh-eating mammal of the northern hemisphere, ancestor of the domestic dog. Gen.: *Canis lupus.*

wolf-fish large, voracious blenny of the North Atlantic. Family: Anarhichadidae.

wolverine large, musteline mammal of northern forests of Eurasia and North America, a predator and scavenger, having dark very thick water-resistant fur. Aka glutton. Sp.: *Gulo gulo.*

wombat (common) Australian bear-like terrestrial marsupial with coarse dark hair and small ears. Sp.: *Vombatus ursinus.*

wombat (hairy nosed) two marsupial species of Queensland and central south Australia, with fine grizzled fur and longer ears than the common wombat. Sp.: *Lasiorhinus krefftii* and *Lasiorhinus latifrons.*

woodchuck reddish-brown and grey North American burrowing marmot. Aka groundhog. Sp.: *Marmota monax.*

woodlouse small, terrestrial, isopod crustacean of the order Oniscoidae, feeding on rotten wood and plant matter, some of them (pill bugs) able to roll into ball. Common woodlouse: *Oniscus asellus.*

yapok see water opossum.

yellowfin tuna fish of warm seas with yellowish fins, widely fished for food. Sp.: *Thunnus albacares.*

yellowtail game fish of coastal waters of southern California and Mexico, having a yellow tail fin. Sp.: *Seriola dorsalis.*

zebra (plains) African quadruped related to the ass and horse, with black and white stripes. Sp.: *Equus burchelli.*

zebu domestic humped ox of Asia and Africa. Sp.: *Bos indicus.*

zorilla flesh-eating African mammal of the weasel family, aka African polecat. Sp.: *Ictonyx striatus.*

Miscellaneous Information

abranchiate having no gills.

amphibian: largest Japanese giant salamander.

anadromous of a fish (e.g. the salmon), swimming up a river from the sea to spawn.

anthrax fatal bacterial disease of sheep and cattle, transmissible to humans and affecting the skin and lungs; aka wool-sorters' disease.

ants: noses five.

apatosaurus: aka Brontosaurus.

ape: smallest gibbon (apes have no tails).

artiodactyl any placental ungulate mammal whose hoofs have an even number of toes – e.g. pigs, sheep, camels, deer, cattle, antelope and hippopotamuses.

batrachian of or relating to frogs or toads.

bees: eyes five.

braxy acute and usually fatal bacterial disease of sheep characterised by high fever, coma and inflammation of the fourth stomach, caused by infection with *Clostridium septicum.*

butterfly: largest Queen Alexandra's birdwing of Papua New Guinea has a wingspan of up to 25 centimetres (10 inches).

butterfly: tastes with back feet.

carnivore: largest the dinosaur Tyrannosaurus is the largest so far known; today the Kodiak bear is largest. The badger is the largest British carnivore.

carnivores: largest molars giant panda.

cat breeds: Abyssinian, Balinese, Birman, Bombay, Burmese, Burmilla, Chartreux, Cornish Rex, Cymric (tailless), Devon Rex, Donskoy, Havana Brown, Javanese, Korat, Manx (tailless), Minskin, Munchkin, Persian, Russian Blue, Siamese (blue, lilac and seal points), Turkish Van (white with patterned colour on head and tail).

catadromous of a fish (e.g. the eel), swimming down a river to the sea to spawn.

chelonian reptiles including turtles, terrapins and tortoises, having upper and lower shells of bony plates – the carapace and plastron – covered with horny scales.

cladistics method of classifying animals and plants on the basis of shared characteristics that indicate the relative recency of common ancestry.

class major taxonomic division of animals that contain one or more orders e.g. Amphibia, Mammalia and Reptilia. The class Mammalia includes the orders Carnivora, Primates and Rodentia.

coarse fish any freshwater fish other than salmon and trout.

crab: lives in cast-off mollusc shell hermit crab.

cricket: ears situated on front legs.

crops: damage boll weevil (cotton); Colorado beetle (potato); locust (most vegetation); phylloxera (vine).

daddy-long-legs: aka cranefly or harvestman (US); the larvae are called leatherjackets.

death-watch beetle the ticking is caused by knocking its head against wood.

dinosaur: heaviest Brachiosaurus (up to 100 tons).

dinosaur: longest Diplodocus (up to 30 metres).

dog breeds: Affenpinscher, Afghan, Airedale, Alaskan Malamute, Alsatian, Basenji (often called the barkless dog), Basset, Beagle, Bearded Collie, Bedlington Terrier, Bichon Frisé, Bloodhound, Borzoi, Boston Terrier, Boxer, Bull, Cairn Terrier, Chihuahua, Chow Chow (bluish tongue), Clumber Spaniel, Dachshund, Dalmatian, Dandy Dinmont, Doberman Pinscher, Fox Terrier, German Shepherd, Golden Retriever, Great Dane, Greyhound, Griffon, Irish Setter, Irish Wolfhound, Jack Russell, Kerry Blue, Labrador, Lhasa Apso, Mexican Hairless, Newfoundland, Norfolk Terrier, Papillon, Pekingese, Pointer, Pomeranian, Poodle, Pug, Rhodesian Ridgeback, Rottweiler, Saluki, Samoyed (white fluffy), Schnauzer, Sealyham, Shar Pei (wrinkled), Shih Tzu, Skye Terrier, St Bernard, Staffordshire Bull, Vizsla, Whippet, Yorkshire Terrier.

dog licences: year abolished 1988.

droppings deer – crotties, hare – currants, otter – spraints.

elephant: teeth number four.

elytron either of the two wing cases of a beetle.

family major taxonomic division of animals that contain one or more genera e.g. Canidae (dogs) and Felidae (cats). The family Canidae includes the genus *Vulpes* (foxes).

fish: fastest cosmopolitan sailfish.

fish: most poisonous stone fish.

fly: wings trues flies (including craneflies, gnat, mosquitos) have two; the four-winged caddis flies, dragonflies, etc., are not true flies.

genus major taxonomic division of animals that contain one or more species e.g. *Vulpes* (foxes). The genus *Vulpes* (foxes) includes the species *Vulpes bengalensis* (Bengal fox).

giant panda: related to raccoons (family Procyonidae).

glanders contagious and fatal disease of horses, mules and donkeys, caused by the bacterium *Actinobacillus mallei* and characterized by swellings below the jaw and mucous discharge from the nostrils.

hedgehog: fleas one hedgehog may have up to 500 fleas, but the hedgehog flea (*Archaeopsylla erinacei*) does not bite humans.

hedgehog: no. of spines usually about 5,000.

hinny offspring of a female donkey and a male horse.

horse: colours bay – brown with black mane and legs; chestnut – reddish-brown; dun – sandy with black mane; palomino – golden with pale mane; piebald – black and white; skewbald – brown and white; strawberry roan – chestnut and white.

insect: heaviest goliath beetle.

insects: segments head, abdomen, thorax (mnemonic: insects wear HATs).

invertebrate: largest giant squid.

kangaroo: name means 'I don't understand'.

kingdom any of the three groups into which natural objects may be divided i.e. animals, plants and minerals.

koala: name means 'no drink' (feeds on eucalyptus leaves).

lobster: colour Bluish but goes red when cooked.

louping-ill viral disease of animals, especially sheep, transmitted by ticks and causing staggering and jumping.

males give birth seahorse, from a pouch where the female deposits her eggs.

mallenders dry, scabby eruption behind a horse's knee.

metazoan any animal of the subkingdom Metazoa, having multicellular and differentiated tissues and comprising all animals except Protozoa and Parazoa (sponges).

mirror: response to the chimpanzee is the only animal, apart from humans, able to recognise itself in a mirror.

mule cross between a male horse and a female donkey or a female horse and male donkey.

murrain infectious disease of cattle caused by parasites.

octopus: hearts three.

omasum the third stomach of a ruminant.

ophidian reptile of the suborder Serpentes, comprising snakes.

order Major taxonomic division of animals that contain one or more families e.g. Carnivora, Primates and Rodentia. The order Carnivore includes the families Canidae (dogs) and Felidae (cats).

pandas: born January (feed on bamboo shoots).

perissodactyl any placental ungulate mammal whose hoofs have an odd number of toes – e.g. horses, tapirs and rhinoceroses.

pets: legal age to buy in Britain 12 years old is the minimum legal age to purchase a pet.

phylum major taxonomic division of animals that contains one or more classes, e.g. Arthropoda and Chordata. The phylum Arthropoda includes the classes, Arachnids, Centipedes, Crustaceans and insects. The phylum Chordata includes the classes, Amphibia, Aves, Mammalia and Reptilia.

pinnipeds: definition carnivorous aquatic mammals with flippers for feet (name means wing-foot).

pismire Middle English name for an ant deriving from the smell of an anthill.

reproduces: young axolotl often reproduces before reaching adult stage itself.

rhinoceros: number of horns Indian and Javan, one; Black, Sumatran and White, two.

rodents: largest capybara (in world), beaver (in Europe), coypu (in UK).

ruminant herbivorous animal that chews the cud.

scrapie fatal disease of sheep and goats, a spongiform encephalopathy producing degeneration of the central nervous system, caused by changes in prion proteins.

sex: changes annually oyster.

silkworm: food mulberry leaves.

snake: heaviest South American anaconda.

spavin disease of a horse's hock with a hard bony swelling or excrescence.

species any of the taxonomic groups into which a genus is divided; e.g. the genus *Vulpes* (foxes) has many different species, such as *Vulpes bengalensis* (Bengal fox) and *Vulpes pallida* (pale fox). Species are denoted by two words, the first being the genus and the second the species.

spider: eyes eight.

stomach: turns inside out starfish.

strangles acute bacterial disease of horses caused by infection with *Streptococcus equi*, characterised by inflammation of the mucous membranes of the respiratory tract. Aka equine distemper.

sunburn: suffers from the pig is the only non-human animal to suffer from sunburn.

taxonomy the branch of biology concerned with the classification of organisms into groups based on similarities of structure, origin and type. Carolus Linnaeus (1707–78) was the first person to structure principles for defining genera and species of organsims and to create a uniform system for naming them. The seven tiers of the hierarchy are kingdom, phylum, class, order, family, genus and species. The first six ranks use a single word to describe their members, but the names of species are binomial. Various intermediary divisions of the seven main ranks have been necessitated by the continuing discovery of new species: the prefixes sub-, super- and infra- are often applied to create new categories, and further tiers are established by using headings such as tribe or cohort. All intermediary divisions use a single word to describe their members, but subspecies become trinomial. Conventionally, the names of superfamilies end in 'oidea', families in idae', subfamilies in 'inae' and tribes in 'ini'.

taxonomy: mnemonic Kingdom, Phylum, Class, Order, Family, Genus, Species (Kent Play Cricket On Fridays, Girls Spectate).

turning sickness affliction of wildebeest whereby loss of balance faculties causes a never-ending walking in circles until death; it happens when bot-flies lay eggs in their nose and larvae find their way into the brain.

twins: consistent production armadillos and salamanders always give birth to twins.

ungulates all mammals with hoofs; they are divided into odd-toed (perissodactyl) and even-toed (artiodactyl).

vision: rear-view giraffes have ability to see behind them without turning.

woodlouse: legs fourteen.

WWF: symbol World Wide Fund for Nature symbol is a giant panda.

zoophyte plantlike animal, e.g. coral, sea anemone or sponge.

Gestation Periods

aardvark	210
alpaca	345
anteater, giant	190
antelope	280
armadillo	60–120
ass	350
baboon	180
badger	100–360
bear, grizzly	230
polar bear	240
beaver	105
bison	280
boar, wild	115
bobcat	63
buffalo	310
bush baby	110–193
capybara	150
cat, domestic	52
cattle	283
chamois	165
cheetah	95
chimpanzee	235
civet	80
coati	77
coyote	63
deer, fallow	230
deer, musk	170
dhole	61
dingo	63
dog, domestic	60
dog, African wild	72
dolphin	350
dormouse	30
dromedary	400
elephant, Asiatic	608
ermine	28
ferret	60
fox, red	63
gazelle	188
gerbil	28
gibbon	230
giraffe	460
goat	150
gorilla	260
guinea pig	63
hamster	25
hare	32
hare, mountain	50
hedgehog	30
hippopotamus	240
horse	350
hyena	93
jackal	63
jaguar	100
kangaroo	180–335
koala	36
lemming	21
lemur	60–160
leopard	100
lion	110
llama	360
lynx	63
macaque	180
marmoset	150
mink	50
mole	35
mongoose	60
moose	264
mouse	25
narwhal	435
ocelot	70
opossum	12
orang-utan	240
otter	55
panda, giant	138
pig	115
porcupine	210
porpoise	183
puma	93
rabbit	30
raccoon	63
rat, black	21
reindeer	225
rhinoceros, black	450
seal, common	245
seal, eared	360
sea lion	350
sheep	148
shrew	18
skunk	63
sloth	180–340
squirrel	40
tapir	370
tiger	103
vole	90
wallaby	40
walrus	460
warthog	172
weasel	40
whale	350
whale, beluga	435
whale, sperm	435
wolf	62
wolverine	270
yak	258
zebra	340
zorilla	43

Maximum Life Spans

Species	*Years*
Marion's tortoise	152
quahog	150
man	123
spur thighed tortoise	116
deep sea clam	100
killer whale	90
sea anemone	90
European eel	88
lake sturgeon	82
freshwater mussel	80
Asiatic elephant	78
tuatara	77
Andean condor	72
African elephant	70
great eagle owl	68
American alligator	66
blue macaw	64
horse	62
ostrich	62
orang-utan	57
chimpanzee	56
pike	55
hippopotamus	54
slow-worm	54
gorilla	53
domestic goose	50
Indian rhinoceros	49
European brown bear	47
grey seal	46
blue whale	45
goldfish	41
common boa	40
common toad	40
Cape giraffe	36
Bactrian camel	35
Hoffmann's sloth	34
domestic cat	34
canary	34
American bison	33
bobcat	32
red kangaroo	30
domestic dog	29
budgerigar	29
lion	29
theraphosid spider	28
domestic pig	27
giant panda	27
red deer	26
tiger	26
grey squirrel	23
domestic goat	20
blue sheep	20
queen ant	18
common rabbit	18
hedgehog	16
land snail	15
guinea pig	14
capybara	12
tree shrew	11
giant centipede	10
golden hamster	10
fat dormouse	8
millipede	7
house mouse	6
moonrat	4
monarch butterfly	1
bedbug	0.5
house fly	0.04

Animal Cries

Animal	Cry	Animal	Cry	Animal	Cry
apes	gibber	falcons	chant	nightingales	pipe, warble, jug-jug
asses	bray	flies	buzz	owls	hoot, screech
bears	growl	foxes	bark, yelp	oxen	low, bellow
bees	hum	frogs	croak	parrots	talk
beetles	drone	geese	cackle, hiss	peacocks	scream
bitterns	boom	grasshoppers	chirp, pitter	peewits	peewit
blackbirds	whistle	guineafowls	come back	pigs	grunt, squeak, squeal
blackcaps	chick-chack	guineapigs	squeak	pigeons	coo
bulls	bellow	grouse	drum	ravens	croak
calves	bleat	hares	squeak	rooks	caw
cats	mew, purr, swear	hawks	scream	sheep	bleat, baa
chaffinches	chirp, pink	hens	cackle, cluck	snakes	hiss
chickens	peep	horses	neigh, whinny	sparrows	chirp
cocks	crow	hyenas	laugh	stags	bellow, call
cows	moo, low	jays	chatter	swallows	twitter
crows	caw	kittens	mew	swans	cry, sing (before death)
cuckoos	cuckoo	lambs	bleat, baa	thrushes	whistle
deer	bell	linnets	chuckle	tigers	roar, growl
dogs	bark, bay, howl, yelp	lions	roar, growl	turkeys	gobble
doves	coo	magpies	chatter	vultures	scream
ducks	quack	mice	squeak, squeal	whitethroat	chirr
eagles	scream	monkeys	chatter, gibber	wolves	howl

Animal Habitations

Animal	Habitation	Animal	Habitation	Animal	Habitation
ant	formicary, ant-hill	fox	earth, lair	rabbit	burrow, warren
ape	tree-nest	hare	form, down	spider	web
badger	set, earth	horse	stable	squirrel	drey
bear	den, lair	lion	den	tiger	lair
beaver	lodge	mole	fortress	wasp	vespiary, nest
bee	apiary, hive	mouse	hole, nest	wolf	lair
bird	nest, aviary	otter	holt		
eagle	eyrie	penguin	rookery		

Animals: Young

Animal	Young	Animal	Young	Animal	Young
ass	foal, hinny	fox	cub	pigeon	squab
bear	cub	frog	tadpole, froglet	pike	jack
beaver	kitten	gnat	bloodworm	rabbit	kit
cat	kitten	goat	kid	roe deer	kid
cod	codling	goose	gosling	salmon	parr, smolt, grilse
cow	calf, heifer	grouse	poult	seal	pup
crane-fly	leather jacket	hare	leveret	sheep	lamb
deer	fawn	hippopotamus	calf	squirrel	kitten
duck	duckling	horse	foal	swan	cygnet
eagle	eaglet	kangaroo	joey	whale	calf
eel	elver	lion	cub	zebra	foal
elephant	calf	otter	whelp		
fish	fry	pig	piglet		

Plants and Trees

abele the white poplar. Sp.: *Populus alba.*

alder betulaceous tree having toothed leaves and cone-like fruits. The bark is used in dying and tanning and the wood for bridges (as it resists under-water rot). Gen.: *Alnus.*

alfalfa leguminous plant with clover-like leaves and flowers, grown for fodder and as a salad vegetable. Aka lucerne. Sp.: *Medicago sativa.*

almond small rosaceous tree native to western Asia with pink flowers and green fruit containing edible nut. Sp.: *Prunus amygdalus.*

aloe vera Caribbean aloe yielding a gelatinous substance used in cosmetics as an emollient. Sp.: *Aloe vera.*

alsike species of clover named after Swedish town. Sp.: *Trifolium hybridum.*

anise umbelliferous plant having aromatic seeds. Sp.: *Pimpinella anisum.*

arum lily tall, lily-like, aroid plant found mainly in Southern Africa. Sp.: *Zantedeschia aethiopica.*

ash oleaceous tree with compound leaves, winged seeds and clusters of greenish flowers. Gen.: *Fraxinus.*

aspen poplar tree with tremulous leaves. Sp.: *Populus tremula.*

balsa bombacaceous tree of tropical America, distinguished by its very light wood. Sp.: *Ochroma lagopus.*

banyan moraceous tree of tropical India and the East Indies, having aerial roots that grow down from the branches into the soil, forming additional trunks. Sp.: *Ficus benghalensis.*

baobab African tree with an enormously thick trunk and large, edible, pulpy fruit hanging down on stalks. Sp.: *Adansonia digitata.*

barley erect, annual, temperate grass with short leaves and bristly flowers used for grain. Sp.: *Hordeum vulgares.*

bayberry North American shrub having aromatic leaves and bearing berries covered in a wax coating. Sp.: *Myrica cerifera and Myrica cerifera.*

beech hardwood tree having smooth, greyish bark. Gen.: *Fagus.*

bee orchid European and North Africa orchid with bee-shaped flowers. Sp.: *Ophrys apifera.*

betony purple-flowered plant. Sp.: *Stachys officinalis.*

bilberry hardy dwarf shrub of North Europe growing on heaths and mountains and having red drooping flowers and dark blue berries. Sp.: *Vaccinium -myrtillus.*

birch hardwood, close-grained tree with thin, peeling bark. Gen.: *Betula.*

black bryony climbing plant with dark tubers and poisonous red berries. Sp.: *Tamus communis.*

black-eyed Susan flower with yellow petals and a dark centre. Gen.: *Rudbeckia.*

bladderwort aquatic plant whose leaves have small bladders for trapping and digesting insects. Gen.: *Utricularia.*

bladderwrack common brown seaweed with fronds containing air bladders that give buoyancy. Sp.: *Fucus vesiculosus.*

bleeding heart plant with heart-shaped, rose pink flowers hanging from an arched stem. Sp.: *Dicentra spectabilis.*

borage plant with bright blue flowers and hairy leaves used as flavouring. Sp.: *Borago officinalis.*

brookweed small, white-flowered plant of the primrose family growing in wet ground. Sp.: *Samolus valerandi.*

buckbean bog plant with white or pinkish hairy flowers. Sp.: *Menyanthes trifoliata.*

buckthorn (common) thorny shrub with berries formerly used as a cathartic. Sp.: *Rhamnus cathartica.*

buckwheat cereal plant with seeds used for fodder and for flour to make bread. Sp.: *Fagopyrum esculentum.*

burdock plant with prickly flowers and dock-like leaves. Gen.: *Arctium.*

busy Lizzie East African plant with abundant red, pink or white flowers, often grown as bedding or house plants. Sp.: *Impatiens walleriana.*

butterbur waterside plant with pale purple flowers and large, soft leaves formerly used to wrap butter. Gen.: *Petasites.*

buttercup yellow-flowered meadow plant of Europe and North America. Gen.: *Ranunculus.*

butterfly bush common name given to buddleia bush. Sp.: *Buddleia davidii.*

calabash tree evergreen tree, bearing fruit in the form of large gourds, native to tropical America. Sp.: *Crescentia cujete.*

calluna common heather native to Europe and North Africa. Sp.: *Calluna vulgaris.*

caper perennial spiny bush native to the area around the Mediterranean Basin. A caper is also the pickled bud of this plant. Gen.: *Capparis.*

carambola small tree native to South-east Asia bearing golden-yellow ribbed fruit. Aka star fruit. Sp.: *Averrhoa carambola.*

cashew bushy evergreen tree native to Central and North America bearing kidney-shaped nuts attached to fleshy fruits. Sp.: *Anacardium occidentale.*

cassava (bitter) plant of the spurge family having starchy tuberous roots. Aka manioc tapioca. Sp.: *Manihot esculenta.*

catmint plant with downy leaves, purple-spotted white flowers, and a mint-like smell attractive to cats. Sp.: *Nepeta cataria.*

cedar coniferous tree having spreading branches, needle-like evergreen leaves and cones. Gen.: *Cedrus.*

celery pine Australasian tree with branchlets like celery leaves. Sp.: *Phyllocladus trichomanoides.*

charlock a wild mustard with yellow flowers. Sp.: *Sinapis arvensis.*

checkerberry North American evergreen shrub of the health family with spiny, scented leaves, white flowers and crimson fruits. Aka wintergreen. Sp.: *Gaultheria procumbens.*

cherry plum tree native to south-western Asia with solitary white flowers and red fruit. Sp.: *Prunus cerasifera.*

chervil umbelliferous plant with small white flowers; its aniseed flavoured leaves used as a herb for flavouring soup and salads. Sp.: *Anthriscus cereifolium.*

chestnut broad-leaved tree, which produces flowers in long catkins and nuts in a prickly bur. Gen.: *Castanea.*

chickpea leguminous plant with short, swollen pods containing yellow-beaked edible seed. Aka garbanza. Sp.: *Cicer arietinum.*

chicory blue-flowered plant cultivated for its salad leaves and its root, which is ground for coffee. Sp.: *Cichorium intybus.*

Chinese water chestnut sedge with rushlike leaves arising from a corm, which is used as food. Sp.: *Eleocharis tuberosa.*

chives small allium with purple-pink flowers and dense tufts of long tubular leaves, which are used as a herb. Sp.: *Allium schoenoprasum.*

Christmas rose small, white-flowered, winter-blooming plant. Sp.: *Helleborus niger.*

cinchona evergreen trees of South America, of the madder family, having fragrant flowers; the bark of this tree contains quinine. Gen.: *Cinchona.*

cineraria plant cultivated for its bright flowers. Sp.: *Pericallis cruenta.*

cloudberry small mountain bramble with a white flower and an orange-coloured fruit. Sp.: *Rubus chamaemorus.*

coco de mer palm tree of the Seychelles producing a large fruit containing a two-lobed, edible nut (world's largest seed). Sp.: *Lodoicea maldivica.*

coltsfoot plant of the daisy family with large leaves and yellow flowers. Sp.: *Tussilago farfara.*

columbine an aquilegia with purple-blue flowers. Sp.: *Aquilegia vulgaris.*

cork oak evergreen Mediterranean oak. Sp.: *Quercus suber.*

cowbane poisonous plant found in marshes. Sp.: *Cicuta virosa.*

cow parsley hedgerow plant having lacelike umbels of flowers. Sp.: *Anthriscus sylvestris.*

cowslip primula with fragrant yellow flowers, which grows in pastures and meadows. Sp.: *Primula veris.*

cranesbill any of various plants of the genus *Geranium*, having pink or purple flowers and long, slender, beaked fruit.

cuckoo flower meadow plant with pale lilac flowers. Aka lady's smock. Sp.: *Cardamine pratensis.*

cuckoo pint wild arum with arrow-shaped leaves and scarlet berries. Sp.: *Arum maculatum.*

daffodil bulbous plant with a yellow, trumpet-shaped corona. Sp.: *Narcissus pseudonarcissus.*

daisy small, low-growing European plant having a rosette of white leaves and yellow centre. Sp.: *Bellis perennis.*

dawn redwood Chinese deciduous coniferous tree of a genus first known only from fossils. Sp.: *Metasequoia glyptostroboides.*

dead man's fingers species of orchid, *Orchis mascula.*

deadly nightshade highly poisonous plant with drooping purple flowers and black, cherry-like fruit. Sp.: *Atropa belladonna.*

death cap poisonous toadstool of deciduous woodland. Sp.: *Amanita phalloides.*

deodar Himalayan cedar with drooping branches bearing large barrel-shaped cones. Tallest of the cedar family. Sp.: *Cedrus deodara.*

destroying angel poisonous white toadstool. Sp.: *Amanita virosa.*

dewberry shrub with bluish fruit similar to a blackberry. Sp.: *Rubus caesius.*

dill umbelliferous herb with yellow flowers and aromatic seeds. Sp.: *Anethum graveolens.*

divi-divi tree native to tropical America, bearing curved pods, which are a source of tannin. Sp.: *Caesalpinia coriaria.*

dog's tooth violet plant of the Liliaceae family with speckled leaves, purple flowers and a toothed perianth. Sp.: *Erythronium dens-canis.*

Douglas fir large conifer over 100m tall of western North America. Sp.: *Pseudotsuga menziesii.*

doum palm tree with edible fruit. Sp.: *Hyphaene thebaica.*

dove's foot type of cranesbill. Sp.: *Geranium molle.*

dragon tree palm-like tree of the Canary Islands. Sp.: *Dracaena draco.*

durian large tree native to South-east Asia, bearing oval spiny fruit containing a creamy pulp with a fetid smell but an agreeable taste. Sp.: *Durio zibethinus.*

Dutchman's breeches plant of eastern North America with white flowers and finely divided leaves. Sp.: *Dicentra cucullaria.*

Dutchman's pipe climbing vine of eastern North America with hooked tubular flowers. Sp.: *Aristolochia durior.*

ebony tree with hard, dark wood often used for cabinetwork. Sometimes called persimmon. Sp.: *Diospyros ebenum.*

eglantine wild rose with small fragrant leaves and flowers. Sp.: *Rosa eglanteria.*

elm tree with serrated leaves and winged fruits (samaras), the wood being hard and heavy. Gen.: *Ulmus.*

endive curly-leaved plant used in salads. Sp.: *Cichorium endivia.*

eucalyptus myrtaceous tree native to Australia; species include blue gum and ironbark. Gen.: *Eucalyptus.*

false acacia the locust tree, often grown for ornament. Sp.: *Robinia pseudoacacia.*

felwort purple-flowered gentian. Sp.: *Gentianella amarella.*

fennel yellow-flowered umbelliferous plant with fragrant seeds and fine leaves used as flavourings. Sp.: *Foeniculum vulgare.*

fenugreek leguminous plant with aromatic seeds, which are often used in curry powder. Sp.: *Trigonella foenum-graecum.*

fern pteridophyte plant having roots, stems and fronds and reproducing by spores formed in structures (sori) on the fronds. Division: Pteridophyta (syn. Filicinophyta).

fever tree yellow-flowered southern African tree. Sp.: *Acacia xanthophloea.*

feverfew aromatic, bushy plant with feathery leaves and white, daisy-like flowers, used to treat migraine and formerly to reduce fever. Sp.: *Tanacetum parthenium.*

figwort plant of the genus *Scrophularia* with dull, purplish-brown flowers, once believed to be useful against scrofula.

flax-lily New Zealand plant of the agave family yielding valuable fibre. Sp.: *Phormium tenax.*

forget-me-not plant with small, yellow-eyed, bright blue flowers. Gen.: *Myosotis.*

foxglove tall plant with erect spikes of purple or white bell-shaped flowers. Sp.: *Digitalis purpurea.*

frangipani deciduous tree of Central America producing flowers ranging from yellow to pink. The tree was named after an Italian perfume used to scent gloves in the 16th century; the perfume itself after its creator, Marquis Frangipani. Gen.: *Plumeria.*

fraxinella aromatic plant of rue family having foliage that emits an ethereal inflammable oil. Aka burning bush. Sp.: *Dictamnus albus.*

gentian plants found in mountainous regions, having violet or blue trumpet-shaped flowers. Gen.: *Gentiana.*

gerbera any plant of the genus *Gerbera*, of Africa or Asia, especially the Transvaal daisy. Gen.: *Gerbera.*

germander any of various plants of the genus *Teucrium*, typically a mildly aromatic, white-felted perennial shrublet with a compact domed shape. The flowers, which appear between April and July, are reddish or purplish in colour. Germander was used in Cypriot folk-medicine as a cure for stomach ailments and jaundice.

germander speedwell creeping plant with germander-like leaves and blue flowers. US name: bird's-eye speedwell. Sp.: *Veronica chamaedrys.*

ginger hot, spicy root, which can be powdered for use in cooking, or preserved in syrup, or candied. Sp.: *Zingiber officinale.*

gladiolus plants of *Iridaceae* family with sword-shaped leaves and brightly coloured flower spikes. Gen.: *Gladiolus.*

goatsbeard Eurasian plant with woolly stems and large heads of yellow-rayed flowers surrounded by large, green bracts. Sp.: *Tragopogon pratensis.*

goatsbeard American rosaceous plant with long spikes of small white flowers. Gen.: *Aruncus.*

goat's-rue Eurasian leguminous plant cultivated for its white, mauve or pinkish flowers. Sp.: *Galega officinalis.*

goat's-rue North American leguminous plant with pink-and-yellow flowers. Sp.: *Tephrosia virginiana.*

good King Henry weed of the goosefoot family. Sp.: *Chenopodium bonus-henricus.*

goosefoot plant that has small greenish flowers and leaves like the foot of a goose. Gen.: *Chenopodium.*

gopher North American tree, yielding yellowish timber aka yellowwood. Not to be confused with the field gopher tree from which Noah's Ark was reputedly built. Sp.: *Cladrastis lutea.*

grass monocotyledonous plants encompassing all the cereal plants as well as reeds and bamboos. Family *Gramineae.*

greenheart tropical American evergreen tree of the laurel family. Gen.: *Ocotea rodiaei.*

guaiacum trees native to tropical America with hard, dense, oily timber. Gen.: *Guaiacum.*

guava small tropical American tree bearing an edible, pale orange fruit with pinky, juicy flesh. Sp.: *Psidium guajava.*

guelder rose deciduous shrub with round bunches of creamy-white flowers. Sp.: *Viburnum opulus.*

guernsey lily nerine, originally from South Africa, with large, pink, lily-like flowers. Sp.: *Nerine sarniensis.*

hare's-foot clover with soft hair on flowers. Sp.: *Trifolium arvense.*

hart's tongue fern with narrow undivided fronds. Sp.: *Phyllitis scolopendrium.*

hawthorn thorny shrub or tree with white, red or pink blossom and small, dark red fruit or haws. Sp.: *Crataegus monogyna.*

hazel small tree bearing round brown edible nuts. Sp.: *Corylus avellana.*

henbane poisonous herbaceous plant with sticky hairy leaves and an unpleasant smell. Sp.: *Hyoscyamus niger.*

henna tropical shrub having small pink, red or white flowers; the reddish dye from its shoots and leaves is used to colour hair. Sp.: *Lawsonia inermis.*

herb Christopher white-flowered baneberry. Sp.: *Actaea spicata.*

herb Paris plant with a single flower and four leaves in a cross shape on an unbranched stem. Sp.: *Paris quadrifolia.*

herb Robert common cranesbill with red-stemmed leaves and pink flowers. Sp.: *Geranium robertianum.*

holly evergreen tree with prickly leaves and red berries, often used as Christmas decorations. Gen.: *Ilex.*

hop climbing plant cultivated for the cones borne by the female, used in brewing. Sp.: *Humulus lupulus.*

hornbeam tree of the genus *Carpinus* with a smooth bark and a hard tough wood. Gen.: *Carpinus.*

horse chestnut Eurasian tree with palmate leaves and inedible nuts enclosed in a spiky bur (conkers). Sp.: *Aesculus hippocastanum.*

horse mushroom large, edible mushroom. Sp.: *Agaricus arvensis.*

horseradish cruciferous plant with long, lobed leaves. Sp.: *Armoracia rusticana.*

hortensia kind of hydrangea (distinct from lacecap) with large, round, infertile flower heads. Sp.: *Hydrangea macrophylla.*

huckleberry North American shrub with blue or black soft fruit. Gen.: *Gaylussacia.*

Iceland poppy Arctic poppy with white or yellow flowers. Sp.: *Papaver nudicaule.*

Indian hemp strong-smelling Asian moraceous plant. Aka marijuana, Cannabis. Sp.: *Cannabis -indica.*

ivy climbing plants having lobed evergreen leaves and black, berry-like fruits. Gen.: *Hedera.*

jack-by-the-hedge white-flowered cruciferous plant of shady places. Sp.: *Alliaria petiolata.*

jackfruit East Indian tree bearing fruit resembling breadfruit. Sp.: *Artocarpus heterophyllus.*

japonica flowering shrub with round white, green or yellow, edible fruit and bright red flowers. Sp.: *Chaenomeles speciosa.*

jarrah the Western Australian mahogany gum tree. Sp.: *Eucalyptus marginata.*

jasmine oleaceous shrub or climbing plant whose fragrant flowers are used in perfumery. Gen.: *Jasminum.*

kangaroo paw Australian plant with irregular woolly flowers. Floral emblem of Western Australia. Sp.: *Anigozanthos manglesii.*

kangaroo vine evergreen climbing plant with serrated leaves. Sp.: *Cissus antarctica.*

kidney vetch yellow-flavoured leguminous plant found in grassland. Aka lady's finger. Sp.: *Anthyllis vulneraria.*

knotweed fast-growing Japanese plant. Sp.: *Fallopia japonica.*

ladino large type of white clover native to Italy and cultivated for fodder. Sp.: *Trifolium repens.*

lamb's ears garden plant with whitish, woolly leaves. Sp.: *Stachys byzantina.*

lemon balm bushy plant with leaves smelling and tasting of lemon. Sp.: *Melissa officinalis.*

lemon geranium lemon-scented pelargonium. Sp.: *Pelargonium crispum.*

lemon verbena shrub with lemon-scented leaves. Aka lemon plant. Sp.: *Aloysia triphylla.*

leopard's bane any plant of the genus *Doronicum* with large, yellow, daisy-like flowers. Sp.: *Doronicum.*

live oak American evergreen tree. Sp.: *Quercus -virginiana.*

loquat tree of the Rosaceae family, bearing small, yellow, egg-shaped fruit. Sp.: *Eriobotrya japonica.*

love-in-a-mist blue-flowered garden plant with many delicate green bracts. Sp.: *Nigella damascena.*

love-lies-bleeding garden plant with drooping spikes of purple-red blooms. Sp.: *Amaranthus caudatus.*

lungwort Eurasian plant with spotted leaves and clusters of blue or purple flowers. Sp.: *Pulmonaria officinalis.*

lungwort (sea) boraginaceous plant of the northern temperate genus *Mertensia*, with drooping clusters of tubular, usually blue flowers. Aka oyster plant. Gen.: *Mertensia maritima.*

madder plant with yellow flowers and red fleshy root. Gen.: *Rubia.*

mahogany tropical tree yielding a hard, reddish-brown wood used for furniture making. Sp.: *Swietenia mahagoni.*

mandrake poisonous plant with white, or purple flowers and large yellow fruit, having emetic and narcotic properties and possessing a root once thought to resemble the human form and to shriek when plucked. Sp.: *Mandragora officinarum.*

mangosteen Malaysian tree bearing a white juicy-pulped fruit with a thick, reddish-brown rind. Sp.: *Garcinia mangostana.*

mangrove any tropical tree or shrub of the genus *Rhizophora* growing in shore-mud with many tangled roots above ground. Gen.: *Rhizophora.*

Manila hemp Philippine plant with a strong fibre used for rope-making. Sp.: *Musa textilis.*

manuka small New Zealand tree with aromatic leaves and hard timber. Sp.: *Leptospermum -scoparium.*
maple any tree or shrub of the genus *Acer,* grown for shade, ornament, wood, or sugar.
marsh mallow herbaceous plant, the roots of which were formerly used to make a sweet confection. Sp.: *Althaea officinalis.*
marsh marigold golden-flowered plant, which grows in moist pastures. Sp.: *Caltha palustris.*
martagon lily with small, purple, turban-like flowers. Sp.: *Lilium martagon.*
marvel of Peru showy garden plant with flowers opening at dusk. Sp.: *Mirabilis jalapa.*
mayapple American herbaceous plant bearing a yellow, egg-shaped fruit in May. Sp.: *Podophyllum peltatum.*
mayflower In North America trailing arbutus that blooms in May. Sp.: *Epigaea repens.*
maz(z)ard the wild sweet cherry of Europe. Sp.: *Prunus avium.*
meadow rue plants of the buttercup family with small yellow or purple flowers. Gen.: *Thalictrum.*
meadow saffron meadow plant resembling a crocus and producing lilac flowers in autumn, while still leafless. Sp.: *Colchicum autumnale.*
meadowsweet plant of the Rosaceae family, common in meadows and damp places, with creamy-white fragrant flowers. Also the name of a North American plant of the genus *Spiraea.* Sp.: *Filipendula ulmaria.*
medlar tree of the rose family bearing small brown apple-like fruits, which are best eaten when overripe. Sp.: *Mespilus germanica.*
mignonette plants of the genus *Reseda,* some -having aromatic grey-green flowers.
mimosa Leguminous shrub having globular yellow flowers and sensitive leaflets, which droop when touched. Sp.: *Mimosa pudica.*
mistletoe parasitic plant growing on apple and other trees and bearing white, glutinous berries in winter. Americans have a related plant of the genus *Phoradendron.* Sp.: *Viscum album.*
mock pennyroyal North American aromatic plant. Sp.: *Hedeoma pulegioides.*
moneywort trailing evergreen plant with round glossy leaves and yellow flowers. Sp.: *Lysimachia nummularia.*
monkey flower short creeping plant with bright yellow flowers. Sp.: *Mimulus guttatus.*
monkey-puzzle coniferous tree native to Chile with downward-pointing branches and small, close-set leaves. Aka Chile pine. Sp.: *Araucaria araucana.*
montbretia hybrid plant of genus *Crocosmia* with bright, orange-yellow, trumpet-shaped flowers.
morning glory any of various twining plants, with trumpet-shaped flowers, of the genus *Ipomoea.*
mother-in-law's tongue plant with long, erect, pointed leaves. Sp.: *Sansevieria trifasciata.*
mung bean leguminous plants of the genus *Vigna,* native to India and yielding a small bean used as food.
musk-rose rambling rose with large, white flowers smelling of musk. Sp.: *Rosa moschata.*
musk thistle nodding thistle whose flowers have a musky fragrance. Sp.: *Carduus nutans.*
musk tree Australian tree with a musky smell. Sp.: *Olearia argyrophylla.*
mustard plant eaten at the seedling stage, often with cress, and whose seeds are crushed and made into a paste and used as a spicy condiment. Sp.: *Sinapis alba.*
mustard plant with slender pods and yellow flowers. Sp.: *Brassica nigra.*
myrtle evergreen shrub with aromatic foliage and white flowers with purple-black ovoid berries. Sp.: *Myrtus communis.*
narcissus yellow, orange or white flowered plants with crown surrounded by spreading segments. Gen.: *Narcissus*
nardoo clover-like plant of Australian origin. Sp.: *Marsilea drummondii.*
nasturtium Any cruciferous plant of the genus Nasturtium, including watercress. Trailing plants of the Americas with rounded edible leaves and bright orange, yellow or red flowers of the genus *Tropaeolum.*
nopal cactus having yellow flowers and purple fruits, sometimes called prickly pear. Gen.: *Opuntia.*
oak any tree of the genus *Quercus,* having lobed leaves and bearing acorns.
obeche West African tree. Sp.: *Triplochiton scleroxylon.*
okra African edible plant of the mallow family. Aka gumbo or ladies' fingers. Sp.: *Abelmoschus esculentus.*
orpin(e) succulent, herbaceous, purple-flowered plant. Sp.: *Sedum telephium.*
ox-eye daisy plant of the daisy family, with large white flowers with yellow centres. Sp.: *Leucanthemum vulgare.*
oxlip woodland primula. Sp.: *Primula elatior.*
ox-tongue plant of daisy family with yellow flowers. Gen.: *Picris.*
palmyra Asian palm with fan-shaped leaves used for matting. Sp.: *Borassus flabellifer.*
parsley biennial herb with white flowers and crinkly aromatic leaves. Sp.: *Petroselinum crispum.*
parsley fern fern with leaves like parsley. Sp.: *Cryptogramma crispa.*
passion flower any climbing plant of the genus *Passiflora* with a flower that was supposed to suggest the instruments of the Crucifixion.
patchouli strongly scented south Asian shrub from which a perfume is made. Gen.: *Pogostemon.*
peanut leguminous plant bearing pods that ripen underground and contain seeds used as food and yielding oil. Sp.: *Arachis hypogaea.*
pedunculate oak a common oak in which clusters of acorns are borne on long stalks. Sp.: *Quercus robur.*
peepul (pipal) moraceous tree of tropical India and the East Indies, resembling the banyan, and thought of as sacred by Buddhists because the founder of the religion is said to have found enlightenment while sitting under its branches. Sp.: *Ficus religiosa.*
pennyroyal creeping mint cultivated for its supposed medicinal properties. Sp.: *Mentha pulegium.*
periwinkle tropical shrub native to Madagascar. Sp.: *Catharanthus roseus.*
periwinkle any of several Eurasian apocynaceous evergreen plants of the genus *Vinca,* having trailing stems and blue flowers. Aka creeping myrtle or trailing myrtle (USA).
pine coniferous evergreen with long, needle-shaped leaves and brown cones. Gen.: *Pinus.*
pinkster flower the pink azalea. Sp.: *Rhododendron periclymenoides.*
piripiri plant of the rose family native to New Zealand and having prickly burs. Sp.: *Acaena anserinifolia.*
poplar salicaceous tree with triangular leaves, light, soft wood and flowers borne in catkins. Gen.: *Populus.*
prickly pear cactus of the genus *Opuntia,* native to arid regions of America and bearing barbed bristles and large, pear-shaped, prickly fruits.
ragged robin pink-flowered campion with spiky, tattered-looking petals. Aka cuckoo flower. Sp.: *Lychnis flos-cuculi.*
rose shrub or climbing plant having prickly stems and fragrant flowers. Gen.: *Rosa.*
rowan tree with delicate pinnate leaves and scarlet berries. Sp.: *Sorbus aucuparia.*
rue dwarf shrub with bipinnate or tripinnate glaucous leaves and yellow flowers. Gen.: *Ruta.*
salsify Mediterranean plant having grass-like leaves, purple flower heads and a long, white edible taproot. Aka oyster plant or vegetable oyster. Sp.: *Tragopogon porrifolius.*
shaddock tree named after Captain Shaddoch who brought the seed to Barbados. Aka pomelo. Sp.: *Citrus maxima.*
shamrock most common shamrock is the wood sorrel, *Oxalis acetosella,* and this is the plant worn on St Patrick's Day. Other trifoliate shamrocks include black medic (*Medicago lupulina*) and white clover (*Trifolium repens*).
snake's head bulbous plant with bell-shaped, pendent flowers. Sp.: *Fritillaria meleagris.*
southernwood bushy kind of wormwood. Sp.: *Artemisia abrotanum.*
sweet marjoram one of two aromatic herbs (the other being wild marjoram) whose fresh dried leaves are used as a flavouring in cookery. Sp.: *Majorana hortensis.*
teak large, verbenaceous tree of East Indies yielding a hard, valuable yellow-brown wood. Sp.: *Tectona grandis.*
tobacco solanaceous plant having hairy leaves, and funnel-shaped, fragrant flowers. Gen.: *Nicotiana.*
tomatillo Mexican ground cherry bearing purplish, edible fruit. Sp.: *Physalis philadelphica.*
tomato plant of the nightshade family bearing glossy red or yellow pulpy edible fruit. Sp.: *Lycopersicon esculentum.*
toothwort parasitic plant with toothlike, root scales. Sp.: *Lathraea squamaria.*
toquilla palm-like tree native to South America. Sp.: *Carludovica palmata.*
trailing arbutus see mayflower.
Transvaal daisy plant of the Asteraceae family. Gen.: *Gerbera.*
traveller's joy wild clematis. Aka old man's beard. Sp.: *Clematis vitalba.*
tree mallow tall, woody-stemmed European mallow of cliffs and rocks. Sp.: *Lavatera arborea.*

tree tomato South American shrub with egg-shaped, red fruit. Sp.: *Cyphomandra betacea.*

tulip bulbous, spring-flowering plant of a variety of colours. The word tulip is derived from the Turkish *Tülbend*, meaning turban, from the shape of the expanded flower. Gen.: *Tulipa.*

tulip tree North American tree with tulip-like flowers and lobed leaves. Gen.: *Liriodendron tulipifera.*

tumbleweed plant of arid areas of North America and Australia. Its globular bush breaks off in late summer and is tumbled about by the wind, spreading its seed. Gen.: *Amaranthus alba.*

turmeric tropical Asian plant of the Zingiberaceae family, yielding aromatic rhizomes used as a spice and for yellow dye. Sp.: *Curcuma longa.*

umbrella plant African sedge having large umbrella--like whorls of slender leaves and widely grown as an ornamental water plant. Sp.: *Cyperus alternifolius.*

umbrella tree North American magnolia having long leaves clustered into an umbrella formation at the ends of the branches and unpleasant-smelling, white flowers. Sp.: *Magnolia tripetala.*

vetch plant largely used for silage and fodder. Sp.: *Vicia sativa.*

violet low-growing plant characterised by horizontal petals and purple, cordate leaves. Gen.: *Viola.*

viper's bugloss bristly blue-flowered plant. Sp.: *Echium vulgare.*

wall fern an evergreen polypody with very large leaves. Sp.: *Polypodium vulgare.*

wallflower spring-flowering garden plant with fragrant yellow, orange-red or dark red flowers. Sp.: *Cheiranthus cheiri.*

wall germander European germander having two-lipped pinkish-purple flowers with a very small upper lip. Sp.: *Teucrium chamaedrys.*

wall rue small fern with leaves like rue, growing on walls and rocks. Aka spleewort. Sp.: *Asplenium ruta-muraria.*

walnut tree having aromatic leaves and drooping catkins, the nut of which contains a wrinkled edible kernel in two halves and enclosed in a green fruit. Gen.: *Juglans.*

wandering jew climbing plant with stemless, variegated leaves. Gen.: *Tradescantia albiflora.*

water chestnut aquatic plant bearing an edible seed. Sp.: *Trapa natans.*

water hyacinth tropical American aquatic plant which is a serious weed of waterways in warm countries. Sp.: *Eichhornia crassipes.*

watercress hardy perennial cress growing in running water, with pungent leaves used in salad. Sp.: *Nasturtium officinale.*

wayfaring tree white-flowered European and Asian shrub, common along roadsides, with berries turning from green through red to black. Sp.: *Viburnum lantana.*

wild marjoram one of two aromatic herbs (the other being sweet marjoram) whose fresh dried leaves are used as a flavouring in cookery. Sp.: *Origanum vulgare.*

wild pansy Eurasian plant having purple, yellow, and pale mauve spurred flowers, aka heartsease, love-in-idleness. Sp.: *Viola tricolor.*

willow white-wood tree with graceful flexible branches and catkins. Gen.: *Salix.*

wintergreen low-growing plants with drooping spikes of white, bell-shaped flowers. Gen.: *Pyrola.*

witch alder American shrub with leaves like that of the alder. Sp.: *Fothergilla gardenii.*

witch hazel North American shrub with yellow flowers, the leaves and bark used to treat bruises. Gen.: *Hamamelis virginiana.*

woad glaucous, yellow-flowered cruciferous plant formerly grown for its blue dye. Sp.: *Isatis tinctoria.*

wolfsbane various ranunculaceous plants with hooded purple or yellow flowers. Aka aconite, monkshood. Gen.: *Aconitum.*

wood anemone wild spring-flowering, anemone. Sp.: *Anemone nemorosa.*

woodruff white-flowered plant grown for the fragrance of its whorled leaves when dried or crushed. Sp.: *Galium odoratum.*

woody nightshade scrambling woody Eurasian plant with purple flowers and recurved petals with protruding cone of yellow anthers and poisonous, red, berry-like fruits. Aka bittersweet. Sp.: *Solanum dulcamara.*

wych elm Eurasian elm with large rough leaves and pliant branches. Sp.: *Ulmus glabra.*

yellow archangel Eurasian yellow-flowered nettle. Sp.: *Lamiastrum galeobdolon.*

yellow flag yellow-flowered iris with slender, sword-shaped leaves. Sp.: *Iris pseudacorus.*

yellow rattle yellow-flowered herb, which is partly parasitic. Sp.: *Rhinanthus minor.*

yellow toadflax plant with narrow leaves like flax and spurred yellow flowers. Sp.: *Linaria vulgaris.*

yerba buena (good herb) North American trailing plant with lilac flowers formally used by Californian Americans to make a medicinal tea. Sp.: *Satureja douglasii.*

yerba santa North American shrub whose leaves are used medicinally. Lit. 'holy herb'. Sp.: *Eriodictyon californicum.*

yew Dark-leaved evergreen coniferous tree having seeds enclosed in a fleshy red aril, and often planted in churchyards. Gen.: *Taxus.*

ylang-ylang / ilang-ilang Malaysian tree from which a fragrant perfume is distilled. Sp.: *Cananga -odorata.*

Yorkshire fog fodder grass. Sp.: *Holcus lanatus.*

yucca plant of Agavaceae family with woody stem and sword-shaped leaves. Aka Adam's needle. Gen.: *Yucca.*

Miscellaneous Information

agriculture: soilless hydroponics.

allogamy cross-fertilisation in plants.

angiosperm flower-producing plants that reproduce by seeds enclosed within a carpel, including herbaceous plants, herbs, shrubs, grasses and most trees.

carnations: types of self (one colour), fancy (multi-coloured), picotee (pale with darker edge).

carnivorous plants pitcher plant, sundew, venus fly trap.

deciduous conifer larch, swamp cypress.

Dutch elm disease disease of elms, often fatal, caused by the fungus *Ceratocystis ulmi* and spread by bark beetles.

entomophily pollination by insects.

entophyte plant growing inside a plant or animal.

epiphyte plant growing on another but not parasitic on it, e.g. a moss on a tree trunk.

fastest growth bamboo (about 38 cm, 15 inches a day).

flower parts female part: pistil male part: stamen Perfect flower: contains male and female parts. Stigma: mouth of the pistil, which receives the pollen in impregnation. Style: neck of the pistil, which contains the stigma. Ovary: swollen basal part of the pistil containg the ovules.

frond the compound leaf of a fern or a palm.

garden city: first Letchworth in Herts (1903), founded by Ebenezer Howard.

gymnosperm any of various plants having seeds unprotected by an ovary, including conifers, cycads and ginkgo.

halophyte plant adapted to saline conditions.

largest living thing a Californian redwood tree, *Sequoia sempervirens*, nicknamed the General Sherman (275 feet high and 1,385 tons in weight).

leaves: types of bract, stipule and pinnate.

mulch half-rotten vegetable matter used to prevent soil erosion.

nettle sting: cause formic acid.

oak apples: caused by wasp eggs.

oldest tree a bristlecone pine (*Pinus longaera*) nicknamed Old Methuselah. Approx 5,000 years old and situated in the White Mountains, California.

osmosis the passage of a solvent through a semipermeable membrane from a less concentrated to a more concentrated solution until both solutions are of the same concentration. Wilhelm Pfeffer, a German plant physiologist, first studied osmosis in 1877, although the term was introduced by the British chemist Thomas Graham in 1854. Osmosis is the method used by plants for water absorption.

pergola arbour or covered walk, formed of growing plants trained over trellis-work.

plant families apple – rose (Rosaceae); ash – olive (Oleaceae); asparagus – lily (Liliaceae); aubergine – nightshade (Solanum); avocado – laurel (Lauraceae); bamboo - grass (Gramineae); barley – grass (Gramineae); blackberry – rose (Rosaceae); bluebell – lily (Liliaceae); breadfruit – mulberry (Moraceae); broccoli – cabbage (Brassica); brussels sprout – cabbage (Brassica); buckwheat – dock (Polygonaceae); camellia – tea (Theaceae); carrot – parsley (Apiaceae); cauliflower – cabbage (Brassica); celery – parsley (Apiaceae); cherry – rose (Rosaceae); chives – lily (Liliaceae); cinnamon – laurel (Lauraceae); coffee – madder (Rubiaceae); cork oak – beech (Fagacrab); cotton – mallow (Malvaceae); dandelion – daisy (Compositae); elder – honeysuckle (Caprifoliaceae); fig – mulberry (Moraceae); garlic – lily (Liliaceae); gooseberry – Grossulariaceae; guelder Rose – (Caprifoliaceae); hemlock – parsley (Apiaceae); hemp - mulberry (Moraceae); hop – mulberry (Moraceae); hyacinth – lily (Liliaceae); jasmine –olive (Oleaceae); Jerusalem artichoke – daisy (Compositae); knotgrass (Aka Allseed) – dock (Polygonaceae); leek – lily (Liliaceae); lemon – rue

(Rutaceae); lettuce – daisy (Compositae); lilac – olive (Oleaceae); lime – rue (Rutaceae); maize – grass (Gramineae); marijuana – mulberry (Moraceae); mustard – cabbage (Brassica); okra – mallow (Malvaceae); onion – lily (Liliaceae); orange – rue (Rutaceae); parsnip – parsley (Apiaceae); peach – rose (Rosaceae); pear – rose (Rosaceae); plum – rose (Rosaceae); potato – nightshade (Solanum); privet – olive (Oleaceae); radish – cabbage (Brassica); rape – cabbage (Brassica); raspberry – rose (Rosaceae); rhubarb – dock (Polygonaceae); rye – grass (Gramineae); shallot – lily (Liliaceae); sorrel – dock (Polygonaceae); strawberry – rose (Rosaceae); swede – cabbage (Brassica); thistle – daisy (Compositae); tobacco – nightshade (Solanum); tomato – nightshade (Solanum); tulip – lily (Liliaceae); turnip – cabbage (Brassica); vanilla – orchid (Orchidaceae); wheat – grass (Gramineae).

plants: products from agar agar – seaweed; amber – pine tree resin; aspirin – willow tree (originally); atropine – deadly nightshade; cocaine – coca plant; cochineal – beetles; copra – coconut; digitalis – foxglove; frankincense (*Olibanum*) – tree bark resin (*Boswellia*); henna dye – leaves of henna plant; heroin – opium poppy; hessian – plant root; linen – spun flax; linseed oil – seeds of flax plant; madder – plant root; morphine – opium poppy; myrrh – myrrh tree resin; opium – opium poppy (*Papaver somniferum*); quinine – cinchona bark; raffia – palm; saffron – crocus; semolina – wheat; tapioca – cassava root; turmeric – curcuma plant; turpentine – coniferous trees (especially pine).

pomegranate: varieties paper-shell, Spanish ruby, wonderful.

roots: types of adventitious, aerial, climbing, contratile, lateral, pneumatophore, prop.

Royal Horticultural Society Founded in 1804 and in its centenary year of 1904 established Wisley as its Show Garden.

sacking: fibre used for jute.

scandents climbing plants.

sweet pea: from Sicily.

tallest tree Douglas fir.

taxonomy classification of living organisms into groups in an organised hierarchy. Largest group is kingdom e.g. Plants (Plantae); Animals (Animalia). Below the Kingdom; in descending order, come: Phylum, Class, Subclass; Order, Family, Genus, Species.

toadstool: most poisonous deathcap.

tomato: original name love apple.

tudor rose conventionalized 5-lobed figure of a rose; the white and the red rose were adopted as the symbols of the Houses of York and Lancaster during the Wars of the Roses.

tulip: named from the Turkish turban *Tülbend.*

underwater: grows rice.

vanilla: family orchid family.

variegation different colourings of a leaf.

xerophyte plant, such as cacti, that grows in dry conditions.

yucca tree: pollination only by the yucca moth, *Pronuba* (Tegetierila) *yuccasella.*

Alternative Names of Flowers, Plants and Trees

Aaron's beard	rose of Sharon, althaea
abele	white poplar
abelmosk	musk mallow
amaryllis	belladonna lily
antirrhinum	snapdragon
aquilegia	columbine
arum lily	calla lily
Australian sword lily	kangaroo paw
baby's breath	gypsophila
baobab	monkey bread tree
bayberry	wax myrtle
belladonna	deadly nightshade, dwale
bluebell	wild hyacinth
bo tree	peepul
bog myrtle	sweet gale
buckbean	bogbean
carnation	gillyflower
catmint	catnip
Chile pine	monkey puzzle
clematis	traveller's joy
cow parsley	Queen Anne's lace
cowslip	marsh marigold (USA)
cranberry	fen-berry
cuckoo flower	ragged Robin, lady's smock
delphinium	larkspur
dogtooth violet	adder's tongue
eglantine	sweet brier
elephant's ear	bergenia, Chinese eddo, dasheen, eddo
field mustard	charlock
frangipani	plumeria
fraxinella	burning bush, dittany, gas plant
French lilac	goat's-rue, (Eurasian plant)
ginkgo	maidenhair tree
gladiolus	sword lily
glory-of-the-snow	chionodoxa
guelder Rose	snowball tree
hawthorn	may, quickthorn, whitethorn
heartsease	Johnny-jump-up (USA) love-in-idleness, wild pansy
iris	fleur-de-lis
Jack-go-to-bed-at-noon	goatsbeard (Eurasian plant)
Jack-in-the-pulpit	cuckoo pint
japonica	Japanese quince
kingcup	marsh marigold
laburnum	golden chain
lady's finger	kidney vetch
larkspur	delphinium
lignum vitae	guaiacum
lime tree	linden tree
livelong	orpin(e)
lords and ladies	cuckoo pint
may apple	mandrake
mayflower	trailing arbutus
meadow saffron	autumn crocus, naked boys, naked ladies
moneywort	wandering sailor
nasturtium	Indian cress
okra	gumbo, ladies' fingers
old man's beard	traveller's joy
periwinkle	creeping myrtle, trailing myrtle
pink azalea	pinkster flower
rowan	mountain ash
salsify	oyster-plant, vegetable oyster, lungwort
scarlet lobelia	cardinal flower
screw-pine	pandanus
southernwood	lad's love
spider plant	chlorophytum
Virginia creeper	woodbine (USA)
wake-Robin	cuckoo pint
water hemlock	cowbane
wild honeysuckle	woodbine
winter cress	yellow rocket
wintergreen	checkerberry

County Flowers

Plantlife International launched a County Flowers campaign in 2002 asking members of the public to nominate a wild flower emblem for their designated areas. The English Bluebell topped the poll but was so far ahead of the competition that it was excluded as a choice. In addition to the present counties of England, the poll also included the traditional counties of Scotland, Wales and Northern Ireland, several of the old English counties plus some other important areas. A total of 50,000 people voted and the results were as follows.

ENGLAND

Bedfordshire: **Bee orchid** (*Ophrys apifera*). The mauve orchids mimic a bumblebee and are seen in disused quarries, on roadsides, even on waste ground in towns.

Berkshire: **Summer snowflake** *(Leucojum aestivum*). Because they grow beside the River Loddon, the tall-stemmed plants with drooping white flowers are known in the county as Loddon lilies.

Birmingham: **Foxglove** (*Digitalis purpurea*). Tall purple flowers found in parks and industrial wastelands. William Withering, the discoverer of the heart drug digitalis, which was derived from the foxglove, was chief physician of Birmingham General Hospital from 1775.

Bristol: **Maltese cross** (*Lychnis chalcedonica*). Introduced to Britain in the 16th century, the delicate red petals can be seen in waste ground and on roadsides. It is known as the Flower of Bristol.

Buckinghamshire: **Chiltern gentian** (*Gentianella germanica*). Grows on the chalk downs of Buckinghamshire and flowers in late summer.

Cambridgeshire: **Pasqueflower** (*Pulsatilla vulgaris*). Has been a famous Cambridgeshire flower since its discovery on the Gog Magog hills by John Ray in 1660. According to legend, the fluffy-stemmed purple plants grow on the graves of Viking warriors.

Cheshire: **Cuckooflower** (*Cardamine pratensis*). Also known as 'milkmaids'. It is a delicate flower of wet meadows and pond margins, befitting a county with more ponds than any other.

Cornwall: **Cornish heath** (*Erica vagans*). Lilac blooms are found on the Lizard moors (exclusively) in late summer.

Cumbria: **Grass-of-Parnassus** (*Parnassia palustris*). The tallish white-petalled flowers appear on the county arms. Legend has it that the cattle of the gods of Mount Parnassus fed on the plant, and so it was given honorary status as a grass.

Derbyshire: **Jacob's ladder** (*Polemonium caeruleum*). The bright blue flowers and delicate ladder-shaped leaves of the wild plant are common in the Peak District and Yorkshire Dales.

Devon: **Primrose** (*Primula vulgaris*). The yellowy-white flowers have a strong presence in Devon's high-banked scenic country lanes. Local papermakers used to present little bunches to their customers to provide a 'breath of Devon'.

Dorset: **Dorset heath** (*Erica ciliaris*). This tall crimson heather is a defining species of Dorset's heathland and bogs.

Durham: **Spring gentian** (*Gentiana verna*). Even if Upper Teesdale had no other plant, botanical die-hards would flock there to see this deep-blue five-petalled favourite.

Essex: **Common poppy** (*Papaver rhoeas*). The unmistakable blood-red flowers still adorn cornfields in the county, though they are just as common on disturbed ground, especially on the chalk.

Gloucestershire: **Wild daffodil** (*Narcissus pseudonarcissus*). The county's golden triangle around the villages of Newent and Dymock is famous for its wild daffodils or Lent lilies. A 10-mile footpath known as 'The Daffodil Way' runs through the heart of Gloucestershire.

Hampshire: **Dog rose** (*Rosa canina*). The lilac-petalled flower has long been the county's emblem.

Herefordshire: **Mistletoe** (*Viscum album*). In Hereford, mistletoe grows on apple trees and hawthorns, from which it can be harvested as a winter crop.

Hertfordshire: **Pasqueflower** (*Pulsatilla vulgaris*). To be seen in abundance on the limestone hillsides.

Huntingdonshire: **Water violet** (*Hottonia palustris*). The dainty five-petalled lilac flowers are hardier than they appear and can survive summer droughts.

Isle of Man: **Fuchsia** (*Fuchsia magellanica*). On the island this exotic plant with its red shrimp-like blossom grows unusually tall.

Isle of Wight: **Pyramidal orchid** (*Anacamptis pyramidalis*). The cone-shaped lilac plant abounds on the undercliff and across the island's hog's-back of chalk in June.

Isles of Scilly: **Thrift** (*Armeria maritima*). The lilac-coloured thrift can be seen on rocks and sea cliffs. The old threepenny bit used to have a depiction of thrift on the reverse.

Kent: **Hop** (*Humulus lupulus*). The pale green and white plants are unobtrusive climbers in hedgerows and thickets.

Lancashire: **Red rose** (*Rosa species*). The Red Rose county since the Middle Ages, when the House of Lancaster adopted the flower as its heraldic badge. The true red rose of Lancashire is supposedly the red rose of the Mediterranean (*Rosa gallica*).

Leeds: **Bilberry** (*Vaccinium myrtillus*). The bulbous purple berries are a symbol of the open air of the hills around Bradford and Leeds.

Leicestershire: **Foxglove** (*Digitalis purpurea*). The foxglove helps to define Leicestershire's uplands, the woods and bracken swards of Charnwood Forest, but is scarce in the agricultural east.

Lincolnshire: **Common dog violet** (*Viola riviniana*). Carpets the great limewoods of Bardney Forest near Lincoln. The term 'dog' denotes its lack of scent and is contrasted to 'sweet' violet.

Liverpool: **Sea holly** (*Eryngium maritimum*). Its powder-blue cone-shaped flowers emerge in July, protected by prickly, wax-covered leaves.

London: **Rosebay willowherb** (*Epilobium angustifolium*). The tall purple flowers mingle with buddleias and Michaelmas daisies on railway banks, walls and waste ground.

Manchester: **Common cotton-grass** (*Eriophorum angustifolium*). The white hairy plumes are an emblem of their boggy habitat and the wide open spaces.

Middlesex: **Wood anemone** (*Anemone nemorosa*). The long-stemmed pale-blue, white or pink unsymmetrical flowers are seen in woods and hedgebanks.

Newcastle upon Tyne: **Monkeyflower** (*Mimulus guttatus*). From midsummer, the banks and shingles of the Tyne are bright with the yellowy-orange, red-spotted 'monkey faces' more common in rural Northumberland.

Norfolk: **Common poppy** (*Papaver rhoeas).* Original choice was Alexanders (*Smyrnium olusatrum*) but natives demanded a re-vote and out of five possible alternatives the poppy won. North Norfolk has long been known as 'poppyland'.

Northamptonshire: **Cowslip** (*Primula veris*). Frequently seen on road verges, quarries and railway banks, the tubular budded long-stemmed flowers adorned with beautiful orangey-yellow petals were chosen by three English counties.

Northumberland: **Bloody crane's-bill** (*Geranium sanguineum*). The vivid magenta flowers adorn coastal cliffs and dunes and spread inland on the rocks of the Whin Sill.

Nottingham: **Nottingham catchfly** (*Silene nutans*). The spider-like flowers were once seen on the walls of the castle but since renovation are not to be found anywhere in Nottingham.

Nottinghamshire: **Autumn crocus** (*Crocus nudiflorus*). The tightly petalled purple flowers used to adorn the meadows of the Trent and were sold at Nottingham market.

Oxfordshire: **Fritillary** (*Fritillaria meleagris*). Some of the best-known fritillary fields are in Oxfordshire, along the flood-meadows of the Thames, the purple bells bowing on their snakey stalks.

Rutland: **Clustered bellflower** (*Campanula glomerata*). The familiar rich-blue flowers of the southern limestone are scarce and therefore highly regarded.

Sheffield: **Wood crane's-bill** (*Geranium sylvaticum*). A much-loved flower of old hay-meadows and damp, open woods near Sheffield, with its distinctive flowers the colour of runny blue ink.

Shropshire: **Round-leaved sundew** *(Drosera rotundifolia*). This crimson-leaved carnivore, with glues and acids to trap and devour careless insects, is a bog plant.

Somerset: **Cheddar pink** (*Dianthus gratianopolitanus*). Discovered on 'Chidderoks' 300 years ago, it grows in several places in the Mendip Hills but nowhere more profusely than the original site at Cheddar Gorge.

Staffordshire: **Heather** (*Calluna vulgaris*). Traditionally a Scottish flower but Staffordshire is proud of its heather moors, blooming purple beyond the Potteries and manufacturing towns.

Suffolk: **Oxlip** (*Primula elatior*). The signature flower of well-established woods on the East Anglian boulder clay. The apricot scents of the drooping yellow blooms made this a popular choice.

Surrey: **Cowslip** (*Primula veris*). In Surrey, cowslips grow in contrasting places – dry chalk downs and damp meadows.

Sussex: **Round-headed rampion** (*Phyteuma orbiculare*). East and West Sussex are considered one county in the survey. Known as the Pride of Sussex, the sharp-blue flowers are common on the South Downs and bear resemblance to a many-tentacled jellyfish ready for its prey.

Warwickshire: **Honeysuckle** (*Lonicera periclymenum*). Honeysuckle is Shakespeare's 'woodbine', mentioned in *A Midsummer Night's Dream*, a play thought to have been set in the Forest of Arden.

Westmorland: **Alpine forget-me-not** *(Myosotis alpestris*). The blue flowers of this prettiest of forget-me-nots are confined in England to a few limestone hill-tops in the North Pennines.

Wiltshire: **Burnt orchid** (*Orchis ustulata*). This dwarf orchid belongs to the chalky core of Wiltshire, its white cone-shaped bloom turning pink and then dark red at the top.

Worcestershire: **Cowslip** (*Primula veris*). In parts of the county there are still small cowslip meadows hidden behind tall hedges. Locals call them 'cowslups'.

Yorkshire: **Harebell** (*Campanula rotundifolia*). It may appear surprising that the white rose was not chosen, but the blue and white blossom of the harebell matches the native folk for toughness and resilience, making it a perfect choice.

SCOTLAND

Aberdeenshire: **Bearberry** (*Arctostaphylos uva-ursi*). This red-berried trailing shrub is widespread at beautiful sites like the Muir of Dinnet.

Angus/Forfarshire: **Alpine catchfly** (*Lychnis alpina*). A single, remote hilltop of Angus boasts almost the whole British population of this pink alpine, although it is also seen in small areas of Cumbria.

Argyll: **Foxglove** (*Digitalis purpurea*). Seen on roadside banks in the mild, humid climate, foxgloves here look bigger and redder than those seen further south.

Ayrshire: **Green-winged orchid** (*Orchis morio*). Vary from pink-purple to almost white, the upper petals marked with dark veins and often suffused green. Unfortunately, although this beautiful flower is seen throughout the British Isles it is rare in Ayrshire.

Banffshire: **Dark-red helleborine** (Epipactis atrorubens). This rare and beautiful wild red orchid is a special plant of old Banff.

Berwickshire: **Rock rose** (*Helianthemum nummularium*). The five-petalled 'solflowers' form spectacular golden banks on some coastal cliffs in early summer.

Bute: **Thrift** (*Armeria maritima*). At its brightest and best on the rocky headlands and islands of the west coast.

Caithness: **Scots primrose** (*Primula scotica*). Scots primrose grows on promontories on the north coast including the most northerly point of mainland Britain, Dunnet Head. The rich purple flower is native to Orkney and Pentland Firth but is found nowhere else.

Clackmannanshire: **Opposite-leaved golden saxifrage** (*Chrysosplenium oppositifolium*). Creeping plant characteristic of the shaded, wooded glens.

Cromarty: **Spring cinquefoil** (*Potentilla neumanniana*). This pretty five-petalled golden trailing flower reaches its northern limit on the sea cliffs.

Dumfriesshire: **Harebell** (*Campanula rotundifolia*). The true bluebell of Scotland, aka the 'cuckoo's shoe'.

Dunbartonshire: **Lesser water-plantain** (*Baldellia ranunculoides*). This pale pink-flowered aquatic brightens a few bays and shores of Loch Lomond, Scotland's first National Park.

East Lothian and Haddingtonshire: **Viper's bugloss** (*Echium vulgare*). Rich blue and black flower found on dry banks and dunes.

Edinburgh: **Sticky catchfly** (*Lychnis viscaria*). The pale purple flower has grown on rocks in Holyrood Park for at least 400 years.

Fife: **Coralroot orchid** (*Corallorrhiza trifida*). This pale yellow claw-fingered flower grows in quarries and disused railway lines.

Glasgow: **Broom** (*Cytisus scoparius*). The pale orange-brown vanilla-scented flowers of broom brighten many braes and railway lines.

Inverness-shire: **Twinflower** (*Linnaea borealis*). A shy species that creeps over the shady floor of mossy pinewoods, its drooping bell-shaped flowers hiding their inner beauty.

Kinross: **Holy-grass** (*Hierochloe odorata*). This delicate, scented grass grows on the banks of Loch Leven, the castle on a small island in the loch being the prison for a year of Mary, Queen of Scots.

Kirkcudbright: **Bog rosemary** (*Andromeda polifolia*). The delicate bulbous pink flowers are a particular feature of the much-reduced bogs of Galloway.

Lanarkshire: **Dune helleborine** (*Epipactis leptochila*). The county's coal 'bings' are home to two exotic orchids: the narrow-lipped or dune helleborine and Young's helleborine.

Moray: **One-flowered wintergreen** (*Moneses uniflora*). This star-shaped white plant needs mossy hollows in undisturbed pinewoods. Aka St Olaf's candle stick.

Nairn: **Chickweed wintergreen** (*Trientalis europaea*). This six-petalled white flower is not a true wintergreen but surprisingly, a relative of the primrose.

Orkney: **Alpine bearberry** (*Arctostaphylos alpinus*). The black berries amid the lightly veined leaves that turn red in autumn are in evidence on the path to the Old Man of Hoy rock stack.

Peebles: **Cloudberry** (*Rubus chamaemorus*). A miniature bramble of high places. The four-petalled, large white flowers with marmalade berries are hard to find but can be seen on the Pentland Hills.

Perthshire: **Alpine gentian** (*Gentiana nivalis*). This sweet 'gentian of the snows' is among the gems of Ben Lawers, the highest of the Perthshire hills.

Renfrewshire: **Bogbean** (*Menyanthes trifoliata*). A plant of dark, moorland waters, the bogbean's feathery flowers somewhat resemble an azalea.

Ross: **Bog asphodel** (*Narthecium ossifragum*). The golden spires of bog asphodel light up dark, peaty places after midsummer.

Roxburghshire: **Maiden pink** (*Dianthus deltoides*). Purple five-petalled scentless flower inhabiting dry banks and hill pastures.

Selkirkshire: **Mountain pansy** (*Viola lutea*). Largest of the native pansies, a flower of upland pastures, sheep and trout becks.

Shetland: **Shetland mouse-ear** (*Cerastium nigrescens*). This white ten-petalled flower is entirely confined to the island of Unst.

Stirlingshire: **Scottish dock** (*Rumex aquaticus*). Confined to the banks of Loch Lomond, the towering russet spires are sometimes called the Loch Lomond dock.

Sutherland: **Grass-of-Parnassus** (*Parnassia palustris*). Increasingly scarce elsewhere, this flower of wet flushes and hollows is still fairly common here.

West Lothian and Linlithgowshire: **Common spotted orchid** (*Dactylorhiza fuchsii*). The lilac spikes and red spotted leaves of this flower enliven many wild places in West Lothian.

Western Isles: **Hebridean spotted orchid** (*Dactylorhiza fuchsii* subspecies *hebridensis*). Believed to be a low-growing form of the much more widespread common spotted orchid, although more conical in shape and a richer lilac in colour.

Wigtownshire: **Yellow iris** (*Iris pseudacorus*). Known locally as 'segg' or 'sword-grass', a reference to the remarkable blade-like leaves. The flagging appearance belies a hardiness demanded by its habitat of wet fields and marshes.

WALES

Anglesey/Sir Fon: **Spotted rock rose** (*Tuberaria guttata*). Yellow five-petalled flower with distinct crimson spots near the base of each petal. Predominant on Anglesey's Holy Island.

Brecknockshire/Sir Frycheiniog: **Cuckooflower** (*Cardamine pratensis*). The delicate tall-stemmed lilac flowers appear in the meadows of Brecknock when the cuckoo returns in mid-April.

Caernarvonshire/Sir Gaernarfon: **Snowdon lily** (*Lloydia serotina*). The pride of Wales, unlike most alpines, blooms alone, and often out of reach, in rock crevices.

Cardiff/Caerdydd: **Wild leek** (*Allium ampeloprasum*). The lilac globes of the flowering wild leek were used to identify Welsh soldiers in battle against the English. The traditional emblem of Wales.

Cardiganshire/Ceredigion: **Bog rosemary** (*Andromeda polifolia*). A speciality of mid-west Wales, with delicate pink bells and rosemary-like foliage. Also chosen by Kirkcudbright.

Carmarthenshire/Sir Gaerfyddin: **Whorled caraway** (*Carum verticillatum*). Found on rough pasture, its frothy blossom symbolises the battle between conservation and intensive agriculture.

Denbighshire/Sir Ddinbych: **Limestone woundwort** (*Stachys alpina*). Grows among rocks by roadsides and is seen only in Denbigh and Gloucestershire.

Flintshire/Sir Fflint: **Bell heather** (*Erica cinerea*). Bell heather announces the brief blaze of colour that lights up the moors at the end of summer.

Glamorgan/Morgannwg: **Yellow whitlow grass** (*Draba aizoides*). Confined to cliffs and old walls on the Gower, this tiny cress flowers in the early spring.

Merioneth/Merionnydd: **Welsh poppy** (*Meconopsis cambrica*). The bright yellow Welsh poppy is a native of rocky gullies and stream sides in Merioneth.

Monmouthshire/Sir Fynwy: **Foxglove** (*Digitalis purpurea*). The foxglove is a common wayside flower in Gwent. Also chosen by Argyll, Birmingham and Leicestershire.

Montgomeryshire/Sir Drefaldwyn: **Spiked speedwell** (*Veronica spicata*). The tall, deep blue spikes of this rock plant are one of the celebrated rarities of Craig Breidden.

Pembrokeshire: **Thrift** (*Armeria maritima*). Thrift brightens up the county's coastline of headlands, rock arches and bays in May. Also chosen by the Isles of Scilly, Bute.

Radnorshire/Sir Faesyfed: **Radnor lily** (*Gagea bohemica*). Aka 'early-star-of-Bethlehem' and sometimes flowering as early as mid-winter.

NORTHERN IRELAND

Antrim: **Harebell** (*Campanula rotundifolia*). Known as the 'goblin's thimble' in Co. Antrim; legend has it that you pick it at your peril. Also chosen by Dumfriesshire and Yorkshire.

Armagh: **Cowbane** (*Cicula virosa*). As its name implies the plant is poisonous to cattle, and it is consequently slowly being eradicated.

Belfast: **Gorse** (*Ulex europaeus*). The bright yellow sweetly scented flowers are ever-present in heathland, waste ground, banks and coastal regions.

Derry: **Purple saxifrage** (*Saxifraga oppositifolia*). Inhabits cliff edges and rocks, and flowers early spring, often amid the lying snow.

Down: **Spring squill** (*Scilla verna*). The lilac petals of the squill inhabit coastal grasslands and cliffs.

Fermanagh: **Globeflower** (*Trollius europaeus*). The distinctive golden puffballs adorn the lake margins of west Fermanagh.

Tyrone: **Bog rosemary** (*Andromeda polifolia*). One of the special plants of the central Irish peat-bogs. Also chosen by Kirkcudbright and Cardiganshire.

Birds

alcid bird of the auk famil, Sp.: *Alcidae.*

Andean condor world's largest bird of prey with a wingspan of 3 metres and body weight of up to 15 kilograms. Sp.: *Vultur gryphus.*

avadavat: green and red South Asian waxbills (aka amadavat). Sp.: *Amandava formosa* and *Amandava amandava.*

avocet white bird with black-patterned head and back; its most notable feature is the upcurved bill. Sp.: *Recurvirostra avosetta.*

bateleur short-tailed African eagle. Sp.: *Terathopius ecaudatus.*

bean goose similar to the pink-footed goose but distinguished by its orange bill and feet. Sp.: *Anser fabalis.*

bee-eater exotic European bird with yellow throat and multi-coloured plumage. Sp.: *Merops apiaster.*

bittern bird of the heron family with a brown and buff plumage barred with black, and famous for its booming call. Sp.: *Botaurus stellaris.*

black grouse spectacular bird with a lyre-shaped tail, the cocks having black plumage and the hens, grey. The black grouse is famous for its courtship display during the mating season. Sp.: *Lyrurus tetrix.*

blackbird aka merle, black bird of the thrush family having a yellow beak, the female having a dark brown plume. Sp.: *Turdus merula.*

blackcap small songbird, nicknamed 'the monk' in Germany because of its grey plumage and distinct black cap. Sp.: *Sylvia atricapilla.*

bobolink North American oriole originally called Bob o' Lincoln. Sp.: *Dolichonyx oryzivorus.*

boobook brown spotted owl, native to Australia and New Zealand. Sp.: *Ninox novaeseelandiae.*

booby tropical marine bird, similar to a gannet, with a straight, stout bill and white plumage with darker markings. Gen.: *Sula.*

bowerbird bird native to Australia and New Guinea; the males construct elaborate bowers of feathers, grasses and shells. Family *Ptilonorhynchidae.*

budgerigar small, green parakeet native to Australia, bred in coloured varieties and often kept as cage birds. Sp.: *Melopsittacus undulatus.*

bulbul Asian or African songbird of dull plumage with contrasting bright patches. Family *Pycnonotidae.*

bullfinch aka nope; small plump finch with black head, grey-blue back and red breast. Sp.: *Pyrrhula pyrrhula.*

bunting: corn. seed-eating bird related to the finches with a streaked, sparrow-like plumage. Sp.: *Emberiza calandra.*

bustard: great large, mainly terrestrial bird with long neck, long legs and stout tapering body. Sp.: *Otis tarda.*

buzzard predatory bird of the hawk family with broad wings, well adapted for soaring flight. Sp.: *Buteo buteo.*

capercaillie largest of the grouse family and extinct in Britain from the late 18th until mid-19th century. Sp.: *Tetrao urogallus.*

cassowary large, flightless bird of Australia and the Malay Archipelago, with heavy body, stout legs, a wattled neck and a bony crest on its forehead. Gen.: *Casuarius.*

chaffinch common European finch, the male of which has a blue-grey head with pinkish cheeks and breast. Sp.: *Fringilla coelebs.*

chough large black bird of the crow family, seen in Europe, Asia and Africa, with a long, downward-curving red bill and red legs. Sp.: *Pyrrhocorax pyrrhocorax.*

chukar red-legged Eurasian partridge. Sp.: *Alectoris chukar.*

collared turtle dove similar to the turtle dove but with a black half moon on the back of its neck, which gives rise to the name. Sp.: *Streptopelia decaocto.*

coot resembles an oversized moorhen, although the breast is grey-black and beak is white rather than yellow and red. Sp.: *Fulica atra.*

cormorant diving seabird with lustrous black plumage. Sp.: *Phalacrocorax carbo.*

corncrake rail with a rasping call, inhabiting grassland and nesting on the ground. Aka land rail Sp.: *Crex crex.*

cotinga any member of the large and varied New World tropical family Cotingidae, many with vivid plumage and unusually modified heel feathers.

cowbird North American oriole which often eats insects stirred up by grazing cattle and is known to lay its eggs in other birds' nests. Gen.: *Molothrus.*

crane long-legged, long-necked wading bird, which inhabits marshes and plains in most parts of the world except South America. Sp.: *Grus grus.*

crested lark often kept as a cage bird, not only for its own song but also for its ability to imitate the calls and cries of other birds. Sp.: *Galerida cristata.*

crossbill finch having a bill with crossed mandibles with which it opens pine cones. Gen.: *Loxia curvirostra.*

crow: carrion common predatory and scavenging European crow, similar to the rook but having a pure black bill. Sp.: *Corvus corone.*

crow: hooded highly intelligent bird with jet black and ashen grey plumage. Sp.: *Corvus cornix.*

cuckoo aka gowk; known as the harbinger of spring, the adult birds are slate blue-grey above, white underneath with dark grey barring. The cuckoo builds no nest of its own but parasitises other birds by laying in their nests. Sp.: *Cuculus canorus.*

curlew bird with brownish plumage that is barred and patterned, and bill that is long and slightly curved downwards. Sp.: *Numenius arquata.*

demoiselle small crane native to Asia and North Africa Sp.: *Anthropoides virgo.*

dipper diving bird of mountain streams. Aka water ouzel. Gen.: *Cinclus.*

dotterel small migratory plover named from the ease with which it is caught (word supposedly signifying stupidity). Sp.: *Eudromias morinellus.*

dowitcher wading bird breeding in North America and related to sandpipers. Gen.: *Limnodromus.*

drongo any insect-eating bird of the family Dicruridae, possessing a long, forked tail, native to Asia, Africa and Australia.

duiker long-tailed cormorant. Sp.: *Phalacrocorax africanus.*

dunlin long-billed sandpiper. Sp.: *Calidris alpina.*

dunnock aka hedge sparrow; small European songbird with brown and grey plumage. Sp.: *Prunella modularis.*

eagle large bird of prey with keen vision and powerful flight. Family Accipitridae.

eider sea duck of which the female's brownish plumage is the source of eiderdown, while the male plumage is white and black. Sp.: *Somateria mollissima.*

emu Australian flightless bird, second in size only to the ostrich, which it resembles, although the emu has three-toed feet as opposed to the ostriches' -two-toed. Sp.: *Dromaius novaehollandiae.*

falcon any diurnal bird of prey of the family Falconidae, having long pointed wings and sometimes trained to hunt small game for sport.

fieldfare large Old World thrush having a pale grey head and rump, brown wings and back and a blackish tail. Sp.: *Turdus pilaris.*

finch any small seed-eating songbird of the family Fringillidae, including canaries, crossbills and chaffinches.

finch: zebra small Australian waxbill with black and white stripes on face, popular as a cage bird. Sp.: *Poephila guttata.*

frigate bird aka man-of-war bird; seabird found in tropical seas, with a wide wingspan and deeply forked tail. Sp.: *Fregata magnificens.*

fulmar gull-like seabird, Britain's longest-lived bird, often reaching 40 years of age. Sp.: *Fulmarus glacialis.*

gadwall brownish-grey freshwater duck. Sp.: *Anas strepera.*

gannet heavily built marine bird, a spectacular diver for fish, having a long stout bill and typically white plumage with dark markings. Sp.: *Sula bassana.*

garganey small duck, the drake of which has a white stripe from the eye to the neck. Sp.: *Anas querquedula.*

gerfalcon (gyrfalcon) large falcon of cold northern regions. Sp.: *Falco rusticolus.*

glaucous gull large gull with typical brown and white speckled plumage, of Arctic coasts. Sp.: *Larus hyperboreus.*

go-away bird any of several touracos of the genus *Corythaixoides.*

godwit wading bird with long legs and a long, straight or slightly upcurved bill. Gen.: *Limosa.*

goldcrest smallest British and European bird, usually growing to a maximum of about 9cm (3 1/2in), with an olive green plumage and yellow or orange crest. Sp.: *Regulus regulus.*

golden eagle large eagle with yellow-tipped head-feathers. Sp.: *Aquila chrysaetos.*

golden-eye black-and-white diving duck of northern waters. Sp.: *Bucephala clangula.*

golden-eye black-and-white diving duck, slightly larger than the above. Sp.: *Bucephala islandica.*

goldfinch exotically coloured bird with an unusual tinkling, twittering song, often compared to little bells. Sp.: *Carduelis carduelis.*

goosander large diving duck with a narrow serrated bill. Sp.: *Mergus merganser.*

goose any of various large waterbirds of the family Anatidae, with short legs, webbed feet and a broad bill.

goose: barnacle an Arctic goose which winters in northern Europe. Sp.: *Branta leucopsis.*

goose: Brent small migratory Arctic-breeding goose with black, grey and white plumage. Sp.: *Branta -bernicla.*

goose: Canada wild goose with brownish-grey plumage and white cheeks and breast, native to northern America. Sp.: *Branta canadensis.*

goshawk large, short-winged hawk often used in -falconry. Sp.: *Accipiter gentilis.*

great crested grebe large Old World grebe with a crest and ear-tufts. Nests on the water's edge. Sp.: *Podiceps cristatus.*

greenfinch aka green linnet; finch with green and yellow plumage. Sp.: *Carduelis chloris.*

greylag goose native to Europe. Sp.: *Anser anser.*

grosbeak Any of various finches and cardinals -having stout conical bills and brightly coloured plumage. The largest species is the pine grosbea,. *Pinicola enucleator.*

guillemot narrow-billed auk, nesting on cliffs or islands. Sp.: *Uria aalge.*

guinea fowl African fowl with slate-coloured white-spotted plumage. Sp.: *Numida meleagris.*

hammerhead heron-like African and Arabian marsh bird with a heavy black bill and an occipital crest. Sp.: *Scopus umbretta.*

harpy eagle South American crested bird of prey, one of the largest of eagles. Sp.: *Harpia harpyja.*

harrier any bird of prey of the genus *Circus* with long wings for swooping over the ground.

hawk any of various diurnal birds of prey of the family Accipitridae, having a curved beak, rounded short wings and a long tail.

heron: grey long-necked wading bird with a blue-grey plumage and yellow beak. Sp.: *Ardea cinerea.*

herring gull becomes progressively greyer as it matures and also changes colour from winter to summer. Sp.: *Larus argentatus.*

hobby small, long-winged falcon, which catches prey on the wing. Sp.: *Falco subbuteo.*

hoopoe Eurasian bird whose crest is held erect at moments of excitement. Sp.: *Upupa epops.*

hornbill tropical Old World bird with a horn-like excrescence on its large curved bill. Family Bucerotidae.

house martin black and white swallow-like bird, which builds a mud nest under the eaves of houses. Sp.: *Delichon urbica.*

ibis any wading bird of the family Threskiornithidae, with a long down-curved bill, long neck and long legs, and nesting in colonies.

Iceland gull although many spend the winter in Iceland the Iceland gull breeds in Greenland and north Alaska. Sp.: *Larus glaucoides.*

jabiru large black-necked stork of Central and South America, with mainly white plumage. Sp.: *Ephippiorhynchus mycteria.*

jacamar small insect-eating bird with partly iridescent plumage, of the tropical South American family Galbulidae.

jacana tropical wading bird with elongated toes and hind claws, which enable them to walk on floating leaves. Family Jacanidae.

jack snipe small snipe often seen in marshy areas. Sp.: *Lymnocryptes minimus.*

jackdaw small grey-headed crow often frequenting rooftops and nesting in tall buildings and noted for its inquisitiveness and magpie tendencies to thieve bright objects. Sp.: *Corvus monedula.*

Java sparrow waxbill native to Java and Bali. Sp.: *Padda oryzivora.*

jay brownish-pink bird of crow family, whose wings are decorated with flashes of blue. Sp.: *Garrulus glandarius.*

kaka large New Zealand parrot with olive-brown plumage. Sp.: *Nestor meridionalis.*

kestrel aka windhover; Britain's most -common true falcon; often mistaken for a sparrowhawk, but is a hoverer rather than a glider and is far less ferocious. Sp.: *Falco tinnunculus.*

killdeer large North American plover with a plaintive song. Sp.: *Charadrius vociferus.*

kingfisher poetically known as halcyon; slightly larger than the house sparrow and brilliantly plumed - a swift flying, swooping bird that feeds on insects and small fish. Sp.: *Alcedo atthis.*

kittiwake small gull that nests on sea cliffs of the north Atlantic and Arctic oceans. Sp.: *Rissa -tridactyla.*

kiwi flightless New Zealand birds with hairlike feathers and a long bill, nesting in burrows. Gen.: *Apteryx.*

knot small northern sandpiper with a short bill and grey plumage. Sp.: *Calidris canutus.*

lammergeier large vulture of Africa, central Asia and southern Europe, with a very large wingspan and dark, beard-like feathers on either side of its beak. Sp.: *Gypaetus barbatus.*

lapwing aka green plover or peewit; plover with black and white plumage, crested head, and a shrill cry. Sp.: *Vanellus vanellus.*

lesser whitethroat slightly smaller than its namesake and tends to be somewhat shyer. Sp.: *Sylvia curruca.*

limpkin wading marsh bird of the Americas whose name derives from its limping gait. Aka courlan. Sp.: *Aramus guarauna.*

linnet small European songbird; grey-brown plumage with red forehead and breast in summer; famous for its wide range of singing voice. Sp.: *Acanthis cannabina.*

little auk small Arctic auk. Sp.: *Plautus alle.*

little grebe aka dabchick; small waterbird of the grebe family. Sp.: *Tachybaptus ruficollis.*

lory any of various brightly coloured Australasian and South-east Asian parrots of the subfamily Loriinae.

lorikeet any of various small brightly coloured parrots of the subfamily Loriinae.

lovebird any of various African and Madagascan parrots. Gen.: *Agapornis.*

lyre-bird either of two Australian birds of the family Menuridae, the male of which has a lyre-shaped tail.

macaw any long-tailed, brightly coloured parrot of the genus *Ara* or *Anodorhynchus,* native to South and Central America.

magpie black and white plumed bird of the crow family, often regarded as a pest by farmers as it has thieving tendencies, especially for bright shiny objects. Sp.: *Pica pica.*

magpie lark Australian bird of the family Grallinidae, in particular a common long-legged black and white bird, Sp.: *Grallina cyanoleuca.*

mallard duck which is common over most of the northern hemisphere, the drake having a bottle green head and rufous markings. The mallard is thought to be the ancestor of all domestic breeds of duck. Sp.: *Anas platyrhynchos.*

mandarin duck originally from eastern Asia but introduced in many other regions; although the female has typical looks, the drake is exotically coloured. Sp.: *Aix galericulata.*

Manx shearwater European oceanic bird with long slender wings and black and white plumage. Sp.: *Puffinus puffinus.*

marabou large West African stork whose down is used as a trimming for hats. Sp.: *Leptoptilos crumeniferus.*

meadow pipit common pipit native to Europe, Asia and Africa. Sp.: *Anthus pratensis.*

meadowlark North American songbirds with a yellow breast. Sp.: *Sturnella magna* and slightly smaller *Sturnella reglecta.*

merganser aka sawbill; any of various diving fish-eating northern ducks of the genus *Mergus,* with a long narrow serrated hooked bill.

merlin small European or N. American falcon that hunts small birds. Sp.: *Falco columbarius.*

mistle (missel) thrush large thrush with a spotted breast that feeds on mistletoe berries. Sp.: *Turdus viscivorus.*

mockingbird long-tailed songbirds of the American family Mimidae noted as mimics of other birds' calls. The common mockingbird of the eastern USA is *Mimus polyglottos.*

Montagu's harrier aka ash-coloured falcon; slender migratory Eurasian bird of prey named after George Montagu 1751–1815, a British naturalist. Sp.: *Circus pygargus.*

moorhen aka marsh hen; black plumage, blue breast and a white line along the flanks. Red & yellow beak. Sp.: *Gallinula chloropus.*

Muscovy musk duck tropical American duck, having a small crest and red markings on its head. Sp.: *Cairina moschata.*

musk duck Australian duck, having a musky smell. Sp.: *Biziura lobata.*

mutton-bird Southern hemisphere birds of the genus *Puffinus,* especially the short-tailed shearwater. Sp.: *Puffinus tenuirostris.*

nightingale aka Philomel; loud songbird with dark brown plumage and lighter underparts. Sp.: *Luscinia megarhynchos.*

nightjar aka goatsucker; nocturnal birds with a cryptic plumage and large eyes - feeds on insects. Sp.: *Caprimulgus.*

nutcracker forest-dwelling Old World bird of the crow family, having speckled plumage. Sp.: *Nucifraga caryocatactes.*

nuthatch small songbird that climbs up and down tree trunks and feeds on nuts and insects. Sp: Sitta europaea.

oriole: golden yellow-plumed Eurasian bird with black wings and red beak. Sp.: *Oriolus oriolus.*

osprey aka fish hawk; bird of prey with a dark back and whitish head and underparts praying on fish. Sp.: *Pandion haliaetus.*

ostrich world's largest living bird can weigh in excess of 180 kilograms and stand 2.5 metres high. The ostrich can attain running speed of 40 mph, which it can sustain for up to 30 minutes. The ostrich lays the largest egg, weighing up to 2 kg and measuring 15 cm in diameter. Sp.: *Struthio camelus.*

ovenbird any Central or South American bird of the family Furnariidae, which build domed nests out of clay or tunnel underground to lay their eggs.

owl: barn aka white owl or yellow owl. Type of owl that likes to nest in barns and other accessible rural buildings. Sp.: *Tyto alba.*

owl: eagle large Eurasian owl with long ear-tufts. Sp.: *Bubo bubo.*

owl: horned North American owl with hornlike feathers over the ears. Sp.: *Bubo virginianus.*

owl: little small owl of Africa and Eurasia, with speckled plumage. Sp.: *Athene noctua.*

owl: long-eared known for its peculiar barking cry, broken by 'yaps'; its long ears are in reality tufts of feathers. Sp.: *Asio otus.*

owl: tawny aka wood owl; familiar owl with rich brown plumage, barred and checked with darker bars and streaks. Sp.: *Strix aluco.*

oystercatcher wading bird with black and white plumage and long laterally compressed orange-red bill. Sp.: *Haematopus ostralegus.*

partridge game bird with light grey plumage, barred and streaked with chestnut. Sp.: *Perdix perdix.*

penguin flightless seabird of the southern hemisphere with black upper parts and white underparts, and wings developed into scaly flippers for swimming underwater. Family Spheniscidae.

penguin: Adélie Most common species of penguin. Sp.: *Pygoscelis adeliae.*

penguin: emperor largest species of penguin, which can grow to a height of 120 cm (4 ft). Sp.: *Aptenodytes forsteri.*

penguin: fairy smallest species of penguin, average height of 41 cm (16 in). Aka little blue penguin. Sp.: *Eudyptula minor.*

penguin: Galápagos unlike the emperor and the Adélie, the Galápagos penguin is confined to the tropics of South America. Sp.: *Spheniscus mendiculus.*

penguin: gentoo abundant in the Falkland and other Atlantic islands. Sp.: *Pygoscelis papua.*

peregrine falcon powerful falcon, breeding on coastal cliffs and much used for falconry. Sp.: *Falco peregrinus.*

petrel small wave-hanging seabirds, blackish with a white rump. Family: Hydrobihdar.

petrel: Wilson's common petrel that breeds around Antarctica but is often seen in the Atlantic. Sp.: *Oceanites oceanicus.*

phalarope any small wading bird or swimming bird of the family Phalaropodidae, with a straight bill and lobed feet.

pheasant game bird introduced to Britain from its native home in south-eastern Europe and
central Asia; the cock birds show a wide colour -variation, with brown and buff common specimens, although some almost black birds have been sighted in recent years. Sp.: *Phasianus colchicus.*

pipit: tree light brown plumed bird of the wagtail family. Sp.: *Anthus trivialis.*

plover: golden a wader noted for its musical but sad rising whistle, the golden plover is a golden -speckled colour with a white or sometimes black underparts. Sp.: *Pluvialis apricaria.*

plover: ringed small chunky wader with brown plumage, white underparts and a black ring round the neck. Sp.: *Charadrius hiaticula.*

pochard familiar diving duck, the male having silvery plumage with chestnut head and black underparts whilst the females are silvery-brown. Sp.: *Aythya ferina.*

ptarmigan high mountain grouse whose grey-brown and black plumage changes to white in the winter. Sp.: *Lagopus mutus.*

puffin aka sea parrot; Britain's most recognisable seabird, with its large multicoloured bill and awkward movement; the main colonies are in north Scotland, the largest on St Kilda, west of the Outer Hebrides. Sp.: *Fratercula arctica.*

quail game bird, which looks like a miniature partridge although its plumage is a red-buff carrying streaks of cream and black. The quail is rarely -sighted, due largely to its habit of taking refuge in grassland when spotted. Sp.: *Coturnix coturnix.*

quetzal spectacular tree bird of central America, a member of the trogon family, with green back and crimson and white under parts; the male's green tail plumes grow to 60 cm (2 feet). Sp.: *Pharomachons mocinno.*

raven large passerine bird of the crow family, having a large,straight, black bill, long, wedge-shaped tail and black plumage. Sp.: *Corvus corax.*

razorbill common auk of the north Atlantic which typically nests in colonies on cliffs. Sp.: *Alca torda.*

red kite once a common scavenger in the streets during Elizabethan and the early Stuart period, this bird of prey gradually died out but has been reintroduced into England and Wales. Sp.: *Milvus milvus.*

redpoll soft striped brown plumed songbird of the finch family. Sp.: *Acanthis flammea.*

redstart similar in size and habit to the robin, with a grey plumage and black throat. Sp.: *Phoenicurus phoenicurus.*

redstart: black darker than its namesake but has similar feeding habits of taking insects, mainly on the wing. Sp.: *Phoenicurus ochruros.*

redwing small European thrush, having a speckled breast, reddish flanks and brown back. Sp.: *Turdus iliacus.*

rhea either of two large flightless birds of South Africa, *Rhea americana* and *Pterocieia pennara*, similar to ostrich but hairy, three-toed feet.

ring ouzel thrush with a white crescent across its breast. Sp.: *Turdus torquatus.*

robin aka poetically as Ruddock; well-loved bird with brown plumage and red breast with yellow throat. Sp.: *Erithacus rubecula.*

roller beautifully coloured migrant from Africa. The plumage shows a brown back, with blue wing coverts, greenish-blue head, blue undersurface and purplish tail and wings. Sp.: *Coracias garrulus.*

rook most common member of the crow family, notable for its jet black plumage and depredations among the eggs of smaller birds. Sp.: *Corvus -frugilegus.*

ruff Eurasian member of the sandpiper family. The males' communal dancing display is called 'lekking'. The female is called a reeve. Sp.: *Philomachus -pugnax.*

Sabine's gull fork-tailed seabird breeding on islets and marshy tundra in Arctic Greenland, Alaska and northern Siberia. Sp.: *Larus sabini.*

sanderling small busy sandpiper of the genus *Calidris* that frequents sandy shores. Sp.: *Calidris alba.*

sand martin slightly smaller than the house martin, with dark brown plumage and a brown band across its white breast. Sp.: *Riparia riparia.*

sandpiper various smallish members of the family Scolopacidae, walkers with long legs and long slender bills, which includes the curlew, dunlin and snipe.

shag aka green cormorant; very similar to the cormorant but smaller and darker green, no white marking on face and more of a crest. Sp.: *Phalacrocorax aristotelis.*

shoveler duck with spoon-shaped bill, a blue patch on each wing, and in the male a green head, white breast and reddish-brown body. Sp.: *Anas clypeata.*

shrike: red-backed chestnut-backed bird with grey head and rump and black ear coverts. Aka butcher bird because it impales its prey on thorn-bushes for storage. Sp.: *Lanius collurio.*

siskin small finch with brownish-green back with -yellow shades and black cap. Sp.: *Carduelis spinus.*

skua: Arctic smaller member of this predatory seabird genus with dark plumage and a hooked bill, all of them famous for harassing terns or gulls into dropping or disgorging fish they have caught. Sp.: *Stercorarius parasiticus.*

skua: great aka bonxie; heavy, broad-winged seabird with brown plumage and wings with white bar on wings. Sp.: *Stercorarius skua.*

skylark like the cuckoo, this ground-dwelling songbird is often thought of as a harbinger of spring; it has a dull brown plumage with white ribbing. Sp.: *Alauda arvensis.*

smew aka white nun; merganser of north Europe and Asia with white plumage with black markings. Sp.: *Mergus albellus.*

snipe bird of the sandpiper family inhabiting marshy areas. Collective noun is a 'wisp'. Sp.: *Gallinago -gallinago.*

snow bunting bunting of northern and arctic regions having a white plumage with dark markings on the wings, back and tail. Sp.: *Plectrophenax nivalis.*

social weaver small gregarious Old World passerine songbird of the chiefly African family Ploceidae, having a short thick bill and a dull plumage. The name derives from the bird's characteristic of building covered nests in trees and living in communities of hundreds. Sp.: *Philetairus socius.*

song thrush aka mavis or throstle; song bird with brown plumage and white underparts speckled brown; its repetitive refrain sounds rather like 'Come out, come out, come out'. Sp.: *Turdus philomelos.*

sparrowhawk fiercest of our native hawks, identified by its rapid flight with long gliding intervals and sudden swoops on prey. Sp.: *Accipiter nisus.*

sparrow: house small common brown and grey bird which nests in the eaves and roofs of houses. Sp.: *Passer domesticus.*

spoonbill wading bird of warm regions, having white plumage and a long, horizontally flattened bill. Sp.: *Platalea leucorodia.*

spotted flycatcher sparrow-sized grey-brown bird with a whitish breast, able to catch insects in flight. Sp.: *Muscicapa striata.*

starling distinctly coloured bird with black, iridescently green-tinged plumage, white flecks throughout its cover, and a yellow beak. Sp.: *Sturnus vulgaris.*

stock dove similar to the wood-pigeon but smaller. Sp.: *Columba oenas.*

storm(y) petrel aka Mother Carey's chicken or witch; Europe's smallest seabird. Sp.: *Hydrobates pelagicus.*

swallow streamlined insect-hunter with a distinctive blue sheen on the back and wings, chestnut throat and white breast. Sp.: *Hirunda rustica.*

swan: Bewick's smallest swan, rarely seen in England outside the Slimbridge Wildfowl Trust and the Ouse Washes. Sp.: *Cygnus columbianus.*

swan: mute commonest Eurasian swan, having white plumage and an orange-red bill with a swollen black base. Sp.: *Cygnus olor.*

swan: trumpeter large North American wild swan. Sp.: *Cygnus buccinator.*

swan: whooper black bill with yellow nose, most of Britain's winter whoopers are from Iceland. Sp.: *Cygnus cygnus.*

swift fast-flying bird with dark brown plumage; it is a summer bird in Britain and spends its winters in Africa. Sp.: *Apus apus.*

teal smallest of Europe's wintering ducks, appearing like a smaller wigeon. Sp.: *Anas crecca.*

tern graceful, slender-winged seabird that dives headlong after small fish. Gen.: *Sterna.*

tern: Arctic greyer than the common or sandwich tern, can be seen at close hand on the Farne Islands. Sp.: *Sterna paradisaea.*

tern: common most familiar tern, with grey-white plumage, black cap and red bill. Sp.: *Sterna hirundo.*

tern: little small tern distinguished from other terns by its yellow bill. Sp.: *Sterna albifrons.*

tern: roseate rare bird with white plumage, black cap and extremely long tail streamers. Sp.: *Sterna dougallii.*

tern: Sandwich largest of the terns found regularly in Britain, distinguished from other terns by its pale white plumage and black bill with yellow tip. Sp.: *Sterna sandvicensis.*

tit: bearded Aka reedling. Eurasian songbird common in reed beds; it has a tawny back and tail and, in the male, a grey and black head. Sp.: *Panurus biarmicus.*

tit: blue aka tinnock, tom tit; gymnastic bird with bright blue cap and yellow underparts, often seen hanging upside down while hunting for food. Sp.: *Parus caeruleus.*

tit: crested chubby bird with dull brown plumage and white crest marked with black, in Britain restricted to the Scottish Highlands but more common on the Continent. Sp.: *Parus cristatus.*

tit: great Eurasian songbird with black-and-white head markings. Sp.: *Parus major.*

tit: long-tailed black and white plumed tit distinguished from other tits by its long tail. Sp.: *Aegithalos caudatus.*

tit: marsh grey-backed tit that inhabits woods and hedges. Sp.: *Parus palustris.*

tit: penduline southern European bird that derives its name from the hanging nest characteristic of the species. Sp.: *Remiz pendulinis.*

tit: willow Eurasian black-capped tit. Sp.: *Parus montanus.*

touraco (turaco) any brightly coloured crested arboreal African bird of the family Musophagidae.

tragopan tree-dwelling Asian pheasant; the male displays erect fleshy horns on its head. Gen.: *Tragopan.*

tree sparrow two distinct species. *Passer montanus* is a Eurasian sparrow inhabiting agricultural land. *Spizella arborea* is a North American sparrow-like bird of the bunting family, breeding on the edge of the tundra.

treecreeper small passerine songbirds of the family Certhiidae of the northern hemisphere, having a brown-and-white plumage and slender downward-curving bill. Named from their characteristic of creeping up trees to feed on insects. Gen.: *Certhia.*

turkey buzzard aka turkey vulture; American vulture, unrelated to the Old World vultures, so called because of its bare reddish head and dark plumage. Sp.: *Cathartes aura.*

turtle dove small slim dove with thin neck, protruding round white head, deep chest and brownish-grey plumage with black marks. Sp.: *Streptopelia turtur.*

umbrella bird cotinga of tropical America, with a large, black, overhanging crest and a long feathered wattle. Gen.: *Cephalopterus.*

Victoria crowned pigeon large blue-crested pigeon of New Guinea. Sp.: *Goura victoria.*

vulture any of various large birds of prey of the distinct Old and New World families Accipitridae and Cathartidae, with the head and neck more or less bare of feathers, feeding mainly on carrion and reputed to gather with others in anticipation of a death.

wagtail: white terrestrial bird, named from the up and down waggings of the tail at each halt that accompany its short darting rushes in a zigzag course. Sp.: *Motacilla alba alba.*

wandering albatross very large white albatross of southern oceans, having very long and narrow black-tipped wings. Sp.: *Diomedea exulans.*

warbler: barred arrives in Europe, from Africa, later than the other warblers and rarely visits Britain. Sp.: *Sylvia nisoria.*

warbler: Cetti's named after an 18th-century Italian Jesuit; it is the only European passerine with 10 tail feathers, rather than 12. Sp.: *Cettia cetti.*

warbler: Dartford until recently Britain's only resident warbler; it was first described from Bexley Heath, near Dartford in Kent, in 1773. Sp.: *Sylvia undata.*

warbler: great reed migrant bird seen frequently in the reed beds of East Anglia and the southern coast. Sp.: *Acrocephalus arundinaceus.*

warbler: icterine migratory warbler with brownish plumage and olive green underparts. Sp.: *Hippolais icterina.*

warbler: reed inconspicuous bird with overall brown colouring with lighter underparts. Sp.: *Acrocephalus scirpaceus.*

water rail highly nervous and secretive bird, more often heard than seen; it hides in its reed-bed home at the slightest disturbance. Sp.: *Rallus aquaticus.*

wattlebird various Australian honeyeaters with a wattle hanging from each cheek. Gen.: *Anthochaera* and *Melidectes.* Also various NZ songbirds of the family Callaeidae, with wattles hanging from the base of the bill, e.g. the saddleback. Sp.: *Creadion carunculatus.*

waxbill any small finch-like bird of the family Estrildidae, with a red bill resembling sealing wax in colour.

waxwing any of three species of crested perching birds of the genus *Bombycilla*, with small tips like red sealing wax to wing feathers.

weka large flightless New Zealand rail. Sp.: *Gallirallus australis.*

whale-headed stork aka shoebill; grey African stork with a large bill shaped like a clog. Sp.: *Balaeniceps rex.*

wheatear small northern thrush having a grey back, black wings and tail, white rump and pale brown underparts. Sp.: *Oenanthe oenanthe.*

whimbrel small migratory curlew with a striped crown and trilling call. Sp.: *Numenius phaeopus.*

whinchat Old World songbird having mottled brown-and-white plumage with pale cream underparts; it is a member of the subfamily of thrushes. Sp.: *Saxicola rubetra.*

white stork widely protected in Europe, a pure white bird with black wing tips and long red beak and legs. Sp.: *Ciconia ciconia.*

whitethroat warbler with greyish plumage, rusty wings and white underparts. Sp.: *Sylvia communis.*

wi(d)geon gregarious duck, the male of which has a reddish-brown head and chest, and grey and white back and wings. Sp.: *Anas penelope.*

woodchat shrike shrike of southern Europe, north Africa and the Middle East, having black and white plumage with a chestnut head. Sp.: *Lanius senator.*

woodcock any game bird of the genus *Scolopax* that inhabits woodlands. The common Eurasian species is *Scolopax rusticola.*

woodpecker any bird of the family Picidae that climbs and taps tree trunks in search of insects.

woodpecker: black largest of the European woodpeckers; the jet-black plumage is broken only by its red cap. Sp.: *Dryocopus martius.*

woodpecker: great spotted black and white plumage with a large red patch on the nape of the neck (male only); noted for its repeated -drumming on the trunks of trees. Sp.: *Dendrocopos major.*

woodpecker: green aka yaffle; large green and yellow European woodpecker with a red crown. Sp.: *Picus viridis.*

woodpecker: pileated large North American woodpecker with a red-topped head. Sp.: *Dryocopus pileatus.*

wood pigeon aka cushat or ring dove; large pigeon, having white patches like a ring round its neck. Sp.: *Columba palumbus.*

wren small light brown bird famous for its building of more than one nest, the hen making her choice and the 'spares' used as roosting spots in bad weather. Sp.: *Troglodytes troglodytes.*

wryneck small bird of the woodpecker family, able to turn its head over its shoulder. Sp.: *Jynx torquilla.*

yellowhammer aka yellow bunting; bunting of which the male has a yellow head, neck and breast. Sp.: *Emberiza -citrinella.*

yellowlegs: greater and lesser two migratory sandpipers with yellow legs. Sp.: *Tringa melanoleuca* and *Tringa flavipes.*

Birds: Miscellaneous Information

altricial of a young bird or animal requiring care and feeding by the parents after hatching or birth

arctic tern: migrates to Antarctica

backwards-flying hummingbird is only bird that can fly backwards

beaks: characteristics insect-eating birds usually have pointed bills while carnivorous birds have hooked bills

bird: smallest bee hummingbird

bird of paradise: from New Guinea (hang upside down)

bird of prey: largest Andean condor

bird of prey: largest UK golden eagle

British bird: biggest mute swan

British bird: fastest runner pheasant (up to 21 mph)

British bird: highest flier whooper swans sighted at 27,000 feet

British bird: largest egg mute swan

British bird: longest-lived Manx shearwater (29.82 years)

British bird: most common wren

British bird: smallest goldcrest (and smallest egg)
British Isles: exclusive to red grouse and Scottish crossbill do not migrate and are found only in the UK
carinate of a bird having a keeled breastbone; opposite of ratite
deepest diving bird emperor penguin
drops bones on rocks to break the bearded vulture (lammergeyer)
ducks: sex that quacks only females
egg: smallest hummingbird (in USA and the world)
extinct birds dodo lived on the island of Mauritius and became extinct in the late 17th century; great auk or Atlantic pigeon became extinct in the - mid-19th century; moa of New Zealand became totally extinct by early 19th century
falconry breeding and training of hawks for sporting purposes. The female is called a falcon, the male is a tiercel
fastest bird peregrine falcon has been timed at 217 mph during swoop as part of the courtship display. The golden eagle has reached speeds exceeding 150 mph during a vertical dive, but the fastest bird in level flight, with recorded speeds exceeding 110 mph, is the Alpine swift
fastest runner ostrich
first known bird archaeopteryx (name means 'ancient wing')
gizzard muscular thick-walled part of a bird's stomach, used for grinding food, usually with the help of grit
grallatorial of or relating to long-legged wading birds e.g. flamingos and storks (from Latin *grallator*, 'stiltwalker')
guano excrement of seabirds found on islands off South America, Africa and the West Indies and used as manure
largest birds ostrich is clearly the largest living bird (moas extinct); the largest flying bird is more contentious but is possibly the kori bustard of sub-Saharan Africa
longest migration Arctic tern (11,222 miles Anglesey to Australia)
nests at end of riverbank tunnels kingfisher
New World: definition term used to differentiate between the time before and after the Americas were discovered. New World relates to the Americas: the western hemisphere – Old World, the eastern
nostrils at tip of beak kiwi
owl: smallest elf owl
painter of USA birds John Audubon
palmiped web-footed bird
ratite of a bird having a keelless breastbone and therefore unable to fly; opposite of carinate
sacred birds quetzal (Aztecs), ibis (Egyptians)
seabird: largest emperor penguin
smells when excited hoopoe emits a foul-smelling liquid
smell: keenest sense of kiwi
snail shells: breaks with stone thrush
sonar-equipped the guacharo, or oilbird, is capable of flying in total darkness in a similar way to bats
strigiformes order of birds that solely includes owls
underwater: longest emperor penguin (up to 18 minutes)
underwater: walks dipper
web-footed bird: smallest petrel
wingspan: longest albatross, although the largest wings belong to the Andean condor

Collective Nouns

actors cast, company, troupe
aeroplanes flight, squadron,
angels host
antelopes herd
ants colony, army
apes shrewdness
arrows sheaf, quiver
asparagus bundle
asses pace
badgers cete
barracuda battery
bass fleet
bears sleuth, sloth
beauties galaxy
beavers colony
bees swarm, grist
bells peal
birds flock, volery
bishops bench
bitterns sedge, siege
bloodhounds sute
boars sounder
books library
bowls set
boy scouts jamboree
boys blush
bread batch, caste
bucks brace, leash
budgerigars chatter
butlers draught
camels caravan, flock
capercaillie tok
capitalists syndicate
cars fleet
cats clowder
cattle herd, drove
chickens brood
choughs chattering
clams bed
clergy assembly, convocation
colts rag
coots covert
corn sheaf
cranes sedge, siege
cricket team eleven
crockery service
crows murder
cubs litter
curlews herd
dancers troupe
deer herd
dogs show, kennel
donkeys drove
dottrel trip
ducks (flight) flush, pump,team
ducks (on ground) badelynge
ducks (in water) paddling
dunlins flight
eagles convocation
eels swarm
eggs clutch
elk gang
falcons cast
ferrets fesnyng, business
finches charm
firewood bundle
fish shoal
flamingos flurry, regiment
flies swarm
foresters stalk
foxes skulk, earth
frogs army, colony
fruit orchard
geese (in flight) skein
geese (on ground) gaggle
girls/women bevy
gnats swarm, cloud
goats herd, tribe, trip
goldfinches charm
goldfish troubling
grapes bunch, cluster
grass tuft
grouse (several broods) pack
grouse (single brood) covey
guardians board
guillemots bazaar
gulls colony
guns battery, park
hares down, husk
harpists melody
hawks cast
hay truss
hedgehogs array
hermits observance
herons sedge, siege
horses haras
hounds pack, mute
hunters blast
hunting dogs cry
ibis crowd
islands archipelago, chain
jellyfish smuck
kangaroos troop
kittens kindle
knaves rayful
labourers gang
lapwings deceit
larks exaltation
leopards leap
lions pride
magistrates bench
magpies tiding, tittering
majors morbidity
mallards flush
mares stud
martens richesse
mice nest
minstrels troupe
moles labour
monkeys troop
mules barren
nightingales watch
onions rope
owls parliament
oxbirds fling
oxen yoke, team
parrots company
partridges covey
passenger pigeons roost
peacocks muster
pearls string, rope
penguins rookery, colony
pheasants nye
pigs litter, drove
plovers congregation, wing
plums basket
pochards rush
polecats chine
police posse. detachment
politicians caucus
porpoises school
poultry run
pups litter
quail bevy
rabbits nest
race horses string
rags bundle
ravens unkindness
rhinoceros crash
roes bevy
rooks clamour, building
sailors crew, deck, watch
sails outfit
saints community
sandpipers fling
sardines family
savages horde
seals herd, pod
servants staff
sheep flock
sheldrakes dopping
ships fleet, flotilla
slaves gang
smelt quantity
snakes den, pit
snipe wisp, walk
soldiers detachment
spiders cluster, clutter
stamps collection
starlings murmuration
stars cluster, constellation
steps flight
sticks faggot
strawberries punnet
subalterns simplicity
swans herd, bevy
swifts flock
swine sounder, drift, dryet
swine (tame) doylt
teals spring
thieves gang
thrush mutation
tigers ambush
toads knot, knab
trees orchard, spinney, thicket
troops brigade, division
trout hover
turkeys rafter
turtles bale, dole
turtle doves pitying
wasps nest
whales school, pod, gam
whelps litter
whiskey case
whiting pod
wigeon company
wild cats dout
wildfowl plump, sord, sute
wine vintage
witches coven
wolves pack
woodcock fall, plump
woodpeckers descent
worshippers congregation

Newspapers

National Newspapers

Name	*Location*	*Founded*	*Details*
Belfast News Letter	Belfast	1737	The UK's oldest surviving daily newspaper
Courier	Dundee	1816	Founded as the *Dundee Courier and Argus*
Daily Courant	London	1702	First successful daily newspaper
Daily Express	London	1900	Founded by C Arthur Pearson. Pro-Conservative. 10 Lower Thames St, London EC3R 6EN. Tel: 0871 434 1010
Daily Herald	London	1911	Merged into the *Sun* in 1964
Daily Mail	London	1896	Founded by Alfred Harmsworth (Lord Northcliffe). Pro-Conservative tabloid. 2 Derry St, Kensington, London W8 5TT. Tel: 020 7938 6000
Daily Mirror	London	1903	Founded by Alfred Harmsworth (Lord Northcliffe). Pro-Labour tabloid. 1 Canada Square, Canary gfWharf, London E14 5AP. Tel: 020 7293 3000
Daily Record	Glasgow	1895	Scottish equivalent of the *Daily Mirror* until the launch of the Scottish *Mirror*
Daily Sketch	London	1909	Merged into the *Daily Mail* in 1971
Daily Sport	Manchester	1989	Founded and owned by David Sullivan, David Gold and Ralph Gold – now online only
Daily Star	London	1978	Owned by United Newspapers (Express Group)
Daily Telegraph	London	1855	Amalgamated in 1937 with *Morning Post.* 111 Buckingham Palace Road, London SW1W 0DT. Tel: 020 7931 2000
European	London	1990	Founded by Robert Maxwell and sold on Thursdays until it ceased publication in 1999.
Evening Standard	London	1827	Owned by Associated Newspapers, part of the Daily Mail Group
Financial News	London	1884	Merged with *Financial Times* in 1945
Financial Times	London	1888	Adopted its pink paper in 1893
Guardian	London	1821	Founded as the *Manchester Guardian* and became a daily in 1855. 119 Farringdon Rd, London EC1R 3ER. Tel: 020 7278 2332
Herald	Glasgow	1783	Founded as *Glasgow Advertiser*, changed name to *Glasgow Herald* 1802–1992
Independent	London	1986	Originally part of the Mirror Group and founded by three *Daily Telegraph* journalists. Independent House, 191 Marsh Wall, London E14 9RS. Tel: 020 7005 2000
Independent on Sunday	London	1990	Originally part of the Mirror Group
Mail on Sunday	London	1982	Sister paper to the *Daily Mail*
News of the World	London	1843	Now defunct – see current affairs section 10 July 2011
Observer	London	1791	Founded by W S Bourne. 119 Farringdon Rd, London EC1R 3ER. Tel: 020 7278 2332
People London E14	London	1881	Founded to support the Conservative cause originally. 1 Canada Square, Canary Wharf, 5AP. Tel: 020 7293 3000
Press and Journal	Aberdeen	1748	Founded by James Chalmers as *Aberdeen's Journal*
Scotland on Sunday	Edinburgh	1988	Sister paper to the *Scotsman*
Scotsman	Edinburgh	1817	First non-London newspaper to open an office in Fleet Street
Sun	London	1964	Founded in 1911 as the *Daily Herald.* 1 Virginia St, London E1 9XR. Tel: 020 7782 4100
Sunday Express	London	1918	Founded by Lord Beaverbrook
Sunday Mirror	London	1963	Founded by Harold Harmsworth as the *Sunday Pictorial* in 1915
Sunday Post	Glasgow	1914	Launched as the *Post Sunday Special*, it is the leading Scottish Sunday paper
Sunday Sport	Manchester	1986	Founded and owned by David Sullivan, David Gold and Ralph Gold
Sunday Telegraph	London	1961	Sister paper to the *Daily Telegraph*
Sunday Times	London	1822	Launched as *The New Observer* and then *The Independent Observer* in 1821
Times	London	1785	Founded by John Walter. 1 Pennington St, London E1 9XN. Tel: 020 7782 5000
Today	London	1986	Founded by Eddie Shah; launched on 4 March 1986. Ceased publication 16 November 1995.

International Newspapers (location and date founded)

ABC (Madrid 1905)
Al-Akhbar (Cairo 1944)
Apogevmatini (Athens 1952)
Avriani (Athens 1980)
Berlingske Tidende (Copenhagen 1749)
Bild am Sonntag (Hamburg 1956)
Boston American (Boston 1904)
B.T. (Copenhagen 1916)
Chicago Sun (Chicago 1941)
Corriere della Sera (Milan 1876)
Diario Popular (Lisbon 1942)
Ethnos (Athens 1891)
Evening Herald (Dublin 1891)
Evening Press (Dublin 1954)
Le Figaro (Paris 1828)
L'Humanité (Paris 1904)
Irish Independent (Dublin 1905)
Irish Times (Dublin 1859)
Izvestiya (Petrograd 1917)
La Lanterne (Brussels 1944)
La Libre (Brussels 1884)
Il Messaggero (Rome 1878)
Le Monde (Paris 1944)
Morgunbladid (Reykavik 1913)
Die Neue Zeitung (Munich 1945)
Neue Zürcher Zeitung (Zurich 1789)
New York Post (New York 1801)
New York Times (New York 1851)
New York World (New York 1860)
L'Osservatore Romano (Vatican 1929)
El Pais (Madrid 1976)
Plain Dealer (Cleveland 1842)
Politiken (Copenhagen 1884)
Pravda (Moscow 1912)
La Repubblica (Rome 1976)
Le Soir (Brussels 1887)
La Stampa (Turin 1867)
Süddeutsche Zeitung (Munich 1945)
Sunday Independent (Dublin 1905)
Sunday Press (Dublin 1949)
Sunday World (Dublin 1973)
Svenska Dagbladet (Stockholm 1884)
Tagesspiegel (Berlin 1945)
Tägliche Rundschau (Berlin 1945)
De Telegraaf (Amsterdam 1893)
Tribune (Chicago 1847)
La Vanguardia (Barcelona 1881)
Wall Street Journal (New York 1889)
Washington Post (Washington DC 1877)
Die Welt (Hamburg 1945)
Ya (Madrid 1935)

Regional Newspapers

Name	Location
Argus	Brighton
Burton Mail	Burton-on-Trent
Chronicle	Bath
Chronicle and Echo	Northampton
Courier and Advertiser	Dundee
Citizen	Gloucester
Daily Echo	Bournemouth
Daily Examiner	Huddersfield
Daily Mail	Hull
Daily Post	Liverpool
Daily Record	Glasgow
Dorset Echo	Weymouth
East Anglian Daily Times	Ipswich
Eastern Daily Press	Norwich
Echo	Lincoln, Liverpool, Sunderland
Essex Chronicle	Chelmsford
Evening Advertiser	Swindon
Evening Chronicle	Newcastle, Oldham
Evening Courier	Halifax
Evening Echo	Weymouth, Basildon
Evening Express	Aberdeen
Evening Gazette	Colchester, Middlesbrough
Evening Herald	Plymouth
Evening Mail	Birmingham
Evening News	Bolton, Cambridge, Edinburgh Manchester, Norwich Scarborough
Evening Post	Bristol, Nottingham, Reading Wigan
Evening Telegraph	Coventry, Derby, Dundee, Grimsby, Peterborough, Scunthorpe
Evening Times	Glasgow
Express and Echo	Exeter
Express Star	Wolverhampton
The Gazette	Blackpool, South Shields
Gloucestershire Echo	Cheltenham
Greenock Telegraph	Dunfermline (head office)
Heartland Evening News	Nuneaton
Herald Express	Torquay
Kent Today	Aylesford
The Journal	Newcastle
Lancashire Evening Post	Preston
Lancashire Evening Telegraph	Blackburn
Mercury	Leicester
News and Star	Carlisle
The News	Portsmouth
Northern Echo	Darlington
Evening Telegraph	Kettering (Northamptonshire)
Observer	Crawley
Oxford Mail	Oxford
Paisley Daily Express	Glasgow
Post	Birmingham
Sentinel	Stoke
Shropshire Star	Telford
South Wales Evening Post	Swansea
Southern Daily Echo	Southampton
Star	Barnsley, Doncaster, Sheffield
Telegraph	Belfast
Telegraph and Argus	Bradford
Western Daily Press	Bristol
Western Mail	Cardiff
Western Morning News	Plymouth
Yorkshire Evening Post	Leeds
Yorkshire Post	Leeds

Editors (as at October 2013)

Daily Express Hugh Whittow
Daily Mail Paul Dacre
Daily Mirror Lloyd Embley
Daily Record Allan Rennie
Daily Sport Pam McVitie
Daily Star Dawn Neesom
Daily Star Sunday Gareth Morgan
Daily Telegraph Tony Gallagher
Evening Standard Sarah Sands
Financial Times Lionel Barber
Guardian Alan Rusbridger
Independent Amol Rajan
Independent on Sunday Lisa Markwell
Mail on Sunday Geordie Greig
Metro Kenny Campbell
Observer John Mulholland
People James Scott
Racing Post Bruce Millington
Radio Times Ben Preston
Spectator Fraser Nelson
Sun David Dinsmore
Sun on Sunday Victoria Newton
Sunday Express Martin Townshend
Sunday Mail Allan Rennie
Sunday Mirror Lloyd Embley
Sunday Sport Nick Appleyard
Sunday Telegraph Ian MacGregor
Sunday Times Martin Ivens
Times John Witherow
Vogue Alexandra Shulman

Agony Aunts, Horoscopes, Crosswords & Chess

Agony Aunts

Virginia Ironside *Independent*
Jane O'Gorman *Daily Star*
Just Joan *Daily Record*
Eve Pollard *Daily Mirror*
Deidre Sanders *Sun*
Kate Saunders *Express*
Miriam Stoppard *Daily Mirror*
Dr Petra Boynton *Telegraph*
Jessica Gorst-Williams *Telegraph*
Sally Brampton *Sunday Times*

Chess

Leonard Barden *Evening Standard*
Raymond Keene *Times*
Jon Speelman *Independent*

Horoscopes

Jonathan Cainer *Daily Mail*
Lynne Ewart *Daily Record*
Russell Grant *Daily Mirror*
Sally Kirkman *Daily Star*
Marjorie Orr *Express*
Mystic Meg *Sun*
Catherine Tennant *Daily Telegraph*
Justin Toper *Daily Express; Daily Star*
Peter Watson *Daily Mail*
Shelley von Strunckel *Sunday Times; Evening Standard*

Crosswords

Peter Watson *Daily Mail*
Aelred *Independent*
Aquila *Independent*
Araucaria *Guardian*
Auctor *Times*
Azed *Observer*
Beelzebub *Sunday Independent*
Bunthorne *Guardian*
Columba *Independent*
Enigmatist *Guardian*
Gemini *Guardian*
Mod *Times*
Monk *Independent*
Pasquale *Guardian*
Paul *Guardian*
Phi *Independent*
Quixote *Sunday Independent*
Roger Squires *Telegraph*
Rufus *Guardian*
Spurios *Independent*

Newspaper Cartoons and Cartoonist(s)

Alisdair *Times* Pugh and Way
Andy Capp *Daily Mirror* and *Sunday Mirror* Reg Smythe
As If *Independent* Sally Ann Lasson
Augusta *Evening Standard* Angus McGill and Dominic Poelsma
Austin *Guardian* Austin
Badlands *Sun* Steve McGarry
Beau Peep *Daily Star* Kettle and Christine
Ben and Katie *Daily Star* Doug Baker and Roca
Bill Caldwell (cartoonist) *Daily Star*
Bogart *Daily Mail* Peter Plant
Bristow *Evening Standard* Frank Dickens
Clogger F.C. *Daily Star* Bill Caldwell
Colonel Blimp *Evening Standard* David Low
Dilbert *Telegraph* and *Express* Scott Adams
Doonesbury *Guardian* Garry Trudeau
Dreadnoughts, The *Sun* Martin Fish
Faith, Hope and Sue *Express* Lisa Wild
Flatmates *Daily Record* Michael Atkinson
Flook (1949–84) *Daily Mail* Trog (Wally Fawkes)
Fred Basset *Daily Mail* Alex Graham
Gambols *Express* Barry Appleby
Garfield *Evening Standard* and *Express* Jim Davis
George & Lynne Sun Conrad and Gual
Giles Daily and Sunday *Express* Carl Ronald Giles
Grandad and the Lad *Daily Record* Bryan Walker
Griffin *Express* Griffin
Hagar the Horrible *Sun* Chris Browne
Heath *Telegraph* Heath
Hector Breeze *Express* Hector Breeze
Horace *Daily Mirror* Kettle and Christine
I Don't Believe It *Daily Mail* Dick Millington
If *Guardian* Steve Bell
Jane *Daily Mirror* Norman Pett (originally)
The Johnsons *Daily Express* Peter Plant
Judge Dredd of 2000 AD *Daily Star* Smith and Rennie
Kipper Williams (cartoonist) *Guardian*
Liberty Meadows *Express* Frank Cho
Livvy *Sun* Bob Maher
Mandy Capp *Daily Mirror* Carla Ostrer and Mahoney
Matt *Telegraph* Matt Pritchett
Modesty Blaise (1963–2001) *Evening Standard* Peter O'Donnell
Morten Morland *Times* Morten Morland (untitled cartoon)
Paul Thomas *Express* Paul Thomas (untitled -cartoon)
Peanuts *Daily Mail* Charles Schulz
Perishers *Daily Mirror* Bill Mevin and Maurice Dodd
Peter Brookes *Times* Peter Brookes (untitled cartoon)
Potto *Evening Standard* Frank Dickens
Psycops *Sun* Wilbur
Real Life *Daily Mirror* Johnston
Rupert Bear *Express* Mary Tourtel (1920–48)
Scorer *Daily Mirror* Tomlinson, Gillat and Pugh
Shuggie and Duggie *Daily Record* Bullimore and Anderson
Steve Bell (cartoonist) *Guardian*
Striker *Sun* Pete Nash & Simon Ravenhill
The Stringalongs *Times* (originally) Mark Boxer
Teenage Mum *Daily Star* Graham Hey
Tim *Independent*
The Ultimate *Daily Sport* Paul Martin
Up and Running *Daily Mail* Gray and Shack
Wallace & Gromit *Sun* Aardman & Titan Comics
Weber Family *Guardian* Posy Simmonds
Wizard of Id *Evening Standard* Parker and Hart

General Information

Asahi Shimbun Japan's leading newspaper has been produced 'untouched by human hands' since 24 September 1980.

***Avanti*: famous editor** Benito Mussolini edited the Milan-based socialist paper from 1912 to 1914. Mussolini subsequently founded the newspaper *Il Popolo d'Italia* in 1914.

Beachcomber Column Began in the *Daily Express* in 1917 under the name 'By the Way' its author inheriting the name 'Beachcomber', J B Morton wrote the column from 1924 to 1975 and the present author is William Hartston.

***Boy's Own*: founded** in 1879 by the Religious Tract Society and ceased in 1967.

cartoon: first drawn by John Wesley Jarvis in 1814 for the Washington Federal Republican.

cartoon: first UK 'The Unknown Tongue' (printed in *Bell's New Weekly Messenger*) 8 Jan. 1832.

Children's Newspaper founded by Arthur Mee in 1919.

***Christian Science Monitor*: founder** Mary Baker Eddy in Boston 1908.

clock on *Times* Diary page always set on 4.30.

colour supplement: first four-page section of the *New York World* 19 November 1893.

colour supplement: first UK Sunday Times Colour Section (became Sunday Times Magazine) 4 February 1962.

comic strip: first *Yellow Kid* by R F Outcault -(published in the *New York World* in 1896).

Corriere della Sera although this newspaper translates as 'Evening Courier', it is a morning daily newspaper.

crossword puzzle: first compiled by Liverpool-born Arthur Wynne (published *New York World* Sunday 21 December 1913).

crossword puzzle: first UK *Sunday Express* 2 November 1924.

crossword puzzle: first *Times* 1 February 1930 and compiled by Adrian Bell (father of ex-MP Martin Bell).

crusader logo introduced on *Express* by Lord Beaverbrook 1930.

daily newspaper: first UK *The Perfect Diurnall* Feb. 1660 (*Daily Courant* of 1702 was first successful daily).

Hitler diaries extracts published by *Stern* magazine in May 1983

daily poem *Independent.*

***Daily Telegraph* editor: former** W F (Bill) Deedes.

***Daily Telegraph*: news first published on front page** 1969.

Daily Worker Communist newspaper founded in 1932. Name changed to *Morning Star* in 1966 but *Daily Worker* revived in 1992.

Der Spiegel the German news magazine was founded in 1947.

Edinburgh Gazette Scottish equivalent of the *London Gazette*, founded in 1699 and appearing twice a week.

***Evening News*: merger** on 31 October 1980 the *Evening News* was merged into the *Evening Standard.*

evening newspaper: first *Dawks's News-Letter* (published in London) 23 June 1696.

famous columnists *Daily Mirror* political cartoonist Vicky and columnist Cassandra.

famous sale Max Aitken sold the Express group to Trafalgar House 30 June 1977 (re-sold to United Newspapers 1985).

Foreign newspapers *El Pais* – Argentina, *Avanti* – Milan, *Exame* – Brazil, *Feral Tribune* – Croatia, *Hihon Keizai Shimbun* – Japan, *La Presse* – Quebec, *Moderna Tider* – Stockholm, *Qianshao* – Hong Kong.

founded as women's paper *Daily Mirror.*

Globe the British paper was suppressed in November 1915 for spreading false rumours about Lord Kitchener's resignation.

***Good Housekeeping*: founded** British magazine was founded in 1922, although the US version was founded much earlier.

Guardian Until 1959, the *Manchester Guardian.* Owned by the Scott Trust and dubbed 'The Grauniad' by *Private Eye* magazine due to the paper's reputation for typographical errors. Socially liberal political bias.

***Harijan*: founder** Mahatma Gandhi founded the Indian weekly publication in 1933.

Hearst, William Randolph: castle San Simeon, California.

Hearst: famous newspapers *Examiner* (1887 his first), *Morning Journal* (1895 later became *Journal-American*).

and considered authentic by historian Hugh Trevor-Roper, but later exposed as a fake produced by a dealer in Nazi memorabilia.

Independent launched by Andreas Whittam-Smith and associates on 7 Oct. 1986 and subsequently acquired by a consortium led by Mirror Group Newspapers, 18 March 1994.

***John Bull*: date commenced** 1906, although the character first appeared in 1712 in a pamphlet by John Arbuthnot (1667–1735).

The Liberator influential anti-slavery weekly newspaper of Abolitionist crusader William Lloyd Garrison between 1831 and 1865, published in Boston.

***Life* magazine: first published** 1936 by Henry Luce, publisher of *Time*. *Life* magazine ceased on 29 December 1972 but was relaunched in October 1978.

***Listener*: founded** by the BBC in 1929 and closed in January 1991.

***London Daily News*: founded by** Robert Maxwell in February 1987 but it folded in July when the *Evening News* was temporarily relaunched.

London Gazette Government's bulletin in which official announcements are made. Founded in 1665 as the *Oxford Gazette* and appearing 4 times a week.

magazine: shortest title *Ms*, the American feminist magazine founded in 1972, may lay claim to that title.

***Marie-Claire*: founded** the French women's magazine was founded in 1954.

Messenger Group: launched by The free news-papers were launched by Eddie Shah in Warrington in 1983 and produced by non-union workers.

Metro Free daily newspaper published by Associated Newspapers (part of Daily Mail Group) across the UK on many public transport services. The paper was launched in 1999.

***New Republic*: founded by** the American paper was founded by H D Croly in 1914.

***New Society*: founded** the weekly sociology magazine was founded in 1962 and merged into the *New Statesman* in 1988.

newspaper: best-selling *News of the World* is Britain's largest-selling newspaper (approx 3 -million).

newspaper: first *Acta Diurna* (Daily Events) dating from 59 BC and attributed to Julius Caesar.

newspaper: first surviving English *Weekly News* 1622. (Newspapers were printed before this date but none survive.)

***New Statesman*: founded by** Beatrice and Sidney Webb in 1913 and aided by leading Fabians such as G B Shaw.

***Now*: founder** the magazine was founded by James Goldsmith in September 1979 and ceased in March 1981.

page 3 girls: year started 1970.

***People*: famous libel case** an article in 1909 alleged that chancellor David Lloyd George had committed adultery and had paid £20,000 to keep the case out of court.

***Picture Post*: first published** 1938 and founded by Edward Hulton. It closed in 1957.

***Playboy*: founded by** Hugh Hefner, December 1953.

***Post*: launched by** Eddie Shah in November 1988 and folded after 33 issues.

Press Council: founded 1953 (replaced by the Press Complaints Commission 1 January 1991).

***Private Eye*: founded** In February 1962 and saved from financial ruin by Peter Cook in April 1962.

Punch first published in 1841 and ceased production on 8 Aril 1992. Aka *The London Charivari*.

***Radio Times*: founded** 1923.

***Radio Times*: first woman editor** Sue Robinson.

***Reader's Digest*: founded** DeWitt Wallace and his wife Lila Acheson published the first issue in Greenwich Village, New York 5 February 1922.

***Scottish Daily News*: founded** launched by a workers' co-operative 5 May 1975 but closed in Oct. 1975 despite intervention by Robert Maxwell.

Sun founded 15 September 1964 when the TUC sold its shares in the *Daily Herald*. Average circulation of almost 3m, the highest in the world for a daily. Pro-Conservative since 2009.

***Sunday Correspondent*: launched** on 17 September 1989 and closed in Nov. 1990.

***Sunday Herald*: founded** in 1915 and -subsequently renamed the *Sunday Graphic*; closed down in 1960.

Tatler founded by Richard Steele in 1709 and assisted by Joseph Addison until its closure in 1711. It was replaced by the non-political *Spectator* in 1711 but the name was revived in 1901 for an illustrated monthly magazine which is still published today.

Telegraph Group moved from Fleet Street to Docklands in 1987 and printed in London and new site (1986) in Manchester. Owned by identical twins David and Frederick Barclay, who also own The Ritz; the newspapers have a Conservative bias.

***Time* magazine: founded by** Henry A Luce and Briton Hadden in 1923.

***Times*: previous name** *Daily Universal Register* until 1788.

***Times*: nickname** *The Thunderer* (the nickname of Thomas Barnes, editor of the *Times* 1817–41).

***Times*: news first appeared on front page** 3 May 1966.

***Today*: date commenced** launched by Eddie Shah 4 March 1986 as Britain's first full-colour, low-cost tabloid, its sales failed to achieve targets and it was subsequently sold to Tiny Rowland's Lonrho Co.

Wapping: exodus to *Times*, *Sunday Times*, *Sun* and *News of the World* moved overnight to a new plant in Wapping 25 Jan. 1986.

William Hickey column pen-name of Tom Driberg when writing for the *Daily Express* between 1928 and 1943. Having become an MP, Driberg later used the name as a columnist with the *Daily Mail* and *New Statesman*. The name derives from a famous 18th century diarist. The *Express* still has a Hickey column, although the 'William' has been dropped.

yellow journalism term coined to describe the sensationalistic reporting and frenzied promotional schemes adopted in the fierce circulation wars between William Randolph Hearst's *Journal* and Joseph Pulitzer's *World*.

NOBEL PRIZE WINNERS

	Physics	*Chemistry*	*Literature*	*Medicine*	*Peace*
1901	Wilhelm Röntgen (Ger.) Discovery of X-rays	Jacobus van't Hoff (Neth.) Laws of chemical dynamics and osmotic pressure	René Sully-Prudhomme (Fr.) Poet	Emil von Behring (Ger.) Work on serum therapy Pioneer in immunology	Jean Henri Dunant (Switz.) Frédéric Passy (Fr.)
1902	Hendrik Lorentz (Neth.) Pieter Zeeman (Neth.) Magnetism on radiation	Emil Fischer (Ger.) Work on sugar and purine syntheses	Theodor Mommsen (Ger.) Historian	Sir Ronald Ross (Brit.) Discovery of how malaria enters an organism	Elie Ducommun (Switz.) Charles Gobat (Switz.)
1903	Antoine-Henri Becquerel (Fr.) Pierre and Marie Curie (Fr.) Radioactivity	Svante Arrhenius (Swed.) Theory of electrolytic dissociation	Björnsterne Björnson (Nor.) Novelist, poet, dramatist	Niels Finsen (Den.) Phototherapy	Sir William Cremer (Brit.) Founder of Workmen's Peace Association
1904	Lord Rayleigh (Brit.) Discovery of argon	Sir William Ramsay (Brit.) Discovery of inert gases	Frédéric Mistral (Fr.) Poet J Echegaray Eizaguirre (Sp.)	Ivan Pavlov (Russ.) Physiology of digestion	Institute of International Law (founded 1873)
1905	Philipp Lenard (Ger.) Research on cathode rays	Adolf von Baeyer (Ger.) Work on organic dyes	H Sienkiewicz (Pol.) Novelist	Robert Koch (Ger.) Tuberculosis research	Bertha von Suttner (Austria)
1906	Sir J J Thomson (Brit.) Research into electrical conductivity of gases	Henri Moissan (Fr.) Isolation of fluorine Moissan furnace	Giosuè Carducci (Ita.) Poet	Camillo Golgi (Ita.) and S Ramon y Cajal (Sp.) Structure of nervous system	Theodore Roosevelt (US)
1907	A A Michelson (US) Spectroscopic and metrological investigations	Eduard Buchner (Ger.) Discovery of non-cellular fermentation	Rudyard Kipling (Brit.) Poet and novelist	Alphonse Laveran (Fr.) Discovery of the role of protozoa in diseases	Ernesto T Moneta (Ita.) Louis Renault (Fr.)
1908	Gabriel Lippman (Fr.) Photographic reproduction of colours	Lord Rutherford (Brit.) Disintegration of elements Chemistry of radioactivity	Rudolf Eucken (Ger.) Philosopher	Paul Ehrlich (Ger.) Ilya Mechnikov (Russ.) Work on immunity	Klas P Arnoldson (Swed.) Fredrik Bajer (Den.)
1909	Guglielmo Marconi (Ita.) Karl Braun (Ger.) Wireless telegraphy	Wilhelm Ostwald (Ger.) Pioneer work on catalysis, chemical equilibrium and reaction velocities	Selma Lagerlöf (Swed.) Novelist	Emil Kocher (Switz.) Physiology, pathology and surgery of thyroid gland	Baron d'Estournelles de Constant (Fr.) Auguste Beernaert (Belg.)
1910	J van Der Waals (Neth.) Gas and liquid equation	Otto Wallach (Ger.) Alicyclic combinations	Paul von Heyse (Ger.) Poet and novelist	Albrecht Kossel (Ger.) Cellular chemistry research	International Peace Bureau (founded 1891)
1911	Wilhelm Wien (Ger.) Discoveries regarding laws governing heat radiation	Marie Curie (Fr.) Discovered/isolated radium Discovered Polonium	Maurice Maeterlinck (Belg.) Dramatist	Allvar Gullstrand (Swed.) Work on dioptrics of the eye	Tobias Asser (Neth.) Alfred Fried (Austria)
1912	Nils Gustaf Dalén (Swed.) Invention of automatic regulators for lighting coastal beacons and light buoys	Victor Grignard (Fr.) Paul Sabatier (Fr.) Discovery of Grignard reagents and hydrogenating organic compounds	Gerhart Hauptmann (Ger.) Dramatist	Alexis Carrel (Fr.) Work on vascular suture Transplantation of organs	Elihu Root (US)

	Physics	*Chemistry*	*Literature*	*Medicine*	*Peace*
1913	H Kamerlingh Onnes (Neth.) Liquid helium production Low temperature properties	Alfred Werner (Switz.) Work on the linkage of atoms in molecules	Sir R Tagore (India) Poet	Charles Richet (Fr.) Work on anaphylaxis	Henri Lafontaine (Belg.)
1914	Max von Laue (Ger.) Discovery of diffraction of X-rays by crystals	Theodore Richards (US) Accurate determination of atomic weights of elements	no award	Robert Barany (Austria) Work on vestibular apparatus	no award
1915	Sir William Bragg (Brit.) Sir Lawrence Bragg (Brit.) Analysis of crystals by means of X-rays	Richard Willstätter (Ger.) Pioneer researches on plant pigments, especially chlorophyll	Romain Rolland (Fr.) Novelist	no award	no award
1916	no award	no award	V von Heidenstam (Swed.) Poet	no award	no award
1917	Charles Barkla (Brit.) Discovery of characteristic X-radiation of elements	no award	Karl Gjellerup (Den.) H Pontoppidan (Den.) Novelists	no award	International Red Cross Committee (founded 1863)
1918	Max Planck (Ger.) Elemental quantum theory	Fritz Haber (Ger.) Synthesis of ammonia	no award	no award	no award
1919	Johannes Stark (Ger.) Doppler effect in positive ions and spectral line division	no award	Carl Spitteler (Switz.) Poet and novelist	Jules Bordet (Belg.) Discoveries in regard to immunity`	Woodrow Wilson (US)
1920	Charles Guillaume (Switz.) Discovery of anomalies in alloys	Walther Nernst (Ger.) Work in thermochemistry	Knut Hamsun (Nor.) Novelist	August Krogh (Den.) Discovery of capillary motor regulating mechanism	Léon Bourgeois (Fr.)
1921	Albert Einstein (Switz.) Services to theoretical physics	Frederick Soddy (Brit.) Chemistry of radioactive substances and occurrence and nature of isotopes	Anatole France (Fr.) Novelist	no award	Karl Branting (Swed.) Christian Louis Lange (Nor.)
1922	Niels Bohr (Den.) Investigation of atomic structure and radiation	Francis Aston (Brit.) Work with mass spectrograph	Jacinto Benavente y Martinez (Spa.) Dramatist	Archibald Hill (Brit.) Discovery relating to heat production in muscles	Fridtjof Nansen (Nor.)
1923	Robert Millikan (US) Work on elementary electric charge	Fritz Pregl (Austria) Method of microanalysis of organic substances	W B Yeats (Ire.) Poet	Sir F G Banting (Can.) J J R Macleod (Brit.) Discovery of insulin	no award
1924	Karl Siegbahn (Swed.) Work in X-ray spectroscopy	no award	Wladyslaw Reymont (Pol.) Novelist	Willem Einthoven (Neth.) Discovery of electro-cardiogram mechanism	no award
1925	James Franck (Ger.) Gustav Hertz (Ger.) Discovery of laws governing impact of electrons upon an atom	Richard Zsigmondy (Austria) Elucidation of hetero-geneous nature of colloidal solutions	George Bernard Shaw (Ire.) Dramatist	no award	Austen Chamberlain (Brit.) Charles G Dawes (US)

	Physics	*Chemistry*	*Literature*	*Medicine*	*Peace*
1926	Jean-Baptiste Perrin (Fr.) Work on discontinuous structure of matter	Theodor Svedberg (Swed.) Work on disperse systems	Grazia Deledda (Ita.) Novelist	Johannes Fibiger (Den.) Contributions to cancer research	Aristide Briand (Fr.) Gustav Stresemann (Ger.)
1927	Arthur Holly Compton (US) Discovery of wave change in diffused X-rays Charles Wilson (Brit.) Visibility of electric particles	Heinrich Wieland (Ger.) Researches into the constitution of bile acids	Henri Bergson (Fr.) Philosopher	J Wagner-Jauregg (Austria) Work on malaria inoculation in dementia paralytica	Ferdinand Buisson (Fr.) Ludwig Quidde (Ger.)
1928	Owen Richardson (Brit.) Richardson's Law	Adolf Windaus (Ger.) Sterols + vitamin connection	Sigrid Undset (Nor.) Novelist	Charles Nicolle (Fr.) Work on typhus	no award
1929	Louis de Broglie (Fr.) Discovery of the wave nature of electrons	Sir Arthur Harden (Brit.) H von Euler-Chelpin (Swed.) Fermentation of sugars and connective enzymes	Thomas Mann (Ger.) Novelist	Christiaan Eijkman (Neth.) Antineuritic vitamin Sir F Hopkins (Brit.) Growth stimulating vitamins	Frank B Kellogg (US)
1930	Sir C Raman (India) Work on light diffusion	Hans Fischer (Ger.) Chlorophyll research	Sinclair Lewis (US) Novelist	Karl Landsteiner (US) Human blood grouping	Nathan Söderblom (Swed.)
1931	no award	Karl Bosch (Ger.) Friedrich Bergius (Ger.) High pressure methods	Erik Axel Karlfeldt (Swed.) Poet	Otto Warburg (Ger.) Discovery of nature and action of respiratory enzyme	Jane Addams (US) Nicholas Murray Butler (US)
1932	Werner Heisenberg (Ger.) Indeterminacy principle of quantum mechanics	Irving Langmuir (US) Discoveries in surface chemistry	John Galsworthy (Brit.) Novelist	Edgar D Adrian (Brit.) Sir C Sherrington (Brit.) Neuron investigations	no award
1933	P A M Dirac (Brit.) Erwin Schrödinger (Austria) Intro of wave equations in quantum mechanics	no award	Ivan Bunin (USSR) Novelist	Thomas Hunt Morgan (US) Heredity transmission functions of chromosomes	Sir Norman Angell (Brit.)
1934	no award	Harold Urey (US) Discovery of heavy hydrogen	Luigi Pirandello (Ita.) Dramatist	George R Minot (US) William P Murphy (US) George H Whipple (US) Anaemia treatments	Arthur Henderson (Brit.)
1935	Sir James Chadwick (Brit.) Discovery of the neutron	Frédéric Joliot-Curie (Fr.) Irène Joliot-Curie (Fr.) Radioactive element theory	no award	Hans Spemann (Ger.) Organizer effect in embryo	Carl von Ossietzky (Ger.)
1936	Victor Hess (Austria) Cosmic radiation discovery Carl Anderson (US) Positron discovery	Peter Debye (Neth.) Work on dipole moments and diffraction of X-rays and electrons in gases	Eugene O'Neill (US) Dramatist	Sir H H Dale (Brit.) Otto Loewi (Ger.) Work on chemical transmission of nerve impulses	Carlos S Lamas (Arg.)
1937	Clinton Davisson (US) George P Thomson (Brit.) Interference phenomenon in crystals irradiated by electrons	Walter Haworth (Brit.) Research on carbohydrates and vitamin C Paul Karrer (Switz.) Research on Carotenoids	Roger Martin du Gard (Fr.) Novelist	Albert Szent-Györgyi (Hung.) Work on biological combustion	Viscount Cecil of Chelwood (Brit.)

	Physics	*Chemistry*	*Literature*	*Medicine*	*Peace*
1938	Enrico Fermi (Ita.) Artificial radioactive element by neutron irradiation	Richard Kuhn (Ger.) Research on carotenoids (declined)	Pearl Buck (US) Novelist	Corneille Heymans (Belg.) Discovery of sinus role in respiration regulation	Nansen International Office for Refugees (founded 1931)
1939	Ernest Lawrence (US) Invented cyclotron	Adolf Butenandt (Ger.) Work on sexual hormones (declined) Leopold Ružička (Switz.) Polymethylenes research	Frans Eemil Sillanpää (Fin.) Novelist	Gerhard Domagk (Ger) Antibacterial effect of Prontosil (declined)	no award
1940	no award	no award	no award	no award	no award
1941	no award	no award	no award	no award	no award
1942	no award	no award	no award	no award	no award
1943	Otto Stern (US) Discovery of the magnetic moment of the proton	George de Hevesy (Hung.) Use of isotopes as tracers in chemical research	no award	Henrik Dam (Den.) Discovery of vitamin K Edward A Doisy (US) Chemical nature of vitamin K	no award
1944	Isidor Rabi (US) Resonance method for registration of magnetic properties of atomic nuclei	Otto Hahn (Ger.) Discovery of the fission of heavy nuclei	J V Jensen (Den.) Novelist	Joseph Erlanger (US) Herbert S Gasser (US) Research on differentiated functions of nerve fibres	International Red Cross Committee (founded 1863)
1945	Wolfgang Pauli (Austria) Discovery of the exclusion principle	Artturi Virtanen (Fin.) Invention of fodder preservation method	Gabriela Mistral (Chile) Poet	Sir Alexander Fleming (Brit.) Ernst B Chain (Brit.) Lord Florey (Aus.) Penicillin discovery	Cordell Hull (US)
1946	Percy Bridgman (US) Discoveries in the domain of high-pressure physics	James Sumner (US) Wendell Stanley (US) John Northrop (US) Enzyme research	Herman Hesse (Switz.) Novelist	Hermann J Muller (US) Production of mutations by X-ray irradiation	Emily Greene Balch (US) John R Mott (US)
1947	Edward Appleton (Brit.) Discovery of Appleton layer in upper atmosphere	Robert Robinson (Brit.) Investigations on alkaloids and other plant products	André Gide (Fr.) Novelist and essayist	Carl F Cori (US) Gerty T Cori (US) Bernardo Houssay (Arg.) Glycogen conversion	American Friends Service Committee (US) Friends Service Council (London)
1948	Patrick Blackett (Brit.) Discoveries in the domain of nuclear physics analysis; serum proteins	Arne Tiselius (Swed.) Researches on electro-phoresis and adsorption	T S Eliot (Brit.) Poet and critic	Paul Müller (Switz.) Properties of DDT	no award
1949	Yukawa Hideki (Jap.) Prediction of the existence of mesons	William Giauque (US) Behaviour of substances at extremely low temps	William Faulkner (US) Novelist	Walter Rudolf Hess (Switz.) Middle brain function Antonio Egas Moniz (Port.) Leucotomy research	Lord Boyd-Orr (Brit.)
1950	Cecil Powell (Brit.) Photographic method of studying nuclear processes; discoveries about mesons	Otto Diels (Ger.) Kurt Alder (Ger.) Discovery and development of diene synthesis	Bertrand Russell (Brit.) Philosopher	Philip S Hench (US) Edward C Kendall (US) Tadeus Reichstein (Switz.) Cortex hormones research	Ralph Bunche (US)

	Physics	*Chemistry*	*Literature*	*Medicine*	*Peace*
1951	John Cockcroft (Brit.) Ernest Walton (Ire.) Atomic nuclei research	Edwin McMillan (US) Glenn Seaborg (US) Transuranium element work	Pär Lagerkvist (Swed.) Novelist	Max Theiler (SA) Yellow fever research	Léon Jouhaux (Fr.)
1952	Felix Bloch (US) Edward Purcell (US) Discovery of nuclear magnetic resonance in solids	Archer Martin (Brit.) Richard Synge (Brit.) Development of partition chromatography	François Mauriac (Fr.) Poet, novelist, dramatist	Selman A Waksman (US) Discovery of streptomycin	Albert Schweitzer (Alsace)
1953	Frits Zernike (Neth.) Method of phase contrast microscopy	Hermann Staudinger (Ger.) Work on macromolecules	Winston Churchill (Brit.) Historian and orator	Fritz A Lipman (US) H A Krebs (Brit.) Discovery of coenzyme A	George C Marshall (US)
1954	Max Born (Brit.) Wave functions studies Walther Bothe (Ger.) Coincidence method	Linus Pauling (US) Study of the nature of the chemical bond	Ernest Hemingway (US) Novelist	John F Enders (US) Thomas H Weller (US) Frederick Robbins (US) Polio virus in tissue culture	Office of the UN High Commisioner for Refugees (founded 1951)
1955	Willis Lamb Jnr (US) Hydrogen spectrum study Polykarp Kusch (US) Magnetic electron study	Vincent du Vigneaud (US) First synthesis of a polypeptide hormone	Halidor Laxness (Ice.) Novelist	Axel Hugo Theorell (Swed.) Nature and mode of action of oxidation enzymes	no award
1956	William Shockley (US) John Bardeen (US) Walter Brattain (US) Discovery of transistor effect	Nikolay Semyonov (USSR) Cyril Hinshelwood (Brit.) Work on the kinetics of chemical reactions	Juan Ramon Jimenez (Spa.) Poet	Werner Forssman (Ger.) Dickinson Richards (US) André F Cournand (US) Heart catheterisation	no award
1957	Tsung-Dao Lee (China) Chen Ning Yang (China) Principle of parity research	Alexander Todd (Brit.) Work on nucleotides and nucleotide coenzymes	Albert Camus (Fr.) Novelist and dramatist	Daniel Bovet (Ita.) Production of curare	Lester B Pearson (Can.)
1958	Pavel A Cherenkov (USSR) Ilya M Frank (USSR) Igor Y Tamm (USSR) Discovery and interpretation of Cherenkov effect	Frederick Sanger (Brit.) Determination of structure of the insulin molecule	Boris Pasternak (USSR) Novelist and poet (declined)	George W Beadle (US) Edward L Tatum (US) Joshua Lederberg (US) Research in genetics	Dominique G Pire (Belg.)
1959	Emilio Segrè (US) Owen Chamberlain (US) Antiproton research	Jaroslav Heyrovsky (Czech) Discovery + development of polarography	Salvatore Quasimodo (Ita.) Poet	Severo Ochoa (US) Arthur Kornberg (US) Nucleic acids research	Philip Noel-Baker (Brit.)
1960	Donald Glaser (US) Development of the bubble chamber	Willard Libby (US) Development of radio-carbon dating	Saint-John Perse (Fr.) Poet	Macfarlane Burnet (Aus.) Peter B Medawar (Brit.) Tissue transplant research	Albert Lutuli (SA)
1961	Robert Hofstadter (US) Atomic nucleon research Rudolf Mössbauer (Ger.) Mössbauer effect	Melvin Calvin (US) Study of chemical steps that take place during photosynthesis	Ivo Andrić (Yug) Novelist	Georg von Békésy (US) Functions of the inner ear	Dag Hammarskjöld (Swed.)
1962	Lev D Landau (USSR) Research into condensed state of matter	John C Kendrew (Brit.) Max F Perutz (Brit.) Hemoprotein research	John Steinbeck (US) Novelist	Francis H C Crick (Brit.) James D Watson (US) Maurice Wilkins (Brit.) DNA molecular structure	Linus Pauling (US)

NOBEL PRIZE WINNERS

	Physics	Chemistry	Literature	Medicine	Peace	Economics
1963	J H D Jensen (Ger.) Maria Goeppert Mayer (US) Eugene Paul Wigner (US) Atomic nuclei research	Giulio Natta (Ita.) Karl Ziegler (Ger.) Research into polymers in the field of plastics	George Seferis (Gre.) Poet	Sir John Eccles (Aus.) Alan Lloyd Hodgkin (Brit.) Andrew Huxley (Brit.) Nerve fibre research	International Red Cross and League of Red Cross (HQ of both in Geneva)	
1964	Charles H Townes (US) Nikolay G Basov (USSR) Aleksandr Prokhorov (USSR) Maser/laser research	Dorothy Hodgkin (Brit.) Determining the structure of biochemical compounds used to control pernicious anaemia	Jean-Paul Sartre (Fr.) Philosopher and dramatist (declined)	Konrad Bloch (US) Feodor Lynen (Ger.) Cholesterol research	Martin Luther King Jr (US)	
1965	Julian Schwinger (US) Richard Feynman (US) Tomonaga Shin'ichiro (Jap.) Quantum electrodynamics	Robert B Woodward (US) Synthesis of chlorophyll	Mikhail Sholokhov (USSR) Novelist	François Jacob (Fr.) Jacques Monod (Fr.) André Lwolf (Fr.) Body cells research	UN Children's Fund (founded 1946)	
1966	Alfred Kastler (Fr.) Optical methods for studying Hertzian resonances in atoms	Robert S Mulliken (US) Research into electronic structure of molecules	Shmuel Yosef Agnon (Isr.) Nelly Sachs (Swed.) Novelist and poet	Charles B Huggins (US) Francis Peyton Rous (US) Cancer research	no award	
1967	Hans A Bethe (US) Discoveries concerning the energy production of stars	Manfred Eigen (Ger.) Ronald G W Norrish (Brit.) George Porter (Brit.) Chemical reaction research	Miguel Angel Asturias (Guat.) Novelist	Haldan Keffer Hartline (US) George Wald (US) Ragnar A Granit (Swed.) Eye research	no award	
1968	Luis W Alvarez (US) Discovered resonance states	Lars Onsager (US) Work on theory of thermo-dynamics of irreversible processes	Kawabata Yasunari (Jap.) Novelist	Robert W Holley (US) H Gobind Khorana (US) Marshall Nirenberg (US) Genetic code deciphering	René Cassin (Fr.)	
1969	Murray Gell-Mann (US) Discoveries concerning the classification of elementary particles	Derek H R Barton (Brit.) Odd Hassel (Nor.) Organic compound research	Samuel Beckett (Ire.) Novelist and dramatist	Max Delbrück (US) Alfred D Hershey (US) Salvador E Luria (US) Research of viruses	International Labour Organization (founded 1919)	Ragnar Frisch (Nor.) Jan Tinbergen (Neth.) Work in econometrics
1970	Hannes Alfvén (Swed.) Louis Néel (Fr.) Work in magnetohydro-dynamics and magnetism	Luis Leloir (Arg.) Discovery of sugar nucleo-tides and their role in the biosynthesis of carbohydrates	A Solzhenitsyn (USSR) Novelist	Julius Axelrod (US) Bernard Katz (Brit.) Ulf von Euler (Swed.) Nerve transmission research	Norman Borlaug (US)	Paul Samuelson (US) Work in scientific analysis of economic theory
1971	Dennis Gabor (Brit.) Holography invention	Gerhard Herzberg (Can.) Molecule structure research	Pablo Neruda (Chile) Poet	Earl W Sutherland Jr (US) Action of hormones	Willy Brandt (Ger.)	Simon Kuznets (US) Economic growth of nations
1972	John Bardeen (US) Leon N Cooper (US) John R Schrieffer (US) Superconductivity theory	Christian B Anfinsen (US) Stanford Moore (US) William H Stein (US) Enzyme chemistry research	Heinrich Böll (Ger.) Novelist	Gerald M Edelman (US) Rodney Porter (Brit.) Research on the chemical structure of antibodies	no award	John Hicks (Brit.) Kenneth J. Arrow (US) Welfare theory and economic equilibrium theory
1973	Leo Esaki (Jap.) Ivar Giaever (US) Brian Josephson (Brit.) Superconductivity research	Ernst Fischer (Ger.) Geoffrey Wilkinson (Brit.) Organometallic chemistry	Patrick White (Aus.) Novelist	Karl von Frisch (Austria) Konrad Lorenz (Austria) Nikolaas Tinbergen (Neth.) Animal behaviour patterns	Henry Kissinger (US) Le Duc Tho (N. Viet.) (declined)	Wassily Leontief (US) Input analysis

	Physics	*Chemistry*	*Literature*	*Medicine*	*Peace*	*Economics*
1974	Sir Martin Ryle (Brit.) Antony Hewish (Brit.) Work in radio astronomy	Paul J Flory (US) Studies of long-chain molecules	Eyvind Johnson (Swed.) Harry Martinson (Swed.) Novelist and poet	Albert Claude (US) Christian R de Duve (Belg.) George E Palade (US) Cell structure research	Sato Eisaku (Jap.) Sean MacBride (Ire.)	Gunnar Myrdal (Swed.) Friedrich von Hayek (Brit.) Economic, social and institutional phenomena
1975	Aage Bohr (Den.) Ben R Mottelson (Den.) L James Rainwater (US) Atomic nucleus research paved way for nuclear fusion	J W Cornforth (Brit.) Vladimir Prelog (Switz.) Work in stereochemistry	Eugenio Montale (Ita.) Poet	Renato Dulbecco (US) Howard M Temin (US) David Baltimore (US) Tumour viruses research	Andrey D Sakharov (USSR)	Leonid Kantorovich (USSR) Tjalling Koopmans (US) Contribution to the theory of optimum allocation of resources
1976	Burton Richter (US) Samuel C C Ting (US) Elementary particles research	William Lipscomb (US) Structure of boranes	Saul Bellow (US) Novelist	Baruch Blumberg (US) D Carleton Gajdusek (US) Infectious diseases research	Mairead Corrigan (N. Ire.) Betty Williams (N. Ire.)	Milton Friedman (US) Consumption analysis and monetary theory
1977	Philip W Anderson (US) Sir Nevill Mott (Brit.) John H Van Vleck (US) Studies into behaviour of electrons in magnetic non-crystalline solids	Ilya Prigogine (Belg.) Widening the scope of thermodynamics	Vicente Aleixandre (Spa.) Poet	Rosalyn S Yalow (US) Roger Guillemin (US) Andrew Schally (US) Development of radio-immunoassay, research on pituitary hormones	Amnesty International (founded 1961)	Bertil Ohlin (Swed.) James Meade (Brit.) Contributions to theory of International trade
1978	Pyotr L Kapitsa (USSR) Invention of helium liquefier Robert W Wilson (US) Arno A Penzias (US) Discovery of cosmic micro-wave background radiation	Peter D Mitchell (Brit.) Formulation of a theory of energy transfer processes in biological systems	Isaac Bashevis Singer (US) Novelist	Werner Arber (Switz.) Daniel Nathans (US) Hamilton O Smith (US) Discovery of enzymes that fragment DNAs	Menachem Begin (Isr.) Anwar Sadat (Egy.)	Herbert A Simon (US) Decision-making processes in economic organisations
1979	Sheldon Glashow (US) Abdus Salam (Pak.) Steven Weinberg (US) Establishment of analogy between electromagnetism and subatomic particles	Herbert C Brown (US) Georg Wittig (Ger.) Introduction of compounds of boron and phosphorus in the synthesis of organic substances	Odysseus Elytis (Greece) Poet	Allan M Cormack (US) Godfrey N Hounsfield (Brit.) Development of computed axial tomography scan	Mother Teresa of Calcutta (India)	W Arthur Lewis (Brit.) Theodore W. Schultz (US) Analyses of economic processes in developing nations
1980	James W Cronin (US) Val L Fitch (US) Demonstration of simul-taneous violation of both charge-conjugation + parity inversion symmetries	Paul Berg (US) 1st preparation of hybrid DNA Walter Gilbert (US) Frederick Sanger (Brit.) Development of chemical analysis of DNA structure	Czeslaw Milosz (US) Poet	Baruj Benacerraf (US) George D Snell (US) Jean Dausset (Fr.) Investigations of genetic control of the response of immunological system to foreign substances	Adolfo Pérez Esquivel (Arg.)	Lawrence R Klein (US) Development and analysis of empirical models of business fluctuations
1981	Kai M Siegbahn (Swed.) Nicolaas Bloembergen (US) Electron spectroscopy for chemical analysis Arthur L Schawlow (US) Applications of lasers in spectroscopy	Fukui Kenichi (Jap.) Roald Hoffmann (US) Orbital symmetry inter-pretation of chemical reactions	Elias Canetti (Bulg.) Novelist and essayist	Roger W Sperry (US) Functions of the cerebral hemispheres Torsten N Wiesel (Swed.) David H Hubel (US) Processing of visual infor-mation by the brain	Office of the United Nations High Commissioner for Refugees (founded 1951)	James Tobin (US) Empirical macro-economic theories

	Physics	Chemistry	Literature	Medicine	Peace	Economics
1982	Kenneth G Wilson (US) Analysis of continuous phase transitions	Aaron Klug (Brit.) Determination of structure of biological substances	Gabriel G Márquez (Col.) Novelist, journalist and social critic	Sune K Bergström (Swe.) Bengt I Samuelsson (Swe.) John R Vane (Brit.) Prostaglandins research	Alva Myrdal (Swed.) Alfonso G. Robles (Mex.)	George Stigler (US) Economic effects of governmental regulation
1983	S Chandrasekhar (US) William A Fowler (US) Research into stars	Henry Taube (Can.) Study of electron transfer reactions	William Golding (Brit.) Novelist	Barbara McLintock (US) Discovery of mobile plant genes affecting heredity	Lech Walesa (Pol.)	Gerard Debreu (US) Mathematical proof of supply and demand theory
1984	Carlo Rubbia (Ita.) Simon van der Meer (Neth.) Discovery of subatomic particles W and Z which supports electro weak theory	Bruce Merrifield (US) Development of a method of polypeptide synthesis	Jaroslav Seifert (Czech.) Poet	Niels K Jerne (Den.) Georges J F Kohler (Ger.) Cesar Milstein (Arg.) Study of monoclonal antibodies	Desmond Tutu (SA)	Richard Stone (Brit.) Development of national income accounting system
1985	Klaus von Klitzing (Ger.) Discovery of quantised Hall effect concerning exact measurement of electrical resistance	Herbert A Hauptman (US) Jerome Karle (US) Mapping chemical structure of small molecules	Claude Simon (Fr.) Novelist	Michael S Brown (US) Joseph L Goldstein (US) Cholesterol metabolism cell receptors	International Physicians for the Prevention of Nuclear War (founded 1980)	Franco Modigliani (US) Financial market theory and household savings
1986	Ernst Ruska (Ger.) Gerd Binnig (Ger.) Heinrich Rohrer (Switz.) Electron microscopes	Dudley Herschbach (US) Yuan T Lee (US) John C Polyani (Can.) Analytical methodology	Wole Soyinka (Nigeria) Playwright and poet	Stanley Cohen (US) Rita Levi-Montalcini (Ita.) Discovery of regulatory agents concerning cell growths	Elie Wiesel (Fr.)	James M Buchanan (US) Political theories advocating limited government role in the economy
1987	J Georg Bednorz (Ger.) K Alex Müller (Switz.) Discovery of new superconducting materials	Charles J Pedersen (US) Donald J Cram (US) Jean-Marie Lehn (Fr.) molecule development	Joseph Brodsky (US) Poet and essayist	Tonegawa Susumu (Jap.) Study of genetic aspects of antibodies	Oscar Arias Sanchez (Costa Rica)	Robert M Solow (US) Economic growth theory
1988	Leon Lederman (US) Melvin Schwartz (US) Jack Steinberger (US) Subatomic particle research	Johann Deisenhofer (Ger.) Robert Huber (Ger.) Hartmut Michel (Ger.) Photosynthesis research	Naguib Mahfouz (Egypt) Novelist	James W Black (Brit.) Gertrude B Elion (US) George H Hitchings (US) Drug research	UN Peacekeeping Forces	Maurice Allais (Fr.) Market theory
1989	Hans Dehmelt (US) Wolfgang Paul (Ger.) Norman Ramsey (US)	Sydney Altman (US) Thomas Cech (US) RNA research	Camilo Jose Cela (Spa.) Poet and novelist	J Michael Bishop (US) Harold E Varmus (US)	Tenzin Gyatso (Tib.) Dalai Lama XIV	Trygve Haavelmo (Nor.) Quantitative economics
1990	Jerome Friedman (US) Henry Kendall (US) Richard Taylor (Can.) Quark model theory	Elias James Corey (US) Retrosynthetic analysis	Octavio Paz (Mex.) Poet	Joseph E Murray (US) E Donnall Thomas (US)	Mikhail Gorbachev (Rus.)	Harry M Markowitz (US) Merton Miller (US) William Sharpe (US) Financial economic theory
1991	Pierre-Gilles de Gennes (Fr.) Superconductivity theory	Richard R Ernst (Switz.) Spectroscopy development	Nadine Gordimer (SA)	Erwin Neher (Ger.) Bert Sakmann (Ger.) Patch-clamp technique	Aung San Suu Kyi (Burma)	Ronald Coase (Brit.) Transaction cost theory
1992	George Charpak (Fr.) Elementary particle study	Rudolph A Marcus (US) Electron transfer	Derek Walcott (St Lucia) Poet	Edmond H Fischer (US) Edwin G Krebs (US) Protein regulation	Rigoberta Menchú (Guat.)	Gary S Becker (US) Microeconomic analysis

	Physics	*Chemistry*	*Literature*	*Medicine*	*Peace*	*Economics*
1993	Russell Hulse (US) Joseph Hooton Taylor (US) Discovery of new type of pulsar	Kary Banks Mullis (US) Polymerase chain reaction Michael Smith (Can.) Mutagenesis theory	Toni Morrison (US) Novelist	Richard Roberts (Brit.) Phillip Allen Sharp (US) Mosaic genes discovery	Nelson Mandela (SA) F W de Klerk (SA)	Robert Fugel (US) Douglas North (US) Quantitative methods as reasons for economic change
1994	Clifford Shull (US) Bertram Brockhouse (Can.) Study of neutron beams	George Olah (US) Carbocations	Kenzaburo Oe (Jap.) Novelist	Martin Rodbell (US) Alfred G Gilman (US) Discovery of G protein	Yasser Arafat (Pal.) Shimon Peres (Isr.) Yitzhak Rabin (Isr.)	John Nash (US) John Harsanyi (US) Reinhard Selten (Ger.) Games theory
1995	Martin L Pearl (US) Tau lepton discovery Frederick Reines (US) Neutrino detection	F Sherwood Rowland (US) Mario Molina (Mex.) Paul Crutzen (Ned.) Ozone layer research	Seamus Heaney (Ire.) Poet	Edward B Lewis (US) Eric F Wieschaus (US) C Nüsslein-Volhard (Ger.) Genes theory	Joseph Rotblat (Brit.) Pugwash Conferences on Science and World Affairs	Robert E Lucas (US) Macroeconomic analysis
1996	David M Lee (US) Douglas D Osheroff (US) Robert C Richardson (US) Discovery of superfluidity in helium-3	Harry Kroto (Brit.) Robert Curl (US) Richard Smalley (US) Discovery of C_{60} molecule	Wislawa Szymborska (Pol.) Poet	Peter C Doherty (Aus.) Rolf M Zinkernagel (Switz.)	Jose Ramos-Horta (E. Timor) Bishop Carlos Belo of Dili	James Mirrlees (Brit.) William Vickrey (Can.)
1997	Steven Chu (US) Claude Cohen-Tannoudji (Fr.) William D Phillips (US) Atom research	John Walker (Brit.) Paul Boyer (US) Jens Skou (Den.) Molecular biology research	Dario Fo (Ita.) Playwright	Stanley B Prusiner (US) Discovery of prions	Ms Jodie Williams (US) and International Campaign to Ban Landmines	Robert Merton (US) Myron Scholes (US) Fischer Black (US) Contribution to economic theory
1998	Robert B Laughlin (US) Horst L Stormer (Ger.) Daniel C Tsui (US) Quantum fluids	John Pople (Brit.) Walter Kohn (USA) Quantum theory application to molecules	José Saramago (Port.) Novelist	Robert S Furghgott (US) Louis J Ignarro (US) Ferid Murad (US) Cardiovascular research	John Hume (N. Ire.) David Trimble (N. Ire.) For 'Good Friday' Agreement	Amartya Sen (India) Welfare economics
1999	Gerardus T Hooft (Neth.) Martinus J G Veltman (Neth.) Study of electro-weak interactions	Ahmed Zewai (Egypt) Femtosecond spectroscopy	Günter Grass (Ger.) Novelist	Günter Blobel (Ger.) Study of proteins	Médecins Sans Frontières (Belg.)	Robert A Mundell (Can.) Fiscal policy analysis
2000	Herbert Kroemer (Ger.) Zhores Alferov (Ger.) Developing semiconductor heterostructures Jack S Kilby (US) Invention of the integrated circuit	Alan J Heeger (US) Alan G MacDiarmid (US) Hideki Shirakawa (Japan) Discovery of conductive polymers	Gao Xingjian (China)	Arvid Carlsson (Sweden) Paul Greengard (US) Eric Kandel (US) Research into signal transduction in the nervous system	Kim Dae Jung (S. Korea) Work in reconciliation with North Korea	James J Heckman (Ger.) Daniel L McFadden (US) Contribution to economic theory and analysis
2001	Eric A Cornell (US) Wolfgang Ketterle (Ger.) Carl E Wieman (US) Bose-Einstein condensation in dilute gases of alkali atoms and studies of the properties of the condensates	William S Knowles (US) Ryoji Noyori (Jap.) Work on chirally catalysed hydro-genation reactions K Barry Sharpless (US) Work on chirally catalysed oxidation reactions	V S Naipaul (Trin.)	Leland H Hartwell (US) R Timothy Hunt (Brit.) Sir Paul M Nurse (Brit.) Discoveries of key regulators of the cell cycle	United Nations Kofi Annan (Gha.) for their work for a better-organised and more peaceful world	George A Akerlof (US) A Michael Spence (US) Joseph E Stiglitz (US) Analyses of markets with asymmetric information

	Physics	Chemistry	Literature	Medicine	Peace	Economics
2002	Raymond Davis Jr (US) Masatoshi Koshiba (Jap.) Detection of cosmic neutrinos Riccardo Giacconi (US) Discovery of cosmic X-ray sources	John B Fenn (US) Koichi Tanaka (Jap.) Soft desorption ionisation methods Kurt Wüthrich (Switz.) Nuclear magnetic resonance spectroscopy	Imre Kertész (Hung.)	Sydney Brenner (Brit.) H Robert Horvitz (US) John E Sulston (Brit.) Study of genetic regulation of organ development and programmed cell death	Jimmy Carter (US) for his efforts to find peaceful solutions to international conflicts	Daniel Kahneman (Isr.) Application of psychological research into economic science Vernon L Smith (US) Experiments in the study of alternative market mechanisms
2003	Alexei A Abrikosov (Rus.) Vitaly L Ginzburg (Rus.) Anthony J Leggett (Brit.) Pioneering contributions to the theory of superconductors and superfluids	Peter Agre (US) Roderick MacKinnon (US) Discoveries concerning channels in cell membranes	John M Coetzee (SA)	Paul C Lauterbur (US) Sir Peter Mansfield (Brit.) Discoveries concerning magnetic resonance imaging	Shirin Ebadi (Iran) For her efforts for democracy and human rights, particularly those of women and children	Robert F Engle III (US) Clive W J Granger (Brit.) Engle: methods of analysing economic time series with time-varying volatility Granger: methods of analysing economic time series with common trends
2004	David J Gross (US) H David Politzer (US) Frank Wilczek (US) Discovery of asymptotic freedom in the theory of the strong interaction	Aaron Ciechanover (Isr.) Avram Hershko (Isr.) Irwin Rose (US) Discovery of ubiquitin-mediated protein degradation	Elfriede Jelinek (Austria)	Richard Axel (US) Linda B Buck (US) Discoveries of odorant receptors and the organisation of the olfactory system	Wangari Maathai (Ken.) For her contribution to sustainable development, democracy and peace	Finn E Kydland (Nor.) Edward C Prescott (US) Contributions to dynamic macroeconomics: the time consistency of economic �policy and the driving forces behind business cycles
2005	Roy J Glauber (US) John L Hall (US) Theodor W Hänsch (US) Glauber awarded half the prize for quantum theory of optical coherence. Hall and Hänsch awarded half for work in precision spectroscopy	Robert Grubbs (US) Richard Schrock (US) Yves Chauvin (Fr.) Work in the field of olefin metathesis	Harold Pinter (Brit.)	Barry J Marshall (Aus.) J Robin Warren (Aus.) Discovery of bacterium *Helicobacter pylori*	Mohamed ElBaradei (Egy.) International Atomic Energy Agency For efforts to prevent nuclear energy from being used by military	Robert Avmann (Isr.) Thomas Schelling (US) Game theory analysis
2006	John C Mather (US) George F Smoot (US) Discovery of the black body form and anisotropy of the cosmic microwave background radiation	Roger D Kornberg (US) Study of the molecular basis of eukaryotic transcription	Orhan Pamuk (Turkey)	Andrew Z Fire (US) Craig C Mello (US) Discovery of RNA interference	Muhammad Yunus (Bang.) Grameen Bank For efforts to create economic and social development	Edmund Phelps (US) Analysis of short-run and long-run effects of economic policy
2007	Albert Fert (Fr.) Peter Grünberg (Ger.) Discovery of giant magnetoresistance which revolutionised read heads in disk drives	Gerhard Ertl (Ger.) Study of chemical processes on solid surfaces	Doris Lessing (Brit.)	Mario Capecchi (US) Martin Evans (Brit.) Oliver Smithies (US) Gene targeting research	Al Gore (US) �Intergovernmental Panel on Climate Change	Leonid Hurwicz (US) Eric Maskin (US) Roger Myerson (US) Mechanism design
2008	Yoichiro Nambu (US) Makoto Kobayashi (Jap.) Toshihide Maskawa (Jap.) Discovery of mechanism of spontaneous broken symmetry in subatomic physics	Osamu Shimomura (Jap.) Martin Chalfie (US) Roger Y Tsien (US) Discovery and development of green fluorescent protein	J M G Le Clézio (Fr.)	Harald zur Hausen (Ger.) Discovery of the role of papilloma viruses Françoise Barré-Sinoussi (Fr.) Luc Montagnier (Fr.) For their discovery of HIV	Martti Ahtisaari (Fin.) �Peace negotiations in Kosovo	Paul Krugman (US) Contributions to New Trade Theory and New Economic Geography

	Physics	*Chemistry*	*Literature*	*Medicine*	*Peace*	*Economics*
2009	Charles K Kao (US) Development and use of fibre optics in telecommunications Willard S Boyle (US) George E Smith (US) Invention of an imaging semiconductor circuit – the CCD sensor. Kao was awarded half the prize and other half was shared	Venkatraman Ramakrishnan (US) Thomas A Steitz (US) Ada E Yonath (Isr.) Study of the structure and function of the ribosome	Herta Müller (Ger.)	Elizabeth Blackburn (US) Carol W Greider (US) Jack W Szostak (US) Chromosome research	Barack Obama (US) Efforts to strengthen international diplomacy	Elinor Ostrom (US) Oliver E Williamson (US) Analysis of economic governance
2010	Andre Geim (Rus.) Konstantin Novoselov (Rus.) groundbreaking experiments regarding two-dimensional material grapheme	Richard F. Heck (US) Ei-ichi Negishi (US) Akira Suzuki (Jap.) palladium-catalyzed cross couplings in organic synthesis	Mario Vargas Llosa (Peru)	Robert G. Edwards (Brit.) development of in vitro fertilization	Liu Xiaobo (China) long struggle for human rights in China	Peter A. Diamond (US) Dale T. Mortensen (US) Christopher A. Pissarides (Brit.) analysis of markets with search frictions
2011	Saul Perlmutter (US) Brian P. Schmidt (US) Adam G. Riess (US) discovery of the accelerating expansion of the Universe	Dan Shechtman (Isr.) discovery of quasicrystals	Tomas Tranströmer (Sweden)	Bruce A. Beutler (US) Jules A. Hoffmann (Fra.) Ralph M. Steinman (US) immunity research	Ellen Johnson Sirleaf (Lib.) Leymah Gbowee (Lib.) Tawakkol Karman (Yem.) women's rights	Thomas J. Sargent (US) Christopher A. Sims (US) empirical research on cause and effect in the macroeconomy
2012	Serge Haroche (Fra.) David J. Wineland (US) measuring and manipulation of individual quantum systems	Robert J. Lefkowitz (US) Brian K. Kobilka (US) studies of G-protein-coupled receptors	Mo Yan (China)	Sir John B. Gurdon (Brit.) Shinya Yamanaka (Jap.) discovery that mature cells can be reprogrammed to become pluripotent	European Union (EU)	Alvin E. Roth (US) Lloyd S. Shapley (US) theory of stable allocations and the practice of market design

NB: Many of the award winners listed above have dual nationalities. The nationality given is therefore not necessarily the country of birth.

General Information

Royal Swedish Academy of Sciences awards the Physics, Chemistry and Economics Prizes.
Swedish Karolinska Institute awards the Medicine Prize.
Swedish Academy of Arts awards the Literature Prize.
The Peace Prize is awarded by a committee of 5 members of the Norwegian Storting.
Nils Dalen, the 1912 Nobel Prizewinner for Physics, was blinded in 1913 by an explosion whilst conducting an experiment.
Eight fathers and sons have won Nobels although William and Lawrence Bragg were the only father and son to win a prize in the same year.
A woman had never won the Economics Prize until 2009.
Jan and Niko Tinbergen are the only siblings to win Nobels.
Husband and wife Pierre and Marie Curie, and their daughter Irene and her husband Frédéric Joliot-Curie, all won Nobels.

NOBEL PRIZE WINNERS

Organisations

Chairmen or Chief Executives (as at October 2013)

Aberdeen Football Club Stewart Milne (C)
Adidas-Salomon Herbert Hainer (CE)
Amstrad Simon Ball (CE)
Ann Summers Jacqueline Gold (CE)
Apple Inc Arthur D. Levinson (C); Tim Cook (CE)
Arsenal Football Club Sir John "Chips" Keswick (C)
Arts Council England Sir Peter Bazalgette (C); Alan Davey (CE)
Aston Villa Football Club Randy Lerner (C)
AT&T Inc Randall Stephenson (C & CE)
@UK (aka ATUK) Ronald Duncan (C); Lyn Duncan (CE)
Barclays Sir David Walker (C); Antony Jenkins (CE)
BAT (British American Tobacco) Richard Burrows (C); Nicandro Durante (CE)
BBC Lord Patten of Barnes (C); Lord Hall of Birkenhead (Director-General)
BMW Dr Norbert Reithofer (CE)
Boeing W James McNerney Jr (C & CE)
Boosey & Hawkes John Minch (CE)
BP Bob Dudley (CE)
Bradford & Bingley Richard Pym (C)
British Airways Keith Williams (CE)
BSkyB Nicholas Ferguson (C); Jeremy Darroch (CE)
BT Sir Michael Rake (C); Gavin Patterson (CE)
BUPA Stuart Fletcher (CE)
Burger King Alexandre Behring (C); Bernardo Hees (CE)
Cadbury Irene Rosenfeld (C & CE)
Camelot Dianne Thompson (CE)
Carillion Philip Rogerson (C); Richard Howson (CE)
Carpetright Lord Harris of Peckham (C); Darren Shapland (CE)
Carrefour Georges Plassat (C & CE)
Centrica Roger Carr (C); Sam Laidlaw (CE)
Channel 4 Lord Burns (C); David Abraham (CE)
Coca Cola Company Muhtar Kent (C & CE)
Coutts and Company Lord Home (C), Rory Tapner (CE)
Daimler Dieter Zetsche (C & CE)
DC Thomson Andrew Thomson (C)
Debenhams Nigel Northridge (C); Michael Sharp (CE)
De La Rue Nicholas Brookes (C); Tim Cobbold (CE)
Diageo (Guinness & Grand Met) Franz Humer (C); Ivan Menezes (CE)
Easyjet Carolyn McCall (CE)
Economist Group, The Rupert Pennant-Rea (C); Chris Stibbs (CE)
EDF Energy Vincent de Rivaz (CE)
Energis Archie Norman (C); John Pluthero (CE)
Eurotunnel PLC Jacques Gounon (C&CE)
Fiat John Elkann (C); Sergio Marchionne (CE)
First City Care Grahame Harding (C)
Ford Motor Company William C. Ford, Jr (C); Alan R. Mulally (CE)
France Telecom Didier Lombard (C&CE)
Friends Provident Trevor Matthews (CE)
Friends Reunited Owned by DC Thomson
FTSE Group Mark Makepeace (CE)
General Motors Daniel Akerson (C & CE)
GKN Roy Brown (C); Nigel Stein (CE)
GlaxoSmithKline Sir Christopher Gent (C); Andrew Witty (CE)
Greene King Timothy Bridge (C); Rooney Anand (CE)
Guardian Media Group Amelia Fawcett (C); Andrew Miller (CE)
GUS Sir Victor Blank (C)
Halfords Matt Davies (CE)
Hanson PLC Patrick O'Shea (CE)
Harrods Michael Ward (CE)
Hays Alan Thomson (C); Alistair Cox (CE)
HBOS Lord Stevenson of Coddenham (C)
House of Fraser Don McCarthy (C); John King (CE)
HSBC Douglas Flint (C); Stuart Gulliver (CE)
IBM Ginni Rometty (C & CE)
Imperial Tobacco Iain Napier (C); Alison Cooper (CE)
ITV PLC Archie Norman (C); Adam Crozier (CE)
J D Wetherspoon Tim Martin (C); John Hutson (CE)
Jessops Peter Jones (C & CE)
J J B Sports Keith Jones (C); David Williams (CE)
Johnson Matthey Tim Stevenson (C); Neil Carson (CE)
John Lewis Partnership Charlie Mayfield (C)
John Menzies Iain Napier (C)
J Sainsbury David Tyler (C); Justin King (CE)
Kellogg James M Jenness (C); John A. Bryant (CE)
KFC Roger Eaton (C & CE)
Kingfisher Daniel Bernard (C); Ian Cheshire (CE)
Laura Ashley Khoo Kay Peng (C); Lilian Tan (CE)
Lego Jørgen Vig Knudstorp (CE)
Leicester City Football Club Vichai Srivaddhanaprabha (C)
Liverpool FC Tom Werner (C)
Lloyds Banking Group Sir Win Bischoff (C); António Horta Osório (CE)
London Stock Exchange Christopher Gibson-Smith (C); Xavier Rolet (CE)
Manchester City PLC Khaldoon Al Mubarak (C)
Manchester United PLC Joel and Avram Glazer (joint C)
Marks & Spencer Robert Swannell (C); Mark Bolland (CE)
Wm Morrison Sir Ian Gibson (C); Dalton Philips (CE)
Motorola Dennis Woodside (C & CE)
National Westminster Bank Sir Philip Hampton (C); Stephen Hester (CE)
Nestlé Peter Brabeck-Letmathe (C); Paul Bulcke (CE)
Newcastle United Mike Ashley (C)
News Corp K R Murdoch (C&CE)
Nissan Carlos Ghosn (C & CE)
Nottingham Forest PLC Fawaz Al-Hasawi (C)
Ocado Michael Grade (C); Tim Steiner (CE)
Old Mutual PLC Patrick O'Sullivan (C)
Orange S.A (formerly France Télécom S.A.) Stéphane Richard (C & CE)
Orange UK Olaf Swantee (CE)
Pearson PLC Glen Moreno (C); John Fallon (CE)
Pension Protection Fund Lady Judge (C); Alan Rubenstein (CE)
Prudential Paul Manduca (C); Tidjane Thiam (CE)
Railway Heritage Trust Sir William McAlpine (C)
Rio Tinto Jan du Plessis (C); Sam Walsh (CE)
Rolls-Royce PLC Simon Robertson (C); John Rishton (CE)
Royal Bank of Scotland Ross McEwan (CE)
Royal Opera House Alex Beard (CE)
Ryanair Michael O'Leary (CE)
Sage Group Donald Brydon (C); Guy Berruyer (CE)
Santander UK Lord Burns (C); Ana Patricia Botín (CE)
Scottish Power Ignacio Sánchez Galán (C); Jose Luis del Valle Doblado (CE)
Siemens Gerhard Cromme (C); Joe Kaeser (CE)
Signet Jewelers Todd Stitzer (C); Terry Burman (CE)
Sony Osamu Nagayama (C); Kazuo Hirai (CE)
Sports Direct Keith Hellawell (C); Dave Forsey (CE)
Tata Steel Europe (formerly Corus) Karl-Ulrich Kohler (CE)
Tate and Lyle Sir Peter Gershon (C); Javed Ahmed (CE)
Taylor Woodrow Norman Askew (C); Ian Smith (CE)
Tesco Sir Richard Broadbent (C); Philip Clarke (CE)
Thomson Reuters David Thomson (C); James C. Smith (CE)
Time Warner Jeffrey Bewkes (C&CE)
Tottenham Hotspur PLC Daniel Levy (C)
Toyota Takeshi Uchiyamada (C); Akio Toyoda (CE)
Unilever Michael Treschow (C); Paul Polman (CE)
Virgin Group Sir Richard Branson (C)
Vodafone Gerard Kleisterlee (C); Vittorio Colao (CE)
Volkswagen Group Ferdinand K. Piëch (C); Martin Winterkorn (CE)
Walmart Samuel Robson Walton (C); Mike Duke (CE)
Wellcome Trust Sir William Castell (C)

Key: C = Chairman; CE = Chief Executive

Organisations, Movements and Bodies

ACP the 68 African, Caribbean and Pacific countries which have special trade relations with the European Union.

Action Directe left wing French revolutionary group formed in 1979 and responsible for numerous bombings.

Agenda 21 blueprint for action adopted at the 1992 Earth Summit in Rio setting out requirements for sustainable development.

Aipac American Israel Public Affairs Committee, Israel's official lobbying arm in the USA and as such part of the influential US Jewish lobby. Based in Washington, DC.

Akali Dal supreme political organisation of the Indian Sikh community. Founded in December 1920 and based in the Punjab.

Alawi Islamic sub-sect signifying followers of the Caliph Ali, revered by Shias. Prominent in Syria, Lebanon and Turkey.

Alfaro Vive Carajo! translates as 'Alfaro Lives, Dammit!' Ecuadorean left-wing nationalist guerrilla group named in memory of the President 1895–1901, 1906–11.

Al-Fatah (Arabic: victory) Movement for the National Liberation of Palestine. Mainstream component of the PLO founded by Yasser Arafat in 1958.

Alpha 66 paramilitary group of anti-Castroites based in Miami. Formed in 1962 and named after its 66 founder members.

Al-Qaeda international terrorist group formed in the late 1980s by Osama bin Laden and Muhammad Atef and dedicated to opposing non-Islamic governments with force and violence.

Amazon Pact signed in July 1978 by Bolivia, Brazil, Colombia, Ecuador, Guyana, Peru, Suriname and Venezuela. Committed to preserving ecological -balance of the Amazon region.

Amnesty International founded in 1961 by Peter Benenson and Sean Macbride Kropotkin, it campaigns for the release of prisoners of -conscience.

ANC African National Congress, South Africa's -principal anti-apartheid organisation, banned 1960–90 but now the majority party in ruling coalition.

Angry Brigade small anarchistic group in the UK in existence in 1968–71, which carried out several bombings.

Anti-Nazi League left wing organisation in the UK formed in the 1970s to combat racist parties and more recently the BNP.

Anzus security pact between Australia, NZ and the USA signed in San Francisco on 1 September 1951. Initially formed as deterrent to Japan but no longer operational.

Apostles Cambridge University Conversation Society founded in 1820. Guy Burgess and Anthony Blunt were recruited from the Apostles by Soviet Intelligence.

Arab League organisation formed in 1945 originally for mutual economic aid but now dealing with the Middle East peace process.

ASEAN Association of South East Asian Nations. Founded in 1967, members include Indonesia, Malaysia, Singapore, Thailand, Philippines and Brunei.

Baader-Meinhof Gang extremist left wing terrorist group active in Germany in the late 1960s; later became the Rote Armee Fraktion.

Ba'ath movement founded in Syria in the 1940s by Michel Aflaq with the aim of creating a single socialist Arab nation.

Band Aid charity formed by Bob Geldof and Midge Ure in December 1984 for the purpose of famine relief in Ethiopia.

BCCI Bank of Credit and Commerce International which collapsed in July 1991. Lord Justice Bingham criticised the Bank of England's supervisory role.

Benelux grouping of Belgium, Netherlands and Luxembourg for a mutually advantageous economic climate. Founded in 1932 by the Convention of Ouchy.

Black Berets élite paramilitary police force formed by the Soviet Interior Ministry in 1987. Aka Omon, they had a reputation for ruthlessness, especially in the Baltic States.

Black Sash South African women's anti-apartheid organisation formed in 1955 as the Women's Defence of the Constitution League in response to the removal of the vote for coloureds. The black sash was worn as a peaceful protest against violation of rights.

Black September Palestinian terrorist group, named in memory of the Jordanian expulsion of Palestinians in Sepember 1970. Responsible for the Munich Olympic massacre of Israeli athletes.

B'Nai B'rith international Jewish organisation founded in 1843 and based in Washington, DC.

BND the German Federal Intelligence Service, founded in 1956 under the ex-Nazi Reinhard Gehlen and based in Munich.

Boss Bureau of State Security, a now defunct branch of the South African Intelligence Service. Founded in 1969 by PM J B Vorster.

Boundaries Commission UK body responsible for defining the boundaries of parliamentary constituencies.

Boys Brigade founded by William Smith in 1883.

Boys' Clubs although boys' clubs were in existence in British cities in the 19th century, the National Association was founded in 1925.

BRA Bougainville Revolutionary Army, a guerrilla force fighting for independence for the mineral-rich island of Bougainville from the state of Papua New Guinea.

Brigate Rosse (Red Brigades) leftwing urban guerrillas responsible for a spate of kidnappings and bombings in the 1970s culminating in the murder of former PM Aldo Moro in 1978.

British Academy Established in 1901; full title 'British Academy for the Promotion of Historical, Philosophical and Philological Studies'.

British Council Established in 1934 and funded by the government for the purpose of representing British culture abroad. With offices in more than 80 countries, it arranges for visits by British artists, lecturers and performers, mounts exhibitions, teaches English and provides libraries of British books.

Brookings Institution Influential US think-tank based in Washington, DC, and comprised of distinguished figures from various fields.

Bruges Group Informal Conservative grouping of 'Eurosceptics', named from a speech made in the Belgian city of Bruges on 20 September 1988 by Margaret Thatcher.

Camorra Network of groups engaged in organised crime in Naples.

Caricom Caribbean Community and Common Market, an alliance of English-speaking Caribbean countries promoting economic, political and cultural unity.

Central African Federation Federation of the British colonies of Northern Rhodesia (Zambia), Southern Rhodesia (Zimbabwe) and Nyasaland (Malawi). Established in 1953 and dissolved in 1963.

Central Committee Organ of the Communist Party of Soviet Union whose full members elected the powerful Politburo and secretariat.

CERM Centre d'Exploitation du Renseignement Militaire (Centre for Exploitation of Military intelligence). French internal security agency, formerly called Deuxième Bureau until 10 Dec. 1971.

CERN European Centre for Nuclear Research, a co-operative agency with 12 member countries founded in 1952 and located outside Geneva.

Charter 88 Pressure group demanding a new constitutional settlement guaranteeing human rights in the UK. In November 2007 it merged with the New Politics Network to form Unlock Democracy.

Chetniks Serbian nationalist army of resistance led by Draza Mihailovic, which occupied parts of east and south Yugoslavia during the second world war. Term now applies to all Serb irregulars.

CHOGM Commonwealth Heads of Government Meeting, the main policy-making body of the Commonwealth, meeting every 2 years.

CIA Central Intelligence Agency, often referred to internally as 'The Company'. Its HQ is at Langley, Virginia.

Civic Forum Czech coalition of parties formed during the Velvet Revolution in November 1989 as opposition to communism.

Club of Rome non-governmental association of industrialists, policy analysts and scientists, seeking to bring their different perspectives to bear on problems of the global economy.

CND Campaign for Nuclear Disarmament, a British organisation which mobilised mass opposition to nuclear weapons in general and the UK's independent nuclear deterrent in particular. Founder members in 1958 include Bertrand Russell.

Comecon Informal name for the Council for Mutual Economic Assistance (CMEA), founded in 1949 as a response to the USA's Marshall Plan. Members included Warsaw Pact countries (excluding Albania) and Cuba, Mongolia and Vietnam.

Committee of 100 Militant offshoot of CND, formed in 1960, headed by Bertrand Russell; its main weapon was 'sit down' protests.

Commonwealth of Nations Voluntary association of 53 member states which evolved from the British Empire, latterly concerned with postcolonial economic and cultural development. Originated with the 1931 Statute of Westminster. Elizabeth II is monarch of sixteen Commonwealth states. Current (2013) Secretary-General is Kamalesh Sharma, a former High Commissioner for India in London.

Confederation of British Industry CBI, formed in 1965 via merger of Federation of British Industries, British Employers' Confederation and National Association of British Manufacturers.

Congress Bicameral legislature of the USA consisting of a 100-member senate elected for 6 years, with a third being renewed every 2 years, and a 435-member House of Representatives (lower house) elected for 2 years. Each state sends 2 senators to the upper house.

Contadora Group Latin American peace initiative in Central America set up by Colombia, Mexico, Panama and Venezuela in January 1983; controversially recognises Nicaraguan Sandinistas.

Contras Nicaraguan counter-revolutionary forces financed during the 1980s by the US Reagan administration, in part illegally, as revealed by the Iran–Contra affair. Many Contras offered allegiance to the dictator Anastasio Somoza, ousted in 1979.

Council of Europe Intergovernmental organisation with its HQ in Strasbourg. Founded on 5 May 1949 to promote civil society and human rights.

CPLA Cordillera People's Liberation Army, a guerrilla group operating in the Philippines until it signed a ceasefire with President Corazon Aquino on 13 Sept. 1986.

Creep Committee to Re-elect the President. Established to re-elect Richard Nixon in 1972 by orchestrating a dirty tricks campaign against his Democratic opponents, which led to Watergate scandal.

Dáil Éireann 166-seat lower house of the legislature of Eire. Members are elected for 5-year term on the basis of proportional representation. Translates as 'Assembly of Ireland'.

Death Squads Rightwing paramilitary groups often associated with conniving governments who assassinate those deemed a threat to the state. Term was coined in the 1960s in Brazil, when the police force used such squads, perhaps financed by the CIA.

Dergue Military ruling body in Ethiopia (1973-91), closely associated with the Marxist-Leninist regime of Lt-Col. Mengistu Haile Mariam.

Deuxième Bureau French internal security agency run by the Ministry of the Interior and Administative Reform. Changed its name to CERM in 1971.

DGSE Direction Générale de la Sécurité Extérieure (General Directorate for External Security), the French foreign secret service established on 4 April 1982.

Diet Japanese bicameral legislature consisting of a House of Representatives (lower chamber) elected for a 4-year term and a House of Councillors (upper chamber), half of whose members are elected every 3 years.

Dina Chilean secret police serving the military junta during 1970s.

DST Direction de la Surveillance du Territoire. The French counterpart to the FBI or MI5.

Duma The name of the parliament of Imperial Russia but now referring to the lower house of the new Russian parliament.

Earth Day Annual worldwide effort on 22 April by pressure groups to focus public attention on environmental issues.

Earth Summit World environmental conference also known as the UN Conference on Environment and Development (UNCED), held in Rio de Janeiro on 3–14 June 1992 and billed as the largest-ever gathering of world leaders.

EBRD European Bank for Reconstruction and Development, founded May 1990 by 39 countries (including USA and Russia), plus the European Commission and the European Investment Bank. Conceived by French president François Mitterrand to aid the Eastern European transition to a market economy.

Economic and Social Council ECOSOC, one of the 6 principal organs of the UN, established under Chapter X of the UN Charter, responsible for co-ordination of UN specialised agencies.

ECSC European Coal and Steel Community, which brought Italy and Benelux countries into Franco-German co-operation framework of 1950 Schuman Plan, forerunner of EEC.

EEC European Economic Community, founded under Treaty of Rome in March 1957 by France, Germany, Italy and Benelux countries; came into operation in January 1958.

EFTA European Free Trade Association, set up in 1960 under the Stockholm Convention. Its 7 original members were UK, Denmark (left in 1973 to join the EC), Portugal (left 1986), Austria, Switzerland, Norway and Sweden.

EMS European Monetary System, an arrangement for closer monetary co-operation within the EC, operational from March 1979.

EMU European Monetary Union, dating back to the Werner report of 1971; works to promote the smooth operation of capital transfers within participating countries.

EOKA National Organisation of Cypriot Fighters, Greek Cypriot movement which from 1955 until the independence of Cyprus in 1960 fought a guerrilla campaign against British rule.

ERM Exchange Rate Mechanism, regarded as the core of the EMS but badly damaged when the UK and Italy pulled out as a result of Black Wednesday in September 1992.

ESA European Space Agency, formed in 1973 as a result of the merger of the European Space Research Organisation and the European Launcher Development Organisation and committed to a European Space policy.

ETA Basque Fatherland and Freedom, militant separatist organisation which fights for the independence of the Basque country from Spain.

EU European Union, currently consisting of 27 member states: Belgium, France, West Germany, Italy, Luxembourg, The Netherlands (1957), Denmark, Eire, UK (1973), Greece (1981), Portugal, Spain (1986), Austria, Finland, Sweden (1995), Cyprus, Czech Republic, Estonia, Hungary, Latvia, Lithuania, Malta, Poland, Slovakia, Slovenia (2004), Bulgaria and Romania (2007). Motto: United in Diversity; anthem: Ode to Joy.

European Communities more generally referred to as the EU since 1 November 1993, the date on which the Maastricht Treaty on the European Union came into force.

European Court of Justice set up in Luxembourg under 1958 Treaty of Rome and responsible for ruling on whether EU member countries are acting in accord with Community Law.

European Parliament one of 3 principal institutions of the EU, with the Council of Ministers and European Commission. Elections held every 5 years and parliament meets in Strasbourg.

Falange Spain's rightwing nationalist party formed in 1937 by General Francisco Franco and formally abolished on 1 April 1977.

Falashas name assigned to Ethiopian Jews, which they themselves reject in favour of the name Beta Israel (House of Israel).

FAO Food and Agricultural Organisation founded in 1945; it aims to combat malnutrition and hunger.

Fascism a 20th-century ideology which has been interpreted as rightwing or centrist in orientation. Derived from the Latin fasces (bundle of rods sometimes including an axe used by Roman magistrates as a symbol of authority), term became prominent following Mussolini's 'March on Rome' in 1922.

FBI Federal Bureau of Investigation, part of US Justice Department dealing with violations of federal law; has its HQ in Washington DC.

FCO Foreign and Commonwealth Office, UK government department responsible for external relations and representation. The FCO was created in 1968 through the merger of the original Foreign Office (formed in 1782) and the Commonwealth Office.

FLN Front de Libération Nationale (National Liberation Front), political organisation during Algeria's independence struggle (1954–62). Founded 1954 under leadership of Ahmed Ben Bella.

FLNC Front de Libération Nationale de la Corse (Corsican National Liberation Front). Formed in May 1976, it is a clandestine extremist group fighting for self-determination from France.

Force de Frappe independent French nuclear weapons strike force instigated by Charles de Gaulle in December 1960 as a protest at the special relationship between the UK and USA.

Four D's democratisation, disarmament, decartelisation and denazification, implemented against the defeated Germans by the Allies and agreed at Potsdam.

Friends of the Earth international environmental pressure group, originating in the USA as an offshoot of the Sierra Club. It supports research on environmental issues, lobbies policy makers, and has been most successful in increasing public awareness.

G8 Group of 8 most powerful industrialised countries: Canada, France, Germany, Italy, Japan, Russia, USA and the UK.

GCHQ Government Communications Headquarters, part of the UK intelligence machinery which provides government departments and military commands with signals intelligence. Established in 1946 as the successor to the Government Code and Cipher School.

Geneva Conventions body of international humanitarian laws adopted in Geneva on 12 August 1949 and endorsed by the UN, which are intended to protect and assist war victims.

Gleneagles Agreement the 1977 decision by Commonwealth heads of government to ban official sporting links with South Africa until the dismantling of apartheid. Named after the golf club in Scotland which was the venue for the meeting.

Gosplan Soviet Union's State Planning Committee established in 1921 to work out a single state economic plan.

Greenpeace pressure group whose members, now organised internationally with a headquarters in Amsterdam, engage in non-violent action to disrupt environmentally damaging projects. Founded 1971 when nuclear tests on Amchitka Island, Alaska were disrupted.

Grey Panthers US pressure group organised to promote the interests of the elderly. Name derived from the Black Panthers.

Guardian Angels US volunteer group founded in 1979 to fight crime in New York City. Wearing red berets, they have been accused of being vigilantes.

Gulag Soviet acronym, Chief Directorate of Labour Camps. Established in 1930, estimates put number of inmates in the 1940s at over 8 million, of whom 85% were political prisoners.

Haganah Jewish defence force which operated from 1920 until the creation of Israel in 1948 to defend Jewish settlements in Palestine.

Hallstein Doctrine West German policy in 1950s and 1960s of severing diplomatic relations with any state recognising East Germany and refusing relations with any communist country except the Soviet Union.

Hamas acronym for Islamic Resistance Movement, a radical islamic group operating in Israeli-occupied territorities. Founded in February 1988 by Sheikh Ahmed Ismail Yassin.

harkis Algerian Muslim auxiliary soldiers in the service of the French army during the French occupation of Algeria 1938–62.

Hezbollah Party of God. The main fundamentalist, Shia movement in Lebanon, operating in the south against Israel.

Human Rights Watch US-based international human rights organisation, the second largest worldwide after Amnesty International. Originated in 1978 with HQ in New York.

IAEA International Atomic Energy Agency, autonomous organisation within the UN which aims to promote the peaceful use of nuclear energy; founded in 1957, and based in Vienna.

IBRD International Bank for Reconstruction and Development, a UN specialised agency more commonly known as the World Bank. Based in Washington, DC, and established in 1945 following the Bretton Woods conference, it is the largest single source of lending for development by its worldwide members.

ICAO International Civil Aviation Organisation, UN specialised agency which aims to establish international standards necessary for the safety and security of air transport.

ICRC International Committee of the Red Cross, founded in 1863 by Swiss philanthropist Henry Dunant after witnessing the battle of Solferino in 1859.

IMF International Monetary Fund, usually deemed synonymous with the World Bank, but to gain access to IBRD funds, member states must be members of the IMF.

Inkatha Zulu word meaning 'Mystical Coil', a reference to the coil worn by African women to help them carry heavy weights on their heads. Conservative South African organisation led by Chief Mangosuthu Buthelezi, founded in 1975 and based in Durban.
International Court of Justice based at The Hague and founded in 1946, the ICJ is the principal judicial organ of the UN and is authorized to resolve disputes between UN member states. It is assisted by a governing body composed of 15 judges of differing nationalities, elected for a 9-year term.
Interpol International Criminal Police Organisation established in 1923 and based in Lyon.
IRA Irish Republican Army, currently the main militant republican movement in Northern Ireland, originally formed in 1919 to fight for Irish independence.
John Birch Society extreme right wing group founded in the USA in 1958 by Robert H W Welch, its name deriving from an American intelligence worker killed by Chinese communists in 1945.
KGB Komitet Gosudarstvennoy Bezopasnosti (Committee of State Security), Soviet Union's security police established in 1954. The KGB was scrapped after the August coup of 1991 and replaced in Russia in Jan. 1994 by the Federal Counterintelligence Service.
Knesset The Israeli unicameral legislature, located in Jerusalem.
KNU Karen National Union - guerrilla organisation in Burma, which has fought for a separate Karen state since the late 1940s.
Ku Klux Klan US white racist paramilitary organisation with long history of violence against blacks. Established in Tennessee at the end of the US Civil War in 1865 and still active.
Lok Sabha lower house of the Indian Parliament.
Mafia in Italy, the network of organised crime, including the Sicilian Mafia, the Neapolitan Camorra and the Calabrian 'Ndrangheta.
Matrix Churchill UK machine tool company at the centre of the events that led to the Scott inquiry established on 15 February 1996, into defence--related exports to Iraq. Paul Henderson, Trevor Abrahams and Peter Allen, executives of the Iraqi-owned Matrix Churchill, were arrested in October 1990 and charged with illegally exporting machine tools to Iraq. All three were acquitted and it emerged that Henderson had acted as an MI6 agent.
Mau Mau secret political society in Kenya which developed into a violent anti-colonial rebellion in the 1950s.
Médecins Sans Frontières founded in Paris by a group of French doctors in 1971 to provide emergency medical aid worldwide, it is funded by donations. MSF has offices in 20 countries worldwide, the international office being in Brussels
MI5 the UK Security Service. The counterintelligence service was originally established in 1909 to assess and combat threats to UK security.
MI6 UK's Secret Intelligence Service. Formed in 1909, its role is to gather intelligence abroad in support of the government's security, defence, foreign and economic policies.
Monday Club right-wing grouping of the UK Conservative Party, formed in 1960. Established in reaction to Harold Macmillan's wind of change speech, the Club was characterised by support for the South African regime, and subsequently the Rhodesian UDI regime, by advocacy of voluntary repatriation of black Commonwealth immigrants, and by opposition to anti-apartheid activities such as sporting boycotts.
Moral Rearmament revivalist movement established in the UK in 1938 by the US-born Lutheran pastor Frank Buchman, which succeeded Buchman's previous 'Oxford Movement', based its teachings on the 4 absolutes of purity, unselfishness, honesty and love, and on the importance of 'life-change'.
Mossad the most important, powerful and prominent of the Israeli intelligence agencies. Founded in 1951 by Isser Harel, who served as its director until 1963, it concerns itself with matters of espionage, intelligence gathering and covert political operations in foreign countries.
Mujaheddin-I-Khalq lay guerrilla organisation representing leftwing Muslim groups in Iran. Founded in the early 1970s, it was banned after the Islamic Revolution for its espousal of a variant of Islamic socialism and its criticism of the regime of Ayatollah Khomeini.
NASA National Aeronautics and Space Administration, the US government agency created in 1958 to co-ordinate civilian activities in space.
National Front fringe UK racist party founded in 1967 from small neo-fascist groups, including League of Empire Loyalists, British National Party, and Racial Preservation Society.
National Health Service UK's state health care system. The architect of the service was Aneurin Bevan, health minister in the Labour government of Clement Attlee, drawing on the Beveridge Report of 1942 on the welfare state. The NHS was officially inaugurated on 5 July 1948.
National Trust National Trust for Places of Historic Interest or Natural Beauty, founded by Octavia Hill in 1895.
Nato North Atlantic Treaty Organisation, based in Brussels and formed in April 1949. Nato came into being during the Soviet blockade of Berlin, taking as its basic tenet that an armed attack on any Nato country would be seen as an attack on them all.
New Jewel Movement leftwing party founded in Grenada in 1973 which in 1979 overthrew the government of Sir Eric Gairy and set up a People's Revolutionary Government under PM Maurice Bishop.
1922 Committee consisting of all Conservative back-bench MPs in the House of Commons. Name commemorates the decision in 1922, forced on the party leadership by Tory backbenchers, to bring down Lloyd George's coalition government. Graham Brady is the chairman
Non-Proliferation Treaty arms control agreement approved by the UN in June 1968 and effective from March 1970.
OECD Organisation for Economic Co-Operation and Development, formed in 1961 as the instrument for international co-operation among member states on economic and social policies. HQ in Paris.
Oireachtas bicameral legislature of the Republic of Ireland, comprising the 166-seat lower house, the Dáil Éireann, and the 60-seat upper house or Senate, the Seanad Éireann.
OPEC Organisation of Petroleum Exporting Countries, Established in Sept. 1960 by Iran, Iraq, Kuwait, Saudi Arabia and Venezuela, subsequently enlarged to include Qatar, Indonesia, Libya, Abu Dhabi, Algeria, Nigeria, Ecuador and Gabon. It aims to unify petroleum policies among member countries in order to ensure stable prices. Ecuador left OPEC in 1993.
Organisation of African Unity established in 1963 by 32 African countries to promote continental unity and solidarity of African states. Headquarters are in Addis Ababa, Ethiopia.
OSS Office for Strategic Services, US intelligence organisation which was the predecessor of the CIA. Established in June 1942.
Oxfam Oxford Committee for Famine Relief, founded in 1942 to aid women and children in Nazi-occupied Greece and based in Oxford, it now has 40 overseas field offices.
PDSA People's Dispensary for Sick Animals, founded by Mary Dickin in 1917.
Pearce Commission UK government body established in Nov. 1971 to investigate whether proposals to settle the dispute with Rhodesia over UDI (Unilateral Declaration of Independence) were acceptable to the Rhodesian people.
Pentagon HQ, in Arlington, VA, of the US Defense Department and the Departments of the Army, Navy and Airforce.
Phalange main right wing Maronite Christian movement in Lebanon. Phalangist Party spearheaded the Christian side in the Lebanese civil war 1975–91, during which they were allied with Israel.
PLO Palestine Liberation Organisation, founded in 1964 as spokesman for all matters concerning the Palestinian people. Yasser Arafat led the PLO between 1969 and 2004 and was succeeded on his death by Mahmoud Abbas (aka Abu Mazen).
Politburo key committee in the leadership structures of most communist parties, elected in the case of the Soviet Union by the central committee of the CPSU.
Quai d'Orsay term used for the French Ministry of Foreign Affairs, whose HQ is located in this street alongside the River Seine in Paris.
Radio Free Europe broadcasting operation covering the countries of Eastern and Central Europe, funded by the US government and operating from Munich under US management. Founded in 1949, it merged with Radio Liberty in 1976 and its aims are to broadcast non-partisan information.
Red Army Russian army formed in 1917 by the Bolsheviks and organised by Leon Trotsky to fight the anti-communist white armies.
Red Guards groups composed of students and schoolchildren in China who as 'Red Guards of the Cultural Revolution' had the task of unmasking revisionists and promoting Maoism. Emerging in 1966, the Red Guard operated for over a year before being disbanded.
Risorgimento the 19th-century movement for the political unification of Italy.
Royal Academy (of Arts) founded in 1768 at Somerset House but eventually moved to Burlington House. First president was Joshua Reynolds.
Royal Automobile Club founded in 1897 and responsible for many aspects of motoring safety and control.
Royal Exchange founded by Thomas Gresham in 1568 and home to various financial institutions. The present building was built by William Tite in 1844.
Royal Geographical Society founded in 1830 as the Geographical Society of London, it has been sited at Kensington Gore since 1912 in a house designed by Norman Shaw.
Royal Horticultural Society established in 1804 and awarded its royal charter in 1861, the RHS holds many shows but is primarily concerned with the Chelsea Flower Show held in Ranelagh Gardens since 1913. The Society has gardens at Wisley, Rosemoor near Great Torrington, Devon, and Hyde Hall, Essex.
Royal Institute of British Architects founded in 1834 under the patronage of William IV and given its Royal Charter in 1837. Membership in excess of 30,000; headquarters at Portland Place, London.
Royal Institution (of GB) established in 1799 by Count Rumford (Benjamin Thompson), this scientific organisation still has its headquarters in Albemarle St, London W1.
Royal Scottish Academy founded in 1826 and occupying a Greek Revival building in Edinburgh built by William Playfair.

Royal Society founded in 1660, early members included Christopher Wren and Samuel Pepys. Isaac Newton was president 1703–27.

SALT Strategic Arms Limitation Talks, held between USSR and USA. Salt I, 1969–72, and Salt II, 1973–4, between Nixon and Brezhnev. Salt II talks were concluded in 1979 by Carter and Brezhnev in Vienna, after which the SALT talks were renamed START.

Samaritans Founded by the Rev Chad Varah in November 1953. At this time Varah was Vicar of St Paul's, Clapham Junction, as well as being the scientific and astronautical consultant to Dan Dare in the *Eagle* comic strip. He was haunted by the suicide of a 14-year-old girl, who killed herself in 1935 when her periods started because she thought she had VD, and when the opportunity arose the helpline phone number of MAN 9000 was set up on 2 November 1953. In 1974 Chad Varah set up Befrienders International, the overseas equivalent of the Samaritans.

Sandinista leftwing Nicaraguan revolutionary movement that overthrew President Anastasio Somoza in 1979. Founded in 1961 and named in honour of Augusto César Sandino, the leader of a small peasant army that waged a campaign (1926–33) against the US occupation of Nicaragua.

SAVAK defunct Iranian security organisation established in 1957 with the aid of USA and Israeli intelligence services, and used to crush opposition to Mohammad Reza Shah Pahlavi.

Save the Children Fund founded by Eglantyne Jebb, an Englishwoman, who saw starving children in Austria (1919). The Princess Royal is the President.

Schengen Group European mainland countries within the EU which are party to the Schengen Agreement on abolishing border controls between their territories while improving police co-operation. The original group which met in Schengen in Luxembourg in June 1985 consisted of the Benelux countries and France and Germany; Spain and Portugal soon -ratified the treaty, followed by Italy, Greece and Austria.

Securitate communist Romania's security police which mounted a brutal defence of the regime of Nicolae Ceausescu during the December 1989 -revolution.

Sejm the lower house of the Polish National Assembly, comprising 460 directly elected members.

SHAPE Supreme Headquarters Allied Powers Europe, the NATO military HQ of Allied Command Europe. SHAPE was moved from Paris to near Mons in Belgium in 1967, after De Gaulle's decision to withdraw France from NATO.

Shin Bet the Israeli internal security agency, aka the General Security Service.

Sierra Club probably the world's first environmental pressure group, formed in 1892 in California by naturalist John Muir.

Sinn Fein (ourselves alone) prominent revolutionary party fighting initially for the republican independence of Ireland, and, since partition, for the reunification of the country.

Situationist International revolutionary group founded by writer Guy Debord and artist Asger Jorn. Active between 1957 and 1972, its ethos was the rejection of capitalism which effectively led to the wildcat strikes of May 1968 in France.

Snowdrop Campaign founded after the killing of 16 children in Dunblane on 13 March 1996 and named after the only flower in bloom that day. The campaign, backed by international film star Sean Connery, aims to ban civilian ownership of firearms.

Solidarity Polish trade union and opposition movement founded in 1980 by striking workers at the Gdansk shipyard. Its first leader was the future President Lech Walesa.

Stasi the Ministry of State Security of communist East Germany, which operated from 1950 to 1990.

Stern Gang British name for the Zionist guerrilla group founded in Palestine in 1940 by Abraham Stern and responsible till 1949 for several terrorist attacks.

Stormont the Northern Ireland parliament buildings in Belfast, the seat of the N.I. parliament from 1932 until the introduction of direct rule in 1972.

Tamil Tigers militant organisation formed in 1976 aiming to achieve and independent Tamil state in northern Sri Lanka.

TASS Soviet Union's state news agency.

Tontons Macoutes (from a Creole word meaning 'Uncle Knapsack', a bogeyman), the notorious Haitian right-wing secret police, set up in 1958 by Papa Doc Duvalier.

TUC Trades Union Congress, the key umbrella employees' organisation in the UK, founded in 1868.

Tulip Revolution Name given to the uprising in the former Soviet republic of Kyrgyzstan in March 2005. Many species of tulip are native to the mountains and steppes of Central Asia.

Tupamaros Uruguayan guerrilla group named after an 18th-century Peruvian Indian chief Tupac Amarú, and founded in 1962 by Raúl Antonaccio, an activist in sugar cane cutters' strikes. The group is still active today under the name 'National Liberation Movement'.

Tynwald parliament of the Isle of Man, a UK Crown Dependency. The principal chamber of Tynwald is the 24-member directly elected House of Keys. Tynwald celebrated its millennium in 1979; only the Althing of Iceland claims to be older (dating back to at least 930).

UN General Assembly established under Chapter IV of the UN Charter to act as the organisation's plenary body, representing all member states, it oversees the work of the UN's subsidiary bodies.

UN Secretariat listed in Chapter III of its Charter, the Secretariat, and the functions of the Secretary-General, are covered in detail in Chapter XV of the Charter. Elected by the Security Council. Secretariatship is usually for a term of 5 years with an automatic option to carry on unless vetoed by a member of the Council. Trygve Lie of Norway took office in Feb. 1946 and his term was extended until he resigned in November 1952, despite a Soviet veto. Other holders have been Dag Hammarskjöld of Sweden (April 1953 until his death in the Congo in September 1961), U Thant of Burma (1961–71), Kurt Waldheim of Austria (1972–81), Javier Pérez de Cuéllar of Peru (1982–91), Boutros Boutros-Ghali of Egypt (1 January 1992 – 1 January 1997, US vetoed continuation), Kofi Annan (1997–2006) and the incumbent Ban Ki-moon of South Korea (from 1 January 2007).

UN Security Council established under Chapter V of the Charter, the Security Council has primary responsibility for the maintenance of international peace and security. It presently has 15 member states, 10 non-permanent members plus China, France, Russia, UK and USA, which are permanent members and carry power of veto.

UNESCO Paris-based UN Educational, Scientific and Cultural Organisation, founded in 1946 to promote international collaboration in those fields of endeavour. USA, UK and Singapore are not members at present after suggestions of financial mismanagement.

UNITA National Union for the Total Independence of Angola. Founded by Jonas Savimbi in March 1966, UNITA fought alongside the Popular Movement for the Liberation of Angola during the struggle against colonial rule, but following the Portuguese withdrawal in 1975 it began a rivalry with the MPLA, backed by South Africa and the USA and not yet concluded. Since the death of Savimbi in February 2002, UNITA has been led by Paulo Lukamba Gato.

United Arab Republic political union of Egypt and Syria proclaimed between 1958 and 1961. Egypt retained the title of UAR until 1971, when it took the name Arab Republic of Egypt.

United Nations Established on 24 Oct. 1945 with its HQ completed in New York in 1952, the UN replaced the inter-war League of Nations, and its 111 articles of the Charter were proposed at the San Francisco Conference from 25 April – 25 June 1945. Its 6 principal organs are the General Assembly, Security Council, Economic and Social Council, Trusteeship Council, International Court of Justice and the Secretariat. Membership has risen from 51 at -inception to 192 as at 31 March 2010. Current Secretary-General is Ban Ki-moon of South Korea.

United Nations Budget Top 5 countries contributing to the UN are USA (24%), Japan (19%), Germany (8.4%), UK (5.96%), France (5.85%) as at 30 April 2005.

Universal Postal Union UN specialised agency based in Berne, Switzerland, first established in 1875 and taken over by the UN in 1948, charged with promoting international collaboration in postal services.

UNPROFOR UN Protection Force, established in January 1992 and dispatched to Croatia in March 1992 to monitor a ceasefire between Croatia and Krajina Serbs.

Velvet Revolution near-bloodless overthrow of Czech communist regime in November–December 1989 resulting in the ousting of the leader, Milos Jakes, and subsequent presidency of Vaclav Havel.

Warsaw Pact Warsaw Treaty Organisation, which was the communist counterpart to NATO during the cold war. Original signatories in May 1955 were Albania, Bulgaria, Czechoslovakia, East Germany, Hungary, Poland, Romania and the USSR. Albania withdrew in 1968 and following the collapse of communism in central and Eastern Europe the Warsaw Pact was dissolved in February 1991.

Women's Institute founded in 1897 at Stoney Creek, Canada.

World Health Organisation UN specialised agency based in Geneva and founded in 1948 with the aim of attaining the highest level of health for mankind.

World Wide Fund for Nature known until 1988 as the World Wildlife Fund, it was formed in 1961 and raises funds for a variety of conservation projects.

Yakuza Japanese criminal organisation comparable to US mafia-type syndicates.

PERFUME

Animal Sources

ambergris found floating on the sea in oily grey lumps; excreted by the sperm whale after feeding on cuttlefish. Used as a base.
castoreum comes from the follicles in the genital areas of both male and female beavers. Used as a fixative.
civet comes from a pouch beneath the tails of both male and female civet cats. Used as a fixative.
hyraceum excreted by the hyrax, a rabbit-like animal of the Middle East. Used in ancient Arabic perfumes but rarely used nowadays.
musk comes from the preputial follicle of the male musk deer. It is used as a fixative and is also thought to be an aphrodisiac. Chinese courtesans were fed bland foods perfumed with musk, so that when aroused the warmth of their bodies released the scent.
propolis a sticky brown fixative which bees collect from trees to use as a cement in their hives.
sweet hoof or onycha an ingredient of incense that comes from the shells of marine snails found around India and the Red Sea.

Plant, Mineral and Synthetic Sources

angelica root of the holy ghost (*Angelica archangelica*). It has a strong musky aroma.
bdellium myrrh (see also opoponax), an aromatic gum.
ben oil an essential oil from the winged seeds of the horseradish tree, used as a base oil for perfumes.
burning bush white dittany. The oil from the plant can vaporise in hot weather and catch fire without harming the plant itself. The fragrant essential oil is used in pot-pourri.
cherry pie heliotrope, used in pot-pourri and in modern perfumes such as 'Lou Lou' (Cacharel).
coumarin a white crystalline substance with a scent of new-mown hay, found in withered herbs and fruits. It is also manufactured synthetically from coal tar.
devil's dung asafoetida, a tall evil-smelling plant used as a fixative.
farnesol manufactured synthetically, but also found in musk. It gives a scent of lily of the valley.
frangipani the first plant to be named after a perfume. In 15th-century Rome, one of the Frangipani family made the perfume from orris, spices, civet and musk digested in wine alcohol. Later, French colonists in the West Indies found a bush (*Plumeria alba*) which had the same smell and named it frangipani.
galbanum small drops of it ooze from the stems of the giant fennel. It is mentioned in the Old Testament. It has a spicy-green scent with a hint of musk and is used in the 'top notes' of quality perfumes like Chanel No. 19.
handflower wallflower. The name 'handflower' comes from the practice, stemming from ancient Greece, of carrying the flowers in the hand as a nosegay during festivals.
indole the synthetic material derived from coal tar used to produce the scent of jasmine and neroli.
ionone the synthetic material used to make the scent of violets.
Labdanum comes from rock-rose shrubs found around the Mediterranean; often gathered by combing the beards of goats which have browsed on the bushes. It was thought to have aphrodisiac qualities. Assyrian kings liked young women who had spent time soaking during a six-month period in baths of labdanum or bdellium, after six months soaking in myrrh.
linalol the synthetic material used to make the scents of lilac, lily and honeysuckle.
love-in-the-mist nigella, a hardy annual which grows to a height of about 1.5 m and has a fragrance of ambrette seeds.
malabathrum a dried aromatic leaf from a species of cinnamon, used by the Romans in the making of unguents.
muguet lily of the valley. It is used in many 'quality' perfumes such as 'Opium' (Yves St Laurent), and 'Florissa' (Floris). Its fragrance is manufactured synthetically as farnesol.
olibanum frankincense, a fragrant gum resin often used as an incense and, in perfumes, as a fixative.
opoponax myrrh (probably the Biblical myrrh collected from the land of Punt). Its oil, with a scent of fenugreek, is distilled from the yellowish lumps which occur on the plant. It is used mainly for incense and pot-pourri.
orris comes from iris roots; has a violet-like scent.
storax originally from the bark of the liquidamber tree which grows in Turkey, Asia Minor and Rhodes, but now manufactured synthetically. It has a smell of cinnamon, and is used as a fixative.
syringa lilac. The flowers are used mainly in pot-pourri, and its oil is used in 'quality' perfumes such as 'Chamade' (Guerlain), 'Florissa' (Floris) and 'Soir de Paris' (Bourjois).
verbena holy wort. The leaves have a lemon scent. It is used mainly in cosmetics and soaps and the leaves are sometimes dried for use in sachets.

Perfumes and Perfume Houses

Alliage	Estée Lauder (1972)
Amarige	Givenchy (1991)
Anaïs Anaïs	Cacharel (1978)
Arpège	Lanvin (1927; relaunched 1994)
Bal à Versailles	Jean Desprez (1962)
Beautiful	Estée Lauder (1985)
Brut	Fabergé (1964)
Cabochard	Grès (1959)
Calandre	Paco Rabanne (1969)
Chamade	Guerlain (1969)
Charlie	Revlon (1973)
Cheap and Chic	Moschino (1996)
Chlöe	Lagerfeld (1975)
Chypre	Coty (1917)
CKOne	Calvin Klein (1994)
Devin	Aramis (1978)
Diva	Ungaro (1983)
Drakkar Noir	Guy Laroche (1982)
Dune	Christian Dior (1991)
Eau de Bonpoint	Annick Goutal (1989)
Eau Sauvage	Dior (1966)
Eden	Cacharel (1994)
Escape	Calvin Klein (1991)
Eternity	Calvin Klein (1988)
Fahrenheit	Dior (1988)
Femme	Rochas (1944)
Fidgi	Guy Laroche (1962)
Fleurs de Fleurs	Nina Ricci (1980)
Gentleman	Givenchy (1974)
Imprévu	Coty (1965)
Intimate	Revlon (1955)
Ivoire	Balmain (1979)
Jardins de Bagatelle	Guerlain (1983)
Je Reviens	Worth (1932)
Jicky	Guerlain (1889)
Joy	Patou (1930)
Knowing	Estée Lauder (1988)
L'Aimant	Coty (1927)
L'Air du Temps	Nina Ricci (1948)
L'Egoïste	Chanel (1990)
Le Jardin	Max Factor (1986)
Lou Lou	Cacharel (1987)
Ma Griffe	Carven (1946)
Mon Parfum	Paloma Picasso / L'Oréal (1984)
Must	Cartier (1981)
Obsession	Calvin Klein (1985)
Old Spice	Shulton (1937)
Only	Julio Iglesias / Myrurgia (1989)
Opium	Yves St Laurent (1977)
Paris	Yves St Laurent (1983)
Parure	Guerlain (1975)
Pleasures	Estée Lauder (1996)
Poême	Lancôme (1995)
Poison	Christian Dior (1985)
Polo	Ralph Lauren (1978)
Red	Giorgio Beverly Hills (1989)
Red Door	Elizabeth Arden (1990; relaunched 1996)
Rive Gauche	Yves St Laurent (1971)
Samsara	Guerlain (1989)
Shalimar	Guerlain (1925)
Shocking	Schiaparelli (1936)
So Pretty	Cartier (1995)
Special No. 127	Floris (1890)
Trésor	Lancôme (1990)
Tweed	Lenthéric (1933)
Vent Vert	Balmain (1947)
Youth Dew	Estée Lauder (1953)
Ysatis	Givenchy (1984)

Miscellaneous

Abir perfumed powder used in India, usually sprinkled on linen. Its ingredients include sandalwood, aloes, cardamon, cloves, civet and rose.
acerra small box used by the Romans to contain incense burned in temples.
alabastrum pot, usually made from alabaster, agate or onyx, used by the Romans to contain perfumed oils.
Aldehyde a group of alcohol-derived chemicals which form other groups of chemicals known as benzoid compounds. Their discovery led to the manufacture of synthetic perfume ingredients.
aqua angeli a perfumed water made from aloewood, nutmeg, clove, storax, benzoin and rosewater, first made for scenting the shirts of Louis XIV of France.
aryballos / ampulla small flask used by the ancient Greeks to contain perfumed oils, often carried hanging from the wrist by a small strap.
Baur Albert Baur was patenter of the first synthetic musk perfume, Musk Baur, in 1988.
Beaux Ernest Beaux developed the first aldehyde-based perfume, Chanel No. 5.
Carles Jean Carles, of Grasse, insured his nose for $1 million. His creations include 'Canoe' in 1935 (for Dana) and 'Shocking' in 1936 (for Schiaparelli). He founded the School of Perfumery in Grasse, Provence.
Chanel No. 5 named because the fragrance chosen by Coco Chanel from specimens supplied by Ernest Beaux was sample No. 5.
Chanel No. 19 named for Coco Chanel's birthday (19 August).
chypre originally a famous Roman perfume made in Cyprus (hence the name). Nowadays used to describe perfumes with fresh top notes of bergamot, with other citrus ingredients such as neroli, lemon and orange, with middle notes of jasmine and rose and a base of oakmoss, with labdanum, storax, civet, patchouli and musk. The first modern chypre perfume was 'Chypre by Coty' (1917).
Cliff Richard: perfume brands Miss You Nights – a warm oriental scent containing rose, jasmine and ylang ylang, combined with sandalwood. Dream Maker – a floral scent, with notes of citrus fruits and a hint of peach.
damask water popular in 16th-century England. It is made mainly from rosewater.
Eau de Bonpoint by Annick Goutal (1989). First fragrance for babies.
eau-de-Cologne first developed by Paul Feminis in Cologne in the early 18th century. Its main ingredients were lavender and citrus, neroli, bergamot and lemon. 4711 Mullhens of Cologne still uses the original formula.
Farina Jean-Marie Farina opened a shop in Paris in 1806 to sell eau-de-Cologne. He sold his business in 1840 to Léonce Collas, who passed it on in 1862 to his cousins, Messrs Roger & Gallet.
Floris Oldest perfume house in the world, founded 1730 as barber's shop in Jermyn Street, London, by Juan Floris from Minorca.
Hermès arose from a harness-making, then glove-making business. Many of its perfumes are named after horse and carriage parts, for example 'Calèche' (a four-wheeled horse-drawn carriage).
Imperial Leather first made in 1768 by Bayleys, the court perfumers in London, as a result of a challenge by the Russian Count Orloff, to make a perfume with the scent of worn leather. It became a favourite of Catherine the Great, under the name 'Eau de Cologne Impériale Russe'. Cussons took over Bayleys and renamed the perfume Imperial Russian Leather, but dropped 'Russian' in 1939.
khaluq unguent made by early Arabs - men were forbidden to use.
kyphi an incense made by the ancient Egyptians, based on wine, honey, raisins, herbs, frankincense, myrrh and juniper berries.
kypros an ancient Greek perfume which contained wine and cardamon and a sweet-scented substance called aspalathus.
L'Interdit launched for Audrey Hepburn in 1957. It was Givenchy's first perfume. The name means 'the forbidden one' – forbidden, at first, to all but Audrey Hepburn, whose face graced the advertisement.
Jicky the first 'modern' perfume, created in 1889 by Aimé Guerlain.
Joy the most expensive perfume on the market soon after its manufacture by Jean Patou in 1930.
magma the dried dregs from unguent bottles which the ancient Greeks and Romans added to scented powders.
olla-podrida pot-pourri made by perfume-makers from their waste materials with which they mixed herbs and lavender and rose petals.
Only launched in 1989 by Myrurgia in association with singer Julio Iglesias.
perfumer's organ not his or her nose! It is the work bench and surrounding ingredients and equipment.
Perkin William Perkin found out how to synthesise coumarin from coal tar, a much-used ingredient with a new-mown-hay fragrance. This was one of the first major discoveries in synthetic perfumery.
pomander a solid ball of perfumed material, such as crushed petals bound with a gum. In Tudor times they were carried to mask unpleasant smells and to ward off infection. In the 16th century it became popular to make them from oranges with cloves pushed into them, then baked. People fastened them to their belts or wrists. Nowadays they are sometimes used to perfume wardrobes.
pouncet box box used since Elizabethan times to contain perfumed powders placed between bedlinen. Originally used to hold pumice stone which was needed in the preparation of parchment for writing.
Special No. 127 created by Floris in 1890 for Grand Duke Orloff of Russia. No. 127 was the page in Floris' Book where he wrote formulae which were created uniquely for individual customers.
tussie-mussie a nosegay dating from Elizabethan times, when it was originally made from flowers and herbs chosen for their symbolic meanings, e.g. rosemary for remembrance, daisy for faithfulness etc.
unguent cone cone made from perfumed fat (usually ox-tallow), which was fixed on to the hair or head-dress so that it melted and ran down the hair and body, perfuming them as it did so.
Vent Vert launched in 1947 by Balmain - the first 'green' perfume.
vinaigrette small metal box whose inner lid was pierced, popular in 18th/19th-century Europe. It held a sponge soaked in aromatic vinegar and was used as a smelling bottle.

Founders

Amouage The Hamood family of the Sultanate of Oman (1983).
Avon David McConnell (1886), Suffern, California. He was a travelling book-salesman who liked to give his customers free gifts of inexpensive perfume. Originally called the California Perfume Co., its name changed to Avon (after Stratford-on-Avon) in 1959.
Cacharel Jean Bosquet (1962), Paris. The name comes from a wild duck found in Provence.
Charles of the Ritz Charles Jundt (1934), New York.
Coty François Sputorno (1905), Paris.
Elizabeth Arden Florence Graham (1910), New York. Name derived from the title of the book *Elizabeth and Her German Garden* by Elizabeth von Arnim.
Fragonard Eugene Fuchs (1783), Grasse - after painter Fragonard.
Lancôme Armand Petitjean (1935), Paris.
Mary Chess Grace Mary Chess Robinson (1932), London.
Revlon Charles and Joseph Revson and Charles Lachmann (1932), Boston, originally to market nail varnish.

Strengths and Forms of Perfume in Descending Order

Concentration	*Name*
15–30% in high-grade alcohol	extrait
15–18% in 80–90% grade alcohol	eau de parfum
4–8% in alcohol	eau de toilette
3–5% in 70% alcohol/water	eau de Cologne
3% in 80% pure alcohol	eau fraiche

Perfume Families or Classification

Perfumes are usually classified according to seven 'family' groups which form a continuum from floral to fougère.
floral mainly made from flower oils. These are light, daytime perfumes, e.g. 'Anaïs Anaïs' (Cacharel), 'L'Air du Temps' (Nina Ricci).
green giving an impression of new-mown grass. Fresh-smelling perfumes which include among their ingredients mosses, ferns, citrus fruits and herbs, e.g. 'Alliage' (Estée Lauder), 'Chanel No. 19' (Chanel).
aldehydic based on synthetic aldehydes. They range from floral through woody to powdery, e.g. 'Chanel No. 5' (Chanel), 'White Linen' (Estée Lauder).
chypre their fragrance is floral or green but with a heavy base such as ambergris, e.g. 'Cabochard' (Grès), 'Chypre' (Coty).
oriental their fragrance is spicy, strong and exotic and has a heavy sweetness which comes from ingredients such as musk, vanilla and sandalwood, e.g. 'Poison' (Christian Dior) and 'Opium' (Yves St Laurent).
tobacco / leather they have a hint of tobacco, leather and woody aromas, e.g. 'Antaeus' (Chanel) and 'Cuir de Russie' (Chanel).
fougère their fragrance is fresh, with a note of lavender, herbs, oakmoss, coumarin and new-mown hay, e.g. 'Drakkar Noir' (Guy Laroche), 'Brut' (Fabergé).

Photography (and Cinematography)

Ansel Easton Adams (1902–84) US photographer who co-founded Group f/64 with Edward Weston (1932) and best-known for his black-and-white landscape photographs of the American West, especially Yosemite National Park.

Diane Arbus (1923–71) US photographer famous for her intense portraits of American social outcasts.

Eugène Atget (1857–1927) French photographer famous for recording the streets and scenes of old Paris.

Richard Avedon (1923–2004) US photographer who made his name as a fashion photographer with *Harper's Bazaar*. His first sitter was Russian pianist-composer Sergei Rachmaninov.

David Royston Bailey (1938–) English photographer who started his professional life as a fashion photographer but developed as a portraitist during the 1960s, specialising in nudes. His 1965 collection *David Bailey's Box of Pin-ups* (1965) included pictures of celebrities of the day, from the Beatles to the Krays.

Billy Bitzer (1874–1944) US motion picture cameraman who, in partnership with director D W Griffiths, developed techniques that set the standard for all future motion pictures. He was the first to use artificial lighting for his work, and his other innovations included the use of soft-focus photography, using a light-diffusion screen in front of the camera lens, the fade-out, and the iris shot, in which the frame is either gradually blacked out in a shrinking circle, thereby ending a scene, or gradually opened in a widening circle, beginning a scene.

Margaret Bourke-White (1904–71) US photo-journalist employed by *Fortune* magazine (1929) and became staff photographer and associate editor on *Life* magazine (1936). First woman photographer to be attached to the US armed forces, producing outstanding reports of the siege of Moscow in 1941, and the opening of the concentration camps in 1944. She married the American author Erskine Caldwell in 1939 but was divorced in 1942.

Mathew Brady (1823–96) New York-born photographer famous for his record of the American Civil War with the Union armies.

Bill Brandt (1904–83) English photographer who studied with Man Ray in London before working for the Ministry of Information and recording conditions during the Blitz. Subsequently found fame with landscapes & nudes. His publications include *The English at Home* (1936), *Perspective of Nudes* (1961) and *Shadows of Light* (1966).

Brassaï (1899–1984) Professional name of Gyula Halász, the Hungarian-born French painter and photographer. His photography included the nightlife of 1930s Paris.

Henri Cartier-Bresson (1908–2004) French photographer who initially studied painting with André Lhote before working as an assistant to film director Jean Renoir. His publications include *The Decisive Moment* (1952) and *The Europeans* (1955). See also Leonor Fini in Art section.

Julia Margaret Cameron (1815–79) British pioneer of portrait photography.

Louis Jacques Mandé Daguerre (1787–1851) French painter and physicist who invented the daguerreotype, requiring exposure of 20 minutes as opposed to Niépce's method requiring 8 hours.

Terence Donovan (1936–96) London-born photographer and film director whose work covered a wide spectrum of contemporary life. He worked for *Vogue*, *Harpers & Queen*, *Elle*, and *Marie Claire*.

George Eastman (1854–1932) US manufacturer who introduced the Kodak camera (1888) and Brownie camera (1900).

Walker Evans (1903–75) US photographer who produced a powerful record of the faces, homes and lives of America's 1930s rural poor.

Roger Fenton (1819–69) English photographer who was famous for his Crimean War pictures.

William Henry Fox Talbot (1800–77) English chemist, linguist and photographer who in 1839 invented the photographic negative and whose *The Pencil of Nature* (1844) was the first photographic book.

William Friese-Greene (1855–1921) British photographer often credited with the invention of cinematography, although Thomas Edison would appear to have a stronger claim. The film, *The Magic Box* (1951) was based on his life.

John Heartfield (1891–1968) Aka Helmut Herzfelde, German pioneer of the photomontage, e.g. *Hurrah, the Butter is Finished* (1935).

Lewis Wickes Hine (1874–1940) US photographer who studied sociology before making a photographic study of Ellis Island immigrants and child labourers. He recorded the construction of the Empire State Building in his survey *Men at Work* (1932).

James Wong Howe (1899–1976) Chinese-born US cinematographer who started work in 1917 as assistant cameraman to Cecil B De Mille. Howe pioneered the use of the wide-angle lens, deep focus, and ceilinged sets to replicate shipboard claustrophobia. He won Oscars for his work on *The Rose Tattoo* (1955) and *Hud* (1963).

Yousuf Karsh (1908–2002) Armenian-born Canadian photographer who was appointed official portrait photographer to the Canadian government in 1935. A 1941 portrait of Sir Winston Churchill led to his reputation of photographing all the world's leading statesmen.

André Kertész (1894–1985) Hungarian-born US photographer famous for his pioneering use of the small hand-held camera

Herbert Land (1909–91) US inventor and physicist whose invention of the Polaroid (one-step) process for developing and printing photographs culminated in a revolution in photography.

Dorothea Lange (1895–1965) US photographer who became famous for her social records of migrant workers during the 1930s.

Lord Patrick Lichfield (1939–2005) British aristocratic photographer known for his royal photographs and nude calendars.

Auguste Lumière (1862–1954), Louis Lumière (1864–1948) French chemist brothers who invented the first successful cine camera and projector (1895) and a process of colour photography. They also produced the first film newsreels, and the first movie, *La Sortie des usines Lumière* (1895).

László Moholy-Nagy (1895–1946) Hungarian-born US photographer famous for his inspirational teaching at the Bauhaus.

Eadweard Muybridge (1830–1904) Original name Edward James Muggeridge. English photographer famous for his landscapes of the American West. Muybridge was employed by the railroad magnate Leland Stanford in 1872 to prove that during a particular moment in trotting, all four legs of a horse are off the ground simultaneously. His studies were interrupted while he was tried for the murder of his wife's lover, but after his acquittal he developed a special shutter giving an exposure of 2/1,000 of a second which proved the theory.

Nadar (1820–1910) Working name of Gaspard-Félix Tournachon, French artist and photographer whose Paris studio became a favourite haunt of the intelligentsia. In 1886 he produced the first photo interview, a series of 21 photographs of the centenarian scientist Eugène Chevreul, each captioned with the sitter's replies to Nadar's questions. He pioneered the use of aerial photographs for map-making and in 1858 took the first pictures from a balloon.

Joseph-Nicéphore Niépce (1765–1833) French inventor who was the first to make a permanent photographic image (1826).

Man Ray (1890–1976) US photographer, painter & film-maker, born Emanuel Rabinovich. He founded the New York Dadaist movement with Marcel Duchamp and Francis Picabia before moving to Paris and working with René Clair. Man Ray pioneered the use of photographic images made without a camera - 'Rayographs'.

Henry Peach Robinson (1830–1901) English photographer who specialised in images of costumed models. He was a founder member of the Linked Ring (1892), a group of photographers seeking to excel in artistic creation.

Alexander Rodchenko (1891–1956) Soviet photographer and photomontagist who introduced 'New Photography' to Russia.

Erich Salomon (1886–1944) German photojournalist who was master of the candid shot whereby he caught politicians and celebrities off guard for new magazines of the 1920s. He died in Auschwitz.

August Sander (1876–1964) German photographer celebrated for his ambitious project 'Man in the Twentieth Century', a picture of the doomed Weimar Republic through the faces of its people.

Aaron Siskind (1903–91) US photographer and teacher; his *Dead End: The Bowery* and *Harlem Document* depicted the depression but in a stylised form. He later photographed the mundane.

W Eugene Smith (1918–78) US photojournalist for *Life* magazine in the 1940s and 50s noted for his impassioned work of the times.

Edward Steichen (1879–1973) Luxembourg-born US photographer who became a member of the Linked Ring in England and made his reputation with his studies of the nude. In 1902 he co-founded the American Photo-Secession Group with Alfred Stieglitz. In WW1 he served as commander of the photographic division of the US army. In the 1920s Steichen became involved in fashion photography. He was head of US Naval Film Services during WW2, and director of photography at the New York Museum of Modern Art 1945-62

Alfred Stieglitz (1864–1946) US photographer who was a major figure in establishing photography as an art form and his gallery of modern art at 291 Fifth Avenue, NY, was the linchpin of his work.

Paul Strand (1890–1976) US photographer and documentary film-maker who studied under Lewis Hine. In 1933 he was appointed chief of photography and cinematography in the government Secretariat of Education in Mexico. Known for his architectural studies and photographic books on regions of the world.

Weegee (1899–1968) Pseudonym of Polish photographer Arthur Fellig, known for his stark black and white street photography. His first collection *Naked City* (1945) became the inspiration for a later movie. His nickname was a corruption of 'ouija' due to his almost supernatural attendance at crime scenes.

Edward Weston (1886–1958) US photographer who produced notable landscapes of the Mojave Desert, and in 1937, with the first-ever award of a Guggenheim Fellowship to a photographer, travelled the American West before touring the Eastern States to illustrate an edition of Walt Whitman's *Leaves of Grass*.

Minor White (1908–76) US photographer and editor who founded the periodicals *Aperture* and *Image*.

Garry Winogrand (1928–84) US photographer who created a highly influential brand of urban street photography, fusing the 'snapshot' approach with a sense of energy and crowded events in his images.

POLITICS

Country -– Name of Governmental Chambers – Type of Government

NB The upper chambers of bicameral parliaments are listed first in this table, and the name of parliaments are the most commonly accepted, e.g. the parliament of Afghanistan is bicameral, the upper house being the Meshrano Jirga and the lower house the Wolesi Jirga. The combined assemblies are generally referred to as the National Assembly. Parliaments are generally elected for a term of years but in some bicameral assemblies the two chambers may have differing lengths of term. In our example of Afghanistan, the lower house is elected for a five-year term but the upper house has a third (34) of its members elected by district councils (one per province) for three-year terms, one-third (34) by provincial councils (one per province) for four-year terms, and one-third (34) are nominated by the president for five-year terms. The membership is the statutory capacity as at October 2013.

Country	*Name of Chamber (members)*	*Name of Parliament*	*Years of Office*
Afghanistan	Meshrano Jirga (House of Elders) (102)	National Assembly	3, 4, & 5
	Wolesi Jirga (House of People) (249)		5
Albania	National Assembly (140)	People's Assembly	4
Algeria	Majlis el-Umma (Council of the Nation) (144)	Majlis	5
	National Assembly (462)		6
American Samoa	Senate (18)	Fono	4
	House of Representatives (21)		2
Andorra	General Council of the Valleys (28)	General Council of the Valleys	4
Angola	National Assembly (220)	National Assembly	4
Anguilla	House of Assembly (11)	National Assembly	5
Antigua and Barbuda	Senate (17)	Parliament	5
	House of Representatives (19)		5
Argentina	Senate (72)	Congress	6
	Chamber of Deputies (257)		4
Armenia	Azgayin Zhoghov (National Assembly) (131)	Azgayin Zhoghov	4
Aruba	Legislative Assembly (21)	Staten	4
Australia	Senate (76)	Federal Parliament	6
	House of Representatives (150)		3
Austria	Bundesrat (Federal Council) (62)	National Assembly	5 & 6
	Nationalrat (National Council) (183)		5
Azerbaijan	Milli-Mejlis (National Council) (125)	Milli-Mejlis	5
Bahamas	Senate (16 members)	Parliament	5
	House of Assembly (38)		5
Bahrain	Consultative Council (40)	Majlis al-Shura	4
	Assembly of Representatives (40)		4
Bangladesh	Jatiya Sangshad (house of the nation) (345)	Jatiya Sangshad	5
Barbados	Senate (21)	Parliament	5
	House of Assembly (30)		5
Belarus	Council of the Republic (64)	National Assembly	5
	House of Representatives (110)		5
Belgium	Senate (71)	Federal Parliament	4
	Chamber of Representatives (150)		4
Belize	Senate (12)	National Assembly	5
	House of Representatives (31)		5
Benin	National Assembly (83)	National Assembly	4
Bermuda	Senate (11)	Parliament	5
	House of Assembly (36)		5
Bhutan	National Council (25)	Gyelong Tshogdu	4
	National Assembly (47)		5
Bolivia	Senate (36)	Congress	5
	Chamber of Deputies (130)		5
Bosnia-Herzegovina	House of Peoples (15- 5 Croat, 5 Muslim, 5 Serb)	Skupština	4
	House of Representatives (42)		4
Botswana	House of Chiefs (35)	National Assembly	5
	National Assembly (63)		5
Brazil	Senate (81)	Congress	8
	Chamber of Deputies (513)		4
Brunei	Sultan rules since a revolt in December 1962.		
Bulgaria	National Assembly (240)	Narodno sabranie	4
Burkina Faso	Assembly of People's Deputies (111)	National Assembly	5
Burundi	Senate (49)	National Assembly	5
	National Assembly (118)		5
Cambodia	Senate (61)	National Assembly	5
	National Assembly (123)		5
Cameroon	National Assembly (180)	National Assembly	5
Canada	Senate (105)	Federal Parliament	4

	House of Commons (308)		4
Cape Verde	National Assembly (102)	National Assembly	5
Central African Republic	National Assembly (100)	National Assembly	5
Chad	National Assembly (155)	National Assembly	4
Channel Islands (less Sark)	States of Deliberation (132)	The States	4
– Sark	Chief Pleas (5)	Chief Pleas	4
Chile	Senate (38)	Congress	8
	Chamber of Deputies (120)		4
China	National People's Congress (2,987)	National People's Congress	5
Colombia	Senate (102)	Congress	4
	House of Representatives (166)		4
Comoros	Assembly of the Union (33)	Assembly of the Union	5
Congo, Dem. Rep. of the	Senate (108)	Parliament	5
	National Assembly (500)		5
Congo, Republic of the	Senate (52)	Parliament	5
	National Assembly (153)		5
Costa Rica	Legislative Assembly (57)	Legislative Assembly	4
Côte d'Ivoire	National Assembly (70)	National Assembly	5
Croatia	Croatian Assembly (151)	Hrvatski sabor	4
Cuba	National Assembly of People's Power (614)	National Assembly	5
Cyprus	House of Representatives (59)	Parliament	5
Czech Republic	Senate (81)	Federal Assembly	6
	Chamber of Deputies (200)		4
Denmark	Folketing (175 + 2 Greenland and 2 Faroes)	Folketing (lit, people's thing)	4
Djibouti	National Assembly (65)	National Assembly	5
Dominica	House of Assembly (21)	National Assembly	5
Dominican Republic	Senate (32)	Congress	4
	Chamber of Deputies (183)		4
East Timor	National Assembly (65)	National Assembly	5
Ecuador	National Assembly (124)	National Assembly	4
Egypt	Consultative Council (Majilis Al-Shura (270)	Majlis	6
	Majlis Ash-Sha'Ab (People's Assembly) (508)		5
El Salvador	Legislative Assembly (84)	Legislative Assembly	3
Equatorial Guinea	National Assembly (100)	National Assembly	5
Eritrea	Hagerawi Baito (National Assembly) (104)	Hagerawi Baito	5
Estonia	Riigikogu (National Assembly) (101)	Riigikogu	4
Ethiopia	Federation Council (112)	Mekir Bet	5
	Council of People's Representatives (547)		5
Falkland Islands	Legislative Council (11)	Legislative Council	4
Faroe Islands	National Assembly (33)	Logting	4
Fiji Islands	Senate (32)	Parliament	5
	House of Representatives (71)		5
Finland	Eduskunta (parliament) (200)	Eduskunta	4
France	Senate (348)	Parliament	6
	National Assembly (577)		5
Gabon	Senate (102)	Parliament	6
	National Assembly (121)		5
Gambia	National Assembly (53)	National Assembly	5
Georgia	Parliament (150)	Parliament	4
Germany	Bundesrat (Federal Council) (69)	Parliament	4
	Bundestag (Federal Assembly) (620)		4
Ghana	Parliament (228)	Parliament	4
Gibraltar	House of Assembly (17)	House of Assembly	4
Greece	Hellenic Parliament (300)	Vouli Ton Ellinon	4
Greenland	National Assembly (31)	Landstinget	4
Grenada	Senate (13)	Parliament	5
	House of Representatives (15)		5
Guatemala	National Congress (158)	Congress	4
Guernsey	Parliament (45 members)	States of Deliberation	4
Guinea	National Assembly (114)	National Assembly	5
Guinea-Bissau	National People's Assembly (100)	National People's Assembly	4
Guyana	National Assembly (65)	National Assembly	5
Haiti	Senate (30)	National Assembly	6
	Chamber of Deputies (99)		4
Honduras	National Congress (128)	Congress	4
Hong Kong	Legislative Council (70 members)	Legislative Council	4
Hungary	Országgyülés (National Assembly) (386)	Országgyülés	4
Iceland	Althingi (Parliament) (63)	Althingi	4
India	Rajya Sabha (Council of States) (250)	Sansad (Parliament)	6
	Lok Sabha (House of the People) (552)		5
Indonesia	Dewan Perwakilan Daerah (132)	Majelis	5
	Dewan Perwakilan Rakyat (560)		5
Iran	Assembly (Majilis) (290)	Majles	4
Iraq	Majlis Watani (Council of the Nation) (325)	Majlis	4
Ireland	Seanad Eireann (Senate) (60)	Oireachtas (parliament)	5
	Dáil Eireann (House of Representatives) (166)		5
Israel	Knesset (Assembly) (120)	Knesset	4
Italy	Senate (315)	Parliament	5
	Chamber of Deputies (630)		5

POLITICS

Jamaica	Senate (20)	Parliament	5
	House of Representatives (63)		5
Japan	Sangiin (House of Councillors) (242)	Kokkai (Diet)	6
	Shugiin (House of Representatives) (480)		4
Jersey	Parliament (55 members)	Assembly of the States	varies
Jordan	Al-Aayan (Senate) (60)	Majlis Al-Umma	6
	Al-Nuwaab (House of Representatives) (120)		4
Kazakhstan	Senate (47)	Mazhilis	6
	Mazhilis (Council) (77)		5
Kenya	Bunge (National Assembly) (224)	Bunge	5
Kiribati	House of Assembly (46)	Maneaba Ni Maungatabu	4
Korea North	Supreme People's Assembly (687)	Ch'oe-go In-min Hoe-ui	5
Korea South	Kuk Hoe (National Assembly) (300)	Gukhoe	4
Kuwait	Majlis Al-Umma (Council of the Nation) (50)	Majlis Al-Umma	4
Kyrgyzstan	Joghorku Kenes (High Council) (120)	Joghorku Kenesh	5
Laos	Sapha Heng Xat (National Assembly) (115)	Sapha Heng Xat	5
Latvia	Saeima (Supreme Council) (100)	Saeima	4
Lebanon	Majlis Al-Nuwwab (Council of Deputies) (128)	Majlis Al-Nuwwab	4
Lesotho	Senate (33)	Parliament	5
	National Assembly (120)		5
Liberia	Senate (30)	National Assembly	9
	House of Representatives (73)		6
Libya	General National Congress (200)	Al-Waṭanī el-Mu'tammar al 'âmm	T.B.A
Liechtenstein	Landtag (25 members)	Landtag	4
Lithuania	Seimas (Supreme Council) (141)	Seimas	4
Luxembourg	Chamber of Deputies (60)	Parliament	5
Macedonia	Sobranie (Assembly) (123)	Sobranie	4
Madagascar	Senate (33)	Antenimieram-Pirenena	5
	National Assembly (160)		
Malawi	National Assembly (194)	National Assembly	5
Malaysia	Dewan Negara (Senate) (70)	Dewan Rakyat	3
	Dewan Rakyat (House of Representatives) (222)		5
Maldives	Majlis (77)	Majlis	5
Mali	National Assembly (160)	National Assembly	5
Malta	House of Representatives (69)	Kamra Tad-Deputati	5
Man, Isle of	Legislative Council (11)	Tynwald	5
	House of Keys (24)		5
Marshall Islands	House of Assembly (33)	Nitijela	4
Mauritania	Majlis-Al-Shuyukh (Senate) (56)	Al Jamiya-Al-Wataniya	6
	National Assembly (81)		5
Mauritius	National Assembly (70)	National Assembly	5
Mexico	Senate (128)	Congress	6
	Chamber of Deputies (500)		3
Micronesia (Federated States)	Congress (14 members, four of whom are elected for four years)	Congress	2
Moldova	Parliament (101)	Parliament	4
Monaco	National Council (24)	National Council	5
Mongolia	Ulsyn Ikh Khural (The Great Hural) (76)	Ulsyn Ikh Khural	4
Montenegro	Skupština (Parliament) (81)	Skupština	4
Morocco	Chamber of Counsellors) (270)	Majlis	9
	Majlis Nawab (Chamber of Representatives (325)		6
Mozambique	People's Assembly (250)	National Assembly	5
Myanmar (Burma)	National Assembly (Amyotha Hluttaw) (224)	Pyidaungsu Hluttaw	5
	People's Assembly (Pyithu Hluttaw) (440)		5
Namibia	National Council (26)	Parliament	6
	National Assembly (78)		5
Nauru	Parliament (18)	Parliament	3
Nepal	Constitutional Assembly (601)	Parliament	5
Netherlands	First Chamber (75)	States General	4
	Second Chamber (150)		4
New Zealand	House of Representatives (120)	Parliament	3
Nicaragua	National Assembly (92)	National Assembly	6
Niger	National Assembly (113)	National Assembly	5
Nigeria	Senate (109)	National Assembly	4
	House of Representatives (360)		4
Norway	Great Assembly (Storting) (169)	Storting	4
Oman	Majlis al-Dawla (Council of State) (83)	Majlis	4
	Majlis al-Shura (Consultative Assembly) (84)		4
Pakistan	Senate (104)	Majlis-e-Shoora	3
	National Assembly (336)		4
Palau	Senate (9)	Olbiil Era Kelulau (Congress)	4
	House of Delegates (16)		4
Panama	Legislative Assembly (71)	Legislative Assembly	5
Papua New Guinea	National Parliament (109)	Parliament	5
Paraguay	Senate (45)	Congress	5
	Chamber of Deputies (80)		5
Peru	National Congress (130)	Congress	5
Philippines	Senate (24)	Congress	6
	House of Representatives (286)		3
Poland	Senate (100)	Sejm	4
	Sejm (Parliament) (460)		4

Country	Chambers	Name	Type
Portugal	Assembly of the Republic (230)	Assembly of the Republic	4
Qatar	Consultative Assembly (35)	Majlis ash-Shura	4
Romania	Senate (137)	Parliament	4
	Chamber of Deputies (326)		4
Russia	Federation Council (166)	Federal Assembly	4
	Duma (450)		4
Rwanda	Senate (Umutwe wa Sena) (26)	Inteko Ishinga Amategeko	5
	Chamber of Deputies (80)		5
Saint Kitts and Nevis	National Assembly (15)	National Assembly	5
Saint Lucia	Senate (11)	National Assembly	5
	National Assembly (17)		5
Saint Vincent and Grenadines	National Assembly (21)	National Assembly	5
Samoa	Legislative Assembly (49)	Legislative Assembly	5
San Marino	Consiglio grande e generale (60)	Consiglio grande e generale	5
São Tomé and Principe	National Assembly (55)	National Assembly	4
Saudi Arabia	Majlis al Shura (Council of State) (150)	Majlis	4
Senegal	Senate (100)	National Assembly	5
	National Assembly (150)		5
Serbia	National Assembly (250)	Narodna Skupština	4
Seychelles	National Assembly (31)	National Assembly	5
Sierra Leone	Parliament (124)	Parliament	5
Singapore	Parliament (99)	Parliament	5
Slovakia	National Council (150)	Národná rada	4
Slovenia	State Council (40)	Državni zbor	5
	National Assembly (90)		4
Solomon Islands	Parliament (50)	Parliament	4
Somalia	Senate (56)	National Assembly	T.B.A.
	House of the People (275)		T.B.A.
South Africa	National Council of Provinces (90)	Volksraad	5
	Volksraad (National Assembly) (400)		5
South Sudan	Council of States (70)	National Legislature	4
	National Legislature Assembly (170)		4
Spain	Congress Senate (266)	Cortes (Courts)	4
	Congress of Deputies (350)		4
Sri Lanka	Parliament (225)	Parliament	6
Sudan	Majlis Welayat (Council of States) (50)	Majlis	4
	Majlis Watani (National Assembly) (450)		4
Suriname	National Assembly (51)	National Assembly	5
Swaziland	Senate (30)	Libandla (Parliament)	5
	House of Assembly (55)		5
Sweden	Riksdag (349)	Riksdag(en)	4
Switzerland	Council of States (46)	Federal Assembly	4
	National Council (200)		4
Syria	Majlis Al-Shaab (250)	Majlis	4
Tadzhikstan	Majlisi Milliy (33)	Majlis Oli (Supreme Council)	5
	Assembly of Representatives (63)		5
Taiwan	Yuan (225 members)	Yuan	3
Tanzania	Bunge (National Assembly) (357)	Bunge	5
Thailand	Wuthisapha (Senate) (150)	Rathasapha (Parliament)	6
	House of Representatives (500)		4
Togo	National Assembly (81)	National Assembly	5
Tonga	Fale Alea (Legislative Assembly) (26)	Fale Alea	3
Trinidad and Tobago	Senate (31)	Parliament	5
	House of Representatives (41)		5
Tunisia	Council of Deputies (217)	Majlis	5
Turkey	Millet Meclisi (National Assembly) (550)	Millet Meclisi	5
Turkmenistan	Mejlis (Council) (125)	Mejlis	5
Tuvalu	Parliament (15)	Parliament	4
Uganda	Parliament (375)	Parliament	5
Ukraine	Supreme Council (450)	Verkhovna Rada	4
United Arab Emirates	Federal National Assembly (40)	Majlis Watani Itihad	2
United Kingdom	House of Lords (765)	Parliament	varies
	House of Commons (650)		5
USA	Senate (100)	Congress	6
	House of Representatives (435)		2
Uruguay	Senate (30)	General Assembly	5
	Chamber of Deputies (99)		5
Uzbekistan	Senate (100)	Oliy Majlis	5
	Legislative Chamber (150)		5
Vanuatu	Parliament (52)	Parliament	4
Vatican City	Pontifical Commission (7)	Pontifical Commission	5
Venezuela	National Assembly (165)	National Assembly	5
Vietnam	Quoc Hoi (National Assembly) (498)	Quoc Hoi	5
Virgin Islands (US)	Senate (15)	Parliament	2
Yemen	Assembly of Representatives (301)	Majlis al-Nuwaab	6
Zambia	House of Assembly (150)	National Assembly	5
Zimbabwe	Senate (40)	National Assembly	5
	House of Assembly (210)		5

British Prime Ministers

	Name	Term of Office	Party	Education	Constituency	Marriage(s)	Buried
1	Sir Robert Walpole (earl of Orford) (1676–1745)	1721–1742	Whig	Eton & Cambridge (King's)	Castle Rising (1701–2) King's Lynn (1702–42)	Catherine Shorter Maria Skerrett	Houghton, Norfolk
2	Sir Spencer Compton (earl of Wilmington) (1673–1743)	1742–1743	Whig	St Pauls & Oxford (Trinity)	Eye (Suffolk) (1698–1710) East Grinstead (1713–15) Sussex (1715–28)	Unmarried	Compton Wynates, Warwickshire
3	Henry Pelham (1695–1754)	1743–1754	Whig	Westminster & Oxford (Hart Hall)	Seaford (1717–22) Sussex (1722–54)	Catherine Manners	Laughton Church, nr Lewes, E. Sussex
4	Thomas Pelham-Holles (duke of Newcastle) (1693–1768)	1754–1756	Whig	Westminster & Cambridge (Clare)	House of Lords	Henrietta Godolphin	Laughton Church, nr Lewes, E. Sussex
5	William Cavendish (duke of Devonshire) (1720–1764)	1756–1757	Whig	private education	Derbyshire (1741–51)	Baroness Clifford	Derby Cathedral
6	Thomas Pelham-Holles (duke of Newcastle) (1693–1768)	1757–1762	Whig	Westminster & Cambridge (Clare)	House of Lords	Henrietta Godolphin	Laughton Church, nr Lewes, E. Sussex
7	John Stuart (earl of Bute) (1713–1792)	1762–1763	Tory	Eton	House of Lords	Mary Wortley-Montagu	Rothesay, Bute
8	George Grenville (1712–1770)	1763–1765	Whig	Eton & Oxford (Christ Church)	Buckingham (1741–70)	Elizabeth Wyndham	Wotton, Bucks
9	Charles Watson Wentworth (marquis of Rockingham) (1730–1782)	1765–1766	Whig	Westminster & Cambridge (St John's)	House of Lords	Mary Bright	York Minster
10	Augustus Henry Fitzroy (duke of Grafton) (1735–1811)	1766–1770	Whig	Westminster & Cambridge (Peterhouse)	Bury St Edmunds (1756)	Anne Liddell Elizabeth Wrottesley	Euston, Suffolk
11	Lord Frederick North (earl of Guildford) (1732–1792)	1770–1782	Tory	Eton, Oxford (Trinity), Leipzig	Banbury (1754–90)	Anne Speke	All Saints, Wroxton, Oxfordshire
12	Charles Watson Wentworth (marquis of Rockingham) (1730–1782)	1782	Whig	Westminster & Cambridge (St John's)	House of Lords	Mary Bright	York Minster
13	William Petty (earl of Shelburne) (1737–1805)	1782–1783	Whig	Oxford (Christ Church)	Chipping Wycombe (1760–61)	Sophia Carteret Louisa FitzPatrick	High Wycombe
14	William Henry Cavendish-Bentinck (duke of Portland) (1738–1809)	1783	Coalition	Eton & Oxford (Christ Church)	Weobly, Herefordshire (1761–2) (as Whig)	Dorothy Cavendish	St Marylebone, London
15	William Pitt the Younger (1759–1806)	1783–1801	Tory	Cambridge (Pembroke Hall)	Appleby (1781–1806)	Unmarried	Westminster Abbey
16	Henry Addington (Viscount Sidmouth) (1757–1844)	1801–1804	Tory	Cheam, Winchester, Lincoln's Inn & Oxford (Brasenose)	Devizes (1784–1805)	Ursula Mary Hammond Marianne Townshend	Mortlake
17	William Pitt the Younger (1759–1806)	1804–1806	Tory	Cambridge (Pembroke Hall)	Appleby (1781–1806)	Unmarried	Westminster Abbey
18	William Wyndham Grenville (1759–1834)	1806–1807	Coalition	Eton, Oxford (Christ Church), Lincoln's Inn	Buckingham (1782–4) Buckinghamshire (1784–90)	Anne Pitt	Burnham, Bucks
19	William Henry Cavendish-Bentinck (duke of Portland) (1738–1809)	1807–1809	Tory	Westminster & Oxford (Christ Church)	Weobly, Herefordshire (1761–2) (as Whig)	Dorothy Cavendish	St Marylebone, London
20	Spencer Perceval (1762–1812)	1809–1812	Tory	Harrow & Cambridge (Trinity)	Northampton	Jane Spencer-Wilson	Charlton
21	Robert Banks Jenkinson (earl of Liverpool) (1770–1828)	1812–1827	Tory	Charterhouse & Oxford (Christ Church)	Rye (1791–1803) elected for Appleby 1790 but too young	Louisa Hervey Mary Chester	Hawkesbury
22	George Canning (1770–1827)	1827	Tory	Eton, Oxford (Christ Church), Lincoln's Inn	see note 4 below	Joan Scott	Westminster Abbey
23	Frederick John Robinson (Viscount Goderich) (1782–1859)	1827–1828	Tory	Harrow, Cambridge (St John's), Lincoln's Inn	Carlow (1806–7) & Ripon (1807–27)	Sarah Hobart	Nocton, Lincs
24	Arthur Wellesley (duke of Wellington) (1769–1852)	1828–1830	Tory	Browns Seminary, King's Rd, Chelsea, Eton, Brussels & Angers Military Acad.	Rye (1806), Newport IOW (1807–9) St Michael (1807)	Catherine Pakenham	St Paul's Cathedral
25	Charles Grey (Earl Grey) (1764–1845)	1830–1834	Whig	Eton, Cambridge (Trinity) & Middle Temple	Northumberland (1786–1807) Appleby (1807), Tavistock (1807)	Mary Elizabeth Ponsonby	Howick House, Northumberland
26	Henry William Lamb (Viscount Melbourne) (1779–1848)	1834	Whig	Eton, Cambridge (Trinity), Glasgow, Lincoln's Inn	see n. 4 below	Caroline Ponsonby	Hatfield

Name	Term of Office	Party	Education	Constituency	Marriage(s)	Buried
27 Robert Peel (1788–1850)	1834–1835	Tory	Harrow, Oxford (Christ Church), Lincoln's Inn	see n. 4 below	Julia Floyd	Drayton Bassett
28 Henry William Lamb (Viscount Melbourne) (1779–1848)	1835–1841	Whig	Eton, Cambridge (Trinity), Glasgow, Lincoln's Inn	see n. 4 below	Caroline Ponsonby	Hatfield
29 Robert Peel (1788–1850)	1841–1846	Conservative	Harrow, Oxford (Christ Church), Lincoln's Inn	see n. 4 below	Julia Floyd	Drayton Bassett
30 John Russell (Earl Russell) (1792–1878)	1846–1852	Whig	Westminster & Edinburgh	see n. 4 below	Abigail Lister Lady Frances Elliot	Chenies, Bucks
31 Edward George Stanley (earl of Derby) (1799–1869)	1852	Conservative	Eton & Oxford (Christ Church)	see n. 4 below	Emma Wilbraham-Bootle	Knowsley, Lancs
32 George Hamilton Gordon (earl of Aberdeen) (1784–1860)	1852–1855	Conservative (Peelite)	Harrow & Cambridge (St John's)	House of Lords	Catherine Hamilton Harriet Douglas	Stanmore, Gtr London
33 Henry John Temple (Viscount Palmerston) (1784–1865)	1855–1858	Liberal	Harrow, Edinburgh, Cambridge (St John's)	see n. 4 below	Emile Lamb the Dowager Countess Cowper	Westminster Abbey
34 Edward George Stanley (earl of Derby) (1799–1869)	1858–1859	Conservative	Eton & Oxford (Christ Church)	see n. 4 below	Emma Wilbraham-Bootle	Knowsley, Lancs
35 Henry John Temple (Viscount Palmerston) (1784–1865)	1859–1865	Liberal	Harrow, Edinburgh, Cambridge (St John's)	see n. 4 below	See above entry	Westminster Abbey
36 John Russell (Earl Russell) (1792–1878)	1865–1866	Liberal	Westminster & Edinburgh	see n. 4 below	Abigail Lister Lady Frances Elliot	Chenies, Bucks
37 Edward George Stanley (earl of Derby) (1799–1869)	1866–1868	Conservative	Eton & Oxford (Christ Church)	see n. 4 below	Emma Wilbraham-Bootle	Knowsley, Lancs
38 Benjamin Disraeli (earl of Beaconsfield) (1804–1881)	1868	Conservative	Lincoln's Inn	Maidstone (1837–41), Shrewsbury (1841–7), Buckinghamshire (1847–76)	Mrs Wyndham Lewis née Mary Ann Evans	Hughenden Manor, Buckinghamshire
39 William Ewart Gladstone (1809–1898)	1868–1874	Liberal	Seaforth Vicarage, Eton, Oxford (Christ Church)	see n. 4 below	Catherine Glynne	Westminster Abbey
40 Benjamin Disraeli (earl of Beaconsfield) (1804–1881)	1874–1880	Conservative	Lincoln's Inn	Maidstone (1837–41), Shrewsbury (1841–7), Buckinghamshire (1847–76)	Mrs Wyndham Lewis née Mary Ann Evans	Hughenden Manor, Buckinghamshire
41 William Ewart Gladstone (1809–1898)	1880–1885	Liberal	Seaforth Vicarage, Eton, Oxford (Christ Church)	see n. 4 below	Catherine Glynne	Westminster Abbey
42 Robert Arthur Talbot Cecil (marquis of Salisbury) (1830–1903)	1885–1886	Conservative	Eton & Oxford (Christ Church)	Stamford (1853–68)	Georgiana Alderson	Hatfield
43 William Ewart Gladstone (1809–1898)	1886	Liberal	Seaforth Vicarage, Eton, Oxford (Christ Church)	see n. 4 below	Catherine Glynne	Westminster Abbey
44 Robert Arthur Talbot Cecil (marquis of Salisbury) (1830–1903)	1886–1892	Conservative	Eton & Oxford (Christ Church)	Stamford (1853–68)	Georgiana Alderson	Hatfield
45 William Ewart Gladstone (1809–1898)	1892–1894	Liberal	Seaforth Vicarage, Eton, Oxford (Christ Church)	see n. 4 below	Catherine Glynne	Westminster Abbey
46 Archibald Philip Primrose (earl of Rosebery) (1847–1929)	1894–1895	Liberal	Eton & Oxford (Christ Church)	House of Lords	Hannah de Rothschild	Dalmeny
47 Robert Arthur Talbot Cecil (marquis of Salisbury) (1830–1903)	1895–1902	Conservative	Eton & Oxford (Christ Church)	Stamford (1853–68)	Georgiana Alderson	Hatfield
48 Arthur Balfour (earl of Balfour) (1848–1930)	1902–1905	Conservative	Eton & Cambridge (Trinity)	Hertford (1874–85), E. Manchester (1885–1906), London (1906–22)	Unmarried	Whittinghame, East Lothian
49 Henry Campbell-Bannerman (1836–1908)	1905–1908	Liberal	Glasgow & Cambridge (Trinity)	Stirling (1868–1908)	Sarah Charlotte Bruce	Meigle, Scotland
50 Herbert Henry Asquith (earl of Oxford) (1852–1928)	1908–1916	Liberal	City of London & Oxford (Balliol)	East Fife (1886–1918), Paisley (1920–4)	Helen Kelsall Melland Emma Tennant	Sutton Courtney Church, Bucks

	Name	Term of Office	Party	Education	Constituency	Marriage(s)	Buried
51	David Lloyd George (earl of Dwyfor) (1863–1945)	1916–1922	Coalition	Llanystumdwy Church School	Caernarvon (1890–1945)	Margaret Owen Frances Stevenson	Bank of River Dwyfor
52	Andrew Bonar Law (1858–1923)	1922–1923	Conservative	Gilbertfield in Hamilton & Glasgow High School	see n. 4 below	Annie Pitcairn Robley	Westminster Abbey
53	Stanley Baldwin (1867–1947) (Earl Baldwin of Bewdley)	1923–1924	Conservative	Harrow & Cambridge (Trinity)	Bewdley, Worcs (1908–37)	Lucy Ridsdale	Worcester Cathedral
54	James Ramsay MacDonald (1866–1937)	1924	Labour	Drainie Parish Board School	see n. 4 below	Margaret Gladstone	Spynie Churchyard, Lossiemouth
55	Stanley Baldwin (1867–1947) (Earl Baldwin of Bewdley)	1924–1929	Conservative	Harrow & Cambridge (Trinity)	Bewdley, Worcs (1908–37)	Lucy Ridsdale	Worcester Cathedral
56	James Ramsay MacDonald (1866–1937)	1929–1935	Labour	Drainie Parish Board School	see n. 4 below	Margaret Gladstone	Spynie Churchyard, Lossiemouth
57	Stanley Baldwin (1867–1947) (Earl Baldwin of Bewdley)	1935–1937	National	Harrow & Cambridge (Trinity)	Bewdley, Worcs (1908–37)	Lucy Ridsdale	Worcester Cathedral
58	Neville Chamberlain (1869–1940)	1937–1940	National	Rugby & Mason College (later Birmingham University)	Ladywood, Birmingham (1918–29) Edgbaston (1929–40)	Annie Vere Cole	Westminster Abbey (ashes)
59	Winston Leonard Spencer Churchill (1874–1965)	1940–1945	Coalition	Harrow & Royal Military College, Sandhurst	see n. 4 below	Clementine Ogilvy Hozier	Bladon, Oxfordshire
60	Clement Attlee (1883–1967)	1945–1951	Labour	Haileybury Coll. & Oxford (University)	Limehouse, Stepney (1922–50) West Walthamstow (1950–5)	Violet Millar	Westminster Abbey
61	Winston Leonard Spencer Churchill (1874–1965)	1951–1955	Conservative	Harrow & Royal Military College, Sandhurst	see n. 4 below	Clementine Ogilvy Hozier	Bladon, Oxfordshire
62	Anthony Eden (earl of Avon) (1897–1977)	1955–1957	Conservative	Eton & Oxford (Christ Church)	Warwick & Leamington (1923–57)	Beatrice Beckett Anne Spencer-Churchill	Alvediston, Wiltshire
63	Maurice Harold Macmillan (earl of Stockton) (1894–1986)	1957–1963	Conservative	Eton & Oxford (Balliol)	Stockton on Tees (1924–9 & 1931–45), Bromley (1945–64)	Dorothy Cavendish	Horsted Keynes
64	Alexander Frederick Douglas-Home (Lord Home of the Hirsel) (1903–1995)	1963–1964	Conservative	Eton & Oxford (Christ Church)	S. Lanark (1931–45), Lanark (1950–1), Kinross & West Perthshire (1963–74)	Elizabeth Alington	Coldstream
65	James Harold Wilson (1916–1995) (Lord Wilson of Rievaulx)	1964–1970	Labour	Milnsbridge, Royds Hall, Wirral, Oxford (Jesus)	Ormskirk (1945–50) Huyton (1950–83)	Gladys Mary Baldwin	Scilly Isles
66	Edward Heath (1916–2005)	1970–1974	Conservative	Chatham House, Ramsgate, Oxford (Balliol)	Bexley (1950–74), Bexley–Sidcup (1974–83), Old Bexley and Sidcup (1983–2001)	Unmarried	Salisbury Cathedral
67	James Harold Wilson (1916–1995) (Lord Wilson of Rievaulx)	1974–1976	Labour	Milnsbridge, Royds Hall, Wirral, Oxford (Jesus)	Ormskirk (1945–50) Huyton (1950–83)	Gladys Mary Baldwin	Scilly Isles
68	Leonard James Callaghan (Lord Callaghan of Cardiff) (1912–2005)	1976–1979	Labour	Portsmouth Northern Sec.	South Cardiff (1945–50), SE Cardiff (1950–83), Cardiff South and Penarth (1983–87)	Audrey Moulton	Cremated privately
69	Margaret Hilda Thatcher (1925–2013) (Baroness Thatcher of Kesteven)	1979–1990	Conservative	Kesteven & Grantham, Oxford (Somerville)	Finchley (1959–74), Barnet, Finchley (1974–92)	Denis Thatcher	Royal Hospital Chelsea (ashes buried)
70	John Major (1943–)	1990–1997	Conservative	Rutlish Grammar	Huntingdon (1983–2001)	Norma Johnson	
71	Tony Blair (1953–)	1997–2007	Labour	Durham Choristers, Fettes (Edinburgh), Oxford (St John's)	Sedgefield (1983–2007)	Cherie Booth	
72	Gordon Brown (1951–)	2007–2010	Labour	Kirkcaldy High School, University of Edinburgh	Dunfermline East (1983–2005) Kirkcaldy & Cowdenbeath (2005–)	Sarah Macaulay	
73	David Cameron (1966–)	2010–	Conservative	Eton & Oxford (Brasenose)	Witney (2001–)	Samantha Sheffield	

Notes

1 Prime Minister Although the office of prime minister is traditionally stated as commencing in 1721, in fact there were chief ministers given this label long before this date, and conversely there have been chief ministers subsequent to this date who did not bear the title of prime minister, e.g. William Pitt the Elder and Charles James Fox, in the mid- and late 18th century. To confuse matters further, Walpole was designated First Lord of the Treasury until 1730, as were some other future prime ministers of the 18th and 19th centuries. It was not until 1905 that the title of prime minister became official.

2 Party A second point of conjecture concerns the designation of the ruling party of the day. Until the first Electoral Reform Act of 1832 and the subsequent rise of the Conservative and Liberal parties, the government of the day was often a coalition of sorts, and the ruling party is given as the party of the prime minister in power, unless unaffiliated.

3 Chief ministers not listed above Sir William Pulteney, earl of Bath, actually kissed the hand of George II on 10 Feb. 1746, but within three days was unable to form a government. James Waldegrave kissed the hand of George II on 8 June 1757 but returned seals on 12 June, unable to form a ministry. Charles James Fox and his erstwhile enemy Lord North were the de facto heads of government in 1783, while the duke of Portland was merely the nominal prime minister. William Pitt the Elder, earl of Chatham, although not included in the table above, was in effect the prime minister from 1756 to 1761 during most of the Seven Years' War, although never taking up official office. From 1766 to 1768 Pitt was also Head of the Government but chose the secondary post of Lord Privy Seal; gout prevented him serving in anything but name for this second term.

4 Constituencies: See numbers in table above

(22) George Canning's: Newport IOW (1793–6 & 1806–7), Wendover (1796–1802), Tralee (1802–6), Hastings (1807–12), Liverpool (1812–23), Harwich (1823–6), Newport IOW (1826–7) & Seaford (1827).

(26) Viscount Melbourne's: Leominster (1806), Haddington Borough (1806–7), Portarlington (1807–12), Peterborough (1816–19), Hertfordshire (1819–26) Newport IOW (1827), Bletchingley (1827–8).

(27) Robert Peel's: Cashel (Tipperary) (1809–12), Chippenham (1812–17), Oxford University (1817–29), Westbury (1829–30), Tamworth (1830–50).

(30) Earl Russell's: Tavistock (1813–17, 1818–20, 1830–1), Huntingdonshire (1820–6), Bandon (1826–30), Devon (1831–2), South Devon (1832–5), Stroud (1835–41), London (1841–61).

(31) Earl of Derby's: Stockbridge (1822–6), Preston (1826–30), Windsor (1831–2), North Lancs (1832–44).

(33) Viscount Palmerston's: Newport IOW (1807–11), Cambridge University (1811–31), Bletchingley (1831–2), South Hants (1832–4), Tiverton (1835–65).

(39) William Gladstone's: Newark (1832–45 Tory), Oxford University (1847–65 as Peelite until 1859 then Liberal), South Lancs (1865–8), Greenwich (1868–80), Midlothian (1880–95).

(52) Andrew Bonar Law's: Blackfriars, Glasgow (1900–6), Dulwich (1906–10), Bootle (1911–18), Central Glasgow (1918–23).

(54) Ramsay MacDonald's: Leicester (1906–18), Aberavon (1922–9), Seaham, Co. Durham (1929–35), Scottish Universities (1936–7).

(59) Winston Churchill's: Oldham (1900–6, Conservative until 1904 then Liberal), NW Manchester (1906–8), Dundee (1908–22), Epping (1924–45), Woodford, Essex (1945–64 as Conservative).

5 Miscellaneous information

(2) Sir Spencer Compton was a Tory until 1704.

(8) George Grenville was nicknamed the Gentle Shepherd.

(9) Charles Watson Wentworth repealed the Stamp Act.

(10) Augustus Henry Fitzroy, the duke of Grafton, was a victim of the pseudonymous Junius letters which attacked various government ministers in the London *Public Advertiser* (1769–72), although the identity of Junius remains unknown. Sir Philip Francis is a possible candidate. He was also a direct descendant of the illegitimate son of Charles II.

(11) Lord Frederick North became a Whig in 1783.

(13) William Petty, the earl of Shelburne, was nicknamed Malagrida, after a notorious scheming Jesuit. He sat in the English House of Lords in his father's English title of Baron Wycombe.

(18) William Wyndham Grenville's administration of February 1806–March 1807 was known as 'The Ministry of All the Talents' and comprised followers of Charles James Fox. Its greatest achievement was the abolition of slavery in March 1807. He was the son of George Grenville (PM 1763–65).

(20) Spencer Perceval was assassinated by John Bellingham in the lobby of the Commons.

(21) Robert Banks Jenkinson was created Lord Hawkesbury in 1803 and earl of Liverpool in 1808.

(22) George Canning fought a duel with Viscount Castlereagh on Putney Heath in September 1809 but was only slightly wounded.

(24) Arthur Wellesley, duke of Wellington, was known as Arthur Wesley until 1804.

(27) Robert Peel created the Metropolitan Police Force in 1829 and drafted the 'Tamworth Manifesto' which laid down the ideology and objectives of the party which became the Conservatives. He died after a fall from a horse.

(30) Abigail Lister, the wife of Lord John Russell, became Baroness Ribblesdale.

(31) Edward George Stanley, the earl of Derby, became a Tory in 1835 (previously a Whig).

(33) Henry John Temple, Viscount Palmerston, was a Tory until 1829, then a Whig, and finally a Liberal. He was the last Prime Minister to die in office.

(42) Robert Arthur Talbot Gascoyne-Cecil was also known as Viscount Cranborne.

(48) Arthur James Balfour was the son of James Balfour MP and his wife, the sister of the third marquess of Salisbury, later the Conservative Prime Minister.

(49) Henry Campbell-Bannerman died at 10 Downing Street, three weeks after resigning.

(50) Herbert Henry Asquith's administration was a coalition from 1915.

(52) Andrew Bonar Law was born in New Brunswick, Canada. His term of office was 209 days.

(53) Stanley Baldwin was related to Rudyard Kipling and Sir Edward Burne-Jones.

(56) Ramsay MacDonald's second administration became a National Government, including Conservatives and Liberals, on 24 August 1931.

(59) Winston Churchill's first administration became Conservative from 23 May 1945.

(62) Anthony Eden's second wife was the niece of the former Prime Minister Winston Churchill.

6 William Pitt (the Elder) (1708–1778) Educated at Eton and Trinity College, Oxford. In 1735 he entered the House of Commons as member for the family borough of Old Sarum. In 1756 Pitt became nominally Secretary of State but was de facto Prime Minister from 1756 until October 1761. The King invited him to form a further government between 1766 and 1768 but he chose the secondary title of Lord Privy Seal while performing Prime Ministerial duties. Chronic gout caused a severe decline in his mental health and he died after making a speech in the House of Lords on 2 April 1778. His second son was William Pitt the Younger.

General Election Results: 6 May 2010 (plus subsequent changes)

Aberavon *Hywel Francis (L)*
Aberconwy *Guto Bebb (C)*
Aberdeen North *Frank Doran (L)*
Aberdeen South *Anne Begg (L)*
Aberdeenshire West and Kincardine *Robert Smith (LD)*
Airdrie and Shotts *Pamela Nash (L)*
Aldershot *Gerald Howarth (C)*
Aldridge-Brownhills *Richard Shepherd (C)*
Altrincham and Sale West *Graham Brady (C)*
Alyn and Deeside *Mark Tami (L)*
Amber Valley *Nigel Mills (C)*
Angus *Mike Weir (SNP)*
Antrim East *Sammy Wilson (DUP)*
Antrim North *Ian Paisley, Jr. (DUP)*
Antrim South *William McCrea (DUP)*
Arfon *Hywel Williams (PC)*
Argyll and Bute *Alan Reid (LD)*
Arundel and South Downs *Nick Herbert (C)*
Ashfield *Gloria De Piero (L)*
Ashford *Damian Green (C)*
Ashton-under-Lyne *David Heyes (L)*
Aylesbury *David Lidington (C)*
Ayr, Carrick and Cumnock *Sandra Osborne (L)*
Ayrshire Central *Brian Donohoe (L)*
Ayrshire North and Arran *Katy Clark (L)*
Banbury *Tony Baldry (C)*
Banff and Buchan *Eilidh Whiteford (SNP)*
Barking *Margaret Hodge (L)*
Barnsley Central *Eric Illsley (L)* replaced by *Dan Jarvis (L)* Mar 2011
Barnsley East *Michael Dugher (L)*
Barrow and Furness *John Woodcock (L)*
Basildon and Billericay *John Baron (C)*
Basildon South and East Thurrock *Stephen Metcalfe (C)*
Basingstoke *Maria Miller (C)*
Bassetlaw *John Mann (L)*
Bath *Don Foster (LD)*
Batley and Spen *Mike Wood (L)*
Battersea *Jane Ellison (C)*
Beaconsfield *Dominic Grieve (C)*
Beckenham *Bob Stewart (C)*
Bedford *Richard Fuller (C)*
Bedfordshire Mid *Nadine Dorries (C)*
Bedfordshire North East *Alistair Burt (C)*
Bedfordshire South West *Andrew Selous (C)*
Belfast East *Naomi Long (APNI)*
Belfast North *Nigel Dodds (DUP)*
Belfast South *Alasdair McDonnell (SDLP)*
Belfast West *Gerry Adams (SF)* replaced by *Paul Maskey (SF)* June 2011
Bermondsey and Old Southwark *Simon Hughes (LD)*
Berwick-upon-Tweed *Alan Beith (LD)*
Berwickshire, Roxburgh and Selkirk *Michael Moore (LD)*
Bethnal Green and Bow *Rushanara Ali (L)*
Beverley and Holderness *Graham Stuart (C)*
Bexhill and Battle *Greg Barker (C)*
Bexleyheath and Crayford *David Evennett (C)*
Birkenhead *Frank Field (L)*
Birmingham, Edgbaston *Gisela Stuart (L)*
Birmingham, Erdington *Jack Dromey (L)*
Birmingham, Hall Green *Roger Godsiff (L)*
Birmingham, Hodge Hill *Liam Byrne (L)*
Birmingham, Ladywood *Shabana Mahmood (L)*
Birmingham, Northfield *Richard Burden (L)*
Birmingham, Perry Barr *Khalid Mahmood (L)*
Birmingham, Selly Oak *Steve McCabe (L)*
Birmingham, Yardley *John Hemming (LD)*
Bishop Auckland *Helen Goodman (L)*
Blackburn *Jack Straw (L)*
Blackley and Broughton *Graham Stringer (L)*
Blackpool North and Cleveleys *Paul Maynard (C)*
Blackpool South *Gordon Marsden (L)*
Blaenau Gwent *Nick Smith (L)*
Blaydon *Dave Anderson (L)*
Blyth Valley *Ronnie Campbell (L)*
Bognor Regis and Littlehampton *Nick Gibb (C)*
Bolsover *Dennis Skinner (L)*
Bolton North East *David Crausby (L)*
Bolton South East *Yasmin Qureshi (L)*
Bolton West *Julie Hilling (L)*
Bootle *Joe Benton (L)*
Boston and Skegness *Mark Simmonds (C)*
Bosworth *David Tredinnick (C)*
Bournemouth East *Tobias Ellwood (C)*
Bournemouth West *Conor Burns (C)*
Bracknell *Phillip Lee (C)*
Bradford East *David Ward (LD)*
Bradford South *Gerry Sutcliffe (L)*
Bradford West *Marsha Singh (L)* replaced by *George Galloway (Respect)* Mar 2012
Braintree *Brooks Newmark (C)*
Brecon and Radnorshire *Roger Williams (LD)*
Brent Central *Sarah Teather (LD)*
Brent North *Barry Gardiner (L)*
Brentford and Isleworth *Mary MacLeod (C)*
Brentwood and Ongar *Eric Pickles (C)*
Bridgend *Madeleine Moon (L)*
Bridgwater and West Somerset *Ian Liddell-Grainger (C)*
Brigg and Goole *Andrew Percy (C)*
Brighton Kemptown *Simon Kirby (C)*
Brighton Pavilion *Caroline Lucas (Green)*
Bristol East *Kerry McCarthy (L)*
Bristol North West *Charlotte Leslie (C)*
Bristol South *Dawn Primarolo (L)*
Bristol West *Stephen Williams (LD)*
Broadland *Keith Simpson (C)*
Bromley and Chislehurst *Bob Neill (C)*
Bromsgrove *Sajid Javid (C)*
Broxbourne *Charles Walker (C)*
Broxtowe *Anna Soubry (C)*
Buckingham *John Bercow (C – Speaker)*
Burnley *Gordon Birtwistle (LD)*
Burton *Andrew Griffiths (C)*
Bury North *David Nuttall (C)*
Bury South *Ivan Lewis (L)*
Bury St Edmunds *David Ruffley (C)*
Caerphilly *Wayne David (L)*
Caithness, Sutherland and Easter Ross *John Thurso (LD)*
Calder Valley *Craig Whittaker (C)*
Camberwell and Peckham *Harriet Harman (L)*
Camborne and Redruth *George Eustice (C)*
Cambridge *Julian Huppert (LD)*
Cambridgeshire North East *Stephen Barclay (C)*
Cambridgeshire North West *Vera Shailesh (C)*
Cambridgeshire South *Andrew Lansley (C)*
Cambridgeshire South East *Jim Paice (C)*
Cannock Chase *Aidan Burley (C)*
Canterbury *Julian Brazier (C)*
Cardiff Central *Jenny Willott (LD)*
Cardiff North *Jonathan Evans (C)*
Cardiff South and Penarth *Alun Michael (L)* replaced by *Stephen Doughty (L)* Nov 2012
Cardiff West *Kevin Brennan (L)*
Carlisle *John Stevenson (C)*
Carmarthen East and Dinefwr *Jonathan Edwards (PC)*
Carmarthen West & South Pembrokeshire *Simon Hart (C)*
Carshalton and Wallington *Tom Brake (LD)*
Castle Point *Rebecca Harris (C)*
Ceredigion *Mark Williams (LD)*
Charnwood *Stephen Dorrell (C)*
Chatham and Aylesford *Tracey Crouch (C)*
Cheadle *Mark Hunter (LD)*
Chelmsford *Simon Burns (C)*
Chelsea and Fulham *Greg Hands (C)*

Cheltenham	*Martin Horwood (LD)*
Chesham and Amersham	*Cheryl Gillan (C)*
Chester, City of	*Stephen Mosley (C)*
Chesterfield	*Toby Perkins (L)*
Chichester	*Andrew Tyrie (C)*
Chingford and Woodford Green	*Iain Duncan Smith (C)*
Chippenham	*Duncan Hames (LD)*
Chipping Barnet	*Theresa Villiers (C)*
Chorley	*Lindsay Hoyle (L)*
Christchurch	*Christopher Chope (C)*
Cities of London and Westminster	*Mark Field (C)*
Clacton	*Douglas Carswell (C)*
Cleethorpes	*Martin Vickers (C)*
Clwyd South	*Susan Elan Jones (L)*
Clwyd West	*David Jones (C)*
Coatbridge, Chryston and Bellshill	*Tom Clarke (L)*
Colchester	*Bob Russell (LD)*
Colne Valley	*Jason McCartney (C)*
Congleton	*Fiona Bruce (C)*
Copeland	*Jamie Reed (L)*
Corby	*Louise Bagshawe (C)* replaced by *Andy Sawford (L) Nov 2012*
Cornwall North	*Dan Rogerson (LD)*
Cornwall South East	*Sheryll Murray (C)*
Cotswolds, The	*Geoffrey Clifton-Brown C)*
Coventry North East	*Bob Ainsworth (L)*
Coventry North West	*Geoffrey Robinson (L)*
Coventry South	*Jim Cunningham (L)*
Crawley	*Henry Smith (C)*
Crewe and Nantwich	*Edward Timpson (C)*
Croydon Central	*Gavin Barwell (C)*
Croydon North	*Malcolm Wicks (L)* d. replaced by *Steve Reed (L)* Nov 2012
Croydon South	*Richard Ottaway (C)*
Cumbernauld, Kilsyth & Kirkintilloch East	*Gregg McClymont (L)*
Cynon Valley	*Ann Clwyd (L)*
Dagenham and Rainham	*Jon Cruddas (L)*
Darlington	*Jenny Chapman (L)*
Dartford	*Gareth Johnson (C)*
Daventry	*Chris Heaton-Harris (C)*
Delyn	*David Hanson (L)*
Denton and Reddish	*Andrew Gwynne (L)*
Derby North	*Chris Williamson (L)*
Derby South	*Margaret Beckett (L)*
Derbyshire Dales	*Patrick McLoughlin (C)*
Derbyshire Mid	*Pauline Latham (C)*
Derbyshire North East	*Natascha Engel (L)*
Derbyshire South	*Heather Wheeler (C)*
Devizes	*Claire Perry (C)*
Devon Central	*Mel Stride (C)*
Devon East	*Hugo Swire (C)*
Devon North	*Nick Harvey (LD)*
Devon South West	*Gary Streeter (C)*
Devon West and Torridge	*Geoffrey Cox (C)*
Dewsbury	*Simon Reevell (C)*
Don Valley	*Caroline Flint (L)*
Doncaster Central	*Rosie Winterton (L)*
Doncaster North	*Ed Miliband (L)*
Dorset Mid and Poole North	*Annette Brooke (LD)*
Dorset North	*Bob Walter (C)*
Dorset South	*Richard Drax (C)*
Dorset West	*Oliver Letwin (C)*
Dover	*Charlie Elphicke (C)*
Down North	*Sylvia Hermon (Ind)*
Down South	*Margaret Ritchie (SDLP)*
Dudley North	*Ian Austin (L)*
Dudley South	*Chris Kelly (C)*
Dulwich and West Norwood	*Tessa Jowell (L)*
Dumfries and Galloway	*Russell Brown (L)*
Dumfriesshire, Clydesdale & Tweeddale	*David Mundell (C)*
Dunbartonshire East	*Jo Swinson (LD)*
Dunbartonshire West	*Gemma Doyle (L)*
Dundee East	*Stewart Hosie (SNP)*
Dundee West	*Jim McGovern (L)*
Dunfermline and West Fife	*Thomas Docherty (L)*
Durham, City of	*Roberta Blackman-Woods (L)*
Durham North	*Kevan Jones (L)*
Durham North West	*Pat Glass (L)*
Dwyfor Meirionydd	*Elfyn Llwyd (PC)*
Ealing Central and Acton	*Angie Bray (C)*
Ealing North	*Stephen Pound (L)*
Ealing Southall	*Virendra Sharma (L)*
Easington	*Grahame Morris (L)*
East Kilbride, Strathaven & Lesmahagow	*Michael McCann (L)*
East Lothian	*Fiona O'Donnell (L)*
Eastbourne	*Stephen Lloyd (LD)*
Eastleigh	*Chris Huhne (LD)* replaced by *Mike Thornton (LD)* Feb 2013
Edinburgh East	*Sheila Gilmore (L)*
Edinburgh North and Leith	*Mark Lazarowicz (L)*
Edinburgh South	*Ian Murray (L)*
Edinburgh South West	*Alistair Darling (L)*
Edinburgh West	*Michael Crockart (LD)*
Edmonton	*Andy Love (L)*
Ellesmere Port and Neston	*Andrew Miller (L)*
Elmet and Rothwell	*Alec Shelbrooke (C)*
Eltham	*Clive Efford (L)*
Enfield North	*Nick de Bois (C)*
Enfield Southgate	*David Burrowes (C)*
Epping Forest	*Eleanor Laing (C)*
Epsom and Ewell	*Chris Grayling (C)*
Erewash	*Jessica Lee (C)*
Erith and Thamesmead	*Teresa Pearce (L)*
Esher and Walton	*Dominic Raab (C)*
Falkirk	*Eric Joyce (L)*
Fareham	*Mark Hoban (C)*
Faversham and Kent Mid	*Hugh Robertson (C)*
Feltham and Heston	*Alan Keen (L)* d. replaced by *Seema Malhotra (L)* Dec 2011
Fermanagh and South Tyrone	*Michelle Gildernew (SF)*
Fife North East	*Menzies Campbell (LD)*
Filton and Bradley Stoke	*Jack Lopresti (C)*
Finchley and Golders Green	*Mike Freer (C)*
Folkestone and Hythe	*Damian Collins (C)*
Forest of Dean	*Mark Harper (C)*
Foyle	*Mark Durkan (SDLP)*
Fylde	*Mark Menzies (C)*
Gainsborough	*Edward Leigh (C)*
Garston and Halewood	*Maria Eagle (L)*
Gateshead	*Ian Mearns (L)*
Gedling	*Vernon Coaker (L)*
Gillingham and Rainham	*Rehman Chishti (C)*
Glasgow Central	*Anas Sarwar (L)*
Glasgow East	*Margaret Curran (L)*
Glasgow North	*Ann McKechin (L)*
Glasgow North East	*Willie Bain (L)*
Glasgow North West	*John Robertson (L)*
Glasgow South	*Tom Harris (L)*
Glasgow South West	*Ian Davidson (L)*
Glenrothes	*Lindsay Roy (L)*
Gloucester	*Richard Graham (C)*
Gordon	*Malcolm Bruce (LD)*
Gosport	*Caroline Dinenage (C)*
Gower	*Martin Caton (L)*
Grantham and Stamford	*Nicholas Boles (C)*
Gravesham	*Adam Holloway (C)*
Great Grimsby	*Austin Mitchell (L)*
Great Yarmouth	*Brandon Lewis C)*
Greenwich and Woolwich	*Nick Raynsford (L)*
Guildford	*Anne Milton (C)*
Hackney North and Stoke Newington	*Diane Abbott (L)*
Hackney South and Shoreditch	*Meg Hillier (L)*
Halesowen and Rowley Regis	*James Morris (C)*
Halifax	*Linda Riordan (L)*
Haltemprice and Howden	*David Davis (C)*
Halton	*Derek Twigg (L)*
Hammersmith	*Andy Slaughter (L)*
Hampshire East	*Damian Hinds (C)*
Hampshire North East	*James Arbuthnot (C)*
Hampshire North West	*George Young (C)*

Hampstead and Kilburn	*Glenda Jackson (L)*
Harborough	*Edward Garnier (C)*
Harlow	*Robert Halfon (C)*
Harrogate and Knaresborough	*Andrew Jones (C)*
Harrow East	*Bob Blackman (C)*
Harrow West	*Gareth Thomas (L)*
Hartlepool	*Iain Wright (L)*
Harwich and Essex North	*Bernard Jenkin (C)*
Hastings and Rye	*Amber Rudd (C)*
Havant	*David Willetts (C)*
Hayes and Harlington	*John McDonnell (L)*
Hazel Grove	*Andrew Stunell (LD)*
Hemel Hempstead	*Mike Penning (C)*
Hemsworth	*John Trickett (L)*
Hendon	*Matthew Offord (C)*
Henley	*John Howell (C)*
Hereford and Herefordshire South	*Jesse Norman (C)*
Herefordshire North	*Bill Wiggin (C)*
Hertford and Stortford	*Mark Prisk (C)*
Hertfordshire North East	*Oliver Heald (C)*
Hertfordshire South West	*David Gauke (C)*
Hertsmere	*James Clappison (C)*
Hexham	*Guy Opperman (C)*
Heywood and Middleton	*Jim Dobbin (L)*
High Peak	*Andrew Bingham (C)*
Hitchin and Harpenden	*Peter Lilley (C)*
Holborn and St Pancras	*Frank Dobson (L)*
Hornchurch and Upminster	*Angela Watkinson (C)*
Hornsey and Wood Green	*Lynne Featherstone (LD)*
Horsham	*Francis Maude (C)*
Houghton and Sunderland South	*Bridget Phillipson (L)*
Hove	*Mike Weatherley (C)*
Huddersfield	*Barry Sheerman (L)*
Hull East	*Karl Turner (L)*
Hull North	*Diana Johnson (L)*
Hull West and Hessle	*Alan Johnson (L)*
Huntingdon	*Jonathan Djanogly (C)*
Hyndburn	*Graham Jones (L)*
Ilford North	*Lee Scott (C)*
Ilford South	*Mike Gapes (L)*
Inverclyde	*David Cairns (L)* d. replaced by *Iain McKenzie (L)* June 2011
Inverness, Nairn, Badenoch & Strathspey	*Danny Alexander (LD)*
Ipswich	*Ben Gummer (C)*
Isle of Wight	*Andrew Turner (C)*
Islington North	*Jeremy Corbyn (L)*
Islington South and Finsbury	*Emily Thornberry (L)*
Islwyn	*Christopher Evans (L)*
Jarrow	*Stephen Hepburn (L)*
Keighley	*Kris Hopkins (C)*
Kenilworth and Southam	*Jeremy Wright (C)*
Kensington	*Malcolm Rifkind (C)*
Kettering	*Philip Hollobone (C)*
Kilmarnock and Loudoun	*Cathy Jamieson (L)*
Kingston and Surbiton	*Ed Davey (LD)*
Kingswood	*Chris Skidmore (C)*
Kirkcaldy and Cowdenbeath	*Gordon Brown (L)*
Knowsley	*George Howarth (L)*
Lagan Valley	*Jeffrey Donaldson (DUP)*
Lanark and Hamilton East	*Jimmy Hood (L)*
Lancashire West	*Rosie Cooper (L)*
Lancaster and Fleetwood	*Eric Ollerenshaw (C)*
Leeds Central	*Hilary Benn (L)*
Leeds East	*George Mudie (L)*
Leeds North East	*Fabian Hamilton (L)*
Leeds North West	*Greg Mulholland (LD)*
Leeds West	*Rachel Reeves (L)*
Leicester East	*Keith Vaz (L)*
Leicester South	*Peter Soulsby (L)* replaced by *Jon Ashworth (L)* May 2011
Leicester West	*Elizabeth Kendall (L)*
Leicestershire North West	*Andrew Bridgen (C)*
Leicestershire South	*Andrew Robathan (C)*
Leigh	*Andy Burnham (L)*
Lewes	*Norman Baker (LD)*
Lewisham Deptford	*Joan Ruddock (L)*
Lewisham East	*Heidi Alexander (L)*
Lewisham West and Penge	*Jim Dowd (L)*
Leyton and Wanstead	*John Cryer (L)*
Lichfield	*Michael Fabricant (C)*
Lincoln	*Karl McCartney (C)*
Linlithgow and East Falkirk	*Michael Connarty (L)*
Liverpool, Riverside	*Louise Ellman (L)*
Liverpool, Walton	*Steve Rotheram (L)*
Liverpool, Wavertree	*Luciana Berger (L)*
Liverpool, West Derby	*Stephen Twigg (L)*
Livingston	*Graeme Morrice (L)*
Llanelli	*Nia Griffith (L)*
Londonderry East	*Gregory Campbell (DUP)*
Loughborough	*Nicky Morgan (C)*
Louth and Horncastle	*Peter Tapsell (C)*
Ludlow	*Philip Dunne (C)*
Luton North	*Kelvin Hopkins (L)*
Luton South	*Gavin Shuker (L)*
Macclesfield	*David Rutley (C)*
Maidenhead	*Theresa May (C)*
Maidstone and The Weald	*Helen Grant (C)*
Makerfield	*Yvonne Fovargue (L)*
Maldon	*John Whittingdale (C)*
Manchester Central	*Tony Lloyd (L)* replaced by *Lucy Powell (L)* Nov 2012
Manchester, Gorton	*Gerald Kaufman (L)*
Manchester, Withington	*John Leech (LD)*
Mansfield	*Alan Meale (L)*
Meon Valley	*George Hollingbery (C)*
Meriden	*Caroline Spelman (C)*
Merthyr Tydfil and Rhymney	*Dai Havard (L)*
Middlesbrough	*Stuart Bell (L)* d. replaced by *Andy McDonald (L)* Nov 2012
Middlesbrough South & East Cleveland	*Tom Blenkinsop (L)*
Midlothian	*David Hamilton (L)*
Milton Keynes North	*Mark Lancaster (C)*
Milton Keynes South	*Iain Stewart (C)*
Mitcham and Morden	*Siobhan McDonough (L)*
Mole Valley	*Paul Beresford (C)*
Monmouth	*David Davies (C)*
Montgomeryshire	*Glyn Davies (C)*
Moray	*Angus Robertson (SNP)*
Morecambe and Lunesdale	*David Morris (C)*
Morley and Outwood	*Ed Balls (L)*
Motherwell and Wishaw	*Frank Roy (L)*
Na h-Eileanan an Iar	*Angus MacNeill (SNP)*
Neath	*Peter Hain (L)*
New Forest East	*Julian Lewis (C)*
New Forest West	*Desmond Swayne (C)*
Newark	*Patrick Mercer (C)*
Newbury	*Richard Benyon (C)*
Newcastle-under-Lyme	*Paul Farrelly (L)*
Newcastle upon Tyne Central	*Chi Onwurah (L)*
Newcastle upon Tyne East	*Nick Brown (L)*
Newcastle upon Tyne North	*Catherine McKinnell (L)*
Newport East	*Jessica Morden (L)*
Newport West	*Paul Flynn (L)*
Newry and Armagh	*Conor Murphy (SF)*
Newton Abbot	*Anne-Marie Morris (C)*
Norfolk Mid	*George Freeman (C)*
Norfolk North	*Norman Lamb (LD)*
Norfolk North West	*Henry Bellingham (C)*
Norfolk South	*Richard Bacon (C)*
Norfolk South West	*Elizabeth Truss (C)*
Normanton, Pontefract and Castleford	*Yvette Cooper (L)*
Northampton North	*Michael Ellis (C)*
Northampton South	*Brian Binley (C)*
Northamptonshire South	*Andrea Leadsom (C)*
Norwich North	*Chloe Smith (C)*
Norwich South	*Simon Wright (LD)*
Nottingham East	*Christopher Leslie (L)*
Nottingham North	*Graham Allen (L)*
Nottingham South	*Lilian Greenwood (L)*
Nuneaton	*Marcus Jones (C)*
Ochil and South Perthshire	*Gordon Banks (L)*
Ogmore	*Huw Irranca-Davies (L)*

Old Bexley and Sidcup	*James Brokenshire (C)*
Oldham East and Saddleworth	*Phil Woolas (L)* replaced by *Debbie Abrahams (L)* Jan 2011
Oldham West and Royton	*Michael Meacher (L)*
Orkney and Shetland	*Alistair Carmichael (LD)*
Orpington	*Joseph Johnson (C)*
Oxford East	*Andrew Smith (L)*
Oxford West and Abingdon	*Nicola Blackwood (C)*
Paisley and Renfrewshire North	*Jim Sheridan (L)*
Paisley and Renfrewshire South	*Douglas Alexander (L)*
Pendle	*Andrew Stephenson (C)*
Penistone and Stocksbridge	*Angela Smith (L)*
Penrith and The Border	*Rory Stewart (C)*
Perth and Perthshire North	*Pete Wishart (SNP)*
Peterborough	*Stewart Jackson (C)*
Plymouth, Moor View	*Alison Seabeck (L)*
Plymouth, Sutton and Devonport	*Oliver Colville (C)*
Pontypridd	*Owen Smith (L)*
Poole	*Robert Syms (C)*
Poplar and Limehouse	*Jim Fitzpatrick (L)*
Portsmouth North	*Penny Mordaunt (C)*
Portsmouth South	*Mike Hancock (LD)*
Preseli Pembrokeshire	*Stephen Crabb (C)*
Preston	*Mark Hendrick (L)*
Pudsey	*Stuart Andrew (C)*
Putney	*Justine Greening (C)*
Rayleigh and Wickford	*Mark Francois (C)*
Reading East	*Rob Wilson (C)*
Reading West	*Alok Sharma (C)*
Redcar	*Ian Swales (LD)*
Redditch	*Karen Lumley (C)*
Reigate	*Crispin Blunt (C)*
Renfrewshire East	*Jim Murphy (L)*
Rhondda	*Chris Bryant (L)*
Ribble Valley	*Nigel Evans (C)*
Richmond	*William Hague (C)*
Richmond Park	*Zac Goldsmith (C)*
Rochdale	*Simon Danczuk (L)*
Rochester and Strood	*Mark Reckless (C)*
Rochford and Southend East	*James Duddridge (C)*
Romford	*Andrew Rosindell (C)*
Romsey and Southampton North	*Caroline Nokes (C)*
Ross, Skye and Lochaber	*Charles Kennedy (LD)*
Rossendale and Darwen	*Jake Berry (C)*
Rother Valley	*Kevin Barron (L)*
Rotherham	*Denis MacShane (L)* replaced by *Sarah Champion (L)* Nov 2012
Rugby	*Mark Pawsey (C)*
Ruislip, Northwood and Pinner	*Nick Hurd (C)*
Runnymede and Weybridge	*Philip Hammond (C)*
Rushcliffe	*Kenneth Clarke (C)*
Rutherglen and Hamilton West	*Tom Greatrex (L)*
Rutland and Melton	*Alan Duncan (C)*
Saffron Walden	*Alan Haselhurst (C)*
St Albans	*Anne Main (C)*
St Austell and Newquay	*Stephen Gilbert (LD)*
St Helens North	*Dave Watts (L)*
St Helens South and Whiston	*Shaun Woodward (L)*
St Ives	*Andrew George (LD)*
Salford and Eccles	*Hazel Blears (L)*
Salisbury	*John Glen (C)*
Scarborough and Whitby	*Robert Goodwill (C)*
Scunthorpe	*Nic Dakin (L)*
Sedgefield	*Phil Wilson (L)*
Sefton Central	*Bill Esterson (L)*
Selby and Ainsty	*Nigel Adams (C)*
Sevenoaks	*Michael Fallon (C)*
Sheffield, Brightside and Hillsborough	*David Blunkett (L)*
Sheffield Central	*Paul Blomfield (L)*
Sheffield, Hallam	*Nick Clegg (LD)*
Sheffield, Heeley	*Meg Munn (L)*
Sheffield South East	*Clive Betts (L)*
Sherwood	*Mark Spencer (C)*
Shipley	*Philip Davies (C)*
Shrewsbury and Atcham	*Daniel Kawczynski (C)*
Shropshire North	*Owen Paterson (C)*
Sittingbourne and Sheppey	*Gordon Henderson (C)*
Skipton and Ripon	*Julian Smith (C)*
Sleaford and North Hykeham	*Stephen Philips (C)*
Slough	*Fiona Mactaggart (L)*
Solihull	*Lorely Burt (LD)*
Somerset North	*Liam Fox (C)*
Somerset North East	*Jacob Rees-Mogg (C)*
Somerton and Frome	*David Heath (LD)*
South Holland and The Deepings	*John Hayes (C)*
South Ribble	*Lorraine Fullbrook (C)*
South Shields	*David Miliband (L)* replaced by *Emma Lewell-Buck (L)* May 2013
Southampton, Itchen	*John Denham (L)*
Southampton, Test	*Alan Whitehead (L)*
Southend West	*David Amess (C)*
Southport	*John Pugh (LD)*
Spelthorne	*Kwasi Kwarteng (C)*
Stafford	*Jeremy Lefroy (C)*
Staffordshire Moorlands	*Karen Bradley (C)*
Staffordshire South	*Gavin Williamson (C)*
Stalybridge and Hyde	*Jonathan Reynolds (L)*
Stevenage	*Stephen McPartland (C)*
Stirling	*Anne McGuire (L)*
Stockport	*Ann Coffey (L)*
Stockton North	*Alex Cunningham (L)*
Stockton South	*James Wharton (C)*
Stoke-on-Trent Central	*Tristram Hunt (L)*
Stoke-on-Trent North	*Joan Walley (L)*
Stoke-on-Trent South	*Rob Flello (L)*
Stone	*Bill Cash (C)*
Stourbridge	*Margot James (C)*
Strangford	*Jim Shannon (DUP)*
Stratford-on-Avon	*Nadhim Zahawi (C)*
Streatham	*Chuka Umunna (L)*
Stretford and Urmston	*Kate Green (L)*
Stroud	*Neil Carmichael (C)*
Suffolk Central and Ipswich North	*Daniel Poulter (C)*
Suffolk Coastal	*Therese Coffey (C)*
Suffolk South	*Tim Yeo (C)*
Suffolk West	*Matthew Hancock (C)*
Sunderland Central	*Julie Elliott (L)*
Surrey East	*Sam Gyimah (C)*
Surrey Heath	*Michael Gove (C)*
Surrey South West	*Jeremy Hunt (C)*
Sussex Mid	*Nicholas Soames (C)*
Sutton and Cheam	*Paul Burstow (LD)*
Sutton Coldfield	*Andrew Mitchell (C)*
Swansea East	*Sian James (L)*
Swansea West	*Geraint Davies (L)*
Swindon North	*Justin Tomlinson (C)*
Swindon South	*Robert Buckland (C)*
Tamworth	*Christopher Pincher (C)*
Tatton	*George Osborne (C)*
Taunton Deane	*Jeremy Browne (LD)*
Telford	*David Wright (L)*
Tewkesbury	*Laurence Robertson (C)*
Thanet North	*Roger Gale (C)*
Thanet South	*Laura Sandys (C)*
Thirsk and Malton*	*Anne McIntosh (C)*
Thornbury and Yate	*Steve Webb (LD)*
Thurrock	*Jackie Doyle-Price (C)*
Tiverton and Honiton	*Neil Parish (C)*
Tonbridge and Malling	*John Stanley (C)*
Tooting	*Sadiq Khan (L)*
Torbay	*Adrian Sanders (LD)*
Torfaen	*Paul Murphy (L)*
Totnes	*Sarah Wollaston (C)*
Tottenham	*David Lammy (L)*
Truro and Falmouth	*Sarah Newton (C)*
Tunbridge Wells	*Greg Clark (C)*
Twickenham	*Vince Cable (LD)*

Constituency	MP	Constituency	MP
Tynemouth	*Alan Campbell (L)*	**Westmorland and Lonsdale**	*Tim Farron (LD)*
Tyneside North	*Mary Glindon (L)*	**Weston-Super-Mare**	*John Penrose (C)*
Tyrone West	*Pat Doherty (SF)*	**Wigan**	*Lisa Nandy (L)*
Ulster Mid	*Martin McGuinness (SF)* replaced by *Francie Molloy (SF)* Mar 2013	**Wiltshire North**	*James Gray (C)*
		Wiltshire South West	*Andrew Murrison (C)*
Upper Bann	*David Simpson (DUP)*	**Wimbledon**	*Stephen Hammond (C)*
Uxbridge and South Ruislip	*John Randall (C)*	**Winchester**	*Steve Brine (C)*
Vale of Clwyd	*Chris Ruane (L)*	**Windsor**	*Adam Afriyie (C)*
Vale of Glamorgan	*Alun Cairns (C)*	**Wirral South**	*Alison McGovern (L)*
Vauxhall	*Kate Hoey (L)*	**Wirral West**	*Esther McVey (C)*
Wakefield	*Mary Creagh (L)*	**Witham**	*Priti Patel (C)*
Wallasey	*Angela Eagle (L)*	**Witney**	*David Cameron (C)*
Walsall North	*David Winnick (L)*	**Woking**	*Jonathan Lord (C)*
Walsall South	*Valerie Vaz (L)*	**Wokingham**	*John Redwood (C)*
Walthamstow	*Stella Creasy (L)*	**Wolverhampton North East**	*Emma Reynolds (L)*
Wansbeck	*Ian Lavery (L)*	**Wolverhampton South East**	*Pat McFadden (L)*
Wantage	*Ed Vaizey (C)*	**Wolverhampton South West**	*Paul Uppal (C)*
Warley	*John Spellar (L)*	**Worcester**	*Robin Walker (C)*
Warrington North	*Helen Jones (L)*	**Worcestershire Mid**	*Peter Luft (C)*
Warrington South	*David Mowat (C)*	**Worcestershire West**	*Harriett Baldwin (C)*
Warwick and Leamington	*Chris White (C)*	**Workington**	*Tony Cunningham (L)*
Warwickshire North	*Dan Byles (C)*	**Worsley and Eccles South**	*Barbara Keeley (L)*
Washington and Sunderland West	*Sharon Hodgson (L)*	**Worthing East and Shoreham**	*Tim Loughton (C)*
Watford	*Richard Harrington (C)*	**Worthing West**	*Peter Bottomley (C)*
Waveney	*Peter Aldous (C)*	**Wrekin, The**	*Mark Pritchard (C)*
Wealden	*Charles Hendry (C)*	**Wrexham**	*Ian Lucas (L)*
Weaver Vale	*Graham Evans (C)*	**Wycombe**	*Steven Baker (C)*
Wellingborough	*Peter Bone (C)*	**Wyre and Preston North**	*Ben Wallace (C)*
Wells	*Tessa Munt (LD)*	**Wyre Forest**	*Mark Garnier (C)*
Welwyn Hatfield	*Grant Shapps (C)*	**Wythenshawe and Sale East**	*Paul Goggins (L)*
Wentworth and Dearne	*John Healey (L)*	**Yeovil**	*David Laws (LD)*
West Bromwich East	*Tom Watson (L)*	**Ynys Môn (Anglesey)**	*Albert Owen (L)*
West Bromwich West	*Adrian Bailey (L)*	**York Central**	*Hugh Bayley (L)*
West Ham	*Lyn Brown (L)*	**York Outer**	*Julian Sturdy (C)*
Westminster North	*Karen Buck (L)*	**Yorkshire East**	*Greg Knight (C)*

Note: Due to death of UKIP candidate John Boakes the Thirsk and Malton result was not decided until 27 May 2010

Miscellaneous Information: After 2010 General Election

Composition of the House of Commons	Conservative Party (10,828,916)	307	(257 men, 50 women)
	Labour Party (8,606,518)	258	(176 men, 82 women)
	Liberal Democrats (6,836,718)	57	(50 men, 7 women)
	Democratic Unionist Party	8	(all men)
	Scottish National Party	6	(5 men, 1 woman)
	Sinn Féin	5	(4 men, 1 woman)
	Plaid Cymru	3	(all men)
	Social Democratic and Labour Party	3	(2 men, 1 woman)
	Green Party of England and Wales	1	(woman)
	Alliance Party of Northern Ireland	1	(woman)
	Independent Unionist (Sylvia Hermon)	1	(woman)
	Speaker	1	(man)

high-profile losers — Charles Clarke (former Labour Home Secretary) in Norwich South; Reg Empey (leader of the Ulster Unionists) in Antrim South; Lembit Opik for the Lib Dems in Montgomeryshire; Peter Robinson (First Minister of Northern Ireland since 5 June 2008 and leader of the DUP since 31 May 2008) in Belfast East; Jacqui Smith (former Labour Home Secretary) in Redditch.

high-profile winners — *Romantic novelist Louise Bagshawe in Corby; millionaire Zac Goldsmith (son of financier Sir James Goldsmith) in Richmond Park; Pamela Nash in Airdrie (at 25 she is the 'Baby of the House'); Caroline Lucas (the Green Party's first-ever MP in the House of Commons of the United Kingdom) in Brighton; Priti Patel (the first Asian female Conservative MP) in Witham; Michelle Gildernew (smallest majority – 4) in Fermanagh and South Tyrone; Helen Grant (first black female Conservative MP) in Maidstone & The Weald; Peter Tapsell (Father of the House – longest serving MP) in Louth & Horncastle.

* **Louise Daphne Bagshawe** (b. 28 June 1971) married Peter Mensch in 2011, retired and relocated to the United States, where her husband took up work. Technically, MPs cannot resign. However, they can effectively do so by requesting to be appointed as Steward of the Chiltern Hundreds or Steward of the Manor of Northstead, which automatically vacates their seat.

NB Several serving MPs have ceased to be a member of their party, but continue to sit in the House of Commons as independents either through choice or because they have had the party whip withdrawn. As at October 2013 these include: **Eric Joyce** (Lab, Falkirk) who was suspended on 23 February 2012 following his arrest on suspicion of assault the night before; **Patrick Mercer** (Con, Newark) who resigned on 31 May 2013 after he was the subject of a journalistic sting exploring his conduct regarding lobbying companies; **Mike Hancock** (LD, Portsmouth South) who resigned on 3 June 2013 until a forthcoming court case, involving allegations of sexual offences made against him, has ended; **David Ward** (LD, Bradford East), who was suspended on 18 July 2013 after questioning the continuing existence of the state of Israel and refusing to apologise for his remarks; **Nigel Evans** (Con, Ribble Valley) who resigned as First Deputy Chairman of Ways and Means and chose to sit as an independent in September 2013 after being charged with offences including sexual assault and rape.

Cabinet Positions (past and present)

The Cabinet is the traditional inner circle of the most senior ministers of Her Majesty's Government in the United Kingdom, composed of the Prime Minister and 22 Cabinet ministers, although recently there has been a trend towards non-Cabinet ministers and even non-members of the Houses of Parliament attending meetings as guests.

The incumbents, frequently entitled Secretaries of State of their various departments, are empowered to form policy and are the public face of their ministries, although the permanent secretaries, who are non-party civil servants, necessarily tend to perform much of the day to day running of the offices.

It is a peculiarity of the UK system that the government of the day heads the departments while the civil servants carrying out its policy might be of a totally opposite political persuasion. This has sometimes been known to cause a certain inertia within departments.

Cabinet members from the Commons are created Privy Councillors on appointment and are addressed as 'The Right Honourable'. Cabinet members from the Lords (a rarity these days) are already Privy Councillors.

The following is a list of the incumbents of the various Cabinet positions in all their guises.

Agriculture, Fisheries and Food

The Ministry of Agriculture, Fisheries and Food was a government department created by the Board of Agriculture Act 1889 and at that time called the Board of Agriculture. In 1903 the department was renamed the Board of Agriculture and Fisheries and by 1919 it became a ministry. It was renamed the Ministry of Agriculture, Fisheries and Food (MAFF) in 1954 after merging with the Ministry of Food which was set up to deal with food rationing in both world wars. Its functions were transferred to a new government department, the Department for Environment, Food and Rural Affairs (Defra), in 2001 although MAFF was not formally disbanded until the following year.

Name	***Period***	***Party***
Henry Chaplin	9 Sept. 1889–11 Aug. 1892	*Conservative*
Herbert Gardner	25 Aug. 1892–21 June 1895	*Liberal*
Walter Hume Long	4 July 1895–16 Nov. 1900	*Conservative*
Robert Hanbury	16 Nov. 1900–28 Apr. 1903	*Conservative*
William Onslow, 4th Earl of Onslow	19 May 1903–12 Mar. 1905	*Conservative*
Ailwyn Fellowes	12 Mar.–4 Dec. 1905	*Conservative*
Charles Robert Wynn Carrington, 1st Earl Carrington	10 Dec. 1905–23 Oct. 1911	*Liberal*
Walter Runciman	23 Oct. 1911–6 Aug. 1914	*Liberal*
Auberon Herbert, 9th Baron Lucas	6 Aug. 1914–25 May 1915	*Liberal*
William Waldegrave Palmer, 2nd Earl of Selborne	25 May 1915–11 July 1916	*Conservative*
David Lindsay, 27th Earl of Crawford	11 July–10 Dec. 1916	*Conservative*
Rowland Edmund Prothero	10 Dec. 1916–15 Aug. 1919	*Conservative*
Arthur Hamilton Lee, 1st Viscount Lee of Fareham	15 Aug. 1919–13 Feb. 1921	*Conservative*
Arthur Griffith-Boscawen	13 Feb. 1921–24 Oct. 1922	*Conservative*
Sir Robert Sanders	24 Oct. 1922–22 Jan. 1924	*Conservative*
Noel Buxton	22 Jan.–3 Nov. 1924	*Labour*
Edward F L Wood	6 Nov. 1924–4 Nov. 1925	*Conservative*
Walter Guinness	4 Nov. 1925–4 June 1929	*Conservative*
Noel Buxton	7 June 1929–5 June 1930	*Labour*
Christopher Addison	5 June 1930–24 Aug. 1931	*Labour*
Sir John Gilmour	25 Aug. 1931–28 Sept. 1932	*Conservative*
Walter Elliot	28 Sept. 1932–29 Oct. 1936	*Conservative*
William Shepherd Morrison	29 Oct. 1936–29 Jan. 1939	*Conservative*
Sir Reginald Dorman-Smith	29 Jan. 1939–14 May 1940	*Conservative*
Robert Hudson	14 May 1940–26 July 1945	*Conservative*
Tom Williams	3 Aug. 1945–26 Oct. 1951	*Labour*
Sir Thomas Dugdale	31 Oct. 1951–20 July 1954	*Conservative*
Derick Heathcoat-Amory	28 July 1954–6 Jan. 1958	*Conservative*
John Hare, 1st Viscount Blakenham	6 Jan. 1958–27 July 1960	*Conservative*
Christopher Soames	27 July 1960–16 Oct. 1964	*Conservative*
Fred Peart	16 Oct. 1964–6 Apr. 1968	*Labour*
Cledwyn Hughes	6 Apr. 1968–19 June 1970	*Labour*
James Prior	20 June 1970–5 Nov. 1972	*Conservative*
Joseph Godber	5 Nov. 1972–4 Mar. 1974	*Conservative*
Fred Peart	5 Mar. 1974–10 Sept. 1976	*Labour*
John Silkin	10 Sept. 1976–4 May 1979	*Labour*
Peter Walker	5 May 1979–11 June 1983	*Conservative*
Michael Jopling	11 June 1983–13 June 1987	*Conservative*
John MacGregor	13 June 1987–24 July 1989	*Conservative*
John Gummer	24 July 1989–27 May 1993	*Conservative*
Gillian Shephard	27 May 1993–20 July 1994	*Conservative*
William Waldegrave	20 July 1994–5 July 1995	*Conservative*
Douglas Hogg	5 July 1995–2 May 1997	*Conservative*
Jack Cunningham	3 May 1997–27 July 1998	*Labour*
Nick Brown	27 July 1998–8 June 2001	*Labour*
Margaret Beckett	8 June 2001–27 Mar. 2002	*Labour*

Board of Trade

The Board of Trade came into existence in 1672 as an amalgamation of the Council of Trade and Council of Foreign Plantations, both formed in 1660. Initially the incumbent was known as First Lord of Trade, but in 1784 Baron Sydney (he who gave his name to cities in Canada and Australia) took office as President of the Committee on Trade and Foreign Plantations. Thereafter the holder was known as President of the Board of Trade until Edward Heath's tenure in 1963, when the job description was widened and he became Secretary of State for Industry, Trade and Regional Development, and President of the Board of Trade. Although the office reverted back to the Board of Trade between 1964 and 1970, both John Davies and Peter Walker were known as Secretary of State for Trade and Industry, and President of the Board of Trade. Between 1974 and 1983 the duties were split and Tony Benn, Eric Varley, Sir Keith Joseph and Patrick Jenkin were Secretaries of State for Industry while the President of the Board of Trade became a secondary title of the Secretary of State for Trade. Between 1983 and 2007 the status quo ante resumed and the offices were again united. From 28 June 2007, the incumbent was known as the Secretary of State for Business, Enterprise and Regulatory Reform, and President of the Board of Trade. Finally, on 5 June 2009, the holder of office became Secretary of State for Business, Innovation and Skills, and President of the Board of Trade.

Name	*Period*	*Party*
Anthony Ashley Cooper, 1st Earl of Shaftesbury	16 Sept. 1672–1676	*Whig*
John Egerton, 3rd Earl of Bridgewater	16 Dec. 1695–9 June 1699	*Whig*
Thomas Grey, 2nd Earl of Stamford	9 June 1699–8 Jan 1702	*Whig*
Thomas Thynne, 1st Viscount Weymouth	8 Jan. 1702–1705	*Whig*
Thomas Grey, 2nd Earl of Stamford	1705–12 June 1711	*Whig*
Charles Finch, 4th Earl of Winchilsea	12 June 1711–15 Sept. 1713	*Whig*
Francis North, 2nd Baron Guilford	15 Sept. 1713–Sept. 1714	*Whig*
William Berkeley, 4th Baron Berkeley	Sept. 1714–12 May 1715	*Whig*
Henry Howard, 6th Earl of Suffolk	12 May 1715–31 Jan. 1718	*Whig*
Robert Darcy, 3rd Earl of Holdernesse	31 Jan. 1718–11 May 1719	*Whig*
Thomas Fane, 6th Earl of Westmorland	11 May 1719–May 1735	*Whig*
Benjamin Mildmay, 1st Earl Fitzwalter	May 1735–June 1737	*Whig*
John Monson, 1st Baron Monson	June 1737–1 Nov. 1748	*Whig*
George Montague-Dunk, 2nd Earl of Halifax	1 Nov. 1748–21 Mar. 1761	*Whig*
Samuel Sandys, 1st Baron Sandys	21 Mar. 1761–1 Mar. 1763	*Whig*
Charles Townshend	1 Mar.–20 Apr. 1763	*Whig*
William Petty, 2nd Earl of Shelburne	20 Apr.–9 Sept. 1763	*Whig*
Wills Hill, 1st Earl of Hillsborough	9 Sept. 1763–20 July 1765	*n/a*
William Legge, 2nd Earl of Dartmouth	20 July 1765–16 Aug. 1766	*n/a*
Wills Hill, 1st Earl of Hillsborough	16 Aug.–Dec. 1766	*n/a*
Robert Nugent, 1st Viscount Clare	Dec. 1766–20 Jan. 1768	*n/a*
Wills Hill, 1st Earl of Hillsborough	20 Jan. 1768–31 Aug. 1772	*n/a*
William Legge, 2nd Earl of Dartmouth	31 Aug. 1772–10 Nov. 1775	*n/a*
Lord George Sackville-Germain	10 Nov. 1775–6 Nov. 1779	*Tory*
Frederick Howard, 5th Earl of Carlisle	6 Nov. 1779–9 Dec. 1780	*Tory*
Thomas Robinson, 2nd Baron Grantham	9 Dec. 1780–11 July 1782	*Whig*
Thomas Townshend, 1st Baron Sydney	5 Mar. 1784–23 Aug. 1786	*Whig*
Charles Jenkinson, 1st Earl of Liverpool	23 Aug. 1786–7 June 1804	*Tory*
James Graham, 3rd Duke of Montrose	7 June 1804–5 Feb. 1806	*n/a*
William Eden, 1st Baron Auckland	5 Feb. 1806–31 Mar. 1807	*n/a*
Henry Bathurst, 3rd Earl Bathurst	31 Mar. 1807–29 Sept. 1812	*Tory*
Richard Le Poer Trench, 2nd Earl of Clancarty	29 Sept. 1812–24 Jan. 1818	*Tory*
Frederick John Robinson	24 Jan. 1818–21 Feb. 1823	*Tory*
William Huskisson	21 Feb. 1823–4 Sept. 1827	*Tory*
Charles Grant	4 Sept. 1827–11 June 1828	*Tory*
William Vesey Fitzgerald	11 June 1828–2 Feb. 1830	*Tory*
John Charles Herries	2 Feb.–22 Nov. 1830	*Tory*
George Eden, 1st Earl of Auckland	22 Nov. 1830–5 June 1834	*Whig*
Charles Edward Poulett Thomson	5 June–14 Nov. 1834	*Whig*
Alexander Baring	15 Dec. 1834–8 Apr. 1835	*Tory*
Charles Edward Poulett Thomson	18 Apr. 1835–29 Aug. 1839	*Whig*
Henry Labouchere	29 Aug. 1839–30 Aug. 1841	*Whig*
Frederick John Robinson, 1st Earl of Ripon	3 Sept. 1841–15 May 1843	*Tory*
William Ewart Gladstone	15 May 1843–5 Feb. 1845	*Peelite*
James Andrew Broun-Ramsay, 10th Earl of Dalhousie	5 Feb. 1845–27 June 1846	*Peelite*
George William Frederick Villiers, 4th Earl of Clarendon	6 July 1846–22 July 1847	*Liberal*
Henry Labouchere	22 July 1847–21 Feb. 1852	*Whig*
Joseph Warner Henley	27 Feb.–17 Dec. 1852	*Liberal*
Edward Cardwell	28 Dec. 1852–31 Mar. 1855	*Peelite*
Edward John Stanley, 2nd Baron Stanley of Alderley	31 Mar. 1855–21 Feb. 1858	*Liberal*
Joseph Warner Henley	26 Feb. 1858–3 Mar. 1859	*Conservative*
Richard John Hely-Hutchinson, 4th Earl of Donoughmore	3 Mar.–11 June 1859	*Conservative*
Thomas Milner Gibson	6 July 1859–26 June 1866	*Liberal*
Sir Stafford Northcote	6 July 1866–8 Mar. 1867	*Conservative*
Charles Henry Gordon-Lennox, 6th Duke of Richmond	8 Mar. 1867–1 Dec. 1868	*Conservative*
John Bright	9 Dec. 1868–14 Jan. 1871	*Liberal*
Chichester Parkinson-Fortescue	14 Jan. 1871–17 Feb. 1874	*Liberal*
Sir Charles Adderley	21 Feb. 1874–4 Apr. 1878	*Conservative*
Dudley Francis Stuart Ryder, Viscount Sandon	4 Apr. 1878–21 Apr. 1880	*Conservative*
Joseph Chamberlain	3 May 1880–9 June 1885	*Liberal*
Charles Henry Gordon-Lennox, 6th Duke of Richmond	24 June–19 Aug. 1885	*Conservative*
Edward Stanhope	19 Aug. 1885–28 Jan. 1886	*Conservative*
Anthony John Mundella	17 Feb.–20 July 1886	*Liberal*
Frederick Stanley, 1st Baron Stanley of Preston	3 Aug. 1886–21 Feb. 1888	*Conservative*

Name	*Period*	*Party*
Sir Michael Hicks Beach	21 Feb. 1888–11 Aug. 1892	*Conservative*
Anthony John Mundella	18 Aug. 1892–28 May 1894	*Liberal*
James Bryce	28 May 1894–21 June 1895	*Liberal*
Charles Thomson Ritchie	29 June 1895–7 Nov. 1900	*Conservative*
Gerald William Balfour	7 Nov. 1900–12 Mar. 1905	*Conservative*
James Edward Hubert Gascoyne-Cecil, 4th Marquess of Salisbury	12 Mar.–4 Dec. 1905	*Conservative*
David Lloyd George	10 Dec. 1905–12 Apr. 1908	*Liberal*
Winston Churchill	12 Apr. 1908–14 Feb. 1910	*Liberal*
Sydney Charles Buxton	14 Feb. 1910–11 Feb. 1914	*Liberal*
John Burns	11 Feb.–5 Aug. 1914	*Liberal*
Walter Runciman	5 Aug. 1914–5 Dec. 1916	*Liberal*
Sir Albert Henry Stanley	10 Dec. 1916–26 May 1919	*Liberal*
Sir Auckland Geddes	26 May 1919–19 Mar. 1920	*Conservative*
Sir Robert Horne	19 Mar. 1920–1 Apr. 1921	*Scottish Unionist*
Stanley Baldwin	1 Apr. 1921–19 Oct. 1922	*Conservative*
Sir Philip Lloyd-Greame	24 Oct. 1922–22 Jan. 1924	*Conservative*
Sidney James Webb	22 Jan.–3 Nov. 1924	*Labour*
Sir Philip Lloyd-Greame*	6 Nov. 1924–4 June 1929	*Conservative*
William Graham	7 June 1929–24 Aug. 1931	*Labour*
Sir Philip Cunliffe-Lister	25 Aug.–5 Nov. 1931	*Conservative*
Walter Runciman	5 Nov. 1931–28 May 1937	*National Liberal*
Oliver Stanley	28 May 1937–5 Jan. 1940	*Conservative*
Sir Andrew Duncan	5 Jan.–3 Oct. 1940	*National*
Oliver Lyttelton	3 Oct. 1940–29 June 1941	*Conservative*
Sir Andrew Duncan	29 June 1941–4 Feb. 1942	*National*
John Llewellin	4–22 Feb. 1942	*Conservative*
Hugh Dalton	22 Feb. 1942–23 May 1945	*Labour*
Oliver Lyttelton	25 May–26 July 1945	*Conservative*
Sir Stafford Cripps	27 July 1945–29 Sept. 1947	*Labour*
Harold Wilson	29 Sept. 1947–23 Apr. 1951	*Labour*
Sir Hartley Shawcross	24 Apr.–26 Oct. 1951	*Labour*
Peter Thorneycroft	30 Oct. 1951–13 Jan. 1957	*Conservative*
Sir David Eccles	13 Jan. 1957–14 Oct. 1959	*Conservative*
Reginald Maudling	14 Oct. 1959–9 Oct. 1961	*Conservative*
Fred Erroll	9 Oct. 1961–20 Oct. 1963	*Conservative*
Edward Heath	20 Oct. 1963–16 Oct. 1964	*Conservative*
Douglas Jay	18 Oct. 1964–29 Aug. 1967	*Labour*
Anthony Crosland	29 Aug. 1967–6 Oct. 1969	*Labour*
Roy Mason	6 Oct. 1969–19 June 1970	*Labour*
Michael Noble	20 June–15 Oct. 1970	*Labour*
John Davies	15 Oct. 1970–5 Nov. 1972	*Conservative*
Peter Walker	5 Nov. 1972–4 Mar. 1974	*Conservative*
Peter Shore	5 Mar. 1974–8 Apr. 1976	*Labour*
Edmund Dell	8 Apr. 1976–11 Nov. 1978	*Labour*
John Smith	11 Nov. 1978–4 May 1979	*Labour*
John Nott	5 May 1979–5 Jan. 1981	*Conservative*
John Biffen	5 Jan. 1981–6 Apr. 1982	*Conservative*
Lord Cockfield	6 Apr. 1982–12 June 1983	*Conservative*
Cecil Parkinson	12 June–11 Oct. 1983	*Conservative*
Norman Tebbit	16 Oct. 1983–2 Sept. 1985	*Conservative*
Leon Brittan	2 Sept. 1985–22 Jan. 1986	*Conservative*
Paul Channon	24 Jan. 1986–13 June 1987	*Conservative*
David Young, Baron Young of Graffham	13 June 1987–24 July 1989	*Conservative*
Nicholas Ridley	24 July 1989–13 July 1990	*Conservative*
Peter Lilley	14 July 1990–10 Apr. 1992	*Conservative*
Michael Heseltine	10 Apr. 1992–5 July 1995	*Conservative*
Ian Lang	5 July 1995–2 May 1997	*Conservative*
Margaret Beckett	2 May 1997–27 July 1998	*Labour*
Peter Mandelson	27 July–23 Dec. 1998	*Labour*
Stephen Byers	23 Dec. 1998–8 June 2001	*Labour*
Patricia Hewitt	8 June 2001–6 May 2005	*Labour*
Alan Johnson	6 May 2005–5 May 2006	*Labour*
Alistair Darling	5 May 2006–27 June 2007	*Labour*
John Hutton	28 June 2007–3 Oct. 2008	*Labour*
Peter Mandelson	3 Oct. 2008–11 May 2010	*Labour*
Vincent Cable	12 May 2010–present	*Lib-Dem*

*On 7 Nov. 1924 Philip Lloyd-Greame changed his surname to Cunliffe-Lister so as to be able to inherit property from his wife's family.

Secretaries of State for Industry

Tony Benn	5 Mar. 1974–10 June 1975	*Labour*
Eric Varley	10 June 1975–4 May 1979	*Labour*
Sir Keith Joseph	7 May 1979–14 Sept. 1981	*Conservative*
Patrick Jenkin	14 Sept. 1981–12 June 1983	*Conservative*

Cabinet Office

The Minister for the Cabinet Office tends to have multi-purpose Cabinet duties in support of the Prime Minister. Hilary Armstrong for instance was Minister for the Cabinet Office, Chancellor of the Duchy of Lancaster and Minister for Social Exclusion during her term of office, and the present incumbent is Minister for the Olympics, Minister for the Cabinet Office and Paymaster General.

Name	*Period*	*Party*
Hilary Armstrong	5 May 2006–27 June 2007	*Labour*
Ed Miliband	28 June 2007–3 Oct. 2008	*Labour*
Liam Byrne	3 Oct. 2008–5 June 2009	*Labour*
Tessa Jowell	5 June 2009–11 May 2010	*Labour*
Francis Maude	12 May 2010–present	*Conservative*

Chancellor of the Duchy of Lancaster

Historically, the incumbent was the chief officer in the management of the considerable lands inherited by John of Gaunt after marriage. The so-called Duchy of Lancaster is still in existence today but is run on behalf of the Crown by a deputy, and the office of Chancellor has become a sinecure for a Cabinet minister without portfolio or an honorary secondary position within the Cabinet.

Name	*Period*	*Party*
Sir Henry de Haydock	1361–1373	*n/a*
Ralph de Ergham	1373–16 Apr. 1377	*n/a*
Thomas de Thelwall	16 Apr. 1377–1378	*n/a*
Sir John De Yerborough	1378–10 Nov. 1382	*n/a*
Sir Thomas Stanley	10–29 Nov. 1382	*n/a*
Sir Thomas Scarle	29 Nov. 1382–Oct. 1383	*n/a*
Sir William Okey	Oct. 1383–1400	*n/a*
John de Wakering	1400	*n/a*
William Burgoyne	1400–15 May 1404	*n/a*
Sir Thomas Stanley	15 May 1404–30 Mar. 1410	*n/a*
John Springthorpe	30 Mar. 1410–4 Apr. 1413	*n/a*
John Wodehouse	4 Apr. 1413–10 June 1424	*n/a*
William Troutbecke	10 June 1424–16 Feb. 1431	*n/a*
Walter Sherington	16 Feb. 1431–3 July 1442	*n/a*
William Tresham	3 July 1442–10 June 1449	*n/a*
John Say	10 June 1449–10 June 1462	*n/a*
Sir Richard Fowler	10 June 1462–3 Nov. 1477	*n/a*
Sir John Say	3 Nov. 1477–2 Apr. 1478	*n/a*
Thomas Thwaites	2 Apr. 1478–7 July 1483	*n/a*
Thomas Metcalfe	7 July 1483–13 Sept. 1486	*n/a*
Sir Reginald Bray	13 Sept. 1486–24 June 1503	*n/a*
Sir John Mordaunt	24 June 1503–3 Oct. 1505	*n/a*
Sir Richard Empson	3 Oct. 1505–14 May 1509	*n/a*
Sir Henry Marney	14 May 1509–14 Apr. 1523	*n/a*
Sir Richard Wingfield	14 Apr. 1523–31 Dec. 1525	*n/a*
Sir Thomas More	31 Dec. 1525–3 Nov. 1529	*n/a*
Sir William Fitzwilliam	3 Nov. 1529–10 May 1533	*n/a*
Sir John Gage	10 May 1533–1 July 1547	*n/a*
Sir William Paget	1 July 1547–7 July 1552	*n/a*
Sir John Gates	7 July 1552–1553	*n/a*
Sir Robert Rochester	1553–1557	*n/a*
Sir Edward Waldegrave	22 June 1558–1559	*n/a*
Sir Ambrose Cave	1559–16 May 1568	*n/a*
Sir Ralph Sadler	16 May 1568–15 June 1587	*n/a*
Sir Francis Walsingham	15 June 1587–1590	*n/a*
Sir Thomas Heneage	1590–7 Oct. 1595	*n/a*
seal in commission	1595–1597	*n/a*
Sir Robert Cecil	8 Oct. 1597–1599	*n/a*
seal in commission	1599–16 Sept. 1601	*n/a*
Sir John Fortescue	16 Sept. 1601–1601	*n/a*
seal in commission	1601	*n/a*
Sir John Fortescue	1601–1607	*n/a*
Sir Thomas Parry	1607–5 June 1616	*n/a*
Sir John Dacombe	27 May 1615–1618	*n/a*
Sir Humphrey May	23 Mar. 1618–16 Apr. 1629	*n/a*
Edward Barrett	16 Apr. 1629–10 Feb. 1644	*n/a*
Francis, Lord Seymour	1644–1645 for the King	*n/a*
Lord Grey of Warke	1645–1648 for the King	*n/a*
William Lenthall	10 Feb. 1644–1648 for Parliament	*n/a*
Sir Gilbert Gerrard	1648–1 Aug. 1649	*n/a*
John Bradshaw	1 Aug. 1649–1653	*n/a*
John Bradshaw	1653–1654	*n/a*
Thomas Fell	1653–1658	*n/a*
John Bradshaw	1658–1659	*n/a*
William Lenthall	1659	*n/a*
Sir Gilbert Gerrard	14 May 1659–9 July 1660	*n/a*
Francis Seymour, 1st Lord Seymour of Trowbridge	9 July 1660–21 July 1664	*n/a*

Name	Period	Party
Sir Thomas Ingram	21 July 1664–22 Feb 1672	n/a
Sir Robert Carr	22 Feb. 1672–21 Nov. 1682	n/a
Sir Thomas Chicheley	21 Nov. 1682–1687	n/a
seal in commission	1687	n/a
Robert Phelipps	1687–21 Mar. 1689	n/a
Robert Bertie, 16th Baron Willoughby of Eresby	21 Mar. 1689–4 May 1697	n/a
Thomas Grey, 2nd Earl of Stamford	4 May 1697–12 May 1702	n/a
Sir John Leveson-Gower	12 May 1702–10 June 1706	n/a
James Stanley, 10th Earl of Derby	10 June 1706–21 Sept. 1710	n/a
William Berkeley, 4th Lord Berkeley of Stratton	21 Sept. 1710–6 Nov. 1714	n/a
Heneage Finch, 1st Earl of Aylesford	6 Nov. 1714–12 Mar. 1716	n/a
Richard Lumley, 1st Earl of Scarborough	12 Mar. 1716–19 June 1717	n/a
Nicolas Lechmere, Baron Lechmere	19 June 1717–17 July 1727	n/a
John Manners, 3rd Duke of Rutland	17 July 1727–21 May 1735	Whig
George Cholmondeley, 3rd Earl of Cholmondeley	21 May 1735–22 Dec. 1742	Whig
Richard Edgcumbe, 1st Lord Edgcumbe of Mount Edgcumbe	22 Dec. 1742–27 Feb. 1759	Whig
Thomas Hay, 9th Earl of Kinnoull	27 Feb. 1759–13 Dec. 1762	Whig
James Stanley, Lord Strange	13 Dec. 1762–14 June 1771	Tory
Thomas Villiers, 1st Earl of Clarendon	14 June 1771–17 Apr. 1782	Whig
John Dunning, 1st Baron Ashburton	17 Apr. 1782–29 Aug. 1783	Whig
Edward Smith-Stanley, 12th Earl of Derby	29 Aug.–31 Dec. 1783	Whig
Thomas Villiers, 1st Earl of Clarendon	31 Dec. 1783–6 Sept. 1786	Whig
Charles Jenkinson, 1st Lord Hawkesbury	6 Sept. 1786–11 Nov. 1803	Tory
Thomas Pelham, Lord Pelham	11 Nov. 1803–6 June 1804	Whig
Henry Phipps	6 June 1804–14 Jan. 1805	Tory
Robert Hobart, 4th Earl of Buckinghamshire	14 Jan.–10 July 1805	Tory
Dudley Ryder, 2nd Lord Harrowby	10 July 1805–12 Feb. 1806	Tory
Edward Smith-Stanley, 12th Earl of Derby	12 Feb. 1806–30 Mar. 1807	Whig
Spencer Perceval	30 Mar. 1807–23 May 1812	Tory
Robert Hobart, 4th Earl of Buckinghamshire	23 May–23 June 1812	Tory
Charles Bathurst	23 June 1812–13 Feb. 1823	Tory
Nicholas Vansittart, 1st Baron Bexley	13 Feb. 1823–26 Jan. 1828	Tory
George Hamilton-Gordon, 4th Earl of Aberdeen	26 Jan.–2 June 1828	Tory
Charles Arbuthnot	2 June 1828–25 Nov. 1830	Tory
Henry Richard Vassall-Fox, 3rd Baron Holland	25 Nov. 1830–14 Nov. 1834	Whig
Charles Watkin Williams-Wynn	26 Dec. 1834–8 Apr. 1835	Tory
Henry Richard Vassall-Fox, 3rd Baron Holland	23 Apr. 1835–31 Oct. 1840	Whig
George William Frederick Villiers, 4th Earl of Clarendon	31 Oct. 1840–23 June 1841	Liberal
Sir George Grey, Bt	23 June–30 Aug. 1841	Whig
Lord Granville Charles Henry Somerset	3 Sept. 1841–27 June 1846	Tory
John Campbell, 1st Baron Campbell of St Andrews	6 July 1846–6 Mar. 1850	Liberal
George William Frederick Howard, 7th Earl of Carlisle	6 Mar. 1850–21 Feb. 1852	Liberal
Robert Adam Christopher	1 Mar.–17 Dec. 1852	Conservative
Edward Strutt	3 Jan. 1853–21 June 1854	Liberal
Granville Leveson-Gower, 2nd Earl Granville	21 June 1854–30 Jan. 1855	Liberal
Dudley Ryder, 2nd Earl of Harrowby	31 Mar.–7 Dec. 1855	Liberal
Matthew Talbot Baines	7 Dec. 1855–21 Feb. 1858	Liberal
James Graham, 4th Duke of Montrose	26 Feb. 1858–11 June 1859	Conservative
Sir George Grey, Bt	22 June 1859–25 July 1861	Whig
Edward Cardwell	25 July 1861–7 Apr. 1864	Liberal
George William Frederick Villiers, 4th Earl of Clarendon	7 Apr. 1864–3 Nov. 1865	Liberal
George Joachim Goschen	26 Jan.–26 June 1866	Liberal
William Reginald Courtenay, 11th Earl of Devon	10 July 1866–26 June 1867	Conservative
John Wilson-Patten	26 June 1867–7 Nov. 1868	Conservative
Thomas Edward Taylor	7 Nov.–1 Dec. 1868	Conservative
Frederick Temple Blackwood, 5th Lord Dufferin	12 Dec. 1868–9 Aug. 1872	Liberal
Hugh Culling Eardley Childers	9 Aug. 1872–30 Sept. 1873	Liberal
John Bright	30 Sept. 1873–17 Feb. 1874	Liberal
Thomas Edward Taylor	2 Mar. 1874–21 Apr. 1880	Conservative
John Bright	28 Apr. 1880–25 July 1882	Liberal
John Wodehouse, 1st Earl of Kimberley	25 July–28 Dec. 1882	Liberal
John George Dodson	28 Dec. 1882–29 Oct. 1884	Liberal
George Otto Trevelyan	29 Oct. 1884–9 June 1885	Liberal
Henry Chaplin	24 June 1885–28 Jan. 1886	Conservative
Edward Heneage	6 Feb.–16 Apr. 1886	Liberal
Sir Ughtred James Kay-Shuttleworth	16 Apr.–20 July 1886	Liberal
Gathorne Hardy, 1st Viscount Cranbrook	3–16 Aug. 1886	Conservative
Lord John Manners	16 Aug. 1886–11 Aug. 1892	Conservative
James Bryce	18 Aug. 1892–28 May 1894	Liberal
Edward Marjoribanks, 2nd Baron Tweedmouth	28 May 1894–21 June 1895	Liberal
Richard Assheton Cross, 1st Viscount Cross	29 June–4 July 1895	Conservative
Sir Henry James	4 July 1895–8 Aug. 1902	Liberal Unionist
Sir William Hood Walrond	8 Aug. 1902–4 Dec. 1905	Conservative
Sir Henry Hartley Fowler	10 Dec. 1905–13 Oct. 1908	Liberal
Edmond Petty-FitzMaurice, 1st Baron FitzMaurice	13 Oct. 1908–25 June 1909	Liberal
Herbert Samuel	25 June 1909–14 Feb. 1910	Liberal
Joseph Albert Pease	14 Feb. 1910–23 Oct. 1911	Liberal
Sir Charles Edward Henry Hobhouse	23 Oct. 1911–11 Feb. 1914	Liberal
Charles Frederick Gurney Masterman	11 Feb. 1914–3 Feb. 1915	Liberal

Name	Period	Party
Edwin Samuel Montagu	3 Feb.–25 May 1915	*Liberal*
Winston Churchill	25 May–25 Nov. 1915	*Liberal*
Herbert Samuel	25 Nov. 1915–11 Jan. 1916	*Liberal*
Edwin Samuel Montagu	11 Jan.–9 July 1916	*Liberal*
Thomas McKinnon Wood	9 July–10 Dec. 1916	*Liberal*
Sir Frederick Cawley	10 Dec. 1916–10 Feb. 1918	*Conservative*
William Maxwell Aitken, 1st Baron Beaverbrook	10 Feb.–4 Nov. 1918	*Liberal Unionist*
William Hayes Fisher, 1st Baron Downham	4 Nov. 1918–10 Jan. 1919	*Conservative*
David Alexander Edward Lindsay, 27th Earl of Crawford and 10th Earl of Balcarres	10 Jan. 1919–1 Apr. 1921	*Conservative*
William Robert Wellesley, 2nd Viscount Peel	1 Apr. 1921–7 Apr. 1922	*Conservative*
Sir William Sutherland	7 Apr.–19 Oct. 1922	*Conservative*
James Edward Hubert Gascoyne-Cecil, 4th Marquess of Salisbury	24 Oct. 1922–25 May 1923	*Conservative*
J C C Davidson	25 May 1923–22 Jan. 1924	*Conservative*
Josiah Wedgwood	22 Jan.–3 Nov. 1924	*Labour*
Robert Cecil, 1st Viscount Cecil of Chelwood	10 Nov. 1924–19 Oct. 1927	*Conservative*
Ronald John McNeill, 1st Baron Cushendun	19 Oct. 1927–4 June 1929	*Conservative*
Sir Oswald Mosley, Bt	7 June 1929–19 May 1930	*Labour*
Clement Attlee	23 May 1930–13 Mar. 1931	*Labour*
Arthur Augustus William Harry Ponsonby, 1st Baron Ponsonby of Shulbrede	13 Mar.–24 Aug. 1931	*Labour*
Philip Kerr, 11th Marquess of Lothian	25 Aug.–10 Nov. 1931	*n/a*
J C C Davidson	10 Nov. 1931–28 May 1937	*Conservative*
Edward Turnour, 6th Earl Winterton	28 May 1937–29 Jan. 1939	*Conservative*
William Shepherd Morrison	29 Jan. 1939–3 Apr. 1940	*Conservative*
George Clement Tryon, 1st Baron Tryon	3 Apr.–14 May 1940	*Conservative*
Maurice Hankey, 1st Baron Hankey	14 May 1940–20 July 1941	*n/a*
Alfred Duff Cooper	20 July 1941–11 Nov. 1943	*Conservative*
Ernest Brown	11 Nov. 1943–25 May 1945	*National Liberal*
Sir Arthur Salter	25 May–26 July 1945	*Conservative*
John Burns Hynd	4 Aug. 1945–17 Apr. 1947	*Labour*
Francis Aungier Pakenham, 1st Baron Pakenham	17 Apr. 1947–31 May 1948	*Labour*
Hugh Dalton	31 May 1948–28 Feb. 1950	*Labour*
Lord Alexander of Hillsborough	28 Feb. 1950–26 Oct. 1951	*Labour Co-Op*
Philip Cunliffe-Lister, 1st Viscount Swinton	31 Oct. 1951–24 Nov. 1952	*Conservative*
Frederick James Marquis, 1st Baron Woolton	24 Nov. 1952–20 Dec. 1955	*Conservative*
George Douglas-Hamilton, 10th Earl of Selkirk	20 Dec. 1955–13 Jan. 1957	*Conservative*
Charles Hill	13 Jan. 1957–9 Oct. 1961	*Conservative*
Iain Macleod	9 Oct. 1961–20 Oct. 1963	*Conservative*
John Hugh Hare, 1st Viscount Blakenham	20 Oct. 1963–16 Oct. 1964	*Conservative*
Douglas Houghton	18 Oct. 1964–6 Apr. 1966	*Labour*
George Thomson	6 Apr. 1966–7 Jan. 1967	*Labour*
Frederick Lee	7 Jan. 1967–6 Oct. 1969	*Labour*
George Thomson	6 Oct. 1969–19 June 1970	*Labour*
Anthony Barber	20 June–28 July 1970	*Conservative*
Geoffrey Rippon	28 July 1970–5 Nov. 1972	*Conservative*
John Davies	5 Nov. 1972–4 Mar. 1974	*Conservative*
Harold Lever	5 Mar. 1974–4 May 1979	*Labour*
Norman St John-Stevas	5 May 1979–5 Jan. 1981	*Conservative*
Francis Pym	5 Jan.–14 Sept. 1981	*Conservative*
Janet Young, Baroness Young	14 Sept. 1981–6 Apr. 1982	*Conservative*
Cecil Parkinson	6 Apr. 1982–11 June 1983	*Conservative*
Francis Cockfield, Baron Cockfield	11 June 1983–11 Sept. 1984	*Conservative*
Alexander Patrick Greysteil Ruthven, 2nd Earl of Gowrie	11 Sept. 1984–3 Sept. 1985	*Conservative*
Norman Tebbit	3 Sept. 1985–13 June 1987	*Conservative*
Kenneth Clarke	13 June 1987–25 July 1988	*Conservative*
Tony Newton	25 July 1988–24 July 1989	*Conservative*
Kenneth Baker	24 July 1989–28 Nov. 1990	*Conservative*
Chris Patten	28 Nov. 1990–10 Apr. 1992	*Conservative*
William Waldegrave	10 Apr. 1992–20 July 1994	*Conservative*
David Hunt	20 July 1994–5 July 1995	*Conservative*
Roger Freeman	5 July 1995–2 May 1997	*Conservative*
David G Clark	3 May 1997–27 July 1998	*Labour*
Jack Cunningham	27 July 1998–11 Oct. 1999	*Labour*
Marjorie 'Mo' Mowlam	11 Oct. 1999–11 June 2001	*Labour*
Gus Macdonald, Baron Macdonald of Tradeston	11 June 2001–13 June 2003	*Labour*
Douglas Alexander	13 June 2003–8 Sept. 2004	*Labour*
Alan Milburn	8 Sept. 2004–6 May 2005	*Labour*
John Hutton	6 May–2 Nov. 2005	*Labour*
Hilary Armstrong	5 May 2006–27 June 2007	*Labour*
Ed Miliband	28 June 2007–3 Oct. 2008	*Labour*
Liam Byrne	3 Oct. 2008–5 June 2009	*Labour*
Janet Royall, Baroness Royall of Blaisdon	5 June 2009–11 May 2010	*Labour*
Thomas Galbraith, 2nd Baron Strathclyde	12 May 2010–7 Jan. 2013	*Conservative*
Jonathan Hopkin Hill, Baron Hill of Oareford	7 Jan. 2013–present	*Conservative*

Chancellor of the Exchequer

The incumbent controls HM Treasury and the position is considered one of the four Great Offices of State (the other three being Prime Minister, Foreign Secretary and Home Secretary); in recent times it has come to be the most powerful office in British politics after the Prime Minister. The Exchequer dates from the reign of Henry I (1100–35) and the first person outside the monarchy to be entrusted with its charge was Eustace de Fauconbridge, Bishop of London, in about 1221, although he was known as Lord High Treasurer. The position was only sporadically filled until 1559 and although Hervey de Stanton is often considered the first holder of office between 1316 and 1327, this title was merely a clerical position and had no political weight. Sir Walter Mildmay was the first incumbent of any significance, although only in the mid-19th century under William Gladstone did the holder become politically powerful – as the Second Lord of the Treasury.

Name	*Period*	*Party*
Sir Walter Mildmay	1559–1589	*n/a*
Sir John Fortescue	1589–1603	*n/a*
George Home, 1st Earl of Dunbar	1603–1606	*n/a*
Sir Julius Caesar	1606–1614	*n/a*
Sir Fulke Greville	1614–1621	*n/a*
Sir Richard Weston	1621–1628	*n/a*
Edward Barrett, 1st Lord Barrett of Newburgh	1628–1629	*n/a*
Francis Cottington, 1st Baron Cottington	1629–1642	*n/a*
Sir John Culpepper	1642–1643	*n/a*
Sir Edward Hyde	19 July 1642–1646	*n/a*
Anthony Ashley Cooper, 1st Earl of Shaftesbury	13 May 1661–22 Nov. 1672	*Country Party*
Sir John Duncombe	22 Nov. 1672–2 May 1676	*Country Party*
Sir John Ernle	2 May 1676–9 Apr. 1689	*Country Party*
Henry Booth, Baron Delamere	9 Apr. 1689–18 Mar. 1690	*Whig*
Richard Hampden	18 Mar. 1690–10 May 1694	*Whig*
Charles Montagu	10 May 1694–2 June 1699	*Whig*
John Smith	2 June 1699–27 Mar. 1701	*Whig*
Henry Boyle	27 Mar. 1701–22 Apr. 1708	*Whig*
John Smith	22 Apr. 1708–11 Aug. 1710	*Whig*
Robert Harley	11 Aug. 1710–4 June 1711	*Whig/Tory*
Robert Benson	4 June 1711–21 Aug. 1713	*Tory*
Sir William Wyndham	21 Aug. 1713–13 Oct. 1714	*Tory*
Sir Richard Onslow	13 Oct. 1714–12 Oct. 1715	*Whig*
Robert Walpole	12 Oct. 1715–15 Apr. 1717	*Whig*
James Stanhope, 1st Viscount Stanhope	15 Apr. 1717–20 Mar. 1718	*Whig*
John Aislabie	20 Mar. 1718–23 Jan. 1721	*Whig*
Sir John Pratt	2 Feb.–3 Apr. 1721	*Whig*
Sir Robert Walpole	3 Apr. 1721–12 Feb. 1742	*Whig*
Samuel Sandys	12 Feb. 1742–12 Dec. 1743	*Whig*
Henry Pelham	12 Dec. 1743–8 Mar. 1754	*Whig*
Sir William Lee	8 Mar.–6 Apr. 1754	*Whig*
Henry Bilson Legge	6 Apr. 1754–25 Nov. 1755	*Whig*
Sir George Lyttelton	25 Nov. 1755–16 Nov. 1756	*Whig*
Henry Bilson Legge	16 Nov. 1756–13 Apr. 1757	*Whig*
William Murray, Baron Mansfield	13 Apr.–2 July 1757	*Whig*
Henry Bilson Legge	2 July 1757–19 Mar. 1761	*Whig*
William Wildman Barrington-Shute	19 Mar. 1761–29 May 1762	*Whig*
Sir Francis Dashwood	29 May 1762–16 Apr. 1763	*Tory*
George Grenville	16 Apr. 1763–16 July 1765	*Whig*
William Dowdeswell	16 July 1765–2 Aug. 1766	*Whig*
Charles Townshend	2 Aug. 1766–4 Sept. 1767	*Whig*
Frederick North, Lord North	11 Sept. 1767–27 Mar. 1782	*Tory*
Lord John Cavendish	27 Mar.–10 July 1782	*Whig*
William Pitt (the Younger)	10 July 1782–31 Mar. 1783	*Whig*
Lord John Cavendish	2 Apr.–19 Dec. 1783	*Whig*
William Pitt (the Younger)	19 Dec. 1783–14 Mar. 1801	*Tory*
Henry Addington	14 Mar. 1801–10 May 1804	*Tory*
William Pitt (the Younger)	10 May 1804–23 Jan. 1806	*Tory*
Lord Henry Petty	5 Feb. 1806–26 Mar. 1807	*Whig*
Spencer Perceval	26 Mar. 1807–12 May 1812	*Tory*
Nicholas Vansittart	12 May 1812–31 Jan. 1823	*Tory*
Frederick John Robinson	31 Jan. 1823–20 Apr. 1827	*Tory*
George Canning	20 Apr.–8 Aug. 1827	*Tory*
Charles Abbott, Baron Tenterden	8 Aug.–3 Sept. 1827	*Tory*
John Charles Herries	3 Sept. 1827–26 Jan. 1828	*Tory*
Henry Goulburn	26 Jan. 1828–22 Nov. 1830	*Tory*
John Spencer, Viscount Althorp	22 Nov. 1830–14 Nov. 1834	*Whig*
Lord Denman	15 Nov.–15 Dec. 1834	*Whig*
Sir Robert Peel	2 Dec. 1834–8 Apr. 1835	*Conservative*
Thomas Spring Rice	18 Apr. 1835–26 Aug. 1839	*Whig*
Sir Francis Thornhill Baring	26 Aug. 1839–30 Aug. 1841	*Whig*
Henry Goulburn	3 Sept. 1841–27 June 1846	*Conservative*
Sir Charles Wood	6 July 1846–21 Feb. 1852	*Whig*
Benjamin Disraeli	27 Feb.–17 Dec. 1852	*Conservative*
William Ewart Gladstone	28 Dec. 1852–28 Feb. 1855	*Peelite*
Sir George Cornewall Lewis	28 Feb. 1855–21 Feb. 1858	*Whig*
Benjamin Disraeli	26 Feb. 1858–11 June 1859	*Conservative*
William Ewart Gladstone	18 June 1859–26 June 1866	*Liberal*
Benjamin Disraeli	6 July 1866–29 Feb. 1868	*Conservative*
George Ward Hunt	29 Feb.–1 Dec. 1868	*Conservative*
Robert Lowe	9 Dec. 1868–11 Aug. 1873	*Liberal*

Name	Period	Party
William Ewart Gladstone	11 Aug. 1873–17 Feb. 1874	*Liberal*
Sir Stafford Henry Northcote	21 Feb. 1874–21 Apr. 1880	*Conservative*
William Ewart Gladstone	28 Apr. 1880–16 Dec. 1882	*Liberal*
Hugh Childers	16 Dec. 1882–9 June 1885	*Liberal*
Sir Michael Hicks Beach	24 June 1885–28 Jan. 1886	*Conservative*
Sir William Vernon Harcourt	6 Feb.–20 July 1886	*Liberal*
Lord Randolph Churchill	3 Aug.–22 Dec. 1886	*Conservative*
George Joachim Goschen	14 Jan. 1887–11 Aug. 1892	*Liberal Unionist*
Sir William Vernon Harcourt	18 Aug. 1892–21 June 1895	*Liberal*
Sir Michael Hicks Beach	29 June 1895–11 Aug. 1902	*Conservative*
Charles Thomson Ritchie	11 Aug. 1902–9 Oct. 1903	*Conservative*
Austen Chamberlain	9 Oct. 1903–4 Dec. 1905	*Liberal Unionist*
Herbert Henry Asquith	10 Dec. 1905–12 Apr. 1908	*Liberal*
David Lloyd George	12 Apr. 1908–25 May 1915	*Liberal*
Reginald McKenna	25 May 1915–10 Dec. 1916	*Liberal*
Andrew Bonar Law	10 Dec. 1916–10 Jan. 1919	*Conservative*
Austen Chamberlain	10 Jan. 1919–1 Apr. 1921	*Conservative*
Sir Robert Stevenson Horne	1 Apr. 1921–19 Oct. 1922	*Conservative*
Stanley Baldwin	27 Oct. 1922–27 Aug. 1923	*Conservative*
Neville Chamberlain	27 Aug. 1923–22 Jan. 1924	*Conservative*
Philip Snowden	22 Jan.–3 Nov. 1924	*Labour*
Winston Churchill	6 Nov. 1924–4 June 1929	*Conservative*
Philip Snowden	7 June 1929–5 Nov. 1931	*Labour*
Neville Chamberlain	5 Nov. 1931–28 May 1937	*Conservative*
Sir John Allsebrooke Simon	28 May 1937–12 May 1940	*National Liberal*
Sir Kingsley Wood	12 May 1940–24 Sept. 1943	*Conservative*
Sir John Anderson	24 Sept. 1943–26 July 1945	*non-party*
Hugh Dalton	27 July 1945–13 Nov. 1947	*Labour*
Sir Stafford Cripps	13 Nov. 1947–19 Oct. 1950	*Labour*
Hugh Gaitskell	19 Oct. 1950–26 Oct. 1951	*Labour*
Richard Austen 'Rab' Butler	28 Oct. 1951–20 Dec. 1955	*Conservative*
Harold Macmillan	20 Dec. 1955–13 Jan. 1957	*Conservative*
Peter Thorneycroft	13 Jan. 1957–6 Jan. 1958	*Conservative*
Derick Heathcoat-Amory	6 Jan. 1958–27 July 1960	*Conservative*
Selwyn Lloyd	27 July 1960–13 July 1962	*Conservative*
Reginald Maudling	13 July 1962–16 Oct. 1964	*Conservative*
James Callaghan	16 Oct. 1964–30 Nov. 1967	*Labour*
Roy Jenkins	30 Nov. 1967–19 June 1970	*Labour*
Iain Macleod	20 June–20 July 1970	*Conservative*
Anthony Barber	25 July 1970–4 Mar. 1974	*Conservative*
Denis Healey	5 Mar. 1974–4 May 1979	*Labour*
Sir Geoffrey Howe	5 May 1979–11 June 1983	*Conservative*
Nigel Lawson	11 June 1983–26 Oct. 1989	*Conservative*
John Major	26 Oct. 1989–28 Nov. 1990	*Conservative*
Norman Lamont	28 Nov. 1990–27 May 1993	*Conservative*
Kenneth Clarke	27 May 1993–2 May 1997	*Conservative*
Gordon Brown	2 May 1997–27 June 2007	*Labour*
Alistair Darling	28 June 2007–11 May 2010	*Labour*
George Osborne	12 May 2010–present	*Conservative*

Chief Secretary to the Treasury

Created in 1961 as the second most significant ministerial role within the Treasury after the Chancellor of the Exchequer. The incumbent's responsibilities include negotiating with departments about budget allocations, public sector pay, welfare reform, and procurement policy.

Name	Period	Party
Henry Brooke	9 Oct. 1961–13 July 1962	*Conservative*
John Boyd-Carpenter	13 July 1962–16 Oct. 1964	*Conservative*
John Diamond	20 Oct. 1964–19 June 1970	*Labour*
Maurice Macmillan	23 June 1970–7 Apr. 1972	*Conservative*
Patrick Jenkin	7 Apr. 1972–8 Jan. 1974	*Conservative*
Thomas Boardman	8 Jan.–4 Mar. 1974	*Labour*
Joel Barnett	7 Mar. 1974–4 May 1979	*Labour*
John Biffen	5 May 1979–5 Jan. 1981	*Conservative*
Leon Brittan	5 Jan. 1981–11 June 1983	*Conservative*
Peter Rees	11 June 1983–2 Sept. 1985	*Conservative*
John MacGregor	2 Sept. 1985–13 June 1987	*Conservative*
John Major	13 June 1987–24 July 1989	*Conservative*
Norman Lamont	24 July 1989–28 Nov. 1990	*Conservative*
David Mellor	28 Nov. 1990–10 Apr. 1992	*Conservative*
Michael Portillo	10 Apr. 1992–20 July 1994	*Conservative*
Jonathan Aitken	20 July 1994–5 July 1995	*Conservative*
William Waldegrave	5 July 1995–2 May 1997	*Conservative*
Alistair Darling	3 May 1997–27 July 1998	*Labour*
Stephen Byers	27 July–23 Dec. 1998	*Labour*
Alan Milburn	23 Dec. 1998–11 Oct. 1999	*Labour*
Andrew Smith	11 Oct. 1999–29 May 2002	*Labour*
Paul Boateng	29 May 2002–6 May 2005	*Labour*
Des Browne	6 May 2005–5 May 2006	*Labour*
Stephen Timms	5 May 2006–27 June 2007	*Labour*

Name	Period	Party
Andy Burnham	28 June 2007–24 Jan. 2008	*Labour*
Yvette Cooper	24 Jan. 2008–5 June 2009	*Labour*
Liam Byrne	5 June 2009–11 May 2010	*Labour*
David Laws	12 May–29 May 2010	*Lib-Dem*
Danny Alexander	29 May 2010–present	*Lib-Dem*

Chief Whip

Chief Whip is not a Cabinet position per se, as all major parties will have such a position. The Government Chief Whip is usually appointed as Parliamentary Secretary to the Treasury so that the holder of office is able to take a seat in the Cabinet. Although the incumbent's official residence is at 12 Downing Street, presently the Chief Whip's office is located at 9 Downing Street. The following is a list of Chief Whips since the turn of the 20th century.

Name	Period	Party
Sir William Hood Walrond	1895–1902	*Conservative*
Sir Alexander Acland-Hood	1902–1905	*Conservative*
George Whiteley	1905–1908	*Liberal*
Joseph Pease	1908–1910	*Liberal*
Alexander Murray, Master of Elibank	1910–1912	*Liberal*
Percy Holden Illingworth	1912–1915	*Liberal*
John William Gulland	1915	*Liberal*
Lord Edmund Talbot	1915–1916 (joint)	*Conservative*
John William Gulland	1915–1916 (joint)	*Liberal*
Lord Edmund Talbot	1916–1921 (joint)	*Conservative*
Neil Primrose	1916–1917 (joint)	*Liberal*
Frederick Guest	1917–1921 (joint)	*Liberal*
Leslie Orme Wilson	1921–1922 (joint)	*Conservative*
Charles McCurdy	1921–1922 (joint)	*Liberal*
Leslie Orme Wilson	1922–1923	*Conservative*
Bolton Eyres-Monsell	1923–1924	*Conservative*
Ben Spoor	1924	*Labour*
Bolton Eyres-Monsell	1924–1929	*Conservative*
Tom Kennedy	1929–1931	*Labour*
David Margesson	1931–1940	*Conservative*
Sir Charles Edwards	1940–1942 (joint)	*Labour*
James Gray Stuart	1941–1945 (joint)	*Conservative*
William Whiteley	1942–1951 (joint until 1945)	*Labour*
Patrick Buchan-Hepburn	1951–1955	*Conservative*
Edward Heath	1955–1959	*Conservative*
Martin Redmayne	1959–1964	*Conservative*
Edward Short	1964–1966	*Labour*
John Silkin	1966–1969	*Labour*
Bob Mellish	1969–1970	*Labour*
Francis Pym	1970–1973	*Conservative*
Humphrey Atkins	1973–1974	*Conservative*
Bob Mellish	1974–1976	*Labour*
Michael Cocks	1976–1979	*Labour*
Michael Jopling	1979–1983	*Conservative*
John Wakeham	1983–1986	*Conservative*
David Waddington	1986–1989	*Conservative*
Tim Renton	1989–1990	*Conservative*
Richard Ryder	1990–1995	*Conservative*
Alastair Goodlad	1995–1997	*Conservative*
Nick Brown	1997–1998	*Labour*
Ann Taylor	1998–2001	*Labour*
Hilary Armstrong	2001–2006	*Labour*
Jacqui Smith	2006–2007	*Labour*
Geoff Hoon	2007–2008	*Labour*
Nick Brown	2008–2010	*Labour*
Patrick McLoughlin	2010–2012	*Conservative*
Andrew Mitchell	Sept 2012–Oct 2012	*Conservative*
Sir George Young, Bt. CH	2012–present	*Conservative*

Communities and Local Government

The post of Secretary of State for Communities and Local Government was created in 2006 by Tony Blair, having previously been under the domain of the Office of the Deputy Prime Minister.

Name	Period	Party
Ruth Kelly	6 May 2006–27 June 2007	*Labour*
Hazel Blears	28 June 2007–5 June 2009	*Labour*
John Denham	5 June 2009–11 May 2010	*Labour*
Eric Pickles	12 May 2010–present	*Conservative*

Culture, Media and Sport

Created in 1992 by John Major as Secretary of State for National Heritage, and took its current title on 14 July 1997.

Name	*Period*	*Party*
David Mellor	11 Apr.–22 Sept. 1992	*Conservative*
Peter Brooke	25 Sept. 1992–20 July 1994	*Conservative*
Stephen Dorrell	20 July 1994–5 July 1995	*Conservative*
Virginia Bottomley	5 July 1995–2 May 1997	*Conservative*
Chris Smith	3 May 1997–8 June 2001	*Labour*
Tessa Jowell	8 June 2001–27 June 2007	*Labour*
James Purnell	28 June 2007–24 Jan. 2008	*Labour*
Andy Burnham	25 Jan. 2008–5 June 2009	*Labour*
Ben Bradshaw	5 June 2009–11 May 2010	*Labour*
Jeremy Hunt	12 May 2010–4 Sept. 2012	*Conservative*
Maria Miller	4 Sept. 2012–present	*Conservative*

Defence

On his appointment as Prime Minister in 1940, Winston Churchill created the new post of Minister of Defence in response to criticism that there was no single minister in charge of the prosecution of the war. Although Churchill carried out his defence duties parallel to the premiership (as he did for four months in his second tenure), by the end of 1946 Clement Attlee had deferred the post to Albert Alexander as a distinct Cabinet position; it thus became the only Cabinet-level post representing the military, with the three service ministers – Secretary of State for War, First Lord of the Admiralty, and Secretary of State for Air – now formally subordinated to the Minister of Defence. The post of Minister of Defence was abolished on 1 April 1964 and replaced by the new post of Secretary of State for Defence.

Name	*Period*	*Party*
Winston Churchill	10 May 1940–23 May 1945	*Conservative*
Clement Attlee	27 July 1945–20 Dec. 1946	*Labour*
A V Alexander	20 Dec. 1946–28 Feb. 1950	*Labour*
Emanuel 'Manny' Shinwell	28 Feb. 1950–26 Oct. 1951	*Labour*
Winston Churchill	28 Oct. 1951–1 Mar. 1952	*Conservative*
Earl Alexander of Tunis	1 Mar. 1952–19 Oct. 1954	*No affiliation*
Harold Macmillan	19 Oct. 1954–7 Apr. 1955	*Conservative*
Selwyn Lloyd	7 Apr.–20 Dec. 1955	*Conservative*
Walter Monckton	20 Dec. 1955–18 Oct. 1956	*Conservative*
Antony Head	18 Oct. 1956–9 Jan. 1957	*Conservative*
Duncan Sandys	13 Jan. 1957–14 Oct. 1959	*Conservative*
Harold Watkinson	14 Oct. 1959–13 July 1962	*Conservative*
Peter Thorneycroft	13 July 1962–16 Oct. 1964	*Conservative*
Denis Healey	16 Oct. 1964–19 June 1970	*Labour*
Lord Carrington	20 June 1970–8 Jan. 1974	*Conservative*
Ian Gilmour	8 Jan.–4 Mar. 1974	*Conservative*
Roy Mason	5 Mar. 1974–10 Sept. 1976	*Labour*
Fred Mulley	10 Sept. 1976–4 May 1979	*Labour*
Francis Pym	5 May 1979–5 Jan. 1981	*Conservative*
John Nott	5 Jan. 1981–6 Jan. 1983	*Conservative*
Michael Heseltine	6 Jan. 1983–7 Jan. 1986	*Conservative*
George Younger	9 Jan. 1986–24 July 1989	*Conservative*
Tom King	24 July 1989–10 Apr. 1992	*Conservative*
Malcolm Rifkind	10 Apr. 1992–5 July 1995	*Conservative*
Michael Portillo	5 July 1995–2 May 1997	*Conservative*
George Robertson	3 May 1997–11 Oct. 1999	*Labour*
Geoff Hoon	11 Oct. 1999–6 May 2005	*Labour*
John Reid	6 May 2005–5 May 2006	*Labour*
Des Browne	5 May 2006–3 Oct. 2008	*Labour*
John Hutton	3 Oct. 2008–5 June 2009	*Labour*
Bob Ainsworth	5 June 2009–11 May 2010	*Labour*
Liam Fox	11 May 2010–14 Oct. 2011	*Conservative*
Philip Hammond	14 Oct. 2011–present	*Conservative*

Deputy Prime Minister

Honorific title conferred, from time to time, by the Prime Minister on a senior member of his Cabinet. Although the honour itself comes with no benefits, and the holder of office does not stand in for the Prime Minister on any official duties, the incumbent's profile and stature is elevated within and without Parliament. The present incumbent is also the leader of the Liberal Democrats within a coalition government with the Conservatives. See also First Secretary of State.

Name	*Period*	*Party*
Clement Attlee	19 Feb. 1942–23 May 1945	*Labour*
Herbert Morrison	26 July 1945–24 Feb. 1951	*Labour*
Sir Anthony Eden	26 Oct. 1951–6 Apr. 1955	*Conservative*
Richard Austen 'Rab' Butler	13 July 1962–18 Oct. 1963	*Conservative*
William Whitelaw	4 May 1979–10 Jan. 1988	*Conservative*
Sir Geoffrey Howe	24 July 1989–1 Nov. 1990	*Conservative*
Michael Heseltine	20 July 1995–2 May 1997	*Conservative*
John Prescott	2 May 1997–27 June 2007	*Labour*
Nick Clegg	11 May 2010–present	*Lib-Dem*

Education

The position of President of the Board of Education was created at the turn of the 20th century. In July 1941, R A 'Rab' Butler became the last minister to hold this title. Butler was responsible for secondary education for all and the Education Act 1944, commonly named after the Conservative politician, prompted the transformation of the Board of Education into the Ministry of Education (3 August 1944) with Butler as its first minister, an office now subordinate to the Secretary of State. The Department of Education and Science was created in 1964 with the merger of the Ministry of Education and the Ministry of Science, Quintin Hogg (formerly Viscount Hailsham) becoming Secretary of State. In 1992 responsibility for science was transferred to the Office of Public Service, and the department was renamed the Department of Education with John Patten as the first Secretary of State. In 1995 the department merged with the Department of Employment to become the Department for Education and Employment (DfEE) and in June 2001 the employment functions were transferred to a newly created Department for Work and Pensions, the DfEE becoming the Department for Education and Skills (DfES). In June 2007 the DfES was split into two new departments: the Department for Children, Schools and Families (DCSF), and the Department for Innovation, Universities and Skills (DIUS), under two new Secretaries of State. In June 2009 the Department for Business, Innovation and Skills (BIS) was created by the merger of the Department for Innovation, Universities and Skills and the Department for Business, Enterprise and Regulatory Reform. The office was again re-established in May 2010 and the incumbent became Secretary of State for Education. The following is a list of Ministers and Secretaries of State since the inception of the office.

Name	*Period*	*Party*
Spencer Cavendish, 8th Duke of Devonshire	1 Apr. 1900–8 Aug. 1902	*Liberal*
Charles Vane-Tempest-Stewart, 6th Marquess of Londonderry	8 Aug. 1902–4 Dec. 1905	*Conservative*
Augustine Birrell	10 Dec. 1905–23 Jan. 1907	*Liberal*
Reginald McKenna	23 Jan. 1907–12 Apr. 1908	*Liberal*
Walter Runciman	12 Apr. 1908–23 Oct. 1911	*Liberal*
Joseph Albert Pease	23 Oct. 1911–25 May 1915	*Liberal*
Arthur Henderson	25 May 1915–18 Aug. 1916	*Labour*
Robert Crewe-Milnes, 1st Marquess of Crewe	18 Aug.–10 Dec. 1916	*Liberal*
Herbert Albert Laurens Fisher	10 Dec. 1916–19 Oct. 1922	*Liberal*
Edward Wood	24 Oct. 1922–22 Jan. 1924	*Conservative*
Charles Philips Trevelyan	22 Jan.–3 Nov. 1924	*Labour*
Lord Eustace Percy	6 Nov. 1924–4 June 1929	*Conservative*
Sir Charles Philips Trevelyan	7 June 1929–2 Mar. 1931	*Labour*
Hastings Lees-Smith	2 Mar.–24 Aug. 1931	*Labour*
Sir Donald Maclean	25 Aug. 1931–15 June 1932	*Liberal*
Edward Wood	15 June 1932–7 June 1935	*Conservative*
Oliver Stanley	7 June 1935–28 May 1937	*Conservative*
James Stanhope, 7th Earl Stanhope	28 May 1937–27 Oct. 1938	*Conservative*
Herbrand Sackville, 9th Earl De La Warr	27 Oct. 1938–3 Apr. 1940	*Labour*
Herwald Ramsbotham	3 Apr. 1940–20 July 1941	*Conservative*
Richard Austen 'Rab' Butler	20 July 1941–25 May 1945	*Conservative*
Richard Law	25 May–26 July 1945	*Conservative*
Ellen Wilkinson	3 Aug. 1945–6 Feb. 1947	*Labour*
George Tomlinson	10 Feb. 1947–26 Oct. 1951	*Labour*
Florence Horsbrugh	2 Nov. 1951–18 Oct. 1954	*Conservative*
David Eccles	18 Oct. 1954–13 Jan. 1957	*Conservative*
Quintin Hogg, 2nd Viscount Hailsham	13 Jan.–17 Sept. 1957	*Conservative*
Geoffrey Lloyd	17 Sept. 1957–14 Oct. 1959	*Conservative*
David Eccles	14 Oct. 1959–13 July 1962	*Conservative*
Sir Edward Boyle	13 July 1962–1 Apr. 1964	*Conservative*
Quintin Hogg	1 Apr.–16 Oct. 1964	*Conservative*
Michael Stewart	18 Oct. 1964–22 Jan. 1965	*Labour*
Anthony Crosland	22 Jan. 1965–29 Aug. 1967	*Labour*
Patrick Gordon Walker	29 Aug. 1967–6 Apr. 1968	*Labour*
Edward Short	6 Apr. 1968–19 June 1970	*Labour*
Margaret Thatcher	20 June 1970–4 Mar. 1974	*Conservative*
Reginald Prentice	5 Mar. 1974–10 June 1975	*Labour*
Fred Mulley	10 June 1975–10 Sept. 1976	*Labour*
Shirley Williams	10 Sept. 1976–4 May 1979	*Labour*
Mark Carlisle	5 May 1979–14 Sept. 1981	*Conservative*
Sir Keith Joseph, Bt	14 Sept. 1981–21 May 1986	*Conservative*
Kenneth Baker	21 May 1986–24 July 1989	*Conservative*
John MacGregor	24 July 1989–2 Nov. 1990	*Conservative*
Kenneth Clarke	2 Nov. 1990–10 Apr. 1992	*Conservative*
John Patten	10 Apr. 1992–20 July 1994	*Conservative*
Gillian Shephard	20 July 1994–2 May 1997	*Conservative*
David Blunkett	2 May 1997–8 June 2001	*Labour*
Estelle Morris	8 June 2001–24 Oct. 2002	*Labour*
Charles Clarke	24 Oct. 2002–15 Dec. 2004	*Labour*
Ruth Kelly	15 Dec. 2004–5 May 2006	*Labour*
Alan Johnson	5 May 2006–27 June 2007	*Labour*
Ed Balls – DCSF	28 June 2007–11 May 2010	*Labour*
John Denham – DIUS	28 June 2007–5 June 2009	*Labour*
Peter Mandelson, Baron Mandelson of Foy and Hartlepool – BIS	5 June 2009–11 May 2010	*Labour*
Michael Gove	12 May 2010–present	*Conservative*

Employment

The department began life as the Ministry of Labour in 1916 but became the Ministry of Labour and National Service between 13 May 1940 and 12 November 1959, resuming under its original name until 6 April 1968. During Barbara Castle's incumbency the office holder was known as Secretary of State for Employment and Productivity; 25 years later in 1995 the post of Secretary of State for Employment was merged with that of Secretary of State for Education to create the position of Secretary of State for Education and Employment.

Name	*Period*	*Party*
John Hodge	10 Dec. 1916–17 Aug. 1917	*Labour*
George Roberts	17 Aug. 1917–10 Jan. 1919	*Labour*
Robert Stevenson Horne	10 Jan. 1919–19 Mar. 1920	*Unionist*
Thomas McNamara	19 Mar. 1920–19 Oct. 1922	*Liberal*
Anderson Montague Barlow	31 Oct. 1922–22 Jan. 1924	*Conservative*
Thomas Shaw	22 Jan.–3 Nov. 1924	*Labour*
Arthur Steel-Maitland	6 Nov. 1924–4 June 1929	*Conservative*
Margaret Bondfield	7 June 1929–24 Aug. 1931	*Labour*
Henry Betterton	25 Aug. 1931–29 June 1934	*Conservative*
Oliver Stanley	29 June 1934–7 June 1935	*Conservative*
Ernest Brown	7 June 1935–13 May 1940	*Liberal*
Ernest Bevin	13 May 1940–23 May 1945	*Labour*
Richard Austen 'Rab' Butler	25 May–26 July 1945	*Conservative*
George Isaacs	3 Aug. 1945–17 Jan. 1951	*Labour*
Aneurin 'Nye' Bevan	17 Jan.–23 Apr. 1951	*Labour*
Alfred Robens	24 Apr.–26 Oct. 1951	*Labour*
Walter Monckton	28 Oct. 1951–20 Dec. 1955	*Conservative*
Iain Macleod	20 Dec. 1955–14 Oct. 1959	*Conservative*
Edward Heath	14 Oct. 1959–27 July 1960	*Conservative*
John Hare	27 July 1960–20 Oct. 1963	*Conservative*
Joseph Godber	20 Oct. 1963–16 Oct. 1964	*Conservative*
Ray Gunter	18 Oct. 1964–6 Apr. 1968	*Labour*
Barbara Castle	6 Apr. 1968–19 June 1970	*Labour*
Robert Carr	20 June 1970–7 Apr. 1972	*Conservative*
Maurice Macmillan	7 Apr. 1972–2 Dec. 1973	*Conservative*
William Whitelaw	2 Dec. 1973–4 Mar. 1974	*Conservative*
Michael Foot	5 Mar. 1974–8 Apr. 1976	*Labour*
Albert Booth	8 Apr. 1976–4 May 1979	*Labour*
James Prior	5 May 1979–14 Sept. 1981	*Conservative*
Norman Tebbit	14 Sept. 1981–16 Oct. 1983	*Conservative*
Tom King	16 Oct. 1983–2 Sept. 1985	*Conservative*
Lord Young	2 Sept. 1985–13 June 1987	*Conservative*
Norman Fowler	13 June 1987–3 Jan. 1990	*Conservative*
Michael Howard	3 Jan. 1990–11 Apr. 1992	*Conservative*
Gillian Shephard	11 Apr. 1992–27 May 1993	*Conservative*
David Hunt	27 May 1993–20 July 1994	*Conservative*
Michael Portillo	20 July 1994–5 July 1995	*Conservative*

Energy and Climate Change

The Department of Energy was created in 1974 following the oil crisis of the year before. Previously, responsibility for energy production came under the auspices of the Department of Trade and Industry (DTI). The department was abolished in 1992, with some of its functions transferred to government watchdog departments and others transferred back to the DTI. The Department of Energy and Climate Change (DECC) was created on 3 October 2008 and took over some of the functions of the Department for Business, Enterprise and Regulatory Reform and Department for Environment, Food and Rural Affairs.

Name	*Period*	*Party*
Lord Carrington	8 Jan.–4 Mar. 1974	*Conservative*
Eric Varley	5 Mar. 1974–10 June 1975	*Labour*
Tony Benn	10 June 1975–4 May 1979	*Labour*
David Howell	5 May 1979–14 Sept. 1981	*Conservative*
Nigel Lawson	14 Sept. 1981–11 June 1983	*Conservative*
Peter Walker	11 June 1983–13 June 1987	*Conservative*
Cecil Parkinson	13 June 1987–24 July 1989	*Conservative*
John Wakeham	24 July 1989–11 Apr. 1992	*Conservative*
Ed Miliband	3 Oct. 2008–11 May 2010	*Labour*
Chris Huhne	12 May 2010–3 Feb 2012	*Lib-Dem*
Ed Davey	3 Feb 2012–present	*Lib-Dem*

Environment, Food and Rural Affairs

The Secretary of State for the Environment was a Cabinet position created in 1970 by Edward Heath as a combination of the Ministry of Housing and Local Government and the Ministry of Public Building and Works. On 2 May 1997, the Department of the Environment was merged with the Department of Transport to form the Department of the Environment, Transport and the Regions (DETR). On 8 June 2001, the environmental protection elements of the DETR were merged with the Ministry of Agriculture, Fisheries and Food (MAFF) to form the Department for Environment, Food and Rural Affairs (Defra). Meanwhile, the transport, housing and planning, and local and regional government aspects went to a new Department for Transport, Local Government and the Regions (DTLR).

Name	Period	Party
Peter Walker	15 Oct. 1970–5 Nov. 1972	*Conservative*
Geoffrey Rippon	5 Nov. 1972–4 Mar. 1974	*Conservative*
Anthony Crosland	5 Mar. 1974–8 Apr. 1976	*Labour*
Peter Shore	8 Apr. 1976–4 May 1979	*Labour*
Michael Heseltine	5 May 1979–6 Jan. 1983	*Conservative*
Tom King	6 Jan.–11 June 1983	*Conservative*
Patrick Jenkin	11 June 1983–2 Sept. 1985	*Conservative*
Kenneth Baker	2 Sept. 1985–21 May 1986	*Conservative*
Nicholas Ridley	21 May 1986–24 July 1989	*Conservative*
Chris Patten	24 July 1989–28 Nov. 1990	*Conservative*
Michael Heseltine	28 Nov. 1990–11 Apr. 1992	*Conservative*
Michael Howard	11 Apr. 1992–27 May 1993	*Conservative*
John Gummer	27 May 1993–2 May 1997	*Conservative*
John Prescott	2 May 1997–8 June 2001	*Labour*
Margaret Beckett	8 June 2001–5 May 2006	*Labour*
David Miliband	5 May 2006–27 June 2007	*Labour*
Hilary Benn	28 June 2007–11 May 2010	*Labour*
Caroline Spelman	12 May 2010–4 Sept. 2012	*Conservative*
Owen Paterson	4 Sept. 2012–present	*Conservative*

First Secretary of State

Honorific title conferred on a senior member of the Cabinet and sometimes preferred to that of Deputy Prime Minister, as it implies seniority over all other Secretaries of State but is more constitutionally sound. In fact both honours amount to the same thing. See also Deputy Prime Minister.

Name	Period	Party
Richard Austen 'Rab' Butler	13 July 1962–18 Oct. 1963	*Conservative*
George Brown	16 Oct. 1964–11 Aug. 1966	*Labour*
Michael Stewart	11 Aug. 1966–6 Apr. 1968	*Labour*
Barbara Castle	6 Apr. 1968–19 June 1970	*Labour*
Michael Heseltine	20 July 1995–2 May 1997	*Conservative*
John Prescott	8 June 2001–27 June 2007	*Labour*
Peter Mandelson, Baron Mandelson of Foy and Hartlepool	5 June 2009–11 May 2010	*Labour*
William Hague	12 May 2010–present	*Conservative*

Foreign and Commonwealth Affairs

The post of Secretary of State for Foreign and Commonwealth Affairs was created on 17 October 1968 with the merger of the Commonwealth Office (dating only from 1966) and the Foreign Office. The Foreign Office itself was created in 1782 by combining the existing Northern and Southern Departments, their domestic responsibilities being assigned at the same time to the Home Office. The headquarters are at King Charles Street, London SW1.

Name	Period	Party
Charles James Fox	27 Mar.–5 July 1782	*Whig*
Thomas Robinson, 2nd Baron Grantham	13 July 1782–2 Apr. 1783	*Whig*
Charles James Fox	2 Apr.–19 Dec. 1783	*Whig*
George Nugent-Temple-Grenville, 1st Marquess of Buckingham	19 Dec.–23 Dec. 1783	*Tory*
Francis Godolphin Osborne, Marquess of Carmarthen	23 Dec. 1783–1 May 1791	*Tory*
William Wyndham Grenville, 1st Baron Grenville	8 June 1791–20 Feb. 1801	*Tory*
Robert Banks Jenkinson, Lord Hawkesbury	20 Feb. 1801–14 May 1804	*Tory*
Dudley Ryder	14 May 1804–11 Jan. 1805	*Tory*
Henry Phipps	11 Jan. 1805–7 Feb. 1806	*Tory*
Charles James Fox	7 Feb.–13 Sept. 1806	*Whig*
Charles Grey	24 Sept. 1806–25 Mar. 1807	*Whig*
George Canning	25 Mar. 1807–11 Oct. 1809	*Tory*
Henry Bathurst	11 Oct.–6 Dec. 1809	*Tory*
Richard Wellesley	6 Dec. 1809–4 Mar. 1812	*Whig*
Robert Stewart, Viscount Castlereagh	4 Mar.–12 Aug. 1822	*Tory*
George Canning	16 Sept. 1822–30 Apr. 1827	*Tory*
John Ward, 1st Earl of Dudley	30 Apr. 1827–2 June 1828	*Tory*
George Hamilton-Gordon, 4th Earl of Aberdeen	2 June 1828–22 Nov. 1830	*Tory*
Henry John Temple, 3rd Viscount Palmerston	22 Nov. 1830–15 Nov. 1834	*Whig*
Arthur Wellesley, 1st Duke of Wellington	15 Nov. 1834–18 Apr. 1835	*Tory*
Henry John Temple, 3rd Viscount Palmerston	18 Apr. 1835–2 Sept. 1841	*Whig*
George Hamilton-Gordon, 4th Earl of Aberdeen	2 Sept. 1841–6 July 1846	*Conservative*
Henry John Temple, 3rd Viscount Palmerston	6 July 1846–26 Dec. 1851	*Whig*
Granville George Leveson-Gower, 2nd Earl Granville	26 Dec. 1851–27 Feb. 1852	*Whig*
James Howard Harris	27 Feb.–28 Dec. 1852	*Conservative*
Lord John Russell	28 Dec. 1852–21 Feb. 1853	*Whig*
George William Frederick Villiers, 4th Earl of Clarendon	21 Feb. 1853–26 Feb. 1858	*Whig*
James Howard Harris	26 Feb. 1858–18 June 1859	*Conservative*
Lord John Russell	18 June 1859–3 Nov. 1865	*Liberal*
George William Frederick Villiers, 4th Earl of Clarendon	3 Nov. 1865–6 July 1866	*Liberal*
Edward Henry Stanley	6 July 1866–9 Dec. 1868	*Conservative*

Name	Period	Party
George William Frederick Villiers, 4th Earl of Clarendon	9 Dec. 1868–6 July 1870	*Liberal*
Granville George Leveson-Gower, 2nd Earl Granville	6 July 1870–21 Feb. 1874	*Liberal*
Edward Henry Stanley	21 Feb. 1874–2 Apr. 1878	*Conservative*
Robert Arthur Talbot Gascoyne-Cecil, 3rd Marquess of Salisbury	2 Apr. 1878–28 Apr. 1880	*Conservative*
Granville George Leveson-Gower, 2nd Earl Granville	28 Apr. 1880–24 June 1885	*Liberal*
Robert Arthur Talbot Gascoyne-Cecil, 3rd Marquess of Salisbury	24 June 1885–6 Feb. 1886	*Conservative*
Archibald Philip Primrose, 5th Earl of Rosebery	6 Feb.–3 Aug. 1886	*Liberal*
Stafford Henry Northcote	3 Aug. 1886–12 Jan. 1887	*Conservative*
Robert Arthur Talbot Gascoyne-Cecil, 3rd Marquess of Salisbury	14 Jan. 1887–11 Aug. 1892	*Conservative*
Archibald Philip Primrose, 5th Earl of Rosebery	18 Aug. 1892–11 Mar. 1894	*Liberal*
John Wodehouse	11 Mar. 1894–21 June 1895	*Liberal*
Robert Arthur Talbot Gascoyne-Cecil, 3rd Marquess of Salisbury	29 June 1895–12 Nov. 1900	*Conservative*
Henry Petty-Fitzmaurice	12 Nov. 1900–4 Dec. 1905	*Liberal Unionist*
Sir Edward Grey	10 Dec. 1905–10 Dec. 1916	*Liberal*
Arthur Balfour	10 Dec. 1916–23 Oct. 1919	*Conservative*
George Nathaniel Curzon	23 Oct. 1919–22 Jan. 1924	*Conservative*
Ramsay MacDonald	22 Jan.–3 Nov. 1924	*Labour*
Austen Chamberlain	6 Nov. 1924–4 June 1929	*Conservative*
Arthur Henderson	7 June 1929–24 Aug. 1931	*Labour*
Rufus Isaacs, 1st Marquess of Reading	25 Aug.–5 Nov. 1931	*Liberal National*
Sir John Allsebrook Simon	5 Nov. 1931–7 June 1935	*Liberal National*
Sir Samuel Hoare	7 June–18 Dec. 1935	*Conservative*
Anthony Eden	22 Dec. 1935–20 Feb. 1938	*Conservative*
Edward Frederick Lindley Wood, 3rd Viscount Halifax	21 Feb. 1938–22 Dec. 1940	*Conservative*
Anthony Eden	22 Dec. 1940–26 July 1945	*Conservative*
Ernest Bevin	27 July 1945–9 Mar. 1951	*Labour*
Herbert Morrison	9 Mar.–26 Oct. 1951	*Labour*
Sir Anthony Eden	28 Oct. 1951–7 Apr. 1955	*Conservative*
Harold Macmillan	7 Apr.–20 Dec. 1955	*Conservative*
Selwyn Lloyd	20 Dec. 1955–27 July 1960	*Conservative*
Alec Douglas-Home, 14th Earl of Home	27 July 1960–20 Oct. 1963	*Conservative*
Richard Austen 'Rab' Butler	20 Oct. 1963–16 Oct. 1964	*Conservative*
Patrick Gordon Walker	16 Oct. 1964–22 Jan. 1965	*Labour*
Michael Stewart	22 Jan. 1965–11 Aug. 1966	*Labour*
George Brown	11 Aug. 1966–16 Mar. 1968	*Labour*
Michael Stewart	16 Mar. 1968–19 June 1970	*Labour*
Sir Alec Douglas-Home	20 June 1970–4 Mar. 1974	*Conservative*
James Callaghan	5 Mar. 1974–8 Apr. 1976	*Labour*
Anthony Crosland	8 Apr. 1976–19 Feb. 1977	*Labour*
Dr David Owen	22 Feb. 1977–4 May 1979	*Labour*
Lord Carrington	5 May 1979–5 Apr. 1982	*Conservative*
Francis Pym	6 Apr. 1982–11 June 1983	*Conservative*
Sir Geoffrey Howe	11 June 1983–24 July 1989	*Conservative*
John Major	24 July–26 Oct. 1989	*Conservative*
Douglas Hurd	26 Oct. 1989–5 July 1995	*Conservative*
Malcolm Rifkind	5 July 1995–2 May 1997	*Conservative*
Robin Cook	2 May 1997–8 June 2001	*Labour*
Jack Straw	8 June 2001–5 May 2006	*Labour*
Margaret Beckett	5 May 2006–28 June 2007	*Labour*
David Miliband	28 June 2007–11 May 2010	*Labour*
William Hague	12 May 2010–present	*Conservative*

Health

Sir Benjamin Hall (who in 1859 gave his name 'Big Ben' to the great bell of the clock at the north end of the Palace of Westminster in London) became the first President of the Board of Health in 1854, but the department was discontinued in 1858 and its powers were eventually merged into the newly formed Local Government Board in 1871. The board was restructured in 1919 and the local government functions were transferred to the Minister of Housing and Local Government, while the Ministry of Health was created with Christopher Addison as First Minister. In 1968 the department was amalgamated with the Ministry of Social Security under Richard Crossman as Secretary of State for Social Services. In July 1988, following the demerger of the Department of Health and Social Security (DHSS), the office was split; John Moore became Secretary of State for Social Security while Kenneth Clarke became Secretary of State for Health.

Name	Period	Party
Sir Benjamin Hall	14 Oct. 1854–13 Aug. 1855	*Whig*
Hon. William Cowper	13 Aug. 1855–9 Feb. 1857	*Liberal*
William Monsell, 1st Baron Emly	9 Feb.–24 Sept. 1857	*Liberal*
Hon. William Cowper	24 Sept. 1857–21 Feb. 1858	*Liberal*
Charles Adderley	8 Mar.–1 Sept. 1858	*Conservative*
James Stansfield	19 Aug. 1871–17 Feb. 1874	*Liberal*
George Sclater-Booth	17 Feb. 1874–3 May 1880	*Conservative*
John George Dodson	3 May 1880–28 Dec. 1882	*Liberal*
Sir Charles Wentworth Dilke	28 Dec. 1882–24 June 1885	*Liberal*
Arthur Balfour	24 June 1885–Feb. 1886	*Conservative*
Joseph Chamberlain	27 Feb.–27 Mar. 1886	*Liberal*

Name	*Period*	*Party*
James Stansfield	3 Apr.–20 July 1886	*Liberal*
Charles Ritchie	20 July 1886–15 Aug. 1892	*Conservative*
Henry Fowler	15 Aug. 1892–2 Mar. 1894	*Liberal*
George John Shaw-Lefevre	2 Mar. 1894–21 June 1895	*Liberal*
Henry Chaplin	29 June 1895–12 Nov. 1900	*Conservative*
Walter Hume Long	12 Nov. 1900–14 Mar. 1905	*Conservative*
Gerald Balfour	14 Mar.–4 Dec. 1905	*Conservative*
John Burns	10 Dec. 1905–11 Feb. 1914	*Liberal*
Herbert Samuel	11 Feb. 1914–25 May 1915	*Liberal*
Walter Hume Long	25 May 1915–28 June 1916	*Conservative*
William Hayes Fisher	28 June 1916–4 Nov. 1918	*Conservative*
Auckland Geddes	4 Nov. 1918–24 June 1919	*Unionist*
Christopher Addison	24 June 1919–1 Apr. 1921	*Liberal*
Alfred Mond	1 Apr. 1921–19 Oct. 1922	*Liberal*
Sir Arthur Griffith-Boscawen	24 Oct. 1922–7 Mar. 1923	*Conservative*
Neville Chamberlain	7 Mar.–27 Aug. 1923	*Conservative*
Sir William Joynson-Hicks	27 Aug. 1923–22 Jan. 1924	*Conservative*
John Wheatley	22 Jan.–3 Nov. 1924	*Labour*
Neville Chamberlain	6 Nov. 1924–4 June 1929	*Conservative*
Arthur Greenwood	7 June 1929–24 Aug. 1931	*Labour*
Neville Chamberlain	25 Aug.–5 Nov. 1931	*Conservative*
Sir Edward Hilton Young	5 Nov. 1931–7 June 1935	*Conservative*
Kingsley Wood	7 June 1935–16 May 1938	*Conservative*
Walter Elliot	16 May 1938–13 May 1940	*Scottish Unionist*
Malcolm MacDonald	13 May 1940–8 Feb. 1941	*Labour*
Ernest Brown	8 Feb. 1941–11 Nov. 1943	*Liberal*
Henry Willink	11 Nov. 1943–26 July 1945	*Conservative*
Aneurin 'Nye' Bevan	3 Aug. 1945–17 Jan. 1951	*Labour*
Hilary Marquand	17 Jan.–26 Oct. 1951	*Labour*
Harry Crookshank	30 Oct. 1951–7 May 1952	*Conservative*
Iain Macleod	7 May 1952–20 Dec. 1955	*Conservative*
Robin Turton	20 Dec. 1955–16 Jan. 1957	*Conservative*
Dennis Vosper	16 Jan.–17 Sept. 1957	*Conservative*
Derek Walker-Smith	17 Sept. 1957–27 July 1960	*Conservative*
Enoch Powell	27 July 1960–20 Oct. 1963	*Conservative*
Anthony Barber	20 Oct. 1963–16 Oct. 1964	*Conservative*
Kenneth Robinson	18 Oct. 1964–1 Nov. 1968	*Labour*
Richard Crossman	1 Nov. 1968–19 June 1970	*Labour*
Sir Keith Joseph, Bt	20 June 1970–4 Mar. 1974	*Conservative*
Barbara Castle	5 Mar. 1974–8 Apr. 1976	*Labour*
David Ennals	8 Apr. 1976–4 May 1979	*Labour*
Patrick Jenkin	5 May 1979–14 Sept. 1981	*Conservative*
Norman Fowler	14 Sept. 1981–13 June 1987	*Conservative*
John Moore	13 June 1987–25 July 1988	*Conservative*
Kenneth Clarke	25 July 1988–2 Nov. 1990	*Conservative*
William Waldegrave	2 Nov. 1990–10 Apr. 1992	*Conservative*
Virginia Bottomley	10 Apr. 1992–5 July 1995	*Conservative*
Stephen Dorrell	5 July 1995–2 May 1997	*Conservative*
Frank Dobson	3 May 1997–11 Oct. 1999	*Labour*
Alan Milburn	11 Oct. 1999–13 June 2003	*Labour*
John Reid	13 June 2003–6 May 2005	*Labour*
Patricia Hewitt	6 May 2005–27 June 2007	*Labour*
Alan Johnson	27 June 2007–5 June 2009	*Labour*
Andy Burnham	5 June 2009–11 May 2010	*Labourr*
Andrew Lansley	12 May 2010–4 Sept. 2012	*Conservative*
Jeremy Hunt	4 Sept. 2012–present	*Conservative*

Home Office

The Home Secretary is responsible for immigration control, security and order within the United Kingdom. He was formerly responsible for the Prison Service and Probation Service, but, since 2007 these are under a newly created Minister of Justice. The Home Office itself was created in 1782 by reallocating the domestic responsibilities of the existing Southern and Northern Departments, their overseas duties being assigned at the same time to the Foreign Office. The headquarters are at Marsham Street, London SW1.

Name	*Period*	*Party*
William Petty, 2nd Earl of Shelburne	27 Mar.–10 July 1782	*Whig*
Thomas Townshend, 1st Viscount Sydney	10 July 1782–2 Apr. 1783	*Whig*
Frederick North, Lord North	2 Apr.–19 Dec. 1783	*Tory*
George Nugent-Temple-Grenville	19 Dec.–23 Dec. 1783	*Whig*
Thomas Townshend, 1st Viscount Sydney	23 Dec. 1783–5 June 1789	*Whig*
William Wyndham Grenville	5 June 1789–8 June 1791	*Tory*
Henry Dundas, 1st Viscount Melville	8 June 1791–11 July 1794	*Tory*
William Henry Cavendish-Bentinck, 3rd Duke of Portland	11 July 1794–30 July 1801	*Tory*
Thomas Pelham, 1st Lord Pelham	30 July 1801–17 Aug. 1803	*Whig*
Charles Philip Yorke	17 Aug. 1803–12 May 1804	*Tory*
Robert Banks Jenkinson	12 May 1804–5 Feb. 1806	*Tory*
George John Spencer	5 Feb. 1806–25 Mar. 1807	*Whig*
Robert Banks Jenkinson	25 Mar. 1807–1 Nov. 1809	*Tory*

POLITICS

Name	*Period*	*Party*
Richard Ryder	1 Nov. 1809–8 June 1812	*Tory*
Henry Addington, 1st Viscount Sidmouth	11 June 1812–17 Jan. 1822	*Tory*
Sir Robert Peel	17 Jan. 1822–10 Apr. 1827	*Tory*
William Sturges-Bourne	30 Apr.–16 July 1827	*Tory*
Henry Petty-Fitzmaurice	16 July 1827–22 Jan. 1828	*Whig*
Sir Robert Peel	26 Jan. 1828–22 Nov. 1830	*Tory*
William Lamb, 2nd Viscount Melbourne	22 Nov. 1830–16 July 1834	*Whig*
John Ponsonby, Viscount Duncannon	19 July–15 Nov. 1834	*Whig*
Arthur Wellesley, 1st Duke of Wellington	15 Nov.–15 Dec. 1834	*Tory*
Henry Goulburn	15 Dec. 1834–18 Apr. 1835	*Conservative*
Lord John Russell	18 Apr. 1835–30 Aug. 1839	*Whig*
Constantine Henry Phipps, 1st Marquess of Normanby	30 Aug. 1839–30 Aug. 1841	*Whig*
Sir James Graham, Bt	6 Sept. 1841–30 June 1846	*Conservative*
Sir George Grey, Bt	6 July 1846–23 Feb. 1852	*Whig*
Spencer Horatio Walpole	27 Feb.–19 Dec. 1852	*Conservative*
Henry John Temple, 3rd Viscount Palmerston	28 Dec. 1852–6 Feb. 1855	*Whig*
Sir George Grey, Bt	8 Feb. 1855–26 Feb. 1858	*Whig*
Spencer Horatio Walpole	26 Feb. 1858–3 Mar. 1859	*Conservative*
Thomas Sotheron-Estcourt	3 Mar.–18 June 1859	*Conservative*
Sir George Cornewall Lewis, Bt	18 June 1859–25 July 1861	*Liberal*
Sir George Grey, Bt	25 July 1861–28 June 1866	*Liberal*
Spencer Horatio Walpole	6 July 1866–17 May 1867	*Conservative*
Gathorne Hardy	17 May 1867–3 Dec. 1868	*Conservative*
Henry Austin Bruce	9 Dec. 1868–9 Aug. 1873	*Liberal*
Robert Lowe	9 Aug. 1873–20 Feb. 1874	*Liberal*
Richard Cross	21 Feb. 1874–23 Apr. 1880	*Conservative*
Sir William Vernon Harcourt	28 Apr. 1880–23 June 1885	*Liberal*
Richard Cross	24 June 1885–1 Feb. 1886	*Conservative*
Hugh Childers	6 Feb.–25 July 1886	*Liberal*
Henry Matthews	3 Aug. 1886–15 Aug. 1892	*Conservative*
Herbert Henry Asquith	18 Aug. 1892–25 June 1895	*Liberal*
Sir Matthew White Ridley	29 June 1895–12 Nov. 1900	*Conservative*
Charles Thomson Ritchie	12 Nov. 1900–12 July 1902	*Conservative*
Aretas Akers-Douglas	12 July 1902–5 Dec. 1905	*Conservative*
Herbert John Gladstone	11 Dec. 1905–19 Feb. 1910	*Liberal*
Winston Churchill	19 Feb. 1910–24 Oct. 1911	*Liberal*
Reginald McKenna	24 Oct. 1911–27 May 1915	*Liberal*
Sir John Allsebrook Simon	27 May 1915–12 Jan. 1916	*Liberal*
Herbert Samuel	12 Jan.–7 Dec. 1916	*Liberal*
George Cave, 1st Viscount Cave	11 Dec. 1916–14 Jan. 1919	*Conservative*
Edward Shortt	14 Jan. 1919–23 Oct. 1922	*Liberal*
William Clive Bridgeman	25 Oct. 1922–22 Jan. 1924	*Conservative*
Arthur Henderson	23 Jan.–4 Nov. 1924	*Labour*
Sir William Joynson-Hicks	7 Nov. 1924–5 June 1929	*Conservative*
John Robert Clynes	8 June 1929–26 Aug. 1931	*Labour*
Sir Herbert Samuel	26 Aug. 1931–1 Oct. 1932	*Liberal*
Sir John Gilmour	1 Oct. 1932–7 June 1935	*Scottish Unionist*
Sir John Simon	7 June 1935–28 May 1937	*National Liberal*
Sir Samuel Hoare	28 May 1937–3 Sept. 1939	*Conservative*
Sir John Anderson	4 Sept. 1939–4 Oct. 1940	*National Independent*
Herbert Morrison	4 Oct. 1940–23 May 1945	*Labour*
Sir Donald Bradley Somervell	25 May–26 July 1945	*Conservative*
James Chuter Ede	3 Aug. 1945–26 Oct. 1951	*Labour*
Sir David Maxwell-Fyfe	27 Oct. 1951–19 Oct. 1954	*Conservative*
Gwilym Lloyd George	19 Oct. 1954–14 Jan. 1957	*Conservative*
Richard Austen 'Rab' Butler	14 Jan. 1957–13 July 1962	*Conservative*
Henry Brooke	13 July 1962–16 Oct. 1964	*Conservative*
Sir Frank Soskice	18 Oct. 1964–23 Dec. 1965	*Labour*
Roy Jenkins	23 Dec. 1965–30 Nov. 1967	*Labour*
James Callaghan	30 Nov. 1967–19 June 1970	*Labour*
Reginald Maudling	20 June 1970–18 July 1972	*Conservative*
Robert Carr	18 July 1972–4 Mar. 1974	*Conservative*
Roy Jenkins	5 Mar. 1974–10 Sept. 1976	*Labour*
Merlyn Rees	10 Sept. 1976–4 May 1979	*Labour*
William Whitelaw	5 May 1979–11 June 1983	*Conservative*
Leon Brittan	11 June 1983–2 Sept. 1985	*Conservative*
Douglas Hurd	2 Sept. 1985–26 Oct. 1989	*Conservative*
David Waddington	26 Oct. 1989–28 Nov. 1990	*Conservative*
Kenneth Baker	28 Nov. 1990–10 Apr. 1992	*Conservative*
Kenneth Clarke	10 Apr. 1992–27 May 1993	*Conservative*
Michael Howard	27 May 1993–2 May 1997	*Conservative*
Jack Straw	2 May 1997–8 June 2001	*Labour*
David Blunkett	8 June 2001–15 Dec. 2004	*Labour*
Charles Clarke	15 Dec. 2004–5 May 2006	*Labour*
John Reid	5 May 2006–27 June 2007	*Labour*
Jacqui Smith	28 June 2007–5 June 2009	*Labour*
Alan Johnson	5 June 2009–11 May 2010	*Labour*
Theresa May	12 May 2010–present	*Conservative*

International Development

The office responsible for promoting development overseas was created in 1997 when the Department for International Development was made independent of the Foreign and Commonwealth Office; Clare Short being the first Secretary of State. The Ministry of Overseas Development was established in 1964 but was conjoined with the Foreign and Commonwealth Office on 15 October 1970. Between 10 June 1975 and 8 October 1979 the Foreign Secretary served as Secretary of State for Foreign and Commonwealth Affairs and Minister for Overseas Development in the Cabinet, while the Minister for Overseas Development held the rank of Minister of State within the Foreign and Commonwealth Office.

Name	*Period*	*Party*
Barbara Castle	18 Oct. 1964–23 Dec. 1965	*Labour*
Anthony Greenwood	23 Dec. 1965–11 Aug. 1966	*Labour*
Arthur Bottomley	11 Aug. 1966–29 Aug. 1967	*Labour*
Reginald Prentice	29 Aug. 1967–6 Oct. 1969	*Labour*
Judith Hart	6 Oct. 1969–19 June 1970	*Labour*
Richard Wood	23 June 1970–4 Mar. 1974	*Conservative*
Judith Hart	7 Mar. 1974–10 June 1975	*Labour*
Reginald Prentice	10 June 1975–21 Dec. 1976	*Labour*
Frank Judd	21 Dec. 1976–21 Feb. 1977	*Labour*
Judith Hart	21 Feb. 1977–4 May 1979	*Labour*
Neil Marten	6 May 1979–6 Jan. 1983	*Conservative*
Tim Raison	6 Jan. 1983–10 Sept. 1986	*Conservative*
Chris Patten	10 Sept. 1986–24 July 1989	*Conservative*
Lynda Chalker	24 July 1989–2 May 1997	*Conservative*
Clare Short	3 May 1997–12 May 2003	*Labour*
Valerie Amos, Baroness Amos	12 May–6 Oct. 2003	*Labour*
Hilary Benn	6 Oct. 2003–27 June 2007	*Labour*
Douglas Alexander	28 June 2007–11 May 2010	*Labour*
Andrew Mitchell	12 May 2010–4 Sept. 2012	*Conservative*
Justine Greening	4 Sept. 2012–present	*Conservative*

Leader of the House of Commons

The office was more often than not held by the Prime Minister until Churchill's wartime Cabinet, but in recent years the post has usually been combined with that of Lord President of the Council. From 2003 it has been combined instead with the office of Lord Privy Seal. The incumbent is responsible for arranging government business in the House of Commons.

Name	*Period*
Henry Pelham	1743–1754
Thomas Robinson	1754–1755
Henry Fox	1755–1756
William Pitt (the Elder)	1756–1761
George Grenville	1763–1765
Henry Seymour Conway	1765–1768
Frederick North, Lord North	1768–1782
Charles James Fox	1782
Thomas Townshend	1782–1783
Charles James Fox and Frederick North, Lord North	1783
William Pitt (the Younger)	1783–1801
Henry Addington	1801–1804
William Pitt (the Younger)	1804–1806
Charles James Fox	1806
Charles Grey, Viscount Howick	1806–1807
Spencer Perceval	1807–1812
Robert Stewart, Viscount Castlereagh	1812–1822
George Canning	1822–1827
William Huskisson	1827–1828
Robert Peel	1828–1830
John Charles Spencer, Viscount Althorp	1830–1834
Lord John Russell	1834
Sir Robert Peel	1834–1835
Lord John Russell	1835–1841
Sir Robert Peel	1841–1846
Lord John Russell	1846–1852
Benjamin Disraeli	1852
Lord John Russell	1852–1855
Henry John Temple, 3rd Viscount Palmerston	1855–1858
Benjamin Disraeli	1858–1859
Henry John Temple, 3rd Viscount Palmerston	1859–1865
William Ewart Gladstone	1865–1866
Benjamin Disraeli	1866–1868
William Ewart Gladstone	1868–1874
Benjamin Disraeli	1874–1876
Sir Stafford Henry Northcote	1876–1880
William Ewart Gladstone	1880–1885
Sir Michael Hicks Beach	1885–1886
William Ewart Gladstone	1886

Lord Randolph Churchill	1886–1887
William Henry Smith	1887–1891
Arthur Balfour	1891–1892
William Ewart Gladstone	1892–1894
Sir William Vernon Harcourt	1894–1895
Arthur Balfour	1895–1905
Sir Henry Campbell-Bannerman	1905–1908
Herbert Henry Asquith	1908–1916
Andrew Bonar Law	1916–1921
Austen Chamberlain	1921–1922
Andrew Bonar Law	1922–1923
Stanley Baldwin	1923–1924
Ramsay MacDonald	1924
Stanley Baldwin	1924–1929
Ramsay MacDonald	1929–1935
Stanley Baldwin	1935–1937
Neville Chamberlain	1937–1940
Winston Churchill	1940–1942
Sir Stafford Cripps	1942
Anthony Eden	1942–1945
Herbert Morrison	1945–1951
James Chuter Ede	1951
Harry Crookshank	1951–1955
Richard Austen 'Rab' Butler	1955–1961
Iain Macleod	1961–1963
Selwyn Lloyd	1963–1964
Herbert Bowden	1964–1966
Richard Crossman	1966–1968
Fred Peart	1968–1970
William Whitelaw	1970–1972
Robert Carr	1972
James Prior	1972–1974
Edward Short	1974–1976
Michael Foot	1976–1979
Norman St John-Stevas	1979–1981
Francis Pym	1981–1982
John Biffen	1982–1987
John Wakeham	1987–1989
Sir Geoffrey Howe	1989–1990
John MacGregor	1990–1992
Tony Newton	1992–1997
Ann Taylor	1997–1998
Margaret Beckett	1998–2001
Robin Cook	2001–2003
John Reid	2003
Peter Hain	2003–2005
Geoff Hoon	2005–2006
Jack Straw	2006–2007
Harriet Harman	2007–2010
Sir George Young	2010–2012
Andrew Lansley	4 Sept.2012-present

Leader of the House of Lords

The incumbent takes charge of the government's business in the House of Lords but is always the holder of a formal Cabinet position, most often Lord President of the Council, Lord Privy Seal or Chancellor of the Duchy of Lancaster. Charles 'Turnip' Townshend, 2nd Viscount Townshend, is sometimes considered the first incumbent in 1721 although his actual title was Secretary of State.

Name	*Period*	*Party*
Charles Watson-Wentworth, 2nd Marquess of Rockingham	1782	*Whig*
William Petty, 2nd Earl of Shelburne	1782–1783	*Whig*
William Cavendish-Bentinck, 3rd Duke of Portland	1783	*Whig*
Thomas Townshend, 1st Viscount Sydney	1783–1789	*Whig*
Francis Godolphin Osborne, 5th Duke of Leeds	1789–1790	*Tory*
William Wyndham Grenville, 1st Baron Grenville	1790–1801	*Whig*
Thomas Pelham, 2nd Baron Pelham	1801–1803	*Whig*
Robert Jenkinson, 2nd Baron Hawkesbury	1803–1806	*Tory*
William Wyndham Grenville, 1st Baron Grenville	1806–1807	*Whig*
Lord Hawkesbury (2nd Earl of Liverpool from 1808)	1807–1827	*Tory*
Frederick John Robinson, 1st Viscount Goderich	1827–1828	*Tory*
Arthur Wellesley, 1st Duke of Wellington	1828–1830	*Tory*
Charles Grey, 2nd Earl Grey	22 Nov. 1830–9 July 1834	*Whig*
William Lamb, 2nd Viscount Melbourne	16 July–14 Nov. 1834	*Whig*
Arthur Wellesley, 1st Duke of Wellington	17 Nov. 1834–8 Apr. 1835	*Tory*
William Lamb, 2nd Viscount Melbourne	18 Apr. 1835–30 Aug. 1841	*Whig*
Arthur Wellesley, 1st Duke of Wellington	3 Sept. 1841–27 June 1846	*Conservative*
Henry Petty-FitzMaurice, 3rd Marquess of Lansdowne	6 July 1846–21 Feb. 1852	*Whig*
Edward Smith-Stanley, 14th Earl of Derby	23 Feb.–17 Dec. 1852	*Conservative*
George Hamilton-Gordon, 4th Earl of Aberdeen	19 Dec. 1852–30 Jan. 1855	*Peelite*
Granville Leveson-Gower, 2nd Earl Granville	8 Feb. 1855–21 Feb. 1858	*Whig*

Name	*Period*	*Party*
Edward Smith-Stanley, 14th Earl of Derby	21 Feb. 1858–11 June 1859	*Conservative*
Granville Leveson-Gower, 2nd Earl Granville	18 June 1859–29 Oct. 1865	*Conservative*
John Russell, 1st Earl Russell	29 Oct. 1865–26 June 1866	*Liberal*
Edward Smith-Stanley, 14th Earl of Derby	28 June 1866–25 Feb. 1868	*Conservative*
James Howard Harris, 3rd Earl of Malmesbury	27 Feb.–1 Dec. 1868	*Conservative*
Granville Leveson-Gower, 2nd Earl Granville	9 Dec. 1868–17 Feb. 1874	*Liberal*
Charles Gordon-Lennox, 6th Duke of Richmond	21 Feb. 1874–21 Aug. 1876	*Conservative*
Benjamin Disraeli, 1st Earl of Beaconsfield	21 Aug. 1876–Apr. 1880	*Conservative*
Granville Leveson-Gower, 2nd Earl Granville	28 Apr. 1880–9 June 1885	*Conservative*
Robert Gascoyne-Cecil, 3rd Marquess of Salisbury	23 June 1885–28 Jan. 1886	*Conservative*
Granville Leveson-Gower, 2nd Earl Granville	6 Feb.–20 July 1886	*Liberal*
Robert Gascoyne-Cecil, 3rd Marquess of Salisbury	25 July 1886–11 Aug. 1892	*Conservative*
John Wodehouse, 1st Earl of Kimberley	18 Aug. 1892–5 Mar. 1894	*Liberal*
Archibald Primrose, 5th Earl of Rosebery	5 Mar. 1894–21 June 1895	*Liberal*
Robert Gascoyne-Cecil, 3rd Marquess of Salisbury	25 June 1895–11 July 1902	*Conservative*
Spencer Cavendish, 8th Duke of Devonshire	12 July 1902–13 Oct. 1903	*Liberal Unionist*
Henry Petty-FitzMaurice, 5th Marquess of Lansdowne	13 Oct. 1903–4 Dec. 1905	*Liberal Unionist*
George Robinson, 1st Marquess of Ripon	10 Dec. 1905–14 Apr. 1908	*Liberal*
Robert Crewe-Milnes, 1st Marquess of Crewe	14 Apr. 1908–10 Dec. 1916	*Liberal*
George Nathaniel Curzon, 1st Marquess Curzon of Kedleston	10 Dec. 1916–22 Jan. 1924	*Conservative*
Richard Burdon Haldane, 1st Viscount Haldane	22 Jan.–3 Nov. 1924	*Labour*
George Nathaniel Curzon, 1st Marquess Curzon of Kedleston	6 Nov. 1924–27 Apr. 1925	*Conservative*
James Gascoyne-Cecil, 4th Marquess of Salisbury	27 Apr. 1925–4 June 1929	*Conservative*
Charles Cripps, 1st Baron Parmoor	7 June 1929–24 Aug. 1931	*Labour*
Rufus Isaacs, 1st Marquess of Reading	25 Aug.–5 Nov. 1931	*Liberal*
Douglas Hogg, 1st Viscount Hailsham	5 Nov. 1931–7 June 1935	*Conservative*
Charles Vane-Tempest-Stewart, 7th Marquess of Londonderry	7 June–22 Nov. 1935	*Conservative*
E F L Wood, 3rd Viscount Halifax	22 Nov. 1935–27 Oct. 1938	*Conservative*
James Stanhope, 7th Earl Stanhope	27 Oct. 1938–14 May 1940	*Conservative*
Thomas Inskip, 1st Viscount Caldecote	14 May–3 Oct. 1940	*Conservative*
E F L Wood, 3rd Viscount Halifax	3 Oct.–22 Dec. 1940	*Conservative*
George Lloyd, 1st Baron Lloyd	22 Dec. 1940–4 Feb. 1941	*Conservative*
Walter Edward Guinness, 1st Baron Moyne	8 Feb. 1941–21 Feb. 1942	*Conservative*
Robert Gascoyne-Cecil, Viscount Cranborne	21 Feb. 1942–26 July 1945	*Conservative*
Christopher Addison, 1st Viscount Addison	3 Aug. 1945–26 Oct. 1951	*Labour*
Robert Gascoyne-Cecil, 5th Marquess of Salisbury	28 Oct. 1951–29 Mar. 1957	*Conservative*
Alec Douglas-Home, 14th Earl of Home	29 Mar. 1957–27 July 1960	*Conservative*
Quintin Hogg, 2nd Viscount Hailsham	27 July 1960–20 Oct. 1963	*Conservative*
Peter Carrington, 6th Baron Carrington	20 Oct. 1963–16 Oct. 1964	*Conservative*
Francis Augier Pakenham, 7th Earl of Longford	18 Oct. 1964–16 Jan. 1968	*Labour*
Edward Shackleton, Baron Shackleton	16 Jan. 1968–19 June 1970	*Labour*
George Jellicoe, 2nd Earl Jellicoe	20 June 1970–23 May 1973	*Conservative*
David Hennessy, 3rd Baron Windlesham	5 June 1973–4 Mar. 1974	*Conservative*
Malcolm Shepherd, 2nd Baron Shepherd	7 Mar. 1974–10 Sept. 1976	*Labour*
Fred Peart, Baron Peart	10 Sept. 1976–4 May 1979	*Labour*
Christopher Soames, Baron Soames	5 May 1979–14 Sept. 1981	*Conservative*
Janet Young, Baroness Young	14 Sept. 1981–11 June 1983	*Conservative*
William Whitelaw, 1st Viscount Whitelaw	11 June 1983–10 Jan. 1988	*Conservative*
John Julian Ganzoni, 2nd Baron Belstead	10 Jan. 1988–28 Nov. 1990	*Conservative*
David Waddington, Baron Waddington	28 Nov. 1990–11 Apr. 1992	*Conservative*
John Wakeham, Baron Wakeham	11 Apr. 1992–20 July 1994	*Conservative*
Robert Gascoyne-Cecil, Viscount Cranborne	20 July 1994–2 May 1997	*Conservative*
Ivor Richard, Baron Richard	2 May 1997–27 July 1998	*Labour*
Margaret Jay, Baroness Jay of Paddington	27 July 1998–8 June 2001	*Labour*
Gareth Williams, Baron Williams of Mostyn	8 June 2001–20 Sept. 2003	*Labour*
Valerie Amos, Baroness Amos	6 Oct. 2003–27 June 2007	*Labour*
Catherine Ashton, Baroness Ashton of Upholland	27 June 2007–2 Oct. 2008	*Labour*
Janet Royall, Baroness Royall of Blaisdon	2 Oct. 2008–11 May 2010	*Labour*
Thomas Galbraith, 2nd Baron Strathclyde	12 May 2010–7 Jan. 2013	*Conservative*
Jonathan Hopkin Hill, Baron Hill of Oareford	7 Jan. 2013–present	*Conservative*

Lord Chancellor

The position of Lord Chancellor dates back to at least the Norman Conquest and until the reign of Elizabeth I was invariably held by a high-ranking church officer. The duties of the Lord Chancellor are varied, including responsibility for constitutional affairs and the effective administration of the court system as well as custodianship of the Great Seal. Reform during the past decade has changed the areas of responsibility of the incumbent and the present holder of the office, Kenneth Clarke, is also Secretary of State for Justice (a position created in May 2007 to replace the Secretary of State for Constitutional Affairs, itself created in 2003 – Lord Falconer being the sole incumbent). Formerly, there were separate Chancellors of England, Scotland and Ireland and although I have listed the English Lord High Chancellors for interest only, the first Lord Chancellor/Lord Keeper of Great Britain was William Cowper in May 1707. Any gaps in the periods of incumbency were when a commission of several men fulfilled the ministerial function.

Name	*Period*	*Party*
Herfast	1068–1070	*n/a*
Osmund	1070–1078	*n/a*
Maurice, Archdeacon of Le Mans	1078–1085	*n/a*
Gerard, Preceptor of Rouen	1085–1092	*n/a*
Robert Blouet	1092–1093	*n/a*

Name	Period	Party
William Giffard	1093–1101	n/a
Roger	1101–1102	n/a
Waldric	1102–1107	n/a
Ranulf	1107–1123	n/a
Geoffrey Rufus	1123–1133	n/a
Robert de Sigillo	1133–1135	n/a
Roger le Poer	1135–1139	n/a
Philip de Harcourt, Dean of Lincoln	1139–1140	n/a
Robert of Ghent, Dean of York	1140–1141	n/a
William FitzGilbert	1141–1142	n/a
William de Vere	1142	n/a
Robert of Ghent, Dean of York	1142–1154	n/a
Thomas Becket, Archdeacon of Canterbury	1155–1162	n/a
Geoffrey Ridel, Archdeacon of Canterbury	1162–1173	n/a
Ralph de Warneville, Treasurer of York	1173–1181	n/a
Geoffrey, the Bastard, Plantagenet	1181–1189	n/a
William Longchamp, Bishop of Ely	1189–1197	n/a
Eustace, Dean of Salisbury	1197–1198	n/a
Eustace, Bishop of Ely	1198–1199	n/a
Hubert Walter, Archbishop of Canterbury	1199–1205	n/a
Walter de Gray	1205–1214	n/a
Richard Marsh	1214–1226	n/a
Ralph Neville	1226–1240	n/a
Richard le Gras, Abbot of Evesham	1240–1242	n/a
Ralph Neville	1242–1244	n/a
Silvester de Everdon, Archdeacon of Chester	1244–1246	n/a
John Maunsell, Provost of Beverley	1246–1247	n/a
Sir John Lexington	1247–1248	n/a
John Maunsell	1248–1249	n/a
Sir John Lexington	1249–1250	n/a
William of Kilkenny	1250–1255	n/a
Henry Wingham	1255–1260	n/a
Nicholas of Ely, Archdeacon of Ely	1260–1261	n/a
Walter de Merton, Archdeacon of Bath	1261–1263	n/a
Nicholas of Ely, Archdeacon of Ely	1263	n/a
John Chishull, Archdeacon of London	1263–1264	n/a
Thomas Cantilupe, Archdeacon of Stafford	1264–1265	n/a
Ralph Sandwich	1265	n/a
Walter Giffard, Bishop of Bath and Wells	1265–1266	n/a
Godfrey Giffard, Archdeacon of Wells	1266–1268	n/a
John Chishull, Dean of St Paul's	1268–1269	n/a
Richard Middleton, Archdeacon of Northumberland	1269–1272	n/a
Walter de Merton, Archdeacon of Bath	1272–1274	n/a
Robert Burnell, Bishop of Bath	1274–1292	n/a
John Langton, Canon of Lincoln	1292–1302	n/a
William Greenfield, Dean of Chichester	1302–1305	n/a
William Hamilton, Dean of York	1305–1307	n/a
Ralph Baldock, Bishop of London	1307	n/a
John Langton, Bishop of Chichester	1307–1310	n/a
Walter Reynolds, Bishop of Worcester	1310–1314	n/a
John Sandall, Canon of Lincoln	1314–1318	n/a
John Hotham, Bishop of Ely	1318–1320	n/a
John Salmon, Bishop of Norwich	1320–1323	n/a
Robert Baldock, Archdeacon of Middlesex	1323–1327	n/a
William Airmyn, Bishop of Norwich	1327–1328	n/a
Henry Burghersh, Bishop of Lincoln	1328–1330	n/a
John de Stratford, Bishop of Winchester	1330–1334	n/a
Richard Bury, Bishop of Durham	1334–1335	n/a
John de Stratford, Archbishop of Canterbury	1335–1337	n/a
Robert de Stratford, Bishop of Chichester	1337–1338	n/a
Richard Bintworth, Bishop of London	1338–1339	n/a
John de Stratford, Archbishop of Canterbury	1340	n/a
Sir Robert Bourchier	1340–1341	n/a
Sir Robert Parning	1341–1343	n/a
Sir Robert Sadington	1343–1345	n/a
John Offord, Dean of Lincoln	1345–1349	n/a
John Thoresby, Bishop of Worcester	1349–1356	n/a
William Edington, Bishop of Winchester	1356–1363	n/a
Simon Langham, Bishop of Ely	1363–1367	n/a
William of Wykeham, Bishop of Winchester	1367–1371	n/a
Sir Robert Thorp	1371–1372	n/a
Sir John Knyvet	1372–1377	n/a
Adam Houghton, Bishop of St David's	1377–1378	n/a
Richard Scrope, 1st Baron Scrope of Bolton	1378–1380	n/a
Simon Sudbury, Archbishop of Canterbury	1380–1381	n/a
Hugh Segrave	1381	n/a
William Courtenay, Bishop of London	1381	n/a
Richard Scrope, 1st Baron Scrope of Bolton	1381–1382	n/a
Robert Braybrook, Bishop of London	1382–1383	n/a

Name	*Period*	*Party*
Michael de la Pole, 1st Earl of Suffolk	1383–1386	*n/a*
Thomas Arundel, Bishop of Ely	1386–1389	*n/a*
William of Wykeham, Bishop of Winchester	1389–1391	*n/a*
Thomas Arundel, Archbishop of York	1391–1396	*n/a*
Edmund Stafford, Bishop of Exeter	1396–1399	*n/a*
Thomas Arundel, Archbishop of Canterbury	1399	*n/a*
John Scarle, Archdeacon of Lincoln	1399–1401	*n/a*
Edmund Stafford, Bishop of Exeter	1401–1403	*n/a*
Henry Beaufort, Bishop of Lincoln	1403–1405	*n/a*
Thomas Langley, Dean of York	1405–1407	*n/a*
Thomas Arundel, Archbishop of Canterbury	1407–1410	*n/a*
Sir Thomas Beaufort	1410–1412	*n/a*
Thomas Arundel, Archbishop of Canterbury	1412–1413	*n/a*
Henry Beaufort, Bishop of Winchester	1413–1417	*n/a*
Thomas Langley, Bishop of Durham	1417–1424	*n/a*
Henry Beaufort, Bishop of Winchester	1424–1426	*n/a*
John Kemp, Archbishop of York	1426–1432	*n/a*
John Stafford, Bishop of Bath	1432–1450	*n/a*
John Kemp, Archbishop of York	1450–1454	*n/a*
Richard Neville, Earl of Salisbury	1454–1455	*n/a*
Thomas Bourchier, Archbishop of Canterbury	1455–1456	*n/a*
William Waynflete, Bishop of Winchester	1456–1460	*n/a*
George Neville, Bishop of Exeter	1460–1467	*n/a*
Richard Stillington, Bishop of Bath	1467–1470	*n/a*
George Neville, Archbishop of York	1470–1471	*n/a*
Richard Stillington, Bishop of Bath	1471–1473	*n/a*
Laurence Booth, Bishop of Durham	1473–1475	*n/a*
John Alcock, Bishop of Rochester	1475	*n/a*
Thomas Rotheram, Bishop of Lincoln	1475–1483	*n/a*
John Russell, Bishop of Lincoln	1483–1485	*n/a*
Thomas Rotheram, Archbishop of York	1485	*n/a*
John Alcock, Bishop of Worcester	1485–1487	*n/a*
John Morton, Archbishop of Canterbury	1487–1500	*n/a*
Henry Deane, Archbishop of Canterbury	1500–1502	*n/a*
William Warham, Archbishop of Canterbury	1502–1515	*n/a*
Thomas Cardinal Wolsey, Archbishop of York	1515–1529	*n/a*
Sir Thomas More	1529–1532	*n/a*
Thomas Audley, 1st Baron Audley of Walden	1532–1544	*n/a*
Thomas Wriothesley, 1st Baron Wriothesley	1544–1547	*n/a*
William Paulet, 1st Baron St John	1547	*n/a*
Richard Rich, 1st Baron Rich	1547–1551	*n/a*
Thomas Goodrich, Bishop of Ely	1552–1553	*n/a*
Stephen Gardiner, Bishop of Winchester	1553–1555	*n/a*
Nicholas Heath, Archbishop of York	1555–1558	*n/a*
Sir Nicholas Bacon	1558–1579	*n/a*
Sir Thomas Bromley	1579–1587	*n/a*
Sir Christopher Hatton	1587–1591	*n/a*
in commission	1591–1592	*n/a*
Sir John Puckering	1592–1596	*n/a*
Sir Thomas Egerton	1596–1617	*n/a*
Francis Bacon, 1st Baron Verulam	1617–1621	*n/a*
in commission	1621	*n/a*
John Williams, Bishop of Lincoln	1621–1625	*n/a*
Thomas Coventry, 1st Baron Coventry	1625–1640	*n/a*
John Finch, 1st Baron Finch	1640–1641	*n/a*
Edward Littleton, 1st Baron Lyttleton of Mounslow	1641–1642	*n/a*
Sir Richard Lane	1645–1653	*n/a*
Sir Edward Herbert	1653–1658	*n/a*
Edward Hyde, 1st Earl of Clarendon	1658–1667	*n/a*
Orlando Bridgeman	1667–1672	*n/a*
Anthony Ashley-Cooper, 1st Earl of Shaftesbury	1672–1673	*n/a*
Heneage Finch, 1st Earl of Nottingham	1673–1682	*n/a*
Francis North, 1st Baron Guilford	1682–1685	*n/a*
George Jeffreys, 1st Baron Jeffreys	1685–1688	*n/a*
in commission	1689–1693	*n/a*
John Somers, 1st Baron Somers	1693–1700	*n/a*
Sir Nathan Wright	1700–1705	*n/a*
William Cowper, 1st Baron Cowper	1705–1708	*Whig*
Simon Harcourt, 1st Baron Harcourt	1710–1714	*Whig*
William Cowper, 1st Baron Cowper	1714–Apr. 1718	*Whig*
Thomas Parker, 1st Earl of Macclesfield	1718–1725	*Whig*
Peter King, 1st Baron King	1725–1733	*Whig*
Charles Talbot, 1st Baron Talbot of Hensol	1733–1737	*Whig*
Philip Yorke, 1st Earl of Hardwicke	1737–1756	*Whig*
Robert Henley, 1st Earl of Northington	1757–1766	*Whig*
Charles Pratt, 1st Baron Camden	1766–1770	*Whig*
Charles Yorke	1770	*Whig*
Henry Bathurst, 1st Baron Apsley	1771–1778	*Tory*
Edward Thurlow, 1st Baron Thurlow	1778–1792	*Tory*

Name	Period	Party
Alexander Wedderburn, 1st Baron Loughborough	1793–1801	*Tory*
John Scott, 1st Baron Eldon	1801–1806	*Tory*
Thomas Erskine, 1st Baron Erskine	1806–1807	*Whig*
John Scott, 1st Earl of Eldon	1807–1827	*Tory*
John Singleton Copley, 1st Baron Lyndhurst	2 May 1827–24 Nov. 1830	*Tory*
Henry Peter Brougham, 1st Baron Brougham and Vaux	22 Nov. 1830–9 July 1834	*Whig*
John Singleton Copley, 1st Baron Lyndhurst	21 Nov. 1834–8 Apr. 1835	*Tory*
Charles Pepys, 1st Baron Cottenham	16 Jan. 1836–30 Aug. 1841	*Whig*
John Singleton Copley, 1st Baron Lyndhurst	3 Sept. 1841–27 June 1846	*Tory*
Charles Pepys, 1st Baron Cottenham	6 July 1846–19 June 1850	*Whig*
Thomas Wilde, 1st Baron Truro	15 July 1850–21 Feb. 1852	*Whig*
Edward Burtenshaw Sugden, 1st Baron St Leonards	27 Feb.–17 Dec. 1852	*Conservative*
Robert Monsey Rolfe, 1st Baron Cranworth	28 Dec. 1852–21 Feb. 1858	*Liberal*
Frederic Thesiger, 1st Baron Chelmsford	26 Feb. 1858–11 June 1859	*Conservative*
John Campbell, 1st Baron Campbell of St Andrews	18 June 1859–24 June 1861	*Liberal*
Richard Bethell, 1st Baron Westbury	26 June 1861–7 July 1865	*Liberal*
Robert Monsey Rolfe, 1st Baron Cranworth	7 July 1865–26 June 1866	*Liberal*
Frederic Thesiger, 1st Baron Chelmsford	6 July 1866–29 Feb. 1868	*Conservative*
Hugh McCalmont Cairns, 1st Baron Cairns	29 Feb.–1 Dec. 1868	*Conservative*
William Page Wood, 1st Baron Hatherley	9 Dec. 1868–15 Oct. 1872	*Liberal*
Roundell Palmer, 1st Baron Selborne	15 Oct. 1872–17 Feb. 1874	*Liberal*
Hugh McCalmont Cairns, 1st Earl Cairns	21 Feb. 1874–21 Apr. 1880	*Conservative*
Roundell Palmer, 1st Earl of Selborne	28 Apr. 1880–9 June 1885	*Liberal*
Hardinge Giffard, 1st Baron Halsbury	24 June 1885–28 Jan. 1886	*Conservative*
Farrer Herschell, 1st Baron Herschell	6 Feb.–20 July 1886	*Liberal*
Hardinge Giffard, 1st Baron Halsbury	3 Aug. 1886–11 Aug. 1892	*Conservative*
Farrer Herschell, 1st Baron Herschell	18 Aug. 1892–21 June 1895	*Liberal*
Hardinge Giffard, 1st Earl of Halsbury	29 June 1895–4 Dec. 1905	*Conservative*
Robert Threshie Reid, 1st Earl of Loreburn	10 Dec. 1905–10 June 1912	*Liberal*
Richard Burdon Haldane, 1st Viscount Haldane	10 June 1912–25 May 1915	*Liberal*
Stanley Buckmaster, 1st Baron Buckmaster	25 May 1915–5 Dec. 1916	*Liberal*
Robert Bannatyne Finlay, 1st Baron Finlay	10 Dec. 1916–10 Jan. 1919	*Liberal*
Frederick Edwin Smith, 1st Earl of Birkenhead	10 Jan. 1919–19 Oct. 1922	*Conservative*
George Cave, 1st Viscount Cave	24 Oct. 1922–22 Jan. 1924	*Conservative*
Richard Burdon Haldane, 1st Viscount Haldane	22 Jan.–6 Nov. 1924	*Labour*
George Cave, 1st Viscount Cave	6 Nov. 1924–28 Mar. 1928	*Conservative*
Douglas Hogg, 1st Baron Hailsham	28 Mar. 1928–4 June 1929	*Conservative*
John Sankey, 1st Viscount Sankey	7 June 1929–7 June 1935	*Labour*
Douglas Hogg, 1st Viscount Hailsham	7 June 1935–9 Mar. 1938	*Conservative*
Frederic Herbert Maugham, 1st Baron Maugham	9 Mar. 1938–3 Sept. 1939	*Conservative*
Thomas Inskip, 1st Viscount Caldecote	3 Sept. 1939–12 May 1940	*Conservative*
John Allsebrook Simon, 1st Viscount Simon	10 May 1940–27 July 1945	*Liberal*
William Allen Jowitt, 1st Viscount Jowitt	27 July 1945–26 Oct. 1951	*Labour*
Gavin Turnbull Simonds, 1st Baron Simonds	30 Oct. 1951–18 Oct. 1954	*Conservative*
David Patrick Maxwell Fyfe, 1st Viscount Kilmuir	18 Oct. 1954–13 July 1962	*Conservative*
Reginald Manningham-Buller, 1st Baron Dilhorne	13 July 1962–16 Oct. 1964	*Conservative*
Gerald Gardiner, Baron Gardiner of Kittisford	16 Oct. 1964–19 June 1970	*Labour*
Quintin Hogg, Baron Hailsham of St Marylebone	20 June 1970–4 Mar. 1974	*Conservative*
Frederick Elwyn Jones, Lord Elwyn-Jones	5 Mar. 1974–4 May 1979	*Conservative*
Quintin Hogg, Baron Hailsham of St Marylebone	4 May 1979–13 June 1987	*Conservative*
Michael Havers, Baron Havers of St Edmundsbury	13 June–26 Oct. 1987	*Conservative*
James Mackay, Baron Mackay of Clashfern	26 Oct.–2 May 1997	*Conservative*
Derry Irvine, Baron Irvine of Lairg	2 May 1997–16 June 2003	*Labour*
Charles Falconer, Baron Falconer of Thoroton	16 June 2003–28 June 2007	*Labour*
Jack Straw	28 June 2007–11 May 2010	*Labour*
Kenneth Clarke	12 May 2010–4 Sept. 2012	*Conservative*
Chris Grayling	4 Sept. 2012–present	*Conservative*

Lord President of the Council

Historically, the fourth of the Great Officers of State, the holder being responsible for presiding over meetings of the Privy Council. In recent years it has been usual for the Lord President also to serve as Leader of the House of Commons. Between 2003 and 2008 the office was combined with that of Leader of the House of Lords. Although Charles Brandon, 1st Duke of Suffolk, is often cited as the first holder of the office in 1530, the honour was conferred sporadically and it was not until 1679 that it became a regular Cabinet position.

Name	Period	Party
Anthony Ashley-Cooper, 1st Earl of Shaftesbury	21 Apr.–15 Oct. 1679	*Whig*
John Robartes, 1st Earl of Radnor	24 Oct. 1679–24 Aug. 1684	*Independent*
Laurence Hyde, 1st Earl of Rochester	24 Aug. 1684–18 Feb. 1685	*Independent*
George Savile, 1st Marquess of Halifax	18 Feb.–4 Dec. 1685	*Independent*
Robert Spencer, 2nd Earl of Sunderland	4 Dec. 1685–Oct. 1688	*Whig*
Richard Graham, 1st Viscount Preston	Oct. 1688–Feb. 1689	*Tory*
Thomas Osborne, 1st Marquess of Carmarthen	14 Feb.–18 May 1699	*Cavalier*
Thomas Herbert, 8th Earl of Pembroke	18 May 1699–29 Jan. 1702	*Whig*
Charles Seymour, 6th Duke of Somerset	29 Jan.–13 July 1702	*Tory*
Thomas Herbert, 8th Earl of Pembroke	13 July 1702–25 Nov. 1708	*Whig*
John Somers, Lord Somers	25 Nov. 1708–21 Sept. 1710	*Whig*
Laurence Hyde, 1st Earl of Rochester	21 Sept. 1710–13 June 1711	*Tory*

Name	Period	Party
John Sheffield, 1st Duke of Buckingham and Normanby	13 June 1711–23 Sept. 1714	*Tory*
Daniel Finch, 2nd Earl of Nottingham	23 Sept. 1714–6 July 1716	*Whig*
William Cavendish, 2nd Duke of Devonshire	6 July 1716–16 Mar. 1718	*Whig*
Charles Spencer, 3rd Earl of Sunderland	16 Mar. 1718–6 Feb. 1719	*Whig*
Evelyn Pierrepont, 1st Duke of Kingston-upon-Hull	6 Feb. 1719–11 June 1720	*Whig*
Charles Townshend, 2nd Viscount Townshend	11 June 1720–25 June 1721	*Whig*
Henry Boyle, 1st Baron Carleton	25 June 1721–27 Mar. 1725	*Whig*
William Cavendish, 2nd Duke of Devonshire	27 Mar. 1725–8 May 1730	*Whig*
Thomas Trevor, 1st Baron Trevor	8 May–19 June 1730	*Whig*
Spencer Compton, 1st Earl of Wilmington	31 Dec. 1730–13 Feb. 1742	*Whig*
William Stanhope, 1st Earl of Harrington	13 Feb. 1742–3 Jan. 1745	*Whig*
Lionel Cranfield Sackville, 1st Duke of Dorset	3 Jan. 1745–17 June 1751	*Whig*
John Carteret, 2nd Earl Granville	17 June 1751–2 Jan. 1763	*Whig/Tory*
John Russell, 4th Duke of Bedford	9 Sept. 1763–12 July 1765	*Whig*
Daniel Finch, 8th Earl of Winchilsea and 3rd Earl of Nottingham	12 July 1765–30 July 1766	*Whig*
Robert Henley, 1st Earl of Northington	30 July 1766–22 Dec. 1767	*Whig*
Granville Leveson-Gower, 2nd Earl Gower	22 Dec. 1767–24 Nov. 1779	*Tory*
Henry Bathurst, 2nd Earl Bathurst	24 Nov. 1779–27 Mar. 1782	*Tory*
Charles Pratt, 1st Baron Camden	27 Mar. 1782–2 Apr. 1783	*Whig*
David Murray, 7th Viscount Stormont	2 Apr.–19 Dec. 1783	*Whig*
Granville Leveson-Gower, 2nd Earl Gower	19 Dec. 1783–1 Dec. 1784	*Tory*
Charles Pratt, 1st Baron Camden	1 Dec. 1784–18 Apr. 1794	*Whig*
William Wentworth-Fitzwilliam, 4th Earl Fitzwilliam	1 July–17 Dec. 1794	*Whig*
David Murray, 7th Viscount Stormont	17 Dec. 1794–21 Sept. 1796	*Whig*
John Pitt, 2nd Earl of Chatham	21 Sept. 1796–30 July 1801	*Tory*
William Henry Cavendish-Bentinck, 3rd Duke of Portland	30 July 1801–14 Jan. 1805	*Tory*
Henry Addington, 1st Viscount Sidmouth	14 Jan.–10 July 1805	*Tory*
John Jeffreys Pratt, 2nd Earl Camden	10 July 1805–19 Feb. 1806	*Tory*
William Wentworth-Fitzwilliam, 4th Earl Fitzwilliam	19 Feb.–8 Oct. 1806	*Whig*
Henry Addington, 1st Viscount Sidmouth	8 Oct. 1806–26 Mar. 1807	*Tory*
John Jeffreys Pratt, 2nd Earl Camden	26 Mar. 1807–8 Apr. 1812	*Tory*
Henry Addington, 1st Viscount Sidmouth	8 Apr.–11 June 1812	*Tory*
Dudley Ryder, 1st Earl of Harrowby	11 June 1812–17 Aug. 1827	*Tory*
William Cavendish-Scott-Bentinck, 4th Duke of Portland	17 Aug. 1827–28 Jan. 1828	*Tory*
Henry Bathurst, 3rd Earl Bathurst	28 Jan. 1828–22 Nov. 1830	*Tory*
Henry Petty-Fitzmaurice, 3rd Marquess of Lansdowne	22 Nov. 1830–15 Dec. 1834	*Whig*
James St Clair Erskine, 2nd Earl of Rosslyn	15 Dec. 1834–18 Apr. 1835	*Tory*
Henry Petty-Fitzmaurice, 3rd Marquess of Lansdowne	18 Apr. 1835–3 Sept. 1841	*Whig*
James Stuart-Wortley-Mackenzie, 1st Baron Wharncliffe	3 Sept. 1841–21 Jan. 1846	*Tory*
Walter Montagu-Douglas-Scott, 5th Duke of Buccleuch	21 Jan.–6 July 1846	*Conservative*
Henry Petty-Fitzmaurice, 3rd Marquess of Lansdowne	6 July 1846–27 Feb. 1852	*Whig*
William Lowther, 2nd Earl of Lonsdale	27 Feb.–28 Dec. 1852	*Tory*
Granville George Leveson-Gower, 2nd Earl Granville	28 Dec. 1852–12 June 1854	*Liberal*
Lord John Russell	12 June 1854–8 Feb. 1855	*Liberal*
Granville George Leveson-Gower, 2nd Earl Granville	8 Feb. 1855–26 Feb. 1858	*Liberal*
James Brownlow William Gascoyne-Cecil, 2nd Marquess of Salisbury	26 Feb. 1858–18 June 1859	*Conservative*
Granville George Leveson-Gower, 2nd Earl Granville	18 June 1859–6 July 1866	*Liberal*
Richard Temple-Nugent-Brydges-Chandos-Grenville, 3rd Duke of Buckingham and Chandos	6 July 1866–8 Mar. 1867	*Conservative*
John Winston Spencer-Churchill, 7th Duke of Marlborough	8 Mar. 1867–9 Dec. 1868	*Conservative*
George Robinson, 1st Marquess of Ripon	9 Dec. 1868–9 Aug. 1873	*Liberal*
Henry Austin Bruce, 1st Baron Aberdare	9 Aug. 1873–21 Feb. 1874	*Liberal*
Charles Gordon-Lennox, 6th Duke of Richmond and Lennox	21 Feb. 1874–28 Apr. 1880	*Conservative*
John Poyntz Spencer, 5th Earl Spencer	28 Apr. 1880–19 Mar. 1883	*Liberal*
Chichester Parkinson-Fortescue	19 Mar. 1883–24 June 1885	*Liberal*
Gathorne Gathorne-Hardy, 1st Viscount Cranbrook	24 June 1885–6 Feb. 1886	*Conservative*
John Poyntz Spencer, 5th Earl Spencer	6 Feb.–3 Aug. 1886	*Liberal*
Gathorne Gathorne-Hardy, 1st Viscount Cranbrook	3 Aug. 1886–18 Aug. 1892	*Conservative*
John Wodehouse, 1st Earl of Kimberley	18 Aug. 1892–10 Mar. 1894	*Liberal*
Archibald Philip Primrose, 5th Earl of Rosebery	10 Mar. 1894–29 June 1895	*Liberal*
Spencer Cavendish, 8th Duke of Devonshire	29 June 1895–19 Oct. 1903	*Liberal*
Charles Vane-Tempest-Stewart, 6th Marquess of Londonderry	19 Oct. 1903–11 Dec. 1905	*Conservative*
Robert Crewe-Milnes, 1st Earl of Crewe	11 Dec. 1905–16 Apr. 1908	*Liberal*
Edward Marjoribanks, 2nd Baron Tweedmouth	16 Apr.–19 Oct. 1908	*Liberal*
Henry Hartley Fowler, 1st Viscount Wolverhampton	19 Oct. 1908–21 June 1910	*Liberal*
William Lygon, 7th Earl Beauchamp	21 June–7 Nov. 1910	*Liberal*
John Morley, 1st Viscount Morley	7 Nov. 1910–5 Aug. 1914	*Liberal*
William Lygon, 7th Earl Beauchamp	5 Aug. 1914–25 May 1915	*Liberal*
Robert Crewe-Milnes, 1st Earl of Crewe	25 May 1915–10 Dec. 1916	*Liberal*
George Nathaniel Curzon, 1st Earl Curzon of Kedleston	10 Dec. 1916–23 Oct. 1919	*Conservative*
Arthur Balfour	23 Oct. 1919–19 Oct. 1922	*Conservative*
James Gascoyne-Cecil, 4th Marquess of Salisbury	24 Oct. 1922–22 Jan. 1924	*Conservative*
Charles Alfred Cripps, 1st Baron Parmoor	22 Jan.–3 Nov. 1924	*Labour*
George Nathaniel Curzon, 1st Earl Curzon of Kedleston	6 Nov. 1924–27 Apr. 1925	*Conservative*
Arthur Balfour, 1st Earl of Balfour	27 Apr. 1925–4 June 1929	*Conservative*
Charles Alfred Cripps, 1st Baron Parmoor	7 June 1929–24 Aug. 1931	*Labour*
Stanley Baldwin	25 Aug. 1931–7 June 1935	*Conservative*

Name	Period	Party
Ramsay MacDonald	7 June 1935–28 May 1937	*Labour*
Edward Frederick Lindley Wood, 3rd Viscount Halifax	28 May 1937–9 Mar. 1938	*Conservative*
Douglas Hogg, 1st Viscount Hailsham	9 Mar.–31 Oct. 1938	*Conservative*
Walter Runciman, 1st Viscount Runciman of Doxford	31 Oct. 1938–3 Sept. 1939	*National Liberal*
James Stanhope, 7th Earl Stanhope	3 Sept. 1939–11 May 1940	*Conservative*
Neville Chamberlain	11 May–3 Oct. 1940	*Conservative*
Sir John Anderson	3 Oct. 1940–24 Sept. 1943	*National*
Clement Attlee	24 Sept. 1943–23 May 1945	*Labour*
Frederick Marquis, 1st Baron Woolton	25 May–26 July 1945	*Conservative*
Herbert Morrison	27 July 1945–9 Mar. 1951	*Labour*
Christopher Addison, 1st Viscount Addison	9 Mar.–26 Oct. 1951	*Labour*
Frederick Marquis, 1st Baron Woolton	28 Oct. 1951–25 Nov. 1952	*Conservative*
Robert Gascoyne-Cecil, 5th Marquess of Salisbury	25 Nov. 1952–29 Mar. 1957	*Conservative*
Alec Douglas-Home, 14th Earl of Home	29 Mar.–17 Sept. 1957	*Conservative*
Quintin Hogg, 2nd Viscount Hailsham	17 Sept. 1957–14 Oct. 1959	*Conservative*
Alec Douglas-Home, 14th Earl of Home	14 Oct. 1959–27 July 1960	*Conservative*
Quintin Hogg, 2nd Viscount Hailsham	27 July 1960–16 Oct. 1964	*Conservative*
Herbert Bowden	16 Oct. 1964–11 Aug. 1966	*Labour*
Richard Crossman	11 Aug. 1966–18 Oct. 1968	*Labour*
Fred Peart	18 Oct. 1968–19 June 1970	*Labour*
William Whitelaw	20 June 1970–7 Apr. 1972	*Conservative*
Robert Carr	7 Apr.–5 Nov. 1972	*Conservative*
James Prior	5 Nov. 1972–4 Mar. 1974	*Conservative*
Edward Short	5 Mar. 1974–8 Apr. 1976	*Labour*
Michael Foot	8 Apr. 1976–4 May 1979	*Labour*
Christopher Soames, Baron Soames	5 May 1979–14 Sept. 1981	*Conservative*
Francis Pym	14 Sept. 1981–7 Apr. 1982	*Conservative*
John Biffen	7 Apr. 1982–11 June 1983	*Conservative*
William Whitelaw, 1st Viscount Whitelaw	11 June 1983–10 Jan. 1988	*Conservative*
John Wakeham	10 Jan. 1988–24 July 1989	*Conservative*
Sir Geoffrey Howe	24 July 1989–1 Nov. 1990	*Conservative*
John MacGregor	2 Nov. 1990–10 Apr. 1992	*Conservative*
Tony Newton	10 Apr. 1992–2 May 1997	*Conservative*
Ann Taylor	3 May 1997–27 July 1998	*Labour*
Margaret Beckett	27 July 1998–8 June 2001	*Labour*
Robin Cook	8 June 2001–18 Mar. 2003	*Labour*
John Reid	4 Apr.–13 June 2003	*Labour*
Gareth Wyn Williams, Lord Williams of Mostyn	13 June –20 Sept. 2003	*Labour*
Valerie Amos, Baroness Amos	6 Oct. 2003–27 June 2007	*Labour*
Catherine Ashton, Baroness Ashton of Upholland	28 June 2007–3 Oct. 2008	*Labour*
Janet Royall, Baroness Royall of Blaisdon	3 Oct. 2008–5 June 2009	*Labour*
Peter Mandelson, Baron Mandelson of Foy and Hartlepool	5 June 2009–11 May 2010	*Labour*
Nick Clegg	11 May 2010–present	*Lib-Dem*

Lord Privy Seal

Historically, the fifth of the Great Officers of State although in recent times the holder has become a Minister without Portfolio, while still attending Cabinet meetings. The list below begins with the English Lords Privy Seal, John Holles, 1st Duke of Newcastle, becoming the first British incumbent after the unification with Scotland in 1707.

Name	Period
William Melton	1307–1312
Roger Northburgh	1312–1316
Thomas Charlton	1316–1320
Robert Baldock	1320–1323
Robert Wodehouse	1323
Robert Ayleston	1323–1324
William Airmyn	1324–1325
Henry Cliff	1325
William Herlaston	1325–1326
Robert Wyvell	1326–1327
Richard Airmyn	1327–1328
Adam Lymbergh	1328–1329
Richard Bury, Bishop of Durham	1329–1334
Robert Ayleston	1334
Robert Tawton	1334–1335
William de la Zouch	1335–1337
Richard Bintworth	1337–1338
William Kilsby	1338–1342
John Offord	1342–1344
Thomas Hatfield	1344–1345
John Thoresby	1345–1347
Simon Islip, Archbishop of Canterbury	1347–1350
Michael Northburgh	1350–1354
Thomas Bramber	1354–1355
John Winwick	1355–1360
John Buckingham, Bishop of Lincoln	1360–1363
William of Wykeham	1363–1367

Name	*Period*
Peter Lacy	1367–1371
Nicholas Carew	1371–1377
John Fordham	1377–1381
William Dighton	1381–1382
Walter Skirclaw, Bishop of Coventry and Lichfield	1382–1386
John Waltham, Bishop of Salisbury	1386–1389
Edmund Stafford, Bishop of Exeter	1389–1396
Guy Mone	1396–1397
Richard Clifford	1397–1401
Thomas Langley	1401–1405
Nicholas Bubwith	1405–1406
John Prophet	1406–1415
John Wakering, Bishop of Norwich	1415–1416
Henry Ware	1416–1418
John Kemp, Bishop of Rochester	1418–1412
John Stafford	1421–1422
William Alnwick, Bishop of Norwich	1422–1432
William Lyndwood, Bishop of St David's	1432–1443
Thomas Beckington, Bishop of Bath and Wells	1443–1444
Adam Moleyns, Bishop of Chichester	1444–1450
Andrew Holes	1450–1452
Thomas Lisieux	1452–1456
Laurence Booth, Bishop of Durham	1456–1460
Robert Stillington, Bishop of Bath and Wells	1460–1467
Thomas Rotheram, Bishop of Rochester	1467–1470
John Hales, Bishop of Coventry and Lichfield	1470–1471
Thomas Rotheram, Bishop of Rochester	1471–1474
John Russell, Bishop of Rochester, later Bishop of Lincoln	1473–1483
John Gunthorp	1483–1485
Peter Courtenay, Bishop of Exeter	1485–1487
Richard Fox, Bishop of Exeter, later Bishop of Bath and Wells, Bishop of Durham and Bishop of Winchester	1487–1516
Thomas Ruthall, Bishop of Durham	1516–1523
Henry Marney, 1st Baron Marney	1523
Cuthbert Tunstall, Bishop of London	1523–1530
Thomas Boleyn, 1st Earl of Wiltshire	1530–1536
Thomas Cromwell, 1st Earl of Essex	1536–1540
William Fitzwilliam, 1st Earl of Southampton	1540–1542
John Russell, 1st Earl of Bedford	1542–1555
William Paget, 1st Baron Paget	1555–1558
William Cecil, 1st Baron Burghley	1571–1572
William Howard, 1st Baron Howard of Effingham	1572–1573
Sir Thomas Smith	1573–1576
Francis Walsingham	1576–1590
William Cecil, 1st Baron Burghley	1590–1598
Robert Cecil, 1st Earl of Salisbury	1598–1608
Henry Howard, 1st Earl of Northampton	1608–1614
Robert Carr, 1st Earl of Somerset	1614–1616
Edward Somerset, 4th Earl of Worcester	1616–1625
Sir John Coke	1625–1628
Sir Robert Naunton	1628
Henry Montagu, 1st Earl of Manchester	1628–1642
Lucius Cary, 2nd Viscount Falkland	1643
Sir Edward Nicholas	1643–1644
Henry Bourchier, 5th Earl of Bath	1644–1654
John Robartes, 2nd Baron Robartes	1661–1673
Arthur Annesley, 1st Earl of Anglesey	1673–1682
George Savile, 1st Marquess of Halifax	1682–1685
Henry Hyde, 2nd Earl of Clarendon	1685–1687
Henry Arundell, 3rd Baron Arundell of Wardour	1687–1688
George Savile, 1st Marquess of Halifax	1689–1690
in commission	1690–1692
Thomas Herbert, 8th Earl of Pembroke	1692–1699
John Lowther, 1st Viscount Lonsdale	1699–1700
Ford Grey, 1st Earl of Tankerville	1700–1701
in commission	1701–1702
John Sheffield, 1st Duke of Buckingham and Normanby	1702–1705
John Holles, 1st Duke of Newcastle	1705–1711
John Robinson, Bishop of Bristol	1711–1713
William Legge, 1st Earl of Dartmouth	1713–1714
Thomas Wharton, 1st Marquess of Wharton	1714–1715
in commission	1715
Charles Spencer, 3rd Earl of Sunderland	1715–1716
Evelyn Pierrepont, 1st Duke of Kingston	1716–1718
Henry Grey, 1st Duke of Kent	1718–1719
Evelyn Pierrepont, 1st Duke of Kingston	1720–1726
Thomas Trevor, 1st Baron Trevor	1726–1730
Spencer Compton, 1st Earl of Wilmington	1730–1731
in commission	1731
William Cavendish, 3rd Duke of Devonshire	1731–1733
Henry Lowther, 3rd Viscount Lonsdale	1733–1735

Name	Period
Francis Godolphin, 2nd Earl of Godolphin	1735–1740
John Hervey, 2nd Baron Hervey	1740–1742
John Leveson-Gower, 2nd Baron Gower	1742–1743
George Cholmondeley, 3rd Earl of Cholmondeley	1743–1744
John Leveson-Gower, 1st Earl Gower	1744–1755
Charles Spencer, 3rd Duke of Marlborough	1755
Granville Leveson-Gower, 2nd Earl Gower	1755–1757
Richard Grenville-Temple, 2nd Earl Temple	1757–1761
John Russell, 4th Duke of Bedford	1761–1763
George Spencer, 4th Duke of Marlborough	1763–1765
Thomas Pelham-Holles, 1st Duke of Newcastle	1765–1766
William Pitt, 1st Earl of Chatham	1766–1768
George William Hervey, 5th Earl of Bristol	1768–1770
George Montague-Dunk, 2nd Earl of Halifax	1770–1771
Henry Howard, 12th Earl of Suffolk	1771
Augustus Henry Fitzroy, 3rd Duke of Grafton	1771–1775
William Legge, 2nd Earl of Dartmouth	1775–1782
Augustus Henry FitzRoy, 3rd Duke of Grafton	1782–1783
Frederick Howard, 5th Earl of Carlisle	1783
Charles Manners, 4th Duke of Rutland	1783–1784
in commission	1784
Granville Leveson-Gower, 1st Marquess of Stafford	1784–1794
George John Spencer, 2nd Earl Spencer	1794
John Pitt, 2nd Earl of Chatham	1794–1798
John Fane, 10th Earl of Westmorland	1798–1806
Henry Addington, 1st Viscount Sidmouth	1806
Henry Richard Vassall-Fox, 3rd Baron Holland	1806–1807
John Fane, 10th Earl of Westmorland	1807–1827
William Cavendish-Scott-Bentinck, 4th Duke of Portland	1827
George Howard, 6th Earl of Carlisle	1827–1828
Edward Law, 2nd Baron Ellenborough	1828–1829
James St Clair-Erskine, 2nd Earl of Rosslyn	1829–1830
John George Lambton, 1st Baron Durham	1830–1833
Frederick John Robinson, 1st Earl of Ripon	1833–1834
George Howard, 6th Earl of Carlisle	1834
Constantine Henry Phipps, 2nd Earl of Mulgrave	1834
James Stuart-Wortley-Mackenzie, 1st Baron Wharncliffe	1834–1835
John William Ponsonby, Viscount Duncannon	1835–1840
George William Frederick Villiers, 4th Earl of Clarendon	1840–1841
Richard Temple-Nugent-Brydges-Chandos-Grenville, 2nd Duke of Buckingham and Chandos	1841–1842
Walter Francis Montagu-Douglas-Scott, 5th Duke of Buccleuch	1842–1846
Thomas Hamilton, 9th Earl of Haddington	1846
Gilbert Elliot-Murray-Kynynmound, 2nd Earl of Minto	1846–1852
James Brownlow William Gascoyne-Cecil, 2nd Marquess of Salisbury	1852
George Douglas Campbell, 8th Duke of Argyll	1853–1855
Dudley Ryder, 2nd Earl of Harrowby	1855–1858
Ulick John de Burgh, 1st Marquess of Clanricarde	1858
Charles Philip Yorke, 4th Earl of Hardwicke	1858–1859
George Douglas Campbell, 8th Duke of Argyll	1859–1866
James Howard Harris, 3rd Earl of Malmesbury	1866–1868
John Wodehouse, 1st Earl of Kimberley	1868–1870
Charles Wood, 1st Viscount Halifax	1870–1874
James Howard Harris, 3rd Earl of Malmesbury	1874–1876
Benjamin Disraeli, 1st Earl of Beaconsfield	1876–1878
Algernon George Percy, 6th Duke of Northumberland	1878–1880
George Douglas Campbell, 8th Duke of Argyll	1880–1881
Chichester Parkinson-Fortescue, 1st Baron Carlingford	1881–1885
Archibald Primrose, 5th Earl of Rosebery	1885
Dudley Ryder, 3rd Earl of Harrowby	1885–1886
William Ewart Gladstone	1886
George Henry Cadogan, 5th Earl Cadogan	1886–1892
William Ewart Gladstone	1892–1894
Edward Marjoribanks, 2nd Baron Tweedmouth	1894–1895
Richard Assheton Cross, 1st Viscount Cross	1895–1900
Robert Arthur Talbot Gascoyne-Cecil, 3rd Marquess of Salisbury	1900–1902
Arthur Balfour	1902–1903
James Edward Hubert Gascoyne-Cecil, 4th Marquess of Salisbury	1903–1905
George Frederick Samuel Robinson, 1st Marquess of Ripon	1905–1908
Robert Crewe-Milnes, 1st Earl of Crewe	1908–1911
Charles Robert Wynn Carrington, 1st Earl Carrington	1911–1912
Robert Crewe-Milnes, 1st Marquess of Crewe	1912–1915
George Nathaniel Curzon, 1st Earl Curzon	1915–1916
David Lindsay, 27th Earl of Crawford	1916–1919
Andrew Bonar Law	1919–1921
Austen Chamberlain	1921–1922
Robert Cecil, 1st Viscount Cecil of Chelwood	1922–1924
John Robert Clynes	1924
James Edward Hubert Gascoyne-Cecil, 4th Marquess of Salisbury	1924–1929
James Henry Thomas	1929–1930
Vernon Hartshorn	1930–1931

Name	Period
Thomas Johnston	1931
William Wellesley Peel, 1st Earl Peel	1931
Philip Snowden, 1st Viscount Snowden	1931–1932
Stanley Baldwin	1932–1934
Anthony Eden	1934–1935
Charles Vane-Tempest-Stewart, 7th Marquess of Londonderry	1935
Edward Frederick Lindley Wood, 3rd Viscount Halifax	1935–1937
Herbrand Sackville, 9th Earl De La Warr	1937–1938
Sir John Anderson	1938–1939
Sir Samuel Hoare	1939–1940
Sir Kingsley Wood	1940
Clement Attlee	1940–1942
Sir Stafford Cripps	1942
Robert Arthur James Gascoyne-Cecil, Viscount Cranborne	1942–1943
William Maxwell Aitken, 1st Baron Beaverbrook	1943–1945
Arthur Greenwood	1945–1947
Philip Inman, 1st Baron Inman	1947
Christopher Addison, 1st Viscount Addison	1947–1951
Ernest Bevin	1951
Richard Stokes	1951
Robert Arthur James Gascoyne-Cecil, 5th Marquess of Salisbury	1951–1952
Harry Crookshank	1952–1955
Richard Austen 'Rab' Butler	1955–1959
Quintin Hogg, 2nd Viscount Hailsham	1959–1960
Edward Heath	1960–1963
Selwyn Lloyd	1963–1964
Francis Aungier Pakenham, 7th Earl of Longford	1964–1965
Sir Frank Soskice	1965–1966
Francis Aungier Pakenham, 7th Earl of Longford	1966–1968
Edward Shackleton, Baron Shackleton	1968
Fred Peart	1968
Edward Shackleton, Baron Shackleton	1968–1970
George Jellicoe, 2nd Earl Jellicoe	1970–1973
David Hennessy, 3rd Baron Windlesham	1973–1974
Malcolm Shepherd, 2nd Baron Shepherd	1974–1976
Fred Peart, Baron Peart	1976–1979
Sir Ian Gilmour	1979–1981
Humphrey Atkins	1981–1982
Janet Young, Baroness Young	1982–1983
John Biffen	1983–1987
John Wakeham	1987–1988
John Ganzoni, 2nd Baron Belstead	1988–1990
David Waddington, Baron Waddington	1990–1992
John Wakeham, Baron Wakeham	1992–1994
Robert Gascoyne-Cecil, Viscount Cranborne	1994–1997
Ivor Richard, Baron Richard	1997–1998
Margaret Jay, Baroness Jay of Paddington	1998–2001
Gareth Wyn Williams, Baron Williams of Mostyn	2001–2003
Peter Hain	2003–2005
Geoff Hoon	2005–2006
Jack Straw	2006–2007
Harriet Harman	2007–2010
Sir George Young	2010–2012
Andrew Lansley	4 Sept.2012–present

Minister without Portfolio

A facility whereby the government of the day can second a prominent politician into the Cabinet despite not heading a particular ministry. In this respect the position is similar to the sinecure positions of Lord Privy Seal and Chancellor of the Duchy of Lancaster.

Name	Period	Party
William Henry Cavendish-Bentinck, 3rd Duke of Portland	1805–1806	*Tory*
William Wentworth-Fitzwilliam, 4th Earl Fitzwilliam	1806–1807	*Whig*
John Jeffreys Pratt, 2nd Earl Camden	1812	*Tory*
Henry Phipps, 1st Earl of Mulgrave	1819–1820	*Tory*
Henry Petty-FitzMaurice, 3rd Marquess of Lansdowne	Apr.–Jul. 1827 and 1852–1858	*Whig*
William Cavendish-Scott-Bentinck, 4th Duke of Portland	Jul.–Sep. 1827	*Tory*
George Howard, 6th Earl of Carlisle	1830–1834	*Whig*
Arthur Wellesley, 1st Duke of Wellington	1841–1846	*Tory*
Lord John Russell	1853–1854	*Whig*
Spencer Horatio Walpole	1867–1868	*Liberal*
Sir Michael Hicks Beach	1887–1888	*Conservative*
Henry Petty-FitzMaurice, 5th Marquess of Lansdowne	1915–1916	*Liberal*
Arthur Henderson	1916–1917	*Labour*
Lord Milner	1916–1918	*Conservative*
Jan Smuts	1917–1919	*n/a*
Sir Edward Carson	1917–1919	*n/a*
George Barnes	1917–1920	*Labour*
Sir Eric Geddes	Jan.–Oct. 1919	*Conservative*

Name	Period	Party
Sir Laming Worthington-Evans	1920–1921	*Conservative*
Christopher Addison	1921–1922	*Liberal*
Anthony Eden	June–Dec. 1935	*Conservative*
Lord Eustace Percy	1935–1936	*Conservative*
Leslie Burgin	Apr.–Jul. 1939	*Liberal*
Lord Hankey	1939–1940	*n/a*
Arthur Greenwood	1940–1942	*Labour*
Sir William Jowitt	1942–1944	*Labour*
A V Alexander	Oct.–Dec. 1946	*Labour*
Arthur Greenwood	Apr.–Sept. 1947	*Labour*
Geoffrey FitzClarence, 5th Earl of Munster	1954–1957	*Conservative*
Percy Herbert Mills, 1st Viscount Mills	1961–1962	*Conservative*
William Francis Deedes	1962–1964	*Conservative*
Lord Carrington	1963–1964	*Conservative*
George Thomson	1968–1969	*Labour*
Lord Drumalbyn	1970–1974	*Conservative*
Lord Young	1984–1985	*Conservative*
Jeremy Hanley	1994–1995	*Conservative*
Brian Mawhinney	1995–1997	*Conservative*
Peter Mandelson	1997–1998	*Labour*
Charles Clarke	2001–2002	*Labour*
John Reid	2002–2003	*Labour*
Ian McCartney	2003–2006	*Labour*
Hazel Blears	2006–2007	*Labour*
Baroness (Sayeeda) Warsi	2010–2012	*Conservative*
Kenneth Clarke and Grant Shapps	4 Sept.2012–present	*Conservatives*

Northern Ireland

The Secretary of State for Northern Ireland is the chief minister in the government of the United Kingdom with responsibilities for Northern Ireland, although the Secretary is responsible only to the Westminster Parliament and not the Northern Ireland Assembly. The office was created following the suspension of the home rule Parliament of Northern Ireland in 1972.

Name	Period	Party
William Whitelaw	24 Mar. 1972–2 Dec. 1973	*Conservative*
Francis Pym	2 Dec. 1973–4 Mar. 1974	*Conservative*
Merlyn Rees	5 Mar. 1974–10 Sept. 1976	*Labour*
Roy Mason	10 Sept. 1976–4 May 1979	*Labour*
Humphrey Atkins	5 May 1979–14 Sept. 1981	*Conservative*
James Prior	14 Sept. 1981–11 Sept. 1984	*Conservative*
Douglas Hurd	11 Sept. 1984–3 Sept. 1985	*Conservative*
Tom King	3 Sept. 1985–24 July 1989	*Conservative*
Peter Brooke	24 July 1989–10 Apr. 1992	*Conservative*
Sir Patrick Mayhew	10 Apr. 1992–2 May 1997	*Conservative*
Marjorie 'Mo' Mowlam	3 May 1997–11 Oct. 1999	*Labour*
Peter Mandelson	11 Oct. 1999–24 Jan. 2001	*Labour*
John Reid	25 Jan. 2001–24 Oct. 2002	*Labour*
Paul Murphy	24 Oct. 2002–6 May 2005	*Labour*
Peter Hain	6 May 2005–27 June 2007	*Labour*
Shaun Woodward	28 June 2007–11 May 2010	*Labour*
Owen Paterson	12 May 2010–4 Sept.2012	*Conservative*
Theresa Villiers	4 Sept.2012–present	*Conservative*

Olympics

The Minister for the Olympics is a temporary position created in July 2005 as a result of the selection of London to host the 2012 Summer Olympics. Not a Cabinet position per se but the incumbent is a Cabinet minister.

Name	Period	Party
Tessa Jowell	6 July 2005–11 May 2010	*Labour*
Jeremy Hunt	12 May 2010–4 Sept.2012	*Conservative*

Scotland

The Secretary of State for Scotland is the chief minister in the government of the United Kingdom with responsibilities for Scotland, although the Secretary is responsible only to the Westminster Parliament and not the Scottish Assembly. The office was originally created for the Scottish Parliament in the 14th century (possibly the most famous incumbent being William Maitland of Lethington, who served Mary Queen of Scots) and only those holders since the Union of the Crowns in 1705 are relevant to British politics. The position was abolished in 1746 following the Jacobite rebellion, Scottish affairs thereafter being managed by the Lord Advocate until 1827, when responsibility passed to the Home Office. In 1885 the post was re-created, with the incumbent usually (though not always) in the Cabinet. In 1926 this post was upgraded to a full Secretary of State appointment but, as with its Welsh and Northern Irish counterparts, its responsibilities have been severely diluted since the introduction of the national assemblies of the home countries.

Name	*Period*	*Party*
John Erskine, 6th Earl of Mar	1705–3 Feb. 1709	*Whig*
James Douglas, 2nd Duke of Queensberry	3 Feb. 1709–6 July 1711	*Scottish Unionist*
John Erskine, 6th Earl of Mar	30 Sept. 1713–24 Sept. 1714	*Whig*
James Graham, 1st Duke of Montrose	24 Sept. 1714–Aug. 1715	*Scottish Unionist*
John Ker, 1st Duke of Roxburghe	13 Dec. 1716–Aug. 1725	*Whig*
John Hay, 4th Marquess of Tweeddale	16 Feb. 1742–3 Jan. 1746	*Whig*
Charles Gordon-Lennox, Duke of Richmond and Gordon	17 Aug. 1885–28 Jan. 1886	*Conservative*
George Otto Trevelyan	8 Feb.–Mar. 1886	*Liberal*
John William Ramsay, Earl of Dalhousie	5 Apr.–20 July 1886	*Liberal*
Arthur Balfour	5 Aug. 1886–11 Mar. 1887	*Conservative*
Schomberg Henry Kerr, Marquess of Lothian	11 Mar. 1887–11 Aug. 1892	*Conservative*
George Otto Trevelyan	18 Aug. 1892–21 June 1895	*Liberal*
Alexander Bruce, Lord Balfour of Burleigh	29 June 1895–9 Oct. 1903	*Conservative*
Andrew Murray	9 Oct. 1903–2 Feb. 1905	*Conservative*
John Adrian Hope, Marquess of Linlithgow	2 Feb.–4 Dec. 1905	*Conservative*
John Sinclair	10 Dec. 1905–13 Feb. 1912	*Liberal*
Thomas McKinnon Wood	13 Feb. 1912–9 July 1916	*Liberal*
Harold Tennant	9 July–5 Dec. 1916	*Coalition*
Robert Munro	10 Dec. 1916–19 Oct. 1922	*Coalition*
Ronald Munro-Ferguson	24 Oct. 1922–22 Jan. 1924	*Liberal*
William Adamson	22 Jan.–3 Nov. 1924	*Labour*
Sir John Gilmour	6 Nov. 1924–7 June 1929	*Conservative*
William Adamson	7 June 1929–24 Aug. 1931	*Labour*
Sir Archibald Sinclair	25 Aug. 1931–28 Sept. 1932	*National Liberal*
Sir Godfrey Collins	28 Sept. 1932–29 Oct. 1936	*National Liberal*
Walter Elliot	29 Oct. 1936–16 May 1938	*Scottish Unionist*
John Colville	6 May 1938–10 May 1940	*National Conservative*
Ernest Brown	14 May 1940–8 Feb. 1941	*Coalition*
Thomas Johnston	8 Feb. 1941–23 May 1945	*Coalition*
Harry Primrose, 6th Earl of Rosebery	25 May–26 July 1945	*National Liberal*
Joseph Westwood	3 Aug. 1945–7 Oct. 1947	*Labour*
Arthur Woodburn	7 Oct. 1947–28 Feb. 1950	*Labour*
Hector McNeil	28 Feb. 1950–26 Oct. 1951	*Labour*
James Stuart	30 Oct. 1951–13 Jan. 1957	*Conservative*
John Maclay	13 Jan. 1957–13 July 1962	*Conservative*
Michael Noble	13 July 1962–16 Oct. 1964	*Conservative*
William Ross	18 Oct. 1964–19 June 1970	*Labour*
Gordon Campbell	20 June 1970–4 Mar. 1974	*Conservative*
William Ross	5 Mar. 1974–8 Apr. 1976	*Labour*
Bruce Millan	8 Apr. 1976–4 May 1979	*Labour*
George Younger	5 May 1979–11 Jan. 1986	*Conservative*
Malcolm Rifkind	11 Jan. 1986–28 Nov. 1990	*Conservative*
Ian Lang	28 Nov. 1990–5 July 1995	*Conservative*
Michael Forsyth	5 July 1995–2 May 1997	*Conservative*
Donald Dewar	3 May 1997–17 May 1999	*Labour*
John Reid	17 May 1999–25 Jan. 2001	*Labour*
Helen Liddell	25 Jan. 2001–13 June 2003	*Labour*
Alistair Darling	13 June 2003–5 May 2006	*Labour*
Douglas Alexander	5 May 2006–27 June 2007	*Labour*
Des Browne	28 June 2007–3 Oct. 2008	*Labour*
Jim Murphy	3 Oct. 2008–11 May 2010	*Labour*
Danny Alexander	12 May–29 May 2010	*Lib-Dem*
Michael Moore	29 May 2010–7 Oct. 2013	*Lib-Dem*
Alistair Carmichael	7 Oct. 2013–present	*Lib-Dem*

Transport

Prior to 2002, the Department for Transport has been variously organised as the Ministry of Transport (1919–41, 1945–53, 1959–70, 1979–81), Ministry of War Transport (1941–45), Ministry of Transport and Civil Aviation (1953–59), Department for the Environment (1970–76), Department of Transport (1976–79, 1981–97, 2002–), Department for the Environment, Transport and the Regions (1997–2001) and Department for Transport, Local Government and the Regions (2001–02). The minister in control of the department has been known under various titles and has not always been a member of the Cabinet. Similarly, after the Cabinet reshuffle of 8 June 2009, Sadiq Khan, serving as Minister of State for Transport (under Lord Adonis as Secretary of State), was given the right to attend Cabinet.

Name	*Period*	*Party*
Eric Campbell Geddes	19 May 1919–7 Nov. 1921	*Conservative*
William Peel, 2nd Viscount Peel	7 Nov. 1921–12 Apr. 1922	*Conservative*
David Lindsay, 27th Earl of Crawford	12 Apr.–31 Oct. 1922	*Conservative*
Sir John Baird	31 Oct. 1922–22 Jan. 1924	*Conservative*
Harry Gosling	24 Jan.–3 Nov. 1924	*Labour*
Wilfrid Ashley	11 Nov. 1924–4 June 1929	*Conservative*
Herbert Morrison	7 June 1929–24 Aug. 1931	*Labour*
Percy John Pybus	3 Sept. 1931–22 Feb. 1933	*Liberal*
Oliver Stanley	22 Feb. 1933–29 June 1934	*Conservative*
Leslie Hore-Belisha	29 June 1934–28 May 1937	*National Liberal*
Leslie Burgin	28 May 1937–21 Apr. 1939	*National Liberal*
Euan Wallace	21 Apr. 1939–14 May 1940	*Conservative*
John Reith	14 May–3 Oct. 1940	*National Independent*

Name	Period	Party
John Moore-Brabazon	3 Oct. 1940–1 May 1941	*Conservative*
Frederick Leathers – Minister of War Transport	1 May 1941–26 July 1945	*Conservative*
Alfred Barnes	3 Aug. 1945–26 Oct. 1951	*Labour*
John Maclay	31 Oct. 1951–7 May 1952	*National Liberal*
Alan Lennox-Boyd	7 May 1952–1 Oct. 1953	*Conservative*
Alan Lennox-Boyd	1 Oct. 1953–28 July 1954	*Conservative*
John Boyd-Carpenter	28 July 1954–20 Dec. 1955	*Conservative*
Harold Watkinson	20 Dec. 1955–14 Oct. 1959	*Conservative*
Ernest Marples	14 Oct. 1959–16 Oct. 1964	*Conservative*
Thomas Fraser	16 Oct. 1964–23 Dec. 1965	*Labour*
Barbara Castle	23 Dec. 1965–6 Apr. 1968	*Labour*
Richard Marsh	6 Apr. 1968–6 Oct. 1969	*Labour*
Fred Mulley	6 Oct. 1969–19 June 1970	*Labour*
John Peyton	23 June 1970–4 Mar. 1974	*Conservative*
Fred Mulley	7 Mar. 1974–12 June 1975	*Labour*
John Gilbert	12 June 1975–10 Sept. 1976	*Labour*
Bill Rodgers	10 Sept. 1976–4 May 1979	*Labour*
Norman Fowler	11 May 1979–14 Sept. 1981	*Conservative*
David Howell	14 Sept. 1981–11 June 1983	*Conservative*
Tom King	11 June–16 Oct. 1983	*Conservative*
Nicholas Ridley	16 Oct. 1983–21 May 1986	*Conservative*
John Moore	21 May 1986–13 June 1987	*Conservative*
Paul Channon	13 June 1987–24 July 1989	*Conservative*
Cecil Parkinson	24 July 1989–28 Nov. 1990	*Conservative*
Malcolm Rifkind	28 Nov. 1990–10 Apr. 1992	*Conservative*
John MacGregor	10 Apr. 1992–20 July 1994	*Conservative*
Brian Mawhinney	20 July 1994–5 July 1995	*Conservative*
Sir George Young, Bt	5 July 1995–2 May 1997	*Conservative*
John Prescott	2 May 1997–8 June 2001	*Labour*
Gavin Strang	3 May 1997–27 July 1998	*Labour*
John Reid	27 July 1998–17 May 1999	*Labour*
Helen Liddell	17 May–29 July 1999	*Labour*
Gus Macdonald, Baron Macdonald of Tradeston	29 July 1999–8 June 2001	*Labour*
Stephen Byers	8 June 2001–29 May 2002	*Labour*
Alistair Darling	29 May 2002–5 May 2006	*Labour*
Douglas Alexander	5 May 2006–27 June 2007	*Labour*
Ruth Kelly	28 June 2007–3 Oct. 2008	*Labour*
Geoff Hoon	3 Oct. 2008–5 June 2009	*Labour*
Andrew Adonis, Baron Adonis	5 June 2009–11 May 2010	*Labour*
Philip Hammond	12 May 2010–14 Oct. 2011	*Conservative*
Justine Greening	14 Oct. 2011–4 Sept. 2012	*Conservative*
Patrick McLoughlin	4 Sept. 2012–present	*Conservative*

Minister of Civil Aviation

Name	Period	Party
Philip Cunliffe-Lister, 1st Viscount Swinton	8 Oct. 1944–26 July 1945	*Conservative*
Reginald Thomas Herbert Fletcher, 1st Baron Winster	4 Aug. 1945–4 Oct. 1946	*Labour*
Harry Louis Nathan	4 Oct. 1946–31 May 1948	*Labour*
Francis Aungier Pakenham, 1st Baron Pakenham	31 May 1948–1 June 1951	*Labour*
David Rees-Williams, 1st Baron Ogmore	1 June–26 Oct. 1951	*Labour*
John Maclay	31 Oct. 1951–7 May 1952	*National Liberal*
Alan Lennox-Boyd	7 May 1952–1 Oct. 1953	*Conservative*

Wales

The Secretary of State for Wales is the chief minister in the government of the United Kingdom with responsibilities for Wales, although the Secretary is responsible only to the Westminster Parliament and not the Welsh Assembly. Created in 1964, its responsibilities have been severely diluted since the introduction of the national assemblies of the home countries.

Name	Period	Party
James Griffiths	18 Oct. 1964–5 Apr. 1966	*Labour*
Cledwyn Hughes	5 Apr. 1966–5 Apr. 1968	*Labour*
George Thomas	5 Apr. 1968–20 June 1970	*Labour*
Peter Thomas	20 June 1970–5 Mar. 1974	*Conservative*
John Morris	5 Mar. 1974–5 May 1979	*Labour*
Nicholas Edwards	5 May 1979–13 June 1987	*Conservative*
Peter Walker	13 June 1987–4 May 1990	*Conservative*
David Hunt	4 May 1990–27 May 1993	*Conservative*
John Redwood	27 May 1993–26 June 1995	*Conservative*
David Hunt	26 June–5 July 1995	*Conservative*
William Hague	5 July 1995–3 May 1997	*Conservative*
Ron Davies	3 May 1997–27 Oct. 1998	*Labour*
Alun Michael	27 Oct. 1998–28 July 1999	*Labour*
Paul Murphy	28 July 1999–24 Oct. 2002	*Labour*
Peter Hain	24 Oct. 2002–24 Jan. 2008	*Labour*
Paul Murphy	24 Jan. 2008–5 June 2009	*Labour*
Peter Hain	5 June 2009–11 May 2010	*Labour*
Cheryl Gillan	12 May 2010–4 Sept. 2012	*Conservative*
David Jones	4 Sept. 2012–present	*Conservative*

Women and Equality

Although not a Cabinet position per se, the holder of office has always been a Cabinet minister with an extra responsibility for ensuring gender equality. The incumbent was entitled the Minister for Women until a reorganisation on 12 October 2007, whereby the Women and Equality Unit, based within the Department for Communities and Local Government, was converted into an independent department supported by the Government Equalities Office (GEO).

Name	*Period*	*Party*
Harriet Harman	1997–1998	*Labour*
Margaret Jay, Baroness Jay of Paddington	1998–2001	*Labour*
Patricia Hewitt	2001–2005	*Labour*
Tessa Jowell	2005–2006	*Labour*
Ruth Kelly	2006–2007	*Labour*
Harriet Harman	2007–2010	*Labour*
Theresa May	2010–4 Sept. 2012	*Conservative*
Maria Miller	2012–present	*Conservative*

Work and Pensions

The Ministry of Pensions was created in 1916 to facilitate the payment of war pensions. On 8 October 1944, a separate Ministry of Social Insurance, under Sir William Jowitt, was formed (renamed the Ministry of National Insurance on 17 November 1944) and the two merged on 3 September 1953 as the Ministry of Pensions and National Insurance. On 6 August 1966 it was renamed Ministry of Social Security, and on 1 November 1968 merged with the Ministry of Health to form the Department of Health and Social Security with the Secretary of State for Social Services as its helmsman. The Department was de-merged on 25 July 1988, creating the separate Department of Health, while the Department of Social Services was renamed the Department of Social Security. On 8 June 2001 it was renamed the Department for Work and Pensions after merging with the Employment element of the Department for Education and Employment.

Name	*Period*	*Party*
George Nicoll Barnes	10 Dec. 1916–17 Aug. 1917	*Labour*
John Hodge	17 Aug. 1917–10 Jan. 1919	*Labour*
Sir Laming Worthington-Evans	10 Jan. 1919–2 Apr. 1920	*Conservative*
Ian Macpherson	2 Apr. 1920–19 Oct. 1922	*Liberal*
George Tryon	31 Oct. 1922–22 Jan. 1924	*Conservative*
Frederick Roberts	23 Jan.–3 Nov. 1924	*Labour*
George Tryon	11 Nov. 1924–4 June 1929	*Conservative*
Frederick Roberts	7 June 1929–24 Aug. 1931	*Labour*
George Tryon	3 Sept. 1931–18 June 1935	*Conservative*
Robert Hudson	18 June 1935–30 July 1936	*Conservative*
Herwald Ramsbotham	30 July 1936–7 June 1939	*Conservative*
Sir Walter Womersley	7 June 1939–26 July 1945	*Conservative*
Wilfred Paling	3 Aug. 1945–17 Apr. 1947	*Labour*
John Hynd	17 Apr.–7 Oct. 1947	*Labour*
George Buchanan	7 Oct. 1947–2 July 1948	*Labour*
Hilary Marquand	2 July 1948–17 Jan. 1951	*Labour*
George Isaacs	17 Jan.–26 Oct. 1951	*Labour*
Derick Heathcoat-Amory	5 Nov. 1951–3 Sept. 1953	*Conservative*
Osbert Peake	3 Sept. 1953–20 Dec. 1955	*Conservative*
John Boyd-Carpenter	20 Dec. 1955–16 July 1962	*Conservative*
Niall Macpherson	16 July 1962–21 Oct. 1963	*Conservative*
Richard Wood	21 Oct. 1963–16 Oct. 1964	*Conservative*
Margaret Herbison	18 Oct. 1964–26 July 1967	*Labour*
Judith Hart	26 July 1967–1 Nov. 1968	*Labour*
Richard Crossman	1 Nov. 1968–19 June 1970	*Labour*
Sir Keith Joseph, Bt	20 June 1970–4 Mar. 1974	*Conservative*
Barbara Castle	5 Mar. 1974–8 Apr. 1976	*Labour*
David Ennals	8 Apr. 1976–4 May 1979	*Labour*
Patrick Jenkin	5 May 1979–14 Sept. 1981	*Conservative*
Norman Fowler	14 Sept. 1981–13 June 1987	*Conservative*
John Moore	13 June 1987–23 July 1989	*Conservative*
Tony Newton	23 July 1989–10 Apr. 1992	*Conservative*
Peter Lilley	10 Apr. 1992–2 May 1997	*Conservative*
Harriet Harman	3 May 1997–27 July 1998	*Labour*
Alistair Darling	27 July 1998–29 May 2002	*Labour*
Andrew Smith	29 May 2002–8 Sept. 2004	*Labour*
Alan Johnson	8 Sept. 2004–6 May 2005	*Labour*
David Blunkett	6 May 2005–2 Nov. 2005	*Labour*
John Hutton	2 Nov. 2005–27 June 2007	*Labour*
Peter Hain	28 June 2007–24 Jan. 2008	*Labour*
James Purnell	24 Jan. 2008–4 June 2009	*Labour*
Yvette Cooper	5 June 2009–11 May 2010	*Labour*
Iain Duncan Smith	12 May 2010–present	*Conservative*

Ministers of Social Insurance/National Insurance

Sir William Jowitt	8 Oct. 1944–23 May 1945	*Labour*
Leslie Hore-Belisha	25 May–26 July 1945	*National Independent*
James Griffiths	4 Aug. 1945–28 Feb. 1950	*Labour*
Edith Summerskill	28 Feb. 1950–26 Oct. 1951	*Labour*
Osbert Peake	31 Oct. 1951–3 Sept. 1953	*Conservative*

PROVERBS

Biblical Proverbs (from the Book of Proverbs)

A wise man will hear, and will increase learning: and a man of understanding shall attain unto wise counsels (1.5).

Listen to the discipline of your father and do not forsake the law of your mother (1.8).

Happy is the man that has found wisdom, and the man that has discernment (3.13).

Do not hold back good from those to whom it is owing, when it happens to be in the power of your hand to do [it] (3.27).

Do not fabricate against your fellow man anything bad, when he is dwelling in a sense of security with you (3.29).

Do not quarrel with a man without cause, if he has rendered no bad to you (3.30).

Do not become envious of a man of violence, nor choose any of his ways (3.31).

Into the path of wicked ones do not enter, and do not walk straight on into the way of bad ones (4.14).

Remove from yourself the crookedness of speech, and the deviousness of lips put far away from yourself (4.24).

Smooth out the course of your foot, and may all your own ways be firmly established (4.26).

Go to the ant, see its ways and become wise (6.6).

Do not reprove a ridiculer, that he may not hate you. Give a reproof to a wise person and he will love you (9.8).

A wise son is one that makes a father rejoice, and a stupid son is the grief of his mother (10.1).

He that is walking in integrity will walk in security, but he that is making his ways crooked will make himself known (10.9).

Hatred is what stirs up contentions, but love covers over even all transgressions (10.12).

The tongue of the righteous person is choice silver, whilst the heart of the wicked one is worth little (10.20).

Deception is in the heart of those fabricating mischief, but those counselling peace have rejoicing (12.20).

A prudent man concealeth knowledge (12.23).

He that walketh with wise men shall be wise: but a companion of fools shall be destroyed (13.20).

He that spareth his rod hateth his son (13.24).

Pride goeth before destruction, and an haughty spirit before a fall (16.18).

General Proverbs

All roads lead to Rome.

An old poacher makes the best keeper.

Beauty is potent but money is omnipotent.

Better be stung by a nettle than pricked by a rose.

Between two stools one falls to the ground.

A bird in the hand is worth two in the bush.

Caesar's wife must be above suspicion.

Cards are the devil's books.

All cats are grey in the dark.

Caveat emptor (Let the buyer beware).

Diligence is the mother of good luck.

A drowning man will catch at a straw.

Enough is as good as a feast.

Every cloud has a silver lining.

Experience is the mistress of fools.

Faint heart never won fair lady.

A fair exchange is no robbery.

Fair words butter no parsnips.

Far fowls have fair feathers.

The folly of one man is the fortune of another.

A fool may ask more questions in an hour than a wise man can answer in seven years.

The fool wanders, the wise man travels.

Give a dog a bad name and hang him.

Go to bed with the lamb, and rise with the lark.

The hand that rocks the cradle rules the world.

He is a fool who makes his doctor his heir.

He should have a long spoon that sups with the devil.

He that sings on Friday will weep on Sunday.

He was a bold man that first ate an oyster.

A heavy purse makes a light heart.

A hedge between keeps friendship green.

If ifs and ands were pots and pans, there'd be no trade for tinkers.

If St Vitus's day [15 June] be rainy weather, it will rain for 30 days together.

If you run after two hares, you will catch neither.

If you sing before breakfast, you'll cry before night.

If you swear, you'll catch no fish.

Keep a thing seven years and you will find a use for it.

Knowledge is power.

A light purse makes a heavy heart.

Lose an hour in the morning and you'll be all day hunting for it.

A mackerel sky is never long dry.

Magpies: one's sorrow, two's mirth, three's a wedding, four's a birth, five's a christening, six a dearth, seven's heaven, eight is hell, and nine's the devil his ane sel'.

March comes in like a lion and goes out like a lamb.

Mighty oaks from little acorns grow.

Monday's child is fair of face,/Tuesday's child is full of grace,/Wednesday's child is full of woe,/Thursday's child has far to go,/Friday's child is loving and giving,/ Saturday's child works hard for living. But the child who is born on the Sabbath day is lucky and happy and good and gay.

Nature abhors a vacuum.

Necessity is the mother of invention.

Needs must when the devil drives.

Never is a long day.

Never trouble trouble till trouble troubles you.

A nod is as good as a wink to a blind horse.

Out of debt, out of danger.

Penny wise, pound foolish.

Prevention is better than cure.

Procrastination is the thief of time

Promises and pie-crusts are made to be broken.

The proof of the pudding is in the eating.

Providence is better than rent.

Rain before seven, fine before eleven.

Red sky at night shepherd's delight, red sky in the morning shepherd's warning.

The road to hell is paved with good intentions.

Salmon and sermon have their season in Lent.

Save your breath to cool your porridge.

Sloth is the key to poverty.

Sneeze on a Monday you sneeze for danger, sneeze on a Tuesday you kiss a stranger, sneeze on a Wednesday you sneeze for a letter, sneeze on a Thursday for something better, sneeze on a Friday you sneeze for sorrow, sneeze on a Saturday see your sweetheart tomorrow, sneeze on a Sunday your safety seek, the devil will have you the whole of the week.

Spare the rod and spoil the child.

Speak well of your friend, of your enemy say nothing.

Still waters run deep.

A tale twice told is cabbage twice sold.

Talk of the devil, and he'll appear.

Tell that to the marines.

Thrift is good revenue.

Time and tide wait for no man.

Virtue is its own reward.

Virtue never grows old.

What can't be cured must be endured.

When the sun is highest he casts the least shadow.

When the wind is in the east it's good for neither man nor beast./When the wind is in the north the skilful fisher goes not forth./When the wind is in the south it blows the bait in the fish's mouth./When the wind is in the west the weather is at the best.

Who knows most says least.

Whom God wishes to destroy, he first makes mad *(Quos Deus vult perdere, prius dementat).*

A wild goose never laid a tame egg.

A wonder lasts but nine days.

You cannot make an omelette without breaking eggs.

You cannot make a silk purse out of a sow's ear.

You cannot teach an old dog new tricks.

Young men may die, old men must.

Zeal without knowledge is fire without light.

Zeal without prudence is frenzy.

NB Some of the proverbs above are corruptions of biblical proverbs. Others were coined by great thinkers and philosophers, and yet others have simply come into general usage through time.

Quotations

All Gaul is divided into three parts.	Julius Caesar
All hope abandon ye who enter. (from *Divine Comedy*)	Dante Alighieri
All is for the best in the best of possible worlds. (from *Candide*)	Voltaire
An archaeologist is the best husband any woman can have – the older she gets the more interested he is in her.	Agatha Christie
And so to bed.	Samuel Pepys
And therefore never send to know for whom the bell tolls; It tolls for thee.	John Donne
Arms and the man I sing. (from the *Aeneid*)	Virgil
Art for art's sake.	Victor Cousin
Attila the hen. (speaking about Margaret Thatcher)	Clement Freud
Balance of power.	Sir Robert Walpole
Bank is a place that will lend you money if you can prove that you don't need it, A	Bob Hope
Because it's there. (when asked why he wanted to climb Mt Everest)	George Mallory
Before God we are all equally wise – and equally foolish.	Albert Einstein
Better to err with Pope, than shine with Pye.	Lord George Byron
Bigger they come the harder they fall, The	Robert Fitzsimmons
Blood is thicker than water.	Commodore Tattnall
Bread and circuses. (*Panem et circenses*, alluding to what the people desired)	Juvenal
Buck stops here, The	Harry S Truman
Bumping pitch and a blinding light, an hour to play and the last man in, A	Sir Henry Newbolt
Candy is dandy - but liquor is quicker.	Ogden Nash
Carthage must be destroyed.	Senator Cato
Cauliflower is nothing but cabbage with a college education.	Mark Twain (from Pudd'nhead Wilson's calendar)
Child is father of the man, The	William Wordsworth
Claret is the liquor for boys, Port for men, but he who aspires to be a hero must drink Brandy.	Dr Samuel Johnson
Classic is something that everybody wants to have read and nobody wants to read, A	Mark Twain
Comedian does funny things; a good comedian does things funny, A	Buster Keaton
Cook was a good cook as cooks go; and as cooks go she went, The	Saki
Cough and the world coughs with you. Fart and you stand alone.	Trevor Griffiths
Desiccated calculating machine, A (writing about Hugh Gaitskell)	Aneurin Bevan
Die is cast, The (on crossing the Rubicon in 49 BC)	Julius Caesar
Don't count your chickens before they are hatched.	Aesop
Don't get mad, get even.	Senator Everett Dirksen
Don't one of you fire until you see the whites of their eyes. (at Bunker Hill in 1775)	US General Israel Putnam
Each man kills the thing he loves. (from *The Ballad of Reading Gaol*)	Oscar Wilde
Ears made him look like a taxi cab with both doors open. (writing about Clark Gable)	Howard Hughes
East is East and West is West and never the twain shall meet.	Rudyard Kipling
England is a nation of shopkeepers.	Napoleon Bonaparte
Eureka (I have found it).	Archimedes
Every man over forty is a scoundrel.	G B Shaw
Experience is the name everyone gives to his mistakes. (from *Lady Windermere's Fan*)	Oscar Wilde
Fair stood the wind for France.	Michael Drayton
Female of the species is more deadly than the male, The	Rudyard Kipling
Fools rush in where angels fear to tread, For	Alexander Pope
From Stettin in the Baltic to Trieste in the Adriatic, an iron curtain has descended across the Continent (describing communism in a speech at Fulton, Missouri (5 Mar. 1946)	Winston Churchill
From the sublime to the ridiculous there is only one step. (1812)	Napoleon Bonaparte (after retreat from Moscow)
Generals January and February. (referring to his chief allies)	Tsar Nicholas I (against Britain & France in Crimea)
Genius is one per cent inspiration and ninety-nine per cent perspiration.	Thomas Alva Edison
Ghost in the machine, The	Gilbert Ryle
Give a man a free hand and he'll run it all over you.	Mae West
Give me a lever long enough and I will move the world.	Archimedes
Give us the tools and we will finish the job.	Winston Churchill
Go and catch a falling star.	John Donne
Go West, young man, and grow up with the country.	Horace Greeley
God does not play dice.	Albert Einstein
God made the country, and man made the town.	William Cowper
God moves in a mysterious way, his wonders to perform.	William Cowper
God's in his heaven – all's right with the world.	Robert Browning
Golf is a good walk spoiled.	Mark Twain
Gondola of London, The (referring to the hansom cab)	Benjamin Disraeli
Good Americans, when they die, go to Paris.	Thomas Gold Appleton
Grain, which in England is generally given to horses but in Scotland supports the People, A (definition of oats)	Dr Samuel Johnson
Great Cham of literature Samuel Johnson, That	Tobias Smollett (in a letter to John Wilkes)
Great fleas have little fleas upon their backs to bite 'em, and little fleas have lesser fleas and so ad infinitum.	Augustus De Morgan
The greatest happiness of the greatest number.	Jeremy Bentham
He can run but he can't hide.	Joe Louis
He makes no friend who never made a foe.	Lord Alfred Tennyson
He nothing common did, or mean, Upon that memorable scene. ('An Horatian Ode upon Cromwell's Return from Ireland')	Andrew Marvell
He speaks to me as if I were a public meeting. (referring to William Gladstone)	Queen Victoria
Heaven has no rage like love to hatred turned, Nor hell a fury like a woman scorned.	William Congreve
Hell is other people.	Jean-Paul Sartre
Here Skugg lies snug as a bug in a rug.	Benjamin Franklin
History is bunk.	Henry Ford
The history of the world is but the biography of great men.	Thomas Carlyle
Hope springs eternal in the human breast.	Alexander Pope
How can they tell? (on being told Calvin Coolidge was dead)	Dorothy Parker
I am his Highness' dog at Kew; Pray tell me sir, whose dog are you?	Alexander Pope
I am just going outside and may be some time.	Capt. Lawrence Oates
I am not afraid of death, I just don't want to be there when it happens.	Woody Allen

I am the State (*L'État, c'est moi*).	Louis XIV
I awoke one morning and found myself famous.	Lord George Byron
I beseech you in the bowels of Christ, think it possible you may be mistaken.	Oliver Cromwell
I can resist everything except temptation. (from *Lady Windermere's Fan*)	Oscar Wilde
I don't want to achieve immortality through my work, I want to achieve it through not dying.	Woody Allen
I fear the Greeks even when they bring gifts. (from the *Aeneid*)	Virgil
I have always thought that every woman should marry, and no man.	Benjamin Disraeli
I have been poor and I have been rich. Rich is better.	Sophie Tucker
I have nothing to declare but my genius. (at US customs)	Oscar Wilde
I have nothing to offer but blood, toil, tears and sweat.	Winston Churchill
I know I have the body of a weak and feeble woman, but I have the heart and stomach of a King.	Elizabeth I
I look upon the world as my parish.	John Wesley
I married beneath me, all women do.	Nancy Astor
I never trust a man unless I've got his pecker in my pocket.	Lyndon B Johnson
I think, therefore I am (*cogito ergo sum*).	René Descartes
I want to be the white man's brother, not his brother-in-law.	Martin Luther King
Ich bin ein Berliner.	John F Kennedy
I'd like that translated, if I may. (reacting to Nikita Khrushchev's banging of shoe on table at the UN)	Harold Macmillan
If God did not exist, it would be necessary to invent him.	Voltaire
If I have seen further it is by standing on the shoulders of giants.	Isaac Newton
If you can keep your head when all about you are losing theirs and blaming it on you.	Rudyard Kipling (from 'If')
If you can meet with triumph and disaster and treat those two impostors just the same	Rudyard Kipling (from 'If')
If you can't annoy somebody, there's little point in writing.	Kingsley Amis
If you can't explain it simply, you don't understand it well enough.	Albert Einstein
If you pay peanuts, you get monkeys.	Sir James Goldsmith
Ignorance is bliss.	Thomas Gray
Ignorance, Madam, pure ignorance. (when asked why he defined pastern as a knee of a horse in his dictionary).	Dr Samuel Johnson
I'm going to spend, spend, spend.	Viv Nicholson
I'm not really a Jew, just Jew-ish, not the whole hog. (*Beyond the Fringe* sketch)	Dr Jonathan Miller
I'm only a beer teetotaller not a champagne teetotaller. (from *Candida*)	G B Shaw
In my sport the quick are too often listed among the dead.	Jackie Stewart
In the future everyone will be famous for fifteen minutes.	Andy Warhol
In the long run we are all dead.	J M Keynes
In this country [England] it is good to kill an admiral from time to time, to encourage the others. (re: shooting of Byng)	Voltaire
In two words, Impossible.	Sam Goldwyn
Include me out.	Sam Goldwyn
Indomitable in retreat; invincible in advance; insufferable in victory.	Winston Churchill (writing of Montgomery)
Into each life some rain must fall.	Henry Wadsworth Longfellow
Into the valley of death rode the six hundred.	Lord Alfred Tennyson
It is better to die on your feet than to live on your knees.	La Pasionaria
It is magnificent but it is not war. (referring to the Charge of the Light Brigade)	General Pierre Bousquet
It is no wonder that people are so horrible when they start their life as children.	Kingsley Amis
It is true that liberty is precious – so precious that it must be rationed.	Lenin
It matters not how a man dies, but how he lives.	Dr Samuel Johnson
It's not the size of the dog in the fight – it's the size of the fight in the dog.	Dwight D Eisenhower
Keep a diary and one day it'll keep you.	Mae West
Kind hearts are more than coronets.	Lord Alfred Tennyson
Knowledge is Power.	Francis Bacon
Lady's not for turning, The	Margaret Thatcher
Lamps are going out all over Europe, The	Edward Gray
Laugh and the world laughs with you; Weep and you weep alone.	Ella Wheeler Wilcox (from her poem 'Solitude')
Let them eat cake.	Marie Antoinette
Let us never negotiate out of fear, but let us never fear to negotiate.	John F Kennedy
Lies, damned lies and statistics.	Benjamin Disraeli
Life is too short to stuff a mushroom.	Shirley Conran
Lion and the calf shall lie down together, but the calf won't get much sleep, The	Woody Allen
Little learning is a dangerous thing, A	Alexander Pope
Love is like the measles, we all have to go through it.	Jerome K Jerome
Love's young dream.	Thomas Moore
Macmillan's role as a poseur was itself a pose.	Harold Wilson
Mad is he? Then I hope he will bite some of my other generals.	George II (on being told General Wolfe was mad)
Man is born free; and everywhere he is in chains. (first line of *The Social Contract*)	Jean-Jacques Rousseau
Man is only as old as the woman he feels, A	Groucho Marx
Man is the hunter, woman is his game.	Lord Alfred Tennyson
Man who dares to waste one hour of time has not discovered the value of life, A	Charles Darwin
Man who knows the price of everything and the value of nothing, A	Oscar Wilde (definition of a cynic)
Manners maketh man.	William of Wykeham
Marriage is a wonderful invention, but then again, so is the bicycle repair kit.	Billy Connolly
Medium is the message, The	Marshall McLuhan
Meek shall inherit the earth, but not its mineral rights, The	J Paul Getty
Men seldom make passes at girls who wear glasses.	Dorothy Parker
Modest little man with much to be modest about, A	Winston Churchill (writing of Clement Attlee)
Mr Balfour's poodle. (referring to the House of Lords)	Lloyd George
Music hath charms to soothe a savage breast.	William Congreve
Never in the field of human conflict was so much owed by so many to so few.	Winston Churchill (referring to Battle of Britain pilots)
Never trust a man with short legs – brains too near their bottom.	Noël Coward
Nice guys finish last. (referring to his baseball team)	Leo Durocher
Night has a thousand eyes and the day but one, The	Francis Bourdillon
No man but a blockhead ever wrote except for money.	Dr Samuel Johnson
No man is an island.	John Donne
No man is justified in doing evil on the ground of expediency.	Theodore Roosevelt
None but the brave deserves the fair.	John Dryden
Nothing is certain but death and taxes.	Benjamin Franklin

Nuts! (replying to von Manteuffel's surrender call during the Battle of the Bulge)	Brigadier General McAuliffe
O what a tangled web we weave when first we practise to deceive.	Sir Walter Scott
Oh liberty! what crimes are committed in your name!	Madame Roland
Old soldiers never die, they simply fade away. (from a popular song of the 1920s)	General MacArthur
One man's wage rise is another man's price increase.	Harold Wilson
One swallow does not make a summer.	Aristotle
Only good Indians I ever saw were dead, The	General Philip Sheridan
Only reason so many people showed up was to make sure that he was dead, The	Sam Goldwyn (of Louis Mayer's funeral)
Only thing we have to fear is fear itself, The	F D Roosevelt
Open my heart and you will see graved inside of it, 'Italy'.	Robert Browning
Patriotism is the last refuge of a scoundrel.	Dr Samuel Johnson
Peace for our time. (on returning from Munich in 1938)	Neville Chamberlain
Peccavi. ('I have sinned' from a telegram sent after capturing Sind in 1834)	Sir Charles Napier
Pen is mightier than the sword, The	Bulwer Lytton
Penny Punch and Judy show, A (referring to television)	Winston Churchill
Politics is the art of the possible.	R A Butler
Power tends to corrupt and absolute power corrupts absolutely.	Lord Acton
Power without responsibility, the privilege of the harlot throughout the ages	Stanley Baldwin (referring to the press)
Procrastination is the thief of time.	Edward Young
Property is theft.	Pierre-Joseph Proudhon
Public be damned, The	Cornelius Vanderbilt
Publish and be damned.	Duke of Wellington
Put your trust in God and keep your powder dry.	Oliver Cromwell
Quoth the Raven, 'Nevermore'. (from 'The Raven')	Edgar Allan Poe
Religion is the opium of the people.	Karl Marx
Remedy is worse than the disease, The	Francis Bacon
Remember that time is money.	Benjamin Franklin
Reports of my death have been greatly exaggerated.	Mark Twain
Riddle wrapped in a mystery inside an enigma, A (referring to the Soviet Union)	Winston Churchill
Rose is a Rose is a Rose, A	Gertrude Stein
Seagreen incorruptible, The (referring to Robespierre)	Thomas Carlyle
Secret of success is sincerity, once you can fake that you've got it made, The	Arthur Bloch
Seize the present day. (*carpe diem*)	Horace
She is the best man in England. (referring to Margaret Thatcher)	Ronald Reagan
Sheep in sheep's clothing, A (writing of Clement Attlee)	Winston Churchill
Sic transit gloria mundi (So passes away the glory of the world).	Thomas à Kempis
Single death is a tragedy, a million deaths is a statistic, A	Joseph Stalin
Speak softly and carry a big stick.	Theodore Roosevelt
Speech is silvern, Silence is golden.	Thomas Carlyle
Stone walls do not a prison make, Nor iron bars a cage. (from 'To Althea from Prison')	Richard Lovelace
Sweet Swan of Avon. (referring to William Shakespeare)	Ben Jonson
Television is an invention that permits you to be entertained in your living room by people you wouldn't have in your home.	Sir David Frost
Tell me the old, old story.	Katherine Hankey
There are two things no man will admit he can't do well: drive and make love.	Stirling Moss
There is no terror in a bang – only in the anticipation of it.	Alfred Hitchcock
There is properly no history; only biography.	Ralph Waldo Emerson
There never was a good war or a bad peace.	Benjamin Franklin
There's a sucker born every minute.	P T Barnum
There's no such thing as a free lunch. (phrase from *The Moon Is a Harsh Mistress*)	Milton Friedman (also used by J K Galbraith)
They also serve who only stand and wait.	John Milton
Thy need is greater than mine. (on giving his water to a soldier at Zutphen)	Sir Philip Sydney
'Tis better to have loved and lost, than never to have loved at all. (from 'In Memoriam')	Lord Alfred Tennyson
To err is human, to forgive, divine.	Alexander Pope
The trouble with Freud is that he never played the Glasgow Empire Saturday night.	Ken Dodd
Turn on, Tune in, Drop out.	Timothy Leary
Unpleasant and unacceptable face of Capitalism. (referring to Lonrho)	Edward Heath
Unspeakable in pursuit of the uneatable, The (referring to foxhunting)	Oscar Wilde
Variety's the spice of life.	William Cowper
Veni, Vidi, Vici (I came, I saw, I conquered). (from a letter written)	Julius Caesar (after his victory at Zela in Asia Minor)
Verbal contract isn't worth the paper it's written on, A	Sam Goldwyn
War is hell.	General Sherman
Warts and everything.	Oliver Cromwell
We are American at puberty. We die French.	Evelyn Waugh
We are not amused.	Queen Victoria
We must indeed all hang together or, most assuredly, we shall all hang separately	Benjamin Franklin (on signing Dec of Independence)
Week is a long time in politics, A	Harold Wilson
What you said hurt me very much. I cried all the way to the bank. (replying to critics)	Liberace
When a man is tired of London he is tired of life.	Dr Samuel Johnson
When a man knows he is to be hanged in a fortnight it concentrates his mind wonderfully.	Dr Samuel Johnson
When the eagles are silent the parrots begin to jabber.	Winston Churchill
Where law ends, tyranny begins.	William Pitt (1st Earl of Chatham)
Whoever is not against us is with us.	Janos Kadar
Will no one rid me of this turbulent priest? (referring to Thomas à Becket)	Henry II
Wind of change is blowing through the continent, The	Harold Macmillan (to South African Parliament 1960)
Winning is not everything. It's the only thing.	Vince Lombardi
Wisest fool in Christendom. (speaking of James I of England and VI of Scotland)	Henry IV of France
Woman is only a woman, but a good cigar is a smoke, A	Rudyard Kipling (from 'The Betrothed')
Women should be obscene and not heard.	John Lennon
Wonders will never cease.	Sir Henry Bate Dudley
Worth seeing, yes; but not worth going to see. (speaking about the Giant's Causeway)	Dr Samuel Johnson
Would you buy a second-hand car from this man? (writing about Richard Nixon)	Mort Sahl
Writer of dictionaries, a harmless drudge, A (definition of a lexicographer)	Dr Samuel Johnson
Ye distant spires, ye antique towers. (from 'Ode on a Distant Prospect of Eton')	Thomas Gray
You can fool all the people some of the time, and some of the people all the time, but you cannot fool all the people all of the time.	Abraham Lincoln
You can have it any colour as long as it's black.	Henry Ford

You can make a throne from bayonets but you can't sit on it long.	Boris Yeltsin
You're either part of the solution or part of the problem.	Eldridge Cleaver
You're not drunk if you can lie on the floor without holding on.	Dean Martin
Youth is wasted on the young.	G B Shaw

Nursery Rhymes

As I was going to St Ives I met a man with seven wives, each wife had seven sacks, each sack had seven cats, each cat had seven kits, kits, cats, sacks and wives, how many going to St Ives?

Baa baa black sheep have you any wool? Yes sir, yes sir, three bags full; one for the master, and one for the dame, and one for the little boy who lives down the lane.

Bobby Shafto's gone to sea, silver buckles on his knee, he'll come back and marry me, bonny Bobby Shafto.

Dance to your daddy, my little babby, dance to your daddy, my little lamb; you shall have a fishy, in a little dishy, you shall have a fishy, when the boat comes in.

Ding, dong, bell, pussy's in the well. Who put her in? Little Johnny Green. Who pulled her out? Little Tommy Stout.

Doctor Foster went to Gloucester, in a shower of rain; he stepped in a puddle, right up to his middle, and never went there again.

Georgie Porgie pudding and pie, kissed the girls and made them cry; when the boys came out to play, Georgie Porgie ran away.

Goosey, goosey gander, where shall I wander? Upstairs and downstairs, in my lady's chamber. There I met an old man who would not say his prayers, I took him by the left leg and threw him down the stairs.

Hey diddle diddle, the cat and the fiddle, the cow jumped over the moon; the little dog laughed to see such sport, and the dish ran away with the spoon.

Hickory, dickory dock, the mouse ran up the clock. The clock struck one, the mouse ran down, hickory, dickory dock.

Humpty Dumpty sat on a wall, Humpty Dumpty had a great fall; all the king's horses and all the king's men couldn't put Humpty together again.

I had a little nut tree, nothing would it bear, but a silver nutmeg, and a golden pear.

If all the world were paper, and all the sea were ink, if all the trees were bread and cheese, what should we have to drink?

Jack be nimble, Jack be quick, Jack jump over the candle stick.

Jack Sprat could eat no fat, his wife could eat no lean, and so between them both, you see, they licked the platter clean.

Little Bo-Peep has lost her sheep, and doesn't know where to find them; leave them alone and they will come home, dragging their tails behind them.

Little Boy Blue, come blow your horn, the sheep's in the meadow, the cow's in the corn. Where is the boy who looks after the sheep? He's under a haystack fast asleep.

Little Jack Horner sat in the corner, eating a Christmas pie; he put in his thumb, and pulled out a plum, and said, What a good boy am I.

Little Miss Muffet sat on a tuffet, eating her curds and whey; along came a spider, who sat down beside her, and frightened Miss Muffet away.

Little Polly Flinders, sat among the cinders, warming her pretty little toes; her mother came and caught her, and whipped her little daughter, for spoiling her nice new clothes.

Little Tommy Tucker sings for his supper; what shall we give him? White bread and butter. How shall he cut it without a knife? How will he marry without a wife?

Lucy Locket lost her pocket, Kitty Fisher found it; not a penny was there in it, only ribbon round it.

Mary had a little lamb, its fleece was white as snow; and everywhere that Mary went the lamb was sure to go.

Mary, Mary, quite contrary, how does your garden grow? With silver bells and cockle shells, and pretty maids all in a row.

Old King Cole was a merry old soul, and a merry old soul was he; he called for his pipe, and he called for his bowl, and he called for his fiddlers three.

Old Mother Hubbard went to the cupboard, to fetch her poor dog a bone; but when she came there, the cupboard was bare, and so the poor dog had none.

On the twelfth day of Christmas my true love sent to me twelve drummers drumming, eleven pipers piping, ten lords a-leaping, nine ladies dancing, eight maids a-milking, seven swans a-swimming, six geese a-laying, five gold rings, four colly birds, three French hens, two turtle doves, and a partridge in a pear tree.

One, two, three, four, five, once I caught a fish alive; six, seven, eight, nine, ten, then I let it go again. Why did you let it go? Because it bit my finger so. Which finger did it bite? This little finger on the right.

Oranges and lemons, say the bells of St Clement's. You owe me five farthings, say the bells of St Martin's. When will you pay me? say the bells of Old Bailey. When I grow rich, say the bells of Shoreditch. When will that be? say the bells of Stepney. I'm sure I don't know, says the great bell at Bow. Here comes the candle to light you to bed, here comes a chopper to chop off your head.

Pat-a-cake, pat-a-cake baker's man, bake me a cake as fast as you can; pat it and prick it and mark it with B, put it in the oven for baby and me.

Pease porridge hot, pease porridge cold, pease porridge in the pot, nine days old.

Polly put the kettle on, Polly put the kettle on, Polly put the kettle on, we'll all have tea. Sukey take it off again, Sukey take it off again, Sukey take it off again, they've all gone away.

Pussy cat, pussy cat, where have you been? I've been to London to visit the Queen. Pussy cat, pussy cat, what did you there? I frightened a little mouse under her chair.

Ride a cock horse to Banbury Cross, to see a fine lady upon a white horse; rings on her fingers and bells on her toes, and she shall have music wherever she goes.

Ring-a-ring o'roses, a pocket full of posies, A-tishoo, A-tishoo, we all fall down.

Rub-a-dub-dub, three men in a tub, and how do you think they got there? The butcher, the baker, the candlestick maker, they all jumped out of a rotten potato, 'twas enough to make a man stare.

See-saw Margery Daw, Johnny shall have a new master; Johnny shall have but a penny a day, because he can't work any faster.

Simple Simon met a pieman, going to the fair; said Simple Simon to the pieman, let me taste your ware. Said the pieman to Simple Simon, show me first your penny; said Simple Simon to the pieman, indeed I have not any.

Sing a song of sixpence, a pocket full of rye; four and twenty blackbirds baked in a pie. When the pie was opened the birds began to sing; wasn't that a dainty dish to set before the king? The king was in his counting-house, counting out his money, the queen was in the parlour, eating bread and honey, the maid was in the garden, hanging out the clothes, along came a blackbird and pecked off her nose.

Solomon Grundy, born on Monday, christened on Tuesday, married on Wednesday, took ill on Thursday, worse on Friday, died on Saturday, buried on Sunday, this is the end of Solomon Grundy.

Taffy was a Welshman, Taffy was a thief, Taffy came to my house and stole a leg of beef. I went to Taffy's house, Taffy wasn't in, I jumped upon his Sunday hat, and poked it with a pin.

The Grand Old Duke of York, he had ten thousand men, he marched them up to the top of the hill, and he marched them down again; and when they were up they were up, and when they were down they were down, and when they were only halfway up, they were neither up nor down.

The man in the moon came down too soon, and asked the way to Norwich; he went by the south, and burnt his mouth, with supping cold plum porridge.

The north wind doth blow, and we shall have snow, and what will poor Robin do then, poor thing? He'll sit in a barn, and keep himself warm, and hide his head under his wing, poor thing.

The Queen of Hearts she made some tarts, all on a summer's day. The Knave of Hearts he stole the tarts, and took them clean away.

There was a crooked man, who walked a crooked mile, he found a crooked sixpence against a crooked stile, he bought a crooked cat, which caught a crooked mouse, and they all lived together in a little crooked house.

There was a man lived in the moon, lived in the moon, lived in the moon, and his name was Aiken Drum, and he played upon a ladle, a ladle, a ladle.

There was an old woman who lived in a shoe, she had so many children she didn't know what to do; she gave them some broth without any bread, she whipped them all soundly and sent them to bed.

This little piggy went to market, this little piggy stayed at home, this little piggy had roast beef, this little piggy had none, and this little piggy went wee-wee-wee, all the way home.

Tom, Tom, the piper's son, stole a pig and away he run; the pig was eat, and Tom was beat, and Tom went howling down the street.

Twinkle, twinkle, little star, how I wonder what you are! Up above the world so high, like a diamond in the sky.

Wee Willie Winkie runs through the town, upstairs and downstairs in his night-gown, rapping at the window, crying through the lock, are the children all in bed, it's past eight o' clock.

What are little boys made of? Snips and snails and puppy-dog tails. What are little girls made of? Sugar and spice and all things nice.

Who killed Cock Robin? I, said the sparrow, with my bow and arrow, I killed Cock Robin. Who saw him die? I, said the fly, with my little eye, I saw him die.

Yankee Doodle came to town, riding on a pony; stuck a feather in his cap, and called it macaroni.

Religion

Popes

	*Popes and antipopes	Dates	Original name, feast day or miscellaneous information
1	St Peter	To 64	feast day 29 June
2	St Linus	*c.* 67–76/79	feast day 23 September
3	St Anacletus	*c.* 76/79–88/91	feast day 26 April
4	St Clement I	*c.* 88/92–97/101	feast day 23 November
5	St Evaristus	*c.* 97–c107	feast day 6 October
6	St Alexander I	*c.* 105/9–115/19	feast day 3 May
7	St Sixtus I	*c.* 115–c125	feast day 3 April
8	St Telesphorus	*c.* 125–c136	feast day 5 January (Greek)
9	St Hyginus	*c.* 136–c140	feast day 11 January (Greek)
10	St Pius I	*c.* 140–c155	feast day 11 July
11	St Anicetus	*c.* 155–c166	feast day 17 April (Syria)
12	St Soter	*c.* 166–c175	feast day 22 April
13	St Eleutherius	*c.* 175–c189	feast day 26 May
14	St Victor I	*c.* 189–c199	feast day 28 July (African)
15	St Zephyrinus	*c.* 199–c217	feast day 26 August
16	St Calixtus I	217–222	feast day 14 October
17	Hippolytus	217–235	first antipope
18	St Urban I	222–230	feast day 25 May
19	St Pontian	230–235	feast day 19 November
20	St Anterus	235–236	feast day 3 January (Greek)
21	St Fabian	236–250	feast day 20 January
22	St Cornelius	251–253	feast day 16 September
23	Novatian	251	Novatianus (antipope)
24	St Lucius I	253–254	feast day 4 March
25	St Stephen I	254–257	feast day 2 August
26	St Sixtus II	257–258	feast day 6 August (Greek)
27	St Dionysius	259–268	feast day 6 December (Greek)
28	St Felix I	269–274	feast day 30 May
29	St Eutychian	275–283	feast day 7 December
30	St Gaius	283–296	feast day 22 April (Dalmatian)
31	St Marcellinus	296–304	feast day 26 April
32	St Marcellus I	308–309	feast day 16 January
33	St Eusebius	309–310	feast day 17 August (Greek)
34	St Miltiades	311–314	feast day 10 December
35	St Sylvester I	314–335	feast day 31 December
36	St Mark	336	feast day 7 October
37	St Julius I	337–352	feast day 12 April
38	Liberius	352–366	
39	Felix II	355–358	antipope 357–8
40	St Damasus I	366–384	feast day 11 December (Latin Mass)
41	Ursinus	366–367	Antipope
42	St Siricius	384–399	feast day 26 November
43	St Anastasius I	399–401	feast day 19 December
44	St Innocent I	401–417	feast day 28 July
45	St Zosimus	417–418	feast day 26 December (Greek)
46	St Boniface I	418–422	feast day 4 September
47	Eulalius	418–419	antipope
48	St Celestine I	422–432	feast day 27 July
49	St Sixtus III	432–440	feast day 28 March
50	St Leo I	440–461	feast day 11 April (Leo the Great)
51	St Hilary	461–468	feast day 28 February
52	St Simplicius	468–483	feast day 10 March
53	St Felix III	483–492	feast day 1 March
54	St Gelasius I	492–496	feast day 21 November
55	Anastasius II	496–498	
56	St Symmachus	498–514	feast day 19 July
57	Laurentius	498	antipope
58	Laurentius	501–505	antipope
59	St Hormisdas	514–523	feast day 6 August
60	St John I	523–526	feast day 27 May
61	Felix IV	526–530	feast day 30 January
62	Dioscorus	530	Egyptian
63	Boniface II	530–532	
64	John II	533–535	Mercurius (first pope to change name)
65	St Agapetus I	535–536	feast day 22 April
66	St Silverius	536–537	feast day 20 June
67	Vigilius	537–555	
68	Pelagius I	556–561	
69	John III	561–574	Catelinus
70	Benedict I	575–579	
71	Pelagius II	579–590	
72	St Gregory I	590–604	feast day 12 March
73	Sabinian	604–606	
74	Boniface III	607	
75	St Boniface IV	608–615	
76	St Deusdedit	615–618	feast day 8 November (aka Adeodatus I)
77	Boniface V	619–625	
78	Honorius I	625–638	
79	Severinus	638–640	
80	John IV	640–642	Dalmatian

81	Theodore I	642–649	Jerusalem
82	St Martin I	649–655	feast day 12 November
83	St Eugenius I	654–657	feast day 2 June
84	St Vitalian	657–672	
85	Adeodatus II	672–676	
86	Donus	676–678	
87	St Agatho	678–681	feast day 10 January
88	St Leo II	681–683	feast day 3 July
89	St Benedict II	684–685	feast day 8 May
90	John V	685–686	Syrian
91	Conon	686–687	
92	St Sergius I	687–701	feast day 8 September
93	Theodore	687	antipope
94	Paschal	687	antipope
95	John VI	701–705	Greek
96	John VII	705–707	Greek
97	Sisinnius	708	
98	Constantine	708–715	
99	St Gregory II	715–731	feast day 11 February
100	St Gregory III	731–741	feast day 28 November (Syrian)
101	St Zacharias	741–752	feast day 15 March
102	Stephen II	752	died after two days
103	Stephen III	752–757	Papal States founder
104	St Paul I	757–767	feast day 28 June
105	Constantine II	767–768	antipope
106	Philip	768	antipope
107	Stephen IV	768–772	
108	Adrian I	772–795	
109	St Leo III	795–816	feast day 12 June (Crowned Charlemagne)
110	Stephen V	816–817	
111	St Paschal I	817–824	feast day 14 May
112	Eugenius II	824–827	
113	Valentine	827	feast day 14 February
114	Gregory IV	827–844	created 1 November All Saints day
115	John	844	antipope
116	Sergius II	844–847	
117	St Leo IV	847–855	feast day 17 July
118	Benedict III	855–858	
119	Anastasius	855	Anastasius the Librarian (antipope)
120	St Nicholas I	858–867	
121	Adrian II	867–872	
122	John VIII	872–882	crowned Charles the Fat Emperor
123	Marinus I	882–884	
124	St Adrian III	884–885	feast day 8 July
125	Stephen VI	885–891	
126	Formosus	891–896	
127	Boniface VI	896	
128	Stephen VII	896–897	
129	Romanus	897	
130	Theodore II	897	
131	John IX	898–900	
132	Benedict IV	900–903	
133	Leo V	903	
134	Christopher	903–904	antipope
135	Sergius III	904–911	
136	Anastasius III	911–913	
137	Lando	913–914	
138	John X	914–928	
139	Leo VI	928	
140	Stephen VIII	929–931	
141	John XI	931–935	
142	Leo VII	936–939	
143	Stephen IX	939–942	
144	Marinus II	942–946	
145	Agapetus II	946–955	
146	John XII	955–964	Ottaviano (crowned Emperor Otto)
147	Leo VIII	963–965	
148	Benedict V	964–966	Benedict the Grammarian
149	John XIII	965–972	
150	Benedict VI	973–974	
151	Boniface VII	974	Franco (first term)
152	Benedict VII	974–983	
153	John XIV	983–984	Pietro Canepanova
154	Boniface VII	984–985	Franco (second term)
155	John XV	985–996	
156	Gregory V	996–999	Bruno of Carinthia (first German pope)
157	John XVI	997–998	Giovanni Filagato (antipope)
158	Sylvester II	999–1003	Gerbert of Aurillac (French)
159	John XVII	1003	Secco
160	John XVIII	1004–1009	Fasano
161	Sergius IV	1009–1012	Pietro Buccaporci
162	Gregory VI	1012	antipope
163	Benedict VIII	1012–1024	Teofilatto
164	John XIX	1024–1032	Romano (crowned Emperor Conrad II)
165	Benedict IX	1032–1044	Teofilatto (12 yrs old)
166	Sylvester III	1045	John of Sabina
167	Benedict IX	1045	Teofilatto (second term)

168	Gregory VI	1045–1046	Giovanni Graziano
169	Clement II	1046–1047	Suidger
170	Benedict IX	1047–1048	Teofilatto (third term)
171	Damasus II	1048	Poppo (Bavarian)
172	St Leo IX	1049–1054	feast day 19 April (aka Bruno of Egisheim)
173	Victor II	1055–1057	Gebhard of Hirschberg
174	Stephen X	1057–1058	Frederick of Lorraine
175	Benedict X	1058–1059	Giovanni Mincio (antipope)
176	Nicholas II	1058–1061	Gerard of Burgundy
177	Alexander II	1061–1073	Anselm of Baggio
178	Honorius II	1061–1072	Cadelo (antipope)
179	St Gregory VII	1073–1085	feast day 25 May 25 (aka Hildebrand)
180	Clement III	1080–1100	Guibert (antipope)
181	Victor III	1086–1087	feast day 16 September
182	Urban II	1088–1099	Odo of Lagery
183	Paschal II	1099–1118	Raniero
184	Theodoric	1100–1102	antipope
185	Albert/Aleric	1102	antipope
186	Sylvester IV	1105–1111	Maginulfo (antipope)
187	Gelasius II	1118–1119	Giovanni da Gaetan
188	Gregory VIII	1118–1121	Maurice Bourdin (antipope)
189	Calixtus II	1119–1124	Guy of Burgundy
190	Honorius II	1124–1130	Lamberto Scannabecchi
191	Celestine II	1124	Theobald Buccapecus
192	Innocent II	1130–1143	Gregorio Papareschi
193	Anacletus II	1130–1138	Pietro Pierleoni (antipope)
194	Victor IV	1138	Gregory Conti (antipope)
195	Celestine II	1143–1144	Guido de Castellis
196	Lucius II	1144–1145	Gherardo Caccianemici
197	Eugenius III	1145–1153	feast day 8 July (aka Bernard of Pisa)
198	Anastasius IV	1153–1154	Corrado di Suburra
199	Adrian IV	1154–1159	Nicholas Breakspear (only English pope)
200	Alexander III	1159–1181	Rolando Bandinelli
201	Victor IV	1159–1164	Ottaviano de Monticello (antipope)
202	Paschal III	1164–1168	Guido da Crema (antipope)
203	Calixtus III	1168–1178	John of Struma (antipope)
204	Innocent III	1179–1180	Lando di Sezze (antipope)
205	Lucius III	1181–1185	Ubaldo Allucingoli
206	Urban III	1185–1187	Uberto Crivelli
207	Gregory VIII	1187	Alberto de Morra
208	Clement III	1187–1191	Paolo Scolari
209	Celestine III	1191–1198	Giacinto Bobo-Orsini
210	Innocent III	1198–1216	Lothair di Segni
211	Honorius III	1216–1227	Cencio Savelli
212	Gregory IX	1227–1241	Ugolino di Segni (excommunicated Frederick II)
213	Celestine IV	1241	Goffredo Castiglioni
214	Innocent IV	1243–1254	Sinibaldo Fieschi
215	Alexander IV	1254–1261	Rinaldo Deisegni
216	Urban IV	1261–1264	Jacques Pantaleon
217	Clement IV	1265–1268	Guido Fulcodi
218	Gregory X	1271–1276	Tebaldo Visconti
219	Innocent V	1276	feast day June 22nd (first Dominican pope)
220	Adrian V	1276	Ottobono Fieschi
221	John XXI	1276–1277	Pedro Hispano (Portuguese)
222	Nicholas III	1277–1280	Giovanni Orsini
223	Martin IV	1281–1285	Simon de Brion
224	Honorius IV	1285–1287	Giacomo Savelli
225	Nicholas IV	1288–1292	Girolamo Masci
226	St Celestine V	1294	feast day 19 May (first pope to abdicate)
227	Boniface VIII	1294–1303	Benedict Caetani
228	Benedict XI	1303–1304	feast day 7 July
229	Clement V	1305–1314	Bertrand de Got (Avignon from 1309)
230	John XXII	1316–1334	Jacques Duese (Babylonian Captivity 1309–77)
231	Nicholas V	1328–1330	Pietro Rainalducci (antipope)
232	Benedict XII	1334–1342	Jacques Fournier (Avignon)
233	Clement VI	1342–1352	Pierre Roger (Avignon)
234	Innocent VI	1352–1362	Etienne Aubert (Avignon)
235	Urban V	1362–1370	feast day 19 December (Avignon)
236	Gregory XI	1370–1378	Pierre de Beaufort (Avignon till 1377)
237	Urban VI	1378–1389	Bartolomeo Prignano (Western Schism 1378–1417)
238	Clement VII	1378–1394	Robert of Geneva (antipope)
239	Boniface IX	1389–1404	Pietro Tomacelli
240	Benedict XIII	1394–1423	Pedro de Luna (antipope)
241	Innocent VII	1404–1406	Cosimo de Migliorati
242	Gregory XII	1406–1415	Angelo Correr
243	Alexander V	1409–1410	Peter of Candia (antipope)
244	John XXIII	1410–1415	Baldassare Cossa (antipope)
245	Martin V	1417–1431	Oddone Colonna
246	Clement VIII	1423–1429	Gil Sanchez Munoz (antipope)
247	Benedict XIV	1425–1433	The Hidden Pope (counter antipope)
248	Eugenius IV	1431–1447	Gabriele Condulmer
249	Felix V	1439–1449	Amadeus VIII the Peaceful (antipope)
250	Nicholas V	1447–1455	Tommaso Parentucelli
251	Calixtus III	1455–1458	Alfonso di Borgia (uncle of Rodrigo)
252	Pius II	1458–1464	Enea Piccolomini
253	Paul II	1464–1471	Pietro Barbo
254	Sixtus IV	1471–1484	Francesco Dellarovere

255	Innocent VIII	1484–1492	Giovanni Battista Cibo
256	Alexander VI	1492–1503	Rodrigo Borgia (father of Lucretia)
257	Pius III	1503	Francesco Piccolomini
258	Julius II	1503–1513	Giuliano Dellarovere (patron of Michelangelo)
259	Leo X	1513–1521	Giovanni de Medici (excommunicated Luther 1521)
260	Adrian VI	1522–1523	Adrian Florenz Boeyens (only Dutch pope)
261	Clement VII	1523–1534	Giulio de Medici
262	Paul III	1534–1549	Alessandro Farnese (called Council of Trent)
263	Julius III	1550–1555	Giovanni del Monte
264	Marcellus II	1555	Marcello Cervini
265	Paul IV	1555–1559	Gian Pietro Carafa
266	Pius IV	1559–1565	Giovanni de Medici (concluded Council of Trent)
267	St Pius V	1566–1572	Antonio Ghislieri (excommunicated Elizabeth I 1570)
268	Gregory XIII	1572–1585	Ugo Boncompagni (Gregorian calendar)
269	Sixtus V	1585–1590	Felice Peretti (excommunicated Henry of Navarre)
270	Urban VII	1590	Giambattista Castagna
271	Gregory XIV	1590–1591	Niccolo Sfondrato
272	Innocent IX	1591	Giovanni Facchinetti
273	Clement VIII	1592–1605	Ippolito Aldobrandini
274	Leo XI	1605	Alessandro de Medici
275	Paul V	1605–1621	Camillo Borghese
276	Gregory XV	1621–1623	Alessandro Ludovisi
277	Urban VIII	1623–1644	Maffeo Barberini (patron of sculptor Bernini)
278	Innocent X	1644–1655	Giovanni Pamphili
279	Alexander VII	1655–1667	Fabio Chigi
280	Clement IX	1667–1669	Giulio Rospiglioso
281	Clement X	1670–1676	Emilio Altieri
282	Innocent XI	1676–1689	feast day 13 August
283	Alexander VIII	1689–1691	Pietro Ottoboni
284	Innocent XII	1691–1700	Antonio Pignatelli
285	Clement XI	1700–1721	Giovanni Albani
286	Innocent XIII	1721–1724	Michelangelo dei Conti (recognised Old Pretender)
287	Benedict XIII	1724–1730	Pietro Maria Orsini
288	Clement XII	1730–1740	Lorenzo Corsini (condemned Freemasonry)
289	Benedict XIV	1740–1758	Prospero Lambertini
290	Clement XIII	1758–1769	Carlo Rezzonico
291	Clement XIV	1769–1774	Giovanni Ganganelli (dissolved Jesuits 1773)
292	Pius VI	1775–1799	Giannangelo Braschi
293	Pius VII	1800–1823	Barnaba Chiaramonti (revived Jesuits 1814)
294	Leo XII	1823–1829	Annibale Della Genga
295	St Pius VIII	1829–1830	Francesco Castiglioni
296	Gregory XVI	1831–1846	Bartolomeo Cappellari (Austrian)
297	Pius IX	1846–1878	Giovanni Mastai-Ferretti (longest reign, 32 yrs)
298	Leo XIII	1878–1903	Vincenzo Pecci
299	St Pius X	1903–1914	feast day 3 September (last to be canonised)
300	Benedict XV	1914–1922	Giacomo Della Chiesa
301	Pius XI	1922–1939	Ambrogio Damiano Ratti
302	Pius XII	1939–1958	Eugenio Maria Pacelli
303	John XXIII	1958–1963	Angelo Giuseppe Roncalli (second Vatican Council)
304	Paul VI	1963–1978	Giovanni Battista Montini (first to visit Asia)
305	John Paul I	1978	Albino Luciani (reigned 34 days)
306	John Paul II	1978–2005	Karol Wojtyla (Polish: first non-Italian since Adrian VI)
307	Benedict XVI	2005–2013	Joseph Alois Ratzinger (German; oldest at election since 1730)
308	Francis	2013–	Jorge Mario Bergoglio (Argentinian; 266th Pope but first Jesuit; feast day 4Oct.)

Popes: Miscellaneous Information

antipope	an alternative claimant to the bishop of Rome who has just cause in disputing the papacy
assassinated	26
boy pope	Benedict IX (12 yrs old)
Britain: first to visit	John Paul II (1982)
British Pope	Adrian IV (Nicholas Breakspear)
Cadaver Synod	Formosus (896) tried and executed after his death!
Celestine II	Theobald Buccapecus, elected pope in 1124, resigned after a few days and is often omitted in lists, hence the duplication.
Council of Trent	19th ecumenical council of RC Church; 1545–63 in northern Italy
crushed to death	John XXI; ceiling of papal palace at Viterbo collapsed
directives called	Papal Bull
double name: first	John Paul I (named after two predecessors)
female pope	Joan (fictional)
Humanae Vitae	encyclical of Paul VI condemning birth control (1968)
Infallibility	doctrine promulgated in July 1870, reaffirmed 1973
John Paul II	archbishop of Cracow
last antipope	the count of Savoy took holy orders and set himself up as Clement XV in 1969 but was never recognised outside his own small circle. Felix X was the last elected antipope.
last non-Italian before John Paul II	Adrian VI (1522) Dutch
last to be canonised	Pius X on 29 May 1954
letters to churches	encyclicals
longest reign	Pius IX (32 yrs)
new pope: how known	White smoke from Vatican chimney
non-existent pope	John XX, due to error in numbering in 10th century
Pacem in Terris	encyclical of John XXIII (Peace on Earth)
Pilgrim Pope	Paul VI (because of his great travelling)
pope's blessing	Urbi et Orbi (To the city and the world)
pope: also called	Sovereign of Vatican City Vicar of Christ on Earth Bishop of Rome Patriarch of the West Primate of Italy
pope: elected by	College of Cardinals: two-thirds majority required
pope: means	father
Redemptor Hominus	encyclical of John Paul II about respect for man
Sacerdotalis Caelibatus	encyclical of Paul VI concerning priestly celibacy
throne	Sedes Gestatoria
Vatican Council: first	1869–70 (convoked by Pius IX)
Vatican Council: second	1962–65 (convoked by John XXIII)

Religion: General Information

Adam's first wife Lilith (according to Jewish folklore).

Adulterer's Bible edition of the Bible of 1631, with the misprinted commandment 'thou shalt commit adultery'. Aka Wicked Bible.

ahimsa law of Reverence for, and non-violence to, every form of life (Hindu, Buddhist and Jainist philosophy).

Angels: hierarchy: 1 Seraphim; 2 Cherubim; 3 Thrones; 4 Dominions / Dominations; 5 Virtues; 6 Powers; 7 Principalities; 8 Archangels; 9 Angels

Black Friars Dominicans (Friar Preachers are a mendicant order founded in 1215).

Black Monks Benedictines (established *c.* AD 535–540).

Buddhism founded by Siddhartha Gautama in the sixth century BC. Buddha means 'Enlightened One'. Two main divisions are Theravada Buddhism and Mahayana Buddhism. The third minor division is Vajrayana or Tantric Buddhism. The Buddha's teachings are described as the Four Noble Truths. The Middle or Noble Eightfold Path is the finding of truth and leads to Nirvana. The ten precepts include five for laymen, i.e. prohibiting killing, stealing, lying, sexual misconduct and drinking intoxicating liquor, and five for monastic novices, i.e. not to eat at certain hours, not to take part in festivals, not to use garlands or perfumes, not to use a luxurious bed and not to accept money for oneself. The birth of the Buddha is celebrated in the festival of Vesak/Wesak. The Buddha's first sermon is celebrated in the festival of Dhamma-cakka.

Cathari Manichean order that flourished in western Europe during the 12th and 13th centuries. The name derives from the Greek 'Katharos' meaning pure.

Christadelphians founded by John Thomas in 1848, although the name was adopted during the US Civil War.

Christian Scientists founded in Boston, Massachusetts, by Mary Baker Eddy (1879).

Church Army founded by Wilson Carlile (1882) in slums of London.

Grey Friars Franciscans (founded *c.* 1207 and affiliated with the Poor Clares since 1212).

Hinduism originated about 4,000 years ago in the land of the Indus River. The Veda is the most ancient body of religious literature.
The power of the Brahmans (priest class) is central to the belief.
Ahimsa is the doctrine of non-injury or the absence of the desire to harm. Brahma (creator), Vishnu (protector) and Siva (destroyer and restorer) constitute the Trimurti.

Islam founded by Mohammed in AD 622 when he fled from Mecca to Medina (flight known as the Hegira). Koran (Qur'ān) is regarded as the word of God given to Mohammed by the angel Gabriel.
Five pillars of Islamic faith are: the Shahādah – there is no god but God and Mohammed is the prophet of God; the salat – the five daily prayer sessions; the zakat – the tax that constitutes the giving of alms; the saum – fasting during daylight hours of Ramadan; hajj – the pilgrimage to Mecca that every Muslim should take at least once in their lifetime. The two major branches of Islam are the Sunnites (largest) and the Shi'ites.

Jainism founded in India in the sixth century BC by Mahavira. Jains practise Ahimsa.

Jehovah's Witnesses founded by Charles Taze Russell (1881).

Jerusalem centre of Islam, Judaism and Christianity. The Wailing Wall is sacred to the Jews, the Dome of the Rock is sacred to Muslims and Church of the Holy Sepulchre is sacred to Christians.

Jesse son of Obed, and father of David.

Judaism the body of Jewish civil and ceremonial law is contained in the Talmud, which comprises the Mishnah and the Gemara. The Hebrew Bible comprises 24 books. The civil calendar begins with the month of Tishri, the first day of which is the holiday of Rosh Hashana (New Year). Other Jewish holidays include Shavuot or Pentecost, which commemorates the revelation of the Torah (Law) at Sinai; Yom Kippur (Day of Atonement), which ends the ten days of penitence from Rosh Hashana; and Sukkot (Tabernacles), in remembrance of the Israelites' wanderings after the Exodus. Yom Kippur, Rosh Hashana, and Sukkot are celebrated in the Jewish month of Tishri. Purim celebrates the story of Esther and is celebrated in the month of Adar. Israeli Jews are divided equally among Ashkenazi (Germanic) and Sephardic (strictly speaking, descendants of Spanish Jews pre-1492; more loosely, non-Ashkenazi), although the Ashkenazim constitute more than 80% of all Jews in the world.

Koran (Qur'an) Sacred book of Islam, regarded by Muslims as the final revelation of God to humankind, passed by the archangel Gabriel in Arabic to Muhammmad, the last of the prophets. It consists of 114 chapters (sūras) containing Christian and Arabic legend as well as Old and New Testament stories. The first translation into English was by George Sale in 1734, although Alexander Ross translated the Koran into English in 1649, but this was from a French translation.

Manich(a)eism religious order founded by the Persian prophet Mani (*c.* 216–274) based on the conflict between goodness and evil. Manicheism also describes any heretical philosophy involving dualistic doctrines.

Menorah seven-branched candelabrum that is now an emblem of Judaism and badge of Israel.

Methodism founded by John Wesley (1738).

Mormons aka Church of Jesus Christ of Latter-Day Saints, founded by Joseph Smith in 1830 and not Brigham Young, who merely led them to Salt Lake City, Utah, in 1847.

Panchen Lama one of the two great Lamas of Tibet. (The other is the Dalai Lama.)

Penitential Psalms seven psalms (i.e. 6, 32, 38, 51, 102, 130, 143) all expressing penitence.

Plymouth Brethren founded in Dublin by the Reverend John Nelson Darby (1827) and named after the Devon town.

Potiphar Pharaoh's official who bought Joseph as a slave.

Premonstratensians religious sect founded in the twelfth century by St Norbert.

religious journals Christian Scientists – *Citadel*, *Monitor*; Jehovah's Witnesses – *Watchtower*; Roman Catholics – *Tablet*, *Universe*, *Herald*; Salvation Army – *War Cry*.

Salvation Army founded by William Booth (1865) as the New Christian Mission; name changed in 1878. Motto: Blood and Fire.

Seven Sorrows of Mary
1 The prophecy of Simeon (that a sword would pierce her soul).
2 The flight into Egypt.
3 The loss of the holy child in Jerusalem.
4 Meeting with the Lord on the road to Calvary.
5 The Crucifixion (when she stood at the foot of the cross).
6 The Deposition (taking down of Christ from the cross).
7 The Entombment (burial of Christ).

Shakers founded by James Wardley and Jane Wardley (1747).

Shinto founded in Japan in the eighth century AD and divided into groups of which the best-known are Jinja and Kyoha.
The sacred texts are *Kojiki* and *Nihonshoki*.
Shinto literally means 'the teaching' or 'the way of the Gods'.

Sikhism founded by the Guru Nanak in the fifteenth century; the holy book is the Adi Granth.

Society of Friends founded by George Fox (1650); aka Quakers.

Society of Jesus founded by Ignatius Loyola (1534).

Stations of the Cross 14 (aka Way of the Cross). Depict the final events in the Passion of Christ. Usually seen portrayed in churches but may also be found in cemeteries, hospitals and mountainsides.
1 Jesus is condemned to death.
2 Jesus is made to bear his cross.
3 Jesus falls the first time.
4 Jesus meets his mother.
5 Simon of Cyrene is made to bear the cross.
6 Veronica wipes Jesus' face.
7 Jesus falls the second time.
8 Women of Jerusalem weep over Jesus.
9 Jesus falls the third time.
10 Jesus is stripped of his garments.
11 Jesus is nailed to the cross.
12 Jesus dies on the cross.
13 Jesus is taken down from the cross.
14 Jesus is placed in the sepulchre.

Ten Commandments listed in Exodus and Deuteronomy.
1 Thou shalt have no other gods before me.
2 Thou shalt not make any graven images or likeness of anything in Heaven.
3 Thou shalt not take the name of the Lord thy God in vain.
4 Remember the Sabbath day, to keep it holy.
5 Honour thy father and thy mother.
6 Thou shalt not kill.
7 Thou shalt not commit adultery.
8 Thou shalt not steal.
9 Thou shalt not bear false witness against thy neighbour.
10 Thou shalt not covet thy neighbour's house, wife, manservant, ox or ass.

Unification Church founded by Reverend Sun Myung Moon (1954).

Visitation the visit of the Virgin Mary to her cousin Elizabeth, mother of John the Baptist.

White Friars Carmelites (mendicant order established *c.* 1155 and approved in 1226 by Pope Honorius III).

White Monks Cistercians (founded in 1098).

Archbishops of York

734	Egberht
767	Æthelberht
780	Eanbald I
796	Eanbald II
808	Wulfsige
837	Wigmund
854	Wulfhere
900	Æthalbald
928	Hrothweard
931	Wulfstan I
956	Osketel
971	Oswald
971	Edwald
992	Ealdwulf
1003	Wulfstan II
1023	Ælfric Puttoc
1041	Æthelric
1051	Cynesige
1061	Ealdred
1070	Thomas I of Bayeux
1100	Gerard
1109	Thomas II
1119	Thurstan
1143	William Fitzherbert
1147	Henry Murdac
1153	William Fitzherbert
1154	Roger of Pont l'Eveque
1191	Geoffrey Plantagenet
1215	Walter de Gray
1256	Sewal de Bovill
1258	Godfrey Ludham
1266	Walter Giffard
1279	William Wickwane
1286	John Romanus
1298	Henry Newark
1300	Thomas Corbridge
1306	William Greenfield
1317	William Melton
1342	William de la Zouche
1352	John Thoresby
1374	Alexander Neville
1388	Thomas Arundel
1396	Robert Waldby
1398	Richard le Scrope
1407	Henry Bowet
1426	John Kempe
1452	William Booth
1464	George Nevill
1476	Lawrence Booth
1480	Thomas Rotherham
1501	Thomas Savage
1508	Christopher Bainbridge
1514	Thomas Wolsey
1531	Edward Lee
1545	Robert Holgate
1555	Nicholas Heath
1561	Thomas Young
1570	Edmund Grindal
1577	Edwin Sandys
1589	John Piers
1595	Matthew Hutton
1606	Tobias Matthew
1628	George Montaigne
1629	Samuel Harsnett
1632	Richard Neile
1641	John Williams
1660	Accepted Frewen
1664	Richard Sterne
1683	John Dolben
1688	Thomas Lamplugh
1691	John Sharp
1714	William Dawes
1724	Lancelot Blackburn
1743	Thomas Herring
1747	Matthew Hutton
1757	John Gilben
1761	Roben Hay Drumond
1777	William Markham
1808	Edward Venables Vernon Harcourt
1847	Thomas Musgrave
1860	Charles Thomas Longley
1863	William Thomson
1891	William Connor Magee
1891	William Dalrymple Maclagan
1909	Cosmo Gordon Lang
1929	William Temple
1942	Cyril Forster Garbett
1956	Arthur Michael Ramsey
1961	Frederick Donald Coggan
1975	Stuart Yarwonh Blanch
1983	John Stapylton Habgood
1995	David Michael Hope*
2005	John Sentamu

*retired in March 2005 to become vicar of St Margaret's in Ilkley, Yorkshire

Patron Saints

accountants	Matthew
actors	Genesius, Vitus
advertising	Bernardino of Siena
airmen	Our Lady of Loretto, Theresa
animals	Francis of Assisi
archers	Sebastian
architects	Thomas, Barbara
Argentina	Our Lady of Lujan
army	Maurice
artists	Luke
astronauts	Joseph of Cupertino
astronomers	Dominic
athletes	Sebastian
Australia	Our Lady Help of Christians
Austria	Leopold
authors	Francis of Sales
bakers	Elizabeth of Hungary, Nicholas of Torentino, Zita
bankers	Matthew
barbers	Cosmas, Damian, Louis
bastards	John Francis Regis
battle	Archangel Michael
beekeepers	Ambrose
beggars	Martin of Tours
Belgium	Joseph
blacksmiths	Dunstan
Bolivia	Our Lady of Capucclana
bookkeepers	Matthew
booksellers	John of God
Brazil	Peter of Alcantara
brewers	Augustine of Hippo, Luke, Nicholas of Myra
bricklayers	Stephen
brides	Nicholas of Myra
bridges	John Nepomucen
broadcasters	Archangel Gabriel
Brussels	Michael
butchers	Anthony the Abbot, Luke, Adrian of Nicomedia
button-makers	Louis
builders	Vincent Ferrer, Barbara, Thomas
cab-drivers	Fiacre
Canada	Joseph, Anne (mother of Mary)
cancer victims	Peregrine Laziosi
caretakers	Joseph of Arimathea
candle-makers	Ambrose
cavalry	Martin of Tours
chaplains	John of Capistrano
charcoal burners	Alexander
childbirth	Gerard Majella, Margaret of Antioch
choirboys	Dominic Savio
church	Joseph
carpenters	Joseph
children	Nicholas
chorea	Vitus
civil servants	Thomas More
clergy	Gabriel Possenti
coffin bearers	Joseph of Arimathea
colleges	Thomas Aquinas
comedians	Vitus
condemned criminals	Dismas
cooks	Lawrence, Martha
craftsmen	Elegius
crippled	Giles
Cuba	Our Lady of Charity
Cyprus	Barnabas
Czech Republic	Wenceslas
dairy workers	Bridgid of Ireland
dancers	Vitus
deacons	Stephen
deaf	Francis of Sales
death	Archangel Michael, Margaret of Antioch
Denmark	Asgar/Canute
dentists	Apollonia
dieticians	Martha
disabled	Giles
disasters	Genevieve
doctors	Luke
domestics	Zita
Dominican Republic	Our Lady of Mercy
doubters	Thomas
drunkards	Martin of Tours
dyers	Maurice
earthquakes	Francis Borgia, Gregory the Wonderworker
ecologists	Francis of Assisi
eczema	Anthony the Abbot
Edinburgh	Giles
editors	John Bosco
Egypt	Mark
El Salvador	Our Lady of Peace
engineers	Patrick, Ferdinand III
England	George
epilepsy	Dympna, Vitus
Europe	Cyril, Benedict
examination candidates	Joseph of Cupertino
farmers	George, Isidore
fathers	Joseph
Finland	Henry
firemen	Florian
flying	Joseph of Cupertino
fishermen	Peter, Andrew
Florence	John the Baptist
florists	Dorothea, Therese
France	Denis
funeral directors	Joseph of Arimathea, Dismas
gardeners	Adelard, Phocas, Tryphon, Dorothea, Fiacre
Germany	Boniface
Glasgow	Kentigern (aka Mungo)
goldsmiths	Dunstan
gravediggers	Anthony, Joseph
Greece	Andrew, Nicholas, Paul
grocers	Michael
Guatemala	James the Greater
gunners	Barbara
haemorrhoids	Fiacre
hairdressers	Martin of Porres
Haiti	Our Lady of Perpetual Help
headaches	Teresa of Avila, Denis
heart patients	John of God
hernia sufferers	Cathal
Holland	Willibrord

horseriders	Martin of Tours
horses	Eligius, Hippolytus
hospitals	John of God, Camillus de Lellis, Vincent de Paul
hoteliers	Gentian, Amand
housewives	Anne, Martha, Zita
Hungary	Stephen
hunters	Eustace, Hubert
ice skaters	Edwina
Iceland	Olaf
India	Our Lady of the Assumption
infantrymen	Maurice
innkeepers	Amand, Martin of Tours, Gentian
Ireland	Patrick
Italy	Francis of Assisi
jewellers	Eligius (Eloi)
Jordan	John the Baptist
journalists	Francis of Sales
judges	John of Capistrano
jumping	Venantius
lame	Giles
lawyers	Genesius, Ivo, Thomas More
lepers	Giles
librarians	Jerome, Catherine of Alexandria
lighthouse keepers	Clement, Venerius
Lisbon	Vincent
London	Paul
lost articles	Anthony of Padua
lost causes	Jude
lovers	Valentine
Madagascar	Vincent de Paul
Madrid	Isidore
magistrates	Ferdinand III of Castile
Malta	Paul
marriage	John Francis Regis
masons	Thomas
mental illness	Dymphna
messengers	Archangel Gabriel
metalworkers	Anastasius, Eligius
Mexico	Joseph
midwives	Raymond Nonnatus
milliners	James the Greater
miners	Barbara, Anne (mother of Mary)
Moscow	Boris
motorcyclists	Our Lady of Grace
motorists	Christopher, Frances of Rome
motorways	John the Baptist
musicians/singers	Cecilia, Dunstan, Gregory
neurological disorders	Vitus
New Zealand	Our Lady Help of Christians
Norway	Olaf
numismatists	Eligius
nurses	Agatha, Raphael, Camillus of Lellis
orphans	Ivo of Kermartin
Oslo	Halivard
painters	Luke
Pakistan	Thomas, Francis Xavier
pallbearers	Joseph of Arimathea
Papua New Guinea	Archangel Michael
paralysed	Giles
paratroopers	Archangel Michael
Paris	Geneviève
pawnbrokers	Nicholas
perfumers	Nicholas of Myra
Peru	Joseph, Rose of Lima
pilots	Mary, Our Lady of Loreto
physicians	Luke
pig herders	Anthony
plasterers	Bartholomew
poets	Cecilia, David, Columbia
Poland	Stanislaus, Casimir
policemen	Michael
politicians	Thomas More
poor	Anthony of Padua, Lawrence
Portugal	George, Anthony
postal workers	Archangel Gabriel
pregnancy	Gerard Majella, Raymond Nonnatus
printers	Augustine of Hippo, John of God
prison officers	Hippolytus
quantity surveyors	Thomas
Quebec	John the Baptist
rabies victims	Hubert
radio	Archangel Gabriel
radiologists	Archangel Michael
Ripon	Wilfred
Rome	Peter
Russia	Andrew, Nicholas
sailors	Christopher, Cuthbert, Francis of Paolo, Dhocas
scholars	Bede, Bridgit, Jerome
scientists	Albert
Scotland	Andrew
scouts	George
sculptors	Claude
secretaries	Genesius
shoemakers	Crispin
singers	Gregory
skiers	Bernard of Montjoux
skin diseases	Anthony
soldiers	George, Joan of Arc, Sebastian
South Africa	Our Lady of the Assumption
Spain	James
speleologists	Benedict
stamp collectors	Archangel Gabriel
statesmen	Thomas More
students	Thomas Aquinas
surgeons	Cosmas, Damian
Sweden	Bridget, Eric
swimmers	Adjutor
Switzerland	Nicholas
tailors	Homobonus
tax collectors	Matthew
teachers	Catherine, Gregory
teenagers	Maria Goretti
telecommunications	Archangel Gabriel
telephone	Gabriel
television	Clare
thieves	Dismas
throat disorders	Blaise
toothache	Apollonia
travellers	Christopher
undertakers	Dismas
unmarried women	Nicholas of Myra
venereal disease	Fiacre
Venice	Mark
vets	Eligius (Eloi)
Vietnam	Joseph
volcanoes	Agatha
Wales	David
West Indies	Gertrude
wine merchants	Amand, Vincent
wine growers	Vincent
wool combers	Blaise
workers	Joseph
writers	Francis of Sales
yachtsmen	Adjutor

NB Almost everyone, everything and everywhere can be included under the auspices of a patron saint. Sometimes the affiliation lies in historical events and sometimes in ancient folklore and, more frequently still, homage is often paid to a particular saint for convenience, for example, cab-drivers call on St Fiacre as their protector because the Hotel St Fiacre in Paris was the first establishment to offer coaches for hire. Confusion often arises in this field as to why a particular saint has been adopted by a particular group. For example, St Martin of Tours is identified with innkeepers and drunks but is often depicted as a young mounted soldier. It should also be noted that many occupations have more than one recognised patron saint, and extra care should therefore be taken when compiling questions on this subject. For example, do not ask who is the patron saint of soldiers unless you are prepared to accept any of the three possible answers.

Archbishops of Canterbury

1	Augustine	597–604
2	Lawrence (Laurentius)	604–619
3	Mellitus	619–624
4	Justus	624–627
5	Honorius	627–653
6	Deusdedit	655–664
7	Theodore of Tarsus	668–690
8	Berhtwald (Beorhtweald)	693–731
9	Tatwine	731–734
10	Nothelm	735–739
11	Cuthbert (Cuthbeorht)	740–760
12	Bregowine (Breguwine)	761–764
13	Jaenberht (Jaenbeorht)	765–792
14	Aethelheard	793–805
15	Wulfred	805–832
16	Feologild	832
17	Ceolnoth	833–870
18	Aethelred	870–889
19	Piegmund	890–914
20	Aethelhelm	914–923
21	Wulfhelm	923–942
22	Oda	942–958
23	Aelfsige	959
24	Beorhthelm	959
25	Dunstan	960–988
26	Aethelgar	988–990
27	Sigeric Serio	990–994
28	Aelfric	995–1005
29	Aelfheah	1005–12
30	Lyfing	1013–20
31	Aethelnoth	1020–38
32	Eadsige	1038–50
33	Robert of Jumièges	1051–52
34	Stigand	1052–70
35	Lanfranc	1070–89
36	Anselm	1093–1109
37	Ralph d'Escures	1114–22
38	William of Corbeil	1123–36
39	Theobald	1138–61
40	Thomas à Becket	1162–70
41	Richard of Dover	1174–84
42	Baldwin	1184–90
43	Hubert Walter	1193–1205
44	Stephen Langton	1206–28

45	Richard le Grant	1229–31
46	Edmund Rich	1233–40
47	Boniface of Savoy	1241–70
48	Robert Kilwardby	1272–78
49	John Pecham	1279–92
50	Robert Winchelsey	1293–1313
51	Walter Reynolds	1313–27
52	Simon Mepham	1327–33
53	John Stratford	1333–48
54	Thomas Bradwardine	1348–49
55	Simon Islip	1349–66
56	Simon Langham	1366–68
57	William Whittlesey	1368–74
58	Simon Sudbury	1375–81
59	William Courtenay	1381–96
60	Thomas Arundel	1396–97
61	Roger Walden	1397–99
60	Thomas Arundel (restored)	1399–1414
62	Henry Chichele	1414–43
63	John Stafford	1443–52
64	John Kempe	1452–54
65	Thomas Bourchier	1454–86
66	John Morton	1486–1500
67	Henry Deane	1501–03
68	William Warham	1503–32
69	Thomas Cranmer	1533–56
70	Reginald Pole	1556–58
71	Matthew Parker	1559–75
72	Edmund Grindal	1575–83
73	John Whitgift	1583–1604
74	Richard Bancroft	1604–10
75	George Abbot	1611–33
76	William Laud	1633–45
77	William Juxon	1660–63
78	Gilbert Sheldon	1663–77
79	William Sancroft	1677–90
80	John Tillotson	1691–94
81	Thomas Tenison	1694–1715
82	William Wake	1715–37
83	John Potter	1737–47
84	Thomas Herring	1747–57
85	Matthew Hutton	1757–58
86	Thomas Secker	1758–68
87	Frederick Cornwallis	1768–83
88	John Moore	1783–1805
89	Charles Manners Sutton	1805–28
90	William Howley	1828–48
91	John Bird Sumner	1848–62
92	Charles Thomas Longley	1862–68
93	Archibald Campbell Tait	1868–82
94	Edward White Benson	1883–96
95	Frederick Temple	1896–1902
96	Randall Thomas Davidson	1903–28
97	Cosmo Gordon Lang	1928–42
98	William Temple	1942–44
99	Geoffrey Francis Fisher	1945–61
100	Arthur Michael Ramsey	1961–74
101	Frederick Donald Coggan	1974–80
102	Robert Alexander Runcie	1980–90
103	George Carey	1990–2002
104	Rowan Williams	2002–2012
105	Justin Welby	2012–

Miscellaneous Information

Archbishop of Canterbury: 100th	Arthur Michael Ramsey
Archbishop: remained bishop	Stigand remained bishop of Worcester
Aristotle philosophies: taught at Oxford	Edmund of Abingdon: first to do so
Augustine landed: where	Isle of Thanet AD 597
buried	SS Peter and Paul (later St Augustine's), Canterbury
converted King	King Aethelbert of Kent
founded church	Christ Church Canterbury
order of monks	Benedictines
Roman prior of	St Andrews Benedictine monastery
welcomed by	King Aethelbert of Kent
Bishop of London	Richard Chartres (132nd) since 26 January 1996. Traditional residence was Fulham Palace but now The Old Deanery, Dean's Court, London
Book of Common Prayer: drew up	Thomas Cranmer
born on Greek island	Frederick Temple
Carthusian monk	Boniface of Savoy
Catholic archbishop: last	Reginald Pole
Charles I: ministered on scaffold	William Juxon
Edmund Rich: also known as	Edmund of Abingdon
English-born archbishop: first	Deusdedit
Father and son: only holders	Frederick and William Temple
Henry Chichele: founded	St John's and All Souls colleges at Oxford 1437
heresy: convicted of	Thomas Cranmer (burned at stake)
high treason: accused of	William Laud (beheaded on Tower Hill)
investiture controversy: resolved by	Synod of Rockingham (temporarily)
Lambeth Conference	decennial meeting of Anglican bishops
Lanfranc: originally trained as	lawyer
secured Crown for	William II (Rufus)
Laurentius' dream	dream of St Peter reminded him of his mission
Lombardy: born	Lanfranc and Anselm
Maidstone Hospital: founder	Boniface of Savoy
married Oliver Cromwell's niece	John Tillotson 1664
Mellitus: prayer legend	caused wind to divert fire from Canterbury church
Morton's Fork:	�rich pay taxes; poor are considered to be concealing wealth
murdered in Canterbury Cathedral	Thomas à Becket
murdered during Peasant's Revolt	Simon Sudbury (first beheading on Tower Hill)
nicknames: John Whitgift	Little black husband (by Elizabeth I)
Matthew Parker	Nosey Parker
official residence of Archbishop of Canterbury	Lambeth Palace, and Old Palace Canterbury
ordination of women	promulgated in the General Synod in Feb. 1994
pallium	a mantle, and symbol of papal approval of archiepiscopal appointment
Piers Gaveston excommunicated by	Robert Winchelsey
plague: died of	Thomas Bradwardine
plot against William I: detected	Lanfranc
position created by	Pope Gregory I
Primate of	All England
prior of Bec Benedictine monastery	Lanfranc, Anselm, Theobald
Protestant archbishop: first	Thomas Cranmer
published *Antiquities of Greece*	John Potter
Queen Elizabeth II: crowned	Geoffrey Fisher
refused oath of allegiance	William Sancroft: to William and Mary
Repton School: former headmasters	William Temple and Geoffrey Fisher

Richard I: governor in absentia	Hubert Walter
Rochester: first bishop of	St Justus
Scholasticism: founder of	St Anselm
Sheldonian Theatre, Oxford: built	Gilbert Sheldon
son-in-law of Archbishop Tait	Randall Thomas Davidson
St Dunstan: secured crown for	St Edward the Martyr AD 975
Stigand: excommunicated by	Pope Nicholas II 1059. Uncanonical behaviour caused Pope to support William I's invasion
succeeded Thomas Arnold at Rugby	Archibald Campbell Tait
Synod of Whitby 663/664	Northumbria decided to follow Roman Church
Tarsus: born in	Theodore
Theobald: patron of	Thomas à Becket, John of Salisbury, Vacarius
Thomas à Becket: also known as	Thomas of London
born	Cheapside, London
shrine despoiled by	Henry VIII
York: first bishop of	St Paulinus

The Bible

Genesis

God creates Adam from dust.
Garden of Eden planted.
Trees of Life and Knowledge.
Adam names all living beasts.
Eve is created from Adam's rib.
Serpent deceives Eve into eating forbidden fruit.
Birth of Cain and Abel.
Cain becomes tiller of the soil, and Abel a shepherd.
Cain kills Abel and when asked by the Lord as to his whereabouts replies, 'Am I my brother's keeper?'
Cain is 'marked' by God and flees to the land of Nod.
Cain's wife gives birth to a son, Enoch, and builds a city in his name.
Adam's third son Seth is fathered at the age of 130 and Adam dies at age 930.
Methuselah is sired by Enoch (descendant of Seth, not Cain) and lives for 969 years.
Methuselah sires Lamech who subsequently sires Noah.
Noah begets three sons: Shem, Ham, and Japheth. He was 500 years old.
God destroys man by bringing great flood but reprieves Noah.
Noah (aged 600) builds an ark of gopher wood (300 x 50 cubits, and 30 cubits high), three storeys in total.
God directs Noah to take aboard seven of each type of clean beast but just two of each unclean.
There were eight humans on the ark, i.e. Noah and his sons plus their wives.
Ark comes to rest on Mt Ararat.
Noah sends forth a raven and then a dove, which comes back with an olive leaf to show that the rains have ceased.
Noah becomes the first 'drunken man' after planting a vineyard.
Noah lives for 350 years after the flood and dies aged 950.
Noah's great grandson, Nimrod, begins to be a mighty one on the earth.
Nimrod's kingdom begins with Babel, Erech, Accad, Calneh and Shinar.
The whole earth is of one language, one speech.
After the tower of Babel is built, the Lord scatters the people abroad to confound their language.
The Lord calls unto Abram and blesses him.
Abram, with his wife Sarai and nephew Lot, journey into the land of Canaan.
Abram and Lot return from Egypt, after Sarai is taken by the Pharaoh.
Lot moves to live in Sodom, but the men of Sodom are wicked and sinners.
Then comes the 'Battle of the Kings'.
At the battle in the vale of Siddim, the kings of Sodom and Gomorrah are beaten and fall into slimepits.
Lot is taken prisoner by the victors.
Abram attacked at Hobah, and gains the release of Lot, all his goods, the women and the people.
Abram's wife Sarai cannot bear him children; she therefore gives Abram her maid Hagar, who bears him Ishmael.
Abram is 86 years old when he fathers Ishmael.
The Lord renames Abram – Abraham.
The Lord makes a covenant with Abraham which states that every male child is to be circumcised at eight days old.
The Lord renames Sarai – Sarah.
At the age of 90, Sarah bears Abraham a son, Isaac.
Two angels come to see Lot at the gates of Sodom.
The men of Sodom are struck blind.
Lot, his wife and two daughters leave Sodom.
They are told not to look behind them.
Sodom and Gomorrah are destroyed by the Lord.
Lot's wife looks behind her and is turned into a pillar of salt.
Lot's two daughters get him drunk so that they may 'lie' with him to preserve his seed.
Lot's elder daughter has a son, Moab.
Lot's younger daughter also has a son called Ben-ammi.
Abraham tells Abimelech, king of Gerar, that Sarah is his sister, and she is taken by Abimelech.
Abraham casts Hagar and his son Ishmael away.
Abimelech makes a covenant with Abraham and returns to the land of the Philistines.
Abraham has his faith tested by the Lord.
Sarah dies at the age of 127.
A wife is sought for Isaac.
Abraham's servant finds and meets Rebekah.
Rebekah consents to go to Isaac; she then becomes his wife.
Abraham takes a second wife, Keturah.
Keturah bears him Zimran, Jokshan, Medan, Midian, Ishbak and Shuah.
Abraham dies aged 175.
Ishmael dies aged 137.
Ishmael has 12 sons - Nebajoth, Kedar, Adbeel, Mibsam, Mishma, Dumah, Massa, Hadar, Tems, Jetur, Naphish, Kedemah.
Rebekah gives birth to twins – Esau (a hunter) and Jacob (a tent-maker).
Esau sells his birthright to Jacob for a mess of pottage (bread and lentil stew).
Jacob deceives his father, Isaac, into believing that he is his brother Esau.
When Esau finds out about the deceit he threatens Jacob.

While searching for a wife, Jacob dreams of the ladder reaching from earth to the heavens.
Jacob dreams of the Angels of God ascending and descending on the ladder.
Jacob meets Rachel.
Jacob works for seven years in order to win Rachel.
Jacob takes both Rachel and her younger sister Leah as his wives.
Rachel is barren, but Leah bears Jacob a son, Reuben.
Leah later bears Simeon, Levi and Judah.
Rachel gives Jacob her handmaiden, Bilhah, to take as a wife.
Bilhah bears Dan and Naphtali.
Leah gives her maid, Zilpah, to Jacob to take as a wife.
Zilpah bears Gad and Asher.
Leah bears Jacob a fifth son, Issachar, a sixth, Zebulun, and a daughter, Dinah.
Rachel herself then conceives and bears a son, Joseph.
Jacob becomes very rich, with many cattle, maidservants, menservants, camels and asses.
Jacob has a vision at Mahanaim.
Jacob sends messengers to Esau, requesting his return to Laban.
Esau comes to meet him with 400 men.
Jacob sends a present to Esau of various animals.
When Jacob meets Esau, Jacob bows seven times.
Esau runs to meet Jacob, and embraces him. They both weep.
Jacob builds an altar at Shalem, and calls it El-elohe-Israel.
Dinah is defiled by Shechem, son of Hamor, the Hivite.
Simeon and Levi slay all the males of the city, and take Dinah from Shechem's house.
Jacob is unhappy with his sons, because the Canaanites and Perizzites will now rise against him.
God tells Jacob to move to Beth-el.
Jacob and his household journey to Beth-el, build an altar and call it El-beth-el.
Jacob is renamed Israel.
Rachel dies while giving birth to Benjamin.
While away from his household, Reuben lies with Bilhah, his father's concubine.
Jacob's sons now number twelve.
Jacob goes to his father, Isaac, at Hebron, where Isaac dies, aged 180.
Jacob favours Joseph over his brothers.
Joseph has dreams which cause his brothers to hate him.
At first Joseph's brothers plot to kill him.
Joseph's brothers sell him into slavery with the Ishmaelites.
The brothers dip Joseph's long garment in goat's blood, and take it to Jacob.
Jacob mourns his son's death.
Judah meets and takes the daughter of a Canaanite, named Shuah.
Shuah bears three sons: Er, Onan and Shelah.
Judah takes a wife for Er, whose name is Tamar.
Er displeases the Lord and He slays him.
Judah tells Onan to marry Tamar, his brother's widow.
Onan spills his seed on the ground; this displeases the Lord also and He slays Onan.
Judah tells Tamar to live in his house and wait until Shelah is grown.
Tamar deceives Judah into thinking she is a harlot.
When Judah hears that Tamar is pregnant, he orders her to be burnt.
She is spared when Judah realises he is the father of her child.
Tamar has twins, Pharez and Zarah.
Joseph is sold in Egypt to Potiphar, an officer of the Pharaoh.
Joseph is promoted to overseer.
Joseph's master's wife asks him to lie with her, but Joseph refuses.
She later pulls his garment off him and Joseph flees.
She lies to Potiphar, saying that Joseph came to her to force her to lie with him.
Joseph is imprisoned in the King's prison.
He interprets the dreams of the Pharaoh's officers.
After being in prison for two years, the Pharaoh has a dream and is told of Joseph.
Joseph interprets the Pharaoh's dream.
Joseph foretells the famine.
Joseph is released from prison and lives in the Pharaoh's house.
The famine is worldwide, but Egypt has stockpiled corn.
All the countries of the world come to Egypt to buy corn.
Jacob sends Joseph's brothers to Egypt to buy corn.
Joseph is now governor of the land.
His brothers come and bow before him.
Joseph recognises his brothers but they not him.
Joseph accuses his brothers of being spies.
Joseph supplies them with food and returns all their money to them.
At an inn the brothers realise that Joseph has returned their money.
Joseph insists that his brothers bring Benjamin to him.
Israel sends all the brothers to Egypt.
All the brothers are taken to Joseph's house for a feast.
Again Joseph fills their sacks with food and also returns their money.
Joseph puts his silver cup in the sack of Benjamin, the youngest brother.
Joseph's stewards find the silver cup and accuse the brothers of theft.
Judah petitions Joseph, asking that Benjamin be allowed to return to his father.
Joseph weeps and makes himself known to his brothers.
Pharaoh commands the brothers to bring back to Egypt all their families.
They tell Israel that Joseph is alive, but Israel does not believe them.
When Israel sees the wagons that Pharaoh has given to them, he believes.
Israel and his entire family return to Egypt to see Joseph.
Joseph meets his father at Goshen.
Israel is given Goshen by Pharaoh.
When people run out of money to buy bread, Joseph sells bread in exchange for livestock.
Joseph buys all the land of Egypt, except the land of the priests.
Joseph gives the people seed to grow their own crops.
The people must give one-fifth of their crops to Pharaoh.
Joseph takes his two sons, Manasseh and Ephraim, to Israel, where Israel blesses them.

Israel prophesies to his twelve sons, then dies, aged 147.
Israel insists that he be buried with his ancestors.
Pharaoh allows Joseph to travel to Canaan for the burial.
Afterwards Joseph and his brothers return to Egypt.
The brothers think that now Israel is dead, Joseph may seek retribution.
Joseph reassures them.
Joseph dies aged 110 and is buried in Egypt.

Exodus

Israel and his sons enter Egypt, each with his household.
Joseph is already in Egypt.
Their offspring multiply at an extraordinary rate until the land is filled with them.
A new king of Egypt becomes worried that the sons of Israel are growing so numerous.
The sons of Israel are oppressed.
The more they are oppressed, the more they multiply.
Eventually the Egyptians make the sons of Israel slaves.
The king of Egypt orders the Hebrew midwives, Shiphrah and Puah, to put to death any male child at birth.
Fearing God, the midwives disobey the Egyptian king.
Finally Pharaoh orders all his people to throw every newborn son into the River Nile.
A man from the house of Levi takes a daughter of Levi, and she becomes pregnant.
She conceals her son for three months.
She then places him in a basket, in the reeds, on the River Nile.
Pharaoh's daughter finds him, and realises he is a child of the Hebrews.
The child grows up and becomes a son to the daughter of Pharaoh.
She names him Moses.
Moses sees an Egyptian striking a Hebrew; he strikes the Egyptian down and kills him.
Pharaoh hears about it and tries to kill Moses.
Moses runs away to the land of Midian.
Moses meets the priest of Midian, who gives his daughter Zipporah to him.
Zipporah bears Moses a son, Gershom.
Moses becomes a shepherd.
While with the flock, Moses comes to Horeb. Here, an Angel appears to him in a flaming bush.
God speaks to Moses, instructing him to bring the sons of Israel out of Egypt.
Moses wants a sign that this is God.
God tells Moses to throw his rod on to the ground and it becomes a serpent.
God then tells Moses to grab the serpent by its tail, and it becomes a rod.
God gives Moses other signs, turning his hand into a leper's hand and restoring it and turning water from the Nile into blood.
Moses meets Aaron, his brother.
Moses returns to Egypt with his wife and family.
Moses and Aaron meet with the elders of the sons of Israel.
Moses and Aaron meet with Pharaoh and ask that the Hebrews may go into the wilderness for a festival.
Pharaoh refuses permission for the Hebrews to go into the wilderness.
Pharaoh makes the sons of Israel work harder.
The officers of the sons of Israel blame Moses and Aaron for this harsh treatment.
Moses promises to deliver the sons of Israel from this oppression.
Moses and Aaron again meet with Pharaoh; Moses is now 80 years old and Aaron 83.
Aaron throws down his rod in front of Pharaoh and it becomes a serpent.
The magic-practising priests of Egypt do the same thing.
Aaron's rod swallows their rods.
Moses meets Pharaoh on the bank of the Nile, strikes the water with his rod and turns the water into blood.
The magic-practising priests proceed to do the same thing.
Moses tells Pharaoh that unless the people are allowed to go into the wilderness, there will be a plague of frogs. Aaron waves his staff over the Nile and a plague of frogs come to land.
The magic-practising priests do the same thing.
Aaron strikes the dust of Egypt, and it all becomes a swarm of gnats.
The magic practising priests attempts to do the same but they fail.
Moses tells Pharaoh that if the people are not released into the wilderness, gadfly will infest every house.
Gadfly infest every house in Egypt.
Finally Pharaoh calls Moses and Aaron and tells them to take their people into the wilderness.
The gadfly disappear, so Pharaoh does not allow the people to go into the wilderness.
Moses tells Pharaoh that if the people are not released, a pestilence will strike every animal in Egypt.
Moses takes a handful of soot, throws it in the air, in sight of Pharaoh, and it becomes boils and blisters upon man and beast.
The magic-practising priests are unable to attempt to copy this because the boils are affecting them.
Moses again goes to Pharaoh and promises a hailstorm that will kill every man and beast in the field .
The next day, a storm of hail, thunder and lightning strikes Egypt.
Pharaoh now calls Moses and Aaron and release the people to go into the wilderness.
Once the storm stops, Pharaoh again refuses to release the people into the wilderness.
Moses and Aaron see Pharaoh and tell him that a plague of locusts will appear tomorrow unless the people are released.
Locusts covers all of the land of Egypt.
Moses stretches out his arm and darkness falls all over Egypt.
The firstborn of every family in Egypt is threatened with death.
Instructions for the feast of the Passover are given to Moses by the Lord.
At midnight, the firstborn of every man and every beast dies.
Finally Pharaoh tells the people to leave.
The exodus takes place.
The people of Israel reach the Red Sea.
A pillar of cloud by daytime and a pillar of fire by night lead them into the wilderness.
Pharaoh proceeds to give chase when he realises that the people are escaping.
When Pharaoh reaches the people they are camped by the sea.
Moses stretches his hand over the sea and it parts, allowing the sons of Israel to walk through the Red Sea. The Egyptians follows them into the Red Sea.
Moses again stretches his hand over the sea and the water returns to its normal state, drowning the Egyptians.
Moses leads the people into the wilderness for three days; they reach Marrah, but cannot drink the water because it is bitter.
The Lord directs Moses to a tree, which he throws into the water and the water becomes sweet.
At the wilderness of Sin, the sons of Israel begin to murmur against Moses and Aaron.
Quails arrive in the evening, and in the morning the wilderness is covered in bread.
By collecting double bread on the sixth day, and resting on the seventh, the Sabbath law is observed.
The sons of Israel eat the manna for 40 years.
At Massah, Moses is instructed to strike a stone with his rod, and water comes out of the rock.

The Amalekites attack the sons of Israel.
Moses instructs Joshua to choose men to go and fight the Amalekites.
Moses watches from the top of a hill.
When Moses lifts his rod, the Israelites are superior.
When Moses lowers his rod, the Amalekites are superior.
Moses' father-in-law, Jethro, along with his wife Zipporah, his two children, Gershom and Eliezer, and Moses' two sons, visits Moses in the wilderness.
Jethro advises Moses to appoint Judges.
Moses takes his advice.
The people go to meet their God on Mount Sinai.
The Lord calls Moses to the top of the mountain.
Moses then returns down the mountain to take Aaron back to the top with him.
Moses is given the Ten Commandments.
Rules on how slaves are treated, including 'eye for eye'.
Further rules covering theft, seduction, sorcery, bestiality, bribery and many more are given to Moses.
Three times a year the Israelites must celebrate a festival to the Lord.
Boundary of the 'promised land' is set, from the Red Sea to the Sea of the Philistines and from the wilderness to the river.
Moses goes up the mountain to receive the stone tablets.
Moses stays on the mountain for 40 days and 40 nights.
The people are instructed to build an ark of acacia wood, two and a half cubits in length, and one and a half cubits deep.
The ark must be overlaid with gold, both inside and outside.
The ark must have four gold rings, two either side.
The people must make two poles of acacia wood and overlay them with gold.
These poles go through the rings in order for the ark to be carried.
The poles must not be removed from the rings.
The commandments must be placed within the ark.
The people are instructed to build a tabernacle, with all its utensils.
The design of the garments to be worn by priests is given to Moses.
Instructions for the installation of priests are given.
Instructions for keeping the Sabbath are given.
When the Lord finishes speaking with Moses on Mount Sinai, he gives to Moses two tablets of stone.
The people are frustrated because Moses is on Mount Sinai for so long.
The people persuade Aaron to make a 'God' for them.
After melting down the people's jewellery, he makes a golden calf.
The making of the golden calf angers the Lord.
When Moses sees the golden calf, he is so angry he smashes the two tablets and destroys the golden calf.
Moses seeks out the loyal people and the sons of Levi gather themselves to him.
Moses sends the sons of Levi back into the camp to kill the sinners; they kill about 3,000.
Moses moves his tent outside the camp and calls it a tent of meeting.
Whenever Moses enters the tent, a pillar of cloud descends and stands at the entrance.
The Lord instructs Moses to carve out two tablets of stone and the Lord will rewrite the commandments.
The Lord will not allow Moses to see his face.
The Lord repeats the terms of the covenant between himself and the people of Israel.
Moses again comes down from Mount Sinai with the two tablets.
The people contribute gifts to the Lord.
Bezalel and Oholiab are selected for special teachings and wisdom.
The people begin to make the cloth and other finery for the tabernacle.
Once completed, the Lord's glory fills the tabernacle.

Leviticus

Instructions for offerings of animals and grain are given to the people of Israel.
All grain offerings must be seasoned with salt.
A young bull must be sacrificed for a sin of a priest.
A young goat must be sacrificed for a sin of a chieftain.
Other sins demand other offerings.
Even unintentional sins must be paid for with offerings.
The eating of fat or blood is forbidden.
Aaron and his sons are installed as priests.
Nadab and Abihu, sons of Aaron, make an offering to the Lord that was not prescribed.
Fire from heaven consumes both.
Instructions as to which animals and fish are clean or unclean are given.
Instructions for the purification of women are given.
Priests are to make leprosy tests; anybody with leprosy is declared unclean.
Garments worn by lepers are also unclean.
Instructions for offerings in the case of a cleansed leper are given.
Uncleanliness in the case of male and female discharges is explained.
Atonement Day procedures are given.
The laws regarding incest are given.
Similarly laws regarding sodomy and bestiality are given.
Laws regarding gleaning of crops are given.
Laws regarding slander, interbreeding, fruit trees and magic are given.
Similarly, laws regarding spiritism, respect of parents and adultery are given.
The law that priests are to be undefiled is explained.
Laws regarding Sabbath, Pentecost, Day of Atonement, festival of Booths and loaves of showbread explained.
The fiftieth year is to become a Jubilee.
The Jubilee year is also a year of restorations. For example, if a man sells his house, he must repurchase it in the fiftieth year.
Laws regarding the help to be given to the poor are explained.
Regarding the poor, money given must bear no usury or interest charges.
No idols or images of the Lord are to be worshipped.
The Lord explains the blessings that the people will enjoy if they keep his laws and commandments.
The Lord explains the chastisements that the people will suffer if they do not keep his laws and commandments.
Values are put on sanctifying your soul, animal, house, field, etc. to the Lord.

Numbers

(Numbers is Bemidbar in Hebrew and means 'In the wilderness'.)
The Lord tells Moses to register every male over 20 years of age.
The Lord also names the assembly; all are chieftains of the tribes of Israel.
The tribes are registered for the army.
All are registered except the Levites.
Moses is told to appoint the Levites over the tabernacle and all the utensils.
When the people set up camp, each tribe must camp with its (three-tribe) division.

Each tribe is designated a place to camp, starting with the (three-tribe) division of Judah eastmost.
The other tribes are designated a place in camp working westwards.
The tribe of Levi must minister to Aaron, and must keep their obligation to him.
Moses registers all the male Levites from the age of one month upwards.
Each of the families of Levi are given a task to perform regarding the tabernacle and the utensils.
Following instructions from Moses, all lepers, persons with discharges and anyone unclean are sent out of the camp.
A water test is explained, to test for jealousy.
If a man or woman takes a special vow to live as a Nazirite, they must stay away from grapes, wine and intoxicating liquor.
Also during the time of living as a Nazirite, no razor should touch a hair.
The further rules of the special vows of living as a Nazirite are explained.
The wording of the Lord's blessing is given to Moses. It is: May the Lord bless you and keep you, May the Lord make his face shine toward you and may he favour you, May the Lord lift up his face toward you and assign peace to you.
Having had all the laws and commandments explained to him, Moses now anoints the tabernacle.
All the chieftains make offerings of grain and cattle, of silver bowls, of other animals, which Moses accepts.
These offerings continue for eleven days.
On the twelfth day an offering by Naphtali is made; this is the inaugural offering at the altar.
The Lord tells Moses to instruct Aaron to light the seven lamps.
Moses is instructed to take the Levites among the people and cleanse them.
Instructions for the cleansing are given.
The Lord explains to Moses the preparation for the Passover.
The Lord instructs Moses to make two trumpets of silver.
These are to be used for convening the assembly or breaking up the camp.
If one trumpet is blown, the chieftains meet with Moses.
If two trumpets are blown, the whole assembly must meet with Moses.
On the twentieth day of the second month, of the third year, the cloud lifts and the people begin to leave the wilderness.
Moses asks Hobab to join the people going to Israel, but Hobab says that he wants to return to his own people.
Moses pleads with Hobab, and he joins Moses and the people.
Some of the people begin to complain about being in the wilderness.
This angers the Lord, and He sends down fire.
The people begin to cry for meat and fish.
Moses asks the Lord for help, because he feels he cannot cope.
The Lord tells Moses to select 70 of the oldest men, take them to the meeting tent, and He will place some of the spirit on them.
The spirit also falls on Eldad and Medad, who were not in the meeting tent, and they begin acting as prophets.
A wind blows quails from the coast to the camp.
Those people who showed selfish craving are slaughtered by the Lord.
Miriam and Aaron begin opposing Moses.
The Lord tells Moses to take Miriam and Aaron to the meeting tent, where He will speak with them.
The Lord is so angry that Miriam is struck with leprosy.
Moses pleads for mercy, and after seven days in quarantine, she is allowed back into the camp.
Moses sends out a man from each tribe, each a chieftain, to spy out the land of Canaan.
After 40 days they return to Moses; ten spies give bad reports.
The people begin to rebel.
The Lord is very angry that the people do not respect Him; He tells Moses that He will strike them with pestilence.
Moses pleads on their behalf.
The punishment for rebellion is to remain in the wilderness for 40 years.
Some of the people decide to leave the camp without Moses and the ark.
These people are defeated by the Amalekites and Canaanites.
Moses is instructed to tell the people of Isreal how they must render up burnt offerings on entering the promised land.
Moses is instructed to tell the people how they must atone for a sin by mistake.
Anyone who commits a deliberate sin must die.
A man collecting pieces of wood on the Sabbath is stoned to death.
Korah, Dathan and Abiram, together with 250 rebels, rise against Moses.
All the rebels are instructed to attend a meeting, each carrying a fire holder.
The earth swallows up Korah, Dathan and Abiram, their households and anything belonging to them.
A fire comes from the Lord and consumes the 250 rebels.
Some of the people still complain, so the Lord brings forth a scourge on them.
Moses tells Aaron to go among them and atone for their sins.
This Aaron does, and eventually stops the scourge.
This scourge kills 14,700 people.
A rod is taken from each of the twelve houses of Israel, placed in the meeting tent, and the Lord chooses one rod to bud.
Aaron's rod, for the house of Levi, has budded.
The Lord explains to Aaron the obligations of Levi.
Moses is instructed again regarding cleansing, especially regarding a man who dies in a tent.
The people move into the wilderness of Zin.
Here Miriam dies and is buried.
The people now have no water and reproach Moses and Aaron.
The Lord instructs Moses to strike a rock and water will come forth.
Moses strikes the rock twice and water enough for all the people and beasts comes forth.
These waters are called the Waters of Meribah.
Moses sends messengers to the king of Edom, to seek permission to pass through his land.
The king of Edom refuses.
The people turn away and travel to Mount Hor.
On Mount Hor, Moses strips Aaron of his clothes and places them on Eleazar (Aaron's son).
Aaron then dies.
The people weep for Aaron for 30 days.
The Canaanite king of Arad begins to attack the people and takes some captives.
The Lord intervenes and strikes down the Canaanites.
The people continue to trek around the land of Edom, but are not happy.
Some of the people rebel, so the Lord sends poisonous serpents among them and many die.
Moses is instructed to make a copper serpent and place it on a pole.
Anyone who was bitten by the serpents will look at the copper serpent and will live.
Moses sends messengers to Sihon, king of the Amorites, requesting permission to pass through his land.
Sihon refuses, and gathers his people and begins to fight the Israelites at Jahaz.
Sihon is defeated and the Israelites take possession of his land.
The Israelites now attack Ogm, the king of Bashan; they defeat him and take possession of his land.
Moab now grows very frightened of the Israelites.
Balak, the king of Moab, sends messengers to Balaam.

Balaam refuses to help.

Balak sends more messengers, more important messengers than at first.

Balaam goes with them to Balak, but on the journey meets with the Lord's angel, which only Balaam's she-ass sees.

Balaam beats his she-ass, and passes by the angel by walking in a field.

The angel reappears at a narrow place; again only Balaam's she-ass sees the angel.

Balaam beats his she-ass and he passes the angel by walking alongside the wall.

The angel reappears at a place where he cannot pass by; the she-ass lies down in the road.

Balaam beats his she-ass again.

The Lord makes the she-ass speak.

She asks Balaam, 'Why have you beaten me three times?'

Balaam says that if he had a sword he would have killed her.

The angel appears to Balaam and asks why he beats his she-ass.

Balaam continues his journey to Moab.

Balaam begins to speak the words that the Lord has put into his mouth.

He orders Balak to build seven altars.

He also orders him to provide seven bulls and seven rams.

A bull and a ram are offered on each altar.

Balaam refuses to help Balak.

Balaam proceeds to utter four proverbial statements, all the word of the Lord.

Balak is foiled.

Israel abides in Shittim and the people begin to commit whoredom with the daughters of Moab.

Israel joins himself unto Baal-peor and the anger of the Lord is blazed against him.

The Lord tells Moses to take the heads of the people and hang them up before him.

Zimri, a child of Israel, brings a Midianite woman into the sight of Moses.

Phinehas, son of Eleazar, son of Aaron, pierces both the man and woman and the plague is scourged.

The Lord tells Moses to vex the Midianites and smite them.

After the plague the Lord tells Moses and Eleazar to take the children of Israel, from 20 years onwards, out of Egypt.

Reuben and his descendants, numbering 250, are swallowed by the earth and become a sign.

The sons of Korah do not die.

Census is taken of eight more tribes and the land is divided.

Joshua is appointed to succeed Moses.

The procedures for various feast days and solemn days are established.

Moses equips an army to slay the Midianites.

The Lord speaks to Moses on the plains of Moab, by the Jordan at Jericho, and tells him to dwell in Canaan.

Deuteronomy The fifth book of the Old Testament is written in the form of a farewell address by Moses to the Israelites before they enter the Promised Land of Canaan. The speeches recall Israel's past, reiterate laws and emphasise that observance of these laws is essential for the well-being of the people. The title Deuteronomy derives from the Greek meaning 'copy', although the Hebrew translation means 'words'.

Joshua The book of Joshua was written while the people of Israel were exiles in Babylonia. It can be divided into three sections, i.e. the conquest of Canaan, the distribution of the land and Joshua's farewell address and death.

This book contains the destruction of the Wall of Jericho.

Judges The book of Judges was written at about the same time as the book of Joshua and the Judges were the leaders of Israel.

Noteworthy events are the death of Joshua and the birth and death of Samson.

Ruth The central character is a Moabite woman who marries the son of a Judaean couple living in Moab.

Ruth moves to Judah with her mother-in-law, Naomi, and becomes the wife of Boaz. She bears Obed, the grandfather of David,

Samuel 1 Samuel anoints Saul as the first King of Israel and the book tells further of the exploits of his son Jonathan.

The book continues with the story of David conquering Goliath and his great friendship with Jonathan.

The book concludes with Abigail giving good counsel to David, Saul visiting the Witch of Endor, and the ultimate death of both Saul and Jonathan on Mount Gilboa.

Samuel 2 David is anointed king at age 30. He rules for a further 40 years.

David commits adultery with Bathsheba, the wife of Uriah the Hittite, and plots his death so he can marry her himself.

The Lord sends Nathan, the anointer of David, to reprove him for his deed by telling him a parable of a ewe lamb.

The Lord takes the life of the first-born of David and Bathsheba as penance.

David and Bathsheba soon have another child, Solomon, and he is loved by the Lord.

David's son Absalom plots the death of his brother Amnon, for forcing his sister Tamar.

Absalom is killed during the civil war and is mourned by David.

Kings 1 Zadok the Priest anoints Solomon as king.

David eventually dies.

The Lord appears to Solomon in a dream and grants a request and is pleased that he asks for wisdom.

Solomon builds a great temple as a place of worship to the Lord and also a great house for himself.

Queen of Sheba visits King Solomon and is impressed by his demeanour and they exchange gifts.

Solomon's heart moves away from the Lord in his old age and he is told the kingship will be removed from his son.

Solomon dies and is succeeded by his son, Rehoboam.

The Lord's words come true as Jeroboam replaces Rehoboam as king of all Israel except Judah.

The divided kingdom of Israel is eventually ruled by Ahab, son of Omri.

Ahab takes Jezebel for a wife and sets up an altar to Baal in Samaria.

Elijah the Tishbite informs Ahab there will be a drought and indeed no rain falls for 3½ years.

Ahab tries to buy the vineyard of Naboth the Jezreelite but is refused.

Ahab's wife Jezebel plots the death of Naboth to gain possession of his vineyard.

Ahab is slain in battle with the Syrians.

Kings 2 Elijah is taken up into heaven by a whirlwind and is succeeded by his pupil, Elisha.

Jezebel is thrown out of a window and killed.

Elisha dies and is buried; a dead man laid on his bones comes to life.

The Lord is incensed by the Israelites and removes them, leaving only the tribe of Judah.

Nebuchadnezzar II, the king of Babylon, destroys Jerusalem.

Chronicles 1 The first book of Chronicles details genealogies from Adam up to and including the reign of David.

The chronicler used the books of Samuel and Kings as his main source, although modifications were made.

Chronicles 2 The second book of Chronicles details the reign of Solomon to the end of the Babylonian exile.

The chronicler has ignored the northern kingdom of Samaria.

Ezra Ezra continues the history of Israel from the end of the Babylonian exile.

The chronicler details the rising of the Persian Empire from its first king, Cyrus the Great.

Nehemiah The chronicler continues the story of Israel in the time of another Jewish leader, Nehemiah, who was released from captivity in *c.* 444 BC, during the reign of Artaxerxes, king of Persia.

The rebuilding of Jerusalem is highlighted and the great wall is built.

Esther Esther is the Jewish wife of the Persian King Ahasuerus (Xerxes I).

Esther persuades the king to retract an order for the general annihilation of Jews throughout the Empire.

The book explains how the feast of Purim came to be celebrated by the Jews.

Job The book of Job is written in the form of a series of speeches whereby Job disputes with three friends and the Lord.
Job proclaims his innocence and injustice of his suffering while his friends (Job's comforters) blame his sin.
Job personifies poverty and patience.

Psalms The book of Psalms consists of 150 sacred poems, which are meant to be sung.
Usually divided into five sections, i.e. psalms 1–41, 42–72, 73–89, 90–106, 107–150.
The best-known psalm is no. 23, 'The Lord is my Shepherd'.
Psalm 51 is often called the 'Neck' verse as its recitation would save the neck of those claiming Benefit of Clergy.
Although the authors are of doubtful origin, 73 psalms are attributed to David.

Proverbs Book of wisdom with moral and ethical relevance, in a similar vein to the book of Job but with more finite thoughts.
At the start of the text the proverbs are attributed to Solomon but it is known that many of them were written after his time.

Ecclesiastes Another book of wisdom, which takes a fatalistic view of life and asks man not to question God's love.
Once again the book alludes to Solomon as being the author, but this is doubtful because of chronologies in the text.

Song of Solomon Collection of love poems spoken alternately by a man and a woman.
This book is the festival scroll for Passover, which celebrates the Exodus of the Israelites from Egypt.
The authorship is unknown and Solomon's name was added at a later date.

Isaiah The prophet Isaiah, son of Amos, reflects on the blasphemy of his people in the eyes of the Lord.
Isaiah calls for a return to the worship of the Lord and talks of 'beating swords into ploughshares'.
Isaiah talks further of peace and his vision of the wolf residing with the lamb.
Isaiah's prophecy of the falling of Babylon comes true.

Jeremiah The Judaean prophet Jeremiah lived during the reign of King Josiah and his ministry lasted until the Babylonian conquest.
Chapters 1–25 consist of prophecies against Judah and Jerusalem.
Chapters 26–45 consist of narratives about Jeremiah and may have been composed by Baruch.
Chapters 46–51 consist of prophecies against foreign nations and chapter 52 is a historical appendix.

Lamentations The poems are laments over the destruction of Judah, Jerusalem and the Temple by the Babylonians in 586 BC.
Lamentations is often called 'Lamentations of Jeremiah', although authorship is uncertain.

Ezekiel The prophet Ezekiel was active during the first quarter of the sixth century BC.
The book was written in exile and is valuable for understanding the lives of exiles in Babylon.

Daniel Daniel interprets Nebuchadnezzar's dream.
Nebuchadnezzar throws Shadrach, Meshach and Abednego into a fiery furnace but the Lord sends an angel to help them.
Belshazzar holds a feast and Daniel interprets the writing on the wall, 'mene, mene, tekel, parsin'.
The interpretation means that the Lord has numbered the days of the Babylonian kingdom and it is to be divided.
King Darius reluctantly throws Daniel into the lions' den but the Lord sends an angel to help Daniel

Hosea The last twelve books of the Old Testament bear the name of the minor prophets and are sometimes known as 'the Twelve'.
The first chapter is a biographical report of the prophet Hosea's marriage to Gomer, a harlot.
A similar marriage is described in Chapter 3, which is thought to allude to the Lord's love for Israel.

Joel Joel reiterates the concept that salvation will come to Judah and Jerusalem only when the people turn to the Lord.

Amos Amos, a Judaean prophet from Tekoa, was active during the reign of Jeroboam II.
Most of the chapters form a collection of individual sayings and reports of visions.
Much of the rest of the text is by way of a moral judgement on the rich and self-indulgent.
The book ends with a promise of restoration for Israel.

Obadiah Shortest book of the Bible, with one chapter of 21 verses.
The book announces that the Day of Judgement is nigh for all nations and that Jews will be restored to their native land.

Jonah The book of Jonah recounts the story of the prophet.
The Lord calls for Jonah to go to the Assyrian city of Nineveh to prophesy.
Jonah is concerned that the city will repent and be forgiven, and tries to escape his bidding.
Jonah is caught in a storm at sea while escaping and is thrown overboard at his own request.
The Lord appoints a great fish to swallow Jonah and he remains in the fish's maw for three days and nights.
Jonah prays for deliverance and is vomited out of the fish and once again told to go to Nineveh.
Jonah becomes angry as his fears of repentance are realised and he sits outside the city awaiting its destruction.
A plant springs up overnight to give him shelter from the heat but it is destroyed by a great worm.
Jonah is bitter about the destruction but the Lord chastises him for his care for a plant rather than people.

Micah The Judaean prophet Micah was active during the last half of the eighth century BC.
Micah's threats and promises are a reiteration of many of the other minor prophets.

Nahum The book is an oracle concerning Nineveh and is attributed to the vision of Nahum of Elkosh.
The fall of the city of Nineveh is the theme of the prophetic oracle.

Habakkuk Similar to the book of Nahum; it is written in a liturgical style and portrays a moral theme.

Zephaniah The dominant theme of the book is the 'Day of the Lord', which the prophet sees as imminent due to the sins of Judah.
The 'Humble' and 'Lowly' will be saved through purification by judgement.

Haggai The book comprises four prophecies delivered over a four-month period in the second year of the reign of Darius I.

Zechariah Chapters 1–8 contain the prophecies of Zechariah; the rest of the book is of unknown attribution.
Zechariah was active from 520 to 518 BC and was a contemporary of Haggai.
He shared the concern of Haggai that the Temple of Jerusalem must be rebuilt.

Malachi Last of the twelve Old Testament books that bear the name of the minor prophets and, indeed, the last book of the OT.
The book comprises four chapters, each in the form of a question-and-answer discussion.
Malachi was probably written in the first half of the fifth century BC and its authorship is unknown.

NB The first five books of the Old Testament are usually called the Pentateuch, or Books of Moses. The contents of the first four of these books have been catalogued in the order that the events took place in the text of the Bible. The remaining books have important events highlighted but have no other great detail about them. The New Testament has been dealt with in a similar manner. The author does not wish to upset any religious denomination and it should be noted that texts can differ slightly from Bible to Bible. There are 39 books of the Old Testament and 27 of the New Testament, totalling 66 in all.

New Testament

Matthew The first of the four New Testament Gospels recounting the life and death of Jesus Christ.
Matthew, Mark and Luke are known as Synoptic Gospels, as they share a similar general view.
The Gospel was composed in Greek *c.* AD 70 and is traditionally attributed to the Apostle Matthew the tax-collector.
Chapters 5–7 describe Jesus's Sermon on the Mount, which includes the Beatitudes and the Lord's Prayer.

Mark The Gospel is attributed to John Mark (Acts 12:12; 15:37), a disciple of Peter and associate of Paul.
Mark is the shortest and earliest of the four Gospels and was probably used by Matthew and Luke to compose their accounts.
More than 90 per cent of the content of Mark's Gospel appears in Matthew's and more than 50 per cent in the Gospel of Luke.

Luke Luke was known as the beloved physician and was a close associate of the Apostle Paul.
Luke gives details of Jesus' infancy and the Ascension as well as Caesar Augustus' census.
Parables include the Good Samaritan and the Prodigal Son.

John John was known as the beloved disciple of Jesus.
John's Gospel covers a different time span than the others, concentrating on Jesus' ministry in Judea.
John's account differs in that it does not record many of the symbolic acts of Jesus but rather portrays Jesus as God's son.

Acts of the Apostles
Acts was traditionally written by Luke, whose Gospel concludes where Acts begins, that is, with Christ's Ascension into heaven.
The early chapters describe the descent of the Holy Spirit on the Apostles at Pentecost, which was the birth of the Church.
Chapter 3 describes Peter's healing of a lame man and chapter 5 the death of Ananias for his false tongue.
Chapter 7 describes the stoning of Stephen.
Chapter 9 describes the healing of Aeneas by Peter and the conversion of Saul to Paul on the road to Damascus.
Chapters 27 and 28 describe Paul's shipwreck in Malta and his successful teaching in Rome.
The underlying theme is the spreading of Christianity to the Gentile world under the influence of the Holy Spirit.

Romans
The proper and full title of this book is 'The Epistle of Paul the Apostle to the Romans'.
The book was probably composed at Corinth in *c.* AD 57 and was addressed to the Christian Church at Rome.
The letter is largely a morality and cautionary tale but is considered important in Lutheran teaching.

Corinthians 1
The proper and full title of this book is 'The First Letter of Paul the Apostle to the Corinthians'.
Written *c.* AD 53 at Ephesus, Asia Minor, and addresses the problems of the early years of the Church.
Paul begins his letter with a reminder that all are servants of Christ and stewards of the mysteries of God.
Paul goes on to address questions of immorality, marriage and celibacy as well as the worthy reception of the Eucharist.
In chapter 13 Paul explains that no gift of God has meaning unless accompanied by love.

Corinthians 2
The proper and full title of this book is 'The Second Letter of Paul the Apostle to the Corinthians'.
Written *c.* AD 55 in Macedonia, possibly after an unsatisfactory visit by Paul to Corinth.
Paul urges the Corinthians to assist the poor of Jerusalem and is gratified when Titus reveals their repentance.

Galatians
The proper and full title of this book is 'The Letter of Paul the Apostle to the Galatians'.
In this book, Paul defends his credentials as a true Apostle of Jesus Christ.

Ephesians
The proper and full title of this book is 'The Letter of Paul the Apostle to the Ephesians'.
Traditionally supposed to have been written while Paul was in prison, but this is doubtful.
The text is in the form of an affirmation that there is one Lord, one faith, one baptism, one God and father of us all.

Philippians
The proper and full title of this book is 'The Letter of Paul the Apostle to the Philippians'.
There is more evidence that this letter was written by Paul in prison (*c.* AD 62) than in the case of his letter to the Ephesians.
His address to the Macedonian people was probably stirred by thoughts of his own mortality as he pondered execution.

Colossians
The proper and full title of this book is 'The Letter of Paul the Apostle to the Colossians'.
Addressed to Christians at Colossae, Asia Minor, whose congregation was founded by Epaphras.
The letter is in the form of a reminder of God's love and a call for repentance for their wayward ways.

Thessalonians 1
The proper and full title of this book is 'The First Letter of Paul the Apostle to the Thessalonians'.
First letter was written after his co-worker, Timothy, returned from Thessalonia to report that the new converts were steadfast.

Thessalonians 2
The proper and full title of this book is 'The Second Letter of Paul the Apostle to the Thessalonians'.
The second letter explains that the final day will not come until after the Antichrist appears and proclaims himself God.

Timothy 1
The proper and full title of this book is 'The First Letter of Paul the Apostle to Timothy'.
The book deals with Church administration and the growth of heresies.

Timothy 2
The proper and full title of this book is 'The Second Letter of Paul the Apostle to Timothy'.
The letter urges Timothy to 'guard the truth that has been entrusted to you by the Holy Spirit'.
The letter urges Timothy to visit soon, although the writer believes he is 'on the point of being sacrificed'.

Ttus
The proper and full title of this book is 'The Letter of Paul the Apostle to Titus'.
Titus was a close friend of Paul and was the organiser of the Church in Crete.
The letter urges Titus to appoint worthy elders to positions of responsibility and to preach sound doctrine.
The letter also warns against the disruptive influence of 'Jewish myths', especially those of the 'circumcision party'.

Philemon
The proper and full title of this book is 'The Letter of Paul the Apostle to Philemon'.
The letter was written to Philemon, a wealthy Christian from Colossae, on behalf of Onesimus, Philemon's former slave.

Hebrews
The proper and full title of this book is 'The Letter of Paul the Apostle to the Hebrews'.
The letter was addressed to a Christian community whose faith was faltering because of strong Jewish influences.
The author concludes that Christianity is superior to Judaism.

James
The letter of James, a Christian Jew, is a moralistic reflection on early Jewish Christianity.
The letter covers topics such as cursing, boasting, oaths, prayers, poverty and endurance under persecution.

Peter 1
The first letter urges persecuted Christians to emulate the suffering Christ in their distress.
He reminded them that after his Passion and death, Jesus rose from the dead and is now in glory.

Peter 2
The second letter is principally concerned with the Second Coming of Christ.
Peter also warns against false teachers, whose conduct is as immoral as their words are deceptive.

John 1
The John in question is the disciple John the Evangelist, son of Zebedee.
His first letter urges the Christian community to repudiate heretical teachings.

John 2
The writer of both the second and the third letters calls himself 'presbyter', i.e. elder.

John 3
Addressed to a certain Gaius and complaining of Diotrephes, who lies to put himself first.

Jude
The letter of Jude, brother of James and a servant of Jesus Christ, warns against false gods.

Revelation
The proper and full title of this book is 'The Revelation of St John the Divine'.
Attributed to John, the beloved disciple, and possibly written at Patmos in the Aegean Sea.
The number 7 is used in a symbolic sense to represent totality or perfection.
Chapter 6 describes the Four Horsemen of the Apocalypse.
Chapter 7 describes the 12 tribes of Israel, which were sealed 12,000 of each, totalling 144,000.
Chapter 13 gives the number of the beast, i.e. 666.
Chapter 14 describes the 144,000 virgins who will have their place in heaven.

SCIENCE

Chemical Elements

Name	*Symbol*	*No.*	*Name source*	*Discovered or isolated by*
actinium	Ac	89	beam	André-Louis Debierne 1899
aluminium	Al	13	alum	Hans Christian Oersted 1825
americium	Am	95	America	Glenn Seaborg, Ralph James, Leon Morgan and Albert Ghiorso at the University of Chicago 1944
antimony	Sb	51	antimonium	known to the ancients, its extraction from stibnite was first discovered by Basil Valentine *c.*1450, although its properties were first described by Nicholas Lémery in 1707
argon	Ar	18	inactive	Lord Rayleigh and W Ramsay 1894
arsenic	As	33	yellow orpiment	Albertus Magnus in the 13th century
astatine	At	85	unstable	Berkeley University, California, 1940
barium	Ba	56	heavy	Humphry Davy 1808
berkelium	Bk	97	university	Berkeley University, California, 1949
beryllium	Be	4	beryl	Nicolas Louis Vauquelin 1797
bismuth	Bi	83	uncertain	Basil Valentine 1450
bohrium	Bh	107	Niels Bohr	Dubna Institute for Nuclear Research 1976
boron	B	5	Arabic, buraq	Gay-Lussac, Thenard and Davy 1808
bromine	Br	35	stench	Antoine-Jérôme Balard 1826
cadmium	Cd	48	zinc ore	Friedrich Stromeyer 1817
caesium	Cs	55	silvery white	Robert Bunsen and G Kirchhoff 1860
calcium	Ca	20	lime	Humphry Davy 1808
californium	Cf	98	California	Berkeley University, California, 1950
carbon	C	6	charcoal	prehistoric
cerium	Ce	58	asteroid Ceres	Hisinger, Klaproth and Berzelius 1803
chlorine	Cl	17	greenish yellow	Humphry Davy 1810
chromium	Cr	24	colour	Nicolas Louis Vauquelin 1797
cobalt	Co	27	goblin	Georg Brandt 1735
copernicium	Cn	112	Nicolaus Copernicus	Darmstadt Institute for Heavy Ion Research 1996
copper	Cu	29	Cyprus	prehistoric
curium	Cm	96	Pierre and Marie Curie	Berkeley University, California, 1944
darmstadtium	Ds	110	Darmstadt, Germany	Dr Jorge Rigol 1994
dubnium	Db	105	Dubna, Russia	Joint Institute for Nuclear Research 1967
dysprosium	Dy	66	hard to get at	P E Lecoq de Boisbaudran 1886
einsteinium	Es	99	Einstein	Albert Ghiorso, Berkeley 1952
erbium	Er	68	Ytterby (Sweden)	Carl Gustav Mosander 1843
europium	Eu	63	Europe	Eugène-Anatole Demarçay 1901
fermium	Fm	100	Enrico Fermi	Albert Ghiorso, Berkeley 1952
flerovium	Fl	114	Flerov Lab, Dubna	Joint Institute for Nuclear Research in Dubna, Russia
fluorine	F	9	flowing	Henri Moissan 1886
francium	Fr	87	France	Marguerite Perey 1939
gadolinium	Gd	64	Johan Gadolin	P E Lecoq de Boisbaudran 1886
gallium	Ga	31	cock	P E Lecoq de Boisbaudran 1875
germanium	Ge	32	Germany	Clemens Winkler 1886
gold	Au	79	colour gold	prehistoric
hafnium	Hf	72	Copenhagen	Dirk Coster and G von Hevesy 1923
hahnium	Ha	105	Otto Hahn	disputed by Russia and USA
hassium	Hs	108	Hesse, Germany	Darmstadt Institute for Heavy Ion Research 1984
helium	He	2	sun	William Ramsay 1895
holmium	Ho	67	Stockholm	Soret, Delafontaine and Cleve 1878/9
hydrogen	H	1	water-producing	Cavendish 1766 but Lavoisier named it
indium	In	49	indigo	Ferdinand Reich and Theo Richter 1863
iodine	I	53	violet	Bernard Courtois 1811
iridium	Ir	77	rainbow (iris)	Smithson Tennant 1804
iron	Fe	26	Anglo-Saxon word	prehistoric
krypton	Kr	36	hidden	W Ramsay and Morris W Travers 1898
lanthanum	La	57	lie unseen	Carl Gustav Mosander 1839
lawrencium	Lr	103	Ernest Lawrence	Berkeley University, California, 1961
lead	Pb	82	Anglo-Saxon word	prehistoric
lithium	Li	3	stone	Johan August Arfvedson 1817
livermorium	Lv	116	Livermore, California	Joint Institute for Nuclear Research in Dubna, Russia
lutetium	Lu	71	Paris	Carl Auer von Welsbach and G Urbain 1907/8
magnesium	Mg	12	magnesia	Humphry Davy 1808
manganese	Mn	25	magnet	Carl W Scheele and Johan Gahn 1774
meitnerium	Mt	109	Lise Meitner	Darmstadt Institute for Heavy Ion Research 1982
mendelevium	Md	101	D I Mendeleyev	Berkeley University, California, 1955
mercury	Hg	80	planet Mercury	prehistoric
molybdenum	Mo	42	lead	Peter Jacob Hjelm 1782
neodymium	Nd	60	new twin	Carl Auer von Welsbach 1885
neon	Ne	10	new	W Ramsay and Morris W Travers 1898
neptunium	Np	93	planet Neptune	Edwin McMillan and Philip Abelson 1940
nickel	Ni	28	copper demon	Baron Axel Frederik Cronstedt 1751
niobium	Nb	41	Tantalus's daughter	discovered by Charles Hatchett 1801; first isolated by C W Blomstrand
nitrogen	N	7	nitre-forming	Daniel Rutherford 1772
nobelium	No	102	Nobel Inst. Stockholm	Berkeley University, California, 1958
osmium	Os	76	smell	Smithson Tennant 1804
oxygen	O	8	acid-producing	Scheele/Priestley 1772/4; Lavoisier name
palladium	Pd	46	asteroid Pallas	William Hyde Wollaston 1803
phosphorus	P	15	light-bringer	Hennig Brand 1669
platinum	Pt	78	silvery element	known to the ancients; first reported by A de Ulloa in South America 1736
plutonium	Pu	94	planet Pluto	Berkeley University, California, 1940
polonium	Po	84	Poland	Marie Curie 1898

potassium	K	19	potash	Humphry Davy 1807
praseodymium	Pr	59	green twin	Carl Auer von Welsbach 1885
promethium	Pm	61	Prometheus	Marinsky, Glendenin and Coryell 1947
protactinium	Pa	91	first actinium	Kasmir Fajans and D Göhring 1913
radium	Ra	88	ray	Pierre and Marie Curie and G Bemont 1898
radon	Rn	86	radium	F Dorn 1901
rhenium	Re	75	rhine	I Tacke, W Noddack and O Berg 1925
rhodium	Rh	45	rose	William Hyde Wollaston 1803
roentgenium	Rg	111	Wilhelm Roentgen	Peter Armbruster and Gottfried Münzenber 1994
rubidium	Rb	37	dark red	R Bunsen and Gustav Kirchhoff 1861
ruthenium	Ru	44	Russia	Karl Klaus 1844 but named by G Osann in its impure form in 1827
rutherfordium	Rf	104	Ernest Rutherford	disputed by Soviet and US scientists
samarium	Sm	62	samarskite	P E Lecoq de Boisbaudran 1879
scandium	Sc	21	Scandinavia	Lars Nilson and Per Teodor Cleve 1879
seaborgium	Sg	106	Glenn T Seaborg	American and Russian Institutes 1974
selenium	Se	34	moon	Jons Jacob Berzelius 1817
silicon	Si	14	hard stone	Jons Jacob Berzelius 1824
silver	Ag	47	colour silver	prehistoric
sodium	Na	11	soda	Humphry Davy 1807
strontium	Sr	38	Strontian (Scotland)	Humphry Davy 1808
sulphur	S	16	sulphur	known to ancients; first recognised as element by Antoine Lavoisier 1777
tantalum	Ta	73	Tantalus	Anders Gustaf Ekeberg 1802
technetium	Tc	43	man-made	discovered by C Perrier and E G Segrè of Italy in a sample of molybdenum at Berkeley University, California, 1937
tellurium	Te	52	Earth	Franz J Müller von Reichenstein 1782
terbium	Tb	65	Ytterby (Sweden)	Carl Gustav Mosander 1843
thallium	Tl	81	green shoot	discovered by Sir William Crookes 1861
thorium	Th	90	Thor	Jons Jacob Berzelius 1828
thulium	Tm	69	Thule	Per Teodor Cleve 1879
tin	Sn	50	Anglo-Saxon word	prehistoric
titanium	Ti	22	Titans	discovered by William Gregor 1771; rediscovered by Martin Heinrich Klaproth (who gave it its present name) 1795
tungsten	W	74	heavy stone	Juan Jose and Fausto Elhuyar 1783
ununoctium	Uuo	118	temporary name	researchers at Lawrence Berkeley National Laboratory
ununpentium	Uup	115	temporary name	researchers at GSI from Lund University in Sweden
ununseptium	Uus	117	temporary name	Joint Institute for Nuclear Research in Dubna, Russia
ununtrium	Uut	113	temporary name	Joint Institute for Nuclear Research in Dubna, Russia
uranium	U	92	planet Uranus	Martin Heinrich Klaproth 1789
vanadium	V	23	Norse goddess	Nils Gabriel Sefström 1830
xenon	Xe	54	stranger	W Ramsay and Morris W Travers 1898
ytterbium	Yb	70	Ytterby (Sweden)	J C G de Marignac 1878
yttrium	Y	39	Ytterby (Sweden)	Johan Gadolin 1794
zinc	Zn	30	German word	known in China and India before 1500
zirconium	Zr	40	golden	discovered by Martin Klaproth 1789; isolated by J J Berzelius in 1824

Periodic Table of Elements

1	hydrogen	H	gas
2	helium	He	gas
3	lithium	Li	metallic solid
4	beryllium	Be	metallic solid
5	boron	B	metallic solid
6	carbon	C	non-metallic solid
7	nitrogen	N	gas
8	oxygen	O	gas
9	fluorine	F	gas
10	neon	Ne	gas
11	sodium	Na	metallic solid
12	magnesium	Mg	metallic solid
13	aluminium	Al	metallic solid
14	silicon	Si	metallic solid
15	phosphorus	P	non-metallic solid
16	sulphur	S	non-metallic solid
17	chlorine	Cl	gas
18	argon	Ar	gas
19	potassium	K	metallic solid
20	calcium	Ca	metallic solid
21	scandium	Sc	metallic solid
22	titanium	Ti	metallic solid
23	vanadium	V	metallic solid
24	chromium	Cr	metallic solid
25	manganese	Mn	metallic solid
26	iron	Fe	metallic solid
27	cobalt	Co	metallic solid
28	nickel	Ni	metallic solid
29	copper	Cu	metallic solid
30	zinc	Zn	metallic solid
31	gallium	Ga	metallic liquid
32	germanium	Ge	metalloid solid
33	arsenic	As	metalloid solid
34	selenium	Se	non-metallic solid
35	bromine	Br	non-metallic liquid
36	krypton	Kr	gas
37	rubidium	Rb	radioactive semi- solid
38	strontium	Sr	metallic solid
39	yttrium	Y	metallic solid
40	zirconium	Zr	metallic solid
41	niobium	Nb	metallic solid
42	molybdenum	Mo	metallic solid
43	technetium	Tc	from molybdenum
44	ruthenium	Ru	metallic solid
45	rhodium	Rh	metallic solid
46	palladium	Pd	metallic solid
47	silver	Ag	metallic solid
48	cadmium	Cd	metallic solid
49	indium	In	metallic solid
50	tin	Sn	metallic solid
51	antinomy	Sb	metallic solid
52	tellurium	Te	non-metallic solid
53	iodine	I	solid but sublimates
54	xenon	Xe	gas
55	caesium	Cs	metallic liquid
56	barium	Ba	metallic solid
57	lanthanum	La	metallic solid
58	cerium	Ce	metallic solid
59	praseodymium	Pr	metallic solid
60	neodymium	Nd	metallic solid
61	promethium	Pm	from uranium
62	samarium	Sm	metallic solid
63	europium	Eu	metallic solid
64	gadolinium	Gd	metallic solid
65	terbium	Tb	metallic solid
66	dysprosium	Dy	metallic solid
67	holmium	Ho	metallic solid
68	erbium	Er	metallic solid
69	thulium	Tm	metallic solid
70	ytterbium	Yb	metallic solid
71	lutetium	Lu	metallic solid
72	hafnium	Hf	metallic solid
73	tantalum	Ta	metallic solid
74	tungsten	W	metallic solid
75	rhenium	Re	metallic solid
76	osmium	Os	metallic solid

77	iridium	Ir	metallic solid	98	californium	Cf	from cerium
78	platinum	Pt	metallic solid	99	einsteinium	Es	from plutonium
79	gold	Au	metallic solid	100	fermium	Fm	from plutonium
80	mercury	Hg	metallic liquid	101	mendelevium	Md	from einsteinium
81	thallium	Tl	metallic solid	102	nobelium	No	from cerium
82	lead	Pb	metallic solid	103	lawrencium	Lr	from californium
83	bismuth	Bi	metallic solid	104	rutherfordium	Rf	synthetic metal
84	polonium	Po	radioactive solid	105	dubnium	Db	metallic solid
85	astatine	At	from bismuth	106	seaborgium	Sg	metallic solid
86	radon	Rn	gas	107	bohrium	Bh	metallic solid
87	francium	Fr	radioactive liquid	108	hassium	Hs	metallic solid
88	radium	Ra	radioactive solid	109	meitnerium	Mt	metallic solid
89	actinium	Ac	from uranium	110	darmstadtium	Ds	metallic solid
90	thorium	Th	metallic solid	111	roentgenium	Rg	metallic solid
91	protactinium	Pa	from thorium	112	copernicium	Cn	transition metal
92	uranium	U	metallic solid	113	Ununtrium	Uut	metallic solid
93	neptunium	Np	from plutonium	114	Flerovium	Fl	non-metallic solid
94	plutonium	Pu	from uranium-238	115	Ununpentium	Uup	metallic solid
95	americium	Am	from plutonium	116	Livermorium	Lv	radioactive solid
96	curium	Cm	from plutonium	117	Ununseptium	Uus	not yet defined
97	berkelium	Bk	from americium	118	Ununoctium	Uuo	not yet defined

Chemistry: General Information

atom and molecule: difference atoms are the smallest part of an element that can take part in a chemical reaction; molecules are the smallest particle of either an element or compound that can exist independently and at the same time keep the properties of original substance, e.g. the smallest unit of water is the water molecule, which is made up of two atoms of hydrogen and one of oxygen.

atom: meaning indivisible.

chemical bonds there are two main types of chemical bonding, covalent and ionic, and two more specialised types, metallic and hydrogen bonding.

chemical groups there are various ways elements can be subdivided, the most common being metallic and non-metallic. Metallic elements, or their oxides, dissolve in acids to form positively charged ions called cations. Non-metallic elements can be further subdivided into the unreactive noble gases, the reactive halogens, and others.

chemical matter: three types compound, mixture or element.

chemistry: definition chemistry is the scientific study of substances.

isotopes atoms of a given element which have the same number of protons and electrons and the same chemical properties, but have a different number of neutrons in their nuclei, and consequently different atomic masses. Isotopes may be either stable or radioactive.

organic compounds all compounds that contain carbon. All other compounds are inorganic.

polymers polymers are long-chain molecules in which a group of atoms are repeated. They can be natural – e.g. cellulose, DNA, fats, proteins and starches – or artificial – e.g. nylon, polystyrene, polythene, PVC, and in fact all by-products of 'plastics'.

states of matter solid, liquid or gas.

sub-atomic particles chemical properties of elements depend on the structure of their atoms, which are made up of three sub-atomic particles, protons (positive charge), neutrons and electrons (negative charge). Protons and neutrons are situated in the nucleus of the atom and the electrons orbit this nucleus. The number of protons in the nucleus of an element determines the atomic number used in the periodic table.

sublimation occurs when chemical matter changes directly from a solid to a gas without first melting into a liquid.

valency property of atoms or groups, equal to the number of atoms of hydrogen that the atom or group will combine with or displace in forming compounds.

Geochemical Abundances of the Elements

		%
Lithosphere	oxygen	46.60
	silicon	27.72
	aluminium	8.13
	iron	5.00
Hydrosphere	oxygen	85.70
	hydrogen	10.80
	chlorine	1.935
	sodium	1.078

	Mohs scale of hardness
1	talc
2	gypsum
3	calcite
4	fluorite
5	apatite
6	orthoclase
7	quartz
8	topaz
9	corundum
10	diamond

Halogens*	**Noble gases†**
fluorine	helium
astatine	argon
bromine	radon
iodine	krypton
chlorine	xenon
	neon

* Mnemonic: Fab(r)ic all end ine.

† Also called inert or rare gases.

NB The table listing the chemical elements in alphabetical order contains the name of the person who discovered or first isolated the element. This may be different from the person who first prepared the chemical, e.g. chlorine was first prepared (from hydrochloric acid and manganese dioxide) by Carl Wilhelm Scheele in 1774 and was considered a compound until Sir Humphry Davy showed that it could not in fact be decomposed and that muriatic (hydrochloric) acid consists of hydrogen and another true element that he named chlorine.

Mathematics: General Information

algebra method of solving mathematical problems by the use of symbols when figures are inadequate due to their size or unknown nature.

angles less than 90° = acute; more than 90° = obtuse; more than 180° = reflex.

Archimedes' principle states that any body submerged in a fluid at rest is acted upon by an upward force equal to the weight of the fluid displaced.

binary numbers Comparison of decimal and binary numbers (decimal first) 1 = 1, 2 = 10, 3 = 11, 4 = 100, 5 = 101, 6 = 110, 7 = 111, 8 = 1000, 9 = 1001, 10 = 1010.

books Euclid – *Elements*; Bertrand Russell (with A N Whitehead) - *Principia Mathematica*; Sir Isaac Newton – *Principia.*

calculus branch of mathematics that permits the manipulation of continuously varying quantities. Subdivided into integral and differential. Calculus (which is Latin for pebble) was independently invented by Gottfried Leibniz and Isaac Newton.

circle: parts of *chord* = a line that joins two points of a circle; *diameter* = the longest chord of a circle; *radius* = point from centre of circle to perimeter; *sector* = portion of circle between centre and two points on perimeter; *segment* = portion of a circle between a chord and the perimeter. Circumference of a circle = 2 x pi x the radius (or pi x the diameter); the area of a circle = pi x radius^2.

complex number number having a real and an imaginary part, e.g. 5 + 3i

coordinates technical names for graph co-ordinates are abscissa (the horizontal *x*) and ordinate (the vertical *y* coordinate).

cylinder solid figure with straight sides and a circular section. Area of a cylinder = 2 x pi x radius x height + 2 x pi x radius squared. Volume = the area of the base x the height.

ellipse an ellipse is a closed conic section with the appearance of a flattened circle. It is formed by an inclined plane that does not intersect the base of the cone.

factorial the factorial of a number is the product of all the whole numbers inclusive between 1 and the number itself; the symbol is ! e.g. 6! = 1 x 2 x 3 x 4 x 5 x 6 = 720.

factors a factor is a number that divides exactly into another number, e.g. 6 divides exactly into 48 eight times; thus both 6 and 8 are factors of 48.

Fibonacci numbers sequence of numbers in which each number is the sum of its two predecessors, e.g. 1, 1, 2, 3, 5, 8, 13, etc.

game theory branch of mathematics used to analyse competitive situations whose outcomes depend not only on one's own choices, and perhaps chance, but also on the choices made by other parties, or 'players'. Modern game theory was created practically at one stroke by the publication in 1944 of *Theory of Games and Economic Behaviour* by the mathematician John von Neumann and the economist Oskar Morgenstern.

geometry branch of mathematics concerned with the properties and relations of points, lines, surfaces, and solids. Euclid's *Elements*, written about 330 BC, is the definitive origin of the subject.

hexadecimal system base 16, uses digits 0–9 plus letters A–F to denote numbers 10 to 15.

imaginary number the square root of –1 is denoted by the letter i, so $i^2 = -1$; real multiples of i, such as 3i, 2.3i, etc., are known as imaginary numbers.

line: definition a line is length without breadth.

logarithms system invented by John Napier whereby multiplication and division of large numbers are made simple by substituting the operations of addition and subtraction.

matrix set of numbers arranged in rows and columns so as to form a rectangular array. The numbers are called the elements, or entries, of the matrix. Term was introduced by C19 English mathematician Arthur Cayley, who developed the algebraic aspect of matrices.

mean in a series of values in a distribution the mean is the average value of all the values: e.g. in a series such as 1, 4, 4, 5, 7, 9, 12 the mean would be 6.

median in a series of values in a distribution the median is the middle value in order of size: e.g. in a series such as 1, 4, 4, 5, 7, 9, 12 the median would be 5. In an even numbered sample the median is the mean of the central two numbers.

mode in a series of values in a distribution the mode is the most frequently occurring value: e.g. in a series such as 1, 4, 4, 5, 7, 9, 12 the mode would be 4.

numbers chiliad – 1,000; myriad – 10,000; lakh – 100,000; crore – 10,000,000; billion – 1,000,000,000,000 (USA 1,000,000,000); googol – one followed by a hundred noughts; googolplex – one followed by a googol of noughts.

octal system base 8; uses digits 0–7: e.g. 31 in base 10 would be 37 in base 8.

parabola curve formed by cutting a right circular cone with a plane parallel to the sloping side of the cone.

parallelogram quadrilateral with opposite pairs of sides equal in length and parallel. When all sides are of the same length it is known as a rhombus. The area of a parallelogram is base · height.

perfect numbers perfect numbers are equal to the sum of all their factors excluding the number itself, e.g. 6, whose factors are 1, 2, and 3. The first five perfect numbers are 6, 28, 496, 8128, and 33,550,336.

pi (π) pi has been measured to many thousands of decimal places but to six places = 3.141592. It is a transcendental number.

polygons the sum of the interior angles = (2n – 4) x 90° where n = the number of sides. The sum of the exterior angles of any polygon = 360° regardless of the number of sides (an exterior angle of a polygon is the angle between one side extended and the adjacent side): e.g. triangle = 180°; quadrilateral = 360°; pentagon = 540°; hexagon = 720°; octagon = 1080°; nonagon = 1260°; decagon = 1440°; hendecagon = 1620°; dodecagon = 1800°; icosagon = 3240°.

polyhedron solid figure with 4 or more faces.

prime number a natural number (over 1) that has no proper factors, i.e. which cannot be divided by any natural numbers other than itself and 1 – e.g. 2, 3, 5, 7, 11, 13, 17

prism solid figure (polyhedron) with 2 equal polygonal faces in parallel planes, other faces being parallelograms. The volume of a prism = the area of either end · the perpendicular distance between the ends.

pyramid a solid figure whose base is a polygon and whose apex is joined to each vertex of the base. Therefore all its faces, apart from the base, are triangles. Any pyramid can be fitted inside a prism so that the base of the pyramid is one end of the prism, and the apex of the pyramid is on the other end of the prism. The volume of a pyramid on a rectangular base = ⅓ length x breadth x height.

Pythagoras' theorem in a right-angled triangle, the square of the hypotenuse is equal to the sum of the squares of the other two sides.

quadratic equation equation containing as its highest power the square of a single unknown variable. Formula is $ax^2 + bx + c = 0$, in which a, b, and c are constants and only the coefficient a cannot equal 0.

rational number number that can be written in the form a/b, where *a* and *b* are integers and *b* is not equal to zero.

Reciprocal (of a quantity) that quantity divided into 1; thus the reciprocal of 2 is ½.

rhombus diamond-shaped plane figure, a parallelogram with four equal sides and no right angles. The area of a rhombus = ½ the product of the diagonals.

simultaneous equations two or more algebraic equations that contain two or more unknown quantities and are simultaneously true, e.g. x + 3y = 6 and 3y – 2x = 4. The solution is to eliminate one of the variables by multiplying the first equation by 2 and adding the two equations to give 9y = 16.

sine in trigonometry, of an angle in a right-angled triangle, the ratio of the length of the side opposite the angle to the length of the hypotenuse.

sphere circular solid with all points on its surface the same distance from its centre. The surface area = 4 x pi x radius squared. Volume = $4/3$ pi x radius cubed A little-known fact about the sphere is that the area of any zone of its curved surface lying between two parallel planes is exactly equal to the curved surface of the surrounding cylinder between the same two planes.

standard deviation in statistics, a measure of the variability (dispersion or spread) of any set of numerical values about their arithmetic mean. It is specifically defined as the square root of the arithmetic mean of the squared deviations.

tetrahedron solid figure with four triangular faces, i.e. a pyramid on a triangular base. The volume of a tetrahedron = ⅓ (the area of the triangular base x height).

topology branch of geometry which deals with those properties of a figure which remain unchanged even when the figure is continuously transformed. A famous topological problem was to prove that only three colours are needed to produce a map to give adjoining areas different colours.

transcendental number real number that is not a root of a polynomial equation with integer coefficients.

trapezium four-sided quadrilateral with two parallel sides of unequal length. The area of a trapezium = ½ the sum of the parallel sides x the perpendicular distance between them. To find the area three measurements have to be taken, i.e. the height between the pair of parallel sides and the length of both of the parallel sides. If a and b are the two sides the formula would be ½ (a + b)h.

triangle Three-sided plane figure; *scalene* triangles have no two sides equal; *isosceles* triangles have two equal sides and angles, *equilateral* triangles have three equal sides and angles. The area of a triangle = ½ base x height, however it is possible to calculate the area from the length of its sides using an Archimedean formula square root of (s(s – a) (s – b) (s – c)) where s = half the sum of the sides.

trigonometry branch of mathematics which solves problems relating to plane and spherical triangles.

vector physical quantity that has both magnitude and direction, such as velocity or acceleration of an object.

Venn diagrams diagram representing sets and the logical relationships between them. Sets are drawn as circles whose overlap contains elements that are common to both sets and thus represent a third set.

Physics: SI Units
(*Système International d'Unités*)

Base units

Quantity	*Unit*	*Symbol*	*Definition*
length	metre	m	1,650,763.73 wavelengths in vacuum of the red-orange light given out by the krypton-86 isotope.
mass	kilogram	kg	Mass of international prototype of the kilogram, at the Bureau International des Poids et Mesures at Sèvres, near Paris.
time	second	s	Duration of 9,192,631,770 periods of the radiation corresponding to the transition between the two hyperfine levels of the ground state of the caesium-133 atom.
electric current	ampere	A	That constant current which, if maintained in two straight parallel conductors of infinite length of negligible circular cross-section, and placed 1 metre apart in a vacuum, would produce between these conductors a force equal to $2 \cdot 10^{-7}$ newtons per metre of length.
thermodynamic temperature	kelvin	K	The fraction $1/273.16$ of the thermodynamic temperature of the triple point of water. The triple point of w-ater is the point where water, ice and water vapour are in equilibrium.
luminous intensity	candela	cd	The luminous intensity, in a given direction, of a source that emits monochromatic radiation of frequency $540 \cdot 10^{12}$ Hz, and has a radiant intensity in that direction of $1/683$ watts per steradian.
amount of substance	mole	mol	Amount of substance of a system that contains as many elementary entities (atoms, molecules, ions, etc.) as there are atoms in 0.012 kilogram of carbon-12.

Supplementary units

plane angle	radian	rad	The plane angle between two radii of a circle that cut off on the circumference an arc equal in length to the radius.
solid angle	steradian	sr	The solid angle that, having its vertex in the centre of a sphere, cuts off an area of the surface of the sphere equal to that of a square having sides of length equal to the radius of the sphere.

Derived Units

Quantity	*Unit*	*Symbol*	*Other SI Units*
area	square metre	m^2	
volume	cubic metre	m^3	
velocity	metre per second	$m \cdot s^{-1}$	
angular velocity	radian per second	rad s^{-1}	
acceleration	metre per second squared	$m \cdot s^{-2}$	
angular acceleration	radian per second squared	rad s^{-2}	
frequency	hertz	Hz	s^{-1}
density	kilogram per cubic metre	$kg \cdot m^{-3}$	
momentum	kilogram metre per second	$kg \cdot m \cdot s^{-1}$	
angular momentum	kilogram metre squared per second	$kg \cdot m^2 \cdot s^{-1}$	
moment of inertia	kilogram metre squared	$kg \cdot m^2$	
force	newton	N	$kg \cdot m \cdot s^{-2}$
pressure (stress)	pascal	Pa	$N \cdot m^{-2} = kg \cdot m^{-1} \cdot s^{-2}$
work (energy)	joule	J	$N \cdot m = kg \cdot m^2 \cdot s^{-2}$
power	watt	W	$J \cdot s^{-1} = kg \cdot m^2 \cdot s^{-3}$
surface tension	newton per metre	$N \cdot m^{-1}$	$kg \cdot s^{-2}$
dynamic viscosity	newton second per metre squared	$N \cdot s \cdot m^{-2}$	$kg \cdot m^{-1} \cdot s^{-1}$
kinematic viscosity	metre squared per second	$m^2 \cdot s^{-1}$	
temperature	degree Celsius	°C	
thermal coefficient of linear expansion	per degree Celsius (or kelvin)	$°C^{-1}$, K^{-1}	
thermal conductivity	watt per metre degree Celsius	$W \cdot m^{-1} \cdot °C^{-1}$	$kg \cdot m \cdot s^{-3} \cdot °C^{-1}$
heat capacity	joule per kelvin	$J \cdot K^{-1}$	$kg \cdot m^2 \cdot s^{-2} \cdot K^{-1}$
specific heat capacity	joule per kilogram kelvin	$J \cdot kg^{-1} \cdot K^{-1}$	$m^2 \cdot s^{-2} K^{-1}$
specific latent heat	joule per kilogram	$J \cdot kg^{-1}$	$m^2\ s^{-2}$
electrical charge	coulomb	C	$A \cdot s$
electromotive force (potential difference)	volt	V	$W \cdot A^{-1} = kg \cdot m^2 \cdot s^{-3} \cdot A^{-1}$
electrical resistance	ohm	▯	$V \cdot A^{-1} = kg \cdot m^2 \cdot s^{-3} \cdot A^{-2}$
electrical conductance	siemens	S	$A \cdot V^{-1} = kg^{-1} \cdot m^{-2} \cdot s^3 \cdot A^2$
electrical capacitance	farad	F	$A \cdot s \cdot V^{-1} = kg^{-1} \cdot m^{-2} \cdot s^4 \cdot A^2$
inductance	henry	H	$V \cdot s \cdot A^{-1} = kg \cdot m^2 \cdot s^{-2} \cdot A^{-2}$
magnetic flux	weber	Wb	$V \cdot s = kg \cdot m^2 \cdot s^{-2} \cdot A^{-1}$
magnetic flux density	tesla	T	$Wb \cdot m^{-2} = kg \cdot s^{-2} \cdot A^{-1}$
magnetomotive force	ampere	A	
luminous flux	lumen	Lm	cd·sr
illumination	lux	Lx	$lm \cdot m^{-2} = cd \cdot sr \cdot m^{-2}$
radiation activity	becquerel	Bq	s^{-1}
radiation absorbed dose	gray	Gy	$J \cdot kg^{-1} = m^2 \cdot s^{-2}$

Physics: General Information

Avogadro's law law stating that equal volumes of gases at the same temperature and pressure contain equal numbers of molecules.

Avogadro's constant the number of atoms or molecules in one mole of a substance.

baryon subatomic particle that has a mass equal to or greater than that of a proton.

Bernoulli's principle the principle that in a liquid flowing through a pipe the pressure difference that accelerates the flow when the bore changes is equal to the product of half the density times the change of the square of the speed, provided friction is negligible. Named after Daniel Bernoulli, Swiss mathematician and physician 1700–82.

Coriolis effect an effect whereby a mass moving in a rotating system is accelerated perpendicular to its motion and to the axis of rotation, which helps to explain why wind patterns are clockwise in the northern hemisphere and anticlockwise in the southern. Named after French engineer G G Coriolis 1792–1843.

Doppler effect phenomenon observed for sound waves and electromagnetic radiation, characterised by a change in the apparent frequency of a wave as a result of relative motion between the observer and the source.

entropy measure of the unavailability of a system's thermal energy for conversion into mechanical work, often interpreted as a measure of the degree of disorder or randomness in the system.

fermion any of several subatomic particles with half-integral spin, e.g. nucleons.

Feynman diagram diagram of interactions between subatomic particles. Named after Richard Feynman, US physicist (1918–88).

Foucault's pendulum pendulum which rotates in relation to the Earth's surface and thus changes its plane in relation to the position of the Earth's rotational plane. The pendulum swings in a clockwise plane in the northern hemisphere and anticlockwise in the southern, and on the equator would therefore be stationary. This mathematical effect explains the trajectory of moving objects through the air. Named after Jean Bernard Foucault (1819–68), who set up the first pendulum.

General relativity Einstein's theory that the effects of acceleration and gravity were equivalent.

Heisenberg uncertainty principle principle that the momentum and position of a particle cannot both be precisely determined at the same time.

Latent heat heat required to convert a solid into a liquid or vapour, or a liquid into vapour, without change of temperature.

Matter: four fundamental forces interactions between matter can be explained by four forces.

1) Gravitational: weakest of the four forces, whereby masses mutually attract. Gravity is the force that holds solar systems and galaxies together.

2) Electromagnetic: force maintaining the magnetic field and the electron-nucleus structure of an atom.

3) Strong: about 100 times stronger than the electromagnetic force, it holds together the protons and neutrons within an atomic nucleus.

4) Weak: force associated with the radioactive beta-decay of some nuclei.

Matter: three fundamental states gas, solid, liquid.

Newton's three laws of motion 1) A body will remain stationary or travelling at a constant velocity unless it is acted upon by an external force.

2) The resultant force exerted on a body is directly proportional to the acceleration produced by the force and takes place in the direction of the force.

3) To every action there is an equal and opposite reaction.

Pauli exclusion principle the assertion that no two electrons in an atom can occupy the same energy state simultaneously, or in other words, that no two fermions can have the same quantum number. Named after Wolfgang Pauli, Austrian physicist (1900–58).

Physics: definition physics is the study of the basic laws that govern matter.

Quantum theory describes the behaviour of particles within atoms and the absorption and emission of electromagnetic radiation by matter in its various states.

Schrödinger's cat hypothetical situation whereby a cat is placed inside a box for one hour with a radioactive atom whose probability of decay is 50% per hour. If the atom decays a Geiger counter triggers a mechanism breaking a cyanide capsule and killing the cat. If the atom does not decay the cat remains alive. Quantum theory suggests that until the box is opened at the end of the hour, the cat is neither alive nor dead.

Special relativity states that nothing can exceed the speed of light, which is the same in all inertial time frames, and that all inertial time frames are equally good for carrying out experiments.

Thermodynamics: three laws 1) First law states that the total amount of energy in any closed system always remains the same.

2) Second law states that heat will always flow from a hotter object to a colder one and not the other way round.

3) Third law states that on approaching absolute zero, extracting energy from a system becomes increasingly harder.

Venturi tube device for measuring fluid flow, consisting of a tube so constricted that the pressure differential produced by fluid flowing through the constriction gives a measure of the rate of flow.

Wheatstone bridge apparatus for measuring electrical resistances by equalising the potential at two points of a circuit.

Young's modulus measure of elasticity equal to the ratio of the stress acting on a substance to the strain produced. Named after Thomas Young, English scientist (1773–1829).

Zeeman effect the splitting of the spectrum line into several components by a magnetic field. Named after Pieter Zeeman, Dutch physicist (1865–1943).

SHAKESPEARE

Plays

1 **All's Well That Ends Well**

The Persons of The Play

The Dowager COUNTESS of Roussillon
BERTRAM, Count of Roussillon, her son
HELEN, an orphan, attending the Countess
LAVATCH, a clown, the Countess's servant
REYNALDO, the Countess's steward
PAROLES, Bertram's companion
LAFEU, an old lord
The KING of France
FIRST LORD DUMAINE
SECOND LORD DUMAINE, his brother
INTERPRETER, a French soldier
The DUKE of Florence
WIDOW Capilet
DIANA, her daughter
MARIANA, a friend of the widow
Lords, attendants, soldiers, citizens

Quotations	Spoken by
A young man married is a man that's marr'd.	Paroles
From lowest place when virtuous things proceed.	King of France
I have an answer will serve all men.	Lavatch
Love all, trust a few, do wrong to none.	Countess of Roussillon
Oft expectation fails and most oft there where most it promises.	Helen
Our remedies oft in ourselves do lie which we ascribe to heaven.	Helen
Praising what is lost makes the remembrance dear.	King of France
The hind that would be mated by the lion must die for love.	Helen
The web of our life is of a mingled yarn.	First Lord Dumaine
There's a place and means for every man alive.	Paroles
'Twere all one that I should love a bright particular star.	Helen

Précis of plot

Helen, the daughter of a poor physician, Gerard de Narbonne, falls in love with Bertram, son of her guardian the Countess of Roussillon. Helen uses her magic to cure the King of France and as a reward he brings about the marriage of Helen and Bertram. The marriage is doomed to fail when Bertram takes flight to the Tuscan wars, and it is only consummated when Bertram seduces Helen in the guise of the Florentine maiden Diana.

Setting

France and Italy in the 14th century

2 **Antony and Cleopatra**

Mark ANTONY, Triumvir of Rome
Friends and followers of Antony:
VENTIDIUS
SILIUS
EROS
CAMIDIUS
SCARUS
DECRETAS
Domitius ENOBARBUS
DEMETRIUS
PHILO
SELEUCUS
Octavius CAESAR, Triumvir of Rome
OCTAVIA, his sister
Friends and followers of Caesar:
MAECENAS
AGRIPPA
TAURUS
DOLABELLA
THIDIAS
GALLUS
PROCULEIUS

LEPIDUS, Triumvir of Rome
Sextus POMPEY (Pompeius)

Friends of Pompey:
MENECRATES
MENAN
VARRIUS

CLEOPATRA, Queen of Egypt
Cleopatra's attendants:
CHARMIAN
IRAS
ALEXAS
DIOMED

MARDIAN, a eunuch

SOOTHSAYER
AMBASSADOR
MESSENGERS
BOY who sings
SENTRY and men of his WATCH
Men of the GUARD
EGYPTIAN
CLOWN
SERVANTS
SOLDIERS
Attendants, eunuchs, soldiers

Quotations	Spoken by
Age cannot wither her, nor custom stale her infinite variety.	Enobarbus
Celerity is never more admired than by the negligent.	Cleopatra
Come thou monarch of the vine, plumpy Bacchus with pink eyne!	Boy (sung)
Dost thou not see my baby at my breast.	Cleopatra
Finish, good lady; the bright day is done, and we are for the dark.	Iras
Give me my robe, put on my crown; I have immortal longings in me.	Cleopatra
He wears the rose of youth upon him.	Antony
His biting is immortal; those that do die of it seldom or never recover.	Clown
His legs bestrid the ocean: his rear'd arm crested the world: his voice was propertied.	Cleopatra
I am dying, Egypt, dying; only I here importune death a while until of many thousand kisses the poor last I lay upon thy lips.	Antony
I found you as a morsel cold upon dead Caesar's trencher.	Antony

I have yet room for six scotches more.	Scarus
I saw her once hop forty paces through the public street; and having lost her breath, she spoke, and panted, that she did make defect perfection.	Enobarbus
I wish you joy o' the worm.	Clown
If thou and nature can so gently part, the stroke of death is as a lover's pinch.	Cleopatra
In nature's infinite book of secrecy little can I read.	Soothsayer
In time we hate that which we often fear.	Charmian
It is well done, and fitting for a princess descended of so many royal kings.	Charmian
Let's have one other gaudy night.	Antony
My salad days, when I was green in judgement, cold in blood.	Cleopatra
Now boast thee, death, in thy possession lies a lass unparalleled.	Charmian
Out, fool – I forgive thee for a witch.	Charmian
O, wither'd is the garland of the war. The soldier's pole is fall'n: young boys and girls are level now with men. The odds is gone.	Cleopatra
Sometime we see a cloud that's dragonish, a vapour sometime like a bear or lion, a towered citadel, a pendant rock, a fork'd mountain, or blue promontory with trees upon't.	Antony
The barge she sat in, like a burnish'd throne, burn'd on the water.	Enobarbus
The nature of bad news infects the teller.	Messenger
There's beggary in the love that can be reckon'd.	Antony
Though I am mad I will not bite him. Call!	Cleopatra
Though it be honest, it is never good to bring bad news.	Cleopatra
To business that we love we rise betime, and go to't with delight	Antony
Unarm, Eros; the long day's task is done, and we must sleep	Antony
What's brave, what's noble, let's do it after the high Roman fashion, and make death proud to take us.	Cleopatra
Where's my serpent of old Nile.	Cleopatra

Précis of plot

The second triumvirate is disintegrating and Mark Antony becomes infatuated with Cleopatra, Queen of Egypt. The play tells of the sea fight between Antony and Octavius near Actium and Antony's subsequent suicide, believing Cleopatra dead. Cleopatra too commits suicide rather than be captured by Octavius.

Setting

Rome and Alexandria in the 1st century BC.

3 As You Like It

DUKE SENIOR, living in banishment
ROSALIND, his daughter, later disguised as Ganymede
AMIENS, Lord attending on Duke Senior
JAQUES, Lord attending on Duke Senior
TWO PAGES
DUKE FREDERICK
CELIA, his daughter, later disguised as Aliena
LE BEAU, a courtier attending on Duke Frederick
CHARLES, Duke Frederick's wrestler
TOUCHSTONE, a jester
OLIVER, eldest son of Sir Rowland de Bois
JAQUES, Oliver's brother
ORLANDO, Oliver's brother
ADAM, a former servant of Sir Rowland
DENIS, Oliver's servant
SIR OLIVER MARTEXT, a country clergyman
CORIN, an old shepherd
SILVIUS, a young shepherd, in love with Phoebe
PHOEBE, a shepherdess
WILLIAM, a countryman, in love with Audrey
AUDREY, a goatherd, betrothed to Touchstone
HYMEN, God of marriage
Lords, pages, and other attendants

Quotations	**Spoken by**
All the world's a stage, and all the men and women merely players.They have their exits and their entrances and one man in his time plays many parts, his acts being seven ages.	Jaques
And rail'd on Lady Fortune in good terms	Jaques
And so, from hour to hour, we ripe and ripe, and then from hour to hour, we rot and rot; and thereby hangs a tale.	Jaques
An ill-favoured thing, sir, but mine own.	Touchstone
Ay, now am I in Ardenne; the more fool I. When I was at home I was in a better place; but travellers must be content.	Touchstone
Beauty provoketh thieves sooner than gold.	Rosalind
Blow, blow, thou winter wind, thou are not so unkind as man's ingratitude.	Amiens (sung)
But whate'er you are that in this desert inaccessible under the shade of melancholy boughs, lose and neglect the creeping hours of time.	Orlando
Chewing the food of sweet and bitter fancy.	Oliver
Dead shepherd, now I find thy saw of might, 'Who ever loved that loved not at first sight?'	Phoebe (quoting Marlowe's 'Hero and Leander')
Down on your knees, and thank heaven, fasting, for a good man's love.	Rosalind
Do you not know I am a woman? when I think I must speak, sweet, say on.	Rosalind
Every one fault seeming monstrous till his fellow-fault came to match it.	Rosalind
Fleet the time carelessly, as they did in the golden world.	Charles
For in my youth I never did apply hot and rebellious liquors to my blood	Adam
Hast any philosophy in thee, shepherd?	Touchstone
He that wants money, means and content is without three good friends.	Corin
He uses his folly like a stalking-horse and under the presentation of that he shoots his wit.	Duke Senior
How now, wit! whither wander you?	Celia
I am not a slut, though I thank the gods I am foul.	Audrey
I can suck melancholy out of a song, as a weasel sucks eggs.	Jaques
I do desire we may be better strangers.	Orlando

Quotation	Speaker
If ever – as that ever may be near – you meet in some fresh cheek the power of fancy, then shall you know the wounds invisible that love's keen arrows make.	
If it be true that good wine needs no bush 'tis true that a good play needs no epilogue.	Rosalind
If thou remember'st not the slightest folly that ever love did make thee run into, thou hast not loved.	Silvius
I had rather have a fool to make me merry than experience to make me sad.	Rosalind
I must have liberty withal, as large a charter as the wind, to blow on whom I please.	Jaques
It is a melancholy of mine own, compounded of many simples, extracted from many objects, and indeed the sundry contemplation of my travels, in which my often rumination wraps me in a most humorous sadness.	Jaques
It is meat and drink to me to see a clown.	Touchstone
It is to be all made of faith and service.	Silvius
It is to be all made of fantasy, all made of passion.	Silvius
It is to be all made of sighs and tears.	Silvius
Men are April when they woo, December when they wed, maids are May when they are maids, but the sky changes when they are wives.	Rosalind
Men have died from time to time and worms have eaten them, but not for love.	Rosalind
Most friendship is feigning, most loving mere folly.	Amiens (sung)
Motley's the only wear.	Jaques
My lungs began to crow like chanticleer, that fools should be so deep-contemplative, and I did laugh sans intermission an hour by his dial.	Jaques
'No sir,' quoth he, 'Call me not fool till heaven hath sent me fortune' and then he drew a dial from his poke, and, looking on it with lack-lustre eye, says very wisely 'it is ten o' clock thus we may see,' quoth he, 'how the world wags.'	Jaques
No sooner met but they looked; no sooner looked but they loved; no sooner loved but they sighed; no sooner sighed but they asked one another the reason, no sooner knew the reason but they sought the remedy.	Rosalind
O, how bitter a thing it is to look into happiness through another man's eyes!	Orlando
O, how full of briers is this working-day world!	Rosalind
O Sir, we quarrel in print, by the book; as you have books for good manners. I will name you the degrees. The first, the Retort Courteous; the second, the Quip Modest; the third, the Reply Churlish; the fourth, the Reproof Valiant; the fifth, the Countercheck Quarrelsome; the sixth, the Lie with Circumstance; the seventh, the Lie Direct.	Touchstone
that, out of all whooping!	
Speak, sad brow and true maid.	Rosalind
Sweep on, you fat and greasy citizens.	First Lord
Sweet are the uses of adversity, which like the toad, ugly and venomous, wears yet a precious jewel in its head; and this our life exempt from public haunt, finds tongues in trees, books in the running brooks, sermons in stones, and good in everything.	Duke Senior
The big round tears coursed one another down his innocent nose in piteous chase.	First Lord
The fair, the chaste and unexpressive she.	Orlando
The horn, the horn, the lusty horn is not a thing to laugh to scorn.	Lords (sung)
Therefore my age is as a lusty winter, frosty, but kindly.	Adam
The 'why' is plain as way to parish church.	Jaques
This is the very false gallop of the verses.	Touchstone
Thou mak'st a testament as worldlings do, giving thy sum of more to that which had too much.	First Lord
Time travels in divers paces with divers persons.	Rosalind
Truly, I would the gods had made thee poetical.	Touchstone
Truly thou art damned, like an ill-roasted egg all on one side.	Touchstone
Under the greenwood tree, who loves to lie with me, and turn his merry note, unto the sweet bird's throat, Come hither, come hither, come hither. Here shall he see: no enemy, but winter and rough weather.	Amiens (sung)
Very good orators, when they are out, they will spit.	Rosalind
We'll have a swashing and a martial outside, as many other mannish cowards have, that do outface it with their semblances.	Rosalind
Well said: that was laid on with a trowel.	Celia
We that are true lovers run into strange capers.	Touchstone
Who doth ambition shun and loves to live i' the sun seeking the food he eats and pleased with what he gets.	Chorus
Your 'if' is the only peacemaker; much virtue in 'if'.	Touchstone

Précis of plot

The story of the love between a high-born maiden, Rosalind, oppressed by her uncle Duke Frederick, who has usurped his elder brother's dukedom, and Orlando, the third and youngest son of Duke Frederick's enemy Sir Rowland de Bois, himself oppressed by his tyrannical elder brother Oliver. Sub-plots include the romantic liaisons between Touchstone and Audrey, Celia and Oliver, and Silvius and Phoebe.

Setting

The Forest of Arden (possibly Ardenne).

4 The Comedy of Errors

Solinus, DUKE of Ephesus
EGEON, father of the Antipholus twins
ANTIPHOLUS OF EPHESUS, Egeon's son
ANTIPHOLUS OF SYRACUSE, twin brother
ANGELO, a goldsmith
BALTHASAR, a merchant
A COURTESAN
Doctor PINCH, a schoolmaster and exorcist

DROMIO OF EPHESUS
DROMIO OF SYRACUSE, his twin brother
ADRIANA, wife of Antipholus of Ephesus
LUCIANA, her sister
NELL, Adriana's kitchen-maid
MERCHANT OF EPHESUS
SECOND MERCHANT, Angelo's creditor
EMILIA, an abbess at Ephesus
Officers and attendants
Jailer, messenger, headsman

Quotations	Spoken by
A wretched soul, bruised with adversity.	Adriana
The pleasing punishment that women bear.	Egeon

Précis of plot
The Comedy of Errors is a true farce, in as much as the unlikely situations stretch the imagination of the audience. But the play itself is probably the most classically constructed of any of Shakespeare's works. The action all takes place within a few hours and revolves around the mistaken identity of twin brothers and their bondmen, who also happen to be twins. The audience are further tested intellectually by the long-lost brothers sharing the same names as do their servants.

Setting
Ephesus circa 14th century.

5 **Coriolanus**
Caius MARTIUS, later surnamed CORIOLANUS
MENENIUS Agrippa
Titus LARTIUS, a General
COMINIUS, a General
VOLUMNIA, Coriolanus' mother
VIRGILIA, his wife
YOUNG MARTIUS, his son
VALERIA, a chaste lady of Rome
SICINIUS Velutus, tribune
Junius BRUTUS, tribune
CITIZENS of Rome
SOLDIERS in the Roman army
Tullus AUFIDIUS, General of the Volscian army
His LIEUTENANT
His SERVINGMEN
CONSPIRATORS with Aufidius
Volscian LORDS
Volscian CITIZENS
SOLDIERS in the Volscian army
ADRIAN, a Roman
NICANOR, a Volscian
A Roman HERALD
MESSENGERS
AEDILES
Gentlewoman, usher, Volscian Senators,
Roman Captains, officers and lictors

Quotations	Spoken by
Bid them wash their faces and keep their teeth clean.	Coriolanus
Chaste as the icicle that's candied by the frost from purest snow and hangs on Diana's temple.	Coriolanus
Hear you this Triton of the minnows?	Coriolanus
His nature is too noble for the world. He would not flatter Neptune for his trident.	Menenius
If you have writ your annals true, 'tis there that, like an eagle in a dove-cote, I fluttered your Volscians in Corioles. Alone I did it. 'Boy'!	Coriolanus
I thank you for your voices, thank you, your most sweet voices.	Third citizen
Look, sir, my wounds, I got them in my country's service when some certain of your brethren roar'd and ran from the noise of our own drums.	Coriolanus
My gracious silence, hail!	Coriolanus
O, a kiss long as my exile, sweet as my revenge!	Coriolanus
You common cry of curs! whose breath I hate.	Coriolanus

Précis of plot
Caius Marcius is granted the cognomen of Coriolanus for his fearlessness in the Roman struggle against the neighbouring Volsci, but this brave but tyrannical warrior ultimately rebels and the subsequent intrigues form the basis of the plot.

Setting
Rome circa 5th century BC, Corioli, Antium.

6 **Cymbeline, King of Britain**
CYMBELINE, King of Britain
Princess INNOGEN, his daughter
GUIDERIUS, Cymbeline's son, known as Polydore
ARVIRAGUS, Cymbeline's son, known as Cadwal
QUEEN, Cymbeline's wife, Innogen's stepmother
Lord CLOTEN, the Queen's son
BELARIUS, a banished Lord, calling himself Morgan
CORNELIUS, a physician
HELEN, a lady attending on Innogen
Two LORDS, attending on Cloten
Two GENTLEMEN
Two British CAPTAINS
Two JAILERS
POSTHUMUS Leonatus, Innogen's husband
PISANIO, his servant
FILARIO, a friend of Posthumus
Filario's friends:
FRENCHMAN
DUTCHMAN
SPANIARD
GIACOMO, an Italian
Caius LUCIUS, ambassador, later General
Two Roman SENATORS
Roman TRIBUNES
Philharmonus, a SOOTHSAYER
JUPITER
Ghost of SICILIUS Leonatus, father of Posthumus
Ghost of the MOTHER of Posthumus
Ghosts of the BROTHERS of Posthumus
Lords attending Cymbeline, ladies attending the
Queen, musicians, messengers, soldiers

Quotations	Spoken by
Fear no more the heat o' th' sun, nor the furious winter' rages. Thou thy worldly task hast done, home art gone and ta'en thy wages. Golden lads and girls all must, as chimney-sweepers, come to dust.	Guiderius
Hark, hark! the lark at heaven's gate sings, and Phoebus gins arise.	Musician (sung)
I have not slept one wink.	Pisanio
Prouder than rustling in unpaid-for silk.	Belarius

Slander, whose edge is sharper than the sword, whose tongue outvenoms all the worms of Nile, whose breath rides on the posting winds and doth belie all corners of the world.	Pisanio
The natural bravery of your isle, which stands as Neptune's park, ribbed and paled in, with banks unscalable and roaring waters.	Queen
There will be many Caesars, ere such another Julius. Britain's a world by itself, and we will nothing pay for wearing our own noses.	Cloten
The sceptre, learning, physic, must all follow this, and come to dust	Arviragus
Weariness can snore upon the flint, when resty sloth finds the down pillow hard.	Belarius
With fairest flowers whilst summer lasts and I live here Fidele, I'll sweeten thy sad grave; thou shalt not lack the flower that's like thy face, pale primrose, nor the azured harebell, like thy veins, no, nor the leaf of eglantine, whom not to slander, out-sweeten'd not thy breath.	Arviragus

Précis of plot
Cymbeline is a tragicomedy full of intrigues and sub-plots, the most notable concerning the wager between Giacomo and Posthumus regarding the chastity of Posthumus' wife Innogen. The subsequent 'death' and awakening of Innogen are central to the events that happily conclude this fantasy.

Setting
Britain and Rome circa 1st century AD.

NB Cymbeline's daughter's name is given in the folio as Imogen, but this is thought to be a misprint.

7 Hamlet

Prince HAMLET, son of King Hamlet and Queen Gertrude	Courtiers:
GHOST of Hamlet, late King of Denmark	VALTEMAND
KING CLAUDIUS, his brother	CORNELIUS
QUEEN GERTRUDE of Denmark, wife of Claudius	OSRIC
POLONIUS, a Lord	GENTLEMEN
LAERTES, son of Polonius	
OPHELIA, a daughter of Polonius	SAILOR
REYNALDO, servant of Polonius	PRIEST
FORTINBRAS, Prince of Norway	
A CAPTAIN in his army	HORATIO
AMBASSADORS from England	ROSENCRANTZ
PLAYERS, who play the Prologue, King and Queen, and	GUILDENSTERN
Lucianus, in 'The Mousetrap'	Soldiers:
Lords, messengers, attendants, guards, soldiers	FRANCISCO
followers of Laertes, sailors	BARNARDO
Two CLOWNS, gravedigger and his companion	MARCELLUS

Quotations	**Spoken by**
A beast, that wants discourse of reason, would have mourned longer.	Hamlet
A certain convocation of political worms are e'en at him.	Hamlet
A countenance more in sorrow than in anger.	Horatio
A king of shreds and patches.	Hamlet
Alas, poor Yorick. I knew him, Horatio – a fellow of infinite jest, of most excellent fancy.	Hamlet
A little more than kin, and less than kind.	Hamlet
A man may fish with the worm that hath eat of a king, and eat of the fish that hath fed of that worm.	Hamlet
A man that fortune's buffets and rewards, hath ta'en with equal thanks.	Hamlet
And then it started like a guilty thing upon a fearful summons.	Horatio
And these few precepts in thy memory keep.	Polonius
And to my mind – though I am native here, and to the manner born, it is a custom more honoured in the breach than the observance.	Hamlet
Angels and ministers of grace defend us.	Hamlet
Assume a virtue, if you have it not.	Hamlet
A was a man. Take him for all in all, I shall not look upon his like again.	Hamlet
Ay, springes to catch woodcocks.	Polonius
Be all my sins remembered.	Hamlet
Beggar that I am, I am even poor in thanks.	Hamlet
Be somewhat scanter of your maiden presence.	Polonius
Be thou as chaste as ice, as pure as snow, thou shalt not escape calumny. Get thee to a nunnery, go, farewell.	Hamlet
Beware of entrance to a quarrel, but being in, bear't that the opposed may be aware of thee.	Polonius
Brevity is the soul of wit.	Polonius
But I am pigeon-liver'd and lack gall to make oppression bitter.	Hamlet
But I have that within which passeth show – these but the trappings and the suits of woe.	Hamlet
But in the gross and scope of my opinion, this bodes some strange eruption to our state.	Horatio
But, look, the morn, in russet mantle clad, walks o'er the dew of yon high eastern hill.	Horatio
But soft! methinks I scent the morning air.	Ghost
But that I am forbid to tell the secrets of my prison-house, I could a tale unfold.	Ghost
Come, give us a taste of your quality.	Hamlet
Cudgel thy brains no more about it.	First Clown
Cut off even in the blossoms of my sin.	Ghost
Do not, as some ungracious pastors do, show me the steep and thorny way to heaven.	Ophelia

Doubt thou the stars are fire; doubt that the sun doth move; doubt truth to be a liar; but never doubt I love.	Polonius
For this relief much thanks; tis bitter cold and I am sick at heart.	Francisco
Frailty thy name is woman.	Hamlet
Give it an understanding but no tongue.	Hamlet
Give me that man that is not passion's slave, and I will wear him in my heart's core, ay, in my heart of heart, as I do thee.	Hamlet
God's bodykins, man, much better. Use every man after his desert, and who should 'scape whipping?	Hamlet
Hath oped his ponderous and marble jaws.	Hamlet
His greatness weighed, his will is not his own.	Laertes
How now, a rat? dead for a ducat, dead.	Hamlet
I am but mad north-north-west; when the wind is southerly, I know a hawk from a handsaw.	Hamlet
I do not set my life at a pin's fee.	Hamlet
I doubt some foul play.	Hamlet
I have heard of your paintings too, well enough. God hath given you one face, and you make yourselves another.	Hamlet
I have thought some of nature's journeymen had made men and not made them well, they impersonated humanity so abominably.	Hamlet
Imperious Caesar, dead, and turn'd to clay. Might stop a hole to keep the wind away.	Hamlet
I must be cruel only to be kind.	Hamlet
In my mind's eye, Horatio.	Hamlet
In the dead waste and middle of the night.	Horatio
It goes so heavily with my disposition that this goodly frame, the earth, seems to me a sterile promontory.	Hamlet
It is not nor it cannot come to good. But break, my heart, for I must hold my tongue.	Hamlet
It out-Herods Herod.	Hamlet
It was as I have seen it in his life, a sable silver'd.	Horatio
It will discourse most excellent music.	Hamlet
I will speak daggers to her, but use none.	Hamlet
Look with what courteous action, it wafts you to a more removed ground.	Marcellus
Marry, this is miching *malhecho.* That means mischief.	Hamlet
More matter, with less art.	Queen Gertrude
Murder most foul, as in the best it is.	Ghost
Must, like a whore, unpack my heart with words.	Hamlet
My words fly up, my thoughts remain below.	King Claudius
Neither a borrower, nor a lender be.	Polonius
Now cracks a noble heart. Goodnight, sweet prince, and flight of angels sing thee to thy rest.	Horatio
O Hamlet, what a falling off was there!	Ghost
O, my offence is rank! it smells to heaven.	King Claudius
O my prophetic soul! mine uncle?	Hamlet
On fortune's cap we are not the very button.	Guildenstern
O, that this too too solid flesh would melt, thaw and resolve itself into a dew	Hamlet
O villain, villain, smiling, damned villain!	Hamlet
O, what a noble mind is here o'erthrown!	Ophelia
O, what a rogue and peasant slave am I.	Hamlet
Rest, rest, perturbed spirit!	Hamlet
Seems, madam? nay, it is; I know not 'seems'.	Hamlet
So excellent a king, that was, to this, Hyperion to a satyr: so loving to my mother, that he might not beteem the winds of heaven visit her face too roughly.	Hamlet
Some say that ever 'gainst that season comes, wherein our saviour's birth is celebrated, the bird of dawning singeth all night long.	Marcellus
Something is rotten in the state of Denmark.	Marcellus
Speak the speech, I pray you, as I pronounced it to you.	Hamlet
Still harping on my daughter.	Polonius
Suit the action to the word, the word to the action.	Hamlet
Take these again; for to the noble mind, rich gifts wax poor when givers prove unkind.	Ophelia
Tear a passion to tatters, to very rags, to split the ears of the groundlings.	Hamlet
That he is mad, 'tis true; 'tis true 'tis pity and pity 'tis 'tis true.	Polonius
The best actors in the world, either for tragedy, comedy, history pastoral, pastorical-comical, historical-pastoral, tragical-historical, tragical-comical-historical-pastoral, scene individable, or poem unlimited. Seneca cannot be too heavy, nor Plautus too light.	Polonius
The chariest maid is prodigal enough if she unmask her beauty to the moon.	Laertes
The glow-worm shows the matin to be near.	Ghost
The lady doth protest too much, methinks.	Queen Gertrude
The mobled queen.	Hamlet
The play, I remember, pleased not the million; 'twas caviare to the general.	Hamlet
The play's the thing wherein I'll catch the conscience of the King.	Hamlet
There are more things in heaven and earth, Horatio, than are dreamt of in your philosophy.	Hamlet
There is nothing either good or bad, but thinking makes it so.	Hamlet
There's rosemary, that's for remembrance. Pray, love, remember. And there is pansies; that's for thoughts.	Ophelia
The rest is silence. O, O, O, O!	Hamlet
These are but wild and whirling words, my lord.	Horatio
The time is out of joint. O cursed spite, that ever I was born to set it right.	Hamlet
They are the abstract and brief chronicles of the time.	Hamlet
This is the very coinage of your brain.	Queen Gertrude
This sweaty haste doth make the night joint-labourer with the day.	Marcellus

Though this be madness, yet there is method in't.	Polonius
Thou know'st 'tis common; all that lives must die.	Queen Gertrude
Thrift, thrift, Horatio! the funeral baked meats did coldly furnish forth the marriage tables.	Hamlet
'Tis now the very witching time of night, when churchyards yawn and hell itself breathes out contagion to this world.	Hamlet
To be, or not to be; that is the question: whether 'tis nobler in the mind to suffer the slings and arrows of outrageous fortune, or to take arms against a sea of troubles, and, by opposing, end them. To die, to sleep – no more, and by a sleep to say we end the heartache and the thousand natural shocks that flesh is heir to – 'tis a consummation devoutly to be wished. To die, to sleep. To sleep, perchance to dream. Ay, there's the rub, for in that sleep of death what dreams may come when we have shuffled off this mortal coil must give us pause.	Hamlet
Unhand me, gentlemen; by heaven, I'll make a ghost of him that lets me.	Hamlet
Very like a whale.	Polonius
We do it wrong, being so majestical, to offer it the show of violence.	Marcellus
We know what we are, but know not what we may be.	Ophelia
What, frighted with false fire?	Hamlet
What may this mean, that thou, dead corpse, again in complete steel, revisit'st thus the glimpses of the moon, making night hideous.	Hamlet
What's Hecuba to him or he to Hecuba, that he should weep for her?	Hamlet
What should such fellows as I do, crawling between earth and heaven.	Hamlet
When sorrows come, they come not single spies, but in battalions.	King Claudius
Whether in sea or fire, in earth or air, the extravagant and erring spirit hies to his confine.	Horatio
While memory holds a seat in this distracted globe.	Hamlet
While one with moderate haste might tell a hundred.	Horatio
Whose sore task does not divide the Sunday from the week.	Marcellus
Why, let the stricken deer go weep, the hart ungalled play, for some must watch, while some must sleep, so runs the world away.	Hamlet
Why, she would hang on him, as if increase of appetite had grown by what it fed on.	Hamlet
With devotion's visage and pious action we do sugar o'er the devil himself.	Polonius
With one auspicious and one dropping eye, with mirth in funeral and with dirge in marriage.	King Claudius

Précis of plot
King Hamlet has been murdered by his brother Claudius, who has usurped the throne and married Gertrude, the King's widow. Prince Hamlet gains his revenge by feigning madness and ultimately killing his would-be assassins and Claudius.

Setting
Denmark.

8 **Henry IV Part 1**

KING HENRY IV
PRINCE HARRY, Prince of Wales, Henry's son
Lord JOHN OF LANCASTER, Henry's son
Earl of WESTMORLAND
Sir Walter BLUNT
Earl of WORCESTER
Percy, Earl of NORTHUMBERLAND, his brother
Henry Percy, known as HOTSPUR, Northumberland's son
Kate, LADY PERCY, Hotspur's wife
Lord Edmund MORTIMER, called Earl of March
LADY MORTIMER, his wife
OWAIN GLYNDWR, Lady Mortimer's father
Mistress Quickly, HOSTESS of an Eastcheap inn
Sir Richard VERNON
Scrope, ARCHBISHOP of York
SIR MICHAEL, member of the Archbishop's household
SIR JOHN Oldcastle
Edward (Ned) POINS
RUSSELL
HARVEY
Earl of DOUGLAS
FRANCIS, a drawer
VINTNER
GADSHILL
CARRIERS
CHAMBERLAIN
OSTLER
TRAVELLERS
SHERIFF
MESSENGERS
SERVANT
Lords and soldiers

Quotations	**Spoken by**
A fellow of no mark nor likelihood.	King Henry
And such a deal of skimble-skamble stuff.	Hotspur
A plague of all cowards, I say.	Sir John
A plague of sighing and grief, it blows a man up like a bladder.	Sir John
Banish plump Jack, and banish all the world.	Sir John
By heaven, methinks it were an easy leap.	Hotspur
Came there a certain lord, neat and trimly dressed, fresh as a bridegroom, and his chin, new reaped, showed like a stubble-land at harvest-home. He was perfumed like a milliner, and 'twixt his finger and his thumb he held a pouncet-box, which ever and anon he gave his nose and took't away again.	Hotspur
Company, villainous company hath been the spoil of me.	Sir John
Domesday is near: die all, die merrily.	Hotspur
Farewell, the latter spring; farewell, All-hallown summer.	Prince Harry
He made me mad, to see him shine so brisk, and smell so sweet, and talk so like a waiting-gentlewoman, of guns and drums, and wounds, God save the mark! and telling me the sovereign'st thing on earth was parmacity for an inward bruise.	Hotspur
He was but as the cuckoo is in June, heard, not regarded.	King Henry
I am bewitched by the rogue's company.	Sir John
I am not in the role of common men.	Glyndwr
I am not yet of Percy's mind, the Hotspur of the North – he that kills me some six or seven dozen of Scots at a breakfast, washes his hands, and says to his wife, 'Fie upon this quiet life! I want work.'	Prince Harry

I could brain him with his lady's fan.	Hotspur
If all the year were playing holidays, to sport would be as tedious as to work.	Prince Harry
If reasons were as plentiful as blackberries.	Sir John
In those holy fields, over whose acres walk'd those blessed feet; which fourteen hundred years ago were nailed, for our advantage, on the bitter cross.	King Henry
I saw young Harry, with his beaver on.	Vernon
It would be argument for a week, laughter for a month, and a good jest forever.	Prince Harry
I understand thy kisses, and thou mine.	Mortimer
Let us be Diana's foresters, gentlemen of the shade, minions of the moon.	Sir John
Look down into the pomegranate, Ralph!	Francis
O, the blood more stirs to rouse a lion than to start a hare!	Hotspur
Old father antic, the law.	Sir John
So shaken as we are, so wan with care.	King Henry
O, thou hast damnable iteration, and art indeed able to corrupt a saint.	Sir John
O, monstrous! eleven buckram men grown out of two!	Prince Harry
Tell truth and shame the devil.	Hotspur
There lives not three good men unhanged in England, and one of them is fat and grows old.	Sir John
There's neither honesty, manhood, nor good fellowship in thee.	Sir John
'Tis my vocation, Hal. 'Tis no sin for a man to labour in his vocation.	Sir John
Two stars keep not their motion in one sphere	Prince Harry
What, in thy quips and thy quiddities.	Sir John
You rogue, they were bound every man of them, or I am a jew else, an Hebrew jew.	Sir John

Précis of plot

The main plot tells of the rebellions against King Henry by Worcester, Hotspur and Glyndwr. However, the sub-plots highlighting the characters of the young Prince Hal and the reprobate Sir John Oldcastle (Falstaff) lend the real substance to the play.

Setting

England in the early 15th century.

9 **Henry IV Part 2**

KING HENRY IV
PRINCE HARRY, later crowned King Henry V
PRINCE JOHN of Lancaster, Henry IV's son
SIR JOHN Falstaff
Bardolf
Poins
Falstaff's Page
Humphrey, Duke of GLOUCESTER, Henry IV's son
Thomas, Duke of CLARENCE, Henry IV's son
Percy, Earl of NORTHUMBERLAND, of the rebels' party
NORTHUMBERLAND'S WIFE
KATE, their son Hotspur's widow
TRAVERS, Northumberland's servant
MORTON, a bearer of news from Shrewsbury
Scrope, ARCHBISHOP of York
Thomas, Lord MOWBRAY, the Earl Marshal
MISTRESS QUICKLY, hostess of a tavern
PORTER of Northumberland's household
Robert SHALLOW, a country justice
DAVY, Shallow's servant
SILENCE, a country justice
Sneak and other musicians
Lord Chief Justice's men, soldiers and attendants
Ensign PISTOL
PETO
DOLL TEARSHEET, a whore
GOWER, a messenger
Sir John Blunt
Sir John Coleville
Lord Hastings
SNARE, a sergeant
FANG, a sergeant
Neville, Earl of WARWICK
Earl of SURREY
Earl of WESTMORLAND
HARCOURT
Ralph MOULDY
Simon SHADOW
Thomas WART
Francis FEEBLE
Peter BULLCALF
DRAWERS
BEADLES
GROOMS
MESSENGER

Quotations	**Spoken by**
A foutre for the world and worldlings base! I speak of Africa and golden joys.	Pistol
A joint of mutton, and any pretty little tiny kickshaws.	Shallow
A man can die but once.	Feeble
A rascally yea-forsooth knave.	Sir John
An habitation giddy and unsure, hath he that buildeth on the vulgar heart.	Archbishop of York
Away, you scullion, you rampallian, you fustilarian! I'll tickle your catastrophe.	Page
By my troth, captain, these are very bitter words.	Mistress Quickly
Death, as the psalmist saith, is certain to all; all shall die. How a good yoke of bullocks at Stamford fair?	Shallow
Even such a man, so faint, so spiritless, so dull, so dead in look, so woe-begone, drew Priam's curtain in the dead of night.	Northumberland
For my voice, I have lost it with hallowing and singing of anthems.	Sir John
He hath eaten me out of house and home.	Mistress Quickly
He was indeed the glass wherein the noble youth did dress themselves.	Lady Percy
I am not only witty in myself, but the cause that wit is in other men.	Sir John
I beseek you now, aggravate your choler.	Mistress Quickly
I can get no remedy against this consumption of the purse. Borrowing only lingers and lingers it out, but the disease is incurable.	Sir John
If I do, fillip me with a three-man beetle.	Sir John
Is it not strange that desire should so many years outlive performance.	Poins
I know thee not old man, fall to thy prayers.	King Harry
It was always yet the trick of our English nation, if they have a good thing, to make it too common.	Sir John
Let the end try the man.	Prince Harry
Lord, Lord, how subject we old men are to this vice of lying.	Sir John

O, sleep, O gentle sleep, nature's soft nurse, how have I frighted thee, that thou no more wilt weigh my eyelids down, and steep my senses in forgetfulness.	King Henry
Past and to come seems best; things present, worst.	Archbishop of York
Thou didst swear to me, upon a parcel-gilt goblet, sitting in my Dolphin-chamber, at the round table, by a sea coal fire, upon Wednesday in Wheeson week.	Mistress Quickly
Under which king, Besonian? speak, or die.	Pistol
Uneasy lies the head that wears a crown.	King Henry
We have heard the chimes at midnight, Master Shallow.	Sir John
We that are in the vanguard of our youth, I must confess, are wags too.	Sir John
Wilt thou upon the high and giddy mast, seal up the ship-boy's eyes, and rock his brains.	King Henry
With all appliances, and means to boot.	King Henry
Yet the first bringer of unwelcome news hath but a losing office, and his tongue sounds ever after as a sullen bell remembered knolling a departing friend.	Northumberland

Précis of plot

The plot of the first part of Henry IV is continued, although there are subtle changes made to certain characters and the historical content is not so highlighted. Hal is still plagued with rebellions, albeit from different spheres, but his anxieties over Prince Harry's behaviour are eventually alleviated in a touching scene, and this change of character is shown to the full in Harry's rejection of Sir John after his crowning.

Setting

England in the early 15th century.

10 Henry V

KING HARRY V of England, claimant to French throne
Duke of GLOUCESTER, the King's brother
Duke of CLARENCE, the King's brother
Duke of EXETER, his uncle
KING CHARLES VI of France
ISABEL, his wife and queen
The DAUPHIN, their son and heir
CATHERINE, their daughter
Archbishop of CANTERBURY
ALICE, an old gentlewoman
Richard, Earl of CAMBRIDGE
Henry, Lord SCROPE of Masham
The CONSTABLE of France
MONTJOY, the French Herald
GOVERNOR of Harfleur
French AMBASSADORS to England
BOY, formerly Falstaff's page
HOSTESS, formerly Mistress Quickly, now Pistol's wife
Captain GOWER, an Englishman
Captain FLUELLEN, a Welshman
Captain MACMORRIS, an Irishman
Captain JAMY, a Scot
Sir Thomas ERPINGHAM
John BATES
Alexander COURT
Michael WILLIAMS
HERALD
Duke of YORK
SALISBURY
WESTMORLAND
WARWICK
Bishop of ELY
Sir Thomas GREY
Duke of BOURBON
Duke of ORLÉANS
Duke of BERRI
Lord RAMBURES
Lord GRANDPRÉ
Duke of BURGUNDY
PISTOL
NIM
BARDOLPH
CHORUS

Quotations	**Spoken by**
All hell shall stir for this.	Pistol
And gentlemen in England now abed, shall think themselves accursed they were not here, and hold their manhoods cheap while any speaks, that fought with us upon Saint Crispin's day.	King Harry
And make your chronicle as rich with praise, as is the ooze and bottom of the sea.	Canterbury
As 'tis ever common that men are merriest when they are from home.	King Harry
Base is the slave that pays.	Pistol
But if it be a sin to covet honour, I am the most offending soul alive.	King Harry
Can this cock-pit hold the vasty fields of France? or may we cram, within this wooden O the very casques that did affright the air at Agincourt?	Chorus
Consideration like an angel came, and whipp'd the offending Adam out of him.	Canterbury
Cry, 'God for Harry! England and Saint George.'	King Harry
Every subject's duty is the king's; but every subject's soul is his own.	King Harry
For so work the honey-bees, creatures that by a rule in nature teach the act of order to a peopled kingdom.	Canterbury
For these fellows of infinite tongue, that can rhyme themselves into ladies' favours, they do always reason themselves out again.	King Harry
From camp to camp through the foul womb of night.	Chorus
He's in Arthur's bosom, if ever man went to Arthur's bosom.	Hostess
I dare not fight, but I will wink and hold out mine iron.	Nim
I see you stand like greyhounds in the slips.	King Harry
If he be not fellow with the best king, thou shalt find the best king of good fellows.	King Harry
If we are marked to die, we are enough to do our country loss; and if to live, the fewer men, the greater share of honour.	King Harry
I thought upon one pair of English legs did march three Frenchmen.	King Harry
Men of few words are the best men.	Boy
Now all the youth of England are on fire, and silken dalliance in the wardrobe lies.	Chorus
O that we now had here, but one ten thousand of those men in England that do no work today!	Warwick
Old men forget, yet all shall be forgot; but he'll remember with advantages, what feats he did that day.	King Harry
Once more unto the breach, dear friends, once more.	King Harry
On, on, you noblest English, whose blood is fet from fathers of war-proof. Fathers that,	King Harry

like so many Alexanders, have in these parts from morn til even fought, and sheathed their swords for lack of argument.	
Self love, my liege, is not so vile a sin as self neglecting.	Dauphin
Tennis balls, my liege.	Exeter
Then shall our names, familiar in his mouth as household words – Harry the King, Bedford and Exeter, Warwick and Talbot, Salisbury and Gloucester – be in their flowing cups, freshly remember'd.	King Harry
There is occasions and causes why and wherefore in all things.	Fluellen
There is some soul of goodness in these evils.	King Harry
This day is called the feast of Crispian. He that outlives this day and comes safe home will stand a-tiptoe when this day is named, and rouse him of the name of Crispian.	King Harry
Though patience be a tired mare, yet she will plod.	Nim
Trust none, for oaths are straws, men's faiths are wafer-cakes, and hold-fast is the only dog, my duck.	Pistol
Turn him to any cause of policy, the Gordian knot of it he will unloose.	Canterbury
We few, we happy few, we band of brothers.	King Harry

Précis of plot
The war against France dominates the play, although Shakespeare stayed loyal to many characters from the two parts of Henry IV to create comic diversion.

Setting
England and France 1414 to 1420.

11 Henry VI Part 1

KING HENRY VI
Duke of GLOUCESTER, Lord Protector, uncle of Henry
Duke of BEDFORD, regent of France
Duke of EXETER
Bishop of WINCHESTER (later Cardinal), uncle of Henry
Duke of SOMERSET
RICHARD PLANTAGENET, later DUKE OF YORK
Duke of BURGUNDY, uncle of King Henry
GENERAL of the French garrison at Bordeaux
RENÉ, Duke of Anjou, King of Naples
MARGARET, his daughter
Sir William GLASDALE
Sir Thomas GARGRAVE
Sir John FASTOLF
Sir William LUCY
CHARLES, Dauphin of France
WOODVILLE, Lieutenant of the Tower of London
Porter, French sergeant, sentinels, scout, herald, officers
Governor of Paris, fiends and soldiers, servingmen
Messengers and keepers of the Tower of London
BASSET
A LAWYER
A LEGATE
Earl of WARWICK
Earl of SALISBURY
Earl of SUFFOLK
Edmund MORTIMER
Duke of ALENÇON
BASTARD of Orléans
Lord TALBOT
JOHN Talbot
COUNTESS of Auvergne
MASTER GUNNER of Orléans
A BOY, his son
JOAN la Pucelle
A SHEPHERD, father of Joan
MAYOR of London
VERNON

Quotations	**Spoken by**
And while I live, I'll ne'er fly from a man.	Joan
Between two hawks, which flies the higher pitch. Between two dogs, which hath the deeper mouth. Between two blades, which bears the better temper. Between two horses, which doth bear him best. Between two girls, which hath the merriest eye. I have perhaps some shallow spirit of judgement.	Warwick
Christ's mother helps me, else I were too weak.	Joan
Unbidden guests are often welcomest when they are gone.	Bedford

Précis of plot
The first part of Henry VI covers the period between the funeral of Henry V and the end of the Hundred Years War, between England and France. As in many of the Shakespearian plays, the historical accuracy comes second to the plot.

Setting
England 1422 to 1453.

12 Henry VI Part 2

KING HENRY VI and QUEEN MARGARET
William de la Pole, Marquis, later Duke of SUFFOLK
Duke Humphrey of GLOUCESTER, the Lord Protector
Dame Eleanor Cobham, the DUCHESS of Gloucester
CARDINAL BEAUFORT, Bishop of Winchester
Duke of BUCKINGHAM
Duke of SOMERSET
Old Lord CLIFFORD and YOUNG CLIFFORD, his son
Duke of YORK
EDWARD, Earl of March, the Duke's son
Crookback RICHARD, the Duke's son
Earl of SALISBURY and Earl of WARWICK, his son
Emmanuel, the CLERK of Chatham
Two or three PETITIONERS
Thomas HORNER, an armourer
PETER Thump, his man
Three NEIGHBOURS, who drink to Horner
Gloucester's SERVANTS
Two SHERIFFS of London
Sir John STANLEY
HERALD
Two MURDERERS
COMMONS
CAPTAIN of a ship
MASTER of that ship
The Master's MATE
Walter WHITMORE
Two GENTLEMEN
Jack CADE, a Kentishman
Dick the BUTCHER
Smith the WEAVER
A sawyer
JOHN
REBELS

Three PRENTICES, who drink to Peter
Sir John HUME, a priest
John SOUTHWELL, a priest
Margery Jordan, a WITCH
Roger BOLINGBROKE, a conjurer
ASNATH, a spirit
Three or four CITIZENS of London
Simon SIMPCOX and SIMPCOX'S WIFE
The MAYOR of Saint Albans
Alexander IDEN, who kills Cade
Aldermen of Saint Albans
Attendants, guards, servants, soldiers, falconers

Sir Humphrey STAFFORD
STAFFORD'S BROTHER
Lord SAYE
Lord SCALES
Matthew Gough
A SERGEANT
A BEADLE of Saint Albans
Townsmen of Saint Albans
VAUX, a messenger
A POST
MESSENGERS
A SOLDIER

Quotations	**Spoken by**
Could I come near your beauty with my nails, I'd set my ten commandments in your face.	Duchess
Is not this a lamentable thing that of the skin of an innocent lamb should be made parchment? that parchment being scribbled o'er should undo a man?	Cade
Sir, he made a chimney in my father's house, and the bricks are alive at this day to testify.	Weaver
Smooth runs the water where the brook is deep.	Suffolk
The first thing we do let's kill all the lawyers.	Dick the Butcher
The gaudy, blabbing, and remorseful day, is crept into the bosom of the sea.	Captain
There shall be in England seven halfpenny loaves sold for a penny, the three-hooped pot shall have ten hoops and I will make it a felony to drink small beer.	Cade
Thou hast most traitorously corrupted the youth of the realm in erecting a grammar school; and, whereas before, our forefathers had no books but the score and tally, thou hast caused printing to be used and, contrary to the King, his crown and dignity, thou hast built a paper mill.	Cade
What stronger breastplate than a heart untainted.	King Henry

Précis of plot
The original title of this play was *The First Part of the Contention of the Two Famous Houses of York and Lancaster*, and Shakespeare has stayed true, to a great extent, to this period of history, which includes the Kentish rebellion led by Jack Cade, and ultimately leads to the Wars of the Roses.

Setting
England 1445 to 1455.

13 Henry VI Part 3
KING HENRY VI
QUEEN MARGARET
PRINCE EDWARD, their son
Duke of SOMERSET
Duke of EXETER
Earl of NORTHUMBERLAND
Earl of WESTMORLAND
Lord CLIFFORD
Lord Stafford
SOMERVILLE
Henry, young Earl of Richmond
A SOLDIER who has killed his father
A HUNTSMAN who guards King Edward
The divided House of Neville:
Earl of WARWICK
Marquis of MONTAGUE, his brother
Earl of OXFORD, their brother-in-law
Lord HASTINGS, their brother-in-law
Of the Duke of York's party:
Richard Plantagenet, Duke of YORK
EDWARD, Earl of March, his son, later KING EDWARD IV
LADY GRAY, a widow, later Edward's wife and queen
Earl RIVERS, Lady Gray's brother

GEORGE, later DUKE OF CLARENCE
RICHARD, later DUKE OF GLOUCESTER
Earl of RUTLAND, Edward's brother
Rutland's TUTOR, a chaplain
SIR JOHN Mortimer, York's uncle
Sir Hugh Mortimer, his brother
Duke of NORFOLK
Sir William Stanley
Earl of Pembroke
Sir John MONTGOMERY
A NOBLEMAN
Two GAMEKEEPERS
Three WATCHMEN
LIEUTENANT of the Tower

The French:
KING LOUIS
LADY BONA, his sister-in-law
Lord Bourbon, the French High Admiral

A SOLDIER who has killed his son
Mayor of Coventry
MAYOR of York
Aldermen of YORK
Soldiers, messengers and attendants

Quotations	**Spoken by**
Didst thou never hear that things ill got had ever bad success?	King Henry
Down, down to hell, and say I sent thee thither.	Richard of Gloucester
Gives not the hawthorn bush a sweeter shade, to shepherds looking on their seely sheep, than doth a rich embroider'd canopy, to Kings that fear their subjects' treachery?	King Henry
My crown is in my heart, not on my head.	King Henry
O God! methinks it were a happy life, to be no better than a homely swain, to sit upon a hill, as I do now; to carve out dials quaintly, point by point, thereby to see the minutes how they run. How many makes the hour full complete, how many hours bring about the day, how many days will finish up the year, how many years a mortal man may live.	King Henry
Oh tiger's heart wrapp'd in a woman's hide!	York
Suspicion always haunts the guilty mind, the thief doth fear each bush an officer.	Richard of Gloucester

Précis of plot

This play chronicles the substantive episodes in the War of the Roses, although the usual Shakespearian anachronisms do not detract from the play's subtleties.

Setting
England 1455 to 1471.

14 Henry VIII (All Is True)

PROLOGUE
KING HENRY VIII
Duke of BUCKINGHAM
Lord ABERGAVENNY
Earl of SURREY
Duke of NORFOLK
Duke of SUFFOLK
LORD CHAMBERLAIN
LORD CHANCELLOR
Lord SANDS (aka Sir William Sands)
Sir Thomas LOVELL
Sir Anthony DENNY
Sir Henry GUILDFORD
CARDINAL WOLSEY
Two SECRETARIES
Buckingham's SURVEYOR
CARDINAL CAMPEIUS
GARDINER, King's secretary, later Bishop of Winchester
His PAGE
Thomas CROMWELL
CRANMER, Archbishop of Canterbury
QUEEN KATHERINE, later KATHERINE, Princess Dowager
GRIFFITH, her gentleman usher
PATIENCE, her waiting woman
Other WOMEN
Six spirits who dance before Katherine in a vision
At Cranmer's trial:
A DOOR-KEEPER
Doctor BUTTS, the King's physician
Pursuivants, pages, footboys, grooms
BRANDON
SERJEANT-AT-ARMS
Sir Nicholas VAUX
Tipstaves, Halberdiers and common people
Appearing at the Legatine Court:
Two vergers
Ladies, gentlemen, a SERVANT, attendants

Archbishop of Canterbury
Bishop of LINCOLN
Bishop of Ely
Bishop of Rochester
Bishop of Saint Asaph
Two priests
Serjeant-at-arms
Two noblemen
A CRIER
Appearing in the Coronation:
Three GENTLEMEN
Two judges
Choristers
Lord Mayor of London
Garter King of Arms
Marquis of Dorset
Four Barons of the Cinque Ports
Stokesley, Bishop of London
Old Duchess of Norfolk
Countesses

A MESSENGER
Lord CAPUTIUS
ANNE Boleyn
An OLD LADY
At the Christening:
A PORTER
His MAN
Two aldermen
Lord Mayor of London
GARTER King of Arms
Six noblemen
Old Duchess of Norfolk, godmother
Princess Elizabeth, the child
Marchioness Dorset, godmother

EPILOGUE
Two SCRIBES

Quotations	**Spoken by**
A peace above all earthly dignities, a still and quiet conscience.	Cardinal Wolsey
Cromwell, I charge thee, fling away ambition. By that sin fell the angels.	Cardinal Wolsey
Had I but serv'd my God with half the zeal I served my King, he would not in mine age have left me naked to mine enemies.	Cardinal Wolsey
Heaven is above all yet – there sits a judge that no king can corrupt.	Queen Katherine
He gave his honours to the world again, his blessed part to heaven, and slept in peace.	Griffith
He was a man of an unbounded stomach.	Katherine
Love thyself last. Cherish those hearts that hate thee.	Cardinal Wolsey
He was a scholar, and a ripe and good one.	Griffith
Men's evil manners live in brass; their virtues we write in water	Griffith
So farewell – to the little good you bear me. Farewell, a long farewell, to all my greatness!	Cardinal Wolsey
So may he rest, his faults lie gently on him.	Katherine
Those twins of learning that he raised in you, Ipswich and Oxford.	Griffith
'Tis better to be lowly born, and range with humble livers in content, than to be perk'd up in a glistering grief and wear a golden sorrow.	Anne
Vain pomp and glory of this world, I hate ye!	Cardinal Wolsey

Précis of plot
The reign of Henry VIII from the opening description of the Field of the Cloth of Gold, of 1520, to the christening of Princess Elizabeth, in 1533.

Setting
England 1521 to 1533.

15 Julius Caesar

Julius CAESAR
CALPURNIA, his wife
Marcus BRUTUS, a noble Roman, opposed to Caesar
PORTIA, his wife
LUCIUS, his servant
Officers and soldiers in Brutus' army:
LUCILLIUS

ARTEMIDORUS
CINNA the Poet
Opposed to Caesar:
Caius CASSIUS
CASCA
TREBONIUS
DECIUS Brutus

MESSALA
VARRUS
CLAUDIO
YOUNG CATO
STRATO
VOLUMNIUS
FLAVIUS
DARDANIUS
CLITUS
Rulers of Rome after Caesar's death:
Mark ANTONY
OCTAVIUS Caesar
LEPIDUS

PINDARUS, Cassius' bondman
TITINIUS, an officer in Cassius' army
POPILLIUS Laena, a Senator
Senators, soldiers and attendants

METELLUS Cimber
CINNA
Caius LIGARIUS

FLAVIUS, a tribune
MURELLUS, a tribune
CICERO, a Senator
PUBLIUS, a Senator

A POET
GHOST of Caesar
A COBBLER
A CARPENTER
Other PLEBEIANS
A MESSENGER
SERVANTS
SOOTHSAYER

Quotations	**Spoken by**
As Caesar loved me, I weep for him.	Brutus
As proper men as ever trod upon neat's leather have gone upon my handiwork.	Cobbler
Between the acting of a dreadful thing and the first motion, all the interim is like a phantasma, or a hideous dream.	Brutus
Beware the ides of March.	Soothsayer
But for your words, they rob the Hybla bees, and leave them honeyless.	Cassius
But I am constant as the Northern Star, of whose true fixed and resting quality, there is no fellow in the firmament.	Caesar
But when I tell him he hates flatterers; he says he does being then most flattered.	Decius
But yesterday the word of Caesar might have stood against the world. Now lies he there, and none so poor to do him reverence.	Antony
Caesar said to me 'Darest thou, Cassius, now leap in with me into this angry flood, and swim to yonder point?' Upon the word, accoutred as I was I plunged in and bade him follow.	Cassius
Cowards die many times before their deaths; the valiant never taste of death but once.	Caesar
Cry 'havoc' and let slip the dogs of war.	Antony
Et tu, Brute? – then fall Caesar.	Caesar (last words)
Fierce fiery warriors fight upon the clouds, in ranks and squadrons and right form of war.	Calpurnia
For Brutus is an honourable man; so are they all, all honourable men.	Antony
For he will never follow anything that other men begin.	Brutus
For I have neither wit, nor words, nor worth, action nor utterance, nor the power of speech, to stir men's blood.	Antony
Friends, Romans, countrymen, lend me your ears.	Antony
He reads much, he is a great observer, and he looks quite through the deeds of men.	Caesar
His life was gentle, and the elements so mixed in him that nature might stand up and say to all the world, 'This was a man'.	Antony
How hard it is for women to keep counsel!	Portia
How many ages hence, shall this our lofty scene be acted over, in states unborn and accents yet unknown.	Cassius
I am no orator as Brutus is; but as you know me all, a plain blunt man.	Antony
I am not gamesome; I do lack some part of that quick spirit that is in Antony.	Brutus
If you have tears, prepare to shed them now.	Antony
I had rather be a dog and bay the moon than such a Roman.	Brutus
Let me have men about me who are fat.	Caesar
Let's carve him as a dish fit for the gods.	Brutus
Lowliness is young ambition's ladder, whereto the climber upward turns his face; but when he once attains the upmost round, he then unto the ladder turns his back, looks in the clouds, scorning the base degrees by which he did ascend.	Brutus
Now in the name of all the gods at once, upon what meat doth this our Caesar feed, that he is grown so great?	Cassius
O judgement, thou art fled to brutish beasts, and men have lost their reasons!	Antony
O pardon me, thou bleeding piece of earth, that I am meek and gentle with these butchers!	Antony
See what a rent the envious Casca made.	Antony
Set honour in one eye and death i'th'other, and I will look on both indifferently.	Brutus
There is a tide in the affairs of men, which, taken at the flood, leads on to fortune.	Brutus
There was a Brutus once that would have brooked the eternal devil to keep his state in Rome, as easily as a king.	Cassius
This was the most unkindest cut of all.	Antony
This was the noblest Roman of them all.	Antony
Well, honour is the subject of my story. I cannot tell what you and other men think of this life; but, for my single self, I had as lief not be, as live to be in awe of such a thing as I myself.	Cassius
When beggars die, there are no comets seen; the heavens themselves blaze forth the death of princes.	Calpurnia
When love begins to sicken and decay, it useth an enforced ceremony.	Brutus
Why, he that cuts off twenty years of life, cuts off so many years of fearing death.	Casca
Why, man, he doth bestride the narrow world like a Colossus.	Cassius
Yet Brutus says he was ambitious, and Brutus is an honourable man.	Antony
Yond Cassius has a lean and hungry look. He thinks too much. Such men are dangerous.	Caesar

You are my true and honourable wife, as dear to me as are the ruddy drops that visit my sad heart.	Brutus
You blocks, you stones, you worse than senseless things!	Murellus

Précis of plot
The play depicts the events that led to the assassination of Julius Caesar and the aftermath thereof. As in many Shakespearian History plays, facts are often altered and rearranged in the interests of dramatic economy and effectiveness.

Setting
Rome, Sardis and near Philippi 44 to 42 BC.

16 King John

KING JOHN of England
QUEEN ELEANOR, his mother
LADY FALCONBRIDGE
Philip the BASTARD, later knighted as Richard Plantagenet, her illegitimate son by King Richard I
Robert FALCONBRIDGE, her legitimate son
James GURNEY, her attendant
Lady BLANCHE of Spain, niece of King John
PRINCE HENRY, son of King John
HUBERT, a follower of King John
LOUIS THE DAUPHIN, his son
ARTHUR, Duke of Brittaine, nephew of King John
Lady CONSTANCE, his mother
Duke of AUSTRIA (Limoges)
CHÂTILLON, ambassador
Cardinal PANDOLF, a legate from the Pope
PETER OF POMFRET, a prophet
Lords, soldiers, attendants
Earl of SALISBURY
Earl of PEMBROKE
Earl of ESSEX
Lord BIGOT
A CITIZEN of Angers
HERALDS
EXECUTIONERS
MESSENGERS
SHERIFF

Quotations	**Spoken by**
And oftentimes excusing of a fault doth make the fault the worser by th' excuse.	Pembroke
Another lean unwashed artificer cuts off his tale, and talks of Arthur's death.	Hubert
For courage mounteth with occasion.	Duke of Austria
Heat me these irons hot.	Hubert
Here is my throne; bid kings come bow to it.	Constance
How oft the sight of means to do ill deeds, make deeds ill done!	King John
Life is as tedious as a twice-told tale, vexing the dull ear of a drowsy man.	Louis the Dauphin
Lord of thy presence, and no land beside?	Queen Eleanor
Saint George that swinged the dragon, and e'er since sits on his horseback at mine hostess' door.	Bastard
This England never did, nor never shall, lie at the proud foot of a conqueror.	Bastard
To gild refined gold, to paint the lily.	Salisbury
When Fortune means to men most good, she looks upon them with a threatening eye.	Pandolf
Zounds! I was never so bethumped with words, since first I called my brother's father, dad.	Bastard

Précis of plot
Selected events from King John's reign are portrayed, although Shakespeare concentrates on Philip Falconbridge, the illegitimate son of Richard I, for his sub-plot; and significant events such as Magna Carta are ignored.

Setting
England and France 1199 to 1216.

17 King Lear

LEAR, King of Britain
GONERIL, Lear's eldest daughter
Duke of ALBANY, her husband
REGAN, Lear's second daughter
Duke of CORNWALL, her husband
CORDELIA, Lear's youngest daughter
King of FRANCE, a suitor of Cordelia
Duke of BURGUNDY, a suitor of Cordelia
Earl of KENT, later disguised as Caius
Earl of GLOUCESTER
EDGAR, later disguised as Tom o' Bedlam
EDMOND, bastard son of Gloucester
OLD MAN, Gloucester's tenant
Lear's FOOL
OSWALD, Goneril's steward
A SERVANT of Cornwall
A KNIGHT
A HERALD
A CAPTAIN
Gentlemen, servants, soldiers, attendants

Quotations	**Spoken by**
And my poor fool is hanged. No, No, no life? Why should a dog, a horse, a rat have life and thou no breath at all?	Lear
As flies to wanton boys are we to the gods, they kill us for their sport	Gloucester
A still soliciting eye, and such a tongue.	Cordelia
Blow, winds, and crack your cheeks! rage, blow, you cataracts and hurricanoes, spout.	Lear
Drinks the green mantle of the standing pool.	Edgar
Fie, foe, and fum; I smell the blood of a British man.	Edgar
Fortune, good night; smile once more; turn thy wheel.	Kent
Howl, howl, howl, howl! O, you are men of stones.	Lear
How sharper than a serpent's tooth it is to have a thankless child.	Lear
I am a man more sinned against than sinning.	Lear

I have seen better faces in my time than stands on any shoulder that I see before me at this instant.	Kent
I have seen the day, with my good biting falchion.	Lear
I'll talk a word with this same learned Theban.	Lear
Ingratitude, thou marble-hearted fiend.	Lear
I tax you not, you elements, with unkindness.	Lear
Mastiff, greyhound, mongrel grim.	Edgar
My cue is villainous melancholy, with a sigh like Tom o' Bedlam.	Edmond
O, that way madness lies. Let me shun that.	Lear
Out-paramoured the Turk.	Edgar
Poor naked wretches, whereso'er you are.	Lear
Poor Tom's a-cold.	Edgar
So young and so untender?	Lear
Take physic, pomp, expose thyself to feel what wretches feel.	Lear
The gods are just, and of our pleasant vices, make instruments to plague us.	Edgar
The little dogs and all, Tray, Blanch, and sweetheart see, they bark at me.	Lear
The prince of darkness is a gentleman.	Edgar
These late eclipses in the sun and moon portend no good to us.	Gloucester
The wheel has come full circle.	Edmond
The worst is not so long as we can say 'This is the worst'.	Edgar
Things that love night, love not such nights as these.	Kent
This is the excellent foppery of the world; that when we are sick in fortune – often the surfeits of our own behaviour – we make guilty of our disasters the sun, the moon, and stars, as if we were villains by necessity, fools by heavenly compulsion, knaves, thieves, and treachers by spherical predominance, drunkards, liars, and adulterers by an enforced obedience of planetary influence; and all that we are evil in by a divine thrusting on.	Edmond
This is the foul fiend Flibbertigibbet; he begins at curfew, and walks 'til the first cock.	Edgar
Thou whoreson Z, thou unnecessary letter.	Kent
'Tis a naughty night to swim in.	Fool
Vex not his ghost, O let him pass.	Kent
You are not worth the dust which the rude wind blows in your face.	Albany

Précis of plot

The story of a king who, angry with the failure of his virtuous youngest daughter, Cordelia, to compete for his favour in a love-test, divides his kingdom between her two malevolent sisters. The sub-plot depicts Lear's madness and the blinding of Gloucester, as well as Edgar's loyalty to his father.

Setting

Britain.

18 Love's Labour's Lost

Ferdinand, KING of Navarre
Lords attending on the King:
BIRON
LONGUEVILLE
DUMAINE

PRINCESS of France
Ladies attending on the Princess:
ROSALINE
KATHERINE
MARIA

BOYET
Two other LORDS
COSTARD, a Clown
JAQUENETTA, a country wench
Sir NATHANIEL, a curate
HOLOFERNES, a schoolmaster
Anthony DULL, a constable
MERCADÉ, a messenger
A FORESTER
Don Adriano de ARMADO, a Spanish braggart
MOTE, his page

Quotations	**Spoken by**
A jest's prosperity lies in the ear of him that hears it, never in the tongue of him that makes it.	Rosaline
A lover's eyes will gaze an eagle blind; a lover's ear will hear the lowest sound.	Biron
At Christmas I no more desire a rose, than wish a snow in May's new-fangled mirth.	Biron
A very beadle to a humorous sigh.	Biron
Devise wit, write pen, for I am for whole volumes, in folio.	Armado
He draweth out the thread of his verbosity finer than the staple of his argument.	Holofernes
He hath never fed of the dainties that are bred in a book.	Nathaniel
In the posteriors of this day, which the rude multitude call the afternoon.	Armado
Light, seeking light, doth light of light beguile.	Biron
Remuneration – O, that's the Latin word for three-farthings.	Costard
Spite of cormorant devouring time.	King
Study is like the heavens' glorious sun, that will not be deep-searched with saucy looks. Small have continual plodders ever won, save base authority from others' books.	Biron
This wimpled, whining, purblind, wayward boy.	Biron
Why, all delights are vain; but that most vain, which with pain purchased, doth inherit pain.	Biron

Précis of plot

The young King of Navarre, and three of his friends, vow to devote the following three years to austere self-improvement, forgoing the company of women. The ensuing farce is both sophisticated and cleverly staged.

Setting

Navarre circa 14th century.

19 Macbeth

KING DUNCAN of Scotland
MALCOLM, King Duncan's son
DONALBAIN, King Duncan's son
A CAPTAIN in Duncan's army
MACBETH, Thane of Glamis, later Thane Cawdor, then King of Scotland
LADY MACBETH, Macbeth's wife
A DOCTOR, attending on Lady Macbeth
A Waiting-GENTLEWOMAN, attending on Lady Macbeth
BANQUO, a Scottish Thane
FLEANCE, his son
MACDUFF, Thane of Fife
LADY MACDUFF, his wife
MACDUFF'S SON
SIWARD, Earl of Northumberland
YOUNG SIWARD, his son
HECATE, Queen of the Witches
A PORTER at Macbeth's castle
Three MURDERERS attending on Macbeth
SEYTON, servant of Macbeth
A show of eight kings, Lords and Thanes

Scottish Thanes:
LENNOX
ROSS
ANGUS
CAITHNESS
MENTEITH

Six WITCHES
An English DOCTOR
A SPIRIT LIKE A CAT
Three APPARITIONS:
an armed head
a bloody child
a child crowned
Other SPIRITS
An OLD MAN
A MESSENGER
MURDERERS
SERVANTS
soldiers, drummers

Quotations	Spoken by
All the perfumes of Arabia will not sweeten this little hand.	Lady Macbeth
Angels are bright still, though the brightest fell.	Malcolm
Be innocent of the knowledge, dearest chuck.	Macbeth
Blow wind, come wrack, at least we'll die with harness on our back.	Macbeth
But screw your courage to the sticking-place, and we'll not fail.	Lady Macbeth
By the pricking of my thumbs, something wicked this way comes.	Second Witch
Canst thou not minister to a mind diseased.	Macbeth
Come what, come may, time and the hour runs through the toughest day.	Macbeth
Consider it not so deeply.	Lady Macbeth
Double, double, toil and trouble, fire burn, and cauldron bubble.	Three Witches
Hang out our banners on the outward walls.	Macbeth
How now, you secret, black, and midnight hags.	Macbeth
I am in blood stepped in so far that, should I wade no more, returning were as tedious as go o'er.	Macbeth
I dare do all that may become a man; who dares do more is none.	Macbeth
If you can look into the seeds of time, and say which grain will grow and which will not.	Banquo
I 'gin to be aweary of the sun.	Macbeth
I had most need of blessing, and Amen stuck in my throat.	Macbeth
I must become a borrower of the night, for a dark hour or twain.	Banquo
Infirm of purpose! give me the daggers.	Lady Macbeth
Is this a dagger which I see before me? the handle towards my hand? come let me clutch thee.	Macbeth
It was the owl that shrieked, the fatal bellman.	Lady Macbeth
I would applaud thee to the very echo.	Macbeth
Look like the innocent flower, but be the serpent under't.	Lady Macbeth
Might be the be-all and the end-all here.	Macbeth
Now good digestion wait on appetite, and health on both.	Macbeth
O, I could play the woman with mine eyes, and braggart with my tongue!	Macduff
Or have we eaten on the insane root, that takes the reason prisoner.	Banquo
Out, damned spot; out, I say.	Lady Macbeth
Shake off this downy sleep, death's counterfeit, and look on death itself!	Macduff
Sleep shall neither night nor day, hang upon his pent-house lid.	First Witch
Stands not within the prospect of belief.	Macbeth
That no compunctious visitings of nature shake my fell purpose.	Lady Macbeth
That which hath made them drunk hath made me bold.	Lady Macbeth
The attempt and not the deed confounds us.	Lady Macbeth
The earth hath bubbles, as the water has, and these are of them.	Banquo
The labour we delight in physics pain.	Macbeth
There's husbandry in heaven, their candles are all out.	Banquo
The Thane of Cawdor lives; why do you dress me in borrow'd robes.	
The weird sisters hand in hand.	Three Witches
This castle hath a pleasant seat; the air nimbly and sweetly recommends itself unto our gentle senses.	King Duncan
Throw physic to the dogs; I'll none of it.	Macbeth
To-morrow, and to-morrow, and to-morrow, creeps in this petty pace from day to day, to the last syllable of recorded time, and all our yesterdays have lighted fools the way to dusty death. Out, out, brief candle! Life's but a walking shadow, a poor player that struts and frets his hour upon the stage and then is heard no more: It is a tale told by an idiot, full of sound and fury, signifying nothing.	Macbeth
We have scotched the snake, not killed it.	Macbeth
What, all my pretty chickens and their dam, at one fell swoop.	Macduff
What are these, so wither'd and so wild in their attire, that look not like the inhabitants o' the earth, and yet are on't.	Banquo
What bloody man is that?	King Duncan
Who can be wise, amazed, temperate and furious, loyal and neutral, in a moment?	Macbeth
Yet I do fear thy nature; it is too full o'th' milk of human kindness.	Lady Macbeth

Yet who would have thought the old man to have had so much blood in him.	Lady Macbeth
Your face, my thane, is as a book where men may read strange matters.	Lady Macbeth

Précis of plot
A story of witchcraft, murder, and retribution, which can also be seen as a study in the philosophy and psychology of evil.

Setting
Scotland and England 1039 to 1057.

20 Measure for Measure

Vincentio, the DUKE of Vienna
ANGELO, appointed his deputy
ESCALUS, an old Lord
CLAUDIO, a young gentleman
JULIET, betrothed to Claudio
ISABELLA, Claudio's sister
LUCIO, 'a fantastic'
Two other such GENTLEMEN
FROTH, a foolish gentleman
MISTRESS OVERDONE, a bawd
POMPEY, her clownish servant
A PROVOST
ELBOW, a simple constable
A JUSTICE
ABHORSON, an executioner
BARNARDINE, a dissolute condemned prisoner
MARIANA, betrothed to Angelo
A BOY, attendant on Mariana
FRIAR PETER
FRANCESCA, a nun
VARRIUS, a Lord, friend to the Duke
Lords, officers, citizens, servants

Quotations	**Spoken by**
Ay, but to die, and go we know not where; to lie in cold obstruction, and to rot.	Claudio
But man, proud man, dressed in a little brief authority, most ignorant of what he's most assured, his glassy essence, like an angry ape, plays such fantastic tricks before high heaven as makes the angels weep.	Isabella
Condemn the fault, and not the actor of it.	Angelo
Every true man's apparel fits your thief.	Abhorson
Heaven doth with us as we with torches do.	Duke of Vienna
If I must die, I will encounter darkness as a bride, and hug it in my arms.	Claudio
I hold you as a thing enskied and sainted.	Lucio
No ceremony that to great ones 'longs. Not the king's crown, nor the deputed sword, the marshal's truncheon, nor the judge's robe, become them with one half so good a grace, as mercy does.	Isabella
O, it is excellent to have a giant's strength, but it is tyrannous to use it like a giant.	Isabella
Our doubts are traitors, and makes us lose the good we oft might win.	Lucio
Some rise by sin, and some by virtue fall.	Escalus
That in the captain's but a choleric word, which in the soldier is flat blasphemy.	Isabella
The jury passing on the prisoner's life, may in the sworn twelve have a thief or two, guiltier than him they try.	Angelo
The miserable have no other medicine; but only hope.	Claudio
They say, best men are moulded out of faults; and for the most, become much more the better, for being a little bad.	Mariana
This will last out a night in Russia, when nights are longest there.	Angelo
Virtue is bold, and goodness never fearful	Duke of Vienna

Précis of plot
The central action revolves around the dilemma of Isabella, a novice nun, whose brother is to be executed unless she succumbs to the attentions of Angelo. *Measure for Measure* is a morality play with similar sentiments to *The Merchant of Venice*, but is far more explicitly concerned with sex, and death.

Setting
Vienna circa 1500.

21 The Merchant of Venice

ANTONIO, a merchant of Venice
BASSANIO, his friend and Portia's suitor
LEONARDO, Bassanio's servant
LANCELOT, a clown and servant
GOBBO, his father
Prince of MOROCCO, Portia's suitor
Prince of ARAGON, Portia's suitor
PORTIA, an heiress
NERISSA, her waiting-gentlewoman
BALTHASAR, Portia's servant
STEFANO, Portia's servant
Jailer, attendants, servants, magnificoes of Venice
SHYLOCK, a Jew
JESSICA, his daughter
LORENZO
GRAZIANO
SALERIO
SOLANIO
DUKE of Venice
TUBAL, a Jew

Quotations	**Spoken by**
A Daniel come to judgement, yea, a Daniel!	Shylock
All that glisters is not gold.	Morocco
And when I ope my lips, let no dog bark.	Graziano
But love is blind and lovers cannot see.	Jessica
But ships are but boards, sailors but men. There be land rats and water rats, water thieves and land thieves.	Shylock
How like a fawning publican he looks. I hate him for he is a Christian.	Shylock
How sweet the moonlight sleeps upon this bank!	Lorenzo
I am never merry when I hear sweet music	Jessica
I dote on his very absence.	Portia

If you prick us do we not bleed? If you tickle us do we not laugh? If you poison us do we not die? and if you wrong us shall we not revenge?	Shylock
It is a wise father that knows his own child.	Lancelot
I would not have given it for a wilderness of monkeys.	Shylock
Mislike me not for my complexion, the shadowed livery of the burnished sun.	Morocco
The quality of mercy is not strained. It droppeth as the gentle rain from heaven, upon the place beneath.	Portia
You call me misbeliever, cut-throat, dog, and spit upon my Jewish gaberdine.	Shylock
You taught me first to beg, and now methinks, you teach me how a beggar should be answered.	Portia

Précis of plot
The central plot involves an irascible Jewish money-lender and his efforts to exact full payment for a debt. The sub-plot involves the method of an heiress, Portia, of testing her suitors. The comedy is created by Shylock, the Jew's, strict adherence to the letter of the law and his ultimate downfall by being hoist by his own petard.

Setting
Venice and Belmont circa 14th century.

22 The Merry Wives of Windsor

MISTRESS Margaret PAGE
Master George PAGE, her husband
ANNE and WILLIAM Page, their children
MISTRESS Alice FORD
Master Frank FORD, her husband
Doctor CAIUS, a French physician
MISTRESS QUICKLY, his housekeeper
John RUGBY, his servant
Master FENTON, in love with Anne Page
Master Abraham SLENDER
Robert SHALLOW, his uncle, a justice
The HOST of the Garter Inn
Sir Hugh EVANS, a Welsh parson
Peter SIMPLE, Slender's servant
Children of Windsor, appearing as fairies
ROBIN, Sir John's page
JOHN, a servant
ROBERT, a servant
SIR JOHN Falstaff
BARDOLPH
PISTOL
NIM

Quotations	Spoken by
A man of my kidney.	Sir John
Faith, thou hast some crotchets in thy head now.	Mistress Ford
Here will be an old abusing of God's patience and the King's English.	Mistress Quickly
I cannot tell what the dickens his name is.	Mistress Page
I have a kind of alacrity in sinking.	Sir John
I hope good luck lies in odd numbers.	Sir John
I will make a Star Chamber matter of it.	Shallow
O, what a world of vile ill-favoured faults.	Anne
There was the rankest compound of villainous smell that ever offended nostril.	Sir John
Vengeance of Jenny's case!	Mistress Quickly
We burn daylight. Here: read, read.	Mistress Ford
Why then, the world's mine oyster, which I with sword will open.	Pistol

Précis of plot
The central plot tells of Sir John Falstaff's unsuccessful attempts to seduce Mistress Page and Mistress Ford, and of the unfounded jealousy of Master Ford. The sub-plot revolves around the wooing of Anne Page and ultimate success of Master Fenton.

Setting
Windsor mid-15th century.

23 A Midsummer Night's Dream

THESEUS, Duke of Athens
HIPPOLYTA, Queen of the Amazons
EGEUS, father of Hermia
HERMIA, daughter of Egeus
LYSANDER, loved by Hermia
DEMETRIUS, suitor to Hermia
HELENA, in love with Demetrius
OBERON, King of the Fairies
TITANIA, Queen of the Fairies
ROBIN GOODFELLOW, a puck
Peter QUINCE, a carpenter
Nick BOTTOM, a weaver
Francis FLUTE, a bellows-mender
Robin STARVELING, a tailor
Attendant Lords and fairies
SNUG, a joiner
Tom SNOUT, a Tinker

Four Fairies:
COBWEB
MOTE
MUSTARDSEED
PEASEBLOSSOM

Quotations	Spoken by
A calendar, a calendar! look in the almanac; find out moonshine, find out moonshine.	Bottom
A lion among ladies is a most dreadful thing; for there is not a more fearful wild-fowl than your lion living.	Bottom
A part to tear a cat in.	Bottom
A proper man, as one shall see in a summer's day.	Quince
And the imperial votaress passed on, in maiden meditation, fancy-free, yet marks I	Oberon

Quotation	Spoken by
where the bolt of Cupid fell: It fell upon a little western flower, before milk-white, now purple with love's wound, and maidens call it love-in-idleness.	
Bless thee, Bottom! bless thee! thou art translated.	Quince
But earthlier happy is the rose distilled than that which, withering on the virgin thorn, grows, lives, and dies in single blessedness.	Theseus
He bravely broach'd his boiling bloody breast.	Quince (as prologue)
I am slow of study.	Snug
I have a reasonable good ear in music. Let's have the tongs and the bones.	Bottom
I have an exposition of sleep come upon me.	Bottom
I know a bank where the wild thyme blows, where oxlips and the nodding violet grows, quite over-canopied with luscious woodbine, with sweet musk-roses and with eglantine.	Oberon
Ill met by moonlight, proud Titania.	Oberon
I'll put a girdle round the earth in forty minutes.	Puck
I will roar you as gently as any sucking dove; I will roar you as 'twere any nightingale.	Bottom
Lord, what fools these mortals be.	Puck
Love looks not with the eyes, but with the mind; and therefore is wing'd Cupid painted blind.	Helena
Masters, spread yourselves.	Bottom
My hounds are bred out of the Spartan kind, so flew'd, so sanded, and their heads are hung, with ears that sweep away the morning dew; crook-knee'd, and dew-lapp'd like Thessalian bulls; slow in pursuit, but match'd in mouth like bells.	Theseus
Oh hell! to choose love by another's eyes.	Hermia
Or in the night, imagining some fear, how easy is a bush supposed a bear.	Theseus
She was a vixen when she went to school; and though she be but little, she is fierce.	Helena
Since once I sat upon a promontory, and heard a mermaid on a dolphin's back uttering such dulcet and harmonious breath that the rude sea grew civil at her song and certain stars shot madly from their spheres, to hear the sea-maid's music.	Oberon
So we grew together, like to a double cherry, seeming parted, but yet an union in partition; two lovely berries moulded on one stem.	Helena
Swift as a shadow, short as any dream, brief as the lightning in the collied night, that, in a spleen, unfolds both heaven and earth, and ere a man hath power to say 'Behold' the jaws of darkness do devour it up.	Lysander
That is the true beginning of our end.	Quince (as prologue)
The best in this kind are but shadows; and the worst are no worse, if imagination amend them.	Theseus
The course of true love never did run smooth.	Lysander
The iron tongue of midnight hath told twelve.	Theseus
The jaws of darkness do devour it up: so quick bright things come to confusion.	Lysander
The lover, all as frantic, sees Helen's beauty in a brow of Egypt. The poet's eye, in a fine frenzy rolling, doth glance from heaven to earth, from earth to heaven.	Theseus
The lunatic, the lover and the poet, are of imagination all compact.	Theseus
This is 'erc'les' vein.	Bottom
Very tragical mirth.	Lysander (reads)
What hempen homespuns have we swaggering here.	Puck

Précis of plot
Theseus, Duke of Athens, prepares to marry Hippolyta, Queen of the Amazons. The sub-plots include the tangled web of love between Lysander, Hermia, Demetrius and Helena, and the production of a play, *Pyramus and Thisbe* (based on Ovid's *Metamorphoses*), for the Duke's wedding.

Setting
Athens and a nearby wood.

24 Much Ado About Nothing

DON PEDRO, Prince of Aragon
BALTHASAR, attendant on Don Pedro, a singer
DON JOHN, the bastard brother of Don Pedro
BORACHIO, follower of Don John
CONRAD, follower of Don John
LEONATO, Governor of Messina
HERO, his daughter
BEATRICE, an orphan, his niece
ANTONIO, an old man, brother of Leonato
MARGARET, attendant on Hero
URSULA, attendant on Hero
DOGBERRY, constable in charge of Watch
VERGES, the Headborough, Dogberry's partner
BENEDICK, of Padua
CLAUDIO, of Florence
FRIAR Francis
A SEXTON
WATCHMEN
A BOY, serving Benedick
Attendants and messengers

Quotations	**Spoken by**
Are you good men and true?	Dogberry
But then there was a star danced, and under that was I born.	Beatrice
Comparisons are odorous.	Dogberry
Disdain and scorn ride sparkling in her eyes.	Hero
Flat burglary, as ever was committed.	Dogberry
For there was never yet philosopher, that could endure the toothache patiently.	Leonato
Friendship is constant in all other things, save in the office and affairs of love.	Claudio
He hath indeed better bettered expectation.	Messenger
He is a very valiant trencherman, he has an excellent stomach.	Beatrice
He wears his faith but as the fashion of his hat.	Beatrice
I have a good eye, uncle, I can see a church by daylight.	Beatrice

I was not born under a rhyming planet.	Benedick
O that he were here to write me down an ass!	Dogberry
O, what men dare do! what men may do! what men daily do, not knowing what they do!	Claudio
Patch grief with proverbs, make misfortune drunk.	Leonato
Taming my wild heart to thy loving hand.	Beatrice
To be a well-favoured man is the gift of fortune, but to write and read comes by nature.	Dogberry
Well, everyone can master a grief but he that has it.	Benedick
What, my dear Lady Disdain! are you yet living?	Benedick
Yes, I thank God, I am as honest as any man living that is an old man and no honester than I.	Verges

Précis of plot

The central plot concerns Don John's deception whereby Claudio believes his beloved Hero unfaithful. However, the sub-plot of the relationship between Beatrice and Benedick adds the real substance to the play, and the gradual realisation of their love for each other has spawned countless works.

Setting

Messina in Sicily.

25 Othello

OTHELLO, the Moor of Venice
DESDEMONA, his wife
Michael CASSIO, his lieutenant
BIANCA, a courtesan, in love with Cassio
IAGO, the Moor's Ensign
EMILIA, Iago's wife
A CLOWN, servant of Othello
BRABANZIO, Desdemona's father, a senator
GRAZIANO, Brabanzio's brother
LODOVICO, kinsman of Brabanzio
RODERIGO, Venetian in love with Desdemona
MONTANO, Governor of Cyprus
Attendants, officers, sailors, gentlemen, musicians

The DUKE of Venice
SENATORS of Venice
A HERALD
A MESSENGER

Quotations	**Spoken by**
A fellow almost damned in a fair wife, that never set a squadron in the field.	Iago
Alas, what ignorant sin have I committed?	Desdemona
And of the cannibals that each other eat, the Anthropophagi, and men whose heads do grow beneath their shoulders.	Othello
Be sure thou prove my love a whore. Be sure of it. Give me the ocular proof.	Othello
But I will wear my heart upon my sleeve, for daws to peck at.	Iago
But men are men, the best sometimes forgot.	Iago
But this denoted a foregone conclusion.	Othello
Excellent wretch! Perdition catch my soul.	Othello
He hath a daily beauty in his life that makes me ugly.	Iago
He that is robbed, not wanting what is stol'n, let him not know it and he's not robbed at all.	Othello
How poor are they that ha' not patience! what wound did ever heal but by degrees?	Iago
I am not merry, but I do beguile.	Desdemona
I do perceive here a divided duty.	Desdemona
If she be black, and thereto have a wit; she'll find a white that shall her blackness fit.	Iago
I have very poor and unhappy brains for drinking, I could well wish courtesy would invent some other custom of entertainment.	Cassio
I would have him nine years a-killing. A fine woman, a fair woman, a sweet woman.	Othello
Keep up your bright swords, for the dew will rust 'em.	Othello
My story being done, she gave me for my pains a world of kisses.	Othello
No hinge, nor loop to hang a doubt on.	Othello
O beware, my lord, of jealousy; it is the green-eyed monster which doth mock the meat it feeds on.	Iago
O God, that men should put an enemy in their mouths to steal away their brains.	Cassio
O most lame and impotent conclusion.	Desdemona
On horror's head horrors accumulate.	Othello
Potations pottle-deep.	Iago
Pride, pomp and circumstance of glorious war!	Othello
Reputation, reputation, reputation! O, I have lost my reputation! I have lost the immortal part of myself, and what remains is bestial.	Cassio
Silence that dreadful bell – It frights the isle from her propriety.	Othello
Take note, take note, O world, to be direct and honest is not safe.	Iago
Then must you speak of one that loved not wisely but too well.	Othello
'Tis neither here nor there.	Emilia
To mourn a mischief that is past and gone, is the next way to draw new mischief on.	Duke of Venice
To suckle fools, and chronicle small beer.	Iago
Your daughter and the Moor are now making the beast with two backs.	Iago
You are one of those that will not serve God, if the devil bids you.	Iago

Précis of plot

The story of a Moorish commander deluded by his ensign into believing that his young wife has been unfaithful to him with another soldier. By subtle innuendo and apparent physical proof, Iago convinces Othello that Desdemona has slept with Cassio, his lieutenant; his deceit results in tragedy.

Setting

Venice and Cyprus circa 1570.

26 Pericles, Prince of Tyre

John GOWER, the Presenter
ANTIOCHUS, King of Antioch
His DAUGHTER
PERICLES, Prince of Tyre
MARINA, Pericles' daughter
CLEON, governor of Tarsus
DIONIZA, his wife
LEONINE, a murderer
CERIMON, a physician of Ephesus
PHILEMON, his servant
KING SIMONIDES of Pentapolis
THAISA, his daughter
Three FISHERMEN, his subjects
Five PRINCES, suitors of Thaisa
LYSIMACHUS, Governor of Mytilene
Lords, ladies, pages, messengers, sailors and gentlemen

THALIART, a villain
HELICANUS
AESCHINES
A MARSHAL
LICHORIDA, Thaisa's nurse
A BAWD
A PANDER
BOULT, a leno
DIANA, Goddess of chastity

Quotations	**Spoken by**
Master, I marvel how the fishes live in the sea.	Third Fisherman
Why, as men do a-land; the great ones eat up the little ones.	First Fisherman (reply)
O you gods! why do you make us love your goodly gifts and snatch them straight away?	Pericles
See where she comes, apparell'd like the spring!	Pericles
'Tis time to fear when tyrants seem to kiss.	Pericles

Précis of plot

Pericles, Prince of Tyre, flees from the court of the King of Antioch after solving a riddle that incriminates the King in an incestuous relationship with his daughter. The play chronicles the ensuing travels of Pericles and culminates in his reunion with his long lost daughter, Marina.

Setting

Antioch, Tyre, Tarsus, Pentapolis, Ephesus, Mitylene.

27 Richard II

KING RICHARD II
The QUEEN, his wife
JOHN OF GAUNT, Duke of Lancaster, Richard's uncle
Harry BOLINGBROKE, his son, later HENRY IV
DUCHESS OF GLOUCESTER
Duke of YORK, King Richard's uncle
DUCHESS OF YORK
Duke of AUMERLE, their son
Thomas MOWBRAY, Duke of Norfolk

Of Bolingbroke's party:
Percy, Earl of NORTHUMBERLAND
HARRY PERCY, his son
Lord ROSS
Of King Richard's party:
Earl of SALISBURY
BISHOP OF CARLISLE
Sir Stephen SCROPE

KEEPER of the prison at Pomfret
GROOM of King Richard's stable

Followers of King Richard:
GREEN
BAGOT
BUSHY

Lord BERKELEY
Lord FITZWATER
Duke of SURREY
Lord WILLOUGHBY
ABBOT OF WESTMINSTER
Sir Piers EXTON
LORD MARSHAL
HERALDS
CAPTAIN of the Welsh army
LADIES attending the Queen
GARDENER
Gardener's MEN
Exton's MEN
Lords, soldiers, attendants

Quotations	**Spoken by**
A jewel in a ten-times barred-up chest is a bold spirit in a loyal breast	Mowbray
Can sick men play so nicely with their names?	King Richard
For God's sake let us sit upon the ground, and tell sad stories of the death of kings: how some have been deposed; some slain in war; some haunted by the ghost they have deposed; some poisoned by their wives; some sleeping kill'd; all murder'd.	King Richard
How long a time lies in one little word!	Bolingbroke
Methinks I am a prophet new-inspired.	John of Gaunt
Mount, mount, my soul; thy seat is up on high, whilst my gross flesh sinks downward, here to die.	Richard (last words)
Not all the water in the rude rough sea, can wash the balm from an anointed king.	King Richard
O call back yesterday, bid time return.	Salisbury
Of comfort no man speak. Let's talk of graves, of worms and epitaphs.	King Richard
Peace shall go sleep with Turks and infidels.	Bishop of Carlisle
That which in mean men we entitle patience is pale cold cowardice in noble breasts.	Duchess of Gloucester
The daintiest last, to make the end most sweet.	Bolingbroke
Things sweet to taste prove in digestion sour.	John of Gaunt
This must my comfort be: the sun that warms you here shall shine on me.	Bolingbroke
This royal throne of kings, this sceptred isle, this earth of majesty, this seat of Mars, this other Eden, demi-paradise, this fortress built by nature for herself against infection and the hand of war, this happy breed of men, this little world, this precious stone set in the silver sea, which serves it in the office of a wall, or as a moat defensive to a house against the envy of less happier lands; this blessed plot, this earth, this realm, this England.	John of Gaunt

Truth hath a quiet breast.	Mowbray
We were not born to sue, but to command.	King Richard
You may my glories and my state depose, but not my griefs; still am I king of those.	Richard

Précis of plot
This tragical history play centres around the time of Richard's enforced abdication. The substance of the play is historically accurate, although elements of fiction do exist to some degree, for example, the murder of Richard by Sir Piers Exton.

Setting
England and Wales at the turn of the 15th century.

28 Richard III

KING EDWARD IV
DUCHESS OF YORK, his mother
PRINCE EDWARD, Edward IV's son
Richard, the young Duke of YORK, Edward IV's son
George, Duke of CLARENCE
RICHARD, Duke of Gloucester, later KING RICHARD
Clarence's SON
Clarence's DAUGHTER
QUEEN ELIZABETH, King Edward's wife
Anthony Woodville, Earl RIVERS, her brother
Marquis of DORSET, her son
Lord GRAY, her son
Sir Thomas VAUGHAN
GHOST OF KING HENRY the Sixth
QUEEN MARGARET, his widow
GHOST OF PRINCE EDWARD, his son
LADY ANNE, Prince Edward's widow
William, LORD HASTINGS, Lord Chamberlain
Lord STANLEY, Earl of Derby, his friend
HENRY EARL OF RICHMOND, later KING HENRY VII
Sir Robert BRACKENBURY, Lieutenant of the Tower
Sir James BLUNT
Sir Walter HERBERT
Duke of BUCKINGHAM
Duke of NORFOLK
Sir Richard RATCLIFF
Sir William CATESBY
Sir James TIRREL
Two MURDERERS
A PAGE
CARDINAL
Bishop of ELY
John, a PRIEST
CHRISTOPHER, a priest
Earl of OXFORD
Lord MAYOR of London
A SCRIVENER
Hastings, a PURSUIVANT
SHERIFF
Aldermen and citizens
Attendants, two bishops, messengers and soldiers

Quotations	**Spoken by**
A horse, a horse, my kingdom for a horse!	King Richard
And thus I clothe my naked villainy, with odd old ends stol'n forth of holy writ, and seem a saint, when I most play the devil.	Richard Gloucester
But soft, here come my executioners.	Richard Gloucester
High-reaching Buckingham grows circumspect.	King Richard
Now is the winter of our discontent, made glorious summer by this son of York.	Richard Gloucester
O coward conscience, how dost thou afflict me?	King Richard
Slave, I have set my life upon a cast, and I will stand the hazard of the die. I think there be six Richmonds in the field. Five have I slain today, instead of him. A horse, a horse, my kingdom for a horse.	King Richard (last words)
So wise so young, they say, do never live long.	Richard Gloucester
Their lips were four red roses on a stalk, and in their summer beauty kissed each other.	Tyrrell
Was ever woman in this humour wooed? Was ever woman in this humour won?	Richard Gloucester

Précis of plot
In this play, Shakespeare demonstrates a more complete artistic control of his historical material than in its predecessors, and historical events are freely manipulated in the interests of an overriding design. The play chronicles the period of about twelve years before Richard's reign, highlighting his bloody progress to the crown and his short two-year reign, culminating in his defeat at Bosworth.

Setting
England 1471 to 1485.

29 Romeo and Juliet

CHORUS
ROMEO
MONTAGUE, his father
MONTAGUE'S WIFE
BENVOLIO, Montague's nephew
ABRAHAM, Montague's servingman
BALTHASAR, Romeo's man
JULIET
CAPULET, her father
CAPULET'S WIFE
TYBALT, her nephew
His page
Escalus, PRINCE of Verona
Other CITIZENS OF THE WATCH
Masquers, guests, gentlewomen, followers
PETER
SAMSON
GREGORY
Other SERVINGMEN
MUSICIANS
PETRUCCIO
MERCUTIO
PARIS
PAGE to Paris
FRIAR LAURENCE
FRIAR JOHN
An APOTHECARY
CHIEF WATCHMAN
CAPULET'S COUSIN
Juliet's NURSE

Quotations	**Spoken by**
A pair of star-crossed lovers take their life.	Chorus
A plague o' both your houses.	Mercutio
For you and I are past our dancing days.	Capulet
I do not bite my thumb at you sir, but I bite my thumb, sir.	Samson
Nay, I am the very pink of courtesy.	Mercutio

O happy dagger, this is thy sheath! there rust, and let me die.	Juliet (last words)
One pain is lessened by another's anguish.	Benvolio
O Romeo, Romeo, wherefore art thou Romeo.	Juliet
O then I see Queen Mab hath been with you.	Mercutio
Parting is such sweet sorrow.	Juliet
See how she leans her cheek upon her hand. O, that I were a glove upon that hand, that I might touch that cheek.	Romeo
Thus with a kiss I die.	Romeo (last words)
True, I talk of dreams, which are the children of an idle brain, begot of nothing but vain fantasy.	Mercutio
What's in a name? That which we call a rose by any other word would smell as sweet.	Juliet
When well-apparelled April on the heel of limping winter treads.	Capulet
With Rosaline, my ghostly father? No, I have forgot that name and that name's woe.	Romeo

Précis of plot
This play tells of the bitter feud between the Montagues and Capulets. Romeo, a Montague, falls in love with Juliet, a Capulet, but their love is doomed from the outset as death and tragedy befall both families.

Setting
Verona and Mantua early in the 14th century.

30 The Taming of the Shrew

In the Induction:
CHRISTOPHER SLY, beggar and tinker
A HOSTESS
A LORD
BARTHOLOMEW, his page
HUNTSMEN, SERVANTS AND PLAYERS
In the play-within-the-play:
BAPTISTA Minola, a gentleman of Padua
KATHERINE, his elder daughter
BIANCA, his younger daughter
PETRUCHIO, a gentleman of Verona, suitor of Katherine
VINCENTIO, Lucentio's father
A PEDANT, schoolmaster from Mantua
Other servants of Baptista and Petruchio
LUCENTIO, disguised as Cambio, a teacher
GREMIO, suitor of Bianca
HORTENSIO, another suitor
TRANIO, a servant
BIONDELLO, a servant
GRUMIO, a servant
CURTIS, a servant
A WIDOW
A TAILOR
A HABERDASHER
An OFFICER
NATHANIEL, a servingman
PHILIP, a servingman
JOSEPH, a servingman
PETER, a servingman

Quotations	**Spoken by**
And as the sun breaks through the darkest clouds, so honour peereth in the meanest habit.	Petruccio
A woman moved is like a fountain troubled, muddy, ill seeming, thick, bereft of beauty.	Katherine
No profit grows where is no pleasure ta'en.	Tranio
This is a way to kill a wife with kindness.	Petruccio

Précis of plot
The play has three main strands. The first shows how a drunken tinker, Christopher Sly, is made to believe himself a lord for whose entertainment a play is to be presented. The second strand is the central plot of the play performed for Sly, in which the shrewish Katherine is wooed, won, and tamed by the fortune-hunting Petruchio. The third strand involves Lucentio, Gremio, and Hortensio, all of them suitors for the hand of Katherine's sister, Bianca.

Setting
Padua and Petruchio's house circa 14th century.

31 The Tempest

PROSPERO, the rightful Duke of Milan
MIRANDA, his daughter
ANTONIO, his brother, the usurping Duke of Milan
ALONSO, King of Naples
SEBASTIAN, his brother
FERDINAND, Alonso's son
GONZALO, an honest old counsellor of Naples
ADRIAN, a Lord
FRANCISCO, a Lord
ARIEL, an airy spirit attendant upon Prospero
CALIBAN, a savage and deformed native, who is also Prospero's slave
TRINCULO, Alonso's jester
STEFANO, Alonso's drunken butler
The MASTER of a ship
BOATSWAIN
MARINERS
SPIRITS
The Masque
Spirits appearing as:
IRIS
CERES
JUNO
Nymphs and reapers

Quotations	**Spoken by**
A very ancient and fish-like smell.	Trinculo
Be not afeard. The isle is full of noises, sounds and sweet airs, that give delight and hurt not.	Caliban
Fie, what a spendthrift is he of his tongue!	Antonio
Full fathom five thy father lies. Of his bones are coral made.	Ariel (sung)
He that dies pays all debts.	Stefano
How beauteous mankind is! O brave new world, that has such people in't!	Miranda
In the dark backward and abyss of time?	Prospero
Knowing I loved my books, he furnished me from mine own library with volumes that I prize above my dukedom.	Prospero
Misery acquaints a man with strange bedfellows.	Trinculo

My library was dukedom large enough.	Prospero
They'll take suggestions as a cat laps milk.	Antonio
We are such stuff as dreams are made on, and our little life is rounded with a sleep.	Prospero
Where the bee sucks, there suck I.	Ariel
You taught me language, and my profit on't is I know how to curse.	Caliban

Précis of plot
The central plot of *The Tempest* is one of witchcraft and connivance. The action takes place on an island after a shipwreck, as Prospero explains to his daughter, Miranda, how they came to the island, some twelve years earlier, and how the shipwreck has brought his enemies, Alonso, King of Naples, and Prospero's own brother, Antonio, face to face with their wrongdoings. The action takes place within a few hours, as in *The Comedy of Errors*.

Setting
A small island off the coast of Tunis.

32 Timon of Athens

TIMON of Athens	FOOL
LUCILIUS, a servant	PAGE
An OLD ATHENIAN	CAPHIS
LORDS and SENATORS of Athens	ISIDORE'S SERVANT
VENTIDIUS, one of Timon's false friends	POET
ALCIBIADES, an Athenian Captain	PAINTER
APEMANTUS, a churlish philosopher	JEWELLER
One dressed as CUPID in the Masque	MERCHANT
LADIES dressed as Amazons in the Masque	Mercer
FLAVIUS, Timon's steward	LUCULLUS' SERVANT
FLAMINIUS, a servant	LUCIUS' SERVANT
SERVILIUS, a servant	TITUS' SERVANT
Other SERVANTS of Timon	HORTENSIUS' SERVANT
LUCULLUS, a flattering Lord	PHILOTUS' SERVANT
LUCIUS, a flattering Lord	PHRYNIA, a whore
SEMPRONIUS, a flatterring Lord	TIMANDRA, a whore
Three STRANGERS, one called Hostilius	The banditti, THIEVES
SOLDIER of Alcibiades' army	
Two of VARRO'S SERVANTS	
Messengers, attendants, soldiers	

Quotations	**Spoken by**
I wonder men dare trust themselves with men.	Apemantus
'Tis not enough to help the feeble up, but to support him after.	Timon

Précis of plot
Timon is a misanthrope because his friends flattered and sponged on him in prosperity but abandoned him in poverty. Timon finds gold once more and his friends return.

Setting
Athens and neighbouring woods.

33 Titus Andronicus

SATURNINUS, later Emperor	CAPTAIN
BASSIANUS, his brother	AEMILIUS
TITUS ANDRONICUS, general against the Goths	Sons of Titus:
SEMPRONIUS, kinsman of Titus	LUCIUS
VALENTINE, kinsman of Titus	QUINTUS
TAMORA, Queen of the Goths, wife of Saturninus	MARTIUS
Her sons:	MUTIUS
ALARBUS	
DEMETRIUS	NURSE
CHIRON	CLOWN
AARON, a Moor, her lover	
LAVINIA, daughter of Titus	
YOUNG LUCIUS, a boy, son of Lucius	
MARCUS ANDRONICUS, a tribune, Titus' brother	
PUBLIUS, his son	
Senators, tribunes, Romans, Goths, soldiers and attendants	

Quotations	**Spoken by**
She is a woman, therefore may be wooed; she is a woman, therefore may be won; she is Lavinia, therefore must be loved.	Demetrius
Sweet mercy is nobility's true badge.	Tamora

Précis of plot
Tamora, Queen of the Goths, seeks revenge on her captor, Titus, for the ritual slaughter of her son, Alarbus; she achieves it when her other sons, Chiron and Demetrius, rape and mutilate Titus' daughter, Lavinia. Later, Titus himself seeks revenge on Tamora and her husband Saturninus, after Tamora's black lover, Aaron, has falsely led him to believe that he can save his sons' lives by allowing his own hand to be chopped off. Though he is driven to madness, Titus, with his brother Marcus and his last surviving son, Lucius, achieves a spectacular sequence of vengeance in which he cuts Tamora's sons' throats, serves their flesh baked in a pie to their mother, kills Lavinia to save her from her shame, and stabs Tamora to death. Then in rapid succession, Saturninus kills Titus and is himself killed by Lucius, who, as the new Emperor, is left with Marcus to bury the dead, to punish Aaron, and to 'heal' Rome.

Setting

Rome 4th century AD.

34 Troilus and Cressida

HELEN, wife of Menelaus, now living with Paris
ALEXANDER, servant of Cressida
Servants of Troilus, musicians
soldiers and attendants
Greeks:
AGAMEMNON, Commander-in-Chief
MENELAUS, his brother
NESTOR
ULYSSES
ACHILLES
PATROCLUS, his companion
DIOMEDES
AJAX
THERSITES
MYRMIDONS, soldiers of Achilles
Servants of Diomedes, soldiers
CASSANDRA, Priam's daughter, a prophetess
ANDROMACHE, wife of Hector
AENEAS, a commander
ANTENOR, a commander
PANDARUS, a Lord
CRESSIDA, his niece
CALCHAS, her father, who has joined the Greeks
PROLOGUE
Trojans:
PRIAM, King of Troy
His sons:
HECTOR
DEIPHOBUS
HELENUS, a priest
PARIS
TROILUS
MARGARETON, a bastard

Quotations	**Spoken by**
For to be wise and love exceeds man's might.	Cressida
I am giddy. Expectation whirls me round. The imaginary relish is so sweet, that it enchants my sense.	Troilus
I have had my labour for my travail.	Pandarus
One touch of nature makes the whole world kin.	Ulysses
The baby figure of the giant mass of things to come at large.	Nestor
Welcome ever smiles, and farewell goes out sighing.	Ulysses

Précis of plot

The war between Greece and Troy has been provoked by the abduction of the Greek, Helen, by the Trojan hero Paris, son of King Priam. Shakespeare's play opens when the Greek forces, led by Menelaus' brother Agamemnon, have already been besieging Troy for seven years. Shakespeare concentrates on the opposition between the Greek hero Achilles and the Trojan Hector. Shakespeare also shows how the war, caused by one love affair, destroys another. The story of the love between the Trojan, Troilus, and the Grecian, Cressida, encouraged by her uncle Pandarus, and of Cressida's desertion of Troilus for the Greek Diomedes.

Setting

Troy and the Greek camp during the Trojan War.

35 Twelfth Night

ORSINO, Duke of Illyria
VALENTINE, attending Orsino
CURIO, attending Orsino
VIOLA, a lady, later disguised as Cesario
SEBASTIAN, her twin brother
ANTONIO, a sea-captain
OLIVIA, a Countess
MARIA, her waiting-gentlewoman
SIR TOBY BELCH, Olivia's kinsman
SIR ANDREW AGUECHEEK
MALVOLIO, Olivia's steward
FABIAN, a member of Olivia's household
FESTE, the clown, her jester
FIRST OFFICER
SECOND OFFICER
CAPTAIN
PRIEST
SERVANT of Olivia
Musicians, sailors, lords, attendants

Quotations	**Spoken by**
Be not afraid of greatness. Some are born great, some achieve greatness, and some have greatness thrust upon 'em.	Malvolio
Cressida was a beggar.	Feste
Farewell, fair cruelty.	Viola
He does it with a better grace, but I do it more natural.	Sir Andrew
He plays o'th' viol-de-gamboys, and speaks three or four languages word for word without book.	Sir Toby
I am a great eater of beef, and I believe that does harm to my wit.	Sir Andrew
I am all the daughters of my father's house, and all the brothers too.	Viola
I am sure care's an enemy to life.	Sir Toby
If music be the food of love, play on.	Orsino
Is it a world to hide virtues in?	Sir Toby
Love sought is good, but given unsought, is better.	Olivia
Many a good hanging prevents a bad marriage.	Feste
My purpose is indeed a horse of that colour.	Maria
No more cakes and ale.	Sir Toby
Not to be a-bed after midnight is to be up betimes.	Sir Toby
O world, how apt the poor are to be proud!	Olivia
Still you keep o'th' windy side of the law.	Fabian
What is the opinion of Pythagoras concerning wildfowl?	Feste
Wherefore are these things hid?	Sir Toby
Why, this is very midsummer madness.	Olivia

Précis of plot
The main plot is of a shipwrecked girl, Viola, who, disguised as a boy, Cesario, serves a young Duke, Orsino, and undertakes love-errands on his behalf to a noble lady, Olivia, who falls in love with her but mistakenly betrothes herself to her twin brother Sebastian.

Setting
Illyria.

36 The Two Gentlemen of Verona

DUKE of Milan
SILVIA, his daughter
PROTEUS, a gentleman of Verona
LANCE, his clownish servant
VALENTINE, a gentleman of Verona
SPEED, his clownish servant
THURIO, a foolish rival to Valentine
EGLAMOUR, agent for Silvia in her escape
ANTONIO, father of Proteus
PANTHINO, his servant
JULIA, beloved of Proteus
LUCETTA, her waiting-woman
HOST, where Julia lodges
OUTLAWS
Servants and musicians

Quotations	Spoken by
How use doth breed a habit in a man!	Valentine
I have no other but a woman's reason, I think him so because I think him so.	Lucetta
O heaven, were man but constant, he were perfect.	Proteus
Who is Silvia? What is she, that all our swains commend her?	Host (sung)

Précis of plot
This play tells of the friendship of Valentine and Proteus and the strain their relationship is put under when they both fall in love with Silvia, the daughter of the Duke of Milan.

Setting
Verona, Milan, and Mantua.

37 The Two Noble Kinsmen

THESEUS, Duke of Athens
HIPPOLYTA, Queen of the Amazons
EMILIA, her sister
PIRITHOUS, friend of Theseus
PALAMON, a noble kinsman
ARCITE, a noble kinsman
Hymen, God of marriage
ARTESIUS, an Athenian soldier
Three QUEENS, widows of kings killed in Thebes
VALERIUS, a Theban
WOMAN, attending Emilia
An Athenian GENTLEMAN
Six KNIGHTS, attending Arcite and Palamon
A JAILER, in charge of Theseus' prison
The WOOER of the jailer's daughter
Two FRIENDS of the jailer
Six COUNTRYMEN, one dressed as a baboon
GERALD, a schoolmaster
NELL, a country wench
Four other country wenches:
Fritz, Madeleine, Luce and Barbara
Timothy, a TABORER
PROLOGUE
A SERVANT
A BOY, who sings
A HERALD
MESSENGERS
A DOCTOR
EPILOGUE

Quotations	Spoken by
New plays and maidenheads are near akin.	Prologue
Your grief is written on your cheek.	Emilia

Précis of plot
This play is based on Chaucer's Knight's Tale, on which Shakespeare had already drawn for episodes of *A Midsummer Night's Dream.* It tells of the conflicting claims of love and friendship between Palamon and Arcite, the Two Noble Kinsmen of the title, who, as in *The Two Gentlemen of Verona*, both fall in love with the same woman, but unlike the earlier play, decide to fight for their love. The play is sometimes not listed as a Shakespearian play, as there is a body of thought that believes it to be, at best, a collaboration with John Fletcher; unlike *Henry VIII*, their other joint work, it was not listed in the 1623 folio of Shakespeare's works.

Setting
Athens.

38 The Winter's Tale

LEONTES, King of Sicily
HERMIONE, his wife
MAMILLIUS, his son
PERDITA, his daughter
POLIXENES, King of Bohemia
FLORIZEL, his son, in love with Perdita, aka Doricles
ARCHIDAMUS, a Bohemian Lord
AUTOLYCUS, a rogue, once in the service of Florizel
PAULINA, Antigonus's wife
EMILIA, a lady attending on Hermione
MOPSA, a shepherdess
DORCAS, a shepherdess
A JAILER
A MARINER
CAMILLO, a Lord
ANTIGONUS, a Lord
CLEOMENES, a Lord
DION, a Lord
CLOWN, his son

Other shepherds and shepherdesses
Twelve countrymen disguised as satyrs
Other Lords and gentlemen, ladies,
Officers and servants at Leontes' court

SERVANT of the old shepherd

TIME, as chorus

Quotations	**Spoken by**
A sad tale's best for winter.	Mamillius
A snapper up of unconsidered trifles.	Autolycus
Exit, pursued by a bear.	Stage direction
For you there's rosemary and rue.	Perdita
Good sooth, she is the queen of curds and cream.	Camillo
I would there were no age between ten and three-and twenty, or that youth would sleep out the rest; for there is nothing in the between but getting wenches with child, wronging the ancientry, stealing, fighting.	Old Shepherd
Jog on, jog on, the footpath way.	Autolycus (sung)
Lawn as white as driven snow.	Autolycus (sung)
Let me have no lying. It becomes none but tradesmen.	Autolycus
We were as twinned lambs that did frisk i' th' sun, and bleat the one at th' other.	Polixenes
When daffodils begin to peer.	Autolycus (sung)

Précis of plot

The improbable tale of King Leontes' suspicions of his wife's adultery with King Polixenes, his childhood friend. Leontes expels his new-born daughter, Perdita, thinking her the fruit of this unholy alliance, and she is brought up as a shepherdess. Perdita falls in love with Florizel, son of Polixenes, her supposed father, but she is eventually re-united with her true father.

Setting

Sicily and Bohemia circa 14th century.

Chronology of Shakespeare's Plays

1589–92	*Henry VI* Parts 1, 2, and 3
1592–93	*Richard III, The Comedy of Errors*
1593–94	*Titus Andronicus, The Taming of the Shrew*
1594–95	*The Two Gentlemen of Verona, Love's Labour's Lost, Romeo and Juliet*
1595–96	*Richard II, A Midsummer Night's Dream*
1596–97	*King John, The Merchant of Venice*
1597–98	*Henry IV* Parts 1 and 2
1598–99	*Much Ado About Nothing, Henry V*
1599–1600	*Julius Caesar, As You Like It*
1600–01	*Hamlet, The Merry Wives of Windsor*
1601–02	*Twelfth Night, Troilus and Cressida*
1602–03	*All's Well That Ends Well*
1604–05	*Measure for Measure, Othello*
1605–06	*King Lear, Macbeth*
1606–07	*Antony and Cleopatra*
1607–08	*Coriolanus, Timon of Athens*
1608–09	*Pericles*
1609–10	*Cymbeline*
1610–11	*The Winter's Tale*
1611–12	*The Tempest*
1612–13	*Henry VIII, The Two Noble Kinsmen*

Other Works

1592–93	*Venus and Adonis*	(narrative poem)
1593–94	*The Rape of Lucrece*	(narrative poem)
1593–1600	*Sonnets*	(154 in total)
1600–01	*The Phoenix and the Turtle*	(67-line elegy)
1609 circa	*A Lover's Complaint*	(329-line poem)
	Various poems	(attributed)

Original Titles

Henry VI Part 2 – *The First Part of the Contention*
Henry VI Part 3 – *Richard Duke of York*
Henry VIII – *All Is True*

Full Titles

Cymbeline, King of Britain
Hamlet, Prince of Denmark
Othello, the Moor of Venice
Pericles, Prince of Tyre
Twelfth Night, or What You Will

NB Shakespeare is generally credited with having penned 37 plays, but it can be argued that this figure could perhaps be just as easily 36, or 38, depending on the treatment given to the final two works, *Henry VIII* and *The Two Noble Kinsmen.* These plays are thought to be collaborations between Shakespeare and John Fletcher, although only *Henry VIII* appears in the First Folio of 1623. Therefore, when one is asked which was the last play Shakespeare wrote, it is true to say that it would be impossible to give an unqualified answer unless the question is very specific. The last play wholly credited to Shakespeare is *The Tempest*; the last play cited in the First Folio is *Henry VIII*; and the last play that Shakespeare wrote ignoring these two provisos is *The Two Noble Kinsmen.*

It should also be noted that as well as doubts as to the degree of Shakespeare's involvement in one or two of the plays, there are also doubts as to their chronological order. There is evidence to suggest, for instance, that Shakespeare's first play was probably not *Henry VI* Part 1, but, *Henry VI* Part 2. However, an answer of *Henry VI* would seem to be the most equitable solution to this one.

Films Based on Shakespearian Works

A Double Life – 1947	based on *Othello* directed by George Cukor
A Midsummer Night's Rave – 2002	based on *A Midsummer Night's Dream* directed by Gil Cates Jr
A Thousand Acres – 1997	based on *King Lear* directed by Jocelyn Moorhouse
All Night Long – 1961	based on *Othello* directed by Basil Dearden
An Honourable Murder – 1959	based on *Julius Caesar* directed by Godfrey Grayson
Angoor – 1992	Bollywood comedy based on *The Comedy of Errors*

	directed by Gulzar
Catch My Soul – 1974	based on *Othello* directed by Patrick McGoohan
Chimes at Midnight – 1966	based on *Henry V* and the plays featuring Falstaff directed by Orson Welles
Deliver Us from Eva – 2003	based on *The Taming of the Shrew* directed by Gary Hardwick
Forbidden Planet – 1956	based on *The Tempest* directed by Fred M Wilcox
Get Over It – 2001	based on *A Midsummer Night's Dream* directed by Tommy O'Haver
King of Texas – 2002	TV film based on *King Lear* directed by Uli Edel
Kiss Me Kate – 1953	musical based on *The Taming of the Shrew* directed by George Sidney
Looking for Richard – 1996	based on *Richard III* directed by Al Pacino
Love + Hate – 2006	based on *Romeo and Juliet* directed by Dominic Savage
Men of Respect – 1990	based on *Macbeth* directed by William Reilly
My Own Private Idaho – 1991	based on *Henry IV* directed by Gus Van Sant
Prospero's Books – 1991	based on *The Tempest* directed by Peter Greenaway
Ran – 1985	Japanese version of *King Lear* three sons cast instead of three daughters written and directed by Akira Kurosawa
Rosencrantz and Guildenstern Are Dead – 1990	based on *Hamlet* written and directed by Tom Stoppard
She's the Man – 2006	based on *Twelfth Night* directed by Andy Fickman
10 Things I Hate About You – 1999	based on *The Taming of the Shrew* directed by Gil Junger
The Boys from Syracuse – 1940	musical based on *The Comedy of Errors* directed by Edward A Sutherland
The Lion King– 1994	animation with themes of Hamlet & Macbeth directed by Roger Allers and Rob Minkoff
The Lion King II: Simba's Pride– 1998	animation loosely based on Romeo and Juliet directed by Darrell Rooney
Throne of Blood – 1957	Japanese version of *Macbeth* directed by Akira Kurosawa
Warm Bodies– 2008	zombie film loose references to Romeo and Juliet directed by Jonathan Levine
Were the World Mine – 2008	based on *A Midsummer Night's Dream* directed by Tom Gustafson
West Side Story – 1961	based on *Romeo and Juliet* directed by Robert Wise
Yellow Sky – 1948	based on *The Tempest* directed by William A Wellman

NB The list above includes only films that do not specifically mention the title of the Shakespeare work: e.g. *Joe Macbeth* is a gangster film that follows a very similar plot to *Men of Respect* but includes a reference to *Macbeth* in the title. There are many films that allude to characters in Shakespeare but do not follow the plot closely enough to be included here. The Orson Welles film *Chimes at Midnight* is sometimes called *Falstaff.*

General Information

As You Like It seven ages of man: 1) infant; 2) schoolboy; 3) lover; 4) soldier; 5) justice; 6) old age; 7) second childhood.

born 23 April 1564 in Stratford-upon-Avon. This may or may not be the actual date, but St George's Day seemed apt.

children three: Susanna, Judith and Hamnet. Susanna born 1582, and twins Hamnet and Judith born 1585. Hamnet died in 1596, aged 11½. Susanna married Dr John Hall and Judith married Thomas Quiney. Shakespeare's line ended in 1670 with the death of Elizabeth, Susanna's daughter.

christened 26 April 1564 at Holy Trinity Church, Stratford-upon-Avon.

chronicler Francis Meres' *Palladis Tamia* listed Shakespeare's works up to 1598.

collaborators John Fletcher and various others.

death 23 April 1616 in Stratford-upon-Avon. Shakespeare therefore, traditionally, died on his birthday, aged 52. There are no names on Shakespeare's gravestone, but these words:

Good friend, for Jesus' sake forbear
To dig the dust enclosed here.
Blest be the man that spares these stones,
And curst be he that moves my bones.

Shakespeare's family erected a monument in Holy Trinity church, Stratford, 1623.

dedicatee Henry Wriothesley, the 3rd Earl of Southampton, had the narrative poems *Venus and Adonis* and *The Rape of Lucrece* dedicated to him.

Falstaff, Sir John based on Sir John Oldcastle, the Protestant martyr. Shakespeare was forced to change the name from Oldcastle to Falstaff after complaints from relatives. *Henry IV* Part 1 is here quoted using the original name. The original names of Sir John's associates Bardolph and Peto have also been listed in *Henry IV* Part 1 in their original form, i.e. Russell and Harvey.

father John Shakespeare, a glover, wool dealer, and sometime Mayor; died 1601.

First Folio John Heminges and Henry Condell produced First Folio 1623.

first play *Henry VI* (see notes at end of plays).

great tragedy the 'four great tragedies' are often listed as *Hamlet*, *King Lear*, *Macbeth*, and *Othello*.

home bought 'New Place' Stratford in 1597 Bishopsgate, and also lived with a French Huguenot family called Mountjoy for a short while during 1604, at Cripplegate.

July: takes place in *Romeo and Juliet.*

kin William was one of eight children of which he was the third child and first son. Only three brothers and a sister survived infancy. William's brother Edmund was also an actor.

last play *The Tempest*, *Henry VIII*, or *The Two Noble Kinsmen* (see notes at end of plays).

lines: most Hamlet has the most lines spoken by any one character in a single play but is only third on the overall list if one takes into consideration other plays that a character may appear in. Richard III has more lines taking into account his appearances in *Henry VI*, but the most lines are spoken by Sir John Falstaff, if one considers that Shakespeare's folio of 1623 had by then changed the name of Sir John Oldcastle in *Henry IV* Part 1.

longest play this can be contentious due to disputed passages, but taking the 1623 folio as the basis of the question, then *Hamlet* is longest followed by *Richard III.*

married Anne Hathaway, a farmer's daughter, from Shottery, near Stratford, 28 November 1582. He was 18, she 26 and pregnant. Anne died in 1623.

mother Mary Arden, from Wilmcote, Warwickshire; died in 1609.

portraits Martin Droeshout's engraving of Shakespeare, first published on the title-page of the First Folio 1623, is one of only two likenesses of Shakespeare; the other is the bust of Shakespeare in his monument, designed by Gheerart Janssen. It is unclear whether these are true likenesses, as it was common practice of many artists to use stencils, and it is thought possible that Droeshout may have used a common stencil of the day, possibly that of Elizabeth I.

shortest play given the criteria used for deciding the longest play, the shortest play is clearly *The Comedy of Errors.*

sobriquet the Sweet Swan of Avon, coined by Ben Jonson.

sonnets published in 1609 by Thomas Thorpe, and dedicated to 'Mr W.H.' The sonnets pertain to a young man, a dark lady, and a rival poet. Sonnets 1 to 17 exhort a young man to marry; Sonnets 1 to 126 are all about a young man; Sonnets 127 to 154 are about the dark lady; Sonnet 126 is not in sonnet form, as it has only 12 lines.

theatres Globe was built in 1599 on Bankside, south of the Thames. James Burbage founded the Lord Chamberlain's Company within the Globe and his son Richard Burbage was the principal actor. Shakespeare bought an interest in the Globe, and also a half share in the Blackfriars Theatre, in 1608, and from then on Shakespeare produced winter plays at the Blackfriars and summer plays at the Globe. The Lord Chamberlain's Men became the King's Men on James I's accession. Opposition to the King's Men came mainly from Edward Alleyne's 'Admiral's Men'. John Fletcher became chief dramatist of the King's Men after Shakespeare. Will Kempe was the leading comedy actor of the King's Men. Richard Tarleton was the leading comedy actor of the rival Admiral's Men. Forerunners of the Lord Chamberlain's Men were the Queen's Men. The Chamberlain's Men first performed at the 'Theatre', in Shoreditch, and then at the 'Curtain'. The Globe caught fire and was destroyed in 1613 during performance of *Henry VIII.*

First and Last Lines of Shakespeare's Plays

(C = Comedy H = History T = Tragedy)

	Play	*First line*	*Spoken by*
C	**All's Well That Ends Well**	In delivering my son from me I bury a second husband.	Dowager Countess of Roussillon
T	**Antony and Cleopatra**	Nay, but this dotage of our General's o'erflows the measure.	Philo
C	**As You Like It**	As I remember, Adam, it was upon this fashion.	Orlando
C	**The Comedy of Errors**	Proceed, Solinus, to procure my fall.	Egeon
T	**Coriolanus**	Before we proceed any further, hear me speak.	first Citizen
C	**Cymbeline, King of Britain**	You do not meet a man but frowns.	first Gentleman
T	**Hamlet**	Who's there?	Barnardo
H	**Henry IV Part 1**	So shaken as we are, so wan with care.	King Henry IV
H	**Henry IV Part 2**	Open your ears; for which of you will stop.	Rumour
H	**Henry V**	O for a muse of fire.	Chorus (as Prologue)
H	**Henry VI Part 1**	Hung be the heavens with black!	Bedford
H	**Henry VI Part 2**	As by your high imperial majesty.	Suffolk
H	**Henry VI Part 3**	I wonder how the King escaped our hands.	Warwick
H	**Henry VIII (All Is True)**	I come no more to make you laugh.	Prologue
T	**Julius Caesar**	Hence, home, you idle creatures, get you home.	Flavius
H	**King John**	Now say, Châtillon, what would France with us?	King John
T	**King Lear**	I thought the King had more affected the Duke of Albany than Cornwall.	Earl of Kent
C	**Love's Labour's Lost**	Let fame, that all hunt after in their lives.	King Ferdinand
T	**Macbeth**	When shall we three meet again? In thunder, lightning, or in rain?	First Witch
C	**Measure for Measure**	Escalus.	Vincentio, Duke of Vienna
C	**The Merchant of Venice**	In sooth, I know not why I am so sad.	Antonio
C	**The Merry Wives of Windsor**	Sir Hugh, persuade me not. I will make a Star Chamber matter of it.	Shallow
C	**A Midsummer Night's Dream**	Now, fair Hippolyta, our nuptial hour draws on apace.	Theseus
C	**Much Ado About Nothing**	I learn in this letter that Don Pedro of Aragon comes this night to Messina.	Leonato
T	**Othello**	Tush, never tell me!	Roderigo
C	**Pericles, Prince of Tyre**	To sing a song that old was sung.	Gower, as Chorus
H	**Richard II**	Old John of Gaunt, time-honoured Lancaster.	King Richard II
H	**Richard III**	Now is the winter of our discontent.	Richard Gloucester
T	**Romeo and Juliet**	Two households, both alike in dignity in fair Verona.	Chorus (as Prologue)
C	**The Taming of the Shrew**	I'll feeze you, in faith.	Christopher Sly

	Play	First line	Spoken by
C	**The Tempest**	Boatswain!	Master of a ship
T	**Timon of Athens**	Good day, sir.	Poet
T	**Titus Andronicus**	Noble patricians, patrons of my right.	Saturninus
C	**Troilus and Cressida**	In Troy there lies the scene. From isles of Greece.	Prologue
C	**Twelfth Night**	If music be the food of love, play on.	Orsino
C	**The Two Gentlemen of Verona**	Cease to persuade, my loving Proteus.	Valentine
C	**The Two Noble Kinsmen**	New plays and maidenheads are near akin.	Prologue
C	**The Winter's Tale**	If you shall chance, Camillo, to visit Bohemia.	Archidamus

	Play	*Last line*	*Spoken by*
C	**All's Well That Ends Well**	The bitter past, more welcome is the sweet.	The King of France (N.B. Epilogue follows)
T	**Antony and Cleopatra**	High order in this great solemnity.	Octavius Caesar
C	**As You Like it**	Proceed, proceed. We'll so begin these rites as we do trust they'll end, in true delights.	Duke Senior (N.B. Epilogue follows)
C	**The Comedy of Errors**	And now let's go hand in hand, not one before another.	Dromio of Ephesus
T	**Coriolanus**	Yet he shall have a noble memory. Assist.	Aufidius
C	**Cymbeline, King of Britain**	Ere bloody hands were washed, with such a peace.	Cymbeline
T	**Hamlet**	Go, bid the soldiers shoot.	Fortinbras
H	**Henry IV Part 1**	Let us not leave till all our own be won.	King Henry IV
H	**Henry IV Part 2**	Come, will you hence?	Prince John (N.B. Epilogue follows)
H	**Henry V**	And may our oaths well kept and prosp'rous be.	King Harry (N.B. Epilogue follows)
H	**Henry VI Part 1**	But I will rule both her, the King, and realm.	Suffolk
H	**Henry VI Part 2**	And more such days as these to us befall!	Warwick
H	**Henry VI Part 3**	For here, I hope, begins our lasting joy.	King Edward IV
H	**Henry VIII (All Is True)**	This little one shall make it holiday.	King Henry VIII
T	**Julius Caesar**	To part the glories of this happy day.	Octavius
H	**King John**	If England to itself do rest but true.	Philip the Bastard
T	**King Lear**	Shall never see so much, nor live so long.	Edgar
C	**Love's Labour's Lost**	The words of Mercury are harsh after the songs of Apollo. You that way, we this way.	Armado
T	**Macbeth**	Whom we invite to see us crowned at Scone.	Malcolm
C	**Measure for Measure**	What's yet behind that's meet you all should know.	Vincentio, Duke of Vienna
C	**The Merchant of Venice**	Well, while I live I'll fear no other thing so sore as keeping safe Nerissa's ring.	Graziano
C	**The Merry Wives of Windsor**	For he tonight shall lie with Mistress Ford.	Master Ford
C	**A Midsummer Night's Dream**	Meet me all by break of day.	Oberon
C	**Much Ado About Nothing**	Think not on him till tomorrow, I'll devise thee brave punishments for him. Strike up, pipers.	Benedick
T	**Othello**	This heavy act with heavy heart relate.	Lodovico
C	**Pericles, Prince of Tyre**	New joy wait on you. Here our play has ending.	Gower
H	**Richard II**	In weeping after this untimely bier.	King Henry IV
H	**Richard III**	That she may long live here, God say 'Amen'.	King Henry VII
T	**Romeo and Juliet**	For never was a story of more woe than this of Juliet and her Romeo.	Escalus
C	**The Taming of the Shrew,**	'Tis a wonder, by your leave, she will be tamed so.	Lucentio
C	**The Tempest**	Please you, draw near.	Prospero (N.B. Epilogue follows)
T	**Timon of Athens**	Let our drums strike.	Alcibiades
T	**Titus Andronicus**	And being dead, let birds on her take pity.	Lucius
C	**Troilus and Cressida**	Hope of revenge shall hide our inward woe.	Troilus
C	**Twelfth Night**	And we'll strive to please you every day.	Feste
C	**The Two Gentlemen of Verona**	One feast, one house, one mutual happiness.	Valentine
C	**The Two Noble Kinsmen**	And bear us like the time.	Theseus (N.B. Epilogue follows)
C	**The Winter's Tale**	We were dissevered. Hastily lead away.	Leontes

Shakespearian Characters

Character	*Play*
AARON, a Moor	*Titus Andronicus*
ABERGAVENNY, Lord	*Henry VIII*
ABHORSON, an executioner	*Measure for Measure*
ABRAHAM, Montague's servingman	*Romeo and Juliet*
ACHILLES	*Troilus and Cressida*
ADAM, a former servant of Sir Rowland	*As You Like It*
ADRIAN, a Lord	*The Tempest*
ADRIAN, a Roman	*Coriolanus*
ADRIANA	*The Comedy of Errors*
AEDILES	*Coriolanus*
AEMILIUS	*Titus Andronicus*
AENEAS, a commander	*Troilus and Cressida*
AESCHINES	*Pericles, Prince of Tyre*
AGAMEMNON, commander in chief	*Troilus and Cressida*
AGRIPPA	*Antony and Cleopatra*
AGUECHEEK, Sir Andrew	*Twelfth Night*
AJAX	*Troilus and Cressida*
ALARBUS, son of Tamora	*Titus Andronicus*
ALBANY, Duke of, Goneril's husband	*King Lear*
ALCIBIADES, an Athenian Captain	*Timon of Athens*
ALENÇON, Duke of	*Henry VI Part 1*

Character	*Play*
ALEXANDER, servant of Cressida	*Troilus and Cressida*
ALEXAS	*Antony and Cleopatra*
ALICE, an old gentlewoman	*Henry V*
ALONSO, King of Naples	*The Tempest*
AMIENS, Lord attending on Duke Senior	*As You Like It*
ANDROMACHE, wife of Hector	*Troilus and Cressida*
ANGELO, a goldsmith	*The Comedy of Errors*
ANGELO, appointed Vincentio's deputy	*Measure for Measure*
ANGUS, a Thane	*Macbeth*
ANNE, Lady	*Richard III*
ANTENOR, a commander	*Troilus and Cressida*
ANTIGONUS, a Lord	*The Winter's Tale*
ANTIOCHUS, King of Antioch	*Pericles, Prince of Tyre*
ANTIPHOLUS OF EPHESUS	*The Comedy of Errors*
ANTIPHOLUS OF SYRACUSE	*The Comedy of Errors*
ANTONIO, a merchant of Venice	*The Merchant of Venice*
ANTONIO, a sea-captain	*Twelfth Night*
ANTONIO, an old man	*Much Ado About Nothing*
ANTONIO, father of Proteus	*The Two Gentlemen of Verona*
ANTONIO, Prospero's brother	*The Tempest*
ANTONY, Mark	*Antony and Cleopatra, Julius Caesar*
APEMANTUS, a churlish philosopher	*Timon of Athens*
APOTHECARY	*Romeo and Juliet*
ARAGON, Prince of	*The Merchant of Venice*
ARCHBISHOP of York, Scrope	*Henry IV Parts 1* and *2*
ARCHIDAMUS, a Bohemian Lord	*The Winter's Tale*
ARCITE, a noble kinsman	*The Two Noble Kinsmen*
ARIEL, an airy spirit	*The Tempest*
ARMADO, Don Adriano de	*Love's Labour's Lost*
ARTEMIDORUS	*Julius Caesar*
ARTESIUS, an Athenian soldier	*The Two Noble Kinsmen*
ARTHUR, Duke of Brittaine	*King John*
ARVIRAGUS	*Cymbeline, King of Britain*
ASNATH, a spirit	*Henry VI Part 2*
AUDREY, a goatherd	*As You Like It*
AUFIDIUS, General	*Coriolanus*
AUMERLE, Duke of	*Richard II*
AUSTRIA (Limoges), Duke of	*King John*
AUSTRINGER	*All's Well That Ends Well*
AUTOLYCUS, a rogue	*The Winter's Tale*
BAGOT	*Richard II*
BALTHASAR, a merchant	*The Comedy of Errors*
BALTHASAR, a singer	*Much Ado About Nothing*
BALTHASAR, Portia's servant	*The Merchant of Venice*
BALTHASAR, Romeo's man	*Romeo and Juliet*
BANDITTI, thieves	*Timon of Athens*
BANQUO, a Scottish Thane	*Macbeth*
BAPTISTA MINOLA	*The Taming of the Shrew*
BARDOLPH	*Henry IV Part 2* and *Henry V* *The Merry Wives of Windsor*
BARNARDINE	*Measure for Measure*
BARNARDO	*Hamlet*
BARTHOLOMEW, a page	*The Taming of the Shrew*
BASSANIO	*The Merchant of Venice*
BASSET	*Henry VI Part 1*
BASSIANUS, Saturninus' brother	*Titus Andronicus*

Character	*Play*
BASTARD of Orleans	*Henry VI Part 1*
BATES, John	*Henry V*
BAWD	*Pericles, Prince of Tyre*
BEADLE of Saint Albans	*Henry VI Part 2*
BEATRICE, an orphan	*Much Ado About Nothing*
BEAUFORT, Cardinal Bishop of Winchester	*Henry VI Part 2*
BEDFORD, Duke of, regent of France	*Henry VI Part 1*
BELARIUS, a banished Lord	*Cymbeline, King of Britain*
BELCH, Sir Toby, Olivia's kinsman	*Twelfth Night*
BENEDICK, of Padua	*Much Ado About Nothing*
BENVOLIO, Montague's nephew	*Romeo and Juliet*
BERKELEY, Lord	*Richard II*
BERRI, Duke of	*Henry V*
BIANCA, a courtesan	*Othello*
BIANCA, Baptista's youngest daughter	*The Taming of the Shrew*
BIGOT, Lord	*King John*
BIONDELLO, a servant	*The Taming of the Shrew*
BIRON	*Love's Labour's Lost*
BLANCHE, Lady, of Spain	*King John*
BLUNT, Sir James	*Richard III*
BLUNT, Sir Walter	*Henry IV Part 1*
BOATSWAIN	*The Tempest*
BOLEYN, Anne	*Henry VIII*
BOLINGBROKE, Harry, Duke of Hereford	*Richard II*
BOLINGBROKE, Roger, a conjurer	*Henry VI Part 2*
BONA, Lady	*Henry VI Part 3*
BORACHIO, follower of Don John	*Much Ado About Nothing*
BOTTOM, a weaver	*A Midsummer Night's Dream*
BOULT	*Pericles, Prince of Tyre*
BOURBON, Duke of	*Henry V*
BOY who sings	*Antony and Cleopatra*
BOY who sings	*The Two Noble Kinsmen*
BOY, attendant on Mariana	*Measure for Measure*
BOY, formerly Falstaff's page	*Henry V*
BOY, serving Benedick	*Much Ado About Nothing*
BOYET	*Love's Labour's Lost*
BRABANZIO, a senator of Venice	*Othello*
BRACKENBURY, Sir Robert	*Richard III*
BRANDON	*Henry VIII*
BRUTUS, Marcus, a noble Roman	*Julius Caesar*
BRUTUS, tribune	*Coriolanus*
BUCKINGHAM, Duke of	*Henry VIII*
BUCKINGHAM, Duke of	*Henry VI Part 2* and *Richard III*
BULLCALF, Peter	*Henry IV Part 2*
BURGUNDY, Duke of	*Henry V* and *Henry VI Part I*
BURGUNDY, Duke of	*King Lear*
BUSHY	*Richard II*
BUTTS, the King's physician	*Henry VIII*
CADE, Jack	*Henry VI Part 2*
CAITHNESS, a Thane	*Macbeth*
CAIUS, a French physician	*The Merry Wives of Windsor*
CALCHAS, Cressida's father	*Troilus and Cressida*
CALIBAN, a deformed savage	*The Tempest*
CALPURNIA	*Julius Caesar*
CAMBRIDGE, Richard, Earl of	*Henry V*
CAMIDIUS	*Antony and Cleopatra*
CAMILLO, a Lord	*The Winter's Tale*
CANTERBURY, Archbishop of	*Henry V*

Character	*Play*
CANTERBURY, Archbishop of	*Henry VIII*
CAPHIS	*Timon of Athens*
CAPTAIN	*King Lear*
CAPTAIN	*Titus Andronicus*
CAPTAIN	*Twelfth Night*
CAPTAIN in Duncan's army	*Macbeth*
CAPTAIN of a ship	*Henry VI Part 2*
CAPTAIN of the Welsh army	*Richard II*
CAPULET'S COUSIN	*Romeo and Juliet*
CAPULET'S WIFE	*Romeo and Juliet*
CAPULET, Juliet's father	*Romeo and Juliet*
CAPUTIUS, Lord	*Henry VIII*
CARDINAL	*Richard III*
CARDINAL CAMPEIUS	*Henry VIII*
CARDINAL WOLSEY	*Henry VIII*
CARLISLE, Bishop of	*Richard II*
CARPENTER	*Julius Caesar*
CARRIERS	*Henry IV Part 1*
CASCA	*Julius Caesar*
CASSANDRA, a prophetess	*Troilus and Cressida*
CASSIO, Michael, a Lieutenant	*Othello*
CASSIUS	*Julius Caesar*
CATESBY, Sir William	*Richard III*
CATHERINE	*Henry V*
CELIA, later disguised as Aliena	*As You Like It*
CERES, a spirit	*The Tempest*
CERIMON, a physician of Ephesus	*Pericles, Prince of Tyre*
CHAMBERLAIN	*Henry IV Part 1*
CHARLES, Dauphin of France	*Henry VI Part 1*
CHARLES, Duke Frederick's wrestler	*As You Like It*
CHARMIAN	*Antony and Cleopatra*
CHÂTILLON, an ambassador	*King John*
CHIEF WATCHMAN	*Romeo and Juliet*
CHILDREN of WINDSOR	*The Merry Wives of Windsor*
CHIRON, son of Tamora	*Titus Andronicus*
CHRISTOPHER, a priest	*Richard III*
CICERO, a senator	*Julius Caesar*
CINNA the conspirator	*Julius Caesar*
CINNA the poet	*Julius Caesar*
CITIZENS OF THE WATCH	*Romeo and Juliet*
CLARENCE, Duke of	*Henry V*
CLARENCE, Duke of	*Richard III*
CLAUDIO	*Julius Caesar*
CLAUDIO, a young gentleman	*Measure for Measure*
CLAUDIO, of Florence	*Much Ado About Nothing*
CLEOMENES, a Lord	*The Winter's Tale*
CLEON, Governor of Tarsus	*Pericles, Prince of Tyre*
CLEOPATRA, Queen of Egypt	*Antony and Cleopatra*
CLIFFORD, Lord	*Henry VI Part 3*
CLIFFORD, Old Lord	*Henry VI Part 2*
CLIFFORD, the younger	*Henry VI Part 2*
CLITUS	*Julius Caesar*
CLOTEN, the Queens' son	*Cymbeline, King of Britain*
CLOWN	*Antony and Cleopatra*
CLOWN	*Titus Andronicus*
CLOWN, Autolycus' son	*The Winter's Tale*
CLOWN, servant of Othello	*Othello*
CLOWNS	*Hamlet*
COBBLER	*Julius Caesar*
COBHAM, Dame Eleanor	*Henry VI Part 2*
COBWEB	*A Midsummer Night's Dream*
COLEVILLE, Sir John	*Henry IV Part 2*
COMINIUS, a General	*Coriolanus*
CONRAD	*Much Ado About Nothing*
CONSTABLE of France	*Henry V*
CONSTANCE, Lady	*King John*
CORDELIA	*King Lear*
CORIN, an old shepherd	*As You Like It*
CORIOLANUS	*Coriolanus*
CORNELIUS	*Hamlet*

Character	*Play*
CORNELIUS, a physician	*Cymbeline, King of Britain*
CORNWALL, Duke of	*King Lear*
COSTARD, a Clown	*Love's Labour's Lost*
COUNTESS of Auvergne	*Henry VI Part 1*
COURT, Alexander	*Henry V*
COURTESAN	*The Comedy of Errors*
CRANMER, Archbishop of Canterbury	*Henry VIII*
CRESSIDA, Pandarus' niece	*Troilus and Cressida*
CRIER	*Henry VIII*
CROMWELL, Thomas	*Henry VIII*
CUPID	*Timon of Athens*
CURIO, attending Orsino	*Twelfth Night*
CURTIS, a servant	*The Taming of the Shrew*
CYMBELINE, King of Britain	*Cymbeline, King of Britain*
DARDANIUS	*Julius Caesar*
DAUPHIN, of France	*Henry V*
DAVY, Shallow's servant	*Henry IV Part 2*
DE LA POLE, William	*Henry VI Part 2*
DECIUS BRUTUS	*Julius Caesar*
DECRETAS	*Antony and Cleopatra*
DEIPHOBUS, son of Priam	*Troilus and Cressida*
DEMETRIUS	*A Midsummer Night's Dream*
DEMETRIUS	*Antony and Cleopatra*
DEMETRIUS	*Titus Andronicus*
DENIS, Oliver's servant	*As You Like It*
DENNY, Sir Anthony	*Henry VIII*
DESDEMONA	*Othello*
DIANA	*All's Well That Ends Well*
DIANA, Goddess of chastity	*Pericles, Prince of Tyre*
DICK the BUTCHER	*Henry VI Part 2*
DIOMED	*Antony and Cleopatra*
DIOMEDES	*Troilus and Cressida*
DION, a Lord	*The Winter's Tale*
DIONIZA, wife of Cleon	*Pericles, Prince of Tyre*
DOCTOR to Lady Macbeth	*Macbeth*
DOCTOR, an Englishman	*Macbeth*
DOGBERRY, the constable	*Much Ado About Nothing*
DOLABELLA	*Antony and Cleopatra*
DOLL TEARSHEET, a whore	*Henry IV Part 2*
DONALBAIN	*Macbeth*
DON JOHN	*Much Ado About Nothing*
DON PEDRO, Prince of Aragon	*Much Ado About Nothing*
DOOR-KEEPER	*Henry VIII*
DORCAS, a shepherdess	*The Winter's Tale*
DORSET, Marchioness of	*Henry VIII*
DORSET, Marquis of	*Henry VIII*
DORSET, Marquis of	*Richard III*
DOUGLAS, Earl of	*Henry IV Part 1*
DROMIO OF EPHESUS	*The Comedy of Errors*
DROMIO OF SYRACUSE	*The Comedy of Errors*
DULL, Anthony, a constable	*Love's Labour's Lost*
DUMAINE	*Love's Labour's Lost*
DUNCAN, King of Scotland	*Macbeth*
DUTCHMAN	*Cymbeline, King of Britain*
EDGAR, aka Tom o' Bedlam	*King Lear*
EDMOND	*King Lear*
EDWARD IV, King	*Richard III*
EDWARD, Earl of March	*Henry VI Parts 2* and *3*
EGEON, merchant of Syracuse	*The Comedy of Errors*
EGEUS, father of Hermia	*A Midsummer Night's Dream*
EGLAMOUR	*The Two Gentlemen of Verona*
EGYPTIAN	*Antony and Cleopatra*
ELBOW, a simple constable	*Measure for Measure*
ELIZABETH, Princess	*Henry VIII*
ELY, Bishop of	*Henry V*
ELY, Bishop of	*Henry VIII*
ELY, Bishop of	*Richard III*
EMILIA	*The Two Noble Kinsmen*
EMILIA, a lady	*The Winter's Tale*
EMILIA, an abbess	*The Comedy of Errors*
EMILIA, Iago's wife	*Othello*
EMMANUEL, Clerk of Chatham	*Henry VI Part 2*
ENOBARBUS, Domitius	*Antony and Cleopatra*
EROS	*Antony and Cleopatra*
ERPINGHAM, Sir Thomas	*Henry V*

Character	Play
ESCALUS, an old Lord	*Measure for Measure*
ESCALUS, Prince of Verona	*Romeo and Juliet*
ESSEX, Earl of	*King John*
EVANS, Sir Hugh, a Welsh parson	*The Merry Wives of Windsor*
EXETER, Duke of	*Henry V*
EXETER, Duke of	*Henry VI Part 1*
EXETER, Duke of	*Henry VI Part 3*
EXTON, Sir Piers	*Richard II*
FABIAN	*Twelfth Night*
FALCONBRIDGE, Lady	*King John*
FALCONBRIDGE, Robert	*King John*
FALSTAFF, Sir John	*Henry IV Part 2* *The Merry Wives of Windsor*
FANG, a sergeant	*Henry IV Part 2*
FASTOLF, Sir John	*Henry VI Part 1*
FEEBLE, Francis	*Henry IV Part 2*
FENTON, Master	*The Merry Wives of Windsor*
FERDINAND	*The Tempest*
FERDINAND, King of Navarre	*Love's Labour's Lost*
FESTE, the clown	*Twelfth Night*
FILARIO	*Cymbeline, King of Britain*
FIRST LORD DUMAINE	*All's Well That Ends Well*
FIRST OFFICER	*Twelfth Night*
FITZWATER, Lord	*Richard II*
FIVE PRINCES	*Pericles, Prince of Tyre*
FLAMINIUS, a servant	*Timon of Athens*
FLAVIUS	*Timon of Athens*
FLAVIUS, a tribune	*Julius Caesar*
FLEANCE	*Macbeth*
FLORENCE, Duke of	*All's Well That Ends Well*
FLORIZEL, aka Doricles	*The Winter's Tale*
FLUELLEN, Captain, a Welshman	*Henry V*
FLUTE, a bellows-mender	*A Midsummer Night's Dream*
FOOL	*King Lear*
FOOL	*Timon of Athens*
FORD, Master Frank	*The Merry Wives of Windsor*
FORD, Mistress Alice	*The Merry Wives of Windsor*
FORESTER	*Love's Labour's Lost*
FORTINBRAS, Prince of Norway	*Hamlet*
FRANCESCA, a nun	*Measure for Measure*
FRANCIS, a drawer	*Henry IV Part 1*
FRANCISCO	*Hamlet*
FRANCISCO, a Lord	*The Tempest*
FREDERICK, Duke	*As You Like It*
FRENCHMAN	*Cymbeline, King of Britain*
FRIAR FRANCIS	*Much Ado About Nothing*
FRIAR JOHN	*Romeo and Juliet*
FRIAR LAURENCE	*Romeo and Juliet*
FRIAR PETER	*Measure for Measure*
FROTH	*Measure for Measure*
GADSHILL	*Henry IV Part 1*
GALLUS	*Antony and Cleopatra*
GARDENER	*Richard II*
GARDINER, later Bishop of Winchester	*Henry VIII*
GARGRAVE, Sir Thomas	*Henry VI Part 1*
GARTER King of Arms	*Henry VIII*
GENERAL of French garrison	*Henry VI Part 1*
GEORGE, Duke of Clarence	*Richard III*
GEORGE, later Duke of Gloucester	*Henry VI Part 3*
GERALD, a schoolmaster	*The Two Noble Kinsmen*
GERTRUDE, Queen of Denmark	*Hamlet*
GHOST of Caesar	*Julius Caesar*
GHOST of Hamlet	*Hamlet*
GHOST of King Henry VI	*Richard III*
GHOST of Mother of Posthumus	*Cymbeline, King of Britain*
GHOST of Prince Edward	*Richard III*
GHOST of Sicilius Leonatus	*Cymbeline, King of Britain*
GHOSTS of brothers of Posthumus	*Cymbeline, King of Britain*

Character	Play
GIACOMO, an Italian	*Cymbeline, King of Britain*
GLASDALE, Sir William	*Henry VI Part 1*
GLOUCESTER, Duchess of	*Richard II*
GLOUCESTER, Duke Humphrey of	*Henry VI Part 2*
GLOUCESTER, Duke of	*Henry V*
GLOUCESTER, Duke of	*Henry VI Part 1*
GLOUCESTER, Earl of	*King Lear*
GLOUCESTER, Humphrey, Duke of	*Henry IV Part 2*
GOBBO	*The Merchant of Venice*
GONERIL	*King Lear*
GONZALO	*The Tempest*
GOODFELLOW, Robin, a puck	*A Midsummer Night's Dream*
GOUGH, Matthew	*Henry VI Part 2*
GOVERNOR of Harfleur	*Henry V*
GOWER, a messenger	*Henry IV Part 2*
GOWER, Captain, an Englishman	*Henry V*
GOWER, John, the Presenter	*Pericles, Prince of Tyre*
GRANDPRÉ, Lord	*Henry V*
GRAY, Lady	*Henry VI Part 3*
GRAY, Lord	*Richard III*
GRAZIANO	*Othello*
GRAZIANO	*The Merchant of Venice*
GREEN	*Richard II*
GREGORY	*Romeo and Juliet*
GREMIO	*The Taming of the Shrew*
GREY, Sir Thomas	*Henry V*
GRIFFITH, a gentleman usher	*Henry VIII*
GROOM of King Richard's stable	*Richard II*
GRUMIO, a servant	*The Taming of the Shrew*
GUIDERIUS, known as Polydore	*Cymbeline, King of Britain*
GUILDENSTERN	*Hamlet*
GUILDFORD, Sir Henry	*Henry VIII*
GURNEY, James	*King John*
HABERDASHER	*The Taming of the Shrew*
HAMLET, Prince	*Hamlet*
HARCOURT	*Henry IV Part 2*
HARVEY	*Henry IV Part 1*
HASTINGS, a pursuivant	*Richard III*
HASTINGS, Lord	*Henry IV Part 2*
HASTINGS, Lord	*Henry VI Part 3*
HECATE, Queen of Witches	*Macbeth*
HECTOR	*Troilus and Cressida*
HELEN	*Cymbeline, King of Britain*
HELEN	*Troilus and Cressida*
HELEN, an orphan	*All's Well That Ends Well*
HELENA	*A Midsummer Night's Dream*
HELENUS, a priest	*Troilus and Cressida*
HELICANUS	*Pericles, Prince of Tyre*
HENRY IV, King	*Henry IV Parts 1* and *2*
HENRY V, King	*Henry V*
HENRY VI, King	*Henry VI Parts 1, 2* and *3*
HENRY VIII, King	*Henry VIII*
HENRY, Earl of Richmond	*Richard III*
HENRY, Lord Scrope of Masham	*Henry V*
HERBERT, Sir Walter	*Richard III*
HERMIA	*A Midsummer Night's Dream*
HERMIONE	*The Winter's Tale*
HERO	*Much Ado About Nothing*
HIPPOLYTA, Queen of the Amazons	*A Midsummer Night's Dream*
HIPPOLYTA, Queen of the Amazons	*The Two Noble Kinsmen*
HOLOFERNES, a schoolmaster	*Love's Labour's Lost*
HORATIO	*Hamlet*
HORNER, Thomas, an armourer	*Henry VI Part 2*
HORTENSIO, a teacher	*The Taming of the Shrew*
HORTENSIUS' SERVANT	*Timon of Athens*
HOST of the Garter Inn	*The Merry Wives of Windsor*

Character	*Play*
HOST, where Julia lodges	*The Two Gentlemen of Verona*
HOSTESS, formerly Mistress Quickly	*Henry V*
HOTSPUR, Henry Percy	*Henry IV Part 1*
HUBERT	*King John*
HUME, Sir John, a priest	*Henry VI Part 2*
HUNTSMAN	*Henry VI Part 3*
HYMEN, God of marriage	*The Two Noble Kinsmen*
HYMEN, God of marriage	*As You Like It*
IAGO, the Moor's ensign	*Othello*
IDEN, Alexander	*Henry VI Part 2*
INNOGEN, Princess	*Cymbeline, King of Britain*
INTERPRETER, a French soldier	*All's Well That Ends Well*
IRAS	*Antony and Cleopatra*
IRIS, a spirit	*The Tempest*
ISABEL	*Henry V*
ISABELLA	*Measure for Measure*
ISIDORE'S SERVANT	*Timon of Athens*
JAILER	*The Two Noble Kinsmen*
JAILER'S BROTHER	*The Two Noble Kinsmen*
JAILER'S DAUGHTER	*The Two Noble Kinsmen*
JAMY, Captain, a Scot	*Henry V*
JAQUENETTA, a country wench	*Love's Labour's Lost*
JAQUES, Lord	*As You Like It*
JESSICA	*The Merchant of Venice*
JEWELLER	*Timon of Athens*
JOAN la Pucelle	*Henry VI Part 1*
JOHN	*Henry VI Part 2*
JOHN OF GAUNT, Duke of Lancaster	*Richard II*
JOHN OF LANCASTER	*Henry IV Part 1*
JOHN, a priest	*Richard III*
JOHN, a servant	*The Merry Wives of Windsor*
JOHN, King of England	*King John*
JOSEPH, a servingman	*The Taming of the Shrew*
JULIA	*The Two Gentlemen of Verona*
JULIET	*Measure for Measure*
JULIET	*Romeo and Juliet*
JULIUS CAESAR	*Julius Caesar*
JUNO, a spirit	*The Tempest*
JUPITER	*Cymbeline, King of Britain*
JUSTICE	*Measure for Measure*
KATE	*Henry IV Part 2*
KATE, Lady Percy	*Henry IV Part 1*
KATHERINE	*Love's Labour's Lost*
KATHERINE	*The Taming of the Shrew*
KEEPER of the prison	*Richard II*
KENT, Earl of	*King Lear*
KING CHARLES VI of France	*Henry V*
KING CLAUDIUS	*Hamlet*
KING of France	*All's Well That Ends Well*
KING of France	*King Lear*
KING PHILIP of France	*King John*
KING SIMONIDES of Pentapolis	*Pericles, Prince of Tyre*
LAERTES	*Hamlet*
LAFEU, an old lord	*All's Well That Ends Well*
LANCE	*The Two Gentlemen of Verona*
LANCELOT, a clown	*The Merchant of Venice*
LARTIUS, a General	*Coriolanus*
LAVATCH, a clown	*All's Well That Ends Well*
LAVINIA	*Titus Andronicus*
LEAR, King of Britain	*King Lear*
LE BEAU	*As You Like It*
LEGATE	*Henry VI Part 1*
LENNOX, a Thane	*Macbeth*
LEONARDO	*The Merchant of Venice*
LEONATO, governor of Messina	*Much Ado About Nothing*
LEONINE, a murderer	*Pericles, Prince of Tyre*
LEONTES, King of Sicily	*The Winter's Tale*
LEPIDUS	*Antony and Cleopatra, Julius Caesar*
LICHORIDA, Thaisa's nurse	*Pericles, Prince of Tyre*
LIEUTENANT of the Tower	*Henry VI Part 3*

Character	*Play*
LIGARIUS	*Julius Caesar*
LINCOLN, Bishop of	*Henry VIII*
LODOVICO	*Othello*
LONGUEVILLE	*Love's Labour's Lost*
LORD CHAMBERLAIN	*Henry VIII*
LORD CHANCELLOR	*Henry VIII*
LORD CHIEF JUSTICE	*Henry IV Part 2*
LORD MARSHAL	*Richard II*
LORD MAYOR OF LONDON	*Henry VIII*
LORD MAYOR OF LONDON	*Richard III*
LORENZO	*The Merchant of Venice*
LOUIS THE DAUPHIN	*King John*
LOUIS, King	*Henry VI Part 3*
LOVELL, Sir Thomas	*Henry VIII*
LUCENTIO, from Pisa	*The Taming of the Shrew*
LUCETTA, a waiting-woman	*The Two Gentlemen of Verona*
LUCIANA	*The Comedy of Errors*
LUCILIUS, a servant	*Timon of Athens*
LUCILLIUS	*Julius Caesar*
LUCIO, 'a fantastic'	*Measure for Measure*
LUCIUS	*Titus Andronicus*
LUCIUS, a flattering Lord	*Timon of Athens*
LUCIUS, a servant	*Julius Caesar*
LUCIUS, an ambassador	*Cymbeline, King of Britain*
LUCIUS' SERVANT	*Timon of Athens*
LUCULLUS, a flattering Lord	*Timon of Athens*
LUCULLUS' SERVANT	*Timon of Athens*
LUCY, Sir William	*Henry VI Part 1*
LYSANDER	*A Midsummer Night's Dream*
LYSIMACHUS, Governor of Mytilene	*Pericles, Prince of Tyre*
MACBETH, Lady	*Macbeth*
MACBETH, Thane of Glamis	*Macbeth*
MACDUFF, Lady	*Macbeth*
MACDUFF, Thane of Fife	*Macbeth*
MACDUFF'S SON	*Macbeth*
MACMORRIS, Captain	*Henry V*
MAECENAS	*Antony and Cleopatra*
MALCOLM, King	*Macbeth*
MALVOLIO, Olivia's steward	*Twelfth Night*
MAMILLIUS	*The Winter's Tale*
MARCELLUS	*Hamlet*
MARCUS ANDRONICUS, a tribune	*Titus Andronicus*
MARDIAN, a eunuch	*Antony and Cleopatra*
MARGARET	*Henry VI Part 1*
MARGARET	*Much Ado About Nothing*
MARGARETON, a bastard	*Troilus and Cressida*
MARIA	*Love's Labour's Lost*
MARIA, a waiting-gentlewoman	*Twelfth Night*
MARIANA	*All's Well That Ends Well*
MARIANA	*Measure for Measure*
MARINA	*Pericles, Prince of Tyre*
MARINER	*The Winter's Tale*
MARSHAL	*Pericles, Prince of Tyre*
MARTEXT, Sir Oliver, a clergyman	*As You Like It*
MARTIUS	*Titus Andronicus*
MASTER of a ship	*Henry VI Part 2*
MASTER of a ship	*The Tempest*
MASTER GUNNER of Orleans	*Henry VI Part 1*
MATE of a ship	*Henry VI Part 2*
MAYOR of London	*Henry VI Part 1*
MAYOR of Saint Albans	*Henry VI Part 2*
MAYOR of York	*Henry VI Part 3*
MELUN, Count	*King John*
MENAN	*Antony and Cleopatra*
MENECRATES	*Antony and Cleopatra*
MENELAUS	*Troilus and Cressida*
MENENIUS Agrippa	*Coriolanus*
MENTEITH, a Thane	*Macbeth*
MERCADE, a messenger	*Love's Labour's Lost*
MERCHANT OF EPHESUS	*The Comedy of Errors*
MERCUTIO	*Romeo and Juliet*
MESSALA	*Julius Caesar*
METELLUS CIMBER	*Julius Caesar*
MICHAEL, Sir	*Henry IV Part 1*

Character	*Play*
MILAN, Duke of	*The Two Gentlemen of Verona*
MIRANDA	*The Tempest*
MONTAGUE, Marquis of	*Henry VI Part 3*
MONTAGUE, Romeo's father	*Romeo and Juliet*
MONTAGUE'S WIFE	*Romeo and Juliet*
MONTANO, Governor of Cyprus	*Othello*
MONTGOMERY, Sir John	*Henry VI Part 3*
MONTJOY, the French Herald	*Henry V*
MOPSA, a shepherdess	*The Winter's Tale*
MOROCCO, Prince of	*The Merchant of Venice*
MORTIMER, aka Earl of March	*Henry IV Part 1*
MORTIMER, Edmund	*Henry VI Part 1*
MORTIMER, Lady	*Henry IV Part 1*
MORTIMER, Sir Hugh	*Henry VI Part 3*
MORTIMER, Sir John	*Henry VI Part 3*
MORTON	*Henry IV Part 2*
MOTE	*A Midsummer Night's Dream*
MOTE, a page	*Love's Labour's Lost*
MOULDY, Ralph	*Henry IV Part 2*
MOWBRAY, Thomas, Duke of Norfolk	*Richard II*
MURELLUS, a tribune	*Julius Caesar*
MUSTARDSEED	*A Midsummer Night's Dream*
MUTIUS	*Titus Andronicus*
MYRMIDONS	*Troilus and Cressida*
NATHANIEL, a servingman	*The Taming of the Shrew*
NATHANIEL, Sir, a curate	*Love's Labour's Lost*
NELL, a country wench	*The Two Noble Kinsmen*
NELL, a kitchen-maid	*The Comedy of Errors*
NERISSA, a waiting-gentlewoman	*The Merchant of Venice*
NESTOR	*Troilus and Cressida*
NICANOR, a Volscian	*Coriolanus*
NIM	*Henry V*
NIM	*The Merry Wives of Windsor*
NORFOLK, Duke of	*Henry VIII*
NORFOLK, Duke of	*Henry VI Part 3* and *Richard III*
NORFOLK, old Duchess of	*Henry VIII*
NORTHUMBERLAND, Earl of	*Henry VI Part 3*
NORTHUMBERLAND'S WIFE	*Henry IV Part 2*
OBERON, King of the Fairies	*A Midsummer Night's Dream*
OCTAVIA	*Antony and Cleopatra*
OCTAVIUS Caesar	*Julius Caesar*
OCTAVIUS CAESAR	*Antony and Cleopatra*
OLD ATHENIAN	*Timon of Athens*
OLDCASTLE, Sir John	*Henry IV Part 1*
OLD MAN	*Macbeth*
OLD MAN, Gloucester's tenant	*King Lear*
OLIVER	*As You Like It*
OLIVIA, a Countess	*Twelfth Night*
OPHELIA	*Hamlet*
ORLANDO	*As You Like It*
ORLÉANS, Duke of	*Henry V*
ORSINO, Duke of Illyria	*Twelfth Night*
OSRIC	*Hamlet*
OSTLER	*Henry IV Part 1*
OSWALD, Goneril's steward	*King Lear*
OTHELLO, the Moor of Venice	*Othello*
OVERDONE, Mistress, a bawd	*Measure for Measure*
OWAIN GLYNDWR	*Henry IV Part 1*
OXFORD, Earl of	*Henry VI Part 3* and *Richard III*
PAGE, Anna	*The Merry Wives of Windsor*
PAGE, Master George	*The Merry Wives of Windsor*
PAGE, Mistress Margaret	*The Merry Wives of Windsor*
PAGE, William	*The Merry Wives of Windsor*
PAINTER	*Timon of Athens*
PALAMON, a noble kinsman	*The Two Noble Kinsmen*
PANDARUS, a Lord	*Troilus and Cressida*

Character	*Play*
PANDER	*Pericles, Prince of Tyre*
PANDOLF, Cardinal	*King John*
PANTHINO, a servant	*The Two Gentlemen of Verona*
PARIS	*Romeo and Juliet*
PARIS	*Troilus and Cressida*
PAROLLES	*All's Well That Ends Well*
PATIENCE, a waiting woman	*Henry VIII*
PATROCLUS	*Troilus and Cressida*
PAULINA	*The Winter's Tale*
PEASEBLOSSOM	*A Midsummer Night's Dream*
PEDANT, schoolmaster from Mantu	*The Taming of the Shrew*
PEMBROKE, Earl of	*King John*
PERCY, Earl of Northumberland	*Henry IV Parts 1* and *2*
PERCY, Earl of Northumberland	*Richard II*
PERCY, Harry	*Richard II*
PERDITA	*The Winter's Tale*
PERICLES, Prince of Tyre	*Pericles, Prince of Tyre*
PETER	*Romeo and Juliet*
PETER, a servingman	*The Taming of the Shrew*
PETER OF POMFRET, a prophet	*King John*
PETER THUMP	*Henry VI Part 2*
PETO	*Henry IV Part 2*
PETRUCCIO	*Romeo and Juliet*
PETRUCHIO, a gentleman of Verona	*The Taming of the Shrew*
PHILEMON, Cerimon's servant	*Pericles, Prince of Tyre*
PHILIP, a servingman	*The Taming of the Shrew*
PHILIP the BASTARD	*King John*
PHILO	*Antony and Cleopatra*
PHILOTUS' SERVANT	*Timon of Athens*
PHOEBE, a shepherdess	*As You Like It*
PHRYNIA, a whore	*Timon of Athens*
PINCH, Doctor, a schoolmaster	*The Comedy of Errors*
PINDARUS	*Julius Caesar*
PIRITHOUS	*The Two Noble Kinsmen*
PISANIO, a servant	*Cymbeline, King of Britain*
PISTOL, Ensign	*Henry V* *The Merry Wives of Windsor* *Henry IV Part 2*
POET	*Julius Caesar*
POET	*Timon of Athens*
POINS, Edward	*Henry IV Parts 1* and *2*
POLIXENES, King of Bohemia	*The Winter's Tale*
POLONIUS, a Lord	*Hamlet*
POMPEY (Pompeius)	*Antony and Cleopatra*
POMPEY, a clownish servant	*Measure for Measure*
POPILIUS Laena, a senator	*Julius Caesar*
PORTER	*Henry IV Part 2*
PORTER at Macbeth's castle	*Macbeth*
PORTER, at the christening	*Henry VIII*
PORTIA, an heiress	*The Merchant of Venice*
PORTIA, Brutus's wife	*Julius Caesar*
POSTHUMUS Leonatus	*Cymbeline, King of Britain*
PRIAM, King of Troy	*Troilus and Cressida*
PRIEST	*Hamlet*
PRIEST	*Twelfth Night*
PRINCE EDWARD	*Henry VI Part 3* and *Richard III*
PRINCE HAL	*Henry IV Parts 1* and *2*
PRINCE HENRY	*King John*
PRINCE JOHN of Lancaster	*Henry IV Part 2*
PRINCESS of France	*Love's Labour's Lost*
PROCULEIUS	*Antony and Cleopatra*
PROSPERO	*The Tempest*
PROTEUS, a gentleman of Verona	*The Two Gentlemen of Verona*
PROVOST	*Measure for Measure*
PUBLIUS	*Titus Andronicus*
PUBLIUS, a senator	*Julius Caesar*
QUEEN, Cymbeline's wife	*Cymbeline, King of Britain*

Character	Play
QUEEN, wife of Richard II	*Richard II*
QUEEN ELEANOR	*King John*
QUEEN ELIZABETH	*Richard III*
QUEEN KATHERINE	*Henry VIII*
QUEEN MARGARET	*Henry VI Parts 2* and *3*
QUEEN MARGARET	*Richard III*
QUICKLY, Mistress	*Henry IV Parts 1* and *2*
QUICKLY, Mistress	*The Merry Wives of Windsor*
QUINCE, a carpenter	*A Midsummer Night's Dream*
QUINTUS	*Titus Andronicus*
RAMBURES, Lord	*Henry V*
RATCLIFF, Sir Richard	*Richard III*
REGAN	*King Lear*
RENÉ, King of Naples	*Henry VI Part 1*
REYNALDO, a servant	*Hamlet*
REYNALDO, a steward	*All's Well That Ends Well*
RICHARD II, King	*Richard II*
RICHARD PLANTAGENET	*Henry VI Parts 1, 2* and *3*
RICHARD, Duke of Gloucester, afterwards King Richard III	*Richard III*
RICHARD, the young	*The Merry Wives of Windsor*
RIVERS, LORD	*Henry VI Part 3*
ROBIN, Sir John's page	*The Merry Wives of Windsor*
ROCHESTER, Bishop of	*Henry VIII*
RODERIGO, a Venetian	*Othello*
ROMEO	*Romeo and Juliet*
ROSALIND	*As You Like It*
ROSALINE	*Love's Labour's Lost*
ROSENCRANTZ	*Hamlet*
ROSS, a Thane	*Macbeth*
ROSS, Lord	*Richard II*
ROUSILLON, Bertram, Count of	*All's Well That Ends Well*
ROUSILLON, Countess of	*All's Well That Ends Well*
RUGBY, John	*The Merry Wives of Windsor*
RUMOUR, the Presenter	*Henry IV Part 2*
RUSSELL	*Henry IV Part 1*
RUTLAND, Earl of	*Henry VI Part 3*
SAINT ASAPH, Bishop of	*Henry VIII*
SALERIO	*The Merchant of Venice*
SALISBURY	*Henry V*
SALISBURY, Earl of	*Henry VI Parts 1* and *2*
SALISBURY, Earl of	*King John*
SALISBURY, Earl of	*Richard II*
SAMSON	*Romeo and Juliet*
SANDS, Lord	*Henry VIII*
SATURNINUS	*Titus Andronicus*
SAWYER	*Henry VI Part 2*
SAYE, Lord	*Henry VI Part 2*
SCALES, Lord	*Henry VI Part 2*
SCARUS	*Antony and Cleopatra*
SCRIVENER	*Richard III*
SCROPE, Sir Stephen	*Richard II*
SEBASTIAN	*The Tempest*
SEBASTIAN	*Twelfth Night*
SECOND LORD DUMAINE	*All's Well That Ends Well*
SECOND MERCHANT	*The Comedy of Errors*
SECOND OFFICER	*Twelfth Night*
SELEUCUS	*Antony and Cleopatra*
SEMPRONIUS	*Titus Andronicus*
SEMPRONIUS, a flattering Lord	*Timon of Athens*
SENIOR, Duke	*As You Like It*
SENTRY and men of his WATCH	*Antony and Cleopatra*
SERGEANT	*Henry VI Part 2*
SERJEANT-AT-ARMS	*Henry VIII*
SERVANT of Cornwall	*King Lear*
SERVANT of Olivia	*Twelfth Night*
SERVANT of the old shepherd	*The Winter's Tale*
SERVILIUS, a servant	*Timon of Athens*
SEXTON	*Much Ado About Nothing*
SEYTON, servant of Macbeth	*Macbeth*
SHADOW, Simon	*Henry IV Part 2*
SHALLOW, Robert, a country justice	*Henry IV Part 2* *The Merry Wives of Windsor*

Character	Play
SHEPHERD, father of Joan	*Henry VI Part 1*
SHERIFF	*Henry IV Part 1*
SHERIFF	*King John*
SHERIFF	*Richard III*
SHYLOCK, a Jew	*The Merchant of Venice*
SICINIUS Velutus, tribune	*Coriolanus*
SILENCE, a country justice	*Henry IV Part 2*
SILIUS	*Antony and Cleopatra*
SILVIA	*The Two Gentlemen of Verona*
SILVIUS, a young shepherd	*As You Like It*
SIMPCOX, Simon	*Henry VI Part 2*
SIMPCOX'S WIFE	*Henry VI Part 2*
SIMPLE, Peter, Slender's servant	*The Merry Wives of Windsor*
SIWARD, Earl of Northumberland	*Macbeth*
SIWARD, the younger	*Macbeth*
SIX COUNTRYMEN	*The Two Noble Kinsmen*
SIX KNIGHTS	*The Two Noble Kinsmen*
SIX SPIRITS	*Henry VIII*
SIX WITCHES	*Macbeth*
SLENDER, Master Abraham	*The Merry Wives of Windsor*
SLY, Christopher, beggar and tinker	*The Taming of the Shrew*
SMITH the WEAVER	*Henry VI Part 2*
SNARE, a sergeant	*Henry IV Part 2*
SNOUT, a tinker	*A Midsummer Night's Dream*
SNUG, a joiner	*A Midsummer Night's Dream*
SOLANIO	*The Merchant of Venice*
SOLDIER of Alcibiades' army	*Timon of Athens*
SOLDIER who has killed his father	*Henry VI Part 3*
SOLDIER who has killed his son	*Henry VI Part 3*
SOLINUS, Duke of Ephesus	*The Comedy of Errors*
SOMERSET, Duke of	*Henry VI Parts 1, 2* and *3*
SOMERVILLE	*Henry VI Part 3*
SOOTHSAYER	*Antony and Cleopatra*
SOOTHSAYER	*Julius Caesar*
SOOTHSAYER, called Philarmonus	*Cymbeline, King of Britain*
SOUTHWELL, John, a priest	*Henry VI Part 2*
SPANIARD	*Cymbeline, King of Britain*
SPEED	*The Two Gentlemen of Verona*
SPIRIT LIKE A CAT	*Macbeth*
STAFFORD, Sir Humphrey	*Henry VI Part 2*
STAFFORD'S BROTHER	*Henry VI Part 2*
STANLEY, Lord, Earl of Derby	*Richard III*
STANLEY, Sir John	*Henry VI Part 2*
STARVELING, a tailor	*A Midsummer Night's Dream*
STEFANO, Alonso's drunken butler	*The Tempest*
STEFANO, Portia's servant	*The Merchant of Venice*
STOKESLEY, Bishop of London	*Henry VIII*
STRATO	*Julius Caesar*
SUFFOLK, Duke of	*Henry VIII*
SUFFOLK, Earl of	*Henry VI Part 1*
SURREY, Duke of	*Richard II*
SURREY, Earl of	*Henry IV Part 2*
SURREY, Earl of	*Henry VIII*
TABORER, called Timothy	*The Two Noble Kinsmen*
TAILOR	*The Taming of the Shrew*
TALBOT, John	*Henry VI Part 1*
TAMORA, Queen of the Goths	*Titus Andronicus*
TAURUS	*Antony and Cleopatra*
THAISA	*Pericles, Prince of Tyre*
THALIART, a villain	*Pericles, Prince of Tyre*
THERSITES	*Troilus and Cressida*
THESEUS, Duke of Athens	*A Midsummer Night's Dream*
THESEUS, Duke of Athens	*The Two Noble Kinsmen*
THIDIAS	*Antony and Cleopatra*
THOMAS, Duke of Clarence	*Henry IV Part 2*
THOMAS, Lord Mowbray	*Henry IV Part 2*
THREE APPARITIONS	*Macbeth*

Character	*Play*
THREE FISHERMEN	*Pericles, Prince of Tyre*
THREE MURDERERS	*Macbeth*
THREE NEIGHBOURS	*Henry VI Part 2*
THREE PRENTICES	*Henry VI Part 2*
THREE QUEENS	*The Two Noble Kinsmen*
THREE STRANGERS	*Timon of Athens*
THURIO	*The Two Gentlemen of Verona*
TIMANDRA, a whore	*Timon of Athens*
TIME, as chorus	*The Winter's Tale*
TIMON of Athens	*Timon of Athens*
TIRREL, Sir James	*Richard III*
TITANIA, Queen of Fairies	*A Midsummer Night's Dream*
TITINIUS, a Roman officer	*Julius Caesar*
TITUS ANDRONICUS	*Titus Andronicus*
TITUS' SERVANT	*Timon of Athens*
TOUCHSTONE, a jester	*As You Like It*
TRANIO, a servant	*The Taming of the Shrew*
TRAVERS, Northumberland's servant	*Henry IV Part 2*
TREBONIUS	*Julius Caesar*
TRINCULO, Alonso's jester	*The Tempest*
TROILUS	*Troilus and Cressida*
TUBAL, a Jew	*The Merchant of Venice*
TUTOR, of Rutland, a chaplain	*Henry VI Part 3*
TWELVE COUNTRYMEN	*The Winter's Tale*
TYBALT	*Romeo and Juliet*
ULYSSES	*Troilus and Cressida*
URSULA, attendant on Hero	*Much Ado About Nothing*
VALENTINE, a gentleman of Verona	*The Two Gentlemen of Verona*
VALENTINE, attending Orsino	*Twelfth Night*
VALENTINE, kinsman of Titus	*Titus Andronicus*
VALERIA	*Coriolanus*
VALERIUS, a Theban	*The Two Noble Kinsmen*
VALTEMAND	*Hamlet*
VARRIUS	*Antony and Cleopatra*
VARRIUS, a Lord	*Measure for Measure*
VARRUS	*Julius Caesar*
VAUGHAN, Sir Thomas	*Richard III*
VAUX, a messenger	*Henry VI Part 2*
VAUX, Sir Nicholas	*Henry VIII*
VENICE, Duke of	*Othello*
VENICE, Duke of	*The Merchant of Venice*
VENTIDIUS	*Antony and Cleopatra*
VENTIDIUS	*Timon of Athens*
VERGES, the Headborough	*Much Ado About Nothing*
VERNON	*Henry VI Part 1*
VERNON, Sir Richard	*Henry IV Part 1*
VINCENTIO, Lucentio's father	*The Taming of the Shrew*
VINCENTIO, The Duke of Vienna	*Measure for Measure*
VINTNER	*Henry IV Part 1*
VIOLA, a lady	*Twelfth Night*
VIRGILIA	*Coriolanus*
VOLUMNIA	*Coriolanus*
VOLUMNIUS	*Julius Caesar*
WAITING-GENTLEWOMAN	*Macbeth*
WART, Thomas	*Henry IV Part 2*
WARWICK	*Henry V*
WARWICK, Earl of	*Henry VI Parts 1, 2* and *3*
WARWICK, Neville, Earl of	*Henry IV Part 2*
WATCHMEN	*Much Ado About Nothing*
WESTMINSTER, Abbot of	*Richard II*
WESTMORLAND	*Henry V*
WESTMORLAND, Earl of	*Henry IV Parts 1, 2* and *3*
WHITMORE, Walter	*Henry VI Part 2*
WIDOW	*The Taming of the Shrew*
WIDOW CAPILET	*All's Well That Ends Well*
WILLIAM, a countryman	*As You Like It*
WILLIAM, Lord Hastings	*Richard III*
WILLIAMS, Michael	*Henry V*
WILLOUGHBY, Lord	*Richard II*
WINCHESTER, Bishop of	*Henry VI Part 1*
WITCH, Margery Jordan	*Henry VI Part 2*
WOMAN, attending Emilia	*The Two Noble Kinsmen*
WOODVILLE, Anthony, Earl RIVERS	*Richard III*
WOODVILLE, Lieutenant of Tower	*Henry VI Part 1*
WOOER of the jailer's daughter	*The Two Noble Kinsmen*
WORCESTER, Earl of	*Henry IV Part 1*
YORK, Duchess of	*Richard II*
YORK, Duchess of	*Richard III*
YORK, Duke of	*Henry V*
YORK, Duke of	*Henry VI Part 2*
YORK, Duke of	*Richard II*
YOUNG CATO	*Julius Caesar*
YOUNG LUCIUS, a boy	*Titus Andronicus*
YOUNG MARTIUS	*Coriolanus*

First Lines of Shakespearian Sonnets

No.	
1	From fairest creatures we desire increase
2	When forty winters shall besiege thy brow
3	Look in thy glass, and tell the face thou viewest
4	Unthrifty loveliness, why dost thou spend
5	Those hours that with gentle work did frame
6	Then let not winter's ragged hand deface
7	Lo, in the orient when the gracious light
8	Music to hear, why hear'st thou music sadly?
9	Is it for fear to wet a widow's eye
10	For shame deny that thou bear'st love to any
11	As fast as thou shalt wane, so fast thou grow'st
12	When I do count the clock that tells the time
13	O that you were yourself! But, love, you are
14	Not from the stars do I my judgement pluck
15	When I consider everything that grows
16	But wherefore do not you a mightier way
17	Who will believe my verse in time to come
18	Shall I compare thee to a summer's day?
19	Devouring time, blunt thou the lion's paws
20	A woman's face with nature's own hand painted
21	So is it not with me as with that muse
22	My glass shall not persuade me I am old
23	As an unperfect actor on the stage
24	Mine eye hath played the painter, and hath steeled
25	Let those who are in favour with their stars
26	Lord of my love, to whom in vassalage
27	Weary with toil I haste me to my bed
28	How can I then return in happy plight
29	When, in disgrace with fortune and men's eyes
30	When to the sessions of sweet silent thought
31	Thy bosom is endeared with all hearts
32	If thou survive my well-contented day
33	Full many a glorious morning have I seen
34	Why didst thou promise such a beauteous day
35	No more be grieved at that which thou hast done
36	Let me confess that we two must be twain
37	As a decrepit father takes delight
38	How can my muse want subject to invent
39	O, how thy worth with manners may I sing
40	Take all my loves, my love, yea, take them all
41	Those pretty wrongs that liberty commits
42	That thou hast her, it is not all my grief
43	When most I wink, then do mine eyes best see
44	If the dull substance of my flesh were thought
45	The other two, slight air and purging fire
46	Mine eye and heart are at a mortal war
47	Betwixt mine eye and heart a league is took
48	How careful was I when I took my way

49 Against that time – if ever that time come
50 How heavy do I journey on the way
51 Thus can my love excuse the slow offence
52 So am I as the rich whose blessed key
53 What is your substance, whereof are you made
54 O how much more doth beauty beauteous seem
55 Not marble nor the gilded monuments
56 Sweet love, renew thy force. Be it not said
57 Being your slave, what should I do but tend
58 That god forbid, that made me first your slave
59 If there be nothing new, but that which is
60 Like as the waves make towards the pebbled shore
61 Is it thy will thy image should keep open
62 Sin of self-love possesseth all mine eye
63 Against my love shall be as I am now
64 When I have seen by time's fell hand defaced
65 Since brass, nor stone, nor earth, nor boundless sea
66 Tired with all these, for restful death I cry
67 Ah, wherefore with infection should he live
68 Thus is his cheek the map of days outworn
69 Those parts of thee that the world's eye doth view
70 That thou are blamed shall not be thy defect
71 No longer mourn for me when I am dead
72 O, lest the world should task you to recite
73 That time of year thou mayst in me behold
74 But be contented when that fell arrest
75 So are you to my thoughts as food to life
76 Why is my verse so barren of new pride
77 Thy glass will show thee how thy beauties wear
78 So oft have I invoked thee for my muse
79 Whilst I alone did call upon thy aid
80 O, how I faint when I of you do write
81 Or I shall live your epitaph to make
82 I grant thou wert not married to my muse
83 I never saw that you did painting need
84 Who is it that says most which can say more
85 My tongue-tied muse in manners holds her still
86 Was it the proud full sail of his great verse
87 Farewell – thou art too dear for my possessing
88 When thou shalt be disposed to set me light
89 Say that thou didst forsake me for some fault
90 Then hate me when thou wilt, if ever, now
91 Some glory in their birth, some in their skill
92 But do thy worst to steal thyself away
93 So shall I live supposing thou art true
94 They that have power to hurt and will do none
95 How sweet and lovely dost thou make the shame
96 Some say thy fault is youth, some wantonness
97 How like a winter hath my absence been
98 From you have I been absent in the spring
99 The forward violet thus did I chide
100 Where art thou, muse, that thou forget'st so long
101 O truant muse, what shall be thy amends
102 My love is strengthened, though more weak in seeming
103 Alack, what poverty my muse brings forth
104 To me, fair friend, you never can be old
105 Let not my love be called idolatry
106 When in the chronicle of wasted time
107 Not mine own fears nor the prophetic soul
108 What's in the brain that ink may character
109 O never say that I was false of heart
110 Alas, 'tis true, I have gone here and there
111 O, for my sake do you with fortune chide
112 Your love and pity doth th'impression fill
113 Since I left you mine eye is in my mind
114 Or whether doth my mind, being crowned with you
115 Those lines that I before have writ do lie
116 Let me not to the marriage of true minds
117 Accuse me thus: that I have scanted all
118 Like as, to make our appetites more keen
119 What potions have I drunk of siren tears
120 That you were once unkind befriends me now
121 'Tis better to be vile than vile esteemed
122 Thy gift, thy tables, are within my brain
123 No, time, thou shalt not boast that I do change!
124 If my dear love were but the child of state
125 Were't aught to me I bore the canopy
126 O thou my lovely boy, who in thy power
127 In the old age black was not counted fair
128 How oft, when thou, my music, music play'st
129 Th' expense of spirit in a waste of shame
130 My mistress' eyes are nothing like the sun
131 Thou art as tyrannous so as thou art
132 Thine eyes I love, and they, as pitying me
133 Beshrew that heart that makes my heart to groan
134 So, now I have confessed that he is thine
135 Whoever hath her wish, thou hast thy Will
136 If thy soul check thee that I come so near
137 Thou blind fool love, what dost thou to mine eyes
138 When my love swears that she is made of truth
139 O, call not me to justify the wrong
140 Be wise as thou art cruel; do not press
141 In faith, I do not love thee with mine eyes
142 Love is my sin, and thy dear virtue hate
143 Lo, as a care-full housewife runs to catch
144 Two loves I have, of comfort and despair
145 Those lips that love's own hand did make
146 Poor soul, the centre of my sinful earth
147 My love is as a fever, longing still
148 O me, what eyes hath love put in my head
149 Canst thou, O cruel, say I love thee not
150 O, from what power hast thou this powerful might
151 Love is too young to know what conscience is
152 In loving thee thou know'st I am forsworn
153 Cupid laid by his brand and fell asleep
154 The little love-god lying once asleep

Kings and Queens of England and Great Britain

	Reign	Date of accession	Born	Died	Marriage(s)
William I aka the Bastard, the Conqueror	1066–1087	25 Dec.	Falaise, France, *c.* 1028, illegitimate son of Robert I, 6th duke of Normandy, by Herleva/ Arlette, daughter of Fulbert the Tanner.	Abdominal injury while riding via Mantes, died 5 weeks later on 9 Sept. 1087 at Rouen. Buried at the Abbey of St Stephen, Caen.	Matilda (died 1083), daughter of Baldwin V, count of Flanders; 4 sons, 5 daughters. Married at Eu *c.* 1053.
William II Rufus	1087–1100	26 Sept.	Normandy, *c.* 1056, 3rd son of William I and Matilda.	Arrow wound while hunting in the New Forest, nr Brockenhurst, Hants, 2 Aug. 1100. Buried in Winchester Cathedral.	Unmarried.
Henry I Beauclerc	1100–1135	5 Aug.	Selby, Yorkshire, 1068, 4th son of William I and Matilda. Buried at Reading Abbey.	Fever, St Denis-le-Ferment, Grisors. Aged 67, 1 Dec. 1135.	Edith (aka Matilda), died 1118, daughter of Malcolm III and Margaret. Married Westminster Abbey, Nov. 1100. Adela, died 1151, daughter of Godfrey VII, count of Louvaine (granddaughter of Edmund Ironside); 1 son, 1 daughter.
Matilda 'Empress Maud'	1141		London, Feb. 1102, only legitimate daughter of Henry I.	Natural causes, Rouen, Normandy. Buried at Fontevraud Abbey church, Anjou.	Henry V, Emperor of Germany, married in 1114, died 1125 Geoffrey V, count of Anjou; 3 sons. Married 1128, died 1151.
Stephen	1135–1154	22 Dec.	Blois, France, *c.* 1096, 3rd son of Stephen aka Henry, count of Blois, and Adela, 5th daughter of William I.	Heart attack, St Martin's Priory, Dover, 25 Oct. 1154. Buried at Faversham Abbey.	Matilda, died 1151, daughter of count of Boulogne and Mary, sister of Matilda (wife of Henry I); 3 sons, 2 daughters. Married 1125.
Henry II Plantagenet Fitzempress Curtmantle	1154–1189	19 Dec.	Le Mans, France, 5 March 1133, eldest son of Geoffrey V, count of Anjou, and Matilda, only daughter of Henry I.	Fever, castle of Chinon, Tours, 6 July 1199. Buried at Fontevraud Abbey in Anjou, reburied Westminster Abbey.	Eleanor (1122–1204), daughter of duke of Aquitaine and divorced wife of Louis VII of France; 5 sons, 3 daughters. Married at Bordeaux, 1152.
Richard I aka Lionheart	1189–1199	3 Sept.	Oxford, 8 Sept. 1157, 3rd son of Henry II and Eleanor.	Arrow wound while besieging the castle of Chalus, Limousin, France, 6 April 1199. Buried at Fontevraud Abbey in Anjou, reburied Westminster Abbey.	Berengaria died *c.*1230, daughter of Sancho VI of Navarre. No issue. Married at Limassol, Cyprus, 1191.
John aka Lackland	1199–1216	27 May	Beaumont Palace, Oxford, 24 Dec. 1167, 5th son of Henry II and Eleanor.	Dysentery, Newark Castle, Notts, Oct. 1216. Buried at Worcester Cathedral.	Isabel, died 1217. Wed 1191 at Marlborough, Wilts; no issue Isabella, died 1246, daughter of count of Angoulême; 2 sons, 3 daughters. Married at Angoulême, Aug. 1200.
Henry III aka the Builder	1216–1272	28 Oct.	Winchester, 1 Oct. 1207, elder son of John and Isabella of Angoulême.	Natural causes, Westminster, aged 65, 16 Nov. 1272. Buried Westminster Abbey Church.	Eleanor, died 1291, daughter of count of Provence, Raymond Berengar. Married at Canterbury, 1236; 2 sons, 3 daughters
Edward I aka Longshanks, Hammer of the Scots	1272–1307	20 Nov.	Westminster, 17 June 1239; eldest son (to survive infancy) of Henry III and Eleanor of Provence. Buried at Westminster Abbey.	Natural causes, Burgh-on-the-Sands nr Carlisle, 7 July 1307, aged 68.	Eleanor, died 1290, daughter of king of Castile, Ferdinand III, 4 sons, 7 daughters. Married Las Huelgas, Oct. 1254. Margaret (1282–1317), daughter of King Philip III of France; 2 sons, 1 daughter. Married Canterbury Sept. 1299.
Edward II	1307–1327	8 July	Caernarfon Castle, Wales, 25 April 1284; 4th and only surviving son of Edward I and Eleanor of Castile.	Murdered Berkeley Castle, Sept. 1327. Buried Gloucester Cathedral.	Isabella (1292–1358), daughter of King Philip IV of France; 2 sons, 2 daughters. Married Boulogne, Jan. 1308.
Edward III	1327–1377	25 Jan.	Windsor Castle, 13 Nov. 1312; elder son of Edward II and Isabella.	Natural causes, Sheen, 21 June 1377. Buried at Westminster Abbey.	Philippa (1314–69) daughter of count of Hainault and Holland; 7 sons, 5 daughters. Married at York, 24 June 1328

	Date of Reign	accession	Born	Died	Marriage(s)
Richard II	1377–1399	22 June	Bordeaux, France, 6 Jan. 1367; 2nd but only surviving son of Edward, the Black Prince, and Joan, the Fair Maid of Kent (granddaughter of Edward I).	Neurasthenia, Pontefract Castle. Buried at Westminster Abbey.	Anne of Bohemia (1366–94), daughter of Emperor Charles I. No issue. Married St Stephens Chapel, 1382. Isabelle (1389–1409), daughter of Charles VI of France. No issue. Wed St Nicholas, Calais, 1396.
Henry IV aka Bolingbroke	1399–1413	30 Sept.	Bolingbroke Castle, Lincolnshire, April 1366; eldest son of John of Gaunt, 4th son of Edward III and Blanche, great-granddaughter of Henry III.	Eczema and gout, Jerusalem Chamber, Westminster. Buried at Westminster Abbey.	Mary de Bohun (1368–94), daughter of Humphrey of Hereford; 5 sons, 2 daughters. Married Rochford, Essex, 1380. Joan (1370–1437), 2nd daughter of King Charles II of Navarre. No issue. Married Winchester, Feb. 1403.
Henry V aka Harry	1413–1422	21 March	Monmouth, Wales, 16 Sept. 1387; 2nd and eldest surviving son of Henry IV and Lady Mary de Bohun.	Dysentery, Bois de Vincennes, aged 34. Buried in Chapel of the Confessor, Westminster Abbey.	Catherine of Valois (1401–37), daughter of Charles VI of France; 1 son. Married church of St John, Troyes, 2 June 1420.
Henry VI	1422–1461	1 Sept.	Windsor, 6 Dec. 1421; only son of Henry V and Catherine of Valois.	Murdered by stabbing, Tower of London, 21 May 1471. Buried at Windsor.	Margaret (1430–82), daughter of René, duke of Anjou; 1 son. Wed Tichfield Abbey, April 1445.
Edward IV	1461–1470	4 March	Rouen, France, 28 April 1442; eldest son of Richard, 3rd duke of York and the Lady Cecily Nevill, daughter of Ralph, earl of Westmorland.	Pneumonia, Westminster, April 1483. Buried at Windsor.	Elizabeth (1437–92), daughter of Sir Richard Woodville; 3 sons, 7 daughters. Wed Grafton, Northants, 1464
Henry VI	1470–1471	6 Oct.	As above.		
Edward IV	1471–1483	11 April	As above.		
Edward V	1483	9 April	Westminster, 2 Nov. 1470, eldest son of Edward IV and Elizabeth Woodville.	Tower of London?	Unmarried.
Richard III aka Crookback	1483–1485	26 June	Fotheringay, Northants, 2 Oct. 1452; 4th and only surviving son of Richard, 3rd duke of York (the Protector), and Cecily Nevill.	Killed Bosworth 22 Aug.1485. Buried at the Abbey of the Grey Friars, Leicester.	Anne (1456–85), daughter of Richard Nevill, earl of Warwick, and widow of Edward, prince of Wales; 1 son. Married 12 July 1472.
Henry VII	1485–1509	22 Aug.	Pembroke Castle, 27 Jan. 1457; only child of Edmund Tudor, 1st earl of Richmond, and Margaret Beaufort, great-great-granddaughter of Edward III.	Rheumatoid arthritis and gout, 21 April 1509, at Richmond. Buried in his own chapel at Westminster.	Elizabeth (1466–1503), daughter of Edward IV; 3 sons, 4 daughters. Married Westminster, Jan. 1486.
Henry VIII aka Bluff King Hal, Old Copper Nose	1509–1547	22 April	Greenwich, 28 June 1491; 2nd and only surviving son of Henry VII and Elizabeth.	Sinusitis and periostitis of the leg at Whitehall, 28 Jan. 1547. Buried at Windsor.	See separate entry.
Edward VI	1547–1553	28 Jan.	Hampton Ct, 12 Oct. 1537; only surviving son of Henry VIII by Jane Seymour.	Tuberculosis at Greenwich. Buried in Henry VII's Chapel, Westminster Abbey.	Unmarried.
Jane aka Nine-Day Queen	1553	10 July	Bradgate Park, Leics, Oct. 1537; eldest daughter of Henry Grey, 3rd marquess of Dorset, and Frances, daughter of Mary Tudor, sister of Henry VIII.	Beheaded Tower of London Feb. 1554. Buried St Peter ad Vincula within the Tower.	Guilford Dudley, son of John Dudley, duke of Northumberland. Married Durham House, London May 1533.

	Reign	Date of accession	Born	Died	Marriage(s)
Mary I aka Bloody Mary	1553–1558	19 July	Greenwich, 18 Feb. 1516; only surviving child of Henry VIII and Catherine of Aragon.	Influenza in London. Buried Westminster Abbey.	Philip, son of Emperor Charles V and later king of Spain in 1554.
Elizabeth I aka Virgin Queen	1558–1603	17 Nov.	Greenwich, 7 Sept. 1533; daughter of Henry VIII and Anne Boleyn.	Sepsis from tonsillar abscess at Richmond. Buried Westminster Abbey.	Unmarried.
James I	1603–1625	26 March	Edinburgh Castle, 19 June 1566; son of Mary queen of Scots (daughter of James V) and Henry Darnley.	Bright's disease, Theobalds Park, Herts. Buried Westminster Abbey.	Anne, daughter of Frederick II of Denmark. Married 20 Aug. 1589, by proxy.
Charles I	1625–1649	27 March	Dunfermline Palace, 19 Nov. 1600; only surviving son of James I and Anne of Denmark.	Beheaded at Whitehall, Jan 1649. Buried at Windsor.	Henrietta Maria, daughter of Henry IV of France. Married Paris, 1 May 1625, by proxy.
Charles II aka Old Rowley	1660–1685	29 May	St James's Palace, 29 May 1630; eldest son of Charles I and Henrietta Maria.	Uraemia and mercurial poisoning, Whitehall. Buried Henry VII's Chapel, Westminster.	Catherine of Braganza, daughter of John. Married Portsmouth, 21 May 1662.
James II	1685–1688	6 Feb.	St James's Palace, 14 Oct. 1633; only surviving son of Charles I and Henrietta Maria.	Cerebral haemorrhage, St Germain, France. Remains were interred at 5 different venues in France. All are now lost except for those at the parish church at St Germain.	Anne Hyde, daughter of Edward Hyde. Married Worcester House, Strand, 3 Sept. 1660. Mary D'este, daughter of duke of Modena. Married Modena, 30 Sept. 1673, by proxy.
William III	1688–1702	13 Feb.	The Hague, 4 Nov. 1650; only son of William II, Prince of Orange, and Mary Stuart, daughter of Charles I.	Pleuro-pneumonia following fracture of right collarbone after falling from his horse near Kensington. Buried Henry VII's Chapel, Westminster.	Mary, daughter of James II and Anne Hyde. Married St James's Palace, 4 Nov. 1677.
Mary II	1688–1694	13 Feb.	St James's Palace, 30 April 1662.	Smallpox at Kensington, 28 Dec. 1694. Buried Henry VII's Chapel, Westminster.	William III.
Anne aka Brandy Nan	1702–1714	8 March	St James's Palace, 6 Feb. 1665, daughter of James II and Anne Hyde.	Brain haemorrhage, Kensington. Buried Henry VII's Chapel, Westminster.	George of Denmark (1653–1708), son of Frederick III of Denmark. Chapel Royal, St James's Palace, 1683.
George I	1714–1727	1 Aug.	Osnabrück, 28 May 1660; son of Ernest, duke of Brunswick-Lüneburg and elector of Hanover, and Sophia, daughter of Elizabeth, queen of Bohemia, eldest daughter of James I.	Thrombosis, Ibbenburen. Buried Hanover.	Sophia Dorothea, daughter of George William, duke of Lüneburg-Celle. Wed 21 Nov. 1682, divorced 1694.
George II	1727–1760	11 Jun.	Hanover, 30 Oct. 1683; son of George I and Sophia Dorothea.	Thrombosis, Palace of Westminster. Buried Henry VII's Chapel, Westminster.	Wilhelmina Charlotte Caroline of Ansbach (1683–1737), daughter of John Frederick, margrave of Brandenburg -Ansbach. Married 22 Aug. 1705.
George III aka Farmer George	1760–1820	25 Oct.	Norfolk House, London, 24 May 1738; son of Frederick Lewis, prince of Wales, and Princess Augusta of Saxe-Gotha.	Senility, Windsor. St George's Chapel, Windsor.	Charlotte Sophia (1744–1818), daughter of Charles Louis Frederick, duke of Mecklenburg-Strelitz, 8 Sept. 1761
George IV	1820–1830	29 Jan.	St James's Palace, 12 Aug. 1762; eldest son of George III and Charlotte.	Stomach rupture and dropsy, Windsor. Buried St George's Chapel, Windsor.	Maria Fitzherbert, 1785, without king's consent and denied by George IV. Caroline of Brunswick, 8 April 1795, Chapel Royal, St James's Palace.

	Reign	*Date of Accession*	*Born*	*Died*	*Marriage(s)*
William IV aka Sailor King	1830–1837	26 June	Buckingham Palace, 21 Aug. 1765; son of George III and Charlotte.	Pneumonia/cirrhosis, Windsor. Buried St George's Chapel, Windsor.	Adelaide, daughter of duke of Saxe- Meiningen. Married 11 July 1818, Kew.
Victoria	1837–1901	20 June	Kensington Palace, 24 May 1819; daughter of Edward duke of Kent, 4th son of George III, and Victoria, daughter of Francis of Saxe-Coburg-Saalfeld.	Senility, Osborne House, IoW. Buried at Frogmore nr Windsor.	Francis Albert (1819–61), 2nd son of Ernest I of Saxe-Coburg-Gotha. Married 10 Feb. 1840, St James's Palace.
Edward VII aka Denmark, Peacemaker	1901–1910	22 Jan.	Buckingham Palace, 9 Nov. 1841; eldest son of Victoria and Albert.	Bronchitis, Buckingham Palace. Buried at St George's Chapel, Windsor.	Alexandra, daughter of Christian IX of Denmark. Married 10 March 1863, St George's Chapel.
George V	1910–1936	6 May	Marlborough House, London, 3 June 1865; 2nd son of Edward and Alexander.	Bronchitis, Sandringham. Buried at St George's Chapel, Windsor.	Mary, daughter of Francis, duke of Teck. Married 6 July 1893, St James's Palace.
Edward VIII aka People's King	1936	20 Jan.	White Lodge, Richmond Park, 23 June 1894; eldest son of George V and Mary.	Throat cancer, Paris, 28 May 1972. Buried at Frogmore, Windsor.	Wallis Simpson née Warfield. Married 3 June 1937 Château de Candé, near Tours, France
George VI	1936–1952	11 Dec.	York Cottage, Sandringham, 14 Dec. 1895; second son of George V and Mary.	Lung cancer, Sandringham. Buried at St George's Chapel, Windsor.	Elizabeth Bowes-Lyon, daughter of 14th earl of Strathmore and Kinghorne. Married 26 April 1922.
Elizabeth II	1952–	6 Feb.	17 Bruton St, London, 21 April 1926; elder daughter of George VI and Elizabeth.	Reigned since 6 Feb. 1952.	Philip, son of Prince Andrew of Greece and Princess Alice. Married in Westminster Abbey, 20 Nov. 1947.

British Royalty: Miscellaneous Details

abdicated: first Edward II (25 January 1327)
Alexandra, Princess (the Hon. Lady Ogilvy)
full name: Alexandra Helen Elizabeth Olga Christabel
born: 25 December 1936, Belgrave Square, London
relationship to Queen: Cousin (sister of Edward, Duke of Kent)
husband: The Rt Hon. Sir Angus Ogilvy (b. 14 Sept. 1928)
children: James Robert Bruce Ogilvy (b. 29 February 1964)
Marina Victoria Alexandra Mowatt (b. 31 July 1966)
house: Thatched House Lodge, Richmond Park, Surrey
Alexandra Rose Day inaugurated in 1912 by Queen Alexandra
Andrew, Prince married Sarah Ferguson in 1986
full name: Andrew Albert Christian Edward
born: 19 February 1960, Buckingham Palace
titles: The Duke of York, Earl of Inverness and Baron Killyleagh
schools: Heatherdown, nr Ascot; Gordonstoun, Morayshire; Lakefield College School, Ontario
children: Beatrice Elizabeth Mary, born 8 August 1988
Eugene Victoria Helena, born 23 March 1990
houses: Sunninghill Park, Ascot; Buckingham Palace, London
Angevin kings Henry II, Richard I, John
Anne, Princess Princess Royal since 1987
born: 15 August 1950, Clarence House
full name: Anne Elizabeth Alice Louise
school: Benenden, Kent
marriages: Captain Mark Phillips (1973–92)
Captain Tim Laurence (1992–)
children: Peter Mark Andrew Phillips (b. 15 November 1977)
Zara Anne Elizabeth Phillips (b. 15 May 1981)
house: Gatcombe Park, Gloucestershire
attempted kidnapping: by Ian Ball in 1974 in the Mall
annus horribilis Queen Elizabeth's name for 1992
anti-smoking tract: published James I
Babington Plot Roman Catholic plot against Elizabeth I in 1586
bald as a young woman Elizabeth I
baldness revealed after execution Mary, queen of Scots
bathed every three months Elizabeth I
battle: died in; last sovereign Richard III
battle: led troops in; last George II (Dettingen)
bigamist George IV
Bill of Rights Act barring Catholics from succession
bodyguard scandal Commander Michael Trestrail resigned as the Queen's bodyguard (19 July 1982) after admitting to his part in a sexual scandal
breast: extra Anne Boleyn
Buckingham Palace: first to live in Queen Victoria
bought by George III in 1762
burnt the cakes (traditionally) King Alfred
Cabal advisers to Charles II: Clifford, Ashley, Buckingham, Arlington and Lauderdale
Cabinet meetings: attended most Queen Anne
Cavalier Parliament Charles II (aka Pensionary Parliament) first English Parliament 8 May 1661
Charles II: illegitimate son Duke of Monmouth, son of Lucy Walter
Charles, Prince married 1981, divorced 1996; remarried 2005
full name: Charles Philip Arthur George
born: 14 November 1948, Buckingham Palace
titles: Duke of Cornwall, Earl of Carrick and Baron Renfrew, Lord of the Isles, Duke of Rothsay, Prince and Great Steward of Scotland
Prince of Wales: title bestowed in 1958; inaugurated in 1969
children: William Arthur Philip Louis, born 21 June 1982
Henry Charles Albert David, born 15 September 1984
houses: St James's Palace, London and Highgrove, Gloucs
Cherry B incident of 1963: Charles bought while under-age, in Outer Hebrides
children's nanny: Tiggy Legge-Bourke
cherry brandy drinker George IV
children: most Henry I (20 acknowledged bastards plus two legitimate)
most legitimate Edward I (18)
Christian: first Ethelbert
Clarence, duke of: last Albert, eldest son of Edward VII
commoner; first to wed Henry IV
corgis Princess Elizabeth was given Susan as a present from her parents on her 18th birthday, April 1944. Ten generations of corgis have been descended from Susan and owned by the Queen. In chronological order their names are Sugar, Honey, Bee, Whisky, Sherry, Heather, Buzz, Foxy, Busy, Tiny, Mask, Rufus, Brush, Cindy, Pickles, Tinker, Socks, Geordie, Jolly, Blackie, Edward, Sweep, Smoky, Chipper, Shadow, Piper, Spark, Myth, Fable, Apollo, Diamond, Kelpie, Ranger, Phoenix, Pharos, Monty, Emma, Linnet, Willow and Holly.
crowned: battlefield Henry VII
crowned: twice Charles II
Defender of the Faith: first Henry VIII
deposed James II
divorced: first John
dukes: royal Cornwall, Edinburgh, Gloucester, Kent, York
education *Prince Charles* Cheam, Gordonstoun, Cambridge. The Prince of Wales also spent the 1966 school year as an exchange student at the Geelong Church of England Grammar School in Melbourne, Australia.
Prince William Mrs Mynors' Nursery School, London, Wetherby School, London, Ludgrove School, Wokingham, Eton College, Berkshire, St Andrews University (Scottish Master of Arts)
Prince Harry Eton College
Princess Beatrice St George's School for Girls, Ascot, Berkshire
Edward, Prince
full name: Edward Antony Richard Louis
born: 10 March 1964, Buckingham Palace
titles: Earl of Wessex, Viscount Severn
schools: Gibbs Preparatory School, Kensington; Heatherdown Preparatory School, nr Ascot; Gordonstoun, Morayshire; Jesus College, Cambridge
marriage: Sophie Helen Rhys-Jones (19 June 1999)
children: Louise Alice Elizabeth Mary, born 8 November 2003
James Alexander Philip Theo, born 17 December 2007
house: Bagshot Park, Surrey
Edward VII: House of Lords speech housing speech given while Prince of Wales
Edward VIII abdication speech written by Walter Monckton
Eleanor Crosses: 12 Marking resting place of Eleanor of Castile's cortege; crosses at Lincoln, Grantham, Stamford, Stratford, Woburn, Dunstable, St Albans, Cheapside, Northampton Geddington and Waltham still standing; last, Charing Cross, is a replica
Elizabeth I: favourite Robert Dudley, Earl of Leicester
Elizabeth II coronation day 2 June 1953
biographer Sarah Bradford (1996)
royal arms insignia Dieu et Mon Droit
aka Lord High Admiral of England
married 20 Nov. 1947
fattest king George IV
finger: extra Anne Boleyn
Five Members Pym, Hampden, Heselrige, Holles and Strode, whom Charles I attempted to arrest on 4 Jan. 1642, as well as Lord Mandeville
gilded coach used by the new Sovereign during Coronation ceremony
Gloucester, Duke of
full name: Richard Alexander Walter George
born: 26 August 1944, Hadley Common, Herts
relationship to Queen: cousin (his father Henry, Duke of Gloucester (1900–74) was the brother of the Queen's father)
wife: Birgitte Eva Van Deurs (born 20 June 1946)
children: Earl of Ulster (Alexander Patrick, born 24 October 1974)
Lady Davina Windsor, born 19 November 1977
Lady Rose Windsor, born 1 March 1980
house: Kensington Palace, London
heirs to throne males are heirs apparent; females are heirs presumptive
Henry, Prince (known as Harry) current military rank: Captain – The Blues and Royals attached to Army Air Corps
Henry VIII: fate of wives divorced, beheaded, died, divorced, beheaded, survived
honours: awarded on New Year's Day & Queen's official birthday

immoral queen Caroline of Brunswick
Irish state coach used by British monarchs for State Opening of Parliaments and by family members at Coronations
jewellers, Crown Garrards
Kent, Duke of
full name: Edward George Nicholas Paul Patrick
born: 9 October 1935, Belgrave Square, London
relationship to Queen: cousin (his father George, Duke of Kent (1902–42), was the brother of the Queen's father)
wife: Katharine Worsley (born 22 Feb. 1933)
children: George, Earl of St Andrews, born 26 June 1962
Lady Helen Taylor, born 28 April 1964
Lord Nicholas Windsor, born 25 July 1970
house: Wren House, Palace Green, London
king over the water Jacobite term for pretenders
Lancaster: House of Henry IV, V, VI
Lollards: suppressed Henry V
mad king George III
madness: bouts of Henry VI
Margaret, Princess married 1960 to Anthony Armstrong Jones (divorced 1978). Margaret died 9 February 2002
full name: Margaret Rose
born: 21 August 1930, Glamis Castle, Scotland
children: David Armstrong Jones (see Viscount Linley)
Sarah (see separate entry)
married kings of England and France Eleanor of Aquitaine (Louis VII and Henry II)
Michael of Kent, Prince
full name: Michael George Charles Franklin
born: 4 July 1942, Coppins, Iver, Bucks
relationship to Queen: cousin (brother of Edward, Duke of Kent)
wife: Baroness Marie-Christine Agnes Hedwig Ida von Reibnitz (born 15 January 1945)
children: Lord Frederick Michael George David Louis Windsor, born 6 April 1979
Lady Gabriella Marina Alexandra Ophelia, born 23 April 1981
houses: Kensington Palace, London
Nether Lypiatt Manor, Gloucestershire
murdered by queen and her lover Edward II
nicknames *Elizabeth II* 'Lilibet' (name originated because she could not pronounce Elizabeth when a child)
Princess Margaret 'Bud' (coined by her sister Elizabeth as a play on her second name of Rose)
oldest on accession William IV (64)
oldest royal residence Windsor Castle
Parliament: first; in the reign of Henry III
pawned Crown jewels Richard II (to pay for wedding)
Philip, Prince
born: 10 June 1921, Corfu, Greece
titles: Duke of Edinburgh, Earl of Merioneth, Baron Greenwich
schools: Cheam, Salem School, Germany, Gordonstoun, Morayshire
Plantagenet: first Henry II
last Richard II, although later kings from Plantagenet line
pot-smoking Prince: Prince Harry (sent to drug rehabilitation clinic to warn him of dangers)
Popish Plot fictitious Jesuit plot of Titus Oates and Israel Tonge against Charles II resulting in the execution of Oliver Plunket, primate of Ireland
premier Duke of Scotland Dukes of Hamilton
pretenders: Henry VII's reign Perkin Warbeck (1498), hanged for treason; Lambert Simnel (1487), became kitchen hand
prince of Wales: longest Edward VII (59 yrs)
last before Charles Edward VIII
last Welsh Llewellyn
Prince Philip: parents Prince Andrew and Princess Alice of Greece
queen never set foot in England Berengaria, wife of Richard I
Richards all died violently
Ridolfi Plot Catholic plot against Elizabeth I in 1571
Roman Catholic monarch: last James II
royal allowance Civil List
rugby Peter Phillips, son of the Princess Royal, played rugby for Scottish schools
Rye House Plot plot to murder Charles II and his brother on the way home from Newmarket races
Sarah Armstrong-Jones daughter of Princess Margaret, born 1 May 1964, Kensington Palace, married Daniel Chatto, 1994
shortest queen Matilda, wife of William I
spoke little English George I
stammered George VI
St Edward's crown made for Charles II's coronation
toilet: died on George II
two queens: father of James II (Mary and Anne)
urinated in font Ethelred the Unready
USA: first to go to George VI
Victoria's gillie John Brown
Viscount Linley son of Princess Margaret, born 3 November 1961, Clarence House
married: Hon. Serena Stanhope, 1993
***White Ship* disaster** William, son of Henry I, drowned at Barfleur, 25 Nov. 1120
wife: met at altar George III (Charlotte Sophia)
William, Prince married Catherine Elizabeth Middleton (b. 9 January 1982) 29 April 2011 at Westminster Abbey
titles: The Duke of Cambridge (in Scotland The Earl of Strathearn) and Baron Carrickfergus
children: George Alexander Louis, born 22 July 2013
Wimbledon: played at George VI
wisest fool in Christendom James I (coined by Henry IV of France)
write name: first to do so Richard II
York, House of Edward IV, V, Richard III

Order of Precedence (England and Wales)

The sovereign	Lord President of the Council
The Prince Philip, duke of Edinburgh	Speaker of the House of Commons
The Prince of Wales	Lord Privy Seal
The sovereign's younger sons	Ambassadors and High Commissioners
The sovereign's grandsons	Lord Great Chamberlain
The sovereign's cousins	Earl Marshal
Archbishop of Canterbury	Lord Steward of the Household
Lord High Chancellor	Lord Chamberlain of the Household
Archbishop of York	Master of the Horse
The Prime Minister	Then dukes, marquesses, earls, viscounts, barons

NB The order of precedence is included in this section to show the distinction between precedence and succession. Precedence is a traditional ceremonial observation and, although closely following the order of succession in areas, is in fact a separate and distinct list.

Order of Succession

1	HRH Prince Charles, The Prince of Wales	11	HRH Princess Anne, Princess Royal
2	HRH Prince William, Duke of Cambridge	12	Peter Phillips, son of Princess Anne
3	HRH Prince George of Cambridge	13	Savannah Phillips (b. 2010)
4	HRH Prince Henry of Wales	14	Isla Phillips (b. 2012)
5	HRH Prince Andrew, duke of Yorkss	15	Zara Tindall, daughter of Princess Anne
6	HRH Princess Beatrice of York	16	Viscount Linley, David Armstrong-Jones
7	HRH Princess Eugenie of York	17	Hon. Charles Armstrong-Jones
8	HRH Edward, Earl of Wessex	18	Hon. Margarita Armstrong-Jones
9	James, Viscount Severn	19	Lady Sarah Chatto (née Armstrong-Jones)
10	Lady Louise Windsor	20	Samuel Chatto (b.1996)

Rulers of the British Isles

Kings and Queens of Scotland

House of Alpin

842–858	Kenneth I (MacAlpin)
858–862	Donald I
862–877	Constantine I
877–878	Aed
878–889	Giric and Eochaid
889–900	Donald II
900–943	Constantine II
943–954	Malcolm I
954–962	Indulf
962–966	Duf
966–971	Culén
971–995	Kenneth II
995–997	Constantine III
997–1005	Kenneth III
1005–1034	Malcolm II

House of Dunkeld

1034–1040	Duncan I

House of Moray

1040–1057	Macbeth
1057–1058	Lulach

House of Dunkeld

1058–1093	Malcolm III (Canmore, aka Big Head)
1093–1097	Donald III
1094	Duncan II
1097–1107	Edgar
1107–1124	Alexander I (the Fierce)
1124–1153	David I (the Saint)
1153–1165	Malcolm IV (the Maiden)
1165–1214	William I (the Lion)
1214–1249	Alexander II
1249–1286	Alexander III

House of Norway

1286–1290	Margaret (Maid of Norway)
1290–1292	interregnum (disputed by 13 competitors)

House of Balliol

1292–1296	John Balliol
1296–1306	interregnum

House of Bruce

1306–1329	Robert I (the Bruce)
1329–1371	David II

House of Balliol

1332–1356	Edward (son of John, abdicated)

House of Stewart

1371–1390	Robert II (Stewart)
1390–1406	Robert III
1406–1437	James I
1437–1460	James II
1460–1488	James III
1488–1513	James IV
1513–1542	James V
1542–1567	Mary
1567–1625	James VI

Rulers of the Principality of Wales

Kingdom of Gwynedd

□□825–844	Merfyn the Freckled
□□844–878	Rhodri I (the Great)
□□878–916	Anarawd
□□916–942	Idwal the Bald
□□942–950	Hywel I (the Good)
□□950–979	Iago I
□□979–985	Hywel II
□□985–986	Cadwallon
□□986–999	Maredudd
□□999–1005	Cynan I
1005–1018	Aeddan
1018–1023	Llywelyn I
1023–1039	Iago II
1039–1063	Gruffydd I
1081–1137	Gruffydd II
1137–1170	Owain
1170–1174	Cynan II
1174–1194	David I (East)
1174–1195	Rhodri II (West)
1174–1200	Gruffydd III (South)
1194–1240	Llywelyn II (The Great)
1240–1246	David II

Principality of Wales

1246–1282	Llywelyn III (ap Gruffydd)
1282–1283	David III

NB Although Llywelyn ap Gruffydd is invariably quoted as the last native prince of Wales, in fact it is true to say that his brother, David ap Gruffydd, was the last native prince of Wales. This confusion arises simply because England did not recognise anyone except Llywelyn as ruler. The Welsh would recognise David as their last prince, and the English Llywelyn. In 1301 the future Edward II became prince of Wales, and subsequently the eldest son of the reigning monarch has been given this title.

The High Kingship of Ireland

House of Ui Néill

445–452	Niall of the Nine Hostages
819–833	Conchobar
1002–1014	Brian Bóruma (king of Munster)
1166–1186	Ruaidri

NB The short list above includes the first and last kings of Ireland and two other famous kings. Many of the other rulers are obscure and were not recognised as such until at least the 9th century.

Other Important Historical Rulers

Israel

1020–1010 BC	Saul
1010–970 BC	David
970–931 BC	Solomon

Kingdom of Judah

930–914 BC	Rehoboam (son of Solomon)

Kingdom of Israel

931–910 BC	Jeroboam I (son of Solomon)

Lydia: last king

560–547 BC	Croesus

Persian Empire

559–530 BC	Cyrus the Great
529–522 BC	Cambyses
522 BC	Smerdis (Bardiya)
521–486 BC	Darius I (The Great)
485–465 BC	Xerxes I
464–424 BC	Artaxerxes I
424 BC	Xerxes II
424 BC	Sogdianus
423–405 BC	Darius II
404–359 BC	Artaxerxes II
358–338 BC	Artaxerxes III
337–336 BC	Arses
335–330 BC	Darius III

Macedonia (selected kings)

399–397 BC	Orestes
359–336 BC	Philip II
336–323 BC	Alexander III (the Great)
179–168 BC	Perseus (the last king)

Visigoth kingdom

395–410	Alaric I (first king of the Visigoths)
711–714	Agila II (last king of the Visigoths)

Anglo-Saxon kingdoms

455–488	Hengest (first ruler of kingdom of Kent)
823–825	Baldred (last ruler of kingdom of Kent)
547–559	Ida (first ruler of Bernicia)
585–592	Hussa (last ruler of Bernicia)
569–599	Aelle (first ruler of Deira)
599–604	Aethelric (last ruler of Deira)
592–616	Aethelfrith (Northumberland: Bernicia and Deira)
913–927	Aldred (last ruler of Northumberland)
633–655	Penda (first ruler of Mercia)
757–796	Offa (kingdom of Mercia)
918–919	Aelfwyn (last ruler of Mercia)
519–534	Cerdic (first ruler of Wessex)
802–839	Egbert (last ruler of Wessex)

Kingdom of France (selected)
Carolingian House
751–768 Pepin the Short (first king of France)
768–814 Charlemagne (Holy Roman Emperor, 800)
840–877 Charles I (the Bald)
877–879 Louis II (the Stammerer)
885–888 Charles II (the Fat)
893–923 Charles III (the Simple)
986–987 Louis V (the Sluggard)

Capetian House
987–996 Hugh Capet
996–1031 Robert II (the Pious)
1108–1137 Louis VI (the Fat)
1137–1180 Louis VII (the Younger)
1223–1226 Louis VIII (the Lion)
1285–1314 Philip IV (the Fair)
1314–1316 Louis X (the Stubborn)
1316–1322 Philip V (the Tall)
1322–1328 Charles IV (the Fair)

House of Valois
1328–1350 Philip VI
1350–1364 John II (the Good)
1364–1380 Charles V (the Wise)
1380–1422 Charles VI (the Mad)
1422–1461 Charles VII (the Victorious)
1483–1498 Charles VIII

House of Angoulême
1515–1547 Francis I
1547–1559 Henry II
1559–1560 Francis II (husband of Mary of Scots)
1560–1574 Charles IX
1574–1589 Henry III

House of Bourbon
1589–1610 Henry IV (Paris is worth a mass)
1610–1643 Louis XIII
1643–1715 Louis XIV (the Sun King)
1715–1774 Louis XV
1774–1792 Louis XVI

First Empire
1804–1814 Napoleon I (king of Italy, 1805)

Second Empire
1852–1870 Napoleon III

Kingdom of Italy
1849–1878 Victor Emmanuel II
1878–1900 Humbert I
1900–1946 Victor Emmanuel III
1946–1946 Humbert II

NB Although Victor Emmanuel III is often thought to be the last king of Italy, in fact, he was the last 'crowned' king. Humbert II (Umberto) was the last incumbent.

Kingdom of Spain (selected)
House of Habsburg
1516–1556 Charles I (Holy Roman Emperor, 1519–58)
1556–1598 Philip II (husband of Bloody Mary)

House of Bourbon
1700–1724 Philip V (grandson of Louis XIV of France)

House of Bonaparte
1808–1813 Joseph Napoleon

House of Bourbon
1975– Juan Carlos I

Kingdom of Portugal (selected)
1139–1185 Afonso I

House of Avis
1385–1433 John I (the Bastard)
1578–1580 Henry (the Cardinal)

House of Braganza
1640–1656 John IV
1706–1750 John V (the Magnanimous)
1834–1853 Maria II

House of Saxe-Coburg-Gotha
1853–1861 Pedro V
1908–1910 Manuel II

Kingdom of Norway (selected)
858–928 Harald I
1957–1991 Olav V
1991– Harald V

Kingdom of Denmark (selected)
940–986 Harald I
1972– Margaret II

Kingdom of Sweden (selected)
980–995 Erik the Victorious

House of Vasa
1523–1560 Gustavus I
1560–1568 Erik XIV
1568–1592 John III
1592–1599 Sigismund

House of Bernadotte
1818–1844 Charles XIV
1973– Charles XVI Gustavus

Kingdom of Netherlands (selected)
1572–1584 William I (the Silent)
1806–1810 Louis Napoleon
1849–1890 William III
1890–1948 Wilhelmina
1948–1980 Juliana
1980–2013 Beatrix
2013– Willem-Alexander

Tsars/Tsarinas of Russia
1462–1505 Ivan III (the Great)
1533–1584 Ivan IV (the Terrible)
1598–1605 Boris Godunov
1613–1645 Michael Romanov
1682–1725 Peter I (the Great)
1725–1727 Catherine I (Martha)
1762–1796 Catherine II (the Great, born Sophie of Anhalt)
1894–1917 Nicholas II

Inca Empire
1532–1533 Atauhualpa
1571–1572 Tupac Amaru

Aztec Empire
1372–1391 Acamapichtli
1427–1440 Itzcoatl

Japanese Empire
0–10 BC Jimmu
1623–1651 Iemitsu
1713–1716 Ietsugu
1853–1858 Iesada
1867–1868 Keiki (Yoshinobu)

Chinese dynasties
18th–12th cent. BC Shang
1111–255 BC Chou
770–221 BC Tung
221–206 BC Ch'in
206–220 AD Han
581–618 Sui
618–907 T'ang
960–1279 Sung
1206–1368 Yüan
1368–1644 Ming
1644–1912 Manchu (Ch'ing)

Last kings/queens of

Romania	Michael (1940–47)
Bulgaria	Simeon II (1943–46)
Albania	Zog I (1928–39)
Afghanistan	Muhammad Zahir Shah (1933–73)
Korea	Sunjong (1907–10)
Burma	Thibaw (1878–85)
Laos	SavangVatthana (1959–75)
Bohemia	Ferdinand I (1526–64)
Cambodia	Sihanouk (1941–55) Monarchy re-established on 23 Sept. 1993
Ethiopia	Asfa Wossen (1974–75)
Madagascar	Ranavalona (1883–96)
Zululand	Dinuzulu (1884–87)
Hawaii	Liliuokalani (1891–93)
Hungary	John Sigismund (1540–70)
Poland	Stanislas II Augustus (1764–95)

Holy Roman Emperors

Charlemagne (Charles I)	800–814
Louis I (the Pious)	814–840
civil war	840–843
Lothair I	843–855
Louis II	855–875
Charles II (the Bald)	875–877
interregnum	877–881
Charles III (the Fat)	881–887
interregnum	887–891
Guido of Spoleto	891–894
Lambert of Spoleto	892–898
Arnulf	898–899
Louis III (the Blind)	901–905
Conrad I	911–918
Berengar	915–924
Henry I	919–936
Otto I (the Great)	936–973
Otto II	973–983
Otto III	983–1002
Henry II (the Saint)	1002–1024
Conrad II	1024–1039
Henry III (the Black)	1039–1056
Henry IV	1056–1106
Rudolf	1077–1080
Hermann	1081–1093
Conrad	1093–1101
Henry V	1106–1125
Lothair II	1125–1137
Conrad III	1138–1152
Frederick I (Barbarossa)	1152–1190
Henry VI	1190–1197
Philip	1198–1208
Otto IV	1198–1214
Frederick II	1215–1250
Henry VII	1220–1235
Henry Raspe	1246–1247
William of Holland	1247–1256
Conrad IV	1250–1254
great interregnum	1254–1273
Richard	1257–1272
Alfonso	1257–1275
Rudolf I	1273–1291
Adolf	1292–1298
Albert I	1298–1308
Henry VII	1308–1313
Frederick III	1314–1326
Louis IV	1314–1346
Charles IV	1346–1378
Wenceslas	1378–1400
Rupert	1400–1410
Jobst	1410–1411
Sigismund	1410–1437
Albert II	1438–1439
Frederick III	1440–1493
Maximillian I	1493–1519
Charles V	1519–1556
Ferdinand I	1556–1564
Maximillian II	1564–1576
Rudolf II	1576–1612
Matthias	1612–1619
Ferdinand II	1619–1637
Ferdinand III	1637–1657
Leopold I	1658–1705
Joseph I	1705–1711
Charles VI	1711–1740
interregnum	1740–1742
Charles VII	1742–1745
Francis I	1745–1765
Joseph II	1765–1790
Leopold II	1790–1792
Francis II	1792–1806

Roman Kings

Romulus	753–715 BC
Numa Pompilius	715–673 BC
Tullus Hostilius	673–642 BC
Ancus Marcius	642–616 BC
Tarquinius Priscus	616–578 BC
Servius Tullius	578–534 BC
Tarquinius Superbus	534–509 BC

NB The traditional seven kings of Rome as listed above are of extremely dubious authenticity and nowadays are only observed as truth in the context of being a very popular quiz question, and to this end the ones to remember are the first, Romulus, and the last, Tarquinius Superbus (Proud Tarquin).

Roman Emperors

Augustus	27 BC–AD 14
Tiberius	14–37
Caligula	37–41
Claudius	41–54
Nero	54–68
Galba	68–69
Otho	69
Vitellius	69
Vespasian	69–79
Titus	79–81
Domitian	81–96
Nerva	96–98
Trajan	98–117
Hadrian	117–138
Antoninus Pius	138–161
Marcus Aurelius	161–180
Commodus	180–192
Pertinax	193
Didius Julianus	193
Septimius Severus	193–211
Geta	211
Caracalla	211–217
Macrinus	217–218
Diadumenian	218
Elagabalus	218–222
Severus Alexander	222–235
Maximinus the Thracian	235–238
Gordian I	238
Gordian II	238
Balbinus	238
Pupienus Maximus	238
Gordian III	238–244
Philip I the Arabian	244–249
Philip II	247–249
Decius	249–251
Herennius Etruscus	251
Hostilian	251
Trebonianus Gallus (co-ruler with Misson Volusian)	251–253
Volusian	251–253
Aemilian	253
Valerian (east)	253–260
Gallienus (west)	253–268
Saloninus	260
Claudius II	268–270
Quintillus	270
Aurelian	270–275
Tacitus	275–276
Florian	276
Probus	276–282
Carus	282–283
Numerian (east)	283–284
Carinus (west)	283–285
Postumus (Gaul)	260–269
Laelian (Gaul)	269
Marius (Gaul)	269
Victorinus (Gaul)	269–271
Tetricus (Gaul)	271–274
Diocletian (see below)	284–305
Maximian (see below)	286–305
Constantius I (see below)	305–306
Galerius (see below)	305–311
Severus (west)	306–307
Maxentius (west)	307–312
Constantine I (west until 324)	307–337
Licinius (Pannonia and east)	308–324
Maximinus II (east)	310–313
Valerius Valens	316–317
Martinian	324
Constantine II (Gaul, Britain, Spain)	337–340
Constans (west)	337–350
Constantius II (east)	337–361
Magnentius (west)	350–353
Julian the Apostate (Gaul until 361)	360–363
Jovian	363–364
Valentinian I (west)	364–375
Valens (east)	364–378
Gratian (west)	375–383
Valentinian II	375–392
Theodosius I (the Great) (east)	379–395
Maximus (west)	383–388
Victor (west)	387–388
Eugenius (west)	392–394

After a short interregnum the Empire split into east and west. Selected entries are as follows:

Western Roman Emperors

Honorius	395–423 (the first)
Romulus Augustus	475–476 (the last)

Eastern Roman Emperors

Arcadius	395–408 (the first)
Justinian I (the Great)	527–565
Constantine XI	1449–1453 (the last)

Turkish capture of Constantinople ultimately ended the Byzantine Empire.

NB The names used in the above table are the ones familiarly adopted by history. The full names are complex and can be depicted in an imperial style or in Latin. It became increasingly impractical to rule over the whole of the Roman Empire and although the empire was not officially split until AD 395, many joint emperors divided their territories between east and west, with further subdivisions into Gaul, Britain, Illyria etc. To use the Diocletian tetrarchy as an example, Galerius, residing in Sirmium, administered Illyria, Achaea, and the Danubian provinces; Maximian,
residing in Milan, administered Italy, Sicily, and Africa; Constantius I, residing in Trier, governed Gaul, Spain, and Britain; and Diocletian, residing in Nicomedia, watched over Thrace, Asia, and Egypt.

AD 69 is often referred to as the year of the four emperors but in AD 238 there were six emperors. Maximinus became the first soldier who had started from the ranks to become Roman emperor, he was replaced by the aged proconsul Gordian, who ruled jointly with his son. Gordian committed suicide on learning of the death of his son in a battle with Capellianus, governor of Numidia. The Roman Senate then proclaimed two elderly senators Balbinus and Pupienus Maximus joint emperors. The imperial guards murdered the Senate's nominees and the grandson of Gordian became emperor as Gordian III, at the age of 13. Valentinian II was proclaimed emperor in Budapest (Aquincum) at the age of 4, and ruled Italy, Africa, Illyricum, through his mother. He was found dead in his palace at Vienna, probably murdered by agents of Arbogast, the usurper in Gaul. In areas likely to confuse, I have added the administrative area in parenthesis. I have omitted usurpers such as Vetranio (abdicated in AD 351) and Procopius (reigned in Constantinople AD 365–6), as this would only confuse matters further.

Sovereigns

General Information on Sovereigns of England and Great Britain

William I Domesday Book of 1086 contained details of the land settlement of England and its purpose was to maximise the land tax yield. It received its name in the 12th century to signify that, like the day of judgement, there could be no appeal from its verdict.

Hereward the Wake ('Watchful One'), a Lincolnshire squire, raided Peterborough Abbey in 1070 as a protest against William's appointment of a Norman abbot. He took refuge on the Isle of Ely and eventually escaped through the Fens.

Bishop Odo of Bayeux was William's half-brother and it was he who commissioned the Bayeux Tapestry (embroidery).

Of William's four sons, Robert became duke of Normandy and Richard died in infancy.

William was Edward the Confessor's cousin by way of his mother Emma, who was the sister of William's grandfather, Count Richard II. Edward the Confessor was Harold II's brother-in-law by way of his marriage to Edith, Harold's sister.

William's invasion forces assembled at the mouth of the Dives river in September 1066 but adverse winds prevented a due-north sailing to the Isle of Wight, so he regrouped at St Valéry on Somme and sailed on 27 September to the south coast of England and took Pevensey and Hastings. unchallenged. Harold was victorious against Tostig and Harald Hardraade at Stamford Bridge, near York, on 25 September and met William at the Battle of Hastings on 14 October. William only had about 7,000 troops but his archers won the day and, when Harold was killed, the English gave up.

William II William was called Rufus because of his ruddy complexion.

Malcolm III of Scotland (Malcolm Canmore, aka Great Head) became king of Scotland in 1057 on the death of Macbeth, who had killed Malcolm's father, Duncan, in 1040. He invaded England five times between 1061 and 1093 and was killed at Alnwick in Northumberland. Four of his sons succeeded him – Duncan, Edgar, Alexander and David.

Traditionally William was shot by an arrow fired by a Norman knight called Walter Tirel, although many believe that William's younger brother Henry was the instigator.

Henry I Henry was the only English-born son of William I.

His brother Robert was paid a pension of 3,000 marks to resign his claim to the English throne and concentrate his attentions on Normandy, but in 1105–6 Henry was forced to make war against his brother's maladministration. Robert was defeated at Tinchebrai in 1106, and was kept a prisoner for life.

In 1120, Henry's only legitimate son, William, was drowned on his way from Normandy to England in what is now known as the *White Ship* disaster.

Matilda Matilda was pledged the throne in 1127 but Stephen became king in 1135. Matilda invaded the kingdom in 1139, landed at Arundel and established a stronghold in the West Country with her half-brother Robert of Gloucester. She captured Stephen at Lincoln and pronounced herself 'Lady of the English'. Her forces were defeated September 14 1141 while besieging the royalist-held Wolvesey Castle in what is known as the 'Rout of Winchester'. Robert Earl of Gloucester was taken prisoner and exchanged for King Stephen. Matilda was never crowned.

Stephen Stephen usurped the crown by declaring Matilda illegitimate, as her father had remarried.

Henry II Henry was the first Plantagenet king of England.

He systematically destroyed the adulterine (unlicensed) castles which had sprung up during the reign of his predecessor.

Henry's conflict with Thomas à Becket was over a written statement made by Henry at Clarendon, near Salisbury, on 30 January 1164 whereby he wanted the benefit of clergy to be lifted and have lay authorities try clerks taking holy orders.

The English pope, Adrian IV, gave Henry authority over the whole of Ireland.

Incited by Queen Eleanor, Prince John and Richard rebelled against Henry and their cause was espoused by the kings of France and Scotland. William the Lion of Scotland was taken prisoner at Alnwick and forced to sign the Treaty of Falaise, 1174, thereby swearing allegiance to Henry.

Henry, the first son of Henry II, died in 1183 and his second son, Geoffrey, was killed in a tournament in Paris in 1185.

Henry's mistress, the fair Rosamond, daughter of Walter Clifford, was said to have borne him two sons – William Longsword, earl of Salisbury, and Geoffrey, archbishop of York – but this is unlikely.

Henry and his two sons were known as Angevin kings, and although Plantagenet was the other name for this royal House, subsequent members are not Angevin. To confuse matters further, although Richard II was traditionally the last king of the House of Plantagenet, the Yorkist Richard III was the last of the direct line.

Henry's second son, Henry (aka FitzHenry), was crowned on 14 June 1170, to rule in association with his father, and was known as Henry III or Henry the Young King; he died of dysentery in 1183.

Richard I Richard was given the Duchy of Aquitaine aged 11, and was enthroned as duke of Aquitaine at Poitiers in 1172.

He departed for the Holy Land to fight the third Crusade in 1190. Richard made a truce for three years with Saladin but was captured on his way home by Duke Leopold in December 1192. He was imprisoned at the duke's castle at Durnstein on the Danube and then handed over to Henry VI of Germany. Richard was released in February 1194 after paying a ransom of nearly 150,000 marks. Richard left Hubert Walter as virtual ruler of England while he was away.

John John became count of Mortain on Richard's accession in 1189.

When Richard recognised his nephew, Arthur, duke of Brittany, as his heir in October 1190, John broke his oath to Richard not to enter England while he was away at the Crusades. Richard finally accepted John as his heir in 1196.

John's first marriage to Isabella of Gloucester was dissolved on the grounds of consanguinity, both parties being great-grandchildren of Henry I. John's second marriage, to Isabella of Angoulême, was largely responsible for the loss of many French territories.

Pope Innocent III excommunicated John in November 1209 because of his refusal to accept Stephen Langton as archbishop of Canterbury.

The Barons' War of 1215–17 ensued after John sealed the Magna Carta of 15 June 1215 but did not abide by it. Magna Carta comprises a preamble and 63 clauses. The most famous clauses are (39), guaranteeing every free man security from illegal interference in his person or property, (40), which guaranteed justice to all, and (12), which stated that the king was not to levy taxes without reference to the 'common council'.

Henry III Henry was 9 years old when he became king, so William Marshal, First Earl of Pembroke and Striguil, acted as his regent for the first three years, followed by Hubert de Burgh for the next eight years.

Henry was forced to agree to the Provisions of Oxford, 1258, which created a council of fifteen barons and formed the first judicial Parliament.

The civil war between Henry III and his barons, led by Simon de Montfort, was called the Second Baron's War (1264–7).

Edward I Edward won great renown as a knight on the eighth, and last, Crusade of 1270 and did not return home for his coronation until 1274.

He campaigned against Llewelyn ap Gruffud, of Gwynedd, and finally forced him into submission in 1276; and after his death in 1282 the principality was formally annexed to the English Crown by the Statute of Wales, 1284.

In 1289 Edward betrothed his infant son to Margaret, the infant Queen of Scotland (Maid of Norway), in order to unite England and Scotland, but Margaret died the following year.

Edward called the 'Model Parliament' of 1295 to allay discontent at home and the following year marched north, stripped John Balliol of his crown and carried the Stone of Scone back to England.

He had a setback at Stirling Bridge in 1297, but the following year he trounced William Wallace at Falkirk.

Edward II In 1301 Edward became the first English Prince of Wales.

His favourite was Piers Gaveston, whom he made duke of Cornwall. When Gaveston was executed in 1312, Edward chose Hugh le Despenser and his son as his new favourites, and they aided in the overthrow of Thomas, earl of Lancaster, in 1321.

Edward was defeated by Robert the Bruce at Bannockburn, 24 June 1314.

Edward's wife, Isabella, despised him and took a lover in Roger de Mortimer. In 1326 she landed on the coast of Suffolk, executed the Despensers and forced Edward to abdicate on 25 January 1327, in favour of his son. He was murdered later that year in Berkeley Castle, Gloucestershire, probably by Isabella and Roger de Mortimer. Edward III was crowned in January 1327, eight months before his father died.

Edward III In 1328 Edward married Philippa of Hainault and two years later put Mortimer to death and banished his mother to Castle Rising.

Charles IV of France died without a son in 1328 and Edward claimed his kingdom by right of his mother, who was Charles's sister. He declared war against Philip VI in 1337, which was in effect the start of the Hundred Years War.

Accompanied by his eldest son, Edward the Black Prince, Edward had a great victory at Crécy in 1346 and another at Poitiers in 1356, where it is said the Black Prince gained his spurs.

Edward's mistress from 1366 onwards was Alice Perrers, his wife's lady-in-waiting, who let the government slip into the hands of Edward's fourth son, John of Gaunt.

The Black Prince died in 1376 and his son by Joan, the Fair Maid of Kent, succeeded Edward III, as Richard II.

Richard II Although a council of twelve was officially entrusted to govern during Richard's minority, in effect John of Gaunt was the regent.

Poll tax of 1380 created national unrest and led to the Peasants' Revolt of 1381, when rebels under Wat Tyler took Rochester Castle in Kent and then marched on London with fellow radicals from Essex. Richard saw the Essex men at Mile End and made extensive promises, and the next day, 14 June, met Wat Tyler's men at Smithfield. Tyler was struck down by the mayor of London, William Walworth, in revenge for the atrocities of the previous day when the archbishop of Canterbury, Simon of Sudbury, was murdered.

John of Gaunt died in 1399 and his son succeeded him as duke of Lancaster. Richard went to Ireland in May 1399 and on 4 July Henry, duke of Lancaster, landed back in England. Although Richard hurried back to England, he submitted to his cousin at Flint on 19 August and was put in the Tower. On 29 September 1399 he resigned the Crown in favour of Henry and he seems to have been murdered at Pontefract Castle, Yorkshire, early in 1400.

Henry IV Henry was the first king of the House of Lancaster.

His surname of Bolingbroke came from his birthplace in Lincolnshire.

Henry defeated Harry Hotspur at Shrewsbury on 21 July 1403, when Hotspur was slain.

Henry V Henry had Richard II's body buried in Westminster Abbey.

Henry thought he had a good claim to the French crown through his great-grandfather, Edward III.

Henry's famous victory at Agincourt was on 25 October 1415.

In 1420 Henry became regent of France via the 'Perpetual Peace' of Troyes.

Henry persecuted the Lollards, would-be Church reformers who had become the first group of English heretics to represent a political threat.

Henry VI Henry was less than a year old when he became king of England, and on the death of his maternal grandfather, King Charles VI, he became king of France when just over 1 year of age. He was officially crowned king of England in 1429 and of France in 1431.

By 1453 the Hundred Years War was effectively over, with England expelled from all France except Calais.

Cade's Rebellion of 1450 was a revolt by Kentish gentry against the high taxes and alleged corruption in Henry's council. On 18 June Cade defeated a royal army at Sevenoaks and then marched on London. He was eventually killed attempting to evade arrest at Heathfield, Sussex.

Edward IV Richard, duke of York, became protector while Henry VI suffered temporary madness in 1454. Richard had in fact a better title to the crown than Henry, as he was descended from Lionel, duke of Clarence, third son of Edward III. When Henry recovered, Richard refused to hand back the throne. He defeated Henry at St Albans on 22 May 1455, thereby starting the Wars of the Roses. Although in the ascendant, York did not claim the Crown until 1460, when he became Henry's heir, resulting in Edward Prince of Wales being disinherited. Richard was killed at Wakefield soon after but his son claimed the Crown as Edward IV, after his victory at Mortimer's Cross, and the second battle at St Albans. After a series of victories at Towton, Hedgeley Moor and Hexham, Edward married Elizabeth Woodvillle and the opposition to this family briefly restored Henry VI to the throne in 1470. Undeterred, Edward regrouped and with only 2,000 men, defeated the Lancastrians and killed Warwick at Barnet on 14 April 1471. Edward carried on to Tewkesbury and on 4 May 1471 his decisive victory and the death of Edward, Prince of Wales, effectively ended the Lancastrian resistance. Henry VI was killed soon after in the Tower of London.

Edward V The 12-year-old King Edward V was escorted from Ludlow by Earl Rivers but Richard, duke of Gloucester, the future Richard III, intercepted him at Northampton, brought him to London on 4 May 1483 and was then made protector. In June, Edward's brother, Richard, duke of York, joined him in the Tower of London and they were never seen again. In 1674 some bones were found and re-interred as theirs in Westminster Abbey.

Richard III Richard became duke of Gloucester in 1461.

On the death of Edward IV on 9 April 1483, Richard became Protector of the Realm for Edward's son and successor, the 12-year-old King Edward V, whom he imprisoned in the Tower of London along with his younger brother Richard on the premise that Edward IV's marriage was invalid and therefore his sons were illegitimate. Richard was proclaimed king in June 1483.

It is possible that Richard had a hand in the murder of Henry VI in the Tower of London on the night of 21 May 1471.

Richard's chief supporter had been Henry Stafford, 2nd duke of Buckingham, but soon after Richard's coronation he entered into a plot with friends of Henry, earl of Richmond, the future Henry VII. The attempt failed and Buckingham was executed. Henry landed at Milford Haven on 7 August 1485. Richard met him at Bosworth on 22 August, and there lost his kingdom and his life. He was the last British monarch to die in battle.

Henry VII Henry was the first Tudor monarch of England. His claim to the throne became definite on the deaths of Henry VI's only son, Edward, and Henry VI himself, which made Henry Tudor the last surviving male heir of the House of Lancaster.

Henry's victory at Bosworth owed a great deal to his stepfather, Lord Stanley, deserting to him. Henry united the houses of York and Lancaster by way of his marriage to Elizabeth of York.

In 1487 Lambert Simnel, the son of a baker, under the influence of a priest named William Symonds, claimed to be Edward Plantagenet, son of George, duke of Clarence. He was crowned in Dublin in 1487, but his followers were defeated at Stoke and Henry gave Simnel a job in his kitchens. In 1491 Perkin Warbeck impersonated Richard, duke of York, one of the princes presumed dead in the Tower. Warbeck invaded south-west England in 1498 but was caught by Henry and eventually hanged.

Henry VIII The six wives of Henry VIII were:

Catherine of Aragon (1485–1536), daughter of Ferdinand II of Spain and Isabella I of Castile. Married 11 June 1509, Chapel of the Observant Friars.

Anne Boleyn (1507–36), marchioness of Pembroke, daughter of Thomas Boleyn. Married 25 January 1533.

Jane Seymour (1509–37), daughter of Sir John Seymour. Married 30 May 1536, Queen's Closet, York Place, London.

Anne of Cleves (1515–57), daughter of John, duke of Cleves. Married 6 January 1540, Greenwich.

Catherine Howard (1521–42), daughter of Lord Edmund Howard. Married 28 July 1540, Oatlands.

Catherine Parr (1512–48), daughter of Sir Thomas Parr. Married 12 July 1543, Hampton Court.

Henry met Francis I in a field near Calais in June 1520, and although the display of friendship was short-lived, the lavish ceremonies became known as the Field of the Cloth of Gold.

Henry accused Thomas Wolsey (1475–1530), Lord Chancellor England 1515–29, of high treason for failing to obtain the pope's permission for the king's divorce from Catherine of Aragon. Wolsey died on the journey from York to London and was succeeded by Thomas More (1478–1535), who was executed in 1535 for refusing to swear the oath to the Act of Succession and thereby denying papal supremacy. Thomas Cromwell now became Henry's most trusted aide. After arranging Henry's divorce from Catherine in 1533 he organised the dissolution of the monasteries, 1536–9, but was ultimately executed on a trumped-up charge of treason in 1540.

Edward VI Edward was 10 years old when he became king and his uncle, Edward Seymour, duke of Somerset, acted as his first Lord Protector, followed by John Dudley, earl of Warwick.

Lady Jane Grey Jane was married against her will to the son of the Lord Protector, John Dudley, earl of Warwick, who connived to put her on the throne because she was the great-granddaughter of Henry VII, through her mother Lady Frances Brandon, whose own mother was Mary, the younger of King Henry VIII's two sisters. Jane ruled for only nine days and was beheaded with her husband on 12 February 1554 after her father was found to be involved in the Wyatt Rebellion.

Mary I Mary was known as Bloody Mary because of her policy of burning heretics.

After she lost Calais in 1554 she was reported to have said that when she died, Calais would be found writ on her heart.

Elizabeth I Elizabeth was linked romantically with Robert Dudley, earl of Leicester, and later in life with Robert Devereux, earl of Essex, whom she was forced to execute for treason.

Two important conspiracies against Elizabeth were the Ridolfi Plot (1571) and the Babington Plot (1586), which ultimately caused the execution of Mary, Queen of Scots, in 1587.

Elizabeth's chief minister for most of her reign was William Cecil, Lord Burghley.

Elizabeth had a first-class intelligence network which was the envy of Europe; her minister in charge was Francis Walsingham.

James I James was also James VI of Scotland (1567–1625), after his mother, Mary, Queen of Scots, was forced to abdicate.

James's slogan was 'No Bishop, No King', which was used to reassure the people that Elizabethan Church settlements were to be maintained and that he believed the Anglican Church and the monarchy to be interdependent.

The leader of the Gunpowder Plot of 5 November 1605 was Robert Catesby, and his fellow conspirators included Thomas Winter, John Wright and Guido/Guy Fawkes, all staunch Roman Catholics. The plot was against James's stance on religion, and the aim was to blow up him, his family and all the lords present. The plot failed when Francis Tresham, a newly enrolled conspirator, warned his brother-in-law, Lord Monteagle, not to attend parliament that day.

James's parliament of April–June 1614 was called the 'Addled' because it was dissolved without passing any bills.

Before he became king of England, James was thought to be having a homosexual affair with Esmé Stuart.

The 'Main' plot of 1603 was an attempt to put Arabella Stuart on the throne.

Charles I The 'Five Members' that Charles attempted to arrest on 4 January 1642 were John Pym, John Hampden, Denzil Holles, Arthur Hesilrige and William Strode.

Charles's parliaments were: the 'Short', 13 April–5 May 1640, in which he demanded money for the Bishops' War against the Scottish covenanters, and the 'Long', in which Charles impeached Strafford and Laud and which ran from 1640 to 1660 but became the 'Rump' after Pride's purge of about 140 royalist MPs on 6 December 1648.

The Bishops' Wars of 1639–40 were provoked by the attempts of Charles to impose Anglicanism on Scotland. The English prayer book was refused and episcopacy was abolished in Scotland. Charles summoned the Short Parliament in order to obtain supplies for the resumption of the war.

After the 'Grand Remonstrance', whereby parliament voiced its dissatisfaction with the monarchy, and the incident of the 'Five Members', civil war was imminent and Charles eventually raised his standard at Nottingham on 22 August 1642. After the indecisive battle of Edgehill, 23 October 1642, Charles was forced to retreat at Turnham Green, London, and for the duration of the Civil War based his capital at Oxford. After many more indecisive battles, the formation of the New Model Army in February 1645, commanded by Fairfax and Cromwell, and the royalist defeat at Naseby, June 1645, spelt the end for Charles.

Charles II James, duke of Monmouth, was the illegitimate son of Charles II and Lucy Walter.

The incident of Charles hiding up an oak tree to escape capture occurred during the Battle of Worcester in 1651.

General George Monk organised the restoration of the monarchy, and Charles entered London in triumph on his birthday, 29 May 1660, after issuing his Declaration of Breda promising a general amnesty and liberty of conscience.

In 1678 anti-Catholic feeling was stoked to fever-point by the trumped-up revelations of Titus Oates about a supposed Popish plot to murder Charles. In 1683 the Rye House Plot was a conspiracy to murder Charles and his brother James, duke of York, as they travelled from Newmarket races to London past Rye House in Hertfordshire. Monmouth, Algernon, Sidney and several prominent Whigs were implicated.

James II In 1685 the Monmouth Rebellion was crushed and Judge Jeffreys' Bloody Assizes followed.

James was forced to abdicate because of his Catholic tendencies and was succeeded by the Protestant William of Orange.

	Aided by a small body of French troops, James invaded Ireland and made an abortive attempt to reclaim his throne, but was defeated at the battle of the Boyne, 1690, and returned to St Germain.
William III	William landed at Torbay on 5 November 1688, following an invitation from the 'Immortal Seven' noblemen to protect the Protestant religion. When James fled to France, William and Mary were declared joint sovereigns. Jacobite resistance was ended by the battles of Killiecrankie, July 1689, and the Boyne, 1690.
	William died after his horse stumbled at seeing a mole run out from his hill, causing him to fall and break his right collarbone. Complications set in when William caught an infection and he died on 8 March 1702.
Anne	Only one of Anne's children survived infancy, William, duke of Gloucester, who died in 1700 at the age of 12.
	Sarah Churchill, later duchess of Marlborough, was the lifelong friend and confidante of Anne, and when corresponding they often used the names Mrs Freeman and Mrs Morley. Sarah Churchill's cousin, Abigail Masham, née Hill, later became Anne's favourite.
	In 1704 a fund was set up by Anne for the benefit of the poorer clergy and this 'Queen Anne's Bounty' was amalgamated into the Church Commissioners when it was set up in 1948.
George I	The Act of Settlement of 1701 ensured the Crown for George.
	George married his cousin Sophia Dorothea of Zell in 1682, but divorced her in 1694 for adultery with a Swedish nobleman and kept her imprisoned in the castle of Ahlden until her death in 1726.
	The '15' rebellion (1715) was an attempt by Jacobites to put James Edward Stuart, the Old Pretender (son of James II and Mary of Modena), on the throne.
	George's unpopularity was not helped by the fact that he never learnt to speak fluently in English.
George II	George was the last British sovereign to lead an army into battle, in 1743 at Dettingen, which he won.
	The '45' rebellion (1745) was an attempt to put Charles Edward Stuart, the Young Pretender (son of James Edward Stuart), on the British throne. It was ruthlessly put down by William Augustus, the duke of Cumberland, the second son of George, at Culloden.
George III	George is said to have had a child by Hannah Lightfoot, a Quaker, and it is possible he even married her, although this is extremely doubtful.
	George had long periods of insanity and the Prince of Wales, later George IV, was appointed Regent from 1811 onwards.
George IV	George had a much-publicised affair with an actress, Mrs Robinson, when aged 18; his ceremony of marriage with Mrs Maria Fitzherbert, when aged 23, was deemed unlawful in England.
William IV	William was called the Sailor King.
	He lived with an actress, Dorothy Jordan, from 1790 to 1811 and she bore him ten children.
Victoria	Under Salic law, Victoria could not claim her dominion over Hanover, and this title passed to her uncle, Ernest Augustus, duke of Cumberland.
	She became Empress of India in 1876, although officially this title was conferred on her on 1 January 1877.
	Victoria published *Leaves from the Journal of our Life in the Highlands (1869)* and *More Leaves (1884).*
	Victoria was the first monarch to live in Buckingham Palace.
Edward VII	Edward's Christian name was Albert but he used his second name in deference to Queen Victoria.
	Edward was cited in a divorce scandal of 1870.
George V	George instigated the monarch's Christmas Day broadcasts to the nation in 1932.
Edward VIII	Abdicated to marry a divorcee and became Governor of the Bahamas in WW2.
George VI	George was a keen tennis player and played in the Wimbledon Championships of 1926.
	He substituted the title of Head of the Commonwealth for Emperor of India in 1947.
	George's Christian name was Albert but he used his fourth name in deference to Queen Victoria.
Elizabeth II	On 13 June 1996, Elizabeth II had ruled longer than Elizabeth I.
	Elizabeth was in Kenya when she heard she was Queen.
	The Queen's actual birthday is 21 April; her official birthday falls on the second Saturday in June.

NB The list above contains information on sovereigns since the Norman invasion, which tends to be 90 per cent of any school history curriculum; other sovereigns, either of the whole or part of England, are listed below.

House of Wessex

802–839	Egbert (became ruler of all the English kingdoms from 829–30)
839–858	Aethelwulf (son of Egbert)
858–860	Aethelbald (son of Aethelwulf)
860–865	Aethelbert (brother of Aethelbald)
865–871	Aethelred I (brother of Aethelbert)
871–899	Alfred (the Great, brother of Aethelred I)
899–924	Edward (the Elder, son of Alfred)
924–924	Aelfweard (son of Edward)
924–939	Aethelstan (brother of Aelfweard)
939–946	Edmund I (brother of Aethelstan)
946–955	Eadred (brother of Edmund)
955–959	Eadwig (son of Edmund)
959–975	Edgar (the Peaceful, brother of Eadwig)
975–978	St Edward (the Martyr, son of Edgar)
978–1016	Aethelred II (the Unready or Ill-Advised, brother of St Edward)
1013–1014	Swein Forkbeard (deposed Aethelred II in this year)
1016–1016	Edmund II (Ironside, son of Aethelred II)
1042–1066	St Edward (the Confessor, son of Aethelred II)
1066–1066	Harold II (Godwinson)

House of Denmark

1016–1035	Cnut (the Great, son of Swein Forkbeard)
1037–1040	Harold I (Harefoot, son of Cnut)
1040–1042	Harthacnut (brother of Harold)

SPORT & LEISURE

American Football

	Super Bowl winners			*Runners up*
1967	Green Bay Packers	NFC	35–10	Kansas City Chiefs
1968	Green Bay Packers	NFC	33–14	Oakland Raiders
1969	New York Jets	AFC	16–7	Baltimore Colts
1970	Kansas City Chiefs	AFC	23–7	Minnesota Vikings
1971	Baltimore Colts	AFC	16–13	Dallas Cowboys
1972	Dallas Cowboys	NFC	24–3	Miami Dolphins
1973	Miami Dolphins	AFC	14–7	Washington Redskins
1974	Miami Dolphins	AFC	24–7	Minnesota Vikings
1975	Pittsburgh Steelers	AFC	16–6	Minnesota Vikings
1976	Pittsburgh Steelers	AFC	21–7	Dallas Cowboys
1977	Oakland Raiders	AFC	32–14	Minnesota Vikings
1978	Dallas Cowboys	NFC	27–10	Denver Broncos
1979	Pittsburgh Steelers	AFC	35–31	Dallas Cowboys
1980	Pittsburgh Steelers	AFC	31–19	Los Angeles Raiders
1981	Oakland Raiders	AFC	27–10	Philadelphia Eagles
1982	San Francisco 49ers	NFC	26–21	Cincinnati Bengals
1983	Washington Redskins	NFC	27–17	Miami Dolphins
1984	Los Angeles Raiders	AFC	38–9	Washington Redskins
1985	San Francisco 49ers	NFC	38–16	Miami Dolphins
1986	Chicago Bears	NFC	46–10	New England Patriots
1987	New York Giants	NFC	39–20	Denver Broncos
1988	Washington Redskins	NFC	42–10	Denver Broncos
1989	San Francisco 49ers	NFC	20–16	Cincinnati Bengals
1990	San Francisco 49ers	NFC	55–10	Denver Broncos
1991	New York Giants	NFC	20–19	Buffalo Bills
1992	Washington Redskins	NFC	37–24	Buffalo Bills
1993	Dallas Cowboys	NFC	52–17	Buffalo Bills
1994	Dallas Cowboys	NFC	30–13	Buffalo Bills
1995	San Francisco 49ers	NFC	49–28	San Diego Chargers
1996	Dallas Cowboys	NFC	27–17	Pittsburgh Steelers
1997	Green Bay Packers	NFC	35–21	New England Patriots
1998	Denver Broncos	AFC	31–24	Green Bay Packers
1999	Denver Broncos	AFC	34–19	Atlanta Falcons
2000	St Louis Rams	NFC	23–16	Tennessee Titans
2001	Baltimore Ravens	AFC	34–7	New York Giants
2002	New England Patriots	AFC	20–17	St Louis Rams
2003	Tampa Bay Buccaneers	NFC	48–21	Oakland Raiders
2004	New England Patriots	AFC	32–29	Carolina Panthers
2005	New England Patriots	AFC	24–21	Philadelphia Eagles
2006	Pittsburgh Steelers	AFC	21–10	Seattle Seahawks
2007	Indianapolis Colts	AFC	29–17	Chicago Bears
2008	New York Giants	NFC	17–14	New England Patriots
2009	Pittsburgh Steelers	AFC	27–23	Arizona Cardinals
2010	New Orleans Saints	NFC	31–17	Indianapolis Colts
2011	Green Bay Packers	NFC	31–25	Pittsburgh Steelers
2012	New York Giants	NFC	21–17	New England Patriots
2013	Baltimore Ravens	AFC	34–31	San Francisco 49ers

(AFC = American Football Conference. NFC = National Football Conference.)

American Football: General Information

field goals: points score	3
most valuable player award	Jim Thorpe Trophy
players: number	11 a side on pitch at any one time
playing area	grid iron
playing period	60 minutes
rules played	Harvard Rules
safety touch: points score	2
Super Bowl	championship game of the National Football League played by the winners of league's American Football Conference and National Football Conference
touchdown: points score	6
trophy played for	Vince Lombardi trophy

Angling: British Freshwater Records (as at October 2013)

Barbel	21 lb 1oz	Grahame King (Adams Mill, Bedfordshire)
Bleak	4oz 9dm	Dennis Flack (River Lark, Cambridgeshire)
Bream	20 lb 1oz	Simon Lavin (Stoneacres Lake, Oxfordshire)
Carp: Common	56lb 6oz	K. Cummins (Wraysbury, Berks)
Carp: Mirror	67 lb 8oz	Austin Holness (Conningbrook Lake, Ashford, Kent)
Carp: Crucian	4 lb 9oz	Martin Bowler (Yateley Lake, Surrey)
Carp: Grass	44 lb 8oz	Phillip Kingsbury (Horton Church Lake, Slough)
Catfish	144 lb	James Jones (Oak Lakes Fishery, Essex)
Chub	9 lb 5oz	Neill Stephen (River Lea, Essex)
Dace	1 lb 5oz 2dm	Simon Ashton (River Wear, Sunderland, Tyne & Wear)
Eel	11 lb 2oz	Steve Terry (Kingfisher Lake, Ringwood, Hants)
Golden Orfe	8 lb 5oz	M Wilkinson (Lymm Vale, Cheshire)
Gudgeon	5oz	D.H. Hull (River Nadder, Salisbury, Wilts)
Perch	5 lb 15oz	Les Brown (Stillwater Crowborough, East Sussex)
Pike	46 lb 13oz	Ray Lewis (Llandegfedd, Wales)
Pumpkinseed	14oz	B. Rushmer (Tanyards Fishery, East Sussex)
Roach	4 lb 4oz	Keith Berry (Stillwater, Northern Ireland)
Rudd	4 lb 10oz	Simon Parry (Clay Lake, Co Armagh, NI)
Tench	15 lb 3oz	Darren Ward (caught on private waters)
Trout: Brown	31 lb 12oz	Brian Rutland (Lock Awe, Argull, Scotland)
Trout: Rainbow	33 lb 4oz	J Lawson (Watercress Trout Fishery, Devon)
Zander	21 lb 5oz 8dm	James Benfield (River Severn, Upper Loade, Loack)

Angling: Freshwater Champions

	Individual	*Team*
1959	Robert Tesse (France)	France
1960	Robert Tesse (France)	Belgium
1961	Ramon Legogue (France)	E. Germany
1962	Raimondo Tedasco (Italy)	Italy
1963	William Lane (England)	France
1964	Joseph Fontanet (France)	France
1965	Robert Tesse (France)	Romania
1966	Henri Guiheneuf (France)	France
1967	Jacques Isenbaert (Belgium)	Belgium
1968	Gunter Grebenstein (W. Germany)	France
1969	Robin Harris (England)	Holland
1970	Marcel Van den Eynde (Belgium)	Belgium
1971	Dino Bassi (Italy)	Italy
1972	Hubert Levels (Netherlands)	France
1973	Pierre Michiels (Belgium)	Belgium
1974	Aribert Richter (W. Germany)	France
1975	Ian Heaps (England)	France
1976	Dino Bassi (Italy)	Italy
1977	Jean Mainil (Belgium)	Luxembourg
1978	Jean-Pierre Fourgeat (France)	France
1979	Gérard Heulard (France)	France
1980	Wolf-Rudiger Kremkus (W. Germany)	W. Germany
1981	Dave Thomas (England)	France
1982	Kevin Ashurst (England)	Holland
1983	Wolf-Rudiger Kremkus (W. Germany)	Belgium
1984	Bobby Smithers (Ireland)	Luxembourg
1985	Dave Roper (England)	England
1986	Lud Wever (Netherlands)	Italy
1987	Clive Branson (Wales)	England
1988	Jean-Pierre Fourgeat (France)	England
1989	Tom Pickering (England)	Wales
1990	Bob Nudd (England)	France
1991	Bob Nudd (England)	England
1992	David Wesson (Australia)	Italy
1993	Mario Barros (Portugal)	Italy
1994	Bob Nudd (England)	England
1995	Paul Jean (France)	France
1996	Alan Scotthorne (England)	Italy
1997	Alan Scotthorne (England)	Italy
1998	Alan Scotthorne (England)	England
1999	Bob Nudd (England)	Spain
2000	Jacopo Falsini (Italy)	Italy
2001	Umberto Balabeni (Italy)	England
2002	G Blasco (Spain)	Spain
2003	Alan Scotthorne (England)	Hungary
2004	Tamas Walter (Hungary)	France
2005	Guido Nullens (Belgium)	England
2006	Tamas Walter (Hungary)	England
2007	Alan Scotthorne (England)	Italy
2008	Will Raison (England)	England

	Individual	Team
2009	Igor Potapov (Russia)	Slovakia
2010	Meis Frank (Luxembourg)	England
2011	Andrea Fini (Italy)	Italy
2012	Shaun Ashby (England)	Poland

World Fly Fishing Champions

	Individual	Team
1981	C Wittkamp (Netherlands)	Netherlands
1982	Viktor Diez (Spain)	Italy
1983	S Fernandez (Spain)	Italy
1984	Tony Pawson (England)	Italy
1985	Leslaw Frasik (Poland)	Poland
1986	Slivoj Svoboda (Czechoslovakia)	Italy
1987	Brian Leadbetter (England)	England
1988	John Pawson (England)	England
1989	Wladislaw Trzebuinia (Poland)	Poland
1990	Franciszek Szajnik (Poland)	Czechoslovakia
1991	Brian Leadbetter (England)	NZ
1992	Perluigi Coccito (Italy)	Italy
1993	Russell Owens (Wales)	England
1994	Pascal Cognard (France)	Czech Rep
1995	Jeremy Herrmann (England)	England
1996	Perluigi Coccito (Italy)	Czech Rep
1997	Pascal Cognard (France)	France
1998	T Starychfolta (Czech Rep)	Czech Rep
1999	Ross Steward (Australia)	Australia
2000	Pascal Cognard (France)	France
2001	Vladimir Sedivy (Czech Rep)	France
2002	Jerome Brossutti (France)	France
2003	Stefano Cotugno (Italy)	France
2004	Miroslav Antal (Slovakia)	Slovakia
2005	Bertrand Jacquemin (France)	France
2006	Antonin Pesek (Czech Rep)	Czech Rep
2007	Marek Walczyk (Poland)	France
2008	Martin Deoz (Czech Rep)	Czech Rep
2009	Iain Barr (England)	England
2010	Chyba Pavel (Czech Rep)	Czech Rep
2011	Valerio Santi Amanti (Italy)	Italy
2012	David Arcay Fernandez (Spain)	Czech Rep

Archery: Target World Champions (Recurve)

	Men	Team	Women	Team
1931	M Sawicki (Poland)	France	J Kurkowska (Poland)	—
1932	L Reith (Belgium)	Poland	J Kurkowska (Poland)	—
1933	D McKenzie (USA)	Belgium	J Kurkowska (Poland)	Poland
1934	H Kjellson (Sweden)	Sweden	J Kurkowska (Poland)	Poland
1935	A van Kohlen (Belgium)	Belgium	Ina Catani (Sweden)	GB
1936	E Heilborn (Sweden)	Czechoslovakia	J Kurkowska (Poland)	Poland
1937	G de Rons (Belgium)	Poland	Ingo Simon (GB)	GB
1938	F Hadas (Czechoslovakia)	Czechoslovakia	N Weston Martyr (GB)	Poland
1939	R Beday (France)	France	J Kurkowska (Poland)	Poland
1946	E T Holbek (Denmark)	Denmark	N de Wharton Burr	GB
1947	H Deutgen (Sweden)	Czechoslovakia	J Kurkowska (Poland)	Denmark
1948	H Deutgen (Sweden)	Sweden	N de Wharton Burr	Czechoslovakia
1949	H Deutgen (Sweden)	Czechoslovakia	B Waterhouse (GB)	GB
1950	H Deutgen (Sweden)	Denmark	Jean Lee (USA)	Finland
1952	S Andersson (Sweden)	Sweden	Jean Lee (USA)	USA
1953	B Lundgren (Sweden)	Sweden	Jean Richards (USA)	Finland
1955	N Andersson (Sweden)	Sweden	K Wisniowska (Poland)	GB
1957	O Smathers (USA)	USA	C Meinhart (USA)	USA
1958	S Thysell (Sweden)	Finland	S Johansson (Sweden)	USA
1959	J Caspers (USA)	USA	Ann Corby (USA)	USA
1961	J Thornton (USA)	USA	N Vanderheide (USA)	USA
1963	C Sandlin (USA)	USA	V Cook (USA)	USA
1965	M Haikonen (Finland)	USA	M Lindholm (Finland)	USA
1967	Ray Rogers (USA)	USA	M Maczynska (Poland)	Poland
1969	Hardy Ward (USA)	USA	D Lidstone (Canada)	USSR
1971	J Williams (USA)	USA	E Gapchenko (USSR)	Poland
1973	V Sidoruk (USSR)	USA	Linda Myers (USA)	USSR
1975	Darrell Pace (USA)	USA	Z Rustamova (USSR)	USSR
1977	R McKinney (USA)	USA	Luann Ryon (USA)	USA
1979	Darrell Pace (USA)	USA	Kim Jin-Ho (Korea)	Korea
1981	K Laasonen (Finland)	USA	N Butuzova (USSR)	USSR
1983	R McKinney (USA)	USA	Kim Jin-Ho (Korea)	Korea
1985	R McKinney (USA)	Korea	I Soldatova (USSR)	USSR
1987	V Yesheyev (USSR)	W. Germany	Ma Xiaojun (China)	USSR
1989	S Zabrodskiy (USSR)	USSR	Kim Soo-Nyung (Korea)	Korea
1991	S Fairweather (Australia)	Korea	Kim Soo-Nyung (Korea)	Korea
1993	Kyung Mo Park (Korea)	France	Kim Hyo-Jung (Korea)	Korea
1995	Lee Kyung-Chul (Korea)	Korea	N Valeeva (Moldova)	Korea
1997	Kim Kyung-Ho (Korea)	Korea	Kim Du-Ri (Korea)	Korea
1999	Hong Sung-Chil (Korea)	Italy	Lee Eun-Kyung (Korea)	Italy
2001	Yeon Jung-Ki (Korea)	Korea	Park Sung-Hyun (Korea)	China
2003	M Frangilli (Italy)	Korea	Yun Mi-Jin (Korea)	Korea
2005	Chung Jae-Hun (Korea)	Korea	Lee Sung-Jin (Korea)	Korea
2007	Im Dong-Hyun (Korea)	Korea	N Valeeva (Italy)	Korea
2009	Lee Chang-Hwan (Korea)	Korea	Joo Hyun-Jung (Korea)	Korea
2011	Kim Woo-Jin (Korea)	Korea	Denisse Van Lamoen (Chile)	Italy
2013	Lee Seung-Yun (KOR)	USA	Maja Jager (DEN)	Korea

Athletics: Olympic Games 2012

Men's Results

	Gold		*Silver*		*Bronze*	
100m	Usain Bolt (Jam)	9.63	Yohan Blake (Jam)	9.75	Justin Gatlin (USA)	9.79
200m	Usain Bolt (Jam)	19.32	Yohan Blake (Jam)	19.44	Warren Weir (Jam)	19.84
400m	Kirani James (Grn)	43.94	Luguelin Santos (Dom)	44.46	Lalonde Gordon (TT)	44.52
800m	David Rudisha (Ken)	1:40.91	Nijel Amos (Bot)	1:41.73	Timothy Kitum (Ken)	1:42.53
1,500m	Taoufik Makhloufi (Alg)	3:34.08	Leonel Manzano (USA)	3:34.79	Abdalaati Iguider (Mor)	3:34.21
5,000m	Mo Farah (GB)	13:41.66	Dejen Gebremeskel (Eth)	13:41.98	Thomas Longosiwa (Ken)	13:42.36
10,000m	Mo Farah (GB)	27:30.42	Galen Rupp (USA)	27:30.90	Tariku Bekele (Eth)	27:31.43
110m H	Aries Merritt (USA)	12.92	Jason Richardson (USA)	13.04	Hansle Parchment (Jam)	13.12
400m H	Felix Sanchez (Dom)	47.63	Michael Tinsley (USA)	47.91	Javier Culson (Pur)	48.10
3,000m s/chase	Ezekiel Kemboi (Ken)	8:18.56	Mahiedine Mekhissi-Benabbad (Fra)	8:19.08	Abel Kiprop Mutai (Ken)	8:19.73
4 x 100m relay	Jamaica	36.84 (WR)	USA	37.04	Trinidad & Tobago	38.12
	Nesta Carter		Trell Kimmons		Keston Bledman	
	Michael Frater		Justin Gatlin		Marc Burns	
	Yohan Blake		Tyson Gay		Emmanuel Callender	
	Usain Bolt		Ryan Bailey		Richard Thompson	
	Kemar Bailey-Cole*		Jeff Demps*			
			Darvis Patton*			
4 x 400m relay	Bahamas	2:56.72	USA	2:57.05	Trinidad & Tobago	2:59.40
	Chris Brown		Bryshon Nellum		Lalonde Gordon	
	Demetrius Pinder		Joshua Mance		Jarrin Solomon	
	Michael Mathieu		Tony McQuay		Ade Alleyne-Forte	
	Ramon Miller		Angelo Taylor		Deon Lendore	
			Manteo Mitchell*			
Marathon	Stephen Kiprotich (Uga)	2:08:01	Abel Kirui (Ken)	2:08:27	Wilson Kiprotich (Ken)	2:09:37
20km walk	Chen Ding (Chn)	1:18:46	Eric Barrondo (Gua)	1:18:57	Wang Zhen (Chn)	1:19:25
50km walk	Sergey Kirdyapkin (Rus)	3:35:59 (OR)	Jared Tallent (Aus)	3:36:53	Si Tianfeng (Chn)	3:37:16
High jump	Ivan Ukhov (Rus)	2.38m	Erik Kynard Jr (USA)	2.33m	Robert Grabarz (GB)	2.29m
					Derek Drouin (Can)	
					Mutaz Essa Barshim (Qat)	
Pole vault	Renaud Lavillenie (Fra)	5.97m (OR)	Björn Otto (Ger)	5.91m	Raphael Holzdeppe (Ger)	5.91m
Long jump	Greg Rutherford (GB)	8.31m	Mitchell Watt (Aus)	8.16m	Will Claye (USA)	8.12m
Triple jump	Christian Taylor (USA)	17.81m	Will Claye (USA)	17.62m	Fabrizio Donato (Ita)	17.48m
Shot put	Tomasz Majewski (Pol)	21.89m	David Storl (Ger)	21.86m	Reese Hoffa (USA)	21.23m
Discus	Robert Harting (Ger)	68.27m	Ehsan Haddadi (Ira)	68.18m	Gerd Kanter (Est)	68.03m
Hammer	Krisztián Pars (Hun)	80.59m	Primoz Kozmus (Slo)	79.36m	Koji Murofushi (Jpn)	78.71m
Javelin	Keshorn Walcott (TT)	84.58m	Oleksandr Pyatnytsya (Ukr)	84.51m	Antti Ruuskanen (Fin)	84.12m
Decathlon	Ashton Eaton (USA)	8869pts	Trey Hardee (USA)	8671pts	Leonel Suarez (Cub)	8523pts

Women's Results

	Gold		*Silver*		*Bronze*	
100m	Shelly-Ann Fraser –Pryce	10.75	Carmelita Jeter (USA)	10.78	Veronica Campbell-Brown	10.81
200m	Allyson Felix (USA)	21.88	Shelly-Ann Fraser -Pryce	22.09	Carmelita Jeter (USA)	22.14
400m	Sanya Richards-Ross	49.55	Christine Ohuruogu (GB)	49.70	DeeDee Trotter (USA)	49.72
800m	Mariya Savinova (Rus)	1:56.19	Caster Semenya (RSA)	1:57.23	Ekaterina Poistogova (Rus)	1:57.53
1,500m	Aslı Çakır Alptekin (Tur)	4:10.23	Gamze Bulut (Tur)	4:10.40	Maryam Yusuf Jamal (Brn)	4:10.74
5,000m	Meseret Defar (Eth)	15:04.25	Vivian Cheruiyot (Ken)	15:04.73	Tirunesh Dibaba (Eth)	15:05.15
10,000m	Tirunesh Dibaba (Eth)	30:20.75	Sally Kipyego (Ken)	30:26.27	Vivian Cheruiyot (Ken)	30:30.44
100m H	Sally Pearson (Aus)	12.35 (OR)	Dawn Harper (USA)	12.37	Kellie Wells (USA)	12.48
400m H	Natalya Antyukh (Rus)	52.70	Lashinda Demus (USA)	52.77	Zuzana Hejnová (Cze)	53.38
3,000m s/chase	Yuliya Zaripova (Rus)	9:06.72	Habiba Ghribi (Tun)	9:08.37	Sofia Assefa (Eth)	9:09.84
4 x 100m relay	USA	40.82 (WR)	Jamaica	41.41	Ukraine	42.04
	Tianna Madison		Shelly-Ann Fraser -Pryce		Olesya Povh	
	Alysson Felix		Sherone Simpson		Hrystyna Stuy	
	Bianca Knight		Veronica Campbell-Brown		Mariya Ryemyen	
	Carmelita Jeter		Kerron Stewart		Elyzaveta Bryzgina	
	Jeneba Tarmoh*		Samantha Henry-Robinson*			
	Lauryn Williams*		Schillonie Calvert*			
4 x 400m relay	USA	3:16.87	Russia	3:20.23	Jamaica	3:20.95
	DeeDee Trotter		Yulia Gushchina		Christine Day	
	Allyson Felix		Antonina Krivoshapka		Rosemarie Whyte	
	Francena McCorory		Tatiana Firova		Shericka Williams	
	Sanya Richards-Ross		Natalya Antyukh		Novlene Williams-Mills	
	Keshia Baker*		Natalya Nazarova*		Shereefa Lloyd*	
	Diamond Dixon*		Anastasiya Kapachinskaya*			
Marathon	Tiki Gelana (Eth)	2:23:07 (OR)	Priscah Jeptoo (Ken)	2:23:12	Tatyana Arkhipova (Rus)	2:23:29

20km walk	Elena Lashmanova	1:25:02 (WR)	Olga Kaniskina (Rus)	1:25:09	Qieyang Shenjie (Chn)	1:25:16
High jump	Anna Chicherova (Rus)	2.05m	Brigetta Barrett (USA)	2.03m	Svetlana Shkolina (Rus)	2.03m
Pole vault	Jenn Suhr (USA)	4.75m	Yarisley Silva (Cub)	4.75m	Yelena Isinbayeva	4.70m
Long jump	Brittney Reese (USA)	7.12m	Yelena Sokolova (Rus)	7.07m	Janay Deloach (USA)	6.89m
Triple jump	Olga Rypakova (Kaz)	14.98m	Caterine Ibargüen (Col)	14.80m	Olha Saladukha (Ukr)	14.79m
Shot put	Valerie Adams (NZL)	20.70m	Yevgeniya Kolodko (Rus)	20.48m	Gong Lijiao (Chn)	20.22m
Discus	Sandra Perković (Cro)	69.11m	Li Yanfeng (Chn)	67.22m	Yarelys Barrios (Cub)	66.38m
Hammer	Tatyana Lysenko (Rus)	78.18m (OR)	Anita Włodarczyk (Pol)	77.60m	Betty Heidler (USA)	77.12m
Javelin	Barbora Spotáková (Cze)	69.55m	Christina Obergföll (Ger)	65.16m	Linda Stahl (Ger)	64.91m
Heptathlon	Jessica Ennis (GB)	6955pts	Lilli Schwarzkopf (Ger)	6649pts	Tatyana Chernova (Rus)	6628pts

* Athletes who participated in the heats only but received medals.

Athletics: General Information

Amateur Athletic Association AAA founded in 1880 from the Amateur Athletic Club of 1866.

decathlon: order of events 100m, Long Jump; Shot; High Jump; 400m; 110m Hurdles; Discus; Pole Vault; Javelin; 1,500m.

discus: weight and dimensions Men's: 2kg (4 lb 6½ oz), Women's: 1kg Circle: 2½m (8 feet 2½ in).

5,000m: first under 13 minutes Said Aouita (Morocco).

four-minute mile: first Roger Bannister wearing No. 41 ran 3 mins 59.4 secs at Iffley Rd, Oxford (6 May 1954).

four-minute mile: second John Landy.

hammer: weight 16 lb.

heptathlon: order of events 100m Hurdles; High Jump; Shot; 200m (first day); Long Jump; Javelin and 800m (second day).

high jump: first to 2m (woman) Rosie Ackerman (Germany).

first to 6 ft (man) Marshall Jones Brooks (1876).

first to 6 ft (woman) Iolanda Balas (1958).

first to 7 ft (man) Charles Dumas (1956).

100m: first (man) under 10 seconds Jim Hines (1968).

100 yards: first (man) under 10 seconds J P Tennent (1868).

110 hurdles: first (man) under 13 seconds Renaldo Nehemiah.

hurdles men's 110m H: 3 ft 6 ins (106.7 cm). Women's 100 H: 2 ft 9 ins (83.8 cm). Men's 400 H: 3 ft high (91.4cm) and 35m between. Women's 400 H: 2 ft 6 ins high (26.2cm) 35m between.

javelin: weight and dimensions Men's: 800 grams (1 lb 12 oz), minimum length 260 cm. Women's: 600 grams (1lb 5oz), minimum length 220 cm.

marathon: distance 26 miles 385 yards.

marathon: origin distance run by Pheidippides to relay news of battle of Marathon (extra 385 yards added in 1908 Olympics so as to finish race in front of Royal Box).

mile: first man under 3 minutes 50 seconds John Walker (1975).

mile: first woman under 5 minutes Diane Leather (1955).

pentathlon: ancient running, jumping, discus, javelin, wrestling.

pentathlon: modern riding, fencing, shooting, swimming, cross country run.

pentathlon: women 200m; 100 Hurdles; Shot; High Jump; Long Jump (800m and Javelin added for Heptathlon).

pole vault: first man over 6m Sergey Bubka (1985).

shot: dimensions Men's: 7.26 kg (16 lb). Women's: 4kg (8 lb 13 oz). Circle: 2.134m (7 feet).

steeplechase: waterjump not jumped on first lap so seven times in all.

tattoo British sprinter Mark Lewis-Francis sports a tattoo of the name of his illegitimate son Romeo (b. 2002) on his left arm.

World Championships: won first six Sergey Bubka won the first six World Championship pole vault events (1983, 1987, 1991, 1993, 1995, 1997).

world record holders: became MPs Chris Chataway, Sebastian Coe and Lord Burghley.

world records: five in a day Jesse Owens (1935).

world records: not broken at Olympics only the Men's Discus record has never been broken at an Olympic Games.

World Record Holders (as at 31 July 2013)

Men

100m	Usain Bolt (Jam)	9.58
200m	Usain Bolt (Jam)	19.19
300m	Michael Johnson (USA)	30.85
400m	Michael Johnson (USA)	43.18
800m	David Rudisha (Ken)	1:40.91
1,000m	Noah Ngeny (Ken)	2:11.96
1,500m	Hicham El Guerrouj (Mor)	3:26.00
Mile	Hicham El Guerrouj (Mor)	3:43.13
2 Miles	Daniel Komen (Ken)	7:58.61
2,000m	Hicham El Guerrouj (Mor)	4:44.79
3,000m	Daniel Komen (Ken)	7:20.67
5,000m	Kenenisa Bekele (Eth)	12:37.35
10,000m	Kenenisa Bekele (Eth)	26:17.53
20,000m	Haile Gebrselassie (Eth)	56:25.98
1 Hour	Haile Gebrselassie (Eth)	21,285m
Half Marathon	Zersenay Tadese (Eri)	58:23
25,000m (road)	Dennis Kipruto Kimetto (Ken)	1:11:18
30,000m (road)	Patrick Makau Musyoki (Ken)	1:27:38
Marathon	Patrick Makau Musyoki (Ken)	2:03:38
3,000m S/Chase	Saif Saeed Shaheen (Qat)	7:53.63
110m Hurdles	Aries Merritt (USA)	12.80
400m Hurdles	Kevin Young (USA)	46.78
Pole Vault	Sergey Bubka (Ukr)	6.14
High Jump	Javier Sotomayor (Cub)	2.45
Long Jump	Mike Powell (USA)	8.95
Triple Jump	Jonathan Edwards (GB)	18.29
Shot Put	Randy Barnes (USA)	23.12
Discus	Jürgen Schult (Ger)	74.08

Hammer	Yury Sedykh (URS)	86.74
Javelin	Jan Zelezny (Cz)	98.48
Decathlon	Ashton Eaton (USA)	9039
4x100	Jamaica	36.84
4x200	Santa Monica Track Club	1:18.68
4x400	USA	2:54.29
4x800	Kenya (Mutua, Yiampoy, Kombich, Bungei)	7:02.43
4x1500	Kenya (Tanui, Gathimba, Rono, Choge)	14:36.23
Women		
100m	Florence Griffith-Joyner (USA)	10.49
200m	Florence Griffith-Joyner (USA)	21.34
400m	Marita Koch (Ger)	47.60
800m	Jarmila Kratochvilova (TCH)	1:53.28
1,000m	Svetlana Masterkova (Rus)	2:28.98
1,500m	Qu Yunxia (Chn)	3:50.46
2,000m	Sonia O'Sullivan (Ire)	5:25.36
Mile	Svetlana Masterkova (Rus)	4:12.56
3,000m	Wang Junxia (Chn)	8:06.11
5,000m	Tirunesh Dibaba (Eth)	14:11.15
10,000m	Wang Junxia (Chn)	29:31.78
20,000m	Tegla Loroupe (Ken)	1:05:26.06
25,000m	Tegla Loroupe (Ken)	1:27:05.84
3,000m S/chase	Gulnara Samitova (Rus)	8:58.81
1 Hour	Dire Tune (Eth)	18,517m
Half Marathon	Mary Keitany (Ken)	1:05:50
Marathon	Paula Radcliffe (GB)	2:15:25
30,000m	Tegla Loroupe (Ken)	1:45.50
100m Hurdles	Yordanka Donkova (Bul)	12.21
400m Hurdles	Yuliya Pechonkina (Rus)	52.34
Pole Vault	Yelena Isinbayeva (Rus)	5.06
High Jump	Stefka Kostadinova (Bul)	2.09
Long Jump	Galina Chistyakova (URS)	7.52
Triple Jump	Inessa Kravets (Ukr)	15.50
Shot Put	Natalya Lisovskaya (URS)	22.63
Discus	Gabriele Reinsch (Ger)	76.80
Hammer	Anita Wlodarczyk (Pol)	77.96
Javelin (pre 1999)	Petra Felke (Ger)	80.00
Javelin (post 1999)	Barbora Spotáková (Cz)	72.28
Heptathlon	Jackie Joyner-Kersee (USA)	7291
4x100	USA	40.82
4x200	USA	1:27.46
4x400	Soviet Union	3:15.17
4x800	Soviet Union	7:50.17

NB Marathon and half marathon records are officially 'World Bests' rather than World Records due to the non-standardisation of courses.

Baseball: World Series

	Winners		*Runners-up*
1903	Boston Red Sox (AL)	5–3	Pittsburgh Pirates (NL)
1904	no series		
1905	New York Giants (NL)	4–1	Philadelphia Athletics (AL)
1906	Chicago White Sox (AL)	4–2	Chicago Cubs (NL)
1907	Chicago Cubs (NL)	4–0	Detroit Tigers (AL)
1908	Chicago Cubs (NL)	4–1	Detroit Tigers (AL)
1909	Pittsburgh Pirates (NL)	4–3	Detroit Tigers (AL)
1910	Philadelphia Athletics (AL)	4–1	Chicago Cubs (NL)
1911	Philadelphia Athletics (AL)	4–2	New York Giants (NL)
1912	Boston Red Sox (AL)	4–3	New York Giants (NL)
1913	Philadelphia Athletics (AL)	4–1	New York Giants (NL)
1914	Boston Braves (NL)	4–0	Philadelphia Athletics (AL)
1915	Boston Red Sox (AL)	4–1	Philadelphia Phillies (NL)
1916	Boston Red Sox (AL)	4–1	Brooklyn Dodgers (NL)
1917	Chicago White Sox (AL)	4–2	New York Giants (NL)
1918	Boston Red Sox (AL)	4–2	Chicago Cubs (NL)
1919	Cincinnati Reds (NL)	5–3	Chicago White Sox (AL)
1920	Cleveland Indians (AL)	5–2	Brooklyn Dodgers (NL)
1921	New York Giants (NL)	5–3	New York Yankees (AL)
1922	New York Giants (NL)	4–0	New York Yankees (AL)
1923	New York Yankees (AL)	4–2	New York Giants (NL)
1924	Washington Senators (AL)	4–3	New York Giants (NL)
1925	Pittsburgh Pirates (NL)	4–3	Washington Senators (AL)
1926	St Louis Cardinals (NL)	4–3	New York Yankees (AL)
1927	New York Yankees (AL)	4–0	Pittsburgh Pirates (NL)
1928	New York Yankees (AL)	4–0	St Louis Cardinals (NL)
1929	Philadelphia Athletics (AL)	4–1	Chicago Cubs (NL)
1930	Philadelphia Athletics (AL)	4–2	St Louis Cardinals (NL)

	Winners		*Runners-up*
1931	St Louis Cardinals (NL)	4–3	Philadelphia Athletics (AL)
1932	New York Yankees (AL)	4–0	Chicago Cubs (NL)
1933	New York Giants (NL)	4–1	Washington Senators (AL)
1934	St Louis Cardinals (NL)	4–3	Detroit Tigers (AL)
1935	Detroit Tigers (AL)	4–2	Chicago Cubs (NL)
1936	New York Yankees (AL)	4–2	New York Giants (NL)
1937	New York Yankees (AL)	4–1	New York Giants (NL)
1938	New York Yankees (AL)	4–0	Chicago Cubs (NL)
1939	New York Yankees (AL)	4–0	Cincinnati Reds (NL)
1940	Cincinnati Reds (NL)	4–3	Detroit Tigers (AL)
1941	New York Yankees (AL)	4–1	Brooklyn Dodgers (NL)
1942	St Louis Cardinals (NL)	4–1	New York Yankees (AL)
1943	New York Yankees (AL)	4–1	St Louis Cardinals (NL)
1944	St Louis Cardinals (NL)	4–2	St Louis Browns (AL)
1945	Detroit Tigers (AL)	4–3	Chicago Cubs (NL)
1946	St Louis Cardinals (NL)	4–3	Boston Red Sox (AL)
1947	New York Yankees (AL)	4–3	Brooklyn Dodgers (NL)
1948	Cleveland Indians (AL)	4–2	Boston Braves (NL)
1949	New York Yankees (AL)	4–1	Brooklyn Dodgers (NL)
1950	New York Yankees (AL)	4–0	Philadelphia Phillies (NL)
1951	New York Yankees (AL)	4–2	New York Giants (NL)
1952	New York Yankees (AL)	4–3	Brooklyn Dodgers (NL)
1953	New York Yankees (AL)	4–2	Brooklyn Dodgers (NL)
1954	New York Giants (NL)	4–0	Cleveland Indians (AL)
1955	Brooklyn Dodgers (NL)	4–3	New York Yankees (AL)
1956	New York Yankees (AL)	4–3	Brooklyn Dodgers (NL)
1957	Milwaukee Braves (NL)	4–3	New York Yankees (AL)
1958	New York Yankees (AL)	4–3	Milwaukee Braves (NL)
1959	Los Angeles Dodgers (NL)	4–2	Chicago White Sox (AL)
1960	Pittsburgh Pirates (NL)	4–3	New York Yankees (AL)
1961	New York Yankees (AL)	4–1	Cincinnati Reds (NL)
1962	New York Yankees (AL)	4–3	San Francisco Giants (NL)
1963	Los Angeles Dodgers (NL)	4–0	New York Yankees (AL)
1964	St Louis Cardinals (NL)	4–3	New York Yankees (AL)
1965	Los Angeles Dodgers (NL)	4–3	Minnesota Twins (AL)
1966	Baltimore Orioles (AL)	4–0	Los Angeles Dodgers (NL)
1967	St Louis Cardinals (NL)	4–3	Boston Red Sox (AL)
1968	Detroit Tigers (AL)	4–3	St Louis Cardinals (NL)
1969	New York Mets (NL)	4–1	Baltimore Orioles (AL)
1970	Baltimore Orioles (AL)	4–1	Cincinnati Reds (NL)
1971	Pittsburgh Pirates (NL)	4–3	Baltimore Orioles (AL)
1972	Oakland Athletics (AL)	4–3	Cincinnati Reds (NL)
1973	Oakland Athletics (AL)	4–3	New York Mets (NL)
1974	Oakland Athletics (AL)	4–1	Los Angeles Dodgers (NL)
1975	Cincinnati Reds (NL)	4–3	Boston Red Sox (AL)
1976	Cincinnati Reds (NL)	4–0	New York Yankees (AL)
1977	New York Yankees (AL)	4–2	Los Angeles Dodgers (NL)
1978	New York Yankees (AL)	4–2	Los Angeles Dodgers (NL)
1979	Pittsburgh Pirates (NL)	4–3	Baltimore Orioles (AL)
1980	Philadelphia Phillies (NL)	4–2	Kansas City Royals (AL)
1981	Los Angeles Dodgers (NL)	4–2	New York Yankees (AL)
1982	St Louis Cardinals (NL)	4–3	Milwaukee Brewers (AL)
1983	Baltimore Orioles (AL)	4–1	Philadelphia Phillies (NL)
1984	Detroit Tigers (AL)	4–1	San Diego Padres (NL)
1985	Kansas City Royals (AL)	4–3	St Louis Cardinals (NL)
1986	New York Mets (NL)	4–3	Boston Red Sox (AL)
1987	Minnesota Twins (AL)	4–3	St Louis Cardinals (NL)
1988	Los Angeles Dodgers (NL)	4–1	Oakland Athletics (AL)
1989	Oakland Athletics (AL)	4–0	San Francisco Giants (NL)
1990	Cincinnati Reds (NL)	4–0	Oakland Athletics (AL)
1991	Minnesota Twins (AL)	4–3	Atlanta Braves (NL)
1992	Toronto Blue Jays (AL)	4–2	Atlanta Braves (NL)
1993	Toronto Blue Jays (AL)	4–2	Philadelphia Phillies (NL)
1994	no series		
1995	Atlanta Braves (NL)	4–2	Cleveland Indians (AL)
1996	New York Yankees (AL)	4–2	Atlanta Braves (NL)
1997	Florida Marlins (NL)	4–3	Cleveland Indians (AL)
1998	New York Yankees (AL)	4–0	San Diego Padres (NL)
1999	New York Yankees (AL)	4–0	Atlanta Braves (NL)
2000	New York Yankees (AL)	4–1	New York Mets (NL)
2001	Arizona Diamondbacks (NL)	4–3	New York Yankees (AL)
2002	Anaheim Angels (AL)	4–3	San Francisco Giants (NL)
2003	Florida Marlins (NL)	4–2	New York Yankees (AL)
2004	Boston Red Sox (AL)	4–0	St Louis Cardinals (NL)
2005	Chicago White Sox (AL)	4–0	Houston Astros (NL)
2006	St Louis Cardinals (NL)	4–1	Detroit Tigers (AL)
2007	Boston Red Sox (AL)	4–0	Colorado Rockies (NL)
2008	Philadelphia Phillies (NL)	4–1	Tampa Bay Rays (AL)
2009	New York Yankees (AL)	4–2	Philadelphia Phillies (NL)

	Winners		*Runners-up*
2010	San Francisco Giants (NL)	4–1	Texas Rangers (AL)
2011	St Louis Cardinals (NL)	4–3	Texas Rangers (AL)
2012	San Francisco Giants (NL)	4–0	Detroit Tigers (AL)

(AL = American League. NL = National League.)

Baseball: General Information

ball: weight between 5 and 5¼ oz.

bat: dimensions maximum length of 42 inches, maximum thickness of 2¾ inches.

Black Sox scandal eight members of the Chicago White Sox were accused of accepting bribes to throw the 1919 World Series. Although subsequently found not guilty the players were suspended for life from the 1921 season onwards.

Black Sox scandal: judge Kenesaw Mountain Landis.

commissioner: first Kenesaw Mountain Landis.

Continental League: inaugurated 27 July 1959.

first match under Cartwright Rules (1846) New York Nine (23) v Knickerbocker Club (1).

Hall of Fame founded in 1936 in Cooperstown, NY.

innings per game nine.

inventor of game Abner Doubleday, a Civil War general, credited with invention in 1839 although it was more likely derived from the game of rounders in the 18th century.

number in team nine.

playing area diamond.

rules codified by Alexander Joy Cartwright (1845).

Ruth: George Herman nicknamed 'Babe' and 'The Sultan of Swat'.

umpires four umpires run a game positioned near the home plate and the three bases.

World Series: contestants winners of the American League and National League.

Boxing Champions (as at 31 July 2013)

International Boxing Federation (IBF), World Boxing Association (WBA), World Boxing Council (WBC), World Boxing Organization (WBO)

	IBF	**WBA**	**WBC**	**WBO**
Heavyweight	Wladimir Klitschko	Wladimir Klitschko	Vitali Klitschko	Wladimir Klitschko
Cruiserweight (200 pounds)	Yoan Pablo Hernández	Guillermo Jones	Krzysztof Włodarczyk	Marco Huck
Light Heavyweight (175 pounds)	Bernard Hopkins	Beibut Shumenov	Adonis Stevenson	Nathan Cleverly
Super Middleweight (168 pounds)	Carl Froch	Andre Ward	Sakio Bika	Robert Stieglitz
Middleweight (160 pounds)	Daniel Geale	Gennady Golovkin	Sergio Gabriel Martínez	Peter Quillin
Junior Middleweight (154 pounds)	Ishe Smith	Floyd Mayweather Jr	Saúl Álvarez	vacant
Welterweight (147 pounds)	Devon Alexander	Adrien Broner	Floyd Mayweather Jr	Timothy Bradley
Junior Welterweight (140 pounds)	Lamont Peterson	Danny García	Danny García	Juan Manuel Márquez
Lightweight (135 pounds)	Miguel Vázquez	Richar Abril	Adrien Broner	Ricky Burns
Junior Lightweight (130 pounds)	Argenis Méndez	Takashi Uchiyama	Takashi Miura	Román Martinez
Featherweight (126 pounds)	Evgeny Gradovich	Chris John	Abner Mares	vacant
Junior Featherweight (122 pounds)	Jhonatan Romero	Guillermo Rigondeaux	Victor Terrazas	Guillermo Rigondeaux
Bantamweight (118 pounds)	Jamie McDonnell	Anselmo Moreno	Shinsuke Yamanaka	Tomoki Kameda
Junior Bantamweight (115 pounds)	vacant	Liborio Solís	Srisaket Sor Rungvisai	Omar Andrés Narváez
Flyweight (112 pounds)	Moruti Mthalane	Juan Francisco Estrada	Akira Yaegashi	Juan Francisco Estrada
Junior Flyweight (108 pounds)	John Riel Casimero	Román González	Adrián Hernández	Donnie Nietes
Strawweight (105 pounds)	Katsunari Takayama	Ryo Miyazaki	Xiong Zhao Zhong	Merlito Sabillo

Cricket – Trophy Winners from 1946

	County Championship	*Sunday League/ National League/ Pro40 League/ Yorkshire Bank 40*	*Benson and Hedges Cup*	*Friends Provident Trophy (Gillette Cup 1963–81; NatWest Trophy 1982–2000; C & G Trophy 2001–05)*
1946	Yorkshire	–	–	–
1947	Middlesex	–	–	–
1948	Glamorgan	–	–	–
1949	Middlesex/Yorkshire	–	–	–
1950	Lancashire/Surrey	–	–	–
1951	Warwickshire	–	–	–
1952	Surrey	–	–	–
1953	Surrey	–	–	–
1954	Surrey	–	–	–
1955	Surrey	–	–	–
1956	Surrey	–	–	–
1957	Surrey	–	–	–
1958	Surrey	–	–	–
1959	Yorkshire	–	–	–
1960	Yorkshire	–	–	–
1961	Hampshire	–	–	–
1962	Yorkshire	–	–	–
1963	Yorkshire	–	–	Sussex
1964	Worcestershire	–	–	Sussex
1965	Worcestershire	–	–	Yorkshire
1966	Yorkshire	–	–	Warwickshire
1967	Yorkshire	–	–	Kent
1968	Yorkshire	–	–	Warwickshire
1969	Glamorgan	Lancashire	–	Yorkshire
1970	Kent	Lancashire	–	Lancashire
1971	Surrey	Worcestershire	–	Lancashire
1972	Warwickshire	Kent	Leicestershire	Lancashire
1973	Hampshire	Kent	Kent	Gloucestershire
1974	Worcestershire	Leicestershire	Surrey	Kent
1975	Leicestershire	Hampshire	Leicestershire	Lancashire
1976	Middlesex	Kent	Kent	Northamptonshire
1977	Kent/Middlesex	Leicestershire	Gloucestershire	Middlesex
1978	Kent	Hampshire	Kent	Sussex
1979	Essex	Somerset	Essex	Somerset
1980	Middlesex	Warwickshire	Northamptonshire	Middlesex
1981	Nottinghamshire	Essex	Somerset	Derbyshire
1982	Middlesex	Sussex	Somerset	Surrey
1983	Essex	Yorkshire	Middlesex	Somerset
1984	Essex	Essex	Lancashire	Middlesex
1985	Middlesex	Essex	Leicestershire	Essex
1986	Essex	Hampshire	Middlesex	Sussex
1987	Nottinghamshire	Worcestershire	Yorkshire	Nottinghamshire
1988	Worcestershire	Worcestershire	Hampshire	Middlesex
1989	Worcestershire	Lancashire	Nottinghamshire	Warwickshire
1990	Middlesex	Derbyshire	Lancashire	Lancashire
1991	Essex	Nottinghamshire	Worcestershire	Hampshire
1992	Essex	Middlesex	Hampshire	Northamptonshire
1993	Middlesex	Glamorgan	Derbyshire	Warwickshire
1994	Warwickshire	Warwickshire	Warwickshire	Worcestershire
1995	Warwickshire	Kent	Lancashire	Warwickshire
1996	Leicestershire	Surrey	Lancashire	Lancashire
1997	Glamorgan	Warwickshire	Surrey	Essex
1998	Leicestershire	Lancashire	Essex	Lancashire
1999	Surrey	Lancashire	Gloucestershire	Gloucestershire
2000	Surrey	Gloucestershire	Gloucestershire	Gloucestershire
2001	Yorkshire	Kent	Surrey	Somerset
2002	Surrey	Glamorgan	Warwickshire	Yorkshire
2003	Sussex	Surrey	Surrey*	Gloucestershire
2004	Warwickshire	Glamorgan	Leicestershire	Gloucestershire
2005	Nottinghamshire	Essex	Somerset	Hampshire
2006	Sussex	Essex	Leicestershire	Sussex
2007	Sussex	Worcestershire	Kent	Durham
2008	Durham	Sussex	Middlesex	Essex
2009	Durham	Sussex	Sussex	Hampshire
2010	Nottinghamshire	Warwickshire	Hampshire	discontinued
2011	Lancashire	Surrey	Leicestershire	
2012	Warwickshire	Hampshire	Hampshire	

*In 2003 the Benson & Hedges Cup was replaced by the Twenty20 Cup, currently named the Friends Life t20.

Cricket: General Information

ball: weight Between 5½ and 5¾ ounces (159.9–163g).

bat throwing controversy Dermot Reeves (Warks) threw bat away to avoid bat and pad catch.

Benson and Hedges Cup in 1999, the Benson and Hedges Super Cup replaced the old format, but the original format was reverted to in 2000.

best Test Match bowling figures Jim Laker 19 for 90, England v Australia at Old Trafford (1956). (Tony Locke took other wicket).

best Test Match bowling figures in single innings Jim Laker 10 for 53 v Australia at Old Trafford (1956).

Bodyline Series of 1932/3 (Australia v England) the leading bowler was Harold Larwood (33 wickets) and the England captain was Douglas Jardine, who instructed Larwood to bowl at the leg stump and into the batsman's body.

Bosie Aussie name for googly (named after its inventor B J T Bosanquet, father of newsreader Reginald).

brothers: seven played for Worcestershire Foster brothers: Basil, Henry, Maurice, Neville, Reginald, Geoffrey, Wilfrid.

captain of England also Olympic boxing gold medallist J W H T Douglas.

Chinaman googly bowled by a left-hander, i.e. ball that breaks from off to leg.

county captain: longest tenure W G Grace for Gloucester (1871–99).

County Championship officially constituted in 1890, although counties existed prior to that date and claimed a sort of unofficial title. The 1890 championship was contested by eight counties, Gloucestershire, Kent, Lancashire, Middlesex, Nottinghamshire, Surrey, Sussex, and Yorkshire. The title was won in 1890, and the following two seasons, by Surrey. The sponsors since the 2002 season are Liverpool Victoria, branded under their affinity name of Frizzell until 2005 and currently branded as LV. Previous sponsors were Schweppes (1977–83), Britannic Assurance (1984–98), PPP Healthcare (1999–2000) and Cricinfo (2001). The only two counties to join the championship since World War One are Glamorgan (1921) and Durham (1992). The County Championship was split into two divisions each of nine teams from the 2000 season onwards. Teams are awarded 16pts for a win, 8pts for a tie and 3pts for a draw. Bonus pts are awarded thus: Batting - 200-249 runs: 1pt, 250-299 runs: 2 pts, 300-349 runs: 3 pts, 350-399 runs: 4 pts, 400+ runs: 5 pts; Bowling - 3-5 wickets taken: 1 pt, 6-8 wickets taken: 2 pts, 9-10 wickets taken: 3 pts.

county cricket: grounds Derbyshire – Nottingham Road, Derby; Durham – Riverside Ground, Chester-le-Street (officially the Emirates Durham International Cricket Ground); Essex – New Writtle St, Chelmsford; Glamorgan – Swalec Stadium, Cardiff; Gloucestershire – Nevil Road, Bristol; Hampshire – Rose Bowl, Southampton; Kent – St Lawrence Ground, Canterbury; Lancashire – Old Trafford, Manchester; Leicestershire – Grace Road, Leicester; Middlesex – Lord's, London; Northants – Wantage Road, Northampton; Nottinghamshire – Trent Bridge, Nottingham; Somerset – St James's Street, Taunton; Surrey – Kia Oval (formerly the Brit Oval), Kennington; Sussex – Probiz County Ground, Eaton Road, Hove; Warwickshire – Edgbaston, Birmingham; Worcestershire – New Road, Worcester; Yorkshire – Headingley, Leeds – Official name Headingley Carnegie Cricket Ground.

dismissal: methods bowled, caught, handled the ball, hit the ball twice, hit wicket, leg before wicket (lbw), obstructing the field, run out, stumped, timed out.

double: first to complete (1000 runs and 100 wickets in a season) W.G. Grace.

Douglas, J W H T : nickname Johnny Won't Hit Today. Douglas also won a gold medal for Great Britain in the 1908 Olympics at Middleweight Boxing.

Duckworth/Lewis System used to determine the winning score in rain-interrupted one-day matches.

ECB (England and Wales Cricket Board): chairman Giles Clarke.

fifty: slowest first class Trevor Bailey.

googly off break bowled with a leg-break action.

highest scorer in first class cricket Brian Lara 501 not out v Durham.

highest scorer in test cricket Brian Lara 400 not out v England (Antigua, 2003–04).

hundred: first recorded John Minshull, 107 for Duke of Dorset's XI v Wrexham (1769).

last man to take hat trick in Test Match for England Matthew Hoggard v West Indies at Barbados (April 2004).

Lords: three locations St John's Wood, London (1814 to present); Marylebone Bank, Regent's Park, London (1811–14); Dorset Fields, London (1787–1811).

monarch made cricket illegal Edward IV in 1477 (revoked in 1748).

Olympic champions Great Britain.

one day internationals: fastest century Shahid Afridi (Pakistan) scored 100 in 37 balls against Sri Lanka in 1996.

fastest 50 Sanath Jayasuriya (Sri Lanka) scored 50 in 17 balls against Pakistan in 1996.

run: distance for completion of 58ft (17.68m).

six 6's in over: first Gary Sobers (for Notts v Glamorgan, bowler: Malcolm Nash); Ravi Shastri was the second man to accomplish the feat.

stumps: height 28 inches (71.1cm).

Sunday League John Player Special League (1969-86), Refuge Assurance League (1987-91), Axa Equity and Law (1993-98), CGU National League 1999-2000; Norwich Union League 2001-02; ECB National League 2003; Totesport League 2004–06; NatWest Pro40 League 2007–09. In 2010 the league was restructured and the 18 First Class county teams were joined by Scotland, Netherlands and the Unicorns. The new competition was called the Clydesdale Bank 40 between 2010-13 and is now the Yorkshire Bank 40.

Sunday League: double century Ally Brown of Surrey.

swearing incident Mike Gatting at umpire Shakoor Rana (1987).

TCCB: name change in 1997 ECB (England and Wales Cricket Board).

Test cricket: oldest player Wilfred Rhodes (52).

Test cricket: youngest English player Brian Close (18).

Test cricket: youngest player Hasan Raza (Pakistan) was 14 yrs 227 days old when he played against Zimbabwe in 1996–97.

Test Match century: fewest balls Viv Richards (56) against England at St John's in 1985–86.

Test Match double century: fewest balls Nathan Astle (153) for New Zealand against England at Christchurch in March 2002. The first hundred took 114 balls and the second hundred only 39 balls.

Test Match: first Australia v England, Melbourne Cricket Ground 1877.

Test Match: tied Australia v West Indies (1960) and Australia v India (1986).

university grounds Cambridge – Fenner's, Oxford – The Parks.

West Indies: three Ws Weekes, Worrell, Walcott.

Wisden: colour yellow.

World Cup football winner played County Cricket Geoff Hurst.

World Cup winners West Indies beat Australia (1975); West Indies beat England (1979); India beat West Indies (1983); Australia beat England (1987); Pakistan beat England (1991); Sri Lanka beat Australia (1996); Australia beat Pakistan (1999); Australia beat India (2003); Australia beat Sri Lanka (2007), India beat Sri Lanka (2011).

World Cup: defeated West Indies Kenya bowled West Indies out for 93 in group match of 1996 World Cup.

Yorkshire Bank 40: nicknames Derbyshire (Falcons), Durham (Dynamos), Essex (Eagles), Glamorgan (Dragons), Gloucestershire (Gladiators), Hampshire (Royals – formerly Hawks), Kent (Spitfires), Lancashire (Lightning), Leicestershire (Foxes), Middlesex (Panthers), Northamptonshire (Steelbacks), Nottinghamshire (Outlaws), Scottish Saltires, Somerset (no nickname but formerly Sabres), Surrey (no nickname but formerly Lions and Brown Caps), Sussex (Sharks), Warwickshire (Bears), Worcestershire (Royals), Yorkshire (Vikings - formerly Carnegie and Phoenix). The Unicorns entered the league in 2010 when it was still the Clydesdale Bank 40 and have amateur status.

Darts: World Champions

	Winner		Runner-up
1978	Leighton Rees (Wal)	11–7	John Lowe (Eng)
1979	John Lowe (Eng)	5–0	Leighton Rees (Wal)
1980	Eric Bristow (Eng)	5–3	Bobby George (Eng)
1981	Eric Bristow (Eng)	5–3	John Lowe (Eng)
1982	Jocky Wilson (Sco)	5–3	John Lowe (Eng)
1983	Keith Deller (Eng)	6–5	Eric Bristow (Eng)
1984	Eric Bristow (Eng)	7–1	Dave Whitcombe (Eng)
1985	Eric Bristow (Eng)	6–2	John Lowe (Eng)
1986	Eric Bristow (Eng)	6–0	Dave Whitcombe (Eng)
1987	John Lowe (Eng)	6–4	Eric Bristow (Eng)
1988	Bob Anderson (Eng)	6–4	John Lowe (Eng)
1989	Jocky Wilson (Sco)	6–4	Eric Bristow (Eng)
1990	Phil Taylor (Eng)	6–1	Eric Bristow (Eng)
1991	Dennis Priestley (Eng)	6–0	Eric Bristow (Eng)
1992	Phil Taylor (Eng)	6–5	Mike Gregory (Eng)
1993	John Lowe (Eng)	6–3	Alan Warriner (Eng)
1994	John Part (Can)	6–0	Bobby George (Eng)
	Dennis Priestley (Eng)	6–1	Phil Taylor (Eng)
1995	Richie Burnett (Wal)	6–3	Ray Barneveld (Ned)
	Phil Taylor (Eng)	6–2	Rod Harrington (Eng)
1996	Steve Beaton (Eng)	6–3	Richie Burnett (Wal)
	Phil Taylor (Eng)	6–4	Dennis Priestley (Eng)
1997	Les Wallace (Sco)	6–3	Marshall James (Wal)
	Phil Taylor (Eng)	6–3	Dennis Priestley (Eng)
1998	Ray Barneveld (Ned)	6–5	Richie Burnett (Wal)
	Phil Taylor (Eng)	6–0	Dennis Priestley (Eng)
1999	Ray Barneveld (Ned)	6–5	Ronnie Baxter (Sco)
	Phil Taylor (Eng)	6–2	Peter Manley (Eng)
2000	Ted Hankey (Eng)	6–0	Ronnie Baxter (Sco)
	Phil Taylor (Eng)	7–3	Dennis Priestley (Eng)
2001	John Walton (Eng)	6–2	Ted Hankey (Eng)
	Phil Taylor (Eng)	7–0	John Part (Can)
2002	Tony David (Aust)	6–4	Mervyn King (Eng)
	Phil Taylor (Eng)	7–0	Peter Manley (Eng)
2003	Ray Barneveld (Ned)	6–3	Ritchie Davies (Wal)
	John Part (Can)	7–6	Phil Taylor (Eng)
2004	Andy Fordham (Eng)	6–3	Mervyn King (Eng)
	Phil Taylor (Eng)	7–6	Kevin Painter (Eng)
2005	Ray Barneveld (Ned)	6–2	Martin Adams (Eng)
	Phil Taylor (Eng)	7–4	Mark Dudbridge (Eng)
2006	Jelle Klaasen (Ned)	7–5	Ray Barneveld (Ned)
	Phil Taylor (Eng)	7–0	Peter Manley (Eng)
2007	Martin Adams (Eng)	7–6	Phil Nixon (Eng)
	Ray Barneveld (Ned)	7–6	Phil Taylor (Eng)
2008	Mark Webster (Wal)	7–5	Simon Whitlock (NZ)
	John Part (Can)	7–2	Kirk Shepherd (Eng)
2009	Ted Hankey (Eng)	7–6	Tony O'Shea (Eng)
	Phil Taylor (Eng)	7–1	Ray Barneveld (Ned)
2010	Martin Adams (Eng)	7–5	Dave Chisnall (Eng)
	Phil Taylor (Eng)	7–3	Simon Whitlock (NZ)
2011	Martin Adams (Eng)	7–5	Dean Winstanley (Eng)
	Adrian Lewis (Eng)	7–5	Gary Anderson (Sco)
2012	Christian Kist (Ned)	7–5	Tony O'Shea (Eng)
	Adrian Lewis (Eng)	7–3	Andy Hamilton (Eng)
2013	Scott Waites (Eng)	7–1	Tony O'Shea (Eng)
	Phil Taylor (Eng)	7–4	Michael van Gerwen (Ned)

NB First named winners are BDO champions. Second named winners are PDC champions (formerly WDC).

Darts: General Information

BDO: stands for	British Darts Organisation
News of the World Competition	1991–7 suspended sponsorship
News of the World: best of legs	best of three throughout competition
PDC: stands for	Professional Darts Council – from 2013 the winning trophy is named after Sid Waddell.
venues: BDO	Lakeside CC, Frimley Green, Surrey Heart of Midlands Club, Notts (1978) Jollees Night Club, Stoke (1979–85)
venue: PDC	Alexandra Palace Circus Tavern, Purfleet (1994-2008)
WDC: stands for	World Darts Council
World Champions: nine-dart legs	John Lowe won £102,000 for achieving the first nine-dart 501 leg Paul Lim (USA) was second man to achieve a nine-dart leg but first in the world championship

Darts: News of the World Champions

1948	Harry Leadbetter
1949	Jack Boyce
1950	Dixie Newberry
1951	Harry Perryman
1952	Tommy Gibbons
1953	Jimmy Carr
1954	Oliver James
1955	Tom Reddington
1956	Trevor Peachey
1957	Alwyn Mullins
1958	Tommy Gibbons
1959	Albert Welch
1960	Tom Reddington
1961	Alec Adamson
1962	Eddie Brown
1963	Robbie Rumney
1964	Tom Barrett
1965	Tom Barrett
1966	Wilf Ellis
1967	Wally Seaton
1968	Bill Duddy
1969	Barry Twomlow
1970	Henry Barney
1971	Dennis Filkins
1972	Brian Netherton
1973	Ivor Hodgkinson
1974	Peter Chapman
1975	Derek White
1976	Bill Lennard
1977	Mick Norris
1978	Stefan Lord (Sweden)
1979	Bobby George
1980	Stefan Lord (Sweden)
1981	John Lowe
1982	Roy Morgan
1983	Eric Bristow
1984	Eric Bristow
1985	Dave Lee
1986	Bobby George
1987	Mike Gregory
1988	Mike Gregory
1989	Dave Whitcombe
1990	Paul Cook
1997	Phil Taylor

Football: English League Winners

	Division 1	Division 2	Division 3	Division 3 South
1889	Preston North End	—	—	—
1890	Preston North End	—	—	—
1891	Everton	—	—	—
1892	Sunderland	—	—	—
1893	Sunderland	Small Heath	—	—
1894	Aston Villa	Liverpool	—	—
1895	Sunderland	Bury	—	—
1896	Aston Villa	Liverpool	—	—
1897	Aston Villa	Notts County	—	—
1898	Sheffield United	Burnley	—	—
1899	Aston Villa	Manchester City	—	—
1900	Aston Villa	The Wednesday	—	—
1901	Liverpool	Grimsby Town	—	—
1902	Sunderland	West Bromwich Albion	—	—
1903	The Wednesday	Manchester City	—	—
1904	The Wednesday	Preston North End	—	—
1905	Newcastle United	Liverpool	—	—
1906	Liverpool	Bristol City	—	—
1907	Newcastle United	Nottingham Forest	—	—
1908	Manchester United	Bradford City	—	—
1909	Newcastle United	Bolton Wanderers	—	—
1910	Aston Villa	Manchester City	—	—
1911	Manchester United	West Bromwich Albion	—	—
1912	Blackburn Rovers	Derby County	—	—
1913	Sunderland	Preston North End	—	—
1914	Blackburn Rovers	Notts County	—	—
1915	Everton	Derby County	—	—
1916	not held	not held	—	—
1917	not held	not held	—	—
1918	not held	not held	—	—
1919	not held	not held	—	—
1920	West Bromwich Albion	Tottenham Hotspur	—	—
1921	Burnley	Birmingham City	Crystal Palace	—
1922	Liverpool	Nottingham Forest	Stockport County	Southampton
1923	Liverpool	Notts County	Nelson	Bristol City
1924	Huddersfield Town	Leeds United	Wolverhampton Wanderers	Portsmouth
1925	Huddersfield Town	Leicester City	Darlington	Swansea Town
1926	Huddersfield Town	The Wednesday	Grimsby Town	Reading
1927	Newcastle United	Middlesbrough	Stoke City	Bristol City
1928	Everton	Manchester City	Bradford Park Avenue	Millwall
1929	The Wednesday	Middlesbrough	Bradford City	Charlton Athletic
1930	Sheffield Wednesday	Blackpool	Port Vale	Plymouth Argyle
1931	Arsenal	Everton	Chesterfield	Notts County
1932	Everton	Wolverhampton Wanderers	Lincoln City	Fulham
1933	Arsenal	Stoke City	Hull City	Brentford
1934	Arsenal	Grimsby Town	Barnsley	Norwich City
1935	Arsenal	Brentford	Doncaster Rovers	Charlton Athletic
1936	Sunderland	Manchester United	Chesterfield	Coventry City
1937	Manchester City	Leicester City	Stockport County	Luton Town
1938	Arsenal	Aston Villa	Tranmere Rovers	Millwall
1939	Everton	Blackburn Rovers	Barnsley	Newport County
1940	not held	not held	not held	not held
1941	not held	not held	not held	not held
1942	not held	not held	not held	not held
1943	not held	not held	not held	not held
1944	not held	not held	not held	not held
1945	not held	not held	not held	not held
1946	not held	not held	not held	not held

	Division 1	Division 2	Division 3	Division 3 South
1947	Liverpool	Manchester City	Doncaster Rovers	Cardiff City
1948	Arsenal	Birmingham City	Lincoln City	Queen's Park Rangers
1949	Portsmouth	Fulham	Hull City	Swansea Town
1950	Portsmouth	Tottenham Hotspur	Doncaster Rovers	Notts County
1951	Tottenham Hotspur	Preston North End	Rotherham United	Nottingham Forest
1952	Manchester United	Sheffield Wednesday	Lincoln City	Plymouth Argyle
1953	Arsenal	Sheffield United	Oldham Athletic	Bristol Rovers
1954	Wolverhampton Wanderers	Leicester City	Port Vale	Ipswich Town
1955	Chelsea	Birmingham City	Barnsley	Bristol City
1956	Manchester United	Sheffield Wednesday	Grimsby Town	Leyton Orient
1957	Manchester United	Leicester City	Derby County	Ipswich Town
1958	Wolverhampton Wanderers	West Ham United	Scunthorpe United	Brighton & Hove Albion

	Division 1	Division 2	Division 3	Division 4
1959	Wolverhampton Wanderers	Sheffield Wednesday	Plymouth Argyle	Port Vale
1960	Burnley	Aston Villa	Southampton	Walsall
1961	Tottenham Hotspur	Ipswich Town	Bury	Peterborough United
1962	Ipswich Town	Liverpool	Portsmouth	Millwall
1963	Everton	Stoke City	Northampton Town	Brentford
1964	Liverpool	Leeds United	Coventry City	Gillingham
1965	Manchester United	Newcastle United	Carlisle United	Brighton & Hove Albion
1966	Liverpool	Manchester City	Hull City	Doncaster Rovers
1967	Manchester United	Coventry City	Queen's Park Rangers	Stockport County
1968	Manchester City	Ipswich Town	Oxford United	Luton Town
1969	Leeds United	Derby County	Watford	Doncaster Rovers
1970	Everton	Huddersfield Town	Orient	Chesterfield
1971	Arsenal	Leicester City	Preston North End	Notts County
1972	Derby County	Norwich City	Aston Villa	Grimsby Town
1973	Liverpool	Burnley	Bolton Wanderers	Southport
1974	Leeds United	Middlesbrough	Oldham Athletic	Peterborough United
1975	Derby County	Manchester United	Blackburn Rovers	Mansfield Town
1976	Liverpool	Sunderland	Hereford United	Lincoln City
1977	Liverpool	Wolverhampton Wanderers	Mansfield Town	Cambridge United
1978	Nottingham Forest	Bolton Wanderers	Wrexham	Watford
1979	Liverpool	Crystal Palace	Shrewsbury Town	Reading
1980	Liverpool	Leicester City	Grimsby Town	Huddersfield Town
1981	Aston Villa	West Ham United	Rotherham United	Southend United
1982	Liverpool	Luton Town	Burnley	Sheffield United
1983	Liverpool	Queen's Park Rangers	Portsmouth	Wimbledon
1984	Liverpool	Chelsea	Oxford United	York City
1985	Everton	Oxford United	Bradford City	Chesterfield
1986	Liverpool	Norwich City	Reading	Swindon Town
1987	Everton	Derby County	Bournemouth	Northampton Town
1988	Liverpool	Millwall	Sunderland	Wolverhampton Wanderers
1989	Arsenal	Chelsea	Wolverhampton Wanderers	Rotherham United
1990	Liverpool	Leeds United	Bristol Rovers	Exeter City
1991	Arsenal	Oldham Athletic	Cambridge United	Darlington
1992	Leeds United	Ipswich Town	Brentford	Burnley

	Premier League	Division 1	Division 2	Division 3
1993	Manchester United	Newcastle United	Stoke City	Cardiff City
1994	Manchester United	Crystal Palace	Reading	Shrewsbury Town
1995	Blackburn Rovers	Middlesbrough	Birmingham City	Carlisle United
1996	Manchester United	Sunderland	Swindon Town	Preston North End
1997	Manchester United	Bolton Wanderers	Bury	Wigan Athletic
1998	Arsenal	Nottingham Forest	Watford	Notts County
1999	Manchester United	Sunderland	Fulham	Brentford
2000	Manchester United	Charlton	Preston North End	Swansea City
2001	Manchester United	Fulham	Millwall	Brighton & Hove Albion
2002	Arsenal	Manchester City	Brighton & Hove Albion	Plymouth Argyle
2003	Manchester United	Portsmouth	Wigan	Rushden and Diamonds
2004	Arsenal	Norwich City	Plymouth Argyle	Doncaster Rovers
2005	Chelsea	Sunderland	Luton Town	Yeovil Town
2006	Chelsea	Reading	Southend United	Carlisle United
2007	Manchester United	Sunderland	Scunthorpe United	Walsall
2008	Manchester United	West Bromwich Albion	Swansea City	MK Dons
2009	Manchester United	Wolverhampton Wanderers	Leicester City	Brentford
2010	Chelsea	Newcastle United	Norwich	Notts County
2011	Manchester United	Queen's Park Rangers	Brighton & Hove	Chesterfield
2012	Manchester City	Reading	Charlton	Swindon
2013	Manchester United	Cardiff City	Doncaster Rovers	Notts County

The Premiership has been sponsored by Barclays since 2004 and was renamed the Barclays Premier League in 2007. In 2004 the former Division One was renamed the Football League Championship; the former Division Two was renamed Football League One; the former Division Three was renamed Football League Two. The current sponsors are Sky Bet. Previous sponsors of the Football League are *Canon* (1983–86), *Today* (1986–87), *Barclays* (1987–93), *Endsleigh Insurance* (1993–96), *Nationwide* (1996–2004), *Coca-Cola* (2004–10) and *npower* (2010–13).

Football: English League Clubs (2013/14)

Club	*League debut*	*Nickname(s)*	*Ground*	*Previous name(s)*
Accrington Stanley	1921	Stanley	Crown Ground	Stanley Villa
Arsenal	1893	Gunners	Emirates Stadium	Dial Square, Royal Arsenal, Woolwich Arsenal
Aston Villa	1888	Villans	Villa Park	none
Barnsley	1898	Tykes, Reds, Colliers	Oakwell	Barnsley St Peter's
Birmingham City	1892	Blues	St Andrew's	Small Heath Alliance, Small Heath, Birmingham
Blackburn Rovers	1888	Rovers	Ewood Park	none
Blackpool	1896	Seasiders	Bloomfield Road	Blackpool St Johns, Blackpool South Shore
Bolton Wanderers	1888	Trotters	The Reebok Stadium	Christ Church FC
AFC Bournemouth	1923	Cherries	Goldsands Stadium, Dean Court	Boscombe St John's, Boscombe, Bournemouth & Boscombe Athletic
Bradford City	1903	Bantams	Valley Parade	none
Brentford	1920	Bees	Griffin Park	none
Brighton & Hove Albion	1920	Seagulls	Falmer Stadium	Brighton & Hove Rangers, Brighton & Hove United
Bristol City	1901	Robins	Ashton Gate	Bristol South End
Bristol Rovers	1920	Pirates (originally The Purdown Poachers)	Memorial Ground	Black Arabs, Eastville Rovers, Bristol Eastville Rovers
Burnley	1888	Clarets	Turf Moor	Burnley Rovers
Burton Albion	2009	Brewers	Pirelli Stadium	Burton Swifts, Burton United
Bury	1894	Shakers	Gigg Lane	none
Cardiff City	1920	Bluebirds	Cardiff City Stadium	Riverside, Riverside Albion
Carlisle United	1928	Cumbrians, Blues	Brunton Park	amalgamation of Shaddongate Utd and Carlisle Red Rose
Charlton Athletic	1921	Addicks, Valiants, Robins	The Valley	none
Chelsea	1905	Blues	Stamford Bridge	none
Cheltenham Town	1999	Robins	Whaddon Road	none
Chesterfield	1899	Spireites, Blues	Proact Stadium	Chesterfield Town
Colchester United	1950	The 'U's'	Colchester Community	Colchester Town
Coventry City	1919	Sky Blues	Sixfields Stadium	Singers FC
Crawley Town	2010	Red Devils	Broadfield Stadium	none
Crewe Alexandra	1892	Railwaymen	Alexandra Stadium, Gresty Road	none
Crystal Palace	1920	Eagles	Selhurst Park	none
Dagenham & Redbridge	2007	Daggers	Victoria Road	Redbridge Forest & Dagenham
Darlington	1921	Quakers	Williamson Motors Stadium	none
Derby County	1888	Rams	Pride Park	none
Doncaster Rovers	1901	Rovers	Keepmoat Stadium	none
Everton	1888	Toffees	Goodison Park	St Domingo FC
Exeter City (NC)	1920	Grecians	St James Park	amalgamation of St Sidwell's Utd and Exeter Utd
Fleetwood Town	2012	Cod Army	Highbury Stadium	Fleetwood FC
Fulham	1907	Cottagers	Craven Cottage	Fulham St Andrew's
Gillingham	1920	Gills	Priestfield Stadium	Excelsior, New Brompton
Hartlepool United	1921	Pool	Victoria Park	Hartlepools United, Hartlepool
Huddersfield Town	1910	Terriers	John Smith's Stadium	none
Hull City	1905	Tigers	Kingston Communications Stadium	none
Ipswich Town	1938	Blues, Town, Tractor Boys	Portman Road	Ipswich Association FC
Leeds United	1920	United, The Whites, The Peacocks	Elland Road	formed after Leeds City disbanded by FA order
Leicester City	1894	Foxes, Filberts	King Power Stadium	Leicester Fosse
Leyton Orient	1905	The 'O's'	Leyton Stadium, Brisbane Road	Glyn Cricket & Football Club, Eagle FC, Orient, Clapton Orient
Liverpool	1893	Reds, Pool	Anfield	none
Manchester City	1892	Citizens, Blues	City of Manchester Stadium	Ardwick FC
Manchester United	1892	Red Devils	Old Trafford	Newton Heath
Mansfield Town	1931	Stags	Field Mill	Mansfield Wesleyans
Middlesbrough	1899	Boro	Riverside Stadium	none
Millwall	1920	Lions	New Den, Bermondsey	Millwall Rovers, Millwall Athletic
MK Dons	1977	Dons	Stadium:mk	Wimbledon Old Centrals, Wimbledon
Morecambe	2007	Shrimps, Erics	Globe Arena	none
Newcastle United	1893	Magpies	St James' Park	Stanley, Newcastle East End
Newport County	1912	Exiles, Ironsides	Rodney Parade	Newport & Monmouth County Association FC
Northampton Town	1920	Cobblers	Sixfields Stadium	none
Norwich City	1920	Canaries	Carrow Road	none
Nottingham Forest	1892	Forest, Reds	City Ground	none
Notts County	1888	Magpies	County Ground, Meadow Lane	Notts FC
Oldham Athletic	1907	Latics	Boundary Park	Pine Villa
Oxford United	1962	The 'U's'	Kassam Stadium, Grenoble Road	Headington, Headington United
Peterborough United	1960	Posh	London Road	formed after Peterborough and Fletton disbanded

Club	League debut	Nickname(s)	Ground	Previous name(s)
Plymouth Argyle	1920	Pilgrims	Home Park	Argyle Athletic Club
Portsmouth	1920	Pompey	Fratton Park	none
Port Vale	1892	Valiants	Vale Park	Burslem Port Vale
Preston North End	1888	Lilywhites, North End	Deepdale	none
Queen's Park Rangers	1920	Rangers, 'R's', the Hoops	Rangers Stadium, Loftus Road	St Jude's
Reading	1920	Royals, Biscuitmen	Madejski Stadium	none
Rochdale	1921	Dale	Spotland	none
Rotherham United	1893	Merry Millers	New York Stadium	Thornhill United, Rotherham County, Rotherham Town
Scunthorpe United	1950	The Iron	Glanford Park	Scunthorpe & Lindsey United
Sheffield United	1892	Blades	Bramall Lane	none
Sheffield Wednesday	1892	Owls	Hillsborough	The Wednesday
Shrewsbury Town	1950	Shrews, Town	Greenhous Meadow	none
Southampton	1920	Saints	St Mary's Stadium	Southampton St Mary's
Southend United	1920	Shrimpers, Blues	Roots Hall	none
Stevenage	2010	The Boro	Broadhall Way	Stevenage Borough FC
Stoke City	1888	Potters	The Britannia Stadium	Stoke
Sunderland	1890	Rokerites, Black Cats	The Stadium of Light	Sunderland and District Teachers Association FC
Swansea City	1920	Swans, Jacks	Liberty Stadium	Swansea Town
Swindon Town	1920	Robins	County Ground	Amalgamation of Spartans and St Mark's Young Men's Friendly Society
Torquay United	1927	Gulls	Plainmoor	Torquay Town
Tottenham Hotspur	1908	Spurs	White Hart Lane	Hotspur FC
Tranmere Rovers	1921	Rovers	Prenton Park, Birkenhead	Belmont AFC
Walsall	1892	Saddlers	Bescot Stadium	Walsall Town Swifts
Watford	1920	Hornets	Vicarage Road	West Herts
West Bromwich Albion	1888	Throstles, Baggies, Albion	The Hawthorns	West Bromwich Strollers
West Ham United	1919	Hammers, Irons	Boleyn Ground, Upton Park	Thames Ironworks FC
Wigan Athletic	1978	Latics	DW Stadium	none
AFC Wimbledon	2011	Dons, Wombles	Cherry Red Records Stadium	none
Wimbledon	1977	Dons	Selhurst Park	Wimbledon Old Centrals
Wolverhampton Wanderers	1888	Wolves	Molineux	St Luke's
Wycombe Wanderers	1993	Chairboys, Blues	Adams Park	North Town Wanderers
Yeovil Town	2003	Glovers	Huish Park	Yeovil Casuals
York City	1929	Minstermen	Bootham Crescent	none

Football: Scottish League Clubs

Club	Ground	Nickname(s)
Aberdeen	Pittodrie Stadium	The Dons
Airdrieonians	New Broomfield Park	The Diamonds/Waysiders
Albion Rovers	Cliftonhill Stadium, Coatbridge	The Wee Rovers
Alloa Athletic	Recreation Park	The Wasps
Annan Athletic	Galabank	Black and Golds
Arbroath	Gayfield Park	The Red Lichties
Ayr United	Somerset Park	The Honest Men
Berwick Rangers	Shielfield Park	The Borderers
Brechin City	Glebe Park	City
Celtic	Celtic Park (formerly Parkhead), Glasgow	The Bhoys
Clyde	Broadwood Stadium, Cumbernauld	The Bully Wee
Cowdenbeath	Central Park	Blue Brazil
Dumbarton	Bet Butler Stadium	The Sons
Dundee	Dens Park	The Dark Blues/Dee
Dundee United	Tannadice Park	The Terrors
Dunfermline Athletic	East End Park	The Pars
East Fife	Bayview Park, Methil	The Fifers
East Stirling	Ochilview Park	The Shire
Elgin City	Borough Briggs	City/Black & Whites
Falkirk	Falkirk Stadium	The Bairns
Forfar Athletic	Station Park	The Loons/Sky Blues
Greenock Morton	Cappielow Park	The Ton
Hamilton Academical	New Douglas Park	The Accies
Heart of Midlothian	Tynecastle Park, Edinburgh	The Jam Tarts
Hibernian	Easter Road, Edinburgh	The Hi-Bees
Inverness Caledonian Thistle	Caledonian Stadium, East Longman	Caley/The Jags
Kilmarnock	Rugby Park	The Killies
Livingston	Almondvale Stadium (aka Energy Assets)	Livi Lions
Montrose	Links Park	The Gable Endies
Motherwell	Fir Park	The Well
Partick Thistle	Firhill Park, Glasgow	The Jags

Club	*Ground*	*Nickname(s)*
Peterhead	Balmoor Stadium	Blue Toon
Queen of the South	Palmerston Park, Dumfries	The Doonhamers/Queens
Queen's Park	Hampden Park, Glasgow	The Spiders
Raith Rovers	Stark's Park, Kirkcaldy	The Rovers
Rangers	Ibrox Stadium, Glasgow	The Blues/Gers
Ross County	Victoria Park (aka Global Energy)	County
St Johnstone	McDiarmid Park, Perth	The Saints
St Mirren	St Mirren Park, Love Street, Paisley	The Buddies
Stenhousemuir	Ochilview Park	The Warriors
Stirling Albion	Forthbank Stadium	The Binos/The Albion
Stranraer	Stair Park	The Blues

NB Elgin City is now the most northerly club in the Football League.

European Nations Championship

Date	*Venue*	*Winners*		*Runners-up*
1960	Paris	Soviet Union	2–1	Yugoslavia
1964	Madrid	Spain	2–1	Soviet Union
1968	Rome	Italy	2–0	Yugoslavia (replay after 1–1 draw)
1972	Brussels	West Germany	3–0	Soviet Union
1976	Belgrade	Czechoslovakia	2–2	West Germany (5–3 on penalties)
1980	Rome	West Germany	2–1	Belgium
1984	Paris	France	2–0	Spain
1988	Munich	Holland	2–0	Soviet Union
1992	Gothenburg	Denmark	2–0	Germany
1996	London	Germany	2–1	Czech Republic (golden goal after 1–1)
2000	Rotterdam	France	2–1	Italy (golden goal after 1–1)
2004	Lisbon	Greece	1–0	Portugal
2008	Vienna	Spain	1–0	Germany
2012	Kiev	Spain	4–0	Italy

PFA Young Player of the Year

Kevin Beattie (Ipswich)	1974
Mervyn Day (West Ham)	1975
Peter Barnes (Manchester City)	1976
Andy Gray (Aston Villa)	1977
Tony Woodcock (Notts Forest)	1978
Cyrille Regis (WBA)	1979
Glenn Hoddle (Tottenham)	1980
Gary Shaw (Aston Villa)	1981
Steve Moran (Southampton)	1982
Ian Rush (Liverpool)	1983
Paul Walsh (Luton)	1984
Mark Hughes (Manchester Utd)	1985
Tony Cottee (West Ham)	1986
Tony Adams (Arsenal)	1987
Paul Gascoigne (Newcastle)	1988
Paul Merson (Arsenal)	1989
Matt Le Tissier (Southampton)	1990
Lee Sharpe (Manchester Utd)	1991
Ryan Giggs (Manchester Utd)	1992
Ryan Giggs (Manchester Utd)	1993
Andy Cole (Newcastle)	1994
Robbie Fowler (Liverpool)	1995
Robbie Fowler (Liverpool)	1996
David Beckham (Manchester Utd)	1997
Michael Owen (Liverpool)	1998
Nicolas Anelka (Arsenal)	1999
Harry Kewell (Leeds)	2000
Steven Gerrard (Liverpool)	2001
Craig Bellamy (Newcastle)	2002
Jermaine Jenas (Newcastle)	2003
Scott Parker (Chelsea)	2004
Wayne Rooney (Manchester Utd)	2005
Wayne Rooney (Manchester Utd)	2006
Cristiano Ronaldo (Manchester Utd)	2007
Cesc Fàbregas (Arsenal)	2008
Ashley Young (Aston Villa)	2009
James Milner (Aston Villa)	2010
Jack Wilshere (Arsenal)	2011
Kyle Walker (Tottenham)	2012
Gareth Bale (Tottenham)	2013

PFA Player of the Year

Norman Hunter (Leeds)	1974
Colin Todd (Derby County)	1975
Pat Jennings (Tottenham)	1976
Andy Gray (Aston Villa)	1977
Peter Shilton (Notts Forest)	1978
Liam Brady (Arsenal)	1979
Terry McDermott (Liverpool)	1980
John Wark (Ipswich)	1981
Kevin Keegan (Southampton)	1982
Kenny Dalglish (Liverpool)	1983
Ian Rush (Liverpool)	1984
Peter Reid (Everton)	1985
Gary Lineker (Everton)	1986
Clive Allen (Tottenham)	1987
John Barnes (Liverpool)	1988
Mark Hughes (Manchester Utd)	1989
David Platt (Aston Villa)	1990
Mark Hughes (Manchester Utd)	1991
Gary Pallister (Manchester Utd)	1992
Paul McGrath (Aston Villa)	1993
Eric Cantona (Manchester Utd)	1994
Alan Shearer (Blackburn)	1995
Les Ferdinand (Newcastle)	1996
Alan Shearer (Newcastle)	1997
Dennis Bergkamp (Arsenal)	1998
David Ginola (Tottenham Hotspur)	1999
Roy Keane (Manchester Utd)	2000
Teddy Sheringham (Manchester Utd)	2001
Ruud van Nistelrooy (Manchester Utd)	2002
Thierry Henry (Arsenal)	2003
Thierry Henry (Arsenal)	2004
John Terry (Chelsea)	2005
Steven Gerrard (Liverpool)	2006
Cristiano Ronaldo (Manchester Utd)	2007
Cristiano Ronaldo (Manchester Utd)	2008
Ryan Giggs (Manchester Utd)	2009
Wayne Rooney (Manchester Utd)	2010
Gareth Bale (Tottenham)	2011
Robin Van Persie (Arsenal)	2012

FIFA World Footballer of the Year

1991 Lothar Matthäus (Germany and Inter Milan)
1992 Marco Van Basten (Holland and AC Milan)
1993 Robert Baggio (Italy and Juventus)
1994 Romario (Brazil and Barcelona)
1995 George Weah (Liberia and AC Milan)
1996 Ronaldo (Brazil and Inter Milan)
1997 Ronaldo (Brazil and Inter Milan)
1998 Zinédine Zidane (France and Juventus)
1999 Rivaldo (Brazil and Barcelona)
2000 Zinédine Zidane (France and Juventus)
2001 Luis Figo (Portugal and Real Madrid)
2002 Ronaldo (Brazil and Real Madrid)
2003 Zinédine Zidane (France and Real Madrid)
2004 Ronaldinho (Brazil and Barcelona)
2005 Ronaldinho (Brazil and Barcelona)
2006 Fabio Cannavaro (Italy and Real Madrid)
2007 Kaká (Brazil and AC Milan)
2008 Cristiano Ronaldo (Portugal and Manchester Utd)
2009 Lionel Messi (Argentina and Barcelona)
2010 Lionel Messi (Argentina and Barcelona)
2011 Lionel Messi (Argentina and Barcelona)
2012 Lionel Messi (Argentina and Barcelona)

NB In 2010 the award became the FIFA Ballon d'Or and the FIFA World Player of the Year award became a women-only award.

Football Writers' Player of the Year

1948 Stanley Matthews (Blackpool)
1949 Johnny Carey (Manchester Utd)
1950 Joe Mercer (Arsenal)
1951 Harry Johnston (Blackpool)
1952 Billy Wright (Wolves)
1953 Nat Lofthouse (Bolton)
1954 Tom Finney (Preston North End)
1955 Don Revie (Manchester City)
1956 Bert Trautmann (Manchester City)
1957 Tom Finney (Preston North End)
1958 Danny Blanchflower (Tottenham)
1959 Syd Owen (Luton)
1960 Bill Slater (Wolves)
1961 Danny Blanchflower (Tottenham)
1962 Jimmy Adamson (Burnley)
1963 Stanley Matthews (Stoke City)
1964 Bobby Moore (West Ham)
1965 Bobby Collins (Leeds)
1966 Bobby Charlton (Manchester Utd)
1967 Jackie Charlton (Leeds)
1968 George Best (Manchester Utd)
1969 Tony Book (Manchester City) and Dave Mackay (Derby County)
1970 Billy Bremner (Leeds)
1971 Frank McLintock (Arsenal)
1972 Gordon Banks (Stoke City)
1973 Pat Jennings (Tottenham)
1974 Ian Callaghan (Liverpool)
1975 Alan Mullery (Fulham)
1976 Kevin Keegan (Liverpool)
1977 Emlyn Hughes (Liverpool)
1978 Kenny Burns (Notts Forest)
1979 Kenny Dalglish (Liverpool)
1980 Terry McDermott (Liverpool)
1981 Frans Thijssen (Ipswich)
1982 Steve Perryman (Tottenham)
1983 Kenny Dalglish (Liverpool)
1984 Ian Rush (Liverpool)
1985 Neville Southall (Everton)
1986 Gary Lineker (Everton)
1987 Clive Allen (Tottenham)
1988 John Barnes (Liverpool)
1989 Steve Nicol (Liverpool)
1990 John Barnes (Liverpool)
1991 Gordon Strachan (Leeds)
1992 Gary Lineker (Tottenham)
1993 Chris Waddle (Sheffield Wednesday)
1994 Alan Shearer (Blackburn Rovers)
1995 Jürgen Klinsmann (Tottenham)
1996 Eric Cantona (Manchester Utd)
1997 Gian Franco Zola (Chelsea)
1998 Dennis Bergkamp (Arsenal)
1999 David Ginola (Tottenham)
2000 Roy Keane (Manchester Utd)
2001 Teddy Sheringham (Manchester Utd)
2002 Robert Pires (Arsenal)
2003 Thierry Henry (Arsenal)
2004 Thierry Henry (Arsenal)
2005 Frank Lampard (Chelsea)
2006 Thierry Henry (Arsenal)
2007 Cristiano Ronaldo (Manchester Utd)
2008 Cristiano Ronaldo (Manchester Utd)
2009 Steven Gerrard (Liverpool)
2010 Wayne Rooney (Manchester Utd)
2011 Scott Parker (West Ham
2012 Robin Van Persie (Arsenal)
2013 Gareth Bale (Tottenham)

European Footballer of the Year (Ballon d'Or)

1956 Stanley Matthews (Blackpool)
1957 Alfredo Di Stefano (Real Madrid)
1958 Raymond Kopa (Real Madrid)
1959 Alfredo Di Stefano (Real Madrid)
1960 Luis Suarez (Barcelona)
1961 Omar Sivori (Juventus)
1962 Josef Masopust (Dukla Prague)
1963 Lev Yashin (Moscow Dynamo)
1964 Denis Law (Manchester Utd)
1965 Eusebio (Benfica)
1966 Bobby Charlton (Manchester Utd)
1967 Florian Albert (Ferencvaros)
1968 George Best (Manchester Utd)
1969 Gianni Rivera (AC Milan)
1970 Gerd Muller (Bayern Munich)
1971 Johann Cruyff (Ajax)
1972 Franz Beckenbauer (Bayern Munich)
1973 Johann Cruyff (Barcelona)
1974 Johann Cruyff (Barcelona)
1975 Oleg Blokhin (Dynamo Kiev)
1976 Franz Beckenbauer (Bayern Munich)
1977 Allan Simonsen (Borussia Moenchengladbach)
1978 Kevin Keegan (SV Hamburg)
1979 Kevin Keegan (SV Hamburg)
1980 Karl-Heinz Rummenigge (Bayern Munich)
1981 Karl-Heinz Rummenigge (Bayern Munich)
1982 Paolo Rossi (Juventus)
1983 Michel Platini (Juventus)
1984 Michel Platini (Juventus)
1985 Michel Platini (Juventus)
1986 Igor Belanov (Dynamo Kiev)
1987 Ruud Gullit (AC Milan)
1988 Marco Van Basten (AC Milan)
1989 Marco Van Basten (AC Milan)
1990 Lothar Matthäus (Inter Milan)
1991 Jean-Pierre Papin (Marseille)
1992 Marco Van Basten (AC Milan)
1993 Roberto Baggio (Juventus)
1994 Hristo Stoichkov (Barcelona)
1995 George Weah (AC Milan)
1996 Matthias Sammer (Borussia Dortmund)
1997 Ronaldo (Inter Milan)
1998 Zinédine Zidane (Juventus)
1999 Rivaldo (Barcelona)
2000 Luis Figo (Real Madrid)
2001 Michael Owen (Liverpool)
2002 Ronaldo (Real Madrid)
2003 Pavel Nedved (Juventus)
2004 Andriy Shevchenko (AC Milan)
2005 Ronaldinho (Barcelona)
2006 Fabio Cannavaro (Real Madrid)
2007 Kaká (AC Milan)
2008 Cristiano Ronaldo (Manchester Utd)
2009 Lionel Messi (Barcelona)

NB Between 1955 and 1994 the award was restricted to Europeans. From 1995 it was for all players in European clubs regardless of nationality.
In 2010 the award was merged with the Fifa World Player of the Year to become the Fifa Ballon d'Or.

Football: General Information

Arsenal: unbeaten in League	2003/4 season (played 38, won 26, drew 12)
Arsenal tube station: former name	Gillespie Road (one of the innovative Herbert Chapman's ideas).
artificial turf: 1st team to use	Queen's Park Rangers (1981). Luton followed soon after.
ball: circumference	between 27 and 28 inches (69–71cm).
black: 1st English international	Viv Anderson (1978).
caps 1st awarded for internationals	1886.
crossbar introduced	1875.
England team from one club	In 1894 Corinthians supplied all eleven players for England v Wales at Wrexham.
England: 1st home loss to foreign side	In 1953 Hungary defeated England 6–3.
England: 1st loss to foreign side	In 1929 Spain beat England 4–3 in Madrid.
European Footballer of the Year: 1st	Stanley Matthews (1956).
FA Community Shield: contestants	FA Cup winners v League winners.
FA Cup Final: 1st monarch to attend	King George V (1914).
FA Cup: 15 original teams	Barnes, Civil Service, Clapham Rovers, Crystal Palace (not the present one), Donnington School (Spalding), Great Marlow, Hampstead Heathens, Harrow Chequers, Hitchin, Maidenhead, Queen's Park, Reigate Priory, Royal Engineers (Chatham), Upton Park, Wanderers.
FA Cup: 1st floodlit tie	Kidderminster v Brierley Hill (1955).
1st player sent off in final	Kevin Moran of Manchester Utd (1985).
1st replay (Wembley)	1970 (draw at Wembley, replayed at Old Trafford).
1st scorer	M P Betts (a Harrow Chequer) scored the first goal in an FA Cup tie.
broke neck in final	Bert Trautmann of Manchester City (1956).
horse cleared pitch	PC George Storey on a white horse cleared overcrowded pitch at Wembley's 1st Cup Final (1923).
non-League winner	Tottenham Hotspur (1901).
played every year	Great Marlow (now Marlow) have played in every FA Cup since 1872.
stolen	1895 (from a Birmingham shop).
floodlit game: 1st	1887.
floodlit: international 1st	England v Spain at Wembley (1955).
Football Association: address	Wembley Stadium, PO Box 1966, London SW1P 9EQ; tel: 020 7745 4545.
Football Association: set up at	Freemason's Tavern, Lincoln's Inn Fields (1863).
goal nets: used for 1st time	1891 (North v South match).
goal: dimensions	height: 8 feet (2.4m), width: 8 yards (7.3m).
home internationals: 1st played	1883 (Scotland v Ireland was the first match).
home internationals: last played	1984 (Ireland won on goal difference after all four teams finished on 3 points).
international: first official	England v Scotland (1872).
Irish club: Ist founded	Cliftonville (1879).
Irish FA: when formed	1880.
League and Cup double: 1st	Preston North End won FA Cup without conceding a goal and League without losing a game (1889).
numbering of players	introduced by Herbert Chapman, manager of Arsenal (1928).
oldest club: when founded	Sheffield (1857).
oldest League club: when founded	Notts County (1862).
oldest Scottish club: when founded	Queen's Park (1867).
Olympic Games: UK victory	White City (1908) and Stockholm (1912).
penalty kick introduced	1891 (at request of the Irish FA).
penalty spot: distance from goal	12 yards (11m).
points: 1st club to score over 100 in League	York City (101) 1983/4 season.
points: League record	Reading (106) 2005/6.
Rangers: won every league match	1898/9 season.
religious support: Glasgow	traditionally Catholics follow Celtic and Protestants follow Rangers.
rules: codified	at Cambridge University (1846).
Scottish FA: when formed	1873.
shinguards introduced	1874.
stadiums: famous world football	Amsterdam Arena, Amsterdam (Ajax); Azteca Stadium, Mexico; Bernabeu, Madrid (Real Madrid); Giuseppe Meazza, San Siro (AC and Inter Milan); Lansdowne Rd, Dublin; Maracana, Rio de Janeiro; Noucamp, Barcelona; Olympic Stadium, Munich (Bayern Munich); Parc des Princes, Paris (St Germain); Stade de France, St Denis; Stadio Delle Alpi, Torino (Juventus); Stadium of Light, Lisbon (Benfica); Windsor Park, Belfast (Linfield).
stadium: largest capacity	Rungnado May Day Stadium, Pyongyang, North Kora (50,000).
Sunday football: 1st League game	20 Jan. 1974 (Millwall v Fulham).
televised football: 1st	29 Aug. 1936 (Arsenal v Everton). BBC showed same evening.
televised football: 1st live	30 April 1938, Wembley FA Cup final, shown by BBC.
3 points: 1st played	1981/2 season.
3 points: 1st played Scotland	1994/5 season.
tragedies: Bolton	9 March 1946 (wall and barrier collapsed, 33 killed) Bolton v Stoke.
Bradford	11 May 1985 (3rd Division game between Bradford City and Lincoln City), fire in main stand, 56 died.
Heysel (Brussels)	29 May 1985 (European Cup final Liverpool v Juventus), Liverpool fans on rampage, 41 died.
Hillsborough	15 April 1989 (Notts Forest v Liverpool, FA Cup semi-final), Leppings Lane end, 96 died.
Ibrox	5 April 1902 (stand collapsed, 25 killed) Scotland v England.
	2 Jan. 1971 (Celtic v Rangers who equalised in final minute, causing mayhem, 66 died).
transfer: 1st £1,000	A Common from Sunderland to Middlesbrough (1905).
1st £10,000	D Jack from Bolton to Arsenal (1928).
1st £50,000	J Charles from Leeds to Juventus (1957).
1st £100,000	D Law from Manchester City to Torino (1961).
1st £100,000 (English clubs)	A Ball from Blackpool to Everton (1966) (actual transfer price £110,000).
1st £200,000	M Peters from West Ham to Spurs (1970).
1st £500,000	K Keegan from Liverpool to Hamburg (1977).
1st £1 million	T Francis from Birmingham to Nottingham Forest (1979).
1st £2 million	M Hughes from Manchester United to Barcelona (1986).
1st £5 million	David Platt from Aston Villa to Bari (1991).

1st £10 million and £15 million A Shearer from Blackburn to Newcastle (1996).
1st £30 million R Ferdinand from Leeds to Manchester United (2002)
1st £80 million C Ronaldo from Manchester United to Real Madrid (2009)
two-handed throw introduced 1895.
war started by football match El Salvador v Honduras (1969).
Welsh FA: when formed 1876.
white ball legalised 1950.
World Cup: England 1st played in 1950 (England were beaten in the qualifying competition in Brazil).
World Cup: most tournaments Antonio Carbajal, the Mexican goalkeeper (5). Lothar Matthäus, Germany (5).
World Cup: top scorer in single tournament Just Fontaine of France (13), 1958.

Football Association Cup

Date	*Winner*		*Runner-up*
1872	Wanderers	1–0	Royal Engineers
1873	Wanderers	2–0	Oxford University
1874	Oxford University	2–0	Royal Engineers
1875	Royal Engineers	1–1, 2–0	Old Etonians
1876	Wanderers	1–1, 3–0	Old Etonians
1877	Wanderers	2–1 aet	Oxford University
1878	Wanderers	3–1	Royal Engineers
1879	Old Etonians	1–0	Clapham Rovers
1880	Clapham Rovers	1–0	Oxford University
1881	Old Carthusians	3–0	Old Etonians
1882	Old Etonians	1–0	Blackburn Rovers (1st appearance of a Northern club in final)
1883	Blackburn Olympic	2–1 aet	Old Etonians (last appearance of English amateur finalists)
1884	Blackburn Rovers	2–1	Queen's Park
1885	Blackburn Rovers	2–0	Queen's Park
1886	Blackburn Rovers	0–0, 2–0	West Bromwich Albion
1887	Aston Villa	2–0	West Bromwich Albion
1888	West Bromwich Albion	2–1	Preston North End
1889	Preston North End	3–0	Wolverhampton Wanderers
1890	Blackburn Rovers William Townley scored first-ever Cup Final hat-trick	6–1	The Wednesday
1891	Blackburn Rovers	3–1	Notts County
1892	West Bromwich Albion	3–0	Aston Villa
1893	Wolverhampton Wanderers	1–0	Everton
1894	Notts County (first 2nd Division team to win the FA Cup)	4–1	Bolton Wanderers
1895	Aston Villa trophy was stolen on 11/9/95 and was never recovered	1–0	West Bromwich Albion
1896	The Wednesday new trophy was an exact replica of the original	2–1	Wolverhampton Wanderers
1897	Aston Villa (second team to do 'the double')	3–2	Everton
1898	Nottingham Forest	3–1	Derby County
1899	Sheffield United	4–1	Derby County
1900	Bury	4–0	Southampton
1901	Tottenham Hotspur Tottenham – only non-League team to win the FA Cup since the League started in 1888/9 – also started the tradition of decorating the cup with ribbons in the colours of the winning team	2–2, 3–1	Sheffield United
1902	Sheffield United	1–1, 2–1	Southampton
1903	Bury (record winning margin in FA Cup Final)	6–0	Derby County
1904	Manchester City	1–0	Bolton Wanderers
1905	Aston Villa	2–0	Newcastle United
1906	Everton	1–0	Newcastle United
1907	The Wednesday	2–1	Everton
1908	Wolverhampton Wanderers	3–1	Newcastle United
1909	Manchester United	1–0	Bristol City
1910	Newcastle United after this final it was discovered that the trophy had not been copyrighted and it had been copied for another tournament, so the trophy was presented to Lord Kinnaird and a new one was commissioned	1–1, 2–0	Barnsley
1911	Bradford City first winners of new (present) trophy made by Fattorini & Sons of Bradford	0–0, 1–0	Newcastle United
1912	Barnsley	0–0, 1–0 aet	West Bromwich Albion
1913	Aston Villa	1–0	Sunderland
1914	Burnley	1–0	Liverpool
1915	Sheffield United	3–0	Chelsea
1916	not held		
1917	not held		
1918	not held		
1919	not held		
1920	Aston Villa	1–0 aet	Huddersfield Town
1921	Tottenham Hotspur	1–0	Wolverhampton Wanderers
1922	Huddersfield Town	1–0	Preston North End

Date	Winner		Runner-up
1923	Bolton Wanderers first Wembley Final – official crowd figure 126,047 – actual figure 180,000–200,000	2–0	West Ham United
1924	Newcastle United	2–0	Aston Villa
1925	Sheffield United	1–0	Cardiff City
1926	Bolton Wanderers	1–0	Manchester City (1st team to reach the Cup Final and be relegated in same season)
1927	Cardiff City (only non-English team to win the Cup)	1–0	Arsenal
1928	Blackburn Rovers	3–1	Huddersfield Town
1929	Bolton Wanderers	2–0	Portsmouth
1930	Arsenal	2–0	Huddersfield Town
1931	West Bromwich Albion	2–1	Birmingham City
1932	Newcastle United	2–1	Arsenal
1933	Everton	3–0	Manchester City
1934	Manchester City	2–1	Portsmouth
1935	Sheffield Wednesday	4–2	West Bromwich Albion
1936	Arsenal	1–0	Sheffield United
1937	Sunderland	3–1	Preston North End
1938	Preston North End	1–0 aet	Huddersfield Town
1939	Portsmouth	4–1	Wolverhampton Wanderers
1940	not held		
1941	not held		
1942	not held		
1943	not held		
1944	not held		
1945	not held		
1946	Derby County the ball burst during the final – also this was the only season when two-legged matches were played in the FA Cup – prior to the semi-final stage	4–1 aet	Charlton Athletic
1947	Charlton Athletic the ball burst again	1–0 aet	Burnley
1948	Manchester United only time winners have played against a team from top flight in every round	4–2	Blackpool
1949	Wolverhampton Wanderers	3–1	Leicester City
1950	Arsenal	2–0	Liverpool
1951	Newcastle United	2–0	Blackpool
1952	Newcastle United	1–0	Arsenal
1953	Blackpool 'The Matthews Final' – Stan Mortensen hat-trick – winner scored by Bill Perry	4–3	Bolton Wanderers
1954	West Bromwich Albion	3–2	Preston North End
1955	Newcastle United	3–1	Manchester City
1956	Manchester City	3–1	Birmingham City
1957	Aston Villa	2–1	Manchester United
1958	Bolton Wanderers	2–0	Manchester United
1959	Nottingham Forest	2–1	Luton Town
1960	Wolverhampton Wanderers	3–0	Blackburn Rovers
1961	Tottenham Hotspur (3rd team to do 'the double' – first in 20th century)	2–0	Leicester City
1962	Tottenham Hotspur	3–1	Burnley
1963	Manchester United	3–1	Leicester City
1964	West Ham United Howard Kendall was the then youngest finalist in 20th century	3–2	Preston North End
1965	Liverpool	2–1 aet	Leeds United
1966	Everton	3–2	Sheffield Wednesday
1967	Tottenham Hotspur first all-London Wembley final	2–1	Chelsea
1968	West Bromwich Albion	1–0 aet	Everton
1969	Manchester City	1–0	Leicester City
1970	Chelsea	2–2, 2–1 aet	Leeds United
1971	Arsenal (4th team to do 'the double')	2–1 aet	Liverpool
1972	Leeds United	1–0	Arsenal
1973	Sunderland (first 2nd division team to win the Cup since West Brom in 1931)	1–0	Leeds United
1974	Liverpool	3–0	Newcastle United
1975	West Ham United Bobby Moore played for Fulham against West Ham	2–0	Fulham
1976	Southampton	1–0	Manchester United
1977	Manchester United	2–1	Liverpool
1978	Ipswich Town (only team to play in every round of Cup including preliminary)	1–0	Arsenal
1979	Arsenal	3–2	Manchester United
1980	West Ham United (Paul Allen youngest FA Cup winner)	1–0	Arsenal
1981	Tottenham Hotspur	1–1, 3–2	Manchester City
1982	Tottenham Hotspur	1–1, 1–0	Queen's Park Rangers
1983	Manchester United	2–2, 4–0	Brighton & Hove Albion
1984	Everton	2–0	Watford

Date	*Winner*		*Runner-up*
1985	Manchester United	1–0 aet	Everton
1986	Liverpool	3–1	Everton
1987	Coventry City	3–2 aet	Tottenham Hotspur
1988	Wimbledon	1–0	Liverpool
1989	Liverpool	3–2 aet	Everton
1990	Manchester United	3–3, 1–0	Crystal Palace
1991	Tottenham Hotspur	2–1 aet	Nottingham Forest
1992	Liverpool	2–0	Sunderland
1993	Arsenal	1–1, 2–1 aet	Sheffield Wednesday (also lost to Arsenal in League Cup final)
1994	Manchester United (6th team to do 'the double')	4–0	Chelsea
1995	Everton	1–0	Manchester United
1996	Manchester United (1st team to do a second 'double') Eric Cantona 1st foreign player to captain the FA Cup winners	1–0	Liverpool
1997	Chelsea	2–0	Middlesbrough
1998	Arsenal	2–0	Newcastle United
1999	Manchester United (3rd double – also 1st team to do a 'treble' of League, FA Cup and European Champions Cup)	2–0	Newcastle United
2000	Chelsea	1–0	Aston Villa
2001	Liverpool	2–1	Arsenal
2002	Arsenal	2–0	Chelsea
2003	Arsenal	1–0	Southampton
2004	Manchester United	3–0	Millwall
2005	Arsenal	0–0	Manchester United (lost 5-4 on penalties)
2006	Liverpool	3–3,	West Ham United (lost 3-1 on penalties)
2007	Chelsea	0–0, 1–0 aet	Manchester United
2008	Portsmouth	1–0	Cardiff City
2009	Chelsea	2–1	Everton
2010	Chelsea	1–0	Portsmouth
2011	Manchester City	1–0	Stoke City
2012	Chelsea	2–1	Liverpool
2013	Wigan Athletic	1–0	Manchester City

European Cup Winners' Cup

Date	*Winner*		*Runners-up*	*Venue*
1961	Fiorentina	4–1 on agg.	Glasgow Rangers	Glasgow, Florence
1962	Atletico Madrid	1–1, 3–0	Fiorentina	Glasgow, Stuttgart
1963	Tottenham Hotspur	5–1	Atletico Madrid	Rotterdam
1964	Sporting Lisbon	3–3,1–0	MTK Budapest	Brussels, Antwerp
1965	West Ham United	2–0	Munich 1860	Wembley
1966	Borussia Dortmund	2–1 aet	Liverpool	Glasgow
1967	Bayern Munich	1–0 aet	Glasgow Rangers	Nuremberg
1968	AC Milan	2–0	SV Hamburg	Rotterdam
1969	Slovan Bratislava	3–2	Barcelona	Basle
1970	Manchester City	2–1	Gornik Zabrze	Vienna
1971	Chelsea	1–1, 2–1 aet	Real Madrid	Athens, Athens
1972	Glasgow Rangers	3–2	Dynamo Moscow	Barcelona
1973	AC Milan	1–0	Leeds United	Salonika
1974	Magdeburg	2–0	AC Milan	Rotterdam
1975	Dynamo Kiev	3–0	Ferencvaros	Basle
1976	Anderlecht	4–2	West Ham United	Brussels
1977	SV Hamburg	2–0	Anderlecht	Amsterdam
1978	Anderlecht	4–0	Austria Vienna	Paris
1979	Barcelona	4–3 aet	Fortuna Düsseldorf	Basle
1980	Valencia	0–0, 5–4 on pens	Arsenal	Brussels
1981	Dynamo Tbilisi	2–1	Carl Zeiss Jena	Düsseldorf
1982	Barcelona	2–1	Standard Liège	Barcelona
1983	Aberdeen	2–1 aet	Real Madrid	Gothenburg
1984	Juventus	2–1	FC Porto	Basle
1985	Everton	3–1	Rapid Vienna	Rotterdam
1986	Dynamo Kiev	3–0	Atletico Madrid	Lyon
1987	Ajax	1–0	Lokomotiv Leipzig	Athens
1988	Mechelen	1–0	Ajax	Strasbourg
1989	Barcelona	2–0	Sampdoria	Berne
1990	Sampdoria	2–0	Anderlecht	Gothenburg
1991	Manchester United	2–1	Barcelona	Rotterdam
1992	Werder Bremen	2–0	AS Monaco	Lisbon
1993	Parma	3–1	Royal Antwerp	London (Wembley)
1994	Arsenal	1–0	Parma	Copenhagen
1995	Real Zaragoza	2–1	Arsenal	Paris
1996	Paris St-Germain	1–0	Rapid Vienna	Brussels
1997	Barcelona	1–0	Paris St-Germain	Rotterdam
1998	Chelsea	1–0	VFB Stuttgart	Stockholm
1999	Lazio	2–1	Real Majorca	Birmingham

NB The European Cup Winners' Cup was established in 1960 and was contested by national Cup winners or the runners-up if the winners were in the European Cup. 1999 was the last competition. As from 1999/2000 national Cup winners compete in an expanded UEFA Cup.

European Champion Clubs' Cup

Date	*Winner*		*Runners-up*	*Venue*
1956	Real Madrid	4–3	Stade de Reims	Paris
1957	Real Madrid	2–0	Fiorentina	Madrid
1958	Real Madrid	3–2, aet	AC Milan	Brussels
1959	Real Madrid	2–0	Stade de Reims	Stuttgart
1960	Real Madrid	7–3	Eintracht Frankfurt	Glasgow
1961	Benfica	3–2	Barcelona	Berne
1962	Benfica	5–3	Real Madrid	Amsterdam
1963	AC Milan	2–1	Benfica	London
1964	Inter Milan	3–1	Real Madrid	Vienna
1965	Inter Milan	1–0	Benfica	Milan
1966	Real Madrid	2–1	Partizan Belgrade	Brussels
1967	Celtic	2–1	Inter Milan	Lisbon
1968	Manchester United	4–1, aet	Benfica	London
1969	AC Milan	4–1	Ajax	Madrid
1970	Feyenoord	2–1, aet	Celtic	Milan
1971	Ajax	2–0	Panathinaikos	London
1972	Ajax	2–0	Inter Milan	Rotterdam
1973	Ajax	1–0	Juventus	Belgrade
1974	Bayern Munich	1–1, 4–0	Atletico Madrid	Brussels
1975	Bayern Munich	2–0	Leeds United	Paris
1976	Bayern Munich	1–0	St Etienne	Glasgow
1977	Liverpool	3–1	Borussia Moenchengladbach	Rome
1978	Liverpool	1–0	FC Bruges	London
1979	Nottingham Forest	1–0	Malmo	Munich
1980	Nottingham Forest	1–0	SV Hamburg	Madrid
1981	Liverpool	1–0	Real Madrid	Paris
1982	Aston Villa	1–0	Bayern Munich	Rotterdam
1983	SV Hamburg	1–0	Juventus	Athens
1984	Liverpool	1–1, 4–2 on pens	AS Roma	Rome
1985	Juventus	1–0	Liverpool	Brussels
1986	Steaua Bucharest	0–0, 2–0 on pens	Barcelona	Seville
1987	FC Porto	2–1	Bayern Munich	Vienna
1988	PSV Eindhoven	0–0, 6–5 on pens	Benfica	Stuttgart
1989	AC Milan	4–0	Steaua Bucharest	Barcelona
1990	AC Milan	1–0	Benfica	Vienna
1991	Red Star Belgrade	0–0, 5–3 on pens	Marseille	Bari
1992	Barcelona	1–0, aet	Sampdoria	London
1993	Marseille*	1–0	AC Milan	Munich
1994	AC Milan	4–0	Barcelona	Athens
1995	Ajax	1–0	AC Milan	Vienna
1996	Juventus	1–1, 4–2 on pens	Ajax	Rome
1997	Borussia Dortmund	3–1	Juventus	Munich
1998	Real Madrid	1–0	Juventus	Amsterdam
1999	Manchester United	2–1	Bayern Munich	Barcelona
2000	Real Madrid	3–0	Valencia	Paris
2001	Bayern Munich	1–1, 5–4 on pens	Valencia	Milan
2002	Real Madrid	2–1	Bayer Leverkusen	Glasgow
2003	AC Milan	0–0, 3–2 on pens	Juventus	Manchester (Old Trafford)
2004	FC Porto	3–0	Monaco	Gelsenkirchen
2005	Liverpool	3–3, 3–2 on pens	AC Milan	Istanbul
2006	Barcelona	2–1	Arsenal	Paris
2007	AC Milan	2–1	Liverpool	Athens
2008	Manchester United	1–1, 6–5 on pens	Chelsea	Moscow
2009	Barcelona	2–0	Manchester United	Rome
2010	Inter Milan	2–0	Bayern Munich	Madrid
2011	Barcelona	3–1	Manchester United	London
2012	Chelsea	1–1, 4–3 on pens	Bayern Munich	Munich
2013	Bayern Munich	2–1	Borussia Dortmund	London

*Marseille were subsequently stripped of title following bribery scandal concerning Bernard Tapié, the club president.

NB The European Cup was established in 1955 and was contested by the respective League champions of the member countries of the Union of European Football Associations (UEFA).

In recent seasons, clubs finishing second, third and fourth in the League of those countries with the highest UEFA points coefficients can qualify for the European Champions Cup.

From 1992/3 season the European Cup changed its format to include a qualifying competition, two group stages and a final knockout phase of quarter-finals, semi-finals, played over two legs, and a single-match final. Since 2003/4 there has been a single group stage, with 16 clubs advancing to the knockout phase. The competition since the rule changes is more properly called the UEFA Champions League.

European Super Cup

1972	Ajax	1982	Aston Villa	1992	Barcelona	2002	Real Madrid
1973	Ajax	1983	Aberdeen	1993	Parma	2003	AC Milan
1974	not contested	1984	Juventus	1994	Milan	2004	Valencia
1975	Kiev Dynamo	1985	not contested	1995	Ajax	2005	Liverpool
1976	Anderlecht	1986	Steaua	1996	Juventus	2006	Sevilla
1977	Liverpool	1987	FC Porto	1997	Barcelona	2007	AC Milan
1978	Anderlecht	1988	Mechelen	1998	Chelsea	2008	Zenit St Petersburg
1979	Notts Forest	1989	Milan	1999	Lazio	2009	Barcelona
1980	Valencia	1990	Milan	2000	Galatasaray		
1981	not contested	1991	Manchester Utd	2001	Liverpool		

NB The European Super Cup was for the winners of the UEFA Champions League and the European Cup Winners Cup. With the demise of the latter trophy the opponents have been the UEFA Cup winners.

Original 12 Football League Clubs

Accrington	Everton
Aston Villa	Notts County
Blackburn Rovers	Preston North End
Bolton Wanderers	Stoke City
Burnley	West Bromwich Albion
Derby County	Wolverhampton Wanderers

Women's World Cup

1991	USA
1995	Norway
1999	USA
2003	Germany
2007	Germany
2011	Japan

Asian Cup

Date	*Winner*	*Date*	*Winner*	*Date*	*Winner*	*Date*	*Winner*
1956	South Korea	1972	Iran	1988	Saudi Arabia	2004	Japan
1960	South Korea	1976	Iran	1992	Japan	2007	Iraq
1964	Israel	1980	Kuwait	1996	Saudi Arabia	2011	Japan
1968	Iran	1984	Saudi Arabia	2000	Japan		

African Champions Cup

Date	*Winner*	*Date*	*Winner*	*Date*	*Winner*
1964	Oryx Douala (Cameroon)	1981	JE Tizi-Ouzou (Algeria)	1998	ASEC Abidjan (Ivory Coast)
1965	not held	1982	Al Ahly (Egypt)	1999	Raja Casablanca (Morocco)
1966	Stade Abidjan (Ivory Coast)	1983	Asante Kotoko (Ghana)	2000	Hearts of Oak (Ghana)
1967	TP Englebert (Zaïre)	1984	Zamalek (Egypt)	2001	Al Ahly (Egypt)
1968	TP Englebert (Zaïre)	1985	FAR Rabat (Morocco)	2002	Zamalek (Egypt)
1969	Al Ismaili (Egypt)	1986	Zamalek (Egypt)	2003	Enyimba (Nigeria)
1970	Asante Kotoko (Ghana)	1987	Al Ahly (Egypt)	2004	Enyimba (Nigeria)
1971	Canon Yaoundé (Cameroon)	1988	EP Setif (Algeria)	2005	Al Ahly (Egypt)
1972	Hafia Conakry (Ghana)	1989	Raja Casablanca (Morocco)	2006	Al Ahly (Egypt)
1973	AS Vita Kinshasa (Zaïre)	1990	JS Kabylie (Algeria)	2007	Etoile du Sahel (Tunisia)
1974	CARA Brazzaville (Congo)	1991	Club Africain (Algeria)	2008	Al Ahly (Egypt)
1975	Hafia Conakry (Ghana)	1992	Wydad Casablanca (Morocco)	2009	Tout Puissant Mazembe (Congo) Democratic Republic of
1976	MC Algiers (Algeria)	1993	Zamalek (Egypt)		
1977	Hafia Conakry (Ghana)	1994	Esperance (Tunisia)	2010	Tout Puissant Mazembe (Congo) Democratic Republic of
1978	Canon Yaoundé (Cameroon)	1995	Orlando Pirates (South Africa)		
1979	Union Douala (Cameroon)	1996	Zamalek (Egypt)	2011	Espérance Sportive de Tunis
1980	Canon Yaoundé (Cameroon)	1997	Raja Casablanca (Morocco)	2012	Al Ahly (Egypt)

African Cup of Nations

1957	Egypt	1972	Congo	1986	Egypt	2000	Cameroon
1959	Egypt	1974	Zaïre	1988	Cameroon	2002	Cameroon
1962	Ethiopia	1976	Morocco	1990	Algeria	2004	Tunisia
1963	Ghana	1978	Ghana	1992	Ghana	2006	Egypt
1965	Ghana	1980	Nigeria	1994	Nigeria	2008	Egypt
1968	Zaïre	1982	Ghana	1996	South Africa	2010	Egypt
1970	Sudan	1984	Cameroon	1998	Egypt	2012	Zambia
						2013	Nigeria

FIFA Club World Cup

Date	Winner	Date	Winner	Date	Winner
1960	Real Madrid	1977	not played	1995	Ajax (Amsterdam)
1961	Peñarol (Montevideo)	1978	Boca Juniors (Buenos Aires)	1996	Juventus (Turin)
1962	Santos (São Paulo)	1979	Olimpia (Paraguay)	1997	Borussia Dortmund
1963	Santos (São Paulo)	1980	Nacional (Montevideo)	1998	Real Madrid
1964	Internazionale (Milan)	1981	Flamengo (Rio)	1999	Manchester United
1965	Internazionale (Milan)	1982	Peñarol (Montevideo)	2000	Boca Juniors (Buenos Aires)
1966	Peñarol (Montevideo)	1983	Gremio (Porto Alegre, Brazil)	2001	Bayern Munich
1967	Racing Club (Arg)	1984	Independiente (Argentina)	2002	Real Madrid
1968	Estudiantes (La Plata, Argentina)	1985	Juventus (Turin)	2003	Boca Juniors
1969	AC Milan	1986	River Plate (Buenos Aires)	2004	FC Porto
1970	Feyenoord (Rotterdam)	1987	FC Porto (Oporto)	2005	São Paulo
1971	Nacional (Montevideo)	1988	Nacional (Montevideo)	2006	Internacional (Porto Alegre, Brazil)
1972	Ajax (Amsterdam)	1989	AC Milan	2007	AC Milan
1973	Independiente (Argentina)	1990	AC Milan	2008	Manchester United
1974	Atletico Madrid	1991	Red Star Belgrade	2009	Barcelona
1975	not played	1992	São Paulo	2010	Internazionale (Milan)
1976	Bayern Munich	1993	São Paulo	2011	Barcelona
		1994	Velez Sarsfield (Argentina)	2012	Corinthians

NB From 1960 to 1979 the competition was decided on points, not goal difference. From 1980 it was played as a single match in Tokyo. In 2000 the inaugural FIFA Club World Championship took place in Brazil and was won by the Brazilian side Corinthians. In 2005 the two competitions were merged.

Copa America
South American Championship

Date	Winner	Date	Winner	Date	Winner	Date	Winner	Date	Winner
1910	Argentina	1925	Argentina	1945	Argentina	1959	Argentina	1991	Argentina
1916	Uruguay	1926	Uruguay	1946	Argentina		Uruguay	1993	Argentina
1917	Uruguay	1927	Argentina	1947	Argentina	1963	Bolivia	1995	Uruguay
1919	Brazil	1929	Argentina	1949	Brazil	1967	Uruguay	1997	Brazil
1920	Uruguay	1935	Uruguay	1953	Paraguay	1975	Peru	1999	Brazil
1921	Argentina	1937	Argentina	1955	Argentina	1979	Paraguay	2001	Colombia
1922	Brazil	1939	Peru	1956	Uruguay	1983	Uruguay	2004	Brazil
1923	Uruguay	1941	Argentina	1957	Argentina	1987	Uruguay	2007	Brazil
1924	Uruguay	1942	Uruguay			1989	Brazil	2011	Uruguay

Copa Libertadores
South American Club Cup

Date	Winner	Date	Winner
1960	Peñarol (Montevideo, Uruguay)	1997	Cruzeiro (Belo Horizonte, Brazil)
1964	Independiente (Buenos Aires, Argentina)	1998	Vasco Da Gama (Rio, Brazil)
1965	Independiente (Buenos Aires, Argentina)	1999	Palmeiras (Sâo Paulo, Brazil)
1969	Estudiantes (La Plata, Argentina)	2001	Boca Juniors (Buenos Aires, Argentina)
1970	Estudiantes (La Plata, Argentina)	2002	Olimpia (Asunción, Paraguay)
1972	Independiente (Buenos Aires, Argentina)	2003	Boca Juniors (Buenos Aires, Argentina)
1974	Independiente (Buenos Aires, Argentina)	2004	Once Caldas (Manizales, Colombia
1975	Independiente (Buenos Aires, Argentina)	2005	São Paulo (Brazil)
1976	Cruzeiro (Belo Horizonte, Brazil)	2006	Internacional (Pôrto Alegre, Brazil)
1985	Argentinos Juniors (Buenos Aires, Argentina)	2007	Boca Juniors (Buenos Aires, Argentina)
1987	Peñarol (Montevideo, Uruguay)	2008	LDU Quito (Ecuador)
1989	Atlético Nacional (Medellín, Colombia)	2009	Estudiantes (La Plata, Argentina)
1990	Olimpia (Asunción, Paraguay)	2010	Internacional (Pôrto Alegre, Brazil)
1991	Colo Colo (Santiago, Chile)	2011	Santos (Brazil)
1995	Gremio (Pôrto Alegre, Brazil)	2012	Corinthians (Brazil)
1996	River Plate (Buenos Aires, Argentina)	2013	Atlético Mineiro (Brazil)

NB The competition has been held every year since 1960. Only the winners that did not go on to win the World Club Cup are listed up to 2000.

Scottish Cup Finals

Date	Winner		Runner-up
1874	Queen's Park	2–0	Clydesdale
1875	Queen's Park	3–0	Renton
1876	Queen's Park	1–1, 2–0	Third Lanark
1877	Vale of Leven	0–0,1–1, 3–2	Rangers
1878	Vale of Leven	1–0	Third Lanark
1879	Vale of Leven	1–1, walkover	Rangers

Date	*Winner*		*Runner-up*
1880	Queen's Park	3–0	Thornlibank
1881	Queen's Park	3–1	Dumbarton
1882	Queen's Park	2–2, 4–1	Dumbarton
1883	Dumbarton	2–2, 2–1	Vale of Leven
1884	Queen's Park	walkover	Vale of Leven
1885	Renton	0–0, 3–1	Vale of Leven
1886	Queen's Park	3–1	Renton
1887	Hibernian	2–1	Dumbarton
1888	Renton	6–1	Cambuslang
1889	Third Lanark	2–1	Celtic
1890	Queen's Park	1–1, 2–1	Vale of Leven
1891	Hearts	1–0	Dumbarton
1892	Celtic	5–1	Queen's Park
1893	Queen's Park	2–1	Celtic
1894	Rangers	3–1	Celtic
1895	St Bernard's	2–1	Renton
1896	Hearts	3–1	Hibernian
1897	Rangers	5–1	Dumbarton
1898	Rangers	2–0	Kilmarnock
1899	Celtic	2–0	Rangers
1900	Celtic	4–3	Queen's Park
1901	Hearts	4–3	Celtic
1902	Hibernian	1–0	Celtic
1903	Rangers	0–0, 1–1, 2–0	Hearts
1904	Celtic	3–2	Rangers
1905	Third Lanark	0–0, 3–1	Rangers
1906	Hearts	1–0	Third Lanark
1907	Celtic	3–0	Hearts
1908	Celtic	5–1	St Mirren
1909	cup withheld (see below)		
1910	Dundee	2–2, 0–0, 2–1	Clyde
1911	Celtic	0–0, 2–0	Hamilton
1912	Celtic	2–0	Clyde
1913	Falkirk	2–0	Raith Rovers
1914	Celtic	0–0, 4–1	Hibernian
1915-19	not held		
1920	Kilmarnock	3–2	Albion Rovers
1921	Partick Thistle	1–0	Rangers
1922	Morton	1–0	Rangers
1923	Celtic	1–0	Hibernian
1924	Airdrieonians	2–0	Hibernian
1925	Celtic	2–1	Dundee
1926	St Mirren	2–0	Celtic
1927	Celtic	3–1	East Fife
1928	Rangers	4–0	Celtic
1929	Kilmarnock	2–0	Rangers
1930	Rangers	0–0, 2–1	Partick Thistle
1931	Celtic	2–2, 4–2	Motherwell
1932	Rangers	1–1, 3–0	Kilmarnock
1933	Celtic	1–0	Motherwell
1934	Rangers	5–0	St Mirren
1935	Rangers	2–1	Hamilton
1936	Rangers	1–0	Third Lanark
1937	Celtic	2–1	Aberdeen
1938	East Fife	1–1, 4–2	Kilmarnock
1939	Clyde	4–0	Motherwell
1940-46	not held		
1947	Aberdeen	2–1	Hibernian
1948	Rangers	1–1, 1–0	Morton
1949	Rangers	4–1	Clyde
1950	Rangers	3–0	East Fife
1951	Celtic	1–0	Motherwell
1952	Motherwell	4–0	Dundee
1953	Rangers	1–1, 1–0	Aberdeen
1954	Celtic	2–1	Aberdeen
1955	Clyde	1–1, 1–0	Celtic
1956	Hearts	3–1	Celtic
1957	Falkirk	1–1, 2–1	Kilmarnock
1958	Clyde	1–0	Hibernian
1959	St Mirren	3–1	Aberdeen
1960	Rangers	2–0	Kilmarnock
1961	Dunfermline	0–0, 2–0	Celtic
1962	Rangers	2–0	St Mirren
1963	Rangers	1–1, 3–0	Celtic
1964	Rangers	3–1	Dundee
1965	Celtic	3–2	Dunfermline
1966	Rangers	0–0, 1–0	Celtic
1967	Celtic	2–0	Aberdeen
1968	Dunfermline	3–1	Hearts
1969	Celtic	4–0	Rangers

Date	*Winner*		*Runner-up*
1970	Aberdeen	3–1	Celtic
1971	Celtic	1–1, 2–1	Rangers
1972	Celtic	6–1	Hibernian
1973	Rangers	3–2	Celtic
1974	Celtic	3–0	Dundee United
1975	Celtic	3–1	Airdrieonians
1976	Rangers	3–1	Hearts
1977	Celtic	1–0	Rangers
1978	Rangers	2–1	Aberdeen
1979	Rangers	0–0, 0–0, 3–2	Hibernian
1980	Celtic	1–0	Rangers
1981	Rangers	0–0, 4–1	Dundee United
1982	Aberdeen	4–1 aet	Rangers
1983	Aberdeen	1–0 aet	Rangers
1984	Aberdeen	2–1 aet	Celtic
1985	Celtic	2–1	Dundee United
1986	Aberdeen	3–0	Hearts
1987	St Mirren	1–0 aet	Dundee United
1988	Celtic	2–1	Dundee United
1989	Celtic	1–0	Rangers
1990	Aberdeen	0–0, 9–8 pens	Celtic
1991	Motherwell	4–3 aet	Dundee United
1992	Rangers	2–1	Airdrieonians
1993	Rangers	2–1	Aberdeen
1994	Dundee United	1–0	Rangers
1995	Celtic	1–0	Airdrieonians
1996	Rangers	5–1	Hearts
1997	Kilmarnock	1–0	Falkirk
1998	Hearts	2–1	Rangers
1999	Rangers	1–0	Celtic
2000	Rangers	4–0	Aberdeen
2001	Celtic	3–0	Hibernian
2002	Rangers	3–2	Celtic
2003	Rangers	1–0	Dundee
2004	Celtic	3–1	Dunfermline Athletic
2005	Celtic	1–0	Dundee United
2006	Hearts	1–1, 4–2 pens	Gretna
2007	Celtic	1–0	Dunfermline Athletic
2008	Rangers	3–2	Queen of the South
2009	Rangers	1–0	Falkirk
2010	Dundee United	3–0	Ross County
2011	Celtic	3–0	Motherwell
2012	Hearts	5–1	Hibernian
2013	Celtic	3–0	Hibernian

NB In 1879 Vale of Leven awarded cup as Rangers failed to appear for replay after 1–1 draw.
In 1881 Dumbarton protested the first result in which Queen's Park won 2–1.
In 1884 Queen's Park awarded the cup after Vale of Leven failed to appear.
In 1889 Scottish FA ordered a replay because of playing conditions after Third Lanark won match 3–0.
In 1892 both teams protested about first game in which Celtic won 1–0.
In 1909 Celtic v Rangers 2–2, 1–1 with riot in extra time – clubs refused to play a third match – cup was withheld by Scottish FA.

World Cup

Date	*Winner*		*Runner-up*		*Venue*
1930	Uruguay	4–2	Argentina		Uruguay
1934	Italy	2–1	Czechoslovakia	after extra time	Italy
1938	Italy	4–2	Hungary		France
1950	Uruguay	2–1	Brazil	deciding match of pool	Brazil
1954	West Germany	3–2	Hungary		Switzerland
1958	Brazil	5–2	Sweden		Sweden
1962	Brazil	3–1	Czechoslovakia		Chile
1966	England	4–2	West Germany	after extra time	England
1970	Brazil	4–1	Italy		Mexico
1974	West Germany	2–1	Holland		West Germany
1978	Argentina	3–1	Holland	after extra time	Argentina
1982	Italy	3–1	West Germany		Spain
1986	Argentina	3–2	West Germany		Mexico
1990	West Germany	1–0	Argentina		Italy
1994	Brazil	0–0	Italy	Brazil won 3–2 on penalties	USA
1998	France	3–0	Brazil		France
2002	Brazil	2–0	Germany		Japan
2006	Italy	1–1	France	Italy won 5–3 on penalties	Germany
2010	Spain	1–0	Holland		South Africa

Inter-Cities Cup (became UEFA Cup in 1972)

Date	Winner		Runner-up
1955–58	Barcelona	8–2 agg.	London
1958–60	Barcelona	4–1 agg.	Birmingham City
1961	AS Roma	4–2 agg.	Birmingham City
1962	Valencia	7–3 agg.	Barcelona
1963	Valencia	4–1 agg.	Dynamo Zagreb
1964	Real Zaragoza	2–1 (in Barcelona)	Valencia
1965	Ferencvaros	1–0 (in Turin)	Juventus
1966	Barcelona	4–3 agg.	Real Zaragoza
1967	Dynamo Zagreb	2–0 agg.	Leeds United
1968	Leeds United	1–0 agg.	Ferencvaros
1969	Newcastle United	6–2 agg.	Ujpest Dozsa
1970	Arsenal	4–3 agg.	Anderlecht
1971	Leeds United	3–3 agg., away goals	Juventus
1972	Tottenham Hotspur	3–2 agg.	Wolverhampton Wanderers
1973	Liverpool	3–2 agg.	Borussia Moenchengladbach
1974	Feyenoord	4–2 agg.	Tottenham Hotspur
1975	Borussia Moenchengladbach	5–1 agg.	Twente Enschede
1976	Liverpool	4–3 agg.	FC Bruges
1977	Juventus	2–2 agg., away goals	Athletic Bilbao
1978	PSV Eindhoven	3–0 agg.	Bastia
1979	Borussia Moenchengladbach	2–1 agg.	Red Star Belgrade
1980	Eintracht Frankfurt	3–3 agg., away goals	Borussia Moenchengladbach
1981	Ipswich Town	5–4 agg.	AZ67 Alkmaar
1982	IFK Gothenburg	4–0 agg.	SV Hamburg
1983	Anderlecht	2–1 agg.	Benfica
1984	Tottenham Hotspur	2–2 agg., 4–3 on pens	Anderlecht
1985	Real Madrid	3–1 agg.	Videoton
1986	Real Madrid	5–3 agg.	Cologne
1987	IFK Gothenburg	2–1 agg.	Dundee United
1988	Bayer Leverkusen	3–3 agg., 3–2 on pens	Espanol
1989	Napoli	5–4 agg.	Stuttgart
1990	Juventus	3–1 agg.	Fiorentina
1991	Inter Milan	2–1 agg.	AS Roma
1992	Ajax	2–2 agg., away goals	Torino
1993	Juventus	6–1 agg.	Borussia Dortmund
1994	Inter Milan	2–0 agg.	Casino Salzburg
1995	Parma	2–1 agg.	Juventus
1996	Bayern Munich	5–1 agg.	Bordeaux
1997	Schalke 04	1–1 agg., 4–1 on pens	Inter Milan
1998	Inter Milan	3–0 (Paris)	Lazio
1999	Parma	3–0 (Moscow)	Marseille
2000	Galatasaray	0–0, 4–1 on pens	Arsenal
2001	Liverpool	5–4 on golden goal (Dortmund)	Alavés
2002	Feyenoord	3–2 (Rotterdam)	Borussia Dortmund
2003	FC Porto	3–2 on golden goal (Seville)	Celtic
2004	Valencia	2–0	Marseille
2005	CSKA Moscow	3–1 (Lisbon)	Sporting Lisbon
2006	Sevilla	4–0 (Eindhoven)	Middlesbrough
2007	Sevilla	2–2, 3–1 on pens (Glasgow)	Espanyol
2008	Zenit St Petersburg	2–0 (Manchester)	Rangers
2009	Shakhtar Donetsk	2–1 aet (Istanbul)	Werder Bremen
2010	Atletico Madrid	2–1 aet (Hamburg)	Fulham
2011	Porto	1–0	Braga
2012	Atletico Madrid	3–0	Athletic Bilbao
2013	Chelsea	2–1	Benfica

NB The 1998 UEFA Cup in Paris was held over one leg for the first time.
Between 1967 and 1971 the competition was known as the European Fairs Cup.
In June 2009 the competiton became the Europa League.

Football League Cup (currently known as the Capital One Cup)

Date	Winner		Runner-up
1961	Aston Villa	3–2 on agg. aet	Rotherham United
1962	Norwich City	4–0 on agg.	Rochdale
1963	Birmingham City	3–1 on agg.	Aston Villa
1964	Leicester City	4–3 on agg.	Stoke City
1965	Chelsea	3–2 on agg.	Leicester City
1966	West Bromwich Albion	5–3 on agg.	West Ham United
1967	Queen's Park Rangers	3–2	West Bromwich Albion
1968	Leeds United	1–0	Arsenal
1969	Swindon Town	3–1	Arsenal
1970	Manchester City	2–1	West Bromwich Albion
1971	Tottenham Hotspur	2–0	Aston Villa
1972	Stoke City	2–1	Chelsea
1973	Tottenham Hotspur	1–0	Norwich City
1974	Wolverhampton Wanderers	2–1	Manchester City
1975	Aston Villa	1–0	Norwich City

Date	*Winner*		*Runner-up*
1976	Manchester City	2–1	Newcastle United
1977	Aston Villa	0–0, 1–1, 3–2 aet	Everton
1978	Nottingham Forest	0–0, 1–0 aet	Liverpool
1979	Nottingham Forest	3–2	Southampton
1980	Wolverhampton Wanderers	1–0	Nottingham Forest
1981	Liverpool	1–1, 2–1	West Ham United
1982	Liverpool	3–1 aet	Tottenham Hotspur
1983	Liverpool	2–1 aet	Manchester United
1984	Liverpool	0–0, 1–0 aet	Everton
1985	Norwich City	1–0	Sunderland
1986	Oxford United	3–0	Queen's Park Rangers
1987	Arsenal	2–1	Liverpool
1988	Luton Town	3–2	Arsenal
1989	Nottingham Forest	3–1	Luton Town
1990	Nottingham Forest	1–0	Oldham Athletic
1991	Sheffield Wednesday	1–0	Manchester United
1992	Manchester United	1–0	Nottingham Forest
1993	Arsenal	2–1	Sheffield Wednesday
1994	Aston Villa	3–1	Manchester United
1995	Liverpool	2–1	Bolton Wanderers
1996	Aston Villa	3–0	Leeds United
1997	Leicester City	1–1, 1–0 aet	Middlesbrough
1998	Chelsea	1–0	Middlesbrough
1999	Tottenham	1–0	Leicester City
2000	Leicester	2–1	Tranmere Rovers
2001	Liverpool	1–1, 5–4 on pens	Birmingham City
2002	Blackburn Rovers	2–1	Tottenham
2003	Liverpool	2–0	Manchester United
2004	Middlesbrough	2–1	Bolton Wanderers
2005	Chelsea	3–2 aet	Liverpool
2006	Manchester United	4–0	Wigan Athletic
2007	Chelsea	2–1	Arsenal
2008	Tottenham Hotspur	2–1 aet	Chelsea
2009	Manchester United	0–0, 4–1 on pens	Tottenham Hotspur
2010	Manchester United	2–1	Aston Villa
2011	Birmingham City	2–1	Arsenal
2012	Liverpool	2-2, 3–2 on pens	Cardiff City
2013	Swansea City	5-0	Bradford City

NB In 1982 the League Cup became the Milk Cup following sponsorship by the Milk Marketing Board. Over the next few seasons it became the Littlewoods, Rumbelows, Coca Cola, Worthington Cup, Carling Cup and is now the Capital One Cup.

Scottish League Cup

	Winners		Runner-up
1947	Rangers	4–0	Aberdeen
1948	East Fife	1–1, 4–1	Falkirk
1949	Rangers	2–0	Raith Rovers
1950	East Fife	3–0	Dunfermline
1951	Motherwell	3–0	Hibernian
1952	Dundee	3–2	Rangers
1953	Dundee	2–0	Kilmarnock
1954	East Fife	3–2	Partick Thistle
1955	Hearts	4–2	Motherwell
1956	Aberdeen	2–1	St Mirren
1957	Celtic	0–0, 3–0	Partick Thistle
1958	Celtic	7–1	Rangers
1959	Hearts	5–1	Partick Thistle
1960	Hearts	2–1	Third Lanark
1961	Rangers	2–0	Kilmarnock
1962	Rangers	1–1, 3–1	Hearts
1963	Hearts	1–0	Kilmarnock
1964	Rangers	5–0	Morton
1965	Rangers	2–1	Celtic
1966	Celtic	2–1	Rangers
1967	Celtic	1–0	Rangers
1968	Celtic	5–3	Dundee
1969	Celtic	6–2	Hibernian
1970	Celtic	1–0	St Johnstone
1971	Rangers	1–0	Celtic
1972	Partick Thistle	4–1	Celtic
1973	Hibernian	2–1	Celtic
1974	Dundee	1–0	Celtic
1975	Celtic	6–3	Hibernian
1976	Rangers	1–0	Celtic
1977	Aberdeen	2–1	Celtic
1978	Rangers	2–1	Celtic
1979	Rangers	2–1	Aberdeen

	Winners		Runner-up
1980	Dundee Utd	0–0, 3–0	Aberdeen
1981	Dundee Utd	3–0	Dundee
1982	Rangers	2–1	Dundee Utd
1983	Celtic	2–1	Rangers
1984	Rangers	3–2	Celtic
1985	Rangers	1–0	Dundee Utd
1986	Aberdeen	3–0	Hibernian
1987	Rangers	2–1	Celtic
1988	Rangers	3–3, 5–3	Aberdeen (lost 5-3 on penalties)
1989	Rangers	3–2	Aberdeen
1990	Aberdeen	2–1	Rangers
1991	Rangers	2–1	Celtic
1992	Hibernian	2–0	Dunfermline
1993	Rangers	2–1	Aberdeen
1994	Rangers	2–1	Hibernian
1995	Raith Rovers	2–2, 6–5	Celtic (lost 6-5 on penalties)
1996	Aberdeen	2–0	Dundee
1997	Rangers	4–3	Hearts
1998	Celtic	3–0	Dundee Utd
1999	Rangers	2–1	St Johnstone
2000	Celtic	2–0	Aberdeen
2001	Celtic	3–0	Kilmarnock
2002	Rangers	4–0	Ayr United
2003	Rangers	2–1	Celtic
2004	Livingston	2–0	Hibernian
2005	Rangers	5–1	Motherwell
2006	Celtic	3–0	Dunfermline
2007	Hibernian	5–1	Kilmarnock
2008	Rangers	2–2, 3–2	Dundee Utd (lost 3-2 on pens)
2009	Celtic	2–0 aet	Rangers
2010	Rangers	1–0	St Mirren
2011	Rangers	2–1 aet	Celtic
2012	Kilmarnock	1–0	Celtic
2013	St Mirren	3–2	Hearts

Scottish League Champions

1892	Dumbarton	1915	Celtic	1938	Celtic	1968	Celtic	1991	Rangers
1893	Celtic	1916	Celtic	1939	Rangers	1969	Celtic	1992	Rangers
1894	Celtic	1917	Celtic	1947	Rangers	1970	Celtic	1993	Rangers
1895	Hearts	1918	Rangers	1948	Hibernian	1971	Celtic	1994	Rangers
1896	Celtic	1919	Celtic	1949	Rangers	1972	Celtic	1995	Rangers
1897	Hearts	1920	Rangers	1950	Rangers	1973	Celtic	1996	Rangers
1898	Celtic	1921	Rangers	1951	Hibernian	1974	Celtic	1997	Rangers
1899	Rangers	1922	Celtic	1952	Hibernian	1975	Rangers	1998	Celtic
1900	Rangers	1923	Rangers	1953	Rangers	1976	Rangers	1999	Rangers
1901	Rangers	1924	Rangers	1954	Celtic	1977	Celtic	2000	Rangers
1902	Rangers	1925	Rangers	1955	Aberdeen	1978	Rangers	2001	Celtic
1903	Hibernian	1926	Celtic	1956	Rangers	1979	Celtic	2002	Celtic
1904	Third Lanark	1927	Rangers	1957	Rangers	1980	Aberdeen	2003	Rangers
1905	Celtic	1928	Rangers	1958	Hearts	1981	Celtic	2004	Celtic
1906	Celtic	1929	Rangers	1959	Rangers	1982	Celtic	2005	Rangers
1907	Celtic	1930	Rangers	1960	Hearts	1983	Dundee Utd	2006	Celtic
1908	Celtic	1931	Rangers	1961	Rangers	1984	Aberdeen	2007	Celtic
1909	Celtic	1932	Motherwell	1962	Dundee	1985	Aberdeen	2008	Celtic
1910	Celtic	1933	Rangers	1963	Rangers	1986	Celtic	2009	Rangers
1911	Rangers	1934	Rangers	1964	Rangers	1987	Rangers	2010	Rangers
1912	Rangers	1935	Rangers	1965	Kilmarnock	1988	Celtic	2011	Rangers
1913	Rangers	1936	Celtic	1966	Celtic	1989	Rangers	2012	Celtic
1914	Celtic	1937	Rangers	1967	Celtic	1990	Rangers	2013	Celtic

Golf: Majors

Year	*British Open*	*US Open*	*US PGA*	*US Masters*
1860	W Park	—	—	—
1861	T Morris Snr	—	—	—
1862	T Morris Snr	—	—	—
1863	W Park	—	—	—
1864	T Morris Snr	—	—	—
1865	A Strath	—	—	—
1866	W Park	—	—	—
1867	T Morris Snr	—	—	—
1868	T Morris Jnr	—	—	—
1869	T Morris Jnr	—	—	—
1870	T Morris Jnr	—	—	—
1871	not held	—	—	—
1872	T Morris Jnr	—	—	—
1873	T Kidd	—	—	—
1874	M Park	—	—	—
1875	W Park	—	—	—
1876	R Martin	—	—	—
1877	J Anderson	—	—	—
1878	J Anderson	—	—	—
1879	J Anderson	—	—	—
1880	R Ferguson	—	—	—
1881	R Ferguson	—	—	—
1882	R Ferguson	—	—	—
1883	W Fernie	—	—	—
1884	J Simpson	—	—	—
1885	R Martin	—	—	—
1886	D Brown	—	—	—
1887	W Park Jnr	—	—	—
1888	J Burns	—	—	—
1889	W Park Jnr	—	—	—
1890	J Ball	—	—	—
1891	H Kirkaldy	—	—	—
1892	H Hilton	—	—	—
1893	W Auchterlonie	—	—	—
1894	J Taylor	—	—	—
1895	J Taylor	H Rawlins	—	—
1896	H Vardon	J Foulis	—	—
1897	H Hilton	J Lloyd	—	—
1898	H Vardon	F Herd	—	—
1899	H Vardon	W Smith	—	—
1900	J Ball	H Vardon	—	—
1901	H Kirkaldy	W Anderson	—	—
1902	A Herd	L Auchterlonie	—	—
1903	H Vardon	W Anderson	—	—
1904	J White	W Anderson	—	—
1905	J Braid	W Anderson	—	—
1906	J Braid	A Smith	—	—
1907	A Massy (France)	A Ross	—	—

Year	*British Open*	*US Open*	*US PGA*	*US Masters*
1908	J Braid	F McLeod	—	—
1909	J Taylor	G Sargent	—	—
1910	J Braid	A Smith	—	—
1911	H Vardon	J McDermott	—	—
1912	Ted Ray	J McDermott	—	—
1913	J Taylor	F Ouimet	—	—
1914	H Vardon	W Hagen	—	—
1915	not held	J Travers	—	—
1916	not held	C Evans Jnr	J Barnes	—
1917	not held	not held	not held	—
1918	not held	not held	not held	—
1919	not held	W Hagen	J Barnes	—
1920	G Duncan	Ted Ray (GB)	J Hutchison	—
1921	J Hutchison	J Barnes	W Hagen	—
1922	W Hagen	G Sarazen	G Sarazen	—
1923	A G Havers	B Jones	G Sarazen	—
1924	W Hagen	C Walker	W Hagen	—
1925	J Barnes	W McFarlane	W Hagen	—
1926	B Jones	B Jones	W Hagen	—
1927	B Jones	T Armour	W Hagen	—
1928	W Hagen	J Farrell	L Diegel	—
1929	W Hagen	B Jones	L Diegel	—
1930	B Jones	B Jones	T Armour	—
1931	T Armour	B Burke	T Creavy	—
1932	G Sarazen	G Sarazen	O Dutra	—
1933	D Shute	J Goodman	G Sarazen	—
1934	T Cotton	O Dutra	P Runyan	H Smith
1935	A Perry	S Parks Jnr	J Revolta	G Sarazen
1936	A Padgham	T Manero	D Shute	H Smith
1937	T Cotton	R Guldahl	D Shute	B Nelson
1938	R Whitcombe	R Guldahl	P Runyan	H Picard
1939	R Burton	B Nelson	H Picard	R Guldahl
1940	not held	L Little	B Nelson	J Demaret
1941	not held	C Wood	V Ghezzi	C Wood
1942	not held	not held	S Snead	B Nelson
1943	not held	not held	not held	not held
1944	not held	not held	B Hamilton	not held
1945	not held	not held	B Nelson	not held
1946	S Snead	L Mangrum	B Hogan	H Keiser
1947	F Daly	L Worsham	J Ferrier	J Demaret
1948	T Cotton	B Hogan	B Hogan	C Harmon
1949	B Locke	C Middlecoff	S Snead	S Snead
1950	B Locke	B Hogan	C Harper	J Demaret
1951	M Faulkner	B Hogan	S Snead	B Hogan
1952	B Locke	J Boros	J Turnesa	S Snead
1953	B Hogan	B Hogan	W Burkemo	B Hogan
1954	P Thompson	E Furgol	C Harbert	S Snead
1955	P Thompson	J Fleck	D Ford	C Middlecoff
1956	P Thompson	C Middlecoff	J Burke	J Burke Jnr
1957	B Locke	D Mayer	L Hebert	D Ford
1958	P Thompson	T Bolt	D Finsterwald	A Palmer
1959	G Player	W Casper	B Rosburg	A Wall Jnr
1960	K Nagle	A Palmer	J Hebert	A Palmer
1961	A Palmer	G Littler	J Barber	G Player
1962	A Palmer	J Nicklaus	G Player	A Palmer
1963	R Charles	J Boros	J Nicklaus	J Nicklaus
1964	T Lema	K Venturi	B Nicholls	A Palmer
1965	P Thompson	G Player	D Marr	J Nicklaus
1966	J Nicklaus	W Casper	A Geiberger	J Nicklaus
1967	R de Vicenzo	J Nicklaus	D January	G Brewer
1968	G Player	L Trevino	J Boros	B Goalby
1969	A Jacklin	O Moody	R Floyd	G Archer
1970	J Nicklaus	A Jacklin	D Stockton	W Caspar
1971	L Trevino	L Trevino	J Nicklaus	C Coody
1972	L Trevino	J Nicklaus	G Player	J Nicklaus
1973	T Weiskopf	J Miller	J Nicklaus	T Aaron
1974	G Player	H Irwin	L Trevino	G Player
1975	T Watson	L Graham	J Nicklaus	J Nicklaus
1976	J Miller	J Pate	D Stockton	R Floyd
1977	T Watson	H Green	L Wadkins	T Watson
1978	J Nicklaus	A North	J Mahaffey	G Player
1979	S Ballesteros	H Irwin	D Graham (Aus)	F Zoeller
1980	T Watson	J Nicklaus	J Nicklaus	S Ballesteros
1981	W Rogers	D Graham (Aus)	L Nelson	T Watson
1982	T Watson	T Watson	R Floyd	C Stadler
1983	T Watson	L Nelson	H Sutton	S Ballesteros
1984	S Ballesteros	F Zoeller	L Trevino	B Crenshaw
1985	S Lyle	A North	H Green	B Langer (Ger)
1986	G Norman	R Floyd	B Tway	J Nicklaus

Year	British Open	US Open	US PGA	US Masters
1987	N Faldo	S Simpson	L Nelson	L Mize
1988	S Ballesteros	C Strange	J Sluman	S Lyle
1989	M Calcavecchia	C Strange	P Stewart	N Faldo
1990	N Faldo	H Irwin	W Grady (Aus)	N Faldo
1991	I Baker-Finch	P Stewart	J Daly	I Woosnam
1992	N Faldo	T Kite	N Price	F Couples
1993	G Norman	L Janzen	P Azinger	B Langer
1994	N Price	E Els	N Price	J M Olazabal
1995	J Daly	C Pavin	S Elkington	B Crenshaw
1996	T Lehman	S Jones	M Brooks	N Faldo
1997	J Leonard	E Els	D Love III	T Woods
1998	M O'Meara	L Janzen	V J Singh	M O'Meara
1999	P Lawrie	P Stewart	T Woods	J M Olazabal
2000	T Woods	T Woods	T Woods	V J Singh
2001	D Duval	R Goosen	D Toms	T Woods
2002	E Els	T Woods	R Beem	T Woods
2003	B Curtis	J Furyk	S Micheel	M Weir
2004	T Hamilton	R Goosen	V Singh	P Mickelson
2005	T Woods	M Campbell (NZ)	P Mickelson	T Woods
2006	T Woods	G Ogilvy (Aus)	T Woods	P Mickelson
2007	P Harrington	A Cabrera	T Woods	Z Johnson
2008	P Harrington	T Woods	P Harrington	T Immelman
2009	S Cink	L Glover	Yang Yong-eun	A Cabrera
2010	L Oosthuizen	G McDowell	M Kaymer	P Mickelson
2011	D Clarke	R McIlroy	K Bradley	C Schwartzel
2012	E Els	W Simpson	R McIlroy	B Watson
2013	P Mickelson	J Rose	J Dufner	A Scott

Golf: World Matchplay Championship

	Winner	Runner-up
1964	Arnold Palmer	Neil Coles
1965	Gary Player	Peter Thomson
1966	Gary Player	Jack Nicklaus
1967	Arnold Palmer	Peter Thomson
1968	Gary Player	Bob Charles
1969	Bob Charles	Gene Littler
1970	Jack Nicklaus	Lee Trevino
1971	Gary Player	Jack Nicklaus
1972	Tom Weiskopf	Lee Trevino
1973	Gary Player	Graham Marsh
1974	Hale Irwin	Gary Player
1975	Hale Irwin	Al Geiberger
1976	David Graham	Hale Irwin
1977	Graham Marsh	Ray Floyd
1978	Isao Aoki	Simon Owen
1979	Bill Rogers	Isao Aoki
1980	Greg Norman	Sandy Lyle
1981	Severiano Ballesteros	Ben Crenshaw
1982	Severiano Ballesteros	Sandy Lyle
1983	Greg Norman	Nick Faldo
1984	Severiano Ballesteros	Bernhard Langer
1985	Severiano Ballesteros	Bernhard Langer
1986	Greg Norman	Sandy Lyle
1987	Ian Woosnam	Sandy Lyle
1988	Sandy Lyle	Nick Faldo
1989	Nick Faldo	Ian Woosnam
1990	Ian Woosnam	Mark McNulty
1991	Severiano Ballesteros	Nick Price
1992	Nick Faldo	Jeff Sluman
1993	Corey Pavin	Nick Faldo
1994	Ernie Els	Colin Montgomerie
1995	Ernie Els	Steve Elkington
1996	Ernie Els	Vijay Singh
1997	Vijay Singh	Ernie Els
1998	Mark O'Meara	Tiger Woods
1999	Colin Montgomerie	Mark O'Meara
2000	Lee Westwood	Colin Montgomerie
2001	Ian Woosnam	Padraig Harrington
2002	Ernie Els	Sergio Garcia
2003	Ernie Els	Thomas Bjorn
2004	Ernie Els	Lee Westwood
2005	Michael Campbell	Paul McGinley
2006	Paul Casey	Shaun Micheel
2007	Ernie Els	Angel Cabrera
2008	No tournament	
2009	Ross Fisher	Anthony Kim
2010	No tournament	
2011	Ian Poulter	Luke Donald
2012	Nicolas Colsaerts	Graeme McDowell
2013	Graeme McDowell	Thongchai Jaidee

Golf: Ryder Cup

	Winner	Venue
1927	USA	Worcester, Massachusetts
1929	GB	Moortown, North Yorkshire
1931	USA	Scioto, Ohio
1933	GB	Southport & Ainsdale, Lancashire
1935	USA	Ridgewood, New Jersey
1937	USA	Southport & Ainsdale, Lancashire
1947	USA	Portland, Oregon
1949	USA	Ganton, Yorkshire
1951	USA	Pinehurst, North Carolina
1953	USA	Wentworth, Surrey
1955	USA	Thunderbird G & C, California
1957	GB	Lindrick, Yorkshire
1959	USA	Eldorado CC, California
1961	USA	Royal Lytham, Lancashire
1963	USA	Atlanta, Georgia
1965	USA	Royal Birkdale, Lancashire
1967	USA	Houston, Texas
1969	tie	Royal Birkdale, Lancashire
1971	USA	St Louis, Missouri
1973	USA	Muirfield, Scotland
1975	USA	Laurel Valley, Pennsylvania
1977	USA	Royal Lytham, Lancashire
1979	USA	Greenbrier, Virginia
1981	USA	Walton Heath
1983	USA	Palm Beach
1985	Europe	Belfry
1987	Europe	Muirfield Village

	Winner	Venue		Winner	Venue
1989	tie	Belfry	2002	Europe	Belfry
1991	USA	Kiawah Island	2004	Europe	Oakland Hills, Michigan
1993	USA	Belfry	2006	Europe	K Club, Co Kildare
1995	Europe	Oak Hill CC	2008	USA	Valhalla, Kentucky
1997	Europe	Valderrama	2010	Europe	Celtic Manor Resort, Newport
1999	USA	Boston, Massachusetts	2012	Europe	Medinah Country Club, Illinois

NB Since 1979 the Ryder Cup has been contested by USA and Europe. The 2001 event was cancelled due to the terrorist attack of 11 September.

Golf: General Information

British Open: correct title	The Open Championship (as it was the first championship open to the world)
oldest winner	Old Tom Morris (46)
youngest winner	Young Tom Morris (17)
youngest winner 20th century	Seve Ballesteros (22)
clubs: maximum allowed	14
Curtis Cup	Biennial tournament instituted in 1932 and played between amateur ladies' teams from the United States and Great Britain and Ireland. Teams consist of six players, two substitutes and a captain.
golf balls: pimples	332
Ryder Cup: father and sons played	Percy and Peter Alliss, Antonio and Ignacio Garrido
Samuel Ryder: profession	seed-merchant
Solheim Cup	Biennial tournament instituted in 1990 and played between professional ladies teams from the United States and Europe. It takes its name from Karsten Solheim, owner of golf club manufacturer Ping. Teams consist of 12 players and a non-playing captain.
US Masters: oldest winner	Jack Nicklaus (46)
youngest winner	Tiger Woods (21)
US Open: oldest winner	Hale Irwin (45)
youngest winner	John McDermott (19)
US PGA: oldest winner	Julius Boros (48)
youngest winner	Gene Sarazen (20)
US Women's Open: first UK winner	Laura Davies (1987)
Walker Cup	Inaugurated in 1921 and played between amateur teams from the United States and the British Isles. It was proposed by George Walker, the then president of the USGA, as the International Challenge Trophy but took its present name in 1922. It became a biennial event in 1924. Teams consist of eight players, two substitutes and a captain.
yips: coined by	Scottish professional Tommy Armour in the 1920s. Term describing inability to release the putter through the ball.

Greyhound Racing

Derby Winners

1980	Indian Joe	1989	Lartigue Note	1998	Tom's the Best	2007	Westmead Lord
1981	Parkdown Jet	1990	Slippy Blue	1999	Chart King	2008	Loyal Honcho
1982	Laurie's Panther	1991	Ballinderry Ash	2000	Rapid Ranger	2009	Kinda Ready
1983	I'm Slippy	1992	Farloe Melody	2001	Rapid Ranger	2010	Bandicoot Tipoki
1984	Whisper Wishes	1993	Ringa Hustle	2002	Allen Gift	2011	Taylors Sky
1985	Pagan Swallow	1994	Moral Standards	2003	Farloe Verdict	2012	Blonde Snapper
1986	Tico	1995	Moaning Lad	2004	Droopys Scholes	2013	Sidaz Jack
1987	Signal Spark	1996	Shanless Slippy	2005	Westmead Hawk		
1988	Hit the Lid	1997	Some Picture	2006	Westmead Hawk		

Horse Racing: British Classics and Grand National Winners

	St Leger		Oaks		Derby	
Year	Horse	Jockey	Horse	Jockey	Horse	Jockey
1776	Allabaculia	J Singleton	—	—	—	—
1777	Bourbon	J Cade	—	—	—	—
1778	Hollandaise	G Hearon	—	—	—	—
1779	Tommy	G Lowrey Snr	Bridget	R Goodison	—	—
1780	Ruler	J Mangle	Teetotum	R Goodison	Diomed	S Arnull
1781	Serina	R Forster	Faith	R Goodison	Young Eclipse	C Hindley
1782	Imperatrix	G Searle	Ceres	S Chifney Snr	Assassin	S Arnull
1783	Phoenomenon	A Hall	Maid of Oakes	S Chifney Snr	Saltram	C Hindley
1784	Omphale	J Kirton	Stella	C Hindley	Sergeant	J Arnull
1785	Cowslip	G Searle	Trifle	J Bird	Aimwell	C Hindley
1786	Paragon	J Mangle	Perdita by Tanden	J Edwards	Noble	J White
1787	Spadille	J Mangle	Annette	Fitzpatrick	Sir Peter Teazle	S Arnull
1788	Young Flora	J Mangle	Nightshade	Fitzpatrick	Sir Thomas	W South
1789	Pewett	J Singleton	Tag	S Chifney Snr	Skyscraper	S Chifney Snr
1790	Ambidexter	G Searle	Hippolyta	S Chifney Snr	Rhadamanthus	J Arnull
1791	Young Traveller	J Jackson	Portia	J Singleton	Eager	Stephenson

Year	St Leger Horse	St Leger Jockey	Oaks Horse	Oaks Jockey	Derby Horse	Derby Jockey
1792	Tartar	J Mangle	Volante	C Hindley	John Bull	F Buckle
1793	Ninety-three	W Peirse	Caelia	J Singleton	Waxy	W Clift
1794	Beningborough	J Jackson	Hermione	S Arnull	Daedalus	F Buckle
1795	Hambletonian	Boyes	Platina	Fitzpatrick	Spreadeagle	A Wheatley
1796	Ambrosio	J Jackson	Parissot	J Arnull	Didelot	J Arnull
1797	Lounger	J Shepherd	Nike	F Buckle	Brown c by fidget	J Singleton
1798	Symmetry	J Jackson	Bellissima	F Buckle	Sir Harry	S Arnull
1799	Cockfighter	T Fields	Bellina	F Buckle	Archduke	J Arnull
1800	Champion	F Buckle	Ephemera	Fitzpatrick	Champion	W Clift
1801	Quiz	J Shepherd	Eleanor	Saunders	Eleanor	Saunders
1802	Orville	J Singleton Jnr	Scotia	F Buckle	Tyrant	F Buckle
1803	Remembrancer	B Smith	Theophania	F Buckle	Ditto	W Clift
1804	Sancho	F Buckle	Pellisse	W Clift	Hannibal	W Arnull
1805	Staveley	J Jackson	Meteora	F Buckle	Cardinal Beaufort	Fitzpatrick
1806	Fyldener	T Carr	Bronze	W Edwards	Paris	J Shepherd
1807	Paulina	W Clift	Briseis	S Chifney	Election	J Arnull
1808	Petronius	B Smith	Morel	W Clift	Pan	Collinson
1809	Ashton	B Smith	Maid of Orleans	J Moss	Pope	T Goodison
1810	Octavian	W Clift	Oriana	W Peirse	Whalebone	W Clift
1811	Soothsayer	B Smith	Sorcery	S Chifney	Phantom	F Buckle
1812	Ottrington	R Johnson	Manuella	W Peirse	Octavius	W Arnull
1813	Altisidora	J Jackson	Music	T Goodison	Smolensko	T Goodison
1814	William	J Shepherd	Medora	Barnard	Blucher	W Arnull
1815	Filho da Puta	J Jackson	Minuet	T Goodison	Whisker	T Goodison
1816	The Duchess	B Smith	Landscape	S Chifney	Prince Leopold	W Wheatley
1817	Ebor	R Johnson	Neva	F Buckle	Azor	J Robinson
1818	Reveller	R Johnson	Corinne	F Buckle	Sam	S Chifney Jnr
1819	Antonio	J Nicholson	Shoveler	S Chifney	Tiresias	W Clift
1820	St Patrick	J Johnson	Caroline	H Edwards	Sailor	S Chifney Jnr
1821	Jack Spiggot	W Scott	Augusta	J Robinson	Gustavus	S Day
1822	Theodore	J Jackson	Pastille	H Edwards	Moses	T Goodison
1823	Barefoot	T Goodison	Zinc	F Buckle	Emilius	F Buckle
1824	Jerry	B Smith	Cobweb	J Robinson	Cedric	J Robinson
1825	Memnon	W Scott	Wings	S Chifney	Middleton	J Robinson
1826	Tarrare	G Nelson	Lilias	T Lye	Lap-dog	G Dockeray
1827	Matilda	J Robinson	Gulnare	F Boyce	Mameluke	J Robinson
1828	The Colonel	W Scott	Turquoise	J B Day	Cadland	J Robinson
1829	Rowton	W Scott	Green Mantle	G Dockeray	Frederick	Forth
1830	Birmingham	P Conolly	Variation	G Edwards	Priam	S Day
1831	Chorister	J B Day	Oxygen	J B Day	Spaniel	W Wheatley
1832	Margrave	J Robinson	Galata	P Conolly	St Giles	W Scott
1833	Rockingham	S Darling	Vespa	J Chapple	Dangerous	J Chapple
1834	Touchstone	G Calloway	Pussy	J B Day	Plenipotentiary	P Conolly
1835	Queen of Trumps	T Lye	Queen of Trumps	T Lye	Mundig	W Scott
1836	Elis	J B Day	Cyprian	W Scott	Bay Middleton	J Robinson
1837	Mango	S Day Jnr	Miss Letty	J Holmes	Phosphorus	G Edwards
1838	Don John	W Scott	Industry	W Scott	Amato	J Chapple
1839	Charles the Twelfth	W Scott	Deception	J B Day	Bloomsbury	S Templeman
1840	Launcelot	W Scott	Crucifix	J B Day	Little Wonder	Macdonald
1841	Satirist	W Scott	Ghuznee	W Scott	Coronation	P Conolly
1842	Blue Bonnett	T Lye	Our Nell	T Lye	Attila	W Scott
1843	Nutwith	J Marson	Poison	F Butler	Cotherstone	W Scott
1844	Foig a Ballagh	H Bell	The Princess	F Butler	Orlando	E Flatman
1845	The Baron	F Butler	Refraction	H Bell	The Merry Monarch	F Bell
1846	Sir Tatton Sykes	W Scott	Mendicant	S Day	Pyrrhus the First	S Day
1847	Van Tromp	J Marson	Miami	S Templeman	Cossack	S Templeman
1848	Surplice	E Flatman	Cymba	S Templeman	Surplice	S Templeman
1849	Flying Dutchman	Marlow	Lady Evelyn	F Butler	Flying Dutchman	Marlow
1850	Voltigeur	J Marson	Rhedycina	F Butler	Voltigeur	J Marson
1851	Newminster	S Templeman	Iris	F Butler	Teddington	J Marson
1852	Stockwell	J Norman	Songstress	F Butler	Daniel O'Rourke	F Butler
1853	West Australian	F Butler	Catherine Hayes	Marlow	West Australian	F Butler
1854	Knight of St George	Basham	Mincemeat	Charlton	Andover	A Day
1855	Saucebox	J Wells	Marchioness	S Templeman	Wild Dayrell	R Sherwood
1856	Warlock	E Flatman	Mincepie	A Day	Ellington	Aldcroft
1857	Imperieuse	E Flatman	Blink Bonny	Charlton	Blink Bonny	Charlton
1858	Sunbeam	L Snowden	Governess	Ashmall	Beadsman	J Wells
1859	Gamester	Aldcroft	Summerside	G Fordham	Musjid	J Wells
1860	St Albans	L Snowden	Butterfly	J Snowden	Thormanby	H Custance
1861	Caller Ou	T Challoner	Brown Duchess	L Snowden	Kettledrum	Bullock
1862	The Marquis	T Challoner	Feu de Joie	T Challoner	Caractacus	J Parsons
1863	Lord Clifden	J Osborne	Queen Bertha	Aldcroft	Macaroni	T Challoner
1864	Blair Atholl	J Snowden	Fille de l'Air	A Edwards	Blair Atholl	J Snowden
1865	Gladiateur	H Grimshaw	Regalia	Norman	Gladiateur	H Grimshaw
1866	Lord Lyon	H Custance	Tormentor	J Mann	Lord Lyon	H Custance

Year	St Leger Horse	St Leger Jockey	Oaks Horse	Oaks Jockey	Derby Horse	Derby Jockey
1867	Achievement	T Challoner	Hippia	J Daley	Hermit	J Daley
1868	Formosa	T Challoner	Formosa	G Fordham	Blue Gown	J Wells
1869	Pero Gomez	J Wells	Brigantine	T Cannon	Pretender	J Osborne
1870	Hawthornden	J Grimshaw	Gamos	G Fordham	Kingcraft	T French
1871	Hannah	C Maidment	Hannah	C Maidment	Favonius	T French
1872	Wenlock	C Maidment	Reine	G Fordham	Cremorne	C Maidment
1873	Marie Stuart	T Osborne	Marie Stuart	T Cannon	Doncaster	F Webb
1874	Apology	J Osborne	Apology	J Osborne	George Frederick	H Custance
1875	Craig Millar	T Challoner	Spinaway	F Archer	Galopin	Morris
1876	Patriarch	J Goater	Enguerrande	Hudson	Kisber	C Maidment
1877	Silvio	F Archer	Placida	H Jeffrey	Silvio	F Archer
1878	Jannette	F Archer	Jannette	F Archer	Sefton	H Constable
1879	Rayon d'Or	J Goater	Wheel of Fortune	F Archer	Sir Bevys	G Fordham
1880	Robert the Devil	T Cannon	Jenny Howlet	J Snowden	Bend Or	F Archer
1881	Iroquois	F Archer	Thebais	G Fordham	Iroquois	F Archer
1882	Dutch Oven	F Archer	Geheimnis	T Cannon	Shotover	T Cannon
1883	Ossian	J Watts	Bonny Jean	J Watts	St Blaise	C Wood
1884	The Lambkin	J Watts	Busybody	T Cannon	St Gatien/ Harvester	C Wood/Loates
1885	Melton	F Archer	Lonely	F Archer	Melton	F Archer
1886	Ormonde	F Archer	Miss Jummy	J Watts	Ormonde	F Archer
1887	Kilwarlin	W Robinson	Reve d'Or	C Wood	Merry Hampton	J Watts
1888	Seabreeze	W Robinson	Seabreeze	W Robinson	Ayrshire	F Barrett
1889	Donovan	F Barrett	L'Abbesse de Jouarre	J Woodburn	Donovan	T Loates
1890	Memoir	J Watts	Memoir	J Watts	Sainfoin	J Watts
1891	Common	G Barrett	Mimi	F Rickaby	Common	G Barrett
1892	La Fleche	J Watts	La Fleche	G Barrett	Sir Hugo	Allsopp
1893	Isinglass	T Loates	Mrs Butterwick	J Watts	Isinglass	T Loates
1894	Throstle	M Cannon	Amiable	W Bradford	Ladas	J Watts
1895	Sir Visto	S Loates	La Sagesse	S Loates	Sir Visto	S Loates
1896	Persimmon	J Watts	Canterbury Pilgrim	F Rickaby	Persimmon	J Watts
1897	Galtee More	C Wood	Limasol	W Bradford	Galtee More	C Wood
1898	Wildfowler	C Wood	Airs and Graces	W Bradford	Jeddah	O'Madden
1899	Flying Fox	M Cannon	Musa	O Madden	Flying Fox	M Cannon
1900	Diamond Jubilee	H Jones	La Roche	M Cannon	Diamond Jubilee	H Jones
1901	Doricles	K Cannon	Cap and Bells II	M Henry	Volodyovski	L Reiff
1902	Sceptre	F W Hardy	Sceptre	H Randall	ard Patrick	J Martin
1903	Rock Sand	D Maher	Our Lassie	M Cannon	Rock Sand	D Maher
1904	Pretty Polly	W Lane	Pretty Polly	W Lane	St Amant	K Cannon
1905	Challacombe	O Madden	Cherry Lass	H Jones	Cicero	D Maher
1906	Troutbeck	G Stern	Keystone II	D Maher	Spearmint	D Maher
1907	Wool Winder	W Halsey	Glass Doll	H Randall	Orby	J Reiff
1908	Your Majesty	W Griggs	Signorinetta	W Bullock	Signorinetta	W Bullock
1909	Bayardo	D Maher	Perola	F Wootton	Minoru	H Jones
1910	Swynford	F Wootton	Rosedrop	C Trigg	Lemberg	B Dillon
1911	Prince Palatine	F O'Neill	Cherimoya	F Winter	Sunstar	G Stern
1912	Tracery	G Bellhouse	Mirska	J Childs	Tagalie	J Reiff
1913	Night Hawk	E Wheatley	Jest	F Rickaby Jnr	Aboyeur	E Piper
1914	Black Jester	W Griggs	Princess Dorrie	W Huxley	Dubar II	M MacGee
1915	Pommern	S Donoghue	Snow Marten	Walter Griggs	Pommern	S Donoghue
1916	Hurry On	C Childs	Fifinella	J Childs	Fifinella	J Childs
1917	Gay Crusader	S Donoghue	Sunny Jane	O Madden	Gay Crusader	S Donoghue
1918	Gainsborough	J Childs	My Dear	S Donoghue	Gainsborough	J Childs
1919	Keysoe	B Carslake	Bayuda	J Childs	Grand Parade	F Templeman
1920	Caligula	A Smith	Charlebelle	A Whalley	Spion Kop	F O'Neill
1921	Polemarch	J Childs	Love in Idleness	J Childs	Humorist	S Donoghue
1922	Royal Lancer	R Jones	Pogram	E Gardner	Captain Cuttle	S Donoghue
1923	Tranquil	T Weston	Brownhylda	V Smyth	Papyrus	S Donoghue
1924	Salmon-Trout	B Carslake	Straitlace	F O'Neill	Sansovino	T Weston
1925	Solario	J Childs	Saucy Sue	F Bullock	Manna	S Donoghue
1926	Coronach	J Childs	Short Story	R A Jones	Coronach	J Childs
1927	Book Law	H Jellis	Beam	T Weston	Call Boy	C Elliot
1928	Fairway	T Weston	Toboggan	T Weston	Felstead	H Wragg
1929	Trigo	M Beary	Pennycomequick	H Jelliss	Trigo	J Marshall
1930	Singapore	G Richards	Rose of England	G Richards	Blenheim	H Wragg
1931	Sandwich	H Wragg	Brulette	E C Elliot	Cameronian	F Fox
1932	Firdaussi	F Fox	Udaipur	M Beary	April the Fifth	F Lane
1933	Hyperion	T Weston	Chatelaine	S Wragg	Hyperion	T Weston
1934	Windsor Lad	C Smirke	Light Brocade	B Carslake	Windsor Lad	C Smirke
1935	Bahram	C Smirke	Quashed	H Jelliss	Bahram	F Fox
1936	Boswell	P Beasley	Lovely Rosa	T Weston	Mahmoud	C Smirke
1937	Chulmleigh	G Richards	Exhibitionist	S Donoghue	Mid-day Sun	M Beary
1938	Scottish Union	B Carslake	Rockfel	H Wragg	Bois Roussel	C Elliot
1939	no race held		Galatea II	R A Jones	Blue Peter	E Smith
1940	Turkhan	G Richards	Godiva	D Marks	Pont L'Eveque	S Wragg
1941	Sun Castle	G Bridgland	Commotion	H Wragg	Owen Tudor	W Nevett

	St Leger		Oaks		Derby	
Year	*Horse*	*Jockey*	*Horse*	*Jockey*	*Horse*	*Jockey*
1942	Sun Chariot	G Richards	Sun Chariot	G Richards	Watling Street	H Wragg
1943	Herringbone	H Wragg	Why Hurry	C E Elliot	Straight Deal	T Carey
1944	Tehran	G Richards	Hycilla	G Bridgland	Ocean Swell	W Nevett
1945	Chamossaire	T Lowrey	Sun Stream	H Wragg	Dante	W Nevett
1946	Airborne	T Lowrey	Steady Aim	H Wragg	Airborne	T Lowrey
1947	Sayajirao	E Britt	Imprudence	W R Johnstone	Pearl Diver	G Bridgland
1948	Black Tarquin	E Britt	Masaka	W Nevett	My Love	W Johnstone
1949	Ridge Wood	M Beary	Musidora	E Britt	Nimbus	C Elliot
1950	Scratch II	W R Johnstone	Asmena	W R Johnstone	Galcador	W R Johnstone
1951	Talma II	W R Johnstone	Neasham Belle	S Clayton	Arctic Prince	C Spares
1952	Tulyar	C Smirke	Frieze	E Britt	Tulyar	C Smirke
1953	Premonition	E Smith	Ambiguity	J Mercer	Pinza	G Richards
1954	Never Say Die	C Smirke	Suncap	W R Johnstone	Never Say Die	L Piggott
1955	Meld	W H Carr	Meld	W H Carr	Phil Drake	F Palmer
1956	Cambremer	F Palmer	Sicarelle	F Palmer	Lavandin	W R Johnstone
1957	Ballymoss	T P Burns	Carrozza	L Piggott	Crepello	L Piggott
1958	Alcide	W Carr	Bella Paola	M Garcia	Hard Ridden	C Smirke
1959	Cantelo	E Hide	Petite Etoile	L Piggott	Parthia	W Carr
1960	St Paddy	L Piggott	Never Too Late	R Poincelet	St Paddy	L Piggott
1961	Aurelius	L Piggott	Sweet Solera	W Rickaby	Psidium	R Poincelet
1962	Hethersett	W Carr	Monade	Y Saint-Martin	Larkspur	N Sellwood
1963	Ragusa	G Bougoure	Noblesse	G Bougoure	Relko	Y Saint-Martin
1964	Indiana	J Lindley	Homeward Bound	G Starkey	Santa Claus	A Breasley
1965	Provoke	J Mercer	Long Look	J Purtell	Sea Bird II	T P Glennon
1966	Sodium	F Durr	Valoris	L Piggott	Charlottown	A Breasley
1967	Ribocco	L Piggott	Pia	E Hide	Royal Palace	G Moore
1968	Ribero	L Piggott	La Lagune	G Thiboeuf	Sir Ivor	L Piggott
1969	Intermezzo	R Hutchinson	Sleeping Partner	J Gorton	Blakeney	E Johnson
1970	Nijinsky	L Piggott	Lupe	A Barclay	Nijinsky	L Piggott
1971	Athens Wood	L Piggott	Altesse Royale	G Lewis	Mill Reef	G Lewis
1972	Boucher	L Piggott	Ginevra	A Murray	Roberto	L Piggott
1973	Peleid	F Durr	Mysterious	G Lewis	Morston	E Hide
1974	Bustino	J Mercer	Polygamy	P Eddery	Snow Knight	B Taylor
1975	Bruni	A Murray	Juliet Marny	L Piggott	Grundy	P Eddery
1976	Crow	Y Saint-Martin	Pawneese	Y Saint-Martin	Empery	L Piggott
1977	Dunfermline	W Carson	Dunfermline	W Carson	The Minstrel	L Piggott
1978	Julio Mariner	E Hide	Fair Salinia	G Starkey	Shirley Heights	G Starkey
1979	Son of Love	A Lequeux	Scintillate	P Eddery	Troy	W Carson
1980	Light Cavalry	J Mercer	Bireme	W Carson	Henbit	W Carson
1981	Cut Above	J Mercer	Blue Wind	L Piggott	Shergar	W Swinburn
1982	Touching Wood	P Cook	Time Charter	W Newmes	Golden Fleece	P Eddery
1983	Sun Princess	W Carson	Sun Princess	W Carson	Teenoso	L Piggott
1984	Comanche Run	L Piggott	Circus Plume	L Piggott	Secreto	C Roche
1985	Oh So Sharp	S Cauthen	Oh So Sharp	S Cauthen	Slip Anchor	S Cauthen
1986	Moon Madness	P Eddery	Midway Lady	R Cochrane	Shahrastani	W Swinburn
1987	Reference Point	S Cauthen	Unite	W Swinburn	Reference Point	S Cauthen
1988	Minster Son	W Carson	Diminuendo	S Cauthen	Kayhasi	R Cochrane
1989	Michelozzo	S Cauthen	Snow Bride	S Cauthen	Nashwan	W Carson
1990	Snurge	A Quinn	Salsabil	W Carson	Quest for Fame	P Eddery
1991	Toulon	P Eddery	Jet Ski Lady	C Roche	Generous	A Munro
1992	User Friendly	G Duffield	User Friendly	G Duffield	Dr Devious	J Reid
1993	Bobs Return	P Robinson	Intrepidity	M Roberts	Commander-in-Chief	M J Kinane
1994	Moonax	P Eddery	Balanchine	L Dettori	Erhaab	W Carson
1995	Classic Cliché	L Dettori	Moonshell	L Dettori	Lammtara	W Swinburn
1996	Shantou	L Dettori	Lady Carla	P Eddery	Shaamit	M Hills
1997	Silver Patriarch	P Eddery	Reams of Verse	K Fallon	Benny the Dip	W Ryan
1998	Nedawi	J Reid	Shahtoush	M J Kinane	High Rise	O Peslier
1999	Mutafaweq	R Hills	Ramruma	K Fallon	Oath	K Fallon
2000	Millenary	T Quinn	Love Divine	T Quinn	Sinndar	J Murtagh
2001	Milan	M J Kinane	Imagine	M J Kinane	Galileo	M J Kinane
2002	Bollin Eric	K Darley	Kazzia	L Dettori	High Chaparral	J Murtagh
2003	Brian Boru	J Spencer	Casual Look	M Dwyer	Kris Kin	K Fallon
2004	Rule of Law	K McEvoy	Ouija Board	K Fallon	North Light	K Fallon
2005	Scorpion	L Dettori	Eswarah	R Hiller	Motivator	J Murtagh
2006	Sixties Icon	L Dettori	Alexandrova	K Fallon	Sir Percy	M Dwyer
2007	Lucarno	J Fortune	Light Shift	T Durcan	Authorized	L Dettori
2008	Conduit	L Dettori	Look Here	S Sanders	New Approach	K Manning
2009	Mastery	T Durcan	Sariska	J Spencer	Sea the Stars	M Kinane
2010	Arctic Cosmos	W Buick	Snow Fairy	R Moore	Workforce	R Moore
2011	Masked Marvel	W Buick	Dancing Rain	J Murtagh	Pour Moi	M Barzalona
2012	Encke	M Barzalona	Was	S Heffernan	Camelot	J O'Brien
2013	Leading Light	J O'Brien	Talent	R Hughes	Ruler of the World	R Moore

Year	2000 Guineas Horse	2000 Guineas Jockey	1000 Guineas Horse	1000 Guineas Jockey	Grand National Horse	Grand National Jockey
1809	Wizard	W Clift	—	—	—	—
1810	Hephestion	F Buckle	—	—	—	—
1811	Trophonius	S Barnard	—	—	—	—
1812	Cwrw	S Chifney	—	—	—	—
1813	Smolensko	H Miller	—	—	—	—
1814	Olive	W Arnold	Charlotte	W Clift	—	—
1815	Tigris	W Arnold	Brown foal by Selim	W Clift	—	—
1816	Nectar	W Arnold	Rhoda	S Barnard	—	—
1817	Manfred	W Wheatley	Neva	W Arnold	—	—
1818	Interpreter	W Clift	Corinne	F Buckle	—	—
1819	Antar	E Edwards	Catgut	F Buckle	—	—
1820	Pindarrie	F Buckle	Rowena	F Buckle	—	—
1821	Reginald	F Buckle	Zeal	F Buckle	—	—
1822	Pastille	F Buckle	Whizgig	F Buckle	—	—
1823	Nicolo	W Wheatley	Zinc	F Buckle	—	—
1824	Schariar	W Wheatley	Cobweb	J Robinson	—	—
1825	Enamel	J Robinson	Tontine	W Alkover	—	—
1826	Dervise	J B Day	Problem	J Day	—	—
1827	Turcoman	F Buckle	Arab	F Buckle	—	—
1828	Cadland	J Robinson	Zoe	J Robinson	—	—
1829	Patron	F Boyce	B foal by Godolphin	Arnull	—	—
1830	Augustus	P Conolly	Charlotte West	J Robinson	—	—
1831	Riddlesworth	J Robinson	Galantine	P Conolly	—	—
1832	Archibald	Pavis	Galata	Arnull	—	—
1833	Clearwell	J Robinson	Tarantella	Wright	—	—
1834	Glencoe	J Robinson	May-Day	J Day	—	—
1835	Ibrahim	J Robinson	Preserve	E Flatman	—	—
1836	Bay Middleton	J Robinson	Destiny	J Day	—	—
1837	Achmet	E Edwards	Chapeau d'Espagne	J Day	The Duke (Maghull)	Mr Potts
1838	Grey Momus	J B Day	Barcarolle	E Edwards	Sir Henry (Maghull)	T Olliver
1839	The Corsair	Wakefield	Cara	G Edwards	Lottery (Liverpool)	Jem Mason
1840	Crucifix	J B Day	Crucifix	J Day	Jerry	Mr Bretherton
1841	Ralph	J B Day	Potentia	J Robinson	Charity	Mr Powell
1842	Meteor	W Scott	Firebrand	S Rogers	Gaylad	T Olliver
1843	Cotherstone	W Scott	Extempore	S Chifney	Vanguard	T Olliver
1844	The Ugly Buck	J Day Jnr	Sorella	J Robinson	Discount	Crickmere
1845	Idas	E Flatman	Pic-nic	W Abdale	Cure-all	W G Loft
1846	Sir Tatton Sykes	W Scott	Mendicant	S Day	Pioneer	Taylor
1847	Conyngham	J Robinson	Clementina	E Flatman	Matthew	D Wynne
1848	Flatcatcher	J Robinson	Canezou	F Butler	Chandler	Capt Little
1849	Nunnykirk	F Butler	Flea	A Day	Peter Simple	T Cunningham
1850	Pitsford	A Day	Chestnut foal by Slane	F Butler	Abdel Kader	C Green
1851	Hernandez	E Flatman	Aphrodite	J Marson	Abdel Kader	T Abbot
1852	Stockwell	Norman	Kate	A Day	Miss Mowbray	Mr A Goodman
1853	West Australian	F Butler	Mentmore Lass	Charlton	Peter Simple	T Olliver
1854	The Hermit	A Day	Virago	J Wells	Bourton	Tasker
1855	Lord of the Isles	Aldcroft	Habena	S Rogers	Wanderer	J Hanlon
1856	Fazzaletto	E Flatman	Manganese	J Osborne	Freetrader	G Stevens
1857	Vedette	J Osborne	Imperieuse	E Flatman	Emigrant	C Boyce
1858	Fitz-Roland	J Wells	Governess	Ashmall	Little Charley	W Archer
1859	The Promised Land	A Day	Mayonnaise	G Fordham	Half Caste	C Green
1860	The Wizard	Ashmall	Sagitta	Aldcroft	Anatis	Mr Thomas
1861	Diophantus	A Edwards	Nemesis	G Fordham	Jealousy	J Kendall
1862	The Marquis	Ashmall	Hurricane	Ashmall	Huntsman	H Lamplugh
1863	Macaroni	T Challoner	Lady Augusta	A Edwards	Emblem	G Stevens
1864	General Peel	Aldcroft	Tomato	J Wells	Emblematic	G Stevens
1865	Gladiateur	H Grimshaw	Siberia	G Fordham	Alcibiade	Capt Coventry
1866	Lord Lyon	Thomas	Repulse	T Cannon	Salamander	Mr A Goodman
1867	Vauban	G Fordham	Achievement	H Custance	Cortolvin	J Page
1868	Moslem	T Challoner	Formosa	G Fordham	The Lamb	Mr Edwards
1869	Pretender	J Osborne	Scottish Queen	G Fordham	The Colonel	G Stevens
1870	Macgregor	J Daley	Hester	J Grimshaw	The Colonel	G Stevens
1871	Bothwell	J Osborne	Hannah	C Maidment	The Lamb	Mr Thomas
1872	Prince Charlie	J Osborne	Reine	H Parry	Casse Tete	J Page
1873	Gang Forward	T Challoner	Cecilia	J Morris	Disturbance	J M Richardson
1874	Atlantic	F Archer	Apology	J Osborne	Reugny	J M Richardson
1875	Camballo	J Osborne	Spinaway	F Archer	Pathfinder	Mr Thomas
1876	Petrarch	Luke	Camelia	T Glover	Regal	J Cannon
1877	Chamant	J Goater	Belphoebe	H Jeffery	Austerlitz	Mr F G Hobson
1878	Pilgrimage	T Cannon	Pilgrimage	T Cannon	Shifnal	J Jones
1879	Charibert	F Archer	Wheel of Fortune	F Archer	The Liberator	G Moore
1880	Petronel	G Fordham	Elizabeth	C Wood	Empress	T Beasley
1881	Peregrine	F Webb	Thebais	G Fordham	Woodbrook	T Beasley
1882	Shotover	T Cannon	St Marguerite	C Wood	Seaman	Lord Manners

	2000 Guineas		*1000 Guineas*		*Grand National*	
Year	*Horse*	*Jockey*	*Horse*	*Jockey*	*Horse*	*Jockey*
1883	Galliard	F Archer	Hauteur	G Fordham	Zoedone	Count Kinsky
1884	Scot-free	Platt	Busybody	T Cannon	Voluptuary	Mr E P Wilson
1885	Paradox	F Archer	Farewell	G Barrett	Roquefort	Mr E P Wilson
1886	Ormonde	G Barrett	Miss Jummy	J Watts	Old Joe	T Skelton
1887	Enterprise	T Cannon	Reve d'Or	C Wood	Gamecock	W Daniells
1888	Ayrshire	J Osborne	Briar-root	W Warne	Playfair	Mawson
1889	Enthusiast	T Cannon	Minthe	J Woodburn	Frigate	T Beasley
1890	Surefoot	Liddiard	Semolina	J Watts	Ilex	A Nightingall
1891	Common	G Barrett	Mimi	F Rickaby	Come Away	H Beasley
1892	Bonavista	W Robinson	La Fleche	G Barrett	Father O'Flynn	Capt Owen
1893	Isinglass	T Loates	Siffleuse	T Loates	Cloister	Dollery
1894	Ladas	J Watts	Amiable	W Bradford	Why Not	A Nightingall
1895	Kirkconnel	J Watts	Galeottia	F Pratt	Wildman From Borneo	J Widger
1896	St Frusquin	T Loates	Thais	J Watts	The Soarer	D Campbell
1897	Galtee More	C Wood	Chelandry	J Watts	Manifesto	T Kavanagh
1898	Disraeli	S Loates	Nun Nicer	S Loates	Drogheda	J Gourley
1899	Flying Fox	M Cannon	Sibola	J T Sloan	Manifesto	G Williamson
1900	Diamond Jubilee	H Jones	Winifreda	S Loates	Ambush II	A Anthony
1901	Handicapper	W Halsey	Aida	D Maher	Grudon	A Nightingall
1902	Sceptre	H Randall	Sceptre	H Randall	Shannon Lass	D Read
1903	Rock Sand	J H Martin	Quintessence	H Randall	Drumcree	P Woodland
1904	St Amant	K Cannon	Pretty Polly	W Lane	Moifaa	A Birch
1905	Vedas	H Jones	Cherry Lass	G McCall	Kirkland	F Mason
1906	Gorgos	H Jones	Flair	B Dillon	Ascetic's Silver	Hon A Hastings
1907	Slieve Gallion	W Higgs	Witch Elm	B Lynham	Eremon	A Newey
1908	Norman III	O Madden	Rhodora	L Lyne	Rubio	H B Bletsoe
1909	Minoru	H Jones	Electra	B Dillon	Lutteur III	G Parfrement
1910	Neil Gow	D Maher	Winkipop	B Lynham	Jenkinstown	R Chadwick
1911	Sunstar	G Stern	Atmah	F Fox	Glenside	J R Anthony
1912	Sweeper II	D Maher	Tagalie	L H Hewitt	Jerry M	E Piggott
1913	Louvois	J Reiff	Jest	F Rickaby Jnr	Covetcoat	P Woodland
1914	Kennymore	G Stern	Princess Dorrie	W Huxley	Sunloch	W J Smith
1915	Pommern	S Donoghue	Vaucluse	F Rickaby Jnr	Ally Sloper	J R Anthony
1916	Clarissimus	J Clark	Canyon	F Rickaby Jnr	Vermouth	J Reardon
1917	Gay Crusader	S Donoghue	Diadem	F Rickaby Jnr	Ballymacad	E Driscoll
1918	Gainsborough	J Childs	Ferry	B Carslake	Poethlyn	E Piggott
1919	The Panther	R Cooper	Roseway	A Whalley	Poethlyn	E Piggott
1920	Tetratema	B Carslake	Cinna	W Griggs	Troytown	J R Anthony
1921	Craig An Eran	J Brennan	Bettina	G Bellhouse	Shaun Spadah	F B Rees
1922	St Louis	G Archibald	Silver Urn	B Carslake	Music Hall	F B Rees
1923	Ellangowan	C Elliot	Tranquil	E Gardner	Sgt Murphy	Capt Bennet
1924	Diophon	G Hulme	Plack	E C Elliott	Master Robert	R Trudgill
1925	Manna	S Donoghue	Saucy Sue	F Bullock	Double Chance	Major Wilson
1926	Colorado	T Weston	Pillion	R Perryman	Jack Horner	W Watkinson
1927	Adam's Apple	J Leach	Cresta Run	A Balding	Sprig	T E Leader
1928	Flamingo	C Elliot	Scuttle	J Childs	Tipperary Tim	W P Dutton
1929	Mr Jinks	H Beasley	Taj Mah	W Sibbritt	Gregalach	R Everett
1930	Diolite	F Fox	Fair Isle	T Weston	Shaun Goilin	T Cullinan
1931	Cameronian	J Childs	Four Course	E C Elliott	Grakle	R Lyall
1932	Orwell	R Jones	Kandy	E C Elliott	Forbra	J Hamey
1933	Rodosto	R Brethes	Brown Betty	J Childs	Kellsboro Jack	D Williams
1934	Colombo	W Johnstone	Campanula	H Wragg	Golden Miller	G Wilson
1935	Bahram	F Fox	Mesa	W R Johnstone	Reynoldstown	F C Furlong
1936	Pay Up	R Dick	Tide-Way	R Perryman	Reynoldstown	F T Walwyn
1937	Le Ksar	C Semblat	Exhibitionist	S Donoghue	Royal Mail	E Williams
1938	Pasch	G Richards	Rockfel	S Wragg	Battleship	Bruce Hobbs
1939	Blue Peter	E Smith	Galatea II	R A Jones	Workman	T Hyde
1940	Djebel	C Elliot	Godiva	D Marks	Bogskar	M Jones
1941	Lambert Simnel	C Elliot	Dancing Time	R Perryman	no race	—
1942	Big Game	G Richards	Sun Chariot	G Richards	no race	—
1943	Kingsway	S Wragg	Herringbone	H Wragg	no race	—
1944	Garden Path	H Wragg	Picture Play	E C Elliott	no race	—
1945	Court Martial	C Richards	Sun Stream	H Wragg	no race	—
1946	Happy Knight	T Weston	Hypericum	D Smith	Lovely Cottage	Capt R Petre
1947	Tudor Minstrel	G Richards	Imprudence	W R Johnstone	Caughoo	E Dempsey
1948	My Babu	C Smirke	Queenpot	G Richards	Sheila's Cottage	A P Thompson
1949	Nimbus	C Elliot	Musidora	E Britt	Russian Hero	L McMorrow
1950	Palestine	C Smirke	Camaree	W R Johnstone	Freebooter	J Power
1951	Ki Ming	A Breasley	Belle Of All	G Richards	Nickel Coin	J A Bullock
1952	Thunderhead II	R Poincelet	Zabara	K Gethin	Teal	A P Thompson
1953	Nearula	E Britt	Happy Laughter	E Mercer	Early Mist	B Marshall
1954	Darius	E Mercer	Festoon	A Breasley	Royal Tan	B Marshall
1955	Our Babu	D Smith	Meld	W H Carr	Quare Times	P Taaffe
1956	Gilles de Retz	F Barlow	Honeylight	E Britt	E.S.B.	D V Dick
1957	Crepello	L Piggott	Rose Royale II	C Smirke	Sundew	F Winter
1958	Pall Mall	D Smith	Bella Paola	S Boullenger	Mr What	A R Freeman
1959	Taboun	G Moore	Petite Etoile	D Smith	Oxo	M Scudamore

Year	2000 Guineas Horse	Jockey	1000 Guineas Horse	Jockey	Grand National Horse	Jockey
1960	Martial	R Hutchinson	Never Too Late	R Poincelet	Merryman II	G Scott
1961	Rockavon	N Stirk	Sweet Solera	W Rickaby	Nicolaus Silver	R Beasley
1962	Privy Councillor	W Rickaby	Abermaid	W Williamson	Kilmore	F Winter
1963	Only For Life	J Lindley	Hula Dancer	R Poincelet	Ayala	P Buckley
1964	Baldric II	W Pyers	Pourparler	G Bougoure	Team Spirit	W Robinson
1965	Niksar	D Keith	Night Off	W Williamson	Jay Trump	T Smith
1966	Kashmir II	J Lindley	Glad Rags	P Cook	Anglo	T Norman
1967	Royal Palace	G Moore	Fleet	G Moore	Foinavon	J Buckingham
1968	Sir Ivor	L Piggott	Caergwrle	A Barclay	Red Alligator	B Fletcher
1969	Right Tack	G Lewis	Full Dress II	R Hutchinson	Highland Wedding	E Harty
1970	Nijinsky	L Piggott	Humble Duty	L Piggott	Gay Trip	P Taaffe
1971	Brigadier Gerard	J Mercer	Altesse Royale	Y Saint-Martin	Specify	J Cook
1972	High Top	W Carson	Waterloo	E Hide	Well To Do	G Thorner
1973	Mon Fils	F Durr	Mysterious	G Lewis	Red Rum	B Fletcher
1974	Nonoalco	Y Saint-Martin	Highclere	J Mercer	Red Rum	B Fletcher
1975	Bolkonski	G Dettori	Nocturnal Spree	J Roe	L'Escargot	T Carberry
1976	Wollow	G Dettori	Flying Water	Y Saint-Martin	Rag Trade	J Burke
1977	Nebbiolo	G Curran	Mrs McArdy	E Hide	Red Rum	T Stack
1978	Roland Gardens	F Durr	Enstone Spark	E Johnson	Lucius	R Davies
1979	Tap on Wood	S Cauthen	One in a Million	J Mercer	Rubstic	M Barnes
1980	Known Fact	W Carson	Quick as Lightning	B Rouse	Ben Nevis	C Fenwick
1981	To-Agori-Mou	G Starkey	Fairy Footsteps	L Piggott	Aldaniti	R Champion
1982	Zino	F Head	On the House	J Reid	Grittar	R Saunders
1983	Lomond	P Eddery	Ma Biche	F Head	Corbiere	B De Haan
1984	El Gran Señor	P Eddery	Pebbles	P Robinson	Hallo Dandy	N Doughty
1985	Shadeed	L Piggott	Oh So Sharp	S Cauthen	Last Suspect	H Davies
1986	Dancing Brave	G Starkey	Midway Lady	R Cochrane	West Tip	R Dunwoody
1987	Don't Forget Me	W Carson	Miesque	F Head	Maori Venture	S Knight
1988	Doyoun	W Swinburn	Ravinella	G Moore	Rhyme 'n Reason	B Powell
1989	Nashwan	W Carson	Musical Bliss	W Swinburn	Little Polveir	J Frost
1990	Tirol	M Kinane	Salsabil	W Carson	Mr Frisk	Mr M Armytage
1991	Mystiko	M Roberts	Shadayid	W Carson	Seagram	N Hawke
1992	Rodrigo De Triano	L Piggott	Hatoof	W Swinburn	Party Politics	C Llewellyn
1993	Zafonic	P Eddery	Sayyedati	W Swinburn	no race	—
1994	Mr Baileys	J Weaver	Las Meninas	J Reid	Minnehoma	R Dunwoody
1995	Pennekamp	T Jarnet	Harayir	R Hills	Royal Athlete	J Titley
1996	Mark of Esteem	L Dettori	Bosra Sham	P Eddery	Rough Quest	M Fitzgerald
1997	Entrepreneur	M J Kinane	Sleepytime	K Fallon	Lord Gyllene	A Dobbin
1998	King of Kings	M J Kinane	Cape Verdi	L Dettori	Earth Summit	C Llewellyn
1999	Island Sands	L Dettori	Wince	K Fallon	Bobbyjo	P Carberry
2000	King's Best	K Fallon	Lahan	R Hills	Papillon	R Walsh
2001	Golan	K Fallon	Ameerat	P Robinson	Red Marauder	R Guest
2002	Rock of Gibraltar	J Murtagh	Kazzia	L Dettori	Bindaree	J Culloty
2003	Refuse to Bend	P Smullen	Russian Rhythm	K Fallon	Monty's Pass	B Geraghty
2004	Haafhd	R Hills	Attraction	K Darley	Amberleigh House	G Lee
2005	Footstepsinthe-sand	K Fallon	Virginia Waters	K Fallon	Hedgehunter	R Walsh
2006	George Washington	K Fallon	Speciosa	M Fenton	Numbersixvalverde	N Madden
2007	Cockney Rebel	O Peslier	Finsceal Beo	K Manning	Silver Birch	R Power
2008	Henrythenavigator	J Murtagh	Natagora	C Lemaire	Comply or Die	T Murphy
2009	Sea the Stars	M Kinane	Ghanaati	R Hills	Mon Mome	L Treadwell
2010	Makfi	C Lemaire	Special Duty	S Pasquier	Don't Push It	A P McCoy
2011	Frankel	T Queally	Blue Bunting	L Dettori	Ballabriggs	J Maguire
2012	Camelot	J O'Brien	Homecoming Queen	R Moore	Neptune Collonges	D Jacob
2013	Dawn Approach	K Manning	Sky Lantern	R Hughes	Auroras Encore	R Mania

Horse Racing: General Information

all weather tracks: UK	Kempton, Lingfield, Southwell, Wolverhampton, Great Leighs (currently closed)
autumn double	Cesarewitch and Cambridgeshire
champion flat jockey: 13 times in a row	E Flatman (1840–52) and Fred Archer (1874–86) but AP McCoy currently has 18 NH in a row
champion jockey: shot himself	Fred Archer (aged 29)
Cheltenham Gold Cup: won five times in row	Golden Miller (1932–36)
classics: jockey won most	Lester Piggott (30)
crash helmets: made compulsory	1924
Derby: inaugurated by	Sir Charles Bunbury
Derby: longest winning distance	Shergar (10 lengths)
Derby: where run during WW2	Newmarket (1940–45)
Ffos Las Racecourse	Situated in Trimsaran, Carmarthenshire; first new NH course in 80 years, opened on 18 June 2009. Also holds flat meetings.
flat jockey: champion most times	Gordon Richards (26)
Fred Archer: nickname	The Tinman
French Derby: run	Chantilly
Gary Bardwell: nickname	The Angry Ant

Grand National winner: future monarch owned Ambush II (King Edward VII in 1900)
Grand National: 1st woman jockey Charlotte Brew (1977)
Grand National: 1st woman jockey to complete Geraldine Rees
Grand National: number of fences 30
Grand National: royal horse that collapsed Devon Loch, ridden by Dick Francis
Grand National: where run during WW1 Gatwick (1916–18) as 'War National Chase' (1917–18), and 'Race Course Association Chase' 1916
Grand National: youngest winning rider Bruce Hobbs on Battleship in 1938 aged 17
harness racing: gaits trotting (striding with horse's left front and right rear leg synchronised)
pacing (moving both legs on one side of body at the same time)
harness racing: vehicle pulled sulky
Harry Wragg: nickname The Head Waiter
Irish Classics: run all at the Curragh
Irish Grand National: run Fairyhouse
Irish Grand National: woman jockey won Ann Ferris
jockey: 1st knighted Gordon Richards
Lester Piggott: 1st winner The Chase (1948)
Lester Piggott: nickname The Long Fellow
mare: age filly becomes five
Melbourne Cup: run Flemington Park
Oaks: where run during WW2 Newmarket (1940–45)
pacing: US Triple Crown William H Cane Futurity (1955); Messenger Stake (1957); Little Brown Jug (1946)
racehorse birthdays 1 January (Northern Hemisphere) and 1 August (Southern Hemisphere)
racehorses: maximum letters in name 18
racing colours: Her Majesty the Queen purple, gold braid, scarlet sleeves, black velvet cap with gold fringe
racing colours: Queen Mother blue, buff stripes, blue sleeves, black cap, gold tassel
Scottish Grand National: run Ayr
spring double Lincoln and Grand National
stallion: age colt becomes five
starting stalls: 1st used in UK Newmarket in 1965 (8 July)
thoroughbred: ancestry Darley Arabian, Byerly Turk, Godolphin Arabian (aka barb)
trotting: US Triple Crown Hambleton (commenced 1926); Yonkers Futurity (1958); Kentucky Futurity (1893)
US Triple Crown Kentucky Derby (1st of the season), Preakness Stakes, Belmont Stakes (last of the season)
virtual racetracks Portman Park (Flat) Steepledown (Jumps)
Welsh Grand National: run Chepstow

Motor Racing: Formula 1 World Champions

Year	*Winning driver*	*Country*	*Car*	*Runner-up*	*Constructor*
1950	Giuseppe Farina	Italy	Alfa Romeo	Juan Manuel Fangio	—
1951	Juan Manuel Fangio	Argentina	Alfa Romeo	Alberto Ascari	—
1952	Alberto Ascari	Italy	Ferrari	Giuseppe Farina	—
1953	Alberto Ascari	Italy	Ferrari	Juan Manuel Fangio	—
1954	Juan Manuel Fangio	Argentina	Maserati/Mercedes	Jose Gonzalez (Argentina)	—
1955	Juan Manuel Fangio	Argentina	Mercedes-Benz	Stirling Moss (GB)	—
1956	Juan Manuel Fangio	Argentina	Lancia-Ferrari	Stirling Moss (GB)	—
1957	Juan Manuel Fangio	Argentina	Maserati	Stirling Moss (GB)	—
1958	Mike Hawthorn	UK	Ferrari	Stirling Moss (GB)	Vanwall
1959	Jack Brabham	Australia	Cooper-Climax	Tony Brooks (GB)	Cooper-Climax
1960	Jack Brabham	Australia	Cooper-Climax	Bruce McLaren (NZL)	Cooper-Climax
1961	Phil Hill	USA	Ferrari	Wolfgang von Trips (W. Germany)	Ferrari
1962	Graham Hill	UK	BRM	Jim Clark	BRM
1963	Jim Clark	UK	Lotus-Climax	Graham Hill	Lotus-Climax
1964	John Surtees	UK	Ferrari	Graham Hill	Ferrari
1965	Jim Clark	UK	Lotus-Climax	Graham Hill	Lotus-Climax
1966	Jack Brabham	Australia	Brabham-Repco	John Surtees	Brabham-Repco
1967	Denny Hulme	New Zealand	Brabham-Repco	Jack Brabham	Brabham-Repco
1968	Graham Hill	UK	Lotus-Ford	Jackie Stewart	Lotus-Ford
1969	Jackie Stewart	UK	Matra-Ford	Jacky Ickx (Belgium)	Matra-Ford
1970	Jochen Rindt	Austria	Lotus-Ford	Jacky Ickx (Belgium)	Lotus-Ford
1971	Jackie Stewart	UK	Tyrrell-Ford	Ronnie Peterson (Sweden)	Tyrrell-Ford
1972	Emerson Fittipaldi	Brazil	Lotus-Ford	Jackie Stewart	Lotus-Ford
1973	Jackie Stewart	UK	Tyrrell-Ford	Emerson Fittipaldi	Lotus-Ford
1974	Emerson Fittipaldi	Brazil	McLaren-Ford	Clay Regazzoni (Switzerland)	McLaren-Ford
1975	Niki Lauda	Austria	Ferrari	Emerson Fittipaldi	Ferrari
1976	James Hunt	UK	McLaren-Ford	Niki Lauda	Ferrari
1977	Niki Lauda	Austria	Ferrari	Jody Scheckter	Ferrari
1978	Mario Andretti	USA	Lotus-Ford	Ronnie Peterson (Sweden)	Lotus-Ford
1979	Jody Scheckter	South Africa	Ferrari	Gilles Villeneuve (Canada)	Ferrari
1980	Alan Jones	Australia	Williams-Ford	Nelson Piquet	Williams-Ford
1981	Nelson Piquet	Brazil	Brabham-Ford	Carlos Reutemann (Argentina)	Williams-Ford
1982	Keke Rosberg	Finland	Williams-Ford	J Watson (GB) and D Pironi (France)	Ferrari
1983	Nelson Piquet	Brazil	Brabham-BMW	Alain Prost	Ferrari
1984	Niki Lauda	Austria	McLaren-TAG	Alain Prost	McLaren-TAG
1985	Alain Prost	France	McLaren-TAG	Michele Alboreto (Italy)	McLaren-TAG
1986	Alain Prost	France	McLaren-TAG	Nigel Mansell	Williams-Honda
1987	Nelson Piquet	Brazil	Williams-Honda	Nigel Mansell	Williams-Honda
1988	Ayrton Senna	Brazil	McLaren-Honda	Alain Prost	McLaren-Honda
1989	Alain Prost	France	McLaren-Honda	Ayrton Senna	McLaren-Honda
1990	Ayrton Senna	Brazil	McLaren-Honda	Alain Prost	McLaren-Honda

Year	*Winning driver*	*Country*	*Car*	*Runner-up*	*Constructor*
1991	Ayrton Senna	Brazil	McLaren-Honda	Nigel Mansell	McLaren-Honda
1992	Nigel Mansell	UK	Williams-Renault	Ricardo Patrese (Italy)	Williams-Renault
1993	Alain Prost	France	Williams-Renault	Ayrton Senna	Williams-Renault
1994	Michael Schumacher	Germany	Benetton-Ford	Damon Hill	Williams-Renault
1995	Michael Schumacher	Germany	Benetton-Renault	Damon Hill	Williams-Renault
1996	Damon Hill	UK	Williams-Renault	Jacques Villeneuve	Williams-Renault
1997	Jacques Villeneuve	Canada	Williams-Renault	Michael Schumacher	Williams-Renault
1998	Mika Hakkinen	Finland	McLaren-Mercedes	Michael Schumacher	McLaren-Mercedes
1999	Mika Hakkinen	Finland	McLaren-Mercedes	Eddie Irvine	Ferrari
2000	Michael Schumacher	Germany	Ferrari	Mika Hakkinen	Ferrari
2001	Michael Schumacher	Germany	Ferrari	David Coulthard (UK)	Ferrari
2002	Michael Schumacher	Germany	Ferrari	Rubens Barrichello (Brazil)	Ferrari
2003	Michael Schumacher	Germany	Ferrari	Kimi Raikkonen (Finland)	Ferrari
2004	Michael Schumacher	Germany	Ferrari	Rubens Barrichello (Brazil)	Ferrari
2005	Fernando Alonso	Spain	Renault	Kimi Raikkonen (Finland)	McLaren-Mercedes
2006	Fernando Alonso	Spain	Renault	Michael Schumacher	Ferrari
2007	Kimi Raikkonen	Finland	Ferrari	Lewis Hamilton	McLaren
2008	Lewis Hamilton	UK	McLaren	Felipe Massa (Brazil)	Ferrari
2009	Jenson Button	UK	Brawn	Sebastian Vettel	Red Bull
2010	Sebastian Vettel	Germany	Red Bull	Fernando Alonso	Red Bull
2011	Sebastian Vettel	Germany	Red Bull	Jenson Button	Red Bull
2012	Sebastian Vettel	Germany	Red Bull	Fernando Alonso	Red Bull

Motor Racing: General Information

circuits: Formula 1 Abu Dhabi – Yas Marina; Argentinian – Buenos Aires; Australian – Adelaide, Melbourne; Austrian – A1 Ring, Spielberg; Bahrain – Bahrain International Circuit; Belgian – Spa-Francorchamps, Zolder; Brazilian – São Paolo, Interlagos (pre-1990 Jacarepagua circuit, Rio de Janeiro); British – Silverstone; Canadian – Montreal; Chinese – Shanghai International; Dutch – Zandvoort; European – Nurburgring, Germany; French – Magny Cours, Dijon; German – Hockenheim; Hungarian – Budapest; Italian – Monza; Japanese – Suzuka; Korean – Yeongam; Malaysian – Sepang; Mexican – Mexico City; Monaco – Monte Carlo; Portuguese – Estoril; San Marino – Imola; Spanish – Catalunya Montjuich (Barcelona); Turkish – Istanbul; US – Detroit, Long Beach, Indianapolis.
Nurburgring is no longer used for German GP but has been the venue of the European GP in recent years. Similarly, Aida in Japan is no longer used for its own GP but has been the venue for Pacific GP.

Formula 1: flags black – disqualification of a driver; black and white chequered – end of race; blue – car about to overtake; red – premature end of race; yellow – danger, no overtaking; yellow and red diagonal stripes – oil on track.

Formula 1: most consecutive wins Alberto Ascari (9).

Formula 1: oldest champion Juan Manuel Fangio (46).

Formula 1: points system From the 2003 season onwards points were awarded for the top eight finishers thus: 10, 8, 6, 5, 4, 3, 2, 1. From 2010 the top ten drivers score poiints thus: 25, 18, 15, 12, 10, 8, 6, 4, 2, 1.

Formula 1: posthumous champion Jochen Rindt (1970).

Formula 1: woman driver, first Maria Teresa de Filippis (1958)

fuel: used in Formula 1 pre 1961 nitro-methane, but since 1961 ordinary commercial fuel has been compulsory, although Indianapolis still uses nitro-methane.

Indianapolis 500: first winner Ray Harroun in Marmon Wasp (1911).

Indianapolis 500: laps 200 (although the race is 500 miles in length, hence the name).

Indianapolis 500: Formula 1 winners Jim Clark (1965), Graham Hill (1966), Mario Andretti (1969), E Fittipaldi (1989 and 1993), J Villeneuve (1995).

land speed record: holder Andy Green in Thrust SSC (760 mph) October 1997. The first over 100 mph: Louis Rigolly in 1904.

Monaco GP: five times winner Graham Hill.

most victories Michael Schumacher – 91 GP wins and 68 pole positions.

motor cycling: nine championships Giacomo Agostini of Italy (eight consecutive 1965–72 and 1975 in the 500 cc class).

speedway championships raced over four laps, the short track world championships commenced in 1936 and long track in 1971.

UK motor racing circuit: first Brooklands.

Olympic Games: Venues

1896	Athens, Greece	1936	Berlin, Germany	1980	Moscow, USSR
1900	Paris, France	1948	London, UK	1984	Los Angeles, USA
1904	St Louis, USA	1952	Helsinki, Finland	1988	Seoul, South Korea
1908	London, UK	1956	Melbourne, Australia	1992	Barcelona, Spain
1912	Stockholm, Sweden	1960	Rome, Italy	1996	Atlanta, USA
1920	Antwerp, Belgium	1964	Tokyo, Japan	2000	Sydney, Australia
1924	Paris, France	1968	Mexico City	2004	Athens, Greece
1928	Amsterdam, Holland	1972	Munich, Germany	2008	Beijing, China
1932	Los Angeles, USA	1976	Montreal, Canada	2012	London, UK
				2016	Rio de Janeiro, Brazil

Winter Olympics: Venues

1924	Chamonix, France	1964	Innsbruck, Austria	1994	Lillehammer, Norway
1928	St Moritz, Switzerland	1968	Grenoble, France	1998	Nagano, Japan
1932	Lake Placid, NY, USA	1972	Sapporo, Japan	2002	Salt Lake City, USA
1936	Garmisch Partenkirchen, Germany	1976	Innsbruck, Austria	2006	Turin, Italy
1948	St Moritz, Switzerland	1980	Lake Placid, NY, USA	2010	Vancouver, Canada
1952	Oslo, Norway	1984	Sarajevo, Yugoslavia	2014	Sochi, Russia
1956	Cortina, Italy	1988	Calgary, Canada	2018	Pyeongchang, South Korea
1960	Squaw Valley, California, USA	1992	Albertville, France		

Olympics: General Information

ancient Olympics: in honour of Zeus.
appearances: most Raymondo d'Inzeo (8).
black power salute Tommie Smith and John Carlos 1968. (Other man on rostrum was Peter Norman of Australia.)
Briton took part in Summer and Winter Olympics Derek Allhusen.
British peer gold medallist The Marquess of Exeter (Lord Burghley) 1928, 400m Hurdles.
cancelled games: intended hosts 1916 – Berlin; 1940 – Tokyo (then Helsinki); 1944 – London.
champions: father and son Imre Nemeth (Hammer) and Miklos Nemeth (Javelin).
champion: five times in row Steve Redgrave (Rowing 1984–2000).
champion: four times in row Al Oerter (Discus 1956–68), Carl Lewis (Long Jump 1984–96)
cheat: Modern Pentathlon Boris Onischenko in Fencing discipline (1976).
country contested every games UK (both Summer and Winter).
diplomas awarded to fourth to eighth places.
equestrian: disqualification Cian O'Connor of Ireland was stripped of his gold medal won in the Individual Show Jumping event in 2004 following a positive drug test on his horse, Waterford Crystal.
equestrian events: 1956 held in Stockholm.
extra lap run in error Steeplechase 1932.
father and son rowing gold medallists Charles and Richard Burnell.
flag: colours blue, yellow, black, green, red rings on a white background. (Rings represent the five major continents.)
gold medals: last given 1912 was the last time solid gold medals were given.
gold medal: received by post Harold Abrahams (1924).
golds: most in single games Mark Spitz (7) (Swimming 1972).
high jump: youngest champion Ulrike Mayfarth (16), who was also the oldest winner aged 28.
host country: no golds Canada (1976).
IOC: presidents Dimitrios Vikélas (1894–96); Baron de Coubertin (1896–1925); Henri de Baillet-La Tour (1925–42); J. Sigfrid Edström (1946–52); Avery Brundage (1956–72); Michael Morris, Lord Killanin (1972–80); Juan António Samaranch (1980–2001); Jacques Rogge (2001–).
marathon: barefoot winner Abebe Bikila (1960).
marathon: distance standardised 1924 (although first run as 26 miles 385 yds in 1908).
medal withheld for professionalism Jim Thorpe in 1912 (he was reinstated in 1973).
modern Olympics: instigator Baron Pierre de Coubertin.
Munich massacre Black September terrorists killing of Israeli athletes (1972).
oldest Briton to win gold medal Jerry Milner (60 years old in 1908 when winning Shooting gold).
Olympiad: definition in ancient Greece the time between games was an Olympiad (four years).
Olympic motto Citius Altius Fortius (Faster, Higher, Stronger).
opening parade always led by Greece and completed by the host country.
original location Olympia (776 BC–AD 393, abolished by Emperor Theodosius I).
POW in World War Two Harold Cassells (1920 Hockey gold medallist).
sex testing: year began 1968.
swimming: first 100m under 1 minute Johnny Weismuller (1924) (59 seconds).
walkover: champion Wyndham Halswelle in the 400m (1908).
woman gold medallist: first Charlotte Cooper (GB) when she won Tennis Singles (1900).
woman: running, throwing, jumping medals Mildred 'Babe' Didrikson won gold in 80m Hurdles and Javelin and silver medal in High Jump (1932).
Zatopek gold medal treble In 1952 Emil Zatopek won 5k, 10k and Marathon.

Summer Olympics: British Gold Medal Winners

Name	*Date*	*Sport*	*Event*
Abrahams, Harold	1924	Athletics	4 x 100m Relay
Adams, Nicola	2012	Boxing	Women's Flyweight
Adlington, Rebecca	2008	Swimming	400m Freestyle
	2008	Swimming	800m Freestyle
Ainslie, Ben	2000	Sailing	Laser Class
	2004	Sailing	Finn Class
	2008	Sailing	Finn Class
	2012	Sailing	Finn Class
Ainsworth-Davis, Jack	1920	Athletics	4 x 400m Relay
Allhusen, Derek	1968	Equestrian	3-Day Event – Team
Amoore, Edward	1908	Shooting	Small-Bore Rifle Team
Applegarth, Willie	1912	Athletics	4 x 100m Relay
Aspin, John	1908	Yachting	12 Metres Class
Astor, J J	1908	Rackets	Doubles
Atkin, Charles	1920	Hockey	
Attrill, Louis	2000	Rowing	Coxed Eight
Ayton, Sarah	2004	Sailing	Yngling Class
	2008	Sailing	Yngling Class
Bacon, Stanley	1908	Wrestling	Middleweight Freestyle
Badcock, Felix	1932	Rowing	Coxless Fours
Bailey, Horace	1908	Football	
Baillie, Timothy	2012	Canoeing	Slalom C-2
Baillon, Louis	1908	Hockey	
Barber, Paul	1988	Hockey	
Barrett, Edward	1908	Tug of War	

Name	*Date*	*Sport*	*Event*
Barrett, Frederick	1920	Polo	
Barrett, Roper	1908	Lawn Tennis	Indoor Men's Doubles
Barridge, J E	1900	Football	
Bartlett, Charles	1908	Cycling	100km Track Race
Batchelor, Steve	1988	Hockey	
Beachcroft, Charles	1900	Cricket	
Bechtolsheimer, Laura	2012	Equestrian	Team Dressage
Beesly, Richard	1928	Rowing	Coxless Fours
Belville, Miles	1936	Yachting	6 Metres Class
Bennett, Charles	1900	Athletics	1500m
	1900	Athletics	5000m Team
Bennett, John	1920	Hockey	
Bentham, Isaac	1912	Swimming	Water Polo Team
Beresford, Jack	1924	Rowing	Single Sculls
	1932	Rowing	Coxless Fours
	1936	Rowing	Double Sculls
Beresford, John	1900	Polo	
Berry, Arthur	1908	Football	
	1912	Football	
Bevan, Edward	1928	Rowing	Coxless Fours
Bhaura, Kulbir	1988	Hockey	
Bingley, Norman	1908	Yachting	7 Metres Class
Birkett, Arthur	1900	Cricket	
Blackstaffe, Harry	1908	Rowing	Single Sculls
Boardman, Chris	1936	Yachting	6 Metres Class
Boardman, Chris	1992	Cycling	4000m Pursuit
Bond, David	1948	Yachting	Swallow Class
Bowerman, Alfred	1900	Cricket	
Brabants, Tim	2008	Canoeing	Flatwater K-1 1000m
Braithwaite, Bob	1968	Shooting	Clay Pigeon
Brash, Scott	2012	Equestrian	Team Showjumping
Brasher, Chris	1956	Athletics	3000m Steeplechase
Brebner, Ron	1912	Football	
Brown, Godfrey	1936	Athletics	4 x 400m Relay
Brownlee, Alistair	2012	Triathlon	Individual
Buchanan, John	1908	Yachting	12 Metres Class
Buckenham, Claude	1900	Football	
Buckley, George	1900	Cricket	
Bucknall, Henry	1908	Rowing	Eights
Budgett, Richard	1984	Rowing	Coxed Fours
Bugbee, Charlie	1912	Swimming	Water Polo Team
	1920	Swimming	Water Polo Team
Bullen, Jane	1968	Equestrian	3-Day Event Team
Bunten, James	1908	Yachting	12 Metres Class
Burchell, Francis	1900	Cricket	
Burgess, Edgar	1912	Rowing	Eights
Burghley, Lord David	1928	Athletics	400m Hurdles
Burke, Steven	2012	Cycling	Team Pursuit
Burn, Tom	1912	Football	
Burnell, Charles	1908	Rowing	Eights
Burnell, Richard	1948	Rowing	Double Sculls
Bushnell, Bertie	1948	Rowing	Double Sculls
Butler, Guy	1920	Athletics	4 x 400m Relay
Campbell, Charles	1908	Yachting	8 Metres Class
Campbell, Colin	1920	Hockey	
Campbell, Darren	2004	Athletics	4 x 100m Relay
Campbell, Luke	2012	Boxing	Bantamweight
Canning, George	1920	Tug of War	
Carnell, Arthur	1908	Shooting	Small-Bore Rifle
Cassels, Harold	1920	Hockey	
Chalk, Alfred	1900	Football	
Chapman, Frederick	1908	Football	
Charles, Peter	2012	Equestrian	Team Showjumping
Christian, Fred	1900	Cricket	
Christie, Linford	1992	Athletics	100m
Clancy, Ed	2008	Cycling	Team Pursuit
	2012	Cycling	Team Pursuit
Clift, Robert	1988	Hockey	
Clive, Lewis	1932	Rowing	Coxless Pairs
Coales, Bill	1908	Athletics	3 Miles Team
Cochrane, Blair	1908	Yachting	8 Metres Class
Coe, Sebastian	1980	Athletics	1,500m
	1984	Athletics	1,500m
Coe, Tom	1900	Swimming	Water Polo Team
Coleman, Robert	1920	Yachting	7 Metres Class
Coode, Ed	2004	Rowing	Coxless Fours
Cook, Stephanie	2000	Modern Pentathlon	Individual Event
Cooke, Harold	1920	Hockey	
Cooke, Nicole	2008	Cycling	Road Race

Name	*Date*	*Sport*	*Event*
Cooper, Charlotte	1900	Lawn Tennis	Women's Singles
	1900	Lawn Tennis	Mixed Doubles
Cooper, Malcolm	1984	Shooting	Small-Bore Rifle, three positions
	1988	Shooting	Small-Bore Rifle, three positions
Copeland, Katherine	2012	Rowing	Women's Lightweight Double Sculls
Corbett, Walter	1908	Football	
Corner, Harry	1900	Cricket	
Cornet, George	1908	Swimming	Water Polo Team
	1912	Swimming	Water Polo Team
Cracknell, James	2000	Rowing	Coxless Fours
	2004	Rowing	Coxless Fours
Crichton, Charles	1908	Yachting	6 Metres Class
Crockford, Eric	1920	Hockey	
Cross, Martin	1984	Rowing	Coxed Fours
Crummack, Rex	1920	Hockey	
Cudmore, Collier	1908	Rowing	Coxless Fours
Cuming, Fred	1900	Cricket	
Currie, Lorne	1900	Yachting	Open Class
	1900	Yachting	0.5–1 Ton Class
Daly, Denis	1900	Polo	
D'Arcy, Vic	1912	Athletics	4 x 100m Relay
Davies, Chris	1972	Yachting	Flying Dutchman Class
Davies, Lynn	1964	Athletics	Long Jump
De Relwyskow, George	1908	Wrestling	Lightweight Freestyle
Deakin, Joe	1908	Athletics	3 Miles Team Race
Dean, Billy	1920	Swimming	Water Polo Team
DeGale, James	2008	Boxing	Middleweight
Dennis, Simon	2000	Rowing	Coxed Eight
Derbyshire, Rob	1900	Swimming	Water Polo Team
	1908	Swimming	4 x 200m Freestyle Relay
Devonish, Marlon	2004	Athletics	4 x 100m Relay
Dines, Joe	1912	Football	
Dixon, Charles	1912	Lawn Tennis	Indoor Mixed Doubles
Dixon, Richard	1908	Yachting	7 Metres Class
Dod, William (brother of Lottie)	1908	Archery	York Round
Dodds, Richard	1988	Hockey	
Doherty, Laurie	1900	Lawn Tennis	Men's Singles
	1900	Lawn Tennis	Men's Doubles
Doherty, Reggie	1900	Lawn Tennis	Men's Doubles
(brother of Laurie Doherty)	1900	Lawn Tennis	Mixed Doubles
	1908	Lawn Tennis	Men's Doubles
Donne, William	1900	Cricket	
Douglas, Johnny	1908	Boxing	Middleweight
Douglas, Rowley	2000	Rowing	Coxed Eight
Downes, Arthur	1908	Yachting	12 Metres Class
Downes, Henry (Arthur's brother)	1908	Yachting	12 Metres Class
Dujardin, Charlotte	2012	Equestrian	Team Dressage
	2012	Equestrian	Individual Dressage
Dunlop, David	1908	Yachting	12 Metres Class
Easte, Philip	1908	Shooting	Clay Pigeon Team
Eastlake-Smith, Gladys	1908	Lawn Tennis	Indoor Women's Singles
Edwards, Jonathan	2000	Athletics	Triple Jump
Edwards, Jumbo	1932	Rowing	Coxless Pairs
	1932	Rowing	Coxless Fours
Eley, Maxwell	1924	Rowing	Coxless Fours
Elliot, Launceston	1896	Weightlifting	One-Handed Lift
Ellison, Adrian	1984	Rowing	Coxed Fours (cox)
Ennis, Jessica	2012	Athletics	Women's Heptathlon
Etherington-Smith, Raymond	1908	Rowing	Eights
Exshaw, William	1900	Yachting	2–3 Ton Class
Farah, Mo	2012	Athletics	5,000mts
	2012	Athletics	10,000mts
Faulds, Richard	2000	Shooting	Double Trap
Faulkner, David	1988	Hockey	
Fenning, John	1908	Rowing	Coxless Pairs
Field-Richards, John	1908	Motor Boating	8 Metres Class
Finnegan, Chris	1968	Boxing	Middleweight
Fleming, John	1908	Shooting	Small-Bore Rifle, moving target
Fleming, Philip	1912	Rowing	Eights
Fletcher, Jennie	1912	Swimming	4 x 100m Freestyle Relay
Forsyth, Charlie	1908	Swimming	Water Polo Team
Foster, Bill	1908	Swimming	4 x 200m Freestyle Relay
Foster, Tim	2000	Rowing	Coxless Fours
Fox, Jim	1976	Modern Pentathlon	Team Event
Freeman, Harry	1908	Hockey	
Garcia, Russell	1988	Hockey	
Gardener, Jason	2004	Athletics	4 x 100m Relay
Garton, Stanley	1912	Rowing	Eights
George, Rowland	1932	Rowing	Coxless Fours

Name	*Date*	*Sport*	*Event*
Gillan, Angus	1908	Rowing	Coxless Fours
	1912	Rowing	Eights
Gladstone, Albert	1908	Rowing	Eights
Glen-Coats, Thomas	1908	Yachting	12 Metres Class
Glover, Helen	2012	Rowing	Women's Coxless Pair
Godfree, Kitty	1920	Lawn Tennis	Women's Doubles
Goodfellow, Fred	1908	Tug of War	
Goodhew, Duncan	1980	Swimming	100m Breaststroke
Goodison, Paul	2008	Sailing	Laser Class
Gordon-Watson, Mary	1972	Equestrian	3-Day Event Team
Gore, Arthur	1908	Lawn Tennis	Indoor Men's Singles
	1908	Lawn Tennis	Indoor Men's Doubles
Gosling, William	1900	Football	
Grace, Fred	1908	Boxing	Lightweight
Grainger, Katherine	2012	Rowing	Women's Double Sculls
Green, Eric	1908	Hockey	
Green, Tommy	1932	Athletics	50km Walk
Gregory, Alex	2012	Rowing	Men's Coxless Four
Gretton, John (serving MP)	1900	Yachting	Open Class
	1900	Yachting	0.5–1 Ton Class
Griffiths, Cecil	1920	Athletics	4 x 400m Relay
Grimley, Martyn	1988	Hockey	
Grinham, Judy	1956	Swimming	100m Backstroke
Grubor, Luka	2000	Rowing	Coxed Eight
Gunn, Dick	1908	Boxing	Featherweight
Gunnell, Sally	1992	Athletics	400m Hurdles
Halswelle, Wyndham	1908	Athletics	400m
Hampson, Tommy	1932	Athletics	800m
Hannam, Edith	1912	Lawn Tennis	Indoor Women's Singles
	1912	Lawn Tennis	Indoor Mixed Doubles
Hanney, Ted	1912	Football	
Hardman, Harry	1908	Football	
Harmer, Russell	1936	Yachting	6 Metres Class
Harrison, Audley	2000	Boxing	Super Heavyweight
Haslam, A	1900	Football	
Haslam, Harry	1920	Hockey	
Hawkes, Robert	1908	Football	
Hemery, David	1968	Athletics	400m Hurdles
Herbert, Garry	1992	Rowing	Coxed Pairs (cox)
Hester, Carl	2012	Equestrian	Team Dressage
Hill, Albert	1920	Athletics	800m
	1920	Athletics	1,500m
Hill, Arthur	1912	Swimming	Water Polo Team
Hill, Bertie	1956	Equestrian	3-Day Event Team
Hillyard, George	1908	Lawn Tennis	Men's Doubles
Hindes, Philip	2012	Cycling	Team Sprint
Hirons, Bill	1908	Tug of War	
Hoare, Gordon	1912	Football	
Hodge, Percy	1920	Athletics	3,000m Steeplechase
Holman, Fred	1908	Swimming	200m Breaststroke
Holmes, Andy	1984	Rowing	Coxed Fours
	1988	Rowing	Coxless Pairs
Holmes, Fred	1920	Tug of War	
Holmes, Kelly	2004	Athletics	800m
	2004	Athletics	1,500m
Horsfall, Ewart	1912	Rowing	Eights
Hosking, Sophie	2012	Rowing	Women's Lightweight Double Sculls
Hoy, Chris	2004	Cycling	1km Sprint
	2008	Cycling	Individual Sprint
	2008	Cycling	Team Sprint
	2008	Cycling	Keirin
	2012	Cycling	Team Sprint
	2012	Cycling	Keirin
Humby, Harry	1908	Shooting	Small-Bore Rifle Team
Humphreys, Fred	1908	Tug of War	
	1920	Tug of War	
Hunt, Kenneth	1908	Football	
Hunt-Davis, Ben	2000	Rowing	Coxed Eight
Hunter, Mark	2008	Rowing	Double Sculls (lightweight)
Ireton, Albert	1908	Tug of War	
Jacobs, David	1912	Athletics	4 x 100m Relay
James, Tom	2008	Rowing	Coxless Fours
	2012	Rowing	Coxless Fours
Jarvis, John Arthur	1900	Swimming	1,000m Freestyle
	1900	Swimming	4,000m Freestyle
Johnson, Victor	1908	Cycling	One-Lap Race
Johnstone, Banner	1908	Rowing	Eights
Jones, Ben	1908	Cycling	5,000m Track Race
	1908	Cycling	Three-Lap Pursuit

Name	*Date*	*Sport*	*Event*
Jones, Ben	1968	Equestrian	3-Day Event Team
Jones, Chris	1920	Swimming	Water Polo Team
Jones, Jade	2012	Taekwondo	Women's 57 kg
Jones, J H	1900	Football	
Joshua, Anthony	2012	Boxing	Super Heavyweight
Keene, Foxhall	1900	Polo	
Kelly, Fred	1908	Rowing	Eights
Kemp, Peter	1900	Swimming	Water Polo Team
Kennaugh, Peter	2012	Cycling	Team Pursuit
Kenny, Jason	2008	Cycling	Team Sprint
	2012	Cycling	Team Sprint
	2012	Cycling	Individual Sprint
Kerly, Sean	1988	Hockey	
King, Danielle	2012	Cycling	Women's Team Pursuit
Kingsbury, Clarrie	1908	Cycling	20km Track Race
	1908	Cycling	Three-Lap Pursuit
Kinnear, Wally	1912	Rowing	Single Sculls
Kirby, Alister	1912	Rowing	Eights
Kirkwood, Jimmy	1988	Hockey	
Knight, Arthur	1912	Football	
Lambert-Chambers, Dolly	1908	Lawn Tennis	Women's Singles
Lance, Tommy	1920	Cycling	2,000m Tandem
Lander, John	1928	Rowing	Coxless Fours
Larner, George	1908	Athletics	3,500m and 10 Mile Walk
Laurie, Ran	1948	Rowing	Coxless Pairs
Law, Leslie	2004	Equestrian	3-Day Event
Laws, Gilbert	1908	Yachting	6 Metres Class
Leaf, Charles	1936	Yachting	6 Metres Class
Leighton, Arthur	1920	Hockey	
Leman, Richard	1988	Hockey	
Lessimore, Edward	1912	Shooting	Small-Bore Rifle Team, 50m
Lewis, Denise	2000	Athletics	Heptathlon
Lewis-Francis, Mark	2004	Athletics	4 x 100m Relay
Liddell, Eric	1924	Athletics	400m
Lindsay, Andrew	2000	Rowing	Coxed Eight
Lindsay, Robert	1920	Athletics	4 x 400m Relay
Lister, Bill	1900	Swimming	Water Polo Team
Littlewort, Henry	1912	Football	
Llewellyn, Sir Harry (Foxhunter)	1952	Equestrian	Prix des Nations Team
Lockett, Vivian	1920	Polo	
Logan, Gerald	1908	Hockey	
Lonsbrough, Anita	1960	Swimming	200m Breaststroke
Lowe, Douglas	1924	Athletics	800m
	1928	Athletics	800m
McBryan, Jack	1920	Hockey	
MacDonald-Smith, Iain	1968	Yachting	Flying Dutchman Class
McGrath, George	1920	Hockey	
Macintosh, Henry	1920	Athletics	4 x 100m Relay
McIntyre, Mike	1988	Yachting	Star Class
Mackay, Frank (USA born)	1900	Polo	
McKeever, Ed	2012	Canoeing	K-1 200 m
McKenzie, John	1908	Yachting	12 Metres Class
MacKinnon, Duncan	1908	Rowing	Coxless Fours
Mackworth-Praed, Cyril	1924	Shooting	Running Deer (double shot)
MacLagen, Gilchrist	1908	Rowing	Eights
McMeekin, Tom	1908	Yachting	6 Metres Class
Macnabb, James	1924	Rowing	Coxless Fours
McNair, Winifred	1920	Lawn Tennis	Women's Doubles
McTaggart, Dick	1956	Boxing	Lightweight
McWhirter, Douglas	1912	Football	
Maddison, W J	1920	Yachting	7 Metres Class
Maher, Ben	2012	Equestrian	Team Showjumping
Mallin, Harry	1920	Boxing	Middleweight
(retired undefeated 300 fights)	1924	Boxing	Middleweight
Manning, Paul	2008	Cycling	Team Pursuit
Marcon, Sholto	1920	Hockey	
Martin, Albert	1908	Yachting	12 Metres Class
Martin, Leonard	1936	Yachting	6 Metres Class
Martin, Steve (played 1 minute)	1988	Hockey	
Matthews, Ken	1964	Athletics	20km Walk
Matthews, M K	1908	Shooting	Small-Bore Rifle Team
Maunder, Alex	1908	Shooting	Clay Pigeon Team
Meade, Richard	1968	Equestrian	3-Day Event Team
	1972	Equestrian	3-Day Event and Team
Melvill, Tim	1920	Polo	
Meredith, Leon	1908	Cycling	Three-Lap Pursuit
Merriman, Fred	1908	Tug of War	
Miller, Charles	1908	Polo	
Miller, George (brother of Charles)	1908	Polo	

Name	*Date*	*Sport*	*Event*
Millner, Jerry	1908	Shooting	Free Rifle
Mills, Edwin	1908	Tug of War	
	1920	Tug of War	
Mitchell, Harry	1924	Boxing	Light-Heavyweight
Moore, Bella	1912	Swimming	4 x 100m Freestyle Relay
Moore, F W	1908	Shooting	Clay Pigeon Team
Moorhouse, Adrian	1988	Swimming	100m Breaststroke
Morris, Stewart	1948	Yachting	Swallow Class
Morrison, Robert	1924	Rowing	Coxless Fours
Morton, Lucy	1924	Swimming	200m Breaststroke
Murray, Andy	2012	Tennis	Singles
Murray, Robert	1912	Shooting	Small-Bore Rifle Team
Neame, Philip (only man to be awarded Victoria Cross, knighthood and Olympic gold)	1924	Shooting	Running Deer (double shot)
Nevinson, George	1908	Swimming	Water Polo Team
Newall, Queenie	1908	Archery	National Round
Nicholas, J	1900	Football	
Nickalls, Guy	1908	Rowing	Eights
Nickalls, Patteson	1908	Polo	
Nightingale, Danny	1976	Modern Pentathlon	Team Event
Noble, Alan	1908	Hockey	
Noel, Evan	1908	Rackets	Singles
Ohuruogu, Christine	2008	Athletics	400m
O'Kelly, Con	1908	Wrestling	Heavyweight, Freestyle
Oldman, Albert	1908	Boxing	Heavyweight
Osborn, John	1976	Yachting	Tornado Class
Ovett, Steve	1980	Athletics	800m
Packer, Ann	1964	Athletics	800m
Page, Edgar	1908	Hockey	
Palmer, Charles	1908	Shooting	Clay Pigeon Team
Pappin, Veryan	1988	Hockey	
Parker, Adrian	1976	Modern Pentathlon	Team Event
Parker, Bridget	1972	Equestrian	3-Day Event Team
Pattisson, Rodney	1968	Yachting	Flying Dutchman Class
	1972	Yachting	Flying Dutchman Class
Payne, Ernest (known as the Worcester Wonder, Payne changed sports to become a Manchester Utd footballer)	1908	Cycling	Three-Lap Pursuit
Peacock, Bill	1920	Swimming	Water Polo Team
Pendleton, Victoria	2008	Cycling	Individual Sprint
	2012	Cycling	Women's Keirin
Pennell, Vane	1908	Rackets	Doubles
Pepe, Joseph	1912	Shooting	Small-Bore Rifle Team, 50m
Percy, Iain	2000	Sailing	Finn Class
	2008	Sailing	Star Class
Perry, Herbert	1924	Shooting	Running Deer (double shot)
Peters, Mary	1972	Athletics	Pentathlon
Phillips, Mark	1972	Equestrian	3-Day Event Team
Pike, J F	1908	Shooting	Clay Pigeon Team
Pimm, William	1908	Shooting	Small-Bore Rifle Team
	1912	Shooting	Small-Bore Rifle Team, 50m
Pinsent, Matthew	1992	Rowing	Coxless Pairs
	1996	Rowing	Coxless Pairs
	2000	Rowing	Coxless Fours
	2004	Rowing	Coxless Fours
Postans, J M	1908	Shooting	Clay Pigeon Team
Potter, Jonathan	1988	Hockey	
Powlesland, Alfred	1900	Cricket	
Pridmore, Reggie	1908	Hockey	
Purcell, Noel (Purcell was also an Irish rugby international)	1920	Swimming	Water Polo Team
Purchase, Zac	2008	Rowing	Double Sculls (lightweight)
Purnell, Clyde	1908	Football	
Quash, Bill	1900	Football	
Queally, Jason	2000	Cycling	Kilometre Sprint
Radmilovic, Paul	1908	Swimming	Water Polo Team
	1908	Swimming	4 x 200m Freestyle Relay
	1912	Swimming	Water Polo Team
	1920	Swimming	Water Polo Team
Rampling, Godfrey	1936	Athletics	4 x 400m Relay
Rand, Mary (Mary won the full set of medals with silver in Pentathlon and bronze in the relay)	1964	Athletics	Long Jump
Rawlinson, Alfred	1900	Polo	
Rawson, Ronald	1920	Boxing	Heavyweight

Name	*Date*	*Sport*	*Event*
Redgrave, Steve	1984	Rowing	Coxed Fours
	1988	Rowing	Coxless Pairs
	1992	Rowing	Coxless Pairs
	1996	Rowing	Coxless Pairs
	2000	Rowing	Coxless Fours
Redwood, Bernard	1908	Motor Boating	8 Metres Class
	1908	Motor Boating	Under 60-Foot Class
Reed, Peter	2008	Rowing	Coxless Fours
	2012	Rowing	Coxless Fours
Rees, Percy	1908	Hockey	
Rhodes, John	1908	Yachting	8 Metres Class
Rimmer, J T	1900	Athletics	4,000m Steeplechase
	1900	Athletics	5,000m Team Race
Ritchie, Major	1908	Lawn Tennis	Men's Singles
Rivett-Carnac, Charles	1908	Yachting	7 Metres Class
Rivett-Carnac, Frances (wife of Charles)	1908	Yachting	7 Metres Class
Roberts, Bill	1936	Athletics	4 x 400m Relay
Robertson, Arthur	1908	Athletics	Three Miles Team Race
Robertson, Arthur	1900	Swimming	Water Polo Team
Robertson, Shirley	2000	Sailing	Europe Dinghy Class
	2004	Sailing	Yngling Class
Robinson, Eric	1900	Swimming	Water Polo Team
Robinson, John	1908	Hockey	
Robinson, Sidney	1900	Athletics	5,000m Team Race
Romero, Rebecca	2008	Cycling	Individual Pursuit
Rook, Laurence	1956	Equestrian	3-Day Event Team
Rowsell, Joanna	2012	Cycling	Women's Team Pursuit
Russell, Arthur	1908	Athletics	3,200m Steeplechase
Rutherford, Greg	2012	Athletics	Long Jump
Ryan, Harry	1920	Cycling	2,000m Tandem
Sanders, Terence	1924	Rowing	Coxless Fours
Sanderson, Ronald	1908	Rowing	Eights
Sanderson, Tessa	1984	Athletics	Javelin
Scarlett, Fred	2000	Rowing	Coxed Eight
Searle, Greg	1992	Rowing	Coxed Pairs
Searle, Jonny	1992	Rowing	Coxed Pairs
Sewell, John	1912	Tug of War	
	1920	Tug of War	
Sharpe, Ivan	1912	Football	
Sheen, Gillian	1956	Fencing	Individual Foil
Shepherd, John	1908	Tug of War	
	1920	Tug of War	
Sherwani, Imran	1988	Hockey	
Shoveller, Stanley	1908	Hockey	
	1920	Hockey	
Simpson, Andrew	2008	Sailing	Star Class
Skelton, Nick	2012	Equestrian	Team Showjumping
Smith, Charles	1908	Swimming	Water Polo Team
	1912	Swimming	Water Polo Team
	1920	Swimming	Water Polo Team
Smith, Faulder	1920	Hockey	
Smith, Herbert	1908	Football	
Somers-Smith, John	1908	Rowing	Coxless Fours
Southwood, Dick	1936	Rowing	Double Sculls
Spackman, F G	1900	Football	
Spiers, Annie	1912	Swimming	4 x 100m Freestyle Relay
Spinks, Terry	1956	Boxing	Flyweight
Staff, Jamie	2008	Cycling	Team Sprint
Stamper, Harry	1912	Football	
Stanning, Heather	2012	Rowing	Women's Coxless Pair
Stapley, Henry	1908	Football	
Steer, Irene	1912	Swimming	4 x 100m Freestyle Relay
Stewart, Douglas	1952	Equestrian	Prix des Nations Team
(only British man to have competed at Olympic eventing and show jumping competitions)			
Stiff, Harry	1920	Tug of War	
Stott, Etienne	2012	Canoeing	Slalom C-2
Strode-Jackson, Arnold	1912	Athletics	1,500m
Styles, William	1908	Shooting	Small-Bore disappearing target
Sutton, Henry	1908	Yachting	8 Metres Class
Swann, Sidney	1912	Rowing	Eights
Symes, John	1900	Cricket	
Tait, Gerald	1908	Yachting	12 Metres Class
Taylor, Henry	1908	Swimming	400m Freestyle
	1908	Swimming	1,500m Freestyle
	1908	Swimming	4 x 200m Freestyle Relay
Taylor, Ian	1988	Hockey	
Thomas, Geraint	2008	Cycling	Team Pursuit
	2012	Cycling	Team Pursuit

Name	*Date*	*Sport*	*Event*
Thomas, Harry	1908	Boxing	Bantamweight
Thompson, Daley	1980	Athletics	Decathlon
	1984	Athletics	Decathlon
Thompson, Don	1960	Athletics	50km Walk
Thomson, Gordon	1908	Rowing	Coxless Pairs
Thorne, Ernie	1920	Tug of War	
Thornycroft, Tom	1908	Motor Boating	8 Metres Class
	1908	Motor Boating	Under 60-Foot Class
Thould, Tom	1908	Swimming	Water Polo Team
	1912	Swimming	Water Polo Team
Toller, Montague	1900	Cricket	
Trapmore, Steve	2000	Rowing	Coxed Eight
Triggs-Hodge, Andy	2008	Rowing	Coxless Fours
	2012	Rowing	Coxless Fours
Trott, Laura	2012	Cycling	Women's Team Pursuit
	2012	Cycling	Women's Omnium
Turnbull, Noel	1920	Lawn Tennis	Men's Doubles
Turner, R R	1900	Football	
Tysoe, Alf	1900	Athletics	800m
	1900	Athletics	5,000m Team Race
Vaile, Bryn	1988	Yachting	Star Class
Voigt, Emil	1908	Athletics	Five Miles
Walden, Harry (also music-hall comic)	1912	Football	
Warriner, Michael	1928	Rowing	Coxless Fours
Watkins, Anna	2012	Rowing	Women's Double Sculls
Webb, Sarah	2004	Sailing	Yngling Class
	2008	Sailing	Yngling Class
Weldon, Frank	1956	Equestrian	Three-Day Event Team
(born in India, Weldon was the only British Olympic gold medal winner to escape from Colditz)			
Wells, Allan	1980	Athletics	100m
Wells, Henry	1912	Rowing	Eights (cox)
West, Kieran	2000	Rowing	Coxed Eight
White, Reg	1976	Yachting	Tornado Class
White, Wilf	1952	Equestrian	Prix des Nations Team
Whitlock, Harold	1936	Athletics	50km Walk
Whitty, Allen	1924	Shooting	Running Deer (double shot)
Wiggins, Bradley	2004	Cycling	4,000m Pursuit
	2008	Cycling	4,000m Pursuit
	2008	Cycling	Team Pursuit
	2012	Cycling	Time Trial
Wilkie, David	1976	Swimming	200m Breaststroke
Wilkinson, Cyril	1920	Hockey	
Wilkinson, George	1900	Swimming	Water Polo Team
	1908	Swimming	Water Polo Team
	1912	Swimming	Water Polo Team
Williams, Steve	2004	Rowing	Coxless Fours
	2008	Rowing	Coxless Fours
Wilson, Herbert	1908	Polo	
Wilson, Jack	1948	Rowing	Coxless Pairs
Wilson, Peter	2012	Shooting	Double Trap
Wilson, Pippa	2008	Sailing	Yngling Class
Wodehouse, Lord John	1920	Polo	
Wolff, Freddie	1936	Athletics	4 x 400m Relay
Wood, Arthur	1908	Yachting	8 Metres Class
Wood, Harvey	1908	Hockey	
Woodward, Vivian	1908	Football	
	1912	Football	
Woosnam, Max	1920	Lawn Tennis	Men's Doubles
(also played football for England and golf and cricket for Cambridge)			
Wormald	1912	Rowing	Eights
Wright, Cyril	1920	Yachting	7 Metres Class
Wright, Dorothy (wife of Cyril)	1920	Yachting	7 Metres Class
Wright, Gordon	1912	Football	
Zealey, Jim	1900	Football	

Rugby League Challenge Cup Winners

Year	**Winners**		**Runners Up**		**Venue**	**Att**	**Man of Match**
1897	Batley	10	St Helens	3	Leeds	13,492	(First awarded in 1946)
1898	Batley	7	Bradford	0	Leeds	27,941	
1899	Oldham	19	Hunslet	9	Manchester	15,763	
1900	Swinton	16	Salford	8	Manchester	17,864	
1901	Batley	6	Warrington	0	Leeds	29,563	
1902	Broughton R	25	Salford	0	Rochdale	15,006	
1903	Halifax	7	Salford	0	Leeds	32,507	
1904	Halifax	8	Warrington	3	Salford	17,041	

Year	Winners		Runners Up		Venue	Att	Man of Match
1905	Warrington	6	Hull KR	0	Leeds	19,638	
1906	Bradford	5	Salford	0	Leeds	15,834	
1907	Warrington	17	Oldham	3	Broughton	18,500	
1908	Hunslet	14	Hull	0	Huddersfield	18,000	
1909	Wakefield T	17	Hull	0	Leeds	23,587	
1910	Leeds	7	Hull	7	Huddersfield	19,413	
replay	Leeds	26	Hull	12	Huddersfield	11,608	
1911	Broughton R	4	Wigan	0	Salford	8,000	
1912	Dewsbury	8	Oldham	5	Leeds	15,271	
1913	Huddersfield	9	Warrington	5	Leeds	22,754	
1914	Hull	6	Wakefield T	0	Halifax	19,000	
1915	Huddersfield	37	St Helens	3	Oldham	8,000	
1920	Huddersfield	21	Wigan	10	Leeds	14,000	
1921	Leigh	13	Halifax	0	Broughton	25,000	
1922	Rochdale H	10	Hull	9	Leeds	32,596	
1923	Leeds	28	Hull	3	Wakefield	29,335	
1924	Wigan	21	Oldham	4	Rochdale	41,831	
1925	Oldham	16	Hull KR	3	Leeds	28,335	
1926	Swinton	9	Oldham	3	Rochdale	27,000	
1927	Oldham	26	Swinton	7	Wigan	33,448	
1928	Swinton	5	Warrington	3	Wigan	33,909	
1929	Wigan	13	Dewsbury	2	Wembley	41,500	
1930	Widnes	10	St Helens	3	Wembley	36,544	
1931	Halifax	22	York	8	Wembley	40,368	
1932	Leeds	11	Swinton	8	Wigan	29,000	
1933	Huddersfield	21	Warrington	17	Wembley	41,874	
1934	Hunslet	11	Widnes	5	Wembley	41,280	
1935	Castleford	11	Huddersfield	8	Wembley	39,000	
1936	Leeds	18	Warrington	2	Wembley	51,250	
1937	Widnes	18	Keighley	5	Wembley	47,699	
1938	Salford	7	Barrow	4	Wembley	51,243	
1939	Halifax	20	Salford	3	Wembley	55,453	
1941	Leeds	19	Halifax	2	Bradford	28,500	
1942	Leeds	15	Halifax	10	Bradford	15,250	
1943	Dewsbury	16	Leeds	9	Dewsbury	10,470	
	Dewsbury	0	Leeds	6	Leeds	16,000	
	(Dewsbury win 16–15 on aggregate)						
1944	Bradford N	0	Wigan	3	Wigan	22,000	
	Bradford N	8	Wigan	0	Bradford	30,000	
	(Bradford win 8–3 on aggregate)						
1945	Huddersfield	7	Bradford N	4	Huddersfield	9,041	
	Huddersfield	6	Bradford N	5	Bradford	17,500	
	(Huddersfield win 13–9 on aggregate)						
1946	Wakefield T	13	Wigan	12	Wembley	54,730	Billy Stott
1947	Bradford N	8	Leeds	4	Wembley	77,605	Willie Davies
1948	Wigan	8	Bradford N	3	Wembley	91,465	Frank Whitcombe
1949	Bradford N	12	Halifax	0	Wembley	95,050	Ernest Ward
1950	Warrington	19	Widnes	0	Wembley	94,249	Gerry Helme
1951	Wigan	10	Barrow	0	Wembley	94,262	Cec Mountford
1952	Workington T	18	Featherstone R	10	Wembley	72,093	Billy Ivison
1953	Huddersfield	15	St Helens	10	Wembley	89,588	Peter Ramsden
1954	Warrington	4	Halifax	4	Wembley	81,841	
replay	Warrington	8	Halifax	4	Bradford	102,569	Gerry Helme
1955	Barrow	21	Workington T	12	Wembley	66,513	Jack Grundy
1956	St Helens	13	Halifax	2	Wembley	79,341	Alan Prescott
1957	Leeds	9	Barrow	7	Wembley	76,318	Jeff Stevenson
1958	Wigan	13	Workington T	9	Wembley	66,109	Rees Thomas
1959	Wigan	30	Hull	13	Wembley	79,811	Brian McTigue
1960	Wakefield T	38	Hull	5	Wembley	79,773	Tommy Harris
1961	St Helens	12	Wigan	6	Wembley	94,672	Dick Huddart
1962	Wakefield T	12	Huddersfield	6	Wembley	81,263	Neil Fox
1963	Wakefield T	25	Wigan	10	Wembley	84,492	Harold Poynton
1964	Widnes	13	Hull KR	5	Wembley	84,488	Frank Collier
1965	Wigan	20	Hunslet	16	Wembley	89,016	Ray Ashby & Brian Gabbitas
1966	St Helens	21	Wigan	2	Wembley	98,536	Len Killeen
1967	Featherstone R	17	Barrow	12	Wembley	76,290	Carl Dooler
1968	Leeds	11	Wakefield T	10	Wembley	87,100	Don Fox
1969	Castleford	11	Salford	6	Wembley	97,939	Mal Reilly
1970	Castleford	7	Wigan	2	Wembley	95,255	Bill Kirkbride
1971	Leigh	24	Leeds	7	Wembley	85,514	Alex Murphy
1972	St Helens	16	Leeds	13	Wembley	89,495	Kel Coslett
1973	Featherstone R	33	Bradford N	14	Wembley	72,395	Steve Nash
1974	Warrington	24	Featherstone R	9	Wembley	77,400	Derek Whitehead
1975	Widnes	14	Warrington	7	Wembley	85,098	Ray Dutton
1976	St Helens	20	Widnes	5	Wembley	89,982	Geoff Pimblett
1977	Leeds	16	Widnes	7	Wembley	80,871	Steve Pitchford
1978	Leeds	14	St Helens	12	Wembley	96,000	George Nicholls
1979	Widnes	12	Wakefield T	3	Wembley	94,218	Dave Topliss

Year	Winners		Runners Up		Venue	Att	Man of Match
1980	Hull KR	10	Hull	5	Wembley	95,000	Brian Lockwood
1981	Widnes	18	Hull KR	9	Wembley	92,496	Mick Burke
1982	Hull	14	Widnes	14	Wembley	92,147	Eddie Cunningham
replay	Hull	18	Widnes	9	Leeds	41,171	
1983	Featherstone R	14	Hull	12	Wembley	84,969	David Hobbs
1984	Widnes	19	Wigan	6	Wembley	80,116	Joe Lydon
1985	Wigan	28	Hull	25	Wembley	97,801	Brett Kenny
1986	Castleford	15	Hull KR	15	Wembley	82,134	Bob Beardmore
1987	Halifax	19	St Helens	18	Wembley	91,267	Graham Eadie
1988	Wigan	32	Halifax	12	Wembley	94,273	Andy Gregory
1989	Wigan	27	St Helens	0	Wembley	78,000	Ellery Hanley
1990	Wigan	36	Warrington	14	Wembley	77,729	Andy Gregory
1991	Wigan	13	St Helens	8	Wembley	75,532	Denis Betts
1992	Wigan	28	Castleford	12	Wembley	77,286	Martin Offiah
1993	Wigan	20	Widnes	14	Wembley	77,684	Dean Bell
1994	Wigan	26	Leeds	16	Wembley	78,348	Martin Offiah
1995	Wigan	30	Leeds	10	Wembley	78,550	Jason Robinson
1996	St Helens	40	Bradford B	32	Wembley	75,994	Robbie Paul
1997	St Helens	32	Bradford B	22	Wembley	78,022	Tommy Martyn
1998	Sheffield E	17	Wigan W	6	Wembley	60,699	Mark Aston
1999	Leeds R	52	London B	16	Wembley	73,242	Leroy Rivett
2000	Bradford N	22	Leeds R	18	Edinburgh	75,356	Henry Paul
2001	St Helens	13	Bradford B	6	Twickenham	68,250	Sean Long
2002	Wigan W	21	St Helens	12	Edinburgh	62,140	Kris Radlinski
2003	Bradford B	22	Leeds R	20	Cardiff	71,212	Gary Connolly
2004	St Helens	32	Wigan W	16	Cardiff	73,734	Sean Long
2005	Hull	25	Leeds R	24	Cardiff	74,213	Kevin Sinfield
2006	St Helens	42	Huddersfield	12	Twickenham	65,187	Sean Long
2007	St Helens	30	Catalans	8	Wembley	84,241	Paul Wellens/Leon Pryce
2008	St Helens	28	Hull	16	Wembley	82,821	Paul Wellens
2009	Warrington	25	Huddersfield	16	Wembley	76,560	Michael Monaghan
2010	Warrington	39	Leeds R	6	Wembley	85,217	Lee Briers
2011	Wigan	28	Leeds R	18	Wembley	78,482	Jeff Lima
2012	Warrington	35	Leeds R	18	Wembley	79,180	Brett Hodgson

Rugby League – Man of Steel

1977 David Ward (Leeds)
1978 George Nicholls (St Helens)
1979 Doug Laughton (Widnes)
1980 George Fairbairn (Wigan)
1981 Ken Kelly (Warrington)
1982 Mick Morgan (Carlisle)
1983 Allan Agar (Featherstone Rovers)
1984 Joe Lydon (Widnes)
1985 Ellery Hanley (Bradford Northern)
1986 Gavin Miller (HKR)
1987 Ellery Hanley (Wigan)
1988 Martin Offiah (Widnes)
1989 Ellery Hanley (Wigan)
1990 Shaun Edwards (Wigan)
1991 Gary Schofield (Leeds)
1992 Dean Bell (Wigan)
1993 Andy Platt (Wigan)
1994 Jonathan Davies (Warrington)
1995 Denis Betts (Wigan)
1996 Andy Farrell (Wigan)
1997 James Lowes (Bradford Bulls)
1998 Iestyn Harris (Leeds Rhinos)
1999 Adrian Vowles (Castleford Tigers)
2000 Sean Long (St Helens)
2001 Paul Sculthorpe (St Helens)
2002 Paul Sculthorpe (St Helens)
2003 Jamie Peacock (Bradford Bulls)
2004 Andy Farrell (Wigan Warriors)
2005 Jamie Lyon (St Helens)
2006 Paul Wellens (St Helens)
2007 James Roby (St Helens)
2008 James Graham (St Helens)
2009 Brett Hodgson (Huddersfield)
2010 Pat Richards (Wigan)
2011 Rangi Chase (Castleford Tigers)
2012 Sam Tomkins (Wigan)

Rugby Union Six Nations Championships

1977 France
1978 Wales
1979 Wales
1980 England
1981 France
1982 Ireland
1983 France / Ireland
1984 Scotland
1985 Ireland
1986 France / Scotland
1987 France
1988 France / Wales
1989 France
1990 Scotland
1991 England
1992 England
1993 France
1994 Wales
1995 England
1996 England
1997 France
1998 France
1999 Scotland (last Five Nations Championship)
2000 England
2001 England
2002 France
2003 England
2004 France
2005 Wales
2006 France
2007 France
2008 Wales
2009 Ireland
2010 France
2011 England
2012 Wales
2013 Wales

Tennis: Wimbledon Champions

	Men	*Women*	*Men's Doubles*	*Women's Doubles*
1877	S W Gore (GB)	—	—	—
1878	P F Hadow (GB)	—	—	—
1879	J T Hartley (GB)	—	—	—
1880	J T Hartley (GB)	—	—	—
1881	W Renshaw (GB)	—	—	—
1882	W Renshaw (GB)	—	—	—
1883	W Renshaw (GB)	—	—	—
1884	W Renshaw (GB)	M Watson (GB)	W Renshaw / E Renshaw	—
1885	W Renshaw (GB)	M Watson (GB)	W Renshaw / E Renshaw	—
1886	W Renshaw (GB)	B Bingley (GB)	W Renshaw / E Renshaw	—
1887	H FLawford (GB)	C Dod (GB)	W Wilberforce / P BLyon	—
1888	E Renshaw (GB)	C Dod (GB)	W Renshaw / E Renshaw	—
1889	W Renshaw (GB)	B Bingley Hillyard (GB)	W Renshaw / E Renshaw	—
1890	W J Hamilton (GB)	H Rice (GB)	J Pim / F O Stoker	—
1891	W Baddeley (GB)	C Dod (GB)	W Baddeley / H Baddeley	—
1892	W Baddeley (GB)	C Dod (GB)	E W Lewis / H S Barlow	—
1893	J Pim (GB)	C Dod (GB)	J Pim / F O Stoker	—
1894	J Pim (GB)	B Hillyard (GB)	W Baddeley / H Baddeley	—
1895	W Baddeley (GB)	C Cooper (GB)	W Baddeley / H Baddeley	—
1896	H S Mahony (GB)	C Cooper (GB)	W Baddeley / H Baddeley	—
1897	R F Doherty (GB)	B Hillyard (GB)	R F Doherty / L H Doherty	—
1898	R F Doherty (GB)	C Cooper (GB)	R F Doherty / L H Doherty	—
1899	R F Doherty (GB)	B Hillyard (GB)	R F Doherty / L H Doherty	—
1900	R F Doherty (GB)	B Hillyard (GB)	R F Doherty / L H Doherty	—
1901	A W Gore (GB)	C Cooper Sterry (GB)	R F Doherty / L H Doherty	—
1902	L H Doherty (GB)	M E Robb (GB)	S H Smith / F L Riseley	—
1903	L H Doherty (GB)	D K Douglass (GB)	R F Doherty / L H Doherty	—
1904	L H Doherty (GB)	D K Douglass (GB)	R F Doherty / L H Doherty	—
1905	L H Doherty (GB)	M Sutton (US)	R F Doherty / L H Doherty	—
1906	L H Doherty (GB)	D K Douglass (GB)	S Smith / F Riseley	—
1907	N E Brookes (Aus)	M Sutton (US)	N E Brookes / A F Wilding	—
1908	A W Gore (GB)	C Sterry (GB)	A F Wilding / M J G Ritchie	—
1909	A W Gore (GB)	D P Boothby (GB)	A W Gore / H Roper Barrett	—
1910	A F Wilding (NZ)	D K Douglass Chambers (GB)	A F Wilding / M J G Ritchie	—
1911	A F Wilding (NZ)	D K Douglass Chambers (GB)	A H Gobert / M Decugis	—
1912	A F Wilding (NZ)	E W Larcombe (GB)	H Roper Barrett / C P Dixon	—
1913	A F Wilding (NZ)	D K Douglass Chambers (GB)	H Roper Barrett / C P Dixon	R J McNair / D P Boothby
1914	N E Brookes (Aus)	D K Douglass Chambers (GB)	N E Brookes / A F Wilding	E Ryan / A M Morton
1915	not held	not held	not held	not held
1916	not held	not held	not held	not held
1917	not held	not held	not held	not held
1918	not held	not held	not held	not held
1919	G L Patterson (Aus)	S Lenglen (Fr)	R V Thomas / P O'Hara Wood	S Lenglen / E Ryan
1920	W T Tilden (US)	S Lenglen (Fr)	R N Williams / C S Garland	S Lenglen / E Ryan
1921	W T Tilden (US)	S Lenglen (Fr)	R Lycett / M Woosnam	S Lenglen / E Ryan
1922	G L Patterson (Aus)	S Lenglen (Fr)	J O Anderson / R Lycett	S Lenglen / E Ryan
1923	W M Johnston (US)	S Lenglen (Fr)	L A Godfree / R Lycett	S Lenglen / E Ryan
1924	J Borotra (Fr)	K McKane (GB)	F T Hunter / V Richards	H Wightman / H N Wills
1925	R Lacoste (Fr)	S Lenglen (Fr)	J Borotra / R Lacoste	S Lenglen / E Ryan
1926	J Borotra (Fr)	K McKane Godfree (GB)	J Brugnon / H Cochet	M K Browne / E Ryan
1927	H Cochet (Fr)	H N Wills (US)	F T Hunter / W T Tilden	H N Wills / E Ryan
1928	R Lacoste (Fr)	H N Wills (US)	J Brugnon / H Cochet	P Saunders / M Watson
1929	H Cochet (Fr)	H N Wills (US)	W L Allison / J Van Ryn	P Saunders Michell/ M Watson
1930	W T Tilden (US)	H N Wills Moody (US)	W L Allison / J Van Ryn	H N Wills Moody/ E Ryan
1931	S B Wood (US)	C Aussem (Ger)	G M Lott / J Van Ryn	P Mudford / D Shepherd-Barron
1932	H E Vines (US)	H N Wills Moody (US)	J Borotra / J Brugnon	D Metaxa / J Sigart
1933	J H Crawford (Aus)	H N Wills Moody (US)	J Borotra / J Brugnon	E Ryan / R Mathieu
1934	F J Perry (GB)	D E Round (GB)	G M Lott / L R Stoefen	E Ryan / R Mathieu
1935	F J Perry (GB)	H N Wills Moody (US)	J H Crawford / A K Quist	F James / K E Stammers
1936	F J Perry (GB)	H H Jacobs (US)	G P Hughes / C R D Tuckey	F James / K E Stammers
1937	J D Budge (US)	D E Round (GB)	J D Budge / G Mako	S Mathieu / B Yorke
1938	J D Budge (US)	H N Wills Moody (US)	J D Budge / G Mako	S Palfrey Fabyan / A Marble
1939	R L Riggs (US)	A Marble (US)	E T Cooke / R L Riggs	S Palfrey Fabyan / A Marble
1940-45	not held	not held	not held	not held
1946	Y Petra (Fr)	P M Betz (US)	T Brown / J A Kramer	L A Brough / M Osborne
1947	J Kramer (US)	M E Osborne (US)	R Falkenburg / J A Kramer	R B Todd / D J Hart
1948	B Falkenburg (US)	A L Brough (US)	J E Bromwich / F A Sedgman	A L Brough / M E Osborne du Pont
1949	T Schroeder (US)	A L Brough (US)	R A Gonzales / F A Parker	A L Brough/ M du Pont
1950	B Patty (US)	A L Brough (US)	J E Bromwich / A K Quist	A L Brough / M du Pont
1951	D Savitt (US)	D J Hart (US)	K B McGregor / F A Sedgman	D J Hart / S J Fry
1952	F Sedgman (Aus)	M Connolly (US)	K B McGregor / F A Sedgman	D J Hart / S J Fry
1953	V Seixas (US)	M Connolly (US)	L A Hoad / K R Rosewall	D J Hart / S J Fry
1954	J Drobny (Cze)	M Connolly (US)	R N Hartwig / M G Rose	A L Brough / M du Pont
1955	M A Trabert (US)	A L Brough (US)	R N Hartwig / L A Hoad	A Mortimer /J A Shilcock
1956	L A Hoad (Aus)	S J Fry (US)	L A Hoad / K R Rosewall	A Buxton / A Gibson

	Men	*Women*	*Men's Doubles*	*Women's Doubles*
1957	L A Hoad (Aus)	A Gibson (US)	J E Patty / G Mulloy	A Gibson / D R Hard
1958	A J Cooper (Aus)	A Gibson (US)	S Davidson / U Schmidt	M E Bueno / A Gibson
1959	A Olmedo (Per)	M E Bueno (Braz)	R Emerson / N A Fraser	J Arth / D R Hard
1960	N A Fraser (Aus)	M E Bueno (Braz)	R H Osuna / R D Ralston	M E Bueno / D R Hard
1961	R G Laver (Aus)	A Mortimer (GB)	R Emerson / N A Fraser	K Hantze / B J Moffitt
1962	R G Laver (Aus)	K Hantze Susman (US)	R A J Hewitt / F S Stolle	B J Moffitt / K Hantze Susman
1963	C R McKinley (US)	M Smith (Aus)	R H Osuna / A Palafox	M E Bueno / D R Hard
1964	R S Emerson (Aus)	M E Bueno (Braz)	R A J Hewitt / F S Stolle	M Smith / L R Turner
1965	R S Emerson (Aus)	M Smith (Aus)	J D Newcombe / A D Roche	M E Bueno / B J Moffitt
1966	M Santana (Spa)	B J Moffitt King (US)	K N Fletcher / J D Newcombe	M E Bueno / N Richey
1967	J D Newcombe (Aus)	B J King (US)	R A J Hewitt / F D McMillan	R Casals / B J Moffitt King
1968	R G Laver (Aus)	B J King (US)	J D Newcombe / A D Roche	R Casals / B J King
1969	R G Laver (Aus)	A Haydon Jones (GB)	J D Newcombe / A D Roche	M Smith Court / J A M Tegart
1970	J D Newcombe (Aus)	M Smith Court (Aus)	J D Newcombe / A D Roche	R Casals / B J King
1971	J D Newcombe (Aus)	E F Goolagong (Aus)	R S Emerson / R G Laver	R Casals / B J King
1972	S R Smith (US)	B J King (US)	R A J Hewitt / F D McMillan	B J King / B Stove
1973	J Kodes (Cze)	B J King (US)	J S Connors / I Nastase	R Casals / B J King
1974	J S Connors (US)	C M Evert (US)	J D Newcombe / A D Roche	E F Goolagong / M Michel
1975	A R Ashe (US)	B J King (US)	V Gerulaitis / A Mayer	A Kiyomura / K Sawamatsu
1976	B Borg (Swe)	C M Evert (US)	B E Gottfried / R Ramirez	C M Evert / M Navratilova
1977	B Borg (Swe)	S V Wade (GB)	R L Case / G Masters	H Gourlay Cawley / J C Russell
1978	B Borg (Swe)	M Navratilova (Cze)	R A J Hewitt / F D McMillan	K Reid / W Turnbull
1979	B Borg (Swe)	M Navratilova (US)	J P McEnroe / P Fleming	B J King / M Navratilova
1980	B Borg (Swe)	E F Goolagong Cawley (Aus)	P McNamara / P McNamee	K Jordan / A E Smith
1981	J P McEnroe (US)	C M Evert Lloyd (US)	J P McEnroe / P Fleming	M Navratilova / P H Shriver
1982	J S Connors (US)	M Navratilova (US)	P McNamara / P McNamee	M Navratilova / P H Shriver
1983	J P McEnroe (US)	M Navratilova (US)	J P McEnroe / P Fleming	M Navratilova / P H Shriver
1984	J P McEnroe (US)	M Navratilova (US)	J P McEnroe / P Fleming	M Navratilova / P H Shriver
1985	B Becker (Ger)	M Navratilova (US)	H P Gunthardt / B Taroczy	K Jordan / E Smylie
1986	B Becker (Ger)	M Navratilova (US)	J Nystrom / M Wilander	M Navratilova / P H Shriver
1987	P Cash (Aus)	M Navratilova (US)	R Seguso / K Flach	C Kohde-Kilsch / H Sukova
1988	S Edberg (Swe)	S Graf (Ger)	R Seguso / K Flach	S Graf / G Sabatini
1989	B Becker (Ger)	S Graf (Ger)	J B Fitzgerald / A Jarryd	J Novotna/H Sukova
1990	S Edberg (Swe)	M Navratilova (US)	R Leach / J Pugh	J Novotna/H Sukova
1991	M Stich (Ger)	S Graf (Ger)	J B Fitzgerald / A Jarryd	L Savchenko / N Zvereva
1992	A Agassi (US)	S Graf (Ger)	J P McEnroe / M Stich	G Fernandez / N Zvereva
1993	P Sampras (US)	S Graf (Ger)	T Woodbridge / M Woodforde	G Fernandez / N Zvereva
1994	P Sampras (US)	C Martinez (Spa)	T Woodbridge / M Woodforde	G Fernandez / N Zvereva
1995	P Sampras (US)	S Graf (Ger)	T Woodbridge / M Woodforde	J Novotna / A Sanchez-Vicario
1996	R Krajicek (Ned)	S Graf (Ger)	T Woodbridge / M Woodforde	M Hingis / H Sukova
1997	P Sampras (US)	M Hingis (Swi)	T Woodbridge / M Woodforde	G Fernandez / N Zvereva
1998	P Sampras (US)	J Novotna (Cze)	J Eltingh / P Haarhuis	M Hingis / J Novotna
1999	P Sampras (US)	L Davenport (US)	M Bhupathi / L Paes	L Davenport / C Morariu
2000	P Sampras (US)	V Williams (US)	T Woodbridge/M Woodforde	V Williams / S Williams
2001	G Ivanisevic (Cro)	V Williams (US)	D Johnson / J Palmer	L Raymond / R Stubbs
2002	L Hewitt (Aus)	S Williams (US)	J Bjorkman / T Woodbridge	V Williams / S Williams
2003	R Federer (Swi)	S Williams (US)	J Bjorkman / T Woodbridge	K Clijsters / A Sugiyama
2004	R Federer (Swi)	M Sharapova (US)	J Bjorkman / T Woodbridge	C Black / R Stubbs
2005	R Federer (Swi)	V Williams (US)	S Huss / W Moodie	C Black / L Huber
2006	R Federer (Swi)	A Mauresmo (Fr)	B Bryan / M Bryan	Z Yan / Zheng Jie
2007	R Federer (Swi)	V Williams (US)	A Clement / M Lodra	C Black / L Huber
2008	R Nadal (Spa)	V Williams (US)	D Nestor / N Zimonjic	V Williams / S Williams
2009	R Federer (Swi)	S Williams (US)	D Nestor / N Zimonjic	V Williams / S Williams
2010	R Nadal (Spa)	S Williams (US)	J Melzer / P Petzschner	V King / Y Shvedova
2011	N Djokovic (Serb)	P Kvitová (Cze)	B Bryan / M Bryan	K Peschke / K Srebotnik
2012	R Federer (Swi)	S Williams (US)	J Marray / F Nielsen	V Williams / S Williams
2013	Andy Murray (GB)	M Bartoli (Fra)	B Bryan / M Bryan	Hsieh Su-wei / Peng Shuai

Tennis: US Open

	Men	*Women*	*Men's Doubles*	*Women's Doubles*
1881	R D Sears (US)	—	C M Clark / F W Taylor	—
1882	R D Sears (US)	—	R D Sears / J Dwight	—
1883	R D Sears (US)	—	R D Sears / J Dwight	—
1884	R D Sears (US)	—	R D Sears / J Dwight	—
1885	R D Sears (US)	—	R D Sears / J S Clark	—
1886	R D Sears (US)	—	R D Sears / J Dwight	—
1887	R D Sears (US)	E Hansell (US)	R D Sears / J Dwight	—
1888	H W Slocum (US)	B L Townsend (US)	O S Campbell / V G Hall	—
1889	H W Slocum (US)	B L Townsend (US)	H W Slocum / H A Taylor	M Ballard / B L Townsend
1890	O S Campbell (US)	E C Roosevelt (US)	V G Hall / C Hobart	E C Roosevelt / G W Roosevelt
1891	O S Campbell (US)	M E Cahill (US)	O S Campbell / R P Huntington	M E Cahill / W F Morgan
1892	O S Campbell (US)	M E Cahill (US)	O S Campbell / R P Huntington	M E Cahill / A M McKinley
1893	R D Wrenn (US)	A M Terry (US)	C Hobart / F H Hovey	A M Terry / H Butler
1894	R D Wrenn (US)	H R Hellwig (US)	C Hobart / F H Hovey	H R Hellwig / J P Atkinson

	Men	*Women*	*Men's Doubles*	*Women's Doubles*
1895	F H Hovey (US)	J P Atkinson (US)	M G Chace / R D Wrenn	H R Hellwig / J P Atkinson
1896	R D Wrenn (US)	E H Moore (US)	C B Neel / S R Neel	E H Moore / J P Atkinson
1897	R D Wrenn (US)	J P Atkinson (US)	L E Ware / G P Sheldon	J P Atkinson / K Atkinson
1898	M D Whitman (US)	J P Atkinson (US)	L E Ware / G P Sheldon	J P Atkinson / K Atkinson
1899	M D Whitman (US)	M Jones (US)	H Ward / D F Davis	J W Craven / M McAteer
1900	M D Whitman (US)	M McAteer (US)	H Ward / D F Davis	E Parker / H Champlin
1901	W A Larned (US)	E H Moore (US)	H Ward / D F Davis	J P Atkinson / M McAteer
1902	W A Larned (US)	M Jones (US)	R F Doherty / H L Doherty	J P Atkinson / M Jones
1903	H L Doherty (GB)	E H Moore (US)	R F Doherty / H L Doherty	E H Moore / C B Neely
1904	H Ward (US)	M G Sutton (US)	H Ward / B C Wright	M G Sutton / M Hall
1905	B C Wright (US)	E H Moore (US)	H Ward / B C Wright	H Homans / C B Neely
1906	W J Clothier (US)	H Homans (US)	H Ward / B C Wright	L S Coe / D S Platt
1907	W A Larned (US)	Evelyn Sears (US)	F B Alexander / B C Wright	M Wimer / C B Neely
1908	W A Larned (US)	M Barger-Wallach (US)	F B Alexander / H H Hackett	Evelyn Sears / M Curtis
1909	W A Larned (US)	H Hotchkiss (US)	F B Alexander / H H Hackett	H V Hotchkiss / E E Rotch
1910	W A Larned (US)	H Hotchkiss (US)	F B Alexander / H H Hackett	H V Hotchkiss / E E Rotch
1911	W A Larned (US)	H Hotchkiss (US)	R D Little / G F Touchard	H V Hotchkiss / Eleanora Sears
1912	M E McLoughlin (US)	K Browne (US)	M E McLoughlin / T C Bundy	D Greene / MK Browne
1913	M E McLoughlin (US)	M K Browne (US)	M E McLoughlin / T C Bundy	M K Browne / L Williams
1914	R N Williams (US)	M K Browne (US)	M E McLoughlin / T C Bundy	M K Browne / L Williams
1915	W M Johnston (US)	M Bjurstedt (Nor)	W M Johnston / C J Griffin	H V Hotchkiss Wightman /Eleanora Sears
1916	R N Williams (US)	M Bjurstedt (Nor)	W M Johnston / C J Griffin	M Bjurstedt / Eleanora Sears
1917	R L Murray (US)	M Bjurstedt (Nor)	F B Alexander / H A Throckmorton	M Bjurstedt / Eleanora Sears
1918	R L Murray (US)	M Bjurstedt (Nor)	W T Tilden / V Richards	M Zinderstein / E E Goss
1919	W M Johnston (US)	H Hotchkiss Wightman (US)	N E Brookes / G L Patterson	M Zinderstein / E E Goss
1920	W T Tilden (US)	M Bjurstedt Mallory (US)	W M Johnston / C J Griffin	M Zinderstein / E E Goss
1921	W T Tilden (US)	M Mallory (US)	W T Tilden / V Richards	M K Browne / L Williams
1922	W T Tilden (US)	M Mallory (US)	W T Tilden / V Richards	M Zinderstein Jessup / H N Wills
1923	W T Tilden (US)	H N Wills (US)	W T Tilden / B I C Norton	K McKane / P L Howkins Covell
1924	W T Tilden (US)	H N Wills (US)	H O Kinsey / R G Kinsey	H Wightman / H N Wills
1925	W T Tilden (US)	H N Wills (US)	R N Williams / V Richards	M K Browne / H N Wills
1926	R Lacoste (Fr)	M Mallory (US)	R N Williams / V Richards	E Ryan / E E Goss
1927	R Lacoste (Fr)	H N Wills (US)	W T Tilden / F T Hunter	K McKane Godfree / E H Harvey
1928	H Cochet (Fr)	H N Wills (US)	G M Lott / J F Hennessey	H Wightman / H N Wills
1929	W T Tilden (US)	H N Wills (US)	G M Lott / J H Doeg	P Watson / P Michel
1930	J H Doeg (US)	B Nuthall (GB)	G M Lott / J H Doeg	B Nuthall / S Palfrey
1931	H E Vines (US)	H N Wills Moody (US)	W L Allison / J Van Ryn	B Nuthall / E Bennett Whittingstall
1932	H E Vines (US)	H H Jacobs (US)	H E Vines / K Gledhill	H H Jacobs / S Palfrey
1933	F J Perry (GB)	H H Jacobs (US)	G M Lott / L R Stoefen	B Nuthall / F James
1934	F J Perry (GB)	H H Jacobs (US)	G M Lott / L R Stoefen	H H Jacobs / S Palfrey
1935	W L Allison (US)	H H Jacobs (US)	W L Allison / J Van Ryn	H H Jacobs / S Palfrey Fabyan
1936	F J Perry (GB)	A Marble (US)	J D Budge / G Mako	M Van Ryn / C A Babcock
1937	J D Budge (US)	A Lizana (Chile)	G Von Cramm / H Henkel	S Palfrey Fabyan / A Marble
1938	J D Budge (US)	A Marble (US)	J D Budge / G Mako	S Palfrey Fabyan / A Marble
1939	R L Riggs (US)	A Marble (US)	A K Quist / J E Bromwich	S Palfrey Fabyan / A Marble
1940	W D McNeill (US)	A Marble (US)	J A Kramer / F R Schroeder	S Palfrey Fabyan / A Marble
1941	R L Riggs (US)	S Palfrey Cooke (US)	J A Kramer / F R Schroeder	S Palfrey Cooke / M E Osborne
1942	F R Schroeder (US)	P M Betz (US)	G Mulloy / W F Talbert	A L Brough / M E Osborne
1943	J R Hunt (US)	P M Betz (US)	J A Kramer / F A Parker	A L Brough / M E Osborne
1944	F A Parker (US)	P M Betz (US)	W D McNeill / R Falkenburg	A L Brough / M E Osborne
1945	F A Parker (US)	S Palfrey Cooke (US)	G Mulloy / W F Talbert	A L Brough / M E Osborne
1946	J A Kramer (US)	P M Betz (US)	G Mulloy / W F Talbert	A L Brough / M E Osborne
1947	J A Kramer (US)	A L Brough (US)	J A Kramer / F R Schroeder	A L Brough / M E Osborne
1948	R A Gonzales (US)	M E Osborne du Pont (US)	G Mulloy / W F Talbert	A L Brough / M E Osborne du Pont
1949	R A Gonzales (US)	M E du Pont (US)	J Bromwich / O W Sidwell	A L Brough / M E du Pont
1950	A Larsen (US)	M E du Pont (US)	J Bromwich / F A Sedgeman	A L Brough / M E du Pont
1951	F A Sedgeman (Aus)	M Connolly (US)	K B McGregor / F A Sedgeman	D J Hart / S J Fry
1952	F A Sedgeman (Aus)	M Connolly (US)	M G Rose / E VSeixas	D J Hart / S J Fry
1953	M A Trabert (US)	M Connolly (US)	R N Hartwig / M G Rose	D J Hart / S J Fry
1954	E V Seixas (US)	D J Hart (US)	E V Seixas / M A Trabert	D J Hart / S J Fry
1955	M A Trabert (US)	D J Hart (US)	K Kamo / A Miyagi	A L Brough / M E du Pont
1956	K R Rosewall (Aus)	S J Fry (US)	L A Hoad / K R Rosewall	A L Brough / M E du Pont
1957	M J Anderson (Aus)	A Gibson (US)	A J Cooper / N A Fraser	A L Brough / M E du Pont
1958	A J Cooper (Aus)	A Gibson (US)	A Olmedo / H Richardson	J M Arth / D R Hard
1959	N A Fraser (Aus)	M E Bueno (Braz)	N A Fraser / R S Emerson	J M Arth / D R Hard
1960	N A Fraser (Aus)	D R Hard (US)	N A Fraser / R S Emerson	M E Bueno / D R Hard
1961	R S Emerson (Aus)	D R Hard (US)	C McKinley / R D Ralston	D R Hard / L Turner
1962	R G Laver (Aus)	M Smith (Aus)	R H Osuna / A Palafox	M E Bueno / D R Hard
1963	R H Osuna (Mex)	M E Bueno (Braz)	C McKinley / R D Ralston	R Ebbern / M Smith
1964	R S Emerson (Aus)	M E Bueno (Braz)	C McKinley / R D Ralston	B J Moffitt / K Hantze Susman
1965	M Santana (Spa)	M Smith (Aus)	R S Emerson / F S Stolle	C A Graebner / N Richey
1966	F S Stolle (Aus)	M E Bueno (Braz)	R S Emerson / F S Stolle	M E Bueno / N Richey
1967	J Newcombe (Aus)	B J Moffitt King (US)	J D Newcombe / A D Roche	R Casals / B J Moffitt King
1968	A R Ashe (US)	S V Wade / B M Smith Court (Aus)	R C Lutz / S R Smith	M E Bueno / B M Smith Court
1969	R G Laver (Aus) / S R Smith (US)	B M Court (Aus)	K R Rosewall / F S Stolle D Crealy / A Stone	F Durr / D R Hard B M Court / S V Wade
1970	K R Rosewall (Aus)	B M Court (Aus)	P Barthes / N Pilic	B M Court / J A M Dalton

	Men	Women	Men's Doubles	Women's Doubles
1971	S R Smith (US)	B J King (US)	J D Newcombe / R Taylor	R Casals / J A M Dalton
1972	I Nastase (Rom)	B J King (US)	C E Drysdale / R Taylor	F Durr / B Stove
1973	J Newcombe (Aus)	B M Court (Aus)	O K Davidson / J D Newcombe	B M Court / S V Wade
1974	J S Connors (US)	B J King (US)	R C Lutz / S R Smith	R Casals / B J King
1975	M Orantes (Spa)	C M Evert (US)	J S Connors / I Nastase	B M Court / S V Wade
1976	J S Connors (US)	C M Evert (US)	T S Okker / M C Riessen	L Boshoff / I Kloss
1977	G Vilas (Arg)	C M Evert (US)	R A J Hewitt / F D McMillan	M Navratilova / B Stove
1978	J S Connors (US)	C M Evert (US)	R C Lutz / S R Smith	B J King / M Navratilova
1979	J P McEnroe (US)	T A Austin (US)	J P McEnroe / P Fleming	W M Turnbull / B Stove
1980	J P McEnroe (US)	C M Evert Lloyd (US)	R C Lutz / S R Smith	B J King / M Navratilova
1981	J P McEnroe (US)	T A Austin (US)	J P McEnroe / P Fleming	K Jordan / A Smith
1982	J S Connors (US)	C M Evert Lloyd (US)	K Curren / S Denton	R Casals / W M Turnbull
1983	J S Connors (US)	M Navratilova (US)	J P McEnroe / P Fleming	M Navratilova / P H Shriver
1984	J P McEnroe (US)	M Navratilova (US)	J B Fitzgerald / T Smid	M Navratilova / P H Shriver
1985	I Lendl (Cze)	H Mandlikova (Cze)	K Flach / R Seguso	C Kohde-Kilsch/ H Sukova
1986	I Lendl (Cze)	M Navratilova (US)	A Gomez / S Zivojinovic	M Navratilova / P H Shriver
1987	I Lendl (Cze)	M Navratilova (US)	S Edberg / A Jarryd	M Navratilova / P H Shriver
1988	M Wilander (Swe)	S Graf (Ger)	S Casal / E Sanchez	G Fernandez / R White
1989	B Becker (Ger)	S Graf (Ger)	J P McEnroe / M Woodforde	H Mandlikova / M Navratilova
1990	P Sampras (US)	G Sabatini (Arg)	P Aldrich / D Visser	G Fernandez / M Navratilova
1991	S Edberg (Swe)	M Seles (Yug)	J B Fitzgerald / A Jarryd	P H Shriver / N Zvereva
1992	S Edberg (Swe)	M Seles (Yug)	J Grabb / R Reneberg	G Fernandez / N Zvereva
1993	P Sampras (US)	S Graf (Ger)	K Flach / R Leach	A Sanchez-Vicario / H Sukova
1994	A Agassi (US)	A Sanchez-Vicario (Spa)	J Eltingh / P Haarhuis	J Novotna / A Sanchez-Vicario
1995	P Sampras (US)	S Graf (Ger)	T Woodbridge / M Woodforde	G Fernandez / N Zvereva
1996	P Sampras (US)	S Graf (Ger)	T Woodbridge / M Woodforde	G Fernandez / N Zvereva
1997	P Rafter (Aus)	M Hingis (Swi)	Y Kafelnikov / D Vacek	J Novotna / L Davenport
1998	P Rafter (Aus)	L Davenport (US)	S Stolle / C Suk	M Hingis / J Novotna
1999	A Agassi (US)	S Williams (US)	S Lareau / A O'Brien	S Williams / V Williams
2000	M Safin (Rus)	V Williams (US)	L Hewitt / M Mirnyi	A Sugiyama / J Halard-Decugis
2001	L Hewitt (Aus)	V Williams (US)	W Black / K Ullyett	L Raymond / R Stubbs
2002	P Sampras (US)	S Williams (US)	M Bhupathi / M Myrnyi	V Ruano Pascual / P Suarez
2003	A Roddick (US)	J Henin-Hardenne (Belg)	J Bjorkman / T Woodbridge	V Ruano Pascual / P Suarez
2004	R Federer (Swi)	S Kuznetsova (Rus)	M Knowles / D Nestor	V Ruano Pascual / P Suarez
2005	R Federer (Swi)	K Clijsters (Belg)	B Bryan / M Bryan	L Raymond / S Stosur
2006	R Federer (Swi)	M Sharapova (Rus)	M Damm / L Paes	N Dechy / V Zvonareva
2007	R Federer (Swi)	J Henin (Belg)	S Aspelin / S Knowle	N Dechy / D Safina
2008	R Federer (Swi)	S Williams (US)	B Bryan / M Bryan	C Black / L Huber
2009	J M Del Potro (Arg)	K Clijsters (Belg)	L Dlouhy / L Paes	S Williams / V Williams
2010	R Nadal (Spa)	K Clijsters (Belg)	B Bryan / M Bryan	V King / Y Shvedova
2011	N Djokovic (Serb)	S Stosur (Aus)	J Melzer / P Petzschner	L Raymond / L Huber
2012	A Murray (GB)	S Williams (US)	B Bryan / M Bryan	S Errani / R Vinci

Tennis: Australian Open

	Men	Women
1905	R W Heath (Aus)	—
1906	A F Wilding (NZ)	—
1907	H M Rice (Aus)	—
1908	F B Alexander (US)	—
1909	A F Wilding (NZ)	—
1910	R W Heath (Aus)	—
1911	N E Brookes (Aus)	—
1912	J C Parke (GB)	—
1913	E F Parker (Aus)	—
1914	A O'Hara Wood (Aus)	—
1915	F G Lowe (GB)	—
1916-18	not held	—
1919	A R F Kingscote (GB)	—
1920	P O'Hara Wood (Aus)	—
1921	R H Gemmell (Aus)	—
1922	J O Anderson (Aus)	M Molesworth (Aus)
1923	P O'Hara Wood (Aus)	M Molesworth (Aus)
1924	J O Anderson (Aus)	S Lance (Aus)
1925	J O Anderson (Aus)	D S Akhurst (Aus)
1926	J B Hawkes (Aus)	D S Akhurst (Aus)
1927	G L Patterson (Aus)	E F Boyd (Aus)
1928	J Borotra (Fr)	D S Akhurst (Aus)
1929	J C Gregory (GB)	D S Akhurst (Aus)
1930	E F Moon (Aus)	D S Akhurst (Aus)
1931	J H Crawford (Aus)	C Buttsworth (Aus)
1932	J H Crawford (Aus)	C Buttsworth (Aus)
1933	J H Crawford (Aus)	J Hartigan (Aus)
1934	F J Perry (GB)	J Hartigan (Aus)
1935	J H Crawford (Aus)	D E Round (GB)
1936	A K Quist (Aus)	J Hartigan (Aus)
1937	V B McGrath (Aus)	N M Wynne (Aus)
1938	J D Budge (US)	D M Bundy (US)
1939	J E Bromwich (US)	E Westacott (Aus)
1940	A K Quist (Aus)	N M Wynne Bolton (Aus)
1941-45	not held	not held
1946	J E Bromwich (US)	N M Bolton (Aus)
1947	D Pails (Aus)	N M Bolton (Aus)
1948	A K Quist (Aus)	N M Bolton (Aus)
1949	F A Sedgman (Aus)	D J Hart (US)
1950	F A Sedgman (Aus)	L A Brough (US)
1951	R Savitt (US)	N M Bolton (Aus)
1952	K B McGregor (Aus)	T Long (Aus)
1953	K R Rosewall (Aus)	M Connolly (US)
1954	M G Rose (Aus)	T Long (Aus)
1955	K R Rosewall (Aus)	B Penrose (Aus)
1956	L G Hoad (Aus)	M Carter (Aus)
1957	A J Cooper (Aus)	S J Fry (US)
1958	A J Cooper (Aus)	A Mortimer (GB)
1959	A Olmedo (Per)	M Carter Reitano (Aus)
1960	R G Laver (Aus)	M Smith (Aus)
1961	R S Emerson (Aus)	M Smith (Aus)
1962	R G Laver (Aus)	M Smith (Aus)
1963	R S Emerson (Aus)	M Smith (Aus)
1964	R S Emerson (Aus)	M Smith (Aus)
1965	R S Emerson (Aus)	M Smith (Aus)
1966	R S Emerson (Aus)	M Smith (Aus)
1967	R S Emerson (Aus)	N Richey (US)
1968	W W Bowrey (Aus)	B J Moffitt King (US)
1969	R G Laver (Aus)	M Smith Court (Aus)
1970	A R Ashe (US)	M Court (Aus)

	Men	*Women*
1971	K R Rosewall (Aus)	M Court (Aus)
1972	K R Rosewall (Aus)	V S Wade (GB)
1973	J D Newcombe (Aus)	M Court (Aus)
1974	J S Connors (US)	E Goolagong (Aus)
1975	J D Newcombe (Aus)	E Goolagong (Aus)
1976	M Edmondson (Aus)	E Goolagong Cawley (Aus)
1977 (Jan)	R Tanner (US)	K Reid (Aus)
1977 (Dec)	V Gerulaitis (US)	E Cawley (Aus)
1978	G Vilas (Arg)	C O'Neill (Aus)
1979	G Vilas (Arg)	B Jordan (US)
1980	B Teacher (US)	H Mandlikova (Cze)
1981	J Kriek (SA)	M Navratilova (US)
1982	J Kriek (SA)	C M Evert Lloyd (US)
1983	M Wilander (Swe)	M Navratilova (US)
1984	M Wilander (Swe)	C M Evert Lloyd (US)
1985	S Edberg (Swe)	M Navratilova (US)
1986	not held	not held
1987	S Edberg (Swe)	H Mandlikova (Cze)
1988	M Wilander (Swe)	S Graf (Ger)
1989	I Lendl (Cze)	S Graf (Ger)
1990	I Lendl (Cze)	S Graf (Ger)

	Men	*Women*
1991	B Becker (Ger)	M Seles (Yug)
1992	J Courier (US)	M Seles (Yug)
1993	J Courier (US)	M Seles (Yug)
1994	P Sampras (US)	S Graf (Ger)
1995	A Agassi (US)	M Pierce (Fra)
1996	B Becker (Ger)	M Seles (US)
1997	P Sampras (US)	M Hingis (Swi)
1998	P Korda (Cze)	M Hingis (Swi)
1999	Y Kafelnikov (Rus)	M Hingis (Swi)
2000	A Agassi (US)	L Davenport (US)
2001	A Agassi (US)	J Capriati (US)
2002	T Johansson (Swe)	J Capriati (US)
2003	A Agassi (US)	S Williams (US)
2004	R Federer (Swi)	J Henin-Hardenne (Belg)
2005	M Safin (Rus)	S Williams (US)
2006	R Federer (Swi)	A Mauresmo (Fr)
2007	R Federer (Swi)	S Williams (US)
2008	N Djokovic (Serb)	M Sharapova (Rus)
2009	R Nadal (Spa)	S Williams (US)
2010	R Federer (Swi)	S Williams (US)
2011	N Djokovic (Serb)	K Clijsters (Belg)
2012	N Djokovic (Serb)	V Azarenka (Bel)
2013	N Djokovic (Serb)	V Azarenka (Bel)

Tennis: French Open

	Men	*Women*
1891	H Briggs	—
1892	J Schopfer (Fr)	—
1893	L Riboulet (Fr)	—
1894	A Vacherot (Fr)	—
1895	A Vacherot (Fr)	—
1896	A Vacherot (Fr)	—
1897	P Aymé (Fr)	C Masson (Fr)
1898	P Aymé (Fr)	C Masson (Fr)
1899	P Aymé (Fr)	C Masson (Fr)
1900	P Aymé (Fr)	Y Prévost (Fr)
1901	A Vacherot (Fr)	P Girod (Fr)
1902	A Vacherot (Fr)	C Masson (Fr)
1903	M Decugis (Fr)	C Masson (Fr)
1904	M Decugis (Fr)	K Gillou (Fr)
1905	M Germot (Fr)	K Gillou (Fr)
1906	M Germot (Fr)	K Fenwick
1907	M Decugis (Fr)	M de Kermel (Fr)
1908	M Decugis (Fr)	K Fenwick
1909	M Decugis (Fr)	J Mattey (Fr)
1910	M Germot (Fr)	J Mattey (Fr)
1911	A H Gobert (Fr)	J Mattey (Fr)
1912	M Decugis (Fr)	J Mattey (Fr)
1913	M Decugis (Fr)	M Broquedis (Fr)
1914	M Decugis (Fr)	M Broquedis (Fr)
1915	not held	not held
1916	not held	not held
1917	not held	not held
1918	not held	not held
1919	not held	not held
1920	A H Gobert (Fr)	S Lenglen (Fr)
1921	J Samazeuilh (Fr)	S Lenglen (Fr)
1922	H Cochet (Fr)	S Lenglen (Fr)
1923	P Blanchy (Fr)	S Lenglen (Fr)
1924	J Borotra (Fr)	D Vlasto (Fr)
1925	R Lacoste (Fr)	S Lenglen (Fr)
1926	H Cochet (Fr)	S Lenglen (Fr)
1927	R Lacoste (Fr)	K Bouman (Ned)
1928	H Cochet (Fr)	H N Wills (US)
1929	R Lacoste (Fr)	H N Wills (US)
1930	H Cochet (Fr)	H N Wills Moody (US)
1931	J Borotra (Fr)	C Aussem (Ger)
1932	H Cochet (Fr)	H N Wills (US)
1933	J H Crawford (Aus)	M C Scriven (GB)
1934	G von Cramm (Ger)	M C Scriven (GB)
1935	F J Perry (GB)	H Sperling (Den)
1936	G von Cramm (Ger)	H Sperling (Den)
1937	H Henkel (Ger)	H Sperling (Den)
1938	J D Budge (US)	S Mathieu (Fr)
1939	W D McNeill (US)	S Mathieu (Fr)
1940-45	not held	not held

	Men	*Women*
1946	M Bernard (Fr)	M E Osborne (US)
1947	J Asboth (Hung)	P Todd (US)
1948	F A Parker (US)	N Landry (Belg)
1949	F A Parker (US)	M E Osborne du Pont (US)
1950	J E Patty (US)	D J Hart (US)
1951	J Drobny (Cze)	S J Fry (US)
1952	J Drobny (Cze)	D J Hart (US)
1953	K R Rosewall (Aus)	M Connolly (US)
1955	M A Trabert (US)	M Connolly (US)
1955	M A Trabert (US)	A Mortimer (GB)
1956	L A Hoad (Aus)	A Gibson (US)
1957	S Davidson (Swe)	S J Bloomer (GB)
1958	M Rose (Aus)	S Kormoczy (Hung)
1959	N Pietrangeli (Ita)	C C Truman (GB)
1960	N Pietrangeli (Ita)	D R Hard (US)
1961	M Santana (Spa)	A S Haydon (GB)
1962	R G Laver (Aus)	M Smith (Aus)
1963	R S Emerson (Aus)	L R Turner (Aus)
1964	M Santana (Spa)	M Smith (Aus)
1965	F S Stolle (Aus)	L R Turner (Aus)
1966	A D Roche (Aus)	A S Haydon Jones (GB)
1967	R S Emerson (Aus)	F Durr (Fr)
1968	K R Rosewall (Aus)	N Richey (US)
1969	R G Laver (Aus)	M Smith Court (Aus)
1970	J Kodes (Cze)	M Court (Aus)
1971	J Kodes (Cze)	E Goolagong (Aus)
1972	A Gimeno (Spa)	B J Moffitt King (US)
1973	I Nastase (Rom)	M Court (Aus)
1974	B Borg (Swed)	C M Evert (US)
1975	B Borg (Swed)	C M Evert (US)
1976	A Panatta (Ita)	S Barker (GB)
1977	G Vilas (Arg)	M Jausovec (Yug)
1978	B Borg (Swed)	V Ruzici (Rom)
1979	B Borg (Swed)	C M Evert Lloyd (US)
1980	B Borg (Swed)	C M Evert Lloyd (US)
1981	B Borg (Swed)	H Mandlikova (Cze)
1982	M Wilander (Swe)	M Navratilova (US)
1983	Y Noah (Fr)	C M Evert Lloyd (US)
1984	I Lendl (Cze)	M Navratilova (US)
1985	M Wilander (Swe)	C M Evert Lloyd (US)
1986	I Lendl (Cze)	C M Evert Lloyd (US)
1987	I Lendl (Cze)	S Graf (Ger)
1988	M Wilander (Swe)	S Graf (Ger)
1989	M Chang (US)	A Sanchez-Vicario (Spa)
1990	A Gomez (Ecu)	M Seles (Yug)
1991	J Courier (US)	M Seles (Yug)
1992	J Courier (US)	M Seles (Yug)
1993	S Bruguera (Spa)	S Graf (Ger)
1994	S Bruguera (Spa)	A Sanchez-Vicario (Spa)
1995	T Muster (Aut)	S Graf (Ger)
1996	Y Kafelnikov (Rus)	S Graf (Ger)

	Men	Women
1997	G Kuerten (Braz)	I Majoli (Croat)
1998	C Moya (Spa)	A Sanchez-Vicario (Spa)
1999	A Agassi (US)	S Graf (Ger)
2000	G Kuerten (Braz)	M Pierce (Fra)
2001	G Kuerten (Braz)	J Capriati (US)
2002	A Costa (Spa)	S Williams (US)
2003	J C Ferrero (Spa)	J Henin-Hardenne (Belg)
2004	G Gaudio (Arg)	A Myskina (Rus)
2005	R Nadal (Spa)	J Henin-Hardenne (Belg)
2006	R Nadal (Spa)	J Henin-Hardenne (Belg)
2007	R Nadal (Spa)	J Henin-Hardenne (Belg)
2008	R Nadal (Spa)	A Ivanovic (Serb)
2009	R Federer (Swi)	S Kuznetsova (Rus)
2010	R Nadal (Spa)	F Schiavone (Ita)
2011	R Nadal (Spa)	Li Na (Chn)
2012	R Nadal (Spa)	M Sharapova (Rus)
2013	R Nadal (Spa)	S Williams (US)

Tennis: General Information

Australian Open: venue	Melbourne Park (formerly known as Flinders Park).
Davis Cup: inaugurated	1900.
most wins	USA.
official title	The International Men's Team Championship of the World.
Federation Cup	women's equivalent of the Davis Cup. Inaugurated in 1963. The United States defeated Australia 2–1 in the first final.
'Four Musketeers'	Jean Borotra, Jacques ('Toto') Brugnon, Henri Cochet, René Lacoste.
French Championships: made Open	before 1925 the French Championships were open only to members of French clubs.
French Open: venue	Roland Garros Stadium, Paris, since 1928.
Grand Slam: definition	winning the four major titles consecutively irrespective of calendar year (formerly had to be achieved in the calendar year).
holders	Donald Budge, Maureen Connolly, Margaret Court, Steffi Graf, Rod Laver (twice) and Martina Navratilova.
junior winner	Earl Buchholz won all four junior titles in 1958 followed by Stefan Edberg in 1983.
Hopman Cup	international mixed teams event first held between 28 December 1988 and 1 January 1989, Czechoslovakia beating Australia in the first championship.
net: height in middle	3 feet (91cm).
nicknames: Bounding Basque	Jean Borotra.
Poker Face	Helen Wills Moody.
Rocket	Rod Laver.
The Ghost	Harold Mahony.
The Two Helens	Helen Wills Moody and Helen Jacobs (great rivals and born on the same street in Berkeley, California).
Olympic champions: 2012	Andy Murray (GB) and Serena Williams (USA).
Olympic Games: ice hockey player	Jaroslav Drobny (Cze, 1948).
tennis challenge: battle of the sexes	Bobby Riggs had beaten Margaret Court but was then beaten by Billie Jean King (and famously presented with a pig).
tennis: original name	sphairistiké.
'Three Musketeers'	Jean Borotra, Henri Cochet, René Lacoste.
US Open: venue	Flushing Meadows, New York, since 1978. Finals showcourt named after Arthur Ashe.
Wimbledon champion: 1st black man	Arthur Ashe (1975).
1st black person	Althea Gibson (1957).
Mixed Doubles: brother and sister	John and Tracy Austin won the 1981 Championship.
man and wife	Mr and Mrs L A Godfree won the 1926 Championship.
boycott year	1973 (due to suspension of Nikki Pilic of Yugoslavia).
champion at first and only attempt	Bobby Riggs (1939) won all three titles on his only appearance at the Championships.
first professional champion	Rod Laver (1968).
last amateur champion	John Newcombe (1967).
longest match	11 hours, 5 minutes: in 2010 John Isner (USA) defeated Nicolas Mahut (Fra) 6–4, 3–6, 6–7(7–9), 7–6(7–3), 70–68, including a final set lasting 8 hours 11 minutes.
oldest men's champion	Arthur Gore (41).
champion later represented Brazil in Davis Cup	Robert Falkenburg.
unseeded champion	Boris Becker (1985).
unseeded player in two finals	Kurt Nielsen (Den) beaten in 1953 and 1955.
youngest champion	Lottie Dod (GB) aged 15.
youngest men's champion	Boris Becker (Ger) aged 17.

Sporting Trophies

Name	*Sport*	*Details*	*First held*
Admirals Cup	yachting	biennial international competition for sailing yachts	1957
Air Canada Silver Broom	curling	formerly the Scotch Whisky Cup, became Air Canada in 1959	1968
America's Cup	yachting	originally called 100 Guineas Cup and raced around the Isle of Wight	1851
Ashes	cricket	England v Australia test matches (since 1882 called 'Ashes')	1877
Baron Matsui Inter-Club Cup	judo	club competition named after the Japanese Ambassador	1928
Bledisloe Cup	rugby union	New Zealand v Australia	1931
Bologna Trophy	swimming	England v Scotland v Wales speed swimming contest	1929

Name	*Sport*	*Details*	*First held*
Borg-Warner Trophy	motor racing	winner of the Indianapolis 500	1932
Bowring Bowl	rugby union	annual Oxbridge Varsity match	1872
Britannia Cup	yachting	for small yachts (under 32ft) of any country to challenge the holder	1951
Britannia Shield	speedway	inter-club challenge competition	1957
Calcutta Cup	rugby union	England v Scotland	1870
Camanachd Cup	shinty	championship of Scotland	1896
Canada Cup	golf	world team championship (two per team)	1953
Cole Cup	fencing	men's sabre	1922
Cowdray Park Gold Cup	polo	international competition	1956
Currie Cup	cricket	South African Provincial competition	1889
Currie Cup	rugby union	South African Provincial Championship	1892
Curtis Cup	golf	amateur women – USA v Great Britain and Ireland	1932
Davis Cup	tennis	The International Lawn Tennis Challenge Trophy	1900
Dewar Cup	rifle shooting	small-bore shooting competition	1909
Diamond Challenge	rowing	blue riband of single sculling	1884
Doggetts Coat & Badge	rowing	sculling contest on the Thames between ex-passenger skiffs	1715
Eisenhower Trophy	golf	biennial international competition	1958
Federation Cup	tennis	women's world amateur team championship	1963
George Hearn Cup	diving	awarded to England's most successful diver	1954
Goldberg-Vass Memorial Trophy	judo	London open competition	1956
Gordon Bennett Trophy	motor racing	forerunner of the Grand Prix	1901
Grand Challenge Cup	rowing	Henley Regatta – eights	1839
Grey Cup	Canadian football	championship game between winners of Eastern and Western Conferences	1909
G Melville Clark Trophy	diving	awarded to England's most successful diving club	1951
Harry Sunderland Trophy	rugby league	man of the Premiership final. T Fogarty of Halifax first winner	1965
Heisman Memorial Trophy	American football	awarded annually by the Downtown Athlete Club of New York City to the outstanding college football player of the United States	1935
Henry Benjamin Trophy	swimming and water polo	awarded to England's most successful swimming and water polo club	1910
Iroquois Cup	lacrosse	English club championship	1890
Jules Rimet Trophy	football	world cup	1930
King George V Gold Cup	showjumping	men's international competition at Hickstead	1934
Kinnaird Cup	Eton fives	public schools' competition	1926
Lance Todd Award	rugby league	man of the match award in Challenge Cup final	1897
Lapham Trophy	squash	Canada v USA	1921
Leonard Trophy	bowls	World team championship	1966
Liam MacCarthy Cup	Hurling	Awarded to winner of All-Ireland Senior Hurling championship	1921
Londonderry Cup	squash	public schools' Old Boys' competition	1934
Lonsdale Belt	boxing	British title – won outright for winning three title fights at the same weight	1909
Lugano Trophy	walking	world championship of race walking	1961
MacRobertson International Shield	croquet	international competition	1925
Manuel Avilla Camacho Cup	polo	Mexico v USA	1941
Marcel Corbillon Cup	table tennis	women's world table tennis team championships	1934
Marchant Cup	rugby fives	London grammar schools competition	1929
Middleton Cup	bowls	inter-county championship	1911
Mosconi Cup	pool	USA v Europe annual event	1994
Norman Brookes Trophy	lawn tennis	awarded to the winner of the men's singles at the Australian Open	1905
Philadelphia Gold Cup	rowing	Olympic single sculling trophy	1908
Pilkington Cup	rugby union	English club knockout cup (prev. National Cup)	1972
Powergen Cup	rugby union	English club knockout cup (formerly John Player Cup, Pilkington Cup, Tetley's Bitter Cup)	1972
Presidents Trophy	golf	USA v Rest of World (Men)	1994
Prince of Wales Cup	yachting	international 14ft dinghy championship	1927
Prince Rainier Cup	fencing	awarded to the nation with best results in World Championships	1950
Princess Elizabeth Cup	rowing	Henley Regatta – eights for public schools	1946
Queen Elizabeth II Cup	showjumping	women's international competition at Hickstead	1949
Queen's Prize	rifle shooting	open competition first competed for at Wimbledon	1860
Ranfurly Shield	rugby union	NZ rugby trophy for provincial teams	1902
Regal Trophy	rugby league	formerly sponsored by John Player, became Regal Trophy in 1989	1971
Russell-Cargill Trophy	rugby union	Awarded to winner of Middlesex Sevens	1951
Ryder Cup	golf	men – USA v Europe (USA v GB and Ire before 1979)	1927
Sam MacGuire Trophy	Gaelic football	All-Ireland Men's Senior Football championship	1928
Scottish Tennant's Cup	rugby union	Scottish club knockout cup	1996
Seawanhaka Cup	yachting	For small yachts (under 25ft) of any country to challenge the holder	1895
Sid Waddell Trophy	darts	PDC World Darts Championship	2013

Name	*Sport*	*Details*	*First held*
Silver Goblets & Nickalls Cup	rowing	Henley Regatta: coxless pairs amateur international	1845
Sir William Burton Trophy	yachting	national 12 ft dinghy championship	1936
Solheim Cup	golf	women – USA v Europe	1990
Stanley Cup	ice hockey	North American ice hockey championship	1894
Strathcona Cup	curling	Canada v Scotland international competition	1903
Subalterns' Cup	polo	inter-services competition	1896
Super 12 Trophy	rugby union	Southern Hemisphere provincial championship	1995
SWALEC Cup	rugby union	Welsh club knockout cup (prev. Welsh Cup, Schweppes Cup)	1972
Swaythling Cup	table tennis	men's world table tennis team championships	1927
Talbot Handicap	crown green bowls	Blackpool-based open competition	1882
Thomas Cup	badminton	men's world badminton team championship	1949
Über Cup	badminton	women's world badminton team championships	1957
Val Barker Trophy	boxing	most stylish boxer at an Olympic Games	1904
Vince Lombardi Trophy	American football	superbowl	1967
Volvo World Cup	showjumping	world championship competition	1979
Walker Cup	golf	amateur men – USA v Great Britain and Ireland	1922
Waterloo Cup	coursing	the 'Derby' of coursing, named after a Liverpool hotel	1836
Waterloo Cup	crown green bowls	Blackpool-based open competition	1907
Webb Ellis Trophy	rugby union	world cup	1987
Westchester Cup	polo	Great Britain v USA	1886
Wheeler-Schebber	motor racing	awarded to the leader of the Indianapolis 500 after 400 miles (160 laps), replaced in 1932 by the Borg-Warner Trophy	
Wightman Cup	tennis	annual team competition between USA and England	1923
Wolfe-Noel Cup	squash	USA v GB women's match	1933
Worrell Trophy	cricket	West Indies v Australia	1931
Wyfold Challenge Cup	rowing	Henley Regatta	1847
Yeaden Memorial Trophy	swimming	awarded to the English swimmer whose performance is adjudged the best	1938
Zurich Premiership Trophy	rugby union	Awarded to winner of English club league championship	1987

NB The inaugural dates given are for the competition; in some cases the trophy has been renamed.

Television Sports Personality of the Year

Chris Chataway	1954	Brendan Foster	1974	Damon Hill	1994
Gordon Pirie	1955	David Steele	1975	Jonathan Edwards	1995
Jim Laker	1956	John Curry	1976	Damon Hill	1996
Dai Rees	1957	Virginia Wade	1977	Greg Rusedski	1997
Ian Black	1958	Steve Ovett	1978	Michael Owen	1998
John Surtees	1959	Sebastian Coe	1979	Lennox Lewis	1999
David Broome	1960	Robin Cousins	1980	Steve Redgrave	2000
Stirling Moss	1961	Ian Botham	1981	David Beckham	2001
Anita Lonsbrough	1962	Daley Thompson	1982	Paula Radcliffe	2002
Dorothy Hyman	1963	Steve Cram	1983	Jonny Wilkinson	2003
Mary Rand	1964	Torvill and Dean	1984	Kelly Holmes	2004
Tommy Simpson	1965	Barry McGuigan	1985	Andrew Flintoff	2005
Bobby Moore	1966	Nigel Mansell	1986	Zara Phillips	2006
Henry Cooper	1967	Fatima Whitbread	1987	Joe Calzaghe	2007
David Hemery	1968	Steve Davis	1988	Chris Hoy	2008
Ann Jones	1969	Nick Faldo	1989	Ryan Giggs	2009
Henry Cooper	1970	Paul Gascoigne	1990	AP McCoy	2010
HRH Princess Anne	1971	Liz McColgan	1991	Mark Cavendish	2011
Mary Peters	1972	Nigel Mansell	1992	Bradley Wiggins	2012
Jackie Stewart	1973	Linford Christie	1993		

Commonwealth Games: Venues

Hamilton, Canada	1930	Kingston, Jamaica	1966	Victoria, Canada	1994
London, England	1934	Edinburgh, Scotland	1970	Kuala Lumpur, Malaysia	1998
Sydney, Australia	1938	Christchurch, NZ	1974	Manchester, England	2002
Auckland, NZ	1950	Edmonton, Canada	1978	Melbourne, Australia	2006
Vancouver, Canada	1954	Brisbane, Australia	1982	Delhi, India	2010
Cardiff, Wales	1958	Edinburgh, Scotland	1986	Glasgow, Scotland	2014
Perth, Australia	1962	Auckland, NZ	1990		

Number of Players in a Team

		Details
polo	4	Up to 8 chukkas of $7\frac{1}{2}$ min
basketball	5	4 periods
ice hockey	6	3 periods of 20 min
volleyball	6	Court size: 30ft x 60ft
kabaddi	7	2 halves of 20 minutes each
netball	7	4 periods of 15 min
water polo	7	blue or white caps (red for goalkeepers)
baseball	9	9 innings
rounders	9	2 innings
American football	11	1 hour
football	11	2 halves of 45 min
cricket	11	see relevant section
hockey	11	field size: 100 yd x 60 yd (goal 4 yd x 7 ft high) men's, 2 halves of 35 min; women's, 2 of 30 min
stoolball	11	girls' game resembling cricket
lacrosse (men's)	10	4 periods of 15 min
lacrosse (women's)	12	4 periods of 15 min
Canadian football	12	field size: 110 yd x 65 yd
shinty	12	field size: 160 yd x 80 yd
rugby league	13	no wing forwards
rugby union	15	2 halves of 40 min
Gaelic football	15	2 periods of 30 min
hurling	15	women's version called 'camogie'
Australian rules	18	4 periods of 25 min

Sportspeople

Aaron, Hank	**baseball**
Abdul-Jabbar, Kareem	**basketball**
Ackland, Janet	**bowls**
Adams, Neil	**judo**
Adams, Nicola	**boxing**
Alexander, Wayne	**boxing**
Allahgreen, Diane	**athletics**
Allan, Alister	**shooting**
Allen, Marcus	**American football**
Alonso, Fernando	**motor racing**
Alsop, Fred	**triple jump**
Altwegg, Jeannette	**figure skating**
Angus, Howard	**rackets**
Aoki, Haruchika	**motor cycling**
Aoki, Isao	**golf**
Appleyard, Bob	**cricket**
Armitstead, Lizzie	**cycling**
Armstrong, Gary	**rugby union**
Ascari, Alberto	**motor racing**
Ashton, Eric	**rugby league**
Aspinall, Nigel	**croquet**
Astbury, Andrew	**swimming**
Atkins, Geoffrey	**rackets**
Atkins, John	**cyclo cross**
Baddeley, Steve	**badminton**
Baddeley, Wilfred & Herbert	**tennis**
Baerlein, Edgar	**rackets**
Baggaley, Andrew	**table tennis**
Bailey, Bill	**cycling**
Bailey, McDonald	**athletics**
Bailey, William James	**cycling**
Baillieu, Chris	**rowing**
Baird, Charlotte	**surfing**
Bairstow, Jonny	**cricket**
Baker, Edwin Percy	**bowls**
Baker, Philip Noel	**athletics**
Baker, Zoe	**swimming**
Bakewell, Enid	**cricket**
Balashov, Alexandr	**ice speedway**
Balding, Gerald	**polo**
Balding, Gerald Matthews	**polo**
Ball, John	**golf**
Ballington, Kork	**motor cycling**
Barber, Bob	**cricket**
Barber, Paul	**hockey**
Barnato, Woolf	**motor racing**
Barras, Sid	**cycling**
Barrichello, Rubens	**motor racing**
Barry, Ernest	**rowing**
Barton, Pam	**golf**
Beamish, George	**rugby union**
Beck, Margaret	**badminton**
Bedell-Sivright, Darkie	**rugby union**
Bell, Diane	**judo**
Beresford, Jack	**rowing**
Berra, Lawrence 'Yogi'	**baseball**
Besford, Jack	**swimming**
Biaggi, Massimiliano	**motor cycling**
Bickers, Dave	**motocross**
Bird, Larry	**basketball**
Black, Dave	**athletics**
Black, Ian	**swimming**
Blankers-Koen, Fanny	**athletics**
Blenkinsop, Ernie	**football**
Bond-Williams, Louise	**fencing**
Boocock, Nigel	**speedway**
Boone, Willie	**rackets**
Bourne, Teddy	**fencing**
Bowman, George	**carriage driving**
Bradley, Caroline	**show jumping**
Bradshaw, Harry	**golf**
Braid, James	**golf**
Braithwaite, Bob	**shooting**
Briggs, Johnny	**cricket**
Briggs, Karen	**judo**
Brinkley, Brian	**swimming**
Brittin, Janette	**cricket**
Brockway, John	**swimming**
Bromfield, Percy	**table tennis**
Bullen, Jane	**three-day event**
Burns, Tommy	**boxing**
Burton, Beryl	**cycling**
Butcher, Don	**squash**
Cacho, Fermin	**athletics**
Cadalora, Luca	**motor cycling**
Caira, Philip Mario	**weightlifting**
Callender, Simone	**judo**
Calvert, David	**shooting**
Calzaghe, Joe	**boxing**
Capirossi, Loris	**motor cycling**
Carnill, Denys	**hockey**
Cazelet, Victor	**squash**
Chamberlain, Wilt	**basketball**
Chapman, Vera	**hockey**
Cheape, Leslie	**polo**
Cheeseborough, Susan	**gymnastics**
Chester, Frank	**cricket**
Chifney, Sam	**horse racing**
Childs, Joe	**horse racing**
Clancy, Ed	**cycling**
Clark, Gillian	**badminton**
Clark, Roger	**rallying**
Clarke, Chris	**croquet**
Cobb, John	**motor racing**
Cobb, Ty	**baseball**
Cockell, Don	**boxing**
Cockett, John	**hockey**
Colclough, Maurice	**rugby union**
Colledge, Cecilia	**figure skating**
Collett, Rebecca	**figure skating**
Collins, Peter	**motor racing**
Collins, Peter	**speedway**
Cook, Kathy (nee Smallwood)	**sprinting**
Cooke, Nicole	**cycling**
Cooke, Rebecca	**swimming**
Cooper, Charlotte	**tennis**
Cooper, Malcolm	**shooting**
Cotter, Edmond	**croquet**
Couch, Jane	**boxing**
Covey, Fred	**real tennis**
Craven, Peter	**speedway**
Creus, Julian	**weightlifting**
Cripps, Norwood	**rackets**
Cronshey, John Dennis	**speed skating**
Crooks, Lee	**rugby league**
Crooks, Tim	**rowing**
Cumming, Arthur	**figure skating**
Curry, Joan	**squash/ tennis**
Curtis, Steve	**powerboating**
Cutler, David	**bowls**
Daley, Tom	**diving**
Daly, Fred	**golf**
Datoo, Camille	**fencing**
Davidge, Chris	**rowing**
Davies, Terry	**rugby union**
Davis, Howard	**hockey**
Dawes, Alison	**show jumping**
De Beaumont, Charles	**fencing**
De Wharton Burr, Nilla	**archery**
Dear, Jim	**racket sports**

Deaton, Nicola	**table tennis**
Dempsey, Jack 'Nonpareil'	**boxing**
Denny, Doreen	**ice dancing**
Didrikson, Babe	**athletics/ golf**
Di Maggio, Joe	**baseball**
Disley, John	**steeplechase**
Dixon, Charles	**tennis**
Dixon, Karen	**three-day event**
Dixon, Robin	**bobsleigh**
Dod, Willie	**archery**
Doherty, Reggie	**tennis**
Donaldson, Walter	**snooker**
Doohan, Michael	**motor cycling**
Doyle, Tony	**cycling**
Driffield, Leslie	**billiards**
Drinkhall, Paul	**table tennis**
Drummond, Des	**rugby league**
Drummond-Hay, Anneli	**show jumping**
Duke, Geoff	**motor cycling**
Dugard, Martin	**speedway**
Dundee, Johnny	**boxing**
Eastman, Howard	**boxing**
Eastwood, Vic	**motocross**
Edwards, Hugh 'Jumbo'	**rowing**
Edwards, Margaret	**swimming**
Egan, Joe	**rugby league**
Egg, Oscar	**cycling**
Elford, Vic	**motor racing**
Ellaby, Alf	**rugby league**
Elliot, Douglas	**rugby union**
Elliot, Helen	**table tennis**
Elliot, Launceston	**weightlifting**
Elwell, Keith	**rugby league**
Engers, Alf	**cycling**
Erhardt, Carl	**ice hockey**
Erskine, Joe	**boxing**
Evans, Mal	**bowls**
Everts, Stefan	**motocross**
Ewing, Patrick	**basketball**
Fahey, Robert	**real tennis**
Fairbrother, Nicola	**judo**
Fairs, Punch	**real tennis**
Fallon, Craig	**judo**
Fangio, Juan Manuel	**motor racing**
Farina, Giuseppe	**motor racing**
Farndon, Tom	**speedway**
Farr, Judy	**walking**
Farr, Tommy	**boxing**
Ferris, Liz	**diving**
Ferris, Sam	**marathon**
Figg, James	**boxing**
Flockhart, Ron	**motor racing**
Fogarty, Carl	**superbikes**
Ford, Bernard	**ice dancing**
Ford, Horace	**archery**
Ford, Trevor	**football**
Fordham, George	**football**
Foster, Bob	**boxing**
Foster, Bob	**motor cycling**
Foster, Jimmy	**ice hockey**
Fox, Jim	**modern pentathlon**
Fox, Neil	**rugby league**
Fox, Richard	**canoeing**
Fox-Pitt, William	**equestrianism**
Foxx, Jimmie	**baseball**
Freeman, Alfred 'Tich'	**cricket**
Frentzen, Heinz-Harold	**motor racing**
Frith, Frederick	**motor cycling**
Froome, Chris	**cycling**
Fulford, Robert	**croquet**
Fulton, Arthur	**shooting**
Funnell, Pippa	**equestrianism**
Furrer, Carl	**trampolining**
Fury, Tyson	**boxing**
Galica, Davina	**skiing & motor racing**
Gallie, Christine	**judo**
Gans, Joe	**boxing**
Gardner, Jason	**athletics**
Gardner, Wayne	**motor cycling**
Gault, Michael	**shooting**
Gee, Kenneth	**rugby league**
George, Walter	**athletics**
Giles, Jack	**squash**
Glen Haig, Mary	**fencing**
Goddard, James	**swimming**
Gordon, Winston	**judo**
Gower, Lily	**croquet**
Grace, Edward Mills	**cricket**
Graham, Leslie	**motor cycling**
Gramigni, Alessandro	**motor cycling**
Green, Tommy	**walking**
Greenwood, Giles	**weightlifting**
Guthrie, Jimmy	**motor cycling**
Haining, Peter	**rowing**
Hakkinen, Mika	**motor racing**
Hale, Jack	**swimming**
Hall, Darren	**badminton**
Hallam, Ian	**cycling**
Hallard, Steve	**archery**
Halliday, Jim	**weightlifting**
Hamill, Billy	**speedway**
Hamilton, Laird	**surfing**
Hancock, Greg	**speedway**
Hand, Tony	**ice hockey**
Hann, Quinten	**snooker**
Harding, Phyllis	**swimming**
Hardisty, Alan	**rugby league**
Hardstaff, Joe	**cricket**
Harlow, Greg	**bowls**
Harper, Ernie	**marathon**
Harris, Lord George	**cricket**
Harris, Reg	**cycling**
Hart, Marvin	**boxing**
Harvey, Len	**boxing**
Hatfield, Jack	**swimming**
Hathorn, Gina	**skiing**
Haughton, Colin	**badminton**
Havelock, Gary	**speedway**
Hawke, Lord Martin	**cricket**
Hawthorn, Mike	**motor racing**
Hayles, Rob	**cycling**
Healey, Donald	**rallying**
Heaney, Julz	**water skiing**
Heaney, Nick	**water skiing**
Heatley, Basil	**marathon**
Heatly, Peter	**diving**
Helme, Gerry	**rugby league**
Hendren, Patsy	**cricket**
Herriott, Maurice	**steeplechaser**
Hicks, Humphrey	**croquet**
Hide, Herbie	**boxing**
Hide, Molly	**cricket**
Hill, Albert	**athletics**
Hill, Phil	**motor racing**
Hiller, Bob	**rugby union**
Hilton, Elliot	**ice skating**
Hipwood, Julian	**polo**
Hocking, Gary	**motor cycling**
Hodgson, Neil	**superbike racing**
Holden, Jack	**marathon**
Holmes, Andrea	**trampolining**
Holmes, Terry	**rugby union**
Horgan, Denis	**shot putter**
Hoskyns, Bill	**fencing**
Howland, Bonzo	**shot putt**
Hulme, Denny	**motor racing**
Hume, Donald	**badminton**
Inkpen, Barbara	**high jump**
Inman, Melbourne	**billiards**
Ireland, Innes	**motor racing**
Ivy, Bill	**motor cycling**
Jackson, Kanukai	**gymnastics**
Jackson, Reggie	**baseball**
James, Carwyn	**rugby union**
Jameson, Andrew	**swimming**
Jameson, Tommy	**squash**
Jarrett, Keith	**rugby**
Jarvis, John	**swimming**
Jay, Allan	**fencing**
Jeeps, Dickie	**rugby union**
Jofre, Eder	**boxing**
Johnson, Ralph	**fencing**
Johnson, Tebbs Lloyd	**walking**
Jones, Cliff	**rugby union**
Jones, Cliff	**football**
Jones, Courtney	**ice dancing**
Jones, Mandy	**cycling**
Jordan, Michael	**basketball**
Jordan, Tony	**badminton**
Joshua, Anthony	**boxer**
Kane, Peter	**boxing**
Kanu, Nwankwo	**football**
Karalius, Vince	**rugby league**
Keane, Moss	**rugby union**
Keenan, Peter	**boxing**
Kelly, Sean	**cycling**
Kelly-Hohmann, Margaret	**swimming**
Kelsey, Jack	**football**
Kendall-Carpenter, John	**rugby union**
Kerly, Sean	**hockey**
Kershaw, Cecil	**rugby union**
King, Dani	**cycling**
King, Norman	**bowls**
King, Shayne	**motocross**
Kingpetch, Pone	**boxing**
Kitchen, Bill	**speedway**
Kluft, Carolina	**athletics**
Knight, Billy	**tennis**
Kocinski, John	**motor cycling**
Laidlaw, Roy	**rugby union**
Langton, Eric	**speedway**
Larcombe, Ethel	**tennis**
Larner, George	**walking**
Latham, Peter	**rackets**
Lawler, Ivan	**canoeing**
Lawson, Eddie	**motor cycling**
Lawton, Barbara	**high jump**
Leather, Diane	**athletics**
Leden, Judy	**hang gliding**
Lee, George	**gliding**
Lee, Michael	**speedway**
Lee, Norvel	**boxing**
Lee, Sidney	**billiards**
Legh, Alice	**archery**
Leman, Richard	**hockey**
Lemon, Meadowlark	**basketball**
Le Moignan, Martine	**squash**
Lennox, Avril	**gymnastics**
Lerwill, Alan	**long jumper**
Lesnevich, Gus	**boxing**
Lessing, Simon	**triathlon**
Levinsky, Battling	**boxing**
Lewis-Francis, Mark	**athletics**
Line, Peter	**bowls**
Lloyd, Emrys	**fencing**
Lombardi, Vincent	**American football**
Long, Liz	**swimming**
Longo, Jeannie	**cycling**
Loram, Mark	**speedway**
Loris, Chris	**speedway**
Lowe, Samantha	**judo**
Lucas, Muriel	**badminton**
Lucchinelli, Marco	**motor cycling**
Lumb, Margot	**squash**
Lumley, Penny	**real tennis**
Lunn family	**skiing**
Lunn, Gladys	**athletics**
Lycett, Randolph	**tennis**
Lydon, Joe	**rugby league**
Lynch, Benny	**boxing**
Mace, Jem	**boxing**
Mack, Curly	**badminton**
Macken, Eddie	**showjumping**
Mackey, Mick	**hurling**
Mackinnon, Esmé	**skiing**
MacLean, Craig	**cycling**
Maduaka, Joice	**athletics**

Maguire, Stephen	snooker
Mahoney, Harold	tennis
Male, James	rackets
Mallin, Frederick	boxing
Mallin, Harry	boxing
Mann, Julia	badminton
Mannion, Wilf	football
Mansergh, Terence	hockey
Mantle, Mickey	baseball
Mapple, Andy	water skiing
Marques, David	rugby union
Marshall, Peter	squash
Martin, Louis	weightlifting
Martin, Stephen	hockey
Matthews, Ken	walking
Mays, Willie	baseball
McAuliffe, Jack	boxing
McAvoy, Jock	boxing
McCoig, Robert	badminton
McConnell, William	hockey
McEvoy, Freddie	bobsleigh
McGregor, Yvonne	cycling
McGwire, Mark	baseball
McIntyre, Bob	motor cycling
McKechnie, Neil	swimming
McKenzie, George	wrestling
McKiernan, Catherina	athletics
McKinlay, Ken	speedway
McLean, William	hockey
McLeod, Hugh	rugby union
McNeill, Carol	orienteering
McQueen, Delroy	weightlifting
McRae, Alister	rallying
McRae, Colin	rallying
McRae, Jimmy	rallying
McTigue, Mike	boxing
Meade, Richard	three-day event
Melandri, Marco	motor cycling
Menu, Alain	touring cars
Meredith, Billy	football
Meredith, Leon	cycling
Miles, Eustace	rackets
Milford, David	rackets
Millar, David	cycling
Millar, Robert	cycling
Miller, David	bowls
Miller, Sammy	motor cycling
Millward, Roger	rugby league
Minter, Derek	motor cycling
Mirra, Dave	BMX
Mitchell, Abe	golf
Mitchell, Beryl	rowing
Mitchell, William	billiards
Monaghan, Terry	speed skating
Montana, Joe	American football
Montgomerie, Robert	fencing
Moore, Ann	show jumping
Moore, Steve	water skiing
Morgan, Janet	squash
Morris, Stewart	yachting
Morton, Lucy	swimming
Moss, Pat	rallying
Mould, Marion	show jumping
Muckelt, Ethel	figure skating
Murphy, Catherine	athletics
Mynn, Alfred	cricket
Namath, Joe	American football
Nash, Tony	bobsleigh
Neale, Denis	table tennis
Nedved, Pavel	football
Neligan, Gwen	fencing
Nettleton, Louise	archery
Netzer, Gunter	football
Nevett, Bill	jockey
Neville, Gary & Phil	football
Neville, Tracey	netball (sister of Gary & Phil)
Newall, Queenie	archery
Newman, Tom	billiards
Nicholas, Alison	golf
Nielsen, Hans	speedway
Nieto, Angel	motor cycling
Noel, Susan	squash
Norman, Wendy	modern pentathlon
Obolensky, Alex	rugby union
Obree, Graeme	cycling
O'Dell, George	motor cycling
Ogogo, Anthony	boxing
O'Keefe, Dan	Gaelic football
Oliver, Alan	show jumping
Oliver, Eric	sidecar racing
Opie, Lisa	squash
O'Reilly, Wilf	speed skating
Ottley, Dave	javelin
Paish, Geoff	tennis
Palmer, Charles	judo
Palmer, Thomas 'Pedlar'	boxing
Panis, Olivier	motor racing
Papke, Billy	boxing
Papp, Lászlό	boxing
Parke, James	tennis & rugby
Parker, Jack	speedway
Pastrano, Willie	boxing
Paterson, Alan	high jump
Pattisson, Rodney	yachting
Patton, Peter	ice hockey
Paul, René	fencing
Payne, Howard	hammer throw
Payne, Rosemary	discus
Paynter, Eddie	cricket
Payton, Walter	American football
Peall, W J	billiards
Peck, Geoff	orienteering
Pedersen, Nicki	speedway
Pedrosa, Dani	motor cycling
Pendleton, Victoria	cycling
Pep, Willie	boxing
Petersen, Jack	boxing
Phelps, Brian	diving & trampolining
Phelps, Richard	modern pentathlon
Phelps, Ted	rowing
Phillips, Mollie	figure skating
Pickering, Jean	long jump
Pickering, Karen	swimming
Pilch, Fuller	cricket
Pinching, Evie	skiing
Platt, Susan	javelin
Pons, Sito	motor cycling
Porter, Hugh	cycling
Potter, Jon	hockey
Potter, Martin	surfing
Prenn, John	rackets
Price, Berwyn	athletics
Price, David	boxing
Price, Sarah	swimming
Price, Tommy	speedway
Probyn, Jeff	rugby union
Pullin, John	rugby union
Queally, Jason	cycling
Quixall, Albert	football
Radford, Peter	athletics
Radmilovic, Paul	swimming & water polo
Raikkonen, Kimi	motor racing
Rainey, Wayne	motor cycling
Randall, Graeme	judo
Ray, Ted	golf
Read, Phil	motor cycling
Reade, Shanaze	cycling
Redman, Jim	motor cycling
Reece, Tom	billiards
Rendle, Sharon	judo
Renshaw, William	tennis
Rhodes, Ronald	canoeing
Rice, Jerry	American football
Richards, Gordon W	horse racing
Richards, Sir Gordon	horse racing
Richards, Tom	marathon
Richardson, Peter	cricket
Richardson, T D	figure skating
Richmond, Ken	wrestling/ judo
Ring, Christy	hurling
Ringer, Anthony	shooting
Riseley, Frank	tennis
Ritchie, Margaret	discus
Roberts, John	billiards
Roberts, Karen	judo
Roberts, Kenny	motor cycling
Roberts, Philippa	water skiing
Robinson, Brian	cycling
Robinson, Jack	baseball
Robinson, Jem	horse racing
Robinson, Val	hockey
Rodman, Dennis	basketball
Rogers, Iris	badminton
Rogers, Michelle	judo
Ronaldson, Chloe	roller skating
Root, Joe	cricketer
Rose, Justin	golf
Ross, Jonathan	bowls
Rossi, Valentino	motor cycling
Round, Dorothy	tennis
Rowe, Arthur	shot putt
Rowe, Diana	table tennis
Rowe, Rosalind	table tennis
Rowsell, Joanna	cycling
Ruffo, Bruno	motor cycling
Russell-Vick, Mary	hockey
Ruth, Babe	baseball
Rutherford, Monica	gymnastics
Salo, Mika	motor racing
Salvadori, Roy	motor racing
Sandford, Cecil	motor cycling
Sarron, Christian	motor cycling
Saunders, Vivien	golf
Savage, David	hockey
Saville, Sammy	hockey
Schofield, Garry	rugby league
Schwantz, Kevin	motor cycling
Scotland, Ken	rugby union
Scott, Peter	yachting & gliding
Scriven, Peggy	tennis
Seaman, Dick	motor racing
Searle, Greg and Johnny	rowing
Seaton, Paul	water skiing
Segrave, Henry	motor racing
Sekjer, Martyn	bowls
Selby, Vera	snooker
Seligman, Edgar	fencing
Sharpe, Graham	figure skating
Shaw, Norma	bowls
Sheen, Gillian	fencing
Sheil, Norman	cycling
Sheppard, Alison	swimming
Sheridan, Eileen	cycling
Shilcock, Anne	tennis
Shotton, Sue	trampolining
Shoveller, Stanley	hockey
Shrubb, Alf	athletics
Simmers, Max	rugby union
Simmonds, Dave	motor cycling
Simmonite, Rachael	rallying
Simmonite, Stephanie	rallying
Simpson, Cyril	rackets
Simpson, Tommy	cycling
Sindelar, Matthias	football
Singleton, Georgina	judo
Singleton, Joey	boxing
Sixsmith, Janet	hockey
Skelton, Matt	boxing
Slawinski, Kendra	netball
Small, Ruth	bowls

Smith, Charles	**water polo**	Thomson, Andy	**bowls**	Warner, Sir Pelham	**cricket**
Smith, Jeff	**motocross**	Thorpe, Dave	**motocross**	Warren, James	**judo**
Smith, Lawrie	**yachting**	Thorpe, Jim	**American football/athletics**	Waterman, Split	**speedway**
Smith, Steve	**cricket**			Watson, Maud	**tennis**
Smith, Steve	**high jump**	Tisdall, Bob	**400m hurdles**	Watson, Willie	**cricket/ football**
Smith, Sydney	**tennis**	Tomes, Alan	**rugby union**	Weah, George	**football**
Smithies, Karen	**cricket**	Tomlins, Freddie	**figure skating**	Webb, Jonathan	**rugby union**
Snode, Chris	**diving**	Tortelli, Sébastien	**motocross**	Webster, Steve	**motor cycling**
Snow, John	**cricket**	Towler, Diane	**ice dancing**	Weetman, Harry	**golf**
Snow, Julian	**real tennis**	Tredgett, Mike	**badminton**	Wells, Billy	**boxing**
Snowball, Betty	**cricket**	Tredgold, Roger	**fencing**	Welsh, Freddie	**boxing**
Solomon, John	**croquet**	Trew, Billy	**rugby union**	Westwood, Jean	**ice dance**
Sopwith, Sir Tommy	**yachting**	Trinidad, Felix	**boxing**	White, Belle	**diving**
Sosa, Samuel	**baseball**	Troke, Helen	**badminton**	White, Wilf	**show jumping**
Spencer, Freddie	**motor cycling**	Trott, Laura	**cycling**	Whitehead, Adam	**swimming**
Springman, Sarah	**triathlon**	Trott, Jonathan	**cricket**	Whiteley, Johnny	**rugby league**
Stammers, Kay	**tennis**	Tucker, Andrew	**shooting**	Whitford, Arthur	**gymnastics**
Starbrook, Dave	**judo**	Tucker, Sam	**rugby union**	Whitlock, Harold	**walking**
Steel, Dorothy	**croquet**	Tuckey, Raymond	**tennis**	Whittle, Harry	**athletics**
Steele, Mavis	**bowls**	Tweddle, Elisabeth	**gymnastics**	Whyte, Jamie	**ice dancing**
Stevens, Ray	**badminton**	Tyler, Dorothy	**high jump**	Wigg, Simon	**speedway**
Stewart-Wood, Jeannette	**water skiing**	Ubbiali, Carlo	**motor cycling**	Wilkinson, Diana	**swimming**
Stoichkov, Hristo	**football**	Uber, Betty	**badminton**	Wilkinson, George	**water polo**
Stoner, Casey	**motor cycling**	Ulyett, George	**cricket**	Williams, Amy	**skeleton bob**
Stoop, Adrian	**rugby union**	Uncini, Franco	**motor cycling**	Williams, Freddie	**speedway**
Sturgess, Colin	**cycling**	Usher, Georgina	**fencing**	Wills, Philip	**gliding**
Sturgess, William	**walking**	Valderrama, Carlos	**football**	Wilson, Justin	**motor racing**
Surtees, William	**rackets**	Verstappen, Jos	**motor racing**	Wonderful Terrific Mons III	**baseball**
Talbot, Derek	**badminton**	Vettel, Sebastian	**motor racing**	Wooderson, Sydney	**athletics**
Tancred, Bill	**discus**	Vickers, Stan	**walking**	Woodgate, W B	**rowing**
Tanner, Haydn	**rugby union**	Vincent, Arnaud	**motor cycling**	Woodward, Clive	**rugby union**
Tarleton, Nelson	**boxing**	Viollet, Denis	**football**	Woodward, Vivian	**football**
Tate, Maurice	**cricket**	Wagstaff, Harold	**rugby league**	Wooller, Wilf	**rugby union**
Tatum, Kelvin	**speedway**	Walker, Stefanie	**ice dancing**	Woosnam, Max	**tennis/ football**
Taylor, Ian	**hockey**	Wallace, Shaun	**cycling**	Yardley, Norman	**cricket**
Terry, Simon	**archery**	Warburg, David	**real tennis**	Young, Cy	**baseball**
Thomas, Neil	**gymnastics**	Ward, David	**bowls**	Zale, Tony	**boxing**
Thompson, Don	**walking**	Ward, Pat	**tennis**		
Thompson, Ian	**marathon**	Wardrop, Jack	**swimming**		

NB The table above is merely a list of perhaps less well-known sports people, due either to their practising a minority sport or to the time elapsed since their success. A more thorough record of their achievements is beyond the scope of this book.

Sporting Terms

adolph *trampolining* three-and-a-half front twisting somersault.
airshot *golf* complete missing of ball which constitutes a stroke (unless mulligan awarded).
albatross *golf* score of 3 under par on a particular hole.
appel *fencing* beating or stamping of foot during contest.
apron *golf* grass cut short between fairway and approach to the green.
Arab spring *gymnastics* cartwheel with a quarter turn.
assist *basketball* final pass given to shooter of a basket.
axel *ice skating* a one-and-a-half turn jump from the forward outside edge of one skate to the backward outside edge of the other (named after Norwegian skater Axel Rudolph Paulser).
back alley *badminton* the area at the back of the court.
bai-hou *karate* white crane stance with one knee raised high (popularised in *Karate Kid* films).
balestra *fencing* attack after an appel.
barani *trampolining* front somersault with half twist.
battery *baseball* originally a term for the pitcher but now incorporates the pitcher and catcher.
baulk *billiards* line from which game begins.
ba(u)lk *baseball* illegal action by a pitcher.
beamer *cricket* ball bowled higher than a full toss so endangering the batsman.
Bernouilli effect *hang-gliding* see venturi effect.
besom *curling* type of broom used to sweep the ice to gain more distance.
bib *netball* tie-up over top with player's position labelled.
birdie *golf* score of 1 under par on a hole.
blind side *rugby* short side between scrum and touch line.
block *volleyball* basic return at the net to counter the opponent's spike.
blocking *basketball* illegal personal contact that impedes the progress of an opponent who does not have the ball.
bogey *golf* score of 1 over par on a hole.
bonk *cycling* tiredness caused by lack of food.
bonspiel *curling* term used for an important match.
boom *yachting* long spar or pole hinged at one end, securing the bottom of a ship's sail.
bosey / bosie *cricket* Australian name for a googly (named after B J T Bosanquet 1877–1936, an English cricketer).
Boston crab *wrestling* manoeuvre whereby one fighter sits on the back of the other with legs tucked under his arms.
bouncer *cricket* ball bowled short and fast in order to cause batsman to take evasive action.
bowling crease *cricket* line extended from the stumps sideways and four feet behind the popping crease; the ball must be delivered between these two lines.
brakeman *bobsleigh* person who operates the brakes in the sleigh.
Brill bend *high jumping* named after Debbie Brill, equivalent to the Fosbury flop.
brush *curling* implement for sweeping the ice, thereby causing the stone to travel further.
bunt *baseball* to let the ball hit the bat without swinging at it.
burgee *yachting* ornamental flag which serves no other purpose.
buttonhook *American football* type of pass for the receiver running straight downfield and then doubling back a few steps to receive it.
bye *cricket* extra gained by batting side when the batsmen run or the ball crosses the boundary after no contact with bat has taken place.
calx *Eton wall game* area behind the goal-line.
caman *shinty* stick used for striking.
cannon *billiards* object ball hitting opponent's ball and the red ball (scores 2 points).
capriole *dressage* horse jumps straight upward with its forelegs drawn in, kicking back with its hind legs horizontal.
catch *real tennis* obsolete former name for the game.
catch a crab *rowing* to get an oar trapped underwater or to miss the water with a stroke.
catenaccio system *football* sweeper system.
checking *ice hockey* legal manoeuvre of physical contact to gain control of puck.

chicane *motor racing* sharp double-bend.
chinaman *cricket* left-handed bowler's googly to a right-handed batsman.
chistera *pelota / jaïi alaïi* curved glove with a chestnut or ash frame, aka Cesta.
christiania *skiing* turn in which the skis are kept in parallel, used for stopping short. Aka christie.
Christmas tree *drag racing* starting system.
Christmas tree *football* descriptive formation.
chui *judo* warning with 3 points deducted.
chukka *polo* each of the 7½-minute periods into which a game is divided. Also spelt 'chucker' or 'chukker'.
close-hauled *wind surfing* area 45 degrees each side of wind direction.
conversion *Canadian football* method of adding to score after touchdown has been scored.
conversion *rugby* method of adding to score after try has been scored (2 points score).
courbet / curvet *dressage* jump forward at the levade.
cover *cricket* fielding position midway between infield and outfield in which a good fielder may save a single.
cover point *cricket* fielding position on the off side and nearer the batsman than the non-striker.
crampon *curling* device formerly used to enable a steady delivery but now obsolete.
crampon *rock-climbing* frame with 10 or 12 metal spikes, strapped to boots to give a firmer footing.
cross buttock *wrestling* throw in which a wrestler throws an opponent head first over his or her hip.
crosse *lacrosse* stick between 40–72 inches long and 4–10 inches wide.
crucifix *gymnastics (rings)* basic position with the arms held outstretched to the sides.
curve ball *baseball* ball which deviates from the path it would otherwise take, because of the spin imparted by the pitcher.
cut line *squash* line above which a served ball must strike the wall.
dan *martial arts* each of the numbered grades of the advanced level of proficiency in many martial arts.
diamond *baseball* the area formed by the four bases within the infield.
dig *volleyball* defensive motion of digging the ball up from below the net height with two hands to counter a spike.
ditch *bowls* the channel around the rink.
dog-leg *golf* hole that bends sharply to one side, so ensuring a positional shot is played.
domestiques *cycling* team members of tour teams who will sacrifice their position for team leaders.
double eagle *golf* score of 3 under par on a particular hole (US term).
down *American football* each of a fixed number of attempts to advance the ball 10 yards.
drop-kick *rugby* kick made by dropping the ball and kicking it as it rebounds from the ground.
drop-line *angling* weighted fishing-line for fishing near the bottom
drop-out *rugby* a drop-kick made from within the defending team's 22-metre (formerly 25yds) line in order to restart play after the ball has gone dead.
dropped goal *rugby* goal scored with a drop-kick that propels the ball over the crossbar.
dummy, sell a *rugby* to successfully feign a pass.
dunk *basketball* shoot a basket by jumping so that the hands are above the ring and the ball is dunked down through the hoop.
eagle *American football* defensive formation.
eagle *golf* score of 2 under par on a hole.
egg position *skiing* tucked position that ensures a good fast glide.
en garde *fencing* call to a fencer to adopt a defensive stance in readiness for an attack or bout.
end *bowls* division of a match whereby after all woods are bowled the next 'end' is played from the other end of the rink.
end *curling* division of a match whereby after all stones are bowled the next 'end' is played from the other end of the rink.
English *pool* north American term for using 'side' on the cueball.
Eskimo roll *canoeing* a 360-degree roll starting and finishing above water but 180 degrees of which is underwater.
expedite *table tennis* rule whereby a match is brought to a conclusion after a series of long rallies or deuces by setting a limit to the number of strokes per point.
extras *cricket* generic name for all types of byes and penalty runs scored other than by the batsman hitting the ball.
face-off *ice hockey* start of game.
fairway *golf* part of golf course between tee and green in which the grass is cut short to reward accuracy.
kinsa *judo* 3 point scoring technique.
feng taidu *kung fu* phoenix stance keeping low on one leg ready to rise.
fine leg *cricket* fielding position between wicket keeper and square leg but deeper.
flèche *archery* obsolete name for an arrow.
flèche *fencing* a running attack.
flic flac *gymnastics* simple back flip.
fliffis *trampolining* double front somersault with twist.
flying mare *wrestling* throw in which one wrestler throws the other over his or her back using the other's arm as a lever.
Fosbury flop *high jumping* technique named after Dick Fosbury, whereby head and shoulders are thrown over the bar first, chest upwards and with legs pulled back to ensure economical clearance.
free throw *basketball* free shot at basket due to an infringement by the opposition.
fukuro shinai *kendo* wooden sword often covered in cloth or leather.
full-nelson *wrestling* two-handed hold whereby the arms are placed under the arms of the opponent and interlocked behind his neck, immobilising the upper body.
gaff *yachting* spar situated on the after side of a mast and supporting the head of a fore-and-aft sail.
garryowen *rugby* another name for an up and under.
genoa *yachting* large jib with a low foot.
gojo-ryu *karate* hard / soft technique.
gokuhi *martial arts* techniques and 'secrets' of masters relayed to gifted students.
googly *cricket* off-break ball bowled with apparent leg-break action.
goosewinged *yachting* square-rigged boats having the topsail spread for scudding under when the wind is strong, the bunt of the sail being hauled up to the yard.
gridiron *American football* the field of play.
gully *cricket* fielding position a little wider than the slips.
gybe *yachting* of a fore-and-aft sail or its boom, to swing from one side of a vessel to the other.
hack *curling* notch made in the ice used to steady the foot when delivering a stone.
hackamore *horse racing* bitless bridle with a hard oval noseband which allows pressure to be exerted on the nose by means of the reins attached just in front of a heavy counterbalancing knot.
half-nelson *wrestling* hold whereby the arm of the opponent is bent behind his back and pushed upwards.
halyard *yachting* rope or tackle for raising or lowering a sail.
hammer grip *table tennis* rarely used method of holding the bat whereby no fingers touch its face.
hand-in *squash* the server.
hand-out *squash* when player loses a point on his service he becomes hand-out.
haute école *dressage* advanced training methods (high school).
head *bowls* the grouping of the woods around the jack.
hecht *gymnastics* dismount from the asymmetric bars head and body first between bars.
held ball *basketball* called when two opponents have one or two hands so firmly upon the ball that neither can gain possession.
herringboning *skiing* method of climbing a slope by walking with the skis pointing outwards.
hikiwake *kendo* a draw in a competitive match.
hog line *curling* line behind which the stone must be delivered.
hog's back *equestrianism* sharp-ridged natural mound for jumping.
honk *cycling* cycling out of the saddle.
hooker *rugby* front row of scrum position player supported between the two props who attemps to hook ball back with his feet to be used by his team.
hoop *basketball* the metal ring of the 'basket'.
hoop *croquet* arch through which the ball must be driven.
house *curling* the round target area of concentric circles.
I formation *American football* offensive formation.
in touch *rugby* out of play.
ippon *judo* full point in Japan (scores 10 points in competition).
Irish whip *wrestling* one-handed throw whereby the arm is whipped back and forth forcing a somersault in the air by the opponent.
jack *bowls* white ball which is the target for the woods.
jib *yachting* triangular staysail stretching from the outer end of the jib-boom to the fore-topmast.
judoka *judo* judo player.
jugogi *judo* judo suit.
jump ball *basketball* method of putting the ball into play whereby the referee tosses it up between two opponents who try to tap it to a teammate.
katame-waza *judo* basic hold.
keikoku *judo* judge's warning with 7 points deducted.
piaffe *dressage* a trot in place.

kip *gymnastics* movement whereby the body is straightened from a piked position by pushing the hips forward and the legs back.
knock-on *rugby* illegal move that knocks the ball forward and on to the ground with hand or arm.
koka *judo* hold between 10 and 20 seconds.
kyu *martial arts* student.
laundry *drag racing* the parachute that slows the cars down.
leg-bye *cricket* run scored after the ball has touched any part of the batsman but his hand.
leg side *cricket* the usual side of the wicket on which the receiving batsman stands.
levade *dressage* horse raises and draws in its forelegs, standing balanced on its bent hind legs.
line-out *rugby* method of throwing ball back into play between two lines of opposing forwards after it has gone out over the touchline.
lock *rugby* one of two forwards in second row of scrum.
long bomb *roller hockey* long pass from defence to set up sudden counter-attack.
long dong *kung fu* eastern dragon position with one hand in front of forehead (palm out) and the other covering abdomen (palm down).
long hop *cricket* ball that is bowled flat and short so as to almost bounce twice before reaching batsman.
luff *yachting* the edge of a fore-and-aft sail next to the mast or stay (among other definitions it is also a term for obstructing the opposition attempting to pass on the windward side by sailing closer to the wind).
lutz *ice skating* jump in which the skater takes off from the outside back edge of one skate and lands, after full rotation, on the outside back edge of the other.
maiden *cricket* an over in which no runs have been scored.
mallet *croquet* the striking implement used to hit the ball
mashie *golf* obsolete colloquial name for a no. 5 iron.
mashie-niblick *golf* obsolete colloquial name for a no. 7 iron.
mata *judo* break of a hold.
maul *rugby* distinguished from ruck by ball being held off the ground.
men *kendo* the armour that covers the head and face.
mid-off *cricket* fielding position on the side opposite to where the facing batsman stands; in the case of a right-handed batsman, to the left of the bowler during his run-up.
mid-on *cricket* fielding position on the side where the facing batsman stands; in the case of a right-handed batsman, to the right of the bowler during his run-up.
mid-wicket *cricket* self-explanatory fielding position whereby if an equilateral triangle was plotted using the 22 yards between the stumps, mid-wicket would lie on the apex.
monkey climb *wrestling* move whereby one wrestler climbs up and wraps himself around the other to immobilise him.
mulligan *golf* free stroke awarded informally after a poor shot, usually an air shot.
nage-waza *judo* basic throw.
niblick *golf* obsolete colloquial name for a sand wedge or sometimes a wedge.
night watchman *cricket* lower-order batsman who comes in up the order to protect a key player if a wicket is lost near close of play.
no side *rugby* official name for end of the game, no longer commonly used.
nock *archery* notch at end of bow to run string through.
nocking point *archery* point of a bowstring to which the notch of an arrow is applied.
Notre Dame shift *American football* offensive move whereby the backs move just before the snap of the ball from their T-formation.
nunchaku *kung fu* rice flail used in exhibitions.
nutmeg *football* to play the ball between the legs of a defender and run around him to collect it.
O'Brien shift *shot putting* common gliding technique named after Parry O'Brien.
Oklahoma *American football* defensive formation.
oxer *equestrianism* brush fence with a guard rail on one side.
ozeki *sumo* the second rank after yokozuna (means 'great barrier').
painter *yachting* short rope or chain by which the shank of an anchor is held fast.
parallelogram *Gaelic football* playing area.
parry *fencing* warding off an attack especially with a counter.
passage *dressage* cadenced high-stepping trot.
pebble *curling* another name for a stone.
penholder grip *table tennis* method of holding the bat like a pencil popularised by the Chinese; quick footwork is essential as backhands are impossible to play. Aka eastern grip.
penthouse *real tennis* sloping roof of the corridor or gallery running around three sides of the court.
shukokai *karate* a karate school.
shuriken *karate* one of various designs of small throwing weapons
pick *basketball* action of a player who, without causing contact, delays or prevents an opponent from reaching his desired position.
pick-up *sprinting* second phase of race after the start during which the head is raised and relaxation starts.
pile-driver *wrestling* up-ending the opponent and driving his head into the canvas.
pinch-hitter *baseball* less technically accomplished player capable of hitting out forcefully.
piste *fencing* total fencing area.
piste *skiing* total skiing area.
pitcher *baseball* specialist thrower of the ball towards the opposing batter.
piton *rock-climbing* eye peg hammered into rock so that a rope can be attached.
pivot *basketball* movement in which a player with the ball steps once or more in any direction with the same foot while the other foot is kept at its point of contact with the floor.
plastron *fencing* padded, leather-covered breastplate.
point *cricket* off-side fielding position wide of gully.
popping crease *cricket* line four feet in front of and parallel to the wicket within which the batsmen must remain unless the ball is dead or they are running.
press *basketball* defensive technique of harassing players into hurried play.
prop *rugby* one of the two forwards in the front row of the scrum who support hooker.
puck *ice hockey* flat rubber disc used in place of ball.
puissance *show jumping* high jump event.
punt *rugby* kick made by dropping the ball and kicking before it hits the ground.
putout *baseball* self-explanatory term meaning to cause a batter or base runner to be out.
quarterback *American football* player stationed behind the centre who directs a team's attacking play.
rack *pool* implement used for setting the red balls at the start of a frame (also the name used for an individual frame).
randolph (randi) *trampolining* two-and-a-half twisting front somersault.
repechage *rowing* a second chance for the best of the losing rowers in eliminating heats to progress to a final.
return crease *cricket* the lines either side of the wicket at right angles to the bowling crease.
riposte *fencing* a lunge or quick thrust after parrying.
rocker *ice skating* a skate with a curved blade.
roquet *croquet* to strike another player's ball with your own.
rover *American football* defensive linebacker assigned to move about to anticipate opponents' plays.
rover *archery* target chosen at random and at an undetermined range (also a mark for long-distance shooting).
rover *Australian rules football* player forming part of the ruck.
rover *croquet* ball that has passed through all the hoops but not pegged out (also a name for a player whose ball has done this).
ruck *rugby* occurs when progress of the ball is checked and two or more players struggle to gain possession. Distinguished from maul by ball being on the ground and legally playable only with the feet.
rush *ice hockey* sudden attack on goal often from a defensive position.
salchow *ice skating* full-turn jump from the inside back edge of one skate to the outside back edge of the other.
schuss *skiing* starting gate or housing.
scissors *high jump* training technique of clearing bar with legs only and no rotation of hips.
scissors *rugby* change of direction of attack by player running in diagonally opposite to the line of attacking play when receiving ball.
screen *basketball* another name for 'pick'.
scrimmage *American football* offense and defense facing each other.
scrum *rugby* formed by eight forwards of each side in three ranks for purpose of gaining possession with the feet. Note: rugby league scrummages contain six players.
serpentine *dressage* series of half-circles alternately to right and left.
shido *judo* judge's warning with no point deducted.
shime-waza *judo* strangulation technique.
shinai *kendo* sword made up of four bamboo sticks bound together.
shobu-ari *kendo* the end of a match.
shopping, going *billiards* potting your opponent's ball.
short leg *cricket* fielding position close to the batsman and on the leg side.
shotgun *American football* offensive formation.
shroud *yachting* set of ropes supporting the mainsail.
tolley *marbles* portmanteau word from 'taw' and 'alley'.
touchdown *American football* equivalent of a try in rugby, except that

often eight-sided and sharp.
side *billiards* off-centre striking of the cueball to make false angle in positional play.
silly mid-off *cricket* close fielding position short of mid-off.
silly mid-on *cricket* close fielding position short of mid-on.
sleeper *wrestling* application of pressure on the nerves in the neck which can cause loss of consciousness.
slip *cricket* fielding position next to the wicket-keeper.
snap *American football* put the ball into play on the ground by a quick backward movement.
soigneur *cycling* general dogsbody of team responsible for its physical and mental preparation.
soop *curling* assist the progress of a curling stone by sweeping the ice in front of it.
southpaw *boxing* boxer who leads with his right hand.
space lob *roller hockey* use of end boards to pass to team mates.
spare *ten pin bowling* knocking down all the pins with two successive bowls.
spider *billiards, snooker* implement used when bridging directly over a ball.
spider *darts* wire frame around the board.
spike *volleyball* one-handed attacking shot from above and across the net. Spike serves are common at the higher levels.
spinnaker *yachting* large triangular sail carried forward of or opposite the mainsail.
spinner *angling* real or artificial bait or lure fixed so as to revolve when pulled through the water.
spinnerama *roller hockey* complicated tactical move to deceive opposition.
spinning *cycling* US term for twiddling now commonly used in UK.
split *ten pin bowling* attempt to knock down pins which are wide apart.
split *weightlifting* action of thrusting forward with one foot and backward with the other to aid leverage during lift.
split T *American football* offensive formation.
spoon *angling* artificial bait in the shape of the bowl of a spoon, used in spinning or trolling.
spoon *golf* any club with a slightly concave wooden head, but often refers to a 3 wood specifically.
stealing bases *baseball* reaching bases without the striker hitting the ball.
stone *curling* the heavy 'top' with a handle which is aimed at the house.
straddle *high jump* similar to western roll, but the straddle jumper keeps legs wide apart and body straight.
strike *baseball* complete miss of the ball.
strike *ten pin bowling* knocking all the pins down with one ball.
suicide squad *American football* specialist players who deliberately block attacks.
sulky *harness racing* vehicle used in harness racing.
sweeper *curling* team member who sweeps the ice to gain distance for stone.
swingtime *trampolining* a series of different moves performed between bounces.
switch-hitting *boxing* changing from orthodox to southpaw during a bout.
tack *equestrianism* saddle, bridle and bit.
tack *yachting* zigzag movement of a boat.
tagged out *baseball* self-explanatory term.
tame-shiwari *karate* exercise for toughening using breaking techniques.
taw *marbles* line from which a player shoots; also another name for the actual game and formerly a name for a large marble.
tee *curling* centre point of the house.
tee *golf* small peg on which to rest the ball when driving; also the name for the area where the initial drive is made.
T formation *American football* offensive formation.
third man *cricket* fielding position deep behind the slip area.
tice *cricket* obsolete term for a yorker.
tice *croquet* stroke tempting an opponent to aim at one's ball.
tiger country *golf* deep rough usually on high ground.
tin *squash* the lower line on the wall above which all shots must be played.
tkachyov *gymnastics* one-handed 360-degree swing on horizontal (high) bar.
the ball need not touch the ground when carried or received inside the opponents' end zone (6 points score).
touché *fencing* an acknowledgment that a scoring hit has been made in a bout.
toucher *bowls* wood that has touched the jack in its travels.
tram lines *tennis* the outer lines at each side of the court which become part of the court in doubles matches.
trapeze *yachting* sliding support used for outboard balancing on a yacht.
travelling *basketball* running with the ball without bouncing it.
triangle *angling* set of three hooks fastened together so that the barbs form a triangle.
triangle *snooker* implement used for setting the red balls at the start of a frame.
troll *angling* fish by drawing bait along in the water.
try *rugby* scoring method by means of touching the ball down in the opponents' goal area behind their goal line (5 points score).
tsuba *kendo* guard of the sword.
tsuka *kendo* handle of the sword.
tsukahara *gymnastics* vault consisting of a quarter or half turn on to the horse followed by one and half somersaults off.
turkey *ten pin bowling* gaining three strikes in successive bowls.
turnover *basketball* loss of possession of the ball by a team before any member has been able to try for a basket.
twiddling *cycling* pedalling fast in a gear with no pressure asserted.
up and under *rugby* kicking the ball up field high and long to make time for the kicker and attacking players to reach the point where it comes down.
uwate-dashi-nage *sumo* one-handed throw.
uwate-nage *sumo* hip throw using both hands.
veer attack *American football* offensive formation.
Venturi effect *hang-gliding* basis for wing design, explaining that air flowing over the upper part of a wing moves faster than the air on the underside of the wing, so that the pressure underneath is greater and hence creates lift. Aka Bernouilli effect.
volley *volleyball* two-handed shot that may go over the net or to another team member to spike.
vorlage *skiing* position in which the skier leans forward without lifting the heels from the skis. It is also a common name for skiing trousers when pluralized.
vorlaufer *skiing* literally meaning 'run on ahead' in German, it is a term used for the pre-competition skiers who test the safety and degree of difficulty of a ski course.
walkover *horse racing* horse having the formality of walking over the line as it is the only entrant in a race.
wall pass *football* pass from one player to another and back to save having to face a defender (also called one-two).
warner single wing *American football* offensive formation.
wazari-ni-chikai-waza *judo* 5-point score (two make an ippon).
wazari *judo* almost point in Japanese (scores 7 points in competition).
western grip *table tennis* traditional method of holding a bat with fingers on face of bat.
western roll *high jumping* technique, rarely used today, whereby the front leg is thrown high over the bar and the body and other leg roll over and parallel to the bar.
wicket maiden *cricket* an over during which no runs have been scored and a wicket has been taken.
wide *cricket* extra given to batting side due to ball being bowled too wide of the batsman.
wipe out *surfing* tumbling off the board, often due to unforeseen wave.
wired *croquet* prevented from taking a particular course by an intervening hoop or peg.
wishbone *yachting* boom composed of two halves that curve outward from the mast on either side of the sail and in again, the clew of the sail between them being attached to the point where they meet aft.
yamashita *gymnastics* flat handspring over the vaulting horse.
yokozuna *sumo* grand champion.
yori kiri *sumo* strong forward push.
yorker *cricket* ball bowled at feet of batsman whether playing back or forward.
yuko *judo* hold between 20 and 25 seconds.

NB This is far from being an exhaustive listing of sporting terminology. Dictionaries of terms are available on many individual sports and so it would be impossible to catalogue all known terms. What I have tried to do is give a good cross-section of technical terms over many sports. I should also point out that some terms will relate to other sports, e.g. billiards-based sports or running ball sports.

Other Sports: World's Strongest Man

The World's Strongest Man competition has been covered by BBC Television almost since the beginning and is based on all aspects of strength and not just the lifting of weights, although most of the very best competitors have also been champion weight-lifters. Geoff Capes of Great Britain ushered in a new breed of athlete: not only very large but also very fit and very quick. The competitions have had many great personalities over the years, from the great bullish Kazmaier to the very extrovert Sigmarsson (sadly no longer with us), with his 'Viking' chant, and of course the other great Icelander Magnusson. Zydrunas Savickas lays claim to be the strongest man that ever lived.

1977 Bruce Wilhelm (United States)
1978 Bruce Wilhelm (United States)
1979 Don Reinhoudt (United States)
1980 Bill Kazmaier (United States)
1981 Bill Kazmaier (United States)
1982 Bill Kazmaier (United States)
1983 Geoff Capes (Great Britain)
1984 Jon Pall Sigmarsson (Iceland)
1985 Geoff Capes (Great Britain)
1986 Jon Pall Sigmarsson (Iceland)
1987 *Jon Pall Sigmarsson (Iceland)
1988 Jon Pall Sigmarsson (Iceland)
1989 Jamie Reeves (Great Britain)
1990 Jon Pall Sigmarsson (Iceland)
1991 Magnus Ver Magnusson (Iceland)
1992 Ted Van Der Parre (Holland)
1993 Gary Taylor (Great Britain)
1994 Magnus Ver Magnusson (Iceland)
1995 Magnus Ver Magnusson (Iceland)
1996 Magnus Ver Magnusson (Iceland)
1997 Jouko Ahola (Finland)
1998 Magnus Samuelsson (Sweden)
1999 Jouko Ahola (Finland)
2000 Janne Virtanen (Finland)
2001 Sven Karlssen (Norway)
2002 Mariusz Pudzianowski (Poland)
2003 Mariusz Pudzianowski (Poland)
2004 Vasil Virastyuk (Ukraine)
2005 Mariusz Pudzianowski (Poland)
2006 Phil Pfister (United States)
2007 Mariusz Pudzianowski (Poland)
2008 Mariusz Pudzianowski (Poland
2009 Zydrunas Savickas (Lithuania)
2010 Zydrunas Savickas (Lithuania)
2011 Brian Shaw (United States)
2012 Zydrunas Savickas (Lithuania)
2013 Brian Shaw (United States)

*Competition known as Pure Strength

Other Sports: The Superstars

The World Superstars competition ran for six years on the BBC and made stars of athletes such as Brian Budd, who treated the competition with the same professional approach as his own sport of soccer. Although Brian Hooper won the last of the competitions, the domestic Superstars was won by fine athletes such as Lynn Davies, Andy Ripley, John Conteh, David Hemery, Keith Fielding, and the most famous of all, judo player Brian Jacks, he of the dip-bar records. And who can ever forget the painful demise of Kevin Keegan on a bike. Austin Healey won the 2001 one-off special. The BBC resurrected the British version in 2003, athlete Duaine Ladejo having a comfortable victory. The series was axed again after the next competition in 2005, won by skier Alain Baxter after a close battle with Ladejo. The champions are listed together with their original sport.

1977 Bob Seagren, USA, Pole Vault
1978 Brian Budd, CAN, Soccer
1979 Brian Budd, CAN, Soccer
1980 Brian Budd, CAN, Soccer
1981 Jody Sheckter, RSA, Racing
1982 Brian Hooper, GBR, Pole Vault

Miscellaneous Information: Sport

Acque Minerale and Tamburello features of Imola and San Marino motor racing circuits.
archery: target colours gold (centre), red, blue, black, white.
Australian rules football: inventor George Ligowsky.
backwards: sports where competitors move back-stroke swimming; rowing; tug of war.
badminton: All-England champion seven successive years Rudy Hartono (1968–74).
badminton: family won 35 All-England titles Frank Devlin and his daughters Judy and Sue.
badminton: origin originally called Shuttlecock and Battledore and named after the country estate of the Duke of Beaufort, where it originated in 1873. It was popularized by army officers in India who played it as an outdoor game.
bagatelle: brief description similar to bar billiards but board has nine holes and nine balls are used (four red, four white and a black ball that scores double).
bagatelle: variations cannon game; Mississippi; sans égal.
basketball: court size 50 ft x 94 ft
basketball: famous US teams Boston Celtics; Houston Rockets; Los Angeles Lakers; Milwaukee Bucks; New York Knickerbockers; Philadelphia 76ers; Phoenix Suns; Portland Trail Blazers; Seattle Supersonics; St Louis Hawks; Washington Bullets.
basketball: inventor Dr James Naismith invented basketball at the YMCA training school in Springfield, Mass. (1891).
beard: not allowed jockeys.
billiards: World Matchplay champion 1998 Mike Russell of England defeated Peter Gilchrist of England 8–5.
boat race: dead heat 1877 (although Oxford are said to have won by about six feet). The actual closest winning margin being the official one foot victory by Oxford in the 2003 race.
boat race: first woman cox Susan Brown in 1981.
boat race: reserve crews Cambridge – Goldie, Oxford – Isis.
bowls: first world champion in 1966 David Bryant (Eng).
bowls: invented by flat green bowls in its modern form began in 1848 when William Mitchell, a Glasgow solicitor, drew up the rules.
boxing: amateur weight limits light fly – 106lb/48kg; fly – 112lb/51kg; bantam – 119lb/54kg; feather – 126lb/57kg; light – 132lb/60kg; light welter – 140lb/63.5kg; welter – 148lb/67kg; light middle – 157lb/71kg; middle – 165lb/75kg; light heavy – 179lb/81kg; heavy – 201lb/91kg; super heavy – 201lb+/91kg+.
champion at eight weights Manny Pacquiao (Philippines).
first champion James Figg is generally regarded as the first modern champion when he set up his school in 1719.
first East European professional Laszlo Papp.
first fight with gloves Gentleman Jim Corbett defeated John L Sullivan in 1892.
first million dollar gate Jack Dempsey v Georges Carpentier in 1921.
four main governing bodies World Boxing Association (WBA), founded 1920; World Boxing Council (WBC), founded 1963; International Boxing Federation (IBF), founded 1983; World Boxing Organization (WBO), founded 1988.
heavyweight champion longest reign Joe Louis (1937–49).
last bareknuckle champion John L Sullivan.
oldest and youngest world champions light heavyweight, Archie Moore (48); light welterweight, Wilfredo Benitez (17).

professional weight limits straw/mini-fly – 105lb/48kg; light fly/jnr fly – 108lb/49kg; fly – 112lb/51kg; super fly/jnr bantam – 115lb/52kg; bantam – 118lb/54kg; super bantam/jnr feather – 122lb/55kg; feather – 126lb/57kg; super feather/jnr light – 130lb/59kg; light – 135lb/61kg; super light/jnr welter – 140lb/64kg; welter – 147lb/67kg; super welter/jnr middle – 154lb/70kg; middle – 160lb/73kg; super middle – 168lb/76kg; light heavy – 175lb/79kg; jnr heavy/cruiser – 190lb/86kg; heavy – 190lb+/86kg+.

Queensberry Rules: first fight under Jim Corbett beat John L Sullivan (1892).

initiated by Jack Broughton devised first rules in 1743, but they were not codified until 1867 by 8th marquess of Queensberry.

undefeated heavyweight champion Rocky Marciano (49 fights).

undisputed heavyweight champions John L Sullivan (1882); James J Corbett (1892); Bob Fitzsimmons (1897); James J Jeffries (1899); Marvin Hart (1905); Tommy Burns (1906); Jack Johnson (1908); Jess Willard (1915); Jack Dempsey (1919); Gene Tunney (1926); Max Schmeling (1930); Jack Sharkey (1932); Primo Carnera (1933); Max Baer (1934); James J Braddock (1935); Joe Louis (1937); Ezzard Charles (1949); Jersey Joe Walcott (1951); Rocky Marciano (1952); Floyd Patterson (1956); Ingemar Johansson (1959); Floyd Patterson (1960); Sonny Liston (1962); Cassius Clay (1964); Joe Frazier (1970); George Foreman (1973); Muhammad Ali (1974); Leon Spinks (1978); Mike Tyson (1987); Lennox Lewis (2000).

youngest world heavyweight champion Mike Tyson.

bullfighting: barbed sticks banderillas.

cape muleta (red one side and yellow the other).

term used for a pass veronica.

terms for fighters matador – principal fighter appointed to kill the bull; picador – horseman who pricks the bull with a banderilla to weaken it; toreador – stock name for any fighter.

croquet four balls used; two to a team; red and yellow play against blue and black; six hoops are used.

cycling: oldest British sprint champion Reg Harris (aged 54).

terms honking – cycling off the saddle; spinning – turning an easy gear very quickly with no effort.

Tour de France, first non-European winner Greg Lemond of USA in 1986.

Tour de France, five times winners Eddie Merckx, Jacques Anquetil, Bernard Hinault, Miguel Indurain.

Tour de France, seven times winner Lance Armstrong of USA (1999–2005).

darts: sponsors Lakeside Country Club sponsor the BDO World Championship while Ladbrokes.com sponsor the WDC Championship.

fatalities: sport with highest rate of angling (fish rather than folk!).

fencing: caught cheating Boris Onischenko of USSR in Modern Pentathlon (1976).

heaviest weapon épée.

target areas foil – body only; épée – no restriction; sabre – over waist.

technical term for guard coquille.

weapons used by women traditionally foil only but nowadays championships exist for sabre and épée.

frisbee: two forms of Ultimate and Guts.

gong: banged for J Arthur Rank Bombardier Billy Wells (1889–1967), British heavyweight boxing champion, was succeeded by Ken Richmond, the wrestling gold medalist at the 1954 Commonwealth Games.

Greyhound Grand National: triple winner Sherry's Prince.

greyhound racing: most consecutive wins Ballyregan Bob (32).

trap colours red – 1; blue – 2; white – 3; black – 4; orange – 5; black and white striped – 6.

grouse shooting: season Glorious Twelfth (August) to 10 December (30 November in Northern Ireland).

gymnastics: exercises for men floor, horizontal bar, parallel bars, pommel horse, rings, vault (lengthwise).

exercises for women floor, asymmetric bars, beam, vault (widthwise).

first perfect score of 10 Nadia Comaneci in 1976.

London Marathon organisers John Disley and Chris Brasher organised first London Marathon in 1981.

martial arts: meanings tae kwon do – way of the foot and fist; judo – gentle way; aikido – way of spirit harmony; karate – way of the empty hand; kyudo – way of the bow; kung fu – leisure time/hobby.

Olympic Games: famous competitors Philip Noel Baker was an Olympic finalist at 1,500m in 1912 and silver medallist in 1920 before winning the Nobel Peace Prize in 1959. Noel Harrison, who took part in Skiing in 1952, is the actor son of Rex Harrison. Harry Llewellyn, who won gold medal for Equestrianism in 1952, is father of Roddy Llewellyn. Charles Simmons, who took part in Gymnastics 1952, is father of Jean Simmons. John Kelly, who won gold medal for Rowing in 1920, was father of Grace Kelly. Prince Albert of Monaco took part in bobsleigh events in 1988. Godfrey Rampling, who ran in the 4 x 400m Relay in 1936, was the father of Charlotte Rampling. Bill Nankeville who ran in the 1500m in 1948, is the father of Bobby Davro. Ioannis Theodoracopulous, who was a hurdler in 1936, was the father of Taki. Arthur Porritt, who accompanied Harold Abrahams in the 1924 Games, was father of Jonathon Porritt the Green politician.

pelota vasca (jai alai): origins invented in Italy as 'longue paume' and introduced to France in 13th century. It is the fastest ball game in the world.

pheasant shooting: season 1 October to 1 February.

polo: pitch dimensions polo has the largest pitch of any sport with a maximum length of 300 yards and width of 200 yards.

racketball: inventors American racketball devised by Joe Sobek in 1949; British racketball was devised by Ian Wright in 1976.

real tennis: origins developed from 'jeu de paume' (game of the palm) and played in Australia, England, France, Scotland and USA. First world champion in 1740 was a Frenchman named Clergé.
World champion since 1994: Robert Fahey (Aus).

roller skating: first rink opened Newport, Rhode Island, in 1866.

rowing: skimming of oar across water feathering.

rugby league: nicknames Australia – Kangaroos; New Zealand – Kiwis; Widnes – Chemics; Warrington – Wires.

rugby union: jersey colours Australia – gold; Barbarians – black and white hoops; England – white; France – blue; Ireland – green; New Zealand – black; Scotland – blue; Wales – red.

nicknames Argentina – Pumas; Australia – Wallabies; New Zealand – All Blacks; South Africa – Springboks.

played both codes at same time Martin Offiah left Wigan August 1996 to play union for Bedford and league for London Broncos.

skiing: Olympic champions who won all titles Toni Sailer (1956) and Jean-Claude Killy (1968).

piste grading black – difficult run; red – intermediate run; blue – easy run; green – beginners' slope.

snooker: first televised 147 maximum by	Steve Davis (1982 Lada Classic).
first to make 147 in World Championships	Cliff Thorburn (1983).
world champions at the Crucible	John Spencer (1977), Ray Reardon (1978), Terry Griffiths (1979), Cliff Thorburn (1980), Steve Davis (1981), Alex Higgins (1982), Steve Davis (1983–84), Dennis Taylor (1985), Joe Johnson (1986), Steve Davis (1987–89), Stephen Hendry (1990), John Parrott (1991), Stephen Hendry 1992–96), Ken Doherty (1997), John Higgins (1998), Stephen Hendry (1999), Mark Williams (2000), Ronnie O'Sullivan (2001), Peter Ebdon (2002), Mark Williams (2003), Ronnie O'Sullivan (2004), Shaun Murphy (2005), Graeme Dott (2006), John Higgins (2007), Ronnie O'Sullivan (2008), John Higgins (2009), Neil Robertson (2010), John Higgins (2011), Ronnie O'Sullivan (2012), Ronnie O'Sullivan (2013).
softball: inventor	George Hancock invented the indoor version of baseball in 1887 in Chicago.
speedway: laps	four
2012 world champion	Chris Holder of Australia.
squash: origins	Harrow school.
world champion sixteen years running	Heather McKay Blundell of Australia.
stop on line: competitors do not pass finishing line	swimming.
substitutes: allowed while game in play	ice hockey.
suicides: famous sportsmen	Fred Archer (1857–86), champion jockey for 13 years 1874–86, shot himself aged 29. George O'Dell (1945–81), a double world champion in side-car racing, took his own life aged 35. Recent sporting suicides include the Yorkshire cricketer David Bairstow, and footballers Justin Fashanu and Robert Enke (German goalkeeper).
table tennis: ball dimensions	from 2001 season ball diameter increased to 40mm.
expedite rule	comes into play in long game and means point must be won within so many strikes or receiver is awarded the point.
ten pin bowling: maximum score in one game	300.
tennis champs: British, venue	Telford.
Vasaloppet	Swedish marathon ski race over 85km between Sălen and Mora, first run in 1922.
volleyball: former name	invented in 1895 by William Morgan of Massachusetts and called 'Mintonette'.
weightlifting: Olympic lifts	clean and jerk, snatch.
weightlifting: power lifts	bench press, dead lift, squat.
wrestling: two styles	freestyle and Greco-Roman.
yachting: famous champion	Peter Scott, son of explorer Robert Falcon Scott, won bronze medal in 1936 Olympics and became British gliding champion in 1963.
Olympic classes	Europe, Finn (solo class), 470, Laser, Mistral, Star, Tornado (catamaran), Soling (three-man crew).

Games: Miscellaneous

baccarat	gambling card game the object of which is to hold cards with values as near to nine as possible.
backgammon	dice number: 5; counters: 15 per player; points on board: 24.
bezique	played with a 64-card double piquet deck, i.e. all cards below 7, except the ace, are removed from two standard 52-card decks.

bingo calls

The origins of Bingo can be traced back to Italy in the year 1530, when a State-run lottery game Lo Giuoco del Lotto d'Italia was originated. 'Le Lotto' migrated to France in the late 1700s in a form similar to the Bingo we know today, with a playing card, tokens and numbers read aloud. Throughout the 1800s these lottery type of games spread quickly throughout Europe and many offshoots of the game were created. In 1929, a game called 'Beano' was played at a carnival near Atlanta, Georgia. A New York toy salesman named Edwin Lowe observed the game, where players exclaimed 'BEANO!' if they filled a line of numbers on their card. Lowe introduced the game to his friends and one of them mistakenly yelled 'BINGO!' in her excitement . 'Lowe's Bingo' was soon very popular and the name stuck.

1 Kelly's eye, Buttered scone, At the beginning, Little Jimmy, Nelson's column, B1 Baby of bingo
2 One little duck, Baby's done it, Doctor Who, Me and you, Little boy blue
3 Dearie me, I'm free, Debbie McGee, You and me, Goodness me, One little flea, Cup of tea
4 The one next door, On the floor, Knock at the door, B4 Crowd says 'and after'
5 Man alive, Jack's alive, Dead alive
6 Tom Mix, Tom's tricks, Chopsticks
7 Lucky seven, God's in heaven, One little crutch
8 Garden gate, Golden gate, Harry Tate, One fat lady
9 Doctor's orders
10 Downing street (UK prime minister's address), Cock and hen (rhyming), Uncle Ben (rhyming), Tony's Den (or whoever is the PM of the day)
11 Legs eleven, Legs – they're lovely, Kelly's Legs Number eleven
12 One dozen, One and two – a dozen, Monkey's cousin (rhymes with 'a dozen')
13 Unlucky for some, Devil's number, Baker's dozen
14 Valentine's day
15 Rugby team, Young and keen
16 Sweet sixteen, She's lovely, Never been kissed
17 Often been kissed, Old Ireland, Dancing queen, The age to catch 'em
18 Key of the door, Now you can vote, Coming of age
19 Goodbye teens
20 One score, Getting plenty, Blind 20
21 Royal salute, Key of the door
22 Two little ducks (suggesting the necks of two swans), Ducks on a pond, Dinky doo, All the twos

23 A duck and a flea, Thee and me, The Lord's My Shepherd (based on 23rd Psalm)
24 Two dozen, Hours from Tulsa
25 Duck and dive
26 Bed and breakfast (traditional price was 2 shillings 6 pence), Half a crown (equivalent to 2 shillings 6 pence), Pick and mix
27 Little duck with a crutch, Gateway to heaven
28 In a state, The old brags, Over weight
29 You're doing fine, Rise and shine
30 Burlington Bertie, Dirty Gertie, Speed limit (in built-up area, UK), Blind 30, Flirty thirty
31 Get up and run
32 Buckle my shoe
33 Dirty knees, All the feathers, All the threes, Gertie Lee, Two little fleas, Sherwood forest (all the trees)
34 Ask for more
35 Jump and jive
36 Three dozen
37 A flea in heaven, More than eleven
38 Christmas cake
39 Those famous steps, All the steps
40 Two score, Life begins at, Blind 40, Naughty 40
41 Life's begun, Time for fun
42 That famous street in Manhattan, Winnie the Poo
43 Down on your knees
44 Droopy drawers, All the fours, Open two doors
45 Halfway house, Halfway there
46 Up to tricks
47 Four and seven
48 Four dozen
49 PC (Police Constable), Copper, Nick nick, Rise and shine
50 Bulls eye, Bung hole, Blind 50, Half a century
51 I love my mum, Tweak of the thumb, The Highland Div[ision]
52 Weeks in a year, The Lowland Div[ision], Danny La Rue
53 Stuck in the tree, The Welsh Div[ision]
54 Clean the floor
55 Snakes alive, All the fives
56 Was she worth it?
57 Heinz varieties, All the beans (Heinz 57 varieties of canned beans)
58 Make them wait, Choo choo Thomas
59 Brighton line
60 Three score, Blind 60, Five dozen
61 Bakers bun
62 Tickety boo, Turn of the screw
63 Tickle me
64 The Beatles number, Red raw
65 Old age pension, Stop work (retirement age)
66 Clickety click, All the sixes
67 Made in heaven, Argumentative number
68 Saving grace
69 The same both ways, your place or mine?, Any way up, Either way up, Any way round, Meal for two
70 Three score and ten, Blind 70
71 Bang on the drum
72 A crutch and a duck, Six dozen, Par for the course (golf)
73 Crutch with a flea, Queen B
74 Candy store
75 Strive and strive
76 Trombones
77 Sunset strip, All the sevens, Two little crutches
78 Heaven's gate
79 One more time
80 Gandhi's breakfast, Blind 80, Eight and blank
81 Fat lady and a little wee, Stop and run
82 Fat lady with a duck, Straight on through
83 Fat lady with a flea, Time for tea, Ethel's Ear
84 Seven dozen
85 Staying alive
86 Between the sticks
87 Fat lady with a crutch, Torquay in Devon
88 Two fat ladies, Wobbly wobbly, All the eights
89 Nearly there, All but one
90 Top of the shop, Top of the house, Blind 90, As far as we go, End of the line

canasta played with two standard decks of 52 cards, plus four jokers, totalling 108 cards. Hands are played until one partnership reaches 5000 points.

Canasta was developed in Uruguay and passed via Argentina to the USA in 1949.

card games: names beggar my neighbour, boston, briscola, calabrasella, donkey, écarté, imperial, klaberjass, loo, michigan, napoleon, oh hell, old maid, Persian pasha, Pope Joan, skat, vint.

cards: Queen depicted Elizabeth of York (wife of Henry VII).

charades parlour game whereby one person mimes and the other players guess the title.

chess: right-hand corner the right-hand corner square as white sets up is white (important to remember).

chess: world champions Wilhelm Steinitz (Austria) (1886–94), Emanuel Lasker (Ger) (1894–1921), Jose Capablanca (Cuba) (1921–27), Alexander Alekhine (USSR) (1927–35), Max Euwe (Neth) (1935–37), Alexander Alekhine (USSR) (1937–46), Mikhail Botvinnik (USSR) (1948–57), Vasily Smyslov (USSR) (1957–58), Mikhail Botvinnik (USSR) (1958–60), Mikhail Tal (USSR) (1960–61), Mikhail Botvinnik (USSR) (1961–63), Tigran Petrosian (USSR) (1963–69), Boris Spassky (USSR) (1969–72), Bobby Fischer (US) (1972–75), Anatoly Karpov (USSR) (1975–1985), Garry Kasparov (USSR/Rus) (1985–2000), Vladimir Kramnik (Rus) (2000–2007), Viswanathan Anand (2007–present).

chicane bridge hand without trumps or without cards of any one suit.

Cluedo: characters Colonel Mustard, Professor Plum, Reverend Green, Mrs Peacock, Miss Scarlet, Mrs White, Dr Black (victim).

weapons knife, revolver, spanner, lead pipe, rope, and candlestick.

crambo game in which a player gives a word or verse line to which each of the others must find a rhyme.

cribbage developed by poet, Sir John Suckling, in the early 17th century and usually played to 121 points.

dominoes 28 tiles in a set with a total of 168 pips (seven doubles).

El Gordo Spanish National Lottery (largest in the world).

euchre played with a 32-card deck (cards below 7 are removed).

fan-tan chinese gambling game in which players try to guess the remainder after the banker has divided a number of hidden objects into four groups.

faro gambling card game in which bets are placed on the order of appearance of the cards. This is the game in which Count Rostov lost a fortune in Tolstoy's *War and Peace*.

frisbee: original name Pluto Platter.

go Japanese board game using terms: false eyes, eyes and armies. Played on a grid of 19 horizontal and 19 vertical lines forming 361interactions.

jai alai South American version of pelota played with large curved wicker baskets.

mahjong Chinese game using terms: pung, kong and chow. 144 tiles are usually used (36 bamboos, 36 circles, 36 characters, 12 honours, 16 winds, 8 flowers and seasons). The name was coined and copyrighted by Joseph P Babcock.

Monopoly: inventor Charles Darrow, a heating engineer.

original properties brown: Old Kent Road (cheapest), Whitechapel; light blue: Angel Islington (pub), Euston Road, Pentonville Road; mauve: Pall Mall, Whitehall, Northumberland Avenue; orange: Bow Street, Marlborough Street, Vine Street (statistically the most 'landed on' square); red: Strand, Fleet Street, Trafalgar Square; yellow: Leicester Square, Coventry Street, Piccadilly; green: Regent Street, Oxford Street, Bond Street; dark blue: Park Lane, Mayfair (most expensive).

stations King's Cross, Marylebone, Fenchurch Street, Liverpool Street.

corners Go, Just Visiting, Free Parking, Go to Jail.

USA version Atlantic City, New Jersey, is used, with 'Boardwalk' the most expensive property.

ombre card game for three players that was popular throughout Europe in the 17th and 18th centuries.

pall-mall game in which a ball is driven by a mallet along an alley and through an iron ring.

patzer poor player at chess.

pelota Basque and Spanish game played in a walled court with a ball and 'basket-like' rackets attached to the hand. Pelota is thought to be the fastest of ball sports outside golf.

pinochle pronounced 'pea knuckle', and played with 48 cards (two decks stripped of cards below 9). Within the game, pinochle stands for the Jack of Diamonds and Queen of Spades. The 9 of trumps is called the dix. Winner is player who first reaches 1000 points.

piquet given the name by Charles I of England to honour Henrietta Maria, his French wife. Piquet deck is 32 cards with all cards below 7 stripped from deck.

poker: best hand royal flush (ace to 10 in the same suit).

roulette: numbers European wheels have 37 divisions (0–36), American wheels have 38 including a double zero.

Scrabble: inventor James Brunot in 1949, first used the name scrabble.

made by Spear Games.

tile values highest Q and Z (10), J and X (8), K (5), Y H V W F (4), P M C B (3), D G (2), others 1 point except blank (0).

original name criss cross (designed by Alfred M Butts, an architect, in 1931).

vigoro Australian ball game combining elements of cricket and baseball.

Yarborough whist or bridge hand with no card above a 9. Named afer the earl of Yarborough who died in 1897, and was said to have bet against its occurrence.

tarot originally 22 cards (the Major Arcana: see below). The Venetians added 56 cards (the Minor Arcana) split into 4 suits: the clubs, symbolising money matters; cups (hearts), symbolising love and friendship; swords (spades), symbolising ill fortune; denari (diamonds), symbolising business and travel.

0	Fool/Joker	11	Fortitude / Strength
1	Magician / Mountebank	12	Hanged Man
2	High Priestess / Popess	13	Death
3	Empress	14	Temperance
4	Emperor	15	Devil
5	Hierophant / Pope	16	Tower
6	Lovers	17	Star
7	Chariot	18	Moon
8	Justice	19	Sun
9	Hermit	20	Judgement
10	Wheel of Fortune	21	World / Universe

NB In some versions of the Major Arcana nos. 8 and 11 are reversed.

Stamps: First Issues

Country	*Year*
Aden	1937
Afghanistan	1870
Andorra	1928
Antigua and Barbuda	1862
Argentina	1858
Armenia	1920
Ascension	1922
Australia	1902
Austria	1850
Azerbaijan	1919
Bahamas	1859
Bahrain	1933
Bangladesh	1971
Barbados	1852
Barbuda	1922
Belgium	1849
Belize	1866
Bermuda	1865
Bolivia	1866
Bosnia-Hercegovina	1879
Botswana	1886
Brazil	1843
British Indian Ocean Territory	1968
British Solomon Isles	1907
Brunei	1906
Bulgaria	1879
Burma/Myanmar	1937
Canada	1851
Cape of Good Hope	1853
Cayman Islands	1900
Channel Isles	1941
Chile	1853
China	1878
Cook Isles	1892
Crete	1900
Cuba	1855
Cyprus	1880
Czech Republic	1918
Danish West Indies	1855
Danzig	1920
Denmark	1851
Dominica	1874
Dominican Republc	1865
Ecuador	1865
Egypt	1866
El Salvador	1867
Estonia	1918
Ethiopia	1894
Faroe Isles	1940
Fiji	1870
Finland	1856
France	1849
Gambia	1869
Georgia	1919
Germany	1872
Ghana	1875
Gibraltar	1886
Great Britain	1840
Greece	1861
Greenland	1938
Grenada	1861
Guatemala	1871
Guyana	1850
Haiti	1881
Hawaii	1851
Heligoland	1867
Honduras	1866
Hong Kong	1862
Hungary	1871
Iceland	1873
India	1852
Ionian Isles	1859
Ireland	1922
Isle of Man	1973
Israel	1948
Italy	1862
Jamaica	1860
Japan	1871
Jordan	1920

Country	*Year*
Kenya	1890
Kiribati	1911
Latvia	1918
Lebanon	1924
Leeward Isles	1890
Liberia	1860
Liechtenstein	1912
Lithuania	1918
Luxembourg	1852
Malawi	1891
Malaysia	1867
Maldives	1906
Malta	1860
Mauritius	1847
Mexico	1856
Monaco	1885
Mongolia	1924
Montserrat	1876
Natal	1857
Nauru	1915
Nepal	1881
Netherlands	1852
New Guinea	1914
New South Wales	1850
New Zealand	1855
Nicaragua	1862
Nigeria	1914
Norfolk Isles	1947
Northern Rhodesia	1925
Norway	1855
Orange Free State	1868
Pakistan	1947
Palestine	1918
Panama	1878
Papua	1901
Papua New Guinea	1952
Paraguay	1870
Philippines	1854
Pitcairn Isles	1940
Portugal	1853
Queensland	1860
Rhodesia	1890
Rhodesia and Nyasaland	1954
Russia	1857
Sabah (North Borneo)	1883
San Marino	1877
Sarawak	1869
Saudi Arabia	1916
Serbia	1866
Seychelles	1890
Sierra Leone	1860
South Africa	1910
South Australia	1855
Southern Rhodesia	1924
South West Africa	1923
South Yemen	1963
Spain	1850
Sri Lanka	1857
St Helena	1856
Sudan	1897
Swaziland	1889
Sweden	1855
Switzerland	1843
Syria	1919
Tasmania	1853
Thailand	1883
Tokelau Isles	1948
Tonga	1886
Transvaal	1869
Turkey	1863
Uganda	1895
Uruguay	1856
USA	1845
USA: Confederacy	1861
Victoria	1850
Western Australia	1854
Yemen	1926
Zambia	1964
Zanzibar	1895
Zimbabwe	1979
Zululand	1888

Television

Programmes

A For Andromeda Julie Christie (Christine/A for Andromeda).

Absolutely Fabulous Jennifer Saunders (Edina Monsoon), Joanna Lumley (Patsy Stone), Julia Sawalha (Saffron), Jane Horrocks (Bubble), June Whitfield (Mother). Shopped at Harvey Nichols and based on Lynne Franks.

Adam Adamant Lives! Gerald Harper (Adam Llewellyn De Vere Adamant), Juliet Harmer (Georgina Jones), Peter Ducrow (the Face). Entombed from 1902 to 1966.

Addams Family, The Carolyn Jones (Morticia), John Astin (Gomez), Jackie Coogan (Uncle Fester Frump), Ted Cassidy (Lurch and Thing), Blossom Rock, sister of Jeanette McDonald (Grandmama). Lived in Cemetery Ridge with assortment of pets including octopus called Aristotle, black widow spider called Homer, man-eating African strangler called Cleopatra.

Adventures of Black Beauty, The Judi Bowker (Victoria Gordon), William Lucas (Dr James Gordon).

Adventures of Robin Hood, The Richard Greene (Robin), Bernadette O'Farrell and Patricia Driscoll (Maid Marian), Archie Duncan and Rufus Cruikshank (Little John), Alexander Gauge (Friar Tuck), Alan Wheatley (Sheriff of Nottingham). Theme sung by Dick James.

Adventures of Tugboat Annie, The Minerva Urecal (Tugboat Annie Brennan, Capt. of *Narcissus*), Walter Sande (Capt. Bullwinkle).

Adventures of William Tell, The Conrad Phillips (Tell), Jennifer Jayne (Hedda), Willoughby Goddard (Landburgher Gessler).

After Henry Prunella Scales (Sarah France), Joan Sanderson (Eleanor Prescott). Originally a BBC radio series, it was transferred to television with the same two stars.

Agony Maureen Lipman (Jane Lucas), Simon Williams (Laurence Lucas). Magazine: *Person Series.* Created by Anna Raeburn and Len Richmond.

Airwolf Jan-Michael Vincent (Stringfellow Hawke, a keen cellist), Ernest Borgnine (Dominic Santini).

Al Murray's Happy Hour Murray's pub landlord act thinly disguised in a chatshow format. Catchphrases include: 'Pint for the fella – Glass of white wine/fruit-based drink for the lady!' and 'I was never confused.'

Albion Market ITV soap set in Manchester; aired between August 1985 and August 1986. Characters include: Alan Curtis (Simon Rouse), Anita Rai (Souad Faress), Carol Broadbent (Barbara Wilshere), Colette Johnson (Nimmy March), Debbie Taylor (Jane Hazlegrove), Derek Owen (David Hargreaves), Geoff Travis (Geoffrey Leesley), Janet Owen (Hetta Charnley), Jaz Sharma (Paul Bhattacharjee), Keith Naylor (Derek Hicks), Larry Rigg (Peter Benson), Lisa O'Shea (Sally Baxter), Louise Todd (Kelly Lawrence), Ly Nhu Chan (Pik-Sen Lim), Lynne Harrison (Noreen Kershaw), Miriam Ransome (Carol Kaye), Morris Ransome (Bernard Spear), Narya Vyas (Rashid Karapiet), Paul O'Donnell (Paul Beringer), Peggy Sagar (Maria Vega), Phil Smith (Burt Caesar), Ralph Friend (David Boyce), Roy Harrison (Jonathan Barlow), Sita Sharma (Seeta Indrani), Ted Pilkington (Anthony Booth), Terry Flynn (Alistair Walker), Tony Fraser (John Michie), Viv Harker (Helen Shapiro).

Alf Alien Life Form (Michu Meszaros wore furry suit and Paul Fusco was the voice of ALF), Max Wright (Willie Tanner). Home planet: Melmac. Neighbours: Ochmoneks. Tanners' pet cat was called Lucky.

Alias Smith and Jones Pete Duel (Hannibal Heyes/Joshua Smith), Ben Murphy (Jed 'Kid' Curry/Thaddeus Jones). Roger Davis was narrator of first series but took over from Pete Duel after he committed suicide and Ralph Story took over voice-overs.

All Creatures Great and Small Christopher Timothy (James Herriot), Robert Hardy (Siegfried Farnon), Tricki Woo (Pekinese), Peter Davison (Tristan Farnon), Carol Drinkwater and Lynda Bellingham (Helen Alderson/Herriot).

All Gas and Gaiters Derek Nimmo (Rev. Mervyn Noote), William Mervyn (Bishop), Robertson Hare (Archdeacon).

All in the Family Carroll O'Connor (Archie Bunker), Jean Stapleton (Edith 'Dingbat' Bunker), Rob Reiner (Mike 'Meathead' Stivic the Pole), Sally Struthers (Gloria). America's answer to Alf Garnett.

All Night Long Keith Barron (Bill Chivers). Sitcom set in a London bakery.

All Our Yesterdays Presenters: James Cameron, Brian Inglis, Bernard Braden.

'Allo 'Allo Gorden Kaye (René Artois), Carmen Silvera (Edith), Vicki Michelle (Yvette), Guy Siner (Lt Gruber), Nicholas Frankou (Flying Officer Carstairs), John D. Collins (Flying Officer Fairfax), Kirsten Cooke (Michelle), Richard Gibson (Herr Flick), Richard Marner (Colonel Von Strohm), Kim Hartman (Helga Geerhart). Created by Jeremy Lloyd and David Croft.

Ally McBeal Calista Flockhart (Ally McBeal), Gil Bellows (Billy Thomas), Courtney Thorne-Smith (Georgia Thomas), Greg Germann (Richard Fish), Peter MacNicol (John Cage), Lucy Liu (Ling Woo).

And Mother Makes Three Wendy Craig (Sally Harrison/Redway). Follow-up series called *And Mother Makes Five.*

Andromeda Breakthrough, The Susan Hampshire (Christine/A for Andromeda). Follow-on series from *A For Andromeda.*

Andy Pandy Created by Freda Lingstrom and Maria Bird. Friends: Teddy and Looby Loo.

Angels Fiona Fullerton (Patricia Rutherford), Julie Dawn Cole (Jo Longhurst), Shirley Cheriton (Kathy Betts), Pauline Quirke (Vicky Smith). Hospital: St Angela's, Battersea.

Animal Hospital Rolf Harris, Shauna Lowry (Hamden Veterinary Hospital in Aylesbury).

Animal Magic Presenters: Johnny Morris, Terry Nutkins.

Antiques Roadshow Presenters: Angela Rippon, Bruce Parker, Arthur Negus, Hugh Scully, Michael Aspel, Fiona Bruce. See *Going For A Song.*

Any Dream Will Do Nationwide talent search to find a male lead for *Joseph and the Amazing Technicolor Dreamcoat.* Panel: Denise van Outen, John Barrowman, Bill Kenwright and Zoe Tyler. Presented by Graham Norton with Andrew Lloyd Webber. Winner: Lee Mead.

Apprentice, The Alan Sugar interviews 14 potential apprentices for his business empire. Winners: Tim Campbell, Michelle Dewberry, Simon Ambrose, Lee McQueen, Yasmina Siadatan, Stella English, Tom Pellereau, Ricky Martin, Leah Totton. Alan Sugar's assistants: Margaret Mountford (replaced by Karren Brady) and Nick Hewer. Donald Trump starred in the American version.

Aquarius Presenters: Humphrey Burton, Russell Harty, Peter Hall.

Are You Being Served? John Inman (Mr Humphries), Mollie Sugden (Mrs Slocombe), Arthur Brough (Mr Grainger), Frank Thornton (Capt. Peacock), Nicholas Smith (Mr Rumbold), Arthur English (Mr Harman), Wendy Richard (Miss Brahms), Mike Berry (Mr Spooner), Trevor Bannister (Mr Lucas). Sequel: *Grace and Favour.*

Army Game, The William Hartnell (CSM Bullimore), Bill Fraser (Sgt Claude Snudge), Michael Medwin (Corporal Springer), Harry Fowler (Corporal 'Flogger' Hoskins), Charles Hawtrey (Pte 'Prof' Hatchett), Bernard Bresslaw (Pte 'Popeye' Popplewell), Alfie Bass (Pte 'Excused Boots' Bisley), Norman Rossington (Pte 'Cupcake' Cook), Frank Williams (Capt. Pocket), Mario Fabrizi (Lance Corporal Ernest 'Moosh' Merryweather), Dick Emery (Pte 'Chubby' Catchpole). Base: Hut 29 of the Surplus Ordnance Depot at Nether Hopping, Staffordshire.

Around the World in 80 Days Michael Palin's reconstruction of Phileas Fogg's journey.

Arthur of the Britons Oliver Tobias (Arthur), Rupert Davies (Cerdig), Jack Watson (Llud), Brian Blessed (Mark of Cornwall), Michael Gothard (Kai).

Ask the Family Brain-teasing quiz between families of four, usually mum and dad and two children. Robert Robinson was host throughout its original run, 1967–84, Alan Titchmarsh hosted a one-off series on UK Gold in 1999 and the series was revived by the BBC in April 2005 with children's presenters Dick and Dom as hosts.

A-Team, The George Peppard (Col. John 'Hannibal' Smith), Lawrence 'Mr T' Tureaud (Sgt Bosco 'BA' Baracus), Dwight Schultz (Capt. H M 'Howling Mad' Murdock), Dirk Benedict (Lt Templeton 'Faceman' Peck), Melinda Culea (Amy Amanda Allen alias Triple A). 'BA' stood for Bad Attitude.

At Last the 1948 Show John Cleese, Tim Brooke-Taylor, Graham Chapman, Marty Feldman, Aimi Macdonald.

Auf Wiedersehen Pet Tim Healy (Denis Patterson), Jimmy Nail ('Oz' Osbourne), Kevin Whately (Neville Hope), Gary Holton (Wayne), Pat Roach (Bomber), Timothy Spall (Barry Taylor), Christopher Fairbank (Moxey). Gary Holton died during filming of the follow-up series in Spain. Pat Roach died after filming series four and did not appear in the Christmas special in 2004.

Avengers, The Patrick MacNee (John Steed), Honor Blackman (Cathy Gale), Diana Rigg (Emma Peel), Linda Thorson (Tara King), Patrick Newell (Mother). Steed lived at 3 Duchess Mews, London. Originally a spin-off of a lesser known series called *Police Surgeon*, starring Ian Hendry as Dr David Keel.

A J Wentworth, BA Arthur Lowe played the absent-minded teacher.

Bagpuss Bagpuss owned by Emily. Narrator and writer: Oliver Postgate.

Ballykissangel Niall Tobin (Father MacAnally), Gary Whelan (Brendan Kearney), Peter Caffrey (Padraig Kelly), Deirdre Donnelly (Siobhan Mehigan), Birdy Sweeney (Eamon), Victoria Smurfit (Orla), Don Wycherley (Father Aidan), Aine Ni Mhuiri (Kathleen), Joe Savino (Liam), Tina Kellegher (Niamh Egan), Lorcan Cranitch (Sean Dillon), Frankie McCafferty (Donal). Original series starred Stephen Tompkinson (Father Clifford) and Dervla Kirwan (Assumpta Fitzgerald) and the late Tony Doyle.

Banacek George Peppard (Thomas Banacek).

Banana Splits, The Voices: Fleegle (Paul Winchell), Bingo (Daws Butler), Drooper (Allan Melvin), Snorky (Don Messick).

Batman Adam West (Batman/Bruce Wayne), Burt Ward (Robin/Dick Grayson), Frank Gorshin and John Astin (Riddler), Julie Newmar, Eartha Kitt, Lee Meriwether (Catwoman), Vincent Price (Egg Head), Tallulah Bankhead (Black Widow), Burgess Meredith (Penguin), Carolyn Jones (Queen of Diamonds), Liberace (Chandel), Cliff Robertson (Shame), Van Johnson (Minstrel), Shelley Winters (Ma Parker), Ida Lupino (Dr Cassandra), Otto Preminger, George Sanders and Eli Wallach (Mr Freeze), Cesar Romero (Joker), Yvonne Craig (Batgirl alias Barbara Gordon).

Battlestar Galactica Lorne Greene (Commander Adama), Dirk Benedict (Lt Starbuck).

Baywatch David Hasselhoff (Lt Mitch Bucannon), Pamela Denise Anderson (C J Parker), Erika Eleniak (Shauni McLain), Nicole Eggert (Summer Quinn), Yasmin Bleeth (Caroline Holden). Story of Los Angeles County Lifeguards working on Malibu Beach. Spin-off from 1989 TV film *Panic at Malibu Beach,* starring David Hasselhoff.

Beadle's About Popular hidden-camera show starring Jeremy Beadle and still shown regularly on Challenge TV. Little-known fact: Jeremy was a trivia buff par excellence and entered the 2002 British Quiz Championships, placing a very respectable 30th.

Beauty and the Beast Vincent (Ron Perlman), Assistant DA Catherine Chandler (Linda Hamilton), Roy Dotrice (Father), Stephen McHattie (Gabriel).

Beiderbecke Affair James Bolam (Trevor Chaplin), Barbara Flynn (Jill Swinburne). The Beiderbecke of the title was Bix Beiderbecke the jazz great, whose music was played by Kenny Baker. Sequels were *The Beiderbecke Tapes* and *The Beiderbecke Connection.*

Ben Casey Vince Edwards (Ben), Sam Jaffe (Dr David Zorba), Ben Piazza (Dr Mike Rogers). Hospital: County General. Produced by Bing Crosby Productions, which discovered Vince Edwards.

Benidorm Steve Pemberton (Mick Garvey), Johnny Vegas (Geoff Maltby aka The Oracle). Sitcom depicting the working-class stereotype of the popular Spanish resort.

Bergerac John Nettles (Det. Sgt Jim Bergerac), Terence Alexander (Charlie Hungerford), Lisa Goddard (Philippa Vale). Story of an alcoholic policeman in Jersey.

Beverly Hillbillies Buddy Ebsen (Jed Clampett), Irene Ryan (Daisy Moses alias Granny), Donna Douglas (Elly May), Max Baer Jnr (Jethro Bodine and Jethrene Bodine), Nancy Kulp (Jane Hathaway), Sharon Tate (Janet Trego).

Beverly Hills 90210 Shannen Doherty (Brenda Walsh), Jason Priestley (Brandon Walsh). Title is a Zip code.

Bewitched Elizabeth Montgomery (Samantha Stephens), Dick York and Dick Sargent (Darren), Agnes Moorhead (Endora), Marion Lorne (Aunt Clara), David White (Larry Tate).

Big Big Talent Show, The Jonathan Ross hosts the star-spotting talent show.

Big Break Snooker-based game show hosted by Jim Davidson and John Virgo.

Big Brother Launched in July 2000. The original ten housemates were Anna, Andrew, Caroline, Craig, Darren, Melanie, Nick, Nichola, Sada and Thomas. Nick Bateman was evicted for cheating and replaced by Claire Strutton. The three finalists were Craig Philips, Anna Nolan and Darren Ramsey. The winner of the £70,000 first prize was Craig. Marjorie was the pet chicken, Juanita the toy baby, and Davina McCall the presenter. Subsequent winners: Brian Dowling (2001), Kate Lawler (2002), Cameron Stout (2003), Nadia Almada (2004), Anthony Hutton (2005), Pete Bennett (2006), Brian Belo (2007), Rachel Rice (2008), Sophie Reade (2009), Josie Gibson (2010), Aaron Allard-Morgan (2011), Luke Anderson (2012), Sam Evans (2013). Celebrity winners: Jack Dee, Mark Owen, Bez, Chantelle Houghton, Shilpa Shetty, Ulrika Jonsson, Alex Reid, Paddy Doherty, Denise Welch, Julian Clary, Ryland Clark. Presenters: Davina McCall, Brian Dowling, Emma Willis.

Bill, The ITV soap (1984-2010). For comprehensive coverage see *The A to Z of British (and Irish) Popular Culture.*

Birds of a Feather Pauline Quirke (Sharon Theodopolopoudos), Linda Robson (Tracey Stubbs), Lesley Joseph (Dorien Green), Peter Polycarpou and David Cardy (Chris Theodopolopoudos). Series created by Laurence Marks and Maurice Gran.

Blackadder Four series written by Rowan Atkinson, Richard Curtis and Ben Elton. Characters included Baldrick (Tony Robinson), Queen Elizabeth I (Miranda Richardson), Melchett (Stephen Fry), Captain Darling/Percy (Tim McInnerny). *Black Adder, The* (set during Wars of the Roses), *Blackadder II* (set in Elizabethan England), *Blackadder the Third* (set in Georgian England), *Blackadder Goes Forth* (set in World War I).

Blake's 7 Gareth Thomas (Blake), Paul Darrow (Kerr Avon), Sally Knyvette (Jenna Stannis), Michael Keating (Vila Restal), Jan Chappell (Cally from Auron), Josette Simon (Dayna Mellanby), David Jackson (Gan Olag), Steven Pacey (Capt. Del Tarrant), Peter Tuddenham (voice of Zen and Orac), Glynis Barber (Soolin), Jacqueline Pearce (Servalan). Spacecraft: Liberator and Scorpio Penal Colony, Cygnus Alpha. Dictatorship name: The Federation. Creator: Terry Nation. Gan Olag was implanted with a 'Brain Limiter' to stop him killing.

Blooming Marvellous Sarah Lancashire (Liz), Clive Mantle (Jack).

Blott on the Landscape David Suchet (Blott), George Cole (Sir Giles Lynchwood MP), Simon Cadell (Dundridge). Adaption by Malcolm Bradbury of Tom Sharpe's black comic novel. Filmed at Stanage Park, near Ludlow.

Blue Peter Original presenters in 1958: Leila Williams and Christopher Trace. Other presenters include Valerie Singleton, Peter Purves, John Noakes, Lesley Judd, Simon Groom, Sarah Greene, Peter Duncan, Janet Ellis, Michael Sundin, Anthea Turner, Diane-Louise Jordan, Caron Keating, John Leslie, Mark Curry, Yvette Fielding, Tim Vincent, Romana D'Annunzio, Richard Bacon, Katy Hill, Konnie Huq, Simon Thomas, Matt Baker, Zoe Salmon, Liz Barker, Gethin Jones, Andy Akinwolere, Helen Skelton, Joel Defries, Barney Harwood, Lindsey Russell, Radzi Chinyanganya.

Bob the Builder Neil Morrissey (voice of Bob). Machines: Scoop the yellow digger, Muck the red bulldozer, Lofty the blue crane, Roley the green steamroller and Dizzy the orange cement mixer.

Bonanza Lorne Greene (Ben Cartwright), Michael Landon (Little Joe Cartwright), Dan Blocker (Eric 'Hoss' Cartwright, Norwegian for good luck), Pernell Roberts (Adam), Victor Sen Yung (Hop Sing), Ray Teal (Sheriff Ray Coffee), David Canary (Mr 'Candy' Canaday), Tim Matheson (Griff King). The three sons had different mothers.

Boon Michael Elphick (Ken Boon), Neil Morrissey (Rocky Cassidy).

Boss Cat Cartoon characters include: Benny the Ball, Choo Choo, Spook, The Brain, Fancy-Fancy, Officer Dibble. Series called *Top Cat* outside UK.

Bottom Rik Mayall (Richie Richard), Adrian Edmondson (Eddie Hitler).

Bouquet of Barbed Wire Frank Finlay (Peter Manson), Sheila Allen (Cassie), Susan Penhaligon (Prue), James Aubrey (Gavin Sorenson).

Boyd QC Michael Denison.

Boys from the Blackstuff Bernard Hill (Yosser Hughes), Michael Angelis (Chrissie Todd), Julie Walters (Angie Todd). Written by Alan Bleasdale. Famous catchphrase: Gi's a job.

Boys from the Bush Tim Healy (Reg Toomer), Chris Haywood (Dennis Tontine).

Brains Trust, The Chairmen: Hugh Ross Willliams, Michael Flanders.

Branded Chuck Connors (Jason McCord), only survivor of Indian massacre at the Battle of Bitter Creek in Wyoming and thought therefore to be a coward. Opening court martial scene is memorable.

Brass Timothy West (Bradley Hardacre), Caroline Blakiston (Patience), Geoffrey Hinsliff and Geoffrey Hutchings (George Fairchild). Set in Utterley.

Bread Peter Howitt and Graham Bickley (Joey Boswell), Jean Boht (Nellie), Ronald Forfar (Freddie), Victor McGuire (Jack), Gilly Coman and Melanie Hill (Aveline), Jonathan Morris (Adrian), Nick Conway (Billy), Rita Tushingham (Celia Higgins). Series created by Carla Lane.

Brideshead Revisited Anthony Andrews (Lord Sebastian Flyte), Jeremy Irons (Charles Ryder), Diana Quick (Lady Julia Flyte), Laurence Olivier (Lord Marchmain), John Gielgud (Edward Ryder), Claire Bloom (Lady Ryder).

Britain's Got Talent Simon Cowell idea began in 2007. Judges include: Simon Cowell, Amanda Holden, Alesha Dixon, David Walliams, Piers Morgan, Kelly Brook, David Hasselhoff, Michael McIntyre. Presented by Ant & Dec. Winners: Paul Potts, George Sampson, Diversity, Spelbound, Jai McDowall, Ashleigh and Pudsey, Attraction.

Brittas Empire, The Chris Barrie (Gordon), Pippa Heywood (Helen), Julia St John (Laura Lancing). Leisure centre: Whitbury Newtown Leisure Centre.

Brookside Soap, first broadcast 2 November 1982. For comprehensive coverage see *The A to Z of British (and Irish) Popular Culture.*

Brothers, The Jean Anderson (Mary Hammond), Glyn Owen and Patrick O'Connell (Edward Hammond), Gabrielle Drake (Jill Hammond), Colin Baker (Paul Merroney), Liza Goddard (April Merroney), Kate O' Mara (Jane Maxwell). Type of business: haulage.

Brush Strokes Karl Howman (Jacko), Mike Walling (Eric), Nicky Croydon (Jean), Howard Lew Lewis (Elmo Putney), Gary Waldhorn (Lionel Bainbridge).

Buck Rogers in the 25th Century Gil Gerard (Buck), Felix Silla (Twiki: voiced by Mel Blanc, Bob Elyea), Henry Silva and Michael Ansara (Kane), Wilfred Hyde-White (Dr Goodfellow), Pamela Hensley (Princess Ardala). Year 2491. Space capsule: Ranger 3, launched in 1987. City: New Chicago. Rivals: Draconians.

Budgie Adam Faith (Budgie Bird), Iain Cuthbertson (Charlie Endell), Lynn Dalby (Hazel), Georgina Hale (Jean Bird), John Rhys-Davies (Laughing Spam Fritter), Rio Fanning (Grogan). Writers: Keith Waterhouse and Willis Hall.

Buffy the Vampire Slayer Sarah Michelle Gellar (Buffy Summers), Alyson Hannigan (Willow Rosenberg), Nicholas Brendon (Xander Harris), Anthony Head (Rupert Giles), Emma Caulfield (Anya), Seth Green (Oz), Marc Blucas (Riley Finn), David Boreanaz (Angel), Charisma Carpenter (Cordelia), James Marsters (Spike).

Bulman Don Henderson (George Bulman). Character first appeared in *The XYY Man* and then in *Strangers*. His quirky nature included his wearing of fingerless gloves, constant use of an inhaler and carrying of a plastic bag whose contents we rarely saw.

Busman's Holiday Presenters: Julian Pettifer, Sarah Kennedy, Elton Welsby

Butterflies Wendy Craig (Ria Parkinson), Geoffrey Palmer (Ben Parkinson, a dentist), Andrew Hall (Russell Parkinson), Nicholas Lyndhurst (Adam Parkinson). Series created by Carla Lane.

By the Sword Divided Sharon Maughan (Anne Lacey/Fletcher), Julian Glover (Sir Martin Lacey), Tim Bentinck (Sir Thomas Lacey). Plot: a family is torn apart by the English Civil War.

Cadfael Derek Jacobi (Cadfael). Story of the former crusading monk with supreme botanical knowledge. Based on stories by Ellis Peters.

Cagney and Lacey Tyne Daly (Mary Beth Lacey), Meg Foster and Sharon Gless (Christine Cagney). Loretta Swit played Cagney in the pilot.

Call My Bluff Presenters: Robert Robinson, Bob Holness, Fiona Bruce, Joe Melia, Peter Wheeler, Robin Ray.

Callan Edward Woodward (Callan), Russell Hunter (Lonely), Ronald Radd, Michael Goodliffe, Derek Bond, William Squire (Hunter), Anthony Valentine (Toby Meres), Patrick Mower (Cross). Series started as an Armchair Theatre production, *A Magnum For Schneider,* with Peter Bowles playing Toby Meres.

Camberwick Green Took over Monday *Watch with Mother* slot from 'Picture Box'. Characters included Capt. Snort, Sgt Major Grout, Windy Miller of Colley's Mill, Mickey Murphy the baker, Dr Mopp, Thomas Tripp the milkman, Mrs Dingle the postmistress, Mrs Honeyman, PC McGarry (No. 452).

Campion Peter Davison (Albert Campion), Brian Glover (Magersfontein Lugg, Campion's manservant).

Candid Camera Presenters: Bob Monkhouse, Jonathan Routh, Peter Dulay.

Captain Pugwash Characters included Capt. Horatio Pugwash (Skipper of the *Black Pig*), Able Seamen Barnabas and Willy, Master Mate (occasionally referred to as Master Bate), Tom and Cutthroat Jake. Theme music 'The Hornblower', performed by Tommy Edmondson. Narrator: Peter Hawkins.

Captain Scarlet and the Mysterons Voices: Francis Matthews (Paul Metcalfe/Capt. Scarlet), Donald Gray (Charles Gray/Col. White), Ed Bishop (Adam Svenson/Capt. Blue), Paul Maxwell (Bradley Holden/Capt. Grey), Sylvia Anderson (Magnolia Jones/Melody Angel), Liz Morgan (Juliette Pointon/Destiny Angel), Janna Hill (Karen Wainwright/Symphony Angel), Liz Morgan (Diane Sims/Rhapsody Angel), Lian-Shin (Chan Kwan/Harmony Angel), Donald Gray (Conrad Turner/Capt. Black), Charles Tingwell (Edward Wilkie/Dr Fawn), Gary Files (Patrick Donaghue/Capt. Magenta), Jeremy Wilkin (Richard Frazier/Capt. Ochre), Cy Grant (Seymour Griffiths/Lt Green), Paul Maxwell (World President). Year: 2068. Spectrum base: Cloudbase Angel. Interceptor aircraft codeword: SIG Spectrum is Green.

Casey Jones Alan Hale Jnr (John Luther 'Casey' Jones). Worked for Illinois Central Railroad. Engine name: Cannonball Express. His faithful dog was called Cinders.

Castaway Original series starred Ben Fogle and his black labrador Inca.

Casualty Medical drama set in Holby City Hospital, first aired 1986. For comprehensive coverage see *The A to Z of British (and Irish) Popular Culture.*

Catherine Tate Show Characters: Lauren the modern day schoolgirl with catchphrase 'Am I bovvered?', Nan Taylor with catchphrase 'What a fucking liberty', Derek the gay man with catchphrase 'How very dare you'.

Cathy Come Home Carol White (Cathy Ward), Ray Brooks (Reg Ward). Written by Jeremy Sandford, directed by Ken Loach. This drama brought Shelter, a campaign for the homeless, to the awareness of many.

Catweazle Geoffrey Bayldon (Catweazle), Robin Davis (Carrot Bennett). Story of an 11th-century wizard stranded in the 20th century.

Celeb Harry Enfield (Gary), Amanda Holden (Debs), Leo Bill (Troy), Rupert Vansittart (Johnson). Sit-com set in the home of a rock superstar. Based on a cartoon in *Private Eye* magazine.

Champions Stuart Damon (Craig Stirling), William Gaunt (Richard Barrett), Alexandra Bastedo (Sharon McCready). Worked for Nemesis, based in Geneva.

Changing Rooms Hosted by Carol Smillie. Designers include Graham Wynne and Linda Barker. DIY expert: Andy Kane.

Charlie's Angels Kate Jackson (Sabrina Duncan), Farrah Fawcett-Majors (Jill Munroe), Jaclyn Smith (Kelly Garrett), Cheryl Ladd (Kris Munroe), Shelley Hack (Tiffany Welles), Tanya Roberts (Julie Rogers). Voice of Charlie Townshend: John Forsythe.

Cheers Ted Danson (Sam Malone), Shelley Long (Diane Chambers), Rhea Perlman (Carla Tortelli/Le Bec), Georg Wendt (Norm the accountant), John Ratzenberger (Cliff the mailman), Kelsey Grammer (Frasier Crane the psychiatrist), Woody Harrelson (Woody), Kirstie Alley (Rebecca Howe).

Chef Lenny Henry (Gareth Blackstock), Caroline Lee Johnson (Janice), Roger Griffiths (Everton). Chef of Le Château Anglais in the Oxfordshire Cotswolds.

Cheyenne Clint Walker (Cheyenne Bodie). Replaced for short time by Ty Hardin as Bronco Lane, who eventually gained his own series.

Chigley Described as a hamlet near Camberwick Green, Trumptonshire. Characters included Mr Clutterbuck the Builder, Chipppy Minton the Carpenter, Lord Belborough, Mr Cresswell the owner of the biscuit factory, Harry Farthing the Potter, Mr Brackett the Butler.

Chinese Detective, The David Yip (Det. Sgt Johnny Ho).

Chips Erik Estrada (Francis 'Ponch' Poncherello), Larry Wilcox (Jonathan Baker). Story of two Los Angeles police motorcyclists working for the California Highway Patrol (Chips).

Circus Boy Notable for the casting of Mickey Braddock (formerly and latterly Dolenz) as Corky.

Cisco Kid, The Duncan Renaldo (Cisco), Leo Carrillo (Pancho). Cisco's horse: Diablo. Pancho's horse: Loco. Pancho was expert with a whip. Based on stories by O'Henry.

Citizen James Sid James (Sidney Balmoral James), Bill Kerr (William 'Bill' Kerr), Liz Fraser (Liz Fraser).

Citizen Smith Robert Lindsay (Walter Henry 'Wolfie' Smith), Mike Grady (Ken), Tony Millan (Tucker), Cheryl Hall (Shirley), Peter Vaughan and Tony Steedman (Charlie Johnson). Leader of the Tooting Popular Front with his catchphrase 'Power to the People'.

Clangers, The Clangers were the pink and woolly, mouse-like creatures who took their names from the sound made when they battened down their dustbin-lid hatches and retreated underground. Other inhabitants of the planet were the Froglets, Soup Dragon and Iron Chicken.

Cleopatras, The Actresses who played the Cleopatras included Michelle Newell, Elizabeth Shepherd, Caroline Mortimer, Sue Holderness, Amanda Boxer, Prue Clarke, Pauline Moran.

Colby's, The (spin-off from *Dynasty* set in Los Angeles; aired between 1985 and 1987) BBC1. Bliss Colby (Claire Yarlett), Constance Colby (Barbara Stanwyck), Fallon Carrington / Colby (Emma Samms), Francesca Scott Colby (Katherine Ross), Jason Colby (Charlton Heston), Miles Colby (Maxwell Caulfield), Monica Colby (Tracy Scoggins), Sable Scott Colby (Stephanie Beacham), Zachary Powers (Ricardo Montalban).

Colditz Jack Hedley (Lt Col. John Preston), Robert Wagner (Flt Lt/Major Phil Carrington), David McCallum (Flt Lt Simon Carter), Bernard Hepton (Kommandant), Anthony Valentine (Major Horst Mohn).

Come Dancing Presenters include McDonald Hobley, Angela Rippon, David Jacobs, Terry Wogan, Rosemarie Ford, Noel Edmonds, Judith Chalmers, Keith Fordyce, Michael Aspel, Peter West and Peter Dimmock.

Compact Ronald Allen (Ian Harmon), Carmen Silvera (Camilla Hope), Vincent Ball (David Rome). Created by Hazel Adair and Peter Ling.

Cool For Cats Britain's first pop music show in 1956 and hosted by Ker Robertson and then Kent Walton.

Coronation Street First broadcast Friday 9 December 1960. See *The A to Z of British (and Irish) Popular Culture* for comprehensive coverage.

Cosby Show Bill Cosby (Heathcliff Huxtable, an obstetrician), Phylicia Ayres-Allen/Rashad (Clair, a lawyer). Their children: Sondra, Rudy, Denise, Theo, Vanessa.

Countdown Words-and-numbers game hosted by Richard Whiteley between 1982 and 2005, Des Lynam (2005–6), Des O'Connor (2007–9), Jeff Stelling (2009–11) and Nick Hewer (2012-present). Carol Vorderman was the co-host between 1982 and 2009 but was then replaced by Rachel Riley. Based on the French version *Des chiffres et des lettres* (literally "numbers and letters").

Cracker Robbie Coltrane (Eddie 'Fitz' Fitzgerald). Created by Jimmy McGovern.

Crackerjack Hosts: Eamonn Andrews, Leslie Crowther, Michael Aspel, Ed Stewart, Stu Francis. Stooges: Peter Glaze, Don Maclean, Leslie Crowther. Game: Double or Drop.

Crime Traveller Michael French (David Wicks in *EastEnders*) starred in this time machine series.

Criss Cross Quiz Popular quiz show hosted by Jeremy Hawk (father of actress Belinda Lang). Format after the American *Tic Tac Dough.*

Crossroads Soap, first aired Monday 2 November 1964. For comprehensive coverage see *The A to Z of British (and Irish) Popular Culture.*

C.A.T.S. Eyes Jill Gascoigne (Maggie Forbes), Rosalyn Landor (Pru Standfast), Leslie Ash (Frederica 'Fred' Smith). C.A.T.S. stood for Covert Activities Thames Section.

Dad's Army Arthur Lowe (Capt. George Mainwaring, a bank manager), John Le Mesurier (Sgt Arthur Wilson), Clive Dunn (L/Corporal Jack Jones, a butcher), John Laurie (Pte James Frazier, an undertaker), James Beck (Pte James Walker, a spiv), Ian Lavender (Pte Frank Pike, a silly boy), Arnold Ridley (Pte Charles Godfrey), Bill Pertwee (ARP Warden William Hodges, a greengrocer), Frank Williams (the vicar), Colin Bean (Pte Sponge), Pamela Cundell (Mrs Fox). Created by Jimmy Perry and David Croft and set in Walmington-on-Sea (supposedly Bexhill).

Dallas Soap, aired from 1978 to 1991) BBC1. Main location Southfork Ranch. John Ross 'JR' Ewing (Larry Hagman), Bobby Ewing (Patrick Duffy), Sue Ellen Ewing (Linda Gray), Ben Stivers / Wes Parmalee (Steve Forrest), Carter McKay (George Kennedy), Clayton Farlow (Howard Keel), Cliff Barnes (Ken Kercheval), Don Lockwood (Ian McShane), Dusty Farlow (Jared Martin), Eleanor Southworth Ewing / Farlow -Miss Ellie- (Barbara Bel Geddes and Donna Reed), Gary Ewing (David Ackroyd and Ted Shackelford), Jenna Wade (Morgan Fairchild, Francine Tacker, Priscilla Presley), Jock Ewing (Jim Davis), Katherine Wentworth (Morgan Brittany), Kristin Shepard (Colleen Camp and Mary Crosby), LeeAnn De La Vega (Barbara Eden), Lucy Ewing / Cooper (Charlene Tilton), Pamela Barnes / Ewing (Victoria Principal), Ray Krebbs (Steve Kanaly), Stephanie Rogers (Lesley Anne Down), Valene Ewing (Joan Van Ark), Willard 'Digger' Barnes (David Wayne and Keenan Wynn).

Dalziel and Pascoe Warren Clarke (Det. Supt Andrew Dalziel), Colin Buchanan (Det. Insp. Peter Pascoe). Written by Stephen Lowe and based on Reginald Hill's books.

Dancing On Ice Celebrity ice skating competition presented by Phillip Schofield and Holly Willoughby (replaced by Christine Bleakley in 2012). Coaches: Jane Torvill and Christopher Dean. Panel: Karen Barber, Nicky Slater, Jason Gardiner and head judge Robin Cousins. Other judges: Ashley Roberts, Karen Kresge, Natalia Bestemianova, Ruthie Henshall, Emma Bunton, Louie Spence, Katarina Witt. Winners: Gaynor Faye, Kyran Bracken, Suzanne Shaw, Ray Quinn, Hayley Tamaddon, Sam Attwater, Matthew Wolfenden, Beth Tweddle. Narrated by Tony Gubba (2006-13), Simon Reed (2013-)

Dangermouse Voices: Dangermouse (David Jason), Penfold (Terry Scott), Stiletto Mafioso (Brian Trueman), Baron Greenback (Edward Kelsey). Created by Mike Harding and Brian Trueman. Written by Brian Trueman and Angus Allen. Narrated by David Jason.

Darling Buds of May, The David Jason (Sidney Charles 'Pop' Larkin), Pam Ferris (Ma Larkin), Catherine Zeta-Jones (Mariette Larkin/Charlton), Philip Franks (Cedric 'Charley' Charlton).

Dawson's Creek Soap, set in Capeside, Massachusetts) C4. Dawson Leery (James Van Der Beek), Josephine 'Joey' Potter (Katie Holmes), Pacey Witter (Joshua Jackson), Andrea 'Andie' McPhee (Meredith Monroe), Audrey Liddell (Busy Philipps), Evelyn 'Grams' Ryan (Mary Beth Peil), Gail Leery (Mary-Margaret Humes), Jack McPhee (Kerr Smith), Jennifer 'Jen' Lindley (Michelle Williams), Mitchell 'Mitch' Leery (John Wesley Shipp).

Deal or No Deal Game show hosted by Noel Edmonds, in which 22 contestants stand over boxes containing amounts from 1p to £250,000. Another contestant opens each box and is offered a deal by the banker depending on the board. To date six people have won the jackpot, Laura Pearce, Alice Munday, Suzanne Mulholland, Tegen Roberts, Nong Skett, and Paddy Roberts. Famous contestants include Olly Murs, Laurence Shahlaei and Shahid Khan, aka Naughty Boy.

Defenders, The E G Marshall (Lawrence Preston), Robert Reed (Kenneth Preston). Father and son lawyers.

Dempsey and Makepeace Michael Brandon (Lt James Dempsey), Glynis Barber (Det. Sgt Harriet Makepeace). Dept: S110.

Department S Peter Wyngarde (Jason King), Joel Fabiani (Stewart Sullivan), Rosemary Nichols (Annabelle Hurst). Department S was a department of Interpol.

Desmond's Norman Beaton (Desmond Ambrose), Carmen Munroe (Shirley Ambrose), Ram John Holder (Pork Pie). Life in a Peckham barber's shop.

Desperate Housewives Marcia Cross (Bree Van De Kamp), Teri Hatcher (Susan Mayer), Felicity Huffman (Lynette Scavo), Eva Longoria (Gabrielle Solis), Nicollette Sheridan (Edie Britt), Brenda Strong (Mary Alice Young), Andrea Bowen (Julie Mayer), Ricardo Antonio Chavira (Carlos Solis), Steven Culp (Rex Van De Kamp), James Denton (Mike Delfino), Cody Kasch (Zach Young), Jesse Metcalfe (John), Mark Moses (Paul Young). Set in Wisteria Lane, a street in the fictional American town of 'Fairview' in the fictional 'Eagle State'. Narrated by Mary Alice Young, a dead neighbour who committed suicide in first episode and is seen in flashback.

Detectives, The Jasper Carrott (Bob Louis), Robert Powell (Dave Briggs), George Sewell (Supt Frank Cottam).

Dial 999 Robert Beatty (Canadian Mountie Mike Maguire), seconded to London on work experience.

Dick Van Dyke Show, The Dick Van Dyke (Rob Petrie), Mary Tyler Moore (Laura), Larry Matthews (Ritchie), Rose Marie (Sally Rogers), Carl Reiner (Alan Brady), Morey Amsterdam (Maurice 'Buddy' Sorrell).

Dinnerladies Victoria Wood (Bren), Thelma Barlow (Dolly), Celia Imrie (Philippa), Maxine Peake (Twinkle), Anne Reid (Jean), Duncan Preston (Stan), Andrew Dunn (Tony), Shobna Gulati (Anita), Julie Walters (Petula), Christopher Greet (Mr Michael), Jane Hazlegrove (Lisa), Sue Devaney (Secretary).

Doctor Finlay Tannochbrae 20 years on (real-life Auchtermuchty in Fife), with Dr Finlay played by David Rintoul and the character's Christian name changed to John.

Dr Finlay's Casebook Bill Simpson (Dr Alan Finlay), Andrew Cruickshank (Dr Angus Cameron), Barbara Mullen (Janet). Set in 1920s Tannochbrae (real-life Callander), the base for practice was Arden House. The stories were based on *The Adventures of a Black Bag* by A J Cronin.

Doctor in the House Barry Evans (Michael Upton), Robin Nedwell (Duncan Waring), Geoffrey Davies (Dick Stuart-Clark), George Layton (Paul Collier). Based on the books by Richard Gordon.

Don't Wait Up Nigel Havers (Dr Tom Latimer), Tony Britton (Dr Toby Latimer). Writer: George Layton.

Doomwatch John Paul (Dr Spencer Quist), Simon Oates (Dr John Ridge), Robert Powell (Tobias 'Toby' Wren).

Dotto Game show hosted by Robert Gladwell, Jimmy Hanley and Shaw Taylor during its two-year run. Based on American show which was taken off as part of the 'Quiz Show Scandal'.

Dr Kildare Richard Chamberlain (Dr James Kildare), Raymond Massey (Dr Leonard Gillespie). Based on Max Brand books. Richard Chamberlain had a hit with the vocal version of the theme tune, 'Three Stars Will Shine Tonight'. Hospital: Blair General.

Dr Who First Dr Who was William Hartnell, followed by Patrick Troughton, Jon Pertwee, Tom Baker, Peter Davison, Colin Baker, Sylvester McCoy. Other Dr Who's have included Richard Hurndall, who took William Hartnell's part in *The Five Doctors*, Paul McGann who played the Doctor in a television film, and Peter Cushing, who appeared as the Doctor in two feature films. The original crew were William Russell (Ian Chesterton), Jacqueline Hill (Barbara Wright) and Carole Ann Ford (Susan Foreman, the Doctor's granddaughter). Other assistants included Peter Purves (Steven Taylor), Nicola Bryant (Perpugilliam 'Peri' Brown), Sophie Aldred (Ace), Louise Jameson (Leela), Frazer Hines (Jamie McCrimmon), Janet Fielding (Tegan Jovanka), Elizabeth Sladen (Sarah Jane Smith), Katy Manning (Jo Grant), Sarah Sutton (Nyssa). The Doctor is from the planet Gallifrey. The six actors who played the Master were (1) Roger Delgado (2) Peter Pratt (3) Geoffrey Beevers (4) Anthony Ainley (5) Eric Roberts (6) John Simm. Tardis: Time And Relative Dimension In Space. The series was axed in 1989 but resurrected in March 2005, the Doctor being played by Christopher Eccleston and his assistant, Rose Tyler, by Billie Piper. Their first adversaries were the Autons and the series was written by Russell T Davies. David Tennant replaced Eccleston in 2006 and Freema Agyeman replaced Piper in 2007. Agyeman was replaced by Catherine Tate (Donna Noble) in 2008. Matt Smith replaced Tennant in 2010 and his assistant was played by Karen Gillan (Amy Pond) and most recently by Jenna-Louise Coleman (Clara Oswald). Peter Capaldi replaced Smith in 2013.

Dragnet Jack Webb (Joe Friday). Episodes began: 'The story you are about to see is true, only the names have been changed to protect the innocent.' Set in Los Angeles. Badge no.: 714.

Dragon's Den Entrepreneurs pitch to gain investment for their ideas. Presenter: Evan Davis. Panel: Duncan Bannatyne, Rachel Elnaugh (replaced by Deborah Meaden), Peter Jones, Doug Richard (replaced by Richard Farleigh and then James Caan), Simon Woodroffe (relaced by Theo Paphitis).

Drop the Dead Donkey Robert Duncan (Gus), Neil Pearson (Dave), Jeff Rawle (George), Stephen Tompkinson (Damien), David Swift (Henry), Victoria Wicks (Sally). Written by Andy Hamilton and Guy Jenkin. Original working title for the show was 'Dead Belgians Don't Count'.

Duchess of Duke Street, The Gemma Jones (Louisa Trotter), Christopher Cazenove (Charles Tyrrell). Loosely based on the life story of Rosa Lewis, a kitchen maid who became manageress of the Cavendish Hotel in Jermyn Street. Hotel in series: Bentinck.

Dukes of Hazzard, The Catherine Bach (Daisy Duke), Tom Wopat (Luke Duke), John Schneider (Bo Duke), Sorrell Booke (Jefferson Davis 'Boss' Hogg). The Dukes were the Robin Hoods of Hazzard County, driving around in their 1969 Dodge Charger named The General Lee. Narration and theme tune by Waylon Jennings.

Dustbinmen, The John Woodvine and Brian Wilde (Bloody Delilah), Bryan Pringle (Cheese and Egg), Graham Haberfield (Winston Platt), Trevor Bannister (Heavy Breathing). Created and produced by Jack Rosenthal. Lorry called Thunderbird Three.

Dynasty Soap, set in Denver, Colorado; aired from 1981 to 1989) BBC1. Alexis Carrington / Colby / Dexter (Joan Collins), Krystle Jennings / Carrington (Linda Evans), Adam Carrington / Michael Torrance (Gordon Thomson), Amanda Carrington (Catherine Oxenburg and Karen Cellini), Ben Carrington (Christopher Cazenove), Blake Carrington (John Forsythe), Caress Morell (Kate O'Mara), Dominique Deveraux (Diahann Carroll), Dr Nick Toscanni (James Farentino), Fallon Carrington / Colby (Pamela Sue Martin and Emma Samms), Jeff Colby (John James), Monica Colby (Tracy Scoggins), Prince Michael (Michael Praed), Sable Colby (Stephanie Beacham), Sammy Jo (Heather Locklear), Steven Carrington (Al Corley and Jack Coleman).

Eastenders Soap, first broadcast 19 February 1985. For comprehensive coverage see *The A to Z of British (and Irish) Popular Culture.*

Edge of Darkness Bob Peck (Ronald Craven), Joanne Whalley (Emma Craven), Joe Don Baker (Darius Jedburgh). Music by Eric Clapton.

Edward and Mrs Simpson Edward Fox (Edward), Cynthia Harris (Mrs Wallis Warfield Simpson), Peggy Ashcroft (Queen Mary), David Waller (Stanley Baldwin).

Edward the Seventh Timothy West (Edward as an adult), Charles Sturridge (Edward as a teenager), Annette Crosbie (Queen Victoria), Robert Hardy (Prince Albert).

Eggheads Hosted by Dermot Murnaghan and Jeremy Vine. Amateur quizzers take on a professional panel of Kevin Ashman, Daphne Fowler, Chris Hughes, Judith Keppel, C J De Mooi, Barry Simmons, Pat Gibson and Dave Rainford.

Eldorado Soap, set in Los Barcos. First aired 6 July 1992 - BBC1. For full coverage see *The A to Z of British (and Irish) Popular Culture.*

Elizabeth R Glenda Jackson (Elizabeth), Robert Hardy (Robert Dudley), Ronald Hines (William Cecil), Daphne Slater (Mary Tudor), Vivian Pickles (Mary, Queen of Scots), John Woodvine (Sir Francis Drake), Nicholas Selby (Sir Walter Raleigh).

Emergency Ward 10 Jill Browne (Carole Young), Charles Tingwell (Dr Alan Dawson), Desmond Carrington (Dr Chris Anderson), John Carlisle (Mr Lester Large), Ray Barrett (Dr Don Nolan), Jane Rossington (Nurse Kate Ford), Paul Darrow (Mr Verity), John Alderton (Dr Richard Moone), Pik-Sen Lim (Nurse Kwai).

Emmerdale (Farm) Soap, first aired 16 October 1972. For comprehensive coverage see *The A to Z of British (and Irish) Popular Culture.*

Empire Road Norman Beaton (Everton Bennett).

Equalizer, The Edward Woodward (Robert McCall).

ER George Clooney (Dr Douglas Ross), Noah Wyle (Dr John Carter), Eriq La Salle (Dr Peter Benton), Julianna Margulies (Nurse Hathaway), Alex Kingston (Dr Elizabeth Corday), Anthony Edwards (Dr Mark Greene), Paul McCrane (Dr Robert Romano), Ming-Na (Dr Jing-Mai Chen), Michael Michele (Dr Cleo Finch), Maura Tiernay (Nurse Abby Lockheart), Laura Innes (Dr Kerry Weaver), Goran Visnjie (Dr Luka Kovac), Erik Palladino (Dr Dave Malucci). Set in Cook County Hospital, Chicago.

Ever-Decreasing Circles Richard Briers (Martin Brice), Penelope Wilton (Ann Brice), Stanley Lebor (Howard Hughes). Creators: John Esmonde and Bob Larbey.

Expert, The Marius Goring (Dr John Hardy).

Extras Ricky Gervais (Andy Millman), Ashley Jensen (Maggie Jacobs), Stephen Merchant (Darren Lamb). Stars playing themselves include Ben Stiller, Kate Winslet, Patrick Stewart, Samuel L Jackson and David Bowie.

Face to Face Presenter: John Freeman.

Fairly Secret Army Geoffrey Palmer (Major Harry Kitchener Wellington Truscott). Army called Queen's Own West Mercian Lowlanders.

Falcon Crest Soap, set in winery in Tuscany Valley, California; aired between 1981 and 1990. Angela Channing / Stavros (Jane Wyman), Apollonia (Patricia 'Apollonia' Kotero), Chase Gioberti (Robert Foxworth), Diana Hunter (Shannon Tweed), Dr Michael Ranson (Cliff Robertson), Emma Channing (Margaret Ladd), Francesca Gioberti (Gina Lollobrigida), Frank Agretti (Rod Taylor), Greg Reardon (Simon MacCorkindale), Jacqueline Perrault (Lana Turner), Jordan Roberts (Morgan Fairchild), Kit Marlowe (Kim Novak), Maggie Gioberti / Channing (Susan Sullivan), Nick Hogan (Roy Thinnes), Peter Stavros (Cesar Romero), Phillip Erikson (Mel Ferrer), Tony Cumson (John Saxon).

Fall and Rise of Reginald Perrin, The Leonard Rossiter (Reginald Iolanthe Perrin/Martin Wellbourne), Pauline Yates (Elizabeth), John Barron (CJ), Sue Nicholls (Joan Greengross), Geoffrey Palmer (Jimmy), John Horsley (Doc Morrissey), Bruce Bould (David Harris-Jones). Created by David Nobbs. Companies: Sunshine Desserts/Grot.

Fame Debbie Allen (Lydia Grant), Erica Gimpel (Coco Hernandez), Gene Anthony Ray (Leroy Johnson), Lori Singer (Julie Miller), Janet Jackson (Cleo Hewitt).

Fame Academy BBC programme showcasing new talent. The first winner in 2002 was David Sneddon, with Ireland's Sinead Quinn runner-up.

Family Affairs Soap, aired at launch of C5 in March 1997. Albie Leach (Martin Herdman), Alex Williams (Jake McCarthy), Amir Sadati (Kayvan Novak), Angus Hart (Ian Cullen), Ania Williams (Elizabeth Holmes-Gwillim), Anna Gregory (Martha Cope), Annie Hart (Liz Crowther), Babs Woods (Jan Harvey), Becky Scott (Chandra Ruegg), Ben Galloway (Peter England), Benji McHugh (Mark McLean), Cameron Davenport (Rupert Hill), Cat Webb (Nicola Duffett), Chloe Costello (Leah Coombes), Chris Hart (Ian Ashpitel), Chris Jacobs (Gemma Wardle), Chrissy Costello (Kazia Pelka), Claire Callan / Toomey (Tina Hall (formerly Russell), Conrad Williams (Simon Merrells), Dan Wilkinson (Charlie Watts), Darren Scott (Ike Hamilton), Dave Matthews (Richard Hawley), David Cash (James Gaddas), Denise Boulter (Claire Perkins), Doug MacKenzie (Gareth Hale), Duncan Hart (Rocky Marshall), Eddie Harris (Tony Scannell), Eileen Day / Callan (Rosie Rowell), Elsa Gates (Delena Kidd), Gary Costello (Gary Webster), Gemma Craig (Angela Hazeldine), Geri Evans (Anna Acton) Ginny Davenport (Joanna Foster), Grace Ellis (Amber and Jade Montague), Graham Parker (Lee Warburton), Holly Hart (Sandra Huggett), Jack Gates (Ken Farrington), Jake Walker (Seb Castang), Jamie Hart (Michael Cole), Jim Webb (Jo Dow), Joe Thorn (Les Dennis), John Stokes (David Michaels), Justin MacKenzie (Ryan Davenport), Karen Ellis (Tanya Franks), Katie Williams (Robyn Page), Kelly Boulter (Carryl Thomas), Kelly Hurst (Nicky Talacko), Kim Davies (Troy Titus-Adams), Matt Ellis (Matthew Jay Lewis), Pete Callan (David Easter), Sadie Hargreaves / Lloyd (Barbara Young), Samantha Cockerill (Tessa Wyatt), Tim Webster (Idris Elba), Vince Farmer (Stephen Yardley), Yasmin Matthews / MacKenzie (Ebony Thomas).

Family at War, A Colin Douglas (Edwin Ashton), Barbara Flynn (Freda Ashton), Coral Atkins (Sheila Ashton), John Nettles (Ian McKenzie).

Family Fortunes Presenters include Bob Monkhouse, Max Bygraves and Les Dennis.

Family, The Fly-on-the-wall look at the Wilkins family from Reading.

Fantasy Football Presenters: Frank Skinner and David Baddiel.

Fantasy Island Ricardo Montalban (Mr Roarke), Herve Villechaize (Tattoo).

Far Pavilions, The Ben Cross (Ashton Pelham-Martyn), Amy Irving (Princess Anjuli), Christopher Lee (Kaka-Ji-Rao), Omar Sharif (Koda Dad), John Gielgud (Cavagnari), Rossano Brazzi (the Rana of Bhithor).

Fast Show, The Paul Whitehouse, Simon Day, Caroline Aherne, John Thomson, Arabella Weir, Mark Williams, Charlie Higson. Sketch show spawning a spin-off, *Ted and Ralph.*

Father Dear Father Patrick Cargill (Patrick Glover), Natasha Pyne (Anna Glover), Ann Holloway (Karen Glover), Noel Dyson (Matilda 'Nanny' Harris).

Fawlty Towers John Cleese (Basil), Prunella Scales (Sybil), Andrew Sachs (Manuel), Connie Booth (Polly Sherman), Ballard Berkeley (Major Gowen). Set in Torquay.

FBI, The Efrem Zimbalist Jnr (Inspector Lewis Erskine).

Fifteen to One General knowledge quiz hosted by William G Stewart. Series winners include Jon Goodwin, Anthony Martin, Kevin Ashman, Mal Collier, Thomas Dyer, Andrew Francis, Barbara Thompson, Leslie Booth, Julian Allen, Martin Riley, Ian Potts, Arnold O'Hara, Trevor Montague, Stanley Miller, Glen Binnie, Bill Francis, Mike Kirby, Nick Terry, Doug Griffiths and Bill McKaig. Mal Collier won the Champion of Champions event held at Christmas 1997.

Filthy, Rich and Catflap Nigel Planer (Filthy Ralph), Rik Mayall (Richard Rich), Adrian Edmondson (Eddie Catflap). Written by Ben Elton.

Fire Crackers Joe Baker (Jumbo). Inept local firemen working in Cropper's End.

Fireball XL5 Characters include Colonel Steve Zodiac, Professor Matthew Matic, Venus Commander Zero, Lt 90, Zoonie, Robert the Robot.

Flamingo Road Soap, set in Truro County, Florida; aired between January 1981 and May 1982. Claude Weldon (Kevin McCarthy), Constance Weldon / Carlyle (Morgan Fairchild), Elmo Tyson (Peter Donat), Eudora Flowers Weldon (Barbara Rush), Fielding Carlyle (Mark Harmon), Lane Ballou Curtis (Cristina Raines), Lute-Mae Sanders (Stella Stevens), Michael Tyronne (David Selby), Sam Curtis (John Beck), Sheriff Titus Semple (Howard Duff).

Flintstones Characters include Fred, Wilma and Pebbles Flintstone, Barney, Betty and Bamm Bamm Rubble, and Dino the pet dinosaur.

Flipper Luke Halpin (Sandy Ricks), Brian Kelly (Porter Ricks). Last star dolphin of seven, called Bebe, died 4 May 1997, aged 40.

Flowerpot Men, The Characters included Bill and Ben, Little Weed and Slowcoach the Tortoise.

Follyfoot Gillian Blake (Dora), Arthur English (Slugger), Desmond Llewellyn (the Colonel), Steve Hodson (Steve).

Food and Drink Presenters include Chris Kelly, Henry Kelly, Susan Grossman, Jilly Goolden, Michael Barry, Oz Clarke, Paul Heiney.

Footballers' Wives Zöe Lucker (Tanya Laslett), Gary Lucy (Kyle Pascoe), Jessie Birdsall (Roger Webb), Ben Price (Conrad Gates), Laila Rouass (Laila Gates), Jamie Davis (Harley Lawson), Sarah Barrand (Shannon Donnelly), Gillian Taylforth (Jackie Pascoe), Caroline Chikezie (Elaine Hardy), Peter Ash (Darius Fry), Alison Newman (Hazel Bailey), Marcel McCalla (Noah Alexander).

Forsyte Saga, The Kenneth More (Jolyon Forsyte), Eric Porter (Soames Forsyte), Nyree Dawn Porter (Irene Heron/Forsyte).

Fortunes of War Kenneth Branagh (Guy Pringle), Emma Thompson (Harriet Pringle).

Fosters, The Notable for an early performance by Lenny Henry as Sonny Foster. First series to feature an all-black cast.

Four Feather Falls Voice of Tex Tucker: Nicholas Parsons. One feather allowed Tex's dog Dusty to speak; another gave speech to his horse, Rocky; the last two controlled the accuracy of his pistols.

Four Just Men, The Jack Hawkins (Ben Manfred MP), Dan Dailey (Tim Collier), Richard Conte (Jeff Ryder), Vittorio De Sica (Ricco Poccari).

Frasier Kelsey Grammer (Frasier Crane), David Hyde Pierce (Niles Crane), Bebe Neuwirth (Lilith), John Mahoney (Martin Crane), Jane Leeves (Daphne Moon), Peri Gilpin (Roz Doyle).

Friends Lisa Kudrow (Phoebe), Matt Le Blanc (Joey), Courtney Cox (Monica), Jennifer Aniston (Rachel Green), David Schwimmer (Ross), Matthew Perry (Chandler). Matt Le Blanc reprised his role in the 2005 spin-off *Joey.*

F Troop Ken Berry (Captain Wilton Parmenter), Forrest Tucker (Sgt Morgan O'Rourke), Larry Storch (Corporal Randolph Agarn), John Mitchum (Trooper Hoffenmuller).

Fugitive, The David Janssen (Dr Richard Kimble), Barry Morse (Lt Philip Gerard), Bill Raisch (Fred Johnson alias the one-armed man).

Game for a Laugh Presenters include Matthew Kelly, Henry Kelly, Sarah Kennedy, Jeremy Beadle, Rustie Lee, Martin Daniels, Debbie Rix, Lee Peck.

Gavin and Stacey Matthew Horne (Gavin Shipman), Joanna Page (Stacey Shipman née West), James Corden (Neil Smith), Ruth Jones (Nessa Jenkins), Alison Steadman (Pam Shipman), Larry Lamb (Mick Shipman), Rob Brydon (Bryn West). Situated in Billericay and Barry. Gavin is a Spurs supporter and Smithy, West Ham. Nessa's catchphrase: 'What's occurring?'

General Hospital Soap aired between Sept 1972 and Jan 1979. For full coverage see *The A to Z of British (and Irish) Popular Culture.*

Generation Game Hosts include Bruce Forsyth, Larry Grayson and Jim Davidson.

Gentle Touch, The Jill Gascoigne (DI Maggie Forbes), Derek Thompson (Det. Sgt Jimmy Fenton).

Get Smart Don Adams (Maxwell Smart, Agent 86), Barbara Feldon (Agent 99). Cover: salesman for Pontiac Greeting Card Co. Series created by Mel Brooks.

Girl From Uncle, The Stefanie Powers (April Dancer), Noel Harrison (Mark Slate), Leo G Carroll (Mr Waverly).

Girls on Top Tracey Ullman (Candice), Dawn French (Amanda), Jennifer Saunders (Jennifer), Ruby Wax (Shelley), Joan Greenwood (Lady Carlton).

Give Us a Break Robert Lindsay (Mickey Noades), Paul McGann (Mo Morris).

Gladiators Presenters: John Fashanu, Jeremy Guscott, Ulrika Jonsson.

Gnomes of Dulwich Terry Scott and Hugh Lloyd continuing their partnership as a big and small gnome. John Clive played the third 'old' gnome.

Going For a Song Presenter: Max Robertson.

Golden Girls, The Beatrice Arthur (Dorothy Zbornak), Rue McClanahan (Blanche Devereaux), Betty White (Rose Nylund), Estelle Getty (Sophia Petrillo).

Golden Shot, The Presenters included Jackie Rae, Bob Monkhouse, Norman Vaughan, Charlie Williams.

Good Afternoon Channel 5 daytime programme featuring the hospital documentary series Liverpool Mums, Pets Go Public, where contestants have to match pets with their owners, and Cryptogram, a general knowledge and word game of which the author has pleasant memories.

Good Life, The Richard Briers (Tom Good), Felicity Kendall (Barbara), Penelope Keith (Margo Leadbeatter), Paul Eddington (Jerry Leadbeatter). Goat: Geraldine.

Goodness Gracious Me Sanjeev Bhaskar, Meera Syal, Kulvinder Ghir, Nina Wadia. Irreverent sketch show that takes a light-hearted look at the Anglo-Asian community.

Goodnight Sweetheart Nicholas Lyndhurst (Gary Sparrow), Dervla Kirwan (Phoebe Bamford), Victor McGuire (Ron Wheatcroft), Christopher Ettridge (PC Reg Deadman), Michelle Holmes (Yvonne Sparrow). Elizabeth Carling and Emma Amos took over leading female roles.

Good Old Days, The Transmitted from the Leeds City Varieties Theatre, compered by Leonard Sachs (originally Don Gemmell). Every show ended with a rendition of 'Down at the Old Bull and Bush'.

Grange Hill Long-running (1978-2008) school drama. Todd Carty (Peter 'Tucker' Jenkins), Susan Tully (Suzanne Ross), Letitia Dean (Lucinda), Peter Moran (Pogo Patterson), Gwyneth Powell (Bridget McCluskey), Mark Savage (Gripper Stebson), Sean Maguire (Tegs Ratcliffe), Terri Dwyer (Miss Adams), Chris Perry-Metcalf (Patrick 'Togger' Johnson), Edward Baker-Duly (Mr Malachay), Holly Mann (Sammy Lee), Georgia May Foote (Alison Simmons), Reece Noi (Taylor Mitchell), Simon O'Brien (Wally Scott), Kacey Barnfield (Maddie Gilks), Jacqui Boatswain (Mrs Bassinger).

Great Antiques Hunt, The Host: Jilly Goolden.

Grimleys, The Brian Conley (Digby), Amanda Holden (Geraldine), Noddy Holder, James Bradshaw.

Gunsmoke/Gun Law James Arness (Matt Dillon), Amanda Blake (Kitty Russell), Milburn Stone (Dr Galen 'Doc' Adams), Dennis Weaver (Chester Goode), Burt Reynolds (Quint Asper), Ken Curtis (Festus).

Happy Days Henry Winkler (Arthur Fonzarelli), Ron Howard (Richie Cunningham), Scott Baio (Charles 'Chachi' Arcola), Suzi Quattro (Leather Tuscadero), Robin Williams (Mork).

Hark at Barker Ronnie Barker (Lord Rustless), David Jason (Dithers).

Harry Enfield Show Characters include the Slobs: Wayne and Waynetta and children Frogmella and Spudulike.

Hart to Hart Robert Wagner (Jonathan Hart), Stefanie Powers (Jennifer Hart), Lionel Stander (Max), Freeway the dog. Occupations: businessman and journalist.

Have Gun Will Travel Richard Boone (Paladin), Kam Tong (Hey Boy), Lisa Lu (Hey Girl).

Have I Got News for You Hosted by Angus Deayton. Team captains are Paul Merton and Ian Hislop. Following the sacking of Angus Deayton a series of guest presenters were used including William Hague, Charlotte Church, Greg Dyke, Charles Kennedy, Liza Tarbuck, Bruce Forsyth, Jack Dee, Kirsty Young, Jeremy Clarkson, Boris Johnson, Dara O'Briain and Alexander Armstrong.

Hawaii Five-O Jack Lord (Steve McGarrett), James MacArthur ('Danno' Williams), Kam Fong (Chin Ho Kelly).

Hawkeye and the Last of the Mohicans John Hart (Nat 'Hawkeye' Cutler), Lon Chaney Jnr (Chingachgook).

Hazell Nicholas Ball (James Hazell), Roddy McMillan (Choc Minty). Created by Terry Venables and Gordon Williams.

Heartbeat Nick Berry (PC Nick Rowan), Derek Fowlds (Sgt Oscar Blaketon), Bill Maynard (Claude Jeremiah Greengrass). Set in 1964 Yorkshire.

Hector's House Adventures of a dog (Hector), a cat (Zaza) and a frog (Mrs Kiki).

Hell's Kitchen Chefs: series one – Gordon Ramsay; series two – Gary Rhodes, Jean-Christophe Novelli; series three and four – Marco Pierre White. Celebrity winners: Jennifer Ellison, Barry McGuigan, Linda Evans.

Herbs, The Garden owners: Sir Bâsil and Lady Rosemary. Other characters include Constable Knapweed, Mr Onion the schoolteacher and his pupils, the Chives, Bayleaf the gardener, Aunt Mint, Sage the owl, Tarragon the dragon, Pashana Bedi the snake-charmer, and Belladonna. The real stars were Dill the dog and Parsley the lion. Gordon Rollings was the narrator and the magic word that opened the gate was 'Herbidacious'.

Here's Lucy Lucille Ball (Lucy Carter), Gale Gordon (Harrison Carter).

Hergé's Adventures of Tin Tin Narrator: Peter Hawkins. Characters include Snowy the white -fox-terrier, Captain Haddock, the Thompson Twins, Professor Calculus and General Alcazar.

Hi-De-Hi Paul Shane (Ted Bovis), Ruth Madoc (Gladys Pugh), Simon Cadell (Jeffrey Fairbrother), David Griffin (Squadron Leader Clive Dempster), Jeffrey Holland (Spike Dixon), Su Pollard (Peggy Ollerenshaw). Holiday camp: Maplins at Crimpton-on-Sea.

Highway to Heaven Michael Landon (Jonathan Smith), Victor French (Mark Gordon).

Hill Street Blues Daniel J Travanti (Captain Frank Furillo), Veronica Hamel (Joyce Davenport), Robert Prosky (Sgt Stanislaus Jablonski).

Hitch-Hiker's Guide to the Galaxy, The Simon Jones (Arthur Dent), David Dixon (Ford Prefect), Sandra Dickinson (Trillian), David Learner (Marvin), Stephen Moore (Marvin's voice), Mark Wing-Davey (Zaphod Beeblebrox), Peter Jones (the book voice).

Hogan's Heroes Bob Crane (Colonel Robert Hogan), Werner Klemperer (Colonel Wilhelm Klink), John Banner (Sgt Hans Schulz), Larry Hovis (Sgt Andrew Carter), Ivan Dixon (Corporal James Kinchloe).

Holby City Soap, spin-off from *Casualty* first aired in January 1999. For comprehensive coverage see *The A to Z of British (and Irish) Popular Culture.*

Holiday Presenters include Frank Bough, Des Lynam, Cliff Michelmore, Joan Bakewell, Jill Dando, Anneka Rice, Eamonn Holmes.

Hollyoaks Soap set in Hollyoaks, Chester, and first aired 1995. For comprehensive coverage see *The A to Z of British (and Irish) Popular Culture.*

Home and Away Soap set in Summer Bay nr Sydney. C4 1989-2000; C5 2001 – . Sally Keating / Fletcher (Kate Ritchie), Alf Stewart (Ray Meagher), Ruth 'Roo' Morgan / Stewart (Justine Clarke and Georgie Parker), Marilyn Chambers / Fisher (Emily Symons), Irene Roberts (Lynne McGranger), Leah Poulos / Patterson (Ada Nicodemou), John Palmer (Shane Withington), Indi Walker (Samara Weaving), Dexter Walker (Charles Cottier), April Scott (Rhiannon Fish), Bianca Scott (Lisa Gormley), Darryl Braxton (Stephen Peacocke), Heath Braxton (Dan Ewing), Casey Braxton (Lincoln Younes), Harvey Ryan (Marcus Graham), Sasha Bezmel (Demi Harman), Jett James (Will McDonald), Kyle Braxton (Nic Westaway), Ricky Sharpe (Bonnie Sveen), Spencer Harrington (Andrew Morley), Maddy Osborne (Kassandra Clementi), Zac MacGuire (Charlie Clausen), Tamara Kingsley (Kelly Paterniti), Adam Cameron (Mat Stevenson), Ailsa Hogan Stewart (Judy Nunn), Al Simpson (Terence Donovan), Angel Brooks / Parish (Melissa George), Barry Hyde (Ivar Kants), Beth Hunter (Clarissa Hous), Celia Stewart (Fiona Spence), Charlotte Best (Annie Campbell), Colleen Smart (Lyn Collingwood), Curtis Reed (Shane Ammann), Damian Roberts (Matt Doran), David Croft (Guy Pearce), Donald 'Flathead' Fisher (Norman Coburn), Emma Jackson (Dannii Minogue), Grant Mitchell (Craig McLachlan), Josh Quong Tart (Miles Copeland), Kane Phillips (Sam Atwell), Nick Smith (Christopher Egan), Noah Lawson (Beau Brady), Peter 'Tug' O'Neale (Tristan Bancks), Shane Withington (John Palmer), Shannon Reed (Isla Fisher).

House of Cards Ian Richardson (Francis Urquhart). Based on Michael Dobbs's novel.

How/How 2 Presenters include Fred Dineage, Jack Hargreaves, Jon Miller, Bunty James, Marian Davies, Carol Vorderman, Gareth Jones.

Howard's Way Maurice Colbourne (Tom Howard), Jan Harvey (Jan Howard), Glyn Owen (Jack Rolfe), Stephen Yardley (Ken Masters), Tony Anholt (Charles Frere), Nigel Davenport (Sir Edward Frere), Kate O'Mara (Laura Wilde). Created by Gerard Glaister and Allan Prior. Yard name: Mermaid.

How Do They Do That? Presenters: Esther McVeigh and Eamonn Holmes.

How Do You Solve A Problem Like Maria? First of Andrew Lloyd Webber's collaborations with the BBC. Graham Norton presented. Three judges: John Barrowman, Zoe Tyler and David Ian. Connie Fisher ultimately won the role of Maria von Trapp.

HR Pufnstuff Jack Wild (Jimmy), Billie Hayes (Witchiepoo).

Huckleberry Hound Show, The Characters included Pixie and Dixie, Jinks the Cat, Yogi Bear and Boo Boo, Hokey Wolf and Ding a Ling. Huckleberry used to sing 'Clementine' constantly.

Human Jungle, The Herbert Lom (Dr Roger Corder), Sally Smith (Jennifer Corder), Mary Yeomans (Nancy Hamilton).

I Claudius Derek Jacobi (Claudius), Siân Phillips (Livia), Brian Blessed (Octavian/Augustus), George Baker (Tiberius), John Hurt (Caligula), Patrick Stewart (Sejanus), Chris Biggins (Nero).

I Love Lucy Lucille Ball (Lucy Ricardo), Desi Arnaz (Ricky Ricardo), Vivian Vance (Ethel Mertz), William Frawley (Fred Mertz). First sit-com to be filmed live in front of a studio audience.

I'm a Celebrity Get Me Out Of Here Presented by Ant & Dec. Winners: Tony Blackburn, Phil Tufnell, Kerry Katona, Joe Pasquale, Carol Thatcher, Matt Willis, Christopher Biggins, Joe Swash, Gino D'Acampo, Stacey Solomon, Dougie Poynter, Charlie Brooks.

In at the Deep End Chris Searle and Paul Heiney took it in turn to learn new skills.

Inside George Webley Roy Kinnear played the depressive character created by Keith Waterhouse and Willis Hall.

Inspector Alleyn Mysteries, The Patrick Malahide (Chief Insp. Roderick Alleyn). Character created by Ngaio Marsh.

Inspector Morse John Thaw (Chief Insp. Endeavour Morse), Kevin Whately (Det. Sgt Robbie Lewis).

Interpol Calling Charles Korvin (Insp. Paul Duval), Edwin Richfield (Insp. Mornay).

Invaders, The Roy Thinnes (David Vincent, an architect). Narrator: William Conrad.

Invisible Man, The In the original series Dr Peter Brady's voice was that of Tim Turner although no actor was billed. David McCallum played the character of Daniel Westin in the 1975 series.

I Spy Robert Culp (Kelly Robinson, tennis pro), Bill Cosby (Alexander Scott, tennis trainer).

It Ain't Half Hot Mum Windsor Davies (RSM B L Williams), Melvyn Hayes (Bombardier 'Gloria' Beaumont), George Layton (Bombardier Solomons), Michael Bates (Rangi Ram), Don Estelle (Gunner 'Lofty' Sugden).

It Takes a Thief Robert Wagner (Alexander Mundy), Fred Astaire (Alister Mundy).

Ivor the Engine Narrated by David Edwards, Anthony Jackson, Olwen Griffiths and Oliver Postgate, who also wrote the stories. Railway: Merioneth and Llantissily Rail Traction Company. Driver: Jones the Steam. Other characters included Owen the Signal and Dai Station, the man who looked after Llaniog Station. Ivor's boiler was fired by Idris the dragon. Jones always aspired to sing in the choir like his pal Evans the Song. Peter Firmin drew all the pictures.

Jackanory First story told by Lee Montague ('Cap of Rushes'). Most prolific story teller: Bernard Cribbins.

The Jamie Kennedy Experiment Actor/comedian Jamie Kennedy, nicknamed JKX for the purposes of this show, combines hidden-camera pranks with sketch comedy to see how everyday people and celebrities behave in unusual situations. JKX is often disguised, and when the joke has run its course he delivers the immortal tag line 'You've been X-ed'. First aired in January 2002 on Channel 4.

Jane Glynis Barber played the wartime cartoon character in the 1982 television adaption.

Jemima Shore Investigates Patricia Hodge played the TV reporter created by Lady Antonia Fraser.

Jesus of Nazareth Robert Powell (Jesus as an adult), Immad Cohen (Jesus as a boy), Olivia Hussey (Virgin Mary), Anne Bancroft (Mary Magdalene), Ian McShane (Judas Iscariot), Rod Steiger (Pontius Pilate), James Mason (Joseph of Arimathea), Peter Ustinov (Herod the Great), Michael York (John the Baptist), Stacy Keach (Barabbas), Laurence Olivier (Nicodemus).

Jetsons, The Jetsons lived in the 21st century in Orbit City. George Jetson worked at Spacely Space Sprockets. The family pet dog was Astro.

Jewel in the Crown, The Peggy Ashcroft (Barbie Batchelor), Geraldine James (Sarah Layton), Stuart Wilson (Major Clark), Tim Pigott-Smith (Ronald Merrick), Art Malik (Hari Kumar), Susan Wooldridge (Daphne Manners), Charles Dance (Sgt Guy Perron), Josephine Welcome (Mira). Based on Paul Scott's novels.

Joe 90 Joe McClaine, alias Joe 90, worked for WIN, the World Intelligence Network, using his father's invention BIGRAT (Brain Impulse Galvanoscope Record And Transfer).

Joking Apart Robert Bathurst (Mark Taylor), Tracie Bennett (Tracy), Fiona Gillies (Becky Taylor).

Jonathan Creek Alan Davies (Jonathan Creek), Caroline Quentin (Madeline Magellan), Julia Sawahla (Carla Borrego).

Juke Box Jury First panel: Alma Cogan, Susan Stranks, Gary Miller and Pete Murray. Presenters: David Jacobs, Noel Edmonds and Jools Holland.

Juliet Bravo Stephanie Turner (Insp. Jean Darblay), Anna Carteret (Insp. Kate Longton). Fictional town: Hartley in Lancashire.

Junior Criss Cross Quiz Hosts included Jeremy Hawk, Bob Holness, Mike Sarne, Bill Grundy and Danny Blanchflower.

Just Good Friends Paul Nicholas (Vince Pinner), Jan Francis (Penny Warrender).

Kavanagh QC John Thaw (James Kavanagh QC), Geraldine James (Eleanor Harker QC).

Keeping Up Appearances Patricia Routledge (Hyacinth Bucket), Geoffrey Hughes (Onslow). Created by Roy Clarke.

Knight Rider David Hasselhoff (Michael Knight, formerly Michael Long), William Daniels (voice of Kitt, the Knight Industries Two Thousand).

Knots Landing Spin-off from Dallas set in California. Abby Cunningham / Ewing / Sumner (Donna Mills), Charles Scott (Michael York), Gary Ewing (Ted Shackleford), Gregory Sumner (William Devane), Joshua Rush (Alec Baldwin), Karen Fairgate / MacKenzie (Michele Lee), Patrick 'Mack' MacKenzie (Kevin Dobson), Ruth Galveston (Ava Gardner), Valene Ewing / Gibson / Waleska (Joan Van Ark),

Kojak Telly Savalas (Lt Theo Kojak), Dan Frazer (Capt. Frank McNeil), Kevin Dobson (Lt Bobby Crocker), George Savalas (Stavros), Mark Russell (Saperstein). Worked in Manhattan South 13th Precinct.

Krypton Factor, The Tough quiz testing both physical and mental faculties. Gordon Burns's name was synonymous with the series. Ben Shephard hosted the show in 2009 after a 14-year break.

The Kumars at No. 42 Sanjeev (Sanjeev Bhaskar), Dad (Vincent Ebrahim), Mum (Indira Joshi), Granny Sushila (Meera Syal). Spoof chat show following the pretext that the Kumars have bulldozed their back garden to build a studio on the back of their house to indulge their spoilt son, Sanjeev, who fancies himself as a celebrity chat-show host.

Kung Fu David Carradine (Kwai Chang Caine), Keye Luke (Master Po), Radames Pera (Caine as a boy). Bruce Lee was rejected for the role and died soon after.

KYTV Angus Deayton (Mike Channel), Geoffrey Perkins (Mike Flex), Helen Atkinson Wood (Anna Daptor).

LA Law Richard Dysart (Leland McKenzie), Harry Hamlin (Michael Kuzak), Corbin Bernsen (Arnie Becker), Michael Tucker (Stuart Markowitz), Diana Muldaur (Rosalind Shays).

Laramie John Smith (Slim Sherman), Robert Fuller (Jess Harper), Hoagy Carmichael (Jonesy), Spring Byington (Daisy Cooper).

Larry Sanders Show, The Garry Shandling (Larry Sanders), Rip Torn (Arthur), Jeffrey Tambor (Hank Kingsley).

Last of the Summer Wine Peter Sallis (Norman Clegg), Bill Owen (Compo Seminite), Michael Bates (Blamire), Brian Wilde (Foggy Dewhurst), Michael Aldridge (Seymour Utterthwaite), Kathy Staff (Nora Batty), Jean Alexander (Auntie Wainwright). Filmed in Holmfirth in Yorkshire. Written by Roy Clarke.

League of Gentlemen, The Jeremy Dyson, Mark Gatiss, Steve Pemberton, Reece Shearsmith. Set in Royston Vazey (the real name of comedian Roy 'chubby' Brown).

Life and Loves of a She Devil, The Julie T Wallace (Ruth Patchett), Dennis Waterman (Bobbo Patchett), Patricia Hodge (Mary Fisher).

Life On Mars John Simm (DI Sam Tyler), Philip Glenister (DCI Gene Hunt). Sam Tyler is transported back to 1973. MARS – Metropolitan Accountability and Reconciliation Strategy. Sequel: *Ashes to Ashes*, set in 1981–3, sees DCI Alex Drake (Keeley Hawes) time-travelling.

Likely Lads, The James Bolam (Terry Collier), Bob Ferris (Rodney Bewes), Sheila Fearn (Audrey Collier), Brigit Forsyth (Thelma Ferris). Written by Dick Clement and Ian La Frenais. Sequel: *Whatever Happened to the Likely Lads.*

Little Britain Radio series written and performed by Matt Lucas and David Walliams, transferred to BBC3 in September 2003 and repeated on BBC2, before winning numerous awards. Characters include Vicky Pollard, the incomprehensible teenager from Darkly Noone; Marjorie Dawes, the rotund leader of Fat Fighters; Lou and Andy, a 'helper' (Walliams) and his apparently wheelchair-bound friend (Lucas); Emily Howard, a totally unconvincing transvestite; and Daffyd, a committed 'homosexualist' residing in the Welsh town of Llanddewi Brefi. His catchphrase 'I'm the only gay in the village' was voted best comedy catchphrase ever in a poll of 3,800 television viewers in January 2005.

Little House on the Prairie Michael Landon (Charles Ingalls), Karen Grassle (Caroline Ingalls), Melissa Gilbert (Laura Ingalls/Wilder), Melissa Sue Anderson (Mary Ingalls/Kendall).

Liver Birds, The Polly James (Beryl Hennessey), Nerys Hughes (Sandra Hutchinson/Paynton), Pauline Collins (Dawn, the original flatmate of Beryl), Elizabeth Estensen (Carol Boswell), Mollie Sugden (Mrs Hutchinson), John Nettles (Paul), Jonathan Lynn (Robert).

London's Burning Mark Arden (Roland 'Vaseline' Cartwright), Glen Murphy (George Green), James Hazeldine (Mike 'Bayleaf' Wilson), Richard Walsh (Bert 'Sicknote' Quigley), Gerard Horan (Leslie 'Charisma' Appleby), Ben Onwukwe (Stuart 'Recall' Mackenzie), Heather Peace (Sally 'Gracie' Fields), Edward Peel (John Coleman), Michael Garner (Geoffrey 'Poison' Pearce), Fuman Dar (Ronnie 'Hi-Ho' Silver), Connor Byrne (Rob 'Hyper' Sharpe), Sam Callis (Adam Benjamin), Al Hunter Ashton (Pit bull). Firefighters of Blue Watch B25, Blackwall, created by Jack Rosenthal.

Lone Ranger, The Initially played by Clayton Moore and then by John Hart before he left to play Hawkeye. Jay Silverheels always played the faithful Tonto. Lone Ranger's horse: Silver. (He would often say 'Hi-ho, Silver, away' when in a hurry.) Tonto's horse: Scout. (Tonto would often call his friend Kemo Sabe, which meant Trusty Scout.) The Lone Ranger's real name was John Reid, a Texas Ranger ambushed and left for dead. It is often said that if you can listen to Rossini's 'William Tell Overture' without thinking of the Lone Ranger (same tune) then you are a real classical music aficionado.

Lord Peter Wimsey Ian Carmichael (Lord Peter Wimsey), Glyn Houston (Bunter, his manservant).

Lost in Space Guy Williams (Professor John Robinson), Jonathan Harris (Zachary Smith), Bob May (the robot), Dick Tufeld (voice of the robot). Spaceship: Jupiter 11. Pet space monkey: the Bloop.

Lotus Eaters, The Ian Hendry (Erik Shepherd), Wanda Ventham (Ann Shepherd). Drama set on Crete.

Lou Grant Edward Asner (Lou), Robert Walden (Joe Rossi). Spin-off from the *Mary Tyler Moore Show.* Newspaper: *Los Angeles Tribune.*

Love Hurts Adam Faith (Frank Carver), Zoë Wanamaker (Tessa Piggott), Jane Lapotaire (Diane Warburg), Tony Selby (Max Taplow).

Love Me Do Game show in which three couples vie for the chance to wed. Host: Shane Richie.

Love Thy Neighbour Jack Smethurst (Eddie Booth), Kate Williams (Joan), Rudolph Walker (Bill Reynolds), Nina Baden Semper (Barbie), Keith Marsh (Jacko Jackson). Jacko's famous saying: 'I'll 'ave 'alf.'

Lovejoy Ian McShane (Lovejoy), Dudley Sutton (Tinker Deal), Chris Jury (Eric Catchpole), Phyllis Logan (Lady Jane Felsham). Lovejoy's Morris Minor: Miriam.

Lovers, The Richard Beckinsale (Geoffrey), Paula Wilcox (Beryl).

Lucy Show, The Lucille Ball (Lucy Carmichael), Gale Gordon (Theodore J Mooney), Vivian Vance (Vivian Bagley).

Lytton's Diary Peter Bowles (Neville Lytton). Incidents in the life of a newspaper diarist.

Magic Roundabout Characters include Dougal (the dog), Ermintrude (the cow), Brian (the snail), Mr Rusty, Mr McHenry, Zebedee, Dylan (the rabbit), Florence. Created by Serge Danot and narrated by Eric Thompson and Nigel Planer.

Magnificent Evans, The Ronnie Barker (Plantagenet Evans), Dyfed Thomas (Home Rule O'Toole), Myfanwy Talog (Bron).

Magnum PI Tom Selleck (Thomas Sullivan Magnum), John Hillerman (Jonathan Quayle Higgins III), Roger E Mosley (Theodore 'TC' Calvin), Orson Welles (voice of Robin Masters).

Magpie Presenters include Susan Stranks, Pete Brady, Tony Bastable, Mick Robertson, Jenny Hanley, Tommy Boyd, Douglas Rae.

Main Chance, The John Stride (David Main), Kate O'Mara (Julia Main). Story of a young, successful lawyer.

Making Out Margi Clarke (Queenie), Shirley Stelfox (Carol May), Tracie Bennett (Norma), Melanie Kilburn (Jill), Keith Allen (Rex), Brian Hibbard (Chunky).

Man About the House Richard O'Sullivan (Robin Tripp), Paula Wilcox (Chrissy Plummer), Sally Thomsett (Jo), Brian Murphy (George Roper), Yootha Joyce (Mildred Roper). Spin-off series were *Robin's Nest* and *George and Mildred.*

Man at the Top Kenneth Haigh (Joe Lampton). Feature film of the same name followed.

Man Called Ironside, A Raymond Burr (Chief Robert T Ironside), Don Galloway (Det. Sgt Ed Brown), Barbara Anderson (Eve Whitfield), Don Mitchell (Mark Sanger), Elizabeth Baur (Fran Belding).

Man From Atlantis Patrick Duffy (Mark Harris; had green eyes), Belinda J Montgomery (Dr Elizabeth Merrill), Victor Buono (Mr Schubert), Robert Lussier (Brent). Submersible name: Cetacean.

Man From Uncle, The Robert Vaughn (Napoleon Solo, agent no. 11), David McCallum (Ilya Kuryakin, agent no. 2), Leo G Carroll (Alexander Waverly, agent no. 1). UNCLE: United Network Command for Law and Enforcement. Secret office: behind Del Floria's Tailor Shop. Enemy: Thrush.

Manhunt Alfred Lynch (Jimmy Porter), Peter Barkworth (Vincent), Cyd Hayman (Nina). Heroic tales of French Resistance in WW2. Theme tune: Beethoven's Fifth Symphony.

Man in a Suitcase Richard Bradford (McGill).

Man in Room 17, The Richard Vernon (Oldenshaw), Michael Aldridge (Dimmock). Criminologists work in office near the Houses of Parliament.

Marcus Welby MD Robert Young (Welby), James Brolin (Dr Steven Kiley).

Mark Saber Donald Gray (Saber), Michael Balfour (Barny O'Keefe). Story of the one-armed detective.

Marriage Lines Richard Briars (George Starling), Prunella Scales (Kate).

Mary Tyler Moore Show Mary Tyler Moore (Mary Richards), Ed Asner (Lou Grant), Valerie Harper (Rhoda Morgenstern), Cloris Leachman (Phyllis Lindstrom). Based in TV Station WJM-TV.

M.A.S.H. Alan Alda (Capt. Benjamin Franklin 'Hawkeye' Pierce), Wayne Rogers (Capt. 'Trapper John' McIntyre), Loretta Swit (Maj. Margaret 'Hot Lips' Houlihan), Larry Linville (Maj. Frank Burns), Gary Burghoff (Corporal Walter 'Radar' O'Reilly), William Christopher (Father Francis Mulcahy), Jamie Farr (Corporal Maxwell Klinger). Hawkeye's tent known as the Swamp. M.A.S.H.: Mobile Army Surgical Hospital.

Masterchef Winners: Joan Bunting, Sue Lawrence, Vanessa Binns, Derek Johns, Gerry Goldwyre, Marion MacFarlane, Neil Hadar, Julie Friend, Lloyd Burgess, Marjorie Lang, Rosa Baden-Powell, Thomasina Miers, Peter Bayless, Steven Wallis, James Nathan, Mat Follas, Dhruv Baker, Tim Anderson, Shelina Permalloo, Natalie Coleman. Judges: Gregg Wallace and Michel Roux, Jr.

Mastermind Ran from 1972 to 1997 with Magnus Magnusson as 'Interrogator' throughout the run. Producer/director David Mitchell. Other producers include Bill Wright, Roger MacKay, Peter Massey, Penelope Cowell Doe. Main researcher: Dee Wallace. Winners: Nancy Wilkinson (1972), Patricia Owen (1973), Elizabeth Horrocks (1974), John Hart (1975), Roger Pritchard (1976), Sir David Hunt (1977), Rosemary James (1978), Dr Philip Jenkins (1979), Fred Housego (1980), Leslie Grout (1981), Sir David Hunt (1982), Christopher Hughes (1983), Margaret Harris (1984), Ian Meadows (1985), Jennifer Keaveney (1986), Dr Jeremy Bradbrooke (1987), David Beamish (1988), Mary-Elizabeth Raw (1989), David Edwards (1990), Stephen Allen (1991), Steve Williams (1992), Gavin Fuller (1993), George Davidson (1994), Kevin Ashman (1995), Richard Sturch (1996), Anne Ashurst (1997). The format transferred to Radio 4 for three years and was hosted by Peter Snow. The winners were Robert Gibson (1998), Rev Kit Carter (1999), Stephen Follows (2000). The Discovery Channel then took over for one season in 2001. The winner was Michael Penrice. The series was revived on the BBC in 2003, the winner being Andy Page. Shaun Wallace became the first black champion in 2004. Other winners: Pat Gibson (2005), Geoff Thomas (2006), David Clark (2008), Nancy Dickman (2009), Jesse Honey (2010), Ian Bayley (2011), Gary Grant (2012), Aidan McQuade (2013). John Humphrys is the current interrogator.

Maverick James Garner (Brett Maverick), Jack Kelly (Bart Maverick), Roger Moore (Cousin Beau).

May to December Anton Rodgers (Alec Callender), Eve Matheson/Lesley Dunlop (Zoe Angell/Callender).

McCloud Dennis Weaver (Sam McCloud), seconded to New York from Taos, New Mexico.

McMillan and Wife Rock Hudson (Commissioner Stewart McMillan), Susan Saint James (Sally McMillan). Based in San Francisco.

Me and My Girl Richard O'Sullivan (Simon Harrap), Joanne Ridley (Samantha Harrap), Joan Sanderson (Nell Cresset), Tim Brooke-Taylor (Derek Yates). Advertising agency: Eyecatchers. Theme song sung by Peter Skellern.

Meet the Wife Thora Hird (Thora Blacklock), Freddie Frinton (Freddie Blacklock). Stemmed from Comedy Playhouse production called *The Bed.*

Me Mammy Milo O'Shea (Bunjy Kennefick), Anna Manahan (Mrs Kennefick), Yootha Joyce (Miss Argyll), David Kelly (Cousin Enda), Ray McAnally (Father Patrick).

Men Behaving Badly Martin Clunes (Gary), Neil Morrissey (Tony), Leslie Ash (Deborah), Caroline Quentin (Dorothy). The first series featured Harry Enfield as Dermot but Neil Morrissey replaced him for series two Although originally an ITV series, by series three it was screened on BBC 1. The writer was Simon Nye, who also created Frank Stubbs.

Metal Mickey The robot Mickey was invented by Ken Wilberforce and played by Ashley Knight. This series is best remembered for the fact that Mickey Dolenz was the producer/director.

Miami Vice Don Johnson (James 'Sonny' Crockett), Philip Michael Thomas (Ricardo Tubbs), Edward James Olmos (Lt Martin Castillo), Sheena Easton (Caitlin Davies).

Midnight Caller Gary Cole (Jack 'Nighthawk' Killian).

Millennium Lance Henriksen (Frank Black), Megan Gallagher (Catherine Black), Chris Ellis (Penseyres). Created by Chris Carter of *X Files* fame.

Minder George Cole (Arthur Daly), Dennis Waterman (Terry McMann), Glynn Edwards (Dave), Patrick Malahide (Det. Sgt Albert 'Charlie' Chisholm), Peter Childs (Sgt Rycott). The theme tune, 'I Could Be So Good For You', was sung by Dennis Waterman.

Mind Your Language Barry Evans (Jeremy Brown), François Pascal (Danielle Favre), Pik-Sen-Lim (Chung Su-Lee).

Miss Marple Joan Hickson (Miss Marple).

Mission Impossible Peter Graves (Jim Phelps), Leonard Nimoy (Paris), Barbara Bain (Cinnamon Carter), Martin Landau (Rollin Hand), Greg Morris (Barney Collier), Steven Hill (Daniel Briggs), Lesley Ann Warren (Dana Lambert), Peter Lupus (Willie Armitage). Voice on the tape: Bob Johnson. Catchprase: 'This tape will self-destruct in five seconds' (occasionally ten seconds).

Mister Ed Alan Young (Wilbur Post). Story of a talking horse.

Mogul Series about an oil company, which later changed its title to *The Troubleshooters.*

Moment of Truth Cilla Black hosted the show in which three contestants have a week to master a given task.

Monkees, The TV Series about a pop group. Micky Dolenz, Mike Nesmith, Peter Tork and Davy Jones.

Monty Python's Flying Circus Messrs Cleese, Idle, Gilliam, Jones, Palin, Chapman and Carol Cleveland.

Moonlighting Bruce Willis (David Addison), Cybill Shepherd (Maddie Hayes). Detective agency: Blue Moon.

Mork and Mindy Robin Williams (Mork from Ork), Pam Dawber (Mindy McConnell), Jonathan Winters (Mearth). Mork gave birth to Mearth, who called Mindy 'Shoe' and Mork 'Mommy'. Series was a spin-off from an episode of *Happy Days.*

Moviedrome Presenters Alex Cox, Mark Cousins.

Mr and Mrs Alternating presenters: Alan Taylor and Derek Batey. Other presenters: Nino Firetto, Julian Clary, Vernon Kay, Fern Britton, Phillip Schofield

Mr Magoo Voice of Magoo (Jim Backus); Waldo was his nephew.

Mr Pastry Richard Hearne, an actor, acrobat and dancer, invented this character. Popular for over 20 years.

Muffin the Mule Presenter: Annette Mills. Puppeteer: Ann Hogarth.

Munsters, The Fred Gwynne (Herman), Yvonne De Carlo (Lily), Al Lewis (Grandpa), Butch Patrick (Eddie), Beverley Owen/Pat Priest (Marilyn). Lived at: 1313 Mockingbird Lane, Mockingbird Heights.

Muppet Show, The Characters include Miss Piggy Lee, Kermit T Frog, Statler and Waldorf, Animal, Gonzo, Fozzie Bear, Zoot, Swedish Chef, Dr Teeth, Robin the Frog. First seen in *Sesame Street.* Created by Jim Henson and Frank Oz.

My Favorite Martian Ray Walston (Uncle Martin), Bill Bixby (Tim O'Hara).

Nearest and Dearest Hylda Baker (Nellie Pledge), Jimmy Jewel (Eli), Madge Hindle (Lily), Edward Malin (Walter).

Neighbours Set in Erinsborough, Melbourne; first aired in 1986. Present cast: Stefan Dennis (Paul Robinson), Tom Oliver (Lou Carpenter), Rebekah Elmaloglou (Terese Willis), Josef Brown (Matt Turner), Saskia Hampele (Georgia Brooks), Colette Mann (Sheila Canning), Eve Morey (Sonya Mitchell), Ashleigh Brewer (Kate Ramsay), Chris Milligan (Kyle Canning), Morgan Baker (Callum Jones), Ryan Moloney (Toadfish Rebecchi), Alan Fletcher (Karl Kennedy). Former cast members: Beth Brennan / Willis (Natalie Imbruglia), Charlene Mitchell / Robinson (Kylie Minogue), Alin Sumarwata (Vanessa Villante), Des Clarke (Paul Keane), Doug Willis (Terence Donovan), Felicity 'Flick' Scully (Holly Valance), Harold Bishop (Ian Smith), Helen Daniels (Anne Haddy), Henry Mitchell (Craig McLachlan), Jim Robinson (Alan Dale), Joe Mangel (Mark Little), Madge Mitchell / Ramsey / Bishop (Anne Charleston), Nell Mangel / Worthington (Vivean Gray), Scott Robinson (Darius Perkins and Jason Donovan), Shane Ramsay (Peter O'Brien), Tadpole 'Tad' Reeves (Jonathon Dutton), Toby Mangel (Finn Greentree-Keane).

Never the Twain Donald Sinden (Simon Peel), Windsor Davies (Oliver Smallbridge), Honor Blackman (Veronica).

New Avengers Joanna Lumley (Purdey), Gareth Hunt (Mike Gambit), Patrick MacNee (John Steed).

New Statesman, The Rik Mayall (Alan Beresford B'Stard), Terence Alexander (Sir Greville), Marsha Fitzalan (Sarah).

Newcomers, The Soap set in Angleton; aired from 1965 to 1969 on BBC1. Andrew Kerr (Robin Bailey), Ellis Cooper (Alan Browning), Joyce Harker (Wendy Richard), Julie Robertson (Deborah Watling), Maria Cooper (Judy Geeson), Robert Malcolm (Conrad Phillips), Vivienne Cooper (Maggie Fitzgibbon).

Nice Time Germaine Greer, Jonathan Routh and Kenny Everett in wacky sketch show produced by John Birt.

Night Fever Channel 5 karaoke programme hosted by Suggs.

99–1 Leslie Grantham (Mick Raynor), Robert Stephens (Commander Oakwood).

No Hiding Place Sequel to *Crimesheet* and *Murder Bag*. Raymond Francis (Superintendent Lockhart), Eric Lander (Sergeant Baxter), Johnny Briggs (Det. Sgt Russell).

No, Honestly John Alderton (Charles 'CD' Danby), Pauline Collins (Clara Danby).

No Place Like Home William Gaunt (Arthur Crabtree), Martin Clunes (Nigel Crabtree), Patricia Garwood (Beryl).

No Problem Judith Jacob (Sensimilia), Janet Kay (Angel), Sarah Lam (Susannah), Victor Romero Evans (Bellamy), Malcolm Frederick (Beast), Angela Wynter (Melba). Written by Farrukh Dhondy and Mustapha Matura and concentrating on the London-based Powell family. The first comedy series specifically to address the lifestyle of the British black community, *No Problem*, was also the first sitcom to be broadcast on Channel 4.

No – That's Me Over Here Ronnie Corbett (Ronnie), Rosemary Leach (Rosemary), Henry McGee (Henry).

Not in Front of the Children Wendy Craig (Jennifer Corner), Paul Daneman/Ronald Hines (Henry Corner).

Not Only But Also Peter Cook and Dudley Moore.

Not the Nine O'Clock News Rowan Atkinson, Chris Langham (replaced by Griff Rhys-Jones), Mel Smith, Pamela Stephenson.

NYPD Blue Dennis Franz (Det. Andy Sipowicz), Rick Schroder (Det. Danny Sorenson), James McDaniel (Lt. Arthur Fancy), Nicholas Turturro (Det. James Martinez), Sharon Lawrence (Asst. DA Sylvia Costas Sipowicz), Gordon Clapp (Det. Greg Medavoy), Mark-Paul Gosselaar (Det. John Clark Jr), Henry Simmons (Det. Baldwin Jones), Bill Brochtrup (PAA John Irvin), Esai Morales (Lt. Tony Rodriguez), Charlotte Ross (Det. Connie McDowell), Garcelle Beauvais-Nilon (ADA Valerie Haywood), Jacqueline Obradors (Det. Rita Ortiz), Sherry Stringfield (Laura Michaels Kelly). Co-created by Steven Bochco and David Milch. NYPD is New York Police Department.

Office, The Ricky Gervais (David Brent), Martin Freeman (Tim Canterbury), Mackenzie Crooke (Gareth Keenan), Lucy Davis (Dawn Tynsley), Ewan Macintosh (Keith), Ralph Ineson (Chris 'Finchy' Finch), Oliver Chris (Ricky), Joel Beckett (Lee), Sally Bretton (Donna), Patrick Baladi (Neil Godwin), Steve Merchant (Nathan aka The Oggmonster or Oggy). Co-written and directed by Ricky Gervais and Steve Merchant. Theme tune: 'Handbags and Gladrags', written by Mike D'abo and arranged and performed by Big George.

Oh Brother/Oh Father Derek Nimmo (Brother/Father Dominic), Felix Aylmer (Father Anselm).

Oh, Doctor Beeching! Su Pollard (Ethel Schumann), Paul Shane (Jack Skinner), Jeffrey Holland (Cecil Parkin), Stephen Lewis (Harry Lambert), Julia Deakin (May Skinner).

Old Grey Whistle Test/Whistle Test Bob Harris, Anne Nightingale, Andy Kershaw, Mark Ellen, Ian Whitcomb, Richard Skinner.

One Foot in the Grave Richard Wilson (Victor Meldrew), Annette Crosbie (Margaret), Angus Deayton (Patrick). Victor killed in hit-and-run accident, the car driver played by Hannah Gordon.

Onedin Line, The Peter Gilmore (Capt. James Onedin), Jane Seymour (Emma Callon), Jill Gascoigne (Letty Gaunt). First ship: *Charlotte Rose*.

Only Fools and Horses David Jason (Del Boy Trotter), Nicholas Lyndhurst (Rodney), Lennard Pearce (Grandad), Buster Merryfield (Uncle Albert), Tessa Peake-Jones (Raquel), Gwyneth Strong (Cassandra), Roger Lloyd Pack (Trigger), John Challis (Boycie), Sue Holderness (Marlene). Pub: Nag's Head. Trotters' address: 368 Nelson Mandela House, Peckham. Company name: Trotter's Independent Trading. Transport: features Del's yellow Reliant Regal Van Mk II. Title from the adage 'Only fools and horses work'. Writer: John Sullivan.

Only When I Laugh James Bolam (Roy Figgis), Peter Bowles (Archie Glover), Richard Wilson (Dr Gordon Thorpe).

On Safari Presenters Armand and Michaela Denis.

On the Buses Reg Varney (Stan Butler), Stephen Lewis (Blakey), Anna Karen (Olive), Michael Robbins (Arthur), Bob Grant (Jack). Bus company: Luxtons.

On the Move Bob Hoskins (Alf), Donald Gee (Bert).

On the Up Dennis Waterman (Tony Carpenter), Sam Kelly (Sam), Joan Sims (Mrs Fiona Wembley).

Opportunity Knocks Presenters: Hughie Green, Bob Monkhouse, Les Dawson.

Other 'Arf, The Lorraine Chase (Lorraine Watts), John Standing (Charles Lattimer), Pat Hodge (Sybil Howarth).

OTT (Over The Top) Adult version of *TISWAS*, with variations such as the three naked balloon dancers.

Our Man at St Mark's Leslie Phillips (Rev. Andrew Parker), Donald Sinden (Rev. Stephen Young).

Outside Edge Robert Daws (Roger Dervish), Brenda Blethyn (Miriam, 'Mim'), Timothy Spall (Kevin Costello), Josie Lawrence (Maggie).

Pallisers, The Susan Hampshire (Lady Glencora McCluskie/Palliser), Philip Latham (Plantagenet Palliser), Jeremy Irons (Frank Tregear), Anthony Andrews (Earl of Silverbridge), Derek Jacobi (Lord Fawn).

Panorama Presenters include Pat Murphy, Richard Dimbleby, Malcolm Muggeridge, David Dimbleby.

Paradise Club Leslie Grantham (Danny Kane), Don Henderson (Frank Kane).

Partridge Family Shirley Jones (Shirley), David Cassidy (Keith), Susan Dey (Laurie), Danny Bonaduce (Chris).

Peak Practice Kevin Whately (Dr Jack Kerruish), Amanda Burton (Dr Beth Glover), Gray O'Brien (Tom Deneley), Gary Mavers (Andrew Attwood), Maggie O'Neill (Alex Redman), Joseph Millson (Sam Morgan). Set in Cardale, Peak District.

Pebble Mill at One Presenters: Bob Langley, Donny MacLeod, Jan Leeming, Anna Ford, Paul Coia, Magnus Magnusson. Pebble Mill was revived after a short break with presenters including Judi Spiers, Alan Titchmarsh, Gloria Hunniford and Ross King.

Peep Show David Mitchell (Mark), Robert Webb (Jeremy). Sitcom where the intimate thoughts of the two lads are made known to the viewer.

Pennies From Heaven Bob Hoskins (Arthur Parker), Cheryl Campbell (Eileen), Gemma Craven (Joan Parker). Written by Dennis Potter.

Perfect Scoundrels Peter Bowles (Guy Buchanan), Bryan Murray (Harry Cassidy). Series created by its stars.

Perry Mason Raymond Burr (Perry Mason), Barbara Hale (Della Street), William Hopper (Paul Drake), William Talman (Hamilton Burger), Ray Collins (Lt Tragg). Set in Los Angeles.

Persuaders, The Tony Curtis (Danny Wilde), Roger Moore (Lord Brett Sinclair), Laurence Naismith (Judge Fulton).

Peter Principle, The Jim Broadbent (Peter), Claire Skinner (Susan), Stephen Moore (Geoffrey), Tracy Keating (Brenda), David Schneider (Bradley), Daniel Flynn (Dave), Janette Legge (Iris). Tale of inept bank manager.

Petrocelli Barry Newman (Tony Petrocelli), Susan Howard (Maggie). Set in fictional San Remo.

Peyton Place Ryan O'Neal (Rodney Harrington), Mia Farrow (Allison McKenzie), Ed Nelson (Dr Mike Rossi), Dorothy Malone (Constance McKenzie), Christopher Connelly (Norman Harrington).

Phil Silvers Show Phil Silvers (Master Sgt Ernest Bilko), Maurice Gosfield (Pte Duane Doberman), Joe E. Ross (Sgt Rupert Ritzik), Billy Sands (Pte Dino Paparelli), Paul Ford (Colonel John Hall), Allan Melvin (Cpl Henshaw), Harvey Lembeck (Cpl Rocco Barbella), Elizabeth Fraser (Joan). Rocco Barbella was the real name of boxer Rocky Graziano, the casting director.

Phoenix Nights Peter Kay plays club boss Brian Potter, who was disabled after being crushed by a fruit machine during a flood, as well as doorman Max and Chorley FM's mullet-haired DJ Paul Le Roy. Series developed from one-off *The Club* and other characters include resident compere Jerry St Clair, real name Jerry Dignan (Dave Spikey), Kenny Senior (Archie Kelly), Kenny Junior (Justin Moorhouse), Holy Mary (Janice Connolly). Resident band: Les Alanos with Alan (Steve Edge) on keyboards and Les (Toby Foster) on drums. Written by Peter Kay, Dave Spikey and Neil Fitzmaurice.

Pie in the Sky Richard Griffiths stars as masterchef and ace detective Henry Crabbe.

Pinky and Perky Creators: Jan and Vlasta Dalibor.

Plane Makers, The Patrick Wymark (John Wilder), Barbara Murray/Ann Firbank (Pamela Wilder), Jack Watling (Don Henderson). Aircraft factory name: Scott Furlong. Follow-on series was called *The Power Game*.

Please Sir John Alderton (Bernard 'Privet' Hedges), Deryck Guyler (Norman Potter), Peter Cleall (Eric Duffy), Joan Sanderson (Doris Ewell), David Barry (Frankie Abbott), Richard Davies (Mr Price), Jill Kerman (Penny Wheeler/Hedges), Spin-off series: *The Fenn Street Gang*.

Poldark Robin Ellis (Ross Poldark), Angharad Rees (Demelza), Ralph Bates (George Warleggan). Based on novels by Winston Graham.

Police Woman Angie Dickinson (Sgt Suzanne 'Pepper' Anderson), Earl Holliman (Lt Bill Crowley).

Popstars Auditions of thousands of young budding pop stars in the quest to put together a five-piece all singing and dancing supergroup. The five winners were Danny Foster, Myleene Klass, Noel Sullivan, Kym Marsh and Suzanne Shaw who became Hear'Say. The show's executive producer was 'Nasty' Nigel Lythgoe.

Porridge Ronnie Barker (Norman Stanley Fletcher), Richard Beckinsale (Lennie Godber), Fulton MacKay (Mr MacKay), Peter Vaughan (Groutie), David Jason (Blanco), Brian Wilde (Mr Barrowclough), Patricia Brake (Ingrid), Chris Biggins (Lukewarm), Maurice Denham (Judge Rawley), Tony Osoba (McLaren), Sam Kelly (Warren). Prison setting: HMP Slade. Sentence: five years. Sequel: *Going Straight*.

Porterhouse Blue David Jason (Skullion), Ian Richardson (Sir Godber Evans), Griff Rhys-Jones (Cornelius Carrington).

Postman Pat Characters include Jess the cat, Mrs Goggins the postmistress and twins Katie and Tom Pottage.

Pot Black Half-hour snooker programme which popularised the game as a television medium. Ran from 1969 to 1986, Ray Reardon was the first champion and Jimmy White the last. The theme tune was 'Ivory Rag'. *Pot Black* was briefly revived for one series. A *Masters Pot Black* was held in 1997, the winner being Joe Johnson.

Potter Arthur Lowe (Redvers Potter), replaced by Robin Bailey when Arthur Lowe died between series.

Price is Right, The Presenters: Leslie Crowther and Bruce Forsyth.

Pride and Prejudice Colin Firth (Fitzwilliam Darcy), Jennifer Ehle (Elizabeth Bennet), Alison Steadman (Mrs Bennet), Julia Sawalha (Lydia Bennet).

Prisoner, The Patrick McGoohan (No. 6). Filmed in Portmeirion, Wales.

Professionals, The Gordon Jackson (George Cowley), Lewis Collins (William Bodie), Martin Shaw (Ray Doyle).

Protectors, The Robert Vaughn (Harry Rule), Nyree Dawn Porter (Contessa di Contini), Tony Anholt (Paul Buchet).

Quantum Leap Scott Bakula (Dr Sam Beckett), Dean Stockwell (Al Calavicci).

Quatermass Reginald Tate/André Morell/John Robinson/John Mills (Professor Bernard Quatermass). Written by Nigel Kneale.

Question of Sport, A Presenters: David Vine, David Coleman, Sue Barker. Current captains: Matt Dawson and Phil Tufnell.

Rab C Nesbit Gregor Fisher's character first appeared in *Naked Video*. Children are Gash and Burney.

Rag Trade, The Peter Jones (Mr Fenner), Reg Varney (Reg), Miriam Karlin (Paddy), Sheila Hancock (Carole), Esma Cannon (Little Lil), Barbara Windsor (Judy), Wanda Ventham (Shirley). A revival series starred Anna Karen as the character she played in *On the Buses*.

Randall and Hopkirk (Deceased) Mike Pratt (Jeff Randall), Kenneth Cope (Marty Hopkirk), Annette Andre (Jean Hopkirk). Revived in the 1990s with Reeves and Mortimer playing Marty and Jeff.

Rawhide Eric Fleming (Gil Favor), Clint Eastwood (Rowdy Yates), Paul Brinegar (Wishbone), Sheb Wooley (Pete Nolan), James Murdock (Harkness 'Mushy' Mushgrove).

Ready Steady Go Presenters Keith Fordyce, Cathy McGowan, David Gell, Michael Aldred.

Red Dwarf Chris Barrie (Arnold J Rimmer BSc, SSC), Craig Charles (Dave Lister), Danny John-Jules (Cat), Norman Lovett/Hattie Hayridge (Holly), David Ross/Robert Llewellyn (Kryten).

Remington Steele Pierce Brosnan, Stephanie Zimbalist (Laura Holt, the owner of Remington Steele Investigations).

Rhoda Valerie Harper (Rhoda Morgenstern/Gerard), Julie Kavner (Brenda Morgenstern), Lorenzo Musoc (Carlton the doorman, voice only). Spin-off from the *Mary Tyler Moore Show*.

Rich Man Poor Man First of the TV 'Best Sellers', based on an Irwin Shaw novel and starring Peter Strauss and Nick Nolte.

Rifleman, The Chuck Connors (Lucas McCain), Johnny Crawford (Mark McCain).

Right to Reply Presenters include: Gus MacDonald, Linda Agran, Brian Hayes, Rory McGrath, Sheena McDonald, Roger Bolton.

Rings on Their Fingers Martin Jarvis (Oliver Pryde), Diane Keen (Sandy Bennett/Pryde).

Rising Damp Leonard Rossiter (Rigsby), Richard Beckinsale (Allan), Frances de la Tour (Miss Jones), Don Warrington (Philip), Vienna the cat. Based on a one-act play, *The Banana Box*.

Robin Hood Short-lived series of 1953 in which Patrick Troughton (second Dr Who) took the lead role.

Robin of Sherwood Michael Praed (Robin of Loxley), Jason Connery (Robert of Huntingdon), Clive Mantle (Little John), Ray Winstone (Will Scarlet), Judi Trott (Maid Marian). Music by Clannad.

Robin's Nest Richard O'Sullivan (Robin Tripp), Tessa Wyatt (Victoria Nicholls), Tony Britton (James Nicholls), David Kelly (Albert Riddle, the one-armed washer-up), Honor Blackman/Barbara Murray (Marion).

Rock Follies Charlotte Cornwell, Julie Covington (Devonia Dee Rhoades), Rula Lenska. Group name: The Little Ladies.

Rockford Files, The James Garner, Noah Beery Jnr (Joseph 'Rocky' Rockford), Joe Santos (Det. Sgt Dennis Becker).

Room 101 Original presenter Nick Hancock, who was followed by Paul Merton and Frank Skinner.

Roseanne Roseanne Barr (Roseanne Conner), John Goodman (Dan), George Clooney (Booker Brooks).

Royle Family, The Caroline Aherne (Denise Best), Ricky Tomlinson (Jim Royle), Sue Johnston (Barbara Royle), Craig Cash (Dave Best), Ralf Little (Anthony Royle), Liz Smith (Norma Speakman).

Rumpole of the Bailey Leo McKern (Horace Rumpole), Patricia Hodge (Phyllida Trant/Erskine-Brown), Peter Bowles (Guthrie Featherstone), Bill Fraser (Justice Bullingham). Wife: Hilda (She who must be obeyed). Winebar: Pomeroy's. Drink: Château Fleet Street).

Saint, The Roger Moore (Simon Templar alias the Saint). Car: Volvo P1800S. Inspector: Claude Eustace Teal. Sequel: *Return of the Saint*, starring Ian Ogilvy.

Sea Hunt Lloyd Bridges (Mike Nelson). Boat: the *Argonaut*.

Secret Army Jan Francis (Lisa Colbert; codename Yvette), Bernard Hepton (Albert Foiret), Clifford Rose (Sturmbannführer Ludwig Kessler). Underground movement: Lifeline.

Secret Diary of Adrian Mole, Aged 13¾ Gian Sammarco (Adrian), Stephen Moore (Mr Mole), Julie Walters and Lulu (Pauline Mole), Lindsey Stagg (Pandora). Based on the Sue Townsend novels.

Seinfeld Jerry Seinfeld (Jerry), Jason Alexander (George), Michael Richards (Kramer), Julia Louis Dreyfus (Elaine).

September Song Michael Williams (Billy Balsam), Russ Abbot (Ted Fenwick), Michael Angelis (Arnie).

77 Sunset Strip Efrem Zimbalist Jnr (Stuart Bailey), Roger Smith (Jeff Spencer), Ed Byrnes (Kookie). Much of the action took place outside Dean Martin's restaurant, Dino's.

Seven Up Documentary first shown in 1964 following the lives of 14 British people from the age of seven to adulthood. Seven-yearly updates are shown, the last in 2005 as *49 Up*.

Sex and the City Sarah Jessica Parker (Carrie Bradshaw), Kim Cattrall (Samantha Jones), Kristin Davis (Charlotte York), Cynthia Nixon (Miranda Hobbes), John Corbett (Aidan), Christopher Orr (Alexander).

Sexton Blake Laurence Payne (Sexton Blake), Roger Foss (Tinker), Dorothea Phillips (Mrs Bardell). Bloodhound: Pedro. White Rolls Royce nicknamed the Grey Panther.

Shameless David Threlfall (Frank Gallagher), Anne-Marie Duff (Fiona Gallagher), Jody Latham (Lip Gallagher), James McAvoy (Steve), Gerard Kearns (Ian Gallagher), Maxine Peake (Veronica), Dean Lennox Kelly (Kev), Maggie O'Neill (Sheila Jackson), Chris Bisson (Kash). Written by Paul Abbott. Set on the Chatsworth Estate.

Sharpe Sean Bean (Richard Sharpe), Daragh O'Malley (Sgt Pat Harper), Peter Postlewaite (Hakeswill), Philip Whitchurch (Frederickson), Liz Hurley (Isabella), Assumpta Sema (Teresa, the first Mrs Sharpe), Abigail Cruttenden (Lady Jane, the second Mrs Sharpe), Cecile Paoli (Lucille Dubert, the third Mrs Sharpe), Louise Germaine (Sally Clayton), John Tams (Hagman) also co-wrote the music. Based on novels by Bernard Cornwell.

Shillingbury Tales Robin Nedwell (Peter Higgins), Diane Keen (Sally Higgins), Lionel Jeffries (Major Langton), Bernard Cribbins (Cuffy), Jack Douglas (Jake).

Shine On Harvey Moon Kenneth Cranham/Nicky Henson (Harvey Moon), Linda Robson (Maggie Moon), Nigel Planer (Lou Lewis), Elizabeth Spriggs (Nan), Pauline Quirke (Veronica), Maggie Steed (Rita Moon). Harvey's occupation: professional footballer.

Simpsons, The Characters include: Homer and Marge Simpson and their children Bart, Lisa and Maggie. The pet dog is called Santa's Little Helper and the cat Snowball II. Other characters include Montgomery Burns, Waylon Smithers, Professor John Frink, Millhouse van Houten, Sideshow Bob, Krusty the Clown, and Chief Wiggum and his son Ralph. Series is set in Springfield and started life as a cartoon short on the *Tracy Ullman Show*.

Singing Detective, The Michael Gambon (Philip E Marlow), Joanne Whalley (Nurse Mills/Carlotta), Patrick Malahide (Mark Binney/Mark Finney/Raymond Binney), Jim Carter (Mr Marlow), Alison Steadman (Beth Marlow/Lili). Hospital ward: Sherpa Tensing. Illness: psoriasis. Written by Dennis Potter.

Sir Francis Drake Terence Morgan (Drake), Jean Kent (Queen Elizabeth), Michael Crawford (John Drake).

Six-Five Special Presenters: Pete Murray, Josephine Douglas, Freddie Mills, Jim Dale. Jack Good was the original producer and Adam Faith made his debut on his way to stardom.

Six Million Dollar Man Lee Majors (Steve Austin), Richard Anderson (Oscar Goldman), Lyndsay Wagner (Jaime Sommers). The opening sequence showing Steve Austin's crash in the Mojave Desert was in fact Donald Campbell's fatal accident while attempting the world water-speed record on Coniston Water.

64,000 Dollar Question, The Questions were guarded every week by Detective Fabian. Bob Monkhouse hosted the British version.

Six Wives of Henry VIII, The Keith Michell (Henry), Annette Crosbie (Catherine of Aragon), Dorothy Tutin (Anne Boleyn), Anne Stallybrass (Jane Seymour), Elvi Hale (Anne of Cleves), Angela Pleasance (Catherine Howard), Rosalie Crutchley (Catherine Parr), Patrick Troughton (Duke of Norfolk). Narrator: Anthony Quayle.

Sliders John Rhys-Davies (Maximillian Arturo), Jerry O'Connell (Quinn Mallory), Sabrina Lloyd (Wade Wells), Cleavant Derricks (Rembrandt Brown). Sliding is the term used for entering parallel universes.

Slinger's Day Bruce Forsyth (Cecil Slinger). The untimely death of Leonard Rossiter precipitated the arrival of Bruce Forsyth to take over the role of the put-upon supermarket manager, his name changed from Tripper to Slinger.

Soap Katherine Helmond (Jessica Tate), Cathryn Damon (Mary Dallas Campbell), Billy Crystal (Jodie Dallas), Robert Guillaume (Benson Dubois), Robert Mandan (Chester Tate).

Soldier, Soldier Jerome Flynn (Paddy Garvey), Robson Green (Dave Tucker), David Haig (Mjr Tom Cadman).

Some Mothers Do 'Ave 'Em Michael Crawford (Frank Spencer), Michele Dotrice (Betty). Daughter: Jessica.

Sopranos, The James Gandolfini (Tony Soprano), Edie Falco (Carmela Soprano), Nancy Marchand (Livia Soprano), Lorraine Bracco (Dr Jennifer Melfi), Jamie-Lynn Sigler (Meadow Soprano), Robert Iler (A J Soprano), Aida Turturro (Janice 'Parvati' Soprano), Dominic Chianese (Corrado Soprano), Tony Sirico (Paulie Walnuts), Steve van Zandt (Silvio Dante), John Ventimiglia (Artie Bucco). Theme tune: 'Woke Up This Morning' by Alabama 3.

Sorry! Ronnie Corbett (Timothy Lumsden, a librarian), Barbara Lott (Mrs Phyllis Lumsden).

South Park Adult cartoon series. Characters include Kenny (who is invariably killed), Kyle, Stan, Cartman, Chef, Mr Garrison, Ned, Uncle Jimbo and Officer Barbrady.

Space: 1999 Martin Landau (John Koenig), Barbara Bain (Dr Helena Russell), Catherine Schell (Maya), Barry Morse (Professor Victor Bergman). Crew of Moonbase Alpha stranded in space.

Space Patrol Voices: Capt. Larry Dart (Dick Vosburgh), Husky and Slim (Ronnie Stevens), Gabblerdictum (Libby Morris), Colonel Raeburn (Murray Kash). Ship: Galasphere 347. Year: 2100. The Space Patrol was the active unit of the United Galactic Organization. Libby Morris was Raeburn's super-efficient blonde secretary from Venus; fortunately there is no such thing as a dumb blonde on Venus.

Special Branch George Sewell (Det. Chief Insp. Alan Craven), Patrick Mower (Det. Chief Insp. Tom Haggerty), Derren Nesbitt (Det. Insp. Jordan), Fulton Mackay (Det. Supt Inman).

Spender Jimmy Nail, Sammy Johnson (Stick), Paul Greenwood (Supt Yelland).

Spenser For Hire Robert Urich (Spenser), Avery Brooks (Hawk), Barbara Stock (Susan Silverman).

Spitting Image Created by Peter Fluck, Roger Law and Michael Lambie-Martin.

St Elsewhere Ed Flanders (Donald Westphall), William Daniels (Mark Craig), Ed Begley Jnr (Victor Ehrlich). Hospital: St Elegius, Boston.

Star Trek William Shatner (James Tiberius Kirk), Leonard Nimoy (Mr Spock – his mother is Amanda, an earth woman, his father is Sarek, a Vulcan), De Forest Kelly (Dr Leonard 'Bones' McCoy), James Doohan (Scottie), George Takei (Mr Sulu), Nichelle Nichols (Lt Uhura), Walter Koenig (Ensign Pavel Chekov), Majel Barrett (Nurse Chapel). Crew size: 430. Decks: 8. Five-year mission to boldly go where no man has gone before. Enterprise no.: NCC 1701A. Shuttle: Galileo. Spock's blood colour: green (T positive).

Star Trek: The Next Generation Patrick Stewart (Captain Jean-Luc Picard), Jonathan Frakes (Commander William Ryker), LeVar Burton (Lt Geordi La Forge), Michael Dorn (Lt Worf), Denise Crosby (Lt Tasha Yar), Gates McFadden (Dr Bev Crusher), Marina Sirtis (Deanna Troi), Brent Spiner (Lt Cmdr Data), Wil Wheaton (Wesley), Diana Muldaur (Dr Katherine Pulaski), Whoopi Goldberg (Guinan). Original *Star Trek* set in the 23rd century; this series was set 78 years later. Enterprise no.: NCC 1701D.

Stars in Their Eyes Presenters: Leslie Crowther, Matthew Kelly, Cat Deeley.

Starsky and Hutch David Soul (Ken Hutchinson), Paul Michael Glaser (Dave Starsky), Antonio Fargas (Huggie Bear).

Steptoe and Son Harry H Corbett (Harold), Wilfred Bramble (Albert), Hercules the horse. American spin-off: *Sandford and Son.*

Stingray Troy Tempest, George 'Phones' Sheridan, Atlanta Shore, Titan, Agent X20. Marina was the mute daughter of Emperor Aphony from Pacifica and her pet seal was called Oink. Organisation: WASP, World Aquanaut Security Patrol, in Marineville. Year: 2000.

Streets of San Francisco, The Karl Malden (Det. Lt Mike Stone), Michael Douglas (Insp. Steve Keller).

Strictly Come Dancing Presented by Bruce Forsyth and Tess Daly. Judges: Len Goodman, Arlene Phillips, Bruno Tonioli, Craig Revel Horwood. Winners: Series one (Natasha Kaplinsky and Brendan Cole); series two (Jill Halfpenny and Darren Bennet); series three (Darren Gough and Lilia Kopylova); series four (Mark Ramprakash and Karen Hardy); series five (Alesha Dixon and Matthew Cutler); series six (Tom Chambers and Camilla Dallerup); series seven (Chris Hollins and Ola Jordan); series eight (Kara Tointon and Artem Chigvintsev); series nine (Harry Judd and Aliona Vilani); series ten (Louis Smith and Flavia Cacace). Arlene Phillips was replaced by Alesha Dixon for series seven and was herself replaced by Darcey Bussell for series ten. Natasha stood in for Tess during the first half of series two while she had a baby. Claudia Winkleman hosted the nightly update show on BBC2. Original dancing pair of Anton du Beke and Erin Boag have never won. Narrated by Alan Dedicoat.

Sullivans, The Soap, made between 1976 and 1982 and set during World War Two. Dave Sullivan (Paul Cronin), Kitty Sullivan (Susan Hannaford), Terry Sullivan (Richard Morgan), Tom Sullivan (Steven Tandy), Grace Sullivan (Lorraine Bayly), Harry Sullivan (Michael Caton), Alice Watkins / Sullivan (Megan Williams), Ida Jessup / Pike (Vivean Gray), Jack Fletcher (Reg Gorman), Jim Sullivan (Andy Anderson), John Sullivan (Andrew McFarlane), Maggie Baker (Vikki Hammond), Norm Baker (Norman Yemm), Rose Sullivan (Maggie Dence), Maureen Sullivan (Fiona Paul), Bert Duggan (Peter Hehir), Cara (Kylie Minogue), Caroline Sullivan (Genevieve Picot), Christopher Merchant (John Waters), Det Sgt Shearer (Noel Trevarthen), Dr Donovan Sullivan (Keith Eden), Ernest 'Erger' O'Keefe (Peter Harvey Wright), Flynn Errol (Peter Ford), Frank Errol (Damon Herriman), Geoff Johnson/Sullivan (Jamie Higgins), Horace 'Orrible' Brown (Nick Waters), Juliana Sleven (Saski Post), Kate Meredith (Ilona Rodgers), Leslie 'Magpie' Maddern (Gary Sweet), Lou Sullivan (Annie Byron), Melina Baker (Chantel Contouri), Patty Spencer / Sullivan (Penny Downie), Robbie McGovern (Graham Harvey).

Sunday Night at the London Palladium Comperes included: Tommy Trinder, Bruce Forsyth, Des O'Connor, Jimmy Tarbuck, Norman Vaughan, Jim Dale, Hughie Green, Alfred Marks, Robert Morley, Dave Allen, Roger Moore, Don Arrol, Arthur Haynes, Dickie Henderson.

Supercar Mike Mercury, Professor Popkiss, Dr Beaker, Masterspy, Mitch the monkey, Zarin.

Supergran Gudrun Ure (Granny Smith), Iain Cuthbertson (Scunner Campbell). Set in Chisleton.

Superman Original series starred George Reeves, who committed suicide after being typecast in this role. The more recent series stars Dean Cain as Superman and Teri Hatcher as Lois Lane.

Surgical Spirit Nichola McAuliffe (Dr Sheila Sabatini), Duncan Preston (Dr Jonathan Haslam). Gillies Hospital.

Sutherland's Law Iain Cuthbertson played Procurator Fiscal Sutherland.

Sweeney, The John Thaw (Det. Inspector Jack Regan), Dennis Waterman (Det. Sgt George Carter).

Sykes Eric Sykes and Hattie Jacques (lived at Sebastopol Terrace), Derek Guyler (Korky), Richard Wattis (Mr Brown).

Sylvania Waters Australian fly-on-the-wall story of the Baker-Donaher family by Paul Watson (*The Family*).

Taggart Mark McManus (Det. Chief Insp. Jim Taggart), Neil Duncan (Det. Sgt Peter Livingstone), Blythe Duff (Det. Sgt. Jackie Reid).

Take Three Girls Angela Down, Liza Goddard, Susan Jameson.

Take Your Pick Presenters: Michael Miles, Des O'Connor. Original man with the gong: Alec Dane.

Taxi Judd Hirsch (Alex Reiger), Jeff Conaway (Bobby Wheeler), Danny de Vito (Louis de Palma), Marilu Henner (Elaine Nardo), Tony Danza (Tony Banta), Andy Kaufman (Latka Gravas), Christopher Lloyd (Reverend Jim 'Iggie' Ignatowski). Cab company: Sunshine Cabs.

Teletubbies Tinky Winky, Dipsy, Laa Laa, Po. Babygros open to reveal televisions. Created by Anne Wood. Looked after by a vacuum cleaner called Noo Noo. Voices include Eric Sykes and Toyah Wilcox.

Tenko Stephanie Beacham (Rose Millar), Stephanie Cole (Dr Beatrice Mason), Bert Kwouk (Yamauchi).

Thank Your Lucky Stars Presenters: Brian Matthews, Jim Dale and Keith Fordyce.

Third Man Michael Rennie (Harry Lime). Popular theme tune played on the zither by Shirley Abicaire.

This Morning Popular daytime magazine hosted live by Richard Madeley and Judy Finnegan.

Thomas the Tank Engine Narrators: Ringo Starr, Michael Angelis. Thomas is a blue engine; Gordon is green. Written by the Reverend Awdry. The Fat Controller became Sir Topham Hat.

Thunderbirds Thunderbird I pilot Scott Tracy (usually first at the scene because of its high-speed capability); Thunderbird 2 pilot Virgil (pod carrier for Thunderbird 4 and any special equipment required); Thunderbird 3 pilot Alan (rocket back-up) – Alan manned the Spacestation occasionally; Thunderbird 4 pilot Gordon (underwater machine which had great versatility); Thunderbird 5 pilot John (the stationery Spacestation). Jeff Tracy was the father and co-ordinator and Kyrano was his oriental assistant. GB agent was Lady Penelope Creighton-Ward and her butler was Parker.

Her Rolls Royce had the registration FAB1; her yacht was FAB2. Technical expert was Hiram Hackenbacker (Brains). Set in the year 2063. The Hood (Kyrano's half-brother) was the arch-enemy who regularly appeared. The Thunderbird pilots were named after famous astronauts.

Till Death Us Do Part Warren Mitchell (Alf Garnett), Anthony Booth (Mike), Dandy Nichols (Else), Una Stubbs (Rita), Patrica Hayes (Min Reed). Written by Johnny Speight.

Time Tunnel, The James Darren (Dr Tony Newman), Robert Colbert (Dr Doug Phillips), Lee Meriwether (Dr Ann McGregor).

Tinker Tailor Soldier Spy Alec Guinness (George Smiley), Bernard Hepton (Toby Esterhase), Beryl Reid (Connie Sachs).

TISWAS Today is Saturday, Watch (wear a) and Smile. Presenters included Chris Tarrant, John Asher, Trevor East, Sally James, Lenny Henry, John Gorman, Clive Webb, Sylvester McCoy, Frank Carson, Fogwell Flax and Bob Carolgees and Spit the dog.

Today's the Day Current affairs quiz programme hosted by Martyn Lewis. Your author, with his chum, Andy Curtis, won the 1997 series.

To the Manor Born Penelope Keith (Audrey Fforbes-Hamilton), Peter Bowles (Richard de Vere), Michael Bilton (Ned), Angela Thorne (Marjory Frobisher), John Rudling (Brabinger), Daphne Heard (Mrs Polouvicka).

Tonight Presenter: Cliff Michelmore. Catchphrase: The next Tonight will be tomorrow night. Notable reporters included Trevor Philpott, Julian Pettifer, Magnus Magnusson, Alan Whicker and the hugely popular Fyfe Robertson.

Top Gear Presenters include William Woolard, Angela Rippon, Barrie Gill, Noel Edmonds, Sue Baker, Jeremy Clarkson, Quentin Willson, Tiff Needell, Chris Goffey, Tony Mason, Janet Trewin, Michele Newman.

Torchwood John Barrowman (Capt Jack Harkness), Eva Myles (Gwen Cooper), Burn Gorman (Owen Harper), Naoko Mori (Toshiko Sato). Spin-off from *Dr Who*.

Triangle Kate O'Mara (Katherine Laker), Michael Craig (John Anderson), Larry Lamb (Matt Taylor). Company: Triangle Lines. Short-lived soap notable for the bikini-clad posing of its star.

Tripper's Day Leonard Rossiter (Norman Tripper); see *Slinger's Day*.

Trumpton Spin-off series from *Camberwick Green* but the action moved from Pippin Fort. Captain Flack's local firemen: Hugh, Pugh, Barney McGrew, Cuthbert, Dibble and Grubb.

Tutti Frutti Robbie Coltrane (Danny McGlone), Emma Thompson (Suzie Kettles). Band: The Majestics.

TW3 That Was The Week That Was, presented by David Frost and produced by Ned Sherrin.

Twin Peaks Kyle MacLachlan (Agent Dale Cooper), Michael Ontkean (Sheriff Harry S Truman), Ray Wise (Leland Palmer), Sheryl Lee (Laura Palmer/Madeleine Ferguson), Piper Laurie (Catherine Martell), Dana Ashbrook (Bobby Briggs), Sherilyn Fenn (Audrey Horne). Characters included a dwarf who talked backwards, the Log Lady and Audrey, who tied knots in cherry stalks with her tongue. Killer was Laura's father, Leland, possessed by 'Bob'.

Two Fat Ladies Jennifer Paterson and Clarissa Dickson Wright. Oversize chefs who ride in a combination motorcycle.

2 Point 4 Children Belinda Lang (Bill Porter), Gary Olsen (Ben Porter).

Two's Company Elaine Stritch (Dorothy McNab), Donald Sinden (Robert Hiller).

UFO Ed Bishop (Commander Edward Straker), George Sewell (Colonel Alec Freeman), Peter Gordeno (Peter Karlin, the captain of the Vipers), Gabrielle Drake (Lt Gay Ellis), Michael Billington (Colonel Paul Foster), Wanda Ventham (Colonel Virginia Lake). Defence unit: SHADO (Supreme Headquarters Alien Defence Organization). Reconnaissance satellite: S.I.D. (Space Intruder Detector). Location: beneath the Harlington-Straker film studios just outside London (and Moonbase).

University Challenge Began in 1962 with Bamber Gascoigne as the presenter. After he bowed out in 1987 the series was resumed in 1995 with Jeremy Paxman as the new presenter. The highest winning score was in a first-round match in 1987 when University College, Oxford, defeated Reading 520-35. Series winners are as follows: 1963 Leicester, 1964 no series this year, 1965 New College, Oxford, 1966 Oriel College, Oxford, 1967 Sussex, 1968 Keele, 1969 Sussex, 1970 Churchill College, Cambridge, 1971 Sidney Sussex College, Cambridge, 1972 University College, Oxford, 1973 Fitzwilliam College, Cambridge, 1974 Trinity College, Cambridge, 1975 Keble College, Oxford, 1976 University College, Oxford, 1977 Durham, 1978 Sidney Sussex College, Cambridge, 1979 Bradford, 1980 Merton College, Oxford, 1981 Queen's University, Belfast, 1982 St Andrews, 1983 Dundee, 1984 Open University 1985 No series this year, 1986 Jesus College, Oxford, 1987 Keble College, Oxford, 1995 Trinity College, Cambridge, 1996 Imperial College, London, 1997 Magdalen College, Oxford, 1998 Magdalen College, Oxford, 1999 Open University, 2000 Durham, 2001 Imperial College, London, 2002 Somerville College, Oxford, 2003 Birkbeck College, London, 2004 Magdalen College, Oxford, 2005 Corpus Christi College, Oxford, 2006 University of Manchester, 2007 University of Warwick, 2008 Christ Church, Oxford, 2009 University of Manchester, 2010 Emmanuel College, Cambridge, 2011 Magdalen College, Oxford, 2012 University of Manchester. 2013 University of Manchester. Corpus Christi College, Oxford won in 2009 but were later disqualified for fielding an ineligible team member, Sam Kay. In 2002 a special 40th anniversary series was made featuring previous champions. Sidney Sussex College, Cambridge, were victorious. In 2003 *University Challenge: The Professionals* began, the Inland Revenue being the first winners; 2004 winners were the British Library and 2005 the Privy Council Office.

Upstairs Downstairs Gordon Jackson (Mr Angus Hudson), Angela Baddeley (Mrs Kate Bridges), Jean Marsh (Rose), David Langton (Lord Richard Bellamy), Simon Williams (Capt. James Bellamy), Nicola Pagett (Elizabeth Bellamy/Kirkbridge), Lesley-Anne Down (Georgina Worsley), Jacqueline Tong (Daisy), Christopher Beeny (Edward), Pauline Collins (Sarah), John Alderton (Thomas). Address: 165 Eaton Place. Spin-off series: *Thomas and Sarah*.

V Marc Singer (Mike Donovan), Jane Badler (Diana: famous scene where she swallowed a mouse), Jenny Beck and Jennifer Cooke (Elizabeth), Michael Ironside (Ham Tyler), Blair Tefkin (Robin Maxwell, who gave birth to Elizabeth).

Very Peculiar Practice, A Peter Davison (Dr Stephen Daker), David Troughton (Dr Bob Buzzard), Barbara Flynn (Dr Rose Marie), Michael J Shannon (Jack B Daniels). Set at Lowlands University. Written by Andrew Davies.

Vicar of Dibley, The Dawn French (Geraldine Granger), Emma Chambers (Alice Tinker), Gary Waldhorn (David Horton), James Fleet (Hugo Horton), Roger Lloyd Pack (Owen Newitt), Trevor Peacock (Jim Trott), John Bluthal (Frank Pickle). Written by Paul Mayhew-Archer and Richard Curtis.

Virginian, The James Drury (Virginian), Doug McClure (Trampas), Lee J Cobb (Judge Henry Garth), Gary Clarke (Steve Hill), John McIntire (Clay Grainger), Stewart Grainger (Alan MacKenzie), Lee Majors (Roy Tate). Series set on the Shiloh Ranch, Medicine Bow, Wyoming.

Vision On Presenters include Tony Hart, Larry Parker, Sylvester McCoy, Pat Keysell, Ben Benison, Wilf Lunn, David Cleveland.

Voyage to the Bottom of the Sea Richard Basehart (Admiral Harriman Nelson), David Hedison (Captain Lee Crane). Nuclear submarine: the *Seaview*. Set in the year 1984.

Wacky Races Eleven cars lined up to win the title 'The World's Wackiest Racer'. Car 1: Boulder Mobile; Rock and Gravel Slag. Car 2: Creepy Coupé; Big and Little Gruesome. Car 3: Ring-a-Ding Convert-a-Car; Prof. Pat Pending. Car 4: Crimson Haybailer; Red Max. Car 5: Compact Pussycat; Penelope Pitstop. Car 6: Army Surplus Special; Gen. Sgt and Private Pinkley. Car 7: Bulletproof Bomb; Clyde and Anthill Mob. Car 8: Arkansas Chugabug; Luke and Blubber Bear. Car 9: Turbo Terrific; All-American Peter Perfect. Car 10: Buzz Wagon; Rufus Ruffcut and Sawtooth. Car 00: Mean Machine driven by Dick Dastardly and his dog Muttley. Spin-off series were *The Perils of Penelope Pitstop* and *Dastardly and Muttley in their Flying Machines*, in which they tried to 'Stop the Pigeon'.

Waltons, The Ralph Waite (John), Michael Learned (Olivia), and their seven children: Richard Thomas and Robert Wightman (John Boy), Judy Norton Taylor (Mary Ellen), Jon Walmsley (Jason), Mary Elizabeth McDonough (Erin), David W Harper (J Robert 'Jim Bob'), Eric Scott (Ben), Kami Cotler (Elizabeth). Their grandparents were played by Will Geer (Zeb) and Ellen Corby (Esther).

Washington Behind Closed Doors Jason Robards (President Richard Monckton).

Watch With Mother Original five: Picture Book (Patricia Driscoll), Andy Pandy, Bill and Ben, Rag, Tag and Bobtail, The Woodentops. Ran from 1952 to 1980. Others included Tales of the Riverbank, Pogles Wood, Bizzy Lizzy and Barnaby.

Watchdog Presenters include Nick Ross, Lynn Faulds Wood, John Stapleton, Anne Robinson, Alice Beer.

Water Margin, The Set in the water margins of Lian Shan Po. The hero was Lin Chung who, with his wife Hsiao, warred against evil in 14th-century China.

Weakest Link, The Presenter Anne Robinson's catchphrase of 'You are the weakest link, goodbye' soon became the ultimate put-down. The popular daytime BBC2 quiz show was given a prime-time slot on BBC1 due to its record viewing figures.

West Wing, The Martin Sheen (President Josiah Bartlet), Allison Janney (C J Cregg), Rob Lowe (Sam Seaborn), John Spencer (Leo McGarry), Janel Maloney (Donna Moss), Richard Schiff (Toby Ziegler), Dulé Hill (Charlie Young), Bradley Whitford (Josh Lyman), Stockard Channing (Abigail).

Whack-O! Jimmy Edwards (Prof. James Edwards), Arthur Howard and Julian Orchard (Mr Oliver Pettigrew). School name: Chiselbury.

What's My Line Presenters include Eamonn Andrews, Emma Forbes, Penelope Keith, David Jacobs. Original panel: Isobel Barnett, David Nixon, Gilbert Harding, Barbara Kelly.

What the Papers Say Presenters include Kingsley Martin, Brian Inglis and Stuart Hall.

When the Boat Comes In James Bolam (Jack Ford), Susan Jameson (Jessie Seaton).

Whiplash Peter Graves (Christopher Cobb). Set in the outback of Australia with a memorable theme tune.

Who Wants to Be a Millionaire? Presenter Chris Tarrant's catchphrases include 'D'you wanna phone a friend?', '50/50', and 'Ask the audience'. The first winner was Judith Keppel and the first man to win the million was David Edwards.

Whoops! Apocalypse Barry Morse (Johnny Cyclops), Richard Griffiths (Premier Dubienkin), Ed Bishop (Jay Garrick), Alexei Sayle (Commissar Solzhenitsyn), Peter Jones (Kevin Pork), John Cleese (Lacrobat).

Wind in the Willows, The Voices were Michael Hordern (Badger), David Jason (Toad), Peter Sallis (Rat), Richard Pearson (Mole).

Winds of War, The Robert Mitchum (Commander Victor 'Pug' Henry), Victoria Tennant (Pamela Tudsbury), Ali MacGraw (Natalie Jastrow), Jan-Michael Vincent (Byron Henry), Ben Murphy (Warren Henry), Howard Lang (Winston Churchill), Gunter Meisner (Hitler). Written by Herman Wouk.

Winston Churchill – The Wilderness Years Robert Hardy (Winston), Siân Phillips (Clementine), Peter Barkworth (Stanley Baldwin), Eric Porter (Neville Chamberlain).

Win, Lose or Draw Hosts: Danny Baker, Shane Richie, Bob Mills.

WKRP in Cincinnati Gary Sandy (Andy Travis), Gordon Jump (Arthur Carlson, 'Big Guy'), Loni Anderson (Jennifer Marlowe), Tim Reid (Gordon Sims, 'Venus Flytrap'), Howard Hesseman (Johnny Caravella, 'Dr Johnny Fever').

Woodentops, The Characters included Daddy and Mummy Woodentop, their twin children Jenny and Willy, Baby Woodentop, Mrs Scrubbit, Sam (the man who helped out in the garden), Buttercup the cow and Spotty the mischievous dog.

World at War World War Two history researched by Noble Frankland, produced by Jeremy Isaacs and narrated by Laurence Olivier.

World's End Short-lived soap opera set around the Mulberry public house, Chelsea, and starring Harry Fowler, Michael Angelis, Paul Brooke, Neville Smith, Primi Townsend.

Worzel Gummidge Jon Pertwee (Worzel), Una Stubbs (Aunt Sally), Geoffrey Bayldon (the Crowman), Lorraine Chase (Dolly Clothes-Peg), Joan Sims (Mrs Bloomsbury-Barton). Written by Keith Waterhouse and Willis Hall from an adaption of Barbara Euphan Todd novels. Worzel was found in Ten Acre Field on Scatterbrook Farm by John and Sue Peters.

Wyatt Earp, The Life and Legend of Hugh O'Brian (Wyatt Earp), Mason Alan Dinehart III (Bat Masterson, Earp's deputy), Douglas Fowley and Myron Healey (Doc Holliday), Lash La Rue (Sheriff John Behan).

Wycliffe Jack Shepherd (Det. Supt Wycliffe), Helen Masters (Det. Insp. Lane), Jimmy Yuill (Det. Insp. Kersey).

Xena: Warrior Princess Lucy Lawless (Xena), New Zealand-made off-shoot series from *Hercules*.

X Factor, The Pop music reality show where the talent is divided into three categories (16–24s, over 25s, groups) mentored by Simon Cowell, Sharon Osbourne and Louis Walsh. First winner in 2004 was Steve Brookstein. Subsequent winners: Shayne Ward (2005), Leona Lewis (2006), Leon Jackson (2007), Alexandra Burke (2008), Joe McElderry (2009), Matt Cardle (2010), Little Mix (2011), James Arthur (2012). In 2007 Dermot O'Leary replaced Kate Thornton as presenter. Other judges include: Dannii Minogue, Cheryl Cole, Tulisa Contostavlos, Kelly Rowland, Gary Barlow, Nicole Scherzinger.

X Files, The David Duchovny (Fox Mulder), Gillian Anderson (Dana Scully), Mitch Pileggi (Skinner), William B Davis (the Cigarette-Smoking Man [C G B Spender]).

XYY Man, The Stephen Yardley (William 'Spider' Scott, who had an extra 'Y' chromosome which appeared to give him a liking for dangerous pursuits, sometimes criminal), Don Henderson (Det. Sgt George Bulman).

Year in Provence, A John Thaw (Peter Mayle), Lindsay Duncan, Christian Luciani.

Yes Minister/Prime Minister Paul Eddington (Jim Hacker, Minister of Administrative Affairs/Prime Minister), Nigel Hawthorne (Sir Humphrey Appleby), Derek Fowlds (Bernard Wooley). Created by Antony Jay and Jonathan Lynn.

You Rang, M'Lord Paul Shane (Alf Stokes), Su Pollard (Ivy Teesdale), Jeffrey Holland (James Twelvetrees). Title song sung by Paul Shane and Bob Monkhouse.

Young Ones, The Rik Mayall (Rick), Nigel Planer (Neil), Adrian Edmondson (Vyvyan), Christopher Ryan (Mike), Alexei Sayle (Jerzy Balowski, and his family). Saying: For Cliff's sake.

You've Been Framed Presenters include Jeremy Beadle and Lisa Riley.

Z Cars Stratford Johns (Det. Chief Insp. Barlow), Frank Windsor (Det. Sgt John Watt), Brian Blessed (PC William 'Fancy' Smith), Joseph Brady (PC John 'Jock' Weir), James Ellis (Sgt Herbert 'Bert' Lynch), Jeremy Kemp (PC Bob Steele), Terence Edmond (PC Ian Sweet), Colin Welland (PC David Graham), Leonard Rossiter (Det. Insp. Bamber), John Slater (Det. Sgt Tom Stone), Alison Steadman (WPC Bayliss). Theme tune based on folk song 'Johnny Todd'. Spin-off series *Softly Softly*, set in Wyvern.

Zoo Gang, The John Mills (Tommy Devon), Brian Keith (Stephen Halliday), Barry Morse (Alec Marlowe), Lili Palmer (Manouche Roget).

Zoo Time Presenters were Desmond Morris, Chris Kelly and Harry Watt.

Zorro Guy Williams (Don Diego de la Vega, 'Zorro'), Gene Sheldon (Bernardo). Zorro means fox in Spanish.

Television, Radio and Media Adverts

A diamond is forever De Beer Consolidated Mines
A little dab'll do ya Brylcreem
Aah . . . Bisto
All human life is there News of the World
All the news that's fit to print *New York Times*
And all because the lady loves . . . Milk Tray
Any time, any place, anywhere Martini (coined by Barry Day)
Appliance of science Zanussi
Are you with . . . No, I'm with the Woolwich
Ask the man from the . . . Pru (Prudential Assurance Co. Ltd)
A . . . works wonders Double Diamond
Australians wouldn't give a xxxx for anything else Castlemaine xxxx lager
Bank that likes to say Yes TSB
Beanz meanz . . . Heinz
Beats as it sweeps as it cleans Hoover vacuum cleaners
Because I'm worth it L'oriel
Because life's complicated enough Abbey National
Beer that made Milwaukee famous Schlitz
Bet you can't eat three Shredded Wheat
B . . . O . . . Lifebuoy soap
Bread with nowt taken out Allinson's bread
. . . Brings express relief Settlers
Builds bonny babies Glaxo
Buy some for Lulu Smarties
. . . calling! Avon
Can you tell . . . from butter? Stork margarine
Central heating for kids Ready Brek
Chocolates with the less fattening centres Maltesers
Chocolates? No . . . Maltesers
Cleans a big, big carpet for less than half a crown 1001
Cleans and polishes in one go Pledge
Clunk click, every trip Jimmy Savile's seat belt campaign (from 1971)
Cool as a mountain stream Consulate cigarettes
Cuts cleaning time in half Flash
Does she or doesn't she? Clairol hair colouring (coined by Shirley Polykoff)
Don't ask the price. It's a penny Marks & Spencer (when first opened)
Don't be vague, ask for . . . Haig whisky
Don't leave home without it American Express
Don't say brown, say . . . Hovis
Don't you just love being in control British Gas, and Mrs Merton and her son, Malcolm
Eveninks and morninks I drink . . . Warninks
Everything you want from a store, and a little bit more Safeways
Finger of Fudge is just enough to give your kids a treat
Fingerlickin' good Kentucky Fried Chicken
First truly feminine cigarette Eve
Fly the flag British Airways
For men who don't have to try too hard Old Spice
Forces grey out, forces white in Fairy Snow
Fortifies the over forties Phyllosan
Fresh as the moment when the pod went pop Birds Eye peas
Full of Eastern promise Fry's Turkish Delight
Genuine article Budweiser
Getting there is half the fun Cunard Steamship Line
Gives a meal man appeal Oxo
Good to the last drop Maxwell House coffee
Gordon's gin (first scented advert) Shown in May 1997 when juniper berries could be smelt in cinema
Go to work on an . . . Egg (slogan is often attributed to Fay Weldon)
Graded grains make finer flour Homepride
Great way to fly Singapore Airlines
Hands that do dishes are as soft as your face with mild, green Fairy Liquid
Have a break, bave a . . . KitKat
Helps you work, rest and play A Mars a day (possibly attributed to Murray Walker)
Hold it up to the light, not a stain and shining bright Surf
I dreamed I . . . in my Maidenform bra
I think you probably are Cockburns Port
I was so impressed I bought the company Remington (said by Victor Kiam)
If you see Sid, tell him British Gas slogan during privatisation
I'm only here for the beer Double Diamond

I'm . . . fly me National Airlines
. . . is good for you Guinness
I never knew it had so much in it TV Times
Is it live, or is it . . . Memorex
Is she or isn't she? Harmony hair spray
It could be you National Lottery
It's for yoo-hoo! British Telecom
It's the real thing Coca-Cola
It's what your right arm's for Courage beer
Keep going well, keep going Shell
Keep your schoolgirl complexion Palmolive
Keynsham – spelt K-E-Y-N-S-H-A-M Horace Batchelor's phrase on Luxembourg's pools advisory service
Kills 99% of all household germs Domestos
King of beers Budweiser
Let's face the music and dance Allied Dunbar
Let your fingers do the walking Yellow Pages (Kirsty MacColl's version of 'Days' was popular theme)
Lion goes from strength to strength Peugeot
Liquid engineering Castrol Motor Oil
Listening Bank The Midland
Looks good, tastes good and by golly it does you good Mackeson
Lot less bovver than a hover Qualcast
Loudest noise comes from the electric clock Rolls Royce
Made by robots, driven by humans Nissan
Made in Scotland from girders Irn Bru
Made to make your mouth water Opal Fruits
Make tea bags make tea Tetley's
Make yourself heard Ericsson
Makes exceedingly good cakes Mr Kipling
Means happy motoring Esso (sign)
Melts in your mouth, not in your hands Treets
Milk from contented cows Carnation
Mint with the hole Polo
Minty bit stronger Trebor Mints
Naughty but nice Original advert about cream cakes (Salman Rushdie coined the phrase)
Never knowingly undersold John Lewis Stores
Nice 'ere 'innit? Campari (Lorraine Chase)
Nice face, shame about the breath Listerine mouthwash
Nice one, Cyril Wonderloaf
Nicole . . . Papa Renault Clio
99 44/100 % Pure Ivory soap
Nissan Almira Parodies of *The Sweeney* and *The Professionals*
Nissan Micra 'No No No' by Nancy Nova
Not everything in black and white makes sense Guinness
Nothing acts faster than . . . Anadin
Nuts! Whole hazelnuts Cadbury's Wholenut
Often a bridesmade – but never a bride Listerine mouthwash
One degree under? Try . . . Aspro
Pizza Hut: appeared in adverts Jonathan Ross, Caprice, Gareth Southgate, Damon Hill, Mikhail Gorbachev, Pamela Anderson
Plink plink fizz Alka Seltzer
Prevents that sinking feeling Bovril
Probably the best lager in the world Carlsberg
Prolongs active life Pal dog food
Promise her anything, but give her . . . Arpège (coined by Edouard Cournand, president of Lanvin Perfumes)
Pure genius Guinness
Put a tiger in your tank Esso
Puts the 'T' in Britain Typhoo tea
Refreshes the parts other beers cannot reach Heineken (coined by Terry Lovelock)
Ring of confidence Colgate toothpaste
. . . satisfy Senior Service cigarettes
Schhh . . . you know who Schweppes
Seven pieces of heaven Fry's Chocolate Cream
Simply years ahead Philips
'Singing in the Rain' (rap version) McDonald's
Snap! crackle! and pop! Kellogg's Rice Crispies
Solutions for a small planet IBM
Splash it on all over Brut
Spreads straight from the fridge Blueband margarine
Station of the Nation Radio Caroline
Stays sharp till the bottom of the glass Harp lager
Stop me and buy one Wall's ice cream
Sweet you can eat between meals Milky Way (without spoiling your appetite)
Takes good care of you BOAC
Tastes as good as it smells Maxwell House Coffee
Tested by dummies, driven by the intelligent Volvo
That's the wonder of... Woollies (Woolworths)
The appetizer Tizer
The bank that listens Midland
The bright one, the right one, it's . . . Martini
The cereal that's shot from guns Quaker Puffed Wheat
The drive of your life Peugeot 106
The real smell of . . . Brut
The shirt you don't iron Rael Brook Toplin
The soluble aspirin Disprin
They came in search of paradise Bounty
They grow on you Roses chocolates
They're bootiful Bernard Matthews's turkeys
They're grrrreat! Frosties
Things go better with . . . Coke (Coca-Cola)
To fly, to serve British Airways
Too good to hurry mints Murray Mints
To our members we're the fourth emergency service AA
Top breeders recommend it Pedigree Chum dog food
Top people read the . . . Times
Try a little VC 10derness British Airways
Vorsprung durch Technik Audi
Watch out there's a Humphrey about Milk
We never forget you have a choice British Caledonian
We sell more cars than Ford, Chrysler, Chevrolet and Buick combined Matchbox toys
We try harder Avis Car Rentals (coined by Doyle, Dane & Bernbach)
We'll take more care of you British Airways
Were you truly wafted here from Paradise? Nah! Luton Airport Campari (Lorraine Chase)
When you fancy a fruity treat, unzip a . . . Banana
When you've got it, flaunt it Braniff Airways
Where do you want to go today Microsoft
Which twin has the Toni? Toni Home Perms
Why does the man in the mask drink . . . Metz
Wodka from Warrington Vladivar
World's favourite airline British Airways
World's finest blade Wilkinson Sword
Wot a lot I got Smarties
Would you give me your last . . .? Rolo
You know what comes between me and my Calvins? Calvin Klein jeans (15-year-old Brooke Shields in 1980)
You'll look a little lovelier each day with fabulous pink Camay soap
You'll wonder where the yellow went .... when you brush your teeth with Pepsodent
You make it what it is BBC
You press the button, we do the rest Kodak
You too can have a body like mine Charles Atlas (Angelo Siciliano)
Your country needs you WW1 army recruitment poster (Kitchener pointing with right hand)
Your flexible friend Access credit card
You're never alone with a . . . Strand (coined by John May)

Television and Radio: Miscellaneous Information

advertisement: first Gibbs SR toothpaste.
advertisement: meerkat Aleksandr Orlov, a fictional anthropomorphic Russian meerkat, began his television appearances in January 2009. Voiced by Simon Greenall, the ad, on behalf of BGL Group, centred on the frustration that 'meerkat' sounded similar to 'market' so people continually visited his website looking for car insurance.
advertisement: shown after death Yul Brynner made anti-smoking advert with the message, 'Hullo, I'm dead; smoking killed me.'
Any Questions/Answers Presenters: Freddy Grisewood, David Jacobs.
Archers First broadcast on BBC on 1 January 1951, although first heard in the Midlands in 1950. The Archers lived on Brookfield Farm in Ambridge, just south of Borchester, Borsetshire. Weddings during the series have been recorded at Hanbury Church in Worcestershire. Princess Margaret as President of the NSPCC visited Ambridge for a fashion show (1984). Eddie Grundy got drunk in Britt Ekland's dressing room at Christmas pantomime (1992). Billing: Everyday story of country folk. Local pub: The Bull.

aspect ratio Normal: 4 x 3. Wide screen: 16 x 9.

BBC announcer: first Leslie Mitchell.

BBC Choice First new BBC channel for 34 years (Clive Anderson opened the proceedings on 23 September 1998).

BBC Director General: first Lord Reith.

BBC Director of Radio Helen Boaden

BBC1 Commenced broadcasting from Alexandra Palace in 1936.

BBC Radio controllers Radio 5 Live – Jonathan Wall; Radio 4 – Gwyneth Williams; Radio 3 – Roger Wright; Radio 2 – Bob Shennan; Radio 1 – Ben Cooper.

BBC Television controllers BBC1 – Charlotte Moore; BBC2 – Janice Hadlow; BBC3 – Zai Bennett; BBC4 – Richard Klein.

BBC Television Director General Tony Hall

BBC3 Digital station. Commenced 9 February 2003 and launched by Johnny Vaughan.

BBC2 Commenced 20 April 1964; mascots were Hullabaloo and Custard (two kangaroos).

Beyond Our Ken Billed as 'A sort of radio show' starred Kenneth Horne.

Brain of Britain Hosted by Robert Robinson and produced by Richard Edis. Questions set by Kevin Ashman (Jorkins). Winners: Martin Dakin (1954), Arthur Maddock (1955), Anthony Carr (1956), Rosemary Watson (1957), David Keys (1958), Dr Reginald Webster (1959), Patrick Bowing (1960), Irene Thomas (1961), Henry Button (1962), Ian Barton (1963), Ian Gillies (1964), Robert Crampsey (1965), Richard Best (1966), Lt Cmdr Loring (1967), Ralph Raby (1968), T D Thomson (1969), Ian Matheson (1970), Fred Morgan (1971), A Lawrence (1972), Glyn Court (1973), Roger Pritchard (1974), Winifred Lawson (1975), Thomas Dyer (1976), Martin Gostelow (1977), James Nesbitt (1978), Arthur Gerard (1979), Tim Paxton (1980), Peter Barlow (1981), John Pusey (1982), Sue Marshall (1983), Peter Bates (1984), Richard Fife (1985), Stephen Gore (1986), Ian Sutton (1987), Paul Monaghan (1988), Barbara Thompson (1989), Jim Eccleson (1990), Chris Wright (1991), Mike Billson (1992), Geoffrey Colton (1993), Ian Wynn-Mackenzie (1994), Ian Kinloch (1995), Kevin Ashman (1996), Daphne Fowler (1997), Guy Herbert (1998), Leslie Duncalf (1999), Mike Smith-Rawnsley (2000), Tom Corfe (2001), Dr David Jones (2002), Dave Steadman (2003), Alan Bennett (2004), Christopher Hughes (2005), Pat Gibson (2006), Mark Bytheway (2007), Geoff Thomas (2008), Ian Bayley (2009), Iwan Thomas (2010), Ray Ward (2011), Barry Simmons (2012).

Brains Trust The first panel were Julian Huxley, C E M Joad and Cmdr A B Campbell. The chairman was Donald McCullough, who was replaced by Gilbert Harding.

Breakfast Television Started 17 January 1983 (*BBC Breakfast Time*).

Broadcasting Standards Authority: first chairman Lord Rees Mogg.

***Byker Grove:* setting** Newcastle upon Tyne.

Carlton TV: fine Carlton Television was fined £2m for faking the documentary *The Connection*.

Channel 4 Started in 1982 (first programme: *Countdown*).

Channel 5 Launched on 30 March 1997 by Dawn Airey and the Spice Girls.

chefs on television See the *A to Z of British (and Irish) Popular Culture* for comprehensive list.

colour television Started in 1967.

Crookes Tube: function Produced cathode rays.

***Desert Island Discs:* first guest** Vic Oliver.

***Desert Island Discs:* presenters** Roy Plomley, Michael Parkinson, Sue Lawley, Kirsty Young.

digital television: advantages Traditional broadcasting is based on electronic signals that rise and fall to represent the shades of black, white and colour in the TV picture. The continuously varying signal is a direct analogue of the image it represents, just as the variations in the grooves of an LP, picked up by the stylus, are an analogue of the music. Analogue broadcasting is spendthrift in its use of the radio spectrum. There is a limited range of frequencies that can be used for TV transmissions, and each analogue station needs a healthy chunk of that space (approx 8 megahertz). Transmitters using the same frequency must be a long way apart, otherwise they interfere with one another, so transmitters closer than a few hundred kilometres to each other must employ different frequencies. As a result, it takes 44 frequencies in the UHF band to provide the four terrestrial channels. Digital broadcasting alters the rules. Instead of representing the image by a continuously variable signal, digital TV encodes it in the same language used by computers, a long stream of binary digits, or 'bits', each of which is either 0 or 1, a pulse or a non-pulse. It takes an enormous number of such bits to encode a TV picture, but it is easier to distinguish a pulse from a non-pulse than it is to discern the varying waveform of an analogue signal. This means that transmitters can be run at a much lower signal strength and still provide a decent picture. This in turn reduces the interference problem for terrestrial broadcasters so that better use can be made of the available frequencies, and picture quality is greatly improved. A full TV picture requires about 216 million bits per second but only the changes from one picture to the next are encoded so as to enable the data to fit into the frequency band

***Hamish Macbeth:* setting** Plockton, on the west coast of Scotland.

House of Lords: first televised 1985.

iconoscope: inventor Vladimir Zworykin (1923).

ITMA (It's That Man Again) Tommy Handley was the title character and Dorothy Summers played Mrs Mopp.

ITN newscaster: first Chris Chataway.

Just a Minute Chairman Nicholas Parsons. Panellists have included: Kenneth Williams, Derek Nimmo, Peter Jones, Clement Freud, Paul Merton, Graham Norton, Lance Percival and Sheila Hancock. The aim is to talk for one minute on a given topic without Hesitation, Deviation or Repetition.

Life with the Lyons Ben Lyon and Bebe Daniels and their children Barbara and Richard.

local radio stations Aire – Leeds, Arrow – Hastings, Beacon – Wolverhampton, BRMB – Birmingham, The Beach – Lowestoft, Broadland – Norwich, Cat – Cheltenham, Centre – Leicester, Chiltern – Luton/Bedford, City – Liverpool, Dream – Colchester, Hallam – Sheffield, Hereward – Peterborough, Kestrel – Basingstoke, Mercia – Coventry, Mercury – Crawley, Oak – Loughborough, Orwell – Ipswich, Pennine – Bradford, Piccadilly – Manchester, Ram – Derby, Silk – Macclesfield, Trent – Nottingham, 2CR – Bournemouth, Viking – Hull, West – Bristol, Wire – Warrington, Wish – Wigan, Wyvern – Hereford and Worcester.

Men from the Ministry, The Wilfrid Hyde Whyte (Roland Hamilton-Jones), Richard Murdoch (Richard Lamb).

Nielsens US equivalent of BARB showing American audience ratings.

OnDigital TV service 30-channel service launched by Ulrika Jonsson on 15 November 1998.

pirate radio station: first Radio Caroline, from 1964 to 1967.

radio play: caused panic Orson Welles's *War of the Worlds* broadcast in 1938.

radio stations: formerly called Radio 4 (Home), Radio 3 (Third), Radio 2 (Light). These were the three main stations. Radio 1 commenced in 1967.

Round Britain Quiz Hosted by Tom Sutcliffe. Former hosts: Gilbert Harding & Lionel Hale, Roy Plomley, Anthony Quinton, Gordon Clough, Nick Clarke.

satellite TV: reception areas Known as Footprints.

S4C: full name Sianel Pedwar Cymru.

SkyDigital Launched on 1 October 1998.

soap opera: first on television *The Appleyards* ran from 1952 to 1957 and is truly the first example of a televised British soap opera. The first adult British soap opera was *The Grove Family* (1954–7). The first daily soap opera was *Sixpenny Corner* (set in the new town of Springwood). This is another controversial area that requires careful attention. *The Appleyards* was shown fortnightly and was a children's soap, while *The Groves* was broadcast weekly and was for adults.

soap opera: why called Term derived from the American radio of the 1930s when soap and detergent companies sponsored the 15-minute daily radio programmes. Proctor and Gamble were a leading light in this field.

Steve Coogan creations Alan Partridge, Paul Calf, Pauline Calf, Tony Farino.

stripping Showing of programme at the same time every day of every week.

swear word: first to use Kenneth Tynan was the first to use the 'f' word on television.

Teletext BBC – Ceefax; ITV – Oracle.

television: inventor John Logie Baird created his first televisor, a contraption made from a tea-chest, a biscuit box and darning needles, in 1923, and gave a first public demonstration in 1926. In 1928 he produced a crude colour system.

television licences: first Licences were first issued in 1946 at £2 each. Cost of a colour licence since April 2010 is £145.50. Black and white is £49.

test card girl: famous Carol Hersey (billed as the most seen person on television).

TV am: launched by David Frost, Michael Parkinson, Robert Kee, Anna Ford, Angela Rippon.

***Twenty Questions:* presenters** Stewart McPherson, Gilbert Harding, Kenneth Horne, Cliff Michelmore.

***Twenty Questions:* mystery voice** Norman Hackforth.

Ulster TV: chairman John B McGuckian.

Ulster TV: location Havelock House, Belfast.

***Variety Playhouse:* MC** Vic Oliver.

weather Laura Greene, Ulrika Jonsson, Sian Lloyd, Trish Williamson (ITV), Ian McCaskill, Bill Giles, Suzanne Charlton, Helen Young, John Kettley, Peter Cockcroft, Michael Fish, Francis Wilson (BBC).

weather: hurricane announcement Michael Fish gave us the good news on 15 October 1987 that the person who rang up saying a hurricane was likely for tomorrow was completely wrong!

***Wogan:* appeared drunk on in 1990** George Best.

World Service Television BBC channel launched in 1991.

Transport: Aircraft

Chronology

1300 Marco Polo reports man-carrying kites in use in China.

1500 Leonardo da Vinci designs helicopters and ornithopters.

1709 A model hot-air balloon demonstrated by Father Laurenço de Gusmao at the court of King John V of Portugal (8 Aug.).

1783 First manned balloon flight by Pilâtre de Rozier and the marquis d'Arlandes in the Bois de Boulogne (21 Nov.). First flight of hydrogen balloon by Professor Jacques Charles (1 Dec.).

1784 First British balloon flight (4 Oct.).

1785 First crossing of the English Channel by balloon piloted by Jean-Pierre Blanchard and John Jeffries (7 Jan.).

1799 Sir George Cayley designs his first glider.

1810 Cayley publishes a paper on the theory of the airplane.

1843 The 'Steam Airplane' patented by William Samuel Henson.

1849 Cayley's 'Boy-Lifter' glider succeeds in lifting a small boy off the ground.

1852 Henri Giffard makes first semi-controlled powered flight in airship (24 Sept.).

1853 Cayley succeeds in making his coachman fly his glider.

1861 Balloons used by Union forces in American Civil War.

1870 Leon Gambetta escapes from a besieged Paris by balloon (7 Oct.).

1890 Clément Ader's *Eole* aircraft makes a short 'hop' near Paris (9 Oct.).

1891 Otto Lilienthal makes his first glider flight.

1894 Sir Hiram Maxim's biplane makes brief uncontrolled ascent (31 July).

1896 Otto Lilienthal dies after glider crash (10 Aug.).

1899 Glider pioneer Percy Pilcher dies following glider crash (2 Oct.).

1900 LZ1 makes first rigid airship flight (Count Zeppelin) (2 July).

1900 Wright brothers begin glider experiments (1 Dec.).

1903 Lebaudy airship makes first fully controlled flight in history (8 May). Samuel Langley's *Aerodrome* aircraft narrowly fails to make first powered flight (7 Oct.). Wright brothers make first powered flight (Orville at the controls) in *Flyer* (17 Dec.).

1906 Alberto Santos-Dumont makes first powered flight in Europe (23 Oct.). French company, Voisin Frères, established for the production of powered aircraft (Nov.).

1907 Breguet gyroplane makes first helicopter 'hop' (19 Sept.). Paul Cornu's helicopter makes first 'hop' (13 Nov.). Lt Thomas W Selfridge becomes first person killed in a plane crash when he and Orville Wright crash at Fort Meyer, Virginia (17 Sept.).

1908 Samuel Cody makes first powered flight in Britain (16 Oct.).

1909 Louis Blériot makes first flight across the English Channel (25 July).

1910 Harry Houdini, the celebrated escapologist and illusionist, makes the first successful flight on the Australian continent in a Voisin biplane (18 March).

1911 Eugene Ely lands Curtiss biplane on USS *Pennsylvania* (18 Jan.). First mail carried by air in UK (9 Sept.). First aerial warfare by Italian Army Aviation Corps over Libya (23 Oct.). Lt Giulio Gavotti makes the first air raid by dropping a 4½ lb bomb on Turks at Ain Zara (1 Nov.). Aircraft used in Mexican Revolution.

1912 Royal Flying Corps (RFC) formed (13 April). Death of Wilbur Wright (30 May). Bulgarian M Popoff becomes first pilot killed in warfare, during a reconnaissance flight (3 Nov.).

1914 Lts V Waterfall and C G G Bayley first British fliers killed in action (22 Aug.). Paris becomes the first capital city to be bombed from the air (30 Aug.). Japanese seaplanes attack the Austro-German fleet at Kiaochow, causing the first ship to be sunk from the air (17 Sept.). HMS *Ark Royal* becomes the world's first aircraft carrier (9 Dec.).

1915 LZ38 airship makes the first air raid on London (31 May). Flt Sub-Lt R A Warneford (VC) downs the LZ37, the first Zeppelin to be shot down (7 June). Katherine Stinson becomes first woman to loop the loop (18 July). Roland Garros is captured in Belgium (20 April). Garros was the first Frenchman to cross the Mediterranean by air, and working with Raymond Saulnier invented deflector plates to enable him to fire a machine gun through the propeller.

1916 Death of Ernst Mach (19 Feb.). Boeing formed as Pacific Aero Products Co (15 July). SL11 airship shot down in North London by Lt W Leefe-Robinson (VC) (2 Sept.). World's first flying bomb, the Hewitt-Sperry, built by Curtiss, is tested (12 Sept.). The airship ace Heinrich Mathy is killed when LZ72 is shot down over Potters Bar (2 Oct.). First British airline, Aircraft Transport &Travel Ltd, registered (5 Oct.).

1917 Baron von Richthofen awarded the 'Pour le Mérite' medal (16 Jan.). Death of Count von Zeppelin (8 March). Billy Mitchell became the first US Army officer to fly over German lines (24 April). Albert Ball killed in France (7 May), awarded posthumous VC (3 June). Sopwith Camel goes into service with Royal Flying Corps (RFC) in France (July). First flight of the Vickers Vimy (30 Nov.).

1918 Air Ministry established and Lord Rothermere is first Sec. of State for Air (2 Jan.). Royal Flying Corps and Royal Naval Air Service combine to create the Royal Air Force (1 April). Baron von Richthofen shot down (21 April). Hermann Goering takes over as leader of Richthofen's squadron (7 July). HMS *Furious*, adapted from cruiser to aircraft carrier, launched six Sopwith Camels against Zeppelin sheds (19 July). Peter Strasser, German commander of airships, shot down in L70 off Cromer (5 Aug.). Roland Garros killed when his SPAD XIII breaks up during a dogfight (5 Oct.). Handley Page 0/400 becomes first plane to fly from Egypt to India (12 Dec.).

1919 Britain's first scheduled air service inaugurated (10 May). US Navy Curtiss flying boat flown by Lt Cmdr Albert Read becomes first aircraft to fly the Atlantic (in stages) (27 May). Alcock and Brown make first non-stop crossing of the Atlantic in a Vickers Vimy (15 June). German Zeppelin fleet scuttled (23 June). First flight of Junkers F13, the first all-metal monoplane airliner (25 June). London's first airport opens at Hounslow Heath (1 July). British airship R34 makes first two-way Atlantic crossing (13 July). Edward Mannock, Britain's most successful ace, posthumously awarded VC (18 July). First flight over the Canadian Rockies by Capt. Ernest Hoy (7 Aug.). KLM founded (7 Oct.). Handley Page Transport provide first in-flight meals (11 Oct.). Ross and Keith Smith make first flight from Britain to Australia in a Vickers Vimy (10 Dec.) .

1920 First flight from Britain to South Africa (20 March). Croydon Airport begins operations, taking over from Hounslow (29 March). Juan de la Cierva is granted a patent for the Autogiro (27 Aug.). Dayton-Wright RB Racer aircraft flown with retractable landing gear. Qantas (Queensland and Northern Territory Aerial Services) founded (16 Nov.). First British airline disaster: Handley Page 0/400 crashes at Cricklewood, killing four (14 Dec.). Airline AT & T goes into liquidation (15 Dec.).

1921 First free flight of a helicopter since 1907, assisted by a balloon (15 Jan.). Orly aerodrome opened in Paris (1 March). Croydon Airport officially opened (31 March). Vickers Vernon, first troop-carrying aircraft, delivered to RAF (1 Aug.). First aerial crop-dusting takes place in Ohio, USA, by Lt John B Macready in a Curtiss JN6 (3 Aug.). Airship R38 crashes in Hull, killing many of Britain's most experienced airshipmen (24 Aug.).

1922 Formation of RAF reserve announced (9 Feb.). Jack Sanderson became first airline steward (2 April). First mid-air collision, between Farman Goliath and Daimler DH18, over Poix in northern France (7 April). First night flight by Grands Express from Le Bourget to Croydon (9 June). First air crossing of South Atlantic by S Cabral and G Coutinho of Portugal (16 June). Dr Albert Taylor and Leo Young make first successful detections of objects by radio observation (23 Sept.). QANTAS flies its first scheduled service, the first passenger being Mr A Kennedy (2 Nov.). First instance of skywriting 'Smoke Lucky Strikes' (28 Nov.).

1923 First public flight of Juan de la Cierva's Autogyro (9 Jan.). First drop tank used (Boeing MB-3A) (5 March). First air troop-transport took place during Kurdish uprising when 280 Sikhs were flown from Kingarban to Kirkuk (April). Etienne Ochmichen makes world's first helicopter closed-circuit flight (1 May). Amelia Earhart receives pilot's certificate from NAA, the first woman to do so (16 May). Sabena Airlines formed in Belgium (23 May). Formation of New Zealand Air Force (14 June). First flight of US airship *Shenandoah* (3 Sept.). Dixmunde disaster over the Mediterranean: 52 killed in airship explosion (21 Dec.).

1924 Royal Canadian Air Force formed (1 April). First sustained forward flight of a helicopter made by Etienne Ochmichen (14 April). Fleet Air Arm established (April). Start of first aeroplane flight round the world by Lts L H Smith and Erik Nelson (24 April–28 Sept.). Formation of Imperial Airways (28 April). First circumnavigation of Australia: Goble and McIntyre in a Fairey IIID (19 May). First flight around Japan: Goto and Yonezawa in a Kawanishi K-6 (31 July). First aerial circumnavigation by two Douglas world cruisers of the US Army Air Service: Smith and Arnold in *Chicago*, Nelson and Harding in *New Orleans* (28 Sept.).

1925 First production DH60 Moth delivered (21 July), maiden flight 22 Feb. First flight of M-17 ELLO, the first Messerschmitt aircraft (16 Aug.). *Shenandoah* breaks up in mid-air over Ohio; 29 dead (3 Sept.).

1926 Alan Cobham flies his DH-50 over Victoria Falls on the way to Cape Town (24 Jan.). Robert Goddard launches first liquid-fuelled rocket (16 March). Formation of Deutsche Luft Hansa A.G. (6 April). Richard G Byrd flies over North Pole in Fokker F.VII (9 May). Amundsen makes first flight over North Pole in an airship (14 May). US Army Air Service becomes US Army Air Corps (2 July). First aircraft launched and recovered by submarine, US *S-1* (28 July). Alan Cobham completes epic flight from London to Australia and back (1 Oct).

1927 Lindbergh makes first non-stop solo Atlantic crossing in *Spirit of St*

Louis (21 May). Lt Dick Bentley makes first solo flight from Britain to Cape Town (28 Sept.).

1928 Inauguration of Flying Doctor service in Australia (15 May). Nobile's *Italia* airship crashes in the Arctic (25 May). Charles Kingsford Smith flies Pacific in *Southern Cross* (9 June). Amelia Earhart becomes first woman to fly the Atlantic (as passenger 18 June). JAL formed in Japan (30 Oct.).

1929 Formation of LOT in Poland (1 Jan.). First scheduled passenger flight from London to India (6 April). First stowaway on transatlantic flight (journalist Arthur Shreiber, 14 June). *Graf Zeppelin* completes first circumnavigation of the globe (29 Aug.). Schneider Trophy retained by Britain, Flying Officer H R D Waghorn in Supermarine S-6B (7 Sept.). Testing of first wireless guidance system for aircraft (1 Oct.). R101 unveiled at Cardington (2 Oct.). First flight of R100 from Howden (16 Nov.).

1930 Whittle applies for patent for his turbojet (16 Jan.). Jack Northrop flies experimental 'Flying Wing', with tail boom (1 May). Ellen Church, a registered nurse from Iowa, became the first air hostess (15 May). Amy Johnson makes first solo flight to Australia by a woman (24 May). Formation of TWA (16 July). Death of Glen Curtiss (23 July). R101 receives Certificate of Airworthiness (2 Oct.). R101 crashes and explodes at Beauvais, France, on way to India (5 Oct.). First demonstration of Handley Page HP42 (17 Nov.).

1931 Iraqi airforce makes inaugural flight (8 April). Wiley Post makes flight around Northern Hemisphere in Lockheed Vega *Winnie Mae* (1 July). 400 mph barrier broken by Flt Lt George Stainforth in Supermarine SGB (29 Sept.). USS *Akron* aircraft carrier airship commissioned (2 Nov.).

1932 Asian mainland attacked from the air for the first time by Japanese bombers (26 Feb.). Aeroflot formed in Moscow (25 March). Amy Johnson and Jim Mollison announce their engagement (9 May). Amelia Earhart becomes first woman to fly Atlantic non-stop solo (21 May). Santos-Dumont commits suicide (23 July). First flight of Model 17, Beech Aircraft Corporation's first aircraft (4 Nov.).

1933 Maiden flight of Boeing 247 (8 Feb.). Formation of Indian airforce (1 April). French Armée de l'Air created (1 April). First flight over Everest (Westland PV3 piloted by marquis of Douglas and Westland Wallace piloted by David McIntyre (3 April). USS *Akron* crashes into the Atlantic off New Jersey; 70 killed (5 April). USS *Macon* (*Akron*'s replacement) commissioned (23 June). First flight of Douglas DC-1 (1 July). Air France inaugurated (31 Oct.).

1934 Deutsche Luft Hansa becomes Lufthansa (1 Jan.). First flight of Boeing P-26 (10 Jan.). DC-2 goes into service with TWA (11 May). De Havilland Comet wins England–Australia air race (24 Oct.).

1935 Amelia Earhart becomes first woman to fly the Pacific alone (12 Jan.). Death of Hugo Junkers (3 Feb.). USS *Macon* crashes into the sea off California (12 Feb.). Goering named as chief of the new Luftwaffe (10 March). First flight of Messerschmitt BF 109 (28 March). Swissair begins regular scheduled service to London (1 April). First flight of privately funded Bristol 142 (Blenheim) (12 April). Successful radar experiment in Suffolk (24 July). First flight of Boeing 299 (Flying Fortress) (28 July). Deaths of Wiley Post and Will Rogers in Alaskan air crash (15 Aug.). First flight of Hurricane (6 Nov.). Charles Kingsford Smith disappears over Indian Ocean (9 Nov.). First air traffic control centre opens in US (1 Dec.). First flight of Douglas DST (DC-3) (12 Dec.).

1936 Death of Billy Mitchell (19 Feb.). Maiden flight of *Hindenburg* (4 March). Supermarine Spitfire makes first flight piloted by Mutt Summers (5 March). Gatwick Airport officially opened (6 June). First flight of Westlander Lysander (10 June). First flight of Vickers Wellington (by Mutt Summers) (15 June). Formation of RAF Volunteer Reserve (30 July). Death of Blériot (8 Aug.). First Short Empire C-Class flying boat goes into service (30 Oct.). DC-2 crashes at Croydon killing 14 including Juan de la Cierva (9 Dec.).

1937 Saab established (2 April). First trials of Whittle's turbojet (13 April). Guernica bombed (26 April). *Hindenburg* explodes at Lakehurst; 36 killed (6 May). Death of R J Mitchell (11 June). Amelia Earhart disappears over the Pacific while attempting a round-the-world flight (navigator: Fred Noonan) (2 July).

1938 First in-flight refuelling of an airliner (Short Empire Flying Boat) (20 Jan.). Short-Mayo composite aircraft separates in flight for the first time (6 Feb.). First flight of Bell XP-3A Airacobra, the first US fighter to feature a cannon (6 April). First flight of Douglas DC-4 (7 June). Spitfire goes into RAF service (4 Aug.). Japanese aircraft shoot down a Chinese DC-2 airliner, the first civil airliner to be lost to hostile air attack (24 Aug.). First flight of Westland Whirlwind (11 Oct.). Germany launches its first aircraft carrier, *Graf Zeppelin* (8 Dec.). First flight of Boeing Stratoliner, the first pressurised airliner (31 Dec.).

1939 First flight of XP-38, Lockheed Lightning (27 Jan.). First flight of Mitsubishi Zero (1 April). Chain Home radar system goes online (4 April). First flight of Short Stirling (14 May). First flight of Focke-Wulf FW 190 (1 June). First flight of rocket-powered Heinkel He 176 at Peenemünde (20 June). Formation of Women's Auxiliary Air Force (28 June). First flight of Bristol Beaufighter (17 July). Formation of BOAC from British Airways and Imperial Airways (4 Aug.). First flight of jet aircraft, Heinkel He 178 (23 Aug.). RAF mobilised (1 Sept.). German paratroops make first-ever offensive parachute drop in Poland (3 Sept.). First 'bombing' raid (of leaflets) by RAF against Germany (4 Sept.). First 'kills' by RAF against German bombers (16 Oct.). First German bomber brought down on British soil since 1918 (28 Oct.). First flight of Heinkel He 177 (19 Nov.). First flight of Consolidated XB-24, Liberator (29 Dec.).

1940 First flight of Hawker Typhoon (24 Feb.). Sikorsky VS-300 helicopter makes first free flight (13 May). First flight of North American B-25 Mitchell (19 Aug.). First RAF raid on Berlin (25 Aug.). Caproni-Campini N.I. experimental jet makes first flight (28 Aug.). Battle of Britain Day; entire strength of RAF Fighter Command committed against Luftwaffe attack (15 Sept.). Eagle Squadron of RAF formed by US volunteer pilots at Church Fenton (19 Sept.). First flight of North American NA-73 (P-51 Mustang) (20 Oct.). First major Italian air raid on Britain (11 Nov.). 20 Fairy Swordfish from HMS *Eagle* and HMS *Illustrious* successfully attack Italian fleet at Taranto (12 Nov.). Coventry bombed (14 Nov.). First flight of DH 98 Mosquito (25 Nov.). First test flight of HS-293A guided bomb (18 Dec.).

1941 Death of Amy Johnson when her Airspeed Oxford crashes in Thames Estuary (5 Jan.). First flight of Avro Lancaster (9 Jan.). First flight of the Heinkel He 280, the world's first multi-jet aircraft (2 April). First flight of Republic P-47 Thunderbolt (6 May). Rudolf Hess parachutes into Scotland from a Messerschmitt Me110 (10 May). First British jet aircraft, a Gloster E-28/39, makes its maiden flight (15 May). Opening of Washington National Airport (16 June). First successful rocket assisted take-off in California (July). Heini Dittmar pilots a Messerschmitt Me 163A Komet at a speed of 623.85 mph (2 Oct.). Japanese attack Pearl Harbor (7 Dec.).

1942 Arthur Harris takes charge of Bomber Command (22 Feb.). First Lancaster mission (3 March). Doolittle raid against Japanese B 25s from USS *Hornet* (21 April). Battle of the Coral Sea (8 May). Battle of Midway (6 June). First flight of Grumman Hellcat (26 June). First flight of Me 262 jet fighter (18 July). First flight of Hawker Tempest (2 Sept.). First flight of B29 Super Fortress (21 Sept.). First flight of Bell XP-59 Airacomet, the first US jet aircraft (1 Oct.). Brabazon Committee (postwar airliners) established (23 Dec.).

1943 First flight of Gloster Meteor, the first British jet fighter (5 March). RAF breaches Mohne and Eder dams using 'bouncing' bomb designed by Barnes Wallis (16 May). Leslie Howard shot down in KLM DC-3 over the English Channel (1 June). First flight of Arado Ar 234, the world's first jet bomber (15 June). *Memphis Belle* becomes first B-17 to complete 25 missions in Europe (19 June). First use by RAF of 'Window', the strips of metal foil dropped to jam radar systems (24 July).

1944 First B29 raid (on Bangkok) (5 June). First V1 hits London (13 June). Marianas Turkey Shoot – Japanese lose 480 aircraft and 3 carriers (20 June). First use of napalm (by Lockheed Lightnings against Coutances, France (17 July). International Civil Aviation conference in Chicago; 52 countries attend. Gives rise to Chicago Convention (1 Nov.–7 Dec.). *Tirpitz* sunk by RAF Lancasters of 617 Squadron (12 Nov.). Glenn Miller disappears in a UC-64 over the English Channel (5 Dec.).

1945 22,000 lb Grand Slam, the heaviest bomb ever dropped, used successfully against the Bielefeld Viaduct (14 March). International Air Transport Association (IATA) formed in Havana (19 April). Atomic bomb tested at Alamogordo (16 July). Atomic bomb 'Little Boy' dropped on Hiroshima by B29 *Enola Gay* (6 Aug.). Atomic bomb 'Fat Man' dropped on Nagasaki by B29 *Bock's Car* (9 Aug.). First flight of turboprop-powered aircraft, a modified Gloster Meteor (20 Sept.). Absolute speed record taken to 606 mph by Gloster Meteor (7 Nov.).

1946 Civil Aviation Act establishes BOAC, BEA and BSAA (British South American Airways), their first commercial departure, made from London Heathrow, a BSAA Lancastrian (1 Jan.). First Pan-Am flight to London from New York (1 June). Air India formed from TATA airlines (29 July). Scandinavian Airline Systems (SAS) formed (31 July). First flight of Convair B-36 (8 Aug.). Aerolinee Italiane Internazionali (Alitalia) established (16 Sept.). Cathay Pacific Airways formed in Hong Kong (24 Sept.). First artificial snowstorm caused by cloud seeding (13 Nov.).

1947 Last DC-3 built by Douglas; it is sold to Sabena but on 2 March 1948 it crashes at Heathrow with loss of 19 lives. First round-the-world air service operated by Pan-Am (12 June). Kenneth Arnold sees nine aircraft moving 'as a saucer would if you skimmed it over the water' at high speed near Mt Rainier, Washington (24 June). First flight of Boeing Stratocruiser (8 July). Last DC-4 built by Douglas delivered to South African Airways (and still in service) (9 Aug.). USAF established as a separate armed service (18 Sept). Captain Charles Yeager becomes first man to break the sound barrier flying at Mach 1.015 at 42,0002 in Bell X-1 (14 Oct.). BEA makes last scheduled flight from Croydon Airport (1 Nov.). Hughes H-4 Hercules (*Spruce Goose*), the largest aircraft in the world, is flown for the first and only time by Howard Hughes, for one mile (2 Nov.).

1948 Death of Orville Wright (30 Jan.). Thirty killed when a Pan-Am Lockheed Constellation crashes near Shannon (15 April). First action by Israeli airforce (20 May). Start of Operation Vittles – the Berlin Airlift (26 June). Thirty-nine killed at Northolt when an RAF Avro York collides with an SAS DC-6 (4 July). First flight of Vickers Viscount (16 July). Idlewild Airport (now JFK) opens in New York (31 July). John Derry breaks sound barrier in UK in a DH 108 (6 Sept.). El Al comes into being (15 Nov.). Wright Flyer goes on display at the Smithsonian Institute (17 Dec.).

1949 Israeli airforce Messerschmitt 109s shoot down four RAF Spitfires near the Egyptian border (7 Jan.). First non-stop round-the-world flight completed by USAF B-50A *Lucky Lady II* (2 March). First flight of English Electric Canberra (13 May). First flight of De Havilland Comet, the world's first jet airliner (27 July). BOAC absorbs BSAA (30 July). First flight of Bristol Brabazon, largest aircraft ever built in Britain (4 Sept.).

1950 World's worst aircrash: 80 killed when Avro Tudor carrying rugby fans crashes in a field near Cardiff (12 March). First glider crossing of the English Channel (Lorne Welch, 12 April). HMS *Ark Royal* launched (3 May). First North Korean aircraft shot down in Korean war by Twin Mustang (27 June). First helicopter rescue of downed pilot behind enemy lines in Korea (4 Sept.). First flight of Lockheed Super Constellation (13 Oct.). Twenty-eight killed as BEA Viking crashes in fog at Heathrow (31 Oct.). World's first jet-against-jet dogfight, F-80 versus Mig-15, the F-80 being successful (8 Nov.). Bell Model 47 helicopters arrive at MASH units in Korea (1 Dec.).

1951 First non-stop unrefuelled crossing of Atlantic by jet, RAF Canberra (21 Feb.). First flight of Vickers Valiant (18 May). First in-flight refuelling under combat conditions in Korea (6 July). First in-flight sweeping of wings – Bell X-5 research aircraft (16 July). JAL reformed in Tokyo (1 Aug.). First flight of Supermarine Swift (5 Aug.). USAF orders nuclear-powered aircraft from Convair (5 Sept.). First mass movement of troops to battlefront by helicopter, in Korea (21 Sept.). Last DC-6 completed and delivered to Braniff Airways (2 Nov.). First flight of Gloster Javelin (26 Nov.). First interception of aircraft by missile at White Sands, New Mexico (27 Nov.). First turbine-engined helicopter, Kaman K-225, makes its maiden flight (10 Dec.). First airline flight over North Pole by Alaska Air (12 Dec.).

1952 First flight of Bristol type 173 twin rotor helicopter (3 Jan.). De Havilland Comet 1 gets first certificate of airworthiness for a jet airliner (22 Jan.). First flight of B-52 (15 April). First successful landing of an aircraft at the North Pole (USAF C-47) (3 May). First scheduled passenger jet service: BOAC Comet 1 from London (3 May). BOAC begins a weekly service from London to Colombo with Comet 1 (11 Aug.). First flight of Bristol Britannia (16 Aug.). First flight of Avro Vulcan (30 Aug.). John Derry and 28 spectators killed when his DH110 crashes at Farnborough (6 Sept.). First doubts about Comet safety after take-off accident in Rome (26 Oct.). First flight of Handley Page Victor (24 Dec.).

1953 Lufthansa revived in Germany (6 Jan.). BOAC Comet crashes near Calcutta killing 43 (2 May). First flight of DC-7 (18 May). Dan-Air established (21 May). 129 killed when USAF C-124 Globemaster II crashes on take-off in Japan (18 June). Neville Duke breaks absolute speed record (727.48 mph) in Hawker Hunter (7 Sept.).

1954 First flight of Lockheed Starfighter (7 Jan.). BOAC Comet *Yoke Peter* crashes off Elba, killing 35 (10 Jan.). Last operational flight of a RAF Spitfire (1 April). South African Airways Comet crashes off Stromboli (8 April). Churchill orders the grounding of all Comets (12 April). First flight of Jet Provost (26 June). First flight of Boeing Model 367-80, prototype of the 707 (15 July). First flight of the Rolls Royce Thrust Measuring Rig, 'The Flying Bedstead' (3 Aug.). First flight of Lockheed Hercules (23 Aug.). Court of Inquiry into Comet crashes concludes that metal fatigue is to blame (19 Oct.).

1955 Pakistan International Airlines (PIA) established (10 Jan.). First operational departure from the central complex at Heathrow (17 April). Fifty-eight killed when a Lockheed Constellation of El Al is shot down by Bulgarian Airforce Mig-15s near the Greek border (27 July). First flight of Republic Thunderchief (22 Oct.). Forty-four killed aboard a United Airlines DC-6B after it blows up in mid-air. It is subsequently proven that the explosion was caused by a bomb, planted to perpetrate an insurance fraud. (Arthur Hailey's *Airport* was based on this incident) (1 Nov.). First flight of Fokker Friendship (24 Nov.).

1956 Death of Lord Trenchard (10 Feb.). Peter Twiss flies Fairey Delta 2 at 1,131.76 mph to take official airspeed record (10 March). First flight of Dassault Super Mystère (15 May). 128 killed when a United Airlines DC-3 collides with a TWA Constellation over the Grand Canyon (30 June). First flight of Fiat G-91 (9 Aug.). First human flight over 100,0002: Iven Kincheloe in Bell X-2 (125,9072) (7 Sept.). Luftwaffe re-established (24 Sept.). First flight of Convair B-58 Hustler (11 Oct.). UK's first atomic bomb dropped in Australia (11 Oct.). Last RAF Lancaster retired (15 Oct.). First aircraft landing at the South Pole: US Navy R4D-5 Skytrain *Que Sera Sera* (31 Oct.). First flight of Dassault Mirage III (17 Nov.).

1957 World's first long-haul airliner, Bristol Britannia, enters service with BOAC (1 Feb.). Death of Richard Byrd (12 March). First flight of Short SC-1 (2 April). UK's first hydrogen bomb dropped near Christmas Island (15 May). First flight of Fairey Rotodyne (6 Nov.). First flight of Boeing 707 (production model) (21 Dec.).

1958 Death of Ernst Heinkel (Jan.). Munich air crash: seven Manchester Utd players killed (6 Feb.). First flight of De Havilland Comet 4 (27 April). First flight of Blackburn Buccaneer (30 April). First flight of McDonnell F-4 Phantom (27 May). First flight of DC-8 (30 May). New Gatwick Airport opens (9 June). First flight of Westland Wessex (20 June). Death of Henri Farman (17 July). NASA created (29 July). Last flying boat operations in UK (Aquila Airways: Southampton to Madeira) (30 Sept.). First jet airliner on Atlantic route (BOAC Comet 4: London–New York–London) (4 Oct.). Last DC-6 built delivered to JAT (Jugoslavian Airlines) (17 Nov.). First production Fokker Friendship delivered to Aer Lingus (29 Nov.).

1959 First flight of A.W. Argosy (8 Jan.). First flight of Convair 880 (27 Jan.). Buddy Holly, Richie Valens and the Big Bopper killed when their Beechcraft Bonanza crashes in Mason City, Iowa (3 Feb.). First flight of Alouette III (28 Feb.). First scheduled passenger flight of Sud-Aviation Caravelle (6 May). Last operational flight of RAF Sunderland (15 May). First flight of X-15 (8 June). First flight of Mirage IV A (17 June). First flight of Northrop F-5 (30 July). Jacqueline Auriol becomes first woman to exceed Mach 2 (in Mirage III) (26 Aug.). Croydon Airport closed (30 Sept.). De Havilland merges with Hawker Siddeley (17 Dec.).

1960 First flight of Grumman A-6 Intruder (19 April). Gary Powers shot down in Lockheed U-2 over Siberia (1 May). Captain Joseph Kittinger free-falls from 102,8002 to 17,5002, the highest parachute jump ever (16 Aug.). First flight of Hawker P-1127 (prototype of Harrier) (21 Oct.). 132 killed when TWA Super Constellation and United DC-8 collide over New York (16 Dec.).

1961 Seventy-three killed when Sabena 707 crashes in Brussels (15 Feb.). VIASA begins operations in Caracas (1 April). Yuri Gagarin becomes first man in space (12 April). X-15 flown at 3,074 mph and 105,1002 by Major Robert White (21 April). Alan Shepherd becomes first US astronaut (5 May). First flight across the Channel by VTOL aircraft, Short SC-1 (27 May). First flight of Aviation Traders ATL-98 Carvair (21 June). Air Congo established (28 June). First flight of Handley Page HP-115 (17 Aug.). Mirage III jet slices through a cable car wire killing six at Chamonix (30 Aug.). Dag Hammarskjöld's DC-6B crashes near Ndola, Northern Rhodesia (18 Sept.).

1962 First flight of Hawker Siddeley Trident (9 Jan.). First use of Agent Orange in defoliant raids in SE Asia (12 Jan.). First US helicopter shot down in Vietnam (4 Feb.). 111 killed when British Caledonian DC-7C crashes at Douala, Cameroon (4 Mar). First flight of Bristol T-188 (14 April). Death of Sir Frederick Handley Page (21 April). First flight of A-12 (prototype of SR-71 Blackbird) (26 April). 130 killed when Air France 707 crashes at Orly (3 June). Air France 707 crashes in Guadeloupe, killing 113 (21 June). X-15A flies at 4,159 mph (27 June). First flight of Vickers VC-10 (29 June). X-15 goes into space: Major Robert White flies it to 314,7502, earning himself 'Astronauts' Wings' (17 July). First flight of HS 125 (13 Aug.). First flight of Aerospace Lines 'Pregnant Guppy' (19 Sept.).

1963 First reference to Anglo-French supersonic airliner as 'Concorde', in speech by De Gaulle (13 Jan.). First flight of Boeing 727 (2 Feb.). BEA introduces first stand-by fares (1 April). Last RAF Mosquitoes retired (8 May). First flight of BAC III (20 Aug.). First flight of HS-748 (21 Dec.). Idlewild Airport renamed John F. Kennedy (24 Dec.).

1964 First flight of Short Belfast (5 Jan.). Death of Maurice Farman (25 Feb.). Jerrie Mock completes first solo aerial circumnavigation by a woman (17 April). VC-10 enters airline service (29 April). First flight of BAC 221 (Concorde research aircraft) (1 May). Actor Roger Moore becomes Air France's 8,000,000th passenger (21 May). First flight of North American XB-70 Valkyrie (21 Sept.). First flight of BAC TSR2 (27 Sept.). First flight of General Dynamics F-111 (21 Dec.). First flight of Lockheed SR-71 (22 Dec.).

1965 First flight of Mirage III V-01 (VTOL aircraft) (12 Feb.). First flight of Douglas DC-9 (25 Feb.). TSR2 cancelled by Wilson government (6 April). Death of Sir Geoffrey De Havilland (26 May).

1966 Four hydrogen bombs fall from a B-52 over southern Spain following a collision with KC-135 tanker; all four are recovered (17 Jan.). Laker Airways launched (8 Feb.). France leaves NATO (7 March). Death of Sir Sydney Camm (12 March). North American XB-70 crashes after colliding with a chase aircraft (8 June). Sheila Scott completes first round-the-world solo flight by a British woman (20 June). X-15 flies at 4,250 mph (Mach 6.33) (18 Nov.).

1967 First flight of Saab 37 Viggen (8 Feb.). Wrecked oil tanker the *Torrey Canyon* bombed by RAF and Royal Navy aircraft (18 March). First flight of Boeing 737 (9 April). First flight of HS Nimrod (23 May). DC-4 charter plane crashes in the Pyrenees, killing 88 (3 June). British Midland Argonaut crashes at Manchester, killing 72 (4 June). Six-day war begins with Israeli air strikes against Egypt, Syria and Jordan (5 June). X-15 attains its fastest speed, 4,534 mph (Mach 6.72), flown by Major William Knight (3 Oct.).

1968 Last Handley Page Hastings retires from RAF (5 Jan.). Yuri Gagarin is killed when his Mig-15 crashes near Moscow (27 March). 121 survive crash of BOAC 707 at Heathrow (8 April). Last Avro Anson retires from RAF after 32 years (28 June). First flight of Sepecat Jaguar (8 Sept.). First flight of TU-144 'Concordski' (31 Dec.).

1969 First flight of Boeing 747 (9 Feb.). First flight of Concorde (001 at Toulouse) (2 March). First flight of Concorde (002 in UK) (9 April). RAF Strike Command formed from Bomber and Fighter Command (30 April). Concorde goes supersonic for the first time (1 Oct.). Nigeria Airways VC-10 crashes in the jungle; 87 killed (20 Nov.).

1970 First wide-bodied airliner landing at Heathrow (Boeing 747 of Pan-Am) (12 Jan.). Death of Mikhail Mil (31 Jan.). Death of Lord Hugh Dowding (15 Feb.). Last Dakota retires from RAF service (4 April). Tullamarine Airport in Melbourne opens (1 July). First flight of McDonnell Douglas DC-10 (29 Aug.). Black September blow up TWA 707, Swissair DC-8 and BOAC VC-10 at Dawson's Field, and a Pan-Am 747 at Cairo (12 Sept.). Concorde 002 lands at Heathrow (13 Sept.). Concorde 001 flies at Mach 2 (4 Nov.). First flight of Lockheed Tristar (16 Nov.). Death of Artem Mikoyan (15 Dec.). Airbus Industrie formally established (18 Dec.). Jeanne M Holm becomes first USAF female general (31 Dec.).

1971 Four members of the Red Arrows killed when two Folland Gnats collide at RAF Kemble (20 Jan.). London Air Traffic Control Centre opens at West Drayton (31 Jan.). First flight of Westland Lynx (21 March). Federal Express founded (17 April). Southwest Airlines begin operations (18 June). 162 killed when ANA Boeing 707 collides with a fighter in Japan (30 July). DC-10 enters airline service (5 Aug.). Civil Aviation Authority established in London (5 Aug.). First flight of Shackleton AEW (30 Sept.). BEA Vanguard breaks up over Belgium; 55 killed (2 Oct.). D B Cooper successfully hijacks a Northwest Boeing 727, demands $200,000 and escapes by parachute (24 Nov.).

1972 President Nixon announces that the space shuttle will be developed (5 Jan.). British Airways Board takes over BOAC, BEA and their subsidiaries (1 April). Lockheed Tristar enters airline service (26 April). First fly-by-wire in the USA: Phantom II (29 April). First flight of Fairchild A-10 (10 May). Japanese terrorists kill 25 at Lod Airport (30 May). 118 killed at Staines when BEA Trident crashes after take-off, Britain's worst air disaster until Lockerbie (18 June). First flight of McDonnell Douglas F15 Eagle (27 July). Ilyushin IL-62 crashes in Berlin; 156 killed (14 Aug.). Prince William of Gloucester is killed when his Piper Cherokee crashes during the Goodwood Trophy air race at Wolverhampton (28 Aug.). Death of Igor Sikorsky (26 Oct.). Death of Andrei Tupolev (23 Dec.).

1973 Libyan Airlines 727 shot down by Israeli fighters over Sinai; 74 killed (21 Feb.). TU-144 crashes at the Paris Air Show following mid-air breakup; 14 killed (3 June). 123 die at Orly when a Varig 707 burns after an emergency landing (11 July). Death of Sir Alan Cobham (21 Oct.). First flight of Dassault-Bregeu Dornier Alpha jet (26 Oct.).

1974 First flight of General Dynamics F-16 (2 Feb.). Last Comet in airline service retires (12 Feb.). World's worst air disaster: 346 killed when a Turkish Airlines DC-10 crashes near Paris (worst until 27 March 1977) (3 March). Airbus A300 enters airline service (23 May). Death of Charles Lindbergh (26 Aug.). First flight of Panavia Tornado (14 Aug.). Fifty-nine killed when Lufthansa 747 crashes in Nairobi, the first ever 747 crash (20 Nov.). First flight of Rockwell B-1 Bomber (23 Dec.).

1975 Death of Air Chief Marshal Sir Keith Park (6 Feb.). Death of Adrienne Bolland (18 March). First flight of DHC Dash 7 (27 March). US helicopters airlift last personnel from embassy roof in Saigon (30 April). First flight of Boeing 747 SP (4 July). Last Lockheed Constellation in airline service retires (16 July). Concorde becomes first aircraft to make four Atlantic crossings in one day (1 Sept.). Graham Hill killed when his aircraft crashes near Elstree (29 Nov.).

1976 First commercial flight of Concorde (Paris–Rio and London–Bahrain) (21 Jan.). Death of Howard Hughes (5 April). Air France and British Airways Concordes land together at Dulles Airport, Washington (24 May). Israeli commandos rescue over 100 passengers from Palestinian terrorists at Entebbe, Uganda (4 July). Viktor Belenko defects to the West in a Mig-25 in Japan (6 Sept.). Worst ever mid-air collision: 176 killed when BA Trident and Yugoslav DC-9 collide over Croatia (10 Sept.).

1977 Death of Sergei Ilyushin (7 Feb.). World's worst ever aircraft disaster: two 747s (KLM and Pan-Am) collide on the ground in Tenerife, 575 killed (27 March). Death of Werner von Braun (16 June). Rockwell B-1 cancelled by President Carter (30 June). First gliding flight of space shuttle *Enterprise* (released from 747) (13 Aug.). Bryan Allen flies *Gossamer Condor*, the first successful man-powered aircraft (23 Aug.). Freddie Laker launches his Skytrain service from London to New York (26 Sept.). GSG 9 successfully storm a hijacked Lufthansa 737 at Mogadishu; 86 saved (17 Oct.).

1978 213 killed when Air India Boeing 747 explodes in mid-air over Bombay (1 Jan.). British Aerospace takes control of British Aircraft Corporation, Hawker Siddeley and Scottish Aviation (1 Jan.). Narita Airport opens in Tokyo amid environmental protests (22 May). First crossing of Atlantic by balloon: *Double Eagle II* (17 Aug.). Death of German aircraft engineer Willy Messerschmitt (15 Sept.). Collision between Pacific Southwest 727 and Cessna in San Diego; 144 killed (25 Sept.). Icelandair DC-8 crashes in Sri Lanka; 202 killed (16 Nov.).

1979 All DC-10 aircraft grounded following crash at Chicago on 25 May which killed 279 (6 June). Bryan Allen flies man-powered aircraft, *Gossamer Albatross*, across the Channel (13 June). Death of Emile Dewoitine (5 July). Death of Sir Barnes Wallis (30 Oct.). 257 killed in Antarctica when Air New Zealand DC-10 crashes near Mt Erebus (29 Nov.).

1980 Air UK formed from British Island Airways and Air Anglia (16 Jan.). Air Zimbabwe created from Air Rhodesia (18 April). Operation Eagle Claw aborted in Iranian desert following collision of CH-53 helicopter with Hercules transport. The operation was intended to free US hostages in Tehran (25 April). HMS *Ark Royal* makes its final voyage, to the breakers yard (22 Sept.). Last commercial flight of Comet 4, a round trip for enthusiasts (9 Nov.).

1981 Last Boeing 707 in Pan-Am service retires (3 Jan.). Death of Donald Douglas (1 Feb.). Death of Jack Northrop (18 Feb.). First flight of Rockwell Space Shuttle *Columbia* (12 April). Israeli airforce bombs Iraqi nuclear reactor at Osirak (7 June). Gulf of Sirte/Sidra incident: two US Navy F-14s shoot down two Libyan SU-22s (19 Aug.). First flight of Boeing 767 (26 Sept.). First flight of Hughes Notar helicopter, i.e. No Tail Rotor (17 Dec.).

1982 Eighty killed when Air Florida 737 crashes into the icy Potomac River in Washington, after wings ice up before take-off (13 Jan.). First flight of Boeing 757 (19 Feb.). First flight of Airbus A310 (3 April). RAF Vulcans take part in the longest bombing runs in history (7,860 miles) from Ascension Island against targets in the Falklands (April–May). Braniff International Airlines files for bankruptcy (13 May). Last Boeing 707 in British Airways service retires (24 May). Last Boeing 707 in Air France service retires (28 Oct.). Last British V-Bomber Squadron disbanded (21 Dec.).

1983 269 killed when a Soviet SU-15 shoots down a Korean Airlines 747 over Sakhalin Island (2 Sept.).

1984 Inaugural flight of Virgin Atlantic Airways (22 June). Last Boeing 727 completed (14 Aug.). First flight of ATR 42 feeder airliner (16 Aug.). First flight of Rockwell B-1B (18 Oct.). First flight of MD-83 (17 Dec.).

1985 TWA 727 hijacked in Rome by AMAL guerrillas; all bar one of the hostages are subsequently released (15 June). 329 killed after an Air India 747 explodes over the Atlantic en route to London (23 June). 520 when JAL 747 crashes into a mountain in Japan (13 Aug). Fifty-four killed at Manchester when a British Airtours 737 catches fire (22 Aug.).

1986 Armed police begin patrolling Heathrow Airport (8 Jan.). *Challenger* disaster: all seven crew are killed when space shuttle explodes shortly after launch (28 Jan.). Terminal 4 opens at Heathrow (12 April). USAF F-IIIs execute air strikes against targets in Libya (15 April). Death of Marcel Bloch (18 April). BA privatised (21 Oct.). Forty-five killed when a BA Chinook ferrying oil workers crashes in the Shetlands (6 Nov.). Dick Rutan and Jeana Yeager fly around the world non-stop and unrefuelled, in specially designed aircraft *Voyager* (23 Dec.).

1987 First flight of Airbus A320 (22 Feb.). Last airworthy Bristol Blenheim crashes at Denham (21 June). BAA privatised (16 July). Richard Branson and Per Lindstrand complete first hot-air balloon crossing of the Atlantic (3 July). BA takes over British Caledonian (16 July). BA takes on first female pilots (31 Oct.). London City Airport opens (5 Nov.).

1988 First ever aircraft registration number retired by FAA, i.e. Amelia Earhart's Lockheed Electra which vanished in July 1937 (8 Feb.). North Terminal opens at Gatwick Airport (18 March). First flight of 'Super-Jumbo' Boeing 747-400 (29 April). Airbus A320 crashes in trees at Mulhouse air show; four killed (26 June). 290 killed when USS Vincennes shoots down Iranian Airbus (3 July). Thirty-three killed at Ramstein when Frecce Tricolori (Italian National Aerobatic Team) aircraft collide above spectators at air show (28 Aug.). Death of Sheila Scott (20 Oct.). F-117A Stealth aircraft formally unveiled by USAF (10 Nov.). Lockerbie disaster: 270 killed after bomb causes Pan-Am Jumbo to crash on houses; worst air disaster in British history (21 Dec.).

1989 Thirty-two killed when British Midland 737 crashes on to the M1 at Kegworth (8 Jan.). First flight of Northrop B-2 Spirit Flying Wing Stealth Bomber (17 July). 107 killed at Sioux City, Iowa, when United Airlines DC-10 crashes on landing (19 July). Death of Alexander Yakovlev (22 Aug.). Bell/Boeing Vertol V-22 Osprey tilt rotor aircraft makes first transition to level flight (14 Sept.).

1990 First flight of Northrop/McDonnell Douglas YF-23 (subsequently dropped in favour of Lockheed YF-22) (27 Aug.). First flight of Rockwell/MBB X-31A low-speed experimental aircraft (11 Oct.). United Airlines takes over Pan-Am's London routes (23 Oct.). Osaka Airport opens in Japan (9 Nov.).

1991 First Boeing 727 retires after 27 years with United Airlines (13 Jan.). Air Europe, based at Gatwick Airport, ceases to operate (17 Jan.). Operation Desert Storm makes large-scale use of Stealth aircraft for the first time (Jan.). First scheduled United Airlines flight to London (4 April). Boeing finally ends production of 707 after 37 years (1 Sept.). First flight of McDonnell Douglas C-17 (15 Sept.). First flight of Airbus A-340 (25 Oct.). First MD-11 delivered (to Finnair) (29 Nov.). Pan-Am ceases operations (4 Dec.).

1992 TWA announces that it is bankrupt (11 Jan.). Piper declared bankrupt (1 April). Plans for MD-12 (4-engine, 600-seat airliner) announced (30 April). BAA announces plans for Terminal 5 at Heathrow (12 May).

1995 First Boeing 777 begins operations at Heathrow (United Airlines) (July).

2003 Air France announces it is to chop its fleet of Concordes on 31 May while British Airways closes down its fleet of seven Concordes at the end of October.

2005 A Boeing 777-200 LR Worldliner completes a 13,422 mile flight across the Pacific in 22 hrs 42 mins, the longest non-stop flight ever.

2008 A new terminal in the shape of a dragon with a ball opens at Beijing Airport, the largest in the world.

2009 Airbus A320 crash lands in the Hudson River after Capt Chesley Sullenberger reports a 'double bird strike'. All 155 passengers are saved.

2010 First Solar Impulse aircraft, HB-SIA, capable of flying both day and night makes its first flight in Payerne, Switzerland charging its batteries in flight.

2011 Space Shuttles - NASA's crewed, partially reusable low Earth orbital spacecraft - operational since 1981, fly for the last time.
KLM becomes the first airline in the world to provide flights using biofuel.

2012 Slovenian pilot Matevž Lenarčič completes a 62,000-mile (99,839-km) solo round-the-world flight in a Pipistrel Virus SW914 ultra-light aircraft.

2013 American Airlines and US Airways announce a merger, creating the world's largest airline, with 900 planes, 3,200 daily flights, and 95,000 employees

Airports: UK

Airport	Location
Aldergrove	Belfast
Ballasalla	Isle of Man
Baltasound	Unst, Shetlands
Barton	Manchester
Benbecula	Hebrides
Birmingham	Solihull
Blackbushe	Camberley
Booker	Wycombe, Bucks
Bournemouth	Dorset
Brize Norton	Oxford (RAF Station)
Brough	East Yorkshire
City	Belfast
City	London
Compton Abbas	Dorset
Conington	Peterborough
Coventry	West Midlands
Dalcross	Inverness
Dyce	Aberdeen
East Midlands	Derbyshire
Eday	Orkneys
Eglinton	Londonderry
Exeter	Devon
Fair Isle	Shetlands
Filton	Bristol
Flotta	Orkneys
Gatwick	West Sussex
Glasgow	Glasgow
Glenegedale	Islay
Goodwood	Chichester
Grimsetter	Orkney
Hatfield	Hertfordshire
Heathrow	London
John Lennon (formerly Speke)	Liverpool
Kidlington	Oxford
Kirkwall	Orkneys
Leeds Bradford	West Yorkshire
Leuchars	Fife (RAF Station)
Linley Hill	Beverley
Lulsgate	Bristol
Lydd	Ashford, Kent
Manchester (formerly Ringway)	Manchester
Manston	Kent
North Bay	Barra, Hebrides
North Denes	Great Yarmouth
North Ronaldsay	Orkneys
Papa Westray	Orkneys
Port Ellen	Islay, Hebrides
Prestwick	Ayrshire
Rhoose	Cardiff
Robin Hood	Doncaster
Roborough	Plymouth
Ronaldsway	Isle of Man
St Angelo	Enniskillen, Fermanagh
St Just	Land's End
St Mary's	Scilly Isles
Sanday	Orkneys
Sandown	Isle of Wight
Scatsa	Shetlands
Scone	Perth
Shoreham	East Sussex
Sibson	Peterborough
Silverstone	Northants
Southampton	Hampshire
Stansted	NE London
Stapleford	Essex
Staverton	Gloucestershire
Stornoway	Hebrides
Stronsay	Orkneys
Sumburgh	Shetlands
Sywell	Northampton
Teeside	Cleveland
Tingwall	Lerwick, Shetlands
Tiree	Hebrides
Tresco	Scillies
Turnhouse	Edinburgh
Unst	Shetlands
Walney Island	Barrow, Cumbria
West Freugh	Dumfries
West Midlands	Birmingham
Westray	Orkneys
Whalsay	Shetlands
Wick	Caithness
Wickenby	Lincolnshire
Woodford	Greater Manchester
Woodvale	Merseyside (RAF Station)
Yeovilton	Somerset (private airfield)

Airlines

Name	*Country*
ACES	Colombia
Aer Lingus	Ireland
Aeroflot	Russia
Aerolineas	Argentina
Air Asia	Malaysia
Air Littoral	France
Air Niugini	PNG
Air UK	UK(Stansted)
Alia	Jordan
Alitalia	Italy
American Airlines	USA
ANA	All Nippon Airways
Augusta Airways	Australia
Avianca	Colombia
Bell-Air	New Zealand
Britannia	UK (Luton)
British Airways	UK
Cargolux	Luxembourg
Cathay Pacific	Hong Kong
Cebo Air	Philippines
Continental	USA
Coyne	UK(Stansted)
CP Air	Canada
Crossair	Switzerland
CSA	Czech Republic
Delta Airlines	USA
DETA	Mozambique
Dragonair	Hong Kong
Eastern Airlines	USA
El Al	Israel
Eva Air	Taiwan
Flitestar	South Africa
Frontie Airlines	USA
Garuda	Indonesia
Gronlandsfly	Greenland
Gulf Air	Bahrain
Iberia	Spain
Interflug	Germany
JAL	Japanese Airlines
JAT	Yugoslavia
Jet	India (Mumbai)
Jetstar Asia	Singapore
KLM	Netherlands
Kyrnair	Corsica
Ladeco	Chile
LAP	Paraguay
Linjeflyg	Sweden
LOT	Poland
Lufthansa	Germany
Malev	Hungary
Maskargo	Malaysia
NFD	Germany
Norontair	Canada
Northwest Airlines	USA
Olympic	Greece
Pan-Am	USA
PIA	Pakistan
Qantas	Australia
Republic Airlines	USA
RyanAir	Ireland
Sabena	Belgium
Sansa	Costa Rica
SAS	Denmark, Norway, Sweden
TAP	Portugal
THY	Turkey
Tiger Airways	Singapore
Tower Air	USA
Transavia Airlines	Netherlands
Transworld Airlines	USA
United Airlines	USA
United Airways	Bangladesh
Varig	Brazil
VIASA	Venezuela
Virgin	UK (Gatwick)
Western Airlines	USA

Airport Codes

Code	Airport	Location
ABD	Abadan	Iran
ABJ	Abidjan	Ivory Coast
ABS	Abu Simnel	Egypt
ABZ	Aberdeen	Scotland
ACE	Arecife	Lanzarote
ACI	Alderney	Channel Islands
ACK	Nantucket, MA	USA
ACT	Waco, Texas	USA
ADD	Addis Ababa	Ethiopia
AGP	Malaga	Spain
AKL	Auckland	New Zealand
ALC	Alicante	Spain
ALH	Albany, WA	Australia
ALP	Aleppo	Syria
ALY	Alexandria	Egypt
AMA	Amarillo, Texas	USA
ANR	Antwerp	Belgium
ASD	Andros	Bahamas
AUH	Abu Dhabi	UAE
BBQ	Barbuda	Leeward Isles
BEB	Benbecula	Scotland
BEY	Beirut	Lebanon
BFS	Belfast	N. Ireland
BGO	Bergen	Norway
BHX	Birmingham	England
BJL	Bangui	Gambia
BKK	Bangkok	Thailand
BKO	Bamako	Mali
BLZ	Blantyre	Malawi
BRN	Berne	Switzerland
BSL	Basle	Switzerland
BTZ	Bursa	Turkey
BUH	Bucharest	Romania
BXO	Bissau	Guinea-Bissau
BZV	Brazzaville	Congo
CAJ	Cairo	Egypt
CCS	Caracas	Venezuela
CCU	Calcutta	India
CDG	Charles de Gaulle	Paris
CER	Cherbourg	France
CFN	Donegal	Eire
CFR	Caen	France
CFU	Kerkyra	Greece
CHC	Christchurch	New Zealand
CMN	Casablanca	Morocco
CPT	Cape Town	South Africa
CXI	Christmas Island	Kiribati
DCA	Washington	USA
DLH	Duluth	Minnesota
DOL	Deauville	France
DTM	Dortmund	Germany
DUD	Dunhedin	New Zealand
DUS	Düsseldorf	Germany
DXB	Dubai	UAE
DYU	Dushanbe	Tadzhikstan
EGC	Bergerac	France
EVN	Yerevan	Armenia
EWR	Newark, NJ	USA
EYW	Key West	Florida
FAO	Faro	Portugal
FBU	Fornebu	Oslo
FCO	Fiumicino	Rome
FIE	Fair Isle	Scotland
FIH	Kinshasa	Dem Rep. of Congo
FNA	Freetown	Sierra Leone
FNC	Funchal	Madeira Islands
FNI	Nîmes	France
FRA	Frankfurt	Germany
GBE	Gaborone	Botswana
GCI	Guernsey	UK
GNB	Grenoble	France
GOA	Genoa	Italy
GOH	Nuuk (Godthaab)	Greenland
GOI	Goa	India
GPS	Galapagos Isles	Ecuador
HAJ	Hanover	Germany
HBA	Hobart	Tasmania
HDO	Hyderabad	Pakistan
HFA	Haifa	Israel
HKT	Phuket	Thailand
HLZ	Hamilton	New Zealand
HND	Haneda	Tokyo
HYD	Hyderabad	India
IAD	Dulles International	Washington
IBZ	Ibiza	Spain
IEV	Kiev	Ukraine
IOM	Isle of Man	UK
IOR	Inishmore	Eire
IPC	Easter Island	Chile
JDH	Jodhpur	India
JFK	John F. Kennedy	New York
JNU	Juneau	Alaska
JRS	Jerusalem	Israel
KEF	Keflavik	Iceland
KEL	Kiel	Germany
KHI	Karachi	Pakistan
KLU	Klagenfurt	Austria
KRK	Krakow	Poland
KTP	Kingston	Jamaica
KTW	Katowice	Poland
KUL	Kuala Lumpur	Malaysia
LAS	McCarran	Las Vegas
LAX	Los Angeles	California
LCA	Larnaca	Cyprus
LEH	Le Havre	France
LFW	Lomé	Togo
LGW	Gatwick	London
LHE	Lahore	Pakistan
LHR	Heathrow	London
LIG	Limoges	France
LTN	Luton	Bedfordshire
LUN	Lusaka	Zambia
LWK	Lerwick	Shetlands
LXR	Luxor	Egypt
MAA	Madras	India
MBJ	Montego Bay	Jamaica
MCM	Monte Carlo	Monaco
MDL	Mandalay	Burma (Myanmar)
MEB	Melbourne	Australia
MFN	Milford Sound	New Zealand
MLH	Mulhouse	France
MMA	Malmö	Sweden
MME	Teesside	England
MOW	Moscow	Russia
MPM	Maputu	Mozambique
MRS	Marseille	France
MXL	Mexicali	Mexico
NBO	Nairobi	Kenya
NCE	Nice	France
NCL	Newcastle	England
NDY	Sanday	Scotland
NQY	Newquay	England
NRT	Narita	Tokyo
NSI	Nsimalen, Yaoundé	Cameroon
NTE	Nantes	France
NTY	Sun City	South Africa
ODE	Odense	Denmark
OPO	Oporto	Portugal
ORD	O'Hare	Chicago
ORK	Cork	Eire
ORN	Oran	Algeria
PAP	Port au Prince	Haiti
PFO	Paphos	Cyprus
PGF	Perpignan	France
PID	Paradise Island	Bahamas
PMO	Palermo	Italy
PNQ	Poona	India
PPG	Pago Pago	American Samoa
PRJ	Capri	Italy
PRY	Pretoria	South Africa
RBA	Rabat	Morocco
REK	Reykjavik	Iceland
RUH	Riyadh	Saudi Arabia
SEL	Seoul	South Korea
SNN	Shannon	Eire
SPK	Sapporo	Japan
STR	Stuttgart	Germany
THR	Tehran	Iran
TIA	Tirana	Albania
URO	Rouen	France
VRN	Verona	Italy
WAW	Warsaw	Poland
WLG	Wellington	New Zealand
YXY	Whitehorse	Canada
YYC	Calgary	Canada
YZF	Yellowknife	Canada
ZAZ	Zaragosa	Spain
ZRH	Zurich	Switzerland

NB The airport codes above are a small-cross section of the thousands of abbreviations used internationally. Most of the codes represent the location of the airport but others denote the name.

Airports: International

Name	Location
Abadan	Iran
Adana	Turkey
Agno	Lugano, Switzerland
Albany County	New York
Alexander Hamilton	St Croix, W Indies
Alfonso Bonilla Aragon	Cali, Colombia
Amausi	Lucknow
Amborovy	Majunga, Madagascar
Amerigo Vespucci	Florence
Amilcar Cabral	Cape Verde
Aminu	Kano, Nigeria
Arlanda	Stockholm
Arnos Vale	St Vincent
Arrecife	Lanzarote
Arturo Marino Benitez	Santiago, Chile
Atuona	Hiva Oa, French Polynesia
Augusto Co Sandino	Managua, Nicaragua

Name	Location
Balice	Krakow, Poland
Baneasa	Bucharest
Bangor	Maine
Banja Luka	Bosnia
Bankstown	New South Wales
Barajas	Madrid
Basle-Mulhouse (Euro Airport)	Basle, Switzerland
Bata	Equatorial Guinea
Beira	Mozambique
Ben Gurion	Tel Aviv
Benina	Benghazi, Libya
Benito Juarez	Mexico City
Bierset	Liège, Belgium
Bilund	Denmark
Blackburne / Plymouth	Montserrat
Blagnac	Toulouse
Blue Danube	Linz
Bole	Addis Ababa
Bonriki	Kiribati
Boukhalef	Tangier, Morocco
Bourgas	Bulgaria
Bradley	Hartford, Connecticut
Brnik	Ljubljana
Bromma	Stockholm
Bulawayo	Zimbabwe
Butmir	Sarajevo
Byrd Field	Richmond, Virginia
Cairns	Queensland
Calabar	Nigeria
Cancun	Mexico
Canefield	Roseau, Dominica
Cannon	Reno, Nevada
Canton	Akron, Ohio
Capodichino	Naples
Cardiff	Rhoose
Carrasco	Montevideo
Carthage	Tunis
Cebu	Philippines
Changi	Singapore
Charleroi	Belgium
Charles B Wheeler	Kansas City, Missouri
Charles de Gaulle	Paris
Charlotte	North Carolina
Chatarpati Shivaji	Bombay / Mumbai
Chek Lap Kok	Hong Kong (new)
Chiang Kai Shek	Taipei, Taiwan
Chileka	Blantyre, Malawi
Ciampino	Rome
Cointrin	Geneva
Collinstown	Dublin
Congonhas	São Paulo, Brazil
Coolidge	Antigua
Costa Smeralda	Olbia, Sardinia
Cotonou	Benin
Cristoforo Colombo	Genoa
Crown Point	Scarborough, Tobago
Cuscatlan	El Salvador
Dabolim	Goa
Dalaman	Turkey
Deurne	Antwerp
D F Malan	Cape Town
Diagoras	Rhodes
Domodedovo	Moscow
Dorval	Montreal
Douala	Cameroon
Dulles	Washington
Dum Dum	Calcutta
Eagle Farm	Brisbane
Ecterdingen	Stuttgart
Eduardo Gomes	Manaus, Brazil
El Alto	La Paz, Bolivia
El Dorado	Bogotá, Colombia
Elat	Israel
Elmas	Cagliari
Eppley Airfield	Omaha, Nebraska
Esenboga	Ankara
Ezeiza	Buenos Aires
Faaa	Tahiti
Faleolo	Apia, Samoa
F D Roosevelt	St Eustatius, W Indies
Ferihegy	Budapest
Findel	Luxembourg
Fiumicino (Leonardo da Vinci)	Rome
Flamingo Field	Bonaire
Flesland	Bergen, Norway
Fontanarossa	Catania, Sicily
Fornebu	Oslo
Fort Myers	Florida
Fort Worth	Dallas, Texas
Frederic Chopin	Warsaw
Freeport	Bahamas
Fua'amotu	Tonga
Fuenterrabia	San Sebastián
Fuerteventura	Canary Islands
Fuhlsbüttel	Hamburg
Galileo Galilei	Pisa
Gardermoen	Oslo
G'Bessia	Conakry
General Manuel Marquez de Leon	Mexico
General Mitchell	Milwaukee
Gillot	Réunion
G. Marconi	Bologna
Golden Rock	St Kitts
Grantley Adams	Barbados
Gulfport-Biloxi	Mississippi
Hahaya	Moroni, Comoros
Halim Perdanakusama	Djakarta
Hanan	Niue
Hancock Field	Syracuse, NY
Haneda	Tokyo
Hartsfield	Atlanta, Georgia
Hato	Curaçao
Hellenikon	Athens
Henderson Field	Honiara, Solomon Isles
Heraklion	Crete
Hewanorra	St Lucia
Heydar Aliyev	Baku
Hongqiao	Shanghai
Hopkins	Cleveland, Ohio
Indira Gandhi	New Delhi
Inezgane	Agadir, Morocco
Ippokratis	Kos
Isla Verde	San Juan, Puerto Rico
Ivanka	Bratislava
Ivato	Antananarivo, Madagascar
Izmir	Turkey
Jackson Field	Port Moresby, PNG
James M Cox	Dayton, Ohio
J F Kennedy	La Paz
Jinnah	Karachi
Johan Adolf Pengel	Paramaribo, Suriname
John F Kennedy	New York
John Foster Dulles	Washington DC
John Paul II	Krakow
John Wayne	Los Angeles, California
Jorge Chavez	Lima, Peru
Jose Martí	Havana, Cuba
Kai Tak	Hong Kong (old)
Kamazu	Lilongwe, Malawi
Kastrup	Copenhagen
Katunayake	Colombo, Sri Lanka
Keflavik	Reykjavik, Iceland
Kent County	Grand Rapids, Michigan
Kerkyra	Corfu
Khon Kaen	Phuket
Khoramaksar	Aden
Khwaja Rawash	Kabul, Afghanistan
Kimpo	Seoul, South Korea
King Khaled	Riyadh
Kingsford Smith	Sydney, Australia
Kitsap	Washington, USA
Klagenfurt	Austria
Kloten	Zurich
Kota Kinabulu	Sabah, Malaysia
Kotoka	Accra, Ghana
Kranebitten	Innsbruck
Kuching	Sarawak, Malaysia
Kungsangen	Norrköping, Sweden
La Aurora	Guatemala
La Coruña	Spain
La Guardia	New York
La Mesa	San Pedro Sula, Honduras
Landvetter	Gothenburg
Larnaca	Cyprus
Las Americas	Dominican Republic
Las Palmas	Gran Canaria
Lawica	Poznan
Le Bourget	Paris
Lech Walesa	Gdansk
Le Lamentin	Martinique
Leonardo da Vinci (Fiumicino)	Rome
Le Raizet	Guadeloupe
Les Angades	Oujda, Morocco
Lesquin	Lille, France
Lester B Pearson	Toronto
Linate	Milan
Lindbergh	San Diego, California
Logan	Boston
Long Beach	California
Loshitsa	Minsk, Belarus
Louis Botha	Durban
Lourdes/Tarbes	Juillan, France
Lubbock	Texas
Lungi	Freetown, Sierra Leone
Lupepau'u	Tonga
Luqa	Malta
M'Poko	Bangui, Central African Republic
Mactan	Cebu, Philippines
Mahon	Menorca
Mais Gate	Haiti
Malmi	Helsinki
Malpensa	Milan
Manas	Bishkek, Kyrgyzstan
Marco Polo	Venice
Mariscal Sucre	Quito, Ecuador
Marsh Harbour	Abaco Island, Bahamas
Matsapha	Manzini, Swaziland
Maturin	Venezuela
Maxglan	Salzburg, Austria
Maya Maya	Brazzaville, Congo
McCarran	Las Vegas
McCoy	Orlando, Florida
McNary Field	Salem, Oregon
Meenambakkam	Madras, India
Mehrabad	Tehran, Iran
Melbourne	Florida
Melita	Djerba, Tunisia

Name	Location
Melsbroek	Brussels
Melville Hall	Dominica
Menara	Marrakesh
Mercedita	Puerto Rico
Merignac	Bordeaux
Midway	Chicago
Ministro Pistarini	Buenos Aires
Mirabel	Montreal
Mohammed V	Casablanca
Monroe County	Rochester, NY
Morelos	Mexico
Münster / Osnabrück	Germany
Murtala Muhammed	Lagos, Nigeria
Nadi	Fiji
Naha	Okinawa (Japan)
Narita	Tokyo
Narssarsuaq	Greenland
N'Djili	Kinshasa
Nejrab	Aleppo, Syria
Netaji Subhas Chandra Bose	Calcutta / Kolkata
Newark	New York
Newcastle	Nevis Island
Ngurah Rai	Denpasar, Bali
Ninoy Aquino	Manila, Philippines
Nis	Yugoslavia
Noi Bai	Hanoi
Norman Manley	Kingston, Jamaica
Norman Rogers	Kingston, Ontario
North Front	Gibraltar
Nouadhibou	Mauritania
Oakland	California
O'Hare	Chicago
Okecie	Warsaw
Olaya Herrera	Medellín, Colombia
Oran	Algeria
Orebro	Sweden
Orly	Paris
Osaka	Japan
Osnabrück (Münster)	Germany
Osvaldo Vieira	Guinea Bissau
Otopeni	Bucharest
Owen Roberts	Grand Cayman
Palese	Bari, Italy
Paphos	Cyprus
Paradisi	Rhodes
Patenga	Bangladesh
Patrick Henry	Norfolk, Virginia
Pearson	Toronto
Pekoa	Vanuatu
Peretola	Florence
Peshawar	Pakistan
Peterson Field	Colorado
Phillip SW Goldson	Belize
Piarco	Trinidad
Pochentong	Cambodia
Point Noire	Congo
Point Salines	Grenada
Polonia	Indonesia
Port Bouet	Ivory Coast
Port Harcourt	Nigeria
Portland	Maine
Princess Beatriz	Aruba
Prince Said Ibrahim	Moroni, Comoros Islands
Provence	Marseille
Pula	Croatia
Pulkovo	St Petersburg
Punta Raisi	Palermo, Sicily
Queen Alia	Jordan
Queen Beatrix	Aruba
Ras Al Khaimah	United Arab Emirates
Rebiechowo	Gdansk, Poland
Reina Beatrix	Aruba
Reina Sofia	Tenerife
Riem	Munich
Robert Mueller	Austin, Texas
Roberts	Monrovia, Liberia
Rochambau	French Guiana
Roskilde	Copenhagen
Ruzyne	Prague
Sainte Foy	Quebec
Sale	Rabat, Morocco
Salgado Filho	Brazil
Salote Pilolevu	Tonga
Sangster	Montego Bay, Jamaica
San Pablo	Seville
Santa Caterina	Funchal, Madeira
Santa Cruz	Bombay
Santa Isabel	Malabo, Guinea
Santos Dumont	Rio
Schiphol	Amsterdam
Schönefeld	Berlin
Schwechat	Vienna
Seeb	Oman
Seewoosagur Ramgoolam	Mauritius
Senou	Mali
Seretse Khama	Gaborone, Botswana
Sfax	Tunisia
Sharjah	U. A. E.
Sheremetyevo	Moscow
Silvio Pettirossi	Paraguay
Simon Bolivar	Ecuador
Simon Bolivar	Caracas, Venezuela
Sir Seretse Khama	Botswana
Skanes	Morocco
Sky Harbour	Phoenix, Arizona
Snilow	Ukraine
Sola	Stavanger, Norway
Sondica	Bilbao
Søndre Srømfjord	Greenland
Spilve	Latvia
Spokane	Washington
Standiford Field	Louisville, Kentucky
Stapleton	Denver, Colorado
St Thomas	Virgin Islands
Sturup	Malmö, Sweden
Sultun Abdul Aziz Shah	Malaysia (Subang)
Sunan	North Korea
Sylmet	Dhaka, Bangladesh
Tacoma	Seattle
Tamatve	Madagascar
Tarbes (Lourdes)	Juillan, France
Tegel	Berlin
Tempelhof	Berlin
Thalerhof	Graz, Austria
Theodore Francis Green	Rhode Island
Timehri	Georgetown, Guyana
Toncontin	Tegucigalpa, Honduras
Tontouta	New Caledonia
Torslanda	Gothenburg
Totegegie	Gambier Island
Townsville	Australia
Treasure Cay	Abaco Island, Bahamas
Tribhuyan	Nepal
Trivandrum	India
Truax Field	Wisconsin
Tullamarine	Melbourne
Turku	Finland
Ulemiste	Estonia
U Michaeli	Haifa, Israel
Unokovo	Moscow
Uplands	Ottawa
VC Bird	Antigua
Vagar	Faeroe Islands
Vantaa	Helsinki
Vigie	St Lucia
Viracopos	São Paulo, Brazil
Vnukovo	Moscow
WA Mozart	Salzburg
Wall Blake	Anguilla
Washington	Baltimore, Maryland
Wattay	Laos
West End	Bahamas
Wichita	Kansas
Wickede	Dortmund
Will Rogers	Oklahoma
William B Hartsfield	Atlanta, Georgia
William P Hobby	Houston, Texas
Willow Run	Detroit, Michigan
WK Kellogg	Battle Creek, Kalamazoo, Michigan
Yeager	Charleston, West Virginia
Yoff	Senegal
Yundam	Gambia
Zarsis	Djerba, Tunisia
Zaventem	Brussels
Zia	Bangladesh
Zvartnots	Yerevan, Armenia

TRANSPORT: CARS

Makes and Models

AC Cars Ace, Aceca, Cobra, Frua, Greyhound, Invacar.

Alfa Romeo Brera, Competizione, GTV, Montreal, 156, Spider .

Aston Martin DB series (David Brown), Lagonda, V8 Vantage. (Aston Martin (Lagonda) Ltd was founded in 1913 by Lionel Martin and Robert Bamford).

Audi A, Q, RS (RennSport), S series, 80, Cabriolet, Quattro.

Austin A90, Cambridge, Healey, Maestro, Metro, Westminster.

Bentley Arnage Mulsanne, Brooklands, Continental T, Zagato (owned since 1998 by the German Volkswagen Group).

BMW 528i, M3, 328i, 1, 3, 4, 5, 6, 7 plus X and Z series.

Cadillac Allante, Ciel, Cien, Escalade, Evoq, Fleetwood, La Salle, SRX (founded in 1902 – a division of General Motors)

Citroën Berlingo, Dyane, Elysee, Mehari, Metropolis, Nemo, Pluriel, Revolte, Saxo 2CV, VTS, Xantia, Xsara (now part of the PSA Peugeot Citroën group)

Daewoo (Korea) Cielo, Espero, Lanos, Leganza, Matiz, Nexia, Nubira (the car division became defunct in 1999).

Daihatsu (Japan) Applause, Copen, Cuore, Materia, Move, Naked, Opti, Rocky, Sonica, Sportrak, Taft, Taruna, Terios, Xenia.

Dodge Charger, Coronet, Dart, Durango, Journey, Power Wagon, Viper (a division of Chrysler Group LLC).

Ferrari Berlinetta, California, Enzo, F355, 458 Italia, 458 Spider, Maranello, 360 Modena, 360 Spider, Testarossa (prancing horse logo)

Fiat Barchetta, Brava, Bravo, Cinquecento, Croma, Doblo, Ducato, Fiorino, Idea, Linea, Marea, Multipla, Panda, Punto, Scudo, Sedici, Seicento, Spider, Stilo, Strada, Tempra, Tipo, Ulysse, Uno (Fabbrica Italiana Automobili Torino was founded in 1899 by a group of investors, including Giovanni Agnelli).

Ford Aerostar, Anglia, Aspire, Bantam, Bronco, Capri, Contour, Cortina, Cougar, Edge, Edsel, Escape, Escort, Expedition, Explorer, Fiesta, Focus, Galaxy, Granada, Ka, Maverick, Model T, Mondeo, Mustang, Pinto, Probe, Puma, Ranger, Sapphire, Scorpio, Taurus, Torino, Thunderbird, Victoria (Ford luxury cars are sold in the USA under the Lincoln brand established in 1917 by Henry M. Leland, who also founded Cadillac 15 years earlier).

Honda Accord, Aerodeck, Civic, CR-V, J-VX, Legend, Odyssey, Passport, Prelude

Hyundai (Korea) Accent, Asta, Avatar, Elantra, Santa Fe, Santro Xing, Sonata, Starex, Terracan, Tiburon, Tucson, Veracruz.

Jaguar E-Type, F-Type, S-Type, XF, XJ12, XK120, XK8, XKR-S (founded as the Swallow Sidecar Company by Sir William Lyons in 1922).

Lada Granta, Kalina, Largus, Niva, Priora, Resolution, Riva, Samara (the Lada badge depicts a Viking sailing ship).

Landrover Defender, Discovery, Freelander, Range Rover Evoque (now part of the Jaguar Land Rover group, a subsidiary of Tata Motors of India).

Lincoln Blackwood, Continental, Cosmopolitan, H K & L series, Navigator, Premiere

Lotus Eclat, Elan, Elise, Elite, Esprit, Europa, Evora, Excel, Exige

Maserati Ghibil, GranCabrio, Levante, Quattroporte (part of FIAT Group - badge is a red trident)

Mercedes C180, CLK, Citan, Malaya, Necar 3, SLK Roadster, SLS- AMG, Viano, Vision SLR (division of the German manufacturer Daimler AG).

Mitsubishi Diamante, Eclipse, Mirage, Montero, Salent, Shogun (based in Tokyo)

Nissan Almira, Altima, Frontier, Leaf, Maxima, Micra, Pathfinder, Patrol, Primera, Quest, QX, Serena, Skyline, 300 ZX, Tirano (based in Yokohama – formerly marketed vehicles under the brand name Datsun).

Peugeot Bipper, Boxer, Expert, 406, Hoggar, Partner, 205 (the Peugeot badge depicts a lion rampant).

Porsche Boxster, Carrera, Cayenne, Cayman, 911, 924, Panamera, Varrera

Proton Exora, Inspira, Perdana, Persona, Prevé, Saga, Satria, Waja (Malaysian company founded in 1983).

Renault Clio, Espace, Extra, Fuego, Kangoo, Laguna, Master, Mégane Alizé, Mégane Scenic, Safranes, Spider, Trafic, Twingo (as part of the Renault-Nissan Alliance, the company is the fourth-largest automotive group in the world behind General Motors, Volkswagen and Toyota).

Rolls Royce Camargue, Corniche, Phantom, Silver Cloud, Silver Dawn, Silver Ghost, Silver Seraph, Silver Shadow, Silver Spirit, Silver Wraith

Saab Carlsson, Sonett (Swedish company founded in 1945).

Seat Alhambra, Arosa, León Mk3, Malaga, Marbella, Toledo

Skoda Fabia, Felicia, Octavia, Superb (Czech company became a wholly owned subsidiary of the Volkswagen Group in 2000).

Subaru Dex, Forester, Impreza, Justy, Legacy, Leone, Loyale, Sumo, Tribeca (based in Tokyo, Subaru is the Japanese name for the Pleiades star cluster)

Suzuki Alto, Baleno, Cappuccino, Every, Jimny, Lapin, Solio, Splash, Swift, Vitaras

Toyota Avalon, Camry Solara, Celica, Corolla, Highlander, Lexus, Prius, RAV4, Scion, Sequoia, Sienna, Supra, Tacoma, Tercel, Tundra

TVR Cerbera, Chimaera, Griffith, Jomar, Trident, Tuscan, Vixen (company name a corruption of first name of founder Trevor Wilkinson).

Vauxhall Adam, Agila, Astra SRi, Belmont SRi, Calibra, Carlton, Cavalier (became Vectra), Chevette, Corsa, Frontera, Insignia, Meriva, Mokka, Monterrey, Nova, Omega, Senator, Tigra Bermuda, Vectra, Zafira

Vauxhall (van) Arena, Astravan, Brava, Combo, Corsavan

Volkswagen Beetle, Cabrio, Cabriolet, Corrado, Eos, Fox, Golf GTi, Jetta, Passat, Phaeton, Polo, Scirocco, Sharan, Thing, Tiguan, Up!, Vento

Volvo C70, 850, 340, S60, S80, V40, V70 (Swedish company based in Gothenburg).

Motorways

M1	London to Leeds	**M20**	Swanley to Folkestone	**M53**	Chester to Wallasey	**M66**	Manchester to Rochdale
M2	Rochester to Faversham	**M23**	Hooley to Crawley	**M54**	M6 to Telford	**M67**	Hyde Bypass
M3	Sunbury to Southampton	**M25**	London Orbital	**M55**	Preston to Blackpool	**M69**	Coventry to Leicester
M4	London to Swansea	**M26**	Sevenoaks to Tonbridge	**M56**	Manchester/Queensferry	**M73**	Glasgow
M5	Birmingham to Exeter	**M27**	Southampton Bypass	**M57**	Liverpool outer ring road	**M74**	Glasgow to Lesmahagow
M6	Rugby to Carlisle	**M32**	Bristol to M4	**M58**	Liverpool to Wigan	**M77**	Ayr
M8	Edinburgh to Erskine Bridge	**M40**	London to Birmingham	**M61**	Manchester to Preston	**M80**	Stepps Bypass
M9	Edinburgh to Dunblane	**M41**	London to West Cross	**M62**	Liverpool to Hull	**M90**	Dunfermline to Perth, Bonnybridge to Kincardine Bridge
M11	London to Cambridge	**M42**	Bromsgrove to Measham	**M63**	Manchester south ring road		
M18	Rotherham to Goole	**M45**	M1 to A45 (Coventry)	**M65**	Calder Valley from M6	**M180**	M18 to Humber Bridge
		M50	Ross to Tewkesbury				

NB The first UK motorway was the Preston Bypass in 1958, now part of the M6.

Vehicle Number Plates

A new registration mark system was introduced on 1 September 2001. The new plates will comprise seven characters: the first two letters to denote the registered office; the next two a numeric age identifier; the final three letters a random element to differentiate vehicles. The age identifier will be subject to change every six months. The tables are reproduced below and the example given by the DVLA is as follows: BD51 SMR where BD indicates the vehicle was registered in the Birmingham office and the 51 indicates a registration date between Sept 2001 and Feb 2002. The typeface was also standardised from 1 September 2001 and only regular block capitals are now allowable.

Letter	Region	Local Offices	DVLA Local Office Identifier
A	Anglia	Peterborough	AA AB AC AD AE AF AG AH AJ AK AL AM AN
		Norwich	AO AP AR AS AT AU
		Ipswich	AV AW AX AY
B	Birmingham	Birmingham	BA – BY
C	Cymru	Cardiff	CA CB CC CD CE CF CG CH CJ CK CL CM CN CO
		Swansea	CP CR CS CT CU CV
		Bangor	CW CX CY
D	Deeside to Shrewsbury	Chester	DA DB DC DD DE DF DG DH DJ DK
		Shrewsbury	DL DM DN DO DP DR DS DT DU DV DW DX DY
E	Essex	Chelmsford	EA – EY
F	Forest & Fens	Nottingham	FA FB FC FD FE FF FG FH FJ FK FL FM FN FP
		Lincoln	FR FS FT FV FW FX FY
G	Garden of England	Maidstone	GA GB GC GD GE GF GG GH GJ GK GL GM GN GO
		Brighton	GP GR GS GT GU GV GW GX GY
H	Hampshire & Dorset	Bournemouth	HA HB HC HD HE HF HG HH HJ
		Portsmouth	HK HL HM HN HO HP HR HS HT HU HV HW HX HY (HW will be used exclusively for Isle of Wight residents)

TRANSPORT : CARS

K		Luton	KA KB KC KD KE KF KG KH KJ KK KL
		Northampton	KM KN KO KP KR KS KT KU KV KW KX KY
L	London	Wimbledon	LA LB LC LD LE LF LG LH LJ
		Stanmore	LK LL LM LN LO LP LR LS LT
M	Manchester & Merseyside	Manchester	MA – MY
N	North	Newcastle	NA NB NC ND NE NG NH NJ NK NL NM NN NO
		Stockton	NP NR NS NT NU NV NW NX NY
O	Oxford	Oxford	OA – OY
P	Preston	Preston	PA PB PC PD PE PF PG PH PJ PK PL PM PN PO PP PR PS PT
		Carlisle	PU PV PW PX PY
R	Reading	Reading	RA – RY
S	Scotland	Glasgow	SA SB SC SD SE SF SG SH SJ
		Edinburgh	SK SL SM SN SO
		Dundee	SP SR SS ST
		Aberdeen	SU SV SW
		Inverness	SX SY
V	Severn Valley	Worcester	VA – VY
W	West of England	Exeter	WA WB WC WD WE WF WG WH WJ
		Truro	WK WL
		Bristol	WM WN WO WP WR WS WT WU WV WW WX WY
Y	Yorkshire	Leeds	YA YB YC YD YE YF YG YH YJ YK
		Sheffield	YL YM YN YO YP YR YS YT YU
		Beverley	YV YW YX YY

Age Identifiers

Code	Date	Code	Date
		51	Sept 2001 – Feb 2002
02	March 2002 – Aug 2002	52	Sept 2002 – Feb 2003
03	March 2003 – Aug 2003	53	Sept 2003 – Feb 2004
04	March 2004 – Aug 2004	54	Sept 2004 – Feb 2005
05	March 2005 – Aug 2005	55	Sept 2005 – Feb 2006
06	March 2006 – Aug 2006	56	Sept 2006 – Feb 2007
07	March 2007 – Aug 2007	57	Sept 2007 – Feb 2008
08	March 2008 – Aug 2008	58	Sept 2008 – Feb 2009
09	March 2009 – Aug 2009	59	Sept 2009 – Feb 2010
10	March 2010 – Aug 2010	60	Sept 2010 – Feb 2011
11	March 2011 – Aug 2011	61	Sept 2011 – Feb 2012
12	March 2012– Aug 2012	62	Sept 2012 – Feb 2013

General Information

Automobile Association founded in 1905; originally formed to warn members of police patrols.

Breathalyser introduced in 1967 by Minister of Transport, Barbara Castle.

car founders and designers: Fiat – Agnelli family; Jaguar – William Lyons; Lotus – Colin Chapman.

driving test initiated in 1935 and L-plates issued in the same year.

Eiffel Tower – served as billboard Between 1925 and 1934 the name Citroen was lit up on the tower at night.

Mini introduced in 1959 and designed by Alex Issigonis.

MoT (Ministry of Transport) testing established in 1960 and compulsory for vehicles over three years old.

number plates first issued in 1903, the first being A1 to Lord Russell.

parking meters first seen in the UK in 1958, the same year that London saw its first traffic wardens.

petrol pumps were first used in 1919 in the UK.

road car: fastest As at April 2010 America's SSC Ultimate Aero TT is the fastest road car in the world with a top speed of 257 mph.

Route 66 runs from Chicago (Illinois) to Los Angeles (California).

Royal Automobile Club founded in 1897, the second largest motoring organisation after the AA.

veteran cars are those built up to the end of 1918; contrast Vintage cars, 1919–30.

TRANSPORT: SHIPS

Famous Ships: Miscellaneous

Aaron Manby first iron steamship, launched in 1822.

Achille Lauro formerly *Willem Ruys*, Italian cruise ship dogged by disaster. Collided with a fishing boat 1971, one crew member killed; fire broke out on board 1981, two passengers killed; hijacked between Alexandria and Port Said by the PLO Oct. 1985, one passenger murdered; gutted by fire and sank in the Indian Ocean Nov. 1994, two passengers killed.

Amoco Cadiz super-tanker that ran aground off the coast of Brittany (March 1978) spilling 220,000 tons of crude oil.

Ancon first ship through the Panama Canal.

Andrea Doria Italian ship which collided with a Swedish ship and sank (1956).

Archimedes first large sea-going steamship driven by a screw-propeller, it weighed 237 tons (Nov. 1838).

Argonaut first submarine to navigate extensively in the open sea. Built in 1897 by the US engineer and naval architect Simon Lake, it was fitted with wheels for travel on the bottom of the sea. In 1898 the *Argonaut* travelled from Norfolk, Virginia, to New York, through heavy storms, proving the seaworthiness of this type of submarine construction.

B&Q 752 long trimaran piloted by Ellen MacArthur in 2005 when the Isle of Wight-based sailor broke the record for a non-stop circumnavigation. Her journey totalled 27,351 miles and took 71 days 14 hrs 18 mins 33 secs.

Black Pig vessel captained by Captain Pugwash in the children's series.

Braer oil tanker that ran aground off the Shetlands (Jan. 1993) spilling 85,000 tons of crude oil.

Britannia launched in April 1953, the Royal Yacht *Britannia* was finally laid to rest in December 1997.

Britannic sister ship of the *Titanic*, sank after hitting a mine in 1916 in the Aegean while employed as a hospital ship.

Californian Leyland liner, accused of ignoring *Titanic*'s distress calls but subsequently found to have no radio operator on duty.

Canberra P&O cruise ship, affectionately nicknamed 'The Great White Whale'; entered service 1961; served as a hospital ship in the Falklands 1982; last cruise 1997.

Carpathia ship that came to the rescue of the *Titanic* when it sank.

Charlotte Dundas first commercially successful paddle-steamer launched in Scotland, 1802, by William Symington for Lord Dundas.

Charlotte Rhodes James Onedin's ship in the TV series *The Onedin Line*.

Christina Aristotle Onassis' yacht named after his daughter.

Cutty Sark famous tea and wool clipper built in 1869, the name deriving from the witch in Burns's *Tam O'Shanter*. It has been on display at Greenwich since 1957.

Don Juan boat in which Percy Bysshe Shelley was drowned in 1822.

Dona Paz Philippine ferry that collided with the tanker *Vector* in the Sibuyan Sea, 20 December 1987. In the subsequent fire both ships sank and a total of 4,386 people lost their lives, only 24 surviving from the *Dona Paz* and two from the *Vector*. The worst-ever peacetime maritime disaster.

Elise first steamboat to cross the English Channel (1816).

ENZA New Zealand catamaran with eight-man crew led by Peter Blake and Robin Knox-Johnston which won the Jules Verne Trophy for sailing non-stop round the world in a record time of 74 days 22 hrs 17 mins, returning on 1 April 1994.

Estonia Swedish-owned ferry that sank in the Baltic in September 1994 when the bow doors broke open, costing 852 lives.

Exxon Valdez super-tanker that ran aground off Alaskan coast (March 1989) spilling 12,000,000 gallons of crude oil.

Forfarshire steamer wrecked off the Farne Islands in 1838, Grace Darling famously helping in the rescue.

Francis Smith first British steamboat fitted with screw-propellers and built by Francis Pettit Smith, a farmer from Hendon (1836). It was 252 long and weighed 5 tons.

Grand Princess the P&O liner is currently being built in Fincantieri, Italy, and is expected to be 9512 long with a gross registered tonnage of 109,000 tons exceeding the *Carnival Destiny* as the largest-ever passenger ship.

Great Britain built by Isambard Kingdom Brunel (1843), it was the first iron-hulled screw-propeller steamship. Since being towed from the Falklands in 1970, where it had been scuttled in 1937, it has been on display in Bristol.

Great Eastern built by Isambard Kingdom Brunel (1858). At 6662 long, it was the world's largest ship until 1899. In 1866, it laid the transatlantic cable. Sold for scrap in 1888.

Great Western built by Isambard Kingdom Brunel (1838), it was the first wooden steamship to make regular transatlantic crossings.

Gypsy Moth IV Francis Chichester became the first Englishman to sail single-handed round the world in this yacht (1966/7). Now on display at Greenwich.

Happy Giant formerly named the *Seawise Giant* and with a deadweight tonnage of 564,763 tons, this was the largest ship afloat, but after extensive damage in the Gulf in Dec. 1987 and May 1988 has been refitted and reduced to 420,000 tons.

Helias Fos this steam-turbine oil tanker is the current largest ship afloat at a deadweight tonnage of 550,051 tons.

Herald of Free Enterprise Townsend Thoresen-owned cross-Channel ferry which capsized near the Belgian port of Zeebrugge due to the bow doors being insecure (6 March 1987); 193 lives were lost as a result.

Hispaniola fictional ship in Robert Louis Stevenson's *Treasure Island*, skippered by Captain Smollet and owned by Squire Trelawney.

Lady Ghislaine yacht owned by Robert Maxwell and named after his daughter, from which he went overboard and drowned (Nov. 1991).

Lake Champlain first British liner with ship's radio (1901), it communicated with the SS *Lucania* mid-Atlantic.

Lenin first nuclear-powered ship. This Soviet naval ice-breaker was launched in 1957.

Little Juliana first steamboat fitted with screw--propellers (May 1804).

Lively Lady yacht in which Alec Rose sailed single-handed round the world, returning to Portsmouth after nearly a year (4 July 1968).

Lusitania Cunard liner sunk by German torpedo off the Irish coast (7 May 1915) with the loss of about 1,200 lives. This was a major factor in the USA's entry into the First World War.

Maiden British yacht with all-female crew skippered by Tracy Edwards; won its class in Whitbread Round the World Race (1989).

Marchioness Thames pleasure steamer rammed and sunk by the dredger *Bowbelle* at Southwark (August 1989); 51 lives were lost.

Mary Celeste US brigantine under command of Ben Briggs, found in Atlantic (1872) with no sign of crew or struggle; cargo was secure.

Mauretania sister ship of the *Lusitania*, built in 1907.

Mayflower carried the 102 Pilgrim Fathers from Plymouth to Cape Cod, Massachusetts (1620), to found the first New England colony. Oceanus Hopkins was born on board the *Mayflower*.

Morning Cloud yacht owned and captained by Edward Heath.

Nautilus Captain Nemo's submarine in Jules Verne's novel *20,000 Leagues Under the Sea*.

Normandie passenger liner destroyed by fire in New York harbour in 1941.

Norway longest passenger liner ever built (formerly called *France*): overall length 10352 222.

Oasis of the Seas As at April 2010 the largest passenger ship in history, 1,1812 long. Gross tonnage: 225,282 tons. Owned by Royal Caribbean International, the cruise ship has 16 passenger decks.

Olympic sister ship of the *Titanic*.

Pequod whaling ship captained by Captain Ahab and destroyed by Moby Dick in Melville's novel.

Pyroscaphe first practical steamboat. Built near Lyon in 1783, it was a 1382-long paddle steamer and weighed 182 tons.

Queen Anne's Revenge Edward Teach's (Blackbeard) ship captured in the Caribbean in 1717 and used for piracy until Jan. 1718.

Queen Elizabeth built in 1938, the *Queen Elizabeth* (Seawise University) was destroyed in Hong Kong Harbour in Jan. 1972.

QEII built in 1968, it is the largest passenger liner in service between Southampton and New York.

Queen Mary now a floating hotel in Long Beach, California, it was built in 1936 and was the flagship of the Cunard line.

Rainbow Warrior Greenpeace ship which was sunk in Auckland Harbour in July 1985 by French intelligence agents, killing one member of the crew.

Rising Star first ship to cross the Atlantic from east to west (1821/2).

Savannah first steamship to cross the Atlantic (1819).

Savannah first commercially successful nuclear-powered ship, launched 1959.

Sea Empress oil tanker which ran aground off Milford Haven (Feb. 1996) spilling 72,000 tons of crude oil.

Speedwell sister ship of the *Mayflower* which left Southampton for New England but was forced into harbour at Plymouth, Devon.

Suhaili yacht in which Robin Knox-Johnston became first man to circumnavigate the world non-stop and single-handed; he returned in April 1969.

Talitha G motor yacht owned by John Paul Getty.

Thomas W Lawson US schooner; the only seven-masted sailing vessel on record. Designed by Bowdoin B Crowninshield and built by the Fore River Ship and Engine Building Co in 1902 for Coastwise Transportation Co. The seven masts were Fore, Main, Mizzen, Number 4, Number 5, Number 6 and Spanker.

Titanic White Star's unsinkable flagship which hit an iceberg on its maiden voyage on the night of 14 April 1912 and capsized in the early hours of 15 April with the loss of 1,513 lives. Wreck was found in 1985.

Torrey Canyon ran aground off Land's End (March 1967) spilling its cargo of 100,000 tons of crude oil.

Turbinia built and demonstrated by Charles Parsons at Spithead (1897), it was the first ship to use turbine engines.

Victoria and Albert name given to three royal yachts; the first was a paddle-steamer of 1843; the last was built in 1899 and used until replaced by *Britannia*.

Famous Ships: Naval

Agamemnon 64-gun ship launched in 1781, commanded by Nelson from 1793 and his favourite ship. Abandoned in 1809 when it ran aground at Maldonado Bay.

Amethyst frigate which in July 1949 escaped under cover of night along the flooded Yangtze.

Arethusa launched 1849; last Royal Navy ship to go into action entirely under sail, at Sebastopol in 1855. From 1874 to 1933 it was a training ship at Greenhithe.

Argus first aircraft carrier, completed in 1918.

Arizona said to be the first US battleship sunk at Pearl Harbor on 7 Dec. 1941.

Ark Royal many ships have had the name but the most famous were probably the flagship of the British Fleet against the Spanish Armada (1588), although it was only the nickname, the aircraft carrier sunk by an Italian torpedo in November 1941, and the present aircraft carrier which is the Royal Navy's largest fighting ship.

Association flagship of Sir Cloudesley Shovell, wrecked off the Scilly Isles in 1707 with all hands lost.

Belfast Europe's largest surviving WW2 warship, displacing 11,500 tons. Commissioned 1939, paid off 1971. The cruiser is now on display on the Thames.

Bellerophon Napoleon Bonaparte surrendered to the British aboard this ship (15 July 1815) after the Battle of Waterloo.

Birmingham US light cruiser from which Eugène Ely took off in a 50 hp Curtiss pusher biplane (10 Nov. 1910) while it was at anchor in Chesapeake Bay, so making it the first ship with a temporary flight-deck.

Bismarck German battleship sunk in the North Atlantic after it had sunk the British battle cruiser HMS *Hood* (May 1941).

Bonhomme Richard John Paul Jones's 40-gun -warship, blown in two off Flamborough Head in 1779.

Bounty ship that while carrying breadfruit trees from Tahiti was the scene of a mutiny (28 April 1789) by Fletcher Christian (settled on Pitcairn Island). Captain William Bligh and 18 crew were set adrift in the Pacific.

Captain experimental British turret ship of 1870 designed by Captain Cowper Coles; sank in the Bay of Biscay shortly after commissioning with the loss of 472 lives.

Constitution American ship of the line, launched 1798. Nicknamed 'Old Ironsides'; on display in Boston.

Coventry sister ship of the *Sheffield* and also sunk by an Argentinian Exocet missile during the Falklands War.

Devastation launched 1871; first British capital ship which did not require sails.

Dreadnought British battleship launched 1906 which revolutionised naval warfare in the early decades of the 20th century.

Dreadnought Britain's first nuclear submarine, launched in 1960.

Elizabeth Bonaventure Drake's flagship in the raid on Cadiz in 1587.

Enterprise first nuclear-powered aircraft carrier.

Excellent home to the naval gunnery school established in 1830; since 1891, a shore base on Whale Island, Portsmouth.

Ganges last British ship of the line; launched 1821, paid off 1861. From 1866 a training ship. Name passed to a shore base near Ipswich in 1905; closed 1976.

General Belgrano Argentine cruiser sunk by the British submarine *Conqueror* during Falklands War (2 May 1982).

Graf Spee German pocket battleship scuttled by her captain off Montevideo Harbour after being harried across the River Plate by the cruisers, *Ajax*, *Achilles* and *Exeter* (Dec. 1939).

Henry, Grâce de Dieu Henry VIII's flagship, built 1514 and carried 186 guns.

Hermes aircraft carrier, last of the old-style carriers operated by the Royal Navy, which was flagship during the Falklands War.

Invincible the second aircraft carrier that was sent to the Falklands after the Argentine invasion (2 April 1982).

Lightning first purpose-built torpedo boat (1877).

Long Beach first nuclear warship, launched in Quincy, Massachusetts (14 July 1959).

Maine American armoured cruiser of 1886; blew up in Havana 1898, resulting in the Spanish-American War.

Mary Rose Henry VIII's favourite ship, launched 1509, sank 1545 but was raised in 1982 and is still being restored at Portsmouth.

Merrimack steam frigate scuttled in Norfolk harbour by Union forces, then raised by the Confederates, converted to an ironclad and renamed *Virginia*; fought a draw with the *Monitor* in Hampton Roads in 1862 and destroyed by her own captain shortly afterwards.

Missouri Japanese surrender terms were signed aboard this ship in Tokyo Bay (2 Sept. 1945).

Monarch First British turret-gunned ship, launched 1868.

Monitor US iron-hulled warship with single gun turret, fought *Merrimack* in Hampton Roads 1862; capsized in a gale shortly after.

Nautilus world's first nuclear-powered submarine, launched by the USA in 1954. The name derived from an early submarine designed by Robert Fulton for Napoleon (1800).

Northumberland third-rate ship of the line which took Napoleon Bonaparte to St Helena in 1815.

PT 109 John F Kennedy's torpedo boat during World War II.

Revenge Drake's ship used during the attack by the Spanish Armada (1588). In 1591, captained by Sir Richard Grenville, fought a fifteen-hour battle singlehandedly against 53 Spanish ships off Flores.

Royal George 100-gun ship of 1756; carried Hawke's flag at Quiberon Bay in 1759; capsized at Spithead in 1782 with loss of 900 lives.

Royal Oak British battleship sunk at Scapa Flow (Orkneys) by a German torpedo (Oct. 1939) with the loss of 833 lives.

Scharnhorst German battlecruiser which escaped from Brest with the *Gneisenau* and *Prinz Eugen* (Feb. 1942) but was sunk at the Battle of North Cape (Dec. 1943).

Sheffield British destroyer hit by an Exocet missile on 4 May 1982 with the loss of 20 lives.

Squirrel Sir Humphrey Gilbert's ship used during the attack by the Spanish Armada (1588).

Temeraire 98-gun ship launched in 1798; fought at Trafalgar; broken up on the Thames 1838 and immortalised on canvas by Turner.

Tiger the ship used by Harold Wilson and Ian Smith during their UDI discussions (1966).

Tirpitz German battleship sunk by RAF bombers in April 1944.

Trincomalee built 1817, renamed *Foudroyant* in 1892 and a training ship in Portsmouth Harbour until 1987 when she was towed to Hartlepool for restoration and given back her original name.

Vanguard iron-hulled frigate accidentally rammed and sunk by her sister ship *Iron Duke* in 1875.

Vanguard Britain's largest battleship. Decommis-sioned 1960 and ran aground on leaving Portsmouth to be scrapped.

Vasa flagship of Gustavus Adolphus of Sweden. Sank in harbour in 1628; recovered intact from seabed and now on display.

Victoria launched 1859; last wooden battleship built for the Royal Navy. Paid off 1867; name used by British battleship of 1887 which sank off Tripoli in 1893 when flagship of Admiral George Tryon. It was accidentally rammed by *Camperdown*, flagship of Tryon's second-in-command, Alfred Markham.

Victory launched at Chatham 1765, Horatio Nelson's flagship at the battle of Trafalgar (21 Oct. 1805); flagship of C-in-C Portsmouth since 1835. Dry-docked and restored in 1922, the *Victory* is now on display at Portsmouth.

Warrior first iron-hulled battleship (and last surviving); built at Blackwall on the Thames (1859/60). When commissioned in 1861, it made every other naval vessel obsolete. On display in Portsmouth since 1987.

Wilton first plastic warship, launched in Southampton 18 Jan. 1972.

Famous Ships: Voyages of Exploration

Adventure James Cook's consort ship to the *Resolution* during his Antarctic voyage 1772–5; converted from a Whitby collier.

Arktika first ship to reach the North Pole, in 1977.

Beagle Charles Darwin's ship which surveyed South American islands and in particular Galapagos (1831–6). Darwin was the science officer, the captain was Robert Fitzroy.

Calypso most famous survey ship of Jacques Cousteau.

Challenger Royal Navy survey ship, sailed 79,000 miles from 1872 to 1876, adding greatly to know-ledge of the seas. Most recent RN ship of that name also an oceanographic vessel.

Discovery Captain James Cook sought the Northwest Passage in 1776–9 with the *Resolution* and the *Discovery*. He was slain on the beach at Kealakekua, Hawaii, by Polynesian natives (1779).

Discovery Robert Falcon Scott's ship used in his British National Antarctic Expedition of 1901–4 in which he was accompanied by Ernest Shackleton. Now on display in Dundee.

Endeavour James Cook's voyage to Australia and New Zealand (1768–71), on which Joseph Banks was chief scientist, was carried out on this converted collier, originally called *Earl of Pembroke*.

Endurance Ernest Shackleton's ship on his Antarctic voyage of 1914–16; sank in the Weddell Sea.

Erebus one of the two ill-fated ships (the other was the *Terror*) used by Sir John Franklin in his search for the Northwest Passage (1845–6).

Fram Norwegian explorer Fridtjof Nansen's ship used on his Arctic explorations (1893–6). Roald Amundsen sailed in *Fram* (which meant 'Forward') on his successful expedition of 1911–12 to the South Pole.

Gjöa Roald Amundsen's ship in which he sailed the Northwest Passage (1902–6) and found the magnetic North Pole.

Golden Hind ship on which Francis Drake became first Englishman to circumnavigate the globe (1580); originally called *Pelican*.

Grenville the schooner that James Cook commanded while surveying the coast of Newfoundland 1763–68.

Kon Tiki Thor Heyerdahl's single-sailed balsa-wood raft on which he crossed the Pacific (1947).

Matthew John Cabot discovered Newfoundland and Nova Scotia (1497) in this 50-ton ship.

Mazurek carried Krystyna Choynowska-Liskievicz on the first female solo circumnavigation of the globe in 1978.

Morning Supply ship that accompanied the *Discovery* in Scott's Antarctic expedition of 1901–4. Ernest Shackleton was invalided home on this ship.

Nimrod Ernest Shackleton's ship on the voyage (1907–9) in which he located the magnetic South Pole, and climbed Mt Erebus but only came within 97 miles of the South Pole.

Quest ship on which Ernest Shackleton died during his third Antarctic voyage (Grytviken, South Georgia 1922).

RA II Thor Heyerdahl's papyrus raft on which he crossed the Atlantic (1970).

Resolute one of Edward Belcher's ships sent to seek the missing (and already dead) John Franklin in 1852; abandoned in 1854 after being locked in ice off Melville Island; found 1,000 miles away in Davis Strait in 1855, still perfectly seaworthy.

Resolution James Cook's flagship during his voyage to Antarctica 1772–5. Cook sought the Northwest Passage 1776–9 in this ship.

Roebuck William Dampier's ship on his voyage to Australia and New Guinea (1699–1700).

Santa Maria Christopher Columbus's flagship during his expedition to the New World (1492–3), accompanied by the caravels *Niña* and *Pinta*.

Spray Joshua Slocum's boat in which he circumnavigated the Earth, the first man to do so solo (1895–8).

Terra Nova Captain Robert Falcon Scott's ship used on his ill-fated Antarctic expedition 1910–12.

Terror one of the two ships (the other was *Erebus*) used by Sir John Franklin in his search for the Northwest Passage (1845–6).

Theodore Roosevelt Robert Peary's ship used when he became first person to reach the North Pole (6 April 1909). Peary's former friend, Frederick Cook, was found to have fraudulently reported his own earlier reaching of the Pole.

Tigris Thor Heyerdahl's third raft.

Trieste bathysphere submarine which holds the record for the deepest descent (10,916 m) on 23 Jan. 1960.

Vega first ship to achieve the Northeast Passage, in 1878–9, under Nils Nordenskjöld.

Victoria first ship to circumnavigate the globe (1519–22). Although Ferdinand Magellan set out with five ships (the flagship *Trinidad, San Antonio, Concepción, Santiago* and *Victoria*) four were lost and he himself was killed in the Philippines (1521). The circumnavigation was completed by the Basque seaman Juan Sebastián del Cano.

Viking Norwegian explorer Fridtjof Nansen's first exploratory ship (1888) in which he first sailed to Greenland.

Windward British Arctic explorer Frederick Jackson's ship on which Fridtjof Nansen briefly journeyed back to Norway in Aug. 1896.

Ships: General Information

binnacle the casing in which the ship's compass is kept.

box the compass to name the points of the compass in proper order.

breeches buoy life-saving device run on a rope stretched from a wrecked vessel to a place of safety.

bulwark that part of the sides of a ship which rises above the upper deck.

caïque long, narrow, light rowing skiff used on the Bosporus.

clipper ship: first *Rainbow* (1845).

dahabeah/dahabeeyah houseboat used on the Nile (from Arabic: the Golden One).

dhow single-masted ship with a very long yard and a lateen sail, used on the Arabian sea.

diesel-powered ship: first *Petit-Pierre.*

distress signals SOS – Morse (formerly CQD, Come Quickly Danger); Mayday – vocal distress shout.

extremities of ship front – bow; back – stern; left side looking front – port (formerly larboard); right side looking front – starboard.

felucca small vessel used in the Mediterranean, propelled by oars or lateen sails, or both.

flotsam goods lost in shipwreck and found floating.

gondola long, narrow Venetian boat with peaked ends, propelled by one oar.

gunwale upper edge of a ship's side next to the bulwarks.

hull: plank types clinker-built – built with overlapping planks fastened with clinched nails; carvel-built – having the planks flush at the edges.

hydrofoil invented by Comte de Lambert in 1897 and developed by Enrico Forlanini in 1898.

jetsam goods thrown overboard in order to lighten a ship in distress, and subsequently washed ashore.

junk flat-bottomed vessel with lugsails, used in the Chinese seas.

kayak Inuit and Alaskan canoe, made of sealskins stretched on a light wooden framework.

kitchen or cook-house galley.

knot one nautical mile per hour. The British nautical mile was 6,080 feet but in 1970 the International nautical mile of 1,852 metres was adopted. The measurement was devised by Richard Norwood in 1673.

lighthouses: UK authority Trinity House.

lights starboard – green; port – red; top at night – white.

masts: how many sloop and cutter (1); ketch, brig, brigantine, yawl (2); barque (3 or more); schooner (2 or more).

oldest surviving ships *Khufu I* and *Khufu II*, built *c.* 2600 BC and buried in pits outside the Great Pyramid of Khufu in Egypt. *Khufu I*, first to be excavated after discovery in 1954, is plank-built and 43 metres long.

P&O: meaning Peninsular and Oriental.

pipe down naval colloquialism derived from the boatswain's call of this name, meaning 'Hands turn in', i.e. 'Lights out'.

piping the side traditional ceremony of blowing the boatswain's pipe when royalty arrive or depart from battleship.

plimsoll line maximum loading mark on hull of ship, named after Samuel Plimsoll (1824–98), promoter of the Merchant Shipping Act 1876.

ports: famous Athens – Piraeus; London – Tilbury; Rome – Ostia.

ports: general biggest – New York; busiest – Rotterdam; largest inland – Montreal.

PT Boat: meaning Patrol Torpedo Boat.

Q-ship merchant ship with concealed guns, used to decoy enemy ships into the range of its weapons. Q stood for 'Query'.

rudder: invented by Chinese, 1st century BC.

sails lateen – triangular.

ships: register of Lloyd's.

ship: largest oil tanker *Jahre Viking* at 1,5042 long and weighing over 564,000 tonnes.

steam turbine: inventor Charles Parsons (1897).

V-shaped hull: pioneer Uffa Fox (who instructed HRH Prince Philip, the Duke of Edinburgh, in the finer points of yachting).

Venice: water bus vaporetto.

watches at sea first watch – 8pm to midnight; middle watch – midnight to 4am; morning watch – 4am to 8am; forenoon – 8am to midday; afternoon watch – midday to 4pm; first dog watch – 4pm to 6pm; second dog watch – 6pm to 8pm.

xebec/zebec small three-masted Mediterranean vessel with both square and lateen sails, formerly used by Algerian pirates.

yachts: famous *Talitha G* – John Paul Getty; *Saratoga* – Humphrey Bogart; *Saxara* – Mohamed Al Fayed.

TRANSPORT: TRAINS

Railway Tunnels: World's Longest

	Span	*Built*	*Railway*	*Length (miles)*
Seikan	Honshu–Hokkaido	1988	Japan Rail	33.5
Channel	Cheriton–Fréthun	1994	BR/French National	30.7
Lötschberg	Frutigen–Raron	2007	Swiss Alp Transit (longest land)	21.5
Guadarrama	Madrid–Valladolid	2007	AVE Trains	17.6
Taihang	Shijiazhuang–Taiyuan	2007	China Rail	17.3
Hakkōda	Tenmabayashi–Aomori	2010	Japan Rail	16.4
Iwate-ichinohe	Morioka–Aomori	2002	Japan Rail	16.1
Wienerwald	Gablitz–Mauerbach	2012	Western Railway (Austria)	14.8
Daishimizu	Jōmō-Kogen–Echigo	1980	Japan Rail	13.9
Lüliangshan	Wucheng–Fenyang	2011	China Rail	12.9

The world's longest tunnel is the Thirlmere Aqueduct a 95.9-mile (154.3 km) section of water supply serving the Manchester area and completed in 1925

Railway Bridges: World's Longest

Location	*Opened*	*Length (ft)*		*Location*	*Opened*	*Length (ft)*	
Danyang	China	2011	540,700	Beijing Grand	China	2011	157,982
Tianjin	China	2011	373,000	**Yangcun**	China	2007	117,493
Weinan Weihe	China	2010	261,588	**Shanghai Maglev**	China	2004	98,123

World's oldest railway bridge is the Causey Arch on the Tanfield Line in County Durham, designed by Ralph Wood and completed in 1727.

London Underground Stations: Name Changes

Current name	*Previous name*	*Current name*	*Previous name*	*Current name*	*Previous name*
Acton Town	Mill Hill Park	**Green Park**	Dover Street	**St Paul's**	Post Office
Arsenal	Gillespie Road	**Kensington (Olympia)**	Addison Road	**Tooting Bec**	Trinity Road
Becontree	Gale Street Halt	**Ladbroke Grove**	Notting Hill	**Tower Hill**	Mark Lane
Charing Cross	Strand	**Marylebone**	Great Central	**West Kensington**	North End (Fulham)
Debden	Chigwell Road	**Moor Park**	Sandy Lodge	**White City**	Wood Lane
Embankment	Charing Cross	**Oakwood**	Enfield West	**Woodside Park**	Torrington Park, Woodside
Euston Square	Gower Street	**Ravenscourt Park**	Shaftesbury Road		
Fulham Broadway	Walham Green	**South Woodford**	George Lane		

Current British Railway Operating Companies

Arriva Trains Wales (owned by Deutsche Bahn)
c2c (Essex Thameside owned by National Express)
Chiltern Railways (owned by Arriva UK Trains)
CrossCountry (owned by Arriva UK Trains)
East Coast (subsidiary of Directly Operated Railways)
East Midlands Trains (owned by Stagecoach Group)
Eurostar (owned by Eurotunnel)
First Capital Connect (Thameslink Great Northern)
First Great Western (serves southern Britain)
First Hull Trains (Hull to King's Cross)
First ScotRail (rebranded as ScotRail in 2008)
First TransPennine Express (above 5 owned by First Group)
Grand Central (owned by Arriva UK Trains)
Greater Anglia (Liverpool St to eastern counties)
Heathrow Connect (Heathrow to Paddington)
Heathrow Express (Heathrow to Paddington)
London Midland (owned by Govia)
London Overground (Transport for London franchise)
Mersey Rail (Northern Line, City Line and Wirral Line)
Northern Rail (owned by Serco-Abellio)
North Yorkshire Moors (largest heritage railway in UK)
Southeastern (owned by Govia)
Southernn (owned by Govia)
South West Trains (owned by Stagecoach Group)
Virgin Trains (owned: Virgin Group (51%) Stagecoach (49%)
West Coast Railways (based at Carnforth, Lancashire)

Railway Stations: Locations

Anhalter	Berlin	**King's Cross**	London	**Saint Lazare**	Paris
Bank Top	Darlington	**Lime Street**	Liverpool	**Shrub Hill**	Worcester
Buchanan Street	Glasgow	**Liverpool Street**	London	**Snow Hill**	Birmingham
Charing Cross	London	**London Rd**	Leicester	**Spa**	Bath
Citadel	Carlisle	**Low Level**	Wolverhampton	**St David's**	Exeter
Connolly	Dublin	**Marine**	Dover	**St Enoch**	Glasgow
Euston	London	**Midland**	Derby	**Temple Meads**	Bristol
Foregate Street	Worcester	**Mumps**	Oldham	**Thorpe**	Norwich
Forster Square	Bradford	**New Street**	Birmingham	**Trent Valley**	Nuneaton
Gare du Nord	Paris	**Paddington**	London	**Union**	Washington
Grand Central	New York	**Paragon**	Hull	**Victoria**	London, Manchester, Bombay
Harbour	Folkestone, Portsmouth	**Parkway**	Bristol		
Haymarket	Edinburgh	**Piccadilly**	Manchester	**Waterloo**	London
High Level	Wolverhampton	**Priory**	Dover	**Waverley**	Edinburgh
High Street	Swansea	**Queen Street**	Cardiff, Glasgow	**Yaroslavl**	Moscow

Railways: General Information

accident: first caused by moving train Rt Hon William Huskisson MP was run down by the *Rocket* at the opening of the Liverpool & Manchester Railway 15 Sept. 1830. He was rushed to Eccles Hospital on the *Northumbrian*. A runaway wagon caused the death of two boys in a Tyne coalpit in 1650. Unfortunately numerous incidents of this kind took place but were not really the work of trains in the accepted sense of the word.

air-brake: designer George Westinghouse (1846–1914) developed the air-brake from the simple non-automatic system of 1866 into the fully automatic (i.e. the brakes are automatically applied should any break in the train air pipe occur). System still in use in most countries. Most British railways used the vacuum brake, which had nothing to do with Westing-house.

APT BR Advanced Passenger Train ran from London to Glasgow in 3 hrs 52 mins 45 secs at an average speed of 103 mph (12 Dec. 1984). This service was abandoned in 1986 due to numerous problems.

British speed records A Eurostar train reached 208mph on a stretch of track between Ashford and Dartford in Kent to create a new UK speed record in July 2003. A Virgin Pendolino tilting train set a record for the non-stop journey between London and Manchester in September 2004. The 184 miles were covered in 1hr 54mins.

broad-gauge railway: last train the *Cornishman* was the last broad-gauge passenger train to run, on 21 May 1892, from Paddington to Penzance.

Chicago rail system nicknamed the 'El', which is short for elevated (several other cities, notably New York, also had elevated railways known as 'Els').

diesel locomotive: first the first diesel locomotive to go into regular service was a Swedish-built metre-gauge Bo Bo type put into operation by Tunisian Railways in 1921.

dining car: first first buffet cars were put into service on the Philadelphia, Wilmington & Baltimore Railroad in 1863.

electric railway: first Brighton seafront, built by Magnus Volk (1851–1937), still known as Volk's Electric Railway.

electrification of railways modern standard system of railway electrification at 25 kV 50 Hz was first used in France in 1950 and in England on the Colchester– Clacton–Walton lines in 1959.

fare-paying customers: first to carry Oystermouth Railway built a railway from Swansea to Mumbles and on 25 March 1807 became first to convey fare-paying passengers. This railway closed in 1960.

father of railways George Stephenson.

father of the locomotive Richard Trevithick.

highest railway station Condor station in Bolivia.

horse-drawn railways Middleton Railway, Leeds, in 1758 was the first to be built under its own Act of Parliament, although other horse-worked railways had been operating in the Tyne coalfield on private land for many years previously.

horse-drawn railways: public the Surrey Iron Railway from Wandsworth to Croydon (opened 26 July 1803) was the first horse-drawn railway opened to the public, inasmuch as it accepted consignments. Passengers were not carried (at least not officially!).

locomotive railway: first Stockton and Darlington, opened in 1825.

locomotive railway: first passenger line Liverpool to Manchester, opened in 1830.

London railway: first Spa Road to Deptford, part of London & Greenwich Railway, opened 8 Feb. 1836.

London Underground: first automatic barrier Stamford Brook.

borne in mind that the term 'Atlantic' properly describes a 4-4-2

London Underground: first line Metropolitan Line, from Bishop's Road to Farringdon Street, 10 Jan. 1863.

longest platform in Great Britain Colchester, at 1981 ft

longest platform in the world Kharagpur Station, West Bengal at 2,733 ft

Mallard LNER 'A4' Class Pacific No. 4468 *Mallard* reached a speed of just over 126 mph for a few seconds on a brake-test trial run between Grantham and Peterborough (3 July 1938). *Mallard* can be seen at the National Railway Museum, York.

monorail: first Charles Lartique's system was used on a demonstration line in France and then on the Listowel and Ballybunion Railway in Ireland, 1883. It was comprised a single rail raised about 4 ft above the ground on an A-frame with two guiding rails about 1 ft off the ground.

National Railway Museum museum opened in York in 1975 and combining the holdings of the British Transport Commission's museum at Clapham and the LNER museum at York.

nationalisation railways were nationalised from 1 Jan. 1948 and were divided into five regions: 1) Scottish, 2) North Eastern, 3) London Midland, 4) Eastern, 5) Western and Southern. (The Eastern and North Eastern were amalgamated on 1 Jan. 1967.)

platforms: most UK Waterloo main line.

Puffing Billy world's first steam locomotive running on smooth rails instead of the previous rack rails. Designed by William Hedley and first put into operation in 1813 from Wylam colliery in Northumberland to the river Tyne. The *Wylam Dilly* was made at much the same time. Note: Trevithick's Penydarren engine had smooth iron wheels running on smooth cast-iron tram plates!

railcar: designer William Bridges Adams designed the 6-wheeled steam railcar *Fairfield* (named from road in Bow where he operated from).

railtrack: longest in straight line Nullarbor Plain, Australia.

railway: first private opened in June 1789 by the Loughborough & Nanpanton Railway Co.

railway king George Hudson.

Railways Act 1921 from 1 Jan. 1923 the amalgamation of the railways meant that four major companies were formed: 1) The Great Western Railway, 2) The London, Midland & Scottish Railway, 3) The London and North Eastern Railway, 4) The Southern Railway.

railways: USA operating co. Amtrak.

Rainhill Trials competition held on 6–14 Oct. 1829 near Liverpool to choose the design of locomotive for Liverpool & Manchester Railway. Robert Stephenson's *Rocket* won the £500 prize by beating Timothy Hackworth's *Sans Pareil* and John Braithwaite and John Ericsson's *Novelty*.

RKB code: meaning the code RKB refers to a single item of rolling stock containing a restaurant seating portion, a buffet counter and a kitchen.

San Francisco rail system BART (Bay Area Rapid Transit).

Schools-Class locomotives introduced by Southern Railway in 1930 and named after famous schools, first being called *Eton*.

Scottish railway: first Kilmarnock and Troon Railway was the first 'proper' railway in Scotland. Opened 6 July 1812.

sleeping cars: European wagons lits.

sleeping car: first the *Chambersburg*, introduced by the Cumberland Valley Railroad on its Pennsylvanian Harrisburg–Chambers route, was the first example of a sleeping car (1836).

standard gauge first used on Willington Colliery wagonway near Newcastle upon Tyne in 1764 and set at 42 8½3 or 1,435 mm, this being an average of the wagon ways in this area. It is thought that the average gauge of between 42 63 and 42 93 was the width of the track required for two horses abreast.

station: largest Grand Central, New York.

station: largest UK Clapham Junction.

station: most northerly in Great Britain Thurso.

steam locomotive: first Richard Trevithick built the first locomotive and ran it on the Penydarren Railway, near Merthyr Tydfil, on 6 Feb. 1804.

TGV Train à Grande Vitesse (High-Speed Train); began a regular hourly service between Paris and Lyon, the 265-mile journey taking 2 hrs 40 mins.

third-class travel redesignated as second class by British Rail in 1956. (The old second class had largely fallen out of use by the turn of the century.)

timetable: national *Bradshaw's Railway Companion* was the first national railway timetable in 1839.

underground: British four British cities with underground railways: London, Glasgow, Liverpool and Newcastle (Metro).

most passengers Moscow.

most stations New York.

names Berlin – U Bahn; Rome – Metropolitana; Stockholm – T-Bana; Paris – Métro.

USSR: terms for first and second class Soft and Hard class.

wheel configurations: nicknames **Atlantic (4-4-2):** name originally applied to a batch of 4-4-2s built by Baldwin of Philadelphia for the Atlantic Coast Railroad in 1894. In the UK, Atlantics were in use for hauling express passenger trains on the Great Northern, North Eastern, North British and London, Brighton & South Coast Railways. It should be locomotive with a separate tender; thus 4-4-2 tank engines, such as were in widespread use in the UK, are not true Atlantics but are more analogous to a 4-4-0 with an additional axle to support a rear bunker. **Mogul (2-6-0):** first true Mogul, with a leading two-wheel Bissell truck, was built by Baldwin of Philadelphia for the Louisville & Nashville Railroad in 1860. In the UK in the twentieth century Moguls were in extensive use on all four of the post-1923 mainline railways, and after 1948, in all regions of British Railways. The term Mogul properly applies to a 2-6-0 with outside cylinders, so that the inside-cylindered 2-6-0s of the Caledonian, and Glasgow and South Western Railways were not true Moguls, being essentially large 0-6-0-s with a leading truck for increased front-end stability. **Pacific (4-6-2):** name seems to have originated because the engines concerned were obviously bigger than Atlantics. In the UK, Pacifics were in general express service on the LNER from the mid-Twenties, the LMS from 1933 and the Southern Railway from 1941. The Great Western Railway had actually built the first UK Pacific (No. 111 *The Great Bear*) in 1908 but found it something of a white elephant. It was scrapped in 1924, and various mechanical components were incorporated in a new 'Castle' class 4-6-0, No. 111 *Viscount Churchill*. **Baltic (4-6-4):** name appears to be of Germanic origin. (To an American, a 4-6-4 is a Hudson.) Only one 4-6-4 tender engine ever ran in the UK. This was Gresley's experimental high-pressure water-tube boiler 4-cylinder compound No. 10000, built for the LNER in 1929. It was rebuilt as a conventional 3-cylinder simple expansion engine and ran until 1959, latterly as British Railways No. 60700. This engine was not a true Baltic, since the rear carrying axles were disposed as a Cartazzi axle and a separate two-wheel radial truck, making the engine technically a 4-6-2-2. Around 1920, however, there was a vogue, particularly on the London Brighton & South Coast, Lancashire & Yorkshire and Glasgow & South Western Railways, for extremely large 4-6-4 tank engines, which, while not true Baltics (*vide supra* under Atlantic), were referred to as Baltics consistently enough to legitimise the usage. **Prairie (2-6-2):** name applied in the American Midwest after first examples were built in 1900 for the Chicago, Burlington & Quincy Railroad. Apart from one curious 8-cylinder experimental engine built as a semi-private venture by Cecil Paget at Derby in 1908, the only 2-6-2 tender engines to run in the UK were Gresley's extremely successful V2-class built from 1936 onwards for the LNER, and his lightweight V4 design of 1941, of which only two examples were built before his death. In the 20th century, several hundred 2-6-2 tank engines were built in the UK, particularly by the Great Western Railway, and, although not true Prairies (being actually Moguls with a rear bunker), they were generally referred to as Prairie tanks. **Consolidation (2-8-0):** name is that carried by the first example of this type, built in 1865 for the Lehigh & Mahanoy Railroad. The name was not much used to describe British 2-8-0s, but it does seem to have attached itself to the 2-8-0 freight locomotives built at Swindon for the Great Western Railway by G J Churchward and his successors. This may be due to Churchward's close following of American locomotive practice resulting in an essentially American designation attaching itself to his engines of the 2-8-0 type. **Mikado (2-8-2):** so named because the first examples were made in the USA for export to Japan. In the UK, the only 2-8-2 tender engines were built by Gresley for the LNER. First, the two heavy freight engines of class P1, built in 1925. These were mechanically a cross between an A1-class Pacific and an O2-class Consolidation. As a small, non-standard class they were both withdrawn in 1945. Second was the magnificent class P2, six examples of which were built 1934–36, for working express passenger trains to Scotland. They were rebuilt as very mediocre Pacifics after Gresley's death. **Decapod:** a curiosity – to an American, a Decapod is a 2-10-0. The only two classes of engines of this type to run in the UK were the 251 examples of the standard-class 9F, built by British Railways between 1954 and 1960, and 25 examples bought secondhand from the Ministry of Supply after WW2. These, however, were never referred to as Decapods (except, presumably, by Americans!). The Decapod, however, was a huge 0-10-0 tank engine built by the Great Eastern Railway in 1903 as part of an experiment in the drastic acceleration of suburban trains. It did everything which was expected of it, but was far too heavy for the track and bridges. It was broken up shortly afterwards and a few components incorporated in a 0-8-0 goods engine. **NB** The following type names are largely in American use only, generally because no locomotives of the type referred to ever ran in the UK. **American (4-4-0):** applies only to the classic outside-cylindered, bar-framed three-point suspension locomotive familiar from countless Western films. **Ten Wheeler (4-6-0):** strictly an American term only. (Casey Jones was driving Illinois Central ten-wheeler No. 382 when he met his death at Vaughan, Mississippi, on 29 April 1900.) **Mastodon (4-8-0):** there were actually two 4-8-0 tender engines on the narrow-gauge Londonderry & Lough Swilly Railway in Ireland. They were used on the desolate Burtonport extension line in north-west Donegal, where I doubt if anyone ever referred to them as Mastodons. **Berkshire (2-8-4):** pronounced 'BurkSHIRE'. **Mountain (4-8-4) Santa Fe (2-10-2):** introduced by the Atchison, Topeka & Santa Fe Railroad in 1903, for working over the Raton Pass. **Texas (2-10-4):** called this in the USA but called 'Selkirk' in Canada.

world speed record 322mph by a French TGV in 1990.

world's longest railway: Trans-Siberian running from Moscow (Yaroslavl Station) to Vladivostok (5,801 miles); opened 3 Nov. 1901

United States

Presidents

	President		*Birthplace*	*Life span*	*Party*	*In office*
1	**Washington**	George	Virginia	1732–1799	Federalist	1789–1797
2	**Adams**	John	Massachusetts	1735–1826	Federalist	1797–1801
3	**Jefferson**	Thomas	Virginia	1743–1826	Republican	1801–1809
4	**Madison**	James	Virginia	1751–1836	Republican	1809–1817
5	**Monroe**	James	Virginia	1758–1831	Republican	1817–1825
6	**Adams**	John Quincy	Massachusetts	1767–1848	Republican	1825–1829
7	**Jackson**	Andrew	South Carolina	1767–1845	Democratic	1829–1837
8	**Van Buren**	Martin	New York	1782–1862	Democratic	1837–1841
9	**Harrison**	William Henry	Virginia	1773–1841	Whig	1841
10	**Tyler**	John	Virginia	1790–1862	Whig	1841–1845
11	**Polk**	James Knox	North Carolina	1795–1849	Democratic	1845–1849
12	**Taylor**	Zachary	Virginia	1784–1850	Whig	1849–1850
13	**Fillmore**	Millard	New York	1800–1874	Whig	1850–1853
14	**Pierce**	Franklin	New Hampshire	1804–1869	Democratic	1853–1857
15	**Buchanan**	James	Pennsylvania	1791–1868	Democratic	1857–1861
16	**Lincoln**	Abraham	Kentucky	1809–1865	Republican	1861–1865
17	**Johnson**	Andrew	North Carolina	1808–1875	Union	1865–1869
18	**Grant**	Ulysses Simpson	Ohio	1822–1885	Republican	1869–1877
19	**Hayes**	Rutherford Birchard	Ohio	1822–1893	Republican	1877–1881
20	**Garfield**	James Abram	Ohio	1831–1881	Republican	1881
21	**Arthur**	Chester Alan	Vermont	1830–1886	Republican	1881–1885
22	**Cleveland**	Stephen Grover	New Jersey	1837–1908	Democratic	1885–1889
23	**Harrison**	Benjamin	Ohio	1833–1901	Republican	1889–1893
24	**Cleveland**	Grover	New Jersey	1837–1908	Democratic	1893–1897
25	**Mckinley**	William	Ohio	1843–1901	Republican	1897–1901
26	**Roosevelt**	Theodore	New York	1858–1919	Republican	1901–1909
27	**Taft**	William Howard	Ohio	1857–1930	Republican	1909–1913
28	**Wilson**	Thomas Woodrow	Virginia	1856–1924	Democratic	1913–1921
29	**Harding**	Warren Gamaliel	Ohio	1865–1923	Republican	1921–1923
30	**Coolidge**	Calvin	Vermont	1872–1933	Republican	1923–1929
31	**Hoover**	Herbert Clark	Iowa	1874–1964	Republican	1929–1933
32	**Roosevelt**	Franklin Delano	New York	1882–1945	Democratic	1933–1945
33	**Truman**	Harry S	Missouri	1884–1972	Democratic	1945–1953
34	**Eisenhower**	Dwight David	Texas	1890–1969	Republican	1953–1961
35	**Kennedy**	John Fitzgerald	Massachusetts	1917–1963	Democratic	1961–1963
36	**Johnson**	Lyndon Baines	Texas	1908–1973	Democratic	1963–1969
37	**Nixon**	Richard Milhous	California	1913–1995	Republican	1969–1974
38	**Ford**	Gerald Rudolph	Nebraska	1913–2006	Republican	1974–1977
39	**Carter**	James Earl	Georgia	1924–	Democratic	1977–1981
40	**Reagan**	Ronald Wilson	Illinois	1911–2004	Republican	1981–1989
41	**Bush**	George Herbert Walker	Massachusetts	1924–	Republican	1989–1993
42	**Clinton**	William Jefferson	Arkansas	1946–	Democratic	1993–2001
43	**Bush**	George Walker	Connecticut	1946–	Republican	2001–2009
44	**Obama**	Barack Hussein	Hawaii	1961–	Democratic	2009–

Vice Presidents

Vice President		*Birthplace*	*In office*	*Vice President to*
Adams	John	Massachusetts	1789–1797	Washington
Jefferson	Thomas	Virginia	1797–1801	Adams
Burr	Aaron	New Jersey	1801–1805	Jefferson
Clinton	George	New York	1805–1812	Jefferson/Madison
Gerry	Elbridge	Massachusetts	1813–1814	Madison
Tompkins	Daniel D	New York	1817–1825	Monroe
Calhoun	John Caldwell	South Carolina	1825–1832	Adams/Jackson
Van Buren	Martin	New York	1833–1837	Jackson
Johnson	Richard Mentor	Kentucky	1837–1841	Van Buren
Tyler	John	Virginia	1841	Harrison
Dallas George Mifflin	Pennsylvania	1845–1849	Polk	
Fillmore	Millard	New York	1849–1850	Taylor
King	William Rufus De Vane	North Carolina	1853	Pierce
Breckinridge	John Cabell	Kentucky	1857–1861	Buchanan
Hamlin	Hannibal	Maine	1861–1865	Lincoln
Johnson	Andrew	North Carolina	1865	Lincoln
Colfax	Schuyler	New York	1869–1873	Grant
Wilson	Henry	New Hampshire	1873–1875	Grant
Wheeler	William A	New York	1877–1881	Hayes
Arthur	Chester A	Vermont	1881	Garfield
Hendricks	Thomas A	Ohio	1885	Arthur
Morton	Levi Parsons	Vermont	1889–1893	Harrison
Stevenson	Adlai E	Kentucky	1893–1897	Cleveland
Hobart	Garret A	New Jersey	1897–1899	McKinley
Roosevelt	Theodore	New York	1901	McKinley
Fairbanks	Charles Warren	Ohio	1905–1909	Roosevelt
Sherman	James Schoolcraft	New York	1909–1912	Taft
Marshall	Thomas R	Indiana	1913–1921	Wilson
Coolidge	Calvin	Vermont	1921–1923	Harding
Dawes	Charles Gates	Ohio	1925–1929	Coolidge

Vice President		*Birthplace*	*In office*	*Vice President to*
Curtis	Charles	Kansas	1929–1933	Hoover
Garner	John Nance	Texas	1933–1941	Roosevelt
Wallace	Henry Agard	Iowa	1941–1945	Roosevelt
Truman	Harry S	Missouri	1945	Roosevelt
Barkley	Alben W	Kentucky	1949–1953	Truman
Nixon	Richard Milhous	California	1953–1961	Eisenhower
Johnson	Lyndon Baines	Texas	1961–1963	Kennedy
Humphrey	Hubert H	South Dakota	1965–1969	Johnson
Agnew	Spiro T	Maryland	1969–1973	Nixon
Ford	Gerald Rudolph	Nebraska	1973–1974	Nixon
Rockefeller	Nelson Aldrich	Maine	1974–1977	Ford
Mondale	Walter F	Minnesota	1977–1981	Carter
Bush	George Herbert Walker	Massachusetts	1981–1989	Reagan
Quayle	J Danforth	Indiana	1989–1993	Bush, G H W
Gore	Albert	Washington DC	1993–2001	Clinton
Cheney	Richard B	Nebraska	2001–2009	Bush, G W
Biden	Joseph Robinette	Pennsylvania	2009–	Obama

Presidents and Vice Presidents: Miscellaneous Information

assassinated Lincoln, Garfield, McKinley, Kennedy.
attempts Jackson (Richard Lawrence 1835), Truman (Griselio Torresola and Oscar Collazo 1950), Ford (5 Sept 1975, Lynette 'Squeaky' Frome; 22 Sept 1975, Sarah Jane More), Reagan (John Hinckley) 1981.
bachelor James Buchanan.
bald Martin Van Buren and Dwight Eisenhower.
bath: got stuck in William Howard Taft.
born in a log cabin Andrew Jackson
broccoli: hated George Bush.
Camelot: nickname of John F Kennedy's regime.
China: first to visit Richard Nixon.
Clinton's cat: named Socks (belonged to daughter Chelsea).
Confederate states: president Jefferson Davis.
cried on television during campaign Edmund Muskie.
Declaration of Independence: drafted by Thomas Jefferson.
Democrat-turned-Republican: first Ronald Reagan.
Democratic Party Headquarters Tammany Hall, New York.
Democratic Party symbol Donkey.
Democratic split during Vietnam War Hawks and Doves.
died in office W Harding, W Harrison, F D Roosevelt, Z Taylor.
divorced: first Ronald Reagan.
duel: killed opponent in Andrew Jackson killed Charles Dickinson in a pistol duel, 30 May 1806.
elected for four terms F D Roosevelt.
elected unanimously by Electoral College George Washington.
elected with one vote against James Monroe.
ex-director of the CIA George Bush.
fathers and sons John Adams and his son John Quincy Adams. George Herbert Walker Bush and his son George 'Dubya' Bush.
father was UK ambassador John F Kennedy's father Joseph.
fireside chats: radio broadcasts F D Roosevelt.
four freedoms Speech, worship, freedom from fear and want. Roosevelt's basis for UN Charter, San Francisco 1945.
Fourteen Points Woodrow Wilson.
Garfield: assassinated by Charles Guiteau 1881.
Gettysburg Address Lincoln's speech of 1863.
grandfather and grandson William Harrison and Benjamin Harrison.
Grand Old Party (GOP) Republican party nickname.
Great Triumvirate statesmen John Calhoun, Henry Clay, Daniel Webster.
hospital: first born in Jimmy Carter.
illegitimate child: accused of having Stephen Grover Cleveland.
impeachment: two In 1868 Andrew Johnson was cleared of breaching Tenure of Office Act. Senate vote fell one short of two-thirds majority. In 1999 Bill Clinton was cleared of high crimes and misdemeanours by the Senate vote on both Articles I and II.
imprisoned by British Andrew Jackson (during War of Independence).
Jefferson: holiday retreat Poplar Row.
Kennedy's attorney general Robert Kennedy, his brother.
Kennedy: assassinated by Lee Harvey Oswald, 1963 (shot by Jack Ruby).
kitchen cabinet Andrew Jackson's unofficial advisers.
knighted by Britain Eisenhower and Reagan.
Lincoln assassinated by John Wilkes Booth (an actor), 1865. Samuel Mudd jailed for setting Booth's leg. Lincoln died in Peterson House, Washington DC.
longest term F D Roosevelt, 12 years.
male model: former Gerald Ford.
McKinley assassinated by Leon Czolgosz, 1901.
minister to Great Britain: first John Adams.
Monroe Doctrine: allegedly drafted by John Quincy Adams.
Monroe: lived Oak Hill.
New Deal F D Roosevelt's 1930s recovery plan.
newspaper publisher Warren Harding – Marion *Star*.
nicknames J Carter – Hot Shot & Toadsy; G H W Bush – Wimp; Andrew Jackson – Old Hickory; Clinton – Comeback Kid; G W Bush – Dubya.
Nobel Peace Prize Theodore Roosevelt, 1906; Woodrow Wilson, 1919; Jimmy Carter, 2002.
not elected as President Gerald Ford (was also not elected Vice President).
occupation: most common lawyer.
oldest to take office Ronald Reagan, aged 69.
pneumonia: died of William Henry Harrison.
President for the day David Atchison – Zachary Taylor would not be sworn in on a Sunday.
prison; presidential candidate ran from Eugene Debs in 1912.
Quakers Herbert Hoover, Richard Nixon.
qualifications required native born,14 years' residence, 35 years old.
re-elected: after losing office Stephen Grover Cleveland.
Republican Party symbol elephant.
residence White House.
resigned Richard Nixon.
resigned as Vice President Spiro Agnew; income tax evasion charge.
Roman Catholic: first John F Kennedy.
Roughriders Roosevelt second in command to Col. Leonard Wood.
Secretary of State Eisenhower's – John Foster Dulles; Nixon's – Henry Kissinger; Carter's – Cyrus Robert Vance; Clinton's – Madeleine Albright; Obama's – Hillary Clinton.
shirt advertisement: appeared in Ronald Reagan.
shortest term William Henry Harrison, about a month.
slogans: presidential Full Dinner Pail – McKinley; Great Society – Lyndon Johnson; New Deal – F D Roosevelt; New Frontier – Kennedy.
slogans: other 'Would you buy a used car from this man?' – said by anti-Nixon protesters. 'The buck stops here' – Truman. 'No taxation without representation' – during dispute with Britain over taxation.
State of the Union presidential speech given annually in January.
stood against Bush- Michael Dukakis; Clinton - Ross Perot & George Bush; Hayes - Samuel Tilde; Hoover - Al Smith; Truman - Thomas Dewey.
terms limitation two, under the 22nd Amendment to Constitution.
Vice President: born James Colbath Henry Wilson.
Crédit Mobilier scandal Schuyler Colfax.
Confederate general John Cabell Breckinridge.
killed Alexander Hamilton Aaron Burr.
letters from London George Mifflin Dallas.
lives at Admiralty Building, Washington.
Nobel Peace Prize 1925 Charles Dawes.
treason trial Aaron Burr.
wrote no. 1 hit single Charles Dawes ('It's all in the Game').
vice-presidential candidate: first female Geraldine Ferraro in 1984.
Virginia plan James Madison.
Washington: lived Mount Vernon.
Washington: Quotation Parson Weems wrote apocryphal stories about Washington, the most famous being when George was six and, given a hatchet, he purportedly chopped down a cherry tree and after his father asked him who had killed it he replied "I cannot tell a lie, I did it with my little hatchet"
Watergate scandal burglary of Democratic HQ in Washington on 17 June 1972.
White House: architect James Hoban.
White House: first occupier John Adams.
wives of presidents George Washington – Martha Custis; Abraham Lincoln – Mary Todd; F D Roosevelt – Eleanor Roosevelt; J F Kennedy – Jacqueline Bouvier; Ronald Reagan – Nancy Davis; George Bush – Barbara Pierce; Bill Clinton – Hillary Rodham; George 'Dubya' Bush – Laura Welch; Barack Obama – Michelle Robinson.
youngest elected president John F Kennedy.
youngest president Theodore Roosevelt (took office following assassination of McKinley).

States

State	*Nickname*	*Motto*	*State tree*	*State bird*	*State flower*	*State capital*	*Post code*
Alabama (Ala.)	Yellowhammer Cotton, Heart of Dixie	We dare defend our rights	southern pine	yellowhammer	camelia	Montgomery	AL
Alaska (Alas.)	Last Frontier Land of the Midnight Sun	North to the future	Sitka spruce	willow ptarmigan	forget-me-not	Juneau	AK
Arizona (Ariz.)	Grand Canyon, Apache	God enriches	paloverde	cactus wren	saguaro cactus blossom	Phoenix	AZ
Arkansas (Ark.)	Natural, Bear, Wonder Land of Opportunity	The people rule	pine	mockingbird	apple blossom	Little Rock	AR
California (Cal.)	Golden	I have found it	Californian redwood	Californian valley quail	golden poppy	Sacramento	CA
Colorado (Colo.)	Centennial	Nothing without providence	Colorado blue spruce	lark bunting	Rocky Mountain columbine	Denver	CO
Connecticut (Conn.)	Constitution Nutmeg	He who transplanted still sustains	white oak	American robin	mountain laurel	Hartford	CT
District of Columbia	DC	Justice for all	scarlet oak	woodthrush	American beauty rose		
Delaware (Del.)	First, Diamond	Liberty and independence	American holly	blue hen chicken	peach blossom	Dover	DE
Florida (Fla.)	Sunshine, Peninsular	In God we trust	sabal palm	mockingbird	orange blossom	Tallahassee	FL
Georgia (Ga.)	Empire State of the South Peach	Wisdom, justice and moderation	live oak	brown thrasher	Cherokee rose	Atlanta	GA
Hawaii (Hi.)	Aloha	The life of the land is perpetuated in righteousness	kukui (candlenut)	nene (Hawaiian goose)	hibiscus	Honolulu	HI
Idaho (Ida.)	Gem	Let it be perpetual	western white pine	mountain bluebird	syringa	Boise	ID
Illinois (Ill.)	Prairie Land of Lincoln	State sovereignty – national union	white oak	cardinal	native violet	Springfield	IL
Indiana (Ind.)	Hoosier	Crossroads of America	tulip tree (yellow poplar)	cardinal	peony	Indianapolis	IN
Iowa (Ia.)	Hawkeye Corn	Our liberties we prize and our rights we will maintain	oak	eastern goldfinch	wild rose	Des Moines	IA
Kansas (Kan.)	Sunflower Jayhawker	To the stars through difficulties	cottonwood	western meadowlark	native sunflower	Topeka	KS
Kentucky (Ky.)	Blue Grass	United we stand, divided we fall	tulip tree (yellow poplar)	cardinal	goldenrod	Frankfort	KY
Louisiana (La.)	Pelican, Sugar Creole, Bayou	Union, justice and confidence	bald cypress	eastern brown pelican	magnolia	Baton Rouge	LA
Maine (Me.)	Pine Tree	I direct	eastern white pine	chickadee	white pine cone and tassel	Augusta	ME
Maryland (Md.)	Free, Old Line	Manly deeds, womanly words	white oak	Baltimore oriole	black-eyed Susan	Annapolis	MD
Massachusetts (Mass.)	Bay Old Colony	By the sword we seek peace but peace only under liberty	American elm	chickadee	mayflower (trailing arbutus)	Boston	MA
Michigan (Mich.)	Wolverine Water Wonderland	If you seek a pleasant peninsula, look about you	white pine	robin	apple blossom	Lansing	MI
Minnesota (Minn.)	North Star, Gopher Land of 10,000 Lakes Land of Sky-Blue Waters	The North Star	red, or Norway pine	loon	pink and white lady's slipper	St Paul	MN

State	*Nickname*	*Motto*	*State tree*	*State bird*	*State flower*	*State capital*	*Post code*
Mississippi (Miss.)	Magnolia	By valor and arms	magnolia	mockingbird	magnolia	Jackson	MS
Missouri (Mo.)	Show Me	The welfare of the people shall be the supreme law	dogwood	bluebird	hawthorn	Jefferson City	MO
Montana (Mont.)	Treasure Big Sky Country	Gold and silver	Ponderosa pine	western meadowlark	bitterroot	Helena	MT
Nebraska (Nebr.)	Cornhusker, Beef Tree Planters	Equality before the law	cottonwood	western meadowlark	goldenrod	Lincoln	NB
Nevada (Nev.)	Sagebrush, Silver Battle Born	All for our country	single-leaf piñon	mountain bluebird	sagebrush	Carson City	NV
New Hampshire (NH)	Granite	Live free or die	white birch	purple finch	purple lilac	Concord	NH
New Jersey (NJ)	Garden	Liberty and prosperity	red oak	eastern goldfinch	purple violet	Trenton	NJ
New Mexico (N. Mex)	Land of Enchantment Sunshine	It grows as it goes	piñon (nut pine)	roadrunner	yucca flower	Santa Fe	NM
New York (NY)	Empire	Ever upward	sugar maple	bluebird	rose	Albany	NY
North Carolina (NC)	Tar Heel Old North	To be rather than to seem	longleaf pine	cardinal	dogwood	Raleigh	NC
North Dakota (N. Dak.)	Flickertail Sioux	Liberty and union, now and forever, one and inseparable	American elm	western meadowlark	wild prairie rose	Bismarck	ND
Ohio (Oh.)	Buckeye	With God, all things are possible	buckeye	cardinal	scarlet carnation	Columbus	OH
Oklahoma (Okla.)	Sooner	Labor conquers all things	redbud	scissor-tailed flycatcher	mistletoe	Oklahoma City	OK
Oregon (Oreg.)	Beaver	The Union	Douglas fir	western meadowlark	Oregon grape	Salem	OR
Pennsylvania (Pa.)	Keystone	Virtue, liberty, and independence	hemlock	ruffed grouse	mountain laurel	Harrisburg	PA
Rhode Island (RI)	Little Rhody Plantation	Hope	red maple	Rhode Island red	violet	Providence	RI
South Carolina (SC)	Palmetto	Prepared in mind and Resources While I breathe, I hope	cabbage palmetto	Carolina wren	yellow jessamine	Columbia	SC
South Dakota (S. Dak.)	Coyote Sunshine	Under God the people rule	Black Hills spruce	ring-necked pheasant	pasqueflower	Pierre	SD
Tennessee (Tenn.)	Volunteer	Agriculture and commerce	tulip poplar	mockingbird	iris	Nashville	TN
Texas (Tex.)	Lone Star	Friendship	pecan	mockingbird	bluebonnet	Austin	TX
Utah (Ut.)	Beehive	Industry	blue spruce	sea gull	sego lily	Salt Lake City	UT
Vermont (Vt.)	Green Mountain	Freedom and unity	sugar maple	hermit thrush	red clover	Montpelier	VT
Virginia (Va.)	Mother of Presidents Old Dominion, Cavalier	Thus always to tyrants	flowering dogwood	cardinal	dogwood	Richmond	VA
Washington (Wash.)	Evergreen, Chinook	By and by	western hemlock	willow goldfinch	western rhododendron	Olympia	WA
West Virginia (W. Va.)	Mountain Panhandle	Mountaineers are always free	sugar maple	cardinal	big rhododendron	Charleston	WV
Wisconsin (Wis.)	Badger	Forward America's Dairyland	sugar maple	robin	wood violet	Madison	WI
Wyoming (Wyo.)	Equality	Equal rights	cottonwood	meadowlark	Indian paintbrush	Cheyenne	WY

States: Bordered by

Alabama Tennessee, Georgia, Mississippi, Florida.
Alaska None.
Arizona California, Nevada, Utah, New Mexico, Colorado.
Arkansas Tennessee, Mississippi, Louisiana, Missouri, Texas, Oklahoma.
California Arizona, Nevada, Oregon.
Colorado Utah, Wyoming, Arizona, New Mexico, Nebraska, Kansas, Oklahoma.
Connecticut Massachusetts, Rhode Island, New York.
Delaware Pennsylvania, New Jersey, Maryland.
Florida Georgia, Alabama.
Georgia South Carolina, Florida, Alabama, Tennessee, North Carolina.
Hawaii None.
Idaho Utah, Nevada, Washington, Wyoming, Oregon, Montana.
Illinois Kentucky, Missouri, Indiana, Wisconsin, Iowa.
Indiana Illinois, Michigan, Ohio, Kentucky.
Iowa Nebraska, Missouri, Illinois, Wisconsin, Minnesota, South Dakota.
Kansas Colorado, Oklahoma, Missouri, Nebraska.
Kentucky Tennessee, Illinois, Virginia, West Virginia, Missouri, Ohio, Indiana.
Louisiana Mississippi, Arkansas, Texas.
Maine New Hampshire.
Maryland Pennsylvania, Virginia, West Virginia, Delaware.
Massachusetts Vermont, New Hampshire, Rhode Island, New York, Connecticut.
Michigan Indiana, Ohio, Wisconsin.
Minnesota North Dakota, South Dakota, Iowa, Wisconsin.
Mississippi Louisiana, Arkansas, Tennessee, Alabama.
Missouri Iowa, Illinois, Kentucky, Tennessee, Arkansas, Oklahoma, Kansas, Nebraska.
Montana Idaho, Wyoming, North Dakota, South Dakota.
Nebraska Colorado, Wyoming, Iowa, South Dakota, Kansas, Missouri.
Nevada California, Utah, Arizona, Idaho, Oregon.
New Hampshire Maine, Massachusetts, Vermont.
New Jersey New York, Pennsylvania, Delaware.
New Mexico Colorado, Oklahoma, Texas, Arizona, Utah.
New York Vermont, Massachusetts, Connecticut, New Jersey, Pennsylvania.
North Carolina South Carolina, Virginia, Georgia, Tennessee.
North Dakota Montana, Minnesota, South Dakota.
Ohio Michigan, Indiana, Kentucky, West Virginia, Pennsylvania.
Oklahoma Texas, Arkansas, Kansas, Missouri, New Mexico, Colorado.
Oregon Washington, Idaho, California, Nevada.
Pennsylvania Delaware, New Jersey, New York, Maryland, West Virginia, Ohio.
Rhode Island Connecticut, Massachusetts.
South Carolina North Carolina, Georgia.
South Dakota North Dakota, Minnesota, Iowa, Nebraska, Wyoming, Montana.
Tennessee Kentucky, Alabama, Mississippi, Missouri, Arkansas, Georgia, Virginia, North Carolina.
Texas Louisiana, New Mexico, Oklahoma, Arkansas.
Utah Colorado, New Mexico, Arizona, Nevada, Wyoming, Idaho.
Vermont Massachusetts, New York, New Hampshire.
Virginia Maryland, West Virginia, Kentucky, Tennessee, North Carolina.
Washington Oregon, Idaho.
West Virginia Virginia, Kentucky, Ohio, Pennsylvania, Maryland.
Wisconsin Illinois, Michigan, Minnesota, Iowa.
Wyoming Montana, South Dakota, Nebraska, Colorado, Utah, Idaho.

Statistical Information

Order of Admission to the Union

1st	Delaware (1787)	**18th**	Louisiana (1812)	**35th**	West Virginia (1863)
2nd	Pennsylvania (1787)	**19th**	Indiana (1816)	**36th**	Nevada (1864)
3rd	New Jersey (1787)	**20th**	Mississippi (1817)	**37th**	Nebraska (1867)
4th	Georgia (1788)	**21st**	Illinois (1818)	**38th**	Colorado (1876)
5th	Connecticut (1788)	**22nd**	Alabama (1819)	**39th**	North Dakota (1889)
6th	Massachusetts (1788)	**23rd**	Maine (1820)	**40th**	South Dakota (1889)
7th	Maryland (1788)	**24th**	Missouri (1821)	**41st**	Montana (1889)
8th	South Carolina (1788)	**25th**	Arkansas (1836)	**42nd**	Washington (1889)
9th	New Hampshire (1788)	**26th**	Michigan (1837)	**43rd**	Idaho (1890)
10th	Virginia (1788)	**27th**	Florida (1845)	**44th**	Wyoming (1890)
11th	New York (1788)	**28th**	Texas (1845)	**45th**	Utah (1896)
12th	North Carolina (1789)	**29th**	Iowa (1846)	**46th**	Oklahoma (1907)
13th	Rhode Island (1790)	**30th**	Wisconsin (1848)	**47th**	New Mexico (1912)
14th	Vermont (1791)	**31st**	California (1850)	**48th**	Arizona (1912)
15th	Kentucky (1792)	**32nd**	Minnesota (1858)	**49th**	Alaska (1959)
16th	Tennessee (1796)	**33rd**	Oregon (1859)	**50th**	Hawaii (1959)
17th	Ohio (1803)	**34th**	Kansas (1861)		

Largest: by size

1st	Alaska	**18th**	North Dakota	**35th**	Tennessee
2nd	Texas	**19th**	Oklahoma	**36th**	Virginia
3rd	California	**20th**	Missouri	**37th**	Kentucky
4th	Montana	**21st**	Washington	**38th**	Indiana
5th	New Mexico	**22nd**	Wisconsin	**39th**	Maine
6th	Arizona	**23rd**	Georgia	**40th**	South Carolina
7th	Nevada	**24th**	Florida	**41st**	West Virginia
8th	Colorado	**25th**	Illinois	**42nd**	Maryland
9th	Wyoming	**26th**	Iowa	**43rd**	Vermont
10th	Michigan	**27th**	Arkansas	**44th**	New Hampshire
11th	Oregon	**28th**	New York	**45th**	Massachusetts
12th	Minnesota	**29th**	North Carolina	**46th**	Hawaii
13th	Utah	**30th**	Alabama	**47th**	New Jersey
14th	Idaho	**31st**	Louisiana	**48th**	Connecticut
15th	Kansas	**32nd**	Mississippi	**49th**	Delaware
16th	Nebraska	**33rd**	Pennsylvania	**50th**	Rhode Island
17th	South Dakota	**34th**	Ohio		

Largest: by population

1st	California	**18th**	Maryland	**35th**	New Mexico
2nd	New York	**19th**	Washington	**36th**	Utah
3rd	Texas	**20th**	Louisiana	**37th**	Nebraska
4th	Florida	**21st**	Minnesota	**38th**	Maine
5th	Pennsylvania	**22nd**	Alabama	**39th**	Hawaii
6th	Illinois	**23rd**	Kentucky	**40th**	New Hampshire
7th	Ohio	**24th**	Arizona	**41st**	Nevada
8th	Michigan	**25th**	South Carolina	**42nd**	Idaho
9th	New Jersey	**26th**	Colorado	**43rd**	Rhode Island
10th	North Carolina	**27th**	Oklahoma	**44th**	Montana
11th	Georgia	**28th**	Connecticut	**45th**	South Dakota
12th	Virginia	**29th**	Iowa	**46th**	North Dakota
13th	Massachusetts	**30th**	Oregon	**47th**	Delaware
14th	Indiana	**31st**	Mississippi	**48th**	Alaska
15th	Missouri	**32nd**	Kansas	**49th**	Vermont
16th	Tennessee	**33rd**	Arkansas	**50th**	Wyoming
17th	Wisconsin	**34th**	West Virginia		

General Information

Alamo: killed in siege of 1836 Davy Crockett and Jim Bowie. **site of siege** Franciscan Mission Hall in San Antonio, Texas. **dates of siege** 23 Feb-ruary to 6 March 1836. **Mexican leader** Santa Anna. **meaning of** poplar (Spanish) or cottonwood tree.

Alaska: purchased from Russia, 1867; known as Seward's Folly.

America: named after Amerigo Vespucci.

anti-communist witch hunts 1950s Senator Joseph McCarthy.

Back to Africa Movement leader Marcus Garvey.

Bay Area Rapid Transit (BART) San Francisco.

Black Muslims: developed movement Elijah Muhammad 1934.

borders with eight other states Missouri and Tennessee.

Boss Tweed Corrupt leader of Tammany Hall Democrats, New York.

Boston Mountains Arkansas and Oklahoma (Ozarks).

Boston Tea Party: date of 16 December 1773. **reason for destruction of tea** protest against British tea tax. **owners of tea** British East India Company. **British retaliation** Intolerable Acts (shut down port, pending payment).

Bretton Woods Conference, NH, 1944: formed IMF and International Bank for Reconstruction.

bus boycott of Montgomery, Alabama: caused by Rosa Parks refusing to give up seat in Dec. 1955.

California: largest city Los Angeles.

Californian gold rush: first prospector James Wilson Marshall, 1848.

first major strike J A Sutter, a Swiss settler, 1849.

capital of America before Washington DC Philadelphia, 1783–9.

Central Park: designers Frederick Law Olmstead and Calvert Vaux.

child: first born of English parents Virginia Dare.

civil rights demo: troops called in Selma, Alabama,1956; Autherine Lucy expelled.

Civil War: dates of outbreak and surrender 15 April 1861 to 9 April 1865. **started: where** Fort Sumter in Charleston Harbour, SC, April 1861. **Lee surrender to Grant: where** Appomattox Court House, Virginia, 9 April 1865. **official ending: on surrender of** Gen. Richard Taylor, 4 May 1865. **first state to secede from Union** South Carolina, December 1860. **second state to secede** Mississippi, January 1861. **antebellum: meaning of** period before the war. **battle above the clouds** Lookout Mountain, Chattanooga, Tennessee. **Confederate capital** Richmond, Virginia.

Colin Powell: autobiography *My American Journey.*

commonwealths: officially called Massachusetts, Kentucky and Virginia.

commonwealth: self-styled Pennsylvania.

Confederate states: antebellum Alabama, Florida, Georgia, Louisiana, Mississippi, South Carolina, Texas. **four joined at outbreak of Civil War** Arkansas, North Carolina, Tennessee, Virginia. **President** Jefferson Davis.

Congress: first woman Jeanette Rankin, 1916.

Constitution of the USA: ratified by New Hampshire's ninth vote, 1788.

constitutional amendments Abolition of Slavery, 13th. Presidential Terms, 22nd. Prohibition, 18th. Votes for Blacks, 15th. Votes for Women, 19th.

coterminous states: high and low point Mt Whitney and Death Valley, both in California.

Coxey's Army unemployed march to Washington DC, 1894.

Dakota: named after Sioux Indian tribe.

Declaration of Independence 4 July 1776.

Delaware: three counties New Castle, Kent, Sussex.

Delaware: largest city Wilmington.

District of Columbia: ceded by Maryland, 1791.

Emancipation proclamation freeing of slaves -during Civil War.

Essex Junto: leader Timothy Pickering. **term coined by** John Hancock, 1778. **supported** Alexander Hamilton. **based** Massachusetts.

first state to join Union Delaware, 7 Dec. 1787.

Florida: largest city Jacksonville.

four corners touching Utah, Colorado, New Mexico, Arizona.

Gadsden purchase of land for USA in 1853 land bought from Mexico, now New Mexico and Arizona.

Georgia: marched through during Civil War General Sherman.

gold on land caused rush 1849 John Sutter.

good neighbour policy 1928 Latin American policy of F D Roosevelt.

Grape Workers Union leader led boycott Cesar Chavez, 1968.

Hartford Convention of 1814–15 began demise of Federalist Party.

Hawaii: European discoverer Captain James Cook, 1778.

Hawaii: former name Sandwich Islands.

Haymarket Massacre of 1886 police fire on crowd at May Day Rally in Chicago.

Homestead Act 1862: Lincoln's aim to provide land free to settlers to cultivate.

Honolulu: island situated Oahu.

honorary citizenship Winston Churchill.

Indian chief surrendered to General Miles Geronimo.

Intolerable Acts enforced embargo of Boston until compensation paid.

Irangate scandal: USA accused of arms for Iran in return for funds to Nicaraguan Contras. **famous testimony** Oliver North.

Ivy League: nickname for Top 8 universities & colleges of USA i.e. Harvard (1636 - Cambridge, Massachusetts), Yale (1701 - New Haven, Connecticut), Pennsylvania (1740 - Philadelphia, Pennsylvania), Princeton (1746 - Princeton, New Jersey), Columbia (1754 - Manhattan, New York City), Brown (1764 - Providence, Rhode Island), Dartmouth (1769 - Hanover, New Hampshire), Cornell (1853 - Ithaca, New York).

Kent State University, Ohio, 1970 National Guard shot dead four students during anti-war demo.

Ku Klux Klan: formed Pulaski, Tennessee, 1866.

Lend-lease Pact: March 1941 Roosevelt signed with Britain for WW2 aid.

Lewis and Clark expedition 1804–6 exploration of western America.

Lewis and Clark: state governors of Louisiana and Missouri Territory respectively.

Los Angeles: name when founded, 1781 the Town of the Queen of the Angels.

Louisiana purchase Mississippi valley bought from France 1803; 828,000 sq miles cost $15 million!
Louisiana: largest city New Orleans.
Louisiana: named in honour of Louis XIV.
Mammoth Cave Kentucky.
Manhattan Island: bought from Indian tribes for trinkets worth 60 guilders.
Manhattan Island: purchaser Peter Minuit.
mapped America Samuel de Champlain, 1605; John Smith, 1614.
Maryland named in honour of wife of Charles I: Henrietta Maria.
Mason–Dixon line: boundaries Pennsylvania– Maryland; border of North and South.
Mason–Dixon line: why drawn disputes of Penn and Calvert families in 1760s.
***Mayflower:* sister ship** *Speedwell*; deemed unseaworthy.
Mexican ceded states of 1848 Texas, New Mexico, California.
Mexican ceded states: clerk responsible Nicholas Trist.
Michigan: two land masses joined by Mackinac Bridge (Big Mac), built 1957.
Michigan: borders on Great Lakes all except Ontario.
Mississippi University: first black to enter James Meredith.
Montana: name means mountain (Spanish).
Mormon Church: founded at Fayette, New York, in 1830.
Nat Turner insurrection 1831 slave uprising in Virginia.
Naval Academy Annapolis, Maryland.
Nebraska: name means flat water.
Nevada: name means snow-clad (Spanish).
New England: named by John Smith, 1614. **6 states** Connecticut, Maine, Massachusetts, New Hampshire, Rhode Island, Vermont.
New Hampshire: named after English county of Hampshire, 1629.
New Orleans: same parallel as Cairo, Delhi, Shanghai.
New York named in honour of duke of York, later James II.
New York City: five boroughs Queens, Bronx, Manhattan, Brooklyn, Staten Island.
New York State: capital's former name Fort Orange, 1624; became Albany.
New York: political differences upstate is Conservative, downstate is Liberal.
North Dakota: largest city Fargo.
Oklahoma: name means red people.
oldest American town St Augustine, Florida, 1565.
Pilgrim Fathers: ship *Mayflower*. **landed** Provincetown in Massachusetts, November 1620.
first to land John Alden. **established** Plymouth Colony. **Indian interpreter** Squanto. **Indian welcomed them** Samoset, a Pemaquid from Maine.
Portsmouth, New Hampshire treaty ended Russo-Japanese war, 1905.
presidential primary: earliest New Hampshire.
rectangular-shaped states Wyoming and Colorado.
Rhode Island: official name The State of Rhode Island and Providence Plantations.
Richmond County: named in honour of Charles Lennox, duke of Richmond, son of Charles II.
Russia: closest point to Diomede Islands, Bering Strait.
San Francisco meeting of United Nations April 1945.
school integration: Federal troops enforced Little Rock, Arkansas, 1957.
Sea Islands: sub-tropical islands of South Carolina.
senator: first black Edward Brooke.
Seneca Falls Convention, 1848 Women's Rights' Movement began.
size of USA doubled by Louisiana purchase.
slave abolitionist leader Harriet Tubman, former slave.
slavery: abolished 1863. **escape network to the North** underground railroad. **last state to abolish** Mississippi.
Spindletop oil well, Texas blew 1901.
Tammany Hall (New York) byword for municipal corruption.
Tarpon Springs, Florida centre for Greek Orthodox religion and sponge industry.
Teapot Dome Affair, aka Elk Hills Scandal Sec. of Interior Albert Fall jailed for corruption.
territories: overseas American Virgin Islands, Commonwealth of Puerto Rico, Guam, Samoa.
terrorism: executed 1927 but pardoned 1977 Sacco and Vanzetti.
Texas: annexed by America, in 1845. **former capital** Houston, until 1839, then Austin. **largest city** Houston.
Townshend Acts 1767 British taxes that sparked revolt.
Vietnam: secret documents Pentagon papers showed USA involvement. **secret documents revealed by** Daniel Ellsberg, 1971.
Virginia: named in honour of Elizabeth I.
War of Independence: started Lexington, Massachusetts, April 1775. **ended** Yorktown, Virginia, October 1781. **rode to warn of British approach** Paul Revere. **traitor for British** Benedict Arnold. **American general** George Washington. **British general** Charles Cornwallis. **Washington's ally** Marquis of Lafayette.
Washington: capital since 1789.
Watts riots Los Angeles, 1965.
witchcraft trials Salem, Massachusetts, 1692 (20 executed).
wobblies Industrial Workers of the World, trade union.
Yellowstone National Park: three states Wyoming, Montana, Idaho.

NB More detailed information pertaining to rivers, mountains and other geographical features of the USA can be found in the Geography section.

Miscellaneous Items of Interest

Units of Length

link (surveying)	7.92 inches (100th part of chain)
span	9 inches (approx span of hand)
hand	4 inches (horse measurement)
cubit	18 inches (biblical measurement)
pace	30 inches (from the stride)
cable	120 fathoms (720 feet; a fathom equals six feet)
nautical mile	6,080 feet (1,852 metres) (1 sec of arc at Equator)

Book Sizes

Crown Quarto	246 x 189 mm
Crown Octavo	186 x 123 mm
Demy Quarto	276 x 219 mm
Demy Octavo	216 x 138 mm
Royal Quarto	312 x 237 mm
Royal Octavo	234 x 156 mm

Paper Sizes

A0	841 x 1189 mm (33⅛ · 46¾ inches)
A1	594 x 841 mm (23⅜ · 33⅛ inches)
A2	420 x 594 mm (16½ · 23⅜ inches)
A3	297 x 420 mm (11¾ · 16½ inches)
A4	210 x 297 mm (8¼ · 11¾ inches)
A5	148 x 210 mm (5⅞ · 8¼ inches)
A6	105 x 148 mm (4⅛ · 5⅞ inches)
A7	74 x 105 mm (2 15/16 · 4⅛ inches)
A8	52 x 74 mm (2 1/16 · 2 15/16 inches)
A9	37 x 52 mm (1 15/32 · 2 1/16 inches)
A10	26 x 37 mm (1 1/32 · 1 15/32 inches)
Elephant	584 x 711 mm (23 · 28 inches)

Morse Code

A	dot dash	**G**	dash dash dot	**M**	dash dash	**S**	dot dot dot	**Y**	dash dot dash dash
B	dash dot dot dot	**H**	dot dot dot dot	**N**	dash dot	**T**	dash	**Z**	dash dash dot dot
C	dash dot dash dot	**I**	dot dot	**O**	dash dash dash	**U**	dot dot dash		
D	dash dot dot	**J**	dot dash dash dash	**P**	dot dash dash dot	**V**	dot dot dot dash		
E	dot	**K**	dash dot dash	**Q**	dash dash dot dash	**W**	dot dash dash		
F	dot dot dash dot	**L**	dot dash dot dot	**R**	dot dash dot	**X**	dash dot dot dash		

Mnemonics

Types of cedars Atlas – Ascending branches, -deodar – drooping branches, Lebanon – level branches.

Can Queen Victoria eat cold apple pie? The seven hills of Rome: Capitoline, Quirinal, Viminal, Esquiline, Caelian, Aventine, Palatine.

Did Mary ever visit Brighton Beach? Order of Nobility: Duke, Marquess, Earl, Viscount, Baron, Baronet.

Bless my dear Aunt Sally Order of operations in algebraic expressions: Brackets, Multiply, Divide, Add, Subtract.

BROM 4689 (Duke of Marlborough's Telephone No.) Marlborough's battles: Blenheim (1704), Ramilies (1706), Oudenarde (1708), Malplaquet (1709).

Men very easily make jugs serve useful nocturnal purposes Planets from the sun: Mercury, Venus, Earth, Mars, Jupiter, Saturn, Uranus, Neptune, Pluto.

Spring forward, fall back Mnemonic to remember whether to put clock forward or back.

Virgins are rare Ohm's Law: Volts = Amps · Resistance.

How I want a drink alcoholic of course after the heavy chapters involving quantum mechanics Mnemonic for remembering pi to 14 places: 3.14159265358979.

No plan like yours to study history wisely British ruling houses: Norman, Plantagenet, Lancaster, York, Tudor, Stuart, Hanover, Windsor

Richard of York gave battle in vain Rainbow colours in order: red, orange, yellow, green, blue, indigo, violet

NB This last little section on mnemonics is a reminder in itself that a sound general knowledge base can only be achieved if facts are committed to memory. There is no shortcut to success in the quiz world; of course, a keen interest taken in things going on around you is desirable, as is a basic level of intelligence, but given that most people share those basic requirements then the secret of success is the amount of data consumed and the way that data is processed. The rate at which information is consumed varies depending on the level of commitment of the reader, but the way that information is stored can be the vital edge required to recall that seemingly long-forgotten nugget or that either/or situation so often encountered by quiz buffs. Mnemonics are an invaluable aid to quiz players, and should be used in some form or other when memorising lists. It does not matter how silly, rude, outlandish or downright inarticulate the mnemonic is, all that matters is that it works.

Colours

alabaster	White
amaranth	Purple
amber	Yellow
argent	Silver
ash	Pale Grey
auburn	Reddish-Brown
aureate	Golden
azure	Sky Blue
bamboo	Yellowish-Brown
bay	Reddish-Brown
bice	Blue
bistre	Brown
bronze	Yellowish-Brown
brunette	Dark Brown
buff	Pale Yellow
cardinal	Red (scarlet)
carmine	Red (crimson)
carnation	Rosy Pink
celandine	Yellow
cerise	Red
cerulean	Blue
chestnut	Reddish-Brown
chocolate	Brown
chrome	Yellow
cinereous	Ash-Grey
cinnabar	Vermilion
cinnamon	Yellowish-Brown
citrine	Lemon Yellow
cobalt	Blue
cochineal	Scarlet
cornelian	Reddish-White
cornflour	Blue
crimson	Purplish-Red
Cyan	Blue-Green
damask	Pinkish-Red
duck-egg	Blue
dun	Greyish-Brown
ebony	Brownish-Black
elephant	Grey
emerald	Green
fallow	Yellow
fawn	Yellowish-Brown
flame	Orangey-Red
foxy	Reddish-Brown
gamboge	Yellow
gentian	Violet
gridelin	Grey-Violet
grizzly	Grey
gules	Red
hazel	Reddish-Brown
heliotrope	Mauve (light purple)
honey	Yellow
indigo	Violet Blue
ivory	Creamy-White
jonquil	Yellow
jupiter	Blue
khaki	Brownish-Yellow

lake	Crimson
lapis lazuli	Blue
lavender	Pale Blue (with trace of red)
lilac	Pinkish-Violet
lily	White
livid	Bluish-Purple
magenta	Mauve (mauvish- crimson)
malachite	Green
maroon	Brownish-Crimson
mazarine	Blue
moon	White
murrey	Purplish-Red
nacarat	Orangey-Red
ochre	Yellow (light browny yellow)
olive	Greyish-Green
or	Gold
peridot	Green (yellowish-green)
pillar-box	Bright Red
plum	Reddish-Purple
primrose	Pale Yellow
puce	Purple-Brown
russet	Reddish-Brown
rust	Reddish-Brown
sable	Black
saffron	Orange-Yellow
sandy	Yellowish-Red
sanguine	Blood Red
sapphire	Blue
scarlet	Bright Red tinged with Orange
sepia	Reddish-Brown
sienna	Yellowish-Brown
solferino	Crimson
sorrel	Reddish-Brown
straw	Pale Yellow
tan	Yellowish-Brown
taupe	Greyish-Brown
teak	Reddish-Brown
teal	Greenish-Blue
topaz	Yellow
turquoise	Greenish-Blue
ultramarine	Blue
umber	Reddish-Brown
verd-antique	Green
vermilion	Red
violet	Bluish-Purple
viridescent	Green
viridian	Bluish-Green
xanthin	Yellow

Angles

	Angles in regular polygon	*Total angles*	*Sides*	*Formula*
triangle	60°	180°	3	(2 x 3 – 4) x 90 = 180
quadrilateral	90°	360°	4	(2 x 4 – 4) x 90 = 360
pentagon	108°	540°	5	(2 x 5 – 4) x 90 = 540
hexagon	120°	720°	6	(2 x 6 – 4) x 90 = 720
heptagon	129°	900°	7	(2 x 7 – 4) x 90 = 900
octagon	135°	1080°	8	(2 x 8 – 4) x 90 = 1080
nonagon	140°	1260°	9	(2 x 9 – 4) x 90 = 1260
decagon	144°	1440°	10	(2 x 10 – 4) x 90 = 1440
hendecagon	147.27°	1620°	11	(2 x 11 – 4) x 90 = 1620
dodecagon	150°	1800°	12	(2 x 12 – 4) x 90 = 1800
isocagon	162°	3240°	20	(2 x 20 – 4) x 90 = 3240

NB Sum of the interior angles of a polygon = (2n – 4) x 90 degrees where n = the number of sides.

Adjectives

	Objects
acicular	needle-like
acinaciform	scimitar-shaped
aciniform	grape-like
alaric	wing-shaped
allantoic	sausage-shaped
amygdaloid	almond-shaped
annular	ring-shaped
arcuate	bow-shaped
baculiform	rod-like
cancroid	crab-like
clavate	club-shaped
cordate	heart-shaped
cricoid	ring-shaped
crinoidal	lily-like
cuneal	wedge-shaped
cyprinoid	carp-like
decussate	cross-shaped
dendroid	tree-shaped
dentoid	tooth-shaped
ethmoid	sieve-like
falciform	sickle-shaped
ganoid	scale-like
hastate	spear-shaped
lenticular	lens-shaped
ligneous	wood-like
linguiform	tongue-shaped
lunate	crescent-shaped
marmoreal	marble-like
navicular	boat-shaped
oculiform	eye-shaped
odontoid	tooth-shaped
oviform	egg-shaped
palmate	palm-shaped
pinnate	feather-like
pyriform	pear-like
reniform	kidney-shaped
sagittate	arrow-shaped
saponaceous	soap-like
scutate	shield-shaped
stellate	star-shaped
toroid	doughnut-shaped
trochal	wheel-shaped
unciform	hook-shaped
verticillate	whorl-shaped
xiphoid	sword-shaped

	Animals
anguine	snake-like
anserine	goose-like
apian	bee-like
aquiline	eagle-like
asinine	ass-like
avian	bird-like
bovine	ox-like
canine	dog-like
caprine	goat-like
cervine	deer-like
columbine	dove-like
corvine	crow-like
equine	horse-like
feline	cat-like
hircine	goat-like
leonine	lion-like
leporine	hare-like
lupine	wolf-like
murine	mouse-like
ovine	sheep-like
ophidian	snake-like
passerine	sparrow-like
pavanine	peacock-like
piscine	fish-like
porcine	pig-like
psittacine	parrot-like
saurian	lizard-like
simian	ape-like
squaloid	shark-like
taurine	bull-like
turdine	thrush-like
ursine	bear-like
vaccine	cow-like
vulpine	fox-like

Roman Roads

Aemilian Way	Rimini to Milan
Akeman Street	Alchester to Cirencester
Appian Way	Rome to Brindisi
Aurelian Way	Rome to Genoa
Casinge Street	Dover to London
Cassian Way	Rome to Florence
Dere Street	Risingham to Hadrian's Wall
Ermine Street	London to York
Flaminian Way	Rome to Rimini
Fosse Way	Lincoln to Exeter
Icknield Way	Wash to Salisbury Plain
Salarian Way	Rome to Ancona
Stane Street (1)	London to Chichester
(2)	Braughing in Herts to Colchester
Watling Street (1)	London to Wroxeter via St Albans
Watling Street (2)	Wroxeter to Abergavenny

Alphabets

	No. of characters	Description
Albanian	36	based on the Tosk language since 1945.
Arabic	28	all consonants; written from right to left.
Aramaic	22	all consonants; written from right to left.
Armenian	38	31 consonants and 7 vowels.
Balinese	27	the Latin alphabet is now used in Bali.
Bassa	29	formerly used in Liberia.
Batak	30	20 consonants, 10 vowels, written from bottom to top.
Braille	63	each made up of 1–6 raised dots arranged in six-position matrix.
Buhid	48	used to write the Tagalog language of the Philippines.
Bulgarian	30	adaptation of the Cyrillic alphabet.
Cyrillic	32	nowadays synonymous with the Russian alphabet.
Ethiopic	26	all consonants; 7 variations of each letter.
Etruscan	20	16 consonants, 4 vowels written left to right then right to left.
Gaelic	18	no J, K, Q, V, W, X, Y, Z.
Georgian	33	used by about 3.5 million people.
Gothic	27	original Gothic alphabet had 25 letters.
Grantha	35	30 consonants and 5 vowels; written left to right.
Greek	24	17 consonants and 7 vowels.
Gujarati	41	34 consonants, 7 vowels each having two variants.
Hebrew	22	all consonants; written from right to left.
Latin (Roman)	26	alphabet used by English speakers. J, U, W not in original Roman alphabet.
Mongolian	33	adaptation of the Cyrillic alphabet.
Ogham	29	also known as beth luis, or beth luis nion.
Phoenician	22	no vowels.
Runic	24	also known as fu(th)ark from its first six letters.
Russian	33	adaptation of the Cyrillic alphabet.
Serbian	29	adaptation of the Cyrillic alphabet.
Tamil	36	24 consonants, 12 vowels.
Telugo	51	35 consonants, 16 vowels.
Ugaritic	30	cuneiform alphabet of 27 consonants and 3 vowels.
Ukrainian	33	adaptation of the Cyrillic alphabet.

US Money

All US bills have a portrait of a famous American on the front and a design on the back as follows:

	Front	Back		Front	Back
$1	Washington	Great Seal of USA	$100	Franklin	Independence Hall
$2	Jefferson	Signers of Declaration	$500	McKinley	Ornate Design
$5	Lincoln	Lincoln Memorial	$1,000	Cleveland	Ornate Design
$10	Hamilton	US Treasury	$5,000	Madison	Ornate Design
$20	Jackson	White House	$10,000	Chase	Ornate Design
$50	Grant	US Capitol	$100,000	Wilson	Ornate Design

British Money

Until 1943 there were white bank notes for values of £10, £20, £50, £100, £500 and £1,000 but these ceased to be legal tender in 1945. The old white £5 note issued between 1945 and 1956 ceased to be legal tender in 1961. The £5 note issued between 1957 and 1963 that coincided with the term of office of Harold MacMillan, and bearing a portrait of Britannia, ceased to be legal tender in 1967. The £5 note issued between 1963 and 1971 was the first of the series to bear a portrait of the Queen. The first note with a portrait of the Queen on the front was a £1 note issued in 1960. The 10 shilling note was replaced by the 50p coin in 1969 and ceased to be legal tender in 1970 (they could however be redeemed if presented at the Head Office of the Bank of England). The £1 note was replaced by a coin in 1983 and ceased to be legal tender in 1988, although the Scottish £1 note is still acceptable in Scotland.

The current notes as at August 2013 portray famous people as follows:

£5	Elizabeth Fry (1780–1845) showing her reading to prisoners in Newgate Prison.
£10	Charles Darwin (1809–82) and the *Beagle* plus a hummingbird.
£20	Adam Smith (1723–90) with an illustration of 'The division of labour in pin manufacturing'
£50	James Watt and Matthew Boulton with steam engine and Boulton's Soho factory.

Series F notes pending include a depiction of Winston Churchill on £5 in 2016 and Jane Austen on £10 in 2017.

The current Chief Cashier of the Bank of England is Andrew Bailey, who replaced Merlyn Lowther.

The current Governor of the Bank of England is Mark Carney, who replaced Mervyn King.

Previous portraits on notes are as follows:

£5	George Stephenson and before him The Duke of Wellington
£10	Charles Dickens and before him Florence Nightingale
£20	Edward Elgar, before him Michael Faraday and before him William Shakespeare
£50	Sir John Houblon (1632–1712) the first Governor of the Bank of England and before him Sir Christopher Wren

British coins ceased to be legal tender as follows:

Farthing (¼d)	1960
Pre-decimal halfpenny	1969
Half-crown (2s 6d)	1970
Threepenny bit	1971
Sixpence (6d = 2½p)	1980
Decimal halfpenny	1984

Confusion often arises when one considers which was the first decimal coin brought into circulation. In 1968 the shilling and two shilling coins were replaced by a new 5p and 10p coin. This pre-empted decimalisation in 1971 and was an exercise in the public becoming used to the new system. The coins were of the same value as previously and did not alter the public perception in any way. In 1969 the new 50p coin was introduced, replacing the ten-shilling note which of course was a vastly different form, hence it often being considered as the first decimal coin introduced.

In 1971 the ½p, 1p, and 2p coins were introduced and in 1982 the 20p coin followed. In 1983 the £1 coin replaced the £1 note and in 1986 the first £2 coin was minted. Decimal coins minted before 1982 had their value in 'New' pence.

UK Telephone STD Codes

0121 Birmingham
0131 Edinburgh
0141 Glasgow
0151 Liverpool
0161 Manchester
0191 Newcastle upon Tyne

Recent changes to STD codes

Cardiff was 01222 now 02920
Coventry was 01203 now 02476
London was 0171 now 0207
London was 0181 now 0208
Portsmouth was 01705 now 02392
Southampton was 01703 now 02380

NB All Northern Ireland numbers have been changed to six-digit numbers, all of which begin 028.

and finally

A few well-known people whose name belies their gender:

Colley Cibber (dramatist) male
Wilkie Collins (novelist) male
Alice Cooper (rock singer) male
Richmal Crompton (novelist) female
George Eliot (novelist) female
Keri Hulme (novelist) female
Julian of Norwich (mystic) female
Harper Lee (novelist) female
Laurie Lee (novelist) male
Marilyn Manson (pop star) male
Ngaio Marsh (novelist) female
Joan Miro (painter) male
Toni Morrison (author) female
Nelly (rapper) male
Andrea Palladio (architect) male
Caryl Phillips (novelist) male
Carol Reed (film director) male
George Sand (novelist) female
Lionel Shriver (novelist) female
Stevie Smith (poet) female
Vesta Tilley (music hall star) female
Evelyn Waugh (novelist) male
Reese Witherspoon (actress) female

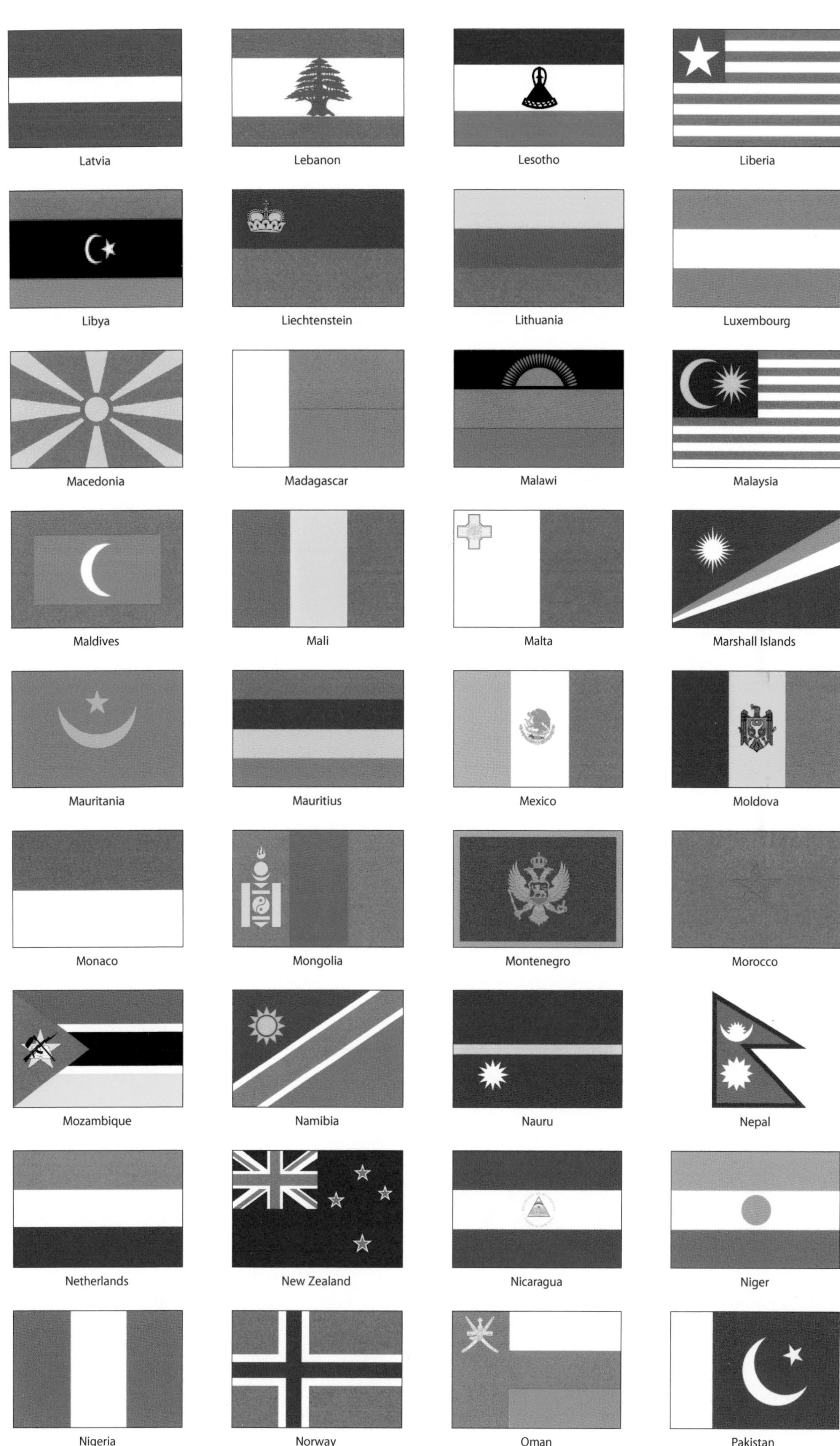
Latvia
Lebanon
Lesotho
Liberia
Libya
Liechtenstein
Lithuania
Luxembourg
Macedonia
Madagascar
Malawi
Malaysia
Maldives
Mali
Malta
Marshall Islands
Mauritania
Mauritius
Mexico
Moldova
Monaco
Mongolia
Montenegro
Morocco
Mozambique
Namibia
Nauru
Nepal
Netherlands
New Zealand
Nicaragua
Niger
Nigeria
Norway
Oman
Pakistan

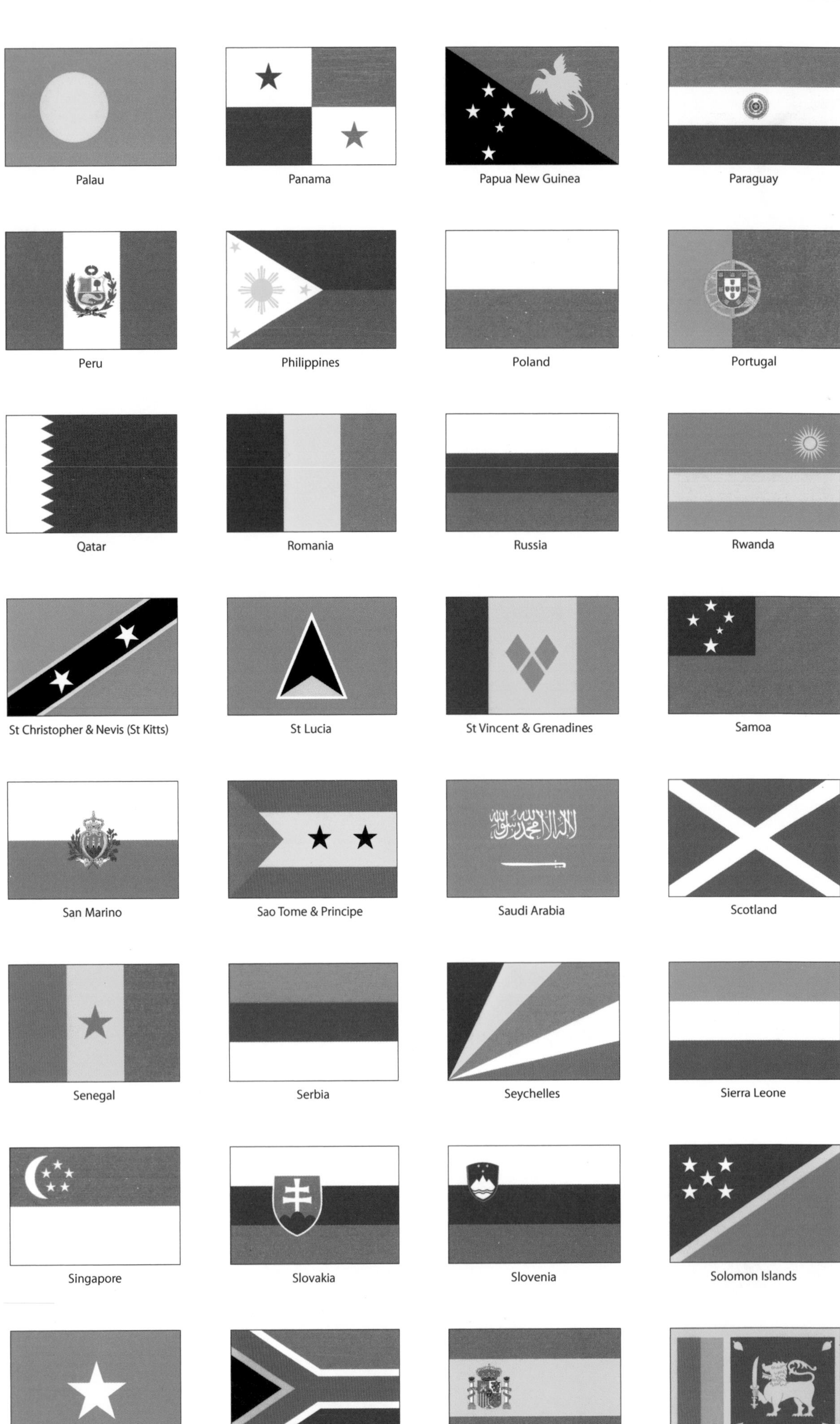
Palau
Panama
Papua New Guinea
Paraguay
Peru
Philippines
Poland
Portugal
Qatar
Romania
Russia
Rwanda
St Christopher & Nevis (St Kitts)
St Lucia
St Vincent & Grenadines
Samoa
San Marino
Sao Tome & Principe
Saudi Arabia
Scotland
Senegal
Serbia
Seychelles
Sierra Leone
Singapore
Slovakia
Slovenia
Solomon Islands
Somalia
South Africa
Spain
Sri Lanka